Merriam-Webster's French-English Dictionary

MERRIAM-WEBSTER, INCORPORATED
Springfield, Massachusetts, U.S.A.

A GENUINE MERRIAM-WEBSTER

The name *Webster* alone is no guarantee of excellence. It is used by a number of publishers and may serve mainly to mislead an unwary buyer.

Merriam-Webster™ is the name you should look for when you consider the purchase of dictionaries or other fine reference books. It carries the reputation of a company that has been publishing since 1831 and is your assurance of quality and authority.

Copyright © 2005 by Merriam-Webster, Incorporated

ISBN-13: 978-0-87779-917-7
ISBN-10: 0-87779-917-2

Merriam-Webster's French-English Dictionary,
principal copyright 2000

All rights reserved. No part of this work covered by the copyrights hereon may be reproduced or copied in any form or by any means—graphic, electronic, or mechanical, including photocopying, recording, taping, or information storage and retrieval systems—without written permission of the publisher.

MADE IN THE UNITED STATES OF AMERICA

12 QWB 07

Contents

Preface	7a
Explanatory Notes	9a
French Grammar	22a
Conjugation of French Verbs	40a
Abbreviations in this Work	59a
Pronunciation Symbols	60a
French–English Dictionary	1
English–French Dictionary	367
Common French Abbreviations	799
French Numbers	803

Preface

MERRIAM-WEBSTER'S FRENCH-ENGLISH DICTIONARY is a completely new dictionary designed to meet the needs of English and French speakers throughout the world. It is intended for language learners, teachers, office workers, tourists, business travelers—anyone who needs to communicate effectively in the French and English languages as they are spoken and written today.

This dictionary provides up-to-date coverage of French words and phrases as they are spoken in France and in other European countries, and special care has been taken to include the unique terminology of French-speaking Canada as well. The English vocabulary and spellings included here reflect North American usage and are primarily those of American English, but British terms and spellings commonly used in Canada are also included.

All of this material is presented in a format that is based firmly upon, and in many ways is similar to, the traditional styling found in other Merriam-Webster dictionaries. The reader who is familiar with Merriam-Webster dictionaries will immediately recognize the style, with its emphasis on clarity and concision of the information, precise discrimination of senses, and the frequent inclusion of example phrases to illustrate idiomatic usage. Also included are pronunciations (in the International Phonetic Alphabet) of the entered words in both languages, extensive coverage of French irregular verbs, a section on basic French grammar, a table of the most common French abbreviations, and a detailed Explanatory Notes section designed to assist readers in the use of this book.

Merriam-Webster's French-English Dictionary represents the combined efforts of many members of the Merriam-Webster Editorial Department, along with the help of consultants outside the company. The primary defining work was done by Anne Eason and Peter A. Sokolowski, with the assistance of Jocelyn Woods; early contributions to the text were also submitted by Jonathan Brook, Ronald Giguère, Lynn A. Prince, and Anna K. Sandström. Anne Eason, Seán O'Mannion-Espejo, and Peter A.

Sokolowski were responsible for preparing the front and back matter in the book. Joanne M. Despres, Ph.D. provided the pronunciations, assisted by Emily B. Arsenault, Deanna M. Chiasson, Kory L. Stamper, and Karen L. Wilkinson. The coordination of typesetting and other production steps was done by Thomas F. Pitoniak, Ph.D., who also offered many helpful suggestions regarding content and format. Proofreading was carried out by Joanne M. Despres, Anne Eason, Seán O'Mannion-Espejo, Thomas F. Pitoniak, Peter A. Sokolowski, Karen L. Wilkinson, and Jocelyn D. Woods. Georgette B. Boucher provided invaluable typing assistance. Madeline L. Novak provided guidance on typographic matters. John M. Morse was responsible for the conception of this book as well as for numerous ideas and continued support along the way.

Eileen M. Haraty
Editor

Explanatory Notes

Entries

1. Main Entries

A boldface letter, word, or phrase appearing flush with the left-hand margin of each column of type is a main entry or entry word. The main entry may consist of letters set solid, of letters joined by a punctuation mark (as a hyphen), or of letters separated by a space:

collant[1], **-lante** . . . *adj* . . .

eye–opener . . . *n* . . .

walk out *vi* . . .

The main entry, together with the material that follows it on the same line and succeeding indented lines, constitutes a dictionary entry.

2. Order of Main Entries

The main entries follow one another in alphabetical order letter by letter without regard to intervening spaces or hyphens; for example, *shake-up* follows *shaker*.

Homographs (words with the same spelling) having different parts of speech are given separate dictionary entries. These entries are distinguished by superscript numerals following the entry word:

mauvais[1] . . . *adv* . . .

mauvais[2], **-vaise** *adj* . . .

salt[1] . . . *vt* . . .

salt[2] *adj* . . .

salt[3] *n* . . .

Numbered homograph entries are listed in the following order: verb, adverb, adjective, noun, conjunction, preposition, pronoun, interjection, article.

Homographs having the same part of speech are normally included at the same dictionary entry, without regard to their different semantic origins. On the English-to-French side, however, separate entries are made if the homographs have distinct pronunciations or if homographic verbs have distinct inflected forms.

3. Guide Words

A pair of guide words is printed at the top of each page, indicating the first and last main entries that appear on that page:

velours • vérifiable

4. Variants

When a main entry is followed by the word *or* and another spelling, the two spellings are variants. Both are standard, and either one may be used according to personal inclination:

jailer *or* **jailor** . . . *n* . . .

lis *or* **lys** . . . *nms & pl* . . .

Occasionally, a variant spelling is used only for a particular sense of a word. In these cases, the variant spelling is listed after the sense number of the sense to which it pertains:

flier . . . *n* . . . **2** *or* **flyer** . . .

Sometimes the entry word is used interchangeably with a longer phrase containing the entry word. For the purposes of this dictionary, such phrases are considered variants of the headword:

bunk[2] *n* **1** *or* **bunk bed** . . .

risée . . . *nf or* **objet de risée** . . .

ward[1] . . . *vt or* **to ward off** . . .

Variant wordings of boldface phrases may also be shown:

table . . . *nf* . . . **4 table de chevet** *or* **table de nuit** . . .

abattre . . . *vt* . . . **5 abattre ses cartes** *or* **abattre son jeu** . . .

5. Run-On Entries

A main entry may be followed by a derivative word in a different part of speech. This is a run-on entry. It is introduced by a boldface dash and has a functional label. It is not defined, however, since its equivalent can be readily derived by adding the corresponding foreign-language suffix to the term or terms used to define the entry word:

illegal . . . *adj* : illégal — **illegally** *adv*

(the French adverb is *illégalement*)

bureaucratie . . . *nf* : bureaucracy — **bureaucratique** . . . *adj*

(the English adjective is *bureaucratic*)

On the French-to-English side of the book, reflexive verbs are sometimes run on undefined:

appauvrir . . . *vt* : to impoverish — **s'appauvrir** *vr*

The absence of a definition indicates that *s'appauvrir* has the simple reflexive meaning "to become impoverished" or "to impoverish oneself."

6. Bold Notes

A main entry may be followed by one or more phrases containing the entry word or an inflected form of it. These are bold notes. Each bold note is defined at its own numbered sense:

abeille . . . *nf* **1** : bee, honeybee **2** **abeille mâle** : drone

hold[1] . . . *vi* . . . **3 to hold forth** : . . . **4** **to hold to** : . . .

If the bold note consists only of the entry word and a single preposition, the entry word is represented by a boldface swung dash ~.

pente . . . *nf* **1** : slope **2 en ~** : sloping

The same bold note phrase may appear at two or more senses if it has more than one distinct meaning:

affaire . . . *nf* . . . **5 affaires** *nfpl* : possessions, belongings **6 affaires** *nfpl* : business <homme d'affaires : businessman> . . .

Pronunciation

Pronunciation of Entry Words

The matter between a pair of brackets [ ] following the entry word indicates the pronunciation. The symbols used are from the International Phonetic Alphabet and are explained in the Pronunciation Symbols chart on page 60a.

The presence of variant pronunciations indicates that not all educated speakers pronounce words the same way. A second-place variant is not to be regarded as less acceptable than the pronunciation that is given first. It may, in fact, be used by as many educated speakers as the first variant, but the requirements of the printed page are such that one must precede the other:

often [ˈɔfən, ˈɔftən] . . .

When a compound word has less than a full pronunciation, the missing part is to be supplied from the pronunciation at the entry for the unpronounced element of the compound:

gamma ray [ˈgæmə] . . .

ray [ˈreɪ] . . .

In general, no pronunciation is indicated for open compounds consisting of two or more English words that are main entries at their own alphabetical place:

smoke detector . . .

smoke[1] [ˈsmok] . . .

detector [dɪˈtɛktər] . . .

Only the first entry in a series of numbered homographs is given a pronunciation if their pronunciations are the same:

dab[1] ['dæb] *vt* . . .

dab[2] *n* . . .

On the English-to-French side, no pronunciation is shown for principal parts of verbs that are formed by regular suffixation, nor for most derivative adverbs formed by the suffix *-ly*.

The aspirate pronunciation of the letter *h* in French is indicated by a symbol ['] preceding the pronunciation of the headword:

habile [abil]

hasard ['azar]

Functional Labels

An italic label indicating a part of speech or some other functional classification follows the pronunciation or, if no pronunciation is given, the main entry. The parts of speech are indicated as follows:

mendier . . . *v* . . .

maintenant . . . *adv* . . .

daily[2] *adj* . . .

jackal . . . *n* . . .

and . . . *conj* . . .

par . . . *prep* . . .

neither[3] *pron* . . .

allô . . . *interj* . . .

le . . . *art*

Verbs that are intransitive are labelled *vi;* verbs that are transitive are labelled *vt*. Entries for verbs that are both transitive and intransitive are labelled *v,* with the labels *vi* and *vt* serving to introduce any transitive and intransitive subdivisions:

necessitate . . . *vt* **-tated; -tating** : nécessiter, exiger

déborder . . . *vi* : to overflow

satisfy . . . *v* **-fied; -fying** *vt* . . . — *vi* . . .

Two other labels are used to indicate functional classifications of verbs: *v aux* (auxiliary verb) and *v impers* (impersonal verb).

may . . . *v aux, past* **might** . . .

aller[1] . . . *vi* . . . — *v aux* : to be going to, to be about to . . . — *v impers* **1** **en ~** : to happen, to go . . .

Gender Labels

In French-to-English noun entries, the gender of the entry word is indicated by an italic *m* (masculine), *f* (feminine), or *mf* (masculine or feminine), immediately following the functional label:

magnésium . . . *nm* . . .

galaxie . . . *nf* . . .

touriste . . . *nmf* . . .

If both the masculine and feminine forms are shown for a noun referring to a person, the label is simply *n*:

directeur[2], **-trice** *n* . . .

French noun equivalents of English entry words are also labeled for gender:

amnesia . . . *n* : amnésie *f*

earache . . . *n* : mal *m* d'oreille

gamekeeper . . . *n* : garde-chasse *m*

Inflected Forms

1. Nouns

The plurals of nouns are shown in this dictionary when they are irregular, when plural suffixation brings about a change in the spelling of the root word, when an English noun ends in a consonant plus *-o* or in *-ey*, when an English noun ends in *-oo*, when an English noun is a compound that pluralizes any element but the last, when a French noun is a hyphenated compound, when a noun has variant plurals, or whenever the dictionary user might have reasonable doubts regarding the spelling of a plural:

tooth . . . *n, pl* **teeth** . . .

madame . . . *nf, pl* **mesdames** . . .

adieu . . . *nm, pl* **adieux** . . .

potato . . . *n, pl* **-toes** . . .

abbey . . . *n, pl* **-beys** . . .

cuckoo[2] *n, pl* **-oos** . . .

brother–in–law . . . *n, pl* **brothers–in–law** . . .

court–circuit . . . *nm, pl* **courts–circuits** . . .

quail[2] *n, pl* **quail** *or* **quails** . . .

récital . . . *nm, pl* **-tals** . . .

Cutback inflected forms are used for most multisyllabic nouns on the English-to-French side, regardless of the number of syllables. On the French-to-English side, cutback inflections are given for nouns that have three or more syllables; plurals for shorter words are written out in full:

shampoo[2] *n, pl* **-poos** . . .

calamity . . . *n, pl* **-ties** . . .

mouse . . . *n, pl* **mice** . . .

terminal[2] *nm, pl* **-naux** . . .

caillou . . . *nm, pl* **cailloux** . . .

If only the masculine gender form has a plural which is irregular, that plural form will be given with the appropriate label:

jumeau, -melle . . . *adj & n, mpl* **jumeaux** : twin

The plurals of nouns are usually not shown when the base word is unchanged by the addition of the regular *-s* plural or when the noun is unlikely to occur in the plural:

apple . . . *n* : pomme *f*

anglais[2] *nm* : English (language)

Nouns that are plural in form and that regularly occur in plural constructions are labeled *npl* (for English nouns), *nmpl* (for French masculine nouns), or *nfpl* (for French feminine nouns):

knickers . . . *npl* . . .

parages . . . *nmpl* . . .

tenailles . . . *nfpl* . . .

Entry words that are unchanged in the plural are labeled *ns & pl* (for English nouns), *nms & pl* (for French masculine nouns), *nfs & pl* (for French feminine nouns), and *nmfs & pl* (for French gender-variable nouns):

deer . . . *ns & pl* . . .

perdrix . . . *nfs & pl* . . .

débours . . . *nms & pl* . . .

après–midi . . . *nmfs & pl* . . .

2. Verbs

ENGLISH VERBS

The principal parts of verbs are shown in English-to-French entries when they are irregular, when suffixation brings about a change in spelling of the root word, when the verb ends in *-ey,* or when there are variant inflected forms:

break[1] . . . *v* **broke** . . . ; **broken** . . . ; **breaking** . . .

drag[1] . . . *v* **dragged; dragging** . . .

imagine . . . *vt* **-ined; -ining** . . .

monkey[1] . . . *vi* **-keyed; -keying** . . .

label[1] . . . *vt* **-beled** *or* **-belled; -beling** *or* **-belling** . . .

Cutback inflected forms are usually used when the verb has two or more syllables:

multiply . . . *v* **-plied; -plying** . . .

bevel[1] . . . *vt* **-eled** *or* **-elled; -eling** *or* **-elling** . . .

forgo *or* **forego** . . . *vt* **-went** . . . ; **-gone** . . . ; **-going** . . .

commit . . . *vt* **-mitted; -mitting** . . .

The principal parts of an English verb are usually not shown when they are regular and the root word is unchanged by suffixation.

delay[1] . . . *vt*

pack[1] . . . *vt*

FRENCH VERBS

The conjugations of French verbs are not shown at the entry but are included in the Conjugation of French Verbs section beginning on page 40a. Regular verbs ending in *-er* or *-ir* have no cross-reference number at their entries, and their conjugations are shown at the beginning of that section. Entries for irregular French verbs are cross-referenced by number to the model conjugations appearing in the Conjugation of French Verbs section:

arranger {17} *vt* . . .

joindre {50} *vt* . . .

Entries for frequently used irregular forms of French verbs are cross-referenced to the corresponding infinitive:

tenu[1] . . . *pp* → **tenir**

joigne . . . , *etc.* → **joindre**

Irregular composite verbs, such as *retenir* and *rejoindre*, do not have cross-referenced forms entered in the dictionary, since their conjugations are based upon the corresponding verbal root.

Adverbs and Adjectives

The comparative and superlative forms of English adjective and adverb main entries are shown when suffixation brings about a change in spelling of the root word, when the inflection is irregular, and when there are variant inflected forms:

fat . . . *adj* **fatter; fattest** . . .

well[2] *adv* **better** . . . ; **best** . . .

evil[1] . . . *adj* **eviler** *or* **eviller; evilest** *or* **evillest** . . .

The superlative forms of adjectives and adverbs of two or more syllables are usually cut back; the superlative is shown in full, however, when it is desirable to indicate the pronunciation of the inflected form:

gaudy . . . *adj* **gaudier; -est** . . .

early[1] . . . *adv* **earlier; -est** . . .

secure[1] . . . *adj* **securer; -est** . . .

but

young[1] . . . *adj* **younger** ['jəŋgər:]; **youngest** ['jəŋgəst] . . .

The absence of the comparative form at an adjective entry indicates that there is no evidence of its use:

mere . . . *adj, superlative* **merest** . . .

The comparative and superlative forms of adjectives and adverbs are usually not shown when the base word is unchanged by suffixation.

quiet[2] *adj* **1** . . .

Usage

1. Usage Labels

The two types of usage labels in this dictionary address a word's regional derivation and register. Words that are limited in use to France, French-speaking Canada, Belgium, Switzerland, or English-speaking Canada are given labels indicating the countries in which they are most commonly used:

bachoter . . . *vi France* : to cram . . .

cocotte . . . *nf* . . . **2** *Can* : pinecone . . .

auditoire . . . *nm* . . . **2** *Bel & Switz* : auditorium

furnace . . . *n* : fourneau *m*, fournaise *f Can*

bloke . . . *n Brit* : type *m*

The following regional labels are used in this book: *Bel* (Belgium), *Brit* (Great Britain and English-speaking Canada), *Can* (French-speaking Canada), *France, Switz* (Switzerland).

A number of French words are given a *fam* (familiar) label as well, indicating that these words are suitable for informal contexts but would not normally be used in formal writing or speaking. The stylistic labels *sometimes offensive* or *usu vulgar* are added for a word which is thought to be vulgar or offensive in many contexts but whose widespread use justifies its inclusion in this book. These labels are intended to warn the reader that the word in question may be inappropriate in polite conversation.

2. Usage Notes

Definitions are sometimes preceded by parenthetical usage notes that give supplementary semantic information:

not . . . *adv* **1** (*used to form a negative*) **:** . . .

when[2] *conj* **1** (*referring to a particular time*)**:** . . .

se . . . *pron* **1** (*used with reflexive verbs*) **:** . . . **2** (*used to indicate reciprocity*) **:** . . .

si[1] . . . *adv* . . . **2** (*used to contradict a negative statement or question*) **:** . . .

Additional semantic orientation is also occasionally given in the form of parenthetical notes appearing within the definition:

calibrate . . . *vt* . . . **:** calibrer (une arme, etc.), étalonner (une balance)

paille . . . *nf* . . . **2 :** (drinking) straw

Occasionally a usage note is used in place of a definition. This is usually done when the entry word has no single foreign-language equivalent. Usage notes of this type will be accompanied by an example or examples of common use:

shall . . . *v aux* . . . **1** (*used to express a command*) <you shall do as I say **:** vous ferez comme je vous dis> . . .

3. Illustrations of Usage

Definitions are sometimes followed by verbal illustrations that show a typical use of the word in context or a common idiomatic usage. These verbal illustrations include a translation and are enclosed in angle brackets:

ici . . . *adv* **1 :** here <ici et là **:** here and there> <par ici **:** this way> . . .

make[1] . . . *vt* . . . **8** EARN **:** gagner <to make a living **:** gagner sa vie> . . .

Sense Division

A boldface colon is used to introduce a definition:

failing[1] . . . *n* **:** défaut *m*

Boldface Arabic numerals separate the senses of a word that has more than one sense:

> **maîtriser** . . . *vt* **1** : to master **2** : to control, to restrain . . .

Whenever some information (such as a synonym, a boldface word or phrase, a usage note, a cross-reference, or a label) follows a sense number, it applies only to that specific numbered sense and not to any other boldface numbered senses:

> **abord** . . . *nm* **1** ACCÈS : . . .
>
> **pile**[1] . . . *vi* **1** *or* **to pile up** : . . .
>
> **caoutchouc** . . . *nm* . . . **2 caoutchoucs** *nmpl* : . . .
>
> **extension** . . . *n* . . . **5 extension cord** : . . .
>
> **myself** . . . *pron* **1** (*used reflexively*) : . . .
>
> **pike** . . . *n* . . . **3** → **turnpike**
>
> **ambitionner** . . . *vt* . . . **2** *Can* : . . .

Cross-References

Three different kinds of cross-references are used in this dictionary: synonymous, cognate, and inflectional. In each instance the cross-reference is readily recognized by the boldface arrow following the entry word.

Synonymous and cognate cross-references indicate that a definition at the entry cross-referred to can be substituted for the entry word:

> **cable**[2] . . . **2** → **cablegram**
>
> **sceptic** . . . → **skeptic**

An inflectional cross-reference is used to identify the entry word as an inflected form of another word (as a noun or verb):

> **aura**[1] . . . , etc. → **avoir**
>
> **mice** → **mouse**

Synonyms

At many entries or senses in this book, a synonym in small capital letters is provided before the boldface colon and the following defining text. These synonyms are all main entries or bold notes elsewhere in the book. They serve as a helpful guide to the meaning of the entry or sense and also give the reader an additional term that might be substituted in a similar context. On the English-to-French side synonyms are particularly abundant, since special care has been taken to guide the English speaker—by means of synonyms, verbal illustrations, or usage notes—to the meaning of the French terms at each sense of a multisense entry.

croiser . . . **3** RENCONTRER : . . .

demand[2] . . . **2** CLAIM : . . .

French Grammar

Accents and Diacritics

French makes use of accents and diacritics to indicate either the phonetic value of a given letter, or to distinguish one word from another which has the same pronunciation and would otherwise share the same spelling. There are three types of accents:

> ***The acute accent*** /´/ ordinarily indicates closed pronunciation.
>
> ***The grave accent*** /`/ ordinarily indicates open pronunciation.
>
> ***The circumflex*** /ˆ/ ordinarily indicates open pronunciation.

In addition to accents, French makes use of the ***diaeresis*** /¨/ which, as in English, indicates that the vowel preceding the marked letter is pronounced separately: *maïs* [mais] (corn) is thus pronounced differently from *mais* [mɛ] (but, however).

> The ***cedilla*** /¸/ indicates soft pronunciation of a *c* /s/ which precedes an *a, o,* or *u* (*ça, rançon, aperçu*).

Diacritics in the French language do not affect word stress.

Capitalization

In French, unlike English, the following words are usually not capitalized:

- Names of days, months, languages, and most religions (*jeudi, octobre, français, judaïsme*).
- Names of holidays composed of two or more words. Unlike English, in French only the distinguishing word and any preceding adjectives are capitalized (*la fête du Travail,* Labor Day; *mercredi des Cendres,* Ash Wednesday).

- French adjectives or nouns derived from proper nouns (*l'équipe sénégalaise, le marxisme*), except for nouns of geographic or national identity, which are usually capitalized (*les Antillais, une Vietnamienne*).

Articles

1. Definite Article

French has three forms of the definite article: *le* (masculine singular), *la* (feminine singular), and the plural article, *les,* which does not distinguish for gender. *Le* and *la* contract to *l'* when they precede a word beginning with a vowel sound (*l'arbre, l'heure*). In some instances an initial *h,* although mute, is considered to be aspirate, in which case the article does not contract (*le héros*). The definite article agrees in gender and number with the noun that follows it (*le bâtiment,* the building; *la rue,* the street; *les bâtiments,* the buildings; *les rues,* the streets).

Whenever the plural article *les* or the singular masculine article *le* immediately follows either *de* or *à,* the two combine to form the contractions *des, aux, du,* and *au* respectively (*les jouets des enfants,* the children's toys; *la maison aux fenêtres larges,* the house with the wide windows; *le cabinet du médecin,* the doctor's office; *elles sont allées au café,* they went to the café). However, if a singular article of either gender is preceded by *de* or *à* and followed by a word with an initial vowel sound, the article becomes *l'* (*le nom de l'église,* the name of the church; *arriver à l'heure,* to arrive on time). The use of *le, la,* and *les* in French corresponds largely to the use of *the* in English; some exceptions are noted below.

The definite article is used:

- With certain geographical regions, including countries and continents (*l'Afrique,* Africa; *le Canada,* Canada; *la Nouvelle-Écosse,* Nova Scotia).
- With languages, except when the language is preceded by *en* or *parler* (*Patti comprend le français,* Patti understands French; *Joseph parle hongrois,* Joseph speaks Hungarian; *c'est en japonais,* it's in Japanese).

- With abstract nouns (*il adore les chiens,* he loves dogs; *l'hiver est long,* winter is long; *le petit déjeuner est inclus,* breakfast is included).
- With body parts (*j'ai mal au bras,* my arm hurts; *elle se brosse les dents,* she's brushing her teeth).

2. Indefinite Article

French has three forms of the indefinite article: *un* (masculine singular), *une* (feminine singular), and the plural article *des,* which is used for both genders. The indefinite article agrees in number and gender with the noun it precedes (*une table,* a table; *un couteau,* a knife; *des verres,* some glasses).

- The use of *un, une,* and *des* in French corresponds largely to the use of *a, an,* and *some* in English (*un oiseau,* a bird; *une poupée,* a doll; *des oranges,* oranges, some oranges). The plural article *des* becomes *de* or *d'* when immediately followed by an adjective (*des amis,* friends; *de bons amis,* good friends). When the adjective begins with a vowel sound, then the article becomes *d'* (*d'énormes quantités,* enormous quantities).
- In a negative statement, the indefinite article is replaced with *de* or, when preceding a word with an initial vowel sound, *d'* (*Marc n'a pas de voiture,* Marc doesn't have a car; *il n'y a plus d'eau,* there is no more water). This rule does not apply to negative statements with the verb *être* (*ce livre n'est pas un roman,* this book is not a novel).

3. Partitive Article

French makes use of the partitive article to indicate that the following noun represents part of an implied, and uncountable, whole. The partitive is formed by *de* plus the definite article, contracting where applicable to *du, de la, de l',* or *des* (*elle écoute de la musique,* she listens to music; *pomper de l'essence,* to pump gas).

Nouns

1. Gender

Nouns in French are either masculine or feminine. Although a noun's gender can be arbitrary and must be learned as one acquires vocabulary, it can often be determined according to the following guidelines:

- Nouns ending in *-age, -èle, -exe, -isme, -oir, -phone,* and *-scope* are usually masculine (*un visage, un modèle, le sexe, le mysticisme, le miroir, un téléphone, un magnétoscope*).
- Nouns deriving from verbs will often signal masculine gender with the ending *-eur* or *-ant*, or feminine gender with the ending *-euse* or *-ante* (*un chanteur, la gagnante*).
- Nouns ending in *-ade, -ance, -ence, -esse, -ette, -ie, -ise, -sion, -té, -tion, -trice, -tude* or *-ure* are usually feminine (*une croisade, la chance, une essence, la jeunesse, une vedette, la patrie, une crise, une décision, l'université, une abstraction, l'empératrice, la similitude, une aventure*).

Most nouns referring to people or animals agree in gender with the subject (*un homme, une femme; le frère, la sœur; le cheval, la jument*). However, some nouns referring to people, including those ending in *-ique* and *-iste,* use the same form for both sexes (*un artiste, une artiste; un diabétique, une diabétique*).

Many names of animals exist in only one gender form (*la souris, le crapaud,* etc.). In these instances, the adjectives *mâle* and *femelle* are sometimes used to distinguish between males and females (*une souris mâle,* a male mouse).

2. Pluralization

Plurals of French nouns are formed as follows:

- As in English, most French nouns are pluralized by adding *-s* (*un médecin, des médecins; l'arbre, les arbres*).
- Nouns ending in *-au* or *-eu* are ordinarily pluralized by adding a final *-x* (*un tuyau, des tuyaux; le feu, les feux*).

- Nouns ending in *-al* are often pluralized by changing the ending to *-aux* (*un animal, des animaux*).
- Singular nouns which end in *-s*, *-x*, or *-z* do not change in the plural (*un matelas, deux matelas; la croix, les croix; un gaz, des gaz*).

Adjectives

1. Gender and Number

Most adjectives agree in gender and number with the nouns or pronouns they modify (*un poète espagnol, des poètes espagnols; elle est espagnole, elles sont espagnoles*). Many adjectives ending in *-e* (*riche*) and most of those ending in *-ble, -ique,* and *-iste* (*probable, fantastique, altruiste*) vary only for number.

Many masculine adjectives add a final *-e* to form the feminine (*petit → petite, français → française*). In some cases, the feminine is formed by modifying the final syllable, according to the following patterns:

-anc → -anche (*franc → franche*)

-el → -elle (*actuel → actuelle*)

-en → -enne (*moyen → moyenne*)

-er → -ère (*passager → passagère*)

-eur → -euse (*frondeur → frondeuse*)

-eux → -euse (*respectueux → respectueuse*)

-if → -ive (*tardif → tardive*)

-il → -ille (*gentil → gentille*)

Some masculine adjectives, including *beau, fou, nouveau,* and *vieux,* modify their ending when immediately followed by a word which begins with a vowel sound:

beau → bel (*un bel arbre,* a beautiful tree)

fou → fol (*un fol appétit,* a tremendous appetite)

nouveau → nouvel (*un nouvel album,* a new album)

vieux → vieil (*un vieil ami,* an old friend)

Adjectives of this type ordinarily form the feminine by adding *-le* to these modified masculine forms:

beau → *bel* → *belle*

vieux → *vieil* → *vieille*

2. Pluralization

Plurals of French adjectives are formed as follows:

- Most adjectives are pluralized by adding *-s* (*de bons livres,* some good books; *des yeux bleus,* blue eyes).
- Masculine adjectives ending in *-au* are ordinarily pluralized by adding a final *-x* (*les beaux arts,* the fine arts; *des mots nouveaux,* new words).
- Masculine adjectives ending in *-al* are often pluralized by changing the ending to *-aux* (*les moyens normaux,* the normal means).

3. Position

Unlike English, most descriptive adjectives in French follow the nouns they modify (*une chose utile, un écrivain célèbre*). Common exceptions include *autre, beau, bon, chaque, faux, gros, jeune, joli, nouveau, petit,* and *vieux,* which usually appear before the noun (*une belle maison, une vieille dame*).

Some adjectives change meaning depending on whether they occur before or after the noun: *un pauvre enfant,* a poor (pitiable) child, *un enfant pauvre,* a poor (not rich) child; *un grand homme,* a great man, *un homme grand,* a tall man; *mes chers amis,* my dear friends; *un ordinateur cher,* an expensive computer.

4. Comparative and Superlative Forms

The comparative of French adjectives is generally rendered as *plus . . . que* (more . . . than) or *moins . . . que* (less . . . than): *je suis plus grande que lui,* I'm taller than he; *ils sont moins intelligents que toi,* they're less intelligent than you.

The superlative of French adjectives usually follows the formula: (definite article + noun) + definite article + *plus/moins* + adjective (*elle est l'étudiante la plus travailleuse,* she is the hardest-working student; *il est le moins connu,* he's the least well-known; *les voitures les plus rapides,* the fastest cars).

Like their English counterparts *good* and *bad,* the adjectives *bon* and *mauvais* have irregular comparative and superlative forms:

Positive	Comparative	Superlative
c'est ***bon,*** it is good	*c'est* ***meilleur*** *que les autres,* it is better than the rest	*c'est* ***le meilleur*** *de tous,* it is the best (one) of all
c'est ***mauvais,*** it is bad	*c'est* ***pire*** *que les autres,* it is worse than the rest	*c'est* ***le pire*** *de tous,* it is the worst (one) of all

The absolute superlative is most often formed by placing *très,* or other adverbs such as *fort, extrêmement,* etc., before the adjective (*elle est très sympathique,* she is very nice; *c'est fort probable,* it is quite likely).

Adverbs

French adverbs are often formed by adding the adverbial suffix *-ment* to an adjective (*facile* → *facilement, prétendu* → *prétendument*). If the masculine form of an adjective ends with a consonant, the suffix is normally added to the feminine form (*ouvert* → *ouverte* → *ouvertement*). Adjectives whose masculine form ends in *-ant* or *-ent* will usually form the adverb by replacing this ending with *-amment* or *-emment* (*indépendant* → *indépendamment, prudent* → *prudemment*). A few adjectives add the acute accent to the final *e* to form the adverb (*énorme* → *énormément, expresse* → *expressément*).

As in English, there are many French adverbs that do not stem from an adjective (*assez,* enough; *bien,* well; *déjà,* already; *très,* very, etc.).

Pronouns

1. Personal (Subject) Pronouns

The personal pronouns in French are:

Person	Singular		Plural	
FIRST	**je**	I	**nous**	we
SECOND	**tu**	you (familiar)	**vous**	you[1]
	vous	you (formal)	**vous**	you[1]
THIRD	**il**	he	**ils,**	they
	elle	she	**elles**	
	on	one (*also* they, someone, you, we, people)		

[1] The pronoun *vous* acts as the plural for both the familiar *tu* and the formal *vous.*

FAMILIAR VS. FORMAL

The second person personal pronouns exist in both familiar and formal forms. The familiar forms are generally used when addressing relatives, friends, and children; the formal forms are ordinarily used to show courtesy, respect, or emotional distance.

USAGE OF *ON*

The third person pronoun *on* is an impersonal subject pronoun and is an approximate equivalent of the impersonal *you* or *they* in English (*comment dit-on ça en russe?,* how do you say it in Russian?; *on a fermé la pharmacie,* they've closed the drugstore).

2. Disjunctive Pronouns

The disjunctive pronouns in French are:

Singular		Plural	
moi	I, me	**nous**	us, we
toi	you	**vous**	you
vous	you (formal)	**vous**	you
lui	him	**eux**	them, they (masculine or mixed)
elle	her	**elles**	them, they (feminine)
soi[1]	oneself		

[1] Used in impersonal constructions (*travailler chez soi,* to work out of one's home)

Disjunctive pronouns are used:

- as the objects of prepositions (*est-ce pour moi?,* is it for me?; *il le leur a donné,* he gave it to them).
- after *c'est* or *ce sont* (*c'est moi,* it is I, it's me; *ce sont elles,* it is they, it's them).
- to add emphasis to, or merely to complement, the subject of a sentence (*c'est elle qui les a achetés,* she's the one who bought them; *il arrive toujours en retard, lui,* he always arrives late).
- in comparisons (*Danielle est plus sportive qu'eux,* Danielle is more athletic than they).
- in compound subjects (*Louis et moi, nous travaillons ensemble,* Louis and I work together).

3. Object Pronouns

DIRECT OBJECT PRONOUNS

Direct object pronouns represent the goal or result of the action of a verb (*Corinne va appeler Charlotte,* Corinne is going to call Charlotte → *Corinne va l'appeler,* Corinne is going to call her; *Jean-Luc a vu Michel et Isabelle,* Jean-Luc saw Michel and Isabelle → *Jean-Luc les a vus,* Jean-Luc saw them). The direct object pronouns in French are:

Singular		Plural	
me, m'[1]	me	**nous**	us
te, t'[1]	you (informal)	**vous**	you (informal and formal)
vous	you (formal)		
le, l'	him, it	**les**	them (masculine, feminine, or mixed)
la, l'	her, it		

[1]These become *moi* or *toi* in affirmative commands: *ne me regarde pas!,* don't look at me!; *regarde-moi!,* look at me!

INDIRECT OBJECT PRONOUNS

Indirect object pronouns represent the secondary goal of the action of a verb (*il m'a donné le cadeau,* he gave me the gift; *je leur ai dit non,* I told them no; *ils lui ont téléphoné hier,* they phoned her yesterday). The indirect object pronouns in French are:

Singular		Plural	
me, m'	(to, for, from) me	**nous**	(to, for, from) us
te, t'	(to, for, from) you	**vous**	(to, for, from) you
lui	(to, for, from) him, her	**leur**	(to, for, from) them

Position of Object Pronouns

The position of the object pronoun in French syntax differs from its English counterpart. The object pronoun can be found before the verb of which it is the object (*je ne peux pas la voir,* I can't see her; *Alice le lit,* Alice is reading it). In affirmative commands, the object pronoun follows the imperative and is linked to it by a hyphen (*écoutez-moi!*, listen to me!). In negative commands, the object pronoun precedes the verb (*ne les achète pas*, don't buy them).

Adverbial Pronouns *y* and *en*

The adverbial pronoun *y* is used to replace many prepositional phrases introduced by *à/dans/en* (+ article and/or adjective) + noun (but not the name of a person). *Y* is ordinarily placed immediately before the verb of which it is the object:

> *il faut répondre à leurs questions*, you have to answer their questions → *il faut y répondre*, you have to answer
>
> *je consens à l'examination*, I consent to the examination → *j'y consens*, I consent, I consent to it

In affirmative commands, *y* appears after the verb and is joined to it by a hyphen:

> *n'y pense pas!* don't think about it! → *penses-y!* think about it!

The pronoun *en* is frequently used to replace phrases consisting of *de* (+ article and/or adjective) + noun. Like *y*, *en* is placed immediately before the verb of which it is the object:

> *nous aurons besoin d'argent*, we'll need money → *nous en aurons besoin*, we'll need some
>
> *ils parlaient des impôts*, they were talking about taxes → *ils en parlaient*, they were talking about it
>
> *combien de pages as-tu lues?* how many pages have you read? → *j'en ai lu une centaine*, I've read about a hundred
>
> *Jean leur a donné de la nourriture*, Jean gave them some food → *Jean leur en a donné*, Jean gave them some

Word Order of Object Pronouns

When several object pronouns precede the verb, the following order applies:

me	→	*le*	→	*lui*	→	*y*	→	*en*	→	*verb*
te		*la*		*leur*						
nous		*les*								
vous										

For example:

ne le lui donne pas, don't give it to him

ne lui en donne pas, don't give any to him, don't give him any

je ne m'y fie plus, I no longer rely on it

When several object pronouns follow the verb (as in affirmative commands), the order is:

verb →	*le* →	*moi* →	*y* →	*en*
	la	*toi*		
	les	*lui*		
		nous		
		vous		
		leur		

For example:

donnez-leur en!, give them some!

envoie-le moi, send it to me

4. Reflexive Pronouns

Reflexive pronouns are used to refer back to the subject of the verb (*je m'habille,* I'm getting dressed, I'm dressing myself; *ils se préparent,* they're getting ready, they're preparing themselves). The reflexive pronouns in French are:

Singular		Plural	
me[1]	myself	**nous**	ourselves
te[1]	yourself	**vous**	yourselves
se[1]	yourself, himself, herself, itself	**se**[1]	yourselves, themselves

[1] These pronouns drop the final *e* when followed by words beginning with a vowel sound: *s'accoutumer, je m'y défends, ils s'habillent,* etc.

Reflexive pronouns normally appear before the verb (*ne t'en fais pas,* don't worry about it; *il faut que tu te dépêches,* you must hurry), but they are placed immediately after the verb in affirmative commands (*dépêchez-vous!* hurry!, hurry up!).

In the plural, reflexive pronouns can indicate reciprocal action (*nous nous voyons fréquemment,* we see each other frequently; *ils ne se parlent plus,* they no longer speak to each other).

It should be noted that many verbs which take reflexive pronouns in French have intransitive equivalents in English (*se coucher,* to lie down; *se réveiller,* to wake up; *s'en aller,* to leave, etc.).

5. Relative Pronouns

Relative pronouns introduce subordinate clauses or modifiers (*les fleurs que nous avons cueillies,* the flowers that we gathered; *les filles dont tu as fait la connaissance,* the girls whom you met). In French, the relative pronouns are:

que[1] (that, which, who, whom)

qui (that, which, who)

quoi (what)

où (where)

lequel, laquelle, lesquels, lesquelles (which)

dont (of which, of whom, whose)

[1]Contracts to *qu'* when followed by a word beginning with a vowel sound

The relative pronoun *qui* refers to the subject of the relative clause, regardless of whether it is a person or thing, while the pronoun *que* refers to its object:

le livre qui est sur le bureau	the book that/ which is on the desk	(*livre* is the subject)
le livre que j'aime	the book (that) I like	(*livre* is the object)

Quoi refers to things only and is used after prepositions:

on aura de quoi causer, people will have plenty to talk about

quelque chose sur quoi s'appuyer, something to lean on

Où also refers exclusively to things and can be used to refer to time as well as place:

le pays d'où tu viens, the country you come from

le jour où nous sommes partis, the day (on which) we left

The pronoun *lequel* varies for gender and number: *lequel* (masculine singular), *laquelle* (feminine singular), *lesquels* (masculine plural), *lesquelles* (feminine plural). Because the first component of this pronoun is the definite article *le,* it observes the same rules of contraction that apply to the masculine singular article *le* and the plural article *les* (see the section Definite Article on page 23a) and combines with the prepositions *à* and *de* to form the following:

à	+	*lequel*	→	*auquel*
à	+	*lesquels*	→	*auxquels*
à	+	*lesquelles*	→	*auxquelles*
de	+	*lequel*	→	*duquel*
de	+	*lesquels*	→	*desquels*
de	+	*lesquelles*	→	*desquelles*

des amis auxquels j'écris souvent, friends to whom I often write

un dîner au cours duquel un prix sera décerné, a dinner in the course of which a prize will be awarded

l'adresse à laquelle vous recevez votre courrier, the address at which you receive your mail

The relative pronoun *dont* can often be used in place of *de qui, de laquelle, duquel, desquels,* and *desquelles,* except after a preposition:

l'organisation dont il est le chef, the organization of which he is the head

tout ce dont elle a envie, all that she desires

les choses dont nous avons parlé, the things we talked about

Possessives

1. Possessive Adjectives

French possessive adjectives precede the nouns they modify. Unlike their English counterparts, they agree in both gender and number with the noun they precede, and not with their possessor (*il a mis sa chemise,* he put on his shirt; *mes chaussures,* my shoes; *notre voiture,* our car; *nos voitures,* our cars). Plural possessive adjectives do not vary for gender (*mes cousins, mes cousines*).

Singular Masculine	Singular Feminine	Plural	English Equivalent
mon	**ma**	**mes**	my
ton	**ta**	**tes**	your (informal)
son	**sa**	**ses**	his, her
notre	**notre**	**nos**	our
votre	**votre**	**vos**	your (formal and/or plural)
leur	**leur**	**leurs**	their

The feminine adjectives *ma, ta,* and *sa* change to the masculine forms *mon, ton,* and *son* when immediately followed by a word with an initial vowel sound (*mon amie, son histoire*).

2. Possessive Pronouns

French possessive pronouns are always preceded by the definite article, and they agree in number and gender with the nouns they replace (*mes clefs,* my keys → *les miennes,* mine; *nos gants,* our gloves → *les nôtres,* ours).

Sing. Masc.	Sing. Fem.	English Equivalent
le mien	**la mienne**	mine
le tien	**la tienne**	yours (informal)

continued

Sing. Masc.	Sing. Fem.	English Equivalent
le sien	**la sienne**	his, hers
le nôtre	**la nôtre**	ours
le vôtre	**la vôtre**	yours (formal and/or plural)
le leur	**la leur**	theirs

Plural Masc.	Plural Fem.	English Equivalent
les miens	**les miennes**	mine
les tiens	**les tiennes**	yours (informal)
les siens	**les siennes**	his, hers
les nôtres	**les nôtres**	ours
les vôtres	**les vôtres**	yours (formal)
les leurs	**les leurs**	theirs

Demonstratives

1. Demonstrative Adjectives

French demonstrative adjectives agree with the nouns they modify in gender and number, and precede them in a sentence. The demonstrative adjectives in French are:

ce masculine singular: *ce mur,* this wall

cet masculine singular, used when the following word begins with a vowel sound: *cet homme,* that man

cette feminine singular: *cette femme,* this woman

ces plural, does not vary for gender: *ces hommes,* these men; *ces femmes,* those women

When the difference between "this" and "that" or "these" and "those" cannot be ascertained from context, or if one wishes to stress the difference, the suffixes *-ci* and *-là* are added to the noun: *cet homme-ci,* this (particular) man; *ces hommes-là,* those (particular) men.

2. Demonstrative Pronouns

Demonstrative pronouns are used in place of a noun modified by *ce, cette,* or *ces* as outlined below:

CELUI AND VARIANTS

Pronouns belonging to the *celui* group always agree in gender and number with the noun which they replace. The pronouns are:

celui	masculine singular
ceux	masculine plural
celle	feminine singular
celles	feminine plural

j'ai reçu deux colis: le tien, et celui de ma sœur, I received two packages: yours, and my sister's

ceux qu'elle préfère sont plus chers, the ones she prefers are more costly

celles qui ont travaillé le plus sont Rose et Marie, the ones who worked the most are Rose and Marie

te souviens-tu de ce qu'elle t'a dit?, do you remember what she told you?

The suffixes *-ci* and *-là* are attached to the pronouns *celui, ceux, celle,* or *celles* for emphasis:

celui-ci est plus important que celui-là, this one is more important than that one

emporte-moi ceux-là, bring me those

CE

Ce does not change for gender and combines with *être* to form a rough equivalent of the English "it is" or "they are," but it differs somewhat in usage and application from its English counterpart. Note that *ce* contracts to *c'* when immediately followed by a vowel sound:

ce sont mes amis, they are my friends

ce sont eux qui me l'ont acheté, they're the ones who bought it for me

c'est chouette!, that's great!

c'est un médecin, he's a doctor, she's a doctor

est-ce vrai?, is it true?

ÇA, CECI, AND *CELA*

The demonstrative pronouns *ça, ceci,* and *cela* act as rough equivalents of the English "this" or "that," with some differences in usage and application:

ça m'est égal, it's all the same to me, it doesn't matter to me

oui, c'est ça!, yes, that's it!

ceci n'est qu'un test, this is only a test

ceci et cela, this and that

Although *cela* and *ça* are often interchangeable, *ça* tends to be used more frequently in spoken French.

Conjugation of French Verbs

Simple Tenses

Tense	Regular verbs ending in -ER PARLER	
PRESENT INDICATIVE	je parle tu parles il parle	nous parlons vous parlez ils parlent
PRESENT SUBJUNCTIVE	je parle tu parles il parle	nous parlions vous parliez ils parlent
PRETERIT INDICATIVE	je parlai tu parlas il parla	nous parlâmes vous parlâtes ils parlèrent
IMPERFECT INDICATIVE	je parlais tu parlais il parlait	nous parlions vous parliez ils parlaient
IMPERFECT SUBJUNCTIVE	je parlasse tu parlasses il parlât	nous parlassions vous parlassiez ils parlassent
FUTURE INDICATIVE	je parlerai tu parleras il parlera	nous parlerons vous parlerez ils parleront
CONDITIONAL	je parlerais tu parlerais il parlerait	nous parlerions vous parleriez ils parleraient
IMPERATIVE	parle, parlez	parlons parlez
PRESENT PARTICIPLE (GERUND)	parlant	
PAST PARTICIPLE	parlé	

Tense	Regular verbs ending in -IR GRANDIR	
PRESENT INDICATIVE	je grandis tu grandis il grandit	nous grandissons vous grandissez ils grandissent
PRESENT SUBJUNCTIVE	je grandisse tu grandisses il grandisse	nous grandissions vous grandissiez ils grandissent
PRETERIT INDICATIVE	je grandis tu grandis il grandit	nous grandîmes vous grandîtes ils grandirent
IMPERFECT INDICATIVE	je grandissais tu grandissais il grandissait	nous grandissions vous grandissiez ils grandissaient
IMPERFECT SUBJUNCTIVE	je grandisse tu grandisses il grandît	nous grandissions vous grandissiez ils grandissent
FUTURE INDICATIVE	je grandirai tu grandiras il grandira	nous grandirons vous grandirez ils grandiront
CONDITIONAL	je grandirais tu grandirais il grandirait	nous grandirions vous grandiriez ils grandiraient
IMPERATIVE	grandis, grandissez	grandissons grandissez
PRESENT PARTICIPLE (GERUND)	grandissant	
PAST PARTICIPLE	grandi	

Perfect Tenses

The perfect tenses are formed with *avoir* and the past participle:

PRESENT PERFECT

j'ai parlé, nous avons parlé, etc. (*indicative*)
j'aie parlé, nous ayons parlé, etc. (*subjunctive*)

PAST PERFECT

j'avais parlé, nous avions parlé, etc. (*indicative*)
j'eusse parlé, nous eussions parlé, etc. (*subjunctive*)

PRETERIT PERFECT

j'eus parlé, nous eûmes parlé, etc.

FUTURE PERFECT

j'aurai parlé, nous aurons parlé, etc.

CONDITIONAL PERFECT

j'aurais parlé, nous aurions parlé, etc.
or
j'eusse parlé, nous eussions parlé, etc.

PAST IMPERATIVE

aie parlé, ayons parlé, ayez parlé

The perfect tenses of the following verbs are formed with *être*:

aller, arriver, décéder, devenir, échoir, éclore, entrer, mourir, naître, partir, repartir, rentrer, rester, retourner, sortir, tomber, venir, revenir, parvenir, survenir

For example, the present perfect of *arriver* would be as follows:

je suis arrivé, nous sommes arrivés, etc. (*indicative*)

Irregular Verbs

The *imperfect subjunctive*, the *conditional*, and the first and second person plural of the *imperative* are not included in the model conjugations list but can be derived from other verb forms:

The *imperfect subjunctive* is formed by using the second person singular of the preterit indicative, removing the final *s*, and adding the following suffixes: *-sse, -sses, -t* (and adding a circumflex accent on the preceding vowel), *-ssions, -ssiez, -ssent*. *Servir* is conjugated as follows:

PRETERIT INDICATIVE, SECOND PERSON SINGULAR	servis – *s* = servi
IMPERFECT SUBJUNCTIVE	je servisse, tu servisses, il servît, nous servissions, vous servissiez, ils servissent

The conditional is formed by using the stem of the future indicative and adding the following suffixes : *-ais, -ais, -ait, -ions, -iez,- aient*. *Prendre* is conjugated as follows:

FUTURE INDICATIVE	je prendrai – *ai* = prendr
CONDITIONAL	je prendrais, tu prendrais, il prendrait, nous prendrions, vous prendriez, ils prendraient

The first and second person plural of the *imperative* are the same as the corresponding forms of the present indicative.

Model Conjugations of Irregular Verbs

The model conjugations below include the following simple tenses : the *present indicative* (*IND*), the *present subjunctive* (*SUBJ*), the *preterit indicative* (*PRET*), the *imperfect indicative* (*IMPF*), the *future indicative* (*FUT*), the second person singular form of the *imperative* (*IMPER*), the *present participle* or *gerund* (*PRP*), and the *past participle* (*PP*). Each set of conjugations is preceded by the corresponding infinitive form of the verb, shown in bold type. Only tenses containing irregularities are listed, and the irregular verb forms within each tense are displayed in bold type.

Also note that some conjugated verbs are labeled *defective verb*. This refers to a verb lacking one or more of the usual forms of grammatical inflection (tense, mood, etc.), for example, in French, the verbs *bruire* and *ouïr*.

Each irregular verb entry in the French-English section of this dictionary is cross-referred by number to one of the following model conjugations. These cross-reference numbers are shown in curly braces { } immediately preceding the entry's functional label.

The three main categories of verbs are:

1) Verbs ending in -ER

2) Verbs ending in -IR

Present indicative endings for verbs in these categories are:

-is, -is, -it, -issons, -issez, -issent

For example, *j'arrondis, nous arrondissons,* etc. for infinitive *arrondir*

3) Verbs ending in -IR/-OIR/-RE

Present indicative endings for verbs in these categories are:

-e, -es, -e, -ons, -ez, -ent

For example, *j'accueille, nous accueillons,* etc. for infinitive *accueillir*

or

-s(x), -s(x), -t(d), -ons, -ez, -ent

For example, *je rends, nous rendons,* etc. for infinitive *rendre*

Note that in the third group there are two different sets of endings for both the present indicative and preterit indicative depending on the verb in question, as shown above for the present indicative. For clarity, these forms are included in the model conjugations in an attempt to prevent the reader from inadvertently choosing the wrong endings.

1 **absoudre :** *IND* **j'absous, tu absous, il absout, nous absolvons, vous absolvez, ils absolvent;** *SUBJ* **j'absolve, tu absolves, il absolve, nous absolvions, vous absolviez, ils absolvent;** *PRET* (*not used*); *IMPF* **j'absolvais, tu absolvais, il absolvait, nous absolvions, vous absolviez, ils absolvaient;** *IMPER* **absous;** *PRP* **absolvant;** *PP* **absous**

2 **accroire** (*defective verb*) *Used only in the infinitive*

3 **accueillir** : *IND* **j'accueille, tu accueilles, il accueille,** nous accueillons, vous accueillez, ils accueillent; *PRET* **j'accueillis, tu accueillis, il accueillit, nous accueillîmes, vous accueillîtes, ils accueillirent;** *FUT* **j'accueillerai, tu accueilleras, il accueillera, nous accueillerons, vous accueillerez, ils accueilleront;** *IMPER* **accueille**

4 **advenir** (*defective verb) Used only in the infinitive and in the following tenses* : *IND* **il advient;** *SUBJ* **il advienne;** *PRET* **il advint;** *IMPF* **il advenait;** *FUT* **il adviendra;** *PRP* **advenant;** *PP* **advenu**

5 **aller** : *IND* **je vais, tu vas, il va, nous allons, vous allez, ils vont;** *SUBJ* **j'aille, tu ailles, il aille, nous allions, vous alliez, ils aillent;** *FUT* **j'irai, tu iras, il ira, nous irons, vous irez, ils iront;** *IMPER* **va**

6 **annoncer** : *IND* j'annonce, tu annonces, il annonce, **nous annonçons,** vous annoncez, ils annoncent; *PRET* **j'annonçai, tu annonças, il annonça, nous annonçâmes, vous annonçâtes, ils annoncèrent;** *IMPF* **j'annonçais, tu annonçais, il annonçait,** nous annoncions, vous annonciez, **ils annonçaient;** *PRP* **annonçant**

7 **apparaître** : *IND* **j'apparais, tu apparais, il apparaît, nous apparaissons, vous apparaissez, ils apparaissent;** *SUBJ* **j'apparaisse, tu apparaisses, il apparaisse, nous apparaissions, vous appparaissiez, ils apparaissent;** *PRET* **j'apparus, tu apparus, il apparut, nous apparûmes, vous apparûtes, ils apparurent;** *IMPF* **j'apparaissais, tu apparaissais, il apparaissait, nous apparaissions, vous apparaissiez, ils apparaissaient;** *IMPER* **apparais;** *PRP* **apparaissant;** *PP* **apparu**

8 **appeler** : *IND* **j'appelle, tu appelles, il appelle,** nous appelons, vous appelez, **ils appellent;** *SUBJ* **j'appelle, tu appelles, il appelle,** nous appelions, vous appeliez, **ils appellent;** *FUT* **j'appellerai, tu appelleras, il appellera, nous appellerons, vous appellerez, ils appelleront;** *IMPER* **appelle**

9 **asseoir** : *IND* **j'assieds** *or* **j'assois, tu assieds** *or* **tu assois, il assied** *or* **il assoit, nous asseyons** *or* **nous assoyons, vous asseyez** *or* **vous assoyez, ils asseyent** *or* **ils assoient;** *SUBJ* **j'asseye** *or* **j'assoie, tu asseyes** *or* **tu assoies, il asseye** *or* **il assoie, nous asseyions** *or* **nous assoyions, vous asseyiez** *or*

vous assoyiez, ils asseyent *or* **ils assoient;** *PRET* **j'assis, tu assis, il assit, nous assîmes, vous assîtes, ils assirent;** *IMPF* **j'asseyais** *or* **j'assoyais, tu asseyais** *or* **tu assoyais, il asseyait** *or* **il assoyait, nous asseyions** *or* **nous assoyions, vous asseyiez** *or* **vous assoyiez, ils asseyaient** *or* **ils assoyaient;** *FUT* (*not used*); *IMPER* **assieds** *or* **assois;** *PRP* **asseyant** *or* **assoyant;** *PP* **assis**

10 **avoir :** *IND* **j'ai, tu as, il a, nous avons, vous avez, ils ont;** *SUBJ* **j'aie, tu aies, il ait, nous ayons, vous ayez, ils aient;** *PRET* **j'eus, tu eus, il eut, nous eûmes, vous eûtes, ils eurent;** *IMPF* **j'avais, tu avais, il avait, nous avions, vous aviez, ils avaient;** *FUT* **j'aurai, tu auras, il aura, nous aurons, vous aurez, ils auront;** *IMPER* **aie, ayons ayez;** *PRP* **ayant;** *PP* **eu**

11 **balayer :** *IND* **je balaie** *or* je balaye, **tu balaies** *or* tu balayes, **il balaie** *or* il balaye, nous balayons, vous balayez, **ils balaient** *or* ils balayent; *SUBJ* **je balaie** *or* je balaye, **tu balaies** *or* tu balayes, **il balaie** *or* il balaye, nous balayions, vous balayiez, **ils balaient** *or* ils balayent; *FUT* **je balaierai** *or* je balayerai, **tu balaieras** *or* tu balayeras, **il balaiera** *or* il balayera, **nous balaierons** *or* nous balayerons, **vous balaierez** *or* vous balayerez, **ils balaieront** *or* ils balayeront; *IMPER* **balaie** *or* balaye

12 **battre :** *IND* **je bats, tu bats, il bat,** nous battons, vous battez, ils battent; *PRET* **je battis, tu battis, il battit, nous battîmes, vous battîtes, ils battirent;** *IMPER* **bats;** *PP* **battu**

13 **boire :** *IND* je bois, tu bois, il boit, **nous buvons, vous buvez, ils boivent;** *SUBJ* **je boive, tu boives, il boive, nous buvions, vous buviez, ils boivent;** *PRET* **je bus, tu bus, il but, nous bûmes, vous bûtes, ils burent;** *IMPF* **je buvais, tu buvais, il buvait, nous buvions, vous buviez, ils buvaient;** *PRP* **buvant;** *PP* **bu**

14 **bouillir :** *IND* **je bous, tu bous, il bout,** nous bouillons, vous bouillez, ils bouillent; *PRET* **je bouillis, tu bouillis, il bouillit, nous bouillîmes, vous bouillîtes, ils bouillirent;** *IMPER* **bous**

15 **braire** (*defective verb*) *Used only in the infinitive and in the following tenses* : *IND* **il brait, ils braient;** *IMPF* **brayait, brayaient;** *FUT* **il braira, ils brairont**

16 **bruire** (*defective verb*) *Used only in the infinitive and in the following tenses* : *IND* **il bruit, ils bruissent;** *SUBJ* (*not used*); *PRET* (*not used*); *IMPF* **il bruissait, ils bruissaient;** *PRP* **bruissant;** *PP* **bruit**

17 **changer** : *IND* je change, tu changes, il change, **nous changeons,** vous changez, ils changent; *PRET* **je changeai, tu changeas, il changea, nous changeâmes, vous changeâtes, ils changèrent;** *IMPF* **je changeais, tu changeais, il changeait,** nous changions, vous changiez, **ils changeaient;** *PRP* **changeant**

18 **choir** (*defective verb*) *Used only in the following tenses* : *IND* **je chois, tu chois, il choit, ils choient;** *SUBJ* (*not used*); *PRET* **il chut;** *IMPF* (*not used*); *FUT* il choira; *IMPER* (*not used*); *PRP* (*not used*); *PP* **chu**

19 **clore** (*defective verb*) *Used only in the following tenses* : *IND* je clos, tu clos, **il clôt, ils closent;** *SUBJ* **je close, tu closes, il close, nous closions, vous closiez, ils closent;** *PRET* (*not used*); *IMPF* (*not used*); *FUT* (*used but regularly formed*); *PRP* **closant;** *PP* **clos**

20 **congeler** : *IND* **je congèle, tu congèles, il congèle,** nous congelons, vous congelez, **ils congèlent;** *SUBJ* **je congèle, tu congèles, il congèle,** nous congelions, vous congeliez, **ils congèlent;** *FUT* **je congèlerai, tu congèleras, il congèlera, nous congèlerons, vous congèlerez, ils congèleront;** *IMPER* **congèle**

21 **conquérir** : *IND* **je conquiers, tu conquiers, il conquiert,** nous conquérons, vous conquérez, **ils conquièrent;** *SUBJ* **je conquière, tu conquières, il conquière,** nous conquérions, vous conquériez, **ils conquièrent;** *PRET* **je conquis, tu conquis, il conquit, nous conquîmes, vous conquîtes, ils conquirent;** *FUT* **je conquerrai, tu conquerras, il conquerra, nous conquerrons, vous conquerrez, ils conquerront;** *IMPER* **conquiers;** *PP* **conquis**

22 **coudre** : *IND* je couds, tu couds, il coud, **nous cousons, vous cousez, ils cousent;** *SUBJ* **je couse, tu couses, il couse, nous cousions, vous cousiez, ils cousent;** *PRET* **je cousis, tu cousis, il cousit, nous cousîmes, vous cousîtes, ils cousirent;** *IMPF* **je cousais, tu cousais, il cousait, nous cousions, vous cousiez, ils cousaient;** *PRP* **cousant;** *PP* **cousu**

23 **courir** : *IND* **je cours, tu cours, il court,** nous courons, vous courez, ils courent; *PRET* **je courus, tu courus, il courut, nous courûmes, vous courûtes, ils coururent;** *FUT* **je courrai, tu courras, il courra, nous courrons, vous courrez, ils courront;** *IMPER* **cours;** *PP* **couru**

24 **croire** : *IND* je crois, tu crois, il croit, **nous croyons, vous croyez,** ils croient; *SUBJ* je croie, tu croies, il croie, **nous croyions, vous croyiez,** ils croient; *PRET* **je crus, tu crus, il crut, nous crûmes, vous crûtes, il crurent;** *IMPF* **je croyais, tu croyais, il croyait, nous croyions, vous croyiez, ils croyaient;** *PRP* **croyant;** *PP* **cru**

25 **croître** : *IND* **je croîs, tu croîs, il croît, nous croissons, vous croissez, ils croissent;** *SUBJ* **je croisse, tu croisses, il croisse, nous croissions, vous croissiez, ils croissent;** *PRET* **je crûs, tu crûs, il crût, nous crûmes, vous crûtes, ils crûrent;** *IMPF* **je croissais, tu croissais, il croissait, nous croissions, vous croissiez, ils croissaient;** *IMPER* **croîs;** *PRP* **croissant;** *PP* **crû**

26 **décevoir** : *IND* **je déçois, tu déçois, il déçoit,** nous décevons, vous décevez, **ils déçoivent;** *SUBJ* **je déçoive, tu déçoives, il déçoive,** nous décevions, vous déceviez, **ils déçoivent;** *PRET* **je déçus, tu déçus, il déçut, nous déçûmes, vous déçûtes, ils déçurent;** *IMPER* **déçois;** *PP* **déçu**

27 **déchoir** (*defective verb*) *Used only in the following tenses* : *IND* je déchois, tu déchois, il déchoit *or* **il déchet, nous déchoyons, vous déchoyez, ils déchoient;** *SUBJ* je déchoie, tu déchoies, il déchoie, **nous déchoyions, vous déchoyiez, ils déchoient;** *PRET* **je déchus, tu déchus, il déchut, nous déchûmes, vous déchûtes, ils déchurent;** *IMPF* (*not used*); *FUT* (*used but regularly formed*); *IMPER* (*not used*); *PRP* (*not used*); *PP* **déchu**

28 **devoir** : *IND* **je dois, tu dois, il doit,** nous devons, vous devez, **ils doivent;** *SUBJ* **je doive, tu doives, il doive,** nous devions, vous deviez, **ils doivent;** *PRET* **je dus, tu dus, il dut, nous dûmes, vous dûtes, ils durent;** *IMPER* **dois;** *PRP* **dû**

29 **dire** : *IND* je dis, tu dis, il dit, **nous disons, vous dites, ils disent;** *SUBJ* **je dise, tu dises, il dise, nous disions, vous disiez, ils disent;** *PRET* **je dis, tu dis, il dit, nous dîmes,**

vous dîtes, ils dirent; *IMPF* **je disais, tu disais, il disait, nous disions, vous disiez, ils disent;** *PRP* **disant;** *PP* **dit**

30 **dormir** : *IND* **je dors, tu dors, il dort,** nous dormons, vous dormez, ils dorment; *PRET* **je dormis, tu dormis, il dormit, nous dormîmes, vous dormîtes, ils dormirent;** *IMPER* **dors**

31 **échoir** (*defective verb*) *Used only in the following tenses* : *IND* **il échoit, ils échoient;** *SUBJ* **il échoie;** *PRET* **il échut, ils échurent;** *IMPF* (not used); *FUT* il échoira *or* **il écherra;** ils échoiront *or* **ils écherront;** *IMPER* (not used); *PRP* **échéant;** *PP* **échu**

32 **éclore** (*defective verb*) *Used only in the following tenses* : *IND* **il éclot;** *PP* **éclos**

33 **écrire** : *IND* j'écris, tu écris, il écrit, **nous écrivons, vous écrivez, ils écrivent;** *SUBJ* **j'écrive, tu écrives, il écrive, nous écrivions, vous écriviez, ils écrivent;** *PRET* **j'écrivis, tu écrivis, il écrivit, nous écrivîmes, vous écrivîtes, ils écrivirent;** *IMPF* **j'écrivais, tu écrivais, il écrivait, nous écrivions, vous écriviez, ils écrivaient;** *PRP* **écrivant;** *PP* **écrit**

34 **enclore** (*defective verb*) *Used only in the following tenses* : *IND* j'enclos, tu enclos, il enclot, **nous enclosons, vous enclosez, ils enclosent;** *SUBJ* **j'enclose, tu encloses, il enclose, nous enclosions, vous enclosiez, ils enclosent;** *PRET* (*not used*); *IMPF* (*not used*); *FUT* (*used but regularly formed*); *IMPER* enclos; *PRP* **enclosant;** *PP* **enclos**

35 **ensuivre (s')** (*defective verb*) *Used only in the following tenses* : *IND* **il s'ensuit;** *SUBJ* **il s'ensuive;** *PRET* **il s'ensuivit;** *IMPF* **il s'ensuivait;** *FUT* **il s'ensuivra;** *PP* **s'ensuivi**

36 **envoyer** : *IND* **j'envoie, tu envoies, il envoie,** nous envoyons, vous envoyez, **ils envoient;** *SUBJ* **j'envoie, tu envoies, il envoie,** nous envoyions, vous envoyiez, **ils envoient;** *FUT* **j'enverrai, tu enverras, il enverra, nous enverrons, vous enverrez, ils enverront;** *IMPER* **envoie**

37 **éteindre** : *IND* **j'éteins, tu éteins, il éteint, nous éteignons, vous éteignez, ils éteignent;** *SUBJ* **j'éteigne, tu éteignes, il éteigne, nous éteignions, vous éteigniez, ils éteignent;** *PRET* **j'éteignis, tu éteignis, il éteignit, nous éteignîmes, vous éteignîtes, ils éteignirent;** *IMPF* **j'éteignais, tu éteignais, il**

éteignait, nous éteignions, vous éteigniez, ils éteignaient; *IMPER* **éteins;** *PRP* **éteignant;** *PP* **éteint**

38 **être :** *IND* **je suis, tu es, il est, nous sommes, vous êtes, ils sont;** *SUBJ* **je sois, tu sois, il soit, nous soyons, vous soyez, ils soient;** *PRET* **je fus, tu fus, il fut, nous fûmes, vous fûtes, ils furent;** *IMPF* **j'étais, tu étais, il était, nous étions, vous étiez, ils étaient;** *FUT* **je serai, tu seras, il sera, nous serons, vous serez, ils seront;** *IMPER* **sois;** *PRP* **étant;** *PP* **été**

39 **exclure :** *IND* **j'exclus, tu exclus, il exclut, nous excluons, vous excluez, ils excluent;** *PRET* **j'exclus, tu exclus, il exclut, nous exclûmes, vous exclûtes, ils exclurent;** *IMPER* **exclus;** *PP* **exclu**

40 **extraire :** *IND* j'extrais, tu extrais, il extrait, **nous extrayons, vous extrayez,** ils extraient; *SUBJ* j'extraie, tu extraies, il extraie, **nous extrayions, vous extrayiez,** ils extraient; *PRET* (not used); *IMPF* **j'extrayais, tu extrayais, il extrayait, nous extrayions, vous extrayiez, ils extrayaient;** *PRP* **extrayant;** *PP* **extrait**

41 **faillir** (*defective verb) Used only in the infinitive and as a* PP **failli**

42 **faire :** *IND* je fais, tu fais, il fait, **nous faisons, vous faites, ils font;** *SUBJ* **je fasse, tu fasses, il fasse, nous fassions, vous fassiez, ils fassent;** *PRET* **je fis, tu fis, il fit, nous fîmes, vous fîtes, ils firent;** *IMPF* **je faisais, tu faisais, il faisait, nous faisions, vous faisiez, ils faisaient;** *FUT* **je ferai, tu feras, il fera, nous ferons, vous ferez, ils feront;** *PRP* **faisant;** *PP* **fait**

43 **falloir** (*defective verb*) *Used only in the following tenses* : *IND* **il faut;** *SUBJ* **il faille;** *PRET* **il fallut;** *IMPF* **il fallait;** *FUT* **il faudra;** *IMPER* (not used); *PRP* (*not used*); *PP* **fallu**

44 **forfaire** (*defective verb) Used only in the infinitive and in the following tenses* : *IND* **il forfait;** *PP* **forfait**

45 **frire** (*defective verb*) *Used only in the following tenses* : *IND* **je fris, tu fris, il frit;** *FUT* je frirai, tu friras, il frira, nous frirons, vous frirez, ils friront; *IMPER* **fris;** *PP* **frit**

46 **fuir :** *IND* je fuis, tu fuis, il fuit, **nous fuyons, vous fuyez, ils fuient;** *SUBJ* je fuie, tu fuies, il fuie, **nous fuyions, vous**

fuyiez, ils fuient; *PRET* je fuis, tu fuis, il fuit, **nous fuîmes, vous fuîtes, ils fuirent**; *IMPF* **je fuyais, tu fuyais, il fuyait, nous fuyions, vous fuyiez, ils fuyaient**; *PRP* **fuyant**; *PP* **fui**

47 **gésir** (*defective verb*) *Used only in the following tenses* : *IND* **je gis, tu gis, il gît, nous gisons, vous gisez, ils gisent**; *IMPF* **je gisais, tu gisais, il gisait, nous gisions, vous gisiez, ils gisaient**; *PRP* **gisant**

48 **haïr** : *IND* **je hais, tu hais, il hait, nous haïssons, vous haïssez, ils haïssent**; *SUBJ* **je haïsse, tu haïsses, il haïsse, nous haïssions, vous haïssiez, ils haïssent**; *PRET* **je haïs, tu haïs, il haït, nous haïmes, vous haïtes, ils haïrent**; *IMPF* **je haïssais, tu haïssais, il haïssait, nous haïssions, vous haïsssiez, ils haïssaient**; *IMPER* **hais**; *PRP* **haïssant**; *PP* **haï**

49 **instruire** : *IND* j'instruis, tu instruis, il instruit, **nous instruisons, vous instruisez, ils instruisent**; *SUBJ* **j'instruise, tu instruises, il instruise, nous instruisions, vous instruisiez, ils instruisent**; *PRET* **j'instruisis, tu instruisis, il instruisit, nous instruisîmes, vous instruisîtes, ils instruisirent**; *IMPF* **j'instruisais, tu instruisais, il instruisait, nous instruisions, vous instruisiez, ils instruisaient**; *PRP* **instruisant**; *PP* **instruit**

50 **joindre** : *IND* **je joins, tu joins, il joint, nous joignons, vous joignez, ils joignent**; *SUBJ* **je joigne, tu joignes, il joigne, nous joignions, vous joigniez, ils joignent**; *PRET* **je joignis, tu joignis, il joignit, nous joignîmes, vous joignîtes, ils joignirent**; *IMPF* **je joignais, tu joignais, il joignait, nous joignions, vous joigniez, ils joignaient**; *IMPERF* **joins**; *PRP* **joignant**; *PP* **joint**

51 **lire** : *IND* je lis, tu lis, il lit, **nous lisons, vous lisez, ils lisent**; *SUBJ* **je lise, tu lises, il lise, nous lisions, vous lisiez, ils lisent**; *PRET* **je lus, tu lus, il lut, nous lûmes, vous lûtes, ils lurent**; *IMPF* **je lisais, tu lisais, il lisait, nous lisions, vous lisiez, ils lisaient**; *PRP* **lisant**; *PP* **lu**

52 **mener** : *IND* **je mène, tu mènes, il mène,** nous menons, vous menez, **ils mènent**; *SUBJ* **je mène, tu mènes, il mène,** nous menions, vous meniez, **ils mènent**; *FUT* **je mènerai, tu mèneras, il mènera, nous mènerons, vous mènerez, ils mèneront**; *IMPER* **mène**

53 **mettre** : *IND* **je mets, tu mets, il met,** nous mettons, vous mettez, ils mettent; *PRET* **je mis, tu mis, il mit, nous mîmes, vous mîtes, il mirent;** *IMPER* **mets;** *PP* **mis**

54 **moudre** : *IND* je mouds, tu mouds, il moud, **nous moulons, vous moulez, ils moulent;** *SUBJ* **je moule, tu moules, il moule, nous moulions, vous mouliez, ils moulent;** *PRET* **je moulus, tu moulus, il moulut, nous moulûmes, vous moulûtes, ils moulurent;** *IMPF* **je moulais, tu moulais, il moulait, nous moulions, vous mouliez, ils moulaient;** *PRP* **moulant;** *PP* **moulu**

55 **mourir** : *IND* **je meurs, tu meurs, il meurt,** nous mourons, vous mourez, **ils meurent;** *SUBJ* **je meure, tu meures, il meure,** nous mourions, vous mouriez, **ils meurent;** *PRET* **je mourus, tu mourus, il mourut, nous mourûmes, vous mourûtes, ils moururent;** *FUT* **je mourrai, tu mourras, il mourra, nous mourrons, vous mourrez, ils mourront;** *IMPER* **meurs;** *PRP* **mourant;** *PP* **mort**

56 **mouvoir** : *IND* **je meus, tu meus, il meut,** nous mouvons, vous mouvez, **ils meuvent;** *SUBJ* **je meuve, tu meuves, il meuve,** nous mouvions, vous mouviez, **ils meuvent;** *PRET* **je mus, tu mus, il mut, nous mûmes, vous mûtes, ils murent;** *IMPER* **meus;** *PP* **mû**

57 **naître** : *IND* **je nais, tu nais, il naît, nous naissons, vous naissez, ils naissent;** *SUBJ* **je naisse, tu naisses, il naisse, nous naissions, vous naissiez, ils naissent;** *PRET* **je naquis, tu naquis, il naquit, nous naquîmes, vous naquîtes, ils naquirent;** *IMPF* **je naissais, tu naissais, il naissait, nous naissions, vous naissiez, ils naissaient;** *IMPER* **nais;** *PRP* **naissant;** *PP* **né**

58 **nettoyer** : *IND* **je nettoie, tu nettoies, il nettoie,** nous nettoyons, vous nettoyez, **ils nettoient;** *SUBJ* **je nettoie, tu nettoies, il nettoie,** nous nettoyions, vous nettoyiez, **ils nettoient;** *FUT* **je nettoierai, tu nettoieras, il nettoiera, nous nettoierons, vous nettoierez, ils nettoieront;** *IMPER* **nettoie**

59 **oindre** (*defective verb*) *Used only in the infinitive and as a* PP **oint**

60 **ouïr** (*defective verb*) *Used only in the infinitive and as a* PP **ouï**

61 **paître** (*defective verb*) *Used only in the following tenses* : *IND* **je pais, tu pais, il paît, nous paissons, vous paissez, ils paissent;** *SUBJ* **je paisse, tu paisses, il paisse, nous paissions, vous paissiez, ils paissent;** *PRET* (*not used*); *IMPF* **je paissais, tu paissais, il paissait, nous paissions, vous paissiez, ils paissaient;** *FUT* (*used but regular*); *IMPER* **pais;** *PRP* **paissant;** *PP* (*not used*)

62 **parfaire** (*defective verb*) *Used only in the infinitive and in the following tenses* *IND* **il parfait;** *PP* **parfait**

63 **perdre** : *IND* je perds, tu perds, **il perd**, nous perdons, vous perdez, ils perdent; *PRET* **je perdis, tu perdis, il perdit, nous perdîmes, vous perdîtes, ils perdirent;** *PP* **perdu**

64 **piéger** : *IND* **je piège, tu pièges, il piège, nous piégeons,** vous piégez, **ils piègent;** *SUBJ* **je piège, tu pièges, il piège,** nous piégions, vous piégiez, **ils piègent;** *PRET* **je piégeai, tu piégeas, il piégea, nous piégeâmes, vous piégeâtes, ils piégèrent;** *IMPF* **je piégeais, tu piégeais, il piégeait,** nous piégions, vous piégiez, **ils piégeaient;** *IMPER* **piège;** *PRP* **piégeant;** *PP* **piégé**

65 **plaindre** : *IND* je plains, tu plains, il plaint, **nous plaignons, vous plaignez, ils plaignent;** *SUBJ* **je plaigne, tu plaignes, il plaigne, nous plagnions, vous plagniez, ils plaignent;** *PRET* **je plaignis, tu plaignis, il plaignit, nous plaignîmes, vous plaignîtes, ils plaignirent;** *IMPF* **je plaignais, tu plaignais, il plaignait, nous plaignions, vous plaigniez, ils plaignaient;** *PRP* **plaignant;** *PP* **plaint**

66 **plaire** : *IND* je plais, tu plais, **il plaît, nous plaisons, vous plaisez, ils plaisent;** *SUBJ* **je plaise, tu plaises, il plaise, nous plaisions, vous plaisiez, ils plaisent;** *PRET* **je plus, tu plus, il plut, nous plûmes, vous plûtes, ils plurent;** *IMPF* **je plaisais, tu plaisais, il plaisait, nous plaisions, vous plaisiez, ils plaisaient;** *PRP* **plaisant;** *PP* **plu**

67 **pleuvoir** (*defective verb*) *Used in the infinitive and in the following tenses* *IND* **il pleut, ils pleuvent** (*only in the figurative*); *SUBJ* **il pleuve, ils pleuvent** (*only in the figurative*); *PRET* **il plut;** *IMPF* **il pleuvait, ils pleuvaient** (*only in the figurative*); *FUT* **il pleuvra;** *IMPER* (not used); *PRP* **pleuvant;** *PP* **plu**

68 **pourvoir** : *IND* **je pourvois, tu pourvois, il pourvoit, nous**

pourvoyons, vous pourvoyez, ils pourvoient; *SUBJ* **je pourvoie, tu pourvoies, il pourvoie, nous pourvoyions, vous pourvoyiez, ils pourvoient;** *PRET* **je pourvus, tu pourvus, il pourvut, nous pourvûmes, vous pourvûtes, ils pourvurent;** *IMPF* **je pourvoyais, tu pourvoyais, il pourvoyait, nous pourvoyions, vous pourvoyiez, ils pourvoyaient;** *FUT* **je pourvoirai, tu pourvoiras, il pourvoira, nous pourvoirons, vous pourvoirez, ils pourvoiront;** *IMPER* **pourvois;** *PRP* **pourvoyant;** *PP* **pourvu**

69 **pouvoir :** *IND* **je peux** *or* **je puis, tu peux, il peut,** nous pouvons, vous pouvez, **ils peuvent;** *SUBJ* **je puisse, tu puisses, il puisse, nous puissions, vous puissiez, ils puissent;** *PRET* **je pus, tu pus, il put, nous pûmes, vous pûtes, ils purent;** *FUT* **je pourrai, tu pourras, il pourra, nous pourrons, vous pourrez, ils pourront;** *IMPER* (*not used*); *PP* **pu**

70 **prendre :** *IND* je prends, tu prends, **il prend, nous prenons, vous prenez, ils prennent;** *SUBJ* **je prenne, tu prennes, il prenne, nous prenions, vous preniez, ils prennent;** *PRET* **je pris, tu pris, il prit, nous prîmes, vous prîtes, ils prirent;** *IMPF* **je prenais, tu prenais, il prenait, nous prenions, vous preniez, ils prenaient;** *PRP* **prenant;** *PP* **pris**

71 **prévaloir :** *IND* **je prévaux, tu prévaux, il prévaut,** nous prévalons, vous prévalez, ils prévalent; *PRET* **je prévalus, tu prévalus, il prévalut, nous prévalûmes, vous prévalûtes, ils prévalurent;** *FUT* **je prévaudrai, tu prévaudras, il prévaudra, nous prévaudrons, vous prévaudrez, ils prévaudront;** *IMPER* **prévaux;** *PP* **prévalu**

72 **rassir** (*defective verb*) *Used only in the infinitive and as a* PP **rassis**

73 **ravoir** (*defective verb*) *Used only in the infinitive*

74 **résoudre :** *INF* **je résous, tu résous, il résout, nous résolvons, vous résolvez, ils résolvent;** *SUBJ* **je résolve, tu résolves, il résolve, nous résolvions, vous résolviez, ils résolvent;** *PRET* **je résolus, tu résolus, il résolut, nous résolûmes, vous résolûtes, ils résolurent;** *IMPF* **je résolvais, tu résolvais, il résolvait, nous résolvions, vous résolviez, ils résolvaient;** *IMPER* **résous;** *PRP* **résolvant;** *PP* **résolu**

75 **résulter** (*defective verb) Used only in the infinitive and in the following tenses* : *IND* **il résulte**; *PRP* **résultant**

76 **rire** : *IND* **je ris, tu ris, il rit, nous rions, vous riez, ils rient**; *SUBJ* je rie, tu ries, il rie, **nous riions, vous riiez**, ils rient; *PRET* **je ris, tu ris, il rit, nous rîmes, vous rîtes, ils rirent**; *IMPER* **ris**; *PP* **ri**

77 **rompre** : *IND* je romps, tu romps, **il rompt**, nous rompons, vous rompez, ils rompent; *PRET* **je rompis, tu rompis, il rompit, nous rompîmes, vous rompîtes, ils rompirent**; *PP* **rompu**

78 **saillir** : *IND* **je saille, tu sailles, il saille**, nous saillons, vous saillez, ils saillent; *PRET* **je saillis, tu sallis, il saillit, nous saillîmes, vous saillîtes, ils saillirent**; *FUT* **je saillerai, tu sailleras, il saillera, nous saillerons, vous saillerez, ils sailleront**; *IMPER* **saille**

79 **savoir** : *IND* **je sais, tu sais, il sait**, nous savons, vous savez, ils savent; *SUBJ* **je sache, tu saches, il sache, nous sachions, vous sachiez, ils sachent**; *PRET* **je sus, tu sus, il sut, nous sûmes, vous sûtes, ils surent**; *FUT* **je saurai, tu sauras, il saura, nous saurons, vous saurez, ils sauront**; *IMPER* **sache, sachons, sachez**; *PRP* **sachant**; *PP* **su**

80 **seoir** (*defective verb*) *Used in the following tenses* : *IND* **il sied, il siéent**; *SUBJ* **il siée, ils siéent**; *PRET* (*not used*); *IMPF* **il seyait, ils seyaient**; *FUT* **il siéra, ils siéront**; *IMPER* (*not used*); *PRP* **séant** *or* **seyant**; *PP* (*not used*)

81 **servir** : *IND* **je sers, tu sers, il sert**, nous servons, vous servez, ils servent; *PRET* **je servis, tu servis, il servit, nous servîmes, vous servîtes, ils servirent**; *FUT* **je servirai, tu serviras, il servira, nous servirons, vous servirez, ils serviront**; *IMPER* **sers**; *PP* **servi**

82 **sortir** : *IND* **je sors, tu sors, il sort**, nous sortons, vous sortez, ils sortent; *PRET* **je sortis, tu sortis, il sortit, nous sortîmes, vous sortîtes, ils sortirent**; *FUT* **je sortirai, tu sortiras, il sortira, nous sortirons, vous sortirez, ils sortiront**; *IMPER* **sors**; *PRP* **sortant**; *PP* **sorti**

83 **souffrir** : *IND* **je souffre, tu souffres, il souffre**, nous souffrons, vous souffrez, ils souffrent; *PRET* **je souffris, tu souf-**

fris, il souffrit, nous souffrîmes, vous souffrîtes, ils souffrirent; *FUT* **je souffrirai, tu souffriras, il souffrira, nous souffrirons, vous souffrirez, ils souffriront;** *IMPER* **souffre;** *PP* **souffert**

84 **sourdre** (*defective verb*) *Used only in the infinitive and in the following tenses* : *IND* **il sourd, ils sourdent;** *IMPF* **il sourdait, ils sourdaient**

85 **stupéfaire** (*defective verb*) *Used only in the following tense* *PP* **stupéfié**

86 **suffire** : *IND* je suffis, tu suffis, il suffit, **nous suffisons, vous suffisez, ils suffisent;** *SUBJ* **je suffise, tu suffises, il suffise, nous suffisions, vous suffisiez, ils suffisent;** *PRET* **je suffis, tu suffis, il suffit, nous suffîmes, vous suffîtes, ils suffirent;** *IMPF* **je suffisais, tu suffisais, il suffisait, nous suffisions, vous suffisiez, ils suffisaient;** *PRP* **suffisant;** *PP* **suffi**

87 **suggérer** : *IND* **je suggère, tu suggères, il suggère,** nous suggérons, vous suggérez, **ils suggèrent;** *SUBJ* **je suggère, tu suggères, il suggère,** nous suggérions, vous suggériez, **ils suggèrent;** *IMPER* **suggère**

88 **suivre** : *IND* **je suis, tu suis, il suit,** nous suivons, vous suivez, ils suivent; *PRET* **je suivis, tu suivis, il suivit, nous suivîmes, vous suivîtes, ils suivirent;** *IMPER* **suis;** *PP* **suivi**

89 **suppléer** : *IND* **je supplée, tu supplées, il supplée, nous suppléons, vous suppléez, ils suppléent;** *SUBJ* **je supplée, tu supplées, il supplée, nous suppléions, vous suppléiez, ils suppléent;** *PRET* **je suppléai, tu suppléas, il suppléa, nous suppléâmes, vous suppléâtes, ils suppléèrent;** *FUT* **je suppléerai, tu suppléeras, il suppléera, nous suppléerons, vous suppléerez, ils suppléeront;** *IMPER* **supplée;** *PP* **suppléé**

90 **surseoir** : *IND* **je sursois, tu sursois, il sursoit, nous sursoyons, vous sursoyez, ils sursoient;** *SUBJ* **je sursoie, tu sursoies, il sursoie, nous sursoyions, vous sursoyiez, ils sursoient;** *PRET* **je sursis, tu sursis, il sursit, nous sursîmes, vous sursîtes, ils sursirent;** *IMPF* **je sursoyais, tu sursoyais, il sursoyait, nous sursoyions, vous sursoyiez, ils sursoyaient;** *FUT* **je surseoirai, tu surseoiras, il surseoira, nous surseoirons, vous surseoirez, ils surseoiront;** *IMPER* **sursois;** *PRP* **sursoyant;** *PP* **sursis**

91 **taire** : *IND* je tais, tu tais, **il tait, nous taisons, vous taisez, ils taisent**; *SUBJ* **je taise, tu taises, il taise, nous taisions, vous taisiez, ils taisent**; *PRET* **je tus, tu tus, il tut, nous tûmes, vous tûtes, ils turent**; *IMPF* **je taisais, tu taisais, il taisait, nous taisions, vous taisiez, ils taisaient**; *PRP* **taisant**; *PP* **tu**

92 **tenir** : *IND* **je tiens, tu tiens, il tient**, nous tenons, vous tenez, **ils tiennent**; *SUBJ* **je tienne, tu tiennes, il tienne**, nous tenions, vous teniez, **ils tiennent**; *PRET* **je tins, tu tins, il tint, nous tînmes, vous tîntes, ils tinrent**; *FUT* **je tiendrai, tu tiendras, il tiendra, nous tiendrons, vous tiendrez, ils tiendront**; *IMPER* **tiens**; *PP* **tenu**

93 **tressaillir** : *IND* **je tressaille, tu tressailles, il tressaille**, nous tressaillons, vous tressaillez, ils tressaillent; *PRET* **je tressaillis, tu tressaillis, il tressaillit, nous tressaillîmes, vous tressaîllites, ils tressaillirent**; *FUT* **je tressaillirai, tu tressailliras, il tressaillira, nous tressaillirons, vous tressaillirez, ils tressailliront**; *IMPF* **tressaille**; *PP* **tressailli**

94 **vaincre** : *IND* **je vaincs, tu vaincs, il vainc, nous vainquons, vous vainquez, ils vainquent**; *SUBJ* **je vainque, tu vainques, il vainque, nous vainquions, vous vainquiez, ils vainquent**; *PRET* **je vainquis, tu vainquis, il vainquit, nous vainquîmes, vous vainquîtes, ils vainquirent**; *IMPF* **je vainquais, tu vainquais, il vainquait, nous vainquions, vous vainquiez, ils vainquaient**; *IMPER* **vaincs**; *PRP* **vainquant**; *PP* **vaincu**

95 **valoir** : *IND* **je vaux, tu vaux, il vaut**, nous valons, vous valez, ils valent; *SUBJ* **je vaille, tu vailles, il vaille**, nous valions, vous valiez, **ils vaillent**; *PRET* **je valus, tu valus, il valut, nous valûmes, vous valûtes, ils valurent**; *FUT* **je vaudrai, tu vaudras, il vaudra, nous vaudrons, vous vaudrez, ils vaudront**; *IMPER* **vaux**; *PP* **valu**

96 **vérifier** : *SUBJ* je vérifie, tu vérifies, il vérifie, **nous vérifiions, vous vérifiiez**, ils vérifient; *IMPF* je vérifiais, tu vérifiais, il vérifiait, **nous vérifiions, vous vérifiiez**, ils vérifiaient

97 **vêtir** : *IND* **je vêts, tu vêts, il vêt**, nous vêtons, vous vêtez, ils vêtent; *PRET* **je vêtis, tu vêtis, il vêtit, nous vêtîmes, vous vêtîtes, ils vêtirent**; *FUT* **je vêtirai, tu vêtiras, il vêtira, nous vêtirons, vous vêtirez, ils vêtiront**; *IMPER* **vêts**; *PP* **vêtu**

98 **vivre :** *IND* **je vis, tu vis, il vit,** nous vivons, vous vivez, ils vivent; *PRET* **je vécus, tu vécus, il vécut, nous vécûmes, vous vécûtes, ils vécurent**; *IMPER* **vis;** *PP* **vécu**

99 **voir :** *IND* je vois, tu vois, il voit, **nous voyons, vous voyez,** ils voient; *SUBJ* je voie, tu voies, il voie, **nous voyions, vous voyiez,** ils voient; *PRET* **je vis, tu vis, il vit, nous vîmes, vous vîtes, ils virent;** *IMPF* **je voyais, tu voyais, il voyait, nous voyions, vous voyiez, ils voyaient;** *FUT* **je verrai, tu verras, il verra, nous verrons, vous verrez, ils verront;** *PRP* **voyant;** *PP* **vu**

100 **vouloir :** *IND* **je veux, tu veux, il veut,** nous voulons, vous voulez, **ils veulent;** *SUBJ* **je veuille, tu veuilles, il veuille,** nous voulions, vous vouliez; **ils veuillent;** *PRET* **je voulus, tu voulus, il voulut, nous voulûmes, vous voulûtes, ils voulurent;** *FUT* **je voudrai, tu voudras, il voudra, nous voudrons, vous voudrez, ils voudront;** *IMPER* **veux** *or* **veuille;** *PP* **voulu**

Abbreviations in this Work

adj	adjective
adv	adverb
art	article
Bel	Belgium
Brit	Great Britain
Can	Canada
conj	conjunction
esp	especially
f	feminine
fam	familiar or colloquial
fpl	feminine plural
France	France
interj	interjection
m	masculine
mf	masculine or feminine
mpl	masculine plural
n	noun
nf	feminine noun
nfpl	feminine plural noun
nfs & pl	invariable singular or plural feminine noun
nm	masculine noun
nmf	masculine or feminine noun
nmfpl	plural noun invariable for gender
nmfs & pl	noun invariable for both gender and number
nmpl	masculine plural noun
nms & pl	invariable singular or plural masculine noun
npl	plural noun
ns & pl	noun invariable for plural
pl	plural
pp	past participle
prep	preposition
pron	pronoun
qqch	quelque chose (something)
qqn	quelqu'un (someone)
s	singular
s.o.	someone
sth	something
Switz	Switzerland
usu	usually
v	verb (transitive and intransitive)
v aux	auxiliary verb
vi	intransitive verb
vi impers	impersonal verb
vr	reflexive verb
vt	transitive verb

Pronunciation Symbols

VOWELS

æ **ask, bat, glad**
ɑ **cot, bomb**
ɑ̃ *French* **chant, ennui**
a *New England* **aunt,** *British* **ask, glass**
ɛ **egg, bet, fed**
ɛ̃ *French* **lapin, main**
ə **about, javelin, Alabama**
ə when italicized as in əl, əm, ən, indicates a syllabic pronunciation of the consonant as in bot**tle**, pris**m**, but**ton**
i **very, any, thirty**
iː **eat, bead, bee**
ɪ **id, bid, pit**
o **Ohio, yellower, potato**
oː **oats, own, zone, blow**
ɔ **awl, maul, caught, paw**
ɔ̃ **ombre, mon**
ʊ **sure, should, could**
uː **boot, two, coo**
ʌ **under, putt, bud**
y *French* **pur,** *German* **fühlen**
eɪ **eight, wade, bay**
aɪ **ice, bite, tie**
aʊ **out, gown, plow**
ɔɪ **oyster, coil, boy**
ø *French* **deux,** *German* **Höhe**
œ *French* **bœuf,** *German* **Gött**
œ̃ *French* **lundi, parfum**

CONSONANTS

b **baby, labor, cab**
d **day, ready, kid**
dʒ **just, badger, fudge**
ð **then, either, bathe**
f **foe, tough, buff**
g **go, bigger, bag**
h **hot, aha**
j **yes, vineyard**
k **cat, keep, lacquer, flock**
l **law, hollow, boil**
m **mat, hemp, hammer, rim**
n **new, tent, tenor, run**
ŋ **rung, hang, swinger**
ɲ *French* **digne, agneau**
p **pay, lapse, top**
r **rope, burn, tar**
s **sad, mist, kiss**
ʃ **shoe, mission, slush**
t **toe, button, mat**
ɾ indicates that some speakers of English pronounce this sound as a voiced alveolar flap, as in **la**ter, **ca**tty, **ba**ttle
tʃ **choose, batch**
θ **thin, ether, bath**
v **vat, never, cave**
w **wet, software**
ɥ *French* **cuir, appui**
x *German* **Bach,** *Scottish* **loch**
z **zoo, easy, buzz**
ʒ **azure, beige**
h, k, p, t when italicized indicate sounds which are present in the pronunciation of some speakers of English but absent in the pronunciation of others, so that *whence* [ˈ*h*wɛn*t*s] can be pronunced as [ˈhwɛns], [ˈhwɛnts], [ˈwɛnts], or [ˈwɛns].

OTHER SYMBOLS

ˈ high stress **pen**manship
ˌ low stress penman**ship**
ʼ aspiration; when used before French words in *h*-, indicates absence of liaison, as in *le héros* [lə ʼero]
( ) indicate sounds that are present in the pronunciation of some speakers of French but absent in that of others, as in *cenellier* [s(ə)nɛlje], *but* [by(t)]

French–English Dictionary

A

a [a] *nm* : a, the first letter of the alphabet
à [a] *prep* **1** : to <je vais à Montréal : I am going to Montreal> <as-tu téléphoné à ton père? : did you call your dad?> <il a donné la clé à son frère : he gave the key to his brother> **2** : at <à deux heures : at two o'clock> <nous sommes à l'aéroport : we are at the airport> **3** : on <à pied : on foot, by foot> <à temps : on time> **4** : with <la fille aux cheveux blonds : the girl with blond hair> **5** (*with infinitive*) : to <ils ont appris à lire : they learned how to read> <problèmes à résoudre : problems to be solved> **6** : from <voler aux riches : to steal from the rich> **7** : per <60 kilomètres à l'heure : 60 kilometers per hour> **8** : in, according to <à leur avis : in their opinion>
abaissement [abɛsmɑ̃] *nm* **1** : lowering **2** DIMINUTION : reduction, drop, fall **3** : abasement, humbling
abaisser [abɛse] *vt* **1** BAISSER : to lower **2** DIMINUER : to reduce **3** : to humble, to abase — **s'abaisser** *vr* **1** : to go down, to slope (down) **2** : to demean oneself, to grovel **3** ~ **à** : to stoop to
abandon [abɑ̃dɔ̃] *nm* **1** : state of neglect **2** : desertion, abandonment **3** : abandon, freedom **4** : surrender, renunciation **5** : withdrawal, retirement (in sports) **6 laisser à l'abandon** : to neglect, to abandon
abandonner [abɑ̃dɔne] *vt* **1** : to abandon **2** : to surrender, to renounce — *vi* : to give up — **s'abandonner** *vr* **1** : to let oneself go, to neglect oneself **2** ~ **à** : to give oneself up to (pleasures, etc.)
abaque [abak] *nm* : abacus
abasourdir [abazurdir] *vt* **1** : to stun **2** : to deafen
abâtardir [abatardir] *vt* : to debase, to degrade — **s'abâtardir** *vr* : to degenerate, to deteriorate
abat-jour [abaʒur] *nm* : lampshade
abats [aba] *nmpl* **1** : entrails, offal **2 abats de volaille** : giblets
abattage [abataʒ] *nm* **1** : felling (of trees) **2** : slaughtering (of animals) **3** : extraction (of metals) **4 avoir de l'abattage** : to be full of vim and vigor
abattant [abatɑ̃] *nm* : flap, leaf (of furniture)
abattement [abatmɑ̃] *nm* **1** : reduction, allowance <abattement à la base : income-tax deduction> **2** : despondency, sadness **3** : weakness, exhaustion
abattis [abati] *nmpl* : giblets
abattoir [abatwar] *nm* : abattoir, slaughterhouse
abattre [abatr] {12} *vt* **1** : to knock down, to cut down, to bring down **2** ÉPUISER : to wear out, to exhaust **3** DÉMORALISER : to demoralize <ne te laisse pas abattre : don't let things get you down> **4** : to slaughter, to kill **5 abattre ses cartes** *or* **abattre son jeu** : to lay one's cards on the table — **s'abattre** *vr* **1** : to come down, to fall, to crash **2** ~ **sur** : to pounce on, to descend on
abattu, -tue [abaty] *adj* : despondent, downcast, dejected
abbaye [abɛi] *nf* : abbey
abbé [abe] *nm* **1** : abbot **2** PRÊTRE : priest
abbesse [abɛs] *nf* : abbess
abcès [apse] *nm* : abscess
abdication [abdikasjɔ̃] *nf* : abdication, renunciation
abdiquer [abdike] *vt* **1** : to abdicate **2** : to renounce — *vi* **1** : to abdicate **2** : to surrender, to give up
abdomen [abdɔmɛn] *nm* : abdomen
abdominal, -nale [abdɔminal] *adj, mpl* **-naux** [-no] : abdominal
abdominaux *nmpl* **les abdominaux** : stomach muscles, abs
abécédaire [abeseder] *nm* : speller, primer
abeille [abɛj] *nf* **1** : bee, honeybee **2 abeille mâle** : drone
aberrant, -rante [aberɑ̃, -rɑ̃t] *adj* **1** : aberrant, abnormal **2** : absurd
aberration [aberasjɔ̃] *nf* : aberration
abêtir [abetir] *vt* : to make stupid — *vi* : to become stupid — **s'abêtir** *vr*
abhorrer [abɔre] *vt* : to abhor, to abominate
abîme [abim] *nm* **1** : abyss, gulf **2 au bord de l'abîme** : on the brink of ruin **3 au fond de l'abîme** : in the depths of despair
abîmer [abime] *vt* DÉTÉRIORER : to damage, to spoil — **s'abîmer** *vr* **1** : to spoil, to become damaged **2** : to sink, to founder <s'abîmer dans la réflexion : to be lost in thought>
abject, -jecte [abʒɛkt] *adj* **1** : despicable, contemptible **2** : abject — **abjectement** [-ʒɛktəmɑ̃] *adv*
abjurer [abʒyre] *vt* : to abjure, to renounce
ablation [ablasjɔ̃] *nf* : removal, excision (in medicine)
ablution [ablysjɔ̃] *nf* : ablution
abnégation [abnegasjɔ̃] *nf* : selflessness, self-denial
aboie [abwa], **aboiera** [abwara], *etc.* → **aboyer**
aboiement [abwamɑ̃] *nm* : barking, baying
abois [abwa] *nmpl* **être aux abois** : to be at bay, to be desperate
abolir [abɔlir] *vt* : to abolish
abolition [abɔlisjɔ̃] *nf* : abolition

abominable [abɔminabl] *adj* : abominable — **abominablement** [-nabləmɑ̃] *adv*
abomination [abɔminasjɔ̃] *nf* : abomination
abominer [abɔmine] *vt* : to abominate, to loathe
abondamment [abɔ̃damɑ̃] *adv* : abundantly
abondance [abɔ̃dɑ̃s] *nf* **1** : abundance **2 en ~** : in plenty, galore
abondant, -dante [abɔ̃dɑ̃, -dɑ̃t] *adj* : abundant
abonder [abɔ̃de] *vi* **1** : to abound, to be plentiful <abonder en bonheur : to be full of happiness> **2 abonder dans le sens de** : to agree wholeheartedly with
abonné, -née [abɔne] *n* : subscriber
abonnement [abɔnmɑ̃] *nm* : subscription
abonner [abɔne] *vt* : to take out a subscription for — **s'abonner** *vr* : to subscribe
abord [abɔr] *nm* **1** ACCÈS : access, approach **2** : manner <il est d'un abord facile : he's very approachable> **3 abords** *nmpl* : surroundings **4 d' ~** : at first, firstly **5 de prime abord** *or* **au premier abord** : at first glance
abordable [abɔrdabl] *adj* **1** ACCESSIBLE : accessible **2** : affordable **3** : approachable
abordage [abɔrdaʒ] *nm* **1** : boarding (of a ship) **2** : collision
aborder [abɔrde] *vt* **1** : to approach **2** : to tackle, to deal with **3** : to board (an enemy ship) — *vi* : to land, to berth <aborder à port : to reach port>
aborigène[1] [abɔriʒɛn] *adj* : aboriginal, indigenous
aborigène[2] *nmf* : aborigine, native
abortif, -tive [abɔrtif, -tiv] *adj* : abortive
aboucher [abuʃe] *vt* : to join (things) end to end — **s'aboucher** *vr* : to get in touch
aboutir [abutir] *vi* **1** RÉUSSIR : to succeed **2 ~ à** *or* **~ dans** : to result in, to end up in
aboutissants [abutisɑ̃] *nmpl* → **tenant**
aboutissement [abutismɑ̃] *nm* : outcome, result
aboyer [abwaje] {58} *vi* : to bark, to bay — *vt* : to bark (out), to shout (an order, etc.)
aboyeur, -yeuse [abwajœr, -jøz] *adj* : barking
abraser [abraze] *vt* : to abrade
abrasif[1], **-sive** [abrazif, -ziv] *adj* : abrasive
abrasif[2] *nm* : abrasive
abrasion [abrazjɔ̃] *nf* : abrasion
abrégé [abreʒe] *nm* : summary, abstract, abridgment <en abrégé : in summary, in brief>
abrègement [abrɛʒmɑ̃] *nm* : summarizing, abridgment
abréger [abreʒe] {64} *vt* : to shorten, to abridge, to abbreviate
abreuver [abrœve] *vt* **1** : to water (an animal) **2** : to soak, to irrigate **3** ACCABLER : to shower, to heap <abreuver qqn de : to overwhelm s.o. with> — **s'abreuver** *vr* : to drink
abreuvoir [abrœvwar] *nm* : watering place (in a river, etc.), drinking trough
abréviation [abrevjasjɔ̃] *nf* : abbreviation
abri [abri] *nm* **1** : shelter, shed <à l'abri : under cover> **2 les sans abri** : the homeless
abricot [abriko] *nm* : apricot
abrier [abrije] {96} *vt Can* : to cover (with a blanket, etc.)
abriter [abrite] *vt* **1** : to shelter, to protect **2** HÉBERGER : to house, to accommodate
abrogation [abrɔgasjɔ̃] *nf* : repeal, abrogation
abroger [abrɔʒe] {17} *vt* : to abrogate, to repeal, to annul
abrupt, -brupte [abrypt] *adj* **1** ESCARPÉ : sheer, steep **2** BRUSQUE : abrupt
abruti, -tie [abryti] *n fam* : fool, idiot
abrutir [abrytir] *vt* **1** ÉTOURDIR : to daze, to stupefy **2** : to wear out, to exhaust **3** ABÊTIR : to make stupid
abrutissant, -sante [abrytisɑ̃, -sɑ̃t] *adj* : exhausting, numbing, stupefying
absence [apsɑ̃s] *nf* : absence
absent[1], **-sente** [apsɑ̃, -sɑ̃t] *adj* : absent
absent[2], **-sente** *n* : absentee
absentéisme [apsɑ̃teism] *nm* : absenteeism
absenter [apsɑ̃te] *v* **s'absenter** *vr* : to leave, to stay away
absinthe [apsɛ̃t] *nf* **1** : absinthe **2** : wormwood
absolu[1], **-lue** [apsɔly] *adj* : absolute — **absolument** [-lymɑ̃] *adv*
absolu[2] *nm* : absolute
absolution [apsɔlysjɔ̃] *nf* : absolution
absorbant, -bante [apsɔrbɑ̃, -bɑ̃t] *adj* **1** : absorbent **2** : absorbing, engrossing
absorber [apsɔrbe] *vt* **1** : to absorb, to engross **2** : to consume, to take up, to absorb — **s'absorber** *vr* **~ dans** : to become engrossed in
absorption [apsɔrpsjɔ̃] *nf* : absorption
absoudre [apsudr] {1} *vt* : to absolve
abstenir [apstənir] {92} *v* **s'abstenir** *vr* **1** : to abstain **2 s'abstenir de faire** : to refrain from doing
abstention [apstɑ̃sjɔ̃] *nf* : abstention
abstinence [apstinɑ̃s] *nf* : abstinence
abstraction [apstraksjɔ̃] *nf* **1** : abstraction **2 faire abstraction de** : to disregard, to set aside
abstraire [apstrɛr] {40} *vt* : to abstract — **s'abstraire** *vr* : to isolate oneself
abstrait[1], **-traite** [apstrɛ, -trɛt] *adj* : abstract — **abstraitement** [-trɛtmɑ̃] *adv*
abstrait[2] *nm* : abstract <dans l'abstrait : in the abstract>

abstrus, -struse [apstry, -stryz] *adj* : abstruse
absurde [apsyrd] *adj* : absurd
absurdité [apsyrdite] *nf* : absurdity
abus [aby] *nm* : abuse, misuse <abus de confiance : breach of trust>
abuser [abyze] *vt* : to deceive, to mislead — *vi* **1** ~ **de** : to misuse **2** ~ **de** : to take advantage of, to exploit — **s'abuser** *vr* : to be mistaken
abuseur [abyzœr] *nm Can* : abuser
abusif, -sive [abyzif, -ziv] *adj* **1** EXAGÉRÉ : excessive <parents abusifs : overprotective parents> **2** IMPROPRE : incorrect, improper — **abusivement** [-zivmɑ̃] *adv*
abyssal, -sale [abisal] *adj, mpl* **-saux** [-so] : abyssal, unfathomable
acabit [akabi] *nm* : sort, type <de tout acabit : of every kind>
acacia [akasja] *nm* : acacia
académicien, -cienne [akademisjɛ̃, -sjɛn] *n* : academician
académie [akademi] *nf* **1** : academy **2** : school district **3** : learned society **4** : nude (in a work of art)
académique [akademik] *adj* : academic
acadien, -dienne [akadjɛ̃, -djɛn] *adj* **1** : Acadian **2** : Cajun
Acadien, -dienne *n* **1** : Acadian **2** : Cajun
acajou [akaʒu] *nm* : mahogany
acariâtre [akarjatr] *adj* : cantankerous
accablant, -blante [akablɑ̃, -blɑ̃t] *adj* : overwhelming, oppressive
accablement [akabləmɑ̃] *nm* : despondency, dejection
accabler [akable] *vt* **1** ÉCRASER : to overwhelm **2** : to condemn
accalmie [akalmi] *nf* : lull, respite
accaparement [akaparmɑ̃] *nm* : monopolizing, hoarding
accaparer [akapare] *vt* **1** MONOPOLISER : to monopolize **2** : to buy up, to hoard
accéder [aksede] {87} *vi* **1** : to gain access, to reach, to obtain **2** : to accede
accélérateur[1], **-trice** [akseleratœr, -tris] *adj* : accelerating
accélérateur[2] *nm* : accelerator
accélération [akselerasjɔ̃] *nf* : acceleration
accélérer [akselere] {87} *v* : to accelerate — **s'accélérer** *vr*
accent [aksɑ̃] *nm* **1** : accent <un accent allemand : a German accent> **2** : stress, emphasis **3** : accent mark <accent aigu : acute accent> **4** NUANCE : hint, tone <un accent plaintif : a plaintive tone>
accentuer [aksɑ̃tɥe] *vt* **1** : to mark with an accent **2** : to stress (a syllable) **3** : to emphasize, to highlight — **s'accentuer** *vr* : to become more pronounced
acceptabilité [akseptabilite] *nf* : acceptability
acceptable [akseptabl] *adj* : acceptable, passable
acceptation [akseptasjɔ̃] *nf* : acceptance
accepter [aksepte] *vt* : to accept, to agree to
acception [aksepsjɔ̃] *nf* **1** : sense, meaning **2 sans acception de** : regardless of
accès [aksɛ] *nm* **1** : access **2** : entry, entrance <accès interdit : no entry> **3** CRISE : fit, attack <accès de fièvre : bout of fever> <accès d'excitation : fit of excitement>
accessibilité [aksesibilite] *nf* : accessibility
accessible [aksesibl] *adj* **1** ABORDABLE : accessible **2 accessible au public** : open to the public
accession [aksesjɔ̃] *nf* AVÈNEMENT : accession, attainment
accessoire[1] [aksɛswar] *adj* : accessory, incidental
accessoire[2] *nm* **1** : accessory **2 accessoires** *nmpl* : props
accessoirement [aksɛswarmɑ̃] *adv* **1** : secondarily, incidentally **2** : if necessary, if need be
accident [aksidɑ̃] *nm* : accident <par accident : by accident, accidentally>
accidenté[1], **-tée** [aksidɑ̃te] *adj* **1** BLESSÉ : injured **2** ENDOMMAGÉ : damaged **3** INÉGAL : uneven, broken <terrain accidenté : uneven ground>
accidenté[2], **-tée** *n* : victim (of an accident), injured person
accidentel, -telle [aksidɑ̃tɛl] *adj* : accidental — **accidentellement** [-tɛlmɑ̃] *adv*
accise [aksiz] *nf Bel, Can* : excise tax
acclamation [aklamasjɔ̃] *nf* : acclamation, cheering
acclamer [aklame] *vt* : to acclaim, to cheer
acclimatation [aklimatasjɔ̃] *nf* : acclimatization
acclimater [aklimate] *vt* : to acclimatize — **s'acclimater** *vr*
accolade [akɔlad] *nf* **1** : accolade **2** EMBRASSADE : embrace **3** : brace, bracket (in printing)
accoler [akɔle] *vt* **1** : to join side by side **2** : to bracket together (in printing)
accommodant, -dante [akɔmɔdɑ̃, -dɑ̃t] *adj* : accommodating, flexible
accommodation [akɔmɔdasjɔ̃] *nf* : accommodation, adaptation
accommodement [akɔmɔdmɑ̃] *nm* : arrangement, compromise, terms
accommoder [akɔmɔde] *vt* : to accommodate, to adapt — **s'accommoder** *vr* ~ **de** : to make do, to put up with
accompagnateur, -trice [akɔ̃paɲatœr, -tris] *n* **1** : accompanist **2** GUIDE : chaperone, guide
accompagnement [akɔ̃paɲmɑ̃] *nm* : accompaniment

accompagner [akɔ̃paɲe] *vt* : to accompany
accompli, -lie [akɔ̃pli] *adj* **1** ACHEVÉ : finished, accomplished **2** CONSOMMÉ : consummate, expert
accomplir [akɔ̃plir] *vt* : to accomplish, to perform, to realize — **s'accomplir** *vr* **1** : to take place **2** : to be fulfilled
accomplissement [akɔ̃plismɑ̃] *nm* : accomplishment, performance
accord [akɔr] *nm* **1** : agreement, understanding <d'accord : in agreement, agreed> <en accord avec : in harmony with> **2** PACTE : pact, agreement, accord (in politics, etc.) **3** : approval, consent **4** : chord (in music)
accordéon [akɔrdeɔ̃] *nm* : accordion
accorder [akɔrde] *vt* **1** : to make agree, to reconcile, to match **2** OCTROYER : to grant, to give **3** : to tune (a musical instrument) — **s'accorder** *vr* : to be in agreement
accordeur [akɔrdœr] *nm* : tuner (of musical instruments)
accoster [akɔste] *vt* **1** ABORDER : to approach, to accost **2** : to come alongside — *vi* : to dock, to land
accotement [akɔtmɑ̃] *nm* : shoulder (of a road)
accoter [akɔte] *vt* : to lean, to rest — **s'accoter** *vr* **~ à** *or* **~ contre** : to lean against
accouchement [akuʃmɑ̃] *nm* : childbirth
accoucher [akuʃe] *vt* : to deliver (a child) — *vi* **1** : to be in labor **2 ~ de** : to give birth to
accoucheur, -cheuse [akuʃœr, -ʃøz] *n* : obstetrician
accoucheuse *nf* SAGE-FEMME : midwife
accouder [akude] *v* **s'accouder** *vr* **1** : to lean on one's elbows **2 ~ à** *or* **~ sur** : to lean (one's elbows) on
accoudoir [akudwar] *nm* : armrest
accouplement [akupləmɑ̃] *nm* **1** : coupling **2** : mating
accoupler [akuple] *vt* **1** : to couple, to link **2** : to mate (of animals) **3** : to yoke (draft animals) — **s'accoupler** *vr* : to mate
accourir [akurir] {23} *vi* : to come running, to run up
accoutrement [akutrəmɑ̃] *nm* : outfit, getup
accoutumance [akutymɑ̃s] *nf* **1** ACCLIMATATION : acclimatization, habituation **2** DÉPENDANCE : dependency, addiction
accoutumé, -mée [akutyme] *adj* : usual, customary
accoutumer [akutyme] *vt* HABITUER : to accustom — **s'accoutumer** *vr* **~ à** : to get accustomed to, to get used to
accréditation [akreditasjɔ̃] *nf* : accreditation
accréditer [akredite] *vt* **1** : to accredit (a person) **2** : to substantiate (a rumor, etc.) — **s'accréditer** *vr* : to gain credibility
accroc [akro] *nm* **1** DÉCHIRURE : rip, tear **2** OBSTACLE : obstacle, hitch, snag
accrochage [akroʃaʒ] *nm* **1** : hanging (for display) **2** : hooking, hitching **3** : (military) skirmish **4** : clash, dispute **5** : minor collision (of an automobile)
accroche [akrɔʃ] *nf* : slogan, catch phrase
accrocher [akrɔʃe] *vt* **1** : to hang up **2** : to hook, to hitch **3** : to get hold of (a person), to catch <accrocher le regard : to catch the eye> <accrocher un client : to buttonhole a client> **4** : to bump into, to hit — *vi* **1** : to catch, to stick, to snag **2** : to attract attention, to catch on — **s'accrocher** *vr* **1** : to hang on, to persevere **2** SE DISPUTER : to quarrel **3 ~ à** : to hold on to, to cling to
accrocheur, -cheuse [akrɔʃœr, -ʃøz] *adj* **1** TENACE : tenacious **2** : catchy, eye-catching
accroire [akrwar] {2} *vt* **en faire accroire à** : to take in, to dupe
accroissement [akrwasmɑ̃] *nm* AUGMENTATION : growth, increase
accroître [akrwatr] {25} *vt* : to increase — **s'accroître** *vr*
accroupir [akrupir] *v* **s'accroupir** *vr* : to squat, to crouch
accueil [akœj] *nm* RÉCEPTION : welcome, reception <faire bon accueil à : to welcome>
accueillant, -lante [akœjɑ̃, -jɑ̃t] *adj* HOSPITALIER : welcoming, hospitable
accueillir [akœjir] {3} *vt* : to greet, to welcome
acculer [akyle] *vt* **1** : to drive, to force **2 ~ à** *or* **~ contre** : to drive (someone) back against **3 ~ dans** : to corner (someone) in
accumulateur [akymylatœr] *nm* : storage battery
accumulation [akymylasjɔ̃] *nf* : accumulation
accumuler [akymyle] *vt* : to accumulate, to amass — **s'accumuler** *vr*
accusateur[1], -trice [akyzatœr, -tris] *adj* : accusatory, incriminating
accusateur[2], -trice *n* : accuser
accusatif [akyzatif] *nm* : accusative (case)
accusation [akyzasjɔ̃] *nf* **1** : accusation **2 l'accusation** : the prosecution **3 mise en accusation** : indictment **4 mettre en accusation** : to indict
accusé[1], -sée [akyze] *adj* : marked, pronounced, prominent
accusé[2], -sée *n* : defendant, accused
accusé[3] *nm* **accusé de réception** : acknowledgment of receipt
accuser [akyze] *vt* **1** : to accuse, to blame **2** : to show (up), to emphasize, to accentuate **3 accuser réception de** : to acknowledge receipt of
acerbe [aserb] *adj* : acerbic, harsh

acéré, -rée [asere] *adj* : sharp
acétate[1] [asetat] *nm* : acetate
acétate[2] *nf Can* : transparency
acétylène [asetilɛn] *nm* : acetylene
achalandage [aʃalɑ̃daʒ] *nm* : clientele
achalandé, -dée [aʃalɑ̃de] *adj* **bien achalandé** : well-stocked
achaler [aʃale] *vt Can fam* : to annoy — **achalant, -lante** [aʃalɑ̃, -lɑ̃t] *adj*
acharné, -née [aʃarne] *adj* : fierce, unremitting, relentless
acharnement [aʃarnəmɑ] *nm* : determination, relentlessness
acharner [aʃarne] *v* **s'acharner** *vr* **1** : to persevere, to persist **2** ~ **sur** : to persecute, to hound
achat [aʃa] *nm* **1** : purchasing, buying <faire des achats : to do some shopping> **2** EMPLETTE : purchase
acheminement [aʃminmɑ̃] *nm* : transporting, dispatch (of goods)
acheminer [aʃmine] *vt* : to transport, to convey — **s'acheminer** *vr* ~ **vers** : to move toward, to head for
acheter [aʃte] {20} *vt* : to buy, to purchase
acheteur, -teuse [aʃtœr, -tøz] *n* ACQUÉREUR : buyer
achèvement [aʃɛvmɑ̃] *nm* : completion
achever [aʃve] {52} *vt* TERMINER : to complete, to finish — **s'achever** *vr* **1** : to reach completion, to end **2** : to draw to a close
achigan [aʃigɑ̃] *nm Can* : black bass
achoppement [aʃɔpmɑ̃] *nm* **pierre d'achoppement** : obstacle, stumbling block
achopper [aʃɔpe] *vi* : to stumble — **s'achopper** *vr*
acide[1] [asid] *adj* : acid, acidic
acide[2] *nm* : acid
acidité [asidite] *nf* : acidity, tartness, sourness
acidulé, -lée [asidyle] *adj* : somewhat acid, tangy
acier [asje] *nm* : steel <acier inoxydable : stainless steel>
aciérie [asjeri] *nf* : steelworks
acné [akne] *nf* : acne
acolyte [akɔlit] *nm* **1** : acolyte (in religion) **2** : accomplice, confederate
acompte [akɔ̃t] *nm* **1** : deposit, down payment **2** : installment
aconit [akɔnit] *nm* : monkshood
acoquiner [akɔkine] *v* **s'acoquiner** *vr* ~ **avec** : to team up with, to gang up with
à-côté [akote] *nm, pl* **à-côtés** **1** : side issue **2** : extra money, perk
à-coup [aku] *nm, pl* **à-coups** : jerk, jolt <par à-coups : in fits and starts>
acoustique[1] [akustik] *adj* : acoustic
acoustique[2] *nf* : acoustics
acquéreur, -reuse [akerœr, -røz] *n* ACHETEUR : buyer
acquérir [akerir] {21} *vt* **1** : to acquire, to obtain **2** : to purchase — **s'acquérir** *vr* : to gain, to win (approval, etc.)
acquière [akjɛr], **acquiert** [akjɛr], *etc.* → **acquérir**
acquiescement [akjɛsmɑ̃] *nm* : acquiescence
acquiescer [akjese] {6} *vi* : to aquiesce, to agree
acquis[1] [aki] *pp* → **acquérir**
acquis[2], **-quise** [aki, -kiz] *adj* **1** : acquired **2** : established, accepted <fait acquis : accepted fact> <tenir pour acquis : to take for granted>
acquis[3] *nms & pl* **1** : knowledge, experience **2** : benefit, gain
acquisition [akizisjɔ̃] *nf* **1** : acquisition **2** : purchase
acquit [aki] *nm* **1** : receipt <par acquit : received> **2 par acquit de conscience** : to put one's mind at ease
acquittement [akitmɑ̃] *nm* **1** : payment (of a debt), fulfillment (of a promise, etc.) **2** : acquittal
acquitter [akite] *vt* **1** : to acquit **2** PAYER : to settle, to pay (off) — **s'acquitter** *vr* ~ **de** : to pay (a debt), to fulfill (an obligation, etc.)
acre [akr] *nf* : acre
âcre [akr] *adj* : acrid, bitter, pungent
âcreté [akrəte] *nf* : bitterness, pungency
acrimonie [akrimɔni] *nf* : acrimony
acrimonieux, -nieuse [akrimɔnjø, -njøz] *adj* : acrimonious — **acrimonieusement** [-njøzmɑ̃] *adv*
acrobate [akrɔbat] *nmf* : acrobat
acrobatie [akrɔbasi] *nf* : acrobatics
acrobatique [akrɔbatik] *adj* : acrobatic
acronyme [akrɔnim] *nm* : acronym
acrylique [akrilik] *adj & nm* : acrylic
acte [akt] *nm* **1** : action, deed <acte gratuit : gratuitous act> <faire acte de présence : to put in an appearance> **2** : act (in a play) **3** : certificate, document <acte de naissance : birth certificate> <acte de vente : bill of sale> **4 actes** *nmpl* : proceedings
acteur, -trice [aktœr, -tris] *n* COMÉDIEN : actor, actress *f*
actif[1], **-tive** [aktif, -tiv] *adj* **1** : active **2** : working <les mères actives : working mothers>
actif[2] *nm* **1** : assets *pl*, credits *pl* **2** : active voice (in grammar)
action [aksjɔ̃] *nf* **1** : action, act <une bonne action : a good deed> <passer à l'action : to go into action> **2** : effect <sous l'action de : due to the effect of, because of> **3** : share (of a security) **4** : lawsuit **5 action de grâce(s)** : thanksgiving (in religion)
actionnaire [aksjɔnɛr] *nmf* : stockholder, shareholder
actionner [aksjɔne] *vt* **1** : to engage, to put into motion, to turn on **2** : to sue
activement [aktivmɑ̃] *adv* : actively, busily
activer [aktive] *vt* **1** : to activate **2** : to speed up — **s'activer** *vr* **1** : to bustle

about, to be busy **2** *fam* : to get a move on
activisme [aktivism] *nm* : activism
activiste [aktivist] *adj & nmf* : activist
activité [aktivite] *nf* : activity <être en activité : to be active, to be in operation>
actrice → acteur
actuaire [aktɥɛr] *nmf* : actuary
actualisation [aktɥalizasjɔ̃] *nf* : updating, modernization
actualiser [aktɥalize] *vt* : to update, to modernize
actualité [aktɥalite] *nf* **1** : current events *pl* **2** : relevance **3 les actualités** : the news
actuel, -tuelle [aktɥɛl] *adj* : current, present — **actuellement** [-tɥɛlmɑ̃] *adv*
acuité [akɥite] *nf* : acuteness
acupuncture [akypɔ̃ktyr] *nf* : acupuncture
adage [adaʒ] *nm* MAXIME : adage
adaptabilité [adaptabilite] *nf* : adaptability
adaptable [adaptabl] *adj* : adaptable, adjustable
adaptateur [adaptatœr] *nm* : adapter
adaptation [adaptasjɔ̃] *nf* : adaptation
adapter [adapte] *vt* : to adapt, to fit — **s'adapter** *vr* **1** : to adapt **2** : to suit, to be appropriate
additif [aditif] *nm* : additive
addition [adisjɔ̃] *nf* **1** : addition **2** NOTE : bill, check (in a restaurant)
additionnel, -nelle [adisjɔnel] *adj* : additional
additionner [adisjɔne] *vt* : to add, to add up
adepte [adɛpt] *nmf* : follower, enthusiast
adéquat, -quate [adekwa, -kwat] *adj* **1** SUFFISANT : adequate **2** CONVENABLE : appropriate — **adéquatement** [-kwatmɑ̃] *adv*
adéquation [adekwasjɔ̃] *nf* : appropriateness, suitability
adhérence [aderɑ̃s] *nf* : adhesion
adhérent[1], -rente [aderɑ̃, -rɑ̃t] *adj* : adhering, sticking
adhérent[2], -rente *n* MEMBRE : member
adhérer [adere] {87} *vi* **1** : to adhere, to stick <adhérer à la route : to stick to the road> **2 ~ à** : to join
adhésif[1], -sive [adezif, -ziv] *adj* : adhesive
adhésif[2] *nm* : adhesive
adhésion [adezjɔ̃] *nf* **1** : adhesion, sticking **2** : adherence, support **3** : joining, membership
adieu [adjø] *nm, pl* **adieux** : farewell, good-bye <faire ses adieux à : to say good-bye to> <un discours d'adieu : a farewell address>
adjacent, -cente [adʒasɑ̃, -sɑ̃t] *adj* : adjacent
adjectif[1], -tive *adj* [adʒɛktif, -tiv] : adjectival
adjectif[2] *nm* : adjective
adjectival, -vale [adʒɛktival] *adj, mpl* **-vaux** [-vo] : adjectival
adjoindre [adʒwɛ̃dr] {50} *vt* **1** : to appoint (as an assistant) **2** : to add, to attach — **s'adjoindre** *vr* **s'adjoindre qqn** : to take s.o. on, to hire s.o.
adjoint, -jointe [adʒwɛ̃, -ʒwɛ̃t] *adj & n* : assistant
adjonction [adʒɔ̃ksjɔ̃] *nf* : addition
adjudant [adʒydɑ̃] *nm* : warrant officer, adjutant
adjudication [adʒydikasjɔ̃] *nf* **1** : auctioning, sale by auction **2** : awarding (of a contract)
adjuger [adʒyʒe] {17} *vt* **1** DÉCERNER : to award **2** : to auction — **s'adjuger** *vr* : to claim, to take for oneself
adjurer [adʒyre] *vt* SUPPLIER : to implore, to beseech
admettre [admɛtr] {53} *vt* **1** : to admit, to let in **2** : to acknowledge, to concede **3** : to permit, to accept
administrateur, -trice [administratœr, -tris] *n* : director, administrator
administratif, -tive [administratif, -tiv] *adj* : administrative — **administrativement** [-tivmɑ̃] *adv*
administration [administrasjɔ̃] *nf* : administration <administration commerciale : business administration>
administrer [administre] *vt* **1** GÉRER : to administer, to manage **2** : to dispense <administrer un médicament : to administer a drug>
admirable [admirabl] *adj* : admirable — **admirablement** [-rabləmɑ̃] *adv*
admirateur, -trice [admiratœr, -tris] *n* : admirer
admiratif, -tive [admiratif, -tiv] *adj* : admiring — **admirativement** [-tivmɑ̃] *adv*
admiration [admirasjɔ̃] *nf* : admiration
admirer [admire] *vt* : to admire
admissible [admisibl] *adj* : admissible, eligible
admission [admisjɔ̃] *nf* **1** : admission **2** : intake, induction
admonester [admɔnɛste] *vt* : to admonish
admonition [admɔnisjɔ̃] *nf* : admonition
ADN [adeɛn] *nm* : DNA
ado [ado] *nmf fam* : adolescent, teenager
adolescence [adɔlesɑ̃s] *nf* : adolescence — **adolescent, -cente** [-lesɑ̃, -sɑ̃t] *adj & n*
adon [adɔ̃] *nm Can* : lucky break
adonner [adɔne] *vi Can fam* : to be convenient <viens me voir si ça adonne : drop by if you get a chance> — **s'adonner** *vr* **1 ~ à** : to devote oneself to **2 ~ avec** *Can* : to get along well with
adopter [adɔpte] *vt* : to adopt
adoptif, -tive [adɔptif, -tiv] *adj* : adoptive, adopted

adoption [adɔpsjɔ̃] *nf* : adoption
adorable [adɔrabl] *adj* : adorable — **adorablement** [-rablǝmɑ̃] *adv*
adoration [adɔrasjɔ̃] *nf* : adoration
adorer [adɔre] *vt* **1** : to adore, to worship **2** : to love
adosser [adose] *vt* **1** : to place back to back **2** ~ **à** *or* ~ **contre** : to lean against — **s'adosser** *vr*
adoucir [adusir] *vt* **1** : to soften, to tone down, to subdue **2** : to sweeten **3** : to alleviate, to ease — **s'adoucir** *vr*
adoucissement [adusismɑ̃] *nm* **1** : softening **2** : sweetening **3** : alleviation, easing, mitigation
adrénaline [adrenalin] *nf* : adrenalin
adresse [adres] *nf* **1** : address **2** HABILETÉ : skill, dexterity <adresse au tir : marksmanship>
adresser [adrese] *vt* **1** : to address (correspondence) **2** : to direct, to aim (remarks, etc.) — **s'adresser** *vr*
adroit, -droite [adrwa, -drwat] *adj* **1** HABILE : skillful **2** : clever, shrewd — **adroitement** [-drwatmɑ̃] *adv*
aduler [adyle] *vt* : to adulate — **adulation** [adylasjɔ̃] *nf*
adulte [adylt] *adj & nmf* : adult, grown-up
adultère[1] [adyltɛr] *adj* : adulterous
adultère[2] *nm* : adultery
adultère[3] *nmf* : adulterer *m*, adulteress *f*
advenir [advǝnir] {4} *v impers* **1** : to occur, to happen <advienne que pourra : whatever happens, come what may> **2** ~ **de** : to become of <qu'est-il advenu de Jeanne? : what(ever) became of Jeanne?>
adverbe [adverb] *nm* : adverb — **adverbial, -biale** [-vɛrbjal] *adj*
adversaire [adversɛr] *nmf* : adversary, opponent
adverse [advers] *adj* **1** : opposing **2** : adverse, unfavorable <circonstances adverses : adverse circumstances>
adversité [adversite] *nf* : adversity
aération [aerasjɔ̃] *nf* **1** : ventilation **2** : aeration
aérer [aere] {87} *vt* **1** VENTILER : to ventilate, to air out **2** : to aerate (soil, etc.) **3** : to lighten, to thin out (a written text) — **s'aérer** *vr* : to get some fresh air
aérien, -rienne [aerjɛ̃, -rjǝn] *adj* **1** : aerial, air <transport aérien : air transport> **2** : overhead, aerial **3** : ethereal, airy
aérobic [aerǝbik] *nm* : aerobics
aérobie [aerǝbi] *adj* : aerobic
aérobique [aerǝbik] *adj Can* : aerobic <danse aérobique : aerobics>
aérodrome [aerǝdrǝm] *nm* : airfield
aérodynamique[1] [aerǝdinamik] *adj* : aerodynamic — **aérodynamiquement** [-mikmɑ̃] *adv*
aérodynamique[2] *nf* : aerodynamics
aérogare [aerǝgar] *nf* : air terminal
aéroglisseur [aerǝglisœr] *nm* : hovercraft
aérogramme [aerǝgram] *nm* : air letter, aerogram
aéronaute [aerǝnǝt] *nmf* : balloonist
aéronautique[1] [aerǝnǝtik] *adj* : aeronautical
aéronautique[2] *nf* : aeronautics
aéronaval, -vale [aerǝnaval] *adj, pl* **-vals** : air and sea
aéronef [aerǝnɛf] *nm* : aircraft
aéroport [aerǝpǝr] *nm* : airport
aéroporté, -tée [aerǝpǝrte] *adj* : airborne
aéropostal, -tale [aerǝpǝstal] *adj, mpl* **-taux** [-to] : airmail
aérosol [aerǝsǝl] *nm* : aerosol
aérospatial, -tiale [aerǝspasjal] *adj, mpl* **-tiaux** [-sjǝ] : aerospace
affabilité [afabilite] *nf* : affability
affable [afabl] *adj* : affable — **affablement** [afablǝmɑ̃] *adv*
affadir [afadir] *vt* **1** : to make bland **2** : to cause to fade — **s'affadir** *vr*
affaiblir [afeblir] *vt* : to weaken — **s'affaiblir** *vr* **1** : to become weak **2** : to diminish, to fade
affaire [afɛr] *nf* **1** : affair, matter, business <ce n'est pas mon affaire : that's none of my business> <affaire de cœur : love affair> **2** : business, enterprise **3** : deal <une (bonne) affaire : a bargain, a good deal> **4** PROCÈS : case, lawsuit **5 affaires** *nfpl* : possessions, belongings **6 affaires** *nfpl* : business <homme d'affaires : businessman> **7 avoir affaire à** : to be faced with, to be dealing with
affairé, -rée [afere] *adj* OCCUPÉ : busy
affairer [afere] *v* **s'affairer** *vr* : to be busy, to bustle about
affaissement [afɛsmɑ̃] *nm* **1** EFFONDREMENT : subsidence (of the earth), caving in **2** : sagging, sinking
affaisser [afɛse] *v* **s'affaisser** *vr* **1** : to collapse **2** : to sag, to sink, to subside
affaler [afale] *v* **s'affaler** *vr* : to collapse, to fall, to slump
affamé, -mée [afame] *adj* : famished, starving
affamer [afame] *vt* : to starve
affectation [afɛktasjɔ̃] *nf* **1** : assignment, appointment **2** : allocation, allotment <affectation des fonds : allocation of funds> **3** : affectation
affecté, -tée [afɛkte] *adj* : mannered, affected
affecter [afɛkte] *vt* **1** : to affect **2** : to assign **3** : to allocate, to allot **4** FEINDRE : to feign
affectif, -tive [afɛktif, -tiv] *adj* : affective, emotional
affection [afɛksjɔ̃] *nf* **1** : affection, caring **2** : ailment, condition <affection respiratoire : respiratory complaint>
affectionner [afɛksjǝne] *vt* AIMER : to like, to be fond of

affectueux, -tueuse [afɛktɥø, -tɥøz] *adj* : affectionate — **affectueusement** [-tɥøzmɑ̃] *adv*
afférent, -rente [aferɑ̃, -rɑ̃t] *adj* ~ **à** : pertaining to, relating to
affermir [afɛrmir] *vt* **1** : to strengthen, to firm up (muscles, etc.) **2** : to reinforce, to consolidate
affermissement [afɛrmismɑ̃] *nm* : strengthening
affichage [afiʃaʒ] *nm* **1** : publicizing, posting **2** : display <affichage numérique : digital display> **3 panneau d'affichage** : bulletin board **4 tableau d'affichage** : scoreboard
affiche [afiʃ] *nf* **1** : poster, notice **2 tenir l'affiche** : to open (of a play, etc.)
afficher [afiʃe] *vt* **1** : to post <défense d'afficher : post no bills> **2** : to show, to display — **s'afficher** *vr*
affidavit [afidavit] *nm* : affidavit
affilé, -lée [afile] *adj* : sharp, keen
affilée [afile] *adv* **d'~** : in a row
affiler [afile] *vt* : to sharpen
affiliation [afiljasjɔ̃] *nf* : affiliation
affilier [afilje] {96} *vt* : to affiliate — **s'affilier** *vr* ~ **à** : to become affiliated with, to join
affiner [afine] *vt* **1** : to refine **2** : to ripen (cheese) — **s'affiner** *vr*
affinité [afinite] *nf* : affinity
affirmatif, -tive [afirmatif, -tiv] *adj* : affirmative — **affirmativement** [-tivmɑ̃] *adv*
affirmation [afirmasjɔ̃] *nf* : affirmation, assertion
affirmative *nf* : affirmative <répondre par l'affirmative : to answer in the affirmative>
affirmer [afirme] *vt* **1** : to maintain, to contend, to affirm **2** : to assert (authority, etc.) — **s'affirmer** *vr* : to assert oneself
affleurement [aflœrmɑ̃] *nm* : outcrop
affleurer [aflœre] *vt* : to make even or flush — *vi* : to come to the surface
affliction [afliksjɔ̃] *nf* : affliction
affligeant, -geante [afliʒɑ̃, -ʒɑ̃t] *adj* : distressing, sorrowful
affliger [afliʒe] {17} *vt* : to afflict, to distress — **s'affliger** *vr*
affluence [aflyɑ̃s] *nf* **1** : crowd **2** ABONDANCE : abundance **3 heure d'affluence** : rush hour
affluent [aflyɑ̃] *nm* : tributary
affluer [aflye] *vi* **1** COULER : to flow, to roll in (of money) **2** : to flock, to surge
afflux [afly] *nm* : influx, rush
affolé, -lée [afɔle] *adj* : panicked, frightened
affolement [afɔlmɑ̃] *nm* : panic
affoler [afɔle] *vt* **1** : to drive crazy **2** EFFRAYER : to frighten — **s'affoler** *vr* : to panic
affranchir [afrɑ̃ʃir] *vt* **1** LIBÉRER : to liberate, to free **2** TIMBRER : to stamp, to postmark
affranchissement [afrɑ̃ʃismɑ̃] *nm* **1** LIBÉRATION : liberation, emancipation **2** : franking, stamping **3** : postage (of a letter, etc.)
affres [afr] *nfpl* : agony, pangs, throes
affrètement [afrɛtmɑ̃] *nm* : renting, chartering
affréter [afrete] {87} *vt* : to charter <vols affrétés : chartered flights>
affreux, -freuse [afrø, -frøz] *adj* : awful, dreadful — **affreusement** [afrøzmɑ̃] *adv*
affrioler [afrijɔle] *vt* : to tempt, to entice — **affriolant, -lante** [-jɔlɑ̃, -lɑ̃t] *adj*
affront [afrɔ̃] *nm* INSULTE : affront
affrontement [afrɔ̃tmɑ̃] *nm* : confrontation, clash
affronter [afrɔ̃te] *vt* : to confront, to brave, to face — **s'affronter** *vr*
affubler [afyble] *vt fam* : to dress up, to deck out — **s'affubler** *vr*
affût [afy] *nm* **1** : carriage (for heavy artillery) **2** : hiding place, blind <être à l'affût de : to lie in wait for, to be on the lookout for>
affûter [afyte] *vt* AIGUISER : to sharpen, to hone
afghan, -ghane [afgɑ̃, -gan] *adj* : Afghan
Afghan, -ghane *n* : Afghan
afin [afɛ̃] *adv* **1** ~ **de** : in order to <afin de trouver une solution : in order to find a solution> **2** ~ **que** : so that <afin que le public comprenne : so that the public understands>
africain, -caine [afrikɛ̃, -kɛn] *adj* : African
Africain, -caine *n* : African
agaçant, -çante [agasɑ̃, -sɑ̃t] *adj* : annoying, irritating
agacement [agasmɑ̃] *nm* IRRITATION : irritation, annoyance
agacer [agase] {6} *vt* ÉNERVER : to annoy, to irritate
agate [agat] *nf* : agate
âge [aʒ] *nm* **1** : age <quel âge avez-vous? : how old are you?> <les gens du troisième âge : senior citizens> **2** : age, era <le Moyen Âge : the Middle Ages>
âgé, -gée [aʒe] *adj* **1** : old, aged, of age <âgé de seize ans : sixteen years old> **2** VIEUX : elderly, old <les personnes âgées : elderly persons>
agence [aʒɑ̃s] *nf* BUREAU : agency, office <agence de voyage : travel agency> <agence immobilière : real estate agency>
agencement [aʒɑ̃smɑ̃] *nm* : layout, arrangement
agencer [aʒɑ̃se] {6} *vt* **1** : to arrange, to lay out **2** : to put together, to construct
agenda [aʒɛ̃da] *nm* **1** : agenda **2** CARNET : appointment book
agenouiller [aʒnuje] *v* **s'agenouiller** *vr* : to kneel

agent[1], **-gente** [aʒɑ̃, -ʒɑ̃t] *n* **1** : agent <agent d'assurances : insurance agent> <agent de change : stockbroker> **2** : officer <agent de police : police officer>
agent[2] *nm* **1** : agent, factor <agents économiques : economic factors> **2** : agent (in chemistry, medicine, etc.)
agglomération [aglɔmerasjɔ̃] *nf* **1** AMAS, ASSEMBLAGE : conglomeration, agglomeration **2** : city, town **3** : urban area
aggloméré [aglɔmere] *nm* **1** : particleboard, fiberboard **2** : briquette, charcoal
agglomérer [aglɔmere] {87} *vt* : to agglomerate, to pile up — **s'agglomérer** *vr* : to aggregate, to gather together
agglutiner [aglytine] *vt* : to stick together — **s'agglutiner** *vr* : to gather
aggravation [agravasjɔ̃] *nf* : aggravation, worsening
aggraver [agrave] *vt* : to aggravate, to make worse — **s'aggraver** *vr* EMPIRER : to worsen, to get worse
agile [aʒil] *adj* : agile — **agilement** [aʒilmɑ̃] *adv*
agilité [aʒilite] *nf* : agility
agir [aʒir] *vi* **1** : to act, to take action **2** : to behave <elle agit comme une sainte : she acts like a saint> **3** : to operate, to take effect <la drogue agira vite : the drug will take effect quickly> — **s'agir** *vr* **1** ~ **de** : to concern, to be a question of <de quoi s'agit-il? : what is it about?> **2** ~ **de** : to be necessary <pour vivre, il s'agit de manger : one must eat to live>
agissements [aʒismɑ̃] *nmpl* : dealings, schemes, machinations
agitation [aʒitasjɔ̃] *nf* **1** : agitation, restlessness **2** : hustle and bustle, activity **3** : (social) unrest **4** : choppiness (of the sea)
agité, -tée [aʒite] *adj* **1** : restless, agitated **2** : rough <eaux agitées : rough waters>
agiter [aʒite] *vt* **1** SECOUER : to agitate, to shake **2** TROUBLER : to disturb **3** DÉBATTRE : to debate — **s'agiter** *vr* **1** : to bustle about **2** : to fidget **3** : to become agitated
agneau [aɲo] *nm, pl* **agneaux** **1** : lamb **2** : lambskin
agnelle [aɲel] *nf* : young ewe
agnostique [agnɔstik] *adj & nmf* : agnostic
agonie [agɔni] *nf* : death throes *pl*
agoniser [agɔnize] *vi* : to be dying
agrafe [agraf] *nf* **1** : hook, fastener **2** : staple **3** : clamp, clip (in medicine)
agrafer [agrafe] *vt* **1** : to fasten **2** : staple **3** *fam* : to catch, to nab
agrafeuse [agraføz] *nf* : stapler
agraire [agrɛr] *adj* : agrarian <réforme agraire : land reform>
agrandir [agrɑ̃dir] *vt* : to enlarge, to expand — **s'agrandir** *vr* : to grow, to be enlarged
agrandissement [agrɑ̃dismɑ̃] *nm* : enlargement, expansion
agréable [agreabl] *adj* : pleasant, agreeable — **agréablement** [-ablɔmɑ̃] *adv*
agréé, agréée [agree] *adj* : accepted, certified <expert-comptable agréé : certified public accountant>
agréer [agree] *vt* {89} **1** ACCEPTER : to accept, to approve <veuillez agréer, l'expression de mes sentiments les meilleurs : yours sincerely> **2** ~ **à** : to suit, to agree with
agrégat [agrega] *nm* : aggregate, mass
agrégation [agregasjɔ̃] *nf* **1** *France* : qualifying exam for a teacher or professor **2** : aggregation
agrégé, -gée [agreʒe] *n France* : certified teacher or professor
agréger [agreʒe] *vt* {64} **1** : to aggregate **2** INTÉGRER : to incorporate, to accept (into a group)
agrément [agremɑ̃] *nm* **1** CONSENTEMENT : consent, authorization **2** : pleasure <voyage d'agrément : pleasure trip> **3** : charm, attractiveness
agrémenter [agremɑ̃te] *vt* ORNER : to decorate, to trim, to embellish
agrès [agrɛ] *nmpl* : apparatus (for gymnastics)
agresser [agrese] *vt* ASSAILLIR : to attack, to assault
agresseur [agrɛsœr] *nm* : attacker, assailant, aggressor
agressif, -sive [agrɛsif, -siv] *adj* : aggressive — **agressivement** [-sivmɑ̃] *adv*
agression [agrɛsjɔ̃] *nf* **1** : attack, assault **2** : aggression
agressivité [agrɛsivite] *nf* : aggressiveness
agricole [agrikɔl] *adj* : agricultural
agriculteur, -trice [agrikyltœr, -tris] *n* : farmer
agriculture [agricyltyr] *nf* : agriculture, farming
agripper [agripe] *vt* : to clutch, to grab — **s'agripper** *vr* : to cling
agrumes [agrym] *nmpl* : citrus fruits
aguets [age] *nmpl* **aux aguets** : on the lookout
aguicher [agiʃe] *vt* : to entice, to allure
ah [a] *interj* : oh <ah oui? : is that so?>
ahuri, -rie [ayri] *adj* **1** : amazed, dumbfounded **2** : dazed, stupefied
ahurir [ayrir] *vt* : to astound, to stun, to daze
ahurissant, -sante [ayrisɑ̃, -sɑ̃t] *adj* : astounding, amazing
ahurissement [ayrismɑ̃] *nm* STUPÉFACTION : amazement, stupefaction
aide[1] [ɛd] *nmf* : assistant
aide[2] *nf* **1** : help, aid <à l'aide! : help!> <à l'aide de : with the help of> **2** *Can* : assist (in sports)

aider [ede] *vt* ASSISTER : to help, to assist
aïe [aj] *interj* : ouch!
aïeul, aïeule [ajœl] *n* : grandfather *m*, grandmother *f*
aïeux [ajø] *nmpl* : ancestors, forefathers
aigle [ɛgl] *nm* **1** : eagle **2 aigle d'Amérique** *or* **aigle à tête blanche** : bald eagle
aiglefin [ɛglə̃fɛ̃] *nm* → **églefin**
aigre [ɛgr] *adj* **1** : sour, tart **2** : sharp, bitter <un vent aigre : a bitter wind>
aigre–doux, -douce [ɛgrədu, -dus] *adj* **1** : bittersweet **2** : sweet and sour
aigrette [ɛgrɛt] *nf* **1** : egret **2** : tuft, spray (of feathers)
aigreur [ɛgrœr] *nf* **1** : sourness, tartness **2** : bitterness
aigrir [ɛgrir] *vt* **1** : to turn sour **2** : to embitter — *vi* : to sour, to become sour — **s'aigrir** *vr*
aigu, -guë [ɛgy] *adj* **1** : sharp, keen **2** : acute, intense <une douleur aiguë : an acute pain> **3** STRIDENT : strident, high-pitched **4** → **accent**
aiguille [eɥij] *nf* **1** : needle **2** : hand (of a clock) <l'aiguille des minutes : the minute hand> **3** PIC : mountain peak **4 aiguille de glace** : icicle **5 travail à l'aiguille** : needlework
aiguiller [eɥije] *vt* **1** : to switch (in railroading) **2** : to steer, to direct
aiguilleur [eɥijœr] *nm* **1** : switchman **2 aiguilleur du ciel** : air traffic controller
aiguillon [eɥijɔ̃] *nm* **1** : goad **2** : stinger **3** : incentive, spur
aiguillonner [eɥijɔne] *vt* **1** : to goad, to prod **2** : to stimulate, to spur
aiguise–crayon [egizkrejɔ̃] *nm, pl* **aiguise–crayons** *Can* : pencil sharpener
aiguiser [egize] *vt* **1** AFFÛTER : to sharpen, to hone **2** : to stimulate, to whet
aiguisoir [egizwar] *nm* : (knife) sharpener
ail [aj] *nm, pl* **ails** *or* **aulx** [o] : garlic
aile [ɛl] *nf* **1** : wing **2** : fender (of an automobile) **3** : **voler de ses propres ailes** : to stand on one's own two feet
aileron [ɛlrɔ̃] *nm* **1** : flap, aileron **2** : fin (of a shark, etc.), wing tip (of a bird)
ailier [elje] *nm* : wing, winger (in sports)
aille [aj], *etc.* → **aller**
ailleurs [ajœr] *adv* **1** : elsewhere **2 d'~** : besides, moreover, by the way **3 par ~** : in addition, what's more
aimable [ɛmabl] *adj* GENTIL : kind, likeable — **aimablement** [ɛmabləmɑ̃] *adv*
aimant[1], -mante [ɛmɑ̃, -mɑ̃t] *adj* : loving, caring
aimant[2] *nm* : magnet
aimanter [ɛmɑ̃te] *vt* : to magnetize
aimer [eme] *vt* **1** : to love **2** *or* **aimer bien** : to like **3 aimer mieux** : to prefer
aine [ɛn] *nf* : groin
aîné[1], -née [ene] *adj* **1** : elder, older **2** : eldest, oldest **3** : senior
aîné[2], -née *n* **1** : elder child, elder son *m*, elder daughter *f* **2** : eldest child, eldest son *m*, eldest daughter *f* **3** : older person, oldest person <il est mon aîné de cinq ans : he's five years older than me>
ainsi [ɛ̃si] *adv* **1** : thus, in this way, in that way <il m'a regardé ainsi : he looked at me like that> **2 ainsi que** : just as <elle l'a fait ainsi que tu disais : she did it just as you said she would> **3 ainsi que** : as well as <mes mains ainsi que mes pieds : my hands as well as my feet> **4 et ainsi de suite** : and so on **5 ainsi soit-il** : so be it, amen **6 pour ainsi dire** : so to speak
air [ɛr] *nm* **1** : air <en plein air : outside, in the open air> <courant d'air : draft> <air conditionné : air-conditioning> **2** MÉLODIE : tune, melody <air d'opéra : aria> **3** : appearance, look <avoir un air distingué : to look distinguished> **4** AMBIANCE : atmosphere, ambience **5 être en air** *Can* : to be ready and willing
aire [ɛr] *nf* **1** : area <aire de repos : rest area> **2** SURFACE : surface, area **3** DOMAINE : field, sphere <aire d'influence : sphere of influence> **4** : aerie
airelle [ɛrɛl] *nf* : blueberry
aisance [ezɑ̃s] *nf* **1** : ease, facility, fluency **2** : affluence, wealth <vivre dans l'aisance : to be well-off>
aise[1] [ɛz] *adj* : pleased
aise[2] *nf* **1** : ease <être mal à l'aise : to be ill at ease> **2** : pleasure **3 aises** *nfpl* : creature comforts
aisé, -sée [eze] *adj* **1** FACILE : easy **2** RICHE : wealthy, well-off **3** : graceful, fluent
aisément [ezemɑ̃] *adv* FACILEMENT : easily
aisselle [ɛsɛl] *nf* : armpit
ajouré, -rée [aʒure] *adj* : openworked, perforated
ajournement [aʒurnəmɑ̃] *nm* **1** : postponement **2** : adjournment, continuance (of a trial)
ajourner [aʒurne] *vt* **1** : to adjourn **2** : to postpone, to defer
ajout [aʒu] *nm* : addition (to a house, etc.)
ajouter [aʒute] *vt* ADDITIONNER : to add
ajustement [aʒystəmɑ̃] *nm* : adjustment
ajuster [aʒyste] *vt* **1** : to adjust, to adapt, to fit **2** : to arrange (hair, etc.) **3** VISER : to aim at <ajuster son tir : to aim, to adjust one's aim>
ajutage [aʒyfaʒ] *nm* : nozzle (of a hose)
alambic [alɑ̃bik] *nm* : still
alambiqué, -quée [alɑ̃bike] *adj* : overcomplicated, convoluted
alangui, -guie [alɑ̃gi] *adj* : languid, listless
alanguir [alɑ̃gir] *vt* : to make languid

alarmant, -mante [alarmɑ̃, -mɑ̃t] *adj* : alarming
alarme [alarm] *nf* **1** ALERTE : alarm <donner l'alarme : to raise the alarm> **2** PEUR : alarm, fear <un état d'alarme : a state of alarm>
alarmer [alarme] *vt* : to alarm, to frighten — **s'alarmer** *vr*
albanais[1], **-naise** [albanɛ, -nɛz] *adj* : Albanian
albanais[2] *nm* : Albanian (language)
Albanais, -naise *n* : Albanian
albâtre [albatr] *nm* : alabaster
albatros [albatros] *nm* : albatross
albinos [albinos] *adj & nmfs & pl* : albino
album [albɔm] *nm* : album
albumen [albymen] *nm* : albumen
albumine [albymin] *nf* : albumin
alcali [alkali] *nm* **1** : alkali **2** AMMONIAQUE : ammonia
alcalin, -line [alkalɛ̃, -lin] *adj* : alkaline <pile alcaline : alkaline battery>
alchimie [alʃimi] *nf* : alchemy — **alchimiste** [-ʃimist] *nmf*
alcool [alkɔl] *nm* : alcohol
alcoolique [alkɔlik] *adj & nmf* : alcoholic — **alcoolisme** [-kɔlism] *nm*
alcoolisé, -sée [alkɔlize] *adj* : alcoholic <boisson non-alcoolisée : nonalcoholic beverage>
alcôve [alkov] *nf* **1** : alcove **2 secrets d'alcôve** : intimate secrets, pillow talk
alcyon [alsjɔ̃] *nm* : kingfisher
aléa [alea] *nm* : hazard, risk
aléatoire [aleatwar] *adj* **1** : uncertain, risky **2** : random
alène [alɛn] *nf* : awl
alentour [alɑ̃tur] *adv* : around, about, surrounding <dans la forêt alentour : in the surrounding forest>
alentours [alɑ̃tur] *nmpl* **1** ENVIRONS : surrounding area, region **2 aux alentours de** : around, in the vicinity of
alerte[1] [alɛrt] *adj* **1** : alert **2** : lively, brisk — **alertement** [alɛrtəmɑ̃] *adv*
alerte[2] *nf* ALARME : alert, warning, alarm
alerter [alɛrte] *vt* PRÉVENIR : to alert, to warn
alésage [alezaʒ] *nm* : bore (of a pipe or tube)
aléser [aleze] {87} *vt* : to bore, to ream
alevin [alvɛ̃] *nm* : young fish, fry
alevinage [alvinaʒ] *nm* : fish farming <station d'alevinage : fish hatchery>
algarade [algarad] *nf* : altercation, quarrel
algèbre [alʒɛbr] *nf* : algebra
algébrique [alʒebrik] *adj* : algebraic — **algébriquement** [-brikmɑ̃] *adv*
algérien, -rienne [alʒerjɛ̃, -rjɛn] *adj* : Algerian
Algérien, -rienne *n* : Algerian
algue [alg] *nf* : alga, seaweed
alias [aljas] *adv* : alias
alibi [alibi] *nm* : alibi
aliénation [aljenasjɔ̃] *nf* **1** : alienation **2** *or* **aliénation mentale** : insanity
aliéné, -née [aljene] *n* : insane person <être reconnu aliéné : to be declared insane>
aliéner [aljene] {87} *vt* **1** : to transfer, to give over **2** : to alienate — **s'aliéner** *vr* : to lose support, esteem, etc.
alignement [aliɲmɑ̃] *nm* **1** : row, line <ne pas être à l'alignement : to be out of line> **2** : alignment
aligner [aliɲe] *vt* : to align, to line up — **s'aligner** *vr* : to fall into line
aliment [alimɑ̃] *nm* **1** : food **2 aliments** *nmpl* : alimony
alimentaire [alimɑ̃tɛr] *adj* **1** : alimentary, food <la chaîne alimentaire : the food chain> **2** : money-making <œuvre alimentaire : potboiler>
alimentation [alimɑ̃tasjɔ̃] *nf* **1** : feeding **2** : nourishment, diet **3** : food <magasin d'alimentation : grocery store, food store> **4** : provision, supply <l'alimentation en eau : the water supply>
alimenter [alimɑ̃te] *vt* **1** NOURRIR : to feed, to nourish **2** APPROVISIONNER : to supply
alinéa [alinea] *nm* **1** : indentation <à l'alinéa : indented> **2** : paragraph
alité, -tée [alite] *adj* : bedridden
alizé [alize] *nm* : trade wind
Allah [ala] *nm* : Allah
allaitement [alɛtmɑ̃] *nm* : feeding, nursing <allaitement maternel : breast-feeding>
allaiter [alete] *vt* : to nurse, to breast-feed
allant[1], **-lante** [alɑ̃, -lɑ̃t] *adj* : active
allant[2] *nm* : drive, spirit
alléchant, -chante [aleʃɑ̃, -ʃɑ̃t] *adj* : tempting, enticing
allécher [aleʃe] {87} *vt* : to allure, to tempt
allée [ale] *nf* **1** : path, passage **2** : road **3** : drive, driveway **4** : aisle **5** *or* **allée de quilles** *Can* : bowling alley **6 allées et venues** : comings and goings
allégation [alegasjɔ̃] *nf* : allegation
allégeance [aleʒɑ̃s] *nf* : allegiance
allègement [aleʒmɑ̃] *nm* : lightening (up), easing
alléger [aleʒe] {64} *vt* **1** : to lighten **2** RÉDUIRE : to reduce **3** : to soothe, to relieve
allégorie [alegɔri] *nf* : allegory
allégorique [alegɔrik] *adj* : allegorical
allègre [alegr] *adj* : lively, cheerful — **allègrement** [alegrəmɑ̃] *adv*
allégresse [alegrɛs] *nf* : exuberance, joy
alléguer [alege] {87} *vt* **1** : to allege, to put forward **2** : to quote, to cite
alléluia [aleluja] *nm & interj* : hallelujah
allemand[1], **-mande** [almɑ̃, -mɑ̃d] *adj* : German
allemand[2] *nm* : German (language)

Allemand, -mande *n* : German
aller[1] [ale] {5} *vi* **1** : to go, to move, to travel <nous allons au cinéma : we're going to the movies> <aller à pied : to go by foot> <allons-y! : let's go!> **2** MARCHER : to work, to run <sa montre ne va pas : his watch isn't working> **3** : to proceed, to get along, to come along <ses études vont mal : her studies are going badly> <comment allez-vous? ça va : how are you? OK, fine> **4 ~ à** : to fit <cette robe me va bien : this dress fits me well> — *v aux* : to be going to, to be about to <il va terminer de bonne heure : he's going to finish early, he'll finish early> <nous allions partir : we were just leaving> — *v impers* **1 en ~** : to happen, to go <il en ira mieux demain : things will go better tomorrow> **2 y aller de** : to be a matter of <il y va de ton bonheur : you're risking your happiness> — **s'en aller** *vr* : to leave, to go <va-t'en! : go away!>
aller[2] *nm* **1** : outward journey **2** *or* **aller simple** : one-way, one-way ticket **3 aller–retour** : round-trip, round-trip ticket
allergène [alɛrʒɛn] *nm* : allergen
allergie [alɛrʒi] *nf* : allergy
allergique [alɛrʒik] *adj* : allergic
alliage [aljaʒ] *nm* : alloy
alliance [aljɑ̃s] *nf* **1** : alliance **2** : wedding ring **3** : marriage, union <tante par alliance : aunt by marriage> **4** : mixture, combination
allié[1], **-liée** [alje] *adj* : allied
allié[2], **-liée** *n* **1** : ally, supporter **2** : relative (by marriage)
allier [alje] {96} *vt* **1** : to mix, to combine **2** : to ally, to unite — **s'allier** *vr*
alligator [aligatɔr] *nm* : alligator
allitération [aliterasjɔ̃] *nf* : alliteration — **allitératif, -tive** [-ratif, -tiv] *adj*
allô [alo] *interj* : hello
allocation [alɔkasjɔ̃] *nf* **1** : allocation, allotment **2** : allowance, benefit <allocation de chômage : unemployment benefit>
allocution [alɔkysjɔ̃] *nf* : short speech, address
allongé, -gée [alɔ̃ʒe] *adj* **1** : elongated <un visage allongé : a long face> **2** : lying down
allongement [alɔ̃ʒmɑ̃] *nm* : lengthening, extension
allonger [alɔ̃ʒe] {17} *vt* **1** : to lengthen, to elongate **2** : to stretch (out) **3** : to thin (a sauce, etc.) **4** : to lay down **5** *fam* : to hand over, to fork over — *vi* : to get longer — **s'allonger** *vr* **1** : to lengthen **2** : to lie down
allouer [alwe] *vt* **1** : to allocate, to allot **2** : to allow, to grant
allumage [alymaʒ] *nm* **1** : lighting (of a fire), switching on (of a lamp, etc.) **2** : ignition (of a motor)
allumer [alyme] *vt* **1** : to light, to ignite **2** : to turn on, to switch on **3** : to excite — **s'allumer** *vr*
allumette [alymɛt] *nf* : match
allure [alyr] *nf* **1** : pace, speed <à toute allure : at full speed> **2** : look, appearance <avoir bonne allure : to look good> **3** : style <avoir de l'allure : to have style, to look stylish>
allusion [alyzjɔ̃] *nf* **1** : allusion **2 faire allusion à** : to allude to
almanach [almana] *nm* : almanac
aloès [alɔɛs] *nms & pl* : aloe
alors [alɔr] *adv* **1** : then, at that time **2** : then, in that case **3** : so, therefore <et alors? : so?, so what?> **4 alors même que** : even if, even though **5 alors que** : while, when, whereas **6 ou alors** : or else
alose [aloz] *nf* : shad
alouette [alwɛt] *nf* **1** : lark **2 alouette des champs** : skylark
alourdir [alurdir] *vt* **1** : to make heavy, to weigh down **2** : to increase — **s'alourdir** *vr* : to grow heavy
alourdissement [alurdismɑ̃] *nm* **1** : heaviness **2** : increase
aloyau [alwajo] *nm, pl* **aloyaux** : sirloin
alpaga [alpaga] *nm* : alpaca
alphabet [alfabɛ] *nm* : alphabet
alphabétique [alfabetik] *adj* : alphabetic, alphabetical — **alphabétiquement** [-tikmɑ̃] *adv*
alphabétisation [alfabetizasjɔ̃] *nf* **1** : alphabetizing **2** : literacy teaching
alphabétiser [alfabetize] *vt* **1** : to alphabetize **2** : to teach to read and write
alpin, -pine [alpɛ̃, -pin] *adj* : alpine
alpinisme [alpinism] *nm* : mountain climbing
alpiniste [alpinist] *nmf* : mountain climber, mountaineer
altération [alterasjɔ̃] *nf* **1** FALSIFICATION : falsification, distortion **2** DÉTÉRIORATION : deterioration **3** : extreme thirst
altercation [alterkasjɔ̃] *nf* : altercation, quarrel
altérer [altere] {87} *vt* **1** FALSIFIER : to falsify, to distort **2** CORROMPRE : to spoil, to impair **3** : to make thirsty — **s'altérer** *vr* : to deteriorate
alternance [alternɑ̃s] *nf* **1** : alternation, rotation **2 en ~** : alternately
alternateur [alternatœr] *nm* : alternator
alternatif, -tive [alternatif, -tiv] *adj* **1** : alternative, alternate **2** : alternating
alternative [alternativ] *nf* : alternative
alternativement [alternativmɑ̃] *adv* : in turn, alternately
alterner [alterne] *v* : to alternate
altesse [altɛs] *nf* : highness <Son Altesse : His Highness, Her Highness>
altier, -tière [altje, -tjɛr] *adj* : haughty
altimètre [altimɛtr] *nm* : altimeter

altitude [altityd] *nf* : altitude <en altitude : at high altitude(s)> <à 2 000 mètres d'altitude : at a height of 2,000 meters>
alto [alto] *nm* **1** : viola **2** : alto (instrument)
altruisme [altrɥism] *nm* : altruism
altruiste[1] [altrɥist] *adj* : altruistic
altruiste[2] *nmf* : altruist
aluminium [alyminjɔm] *nm* : aluminum
alun [alœ̃] *nm* : alum
alunir [alynir] *vi* : to land on the moon
alvéole [alveɔl] *nmf* **1** : alveolus, cell <alvéole dentaire : tooth socket> **2** : pit, cavity (in geology)
alvéolé, -lée [alveɔle] *adj* : honeycombed
amabilité [amabilite] *nf* **1** : kindness <avoir l'amabilité de : to be so kind as to> **2** : politeness <avec amabilité : courteously> **3 amabilités** *nfpl* : civilities, polite remarks
amadou [amadu] *nm* : tinder
amadouer [amadwe] *vt* **1** : to coax, to cajole **2** : to mollify
amaigrir [amegrir] *vt* : to make thin
amaigrissement [amegrismɑ̃] *nm* **1** : reducing, slimming **2** : weight loss, emaciation
amalgame [amalgam] *nm* **1** : amalgam **2** MÉLANGE : mixture
amalgamer [amalgame] *vt* **1** : to amalgamate **2** : to mix, to combine — **s'amalgamer** *vr*
amande [amɑ̃d] *nf* **1** : almond **2** : kernel (of a fruit or nut)
amant, -mante [amɑ̃, -mɑ̃t] *n* : lover
amarrage [amaraʒ] *nm* : mooring <poste d'amarrage : anchorage, berth>
amarrer [amare] *vt* **1** : to moor **2** : to tie (up), to secure — **s'amarrer** *vr*
amaryllis [amarilis] *nf* : amaryllis
amas [ama] *nm* **1** : pile, heap **2** : cluster (in astronomy), mass (in mineralogy)
amasser [amase] *vt* ACCUMULER : to amass, to pile up — **s'amasser** *vr* : to build up
amateur[1] [amatœr] *adj* : amateur
amateur[2] *nm* **1** : connoisseur, enthusiast **2** : amateur
amazone [amazon] *nf* **1** : horsewoman **2 monter en amazone** : to ride sidesaddle
ambages [ɑ̃baʒ] *nfpl* **sans ~** : plainly, unambiguously
ambassade [ɑ̃basad] *nf* : embassy
ambassadeur, -drice [ɑ̃basadœr, -dris] *n* : ambassador
ambiance [ɑ̃bjɑ̃s] *nf* : ambience, atmosphere
ambiant, -biante [ɑ̃bjɑ̃, -bjɑ̃t] *adj* : ambient, surrounding
ambidextre [ɑ̃bidekstr] *adj* : ambidextrous
ambigu, -guë [ɑ̃bigy] *adj* : ambiguous — **ambiguïté** [ɑ̃biguite] *nf*
ambitieux, -tieuse [ɑ̃bisjø, -sjøz] *adj* : ambitious — **ambitieusement** [-sjøzmɑ̃] *adv*
ambition [ɑ̃bisjɔ̃] *nf* **1** : ambition **2** : claim, pretension
ambitionner [ɑ̃bisjɔne] *vt* **1** : to aim for, to aspire to **2** *Can* : to exaggerate, to go overboard
ambivalence [ɑ̃bivalɑ̃s] *nf* : ambivalence — **ambivalent, -lente** [-valɑ̃, -lɑ̃t] *adj*
ambler [ɑ̃ble] *vi* : to amble — **amble** [ɑ̃bl] *nm*
ambre [ɑ̃br] *nm* **1** : amber **2 ambre gris** : ambergris
ambroisie [ɑ̃brwazi] *nf* : ragweed
ambulance [ɑ̃bylɑ̃s] *nf* : ambulance
ambulancier, -cière [ɑ̃bylɑ̃sje, -sjɛr] *n* : ambulance driver
ambulant, -lante [ɑ̃bylɑ̃, -lɑ̃t] *adj* : traveling, itinerant <cirque ambulant : traveling circus>
ambulatoire [ɑ̃bylatwar] *adj* : ambulatory
âme [am] *nf* **1** : soul, spirit <rendre l'âme : to breathe one's last, to give up the ghost> <âme sœur : soul mate, kindred spirit> **2 état d'âme** : state of mind
amélioration [ameljɔrasjɔ̃] *nf* : amelioration, improvement
améliorer [ameljɔre] *vt* : to ameliorate, to improve — **s'améliorer** *vr*
amen [amen] *interj* : amen
aménagement [amenaʒmɑ̃] *nm* **1** : development, planning <l'aménagement urbain : urban development> **2** : conversion (of rooms, buildings, etc.) **3** : equipping, fitting out <aménagements intérieurs : fittings, fixtures> **4** : adjustment (of taxes, schedules, etc.)
aménager [amenaʒe] {17} *vt* **1** : to plan, to lay out **2** : to convert <une grange aménagée : a converted barn> **3** : to equip, to fit out **4** : to adjust, to arrange
amende [amɑ̃d] *nf* **1** : fine, penalty **2 faire amende honorable** : to make amends
amendement [amɑ̃dmɑ̃] *nm* : amendment
amender [amɑ̃de] *vt* **1** : to amend **2** AMÉLIORER : to improve — **s'amender** *vr* : to mend one's ways
amener [amne] {52} *vt* **1** : to bring, to take **2** : to bring about, to cause **3** : to bring up — **s'amener** *vr fam* : to show up, to turn up
amenuiser [amənɥize] *vt* : to reduce — **s'amenuiser** *vr* : to diminish, to dwindle
amer, -mère [amɛr] *adj* : bitter — **amèrement** [amɛrmɑ̃] *adv*
américain, -caine [amerikɛ̃, -kɛn] *adj* : American

Américain, -caine *n* : American
américanisme [amerikanism] *nm* : Americanism
amertume [amɛrtym] *nf* : bitterness
améthyste [ametist] *nf* : amethyst
ameublement [amœbləmɑ̃] *nm* **1** : furnishing **2** MEUBLES : furniture
ameuter [amøte] *vt* : to stir up, to rouse — **s'ameuter** *vr* : to form a mob
ami[1], **-mie** [ami] *adj* : friendly
ami[2], **-mie** *n* **1** : friend <ami intime : close friend> <ami des bêtes : animal lover> <ami des arts : patron of the arts> **2** *or* **petit ami** : boyfriend **3** *or* **petite amie** : girlfriend
amiable [amjabl] *adj* **à l'amiable** : amicable, private <un accord à l'amiable : a settlement out of court>
amiante [amjɑ̃t] *nm* : asbestos
amibe [amib] *nf* : amoeba
amibien, -bienne [amibjɛ̃, -bjɛn] *adj* : amoebic
amical, -cale [amikal] *adj, mpl* **-caux** [-ko] : friendly
amicalement [amikalmɑ̃] *adv* **1** : amicably, in a friendly manner **2** (*used in correspondence*) : yours (truly), best wishes
amidon [amidɔ̃] *nm* : starch
amidonner [amidɔne] *vt* : to starch
amincir [amɛ̃sir] *vt* : to make thinner — **s'amincir** *vr*
aminé [amine] *adj* **acide aminé** : amino acid
amiral [amiral] *nm, pl* **-raux** [-ro] : admiral
amitié [amitje] *nf* **1** : friendship <prendre en amitié : to befriend, to take a liking to> **2** : kindness, favor **3** **amitiés** *nfpl* : best wishes, best regards
ammoniac [amɔnjak] *nm* : ammonia (gas)
ammoniaque [amɔnjak] *nf* : ammonia, ammonia water
amnésie [amnezi] *nf* : amnesia
amnésique [amnezik] *adj & nmf* : amnesiac, amnesic
amnistie [amnisti] *nf* : amnesty
amocher [amɔʃe] *vt fam* : to bash
amoindrir [amwɛ̃drir] *vt* RÉDUIRE : to reduce, to diminish, to undermine — **s'amoindrir** *vr* : to lessen, to diminish
amoindrissement [amwɛ̃drismɑ̃] *nm* : reduction
amollir [amɔlir] *vt* : to soften — **s'amollir** *vr* **1** : to become soft **2** : to weaken
amonceler [amɔ̃sle] {8} *vt* : to pile up, to accumulate — **s'amonceler** *vr*
amoncellement [amɔ̃selmɑ̃] *nm* : pile, heap, mass
amont [amɔ̃] *nm* **en ~** : upstream, uphill
amoral, -rale [amɔral] *adj, mpl* **-raux** [-ro] : amoral
amorce [amɔrs] *nf* **1** : beginning(s), start <l'amorce de récession : the beginnings of recession> **2** APPÂT : bait **3** : detonator, cap
amorcer [amɔrse] {6} *vt* **1** : to begin **2** APPÂTER : to bait, to entice **3** : to prime **4** : to boot (a computer) — **s'amorcer** *vr* : to begin
amorphe [amɔrf] *adj* **1** APATHIQUE : apathetic, passive **2** : amorphous
amorti [amɔrti] *nm Can* : bunt (in baseball) <amorti-sacrifice : sacrifice bunt>
amortir [amɔrtir] *vt* **1** : to absorb, to cushion (a blow, etc.), to deaden (sound) **2** : to make (something) pay for itself **3** : to pay off, to amortize
amortissement [amɔrtismɑ̃] *nm* **1** : absorption, cushioning **2** : amortization
amortisseur [amɔrtisœr] *nm* : shock absorber
amour [amur] *nm* **1** : love, affection, passion <l'amour du prochain : love of one's neighbor> <faire l'amour : to make love> **2** : romance, love affair
amoureusement [amurøzmɑ̃] *adv* : lovingly, amorously
amoureux[1], **-reuse** [amurø, -røz] *adj* **1** : in love, amorous **2** : loving
amoureux[2], **-reuse** *n* : lover
amour-propre [amurprɔpr] *nm* : self-esteem
amovible [amɔvibl] *adj* : removable, detachable
ampère [ɑ̃pɛr] *nm* : ampere
ampèremètre [ɑ̃pɛrmɛtr] *nm* : ammeter
amphétamine [ɑ̃fetamin] *nf* : amphetamine
amphibie [ɑ̃fibi] *adj* : amphibious
amphibien [ɑ̃fibjɛ̃] *nm* : amphibian
amphithéâtre [ɑ̃fiteatr] *nm* **1** : amphitheater **2** : lecture hall, auditorium
ample [ɑ̃pl] *adj* : ample, full, generous — **amplement** [ɑ̃pləmɑ̃] *adv*
ampleur [ɑ̃plœr] *nf* **1** : size, scale, extent **2** : fullness (of clothing)
amplificateur [ɑ̃plifikatœr] *nm* : amplifier
amplification [ɑ̃plifikasjɔ̃] *nf* **1** : amplification **2** : development, expansion
amplifier [ɑ̃plifje] {96} *vt* **1** : to amplify, to enlarge, to magnify **2** : to expand, to increase — **s'amplifier** *vr*
amplitude [ɑ̃plityd] *nf* : amplitude
ampoule [ɑ̃pul] *nf* **1** : lightbulb **2** : blister **3** : vial
ampoulé, -lée [ɑ̃pule] *adj* : pompous, bombastic
amputation [ɑ̃pytasjɔ̃] *nf* : amputation
amputer [ɑ̃pyte] *vt* **1** : to amputate **2** : to cut drastically
amulette [amylɛt] *nf* : amulet
amusant, -sante [amyzɑ̃, -zɑ̃t] *adj* : amusing
amuse-gueule [amyzgœl] *nms & pl* : appetizer, canapé
amusement [amyzmɑ̃] *nm* **1** : amusement **2** : diversion, pastime

amuser [amyze] *vt* DIVERTIR : to amuse — **s'amuser** *vr* **1** : to play **2** : to enjoy oneself, to have fun
amuseur, -seuse [amyzœr, -zøz] *n* : entertainer
amygdale [amidal] *nf* : tonsil
amygdalite [amidalit] *nf* : tonsilitis
an [ɑ̃] *nm* **1** : year <elle a treize ans : she is thirteen years old> <l'an prochain : next year> **2 bon an, mal an** : year in, year out **3 le Jour de l'an** *or* **le Nouvel An** : New Year's Day
anachronique [anakrɔnik] *adj* : anachronistic
anachronisme [anakrɔnism] *nm* : anachronism
anaconda [anakɔ̃da] *nm* : anaconda
anagramme [anagram] *nf* : anagram
anal, -nale [anal] *adj, mpl* **anaux** [ano] : anal
analgésique [analʒezik] *adj & nm* : analgesic
analogie [analɔʒi] *nf* : analogy
analogique [analɔʒik] *adj* : analog
analogue [analɔg] *adj* : analogous, similar
analphabète [analfabet] *adj & nmf* : illiterate
analphabétisme [analfabetism] *nm* : illiteracy
analyse [analiz] *nf* **1** : analysis **2** : test <analyse du sang : blood test>
analyser [analize] *vt* **1** : to analyze **2** : to test (in medicine)
analyste [analist] *nmf* : analyst
analytique [analitik] *adj* : analytic, analytical — **analytiquement** [-tikmɑ̃] *adv*
ananas [anana(s)] *nms & pl* : pineapple
anarchie [anarʃi] *nf* : anarchy — **anarchique** [anarʃik] *adj*
anarchiste[1] [anarʃist] *adj* : anarchist, anarchistic
anarchiste[2] *nmf* : anarchist
anathème [anatɛm] *nm* : anathema
anatife [anatif] *nm* : barnacle
anatomie [anatɔmi] *nf* : anatomy
anatomique [anatɔmik] *adj* : anatomic, anatomical — **anatomiquement** [-mikmɑ̃] *adv*
ancestral, -trale [ɑ̃sɛstral] *adj, mpl* **-traux** [-tro] : ancestral
ancêtre [ɑ̃sɛtr] *nmf* : ancestor
anche [ɑ̃ʃ] *nf* : reed (of a musical instrument)
anchois [ɑ̃ʃwa] *nms & pl* : anchovy
ancien[1], **-cienne** [ɑ̃sjɛ̃, -sjɛn] *adj* **1** : former <anciens combattants : veterans> **2** VIEUX : ancient, old **3 ancien elève, ancienne elève** : alumnus *m*, alumna *f*
ancien[2] *nm* **1** : elder, old man **2 l'ancien** : antiques *pl* **3 les anciens** *nmpl* : the ancients
anciennement [ɑ̃sjɛnmɑ̃] *adv* : formerly
ancienneté [ɑ̃sjɛnte] *nf* **1** : seniority **2** : antiquity **3** : oldness, age
ancrage [ɑ̃kraʒ] *nm* : anchorage
ancre [ɑ̃kr] *nf* : anchor <jeter l'ancre : to drop anchor>
ancrer [ɑ̃kre] *vt* **1** : to anchor **2** : to fix firmly, to root — **s'ancrer** *vr*
andorran, -rane [ɑ̃dɔrɑ̃, -ran] *adj* : Andorran
Andorran, -rane *n* : Andorran
andouille [ɑ̃duj] *nf* **1** : andouille (sausage made from chitterlings) **2** *fam* : fool
androgyne [ɑ̃drɔʒin] *adj* : androgynous
âne [an] *nm* **1** : ass, donkey **2** IMBÉCILE : fool, idiot
anéantir [aneɑ̃tir] *vt* **1** DÉTRUIRE : to destroy, to wipe out **2** : to overwhelm, to exhaust — **s'anéantir** *vr* : to be dashed, to be shattered
anéantissement [aneɑ̃tismɑ̃] *nm* : annihilation, destruction
anecdote [anɛkdɔt] *nf* : anecdote
anecdotique [anɛkdɔtik] *adj* : anecdotal
anémie [anemi] *nf* : anemia — **anémique** [anemik] *adj*
anémone [anemɔn] *nf* : anemone
ânerie [anri] *nf* **1** BÊTISE : blunder, stupid mistake **2** : stupidity **3** : stupid remark, nonsense
anesthésie [anɛstezi] *nf* : anesthesia
anesthésier [anɛstezje] {96} *vt* : to anesthetize
anesthésique [anɛstezik] *adj & nm* : anesthetic
anesthésiste [anɛstezist] *nmf* : anesthetist
aneth [anet] *nm* : dill
anfractuosité [ɑ̃fraktɥɔzite] *nf* : crevice
ange [ɑ̃ʒ] *nm* : angel <ange gardien : guardian angel>
angélique [ɑ̃ʒelik] *adj* : angelic, angelical — **angéliquement** [-likmɑ̃] *adv*
angelot [ɑ̃ʒlo] *nm* : cherub
angine [ɑ̃ʒin] *nf* **1** : sore throat, throat infection **2** *or* **angine rouge** : tonsillitis **3** *or* **angine de poitrine** : angina
anglais[1], **-glaise** [ɑ̃glɛ, -glɛz] *adj* : English
anglais[2] *nm* : English (language)
Anglais, -glaise *n* : Englishman *m*, Englishwoman *f*
angle [ɑ̃gl] *nm* **1** : angle <angle droit : right angle> <angle aigu : acute angle> **2** COIN : corner
anglicisme [ɑ̃glisism] *nm* : anglicism
anglophone[1] [ɑ̃glɔfɔn] *adj* : English-speaking
anglophone[2] *nmf* : English speaker
anglo-saxon[1], **-saxonne** [ɑ̃glɔsaksɔ̃, -saksɔn] *adj* : Anglo-Saxon
anglo-saxon[2] *nm* : Anglo-Saxon (language)
Anglo-Saxon, -Saxonne *n* : Anglo-Saxon
angoissant, -sante [ɑ̃gwasɑ̃, -sɑ̃t] *adj* : agonizing
angoisse [ɑ̃gwas] *nf* : anguish

angoisser [ãgwase] *vt* : to distress, to worry
angolais, -laise [ãgɔlɛ, -lɛz] *adj* : Angolan
Angolais, -laise *n* : Angolan
angora [ãgɔra] *nm* : angora
anguille [ãgij] *nf* **1** : eel **2 il y a anguille sous roche** : there's something fishy going on
angulaire [ãgylɛr] *adj* : angular
anguleux, -leuse [ãgylø, -løz] *adj* : angular, sharp
anicroche [anikrɔʃ] *nf* ACCROC : snag, small problem
animal[1], **-male** [animal] *adj, mpl* **-maux** [-mo] : animal <le règne animal : the animal kingdom>
animal[2] *nm, pl* **-maux** : animal
animalier, -lière [animalje, -ljɛr] *adj* : animal <un peintre animalier : a wildlife painter>
animateur, -trice [animatœr, -tris] *n* **1** : leader, organizer **2** : host <animateur d'une émission de télévision : television show host> **3** : (cartoon) animator
animation [animasjɔ̃] *nf* **1** : organizing, coordinating **2** : liveliness, vivacity **3** : animation (in movies)
animé, -mée [anime] *adj* **1** : lively, animated **2** : living, animate
animer [anime] *vt* **1** : to enliven, to brighten up **2** : to drive, to impel **3** : to host, to present **4** : to animate, to bring to life — **s'animer** *vr* **1** : to become lively **2** : to come to life
animosité [animɔzite] *nf* : animosity
anis [ani(s)] *nm* : anise
ankyloser [ãkiloze] *v* **s'ankyloser** *vr* : to stiffen (up)
ankylostome [ãkilɔstɔm] *nm* : hookworm
annales [anal] *nfpl* : annals
anneau [ano] *nm, pl* **anneaux** : ring
année [ane] *nf* : year <année bissextile : leap year> <souhaiter la bonne année à qqn : to wish s.o. a happy New Year>
année–lumière [anelymjɛr] *nf, pl* **années–lumière** : light-year
annexe[1] [anɛks] *adj* **1** : related, associated **2** : appended, attached
annexe[2] *nf* **1** : annex (of a building) **2** : appendix, annex (of a document)
annexer [anɛkse] *vt* **1** : to annex **2** : to append
annexion [anɛksjɔ̃] *nf* : annexation
annihilation [aniilasjɔ̃] *nf* : destruction, annihilation
annihiler [aniile] *vt* : to destroy, to annihilate
anniversaire [anivɛrsɛr] *nm* **1** : anniversary **2** : birthday
annonce [anɔ̃s] *nf* **1** : announcement, notice **2** : advertisement <petite annonce : classified ad> <annonce publicitaire : commercial>
annoncer [anɔ̃se] {6} *vt* **1** DÉCLARER : to announce **2** PRÉDIRE : to predict — **s'annoncer** *vr* **1** : to be looming **2** : to look (to be) <les négociations s'annoncent difficiles : the negotiations promise to be difficult>
annonceur, -ceuse [anɔ̃sœr, -søz] *n* **1** : advertiser **2** *Can* : announcer (on radio, television, etc.)
annonciateur, -trice [anɔ̃sjatœr, -tris] *adj* : heralding, presaging
annoter [anɔte] *vt* : to annotate — **annotation** [anɔtasjɔ̃] *nf*
annuaire [anɥɛr] *nm* **1** : directory <annuaire téléphonique : telephone directory> **2** : yearbook
annuel, -nuelle [anɥɛl] *adj* : annual — **annuellement** [anɥɛlmã] *adv*
annulaire [anylɛr] *nm* : ring finger
annulation [anylasjɔ̃] *nf* **1** : cancellation **2** : annulment
annuler [anyle] *vt* **1** : to cancel, to call off **2** : to revoke, to annul
anode [anɔd] *nf* : anode
anodin, -dine [anɔdɛ̃, -din] *adj* **1** INSIGNIFIANT : insignificant **2** : harmless, innocuous
anomalie [anɔmali] *nf* : anomaly
ânonner [anɔne] *vt* : to stumble through (a speech) — *vi* : to hem and haw, to drone on
anonymat [anɔnima] *nm* : anonymity, obscurity
anonyme [anɔnim] *adj* : anonymous — **anonymement** [-nimmã] *adv*
anorexie [anɔrɛksi] *nf* : anorexia — **anorexique** [-rɛksik] *adj*
anormal, -male [anɔrmal] *adj, mpl* **-maux** [-mo] : abnormal — **anormalement** [-malmã] *adv*
anormalité [anɔrmalite] *nf* : abnormality
anse [ãs] *nf* **1** : handle **2** : cove
antagonisme [ãtagɔnism] *nm* : antagonism
antagoniste[1] [ãtagɔnist] *adj* : antagonistic
antagoniste[2] *nmf* : antagonist
antan [ãtã] *nm* **d'~** : of old, of yesteryear
antarctique [ãtarktik] *adj* : antarctic
antécédent[1], **-dente** [ãtesedã, -dãt] *adj* : previous
antécédent[2] *nm* **1** : antecedent **2** : history, record <antécédents médicaux : medical history>
antenne [ãtɛn] *nf* **1** : antenna <antenne parabolique : satellite dish> **2** : antenna, feeler (of an insect)
antérieur, -rieure [ãterjœr] *adj* **1** PRÉCÉDENT : prior, previous <engagements antérieurs : previous engagements> **2** : front
antérieurement [ãterjœrmã] *adv* : previously <antérieurement à : prior to>
anthère [ãtɛr] *nf* : anther
anthologie [ãtɔlɔʒi] *nf* FLORILÈGE : anthology

anthracite [ɑ̃tʀasit] *nm* : anthracite
anthropoïde[1] [ɑ̃tʀapɔid] *adj* : anthropoid
anthropoïde[2] *nm* : anthropoid, large ape
anthropologie [ɑ̃tʀɔpɔlɔʒi] *nf* : anthropology
anthropologique [ɑ̃tʀɔpɔlɔʒik] *adj* : anthropological
anthropologiste [ɑ̃tʀɔpɔlɔʒist] *or* **anthropologue** [-pɔlɔg] *nmf* : anthropologist
anthropophage[1] [ɑ̃tʀɔpɔfaʒ] *adj* : cannibalistic
anthropophage[2] *nmf* CANNIBALE : cannibal
anthropophagie [ɑ̃tʀɔpɔfaʒi] *nf* : cannibalism
antiadhésif, -sive [ɑ̃tiadesif, -siv] *adj* : antiadhesive, nonstick
antiaérien, -rienne [ɑ̃tiaeʀjɛn] *adj* : antiaircraft
antibiotique [antibiɔtik] *adj & nm* : antibiotic
antiblocage [ɑ̃tibloka3] *adj* : antilock
antichambre [ɑ̃ti[ɑ̃bʀ] *nf* : anteroom
anticipation [ɑ̃tisipasjɔ̃] *nf* **1** : anticipation **2 par ~** : in advance
anticiper [ɑ̃tisipe] *vt* **1** PRÉVOIR : to anticipate, to foresee **2** : to do or pay in advance — *vi* : to think ahead
anticlérical, -cale [ɑ̃tiklerikal] *adj, mpl* **-caux** [-ko] : anticlerical
anticommuniste [ɑ̃tikɔmynist] *adj & nmf* : anticommunist
anticonceptionnel, -nelle [ɑ̃tikɔ̃sɛpsjɔnɛl] *adj* CONTRACEPTIF : contraceptive
anticorps [ɑ̃tikɔʀ] *nms & pl* : antibody
antidater [ɑ̃tidate] *vt* : to antedate, to predate
antidémocratique [ɑ̃tidemɔkratik] *adj* : antidemocratic, undemocratic
antidépresseur [ɑ̃tidepʀesœʀ] *adj & nm* : antidepressant
antidérapant, -pante [ɑ̃tiderapɑ̃, -pɑ̃t] *adj* : nonskid
antidote [ɑ̃tidɔt] *nm* : antidote
antidrogue [ɑ̃tidʀɔg] *adj* : antidrug
antifasciste [ɑ̃tifaʃist] *adj* : antifascist
antigel [ɑ̃tiʒɛl] *nm* : antifreeze
antihistaminique [ɑ̃tiistaminik] *nm* : antihistamine
anti-inflammatoire [ɑ̃tiɛ̃flamatwaʀ] *adj* : anti-inflammatory
antillais, -laise [ɑ̃tijɛ, -jɛz] *adj* : West Indian
Antillais, -laise *n* : West Indian
antilope [ɑ̃tilɔp] *nf* : antelope
antimite [ɑ̃timit] *adj* **boules antimites** : mothballs
antimoine [ɑ̃timwan] *nm* : antimony
antinucléaire [ɑ̃tinykleeʀ] *adj* : antinuclear
antioxydant [antiɔksidɑ̃] *nm* : antioxidant — **antioxydant, -dante** [-sidɑ̃, -dɑ̃t] *adj*
antipathie [ɑ̃tipati] *nf* AVERSION : antipathy
antipode [ɑ̃tipɔd] *nm* **1** : antipode **2 être aux antipodes de** : to be diametrically opposed to
antiquaire [ɑ̃tikɛʀ] *nmf* : antique dealer
antique [ɑ̃tik] *adj* **1** : ancient **2** : antique **3** : old-fashioned, antiquated
antiquité [ɑ̃tikite] *nf* **1** : antiquity **2** : antique
antirabique [ɑ̃tirabik] *adj* : rabies <vaccin antirabique : rabies vaccine>
antirévolutionnaire [ɑ̃tirevɔlysjɔnɛʀ] *adj* : antirevolutionary
antisémite [ɑ̃tisemit] *adj* : anti-Semitic
antisémitisme [ɑ̃tisemitism] *nm* : anti-Semitism
antiseptique [ɑ̃tiseptik] *adj & nm* : antiseptic
antisocial, -ciale [ɑ̃tisɔsjal] *adj, mpl* **-ciaux** [-sjo] : antisocial
antitabac [ɑ̃titaba] *adj* : antismoking
antithèse [ɑ̃titɛz] *nf* : antithesis
antitoxine [ɑ̃titɔksin] *nf* : antitoxin
antitrust [ɑ̃titʀœst] *adj* : antitrust
antitussif, -sive [ɑ̃titysif, -siv] *adj* : cough <sirop antitussif : cough syrup>
antivol [ɑ̃tivɔl] *adj* : antitheft
antonyme [ɑ̃tɔnim] *nm* : antonym
antre [ɑ̃tʀ] *nm* **1** : den, lair **2** : cave
anus [anys] *nms & pl* : anus
anxiété [ɑ̃ksjete] *nf* : anxiety
anxieux, anxieuse [ɑ̃ksjø, -sjøz] *adj* : anxious — **anxieusement** [-sjøzmɑ̃] *adv*
aorte [aɔʀt] *nf* : aorta
août [u(t)] *nm* : August
apaisement [apɛzmɑ̃] *nm* **1** : calming (down), soothing **2** : appeasement (in politics) **3 apaisements** *nmpl* : reassurances
apaiser [apeze] *vt* **1** : to pacify, to appease **2** : to assuage (hunger, thirst, etc.) **3** : to soothe, to calm, to mollify — **s'apaiser** *vr* : to die down, to calm down, to abate
apanage [apanaʒ] *nm* : prerogative
aparté [aparte] *nm* **1** : aside (in theater) **2** : private conversation
apartheid [apartɛd] *nm* : apartheid
apathie [apati] *nf* : apathy
apathique [apatik] *adj* : apathetic
apercevoir [apɛʀsəvwaʀ] {26} *vt* : to perceive, to see — **s'apercevoir** *vr* **1** : to catch sight of each other **2 ~ de** : to notice, to become aware of **3 ~ que** : to notice that, to realize that
aperçu [apɛʀsy] *nm* **1** : glimpse **2** : outline, general idea <avoir des aperçus sur : to have some insight into>
apéritif [aperitif] *nm* : aperitif
apesanteur [apəzɑ̃tœʀ] *nf* : weightlessness
à-peu-près [apøpʀe] *nms & pl* : approximation

apeuré, -rée [apœre] *adj* : frightened, scared
apex [apɛks] *nms & pl* : apex
aphorisme [afɔrism] *nm* : aphorism
aphrodisiaque [afrɔdizjak] *adj & nm* : aphrodisiac
apiculteur, -trice [apikyltœr, -tris] *n* : beekeeper
apitoiement [apitwamɑ̃] *nm* : pity, compassion
apitoyer [apitwaje] {58} *vt* : to move (someone) to pity — **s'apitoyer** *vr* ~ **sur** : to feel sorry for
aplanir [aplanir] *vt* **1** : to plane, to level **2** : to iron out, to resolve (a problem) — **s'aplanir** *vr*
aplatir [aplatir] *vt* : to flatten — **s'aplatir** *vr*
aplomb [aplɔ̃] *nm* **1** : aplomb, composure <perdre son aplomb : to lose one's nerve> **2** : perpendicularity **3 d'aplomb** : steady, balanced, upright
apocalypse [apɔkalips] *nf* : apocalypse
apocalyptique [apɔkaliptik] *adj* : apocalyptic
apocryphe [apɔkrif] *nm* **les Apocryphes** : the Apocrypha
apogée [apɔʒe] *nm* **1** : peak, culmination **2** : apogee (in astronomy)
apolitique [apɔlitik] *adj* : apolitical
apologie [apɔlɔʒi] *nf* : defense, justification
apoplexie [apɔpleksi] *nf* : apoplexy — **apoplectique** [-plɛktik] *adj*
apostolique [apɔstɔlik] *adj* : apostolic
apostrophe [apɔstrɔf] *nf* **1** : direct address (in grammar) **2** : invective, rude remark **3** : apostrophe (sign of punctuation)
apostropher [apɔstrɔfe] *vt* : to shout at, to address rudely
apothéose [apɔteoz] *nf* **1** : highlight, crowning moment, grand finale **2** : apotheosis
apôtre [apotr] *nm* : apostle
apparaître [aparetr] {7} *vi* : to appear — *v impers* : to appear, to seem <il apparaît que : it seems that>
apparat [apara] *nm* **1** CÉRÉMONIE : pomp **2 d'~** : ceremonial
appareil [aparej] *nm* **1** : apparatus, device, appliance <appareil de télévision : television set> <appareil photo : camera> <appareil auditif : hearing aid> <appareil de chauffage : heater> **2** : telephone **3** : system <appareil digestif : digestive system>
appareillage [apareja3] *nm* **1** : outfitting, equipment **2** : casting off (of a ship)
appareiller [apareje] *vt* **1** : to fit out (a ship, etc.) **2** : to match up, to pair — *vi* : to get under way
apparemment [aparamɑ̃] *adv* : apparently
apparence [aparɑ̃s] *nf* **1** ASPECT : appearance, appearing, guise **2 en ~** : apparently
apparent, -rente [aparɑ̃, -rɑ̃t] *adj* : apparent
apparenté, -tée [aparɑ̃te] *adj* : related
apparier [aparje] {96} *vt* : to pair, to match (up)
apparition [aparisjɔ̃] *nf* **1** : appearance **2** : apparition, ghost
appartement [apartəmɑ̃] *nm* : apartment
appartenance [apartənɑ̃s] *nf* : membership, affiliation, belonging
appartenir [apartənir] {92} *vi* **1 ~ à** : to belong to <ça m'appartient : that belongs to me> **2 ~ à** : to be a member of — *v impers* : to be up to <il appartient à vous de le faire : it's up to you to do it>
appât [apa] *nm* : bait, lure <mordre à l'appât : to take the bait>
appâter [apate] *vt* **1** : to bait **2** : to lure, to entice
appauvrir [apovrir] *vt* : to impoverish — **s'appauvrir** *vr*
appauvrissement [apovrismɑ̃] *nm* : impoverishment
appeau [apo] *nm, pl* **appeaux** : decoy
appel [apɛl] *nm* **1** : call <un appel téléphonique : a telephone call> <cri d'appel : call for help> **2** : appeal
appelé [aple] *nm* : draftee
appeler [aple] {8} *vt* **1** : to call <appeler au secours : to call for help> <tu m'appelleras au téléphone ce soir? : you'll phone me tonight?> **2** : to summon <faire appeler le médecin : to send for the doctor> **3** EXIGER : to require, to call for **4** NOMMER : to name **5 en appeler à** : to appeal to **6 en appeler de** : to appeal against, to dispute — **s'appeler** *vr* : to be named, to be called <je m'appelle Isabelle : my name is Isabelle>
appellation [apelasjɔ̃] *nf* **1** : name, designation **2 appellation contrôlée** : guaranteed vintage (of wine)
appelle [apɛl], **appellera** [apɛlərа], *etc.* → **appeler**
appendice [apɑ̃dis] *nm* **1** : appendix (of a book) **2** : appendix (in anatomy) **3** : appendage, annex
appendicectomie [apɛ̃disɛktɔmi] *nf* : appendectomy
appendicite [apɑ̃disit] *nf* : appendicitis
appentis [apɑ̃ti] *nm* : lean-to, shed
appesantir [apəzɑ̃tir] *vt* : to weigh down, to slow down, to dull <les sens appesantis par l'épuisement : senses dulled by fatigue> — **s'appesantir** *vr* **1** : to grow heavier **2 ~ sur** : to dwell upon
appétissant, -sante [apetisɑ̃, -sɑ̃t] *adj* : appetizing
appétit [apeti] *nm* : appetite <bon appétit! : enjoy your meal!> <ouvrir l'appétit de qqn : to whet s.o.'s appetite>
applaudir [aplodir] *vt* : to applaud <applaudir une décision : to applaud a

decision> — *vi* : to applaud, to clap — **s'applaudir** *vr* : to congratulate oneself

applaudissements [aplodismɑ̃] *nmpl* : applause

applicable [aplikabl] *adj* : applicable — **applicabilité** [-kabilite] *nf*

applicateur [aplikatœr] *nm* : applicator

application [aplikasjɔ̃] *nf* **1** : applying (of paint, etc.) **2** : application, practicing <mettre en application : to put into practice> **3** : care <avec application : diligently, industriously>

applique [aplik] *nf* : appliqué

appliqué, -quée [aplike] *adj* : careful, industrious, diligent

appliquer [aplike] *vt* : to apply — **s'appliquer** *vr* **1** : to apply oneself, to take pains **2** ~ **à** : to apply to <la loi s'applique à tous : the law applies to all>

appoint [apwɛ̃] *nm* **1** : change <faire l'appoint : to make exact change> **2** : contribution, support **3 d'**~ : supplementary, extra

appointements [apwɛ̃tɔmɑ̃] *nmpl* : salary

appointer [apwɛ̃te] *vt* **1** : to pay a salary to **2** : to sharpen

apport [apɔr] *nm* **1** : contribution **2** : intake, supply

apporter [apɔrte] *vt* **1** AMENER : to bring **2** : to provide, to supply

apposer [apoze] *vt* : to put, to affix <apposez votre signature ici : sign here>

appréciable [apresjabl] *adj* : appreciable, considerable

appréciatif, -tive [apresjatif, -tiv] *adj* : appreciative

appréciation [apresjasjɔ̃] *nf* **1** : assessment, judgment **2** : appraisal, estimate **3** : appreciation (in value)

apprécier [apresje] {96} *vt* **1** : to appreciate, to value **2** ESTIMER : to appraise, to estimate — **s'apprécier** *vr* : to appreciate in value

appréhender [apreɑ̃de] *vt* **1** ARRÊTER : to apprehend, to arrest **2** : to dread

appréhension [apreɑ̃sjɔ̃] *nf* **1** : arrest **2** : dread

apprenait [aprɔnɛ] *etc.* → **apprendre**

apprendre [aprɑ̃dr] {70} *vt* **1** : to learn <j'apprends à parler l'anglais : I am learning to speak English> **2** : to hear, to learn of **3** : to teach <il m'a appris à jouer : he taught me how to play> **4** : to inform of, to tell — *vi* : to apprehend — **s'apprendre** *vr* : to be learned

apprenne [aprɛn] *etc.* → **apprendre**

apprenti, -tie [aprɑ̃ti] *n* : apprentice

apprentissage [aprɑ̃tisaʒ] *nm* **1** : apprenticeship <mettre en apprentissage : to apprentice> **2** : learning <faire l'apprentissage de : to learn about>

apprêt [aprɛ] *nm* **1** : finish, sizing, primer **2** : affectation <sans apprêt : unaffectedly> **3 apprêts** *nmpl* : preparations

apprêté, -tée [aprɛte] *adj* : affected, mannered

apprêter [aprɛte] *vt* **1** : to finish, to size, to dress **2** PRÉPARER : to prepare — **s'apprêter** *vr* : to get ready

appris [apri] *pp* → **apprendre**

apprivoiser [aprivwaze] *vt* : to tame — **s'apprivoiser** *vr* : to become tame, to become more sociable

approbateur, -trice [aprɔbatœr, -tris] *adj* : approving

approbation [aprɔbasjɔ̃] *nf* : approbation, approval

approchant, -chante [aprɔʃɑ̃, -ʃɑ̃t] *adj* : similar <qqch d'approchant : sth like that>

approche [aprɔʃ] *nf* **1** : approach <à l'approche du printemps : at the coming of spring> **2 approches** *nfpl* : surrounding area, vicinity

approcher [aprɔʃe] *vt* : to approach, to draw near to — *vi* **1** : to come near, to get nearer **2** ~ **de** : to approach, to near <nous approchons de la fin : we're nearing the end> — **s'approcher** *vr* : to approach <il s'est approché de moi : he came up to me, he approached me>

approfondi, -die [aprɔfɔ̃di] *adj* : thorough, detailed

approfondir [aprɔfɔ̃dir] *vt* **1** : to deepen **2** : to enter deeply into, to delve into

approfondissement [aprɔfɔ̃dismɑ̃] *nm* : deepening

appropriation [aprɔprijasjɔ̃] *nf* : appropriation (of property, etc.)

approprié, -priée [aprɔprije] *adj* : appropriate, suitable

approprier [aprɔprije] {96} *vt* : to adapt — **s'approprier** *vr* **1** : to appropriate **2** S'ADAPTER : to be appropriate, to be suited

approuver [apruve] *vt* **1** : to approve, to pass **2** : to approve of

approvisionnement [aprɔvizjɔnmɑ̃] *nm* : provision, supply

approvisionner [aprɔvizjɔne] *vt* **1** : to supply, to stock **2** : to pay money into (an account, etc.) — **s'approvisionner** *vr* : to stock up

approximatif, -tive [aprɔksimatif, -tiv] *adj* : approximate — **approximativement** [-tivmɑ̃] *adv*

approximation [aprɔksimasjɔ̃] *nf* : approximation

appui [apɥi] *nm* **1** SOUTIEN : support <à l'appui de : in support of> <prendre appui sur : to lean on> **2 appui de fenêtre** : windowsill

appui–bras [apɥibra] *nm, pl* **appuis–bras** : armrest

appuie [apɥi], **appuiera** [apɥira], *etc.* → **appuyer**

appui–livres [apɥilivr] *nm, pl* **appuis–livres** *Can* : bookend

appuyer [apɥije] {58} *vt* **1** : to rest, to lean **2** : to support, to back up — *vi* **1 ~ sur** : to push, to press **2 ~ sur** : to emphasize, to stress **3 ~ sur** : to bear <appuyer sur la droite : to bear right> — **s'appuyer** *vr* **1** : to lean **2 ~ à** *or* **~ contre** : to rest against **3 ~ sur** : to depend on, to rely on

âpre [apr] *adj* **1** : sour, acrid **2** : harsh, bitter <après un âpre débat : following a bitter debate> **3 âpre au gain** AVIDE : acquisitive, greedy

après¹ [apre] *adv* **1** : afterwards, later **2** : after, farther on (in space) **3** : next <qui est après? : who's next?>

après² *prep* **1** : after <jour après jour : day after day> <tournez après le pont : turn after the bridge> **2** : at, with <crier après qqn : to shout at s.o.> <je suis furieux après toi : I'm angry with you> **3 après coup** : afterwards **4 après que** : after <après qu'il a parlé : after he spoke> **5 après tout** : after all **6 d'~** : according to, from <d'après lui : in his opinion>

après–demain [apredmɛ̃] *adv* : the day after tomorrow

après–guerre [apreɡɛr] *nm* : postwar period

après–midi [apremidi] *nmfs & pl* : afternoon

âpreté [aprəte] *nf* **1** : bitterness, harshness **2** : tartness, pungency

à–propos [aprɔpo] *nm* : appropriateness, aptness <faire preuve d'à-propos : to show presence of mind> <avec à-propos : aptly, suitably>

apte [apt] *adj* : capable, fit

aptitude [aptityd] *nf* : aptitude

aquarelle [akwarɛl] *nf* : watercolor

aquarium [akwarjɔm] *nm* : aquarium

aquatique [akwatik] *adj* : aquatic <plantes aquatiques : aquatic plants>

aqueduc [akdyk] *nm* : aqueduct

aquilin [akilɛ̃] *adj m* : aquiline

ara [ara] *nm* : macaw

arabe¹ [arab] *adj* : Arab, Arabian, Arabic

arabe² *nm* : Arabic (language)

Arabe *nmf* : Arab, Arabian

arabesque [arabɛsk] *nf* : arabesque

arable [arabl] *adj* : arable

arachide [araʃid] *nf* : peanut

araignée [arene] *nf* **1** : spider **2 araignée de mer** : spider crab

arbalète [arbalɛt] *nf* : crossbow

arbitrage [arbitraʒ] *nm* **1** : arbitration **2** : refereeing, umpiring

arbitraire [arbitrɛr] *adj* : arbitrary — **arbitrairement** [-trɛrmɑ̃] *adv*

arbitre [arbitr] *nm* **1** : arbitrator **2** : umpire, referee **3** : arbiter <un arbitre du goût : an arbiter of taste> **4 libre arbitre** : free will

arbitrer [arbitre] *vt* **1** : to arbitrate **2** : to referee, to umpire — *vi* **~ entre** : to arbitrate between

arborer [arbore] *vt* **1** PORTER : to wear, to sport **2** : to bear, to display (a flag, etc.)

arboricole [arbɔrikɔl] *adj* : arboreal

arbre [arbr] *nm* **1** : tree <arbre de Noël : Christmas tree> <arbre généalogique : family tree> **2** : shaft

arbrisseau [arbriso] *nm* : shrub

arbuste [arbyst] *nm* : small shrub, bush

arc [ark] *nm* **1** : arc, curve **2** ARCHE : arch **3** : bow (in archery)

arcade [arkad] *nf* **1** : arch <arcade dentaire : dental arch> **2** : arcade

arcanes [arkan] *nmpl* : mysteries

arc–boutant [arkbutɑ̃] *nm, pl* **arcs–boutants** : flying buttress

arc–en–ciel [arkɑ̃sjɛl] *nm, pl* **arcs–en–ciel** : rainbow

archaïque [arkaik] *adj* : archaic

archange [arkɑ̃ʒ] *nm* : archangel

arche [arʃ] *nf* **1** : arch **2** : ark <l'arche de Noé : Noah's ark>

archéologie [arkeɔlɔʒi] *nf* : archaeology

archéologique [arkeɔlɔʒik] *adj* : archaeological

archéologue [arkeɔlɔg] *nmf* : archaeologist

archer [arʃe] *nm* : archer

archet [arʃɛ] *nm* : bow <archet de violon : violin bow>

archétype [arketip] *nm* : archetype

archevêque [arʃəvɛk] *nm* : archbishop

archidiocèse [arʃidjɔsɛz] *nm* : archdiocese

archipel [arʃipɛl] *nm* : archipelago

architecte [arʃitɛkt] *nmf* : architect

architecture [arʃitɛktyr] *nf* : architecture — **architectural, -rale** [-tyral] *adj, mpl* **-raux** [-ro]

archives [arʃiv] *nfpl* : archives

archiviste [arʃivist] *nmf* : archivist

arctique [arktik] *adj* : arctic <cercle arctique : arctic circle>

ardemment [ardamɑ̃] *adv* : ardently, passionately

ardent, -dente [ardɑ̃, -dɑ̃t] *adj* **1** : burning, glowing, blazing **2** : ardent, passionate

ardeur [ardœr] *nf* **1** : heat **2** : ardor, fervor

ardillon [ardijɔ̃] *nm* **1** : prong (of a buckle) **2** : barb (of a fishhook, etc.)

ardoise [ardwaz] *nf* : slate

ardu, -due [ardy] *adj* **1** : arduous, difficult **2** : steep

aréna [arena] *nm Can* : arena

arène [arɛn] *nf* **1** : arena **2 arènes** *nfpl* : amphitheater, bullring

arête [arɛt] *nf* **1** : fish bone **2** : edge, ridge **3 l'arête du nez** : the bridge of the nose

argent [arʒɑ̃] *nm* **1** : money <payer en argent comptant : to pay in cash> **2** : silver

argenté, -tée [arʒɑ̃te] *adj* **1** : silver-plated **2** : silvery **3** *fam* : loaded, well-heeled

argenterie [arʒɑ̃tri] *nf* : silverware
argentin, -tine [arʒɑ̃tɛ̃, -tin] *adj* **1** : silvery **2** : Argentine, Argentinean, Argentinian
Argentin, -tine *n* : Argentine, Argentinean, Argentinian
argile [arʒil] *nf* : clay
argileux, -leuse [arʒilø, -løz] *adj* : clayey
argon [argɔ̃] *nm* : argon
argot [argo] *nm* : argot, slang
argotique [argɔtik] *adj* : slang, slangy
arguer [argɥe] *vt* **1** : to deduce, to infer **2** ~ **de** : to use as a pretext **3** ~ **que** : to argue that, to protest that
argument [argymɑ̃] *nm* : argument
argumentation [argymɑ̃tasjɔ̃] *nf* : argumentation, rationale
argumenter [argymɑ̃te] *vi* : to argue, to debate
argutie [argysi] *nf* : quibble
aria [arja] *nf* : aria
aride [arid] *adj* **1** : arid, dry **2** : dull, uninteresting
aridité [aridite] *nf* : aridity
aristocrate [aristɔkrat] *nmf* : aristocrat — **aristocratique** [-kratik] *adj*
aristocratie [aristɔkrasi] *nf* : aristocracy
arithmétique[1] [aritmetik] *adj* : arithmetic, arithmetical
arithmétique[2] *nf* : arithmetic
arithmétiquement [aritmetikmɑ̃] *adv* : arithmetically
arlequin [arlɔkɛ̃] *nm* : harlequin
armada [armada] *nf* : armada
armature [armatyr] *nf* : frame, framework, reinforcement
arme [arm] *nf* **1** : weapon, arm <arme à feu : firearm> <prendre les armes : to take up arms> **2 armes** *nfpl* : coat of arms
armée [arme] *nf* : army
armement [armɔmɑ̃] *nm* **1** : arming, equipping (of a military force) **2** : armament, weaponry, arms *pl* <la course aux armements : the arms race>
arménien[1], **-nienne** [armenjɛ̃, -njɛn] *adj* : Armenian
arménien[2] *nm* : Armenian (language)
Arménien, -nienne *n* : Armenian
armer [arme] *vt* **1** : to arm **2** : to cock (a gun) **3** : to reinforce
armistice [armistis] *nm* : armistice
armoire [armwar] *nf* : cupboard, cabinet, wardrobe <armoire à pharmacie : medicine cabinet>
armoiries [armwari] *nfpl* : coat of arms
armoise [armwaz] *nf* : sagebrush
armure [armyr] *nf* : armor
arnaque [arnak] *nf fam* : swindle, gyp
arnaquer [arnake] *vt fam* : to rip off, to swindle, to gyp
arnaqueur, -queuse [arnakœr, -køz] *n fam* : swindler
aromate [arɔmat] *nm* : spice, herb
aromatique [arɔmatik] *adj* : aromatic
aromatiser [arɔmatize] *vt* : to flavor
arôme [arom] *nm* **1** : aroma, fragrance **2** : flavor, flavoring
arpège [arpɛʒ] *nm* : arpeggio
arpentage [arpɑ̃taʒ] *nm* : surveying
arpenter [arpɑ̃te] *vt* **1** : to pace, to stride along **2** : to survey
arpenteur, -teuse [arpɑ̃tœr, -tøz] *n* : surveyor
arqué, -quée [arke] *adj* : arched, curved <jambes arquées : bandy legs>
arrache-pied [araʃpje] *adv* **d'arrache-pied** : nonstop, relentlessly
arracher [araʃe] *vt* **1** : to uproot, to tear out **2** : to extract, to pull out <arracher une dent : to extract a tooth> **3** : to snatch, to grab — *vi* **en** ~ *Can* : to have difficulty, to have problems — **s'arracher** *vr* **1** : to pull out, to pluck <s'arracher les cheveux : to tear one's hair> **2** : to fight over **3** ~ **de** : to tear oneself away from
arraisonner [arezɔne] *vt* : to board and inspect (a ship, plane, etc.)
arrangeant, -geante [arɑ̃ʒɑ̃, -ʒɑ̃t] *adj* : accommodating, obliging
arrangement [arɑ̃ʒmɑ̃] *nm* : arrangement
arranger [arɑ̃ʒe] {17} *vt* **1** : to arrange 2 RÉPARER : to repair, to fix 3 CONVENIR : to suit, to please <cette idée arrangera tout le monde : that idea will please everyone> **4** : to settle, to sort out — **s'arranger** *vr* **1** : to come to an agreement **2** : to get better, to improve <cela va s'arranger : things will turn out all right> **3 s'arranger pour faire** : to make sure something gets done
arrérages [areraʒ] *nmpl* : arrears
arrestation [arɛstasjɔ̃] *nf* : arrest
arrêt [are] *nm* **1** : stopping, halt <sans arrêt : nonstop> **2** : stop <arrêt d'autobus : bus stop> **3** : ruling, decree **4** : save (in sports) **5 arrêts** *nmpl* : arrest (in the military) **6 arrêt du cœur** : heart failure, cardiac arrest
arrêt-court [arɛkur] *nm* : shortstop
arrêté[1], **-tée** [arete] *adj* : fixed, decided
arrêté[2] *nm* **1** : order, decree **2 arrêté de comptes** : settlement of accounts
arrêter [arete] *vt* **1** : to stop, to halt **2** : to switch off <arrêtez la radio : turn off the radio> **3** : to give up, to discontinue **4** : to arrest **5** : to decide upon, to fix — *vi* : to stop — **s'arrêter** *vr* **1** : to stop, to come to a halt **2** ~ **à** : to dwell on **3** ~ **de** : to give up <s'arrêter de fumer : to give up smoking>
arrhes [ar] *nfpl France* : deposit, down payment
arrière[1] [arjer] *adj* : back, rear <siège arrière : back seat>
arrière[2] *nm* **1** : back, rear <à l'arrière : in the back, at the rear, astern> <en arrière : backwards, back> <en arrière de : behind> **2** : fullback, back (in sports) **3 arrières** *nmpl* : rear (in

the military) **4 prendre de l'arrière** *Can* : to be slow <ma montre prend de l'arrière : my watch is slow>
arriéré¹, -rée [arjere] *adj* **1** : late, overdue **2** : backward <être arriéré : to be behind the times> **3** : (mentally) retarded
arriéré² *nm* **1** : arrears *pl* **2** : backlog
arrière-cours [arjɛrkur] *nf* : backyard
arrière-garde [arjɛrgard] *nf* : rear guard
arrière-goût [arjɛrgu] *nm* : aftertaste
arrière-grand-mère [arjɛrgrɑ̃mɛr] *nf, pl* **arrière-grands-mères** : great-grandmother
arrière-grand-père [arjɛrgrɑ̃pɛr] *nm, pl* **arrière-grands-pères** : great-grandfather
arrière-grands-parents [arjɛrgrɑ̃parɑ̃] *nmpl* : great-grandparents
arrière-pays [arjɛrpei] *nms & pl* : hinterland
arrière-pensée [arjɛrpɑ̃se] *nf* : ulterior motive
arrière-petite-enfante *f* : great-granddaughter
arrière-petit-enfant *m* : great-grandson
arrière-plan [arjɛrplɑ̃] *nm* : background
arrière-saison [arjɛrsezɔ̃] *nf* : late autumn
arrière-train [arjɛrtrɛ̃] *nm* **1** : hindquarters **2** *fam* : buttocks, bottom
arrimer [arime] *vt* **1** : to stow **2** : to secure, to fix
arrivage [arivaʒ] *nm* **1** : delivery **2** : arrival, influx (of persons)
arrivant, -vante [arivɑ̃, -vɑ̃t] *n* : newcomer, new arrival
arrivée [arive] *nf* **1** : arrival **2** : finish <ligne d'arrivée : finish line> **3** : inlet, intake (for air, gas, etc.)
arriver [arive] *vi* **1** : to arrive, to come <j'arrive! : I'm coming!> <arriver en retard : to be late> **2** : to succeed <arriver à sa fin : to achieve one's goal> <arriver à faire : to succeed in doing> **3** : to happen, to occur <cela m'est arrivé : that happened to me> <il arrive que : it happens that> **4 ~ à** ATTEINDRE : to reach
arriviste¹ [arivist] *adj* : (overly) ambitious, pushy
arriviste² *nmf* : upstart, go-getter
arrogance [arɔgɑ̃s] *nf* : arrogance
arrogant, -gante [arɔgɑ̃, -gɑ̃t] *adj* : arrogant
arroger [arɔʒe] {17} *v* **s'arroger** *vr* : to assume, to take upon oneself
arrondi [arɔ̃di] *nm* **1** : roundness **2** : hemline
arrondir [arɔ̃dir] *vt* **1** : to round, to make round **2** : to round off **3** AUGMENTER : to increase **— s'arrondir** *vr*
arrondissement [arɔ̃dismɑ̃] *nm* : district, subdivision
arrosage [arozaʒ] *nm* : watering, spraying
arroser [aroze] *vt* **1** : to water, to sprinkle, to spray **2** : to wash down (with wine), to drink to (a success, etc.) **3** : to baste (in cooking)
arroseur [arozœr] *nm* : sprinkler
arrosoir [arozwar] *nm* : watering can
arsenal [arsɔnal] *nm, pl* **-naux** [-no] **1** : arsenal, armory **2** : (naval) shipyard **3** : gear, equipment
arsenic [arsɔnik] *nm* : arsenic
art [ar] *nm* **1** : art <musée des beaux arts : museum of fine arts> <un œuvre d'art : a work of art> **2** : technique, skill
artère [artɛr] *nf* **1** : artery <durcissement des artères : hardening of the arteries> **2** : main road, thoroughfare
artériel, -rielle [arterjɛl] *adj* : arterial
artériosclérose [arterjɔskleroz] *nf* : arteriosclerosis
arthrite [artrit] *nf* : arthritis
arthritique [artritik] *adj* : arthritic
arthropode [artrɔpɔd] *nm* : arthropod
artichaut [artiʃo] *nm* : artichoke
article [artikl] *nm* **1** : article (in a publication) <article de fond : feature (article)> **2** : clause, section, article **3** : item (in commerce) <articles de toilette : toiletries> **4** : dictionary entry **5** : article (in grammar) <l'article indéfini : the indefinite article>
articulation [artikylasjɔ̃] *nf* **1** : articulation **2** JOINTURE : joint (in anatomy)
articuler [artikyle] *vt* **1** PRONONCER : to articulate, to state, to pronounce **2** : to join, to hinge **— s'articuler** *vr* : to connect <s'articuler autour de : to be based on, to hinge on>
artifice [artifis] *nm* **1** : trick, ruse **2** : artifice, device
artificiel, -cielle [artifisjɛl] *adj* : artificial, false **— artificiellement** [-sjɛlmɑ̃] *adv*
artificieux, -cieuse [artifisjø, -sjøz] *adj* : deceitful, cunning
artillerie [artijri] *nf* : artillery, gunnery
artilleur [artijœr] *nm* **1** : artilleryman, gunner **2** *Can* : pitcher (in baseball)
artisan, -sane [artizɑ̃, -zan] *n* **1** : artisan, craftsman *m*, craftswoman *f* **2** : maker, architect <artisan de la paix : peacemaker>
artisanat [artizana] *nm* **1** : artisans **2** : craft industry
artiste [artist] *nmf* : artist
artistique [artistik] *adj* : artistic **— artistiquement** [-tikmɑ̃] *adv*
as [as] *nm* **1** : ace <l'as de pique : the ace of spades> **2** : champion, ace (in sports)
ascaride [askarid] *nm* : roundworm
ascendance [asɑ̃dɑ̃s] *nf* **1** : descent, ancestry <d'ascendance égyptienne : of Egyptian descent> **2** : ascent, rising (in astronomy)

ascendant[1], **-dante** [asɑ̃dɑ̃, -dɑ̃t] *adj* : rising, ascending
ascendant[2] *nm* **1** : ascendancy, influence **2** : ascendant (in astronomy) **3 ascendants** *nmpl* : ancestors
ascenseur [asɑ̃sœr] *nm* : elevator
ascension [asɑ̃sjɔ̃] *nf* : ascent, climb
ascensionnel, -nelle [asɑ̃sjɔnɛl] *adj* : upward
ascète [aset] *nmf* : ascetic
ascétique [asetik] *adj* : ascetic
ascétisme [asetism] *nm* : asceticism
aseptique [aseptik] *adj* : aseptic
aseptiser [aseptize] *vt* : to sterilize, to disinfect
asiatique [azjatik] *adj* : Asian
Asiatique *nmf* : Asian
asile [azil] *nm* **1** : asylum, refuge <asile politique : political asylum> **2** : retreat, shelter <un asile de paix : a peaceful retreat> <asile pour la nuit : shelter for the night>
aspect [aspɛ] *nm* **1** : aspect, side **2** APPARENCE : appearance, look
asperge [aspɛrʒ] *nf* : asparagus (spear)
asperger [aspɛrʒe] *vt* {17} : to spray, to sprinkle, to splash
aspérité [asperite] *nf* **1** : bump, protrusion **2** : harshness, asperity
asphalte [asfalt] *nm* : asphalt
asphyxie [asfiksi] *nf* : asphyxiation
asphyxier [asfiksje] {96} *vt* **1** : to asphyxiate, to suffocate **2** : to stifle — **s'asphyxier** *vr*
aspic [aspik] *nm* **1** : asp **2** : aspic
aspirant, -rante [aspirɑ̃, -rɑ̃t] *n* : aspirant
aspirateur [aspiratœr] *nm* **1** : vacuum cleaner **2 passer l'aspirateur** : to vacuum
aspiration [aspirasjɔ̃] *nf* **1** : aspiration, hope **2** : suction **3** : inhaling
aspirer [aspire] *vt* **1** : to aspirate, to suck up **2** : to inhale — *vi* : to aspire <aspirer à une carrière politique : to aspire to a political career>
aspirine [aspirin] *nf* : aspirin
assagir [asaʒir] *vt* **1** : to make wiser **2** : to calm, to quiet down — **s'assagir** *vr* : to settle down
assaillant, -lante [asajɑ̃, -jɑ̃t] *n* : assailant, attacker
assaillir [asajir] {93} *vt* ATTAQUER : to assail, to attack
assainir [asenir] *vt* **1** : to clean, to purify **2** : to stabilize (an economy, etc.) — **s'assainir** *vr*
assainissement [asenismɑ̃] *nm* **1** : cleaning up, purification **2** : stabilization
assaisonnement [asɛzɔnmɑ̃] *nm* : seasoning
assaisonner [asɛzɔne] *vt* : to season
assassin[1], **-sine** [asasɛ̃, -sin] *adj* **1** : murderous **2** : provocative
assassin[2] *nm* : murderer, assassin
assassinat [asasina] *nm* : murder, assassination
assassiner [asasine] *vt* : to murder, to assassinate
assaut [aso] *nm* **1** : assault, attack <prendre d'assaut : to storm, to take by storm> **2** : match (in fencing)
assécher [aseʃe] {87} *vt* **1** : to drain **2** : to dry (up)
assemblage [asɑ̃blaʒ] *nm* **1** : assembling, combining **2** : assembly, collection **3** : joint
assemblée [asɑ̃ble] *nf* **1** RÉUNION : meeting **2** : gathering <assemblée des fidèles : congregation> **3** : assembly, parliament
assembler [asɑ̃ble] *vt* : to assemble, to bring together, to put together — **s'assembler** *vr* : to gather <s'assembler en troupeau : to herd together>
asséner [asene] {87} *vt* : to strike <asséner un coup : to deal a blow>
assentiment [asɑ̃timɑ̃] *nm* : assent, consent
asseoir [aswar] {9} *vt* **1** : to seat, to sit (someone) up, to sit (someone) down **2** : to set up, to establish — **s'asseoir** *vr* : to sit down
assermentation [asɛrmɑ̃tasjɔ̃] *nf Can* : swearing in
assermenté, -tée [asɛrmɑ̃te] *adj* : sworn
assertion [asɛrsjɔ̃] *nf* : assertion
asservir [asɛrvir] *vt* **1** : to enslave **2** : to control
asservissement [asɛrvismɑ̃] *nm* **1** : enslavement **2** : subservience
assez [ase] *adv* **1** SUFFISAMMENT : enough, sufficiently <il ne rit pas assez : he doesn't laugh enough> **2** : rather, quite <elle le fait assez bien : she does it fairly well> **3 ~ de** : enough of, sufficient
assidu, -due [asidy] *adj* **1** ZÉLÉ : diligent, zealous **2** FRÉQUENT : constant, regular — **assidûment** [-dymɑ̃] *adv*
assiduité [asiduite] *nf* **1** APPLICATION : assiduousness, diligence **2** FRÉQUENTATION : regular attendance **3 assiduités** *nfpl* : attentions
assiéger [asjeʒe] {64} *vt* ASSAILLIR : to besiege, to assail
assiette [asjɛt] *nf* **1** : plate, dish **2** : seat (on a horse) **3** : tax base **4 ne pas être dans son assiette** : to feel unwell
assiettée [asjete] *nf* : plateful
assignation [asiɲasjɔ̃] *nf* **1** : assignment, allocation **2** : summons, subpoena
assigner [asiɲe] *vt* **1** : to assign, to allot **2** : to summon, to subpoena
assimilation [asimilasjɔ̃] *nf* : assimilation
assimiler [asimile] *vt* **1** INTÉGRER : to assimilate, to integrate **2** APPRENDRE : to learn **3** IDENTIFIER : to liken, to compare, to consider the equivalent of — **s'assimiler** *vr* : to become assimilated
assis[1] [asi] *pp* → **asseoir**
assis[2], **-sise** [asiz] *adj* : seated, sitting down

assise *nf* **1** BASE : foundation, base **2** COUCHE : layer, stratum **3 assises** *nfpl* RÉUNION : meeting, conference **4 assises** *nfpl* : court <assises criminelles : criminal court>
assistance [asistãs] *nf* **1** AIDE : assistance, aid **2** : attendance **3** : audience
assistant, -tante [asistã, -tãt] *n* **1** ADJOINT : assistant <assistante sociale : social worker> **2** : spectator, audience member
assister [asiste] *vt* AIDER : to assist — *vi* ~ **à** : to attend, to be present at
association [asɔsjasjɔ̃] *nf* **1** : association **2** : partnership
associé, -ciée [asɔsje] *n* : associate, partner
associer [asɔsje] {96} *vt* **1** : to associate, to bring together, to join <associer des idées : to associate ideas> **2 associer qqn à** : to include s.o. in — **s'associer** *vr* **1** : to join together, to be combined **2** ~ **à** : to share in
assoie [aswa], **assoit** [aswa], *etc.* → **asseoir**
assoiffé, -fée [aswafe] *adj* : thirsty
assombrir [asɔ̃brir] *vt* **1** : to darken **2** : to cast a shadow over, to make gloomy — **s'assombrir** *vr*
assommant, -mante [asɔmã, -mãt] *adj* : boring, tiresome
assommer [asɔme] *vt* **1** : to stun, to knock out **2** *fam* : to bore stiff
assommoir [asɔmwar] *nm* : bludgeon, blackjack
assorti, -tie [asɔrti] *adj* : assorted
assortiment [asɔrtimã] *nm* **1** : assortment, collection, set **2** : matching, harmony (of colors, etc.) **3** : stock, inventory
assortir [asɔrtir] *vt* **1** : to match **2** APPROVISIONNER : to stock **3** ~ **de** : to combine with, to add to — **s'assortir** *vr*
assoupir [asupir] *vt* **1** ENDORMIR : to make drowsy **2** ENGOURDIR : to dull, to numb — **s'assoupir** *vr* **1** : to doze off **2** : to wane, to die down
assoupissement [asupismã] *nm* : drowsiness
assouplir [asuplir] *vt* **1** : to make supple, to soften **2** : to ease, to relax, to limber up — **s'assouplir** *vr*
assouplisseur [asuplisœr] *nm* : fabric softener
assourdir [asurdir] *vt* **1** : to deafen **2** : to deaden, to muffle
assouvir [asuvir] *vt* : to appease, to satisfy, to satiate
assoyait [aswaje], *etc.* → **asseoir**
assujettir [asyʒetir] *vt* **1** : to subjugate **2** FIXER : to fix, to fasten **3** ~ **à** : to subject to — **s'assujettir** *vr* : to submit
assujettissement [asyʒetismã] *nm* : subjugation
assumer [asyme] *vt* **1** : to assume, to take on **2** : to accept, to endure <le diagnostic était difficile à assumer : the diagnosis was difficult to accept>
assurance [asyrãs] *nf* **1** : insurance **2** PROMESSE : assurance, promise **3** CONFIANCE : confidence, self-confidence
assurance–vie *nf, pl* **assurances–vie** [asyrãsvi] : life insurance
assuré[1], **-rée** [asyre] *adj* **1** : certain, sure **2** : assured, self-confident
assuré[2], **-rée** *n* : insured person
assurément [asyremã] *adv* : certainly, definitely, assuredly
assurer [asyre] *vt* **1** GARANTIR : to assure, to guarantee **2** POURVOIR : to provide, to supply **3** : to insure **4** : to secure, to steady — **s'assurer** *vr* **1** : to make sure **2** : to secure, to get
assureur [asyrœr] *nm* : insurance agent
aster [aster] *nm* : aster
astérisque [asterisk] *nm* : asterisk
astéroïde [asterɔid] *nm* : asteroid
asthmatique [asmatik] *adj & nmf* : asthmatic
asthme [asm] *nm* : asthma
asticot [astiko] *nm* : maggot
astigmate [astigmat] *adj* : astigmatic
astigmatisme [astigmatism] *nm* : astigmatism
astiquer [astike] *vt* : to polish
astral, -trale [astral] *adj, mpl* **astraux** [astro] : astral
astre [astr] *nm* : star
astreignant, -gnante [astrɛɲã, -ɲãt] *adj* : demanding, exacting
astreindre [astrɛ̃dr] {37} *vt* : to oblige, to compel, to force — **s'astreindre** *vr*
astringent, -gente [astrɛ̃ʒã, -ʒãt] *adj* : astringent
astrologie [astrɔlɔʒi] *nf* : astrology
astrologique [astrɔlɔʒik] *adj* : astrological
astrologue [astrɔlɔg] *nmf* : astrologer
astronaute [astrɔnot] *nmf* : astronaut
astronautique [astrɔnotik] *nf* : astronautics
astronome [astrɔnɔm] *nmf* : astronomer
astronomie [astrɔnɔmi] *nf* : astronomy
astronomique [astrɔnɔmik] *adj* : astronomical — **astronomiquement** [-mikmã] *adv*
astuce [astys] *nf* **1** : astuteness, cleverness **2** TRUC : trick, maneuver **3** PLAISANTERIE : joke, pun
astucieux, -cieuse [astysjø, -sjøz] *adj* : astute, clever — **astucieusement** [-sjøzmã] *adv*
asymétrie [asimetri] *nf* : asymmetry
asymétrique [asimetrik] *adj* : asymmetrical, asymmetric
asymptomatique [asɛ̃ptomatik] *adj* : asymptomatic
atavique [atavik] *adj* : atavistic
atelier [atəlje] *nm* **1** : studio **2** : workshop
atermoiements [atɛrmwamã] *nmpl* : procrastination

atermoyer [atɛrmwaje] {58} *vi* : to procrastinate
athée[1] [ate] *adj* : atheistic
athée[2] *nmf* : atheist
athéisme [ateism] *nm* : atheism
athlète [atlɛt] *nmf* : athlete
athlétique [atletik] *adj* : athletic
athlétisme [atletism] *nm* : athletics
atlantique [atlɑ̃tik] *adj* : Atlantic
atlas [atlas] *nm* : atlas
atmosphère [atmɔsfɛr] *nf* : atmosphere
atmosphérique [atmɔsferik] *adj* : atmospheric
atoca *or* **atocas** [atɔka] *nm Can* : cranberry
atoll [atɔl] *nm* : atoll
atome [atom] *nm* **1** : atom **2 avoir des atomes crochus avec qqn** : to hit it off with s.o.
atomique [atɔmik] *adj* : atomic
atomiseur [atɔmizœr] *nm* BOMBE : spray bottle, atomizer
atone [atɔn] *adj* **1** : dull, lifeless **2** : expressionless **3** : unaccented
atours [atur] *nmpl* : finery
atout [atu] *nm* **1** : trump (card) **2** AVANTAGE : advantage, asset
âtre [atr] *nm* : hearth
atroce [atrɔs] *adj* HORRIBLE : atrocious, horrible **— atrocement** [atrɔsmɑ̃] *adv*
atrocité [atrɔsite] *nf* : atrocity
atrophie [atrɔfi] *nf* : atrophy
atrophier [atrɔfje] {96} *vt* : to atrophy **— s'atrophier** *vr*
attabler [atable] *v* **s'attabler** *vr* : to sit down at the table
attachant, -chante [ataʃɑ̃, -ʃɑ̃t] *adj* : appealing, likeable
attache [ataʃ] *nf* **1** : fastener, string, strap **2** LIEN : tie, bond
attaché, -chée [ataʃe] *n* : attaché
attaché–case [ataʃekɛz] *nm, pl* **attachés–cases** : attaché case
attachement [ataʃmɑ̃] *nm* : attachment, close tie
attacher [ataʃe] *vt* **1** : to tie, to attach, to fasten **2** : to tie up **—** *vi* : to stick **— s'attacher** *vr* **1** : to fasten (up), to be buttoned **2** : to adhere, to cling **3 s'attacher à faire** : to apply oneself to doing
attaquant, -quante [atakɑ̃, -kɑ̃t] *n* **1** : attacker **2** : forward (in sports)
attaque [atak] *nf* **1** : attack **2** : stroke, fit, attack (in medicine)
attaquer [atake] *vt* **1** : to attack, to assault **2** : to tackle, to get started on **— s'attaquer** *vr* **~ à** : to attack
attardé [atarde] *adj* **1** : late **2** : retarded **3** ARRIÉRÉ : backward, old-fashioned
attarder [atarde] *vt* : to delay, to slow down **— s'attarder** : to linger
atteignait [atenɛ], **atteignions** [atenjiɔ̃], *etc.* → **atteindre**
atteigne [atenɔ], *etc.* → **atteindre**
atteindre [atɛ̃dr] {37} *vt* **1** : to reach, to attain, to achieve **2** : to strike, to hit **3** : to affect **4** : to contact, to get in touch with
atteinte [atɛ̃t] *nf* **1** : attack <porter atteinte à : to undermine> **2 hors d'atteinte** : out of reach
attelage [atlaʒ] *nm* : team (of animals)
atteler [atle] {8} *vt* : to harness, to yoke **— s'atteler** *vr* **~ à** : to apply oneself to
attelle [atɛl] *nf* : splint
attenant, -nante [atnɑ̃, -nɑ̃t] *adj* : adjacent, adjoining
attendre [atɑ̃dr] {63} *vt* **1** : to wait for, to await <je l'attends : I'm waiting for him> <attendez voir : let's wait and see> **2** : to expect, to anticipate <attendre un bébé : to be expecting (a baby)> **3** : to be ready for <le dîner t'attend : your dinner's ready> **4** : to be in store for **—** *vi* **1** : to wait <faire attendre qqn : to keep s.o. waiting> **2 ~ après** : to be in a hurry for **3 en attendant** : in the meantime **— s'attendre** *vr* **~ à** : to expect
attendri, -drie [atɑ̃dri] *adj* : tender
attendrir [atɑ̃drir] *vt* **1** ÉMOUVOIR : to move, to touch **2** : to tenderize, to soften **— s'attendrir** *vr*
attendrissant, -sante [atɑ̃drisɑ̃, -sɑ̃t] *adj* ÉMOUVANT : moving, touching
attendrissement [atɑ̃drismɑ̃] *nm* **1** : compassion **2** : tenderness
attendu[1], **-due** [atɑ̃dy] *adj* **1** : expected **2** : long-awaited
attendu[2] *prep* **1** : considering, given <attendu sa pauvreté, il s'habille bien : considering his poverty, he dresses well> **2 attendu que** : considering that, seeing that
attentat [atɑ̃ta] *nm* **1** : attack, assault <attentat à la pudeur : indecent assault> **2** : murder attempt, assassination attempt
attente [atɑ̃t] *nf* **1** : wait, waiting <dix minutes d'attente : a ten-minute wait> **2** : expectation, hope
attenter [atɑ̃te] *vi* **~ à** : to make an attempt on (someone's life), to violate (rights, etc.)
attentif, -tive [atɑ̃tif, -tiv] *adj* **1** : attentive <être attentif à : to pay attention to> **2** : careful, scrupulous **— attentivement** [-tivmɑ̃] *adv*
attention [atɑ̃sjɔ̃] *nf* **1** : attention <faire attention : to pay attention> **2 attention!** : look out!, beware!
attentionné, -née [atɑ̃sjɔne] *adj* : considerate, attentive
atténuant, -nuante [atenɥɑ̃, -nɥɑ̃t] *adj* : extenuating, mitigating <circonstances atténuantes : extenuating circumstances>
atténuation [atenɥasjɔ̃] *nf* : reduction, easing, mitigation
atténuer [atenɥe] *vt* : to ease, to tone down, to reduce **— s'atténuer** *vr*
atterrer [atere] *vt* : to dismay, to appall

atterrir [aterir] *vi* : to land, to make a landing
atterrissage [aterisaʒ] *nm* : landing <atterrissage d'urgence : emergency landing>
attestation [atɛstasjɔ̃] *nf* **1** : affidavit, attestation **2** : certificate
attester [atɛste] *vt* : to attest, to vouch for, to testify to
attiédir [atjedir] *vt* : to make lukewarm, to cool down
attifer [atife] *vt fam* : to deck out, to doll up
attirail [atiraj] *nm* **1** : gear, equipment **2** *fam* : paraphernalia
attirance [atirɑ̃s] *nf* : attraction
attirant, -rante [atirɑ̃, -rɑ̃t] *adj* ATTRAYANT : attractive
attirer [atire] *vt* **1** : to attract **2** : to lure, to entice **3 attirer des ennuis à** : to make trouble for
attiser [atize] *vt* : to stir up, to fuel <attiser le feu : to fan the flames>
attitré, -trée [atitre] *adj* **1** OFFICIEL : official, authorized **2** HABITUEL : regular
attitude [atityd] *nf* **1** : attitude **2** : posture, bearing
attouchement [atuʃmɑ̃] *nm* : touching, fondling
attraction [atraksjɔ̃] *nf* **1** : attraction <l'attraction magnétique : magnetic force> **2 attractions** *nfpl* : attractions, amusements
attrait [atre] *nm* **1** : appeal, attraction **2 attraits** *nmpl* : charms
attrape [atrap] *nm* : trick, joke, catch
attrape–nigaud [atrapnigo] *nm fam* : con, con game
attraper [atrape] *vt* : to capture, to catch <attraper un rhume : to catch a cold> **— s'attraper** *vr*
attrayant, -trayante [atrejɑ̃, -trɛjɑ̃t] *adj* ATTIRANT : attractive <peu attrayant : unappealing, unattractive>
attribuable [atribɥabl] *adj* : attributable, ascribable
attribuer [atribɥe] *vt* **1** : to attribute, to ascribe **2** : to assign **— s'attribuer** *vr* : to claim, to appropriate
attribut [atriby] *nm* : attribute
attribution [atribysjɔ̃] *nf* **1** : attribution **2** : awarding, allotment, allocation
attrister [atriste] *vt* : to sadden
attroupement [atrupmɑ̃] *nm* : crowd
attrouper [atrupe] *v* **s'attrouper** *vr* : to gather (together)
au [o] **→ à, le**
aubaine [obɛn] *nf* **1** : godsend, windfall **2** : good deal, bargain
aube [ob] *nf* **1** AURORE : dawn **2** : paddle, blade <bateaux à aubes : paddle boat>
aubépine [obepin] *nf* : hawthorn
auberge [obɛrʒ] *nf* : inn <auberge de jeunesse : youth hostel>
aubergine [obɛrʒin] *nf* : eggplant
aubergiste [obɛrʒist] *nmf* : innkeeper
aucun¹, -cune [okœ̃, -kyn] *adj* **1** (*in negative constructions*) : no, none, not any <il n'y a aucun doute : there is no doubt> **2** : any <plus qu'aucun autre : more than any other>
aucun², -cune *pron* **1** : none, not any <aucune de ses idées n'est bonne : none of his ideas is good> **2** : any, anyone <il travaille plus qu'aucun de ses amis : he works more than any of his friends> **3 d'aucuns** : some, some people
aucunement [okynmɑ̃] *adv* NULLEMENT : not at all, in no way
audace [odas] *nf* **1** : audacity, nerve **2** COURAGE : boldness, daring
audacieux, -cieuse [odasjø, -jøz] *adj* **1** : audacious **2** HARDI : bold, daring **— audacieusement** [odasjøzmɑ̃] *adv*
au–dedans [odədɑ̃] *adv* **1** : inside **2 ~ de** : inside (of), within <au-dedans du bâtiment : inside the building>
au–dehors [odəɔr] *adv* **1** : outside **2 ~ de** : outside (of) <au-dehors de la ville : outside the city>
au–delà¹ [odəla] *adv* **1** : beyond **2 ~ de** : beyond <au-delà de l'horizon : beyond the horizon>
au–delà² *nm* **l'au–delà** : eternity, the afterlife
au–dessous [odsu] *adv* **1** : below **2 ~ de** : beneath, below, under <au-dessous de la table : under the table>
au–dessus [odsy] *adv* **1** : above **2 ~ de** : above, over <au-dessus de la terre : above ground>
au–devant [odvɑ̃] *adv* : ahead <aller au-devant de qqn : to go to meet s.o.> <aller au-devant des demandes : to anticipate requests> <aller au-devant du danger : to court danger>
audible [odibl] *adj* : audible **— audibilité** [-bilite] *nf*
audience [odjɑ̃s] *nf* **1** PUBLIC : audience **2** : hearing, session <audiences publiques : public hearings>
audio [odjo] *adj* : audio
audiovisuel, -suelle [odjɔvizɥɛl] *adj* : audiovisual
audit [odit] *nm* : audit
auditer [odite] *vt* : to audit
auditeur, -trice [oditœr, -tris] *n* **1** : listener <les auditeurs : the audience> **2** : auditor
auditif, -tive [oditif, -tiv] *adj* : auditory, hearing
audition [odisjɔ̃] *nf* **1** : hearing (sense) **2** : audition **3** : examination, (judicial) hearing
auditionner [odisjɔne] *v* : to audition
auditoire [oditwar] *nm* **1** PUBLIC : audience **2** *Bel & Switz* : auditorium
auditorium [oditɔrjɔm] *nm* : auditorium
auge [oʒ] *nf* : trough
augmentation [ogmɑ̃tasjɔ̃] *nf* **1** ACCROISSEMENT : augmentation, increase **2** : raise (in salary, prices, etc.)

augmenter [ogmãte] *vt* : to augment, to increase, to raise — *vi* : to increase, to rise
augure [ogyr] *nm* **1** : omen <c'est de bon augure : that's a good omen> **2** : oracle, soothsayer
augurer [ogyre] *vt* : to augur, to bode <cela augure mal pour lui : that doesn't bode well for him>
auguste [ogyst] *adj* : august, noble, majestic
aujourd'hui [oʒurdɥi] *adv & nm* : today <il y a aujourd'hui un mois : a month ago today>
aulne [on] *nm* : alder
aulx → **ail**
aumône [omon] *nf* : alms *pl* <faire l'aumône à : to give alms to>
aumônier [omonje] *nm* : chaplain
auparavant [oparavã] *adv* **1** AVANT : before, previously **2** : beforehand, first
auprès [oprɛ] *adv* ~ **de 1** : beside, near, next to **2** : with, on, over <avoir de l'influence auprès de qqn : to have influence over s.o.> **3** : to <ambassadeur auprès des Nations Unies : ambassador to the United Nations> **4** : compared with **5** : in the opinion of
auquel [okɛl] → **lequel**
aura[1] [ɔra] *pp* → **avoir**
aura[2] [ora] *nf* : aura
auréole [oreɔl] *nf* **1** : halo **2** TACHE : spot, ring
auriculaire *nm* [orikylɛr] : little finger, pinkie
aurique [orik] *adj* : fore-and-aft
aurore [ɔrɔr] *nf* **1** : aurora <aurore boréale : aurora borealis, northern lights> **2** AUBE : dawn
ausculter [oskylte] *vt* : to examine (with a stethoscope), to sound
auspices [ospis] *nmpl* : auspices <sous les auspices de : under the auspices of>
aussi[1] [osi] *adv* **1** : too, also, as well **2** TELLEMENT : so <je ne savais pas qu'elle était aussi occupée : I didn't know she was so busy> **3** : as <il est aussi grand que moi : he is as tall as me> <aussi difficile qu'il soit : however difficult it may be> **4 aussi bien que** : as well as
aussi[2] *conj* **1** : so, therefore **2** D'AILLEURS : but, in any case
aussitôt [osito] *adv* **1** : immediately **2 aussitôt que** : as soon as
austère [oster] *adj* : austere — **austèrement** [ostermã] *adv*
austérité [osterite] *nf* : austerity
austral, -trale [ostral] *adj, mpl* **australs** : southern
australien, -lienne [ostraljɛ̃, -jɛn] *adj* : Australian
Australien, -lienne *n* : Australian
autant [otã] *adv* **1** : as much, as many, so much, so many <il n'en a jamais vu autant : he never saw so much of it> **2** ~ **de** : as much, as many, so much, so many <autant d'enfants que d'adultes : as many children as adults> **3** ~ **que** : as much as, as many as, as far as <j'en ai autant que vous : I have as much as you do> <(pour) autant que je sache : as far as I know> **4 autant comme autant** *Can* : time and time again **5 d'autant plus** : all the more **6 pour autant** : for all that **7 pour autant que** : insofar as, as far as
autel [otɛl] *nm* : altar
auteur [otœr] *nm* **1** : author, composer, artist <auteur dramatique : playwright> **2** : originator, inventor **3** : perpetrator
auteure [otœr] *nf Can* : author
authenticité [otãtisite] *nf* : authenticity
authentifier [otãtifje] {96} *vt* : to authenticate
authentique [otãtik] *adj* : authentic — **authentiquement** [-tikmã] *adv*
autisme [otism] *nm* : autism
autiste [otist] *or* **autistique** [otistik] *adj* : autistic
auto [oto] *nf* : car, automobile
autobiographie [otobjɔgrafi] *nf* : autobiography
autobiographique [otobjɔgrafik] *adj* : autobiographical
autobus [otobys] *nm* BUS : bus
autocar [otokar] *nm* : bus, coach
autochtone [otokton] *adj & nmf* : native
autocollant[1], **-lante** [otokɔlã, -lãt] *adj* : self-adhesive
autocollant[2] *nm* : sticker, bumper sticker
autocrate [otokrat] *nmf* : autocrat — **autocratique** [-kratik] *adj*
autocratie [otokrasi] *nf* : autocracy
autocritique [otokritik] *nf* : self-criticism
autocuiseur [otokɥizœr] *nm* : pressure cooker
autodéfense [otodefãs] *nf* : self-defense
autodestructeur, -trice [otodɛstryktœr, -tris] *adj* : self-destructive
autodétermination [otodeterminasjõ] *nf* : self-determination
autodidacte[1] [otodidakt] *adj* : self-taught
autodidacte[2] *nmf* : autodidact, self-taught person
autodiscipline [otodisiplin] *nf* : self-discipline
autographe [otograf] *nm* : autograph
auto-infligé, -gée [otoɛ̃fliʒe] *adj* : self-inflicted
automate [otomat] *nm* : automaton
automation [otomasjõ] *nf* : automation
automatique [otomatik] *adj* : automatic — **automatiquement** [-tikmã] *adv*
automatisation [otomatizasjõ] *nf* : automation, automating
automatiser [otomatize] *vt* : to automate

automnal, -nale [otɔnal] *adj, mpl* **-naux** [-no] : autumnal
automne [otɔn] *nm* : autumn, fall
automobile[1] [otɔmɔbil] *adj* : automotive, motor <l'industrie automobile : the motor industry>
automobile[2] *nf* : automobile, car
automobiliste [otɔmɔbilist] *nmf* : motorist, driver
autonome [otɔnɔm] *adj* : autonomous
autonomie [otɔnɔmi] *nf* : autonomy
autoportrait [otɔpɔrtrɛ] *nm* : self-portrait
autopropulsé, -sée [otɔprɔpylsi] *adj* : self-propelled
autopsie [otɔpsi] *nf* : autopsy — **autopsier** [-sje] *vt*
autoradio [otɔradjo] *nm* : car radio
autorisation [otɔrizasjɔ̃] *nf* **1** : authorization, permission **2** : license, permit
autorisé, -sée [otɔrize] *adj* **1** : permitted, allowed **2** : authoritative
autoriser [otɔrize] *vt* : to authorize, to give permission for, to empower
autoritaire [otɔritɛr] *adj* : authoritative — **autoritairement** [-tɛrmɑ̃] *adv*
autorité [otɔrite] *nf* : authority <faire autorité : to be authoritative>
autoroute [otɔrut] *nf* : (interstate) highway, freeway <autoroute à péage : turnpike>
auto–stop [otɔstɔp] *nm* **1** : hitchhiking **2 faire de l'auto-stop** : to hitchhike
auto–stoppeur, -peuse [otɔstɔpœr, -pøz] *n* : hitchhiker
autosuffisance [otɔsyfizɑ̃s] *nf* : self-sufficiency, self-reliance
autosuffisant, -sante [otɔsyfizɑ̃, -zɑ̃t] *adj* : self-sufficient
autour [otur] *adv* **1** : around, about <tout autour : all around> **2 ~ de** : around, about <autour de la table : around the table> <autour de six heures : about six o'clock>
autre[1] [otr] *adj* **1** : other, different <l'autre jour : the other day> <un autre problème : another problem> <se sentir autre : to feel different> **2 autre chose** : something else, something different **3 autre part** : somewhere else
autre[2] *pron* : other, another <suivons les autres : let's follow the others> <prenez-en un autre : take another one>
autrefois [otrəfwa] *adv* **1** JADIS : formerly, in the past **2 d'~** : of old, of the past <ma vie d'autrefois : my past life>
autrement [otrəmɑ̃] *adv* **1** : otherwise, differently <elle ne pouvait pas faire autrement : she couldn't act differently> <autrement dit : in other words> **2** : otherwise, if not <autrement vous le regretterez : otherwise you will be sorry> **3** : far (more) <c'est autrement moins sérieux : it's much less serious> **4 pas autrement** : not especially
autrichien, -chienne [otriʃjɛ̃, -ʃjɛn] *adj* : Austrian
Autrichien, -chienne *n* : Austrian
autruche [otryʃ] *nf* : ostrich
autrui [otrɥi] *pron* : others, other people
auvent [ovɑ̃] *nm* : canopy, awning
aux [o] → **à, les**
auxiliaire[1] [oksiljɛr] *adj* : auxiliary
auxiliaire[2] *nmf* : auxiliary
auxiliaire[3] *nm* : auxiliary (verb)
auxquels, auxquelles [okɛl] → **lequel**
avachi, -chie [avaʃi] *adj* **1** : shapeless, misshapen **2** : limp, flabby
aval [aval] *nm* **1** : endorsement (in law and finance) **2** : SOUTIEN : support, backing **3 : en ~** : downstream, lower down
avalanche [avalɑ̃ʃ] *nf* : avalanche
avaler [avale] *vt* **1** : to swallow **2** : to inhale
avaliser [avalize] *vt* : to endorse, to support
avance [avɑ̃s] *nf* **1** : advance **2** : lead **3 à l'avance** : in advance, ahead of schedule **4 d'avance** *or* **par ~** : in advance, already **5 en ~** : early **6 avances** *nfpl* : advances, overtures
avancé, -cée [avɑ̃se] *adj* **1** : advanced **2** : progressive
avancée *nf* : overhang, projection
avancement [avɑ̃smɑ̃] *nm* **1** : advancement, progress **2** : promotion
avancer [avɑ̃se] {6} *vt* **1** : to advance, to put forward **2** : to promote, to further — *vi* **1** : to advance, to go forward **2** : to be ahead of time <ma montre avance de trois minutes : my watch is three minutes fast> — **s'avancer** *vr* **1** : to advance, to move forward **2** : to progress, to get ahead **3** : to project, to protrude
avanie [avani] *nf* : snub
avant[1] [avɑ̃] *adv* **1** : before <quelques semaines avant : a few weeks before> <la page d'avant : the preceding page> **2** : first <tu devrais manger avant : you should eat first> **3** : far, deep <avant dans la forêt : deep within the forest> **4** : in front <elle marchait avant : she was walking in front> **5 ~ de** : before <avant de partir : before leaving> **6 avant que** : before, until <ne parlez pas avant qu'il ne le fasse : don't speak until he does>
avant[2] *adj* : front <la roue avant : the front wheel>
avant[3] *nm* **1** : front **2** : forward (in sports) **3 en ~** : forward, ahead **4 en avant de** : ahead of
avant[4] *prep* **1** : before, by <avant la fin : before the end> <avant huit heures : by eight o'clock> <avant peu : shortly> **2 avant tout** : first and foremost, above all

avantage [avɑ̃taʒ] *nm* **1** : advantage <tirer avantage de : to take advantage of> **2** : benefit <avantages sociaux : fringe benefits> **3 être à son avantage** : to look one's best
avantager [avɑ̃taʒe] {17} *vt* **1** FAVORISER : to favor, to give an advantage to **2** : to flatter, to show to advantage
avantageux, -geuse [avɑ̃taʒø, -ʒøz] *adj* **1** : advantageous, attractive <prix avantageux : attractive prices> **2** : flattering — **avantageusement** [-ʒøzmɑ̃] *adv*
avant–bras [avɑ̃bra] *nm* : forearm
avant–coureur [avɑ̃kurœr] *adj* : precursory, early
avant–dernier, -nière [avɑ̃dɛrnje, -njɛr] *adj* : next to last
avant–garde [avɑ̃gard] *nf* **1** : vanguard **2** : avant-garde
avant–goût [avɑ̃gu] *nm* : foretaste
avant–hier [avɑ̃tjɛr] *adv* : the day before yesterday
avant–midi [avɑ̃midi] *nf & pl Can nms & pl Belg* : morning
avant–poste [avɑ̃pɔst] *nm* : outpost
avant–première [avɑ̃prəmjɛr] *nf* : preview
avant–projet [avɑ̃prɔʒe] *nm* : (rough) draft
avant–propos [avɑ̃prɔpo] *nms & pl* : foreword
avant–toit [avɑ̃twa] *nm* : eaves *pl*
avare[1] [avar] *adj* : miserly, greedy
avare[2] *nmf* : miser
avarice [avaris] *nf* : avarice, miserliness
avaricieux, -cieuse [avarisjø, -sjøz] *adj* : miserly, stingy
avarie [avari] *nf* : damage (in shipping)
avatar [avatar] *nm* **1** : mishap **2** : metamorphosis, transformation **3** : avatar
avec[1] [avɛk] *adv fam* : with it, with that, with them <voulez-vous du vin avec? : would you like wine with that?>
avec[2] *prep* : with
aveline [avlin] *nf* : filbert (nut)
avenant[1], **-nante** [avnɑ̃, -nɑ̃t] *adj* : pleasant, attractive
avenant[2] *nm* **1** : endorsement **2** : codicil **3 à l'avenant** : in keeping, in conformity
avènement [avɛnmɑ̃] *nm* **1** : accession (to a throne) **2** : coming, advent
avenir [avnir] *nm* : future <à l'avenir : in the future>
avent [avɑ̃] *nm* **l'avent** : Advent
aventure [avɑ̃tyr] *nf* **1** : adventure **2** : venture **3** LIAISON : love affair **4 d'~** : by chance
aventurer [avɑ̃tyre] *vt* : to risk — **s'aventurer** *vr* : to venture
aventureux, -reuse [avɑ̃tyrø, -røz] *adj* **1** : adventurous, venturesome **2** : risky
aventurier, -rière [avɑ̃tyrje, -rjɛr] *n* : adventurer
avenu, -nue [avny] *adj* **nul et non avenu** : null and void
avenue *nf* : avenue
avéré, -rée [avere] *adj* : acknowledged, recognized
avérer [avere] {87} *v* **s'avérer** *vr* : to prove to be, to turn out to be
averse [avɛrs] *nf* : shower, storm
aversion [avɛrsjɔ̃] *nf* : aversion, dislike
avertir [avɛrtir] *vt* **1** : to warn **2** AVISER : to advise, to inform
avertissement [avɛrtismɑ̃] *nm* **1** : warning **2** : official notice, reprimand **3** : foreword (of a book)
avertisseur [avɛrtisœr] *nm* **1** : (car) horn **2** : alarm <avertisseur de fumée : smoke alarm>
aveu [avø] *nm, pl* **aveux** : confession, admission <passer aux aveux : to confess>
aveuglant, -glante [avœglɑ̃, -glɑ̃t] *adj* : blinding, glaring
aveugle[1] [avœgl] *adj* : blind
aveugle[2] *nmf* : blind person
aveuglement [avœgləmɑ̃] *nm* : blindness
aveuglément [avœglemɑ̃] *adv* : blindly
aveugler [avœgle] *vt* **1** : to blind, to dazzle **2** : to block, to stop up — **s'aveugler** *vr* **~ sur** : to turn a blind eye to
aveuglette [avœglɛt] *adv* **à l'aveuglette** : blindly <avancer à l'aveuglette : to grope one's way>
aviateur, -trice [avjatœr, -tris] *n* : aviator, pilot
aviation [avjasjɔ̃] *nf* : aviation
aviculture [avikyltyr] *nf* : poultry farming
avide [avid] *adj* **1** : greedy **2** : eager — **avidement** [avidmɑ̃] *adv*
avidité [avidite] *nf* **1** : greed **2** : eagerness
avilir [avilir] *vt* : to degrade, to debase — **s'avilir** *vr*
avilissement [avilismɑ̃] *nm* : degradation, debasement
aviné, -née [avine] *adj* : inebriated
avion [avjɔ̃] *nm* : airplane <avion à réaction : jet plane> <avion de ligne : airliner> <avion de chasse : fighter plane>
avion–cargo [avjɔ̃kargo] *nm, pl* **avions–cargos** : cargo plane, freighter
aviron [avirɔ̃] *nm* **1** RAME : oar **2** *Can* : paddle **3** : rowing
avis [avis] *nm* **1** : opinion <à mon avis : in my opinion> <changer d'avis : to change one's mind> **2** ANNONCE : notice, notification **3** CONSEIL : advice
avisé, -sée [avize] *adj* : prudent, sensible
aviser [avize] *vt* INFORMER : to advise, to inform, to notify — *vi* RÉFLÉCHIR : to think things over, to decide — **s'aviser** *vr* : to realize, to take notice
aviver [avive] *vt* **1** : to revive, to stir up **2** : to brighten, to liven up
avocat[1], **-cate** [avɔka, -kat] *n* **1** : lawyer, attorney **2** : advocate

avocat[2] *nm* : avocado
avoine [avwan] *nf* : oats *pl*
avoir[1] [avwar] {10} *vt* **1** : to have <il a de l'argent : he has money> <elle va avoir un enfant : she's going to have a baby> **2** : to get <j'ai eu mes billets hier : I got my tickets yesterday> **3** : to be (a particular age) <j'ai seize ans : I'm sixteen years old> **4** : to suffer, to feel <qu'est-ce que tu as? : what's wrong?> <j'ai mal : I'm hurt> **5 ~ à** : to have to <j'ai à vous parler : I must speak to you> **6 se faire avoir** *fam* : to be had, to be conned — *v impers* **il y a** : there is, there are — *v aux* : to have <je l'ai écrit : I wrote it, I have written it, I did write it> <elle y avait été : she had been there> <ils auront fini demain : they will have finished tomorrow>
avoir[2] *nm* **1** : assets *pl*, property **2** : credit
avoirdupoids [avwardypwa] *nm* : avoirdupois
avoisiner [avwazine] *vt* : to neighbor, to be near
avortement [avɔrtəmɑ̃] *nm* **1** : abortion <avortement spontané : miscarriage> **2** : failure, collapse
avorter [avɔrte] *vi* **1** : to abort, to miscarry **2** : to fail, to abort
avorton [avɔrtɔ̃] *nm* : runt
avoué[1], **-vouée** [avwe] *adj* : avowed, declared
avoué[2] *nm* : attorney
avouer [avwe] *vt* : to admit, to confess to — *vi* : to own up — **s'avouer** *vr* : to admit <s'avouer coupable : to admit one's guilt>
avril [avril] *nm* : April
axe [aks] *nm* **1** : axis **2** : axle **3** : major road, highway **4** : main line, mainstream (in politics, etc.)
axer [akse] *vt* : to center, to focus
axiomatique [aksjɔmatik] *adj* : axiomatic
axiome [aksjom] *nm* : axiom
axis [aksis] *nms & pl* : axis
ayoye *or* **ayoille** [ajɔj] *interj Can* : ouch!
azalée [azale] *nf* : azalea
azimut [azimyt] *nm* **1** : azimuth **2 tous azimuts** : all out, total **3 dans tous les azimuts** : all over the place
azote [azɔt] *nm* : nitrogen
azur [azyr] *nm* : azure
azyme [azim] *adj* : unleavened

B

b [be] *nm* : b, the second letter of the alphabet
babeurre [babœr] *nm* : buttermilk
babiche [babiʃ] *nf Can* : leather lacing (for moccasins, snowshoes, etc.)
babillage [babijaʒ] *nm* : babbling, prattle
babillard [babijar] *nm Can* : bulletin board
babiller [babije] *vi* : to babble, to chatter
babines [babin] *nfpl* : chops <se lécher les babines : to lick one's chops>
babiole [babjɔl] *nf* : bauble, trinket
bâbord [babɔr] *nm* : port (side), larboard
babouin [babwɛ̃] *nm* : baboon
baboune [babun] *nf Can fam* **faire la baboune** : to sulk
baby–sitter [bebisitœr] *nmf, pl* **baby–sitters** *France* : baby-sitter
baby–sitting [bebisitiŋ] *nm France* : baby-sitting
bac [bak] *nm* **1** : ferry **2** : tub, vat <bac à glace : ice tray> **3** *fam* → **baccalauréat**
baccalauréat [bakalɔrea] *nm* **1** *France* : school-leaving certificate **2** *Can* : bachelor's degree
bâche [baʃ] *nf* : tarpaulin
bachelier, -lière [baʃalje, -ljɛr] *n* : person who holds a *baccalauréat*
bachot [baʃo] *nm France fam* → **baccalauréat**
bachoter [baʃɔte] *vi France* : to cram (for an exam)
bacille [basil] *nm* : bacillus
bâcler [bakle] *vt* : to rush through, to dash off <travail bâclé : slapdash job, botched-up work>
bacon [bekɔn] *nm* : bacon
bactérie [bakteri] *nf* : bacterium
bactérien, -rienne [bakterjɛ̃, -rjɛn] *adj* : bacterial
bactériologie [bakterjɔlɔʒi] *nf* : bacteriology — **bactériologiste** [-lɔʒist] *nmf*
badaud, -daude [bado, -dod] *n* **1** : stroller, passerby **2** : (curious) onlooker
badge [badʒ] *nm* : badge
badigeonner [badiʒɔne] *vt* **1** : to daub, to smear **2** : to whitewash **3** : to paint (in medicine)
badin, -dine [badɛ̃, -din] *adj* : playful, jocular
badinage [badinaʒ] *nm* : banter, joking
badine [badin] *nf* : switch, cane
badiner [badine] *vi* **1** : to joke, to jest **2 ~ avec** : to trifle with, to toy with
badminton [badmintɔn] *nm* : badminton
bâdrer [badre] *vt Can fam* : to bother, to annoy

baffe [baf] *nf fam* : slap, smack
bafouer [bafwe] *vt* RIDICULISER : to ridicule, to scorn
bafouillage [bafujaʒ] *nm* **1** : mumbling, stammering **2** : gibberish
bafouiller [bafuje] *v* : to mumble, to stammer
bâfrer [bafre] *vt fam* : to gobble, to guzzle — *vi fam* : to stuff oneself
bagage [bagaʒ] *nm* **1** : baggage, luggage <bagages à main : hand luggage> <plier bagage : to pack up and leave> **2** : knowledge, background
bagarre [bagar] *nf* : fight, brawl
bagarrer [bagare] *vi* : to fight, to brawl — **se bagarrer** *vr*
bagarreur, -reuse [bagarœr, -røz] *n* : fighter, brawler
bagatelle [bagatɛl] *nf* **1** : trifle, trinket **2** : trifling sum
bagnard [baɲar] *nm* : convict
bagne [baɲ] *nm* **1** : penal colony **2** : hard labor
bagnole [baɲɔl] *nf fam* : jalopy, car
bague [bag] *nf* **1** : ring <bague de fiançailles : engagement ring> **2** : band, circlet
baguette [bagɛt] *nf* **1** : stick, rod, baton <baguette à fusil : ramrod> <baguette de tambour : drumstick> <baguette magique : magic wand> **2** : baguette (loaf of French bread) **3** **baguettes** *nfpl* : chopsticks
bahreïni, -nie [bareini] *adj* : Bahraini
Bahreïni, -nie *n* : Bahraini
baie [bɛ] *nf* **1** : bay **2** : berry **3** *or* **baie vitrée** : picture window
baignade [bɛɲad] *nf* : swimming, bathing
baigner [bɛɲe] *vt* : to bathe, to wash — *vi* : to soak, to steep — **se baigner** *vr* **1** : to take a bath **2** : to go swimming
baigneur, -gneuse [bɛɲœr, -ɲøz] *n* : swimmer, bather
baignoire [bɛɲwar] *nf* : bathtub
bail [baj] *nm, pl* **baux** [bo] : lease
bâillement [bajmɑ̃] *nm* : yawn
bâiller [baje] *vi* **1** : to yawn **2** : to gape (open)
bailleur, -leresse [bajœr, -jrɛs] *n* **1** : lessor **2** **bailleur de fonds** : financial backer
bâillon [bajɔ̃] *nm* : gag
bâillonner [bajɔne] *vt* **1** : to gag **2** : to silence
bain [bɛ̃] *nm* **1** : bath <bain de bouche : mouthwash> <bain de sang : bloodbath> <bain de soleil : sunbath> <prendre un bain : to take a bath> **2** : swim **3** **se mettre dans le bain** : to get into the swing of things
bain-marie [bɛ̃mari] *nm, pl* **bains-marie** : double boiler
baïonnette [bajɔnɛt] *nf* : bayonet
baiser[1] [beze] *vt* : to kiss
baiser[2] *nm* : kiss
baisse [bɛs] *nf* **1** : fall, drop, decline **2** **à la baisse** : downward
baisser [bese] *vt* **1** : to let down, to lower <baisser les yeux : to look down> <baisser les bras : to give up> **2** : to reduce (volume, light) — *vi* : to go down, to drop, to decline — **se baisser** : to bend down, to stoop, to duck
bajoues [baʒu] *nfpl* : chops, jowls
bal [bal] *nm* : ball, dance
balade [balad] *nf* PROMENADE : stroll, walk
balader [balade] *vt* : to take for a walk — *vi* : to stroll, to saunter — **se balader** *vr* : to go for a walk, to stroll about, to gallivant (around)
baladeur [baladœr] *nm* : portable radio–cassette player
balafre [balafr] *nf* **1** : gash, slash **2** CICATRICE : scar
balai [balɛ] *nm* **1** : broom, brush <passer le balai : to sweep the floor> **2** : windshield-wiper blade
balaie [bale], **balaiera** [balera], *etc.* → **balayer**
balance [balɑ̃s] *nf* **1** : scale, scales *pl* <faire pencher la balance : to tip the scales> **2** : balance <balance de commerce : balance of trade> **3** *Can* : difference, remainder <la balance de : the rest of>
Balance *nf* : Libra
balancement [balɑ̃smɑ̃] *nm* : swaying, swinging
balancer [balɑ̃se] {6} *vt* **1** : to sway, to swing, to rock **2** *fam* : to fling, to chuck, to junk — *vi* **1** : to sway **2** : to waver, to hesitate — **se balancer** *vr* : to rock, to swing, to sway
balancier [balɑ̃sje] *nm* : pendulum
balançoire [balɑ̃swar] *nf* **1** : swing **2** BASCULE : seesaw
balayage [balejaʒ] *nm* : sweeping
balayer [baleje] {11} *vt* **1** : to sweep, to sweep away **2** : to scan
balayeur, balayeuse [balejœr, balejøz] *n* : street sweeper
balayeuse [balejøz] *nf* **1** : street-cleaning truck **2** *Can* : vacuum cleaner
balbutiement [balbysimɑ̃] *nm* **1** : stammering, stuttering **2** **balbutiements** *nmpl* : early stages, beginnings
balbutier [balbysje] {96} *v* : to stammer, to stutter
balbuzard [balbyzar] *nm or* **balbuzard pêcheur** : osprey
balcon [balkɔ̃] *nm* : balcony
baldaquin [baldakɛ̃] *nm* : canopy
baleine [balɛn] *nf* **1** : whale **2** : rib (of an umbrella)
baleinier [balenje] *nm* : whaler (ship or person)
baleinière [balenjɛr] *nf* : whaleboat
balise [baliz] *nf* **1** : buoy, beacon **2** : signpost, marker
baliser [balize] *vt* : to mark (with beacons or signs)
balistique[1] [balistik] *adj* : ballistic
balistique[2] *nf* : ballistics

balivernes [balivɛrn] *nfpl* SORNETTES : nonsense, humbug
ballade [balad] *nf* : ballad
ballant[1], **-lante** [balɑ̃, -lɑ̃t] *adj* : dangling
ballant[2] *nm* : slack, looseness
ballast [balast] *nm* : ballast
balle [bal] *nf* **1** : ball <balle de tennis : tennis ball> <renvoyer la balle : to pass the buck> **2** : bullet **3** : bale, bundle **4** : husk, chaff **5** *France fam* : franc
balle–molle [balmɔl] *nf Can* : softball
ballerine [balrin] *nf* : ballerina
ballet [balɛ] *nm* : ballet
ballon [balɔ̃] *nm* **1** : ball <ballon de football : football, soccer ball> **2** : balloon **3** : wine glass, brandy glass **4 ballon d'oxygène** : oxygen tank
ballonner [balɔne] *vt* : to bloat, to distend (the stomach)
ballon–panier [balɔ̃panje] *nm Can* : basketball (game)
ballot [balo] *nm* **1** BALUCHON : pack, bundle **2** *fam* : chump, fool
ballottage [balɔtaʒ] *nm* : second ballot
ballotter [balɔte] *vt* SECOUER : to shake, to toss about — *vi* : to toss, to roll around
balloune [balun] *nf Can* **1** : balloon **2** : bubble <gomme balloune : bubble gum>
balluchon [balyʃɔ̃] → **baluchon**
balnéaire [balneɛr] *adj* : seaside <station balnéaire : seaside resort>
balourd[1], **-lourde** [balur, -lurd] *adj* : awkward, clumsy, stupid
balourd[2], **-lourde** *n* : clumsy oaf, dolt
balourdise [balurdiz] *nf* **1** : awkwardness, clumsiness **2** : gaffe, blunder
balsa [balza] *nm* : balsa
balsamine [balzamin] *nf* : balsam fir
balte [balt] *adj* : Baltic
baluchon [balyʃɔ̃] *nm* BALLOT : pack, bundle <faire son baluchon : to pack one's bag>
balustrade [balystrad] *nf* **1** : balustrade **2** : railing, bannister
balustre [balystr] *nf* : baluster
bambin, -bine [bɑ̃bɛ̃, -bin] *n* : child, toddler
bambou [bɑ̃bu] *nm* : bamboo
ban [bɑ̃] *nm* **1** : round of applause **2 bans** *nmpl* : banns **3 mettre au ban** : to banish, to ostracize
banal, -nale [banal] *adj, mpl* **banals 1** ORDINAIRE : commonplace, ordinary **2** : banal, trite
banaliser [banalize] *vt* **1** : to make commonplace **2 voiture banalisée** : unmarked car
banalité [banalite] *nf* **1** : banality, triteness **2** : platitude, cliché
banane [banan] *nf* : banana
bananier [bananje] *nm* : banana tree
banc [bɑ̃] *nm* **1** : bench <banc des accusés : dock (in court)> <banc d'église : pew> **2** : shoal, school (of fish) **3** : bank <banc de sable : sandbank> <banc de neige *Can* : snowbank>
bancaire [bɑ̃kɛr] *adj* : banking, bank <compte bancaire : bank account>
bancal, -cale [bɑ̃kal] *adj, mpl* **bancals** : shaky, wobbly
bandage [bɑ̃daʒ] *nm* **1** : bandaging **2** PANSEMENT : bandage, dressing
bande [bɑ̃d] *nf* **1** : gang, group, troop **2** : pack (of animals) **3** : band, strip <bande dessinée : comic strip> **4** : tape, (reel of) film <bande vidéo : videotape> <bande sonore : soundtrack> **5 donner de la bande** : to list (of a ship)
bandeau [bɑ̃do] *nm, pl* **bandeaux 1** : blindfold **2** : headband
bandelette [bɑ̃dlɛt] *nf* : narrow strip (of cloth, etc.)
bander [bɑ̃de] *vt* **1** : to bandage **2** : to bend (a bow) **3** : to flex, to tense **4 bander les yeux à** : to blindfold
banderole [bɑ̃drɔl] *nf* : banner, pennant
bandit [bɑ̃di] *nm* **1** VOLEUR : bandit, robber **2** : scoundrel **3** *or* **petit bandit** : rascal
banditisme [bɑ̃ditism] *nm* : banditry
bandoulière [bɑ̃duljɛr] *nf* : shoulder strap <en bandoulière : slung over one's shoulder>
bangladais, -daise [bɑ̃gladɛ, -dɛz] *adj* : Bangladeshi
Bangladais, -daise *n* : Bangladeshi
banjo [bɑ̃(d)ʒo] *nm* : banjo
banlieue [bɑ̃ljø] *nf* : suburb(s) <de banlieue : suburban>
banlieusard[1], **-sarde** [bɑ̃ljøzar, -zard] *adj* : suburban
banlieusard[2], **-sarde** *n* : suburbanite, suburban commuter
banni[1], **-nie** [bani] *adj* : exiled, banished
banni[2], **-nie** *n* : exile
bannière [banjɛr] *nf* : banner
bannir [banir] *vt* : to banish, to exile
bannissement [banismɑ̃] *nm* : banishment
banque [bɑ̃k] *nf* **1** : bank <banque commerciale : commercial bank> <banque du sang : blood bank> **2** : banking
banqueroute [bɑ̃krut] *nf* **1** : bankruptcy **2 faire banqueroute** : to go bankrupt
banquet [bɑ̃kɛ] *nm* FESTIN : banquet, feast
banquette [bɑ̃kɛt] *nf* : bench, seat (in a booth or vehicle) <banquette arrière : back seat>
banquier, -quière [bɑ̃kje, -kjɛr] *n* : banker
banquise [bɑ̃kiz] *nf* : ice floe
bans [bɑ̃] *nmpl* : banns (of marriage)
baptême [batɛm] *nm* : baptism, christening
baptiser [batize] *vt* : to baptize, to christen

baptismal, -male [batismal] *adj, mpl* **-maux** [-mo] : baptismal
baptistaire [batister] *nm Can* : certificate of baptism
bar [bar] *nm* **1** : bar **2** : sea bass
baragouin [baragwɛ̃] *nm* : gibberish, gobbledegook
baragouiner [baragwine] *vi* : to talk gibberish — *vt* : to speak (a language) badly <baragouiner l'anglais : to speak broken English>
baraque [barak] *nf* **1** BICOQUE : hut, shack **2** : stall, stand (at a fair, etc.)
baraquement [barakmɑ̃] *nm* : group of shacks
baratin [baratɛ̃] *nm* : smooth talk, sales patter
baratte [barat] *nf* : churn
baratter [barate] *vt* : to churn
barauder [barode] *vt Can* : to move back and forth, to skid (on ice, etc.)
barbant, -bante [barbɑ̃, -bɑ̃t] *adj fam* RASANT : boring
barbare[1] [barbar] *adj* : barbarous, barbaric
barbare[2] *nmf* : barbarian
barbarie [barbari] *nf* : barbarity, barbarism
barbarisme [barbarism] *nm* : barbarism (in language, manners, etc.)
barbe [barb] *nf* **1** : beard **2** : barb (of a feather, of metal) **3** : tuft, awn (of a plant) **4** *fam* : bore <quelle barbe! : what a bore!>
barbecue [barbɔkju] *nm* : barbecue
barbelé[1], **-lée** [barbəle] *adj* : barbed
barbelé[2] *nm* : barbed wire
barber [barbe] *vt fam* : to bore — **se barber** *vr*
barbiche [barbiʃ] *nf* **1** : goatee **2** : beard (of a goat)
barbier [barbje] *nm Can* : barber
barbiturique [barbityrik] *nm* : barbiturate
barboter [barbɔte] *vi* : to paddle, to splash around — *vt fam* : to filch
barboteuse [barbɔtøz] *nf Can* : wading pool
barbouillage [barbujaʒ] *nm* : daub, smear
barbouiller [barbuje] *vt* **1** : to smear, to daub **2** : to scribble **3** : to nauseate, to make sick <ça me barbouille le coeur : it turns my stomach>
barbu, -bue [barby] *adj* : bearded
barda [barda] *nm fam* : gear, stuff
bardane [bardan] *nf* : bur, burr (in botany)
barde [bard] *nm* : bard
bardeau [bardo] *nm, pl* **bardeaux 1** : shingle **2 manquer un bardeau** *Can fam* : to be a little crazy
barder [barde] *vt* : to bard (in cooking) — *v impers* **ça va barder!** *fam* : there's going to be trouble!, sparks will fly!
barème [barɛm] *nm* : scale, table <barème de salaires : salary scale>
baril [baril] *nm* TONNELET : barrel, keg
barillet [barije] *nm* **1** : small barrel **2** : cylinder (of a revolver)
bariolé, -lée [barjɔle] *adj* MULTICOLORE : multicolored
barman [barman] *nm, pl* **barmans** *or* **barmen** : bartender
baromètre [barɔmetr] *nm* : barometer — **barométrique** [-metrik] *adj*
baron, -ronne [barɔ̃, -rɔn] *n* : baron *m*, baroness *f*
baroque [barɔk] *adj* **1** : baroque **2** BIZARRE : weird, odd
baroud [barud] *nm fam* : fight, set-to <baroud d'honneur : last stand>
barque [bark] *nf* : small boat
barracuda [barakyda] *nm* : barracuda
barrage [baraʒ] *nm* **1** : dam **2** : roadblock, barricade
barre [bar] *nf* **1** : bar, rod **2** : (written) line, stroke **3** : mark <sous la barre des deux pour cent : below the two percent mark> **4** : helm <prendre la barre : to take the helm, to take charge> **5** : bar (in law) **6** : sandbar **7 ~ d'outils** : toolbar
barreau [baro] *nm, pl* **barreaux 1** : bar <derrière les barreaux : behind bars> **2** : rung (of a ladder, etc.) **3 le barreau** : the bar, the legal profession
barrer [bare] *vt* **1** : to bar, to block **2** : to mark, to cross, to cross out **3** : to steer (a boat) **4** *Can* : to lock (a door) — **se barrer** *vr fam* : to clear out <barrez-vous! : get out of here!>
barrette [baret] *nf* **1** : barrette **2** : biretta
barricade [barikad] *nf* : barricade
barricader [barikade] *vt* : to barricade — **se barricader** *vr* : to barricade oneself, to shut oneself away
barrière [barjɛr] *nf* **1** OBSTACLE : barrier <barrières douanières : trade barriers> **2** : fence, gate
barrique [barik] *nf* TONNEAU : barrel, cask
barrir [barir] *vi* : to trumpet (of an elephant)
baryton [baritɔ̃] *nm* : baritone
baryum [barjɔm] *nm* : barium
bas[1] [ba] *adv* **1** : low <tomber bas : to sink low> **2** : softly, quietly
bas[2], **basse** [ba, baz (*before a vowel or mute h*), bas] *adj* **1** : low **2** : base, vile **3** : bass
bas[3] *nms & pl* **1** : bottom, lower part <de haut en bas : from top to bottom> <à bas : down with> <en bas : downstairs, below, at the bottom> <en bas de : at the bottom of, beneath> **2** : stocking **3** : bass (part)
basalte [bazalt] *nm* : basalt
basané, -née [bazane] *adj* **1** : tanned, sunburned **2** : swarthy
bascule [baskyl] *nf* **1** : balance, scales *pl* **2** : rocker <fauteuil à bascule : rocking chair> **3** BALANÇOIRE : seesaw

basculer [baskyle] *vi* **1** : to tip, to topple over **2** : to rock, to swing
base [baz] *nf* **1** : base <à la base de : at the root of> <base de lancement : launching site> **2** : basis **3 base de données** : database
baseball *or* **base–ball** [bɛzbol] *nm* : baseball
baseballeur, -leuse [bɛzbolœr, -løz] *n Can* : baseball player
baser [baze] *vt* FONDER : to base, to found
bas–fond [bafɔ̃] *nm* **1** : shallows *pl* **2** : lowland **3 bas–fonds** *nmpl* : dregs (of society), slums
basilic [bazilik] *nm* : basil
basilique [bazilik] *nf* : basilica
basique [bazik] *adj* : basic (in chemistry)
basket [basket] *or* **basket-ball** *or* **basketball** [basketbol] *nm* : basketball
basketteur, -teuse [basketœr, -tøz] *n* : basketball player
basque[1] [bask] *adj* : Basque
basque[2] *nm* : Basque (language)
Basque *nmf* : Basque
bas–relief [barəljef] *nm, pl* **bas–reliefs** : bas-relief
basse [bas] *nf* **1** → **bas**[2] **2** : bass (in music)
basse–cour [baskur] *nf, pl* **basses–cours 1** : farmyard, barnyard **2** : poultry
bassesse [basɛs] *nf* : baseness, meanness
basset [basɛ] *nm* : basset hound
bassin [basɛ̃] *nm* **1** : basin (of a river) **2** : lake, pond, pool **3** : pelvis
bassine [basin] *nf* **1** : large bowl, basin **2** *Can* : bedpan **3** : bowlful
basson [basɔ̃] *nm* : bassoon
bastion [bastjɔ̃] *nm* : bastion
bas–ventre [bavɑ̃tr] *nm, pl* **bas–ventres** : lower abdomen
bât [ba] *nm* **1** : packsaddle **2 c'est là où le bât blesse** : that's where the shoe pinches
bataclan [bataklɑ̃] *nm fam* **1** : stuff, gear **2 tout le bataclan** : the whole kit and caboodle
bataille [bataj] *nf* **1** : battle, fight **2 en ~** : in disarray, disheveled
batailler [bataje] *vi* : to fight
batailleur[1], **-leuse** [batajœr, -jøz] *adj* : quarrelsome, belligerent
batailleur[2], **-leuse** *n* : fighter
bataillon [batajɔ̃] *nm* : battalion
bâtard[1], **-tarde** [batar, -tard] *adj* **1** : hybrid, crossbred **2** : bastard
bâtard[2], **-tarde** *n* : bastard
bâtard[3] *nm France* : small loaf of bread
bateau[1] [bato] *adj, s & pl* **bateau** : hackneyed
bateau[2] *nm, pl* **bateaux 1** : boat, ship <bateau de pêche : fishing boat> <bateau amiral : flagship> <bateau de guerre : warship> <bateau de plaisance : launch> <bateau à voile : sailboat> **2 faire du bateau** : to go sailing
bateau–mouche [batomuʃ] *nm, pl* **bateaux–mouches** : sightseeing boat
bateleur, -leuse [batlœr, -løz] *n* **1** : juggler, tumbler **2** : fool, buffoon
batelier, -lière [batəlje, -ljɛr] *n* : boatman
bâti [bati] *nm* **1** : framework, support **2** : tacking, basting (in sewing)
batifoler [batifɔle] *vi* : to frolic, to romp
bâtiment [batimɑ̃] *nm* **1** : building **2** : building trade **3** : ship <bâtiment de guerre : man-of-war>
bâtir [batir] *vt* **1** CONSTRUIRE : to build, to erect **2** : to build up, to develop **3** : to baste, to tack
bâtisseur, -seuse [batisœr, -søz] *n* : builder
bâton [batɔ̃] *nm* **1** : rod, pole <bâton de ski : ski pole> **2** : piece, stick <bâton de rouge (à lèvres) : lipstick> **3** : nightstick **4** : baton **5** *Can* : bat <bâton de baseball : baseball bat>
bâtonnet [batɔnɛ] *nm* : short stick, rod
battage [bataʒ] *nm* **1** : beating, threshing **2** : hype **3** : shuffle, shuffling (of playing cards)
battant[1], **-tante** [batɑ̃, -tɑ̃t] *adj* : beating, driving, banging <pluie battante : driving rain> <le cœur battant : with a pounding heart>
battant[2] *nm* **1** : flap, section (of a door, window, etc.) **2** : clapper (of a bell)
battant[3], **-tante** [batɑ̃, -tɑ̃t] *nmf* : fighter, go-getter
batte [bat] *nf* : bat (in sports)
battement [batmɑ̃] *nm* **1** : beating, fluttering, blinking **2** : clapping, tapping, banging **3** : interval, wait
batterie [batri] *nf* **1** : set, group, battery <une batterie de tests : a string of tests> **2** : battery (of artillery) **3** : drums, drum set **4** : battery (of a motor vehicle)
batteur [batœr, -tøz] *nm* **1** : (egg) whisk, eggbeater <batteur électrique : electric mixer> **2** : drummer **3** : batter (in sports)
batteuse [batøz] *nf* : thresher, threshing machine
battre [batr] {12} *vt* **1** FRAPPER : to hit, to strike, to beat **2** VAINCRE : to defeat <battre à plates coutures : to defeat soundly, to wallop> **3** : to shuffle (playing cards) — *vi* : to beat — **se battre** *vr* : to fight
batture [batyr] *nf Can* : sandbar
baudet [bodɛ] *nm fam* : jackass
baudrier [bodrije] *nm* BANDOULIÈRE : shoulder strap
bauge [boʒ] *nf* : wallow (for animals)
baume [bom] *nm* **1** : balm, balsam **2 mettre du baume au cœur** : to be of comfort
baux → bail

bavard[1], **-varde** [bavar, -vard] *adj* : talkative
bavard[2], **-varde** *n* : talkative person, chatterbox
bavardage [bavardaʒ] *nm* : idle talk, chatter
bavarder [bavarde] *vi* **1** : to chatter **2** : to gossip
bavarois, -roise [bavarwa, -rwaz] *adj* : Bavarian
Bavarois, -roise *n* : Bavarian
bave [bav] *nf* : dribble, drool, spittle
baver [bave] *vi* **1** : to dribble, to drool **2** : to run, to leak **3 ~ en** : to have a hard time of it **4 ~ sur** : to slander
bavette [bavɛt] *nf* **1** : bib **2** : flank (of beef) **3** : mudguard
baveux[1], **-veuse** [bavø, -vøz] *adj* **1** : dribbling, drooling **2** : runny (of an omelette, etc.)
baveux[2], **-veuse** *n Can fam* : pain in the neck, annoying person
bavoir [bavwar] *nm* : bib (for babies)
bavure [bavyr] *nf* **1** : smudge, blur **2** : error, blunder
bayer [baje] {11} *vi* **bayer aux corneilles** : to gape, to gaze into space
bayou [baju] *nm* : bayou
bazar [bazar] *nm* **1** : bazaar **2** : general store **3** : clutter, mess
bazou [bazu] *nm Can fam* : jalopy
beagle [bigœl] *nm* : beagle
béant, béante [beã, beãt] *adj* : gaping
béat, béate [bea, beat] *adj* **1** : blissful **2** : self-satisfied, smug
béatement [beatmã] *adv* : blissfully
béatitude [beatityd] *nf* **1** : bliss **2** : beatitude
beau[1] [bo] *adv* **1 avoir beau** : to do (something) in vain <j'ai beau essayer : it's useless for me to try> **2 faire beau** : to be fine, to be fair <il fait beau : it's nice outside>
beau[2] **(bel** [bɛl] *before vowel or mute h*), **belle** [bɛl] *adj, mpl* **beaux** [bo] **1** : beautiful, handsome **2** : good, noble **3** : fine, fair <beau temps : nice weather> **4** : excellent, desirable <belle santé : good health> **5** : considerable, great (in quantity) <un bel âge : a ripe old age> <une belle somme : a tidy sum> **6 bel et bien** : for sure, truly
beau[3] *nm* **1 le beau** : the beautiful, beauty **2 faire le beau** : to sit up and beg (of a dog)
beaucoup [boku] *adv* **1** : much, a lot <je t'aime beaucoup : I love you very much> **2 ~ de** : much, many, a lot of <beaucoup de livres : a lot of books> **3 de ~** : by far
beau-fils [bofis] *nm, pl* **beaux-fils 1** : son-in-law **2** : stepson
beau-frère [bofrɛr] *nm, pl* **beaux-frères 1** : brother-in-law **2** : stepbrother
beau-père [boper] *nm, pl* **beaux-pères 1** : father-in-law **2** : stepfather
beauté [bote] *nf* : beauty
beaux-arts [bozar] *nmpl* : fine arts
beaux-parents [boparã] *nmpl* : in-laws
bébé [bebe] *nm* : baby, infant
bebelle [bəbɛl] *nf Can fam* **1** : gadget **2 bebelles** *nfpl* : things <tes bebelles puis dans ta cour : pack your things and go>
bébête [bebɛt] *adj* : silly, babyish
bébite [bebit] *nf Can fam* : bug, insect
bec [bɛk] *nm* **1** : beak, bill **2** *fam* : mouth, nose, face **3** EMBOUCHURE : mouthpiece **4** : burner <bec à gaz : gas burner> **5** : point, nib **6** : spout, lip (of a jug, etc.) **7** *Belg, Can, Switz fam* : kiss **8 bec fin** : gourmet **9 tomber sur un bec** : to run into a snag
bécane [bekan] *nf fam* : bike
bécasse [bekas] *nf* **1** : woodcock **2** *fam* : featherbrain, silly goose
bécasseau [bekaso] *nm* : sandpiper
bécassine [bekasin] *nf* : snipe
bec-de-lièvre [bɛkdəljɛvr] *nm, pl* **becs-de-lièvre** : harelip
bêche [bɛʃ] *nf* : spade
bêcher [beʃe] *vt* **1** : to dig (up) **2** : to criticize
bêcheur[1], **-cheuse** [bɛʃœr, -ʃøz] *adj* : stuck-up
bêcheur[2], **-cheuse** *n* : stuck-up person, snob
becqueter [bekte] {8} *vt* **1** : to peck at **2** *fam* : to eat
bedaine [bədɛn] *nf* : paunch, potbelly
bedonnant, -nante [bədɔnã, -nãt] *adj* : paunchy, portly, potbellied
bédouin, -douine [bedwẽ, -dwin] *n* : bedouin
bée [be] *adj* **bouche bée** : open-mouthed <être bouche bée devant : to gape at>
beffroi [befrwa] *nm* : belfry
bégaie [bege], **bégaiera** [begera], *etc.* → **bégayer**
bégaiement [begɛmã] *nm* : stuttering, stammering
bégayer [begeje] {11} *v* : to stutter, to stammer
bégonia [begɔnja] *nm* : begonia
bégueule [begœl] *nmf* : prude
béguin [begɛ̃] *nm fam* : crush, infatuation
beige [bɛʒ] *adj & nm* : beige
beigne[1] [bɛɲ] *nf fam* : smack, sock, punch
beigne[2] *nm Can* : doughnut
beignet [bɛɲe] *nm* **1** : doughnut **2** : fritter
bel → beau
bêlement [bɛlmã] *nm* : bleat
bêler [bele] *vi* : to bleat
belette [bəlɛt] *nf* : weasel
belge [bɛlʒ] *adj* : Belgian
Belge *nmf* : Belgian
bélier [belje] *nm* **1** : ram **2** : battering ram
Bélier *nm* : Aries

bélizien, -zienne [belizjɛ̃] *adj* : Belizean
Bélizien, -zienne *n* : Belizean
belladone [beladɔn] *nf* : belladonna
belle[1] → **beau**
belle[2] *nf* : beauty, belle
belle–famille [bɛlfamij] *nf, pl* **belles–familles** : in-laws *pl*
belle–fille [bɛlfij] *nf, pl* **belles–filles 1** : daughter-in-law **2** : stepdaughter
belle–mère [bɛlmɛr] *nf, pl* **belles–mères 1** : mother-in-law **2** : stepmother
belle–sœur [bɛlsœr] *nf, pl* **belles–sœurs** : sister-in-law
bellicisme [bɛlisism] *nm* : bellicosity, warmongering
belliciste[1] [bɛlisist] *adj* : bellicose, warmongering
belliciste[2] *nmf* : warmonger
belligérant, -rante [beliʒerɑ̃, -rɑ̃t] *adj & n* : belligerent — **belligérance** [-ʒerɑ̃s] *nf*
belliqueux, -queuse [bɛlikø, -køz] *adj* GUERRIER : warlike
bémol [bemɔl] *adj & nm* : flat (in music)
bénédicité [benedisite] *nm* : grace <dire le bénédicité : to say grace>
bénédictin, -tine [benediktɛ̃, -tin] *adj & n* : Benedictine
bénédiction [benediksjɔ̃] *nf* **1** : blessing, benediction **2** AUBAINE : godsend
bénéfice [benefis] *nm* **1** AVANTAGE : benefit, advantage **2** : profit <faire du bénéfice : to make a profit>
bénéficiaire[1] [benefisjɛr] *adj* : profitable <marge bénéficiaire : profit margin>
bénéficiaire[2] *nmf* : beneficiary, payee
bénéficier [benefisje] {96} *vi* ~ **de** : to profit from, to receive the benefits of
bénéfique [benefik] *adj* : beneficial, advantageous
bénêt[1] [bɔnɛ] *adj* : simpleminded, silly
bénêt[2] *nm* : simpleton
bénévolat [benevɔla] *nm* : volunteer work
bénévole[1] [benevɔl] *adj* : voluntary, volunteer
bénévole[2] *nmf* : volunteer
bengali[1] [bɛ̃gali] *adj* : Bengali
bengali[2] *nm* : Bengali (language)
Bengali *nmf* : Bengali
bénin, -nigne [benɛ̃, beniɲ] *adj* **1** : slight, minor **2** : benign
béninois, -noise [beninwa, -nwaz] *adj* : Beninese
Béninois, -noise *n* : Beninese
bénir [benir] *vt* : to bless
bénit, -nite [beni, -nit] *adj* : blessed, consecrated <eau bénite : holy water>
bénitier [benitje] *nm* : holy water font
benjamin, -mine [bɛ̃ʒamɛ̃, -min] *n* CADET : youngest child
benzène [bɛ̃zɛn] *nm* : benzene
béotien, -tienne [beɔsjɛ̃, -sjɛn] *adj & n* : philistine
béquille [bekij] *nf* **1** : crutch **2** : kickstand
bercail [bɛrkaj] *nm* : fold <rentrer au bercail : to return to the fold>
berçante [bɛrsɑ̃t] *nf or* **chaise berçante** *Can* : rocking chair
berceau [bɛrso] *nm, pl* **berceaux** : cradle
bercer [bɛrse] {6} *vt* **1** : to rock (a baby) **2** : to soothe, to lull — **se bercer** *vr* **1** : to rock, to swing **2** : to delude oneself
berceuse [bɛrsøz] *nf* **1** : lullaby **2** : rocking chair
béret [bɛre] *nm* : beret
berge [bɛrʒ] *nf* RIVE : bank (of a river, etc.)
berger[1], **-gère** [bɛrʒe, -ʒɛr] *n* : shepherd, shepherdess *f*
berger[2] *nm* : sheepdog <berger allemand : German shepherd>
bergerie [bɛrʒəri] *nf* : sheepfold
berline [bɛrlin] *nf* : sedan
berlingot [bɛrlɛ̃go] *nm* **1** : carton (for milk, etc.) **2** : hard candy
berlue [bɛrly] *nf* **avoir la berlue** : to be seeing things, to delude oneself
berne [bɛrn] *nf* **en** ~ : at half mast
berner [bɛrne] *vt* : to fool, to deceive
besogne [bəzɔɲ] *nf* : task, job
besogner [bəzɔɲe] *vi* : to drudge, to slave away
besogneux, -gneuse [bəzɔɲø, -ɲøz] *adj* **1** : poor, needy **2** : plodding, hard-working
besoin [bəzwɛ̃] *nm* **1** : need, requirement <besoins essentiels : basic needs> **2** : neediness, want <enfants dans le besoin : needy children> **3 au** ~ *or* **si besoin est** : if necessary, if need be **4 avoir besoin de** : to need
bestial, -tiale [bɛstjal] *adj, mpl* **bestiaux** [bɛstjo] : brutish, bestial — **bestialement** [bɛstjalmɑ̃] *adv*
bestialité [bɛstjalite] *nf* : brutishness
bestiaux [bɛstjo] *nmpl* BÉTAIL : livestock, cattle
bestiole [bɛstjɔl] *nf* : bug, tiny creature
bétail [betaj] *nm* : livestock, cattle *pl*
bête[1] [bɛt] *adj* **1** STUPIDE : stupid, foolish **2** : simple <c'est tout bête! : there's nothing to it!> — **bêtement** [bɛtmɑ̃] *adv*
bête[2] *nf* **1** ANIMAL : animal <bête de somme : beast of burden> <bête sauvage : wild animal> **2** BESTIOLE : insect, creature <bête à bon Dieu : ladybug> **3** : fool, idiot **4 bête noire** : pet peeve **5 bête puante** *Can* : skunk
bêtise [bɛtiz] *nf* **1** : stupidity, foolishness **2** : nonsense **3** : stupid mistake
béton [betɔ̃] *nm* : concrete
bétonnière [betɔnjɛr] *nf* : cement mixer

bette [bɛt] *nf* **1** : Swiss chard **2** *Can fam* : face <se montrer la bette : to show one's face>
betterave [bɛtrav] *nf* : beet
beuglement [bøgləmɑ̃] *nm* **1** : bellow **2** : blare (of a radio, etc.)
beugler [bøgle] *vi* : to low, to moo, to bellow — *vt* : to bellow out <beugler une chanson : to bellow out a song>
beurre [bœr] *nm* : butter
beurrée [bœre] *nf Can* : slice of bread and butter topped with jam or maple sugar
beurrer [bœre] *vt* : to butter
beurrier [bœrje] *nm* : butter dish
beuverie [bœvri] *nf* : drinking bout, binge
bévue [bevy] *nf* BOURDE : blunder
biais [bjɛ, bjɛz] *nm* **1** : means, way <par le biais de : by means of, via> **2** : bias, slant
biaiser [bjeze] *vi* : to hedge, to dodge the issue
bibelot [biblo] *nm* : trinket, curio
biberon [bibrɔ̃] *nm* : bottle (for a baby)
bible [bibl] *nf* **1** : bible **2 la Bible** : the Bible
bibliobus [biblijɔbys] *nm* : bookmobile
bibliographe [biblijɔgraf] *nmf* : bibliographer
bibliographie [biblijɔgrafi] *nf* : bibliography
bibliographique [biblijɔgrafik] *adj* : bibliographic
bibliothécaire [biblijɔtekɛr] *nmf* : librarian
bibliothèque [biblijɔtɛk] *nf* **1** : library **2** : bookcase
biblique [biblik] *adj* : biblical, scriptural
bicaméral, -rale [bikameral] *adj, mpl* **-raux** [-ro] : bicameral
bicarbonate [bikarbɔnat] *nm* : bicarbonate <bicarbonate de soude : baking soda>
bicentenaire [bisɑ̃tnɛr] *nm* : bicentennial
biceps [biseps] *nms & pl* : biceps
biche [biʃ] *nf* **1** : doe **2 ma biche** *fam* : my darling
bicher [biʃe] *vi France fam* : to get on well <ça biche? : how's it going?>
bichonner [biʃɔne] *vt* **1** : to pamper **2** : to spruce up, to doll up — **se bichonner** *vr* : to preen oneself
bicolore [bikɔlɔr] *adj* : two-colored, two-tone
bicoque [bikɔk] *nf* BARAQUE : shack, hut
bicorne [bikɔrn] *nm* : cocked hat
bicyclette [bisiklɛt] *nf* : bicycle <faire de la bicyclette : to ride a bicycle>
bidet [bide] *nm* : bidet
bidon[1] [bidɔ̃] *adj fam* : bogus, phoney
bidon[2] *nm* **1** : can, (oil) drum **2** : flask, canteen **3** *fam* : belly, gut **4** *fam* : nonsense, hot air <c'est du bidon! : that's baloney!>
bidonner [bidɔne] *v* **se bidonner** *vr fam* : to laugh one's head off
bidonville [bidɔ̃vil] *nm* : shantytown
bidule [bidyl] *nm fam* MACHIN : thingamajig
bien[1] [bjɛ̃] *adv* **1** : well, satisfactorily **2** : very, quite <bien souvent : quite often> **3** : definitely, really **4** : readily, happily <j'aimerais bien un café : I could go for a coffee> **5** : at least <il y avait bien dix personnes : there were at least ten people> **6 ~ de** : a good many, many more <bien des fois : many times> **7 bien que** : although <bien que malade, elle travaille : though ill, she is working> **8 bien sûr** : of course
bien[2] *adj* **1** : good, fine, satisfactory **2** : well, in good health <je me sens bien : I feel good> **3** : good-looking **4** : nice, decent, respectable <un voisinage bien : a nice neighborhood> **5** : comfortable
bien[3] *nm* **1** : good <faire le bien : to do good> **2 biens** *nmpl* : possessions, property <biens de consommation : consumer goods> <biens immobiliers : real estate>
bien[4] *interj* : OK, all right, good, very well <bien, allons-nous-en : OK, let's go> <bien! bien! j'entends : all right! all right! I understand> <bien, je le prendrai : good! I'll take it>
bien-aimé, -aimée [bjɛ̃neme] *adj & n* : beloved
bien-être [bjɛ̃nɛtr] *nm* **1** : well-being **2** : comfort **3 bien-être social** *Can* : (public) welfare
bienfaisance [bjɛ̃fəzɑ̃s] *nf* : charity, beneficence
bienfaisant, -sante [bjɛ̃fəzɑ̃, -zɑ̃t] *adj* **1** : charitable, beneficent **2** : beneficial
bienfait [bjɛ̃fɛ] *nm* **1** : act of kindness **2** AVANTAGE : benefit, advantage
bienfaiteur, -trice [bjɛ̃fɛtœr, -tris] *n* : benefactor, benefactress *f*
bien-fondé [bjɛ̃fɔ̃de] *nm* **1** : validity, soundness **2** LÉGITIMITÉ : legitimacy (in law)
bienheureux, -reuse [bjɛ̃nøʀø, -ʀøz] *adj* **1** : happy, joyful **2** : blessed
biennal, -nale [bjenal] *adj, mpl* **-naux** [-no] : biennial — **biennalement** [-nalmɑ̃] *adv*
bien-pensant, -sante [bjɛ̃pɑ̃sɑ̃, -sɑ̃t] *adj* : right-minded, conformist
bienséance [bjɛ̃seɑ̃s] *nf* : propriety, decorum
bienséant, -séante [bjɛ̃seɑ̃, -seɑ̃t] *adj* : proper, seemly
bientôt [bjɛ̃to] *adv* **1** : soon <à bientôt! : see you soon!> **2** : nearly <il est bientôt trois heures : it's nearly three o'clock>
bienveillance [bjɛ̃vejɑ̃s] *nf* : kindness, benevolence
bienveillant, -lante [bjɛ̃vejɑ̃, -jɑ̃t] *adj* : kind, benevolent

bienvenu[1], **-nue** [bjɛ̃vny] *adj* : welcome, opportune
bienvenu[2], **-nue** *n* **être le bienvenu** : to be welcome
bienvenue *nf* **1** : welcome <souhaiter la bienvenue à : to welcome> **2 bienvenue** *Can fam* : you're welcome!
bière [bjɛr] *nf* **1** : beer <bière pression : draft beer> <bière blonde : lager> **2** : casket, coffin
biffer [bife] *vt* : to cross out
bifteck [biftɛk] *nm* : steak
bifurcation [bifyrkasjɔ̃] *nf* : fork, junction
bifurquer [bifyrke] *vi* : to fork, to branch off
bigame[1] [bigam] *adj* : bigamous — **bigamie** [-gami] *nf*
bigame[2] *nmf* : bigamist
bigarré [bigare] *adj* MULTICOLORE : multicolored, variegated
bigot[1], **-gote** [bigo, -gɔt] *adj* : overly devout, sanctimonious
bigot[2], **-gote** *n* : zealot, (religious) bigot
bigoterie [bigɔtri] *nf* : (religious) bigotry
bigoudi [bigudi] *nm* : hair curler, roller
bijou [biʒu] *nm, pl* **bijoux 1** : jewel, piece of jewelry **2** : gem, marvel
bijouterie [biʒutri] *nf* **1** BIJOUX : jewelry, jewels *pl* **2** : jewelry store
bijoutier, -tière [biʒutje, -tjɛr] *n* JOAILLIER : jeweler
bikini [bikini] *nm* : bikini
bilan [bilɑ̃] *nm* **1** : assessment, appraisal <faire le bilan de : to take stock of> **2** : balance sheet <déposer son bilan : to declare bankruptcy> **3** *or* **bilan de santé** : (medical) check-up
bilatéral, -rale [bilateral] *adj, mpl* **-raux** [-ro] : bilateral — **bilatéralement** [-ralmɑ̃] *adv*
bile [bil] *nf* **1** : bile **2 se faire de la bile** : to worry, to fret
biliaire [biljɛr] *adj* → **vésicule**
bilieux, -lieuse [biljø, -ljøz] *adj* : bilious, irritable
bilingue [bilɛ̃g] *adj* : bilingual
billard [bijar] *nm* : billiards *pl*
bille [bij] *nf* **1** : marble <jouer aux billes : to play marbles> **2** : billiard ball **3** : log **4** → **roulement**
billet [bijɛ] *nm* **1** : bill, banknote <un billet de vingt dollars : a twenty-dollar bill> **2** TICKET : ticket **3 billet doux** : love letter
billetterie [bijɛtri] *nf* **1** : ticket office, ticket agency **2** : automatic teller machine
billion [biljɔ̃] *nm* : trillion (United States), billion (Great Britain)
billot [bijo] *nm* **1** : block **2** *Can* : log
bimensuel, -suelle [bimɑ̃sɥɛl] *adj* : semimonthly, twice a month
binaire [binɛr] *adj* : binary
bine [bin] *nf Can* : white bean, broad bean
biner [bine] *vt* : to hoe, to harrow
binette [binɛt] *nf* : hoe
bingo [bingo] *nm Can* : bingo
binoculaire [binɔkylɛr] *adj* : binocular
biochimie [bjɔʃimi] *nf* : biochemistry — **biochimiste** [-ʃimist] *nmf*
biochimique [bjɔʃimik] *adj* : biochemical
biodégradable [bjɔdegradabl] *adj* : biodegradable
biographe [bjɔgraf] *nmf* : biographer
biographie [bjɔgrafi] *nf* : biography
biographique [bjɔgrafik] *adj* : biographical
biologie [bjɔlɔʒi] *nf* : biology — **biologiste** [-lɔʒist] *nmf*
biologique [bjɔlɔʒik] *adj* : biological
biophysicien, -cienne [bjɔfizisjɛ̃, -sjɛn] *n* : biophysicist
biophysique [bjɔfizik] *nf* : biophysics
biopsie [bjɔpsi] *nf* : biopsy
biosphère [bjɔsfɛr] *nf* : biosphere
biotechnologie [bjɔtɛknɔlɔʒi] *nf* : biotechnology
bip [bip] *nm* **1** : beep **2** *fam* : beeper
bipartite [bipartit] *adj* : bipartite, bipartisan
bipède [bipɛd] *adj & nm* : biped
bipolaire [bipɔlɛr] *adj* : bipolar
birman, -mane [birmɑ̃, -man] *adj* : Burmese
Birman, -mane *n* : Burmese
bis[1] [bis] *adv* **1** : twice, repeat (in music) **2** : A (in an address) <14 bis : 14A>
bis[2], **bise** [bi, biz] *adj* : grayish brown
bis[3] [bis] *nm & interj* : encore
bisannuel, -nuelle [bizanyɛl] *adj & nf* : biannual, biennial — **bisannuellement** [-nɥɛlmɑ̃] *adv*
bisbille [bizbij] *nf fam* : squabble, tiff
biscornu, -nue [biskɔrny] *adj* **1** : misshapen, crooked **2** : quirky, bizarre
biscotte [biskɔt] *nf* : zwieback
biscuit [biskɥi] *nm* **1** : cookie **2** : sponge cake
bise [biz] *nf* **1** : north wind **2** *fam* : kiss, smack <faire la bise : to kiss on the cheeks>
biseau [bizo] *nm* **1** : bevel **2 en ~** : beveled
biseauter [bizote] *vt* : to bevel
bisexuel, -sexuelle [biseksɥɛl] *adj* : bisexual — **bisexualité** [-seksɥalite] *nf*
bismuth [bismyt] *nm* : bismuth
bison [bizɔ̃] *nm* : bison, buffalo
bisser [bise] *vt* : to encore
bissextile [bisɛkstil] *adj* **année bissextile** : leap year
bistouri [bisturi] *nm* : lancet
bistro *or* **bistrot** [bistro] *nm* : bistro, café
bit [bit] *nm* : bit (unit of information)
bitume [bitym] *nm* **1** : bitumen **2** : blacktop, asphalt
bitumineux, -neuse [bityminø, -nøz] *adj* : bituminous
bivalve [bivalv] *adj & nm* : bivalve

bivouac [bivwak] *nm* : bivouac
bivouaquer [bivwake] *vi* : to bivouac
bizarre [bizar] *adj* : bizarre, strange, odd — **bizarrement** [-zarmɑ̃] *adv*
bizarrerie [bizarri] *nf* **1** : strangeness **2** : eccentricity, peculiarity
blackbouler [blakbule] *vt* : to blackball
blafard, -farde [blafar, -fard] *adj* : pale, pallid
blague [blag] *nf* PLAISANTERIE : joke, trick, fib <sans blague! : no kidding!>
blaguer [blage] *vi* PLAISANTER : to joke, to kid, to fib
blagueur, -gueuse [blagœr, -gøz] *n fam* : joker, prankster
blaireau [blɛro] *nm, pl* **blaireaux 1** : badger **2** : shaving brush
blairer [blɛre] *vt fam* : to stand, to stomach <personne ne peut la blairer : no one can stand her>
blamable [blamabl] *adj* : blameworthy
blâme [blam] *nm* **1** : blame, censure **2** : reprimand
blâmer [blame] *vt* **1** : to blame, to censure **2** : to reprimand
blanc[1], **blanche** [blɑ̃, blɑ̃ʃ] *adj* **1** : white **2** PÂLE : light-colored, pale **3** : blank **4** : pure, innocent
blanc[2] *nm* **1** : white **2** INTERVALLE : gap, blank space **3 blanc d'œuf** : egg white
blanc–bec [blɑ̃bɛk] *nm, pl* **blancs–becs** : greenhorn
blanchâtre [blɑ̃ʃatr] *adj* : whitish, off-white
blancheur [blɑ̃ʃœr] *nf* : whiteness
blanchiment [blɑ̃ʃimɑ̃] *nm* **1** : whitening, bleaching **2** : money laundering
blanchir [blɑ̃ʃir] *vt* **1** : to whiten, to bleach **2** : to launder **3** : to blanch, to parboil (vegetables) **4** : to clear (someone's name) **5** *Can* : to shut out (in sports) — *vi* : to turn white — **se blanchir** *vr* : to clear one's name
blanchissage [blɑ̃ʃisaʒ] *nm* **1** : washing, laundering **2** : refining (of sugar, etc.) **3** *Can* : shutout (in sports)
blanchisserie [blɑ̃ʃisri] *nf* : laundry
blanchisseur, -seuse [blɑ̃ʃisœr, -søz] *n* : laundry worker
blasé, -sée [blaze] *adj* : blasé, jaded
blason [blazɔ̃] *nm* **1** : coat of arms **2 redorer son blason** : to restore one's good name
blasphématoire [blasfematwar] *adj* : blasphemous
blasphème [blasfɛm] *nm* : blasphemy
blasphémer [blasfeme] {87} *v* : to blaspheme
blatte [blat] *nf France* : cockroach
blazer [blazɛr] *nm* : blazer (jacket)
blé [ble] *nm* **1** : wheat **2 blé d'Inde** *Can* : Indian corn, maize **3 blé noir** SARRASIN : buckwheat
bled [bled] *nm fam* : small village, boondocks *pl*
blême [blɛm] *adj* : pale, wan, pallid
blennorragie [blenɔraʒi] *nf* : gonorrhea
bléser [bleze] {87} *vi* : to lisp
blessé, -sée [blese] *n* : casualty, injured person
blesser [blese] *vt* : to injure, to wound, to hurt
blessure [blesyr] *nf* : injury, wound
bleu[1], **bleue** [blø] *adj* **1** : blue <des yeux bleus : blue eyes> **2** : very rare (of steak, etc.)
bleu[2] *nm* **1** : blue **2** : bruise <se faire un bleu : to bruise oneself> <couvert de bleus : black-and-blue> **3** *or* **fromage bleu** : blue cheese **4** : blueprint
bleuâtre [bløatr] *adj* : bluish
bleuet [bløɛ] *nm* **1** : cornflower **2** *Can* : blueberry
bleuir [bløir] *v* : to turn blue
bleuté, -tée [bløte] *adj* : bluish
blindage [blɛ̃daʒ] *nm* : armor (plating)
blindé[1], **-dée** [blɛ̃de] *adj* : armored
blindé[2] *nm* : armored vehicle
bloc [blɔk] *nm* **1** : block (of wood) **2** : bloc (in politics) **3** : pad (of paper) **4** *Can* : block <faire le tour du bloc en courant : to run around the block> **5 en ~** : as a whole, outright
blocage [blɔkaʒ] *nm* **1** : locking, jamming (of mechanisms) **2** : mental block **3** : freezing (of prices, wages, etc.)
blocus [blɔkys] *nm* : blockade
blond, blonde [blɔ̃, blɔ̃d] *adj & n* : blond
blonde *nf Can fam* : girlfriend
blondeur [blɔ̃dœr] *nf* : blondness, fairness
bloquer [blɔke] *vt* **1** : to block **2** : to freeze (a bank account), to stop (a check) **3** : to jam, to lock — **se bloquer** *vr*
bloquiste [blɔkist] *nmf Can* : member of the Bloc québécois party
blottir [blɔtir] *v* **se blottir** *vr* : to nestle, to cuddle, to snuggle up
blouse [bluz] *nf* **1** CHEMISIER : blouse **2** SARRAU : smock **3** : pocket (in billiards)
blouson [bluzɔ̃] *nm* : jacket <blouson d'aviateur : bomber jacket>
blue–jean [bludʒin] *nm, pl* **blue–jeans** : jeans *pl*, blue jeans *pl*
bluff [blœf] *nm* : bluff <c'est du bluff : he's just bluffing>
bluffer [blœfe] *v* : to bluff
boa [bɔa] *nm* : boa
bob [bɔb] *nm* → **bobsleigh**
bobard [bɔbar] *nm fam* : fib, tall tale
bobine [bɔbin] *nf* **1** : spool, reel, bobbin <bobine de pellicule : roll of film> **2** : electric coil
bobo [bobo] *nm fam* : boo-boo, scratch
bobsleigh [bɔbsleg] *nm* : bobsled
bocal [bɔkal] *nm, pl* **bocaux** [bɔko] : jar
bock [bɔk] *nm* **1** CHOPE : beer glass **2** : glass of beer
bœuf [bœf] *nm, pl* **bœufs** [bø] **1** : beef **2** : steer, ox

bohème [bɔɛm] *adj & nmf* : bohemian
bohémien, -mienne [bɔemjɛ̃, -mjɛn] *n* : Bohemian, gypsy
boire[1] [bwar] {13} *vt* **1** : to drink <boire un coup : to have a drink> **2** : to absorb, to soak up — *vi* **1** : to drink **2** ~ **à** : to toast
boire[2] *nm* : drink <le boire et le manger : food and drink>
bois [bwa] *nms & pl* **1** : wood <bois à brûler : firewood> <bois dur : hardwood> <petit bois : kindling> **2** FORÊT : woods *pl* **3** : woodcut **4 bois** *nmpl* : antlers **5 bois** *nmpl* : woodwinds
boisé[1], **-sée** [bwaze] *adj* : wooded
boisé[2] *nm Can* : woods *pl*, wooded area
boisement [bwazmɑ̃] *nm* : afforestation
boiserie [bwazri] *nf* **1** : woodwork **2 boiseries** *nfpl* : paneling
boisseau [bwaso] *nm* : bushel
boisson [bwasɔ̃] *nf* **1** : drink, beverage <boisson gazeuse : pop, soda> **2 en** ~ *Can* : drunk
boîte [bwat] *nf* **1** : (tin) can <mettre en boîte : to can> **2** : box <boîte à gantes : glove compartment> <boîte aux lettres : mailbox> **3** *fam* : nightclub **4 boîte de vitesses** : transmission (of a motor vehicle)
boiter [bwate] *vi* **1** : to limp **2** : to wobble
boiterie [bwatri] *nf* : limp
boiteux, -teuse [bwatø, -tøz] *adj* **1** : lame **2** : wobbly, shaky
boîtier [bwatje] *nm* : casing, housing
boitillement [bwatijmɑ̃] *nm* : hobble, (slight) limp
boitiller [bwatije] *vi* : to limp slightly
bol [bɔl] *nm* **1** : bowl **2** : bowlful <un bol d'air : a breath of fresh air> **3 coup de bol** : stroke of luck
boléro [bɔlero] *nm* : bolero
bolide [bɔlid] *nm* **1** : meteorite **2** : racing car
bolivien, -vienne [bɔlivjɛ̃, -vjɛn] *adj* : Bolivian
Bolivien, -vienne *n* : Bolivian
bombarde [bɔ̃bard] *nf* : Jew's harp
bombardement [bɔ̃bardəmɑ̃] *nm* : bombing, bombardment
bombarder [bɔ̃barde] *vt* **1** : to bomb **2** : to bombard, to pelt
bombardier [bɔ̃bardje] *nm* **1** : bomber **2** : bombardier
bombe [bɔ̃b] *nf* **1** : bomb **2** ATOMISEUR : aerosol spray, atomiser **3 faire la bombe** *fam* : to live it up, to go on a spree
bomber [bɔ̃be] *vt* **1** GONFLER : to puff up, to stick out <bomber le torse : to swell with pride> **2** : to spray (paint) — *vi* : to bulge out
bon[1] [bɔ̃, bɔn *before a vowel or mute h*] *adv* **1 faire bon** : to be nice, to be good, to be acceptable <il fait bon ici : it's nice here> <il ne ferait pas bon l'arrêter : it would be unwise to stop him> **2 tenir bon** : to hold firm, to stand fast
bon[2], **bonne** [bɔ̃ (bon *before a vowel or mute h*), bɔn] *adj* **1** : good, honest, upright **2** : sound, high-quality **3** : pleasant, desirable <bonne chance! : good luck!> <ça sent bon : that smells good> **4** : correct, proper **5** : capable, knowledgeable <bon en science : good at science> **6** : good, profitable <être bon à faire : to be worth doing> **7** : effective <bon contre la douleur : good for pain> **8** (*used as an intensive*) <un bon nombre : a good many> <trois bonnes heures : three solid hours> **9 bon enfant** : easygoing **10 bon marché** : cheap, inexpensive **11 bon mot** : witticism **12 bonne femme** *fam* : woman, old lady **13 bonne sœur** : nun **14 bon sens** : common sense **15 de bonne heure** : early **16 pour de bon** : really, for good <il est parti pour de bon : he's gone for good>
bon[3] *nm* **1** : good thing, good person <les bons : the good> <avoir du bon : to have (some) good points> **2** : voucher, coupon **3** : bond <bon du Trésor : treasury bond> <bon de commande : purchase order>
bon[4] *interj* **1** : right, OK, fine <bon, mangeons : OK, let's eat> **2** : so, now, well <bon, où en étions-nous? : now, where were we?>
bonasse [bɔnas] *adj* : meek
bonbon [bɔ̃bɔ̃] *nm* : candy
bonbonnière [bɔ̃bɔnjɛr] *nf* : candy box
bond [bɔ̃] *nm* **1** : bound, jump, leap <faire un bond : to leap> <bond en avant : leap forward, breakthrough> **2** : bounce
bondé, -dée [bɔ̃de] *adj* : crammed, jam-packed
bondir [bɔ̃dir] *vi* **1** SAUTER : to jump, to leap **2** : to rush, to dash
bonheur [bɔnœr] *nm* **1** : happiness **2** : pleasure **3** : luck, good fortune <par bonheur : fortunately>
bonhomie [bɔnɔmi] *nf* : good-naturedness, cordiality
bonhomme[1] [bɔnɔm] *adj, pl* **bonshommes** : affable, good-natured
bonhomme[2] *nm, pl* **bonshommes 1** *fam* : fellow, guy **2 bonhomme de neige** : snowman
boni [bɔni] *nm* **1** : bonus **2** : surplus
bonification [bɔnifikasjɔ̃] *nf* **1** : improvement (of land, etc.) **2** : bonus points *pl* (in sports)
bonifier [bɔnifje] {96} *vt* : to improve — **se bonifier** *vr*
boniment [bɔnimɑ̃] *nm* **1** : sales pitch **2** *fam* : tall story **3** *Can* : short speech
bonimenteur [bɔnimɑ̃tœr] *nm* : barker (at a fair)

bonjour [bɔ̃ʒur] *nm* **1** : hello, good morning, good afternoon **2** *Can* : good-bye
bonne [bɔn] *nf* **1** DOMESTIQUE : maid **2 bonne d'enfants** : nanny
bonnement [bɔnmɑ̃] *adv* **tout bonnement** : quite simply
bonnet [bɔne] *nm* **1** : cap, bonnet **2** : cup (of a brassiere) **3 c'est blanc bonnet et bonnet blanc** : it's six of one, half dozen of the other **4 gros bonnet** *fam* : bigwig, big shot
bonneterie [bɔnetri] *nf* : hosiery
bonsoir [bɔ̃swar] *nm* : good evening, good night
bonté [bɔ̃te] *nf* : goodness, kindness
bookmaker [bukmekœr] *nm* : bookmaker
boom [bum] *nm* : boom (in economics)
boomerang [bumrɑ̃g] *nm* : boomerang
bord [bɔr] *nm* **1** : edge **2** : bank, shore **3** : border (of fabric, etc.) **4** : rim, brim **5** CÔTÉ : side **6 à ~** : on board, aboard **7 au bord de** : on the verge of, on the brink of **8 par–dessus ~** : overboard
bordeaux [bɔrdo] *nm* **1** : Bordeaux (wine) **2** : maroon
bordée [bɔrde] *nf* **1** : broadside, volley <une bordée d'injures : a volley of abuse> **2** : tack (of a ship) <faire une bordée : to tack> **3 bordée de neige** *Can* : snowstorm
bordel [bɔrdɛl] *nm fam* **1** : brothel **2** : mess, shambles
bordelais, -laise [bɔrdəlɛ, -lɛz] *adj* : of or from Bordeaux
border [bɔrde] *vt* **1** : to border, to line, to ring **2** : to tuck in
bordereau [bɔrdəro] *nm, pl* **-reaux** [-ro] : statement (of an account), note, slip <bordereau de dépôt : deposit slip>
bordure [bɔrdyr] *nf* **1** BORD : border, edge **2** : side (of a road), curb
bore [bɔr] *nm* : boron
boréal, boréale [bɔreal] *adj, mpl* **boréaux** [bɔreo] **1** : boreal, northern **2 → aurore**
borgne [bɔrɲ] *adj* : one-eyed
borique [bɔrik] *adj* : **acide borique** : boric acid
borne [bɔrn] *nf* **1** : milestone, landmark **2** *France fam* : kilometer **3** : terminal (in electricity) **4 bornes** *nfpl* : limits, boundaries **5 borne d'incendie** : fire hydrant
borné, -née [bɔrne] *adj* : narrow-minded
borne–fontaine [bɔrnfɔ̃ten] *nf Can* : fire hydrant
borner [bɔrne] *vt* **1** : to mark out the boundaries of **2** LIMITER : to limit, to restrict — **se borner** *vr*
bosniaque [bɔsnjak] *adj* : Bosnian
Bosniaque *nmf* : Bosnian
bosquet [bɔske] *nm* : grove, copse
bosse [bɔs] *nf* **1** : hump (of a person or animal) **2** : lump, bump, dent **3 avoir la bosse de** : to have a flair for
bosseler [bɔsle] {8} *vt* **1** : to emboss **2** : to dent
bosser [bɔse] *vi France fam* : to work, to slave away
bossu[1], **-sue** [bɔsy] *adj* : hunchbacked
bossu[2], **-sue** *n* : hunchback (person)
botanique[1] [bɔtanik] *adj* : botanical
botanique[2] *nf* : botany — **botaniste** [-tanist] *nmf*
botte [bɔt] *nf* **1** : boot **2** : bunch, sheaf, bale **3** : thrust, lunge (in fencing)
botter [bɔte] *vt* **1** : to put boots on **2** : to kick (in sports)
botteur, -teuse [bɔtœr, -tøz] *n* : kicker (in sports)
bottillon [bɔtijɔ̃] *nm* : bootee
bottin [bɔtɛ̃] *nm* : telephone directory
bottine [bɔtin] *nf* : ankle boot
botulisme [bɔtylism] *nm* : botulism
bouc [buk] *nm* **1** : goat, billy goat **2** : goatee **3 bouc émissaire** : scapegoat
boucan [bukɑ̃] *nm fam* : din, racket
boucane [bukan] *nf Can* : smoke
boucanier [bukanje] *nm* : buccaneer
bouche [buʃ] *nf* **1** : mouth <de bouche à l'oreille : confidentially> **2** : opening, entrance <bouche d'égout : manhole> **3 le bouche à bouche** : mouth-to-mouth resuscitation **4 bouche d'incendie** : fire hydrant **5 faire la fine bouche** : to turn up one's nose **6 → bée**
bouchée [buʃe] *nf* : mouthful
boucher[1] [buʃe] *vt* : to stop up, to plug, to block — **se boucher** *vr* **1** : to get blocked **2 se boucher le nez** : to hold one's nose
boucher[2], **-chère** [buʃe, -ʃɛr] *n* : butcher
boucherie [buʃri] *nf* **1** : butcher's shop **2** MASSACRE : butchery, slaughter
bouche–trou [buʃtru] *nm, pl* **bouche–trous** : stand-in, stopgap
bouchon [buʃɔ̃] *nm* **1** : cork, stopper **2** : float (in fishing) **3** : traffic jam, gridlock
boucle [bukl] *nf* **1** : buckle, loop **2** : curl, loop **3 boucle d'oreille** : earring
boucler [bukle] *vt* **1** : to buckle, to fasten **2** : to complete, to finish off <boucler la boucle : to come full circle> **3** *fam* : to lock up, to imprison — *vi* : to curl
bouclier [buklije] *nm* : shield
bouddhisme [budism] *nm* : Buddhism — **bouddhiste** [budist] *adj & nmf*
bouder [bude] *vt* : to avoid, to be cool towards — *vi* : to sulk, to pout
bouderie [budri] *nf* : sulking, sulkiness
boudeur, -deuse [budœr, -døz] *adj* : sulky
boudin [budɛ̃] *nm* **1** : blood sausage **2** : flange (on a wheel)

boudiné, -née [budine] *adj* **1** : pudgy (of fingers, etc.) **2** ~ **dans** : squeezed into, bulging out of

boue [bu] *nf* : mud

bouée [bwe] *nf* **1** : buoy **2 bouée de sauvetage** : life preserver

bouette [bwɛt] *nf Can fam* : mud

boueux, boueuse [buø, buøz] *adj* : muddy

bouffant, -fante [bufɑ̃, -fɑ̃t] *adj* **1** : puffed out, baggy **2** : bouffant

bouffe [buf] *nf fam* : grub, chow

bouffée [bufe] *nf* **1** : puff, gust **2** : surge, fit (of pride, etc.)

bouffer [bufe] *vt fam* : to eat, to gobble up

bouffi, -fie [bufi] *adj* : puffy, swollen

bouffir [bufir] *v* : to puff up

bouffisure [bufisyr] *nf* : puffiness (of the face, etc.)

bouffon[1], **-fonne** [bufɔ̃, bufɔn] *adj* : farcical, comical

bouffon[2] *nm* : clown, buffoon, jester

bouffonnerie [bufɔnri] *nf* : buffoonery, antics *pl*

bouge *nm* [buʒ] **1** : hovel, dump **2** : dive, seedy café

bougeoir [buʒwar] *nm* : candlestick

bougeotte [buʒɔt] *nf* : fidgets *pl* <avoir la bougeotte : to be fidgety>

bouger [buʒe] {17} *vt* : to move — *vi* : to budge, to stir — **se bouger** *vr*

bougie [buʒi] *nf* **1** : candle **2** : spark plug

bougonner [bugɔne] *vi* : to grumble, to complain

bougre [bugr] *nm fam* : guy, fellow

bougrement [bugrəmɑ̃] *adv fam* : awfully, damned

bouillabaisse [bujabɛs] *nf* : bouillabaisse, fish soup

bouillie [buji] *nf* : baby cereal, gruel

bouillir [bujir] {14} *vi* **1** : to boil **2** : to seethe (with anger, etc.)

bouilloire [bujwar] *nf* : kettle, teakettle

bouillon [bujɔ̃] *nm* **1** : broth, stock **2** : bubble

bouillonnant, -nante [bujɔnɑ̃, -nɑ̃t] *adj* **1** : bubbling, foaming **2** : lively

bouillonnement [bujɔnmɑ̃] *nm* **1** : bubbling, foaming **2** : agitation, ferment

bouillonner [bujɔne] *vi* **1** : to bubble, to foam **2** : to seethe

boulanger, -gère [bulɑ̃ʒe, -ʒɛr] *n* : baker

boulangerie [bulɑ̃ʒri] *nf* : bakery

boule [bul] *nf* **1** : ball <boule de neige : snowball> **2 se mettre en boule** *fam* : to blow one's top

bouleau [bulo] *nm, pl* **bouleaux** : birch

bouledogue [buldɔg] *nm* : bulldog

boulet [bulɛ] *nm* **1** : cannonball **2** : ball and chain **3** : fetlock (of a horse)

boulette [bulɛt] *nf* **1** : pellet **2** *fam* : blunder **3 boulette de pâte** : dumpling **4 boulette de viande** : meatball

boulevard [bulvar] *nm* : boulevard

bouleversant, -sante [bulvɛrsɑ̃, -sɑ̃t] *adj* : distressing, upsetting

bouleversement [bulvɛrsəmɑ̃] *nm* : upheaval, upset

bouleverser [bulvɛrse] *vt* **1** : to overwhelm, to upset **2** : to disrupt, to turn upside down

boulier [bulje] *nm* : abacus

boulimie [bulimi] *nf* : bulimia — **boulimique** [-limik] *adj*

boulon [bulɔ̃] *nm* : bolt

boulot[1], **-lotte** [bulo, -lɔt] *adj* : plump, chubby

boulot[2] *nm fam* **1** : work, task **2** : job <petit boulot : odd job>

boum[1] [bum] *nm* **1** : bang **2** : boom (of business, births, etc.)

boum[2] *nf France* : party

bouquet [bukɛ] *nm* **1** : bouquet, bunch (of flowers, etc.) **2** : clump (of trees) **3** : bouquet (of wine) **4** : crowning event <ça, c'est le bouquet! : that takes the cake!>

bouquetin [buktɛ̃] *nm* : ibex

bouquin [bukɛ̃] *nm fam* : book

bouquiner [bukine] *v fam* : to read

bouquiniste [bukinist] *nmf* : second-hand bookseller

bourbeux, -beuse [burbø, -bøz] *adj* : muddy, swampy

bourbier [burbje] *nm* : swamp, quagmire

bourbon [burbɔ̃] *nm* : bourbon

bourde [burd] *nf* BÉVUE : blunder

bourdon [burdɔ̃] *nm* **1** : bumblebee **2 avoir le bourdon** *fam* : to have the blues

bourdonnement [burdɔnmɑ̃] *nm* **1** : buzzing, droning **2 bourdonnement d'oreilles** : ringing in the ears

bourdonner [burdɔne] *vi* : to buzz, to hum, to drone

bourg [bur] *nm* : market town

bourgade [burgad] *nf* : small town, village

bourgeois, -geoise [burʒwa, -ʒwaz] *adj & n* : bourgeois

bourgeoisie [burʒwazi] *nf* : bourgeoisie, middle class

bourgeon [burʒɔ̃] *nm* : bud

bourgeonner [burʒɔne] *vi* : to bud

bourgogne [burgɔɲ] *nm* : Burgundy (wine)

bourguignon, -gnonne [burgiɲɔ̃, -ɲɔn] *adj* **1** : Burgundian **2 bœuf bourguignon** : beef bourguignon

bourrage [buraʒ] *nm* **1** : filling, stuffing **2** : cramming (for an exam) **3 bourrage de crâne** : brainwashing

bourrasque [burask] *nf* : squall, gust (of wind), flurry (of snow)

bourrasser [burase] *vt Can fam* : to be rough with, to push around

bourre [bur] *nf* : stuffing, padding, wad

bourreau [buro] *nm, pl* **bourreaux 1** : executioner, hangman **2** : torturer, tormentor **3 bourreau de travail** : workaholic

bourrée [bure] *nf Can* : spurt <travailler par bourrées : to work in spurts>
bourrelet [burlɛ] *nm* **1** : weather strip **2** : roll (of fat)
bourrer [bure] *vt* : to fill, to stuff, to cram — *vi* : to be filling — **se bourrer** *vr* : to stuff oneself
bourrique [burik] *nf* **1** ÂNE : ass, donkey **2** *fam* : stubborn fool
bourru, -rue [bury] *adj* : gruff
bourrure [buryr] *nf Can* : stuffing, padding
bourse [burs] *nf* **1** PORTE-MONNAIE : change purse **2** : scholarship, grant **3 la Bourse** : the stock market
boursier[1], **-sière** [bursje, -sjɛr] *adj* : stock, stock-market
boursier[2], **-sière** *n* **1** : scholarship holder, scholar **2** : stock-market trader
boursouflé, -flée [bursufle] *adj* **1** : puffy, bloated **2** : bombastic
boursoufler [bursufle] *vt* : to puff up, to cause to swell — **se boursoufler** *vr* **1** : to swell (up) **2** : to blister (of paint)
boursouflure [bursuflyr] *nf* **1** : swelling, puffiness **2** : pomposity **3** : blister (on paint, etc.)
bousculade [buskylad] *nf* **1** : crush, jostling **2** : rush, scramble
bousculer [buskyle] *vt* **1** : to bump into, to jostle, to shove **2** : to rush, to hurry — **se bousculer** *vr* : to bump into each other
bouse [buz] *nf* : cow dung, cowpat
bousiller [buzije] *vt fam* **1** : to bungle, to botch **2** : to wreck **3** : to bump off, to kill
bousilleur, -leuse [busijœr, -jøz] *n fam* : bungler
boussole [busɔl] *nf* : compass
bout[1] [bu], *etc.* → **bouillir**
bout[2] [bu] *nm* **1** EXTRÉMITÉ : end, tip <bout de doigt : fingertip> <bout de la table : head of the table> **2** : bit, piece **3 à bout portant** : point-blank **4 au bout de** : after <au bout de cinq minutes : after five minutes> **5 au bout du compte** : in the end, ultimately **6 être à bout** : to be exhausted <ma patience est à bout : my patience has run out>
boutade [butad] *nf* PLAISANTERIE : joke, witticism
bouteille [butɛj] *nf* : bottle
boutique [butik] *nf* : store, shop, boutique
boutiquier, -quière [butikje, -kjɛr] *n* : shopkeeper
bouton [butɔ̃] *nm* **1** : button **2** BOURGEON : bud **3** : pimple **4 bouton de porte** : doorknob
bouton-d'or [butɔ̃dɔr] *nm, pl* **boutons-d'or** : buttercup
boutonner [butɔne] *vt* : to button — **se boutonner** *vr* : to button up
boutonneux, -neuse [butɔnø, -nøz] *adj* : pimply
boutonnière [butɔnjɛr] *nf* : buttonhole
bouton-pression [butɔ̃presjɔ̃] *nm, pl* **boutons-pression** : snap (fastener)
bouture [butyr] *nf* : cutting (from a plant)
bouvier, -vière [buvje, -vjɛr] *n* : cowherd
bovin, -vine [bɔvɛ̃, -vin] *adj* : bovine
bovins [bɔvɛ̃] *nmpl* : cattle
bowling [bulin] *nm* **1** : bowling **2** : bowling alley
box [bɔks] *nm, pl* **boxes 1** : stall, alcove, cubicle **2 box des accusés** : dock (in court)
boxe [bɔks] *nf* : boxing
boxer[1] [bɔkse] *vi* : to box — *vt fam* : to strike, to punch
boxer[2] [bɔksɛr] *nm* : boxer (dog)
boxeur [bɔksœr] *nm* : boxer, fighter
box-office [bɔksɔfis] *nm, pl* **box-offices** : box office
boyau [bwajo] *nm, pl* **boyaux 1** TUYAU : hose, tube **2** INTESTIN : intestine, gut **3** : narrow passageway **4 boyau d'arrosage** *Can* : hose
boycott [bɔjkɔt] *or* **boycottage** [bɔjkɔtaʒ] *nm* : boycott
boycotter [bɔjkɔte] *vt* : to boycott
bozo [bozo] *nm Can fam* : idiot, fool
bracelet [braslɛ] *nm* **1** : bracelet **2** *or* **bracelet de montre** : watchband
bracelet-montre [braslɛmɔ̃tr] *nm, pl* **bracelets-montres** : wristwatch
braconner [brakɔne] *vi* : to poach
braconnier, -nière [brakɔnje, -njɛr] *n* : poacher
brader [brade] *vt* : to sell (off) cheaply
braderie [bradri] *nf* : clearance sale
braguette [braget] *nf* : fly (of pants, etc.)
braille [braj] *nm* : braille
brailler [braje] *vi fam* : to bawl, to yell, to howl — *vt fam* : to bellow out
braiment [brɛmɑ̃] *nm* : bray, braying
braire [brɛr] {15} *vi* : to bray
braise [brɛz] *nf* : embers *pl*, coals *pl*
braiser [brɛze] *vt* : to braise
bran [brɑ̃] *nm* **1** : bran **2 bran de scie** : sawdust
brancard [brɑ̃kar] *nm* **1** CIVIÈRE : stretcher **2** : shaft (of a carriage, etc.)
branche [brɑ̃ʃ] *nf* **1** : branch, bough (of a tree) **2** : branch (of a family, a river, etc.) **3** : field (of activity) **4** : sidepiece (of eyeglasses)
branché, -chée [brɑ̃ʃe] *adj fam* : fashionable, trendy, in
brancher [brɑ̃ʃe] *vt* **1** : to connect up (a utility) **2** : to plug in **3** *fam* : to interest, to turn on <le rock, ça ne me branche pas : I'm not into rock music>
branchie [brɑ̃ʃi] *nf* : gill (of a fish, etc.)
brandir [brɑ̃dir] *vt* : to brandish, to wave about

branlant, -lante [brɑ̃lɑ̃, -lɑ̃t] *adj* : shaky, wobbly, unsteady
branle [brɑ̃l] *nm* **1** : oscillation, swing **2** : impetus, momentum <mettre en branle : to set in motion>
branle–bas [brɑ̃lba] *nms & pl* : commotion, bustle
branler [brɑ̃le] *vi* : to wobble, to be loose
branleux, -leuse [brɑ̃lø, -løz] *adj Can fam* **1** : lazy **2** : indecisive
braquer [brake] *vt* **1** : to aim, to point, to fix on **2** : to turn (a steering wheel) **3** : to antagonize — *vi* : to turn the steering wheel
bras [bra] *nms & pl* **1** : arm **2 bras** *nmpl* : workers, manpower **3 bras de mer** : inlet **4 bras droit** : right-hand man
brasero [brazero] *nm* : brazier
brasier [brazje] *nm* : blaze, inferno
bras–le–corps [bralkɔr] **à bras–le–corps** *adv* **1** : bodily **2** : head-on
brassage [brasaʒ] *nm* **1** : mixing, intermingling **2** : brewing
brasse [bras] *nf* **1** : breaststroke **2** : fathom
brassée [brase] *nf* **1** : armful **2** *Can* : load (of laundry)
brasser [brase] *vt* **1** : to mix, to toss, to shuffle **2** : to brew (beer)
brasserie [brasri] *nf* **1** : large café, restaurant **2** : brewery
brasseur, -seuse [brasœr, -søz] *n* **1** : brewer **2 brasseur d'affaires** : tycoon, financier
brassière [brasjɛr] *nf Can* : bra, brassiere
bravade [bravad] *nf* : bravado
brave[1] [brav] *adj* **1** GENTIL : good, decent, nice <c'est un brave homme : he's a good man> **2** : brave, courageous <c'est une femme brave : she's a brave woman>
brave[2] *nmf* : brave person, hero
bravement [bravmɑ̃] *adv* : bravely, boldly
braver [brave] *vt* : to defy, to challenge
bravo [bravo] *nm & interj* : bravo
bravoure [bravur] *nf* : bravery
break [brek] *nm* **1** *France* : station wagon **2** : break (in music, sports, etc.) **3 prendre un break** *Can* : to take a break
brebis [brəbi] *nf* **1** : ewe **2 brebis** *nfpl* : flock (in religion) **3 brebis galeuse** : black sheep
brèche [brɛʃ] *nf* **1** : hole, gap **2** : breach
bréchet [breʃɛ] *nm* : wishbone
bredouille [brəduj] *adj* : empty-handed
bredouiller [brəduje] *v* : to mumble, to mutter
bref[1] [brɛf] *adv or* **en bref** : briefly, in short
bref[2], **brève** [brɛf, brɛv] *adj* : brief, short
breloque [brəlɔk] *nf* : charm (on a bracelet)
brésilien, -lienne [breziljɛ̃, -ljɛn] *adj* : Brazilian
Brésilien, -lienne *n* : Brazilian
bretelle [brətɛl] *nf* **1** : strap, shoulder strap **2** : ramp <bretelle de sortie : exit ramp> **3 bretelles** *nfpl* : suspenders
breton, -tonne [brətɔ̃, brətɔn] *adj* : Breton
bretzel [brɛtzɛl] *nm* : pretzel
breuvage [brœvaʒ] *nm* : beverage, drink
brevet [brəve] *nm* **1** : patent **2** : diploma, certificate **3** : commission (in the armed forces)
breveté, -tée [brəvte] *adj* **1** : patented **2** : qualified, certified
breveter [brəvte] {8} *vt* : to patent
bréviaire [brevjɛr] *nm* : breviary
bribes [brib] *nfpl* : bits, pieces <bribes de conversation : snatches of conversation>
bric–à–brac [brikabrak] *nms & pl* : bric-a-brac, odds and ends
brick [brik] *nm* : brig (ship)
bricolage [brikɔlaʒ] *nm* **1** : do-it-yourself work **2** : makeshift repairs
bricole [brikɔl] *nf* **1** : trifle, trinket **2 bricoles** *nfpl* : bits and pieces
bricoler [brikɔle] *vi* **1** : to fix things up **2** : to do odd jobs, to putter — *vt* **1** : to fix up, to mend **2** : to tinker with
bricoleur, -leuse [brikɔlœr, -løz] *n* **1** : handyman **2** : do-it-yourselfer
bride [brid] *nf* **1** : bridle <tenir en bride : to keep a tight rein on> **2** : flange (of a pipe, etc.)
brider [bride] *vt* **1** : to bridle (a horse) **2** : to keep in check
bridge [bridʒ] *nm* **1** : bridge (card game) **2** *or* **bridge dentaire** : denture, bridgework
brièvement [brijɛvmɑ̃] *adv* : briefly
brièveté [brijɛvte] *nf* : brevity
brigade [brigad] *nf* **1** : brigade **2** : squad, team
brigadier[1] [brigadje] *nm* **1** : corporal (in the military) **2** : police sergeant
brigadier[2], **-dière** [brigadje, -djɛr] *n Can* : crossing guard
brigand [brigɑ̃] *nm* : robber, thief
brigandage [brigɑ̃daʒ] *nm* : armed robbery
briguer [brige] *vt* **1** : to aspire to **2** : to solicit, to seek
brillamment [brijamɑ̃] *adv* : brilliantly
brillant, -lante [brijɑ̃, -jɑ̃t] *adj* **1** : brilliant, outstanding **2** : bright, sparkling, shiny
briller [brije] *vi* : to shine, to sparkle
brimade [brimad] *nf* : bullying, harassment, hazing
brimer [brime] *vt* : to bully, to haze
brin [brɛ̃] *nm* **1** : blade (of grass), sprig, twig **2** : touch, little bit <il est un brin ennuyeux : he's rather boring> **3** : iota **4** : strand (of wool, thread, etc.)
brindille [brɛ̃dij] *nf* : twig

bringue [brɛ̃g] *nf fam* : binge <faire la bringue : to go on a binge>
brio [brijo] *nm* **1** : brilliance, panache **2 avec ~** : brilliantly
brioche [brijɔʃ] *nf* **1** : brioche **2** *fam* : paunch
brique [brik] *nf* : brick
briquet [brikɛ] *nm* **1** : (cigarette) lighter **2** : beagle
bris [bri] *nms & pl* : breaking, breakage
brise [briz] *nf* : breeze
brise–glace [brizglas] *nms & pl* : icebreaker
brise–lames [brizlam] *nms & pl* : breakwater
briser [brize] *vt* **1** : to break, to smash **2** : to ruin, to wreck, to crush <des faux bruits ont brisé sa carrière : false rumors wrecked his career> — *vi* : to break <briser avec la tradition : to break with tradition> — **se briser** *vr* **1** : to shatter, to break up, to break down **2** : to break <son cœur se brisait : her heart was breaking>
briseur, -seuse [brizœr, -zøz] *n* **1** : wrecker **2 briseur de grève** : strikebreaker
brise–vent [brizvɑ̃] *nms & pl* : windbreak
brisure [brizyr] *nf* : break, crack
britannique [britanik] *adj* : British
Britannique *nmf* : British person, Briton
broc [bro] *nm* : jug, pitcher
brocante [brɔkɑ̃t] *nf* **1** : secondhand trade **2** : flea market
brocanteur, -teuse [brɔkɑ̃tœr, -tøz] *n* : secondhand dealer
brocart [brɔkar] *nm* : brocade
broche [brɔʃ] *nf* **1** : brooch **2** : spit, skewer **3** : spindle (on a spinning machine) **4** *Can* : wire <broche piquante : barbed wire>
broché, -chée [brɔʃe] *adj* : paperbound
brochet [brɔʃɛ] *nm* : pike (fish)
brochette [brɔʃɛt] *nf* **1** : skewer **2** : shish kebab
brochure [brɔʃyr] *nf* : brochure, pamphlet, booklet
brocoli [brɔkɔli] *nm* : broccoli
broder [brɔde] *vt* : to embroider — *vi* **~ sur** : to elaborate on, to embellish
broderie [brɔdri] *nf* : embroidery
broie [brwa], **broiera** [brwara], *etc.* → **broyer**
brome [brom] *nm* : bromine
broncher [brɔ̃ʃe] *vi* **1** : to flinch **2** : to stumble (of a horse)
bronches [brɔ̃ʃ] *nfpl* : bronchial tubes
bronchite [brɔ̃ʃit] *nf* : bronchitis
bronzage [brɔ̃zaʒ] *nm* : suntan
bronze [brɔ̃z] *nm* : bronze
bronzé, -zée [brɔ̃ze] *adj* : tanned, suntanned
bronzer [brɔ̃ze] *vt* **1** : to tan **2** : to bronze (metals) — *vi* : to get a suntan
brossage [brɔsaʒ] *nm* : brushing
brosse [brɔs] *nf* **1** : brush <brosse à cheveux : hairbrush> <brosse à dents : toothbrush>
brosser [brɔse] *vt* **1** : to brush **2** : to paint (a picture) — **se brosser** *vr* : to brush oneself <se brosser les cheveux : to brush one's hair>
broue [bru] *nf Can* **1** : froth **2 péter de la broue** *fam* : to show off
brouette [bruet] *nf* : wheelbarrow
brouhaha [bruaa] *nm* : brouhaha, hubbub
brouillard [brujar] *nm* **1** : fog, mist **2 être dans un brouillard** : to be in a fog
brouille [bruj] *nf* **1** : quarrel, misunderstanding **2** : discord
brouiller [bruje] *vt* **1** : to mix up, to shuffle (cards), to scramble (eggs, etc.) **2** : to blur, to cloud **3** : to interfere with (radio transmission, etc.) **4** : to turn against, to fall out with — **se brouiller** *vr* **1** : to quarrel, to fall out **2** : to become confused **3** : to cloud over
brouillon[1], -lonne [brujɔ̃, -jɔn] *adj* **1** DÉSORGANISÉ : disorganized **2** DÉSORDONNÉ : untidy
brouillon[2] *nm* : rough draft
broussaille [brusaj] *nf* : undergrowth
broussailleux, -leuse [brusajø, -jøz] *adj* : bushy, scrubby
brousse [brus] *nf* **1** : brush (vegetation) **2** *fam* : boondocks <en pleine brousse : in the middle of nowhere>
brouter [brute] *vt* : to graze on, to nibble on — *vi* : to graze
broutille [brutij] *nf* : trifle
broyer [brwaje] {58} *vt* **1** : to grind, to crush **2 broyer du noir** : to be in the doldrums, to brood, to mope
broyeur *nm* [brwajœr] **1** : grinder, crusher **2 broyeur à ordures** : garbage disposal unit
bru [bry] *nf* : daughter-in-law
bruant [bryɑ̃] *nm* : bunting, small finch
brucelles [brysɛl] *nfpl* : tweezers
brugnon *nm* [brynɔ̃] : nectarine
bruine [bryin] *nf* : drizzle — **bruiner** [bryine] *vi*
bruire [bryir] {16} *vi* **1** : to rustle (of leaves, etc.) **2** : to murmur, to hum, to drone, to buzz
bruissement [bryismɑ̃] *nm* : rustling, murmuring, humming
bruit [bryi] *nm* **1** : noise, sound <faire du bruit : to make noise, to be noisy> <bruit de fond : background noise> **2** : commotion, fuss, uproar **3** : rumor, gossip
bruitage [bryitaʒ] *nm* : sound effects *pl*
brûlant, -lante [brylɑ̃, -lɑ̃t] *adj* **1** : burning hot **2** : passionate, fervent **3** : urgent <un sujet brûlant : a burning issue>
brûlé, -lée [bryle] *adj Can fam* : worn-out, beat

brûler [bryle] *vt* **1** : to burn, to scald **2** : to run (a red light) — *vi* **1** : to burn (up), to be on fire **2** ~ **de** : to long for, to be consumed with — **se bruler** *vr* : to burn oneself
brûleur [brylœr] *nm* : burner (of a stove)
brulôt [brylo] *nm Can* : gnat
brûlure [brylyr] *nf* **1** : burn **2** : burning <brûlures d'estomac : heartburn>
brume [brym] *nf* : mist, haze
brumeux, -meuse [brymø, -møz] *adj* : misty, foggy, hazy
brun[1], **brune** [brœ̃, bryn] *adj* : brown
brun[2], **brune** *n* : brown-haired person, brunet
brun[3] *nm* : brown
brunante [brynãt] *nf Can* : dusk
brunâtre [brynatr] *adj* : brownish
brunch [brœnʃ] *nm* : brunch
brunette [brynɛt] *nf* : brunette
brunir [brynir] *vt* **1** : to burnish **2** BRONZER : to tan — *vi* **1** : to get tan **2** : to darken, to brown
brusque [brysk] *adj* : brusque, abrupt, curt — **brusquement** [bryskəmã] *adv*
brusquer [bryske] *vt* **1** : to be brusque with **2** : to rush, to hurry
brusquerie [bryskəri] *nf* **1** : brusqueness **2** : suddenness
brut, brute [bryt] *adj* **1** : raw, crude, rough **2** : dry (of wine) **3** : total, gross <poids brut : gross weight>
brutal, -tale [brytal] *adj, mpl* **brutaux** [bryto] **1** : brutal, violent **2** : sudden, sharp **3** : blunt, stark — **brutalement** [-talmã] *adv*
brutaliser [brytalize] *vt* : to abuse, to mistreat
brutalité [brytalite] *nf* **1** : brutality **2** : suddenness
brute [bryt] *nf* : brute, beast
bruxellois, -loise [brysɛlwa, -lwaz] *adj* : of or from Brussels
Bruxellois, -loise *n* : person from Brussels
bruyamment [brɥijamã] *adv* : loudly, noisily
bruyant, bruyante [brɥijã, -jãt] *adj* : noisy
bruyère [bryjɛr] *nf* **1** : heather **2** : heath, moor
bu [by] *pp* → **boire**
buanderie [byãdri] *nf* **1** : laundry room **2** *Can* : self-service laundry
buandier, -dière [byãdje, -djɛr] *n Can* : laundry worker
buccal, -cale [bykal] *adj, mpl* **buccaux** [byko] : oral
buccin [byksɛ̃] *nm* : whelk
bûche [byʃ] *nf* : log
bûcher[1] [byʃe] *vt* **1** *fam* : to plod away at **2** *Can* : to chop down (trees) — *vi* **1** *fam* : to keep working, to slave away **2** *Can* : to fell trees
bûcher[2] *nm* **1** : stake, pyre **2** : woodshed
bûcheron, -ronne [byʃrɔ̃, -rɔn] *n* : logger, lumberjack
bûcheur[1], **-cheuse** [byʃœr, -ʃøz] *adj fam* : hardworking
bûcheur[2], **-cheuse** *n fam* : grind, hard worker
bucolique [bykɔlik] *adj* : bucolic
budget [bydʒɛ] *nm* : budget
budgétaire [bydʒetɛr] *adj* : budgetary
budgétiser [bydʒetize] *vt* : to budget
buée [byɛ] *nf* : steam, mist, condensation
buffet [byfɛ] *nm* **1** : sideboard **2** : buffet-style meal or restaurant
buffle [byfl] *nm* : Cape buffalo, water buffalo
buis [bɥi] *nm* : box (plant), boxwood
buisson [bɥisɔ̃] *nm* : bush, shrub
buissonnière [bɥisɔnjɛr] *adj* **faire l'école buissonnière** : to skip school
bulbe [bylb] *nm* : bulb (of a plant)
bulbeux, -beuse [bylbø, -bøz] *adj* : bulbous
bulgare[1] [bylgar] *adj* : Bulgarian
bulgare[2] *nm* : Bulgarian (language)
Bulgare *nmf* : Bulgarian
bulldozer [byldozɛr] *nm* : bulldozer
bulle [byl] *nf* **1** : bubble **2** : balloon (in a comic strip) **3** : papal bull
bulletin [byltɛ̃] *nm* **1** : report, bulletin, newsletter <bulletin météorologique : weather forecast> <bulletin scolaire : report card> **2** : certificate <bulletin de naissance : birth certificate> **3** : form, slip, ticket <bulletin de commande : order form> **4** *or* **bulletin de vote** : ballot (form)
bureau [byro] *nm, pl* **bureaux 1** : office, study **2** : desk **3** : department, agency, bureau <bureau de poste : post office> <bureau de placement : employment agency> **4** : board, committee
bureaucrate [byrokrat] *nmf* : bureaucrat
bureaucratie [byrokrasi] *nf* : bureaucracy — **bureaucratique** [-kratik] *adj*
bureautique [byrotik] *nf* : office automation
burette [byrɛt] *nf* **1** : cruet **2** : oilcan
buriné, -née [byrine] *adj* : furrowed, deeply lined <un visage buriné : a craggy face>
burlesque[1] [byrlɛsk] *adj* : farcical, ludicrous
burlesque[2] *nm* : burlesque
burundais, -daise [burundɛ, -dɛz] *adj* : Burundian
Burundais, -daise *n* : Burundian
bus [bys] *nm* AUTOBUS : bus
buse [byz] *nf* : buzzard
buste [byst] *nm* **1** : chest **2** : bust (in sculpture) **3** : bust, bosom (of a woman)
but [by(t)] *nm* **1** : aim, objective <aller droit au but : to go straight to the point> <sans but : aimlessly> **2** : goal,

target, touchdown **3** *Can* : base (in baseball) <but sur balles : base on balls, walk> **4 de but en blanc** : point-blank, bluntly

butane [bytan] *nm* : butane

buté, -tée [byte] *adj* : obstinate, stubborn

butée [byte] *nf* : abutment

buter [byte] *vi* **1 ~ contre** *or* **~ sur** : to stumble on, to trip over **2 ~ contre** : to rest on, to abut — *vt* **1** : to prop up **2** : to antagonize, to make (someone) stubborn **3** *fam* : to kill, to bump off

butin [bytɛ̃] *nm* : booty, loot, spoils *pl*

butiner [bytine] *vt* **1** : to gather (nectar) **2** : to glean, to pick up (ideas, information)

butoir [bytwar] *nm* **1** : buffer, stop <butoir de porte : doorstop> **2** *or* **date butoir** : deadline

butor [bytɔr] *nm* : bittern

butte [byt] *nf* **1** : small hill, mound **2 être en butte à** : to come up against

buvable [byvabl] *adj* POTABLE : drinkable, potable

buvard [byvar] *nm* : blotter

buveur, -veuse [byvœr, -vøz] *n* : drinker

buvons [byvɔ̃], *etc.* → **boire**

byzantin, -tine [bizɑ̃tɛ̃, -tin] *adj* : Byzantine

C

c [se] *nm* : c, the third letter of the alphabet

ça[1] [sa] *pron* **1** : that, this <je n'aime pas ça : I don't like that> <ça coûte combien? : how much does this cost?> **2** : it, that <ça va? : how's it going?> <c'est ça : that's it, that's right> **3 ça alors!** : well!, really! **4 ça y est** : there, that's it **5 et avec ça?** : anything else?

ça[2] *nm* **le ça** : the id

çà [sa] *adv* **çà et là** : here and there

cabale [kabal] *nf* : cabal

cabane [kaban] *nf* **1** HUTTE : cabin, hut **2** ABRI : shelter <cabane à lapins : rabbit hutch> **3** *or* **cabane à sucre** *Can* : sugarhouse **4 en ~** *fam* : in jail, in the clink

cabanon [kabanɔ̃] *nm* **1** ABRI : shed **2** : country cottage (in Provence)

cabaret [kabarɛ] *nm* : cabaret, nightclub

cabas [kaba] *nms & pl France* : shopping bag

cabestan [kabɛstɑ̃] *nm* : capstan

cabillaud [kabijo] *nm* : cod

cabine [kabin] *nf* : cabin, cubicle, cab (of a truck, etc.), booth <cabine téléphonique : telephone booth> <cabine de pilotage : cockpit>

cabinet [kabinɛ] *nm* **1** *or* **cabinet de travail** BUREAU : office **2** *or* **cabinet médical** : doctor's office **3** : cabinet (in government) **4 cabinet de toilette** *France* : toilet, bathroom

câblage [kablaʒ] *nm* : wiring

câble [kabl] *nm* **1** : cable, line, rope **2** : cable television **3** : cablegram

câbler [kable] *vt* : to cable

câblodistribution [kablɔdistribysjɔ̃] *nf* : cable television

câblogramme [kablɔɡram] *nm* : cablegram

cabochard, -charde [kabɔʃar, -ʃard] *adj fam* : stubborn, pigheaded

caboche [kabɔʃ] *nf* **1** : hobnail **2** *fam* : head, nut

cabosser [kabɔse] *vt* : to dent <un chapeau cabossé : a battered hat>

cabotin, -tine [kabɔtɛ̃, -tin] *n* : ham actor, show-off

cabrer [kabre] *v* **se cabrer** *vr* **1** : to rear up (of a horse), to climb steeply (of a plane) **2** : to rebel, to protest

cabriole [kabrijɔl] *nf* **1** : capering (about) **2 faire des cabrioles** : to caper, to gambol, to cavort, to prance

cabriolet [kabrijɔle] *nm* DÉCAPOTABLE : convertible

caca [kaka] *nm fam* : excrement

cacahuète [kakaɥɛt] *nf* : peanut

cacao [kakao] *nm* **1** : cocoa **2** : cocoa bean

cacarder [kakarde] *vi* : to honk (of a goose)

cacatoès [kakatɔɛs] *nm* : cockatoo

cache [kaʃ] *nf* : hiding place, cache

cache-cache [kaʃkaʃ] *nms & pl* : hide-and-seek <jouer à cache-cache : to play hide-and-seek>

cache-col [kaʃkɔl] *nms & pl* : scarf

cachemire [kaʃmir] *nm* : cashmere

cache-nez [kaʃne] *nms & pl* : scarf, muffler

cache-pot [kaʃpo] *nm* : planter, container for a flowerpot

cacher [kaʃe] *vt* **1** : to hide, to conceal **2** : to cover up, to mask — **se cacher** *vr*

cachet [kaʃɛ] *nm* **1** COMPRIMÉ : tablet, pill **2** : seal, stamp <cachet de la poste : postmark> **3** : fee **4** : style, character, charm

cacheter [kaʃte] {8} *vt* SCELLER : to seal

cachette [kaʃɛt] *nf* **1** CACHE : hiding place, hideout **2** *Can* : hide-and-seek <jouer à la cachette : to play hide-and-seek> **3 en ~** : secretly

cachot [kaʃo] *nm* **1** : prison, dungeon **2** *Can* : penalty box (in hockey)

cachotterie [kaʃɔtri] *nf* : little secret

cachottier, -tière [kaʃotje, -tjɛr] *adj* : secretive

cacophonie [kakɔfɔni] *nf* : cacophony
cactus [kaktys] *nms & pl* : cactus
cadastre [kadastr] *nm* : land office
cadavérique [kadaverik] *adj* : deathly (pale)
cadavre [kadavr] *nm* : corpse, cadaver
caddie *or* **caddy** [kadi] *nm* : caddie, caddy
cadeau [kado] *nm, pl* **cadeaux** : gift, present <cadeau de Noël : Christmas present> <faire un cadeau à : to give a gift to>
cadenas [kadna] *nm* : padlock — **cadenasser** [-nase] *vt*
cadence [kadɑ̃s] *nf* **1** RYTHME : cadence, rhythm **2** : rate, pace
cadet[1], **-dette** [kade, -dɛt] *adj* : younger, youngest
cadet[2], **-dette** *n* **1** : younger (son, daughter, child), youngest (son, daughter, child) **2** : junior <elle est son cadet de quatre ans : she is four years his junior> **3** : cadet **4 c'est le cadet de mes soucis** : that's the least of my worries
cadmium [kadmjɔm] *nm* : cadmium
cadran [kadrɑ̃] *nm* **1** : dial, face **2** *Can fam* : alarm clock **3 cadran solaire** : sundial
cadre [kadr] *nm* **1** : frame **2** : setting, surroundings *pl* **3** : framework, structure **4** : manager, executive
cadrer [kadre] *vt* : to center (an image, etc.) — *vi* : to fit, to correspond
caduc, -duque [kadyk] *adj* **1** : obsolete, outmoded **2** : null and void **3** : deciduous **4** : mute, silent <e caduc : silent e>
cafard[1] [kafar] *nm* **1** BLATTE : cockroach **2** : melancholy, blues <avoir le cafard : to be down in the dumps>
cafard[2], **-farde** [kafar, -fard] *n fam* : sneaky person, squealer
café [kafe] *nm* **1** : coffee <café en poudre : instant coffee> **2** : café, bar
caféine [kafein] *nf* : caffeine
cafétéria [kafeterja] *nf* : cafeteria
cafetière [kaftjɛr] *nf* **1** : coffeepot, coffeemaker **2 cafetière à pression** : percolator
cafouillage [kafujaʒ] *nm fam* : mess, confusion
cafouiller [kafuje] *vi fam* : to get into a mess, to flounder around
cage [kaʒ] *nf* **1** : cage <cage à oiseaux : birdcage> <cage thoracique : rib cage> **2 cage d'ascenseur** : elevator shaft **3 cage d'escalier** : stairwell
cageot [kaʒo] *nm* : crate
cagibi [kaʒibi] *nm* : storeroom
cagneux, -gneuse [kaɲø, -ɲøz] *adj* : knock-kneed
cagnotte [kaɲɔt] *nf* : pool, kitty
cagoulard, -larde [kagular, -lard] *n Can* : masked robber
cagoule [kagul] *nf* : hood, cowl
cahier [kaje] *nm* **1** : notebook **2** : section, supplement (of a periodical) **3 cahiers** *nmpl* : journal
cahin–caha [kaɛ̃kaa] *adv* **aller cahin–caha** : to struggle along
cahot [kao] *nm* SECOUSSE : bump, jolt
cahoter [kaɔte] *vi* : to bump around, to jolt along
cahoteux, -teuse [kaɔtø, -tøz] *adj* : rough, bumpy
cahute [kayt] *nf* : shack, hut
caïd [kaid] *nm fam* : ring leader, big shot
caille [kaj] *nf* : quail
caillé [kaje] *nm* : curds *pl*
cailler [kaje] *vt* : to curdle — *vi* **1** : to curdle, to congeal **2 ça caille** *fam* : it's freezing — **se cailler** *vr*
caillot [kajo] *nm* : clot
caillou [kaju] *nm, pl* **cailloux** : pebble, stone
caillouteux, -teuse [kajutø, -tøz] *adj* : pebbly, stony
cailloutis [kajuti] *nm* : gravel, crushed stone
caisse [kɛs] *nf* **1** BOÎTE : box, crate **2** : case, casing, body (of a vehicle) **3** *or* **caisse enregistreuse** : till, cash register **4** : fund, funding organization <caisse de retraite : pension fund> <caisse populaire *Can* : cooperative bank> **5** : drum <caisse claire : snare drum>
caissier, -sière [kesje, -sjɛr] *n* **1** : cashier, sales clerk **2** : (bank) teller
caisson [kɛsɔ̃] *nm* **1** : caisson **2 la maladie des caissons** : caisson disease, the bends
cajoler [kaʒɔle] *vt* **1** : to fuss over, to cuddle **2** : to cajole, to wheedle
cajolerie [kaʒɔlri] *nf* : cuddling
cajou [kaʒu] *nm* **noix de cajou** : cashew nut
cajun [kaʒœ̃] *adj* : Cajun
Cajun *nmf* : Cajun
cake [kɛk] *nm* : fruitcake
cal [kal] *nm, pl* **cals** : callus
calamine [kalamin] *nf* : calamine
calamité [kalamite] *nf* DÉSASTRE : calamity
calandre [kalɑ̃dr] *nf* : radiator grill (of an automobile)
calcaire[1] [kalkɛr] *adj* : chalky, hard (of water)
calcaire[2] *nm* : limestone
calciner [kalsine] *vt* : to char, to burn to a crisp
calcium [kalsjɔm] *nm* : calcium
calcul [kalkyl] *nm* **1** : calculation, sum (in mathematics) **2** : arithmetic **3** : calculus **4** : stone <calcul rénal : kidney stone> <calcul bilaire : gallstone>
calculateur, -trice [kalkylatœr, -tris] *adj* : calculating
calculatrice *nf* : calculator
calculer [kalkyle] *vt* : to calculate, to compute

cale [kal] *nf* **1** : wedge, chock **2** : hold (of a ship) **3 cale sèche** : dry dock
calé, -lée [kale] *adj fam* **1** : brainy, clever **2** : tough (of a problem, etc.)
calebasse [kalbas] *nf* : calabash
calèche [kaleʃ] *nf* : (horse-drawn) carriage
caleçon [kalsɔ̃] *nm* **1** : boxer shorts *pl* **2** *or* **caleçons de bain** : swimming trunks **3** : leggings
calembour [kalɑ̃bur] *nm* : pun
calendes [kalɑ̃d] *nfpl* **renvoyer aux calendes grecques** : to put something off indefinitely
calendrier [kalɑ̃drije] *nm* : calendar
calepin [kalpɛ̃] *nm* : notebook
caler [kale] *vt* **1** : to wedge **2** : to prop up **3** *fam* : to fill up (one's stomach) **4** *Can fam* : to gulp down — *vi* **1** : to stall out **2** : to give up **3** *Can* : to sink (in snow, etc.)
calfeutrer [kalføtre] *vt* : to seal, to make draftproof — **se calfeutrer** *vr* : to make oneself snug
calibre [kalibr] *nm* **1** : caliber, bore **2** : grade, size **3** : class, stature
calibrer [kalibre] *vt* : to calibrate, to grade
calice [kalis] *nm* **1** : chalice **2** : calyx
calicot [kaliko] *nm* : calico
calife [kalif] *nm* : caliph
califourchon [kalifurʃɔ̃] **à califourchons** : astride, astraddle
câlin, -line [kalɛ̃, -lin] *adj* : tender, affectionate
câliner [kaline] *vt* : to cuddle — **se câliner** *vr*
calleux, -leuse [kalø, -løz] *adj* : calloused, hard
calligraphie [kaligrafi] *nf* : calligraphy — **calligraphique** [-grafik] *adj*
callosité [kalɔzite] *nf* : callus
calmant[1], **-mante** [kalmɑ̃, -mɑ̃t] *adj* : soothing
calmant[2] *nm* : sedative
calmar [kalmar] *nm* : squid, calamari
calme[1] [kalm] *adj* TRANQUILLE : calm — **calmement** [kalmɑ̃mɑ̃] *adv*
calme[2] *nm* **1** : calm, peace <calme plat : dead calm> **2 garder son calme** : to keep one's head
calmer [kalme] *vt* **1** APAISER : to calm **2** : to ease, to soothe — **se calmer** *vr* : to calm down
calomnie [kalɔmni] *nf* DIFFAMATION : slander, libel
calomnier [kalɔmnje] {96} *vt* : to slander, to libel
calomnieux, -nieuse [kalɔmnjø, -njøz] *adj* : slanderous, libelous
calorie [kalɔri] *nf* : calorie
calorifère[1] [kalɔrifer] *adj* : heating, heat-carrying
calorifère[2] *nm* **1** : heater, stove **2** *Can* : room radiator
calorique [kalɔrik] *adj* : caloric
calotte [kalɔt] *nf* **1** : skullcap **2** *Can* : cap **3 calotte glaciaire** : ice cap
calque [kalk] *nm* **1** DESSIN : tracing <papier calque : tracing paper> **2** : exact copy, replica
calquer [kalke] *vt* **1** : to trace **2** IMITER : to copy exactly, to imitate
calumet [kalymɛ] *nm* : peace pipe
calvaire [kalvɛr] *nm* **1** : wayside cross **2** : ordeal, suffering
calvitie [kalvisi] *nf* : baldness
calypso [kalipso] *nm* : calypso
camarade [kamarad] *nmf* : comrade, friend <camarade de classe : classmate>
camaraderie [kamaradri] *nf* : camaraderie, friendship
cambiste [kɑ̃bist] *nm* : exchange broker, money changer
cambodgien[1], **-dgienne** [kɑ̃bɔdʒjɛ̃, -dʒjɛn] *adj* : Cambodian
cambodgien[2] *nm* : Cambodian (language)
Cambodgien, -dgienne *n* : Cambodian
cambrer [kɑ̃bre] *vt* : to bend, to arch <cambrer les reins : to arch one's back> — **se cambrer** *vr* : to arch one's back
cambriolage [kɑ̃brijɔlaʒ] *nm* : burglary
cambrioler [kɑ̃brjɔle] *vt* : to burglarize
cambrioleur, -leuse [kɑ̃brijɔlœr, -løz] *n* : burglar
cambrure [kɑ̃bryr] *nf* **1** : arch, curve **2 cambrure des pieds** : instep
came [kam] *nf* : cam <arbre à cames : camshaft>
camée [kame] *nm* : cameo
caméléon [kameleɔ̃] *nm* : chameleon
camélia [kamelja] *nf* : camelia
camelot [kamlo] *nm* **1** : street vendor **2** *Can* : paperboy
camelote [kamlɔt] *nf fam* : trash, junk
camembert [kamɑ̃bɛr] *nm* : Camembert
caméra [kamera] *nf* : movie camera, television camera
camerounais, -naise [kamrunɛ, -nɛz] *adj* : Cameroonian
Camerounais, -naise *n* : Cameroonian
caméscope [kameskɔp] *nm* : camcorder
camion [kamjɔ̃] *nm* : truck
camionnage [kamjɔnaʒ] *nm* : trucking
camionner [kamjne] *vt* : to transport (by truck)
camionnette [kamjɔnɛt] *nf* : van, pickup truck
camionneur, -neuse [kamjɔnœr, -nøz] *n* ROUTIER : truck driver, trucker
camisole [kamizɔl] *nf* **1** : camisole **2 camisole de force** : straitjacket
camomille [kamɔmij] *nf* : camomile
camouflage [kamuflaʒ] *nm* : camouflage
camoufler [kamufle] *vt* : to camouflage
camp [kɑ̃] *nm* **1** CAMPEMENT : camp <lever le camp : to strike camp> <camp de concentration : concentra-

tion camp> **2** PARTI : side, team, faction

campagnard[1], **-gnarde** [kɑ̃paɲar, -ɲard] *adj* : country, rustic

campagnard[2], **-gnarde** *n* : countryman *m*, countrywoman *f*

campagne [kɑ̃paɲ] *nf* **1** : country, countryside **2** : campaign <faire campagne contre : to agitate against>

campagnol [kɑ̃paɲɔl] *nm* : vole

campement [kɑ̃pmɑ̃] *nm* : camp, encampment

camper [kɑ̃pe] *vt* **1** : to encamp **2** POSER : to place firmly **3** : to portray (a character) — *vi* : to camp — **se camper** *vr* : to stand firmly

campeur, -peuse [kɑ̃pœr, -pøz] *n* : camper

camphre [kɑ̃fr] *nm* : camphor

camping [kɑ̃piŋ] *nm* **1** : camping <faire du camping : to go camping> **2** : campground, campsite

campus [kɑ̃pys] *nm* : campus

camus, -muse [kamy, -myz] *adj* **nez camus** : pug nose

canadien, -dienne [kanadjɛ̃, -djɛn] *adj* : Canadian

Canadien, -dienne *n* : Canadian

canadien–français, canadienne–française *adj*, *pl* **canadiens–français, canadiennes–françaises** : French-Canadian

canaille [kanaj] *nf* **1** : rabble, riffraff **2** : scoundrel, rascal

canal [kanal] *nm, pl* **canaux** [kano] **1** : canal **2** : channel

canaliser [kanalize] *vt* : to channel

canapé [kanape] *nm* **1** : sofa, couch **2** : canapé

canapé–lit [kanapeli] *n, pl* **canapés–lits** : sofa bed

canard [kanar] *nm* **1** : duck **2** : false note (in music) **3** *fam* : rag, newspaper

canari [kanari] *nm* : canary

canasson [kanasɔ̃] *nm fam* : nag (horse)

cancan [kɑ̃kɑ̃] *nm* **1** : cancan **2** : rumor, gossip

cancaner [kɑ̃kane] *vi* **1** : to quack **2** : to spread gossip

cancanier, -nière [kɑ̃kanje, -njɛr] *n* : gossip

cancer [kɑ̃sɛr] *nm* : cancer

Cancer *nm* : Cancer

cancéreux[1], **-reuse** [kɑ̃serø, -røz] *adj* : cancerous

cancéreux[2], **-reuse** *n* : cancer patient

cancérigène [kɑ̃serizɛn] *adj* : carcinogenic

cancre [kɑ̃kr] *nm fam* : dunce

candélabre [kɑ̃delabr] *nm* : candelabrum

candeur [kɑ̃dœr] *nf* INGÉNUITÉ : ingenuousness

candidat, -date [kɑ̃dida, -dat] *n* : candidate

candidature [kɑ̃didatyr] *nf* : candidacy

candide [kɑ̃did] *adj* : ingenuous, naïve

cane [kan] *nf* : (female) duck

caneton [kantɔ̃] *nm* : duckling

canette [kanɛt] *nf* **1** BOUTEILLE : (small) bottle **2** BOÎTE : can (of a beverage) **3** : spool **4** : (female) duckling

canevas [kanva] *nms & pl* **1** : canvas **2** : framework

caniche [kaniʃ] *nm* : poodle

canicule [kanikyl] *nf* : heat wave

canidé [kanide] *nm* : canine

canif [kanif] *nm* : jackknife, pocketknife

canin, -nine [kanɛ̃, -nin] *adj* : canine

canine *nf* : canine (tooth)

caniveau [kanivo] *nm, pl* **-veaux** : (street) gutter

cannabis [kanabis] *nm* : cannabis

canne [kan] *nf* **1** : cane, walking stick **2** : cane (in botany) <canne à sucre : sugarcane> **3 canne à pêche** : fishing rod

canneberge [kanbɛrʒ] *nf* : cranberry

cannelé, -lée [kanle] *adj* : fluted, grooved

canneler [kanle] {8} *vt* : to groove

cannelle [kanɛl] *nf* : cinnamon

cannette [kanɛt] *nf* → **canette**

cannibale [kanibal] *nmf* : cannibal — **cannibalisme** [-balism] *nm*

canoë [kanɔe] *nm* : canoe

canon [kanɔ̃] *nm* **1** : cannon **2** : barrel, muzzle (of a gun) **3** : canon, rule **4** : shank (of a horse)

canoniser [kanɔnize] *vt* : to canonize — **canonisation** [-nizasjɔ̃] *nf*

canonnière [kanɔnjɛr] *nf* : gunboat

canot [kano] *nm* **1** *France* : boat, dinghy **2** *Can* : canoe **3 canot de sauvetage** : lifeboat

canotage [kanɔtaʒ] *nm* **1** *France* : boating **2** *Can* : canoeing

cantaloup [kɑ̃talu] *nm* : cantaloupe

cantate [kɑ̃tat] *nf* : cantata

cantatrice [kɑ̃tatris] *nf* : opera singer

cantilever [kɑ̃tilevœr] *adj & nm* : cantilever

cantine [kɑ̃tin] *nf* : canteen, cafeteria

cantique [kɑ̃tik] *nm* HYMNE : canticle, hymn

canton [kɑ̃tɔ̃] *nm* **1** *Can* : township <les cantons de l'Est : the Eastern Townships> **2** *France* : district

cantonnement [kantɔnmɑ̃] *nm* : billet, billeting

cantonner [kɑ̃tɔne] *v* **1** : to confine, to limit **2** : to station, to billet — **se cantonner** *vr* SE CONFINER : to confine oneself, to lock oneself away

cantonnière [kɑ̃tɔnjɛr] *nf* : valance

canular [kanylar] *nm* : hoax, practical joke

canyon [kaɲɔ̃] *nm* : canyon

caoutchouc [kautʃu] *nm* **1** : rubber **2 caoutchoucs** *nmpl* : galoshes

caoutchouteux, -teuse [kautʃutø, -tøz] *adj* : rubbery

cap [kap] *nm* **1** PROMONTOIRE : cape, headland **2** : mark, milestone **3** DIRECTION : course, direction
capable [kapabl] *adj* **1** : capable, able **2** : likely **3** *Can* : strong, robust
capacité [kapasite] *nf* **1** : capacity **2** APTITUDE : ability
cape [kap] *nf* : cape, cloak
capillaire[1] [kapilɛr] *adj* **1** : capillary **2** : hair <lotion capillaire : hair lotion>
capillaire[2] *nm* : capillary
capitaine [kapitɛn] *nm* **1** : captain **2** **capitaine de corvette** : lieutenant commander
capital[1], **-tale** [kapital] *adj, mpl* **-taux** [-to] **1** : major, crucial **2** : capital <peine capitale : capital punishment>
capital[2] *nm, pl* **-taux** : capital, assets *pl*
capitale *nf* : capital (city)
capitaliser [kapitalize] *vt* : to capitalize (in finance) — *vi* : to save
capitalisme [kapitalism] *nm* : capitalism
capitaliste[1] [kapitalist] *adj* : capitalist, capitalistic
capitaliste[2] *nmf* : capitalist
capiteux, -teuse [kapitø, -tøz] *adj* : heady, intoxicating
capitole [kapitɔl] *nm* : capitol
capitonner [kapitɔne] *vt* : to pad
capitulation [kapitylasjɔ̃] *nf* : capitulation, surrender
capituler [kapityle] *vi* : to capitulate, to surrender
caporal–chef [kapɔralʃɛf] *nm, pl* **caporaux–chefs** [-ro] : corporal
capot [kapo] *nm* **1** : cover, casing **2** : hood (of an automobile)
capote [kapɔt] *nf* **1** : greatcoat **2** : top (of a convertible)
capoter [kapɔte] *vi* **1** CHAVIRER : to capsize, to overturn **2** *fam* : to fall through, to come to nothing **3** *Can fam* : to lose one's head
câpre [kapr] *nf* : caper
caprice [kapris] *nm* **1** : caprice, whim **2** : tantrum <faire un caprice : to throw a tantrum>
capricieux, -cieuse [kaprisjø, -sjøz] *adj* : capricious, temperamental — **capricieusement** [-sjøzmɑ̃] *adv*
Capricorne [kaprikɔrn] *nm* : Capricorn
capsule [kapsyl] *nf* **1** : capsule <capsule spatiale : space capsule> **2** : top, cap **3** : capsule (in pharmacy)
capter [kapte] *vt* **1** RECEVOIR : to receive, to pick up (radio or television signals) **2** : to capture, to catch <capter l'attention de : to capture the attention of>
capteur [kaptœr] *nm* : sensor
captieux, -tieuse [kapsjø, -sjøz] *adj* FALLACIEUX : fallacious, misleading
captif, -tive [kaptif, -tiv] *adj & n* : captive
captivant, -vante [kaptivɑ̃, -vɑ̃t] *adj* FASCINANT : fascinating, captivating
captiver [kaptive] *vt* : to captivate, to fascinate
captivité [kaptivite] *nf* : captivity
capture [kaptyr] *nf* **1** : capture, seizure **2** PRISE : catch
capturer [kaptyre] *vt* : to capture, to catch
capuche [kapyʃ] *nf* : hood
capuchon [kapyʃɔ̃] *nm* **1** : hood **2** : cap, top (of a pen, etc.)
capucine [kapysin] *nf* : nasturtium
cap–verdien, -dienne [kapvɛrdjɛ̃, -djɛn] *adj* : Cape Verdean
Cap–verdien, -dienne *n* : Cape Verdean
caquet [kakɛ] *nm* **1** : cackle, cackling **2** BAVARDAGE : chatter, prattle
caqueter [kakte] {8} *vi* **1** : to cackle **2** BAVARDER : to chatter, to prattle
car[1] [kar] *nm* AUTOCAR : bus, coach
car[2] *conj* : for, because
carabine [karabin] *nf* : carbine, rifle
caracoler [karakɔle] *vt* **1** : to prance (of a horse) **2** : to gambol, to skip
caractère [karakter] *nm* **1** : letter, character, graphic sign <en gros caractères : in large print> **2** : character, nature, disposition <avoir mauvais caractère : to be ill-tempered> **3** : characteristic, feature
caractériser [karakterize] *vt* : to characterize, to describe — **caractérisation** [-rizasjɔ̃] *nf*
caractéristique [karakteristik] *adj & nf* : characteristic
carafe [karaf] *nf* : carafe, decanter
caraïbe[1] [karaib] *adj* : Caribbean
caraïbe[2] *nm* : Carib (language)
carambolage [karɑ̃bɔlaʒ] *nm* **1** : pileup, multicar accident **2** : carom (in billiards, etc.)
caramboler [karɑ̃bɔle] *vi* : to carom (in billiards) — *vt* : to collide with, to crash into (an automobile)
caramel [karamɛl] *nm* : caramel
carapace [karapas] *nf* : shell
carat [kara] *nm* : carat
caravane [karavan] *nf* **1** : caravan **2** : trailer
carbone [karbɔn] *nm* **1** : carbon **2** *or* **papier carbone** : carbon paper
carbonique [karbɔnik] *adj* **1** **gaz carbonique** : carbon dioxide **2** **neige carbonique** : dry ice
carboniser [karbɔnize] *vt* : to char
carburant [karbyrɑ̃] *nm* : fuel
carburateur [karbyratœr] *nm* : carburetor
carcan [karkɑ̃] *nm* **1** : constraint, yoke **2** : iron collar
carcasse [karkas] *nf* **1** : carcass **2** : frame (of a building, vehicle, etc.)
carcéral, -rale [karseral] *adj, mpl* **-raux** [-ro] : prison
carcinogène [karsinɔʒɛn] *adj* : carcinogenic
carcinome [karsinom] *nm* : carcinoma
carder [karde] *vt* : to card (fibers)

cardiaque [kardjak] *adj* : cardiac
cardigan [kardigɑ̃] *nm* : cardigan
cardinal[1], **-nale** [kardinal] *adj, mpl* **-naux** [-no] : cardinal, chief
cardinal[2] *nm, pl* **-naux 1** : cardinal (in religion) **2** : cardinal number **3** : cardinal, redbird
cardiologie [kardjolɔʒi] *nf* : cardiology
cardiologue [kardjolɔg] *nmf* : cardiologist
cardio–vasculaire [kardjovaskylɛr] *adj* : cardiovascular
carême [karɛm] *nm* : Lent
carence [karɑ̃s] *nf* **1** ABSENCE : lack, deficiency **2** : shortcomings *pl* **3** : insolvency
carène [karɛn] *nf* : hull (of a ship)
caréner [karene] {87} *vt* **1** : to careen (a ship) **2** : to streamline
caressant, -sante [karesɑ̃, -sɑ̃t] *adj* : affectionate, tender
caresse [karɛs] *nf* : caress
caresser [karese] *vt* **1** : to caress **2** : to cherish, to entertain (hopes, etc.)
cargaison [kargɛzɔ̃] *nf* : cargo, freight
cargo [kargo] *nm* : freighter
cari [kari] *nm* → **curry**
caribou [karibu] *nm* : caribou
caricature [karikatyr] *nf* : caricature, cartoon
caricaturer [karikatyre] *vt* : to caricature — **caricaturiste** [-tyrist] *nmf*
carie [kari] *nf* **1** : blight (in botany) **2** *or* **carie dentaire** : caries, tooth decay <une carie : a cavity>
carier [karje] {96} *vt* : to rot, to decay — **se carier** *vr*
carillon [karijɔ̃] *nm* : bell, chime
carillonnement [karijɔnmɑ̃] *nm* : peal
carillonner [karijɔne] *v* : to chime, to peal
caritatif, -tive [karitatif, -tiv] *adj* : charitable
carlin [karlɛ̃] *nm* : pug (dog)
carlingue [karlɛ̃g] *nf* : cabin (of an airplane)
carmin [karmɛ̃] *adj & nm* : carmine (red)
carnage [karnaʒ] *nm* TUERIE : carnage, slaughter
carnassier[1], **-sière** [karnasje, -sjɛr] *adj* : carnivorous
carnassier[2] *nm* : carnivore
carnaval [karnaval] *nm, pl* **-vals** : carnival
carnet [karnɛ] *nm* **1** : notebook **2** : book (of stamps, tickets, etc.) <carnet de chèques : checkbook>
carnivore[1] [karnivɔr] *adj* : carnivorous
carnivore[2] *nm* : carnivore
carotte [karɔt] *nf* : carrot
carotter [karɔte] *vt fam* : to swindle, to chisel, to cheat
caroubier [karubje] *nm* : locust (tree)
carpe [karp] *nf* : carp
carpelle [karpɛl] *nm* : carpel
carpette [karpɛt] *nf* : rug
carquois [karkwa] *nm* : quiver
carré[1], **-rée** [kare] *adj* **1** : square **2** : straightforward, forthright
carré[2] *nm* **1** : square **2** : plot, patch (of land) **3** : (square) scarf **4** : four of a kind <un carré d'as : four aces>
carreau [karo] *nm, pl* **carreaux 1** : tile **2** VITRE : windowpane **3** : square, check <à carreaux : checkered> **4** : diamond (in playing cards)
carreauté, -tée [karote] *adj Can* : checkered, checked
carrefour [karfur] *nm* : intersection, crossroads
carrelage [karlaʒ] *nm* : tile, tiled floor
carreler [karle] {8} *vt* : to tile
carrément [karemɑ̃] *adv* **1** : squarely, firmly **2** : bluntly, straight out
carrer [kare] *v* **se carrer** *vr* : to settle oneself
carrière [karjɛr] *nf* **1** : career **2** : stone quarry
carriole [karjɔl] *nf* **1** : cart **2** *Can* : sleigh
carrossable [karɔsabl] *adj* : suitable for motor vehicles
carrosse [karɔs] *nm* **1** : carriage, coach **2** *Can* : baby carriage
carrosserie [karɔsri] *nf* **1** : body (of a car) **2** : (automobile) bodywork
carrousel [karuzɛl] *nm* : carousel
carrure [karyr] *nf* **1** : build, shoulder width **2** STATURE : stature, caliber
carry [kari] *nm* → **curry**
carte [kart] *nf* **1** : card <carte postale : postcard> <carte de crédit : credit card> <carte d'identité : identification card> **2** : map <carte routière : road map> **3** : menu <carte de vins : wine list> **4** *or* **carte à jouer** : playing card <jouer cartes sur table : to lay one's cards on the table>
cartel [kartɛl] *nm* : cartel
cartilage [kartilaʒ] *nm* : cartilage, gristle
cartilagineux, -neuse [kartilaʒinø, -nøz] *adj* : gristly, cartilaginous
cartographe [kartɔgraf] *nmf* : cartographer
cartographie [kartɔgrafi] *nf* : cartography
cartomancie [kartɔmɑ̃si] *nf* : fortune-telling (with cards)
cartomancien, -cienne [kartɔmɑ̃sjɛ̃, -sjɛn] *n* : fortune-teller (with cards)
carton [kartɔ̃] *nm* **1** : cardboard **2** : cardboard box, carton
carton–pâte [kartɔ̃pat] *nm* : pasteboard
cartouche [kartuʃ] *nf* **1** : cartridge <cartouche d'encre : fountain-pen refill> **2** : carton (of cigarettes, etc.)
carvi [karvi] *nm* : caraway
cas [ka] *nms & pl* **1** : case **2 en cas de** : in case of <en cas de bien : if need be> **3 en tout cas** : in any case **4** → **limite**
casanier, -nière [kazanje, -njɛr] *n* : homebody

cascade [kaskad] *nf* **1** : stream, cascade, torrent **2** CHUTE : waterfall **3** : stunt (in movies)
case [kaz] *nf* **1** : box (on a form or questionnaire) **2** : compartment **3** CABANE : hut **4** : square (in a board game) <retourner à la case départ : to go back to square one> **5 case postale** : post office box
caser [kaze] *vt* **1** PLACER : to put **2** *fam* : to put up, to lodge **3** *fam* : to marry off **4** *fam* : to find a job for
caserne [kazɛrn] *nf France* **1** : barracks *pl* **2 caserne de pompiers** : fire station
casher [kaʃɛr] → **kascher**
casier [kazje] *nm* **1** : compartment, pigeonhole **2** : rack (for bottles, etc.) **3 casier judiciaire** : police record
casino [kazino] *nm* : casino
casque [kask] *nm* **1** : helmet **2** : headphones *pl* **3** *Can* : fur cap
casquette [kasket] *nf* : cap
cassable [kasabl] *adj* : breakable
cassant, -sante [kasɑ̃, -sɑ̃t] *adj* **1** : brittle **2** : abrupt, curt
casse [kas] *nf* **1** : breakage, damage **2** : scrap yard **3** : case (in printing) <haut de casse : uppercase>
cassé, -sée [kase] *adj fam* : out of money, broke
casse-cou [kasku] *nms & pl* **1** : danger spot **2** : daredevil
casse-croûte [kaskrut] *nms & pl* **1** : snack, lunch **2** *Can* : restaurant, snack bar
casse-noisettes [kasnwazɛt] *nms & pl* : nutcracker
casse-noix [kasnwa] *nms & pl* : nutcracker
casse-pieds [kaspje] *nmfs & pl fam* : pain in the neck, bore
casser [kase] *vt* **1** BRISER : to break **2** DÉGRADER : to demote **3** ANNULER : to quash, to annul — *vi* : to break — **se casser** *vr* **1** : to break <se casser le cou : to break one's neck> **2** *fam* : to go away <casse-toi! : get out of here!>
casserole [kasrɔl] *nf* : saucepan
casse-tête [kastɛt] *nms & pl* **1** : puzzle **2** : problem, headache
cassette [kaset] *nf* : cassette
cassonade [kasɔnad] *nf* : brown sugar
cassure [kasyr] *nf* **1** : break **2** : crack, fissure
castagnettes [kastaɲɛt] *nfpl* : castanets
caste [kast] *nf* : caste
castor [kastɔr] *nm* : beaver
castration [kastrasjɔ̃] *nf* : castration
castrer [kastre] *vt* : to castrate, to neuter
cataclysme [kataklism] *nm* : cataclysm
catacombes [katakɔ̃b] *nfpl* : catacombs
catafalque [katafalk] *nm* : bier (stand)
catalogue [katalɔg] *nm* : catalog
cataloguer [katalɔge] *vt* **1** : to catalog **2** : to categorize, to label (as)
catalyseur [katalizœr] *nm* : catalyst
catalytique [katalitik] *adj* : catalytic
catamaran [katamarɑ̃] *nm* : catamaran
cataplasme [kataplasm] *nm* : poultice
catapulte [katapylt] *nf* : catapult
catapulter [katapylte] *vt* : to catapult
cataracte [katarakt] *nf* **1** : cataract, falls **2** : cataract (in medicine)
catarrhe [katar] *nm* : catarrh
catastrophe [katastrɔf] *nf* : disaster, catastrophe
catastrophique [katastrɔfik] *adj* : disastrous, catastrophic
catch [katʃ] *nm* **1** : wrestling **2 faire du catch** : to wrestle
catéchisme [kateʃism] *nm* : catechism
catégorie [kategɔri] *nf* **1** : category **2** : grade, quality (of meat, etc.)
catégorique [kategɔrik] *adj* : categorical — **catégoriquement** [-rikmɑ̃] *adv*
catharsis [katarsis] *nf* : catharsis — **cathartique** [-tartik] *adj*
cathédrale [katedral] *nf* : cathedral
cathéter [kateter] *nm* : catheter
cathode [katɔd] *nf* : cathode
catholicisme [katɔlisism] *nm* : Catholicism
catholique[1] [katɔlik] *adj* **1** : Roman Catholic **2** : **pas (très) catholique** : dubious, questionable
catholique[2] *nmf* : Roman Catholic
catimini [katimini] **en ~** : stealthily, on the sly
caucasien, -sienne [kokazjɛ̃, -zjɛn] *adj* : Caucasian
cauchemar [kɔʃmar] *nm* : nightmare
cauchemardesque [kɔʃmardɛsk] *adj* : nightmarish
cause [koz] *nf* **1** : cause, reason <à cause de : because, on account of> <pour cause de : owing to> **2** AFFAIRE : case, lawsuit <être en cause : to be at issue, to be involved>
causer [koze] *vt* PROVOQUER : to cause — *vi* : to chat <causer de : to talk about>
causerie [kozri] *nf* : talk, chat
causette [kozɛt] *nf fam* : chat, chitchat <faire la causette à : to have a chat with>
causeur[1], **-seuse** [kozœr, -zøz] *adj* : talkative, chatty
causeur[2], **-seuse** *n* : conversationalist, talker
causeuse *nf* : love seat
caustique [kostik] *adj* : caustic
cauteleux, -leuse [kotlø, -løz] *adj* : sly, wily
cautériser [koterize] *vt* : to cauterize — **cautérisation** [-rizasjɔ̃] *nf*
caution [kosjɔ̃] *nf* **1** : security, guarantee **2 libérer sous caution** : to release on bail
cautionnement [kosjɔnmɑ̃] *nm* : bail, guarantee
cautionner [kosjɔne] *vt* **1** : to guarantee **2** : to support, to sanction

cavalcade [kavalkad] *nf* **1** : cavalcade **2** : stampede, rush
cavale [kaval] *nf fam* **en ~** : on the run
cavalerie [kavalri] *nf* : cavalry
cavalier[1], **-lière** [kavalje, -ljɛr] *adj* : cavalier, offhand
cavalier[2], **-lière** *n* **1** : rider, horseman *m*, horsewoman *f* **2** : dance partner, escort <faire cavalier seul : to go it alone>
cavalier[3] *nm* **1** : cavalryman **2** : knight (in chess)
cave[1] [kav] *adj* : hollow, sunken
cave[2] *nf* **1** : cellar **2 de la cave au grenier** : from top to bottom, high and low
caveau [kavo] *nm, pl* **caveaux 1** : small cellar **2** : burial vault
caverne [kavɛrn] *nf* GROTTE : cave, cavern
caverneux, -neuse [kavɛrnø, -nøz] *adj* : cavernous
caviar [kavjar] *nm* : caviar
cavité [kavite] *nf* : cavity
CD [sede] *nm* : CD (compact disc)
ce[1] [sə] (**cet** [sɛt] *before a vowel or mute h*), **cette** [sɛt] *adj, pl* **ces** [se] **1** : this, that, these, those <un de ces jours : one of these days> <cette fois-ci : this time> <cet homme-là : that man> <ces livres sur la table : those books on the table> **2** (*used for emphasis*) <cette idée! : what an idea!>
ce[2] (**c'** [s] *before a vowel*) *pron* **1** : it, that, these, those <c'est lui : it's him, that's him> <qui est-ce? : who is it?, who's that?> <ce sont mes amis : these are my friends, they are my friends> <c'est cela : that's right> **2 ce que, ce qui, ce dont** : what, which <il comprend ce que je lui dis : he understands what I'm telling him> <montrez-moi ce que vous avez fait : show me what you did> <ce dont on parle : what they're talking about> <il faut être patient, ce que je ne suis pas : you have to be patient, which I'm not> **3 ce faisant** : in so doing **4 pour ce faire** : to this end
ceci [səsi] *pron* **1** : this <écoutez ceci : listen to this> **2 à ceci près que** : except that
cécité [sesite] *nf* : blindness
céder [sede] {87} *vt* : to give up, to yield, to cede — *vi* : to give in
cédille [sedij] *nf* : cedilla
cédrat [sedra] *nm* : citron (fruit)
cèdre [sɛdr] *nm* : cedar
cégep [seʒep] (**collège d'enseignement général et professionnel**) *nm Can* : junior college
cégépien, -pienne [seʒepjɛ̃, -pjɛn] *n Can* : junior college student
ceindre [sɛ̃dr] {37} *vt* : to gird, to put on
ceinture [sɛ̃tyr] *nf* **1** : belt <ceinture de sauvetage : life belt> <ceinture de sécurité : safety belt> **2** : waist (in anatomy) **3** : waistband **4** : ring, belt, circle
ceinturer [sɛ̃tyre] *vt* ENTOURER : to surround
cela [səla] *pron* **1** : that <cela dit : that said> <malgré cela : in spite of that, nonetheless> **2** : it <cela ne fait rien : it doesn't matter>
célébration [selebrasjɔ̃] *nf* : celebration
célèbre [selebr] *adj* FAMEUX : famous
célébrer [selebre] {87} *vt* **1** : to celebrate **2** : to extol, to praise
célébrité [selebrite] *nf* **1** RENOMMÉE : fame, renown **2** : celebrity, famous person
celer [səle] {20} *vt* : to conceal
céleri [sɛlri] *nm* : celery
célérité [selerite] *nf* VITESSE : swiftness, speed
céleste [selɛst] *adj* : celestial, heavenly
célibat [seliba] *nm* **1** : unmarried life **2** : celibacy
célibataire[1] [selibatɛr] *adj* : single, unmarried
célibataire[2] *nmf* : single person, bachelor *m*, spinster *f*
celle, celles → **celui**
cellier [selje] *nm* : storeroom
cellophane [selɔfan] *nf* : cellophane
cellulaire [selyler] *adj* : cellular
cellule [selyl] *nf* : cell
cellulose [selyloz] *nf* : cellulose
Celsius [sɛlsjys] *adj s & pl* : Celsius
celte [sɛlt] *adj* : Celtic
Celte *nmf* : Celt
celtique [sɛltik] *adj* : Celtic
celui [səlɥi], **celle** [sɛl] *pron, pl* **ceux** [sø], **celles** [sɛl] **1** : the one(s), those <mon livre et celui de Jean : my book and John's> <les récipients en acier et ceux en plastique : steel containers and plastic ones> **2** : he, she, those <celui qui danse : he who dances> <ceux d'entre vous : those among you>
celui–ci [səlɥisi], **celle–ci** [sɛlsi] *pron, pl* **ceux–ci** [søsi], **celles–ci** [sɛlsi] **1** : this (one), these **2** : the latter **3** : one <celle-ci chante, celle-là joue de la guitare : one sings, another plays the guitar>
celui–là [səlɥila], **celle–là** [sɛlla] *pron, pl* **ceux–là** [søla], **celles–là** [sɛlla] **1** : that (one), those **2** : the former **3** : another <celui-ci fait la cuisine, celui-là fait la vaisselle : one cooks, another washes the dishes>
cénacle [senakl] *nm* : circle, (literary) club
cendre [sɑ̃dr] *nf* **1** : ashes *pl*, cinders *pl* **2 cendres** *nfpl* : ashes, remains (of the dead)
cendreux, -dreuse [sɑ̃drø, -drøz] *adj* **1** : ashen, pale **2** : ashy
cendrier [sɑ̃drije] *nm* : ashtray
cène [sɛn] *nf* **la Cène** : the Last Supper

cenellier [s(ə)nɛlje] *nm Can* : hawthorn (tree)
censé, -sée [sɑ̃se] *adj* : supposed <elle est censée arriver lundi : she is supposed to arrive on Monday>
censément [sɑ̃semɑ̃] *adv* : supposedly
censeur [sɑ̃sœr] *nm* **1** : censor **2** : critic
censure [sɑ̃syr] *nf* **1** : censorship **2** : censure
censurer [sɑ̃syre] *vt* **1** : to censor, to ban **2** : to censure
cent[1] [sɑ̃] *adj* : a hundred, one hundred <trois cents hommes : three hundred men>
cent[2] *nm* **1** : hundred <un cent de livres : one hundred books> **2** : cent, 1/100 of a dollar **3 pour ~** : percent
centaine [sɑ̃ten] *nf* : hundred <une centaine de chaises : about a hundred chairs> <des centaines de fleurs : hundreds of flowers>
centaure [sɑ̃tɔr] *nm* : centaur
centenaire[1] [sɑ̃tnɛr] *adj* : hundred-year-old
centenaire[2] *nm* : centennial
centenaire[3] *nmf* : centenarian
centième[1] [sɑ̃tjɛm] *adj & nmf & nm* : hundredth
centième[2] *nf* : hundredth performance
centigrade [sɑ̃tigrad] *adj* : centigrade, Celsius
centigramme [sɑ̃tigram] *nm* : centigram
centime [sɑ̃tim] *nm* : centime <il n'a pas un centime : he hasn't got a cent>
centimètre [sɑ̃timɛtr] *nm* **1** : centimeter **2** : tape measure
central[1], **-trale** [sɑ̃tral] *adj, mpl* **centraux** [sɑ̃tro] **1** : central **2** : main
central[2] *nm* **central téléphonique** : telephone exchange
centrale *nf* **1** : generating station <centrale électrique : electric power plant> **2** : confederation <centrales syndicales : labor unions>
centraliser [sɑ̃tralize] *vt* : to centralize **— centralisation** [-zasjɔ̃] *nf*
centraméricain, -caine [sɑ̃tramerikɛ̃, -kɛn] *adj* : Central American
Centraméricain, -caine *n* : Central American
centre [sɑ̃tr] *nm* **1** : center <centre de gravité : center of gravity> **2 centre commercial** : shopping center, shopping mall **3 centre communautaire** *Can* : community center **4 centre d'accueil** *Can* : nursing home **5 centres vitaux** : vital organs
centrer [sɑ̃tre] *vt* : to center
centre–ville [sɑ̃trəvil] *nm, pl* **centres–villes** : downtown
centrifuge [sɑ̃trifyʒ] *adj* : centrifugal
centripète [sɑ̃tripɛt] *adj* : centripetal
centuple [sɑ̃typl] *nm* **1 au ~** : a hundredfold **2 être le centuple de** : to be a hundred times (a number)
centupler [sɑ̃typle] *v* : to increase a hundredfold
cépage [sepaʒ] *nm* : vine
cependant [səpɑ̃dɑ̃] *conj* **1** : however, yet **2 cependant que** : while, whereas
céramique[1] [seramik] *adj* : ceramic
céramique[2] *nf* : ceramics
cerbère [sɛrbɛr] *nm* **1** : strict doorkeeper, watchdog **2** *Can* : goalkeeper, goalie
cerceau [sɛrso] *nm, pl* **cerceaux** : hoop
cercle [sɛrkl] *nm* **1** : circle <cercle vicieux : vicious circle> **2** : group, set (of friends, etc.) **3** : club **4** : range, scope **5** : hoop
cercueil [sɛrkœj] *nm* : coffin, casket
céréale [sereal] *nf* : cereal
céréalier, -lière [serealje, -ljɛr] *adj* : cereal
cérébral, -brale [serebral] *adj, mpl* **-braux** [-bro] : cerebral
cérémonial [seremɔnjal] *nm, pl* **-nials** : ceremonial
cérémonie [seremɔni] *nf* : ceremony
cérémoniel, -nielle [seremɔnjɛl] *adj* : ceremonial, ceremonious
cérémonieux, -nieuse [seremɔnjø, -njøz] *adj* : ceremonious, formal **— cérémonieusement** [-njøzmɑ̃] *adv*
cerf [sɛr] *nm* **1** : stag, red dear **2 cerf de Virginie** *Can* → **chevreuil**
cerf–volant [sɛrvɔlɑ̃] *nm* : kite <faire voler un cerf-volant : to fly a kite>
cerise[1] [sərиz] *adj or* **rouge cerise** : cerise, cherry-colored
cerise[2] *nf* : cherry
cerisier [sərizje] *nm* : cherry tree
cerne [sɛrn] *nm* : ring <avoir des cernes : to have rings under one's eyes>
cerner [sɛrne] *vt* **1** : to surround **2** : to define, to determine
certain, -taine [sɛrtɛ̃, -tɛn] *adj* **1** : certain, sure, definite <c'est une chose certaine : there's no doubt about it> **2** : certain <une certaine aptitude : a certain aptitude, some aptitude> <dans un certain sens : in a way> <à certains moments : at certain times, sometimes>
certainement [sɛrtɛnmɑ̃] *adv* : certainly, surely
certains, certaines [sɛrtɛ̃, -tɛn] *pron pl* : some (people), certain (ones)
certes [sɛrt] *adv* : of course, indeed
certificat [sɛrtifika] *nm* : certificate <certificat de naissance : birth certificate>
certifier [sɛrtifje] {96} *vt* : to certify, to attest to, to notarize
certitude [sɛrtityd] *nf* : certainty, certitude
cérumen [serymɛn] *nm* : earwax
cerveau [sɛrvo] *nm, pl* **cerveaux 1** : brain, cerebrum **2** : mind, intellect
cervelet [sɛrvəlɛ] *nm* : cerebellum

cervelle [sɛrvɛl] *nf* **1** : brain (in anatomy) **2** : brains *pl* <se creuser la cervelle : to rack one's brains>
cervical, -cale [sɛrvikal] *adj, mpl* **-caux** [-ko] : cervical
ces → ce¹
césarienne [sezarjɛn] *nf* : caesarean section
césium [sezjɔm] *nm* : cesium
cessation [sɛsasjɔ̃] *nf* : cessation, suspension
cesse [sɛs] *nf* **sans ~** : unceasingly, incessantly, constantly
cesser [sɛse] *v* : to cease, to stop
cessez–le–feu [seselfø] *nms & pl* : cease-fire
cession [sɛsjɔ̃] *nf* : transfer
c'est–à–dire [sɛtadir] *conj* **1** : that is (to say) **2 c'est–à–dire que** : which means (that) <il s'est endormi tard hier soir, c'est-à-dire qu'il sera fatigué aujourd'hui : he went to bed late last night, which means he'll be tired today>
cet, cette → ce
ceux → celui
ceux–ci → celui–ci
ceux–là → celui–là
chacal [ʃakal] *nm, pl* **chacals** : jackal
chacun, chacune [ʃakœ̃, -kyn] *pron* **1** : each (one) **2** : everybody, everyone <chacun pour soi : everybody for himself>
chagrin¹, -grine [ʃagrɛ̃, -grin] *adj* **1** : sorrowful, doleful **2** : peevish, ill-humored
chagrin² *nm* PEINE : grief, sorrow
chagriner [ʃagrine] *vt* **1** PEINER : to grieve, to distress **2** CONTRARIER : to annoy, to bother
chahut [ʃay] *nm* : uproar, racket, rumpus
chahuter [ʃayte] *vi* : to create an uproar — *vt* : to heckle
chaîne [ʃɛn] *nf* **1** : chain **2** : series, range <chaîne de montagnes : mountain range> <chaîne d'idées : train of thought> **3** : (television) channel **4** : audio system <chaîne hi-fi : hi-fi (system)> **5** : warp (in weaving)
chaînon [ʃɛnɔ̃] *nm* : link <chaînon manquant : missing link>
chair [ʃɛr] *nf* **1** : flesh **2** : meat **3 chair de poule** : goose bumps
chaire [ʃɛr] *nf* **1** : (university) chair **2** : pulpit
chaise [ʃɛz] *nf* **1** : chair, seat **2 chaise roulante** : wheelchair
chaland [ʃalɑ̃] *nm* : barge, scow
châle [ʃal] *nm* : shawl
chalet [ʃale] *nm* **1** : chalet **2** *Can* : cottage
chaleur [ʃalœr] *nf* **1** : heat **2** : warmth, fervor
chaleureux, -reuse [ʃalœrø, -røz] *adj* : warm, cordial — **chaleureusement** [-røzmɑ̃] *adv*
challenge [ʃalɑ̃ʒ] *nm* **1** DÉFI : challenge **2** : tournament
chaloupe [ʃalup] *nf* **1** : launch <chaloupe de sauvetage : lifeboat> **2** : rowboat
chalumeau [ʃalymo] *nm, pl* **-meaux 1** : blowtorch **2** *Can* : tap (for collecting sap from a tree)
chalut [ʃaly] *nm* : trawl
chalutier [ʃalytje] *nm* : trawler
chamade [ʃamad] *nf* **battre la chamade** : to beat wildly, to pound
chamailler [ʃamaje] *v* **se chamailler** *vr* : to squabble, to bicker
chamarrer [ʃamare] *vt* : to adorn
chambardement [ʃɑ̃bardəmɑ̃] *nm fam* **1** : upheaval, shake-up **2** : mess
chambarder [ʃɑ̃barde] *vt fam* **1** : to mess up, to turn upside down **2** : to shake up
chambouler [ʃɑ̃bule] *vt fam* : to mess up, to turn upside down
chambranle [ʃɑ̃brɑl] *nm* **1** : frame (of a door or window) **2** : mantelpiece
chambre [ʃɑ̃br] *nf* **1** : room, bedroom **2** : chamber (of a gun, etc.) **3** : (legislative) chamber, house **4 musique de chambre** : chamber music
chambrée [ʃɑ̃bre] *nf* : barracks
chambreur, -breuse [ʃɑ̃brœr, -brøz] *n Can* : roomer
chameau [ʃamo] *nm, pl* **chameaux** : camel
chamois¹ [ʃamwa] *adj s & pl* : buff(-colored)
chamois² *nms & pl* **1** : chamois (animal) **2** : buff (color)
champ [ʃɑ̃] *nm* **1** : field, land area <champ de maïs : cornfield> <champ de courses : racecourse, racetrack> <champ de bataille : battlefield> <petit champ : infield> **2** : area, domain <champ d'action : sphere of activity> **3** : field (in physics, physiology, mathematics) <champ magnétique : magnetic field> <champ visuel : visual field> **4 champs** *nmpl* : countryside, country **5 → sur–le–champ**
champagne [ʃɑ̃pan] *nm* : champagne
champêtre [ʃɑ̃pɛtr] *adj* : rustic, rural
champignon [ʃɑ̃piɲɔ̃] *nm* : mushroom
champion¹, -pionne [ʃɑ̃pjɔ̃, -pjɔn] *adj fam* : great, terrific
champion², -pionne *n* : champion
championnat [ʃɑ̃pjɔna] *nm* : championship
champlure [ʃɑ̃plyr] *nf Can* : faucet
chance [ʃɑ̃s] *nf* **1** : luck, fortune <coup de chance : stroke of luck> <par chance : fortunately, luckily> **2** : chance, opportunity **3** : possibility, likelihood
chancelant, -lante [ʃɑ̃slɑ̃, -lɑ̃t] *adj* **1** : unsteady, groggy **2** : flagging, faltering
chanceler [ʃɑ̃sle] {8} *vi* **1** : to totter **2** : to waver, to falter
chancelier [ʃɑ̃səlje] *nm* : chancellor

chanceux, -ceuse [ʃɑ̃sø, -søz] *adj* : lucky, fortunate
chancre [ʃɑ̃kr] *nm* : chancre (in medicine)
chandail [ʃɑ̃daj] *nm* : sweater, pullover
chandelier [ʃɑ̃dəlje] *nm* **1** : candlestick **2** : candelabrum
chandelle [ʃɑ̃dɛl] *nf* : candle
change [ʃɑ̃ʒ] *nm* **1** : exchange, exchange rate **2 donner le change à qqn** : to throw s.o. off the trail
changeant, -geante [ʃɑ̃ʒɑ̃, -ʒɑ̃t] *adj* **1** : changing **2** : fickle, changeable
changement [ʃɑ̃ʒmɑ̃] *nm* **1** : change **2 changement de vitesse** : gears *pl* (of an automobile)
changer [ʃɑ̃ʒe] {17} *vt* **1** : to change, to exchange, to replace **2** : to alter, to transform — *vi* **1** : to undergo change **2 ~ de** : to change <changer d'avis : to change one's mind> <changer de vitesse : to change gears> — **se changer** *vr* **1** : to change (one's clothes) **2** : to be transformed
changeur, -geuse [ʃɑ̃ʒœr, -ʒøz] *n* : money changer
chanoine [ʃanwan] *nm* : canon (in religion)
chanson [ʃɑ̃sɔ̃] *nf* : song
chansonnette [ʃɑ̃sɔnɛt] *nf* : simple song, ditty
chansonnier, -nière [ʃɑ̃sɔnje, -njɛr] *n Can* : songwriter
chant [ʃɑ̃] *nm* **1** : song <chant de Noël : Christmas carol> **2** : singing **3** : canto, ode **4** : edge <de chant, sur chant : edgewise, on edge>
chantage [ʃɑ̃taʒ] *nm* : blackmail
chantant, -tante [ʃɑ̃tɑ̃, -tɑ̃t] *adj* **1** : singsong, lilting **2** : tuneful, catchy
chanter [ʃɑ̃te] *vt* **1** : to sing **2** : to relate, to tell of — *vi* **1** : to sing **2** : to chirp, to crow **3 ~ à** *fam* : to appeal to, to catch the fancy of **4 faire chanter** : to blackmail
chanteur, -teuse [ʃɑ̃tœr, -tøz] *n* : singer
chantier [ʃɑ̃tje] *nm* **1** : (construction) site **2** : depot, yard <chantier naval : shipyard> **3 mettre en chantier** : to start work on, to undertake
chantonner [ʃɑ̃tɔne] *v* : to croon, to hum
chantre [ʃɑ̃tr] *nm* : cantor
chanvre [ʃɑ̃vr] *nm* : hemp
chaos [kao] *nm* : chaos
chaotique [kaɔtik] *adj* : chaotic
chaparder [ʃaparde] *vt fam* PIQUER : to pilfer, to swipe
chapeau [ʃapo] *nm, pl* **chapeaux 1** : hat, cap <tirer son chapeau à : to take one's hat off to> **2 chapeau!** : well done!
chapeauter [ʃapote] *vt* : to head, to lead
chapelain [ʃaplɛ̃] *nm* : chaplain
chapelet [ʃaple] *nm* **1** : rosary **2** : series, string <un chapelet d'îlots : a chain of small islands>
chapelier, -lière [ʃapəlje, -ljɛr] *n* : hatter
chapelle [ʃapɛl] *nf* : chapel
chapelure [ʃaplyr] *nf* : bread crumbs *pl*
chaperon [ʃaprɔ̃] *nm* : chaperon, chaperone
chaperonner [ʃaprɔne] *vt* : to chaperon
chapiteau [ʃapito] *nm, pl* **-teaux 1** : capital (of a column) **2** : big top, circus tent
chapitre [ʃapitr] *nm* **1** : chapter (of a book) **2** : topic, subject matter **3** : item, heading (in a budget)
chapon [ʃapɔ̃] *nm* : capon
chaque [ʃak] *adj* : each, every <chaque personne : each person, everyone> <cent dollars chaque : a hundred dollars each>
char [ʃar] *nm* **1** : cart, wagon **2** : chariot **3** *Can fam* : car **4** *or* **char d'assaut** : tank
charabia [ʃarabja] *nm fam* : gibberish, gobbledegook
charade [ʃarad] *nf* **1** : riddle **2** : charades (game)
charançon [ʃarɑ̃sɔ̃] *nm* : weevil
charbon [ʃarbɔ̃] *nm* **1** : coal **2** : smut (of grains) **3 charbon ardent** : ember **4 charbon de bois** : charcoal
charcuterie [ʃarkytri] *nf* **1** : delicatessen, pork butcher's shop **2** : cooked pork products
charcutier, -tière [ʃarkytje, -tjɛr] *n* : pork butcher
chardon [ʃardɔ̃] *nm* : thistle
chardonneret [ʃardɔnrɛ] *nm* : goldfinch
charge [ʃarʒ] *nf* **1** : load, weight <charge limite : maximum load> **2** : responsibility, job <à charge de : dependent on> <charge de travail : workload> **3** : office <charge élective : elective office> **4** : charge (of explosives or electricity) **5** : assault, (military) charge **6** : cost, expense <charges de l'état : government expenditures> **7** : accusation, indictment **8** : emotional burden **9** : caricature
chargé¹, -gée [ʃarʒe] *adj* **1** : full, loaded, heavy **2** : busy, full
chargé², -gée *n* **1 chargé d'affaires** : chargé d'affaires **2 chargé de cours** : (university) lecturer
chargement [ʃarʒəmɑ̃] *nm* **1** : loading **2** : load, cargo
charger [ʃarʒe] {17} *vt* **1** : to load, to fill (up), to overload **2** : to load (a gun, etc.), to charge (with electricity) **3** : to charge at, to attack **4 ~ de** : to put in charge of, to give responsibility for, to command — *vi* : to charge, to attack — **se charger** *vr* **~ de** : to take responsibility for
chargeur [ʃarʒœr] *nm* **1** : magazine, clip (of a firearm) **2** : shipper, shipping agent

chariot [ʃarjo] *nm* **1** : cart, wagon <chariot de supermarché : shopping cart> **2** : truck <chariot élévateur : forklift truck> **3** : carriage (of a typewriter)
charisme [karism] *nm* : charisma — **charismatique** [-rismatik] *adj*
charitable [ʃaritabl] *adj* : charitable — **charitablement** [-bləmɑ̃] *adv*
charité [ʃarite] *nf* : charity
charivari [ʃarivari] *nm* : racket, hullaballoo
charlatan [ʃarlatɑ̃] *nm* : charlatan, quack
charmant, -mante [ʃarmɑ̃, -mɑ̃t] *adj* : charming, delightful
charme [ʃarm] *nm* **1** : charm, attraction **2** : spell
charmer [ʃarme] *vt* : to charm
charmeur[1], -meuse [ʃarmœr, -møz] *adj* : charming
charmeur[2], -meuse *n* : charmer
charnel, -nelle [ʃarnɛl] *adj* : carnal
charnier [ʃarnje] *nm* : mass grave
charnière[1] [ʃarnjɛr] *adj* : transitional, pivotal
charnière[2] *nf* **1** : hinge **2** : turning point
charnu, -nue [ʃarny] *adj* : fleshy, plump
charognard [ʃarɔɲar] *nm* : scavenger (animal)
charogne [ʃarɔɲ] *nf* **1** : carrion **2** *fam* : bastard
charpente [ʃarpɑ̃t] *nf* **1** : framework, structure **2** : frame, build (of the body)
charpenté, -tée [ʃarpɑ̃te] *adj* : built, constructed
charpenterie [ʃarpɑ̃tri] *nf* : carpentry
charpentier [ʃarpɑ̃tje] *nm* : carpenter
charpie [ʃarpi] *nf* **1** : lint **2 en ~** : in shreds
charrette [ʃarɛt] *nf* : cart <charrette à bras : pushcart>
charrier [ʃarje] {96} *vt* **1** : to cart, to carry along **2** *fam* : to poke fun at — *vi* : to exaggerate, to go too far
charrue [ʃary] *nf* : plow
charte [ʃart] *nf* : charter
charter [ʃarte] *nm* **1** : charter flight **2** : chartered plane
chas [ʃa] *nm* : eye (of a needle)
chasse [ʃas] *nf* **1** : hunting <aller à la chasse : to go hunting> **2** POURSUITE : chase <donner chasse à : to chase> <chasse à l'homme : manhunt> **3** *or* **chasse d'eau** : flush (of a toilet) <actionner la chasse d'eau : to flush the toilet>
chassé–croisé [ʃasekrwaze] *nm, pl* **chassés–croisés** : coming and going, moving back and forth
chasse–neige [ʃasnɛʒ] *nms & pl* : snowplow
chasser [ʃase] *vt* **1** : to hunt, to chase **2** : to chase away, to drive away **3** : to dispel — *vi* **1** : to go hunting, to hunt **2** : to skid
chasseur[1], -seuse [ʃasœr, -søz] *n* **1** : hunter **2 chasseur de têtes** : headhunter
chasseur[2] *nm* **1** : fighter <chasseur-bombardier : fighter-bomber> **2** : bellhop, bellboy
châssis [ʃasi] *nm* **1** : frame (of a window, etc.) **2** : chassis
chaste [ʃast] *adj* : chaste — **chastement** [ʃastmɑ̃] *adv*
chasteté [ʃastəte] *nf* : chastity
chasuble [ʃazybl] *nf or* **robe chasuble** : pinafore (dress)
chat, chatte [ʃa, ʃat] *n* **1** : cat **2 chat sauvage** : wildcat **3 chat sauvage** *Can* : raccoon
châtaigne [ʃatɛɲ] *nf* : chestnut
châtaignier [ʃatɛɲe] *nm* : chestnut tree
châtain [ʃatɛ̃] *adj* : chestnut brown
château [ʃato] *nm, pl* **châteaux 1** : castle **2 château fort** : fortified castle, stronghold
châtier [ʃatje] {96} *vt* **1** : to chastise, to punish **2** : to polish, to refine (style, etc.)
châtiment [ʃatimɑ̃] *nm* PUNITION : punishment
chaton [ʃatɔ̃] *nm* **1** : kitten **2** : catkin (in botany) **3** : setting (of a ring)
chatouillement [ʃatujmɑ̃] *nm* : tickle, tickling
chatouiller [ʃatuje] *vt* **1** : to tickle **2** : to titillate (the senses), to pique (curiosity, pride, etc.)
chatouilleux, -leuse [ʃatujø, -jøz] *adj* **1** : ticklish **2** : sensitive, touchy
chatoyant, -yante [ʃatwajɑ̃, -jɑ̃t] *adj* : iridescent, shimmering
chatoyer [ʃatwaje] {58} *vi* : to shimmer
châtrer [ʃatre] *vt* : to castrate, to neuter
chaud[1] [ʃo] *adv* **1 avoir chaud** : to feel warm, to feel hot **2 boire chaud** : to drink something hot **3 il fait chaud** : it's warm, it's hot **4 manger chaud** : to eat hot food
chaud[2], chaude [ʃo, ʃod] *adj* **1** : warm, hot **2** : enthusiastic, keen **3** : heated, tense
chaud[3] *nm* : heat, warmth
chaudement [ʃodmɑ̃] *adv* **1** : warmly **2** : heartily
chaudière [ʃodjɛr] *nf* : boiler
chaudron [ʃodrɔ̃] *nm* : cauldron
chauffage [ʃofaʒ] *nm* : heating <chauffage central : central heating>
chauffard [ʃofar] *nm* : reckless driver
chauffe–eau [ʃofo] *nms & pl* : water heater
chauffer [ʃofe] *vt* : to heat, to warm — *vi* : to become warm, to warm up — **se chauffer** *vr*
chaufferette [ʃofrɛt] *nf Can* **1** : space heater **2** : heater (in a car)
chaufferie [ʃofri] *nf* : boiler room
chauffeur [ʃofœr] *nm* **1** CONDUCTEUR : driver **2** : chauffeur **3** : stoker, fireman

chaume [ʃom] *nm* **1** : thatch **2** : stubble (of grain)
chaumière [ʃomjɛr] *nf* : (thatched) cottage
chaussée [ʃose] *nf* : roadway, causeway
chausser [ʃose] *vt* **1** : to put on (boots, skis, etc.) **2** : to put shoes on (s.o.) **3** : to fit (with shoes) — *vi* ~ **de** : to take (a shoe size) — **se chausser** *vr* : to put on shoes
chausse–trape *or* **chausse–trappe** [ʃostrap] *nf* : trap, pitfall
chaussette [ʃosɛt] *nf* : sock
chausseur [ʃosœr] *nm* : shoemaker
chausson [ʃosɔ̃] *nm* **1** : slipper **2** : turnover <chausson aux pommes : apple turnover>
chaussure [ʃosyr] *nf* **1** : shoe **2** : footwear industry
chauve [ʃov] *adj* : bald
chauve–souris [ʃovsuri] *nf, pl* **chauves–souris** : bat (animal)
chauvin[1], **-vine** [ʃovɛ̃, -vin] *adj* : chauvinistic — **chauvinisme** [ʃovinism] *nm*
chauvin[2], **-vine** *n* : chauvinist
chaux [ʃo] *nf* **1** : lime **2 lait de chaux** : whitewash
chavirer [ʃavire] *vt* **1** CAPOTER : to capsize, to overturn, to keel over **2** ÉMOUVOIR : to upset, to overwhelm — *vi* : to capsize
cheddar [ʃedar] *nm* : cheddar
chef [ʃɛf] *nm* **1** : leader, boss, head **2** *or* **chef cuisinier** : chef **3 au premier chef** : above all, primarily **4 chef d'accusation** : charge, count (in law) **5 chef d'orchestre** : conductor **6 en chef** : chief, head
chef–d'oeuvre [ʃɛdœvr] *nm, pl* **chefs–d'oeuvre** : masterpiece
chefferie [ʃefri] *nf Can* : leadership (of a political party)
cheikh *or* **cheik** [ʃɛk] *nm* : sheikh
chemin [ʃəmɛ̃] *nm* **1** : way, road, path **2 chemin de fer** : railroad
cheminée [ʃəmine] *nf* **1** : fireplace **2** : chimney **3** : mantel, mantelpiece
cheminement [ʃəminmɑ̃] *nm* **1** AVANCE : advance, progress **2** : development
cheminer [ʃəmine] *vi* **1** : to walk along **2** : to advance, to progress
cheminot [ʃəmino] *nm* : railroad worker, railroader
chemise [ʃəmiz] *nf* **1** : shirt **2** : folder **3 chemise de nuit** : nightgown
chemisier [ʃəmizje] *nm* CORSAGE : blouse
chenal [ʃənal] *nm, pl* **chenaux** [ʃəno] : channel (in a river, harbor, etc.)
chêne [ʃɛn] *nm* : oak
chéneau [ʃeno] *nm, pl* **chéneaux** : gutter (of a roof)
chenet [ʃənɛ] *nm* : andiron
chenil [ʃənil] *nm* : kennel
chenille [ʃənij] *nf* **1** : caterpillar **2** : chenille (fabric)
chenu, -nue [ʃəny] *adj* : white-haired, hoary
cheptel [ʃɛptɛl] *nm* : livestock
chèque [ʃɛk] *nm* : check <chèque en blanc : blank check> <chèque de voyage : traveler's check>
chèque–cadeau [ʃɛkkado] *nm, pl* **chèques–cadeaux** : gift certificate
cher[1] [ʃɛr] *adv* **1 coûter cher** : to cost a lot **2 payer cher** : to pay dearly
cher[2], **chère** [ʃɛr] *adj* **1** : dear, beloved **2** COÛTEUX : expensive
cher[3], **chère** *n* : dear <ma chère : my dear>
chercher [ʃɛrʃe] *vt* **1** : to look for, to seek **2 chercher à faire** : to try to do **3 aller chercher** : to go and get
chercheur[1], **-cheuse** [ʃɛrʃœr, -ʃøz] *adj* : inquiring
chercheur[2], **-cheuse** *n* : researcher
chercheur[3] *nm* : finder (of a telescope, etc.)
chère [ʃɛr] *nf* : food, fare
chèrement *adv* [ʃɛrmɑ̃] : dearly, at great cost
chéri, -rie [ʃeri] *adj & n* : darling, dear
chérir [ʃerir] *vt* : to cherish
cherté [ʃɛrte] *nf* : expensiveness, high cost
chérubin [ʃerybɛ̃] *nm* : cherub
chétif, -tive [ʃetif, -tiv] *adj* **1** : sickly, weak **2** MALINGRE : puny
cheval [ʃəval] *nm, pl* **chevaux** [ʃəvo] **1** : horse <à cheval : on horseback> **2** *or* **cheval–vapeur** : horsepower
chevaleresque [ʃəvalrɛsk] *adj* : chivalrous, knightly
chevalerie [ʃəvalri] *nf* **1** : chivalry **2** : knighthood
chevalet [ʃəvalɛ] *nm* **1** : easel **2** : rack (instrument of torture) **3** : stand, trestle, sawhorse
chevalier [ʃəvalje] *nm* : knight
chevalin, -line [ʃəvalɛ̃, -lin] *adj* **1** : equine **2** : horsey
cheval–vapeur [ʃəvalvapœr] *nm, pl* **chevaux–vapeur** → **cheval**
chevauchée [ʃəvoʃe] *nf* : ride
chevauchement [ʃəvoʃmɑ̃] *nm* : overlap
chevaucher [ʃəvoʃe] *vt* **1** : to straddle **2** : to overlap — *vi* : to overlap
chevelu, -lue [ʃəvly] *adj* : hairy
chevelure [ʃəvlyr] *nf* CHEVEUX : hair
chevet [ʃəvɛ] *nm* : bedside, head (of a bed) <rester au chevet de qqn : to stay at s.o.'s bedside>
cheveu [ʃəvø] *nm, pl* **cheveux 1** POIL : hair <être à un cheveu de : to be within a hair's breadth of> **2 cheveux** *nmpl* : hair, head of hair
cheville [ʃəvij] *nf* **1** : ankle **2** : pin, peg **3 cheville ouvrière** : kingpin
chèvre [ʃɛvr] *nf* : goat
chevreau [ʃəvro] *nm, pl* **chevreaux** : kid, young goat (male)
chèvrefeuille [ʃɛvrəfœj] *nm* : honeysuckle

chevrette [ʃəvrɛt] *nf* : kid, young goat (female)
chevreuil [ʃəvrœj] *nm* **1** : roe deer **2** : venison **3** *Can* : white-tailed deer
chevron [ʃəvrɔ̃] *nm* **1** : rafter **2** : chevron
chevronné, -née [ʃəvrɔne] *adj* : seasoned, experienced
chevrotement [ʃəvrɔtmɑ̃] *nm* : quavering
chevroter [ʃəvrɔte] *vi* : to quaver
chevrotine [ʃəvrɔtin] *nf* : buckshot
chewing-gum [ʃwiŋgɔm] *nm France* : chewing gum
chez [ʃe] *prep* **1** : at the home, business, or practice of <chez elle : at her house> <chez le dentiste : at the dentist's office> **2** : among, in <chez les Suisses : among the Swiss> <chez les Québécois : in Quebec> **3** : in the works of <chez Victor Hugo : in Victor Hugo's writing> **4** : in (a person) <le meilleur trait chez lui, c'est sa gentillesse : his best trait is his kindness>
chez-soi [ʃeswa] *nm* : place of one's own, home
chialer [ʃiale] *vi* **1** *fam* : to blubber, to snivel **2** *Can fam* : to whine, to complain
chic[1] [ʃik] *adj s & pl* **1** : chic, stylish **2** : nice
chic[2] *nm* **1** : stylishness, elegance **2** **avoir le chic pour** : to have a knack for
chicane [ʃikan] *nf* : bickering, squabble, quibble
chicaner [ʃikane] *vt* : to quibble with — *vi* : to bicker, to squabble <chicaner sur : to quibble over>
chiche [ʃiʃ] *adj* **1** AVARE : stingy, mean **2** : meager, scanty — **chichement** [ʃiʃmɑ̃] *adv*
chichi [ʃiʃi] *nm fam* **1** : affectation, airs **2** **faire des chichis** : to make a fuss
chicorée [ʃikɔre] *nf* **1** : endive **2** : chicory (for coffee)
chicoter [ʃikɔte] *vt Can fam* : to worry, to bother
chien[1], **chienne** [ʃiɛ̃, -ʃjɛn] *n* **1** : dog, bitch *f* **2** **chien d'arrêt** : bird dog, pointer, retriever **3** **chien de berger** : sheepdog **4** **chien de chasse** : retriever, hunting dog **5** **chien courant** : hound **6** **chien esquimau** : husky **7** **chien de garde** : watchdog **8** **chien de meute** : hound **9** **chien de prairie** : prairie dog
chien[2] *nm* : hammer (of a firearm)
chien-loup [ʃjɛ̃lu] *nm, pl* **chiens-loups** : German shepherd
chiffe [ʃif] *nf* : spineless person
chiffon [ʃifɔ̃] *nm* : rag, dustcloth
chiffonner [ʃifɔne] *vt* **1** : to crease, to crumple **2** : to bother
chiffre [ʃifr] *nm* **1** : numeral <chiffre romain : Roman numeral> **2** : amount, sum <chiffre d'affaires : turnover> **3** : cipher, code **4** : monogram
chiffrer [ʃifre] *vt* **1** : to number (pages, etc.) **2** : to calculate, to assess **3** : to encode **4** : to mark, to monogram — **se chiffrer** *vr* **~ à** : to amount to
chignon [ʃiɲɔ̃] *nm* : chignon, (hair) bun
chilien, -lienne [ʃiljɛ̃, -jɛn] *adj* : Chilean
Chilien, -lienne *n* : Chilean
chimère [ʃimɛr] *nf* **1** : Chimera (in mythology) **2** : illusion, pipe dream
chimérique [ʃimerik] *adj* : illusory, fanciful
chimie [ʃimi] *nf* : chemistry
chimique [ʃimik] *adj* : chemical — **chimiquement** [-mikmɑ̃] *adv*
chimiste [ʃimist] *nmf* : chemist
chimpanzé [ʃɛ̃pɑ̃ze] *nm* : chimpanzee
chinchilla [ʃɛ̃ʃila] *nm* : chinchilla
chine [ʃin] *nm* **1** : china, porcelain ware **2** : rice paper
chinois[1], **-noise** [ʃinwa, -nwaz] *adj* : Chinese
chinois[2] *nm* : Chinese (language)
Chinois, -noise *n* : Chinese
chinoiserie [ʃinwazri] *nf* **1** : chinoiserie, Chinese curio **2** **chinoiseries administratives** : red tape
chintz [ʃints] *nm* : chintz
chiot [ʃjo] *nm* : puppy
chiper [ʃipe] *vt fam* : to pinch, to swipe
chipie [ʃipi] *nf* : shrew, vixen
chipoter [ʃipɔte] *vi* **1** : to haggle, to quibble **2** : to pick at one's food
chips [ʃips] *nfpl* : potato chips
chiquenaude [ʃiknod] *nf* : flick (with the finger)
chiquer [ʃike] *vt* : to chew (tobacco) — *vi* : to chew tobacco
chiropraticien, -cienne [kirɔpratisjɛ̃, -sjɛn] *n* : chiropractor
chiropratique [kirɔpratik] *nf Can* : chiropractic
chiropraxie [kirɔpraksi] *or* **chiropractie** [kirɔprakti] *nf* : chiropractic
chirurgical, -cale [ʃiryrʒikal] *adj, mpl* **-caux** [-ko] : surgical
chirurgie [ʃiryrʒi] *nf* : surgery <chirurgie plastique *or* chirurgie esthétique : plastic surgery>
chirurgien, -gienne [ʃiryrʒjɛ̃, -ʒjɛn] *n* : surgeon
chirurgien-dentiste [ʃiryrʒjɛ̃dɑ̃tist] *nm, pl* **chirurgiens-dentistes** : oral surgeon
chlore [klɔr] *nm* : chlorine
chloroforme [klɔrɔfɔrm] *nm* : chloroform
chloroformer [klɔrɔfɔrme] *vt* : to chloroform
chlorophylle [klɔrɔfil] *nf* : chlorophyll
chlorure [klɔryr] *nm* : chloride
choc [ʃɔk] *nm* **1** : shock **2** : impact, crash **3** : clash (of opinions, etc.)
chocolat [ʃɔkɔla] *nm* : chocolate
chœur [kœr] *nm* **1** : choir **2** : chorus (song)

choir [ʃwar] {18} *vi* : to drop, to fall
choisi [ʃwazi] *adj* **1** : selected **2** : select, choice
choisir [ʃwazir] *vt* : to choose, to select
choix [ʃwa] *nm* **1** : choice, selection **2 de (premier) choix** : select, choice, first-rate
choléra [kɔlera] *nm* : cholera
cholestérol [kɔlɛsterɔl] *nm* : cholesterol
chômage [ʃomaʒ] *nm* : unemployment
chômer [ʃome] *vi* : to be unemployed, to be idle
chômeur, -meuse [ʃomœr, -møz] *n* : unemployed person
chope [ʃɔp] *nf* : (beer) mug, tankard
choquant, -quante [ʃɔkã, -kãt] *adj* : shocking
choquer [ʃɔke] *vt* **1** HEURTER : to knock, to bump **2** OFFUSQUER : to shock, to offend **3** : to shake up, to devastate **— se choquer** *vr* **1** : to be shocked **2** *Can* : to get angry
choral[1], **-rale** [kɔral] *adj, mpl* **chorals** or **choraux** [kɔro] : choral
choral[2] *nm, pl* **chorals** : chorale
chorale *nf* : choir
chorégraphe [kɔregraf] *nmf* : choreographer **— chorégraphique** [-grafik] *adj*
chorégraphie [kɔregrafi] *nf* : choreography **— chorégraphier** [-grafie] *vt*
choriste [kɔrist] *n* : choir member, chorus member
chose[1] [ʃoz] *adj fam* : peculiar, funny <se sentir tout chose : to feel out of sorts>
chose[2] *nf* **1** : thing <choses à faire : things to do> **2** : matter, affair <avant toute chose : above all, before all else>
chose[3] *nm fam* **1** : thingamajig **2** : what's-his-name, what's-her-name
chou[1] [ʃu] *adj fam* : sweet, nice, cute
chou[2], **choute** *n fam* : darling, dear
chou[3] *nm, pl* **choux 1** : cabbage **2 chou frisé** : kale
chouchou, -choute [ʃuʃu, -ʃut] *n fam* : pet, favorite <chouchou du prof : teacher's pet>
choucroute [ʃukrut] *nf* : sauerkraut
chouette[1] [ʃwɛt] *adj fam* : great, terrific, neat
chouette[2] *nf* **1** : owl **2** *fam* : goody, neat thing **3 ma chouette** *Can* : sweetheart, darling
chou–fleur [ʃuflœr] *nm, pl* **choux–fleurs** : cauliflower
chou–rave [ʃurav] *nm* : kohlrabi
chow–chow [ʃoʃo] *nm, pl* **chows–chows** : chow (dog)
choyer [ʃwaje] {58} *vt* : to pamper, to coddle
chrétien, -tienne [kretjẽ, -tjɛn] *adj & n* : Christian
chrétienté [kretjẽte] *nf* : Christendom
christianisme [kristjanism] *nm* : Christianity
chromatique [krɔmatik] *adj* : chromatic
chrome [krom] *nm* **1** : chromium **2 chromes** *nmpl* : chrome (of an automobile)
chromé, -mée [krome] *adj* : chrome-plated
chromosome [krɔmɔzom] *nm* : chromosome
chronique[1] [krɔnik] *adj* : chronic
chronique[2] *nf* **1** : chronicle **2** : column (in a newspaper), report (in radio or television)
chroniqueur, -queuse [krɔnikœr, -køz] *n* **1** : chronicler **2** : columnist, commentator
chronologie [krɔnɔlɔʒi] *nf* : chronology
chronologique [krɔnɔlɔʒik] *adj* : chronological **— chronologiquement** [-ʒikmã] *adv*
chronomètre [krɔnɔmetr] *nm* **1** : chronometer **2** : stopwatch
chronométrer [krɔnɔmetre] {87} *vt* : to time
chronométreur, -treuse [krɔnɔmetrœr, -trøz] *n* : timekeeper
chrysalide [krizalid] *nf* : chrysalis
chrysanthème [krizãtɛm] *nm* : chrysanthemum
chu [ʃy] *pp* → **choir**
chuchotement [ʃyʃɔtmã] *nm* : whisper, murmur
chuchoter [ʃyʃɔte] *v* : to whisper, to murmur
chuintement [ɥɛ̃tmã] *nm* : hiss
chuinter [ɥɛ̃te] *vi* **1** : to hoot **2** : to hiss
chum[1] [tʃɔm] *nmf Can fam* : friend, pal
chum[2] *nm Can fam* : boyfriend
chut [ʃyt] *interj* : sh!, hush!
chute [ʃyt] *nf* **1** : fall <faire une chute : to take a fall> <chute de cheveux : hair loss> <chute du jour : nightfall> <chute de neige : snowfall> <chute de pluie : rainfall> **2** *or* **chute d'eau** CASCADE : waterfall **3 chute des reins** : small of the back
chuter [ʃyte] *vi fam* **1** : to fall down **2** : to fail, to flop
chypriote [ʃipriɔt] *adj* : Cypriot
Chypriote *nmf* : Cypriot
ci[1] [si] *adv* **1** (*used with* **ce, cette, ces, celui, celle, ceux**) <ce livre-ci : this book> <ceux-ci : these ones> **2** : here <par-ci par-là : here and there>
ci[2] *pron* **1** : this <ci et ça : this and that> **2** → **comme**
ci–après [siapre] *adv* : below, hereafter, herein
ci–bas [siba] *adv* : below
cible [sibl] *nf* : target, mark
cibler [sible] *vt* : to target
ciboule [sibul] *nf* : scallion
ciboulette [sibulɛt] *nf* : chive
cicatrice [sikatris] *nf* : scar
cicatriser [sikatrize] *v* : to heal, to scar over **— se cicatriser** *vr* : to scar
ci–contre [sikɔ̃tr] *adv* : opposite

ci–dessous [sidəsu] *adv* : below <voir ci-dessous : see below>
ci–dessus [sidəsy] *adv* : above <voir ci-dessus : see above>
ci–devant [sidəvɑ̃] *adv* : formerly, previously
cidre [sidr] *nm* : cider
cidrerie [sidrəri] *nf* **1** : cider house **2** : cidermaking
ciel [sjɛl] *nm* **1** *pl* **ciels** : sky (in meteorology) **2** *pl* **cieux** [sjø] : sky <à ciel ouvert : open-air> **3** *pl* **cieux** : heaven **4 en plein ciel** : midair
cierge [sjɛrʒ] *nm* **1** : candle (in a church) **2 cierge magique** : sparkler
cigale [sigal] *nf* : cicada
cigare [sigar] *nm* : cigar
cigarette [sigaret] *nf* : cigarette
ci–gît [siʒi] *adv* : here lies
cigogne [sigɔɲ] *nf* : stork
ciguë [sigy] *nf* : hemlock (plant)
ci–inclus[1] [siɛ̃kly] *adv* : enclosed
ci–inclus[2], **-cluse** [siɛ̃kly, -klyz] *adj* : enclosed, included
ci–joint[1] [siʒwɛ̃] *adv* : enclosed, attached
ci–joint[2], **-jointe** [siʒwɛ̃, -ʒwɛ̃t] *adj* : enclosed, attached
cil [sil] *nm* : eyelash
ciller [sije] *vi* : to blink
cime [sim] *nf* SOMMET : summit, top, peak
ciment [simɑ̃] *nm* : cement
cimenter [simɑ̃te] *vt* : to cement
cimetière [simtjɛr] *nm* **1** : cemetery, graveyard **2** : churchyard
cinéaste [sineast] *nmf* : film director, filmmaker
cinéma [sinema] *nm* **1** : movie theater <aller au cinéma : to go to the movies> **2** : cinema, filmmaking
cinémathèque [sinematɛk] *nf* : film library
cinématographie [sinematɔgrafi] *nf* : cinematography
cinématographique [sinematɔgrafik] *adj* : film, movie, cinematic <œuvres cinématographiques : films, movies>
ciné–parc [sinepark] *nm Can, pl* **ciné–parcs** : drive-in theater
cinéphile [sinefil] *nmf* : movie buff
cinglant, -glante [sɛ̃glɑ̃, -glɑ̃t] *adj* : cutting, biting, scathing
cinglé, -glée [sɛ̃gle] *adj fam* : crazy, nuts
cingler [sɛ̃gle] *vt* : to whip, to lash — *vi* ~ **vers** : to head for
cinq[1] [sɛ̃k] *adj* **1** : five **2** : fifth <le cinq juin : the fifth of June>
cinq[2] *nms & pl* : five
cinquantaine [sɛ̃kɑ̃tɛn] *nf* **une cinquantaine de** : about fifty
cinquante [sɛ̃kɑ̃t] *adj & nms & pl* : fifty
cinquantenaire [sɛ̃kɑ̃tnɛr] *nm* : fiftieth anniversary
cinquantième [sɛ̃kɑ̃tjɛm] *adj & nmf & nm* : fiftieth
cinquième[1] [sɛ̃kjɛm] *adj & nmf* : fifth
cinquième[2] *nm* **1** : fifth floor **2** : fifth (in mathematics)
cintre [sɛ̃tr] *nm* **1** : curve, bend **2** : arch <arc en plein cintre : semicircular arch> **3** : coat hanger
cintré, -trée [sɛ̃tre] *adj* **1** : arched, vaulted **2** : fitted, tailored
cirage [siraʒ] *nm* **1** : waxing, polishing **2** : shoe polish **3 être dans le cirage** *fam* : to be in a daze
circoncire [sirkɔ̃sir] {86} *vt* : to circumcise
circoncision [sirkɔ̃sizjɔ̃] *nf* : circumcision
circonférence [sirkɔ̃ferɑ̃s] *nf* : circumference
circonflexe [sirkɔ̃flɛks] *adj* **accent circonflexe** : circumflex (accent)
circonlocution [sirkɔ̃lɔkysjɔ̃] *nf* : circumlocution
circonscription [sirkɔ̃skripsjɔ̃] *nf* : district, ward <circonscription électorale : electoral district>
circonscrire [sirkɔ̃skrir] {33} *vt* **1** DÉLIMITER : to define, to mark out **2** : to contain (a fire, etc.)
circonspect, -specte [sirkɔ̃spɛ, -spɛkt] *adj* : circumspect, cautious, wary
circonspection [sirkɔ̃spɛksjɔ̃] *nf* : circumspection, caution
circonstance [sirkɔ̃stɑ̃s] *nf* : circumstance <circonstances atténuantes : mitigating circumstances> <être de circonstance : to be fitting>
circonstancié, -ciée [sirkɔ̃stɑ̃sje] *adj* : detailed
circonstanciel, -cielle [sirkɔ̃stɑ̃sjɛl] *adj* **complément circonstanciel** : adverbial phrase
circonvenir [sirkɔ̃vnir] {92} *vt* : to circumvent
circuit [sirkɥi] *nm* **1** : circuit <circuit intégré : integrated circuit> **2** : tour, trip **3** *or* **coup de circuit** *Can* : home run (in baseball)
circulaire [sirkylɛr] *adj & nf* : circular
circulation [sirkylasjɔ̃] *nf* **1** : circulation **2** : traffic
circulatoire [sirkylatwar] *adj* : circulatory
circuler [sirkyle] *vi* **1** : to circulate (of air, blood, etc.) **2** : to move along, to get around **3** : to run (of buses, etc.) **4 faire circuler** : to circulate, to spread (rumors, etc.)
cire [sir] *nf* **1** : wax **2 cire d'abeille** : beeswax
ciré [sire] *nm* : oilskin
cirer [sire] *vt* : to wax, to polish
cireux, -reuse [sirø, -røz] *adj* **1** : waxen, pale **2** : waxy
cirque [sirk] *nm* **1** : circus **2** *fam* : disorder, shambles
cirrhose [siroz] *nf* : cirrhosis
cirrus [sirys] *nms & pl* : cirrus
cisailler [sizaje] *vt* **1** : to cut, to snip **2** : to prune
cisailles [sizaj] *nfpl* : shears

ciseau [sizo] *nm, pl* **ciseaux 1** : chisel **2 ciseaux** *nmpl* : scissors
ciseler [sizle] {20} *vt* : to engrave, to carve
ciselure [sizlyr] *nf* **1** : engraving **2** : carving
citadelle [sitadɛl] *nf* : citadel, stronghold
citadin, -dine [sitadɛ̃, -din] *n* : city dweller
citation [sitasjɔ̃] *nf* **1** : citation, quotation **2** : summons (to court), subpoena **3** : (military) citation
cité [site] *nf* **1** : city **2 cité universitaire** *France* : college dormitories *pl* **3 cité universitaire** *Can* : college campus
citer [site] *vt* **1** : to quote **2** : to cite, to mention **3** : to summon, to subpoena
citerne [sitɛrn] *nf* : cistern, tank, reservoir
cithare [sitar] *nf* : zither
citoyen, citoyenne [sitwajɛ̃, -jɛn] *n* : citizen
citoyenneté [sitwajente] *nf* : citizenship
citron[1] [sitrɔ̃] *adj* : lemon, lemon yellow
citron[2] *nm* **1** : lemon **2 citron vert** : lime
citronnade [sitrɔnad] *nf* : lemonade
citronné, -née [sitrɔne] *adj* : lemon-flavored, lemony
citronnier [sitrɔnje] *nm* : lemon tree
citrouille [sitruj] *nf* **1** : pumpkin **2** *fam* : head
cive [siv] *nf* : chive
civet [sive] *nm* : stew <civet de lapin : rabbit stew>
civière [sivjɛr] *nf* : stretcher
civil[1], **-vile** [sivil] *adj* **1** : civil <droit civil : civil law> **2** : civilian, secular **3** : polite, civil
civil[2], **-vile** *n* : civilian
civilement [sivilmɑ̃] *adv* **1** : civilly, politely **2 se marier civilement** : to have a civil marriage
civilisation [sivilizasjɔ̃] *nf* : civilization
civiliser [sivilize] *vt* : to civilize
civilité [sivilite] *nf* : civility
civique [sivik] *adj* **1** : civic **2 instruction civique** *or* **éducation civique** : civics
civisme [sivism] *nm* : good citizenship
clair[1] [klɛr] *adv* **1** : clearly <voir clair : to see clearly> **2 il fait clair** : it's light, it's getting light (outside)
clair[2], **claire** [klɛr] *adj* **1** : clear **2** : light, bright **3** : light-colored
clair[3] *nm* **1** : light <clair de lune : moonlight> **2** : light color **3 mettre au clair** : to make clear, to shed light on
clairement [klɛrmɑ̃] *adv* : clearly
claire–voie [klɛrvwa] *nf, pl* **claires–voies** : openwork fence <à claire-voie : openwork, open-worked>
clairière [klɛrjɛr] *nf* : clearing, glade
clair–obscur [kleropskyr] *nm, pl* **clairs–obscurs** : twilight
clairon [klɛrɔ̃] *nm* **1** : bugle **2** : bugler
clironnant [klɛrɔnɑ̃] *adj* : resonant, strident
clironner [klɛrɔne] *vt* : to trumpet, to broadcast (news, etc.)
clairsemé, -mée [klɛrsɔme] *adj* : scattered, sparse
clairvoyant, -voyante [klɛrvwajɑ̃, -jɑ̃t] *adj* : clairvoyant — **clairvoyance** [-vwajɑ̃s] *nf*
clamer [klame] *vt* : to shout out, to proclaim
clameur [klamœr] *nf* : clamor, outcry
clan [klɑ̃] *nm* : clan, clique
clandestin[1], **-tine** [klɑ̃dɛstɛ̃, -tin] *adj* **1** : clandestine, covert, underground **2 passager clandestin** : stowaway
clandestin[2], **-tine** *n* : illegal alien
clapoter [klapɔte] *vi* : to lap (of waves)
clapotis [klapɔti] *nm* : lapping (of the waves)
claque [klak] *nf* **1** : slap, smack **2 claques** *nfpl Can* : rubbers, galoshes
claqué, -quée [klake] *adj fam* : dog-tired, exhausted
claquement [klakmɑ̃] *nm* : slamming, slapping, snapping, flapping
claquemurer [klakmyre] *v* **se claquemurer** *vr* : to shut oneself away
claquer [klake] *vt* **1** GIFLER : to slap **2** : to slam **3** *fam* : to spend, to squander **4** *fam* : to exhaust **5** : to strain (a muscle) — *vi* **1** : to make a clicking sound <ses dents claquent : his teeth are chattering> <faire claquer ses doigts : to snap one's fingers> **2** : to slam, to bang **3** *fam* : to wear out, to conk out, to fall through
claquettes [klaket] *nfpl* : tap dancing
clarifier [klarifje] {96} *vt* : to clarify — **clarification** [-rifikasjɔ̃] *nf*
clarinette [klarinet] *nf* : clarinet — **clarinettiste** [-netist] *nf*
clarté [klarte] *nf* **1** : clearness **2** : clarity, lucidity **3** : brightness, light (of the moon, etc.)
classe [klas] *nf* **1** : class, category, rank <première classe : first class> <classe moyenne : middle class> **2** : class, classroom (in a school) <aller en classe : to go to school>
classement [klasmɑ̃] *nm* **1** : classification **2** : place, ranking
classer [klase] *vt* : to class, to classify, to rate — **se classer** *vr* : to be classified, to rank
classeur [klasœr] *nm* **1** : binder, loose-leaf file **2** : filing cabinet
classicisme [klasisism] *nm* : classicism
classification [klasifikasjɔ̃] *nf* : classification
classifier [klasifje] {96} *vt* : to classify
classique[1] [klasik] *adj* : classic, classical
classique[2] *nm* **1** : classic **2** : classical author **3** : classical art, music, etc.
claudication [klodikasjɔ̃] *nf* : lameness
clause [kloz] *nf* : clause

claustrophobe [klostrɔfɔb] *adj* : claustrophobic
claustrophobie [klostrɔfɔbi] *nf* : claustrophobia
clavecin [klavsɛ̃] *nm* : harpsichord
clavicule [klavikyl] *nf* : collarbone, clavicle
clavier [klavje] *nm* **1** : keyboard **2** : range, gamut
clé *or* **clef**[1] [kle] *adj* : key, important
clé *or* **clef**[2] *nf* **1** : key <clé de contact : ignition key> <sous clé : under lock and key> **2** : clue, means, solution <la clé du bonheur : the key to happiness> **3** : clef <clé de sol : treble clef> **4 clé à molette** : monkey wrench **5 clé de voûte** : keystone
clémence [klemɑ̃s] *nf* : clemency, leniency
clément, -mente [klemɑ̃, -mɑ̃t] *adj* **1** : lenient **2** : mild, clement
clémentine [klemɑ̃tin] *nf* : tangerine
clenche [klɑ̃ʃ] *nf* : latch
clencher [klɑ̃ʃe] *vt Can* : to latch
cleptomanie [kleptɔmani] *nf* → **kleptomanie**
clerc [klɛr] *nm* **1** : clerk **2** : cleric
clergé [klɛrʒe] *nm* : clergy
clérical, -cale [klerikal] *adj, mpl* **-caux** [-ko] : clerical
clic [klik] *nm* : click, clicking
cliché [kliʃe] *nm* **1** : negative (in photography) **2** : cliché
client, cliente [kliɑ̃, kliɑ̃t] *n* **1** : customer, client **2** : patient **3** : guest (in a hotel)
clientèle [kliɑ̃tɛl] *nf* **1** : clientele, customers *pl* **2** : practice (of a doctor)
cligner [kliɲe] *vi* **1** : to squint, to blink **2 cligner de l'œil** : to wink
clignotant *nm* [kliɲɔtɑ̃] : blinker, turn signal
clignoter [kliɲɔte] *vi* **1** : to flash, to twinkle, to flicker **2** : to blink
climat [klima] *nm* : climate
climatique [klimatik] *adj* : climatic
climatisation [klimatizasjɔ̃] *nf* : air-conditioning
climatisé, -sée [klimatize] *adj* : air-conditioned
climatiseur [klimatizœr] *nm* : air conditioner
clin [klɛ̃] *nm* **1 clin d'œil** : wink **2 en un clin d'œil** : in a flash
clinique[1] [klinik] *adj* : clinical — **cliniquement** [-nikmɑ̃] *adv*
clinique[2] *nf* : clinic, private hospital
clinquant[1], **-quante** [klɛ̃kɑ̃, -kɑ̃t] *adj* : flashy
clinquant[2] *nm* **1** : tinsel **2** : flashiness
clip [klip] *nm* **1** : (music) video **2** : brooch
clique [klik] *nf* **1** : clique **2** : (military) band **3 prendre ses cliques et ses claques** : to pack up and go
cliquer [klike] *vi* : to click (on a computer)
cliqueter [klikte] {8} *vi* : to clink, to clack, to rattle, to jingle
cliquetis [klikti] *nm* : clink, clack, rattle, jingle
clitoris [klitɔris] *nm* : clitoris
clivage [klivaʒ] *nm* **1** : cleaving, split **2** : cleavage
cloaque [klɔak] *nm* : cesspool
clochard, -charde [klɔʃar, -ʃard] *n* : tramp, hobo
cloche [klɔʃ] *nf* **1** : bell **2** *fam* : dope, idiot
cloche–pied [klɔʃpje] **sauter à cloche–pied** : to hop
clocher[1] [klɔʃe] *vi fam* : to go wrong
clocher[2] *nm* **1** : belfry, bell tower **2 de ~** : parochial, small-town
clochette [klɔʃet] *nf* : small bell
cloison [klwazɔ̃] *nf* **1** : partition, divider <mur de cloison : dividing wall> **2** : bulkhead **3** : septum
cloisonner [klwazɔne] *vt* : to partition (off)
cloître [klwatr] *nm* : cloister — **cloîtrer** [klwatre] *vt*
clone [klon] *nm* : clone
cloner [klone] *vt* : to clone
clopin–clopant [klɔpɛ̃klɔpɑ̃] *adv* **aller clopin–clopant** *fam* : to hobble along
clopiner [klɔpine] *vi* : to hobble (along)
cloquer [klɔke] *vi* : to blister
clore [klɔr] {19} *vt* : to close, to conclude
clos[1], **close** [klo, -kloz] *adj* **1** : closed, shut **2** : concluded
clos[2] *nm* **1** : enclosure, enclosed field **2** *or* **clos de vigne** : vineyard
clôture [klotyr] *nf* **1** BARRIÈRE : enclosure, fence **2** : closure
clôturer [klotyre] *vt* **1** : to enclose **2** : to bring to a close
clou [klu] *nm, pl* **clous 1** : nail **2** : feature, attraction **3** FURONCLE : boil **4 clou de girofle** : clove **5 clous** *nmpl France fam* : crosswalk **6 au clou** *fam* : in hock **7 cogner des clous** *Can* : to nod off
clouer [klue] *vt* **1** : to nail **2** : to pin down <être cloué au lit : to be bedridden> **3 clouer le bec à qqn** *fam* : to shut s.o. up
clouté, -tée [klute] *adj* **1** : studded **2 passage clouté** *France* : crosswalk
clown [klun] *nm* : clown <faire le clown : to clown around, to play the fool>
club [klœb] *nm* : club
coaguler [kɔagyle] *vt* : to coagulate — **se coaguler** *vr* : to coagulate, to clot — **coagulation** [-gylasjɔ̃] *nf*
coaliser [kɔalize] *v* **se coaliser** *vr* : to unite, to form a coalition
coalition [kɔalisjɔ̃] *nf* : coalition
coassement [kɔasmɑ̃] *nm* : croaking
coasser [kɔase] *vi* : to croak
cobalt [kɔbalt] *nm* **1** : cobalt **2 bleu de cobalt** : cobalt blue
cobaye [kɔbaj] *nm* : guinea pig
cobra [kɔbra] *nm* : cobra

cocagne [kɔkaɲ] *nf* **pays de cocagne** : land of plenty
cocaïne [kɔkain] *nf* : cocaine
cocarde [kɔkard] *nf* : rosette
cocasse [kɔkas] *adj* : comical
coccinelle [kɔksinɛl] *nf* : ladybug
coche [kɔʃ] *nf* **1** : notch, mark **2 être à côté de la coche** *Can* : to be wrong, to be mistaken
cocher[1] [kɔʃe] *vt* **1** ENTAILLER : to notch **2** POINTER : to check (off)
cocher[2] *nm* : coachman
cochon[1], **-chonne** [kɔʃɔ̃, -ʃɔn] *adj fam* **1** : smutty, indecent **2** : dirty, messy
cochon[2], **-chonne** *n fam* : slob, dirty pig
cochon[3] *nm* **1** : pig **2 cochon d'Inde** : guinea pig **3 cochon de mer** : porpoise
cochonnerie [kɔʃɔnri] *nf* **1** : junk, trash **2** : filthiness, mess **3** : smut **4** : dirty trick
cockpit [kɔkpit] *nm* : cockpit
cocktail [kɔktɛl] *nm* : cocktail
coco [kɔko] *nm or* **noix de coco** : coconut
cocon [kɔkɔ̃] *nm* : cocoon
cocotier [kɔkɔtje] *nm* : coconut palm
cocotte [kɔkɔt] *nf* **1** : casserole dish **2** *Can* : pinecone **3** *fam* : chicken (in baby talk) **4 ma cocotte** *fam* : my sweetie
code [kɔd] *nm* : code <code à barres : bar code> <code postal : zip code> <code d'honneur : code of honor>
codéine [kɔdein] *nf* : codeine
coder [kɔde] *vt* : to code, to encode
codicille [kɔdisil] *nm* : codicil
codifier [kɔdifje] {96} *vt* : to codify
coefficient [kɔefisjã] *nm* : coefficient <coefficient d'erreur : margin of error>
coéquipier, -pière [kɔekipje, -jɛr] *n* : teammate
coercitif, -tive [kɔɛrsitif, -tiv] *adj* : coercive
coercition [kɔɛrsisjɔ̃] *nf* : coercion
cœur [kœr] *nm* **1** : heart <maladie de cœur : heart disease> **2** : stomach <mal au cœur : upset stomach, nausea> **3** : spirit, courage <de bon cœur : with good spirits, willingly> **4** : heart, feelings *pl*, mind <avoir bon cœur : to be kindhearted> <à cœur joie : to one's heart's content> <apprendre par cœur : to learn by heart> **5** : center, middle <au cœur de la nuit : in the dead of night> <le cœur de l'été : the height of summer> **6** : core (of a fruit) **7** : hearts *pl* (in playing cards)
coexister [kɔɛgziste] *vi* : to coexist — **coexistence** [-zistãs] *nf*
coffre [kɔfr] *nm* **1** : chest, bin <coffre à jouets : toy chest> **2** : safe, strongbox **3** : trunk (of a car)
coffre–fort [kɔfrəfɔr] *nm, pl* **coffres–forts** : safe
coffrer [kɔfre] *vi Can* : to warp (of wood)
coffret [kɔfrɛ] *nm* : small box, case <coffret à bijoux : jewelry box>
cogiter [kɔʒite] *vi* RÉFLÉCHIR : to cogitate, to reflect
cognac [kɔɲak] *nm* : cognac
cogner [kɔɲe] *vt* : to knock, to bang — *vi* **cogner contre** : to bump against — **se cogner** *vr* : to bump oneself <se cogner la tête : to hit one's head>
cohabiter [kɔabite] *vi* : to live together
cohérent, -rente [kɔerã, -rãt] *adj* : coherent — **cohérence** [-erãs] *nf*
cohésion [kɔezjɔ̃] *nf* : cohesion, cohesiveness
cohorte [kɔɔrt] *nf fam* : band, troop
cohue [kɔy] *nf* **1** FOULE : crowd **2** BOUSCULADE : crush
coi, coite [kwa, kwat] *adj* SILENCIEUX : silent, speechless <se tenir coi : to keep quiet>
coiffe [kwaf] *nf* : headdress
coiffer [kwafe] *vt* **1** : to top, to cover **2** : to head **3 coiffer qqn** : to do s.o's hair — **se coiffer** *vr* : to do one's hair
coiffeur, -feuse [kwafœr, -føz] *n* : hairdresser, barber
coiffeuse [kwaføz] *nf* : vanity, dressing table
coiffure [kwafyr] *nf* **1** : hat, headdress **2** : hairdo **3** : hairdressing
coin [kwɛ̃] *nm* **1** : corner <au coin du feu : by the fireside> <regard en coin : sidelong glance> **2** : place, spot <un coin de ciel : a patch of sky> **3** : wedge
coincé, -cée [kwɛ̃se] *adj fam* : repressed, uptight
coincer [kwɛ̃se] {6} *vt* **1** : to wedge, to jam **2** : to catch (out), to get someone stuck — *vi* : to jam, to get stuck — **se coincer** *vr*
coïncidence [kɔɛ̃sidãs] *nf* : coincidence
coïncider [kɔɛ̃side] *vi* : to coincide, to tally
coin–coin [kwɛ̃kwɛ̃] *nm* : quack
coing [kwɛ̃] *nm* : quince
coït [kɔit] *nm* : coitus
coke [kɔk] *nm* : coke
col [kɔl] *nm* **1** : collar <col roulé : turtleneck> **2** : neck (of bottle) **3** : mountain pass, gap **4** *or* **col de l'utérus** : cervix
coléoptère [kɔleɔptɛr] *nm* : beetle
colère [kɔlɛr] *nf* **1** : anger **2 en ~** : angry <se mettre en colère : to get angry>
coléreux, -reuse [kɔlerø, -røz] *adj* : bad-tempered, irritable
colérique [kɔlerik] → **coléreux**
colibri [kɔlibri] *nm* : hummingbird
colifichet [kɔlifiʃɛ] *nm* : trinket
colimaçon [kɔlimasɔ̃] *nm* **1** : snail **2 en ~** : spiral
colin [kɔlɛ] *nm* : hake (for cooking)
colique [kɔlik] *nf* **1** : diarrhea **2** *or* **coliques** *nfpl* : colic, stomachache **3** *fam* : hassle, pain in the neck

colis [kɔli] *nm* PAQUET : parcel, package <colis postal : parcel post>
collaborateur, -trice [kɔlabɔratœr, -tris] *n* **1** COLLÈGUE : colleague, coworker **2** : contributor **3** : collaborator
collaborer [kɔlabɔre] *vi* : to collaborate — **collaboration** [-bɔrasjɔ̃] *nf*
collage [kɔlaʒ] *nm* : collage
collant[1], **-lante** [kɔlɑ̃, -lɑ̃t] *adj* **1** : sticky, tacky **2** : tight-fitting
collant[2] *nm* **1** : panty hose *pl* **2** *or* **collants** *mpl* : leotard, leggings *pl*, tights *pl* **3** *Can* : sticker
collation [kɔlasjɔ̃] *nf* : snack
collationner [kɔlasjɔne] *vt* : to collate
colle [kɔl] *nf* **1** : paste, glue **2 poser une colle** *fam* : to ask a trick question (on an exam)
collecte [kɔlɛkt] *nf* : collection
collecter [kɔlɛkte] *vt* : to collect
collecteur[1], **-trice** [kɔlɛktœr, -tris] *n* : collector
collecteur[2] *nm* **1** : main sewer **2** : manifold (of an automobile)
collectif, -tive [kɔlɛktif, -tiv] *adj* : collective, joint — **collectivement** [-tivmɑ̃] *adv*
collection [kɔlɛksjɔ̃] *nf* : collection
collectionner [kɔlɛksjɔne] *vt* : to collect <collectionner les timbres : to collect stamps>
collectionneur, -neuse [kɔlɛksjɔnœr, -nøz] *n* : collector
collectivité [kɔlɛktivite] *nf* : community
collège [kɔlɛʒ] *nm* **1** *France* : junior high school **2** *Can* : junior college, vocational college **3** : college <collège électoral : electoral college>
collégial, -giale [kɔleʒjal] *adj, mpl* **-giaux** [-ʒjo] : collegiate
collégien, -gienne [kɔleʒjɛ̃, -ʒjɛn] *n* **1** *France* : schoolboy *m*, schoolgirl *f* **2** *Can* CÉGÉPIEN : junior-college student
collègue [kɔlɛg] *nmf* : colleague
coller [kɔle] *vt* **1** : to stick, to glue **2** APPUYER : to press <coller son visage contre la fenêtre : to press one's face against the window> — *vi* **1** : to adhere, to cling **2** ~ **à** : to stick close to — **se coller** *vr* ~ **à** : to press oneself (up) against
collet [kɔlɛ] *nm* **1** : snare, noose **2** : collar, neck <être collet monté : to be prim, to be straight-laced>
colleter [kɔlte] {8} *vt* : to collar — **se colleter** *vr* ~ **avec** : to fight with, to grapple with
colley [kɔle] *nm* : collie
collier [kɔlje] *nm* **1** : necklace **2** : collar (of an animal, a machine, etc.) **3** *or* **collier de barbe** : short close beard
collimateur [kɔlimatœr] *nm* **avoir qqn dans le collimateur** : to have s.o. in one's sights
colline [kɔlin] *nf* : hill
collision [kɔlizjɔ̃] *nf* : collision <entrer en collision avec : to collide with>
colloque [kɔlɔk] *nm* : colloquium, symposium
collusion [kɔlyzjɔ̃] *nf* : collusion
collyre [kɔlir] *nm* : eye drops *pl*
colmater [kɔlmate] *vt* : to fill in, to seal up, to plug
colombe [kɔlɔ̃b] *nf* : dove
colombien, -bienne [kɔlɔ̃bjɛ̃, -bjɛn] *adj* : Colombian
Colombien, -bienne *n* : Colombian
colon [kɔlɔ̃] *nm* : colonist, settler
côlon [kolɔ̃] *nm* : colon
colonel [kɔlɔnɛl] *nm* : colonel
colonial[1], **-niale** [kɔlɔnjal] *adj, mpl* **-niaux** [-njo] : colonial — **colonialisme** [-njalism] *nm*
colonial[2], **-niale** *n, mpl* **-niaux** [-njo] : colonial (person)
colonie [kɔlɔni] *nf* : colony
colonisateur, -trice [kɔlɔnizatœr, -tris] *n* : colonist, settler
colonisation [kɔlɔnizasjɔ̃] *nf* : colonization
coloniser [kɔlɔnize] *vt* : to colonize, to settle
colonnade [kɔlɔnad] *nf* : colonnade
colonne [kɔlɔn] *nf* **1** : column <en colonne par quatre : four abreast> **2** : pillar, column (in architecture) **3** **colonne vertébrale** : spinal column, backbone
colophane [kɔlɔfan] *nf* : rosin
colorant[1], **-rante** [kɔlɔrɑ̃, -rɑ̃t] *adj* : coloring
colorant[2] *nm* : dye, stain
coloration [kɔlɔrasjɔ̃] *nf* : coloring
coloré, -rée [kɔlɔre] *adj* **1** : colored **2** : colorful, lively
colorer [kɔlɔre] *vt* : to color, to tint — **se colorer** *vr* : to flush, to blush
colorier [kɔlɔrje] {96} *vt* : to color
coloris [kɔlɔri] *nm* **1** : color, shade **2** : colors *pl*, color scheme
colossal, -sale [kɔlɔsal] *adj, mpl* **-saux** [-so] ÉNORME : colossal, enormous
colosse [kɔlɔs] *nm* GÉANT : colossus, giant
colporter [kɔlpɔrte] *vt* : to hawk, to peddle
colporteur, -teuse [kɔlpɔrtœr, -tøz] *n* : peddler
coltiner [kɔltine] *vt* : to carry, to lug — **se coltiner** *vr* **1** : to lug around **2** : to get stuck with
colvert [kɔlvɛr] *nm* : mallard (duck)
colza [kɔlza] *nm* : rapeseed, rape (plant)
coma [kɔma] *nm* : coma
comateux, -teuse [kɔmatø, -tøz] *adj* : comatose
combat [kɔ̃ba] *nm* **1** : combat, fighting <combat de boxe : boxing match> **2** : conflict, struggle
combatif, -tive [kɔ̃batif, -tiv] *adj* : combative, aggressive

combattant, -tante [kɔ̃batɑ̃, -tɑ̃t] *n* : combatant, fighter
combattre [kɔ̃batr] {12} *v* : to fight
combien [kɔ̃bjɛ̃] *adv* **1** : how much, how many <combien coûte cela : how much does that cost?> <combien sont-ils? : how many (of them) are there?> **2 ~ de** : how much, how many <combien de temps : how long> <combien de livres : how many books>
combinaison [kɔ̃binɛzɔ̃] *nf* **1** : combination **2** : (full-length) slip **3** : suit, overalls <combinaison spatiale : space suit> **4** : plan, scheme
combine [kɔ̃bin] *nf fam* : scheme, trick
combiné [kɔ̃bine] *nm* : (telephone) receiver
combiner [kɔ̃bine] *vt* **1** : to combine **2** : to contrive, to work out (a plan, etc.) **— se combiner** *vr* : to combine
comble[1] [kɔ̃bl] *adj* : packed, filled up
comble[2] *nm* **1** : extreme point <le comble de la joie : the height of joy> <c'est le comble! : that takes the cake!> **2 combles** *nmpl* : attic **3 de fond en comble** : from top to bottom
combler [kɔ̃ble] *vt* **1** : to fill in, to fill up **2** : to fulfill, to satisfy
combustible[1] [kɔ̃bystibl] *adj* : combustible, inflammable
combustible[2] *nm* : fuel
combustion [kɔ̃bystjɔ̃] *nf* : combustion
comédie [kɔmedi] *nf* **1** : comedy <comédie musicale : musical> **2** : playacting, pretense
comédien, -dienne [kɔmedjɛ̃, -djɛn] *n* **1** ACTEUR : actor *m*, actress *f* **2** : comedian **3** HYPOCRITE : sham
comestible [kɔmɛstibl] *adj* : edible
comestibles *nmpl* : food
comète [kɔmɛt] *nf* : comet
comique[1] [kɔmik] *adj* **1** : comic **2** : comical, funny
comique[2] *nmf* : comedian, comic
comique[3] *nm* **1** : comedy **2** : funny thing, funny part
comité [kɔmite] *nm* : committee
commandant [kɔmɑ̃dɑ̃] *nm* **1** : commandant, commander **2** : major (in the army) **3 commandant de bord** : captain (in the navy or air force)
commande [kɔmɑ̃d] *nf* **1** : order <passer une commande : to place an order> **2 commande à distance** : remote control **3 fait sur commande** : made-to-order
commandement [kɔmɑ̃dmɑ̃] *nm* **1** ORDRE : command, order **2** AUTORITÉ : authority, control **3** : commandment (in religion)
commander [kɔmɑ̃de] *vt* **1** : to command **2** : to commission, to order (a meal, etc.) **— *vi*** : to be in command
commanditaire [kɔmɑ̃ditɛr] *nm* : sponsor, backer
commandite [kɔmɑ̃dit] *nf* : limited partnership
commanditer [kɔmɑ̃dite] *vt* : to finance, to back
commando [kɔmɑ̃do] *nm* : commando
comme[1] [kɔm] *adv* **1** : how <comme c'est beau! : how beautiful it is!> **2 comme de bonne** *Can* : naturally, as one might expect **3 comme du monde** *Can fam* : properly
comme[2] *conj* **1** : as, like <faites comme moi : do as I do> <blanc comme la neige : white as snow> **2** : since <comme elle se sentait malade, elle est partie : since she felt ill, she left> **3** : when, as <comme il disait au revoir, elle pleurait : as he said goodbye, she cried> **4 comme ci, comme ça** : so-so **5 comme il faut** : properly **6 comme si** : as if, as though
comme[3] *prep* **1** : like <un visage comme un masque : a face like a mask> **2** : as, in the capacity of <il travaille comme rédacteur : he works as an editor>
commémoration [kɔmemɔrasjɔ̃] *nf* : commemoration
commémorer [kɔmemɔre] *vt* : to commemorate **— commémoratif, -tive** [-mɔratif, -tiv] *adj*
commencement [kɔmɑ̃smɑ̃] *nm* **1** : beginning, start **2 au commencement** : in the beginning, at first
commencer [kɔmɑ̃se] {6} *v* : to begin, to start
comment[1] [kɔmɑ̃] *adv* **1** : how <comment ça va? : how is it going?> <je me demande comment elle va en finir : I wonder how she'll end up> **2** : what <comment! tu n'as pas d'argent? : what! you have no money?> **3** : sorry, who, what <Anne comment? : Anne who?> **4 comment donc** : of course, by all means
comment[2] *nm inv* **1 le comment** : the how **2 → pourquoi**
commentaire [kɔmɑ̃tɛr] *nm* **1** REMARQUE : comment, remark **2** : commentary
commentateur, -trice [kɔmɑ̃tatœr, -tris] *n* : commentator
commenter [kɔmɑ̃te] *vt* : to comment on
commérage [kɔmeraʒ] *nm fam* : gossip
commerçant[1], **-çante** [kɔmɛrsɑ̃, -sɑ̃t] *adj* : commercial, shopping
commerçant[2], **-çante** *n* : merchant, storekeeper
commerce [kɔmɛrs] *nm* : business, commerce, trade <faire du commerce : to be in business> <commerce en gros : wholesale trade>
commercer [kɔmɛrse] {6} *vi* : to trade, to deal
commercial [kɔmɛrsjal] *adj, mpl* **-ciaux** [-sjo] : commercial **— commercialement** [-sjalmɑ̃] *adv*
commercialisation [kɔmɛrsjalizasjɔ̃] *nf* : marketing

commercialiser [kɔmɛrsjalize] *vt* : to market
commère [kɔmɛr] *nf fam* : gossip (person)
commettre [kɔmɛtr] {53} *vt* **1** : to commit (a crime, etc.), to make (an error) **2** : to appoint, to nominate
commis [kɔmi] *nm* **1** : clerk **2 commis voyageur** : traveling salesman
commisération [kɔmizerasjɔ̃] *nf* : commiseration
commissaire [kɔmiser] *nm* : superintendent, commissioner
commissaire–priseur [kɔmiserprizœr] *nm, pl* **commissaires–priseurs** : auctioneer
commissariat [kɔmisarja] *nm* **commissariat de police** : police station
commission [kɔmisjɔ̃] *nf* **1** : commission, committee **2** : commission, percentage **3** MESSAGE : message **4** COURSE : errand **5 commissions** *nfpl* : shopping
commissionnaire [kɔmisjɔnɛr] *nm* **1** : agent, broker **2** : messenger
commissionner [kɔmisjɔne] *vt* : to commission
commode[1] [kɔmɔd] *adj* **1** : convenient, handy, useful **2** FACILE : easy <ce n'est pas commode! : it's not easy!> **3** AIMABLE : easy to get along with
commode[2] *nf* : chest of drawers
commodément [kɔmɔdemɑ̃] *adv* : comfortably, conveniently
commodité [kɔmɔdite] *nf* : comfort, convenience
commotion [kɔmɔsjɔ̃] *nf* **1** : shock **2 commotion cérébrale** : concussion
commuer [kɔmɥe] *vt* : to commute, to reduce (a legal penalty)
commun[1], **-mune** [kɔmœ̃, -myn] *adj* **1** : common, joint **2** : mutual, shared **3** : usual, ordinary
commun[2] *nm* **1** : ordinary (one), average person or thing <le commun des lecteurs : the average reader> <hors du commun : out of the ordinary> **2 en ~** : in common, jointly
communautaire [kɔmynotɛr] *adj* : community, communal
communauté [kɔmynote] *nf* **1** : community **2** : commune
commune [kɔmyn] *nf* **1** : village, town **2** *Can* : rural area used in common
communément [kɔmynemɑ̃] *adv* : commonly, generally
communicable [kɔmynikabl] *adj* : communicable
communicatif, -tive [kɔmynikatif, -tiv] *adj* **1** : communicative, talkative **2** CONTAGIEUX : contagious, infectious
communication [kɔmynikasjɔ̃] *nf* **1** : communication, report **2** : communication(s), communicating <la communication de masse : mass media> **3 communication téléphonique** : telephone call
communier [kɔmynje] {96} *vi* **1** : to receive Communion **2 ~ avec** : to commune with
communion [kɔmynjɔ̃] *nf* **1** : Communion **2 être en communion avec** : to be in communion with, to be of the same mind as
communiqué [kɔmynike] *nm* : communiqué, press release
communiquer [kɔmynike] *vt* : to communicate, to pass on, to transmit — *vi* **~ avec** : to communicate with
communisme [kɔmynism] *nm* : communism, Communism
communiste [kɔmynist] *adj & nmf* : communist, Communist
commutateur [kɔmytatœr] *nm* : switch
commutation [kɔmytasjɔ̃] *nf* **1** : commutation (in law) **2** : switching
compact[1], **-pacte** [kɔ̃pakt] *adj* : compact, dense
compact[2] *nm* : compact disc
compacte *nf* : compact (car)
compacter [kɔ̃pakte] *vt* : to compact
compagne [kɔ̃paɲ] *nf* : (female) companion, partner
compagnie [kɔ̃paɲi] *nf* **1** : company, companionship <tenir compagnie à qqn : to keep s.o. company> **2** : company, firm <compagnie d'assurances : insurance company> **3** : company (in the military, in theater) **4 en compagnie de** : with, accompanied by
compagnon [kɔ̃paɲɔ̃] *nm* **1** CAMARADE : companion, comrade **2** : journeyman, apprentice
comparable [kɔ̃parabl] *adj* : comparable
comparaison [kɔ̃parezɔ̃] *nf* **1** : comparison **2** : simile
comparaître [kɔ̃paretr] {7} *vi* : to appear (before a court)
comparatif[1], **-tive** [kɔ̃paratif, -tiv] *adj* : comparative — **comparativement** [-tivmɑ̃] *adv*
comparatif[2] *nm* : comparative (case)
comparer [kɔ̃pare] *vt* : to compare
comparse [kɔ̃pars] *nmf* **1** : sidekick **2** FIGURANT : extra, bit player
compartiment [kɔ̃partimɑ̃] *nm* : compartment
compartimenter [kɔ̃partimɑ̃te] *vt* **1** : to partition **2** : to compartmentalize
comparution [kɔ̃parysjɔ̃] *nf* : appearance (in court)
compas [kɔ̃pa] *nms & pl* : compass
compassion [kɔ̃pasjɔ̃] *nf* : compassion
compatibilité [kɔ̃patibilite] *nf* : compatibility
compatible [kɔ̃patibl] *adj* : compatible
compatir [kɔ̃patir] *vi* **~ à** : to sympathize with
compatissant, -sante [kɔ̃patisɑ̃, -sɑ̃t] *adj* : compassionate, sympathetic
compatriote [kɔ̃patrijɔt] *nmf* : compatriot, fellow countryman, fellow countrywoman *f*

compensateur, -trice [kɔ̃pɑ̃satœr, -tris] *adj* : compensatory
compensation [kɔ̃pɑ̃sasjɔ̃] *nf* : compensation
compensatoire [kɔ̃pɑ̃satwar] *adj* : compensatory
compenser [kɔ̃pɑ̃se] *vt* : to compensate for, to make up for
compère [kɔ̃pɛr] *nm* : accomplice
compétent, -tente [kɔ̃petɑ̃, -tɑ̃t] *adj* : competent — **compétence** [-petɑ̃s] *nf*
compétiteur, -trice [kɔ̃petitœr, -tris] *n* : competitor, rival
compétitif, -tive [kɔ̃petitif, -tiv] *adj* : competitive
compétition [kɔ̃petisjɔ̃] *nf* **1** RIVALITÉ : rivalry **2** CONCOURS : competition, competitive event
compétitivité [kɔ̃petitivite] *nf* : competitiveness
compilateur, -trice [kɔ̃pilatœr] *n* : compiler
compilation [kɔ̃pilasjɔ̃] *nf* : compilation
compiler [kɔ̃pile] *vt* : to compile
complainte [kɔ̃plɛ̃t] *nf* : lament
complaire [kɔ̃plɛr] {66} *vi* **~ à** : to please — **se complaire** *vr* **1 ~ dans** : to delight in (something) **2 ~ à faire** : to delight in doing
complaisance [kɔ̃plɛzɑ̃s] *nf* **1** : obligingness, kindness **2** : complacency **3** : indulgence, leniency
complaisant, -sante [kɔ̃plɛzɑ̃, -zɑ̃t] *adj* **1** : obliging, kind **2** : complacent, smug **3** : indulgent — **complaisamment** [-zamɑ̃] *adv*
complément [kɔ̃plemɑ̃] *nm* : complement
complémentaire [kɔ̃plemɑ̃tɛr] *adj* **1** : complementary **2** ADDITIONNEL : supplementary
complet¹, -plète [kɔ̃plɛ, -plɛt] *adj* **1** : complete **2** PLEIN : full (of a hotel, theater, etc.)
complet² *nm* : suit
complètement [kɔ̃plɛtmɑ̃] *adv* **1** : completely, totally **2** : fully, thoroughly
compléter [kɔ̃plete] {87} *vt* **1** : to complete **2** : to complement, to supplement — **se compléter** *vr* : to complement one another
complexe [kɔ̃pleks] *adj & nm* : complex
complexé, -plexée [kɔ̃plɛkse] *adj* : full of complexes, neurotic
complexité [kɔ̃pleksite] *nf* : complexity, intricacy
complication [kɔ̃plikasjɔ̃] *nf* : complication
complice¹ [kɔ̃plis] *adj* **1** : knowing (of a look, etc.) **2** : accessory
complice² *nmf* : accomplice
complicité [kɔ̃plisite] *nf* : complicity
compliment [kɔ̃plimɑ̃] *nm* **1** : compliment **2 compliments** *nmpl* FÉLICITATIONS : compliments, congratulations
complimenter [kɔ̃plimɑ̃te] *vt* : to compliment, to congratulate
compliqué, -quée [kɔ̃plike] *adj* : complicated, complex
compliquer [kɔ̃plike] *vt* : to complicate — **se compliquer** *vr*
complot [kɔ̃plo] *nm* MACHINATION : plot, conspiracy
comploter [kɔ̃plɔte] *v* : to plot, to conspire
comploteur, -teuse [kɔ̃plɔtœr, -tøz] *n* : plotter, schemer
comportement [kɔ̃pɔrtəmɑ̃] *nm* **1** : behavior, conduct **2** : performance
comporter [kɔ̃pɔrte] *vt* **1** : to include **2** : to comprise, to consist of **3** : to entail (risks, etc.) — **se comporter** *vr* : to behave, to perform
composant¹, -sante [kɔ̃pozɑ̃, -zɑ̃t] *adj* : component, constituent
composant² *nm* ÉLÉMENT : component, constituent
composante *nf* : (mathematical) component, constituent
composé¹, -sée [kɔ̃poze] *adj* : compound
composé² *nm* : compound
composer [kɔ̃poze] *vt* **1** : to compose (music, writings, etc.) **2** : to constitute, to make up **3** : to dial (a number) **4** : to typeset — *vi* : to compromise — **se composer** *vr* : to be made up of
composite¹ [kɔ̃pozit] *adj* **1** : composite **2** : varied, heterogeneous
composite² *nm* : composite
compositeur, -trice [kɔ̃pozitœr, -tris] *n* **1** : composer **2** : typesetter
composition [kɔ̃pozisjɔ̃] *nf* **1** : composition **2** : typesetting **3 de bonne composition** : good-natured, accommodating
compost [kɔ̃pɔst] *nm* : compost
composter [kɔ̃pɔste] *vt* **1** : to compost **2** : to stamp, to validate (a ticket, etc.)
compote [kɔ̃pɔt] *nf* **1** : stewed fruit **2 compote de pommes** : apple sauce
compréhensible [kɔ̃preɑ̃sibl] *adj* : comprehensible
compréhensif, -sive [kɔ̃preɑ̃sif, -siv] *adj* **1** : comprehensive **2** : understanding
compréhension [kɔ̃preɑ̃sjɔ̃] *nf* : understanding
comprenait [kɔ̃prənɛ], *etc.* → **comprendre**
comprendre [kɔ̃prɑ̃dr] {70} *vt* **1** : to comprise, to consist of **2** : to include **3** : to understand <mal comprendre : to misunderstand> — **se comprendre** *vr* **1** : to understand each other **2** : to be understandable
comprenne [kɔ̃prɛn], *etc.* → **comprendre**
compresse [kɔ̃prɛs] *nf* : compress

compresseur [kɔ̃prɛsœr] *nm* : compressor
compression [kɔ̃prɛsjɔ̃] *nf* **1** : compression **2** : reduction
comprimé¹ [kɔ̃prime] *adj* : compressed <air comprimé : compressed air>
comprimé² *nm* : tablet, pill
comprimer [kɔ̃prime] *vt* **1** : to compress **2** : to reduce, to cut **3** : to repress
compris¹ [kɔ̃pri] *pp* → **comprendre**
compris², -prise [kɔ̃pri, -priz] *adj* **1** : understood **2** INCLUS : included <tout compris : inclusive, in total> <y compris : including>
compromettant, -tante [kɔ̃prɔmetɑ̃, -tɑ̃t] *adj* : compromising, incriminating
compromettre [kɔ̃prɔmetr] {53} *vt* **1** : to compromise, to implicate, to involve **2** : to endanger — **se compromettre** *vr* : to compromise oneself
compromis [kɔ̃prɔmi] *nm* : compromise
compromission [kɔ̃prɔmisjɔ̃] *nf* : compromising, (shady) deal
comptabiliser [kɔ̃tabilize] *vt* **1** : to count **2** : to enter into the books
comptabilité [kɔ̃tabilite] *nf* : accounting, bookkeeping
comptable¹ [kɔ̃tabl] *adj* **1** : accounting **2** : accountable
comptable² *nmf* : accountant, bookkeeper
comptant [kɔ̃tɑ̃] *adv & adj* **1** : cash <payer comptant : to pay cash> <500 francs comptant : 500 francs cash> **2 au comptant** : in cash, for cash
compte [kɔ̃t] *nm* **1** : account <compte bancaire : bank account> **2 à bon compte** : cheap, cheaply **3 au bout du compte** : when all is said and done **4 compte à rebours** : countdown **5 compte rendu** : report, review **6 en fin de compte** : all things considered **7 se rendre compte de** : to notice, to realize **8 tenir compte de** : to take into account, to allow for <sans tenir compte de : irrespective of>
compte–gouttes [kɔ̃tgut] *nms & pl* : dropper
compter [kɔ̃te] *vt* **1** : to count **2** : to allow (for) **3** INCLURE : to include, to count **4** : to have **5** : to charge (for) **6** : to intend **7** : to expect — *vi* **1** : to count **2** : to matter **3 à compter de** : as from, as of **4 compter sur** : to count on
compte–rendu [kɔ̃trɑ̃dy] *nm, pl* **comptes–rendus** → **compte**
compteur¹ [kɔ̃tœr] *nm* **1** : meter **2 compteur de vitesse** : speedometer **3 compteur Geiger** : Geiger counter
compteur², -teuse [kɔ̃tœr, -tøz] *n Can* : scorer
comptoir [kɔ̃twar] *nm* **1** : counter, bar **2** : trading post **3** SUCCURSALE : branch (of a bank)
compulsion [kɔ̃pylsjɔ̃] *nf* : compulsion — **compulsif, -sive** [-pylsif, -siv] *adj*
comte, -tesse [kɔ̃t, -tɛs] *n* : count *m*, countess *f*
comté [kɔ̃te] *nm* : county
con¹, conne [kɔ̃, kɔn] *adj, usu vulgar* : stupid, idiotic
con², conne *n, usu vulgar* : stupid idiot, fool
concasser [kɔ̃kase] *vt* : to crush, to grind
concave [kɔ̃kav] *adj* : concave
concéder [kɔ̃sede] {87} *vt* : to concede, to grant
concentration [kɔ̃sɑ̃trasjɔ̃] *nf* : concentration
concentré¹, -trée [kɔ̃sɑ̃tre] *adj* **1** : concentrated, condensed **2** ATTENTIF : concentrating
concentré² *nm* : concentrate <concentré de tomate : tomato paste>
concentrer [kɔ̃sɑ̃tre] *vt* : to concentrate — **se concentrer** *vr*
concentrique [kɔ̃sɑ̃trik] *adj* : concentric
concept [kɔ̃sɛpt] *nm* : concept
concepteur, -trice [kɔ̃sɛptœr, -tris] *n* : designer
conception [kɔ̃sɛpsjɔ̃] *nf* : conception
concernant [kɔ̃sɛrnɑ̃] *prep* : concerning, regarding
concerner [kɔ̃sɛrne] *vt* : to concern, to affect <en ce qui me concerne : as far as I'm concerned>
concert [kɔ̃ser] *nm* **1** : concert **2 de ~** : together, jointly, in unison
concertation [kɔ̃sertasjɔ̃] *nf* : dialogue, consultation
concerté, -tée [kɔ̃serte] *adj* : concerted
concerter [kɔ̃serte] *vt* : to devise, to plan (out) — **se concerter** *vr* : to consult (each other)
concerto [kɔ̃serto] *nm* : concerto
concession [kɔ̃sesjɔ̃] *nf* **1** COMPROMIS : concession, compromise **2** : dealership **3** : plot (in a cemetery)
concessionnaire [kɔ̃sesjɔner] *nmf* : dealer, agent
concevoir [kɔ̃səvwar] {26} *vt* **1** : to conceive (a child) **2** : to conceive of, to design, to imagine **3** : to understand — **se concevoir** *vr* **1** : to be imagined **2** : to be understandable
concierge [kɔ̃sjerʒ] *nmf* : concierge, superintendent
conciliant, -liante [kɔ̃siljɑ̃, -ljɑ̃t] *adj* : conciliatory
conciliateur, -trice [kɔ̃siljatœr, -tris] *adj* : conciliatory (of a person)
conciliation [kɔ̃siljasjɔ̃] *nf* **1** : conciliation **2** : reconciliation
concilier [kɔ̃silje] {96} *vt* : to reconcile — **se concilier** *vr* : to gain, to win (over)
concis, -cise [kɔ̃si, -siz] *adj* : concise
conclave [kɔ̃klav] *nm* : conclave
concluant, -cluante [kɔ̃klyɑ̃, -klyɑ̃t] *adj* : conclusive

conclure [kɔ̃klyr] {39} *vt* **1** : to conclude, to decide **2** : to conclude, to end **3** : to finish up, to settle <conclure un marché : to clinch a deal>
conclusion [kɔ̃klyzjɔ̃] *nf* : conclusion
concocter [kɔ̃kɔkte] *vt* : to concoct
conçoit [kɔ̃swa], **conçoive** [kɔ̃swav], *etc.* → **concevoir**
concombre [kɔ̃kɔ̃br] *nm* : cucumber
concomitant, -tante [kɔ̃kɔmitɑ̃, -tɑ̃t] *adj* : concomitant
concordance [kɔ̃kɔrdɑ̃s] *nf* **1** : similarity, agreement **2** : index, concordance
concordant, -dante [kɔ̃kɔrdɑ̃, -dɑ̃t] *adj* : conforming, corresponding
concorde [kɔ̃kɔrd] *nf* : concord, harmony
concorder [kɔ̃kɔrde] *vi* : to agree, to tally
concourir [kɔ̃kurir] {23} *vi* **1** : to compete **2** ~ **à** : to work toward
concours [kɔ̃kur] *nm* **1** COMPÉTITION : competition, contest **2** AIDE : assistance, aid **3 concours de circonstances** : combination of circumstances
concret, -crète [kɔ̃krɛ, -krɛt] *adj* : concrete
concrètement [kɔ̃krɛtmɑ̃] *adv* : in concrete terms
concrétiser [kɔ̃kretize] *vt* : to put in concrete form, to realize
conçu [kɔ̃sy] *pp* → **concevoir**
concubin, -bine [kɔ̃kybɛ̃, -bin] *n* : common-law spouse, partner
concupiscent, -cente [kɔ̃kypisɑ̃, -sɑ̃t] *adj* : lustful
concurremment [kɔ̃kyramɑ̃] *adv* : jointly, concurrently
concurrence [kɔ̃kyrɑ̃s] *nf* **1** RIVALITÉ : competition, rivalry <concurrence déloyale : unfair competition> <faire concurrence à : to compete with> **2 jusqu'à concurrence de** : up to, not exceeding
concurrencer [kɔ̃kyrɑ̃se] {6} *vt* : to rival, to compete with
concurrent[1], **-rente** [kɔ̃kyrɑ̃, -rɑ̃t] *adj* : competing, rival
concurrent[2], **-rente** *n* : competitor
concurrentiel, -tielle [kɔ̃kyrɑ̃sjɛl] *adj* : competitive
condamnable [kɔ̃danabl] *adj* RÉPRÉHENSIBLE : reprehensible
condamnation [kɔ̃danasjɔ̃] *nf* **1** : condemnation **2** PEINE : conviction, sentence
condamné, -née [kɔ̃dane] *n* : convict
condamner [kɔ̃dane] *vt* **1** : to condemn **2** : to sentence <condamner qqn à une amende : to fine s.o.> **3** : to block up, to seal off
condensation [kɔ̃dɑ̃sasjɔ̃] *nf* : condensation
condensé [kɔ̃dɑ̃se] *nm* : digest, summary
condenser [kɔ̃dɑ̃se] *vt* : to condense — **se condenser** *vr*
condescendance [kɔ̃desɑ̃dɑ̃s] *nf* : condescension
condescendant, -dante [kɔ̃desɑ̃dɑ̃, -dɑ̃t] *adj* : condescending
condescendre [kɔ̃desɑ̃dr] {63} *vi* ~ **à** : to condescend to
condiment [kɔ̃dimɑ̃] *nm* : condiment, seasoning
condisciple [kɔ̃disipl] *nmf* : schoolmate, fellow student
condition [kɔ̃disjɔ̃] *nf* **1** : condition, stipulation <sans conditions : unconditionally> <sous condition que : on the condition that> **2** FORME : condition, shape <se mettre en condition : to get in shape> **3** : social status, background, walk of life **4 conditions** *nfpl* : conditions, circumstances <conditions de vie : living conditions>
conditionné, -née [kɔ̃disjɔne] *adj* **1** : conditioned **2** : packaged <conditionné sous vide : vacuum-packed>
conditionnel, -nelle [kɔ̃disjɔnɛl] *adj* : conditional — **conditionnellement** [-nɛlmɑ̃] *adv*
conditionner [kɔ̃disjɔne] *vt* **1** : to condition **2** : to determine, to govern **3** EMBALLER : to package
condoléances [kɔ̃dɔleɑ̃s] *nfpl* : condolences
condom [kɔ̃dɔm] *nm* PRÉSERVATIF : condom
condominium [kɔ̃dɔminjɔm] *nm* : condominium
conducteur[1], **-trice** [kɔ̃dyktœr, -tris] *n* **1** : driver **2** : operator (of a machine, etc.)
conducteur[2] *nm* : conductor (of electricity)
conduction [kɔ̃dyksjɔ̃] *nf* : conduction
conductivité [kɔ̃dyktivite] *nf* : conductivity
conduire [kɔ̃duir] {49} *vt* **1** : to drive **2** MENER : to lead **3** DIRIGER : to run, to manage — **se conduire** *vr* : to behave
conduisait [kɔ̃duize], **conduisions** [kɔ̃duizjɔ̃], *etc.* → **conduire**
conduise [kɔ̃duiz], *etc.* → **conduire**
conduit [kɔ̃dui] *nm* **1** : conduit, duct <conduit de fumée : flue> **2** : canal (in anatomy)
conduite [kɔ̃duit] *nf* **1** : conduct, behavior **2** : conducting, leading **3** : driving <conduite à droite : right-hand drive> **4** : pipe <conduite d'eau : water main>
cône [kon] *nm* : cone
confection [kɔ̃feksjɔ̃] *nf* **1** ÉLABORATION : making, preparation **2 la confection** : the clothing industry
confectionner [kɔ̃fɛksjɔne] *vt* : to make, to prepare
confédération [kɔ̃federasjɔ̃] *nf* : confederation, confederacy

confédérer [kɔ̃federe] {87} *vt* : to confederate — **se confédérer** *vr*
conférence [kɔ̃ferɑ̃s] *nf* **1** : conference <conférence de presse : press conference> **2** : lecture
conférencier, -cière [kɔ̃ferɑ̃sje, -sjɛr] *n* : lecturer
conférer [kɔ̃fere] {87} *v* : to confer
confesser [kɔ̃fese] *vt* : to confess
confession [kɔ̃fesjɔ̃] *nf* **1** : confession **2** : faith, denomination
confessionnal [kɔ̃fesjɔnal] *nm, pl* **-naux** [-no] : confessional
confessionnel, -nelle [kɔ̃fesjɔnɛl] *adj* : denominational
confetti [kɔ̃feti] *nm* : (piece of) confetti <des confettis : confetti>
confiance [kɔ̃fjɑ̃s] *nf* **1** : confidence, trust, faith <avoir confiance en : to have confidence in> <faire confiance à : to trust> **2 confiance en soi** : self-confidence **3 de confiance** : trustworthy, reliable
confiant, -fiante [kɔ̃nfjɑ̃, -fjɑ̃t] *adj* **1** : confident **2** : trusting, trustful **3** ASSURÉ : self-confident
confidence [kɔ̃fidɑ̃s] *nf* : confidence, secret <être dans la confidence : to be in the know> <faire des confidences à qqn : to confide in s.o.>
confident, -dente [kɔ̃fidɑ̃, -dɑ̃t] *n* : confidant, confidante *f*
confidentiel, -tielle [kɔ̃fidɑ̃sjɛl] *adj* SECRET : confidential, secret — **confidentiellement** [-sjɛlmɑ̃] *adv*
confier [kɔ̃fje] {96} *vt* **1 confier (qqch) à qqn** : to entrust (sth) to s.o. **2 confier à qqn** : to confide to s.o. — **se confier** *vr* **se confier à qqn** : to confide in s.o.
configuration [kɔ̃figyrasjɔ̃] *nf* : configuration
configurer [kɔ̃figyre] *vt* : to configure
confiner [kɔ̃fine] *vt* **1** : to confine **2 confiner qqn à** : to restrict s.o. to — *vi* **~ à** : to border on — **se confiner** *vr* **1** : to shut oneself away **2 ~ à** *or* **dans** : to confine oneself to
confins [kɔ̃fɛ̃] *nmpl* : borders, confines
confire [kɔ̃fir] {86} *vt* : to preserve, to candy, to pickle
confirmation [kɔ̃firmasjɔ̃] *nf* : confirmation
confirmer [kɔ̃firme] *vt* : to confirm
confiscation [kɔ̃fiskasjɔ̃] *nf* : confiscation, seizure
confiserie [kɔ̃fizri] *nf* **1** : candy store **2** : candy, confection
confisquer [kɔ̃fiske] *vt* : to confiscate
confit, -fite [kɔ̃fi, -fit] *adj* : candied, crystallized
confiture [kɔ̃fityr] *nf* : jam, preserves
conflagration [kɔ̃flagrasjɔ̃] *nf* : conflagration
conflictuel, -tuelle [kɔ̃fliktɥɛl] *adj* : conflicting
conflit [kɔ̃fli] *nm* : conflict, struggle
confluence [kɔ̃flyɑ̃s] *nf* : confluence, convergence
confluer [kɔ̃flye] *vi* : to meet, to converge
confondre [kɔ̃fɔ̃dr] {63} *vt* **1** : to confuse **2** MÉLANGER : to merge, to intermingle **3** ÉTONNER : to astound **4** DÉMASQUER : to expose — **se confondre** *vr* **1** : to merge **2 se confondre en excuses** : to apologize profusely
conforme [kɔ̃fɔrm] *adj* **1 ~ à** : corresponding to, in keeping with **2 ~ à** : true to <une copie conforme à l'original : an exact copy>
conformé, -mée [kɔ̃fɔrme] *adj* : formed, shaped <bien conformé : well-formed> <mal conformé : misshapen>
conformément [kɔ̃fɔrmemɑ̃] *adv* **~ à** : in accordance with, in compliance with
conformer [kɔ̃fɔrme] *vt* : to conform, to shape — **se conformer** *vr* **~ à** : to conform to
conformiste [kɔ̃fɔrmist] *nmf* : conformist
conformité [kɔ̃fɔrmite] *nf* **1** : conformity, conventionality **2** RESSEMBLANCE : similarity
confort [kɔ̃fɔr] *nm* **1** : comfort **2 tout confort** : with all (modern) conveniences
confortable [kɔ̃fɔrtabl] *adj* : comfortable — **confortablement** [-tabləmɑ̃] *adv*
conforter [kɔ̃fɔrte] *vt* : to strengthen, to reinforce
confrère [kɔ̃frɛr] *nm* : colleague
confrérie [kɔ̃freri] *nf* : brotherhood, association
confrontation [kɔ̃frɔ̃tasjɔ̃] *nf* **1** : confrontation **2** : comparison
confronter [kɔ̃frɔ̃te] *vt* **1** : to confront **2** : to compare
confus [kɔ̃fy] *adj* **1** : confused **2** : embarrassed <je suis vraiment confus : I'm truly sorry>
confusément [kɔ̃fyzemɑ̃] *adv* **1** : indistinctly, vaguely **2** : confusedly
confusion [kɔ̃fyzjɔ̃] *nf* **1** DÉSORDRE : confusion, disarray **2** GÊNE : embarrassment **3** MÉPRISE: confusion, mix-up
congé [kɔ̃ʒe] *nm* **1** VACANCES : vacation **2** : leave <congé de maladie : sick leave> **3** : notice <donner son congé à : give (one's) notice to> **4 prendre congé de** : to take leave of
congédier [kɔ̃ʒedje] {96} *vt* : to dismiss, to give notice to
congélateur [kɔ̃ʒelatœr] *nm* : freezer
congeler [kɔ̃ʒle] {20} *vt* : to freeze — **se congeler** *vr*
congénère [kɔ̃ʒenɛr] *nmf* : fellow creature
congénital, -tale [kɔ̃ʒenital] *adj, mpl* **-taux** [-to] : congenital

congère [kɔ̃ʒɛr] *nf France* : snowdrift, snowbank
congestion [kɔ̃ʒɛstjɔ̃] *nf* : congestion
congestionner [kɔ̃ʒɛstjɔne] *vt* **1** : to congest **2** : to make (one's face) flushed **— se congestionner** *vr* : to flush
conglomérat [kɔ̃glɔmera] *nm* : conglomerate, conglomeration
conglomeré, -rée [kɔ̃glɔmere] *adj* : conglomerate
congolais, -laise [kɔ̃gɔlɛ, -lɛz] *adj* : Congolese
Congolais, -laise *n* : Congolese
congratuler [kɔ̃gratyle] *vt* : to congratulate
congrès [kɔ̃grɛ] *nm* CONFÉRENCE : congress, conference, convention
congru, -grue [kɔ̃gry] *adj* : congruent (in mathematics)
conifère[1] [kɔnifɛr] *adj* : coniferous
conifère[2] *nm* : conifer
conique [kɔnik] *adj* : conic, conical
conjecture [kɔ̃ʒɛktyr] *nf* SUPPOSITION : conjecture, guess
conjecturer [kɔ̃ʒɛktyre] *vt* PRÉSUMER : to conjecture, to presume
conjoint[1], **-jointe** [kɔ̃ʒwɛ̃, -ʒwɛ̃t] *adj* : joint, conjoint **— conjointement** [-ʒwɛ̃tmɑ̃] *adv*
conjoint[2], **-jointe** *n* ÉPOUX : spouse
conjonctif, -tive [kɔ̃ʒɔ̃ktif, -tiv] *adj* **1** : conjunctive **2** → **tissu**
conjonction [kɔ̃ʒɔ̃ksjɔ̃] *nf* : conjunction
conjonctivite [kɔ̃jɔ̃ktivit] *nf or* **conjonctivite aiguë contagieuse** : pinkeye
conjoncture [kɔ̃jɔ̃ktyr] *nf* : circumstances *pl*, situation
conjugaison [kɔ̃ʒygɛzɔ̃] *nf* **1** : conjugation **2** : combination, uniting
conjugal, -gale [kɔ̃ʒygal] *adj, mpl* **-gaux** [-go] : conjugal, marital
conjuguer [kɔ̃ʒyge] *vt* **1** : to conjugate (a verb) **2** COMBINER, UNIR : to combine, to unite **— se conjuguer** *vr*
conjuration [kɔ̃ʒyrasjɔ̃] *nf* COMPLOT : conspiracy
conjuré, -rée [kɔ̃ʒyre] *n* : conspirator
conjurer [kɔ̃ʒyre] *vt* **1** : to avert, to ward off **2** IMPLORER : to beseech, to implore **— se conjurer** *vr* : to conspire
connaissable [kɔnɛsabl] *adj* : knowable
connaissait [kɔnɛsɛ], *etc.* → **connaître**
connaissance [kɔnɛsɑ̃s] *nf* **1** : knowledge, understanding <à ma connaissance : to the best of my knowledge> <connaissance anticipée : foreknowledge> **2** : acquaintance <faire connaissance avec qqn : to meet s.o.> **3** CONSCIENCE : consciousness <avoir connaissance de : to be aware of> **4 connaissances** *nfpl* : knowledge, learning
connaisse [kɔnɛs], *etc.* → **connaître**
connaisseur[1], **-seuse** [kɔnɛsœr, -søz] *adj* : knowledgeable, expert
connaisseur[2], **-seuse** *n* : connoisseur, expert
connaître [kɔnɛtr] {7} *vt* **1** : to know <il faut connaître la vérité : we need to know the truth> <faire connaître : to make known> **2** : to be acquainted with, to know <je connais bien cette ville : I know this city well> **3** : to experience (sensation, emotion), to enjoy (success), to have (problems) **— se connaître** *vr* **1** : to know each other **2** : to know oneself **3 s'y connaître en** : to know about, to be an expert in
connecter [kɔnɛkte] *vt* : to connect
connerie [kɔnri] *nf fam* : blunder, stupid remark
connexe [kɔnɛks] *adj* : connected, related
connivence [kɔnivɑ̃s] *nf* COMPLICITÉ : connivance, complicity
connu[1] [kɔny] *pp* → **connaître**
connu[2], **-nue** [kɔny] *adj* : well-known
conque [kɔ̃k] *nf* : conch
conquérant, -rante [kɔ̃kerɑ̃, -rɑ̃t] *n* : conqueror
conquérir [kɔ̃kerir] {21} *vt* **1** : to conquer, to capture **2** : to win, to win over
conquête [kɔ̃kɛt] *nf* : conquest
conquière [kɔ̃kjɛr], **conquiert** [kɔ̃kjɛr], *etc.* → **conquérir**
conquis [kɔ̃ki] *pp* → **conquérir**
consacrer [kɔ̃sakre] *vt* **1** : to consecrate **2** : to sanction **3** ~ **à** : to devote to **— se consacrer** *vr* ~ **à** : to dedicate oneself to
consciemment [kɔ̃sjamɑ̃] *adv* : consciously
conscience [kɔ̃sjɑ̃s] *nf* **1** : conscience **2** : consciousness, awareness <avoir conscience de : to become aware of>
consciencieux, -cieuse [kɔ̃sjɑ̃sjø, -sjøz] *adj* : conscientious **— consciencieusement** [-sjøzmɑ̃] *adv*
conscient, -ciente [kɔ̃sjɑ̃, -sjɑ̃t] *adj* : conscious, aware
conscrit [kɔ̃skri] *nm* : conscript, draftee
consécration [kɔ̃sekrasjɔ̃] *nf* **1** : sanctioning, recognition **2** : consecration (in religion)
consécutif, -tive [kɔ̃sekytif, -tiv] *adj* : consecutive **— consécutivement** [-tivmɑ̃] *adv*
conseil [kɔ̃sɛj] *nm* **1** : counsel, (piece of) advice <donner un conseil à qqn : to give s.o. advice> <des conseils : advice> **2** : council <conseil d'administration : board of directors>
conseiller[1] [kɔ̃seje] *vt* **1** : to counsel, to give advice to **2** : to recommend, to advise
conseiller[2], **-lère** [kɔ̃seje, -jɛr] *n* **1** : counselor, advisor **2** : councillor
consensus [kɔ̃sɛ̃sys] *nm* : consensus

consentant, -tante [kɔ̃sɑ̃tɑ̃, -tɑ̃t] *adj* : consenting, willing
consentement [kɔ̃sɑ̃tmɑ̃] *nm* : consent
consentir [kɔ̃sɑ̃tir] {82} *vi* : to consent, to agree — *vt* : to grant
conséquence [kɔ̃sekɑ̃s] *nf* **1** : consequence, outcome **2 agir en conséquence** : to act accordingly
conséquent[1], **-quente** [kɔ̃sekɑ̃, -kɑ̃t] *adj* **1** : consistent, logical **2** *fam* : substantial, important
conséquent[2] *nm* **par ~** : consequently, therefore
conservateur[1], **-trice** [kɔ̃servatœr, -tris] *adj* : conservative
conservateur[2], **-trice** *n* **1** : conservative **2** : curator
conservation [kɔ̃servasjɔ̃] *nf* PRÉSERVATION : preservation, conservation
conservatisme [kɔ̃servatism] *nm* : conservatism
conservatoire [kɔ̃servatwar] *nm* : academy, conservatory
conserve [kɔ̃serv] *nf* **1** : canned food <en conserve : canned> **2 de ~** : in concert, together
conserver [kɔ̃serve] *vt* **1** GARDER : to keep **2** : to preserve, to conserve (food) — **se conserver** *vr* : to keep, to store
conserverie [kɔ̃servəri] *nf* : cannery
considérable [kɔ̃siderabl] *adj* : considerable — **considérablement** [-rablemɑ̃] *adv*
considération [kɔ̃siderasjɔ̃] *nf* **1** : consideration <en considération de : because of, in view of> **2** : respect, consideration
considérer [kɔ̃sidere] {87} *vt* **1** : to consider <tout bien considéré : all things considered> **2** : to think highly of, to regard
consigne [kɔ̃siɲ] *nf* **1** : instructions *pl*, orders *pl* **2** : checkroom **3** : deposit
consigner [kɔ̃siɲe] *vt* **1** : to record, to write down **2** : to check (luggage, etc.) **3** : to deposit
consistance [kɔ̃sistɑ̃s] *nf* **1** : consistency <prendre consistance : to thicken> **2** : substance, strength <sans consistance : unfounded, groundless>
consistant, -tante [kɔ̃sistɑ̃, -tɑ̃t] *adj* **1** : thick (of sauce, paint, etc.) **2** : substantial, nourishing **3** : solid, well-founded (of an argument, etc.)
consister [kɔ̃siste] *vi* **1 ~ dans** *or* **~ à** : to lie in, to consist in <le bonheur consiste dans la modération : happiness lies in moderation> <son devoir consiste à partir : it is her duty to leave> **2 ~ en** : to be composed of, to consist of
consolation [kɔ̃sɔlasjɔ̃] *nf* : consolation
console [kɔ̃sɔl] *nf* : console
consoler [kɔ̃sɔle] *vt* : to console, to comfort, to soothe — **se consoler** *vr*
consolidation [kɔ̃sɔlidasjɔ̃] *nf* : consolidation
consolider [kɔ̃sɔlide] *vt* : to consolidate, to strengthen — **se consolider** *vr* : to grow stronger
consommateur, -trice [kɔ̃sɔmatœr, -tris] *n* **1** : consumer **2** : customer (in a café, etc.)
consommation [kɔ̃sɔmasjɔ̃] *nf* **1** : consumption **2** BOISSON : drink **3** : consummation (of a marriage) **4** PERPÉTRATION : perpetration (of a crime)
consommé[1], **-mée** [kɔ̃sɔme] *adj* : consummate
consommé[2] *nm* : consommé, clear soup
consommer [kɔ̃sɔme] *vt* **1** : to consume **2** : to consummate — *vi* : to have a drink
consonance [kɔ̃sɔnɑ̃s] *nf* : consonance (in music or poetry)
consonne [kɔ̃sɔn] *nf* : consonant
corsortium [kɔ̃sɔrsjɔm] *nm* : consortium, syndicate
conspirateur, -trice [kɔ̃spiratœr, -tris] *n* : conspirator, plotter
conspiration [kɔ̃spirasjɔ̃] *nf* : conspiracy
conspirer [kɔ̃spire] *vi* : to conspire, to plot
constant, -tante [kɔ̃stɑ̃, -tɑ̃t] *adj* **1** : constant, unchanging **2** : continual **3** : firm, steadfast — **constamment** [kɔ̃stamɑ̃] *adv*
constante [kɔ̃stɑ̃t] *nf* : constant
constat [kɔ̃sta] *nm* **1** : affidavit, official report **2** : acknowledgment
constatation [kɔ̃statasjɔ̃] *nf* OBSERVATION : observation, noticing
constater [kɔ̃state] *v* **1** : to notice, to observe **2** : to certify, to state
constellation [kɔ̃stelasjɔ̃] *nf* : constellation
consternation [kɔ̃sternasjɔ̃] *nf* : consternation, dismay
consterner [kɔ̃sterne] *vt* : to dismay, to distress
constiper [kɔ̃stipe] *vt* : to constipate — **constipation** [-stipasjɔ̃] *nf*
constituant, -tuante [kɔ̃stituɑ̃, -tɥɑ̃t] *adj* : constituent
constituer [kɔ̃stitɥe] *vt* **1** : to constitute, to make up, to impanel (a jury) **2** : to set up, to form **3** : to settle (in law)
constitutif, -tive [kɔ̃stitytif, -tiv] *adj* : constituent
constitution [kɔ̃stitysjɔ̃] *nf* **1** : establishment, setting up **2** : constitution (in politics or physiology) **3** : composition, makeup
constitutionnel, -nelle [kɔ̃stitysjɔnɛl] *adj* : constitutional
constructeur, -trice [kɔ̃stryktœr, -tris] *n* **1** : builder **2** : manufacturer (of automobiles, etc.)
constructif, -tive [kɔ̃stryktif, -tiv] *adj* : constructive
construction [kɔ̃stryksjɔ̃] *nf* : building, construction

construire [kɔ̃strɥir] {49} *vt* : to construct, to build — **se construire** *vr Can* : to build <il se construit à Québec : he's building in Quebec>
consul [kɔ̃syl] *nm* : consul
consulat [kɔ̃syla] *nm* : consulate
consultant, -tante [kɔ̃syltɑ̃, -tɑ̃t] *n* : consultant
consultatif, -tive [kɔ̃syltatif, -tiv] *adj* : advisory
consultation [kɔ̃syltasjɔ̃] *nf* **1** : consulting, checking **2** : consultation (with an expert, a doctor, etc.) <heures de consultation : office hours> <aller à la consultation : to go to the doctor's> <entrer en consultation avec : to consult with> **3 consultation électorale** : election, voting
consulter [kɔ̃sylte] *vt* **1** : to consult, to seek advice from **2** : to refer to — *vi France* : to see patients — **se consulter** *vr* : to confer
consumer [kɔ̃syme] *vt* **1** : to consume **2** : to burn, to destroy — **se consumer** *vr* **1** : to burn (up, out) **2** : to waste away
contact [kɔ̃takt] *nm* **1** : contact, touch <rester en contact : to keep in touch> **2** : electrical contact, switch <couper le contact : to switch off the ignition> **3** : contact, connection (person)
contacter [kɔ̃takte] *vt* : to contact <j'ai contacté ma sœur : I got in touch with my sister>
contagion [kɔ̃taʒjɔ̃] *nf* : contagion — **contagieux, -gieuse** [-taʒjœ, -ʒjøz] *adj*
contaminer [kɔ̃tamine] *vt* **1** POLLUER : to contaminate, to pollute **2** INFECTER : to infect — **contamination** [-minasjɔ̃] *nf*
conte [kɔ̃t] *nm* **1** HISTOIRE : tale, story **2 conte de fées** : fairy tale
contempler [kɔ̃tɑ̃ple] *vt* **1** : to contemplate, to gaze at **2** : to reflect upon — **contemplation** [-tɑ̃plasjɔ̃] *nf*
contemporain, -raine [kɔ̃tɑ̃pɔʀɛ̃, -ʀɛn] *adj & n* : contemporary
contenance [kɔ̃tnɑ̃s] *nf* **1** CAPACITÉ : capacity (of a container) **2** AIR : bearing, attitude <perdre contenance : to lose (one's) composure>
contenant [kɔ̃tnɑ̃] *nm* RÉCIPIENT : container
contenir [kɔ̃tnir] {92} *vt* **1** : to contain, to hold **2** : to restrain — **se contenir** *vr* : to control oneself
content, -tente [kɔ̃tɑ̃, -tɑ̃t] *adj* HEUREUX : content, pleased, happy
contentable [kɔ̃tɑ̃tabl] *adj* **il n'est pas contentable** *Can* : he can't be satisfied
contentement [kɔ̃tɑ̃tmɑ̃] *nm* SATISFACTION : contentment, satisfaction
contenter [kɔ̃tɑ̃te] *vt* SATISFAIRE : to satisfy, to please — **se contenter** *vr* **~ de** : to be contented with
contentieux[1], **-tieuse** [kɔ̃tɑ̃sjø, -sjøz] *adj* : contentious
contentieux[2] *nm* **1** : dispute **2** : legal department **3** : litigation
contenu [kɔ̃tny] *nm* : contents *pl*
conter [kɔ̃te] *vt* **1** RELATER : to tell, to relate **2 s'en laisser conter** : to be fooled, to be taken in
contestable [kɔ̃tɛstabl] *adj* : contestable, debatable
contestation [kɔ̃tɛstasjɔ̃] *nf* **1** : challenging, questioning **2** DISPUTE : dispute **3** : (political) protest
contester [kɔ̃tɛste] *vt* : to contest, to dispute — *vi* : to protest
conteur, -teuse [kɔ̃tœr, -tøz] *n* : storyteller, narrator
contexte [kɔ̃tɛkst] *nm* : context
contigu, -guë [kɔ̃tigy] *adj* : adjacent
continence [kɔ̃tinɑ̃s] *nf* : self-restraint, continence — **continent, -nente** [-tinɑ̃, -nɑ̃t] *adj*
continent [kɔ̃tinɑ̃] *nm* **1** : continent **2 le continent** : the mainland — **continental, -tale** [-nɑ̃tal] *adj, mpl* **-taux** [-to]
contingence [kɔ̃tɛ̃ʒɑ̃s] *nf* : contingency
contingent [kɔ̃tɛ̃ʒɑ̃] *nm* : contingent
continu, -nue [kɔ̃tiny] *adj* : continuous, ongoing
continuation [kɔ̃tinɥasjɔ̃] *nf* **1** : continuation **2 bonne continuation!** : carry on!
continuel, -nuelle [kɔ̃tinɥɛl] *adj* **1** : continuous **2** : continual, constant — **continuellement** [kɔ̃tinɥɛlmɑ̃] *adv*
continuer [kɔ̃tinɥe] **1** : to continue, to keep up **2** PROLONGER : to extend — *vi* : to continue, to carry on — **se continuer** *vr*
continuité [kɔ̃tinɥite] *nf* : continuity
contorsion [kɔ̃tɔrsjɔ̃] *nf* : contortion, twisting
contorsionner [kɔ̃tɔrsjɔne] *v* **se contorsionner** *vr* : to contort oneself, to writhe
contour [kɔ̃tur] *nm* : contour, outline
contourner [kɔ̃turne] *vt* **1** : to skirt, to bypass **2** : to get around (a difficulty, a law, etc.)
contraceptif[1], **-tive** [kɔ̃trasɛptif, -tiv] *adj* : contraceptive
contraceptif[2] *nm* : contraceptive
contraception [kɔ̃trasɛpsjɔ̃] *nf* : contraception
contracter [kɔ̃trakte] *vt* **1** : to contract, to tense **2** : to incur (a debt) **3** : to contract, to catch (a cold, etc.) **4** : to shorten, to contract (a word)
contracteur, -teuse [kɔ̃traktœr, -tøz] *nm Can* : contractor
contraction [kɔ̃traksjɔ̃] *nf* **1** CRISPATION : contraction, tensing **2** : contraction, shortening (of a word) **3 contraction de texte** : summary, précis

contractuel, -tuelle [kɔ̃traktɥɛl] *adj* : contractual — **contractuellement** [-tɥɛlmɑ̃] *adv*
contradiction [kɔ̃tradiksjɔ̃] *nf* : contradiction
contradictoire [kɔ̃tradiktwar] *adj* : conflicting, contradictory
contraignait [kɔ̃trɛɲɛ], **contraignions** [kɔ̃trɛɲɔ̃], *etc.* → **contraindre**
contraigne, *etc.* → **contraindre**
contraindre [kɔ̃trɛ̃dr] {65} *vt* **1** : to compel, to constrain <elle l'a contraint à agir : she compelled him to act> <j'étais contraint de parler : I was forced to speak> **2** : to restrain — **se contraindre** *vr*
contraint, -trainte [kɔ̃trɛ̃, -trɛ̃t] *adj* **1** : strained, forced **2 contraint et forcé** : under duress
contrainte *nf* **1** : constraint, restraint <sans contrainte : freely> **2** : pressure, coercion
contraire [kɔ̃trɛr] *adj & nm* : contrary, opposite <au contraire : on the contrary>
contrairement [kɔ̃trɛrmɑ̃] *adv* ~ **à** : contrary to
contralto[1] [kɔ̃tralto] *nmf* : alto, contralto (singer)
contralto[2] *nm* : alto, contralto (voice)
contrariant, -riante [kɔ̃trarjɑ̃, -rjɑ̃t] *adj* **1** : contrary, balky **2** : annoying
contrarier [kɔ̃trarje] {96} *vt* **1** : to annoy, to vex **2** : to thwart
contrariété [kɔ̃trarjete] *nf* : annoyance, vexation
contraste [kɔ̃trast] *nm* : contrast
contraster [kɔ̃traste] *v* : to contrast
contrat [kɔ̃tra] *nm* **1** : contract, agreement **2 passer un contrat avec** : to enter into a contract with
contravention [kɔ̃travɑ̃sjɔ̃] *nf* **1** : infraction **2** : ticket, violation notice
contre[1] [kɔ̃tr] *adv* : being against <je m'appuyais contre : I was leaning against it> <parler contre : to speak in opposition>
contre[2] *nm* **1** : opposition <le pour et le contre : the pros and cons> **2** : counterattack (in sports) **3 par contre** : on the other hand
contre[3] *prep* **1** : against <contre le mur : against the wall> <contre la guerre : against the war> **2** : (in exchange) for <envoi contre remboursement : cash on delivery> **3** : (in proportion) to <trois contre un : three to one> **4** : from <se protéger contre le danger : to protect oneself from danger> **5** : in spite of
contre–amiral [kɔ̃tramiral] *nm, pl* **-raux** [-ro] : rear admiral
contre–attaque [kɔ̃tratake] *nf, pl* **-attaques** : counterattack — **contre–attaquer** [kɔ̃tratake] *vi*
contrebalancer [kɔ̃trəbalɑ̃se] {6} *vt* : to counterbalance, to offset — **se contrebalancer** *vr* **1** : to offset each other **2** *fam* : not to give a damn <je m'en contrebalance : I couldn't care less>
contrebande [kɔ̃trəbɑ̃d] *nf* **1** : smuggling **2** : contraband, smuggled goods
contrebandier, -dière [kɔ̃trəbɑ̃dje, -djɛr] *n* : smuggler
contrebas [kɔ̃trəba] **en contrebas** : (down) below
contrebasse [kɔ̃trəbas] *nf* : double bass
contrecarrer [kɔ̃trəkare] *vt* : to thwart
contrecœur [kɔ̃trəkœr] **à** ~ : unwillingly, grudgingly
contrecoup [kɔ̃trəku] *nm* : repercussion, consequence
contre–courant [kɔ̃trəkurɑ̃] *nm, pl* **-courants 1** : countercurrent **2 à** ~ : upstream, against the current
contredire [kɔ̃trədir] {29} *vt* : to contradict — **se contredire** *vr*
contredit [kɔ̃trədi] **sans** ~ : indisputably, without question
contrée [kɔ̃tre] *nf* : country, land, region
contre–espionnage [kɔ̃trɛspjɔnaʒ] *nm* : counterespionage
contrefaçon [kɔ̃trəfasɔ̃] *nf* **1** : counterfeiting **2** : forgery
contrefaire [kɔ̃trəfɛr] {42} *vt* **1** : to imitate, to mimic **2** : to counterfeit **3** : to disguise (one's voice, etc.)
contrefait, -faite [kɔ̃trəfɛ, -fɛt] *adj* **1** : counterfeit, forged **2** DIFFORME : deformed
contrefort [kɔ̃trəfɔr] *nm* **1** : buttress, abutment **2 contreforts** *nmpl* : foothills
contre–indiqué, -quée [kɔ̃trɛ̃dike] *adj* : inadvisable, unwise
contre–interrogatoire [kɔ̃trɛ̃terɔgatwar] *nm, pl* **-toires** : cross-examination
contremaître, -maîtresse [kɔ̃trəmɛtr, -mɛtrɛs] *n* : foreman *m*, forewoman *f*
contrepartie [kɔ̃trəparti] *nf* **1** : compensation <en contrepartie : in compensation, in return> **2** : opposing view
contre–performance [kɔ̃trəperfɔrmɑ̃s] *nf, pl* **-mances** : poor performance
contre–pied [kɔ̃trəpje] *nm, pl* **-pieds 1** : opposite opinion **2 prendre qqn à contre–pied** : to catch s.o. off balance
contre–plaqué [kɔ̃trəplake] *nm, pl* **-plaqués** : plywood
contrepoids [kɔ̃trəpwa] *nm* : counterweight, counterbalance
contrepoint [kɔ̃trəpwɛ̃] *nm* : counterpoint
contrepoison [kɔ̃trəpwazɔ̃] *nm* : antidote
contrer [kɔ̃tre] *vt* : to counter, to block
contre–révolution [kɔ̃trərevɔlysjɔ̃] *nf* : counterrevolution — **contre–révolutionnaire** [-sjɔnɛr] *adj & nmf*
contresens [kɔ̃trəsɑ̃s] *nm* **1** : misinterpretation, mistranslation **2 à** ~ : the wrong way, in the opposite direction

contresigner [kɔ̃trəsiɲe] *vt* : to countersign
contretemps [kɔ̃trətɑ̃] *nm* **1** : mishap, hitch **2** : offbeat (in music) **3 à ~** : inopportunely
contre-torpilleur [kɔ̃trətɔrpijœr] *nm* : destroyer (ship)
contrevenant¹, -nante [kɔ̃trəvnɑ̃, -vnɑ̃t] *adj* : contravening, offending
contrevenant², -nante *n* : offender, lawbreaker
contrevenir [kɔ̃trəvnir] {92} *vi* **~ à** : to contravene, to infringe
contrevent [kɔ̃trəvɑ̃] *nm* : window shutter
contribuable [kɔ̃tribɥabl] *nmf* : taxpayer
contribuer [kɔ̃tribɥe] *vi* : to contribute
contribution [kɔ̃tribysjɔ̃] *nf* **1** : contribution **2 contributions** *nfpl* IMPÔTS : taxes, taxation
contrit, -trite [kɔ̃tri, -trit] *adj* : contrite
contrôle [kɔ̃trol] *nm* **1** : control <contrôle des naissances : birth control> <contrôle de soi-même : self-control> **2** : checking, monitoring, auditing <contrôle de sécurité : security check>
contrôler [kɔ̃trole] *vt* **1** : to control **2** : to check, to inspect **3** SUPERVISER : to supervise, to monitor
contrôleur, -leuse [kɔ̃trolœr, -løz] *n* **1** : inspector, assessor **2** : controller <contrôleur aérien : air-traffic controller>
controverse [kɔ̃trɔvɛrs] *nf* : controversy
controversé, -sée [kɔ̃trɔverse] *adj* : controversial
contusion [kɔ̃tyzjɔ̃] *nf* : contusion, bruise
convaincant, -cante [kɔ̃vɛ̃kɑ̃, -kɑ̃t] *adj* : persuasive, convincing
convaincre [kɔ̃vɛ̃kr] {94} *vt* **1** PERSUADER : to convince, to persuade **2** : to convict
convalescence [kɔ̃valesɑ̃s] *nf* : convalescence
convalescent, -cente [kɔ̃valesɑ̃, -sɑ̃t] *adj & n* : convalescent
convenable [kɔ̃vnabl] *adj* **1** APPROPRIÉ : suitable, appropriate **2** ACCEPTABLE : acceptable, adequate **3** : proper, decent **— convenablement** [-vnablamɑ̃] *adv*
convenance [kɔ̃vnɑ̃s] *nf* **1** : suitability **2 convenances** *nfpl* : conventions, proprieties
convenir [kɔ̃vnir] {92} *vt* : to agree, to admit <je conviens que j'ai eu tort : I admit that I was wrong> — *vi* **1 ~ à** : to suit, to fit **2 ~ de** : to acknowledge, to admit — *v impers* **il convient de** : it is advisable to <il convient de partir maintenant : we should leave now>
convention [kɔ̃vɑ̃sjɔ̃] *nf* **1** : convention, norm <de convention : conventional> **2** : agreement <convention collective : collective (labor) agreement> **3** : (political) convention
conventionnel, -nelle [kɔ̃vɑ̃sjɔnɛl] *adj* : conventional — **conventionnellement** [-nɛlmɑ̃] *adv*
convenu, -nue [kɔ̃vny] *adj* **1** : agreed **2** : conventional
converger [kɔ̃vɛrʒe] {17} *vi* **1** : to converge **2** : to meet, to agree <nos avis convergent : our opinions tend in the same direction>
conversation [kɔ̃vɛrsasjɔ̃] *nf* : conversation, talk
converser [kɔ̃vɛrse] *vi* : to converse, to talk
conversion [kɔ̃vɛrsjɔ̃] *nf* : conversion
convertible [kɔ̃vɛrtibl] *adj* : convertible
converti, -tie [kɔ̃vɛrti] *n* : convert (to a religion)
convertir [kɔ̃vɛrtir] *vt* **1** : to convert **2 ~ en** : to transform into **— se convertir** *vr*
convertisseur [kɔ̃vɛrtisœr] *nm* : converter
convexe [kɔ̃vɛks] *adj* : convex
conviction [kɔ̃viksjɔ̃] *nf* CERTITUDE : conviction
convier [kɔ̃vje] {96} *vt* **1** INVITER : to invite **2** : to urge
convive [kɔ̃viv] *nmf* : guest (at a meal)
convivial, -viale [kɔ̃vivjal] *adj, mpl* **-viaux** [-vjo] **1** : convivial **2** : user-friendly **— convivialité** [-vjalite] *nf*
convocation [kɔ̃vɔkasjɔ̃] *nf* **1** : inviting, summoning **2** : notification (to attend), summons
convoi [kɔ̃vwa] *nm* **1** : convoy **2** *or* **convoi funèbre** : funeral procession
convoiter [kɔ̃vwate] *vt* : to covet
convoitise [kɔ̃vwatiz] *nf* **1** : covetousness, greed **2** : lust
convoluté, -tée [kɔ̃vɔlyte] *adj* : coiled, convoluted
convoquer [kɔ̃vɔke] *vt* **1** : to convoke, to convene **2** : to summon
convoyer [kɔ̃vwaje] {58} *vt* : to escort
convoyeur [kɔ̃vwajœr] *nm* **1** : convoy, escort (ship) **2** : conveyor
convulser [kɔ̃vylse] *vt* : to convulse, to distort (one's face, etc.)
convulsif, -sive [kɔ̃vylsif, -siv] *adj* : convulsive
convulsion [kɔ̃vylsjɔ̃] *nf* : convulsion
coopératif, -tive [kɔɔperatif, -tiv] *adj* : cooperative
coopérative *nf* : cooperative
coopérer [kɔɔpere] {87} *vi* : to cooperate **— coopération** [-perasjɔ̃] *nf*
coopter [kɔɔpte] *vt* : to co-opt
coordination [kɔɔrdinasjɔ̃] *nf* : coordination
coordonnateur¹, -trice [kɔɔrdɔnatœr, -tris] *adj* : coordinating
coordonnateur², -trice *n* : coordinator
coordonné, -née [kɔɔrdɔne] *adj* **1** : coordinated **2** : coordinate <prop-

osition coordonnée : coordinate clause>

coordonnées [kɔɔrdɔne] *nfpl* **1** : (mathematical) coordinates *pl* **2** *fam* : address and telephone number

coordonner [kɔɔrdɔne] *vt* : to coordinate

copain, -pine [kɔpɛ̃, -pin] *n* **1** : friend, pal, buddy **2** *or* **petit copain, petite copine** : boyfriend *m*, girlfriend *f*

copeau [kɔpo] *nm* : chip, flake (of wood, metal, etc.)

copie [kɔpi] *nf* **1** : copy, duplicate **2** IMITATION : imitation **3** : manuscript, printer's copy **4** : paper, schoolwork

copier [kɔpje] {96} *vt* **1** : to copy, to transcribe **2** REPRODUIRE : to reproduce **3** : to copy (s.o.'s schoolwork)

copieux, -pieuse [kɔpjø, -pjøz] *adj* : copious — **copieusement** [-pjøzmɑ̃] *adv*

copilote [kɔpilɔt] *nmf* : copilot

copine → **copain**

copiste [kɔpist] *nmf* : copyist

copropriété [kɔprɔprijete] *nf* : joint ownership

copuler [kɔpyle] *vi* : to copulate — **copulation** [-pylasjɔ̃] *nf*

copyright [kɔpirajt] *nm* : copyright

coq [kɔk] *nm* : rooster

coq–à–l'âne [kɔkalan] *nm, pl* **coqs–à–l'âne** : abrupt change of subject

coq–l'oeil[1] [kɔklœj] *adj Can* **1** : one-eyed **2** : cross-eyed

coq–l'oeil[2] *nmf Can* **1** : one-eyed person **2** : cross-eyed person

coque [kɔk] *nf* **1** : cockle **2** : shell (of a nut) **3** : bow, loop, curl (of hair) **4** : hull (of a boat) **5 œuf à la coque** : soft-boiled egg

coquelicot [kɔkliko] *nm* : poppy

coqueluche [kɔkly(ʃ)] *nf* **1** : whooping cough **2** *fam* : idol (in entertainment, sports, etc.)

coquerelle [kɔkrɛl] *nf Can* : cockroach

coquet, -quette [kɔke, -kɛt] *adj* **1** : stylish **2** : charming, pretty **3** *fam* : considerable <une coquette somme : a substantial sum>

coquette *nf* : coquette, flirt

coquetterie [kɔkɛtri] *nf* **1** : affectation **2** : flirtatiousness **3** : clothes-consciousness, stylishness

coquillage [kɔkijaʒ] *nm* **1** : shellfish **2** COQUILLE : shell

coquille [kɔkij] *nf* **1** : shell <coquille de noix : nutshell> **2** FAUTE : misprint **3 coquille Saint–Jacques** : scallop

coquin[1], **-quine** [kɔkɛ̃, -kin] *adj* ESPIÈGLE : mischievous, naughty

coquin[2], **-quine** *n* : little rascal, scamp

cor [kɔr] *nm* **1** : horn <cor anglais : English horn> **2** : corn (on one's foot)

corail [kɔraj] *nm, pl* **coraux** [kɔro] : coral

Coran [kɔrɑ̃] *nm* **le Coran** : the Koran

corbeau [kɔrbo] *nm, pl* **corbeaux 1** : crow **2** *or* **grand corbeau** : raven

corbeille [kɔrbɛj] *nf* **1** : basket <corbeille à papier : wastepaper basket> **2 corbeille de mariage** : wedding presents *pl*

corbillard [kɔrbijar] *nm* : hearse

cordage [kɔrdaʒ] *nm* **1** : rope **2 cordages** *nmpl* : rigging

corde [kɔrd] *nf* **1** : rope, cord <corde raide : tightrope> **2** : string <instrument à cordes : stringed instrument> **3 corde dorsal** : spinal cord **4 cordes vocales** : vocal cords **5 usé jusqu'à la corde** : threadbare

cordée [kɔrde] *nf* **1** : cord (of wood) **2** : roped party (of climbers)

cordial[1], **-diale** [kɔrdjal] *adj, mpl* **-diaux** [-djo] : cordial — **cordialement** [-djalmɑ̃] *adv*

cordial[2] *nm, pl* **cordiaux** : cordial

cordialité [kɔrdjalite] *nf* : cordiality, geniality

cordon [kɔrdɔ̃] *nm* **1** : cord, string, lace <cordon ombilical : umbilical cord> <cordon de soulier : shoelace> **2** : cordon (of police, etc.)

cordon–bleu [kɔrdɔ̃blø] *nm, pl* **cordons–bleus** : cordon-bleu chef

cordonnerie [kɔrdɔnri] *nf* **1** : cobbler's shop **2** : shoemaking, shoe repair

cordonnier, -nière [kɔrdɔnje, -njɛr] *n* : shoemaker, cobbler

coréen[1], **-réenne** [kɔreɛ̃, -reɛn] *adj* : Korean

coréen[2] *nm* : Korean (language)

Coréen, -réenne *n* : Korean

coriace [kɔrjas] *adj* DUR : tough

coriandre [kɔrjɑ̃dr] *nf* : coriander

cormoran [kɔrmɔrɑ̃] *nm* : cormorant

corne [kɔrn] *nf* **1** : antler, horn **2** : horny substance, tortoiseshell **3** : callus **4** : horn (instrument) <corne de brume : foghorn> **5 corne d'abondance** : cornucopia, horn of plenty

corned–beef [kɔrnbif] *nms & pl* : corned beef

cornée [kɔrne] *nf* : cornea

corneille [kɔrnɛj] *nf* : crow, rook

cornemuse [kɔrnɔmyz] *nf* : bagpipes *pl*

corner [kɔrne] *vt* : to turn down (the corner of a page) — *vi* KLAXONNER : to honk, to toot

cornet [kɔrnɛ] *nm* **1** : cone <cornet de crème glacée : ice-cream cone> **2 cornet à pistons** : cornet

corniche [kɔrniʃ] *nf* **1** : cornice **2** : ledge, cliff road

cornichon [kɔrniʃɔ̃] *nm* **1** : gherkin **2** *fam* : idiot, dope

cornouiller [kɔrnuje] *nm* : dogwood

cornu, -nue [kɔrny] *adj* : horned

corollaire [kɔrɔlɛr] *nm* : corollary

corolle [kɔrɔl] *nf* : corolla

coronaire [kɔrɔnɛr] *adj* : coronary <artère coronaire : coronary artery>

coroner [kɔrɔnɛr] *nm* : coroner

corporatif, -tive [kɔrpɔratif, -tiv] *adj* : corporate

corporation [kɔrpɔrasjɔ̃] *nf* : corporation
corporel, -relle [kɔrpɔrɛl] *adj* : bodily, corporeal
corps [kɔr] *nm* **1** : body <corps à corps : hand to hand> **2** : corps (in the army, etc.), professional body <corps médical : medical profession> **3** : substance, body <corps étranger : foreign body> <prendre corps : to take shape> **4** *Can* : undershirt **5 à corps perdu** : headlong, with all one's might **6 à son corps défendant** : unwillingly, despite oneself **7 corps à corps** : hand-to-hand combat, clinch (in boxing)
corpulence [kɔrpylɑ̃s] *nf* : corpulence, stoutness — **corpulent, -lente** [kɔrpylɑ̃, -lɑ̃t] *adj*
corpuscule [kɔrpyskyl] *nm* : corpuscle
correct, -recte [kɔrɛkt] *adj* : correct — **correctement** [-rɛktəmɑ̃] *adv*
correcteur[1], **-trice** [kɔrɛktœr, -tris] *adj* : corrective
correcteur[2], **-trice** *n* **1** : corrector, grader **2** : proofreader
correctif, -tive [kɔrɛktif, -tiv] *adj* : corrective
correction [kɔrɛksjɔ̃] *nf* **1** : correction **2** : grading, marking **3** : thrashing, punishment **4** : correctness **5** : proofreading
correctionnel, -nelle [kɔrɛksjɔnɛl] *adj* : correctional
corrélation [kɔrelasjɔ̃] *nf* **1** : correlation **2 mettre en corrélation** : to interrelate
correspondance [kɔrɛspɔ̃dɑ̃s] *nf* **1** : correspondence **2** : connection (of a plane, bus, etc.)
correspondant, -dante [kɔrɛspɔ̃dɑ̃, -dɑ̃t] *n* **1** : correspondent, letter writer **2** : person being called (on the telephone) **3** : press correspondent
correspondre [kɔrɛspɔ̃dr] {63} *vi* **1** : to correspond, to write <elle correspond avec lui : she writes to him> **2** : to communicate (by telephone, etc.) **3 ~ à** : to correspond to, to match
corrida [kɔrida] *nf* : bullfight
corridor [kɔridɔr] *nm* : corridor, passageway
corrigé [kɔriʒe] *nm* : correct version
corriger [kɔriʒe] {17} *vt* **1** : to correct, to mark, to proofread **2** : to alleviate, to remedy **3** : to thrash — **se corriger** *vr* **~ de** : to cure oneself of
corroborer [kɔrɔbɔre] *vt* : to corroborate — **corroboration** [-bɔrasjɔ̃] *nf*
corroder [kɔrɔde] *vt* : to corrode
corrompre [kɔrɔ̃pr] {77} *vt* **1** PERVERTIR : to corrupt **2** SOUDOYER : to bribe
corrompu, -pue [kɔrɔ̃py] *adj* : corrupt
corrosif, -sive [kɔrɔzif, -ziv] *adj* : corrosive
corrosion [kɔrɔzjɔ̃] *nf* : corrosion
corruption [kɔrypsjɔ̃] *nf* **1** : corruption **2** : bribery
corsage [kɔrsaʒ] *nm* **1** CHEMISIER : blouse **2** : bodice (of a dress)
corsaire [kɔrsɛr] *nm* : privateer
corse [kɔrs] *adj* : Corsican
Corse *nmf* : Corsican
corsé, -sée [kɔrse] *adj* **1** ÉPICÉ : spicy **2** DIFFICILE : tough, tricky **3** : full-bodied (of wine), strong (of coffee, etc.)
corser [kɔrse] *vt* **1** : to add spice to **2** : to aggravate <pour corser l'affaire : to complicate matters> **3** : to liven up **4** : to spike (a drink) — **se corser** *vr* : to get more complicated <l'affaire se corse : the plot thickens>
corset [kɔrsɛ] *nm* : corset
cortège [kɔrtɛʒ] *nm* : procession, cortege
cortex [kɔrtɛks] *nm* : cortex
cortisone [kɔrtizɔn] *nf* : cortisone
corvée [kɔrve] *nf* **1** : chore **2** : duty (in the military)
cosignataire [kɔsiɲatɛr] *nmf* : cosigner, cosignatory
cosigner [kɔsiɲe] *vt* : to cosign
cosmétique [kɔsmetik] *adj* : cosmetic
cosmétiques *nmpl* : cosmetics, beauty products
cosmique [kɔsmik] *adj* : cosmic
cosmonaute [kɔsmɔnot] *nmf* : cosmonaut
cosmopolite [kɔsmɔpɔlit] *adj* : cosmopolitan
cosmos [kɔsmos] *nm* : cosmos
cosse [kɔs] *nf* : pod, husk
cossins [kɔsɛ̃] *nmpl Can fam* : things, stuff <ramasse tes cossins : pick up your things>
cossu, -sue [kɔsy] *adj* **1** : well-to-do, affluent **2** : opulent, posh
costaricain, -caine [kɔstarikɛ̃, -kɛn] *adj* : Costa Rican
Costaricain, -caine *n* : Costa Rican
costaud, -taude [kɔsto, -tod] *adj fam* : strong, sturdy, robust
costume [kɔstym] *nm* **1** : suit **2** : costume, dress
costumer [kɔstyme] *vt* : to dress up — **se costumer** *vr* **~ en** : to get dressed up as
cotation [kɔtasjɔ̃] *nf* : quotation (in finance)
cote [kɔt] *nf* **1** : quotation, quoted value **2** : rating, standing <cote de popularité : popularity rating> **3** : odds **4** : dimension (in construction) **5** : height <cote d'alerte : flood level> **6** : call number (of a library book)
côte [kot] *nf* **1** : coast, shore **2** : rib **3** : side <côte à côte : side by side> **4** : chop, cutlet **5** : hill, slope
côté [kote] *nm* **1** : side <se coucher sur le côté : to lie on one's side> **2** ASPECT : aspect, point of view <d'un autre côté : on the other hand> <de mon côté : for my part> **3** : way,

direction <de quel côté? : which way?> **4 à ~** : nearby **5 à côté de** : next to **6 de côté** : sideways, sidelong **7 de ~** : aside, to one side <mettre de côté : to put aside> **8 du côté de** : toward <allons du côté de la plage : let's head for the beach>

coteau [kɔto] *nm, pl* **coteaux 1** PENTE, VERSANT : slope, hillside **2** COLLINE : hill

côtelé, -lée [kotle] *adj* **1** : ribbed **2 velours côtelé** : corduroy

côtelette [kotlet] *nf* : chop

coter [kɔte] *vt* **1** : to classify (books) **2** : to quote, to value (in finance)

coterie [kɔtri] *nf* : clique, set (of cronies)

côteux, -teuse [kotø, -tøz] *adj Can* : hilly

côtier, -tière [kotje, -tjɛr] *adj* : coastal

cotisation [kɔtizasjɔ̃] *nf* : dues *pl*, fee

cotiser [kɔtize] *vi* **1** : to subscribe, to pay one's dues **2** : to contribute (to a fund)

coton [kɔtɔ̃] *nm* : cotton

cotonnade [kɔtɔnad] *nf* : cotton fabric

cotonneux, -neuse [kɔtɔnø, -nøz] *adj* : fleecy, fluffy

côtoyer [kotwaye] {58} *vt* **1** : to skirt, to run alongside **2** : to be close to, to mix with

cotre [kɔtr] *nm* : cutter (boat)

cottage [kɔtaʒ] *nm* **1** *France* : cottage **2 → fromage**

cotte [kɔt] *nf* **1** *France* : overalls *pl* **2 cotte de mailles** : coat of mail

cou [ku] *nm* : neck

couard[1], **couarde** [kwar, kward] *adj* POLTRON : cowardly

couard[2], **couarde** *n* : coward

couardise [kwardiz] *nf* : cowardice

couchage [kuʃaʒ] *nm* **1** : bed, sleeping arrangements **2 → sac**

couchant[1], **-chante** [kuʃɑ̃, -ʃɑ̃t] *adj* : setting <le soleil couchant : the setting sun>

couchant[2] *nm* **1** : sunset **2** : west

couche [kuʃ] *nf* **1** : layer, stratum <couche d'ozone : ozone layer> <couche sociale : social stratum> **2** : coat (of paint) **3** : diaper **4 couches** *nfpl* : childbirth **5 → faux**

coucher[1] [kuʃe] *vt* **1** : to put up, to provide a bed for **2** : to put to bed **3** : to lay down flat, to flatten **4** : to put in writing **— *vi*** **1** : to sleep, to spend the night **2 ~ avec** : to sleep with **— se coucher** *vr* : to lie down, to go to bed

coucher[2] *nm* **1** : bedtime **2 coucher du soleil** : sunset

couchette [kuʃɛt] *nf* **1** : cot (for a child) **2** : berth, bunk (in a train or ship)

coucou [kuku] *nm* **1** : cuckoo <coucou terrestre : roadrunner> **2** : cuckoo clock **3** : cowslip

coude [kud] *nm* **1** : elbow **2** : bend, angle **3 coude à coude** : side by side, shoulder to shoulder

coudée [kude] *nf* **avoir les coudées franches** : to have elbow room

cou-de-pied [kudpje] *nm, pl* **cous-de-pied** : instep

coudon [kudɔ̃] *interj Can fam* : come on! <coudon, que'est-ce qu'ils font? : what on earth are they doing?>

coudoyer [kudwaje] {58} *vt* : to rub shoulders with

coudre [kudr] {22} *v* : to sew

coudrier [kudrije] *nm* : hazel (tree)

couenne [kwan] *nf* **1** : pork rind **2 avoir la couenne dure** *Can* : to be resilient, to be hard-shelled

couette [kwɛt] *nf* **1** : comforter, duvet **2 couettes** *nfpl* : pigtails

couguar [kug(w)ar] *nm* PUMA : cougar, puma

couinement [kwinmɑ̃] *nm* : squeaking, squealing

couiner [kwine] *vt* : to squeak, to squeal

coulant[1], **-lante** [kulɑ̃, -lɑ̃t] *adj* **1** : flowing (of style, etc.) **2** : runny <fromage coulant : runny cheese> **3** : easygoing

coulant[2] *nm* : runner (of a plant)

coulée [kule] *nf* **1** : flow, slide <coulée de lave : lava flow> **2** : casting (of metal) **3** *Can* : ravine, gully

couler [kule] *vt* **1** : to sink (a ship) **2** : to pour, to cast **3** : to ruin, to cause to fail **4** : to spend, to pass (time) **— *vi*** **1** : to flow, to run **2** : to slide, to slip **3** : to leak **4** : to sink **— se couler** *vr* **1 ~ dans** : to slip into **2 se la couler douce** *fam* : to have an easy time of it

couleur [kulœr] *nf* **1** : color **2** : suit (of cards)

couleuvre [kulœvr] *nf* : grass snake

coulisse [kulis] *nf* **1** : groove, slot **2** : slide (of a trombone) **3** *Can* : trickle, drip (of paint, sap, water, etc.) **4 coulisses** *nfpl* : backstage, wings (in a theater)

coulisser [kulise] *vi* : to slide, to run (in a groove)

couloir [kulwar] *nm* **1** : corridor, passage **2** : lane (in sports or transportation) **3** : gully

coup [ku] *nm* **1** : knock, blow <coup de pied : kick> <coup de poing : punch> **2** : shock <ça lui a donné un coup : that gave him a shock> **3** : shot <coup de feu : gunshot> **4** : movement <un coup d'œil : a glance> **5** : stroke, shot (in sports) <coup droit : forehand (drive)> **6** : action, effect <coup de soleil : sunburn> <coup de téléphone : telephone call> <coup de foudre : love at first sight> **7** : (political) coup <coup d'État : coup d'état> **8 à coup sûr** : definitely, for sure **9 après coup** : afterwards **10 coups et blessures** : assault and battery **11 coup sûr** *Can* : base hit **12 coup sur coup** : one af-

ter another **13 du coup** : as a result **14 tout à coup** : suddenly
coupable[1] [kupabl] *adj* : guilty
coupable[2] *nmf* : culprit
coupant, -pante [kupɑ̃, -pɑ̃t] *adj* **1** : sharp **2** TRANCHANT : cutting, curt (of a remark, etc.)
coupe [kup] *nf* **1** : goblet, fruit dish **2** : cup (in sports) **3** : cut, cutting <coupe (de cheveux) : haircut> **4** : section (in biology)
coupé [kupe] *nm* : coupé, coupe
coupe–circuit [kupsirkɥi] *nms & pl* : circuit breaker
coupée [kupe] *nf* : gangway
coupe–feu [kupfø] *nms & pl* : firebreak
coupe–ongles [kupɔ̃gl] *nms & pl* : nail clippers
coupe–papier [kuppapje] *nms & pl* : letter opener
couper [kupe] *vt* **1** : to cut, to cut up, to cut down **2** : to cut off, to break off, to block off **3** : to cut across, to intersect **4** : to dilute (wine, etc.) — *vi* **1** : to cut **2** : to take a shortcut **3 couper à court** : to cut short, to curtail — **se couper** *vr* **1** : to cut oneself <il s'est coupé le doigt : he cut his finger> <se couper les cheveux : to cut one's hair> **2** : to intersect **3** ~ **de** : to cut oneself off from
couperet [kupre] *nm* **1** : cleaver **2** : blade (of a guillotine)
couperosé, -sée [kuproze] *adj* : blotchy
coupe–vent [kupvɑ̃] *nms & pl* : windbreaker
couplage [kuplaʒ] *nm* : (mechanical) coupling
couple [kupl] *nm* : couple, pair
coupler [kuple] *vt* : to couple, to pair (up)
couplet [kuple] *nm* : verse
coupoir [kupwar] *nm* : cutter (tool)
coupole [kupɔl] *nf* : cupola, dome
coupon [kupɔ̃] *nm* **1** : coupon **2** : remnant (of cloth) **3** : ticket, pass
coupure [kupyr] *nf* **1** : cut <coupure profonde : deep cut> <coupure du salaire : salary cut> **2** : gap **3** : break <coupure publicitaire : commercial break> **4** BILLET : banknote **5 coupure de presse** : newspaper clipping
cour [kur] *nf* **1** : court <Cour suprême : Supreme Court> **2** : courtyard <cour de récréation : playground> **3** : courtship **4 cour martiale** : court-martial
courage [kuraʒ] *nm* **1** : courage **2** : will, spirit <bon courage! : stick to it!, good luck!>
courageux, -geuse [kuraʒø, -ʒøz] *adj* **1** : courageous, brave **2** : energetic — **courageusement** [-ʒøzmɑ̃] *adv*
courailler [kuraje] *vi Can fam* : to run around from one place to another
couramment [kuramɑ̃] *adv* **1** : fluently **2** : commonly
courant[1], **-rante** [kurɑ̃, -rɑ̃t] *adj* **1** : current **2** : common, frequent **3** COMMUN : usual, ordinary
courant[2] *nm* **1** : current <courant continu : direct current> <courant alternatif : alternating current> <courant d'air : draft> <contre le courant : against the tide> **2** : trend **3** : movement (of populations, etc.) **4** : course <dans le courant de l'année : in the course of the year> **5 au courant** : up-to-date, in the know
courbature [kurbatyr] *nf* : stiffness, ache, charley horse
courbaturé, -rée [kurbatyre] *adj* : aching
courbe[1] [kurb] *adj* : curved
courbe[2] *nf* **1** : (graphic) curve **2** : bend, curve
courber [kurbe] *vt* **1** : to bend, to curve **2** : to bow — *vi* : to bend (over), to bow — **se courber** *vr*
courbette [kurbɛt] *nf* : low bow <faire des courbettes à : to kowtow to>
courbure [kurbyr] *nf* : curvature
coureur[1], **-reuse** [kurœr, -røz] *n* **1** : runner **2** : racer <coureur cycliste : bicycle racer> <coureur automobile : race car driver>
coureur[2] *nm or* **oiseau coureur** : flightless bird
courge [kurʒ] *nf* : gourd, squash
courgette [kurʒɛt] *nf* : zucchini
courir [kurir] {23} *vt* **1** : to run <courir le risque : to run the risk> **2** : to go around, to roam **3** FRÉQUENTER : to frequent **4** POURSUIVRE : to run after, to pursue — *vi* **1** : to run **2** : to race **3** : to rush **4 le bruit court** : rumor has it **5 par les temps qui courent** : nowadays, at the present time
courlis [kurli] *nm* : curlew
couronne [kurɔn] *nf* **1** : crown **2** : wreath **3** : corona
couronnement [kurɔnmɑ̃] *nm* **1** : coronation, crowning **2** : crowning achievement
couronner [kurɔne] *vt* : to crown
courra [kura], *etc.* → **courir**
courriel [kurjɛl] *nm* : e-mail, electronic mail
courrier [kurje] *nm* : mail, correspondence <courrier des lecteurs : letters to the editor> <courrier électronique : electronic mail>
courroie [kurwa] *nf* **1** : strap **2** : belt <courroie de ventilateur : fan belt>
courroucé, -cée [kuruse] *adj* : wrathful, infuriated
courroux [kuru] *nm* COLÈRE : anger, wrath
cours [kur] *nm* **1** : course <au cours de : in the course of, during> **2** : course, class, lesson <suivre un cours : to take a class> **3** : school <cours du soir : night school> **4** MANUEL : textbook **5** : flow, current <cours d'eau : riv-

er, stream> **6** : rate, price <cours des devises : foreign exchange rate> <avoir cours : to be legal tender, to be current, to be used> **7 en ~** : current, in progress

course [kurs] *nf* **1** : run, running **2** : race <course cycliste : bicycle race> <course contre la montre : race against time> **3** : errand <faire des courses : to go shopping> **4** : course, path **5** : journey, ride (in a taxi)

coursier[1], **-sière** [kursje, -sjɛr] *n* : messenger

coursier[2] *nm* : steed

court[1] [kur] *adv* **1** : short <s'arrêter court : to stop short> **2 à court de** : short of **3 tout court** : simply

court[2], **courte** [kur, kurt] *adj* **1** : short (in height), narrow **2** : brief, quick

court[3] *nm* : court <court de tennis : tennis court> <tenir court : to hold court>

courtage [kurtaʒ] *nm* : brokerage

court–circuit [kursirkɥi] *nm, pl* **courts–circuits** : short circuit

court–circuiter [kursirkɥite] *vt* **1** : to short-circuit **2** : to bypass

courtepointe [kurtəpwɛ̃t] *nf* : duvet, quilt

courtesane [kurtizan] *nf* : courtesan

courtier, -tière [kurtje, -tjɛr] *n* : broker, agent

courtisan [kurtizɑ̃] *nm* **1** : sycophant, flatterer **2** : courtier

courtiser [kurtize] *vt* : to court, to woo

court–métrage [kurmetraʒ] *nm* : short (film)

courtois, -toise [kurtwa, -twaz] *adj* : courteous — **courtoisement** [-twazmɑ̃] *adv*

courtoisie [kurtwazi] *nf* : courtesy

cousait [kuzɛ], *etc.* → **coudre**

couse [kuz], *etc.* → **coudre**

cousin[1], **-sine** [kuzɛ̃, -zin] *n* : cousin <cousin germain : first cousin>

cousin[2] *nm* : mosquito

coussin [kusɛ̃] *nm* **1** : cushion **2** *Can* : base (in baseball)

cousu [kuzy] *pp* → **coudre**

coût [ku] *nm* : cost <le coût de la vie : the cost of living>

coûtant [kutɑ̃] *adj* **à prix coûtant** : at cost

couteau [kuto] *nm, pl* **couteaux** : knife <couteau de poche : pocketknife, jacknife>

coutelas [kutla] *nm* **1** : cutlass **2** : butcher knife

coutellerie [kutɛlri] *nf* **1** : cutlery, knives **2** *Can* : silverware (set)

coûter [kute] *vt* : to cost <coûter cher : to be expensive> <ça coûte combien? : how much is it?> — *vi* : to cost

coûteux, -teuse [kutø, -tøz] *adj* : costly

coutume [kutym] *nf* **1** : custom **2 de coutume** : usual, customary

coutumier, -mière [kutymje, -mjɛr] *adj* : customary

couture [kutyr] *nf* **1** : sewing, needlework **2** : dressmaking **3** : seam

couturier [kutyrje] *nm* : fashion designer

couturière [kutyrjɛr] *nf* : dressmaker

couvée [kuve] *nf* : brood

couvent [kuvɑ̃] *nm* : convent, monastery

couver [kuve] *vt* **1** : to brood, to hatch **2** : to overprotect — *vi* **1** : to smolder, to be brewing **2** : to brood

couvercle [kuvɛrkl] *nm* **1** : lid, cover **2** : top, cap (of a spray can, etc.)

couvert[1] [kuvɛr] *pp* → **couvrir**

couvert[2], **-verte** [kuvɛr, -vɛrt] *adj* **1** : covered, indoor <piscine couverte : indoor swimming pool> **2** : overcast, cloudy

couvert[3] *nm* **1** : place setting (at a table) <couverts : eating utensils, flatware> **2** ABRI : shelter, cover **3** : cover charge

couverture [kuvɛrtyr] *nf* **1** : cover (of a book, etc.) **2** : blanket **3** : coverage **4** : roofing

couveuse [kuvøz] *nf* **1** : brood hen **2** : incubator

couvoir [kuvwar] *nm* : hatchery (for chickens, etc.)

couvre–chef [kuvrəʃɛf] *nm, pl* **couvre–chefs** : headgear

couvre–feu [kuvrəfø] *nm, pl* **couvre–feux** : curfew

couvre–lit [kuvrəli] *nm, pl* **couvre–lits** : bedspread

couvre–pieds [kuvrəpje] *nms & pl* : quilt, coverlet

couvre–plancher [kuvrəplɑ̃ʃe] *nm, pl* **couvre–planchers** *Can* : flooring

couvrir [kuvrir] {83} *vt* **1** : to cover **2** : to cover up for, to shield **3** : to drown out (sound) — **se couvrir** *vr* **1** : to wrap (oneself) up **2** : to cover oneself **3** : to cloud over **4 ~ de** : to be covered with

covoiturage [kovwatyraʒ] *nm Can* : car pool(ing)

cow–boy [kɔbɔj] *nm, pl* **cow–boys** : cowboy

coyote [kɔjɔt] *nm* : coyote

crabe [krab] *nm* : crab

crachat [kraʃa] *nm* : spittle

craché, -chée [kraʃe] *adj fam* **être (qqn) tout craché** : to be the spitting image (of s.o.)

cracher [kraʃe] *vt* **1** : to spit (out) **2** : to belch out (smoke, lava, etc.) **3** *fam* : to cough up (money, etc.) — *vi* : to spit

crachin [kraʃɛ̃] *nm* : drizzle — **crachiner** [kraʃine] *vi*

crachoir [kraʃwar] *nm* : spittoon

crack [krak] *nm* **1** : crack (cocaine) **2** *fam* : whiz, ace <c'est un crack aux échecs : he's a whiz at chess>

craie [krɛ] *nf* : chalk

craignait [krɛnɛ], **craignions** [krɛniɔ̃], *etc.* → **craindre**

craigne [krɛɲ], *etc.* → **craindre**
craindre [krɛ̃dr] {65} *vt* **1** REDOUTER : to fear, to be afraid of **2 ~ que** : to regret that, to fear that **3** : to be susceptible to
crainte [krɛ̃t] *nf* : fear, dread <de crainte que : lest>
craintif, -tive [krɛ̃tif, -tiv] *adj* : fearful, timid — **craintivement** [-tivmɑ̃] *adv*
cramoisi [kramwazi] *nm* : crimson
crampe [krɑ̃p] *nf* : cramp, spasm
crampon [krɑ̃pɔ̃] *nm* **1** : clamp **2** : cleat
cramponner [krɑ̃pɔne] *vt* **1** : to clamp together **2** *fam* : to pester — **se cramponner** *vr* **~ à** : to hold on to, to cling to
cran [krɑ̃] *nm* **1** : notch, hole (in a belt) **2** *fam* : courage <avoir du cran : to have guts>
crâne [kran] *nm* **1** : cranium, skull **2 bourrer le crâne à qqn** *fam* : to brainwash s.o.
crâner [krane] *vi fam* : to show off
crâneur[1], **-neuse** [kranœr, -øz] *adj fam* : boastful
crâneur[2], **-neuse** *n fam* : show-off
crânien, -nienne [kranjɛ̃, -njɛn] *adj* **1** : cranial **2 boîte crânienne** : cranium, skull
crapaud [krapo] *nm* : toad
crapule [krapyl] *nf* : scoundrel, crook
crapuleux, -leuse [krapylø, -løz] *adj* : crooked, villainous
craque [krak] *nf Can* : crack, crevasse
craquement [krakmɑ̃] *nm* : crack, crunch, creak
craquer [krake] *vi* **1** : to crack, to crunch, to creak **2** SE DÉCHIRER : to burst apart, to tear **3** *fam* : to collapse, to break down — *vt* **1** : to tear, to rip **2** : to strike (a match)
crasse[1] [kras] *adj* : crass, gross — **crassement** [krasmɑ̃] *adv*
crasse[2] *nf* **1** : filth, grime **2** : dross, slag **3 faire une crasse** : to play a dirty trick
crasseux, -seuse [krasø, -søz] *adj* : filthy, grimy
cratère [kratɛr] *nm* : crater
cravache [kravaʃ] *nf* : whip, crop
cravacher [kravaʃe] *vt* : to horsewhip
cravate [kravat] *nf* : necktie, cravat
crayeux, crayeuse [krɛjø, -jøz] *adj* : chalky (of the complexion)
crayon [krɛjɔ̃] *nm* **1** : pencil <crayon de couleur : colored pencil> **2 crayon à bille** : ballpoint pen **3 crayon de cire** : crayon
crayonner [krɛjɔne] *vt* **1** : to scribble, to jot down (in pencil) **2** : to sketch
créance [kreɑ̃s] *nf* **1** : debt **2** : letter of credit **3** : credence, credibility
créancier, -cière [kreɑ̃sje, -sjɛr] *n* : creditor
créateur[1], **-trice** [kreatœr, -tris] *adj* : creative
créateur[2], **-trice** *n* : creator, originator
création [kreasjɔ̃] *nf* : creation
créativité [kreativite] *nf* : creativity
créature [kreatyr] *nf* : creature
crécelle [kresɛl] *nf* : noisemaker
crèche [krɛʃ] *nf* **1** : crèche, Nativity scene **2** *France* : day-care center, nursery
crédible [kredibl] *adj* : credible — **crédibilité** [-dibilite] *nf*
crédit [kredi] *nm* **1** : credit <acheter à crédit : to buy on credit> **2** : credence, credibility **3 crédits** *nmpl* : funds
crédit-bail [kredibaj] *nm, pl* **crédits-bails** : leasing
créditer [kredite] *vt* : to credit
créditeur, -trice [kreditœr, -tris] *n* **1** : creditor **2 être crediteur** : to be in the black
crédo [kredo] *nm* : creed
crédule [kredyl] *adj* NAIF : credulous, gullible — **crédulité** [-dylite] *nf*
créer [kree] {89} *vt* **1** : to create **2** : to set up, to establish
crémage [krɛ(e)mɑʒ] *nm Can* : icing (on a cake)
crème [krɛm] *nf* **1** : cream <crème hydratante : moisturizer> **2 crème glacée** *Can* : ice cream
crémerie [krɛmri] *nf France* : dairy shop
crémeux, -meuse [kremø, -møz] *adj* : creamy
créneau [kreno] *nm, pl* **créneaux 1** : slot, gap, window (of time) **2** : niche, share <créneau du marché : market share> **3** : crenellation, battlement **4 faire un créneau** : to back into a parking space
créole[1] [kreɔl] *adj* : creole
créole[2] *nm* : Creole (language)
Créole *nmf* : Creole
créosote [kreɔzɔt] *nf* : creosote
crêpe[1] [krɛp] *nf* : pancake, crepe
crêpe[2] *nm* : crepe (fabric)
crépitement [krɛpitmɑ̃] *nm* : crackling, clacking, patter (of rain)
crépiter [krɛpite] *vi* : to crackle, to splutter, to patter
crépuscule [krɛpyskyl] *nm* : twilight, dusk
crescendo [krɛʃɛndo, krɛʃɛ̃do] *nms & pl* : crescendo
cresson [krɛsɔ̃] *nm* : cress, watercress
crête [krɛt] *nf* **1** : crest, peak **2** : comb, crest
crétin, -tine [kretɛ̃, -tin] *n* IDIOT : idiot, moron
cretons [krətɔ̃] *nmpl Can* : pâté made with pork and veal
creusement [krøzmɑ̃] *nm* : digging, excavation
creuser [krøze] *vt* **1** : to dig, to hollow out, to furrow **2** : to study in depth **3** : to flex, to bend <creuser le dos : to arch one's back> **4 ça creuse!** *fam* : that gives one an appetite! — *vi* : to dig, to excavate — **se creuser**

vr **se creuser la tête** *fam* : to rack one's brains
creuset [krøzɛ] *nm* **1** : crucible **2** : melting pot
creux[1], **creuse** [krø, krøz] *adj* **1** VIDE : hollow, empty **2** CONCAVE : concave, sunken **3** : shallow, superficial
creux[2] *nm* : hollow, hole, cavity <le creux de l'estomac : the pit of the stomach>
crevaison [krəvɛzɔ̃] *nf* : flat tire, puncture
crevasse [krəvas] *nf* **1** : crevasse **2** : crack, crevice **3 avoir des crevasses aux mains** : to have chapped hands
crevé, -vée [krəve] *adj* **1** : punctured, flat (of a tire) **2** : dead **3** *fam* : exhausted, dead tired
crève–cœur [krɛvkœr] *nms & pl* : heartbreak
crever [krəve] {52} *vt* **1** : to burst, to puncture **2** *fam* : to wear out **3 crever de faim** : to be starving — *vi* **1** : to burst **2** *fam* : to die — **se crever** *vr fam* : to wear oneself out
crevette [krəvɛt] *nf* : shrimp, prawn
cri [kri] *nm* **1** : cry, shout <à grands cris : at the top of one's lungs> **2 le dernier cri** : the latest thing
criaillement [kriajmɑ̃] *nm* : squawking, screeching, honking
criailler [kriaje] *vi* **1** : to squawk, to screech, to honk **2** : to complain, to grumble
criant, criante [krijɑ̃, krijɑ̃t] *adj* : obvious, flagrant, striking
criard, criarde [krijar, krijard] *adj* **1** : shrill **2** : loud, garish
crible [kribl] *nm* **1** : sieve, screen **2 passer au crible** : to screen, to examine closely
cribler [krible] *vt* **1** : to sift, to screen **2** : to riddle, to fill with holes
cric [krik] *nm* VÉRIN : jack
cricket [krikɛt] *nm* : cricket (sport)
criée [krije] *nf* : auction
crier [krije] {96} *vi* **1** : to shout, to cry out **2** : to squeal, to squeak — *vt* **1** : to shout **2** : to proclaim, to protest
crieur, crieuse [krijœr, krijøz] *n* : hawker, peddler
crime [krim] *nm* **1** : crime **2** : murder
criminel[1], **-nelle** [kriminɛl] *adj* : criminal — **criminellement** [-nɛlmɑ̃] *adv*
criminel[2], **-nelle** *n* **1** : criminal **2** MEURTRIER : murderer
crin [krɛ̃] *nm* **1** : horsehair **2 à tout crin** : die-hard, fanatical
crinière [krinjɛr] *nf* : mane
crique[1] [krik] *nf* : cove, inlet
crique[2] *nm Can* : creek
criquet [krikɛ] *nm* **1** *or* **criquet migrateur** : locust (insect) **2** *Can* : cricket (insect)
crise [kriz] *nf* **1** : crisis **2** ACCÈS : fit, outburst <crise de désespoir : fit of despair> **3** ATTAQUE : attack (in medicine) <crise cardiaque : heart attack>
crispant, -pante [krispɑ̃, -pɑ̃t] *adj* AGAÇANT : aggravating, annoying
crispation [krispasjɔ̃] *nf* CONTRACTION : tension, contraction
crispé, -pée [krispe] *adj* : tense, strained, nervous
crisper [krispe] *vt* **1** CONTRACTER : to tense, to contract **2** *fam* : to irritate <sa voix me crispe : her voice gets on my nerves>
crissement [krismɑ̃] *nm* **1** : screeching, squealing **2** : grating, grinding **3** : crunching
crisser [krise] *vi* **1** : to screech, to squeal **2** : to grate, to grind **3** : to crunch
cristal [kristal] *nm, pl* **cristaux** [kristo] : crystal — **cristallin, -line** [-stalɛ̃, -lin] *adj*
cristallin [kristalɛ̃] *nm* : lens (of the eye)
cristalliser [kristalize] *v* : to crystallize — **se cristalliser** *vr*
critère [kriter] *nm* : criterion
critérium [kriterjɔm] *nm* : heat (in sports)
critiquable [kritikabl] *adj* : open to criticism, questionable
critique[1] [kritik] *adj* : critical
critique[2] *nmf* : critic
critique[3] *nf* **1** : criticism, reproach **2** : critique, review
critiquer [kritike] *vt* : to criticize
critiqueur, -queuse [kritikœr, -køz] *n* : faultfinder
croassement [krɔasmɑ̃] *nm* : caw, croak
croasser [krɔase] *vi* : to croak, to caw
croate [krɔat] *adj* : Croatian
Croate *nmf* : Croat, Croatian
croc [kro] *nm* **1** CROCHET : hook **2** : fang
croc–en–jambe [krɔkɑ̃ʒɑ̃b] *nm, pl* **crocs–en–jambe** : tripping <faire un croc-en-jambe à qqn : to trip s.o. up>
croche[1] [krɔʃ] *adj Can* **1** : bent, crooked **2** : dishonest
croche[2] *nf* : eighth note
croche–pied [krɔʃpje] *nm fam* → **croc–en–jambe**
crochet [krɔʃɛ] *nm* **1** : hook **2** : crochet, crocheting <faire du crochet : to crochet> **3** : crochet hook **4** : square bracket **5** : detour <faire un crochet : to make a detour> **6** : fang (of a snake) **7 vivre aux crochets de qqn** : to scrounge off s.o.
crocheter [krɔʃte] {20} *vt* **1** : to pick (a lock) **2** : to crochet
crochir [krɔʃir] *vt Can* : to bend (out of shape), to distort
crochu, -chue [krɔʃy] *adj* : hooked, bent, crooked
crocodile [krɔkɔdil] *nm* : crocodile
crocus [krɔkys] *nm* : crocus
croire [krwar] {24} *v* **1** : to believe, to trust **2** PENSER : to think <tu crois?

: do you think so?> — *vi* **1** : to believe (in religion) **2 ~ à** *or* **~ en** : to believe in, to have confidence in — **se croire** *vr* : to consider oneself
croisade [krwazad] *nf* : crusade
croisé[1], **-sée** [krwaze] *adj* **1** : crossed **2** : double-breasted
croisé[2] *nm* **1** : crusader **2** : twill
croisée *nf* **1** : crossroads, crossing **2** : casement (window)
croisement [krwazmɑ̃] *nm* **1** : crossing, intersection <croisement en trêfle : cloverleaf> **2** : crossbreeding
croiser [krwaze] *vt* **1** : to cross <croiser les bras : to fold one's arms> **2** : to intersect **3** RENCONTRER : to pass, to meet **4** : to crossbreed — *vi* : to cruise (of a ship) — **se croiser** *vr* **1** : to intersect **2** : to pass each other
croiseur [krwazœr] *nm* : cruiser (ship)
croisière [krwazjɛr] *nf* **1** : cruise **2 vitesse de croisière** : cruising speed
croissait [krwasɛ], *etc.* → **croître**
croissance [krwasɑ̃s] *nf* : growth
croissant[1], **-sante** [krwasɑ̃, -sɑ̃t] *adj* : growing, increasing
croissant[2] *nm* **1** : crescent **2** : croissant
croître [krwatr] {25} *vi* : to grow, to increase
croix [krwa] *nf* : cross
croquant, -quante [krɔkɑ̃, -kɑ̃t] *adj* : crisp, crunchy
croque–mitaine [krɔkmitɛn] *nm, pl* **croque–mitaines** : bogey, bogeyman
croque–monsieur [krɔkməsjø] *nms & pl* : grilled ham and cheese sandwich
croque–mort [krɔkmɔr] *nm, pl* **croque–morts** *fam* : undertaker
croquer [krɔke] *vt* **1** : to crunch, to munch **2** ESQUISSER : to sketch **3** *fam* : to squander — *vi* **1** : to be crunchy **2 ~ dans** : to bite into (an apple, etc.)
croquet [krɔkɛ] *nm* : croquet
croquette [krɔkɛt] *nf* : croquette
croquis [krɔki] *nm* ESQUISSE : sketch, drawing
cross [krɔs] *or* **cross–country** [krɔskuntri] *nm* : cross-country run, cross-country race
crosse [krɔs] *nf* **1** : butt, grip (of a gun) **2** : stick, lacrosse stick <crosse de hockey : hockey stick> **3** LACROSSE : lacrosse **4** : crosier, crook
crotale [krɔtal] *nm* : rattlesnake
crotte [krɔt] *nf* : droppings *pl,* dung
crotté, -tée [krɔte] *adj* : muddy
crottin [krɔtɛ̃] *nm* : (horse) manure
crouler [krule] *vi* : to collapse, to crumble
croupe [krup] *nf* **1** : rump (of a horse) **2** : crest, summit
croupir [krupir] *vi* **1** : to stagnate **2** : to wallow <croupir dans l'ignorance : to wallow in ignorance>
croustillant, -lante [krustijɑ̃, -jɑ̃t] *adj* **1** : crisp, crunchy **2** : spicy, bawdy
croustiller [krustije] *vi* : to crunch, to be crispy
croûte [krut] *nf* **1** : crust **2** : scab **3 casser la croûte** : to have a snack
croûteux, -teuse [krutø, -tøz] *adj* : scabby
croûton [krutɔ̃] *nm* **1** : crust, heel (of bread) **2** : crouton
croyable [krwajabl] *adj* : credible, believable
croyait [krwajɛ], *etc.* → **croire**
croyance [krwajɑ̃s] *nf* : belief
croyant[1], **croyante** [krwajɑ̃, -jɑ̃t] *adj* : believing <être croyant : to be a believer>
croyant[2], **croyante** *n* : believer
cru[1] [kry] *pp* → **croire**
cru[2], **crue** [kry] *adj* **1** : raw, uncooked **2** : crude, harsh **3 à ~** : bareback, barebacked
cru[3] *nm* **1** VIGNOBLE : vineyard **2** : vintage (of wine) **3 du ~** : local
crû [kry] *pp* → **croître**
cruauté [kryote] *nf* : cruelty
cruche [kryʃ] *nf* **1** : jug, pitcher **2** *fam* : nitwit, dumbell
crucial, -ciale [krysjal] *adj, pl* **-ciaux** [-sjo] : crucial
crucifier [krysifje] {96} *vt* : to crucify
crucifix [krysifi] *nms & pl* : crucifix
crucifixion [krysifiksjɔ̃] *nf* : crucifixion
crudité [krydite] *nf* **1** : crudeness **2 crudités** *nfpl* : raw vegetables (as hors d'oeuvres)
crue [kry] *nf* : rising (of waters), flood
cruel, cruelle [kryɛl] *adj* : cruel — **cruellement** [-ɛlmɑ̃] *adv*
crûment [krymɑ̃] *adv* **1** : crudely, coarsely **2** : bluntly
crustacé [krystase] *nm* **1** : crustacean **2 crustacés** *npl* : shellfish
crypte [kript] *nf* : crypt
cryptographie [kriptɔgrafi] *nf* : cryptography
cubain, -baine [kybɛ̃, -bɛn] *adj* : Cuban
Cubain, -baine *n* : Cuban
cube[1] [kyb] *adj* : cubic <mètre cube : cubic meter>
cube[2] *nm* : cube
cubique [kybik] *adj* : cubic
cubitus [kybitys] *nm* : ulna
cueillette [kœjɛt] *nf* : gathering, picking
cueillir [kœjir] {3} *vt* **1** : to pick, to gather **2** *fam* : to catch, to nab **3 être cueilli à froid** : to be caught off guard
cuillère *or* **cuiller** [kɥijɛr] *nf* **1** : spoon **2** : spoonful **3 cuillère à thé** *or* **cuillère à café** : teaspoon
cuillerée [kɥijere] *nf* **1** : spoonful **2 cuillerée à café** : teaspoonful
cuir [kɥir] *nm* **1** : leather **2** : hide <cuir brut : rawhide> **3 cuir chevelu** : scalp
cuirasse [kɥiras] *nf* **1** : breastplate **2** : armor (of a tank, etc.)
cuirassé [kɥirase] *nm* : battleship
cuirasser [kɥirase] *vt* **1** : to armor **2** : to harden — **se cuirasser** *vr* : to harden oneself

cuire [kɥir] {49} *vt* **1** : to cook, to bake **2** : to fire (pottery) — *vi* **1** : to cook **2** : to sting, to burn
cuisait [kɥizɛ], **cuisions** [kɥizjɔ̃], *etc.* → **cuire**
cuisant, -sante [kɥizɑ̃, -zɑ̃t] *adj* **1** : stinging, smarting **2** : bitter
cuise [kɥiz], *etc.* → **cuire**
cuisine [kɥizin] *nf* **1** : kitchen **2** : cooking, cuisine **3 faire la cuisine** : to cook
cuisiné, -née [kɥizine] *adj* **plat cuisiné** : prepared food
cuisiner [kɥizine] *vt* **1** : to cook **2** *fam* : to grill, to interrogate — *vi* : to cook
cuisinette [kɥizinɛt] *nf* : kitchenette
cuisinier, -nière [kɥizinje, -njɛr] *n* : chef, cook
cuisinière *nf* : stove
cuisse [kɥis] *nf* **1** : thigh **2** : leg <cuisses de grenouilles : frogs' legs>
cuisson [kɥisɔ̃] *nf* : cooking, baking
cuit, cuite [kɥi, kɥit] *adj* **1** : cooked <bien cuit : well-done> **2 être cuit** *fam* : to be done for, to have had it
cuite *nf* **prendre une cuite** *fam* : to get drunk
cuivre [kɥivr] *nm* **1** *or* **cuivre rouge** : copper **2** *or* **cuivre jaune** : brass **3 cuivres** *nmpl* : brass (musical instruments)
cuivré, -vrée [kɥivre] *adj* **1** : copper-colored, bronzed **2** : resonant
culbute [kylbyt] *nf* **1** : somersault **2** CHUTE : tumble, fall
culbuter [kylbyte] *vt* **1** : to knock over **2** : to overthrow — *vi* **1** : to somersault **2** TOMBER : to tumble, to fall
cul-de-sac [kydsak] *nm, pl* **culs-de-sac** : dead end, cul-de-sac
culinaire [kylinɛr] *adj* : culinary
culminant, -nante [kylminɑ̃, -nɑ̃t] *adj* **point culminant** : high point, peak
culminer [kylmine] *vi* **1** : to culminate, to peak **2** DOMINER : to dominate, to tower
culot [kylo] *nm fam* : impudence, cheek <avoire du culot : to have a lot of nerve>
culotte [kylɔt] *nf* **1** PANTALON : pants *pl*, trousers *pl* **2** : panties *pl*
culotté, -tée [kylɔte] *adj fam* : sassy, cheeky
culpabiliser [kylpabilize] *vt* ~ **qqn** : to make someone feel guilty — *vi* : to feel guilty
culpabilité [kylpabilite] *nf* : guilt
culte [kylt] *nm* **1** : worship, cult <liberté de culte : freedom of worship> <le culte de personalité : the cult of personality> **2** : religion, creed **3** : (Protestant) service
cultivateur, -trice [kyltivatœr, -tris] *n* AGRICULTEUR : farmer
cultivé, -vée [kyltive] *adj* **1** : cultivated **2** : cultured
cultiver [kyltive] *vt* : to cultivate — **se cultiver** *vr*
culture [kyltyr] *nf* **1** : culture **2** : cultivation, growing **3 culture physique** : physical education
culturel, -relle [kyltyrɛl] *adj* : cultural — **culturellement** [-rɛlmɑ̃] *adv*
culturisme [kyltyrism] *nm* : bodybuilding
cumin [kymɛ̃] *nm* : cumin
cumul [kymyl] *nm* **1** : holding concurrently <cumul de fonctions : holding several offices at the same time> **2** : accumulation
cumulatif, -tive [kymylatif, -tiv] *adj* : cumulative
cumuler [kymyle] *vt* **1** : to hold concurrently **2** ACCUMULER : to accumulate, to pile up — **se cumuler** *vr* : to accrue
cumulus [kymylys] *nms & pl* : cumulus
cupide [kypid] *adj* : greedy
cupidité [kypidite] *nf* : greed
curatif, -tive [kyratif, -tiv] *adj* : curative
cure [kyr] *nf* **1** : treatment, cure **2** : parish, vicarage **3 n'avoir cure de** : to have little concern for <elle n'en a cure : she doesn't care about it>
curé [kyre] *nm* : pastor, parish priest
cure-dent *or* **cure-dents** [kyrdɑ̃] *nm, pl* **cure-dents** : toothpick
curer [kyre] *vt* : to clean out, to scrape out — **se curer** *vr* : to clean (one's nails, etc.)
curieusement [kyrjøzmɑ̃] *adv* : curiously, strangely
curieux[1], **-rieuse** [kyrjø, -rjøz] *adj* **1** : curious, inquisitive **2** : strange, odd
curieux[2], **-rieuse** *n* **1** : onlooker **2** : busybody
curieux[3] *nm* : curious thing, oddity <le curieux dans tout ça : the strange thing in all that>
curiosité [kyrjɔzite] *nf* : curiosity
curry [kyri] *nm* : curry
curseur [kyrsœr] *nm* : cursor
cuspide [kyspid] *nf* : cusp
cutané, -née [kytane] *adj* : cutaneous, skin
cuve [kyv] *nf* : tub, tank, vat
cuvée [kyve] *nf* : vintage
cuver [kyve] *vi* : to ferment
cuvette [kyvɛt] *nf* **1** : bowl, washbasin **2** : basin (in geology)
cyanure [sjanyr] *nm* : cyanide
cyberespace [siberɛspas] *nm* : cyberspace
cyclable [siklabl] *adj* **piste cyclable** : bicycle path
cycle [sikl] *nm* : cycle
cyclique [siklik] *adj* : cyclic, cyclical
cyclisme [siklism] *nm* : cycling, bicycling
cycliste[1] [siklist] *adj* : cycle, bicycle <course cycliste : bicycle race>
cycliste[2] *nmf* : cyclist, bicyclist
cyclomoteur [sikləmɔtœr] *nm* : moped
cyclone [siklon] *nm* : cyclone
cygne [siɲ] *nm* : swan

cylindre [silɛ̃dr] *nm* : cylinder
cylindrée [silɛ̃dre] *nf* : capacity (of an engine)
cylindrique [silɛ̃drik] *adj* : cylindrical
cymbale [sɛ̃bal] *nf* : cymbal
cynique[1] [sinik] *adj* : cynical — **cyniquement** [-nikmɑ̃] *adv*
cynique[2] *nmf* : cynic
cynisme [sinism] *nm* : cynicism
cyprès [sipre] *nm* : cypress
cypriote [siprijɔt] *adj* : Cypriot
Cypriote *nmf* : Cypriot
cytoplasme [sitɔplasm] *nm* : cytoplasm

D

d [de] *nm* : d, the fourth letter of the alphabet
d'abord [dabɔr] → **abord**
d'accord [dakɔr] → **accord**
dactylo[1] [daktilo] *or* **dactylographe** [daktilɔgraf] *nmf* : typist
dactylo[2] *nf* **1** → **dactylographie 2** *Can* : typewriter
dactylographie [daktilɔgrafi] *nf* : typing
dactylographier [daktilɔgrafje] {96} *vt* : to type
dada [dada] *nm* **1** *fam* : hobbyhorse, pet subject **2** : Dada
dadais [dadɛ] *nms & pl* : silly fool, oaf
dague [dag] *nf* : dagger
dahlia [dalja] *nm* : dahlia
daigner [deɲe] *vt* : to deign, to condescend <il n'a pas daigné répondre : he didn't deign to reply>
daim [dɛ̃] *nm* **1** : fallow deer **2** : suede
dais [dɛ] *nms & pl* : canopy
dallage [dalaʒ] *nm* **1** : paving **2** : pavement
dalle [dal] *nf* **1** : paving stone, flagstone **2** : slab (of stone or concrete)
daller [dale] *vt* : to pave
dalmatien [dalmasjɛ̃] *nm* : dalmatian (dog)
daltonien, -nienne [daltɔnjɛ̃, -njɛn] *adj* : color-blind
dam [dam] *nm* **au grand dam de** : much to the detriment of, to the great displeasure of
damas [damɑs] *nms & pl* : damask
dame [dam] *nf* **1** : lady **2** : queen (in chess or card games) **3 dames** *nfpl or* **jeu de dames** : checkers
damer [dame] *vt* **1** : to pack down **2** : to crown (in checkers) **3 damer le pion à** : to get the better of
damier [damje] *nm* : checkerboard
damnation [danasjɔ̃] *nf* : damnation
damné[1], **-née** [dane] *adj* : damned, cursed
damné[2], **-née** *n* : damned person
damner [dane] *vt* : to damn
dandinement [dɑ̃dinmɑ̃] *nm* : waddling, waddle
dandiner [dɑ̃dine] *v* **se dandiner** *vr* : to waddle
dandy [dɑ̃di] *nm* : dandy
danger [dɑ̃ʒe] *nm* : danger
dangereux, -reuse [dɑ̃ʒrø, -røz] *adj* : dangerous — **dangereusement** [-røzmɑ̃] *adv*
danois[1], **-noise** [danwa, -waz] *adj* : Danish
danois[2] *nm* **1** : Danish (language) **2** : Great Dane
Danois, -noise *n* : Dane
dans [dɑ̃] *prep* **1** : in <dans la boîte : in the box> <dans dix jours : in ten days> **2** : into <monter dans l'auto : to get into the car> **3** : from, out of <elle buvait dans une tasse : she was drinking from a cup>
dansant, -sante [dɑ̃sɑ̃, -sɑ̃t] *adj* : dancing <soirée dansante : dance (party)>
danse [dɑ̃s] *nf* : dance, dancing
danser [dɑ̃se] *v* : to dance
danseur, -seuse [dɑ̃sœr, -søz] *n* : dancer
dard [dar] *nm* **1** AIGUILLON : stinger **2** : spear, javelin **3** *Can* : dart <jouer aux dards : to play darts>
darder [darde] *vt* : to shoot forth, to hurl
date [dat] *nf* **1** : date <date de naissance : date of birth> **2** : time <de longue date : long-standing> **3** → **limite**
dater [date] *vt* : to date — *vi* **1** : to be dated, to be old-fashioned **2** ~ **de** : to date from, to date back to
datte [dat] *nf* : date (fruit)
daube [dob] *nf* : casserole, stew
dauphin [dofɛ̃] *nm* **1** : dolphin **2** : dauphin, heir apparent
davantage [davɑ̃taʒ] *adv* **1** : more <elle ne se souvient pas davantage : she doesn't remember more> **2** : longer, any longer <je voudrais rester davantage : I'd like to stay longer>
DDT [dedete] *nm* : DDT
de [də] (**d'** *before vowels and mute h*) *prep* **1** : from <de Québec à Montréal : from Quebec to Montreal> **2** : by <de nuit : by night> <une comédie de Molière : a play by Molière> **3** : of <au bout du monde : at the ends of the earth> **4** : with <je tombe de fatigue : I'm completely worn out> **5** (*before infinitive*) : to, of <il craint d'être en retard : he's afraid of being late> **6 de la, du, des** : some, any <voulez-vous des haricots? : would you like some beans?>
dé [de] *nm* **1** : die, dice *pl* **2** *or* **dé à coudre** : thimble

déambuler [deɑ̃byle] *vi* : to stroll, to wander about
débâcle [debakl] *nf* : debacle, fiasco
déballer [debale] *vt* **1** : to unpack, to unwrap **2** : to display (merchandise)
débandade [debɑ̃dad] *nf* **1** : rout, stampede **2 à la débandade** : in disarray
débarbouiller [debarbuje] *v* **se débarbouiller** *vr* : to wash one's face
débarbouillette [debarbujet] *nf Can* : washcloth, facecloth
débarcadère [debarkadɛr] *nm* : wharf, dock
débardeur [debardœr] *nm* : longshoreman
débarquement [debarkəmɑ̃] *nm* **1** : unloading **2** : landing, disembarcation
débarquer [debarke] *vt* **1** : to unload (goods) **2** : to land (troops, etc.) — *vi* : to disembark
débarrasser [debarase] *vt* **1** : to clear **2** ~ **de** : to relieve of, to free from — **se débarrasser** *vr* ~ **de** : to get rid of
débarrer [debare] *vt Can* : to unlock
débat [deba] *nm* **1** : debate, discussion **2 débats** *nmpl* : proceedings
débattre [debatr] {12} *vt* : to debate, to discuss — *vi Can* : to pound, to race (of the heart) — **se débattre** *vr* : to struggle, to thrash about
débauche [deboʃ] *nf* : debauchery, vice
débauché[1], **-chée** [deboʃe] *adj* : debauched
débauché[2], **-chée** *n* : debauched person, libertine
débaucher [deboʃe] *vt* **1** CORROMPRE : to corrupt **2** LICENCIER : to lay off **3** : to cause to go on strike
débile [debil] *adj* **1** : weak, feeble **2** *fam* : stupid, idiotic
débilité [debilite] *nf* **1** : debility **2** *fam* : silliness, stupidity
débiliter [debilite] *vt* **1** : to debilitate **2** : to demoralize
débiner [debine] *vt Can fam* : to disconcert
débit [debi] *nm* **1** : debit **2** : turnover (of merchandise, etc.) **3** : (rate of) flow, discharge **4** ÉLOCUTION : delivery, speech **5** *France* : shop <débit de boissons : bar>
débiter [debite] *vt* **1** : to debit **2** : to sell, to retail **3** : to produce, to yield **4** : to cut up **5** : to discharge, to flow (out) **6** : to drone, to reel off
débiteur[1], **-trice** [debitœr, -tris] *adj* : debit <compte débiteur : debit account>
débiteur[2], **-trice** *n* : debtor
déblai [deble] *nm* **1** : excavation **2 déblais** *nmpl* DÉCOMBRES : rubble, debris
déblaiement [deblɛmɑ̃] *nm* : clearing (of earth)
déblatérer [deblatere] {87} *vi* ~ **contre** : to rant against
déblayer [debleje] {11} *vt* **1** : to clear (away) **2** : to prepare, to sort out
débloquer [debloke] *vt* **1** : to free, to release **2** : to unfreeze (funds), to release — *vi fam* **1** : to talk nonsense **2** : to be out of one's mind
déboguer [debɔge] *vt* : to debug
déboires [debwar] *nmpl* **1** DÉCEPTIONS : disappointments **2** ENNUIS : difficulties, tribulations
déboiser [debwaze] *vt* : to deforest
déboîtement [debwatmɑ̃] *nm* : dislocation
déboîter [debwate] *vt* **1** : to dislocate (in medicine) **2** : to disconnect, to unfasten — *vi* : to pull out, to change lanes (in an automobile) — **se déboîter** *vr* : to dislocate (one's shoulder, etc.)
débonnaire [debɔnɛr] *adj* : easygoing, good-natured
débordant, -dante [debɔrdɑ̃, -dɑ̃t] *adj* : overflowing, brimming <débordant d'énergie : bursting with energy>
débordé, -dée [debɔrde] *adj* : overwhelmed, overloaded (with work, etc.)
débordement [debɔrdəmɑ̃] *nm* : overflow, excess
déborder [debɔrde] *vi* : to overflow — *vt* **1** : to jut out from, to extend beyond **2** : to overwhelm **3** : to overflow
débouché [debuʃe] *nm* **1** : outlet, market **2** : opportunity, prospect
déboucher [debuʃe] *vt* **1** : to clear, to unblock **2** : to uncork, to open — *vi* **1** ~ **de** : to emerge from, to come out of **2** ~ **sur** : to open onto, to lead to — **se déboucher** : to become unblocked
déboucler [debukle] *vt* : to unbuckle, to undo
débouler [debule] *vi* **1** *fam* : to tumble down **2** : to bolt, to shoot out — *vt* : to charge down (a stairway, etc.)
débours [debur] *nms & pl* : expense, outlay
débourser [deburse] *vt* : to pay out, to spend <sans rien débourser : without paying a penny>
déboussolé, -lée [debusɔle] *adj fam* : disoriented, confused
debout [dəbu] *adv* **1** : standing up **2** : upright, on end **3** : up, out of bed **4 tenir debout** : to stand up to examination, to hold water
déboutonner [debutɔne] *vt* : to unbutton, to undo — **se déboutonner** *vr*
débraillé, -lée [debraje] *adj* : disheveled, slovenly
débrancher [debrɑ̃ʃe] *vt* : to unplug, to disconnect
débrayage [debrɛjaʒ] *nm* **1** : disengaging the clutch **2** : strike, walkout
débrayer [debreje] {1} *vi* **1** : to disengage the clutch **2** : to go on strike
débridé, -dée [debride] *adj* : unbridled, unrestrained

débris [debri] *nms & pl* **1** : fragment **2** **débris** *nmpl* : rubbish, scraps, remains
débrouillard, -larde [debrujar, -jard] *adj fam* : resourceful
débrouillardise [debrujardiz] *nf fam* : resourcefulness
débrouiller [debruje] *vt* **1** DÉMÊLER : to disentangle **2** : to unravel, to solve — **se débrouiller** *vr* **1** : to manage <se débrouiller pour obtenir : to wangle, to finagle> **2** : to get by <il se débrouille bien : he's getting along all right>
débroussailler [debrusaje] *vt* **1** : to clear (land) **2** : to lay the groundwork for
débusquer [debyske] *vt* : to flush, to drive out (from hiding)
début [deby] *nm* **1** : beginning, start <au début : at the beginning> <dès le début : from the start> **2** (*used in expressions of time*) <début juin : in early June> **3 débuts** *nmpl* : debut, early stages <faire ses débuts : to make one's debut> **4 au début** : to begin with, at first
débutant, -tante [debytã, -tãt] *n* : beginner, novice, learner
débutante *nf* : debutante
débuter [debyte] *v* : to begin, to start
deçà [dəsa] *adv* **1 deçà, delà** : here and there **2 en deçà de** : on this side of **3 en deçà de** : short of, below
décacheter [dekaʃte] {8} *vt* : to unseal (an envelope)
décade [dekad] *nf* **1** : period of ten days **2** : decade
décadence [dekadãs] *nf* : decadence
décadent, -dente [dekadã, -dãt] *adj* : decadent
décaféiné, -née [dekafeine] *adj* : decaffeinated
décalage [dekalaʒ] *nm* **1** : discrepancy **2** : gap, space **3** : interval <décalage horaire : time difference>
décalcomanie [dekalkɔmani] *nf* : decal
décaler [dekale] *vt* **1** : to move forward or back (a time, a date) **2** : to move, to shift (an object)
décamper [dekãpe] *vi* : to clear out, to decamp
décanter [dekãte] *vt* **1** : to allow (a liquid) to settle **2** : to clarify (ideas, etc.) — **se décanter** *vr*
décapant[1], **-pante** [dekapã, -pãt] *adj* : caustic, abrasive
décapant[2] *nm* **1** : scouring agent **2** : paint stripper
décaper [dekape] *vt* **1** : to clean, to scour **2** : to strip (paint, etc.)
décapiter [dekapite] *vt* : to decapitate, to behead
décapotable [dekapɔtabl] *adj & nf* : convertible
décapsuleur [dekapsylœr] *nm* : bottle opener
décati, -tie [dekati] *adj* : decrepit
décédé, -dée [desede] *adj* : deceased
décéder [desede] {87} *vi* : to die, to pass away
déceler [desle] {20} *vt* **1** DÉCOUVRIR : to detect, to uncover **2** RÉVÉLER : to indicate, to reveal
décélération [deselerasjõ] *nf* : deceleration
décembre [desãbr] *nm* : December
décemment [desamã] *adv* : decently
décence [desãs] *nf* : decency
décennie [deseni] *nf* : decade
décent, -cente [desã, -sãt] *adj* : decent
décentraliser [desãtralize] *vt* : to decentralize — **décentralisation** [-lizasjõ] *nf*
déception [desepsjõ] *nf* : disappointment
décerner [deserne] *vt* **1** : to award **2** : to issue (a writ)
décès [dese] *nm* : death
décevant, -vante [desəvã, -vãt] *adj* : disappointing
décevoir [desəvwar] {26} *vt* : to disappoint
déchaîné, -née [deʃene] *adj* : raging, unbridled
déchaînement [deʃɛnmã] *nm* **1** : fury, raging (of the elements) **2** EXPLOSION : outburst (of emotion)
déchaîner [deʃene] *vt* : to unleash, to arouse — **se déchaîner** *vr* : to erupt, to burst out
déchanter [deʃãte] *vi* : to become disillusioned
décharge [deʃarʒ] *nf* **1** : discharge (of a firearm) **2** : garbage dump **3 décharge électrique** : electric shock
déchargement [deʃarʒəmã] *nm* : unloading
décharger [deʃarʒe] {17} *vt* **1** : to unload **2** : to discharge (a firearm, etc.) **3** : to relieve, to unburden **4** : to exonerate, to clear **5** : to give vent to
décharné, -née [deʃarne] *adj* : emaciated, bony
déchausser [deʃose] *v* **se déchausser** *vr* : to take off one's shoes
déchéance [deʃeãs] *nf* : decay, decline
déchet [deʃɛ] *nm* **1** : scrap **2** : waste, wastage **3 déchets** *nmpl* : refuse, waste (materials) <déchets toxiques : toxic waste>
déchiffrer [deʃifre] *vt* **1** : to decipher **2** : to sight-read (music)
déchiqueté, -tée [deʃikte] *adj* : jagged, ragged
déchiqueter [deʃikte] {8} *vt* : to tear into pieces
déchirant, -rante [deʃirã, -rãt] *adj* : heartbreaking, heartrending
déchirement [deʃirmã] *nm* **1** : tearing **2** : heartbreak **3** : rift, split
déchirer [deʃire] *vt* **1** : to tear up, to rip **2** : to tear apart, to split — **se déchirer** *vr*
déchirure [deʃiryr] *nf* : tear <déchirure ligamentaire : torn ligament>

déchoir [deʃwar] {27} *vi* **1** : to demean oneself **2** : to fall, to decline (in prestige)
déchu[1] [deʃy] *pp* → **décevoir**
déchu[2], **-chue** [deʃy] *adj* **1** : fallen (from grace or favor) **2** : deposed
décibel [desibɛl] *nm* : decibel
décidé, -dée [deside] *adj* **1** : decided, settled **2** DÉTERMINÉ : determined, resolved
décidément [desidemɑ̃] *adv* : definitely, really
décider [deside] *vt* **1** : to decide <j'ai décidé de partir : I decided to leave> **2** CONVAINCRE : to persuade **3 ~ de** : to decide on, to determine <nous avons décidé d'une date : we've set a date> — **se décider** *vr* : to make up one's mind
décimal, -male [desimal] *adj, mpl* **-maux** [-mo] : decimal
décimale *nf* : decimal
décimer [desime] *vt* : to decimate
décisif, -sive [desizif, -ziv] *adj* : decisive — **décisivement** [-zivmɑ̃] *adv*
décision [desizjɔ̃] *nf* **1** : decision <prendre une decision : to make a decision> **2** : decisiveness
déclamer [deklame] *vi* : to declaim
déclaratif, -tive [deklaratif, -tiv] *adj* : declarative
déclaration [deklarasjɔ̃] *nf* **1** : declaration, statement <déclaration de guerre : declaration of war> <faire sa déclaration : to declare one's love> **2** : (official) notification <déclaration d'impôts : income tax return> **3** : testimony, statement (in court)
déclarer [deklare] *vt* **1** : to declare, to announce **2** : to claim, to register (births, deaths, etc.) <déclarer qqch à la douane : to declare sth at customs> — **se déclarer** *vr* **1** : to declare oneself **2** : to declare one's love **3** : to break out, to show itself (of a disease, a fire, etc.)
déclassement [deklasmɑ̃] *nm* : downgrading, demotion
déclasser [deklase] *vt* **1** : to demote, to downgrade **2** : to get out of order, to disarrange **3** : to demean
déclenchement [deklɑ̃ʃmɑ̃] *nm* : start, launching
déclencher [deklɑ̃ʃe] *vt* **1** : to release, to set off **2** PROVOQUER : to trigger, to prompt **3** : to launch, to begin
déclencheur [deklɑ̃ʃœr] *nm* **1** : release mechanism **2** : trigger
déclic [deklik] *nm* **1** : trigger (mechanism) **2** : click
déclin [deklɛ̃] *nm* **1** : decline, waning **2** : close <le déclin du jour : the close of day>
déclinaison [deklinezɔ̃] *nf* : declension
décliner [dekline] *vi* : to decline, to wane — *vt* **1** : to refuse **2** : to decline (a noun) **3** : to state, to give (one's name, address, etc.)
déclivité [deklivite] *nf* : slope, incline
décloisonner [deklwazɔne] *vt* : to open up, to decompartmentalize
décocher [dekɔʃe] *vt* **1** : to shoot, to hurl **2** : to flash, to dart <il a décoché un sourire : he flashed a smile>
décoder [dekɔde] *vt* : to decode
décoiffer [dekwafe] *vt* **décoiffer qqn** : to mess up s.o.'s hair — *vi* **ça décoiffe** *fam* : it takes your breath away
décoincer [dekwɛ̃se] {6} *vt* **1** : to loosen, to unjam **2** *fam* : to loosen (someone) up — **se décoincer** *vr*
déçoit [deswa], **déçoive** [deswav], *etc.* → **décevoir**
décolérer [dekɔlere] {87} *vi* : to calm down, to cool off
décollage [dekɔlɑtaʒ] *nm* : takeoff
décoller [dekɔle] *vt* : to unstick, to remove — *vi* : to take off (of an airplane, a project, etc.)
décolleté[1], **-tée** [dekɔlte] *adj* : low-cut
décolleté[2] *nm* **1** : low neckline **2** : cleavage
décolorant [dekɔlɔrɑ̃, -rɑt] *nm* : bleach
décoloration [dekɔlɔrasjɔ̃] *nf* **1** : fading, discoloration **2** : bleaching
décolorer [dekɔlɔre] *vt* : to bleach, to cause to fade — **se décolorer** *vr* **1** : to fade **2** : to bleach one's hair
décombres [decɔ̃br] *nmpl* : rubble, debris
décommander [dekɔmɑ̃de] *vt* : to cancel — **se décommander** *vr* : to cancel one's appointment
décomposer [dekɔ̃poze] *vt* **1** : to break down, to break up **2** POURRIR : to rot, to cause to decompose **3** : to contort, to distort (one's face) — **se décomposer** *vr*
décomposition [dekɔ̃pozisjɔ̃] *nf* : decomposition, rotting
décompresser [dekɔ̃prese] *vt* : to decompress — *vi* : to relax, to unwind
décompte [dekɔ̃t] *nm* **1** : account, statement **2** : breakdown, count **3** : deduction, discount
décompter [dekɔ̃te] *vt* **1** : to deduct **2** : to calculate, to count — *vi* : to strike the wrong hour
déconcentration [dekɔ̃sɑ̃trasjɔ̃] *nf* **1** : decentralization **2** : distraction, loss of concentration
déconcentrer [dekɔ̃sɑ̃tre] *vt* **1** : to decentralize **2** : to distract — **se déconcentrer** *vr* : to lose one's concentration
déconcerter [dekɔ̃serte] *vt* : to disconcert
déconfit, -fite [dekɔ̃fi, -fit] *adj* : downcast, crestfallen
déconfiture [dekɔ̃fityr] *nf* **1** : failure, collapse, defeat **2** : insolvency, bankruptcy
décongeler [dekɔ̃ʒle] {20} *vt* : to thaw, to defrost
décongestif [dekɔ̃ʒestif, -tiv] *nm* : decongestant

décongestionnant[1], **-nante** [dekɔ̃ʒɛstjɔnɑ̃, -nɑ̃t] *adj* : decongestant
décongestionnant[2] *nm* : decongestant
décongestionner [dekɔ̃ʒɛstjɔne] *vt* : to relieve congestion in, to decongest
déconnecter [dekɔnɛkte] *vt* : to disconnect
déconner [dekɔne] *vi fam* **1** : to talk nonsense **2** : to mess around **3** : to be on the blink
déconseiller [dekɔ̃seje] *vt* : to dissuade, to advise against <elle m'a déconseillé d'y aller : she advised me not to go>
déconsidération [dekɔ̃siderasjɔ̃] *nf* : discredit
déconsidérer [dekɔ̃sidere] {87} *vt* : to discredit — **se déconsidérer** *vr*
décontaminer [dekɔ̃tamine] *vt* : to decontaminate
décontenancer [dekɔ̃tnɑ̃se] {6} *vt* : to disconcert — **se décontenancer** *vr* : to lose one's composure
décontracté, -tée [dekɔ̃trakte] *adj* **1** : relaxed **2** : casual, laid-back
décontracter [dekɔ̃trakte] *vt* : to relax — **se décontracter** *vr*
déconvenue [dekɔ̃vny] *nf* DÉCEPTION : disappointment
décor [dekɔr] *nm* **1** : decor **2** : scenery **3** : set, scenery (of movies or theater) **4 dans le décor** : off the road <il est rentré dans le décor : he drove off the road>
décorateur, -trice [dekɔratœr, -tris] *n* **1** : interior decorator **2** : set designer
décoratif, -tive [dekɔratif, -tiv] *adj* : decorative, ornamental
décorer [dekɔre] *vt* ORNER : to decorate — **décoration** [-kɔrasjɔ̃] *nf*
décortiquer [dekɔrtike] *vt* **1** : to shell, to hull **2** : to dissect, to analyze
décorum [dekɔrɔm] *nm* : decorum, propriety
découcher [dekuʃe] *vi* : to stay out all night
découdre [dekudr] {22} *vt* : to unstitch, to rip — *vi* **en ~** : to fight
découler [dekule] *vi* : to result, to follow, to ensue
découpage [dekupaʒ] *nm* **1** : cutting up, carving **2** : cutout **3** : shooting script (of a film) **4 découpage électoral** : districting
découper [dekupe] *vt* **1** : to cut up, to carve **2** : to cut out **3** : to indent (landforms, etc.) — **se découper** *vr* : to stand out
découplé, -plée [dekuple] *adj* **bien découplé** : well-built, well-proportioned
découpure [dekupyr] *nf* **1** : cutting **2** : indented outline
découragement [dekuraʒmɑ̃] *nm* : discouragement, despondency
décourager [dekuraʒe] {17} *vt* **1** : to discourage, to dishearten **2** : to deter, to put off
décousu, -sue [dekusy] *adj* **1** : unstitched **2** : disjointed, disconnected
découvert[1], **-verte** [dekuvɛr, -vɛrt] *adj* : bare, uncovered, exposed
découvert[2] *nm* : overdraft <être à découvert : to be overdrawn>
découverte *nf* : discovery, find
découvreur, -vreuse [dekuvrœr, -vrøz] *n* : discoverer, finder
découvrir [dekuvrir] {83} *vt* **1** : to discover **2** : to uncover **3** : to disclose, to reveal **4** : to catch sight of, to see — **se découvrir** *vr* **1** : to doff one's hat **2** : to undress, to uncover oneself **3** : to understand oneself **4** : to expose oneself to attack **5** : to clear up (of weather)
décrasser [dekrase] *vt* **1** : to clean, to scrub **2** : to polish, to remove the rough edges from (a person) — **se décrasser** *vr*
décrépit, -pite [dekrepi, -pit] *adj* : decrepit
décrépitude [dekrepityd] *nf* : decrepitude
décret [dekrɛ] *nm* : decree, edict
décréter [dekrete] {87} *vt* : to decree, to order
décrier [dekrije] {96} *vt* : to decry, to disparage
décrire [dekrir] {33} *vt* : to describe
décrocher [dekrɔʃe] *vt* **1** : to unhook, to take down, to undo <décrocher le téléphone : to pick up the telephone> **2** *fam* : to get, to land <décrocher une bonne situation : to land a good job> — *vi* **1** *fam* : to drop out, to give up **2** *fam* : to tune out, to stop paying attention **3** : to fall behind
décrocheur, -cheuse [dekrɔʃœr, -ʃøz] *n* *Can* : high school dropout
décroissance [dekrwasɑ̃s] *nf* : decrease, decline
décroître [dekrwatr] {25} *vi* : to decrease, to decline
décrotter [dekrɔte] *vt* : to scrape mud off
décrue [dekry] *nf* : drop in the water level
décrypter [dekripte] *vt* : to decipher
déçu[1] [desy] *pp* → **décevoir**
déçu[2], **-çue** [desy] *adj* : disappointed
décupler [dekyple] *v* : to increase tenfold
dédaigner [dedeɲe] *vt* : to disdain, to scorn
dédaigneux, -neuse [dedeɲø, -ɲøz] *adj* : disdainful, scornful — **dédaigneusement** [-ɲøzmɑ̃] *adv*
dédain [dedɛ̃] *nm* MÉPRIS : disdain, scorn
dédale [dedal] *nm* : maze, labyrinth
dedans[1] [dədɑ̃] *adv* **1** : inside, in **2 de ~** : from within **3 en ~** : on the inside, inwardly, within
dedans[2] *nm* : inside, interior <du dehors vers le dedans : from the outside in>

dédicace [dedikas] *nf* : dedication, inscription (in a book, etc.)

dédicacer [dedikase] {6} *vt* : to inscribe, to autograph, to dedicate

dédier [dedje] {96} *vt* **1** : to dedicate (a work of art, etc.) **2** : to devote, to dedicate

dédire [dedir] {29} *v* **se dédire** *vr* **1** : to retract (a statement) **2 ~ de** : to go back on, to fail to honor

dédit [dedi] *nm* **1** : retraction **2** : penalty (for breach of contract)

dédommagement [dedɔmɔʒmɑ̃] *nm* INDEMNITÉ : compensation

dédommager [dedɔmaʒe] {17} *vt* **1** : to compensate **2** : to repay, to make up for

dédouaner [dedwane] *vt* **1** : to clear through customs **2** : to clear (one's name), to rehabilitate

dédoubler [deduble] *vt* **1** : to divide, to split in two **2** : to remove the lining of (a garment) — **se dédoubler** *vr* **1** : to split (up), to come apart **2** : to be in two places at once

déductible [dedyktibl] *adj* : deductible

déduction [dedyksjɔ̃] *nf* **1** : deduction **2** : conclusion, inference

déduire [deduir] {49} *vt* **1** : to deduct **2** : to deduce, to infer

déesse [deɛs] *nf* : goddess

défaillance [defajɑ̃s] *nf* **1** : failure, fault **2** : failing, weakness **3** ÉVANOUISSEMENT : blackout, fainting fit

défaillant, -lante [defajɑ̃, -jɑ̃t] *adj* **1** : failing, unsteady **2** : weak, faint

défaillir [defajir] {93} *vi* **1** : to faint **2** : to weaken, to falter

défaire [defɛr] {42} *vt* **1** : to undo, to untie, to unravel **2** : to unpack **3** DÉMONTER : to dismantle, to take down, to break up **4 défaire le lit** : to strip the bed — **se défaire** *vr* **1** : to come undone, to come apart **2 ~ de** : to part with

défait, -faite [defɛ, -fɛt] *adj* **1** : undone **2** : defeated **3** : haggard

défaite *nf* : defeat

défaitisme [defetism] *nm* : defeatism — **défaitiste** [-fetist] *adj & nmf*

défalquer [defalke] *vt* : to deduct — **défalcation** [-falkasjɔ̃] *nf*

défausser [defose] *vt* : to straighten — **se défausser** *vr* : to discard (in card games)

défaut [defo] *nm* **1** IMPERFECTION : flaw, defect <défaut d'élocution : speech impediment> **2** FAIBLESSE : fault, shortcoming **3** MANQUE : lack, shortage <faire défaut : to be lacking> **4 à défaut de** : for lack of

défaveur [defavœr] *nf* : disfavor

défavorable [defavɔrabl] *adj* : unfavorable — **défavorablement** [-rabləmɑ̃] *adv*

défavoriser [defavɔrize] *vt* DÉSAVANTAGER : to put at a disadvantage

défection [defɛksjɔ̃] *nf* **1** : defection, desertion **2 faire défection** : to defect

défectueux, -tueuse [defɛktɥø, -tɥøz] *adj* : defective, faulty

défectuosité [defɛktɥozite] *nf* **1** : defectiveness **2** : defect, fault

défendable [defɑ̃dabl] *adj* : defensible, justifiable

défendeur, -deresse [defɑ̃dœr, -drɛs] *n* : defendant

défendre [defɑ̃dr] {63} *vt* **1** SOUTENIR : to defend, to champion **2** PROTÉGER : to protect, to safeguard **3** INTERDIRE : to forbid, to prohibit <il est défendu de fumer : smoking is prohibited> — **se défendre** *vr* **1** : to defend oneself **2** : to make sense <ses raisons se défendent : he's got a point> **3** *fam* : to get by, to manage **4 ~ de** : to refrain from **5 ~ de** : to deny

défense [defɑ̃s] *nf* **1** : defense **2** INTERDICTION : prohibition <défense d'entrer : no admittance> **3** : tusk

défenseur [defɑ̃sœr] *nm* **1** : defender, advocate **2** : defender (in sports) **3** : defense attorney

défensif, -sive [defɑ̃sif, -siv] *adj* : defensive — **défensivement** [-sivmɑ̃] *adv*

défensive *nf* : defensive <se tenir sur la défensive : to be on the defensive>

déféquer [defeke] {87} *vi* : to defecate

déférence [deferɑ̃s] *nf* : deference

déférent, -rente [deferɑ̃, -rɑ̃t] *adj* RESPECTUEUX : deferential, respectful

déférer [defere] {87} *vt* : to refer (a case) to a court — *vi* **~ à** : to defer to

déferlement [deferləmɑ̃] *nm* **1** : surge, breaking (of waves) **2** : surge, wave (of emotion)

déferler [deferle] *vt* : to unfurl — *vi* **1** : to break (of waves) **2** : to flood in <les spectateurs déferlent dans le théâtre : the audience is streaming into the theater>

défi [defi] *nm* **1** : challenge, dare **2** : (act of) defiance

défiance [defjɑ̃s] *nf* : distrust

défiant, -fiante [defjɑ̃, -fjɑ̃t] *adj* : distrustful

déficeler [defisle] {8} *vt* : to untie (a package) — **se déficeler** *vr*

déficience [defisjɑ̃s] *nf* : deficiency

déficient, -ciente [defisjɑ̃, -sjɑ̃t] *adj* : deficient

déficit [defisit] *nm* **1** : deficit **2** MANQUE : deficiency, lack

déficitaire [defisitɛr] *adj* **1** : in deficit **2** : meager, poor <une récolte déficitaire : a poor harvest>

défier [defje] {96} *vt* **1** : to challenge **2** : to defy — **se défier** *vr* **~ de** : to distrust

défigurement [defigyrmɑ̃] *n* : disfigurement

défigurer [defigyre] *vt* **1** : to disfigure **2** : to distort <défigurer les faits : to distort the facts>
défilé [defile] *nm* **1** : parade **2** : stream <défilé de pensées : stream of thoughts> **3** : gorge, pass
défiler [defile] *vi* **1** : to march, to parade **2** : to succeed one another <les heures défilent : the hours pass one after the other> **3** : to stream past **4** : to scroll (on a computer) — **se défiler** *vr* : to sneak off, to slip away
défini, -nie [defini] *adj* **1** : defined <bien défini : well-defined> **2** : definite <article défini : definite article>
définir [definir] *vt* : to define — **se définir** *vr*
définitif, -tive [definitif, -tiv] *adj* : definitive, final
définition [definisjɔ̃] *nf* **1** : definition **2** : clue (in a crossword puzzle) **3** : resolution (of a televised image)
définitive *nf* **en ~** : finally, in the final analysis
définitivement [definitivmɑ̃] *adv* **1** : definitively, permanently **2** : definitely
déflagration [deflagrasjɔ̃] *nf* : explosion, combustion
déflation [deflasjɔ̃] *nf* : deflation
déflorer [deflɔre] *vt* **1** : to deflower **2** : to spoil <la répétition a défloré la plaisanterie : repetition made the joke stale>
défoncer [defɔ̃se] {6} *vt* **1** : to smash, to demolish, to break **2** : to knock the bottom out of — **se défoncer** *vr fam* **1** : to give it one's all **2** : to get high (on drugs)
déforestation [deforestasjɔ̃] *nf* : deforestation
déformation [deformasjɔ̃] *nf* **1** : deformation, distortion **2 déformation professionnelle** : conditioning by one's job, force of habit
déformer [deforme] *vt* **1** : to bend (out of shape) **2** : to deform, to distort — **se déformer** *vr* : to lose its shape
défoulement [defulmɑ̃] *nm* : release, letting off of steam
défouler [defule] *v* **se défouler** *vr* **1** : to unwind, to relax **2** : to vent (one's anger, etc.)
défraîchi, -chie [defreʃi] *adj* : faded, dingy, shopworn
défrayer [defreje] {11} *vt* **1** : to defray, to pay **2 défrayer la chronique** : to be in the news
défricher [defriʃe] *vt* **1** : to clear, to reclaim (land) **2** : to do the spadework for
défriser [defrize] *vt* **1** : to straighten (hair) **2** *fam* : to annoy, to bug
défroisser [defrwase] *vt* : to smooth out
défunt, -funte [defœ̃, -fœt] *adj & n* : deceased
dégagé, -gée [degaʒe] *adj* **1** : clear, open, bare **2** LIBRE : casual, free and easy
dégager [degaʒe] {17} *vt* **1** DÉLIVRER : to release, to free **2** : to clear <dégagez la voie! : clear the way!> **3** : to make (funds) available <dégager des profits : to show a profit> **4** EXTRAIRE : to bring out, to extract **5** ÉMETTRE : to emit, to give off — **se dégager** *vr* **1** : to emanate **2** : to clear (up) **3 ~ de** : to get free of, to extricate oneself from
dégaine [degɛn] *nf* : odd gait, gawky appearance
dégainer [degene] *vt* : to draw (a weapon)
dégarnir [degarnir] *vt* **1** VIDER : to empty, to clear **2** : to withdraw (troops) — **se dégarnir** *vr* **1** : to empty, to be cleared out **2** : to go bald **3** : to lose its leaves
dégâts [dega] *nmpl* : damage <dégâts des eaux : flood damage>
dégel [deʒɛl] *nm* : thaw
dégeler [deʒle] {20} *vt* **1** : to thaw out, to defrost **2** : to unfreeze (assets) **3** *fam* : to relax, to loosen up — *vi* : to thaw
dégêner [deʒɛne] *vt Can* : to put at ease — **se dégêner** *vr* : to come out of one's shell
dégénéré, -rée [deʒenere] *adj* : degenerate
dégénérer [deʒenere] {87} *vi* : to degenerate
dégénérescence [deʒeneresɑ̃s] *nf* : degeneration
dégingandé, -dée [deʒɛ̃gɑ̃de] *adj* : lanky, gangling
dégivrer [deʒivre] *vt* : to defrost, to deice
dégivreur [deʒivrœr] *nm* : defroster, deicer
déglinguer [deglɛ̃ge] *vt fam* : to bust, to break — **se déglinguer** *vr fam* : to break down, to go on the blink
déglutir [deglytir] *vi* : to swallow
déglutition [deglytisjɔ̃] *nf* : swallowing
dégommer [degɔme] *vt fam* : to sack, to fire
dégonflement [degɔ̃fləmɑ̃] *nm* : deflation (of a tire, etc.)
dégonfler [degɔ̃fle] *vt* **1** : to deflate **2** : to reduce (swelling) **3** *fam* : to debunk — **se dégonfler** *vr* **1** : to deflate, to go flat **2** : to go down **3** *fam* : to chicken out, to lose one's nerve
dégorger [degɔrʒe] {17} *vt* **1** : to disgorge (liquid) **2** : to unblock, to clear **3** : to soak clean — *vi* **1** : to run (of fabric) **2 faire dégorger** : to soak
dégouliner [deguline] *vi* **1** : to trickle **2** : to drip
dégourdi, -die [degurdi] *adj* : smart, clever
dégourdir [degurdir] *vt* **1** : to warm up, to loosen up (one's legs, etc.) **2** *fam* : to bring (s.o.) out, to make less timid — **se dégourdir** *vr* **1** : to move about

<se dégourdir les jambes : to stretch one's legs> **2** *fam* : to wise up
dégoût [degu] *nm* **1** : disgust, repugnance **2 dégoût de la vie** : weariness
dégoûtant, -tante [degutɑ̃, -tɑ̃t] *adj* : disgusting, revolting
dégoûté, -tée [degute] *adj* **1** : disgusted **2** DIFFICILE : fastidious <il n'est pas dégoûté : he's not fussy>
dégoûter [degute] *vt* : to disgust — **se dégoûter** *vr* ~ **de** : to get sick of
dégoutter [degute] *vi* : to drip
dégradation [degradasjɔ̃] *nf* **1** : degradation, deterioration **2** : decline (of conditions, morals, etc.) **3** : damage **4 dégradation civique** : loss of civil rights
dégradé [degrade] *nm* : gradation, shading (of colors)
dégrader [degrade] *vt* **1** : to degrade **2** ABÎMER : to damage, to spoil — **se dégrader** *vr*
dégrafer [degrafe] *vt* : to unhook, to unclasp
dégraissage [degrɛsaʒ] *nm* **1** : downsizing, cutbacks *pl* **2** : removal of grease stains **3** : trimming (of meat)
dégraisser [degrɛse] *vt* **1** : to downsize **2** : to remove grease marks from **3** : to trim the fat from
degré [dəgre] *nm* **1** : degree <un angle de 90 degrés : a 90-degree angle> **2** : proof (of alcohol) **3** : level, extent <une brûlure du premier degré : a first-degree burn> <cousins au second degré : second cousins> **4** : step <les degrés de l'échelle sociale : the rungs of the social ladder> **5 par degrés** : gradually
dégressif, -sive [degrɛsif, -siv] *adj* : graduated (of taxes, etc.)
dégrèvement [degrɛvmɑ̃] *nm* : tax relief
dégringolade [degrɛ̃gɔlad] *nf fam* : tumble, collapse
dégringoler [degrɛ̃gɔle] *fam vt* : to tumble down, to rush down — *vi* : to fall, to tumble
déguerpir [degɛrpir] *vi* **1** : to clear out **2 faire déguerpir** : to drive away
dégueulasse [degœlas] *adj fam* : disgusting
déguisement [degizmɑ̃] *nm* : disguise
déguiser [degize] *vt* : to disguise — **se déguiser** *vr* ~ **en** : to dress up as, to masquerade as
dégustateur, -trice [degystatœr, -tris] *n* : taster
déguster [degyste] *vt* **1** : to taste, to sample **2** : to savor, to enjoy
dehors[1] [dəɔr] *adv* **1** : outside, outdoors **2** : out <allons dehors ce soir : let's go out tonight> **3 en** ~ : (toward the) outside **4 en dehors de** : outside of, apart from
dehors[2] *nms & pl* **1** : outside, exterior **2 les dehors** : appearances
déifier [deifje] {96} *vt* : to deify
déjà [deʒa] *adv* **1** : already **2** : before, previously **3** *fam* : again <tu viens quand, déjà? : tell me again when you're coming?> **4** (*used for reinforcement*) <ce n'est déjà pas si mal : it's not all that bad>
déjeté, -tée [deʒte] *adj* : warped, lopsided
déjeuner[1] [deʒœne] *vi* **1** : to have lunch **2** *Bel, Can, Switz* : to have breakfast
déjeuner[2] *nm* **1** : lunch **2** *Bel, Can, Switz* : breakfast
déjouer [deʒwe] *vt* : to thwart, to outsmart
delà [dəla] *adv* **1 → deça 2 → au–delà, par–delà**
délabré, -rée [delabre] *adj* : dilapidated
délabrement [delabrəmɑ̃] *nm* **1** : dilapidation, deterioration **2** : ruin (of reputation, health, etc.)
délabrer [delabre] *vt* : to ruin — **se délabrer** *vr* : to deteriorate
délai [delɛ] *nm* **1** : time limit, deadline **2** : extension (of time) **3** : waiting period <sans délai : immediately, without delay>
délaissement [delɛsmɑ̃] *nm* : abandonment, desertion, neglect
délaisser [delɛse] *vt* **1** ABANDONNER : to abandon, to desert **2** : to neglect
délassement [delasmɑ̃] *nm* : relaxation
délasser [delase] *vt* : to relax — **se délasser** *vr*
délateur, -trice [delatœr, -tris] *n* : informer
délation [delasjɔ̃] *nf* : informing, denunciation
délavé, -vée [delave] *adj* : faded
délayage [deleja3] *nm* **1** : mixing **2** : dragging out (of a speech, etc.)
délayer [deleje] {11} *vt* **1** : to dilute, to mix **2** : to pad out, to drag out (a speech, etc.)
délectable [delɛktabl] *adj* : delectable, delicious
délectation [delɛktasjɔ̃] *nf* : delight
délecter [delɛkte] *v* **se délecter** *vr* ~ **de** : to delight in
délégation [delegasjɔ̃] *nf* **1** : delegation, assignment **2** : group of delegates
délégué, -guée [delege] *n* : delegate, representative
déléguer [delege] {87} *vt* : to delegate
délester [deleste] *vt* **1** : to remove ballast from, to unload **2** : to relieve, to unburden **3** : to divert traffic away from **4** *fam* : to rob
délibération [deliberasjɔ̃] *nf* : deliberation
délibéré, -rée [delibere] *adj* **1** INTENTIONNEL : deliberate **2** DÉCIDÉ : resolute, determined — **délibérément** [-remɑ̃] *adv*
délibérer [delibere] {87} *vi* : to deliberate
délicat, -cate [delika, -kat] *adj* **1** : delicate, sensitive, tender **2** : dainty, re-

fined, delicious **3** : considerate, tactful **4** : awkward, tricky **5** : scrupulous **6** : fussy, difficult

délicatement [delikatmɑ̃] *adv* **1** : delicately, gently, daintily **2** : thoughtfully, tactfully

délicatesse [delikatɛs] *nf* **1** : delicacy, tenderness **2** : fineness **3** : tactfulness **4** : awkwardness, difficulty **5** : scrupulousness

délice [delis] *nm* : delight

délicieux, -cieuse [delisjø, -sjøz] *adj* : delicious, delightful — **délicieusement** [-sjøzmɑ̃] *adv*

délictueux, -tueuse [deliktɥø, -tɥøz] *adj* : criminal

délié, -liée [delje] *adj* **1** : slender, fine **2** : nimble

délier [delje] {96} *vt* **1** : to untie **2** : to loosen (up) <l'alcool a délié sa langue : alcohol loosened his tongue> **3** ~ **de** : to release from — **se délier** *vr*

délimitation [delimitasjɔ̃] *nf* : delimitation, boundary

délimiter [delimite] *vt* **1** : to delimit, to demarcate **2** : to define, to determine

délinquance [delɛ̃kɑ̃s] *nf* : crime, delinquency <délinquance juvenile : juvenile delinquency>

délinquant, -quante [delɛ̃kɑ̃, -kɑ̃t] *adj & n* : delinquent, offender

délirant, -rante [deliRɑ̃, -Rɑ̃t] *adj* **1** : delirious **2** : frenzied, wild

délire [delir] *nm* **1** : delirium **2 en** ~ : delirious, frenzied

délirer [delire] *vi* **1** : to be delirious **2** : to rave, to be out of one's mind

délit [deli] *nm* : crime, offense

délivrance [delivRɑ̃s] *nf* **1** : freeing, release **2** : delivery, issue **3** : relief

délivrer [delivre] *vt* **1** : to set free **2** : to issue, to award, to hand over **3** ~ **de** : to relieve of — **se délivrer** *vr* ~ **de** : to rid oneself of

déloger [deloʒe] {17} *vt* **1** : to evict, to throw out **2** : to remove, to dislodge — *vi* : to leave home, to move out

déloyal, déloyale [delwajal] *adj, mpl* **déloyaux** [-jo] **1** : disloyal **2** : unfair, dishonest — **déloyalement** [-mɑ̃] *adv*

déloyauté [delwajote] *nf* : disloyalty

delta [delta] *nm* : delta

déluge [delyʒ] *nm* **1** : deluge, flood **2** : downpour

déluré, -rée [delyre] *adj* **1** : sharp, smart **2** : forward, brazen

démagogie [demagɔʒi] *nf* : demagogy — **démagogique** [-gɔʒik] *adj*

démagogue [demagɔg] *nmf* : demagogue

demain[1] [dəmɛ̃] *adv* **1** : tomorrow <demain soir : tomorrow evening> **2** : in the future

demain[2] *nm* **1** : tomorrow <à demain : see you tomorrow!> **2** : the future <le monde de demain : the world of the future, tomorrow's world>

démancher [demɑ̃ʃe] *vt Can* : to take apart, to dismantle

demande [dəmɑ̃d] *nf* **1** : request <demande en mariage : marriage proposal> **2** : application <demande d'emploi : job application> **3** : demand <l'offre et la demande : supply and demand> **4** : claim (in law)

demander [dəmɑ̃de] *vt* **1** : to ask for, to request **2** : to call for <on vous demande au téléphone : you are wanted on the telephone> **3** : to ask (about) <demander son chemin : to ask directions> **4** EXIGER : to demand, to ask <il m'en demande trop : he asks too much of me> **5** NÉCESSITER : to require, to need **6** : to send for (a doctor, etc.) — *vi* ~ **à** : to ask to — **se demander** *vr* : to wonder

demandeur[1], **-deuse** [dəmɑ̃dœR, -døz] *n* : applicant <demandeur d'emploi : job applicant>

demandeur[2], **-deresse** [dəmɑ̃dœR, -dRɛs] *n* : plaintiff

démangeaison [demɑ̃ʒɛzɔ̃] *nf* **1** : itch, itching **2** : urge

démanger [demɑ̃ʒe] {17} *vt* : to itch, to make itchy

démanteler [demɑ̃tle] {20} *vt* **1** : to demolish **2** : to break up, to dismantle

démaquillant [demakijɑ̃, -jɑ̃t] *nm* : makeup remover, cleansing cream

démaquiller [demakije] *v* **se démaquiller** *vr* : to remove one's makeup

démarcation [demarkasjɔ̃] *nf* : demarcation

démarchage [demarʃaʒ] *nm* : door-to-door solicitation <démarchage électoral : canvassing>

démarche [demarʃ] *nf* **1** : gait, walk **2** : step, action <faire des démarches : to take steps> **3** : approach, thought process

démarquer [demarke] *vt* **1** : to mark down (merchandise) **2** : to plagiarize — **se démarquer** *vr* : to distance oneself

démarrage [demaraʒ] *nm* : starting up

démarrer [demare] *vi* **1** : to start up (an automobile) **2** : to start, to launch (a project) — *vi* **1** : to start up (of an automobile) **2** : to drive off (of a driver) **3** : to get under way

démarreur [demarœR] *nm* : starter (of an automobile)

démasquer [demaske] *vt* : to unmask — **se démasquer** *vr* : to drop one's mask

démêlé [demele] *nm* **1** : quarrel **2 démêlés** *nmpl* : problems <avoir des démêlés avec la justice : to get in trouble with the law>

démêler [demele] *vt* **1** : to disentangle, to untangle **2** : to clear up, to sort out — **se démêler** *vr* ~ **de** : to extricate oneself from (a problem, etc.)

démembrer [demɑ̃bre] *vt* **1** : to dismember, to cut up **2** : to divide up
déménagement [demenaʒmɑ̃] *nm* : moving, relocation
déménager [demenaʒe] {17} *v* : to move, to relocate
déménageur, -geuse [demenaʒœr, -ʒøz] *n* : (furniture) mover
démence [demɑ̃s] *nf* : madness, insanity
démener [demne] {52} *v* **se démener** *vr* **1** : to thrash about, to struggle **2** : to exert oneself
dément[1], **-mente** [demɑ̃, -mɑ̃t] *adj* **1** : demented, insane **2** *fam* : incredible, fantastic
dément[2], **-mente** *n* : demented person
démenti [demɑ̃ti] *nm* : denial
démentiel, -tielle [demɑ̃sjel] *adj* : insane
démentir [demɑ̃tir] {82} *vt* **1** : to deny **2** CONTREDIRE : to refute, to contradict
démérite [demerit] *nm* : demerit
démériter [demerite] *vi* **1** : to show oneself unworthy **2 démériter auprès de qqn** : to lose s.o.'s esteem
démesuré, -rée [demɔzyre] *adj* : excessive, immoderate — **démesurément** [-remɑ̃] *adv*
démettre [demɛtr] {53} *vt* **1** DESTITUER : to dismiss, to fire **2** : to dislocate (in medicine) — **se démettre** *vr* **1** : to resign **2 se démettre l'épaule** : to dislocate one's shoulder
demeurant [dəmœrɑ̃] *adv* **au ~** : after all, for all that
demeure [dəmœr] *nf* **1** : residence, abode **2 à ~** : permanently **3 mettre en demeure** : to require **4 mise en demeure** : summons, demand
demeurer [dəmœre] *vi* **1** (*with auxiliary verb* **être**) : to remain **2** (*with auxiliary verb* **avoir**) : to reside **3 il n'en demeure pas moins** : the fact remains, nonetheless
demi[1] [dəmi] *adv* **1** : half <demi-cuit : half-cooked> **2 à ~** : halfway <faire les choses à demi : to do things by halves>
demi[2], **-mie** *adj* **1** : half <un demi pain : half a loaf> **2 et ~** : and a half <sept litres et demi : seven and a half liters> <à cinq heures et demie : at five-thirty>
demi[3], **-mie** *n* : half <voulez-vous une bouteille? non, une demie : do you want a bottle? no, (just) a half>
demi[4] *nm* **1** : half <trois demis : three halves> **2** *France* : half-pint (of beer) **2** : halfback
demi–bas [dəmiba] *nms & pl* : kneesock
demi–bouteille [dəmibutɛj] *nf, pl* **demi–bouteilles** : half-bottle
demi–cercle [dəmisɛrkl] *nm, pl* **demi–cercles** : semicircle — **demi–circulaire** [-sirkylɛr] *adj*
demi–dieu [dəmidjø] *nm, pl* **demi–dieux** : demigod
demi–douzaine [dəmiduzɛn] *nf, pl* **demi–douzaines** : half a dozen
demie *nf* : half hour <la cloche a sonné la demie : the bell rang the half hour> <à la demie : at half past>
demi–finale [dəmifinal] *nf, pl* **demi–finales** : semifinal — **demi–finaliste** [-nalist] *nmf*
demi–frère [dəmifrɛr] *nm, pl* **demi–frères** : half brother
demi–heure [dəmijœr] *nf, pl* **demi–heures** : half hour
demi–jour [dəmiʒur] *nm, pl* **demi–jours** : half-light
demi–journée [dəmiʒurne] *nf, pl* **demi–journées** : half a day, half day
demi–litre [dəmilitr] *nm, pl* **demi–litres** : half-liter
demi–lune [dəmilyn] *nf, pl* **demi–lunes** **1** : half-moon **2 en ~** : semicircular
demi–mal [dəmimal] *nm* **il n'y a que demi–mal** : things could be worse
demi–mesure [dəmiməzyr] *nf, pl* **demi–mesures** : half measure
demi–mot [dəmimo] **à ~** : without having to spell things out
demi–pension [dəmipɑ̃sjɔ̃] *nf, pl* **demi–pensions** : half board (one meal furnished daily)
demi–place [dəmiplas] *nf, pl* **demi–places** **1** : half-price seat (at the theater) **2** : half-price fare (on a train, etc.)
demi–saison [dəmisɛzɔ̃] *nf* **vêtements de demi–saison** : spring or fall clothing
demi–sel [dəmisɛl] *nms & pl* : slightly salted (cheese, butter, etc.)
demi–sœur [dəmisœr] *nf, pl* **demi–sœurs** : half sister
démission [demisjɔ̃] *nf* **1** : resignation **2** : abdication of responsibility
démissionnaire [demisjɔnɛr] *adj* : outgoing, resigning
démissionner [demisjɔne] *vi* **1** : to resign **2** : to give up <je démissionne après cet essai : I'm giving up after this try> — *vt fam* : to oust
demi–tarif [dəmitarif] *nm, pl* **demi–tarifs** : half-price ticket
demi–teinte [dəmitɛ̃t] *nf, pl* **demi–teintes** : halftone
demi–tour [dəmitur] *nm, pl* **demi–tours** **1** : half turn <faire un demi-tour : to turn back> **2** : about-face **3** : U-turn
demi–vie [dəmivi] *nf, pl* **demi–vies** : half-life
démobiliser [demɔbilize] *vt* : to demobilize — **démobilisation** [-lizasjɔ̃] *nf*
démocrate[1] [demɔkrat] *adj* : democratic
démocrate[2] *nmf* : democrat
démocratie [demɔkrasi] *nf* : democracy

démocratique [demɔkratik] *adj* : democratic — **démocratiquement** [-tikmɑ̃] *adv*
démodé, -dée [demɔde] *adj* : old-fashioned, out-of-date
démographie [demɔgrafi] *nf* : demography — **démographique** [-grafik] *adj*
demoiselle [dəmwazɛl] *nf* **1** : young lady **2 demoiselle d'honneur** : bridesmaid
démolir [demɔlir] *vt* **1** : to demolish, to tear down **2** : to destroy, to ruin
démolition [demɔlisjɔ̃] *nf* **1** : demolition **2** : destruction, ruin
démon [demɔ̃] *nm* **1 le démon** : the devil **2** : demon, evil spirit **3 être en démon** *Can fam* : to be furious
démoniaque [demɔnjak] *adj* : fiendish, diabolical
démonstrateur, -trice [demɔ̃stratœr, -tris] *n* : demonstrator
démonstratif, -tive [demɔ̃stratif, -tiv] *adj* : demonstrative
démonstration [demɔ̃strasjɔ̃] *nf* **1** MANIFESTATION : demonstration, show <une démonstration de force : a show of strength> **2** PREUVE : proof
démontable [demɔ̃tabl] *adj* : collapsible, able to be dismantled
démonter [demɔ̃te] *vt* **1** : to dismantle **2** : to remove, to take down **3** : to disconcert — **se démonter** *vr*
démontrer [demɔ̃tre] *vt* : to demonstrate, to show, to prove
démoralisant, -sante [demɔralizɑ̃, -zɑ̃t] *adj* : demoralizing
démoraliser [demɔralize] *vt* : to demoralize — **se démoraliser** *vr*
démordre [demɔrdr] {63} *vt* **ne pas démordre de** : to stick to, to refuse to give up
démuni, -nie [demyni] *adj* **1** : poor, impoverished **2** : powerless
démunir [demynir] *vt* : to deprive — **se démunir** *vr* ~ **de** : to part with
démystifier [demistifje] {96} *vt* **1** : to demystify **2** : to disabuse
dénaturé, -rée [denatyre] *adj* **1** : denatured **2** : unnatural
dénaturer [denatyre] *vt* **1** : to distort, to misrepresent **2** : to denature, to alter completely
dénégation [denegasjɔ̃] *nf* : denial
déneigement [deneʒmɑ̃] *nm* : snow removal
déneiger [deneʒe] {17} *vt* : to clear snow from
déni [deni] *nm* : denial
dénicher [deniʃe] *vt* **1** : to unearth, to discover **2** : to take (a bird) from the nest — *vi* : to leave the nest
denier [dənje] *nm* **deniers publics** : public funds
dénier [denje] {96} *vt* : to deny
dénigrement [denigrəmɑ̃] *nm* : disparagement
dénigrer [denigre] *vt* : to denigrate, to disparage
denim [dənim] *nm* : denim
dénivellation [denivɛlasjɔ̃] *nf* **1** : difference in altitude or level **2** : gradient, slope
dénivellement [denivɛlmɑ̃] *nm* → **dénivellation**
dénombrement [denɔ̃brəmɑ̃] *nm* : counting, count
dénombrer [denɔ̃bre] *vt* : to count
dénominateur [denɔminatœr] *nm* : denominator <dénominateur commun : common denominator>
dénomination [denɔminasjɔ̃] *nf* **1** : naming **2** : name, designation
dénommé, -mée [denɔme] *n* **un dénommé** : a person by the name of <une dénommée Marie : a certain Marie>
dénommer [denɔme] *vt* : to name, to call
dénoncer [denɔ̃se] {6} *vt* : to denounce, to inform on — **se dénoncer** *vr* : to give oneself up
dénonciation [denɔ̃sjasjɔ̃] *nf* : denunciation
dénoter [denɔte] *vt* : to denote, to indicate
dénouement [denumɑ̃] *nm* **1** : denouement (in theater) **2** : outcome
dénouer [denwe] *vt* **1** : to untie **2** : to unravel, to resolve — **se dénouer** *vr*
dénoyauter [denwajote] *vt* : to pit (a fruit)
denrée [dɑ̃re] *nf* : commodity <denrées alimentaires : foods> <une denrée rare : a rare commodity>
dense [dɑ̃s] *adj* : dense — **densément** [dɑ̃semɑ̃] *adv*
densité [dɑ̃site] *nf* : density, denseness
dent [dɑ̃] *nf* **1** : tooth <dents de sagesse : wisdom teeth> <dents de lait : baby teeth> **2** : cog (of a wheel, etc.) **3** : prong, tine (of a fork) **4 avoir une dent contre** : to hold a grudge against **5 en dents de scie** : serrated **6 faire ses dents** : to teethe
dentaire [dɑ̃tɛr] *adj* : dental
dent-de-lion [dɑ̃dəljɔ̃] *nf, pl* **dents-de-lion** : dandelion
denté, -tée [dɑ̃te] *adj* : toothed
dentelé, -lée [dɑ̃tle] *adj* : serrated, jagged, indented
dentelle [dɑ̃tɛl] *nf* : lace
dentier [dɑ̃tje] *nm* : dentures *pl*
dentifrice [dɑ̃tifris] *nm* : toothpaste
dentiste [dɑ̃tist] *nmf* : dentist
dentisterie [dɑ̃tistəri] *nf* : dentistry
dentition [dɑ̃tisjɔ̃] *nf* : teeth *pl*, dentition <avoir une belle dentition : to have nice teeth>
dénudé, -dée [denyde] *adj* **1** : bare **2** : bald
dénuder [denyde] *vt* **1** : to bare **2** : to strip (off) — **se dénuder** *vr* **1** : to strip **2** : to go bald
dénué, -nuée [denɥe] *adj* ~ **de** : devoid of, lacking in

dénuement [denymɑ̃] *nm* : destitution
déodorant [deɔdɔrɑ̃] *adj & nm* : deodorant
dépanner [depane] *vt* **1** : to fix, to repair **2** : to help out
dépanneur[1], **-neuse** [depanœr, -nøz] *n* : repairman, repairwoman
dépanneur[2] *nm Can* : convenience store
dépanneuse *nf* : tow truck, wrecker
dépareillé, -lée [depareje] *adj* **1** : incomplete **2** : odd, unpaired
déparer [depare] *vt* : to spoil, to mar
déparler [deparle] *vi Can fam* : to rave, to talk nonsense
départ [depar] *nm* **1** : departure **2** : start (in sports) <ligne de départ : starting line> **3 au départ** : at first, initially **4 être sur le départ** : to be about to leave
départager [departaʒe] {17} *vt* : to decide between
département [departəmɑ̃] *nm* **1** : department **2** : territorial division in France — **départemental, -tale** [-mɑ̃tal] *adj*
départir [departir] {82} *vt* : to assign, to allot — **se départir** *vr* : to abandon, to give up
dépassé, -sée [depase] *adj* : outdated, outmoded
dépassement [depasmɑ̃] *nm* **1** : passing (with an automobile) **2** : excess, overrun
dépasser [depase] *vt* **1** : to pass, to go past **2** EXCÉDER : to exceed, to go beyond <l'addition a depassé la somme prévue : the bill exceeded the expected amount> **3** : to outshine, to surpass **4 cela me dépasse!** : that's beyond me! — *vi* : to show, to stick out <ton jupon dépasse : your slip is showing>
dépaysement [depeizmɑ̃] *nm* **1** : disorientation **2** : change of scenery
dépayser [depeize] *vt* **1** : to disorient **2** : to provide with a change of scenery
dépecer [depɔse] {6} *and* {52} *vt* : to carve up, to cut up
dépêche [depɛʃ] *nf* **1** : dispatch **2** *or* **dépêche télégraphique** : telegram
dépêcher [depeʃe] *vt* : to dispatch — **se dépêcher** *vr* SE HÂTER : to hurry
dépeindre [depɛ̃dr] {37} *vt* : to depict, to describe
dépendamment [depɑ̃damɑ̃] *adv* **~ de** *Can* : depending on
dépendance [depɑ̃dɑ̃s] *nf* **1** : dependence **2** : dependency (on drugs, etc.) **3** : outbuilding
dépendant, -dante [depɑ̃dɑ̃, -dɑ̃t] *adj* : dependent
dépendre [depɑ̃dr] {63} *vi* **1 ~ de** : to depend on **2 ~ de** : to belong to — *vt* : to take down
dépens [depɑ̃] *nmpl* **aux dépens de** : at the expense of
dépense [depɑ̃s] *nf* **1** : spending, expenditure **2** : expense **3** : consumption
dépenser [depɑ̃se] *vt* **1** : to spend **2** : to use up, to expend <j'ai dépensé toute mon énergie : I've used up all my energy> — **se dépenser** *vr* : to exert oneself
dépensier[1], **-sière** [depɑ̃sje, -sjɛr] *adj* : extravagant, wasteful
dépensier[2], **-sière** *n* : spendthrift
déperdition [deperdisjɔ̃] *nf* : loss
dépérir [deperir] *vi* **1** : to wither (of a plant) **2** : to waste away (of persons) **3** : to be on the decline
dépêtrer [depetre] *v* **se dépêtrer** *vr* **~ de** : to extricate oneself from
dépeupler [depœple] *vt* : to depopulate
déphasé, -sée [defaze] *adj* : out of touch (with reality), out of it
dépilatoire [depilatwar] *adj* : depilatory
dépiler [depile] *vt* : to remove hair from
dépistage [depistaʒ] *nm* : screening, testing <dépistage précoce : early detection>
dépister [depiste] *vt* **1** : to detect (a disease) **2** : to track down
dépit [depi] *nm* **1** : pique, vexation **2 en dépit de** MALGRÉ : in spite of, despite <en dépit de sa bonne volonté : despite his good will>
déplacé, -cée [deplase] *adj* **1** MALVENU : out of place, uncalled-for **2** : displaced <personnes déplacées : displaced persons>
déplacement [deplasmɑ̃] *nm* **1** : displacement **2** : moving, shifting **3** : trip, traveling <frais de déplacement : travel expenses> <être en déplacement : to be away on business>
déplacer [deplase] {6} *vt* **1** : to move, to shift, to change **2** : to displace — **se déplacer** *vr*
déplaire [depler] {66} *vi* **1** : to be disliked **2 ~ à** : to put off, to repel <cela me déplaît : I don't like it> **3 ~ à** : to annoy, to offend <ne t'en déplaise : whether you like it or not>
déplaisant, -sante [deplezɑ̃, -zɑ̃t] *adj* : unpleasant, disagreeable
déplaisir [deplezir] *nm* : annoyance, displeasure
déplantoir [deplɑ̃twar] *nm* : (garden) trowel
dépliant [deplijɑ̃, -jɑ̃t] *nm* : brochure, pamphlet
déplier [deplije] {96} *vt* : to unfold — **se déplier** *vr*
déplisser [deplise] *vt* : to smooth out, to remove the pleats from
déploiement [deplwamɑ̃] *nm* **1** : deployment **2** : unfolding, spreading **3** : display
déplorable [deplɔrabl] *adj* : deplorable — **déplorablement** [-rabləmɑ̃] *adv*
déplorer [deplɔre] *vt* : to deplore, to lament

déployer [deplwaje] {58} *vt* **1** : to deploy **2** : to unfold, to spread out **3** : to display, to exhibit
déplumer [deplyme] *vt* : to pluck (a bird) — **se déplumer** *vr* **1** : to molt **2** *fam* : go bald
dépoli, -lie [depɔli] *adj* **verre dépoli** : frosted glass
déporter [deporte] *vt* **1** : to inter in a concentration camp **2** DÉVIER : to divert, to carry off course — **se déporter** *vr* : to swerve
déposant, -sante [depozɑ̃, -zɑ̃t] *n* **1** : depositor **2** : witness (in law)
déposé, -sée [depoze] *adj* : registered <marque déposée : registered trademark>
déposer [depoze] *vt* **1** : to lay down, to put down **2** : to deposit **3** : to drop off, to leave **4** : to register, to file **5** : to depose **6** : to remove, to take down — *vi* **1** : to settle, to form a sediment **2** : to give evidence (in court) — **se déposer** *vr* : to settle
dépositaire [depɔziter] *nmf* **1** : agent, dealer **2** : trustee **3** : repository (of a secret, etc.)
déposition [depozisjɔ̃] *nf* : evidence, testimony (in court)
déposséder [depɔsede] {87} *vt* : to dispossess
dépôt [depo] *nm* **1** : deposit, depository <dépôt en coffre-fort : safe deposit> **2** ENTREPÔT : warehouse, depot **3** : (retail) outlet **4** : registration, filing (of documents) **5** : sediment, (geological) deposit
dépotoir [depɔtwar] *nm* : dump
dépouille [depuj] *nf* **1** : hide, skin **2** *or* **dépouille mortelle** : mortal remains *pl* **3 dépouilles** *nfpl* : spoils
dépouillement [depujmɑ̃] *nm* **1** : austerity, soberness **2** : counting, perusal <dépouillement du scrutin : tally of votes>
dépouiller [depuje] *vt* **1** : to strip (off) **2** : to dispossess, to despoil **3** : to peruse, to scrutinize <dépouiller le scrutin : to tally the votes> **4** : to skin — **se dépouiller** *vr* ~ **de** : to divest oneself of
dépourvu, -vue [depurvy] *adj* **1** ~ **de** : lacking in, devoid of, without **2 au** ~ : by surprise
dépravation [depravasjɔ̃] *nf* : depravity
dépraver [deprave] *vt* : to deprave — **dépravé, -vée** [-ve] *adj*
dépréciation [depresjasjɔ̃] *nf* : depreciation
déprécier [depresje] {96} *vt* **1** : to depreciate **2** : to disparage, to belittle — **se déprécier** *vr* **1** : to depreciate **2** : to put oneself down
déprédations [depredasjɔ̃] *nfpl* : damage
dépresseur [depresœr] *nm* : depressant
dépressif, -sive [depresif, -siv] *adj & n* : depressive
dépression [depresjɔ̃] *nf* **1** : depression **2 dépression nerveuse** : nervous breakdown
déprimant, -mante [deprimɑ̃, -mɑ̃t] *adj* : depressing
déprimé, -mée [deprime] *adj* : depressed, dejected
déprimer [deprime] *vt* **1** : to depress, to demoralize **2** : to press in, to indent — *vi fam* : to be depressed
depuis[1] [dəpɥi] *adv* **1** : since (then) <nous ne les avons pas revus depuis : we've never seen them since> **2 depuis que** : (ever) since <depuis qu'ils sont partis : ever since they left>
depuis[2] *prep* **1** : since <depuis 1831 : since 1831> **2** : from <depuis le matin jusqu'au soir : from morning till night> <depuis Londres à New York : from London to New York> **3** : for <en fonction depuis deux ans : in office for two years>
députation [depytasjɔ̃] *nf* **1** : deputation **2** : position of deputy
député, -tée [depyte] *n* **1** : deputy, representative (in government) **2** : delegate
députer [depyte] *vt* : to delegate, to appoint as representative, to deputize
déraciner [derasine] *vt* **1** ARRACHER : to uproot **2** : to eradicate
déraillement [derajmɑ̃] *nm* : derailment
dérailler [deraje] *vi* : to derail
déraisonnable [derezɔnabl] *adj* : unreasonable — **déraisonnablement** [-nabləmɑ̃] *adv*
déraisonner [derezɔne] *vi* : to talk nonsense
dérangement [derɑ̃ʒmɑ̃] *nm* **1** : trouble **2** : disorder, breakdown <en dérangement : out of order>
déranger [derɑ̃ʒe] {17} *vt* **1** : to bother, to disturb <ne vous dérangez pas : don't bother> **2** : to disrupt, to upset — **se déranger** *vr* **1** : to get up, to go out **2** : to put oneself out
dérapage [derapaʒ] *nm* **1** : skid, slip **2** : blunder **3** : loss of control
déraper [derape] *vi* **1** : to skid, to slip **2** : to get out of hand
derby [derbi] *nm, pl* **derbys** *or* **derbies** : derby (horse race)
déréglé, -lée [deregle] *adj* **1** : out of order **2** : dissolute
déréglementer [deregləmɑ̃te] *vt* : to deregulate — **déréglementation** [-mɑ̃tasjɔ̃] *nf*
dérégler [deregle] {87} *vt* **1** : to put out of order **2** : to upset, to disturb — **se dérégler** *vr* : to go wrong
dérhumer *v* **se dérhumer** *vr Can fam* : to clear one's throat
dérider [deride] *vt* : to cheer up
dérision [derizjɔ̃] *nf* MÉPRIS : derision
dérisoire [derizwar] *adj* **1** : ridiculous, laughable **2** : trivial, pathetic

dérivation [derivasjɔ̃] *nf* : derivation
dérivatif[1], **-tive** [derivatif, -tiv] *adj* : derivative
dérivatif[2] *nm* : distraction, diversion
dérive [deriv] *nf* **1** : drift **2 à la dérive** : adrift
dérivé [derive] *nm* **1** : derivation (of a word) **2** SOUS-PRODUIT : by-product
dériver [derive] *vt* **1** : to divert **2 ~ de** : to derive from — *vi* : to drift, to be adrift
dermatologie [dɛrmatɔlɔʒi] *nf* : dermatology
dermatologique [dɛrmatɔlɔʒik] *adj* : dermatologic, dermatological
dermatologue [dɛrmatɔlɔg] *nmf* : dermatologist
dernier[1], **-nière** [dɛrnje, -njɛr] *adj* **1** : last, previous <l'année dernière : last year> **2** : latest **3** : final, last **4** : highest <le dernier degré de : the height of> **5** : lowest <la dernière marche : the bottom step>
dernier[2], **-nière** *n* **1** : last (one) **2 ce dernier, cette dernière** : the latter
dernier[3] *nm* **en ~** : last <il est arrivé en dernier : he arrived last>
dernièrement [dɛrnjɛrmɑ̃] *adv* : recently, lately
dernier–né, dernière–née [dɛrnjene, dɛrnjɛrne] *n* : last-born child
dérobade [derɔbad] *nf* : evasion
dérobé, -bée [derɔbe] *adj* **1** : concealed, hidden **2 à la dérobée** : surreptitiously
dérober [derɔbe] *vt* **1** : to steal **2** MASQUER : to conceal, to hide — **se dérober** *vr* **1** : to shy away, to be evasive **2** : to give way, to collapse **3 ~ à** : to avoid, to shirk
dérogation [derɔgasjɔ̃] *nf* : dispensation, exemption
déroger [derɔʒe] {17} *vi* **~ à** : to depart from
dérougir [deruʒir] *vi Can fam* **ne pas dérougir** : to continue without interruption <le téléphone n'a pas dérougi : the phone rang off the hook>
dérouiller [deruje] *vt fam* : to beat up — *vi France fam* : to have a hard time — **se dérouiller** *vr* SE DÉGOURDIR : to limber up, to stretch (one's legs, etc.)
déroulement [derulmɑ̃] *nm* **1** : unwinding, unrolling **2** : development, progress
dérouler [derule] *vt* : to unwind, to unroll — **se dérouler** *vr* **1** : to take place **2** : to develop, to progress **3** : to unwind
déroute [derut] *nf* **1** : rout **2 en ~** : routed, in full flight
dérouter [derute] *vt* **1** : to reroute, to divert **2** : to disconcert, to confuse
derrière[1] [dɛrjɛr] *adv & prep* : behind
derrière[2] *nm* **1** : back, rear <le derrière de l'édifice : the back of the building> **2** : rump, haunches *pl* (of an animal) **3** *fam* : buttocks *pl*, bottom
des[1] [de] → **de, le**
des[2] → **un**
dès [dɛ] *prep* **1** : from <dès le début : from the start> <dès Boston jusqu'à Portland : from Boston to Portland> <dès son arrivée : as soon as he arrived> **2 dès lors** : from then on **3 dès lors que** : from the moment that, since **4 dès que** : as soon as
désabusé, -sée [dezabyze] *adj* : disillusioned, disenchanted
désaccord [dezakɔr] *nm* **1** DIFFÉREND : disagreement **2** : discrepancy
désaccoutumer [dezakutyme] *vt* **désaccoutumer qqn de** : to cure s.o. of the habit of — **se désaccoutumer** *vr* **~ de** : to get out of the habit of
désaffecté, -tée [dezafɛkte] *adj* : disused
désaffection [dezafɛksjɔ̃] *nf* : disaffection
désagréable [dezagreabl] *adj* DÉPLAISANT : disagreeable, unpleasant — **désagréablement** [-abləmɑ̃] *adv*
désagrégation [dezagregasjɔ̃] *nf* : disintegration, breakup
désagréger [dezagreʒe] {64} *vt* : to break up — **se désagréger** *vr* : to disintegrate
désagrément [dezagremɑ̃] *nm* : inconvenience, annoyance
désaligné, -née [dezaliɲe] *adj* : out of alignment
désaltérant, -rante [dezalterɑ̃, -rɑ̃t] *adj* : thirst-quenching
désaltérer [dezaltere] {87} *vt* : to quench the thirst of — **se désaltérer** *vr* : to quench one's thirst
désamorcer [dezamɔrse] {6} *vt* : to defuse
désappointer [dezapwɛ̃te] *vt* : to disappoint — **désappointement** [-pwɛ̃tmɑ̃] *nm*
désapprobateur, -trice [dezaprɔbatœr, -tris] *adj* : disapproving
désapprobation [dezaprɔbasjɔ̃] *nf* : disapproval
désapprouver [dezapruve] *vt* : to disapprove of
désarçonner [dezarsɔne] *vt* **1** : to throw (a rider), to unseat **2** : to nonplus
désargenté, -tée [dezarʒɑ̃te] *adj fam* : short of cash, broke
désarmant, -mante [dezarmɑ̃, -mɑ̃t] *adj* : disarming
désarmement [dezarməmɑ̃] *nm* : disarmament
désarmer [dezarme] *vt* : to disarm — *vi* **1** : to disarm **2** : to relent, to abate
désarroi [dezarwa] *nm* : confusion, distress, dismay
désassembler [dezasɑ̃ble] *vt* : to disassemble
désastre [dezastr] *nm* : disaster
désastreux, -treuse [dezastrø, -trøz] *adj* : disastrous

désavantage [dezavɑ̃taʒ] *nm* : disadvantage, drawback
désavantager [dezavɑ̃taʒe] {17} *vt* : to put at a disadvantage
désavantageux, -geuse [dezavɑ̃taʒø, -øz] *adj* : disadvantageous, unfavorable
désaveu [dezavø] *nm, pl* **-veux 1** : repudiation **2** : disavowal, denial
désavouer [dezavwe] *vt* **1** : to deny **2** : to disown
désaxé, désaxée [dezakse] *adj* : (mentally) unbalanced
descendance [desɑ̃dɑ̃s] *nf* **1** : lineage, descent <de descendance irlandaise : of Irish descent> **2** PROGÉNITURE : offspring, descendants *pl*
descendant[1], **-dante** [desɑ̃dɑ̃, -dɑ̃t] *adj* : descending, downward
descendant[2], **-dante** *n* : descendant
descendre [dəsɑ̃dr] {63} *vt* **1** : to descend, to go down **2** : to take down, to bring down **3** : to lower — *vi* **1** : to descend, to go down, to come down **2** : to get off, to get out, to disembark, to dismount **3** ~ **à** : to stay at (a hotel, etc.) **4** ~ **de** : to be descended from
descente [desɑ̃t] *nf* **1** : descent **2** : (police) raid **3** : slope
descriptif, -tive [deskriptif, -tiv] *adj* : descriptive
description [deskripsjɔ̃] *nf* : description
désemparé, -rée [dezɑ̃pare] *adj* **1** : distraught, at a loss **2** : disabled (of a plane, ship, etc.)
désemparer [dezɑ̃pare] *vi* **sans** ~ : without interruption, continuously
désenchanter [dezɑ̃ʃɑ̃te] *vt* : to disenchant, to disillusion — **désenchantement** [-ʃɑ̃tmɑ̃] *nm*
désencombrer [dezɑ̃kɔ̃bre] *vt* : to unblock, to clear
désenfler [dezɑ̃fle] *vi* : to become less swollen, to go down
désengagement [dezɑ̃gaʒmɑ̃] *nm* : disengagement, withdrawal
désengager [dezɑ̃gaʒe] {17} *vt* : to disengage, to release — **se désengager** *vr* : to withdraw
désenivrer [dezɑ̃nivre] *vt* : to sober up — **se désenivrer** *vr*
déséquilibre [dezekilibr] *nm* **1** : lack of balance, instability **2** : imbalance
déséquilibrer [dezekilibre] *vt* : to unbalance — **déséquilibré, -brée** [dezekilibre] *adj*
désert[1], **-serte** [dezɛr, -zɛrt] *adj* : uninhabited, deserted <île déserte : desert island>
désert[2] *nm* : desert
déserter [dezɛrte] *v* : to desert
déserteur [dezɛrtœr] *nm* : deserter
désertion [dezɛrsjɔ̃] *nf* : desertion
désertique [dezɛrtik] *adj* **1** : desert **2** : barren
désespérance [dezɛsperɑ̃s] *nf* : despair
désespérant, -rante [dezɛsperɑ̃, -rɑ̃t] *adj* **1** : hopeless, despairing **2** : appalling, terrible
désespéré, -rée [dezɛspere] *adj* **1** : desperate **2** : hopeless
désespérément [dezɛsperemɑ̃] *adv* : desperately, hopelessly, helplessly
désespérer [dezɛspere] {87} *vi* : to despair <elle désespère d'une carrière : she has given up hope for a career> — *vt* : to drive to despair
désespoir [dezɛspwar] *nm* **1** : despair, desperation **2 en désespoir de cause** : as a last resort, in sheer desperation
déshabillé [dezabije] *nm* : negligee
déshabiller [dezabije] *vt* : to undress — **se déshabiller** *vr*
déshabituer [dezabituɛ] *vt* **déshabituer qqn de** : to break s.o. of the habit of — **se déshabituer** *vr* ~ **de** : to get out of the habit of
désherber [dezɛrbe] *v* : to weed
déshérité[1], **-tée** [dezerite] *adj* **1** : disinherited **2** : deprived, underprivileged
déshérité[2], **-tée** *n* **les déshérités** : the underprivileged
déshériter [dezerite] *vt* : to disinherit
déshonneur [dezɔnœr] *nm* : disgrace
déshonorant, -rante [dezɔnɔrɑ̃, -rɑ̃t] *adj* : dishonorable
déshonorer [dezɔnɔre] *vt* : to dishonor, to disgrace — **se déshonorer** *vr* : to disgrace oneself
déshumaniser [dezymanize] *vt* : to dehumanize
déshydratation [dezidratasjɔ̃] *nf* : dehydration
déshydrater [dezidrate] *vt* : to dehydrate — **se déshydrater** *vr*
design [dizajn] *nm* : design
désignation [deziɲasjɔ̃] *nf* **1** : designation, name **2** NOMINATION : appointment, nomination
designer [dizajnœr] *nmf* : designer
désigner [deziɲe] *vt* **1** : to designate, to indicate **2** NOMMER : to name, to appoint
désillusion [dezilyzjɔ̃] *nf* : disillusionment
désillusionner [dezilyzjɔne] *vt* : to disillusion
désincarné, -née [dezɛ̃karne] *adj* : disembodied
désinfectant[1], **-tante** [dezɛ̃fɛktɑ̃, -tɑ̃t] *adj* : disinfectant
désinfectant[2] *nm* : disinfectant
désinfecter [dezɛ̃fɛkte] *vt* : to disinfect
désinformation [dezɛ̃fɔrmasjɔ̃] *nf* : disinformation
désinstaller [dezɛ̃stale] *vt* : uninstall
désintégrer [dezɛ̃tegre] {87} *vt* : to disintegrate, to break up — **se désintégrer** *vr* — **désintégration** [-tegrasjɔ̃] *nf*
désintéressé, -sée [dezɛ̃terese] *adj* : disinterested, impartial

désintéressement [dezɛ̃tɛresmɑ̃] *nm* : disinterestedness
désintérêt [dezɛ̃tɛrɛ] *nm* : lack of interest
désinvolte [dezɛ̃vɔlt] *adj* **1** : casual, unself-conscious **2** : offhand, flippant, glib
désinvolture [dezɛ̃vɔltyr] *nf* **1** : casualness, nonchalance **2** : offhand manner, flippancy, glibness
désir [dezir] *nm* : desire
désirable [dezirabl] *adj* : desirable
désirer [dezire] *vt* **1** : to want, to wish for **2** : to desire (sexually) **3 laisser à désirer** : to leave something to be desired
désireux, -reuse [dezirø, -røz] *adj* : anxious, desirous
désistement [dezistəmɑ̃] *nm* : withdrawal
désister [deziste] *v* **se désister** *vr* : to withdraw
désobéir [dezɔbeir] *vi* : to disobey <désobéir à ses parents : to disobey one's parents>
désobéissance [dezɔbeisɑ̃s] *nf* : disobedience
désobéissant, -sante [dezɔbeisɑ̃, -sɑ̃t] *adj* : disobedient
désobligeant, -geante [dezɔbliʒɑ̃, -ʒɑ̃t] *adj* : disagreeable, unpleasant
désobliger [dezɔbliʒe] {17} *vt* : to offend
désodorisant [dezɔdorizɑ̃] *nm* : air freshener, deodorizer
désodoriser [dezɔdɔrize] *vt* : to deodorize
désœuvré, -vrée [dezœvre] *adj* : idle
désœuvrement [dezœvrəmɑ̃] *nm* : idleness
désolant, -lante [dezɔlɑ̃, -lɑ̃t] *adj* : distressing
désolation [dezɔlasjɔ̃] *nf* **1** : desolation, devastation **2** : distress, grief
désolé, -lée [dezɔle] *adj* **1** : bleak, desolate **2** : contrite <je suis désolé : I'm sorry>
désoler [dezɔle] *vt* : to upset, to distress **— se désoler** *vr*
désolidariser [desɔlidarize] *v* **se désolidariser** *vr* **~ de** : to dissociate oneself from
désopilant, -lante [dezɔpilɑ̃, -lɑ̃t] *adj* : hilarious
désordonné, -née [dezɔrdɔne] *adj* **1** : disorganized **2** : untidy
désordre [dezɔrdr] *nm* **1** : confusion, disorder **2** : untidiness <en désordre : in a mess>
désorganiser [dezɔrganize] *vt* : to disorganize **— désorganisation** [-nizasjɔ̃] *nf*
désorienter [dezɔrjɑ̃te] *vt* **1** : to disorient **2** : to bewilder, to confuse
désormais [dezɔrmɛ] *adv* : henceforth, from now on
désosser [dezɔse] *vt* : to bone (meat)
despote [dɛspɔt] *nm* : despot **— despotisme** [-pɔtism] *nm*
despotique [dɛspɔtik] *adj* : despotic
desquels, desquelles [dekɛl] **→ lequel**
dessécher [deseʃe] {87} *vt* **1** : to dry up, to desiccate, to parch **2** : to harden (one's heart)
dessein [desɛ̃] *nm* **1** : design, plan, intention **2 à ~** : intentionally, on purpose
desserrer [desere] *vt* **1** : to loosen **2** : to release (a brake) **3** RELÂCHER : to relax, to unclench
dessert [desɛr] *nm* : dessert
desserte [desɛrt] *nf* **1** : (transportation) service <desserte par bus : bus service> **2** : sideboard, serving table
desservir [deservir] {81} *vt* **1** : to serve **2** : to lead into <deux portes desservent la salle de bain : two doors lead into the bathroom> **3** : to clear (the table) **4** : to do a disservice to
dessin [desɛ̃] *nm* **1** : drawing **2** : design, pattern **3** : outline **4 dessin animé** : (animated) cartoon
dessinateur, -trice [desinatœr, -tris] *n* **1** : artist, draftsman **2** : designer **3 dessinateur humoristique** : cartoonist
dessiner [desine] *vt* **1** : to draw **2** : to design **3** : to outline — *vi* : to draw, to sketch **— se dessiner** *vr* **1** : to stand out **2** : to take shape
dessoûler [desule] *v* : to sober up
dessous[1] [dəsu] *adv* : underneath
dessous[2] *nms & pl* **1** : underneath, underside **2 dessous** *nmpl* : underwear, lingerie **3 de ~** : from underneath **4 en ~** : underneath, down below **5 en dessous de** : below, beneath **6 → au–dessous, par–dessous**
dessous–de–verre [d(ə)sudvɛr] *nms & pl* : coaster
dessus[1] [dəsy] *adv* : on top, on
dessus[2] *nms & pl* **1** : top **2** : upper (of a shoe) **3** : upper floor, upstairs **4 de ~** : off, from **5 en ~** : on top, above **6 avoir le dessus** : to have the upper hand **7 → au–dessus, par–dessus**
déstabiliser [destabilize] *vt* : to destabilize
destin [destɛ̃] *nm* : fate, destiny
destinataire [destinatɛr] *nmf* **1** : addressee **2** : payee, beneficiary
destination [destinasjɔ̃] *nf* **1** : destination **2 à destination de** : bound for
destinée [destine] *nf* : fate, destiny
destiner [destine] *vt* **1** : to intend **2** : to destine **— se destiner** *vr* **~ à** : to intend to become
destituer [destitue] *vt* **1** DÉMETTRE : to dismiss, to discharge **2** : to depose
destructeur[1], **-trice** [destryktœr, -tris] *adj* : destructive
destructeur[2], **-trice** *n* : destroyer, wrecker
destructible [destryktibl] *adj* : destructible

destructif, -tive [dɛstryktif, -tiv] *adj* : destructive
destruction [dɛstryksjɔ̃] *nf* : destruction
désuet, -suète [dezɥɛ, -zɥɛt] *adj* : outdated, obsolete
désuétude [dezɥetyd] *nf* : obsolescence <tomber en désuétude : to fall into disuse>
désuni, -nie [dezyni] *adj* : disunited, divided
désunion [dezynjɔ̃] *nf* : disunity, dissension
désunir [dezynir] *vt* : to separate, to divide
détaché, -chée [detaʃe] *adj* **1** : detached **2** : transferred
détachement [detaʃmɑ̃] *nm* : detachment
détacher [detaʃe] *vt* **1** : to detach, to tear off **2** : to untie, to unfasten **3** DÉTOURNER : to turn (one's eyes, attention, etc.) away from **4** : to transfer **5** : to make stand out — **se détacher** *vr* **1** : to come undone **2** ~ **de** : to grow away from, to lose interest in **3** ~ **sur** : to stand out against
détail [detaj] *nm* **1** : detail <entrer dans les détails : to go into detail> **2** : retail <ventes au détail : retail sales>
détaillant, -lante [detajɑ̃, -jɑ̃t] *n* : retailer
détaillé, -lée [detaje] *adj* : detailed
détailler [detaje] *vt* **1** : to retail **2** ÉNUMÉRER : to detail, to itemize **3** : to scrutinize
détecter [detɛkte] *vt* : to detect
détecteur [detɛktœr] *nm* : detector, sensor <détecteur de mensonges : lie detector>
détection [detɛksjɔ̃] *nf* : detection
détective [detɛktiv] *nm* : detective <détective privé : private detective>
déteindre [detɛ̃dr] {37} *vt* : to make fade — *vi* **1** : to fade **2** : to run (of colors) **3** ~ **sur** : to rub off on
détendre [detɑ̃dr] {63} *vt* **1** : to slacken, to loosen **2** : to relax, to ease — **se détendre** *vr* : to relax, to ease up
détendu, -due [detɑ̃dy] *adj* : relaxed
détenir [detnir] {92} *vt* **1** POSSÉDER : to hold, to be in possession of <détenir un secret : to have a secret> **2** : to detain, to hold (a prisoner)
détente [detɑ̃t] *nf* **1** : relaxation **2** : détente **3** : trigger
détenteur, -trice [detɑ̃tœr, -tris] *n* : holder <détenteur du record : record holder>
détention [detɑ̃sjɔ̃] *nf* **1** : possession, holding <détention de stupéfiants : drug possession> **2** EMPRISONNEMENT : detention, imprisonment
détenu, -nue [detny] *n* : prisoner
détergent [deterʒɑ̃] *nm* : detergent
détérioration [deterjɔrasjɔ̃] *nf* : deterioration
détériorer [deterjɔre] *vt* : to damage, to harm — **se détériorer** *vr* : to deteriorate
déterminant, -nante [determinɑ̃, -nɑ̃t] *adj* : decisive, determining <un facteur déterminant : a determining factor>
détermination [determinasjɔ̃] *nf* **1** : determination, resoluteness **2** RÉSOLUTION : decision
déterminé, -née [determine] *adj* **1** : determined, resolute **2** : specified, definite
déterminer [determine] *vt* **1** : to determine, to specify **2** : to encourage, to incite **3** : to cause — **se déterminer** *vr* : to decide, to make up one's mind
déterrer [detere] *vt* : to dig up, to unearth
détersif [detersif, -siv] *nm* DÉTERGENT : detergent
détestable [detestabl] *adj* : detestable, foul, hateful — **détestablement** [-bləmɑ̃] *adv*
détester [deteste] *vt* : to detest, to hate — **se détester** *vr*
détonant, -nante [detɔnɑ̃, -nɑ̃t] *adj* : explosive
détonateur [detɔnatœr] *nm* : detonator
détonation [detɔnasjɔ̃] *nf* : detonation, explosion
détoner [detɔne] *vi* : to detonate, to explode
détonner [detɔne] *vi* **1** : to be out of tune **2** : to clash
détordre [detɔrdr] {63} *vt* : to untwist, to unbend
détour [detur] *nm* **1** : curve, bend **2** DÉVIATION : detour **3** **sans** ~ : directly, frankly
détourné, -née [deturne] *adj* : indirect, roundabout, circuitous
détournement [deturnəmɑ̃] *nm* **1** : diversion, rerouting **2** : hijacking **3** **détournement de fonds** : embezzlement, misappropriation of funds **4** **détournement de mineur** : corruption of a minor
détourner [deturne] *vt* **1** : to divert, to reroute **2** : to turn aside <détourner les soupçons : to avert suspicion> <détourner la conversation : to change the subject> **3** : to hijack **4** : to misappropriate, to embezzle **5** : to twist, to distort, to corrupt
détracteur, -trice [detraktœr, -tris] *n* : detractor, faultfinder
détraqué, -quée [detrake] *adj* **1** : broken-down, out of order **2** *fam* : deranged, crazy
détraquer [detrake] *vt* **1** : to put out of order, to make go wrong **2** *fam* : to upset (one's stomach, etc.), to unhinge (mentally) — **se détraquer** *vr* : to break down, to go wrong
détremper [detrɑ̃pe] *vt* **1** : to soak, to saturate **2** : to dilute
détresse [detrɛs] *nf* : distress

détriment [detrimɑ̃] *nm* **au détriment de** : to the detriment of
détritus [detrityˢ] *nmpl* : waste, garbage, litter
détroit [detrwa] *nm* : strait <le détroit de Gibraltar : the strait of Gibraltar>
détromper [detrɔ̃pe] *vt* : to set straight, to disabuse — **se détromper** *vr* : to set oneself straight <détrompez-vous! : think again!>
détrôner [detrone] *vt* **1** : to depose, to dethrone **2** : to oust
détruire [detruir] {49} *vt* : to destroy — **se détruire** *vr*
dette [det] *nf* : debt
deuil [dœj] *nm* : bereavement, mourning <porter le deuil : to be in mourning>
deux[1] [dø] *adj* **1** : two <deux cents : two hundred> <les deux côtés : both sides> **2** : second <le deux mai : May second> **3 à deux pas** : nearby, close **4 deux fois** : twice **5 tous les deux jours** : every other day
deux[2] *nm* **1** : two <couper en deux : to cut in two> **2 tous les deux** : both (of them)
deuxième [døzjem] *adj & nmf* : second
deuxièmement [døzjemmɑ̃] *adv* : secondly, second
deux–pièces [døpjɛs] *nms & pl* **1** : two-piece suit, two-piece swimsuit **2** : two-room apartment
deux–points [døpwɛ̃] *nms & pl* : colon
deux–roues [dəru] *nms & pl* : two-wheeled vehicle
dévaler [devale] *vt* : to hurtle down
dévaliser [devalize] *vt* : to rob
dévalorisation [devalɔrizasjɔ̃] *nf* : depreciation
dévaloriser [devalɔrize] *vt* **1** : to devalue **2** : to belittle
dévaluation [devalɥasjɔ̃] *nf* : devaluation
dévaluer [devalɥe] *vt* : to devalue
devancer [dəvɑ̃se] {6} *vt* **1** : to be ahead of <devancer ses rivaux : to be ahead of one's rivals> **2** PRÉCÉDER : to arrive before **3** : to anticipate
devant[1] [dəvɑ̃] *adv* : in front, ahead, before <il marche devant : he is walking ahead>
devant[2] *nm* **1** : front <le devant de la maison : the front of the house> **2 prendre les devants** : to take the initiative
devant[3] *prep* **1** : in front of <devant chez toi : in front of your house> <jurer devant témoins : to swear before witnesses> **2** : ahead of <avoir du temps devant soi : to have time to spare> **3** : in the face of <sans peur devant le danger : fearless in the face of danger>
devanture [dəvɑ̃tyr] *nf* **1** : storefront **2** : shopwindow **3 en ~** : on display
dévastateur, -trice [devastatœr, -tris] *adj* : devastating, destructive
dévastation [devastasjɔ̃] *nf* : devastation
dévaster [devaste] *vt* : to devastate, to ravage
développement [devlɔpmɑ̃] *nm* **1** : development **2** CROISSANCE : growth, expansion **3** : developing (of photographic film)
développer [devlɔpe] *vt* : to develop — **se développer** *vr*
devenir [dəvnir] {92} *vi* : to become <je deviens vieux : I'm growing old> <qu'est-il devenu? : what has become of him?> <qu'est-ce que tu deviens? : what are you up to?>
déverrouiller [deveruje] *vt* : to unbolt
déverser [deverse] *vt* : to pour (out), to dump — **se déverser** *vr* **~ dans** : to flow into
dévêtir [devetir] {97} *vt* : to undress — **se dévêtir** *vr*
déviation [devjasjɔ̃] *nf* **1** : deviation **2** DÉTOUR : detour
dévider [devide] *vt* : to unwind
dévier [devje] {96} *vi* **1** : to veer, to swerve **2 ~ de** : to deviate from — *vt* : to deflect, to divert <dévier la circulation : to divert traffic>
devin, -vineresse [dəvɛ̃,-vinres] *n* : soothsayer, fortune-teller
deviner [dəvine] *vt* **1** : to guess **2** APERCEVOIR : to perceive, to sense **3** PRÉDIRE : to foretell
devinette [dəvinet] *nf* : riddle
devis [dəvi] *nms & pl* : estimate
dévisager [devizaʒe] {17} *vt* : to stare at
devise [dəviz] *nf* **1** : motto, slogan **2** : currency (money)
deviser [dəvize] *vi* : to converse
dévisser [devise] *vt* : to unscrew
dévoiler [devwale] *vt* : to unveil, to reveal
devoir[1] [dəvwar] {28} *vt* : to owe — *v aux* **1** : to have to, to be compelled to <il doit le faire : he must do it> **2** : to be advised to <tu dois lire les instructions : you should read the instructions> <elle doit répondre : she ought to reply> **3** : to be presumed to <il a dû payer : he must have paid> **4** : to be expected to <elles devaient se rencontrer plus tard : they were supposed to meet later> — **se devoir** *vr* **1** : to be obligated to each other **2 se devoir de faire** : to be duty bound to do (sth)> **3 comme il se doit** : as is proper, as might be expected
devoir[2] *nm* **1** : duty **2 devoirs** *nmpl* : homework
dévolu[1], **-lue** [devɔly] *adj* **~ à** : allotted to
dévolu[2] *nm* **jeter son dévolu sur** : to set one's sights on
dévorer [devɔre] *vt* **1** : to devour <être dévoré de : to be eaten up by> **2** CONSUMER : to consume
dévot, -vote [devo, -vɔt] *adj* : devout, pious

dévotion [devosjɔ̃] *nf* **1** : devotion <avec dévotion : devotedly> **2** : devoutness
dévoué, -ouée [devwe] *adj* : devoted
dévouement [devumɑ̃] *nm* : dedication, devotion
dévouer [devwe] *vt* : to devote — **se dévouer** *vr* **1** : to devote oneself **2** : to sacrifice oneself
dévoyé, -yée [devwaje] *adj & n* : delinquent
devra [dəvra], *etc.* → **devoir**
dextérité [dɛksterite] *nf* : dexterity, skill
diabète [djabɛt] *nm* : diabetes
diabétique [djabetik] *adj & nmf* : diabetic
diable [djabl] *nm* **1** : devil <avoir le diable au corps : to be the very devil> <ce n'est pas le diable : it's not all that bad> **2 à la diable** : any old way **3 au ~** : to hell with **4 en ~** : devilishly, terribly **5 mener le diable** *Can fam* : to make a racket **6 où (quand, qui, pourquoi) diable** : where (when, who, why) the devil
diablement [djabləmɑ̃] *adv fam* : very, extremely, awfully
diablerie [djabləri] *nf* : mischief
diablotin [djablotɛ̃] *nm* : little demon, imp
diabolique [djabɔlik] *adj* : diabolical, diabolic, devilish — **diaboliquement** [-likmɑ̃] *adv*
diachylon [djaʃilɔ̃] *nm Can* : adhesive bandage
diacre [djakr] *nm* : deacon
diadème [djadɛm] *nm* : diadem
diagnostic [djagnɔstik] *nm* : diagnosis — **diagnostique** [-nɔstik] *adj*
diagnostiquer [djagnɔstike] *vt* : to diagnose
diagonal, -nale [djagɔnal] *adj, mpl* **-naux** [-no] : diagonal
diagonale *nf* **1** : diagonal **2 en ~** : diagonally
diagramme [djagram] *nm* : graph, chart
dialecte [djalɛkt] *nm* : dialect
dialogue [djalɔg] *nm* : dialogue
dialoguer [djalɔge] *vi* **1** : to converse **2** : to engage in dialogue, to have talks
dialyse [djaliz] *nf* : dialysis
diamant [djamɑ̃] *nm* : diamond
diamétralement [djametralmɑ̃] *adv* : diametrically
diamètre [djametr] *nm* : diameter
diapason [djapazɔ̃] *nm* **1** : tuning fork **2 être au même diapason** : to be on the same wavelength
diaphane [djafan] *adj* : diaphanous
diaphragme [djafragm] *nm* : diaphragm
diapositive [djapɔzitiv] *nf* : slide, transparency
diarrhée [djare] *nf* : diarrhea
diatribe [djatrib] *nf* : diatribe
dichotomie [dikɔtɔmi] *nf* : dichotomy
dictateur [diktatœr] *nm* : dictator
dictatorial, -riale [diktatɔrjal] *adj, mpl* **-riaux** [-rjo] : dictatorial
dictature [diktatyr] *nf* : dictatorship
dictée [dikte] *nf* : dictation
dicter [dikte] *vt* : to dictate
diction [diksjɔ̃] *nf* : diction
dictionnaire [diksjɔnɛr] *nm* : dictionary
dicton [diktɔ̃] *nm* : saying
didactique [didaktik] *adj* : didactic
dièse [djɛz] *adj & nm* : sharp (in music)
diesel [djezɛl] *adj & nm* : diesel
diète [djɛt] *nf* RÉGIME : diet — **diététique** [djetetik] *adj*
diététicien, -cienne [djetetisjɛ̃, -sjɛn] *n* : dietician
dieu [djø] *nm, pl* **dieux** : god
Dieu *nm* : God
diffamation [difamasjɔ̃] *nf* CALOMNIE : slander, libel
diffamatoire [difamatwar] *adj* : slanderous, defamatory
diffamer [difame] *vt* CALOMNIER : to defame, to slander, to libel
différé, -rée [difere] *adj* **1** : postponed, deferred **2 en ~** : prerecorded
différemment [diferamɑ̃] *adv* : differently
différence [diferɑ̃s] *nf* **1** : difference <faire la différence : to tell the difference> **2 à la différence de** : unlike
différencier [diferɑ̃sje] {96} *vt* DISTINGUER : to differentiate — **se différencier** *vr* **~ de** : to differ from
différend [diferɑ̃] *nm* : disagreement, difference (of opinion)
différent, -rente [diferɑ̃, -rɑ̃t] *adj* **1** : different, various **2 ~ de** : different from, unlike
différentiel, -tielle [diferɑ̃sjɛl] *adj* : differential
différer [difere] {87} *vt* : to defer, to postpone — *vi* **1** : to differ, to vary **2 ~ de** : to differ from
difficile [difisil] *adj* **1** : difficult, hard **2** : choosy, hard to please
difficilement [difisilmɑ̃] *adv* : with difficulty
difficulté [difikylte] *nf* **1** : difficulty **2** : problem <en difficulté : in trouble>
difforme [difɔrm] *adj* : deformed, misshapen
difformité [difɔrmite] *nf* : deformity
diffus, -fuse [dify, -fyz] *adj* : diffuse
diffuser [difyze] *vt* **1** : to broadcast **2** : to spread, to distribute **3** : to diffuse (light, etc.) — **se diffuser** *vr*
diffuseur [difyzœr] *nm* **1** : distributor **2** : broadcaster
diffusion [difyzjɔ̃] *nf* **1** : distribution **2** : diffusion **3** RADIODIFFUSION : broadcasting
digérer [diʒere] {87} *vt* **1** : to digest **2** : to assimilate **3** : to accept, to put up with

digeste [diʒɛst] *adj* : (easily) digestible
digestible [diʒɛstibl] *adj* : digestible
digestif, -tive [diʒɛstif, -tiv] *adj* : digestive
digestion [diʒɛstjɔ̃] *nf* : digestion
digital, -tale [diʒital] *adj, mpl* **-taux** [-to] **1** : digital **2** → **empreinte**
digitale [diʒital] *nf* **1** : digitalis **2** *or* **digitale pourprée** : foxglove
digne [diɲ] *adj* **1** : worthy <digne de foi : trustworthy> **2** : dignified
dignement [diɲmɑ̃] *adv* **1** : with dignity **2** : suitably, justly
dignitaire [diɲitɛr] *nm* : dignitary
dignité [diɲite] *nf* : dignity
digression [digresjɔ̃] *nf* : digression
digue [dig] *nf* **1** : dike, seawall **2** : barrier
dilapider [dilapide] *vt* : to squander, to waste
dilater [dilate] *vt* : to dilate, to expand — **se dilater** *vr*
dilatoire [dilatwar] *adj* : dilatory, delaying
dilemme [dilɛm] *nm* : dilemma
dilettante [diletɑ̃t] *nmf* : dilettante, amateur
diligence [diliʒɑ̃s] *nf* **1** : dispatch <faire diligence : to make haste> **2** : stagecoach
diligent, -gente [diliʒɑ̃, -ʒɑ̃t] *adj* : prompt, speedy
diluant [dilɥɑ̃] *nm* : thinner
diluer [dilɥe] *vt* : to dilute — **dilution** [dilysjɔ̃] *nf*
dimanche [dimɑ̃ʃ] *nm* : Sunday
dîme [dim] *nf* : tithe
dimension [dimɑ̃sjɔ̃] *nf* **1** : dimension, measurement **2** : aspect **3 dimensions** *nfpl* : dimensions, size
diminuer [diminɥe] *vt* RÉDUIRE : to lower, to reduce — *vi* : to diminish, to decrease, to drop
diminution [diminysjɔ̃] *nf* : reduction, decreasing
dinde [dɛ̃d] *nf* **1** : (female) turkey **2** : stupid woman
dindon [dɛ̃dɔ̃] *nm* **1** : (male) turkey **2 être le dindon de la farce** : to be made a fool of
dîner[1] [dine] *vi* **1** : to dine, to have dinner **2** *Bel, Can, Switz* : to have lunch
dîner[2] *nm* **1** : dinner **2** *Bel, Can, Switz* : lunch
dîneur, -neuse [dinœr, -nœz] *n* : diner (person)
dingue [dɛ̃g] *adj fam* **1** : crazy, nuts, goofy **2** : incredible
dinosaure [dinozɔr] *nm* : dinosaur
diocèse [djɔsɛz] *nm* : diocese
diphtérie [difteri] *nf* : diphtheria
diphtongue [diftɔ̃g] *nf* : diphthong
diplomate[1] [diplɔmat] *adj* : diplomatic
diplomate[2] *nmf* : diplomat
diplomatie [diplɔmasi] *nf* : diplomacy
diplomatique [diplɔmatik] *adj* : diplomatic — **diplomatiquement** [-tikmɑ̃] *adv*
diplôme [diplom] *nm* **1** : diploma, certificate, degree **2** : (qualifying) exam
diplômé[1], **-mée** [diplome] *adj* **1** : qualified, certified **2 être diplômé de** : to be a graduate of
diplômé[2], **-mée** *n* : graduate
dire[1] [dir] {29} *vt* **1** : to say <comme on dit : as they say> <cela va sans dire : that goes without saying> <sans dire mot : without saying a word> **2** : to tell <dire la vérité : to tell the truth> <c'est ce qu'on m'a dit : so I've been told> **3** : to think <qu'en dis-tu? : what do you think?> <on dirait qu'il est perdu : he seems lost> **4** : to show, to indicate <dire l'heure : to tell the time> **5** : to appeal to <cela vous dit d'aller dehors? : do you feel like going outside?> **6 pour ainsi dire** : so to speak **7 vouloir dire** ; to mean <que veut dire ce mot? : what does this word mean?> — **se dire** *vr* **1** : to tell oneself **2** : to say to each other <se dire au revoir : to say good-bye (to each other)> **3** : to claim to be <elle se dit malade : she says she's sick> **4** : to say (in another language) <comment se dit *chien* en russe? : how do you say *dog* in Russian?> **5** : to be said <cela ne se dit pas : we shouldn't say that>
dire[2] *nm* **1 au dire de** : according to **2 avoir pour son dire** *Can* : to be in the habit of saying **3 dires** *nmpl* : statements
direct[1], **-recte** [direkt] *adj* : direct — **directement** [-tɔmɑ̃] *adv*
direct[2] *nm* **1** : express train **2** : jab (in boxing) **3 en ~** : live, in person
directeur[1], **-trice** [direktœr, -tris] *adj* **1** : directing, guiding <ligne directrice : guideline> **2** : main <idée directrice : main idea>
directeur[2], **-trice** *n* **1** : manager, director **2 directeur général** : general manager, chief executive officer **3 directeur d'école** : principal
direction [direksjɔ̃] *nf* **1** : direction **2** GESTION : management, supervision, leadership <la direction du parti : party management> **3** : steering <direction assistée : power steering>
directive [direktiv] *nf* ORDRE : order, directive
directorial, -riale [direktɔrjal] *adj, pl* **-riaux** [-rjo] : managerial, directorial
dirigeable [diriʒabl] *nm* : airship, dirigible
dirigeant[1], **-geante** [diriʒɑ̃, -ʒɑ̃t] *adj* : ruling <la classe dirigeante : the ruling class>
dirigeant[2], **-geante** *n* **1** : leader (of a country, etc.) **2** : manager
diriger [diriʒe] {17} *vt* **1** : to direct, to manage <diriger une entreprise : to run a company> **2** : to aim, to direct (one's attention, efforts, etc.) **3** : to

steer **4** : to conduct (an orchestra) — **se diriger** *vr* **1** : to find one's way **2** ~ **vers** : to head toward

disait [dizɛ], **disions** [dizjɔ̃], *etc.* → **dire**

discernement [disɛrnəmɑ̃] *nm* : discernment, judgment

discerner [diserne] *vt* : to discern, to distinguish

disciple [disipl] *nm* : follower, disciple

disciplinaire [disiplinɛr] *adj* : disciplinary

discipline [disiplin] *nf* : discipline

discipliner [disipline] *vt* : to discipline — **se discipliner** *vr*

disc–jockey [diskʒɔkɛ] *nmf, pl* **disc–jockeys** : disc jockey

discontinu, -nue [diskɔ̃tiny] *adj* **1** : broken, dotted **2** : intermittent

discontinuer [diskɔ̃tinɥe] *vi* **sans** ~ : without interruption

discordance [diskɔrdɑ̃s] *nf* **1** : clash, conflict **2** : dissonance

discordant, -dante [diskɔrdɑ̃, -dɑ̃t] *adj* **1** : conflicting, clashing **2** : dissonant

discorde [diskɔrd] *nf* **1** : discord, dissension **2 pomme de discorde** : bone of contention

discothèque [diskɔtɛk] *nf* **1** : disco, nightclub **2** : record library

discourir [diskurir] {23} *vi* **1** : to discourse, to talk at length **2** ~ **sur** : to hold forth on

discours [diskur] *nms & pl* **1** : speech, address **2** : discourse, speech (in grammar) <discours indirect : indirect discourse>

discourtois, -toise [diskurtwa, -twaz] *adj* : discourteous — **discourtoisement** [-twazmɑ̃] *adv*

discrédit [diskredi] *nm* : discredit

discréditer [diskredite] *vt* : to discredit, to disparage — **se discréditer** *vr*

discret, -crète [diskrɛ, -krɛt] *adj* **1** : discreet **2** : unassuming, unobtrusive

discrètement [diskrɛtmɑ̃] *adv* : discreetly

discrétion [diskresjɔ̃] *nf* **1** : discretion **2 à** ~ : unlimited, as much as one wants

discrétionnaire [diskresjɔnɛr] *adj* : discretionary

discrimination [diskriminasjɔ̃] *nf* **1** : discrimination **2 sans** ~ : indiscriminately

discriminatoire [diskriminatwar] *adj* : discriminatory

disculper [diskylpe] *vt* : to exonerate — **se disculper** *vr* : to vindicate oneself

discussion [diskysjɔ̃] *nf* **1** : discussion **2** : argument, debate

discutable [diskytabl] *adj* **1** : debatable, arguable **2** : questionable, doubtful

discuté, -tée [diskyte] *adj* : controversial

discuter [diskyte] *vt* **1** : to discuss, to debate **2** : to question — *vi* **1** : to talk **2** : to argue **3** ~ **de** : to discuss

dise [diz], *etc.* → **dire**

disette [dizɛt] *nf* : shortage of food

diseur, -seuse [dizœr, -zøz] *n* **diseur de bonne aventure** : fortune-teller

disgrâce [disgras] *nf* **1** : disgrace, disfavor **2** : misfortune

disgracieux, -cieuse [disgrasjø, -sjøz] *adj* **1** : awkward, ungainly **2** : ugly

disjoindre [disʒwɛ̃dr] {50} *vt* **1** : to take apart **2** : to separate (out) — **se disjoindre** *vr* : to come apart

disjoncteur [disʒɔ̃ktœr] *nm* : circuit breaker

dislocation [dislɔkasjɔ̃] *nf* **1** : dislocation (in medicine) **2** : breaking up

disloquer [dislɔke] *vt* **1** LUXER : to dislocate (in medicine) **2** : to break up, to dismantle

disparaître [disparɛtr] {7} *vi* **1** : to disappear **2** MOURIR : to die (out) **3 faire disparaître** : to get rid of

disparate [disparat] *adj* **1** : disparate, dissimilar **2** : clashing

disparité [diparite] *nf* : disparity

disparition [disparisjɔ̃] *nf* **1** : disappearance **2** : extinction, death

disparu[1], **-rue** [dispary] *adj* **1** : missing **2** : lost, vanished, extinct

disparu[2], **-rue** *n* **1** : missing person **2** : dead person <notre cher disparu : our dear departed>

dispendieux, -dieuse [dispɑ̃djø, -djøz] *adj* COÛTEUX : expensive, costly

dispensaire [dispɑ̃sɛr] *nm* : dispensary, free clinic

dispense [dispɑ̃s] *nf* : exemption, dispensation

dispenser [dispɑ̃se] *vt* **1** : to exempt, to excuse **2** : to dispense, to bestow — **se dispenser** *vr* ~ **de** : to avoid, to get out of

disperser [disperse] *vt* ÉPARPILLER : to disperse, to scatter — **se disperser** *vr*

dispersion [dispersjɔ̃] *nf* : scattering, dispersal

disponibilité [disponibilite] *nf* **1** : availability **2 en** ~ : on leave of absence **3 disponibilités** *nfpl* : liquid assets

disponible [disponibl] *adj* : available

dispos, -pose [dispo, -poz] *adj* **1** : refreshed **2 frais et dispos** : as fresh as a daisy

disposé, -sée [dispoze] *adj* **1** : arranged **2** ~ **à** : disposed to, willing to **3 bien disposé envers** : well-disposed toward

disposer [dispoze] *vt* **1** PLACER : to arrange, to place **2** : to incline, to dispose — *vi* **1** : to leave <ils peuvent disposer : they may leave> **2** ~ **de** : to have at one's disposal — **se disposer** *vr* **se disposer à faire** : to be about to do

dispositif [dispozitif] *nm* **1** : device, mechanism <dispositif de sûreté : safeguard> **2** : plan of action

disposition [dispozisjɔ̃] *nf* **1** : arrangement, layout **2** : aptitude **3** : tendency

4 à la disposition de : at the disposal of **5 dispositions** *nfpl* : mood, state of mind **6 dispositions** *nfpl* : steps, measures

disproportion [disprɔpɔrsjɔ̃] *nf* : disproportion

disproportionné, -née [disprɔpɔrsjɔne] *adj* : disproportionate

dispute [dispyt] *nf* : argument, quarrel

disputer [dispyte] *vt* **1** : to compete in, to play **2** : to contend with, to fight **3** *fam* : to tell off **4** *Can* : to scold, to chide — **se disputer** *vr* : to quarrel, to fight

disqualifier [diskalifje] {96} *vt* : to disqualify — **disqualification** [-lifikasjɔ̃] *nf*

disque [disk] *nm* **1** : record, disc <disque compact : compact disc> <disque vidéo : videodisc> **2** : disk (in anatomy, astronomy, etc.) **3** : discus

disquette [diskɛt] *nf* : diskette, floppy disk

dissection [diseksjɔ̃] *nf* : dissection

dissemblable [disɑ̃ablə̃] *adj* : dissimilar

dissemblance [disɑ̃blɑ̃s] *nf* : dissimilarity, difference

dissémination [diseminasjɔ̃] *nf* **1** : scattering, dispersal **2** : dissemination, spread (of ideas, etc.)

disséminer [disemine] *vt* **1** : to scatter **2** : to disseminate, to spread

dissension [disɑ̃sjɔ̃] *nf* : dissension, disagreement

dissentiment [disɑ̃timɑ̃] *nm* : dissent

disséquer [diseke] {87} *vt* : to dissect

dissertation [disɛrtasjɔ̃] *nf* : essay (in school)

dissident, -dente [disidɑ̃, -dɑ̃t] *adj & n* : dissident — **dissidence** [-sidɑ̃s] *nf*

dissimulation [disimylasjɔ̃] *nf* **1** : dissimulation, dissembling **2** : concealment

dissimulé, -lée [disimyle] *adj* **1** : hidden, concealed **2** : secretive

dissimuler [disimyle] *vt* CACHER : to conceal, to hide — **se dissimuler** *vr*

dissipation [disipasjɔ̃] *nf* **1** : dissipation **2** : squandering, wasting

dissipé, -pée [disipe] *adj* **1** : undisciplined, unruly **2** : dissipated, dissolute

dissiper [disipe] *vt* **1** : to disperse, to clear, to dispel **2** : to squander — **se dissiper** *vr* **1** : to clear (up), to vanish **2** : to become unruly

dissocier [disɔsje] {96} *vt* : to dissociate, to separate — **se dissocier** *vr*

dissolu, -lue [disɔly] *adj* : dissolute

dissolution [disɔlysjɔ̃] *nf* **1** : dissolution, breakup **2** : dissolving

dissolvant [disɔlvɑ̃] *nm* **1** : solvent **2** : nail polish remover

dissonant, -nante [disɔnɑ̃, -nɑ̃t] *adj* : dissonant, discordant — **dissonance** [-sɔnɑ̃s] *nf*

dissoudre [disudr] {1} *vt* : to dissolve — **se dissoudre** *vr*

dissuader [disɥade] *vt* : to dissuade

dissuasif, -sive [disɥazif, -ziv] *adj* : deterrent, dissuasive

dissuasion [disɥazjɔ̃] *nf* : dissuasion, deterrence

distance [distɑ̃s] *nf* **1** : distance <à distance : at a distance> <garder ses distances : to keep one's distance> **2** : gap, interval **3 distance focale** : focal length

distancer [distɑ̃se] {6} *vt* : to outdistance, to outrun, to outstrip

distancier [distɑ̃sje] {96} *v* **se distancier** *vr* ~ **de** : to distance oneself from

distant, -tante [distɑ̃, -tɑt] *adj* **1** : distant <une ville distante de deux kilomètres : a town two kilometers away> **2** : distant, aloof

distendre [distɑ̃dr] {63} *vt* : to distend, to stretch, to strain — **se distendre** *vr* **1** : to distend **2** : to slacken

distillation [distilasjɔ̃] *nf* : distillation

distiller [distile] *vt* **1** : to distill **2** : to secrete, to exude

distillerie [distilri] *nf* : distillery

distinct, -tincte [distɛ̃, -tɛ̃kt] *adj* : distinct — **distinctement** [-tɛ̃ktɔmɑ̃] *adv*

distinctif, -tive [distɛ̃ktif, -tiv] *adj* : distinctive, distinguishing

distinction [distɛ̃ksjɔ̃] *nf* **1** : distinction **2 distinction honorifique** : award

distingué, -guée [distɛ̃ge] *adj* : distinguished

distinguer [distɛ̃ge] *vt* **1** : to distinguish, to differentiate **2** : to discern **3** : to set apart — *vi* : to distinguish, to make a distinction — **se distinguer** *vr* **1** : to stand out **2** : to distinguish oneself

distorsion [distɔrsjɔ̃] *nf* : distortion

distraction [distraksjɔ̃] *nf* **1** : distraction, absentmindedness **2** : recreation, amusement

distraire [distrɛr] {40} *vt* **1** : to distract **2** DIVERTIR : to amuse, to entertain — **se distraire** *vr* : to amuse oneself

distrait, -traite [distrɛ, -trɛt] *adj* : absentminded — **distraitement** [-trɛtmɑ̃] *adv*

distrayant, -trayante [distrɛjɑ̃, -trɛjɑ̃t] *adj* : entertaining

distribuer [distribɥe] *vt* **1** : to distribute, to deal out **2** : to assign, to allocate **3** : to supply (water, etc.)

distributeur[1], **-trice** [distribytœr, -tris] *n* : distributor

distributeur[2] *nm* **1** : distributor (of an automobile) **2** *or* **distributeur automatique** : dispenser, vending machine

distribution [distribysjɔ̃] *nf* **1** : distribution **2** : supplying (of utilities, etc.) **3** : casting (of a movie or play)

district [distrikt] *nm* : district

dit, dite [di, dit] *adj* **1** : agreed upon, stated <à l'heure dite : at the appointed time> **2** : called, known as

dites [dit] → **dire**

diurétique [djyretik] *adj & nm* : diuretic
diurne [djym] *adj* : diurnal, daytime
divagation [divagasjɔ̃] *nf* : rambling, raving
divaguer [divage] *vi* **1** : to ramble (on) **2** : to rave
divan [divɑ̃] *nm* : divan, couch
divergent, -gente [divɛrʒɑ̃, -ʒɑ̃t] *adj* : divergent — **divergence** [-vɛrʒɑ̃s] *nf*
diverger [divɛrʒe] {17} *vi* : to diverge
divers, -verse [divɛr, -vɛrs] *adj* **1** VARIÉ : diverse, varied **2** PLUSIEURS : various, sundry <en diverses occasions : on various occasions> **3** : miscellaneous
diversification [diversifikasjɔ̃] *nf* : diversification
diversifier [diversifje] {96} *vt* : to diversify, to vary — **se diversifier** *vr*
diversion [diversjɔ̃] *nf* : diversion
diversité [diversite] *nf* : diversity, variety
divertir [divɛrtir] *vt* : to amuse, to entertain — **se divertir** *vr*
divertissement [divɛrtismɑ̃] *nm* : entertainment, pastime
dividende [dividɑ̃d] *nm* : dividend
divin, -vine [divɛ̃, -vin] *adj* : divine — **divinement** [-vinmɑ̃] *adv*
divinité [divinite] *nf* : divinity
diviser [divize] *vt* **1** : to divide (in mathematics) <diviser 10 par 2 : to divide 10 by 2> **2** : to divide, to split up — **se diviser** *vr*
diviseur [divizœr] *nm* : divisor
divisible [divizibl] *adj* : divisible
division [divizjɔ̃] *nf* : division
divorce [divɔrs] *nm* : divorce
divorcé, -cée [divɔrse] *n* : divorced person, divorcé *m*, divorcée *f*
divorcer [divɔrse] {6} *vi* **1** : to get a divorce **2** ~ **avec** *or* ~ **d'avec** *or* ~ **de** : to divorce (s.o.)
divulgation [divylgasjɔ̃] *nf* : disclosure
divulguer [divylge] *vt* : to divulge, to disclose
dix[1] [dis, *bef. consonant* di, *bef. vowel or mute h* diz] *adj* **1** : ten **2** : tenth <le dix avril : April tenth>
dix[2] *nms & pl* : ten
dix-huit[1] [dizɥit] *adj* **1** : eighteen **2** : eighteenth <le dix-huit juin : June eighteenth>
dix-huit[2] *nms & pl* : eighteen
dix-huitième [dizɥitjɛm] *adj & nmf & nm* : eighteenth
dixième [dizjɛm] *adj & nmf & nm* : tenth
dix-neuf[1] [diznœf] *adj* **1** : nineteen **2** : nineteenth <le dix-neuf mai : May nineteenth>
dix-neuf[2] *nms & pl* : nineteen
dix-neuvième [diznœvjɛm] *adj & nmf & nm* : nineteenth
dix-sept[1] [diset] *adj* **1** : seventeen **2** : seventeenth <le dix-sept avril : April seventeenth>
dix-sept[2] *nms & pl* : seventeen
dix-septième [disetjɛm] *adj & nmf & nm* : seventeenth
dizaine [dizɛn] *nf* **1** : ten **2** : about ten, ten or so
docile [dɔsil] *adj* : docile, obedient — **docilement** [-silmɑ̃] *adv*
dock [dɔk] *nm* : dock, berth (for a ship)
docker [dɔkɛr] *nm* : longshoreman, stevedore
docteur [dɔktœr] *nm* : doctor
doctorat [dɔktɔra] *nm* : doctorate
doctrine [dɔktrin] *nf* : doctrine
document [dɔkymɑ̃] *nm* : document
documentaire[1] [dɔkymɑ̃tɛr] *adj* **1** : documentary **2 à titre documentaire** : for your information
documentaire[2] *nm* : documentary (film)
documentation [dɔkymɑ̃tasjɔ̃] *nf* **1** : documentation, information **2** : research
documenter [dɔkymɑ̃te] *vt* : to inform, to provide with evidence — **se documenter** *vr* ~ **sur** : to research
dodo [dodo] *nm* **1** : dodo (bird) **2 faire dodo** : to go to bed (in baby talk)
dodu, -due [dɔdy] *adj* : plump, chubby
dogmatique [dɔgmatik] *adj* : dogmatic
dogmatisme [dɔgmatism] *nm* : dogmatism
dogme [dɔgm] *nm* : dogma
dogue [dɔg] *nm* : mastiff
doigt [dwa] *nm* **1** : finger <bout du doigt : fingertip> **2 doigt de pied** : toe **3 montrer du doigt** : to point at **4 se mordre les doigts** : to regret
doigté [dwate] *nm* **1** TACT : diplomacy, tact **2** : fingering (in music)
doit [dwa], **doive** [dwav], *etc.* → **devoir**
doléance [dɔleɑ̃s] *nf* : grievance, complaint
dolent, -lente [dɔlɑ̃, -lɑ̃t] *adj* : doleful, plaintive
dollar [dɔlar] *nm* : dollar
domaine [dɔmɛn] *nm* **1** PROPRIÉTÉ : estate, property **2** SPÉCIALITÉ : field, domain **3 domaine public** : public domain
dôme [dom] *nm* : dome
domestique[1] [dɔmɛstik] *adj* **1** : domestic, home **2** : domesticated
domestique[2] *nmf* : domestic, servant
domestiquer [dɔmɛstike] *vt* **1** APPRIVOISER : to domesticate **2** : to harness (energy)
domicile [dɔmisil] *nm* : residence, home
domicilié, -liée [dɔmisilje] *adj* **être domicilié à** : to be a resident in
dominance [dɔminɑ̃s] *nf* : dominance
dominant, -nante [dɔminɑ̃, -nɑ̃t] *adj* **1** : dominant, ruling **2** : predominant
dominateur, -trice [dɔminatœr, -tris] *adj* : domineering, overbearing
domination [dɔminasjɔ̃] *nf* : domination

dominer [dɔmine] *vt* **1** : to dominate **2** MAÎTRISER : to master, to control **3** : to outclass, to surpass **4** : to tower over — *vi* **1** : to be in a dominant position **2** : to prevail — **se dominer** *vr* : to control oneself

dominicain, -caine [dɔminikɛ̃, -kɛn] *adj* : Dominican

Dominican, -caine *n* : Dominican

domino [dɔmino] *nm* : domino

dommage [dɔmaʒ] *nm* **1** PRÉJUDICE : harm, injury **2** DÉGÂTS : damage **3** **c'est dommage** : that's a pity, that's too bad

dommageable [dɔmaʒabl] *adj* : detrimental, harmful

dompter [dɔ̃te] *vt* : to tame, to subdue

dompteur, -teuse [dɔ̃tœr, -tøz] *n* : trainer, (wild-animal) tamer

don [dɔ̃] *nm* **1** CADEAU : gift **2** : donation **3** : talent **4 don de soi** : self-sacrifice

donateur, -trice [dɔnatœr, -tris] *n* : donor, giver

donation [dɔnasjɔ̃] *nf* : donation

donc [dɔ̃k] *conj* **1** : so, therefore, consequently <je pense, donc je suis : I think, therefore I am> **2** : so, then <vous venez donc? : so you're coming?> **3** (*used for emphasis*) <écoute-moi donc! : would you listen to me!> <quoi donc? : what was that?>

donjon [dɔ̃ʒɔ̃] *nm* : keep (of a castle)

donne [dɔn] *nf* : deal (in card games)

donné, -née [dɔne] *adj* **1** : given <étant donné que : given that, considering that> **2 c'est donné** : it's a bargain

donnée *nf* **1** : fact, piece of information **2 données** *nfpl* : data <les données informatiques : computer data>

donner [dɔne] *vt* **1** : to give, to hand out, to donate **2** ATTRIBUER : to attribute to, to assign <quel âge lui donnez-vous? : how old would you say he is?> **3** : to provide, to transmit <donner un bon exemple : to set a good example> <donner un rhume à : to give a cold to> **4** CAUSER : to cause <donner du souci : to cause concern> <ça me donne froid : that makes me cold> **5** : to show, to put on (a film, play, etc.) **6** : to deal (cards) — *vi* **1** : to produce, to yield a crop **2 ~ contre** : to hit, to run into **3 ~ dans** : to lead toward (a place), to fall into (a trap), to tend toward (an opinion, etc.) — **se donner** *vr* **1** : to give to oneself, to have <se donner du bon temps : to have a good time> **2 ~ à** : to devote oneself to **3 ~ pour** : to pretend to be

donneur, -neuse [dɔnœr, -nøz] *n* **1** : donor **2** : dealer (in card games)

dont [dɔ̃] *pron* : of which, of whom, whose <la famille dont je sors : the family I come from> <ce dont il s'agit : what it's all about> <la fille dont la chevelure est bouclée : the girl whose hair is curly>

doper [dɔpe] *vt* : to dope

doré, -rée[1] [dɔre] *adj* **1** : gilded, gilt **2** : golden

dorénavant [dɔrenavɑ̃] *adv* : henceforth

dorer [dɔre] *vt* **1** : to gild **2** : to turn golden, to tan **3** : to glaze — *vi* : to brown (in cooking) — **se dorer** *vr* **se dorer au soleil** : to sunbathe, to tan

doris [dɔris] *nm* : dory (boat)

dorloter [dɔrlɔte] *vt* : to pamper, to baby

dormant, -mante [dɔrmɑ̃, -mɑ̃t] *adj* **1** : still, unmoving **2** : dormant (in botany)

dormeur, -meuse [dɔrmœr, -møz] *n* : sleeper

dormir [dɔrmir] {30} *vi* **1** : to sleep, to be asleep **2** : to be dormant, to be still, to lie idle

dorsal, -sale [dɔrsal, -sal] *adj, mpl* **dorsaux** [dɔrso] : dorsal

dort [dɔr], *etc.* → **dormir**

dortoir [dɔrtwar] *nm* : dormitory

dorure [dɔryr] *nf* **1** : gilt **2** : gilding

dos [do] *nms & pl* **1** : back <dos à dos : back to back> **2** : spine (of a book) **3 de ~** : from behind

dos–d'âne [dodan] *nm* : speed bump

dose [doz] *nf* : dose

doser [doze] *vt* : to measure out (a dose of medicine, etc.), to apportion

doseur [dozœr] *nm* **1** : measure **2** *or* **bouchon doseur** : measuring cup

dossard [dosar] *nm* : number (worn by an athlete)

dossier [dosje] *nm* **1** : file, dossier <dossier criminel : criminal record> **2** : back (of a chair, etc.)

dot [dɔt] *nf* : dowry

dotation [dɔtasjɔ̃] *nf* : endowment

doter [dɔte] *vt* **1** : to endow **2** ÉQUIPER : to equip **3** : to allocate

douane [dwan] *nf* **1** : customs **2** : (import) duty

douanier[1], **-nière** [dwanje, -njɛr] *adj* : customs <tarif douanier : customs tariff>

douanier[2] *nm* : customs officer

doublage [dublaʒ] *nm* **1** : acting as an understudy **2** : lining **3** : dubbing

double[1] [dubl] *adv & adj* : double

double[2] *nm* **1** : double <le double de : twice as much as> <plus du double : more than double> **2** : copy, duplicate <un double de clés : a spare set of keys>

doublement[1] [dubləmɑ̃] *adv* : doubly

doublement[2] *nm* : doubling

doubler [duble] *vt* **1** : to double **2** : to line **3** : to dub (a film, etc.) **4** : to pass, to overtake **5** : *fam* : to double–cross — *vi* : to double, to increase twofold

doublure [dublyr] *nf* **1** : lining **2** : understudy, stand-in

doucement [dusmɑ̃] *adv* **1** : gently, softly **2** : slowly **3** : meekly
doucereux, -reuse [dusrø, -røz] *adj* **1** MIELLEUX : smooth, unctuous **2** : sugary, saccharine
douceur [dusœr] *nf* **1** : softness, smoothness **2** : gentleness, mildness, meekness **3 douceurs** *nfpl* : candy, sweets **4 en ~** : gently, smoothly
douche [duʃ] *nf* **1** : shower <prendre une douche : to take a shower> **2** : douche (in medicine) **3 douche froide** : letdown
doucher [duʃe] *vt* **1** : to give a shower to **2** : to soak, to drench **— se doucher** *vr* : to take a shower
doué, douée [dwe] *adj* **1** : gifted, talented **2 ~ de** : endowed with
douille [duj] *nf* **1** : cartridge case **2** : electric socket
douillet, -lette [dujɛ, -jɛt] *adj* **1** : cozy **2** : oversensitive
douillette *nf Can* : comforter (for a bed)
douleur [dulœr] *nf* **1** : pain, ache **2** CHAGRIN : sorrow, grief
douloureusement [dulurøzmɑ̃] *adv* **1** : grievously, terribly **2** : painfully
douloureux, -reuse [dulurø, -røz] *adj* **1** : painful, sore **2** : distressing **3** : sorrowful, sad
doute [dut] *nm* : doubt
douter [dute] *vt* **1** : to doubt **2 ~ de** : to question <douter de l'honnêteté de : to question the honesty of> **— se douter** *vr* **~ de** : to suspect <je ne me doutais de rien : I didn't suspect a thing>
douteux, -teuse [dutø, -tøz] *adj* **1** INCERTAIN : doubtful, uncertain **2** : questionable, dubious **3** : ambiguous
douve [duv] *nf* **1** : moat **2** : stave (of a barrel)
doux, douce [du, dus] *adj* **1** : sweet **2** : soft <une peau douce : soft skin> **3** : mild, gentle <un hiver doux : a mild winter> **4** : meek **5 en ~** : quietly, secretly
douzaine [duzɛn] *nf* **1** : dozen **2 une douzaine de** : about twelve
douze[1] [duz] *adj* **1** : twelve **2** : twelfth <le douze avril : April twelfth>
douze[2] *nms & pl* : twelve
douzième [duzjɛm] *adj & nmf & nm* : twelfth
doyen, doyenne [dwajɛ̃, -jɛn] *n* **1** : dean **2 doyen d'âge** : oldest person
draconien, -nienne [drakɔnjɛ̃, -njɛn] *adj* : draconian, harsh
dragage [dragaʒ] *nm* : dredging
dragée [draʒe] *nf* **1** *France* : sugar-coated almond **2** : pill
dragon [dragɔ̃] *nm* : dragon
drague [drag] *nf* : dredge
draguer [drage] *vt* **1** : to dredge **2** *fam* : to cruise, to try to pick up <il drague les filles : he's trying to pick up girls>
drainage [drɛnaʒ] *nm* : drainage, draining
drainer [drɛne] *vt* : to drain
dramatique [dramatik] *adj* **1** : dramatic **2** : tragic
dramatiquement [dramatikmɑ̃] *adv* : tragically
dramatisation [dramatizasjɔ̃] *nf* : dramatization
dramatiser [dramatize] *v* : to dramatize
dramaturge [dramatyrʒ] *nmf* : playwright, dramatist
drame [dram] *nm* **1** : drama **2** : tragedy
drap [dra] *nm* **1** : woolen fabric **2** *or* **drap de lit** : bed sheet **3 drap fin** : broadcloth **4 drap mortuaire** : pall
drapé [drape] *nm* : drape, hang (of fabric)
drapeau [drapo] *nm, pl* **drapeaux** : flag
draper [drape] *vt* : to drape **— se draper** *vr* **~ dans** : to drape oneself in
draperie [drapri] *nf* **1** : drapery, wall hanging **2** : cloth industry
drastique [drastik] *adj* : drastic
drave [drav] *nf Can* : drive (of logs)
draver [drave] *vt Can* : to drive (logs down a stream)
dressage [drɛsaʒ] *nm* : (animal) training
dresser [drɛse] *vt* **1** LEVER : to raise **2** ÉRIGER : to put up, to erect **3** : to lay out, to set (up) **4** : to draft, to draw up <dresser une liste : to draw up a list> **5** : to train <dresser un chien : to train a dog> **6 dresser qqn contre** : to set s.o. against **— se dresser** *vr* **1** : to stand up **2** : to rise up, to tower **3 ~ contre** : to rebel against
dresseur, -seuse [drɛsœr, -søz] *n* : trainer, tamer <dresseur de lions : lion tamer>
dressoir [drɛswar] *nm* : cupboard, sideboard
dribble [dribl] *nm* : dribble (in basketball)
dribbler [drible] *vi* : to dribble (in basketball)
drille [drij] *nm* **un joyeux drille** : a cheerful fellow
drogue [drɔg] *nf* : drug
drogué, -guée [drɔge] *n* : drug addict
droguer [drɔge] *vt* : to drug **— se droguer** *vr* : to take drugs
droit[1] [drwa] *adv* : straight, directly <droit au but : straight to the point>
droit[2], **droite** [drwa, drwat] *adj* **1** : right, right-hand **2** : straight, direct **3** : upright, vertical **4** : honest, upright
droit[3] *nm* **1** : right <les droits de l'homme : human rights> <avoir droit à : to have the right to, to be eligible for> **2** : fee <droit d'entrée : entrance fee> **3** : law <droit pénal : criminal law> **4 droits d'auteur** : copyright, royalties **5 à qui de droit** : to whom it may concern
droite *nf* **1** : right, right-hand side **2 la droite** : the right, the right wing

droitier[1], **-tière** [drwatje, -tjɛr] *adj* : right-handed
droitier[2], **-tière** *n* : right-handed person
droiture [drwatyr] *nf* : uprightness, integrity
drôle [drol] *adj* **1** COMIQUE : funny, droll **2** BIZARRE : strange, odd **3 ~ de** : funny, strange <un drôle de chapeau : a strange hat> <une drôle d'idée : a funny idea>
drôlement [drolmɑ̃] *adv* **1** : amusingly, comically **2** : strangely, oddly **3** *fam* : really, awfully <les prix sont drôlement élevés : prices are terribly high>
drôlerie [drolri] *nf* **1** : drollness **2** : funny remark
dromadaire [drɔmadɛr] *nm* : dromedary
dru[1] [dry] *adv* : thickly, heavily
dru[2], **drue** [dry] *adj* **1** : thick, dense, bushy <avoir la barbe drue : to have a thick beard> **2** : heavy <une pluie drue : heavy rain>
du [dy] → **de, le**
dû[1] [dy] *pp* → **devoir**
dû[2], **due** [dy] *adj* **1** : due, owing **2** : proper, appropriate **3 ~ à** : due to
dû[3] *nm* : due <réclamer son dû : to claim one's due>
dubitatif, -tive [dybitatif, -tiv] *adj* : dubious, skeptical
duc [dyk] *nm* : duke
duchesse [dyʃɛs] *nf* : duchess
duel [dɥɛl] *nm* : duel
dûment [dymɑ̃] *adv* : duly
dune [dyn] *nf* : dune
duo [dyo] *nm* **1** : duet **2** : duo, pair
dupe [dyp] *nf* : dupe
duper [dype] *vt* : to dupe, to deceive
duplex [dypleks] *nm* **1** : duplex apartment **2** : (radio or television) linkup
duplicata [dyplikata] *nms & pl* : duplicate
duplicité [dyplisite] *nf* : duplicity
duquel → **lequel**
dur[1] [dyr] *adv* : hard <travailler dur : to work hard>
dur[2], **dure** [dyr] *adj* **1** : hard, stiff **2** : difficult **3** : harsh
dur[3] *nm* **1** : solid structure <construire en dur : to build with permanent materials> **2** *fam* : toughie, roughneck
durabilité [dyrabilite] *nf* : durability
durable [dyrabl] *adj* : durable, lasting
durant [dyrɑ̃] *prep* **1** : for <durant dix jours : for ten days> **2** : during
durcir [dyrsir] *v* : to harden — **se durcir** *vr*
durcissement [dyrsismɑ̃] *nm* : hardening
dure *nf* **1 à la dure** : the hard way **2 coucher sur la dure** : to sleep on the ground
durée [dyre] *nf* **1** : duration, length **2 de longue durée** : long-term, long-lasting
durement [dyrmɑ̃] *adv* : harshly, severely
durer [dyre] *vi* : to last, to go on
dureté [dyrte] *nf* **1** : hardness, arduousness **2** : harshness
durillon [dyrijɔ̃] *nm* CAL : callus
duvet [dyvɛ] *nm* **1** : down (feathers) **2** : sleeping bag
duveteux, -teuse [dyvtø, -tøz] *adj* : downy, fluffy, fuzzy
DVD [devede] *nm* : DVD (digital video disc)
dynamique[1] [dinamik] *adj* : dynamic — **dynamiquement** [-mikmɑ̃] *adv*
dynamique[2] *nf* : dynamics *pl*
dynamisme [dinamism] *nm* : dynamism
dynamite [dinamit] *nf* : dynamite
dynamiter [dinamite] *vt* : to dynamite, to blast
dynamo [dinamo] *nf* : dynamo
dynastie [dinasti] *nf* : dynasty — **dynastique** [-nastik] *adj*
dysenterie [disɑ̃tri] *nf* : dysentery
dyslexie [dislɛksi] *nf* : dyslexia — **dyslexique** [-lɛksik] *adj*
dyspepsie [dispɛpsi] *nf* : dyspepsia — **dyspepsique** [-pɛpsik] *or* **dyspeptique** [-pɛptik] *adj*
dystrophie [distrɔfi] *nf* **1** : dystrophy **2 dystrophie musculaire** : muscular dystrophy

E

e [ø] *nm* : e, fifth letter of the alphabet
eau [o] *nf, pl* **eaux 1** : water <eau douce : freshwater> <eau de pluie : rainwater> <eau bénite : holy water> <les eaux territoriales : territorial waters> **2 eau de Cologne** : cologne **3** → **Javel 4 eau oxygénée** : hydrogen peroxide **5 faire eau** : to leak **6 mettre l'eau à la bouche** : to make one's mouth water
eau–de–vie [odvi] *nf, pl* **eaux–de–vie** : brandy
eau–forte [ofɔrt] *nf, pl* **eaux–fortes** : etching
ébahi, -hie [ebai] *adj* : flabbergasted, dumbfounded
ébahir [ebair] *vt* ÉBERLUER : to astound, to dumbfound — **s'ébahir** *vr*
ébahissement [ebaismɑ̃] *nm* : astonishment

ébats [eba] *nmpl* GAMBADES : frolicking
ébattre [ebatr] {12} *v* **s'ébattre** *vr* : to frolic
ébauche [eboʃ] *nf* : outline, rough draft, sketch
ébaucher [eboʃe] *vt* : to sketch out, to outline — **s'ébaucher** *vr* : to form, to take shape
ébène [ebɛn] *nf* : ebony
ébéniste [ebenist] *nmf* : cabinetmaker
ébénisterie [ebenistəri] *nf* : cabinetmaking
éberluer [eberlɥe] ÉBAHIR *vt* : to astonish, to astound
éblouir [ebluir] *vt* **1** : to dazzle **2** : to stun, to amaze — **éblouissant, -sante** [-isɑ̃, -sɑ̃t] *adj*
éblouissement [ebluismɑ̃] *nm* **1** ÉMERVEILLEMENT : amazement, wonder **2** VERTIGE : dizzy spell
éborgner [ebɔrɲe] *vt* **1** : to blind (in one eye) **2** *Can* : to chip (a glass, plate, etc.)
éboueur [ebwœr] *nm* : garbage collector, garbageman
ébouillanter [ebujãte] *vt* **1** : to scald, to burn (one's hands, etc.) **2** : to blanch (in cooking) — **s'ébouillanter** *vr*
éboulement [ebulmɑ̃] *nm* **1** : crumbling, collapse **2** : heap of fallen rocks or earth <éboulement de terre : landslide>
ébouler [ebule] *v* **s'ébouler** *vr* : to cave in, to collapse
éboulis [ebuli] *nms & pl* : heap of rocks or earth, debris
ébouriffer [eburife] *vt* **1** : to tousle, to ruffle **2** *fam* : to amaze, to stun
ébrancher [ebrɑ̃ʃe] *vt* ÉLAGUER : to prune
ébranlement [ebrɑ̃lmɑ̃] *nm* **1** : shaking, rattling **2** : shock
ébranler [ebrɑ̃le] *vt* **1** : to shake, to rattle **2** : to weaken, to undermine — **s'ébranler** *vr* : to move off
ébrécher [ebreʃe] {87} *vt* : to chip, to nick — **s'ébrécher** *vr*
ébréchure [ebreʃyr] *nf* : nick, chip, flaw
ébriété [ebrijete] *nf* : inebriation, drunkenness
ébrouer [ebrue] *v* **s'ébrouer** *vr* **1** : to snort **2** : to shake oneself
ébruiter [ebrɥite] *vt* : to spread, to divulge — **s'ébruiter** *vr* : to become known
ébullition [ebylisjɔ̃] *nf* **1** : boil, boiling <point d'ébullition : boiling point> **2 en état d'ébullition** : in a fever of excitement, in turmoil
écaille [ekaj] *nf* **1** : scale (of fish, reptiles, etc.) **2** : oyster shell **3** : tortoiseshell **4** : flake, chip
écailler [ekaje] *vt* **1** : to scale (fish) **2** : to open (a shell) **3** : to chip (paint) — **s'écailler** *vr* : to flake off
écailleux, -leuse [ekajø, -jøz] *adj* : scaly, flaky
écale [ekal] *nf* : husk, hull
écaler [ekale] *vt* : to husk, to hull (nuts, etc.)
écarlate [ekarlat] *adj & nf* : scarlet
écarquiller [ekarkije] *vt* **écarquiller les yeux** : to open one's eyes wide
écart [ekar] *nm* **1** DISTANCE : distance, gap, interval **2** DIFFÉRENCE : difference, disparity, deviation **3** : lapse (in behavior, etc.) **4** : swerving <faire un écart : to swerve, to shy, to step aside> **5 à l'écart** : apart, away <se tenir à l'écart : to stand apart, to keep to oneself> **6 faire le grand écart** : to do the split (in gymnastics)
écarté, -tée [ekarte] *adj* **1** ISOLÉ : remote, secluded **2** : wide apart <avec les bras écartés : with arms outstretched>
écarteler [ekartəle] {20} *vt* **1** : to tear apart **2 être écartelé entre** : to be torn between
écartement [ekartəmɑ̃] *nm* ESPACE : space, gap
écarter [ekarte] *vt* **1** : to spread, to open **2** ÉLOIGNER : to move aside, to push away **3** EXCLURE : to dismiss, to rule out **4** DÉTOURNER : to divert, to distract **5** *Can* : to lose **6** *France* : to discard (in card games) — **s'écarter** *vr* **1** : to move away, to deviate, to digress **2** : to part, to separate **3 ~ de** : to stray from
écartiller [ekartije] *vt Can fam* : to open, to spread <il a écartillé les bras pour les accueillir : he opened his arms to welcome them>
ecchymose [ekimoz] *nf* : bruise
ecclésiastique[1] [eklezjastik] *adj* : ecclesiastical
ecclésiastique[2] *nm* : clergyman
écervelé, -lée [eservəle] *adj* ÉTOURDI : scatterbrained, empty-headed
échafaud [eʃafo] *nm* : scaffold
échafaudage [eʃafodaʒ] *nm* **1** : scaffolding **2** AMAS : heap, pile
échafauder [eʃafode] *vi* : to erect scaffolding — *vt* **1** : to stack, to pile up **2** : to construct, to build up (plans, theories, etc.)
échalier [eʃalje] *nm* **1** : gate **2** : stile
échalote [eʃalɔt] *nf* **1** : shallot **2** *Can* : scallion
échancré, -crée [eʃɑ̃kre] *adj* **1** : low-cut (of clothing) **2** : indented <un littoral échancré : a jagged coastline>
échancrure [eʃɑ̃kryr] *nf* **1** : low neckline **2** : indentation (of a coastline)
échange [eʃɑ̃ʒ] *nm* **1** : exchange <en échange de : in return for> **2** : trade <échange libre : free trade> <échanges internationaux : international trade>
échanger [eʃɑ̃ʒe] {17} *vt* : to exchange, to trade
échangeur [eʃɑ̃ʒœr] *nm* : interchange, junction (of highways)

échantillon [eʃɑ̃tijɔ̃] *nm* : sample, specimen
échantillonnage [eʃɑ̃tijɔnaʒ] *nm* **1** : sampling **2** : selection (of samples)
échappatoire [eʃapatwar] *nf* : way out, loophole
échappée [eʃape] *nf* **1** : breakaway (in sports) **2** VUE : vista, view **3** : brief period, break **4** : space, gap
échappement [eʃapmɑ̃] *nm* **1** : escapement (of a watch) **2** : exhaust (of an automobile) **3** → **pot**
échapper [eʃape] *vi* **1** ~ **à** : to escape from (a person, a situation), to escape (danger, etc.) **2** ~ **à** : to elude, to evade <rien ne lui échappe : nothing gets by him> **3 échapper à qqn** : to slip out (of s.o.'s hands) <le stylo lui a échappé des mains : the pen slipped out of his hands> <son nom m'échappe : her name escapes me> **4 laisser échapper** : to let out (a cry, a sigh, etc.) **5 échapper belle** : to have a narrow escape — *vt Can* : to drop <échapper un colis : to drop a parcel> — **s'échapper** *vr* : to escape
écharde [eʃard] *nf* : splinter
écharpe [eʃarp] *nf* **1** : scarf **2** : sash (of office) **3** : sling **4 prendre en écharpe** : to sideswipe
échasse [eʃas] *nf* : stilt
échassier [eʃasje] *nm* : wading
échauder [eʃode] *vt* **1** : to scald **2** : to teach a lesson, to make wary <échaudé par expérience : burned by experience>
échauffement [eʃofmɑ̃] *nm* **1** : heating up **2** : warm-up (in sports) **3** : overexcitement
échauffer [eʃofe] *vt* **1** : to make hot, to overheat **2** : to warm up (in sports) **3** EXCITER : to excite, to stimulate — **s'échauffer** *vr* : to warm up
échauffourée [eʃofure] *nf* **1** ESCARMOUCHE : skirmish **2** BAGARRE : brawl
échéance [eʃeɑ̃s] *nf* **1** : due date, expiration (date) <venir à échéance : to fall due> **2** : financial obligation, payment **3** : term <à longue échéance : in the long run>
échéancier [eʃeɑ̃sje] *nm* **1** : payment schedule **2** : schedule, calendar
échéant [eʃeɑ̃] *adv* **le cas échéant** : if need be
échec [eʃek] *nm* **1** : failure, setback **2 échecs** *nmpl* : chess **3 échec et mat** : checkmate **4 mise en échec** *Can* : check (in hockey) **5 tenir en échec** : to hold in check, to thwart
échelle [eʃɛl] *nf* **1** : ladder **2** : scale <carte à grande échelle : large-scale map> <échelle de salaires : pay scale> **3** GAMME : scale (in music) **4** : run, ladder (in stockings)
échelon [eʃlɔ̃] *nm* **1** : rung (of a ladder) **2** : step, grade, level **3** : echelon
échelonner [eʃlɔne] *vt* : to space out, to spread out — **s'échelonner** *vr*
écheveau [eʃvo] *nm, pl* **-veaux 1** : skein, hank **2** ENCHEVÊTREMENT : tangle
échevelé, -lée [eʃəvle] *adj* **1** : disheveled **2** : wild, disorderly
échine [eʃin] *nf* : backbone, spine
échiner [eʃine] *v* **s'échiner** *vr* : to work oneself to the bone
échiquier [eʃikje] *nm* : chessboard
écho [eko] *nm* **1** : echo **2** : repeating <se faire l'écho de : to repeat, to spread> **3** : response <recevoir un écho : to get a response> **4 échos** *nmpl* : gossip, rumors *pl*
échographie [ekografi] *nf* : ultrasound
échoir [eʃwar] {31} *vi* **1** : to expire **2** : to fall due **3** ~ **à** : to fall to <le travail qui m'est échu : the task that fell to me>
échoppe [eʃɔp] *nf* : booth, stall
échouer [eʃwe] *vi* **1** : to run (a ship) aground **2** : to fail, to fall through — *vt* : to beach — **s'échouer** *vr* : to run aground
éclabousser [eklabuse] *vt* **1** : to splash, to spatter **2** : to stain, to smear (a reputation)
éclaboussure [eklabusyr] *nf* **1** : splash, spattering **2** : smear, blemish (on a reputation)
éclair [eklɛr] *nm* **1** : flash of lightning **2** : flash **3** : éclair
éclairage [eklɛraʒ] *nm* : lighting, illumination
éclaircie [eklɛrsi] *nf* **1** EMBELLIE : sunny spell **2** : clearing, glade
éclaircir [eklɛrsir] *vt* **1** : to lighten **2** CLARIFIER : to clarify, to shed light on **3** : to thin (in cooking) — **s'éclaircir** *vr* **1** : to clear <le temps s'éclaircit : the weather is clearing up> <s'éclaircir la gorge : to clear one's throat> **2** : to thin out **3** : to become clearer (of a situation, etc.)
éclaircissement [eklɛrsismɑ̃] *nm* : explanation, clarification
éclairer [eklɛre] *vt* **1** : to light, to light up **2** : to enlighten **3** CLARIFIER, EXPLIQUER : to shed light on, to clarify — *vi* : to give light — *v impers* **il éclaire** *Can* : it's thundering and lightening — **s'éclairer** *vr* **1** : to light up **2** : to become clearer
éclaireur[1], **-reuse** [eklɛrœr, -røz] *n* : boy scout *m*, girl scout *f*
éclaireur[2] *nm* : scout (in the military)
éclat [ekla] *nm* **1** : splinter, chip <voler en éclats : to fly into pieces> **2** : brilliance, radiance **3** : splendor, magnificence <coup d'éclat : remarkable feat> **4** : outburst, uproar <éclat de rire : burst of laughter> <éclats de voix : shouts, cries>
éclatant, -tante [eklatɑ̃, -tɑ̃t] *adj* **1** BRILLANT : bright, brilliant **2** RETENTISSANT : resounding <un succès écla-

tant : a resounding success> **3** : loud, piercing

éclatement [eklatmɑ̃] *nm* **1** EXPLOSION : explosion, bursting **2** : blowout (of a tire) **3** : rupture, split

éclater [eklate] *vi* **1** EXPLOSER : to burst, to explode **2** : to break up, to splinter **3** : to break out <la guerre a éclaté : war broke out> — **s'éclater** *vr fam* : to have a great time

éclectique [eklɛktik] *adj* : eclectic

éclipse [eklips] *nf* : eclipse

éclipser [eklipse] *vt* : to eclipse, to outshine — **s'éclipser** *vr* S'ESQUIVER : to slip away

éclopé, -pée [eklɔpe] *adj* : lame

éclore [eklɔr] {32} *vi* **1** : to hatch **2** : to open out, to blossom

éclosion [eklozjɔ̃] *nf* **1** : hatching **2** : blossoming

écluse [eklyz] *nf* : lock (of a canal)

écluser [eklyze] *vt* **1** : to provide with locks **2** *fam* : to swill down

écœurant, -rante [ekœrɑ̃, -rɑ̃t] *adj* **1** NAUSÉABOND : sickening, nauseating **2** : disgusting

écœuranterie [ekœrɑ̃tri] *nf Can fam* : dirty trick

écœurement [ekœrmɑ̃] *nm* **1** NAUSÉE : nausea **2** : disgust, distaste **3** DÉCOURAGEMENT : discouragement

écœurer [ekœre] *vt* **1** : to nauseate, to sicken **2** : to disgust **3** DÉCOURAGER : to discourage

école [ekɔl] *nf* **1** : school <école maternelle *France* : nursery school> <école maternelle *Can* : kindergarten> <école primaire : grade school> <école secondaire *Can* : high school> **2** : schooling, education **3** : training, experience <être à bonne école : to be in good hands> <être à rude école : to learn the hard way> **4** : movement, school (of artists, etc.)

écolier, -lière [ekɔlje, -ljɛr] *n* : schoolboy *m*, schoolgirl *f*

écologie [ekɔlɔʒi] *nf* : ecology

écologique [ekɔlɔʒik] *adj* : ecological — **écologiquement** [-ʒikmɑ̃] *adv*

écologiste [ekɔlɔʒist] *nmf* : ecologist, environmentalist

éconduire [ekɔ̃duir] {49} *vt* : to reject, to dismiss

économe[1] [ekɔnɔm] *adj* : thrifty, economical

économe[2] *nmf* : bursar

économie [ekɔnɔmi] *nf* **1** : economy **2** : economics **3** : saving, thrift <faire une économie de temps : to save time> **4 économies** *nfpl* : savings

économique [ekɔnɔmik] *adj* **1** : economic **2** : economical, inexpensive — **économiquement** [-mikmɑ̃] *adv*

économiser [ekɔnɔmize] *vt* : to economize, to save, to conserve — *vi* : to economize, to save money

économiste [ekɔnɔmist] *nmf* : economist

écoper [ekɔpe] *vt* : to bail out (a boat) — *vi fam* ~ **de** : to get <écoper de trois ans de prison : to get a three-year sentence>

écorce [ekɔrs] *nf* **1** : bark **2** : peel, rind **3 l'écorce terrestre** : the earth's crust

écorcher [ekɔrʃe] *vt* **1** DÉPOUILLER : to skin **2** ÉRAFLER : to scratch, to graze, to chafe **3** : to mispronounce

écorchure [ekɔrʃyr] *nf* : graze, scratch, chafing

écorner [ekɔrne] *vt* **1** : to chip the corner off (furniture), to dog-ear (a page) **2** : to make a dent in (one's fortune, etc.) — **s'écorner** *vr*

écornifler [ekɔrnifle] *vt Can fam* : to spy on — *vi Can fam* : to snoop around

écossais[1], **-saise** [ekɔsɛ, -sɛz] *adj* **1** : Scottish **2 tissu écossais** : tartan, plaid **3 whisky écossais** : Scotch (whiskey)

écossais[2] *nm* **1** : Scots (language) **2** : tartan

Écossais, -saise *n* : Scot, Scottish person

écosser [ekɔse] *vt* : to shell

écosystème [ekɔsistɛm] *nm* : ecosystem

écot [eko] *nm* **payer son écot** : to pay one's share

écoulement [ekulmɑ̃] *nm* **1** : flowing, streaming **2** : discharge <écoulement sanguin : bleeding> **3** : dispersal (of a crowd) **4** : selling (of merchandise)

écouler [ekule] *vt* **1** : to sell **2** : to pass (into circulation) — **s'écouler** *vr* **1** : to flow (out) **2** : to drift away, to disperse **3** : to pass, to elapse <les minutes s'écoulent : the minutes pass by>

écourter [ekurte] *vt* : to cut short, to curtail

écoute [ekut] *nf* **1** : listening (in radio and television) <être aux écoutes : to be listening, to be tuned in> <les heures de grande écoute : prime time> **2** : listening (in) <écoutes téléphoniques : phone tapping> <poste d'écoute : listening post>

écouter [ekute] *vt* : to listen to — *vi* **1** : to listen **2 écouter aux portes** : to eavesdrop — **s'écouter** *vr*

écouteur [ekutœr] *nm* **1** : receiver (of a telephone) **2 écouteurs** *nmpl* : headphones, earphones

écoutille [ekutij] *nf* : hatchway

écrabouiller [ekrabuje] *vt fam* : to crush, to squash

écran [ekrɑ̃] *nm* : screen <le petit écran : television>

écrasant, -sante [ekrazɑ̃, -zɑ̃t] *adj* : crushing, overwhelming

écraser [ekraze] *vt* **1** : to crush, to squash, to mash **2** : to run over **3** ACCABLER : to overwhelm — **s'écraser** *vr* **1** : to get crushed **2** : to crash **3** *Can fam* : to collapse, to sink <elle s'est

écrasée sur le divan : she collapsed onto the sofa>

écrémer [ekreme] {87} *vt* : to skim (milk)

écrevisse [ekrevis] *nf* : crayfish

écrier [ekrije] {96} *v* **s'écrier** *vr* : to exclaim

écrin [ekrɛ̃] *nm* : case, box

écrire [ekrir] {33} *vt* **1** : to write **2** ÉPELER : to spell <comment écrivez-vous ce mot? : how do you spell this word?> — *vi* : to write — **s'écrire** *vr* **1** : to be written, to be spelled **2** : to write to each other

écrit [ekri] *nm* **1** : writing, written work **2** : written exam **3 écrits** *nmpl* : writings, works **4 par ~** : in writing

écriteau [ekrito] *nm, pl* **-teaux** : notice, sign

écriture [ekrityr] *nf* **1** : handwriting, penmanship **2** : writing, script **3 écritures** *nfpl* : accounts, books **4 les Écritures** : the Scriptures

écrivaillon [ekrivajõ] *nm fam* : hack (writer)

écrivain [ekrivɛ̃] *nm* : writer

écrivaine [ekrivɛn] *nf Can* : (female) writer

écrivait [ekrivɛ], **écrivions** [ekrivjõ], *etc.* → **écrire**

écrive [ekriv], *etc.* → **écrire**

écrou [ekru] *nm* : nut <écrou à ailettes : wing nut>

écrouer [ekrue] *vt* : to imprison

écroulement [ekrulmã] *nm* : collapse

écrouler [ekrule] *v* **s'écrouler** *vr* : to collapse, to fail, to fold

écru, -crue [ekry] *adj* **1** : raw, unbleached, natural <soie écrue : raw silk> **2** : ecru (color)

écu [eky] *nm* **1** BOUCLIER : shield **2** : crown (monetary unit)

écueil [ekœj] *nm* **1** RÉCIF : reef **2** : pitfall

écuelle [ekɥɛl] *nf* **1** : bowl **2** : bowlful

éculé, -lée [ekyle] *adj* **1** : worn at the heel **2** : hackneyed

écume [ekym] *nf* **1** : foam, froth **2** : scum

écumer [ekyme] *vt* **1** : to skim **2** PILLER : to plunder **3** : to search through, to scour — *vi* : to foam, to froth

écumeur, -meuse [ekymœr, -møz] *adj* : foamy, frothy

écureuil [ekyrœj] *nm* : squirrel

écurie [ekyri] *nf* : stable

écusson [ekysõ] *nm* : badge

écuyer, -yère [ekɥije, -jɛr] *n* : horseman *m*, horsewoman *f*, rider

eczéma [egzema] *nm* : eczema

éden [edɛn] *nm* : Eden, paradise

édenté, -tée [edãte] *adj* : toothless

édicter [edikte] *vt* : to decree

édifiant, -fiante [edifjã, -fjãt] *adj* : edifying

édification [edifikasjõ] *nf* **1** : edification **2** : construction, building

édifice [edifis] *nm* : edifice, building

édifier [edifje] {96} *vt* **1** CONSTRUIRE : to erect, to build **2** : to edify

édit [edi] *nm* : edict

éditer [edite] *vt* **1** : to publish **2** : to edit

éditeur[1], **-trice** [editœr, -tris] *n* **1** : publisher **2** : editor

éditeur[2] *nm* **éditeur de textes** : text editing program

édition [edisjõ] *nf* **1** : publishing <maison d'édition : publishing house> **2** : edition <nouvelle édition : new edition> **3** : editing

éditorial[1], **-riale** [editɔrjal] *adj, mpl* **-riaux** [-rjo] : editorial

éditorial[2] *nm, pl* **-riaux** : editorial

éditorialiste [editɔrjalist] *nmf* : editorial writer

édredon [edrədõ] *nm* : comforter, eiderdown

éducateur[1], **-trice** [edykatœr, -tris] *adj* : educational

éducateur[2], **-trice** *n* : teacher, educator

éducatif, -tive [edykatif, -tiv] *adj* : educational

éducation [edykasjõ] *nf* **1** ENSEIGNEMENT : education **2** : upbringing, breeding <avoir de l'éducation : to have good manners> **3** : training

édulcorant [edylkɔrã] *nm* : sweetener

édulcorer [edylkɔre] *vt* **1** SUCRER : to sweeten **2** ATTÉNUER : to tone down

éduquer [edyke] *vt* **1** : to educate **2** ÉLEVER : to bring up, to raise **3** : to train

efface *nf Can* [efas] : eraser

effacé, -cée [efase] *adj* **1** : faded **2** : retiring, self-effacing

effacement [efasmã] *nm* : erasing, obliteration

effacer [efase] {6} *vt* **1** : to erase, to delete **2** : to wipe out, to obliterate **3** : to outshine — **s'effacer** *vr* **1** : to wear off **2** : to fade, to diminish **3** : to stand aside

effarant, -rante [efarã, -rãt] *adj* : startling, alarming

effarement [efarmã] *nm* : alarm

effarer [efare] *vt* : to alarm

effaroucher [efaruʃe] *vt* **1** : to frighten, to scare away **2** : to alarm — **s'effaroucher** *vr*

effectif[1], **-tive** [efɛktif, -tiv] *adj* : effective, real

effectif[2] *nm* : size, strength, total number <un effectif de 160 personnes : a total of 160 people>

effectivement [efɛktivmã] *adv* **1** RÉELLEMENT : actually, really **2** : indeed, in fact

effectuer [efɛktɥe] *vt* EXÉCUTER : to carry out, to make <effectuer une enquête : to carry out an investigation>

efféminé, -née [efemine] *adj* : effeminate

effervescence [efɛrvesãs] *nf* **1** : effervescence **2** : agitation, turmoil <être en effervescence : to be all excited>
effervescent, -cente [efɛrvesɑ̃, -sãt] *adj* : effervescent
effet [efɛ] *nm* **1** : effect, result <faire de l'effet : to have an effect, to be effective> **2** : impression <il fait bon effet : he makes a good impression> **3** : operation, action <mettre à effet : to put into action> **4 à cet effet** : for that purpose **5 en ~** : indeed, actually **6 effets** *nmpl* : things, belongings
efficace [efikas] *adj* **1** : efficient **2** : efficacious, effective — **efficacement** [-kasmã] *adv*
efficacité [efikasite] *nf* **1** : efficiency **2** : effectiveness
efficience [efisjãs] *nf* : efficiency
effigie [efiʒi] *nf* : effigy
effilé, -lée [efile] *adj* **1** : sharp **2** : slim, slender **3** : frayed
effiler [efile] *vt* **1** : to make pointed, to taper **2** : to fray, to unravel — **s'effiler** *vr* : to fray
effiloche [efilɔʃ] *nf* : fraying, ravel
effilocher [efilɔʃe] *vt* : to shred, to fray — **s'effilocher** *vr* : to fray, to unravel
efflanqué, -quée [eflãke] *adj* : emaciated
effleurement [eflœrmã] *nm* : light touch, caress
effleurer [eflœre] *vt* **1** FRÔLER : to touch lightly, to brush against **2** : to touch on (an idea, etc.) <ça m'a effleuré l'esprit : it crossed my mind>
effluve [eflyv] *nm* ÉMANATION : emanation, odor
effondrement [efɔ̃drəmã] *nm* : collapse
effondrer [efɔ̃dre] *v* **s'effondrer** *vr* : to sink, to collapse
efforcer [efɔrse] {6} *v* **s'efforcer** *vr* : to strive, to endeavor
effort [efɔr] *nm* **1** : effort <sans effort : effortless> **2** : stress (in engineering)
effraction [efraksjɔ̃] *nf* : housebreaking, breaking and entering
effraie [efrɛ], **effraiera** [efrɛra], *etc.* → **effrayer**
effranger [efrãʒe] {17} *vt* : to fray — **s'effranger** *vr*
effrayant, -yante [efrɛjã, -jãt] *adj* **1** : frightening, scary **2** *fam* : terrible, frightful
effrayer [efreje] {11} *vt* **1** : to frighten, to scare **2** REBUTER : to put off, to scare away — **s'effrayer** *vr*
effréné, -née [efrene] *adj* **1** DÉCHAÎNÉ : unbridled, unrestrained **2** : frantic
effritement [efritmã] *nm* : crumbling, disintegration
effriter [efrite] *vt* : to crumble — **s'effriter** *vr* : to crumble away, to disintegrate
effroi [efrwa] *nm* TERREUR : terror, dread
effronté, -tée [efrɔ̃te] *adj* INSOLENT : insolent, impudent — **effrontément** [-temã] *adv*
effronterie [efrɔ̃tri] *nf* INSOLENCE : insolence, impudence
effroyable [efrwajabl] *adj* AFFREUX : dreadful, appalling
effroyablement [efrwajablə̃mã] *adv* **1** : appallingly **2** : extremely, terribly
effusion [efyzjɔ̃] *nf* **1** : effusion **2 effusion de sang** : bloodshed
égailler [egaje] *v* **s'égailler** *vr* : to disperse, to scatter
égal[1], **-gale** [egal] *adj, mpl* **égaux** [ego] **1** : equal **2** RÉGULIER : steady, regular <un pouls égal : a steady heartbeat> **3** : level, even **4 ça m'est égal** : it makes no difference to me
égal[2], **-gale** *n* **1** : equal **2 sans égal** : unequaled, matchless
également [egalmã] *adv* **1** : equally **2** AUSSI : also, as well, too
égaler [egale] *vt* **1** : to equal, to be equal to <deux plus deux égalent quatre : two plus two equals four> **2** : to match, to rival <personne ne l'égale : no one can match him>
égalisateur, -trice [egalizatœr, -tris] *adj* **1** : equalizing **2** : tying <le but égalisateur : the tying goal>
égaliser [egalize] *vt* **1** : to equalize **2** : to level (out), to even up — *vi* : to tie (in sports)
égalitaire [egaliter] *adj* : egalitarian
égalitarisme [egalitarism] *nm* : egalitarianism
égalité [egalite] *nf* **1** : equality **2** : evenness **3 à ~** : tied (in sports)
égard [egar] *nm* **1** : regard, consideration <sans égard pour les autres : without considering others> <par égard pour : out of deference to> **2 à l'égard de** : toward, with regard to **3 à cet égard** : in this respect **4 eu égard à** : in view of **5 égards** *nmpl* : consideration, respect
égaré, -rée [egare] *adj* **1** : lost, stray **2** : distraught
égarement [egarmã] *nm* **1** : distraction **2** : derangement, folly
égarer [egare] *vt* **1** : to lead astray **2** : to lose, to misplace — **s'égarer** *vr* **1** : to lose one's way **2** : to be misplaced **3** : to ramble, to digress
égayer [egeje] {11} *vt* : to cheer up, to brighten — **s'égayer** *vr*
égide [eʒid] *nf* : aegis <sous l'égide de : under the aegis of>
églantier [eglãtje] *nm* : wild rose (bush)
églantine [eglãtin] *nf* : wild rose
églefin [eglə̃fɛ̃] *nm* : haddock
église [egliz] *nf* : church
ego [ego] *nm* : ego
égocentrique [egɔsãtrik] *adj* : egocentric, self-centered
égoïsme [egɔism] *nm* : selfishness, egoism

égoïste[1] [egɔist] *adj* : selfish, egoistic — **égoïstement** [-istəmɑ̃] *adv*
égoïste[2] *nmf* : selfish person, egoist
égorger [egɔrʒe] {17} *vt* : to cut the throat of
égosiller [egɔzije] *v* **s'égosiller** *vr* **1** : to shout oneself hoarse **2** : to sing at the top of one's lungs
égotisme [egɔtism] *nm* : egotism
égotiste[1] [egɔtist] *adj* : egotistic, egotistical
égotiste[2] *nmf* : egotist
égout [egu] *nm* **1** : sewer **2 eaux d'égout** : sewage
égoutter [egute] *vt* : to allow to drip, to drain — **s'égoutter** *vr*
égouttoir [egutwar] *nm* **1** : dish drainer **2** : strainer, colander
égratigner [egratiɲe] *vt* ÉRAFLER : to scratch, to graze — **s'égratigner** *vr*
égratignure [egratiɲyr] *nf* : scratch
égrener [egrəne] {52} *vt* **1** : to shell (peas, etc.), to seed (grains, fruit), to gin (cottton) **2 égrener son chapelet** : to say one's rosary **3 égrener les heures** : to mark the hours
égreneuse [egrənøz] *nf* : cotton gin
égrillard, -larde [egrijar, -jard] *adj* : ribald, bawdy
égyptien, -tienne [eʒipsjɛ̃, -sjɛn] *adj* : Egyptian
Égyptien, -tienne *n* : Egyptian
eh [e] *interj* **1** : hey! **2 eh bien** : well <eh bien, allons-y : well, let's go>
éhonté, -tée [eɔ̃te] *adj* : shameless, brazen
éjaculation [eʒakylasjɔ̃] *nf* : ejaculation
éjaculer [eʒakyle] *vt* : to ejaculate
éjecter [eʒekte] *vt* **1** : to eject **2** *fam* : to kick out
éjection [eʒeksjɔ̃] *nf* : ejection
élaboration [elabɔrasjɔ̃] *nf* : development, making, drawing up
élaborer [elabɔre] *vt* : to develop, to put together
élagage [elagaʒ] *nm* : pruning
élaguer [elage] *vt* ÉMONDER : to prune, to lop
élan [elɑ̃] *nm* **1** : momentum **2** : burst, rush, surge <un élan de colère : a burst of anger> <avec élan : enthusiastically> **3** : (European) elk **4** *Can* : swing (in baseball) **5 élan d'Amérique** *Can* → **orignal**
élancé, -cée [elɑ̃se] *adj* : slender
élancement [elɑ̃smɑ̃] *nm* : shooting pain
élancer [elɑ̃se] {6} *vi* : to give shooting pains — **s'élancer** *vr* **1** SE PRÉCIPITER : to dash forward, to rush **2** : to soar **3** *Can* : to swing (in baseball)
élargir [elarʒir] *vt* **1** : to widen, to broaden, to extend **2** LIBÉRER : to release, to discharge — **s'élargir** *vr* : to broaden, to expand
élargissement [elarʒismɑ̃] *nm* **1** : widening, broadening **2** LIBÉRATION : release, discharge
élasticité [elastisite] *nf* **1** : elasticity **2** : flexibility
élastique[1] [elastik] *adj* FLEXIBLE : elastic, flexible
élastique[2] *nm* **1** : elastic **2** : rubber band **3** : bungee cord
électeur, -trice [elektœr, -tris] *n* : voter, elector
électif, -tive [elektif, -tiv] *adj* : elective
élection [eleksjɔ̃] *nf* **1** : election **2** CHOIX : choice
électoral, -rale [elektɔral] *adj, mpl* **-raux** [-ro] : electoral, election
électorat [elektɔra] *nm* : electorate
électricien, -cienne [elektrisjɛ̃, -sjɛn] *n* : electrician
électricité [elektrisite] *nf* : electricity
électrifier [elektrifje] {96} *vt* : to electrify — **électrification** [-trifikasjɔ̃] *nf*
électrique [elektrik] *adj* : electric, electrical — **électriquement** [-trikmɑ̃] *adv*
électrisant, -sante [elektrizɑ̃, -zɑ̃t] *adj* : electrifying, thrilling
électriser [elektrize] *vt* : to electrify
électroaimant [elektrɔɛmɑ̃] *nm* : electromagnet
électrocardiogramme [elektrɔkardjɔgram] *nm* : electrocardiogram
électrocardiographe [elektrɔkardjɔgraf] *nm* : electrocardiograph
électrocuter [elektrɔkyte] *vt* : to electrocute — **électrocution** [-trɔkysjɔ̃] *nf*
électrode [elektrɔd] *nf* : electrode
électrolyse [elektrɔliz] *nf* : electrolysis
électrolyte [elektrɔlit] *nm* : electrolyte
électromagnétisme [elektrɔmaɲetism] *nm* : electromagnetism — **électromagnétique** [-ɲetik] *adj*
électroménager[1] [elektrɔmenaʒe] *adj* **appareil électroménager** : household (electrical) appliance
électroménager[2] *nm* **l'électroménager** : household (electrical) appliances
électron [elektrɔ̃] *nm* : electron
électronicien, -cienne [elektrɔnisjɛ̃, -sjɛn] *n* : electronics engineer
électronique[1] [elektrɔnik] *adj* : electronic — **électroniquement** [-nikmɑ̃] *adv*
électronique[2] *nf* : electronics
élégamment [elegamɑ̃] *adv* : elegantly
élégance [elegɑ̃s] *nf* : elegance
élégant, -gante [elegɑ̃, -gɑ̃t] *adj* : elegant
élégiaque [eleʒjak] *adj* : elegiac
élégie [eleʒi] *nf* : elegy
élément [elemɑ̃] *nm* **1** : element **2** COMPOSANT : component, ingredient, part **3** : cell (of a battery) **4 éléments** *nmpl* : rudiments, basics
élémentaire [elemɑ̃tɛr] *adj* : elementary, basic
éléphant [elefɑ̃] *nm* : elephant

éléphantesque [elefɑ̃tɛsk] *adj* : elephantine, gigantic
élevage [elvaʒ] *nm* **1** : breeding, raising <l'élevage de chevaux : horse breeding> **2** : ranch, livestock farm
élévateur [elevatœr] *nm* : (grain) elevator
élévation [elevasjɔ̃] *nf* **1** : elevation **2** : rise, increase **3** : raising
élève [elɛv] *nmf* : pupil, student
élevé, -vée [elve] *adj* **1** : high **2** : elevated, noble **3 bien élevé** : well-mannered, well brought up
élever [elve] {52} *vt* **1** : to raise, to increase **2** ÉRIGER : to erect, to build **3** : to elevate (mind, spirit, etc.) **4** : to bring up, to raise <élever un enfant : to raise a child> — **s'élever** *vr* **1** : to rise, to go up **2** : to be built, to stand **3** : to arise, to come up **4 ~ à** : to amount to, to come to **5 ~ contre** : to rise (up) against, to protest
éleveur, -veuse [elvœr, -vøz] *n* : rancher, breeder
elfe [ɛlf] *nm* : elf
élider [elide] *vt* : to elide
éligibilité [eliʒibilite] *nf* : eligibility
éligible [eliʒibl] *adj* : eligible
élimé, -mée [elime] *adj* : threadbare, worn
élimination [eliminasjɔ̃] *nf* : elimination
éliminatoire[1] [eliminatwar] *adj* : qualifying
éliminatoire[2] *nf* : heat (in sports)
éliminer [elimine] *vt* : to eliminate
élire [elir] {51} *vt* **1** : to elect **2 élire domicile** : to take up residence
élision [elizjɔ̃] *nf* : elision
élite [elit] *nf* : elite
élixir [eliksir] *nm* : elixir
elle [ɛl] *pron* **1** : she, it <elle est heureuse : she's happy> <elle est toute neuve : it is brand new> **2** : her <c'était son idée à elle : it was her idea> **3 elles** *pron pl* : they, them <elles se trompent : they're mistaken> <selon elles : according to them>
elle-même [ɛlmɛm] *pron* **1** : herself, itself **2 elles-mêmes** *pron pl* : themselves
ellipse [elips] *nf* **1** OVALE : ellipse, oval **2** : ellipsis
elliptique [eliptik] *adj* : elliptical, elliptic
élocution [elɔkysjɔ̃] *nf* : elocution, diction
éloge [elɔʒ] *nm* **1** : eulogy **2** LOUANGE : praise
élogieux, -gieuse [elɔʒjø, -ʒjøz] *adj* : full of praise, laudatory
éloigné, -gnée [elwaɲe] *adj* : distant, remote
éloignement [elwaɲmɑ̃] *nm* **1** DISTANCE : remoteness, distance (in space or time) **2** : removal **3** : absence
éloigner [elwaɲe] *vt* **1** ÉCARTER : to push aside, to move away **2** DÉTOURNER : to divert, to turn away **3** : to postpone, to put off — **s'éloigner** *vr* : to move away, to go away
éloquence [elɔkɑs] *nf* : eloquence
éloquent, -quente [elɔkɑ̃, -kɑt] *adj* : eloquent — **éloquemment** [elɔkamɑ̃] *adv*
élu[1], **-lue** [ely] *adj* **1** : elect, future **2** : elected
élu[2], **-lue** *n* **1** : elected representative **2** : chosen one <l'élu de mon cœur : my beloved> <les élus : the elect>
élucider [elyside] *vt* CLARIFIER : to clarify, to elucidate — **élucidation** [-sidasjɔ̃] *nf*
élucubrations [elykybrasjɔ̃] *nfpl* : rantings, wild imaginings
éluder [elyde] *vt* : to elude, to evade
élusif, -sive [elyzif, -ziv] *adj* : elusive, evasive
émaciation [emasjasjɔ̃] *nf* : emaciation
émacié, -ciée [emasje] *adj* : emaciated
émail [emaj] *nm, pl* **émaux** [emo] **1** : enamel **2** *Can* : latex (paint)
émailler [emaje] *vt* **1** : to enamel **2** PARSEMER : to scatter, to sprinkle
émanation [emanasjɔ̃] *nf* **1** : emanation <émanations toxiques : toxic fumes> **2** : expression, manifestation
émancipation [emɑ̃sipasjɔ̃] *nf* : emancipation
émanciper [emɑ̃sipe] *vt* AFFRANCHIR : to emancipate, to liberate — **s'émanciper** *vr*
émaner [emane] *vi* **~ de** : to emanate from
émarger [emarʒe] {17} *vt* **1** : to sign, to initial **2** : to trim the margins of — *vi* **~ à** : to be paid from
émasculer [emaskyle] *vt* CASTRER : to emasculate
emballage [ɑ̃balaʒ] *nm* : packing, wrapping <papier d'emballage : wrapping paper>
emballement [ɑ̃balmɑ̃] *nm* **1** : surge, burst <un emballement d'enthousiasme : a burst of enthusiasm> **2** : racing (of an engine)
emballer [ɑ̃bale] *vt* **1** EMPAQUETER : to pack, to wrap **2** *fam* : to thrill <ça ne m'emballe pas : it doesn't thrill me> — **s'emballer** *vr* **1** : to surge **2** : to race (of an engine), to bolt (of a horse) **3** *fam* : to get carried away
embarcadère [ɑ̃barkader] *nm* : wharf, pier
embarcation [ɑ̃barkasjɔ̃] *nf* BARQUE : small boat
embardée [ɑ̃barde] *nf* : swerve, lurch <faire une embardée : to swerve>
embargo [ɑ̃bargo] *nm* **1** : embargo **2 mettre l'embargo sur** : to embargo
embarquement [ɑ̃barkəmɑ̃] *nm* **1** : boarding, embarkation <carte d'embarquement : boarding pass> **2** CHARGEMENT : loading (on board)

embarquer [ɑ̃barke] *vt* **1** : to embark **2** : to load **3** *fam* : to start on, to get involved with — *vi* **1** : to board **2** ~ **dans** *Can* : to get in, to climb in <embarque dans la voiture : get in the car> **3** ~ **sur** *Can fam* : to climb (up) on — **s'embarquer** *vr* **1** : to board **2** ~ **dans** *fam* : to get involved in, to launch into

embarras [ɑ̃bara] *nms & pl* **1** DIFFICULTÉ : difficulty, trouble <embarras financiers : financial problems> **2** GÊNE : embarrassment **3** : awkward situation, predicament <un embarras de choix : too much to choose from> **4 embarras gastrique** : stomach upset

embarrassant, -sante [ɑ̃barasɑ̃, -sɑ̃t] *adj* **1** : embarrassing, awkward **2** ENCOMBRANT : cumbersome

embarrasser [ɑ̃barase] *vt* **1** ENCOMBRER : to clutter **2** : to hinder, to hamper **3** GÊNER : to embarrass — **s'embarrasser** *vr* **1** ~ **dans** : to get tangled up in (lies, etc.) **2** ~ **de** : to burden oneself with, to worry over

embarrer [ɑ̃bare] *vt Can* : to lock <ils l'ont embarré dans la chambre : they locked him in the room> — **s'embarrer** *vr Can* ~ **dans** : to lock oneself in

embauche [ɑ̃boʃ] *nf* : hiring, employment

embaucher [ɑ̃boʃe] *vt* ENGAGER : to hire

embaumer [ɑ̃bome] *vt* **1** : to embalm **2** PARFUMER : to make fragrant, to scent — *vi* : to smell good

embellie [ɑ̃beli] *nf* **1** ÉCLAIRCIE : clear spell, bright spell **2** ACCALMIE : lull

embellir [ɑ̃belir] *vt* **1** ENJOLIVER : to make more attractive, to beautify **2** : to embellish (a story, etc.) — *vi* : to become more attractive

embellissement [ɑ̃belismɑ̃] *nm* **1** : embellishment **2** : improvement

embêtant, -tante [ɑ̃bɛtɑ̃, -tɑ̃t] *adj* **1** : annoying **2** : awkward, tricky

embêtement [ɑ̃bɛtmɑ̃] *nm* : hassle, trouble, bother

embêter [ɑ̃bɛte] *vt* **1** : to annoy, to bother **2** : to bore — **s'embêter** *vr* : to be bored

emblée [ɑ̃ble] **d'**~ : right away

emblématique [ɑ̃blemat'k] *adj* : emblematic

emblème [ɑ̃blɛm] *nm* : emblem

embobiner [ɑ̃bɔbine] *vt fam* : to bamboozle, to trick

emboîter [ɑ̃bwate] *vt* **1** : to fit together **2** ~ **dans** : to fit into **3 emboîter le pas à qqn** : to follow close behind s.o. — **s'emboîter** *vr*

embolie [ɑ̃bɔli] *nf* : embolism

embonpoint [ɑ̃bɔ̃pwɛ̃] *nm* CORPULENCE : stoutness, corpulence

embouchure [ɑ̃buʃyr] *nf* **1** : mouth (of a river) **2** : mouthpiece

embourber [ɑ̃burbe] *v* **s'embourber** *vr* **1** : to get stuck in the mud **2** S'EMPÊTRER : to get bogged down

embourgeoiser [ɑ̃burʒwaze] *v* **s'embourgeoiser** *vr* : to become middle-class

embouteillage [ɑ̃butɛjaʒ] *nm* **1** : bottling **2** : bottleneck, traffic jam

embouteiller [ɑ̃buteje] *vt* **1** : to bottle **2** : to block, to jam <la circulation est très embouteillée : traffic is very congested>

emboutir [ɑ̃butir] *vt* **1** : to stamp, to press (metal) **2** : to crash into, to ram

embranchement [ɑ̃brɑ̃ʃmɑ̃] *nm* **1** CARREFOUR : junction, fork <à l'embranchement des deux routes : at the fork in the road> **2** : branching **3** : branch (in botany and zoology) **4** : side street

embraser [ɑ̃braze] *vt* **1** : to set ablaze **2** ILLUMINER : to illuminate **3** : to inflame, to fire up (passion, enthusiasm, etc.) — **s'embraser** *vr* **1** : to catch fire **2** : to flare up

embrassade [ɑ̃brasad] *nf* : embrace, hugging and kissing

embrasser [ɑ̃brase] *vt* **1** : to kiss **2** ÉTREINDRE : to embrace, to hug **3** : to adopt, to take up (a cause, etc.) — **s'embrasser** *vr* : to kiss (each other)

embrasure [ɑ̃brazyr] *nf* OUVERTURE : opening <embrasure de la porte : doorway>

embrayage [ɑ̃brɛjaʒ] *nm* : clutch (of an automobile)

embrayer [ɑ̃breje] {11} *vi* **1** : to engage the clutch **2** ~ **sur** *fam* : to get going on, to launch oneself into **3 embraye** *Can fam* : get a move on!, hurry up!

embrigader [ɑ̃brigade] *vt* ENRÔLER : to recruit, to enlist

embrocher [ɑ̃brɔʃe] *vt* : to skewer, to put on a spit

embrouillamini [ɑ̃brujamini] *nm fam* : muddle, confusion

embrouillé, -lée [ɑ̃bruje] *adj* : confused, muddled

embrouiller [ɑ̃bruje] *vt* **1** : to tangle up **2** : to confuse, to mix up — **s'embrouiller** *vr*

embroussaillé, -lée [ɑ̃brusaje] *adj* **1** : overgrown (with plants) **2** : shaggy, bushy

embrumé, -mée [ɑ̃bryme] *adj* : misty

embruns [ɑ̃brœ̃] *nmpl* : sea spray

embryologie [ɑ̃brijɔlɔʒi] *nf* : embryology

embryon [ɑ̃brijɔ̃] *nm* : embryo

embryonnaire [ɑ̃brijɔnɛr] *adj* : embryonic

embûche [ɑ̃byʃ] *nf* : trap, pitfall

embuer [ɑ̃bue] *vt* : to mist up, to fog up <les yeux embués de larmes : eyes misty with tears> — **s'embuer** *vr*

embuscade [ɑ̃byskad] *nf* : ambush

embusquer [ɑ̃byske] *v* **s'embusquer** *vr* : to lie in ambush
éméché, -chée [emeʃe] *adj fam* : tipsy
émeraude[1] [emrod] *adj* : emerald green
émeraude[2] *nf* : emerald (stone)
émeraude[3] *nm* : emerald (color)
émergence [emɛrʒɑ̃s] *nf* : emergence
émerger [emɛrʒe] {17} *vi* **1** : to emerge **2** : to come to the fore, to stand out
émeri [emri] *nm* : emery
émérite [emerit] *adj* : eminent, outstanding
émerveillement [emɛrvɛjmɑ̃] *nm* ÉBLOUISSEMENT : amazement, wonder
émerveiller [emɛrveje] *vt* ÉBLOUIR : to amaze — **s'émerveiller** *vr* ~ **de** : to marvel at, to be amazed at
émétique [emetik] *adj & nm* : emetic
émetteur[1], **-trice** [emetœr, -tris] *adj* **1** : transmitting **2** : issuing <banque émettrice : issuing bank>
émetteur[2], **-trice** *nm* **1** : transmitter **2** : issuer
émetteur[3] *n* : (radio or television) transmitter
émettre [emetr] {53} *vt* **1** PRODUIRE : to produce, to give off **2** DISTRIBUER : to issue **3** TRANSMETTRE : to transmit, to broadcast **4** EXPRIMER : to express
émeu [emø] *nm* : emu
émeute [emøt] *nf* : riot
émeutier, -tière [emøtje] *n* : rioter
émietter [emjete] *vt* **1** : to crumble, to flake **2** MORCELER : to break up, to disperse — **s'émietter** *vr*
émigrant, -grante [emigrɑ̃, -grɑ̃t] *n* : emigrant
émigration [emigrasjɔ̃] *nf* : emigration
émigré, -grée [emigre] *n* : emigrant, émigré
émigrer [emigre] *vi* **1** : to emigrate **2** : to migrate
éminemment [eminamɑ̃] *adv* : eminently
éminence [eminɑ̃s] *nf* **1** : eminence <Votre Éminence : Your Eminence> **2** COLLINE : hill **3** PROTUBÉRANCE : protuberance (in anatomy)
éminent, -nente [eminɑ̃, -nɑ̃t] *adj* : eminent, distinguished
émir [emir] *nm* : emir
émirat [emira] *nm* : emirate
émissaire [emisɛr] *nm* : emissary
émission [emisjɔ̃] *nf* **1** : emission **2** : transmission, broadcasting **3** : program, broadcast **4** : issue, issuing
emmagasinage [ɑ̃magazinaʒ] *nm* : storage
emmagasiner [ɑ̃magazine] *vt* **1** ENGRANGER : to store **2** ACCUMULER : to store up, to stockpile
emmailloter [ɑ̃majote] *vt* : to wrap up
emmêler [ɑ̃mele] *vt* **1** : to tangle up, to mat **2** : to muddle, to mix up — **s'emmêler** *vr*
emménager [ɑ̃menaʒe] {17} *vi* : to move in
emmener [ɑ̃mne] {52} *vt* **1** AMENER : to take <ils l'ont emmené au poste de police : they took him to the police station> **2** TRANSPORTER : to carry, to transport
emmitoufler [ɑ̃mitufle] *vt* : to wrap up, to bundle up — **s'emmitoufler** *vr*
emmurer [ɑ̃myre] *vt* : to wall in, to immure
émoi [emwa] *nm* **1** : agitation, strong emotion <en émoi : in a state, all agog> **2** : commotion, turmoil
émoluments [emɔlymɑ̃] *nmpl* : remuneration, salary
émonder [emɔ̃de] *vt* ÉLAGUER : to prune, to trim
émotif, -tive [emɔtif, -tiv] *adj* : emotional
émotion [emosjɔ̃] *nf* **1** : emotion, feeling **2 donner des émotions à qqn** *fam* : to give s.o. a fright
émotionnel, -nelle [emosjɔnɛl] *adj* : emotional
émousser [emuse] *vt* : to blunt, to dull — **s'émousser** *vr*
émoustiller [emustije] *vt* **1** : to exhilarate **2** : to titillate, to arouse
émouvant, -vante [emuvɑ̃, -vɑ̃t] *adj* TOUCHANT : moving, touching
émouvoir [emuvwar] {56} *vt* **1** TOUCHER : to move, to touch, to stir **2** TROUBLER : to disturb, to upset — **s'émouvoir** *vr*
empailler [ɑ̃paje] *vt* : to stuff
empaler [ɑ̃pale] *vt* : to impale
empaquetage [ɑ̃paktaʒ] *nm* EMBALLAGE : packaging, wrapping
empaqueter [ɑ̃pakte] {8} *vt* EMBALLER : to package, to wrap up
emparer [ɑ̃pare] *v* **s'emparer** *vr* ~ **de** : to seize, to take hold of <s'emparer du pouvoir : to seize power>
empâté, -tée [ɑ̃pate] *adj Can* : spineless, weak
empâter [ɑ̃pate] *vt* **1** : to fatten out (the body) **2** : to thicken, to coat (the tongue) — **s'empâter** : to put on weight
empathie [ɑ̃pati] *nf* : empathy
empattement [ɑ̃patmɑ̃] *nm* **1** : footing, base (of a wall, etc.) **2** : wheelbase
empêchement [ɑ̃peʃmɑ̃] *nm* : unexpected obstacle, hitch, holdup
empêcher [ɑ̃peʃe] *vt* **1** : to prevent, to stop **2 il n'empêche que** : nevertheless, still — **s'empêcher** *vr* : to refrain, to stop oneself <il ne pouvait s'empêcher de rire : he couldn't keep from laughing>
empêcheur, -cheuse [ɑ̃peʃœr, -ʃøz] *n* **empêcheur de tourner en rond** : spoilsport, killjoy
empeigne [ɑ̃peɲ] *nf* : upper (of a shoe)
empereur [ɑ̃prœr] *nm* : emperor
empesé, -sée [ɑ̃peze] *adj* **1** : starched **2** : stiff, affected
empeser [ɑ̃peze] {52} *vt* AMIDONNER : to starch

empester [ãpɛste] *vt* **1** EMPUANTIR : to stink up **2** : to reek of — *vi* : to stink, to reek
empêtrer [ãpɛtre] *vt* : to entangle, to involve — **s'empêtrer** *vr* **1** : to become entangled **2** ~ **dans** : to get bogged down in
emphase [ãfaz] *nf* GRANDILOQUENCE : pomposity, bombast
emphatique [ãfatik] *adj* **1** : pompous **2** : emphatic — **emphatiquement** [-tikmã] *adv*
empiècement [ãpjɛsmã] *nm* : yoke (of a garment)
empiéter [ãpjete] {87} *vi* ~ **sur** : to encroach upon, to infringe on
empiffrer [ãpifre] *v* **s'empiffrer** *vr fam* : to stuff oneself
empilade [ãpilad] *nf Can* : pileup
empiler [ãpile] *vt* : to pile up, to stack — **s'empiler** *vr*
empire [ãpir] *nm* **1** : empire **2 sous l'empire de** : under the influence of
empirer [ãpire] *vt* AGGRAVER : to worsen, to make worse — *vi* : to worsen, to deteriorate
empirique [ãpirik] *adj* : empirical — **empiriquement** [-rikmã] *adv*
emplacement [ãplasmã] *nm* : site, location
emplâtre [ãplatr] *nm* **1** : (medical) plaster **2** : patch (for a tire) **3** *fam* : clumsy oaf, clod
emplette [ãplɛt] *nf* **1** ACHAT : purchase **2 faire ses emplettes** : to go shopping
emplir [ãplir] *vt* **1** : REMPLIR : to fill **2 faire emplir** *Can* : to bamboozle, to trick — **s'emplir** *vr* : to fill up
emploi [ãplwa] *nm* **1** UTILISATION : use <mode d'emploi : instructions, directions> **2** TRAVAIL : employment, job **3** USAGE : usage (of language) **4 emploi du temps** : schedule, timetable
emploie [ãplwa], **emploiera** [ãplwara], *etc.* → **employer**
employé, -yée [ãplwaje] *n* : employee
employer [ãplwaje] {58} *vt* **1** UTILISER : to use **2** : to employ, to provide jobs for — **s'employer** *vr* **1** : to be used **2** : to apply oneself
employeur, -ployeuse [ãplwajœr, -plwajøz] *n* : employer
empocher [ãpɔʃe] *vt* : to pocket
empoignade [ãpwaɲad] *nf* : altercation, row
empoigner [ãpwaɲe] *vt* **1** SAISIR : to seize, to grasp **2** ÉMOUVOIR : to thrill, to grip — **s'empoigner** *vr* : to quarrel, to come to blows
empois [ãpwa] *nms & pl* : (laundry) starch
empoisonnement [ãpwazɔnmã] *nm* **1** : poisoning **2** *fam* : nuisance, trouble
empoisonner [ãpwazɔne] *vt* **1** : to poison **2** EMPUANTIR : to stink up **3** *fam* : to annoy, to bug — **s'empoisonner** *vr* **1** : to poison oneself **2** *fam* : to be bored stiff
emporté, -tée [ãpɔrte] *adj* : quick-tempered
emportement [ãpɔrtəmã] *nm* **1** : fit of anger, rage **2** : ardor, fervor
emporter [ãpɔrte] *vt* **1** : to take, to take away <plats à emporter : food to go> **2** : to carry away, to sweep away **3** : to carry off, to cause (a sick person) to die **4** : to carry, to win <l'emporter sur : to get the better of> — **s'emporter** *vr* : to lose one's temper
empoté, -tée [ãpɔte] *adj fam* : clumsy, awkward
empoter [ãpɔte] *vt* : to pot (a plant)
empourprer [ãpurpre] *vt* : to turn crimson — **s'empourprer** *vr*
empreint, -preinte [ãprɛ̃, -prɛ̃t] *adj* ~ **de** : marked with, stamped with <empreint de douleur : imbued with sadness>
empreinte *nf* **1** : print, track <empreinte de pied : footprint> <empreinte digitale : fingerprint> **2** IMPRESSION : impression, stamp, imprint
empressé, -sée [ãprese] *adj* : attentive, eager (to please)
empressement [ãpresmã] *nm* **1** : attentiveness **2** ENTHOUSIASME : eagerness, enthusiasm, haste
empresser [ãprese] *v* **s'empresser** *vr* **1 s'empresser auprès de** : to be attentive toward **2** ~ **de** : to be in a hurry to <elle s'est empressée de partir : she hastened to leave>
emprise [ãpriz] *nf* : influence, hold <sous l'emprise de : under the influence of>
emprisonnement [ãprizɔnmã] *nm* : imprisonment
emprisonner [ãprizɔne] *vt* **1** : to imprison **2** : to hold tightly, to grip
emprunt [ãprœ̃] *nm* **1** : loan **2** : borrowing **3** : word <un emprunt à l'allemand : a borrowing from the German> **4 d'**~ : borrowed <nom d'emprunt : assumed name>
emprunté, -tée [ãprœ̃te] *adj* **1** : awkward, self-conscious **2** : sham, feigned
emprunter [ãprœ̃te] *vt* **1** : to borrow **2** PRENDRE : to take, to follow <empruntez la nouvelle route : take the new road> **3** : to assume, to take on <emprunter un nom : to assume a name>
empuantir [ãpɥãtir] *vt* : to stink up
ému, -mue [emy] *adj* : moved, touched
émulation [emylasjɔ̃] *nf* : competition, emulation
émule [emyl] *nmf* : imitator, emulator
émulsion [emylsjɔ̃] *nf* : emulsion
émulsionner [emylsjɔne] *vt* : to emulsify
en[1] [ã] *prep* **1** : in <j'habite en ville : I live in town> <en français : in

French> <en 1847 : in 1847> **2** : to <elle va en Belgique : she's going to Belgium> <de mal en pis : from bad to worse> **3** : by <elle va en voiture : she's going by car> **4** : of <fait en plastique : made of plastic> **5** : at <en guerre : at war> **6** : as <je te parle en ami : I'm speaking to you as a friend> <il est habillé en militaire : he is dressed as a soldier> **7** : into <traduit en français : translated into French>

en² *pron* **1** (*representing a noun governed by* de) <je m'en souviens : I remember it> <qu'est-ce que tu en sais? : what do you know about it?> **2** (*used with expressions of quantity*) <j'en ai plusieurs : I have several> **3** (*used to replace the possessive*) <j'en ai perdu la clef : I lost its key> **4** (*used to replace a phrase*) <il n'a pas joué mais il en est capable : he didn't play but he can> **5** (*used in partitive constructions*) <en avez-vous? : do you have some?> <j'en connais : I know a few>

enamourer [ɑ̃namure] *v* **s'enamourer** *vr* : to fall in love, to become enamored

encadrement [ɑ̃kadrəmɑ̃] *nm* **1** : frame **2** : staff <l'encadrement administratif : the administrative staff> **3** : supervision <les étudiants manquent d'encadrement : the students lack supervision> **4** : restriction, control (of prices, credit, etc.)

encadrer [ɑ̃kadre] *vt* **1** : to frame **2** : to surround, to flank **3** : to supervise, to train

encaisse [ɑ̃kɛs] *nf* : cash in hand

encaissé, -sée [ɑ̃kese] *adj* : steep-sided

encaisser [ɑ̃kese] *vt* **1** : to cash (a check), to collect (money) **2** *fam* : to take, to tolerate <encaisser un coup : to take a beating> <je ne peux pas l'encaisser! : I can't take it!>

encan [ɑ̃kɑ̃] *nm* : auction <vendre à l'encan : to auction off, to sell at auction>

encanailler [ɑ̃kanaje] *v* **s'encanailler** *vr* : to slum, to keep bad company

encanter [ɑ̃kɑ̃te] *vt Can* : to auction

encanteur, -teuse [ɑ̃kɑ̃tœr] *n Can* : auctioneer

encart [ɑ̃kar] *nm* : insert, pamphlet <encart publicitaire : advertising insert>

en–cas [ɑ̃ka] *nms & pl* : snack

encastré, -trée [ɑ̃kastre] *adj* : built-in <un four encastré : a built-in oven>

encastrer [ɑ̃kastre] *vt* : to fit, to embed, to build in — **s'encastrer** *vr*

encaustique [ɑ̃kɔstik] *nf* CIRE : polish, wax — **encaustiquer** [-stike] *vt*

enceinte¹ [ɑ̃sɛ̃t] *adj* : pregnant

enceinte² *nf* **1** : surrounding wall, fence **2** ESPACE : interior, enclosure <dans l'enceinte du tribunal : inside the courtroom> **3** **enceinte acoustique** : speaker

encens [ɑ̃sɑ̃] *nm* : incense

encenser [ɑ̃sɑ̃se] *vt* **1** : to perfume (with incense) **2** FLATTER : to flatter

encensoir [ɑ̃sɑ̃swar] *nm* : censer

encercler [ɑ̃sɛrkle] *vt* ENTOURER : to surround, to encircle

enchaînement [ɑ̃ʃɛnmɑ̃] *nm* **1** SÉRIE : series, sequence **2** LIAISON : link, connection

enchaîner [ɑ̃ʃene] *vt* **1** : to chain (up) **2** LIER : to link, to connect — *vi* : to continue, to move on — **s'enchaîner** *vr* : to link up, to be connected

enchanté, -tée [ɑ̃ʃɑ̃te] *adj* **1** MAGIQUE : magic, enchanted **2** RAVI : delighted, pleased <enchanté de faire votre connaissance : pleased to meet you>

enchantement [ɑ̃ʃɑ̃tmɑ̃] *nm* **1** : enchantment **2** : delight

enchanter [ɑ̃ʃɑ̃te] *vt* **1** ENSORCELER : to enchant, to bewitch **2** RAVIR : to delight

enchanteur¹, -teresse [ɑʃɑ̃tœr, -trɛs] *adj* CHARMANT : enchanting, charming

enchanteur², -teresse *n* : enchanter *m*, enchantress *f*

enchâssement [ɑ̃ʃɑsmɑ̃] *nm* : setting, mounting (of gems)

enchâsser [ɑ̃ʃase] *vt* **1** : to mount, to set **2** INSÉRER : to insert (a word, etc.)

enchère [ɑ̃ʃɛr] *nf* **1** : bid, bidding **2** **vente aux enchères** : auction

enchérisseur, -seuse [ɑ̃ʃerisœr, -søz] *n* : bidder

enchevêtrement [ɑ̃ʃəvɛtrəmɑ̃] *nm* **1** : tangle **2** : confusion

enchevêtrer [ɑ̃ʃəvɛtre] *vt* **1** : to tangle up **2** : to muddle, to confuse — **s'enchevêtrer** *vr*

enclave [ɑ̃klav] *nf* : enclave

enclaver [ɑ̃klave] *vt* **1** ENTOURER : to enclose, to surround **2** : to fit together, to interlock

enclencher [ɑ̃klɑ̃ʃe] *vt* **1** : to engage (a mechanism) **2** : to set in motion, to get under way — **s'enclencher** *vr*

enclin, -cline [ɑ̃klɛ̃, -klin] *adj* **~ à** : inclined to, prone to

enclore [ɑ̃klɔr] {34} *vt* : to enclose

enclos [ɑ̃klo] *nm* : enclosure

enclume [ɑ̃klym] *nf* : anvil

encoche [ɑ̃kɔʃ] *nf* : notch

encocher [ɑ̃kɔʃe] *vt* : to notch

encoder [ɑ̃kɔde] *vt* : to encode

encoignure [ɑ̃kwaɲyr] *nf* : corner (of a room)

encoller [ɑ̃kɔle] *vt* : to paste, to glue

encolure [ɑ̃kɔlyr] *nf* **1** COU : neck **2** : collar (size)

encombrant, -brante [ɑ̃kɔ̃brɑ̃, -brɑ̃t] *adj* : cumbersome

encombre [ɑ̃kɔ̃br] *adv* **sans ~** : without mishap, without a hitch

encombrement [ɑ̃kɔ̃brəmɑ̃] *nm* **1** : clutter **2** : overall size, bulk **3** : blocking, jamming **4** : traffic jam **5** : congestion (in medicine)

encombrer [ɑ̃kɔ̃bre] *vt* **1** : to clutter up, to congest **2** : to block, to jam **3** : to burden, to encumber — **s'encombrer** *vr* ~ **de** : to burden oneself with

encontre [ɑ̃kɔ̃tr] **à l'encontre de** : against, counter to, contrary to

encore [ɑ̃kɔr] *adv* **1** TOUJOURS : still <je travaille encore ici : I'm still working here> **2** DAVANTAGE : more, again <encore une fois : once more, once again> <il m'a encore parlé : he spoke to me again> **3** : yet <pas encore : not yet> <encore mieux : better yet> **4** : another <pendant encore trois mois : for another three months> **5 encore que** : although **6 si encore** *or* **encore si** : if only

encorner [ɑ̃kɔrne] *vt* : to gore

encornet [ɑ̃kɔrnɛ] *nm* : squid

encouragement [ɑ̃kuraʒmɑ̃] *nm* : encouragement

encourager [ɑ̃kuraʒe] {17} *vt* : to encourage

encourir [ɑ̃kurir] {23} *vt* : to incur

encrasser [ɑ̃krase] *vt* **1** SALIR : to dirty **2** OBSTRUER : to clog up — **s'encrasser** *vr*

encre [ɑ̃kr] *nf* : ink

encrer [ɑ̃kre] *vt* : to ink

encrier [ɑ̃krije] *nm* : inkwell

encroûter [ɑ̃krute] *v* **s'encroûter** *vr* : to get in a rut <encroûté dans ses habitudes : set in one's ways>

encyclique [ɑ̃siklik] *nf* : encyclical

encyclopédie [ɑ̃siklɔpedi] *nf* : encyclopedia — **encyclopédique** [-pedik] *adj*

endémique [ɑ̃demik] *adj* : endemic

endetté, -tée [ɑ̃dete] *adj* : in debt

endettement [ɑ̃detmɑ̃] *nm* : debt

endetter [ɑ̃dete] *v* **s'endetter** *vr* : to get into debt

endeuiller [ɑ̃dœje] *vt* **1** : to plunge into mourning **2** : to cast gloom over (an event, etc.)

endiablé, -blée [ɑ̃djable] *adj* **1** : wild, furious **2** : boisterous

endiguer [ɑ̃dige] *vt* **1** : to dam up **2** RETENIR : to check, to hold back, to contain

endimanché, -chée [ɑ̃dimɑ̃ʃe] *adj* : in one's Sunday best

endisquer [ɑ̃diske] *vt Can* : to record (a CD)

endive [ɑ̃div] *nf* : endive, chickory

endocrine [ɑ̃dɔkrin] *adj* : endocrine

endoctrinement [ɑ̃dɔktrinmɑ̃] *nm* : indoctrination

endoctriner [ɑ̃dɔktrine] *vt* : to indoctrinate

endolori, -rie [ɑ̃dɔlori] *adj* : painful, sore

endommager [ɑ̃dɔmaʒe] {17} *vt* : to damage

endormant, -mante [ɑ̃dɔrmɑ̃, -mɑ̃t] *adj* ENNUYEUX : boring

endormi, -mie [ɑ̃dɔrmi] *adj* **1** : asleep, sleeping **2** LÉTHARGIQUE : sluggish, lethargic

endormir [ɑ̃dɔrmir] {30} *vt* **1** : to put to sleep **2** ANESTHÉSIER : to anesthetize, to numb **3** : to allay, to calm — **s'endormir** *vr* **1** : to fall asleep **2** : to slack off **3** : to subside, to die down **4** : to pass away, to die

endossement [ɑ̃dɔsmɑ̃] *nm* : endorsement

endosser [ɑ̃dɔse] *vt* **1** : to take on, to shoulder **2** : to endorse, to sign **3** : to don, to put on (clothes)

endroit [ɑ̃drwa] *nm* **1** : place, spot, locale **2** : right side (of a garment, etc.) <à l'endroit : right side up> **3 à l'endroit de** : toward, with regard to **4 par endroits** : here and there, in places

enduire [ɑ̃duir] {49} *vt* : to coat, to cover — **s'enduire** *vr*

enduit [ɑ̃dui] *nm* : coating

endurance [ɑ̃dyrɑ̃s] *nf* : endurance

endurant, -rante [ɑ̃dyrɑ̃, -rɑ̃t] *adj* : hardy, tough

endurci, -cie [ɑ̃dyrsi] *adj* **1** DUR : hard **2** INVÉTÉRÉ : hardened, inveterate

endurcir [ɑ̃dyrsir] *vt* **1** : to toughen, to strengthen **2** : to harden — **s'endurcir** *vr*

endurer [ɑ̃dyre] *vt* SUPPORTER : to endure

énergétique [enerʒetik] *adj* **1** : energy <ressources énergétiques : energy resources> **2** : energizing

énergie [enerʒi] *nf* : energy

énergique [enerʒik] *adj* **1** : energetic **2** : vigorous, forceful, emphatic — **énergiquement** [-ʒikmɑ̃] *adv*

énervant, -vante [enervɑ̃, -vɑ̃t] *adj* AGAÇANT : irritating, annoying

énervement [enervəmɑ̃] *nm* **1** AGACEMENT : irritation **2** : agitation, edginess

énerver [enerve] *vt* AGACER : to irritate, to annoy — **s'énerver** *vr* **1** : to become annoyed **2** : to get worked up

enfance [ɑ̃fɑ̃s] *nf* **1** : childhood **2** DÉBUT : infancy, beginning **3** : children *pl*

enfant[1] [ɑ̃fɑ̃] *adj* : childish, childlike <il est resté très enfant : he's still very childlike>

enfant[2] *nmf* **1** : child <faire l'enfant : to act childishly> <enfant prodige : child prodigy> <enfant trouvé : foundling> **2** : offspring, child <un enfant unique : an only child> **3 bon enfant** : good-natured **4 enfant de chœur** : altar boy

enfantement [ɑ̃fɑ̃tmɑ̃] *nm* : childbirth

enfanter [ɑ̃fɑ̃te] *vt* : to give birth to

enfantillage [ɑ̃fɑ̃tijaʒ] *nm* : childishness

enfantin, -tine [ɑ̃fɑ̃tɛ̃, -tin] *adj* **1** : childlike **2** : simple <c'est enfantin : it's child's play> **3** PUÉRIL : childish

enfarger [ɑ̃farʒe] {17} *vt Can* : to make (someone) trip — **s'enfarger** *vr* : to trip, to stumble
enfer [ɑ̃fɛr] *nm* **1** : hell **2 d'~** : infernal, hellish
enfermer [ɑ̃ferme] *vt* **1** : to shut up, to lock up **2** ENTOURER : to enclose, to surround — **s'enfermer** *vr* **1** : to shut oneself away **2 ~ dans** : to retreat into
enferrer [ɑ̃fere] *v* **s'enferrer** *vr* **~ dans** : to get tangled up in
enfilade [ɑ̃filad] *nf* : row, succession
enfiler [ɑ̃file] *vt* **1** METTRE : to slip on, to put on <enfiler un chandail : to put on a sweater> **2** : to thread, to string **3** : to take, to go down (a street, corridor, etc.) — **s'enfiler** *vr* **1** *fam* : to guzzle, to devour **2 ~ dans** : to disappear into (a doorway, etc.)
enfin [ɑ̃fɛ̃] *adv* **1** : finally, at last <enfin seuls! : alone at last!> **2** : lastly <enfin et surtout : last but not least> **3** : in short, in a word **4** : well, at least <enfin, je crois : at least I think so> **5** : anyhow, after all **6** (*used to show impatience*) <mais enfin, donne-le-moi! : come on, give it to me!>
enflammé, -mée [ɑ̃flame] *adj* **1** BRÛLANT : burning **2** PASSIONNÉ : passionate **3** : inflamed (in medicine)
enflammer [ɑ̃flame] *vt* **1** ALLUMER : to ignite, to set fire to **2** : to inflame — **s'enflammer** *vr* : to catch fire
enfler [ɑ̃fle] *vt* **1** : to cause to swell **2** : to increase the volume of (a sound, one's voice) — *vi* : to swell (up) — **s'enfler** *vr*
enflure [ɑ̃flyr] *nf* : swelling
enfoncé, -cée [ɑ̃fɔ̃se] *adj* : sunken, deep-set
enfoncer [ɑ̃fɔ̃se] {6} *vt* **1** : to drive in (a nail, etc.) **2** : to push in, to insert <enfoncer ses mains dans ses poches : to thrust one's hands in one's pockets> **3** : to break open, to break down — *vi* : to sink — **s'enfoncer** *vr* **1** CÉDER : to yield, to give way **2** PÉNÉTRER : to penetrate, to sink in **3 ~ dans** : to disappear into
enfouir [ɑ̃fwir] *vt* **1** : to bury **2** CACHER : to hide, to tuck away — **s'enfouir** *vr* **~ dans** : to bury oneself in
enfouissement [ɑ̃fwismɑ̃] *nm* : burying
enfourcher [ɑ̃furʃe] *vt* : to mount, to get on, to straddle
enfourner [ɑ̃furne] *vt* **1** : to put in the oven **2** *fam* : to gobble up
enfreindre [ɑ̃frɛ̃dr] {37} *vt* : to infringe, to violate <enfreindre la loi : to break the law>
enfuir [ɑ̃fɥir] {46} *v* **s'enfuir** *vr* S'ÉCHAPPER : to run away, to escape, to flee
enfumer [ɑ̃fyme] *vt* : to fill with smoke
engagé, -gée [ɑ̃gaʒe] *adj* **1** : committed, involved **2** *Can fam* : busy <la ligne est engagée : the line is busy>
engageant, -geante [ɑ̃gaʒɑ̃, -ʒɑ̃t] *adj* : engaging, attractive
engagement [ɑ̃gaʒmɑ̃] *nm* **1** PROMESSE : commitment, promise **2** : engagement, contract, enlistment (in the military) **3** DÉBUT : start **4** : involvement, participation **5** : (military) engagement
engager [ɑ̃gaʒe] {17} *vt* **1** : to bind, to commit **2** RECRUTER : to hire, to take on **3** IMPLIQUER : to involve **4** : to invest, to lay out (capital, etc.) **5** EXHORTER : to urge **6** COMMENCER : to start, to begin **7** INTRODUIRE : to insert — **s'engager** *vr* **1** : to commit oneself, to undertake **2** : to enlist, to join up **3** : to begin, to start up **4 ~ dans** : to enter, to turn into (a street, etc.)
engelure [ɑ̃ʒlyr] *nf* : chilblain
engendrer [ɑ̃ʒɑ̃dre] *vt* **1** : to engender, to generate **2** : to father, to beget
engin [ɑ̃ʒɛ̃] *nm* **1** APPAREIL : machine, device <engin explosif : explosive device> **2** VÉHICULE : vehicle <engin blindé : armored vehicle> **3** MISSILE : missile **4** *fam* MACHIN : gadget, contraption
englober [ɑ̃glɔbe] *vt* : to include
engloutir [ɑ̃glutir] *vt* **1** : to gobble up, to devour **2** : to engulf, to swallow up **3** : to squander
engoncé, -cée [ɑ̃gɔ̃se] *adj* **~ dans** : squeezed into
engorgement [ɑ̃gɔrʒəmɑ̃] *nm* : blocking (up), congestion
engorger [ɑ̃gɔrʒe] {17} *vt* **1** : to block, to jam up **2** : to congest (in medicine)
engouement [ɑ̃gumɑ̃] *nm* : infatuation
engouer [ɑ̃gwe] *v* **s'engouer** *vr* **~ de** : to become infatuated with
engouffrer [ɑ̃gufre] *vt* **1** : to engulf, to swallow up **2** : to gobble up, to devour — **s'engouffrer** *vr* **~ dans** : to rush into
engourdi, -die [ɑ̃gurdi] *adj* **1** : numb **2** : dulled, lethargic
engourdir [ɑ̃gurdir] *vt* **1** : to numb **2** : to dull — **s'engourdir** *vr*
engourdissement [ɑ̃gurdismɑ̃] *nm* **1** : numbness **2** : dullness, torpor
engrais [ɑ̃grɛ] *nm* **1** : fertilizer, manure **2 mettre à l'engrais** : to fatten
engraisser [ɑ̃grese] *vt* **1** : to fatten **2** : to fertilize — *vi* GROSSIR : to get fat, to put on weight — **s'engraisser** *vr*
engranger [ɑ̃grɑ̃ʒe] {17} *vt* **1** : to garner, to gather **2** EMMAGASINER : to store
engrenage [ɑ̃grənaʒ] *nm* **1** : gears *pl* **2 être pris dans l'engrenage** : to be caught up in the system
engrener [ɑ̃grəne] {52} *vt* : to engage, to mesh (gears) — **s'engrener** *vr*

engueulade [ãgœlad] *nf fam* : argument, shouting match
engueuler [ãgœle] *vt fam* : to yell at, to bawl out — **s'engueler** *vr*
enguirlander [ãgirlãde] *vt* : to garland, to adorn with garlands
énième [enjɛm] *adj* : nth, umpteenth <pour l'énième fois : for the umpteenth time>
énigmatique [enigmatik] *adj* : enigmatic — **énigmatiquement** [-tikmã] *adv*
énigme [enigm] *nf* : enigma, riddle
enivrant, -vrante [ãnivrã, -vrãt] *adj* : intoxicating
enivrement [ãnivrəmã] *nm* : intoxication
enivrer [ãnivre] *vr* **1** : to intoxicate, to make drunk **2** : to elate, to exhilarate — **s'enivrer** *vr*
enjambée [ãʒãbe] *nf* : stride
enjamber [ãʒãbe] *vt* **1** : to step over **2** : to span, to straddle
enjeu [ãʒø] *nm, pl* **enjeux 1** : issue <les enjeux politiques : political issues> **2** : stake <son emploi est à l'enjeu : his job is at stake>
enjoindre [ãʒwẽdr] {50} *vt* : to enjoin, to order <enjoindre à qqn de faire qqch : to enjoin s.o. to do sth>
enjôler [ãʒole] *vt* : to cajole, to wheedle
enjoliver [ãʒɔlive] *vt* : to embellish
enjoliveur [ãʒɔlivœr] *nm* : hubcap
enjoué, -jouée [ãʒwe] *adj* : cheerful, light-hearted
enjouement [ãʒumã] *nm* : playfulness, gaiety
enlacement [ãlasmã] *nm* **1** : embrace **2** : intertwining
enlacer [ãlase] {6} *vt* **1** ÉTREINDRE : to embrace, to hug **2** ENTRELACER : to entwine, to enlace — **s'enlacer** *vr*
enlaidir [ãledir] *vt* : to make ugly — *vi* : to grow ugly — **s'enlaidir** *vr*
enlevant, -vante [ãlvã, -vãt] *adj Can* : lively, spirited
enlevé, -vée [ãlve] *adj* : lively, spirited
enlèvement [ãlɛvmã] *nm* **1** : kidnapping, abduction **2** : removal <enlèvement des ordures ménagères : garbage collection>
enlever [ãlve] {52} *vt* **1** : to remove, to take off, to take away **2** LEVER : to raise, to lift **3** KIDNAPPER : to abduct, to kidnap **4** GAGNER : to carry off, to win — **s'enlever** *vr* : to come off, to come out
enlisement [ãlizmã] *nm* : sinking, bogging down
enliser [ãlize] *v* **s'enliser** *vr* **1** : to sink, to get stuck **2** : to get bogged down
enneigé, -gée [ãneʒe] *adj* : snow-covered
enneigement [ãneʒmã] *nm* : snow accumulation, snow cover
ennemi[1], -mie [ɛnmi] *adj* : enemy, hostile <en pays ennemi : in enemy territory>
ennemi[2], -mie *n* : enemy
ennoblir [ãnɔblir] *vt* : to ennoble
ennui [ãnɥi] *nm* **1** PROBLÈME : trouble, problem <avoir des ennuis : to have problems> **2** : boredom, ennui
ennuie [ãnwi], **ennuiera** [ãnwira], *etc.* → **ennuyer**
ennuyant, ennuyante [ãnɥijã, ãnɥijãt] *adj Can* **1** : annoying, irritating **2** : boring
ennuyer [ãnɥije] {58} *vt* **1** AGACER : to annoy **2** : to bore — **s'ennuyer** *vr* : to be bored
ennuyeux, ennuyeuse [ãnɥijø, ãnɥijøz] *adj* **1** AGAÇANT : annoying, irritating **2** LASSANT : boring, tedious
énoncé [enɔ̃se] *nm* **1** : statement, declaration **2** : terms *pl*, wording **3** : utterance
énoncer [enɔ̃se] {6} *vt* : to express, to state — **s'énoncer** *vr*
énonciation [enɔ̃sjasjɔ̃] *nf* : stating, statement
enorgueillir [ãnɔrgœjir] *vt* : to make proud — **s'enorgueillir** *vr* : to pride oneself
énorme [enɔrm] *adj* : enormous, huge
énormément [enɔrmemã] *adv* **1** : enormously, tremendously **2** ~ **de** : a great number of
énormité [enɔrmite] *nf* **1** : enormity, hugeness **2** : outrageous remark
enquérir [ãkerir] {21} *v* **s'enquérir** *vr* ~ **de** : to inquire about
enquête [ãkɛt] *nf* **1** INVESTIGATION : investigation, inquiry, inquest **2** SONDAGE : poll, survey
enquêter [ãkete] *vi* : to investigate, to hold an inquiry
enquiquiner [ãkikine] *vt fam* : to irritate, to pester, to nag at
enraciner [ãrasine] *vt* **1** : to root **2** : to entrench, to establish — **s'enraciner** *vr* : to take root
enragé, -gée [ãraʒe] *adj* **1** : rabid **2** : furious
enrageant, -geante [ãraʒã, -ʒãt] *adj* : infuriating
enrager [ãraʒe] {17} *vi* **1** : to be furious, to be in a rage **2 faire enrager** : to enrage
enrayer [ãreje] {11} *vt* **1** : to check, to stop, to curb <enrayer une maladie : to bring a disease under control> **2** BLOQUER : to jam — **s'enrayer** *vr*
enrégimenter [ãreʒimãte] *vt* : to regiment
enregistrement [ãrəʒistrəmã] *nm* **1** : registration **2** : recording <enregistrement magnétique : tape recording> **3** : checking in <enregistrement des bagages : luggage check-in>
enregistrer [ãrəʒistre] *vt* **1** INSCRIRE : to register **2** : to record, to tape **3** : to check in

enregistreur[1], **-treuse** [ãrəʒistrœr, -trøz] *adj* **1** : recording **2 caisse enregistreuse** : cash register
enregistreur[2] *nm* : recorder <enregistreur de vol : flight recorder>
enrhumé, -mée [ãryme] *adj* **être enrhumé** : to have a cold
enrhumer [ãryme] *v* **s'enrhumer** *vr* : to catch a cold
enrichi, -chie [ãriʃi] *adj* : enriched, fortified <farine enrichie : enriched flour>
enrichir [ãriʃir] *vt* **1** : to make rich **2** : to enrich — **s'enrichir** *vr*
enrichissant, -sante [ãriʃisã, -sãt] *adj* : enriching, rewarding
enrichissement [ãriʃismã] *nm* : enrichment
enrobage [ãrɔbaʒ] *nm* : coating
enrober [ãrɔbe] *vt* **1** RECOUVRIR : to coat **2** : to wrap up, to dress up (words, etc.)
enrôlement [ãrolmã] *nm* : enrollment, enlistment
enrôler [ãrole] *vt* : to enroll, to enlist — **s'enrôler** *vr*
enroué, -rouée [ãrwe] *adj* : hoarse, husky
enrouer [ãrwe] *vt* : to make hoarse — **s'enrouer** *vr*
enrouler [ãrule] *vt* : to wind, to coil, to roll up — **s'enrouler** *vr* **1 ~ dans** : to wrap oneself up in **2 ~ sur** : to wind around
ensabler [ãsable] *v* **s'ensabler** *vr* **1** : to get stuck in the sand **2** : to silt up
ensacher [ãsaʃe] *vt* : to bag (merchandise)
ensanglanté, -tée [ãsãglãte] *adj* : covered with blood, bloodstained
enseignant[1], **-gnante** [ãsɛɲã, -ɲãt] *adj* : teaching
enseignant[2], **-gnante** *n* : teacher
enseigne[1] [ãsɛɲ] *nf* **1** : sign <enseigne lumineuse : neon sign> **2** DRAPEAU : flag, ensign **3 être logé à la même enseigne** : to be in the same boat
enseigne[2] *nm* **1** : ensign **2 enseigne de vaisseau** : midshipman
enseignement [ãsɛɲmã] *nm* **1** : teaching **2** : education **3** LEÇON : lesson, lecture
enseigner [ãsɛɲe] *v* : to teach
ensemble[1] [ãsãbl] *adv* : together
ensemble[2] *nm* **1** : group (of persons), set (of objects), series (of ideas, etc.) **2** : whole <dans l'ensemble : on the whole> **3** : unity <avec un ensemble parfait : simultaneously, in perfect unison> **4** : ensemble (in music) **5** : suit (of clothing), outfit **6** : set (in mathematics) **7 d'~** : overall, general **8 dans l'ensemble** : on the whole **9 grand ensemble** : housing development
ensemblier [ãsãblije] *nm* : interior decorator
ensemencer [ãsɑ̃mãse] {6} *vt* : to sow, to seed
enserrer [ãsere] *vt* **1** : to fit tightly around, to encircle **2** SERRER : to clasp, to grip
ensevelir [ãsɑ̃vlir] *vt* ENTERRER : to bury
ensoleillé, -lée [ãsɔleje] *adj* : sunny
ensoleillement [ãsɔlejmã] *nm* : (amount of) sunshine
ensommeillé, -lée [ãsɔmeje] *adj* : sleepy, drowsy
ensorceler [ãsɔrsəle] {8} *vt* : to bewitch, to charm
ensorcellement [ãsɔrselmã] *nm* : bewitchment, enchantment
ensuite [ãsɥit] *adv* **1** : then, next **2** : afterwards, later
ensuivre [ãsɥivr] {35} *v* **s'ensuivre** *vr* : to ensue, to follow <il s'ensuit que . . . : it follows that . . . >
entacher [ãtaʃe] *vt* **1** : to mar, to sully **2 entaché de nullité** : null and void
entaille [ãtaj] *nf* **1** : cut, gash **2** ENCOCHE : notch
entailler [ãtaje] *vt* : to gash, to slash, to cut (into) — **s'entailler** *vr* : to get a gash in
entamer [ãtame] *vt* **1** : to cut into, to make inroads into **2** : to start, to initiate **3** : to damage, to sully **4** : to shake, to undermine
entassement [ãtasmã] *nm* **1** : piling up **2** : pile, heap
entasser [ãtase] *vt* **1** : to pile up, to accumulate **2** : to cram, to pack together — **s'entasser** *vr* : to pile up
entendement [ãtãdmã] *nm* : understanding
entendeur [ãtãdœr] *nm* **à bon entendeur, salut!** : a word to the wise!
entendre [ãtãdr] {63} *vt* **1** : to hear **2** SIGNIFIER : to mean, to intend **3** COMPRENDRE : to understand <laisser entendre : to intimate> **4 entendre dire que** : to hear that **5 entendre parler de** : to hear of — *vi* **1** : to hear **2** : to understand — **s'entendre** *vr* **1** : to get along, to understand one another **2** : to agree **3** : to be understood <cela s'entend : it goes without saying> **4** : to be heard <cela s'entend à peine : it's barely audible> **5 ~ à** : to know about, to be good at
entendu, -due [ãtãdy] *adj* **1** : agreed, understood <entendu! : OK!> **2** : knowing, understanding <d'un air entendu : knowingly> **3 bien entendu** : of course
entente [ãtãt] *nf* **1** : harmony **2** : agreement, understanding **3 à double entente** : with a double meaning
entériner [ãterine] *vt* : to ratify, to confirm
enterrement [ãtɛrmã] *nm* **1** INHUMATION : burial, interment **2** FUNÉRAILLES : funeral **3** : funeral procession **4** : end, death <l'enterrement

de mon projet : the shelving of my project>

enterrer [ɑ̃tere] *vt* **1** : to bury, to inter **2** : to leave behind, to lay aside — **s'enterrer** *vr* : to bury oneself (away)

en–tête [ɑ̃tɛt] *nm, pl* **en–têtes 1** : letterhead **2** : heading

entêté[1], **-tée** [ɑ̃tete] *adj* : stubborn, obstinate

entêté[2], **-tée** *n* : stubborn person

entêtement [ɑ̃tetmɑ̃] *nm* : stubbornness, obstinacy

entêter [ɑ̃tete] *v* **s'entêter** *vr* : to persist

enthousiasmant, -mante [ɑ̃tuzjasmɑ̃, -mɑ̃t] *adj* : exciting

enthousiasme [ɑ̃tuzjasm] *nm* **1** : enthusiasm **2 avec ~** : enthusiastically

enthousiasmer [ɑ̃tuzjasme] *vt* : to fill with enthusiasm, to excite — **s'enthousiasmer** *vr* **~ pour** : to get enthusiastic about

enthousiaste[1] [ɑ̃tuzjast] *adj* : enthusiastic

enthousiaste[2] *nmf* : enthusiast

enticher [ɑ̃tiʃe] *v* **s'enticher** *vr* : to become infatuated <être entiché de : to be infatuated with>

entier[1], **-tière** [ɑ̃tje, -tjɛr] *adj* **1** : entire, whole <la ville entière : the whole town> <pendant des heures entières : for hours on end> **2** : complete, full <leur entière coopération : their full cooperation> **3** : intact, unaltered <rester entier : to remain unresolved> **4 tout entier** : completely, wholeheartedly <se donner tout entier : to devote oneself wholeheartedly>

entier[2] *nm* **1** : integer, whole number **2 en ~** : all of it, in its entirety

entièrement [ɑ̃tjɛrmɑ̃] *adv* : entirely, wholly, completely

entièreté [ɑ̃tjɛrte] *nf* : entirety, wholeness

entité [ɑ̃tite] *nf* : entity

entomologie [ɑ̃tɔmɔlɔʒi] *nf* : entomology — **entomologiste** [-lɔʒist] *nmf*

entomologique [ɑ̃tɔmɔlɔʒik] *adj* : entomological

entonner [ɑ̃tɔne] *vt* : to strike up (a song), to start singing

entonnoir [ɑ̃tɔnwar] *nm* **1** : funnel **2** : crater

entorse [ɑ̃tɔrs] *nf* **1** FOULURE : sprain <se faire une entorse à la cheville : to sprain one's ankle> **2** : infringement <faire une entorse à : to break (a law), to bend (a rule), to distort (the truth)>

entortiller [ɑ̃tɔrtije] *vt* **1** : to twist, to wind, to wrap (up) **2** : to tangle up, to complicate **3** *fam* : to hoodwink

entour [ɑ̃tur] *nm* **à l'entour** : in the vicinity, around

entourage [ɑ̃turaʒ] *nm* : circle, entourage

entouré, -rée [ɑ̃ture] *adj* **1** : popular **2 ~ de** : surrounded by

entourer [ɑ̃ture] *vt* **1** ENCERCLER : to surround, to encircle **2** : to rally around — **s'entourer** *vr* **~ de** : to surround oneself with <s'entourer de précautions : to take every possible precaution>

entourloupette [ɑ̃turlupet] *nf* : dirty trick

entournure [ɑ̃turnyr] *nf* **1** : armhole **2 être gêné aux entournures** : to be ill at ease, to be in awkward straits

entracte [ɑ̃trakt] *nm* : intermission

entraide [ɑ̃trɛd] *nf* : mutual aid

entraider [ɑ̃trede] *v* **s'entraider** *vr* : to help one another

entrailles [ɑ̃traj] *nfpl* **1** : entrails, guts **2** : womb **3** : depths, bowels, heart <les entrailles de la terre : the bowels of the earth> <sans entrailles : heartless>

entrain [ɑ̃trɛ̃] *nm* : liveliness, spirit

entraînant, -nante [ɑ̃trɛnɑ̃, -nɑ̃t] *adj* : lively

entraînement [ɑ̃trɛnmɑ̃] *nm* **1** : training <manquer d'entraînement : to be out of training> **2** : practice

entraîner [ɑ̃trene] *vt* **1** EMPORTER : to carry away <se laisser entraîner dans : to get carried away with> **2** PROVOQUER : to lead to, to provoke <cela pourrait entraîner des problèmes : that could lead to problems> **3** FORMER : to train, to coach — **s'entraîner** *vr* : to train, to practice

entraîneur, -neuse [ɑ̃trɛnœr, -nøz] *n* : trainer, coach

entrapercevoir *or* **entr'apercevoir** [ɑ̃trapɛrsəvwar] {26} *vt* : to catch a glimpse of

entrave [ɑ̃trav] *nf* **1** : hobble, shackle **2** : hindrance **3 sans entraves** : unfettered

entraver [ɑ̃trave] *vt* **1** : to shackle, to fetter **2** GÊNER : to hold up, to hinder

entre [ɑ̃tr] *prep* **1** : between <entre nous : between ourselves, between you and me> <entre les deux : in between> **2** PARMI : among <l'un d'entre eux : one of them> <entre autres : among others, among other things>

entrebâillement [ɑ̃trəbajmɑ̃] *nm* : gap, opening <par l'entrebâillement de la porte : through the half-open door>

entrebâiller [ɑ̃trəbaje] *vt* : to open halfway — **s'entrebâiller** *vr*

entrechoquer [ɑ̃trəʃɔke] *vt* : to bang together — **s'entrechoquer** *vr* **1** : to clink, to clatter, to chatter (of teeth) **2** : to clash (of ideas, etc.)

entrecôte [ɑ̃trəkot] *nf* : rib steak

entrecouper [ɑ̃trəkupe] *vt* **1** : to intersperse **2** : to interrupt — **s'entrecouper** *vr* : to intersect

entrecroiser [ɑ̃trəkrwaze] *vt* : to intertwine, to interlace — **s'entrecroiser** *vr* : to intersect
entre–deux [ɑ̃trədø] *nms & pl* : space, gap, interval
entrée [ɑ̃tre] *nf* **1** : entrance, entry **2** : admission, admittance <entrée libre : free admission> **3** PLACE : ticket, seat **4** : first course (of a meal) **5** VESTIBULE : hall, lobby **6** : entry (in a reference book), input (in a computer) **7** DÉBUT : beginning **8 d'~ (de jeu)** : from the start, right off
entrefaite [ɑ̃trəfɛt] *nf* **sur ces entrefaites** : at the moment
entrefilet [ɑ̃trəfile] *nm* : paragraph, news item
entregent [ɑ̃trəʒɑ̃] *nm* : tact, diplomacy
entre–jambes *or* **entrejambes** [ɑ̃trəʒɑ̃b] *nms & pl* : crotch
entrelacer [ɑ̃trəlase] {6} *vt* : to intertwine, to interlace — **s'entrelacer** *vr*
entremêler [ɑ̃trəmele] *vt* : to mix together, to intermingle — **s'entremêler** *vr*
entremets [ɑ̃trəme] *nms & pl* : dessert
entremetteur, -teuse [ɑ̃trəmetœr, -tøz] *n* **1** : go-between **2** : procurer, pimp
entremettre [ɑ̃trəmetr] {53} *v* **s'entremettre** *vr* : to intervene
entremise [ɑ̃trəmiz] *nf* : intervention <par l'entremise de son avocat : through his lawyer>
entreposage [ɑ̃trəpozaʒ] *nm* : storage
entreposer [ɑ̃trəpoze] *vt* **1** : to store **2** : to bond (in commerce)
entrepôt [ɑ̃trəpo] *nm* : warehouse
entreprenant, -nante [ɑ̃trəprənɑ̃, -nɑ̃t] *adj* **1** : enterprising **2** : forward, brash
entreprendre [ɑ̃trəprɑ̃dr] {70} *vt* : to undertake, to start, to embark on
entrepreneur, -neuse [ɑ̃trəprənœr, -nøz] *n* **1** : contractor **2** : entrepreneur **3 entrepreneur de pompes funèbres** : undertaker, funeral director
entreprise [ɑ̃trəpriz] *nf* **1** : enterprise, undertaking, venture **2** FIRME : business, firm **3** CONTRAT : contract
entrer [ɑ̃tre] *vt* **1** : to take in, to bring in <entrer les meubles : to bring in the furniture> **2** ENFONCER : to push in, to stick **3** : to enter (in a computer) — *vi* **1** : to enter, to go in, to come in <il est entré dans la pièce : he entered the room> <entrer à l'hôpital : to go into the hospital> <entrez! : come in!> **2** : to fit <cette clé n'entre pas dans la serrure : this key doesn't fit in the lock> **3 ~ dans** : to join, to go into <entrer dans l'armée : to join the army> **4 ~ en** : to begin <entrer en ébullition : to start boiling>
entresol [ɑ̃trəsɔl] *nm* : mezzanine
entre–temps [ɑ̃trətɑ̃] *adv* : meanwhile, in the meantime
entretenir [ɑ̃trətnir] {92} *vt* **1** MAINTENIR : to maintain, to keep up **2** : to keep alive, to cherish, to harbor <entretenir des doutes : to entertain doubts> **3** : to support, to look after **4** : to speak to, to address — **s'entretenir** *vr*
entretenu, -nue [ɑ̃trətny] *adj* : kept, maintained <mal entretenu : poorly maintained>
entretien [ɑ̃trətjɛ̃] *nm* **1** : maintenance, upkeep **2** : discussion, talk, interview <entretien d'embauche : job interview> **3** : support, (financial) maintenance
entrevoir [ɑ̃trəvwar] {99} *vt* **1** APERCEVOIR : to glimpse, to perceive **2** PRÉVOIR : to foresee, to anticipate
entrevue [ɑ̃trəvy] *nf* : meeting, interview
entrouvert, -verte [ɑ̃truvɛr, -vɛrt] *adj & adv* : half open, ajar
entrouvrir [ɑ̃truvrir] {83} *vt* : to open halfway — **s'entrouvrir** *vr* : to be half open
énumérer [enymere] {87} *vt* : to enumerate — **énumération** [-merasjɔ̃] *nf*
envahir [ɑ̃vair] *vt* **1** : to invade **2** : to overcome <envahi par le chagrin : overcome by grief>
envahissant, -sante [ɑ̃vaisɑ̃, -sɑ̃t] *adj* **1** : intrusive, invasive **2** : pervasive
envahissement [ɑ̃vaismɑ̃] *nm* : invasion
envahisseur, -seuse [ɑ̃vaisœr, -søz] *n* : invader
enveloppe [ɑ̃vlɔp] *nf* **1** : envelope **2** : cover, casing, shell, husk (of corn, etc.) **3** : exterior **4** : sum of money, budget
envelopper [ɑ̃vlɔpe] *vt* **1** : to envelop, to shroud **2** RECOUVRIR : to wrap up, to cover — **s'envelopper** *vr*
envenimer [ɑ̃vnime] *vt* **1** INFECTER : to infect **2** : to inflame, to aggravate
envergure [ɑ̃vɛrgyr] *nf* **1** : wingspan **2** ÉTENDUE : breadth, scope, scale <de grande envergure : large-scale> **3** CALIBRE : caliber, stature
enverra [ɑ̃vera], *etc.* → **envoyer**
envers[1] [ɑ̃vɛr] *prep* **1** : toward, with regard to **2 envers et contre tout** : in spite of everything, against all opposition **3 être tout à l'envers** *Can* : to be very upset
envers[2] *nm* **1** REVERS : back, reverse **2 à l'envers** : inside out, upside down, backward
enviable [ɑ̃vjabl] *adj* : enviable
envie [ɑ̃vi] *nf* **1** JALOUSIE : envy, jealousy **2** DÉSIR : desire, wish, longing <avoir envie de : to feel like, to want> **3** : birthmark **4** : hangnail
envier [ɑ̃vje] {96} *vt* : to envy
envieux, -vieuse [ɑ̃vjø, -vjøz] *adj* : envious, jealous — **envieusement** [ɑ̃vjøzmɑ̃] *adv*
environ [ɑ̃virɔ̃] *adv* : about, around, approximately <viens dans environ une heure : come in an hour or so>

environnant, -nante [ãvirɔnã, -nãt] *adj* : surrounding
environnement [ãvirɔnmã] *nm* : environment
environnemental, -tale [ãvirɔnmãtal] *adj, pl* **-taux** [-to] : environmental
environnementaliste [ãvirɔnmãtalist] *nmf* : environmentalist
environner [ãvirɔne] *vt* : to surround
environs [ãvirɔ̃] *nmpl* **1** : surroundings, vicinity **2 aux environs de** : around <aux environs de Pâques : around Easter>
envisager [ãvizaʒe] {17} *vt* **1** : to envisage, to contemplate **2 envisager de faire** : to plan to do, to consider doing
envoi [ãvwa] *nm* **1** : sending, dispatching <envoi contre remboursement : cash on delivery> **2** COLIS : parcel, package **3 coup d'envoi** : kickoff
envoie [ãvwa], *etc.* → **envoyer**
envol [ãvɔl] *nm* : takeoff
envolée [ãvɔle] *nf* **1** : takeoff, flight **2** *or* **envolée de l'imagination** : flight of fancy, inspired discourse **3** : rise, surge (in value, etc.)
envoler [ãvɔle] *v* **s'envoler** *vr* **1** : to take off **2** : to fly away **3** : to blow away **4** DISPARAÎTRE : to disappear, to vanish **5** : to surge (of prices, values, etc.)
envoûtement [ãvutmã] *nm* : spell, bewitchment
envoûter [ãvute] *vt* : to bewitch, to cast a spell over
envoyé, -voyée [ãvwaje] *n* **1** : messenger **2** : envoy **3 envoyé spécial** : special (press) correspondent
envoyer [ãvwaje] {36} *vt* **1** : to send, to send out <envoyer par la poste : to mail> **2** LANCER : to throw, to hurl **3 envoyer promener** *fam* : to send packing — **s'envoyer** *vr* **1** : to send to each other, to exchange **2** *fam* : to guzzle, to wolf down
envoyeur, -voyeuse [ãvwajœr, -vwajøz] *n* : sender
enzyme [ãzim] *nf* : enzyme
épagneul, -gneule [epaɲœl] *n* : spaniel
épais, épaisse [epɛ, -pɛs] *adj* : thick
épaisseur [epɛsœr] *nf* **1** : thickness **2** : layer
épaissir [epesir] *v* : to thicken — **s'épaissir** *vr* **1** : to thicken (up) **2** : to deepen <le mystère s'est épaissi : the mystery deepened>
épaississant [epesisã] *nm* : thickener
épaississement [epesismã] *nm* : thickening
épanchement [epãʃmã] *nm* **1** : effusion, outpouring **2 épanchement de synovie** : water on the knee
épancher [epãʃe] *vt* : to give vent to, to pour out (one's feelings, etc.) — **s'épancher** *vr* : to pour one's heart out
épandage [epãdaʒ] *nm* : spreading
épandre [epãdr] {63} *vt* : to spread
épanoui, -nouie [epanwi] *adj* **1** : in full bloom **2** : radiant **3** : fully developed (of the body, etc.)
épanouir [epanwir] *vt* **1** : to make bloom **2** : to light up, to brighten — **s'épanouir** *vr* **1** : to bloom **2** : to light up **3** : to develop, to blossom, to flourish
épanouissement [epanwismã] *nm* **1** : blooming, flowering **2** : brightening, lighting up
épargnant, -gnante [eparɲã, -ɲãt] *n* : saver, investor
épargne [eparɲ] *nf* **1** ÉCONOMIE : saving, economy **2** : savings *pl*
épargner [eparɲe] *vt* **1** ÉCONOMISER : to save **2** : to spare — **s'épargner** *vr* : to spare oneself (trouble, etc.)
éparpillement [eparpijmã] *nm* : scattering, dispersal
éparpiller [eparpije] *vt* **1** : to scatter, to disperse **2** : to dissipate (efforts, etc.) — **s'éparpiller** *vr*
épars, éparse [epar, -pars] *adj* : scattered
épatant, -tante [epatã, -tãt] *adj fam* : great, fantastic
épater [epate] *vt fam* **1** ÉTONNER : to amaze **2** IMPRESSIONNER : to impress — **s'épater** *vr*
épaule [epol] *nf* : shoulder
épaulement [epolmã] *nm* **1** : retaining wall **2** : escarpment
épauler [epole] *vt* **1** AIDER : to back, to support **2** : to raise (a firearm), to take aim with — *vi* : to take aim
épaulette [epolet] *nf* **1** : epaulet **2** BRETELLE : shoulder strap **3** : shoulder pad
épave [epav] *nf* **1** : wreck (of a ship) **2 épave flottante** : flotsam
épée [epe] *nf* **1** : sword **2 coup d'épée dans l'eau** : wasted effort
épeler [eple] {8} *vt* : to spell — **s'épeler** *vr*
épelle [epɛl], **épellera** [epɛlra], *etc.* → **épeler**
épépiner [epepine] *vt* : to seed, to remove the seeds from
éperdu, -due [eperdy] *adj* **1** PASSIONNÉ : passionate, intense **2** : frantic, overwhelmed <éperdu de peur : overcome with fear>
éperdument [eperdymã] *adv* **1** : frantically, desperately <éperdument amoureux : madly in love> **2 je m'en moque éperdument** : I couldn't care less
éperlan [eperlã] *nm* : smelt
éperon [eprɔ̃] *nm* : spur
éperonner [eprɔne] *vt* : to spur (on)
épeurant, -rante [epœrã, -rãt] *adj Can* : scary, frightening
éphémère[1] [efemɛr] *adj* : ephemeral, fleeting
éphémère[2] *nm* : mayfly

épi [epi] *nm* **1** : ear, cob <épi de maïs : corncob> **2** : tuft (of hair) **3 se garer en épi** : to park at an angle
épice [epis] *nf* : spice
épicé, -cée [epise] *adj* : highly spiced, spicy
épicéa [episea] *nm France* : spruce
épicentre [episɑ̃tr] *nm* : epicenter
épicer [epise] {6} *vt* : to spice
épicerie [episri] *nf* **1** : grocery store **2** : groceries *pl*
épicier, -cière [episje, -sjɛr] *n* : grocer
épicurien[1], **-rienne** [epikyrjɛ̃, -rjɛn] *adj* : epicurean
épicurien[2], **-rienne** *n* : epicure
épidémie [epidemi] *nf* : epidemic — **épidémique** [-demik] *adj*
épiderme [epidɛrm] *nm* : epidermis
épidermique [epidɛrmik] *adj* **1** : epidermal, skin **2 réaction épidermique** : automatic reaction, gut feeling
épier [epje] {96} *vt* **1** OBSERVER : to spy on, to watch closely **2** ATTENDRE : to watch out for
épigramme [epigram] *nf* : epigram
épilepsie [epilɛpsi] *nf* : epilepsy
épileptique [epileptik] *adj & nmf* : epileptic
épiler [epile] *vt* : to remove hair from, to pluck
épilogue [epilɔg] *nm* **1** : epilogue **2** : conclusion, outcome
épiloguer [epilɔge] *vt* **~ sur** : to hold forth on, to go on and on about
épinard [epinar] *nm* **1** : spinach (plant) **2 épinards** *nmpl* : spinach (for eating)
épine [epin] *nf* **1** : thorn, prickle **2 épine dorsale** : spine, backbone
épinette [epinɛt] *nf* **1** : spinet **2** *Can* : spruce
épineux, -neuse [epinø, -nøz] *adj* : thorny, prickly
épingle [epɛ̃gl] *nf* **1** : pin <épingle de sûreté : safety pin> <épingle à linge : clothespin> <épingle à cheveux : hairpin> **2 tiré à quatre épingles** : impeccably dressed **3 tirer son épingle du jeu** : to extricate oneself, to pull out in time
épingler [epɛ̃gle] *vt* **1** : to pin **2** *fam* : to nab
épingletta [epɛ̃glɛt] *nf Can* **1** : brooch **2** : pin, button, badge
épinière [epinjɛr] *adj* → **moelle**
épique [epik] *adj* : epic
episcopal, -pale [episkɔpal] *adj, mpl* **-paux** [-po] : episcopal
épisode [epizɔd] *nm* : episode
épisodique [epizɔdik] *adj* : episodic — **épisodiquement** [-dikmɑ̃] *adv*
épisser [epise] *vt* : to splice
épissure [episyr] *nf* : splice
épistolaire [epistɔlɛr] *adj* : epistolary <avoir des relations épistolaires avec : to correspond with>
épitaphe [epitaf] *nf* : epitaph
épithète [epitɛt] *nf* : epithet
épître [epitr] *nf* : epistle
éploré, -rée [eplɔre] *adj* : tearful, in tears
éplucher [eplyʃe] *vt* **1** PELER : to peel **2** DÉCORTIQUER : to analyze, to scrutinize, to plow through (a text, etc.)
épluchure [eplyʃyr] *nf* : peel, peelings (of potatoes, etc.)
épointer [epwɛ̃te] *vt* : to blunt
éponge [epɔ̃ʒ] *nf* **1** : sponge **2 jeter l'éponge** : to throw in the towel **3 passer l'éponge** : to forget about it, to let bygones be bygones
éponger [epɔ̃ʒe] {17} *vt* **1** : to sponge up, to mop up **2** : to soak up, to absorb **3 éponger ses dettes** : to pay off one's debts — **s'éponger** *vr* **s'éponger le front** : to mop one's brow
épopée [epɔpe] *nf* : epic
époque [epɔk] *nf* **1** : epoch, era, age **2** : time, period <à cette époque : at that time>
épouse [epuz] *nf* → **époux**
épouser [epuze] *vt* **1** : to marry, to wed **2** : to espouse (an idea, etc.) **3** MOULER : to take the shape of, to fit closely
époussetage [epustaʒ] *nm* : dusting
épousseter [epuste] {8} *vt* : to dust
époustouflant, -flante [epustuflɑ̃, -flɑ̃t] *adj fam* : amazing, mind-boggling
époustoufler [epustufle] *vt* : to amaze, to flabbergast
épouvantable [epuvɑ̃tabl] *adj* : dreadful, horrible — **épouvantablement** [-tabləmɑ̃] *adv*
épouvantail [epuvɑ̃taj] *nm* **1** : scarecrow **2** : bogey(man)
épouvante [epuvɑ̃t] *nf* : terror, horror <roman d'épouvante : horror story>
épouvanter [epuvɑ̃te] *vt* TERRIFIER : to terrify, to fill with dread — **s'épouvanter** *vr* : to get frightened
époux, épouse [epu, epuz] *n* : spouse, husband *m*, wife *f*
éprendre [eprɑ̃dr] {70} *v* **s'éprendre** *vr* **~ de** : to fall in love with, to be taken with
épreuve [eprœv] *nf* **1** : test <mettre à l'épreuve : to put to the test> <épreuve de force : test of strength, showdown> **2** : ordeal, trial **3** : examination, test <épreuve écrite : written exam> **4** : event (in sports) **5** : proof, print (in printing, photography, etc.) **6 à l'épreuve de** : proof against
épris, éprise [epri, epriz] *adj* **~ de** : in love with
éprouvant, -vante [epruvɑ̃, -vɑ̃t] *adj* : trying, difficult to endure
éprouver [epruve] *vt* **1** TESTER : to test, to try (out) **2** RESSENTIR : to feel, to experience **3** : to suffer, to endure (a loss) **4** : to distress **5** : to try, to make suffer
éprouvette [epruvɛt] *nf* : test tube

épuisant, -sante [epɥizɑ̃, -zɑ̃t] *adj* : exhausting
épuisé, -sée [epɥize] *adj* **1** : exhausted **2** : out of stock
épuisement [epɥizmɑ̃] *nm* **1** : exhaustion, fatigue **2** : depletion (of stock, etc.)
épuiser [epɥize] *vt* **1** FATIGUER : to tire out, to wear out, to fatigue **2** : to exhaust, to use up — **s'épuiser** *vr*
épuration [epyrasjɔ̃] *nf* **1** : purification (of substances) **2** : refinement (of style, morals, etc.) **3** : purge (in politics)
épurer [epyre] *vt* **1** : to purify, to filter **2** : to refine (language, etc.) **3** : to purge (in politics)
équanimité [ekwanimite] *nf* : equanimity
équarrir [ekarir] *vt* **1** : to quarter (an animal) **2** : to square off
équateur [ekwatœr] *nm* : equator
équation [ekwasjɔ̃] *nf* : equation
équatorial, -riale [ekwatɔrjal] *adj, mpl* **-riaux** [-rjo] : equatorial
équatorien, -rienne [ekwatɔrjɛ̃, -rjɛn] *adj* : Ecuadoran, Ecuadorean, Ecuadorian
Équatorien, -rienne *n* : Ecuadoran, Ecuadorean, Ecuadorian
équerre [ekɛr] *nf* **1** : square <équerre en T : T square> **2 d'~** : square, straight **3 en ~** : at right angles **4 mettre d'équerre** : to square, to true
équestre [ekɛstr] *adj* : equestrian
équilatéral, -rale [ekɥilateral] *adj, mpl* **-raux** [-ro] : equilateral
équilibre [ekilibr] *nm* : equilibrium, balance <en équilibre : balanced, stable> <perdre l'équilibre : to lose one's balance> <équilibre sur les mains : handstand>
équilibré, -brée [ekilibre] *adj* : well-balanced, levelheaded
équilibrer [ekilibre] *vt* : to balance — **s'équilibrer** *vr*
équilibriste [ekilibrist] *nmf* **1** ACROBATE : acrobat **2** FUNAMBULE : tightrope walker
équinoxe [ekinɔks] *nm* : equinox
équipage [ekipaʒ] *nm* : crew
équipe [ekip] *nf* **1** : team <esprit d'équipe : team spirit> <faire équipe avec : to team up with> **2** : crew, gang, squad <équipe de nuit : night crew, night shift> <équipe de secours : rescue squad>
équipée [ekipe] *nf* **1** : escapade **2** : outing, jaunt
équipement [ekipmɑ̃] *nm* **1** MATÉRIEL : equipment **2 équipements** *nmpl* : facilities, installations <équipements sportifs : sports facilities>
équiper [ekipe] *vt* : to equip, to outfit — **s'équiper** *vr*
équipier, -pière [ekipje, -pjɛr] *n* : team member
équitable [ekitabl] *adj* : fair, equitable — **équitablement** [-tablemɑ̃] *adv*
équitation [ekitasjɔ̃] *nf* : horseback riding, horsemanship
équité [ekite] *nf* : equity
équivalence [ekivalɑ̃s] *nf* : equivalence
équivalent[1], -lente [ekivalɑ̃, -lɑ̃t] *adj* : equivalent
équivalent[2] *nm* : equivalent
équivaloir [ekivalwar] {95} *vi* **~ à** : to be equivalent to, to be tantamount to
équivoque[1] [ekivɔk] *adj* **1** AMBIGU : equivocal, ambiguous **2** DOUTEUX : questionable, doubtful
équivoque[2] *nf* **1** AMBIGUÏTÉ : ambiguity, uncertainty **2** MALENTENDU : misunderstanding **3 sans ~** : unequivocal, unequivocally
érable [erabl] *nm* : maple <sirop d'érable : maple syrup>
éradication [eradikasjɔ̃] *nf* : eradication
éradiquer [eradike] *vt* : to eradicate
érafler [erafle] *vt* **1** : to graze, to scratch (the skin) **2** : to scrape (a surface)
éraflure [eraflyr] *nf* : scratch, scrape
éraillé, -lée [eraje] *adj* **1** : hoarse, rasping **2** : frayed **3 avoir les yeux éraillés** : to have bloodshot eyes
ère [ɛr] *nf* : era
érection [erɛksjɔ̃] *nf* : erection
éreintant, -tante [erɛ̃tɑ̃, -tɑ̃t] *adj* : back-breaking, exhausting
éreinter [erɛ̃te] *vt* **1** ÉPUISER : to exhaust, to wear out **2** CRITIQUER : to criticize, to pan — **s'éreinter** *vr* : to wear oneself out
ergonomie [ergɔnɔmi] *nf* : ergonomics
ergonomique [ergɔnɔmik] *adj* : ergonomic
ergot [ergo] *nm* **1** : spur (of a rooster) **2 se dresser sur ses ergots** : to get up on one's high horse
ergoter [ergote] *vi* : to quibble
ergoteur, -teuse [ergɔtœr, -tøz] *adj* : quibbling, argumentative
ergothérapeute [ergɔterapøt] *nmf* : occupational therapist
ergothérapie [ergɔterapi] *nf* : occupational therapy
ériger [eriʒe] {17} *vt* **1** : to erect **2** : to establish, to set up — **s'ériger** *vr* **~ en** : to set oneself up as
ermitage [ermitaʒ] *nm* **1** : hermitage **2** : retreat
ermite [ɛrmit] *nm* : hermit
éroder [erɔde] *vt* : to erode, to eat away — **s'éroder** *vr*
érogène [erɔʒɛn] *adj* : erogenous
érosion [erozjɔ̃] *nf* : erosion
érotique [erɔtik] *adj* : erotic — **érotiquement** [-tikmɑ̃] *adv*
érotisme [erɔtism] *nm* : eroticism
errant, -rante [erɑ̃, -rɑ̃t] *adj* : wandering <un chien errant : a stray dog>
errata [erata] *nms & pl* : errata

erratique [ɛratik] *adj* : erratic (in geology or medicine)
errements [ɛrmɑ̃] *nmpl* : transgressions, bad habits
errer [ɛre] *vi* **1** : to wander, to stray, to roam **2** : to err
erreur [ɛrœr] *nf* : error, mistake <être dans l'erreur : to be wrong, to be mistaken> <par erreur : by mistake>
erroné, -née [ɛrɔne] *adj* : erroneous, wrong — **erronément** [-nemɑ̃] *adv*
éructer [erykte] *vi* : to belch
érudit[1], **-dite** [erydi, -dit] *adj* : erudite, learned
érudit[2], **-dite** *n* : scholar
érudition [erydisjɔ̃] *nf* : erudition
éruption [erypsjɔ̃] *nf* **1** : eruption (of a volcano) **2** : eruption, rash **3** : outburst <une éruption de colère : a fit of anger>
erythréen, -thréenne [eritreɛ̃, -treɛn] *adj* : Eritrean
Erythréen, -thréenne *n* : Eritrean
ès [ɛs] *prep* **docteur ès lettres** : doctor of letters, Ph.D.
esbroufe [ɛzbruf] *nf fam* : showing off, swagger
escabeau [ɛskabo] *nm, pl* **-beaux 1** TABOURET : stool **2** : stepladder
escadre [ɛskadr] *nf* : squadron
escadrille [ɛskadrij] *nf* : squadron
escadron [ɛskadrɔ̃] *nm* **1** : squad, squadron <escadron de la mort : death squad> **2** : crowd, bunch
escalade [ɛskalad] *nf* **1** : climbing, scaling **2** : escalation
escalader [ɛskalade] *vt* : to climb, to scale
escalator [ɛskalatɔr] *nm* : escalator
escale [ɛskal] *nf* **1** : port of call **2** : stopover
escalier [ɛskalje] *nm* : stairs, steps <escalier en colimaçon : spiral staircase> <escalier mécanique : escalator> <escalier de secours : fire escape>
escalope [ɛskalɔp] *nf* : cutlet <escalope de veau : veal cutlet>
escamotable [ɛskamɔtabl] *adj* **1** : retractable **2** : foldaway, collapsible
escamoter [ɛskamɔte] *vt* **1** : to cause to disappear **2** : to retract, to fold away **3** VOLER : to snatch, to filch **4** SAUTER : to leave out, to skip **5** ÉLUDER : to dodge, to evade
escampette [ɛskɑ̃pet] *nf* **prendre la poudre d'escampette** *fam* : to take to one's heels
escapade [ɛskapad] *nf* : escapade, jaunt <faire une escapade : to run away>
escarbille [ɛskarbij] *nf* : cinder
escargot [ɛskargo] *nm* : snail
escarmouche [ɛskarmuʃ] *nf* : skirmish
escarpé, -pée [ɛskarpe] *adj* : steep
escarpement [ɛskarpəmɑ̃] *nm* : escarpment, steep slope
escarpin [ɛskarpɛ̃] *nm* : pump (shoe)
escient [ɛsjɑ̃] *nm* **1 à bon escient** : judiciously, advisedly **2 à mauvais escient** : injudiciously, unwisely
esclaffer [ɛsklafe] *v* **s'esclaffer** *vr* : to burst out laughing, to guffaw
esclandre [ɛsklɑ̃dr] *nm* : scene, fracas
esclavage [ɛsklavaʒ] *nm* : slavery
esclave [ɛsklav] *adj & nmf* : slave
escompte [ɛskɔ̃t] *nm* : discount
escompter [ɛskɔ̃te] *vt* **1** : to discount **2** ANTICIPER : to expect, to anticipate
escopette [ɛskɔpet] *nf* : blunderbuss
escorte [ɛskɔrt] *nf* : escort
escorter [ɛskɔrte] *vt* : to escort
escorteur [ɛskɔrtœr] *nm* : escort ship
escouade [ɛskwad] *nf* **1** ESCADRON : squad **2** GROUPE : gang, group
escrime [ɛskrim] *nf* : fencing <faire de l'escrime : to fence>
escrimer [ɛskrime] *v* **s'escrimer** *vr* **1 s'escrimer à faire** : to wear oneself out doing **2 ~ sur** : to struggle with, to work away at
escrimeur, -meuse [ɛskrimœr, -møz] *n* : fencer
escroc [ɛskro] *nm* : swindler, crook
escroquer [ɛskrɔke] *vt* : to swindle, to defraud, to gyp
escroquerie [ɛskrɔkri] *nf* : swindle, fraud, gyp
eskimo [ɛskimo] → **esquimau**
ésotérique [ezɔterik] *adj* : esoteric
espace[1] [ɛspas] *nm* **1** : space, outer space **2** PLACE : area, room, space **3** : interval, gap <laissez un espace entre les deux : leave a space between the two> <en l'espace de dix minutes : within the space of ten minutes> **4 espaces verts** : parks, gardens
espace[2] *nf* : space (in printing)
espacer [ɛspase] {6} *vt* : to space (out)
espadon [ɛspadɔ̃] *nm* : swordfish
espadrille [ɛspadrij] *nf* **1** : espadrille **2 espadrilles** *nfpl Can* : sneakers
espagnol[1], **-gnole** [ɛspaɲɔl] *adj* : Spanish
espagnol[2] *nm* : Spanish (language)
Espagnol, -gnole *n* **1** : Spaniard **2 les Espagnols** : the Spanish
espar [ɛspar] *nm* : spar
espèce [ɛspɛs] *nf* **1** : species **2** SORTE : sort, kind <de toute espèce : of every kind> <espèce d'idiot! : you idiot!> **3 espèces** *nfpl* : cash <payer en espèces : to pay in cash>
espérance [ɛsperɑ̃s] *nf* **1** : hope, expectation **2** : expectancy <espérance de vie : life expectancy>
espérer [ɛspere] {87} *vt* **1** : to hope, to hope for <je l'espère bien : I hope so> **2** : to expect — *vi* **1** : to hope **2 ~ en** : to trust in
esperluette [ɛsperlyet] *nf* : ampersand
espiègle [ɛspjɛgl] *adj* : mischievous, impish
espièglerie [ɛspjɛglɔri] *nf* **1** : mischievousness, impishness **2** : prank, mischief

espion, -pionne [ɛspjɔ̃, -pjɔn] *n* : spy
espionnage [ɛspjɔnaʒ] *nm* : espionage
espionner [ɛspjɔne] *vt* : to spy on
espoir [ɛspwar] *nm* : hope <avoir bon espoir : to be confident, to have high hopes> <un cas sans espoir : a hopeless case>
esprit [ɛspri] *nm* **1** CERVEAU : mind, intellect <venir à l'esprit : to come to mind> **2** CARACTÈRE : character, mentality <avoir l'esprit étroit : to be narrow-minded> **3** HUMOUR : wit <avoir de l'esprit : to be witty> **4** HUMEUR : mood, disposition **5** PERSONNE : person **6** FANTÔME : spirit, ghost <esprit frappeur : poltergeist>
esquif [ɛskif] *nm* : skiff
esquimau[1], **-maude** [ɛskimo, -mod] *adj, mpl* **-maux** [-mo] : Eskimo
esquimau[2] *nm* : Eskimo (language)
Esquimau, -maude *n, mpl* **-maux** : Eskimo
esquinter [ɛskɛ̃te] *vt fam* **1** : to ruin, to mess up **2** : to pan — **s'esquinter** *vr* **s'esquinter à faire qqch** : to knock oneself out doing sth
esquisse [ɛskis] *nf* : sketch, outline, summary
esquisser [ɛskise] *vt* **1** : to sketch, to outline **2** : to give a hint of <esquisser un sourire : to give a slight smile>
esquive [ɛskiv] *nf* **1** : dodge (in sports) **2** : evasion, sidestepping
esquiver [ɛskive] *vt* : to avoid, to dodge, to evade — **s'esquiver** *vr* : to slip away
essai [ɛsɛ] *nm* **1** TENTATIVE : attempt, try **2** : trial, test <essai nucléaire : nuclear test> <mettre à l'essai : to put to the test> **3** : essay
essaie [ɛsɛ], **essaiera** [ɛsɛra], *etc.* → **essayer**
essaim [ɛsɛ̃] *nm* : swarm
essaimer [ɛseme] *vt* **1** : to swarm **2** : to spread (out), to expand
essayage [ɛseja3] *nm* : fitting, trying on <cabine d'essayage : fitting room>
essayer [ɛseje] {11} *vt* **1** TENTER : to try, to attempt **2** : to test, to try out **3** : to try on **4** : to assay (metals) — *vi* : to try — **s'essayer** *vr* ~ **à** : to try one's hand at
essayeur, essayeuse [ɛsejœr, esejøz] *n* : tester, fitter
essayiste [ɛsejist] *nmf* : essayist
essence [ɛsɑ̃s] *nf* **1** : gasoline <essence sans plomb : unleaded gas> **2** : essence <par essence : in essence, essentially>
essentiel[1], **-tielle** [ɛsɑ̃sjɛl] *adj* : essential — **essentiellement** [-sjɛlmɑ̃] *adv*
essentiel[2] *nm* **1** : main part, main thing, gist **2** : essentials *pl*, basics *pl*
esseulé, -lée [ɛsœle] *adj* : forlorn
essieu [ɛsjø] *nm, pl* **essieux** : axle
essor [ɛsɔr] *nm* **1** : flight (of a bird) <prendre son essor : to take flight, to soar> **2** : expansion, growth, development <prendre son essor : to grow, to expand rapidly> <être en plein essor : to be booming>
essorer [ɛsɔre] *vt* : to wring out, to spin dry
essoreuse [ɛsɔrøz] *nf* : wringer
essoufflement [ɛsufləmɑ̃] *nm* : breathlessness
essouffler [ɛsufle] *vt* : to make breathless, to wind — **s'essouffler** *vr* **1** : to get out of breath **2** : to become exhausted, to run out of steam
essuie [ɛsɥi], **essuiera** [ɛsɥira], *etc.* → **essuyer**
essuie-glace [ɛsɥiglas] *nm, pl* **essuie-glaces** : windshield wiper
essuie-mains [ɛsɥimɛ̃] *nms & pl* : hand towel
essuie-tout [ɛsɥitu] *nms & pl* : paper towel
essuyer [ɛsɥije] {58} *vt* **1** : to wipe, to dry **2** SUBIR : to suffer, to endure — **s'essuyer** *vr* : to dry oneself
est[1] [ɛ], *etc.* → **être**
est[2] [ɛst] *adj* : east, eastern
est[3] *nm* **1** : east <le vent d'est : the east wind> <vers l'est : eastward> **2 l'Est** : the East
estafilade [ɛstafilad] *nf* : gash, slash
estampe [ɛstɑ̃p] *nf* : engraving, print
estamper [ɛstɑ̃pe] *vt* **1** : to stamp **2** *fam* : to swindle, to rip off
estampille [ɛstɑ̃pij] *nf* **1** : stamp (on a document) **2** : trademark, label (on merchandise)
est-ce que [ɛska] *adv* (*used to introduce questions*) <est-ce qu'elle aime le café? : does she like coffee?> <est-ce qu'il y était? : was he there?> <pourquoi est-ce que tu pleures? : why are you crying?>
ester [ɛste] *nm* : ester
esthète [ɛstɛt] *nmf* : aesthete
esthéticien, -cienne [ɛstetisjɛ̃, -sjɛn] *n* : beautician
esthétique[1] [ɛstetik] *adj* **1** : aesthetic **2** : aesthetically pleasing, attractive — **esthétiquement** [-tikmɑ̃] *adv*
esthétique[2] *nf* : aesthetics
estimable [ɛstimabl] *adj* **1** : estimable, respected **2** : decent, sound
estimation [ɛstimasjɔ̃] *nf* **1** ÉVALUATION : valuation, appraisal **2** : estimate, reckoning
estime [ɛstim] *nf* : esteem, respect
estimer [ɛstime] *vt* **1** ÉVALUER : to assess, to appraise **2** : to estimate, to reckon **3** RESPECTER : to esteem, to respect **4 estimer que** : to consider that, to judge that — **s'estimer** *vr* SE JUGER : to consider oneself <je m'estime heureux : I consider myself fortunate>
estival, -vale [ɛstival] *adj, mpl* **-vaux** [-vo] : summer <la saison estivale : the summer season>
estivant, -vante [ɛstivɑ̃, -vɑ̃t] *n* : summer vacationer

estocade [ɛstɔkad] *nf* : deathblow, final thrust

estomac [ɛstɔma] *nm* **1** : stomach <mal à l'estomac : stomachache> **2 avoir de l'estomac** *fam* : to have guts **3 avoir l'estomac dans les talons** *fam* : to be famished

estomaqué, -quée [ɛstɔmake] *adj fam* : astounded, flabbergasted

estomper [ɛstɔ̃pe] *vt* : to blur, to dim — **s'estomper** *vr* : to fade away, to diminish

estonien[1], **-nienne** [ɛstɔnjɛ̃, -njɛn] *adj* : Estonian

estonien[2] *nm* : Estonian (language)

Estonien, -nienne *n* : Estonian

estrade [ɛstrad] *nf* : platform, dais

estragon [ɛstragɔ̃] *nm* : tarragon

estrogène [ɛstrɔʒɛn] *nm* : estrogen

estropié[1], **-piée** [ɛstrɔpje] *adj* : crippled, maimed

estropié[2], **-piée** *n* : cripple, disabled person

estropier [ɛstrɔpje] {96} *vt* **1** : to cripple, to maim **2** : to mispronounce, to misspell, to misquote

estuaire [ɛstɥɛr] *nm* : estuary

estudiantin, -tine [ɛstydjɑ̃tɛ̃, -tin] *adj* : student

esturgeon [ɛstyrʒɔ̃] *nm* : sturgeon

et [e] *conj* **1** : and <mon père et moi : my father and me> <et moi? : what about me?> **2 et . . . et . . .** : both . . . and . . . **3** (*used in numbers and fractions*) <vingt et un : twenty-one> <trois heures et demie : three-thirty, half past three>

étable [etabl] *nf* : cowshed

établi[1], **-blie** [etabli] *adj* : established

établi[2] *nm* : workbench

établir [etablir] *vt* **1** INSTITUER : to set up, to establish **2** : to draw up, to make out **3** PROUVER : to prove (guilt, innocence) **4** : to set (a record) — **s'établir** *vr* **1** : to get established, to set oneself up **2** : to settle

établissement [etablismɑ̃] *nm* **1** : establishment, setting up **2** : institution, establishment <établissement industriel : factory> <établissement scolaire : school>

étage [etaʒ] *nm* **1** : story, floor **2** : stage (of a rocket) **3** : tier, level

étager [etaʒe] {17} *vt* **1** : to lay out in tiers **2** : to stagger, to alternate — **s'étager** *vr*

étagère [etaʒɛr] *nf* **1** : shelf **2** : shelves *pl*, shelving unit

étai [ete] *nm* : prop, support

étain [etɛ̃] *nm* **1** : tin **2** : pewter

était [ete], *etc.* → **être**

étal [etal] *nm, pl* **étals** [etal] *or* **étaux** [eto] **1** ÉVENTAIRE : stall (in a market) **2** : butcher's block

étalage [etalaʒ] *nm* **1** : display <faire étalage de : to show off, to flaunt> **2** DEVANTURE : window display

étaler [etale] *vt* **1** : to lay out, to spread out, to display **2** : to spread (on), to apply **3** ÉCHELONNER : to space out, to stagger **4** : to show off, to flaunt — **s'étaler** *vr* **1** : to spread <cette peinture s'étale mal : this paint doesn't spread well> **2** : to be spread, to extend (in time) **3** *fam* : to sprawl **4** *fam* : to fall on one's face

étalon [etalɔ̃] *nm* **1** : stallion **2** MODÈLE : standard, yardstick <l'étalon-or : the gold standard>

étalonner [etalɔne] *vt* **1** : to standardize **2** : to calibrate

étamine [etamin] *nf* **1** : stamen **2** : cheesecloth, muslin, bunting

étanche [etɑ̃ʃ] *adj* **1** : watertight, waterproof **2** *or* **étanche à l'air** : airtight

étancher [etɑ̃ʃe] *vt* **1** : to stem, to staunch **2** : to seal, to make watertight **3 étancher sa soif** : to quench one's thirst

étang [etɑ̃] *nm* : pond

étape [etap] *nf* **1** HALTE : stop, halt **2** : stage, leg (of a journey) **3** PHASE : step, stage, phase <les étapes de la vie : the stages of life>

état [eta] *nm* **1** : state, condition <en bon état : in good condition> <hors d'état : out of order> <état d'esprit : state of mind> <en état d'urgence : in a state of emergency> **2** : statement, inventory <états de comptes : financial statements> <faire état de : to give an account of> **3** : occupation, lot in life <de son état : by profession> **4 état civil** : civil status <bureau d'état civil : registry office>

État *nm* **1** : state, State <homme d'État : statesman> **2** : central government <monopole d'État : state monopoly>

étatique [etatik] *adj* : state, state-controlled

étatisation [etatizasjɔ̃] *nf* : state control, nationalization

étatiser [etatize] *vt* : to bring under state control

étatisme [etatism] *nm* : state control

état-major [etamaʒɔr] *nm, pl* **états-majors 1** : general staff (in the military) **2** : senior staff, management (in business, politics, etc.)

étau [eto] *nm, pl* **étaux** : vise

étayer [eteje] {11} *vt* **1** SOUTENIR : to prop up, to shore up **2** APPUYER : to support, to back up

et cætera *or* **et cetera** [etsetera] : et cetera, and so on

été [ete] *nm* : summer

éteignait [eteɲɛ], **éteignions** [eteɲiɔ̃], *etc.* → **éteindre**

éteigne [eteɲ], *etc.* → **éteindre**

éteindre [etɛ̃dr] {37} *vt* **1** : to extinguish, to put out **2** : to turn off, to switch off — **s'éteindre** *vr* **1** : to go out, to die out **2** S'AFFAIBLIR : to subside, to fade **3** MOURIR : to die

étendard [etɑ̃dar] *nm* : standard, flag
étendre [etɑ̃dr] {63} *vt* **1** ÉTALER : to spread, to spread out **2** PENDRE : to hang up (laundry, etc.) **3** ALLONGER : to stretch (out) **4** ÉLARGIR : to extend, to expand, to widen **5** DILUER : to dilute, to thin — **s'étendre** *vr* **1** : to stretch **2** : to lie down **3** : to spread **4 ~ sur** : to elaborate on
étendu, -due [etɑ̃dy] *adj* **1** VASTE : extensive, wide **2** ALLONGÉ : outstretched, spread
étendue *nf* **1** : area, expanse **2** : extent, range, scope
éternel, -nelle [eternɛl] *adj* : eternal — **éternellement** [-nɛlmɑ̃] *adv*
éterniser [eternize] *vt* **1** PERPÉTUER : to perpetuate **2** PROLONGER : to drag out, to prolong — **s'éterniser** *vr* : to go on and on
éternité [eternite] *nf* : eternity <il y a une éternité que . . . : it's been ages since . . . > <de toute éternité : from time immemorial>
éternuement [eternymɑ̃] *nm* : sneeze
éternuer [eternɥe] *vi* : to sneeze
éthane [etan] *nm* : ethane
éther [eter] *nm* : ether
éthéré, -rée [etere] *adj* : ethereal
éthiopien, -pienne [etjɔpjɛ̃, -pjɛn] *adj* : Ethiopian
Éthiopien, -pienne *n* : Ethiopian
éthique[1] [etik] *adj* : ethical
éthique[2] *nf* : ethics
ethnie [etni] *nf* : ethnic group
ethnique [etnik] *adj* : ethnic
ethnologie [etnɔlɔʒi] *nf* : ethnology
ethnologue [etnɔlɔg] *nmf* : ethnologist
étincelant, -lante [etɛ̃slɑ, -lɑ̃t] *adj* : sparkling, glittering
étinceler [etɛ̃sle] {8} *vi* : to sparkle, to glitter
étincelle [etɛ̃sɛl] *nf* **1** : spark **2** : sparkle, flash
étioler [etjɔle] *v* **s'étioler** *vr* **1** : to wilt **2** : to weaken, to become sickly
étique [etik] *adj* : skinny, scrawny
étiqueter [etikte] {8} *vt* **1** : to label (merchandise) **2 ~ comme** : to label as, to classify as
étiquette [etiket] *nf* **1** : label **2** : etiquette
étirer [etire] *vt* : to stretch — **s'étirer** *vr*
étoffe [etɔf] *nf* **1** TISSU : material, fabric **2** : substance, stuff <l'étoffe d'un héros : the stuff heroes are made of> <avoir l'étoffe de : to have the makings of>
étoffer [etɔfe] *vt* : to flesh out, to give substance to — **s'étoffer** *vr* : to fill out
étoile [etwal] *nf* **1** : star (in astronomy) <étoile filante : shooting star> <étoile polaire : North Star> **2** : star (of movies, sports, etc.) **3** : starlike object <général à quatre étoiles : four-star general> <en étoile : star-shaped> **4 à la belle étoile** : outdoors, under the stars **5 étoile de mer** : starfish
étoilé, -lée [etwale] *adj* : starry
étole [etɔl] *nf* : stole
étonnant, -nante [etɔnɑ̃, -nɑ̃t] *adj* : surprising, astonishing, amazing — **étonnamment** [-namɑ̃] *adv*
étonné, -née [etɔne] *adj* : surprised, astonished, amazed
étonnement [etɔnmɑ̃] *nm* : surprise, astonishment
étonner [etɔne] *vt* : to surprise, to astonish, to amaze — **s'étonner** *vr*
étouffant, -fante [etufɑ̃, -fɑ̃t] *adj* : stifling
étouffée [etufe] *nf* **à l'étouffée** : braised, steamed
étouffement [etufmɑ̃] *nm* **1** RÉPRESSION : suppression **2** ASPHYXIE : suffocation, asphyxiation
étouffer [etufe] *vt* **1** RÉPRIMER : to stifle, to suppress **2** ASPHYXIER : to suffocate, to smother **3** : to muffle <étouffer ses pas : to muffle one's footsteps> **4** : to hush up — **s'étouffer** *vr* **1** : to choke **2** : to suffocate
étourderie [eturdəri] *nf* **1** : careless mistake **2** : carelessness, thoughtlessness
étourdi[1], **-die** [eturdi] *adj* : absent-minded, scatterbrained
étourdi[2], **-die** *n* : scatterbrain
étourdir [eturdir] *vt* **1** ASSOMMER : to stun, to daze **2** GRISER : to make dizzy, to overpower <les louanges l'étourdissaient : the praise was going to his head> — **s'étourdir** *vr* : to lose oneself <s'étourdir de paroles : to get drunk on words>
étourdissant, -sante [eturdisɑ̃, -sɑ̃t] *adj* **1** : deafening **2** : stunning, exhilarating
étourdissement [eturdismɑ̃] *nm* **1** VERTIGE : dizziness **2** GRISERIE : exhilaration
étourneau [eturno] *nm, pl* **-neaux** [-no] : starling
étrange [etrɑ̃ʒ] *adj* : strange — **étrangement** [etrɑ̃ʒmɑ̃] *adv*
étranger[1], **-gère** [etrɑ̃ʒe, -ʒɛr] *adj* **1** : foreign **2** : strange, unfamiliar
étranger[2], **-gère** *n* **1** : foreigner **2** : stranger **3 à l'étranger** : abroad
étrangeté [etrɑ̃ʒte] *nf* : strangeness, oddity
étranglement [etrɑ̃gləmɑ̃] *nm* **1** : strangulation **2** : narrowing, constriction
étrangler [etrɑ̃gle] *vt* **1** : to strangle **2** : to constrict — **s'étrangler** *vr* : to choke
étrangleur, -gleuse [etrɑ̃glœr, -gløz] *n* : strangler
être[1] [etr] {38} *vi* **1** : to be <il est mon frère : he is my brother> <Denise est belle : Denise is pretty> <sois sage! : be good!> <nous sommes à Paris : we're in Paris> **2** : to exist, to live <être ou ne pas être : to be or not to

be> **3** (*used with expressions of time, date, season*) <nous sommes le 15 mai : it is May 15th> <il est 10 heures : it is 10 o'clock> **4** (*used in formal expressions*) <il est des moments pareils : there are such moments> <il était une fois : once upon a time> **5 ~ à** : to belong to <ce livre est à moi : this book is mine> **6** (*indicating a state of action*) <j'étais à travailler : I was working> <tu es toujours à apprendre qqch : you're always learning sth> **7 soit . . . soit** : either . . . or — *v aux* **1** (*used in composite constructions*) <je serais partie : I would have left> <merci d'être venus! : thanks for coming!> **2** (*used in passive constructions*) <je suis passé te voir : I stopped by to see you> <elle a été blessée : she was injured> <il est né en 1938 : he was born in 1938> **3** (*used with an infinitive to indicate obligation*) <c'est un film à voir : it's a film you must see> <ses avis sont à entendre : her opinions should be heard>

être² *nm* **1** : organism, being <être humain : human being> **2** : person <un être cher : a loved one> **3** : soul, heart, being <au fond de mon être : deep in my heart>

étreindre |etrẽdr| {37} *vt* **1** : to embrace, to hug **2** : to grip, to seize — **s'étreindre** *vr* : to embrace each other

étreinte |etrẽt| *nf* **1** : embrace, hug **2** : grip, grasp <sous l'étreinte de la misère : in the grip of poverty>

étrenner |etrene| *vt* : to use for the first time

étrennes |etrɛn| *nfpl* : Christmas or New Year's present

étrier |etrije| *nm* : stirrup

étriller |etrije| *vt* **1** : to curry, to brush **2** : to criticize harshly, to pan

étriper |etripe| *vt* **1** : to gut, to disembowel **2** *fam* : to slaughter, to tear into (a person) — **s'étriper** *vr fam* : to tear each other to pieces

étriqué, -quée |etrike| *adj* **1** : skimpy, tight **2** : narrow, petty

étroit, étroite |etrwa, etrwat| *adj* **1** : narrow **2** ÉTRIQUÉ : tight **3** RIGOUREUX : strict **4** INTIME : close <étroite collaboration : close collaboration> **5 à l'étroit** : cramped

étroitement |etrwatmɑ̃| *adv* **1** : tightly, closely **2** : strictly

étroitesse |etrwatɛs| *nf* **1** : narrowness **2 étroitesse d'esprit** : narrow-mindedness

étude |etyd| *nf* **1** : study, studying <l'étude de la médecine : the study of medicine> <faire des études : to study> **2** : study, (research) paper **3** BUREAU : office **4** CLIENTÈLE : (professional) practice **5** : consideration <mettre à l'étude : to take under consideration> **6** : étude (in music)

étudiant, -diante |etydjɑ̃, -djɑ̃t| *adj & n* : student

étudié, -diée |etydje| *adj* **1** : carefully designed **2** AFFECTÉ : studied, affected

étudier |etydje| {96} *vt* **1** : to study, to learn **2** : to consider **3** : to devise, to design — *vi* : to study

étui |etɥi| *nm* : case <étui à lunettes : glasses case> <étui de révolver : holster>

étuve |etyv| *nf* **1** : steam room **2** : sterilizer

étymologie |etimɔlɔʒi| *nf* : etymology

étymologique |etimɔlɔʒik| *adj* : etymological — **étymologiquement** |-ʒikmɑ̃| *adv*

eu |ø| *pp* → **avoir**

eucalyptus |økaliptys| *nms & pl* : eucalyptus

Eucharistie |økaristi| *nf* : Eucharist

eunuque |ønyk| *nm* : eunuch

euphémique |øfemik| *adj* : euphemistic — **euphémiquement** |-mikmɑ̃| *adv*

euphémisme |øfemism| *nm* : euphemism

euphonie |øfɔni| *nf* : euphony

euphorie |øfɔri| *nf* : euphoria

euphorique |øfɔrik| *adj* : euphoric

eurasien, -sienne |ørazjɛ̃, -zjɛn| *adj* : Eurasian

Eurasien, -sienne *n* : Eurasian

euro |øro| *nm* : euro (monetary unit)

européen, -péenne |ørɔpeɛ̃, -peɛn| *adj* : European

Européen, -péenne *n* : European

eut |ø|, *etc.* → **avoir**

euthanasie |øtanazi| *nf* : euthanasia

eux |ø| *pron* : they, them <ce sont eux : they're the ones> <sans eux : without them> <eux deux : both of them>

eux-mêmes |ømɛm| *pron* : themselves

évacuation |evakɥasjɔ̃| *nf* **1** : evacuation **2** : draining, discharge

évacuer |evakɥe| *vt* **1** : to evacuate, to clear out **2** : to drain, to discharge

évadé, -dée |evade| *n* : fugitive, escapee

évader |evade| *v* **s'évader** *vr* : to escape

évaluateur, -trice |evalɥatœr, -tris| *n Can* : appraiser

évaluation |evalɥasjɔ̃| *nf* : evaluation, assessment, appraisal

évaluer |evalɥe| *vt* : to evaluate, to assess, to appraise

évangélique |evɑ̃ʒelik| *adj* : evangelical

évangéliste |evɑ̃ʒelist| *nm* **1** : Evangelist **2** : evangelist, preacher

évangile |evɑ̃ʒil| *nm* **1** : gospel **2 l'Évangile** : the Gospel

évanouir |evanwir| *v* **s'évanouir** *vr* **1** : to faint **2** DISPARAÎTRE : to vanish, to disappear

évanouissement |evanwismɑ̃| *nm* **1** : fainting, faint **2** DISPARITION : vanishing, disappearance

évaporation [evapɔrasjɔ̃] *nf* : evaporation
évaporé, -rée [evapɔre] *adj* : giddy, scatterbrained
évaporer [evapɔre] *v* **s'évaporer** *vr* **1** : to evaporate **2** *fam* : to vanish, to disappear
évasé, -sée [evaze] *adj* : flared, bell-shaped
évaser [evaze] *vt* : to widen, to flare — **s'évaser** *vr*
évasif, -sive [evazif,-ziv] *adj* : evasive — **évasivement** [-zivmɑ̃] *adv*
évasion [evazjɔ̃] *nf* **1** : escape **2 évasion fiscale** : tax evasion
évêché [eveʃe] *nm* : bishopric
éveil [evɛj] *nm* **1** : awakening **2 donner l'éveil** : to arouse suspicions **3 en ~** : on the alert
éveillé, -lée [eveje] *adj* **1** : awake **2** : bright, alert
éveiller [eveje] *vt* **1** RÉVEILLER : to awaken **2** STIMULER : to stimulate, to arouse (curiosity, suspicion, etc.) — **s'éveiller** *vr*
événement [evɛnmɑ̃] *nm* : event
éventail [evɑ̃taj] *nm* **1** : fan **2** : range, spread
éventaire [evɑ̃tɛr] *nm* : stall, stand
éventé, -tée [evɑ̃te] *adj* **1** : stale, flat **2** : exposed to the wind, breezy
éventer [evɑ̃te] *vt* **1** : to air (out) **2** : to fan **3** : to find out, to discover — **s'éventer** *vr* **1** : to fan oneself **2** : to go stale, to go flat
éventrer [evɑ̃tre] *vt* **1** : to disembowel **2** : to gore **3** : to tear open
éventualité [evɑ̃tɥalite] *nf* : eventuality, possibility
éventuel, -tuelle [evɑ̃tɥɛl] *adj* : possible — **éventuellement** [-tɥɛlmɑ̃] *adv*
évêque [evɛk] *nm* : bishop
évertuer [evɛrtɥe] *v* **s'évertuer** *vr* : to strive, to try one's best
éviction [eviksjɔ̃] *nf* **1** : eviction **2** : expulsion, ousting
évidemment [evidamɑ̃] *adv* : obviously, of course
évidence [evidɑ̃s] *nf* **1** : obviousness, clearness <de toute évidence : obviously> **2 mettre en évidence** : to display, to highlight **3 se mettre en évidence** : to come to the fore
évident, -dente [evidɑ̃, -dɑ̃t] *adj* : obvious, evident
évider [evide] *vt* : to hollow out, to scoop out
évier [evje] *nm* : (kitchen) sink
évincer [evɛ̃se] {6} *vt* **1** : to oust **2** : to evict
évitable [evitabl] *adj* : avoidable
éviter [evite] *vt* **1** : to avoid **2** : to dodge, to evade
évocateur, -trice [evɔkatœr, -tris] *adj* : evocative, suggestive
évocation [evɔkasjɔ̃] *nf* : evocation
évolué, -luée [evɔlɥe] *adj* : highly developed, advanced
évoluer [evɔlɥe] *vi* **1** : to evolve, to develop **2** : to maneuver, to move about
évolutif, -tive [evɔlytif, -tiv] *adj* : developing, progressive
évolution [evɔlysjɔ̃] *nf* **1** : evolution (in biology) **2** : development, advancement, change
évoquer [evɔke] *vt* **1** : to recall **2** : to mention **3** : to evoke, to conjure up
exacerber [ɛgzasɛrbe] *vt* : to exacerbate
exact, exacte [ɛgzakt] *adj* **1** PRÉCIS : exact, precise **2** JUSTE : accurate, correct <c'est exact : that's right> **3** PONCTUEL : punctual
exactement [ɛgzaktəmɑ̃] *adv* : exactly, precisely
exaction [ɛgzaksjɔ̃] *nf* : exaction, extortion
exactitude [ɛgzaktityd] *nf* **1** : exactness, accuracy **2** PONCTUALITÉ : punctuality
ex æquo [ɛgzeko] *adv* : equal, equally placed <ex æquo à la première place : tied for first place>
exagération [ɛgzaʒerasjɔ̃] *nf* : exaggeration
exagéré, -rée [ɛgzaʒere] *adj* : exaggerated, excessive — **exagérément** [-remɑ̃] *adv*
exagérer [ɛgzaʒere] {87} *vt* : to exaggerate — *vi* : to go too far, to overdo it
exaltant, -tante [ɛgzaltɑ̃, -tɑ̃t] *adj* : exciting, stirring
exaltation [ɛgzaltasjɔ̃] *nf* **1** GLORIFICATION : exalting, extolling **2** EXCITATION : excitement, enthusiasm
exalté, -tée [ɛgzalte] *adj* : excited, inflamed, hotheaded
exalter [ɛgzalte] *vt* **1** GLORIFIER : to exalt, to extol **2** EXCITER : to excite, to thrill — **s'exalter** *vr* : to get excited
examen [ɛgzamɛ̃] *nm* : examination <réussir à un examen : to pass an exam>
examinateur, -trice [ɛgzaminatœr, -tris] *n* : examiner
examiner [ɛgzamine] *vt* **1** : to examine **2** PESER : to consider — **s'examiner** *vr*
exaspération [ɛgzasperasjɔ̃] *nf* : exasperation
exaspérer [ɛgzaspere] {87} *vt* **1** IRRITER : to exasperate, to infuriate **2** AGGRAVER : to aggravate, to make worse — **s'exaspérer** *vr*
exaucer [ɛgzose] {6} *vt* : to fulfill, to grant
excavateur [ɛkskavatœr] *nm* : excavator, steam shovel
excavation [ɛkskavasjɔ̃] *nf* : excavation
excavatrice [ɛkskavatris] *nf* : excavator, steam shovel
excaver [ɛkskave] *vt* : to excavate
excédent [ɛksedɑ̃] *nm* : surplus, excess <excédent commercial : trade sur-

plus> <excédent de bagages : excess baggage>
excédentaire [ɛksedɑ̃tɛr] *adj* : surplus, excess
excéder [ɛksede] {87} *vt* **1** DÉPASSER : to exceed **2** EXASPÉRER : to exasperate, to infuriate
excellence [ɛkselɑ̃s] *nf* **1** : excellence **2** : excellency <Votre Excellence : Your Excellency>
excellent, -lente [ɛkselɑ̃, -lɑ̃t] *adj* : excellent
exceller [ɛksele] *vi* : to excel
excentricité [ɛksɑ̃trisite] *nf* **1** : eccentricity **2** : remoteness
excentrique[1] [ɛksɑ̃trik] *adj* **1** : eccentric, odd **2** : remote, outlying
excentrique[2] *nmf* : eccentric
excentriquement [ɛksɑ̃trikmɑ̃] *adv* : eccentrically
excepté [ɛksɛpte] *prep* SAUF : except, apart from
excepter [ɛksɛpte] *vt* : to except, to exclude
exception [ɛksɛpsjɔ̃] *nf* **1** : exception **2 à l'exception de** : except for, with the exception of **3 d'~** : exceptional, special
exceptionnel, -nelle [ɛksɛpsjɔnɛl] *adj* : exceptional, special
exceptionnellement [ɛksɛpsjɔnɛlmɑ̃] *adv* **1** : exceptionally, extremely **2** : by way of exception, in this instance
excès [ɛksɛ] *nm* **1** : excess <sans excès : in moderation> **2 à l'excès** : to excess, excessively **3 excès de vitesse** : speeding
excessif, -sive [ɛksɛsif, -siv] *adj* : excessive — **excessivement** [-sivmɑ̃] *adv*
exciser [ɛksize] *vt* : to excise, to cut out
excision [ɛksizjɔ̃] *nf* : excision
excitable [ɛksitabl] *adj* **1** : irritable, edgy **2** : excitable (in physiology)
excitant[1], **-tante** [ɛksitɑ̃, -tɑ̃t] *adj* : exciting, stimulating
excitant[2] *nm* : stimulant
excitation [ɛksitasjɔ̃] *nf* : excitement, arousal
excité[1], **-tée** [ɛksite] *adj* : excited
excité[2], **-tée** *n* : hothead
exciter [ɛksite] *vt* **1** ENTHOUSIASMER : to excite, to thrill **2** STIMULER : to stimulate, to arouse **3** INCITER : to incite, to stir up — **s'exciter** *vr* : to get excited
exclamatif, -tive [ɛksklamatif, -tiv] *adj* : exclamatory
exclamation [ɛksklamasjɔ̃] *nf* : exclamation
exclamer [ɛksklame] *v* **s'exclamer** *vr* : to exclaim
exclu, -clue [ɛksklу] *adj* **1** : excluded **2 il n'est pas exclu que** : it is not impossible that
exclure [ɛksklyr] {39} *vt* **1** EXPULSER : to expel **2** EXCEPTER : to exclude, to rule out — **s'exclure** *vr*
exclusif, -sive [ɛksklyzif, -ziv] *adj* **1** : exclusive **2** : sole — **exclusivement** [-sivmɑ̃] *adv*
exclusion [ɛksklyzjɔ̃] *nf* **1** : expulsion **2** : exclusion **3 à l'exclusion de** : with the exception of, except for
exclusivité [ɛksklyzivite] *nf* **1** : exclusive rights *pl* **2** : exclusive object, product, etc. **3 en ~** : exclusively
excommunier [ɛkskɔmynje] {96} *vt* : to excommunicate
excréments [ɛkskremɑ̃] *nmpl* : excrement, feces
excréter [ɛkskrete] {87} *vt* : to excrete
excrétion [ɛkskresjɔ̃] *nf* : excretion
excroissance [ɛkskrwasɑ̃s] *nf* : outgrowth, excrescence
excursion [ɛkskyrsjɔ̃] *nf* : excursion, trip <faire une excursion : to go on a trip>
excursionniste [ɛkskyrsjɔnist] *nmf* : vacationer, tourist
excusable [ɛkskyzabl] *adj* : excusable
excuse [ɛskyz] *nf* **1** : excuse **2** : apology <présenter des excuses : to apologize>
excuser [ɛskyze] *vt* **1** PARDONNER : to forgive, to pardon <excusez-moi : I'm sorry, forgive me> **2** JUSTIFIER : to justify **3** : to excuse <se faire excuser : to ask to be excused> — **s'excuser** *vr* : to apologize <je m'excuse : I apologize>
exécrable [ɛgzekrabl] *adj* : atrocious, awful
exécrer [ɛgzekre] {87} *vt* : to abhor, to loathe
exécutant, -tante [ɛgzekytɑ̃, -tɑ̃t] *n* : performer
exécuter [ɛgzekyte] *vt* **1** : to execute, to carry out **2** : to perform (music, etc.) **3** : to execute, to put to death — **s'exécuter** *vr* : to comply
exécuteur[1], **-trice** [ɛgzekytœr, -tris] *n* **exécuteur testamentaire** : executor (of a will)
exécuteur[2] *nm* : executioner
exécutif[1], **-tive** [ɛgzekytif, -tiv] *adj* : executive
exécutif[2] *nm* **l'exécutif** : executive power (of government)
exécution [ɛgzekysjɔ̃] *nf* **1** : execution, performance <mettre à exécution : to carry out> **2** : execution, putting to death
exécutoire [ɛgzekytwar] *adj* : enforceable, binding
exemplaire[1] [ɛgzɑ̃plɛr] *adj* : exemplary
exemplaire[2] *nm* **1** : copy **2** : specimen, example
exemple [ɛgzɑ̃pl] *nm* **1** : example <pour l'exemple : as an example> <donner l'exemple : to set an example> **2 par ~** : for example, for instance
exemplifier [ɛgzɑ̃plifje] {96} *vt* : to exemplify

exempt, exempte [ɛgzɑ̃, ɛgzɑ̃t] *adj* : exempt <exempt de taxes : tax-exempt>
exempter [ɛgzɑ̃te] *vt* : to exempt
exemption [ɛgzɑ̃psjɔ̃] *nf* : exemption
exercé, -cée [ɛgzɛrse] *adj* : trained, experienced
exercer [ɛgzɛrse] {6} *vt* **1** : to exercise, to train **2** : to exert (control, influence, etc.) **3** : to practice (a profession) — *vi* : to practice, to be in practice — **s'exercer** *vr*
exercice [ɛgzɛrsis] *nm* **1** : (physical or mental) exercise **2** : practice <en exercice : in office, in practice> **3** : exercising, carrying out **4 exercice budgétaire** : fiscal year
exerciseur [ɛgzɛrsizœr] *nm* : exercise machine
exergue [ɛgzɛrg] *nm* **1** : inscription, epigraph **2 mettre en exergue** : to highlight, to emphasize
exhalaison [ɛgzalɛzɔ̃] *nf* : odor, fume
exhaler [ɛgzale] *vt* **1** : to exhale (breath) **2** : to give off, to emit **3** : to utter, to give vent to
exhausser [ɛgzose] *vt* : to raise (up)
exhaustif, -tive [ɛgzostif, -tiv] *adj* : exhaustive
exhiber [ɛgzibe] *vt* **1** : to show, to exhibit **2** : to show off, to flaunt — **s'exhiber** *vr* : to make an exhibition of
exhibition [ɛgzibisjɔ̃] *nf* **1** : display, exhibition **2** : presentation **3** : flaunting
exhibitionnisme [ɛgzibisjɔnism] *nm* : exhibitionism
exhibitionniste [ɛgzibisjɔnist] *nmf* : exhibitionist
exhortation [ɛgzɔrtasjɔ̃] *nf* : exhortation
exhorter [ɛgzɔrte] *vt* : to exhort, to urge
exhumer [ɛgzyme] *vt* : to exhume, to dig up
exigeant, -geante [ɛgziʒɑ̃, -ʒɑ̃t] *adj* : demanding
exigence [ɛgziʒɑ̃s] *nf* : demand, requirement
exiger [ɛgziʒe] {17} *vt* : to demand, to require
exigu, -guë [ɛgzigy] *adj* : cramped, tiny
exiguïté [ɛgziguite] *nf* : smallness, narrowness
exil [ɛgzil] *nm* : exile <en exil : in exile>
exilé, -lée [ɛgzile] *n* : exile
exiler [ɛgzile] *vt* : to exile — **s'exiler** *vr* : to go into exile, to isolate oneself
existant, -tante [ɛgzistɑ̃, -tɑ̃t] *adj* : existing, extant
existence [ɛgzistɑ̃s] *nf* : existence
existentialisme [ɛgzistɑ̃sjalism] *nm* : existentialism
existentiel, -tielle [ɛgzistɑ̃sjɛl] *adj* : existential
exister [ɛgziste] *vi* : to exist
exode [ɛgzɔd] *nm* : exodus
exonération [ɛgzɔnerasjɔ̃] *nf* : exemption <exonération d'impôts : tax exemption>
exonérer [ɛgzɔnere] {87} *vt* EXEMPTER : to exempt
exorbitant, -tante [ɛgzɔrbitɑ̃, -tɑ̃t] *adj* : exorbitant
exorbité, -tée [ɛgzɔrbite] *adj* : bulging
exorciser [ɛgzɔrsize] *vt* : to exorcize — **exorcisme** [-zɔrsism] *nm*
exotique [ɛgzɔtik] *adj* : exotic
expansif, -sive [ɛkspɑ̃sif, -siv] *adj* : expansive, outgoing
expansion [ɛkspɑ̃sjɔ̃] *nf* : expansion
expansivité [ɛkspɑ̃sivite] *nf* : expansiveness
expatrié, -triée [ɛkspatrije] *adj & n* : expatriate
expatrier [ɛkspatrije] {96} *vt* : to expatriate, to deport — **s'expatrier** *vr* : to emigrate
expectative [ɛkspɛktativ] *nf* : expectation <être dans l'expectative : to be waiting to see>
expectorant[1], -rante [ɛkspɛktɔrɑ̃, -rɑ̃t] *adj* : expectorant <sirop expectorant : expectorant cough syrup>
expectorant[2] *nm* : expectorant
expédient[1], -diente [ɛkspedjɑ̃, -djɑ̃t] *adj* : expedient
expédient[2] *nm* : expedient <vivre d'expédients : to live by one's wits>
expédier [ɛkspedje] {96} *vt* **1** : to dispatch, to send **2** : to send (someone) off **3** : to deal with, to make short work of
expéditeur, -trice [ɛkspeditœr, -tris] *n* : sender, forwarder
expéditif, -tive [ɛkspeditif, -tiv] *adj* : expeditious, quick
expédition [ɛkspedisjɔ̃] *nf* **1** ENVOI : sending, dispatching **2** : shipment **3** : expedition
expérience [ɛksperjɑ̃s] *nf* **1** PRATIQUE : experience, practice **2** ESSAI : experiment
expérimental, -tale [ɛksperimɑ̃tal] *adj, mpl* **-taux** [-to] : experimental — **expérimentalement** [-talmɑ̃] *adv*
expérimentation [ɛksperimɑ̃tasjɔ̃] *nf* : experimentation
expérimenté, -tée [ɛksperimɑ̃te] *adj* : experienced
expérimenter [ɛksperimɑ̃te] *vt* **1** ESSAYER : to test **2** ÉPROUVER : to experience — *vi* : to experiment
expert, -perte [ɛkspɛr, -pɛrt] *adj & n* : expert — **expertement** [-pɛrtəmɑ̃] *adv*
expert–comptable [ɛksperkɔ̃tabl] *nm, pl* **experts–comptables** : certified public accountant
expertise [ɛkspɛrtiz] *nf* **1** : expertise **2** : expert evaluation, appraisal
expertiser [ɛkspɛrtize] *vt* : to appraise, to assess
expiation [ɛkspjasjɔ̃] *nf* : atonement

expier [ɛkspje] {96} *vt* : to expiate, to atone for
expiration [ɛkspirasjɔ̃] *nf* **1** ÉCHÉANCE : expiration <venir à expiration : to expire> **2** : exhalation, breathing out
expirer [ɛkspire] *vi* **1** EXHALER : to exhale **2** : to expire <un bail qui expire le 30 juin : a lease which expires on June 30> — *vt* : to breathe out (air), to exhale
explicable [ɛksplikabl] *adj* : explicable
explicatif, -tive [ɛksplikatif, -tiv] *adj* : explanatory, illustrative
explication [ɛksplikasjɔ̃] *nf* **1** : explanation **2 explication de texte** : literary criticism
explicite [ɛksplisit] *adj* : explicit — **explicitement** [-sitmɑ̃] *adv*
expliciter [ɛksplisite] *vt* : to make explicit
expliquer [ɛksplike] *vt* : to explain — **s'expliquer** *vr* **1** : to explain oneself **2** : to understand <je m'explique mal sa réussite : I can't understand his success>
exploit [ɛksplwa] *nm* : exploit, feat
exploitable [ɛksplwatabl] *adj* : exploitable <exploitable par machine : machine-readable>
exploitant, -tante [ɛksplwatɑ̃, -tɑ̃t] *n* **1** : farmer **2** : manager of a movie theater
exploitation [ɛksplwatasjɔ̃] *nf* **1** : exploitation, utilizing **2** : running, operating, management **3 exploitation agricole** : farm
exploiter [ɛksplwate] *vt* **1** : to exploit **2** : to run, to operate, to manage
explorateur, -trice [ɛksplɔratœr, -tris] *n* : explorer
exploration [ɛksplɔrasjɔ̃] *nf* : exploration
exploratoire [ɛksplɔratwar] *adj* : exploratory
explorer [ɛksplɔre] *vt* : to explore
exploser [ɛksploze] *vi* **1** : to explode <faire exploser : to detonate, to blow up> **2** : to burst out, to flare up (with anger, etc.)
explosif[1], **-sive** [ɛksplozif, -ziv] *adj* : explosive
explosif[2] *nm* : explosive
explosion [ɛksplozjɔ̃] *nf* **1** : explosion **2** : outburst
exportateur[1], **-trice** [ɛkspɔrtatœr, -tris] *adj* : export, exporting
exportateur[2], **-trice** *n* : exporter
exportation [ɛkspɔrtasjɔ̃] *nf* : export, exportation
exporter [ɛkspɔrte] *vt* : to export
exposant[1], **-sante** [ɛkspozɑ̃, -zɑ̃t] *n* : exhibitor
exposant[2] *nm* : exponent
exposé[1], **-sée** [ɛkspoze] *adj* : exposed, oriented <exposé au nord : facing north>
exposé[2] *nm* **1** : lecture, talk **2** : account, report <un exposé des faits : an account of the facts>
exposer [ɛkspoze] *vt* **1** PRÉSENTER : to display, to exhibit **2** EXPLIQUER : to explain, to set out **3** ORIENTER : to orient, to set facing **4** : to endanger <exposer sa vie : to risk one's life> — **s'exposer** *vr* : to expose oneself (to the sun, to criticism, etc.)
exposition [ɛkspozisjɔ̃] *nf* **1** : display, exhibition <exposition d'art : art exhibition> **2** PRÉSENTATION : exposition, presentation (of facts, etc.) **3** : exposition (in literature or music) **4** : exposure **5** : orientation, aspect
exprès[1] [ɛkspre] *adv* **1** : on purpose, intentionally **2** SPÉCIALEMENT : specially, especially <une robe fabriquée exprès pour moi : a dress made specially for me>
exprès[2], **-presse** [ɛkspres] *adj* FORMEL : express, strict <défense expresse de nager : swimming strictly forbidden>
exprès[3] *adj* : special-delivery <lettre exprès : special-delivery letter> <envoyer en exprès : to send (as) special-delivery>
express[1] [ɛkspres] *adj* **1** : express <autobus express : express bus> **2** : espresso
express[2] *nms & pl* **1** : express **2** : espresso
expressément [ɛkspresemɑ̃] *adv* **1** : expressly, explicitly **2** : specially
expressif, -sive [ɛkspresif, -siv] *adj* : expressive
expression [ɛkspresjɔ̃] *nf* : expression <expression toute faite : set phrase, cliché> <sans expression : expressionless>
expressivité [ɛkspresivite] *nf* : expressiveness
exprimer [ɛksprime] *vt* **1** : to express **2** EXTRAIRE : to squeeze, to extract (juice, etc.) — **s'exprimer** *vr* : to express oneself
exproprier [ɛksprɔprije] {96} *vt* : to expropriate — **expropriation** [-prijasjɔ̃] *nf*
expulser [ɛkspylse] *vt* : to expel, to evict
expulsion [ɛkspylsjɔ̃] *nf* : expulsion, eviction, ouster
expurger [ɛkspyrʒe] {17} *vt* : to expurgate
exquis, -quise [ɛkski, -kiz] *adj* : exquisite, delightful
exsangue [ɛksɑ̃g] *adj* **1** : bloodless **2** : ashen, deathly pale
exsuder [ɛksyde] *v* : to exude
extase [ɛkstaz] *nf* : ecstasy
extasié, -siée [ɛkstazje] *adj* : rapturous, ecstatic
extasier [ɛkstazje] {96} *v* **s'extasier** *vr* : to be in ecstasy
extatique [ɛkstatik] *adj* : ecstatic, enraptured

extensible [ɛkstɑ̃sibl] *adj* : extendable, tensile
extensif, -sive [ɛkstɑ̃sif, -siv] *adj* **1** : extensive **2** : wider, extended <dans son sens extensif : in its extended sense>
extension [ɛkstɑ̃sjɔ̃] *nf* **1** : stretching (of a muscle, etc.) **2** : extension, expansion
exténuant, -ante [ɛkstenɥɑ, -ɥɑ̃t] *adj* : exhausting
exténuer [ɛkstenɥe] *vt* : to exhaust, to tire out
extérieur[1], **-rieure** [ɛksterjœr] *adj* **1** : exterior, external, outside <activités extérieures : outside activities> **2** : outward, apparent <signes extérieurs : outward signs> **3** : foreign <commerce extérieur : foreign trade>
extérieur[2] *nm* **1** : exterior, outside **2 à l'extérieur** : abroad **3 match à l'extérieur** : away game
extérieurement [ɛksterjœrmɑ̃] *adv* **1** : externally **2** : outwardly
extérioriser [ɛksterjɔrize] *vt* : to show, to express (one's feelings, etc.) — **s'extérioriser** *vr* : to express oneself
exterminateur, -trice [ɛksterminatœr, -tris] *n* : exterminator
extermination [ɛksterminasjɔ̃] *nf* : extermination
exterminer [ɛksterminе] *vt* : to exterminate, to wipe out — **s'exterminer** *fam* : to knock oneself out (doing something)
externat [ɛksterna] *nm* : day school
externe[1] [ɛkstern] *adj* : external
externe[2] *nmf* : day student
extincteur [ɛkstɛ̃ktœr] *nm* : fire extinguisher
extinction [ɛkstɛ̃ksjɔ̃] *nf* **1** : extinction **2** : extinguishing **3 extinction de voix** : loss of voice
extirper [ɛkstirpe] *vt* **1** : to uproot (a plant) **2** : to root out, to eradicate
extorquer [ɛkstɔrke] *vt* : to extort
extorsion [ɛkstɔrsjɔ̃] *nf* : extortion
extra[1] [ɛkstra] *adj* **1** : first-rate, top-quality **2** *fam* : great, fantastic
extra[2] *nms & pl* **1** : extra person **2** : extra thing or amount **3 un petit extra** : a little extra, a treat
extraconjugal, -gale [ɛkstrakɔ̃ʒygal] *adj, pl* **-gaux** [-go] : extramarital
extraction [ɛstraksjɔ̃] *nf* : extraction
extrader [ɛkstrade] *vt* : to extradite — **extradition** [-stradisjɔ̃] *nf*
extraire [ɛkstrɛr] {40} *vt* **1** : to extract **2** : to excerpt — **s'extraire** *vr* : to extricate oneself
extrait [ɛkstrɛ] *nm* **1** : extract **2** : excerpt **3** : certificate, certified copy <extrait de naissance : birth certificate>
extraordinaire [ɛkstraɔrdinɛr] *adj* **1** : extraordinary **2 par ~** : by some unlikely chance
extraordinairement [ɛkstraɔrdinɛrmɑ̃] *adv* : extraordinarily, amazingly
extrapoler [ɛkstrapɔle] *vt* : to extrapolate — **extrapolation** [-pɔlasjɔ̃] *nf*
extrasensoriel, -rielle [ɛkstrasɑ̃sɔrjɛl] *adj* : extrasensory
extraterrestre [ɛkstraterɛstr] *adj & nmf* : extraterrestrial
extravagant, -gante [ɛkstravagɑ̃, -gɑ̃t] *adj* : extravagant — **extravagance** [-vagɑ̃s] *nf*
extraverti[1], **-tie** [ɛkstravɛrti] *adj* : extroverted
extraverti[2], **-tie** *n* : extrovert
extrême[1] [ɛkstrɛm] *adj* **1** : far, farthest, extreme <à l'extrême limite : to the farthest point> <l'extrême droite : the far right> **2** : extreme, great <avec extrême difficulté : with very great difficulty> **3** : extreme, excessive <il fait une chaleur extrême : it's extremely hot>
extrême[2] *nm* : extreme <pousser à l'extrême : to take to extremes> <passer d'un extrême à l'autre : to go from one extreme to the other>
extrêmement [ɛkstrɛmmɑ̃] *adv* : extremely
extrême-onction [ɛkstrɛmɔ̃ksjɔ̃] *nf, pl* **extrêmes-onctions** : extreme unction
Extrême-Orient [ɛkstrɛmɔrjɑ̃] *nm* : Far East
extrémisme [ɛkstremism] *nm* : extremism — **extrémiste** [-tremist] *adj & nmf*
extrémité [ɛkstremite] *nf* **1** : extremity, end **2** : extreme (act) <pousser à des extrémités : to drive to extremes> **3** : plight, straits *pl* <à la dernière extrémité : at the point of death> **4 extrémités** *nfpl* : extremities (in anatomy)
extruder [ɛkstryde] *vt* : extrude
exubérant, -rante [ɛgzyberɑ̃, -rɑ̃t] *adj* : exuberant — **exubérance** [-berɑ̃s] *nf*
exulter [ɛgzylte] *vi* : to exult — **exultation** [ɛgzyltasjɔ̃] *nf*
exutoire [ɛgzytwar] *nm* : outlet, release
ex-voto [ɛksvɔto] *nm* : commemorative plaque

F

f [ɛf] *nm* : f, the sixth letter of the alphabet
fable [fabl] *nf* **1** : fable **2** MENSONGE : story, lie
fabricant, -cante [fabrikɑ̃, -kɑ̃t] *n* : manufacturer
fabrication [fabrikasjɔ̃] *nf* : manufacture, making <de fabrication artisanale : handmade>
fabrique [fabrik] *nf* **1** USINE : factory, mill **2 marque de fabrique** : trademark
fabriquer [fabrike] *vt* **1** : to make, to manufacture **2** : to fabricate (a story), to forge (documents, money, etc.)
fabulation [fabylasjɔ̃] *nf* : fabrication, lie
fabuleusement [fabyløzmɑ̃] *adv* : fabulously
fabuleux, -leuse [fabylø, -løz] *adj* **1** EXTRAORDINAIRE : fabulous, extraordinary **2** : mythical
fac [fak] *nf France fam* : university
façade [fasad] *nf* **1** : facade, front **2** APPARENCE : appearance, pretense
face [fas] *nf* **1** VISAGE : face <face à face : face to face> **2** : side, facet <pile ou face : heads or tails> **3 de ~** : from the front, head-on **4 d'en face** : facing, opposite **5 en ~** : opposite, across the street, opposing **6 faire face à** : to face towards, to face up to **7 sauver la face** : to save face
facétie [fasesi] *nf* **1** : joke, witticism **2** FARCE : prank
facétieux, -tieuse [fasesjø, -sjøz] *adj* : mischievous, facetious — **facétieusement** [fasesjøzmɑ̃] *adv*
facette [faset] *nf* : facet, aspect
fâché, -chée [faʃe] *adj* **1** : angry **2** DÉSOLÉ : sorry
fâcher [faʃe] *vt* : to anger — **se fâcher** *vr* : to get angry, to lose one's temper
fâcherie [faʃri] *nf* : quarrel, disagreement
fâcheux, -cheuse [faʃø, -ʃøz] *adj* **1** ENNUYEUX : annoying **2** REGRETTABLE : unfortunate — **fâcheusement** [-ʃøzmɑ̃] *adv*
facial, -ciale [fasjal] *adj, mpl* **faciaux** [fasjo] : facial
facile [fasil] *adj* **1** : easy **2** *or* **facile à vivre** : easygoing **3** : superficial, facile
facilement [fasilmɑ̃] *adv* : easily, readily
facilité [fasilite] *nf* **1** : easiness **2** MOYEN : means, opportunity **3** : aptitude **4 facilités de paiement** : easy terms (of payment)
faciliter [fasilite] *vt* : to facilitate, to make easier
façon [fasɔ̃] *nf* **1** : way, manner <de cette façon : in this way, thus> <façon de parler : manner of speaking> **2** : fashioning, making (of clothing, etc.) **3** : imitation <façon cuir : imitation leather> **4 façons** *nfpl* : behavior, manners <faire des façons : to put on airs> <sans façon : without a fuss, plain, simple> **5 de façon à** : so as to **6 de toute façon** : in any case **7 faire de la façon à qqn** *Can fam* : to be nice to s.o.
façonner [fasɔne] *vt* **1** : to shape, to fashion **2** FABRIQUER : to manufacture, to make
fac-similé [faksimile] *nm, pl* **fac-similés 1** REPRODUCTION : facsimile, copy **2** : fax
facteur[1], **-trice** [faktœr, -tris] *n* : letter carrier, mailman *m*
facteur[2] *nm* **1** : factor, element <le facteur chance : the element of chance> **2** : factor (in mathematics) **3** : builder, maker (of organs, pianos, etc.)
factice [faktis] *adj* : artificial, imitation, false
faction [faksjɔ̃] *nf* **1** : faction **2** : guard duty, watch
factionnaire [faksjɔner] *nm* : sentry
factuel, -tuelle [faktyɛl] *adj* : factual
facturation [faktyrasjɔ̃] *nf* : billing, invoicing
facture [faktyr] *nf* **1** : bill, invoice **2** : workmanship, technique
facturer [faktyre] *vt* : to bill, to invoice
facultatif, -tive [fakyltatif, -tiv] *adj* : optional
faculté [fakylte] *nf* **1** : faculty, ability **2** : right, option <la faculté de choisir : freedom of choice> **3** : faculty (of a college or university) **4** : department, school <faculté de droit : school of law>
fadaises [fadɛz] *nfpl* : drivel, nonsense
fade [fad] *adj* **1** : dull, drab **2** : tasteless, insipid
fadeur [fadœr] *nf* : blandness, dullness
fafiner [fafine] → **farfiner**
fagot [fago] *nm* : bundle of firewood
fagoté, -tée [fagɔte] *adj fam* : badly dressed, frumpy
Fahrenheit [farenajt] *adj* : Fahrenheit
faible[1] [fɛbl] *adj* **1** : weak, feeble <avoir la vue faible : to have weak eyes> <faible d'esprit : feebleminded> **2** : small, low <une faible quantité : a small quantity> <à faible revenu : low-income> **3** : faint, slight <un faible bruit : a faint sound> — **faiblement** [fɛbləmɑ̃] *adv*
faible[2] *nmf* : weak-willed person
faible[3] *nm* : weakness, partiality <avoir un faible pour : to have a soft spot for>
faiblesse [fɛbles] *nf* **1** : weakness, frailty **2** DÉFAUT : inadequacy, shortcoming **3** : faintness, dimness

faiblir [feblir] *vi* **1** : to weaken **2** DIMINUER : to diminish, to die down
faïence [fajɑ̃s] *nf* : earthenware
faille[1] [faj] → **falloir**
faille[2] [faj] *nf* **1** : fault (in geology) **2** : flaw, weakness
failli[1], **-lie** [faji] *adj* : bankrupt
failli[2], **-lie** *n* : bankrupt (person)
faillible [fajibl] *adj* : fallible
faillir [fajir] {41} *vi* : to fail <faillir à son devoir : to fail to do one's duty> — *vt* MANQUER : to barely escape, to narrowly miss <j'ai failli m'évanouir : I nearly fainted>
faillite [fajit] *nf* **1** ÉCHEC : failure **2** : bankruptcy <faire faillite : to go bankrupt>
faim [fɛ̃] *nf* : hunger <avoir faim : to be hungry> <mourir de faim : to be starving> <rester sur sa faim : to be disappointed>
fainéant[1], **fainéante** [feneɑ̃, -neɑ̃t] *adj* : lazy
fainéant[2], **fainéante** *n* : loafer, idler
fainéanter [feneɑ̃te] *vi* : to laze about, to bum around
faire [fɛr] {42} *vt* **1** : to do <que faites-vous comme métier? : what do you do for a living?> <elle fait ses études ici : she studies here> **2** : to make <tu fais une erreur : you're making a mistake> <faire savoir : to make known, to inform> **3** : to be <faire le difficile : to be fussy> <il fait soleil : it's sunny> **4** : to amount to, to measure <deux et deux font quatre : two plus two equals four> <la salle fait 7 mètres de long : the room is 7 meters long> **5** : to say <«eh bien,» fit-il : «well,» he said> **6 cela ne fait rien** : it doesn't matter **7 faire jeune** : to look young **8 faire mal à** : to hurt — **se faire** *vr* **1 ça ne se fait pas** : it's not done **2 s'en faire** : to worry, to be bothered **3 se faire à** : to get used to
faire–part [fɛrpar] *nms & pl* : announcement (of birth, death, marriage, etc.)
faire–valoir [fɛrvalwar] *nms & pl* : foil, straight man
faisable [fəzabl] *adj* : feasible — **faisabilité** [-zabilite] *nf*
faisait [fəzɛ], **faisions** [fəzjɔ̃], *etc.* → **faire**
faisan, -sane [fəzɑ̃] *n* : pheasant
faisandé, -dée [fəzɑ̃de] *adj* : gamy
faisceau [fɛso] *nm, pl* **faisceaux 1** : beam (of light) **2** : bundle
faiseur, -seuse [fəzœr, -zøz] *n* : maker, doer <faiseur d'intrigues : schemer>
fait[1], **faite** [fɛ, fɛt] *adj* **1** : made, done <bien fait : well done> **2** : ripe (of cheese) **3** : mature <un homme fait : a grown man> **4 tout fait** : ready-made
fait[2] *nm* **1** : fact **2** ACTE : act, deed **3** EXPLOIT : exploit, feat **4** ÉVÉNEMENT : event **5 au fait** : by the way, incidentally **6 au fait de** : informed about **7 comme de fait** *Can* : indeed **8 en fait de** : as regards
faîte [fɛt] *nm* **1** SOMMET : summit, top **2** APOGÉE : pinnacle <le faîte de la gloire : the height of glory>
fakir [fakir] *nm* : fakir
falaise [falɛz] *nf* : cliff
fallacieux, -cieuse [falasjø, -sjøz] *adj* CAPTIEUX : fallacious, misleading
falloir [falwar] {43} *v impers* **1** (*indicating a need*) <il faut partir : we must go> <il faut que je le fasse : I need to do it> **2** (*indicating an obligation*) <il fallait le faire : we had to do it> <j'y vais, il le faut : I'm going, I have to> <il fallait me le dire! : you should have said so!> **3** (*indicating a probability*) <il faut avoir été fou : he must have been out of his mind> **4 comme il faut** : proper, properly — **s'en falloir** *vr* **1 il s'en faut de peu** *or* **peu s'en faut** : very nearly, only just **2 il s'en faut de beaucoup** : (very) far from it
falot[1], **-lote** [falo, -lɔt] *adj* : colorless, insipid
falot[2] *nm* : lantern
falsification [falsifikasjɔ̃] *nf* : falsification, forgery, faking
falsifier [falsifje] {96} *vt* **1** : to falsify **2** : to adulterate
famé, -mée [fame] *adj* **mal famé** : disreputable
famélique [famelik] *adj* : half-starved, scrawny
fameusement [famøzmɑ̃] *adv fam* : really <c'est fameusement bien fait : it's really well done>
fameux, -meuse [famø, -møz] *adj* **1** CÉLÈBRE : famous **2** : excellent, first-rate **3** : real, remarkable <c'est un fameux mensonge : it's a whopping lie> **4 pas fameux** *fam* : not very good
familial, -liale [familjal] *adj, mpl* **-liaux** [-ljo] : family <revenu familial : family income>
familiale *nf* : station wagon
familiariser [familjarize] *vt* : to familiarize — **se familiariser** *vr*
familiarité [familjarite] *nf* **1** : familiarity **2 familiarités** *nfpl* : liberties, forwardness
familier, -lière [familje, -ljɛr] *adj* **1** : familiar, known **2** : informal, (overly) friendly **3** : colloquial, informal (of language) **4 animal familier** : pet
famille [famij] *nf* : family <c'est de famille : it runs in the family> <en famille : at home, with one's family>
famine [famin] *nf* : famine
fan [fan] *nmf* : fan, enthusiast
fana [fana] *nmf fam* : fanatic, freak
fanal [fanal] *nm, pl* **fanaux** [fano] : lantern
fanatique[1] [fanatik] *adj* : fanatic, fanatical

fanatique[2] *nmf* : fanatic — **fanatisme** [-natism] *nm*
faner [fane] *vt* **1** : to fade **2** : to wither — *vi* **1** : to fade **2** : to make hay (in agriculture) — **se faner** *vr* **1** : to wilt, to wither **2** : to fade (away)
fanfare [fɑ̃far] *nf* **1** : fanfare **2** : brass band
fanfaron[1], **-ronne** [fɑ̃farɔ̃, -rɔn] *adj* : boastful
fanfaron[2], **-ronne** *n* : braggart
fanfaronnade [fɑ̃farɔnad] *nf* : bragging, boasting
fanfaronner [fɑ̃farɔne] *vi* : to brag, to boast
fange [fɑ̃ʒ] *nf* : mire <traîner dans la fange : to drag through the mire>
fanion [fanjɔ̃] *nm* : pennant
fanon [fanɔ̃] *nm* **1** : whalebone **2** : wattle, dewlap **3** : fetlock (of a horse)
fantaisie [fɑ̃tezi] *nf* **1** : fantasy, imagination **2** CAPRICE : fancy, whim **3** : fantasia (in music)
fantaisiste [fɑ̃tezist] *adj* **1** : far-fetched, fanciful **2** : eccentric
fantasme [fɑ̃tasm] *nm* : fantasy
fantasmer [fɑ̃tasme] *vi* : to fantasize
fantasque [fɑ̃task] *adj* **1** : whimsical, capricious **2** BIZARRE : strange, weird
fantassin [fɑ̃tasɛ̃] *nm* : infantryman
fantastique [fɑ̃tastik] *adj* : fantastic — **fantastiquement** [-tikmɑ̃] *adv*
fantoche[1] [fɑ̃tɔʃ] *adj* : puppet <gouvernement fantoche : puppet government>
fantoche[2] *nm* MARIONNETTE : puppet
fantomatique [fɑ̃tɔmatik] *adj* : ghostly
fantôme [fɑ̃tom] *nm* SPECTRE : ghost, phantom
faon [fɑ̃] *nm* : fawn
faramineux, -neuse [faraminø, -nøz] *adj fam* : incredible, fantastic <une somme faramineuse : a staggering sum>
farce [fars] *nf* **1** : farce (in theater) **2** BLAGUE : practical joke, prank **3** : stuffing (in cooking)
farceur, -ceuse [farsœr, -søz] *n* : practical joker, prankster
farcir [farsir] *vt* **1** : to stuff (in cooking) **2** ~ **de** *fam* : to cram with — **se farcir** *fam* : to have to put up with, to get stuck with
fard [far] *nm* **1** : makeup **2 sans** ~ : plainly, openly
fardeau [fardo] *nm, pl* **fardeaux 1** : load **2** : burden, responsibility
farder [farde] *vt* **1** : to put makeup on **2** : to disguise, to conceal — **se farder** *vr* : to put on makeup
fardoches [fardɔʃ] *nfpl Can* : undergrowth, brush
farfelu, -lue [farfəly] *adj fam* : harebrained, wacky
farfiner [farfine] *vi Can fam* : to dawdle, to dillydally
farfouiller [farfuje] *vi fam* : to rummage (around)
farine [farin] *nf* : flour <farine d'avoine : oatmeal> <farine de maïs : cornmeal>
fariner [farine] *vt* : to flour
farineur, -neuse [farinœr, -nøz] *adj* **1** : covered with flour **2** : starchy, mealy
farouche [faruʃ] *adj* **1** SAUVAGE : wild, savage **2** TIMIDE : shy, timid **3** : fierce, unyielding
farouchement [faruʃmɑ̃] *adv* : fiercely
fart [far(t)] *nm* : (ski) wax
fascicule [fasikyl] *nm* **1** : installment, fascicle **2** : booklet
fascinant, -nante [fasinɑ̃, -nɑ̃t] *adj* : fascinating
fascination [fasinasjɔ̃] *nf* : fascination
fasciner [fasine] *vt* CAPTIVER : to fascinate
fascisme [faʃism] *nm* : fascism — **fasciste** [faʃist] *adj & nmf*
fasse [fas], *etc.* → **faire**
faste[1] [fast] *adj* : auspicious, lucky
faste[2] *nm* : pomp, splendor
fastidieux, -dieuse [fastidjø, -djøz] *adj* : tedious — **fastidieusement** [-djøzmɑ̃] *adv*
fastueux, -tueuse [fastɥø, -tɥøz] *adj* : luxurious, sumptuous
fatal, -tale [fatal] *adj, mpl* **fatals 1** MORTEL : fatal **2** INÉVITABLE : inevitable
fatalement [fatalmɑ̃] *adv* : inevitably
fatalisme [fatalism] *nm* : fatalism
fataliste[1] [fatalist] *adj* : fatalistic
fataliste[2] *nmf* : fatalist
fatalité [fatalite] *nf* **1** DESTIN : fate **2** : bad luck, misfortune **3** : inevitability
fatidique [fatidik] *adj* : fateful
fatigant, -gante [fatigɑ̃, -gɑ̃t] *adj* **1** : tiring **2** : tiresome
fatigue [fatig] *nf* : fatigue
fatigué, -guée [fatige] *adj* : tired, weary
fatiguer [fatige] *vt* **1** : to tire out **2** IMPORTUNER : to bother, to annoy **3** : to strain (an engine, a structure, etc.) — *vi* **1** : to labor (of an engine) **2** : to undergo strain — **se fatiguer** *vr* : to grow tired, to wear oneself out
fatras [fatra] *nm* : jumble
fatuité [fatɥite] *nf* : smugness, self-satisfaction
faubourg [fobur] *nm* BANLIEUE : suburb
fauché, -chée [foʃe] *adj fam* : broke <être complètement fauché : to be flat broke>
faucher [foʃe] *vt* **1** : to mow, to cut **2** : to mow down, to knock down **3** *fam* : to swipe, to pinch
faucheuse [foʃøz] *nf* : reaper, mowing machine
faucheux [foʃø] *nm* : harvestman, daddy longlegs
faucille [fosij] *nf* : sickle
faucon [fokɔ̃] *nm* : falcon, hawk
fauconnerie [fokɔnri] *nf* : falconry

faudra [fodra] → **falloir**
faufiler [fofile] *vt* : to baste (in sewing) — **se faufiler** *vr* : to thread one's way, to slip, to sneak
faune[1] [fon] *nf* : fauna, wildlife
faune[2] *nm* : faun
faunique [fonik] *adj* **réserve faunique** *Can* : wildlife reserve
faussaire [fosɛr] *nmf* : forger, counterfeiter
fausse → **faux**
faussement [fosmɑ̃] *adv* **1** : falsely **2** : wrongfully
fausser [fose] *vt* **1** : to falsify, to distort **2** DÉFORMER : to bend out of shape
fausset [fose] *nm* **voix de fausset** : falsetto voice
fausseté [foste] *nf* **1** : falseness, falsity **2** : duplicity
faut [fo] → **falloir**
faute [fot] *nf* **1** : fault **2** : misdeed, transgression <faute professionnelle : malpractice> **3** ERREUR : mistake, error, foul (in sports) **4** MANQUE : lack, want <faute de mieux : for lack of anything better>
fauteuil [fotœj] *nm* **1** : armchair, easy chair **2** : seat (in a theater) **3** : chair, seat (in government or an organization) **4 fauteuil roulant** : wheelchair
fauteur, -trice [fotœr, -tris] *n* **fauteur de troubles** : troublemaker, agitator
fautif, -tive [fotif, -tiv] *adj* **1** : at fault **2** : faulty, inaccurate
fauve[1] [fov] *adj* : tawny, fawn
fauve[2] *nm* **1** : big cat **2** : fawn (color)
fauvette [fovɛt] *nf* : warbler
faux[1] [fo] *adv* **1** : out of tune **2** : false, wrong <ça sonne faux : that doesn't ring true>
faux[2], **fausse** [fo, fos] *adj* **1** : false, inaccurate **2** : wrong <faire un faux pas : to stumble> **3** : imitation, counterfeit, fake **4** : deceitful <un faux frère : a false friend> **5 fausse couche** : miscarriage **6 faux nom** : assumed name, alias **7 faux témoignage** : perjury
faux[3] *nm* **1** : forgery, fake **2 le faux** : the false, falsehood
faux[4] *nf* : scythe
faux-filet [fofilɛ] *nm, pl* **faux-filets** : sirloin
faux-fuyant [fofɥijɑ̃] *nm, pl* **faux-fuyants** : pretext, subterfuge
faux-monnayeur [fomɔnɛjœr] *nm, pl* **faux-monnayeurs** : counterfeiter, forger
faux-semblant [fosɑ̃blɑ̃] *nm, pl* **faux-semblants** : sham, pretense, pose
faux-sens [fosɑ̃s] *nms & pl* : mistranslation
faveur [favœr] *nf* **1** : favor **2 à la faveur de** : thanks to **3 en faveur de** : in favor of, on behalf of
favorable [favɔrabl] *adj* : favorable — **favorablement** [-rabləmɑ̃] *adv*
favori[1], **-rite** [favɔri, -rit] *adj* : favorite
favori[2], **-rite** *n* : favorite
favoris *nmpl* : sideburns
favoriser [favɔrize] *vt* **1** : to favor, to prefer **2** : to promote, to encourage
favoritisme [favɔritism] *nm* : favoritism
fax [faks] *nm* : fax
faxer [fakse] *vt* : to fax
fébrile [febril] *adj* : feverish, febrile — **fébrilement** [-brilmɑ̃] *adv*
fébrilité [febrilite] *nf* : feverishness
fécal, -cale [fekal] *adj, mpl* **fécaux** [-ko] : fecal
fèces [fɛs] *nfpl* : feces
fécond, -conde [fekɔ̃, -kɔ̃d] *adj* FERTILE : fecund, fertile — **fécondité** [fekɔ̃dite] *nf*
fécondation [fekɔ̃dasjɔ̃] *nf* **1** : fertilization **2 fécondation artificielle** : artificial insemination
féconder [fekɔ̃de] *vt* **1** : to fertilize **2** : to impregnate, to inseminate **3** : to pollinate
fécondité [fekɔ̃dite] *nf* FERTILITÉ : fecundity, fertility
fécule [fekyl] *nf* **1** : starch **2 fécule de maïs** : cornstarch
féculent[1], **-lente** [fekylɑ̃, -lɑ̃t] *adj* : starchy
féculent[2] *nm* : starchy food
fédéral, -rale [federal] *adj, mpl* **-raux** [-ro] : federal
fédéralisme [federalism] *nm* : federalism — **fédéraliste** [-ralist] *adj & nmf*
fédération [federasjɔ̃] *nf* : federation
fédérer [federe] {87} *vt* : to federate
fée [fe] *nf* : fairy
feed-back [fidbak] *nms & pl* : feedback
féerie [fe(e)ri] *nf* **1** : enchantment **2** : extravaganza, spectacular
féerique [fe(e)rik] *adj* : magical, enchanting
feignait [fɛɲɛ], **feignions** [fɛɲɔ̃], *etc.* → **feindre**
feigne [fɛɲ], *etc.* → **feindre**
feindre [fɛ̃dr] {37} *vt* : to feign — *vi* : to pretend, to dissemble
feinte [fɛ̃t] *nf* **1** : feint, fake (in sports) **2** PIÈGE : trick, ruse
feinter [fɛ̃te] *vt* : to fake, to feint at (in sports) — *vi* : to fake, to feint (in sports)
fêlé[1], **-lée** [fele] *adj* **1** : cracked **2 avoir la tête fêlée** *fam* : to be a little crazy
fêlé[2], **-lée** *n fam* : crackpot
fêler [fele] *vt* : to crack — **se fêler** *vr*
félicitations [felisitasjɔ̃] *nfpl* : congratulations
félicité [felisite] *nf* : bliss, happiness
féliciter [felisite] *vt* CONGRATULER : to congratulate — **se féliciter** *vr* ~ **de** : to be very pleased about
félin[1], **-line** [felɛ̃, -lin] *adj* : feline
félin[2] *nm* : feline, cat
félon[1], **-lonne** [felɔ̃, -lɔn] *adj* : disloyal, treacherous
félon[2], **-lonne** *n* : traitor

félonie [felɔni] *nf* : treachery
fêlure [felyr] *nf* : crack
femelle [fəmɛl] *adj & nf* : female
féminin[1], **-nine** [feminɛ̃, -nin] *adj* : feminine
féminin[2] *nm* : feminine (in grammar)
féminisme [feminism] *nm* : feminism
féministe [feminist] *adj & nmf* : feminist
féminité [feminite] *nf* : femininity
femme [fam] *nf* **1** : woman **2** ÉPOUSE : wife **3 femme au foyer** : homemaker **4 femme d'affaires** : businesswoman **5 femme de chambre** : maid, chambermaid
fémoral, -rale [femɔral] *adj, mpl* **-raux** [-ro] : femoral
fémur [femyr] *nm* : femur, thighbone
fendant, -dante [fɑ̃dɑ̃, -dɑ̃t] *adj Can* : arrogant, pretentious
fendiller [fɑ̃dije] *vt* : to crack — **se fendiller** *vr* **1** SE GERCER : to chap **2** : to crack, to craze
fendre [fɑ̃dr] {63} *vt* **1** : to split <fendre le cœur : to break one's heart> **2** : to crack — **se fendre** *vr* : to crack, to split
fenêtre [fənɛtr] *nf* : window
fenouil [fənuj] *nm* : fennel
fente [fɑ̃t] *nf* **1** : slot, slit **2** : crack
féodal, -dale [feɔdal] *adj, mpl* **-daux** [-do] : feudal — **féodalisme** [-dalism] *nm*
fer [fɛr] *nm* **1** : iron <de fer : iron, strong> **2 fer à cheval** : horseshoe **3 fer à repasser** : iron (for pressing clothes) **4 fer de lance** : spearhead **5 fers** *nmpl* : irons, shackles
fera [fəra], *etc.* → **faire**
fer–blanc [fɛrblɑ̃] *nm, pl* **fers–blancs** : tinplate
férié, -riée [ferje] *adj* **jour férié** : holiday
ferme[1] [fɛrm] *adv* : firmly, hard <tiens ferme! : hold your ground!>
ferme[2] *adj* **1** : firm **2** : steady — **fermement** [fɛrməmɑ̃] *adv*
ferme[3] *nf* **1** : farm **2** *or* **maison de ferme** : farmhouse
fermé, -mée [fɛrme] *adj* **1** : closed **2** IMPÉNÉTRABLE : inscrutable, impassive **3** EXCLUSIF : exclusive
ferment [fɛrmɑ̃] *nm* : ferment
fermentation [fɛrmɑ̃tasjɔ̃] *nf* **1** : fermentation **2** AGITATION : agitation, ferment
fermenter [fɛrmɑ̃te] *vi* : to ferment
fermer [fɛrme] *vt* **1** : to close, to shut <fermer les rideaux : to draw the curtains> <fermer à clef : to lock up> <fermer au loquet : to latch> **2** : to close down, to shut down <fermer boutique : to close up shop> **3** : to close off, to block **4** ÉTEINDRE : to turn off, to switch off **5** CLORE : to conclude — *vi* : to close — **se fermer** *vr* **1** : to close up, to fasten **2** ~ **à** : to be closed to
fermeté [fɛrməte] *nf* : firmness
fermeture [fɛrmətyr] *nf* **1** : closing, shutting **2** : latch, clasp, fastener **3 fermeture à glissière** : zipper
fermier[1], **-mière** [fɛrmje, -mjɛr] *adj* : farming, farm
fermier[2], **-mière** *n* : farmer
fermoir [fɛrmwar] *nm* : clasp
féroce [ferɔs] *adj* : ferocious — **férocement** [-rɔsmɑ̃] *adv*
férocité [ferɔsite] *nf* : ferocity, ferociousness
ferraille [feraj] *nf* **1** : scrap iron **2** : scrapheap, scrapyard **3** *fam* : small change
ferré, -rée [fɛre] *adj* **1** : ironclad, iron-tipped **2** : hobnailed **3** : shod (of a horse) **4 être ferré sur** *fam* : to be well up on, to be in the know about
ferrer [fɛre] *vt* **1** : to shoe (a horse) **2** : to tip with metal **3** : to catch (a fish on a hook)
ferreux, -reuse [ferø, -røz] *adj* : ferrous
ferrique [ferik] *adj* : ferric
ferronnerie [ferɔnri] *nf* **1** : ironworks **2** : metalwork, wrought iron
ferroviaire [ferɔvjɛr] *adj* : rail, railroad
ferry–boat [feribot] *nm, pl* **ferry–boats** : ferry
fertile [fɛrtil] *adj* **1** : fertile **2** : productive <fertile en événements : eventful>
fertilisant [fɛrtilizɑ̃] *nm* : fertilizer
fertiliser [fɛrtilize] *vt* : to fertilize — **fertilisation** [-lizasjɔ̃] *nf*
fertilité [fɛrtilite] *nf* : fertility
féru, -rue [fery] *adj* **être féru de** : to be passionately interested in
férule [feryl] *nf* **être sous la férule de qqn** : to be under s.o.'s authority
fervent[1], **-vente** [fɛrvɑ̃, -vɑ̃t] *adj* : fervent
fervent[2], **-vente** *n* : enthusiast, devotee
ferveur [fɛrvœr] *nf* : fervor
fesse [fɛs] *nf* **1** : buttock **2 fesses** *nfpl* : buttocks, bottom
fessée [fese] *nf* : spanking
fesser [fese] *vt* : to spank
festin [fɛstɛ̃] *nm* BANQUET : feast, banquet
festival [fɛstival] *nm, pl* **-vals** : festival
festivités [fɛstivite] *nfpl* : festivities
feston [fɛstɔ̃] *nm* : festoon
festonner [fɛstɔne] *vt* : to festoon
festoyer [fɛstwaje] {58} *vi* : to feast
fêtard, -tarde [fɛtar, -tard] *n fam* : merrymaker, reveler
fête [fɛt] *nf* **1** : party **2** : holiday <la fête des Mères : Mother's Day> **3** : festival <fête foraine : fair> **4 de** ~ : festive **5 faire la fête** : to have a good time
fêter [fete] *vt* : to celebrate
fétiche [feti∫] *nm* : fetish
fétide [fetid] *adj* : foul, fetid
fétu [fety] *nm* **fétu de paille** : wisp of straw

feu[1], **feue** [fø] *adj* : late <feu la reine, la feue reine : the late queen>
feu[2] *nm, pl* **feux 1** : fire <prendre feu : to catch fire> <mettre le feu à : to set fire to> <feu de camp : campfire> <feu de joie : bonfire> **2** : light <feu de circulation : traffic light> <feux de la rampe : footlights> **3** : burner (of a stove) **4** : light (for a cigarette, etc.) <avez-vous du feu? : have you got a light?> **5** : fire, shooting <faire feu : to fire> <coup de feu : shot> **6** : passion, ardor <avec feu : passionately, heatedly> **7 feux d'artifice** : fireworks
feuillage [fœjaʒ] *nm* : foliage
feuille [fœj] *nf* **1** : leaf <feuille de nénuphar : lily pad> **2** : sheet (of paper or metal), foil **3** : form <feuille d'impôts : tax return>
feuillet [fœje] *nm* : page, leaf
feuilleté[1], **-tée** [fœjte] *adj* **1** : laminated **2 pâte feuilletée** : puff pastry
feuilleté[2] *nm* : puff pastry
feuilleter [fœjte] {8} *vt* **1** : to leaf through (a book) **2** : to roll and fold (dough) **3** : to laminate (glass)
feuilleton [fœjtɔ̃] *nm* : series, serial
feuillu, -lue [fœjy] *adj* **1** : leafy **2** : broad-leaved
feutre [føtr] *nm* **1** : felt **2** → **stylo-feutre**
feutré, -trée [føtre] *adj* **1** : felt, feltlike **2** : muffled
fève [fɛv] *nf* : broad bean
février [fevrije] *nm* : February
fez [fɛz] *nm* : fez
fi [fi] *interj* **faire fi de** : to scorn, to turn up one's nose at
fiable [fjabl] *adj* : reliable — **fiabilité** [fjabilite] *nf*
fiacre [fjakr] *nm* : (horse-drawn) carriage, hackney
fiançailles [fijɑ̃saj] *nfpl* : engagement
fiancé, -cée [fijɑ̃se] *n* : fiancé *m*, fiancée *f*
fiancer [fijɑ̃se] {6} *v* **se fiancer** *vr* : to get engaged
fiasco [fjasko] *nm* : fiasco
fibre [fibr] *nf* **1** : fiber **2 fibre de verre** : fiberglass **3 fibres alimentaires** : roughage
fibreux, -breuse [fibrø, -brøz] *adj* : fibrous
ficeler [fisle] {8} *vt* : to tie up
ficelle [fisɛl] *nf* **1** : string, twine **2** : trick <les ficelles du métier : the tricks of the trade>
fiche [fiʃ] *nf* **1** : index card, slip (of paper) **2** FORMULAIRE : form **3** : (electric) plug
ficher [fiʃe] *vt* **1** ENFONCER : to drive in, to stick **2** : to put on file **3** *fam* : to do <qu'est-ce qu'elle fiche? : what's she doing?> **4** *fam* : to put, to push <fiche-le dehors! : kick him out!> **5** *fam* : to give <ficher une claque à qqn : to give s.o. a slap> — **se ficher** *vr* **1** ~ **dans** : to stick into **2** ~ **de** *fam* : to make fun of **3 je m'en fiche** *fam* : I don't give a damn
fichier [fiʃje] *nm* **1** : file, index **2** : index card box, filing cabinet
fichu[1] [fiʃy] *pp* → **ficher 3, 4, 5**
fichu[2], **-chue** *adj fam* **1** : rotten, awful <quelle fichue température! : what rotten weather!> **2** : done for, sunk **3** ~ **de** : capable of
fichu[3] *nm* : scarf, shawl
fichument [fiʃymɑ̃] *adv Can fam* : really, extremely <fichument content : really pleased>
fictif, -tive [fiktif, -tiv] *adj* : fictional, fictitious — **fictivement** [-tivmɑ̃] *adv*
fiction [fiksjɔ̃] *nf* : fiction
fidèle[1] [fidɛl] *adj* **1** LOYAL : loyal **2** CONSTANT : faithful **3** : true, accurate — **fidèlement** [-dɛlmɑ̃] *adv*
fidèle[2] *nmf* **1** : believer <les fidèles : the faithful> **2** : supporter, follower **3** : regular (customer)
fidélité [fidelite] *nf* : fidelity, faithfulness
fidjien[1], **-jienne** [fidʒjɛ̃, -dʒjɛn] *adj* : Fijian
fidjien[2] *nm* : Fijian (language)
Fidjien, -jienne *n* : Fijian
fiduciaire[1] [fidysjɛr] *adj* : fiduciary
fiduciaire[2] *nmf* : trustee
fiducie [fidysi] *nf* : trust <société de fiducie : trust company>
fief [fjɛf] *nm* **1** : fief **2** : stronghold
fiel [fjɛl] *nm* **1** : gall, bile **2** : bitterness, acrimony
fier[1] [fje] *v* **se fier** *vr* ~ **à** : to trust, to rely on
fier[2], **fière** [fjɛr] *adj* : proud — **fièrement** [fjɛrmɑ̃] *adv*
fierté [fjɛrte] *nf* : pride
fièvre [fjɛvr] *nf* : fever <avoir de la fièvre : to have a high fever> <fièvre jaune : yellow fever>
fiévreux, -vreuse [fjevrø, -vrøz] *adj* : feverish — **fiévreusement** [-vrøzmɑ̃] *adv*
fifre [fifr] *nm* : fife
figer [fiʒe] {17} *vt* **1** : to congeal, to coagulate **2** : to freeze, to paralyze <être figé sur place : to be rooted to the spot> — **se figer** *vr* **1** : to congeal **2** S'IMMOBILISER : to freeze <son sang se figea : his blood froze>
fignoler [fiɲɔle] *vt* : to refine, to put the finishing touch upon
figue [fig] *nf* : fig
figuier [figje] *nm* : fig tree
figurant, -rante [figyrɑ̃, -rɑ̃t] *n* COMPARSE : extra, bit player
figuratif, -tive [figyratif, -tiv] *adj* : figurative, representational
figuration [figyrasjɔ̃] *nf* **faire de la figuration** : to work as an extra
figurativement [figyrativmɑ̃] *adv* : figuratively
figure [figyr] *nf* **1** VISAGE : face **2** : appearance <faire bonne figure : to put

on a good show> **3** PERSONNAGE : figure, person **4** : illustration, figure (in a text) **5** : expression <figure de rhétorique : figure of speech>

figuré, -rée [figyre] *adj* : figurative

figurer [figyre] *vi* : to appear — *vt* REPRÉSENTER : to represent — **se figurer** *vr* : to imagine

figurine [figyrin] *nf* : figurine

fil [fil] *nm* **1** : thread, yarn <fil à coudre : sewing thread> <fil dentaire : dental floss> **2** : wire, cable <fil électrique : electric wire> <fil à pêche : fishing line> **3** : current, stream <le fil des événements : the chain of events> <au fil du temps : as time goes by> **4 coup de fil** *fam* : phone call

filament [filamɑ̃] *nm* : filament

filandreux, -dreuse [filɑ̃drø, -drøz] *adj* **1** : stringy **2** : rambling

filant, -lante [filɑ̃, -lɑ̃t] *adj* **1** : runny (in cooking) **2** → **étoile**

filature [filatyr] *nf* **1** FABRIQUE : mill **2** : spinning **3 prendre en filature** : to shadow, to tail

file [fil] *nf* **1** : line, file, row <prendre la file : to get in line> <file indienne : single file> **2** : lane (of a paved road) **3 en ~** *or* **à la file** : one after another

filée [file] *nf Can fam* : line, queue

filer [file] *vt* **1** : to spin (yarn) **2** : to shadow, to tail **3** *fam* : to give <je lui ai filé un billet de 100 francs : I slipped him a 100 franc note> — *vi* **1** : to trickle, to run **2** : to run (of stockings) **3** *fam* : to dash off, to rush away **4** *fam* : to fly by, to slip away <le temps filait : time was flying> **5 filer bien** *Can fam* : to be doing fine

filet [file] *nm* **1** : net **2** : fillet **3** : trickle (of water)

filial, -liale [filjal] *adj, mpl* **-liaux** [-ljo] : filial

filiale *nf* : subsidiary (company)

filiation [filjasjɔ̃] *nf* **1** : line of descent **2** : relationship (of ideas, etc.)

filière [filjɛr] *nf* **1** : (official) channels *pl* **2** : field, line (of study or work) **3** : network, ring (of criminals)

filigrane [filigran] *nm* **1** : watermark **2** : filigree **3 lire en filigrane** : to read between the lines

fille [fij] *nf* **1** : girl **2** : daughter

fillette [fijɛt] *nf* : little girl

filleul, -leule [fijœl] *n* : godchild, godson *m*, goddaughter *f*

film [film] *nm* **1** : film, movie <film d'animation : cartoon> <film (pour projection) fixe : filmstrip> **2** PELLICULE : movie film **3** : film coating **4** : course, sequence (of events, etc.)

filmer [filme] *vt* : to film

filon [filɔ̃] *nm* **1** : vein, lode **2 trouver le filon** *fam* : to strike it rich

filou [filu] *nm* : crook, swindler

fils [fis] *nm* : son

filtrage [filtraʒ] *nm* **1** : filtering **2** : screening

filtration [filtrasjɔ̃] *nf* : filtration, filtering

filtre [filtr] *nm* : filter

filtrer [filtre] *vt* **1** : to filter **2** : to screen — *vi* : to filter through

fin[1] [fɛ̃] *adv* **1** : finely, thinly, sharply **2 être fin prêt** : to be ready, to be all set

fin[2], **fine** *adj* **1** : fine, delicate <cheveux fins : fine hair> **2** : thin <tranches fines : thin slices> **3** : excellent, first-rate **4** : sharp, keen <avoir le nez fin : to have a keen sense of smell> **5** *Can* : nice **6** : ultimate, very <au fin fond : at the very bottom>

fin[3] *nf* **1** : end <mettre fin à : to put an end to> <prendre fin : to come to an end> <sans fin : endless, endlessly> **2** MORT : death, end <une fin prématurée : an untimely death> **3** BUT : aim, purpose, end **4 à la fin** : eventually, in the end **5 à toutes fins utiles** : for all practical purposes

final, -nale [final] *adj, mpl* **finals** *or* **finaux** [fino] : final, last

finale[1] *nm* : finale

finale[2] *nf* : final, finals *pl* (in sports)

finalement [finalmɑ̃] *adv* **1** : finally, at last **2** : after all, in fact

finaliser [finalize] *vt* : to finalize

finaliste [finalist] *nmf* : finalist

finance [finɑ̃s] *nf* **1** : finance **2 finances** *nfpl* : finances, resources

financement [finɑ̃smɑ̃] *nm* : financing

financer [finɑ̃se] {6} *vt* : to finance

financier[1], **-cière** [finɑ̃sje,-sjɛr] *adj* : financial — **financièrement** [-sjɛrmɑ̃] *adv*

financier[2] *nm* : financier

finasser [finase] *vi* : to scheme, to wheel and deal

finaud, -naude [fino, -nod] *adj* : cunning, crafty

finement [finmɑ̃] *adv* **1** : finely **2** : shrewdly, subtly **3** : precisely

finesse [finɛs] *nf* **1** : finesse, delicacy **2** : fineness, thinness **3** : subtlety, shrewdness

fini[1], **-nie** [fini] *adj* **1** : finished, ended, complete **2** : finite

fini[2] *nm Can* : finish (of a surface)

finir [finir] *vt* **1** : to finish, to end **2** : to use up — *vi* **1** : to finish, to come to an end **2 à n'en plus finir** : endless, never-ending **3 en finir avec** : to be done with **4 finir par faire** : to end up doing

finition [finisjɔ̃] *nf* : finish, finishing touches

finlandais[1], **-daise** [fɛ̃lɑ̃dɛ, -dɛz] *adj* : Finnish

finlandais[2] *nm* : Finnish (language)

Finlandais, -daise *n* : Finn

finnois[1], **-noise** [finwa, -nwaz] *adj* : Finnish

finnois[2] *nm* : Finnish (language)

fiole [fjɔl] *nf* : vial
fiord → fjord
fioriture [fjɔrityr] *nf* : ornament, embellishment
fioul [fjul] *nm* : fuel oil
firmament [firmamɑ̃] *nm* : firmament, heavens *pl*
firme [firm] *nf* : firm, company
fisc [fisk] *nm* : tax collection agency
fiscal, -cale [fiskal] *adj, mpl* **fiscaux** [fisko] : fiscal <fraude fiscale : tax evasion> **— fiscalement** [-kalmɑ̃] *adv*
fiscaliser [fiskalize] *vt* : to subject to tax
fiscalité [fiskalite] *nf* : tax system
fission [fisjɔ̃] *nf* : fission
fissure [fisyr] *nf* : fissure, crack
fiston [fistɔ̃] *nm fam* : son, youngster
fixatif [fiksatif] *nm* **1** : fixative **2** *Can* : hair spray
fixation [fiksasjɔ̃] *nf* **1** : fixing, fastening, attachment **2** : fixation (in psychology) **3** : ski binding
fixe [fiks] *adj* **1** IMMOBILE : fixed **2** : permanent, steady **3** : regular <à heure fixe : at a set time>
fixement [fiksmɑ̃] *adv* : fixedly
fixer [fikse] *vt* **1** : to fix, to fasten **2** DÉTERMINER : to determine, to set **3** ÉTABLIR : to establish **4** : to focus <fixer son regard sur : to fix one's gaze on> **5** : to stare at **— se fixer** *vr* **1** : to settle down **2** : to decide (on something), to set (for) oneself
fjord *or* **fiord** [fjɔrd] *nm* : fjord
flaccidité [flaksidite] *nf* : flaccidity, flabbiness
flacon [flakɔ̃] *nm* : flask, small bottle
flagellation [flaʒɛlasjɔ̃] *nf* : flogging, whipping
flageller [flaʒɛle] *vt* FOUETTER : to flog, to whip **— se flageller** *vr*
flageoler [flaʒɔle] *vi* : to feel unsteady, to tremble <flageoler sur ses jambes : to be quaking in one's boots>
flageolet [flaʒɔlɛ] *nm* : flageolet, dwarf kidney bean
flagorneur, -neuse [flagɔrnœr, -nøz] *n* : toady, flatterer
flagrant [flagrɑ̃] *adj* **1** : flagrant, blatant **2 en flagrant délit** : red-handed
flair [flɛr] *nm* **1** ODORAT : sense of smell, nose **2** INTUITION : intuition
flairer [flɛre] *vt* **1** : to sniff, to smell **2** : to sniff out, to detect
flamand[1], **-mande** [flamɑ̃, -mɑ̃d] *adj* : Flemish
flamand[2] *nm* : Flemish (language)
Flamand, -mande *n* **1** : Fleming **2 les Flamands** : the Flemish
flamant [flamɑ̃] *nm* : flamingo
flambant, -bante [flɑ̃bɑ̃, -bɑ̃t] *adj* **1** : flaming **2 flambant neuf** : brand-new
flambeau [flɑ̃bo] *nm, pl* **flambeaux 1** TORCHE : torch **2** CHANDELIER : candlestick
flambée [flɑ̃be] *nf* **1** : blaze, fire **2** : outburst, explosion (of anger, etc.) **3** : sudden increase <une flambée des prix : skyrocketing prices>
flamber [flɑ̃be] *vt* **1** : to singe, to char **2** : to sterilize **— *vi*** **1** : to flame, to burn **2** : to soar, to skyrocket
flamboiement [flɑ̃bwamɑ̃] *nm* : blaze, flash
flamboyant, -boyante [flɑ̃bwajɑ̃, -bwajɑ̃t] *adj* **1** : blazing **2** : flamboyant (in architecture)
flamboyer [flɑ̃bwaje] {58} *vi* : to blaze, to flash
flamme [flam] *nf* **1** : flame <en flammes : in flames> **2** : passion, fervor **3** : pennant (of a ship)
flammèche [flamɛʃ] *nf* : spark
flan [flɑ̃] *nm* : baked custard
flanc [flɑ̃] *nm* : side, flank
flancher [flɑ̃ʃe] *vi fam* **1** : to flinch, to waver **2** : to fail, to give out
flanelle [flanɛl] *nf* : flannel
flanellette [flanɛlɛt] *nf Can* : brushed cotton, cotton flannel
flâner [flane] *vi* **1** SE BALADER : to stroll **2** PARESSER : to loaf around, to idle
flâneur, -neuse [flanœr, -nøz] *n* : idler, loiterer
flanquer [flɑ̃ke] *vt* **1** : to flank **2** *fam* : to fling **3** *fam* : to give <flanquer la frousse à qqn : to give s.o. a fright> <flanquer un coup de poing : to land a blow>
flanqueur [flɑ̃kœr] *nm Can* : wing (in sports)
flaque [flak] *nf* : puddle, pool
flash [flaʃ] *nm, pl* **flashes 1** : flash (in photography) **2** : news flash
flasque[1] [flask] *adj* : flabby, limp
flasque[2] *nf* FLACON : flask
flatter [flate] *vt* **1** : to flatter <flatter bassement qqn : to pander to s.o.> **2** : to please, to delight **3** : to pat, to stroke (an animal) **— se flatter** *vr* : to pride oneself
flatterie [flatri] *nf* : flattery
flatteur[1], **-teuse** [flatœr, -tøz] *adj* : flattering
flatteur[2], **-teuse** *n* : flatterer
flatulence [flatylɑ̃s] *nf* : flatulence
flatulent, -lente [flatylɑ̃, -lɑ̃t] *adj* : flatulent
fléau [fleo] *nm, pl* **fléaux 1** : calamity, scourge **2** : flail (in agriculture)
flèche [flɛʃ] *nf* **1** : arrow <monter en flèche : to shoot up, to soar> **2** : spire
fléchette [fleʃɛt] *nf* **1** : dart **2 fléchettes** *nfpl* : darts (game)
fléchir [fleʃir] *vt* **1** COURBER : to bend, to flex **2** : to sway, to move **— *vi*** **1** : to bend, to give way **2** : to diminish, to fall off **3** : to yield, to relent
fléchissement [fleʃismɑ̃] *nm* **1** : weakening, fall, drop **2** : yielding, bending
flegmatique [flɛgmatik] *adj* : phlegmatic

flegme [flɛgm] *nm* : composure <avec flegme : coolly, phlegmatically>
flemme [flɛm] *nf France fam* : laziness
flet [flɛt] *nm* : flounder
flétan [fletɑ̃] *nm* : halibut
flétrir [fletrir] *vt* **1** : to wither, to fade **2** : to blacken (a reputation, etc.), to condemn — **se flétrir** *vr* : to wither, to fade
fleur [flœr] *nf* **1** : flower, blossom **2 fleur bleue** : sentimental **3 faire une fleur à qqn** : to do s.o. a favor **4 fleur de lis** *or* **fleur de lys** : fleur-de-lis
fleurdelisé[1] [flœrdəlize] *adj* : adorned with the fleur-de-lis
fleurdelisé[2] *nm* : the provincial flag of Quebec
fleurer [flœre] *vt* : to smell of
fleuret [flœrɛ] *nm* : foil (in fencing)
fleuri, -rie [flœri] *adj* **1** : flowered, flowery **2** : florid, ruddy **3** : ornate
fleurir [flœrir] *vt* : to decorate with flowers — *vi* **1** : to flower, to blossom **2** : to flourish
fleuriste [flœrist] *nmf* : florist
fleuron [flœrɔ̃] *nm* **1** : floret **2** : jewel <le fleuron de ma collection : the jewel of my collection>
fleuve [flœv] *nm* : river
flexibilité [flɛksibilite] *nf* : flexibility
flexible [flɛksibl] *adj* : flexible
flexion [flɛksjɔ̃] *nf* **1** : bending, flexing **2** : inflection (in grammar)
flic [flik] *nm fam* : cop
flirt [flœrt] *nm* : flirtation, fling
flirter [flœrte] *vi* : to flirt
flo [flo] → **flot**
flocon [flɔkɔ̃] *nm* : flake <flocon de neige : snowflake> <flocons de maïs : cornflakes>
flopée [flɔpe] *nf fam* **une flopée de** : a whole bunch of
floraison [flɔrɛzɔ̃] *nf* : flowering, blossoming
floral, -rale [flɔral] *adj, mpl* **floraux** [flɔro] : floral
flore [flɔr] *nf* : flora
florilège [flɔrilɛʒ] *nm* : anthology
florissant, -sante [flɔrisɑ̃, -sɑ̃t] *adj* : flourishing
flot [flo] *nm* **1** : tide **2** : flood, stream, torrent <entrer à flots : to stream in> **3 à ~** : afloat <être à flot : to be on an even keel> **4** *or* **flo** *Can* : young boy, kid **5 flots** *nmpl* : waves (in the ocean)
flottabilité [flɔtabilite] *nf* : buoyancy
flottable [flɔtabl] *adj* : buoyant
flottaison [flɔtɛzɔ̃] *nf* **1** : floating **2 ligne de flottaison** : waterline
flottant, -tante [flɔtɑ̃, -tɑ̃t] *adj* **1** : floating **2** : flowing, loose **3** : indecisive
flotte [flɔt] *nf* **1** : fleet **2** *fam* : water, rain
flottement [flɔtmɑ̃] *nm* **1** INDÉCISION : hesitation, indecision **2** : fluttering, flapping **3** : fluctuation (in finance)
flotter [flɔte] *vi* **1** : to float **2** : to fly, to flutter, to drift **3** : to fluctuate
flotteur [flɔtœr] *nm* : float
flottille [flɔtij] *nf* : flotilla
flou[1], **floue** [flu] *adj* **1** : blurred, fuzzy **2** : loose, soft **3** : vague, hazy (of ideas, etc.)
flou[2] *nm* **1** IMPRÉCISION : vagueness **2** : fuzziness (of focus, outline, etc.)
fluctuer [flyktɥe] *vi* : to fluctuate — **fluctuation** [flyktɥasjɔ̃] *nf*
fluet, fluette [flyɛ, flyɛt] *adj* GRÊLE : thin, slender
fluide[1] [flɥid] *adj* **1** : fluid **2** : smooth, flowing freely
fluide[2] *nm* **1** : fluid **2** : (occult) force, psychic powers *pl*
fluidité [flɥidite] *nf* **1** : fluidity, (free) flow **2** : flexibility
fluor [flyɔr] *nm* : fluorine
fluoration [flyɔrasjɔ̃] *nf* : fluoridation
fluoré, -rée [flyɔre] *adj* : fluoridated
fluorescent, -cente [flyɔresɑ̃, -sɑ̃t] *adj* : fluorescent — **fluorescence** [-sɑ̃s] *nf*
fluorure [flyɔryr] *nm* : fluoride
flûte[1] [flyt] *nf* **1** : flute <flûte à bec : recorder> <petite flûte : piccolo> **2** : baguette **3** : tall champagne glass
flûte[2] *interj* **flûte alors**! : fiddlesticks!, nonsense!
flûtiste [flytist] *nmf* : flutist
fluvial, -viale [flyvjal] *adj, mpl* **-viaux** [-vjo] : river <eau fluviale : river water>
flux [fly] *nm* **1** : flow **2** FLOT : flood, influx <un flux d'appels : a flood of calls> **3** : flood tide <le flux et reflux : the ebb and flow> **4** : flux (in medicine and physics)
foc [fɔk] *nm* : jib
focal, -cale [fɔkal] *adj* : focal
focaliser [fɔkalize] *vt* : to focus
fœtal, -tale [fetal] *adj, mpl* **fœtaux** [feto] : fetal
fœtus [fetys] *nms & pl* : fetus
foi [fwa] *nf* **1** : faith **2** : trust, confidence <digne de foi : reliable, trustworthy> **3 bonne foi** : sincerity, honesty **4 mauvaise foi** : dishonesty, insincerity **5 faire foi de** : to be proof of **6 ma foi** ! : well! **7 sous la foi du serment** : under oath
foie [fwa] *nm* **1** : liver <crise de foie : indigestion> **2** : liver (in cooking) <foies de volaille : chicken livers>
foin [fwɛ̃] *nm* **1** : hay **2** *Can fam* : money <avoir du foin : to be well off> **3** → **rhume**
foire [fwar] *nf* : fair, market
fois [fwa] *nf* **1** : time <cette fois-ci : this time> <à chaque fois : each time> **2 il était une fois** : once upon a time **3 maintes et maintes fois** : time and time again **4 une fois pour toutes** : once and for all
foison [fwazɔ̃] **à ~** : in abundance, aplenty
foisonnant, -nante [fwazɔnɑ̃, -nɑ̃t] *adj* : abundant, plentiful

foisonnement [fwazɔnmɑ̃] *nm* **1** : profusion, abundance **2** : swelling, expansion
foisonner [fwazɔne] *vi* **1** ABONDER : to abound **2** : to expand
fol → fou
folâtre [fɔlatr] *adj* : playful, frolicsome
folâtrer [fɔlatre] *vi* : to frolic, to gambol
folichon, -chonne [fɔliʃɔ̃, -ʃɔn] *adj* **ça n'est pas folichon** : it's not much fun
folie [fɔli] *nf* **1** : craziness, madness <la folie des grandeurs : delusions of grandeur> **2** : folly **3 à la folie** : madly, passionately <aimer à la folie : to be madly in love with>
folio [fɔljo] *nm* : folio
folk [fɔlk] *or* **folksong** [fɔlksɔ̃g] *nm* : folk music
folklore [fɔlklɔr] *nm* : folklore
folklorique [fɔlklɔrik] *adj* **1** : folk <danse folklorique : folk dancing> **2** *fam* : bizarre, eccentric
folle → fou
follement [fɔlmɑ̃] *adv* : madly, wildly
follicule [fɔlikyl] *nm* : follicle
fomenter [fɔmɑ̃te] *vt* : to foment, to stir up
foncé, -cée [fɔ̃se] *adj* : dark <un bleu foncé : a dark blue>
foncer [fɔ̃se] {6} *vt* ASSOMBRIR : to darken — *vi* **1** : to rush, to charge **2** *fam* : to tear along **3** S'ASSOMBRIR : to darken
fonceur[1], **-ceuse** [fɔ̃sœr, -søz] *adj fam* : dynamic, driven
fonceur[2], **-ceuse** *n fam* : dynamic person, go-getter
foncier, -cière [fɔ̃sje, -sjɛr] *adj* **1** : land <propriétaire foncier : landowner> <impôt foncier : property tax> **2** INNÉ : innate, inherent
foncièrement [fɔ̃sjɛrmɑ̃] *adv* : fundamentally, inherently
fonction [fɔ̃ksjɔ̃] *nf* **1** : function **2** : job, duties *pl*, position <faire fonction de : to serve as> **3 en fonction de** : according to **4 fonction publique** : civil service
fonctionnaire [fɔ̃ksjɔnɛr] *nmf* : official, civil servant
fonctionnel, -nelle [fɔ̃ksjɔnɛl] *adj* : functional — **fonctionnellement** [-nɛlmɑ̃] *adv*
fonctionnement [fɔ̃ksjɔnmɑ̃] *nm* : functioning, working <bon fonctionnement : good working order>
fonctionner [fɔ̃ksjɔne] *vi* : to function, to work
fond [fɔ̃] *nm* **1** : bottom, back <au fond de : at the bottom of, at the back of, in the depths of> <sans fond : bottomless> **2** : root, heart, essence **3** : background <sur fond bleu : on a blue background> <fond sonore : background music> **4 à ~** : completely, deeply **5 au fond** : in fact, basically **6 de fond en comble** : from top to bottom, thoroughly **7 fond de teint** : foundation (makeup)
fondamental, -tale [fɔ̃damɑ̃tal] *adj, mpl* **-taux** [-to] : fundamental — **fondamentalement** [-talmɑ̃] *adv*
fondamentalisme [fɔ̃damɑ̃talism] *nm* : fundamentalism
fondateur, -trice [fɔ̃datœr, -tris] *n* : founder
fondation [fɔ̃dasjɔ̃] *nf* **1** : founding, establishment **2** : foundation, endowment **3 fondations** *nfpl* : foundation(s) (in construction)
fondé, -dée [fɔ̃de] *adj* : well-founded, justified <mal fondé : groundless>
fondement [fɔ̃dmɑ̃] *nm* **1** : foundation, basis <sans fondement : unfounded, groundless> **2** *fam* : bottom, buttocks
fonder [fɔ̃de] *vt* **1** : to found, to establish **2** : to base — **se fonder** *vr* **~ sur** : to be based on
fonderie [fɔ̃dri] *nf* : foundry
fondre [fɔ̃dr] {63} *vt* **1** : to melt, to smelt **2** : to dissolve <fondre en larmes : to dissolve into tears> **3** : to cast (a statue, etc.) **4** : to merge, to blend — *vi* **1** : to melt **2** : to dissolve **3 ~ sur** : to swoop down on — **se fondre** *vr* : to merge, to blend
fondrière [fɔ̃drijɛr] *nf* : pothole
fonds [fɔ̃] *nms & pl* **1** : collection (in a museum, etc.) **2** : fund <Fonds Monétaire International : International Monetary Fund> **3** *or* **fonds de commerce** : business **4 fonds** *nmpl* : funds, capital
fondue [fɔ̃dy] *nf* : fondue
fongicide[1] [fɔ̃ʒisid] *adj* : fungicidal
fongicide[2] *nm* : fungicide
fontaine [fɔ̃tɛn] *nf* **1** : fountain **2** SOURCE : spring
fonte [fɔ̃t] *nf* **1** : melting, smelting **2** : casting **3** : cast iron **4** : font (in printing)
fonts [fɔ̃] *nmpl* **fonts baptismaux** : baptismal font
foot [fut] *nm fam* : soccer
football [futbol] *nm* **1** : soccer **2** *Can* : football **3 football américain** : football
footballeur, -leuse [futbolœr, -løz] *n* : soccer player, football player
footing [futiŋ] *nm France* : jogging
for [fɔr] *nm* **en son for intérieur** : in one's heart of hearts, inwardly
forage [fɔraʒ] *nm* : drilling, boring
forain, -raine [fɔrɛ̃, -rɛn] *adj* : fairground <marchand forain : fairground merchant>
forban [fɔrbɑ̃] *nm* **1** PIRATE : pirate, freebooter **2** ESCROC : crook
forçat [fɔrsa] *nm* **1** : convict, galley slave **2 travail de forçat** : drudgery, hard work
force [fɔrs] *nf* **1** : strength <reprendre des forces : to regain one's strength> <force de caractère : strength of

character> <force d'âme : fortitude> <force vitale : lifeblood> **2** : force <entrer de force dans : to force one's way into> <la force de l'habitude : the force of habit> **3** : force (in physics) <force électromagnétique : electromagnetic force> **4** : (military or security) force <les forces armées : the armed forces> <les forces de l'ordre : the police> **5 à force de** : as a result of, by dint of **6 à toute force** : at all costs **7 par la force des choses** : of necessity, inevitably

forcé, -cée [fɔrse] *adj* **1** : forced **2** : inevitable

forcément [fɔrsemɑ̃] *adv* : necessarily, inevitably

forcené[1], **-née** [fɔrsəne] *adj* : frantic, frenzied

forcené[2] *nm* : maniac

forceps [fɔrseps] *nms & pl* : forceps *pl*

forcer [fɔrse] {6} *vt* **1** : to force, to compel **2** : to force open, to force through **3** : to strain, to overtax — *vi* : to strain, to overdo it — **se forcer** *vr* : to force oneself, to make an effort

forclusion [fɔrklyzjɔ̃] *nf* : foreclosure

forer [fɔre] *vt* : to drill, to bore

foresterie [fɔrestəri] *nf* : forestry

forestier[1], **-tière** [fɔrestje, -tjɛr] *adj* : forest, forested

forestier[2], **-tière** *n* : forester

foret [fɔre] *nm* : (manual) drill

forêt [fɔre] *nf* : forest

foreuse [fɔrøz] *nf* : drill

forfaire [fɔrfɛr] {44} *vi* ~ **à** : to fail in, to be false to

forfait [fɔrfɛ] *nm* **1** : fixed price, package deal **2** : default <déclarer forfait : to withdraw, to give up> **3** : heinous crime

forfaitaire [fɔrfɛtɛr] *adj* : inclusive

forfanterie [fɔrfɑ̃tri] *nf* : bragging, boastfulness

forge [fɔrʒ] *nf* : forge

forgé, -gée [fɔrʒe] *adj* **1** : fabricated, made up **2 fer forgé** : wrought iron

forger [fɔrʒe] {16} *vt* **1** : to forge **2** : to form, to build (character, etc.) **3** : to concoct, to invent <c'est forgé de toutes pièces : it's a total fabrication>

forgeron [fɔrʒərɔ̃] *nm* : blacksmith

formaldéhyde [fɔrmaldeid] *nm* : formaldehyde

formaliser [fɔrmalize] *vt* : to formalize — **se formaliser** *vr* : to take offense

formalisme [fɔrmalism] *nm* : formalism

formalité [fɔrmalite] *nf* : formality

format [fɔrma] *nm* : format

formater [fɔrmate] *vt* : to format (a computer disk)

formateur[1], **-trice** [fɔrmatœr, -tris] *adj* : formative

formateur[2], **-trice** *n* : trainer

formation [fɔrmasjɔ̃] *nf* **1** : formation **2** : education, training <formation professionnelle : vocational training>

forme [fɔrm] *nf* **1** : form, shape <prendre forme : to take shape> <sans forme : formless, shapeless> **2** : method, way <forme de pensée : way of thinking> **3** : form, procedure <pour la forme : as a matter of form> **4** : form, fitness <être en pleine forme : to be in great shape> **5** : last (of shoes) **6 formes** *nfpl* : figure (of the human body), lines (of an object) **7 formes** *nfpl* : proprieties, conventions <y mettre les formes : to be tactful>

formel, -melle [fɔrmɛl] *adj* **1** : formal **2** CATÉGORIQUE : definitive, categorical, express — **formellement** [-mɛlmɑ̃] *adv*

former [fɔrme] *vt* **1** : to form, to shape **2** : to develop **3** : to constitute **4** : to train, to educate — **se former** *vr*

formidable [fɔrmidabl] *adj* **1** ÉNORME : tremendous <un formidable défi : a tremendous challenge> **2** *fam* : great, terrific **3** *fam* : incredible — **formidablement** [-dabləmɑ̃] *adv*

formulaire [fɔrmylɛr] *nm* : form, questionnaire

formulation [fɔrmylasjɔ̃] *nf* : formulation

formule [fɔrmyl] *nf* **1** : formula **2** : expression, phrase <formule de politesse : polite phrase, closing (of a letter)> **3** : method, way, option <formule de paiement : method of payment> **4** FORMULAIRE : (printed) form

formuler [fɔrmyle] *vt* **1** : to formulate, to express **2** : to draw up, to write out

fornication [fɔrnikasjɔ̃] *nf* : fornication

forniquer [fɔrnike] *vi* : to fornicate

fort[1] [fɔr] *adv* **1** TRÈS : very, extremely <vous savez fort bien : you know full well> **2** BEAUCOUP : greatly, very much <j'en doute fort : I doubt it very much> **3** : strongly, loudly, hard <frapper fort : to strike hard>

fort[2], **forte** [fɔr, fɔrt] *adj* **1** : strong, powerful <fort comme un bœuf : strong as an ox> <café fort : strong coffee> <c'est plus fort que moi : I can't help it> **2** : intense, loud, bright **3** : large, heavy, stout **4** : able, gifted <être fort de : to be good at> **5 c'est un peu fort!** *fam* : that's a bit much!

fort[3] *nm* **1** : strength, strong point **2** : strong person **3** : fort, fortress **4 au fort de** : at the height of, in the midst of, in the depths of

fortement [fɔrtəmɑ̃] *adv* : strongly, deeply, intensely

forteresse [fɔrtəres] *nf* : fortress

fortification [fɔrtifikasjɔ̃] *nf* : fortification

fortifier [fɔrtifje] {96} *vt* : to fortify, to strengthen — **se fortifier** *vr*

fortuit, -tuite [fɔrtɥi, -tɥit] *adj* : fortuitous, chance
fortuitement [fɔrtɥitmɑ̃] *adv* : fortuitously, by chance
fortune [fɔrtyn] *nf* **1** : fortune <faire fortune : to make one's fortune> **2** CHANCE : chance, luck **3 de ~** : makeshift
fortuné, -née [fɔrtyne] *adj* **1** : fortunate **2** RICHE : wealthy
forum [fɔrɔm] *nm* **1** : forum **2** : newsgroup (on the Internet)
fosse [fos] *nf* **1** : pit <fosse septique : septic tank> <fosse d'aisances : cesspool> <fosse d'orchestre : orchestra pit> **2** TOMBE : grave
fossé [fose] *nm* **1** : ditch, trench **2** : gulf, gap <fossé de générations : generation gap>
fossette [fosɛt] *nf* : dimple
fossile[1] [fɔsil] *adj* : fossil, fossilized
fossile[2] *nm* : fossil
fossiliser [fɔsilize] *vt* : to fossilize — **se fossiliser** *vr*
fossoyeur [fɔswajœr] *nm* : gravedigger
fou[1] [fu] (**fol** [fɔl] *before a vowel or mute h*), **folle** [fɔl] *adj* **1** : crazy, insane <devenir fou : to go mad> <il est fou d'elle : he's crazy about her> **2** : silly, ridiculous **3** : tremendous, extreme <avoir un talent fou : to be extremely talented> **4 ~ de** : crazy with <fou de joie : jumping for joy> <fou de jalousie : green with envy>
fou[2], **folle** *n* **1** : crazy person, lunatic **2 comme un fou** *fam* : like crazy
fou[3] *nm* **1** : bishop (in chess) **2** : fool, jester **3 fou de Bassan** : gannet
foudre [fudr] *nf* **1** : lightning **2 foudres** *nfpl* : wrath
foudroyant, foudroyante [fudrwajɑ̃, fudrwajɑ̃t] *adj* **1** : overwhelming, crushing **2** : violent (of an illness) <une mort foudroyante : a sudden death>
foudroyer [fudrwaje] {58} *vt* : to strike down
fouet [fwɛ] *nm* **1** : whip **2** : whisk <fouet à œufs : egg whisk> **3 de plein fouet** : full-force, head-on
fouetter [fwete] *vt* **1** : to whip, to lash **2** : to whisk <crème fouettée : whipped cream>
fougère [fuʒɛr] *nf* : fern, bracken
fougue [fug] *nf* : ardor, spirit, passion
fougueusement [fugøzmɑ̃] *adv* : with spirit, ardently
fougueux, -geuse [fugø, -gøz] *adj* : ardent, spirited
fouille [fuj] *nf* **1** : digging **2** : search **3 fouilles** *nfpl* : excavations, (archaeological) dig
fouiller [fuje] *vt* **1** : to search, to go through (baggage, pockets, etc.) **2** : to excavate, to dig — *vi* **1** : to dig, to root (of a pig) **2 ~ dans** : to rummage through, to delve into
fouillis [fuji] *nm* : jumble, mess
fouiner [fwine] *vi fam* : to be nosy, to snoop around
fouineur[1], **-neuse** [fwinœr, -nøz] *adj* : inquisitive, nosy
fouineur[2], **-neuse** *n* **1** : busybody **2** : bargain hunter
fouir [fwir] *vt* : to burrow, to dig
foulard [fular] *nm* : scarf, neckerchief
foule [ful] *nf* **1** : crowd, mob **2 une foule de** : masses of, lots of
foulée [fule] *nf* **1** : stride **2 dans la foulée** : while I was (he was, etc.) at it **3 dans la foulée de** : on the heels of, in the wake of
fouler [fule] *vt* **1** : to press **2** : to tread, to set foot on <fouler aux pieds : to trample on> **3** : to sprain — *vi Can* : to shrink <mes pantalons ont foulé : my pants shrank> — **se fouler** *vr* **1** : to sprain **2** *fam* : to strain oneself
foulure [fulyr] *nf* ENTORSE : sprain
four [fur] *nm* **1** : oven <four à micro-ondes : microwave (oven)> **2** : kiln **3** *fam* : flop (in theater, etc.)
fourbe [furb] *adj* : deceitful
fourberie [furbəri] *nf* : deceit
fourbir [furbir] *vt* **1** : to polish up **2 fourbir ses armes** : to prepare for battle
fourbu, -bue [furby] *adj* : exhausted
fourche [furʃ] *nf* **1** : pitchfork **2** : fork, branching
fourcher [furʃe] *vi* **1** : to fork **2 ma (sa) langue a fourché** : it was a slip of the tongue — *vt* : to fork (in agriculture)
fourchette [furʃɛt] *nf* **1** : fork **2** : range, bracket
fourchu, -chue [furʃy] *adj* forked, split
fourgon [furgɔ̃] *nm* **1** : van **2** : freight car, baggage car <fourgon de queue : caboose> **3** : poker (for a fireplace)
fourgonnette [furgɔnɛt] *nf* : minivan
fourmi [furmi] *nf* : ant
fourmilier [furmilje] *nm* : anteater
fourmilière [furmiljɛr] *nf* : anthill
fourmillement [furmijmɑ̃] *nm* **1** : swarming **2** : tingling, pins and needles *pl*
fourmiller [furmije] *vi* **1** : to swarm, to mill about **2** : to abound <fourmiller de : to be teeming with> **3** : to tingle, to have pins and needles
fournaise [furnɛz] *nf Can* : furnace
fourneau [furno] *nm, pl* **fourneaux** [furno] **1** : stove **2** : furnace
fournée [furne] *nf* : batch
fourni, -nie [furni] *adj* **1** : thick, bushy **2 bien fourni** : well-stocked
fournil [furnil] *nm* : bakery
fournir [furnir] *vt* **1** : to supply, to provide (with) **2** : to produce (wine, etc.) **3 fournir un effort** : to make an effort — *vi* **~ à** : to provide for — **se fournir** *vr* **~ chez** : to shop at
fournisseur, -seuse [furnisœr, -søz] *n* : supplier, dealer, purveyor
fourniture [furnityr] *nf* **1** : furnishing **2 fournitures** *nfpl* : equipment, sup-

plies <fournitures de bureaux : office supplies>
fourrage [furaʒ] *nm* : feed, fodder
fourrager [furaʒe] {17} *vi* : to rummage, to forage
fourré[1], **-rée** [fure] *adj* **1** : fur-lined **2** : filled (of candies)
fourré[2] *nm* : thicket
fourreau [furo] *nm, pl* **fourreaux 1** : sheath, case, scabbard **2** *or* **robe fourreau** : sheath dress
fourrer [fure] *vt* **1** : to line with fur **2** : to stuff, to fill **3** *fam* : to thrust, to stick **— se fourrer** *vr* **1** *fam* : to get, to put oneself <se fourrer sous les couvertures : to crawl under the covers> **2** *Can fam* : to mess up
fourre–tout [furtu] *nms & pl* : tote bag, carryall
fourreur, -reuse [furœr, -røz] *n* : furrier
fourrière [furjɛr] *nf* : pound (for animals or vehicles)
fourrure [furyr] *nf* **1** : fur **2** : coat (of an animal)
fourvoyer [furvwaje] {58} *vt* : to lead astray **— se fourvoyer** *vr* **1** : to make an error, to go astray **2 ~ dans** : to stray into, to get involved in
foyer [fwaje] *nm* **1** : hearth, fireplace **2** RÉSIDENCE : home <femme au foyer : housewife> <sans foyer : homeless> **3** : home (for the elderly, etc.) **4** : focus <lunettes à double foyer : bifocals> **5** : center, seat, source
fracas [fraka] *nms & pl* : crash, din
fracassant, -sante [frakasɑ̃, -sɑ̃t] *adj* **1** : deafening, thunderous **2** : sensational <un succès fracassant : a stunning success>
fracasser [frakase] *vt* : to shatter, to smash **— se fracasser** *vr*
fraction [fraksjɔ̃] *nf* : fraction
fractionnaire [fraksjɔnɛr] *adj* : fractional
fractionner [fraksjɔne] *vt* : to divide, to split (up) **— se fractionner** *vr*
fracture [fraktyr] *nf* : fracture <fracture du crâne : fractured skull>
fracturer [fraktyre] *vt* **1** : to fracture, to break **2** : to break open
fragile [fraʒil] *adj* **1** CASSABLE : fragile, breakable **2** FAIBLE : sensitive, weak, frail
fragiliser [fraʒilize] *vt* : to weaken, to make fragile
fragilité [fraʒilite] *nf* **1** : fragility **2** : frailty
fragment [fragmɑ̃] *nm* **1** : fragment, bit **2** : passage (from a book), snatch (of a conversation)
fragmentaire [fragmɑ̃tɛr] *adj* : fragmentary, sketchy
fragmenter [fragmɑ̃te] *vt* : to fragment, to break up **— se fragmenter** *vr*
fragmentation [fragmɑ̃tasjɔ̃] *nf* : fragmentation, splitting up
frai [frɛ] *nm* **1** : fry **2** : fish eggs, spawn
fraîchement [frɛʃmɑ̃] *adv* **1** : freshly, newly <fraises fraîchement cueillies : freshly picked strawberries> **2** : coolly <fraîchement reçu : coolly received>
fraîcheur [frɛʃœr] *nf* **1** : freshness **2** : coolness
fraîchir [frɛʃir] *vi* **1** : to cool off **2** : to freshen
frais[1] [frɛ] *adv* **1** : freshly, recently **2 il fait frais** : it's cool outside
frais[2], **fraîche** [frɛ, frɛʃ] *adj* **1** : fresh <fruits frais : fresh fruit> **2** RÉCENT : new, recent <nouvelles fraîches : recent news> **3** : cool <températures plus fraîches : cooler temperatures> **4 peinture fraîche** : wet paint
frais[3] *nm* **1 mettre au frais** : to put in a cool place **2 prendre le frais** : to take a breath of fresh air **3 frais** *nmpl* : expenses, fees, charges
fraise [frɛz] *nf* **1** : strawberry **2** : (dentist's) drill
fraiser [frɛze] *vt* : to ream
framboise [frɑ̃bwaz] *nf* : raspberry
franc[1] [frɑ̃] *adv* **à parler franc** : frankly, to be quite frank
franc[2], **franche** [frɑ̃, frɑ̃ʃ] *adj* **1** : frank, straightforward **2** : pure (of colors, etc.) **3** : absolute, downright **4** : free, exempt <port franc : duty-free port>
franc[3] *nm* : franc
français[1], **-çaise** [frɑ̃se, -sɛz] *adj* : French
français[2] *nm* : French (language)
Français, -çaise *n* : Frenchman *m*, Frenchwoman *f*
franchement [frɑ̃ʃmɑ̃] *adv* **1** : frankly, candidly **2** : clearly, definitely **3** : boldly, firmly **4** : downright <c'est franchement ridicule! : it's really silly!>
franchir [frɑ̃ʃir] *vt* **1** : to cross over, to surmount, to clear **2** : to cover (a distance) **3** : to last through (a period of time)
franchise [frɑ̃ʃiz] *nf* **1** : frankness **2** : exemption <en franchise douanière : duty-free> <franchise postale : postage paid> **3** : deductible **4** : franchise
franchissement [frɑ̃ʃismɑ̃] *nm* : crossing, clearing
franciscain, -caine [frɑ̃siskɛ̃, -kɛn] *adj & n* : Franciscan
franciser [frɑ̃size] *vt* : to frenchify
franc–jeu [frɑ̃ʒø] *nm* : fair play
franc–maçon [frɑ̃masɔ̃] *nm* : Freemason **— franc–maçonnerie** [frɑ̃masɔnri] *nf*
franco–canadien[1], **-dienne** [frɑ̃kokanadjɛ̃,-djɛn] *adj* : French-Canadian
franco–canadien[2], **-dienne** *n* : Canadian French
francophile [frɑ̃kɔfil] *adj & nmf* : francophile

francophone[1] |frɑ̃kɔfɔn| *adj* : French-speaking
francophone[2] *nmf* : French speaker
francophonie |frɑ̃kɔfɔni| *nf* : French-speaking community
franc–parler |frɑ̃parle| *nm, pl* **franc–parlers** : frankness <avoir son franc-parler : to speak one's mind>
franc–tireur |frɑ̃tirœr| *nm, pl* **francs–tireurs 1** : irregular (soldier), guerrilla **2** : maverick <agir en franc-tireur : to act independently>
frange |frɑ̃ʒ| *nf* **1** : fringe **2** : bangs (of hair)
franger |frɑ̃ʒe| {17} *vt* : to fringe
frangin, -gine |frɑ̃ʒɛ̃, -ʒin| *n France fam* : brother *m*, sister *f*
franquette |frɑ̃kɛt| *nf* **à la bonne franquette** : without ceremony, informally
frappant, -pante |frapɑ̃, -pɑ̃t| *adj* : striking <un contraste frappant : a striking contrast>
frappe |frap| *nf* **1** : impression, stamp **2** : typing
frapper |frape| *vt* **1** : to strike, to hit **2** : to strike, to impress, to astonish **3** : to mint **4** : to ice, to chill **5 frapper d'ostracisme** : to ostracize — *vi* **1** : to hit, to knock, to bang **2** : to clap <frapper dans ses mains : to clap one's hands> — **se frapper** *vr* : to get all worked up
frappeur, -peuse |frapœr, -pøz| *n Can* : hitter, batter <frappeur désigné : designated hitter>
frasque |frask| *nf* : prank, escapade <faire des frasques : to get into mischief>
fraternel, -nelle |fraternɛl| *adj* : fraternal — **fraternellement** |-nɛlmɑ̃| *adv*
fraterniser |fraternize| *vi* : to fraternize — **fraternisation** |-nizasjɔ̃| *nf*
fraternité |fraternite| *nf* : fraternity, brotherhood
fratricide[1] |fratrisid| *adj* : fratricidal
fratricide[2] *nm* : fratricide
fraude |frod| *nf* **1** : fraud <fraude fiscale : tax evasion> **2 passer en fraude** : to smuggle in
frauder |frode| *v* : to cheat
fraudeur, -deuse |frodœr, -døz| *n* : cheat, swindler
frauduleux, -leuse |frodylø, -løz| *adj* : fraudulent — **frauduleusement** |-løzmɑ̃| *adv*
frayer |freje| {11} *vt* : to open up, to clear — *vi* **1** : to spawn **2** ~ **avec** : to associate with — **se frayer** *vr* **se frayer un chemin** : to make one's way
frayeur |frejœr| *nf* : fright
fredaine |frədɛn| *nf* : prank, escapade
fredonner |frədɔne| *vt* : to hum
freezer |frizœr| *nm* : freezer (of a refrigerator)
frégate |fregat| *nf* : frigate
frein |frɛ̃| *nm* **1** : brake **2** : check, restraint <mettre un frein à : to curb, to block> <sans frein : unrestrained, unbridled>
freinage |frɛnaʒ| *nm* : braking
freiner |frene| *vt* : to slow down, to check — *vi* : to brake
frelaté, -tée |frəlate| *adj* **1** : adulterated **2** : unnatural, artificial, corrupt
frêle |frɛl| *adj* **1** : weak, flimsy **2** : frail
frelon |frəlɔ̃| *nm* : hornet
frémir |fremir| *vi* **1** FRISSONNER : to tremble, to shiver, to shudder **2** : to quiver, to flutter **3** : to start to boil, to simmer
frémissant, -sante |fremisɑ̃, -sɑ̃t| *adj* : quivering, trembling
frémissement |fremismɑ̃| *nm* : trembling, shivering, shuddering
frêne |frɛn| *nm* : ash (tree or wood)
frénésie |frenezi| *nf* : frenzy
frénétique |frenetik| *adj* : frantic, frenetic — **frénétiquement** |-tikmɑ̃| *adv*
fréquemment |frekamɑ̃| *adv* : frequently
fréquence |frekɑ̃s| *nf* : frequency
fréquent, -quente |frekɑ̃, -kɑ̃t| *adj* : frequent
fréquentation |frekɑ̃tasjɔ̃| *nf* **1** : frequenting **2** : attendance <taux de fréquentation : attendance rate> **3** RELATION : acquaintance <mauvaises fréquentations : bad company> **4 fréquentations** *nfpl Can* : dating, courting
fréquenter |frekɑ̃te| *vt* **1** : to frequent **2** : to attend **3** : to associate with, to consort with — **se fréquenter** *vr* **1** : to see each other **2** : to go out (with each other), to date
frère |frɛr| *nm* **1** : brother **2** : friar, brother (in religion)
fresque |fresk| *nf* : fresco
fret |frɛ(t)| *nm* : freight
fréter |frete| {87} *vt* : to charter
frétillement |fretijmɑ̃| *nm* : wagging, wag (of a tail)
frétiller |fretije| *vi* **1** : to wriggle, to quiver <frétillant de joie : quivering with delight> **2** : to wag <sa queue frétille : its tail is wagging>
fretin |fratɛ̃| *nm* **menu fretin** : small fry
freux |frø| *nm* CORBEAU : rook
friable |frijabl| *adj* : crumbly
friand, friande |frijɑ̃, -jɑ̃d| *adj* ~ **de** : partial to, fond of
friandise |frijɑ̃diz| *nf* **1** BONBON : candy **2** : delicacy
fric |frik| *nm fam* : dough, cash
fricassée |frikase| *nf* : fricassee — **fricasser** |frikase| *vt*
friche |friʃ| *nf* : fallow land, wasteland <en friche : fallow>
friction |friksjɔ̃| *nf* **1** : friction **2** MASSAGE : massage, rubdown
frictionner |friksjɔne| *vt* : to rub (down), to massage — **se frictionner** *vr*

frigide [frizid] *adj* : frigid — **frigidité** [-ʒidite] *nf*
frigo [frigo] *nm fam* : fridge
frigorifier [frigɔrifje] {96} *vt* **1** : to refrigerate **2 être frigorifié** *fam* : to be frozen stiff
frigorifique [frigɔrifik] *adj* : refrigerated (of a truck, etc.)
frileux, -leuse [frilø. -øz] *adj* **1** : sensitive to cold **2** : cautious, timid
frimas [frima] *nms & pl* : hoarfrost
frime [frim] *nf fam* : sham, pretense <c'est pour la frime : it's just for show>
frimer [frime] *vi fam* : to put on an act
frimousse [frimus] *nf fam* : pretty little face
fringale [frɛ̃gal] *nf fam* **1 avoir la fringale** : to be starving **2 avoir une fringale de** : to have a craving for
fringant, -gante [frɛ̃gɑ̃. -gɑ̃t] *adj* **1** : dashing **2** : spirited (of a horse)
fringillidé [frɛ̃ʒilide] *nm* : finch
fringues [frɛ̃g] *nfpl fam* : gear, duds
friper [fripe] *vt* : to wrinkle, to crumple — **se friper** *vr*
friperie [fripri] *nf France* **1** : secondhand clothes shop **2** : secondhand clothes
fripon[1], **-ponne** [fripɔ̃. -pɔn] *adj* COQUIN : mischievous
fripon[2], **-ponne** *n* : rascal
fripouille [fripuj] *nf fam* : scoundrel, crook
frire [frir] {45} *v* : to fry
frise [friz] *nf* : frieze
friser [frize] *vt* **1** : to curl **2** : to graze, to skim (a surface) **3** : to border on <elle doit friser la quarantaine : she must be close to forty> — *vi* : to curl — **se friser** *vr* **se faire friser** : to have one's hair curled
frisette [frizɛt] *nf* : ringlet
frisquet, -quette [friskɛ. -kɛt] *adj* : chilly, nippy
frisson [frisɔ̃] *nm* **1** : shiver, shudder **2** : ripple (of water, etc.), rustle (of leaves)
frissonnement [frisɔnmɑ̃] *nm* **1** : shiver, shudder **2** : rippling, rustling
frissonner [frisɔne] *vi* **1** : to shiver, to shudder **2** : to rustle, to ripple
frites [frit] *nfpl* : french fries
friture [frityr] *nf* **1** : frying **2** : deep fat, oil **3** : fried food
frivole [frivɔl] *adj* : frivolous, trivial — **frivolement** [-vɔlmɑ̃] *adv*
frivolité [frivɔlite] *nf* : frivolity
froc [frɔk] *nm* **1** : (religious) habit **2** *fam* : pants *pl*, trousers *pl*
froid[1] [frwa] *adv* **il fait froid** : it's cold (outside)
froid[2], **froide** [frwa. frwad] *adj* **1** : cold **2** : unfeeling, insensitive
froid[3] *nm* **1** : cold <un grand froid : intense cold> <avoir froid : to feel cold> <conservez au froid : keep in a cold place> **2** : cold (illness) <prendre froid : to catch cold> **3** : coolness, chill <être en froid avec : to be on bad terms with> **4 à ~** : calmly, cooly **5 à ~** : without preparation, spontaneous(ly)
froidement [frwadmɑ̃] *adv* : coldly, coolly
froideur [frwadœr] *nf* : coldness, coolness
froissement [frwasmɑ̃] *nm* **1** : crumpling, creasing **2** : rustle, rustling
froisser [frwase] *vt* **1** : to crumple, to crease, to muss up **2** BLESSER : to hurt, to offend, to upset — **se froisser** *vr* **1** : to crease, to crumple (up) **2 se froisser un muscle** : to strain a muscle
frôler [frole] *vt* EFFLEURER : to touch lightly, to brush, to graze
fromage [frɔmaʒ] *nm* **1** : cheese **2 fromage blanc** *or* **fromage cottage** : cottage cheese
fromager[1], **-gère** [frɔmaʒe. -ʒɛr] *adj* : cheese <l'industrie fromagère : the cheese industry>
fromager[2], **-gère** *n* : cheese maker, cheese merchant
fromagerie [frɔmaʒri] *nf* : cheese store
froment [frɔmɑ̃] *nm* : wheat
fronce [frɔ̃s] *nf* : gather (of fabric)
froncement [frɔ̃smɑ̃] *nm* **froncement de sourcils** : frown
froncer [frɔ̃se] {6} *vt* **1** : to gather (fabric) **2** : to wrinkle, to pucker <froncer les sourcils : to knit one's brow, to frown>
frondaison [frɔ̃dɛzɔ̃] *nf* : foliage
fronde [frɔ̃d] *nf* **1** : rebellion, revolt **2** : slingshot **3** : frond
frondeur, -deuse [frɔ̃dœr. -døz] *adj* : rebellious
front [frɔ̃] *nm* **1** : forehead, brow **2** : front (in meorology, politics, war, etc.) **3** : audacity, effrontery <avoir le front de faire : to have the nerve to do> **4 de ~** : without hesitation, head-on **5 de ~** : abreast <à cinq de front : five abreast> **6 faire front à** : to confront, to face up to
frontal, -tale [frɔ̃tal] *adj, mpl* **frontaux** [frɔ̃to] : frontal
frontalier, -lière [frɔ̃talje. -ljɛr] *adj* : frontier, border
frontière [frɔ̃tjɛr] *nf* **1** : frontier, border **2** : boundary
frontispice [frɔ̃tispis] *nm* : frontispiece
fronton [frɔ̃tɔ̃] *nm* : pediment
frottement [frɔtmɑ̃] *nm* **1** : rubbing, scraping **2 frottements** *nmpl* : friction, disagreement
frotter [frɔte] *vt* **1** : to rub <frotter une allumette : to strike a match> **2** : to polish, to scrub — *vi* : to rub — **se frotter** *vr* **1** : to rub <ne te frotte pas les yeux : don't rub your eyes> **2** : to scrub oneself **3 ~ à** : to face up to, to take on

frou–frou *or* **froufrou** [frufru] *nm, pl* **frou–frous** *or* **froufrous** : rustle, swish
froufrouter [frufrute] *vi* : to rustle, to swish
frousse [frus] *nf fam* : scare, fright, jitters *pl*
fructifier [fryktifje] {96} *vi* **1** : to bear fruit **2** : to yield a profit
fructueux, -tueuse [fryktyø, -tyøz] *adj* **1** : fruitful, productive **2** RENTABLE : profitable
frugal, -gale [frygal] *adj, mpl* **frugaux** [frygo] : frugal — **frugalement** [-galmɑ̃] *adv*
frugalité [frygalite] *nf* : frugality
fruit [fryi] *nm* **1** : fruit <jus de fruits : fruit juice> **2 fruits de mer** : seafood
fruité, -tée [fryite] *adj* : fruity
fruitier[1], **-tière** [fryitje, -tjɛr] *adj* : fruit <arbre fruitier : fruit tree>
fruitier[2], **-tière** *n* : fruit merchant
fruste [fryst] *adj* **1** : worn **2** GROSSIER : rough, uncouth
frustrant, -trante [frystrɑ̃, -trɑ̃t] *adj* : frustrating
frustration [frystrasjɔ̃] *nf* : frustration
frustrer [frystre] *vt* **1** DÉCEVOIR : to frustrate, to disappoint **2** PRIVER : to deprive
fuel [fjul] → **fioul**
fugace [fygas] *adj* ÉPHÉMÈRE : fleeting
fugitif[1], **-tive** [fyʒitif, -tiv] *adj* **1** : escaped, fugitive **2** : fleeting, elusive
fugitif[2], **-tive** *n* **1** : fugitive, escapee **2** : runaway
fugue [fyg] *nf* **1** : running away <faire une fugue : to run away (from home)> <fugue amoureuse : elopement> **2** : fugue
fuguer [fyge] *vi* : to run away
fugueur, -gueuse [fygœr, -gøz] *adj & n* : runaway
fuir [fuir] {46} *vi* **1** : to flee **2** : to leak — *vt* **1** : to shun, to avoid **2** : to flee, to run away from
fuite [fuit] *nf* **1** : flight, escape **2** : leak
fulgurant, -rante [fylgyrɑ̃, -rɑ̃t] *adj* **1** ÉBLOUISSANT : dazzling **2** : shooting, searing, intense
fulminant, -nante [fylminɑ̃, -nɑ̃t] *adj* : furious, enraged
fulminer [fylmine] *vt* : to bellow out (threats, etc.) — *vi* ENRAGER : to be enraged, to fulminate
fumé, -mée [fyme] *adj* **1** : smoked **2** : tinted
fumée *nf* **1** : smoke **2** : steam
fumer [fyme] *vt* **1** : to smoke **2** : to manure — *vi* **1** : to smoke **2** : to steam **3** : to fume (with anger)
fumet [fymɛ] *nm* : aroma (of food or wine)
fumier [fymje] *nm* : dung, manure
fumigation [fymigasjɔ̃] *nf* : fumigation
fumiste [fymist] *nmf fam* **1** : shirker **2** : phoney
fumisterie [fymistəri] *nf fam* **1** : joke, farce **2** : sham
fumoir [fymwar] *nm* **1** : smokehouse **2** : smoking room
fun [fœn] *nm Can fam* : fun <j'ai eu du fun : I had fun>
funambule [fynɑ̃byl] *nmf* ÉQUILIBRISTE : tightrope walker
funèbre [fynɛbr] *adj* **1** FUNÉRAIRE : funeral **2** LUGUBRE : funereal, gloomy
funérailles [fyneraj] *nfpl* : funeral
funéraire [fynerɛr] *adj* **1** : funeral, funerary **2 salon funéraire** *Can* : funeral home
funeste [fynɛst] *adj* **1** : fatal, deathly **2** CATASTROPHIQUE : disastrous, dire
fur [fyr] *nm* **au fur et à mesure** : little by little, as one goes along
furet [fyre] *nm* : ferret
fureter [fyrte] {20} *vi* : to ferret around, to nose about
fureteur, -teuse [fyrtœr, -tøz] *adj* : inquisitive, prying
fureur [fyrœr] *nf* **1** RAGE : rage, fury **2 faire fureur** : to be all the rage
furibond, -bonde [fyribɔ̃, -bɔ̃d] *adj* : furious, livid
furie [fyri] *nf* **1** : fury, rage **2 avec ~** : furiously, violently
furieusement [fyrjøzmɑ̃] *adv* **1** : furiously **2** : extremely, tremendously
furieux, -rieuse [fyrjø, -jøz] *adj* **1** : furious, angry **2** : fierce, intense
furoncle [fyrɔ̃kl] *nm* : boil, carbuncle
furtif, -tive [fyrtif, -tiv] *adj* : furtive, sly — **furtivement** [-tivmɑ̃] *adv*
fusain [fyzɛ̃] *nm* **1** : spindle tree **2** : charcoal (for drawing) **3** : charcoal drawing
fuseau [fyzo] *nm, pl* **fuseaux 1** : spindle, bobbin **2 fuseau horaire** : time zone **3 pantalon fuseau** : ski pants
fusée [fyze] *nf* **1** : rocket **2 fusée éclairante** : flare
fuselage [fyzlaʒ] *nm* : fuselage
fuselé, -lée [fyzle] *adj* : slender, tapering
fuser [fyze] *vi* **1** : to stream out, to gush out **2** JAILLIR : to burst forth (of laughter, etc.)
fusible [fyzibl] *nm* : fuse <faire sauter un fusible : to blow a fuse>
fusil [fyzi] *nm* **1** : gun, rifle **2** : marksman
fusilier [fyzilje] *nm* **1** : rifleman **2 fusilier marin** : marine
fusillade [fyzijad] *nf* **1** : gunfire **2** : shooting
fusiller [fyzije] *vt* **1** : to shoot, to execute **2 fusiller du regard** : to look daggers at
fusil–mitrailleur [fyzimitrajœr] *nm, pl* **fusils–mitrailleurs** : automatic rifle, machine gun
fusion [fyzjɔ̃] *nf* **1** : fusion **2** : melting <roche en fusion : molten rock> **3** : merger
fusionner [fyzɔnje] *v* : to merge

fustiger |fystiʒe| {17} *vt* : to castigate, to censure
fut |fy|, *etc.* → **être**
fût |fy| *nm* **1** TONNEAU : barrel, cask <bière en fût : draft beer> **2** : shaft (of a column) **3** : trunk (of a tree)
futaie |fytɛ| *nf* : forest (of tall trees)
futé, -tée |fyte| *adj* : cunning, crafty
futile |fytil| *adj* **1** : futile **2** FRIVOLE : trivial, frivolous
futilité |fytilite| *nf* : futility
futur[1], **-ture** |fytyr| *adj* : future
futur[2] *nm* **1** : future **2** : future tense
futuriste |fytyrist| *adj* : futuristic
fuyait |fɥijɛ|, **fuyions** |fɥijɔ̃|, *etc.* → **fuir**
fuyant, fuyante |fɥijɑ̃, fɥijɑ̃t| *adj* **1** INSAISISSABLE : elusive, shifty **2** : receding
fuyard, fuyarde |fɥijar, fɥijard| *n* **1** : runaway **2** : deserter (in the military)

G

g |ʒe| *nm* : g, the seventh letter of the alphabet
gabardine |gabardin| *nf* : gabardine
gabarit |gabari| *nm* **1** : template, gauge **2** : size, dimensions *pl* **3** *fam* : (physical) build **4** *fam* : caliber, sort <du même gabarit : of the same ilk>
gabonais, -naise |gabɔnɛ, -nɛz| *adj* : Gabonese
Gabonais, -naise *n* : Gabonese
gâcher |gaʃe| *vt* **1** : to spoil, to ruin **2** GASPILLER : to waste, to squander **3** : to mix (plaster, mortar, etc.)
gâchette |gaʃɛt| *nf* : trigger
gâchis |gaʃi| *nm* **1** DÉSORDRE : mess <faire du gâchis : to make a mess> **2** GASPILLAGE : waste
gadelle |gadɛl| *nf Can* : currant
gadget |gadʒɛt| *nm* **1** : gimmick, gadget **2 gadgets** *nmpl* : gadgetry
gadoue |gadu| *nf* **1** : mud, muck **2** *Can* : slush
gaélique[1] |gaelik| *adj* : Gaelic
gaélique[2] *nm* : Gaelic (language)
gaffe |gaf| *nf* **1** : boat hook **2** *fam* : blunder, stupidity, goof
gaffer |gafe| *vi fam* : to blunder, to goof (up)
gaffeur, -feuse |gafœr, -føz| *n fam* : blunderer
gag |gag| *nm* : gag, joke
gage |gaʒ| *nm* **1** : security <mettre en gage : to pawn> **2** : pledge, guarantee <en gage d'amitié : as a token of our friendship> **3** : forfeit (in games) **4 gages** *nmpl* : wages, pay
gager |gaʒe| {17} *vt* **1** : to bet, to wager **2** : to guarantee (a loan, etc.)
gageure |gaʒœr| *nf* **1** : challenge **2** *Can* : bet, wager
gagnant[1], **-gnante** |gaɲɑ̃, -ɲɑ̃t| *adj* : winning <billet gagnant : winning ticket>
gagnant[2], **-gnante** *n* : winner
gagne-pain |gaɲpɛ̃| *nms & pl* : job, livelihood
gagner |gaɲe| *vt* **1** : to win **2** : to earn <gagner sa vie : to earn one's living> **3** : to gain <gagner du terrain : to gain ground> <gagner de la vitesse : to pick up speed> **4** ÉCONOMISER : to save (time, space, etc.) **5** ATTEINDRE : to reach, to arrive at **6** : to win (someone) over **7** : to overcome — *vi* **1** : to win **2** : to gain, to advance, to encroach **3** : to increase <gagner en longueur : to grow longer> **4** ~ **à** : to gain by <gagner à vieillir : to improve with age> **5 y gagner** : to be better off <ils y gagnent : it's to their advantage>
gai, gaie |gɛ| *adj* **1** JOYEUX : cheerful, happy, merry **2** HOMOSEXUEL : gay, homosexual
gaiement |gemɑ̃| *adv* : gaily, merrily
gaieté |getɛ| *nf* : cheerfulness, mirth
gaillard[1], **-larde** |gajar, -jard| *adj* **1** : lively, sprightly **2** GRIVOIS : ribald, bawdy
gaillard[2], **-larde** *nmf* : sturdy fellow *m*, strapping individual
gaillard[3] *nm* **gaillard d'avant** : forecastle
gaillardement |gajardəmɑ̃| *adv* : cheerfully
gain |gɛ̃| *nm* **1** : earnings *pl* **2** : saving (of time, space, etc.) **3** : gain (in finance) **4** : winning <avoir gain de cause : to win the case>
gaine |gɛn| *nf* **1** : girdle, corset **2** : sheath
gainer |gene| *vt* : to cover, to sheathe
gala |gala| *nm* : gala, reception
galactique |galaktik| *adj* : galactic
galamment |galamɑ̃| *adv* : gallantly
galant[1], **-lante** |galɑ̃, -lɑ̃t| *adj* **1** : courteous, gallant **2 en galante compagnie** : with a person of the opposite sex **3 homme galant** : ladies' man
galant[2] *nm* : beau, suitor
galanterie |galɑ̃tri| *nf* : gallantry
galaxie |galaksi| *nf* : galaxy
galbe |galb| *nm* : curve, shapeliness
gale |gal| *nf* **1** : scabies **2** : mange **3** *Can* : scab
galéjade |galeʒad| *nf* : tall story
galère |galɛr| *nf* **1** : galley (ship) **2** *fam* : hard time, hassle
galerie |galri| *nf* **1** : gallery **2** : balcony (in a theater) **3** : roof rack (of an automobile) **4** *Can* : porch **5 galerie marchande** : shopping mall

galet [galɛ] *nm* CAILLOU : pebble
galette [galɛt] *nf* **1** : flat round cake **2** : pancake **3** *Can* : soft cookie <galette à la mélasse : molasses cookie> **4** *fam* : dough, cash
galeux, -leuse [galø, -øz] *adj* : mangy
galimatias [galimatja] *nm* : gibberish, nonsense
galion [galjɔ̃] *nm* : galleon
galipette [galipɛt] *nf fam* : somersault <faire des galipettes : to turn somersaults>
galipote [galipɔt] *nf* **courir la galipote** *Can* : to gallivant
galle [gal] *nf* : gall (in botany)
gallicisme [galisism] *nm* **1** : French idiom **2** : gallicism
gallium [galjɔm] *nm* : gallium
gallois[1], **-loise** [galwa, -lwaz] *adj* : Welsh
gallois[2] *nm* : Welsh (language)
Gallois, -loise *n* : Welshman *m*, Welshwoman *f*
gallon [galɔ̃] *nm* : gallon
galoche [galɔʃ] *nf* **1** SABOT : clog **2** : overshoe
galon [galɔ̃] *nm* **1** : braid (on fabric) **2** : stripe (in the military) <prendre du galon : to be promoted> **3** *Can* : measuring tape
galop [galo] *nm* : gallop <au galop : at a gallop>
galopant, -pante [galɔpɑ̃, -pɑ̃t] *adj* : runaway, galloping
galoper [galɔpe] *vi* **1** : to gallop **2** : to run about **3** : to run wild <son imagination galope : his imagination is running riot>
galopin [galɔpɛ̃] *nm* : rascal
galvaniser [galvanize] *vt* : to galvanize
galvauder [galvode] *vt* **1** : to tarnish, to sully **2** : to debase <une expression galvaudée : a hackneyed phrase> — **se galvauder** *vr*
gambade [gɑ̃bad] *nf* : leap, skip
gambader [gɑ̃bade] *vi* : to leap about, to gambol
gambien, -bienne [gɑ̃bjɛ̃, -bjɛn] *adj* : Gambian
Gambien, -bienne *n* : Gambian
gambit [gɑ̃bi] *nm* : gambit
gamelle [gamɛl] *nf* : mess kit
gamète *nm* [gamɛt]: gamete
gamin[1], **-mine** [gamɛ̃, -min] *adj* **1** ESPIÈGLE : mischievous, playful **2** PUÉRIL : childish
gamin[2], **-mine** *n fam* : kid, youngster
gaminerie [gaminri] *nf France* : childishness
gamme [gam] *nf* **1** : scale (in music) **2** SÉRIE : range (of colors, products, etc.), gamut (of emotions)
gang[1] [gɑ̃g] *nm France* : gang
gang[2] *nf Can fam* : gang, group <la gang du bureau : the gang in the office>
ganglion [gɑ̃glijɔ̃] *nm* **1** : ganglion **2** **avoir des ganglions** *fam* : to have swollen glands
gangrène [gɑ̃grɛn] *nf* **1** : gangrene **2** : scourge, corrupting influence
gangreneux, -neuse [gɑ̃grənø, -nøz] *adj* : gangrenous
gangster [gɑ̃gstɛr] *nm* : gangster
gannet [ganɛ] *nm* : gannet
ganse [gɑs] *nf* : braid (in sewing)
gant [gɑ̃] *nm* **1** : glove <gant de boxe : boxing glove> **2** **gant de toilette** : washcloth **3** **jeter le gant** : to throw down the gauntlet **4** **prendre des gants pour** *or* **mettre des gants pour** : to handle with kid gloves
gantelet [gɑ̃tlɛ] *nm* : gauntlet
garage [garaʒ] *nm* **1** : garage <garage d'autobus : bus depot> <garage d'avions : hangar> **2** STATION-SERVICE : service station, repair shop
garagiste [garaʒist] *nmf* **1** : garage owner **2** : garage mechanic
garant[1], **-rante** [garɑ̃, -rɑ̃t] *n* **1** : guarantor, surety **2** **se porter garant de** : to be answerable for, to vouch for
garant[2] *nm* : guarantee, assurance
garantie [garɑ̃ti] *nf* : guarantee, warranty
garantir [garɑ̃tir] *vt* **1** ASSURER : to guarantee, to assure **2** **~ de** : to protect from
garçon [garsɔ̃] *nm* **1** : boy, young man **2** SERVEUR : waiter **3** CÉLIBATAIRE : bachelor **4** **garçon manqué** : tomboy
garçonnet [garsɔnɛ] *nm* : little boy
garde[1] [gard] *nm* **1** : guard, warden **2** **garde côtière** *Can* : coast guard **3** **garde du corps** : bodyguard **4** **garde de nuit** : night watchman **5** **garde forestier** : forest ranger
garde[2] *nf* **1** : nurse **2** : (military) guard, watch **3** : custody, care <avoir la garde des enfants : to have custody of the children> **4** : duty <être de garde : to be on duty> **5** **chien de garde** : watchdog **6** **mettre en garde** : to warn **7** **prendre garde** : to be careful
garde-à-vous [gardavu] *nms & pl* : standing at attention
garde-boue [gardəbu] *nms & pl* : mudguard
garde-chasse [gardəʃas] *nm, pl* **gardes-chasse(s)** : gamekeeper, game warden
garde-feu [gardəfø] *nms & pl* **1** : fire screen **2** *Can* : fire warden
garde-fou [gardəfu] *nm, pl* **garde-fous** PARAPET : railing, parapet
garde-malade [gardəmalad] *nmf* **gardes-malade(s)** INFIRMIER : nurse
garde-manger [gardəmɑ̃ʒe] *nms & pl* : pantry
gardénia [gardenja] *nm* : gardenia
garde-pêche [gardəpɛʃ] *nm, pl* **gardes-pêche** : fish warden

garder [garde] *vt* **1** CONSERVER : to keep **2** : to keep on (clothing) **3** : to keep (oneself) in <garder le lit : to stay in bed> **4** SURVEILLER : to guard, to watch over <garder des enfants : to look after children, to baby-sit> **5 ~ de** : to protect from **— se garder** *vr* **1** SE CONSERVER : to keep **2 ~ de** : to be careful not to <gardez-vous de parler : be careful not to talk>

garderie [gardəri] *nf Can* : day-care center, nursery

garde–robe[1] [gardərɔb] *nf, pl* **garde–robes** : wardrobe, clothes

garde–robe[2] *nmf Can* : wardrobe, closet

gardien[1], **-dienne** [gardjɛ̃, -djɛn] *n* **1** : caretaker, attendant, custodian **2** : guardian, keeper <gardien des droits humains : guardian of human rights>

gardien[2] *nm* **1 gardien de but** : goalkeeper **2 gardien de la paix** *France* : police officer, policeman **3 gardien de troupeau** : herdsman

gardienne *nf* **gardienne d'enfants** : day-care worker, baby-sitter

gare[1] [gar] *nf* **1** : railroad station **2 gare d'autobus** *Can or* **gare routière** *France* : bus station

gare[2] *interj* **1 gare à vous!** : watch out! **2 sans crier gare** : without warning

garenne [garɛn] *nf* : (rabbit) warren

garer [gare] *vt* STATIONNER : to park **— se garer** *vr* **1** : to park **2** SE RANGER : to pull over

gargantuesque [gargãtyɛsk] *adj* : gargantuan

gargariser [gargarize] *v* **se gargariser** *vr* **1** : to gargle **2 ~ de** *fam* : to revel in

gargarisme [gargarism] *nm* **1** : gargling **2** : gargle (product)

gargote [gargɔt] *nf* : cheap restaurant

gargouille [garguj] *nf* : gargoyle

gargouillement [gargujmã] *nm* : rumble, rumbling

gargouiller [garguje] *vi* : to gurgle (of water), to rumble (of one's stomach)

garnement [garnəmã] *nm* : rascal

garni, -nie [garni] *adj* : garnished (in cooking) <plat garni : meal with vegetables> <hamburger garni : hamburger with all the trimmings>

garnir [garnir] *vt* **1** REMPLIR : to fill **2** : to cover **3** : to decorate, to trim **4** : to garnish (a dish) **— se garnir** *vr* : to fill up

garnison [garnizɔ̃] *nf* : garrison

garniture [garnityr] *nf* **1** : filling, garnish (in cooking) <sans garniture : without vegetables> **2** : trimming **3 garniture de frein** : brake lining

garrocher [garɔʃe] *vt Can fam* : to throw

garrot [garo] *nm* **1** : tourniquet **2** : garrote **3** : withers (of a horse)

garrotter [garɔte] *vt* **1** LIGOTER : to tie up, to bind **2** BÂILLONNER : to gag, to stifle

gars [ga] *nm fam* **1** : boy, lad **2** TYPE : guy, fellow

gascon, -conne [gaskɔ̃, -skɔn] *adj* : Gascon

Gascon, -conne *n* : Gascon

gaspillage [gaspijaʒ] *nm* : waste

gaspiller [gaspije] *vt* : to waste, to squander

gaspilleur, -leuse [gaspijœr, -jøz] *adj* : wasteful

gastrique [gastrik] *adj* : gastric

gastronome [gastrɔnɔm] *nmf* : gourmet

gastronomie [gastrɔnɔmi] *nf* : gastronomy

gastronomique [gastrɔnɔmik] *adj* : gastronomic, gourmet

gâteau [gato] *nm, pl* **gâteaux 1** : cake <gâteau d'anniversaire : birthday cake> **2 gâteau sec** *France* : cookie **3 c'est du gâteau** *fam* : it's a piece of cake

gâter [gate] *vt* **1** CHOYER : to spoil, to pamper **2** : to spoil, to ruin **— se gâter** *vr* **1** : to go bad **2** : to deteriorate, to change for the worse

gâterie [gatri] *nf* : little treat, delicacy

gâteux, -teuse [gatø, -tøz] *adj* : senile

gâtisme [gatism] *nm* : senility

gauche[1] [goʃ] *adj* **1** : left <tourner à gauche : to make a left turn> <du côté gauche : on the left-hand side> **2** MALADROIT : awkward, clumsy **3** : warped

gauche[2] *nf* **1** : left <à gauche de : to the left of> **2 la gauche** : the Left, the left wing

gauchement [goʃmã] *adv* : awkwardly, clumsily

gaucher[1], **-chère** [goʃe, -ʃɛr] *adj* : left-handed

gaucher[2], **-chère** *n* : left-handed person

gaucherie [goʃri] *nf* : awkwardness, clumsiness

gauchir [goʃir] *vt* **1** : to warp **2** : to distort (facts, etc.) **—** *vi* : to warp

gauchissement [goʃismã] *nm* **1** : warp, warping **2** : distortion

gauchiste [goʃist] *adj & nmf* : leftist **— gauchisme** [goʃism] *nm*

gaufre[1] [gofr] *nm Can* : gopher

gaufre[2] *nf* **1** : waffle **2** : honeycomb

gaufrer [gofre] *vt* **1** : to emboss **2** : to crinkle

gaufrette [gofrɛt] *nf* : wafer

gaufrier [gofrije] *nm* : waffle iron

gaulois, -loise [golwa, -lwaz] *adj* **1** : Gallic **2** GRIVOIS : bawdy

gauloiserie [galwazri] *nf* **1** : bawdy joke **2** : bawdiness

gaulthérie [golteri] *nf* : wintergreen

gausser [gose] *v* **se gausser** *vr* SE MOQUER : to deride, to make fun of

gaver [gave] *vt* **1** : to force-feed **2** : to fill up — **se gaver** *vr* SE BOURRER : to stuff oneself
gay [gɛ] → **gai**
gaz [gaz] *nms & pl* **1** : gas <gaz carbonique : carbon dioxide> <gaz lacrymogène : tear gas> <gaz naturel : natural gas> **2** *Can fam* : gasoline **3 mettre le gaz** *fam* : to step on the gas
gaze [gaz] *nf* : gauze
gazéifié, -fiée [gazeifje] *adj* : carbonated
gazelle [gazɛl] *nf* : gazelle
gazer [gaze] *vt* : to gas — *vi fam* : to be going well <ça gaze? : how are things going?>
gazette [gazɛt] *nf fam* : newspaper
gazeux, -zeuse [gazø, -øz] *adj* **1** : gaseous **2 eau gazeuse** : sparkling water **3 boisson gazeuse** : soft drink
gazoduc [gazɔdyk] *nm* : gas pipeline
gazon [gazɔ̃] *nm* **1** : grass, turf, sod **2** PELOUSE : lawn
gazouillement [gazujmɑ̃] *nm* **1** : chirping, twittering **2** : babbling, gurgling
gazouiller [gazuje] *vi* **1** : to chirp **2** : to babble, to gurgle
gazouillis [gazuji] *nms & pl* **1** : chirp, twittering **2** : babbling
geai [ʒɛ] *nm* : jay
géant[1], **géante** [ʒeɑ̃, -ɑ̃t] *adj* : giant, gigantic
géant[2], **géante** *n* **1** : giant **2 à pas de géant** : with giant strides, rapidly
geignard, -narde [ʒɛɲar, -ɲard] *adj fam* : whiny, whining
geignement [ʒɛɲəmɑ̃] *nm* : moaning, groaning
geindre [ʒɛ̃dr] {37} *vi* **1** : to groan, to moan **2** : to whine, to whimper
gel [ʒɛl] *nm* **1** : frost **2** : freeze, freezing **3** : gel <gel coiffant : hair gel>
gélatine [ʒelatin] *nf* : gelatine
gélatineux, -neuse [ʒelatinø, -nøz] *adj* : jelly-like, gelatinous
gelé, -lée [ʒəle] *adj* **1** : frozen **2** : frost-bitten
gelée *nf* **1** : frost <gelée blanche : hoarfrost> **2** : jelly
geler [ʒəle] {20} *v* : to freeze — *v impers* : to freeze <il gèle! : it's freezing!> — **se geler** *vr*
gélifier [ʒelifje] {96} *vt* : to jell — **se gélifier** *vr* : to jell
gélule [ʒelyl] *nf* : capsule
gelure [ʒəlyr] *nf* : frostbite
Gémeaux [ʒemo] *nmpl* : Gemini
gémir [ʒemir] *vi* **1** : to groan, to moan **2** : to wail (of wind, etc.), to creak **3 ~ sur** : to bemoan
gémissement [ʒemismɑ̃] *nm* **1** : groan, moan **2** : creaking
gemme[1] [ʒɛm] *adj* **sel gemme** : rock salt
gemme[2] *nf* : gem, precious stone
gênant, -nante [ʒenɑ̃, -nɑ̃t] *adj* **1** EMBARRASSANT : embarrassing, awkward **2** ENCOMBRANT : cumbersome, in the way **3** ENNUYEUX : annoying, intrusive **4** *Can* : intimidating, imposing
gencives [ʒɑ̃siv] *nfpl* : gums
gendarme [ʒɑ̃darm] *nm* **1** *France* : gendarme, police officer **2** *Can* : federal police officer (member of the Royal Canadian Mounted Police)
gendarmerie [ʒɑ̃darmərі] *nf* **1** *France* : police force **2** *France* : police station **3** *Can* : federal police force **3 gendarmerie maritime** *France* : coast guard
gendre [ʒɑ̃dr] *nm* : son-in-law
gène [ʒɛn] *nm* : gene
gêne [ʒɛn] *nf* **1** NUISANCE : inconvenience, bother **2** CONFUSION : embarrassment **3** : difficulty, (physical) discomfort **4** PAUVRETÉ : poverty
gêné, -née [ʒene] *adj* **1** : embarrassed **2** : short of money **3** : uncomfortable **4** *Can* : shy
généalogie [ʒenealɔʒi] *nf* : genealogy
généalogique [ʒenealɔʒik] *adj* : genealogical
gêner [ʒene] *vt* **1** : to embarrass, to make uncomfortable **2** DÉRANGER : to bother **3** : to hamper, to restrict, to disrupt — **se gêner** *vr* **1** : to get in each other's way **2** : to put oneself out <ne te gêne pas! : don't mind me!>
général[1], **-rale** [ʒeneral] *adj, mpl* **-raux** [-ro]: general <en général : in general, for the most part> — **généralement** [-ralmɑ̃] *adv*
général[2] *nm, pl* **-raux** : general <général de brigade : brigadier general>
générale *nf* **1** : general's wife **2** : dress rehearsal
généralisation [ʒeneralizasjɔ̃] *nf* **1** : general application, spreading **2** : generalization
généraliser [ʒeneralize] *vt* : to make general, to put to general use — *vi* : to generalize — **se généraliser** *vr* : to become widespread
généraliste[1] [ʒeneralist] *adj* : general, nonspecialist
généraliste[2] *nmf* : general practitioner
généralité [ʒeneralite] *nf* : generality
générateur[1], **-trice** [ʒeneratœr, -tris] *adj* : generating, generative
générateur[2] *nm* : generator, producer
génération [ʒenerasjɔ̃] *nf* : generation
génératrice *nf* : generator (of electricity)
générer [ʒenere] {87} *vt* : to generate
généreux, -reuse [ʒenerø, -røz] *adj* : generous — **généreusement** [-røzmɑ̃] *adv*
générique[1] [ʒenerik] *adj* : generic
générique[2] *nm* : credits *pl* (in movies)
générosité [ʒenerɔzite] *nf* : generosity
genèse [ʒənɛz] *nf* : genesis
genêt [ʒənɛ] *nm* : broom (plant)

généticien, -cienne [ʒenetisjɛ̃] *n* : geneticist
génétique¹ [ʒenetik] *adj* : genetic — **génétiquement** [-tikmɑ̃] *adv*
génétique² *nf* : genetics
genévrier [ʒənevrije] *nm* : juniper
génial, -niale [ʒenjal] *adj, mpl* **-niaux** [-njo] **1** : of genius, brilliant **2** *fam* : fantastic, great
génie [ʒeni] *nm* **1** : genius **2** : genie **3** : engineering <génie civil : civil engineering>
génisse [ʒenis] *nf* **1** : heifer **2** *Can* : female calf
génital, -tale [ʒenital] *adj, mpl* **-taux** [-to] : genital
génitif [ʒenitif] *nm* : genitive (in grammar)
génocide [ʒenɔsid] *nm* : genocide
genou [ʒənu] *nm, pl* **genoux 1** : knee **2 se mettre à genoux** : to kneel down
genre [ʒɑ̃r] *nm* **1** SORTE : kind, sort, type **2** : style, manner **3** : gender **4** : genre (in art, etc.) **5** : genus
gens [ʒɑ̃] *nmfpl* **1** : people <la plupart des gens : most people> <vieilles gens : old folk> <jeunes gens : young people, teenagers> **2 gens d'affaires** : businessmen *m*, businesswomen *f* **3 gens de lettres** : writers, scholars
gentil¹, -tille [ʒɑ̃ti, -tij] *adj* **1** AIMABLE : kind, nice **2** SAGE : good, well-behaved **3** AGRÉABLE : pleasant **4** : fair <une gentille somme : a tidy sum>
gentil² [ʒɑ̃ti] *nm* : gentile
gentilhomme [ʒɑ̃tijɔm] *nm, pl* **gentilshommes** : gentleman
gentillesse [ʒɑ̃tijɛs] *nf* AMABILITÉ : kindness, niceness
gentiment [ʒɑ̃timɑ̃] *adv* : nicely, kindly
gentleman [dʒɛntləman] *nm, pl* **gentlemen** [-tləmɛn] : gentleman
génuflexion [ʒenyflɛksjɔ̃] *nf* : genuflexion
géochimie [ʒeɔʃimi] *nf* : geochemistry
géodésique [ʒeɔdezik] *adj* : geodesic
géographe [ʒeɔgraf] *nmf* : geographer
géographie [ʒeɔgrafi] *nf* : geography
géographique [ʒeɔgrafik] *adj* : geographic, geographical — **géographiquement** [-fikmɑ̃] *adv*
geôlier, -lière [ʒolje, -ljɛr] *n* : jailer
géologie [ʒeɔlɔʒi] *nf* : geology
géologique [ʒeɔlɔʒik] *adj* : geologic, geological — **géologiquement** [-ʒikmɑ̃] *adv*
géologue [ʒeɔlɔg] *nmf* : geologist
géomagnétique [ʒeɔmaɲetik] *adj* : geomagnetic
géomètre [ʒeɔmɛtr] *nmf or* **arpenteur géomètre** : surveyor
géométrie [ʒeɔmetri] *nf* : geometry
géométrique [ʒeɔmetrik] *adj* : geometrical
gérance [ʒerɑ̃s] *nf* : management
géranium [ʒeranjɔm] *nm* : geranium
gérant, -rante [ʒerɑ̃, -rɑ̃t] *n* : manager
gerbe [ʒɛrb] *nf* **1** : sheaf (of wheat) **2** : bunch (of flowers, etc.) **3** : spray, burst (of water, sparks, etc.)
gerbille [ʒɛrbij] *nf* : gerbil
gercer [ʒɛrse] {6} *vt* : to chap, to crack — **se gercer** *vr*
gerçure [ʒɛrsyr] *nf* : chapping, crack (in the skin)
gérer [ʒere] {87} *vt* : to manage, to run, to handle
gériatrie [ʒerjatri] *nf* : geriatrics
gériatrique [ʒerjatrik] *adj* : geriatric
germain, -maine [ʒɛrmɛ̃, -mɛn] *adj* **cousin germain** : first cousin
germanium [ʒɛrmanjɔm] *nm* : germanium
germe [ʒɛrm] *nm* **1** : germ **2** : sprout **3** : seed (of an idea, etc.)
germer [ʒɛrme] *vi* **1** : to sprout, to germinate **2** : to form (of ideas, hopes, etc.)
germination [ʒɛrminasjɔ̃] *nf* : germination
gérondif [ʒerɔ̃dif] *nm* : gerund
gérontologie [ʒerɔ̃tɔlɔʒi] *nf* : gerontology
gérontologue [ʒerɔ̃tɔlɔg] *nmf* : gerontologist
gésier [ʒezje] *nm* : gizzard
gésir [ʒezir] {47} *vi* : to lie, to be lying
gestation [ʒestasjɔ̃] *nf* : gestation
geste [ʒɛst] *nm* : gesture, movement <ne faites pas un geste : don't move>
gestion [ʒɛstjɔ̃] *nf* : management <gestion de fichiers : file management>
gestionnaire [ʒɛstjɔnɛr] *nmf* : administrator
geyser [ʒezɛr] *nm* : geyser
ghanéen, -néenne [ganeɛ̃, -neɛn] *adj* : Ghanaian
Ghanéen, -néenne *n* : Ghanaian
ghetto [geto] *nm* : ghetto
gibbon [jibɔ̃] *nm* : gibbon
gibecière [jibɛsjɛr] *nf* **1** : game bag **2** : shoulder bag
gibet [jibɛ] *nm* : gallows
gibier [jibje] *nm* **1** : game (animals) **2** : prey <un gibier facile : an easy target>
giboulée [jibule] *nf* : sudden shower <les giboulées de mars : April showers>
giclée [jikle] *nf* : spurt, squirt
gicler [jikle] *vi* : to spurt, to squirt, to spatter
gicleur [jiklœr] *nm Can* : sprinkler (for fire)
gifle [jifl] *nf* : slap (in the face)
gifler [jifle] *vt* : to slap
gigantesque [jigɑ̃tɛsk] *adj* : gigantic, huge
gigogne [jigɔɲ] *adj* **1 lit gigogne** : trundle bed **2 tables gigognes** : nest of tables
gigot [jigo] *nm* : leg of lamb
gigoter [jigɔte] *vi fam* : to wriggle, to fidget
gigue [jig] *nf* : jig

gilet [ʒilɛ] *nm* **1** : vest <gilet pare-balles : bulletproof vest> <gilet de sauvetage : life jacket> **2** : cardigan (sweater)
gin [dʒin] *nm* : gin
gingembre [ʒɛ̃ʒɑbr] *nm* : ginger
ginseng [ʒinsɑ̃g] *nm* : ginseng
girafe [ʒiraf] *nf* : giraffe
giratoire [ʒiratwar] *adj* **sens giratoire** : rotary, traffic circle
girofle [ʒirɔfl] *nm* **clou de girofle** : clove
giroflée [ʒirɔfle] *nf* : wallflower
giron [ʒirɔ̃] *nm* **1** : lap **2** : bosom <dans le giron familial : in the bosom of one's family>
girouette [ʒirwɛt] *nf* : weather vane
gisement [ʒizmɑ̃] *nm* : deposit, bed (in geology)
gitan, -tane [ʒitɑ̃, -tan] *n* : Gypsy
gîte[1] [ʒit] *nm* **1** : shelter, lodging <le gîte et le couvert : room and board> **2** : shank (of beef, etc.)
gîte[2] *nf* : list, listing (of a boat)
gîter [ʒite] *vi* : to heel, to list (of a ship)
givre [ʒivr] *nm* : frost
givrer [ʒivre] *vt* : to cover with frost — *vi* : to ice up — **se givrer** *vr*
glabre [glabr] *adj* **1** : hairless **2** : clean-shaven
glaçage [glasaʒ] *nm* **1** : glazing (of fabric, etc.) **2** : icing (on cake)
glace [glas] *nf* **1** : ice **2** *France* : ice cream **3** VITRE : glass **4** MIROIR : mirror **5 glaces** *nfpl* : ice sheets **6 rester de glace** : to remain unmoved
glacé, -cée [glase] *adj* **1** GLACIAL : icy **2** : iced <thé glacé : iced tea> **3** GELÉ : frozen **4** : glossy (of paper, etc.)
glacer [glase] {6} *vt* **1** : to freeze, to chill **2** : to frost (a cake) **3** : to glaze, to give a shiny finish to **4** INTIMIDER : to intimidate
glacial, -ciale [glasjal] *adj, mpl* **-cials** *or* **-ciaux** [-sjo] : icy, frigid — **glacialement** [-sjalmɑ̃] *adv*
glaciaire [glasjɛr] *adj* : glacial (in geology)
glacier [glasje] *nm* : glacier
glacière [glasjɛr] *nf* : cooler, ice chest
glaçon [glasɔ̃] *nm* **1** : icicle **2** : ice cube
gladiateur [gladjatœr] *nm* : gladiator
glaïeul [glajœl] *nm* : gladiolus
glaire [glɛr] *nf* **1** : white of an egg **2** : mucus
glaise [glɛz] *nf* : clay
glaive [glɛv] *nm* : sword
gland [glɑ̃] *nm* **1** : acorn **2** : tassel
glande [glɑd] *nf* : gland — **glandulaire** [-dylɛr] *adj*
glaner [glane] *v* : to glean
glapir [glapir] *vi* : to yelp
glapissement [glapismɑ̃] *nm* : yelp
glas [gla] *nm* **1** : toll, knell **2 sonner le glas de** : to sound the death knell for
glaucome [glokom] *nm* : glaucoma
glauque [glok] *adj* **1** : dull blue-green **2** LUGUBRE : gloomy, dreary
glissade [glisad] *nf* **1** : slide, sliding **2** CHUTE : fall, slip
glissant, -sante [glisɑ̃, -sɑ̃t] *adj* : slippery
glissement [glismɑ̃] *nm* **1** : sliding, gliding **2** : shift <glissement politique vers la droite : political shift to the right> **3 glissement de terrain** : landslide
glisser [glise] *vi* **1** : to slide **2** : to slip **3** DÉRAPER : to skid — *vt* **1** : to slip, to sneak <glissez la lettre sous la porte : slip the letter under the door> **2** : to drag <glisser-déposer : drag and drop> — **se glisser** *vr* : to slip, to creep
glissière [glisjɛr] *nf* **1** : slide, groove **2 porte à glissière** : sliding door
glissoire [gliswar] *nf* : slide
global, -bale [glɔbal] *adj, mpl* **globaux** [glɔbo] : overall, total
globalement [glɔbalmɑ̃] *adv* : as a whole
globe [glɔb] *nm* **1** : globe **2 globe oculaire** : eyeball **3 globe terrestre** : the earth
globulaire [glɔbylɛr] *adj* : globular
globule [glɔbyl] *nm* : corpuscle, blood cell <globules blancs : white blood cells>
globuleux, -leuse [glɔbylø, -løz] *adj* : protruding (of eyes)
gloire [glwar] *nf* **1** RENOMMÉE : glory, fame **2** MÉRITE : distinction, credit **3** HOMMAGE : praise, homage **4** : celebrity, star
glorieux, -rieuse [glɔrjø, -rjøz] *adj* : glorious — **glorieusement** [-jøzmɑ̃] *adv*
glorification [glɔrifikasjɔ̃] *nm* : glorification
glorifier [glɔrifje] {96} *vt* : to glorify, to extol — **se glorifier** *vr* ~ **de** : to glory in
gloriole [glɔrjɔl] *nf* : vainglory
glose [gloz] *nf* : gloss, annotation
gloser [gloze] *vt* : to annotate, to gloss — *vi* ~ **sur** : to ramble on about
glossaire [glɔsɛr] *nm* : glossary
glouglou [gluglu] *nm* **1** *fam* : gurgling **2** : gobbling (of a turkey)
glougloter [gluglute] *vi* **1** *fam* : to gurgle **2** : to gobble (of a turkey)
gloussement [glusmɑ̃] *nm* : **1** clucking **2** : chuckling, chortling
glousser [gluse] *vi* **1** : to cluck **2** : to chuckle, to chortle
glouton[1], **-tonne** [glutɔ̃, -tɔn] *adj* : gluttonous, greedy
glouton[2], **-tonne** *n* : glutton
glouton[3] *nm* : wolverine
gloutonnerie [glutɔnri] *nf* : gluttony
gluant, gluante [glyɑ̃, -ɑ̃t] *adj* COLLANT : sticky, gummy, glutinous
glucose [glykoz] *nm* : glucose
gluten [glytɛn] *nm* : gluten
glutineux, -neuse [glytinø, -nøz] *adj* : glutinous
glycérine [gliserin] *nf* : glycerine

glycine [glisin] *nf* : wisteria
gnôle [ɲol] *nf France fam* : booze
gnome [ɡnom] *nm* : gnome
gnou [ɡnu] *nm* : gnu
go [ɡo] *adv France fam* **tout de go** : straightaway, at once
gobelet [ɡɔblɛ] *nm* : tumbler, beaker
gober [ɡɔbe] *vt* **1** : to swallow whole **2** *fam* : to swallow, to fall for
godasse [ɡɔdas] *nf fam* : shoe
godet [ɡɔde] *nm* **1** : jar, small pitcher **2** : pucker (in clothing)
godille [ɡɔdij] *nf* : scull, paddle
godiller [ɡɔdije] *vi* : to scull
goéland [ɡɔelɑ̃] *nm* : gull
goélette [ɡɔelɛt] *nf* : schooner
goglu [ɡɔɡly] *nm Can* : bobolink
gogo [ɡoɡo] *nm fam* **à ~** : galore
goguenard, -narde [ɡɔɡnar, -nard] *adj* MOQUEUR : mocking
goinfre [ɡwɛ̃fr] *nm fam* : pig, glutton
goitre [ɡwatr] *nm* : goiter
golf [ɡɔlf] *nm* : golf
golfe [ɡɔlf] *nm* : gulf, bay
golfeur, -feuse [ɡɔlfœr, -føz] *n* : golfer
gombo [ɡɔ̃bo] *nm* : gumbo
gomme [ɡɔm] *nf* **1** : gum, resin **2** : eraser **3 gomme à mâcher** : chewing gum
gommer [ɡɔme] *vt* **1** : to gum <papier gommé : gummed paper> **2** EFFACER : to erase
gond [ɡɔ̃] *nm* **1** : hinge **2 sortir de ses gonds** *fam* : to fly off the handle
gondole [ɡɔ̃dɔl] *nf* : gondola
gondoler [ɡɔ̃dɔle] *v* **se gondoler** *vr* **1** : to warp, to buckle **2** *fam* : to laugh, to be in stitches
gonflable [ɡɔ̃flabl] *adj* : inflatable
gonflé, -flée [ɡɔ̃fle] *adj* **1** : swollen, bloated **2 être gonflé** *fam* : to have a nerve
gonflement [ɡɔ̃fləmɑ̃] *nm* **1** : inflation **2** : swelling
gonfler [ɡɔ̃fle] *vt* **1** : to blow up, to inflate (a balloon, a tire, etc.) **2** : to swell <avoir les yeux gonflés : to have swollen eyes> **3** : to inflate, to exaggerate <prix gonflés : inflated prices> — *vi* : to swell, to rise — **se gonfler** *vr* **1** : to swell **2 ~ de** : to swell up with, to be filled with
gonfleur [ɡɔ̃flœr] *nm* : (air) pump
gong [ɡɔ̃ɡ] *nm* : gong
goret [ɡɔrɛ] *nm* : piglet
gorge [ɡɔrʒ] *nf* **1** : throat <mal de gorge : sore throat> <avoir la gorge serrée : to have a lump in one's throat> **2** : bosom, chest **3** : gorge (in geography) **4** : groove, channel
gorgée [ɡɔrʒe] *nf* : mouthful, sip, gulp
gorger [ɡɔrʒe] {17} *vt* : to fill, to stuff — **se gorger** *vr* **1** : to fill up **2** SE BOURRER : to stuff oneself
gorille [ɡɔrij] *nm* **1** : gorilla **2** *fam* : bodyguard
gosier [ɡozje] *nm* : throat
gosse [ɡɔs] *nmf France fam* : kid, youngster
gosser [ɡɔse] *vt Can fam* : to whittle
gothique [ɡɔtik] *adj* : Gothic
gouache [ɡwaʃ] *nf* : poster paint
gouaille [ɡwaj] *nf* : cocky humor, cheek
goudron [ɡudrɔ̃] *nm* : tar
goudronner [ɡudrɔne] *vt* : to tar (a road)
gouffre [ɡufr] *nm* **1** : gulf, abyss **2 au bord du gouffre** : on the brink of despair
gouge [ɡuʒ] *nf* : gouge, chisel
goujat [ɡuʒa] *nm* : boor
goujon [ɡuʒɔ̃] *nm* : dowel
goulasch *or* **goulache** [ɡulaʃ] *nmf* : goulash
goule [ɡul] *nf* : ghoul
goulet [ɡulɛ] *nm* **1** : gully **2** : narrows **3 goulet d'étranglement** : bottleneck
goulot [ɡulo] *nm* **1** : neck (of a bottle) <boire au goulot : to drink from the bottle> **2 goulot d'étranglement** : bottleneck, obstacle
goulu[1], **-lue** [ɡuly] *adj* : greedy, gluttonous — **goulûment** [-lymɑ̃] *adv*
goulu[2], **-lue** *n* : glutton
goupille [ɡupij] *nf* : pin
gourbi [ɡurbi] *nm* : foxhole
gourd, gourde [ɡur, ɡurd] *adj* : numb (with cold)
gourde [ɡurd] *nf* **1** : canteen, flask **2** : gourd **3** *fam* : dope, blockhead
gourdin [ɡurdɛ̃] *nm* : cudgel, club
gourmand[1], **-mande** [ɡurmɑ̃, -mɑ̃d] *adj* **1** : greedy **2** : fond of eating
gourmand[2], **-mande** *n* **1** : glutton **2** : gourmet, epicure
gourmandise [ɡurmɑ̃diz] *nf* **1** : greed **2** : gluttony **3 gourmandises** *nfpl* : sweets, delicacies
gourmet [ɡurmɛ] *nm* GASTRONOME : gourmet
gourmette [ɡurmɛt] *nf* : chain bracelet
gourou [ɡuru] *nm* : guru
gousse [ɡus] *nf* **1** : pod **2 gousse d'ail** : clove of garlic
gousset [ɡusɛ] *nm* : vest pocket, watch pocket
goût [ɡu] *nm* **1** : taste (sense) **2** SAVEUR : flavor **3** : taste, discernment <avoir du goût : to have good taste> <de mauvais goût : tasteless, in bad taste> **4** : liking, fondness <prendre goût à : to develop a liking for>
goûter[1] [ɡute] *vt* **1** : to taste **2** : to relish, to enjoy — *vi* **1** : to have an afternoon snack **2 ~ à** *or* **~ de** : to try out, to sample **3 ~ à** *or* **~ de** : to get a taste of
goûter[2] *nm* : afternoon snack
goutte [ɡut] *nf* **1** : drop <une goutte de sang : a drop of blood> <tomber goutte à goutte : to drip> **2** : gout **3 gouttes** *nfpl* : drops (in medicine)
gouttelette [ɡutlɛt] *nf* : droplet, globule
goutter [ɡute] *vi* : to drip

gouttière [gutjɛr] *nf* **1** : gutter (on a roof) **2** : downspout **3** : cast, splint
gouvernail [guvɛrnaj] *nm* **1** : rudder **2** BARRE : helm <tenir le gouvernail : to take the helm>
gouvernante [guvɛrnɑ̃t] *nf* **1** : governess **2** : housekeeper
gouverne [guvɛrn] *nf* **1 gouverne de direction** : rudder (of an airplane) **2 pour votre gouverne** : for your information
gouvernement [guvɛrnəmɑ̃] *nm* : government — **gouvernemental, -tale** [-mɑ̃tal] *adj*
gouverner [guvɛrne] *vt* **1** DIRIGER : to steer (a ship) **2** : to govern, to rule **3** MAÎTRISER : to control (one's emotions, etc.) — *vi* : to steer
gouverneur [guvɛrnœr] *nm* **1** : governor **2 gouverneur général** *Can* : governor-general
goyave [gɔjav] *nf* : guava (fruit)
grabat [graba] *nm* : pallet (bed)
grabataire[1] [grabatɛr] *adj* : bedridden
grabataire[2] *n* : (bedridden) invalid
grabuge [grabyʒ] *nm fam* BAGARRE : brawl, fighting
grâce [gras] *nf* **1** : gracefulness, charm <avec grâce : gracefully> **2** : willingness <de bonne grâce : with good grace, willingly> **3** : favor <accorder une grâce : to grant a favor> **4** : mercy, pardon **5 ~ à** : thanks to **6 grâces** *nfpl* : grace <dire les grâces : to say grace>
gracier [grasje] {96} *vt* : to pardon
gracieuseté [grasjøzte] *nf* **1** : kindliness **2** : free gift
gracieux, -cieuse [grasjø, -sjøz] *adj* **1** : graceful **2** AIMABLE : gracious, kind **3** GRATUIT : free — **gracieusement** [-sjøzmɑ̃] *adv*
gracile [grasil] *adj* ÉLANCÉ : slender
gradation [gradasjɔ̃] *nf* : gradation
grade [grad] *nm* **1** : rank <monter en grade : to be promoted> **2** : university degree, title **3** : grade (of oil)
gradin [gradɛ̃] *nm* **1** : tier **2 gradins** *nmpl* : bleachers, stands
graduel, -duelle [gradyɛl] *adj* : gradual, progressive — **graduellement** [-dyɛlmɑ̃] *adv*
graduer [gradye] *vt* **1** : to graduate (a measuring instrument) **2** : to increase gradually
graffiti [grafiti] *nmpl* : graffiti
grafigne [grafiɲ] *or* **grafignure** [grafiɲyr] *nf Can* : scratch, scrape
grafigner [grafiɲe] *vt Can* : to scratch, to scrape
grain [grɛ̃] *nm* **1** : (cereal) grain **2** : seed, berry <grain de café : coffee bean> <grain de poivre : peppercorn> <grain de raisin : grape> **3** : bead **4** : speck, particle <grain de sable : grain of sand> <un grain d'originalité : a touch of originality> **5 grain de beauté** : mole
graine [grɛn] *nf* **1** : seed <monter en graine : to go to seed> **2 être de la mauvaise graine** : to be incorrigible, to be a bad lot
graisse [grɛs] *nf* **1** : grease **2** : fat **3 graisse de baleine** : blubber
graisser [grɛse] *vt* **1** : to lubricate, to grease, to oil **2** : to stain with grease
graisseux, -seuse [grɛsø, -søz] *adj* **1** : greasy **2** : fatty (in medicine)
grammaire [gramɛr] *nf* : grammar
grammatical, -cale [gramatikal] *adj, mpl* **-caux** [-ko] : grammatical — **grammaticalement** [-kalmɑ̃] *adv*
gramme [gram] *nm* : gram
granade [granad] *nf* : pomegranate
grand[1] [grɑ̃] *adv* **1** : wide <ouvrir grand : to open wide> **2 voir grand** : to think big **3 en ~** : on a large scale, in a big way
grand[2], **grande** [grɑ̃, grɑ̃d] *adj* **1** : tall, long, wide **2** GROS : big, large **3** : abundant <un grand monde : many people> <au grand jour : in broad daylight> **4** : great <grandes distances : great distances> <c'est une grande travailleuse : she works very hard> **5** PRINCIPAL : main, principal **6** : important <un grand homme : a great man> **7** : elder, older, grown-up <ma grande sœur : my older sister> <les grandes personnes : grown-ups, adults> **8** : extreme, intense <avoir grand faim : to be very hungry> <il est grand temps que : it's high time that>
grand[3] *nm* : important person, leader, big power
grand-angle [grɑ̃tɑ̃gl] *or* **grand-angulaire** [-ɑ̃gylɛr] *nm, pl* **grands-angles** [grɑ̃zɑ̃gl] *or* **grands-angulaires** [grɑ̃zɑ̃gylɛr] : wide-angle lens
grand-chose [grɑ̃ʃoz] *pron* **pas grand-chose** : not much
grandement [grɑ̃dmɑ̃] *adv* **1** BEAUCOUP : greatly, a lot **2** : extremely
grandeur [grɑ̃dœr] *nf* **1** : size, scale, magnitude <grandeur nature : life-size> **2** NOBLESSE : greatness, nobility **3** SPLENDEUR : splendor, glory
grandiloquence [grɑ̃dilɔkɑ̃s] *nf* : pomposity, bombast
grandiloquent, -quente [grɑ̃dilɔkɑ̃, -kɑ̃t] *adj* : grandiloquent, pompous
grandiose [grɑ̃djoz] *adj* : grandiose
grandir [grɑ̃dir] *vt* **1** : to magnify, to make look taller **2** EXAGÉRER : to exaggerate **3** ENNOBLIR : to increase the stature of — *vi* **1** : to grow **2** AUGMENTER : to increase
grand-mère [grɑ̃mɛr] *nf, pl* **grands-mères** : grandmother
grand-oncle [grɑ̃tɔ̃kl] *nm, pl* **grands-oncles** [grɑ̃zɔ̃kl] : great-uncle
grand-peine [grɑ̃pɛn] *nf* **à ~** : with great difficulty
grand-père [grɑ̃pɛr] *nm, pl* **grands-pères** : grandfather

grands–parents [grɑ̃parɑ̃] *nmpl* : grandparents
grand–tante [grɑ̃tɑ̃t] *nf, pl* **grand(s)–tantes** : great-aunt
grand–voile [grɑ̃vwal] *nf, pl* **grand(s)–voiles** : mainsail
grange [grɑ̃ʒ] *nf* : barn
granit *or* **granite** [granit] *nm* : granite
granule [granyl] *nm* : small pill
granulé [granyle] *nm* : granule
granuleux, -leuse [granylø, -løz] *adj* : granular
graphique[1] [grafik] *adj* : graphic — **graphiquement** [-fikmɑ̃] *adv*
graphique[2] *nm* : graph
graphisme [grafism] *nm* **1** : writing, handwriting **2** : graphic arts *pl*
graphiste [grafist] *nmf* : graphic artist
graphite [grafit] *nm* : graphite
grappe [grap] *nf* : cluster <grappe de raisins : bunch of grapes>
grappiller [grapije] *vt* : to gather, to glean
grappin [grapɛ̃] *nm* **1** : grapnel **2 mettre le grappin sur** : to get one's hooks into
gras[1] [gra] *adv* **1 faire gras** : to eat meat (in religion) **2 manger gras** : to eat fatty foods **3 parler gras** : to talk coarsely
gras[2], **grasse** [gra, gras] *adj* **1** : fatty <matières grasses : fats> **2** GROS : fat (of persons) **3** HUILEUX : greasy, oily **4** : sticky, slimy **5** : throaty (of the voice), loose (of a cough) **6** VULGAIRE : crude, coarse **7** : lush, abundant **8** : bold (of type)
gras[3] *nm* **1** : fat **2** : grease **3** : fleshy part <gras de la jambe : calf>
grassement [grasmɑ̃] *adv* : highly, handsomely <grassement payé : well paid>
grassouillet, -lette [grasujɛ, -jɛt] *adj* POTELÉ : pudgy, plump
gratifiant, -fiante [gratifjɑ̃, -jɑ̃t] *adj* : gratifying, rewarding
gratification [gratifikasjɔ̃] *nf* **1** : bonus **2** : gratification
gratifier [gratifje] {96} *vt* **1** : to reward **2** : to gratify
gratin [gratɛ̃] *nm* **1** : dish baked with cheese or crumb topping **2** *fam* : upper crust (of society)
gratiné, -née [gratine] *adj* **1** : au gratin, browned **2** *fam* : extreme, difficult, weird
gratis [gratis] *adv* : free
gratitude [gratityd] *nf* : gratitude, gratefulness
gratte [grat] *nf Can* CHASSE-NEIGE : snowplow
gratte–ciel [gratsjɛl] *nms & pl* : skyscraper
grattement [gratmɑ̃] *n* : scratching (sound)
gratte–papier [gratpapje] *nms & pl* : pencil pusher, office drudge
gratte–pieds [gratpje] *nms & pl* : doormat
gratter [grate] *vt* **1** : to scratch **2** : to scrape (a surface) **3** *fam* : to scrape together **4** *fam* : to overtake **5 gratter (de) la guitare** : to strum a guitar — *vi* : to scratch — **se gratter** *vr* : to scratch oneself
gratteux, -teuse [gratø, -tøz] *adj Can fam* : stingy, cheap
grattoir [gratwar] *nm* : scraper
gratuit, -tuite [gratɥi, -tɥit] *adj* **1** : free **2** : gratuitous — **gratuitement** [-tɥitmɑ̃] *adv*
gratuité [gratɥite] *nf* **1** : exemption from payment **2** : gratuitousness
gravats [grava] *nmpl* : rubble
grave [grav] *adj* **1** SÉRIEUX : grave, serious **2** : solemn **3** : deep, low-pitched
graveleux, -leuse [gravlø, -løz] *adj* **1** : gravelly **2** : gritty **3** : indecent, smutty
gravelle [gravɛl] *nf Can* : fine gravel
gravement [gravmɑ̃] *adv* **1** : gravely, solemnly **2** : seriously
graver [grave] *vt* **1** : to engrave, to carve **2** : to fix, to etch <gravé dans ma mémoire : etched in my memory>
graveur, -veuse [gravœr, -vøz] *n* : engraver
gravier [gravje] *nm* : gravel, grit
gravillon [gravijɔ̃] *nm* : (fine) gravel
gravir [gravir] *vt* : to climb (up)
gravitation [gravitasjɔ̃] *nf* : gravitation
gravité [gravite] *nf* **1** : gravity **2** : seriousness, importance
graviter [gravite] *vi* : to gravitate, to revolve
gravure [gravyr] *nf* **1** : engraving <gravure sur bois : woodcutting> <gravure à l'eau forte : etching> **2** : print, plate
gré [gre] *nm* **1** VOLONTÉ : will <de plein gré : willingly> <contre son gré : unwillingly> **2** GOÛT : taste, liking <à votre gré : as you wish> **3 bon gré mal gré** : like it or not **4 savoir (bien) gré à** : to be grateful to
grèbe [grɛb] *nm* : grebe
grébiche [grebiʃ] *nf Can* : crone, hag
grec[1], **grecque** [grɛk] *adj* : Greek
grec[2] *nm* : Greek (language)
Grec, Grecque *n* : Greek
gréement [gremɑ̃] *nm* : rigging
gréer [gree] {89} *vt* : to rig (a ship)
greffe [grɛf] *nf* **1** : graft (in botany) **2** : graft, transplant (in medicine)
greffer [grɛfe] *vt* **1** : to graft **2** : to transplant (an organ) — **se greffer** *vr* : to come along, to arise
greffier, -fière [grɛfje, -fjɛr] *nm* : clerk of court
grégaire [greger] *adj* : gregarious
grège [grɛʒ] *adj* : raw, unbleached
grêle[1] [grɛl] *adj* **1** : lanky, spindly **2** : high-pitched, shrill
grêle[2] *nf* : hail
grêlé, -lée [grele] *adj* : pockmarked

grêler [grele] *v impers* **il grêle** : it's hailing
grêlon [grɛlɔ̃] *nm* : hailstone
grelot [grəlo] *nm* : small bell, sleigh bell
grelotter [grəlɔte] *vi* **1** TREMBLER : to shiver **2** : to tinkle, to jingle
grenade [grənad] *nf* **1** : pomegranate **2** : grenade <grenade à main : hand grenade>
grenadin, -dine [grənadɛ̃, -din] *adj* : Grenadian
Grenadin, -dine *n* : Grenadian
grenadine [grənadin] *nf* : grenadine
grenat[1] [grəna] *adj* : dark red
grenat[2] *nm* : garnet
grenier [grənje] *nm* **1** : attic, loft <grenier à foin : hayloft> **2** *or* **grenier à blé** : breadbasket (region)
grenouille [grənuj] *nf* : frog
grès [grɛ] *nm* **1** : sandstone **2** : stoneware
grésil [grezil] *nm* : fine hail, sleet
grésillement [grezijmɑ̃] *nm* **1** : crackling (of a telephone, radio, etc.) **2** : sizzling
grésiller [grezije] *vi* : to crackle, to sizzle — *v impers* : to sleet, to hail
grève [grɛv] *nf* **1** PLAGE : shore **2** : strike <grève de la faim : hunger strike>
grever [grəve] {52} *vt* : to burden, to put a (financial) strain on
gréviste[1] [grevist] *adj* : striking
gréviste[2] *nmf* : striker
gribouillage [gribujaʒ] *nm* : scribble, scrawl
gribouiller [gribuje] *vt* : to scribble — *vi* : to doodle, to scribble
gricher [grife] *vt Can fam* : to grind (one's teeth)
grief [grijef] *nm* : grievance
grièvement [grijɛvmɑ̃] *adv* : seriously, severely
griffe [grif] *nf* **1** : claw <sortir ses griffes : to show one's claws> <les griffes de la mort : the jaws of death> **2** : signature, label (of a product)
griffer [grife] *vt* : to scratch — **se griffer** *vr*
griffonner [grifɔne] *vt* : to scribble, to jot down
griffure [grifyr] *nf* : scratch
grignoter [grinɔte] *vt* **1** : to nibble **2** : to eat away at **3** : to gain, to acquire gradually — *vi* **1** : to gnaw **2** : to nibble
gril [gril] *nm* **1** : broiler **2** : grill (for cooking)
grill [gril] *nm* : grill (restaurant)
grillade [grijad] *nf* **1** : grilled meat, grill **2 faire des grillades** : to have a barbecue
grillage [grijaʒ] *nm* : wire fencing
grille [grij] *nf* **1** : metal fencing or gate **2** : bars *pl* **3** : grate **4** : grid, squares *pl* **5** : scale, table <grille des salaires : salary scale>
grille–pain [grijpɛ̃] *nms & pl* : toaster
griller [grije] *vt* **1** : to toast, to roast (nuts, etc.) **2** : to grill, to broil **3** : to burn out **4 griller un feu rouge** : to go through a red light — *vi* **1** : to broil **2 se faire griller** *Can fam* : to get a suntan
grillon [grijɔ̃] *nm* : cricket
grimace [grimas] *nf* : grimace, face <faire des grimaces : to make faces> <faire la grimace : to make a (long) face, to scowl>
grimacer [grimase] {6} *vi* : to grimace
grimper [grɛ̃pe] *vi* **1** : to climb **2** : to be steep **3** *fam* : to soar, to rocket — *vt* : to climb
grimpeur, -peuse [grɛ̃pœr, -pøz] *n* : climber
grinçant, -çante [grɛ̃sɑ̃, -sɑ̃t] *adj* **1** : creaking, grating **2** : caustic <humour grinçant : caustic wit>
grincement [grɛ̃smɑ̃] *nm* : creak, squeak
grincer [grɛ̃se] {6} *vi* **1** : to creak, to grate, to grind **2 grincer des dents** : to grind one's teeth
grincheux, -cheuse [grɛ̃ʃø, -ʃøz] *adj* GROGNON : grumpy
gringalet [grɛ̃galɛ] *nm* : puny person, weakling
grippe [grip] *nf* **1** : flu, influenza **2 prendre qqn en grippe** : to take a sudden dislike to s.o.
grippé, -pée [gripe] *adj* **être grippé** : to have the flu
gripper [gripe] *v* : to jam — **se gripper** *vr* : to seize up
grippe–sou [gripsu] *nm, pl* **grippe–sous** *fam* : tightwad, skinflint
gris[1], **grise** [gri, griz] *adj* **1** : gray **2** MORNE : dull, dreary <un temps gris : a gray day> **3** *fam* : tipsy
gris[2] *nm* : gray
grisaille [grizaj] *nf* **1** : grayness **2** MONOTONIE : dullness
grisant, -sante [grizɑ̃, -zɑ̃t] *adj* ENIVRANT : exhilarating, intoxicating
grisâtre [grizatr] *adj* : grayish
griser [grize] *vt* **1** ENIVRER : to intoxicate **2** : to exhilarate — **se griser** *vr*
griserie [grizri] *nf* : exhilaration
grisonnant [grizɔnɑ̃] *adj* : grizzled
grisonner [grizɔne] *vi* : to turn gray, to go gray
grive [griv] *nf* : thrush
grivois, -voise [grivwa, -waz] *adj* : bawdy, risqué
grizzli *or* **grizzly** [grizli] *nm* : grizzly bear
Groenlandais, -daise [grɔenlɑ̃dɛ, -dɛz] *n* : Greenlander
grog [grɔg] *nm* : grog
grogne [grɔɲ] *nf* : grumbling, discontent
grognement [grɔɲmɑ̃] *nm* **1** : growl, grunt **2** : grumble
grogner [grɔɲe] *vi* **1** : to growl, to grunt **2** : to grumble, to grouch

grognon, -gnonne [grɔɲɔ̃, -ɲɔn] *adj* : grumpy, grouchy
groin [grwɛ̃] *nm* : snout (of a pig)
grommeler [grɔmle] {8} *vt* : to mutter — *vi* **1** : to groan, to grumble **2** : to snort
grondement [grɔ̃dmɑ̃] *nm* **1** : rumble, roar **2** : growl
gronder [grɔ̃de] *vt* RÉPRIMANDER : to scold — *vi* **1** : to rumble, to roar **2** GROGNER : to growl **3** : to be brewing
gros[1] [gro] *adv* **1** BEAUCOUP : a great deal <coûter gros : to cost a lot> **2 écrire gros** : to write in big letters
gros[2], **grosse** [gro, gros] *adj* **1** : big, large **2** : thick, bulky **3** : fat **4** : great, considerable <de gros dégâts : considerable damage> **5** : serious, major **6** : loud <une grosse voix : a booming voice> **7** : heavy <un gros fumeur : a heavy smoker> **8** : coarse, crude, rough **9 gros lot** : jackpot **10 gros plan** : close-up **11 gros titre** : headline **12 grosse caisse** : bass drum
gros[3], **grosse** *n* **1** : fat person **2** : rich person
gros[4] *nm* **1** : bulk, main part <le gros des étudiants : most of the students> **2** : wholesale business **3 en ~** : roughly, in general
groseille [grozɛj] *nf* **1** : currant **2 groseille à maquereau** : gooseberry
gros-porteur [groporter] *nm, pl* **gros-porteurs** : jumbo jet, liner
grosse [gros] *nf* : gross, twelve dozen
grossesse [grosɛs] *nf* : pregnancy
grosseur [grosœr] *nf* **1** : fatness, corpulence **2** : size **3** : lump, tumor
grossier, -sière [grosje, -sjɛr] *adj* **1** : coarse, rough **2** : crude, vulgar **3** : flagrant, glaring (of an error, etc.)
grossièrement [grosjɛrmɑ̃] *adv* **1** IMPOLIMENT : rudely **2** LOURDEMENT : grossly <se tromper grossièrement : to be grossly mistaken> **3** : roughly, crudely, coarsely **4** : approximately
grossièreté [grosjɛrte] *nf* **1** : rudeness **2** : crudeness **3** : coarseness, vulgarity
grossir [grosir] *vt* **1** AUGMENTER : to increase **2** EXAGÉRER : to exaggerate **3** AGRANDIR : to magnify, to enlarge **4** : to make appear fatter — *vi* **1** ENGRAISSER : to put on weight **2** : to grow larger
grossissant, -sante [grosisɑ̃, -sɑ̃t] *adj* **1** : magnifying <verre grossissant : magnifying glass> **2** : swelling, growing
grossissement [grosismɑ̃] *nm* **1** : enlargement **2** : magnification
grossiste [grosist] *nmf* : wholesaler, jobber
grosso modo [grosomodo] *adv* : more or less, roughly
grotesque [grɔtɛsk] *adj* **1** : grotesque **2** : ridiculous — **grotesquement** [-tɛskmɑ̃] *adv*
grotte [grɔt] *nf* : cave, grotto
grouiller [gruje] *vi* **~ de** : to swarm with, to teem with — **se grouiller** *vr fam* : to hurry, to get a move on
groupe [grup] *nm* **1** : group (of persons or objects) <groupe ethnique : ethnic group> <groupe de pression : pressure group, lobby> <groupe d'arbres : clump of trees> **2 groupe sanguin** : blood type
groupement [grupmɑ̃] *nm* **1** : grouping, group **2** : association
grouper [grupe] *vt* : to group, to pool (resources, etc.) — **se grouper** *vr* : to gather, to get together
groupuscule [grupyskyl] *nm* : faction, (political) clique
grouse [gruz] *nf* : grouse (bird)
gruau [gryo] *nm* **1** : (fine) wheat flour **2** : groats <gruau de maïs : grits> **3** *Can* : oatmeal, porridge
grue [gry] *nf* : crane
gruger [gryʒe] {17} *vt* **1** : to dupe, to swindle **2** *Can fam* : to eat away at
grumeau [grymo] *nm, pl* **grumeaux** : lump (in sauce, etc.)
grumeleux, -leuse [grymlø, -løz] *adj* : lumpy
gruyère [gryjɛr] *nm* : Gruyère (cheese)
guatémaltèque [gwatemaltɛk] *adj* : Guatemalan
Guatémaltèque *nmf* : Guatemalan
gué [ge] *nm* : ford, crossing <passer à gué : to ford>
guenille [gənij] *nf* **1** *Can* : rag **2 guenilles** *nfpl* : rags and tatters (clothing)
guenon [gənɔ̃] *nf* : female monkey
guépard [gepar] *nm* : cheetah
guêpe [gɛp] *nf* : wasp
guêpier [gɛpje] *nm* **1** : wasps' nest **2** : sticky situation, trap
guère [gɛr] *adv* **1 ne . . . guère** : hardly, scarcely <elle n'est guère aimable : she's not very kind> <il n'y a guère de voitures : there are hardly any cars> **2 ne . . . guère** : not for long, not often <il ne vient guère me voir : he rarely comes to see me>
guérilla [gerija] *nf* : guerrilla warfare, guerrillas *pl* (fighters)
guérillero [gerijero] *nm* : guerrilla
guérir [gerir] *vt* : to cure, to heal — *vi* **1** SE RÉTABLIR : to get better, to recover **2** : to heal — **se guérir** *vr* **1** : to be cured **2** : to break oneself of, to get over
guérison [gerizɔ̃] *nf* **1** : cure, healing **2** RÉTABLISSEMENT : recovery
guérissable [gerisabl] *adj* : curable
guérisseur, -seuse [gerisœr, -søz] *n* : healer
guérite [gerit] *nf* **1** : sentry box **2** *France* : workman's hut

guerre [gɛr] *nf* : war <faire la guerre à : to wage war against> <guerre chimique : chemical warfare>
guerrier[1], **-rière** [gɛrje, -jɛr] *adj* : warlike, martial
guerrier[2], **-rière** *n* : warrior
guerroyer [gerwaje] {58} *vi* : to wage war
guet [gɛ] *nm* : watch, lookout <faire le guet : to be on the lookout>
guet–apens [getapɑ̃] *nm, pl* **guets–apens** : ambush
guetter [gete] *vt* **1** ÉPIER : to watch intently **2** ATTENDRE : to watch out for, to lie in wait for
guetteur [getœr] *nm* : lookout
gueule [gœl] *nf* **1** : mouth (of an animal, a tunnel, etc.) **2** *fam* : mouth, trap <(ferme) ta gueule! : shut up!> **3** *fam* : face <faire la gueule : to pull a face, to look sulky> **4 gueule de bois** : hangover
gueule–de–loup [gœldəlu] *nf, pl* **gueules–de–loup** : snapdragon
gueuler [gœle] *v fam* : to bawl, to bellow
gueuleton [gœltɔ̃] *nm fam* : feast, spread
gui [gi] *nm* **1** : mistletoe **2** : boom (of a ship)
guichet [giʃɛ] *nm* **1** : window, counter **2** : box office <jouer à guichets fermés : to play to a full house> **3 guichet automatique** : automatic teller machine
guichetier, -tière [giʃtje, -tjɛr] *n* : counter clerk
guide[1] [gid] *nmf* **1** : guide <guide de montagne : mountain guide> **2** CONSEILLER : counselor, advisor
guide[2] *nm* **1** : guide **2** : guidebook <guide touristique : tourist guide>
guide[3] *nf* **1** : girl scout **2 guides** *nfpl* : reins
guider [gide] *vt* : to guide
guidon [gidɔ̃] *nm* : handlebars *pl*
guigne [giɲ] *nf fam* : bad luck <avoir la guigne : to be jinxed>
guigner [giɲe] *vt* : to eye, to take a look at
guignol [giɲɔl] *nm* **1** : puppet show <c'est du guignol : it's a complete farce> **2** : silly person, clown, fool
guillemets [gijmɛ] *nmpl* : quotation marks
guilleret, -rette [gijrɛ, -rɛt] *adj* : sprightly, perky
guillotine [gijɔtin] *nf* : guillotine — **guillotiner** *vt*
guimauve [gimov] *nf* **1** : marshmallow **2** *fam* : sentimentality, mush
guimbarde [gɛ̃bard] *nf* **1** : Jew's harp **2** *fam* : jalopy
guindé, -dée [gɛ̃de] *adj* : stiff, affected, prim
guindeau [gɛ̃d] *nm* : windlass
guinéen, -néenne [gineɛ̃, -neɛn] *adj* : Guinean
Guinéen, -néenne *n* : Guinean
guingois [gɛ̃gwa] **de ~** : askew <être de guingois : to be lopsided>
guinguette [gɛ̃get] *nf France* : café featuring music and dancing
guirlande [girlɑ̃d] *nf* **1** : garland **2 guirlandes de Noël** : tinsel
guise [giz] *nf* **1 à ta guise** : as you wish **2 en guise de** : by way of
guitare [gitar] *nf* : guitar
guitariste [gitarist] *nmf* : guitarist
guppy [gypi] *nm* : guppy
gustatif, -tive [gystatif, -tiv] *adj* : gustatory, of taste
guttural, -rale [gytyral] *adj, mpl* **-raux** [-ro] : guttural
guyanais, -naise [gɥijanɛ, -nɛz] *adj* : Guyanese
Guyanais, -naise *n* : Guyanese
gymnase [ʒimnaz] *nm* : gymnasium
gymnaste [ʒimnast] *nmf* : gymnast
gymnastique[1] [ʒimnastik] *adj* : gymnastic
gymnastique[2] *nf* : gymnastics
gynécologie [ʒinekɔlɔʒi] *nf* : gynecology
gynécologique [ʒinekɔlɔʒik] *adj* : gynecologic, gynecological
gynécologue [ʒinekɔlɔg] *nmf* : gynecologist
gypse [ʒips] *nm* : gypsum
gyrophare [ʒirɔfar] *nm* : revolving flashing light (on a vehicle)
gyroscope [ʒirɔskɔp] *nm* : gyroscope

H

h [aʃ] *nm* : h, the eighth letter of the alphabet
ha [ʾa] *interj* **ha ha** : ha-ha, very funny
habile [abil] *adj* **1** ADROIT : skillful **2** : clever — **habilement** [abilmɑ̃] *adv*
habileté [abilte] *nf* **1** : skill, skillfulness **2** : cleverness
habilité, -tée [abilite] *adj* **~ à** : entitled to, authorized to
habiliter [abilite] *vt* : to entitle, to empower
habillage [abijaʒ] *nm* **1** : dressing, getting dressed **2** : packaging, covering, casing
habillé, -lée [abije] *adj* **1** : dressed <tout habillé : fully clothed> **2** CHIC : smart, stylish
habillement [abijmɑ̃] *nm* **1** : clothes *pl*, clothing **2** : clothing industry

habiller [abije] *vt* **1** : to dress, to clothe **2** : to fit, to suit <cette robe vous habille bien : that dress really suits you> **3** REVÊTIR : to cover **— s'habiller** *vr* **1** : to get dressed <comment vais-je m'habiller? : what will I wear?> **2 ~ chez** : to buy one's clothes from **3 ~ en** : to dress up as

habit [abi] *nm* **1** : outfit, costume **2** : (religious) habit **3** *or* **habit de soirée** : evening dress, tails *pl* **4 habits** *nmpl* : clothes

habitable [abitabl] *adj* : habitable, inhabitable

habitacle [abitakl] *nm* : cockpit

habitant[1], **-tante** [abitɑ̃, -tɑ̃t] *n* **1** : inhabitant, resident **2** : occupant, dweller

habitant[2] *nm Can* : farmer

habitat [abita] *nm* **1** : housing **2** : habitat

habitation [abitasjɔ̃] *nf* **1** : living <conditions d'habitation : living conditions> **2** : house, dwelling **3** : residence, home

habiter [abite] *vt* **1** : to live in, to inhabit **2** : to dwell in (one's heart, etc.) **—** *vi* DEMEURER : to live, to reside <habiter à l'étranger : to live abroad>

habitude [abityd] *nf* **1** : habit <j'ai l'habitude de travailler dur : I'm used to working hard> **2** COUTUME : custom **3 comme d'habitude** : as usual **4 d'~** : usually **5 par habitude** : out of habit

habitué[1], **-tuée** [abituɥe] *adj* **~ à** : used to, accustomed to

habitué[2], **-tuée** *n* : regular (customer)

habituel, -tuelle [abituɛl] *adj* : usual, regular **— habituellement** [-tuɛlmɑ̃] *adv*

habituer [abituɥe] *vt* ACCOUTUMER : to accustom **— s'habituer** *vr* **~ à** : to get used to

hableur[1], **-bleuse** [ˈablœr, -bløz] *adj* : boastful

hableur[2], **-bleuse** *n* : braggart

hache [ˈaʃ] *nf* **1** : ax **2 hache d'armes** : battle-ax

haché, -chée [ˈaʃe] *adj* **1** : ground, chopped, minced <biftek haché : ground beef> **2** : jerky, disjointed

hacher [ˈaʃe] *vt* **1** : to chop, to mince **2** : to cut to pieces

hachette [aʃɛt] *nf* : hatchet

hache-viande [ˈaʃvjɑd] *nms & pl* : meat grinder

hachis [ˈaʃi] *nms & pl* : ground or minced food, hash <hachis de viande : ground meat>

hachisch [ˈaʃiʃ]→ **haschish**

hachoir [ˈaʃwar] *nm* **1** : meat grinder **2** : chopper, cleaver **3** : cutting board

hachure [ˈaʃyr] *nf* : shading, hatching

hachurer [aʃyre] *vt* : to shade in

hagard, -garde [ˈagar, -gard] *adj* : distraught, wild, frantic

haie [ˈɛ] *nf* **1** : hedge **2** : hurdle (in sports) **3** : row, line <haie d'honneur : honor guard>

haillons [ˈajɔ̃] *nmpl* : rags, tatters

haine [ˈɛn] *nf* : hatred, hate

haineux, -neuse [ˈɛnø, -nøz] *adj* : full of hatred

haïr [ˈair] {48} *vt* : to hate **— se haïr** *vr*

haïssable [ˈaisabl] *adj* : hateful, detestable

haïtien, -tienne [aisjɛ̃, -sjɛn] *adj* : Haitian

Haïtien, -tienne *n* : Haitian

hâle [ˈal] *nm* : suntan

hâlé, -lée [ˈale] *adj* : tanned, sunburned

haleine [alɛn] *nf* **1** : breath <avoir mauvaise haleine : to have bad breath> <hors d'haleine : out of breath> **2 de longue haleine** : long-term **3 tenir en haleine** : to hold spellbound

haler [ˈale] *vt* : to haul (in), to tow

haletant, -tante [ˈaltɑ̃, -tɑ̃t] *adj* : panting, breathless

halètement [ˈaletmɑ̃] *nm* : gasp

haleter [ˈalte] {20} *vi* **1** : to pant, to gasp for breath **2** : to puff, to chug (of an engine)

hall [ˈol] *nm* : (entrance) hall, lobby

halle [ˈal] *nf France* : (covered) market

hallier [ˈalje] *nm* : thicket, brush

Halloween [alowin] *nf* : Halloween

hallucinant, -nante [alysinɑ̃, -nɑ̃t] *adj* : extraordinary, astounding

hallucination [alysinasjɔ̃] *nf* : hallucination <avoir des hallucinations : to hallucinate>

hallucinogène[1] [alysinɔʒɛn] *adj* : hallucinogenic

hallucinogène[2] *nm* : hallucinogen

halo [ˈalo] *nm* : halo

halogène [alɔʒɛn] *nm* : halogen <lampe (à) halogène : halogen lamp>

halte [ˈalt] *nf* **1** ARRÊT : stop, halt **2** : stopping place **3 halte routière** *Can* : rest stop (on a highway)

haltère [altɛr] *nm* : dumbbell, barbell

haltérophilie [alterɔfili] *nf* : weightlifting

hamac [ˈamak] *nm* : hammock

hamamélis [amamelis] *nm* : witch hazel

hamburger [ˈɑ̃bœrgœr] *nm* : hamburger (cooked)

hameau [ˈamo] *nm, pl* **hameaux** : hamlet

hameçon [amsɔ̃] *nm* : fishhook

hampe [ˈamp] *nf* **1** : pole (for a flag, etc.) **2** : shaft **3** : flank (of beef)

hamster [ˈamstɛr] *nm* : hamster

hanche [ˈɑ̃ʃ] *nf* **1** : hip **2** : haunch (of a horse)

handball [ˈɑ̃dbal] *nm* : handball

handicap [ˈɑ̃dikap] *nm* : handicap

handicapé[1], **-pée** [ˈɑ̃dikape] *adj* : handicapped, disabled

handicapé², **-pée** *n* : handicapped person, disabled person
handicaper [ˈɑ̃dikape] *vt* : to handicap
hangar [ˈɑ̃gar] *nm* **1** : (large) shed **2** : hangar
hanter [ˈɑ̃te] *vt* : to haunt
hantise [ˈɑ̃tiz] *nf* : obsessive fear, dread
happer [ˈape] *vt* **1** : to seize, to snatch **2 être happé par** : to be hit by (a car, train, etc.)
harangue [ˈarɑ̃g] *nf* : harangue — **haranguer** [ˈarɑ̃ge] *vt*
harasser [ˈarase] *vt* EXTÉNUER : to exhaust, to tire out
harcèlement [ˈarselmɑ̃] *nm* : harassment
harceler [ˈarsəle] {8 *and* 20} *vt* **1** : to harass, to harry **2** : to pester
hardes [ˈard] *nfpl* : rags, old clothes
hardi, **-die** [ˈardi] *adj* : bold, daring — **hardiment** [-dimɑ̃] *adv*
hardiesse [ˈardjɛs] *nf* : boldness, audacity
harem [ˈarɛm] *nm* : harem
hareng [ˈarɑ̃] *nm* **1** : herring **2 hareng saur** : smoked herring, kipper
hargne [ˈarɲ] *nf* : aggressiveness, bad temper
hargneux, **-gneuse** [ˈarɲø, -ɲøz] *adj* : quarrelsome, bad-tempered
haricot [ˈariko] *nm* : bean <haricot de Lima : lima bean> <haricot rouge : kidney bean> <haricot vert : green bean, string bean>
harmonica [armɔnika] *nm* : harmonica
harmonie [armɔni] *nf* : harmony
harmonieux, **-nieuse** [armɔnjø, -njøz] *adj* : harmonious — **harmonieusement** [-njøzmɑ̃] *adv*
harmonique [armɔnik] *adj* : harmonic — **harmoniquement** [-nikmɑ̃] *adv*
harmoniser [armɔnize] *vt* **1** : to harmonize **2** : to bring into line, to reconcile — **s'harmoniser** *vr* : to coordinate, to go well together
harnachement [ˈarnaʃmɑ̃] *nm* **1** : harness, harnessing **2** *fam* : outfit, getup
harnacher [ˈarnaʃe] *vt* **1** : to harness (an animal) **2** *fam* : to rig out (a person)
harnais [ˈarnɛ] *nm* : harness
harpe [ˈarp] *nf* : harp — **harpiste** [ˈarpist] *nmf*
harpie [ˈarpi] *nf* : harpy
harpon [ˈarpɔ̃] *nm* : harpoon
harponner [ˈarpɔne] *vt* **1** : to harpoon **2** *fam* : to nab, to collar
hasard [ˈazar] *nm* **1** : chance, luck, coincidence <un heureux hasard : a stroke of luck> <à tout hasard : on the off chance, just in case> <au hasard : at random> **2** SORT : fate, destiny **3 hasards** *nmpl* : dangers, hazards
hasarder [ˈazarde] *vt* RISQUER : to risk, to venture — **se hasarder** *vr* **1 se hasarder à faire** : to risk doing **2 ~ dans** : to venture into
hasardeux, **-deuse** [ˈazardø, -døz] *adj* : hazardous, risky
haschisch [ˈaʃiʃ] *nm* : hashish
hâte [ˈat] *nf* **1** : haste, hurry **2 à la hâte** : hurriedly, hastily **3 avoir hâte de** : to be eager to
hâter [ˈate] *vt* : to hasten, to hurry — **se hâter** *vr*
hâtif, **-tive** [ˈatif, -tiv] *adj* **1** : hurried **2** : hasty, rash **3** : early <une hâtive récolte : an early harvest>
hâtivement [ˈativmɑ̃] *adv* : hurriedly, hastily
hausse [ˈos] *nf* **1** : rise, increase **2 à la hausse** *or* **en ~** : rising, up
haussement [ˈosmɑ̃] *nm* **1** : raising, increasing **2** : **haussement d'épaules** : shrug
hausser [ˈose] *vt* : to raise <hausser la voix : to raise one's voice> <hausser les épaules : to shrug one's shoulders>
haut¹ [ˈo] *adv* **1** : high <voler haut : to fly high> <haut placé : in a high position, highly placed> **2** : loud, loudly <penser tout haut : to think out loud> **3 plus haut** : above, earlier (in a text)
haut², **haute** [ˈo, ˈot] *adj* **1** : high, tall <haut de cinq mètres : five meters high> <à mer haute : at high tide> **2** : high (up) <haut dans le ciel : high in the sky> <l'étagère la plus haute : the top shelf> **3** : high, advanced, increased <haute fréquence : high frequency> <haute pression : high blood pressure> <à haute voix : aloud, out loud> **4** : early <de la plus haute antiquité : from the earliest times> **5** : upper <le haut Nil : the Upper Nile>
haut³ *nm* **1** HAUTEUR : height <un mètre de haut : one meter high> **2** SOMMET : top <l'étage du haut : the top floor> <de haut en bas : from top to bottom> **3 avoir des hauts et des bas** : to have one's ups and downs **4 en ~** : upstairs **5 en ~** : on the top, atop
hautain, **-taine** [ˈotɛ̃, -tɛn] *adj* : haughty
hautbois [ˈobwa] *nms & pl* : oboe — **hautboïste** [ˈobɔist] *nmf*
haute-fidélité [ˈotfidelite] *nf, pl* **hautes-fidélités** : high fidelity
hautement [ˈotmɑ̃] *adv* **1** FORTEMENT : highly, extremely **2** OUVERTEMENT : openly
hauteur [ˈotœr] *nf* **1** : height <prendre de la hauteur : to take on height, to climb> <à la hauteur de : (on a) level with> **2** NOBLESSE : nobility, loftiness **3** : haughtiness **4** : hill, height (in geography)
haut-le-cœur [ˈolkœr] *nms & pl* : retching <avoir des haut-le-cœur : to retch, to gag>

haut–le–corps [ˈolkɔr] *nms & pl* : start, jump
haut–parleur [ˈoparlœr] *nm, pl* **haut–parleurs** : loudspeaker
hâve [ˈav] *adj* : gaunt
havre [ˈavr] *nm* : haven, refuge
hawaïen[1], **-waïenne** [awajɛ̃, -jɛn] *adj* : Hawaiian
hawaïen[2] *nm* : Hawaiian (language)
Hawaïen, -waïenne *n* : Hawaiian
hayon [ˈajɔ̃] *nm* : tailgate
hé [ˈe] *interj* **1** : hey **2 hé, hé!** : well! well!
hebdomadaire [ebdɔmadɛr] *adj & nm* : weekly
hébergement [ebɛrʒəmɑ̃] *nm* : accommodations *pl*, lodging
héberger [ebɛrʒe] {17} *vt* **1** : to accommodate, to put up **2** : to take in (a refugee, etc.)
hébété, -tée [ebete] *adj* AHURI : dazed, stupefied
hébéter [ebete] {87} *vt* : to daze, to stupefy
hébétude [ebetyd] *nf* : stupor
hébraïque [ebraik] *adj* : Hebrew, Hebraic
hébreu[1] (*masculine only*) [ebrø] *adj, pl* **hébreux** : Hebrew
hébreu[2] *nm* : Hebrew (language)
Hébreu *nm, pl* **Hébreux** : Hebrew
hédoniste [edɔnist] *adj* : hedonistic
hégémonie [eʒemɔni] *nf* : hegemony
hein [ˈɛ̃] *interj* : eh?, what?
hélas [ˈelas] *interj* : alas!
héler [ˈele] {87} *vt* : to hail, to summon
hélice [elis] *nf* **1** : helix **2** : propeller
hélicoptère [elikɔptɛr] *nm* : helicopter
héliotrope [eljɔtrɔp] *nm* : heliotrope
héliport [elipɔr] *nm* : heliport
hélium [eljɔm] *nm* : helium
hématologie [ematɔlɔʒi] *nf* : hematology
hémisphère [emisfɛr] *nm* : hemisphere
hémisphérique [emisferik] *adv* : hemispheric, hemispherical
hémoglobine [emɔglɔbin] *nf* : hemoglobin
hémophile [emɔfil] *adj & nmf* : hemophiliac
hémophilie [emɔfili] *nf* : hemophilia
hémorragie [emɔraʒi] *nf* : bleeding, hemorrhage <faire une hémorragie : to hemorrhage>
hémorroïdes [emɔroid] *nfpl* : hemorrhoids
henné [ˈene] *nm* : henna
hennir [ˈenir] *vi* : to neigh, to whinny
hennissement [ˈenismɑ̃] *nm* : neighing, whinny
hépatique [epatik] *adj* : hepatic, liver
hépatite [epatit] *nf* : hepatitis
héraldique[1] [eraldik] *adj* : heraldic
héraldique[2] *nf* : heraldry
héraut [ˈero] *nm* : herald, messenger
herbacé, -cée [ɛrbase] *adj* : herbaceous
herbage [ɛrbaʒ] *nm* : pasture
herbe [ɛrb] *nf* **1** : grass **2** : herb (in cooking) **3 en ~** : budding, in the making **4 herbe à (la) puce** *Can* : poison ivy, poison sumac **5 herbe aux chats** : catnip **6 mauvaise herbe** : weed
herbeux, -beuse [ɛrbø, -bøz] *adj* : grassy
herbicide [ɛrbisid] *nm* : herbicide, weed killer
herbivore[1] [ɛrbivɔr] *adj* : herbivorous
herbivore[2] *nm* : herbivore
herboriste [ɛrbɔrist] *nmf* : herbalist
herculéen, -léenne [ɛrkyleɛ̃, -ɛn] *adj* : herculean
hère [ˈɛr] *nm* **pauvre hère** : poor wretch
héréditaire [ereditɛr] *adj* : hereditary
hérédité [eredite] *nf* : heredity
hérésie [erezi] *nf* : heresy
hérétique[1] [eretik] *adj* : heretical
hérétique[2] *nmf* : heretic
hérissé, -sée [ˈerise] *adj* : standing on end, bristling
hérisser [ˈerise] *vt* **1** : to ruffle up (fur, feathers, etc.) **2 ~ de** : to spike with, to stud with <herissé de difficultés : fraught with problems> **3 hérisser qqn** *fam* : to ruffle s.o.'s feathers, to irritate s.o. **— se hérisser** *vr* **1** : to stand on end **2** *fam* : to bristle (with annoyance)
hérisson [ˈerisɔ̃] *nm* : hedgehog
héritage [eritaʒ] *nm* **1** : inheritance **2** : heritage, legacy
hériter [erite] *vi* **~ de** : to inherit <j'ai hérité de la maison : I inherited the house> **—** *vt* : to inherit
héritier, -tière [eritje, -tjɛr] *n* : heir, heiress *f*, inheritor
hermaphrodite [ɛrmafrɔdit] *nmf* : hermaphrodite
hermétique [ɛrmetik] *adj* **1** ÉTANCHE : airtight, watertight **2** OBSCUR : obscure, abstruse, hermetic
hermétiquement [ɛrmetikmɑ̃] *adv* : hermetically
hermine [ɛrmin] *nf* : ermine
herminette [ɛrminet] *nf* : adze
hernie [ˈɛrni] *nf* : hernia
héroïne [erɔin] *nf* **1** : heroine **2** : heroin
héroïque [erɔik] *adj* : heroic **— héroïquement** [-ikmɑ̃] *adv*
héroïsme [erɔism] *nm* : heroism
héron [ˈerɔ̃] *nm* : heron
héros [ˈerɔ] *nm* : hero
herpès [ɛrpɛs] *nms & pl* : herpes
herpétologie [ɛrpetɔlɔʒi] *nf* : herpetology
herse [ˈɛrs] *nf* : harrow
herser [ˈɛrse] *vt* : to harrow
hertz [ˈɛrts] *nm & pl* : hertz
hésitant, -tante [ezitɑ̃, -tɑ̃t] *adj* **1** : hesitant **2** : faltering, wavering
hésitation [ezitasjɔ̃] *nf* **1** : hesitation <avec hésitation : hesitantly> **2** : indecision, hesitancy

hésiter [ezite] *vi* **1** : to hesitate **2** : to vacillate, to waver
hétéroclite [eterɔklit] *adj* : disparate, sundry
hétérogène [eterɔʒɛn] *adj* : heterogeneous
hétérosexuel, -sexuelle [eterɔseksyɛl] *adj & n* : heterosexual — **hétérosexualité** [-seksualite] *nf*
hêtre [ˈɛtr] *nm* : beech
heure [œr] *nf* **1** : time <quelle heure est-il? : what time is it?> <avez-vous l'heure? : do you have the time?> **2** : hour <une demi-heure : half an hour> <cent kilomètres à l'heure : sixty miles per hour> **3 à l'~** : on time **4 de bonne heure** : early **5 heure avancée** *Can* : daylight saving time **6 heure d'été** : daylight saving time **7 heure de pointe** : rush hour **8 heure normale** *Can* : standard time **9 heures supplémentaires** : overtime **10 tout à l'heure** : later on
heureusement [œrøzmɑ̃] *adv* : fortunately, luckily
heureux, -reuse [œrø, -røz] *adj* **1** : happy, cheerful <vivre heureux : to live happily> **2** : glad, pleased <heureux de te revoir : glad to see you again> **3** : fortunate, lucky <heureux en amour : lucky in love> **4** : apt, pleasing
heurt [ˈœr] *nm* **1** : collision, crash **2** CONFLIT : clash, conflict **3 sans heurts** : smoothly, smooth
heurter [ˈœrte] *vt* **1** : to strike, to hit, to collide with **2** : to conflict with, to go against **3** : to offend — *vi* : to hit, to collide <heurter contre : to strike> — **se heurter** *vr* **1** : to collide **2 ~ à** : to come up against
heurtoir [ˈœrtwar] *nm* : (door) knocker
hexagonal, -nale [ɛgzagɔnal] *adj, mpl* **-naux** [-no] : hexagonal
hexagone [ɛgzagɔn] *nm* **1** : hexagon **2 l'Hexagone** : France
hiatus [jatys] *nms & pl* : hiatus
hiberner [ibɛrne] *vi* : to hibernate — **hibernation** [ibɛrnasjɔ̃] *nf*
hibou [ˈibu] *nm, pl* **hiboux** [ibu] : owl
hic [ˈik] *nm fam* : snag <voilà le hic! : that's the trouble!>
hickory [ˈikɔri] *nm* : hickory
hideux, -deuse [ˈidø, -døz] *adj* : hideous — **hideusement** [-døzmɑ̃] *adv*
hier [ijɛr] *adv* : yesterday <hier matin : yesterday morning> <comme si s'était hier : as if it were yesterday>
hiérarchie [ˈjerarʃi] *nf* : hierarchy
hiérarchique [ˈjerarʃik] *adj* : hierarchical
hiéroglyphe [jerɔglif] *nm* : hieroglyph, hieroglyphic
hilarant, -rante [ilarɑ̃, -rɑ̃t] *adj* : hilarious
hilare [ilar] *adj* : merry, mirthful
hilarité [ilarite] *nf* : hilarity, mirth
hindou, -doue [ɛ̃du] *adj* : Hindu
Hindou, -doue *n* : Hindu
hindouisme [ɛ̃duism] *nm* : Hinduism
hippie *or* **hippy** [ˈipi] *nmf, pl* **hippies** : hippie
hippique [ipik] *adj* : equestrian, horse <course hippique : horse race>
hippisme [ipism] *nm* : (horseback) riding
hippocampe [ipɔkɑ̃p] *nm* : sea horse
hippodrome [ipɔdrom] *nm* : racecourse
hippopotame [ipɔpɔtam] *nm* : hippopotamus
hirondelle [irɔ̃dɛl] *nf* **1** : swallow **2 hirondelle de mer** : STERNE : tern
hirsute [irsyt] *adj* **1** : tousled, disheveled **2** : hairy, shaggy
hispanique[1] [ispanik] *adj* : Hispanic
hispanique[2] *nmf* : Hispanic (person)
hispano-américain, -caine [ispanoamerikɛ̃, -kɛn] *adj* : Spanish-American
Hispano-Américain, -caine *n* : Spanish American
hisser [ˈise] *vt* : to hoist, to haul up — **se hisser** *vr* : to raise oneself up <se hisser sur la pointe des pieds : to stand on tiptoe>
histogramme [istɔgram] *nm* : bar graph
histoire [istwar] *nf* **1** : history **2** : story **3** : affair, matter <c'est toujours la même histoire : it's always the same old story> **4 histoires** *nfpl* ENNUIS : trouble, problems <s'attirer des histoires : to be asking for trouble> **5 ~ de** : just <histoire de voir : just to see> **6 histoire naturelle** : natural history
historien, -rienne [istɔrjɛ̃, -rjɛn] *n* : historian
historique[1] [istɔrik] *adj* **1** : historical **2** : historic <champs de batailles historiques : historic battlefields> — **historiquement** [-rikmɑ̃] *adv*
historique[2] *nm* : account, story, history
hiver [ivɛr] *nm* : winter
hivernal, -nale [ivɛrnal] *adj, mpl* **-naux** [-no] : winter, wintry
hiverner [ivɛrne] *vi* : to winter
hochement [ˈɔʃmɑ̃] *nm* **hochement de tête** : shake of the head, nod
hocher [ˈɔʃe] *vt* **hocher la tête** : to nod, to shake one's head
hochet [ˈɔʃɛ] *nm* : rattle
hockey [ˈɔkɛ] *nm* : hockey
holà [ˈɔla] *interj* **1** : stop!, whoa! **2** : hey! **3 mettre le holà à** : to put a stop to
hold-up [ˈoldœp] *nms & pl* : holdup, robbery
holistique [ɔlistik] *adj* : holistic
hollandais[1], **-daise** [ˈɔlɑ̃de, -dɛz] *adj* : Dutch
hollandais[2] *nm* : Dutch (language)
Hollandais, -daise *n* **1** : Dutchman *m*, Dutchwoman *f* **2 les Hollondais** : the Dutch

holocauste [ɔlɔkost] *nm* : holocaust
hologramme [ɔlɔgram] *nm* : hologram
homard ['ɔmar] *nm* : lobster
homélie [ɔmeli] *nf* : homily, sermon
homéopathie [ɔmeɔpati] *nf* : homeopathy — **homéopathique** [ɔmeɔpatik] *adj*
homicide[1] [ɔmisid] *adj* : homicidal
homicide[2] *nm* **1** : homicide **2 homicide involontaire** : manslaughter
hommage [ɔmaʒ] *nm* : homage, tribute <rendre hommage à : to pay tribute to>
hommasse [ɔmas] *adj* : mannish
homme [ɔm] *nm* **1** : man **2 l'homme** : man, mankind **3 homme d'affaires** : businessman **4 homme à tout faire** : handyman
homme–grenouille [ɔmgrənuj] *nm, pl* **hommes–grenouilles** : frogman
homogène [ɔmɔʒɛn] *adj* : homogeneous
homogénéiser [ɔmɔʒeneize] *vt* : to homogenize — **homogénéisé, -sée** [-ize] *adj*
homogénéité [ɔmɔʒeneite] *nf* : homogeneity
homographe [ɔmɔgraf] *nm* : homograph
homologation [ɔmɔlɔgasjɔ̃] *nf* : probate, ratification
homologue [ɔmɔlɔg] *nmf* : counterpart, opposite number
homologuer [ɔmɔlɔge] *vt* **1** : to ratify, to approve **2** : to probate (a will)
homonyme [ɔmɔnim] *nm* **1** : homonym **2** : namesake
homophone [ɔmɔfɔn] *nm* : homophone
homosexualité [ɔmɔseksyalite] *nf* : homosexuality
homosexuel, -sexuelle [ɔmɔseksyɛl] *adj & n* : homosexual
hondurien, -rienne ['ɔ̃dyrjɛ̃, -rjɛn] *adj* : Honduran
Hondurien, -rienne *n* : Honduran
hongrois[1], **-groise** ['ɔ̃ngrwa, -grwaz] *adj* : Hungarian
hongrois[2] *nm* : Hungarian (language)
Hongrois, -groise *n* : Hungarian
honnête [ɔnɛt] *adj* **1** INTÈGRE : honest, honorable **2** JUSTE : reasonable, fair **3** RESPECTABLE : decent, respectable — **honnêtement** [ɔnɛtmɑ̃] *adv*
honnêteté [ɔnɛtte] *nf* : honesty
honneur [ɔnœr] *nm* : honor <avoir l'honneur de : to have the honor of> <en l'honneur de : in honor of> <se faire l'honneur de : to pride oneself on>
honorable [ɔnɔrabl] *adj* **1** : honorable **2** : decent, satisfactory <un salaire honorable : a decent salary> **3** : creditable, worthy — **honorablement** [-rabləmɑ̃] *adv*
honoraire [ɔnɔrɛr] *adj* : honorary
honoraires *nmpl* : fees
honorer [ɔnɔre] *vt* **1** : to honor **2** : to be a credit to **3** : to honor (a debt), to pay — **s'honorer** *vr* **1** : to gain distinction **2 ~ de** : to pride oneself on
honorifique [ɔnɔrifik] *adj* : honorary
honte ['ɔ̃t] *nf* : shame, disgrace <avoir honte : to be ashamed> <faire honte à : to put to shame>
honteux, -teuse ['ɔ̃tø, -tøz] *adj* **1** : ashamed **2** : shameful — **honteusement** ['ɔ̃tøzmɑ̃] *adv*
hôpital [ɔpital] *nm, pl* **-taux** [-to] : hospital
hoquet ['ɔkɛ] *nm* : hiccup <avoir le hocquet : to have the hiccups>
hoqueter ['ɔkte] {8} *vi* : to hiccup
horaire[1] [ɔrɛr] *adj* : hourly
horaire[2] *nm* : timetable, schedule
horde ['ɔrd] *nf* : horde
horizon [ɔrizɔ̃] *nm* **1** : horizon <à l'horizon : on the horizon> **2** PAYSAGE : view, landscape **3** : outlook, prospect <horizons économiques : economic prospects> **4** : field of activity <ouvrir ses horizons : to broaden one's horizons>
horizontal, -tale [ɔrizɔ̃tal] *adj, mpl* **-taux** [-to] : horizontal — **horizontalement** [-talmɑ̃] *adv*
horizontale *nf* **à l' horizontale** : in a horizontal position
horloge [ɔrlɔʒ] *nf* : clock
horloger, -gère [ɔrlɔrʒe, -ʒɛr] *n* : watchmaker
hormis ['ɔrmi] *prep* : except, save
hormonal, -nale [ɔrmɔnal] *adj, mpl* **-naux** [-no] : hormonal
hormone [ɔrmɔn] *nf* : hormone
horoscope [ɔrɔskɔp] *nm* : horoscope
horreur [ɔrœr] *nf* **1** ÉPOUVANTE : horror, fear **2** ATROCITÉ : horror, atrocity **3** AVERSION : loathing, repugnance <avoir horreur de : to loathe, to detest> <quelle horreur! : how sickening!>
horrible [ɔribl] *adj* : horrible — **horriblement** [ɔribləmɑ̃] *adv*
horrifiant, -fiante [ɔrifjɑ̃, -fjɑ̃t] *adj* : horrifying
horrifier [ɔrifje] {96} *vt* : to horrify
horripiler [ɔripile] *vt* : to exasperate
hors ['ɔr] *prep* **1** : except for, save **2** : outside, beyond <hors normes : nonstandard> <hors pair : outstanding, exceptional> <hors service : out of service> <hors tout : overall> **3 ~ de** : out of <hors d'atteinte : out of reach> <hors de doute : beyond doubt> <hors de question : out of the question> <hors de la ville : outside of town> **4 être hors de soi** : to be beside oneself
hors–bord ['ɔrbɔr] *nms & pl* **1** : outboard motor **2** : speedboat
hors–concours ['ɔrkɔ̃kur] *nms & pl* : disqualification
hors–d'œuvre ['ɔrdœvr] *nms & pl* : hors d'oeuvre

hors–la–loi [ˈɔrlalwa] *nms & pl* : outlaw
hors–taxe [ˈɔrtaks] *nms & pl* : duty-free articles
hors–texte [ˈɔrtɛkst] *nms & pl* : plate (in a book)
horticole [ɔrtikɔl] *adj* : horticultural
horticulture [ɔrtikyltyr] *nf* : horticulture
hosanna [ozana] *nm & interj* : hosanna
hospice [ɔspis] *nm France* **1** : home (for the elderly, etc.) **2** : hospice
hospitalier, -lière [ɔspitalje, -jɛr] *adj* **1** : hospital <services hospitaliers : hospital services> **2** : hospitable
hospitalisation [ɔspitalizasjɔ̃] *nf* : hospitalization
hospitaliser [ɔspitalize] *vt* : to hospitalize
hospitalité [ɔspitalite] *nf* : hospitality
hostie [ɔsti] *nf* : host, eucharistic bread
hostile [ɔstil] *adj* : hostile — **hostilement** [ɔstilmɑ̃] *adv*
hostilité [ɔstilite] *nf* **1** : hostility **2 hostilités** *nfpl* : hostilities, war
hot–dog [ˈɔtdɔg] *nm, pl* **hot–dogs** : hot dog
hôte[1], **hôtesse** [ot, otɛs] *n* : host, hostess *f*
hôte[2] *nmf* **1** INVITÉ : guest **2** : occupant, guest (in a hotel, etc.)
hôte[3] *nm* : host (in biology)
hôtel [otɛl] *nm* **1** : hotel **2 hôtel de ville** : town hall **3 hôtel particulier** : mansion, townhouse
hôtelier[1], **-lière** [otəlje, -jɛr] *adj* : hotel
hôtelier[2], **-lière** *n* : hotelier, hotel manager
hôtellerie [otɛlri] *nf* : hotel business
hôtesse [otɛs] *nf* **1** → **hôte**[1] **2** *or* **hôtesse de l'air** : stewardess, flight attendant **3** *or* **hôtesse d'accueil** : receptionist
hotte [ˈɔt] *nf* **1** : basket (carried on the back) **2** : hood (of a chimney) **3** *or* **hotte aspirante** : range hood, ventilator
houblon [ˈublɔ̃] *nm* **1** : hop (plant) **2** : hops *pl*
houe [ˈu] *nf* : hoe
houille [ˈuj] *nf* **1** : coal **2 houille blanche** : hydroelectric power
houiller, -ière [ˈuje, -jɛr] *adj* : coal, coal-mining
houillère *nf* : coal mine
houle [ˈul] *nf* : swell, surge
houlette [ˈulɛt] *nf* **1** : crook, staff (of a shepherd) **2 sous la houlette de** : under the guidance of
houleux, -leuse [ˈulø, -løz] *adj* **1** : rough (of the sea) **2** : stormy, turbulent <débats houleux : stormy debates>
houppe [ˈup] *nf* **1** *or* **houppette** : powder puff **2** : tuft (of hair)
hourra [ˈura] *nm & interj* : hurrah
houspiller [ˈuspije] *vt* RÉPRIMANDER : to scold
housse [ˈus] *nf* : cover, slipcover, dust cover
houx [ˈu] *nms & pl* : holly
huard *or* **huart** [ˈyar] *nm Can* : loon
hublot [ˈyblo] *nm* : porthole
huche [ˈyʃ] *nf* **1** COFFRE : chest **2 huche à pain** : bread box
huées [ˈɥe] *nfpl* : boos
huer [ˈɥe] *vt* : to boo — *vi* : to hoot
huile [ɥil] *nf* **1** : (cooking) oil <huile d'olive : olive oil> **2** : oil, lubricant <huile moteur : motor oil> <huile de coude : elbow grease> **3** : oil (in pharmacy) <huile solaire : suntan lotion> **4** : oil (painting) **5 mer d'huile** : calm sea, sea of glass
huiler [ɥile] *vt* : to oil
huileux, -leuse [ɥilø, -løz] *adj* : oily
huilier [ɥilje] *nm* : cruet
huis [ɥi] *nm* **à huis clos** : behind closed doors
huissier [ɥisje] *nm* **1** : usher (in a court of law) **2** : bailiff
huit[1] [ˈɥit, *before consonant* ˈɥi] *adj* **1** : eight <huit jours : a week> **2** : eighth <le huit décembre : December eighth>
huit[2] *nms & pl* : eight
huitaine [ˈɥitɛn] *nf* **1** : about a week **2** : about eight
huitième [ˈɥitjɛm] *adj & nmf & nm* : eighth
huître [ɥitr] *nf* : oyster
hululement [ˈylylmɑ̃] *nm* : hoot
hululer [ˈylyle] *vi* : to hoot
humain[1], **-maine** [ymɛ̃, -mɛn] *adj* **1** : human <la nature humaine : human nature> **2** : humane — **humainement** [-mɛnmɑ̃] *adv*
humain[2] *nm* : human being
humaniser [ymanize] *vt* : to humanize
humanisme [ymanism] *nm* : humanism
humaniste[1] [ymanist] *adj* : humanist, humanistic
humaniste[2] *nmf* : humanist
humanitaire [ymanitɛr] *adj* : humanitarian
humanitarisme [ymanitarism] *nm* : humanitarianism
humanité [ymanite] *nf* : humanity
humanoïde [ymanɔid] *adj & nmf* : humanoid
humble [œ̃bl] *adj* : humble — **humblement** [œ̃bləmɑ̃] *adv*
humecter [ymɛkte] *vt* : to dampen, to moisten — **s'humecter** *vr*
humer [ˈyme] *vt* **1** : to breathe in, to inhale **2** : to smell
humérus [ymerys] *nms & pl* : humerus
humeur [ymœr] *nf* **1** : mood, humor <de bonne humeur : in a good mood> <sautes d'humeur : mood swings> **2** : temperament, temper <d'humeur égale : even-tempered> **3** : ill humor, bad temper <accès d'humeur : fit of bad temper>
humide [ymid] *adj* **1** : moist, damp **2** : humid, muggy
humidificateur [ymidifikatœr] *nm* : humidifier

humidifier [ymidifje] {96} *vt* : to humidify
humidité [ymidite] *nf* **1** : humidity **2** : dampness, moisture
humiliant, -liante [ymiljã, -jãt] *adj* : humiliating
humiliation [ymiljasjõ] *nf* : humiliation
humilier [ymilje] {96} *vt* : to humiliate — **s'humilier** *vr* : to humble oneself
humilité [ymilite] *nf* : humility
humoriste [ymɔrist] *nmf* : humorist
humoristique [ymɔristik] *adj* : humorous
humour [ymur] *nm* : humor, wit <avoir de l'humour : to have a sense of humor>
humus [ymys] *nms & pl* : humus
huppé, -pée ['ype] *adj* **1** : tufted, crested **2** *fam* : posh, high-class
hurlement ['yrləmã] *nm* : howl, yell
hurler ['yrle] *vt* : to yell out — *vi* **1** : to howl, to roar **2** : to yell, to shout
hurluberlu, -lue [yrlybɛrly] *n* : oddball, crank
hurrah ['ura] → **hourra**
hutte ['yt] *nf* : hut
hyacinthe [jasɛ̃t] *nf* : hyacinth
hybride[1] [ibrid] *adj* : hybrid
hybride[2] *nm* : hybrid
hydratant[1], **-tante** [idratã, -tãt] *adj* : moisturizing
hydratant[2] *nm* : moisturizer
hydrate [idrat] *nm* **hydrate de carbon** : carbohydrate
hydraulique[1] [idrolik] *adj* : hydraulic
hydraulique[2] *nf* : hydraulics
hydravion [idravjõ] *nm* : seaplane
hydrocarbure [idrɔkarbyr] *nm* : hydrocarbon
hydroélectrique *or* **hydro–électrique** [idroelektrik] *adj* : hydroelectric
hydrogène [idrɔʒɛn] *nm* : hydrogen
hydroglisseur [idrɔglisœr] *nm* : hydroplane (boat)
hyène [jɛn] *nf* : hyena
hygiène [iʒjɛn] *nf* : hygiene <hygiène publique : public health>
hygiénique [iʒjenik] *adj* : hygienic
hygiéniste [iʒjenist] *nmf* : hygienist
hygromètre [igrɔmetr] *nm* : hygrometer
hymne [imn] *nm* **1** : hymn **2 hymne nationale** : national anthem
hyperactif, -tive *adj* : hyperactive
hyperbole [iperbɔl] *nf* : hyberbole
hypermétrope [ipermetrɔp] *adj* PRESBYTE : farsighted
hypermétropie [ipermetrɔpi] *nf* PRESBYTIE : farsightedness
hypersensible [ipersãsibl] *adj* : hypersensitive
hypertension [ipertãsjõ] *nf* : high blood pressure, hypertension
hypertexte [ipertekst] *nm* : hypertext
hypnose [ipnoz] *nf* : hypnosis
hypnotique [ipnɔtik] *adj* : hypnotic
hypnotiser [ipnɔtize] *vt* : to hypnotize
hypnotiseur [ipnɔtizœr] *nm* : hypnotist
hypnotisme [ipnɔtism] *nm* : hypnotism
hypocondriaque[1] [ipɔkõdrijak] *adj* : hypochondriacal, hypochondriac
hypocondriaque[2] *nmf* : hypochondriac
hypocondrie [ipɔkõdri] *nf* : hypochondria
hypocrisie [ipɔkrizi] *nf* : hypocrisy
hypocrite[1] [ipɔkrit] *adj* : hypocritical — **hypocritement** [-kritmã] *adv*
hypocrite[2] *nmf* : hypocrite
hypodermique [ipɔdɛrmik] *adj* : hypodermic <seringue hypodermique : hypodermic needle>
hypotension [ipɔtãsjõ] *nf* : low blood pressure, hypotension
hypoténuse [ipɔtenyz] *nf* : hypotenuse
hypothécaire [ipɔtekɛr] *adj* : mortgage <prêt hypothécaire : mortgage loan>
hypothèque [ipɔtɛk] *nf* : mortgage
hypothéquer [ipɔteke] {87} *vt* : to mortgage
hypothermie [ipɔtɛrmi] *nf* : hypothermia
hypothèse [ipɔtɛz] *nf* : hypothesis
hypothétique [ipɔtetik] *adj* : hypothetical — **hypothétiquement** [-tikmã] *adv*
hystérectomie [isterektɔmi] *nf* : hysterectomy
hystérie [isteri] *nf* : hysteria
hystérique [isterik] *adj* : hysterical — **hystériquement** [-rikmã] *adj*

I

i [i] *nm* : i, the ninth letter of the alphabet
ibis [ibis] *nms & pl* : ibis
iceberg [ajsberg] *nm* : iceberg
ichtyologie [iktjɔlɔʒi] *nf* : ichthyology
ici [isi] *adv* **1** : here <ici et là : here and there> <par ici : this way> **2** : now <jusqu'ici : up until now> <d'ici là : by then> **3 d'ici** : hence, therefore <d'ici six ans : six years hence>
ici–bas [isiba] *adv* : here below, on earth
icône [ikon] *nf* : icon

iconoclasme [ikɔnɔklasm] *nm* : iconoclasm
iconoclaste[1] [ikɔnɔklast] *adj* : iconoclastic
iconoclaste[2] *nmf* : iconoclast
idéal[1], **idéale** [ideal] *adj, mpl* **idéals** *or* **idéaux** [ideo] : ideal — **idéalement** [-almɑ̃] *adv*
idéal[2] *nm* : ideal
idéaliser [idealize] *vt* : to idealize — **idéalisation** [-lizasjɔ̃] *nf*
idéalisme [idealism] *nm* : idealism
idéaliste[1] [idealist] *adj* : idealistic
idéaliste[2] *nmf* : idealist
idée [ide] *nf* **1** : idea <changer d'idée : to change one's mind> <se faire des idées : to imagine things> **2 idée de génie** : brainwave **3 idée fixe** : obsession **4 idée reçue** : accepted opinion, commonplace
idem [idɛm] *adv* : ditto, idem
identifiable [idɑ̃tifjabl] *adj* : identifiable
identification [idɑ̃tifikasjɔ̃] *nf* : identification
identifier [idɑ̃tifje] {96} *vt* **1** : to identify, to recognize **2** ASSIMILER : to liken, to consider equivalent — **s'identifier** *vr* ~ **avec** : to identify with
identique [idɑ̃tik] *adj* : identical — **identiquement** [-tikmɑ̃] *adv*
identité [idɑ̃tite] *nf* : identity
idéologie [ideɔlɔʒi] *nf* : ideology
idéologique [ideɔlɔʒik] *adj* : ideological
idiomatique [idjɔmatik] *adj* : idiomatic
idiome [idjom] *nm* : idiom
idiosyncrasie [idjɔsɛ̃krazi] *nf* : idiosyncrasy
idiot[1], **-diote** [idjo, -djɔt] *adj* : idiotic — **idiotement** [idjɔtmɑ̃] *adv*
idiot[2], **-diote** *n* : idiot, fool
idiotie [idjɔsi] *nf* **1** : idiocy **2** : idiotic action or remark
idiotisme [idjɔtism] *nm* : idiom, idiomatic expression
idoine [idwan] *adj* : suitable, fitting
idolâtrer [idɔlatre] *vt* : to idolize
idolâtrie [idɔlatri] *nf* : idolatry
idole [idɔl] *nf* : idol
idylle [idil] *nf* **1** : romance, love affair **2** : idyll (poem)
idyllique [idilik] *adj* : idyllic
if [if] *nm* : yew
igloo [iglu] *nm* : igloo
igname [iɲam] *nf* : yam
ignare[1] [iɲar] *adj* : ignorant
ignare[2] *nmf* : ignoramus
ignifuge [iɲifyʒ] *adj* : fireproof
ignifuger [iɲifyʒe] {17} *vt* : to fireproof
ignoble [iɲɔbl] *adj* **1** INFÂME : base, vile **2** RÉPUGNANT : revolting, repugnant
ignominie [iɲɔmini] *nf* **1** : ignominy **2** : shameful act
ignominieux, -nieuse [iɲɔminjø, -njøz] *adj* : ignominious — **ignominieusement** [-njøzmɑ̃] *adv*
ignorance [iɲɔrɑ̃s] *nf* : ignorance
ignorant, -rante [iɲɔrɑ̃, -rɑ̃t] *adj* : ignorant
ignorer [iɲɔre] *vt* **1** : to be unaware of <je l'ignore : I don't know> **2** : to ignore
iguane [igwan] *nm* : iguana
il [il] *pron* **1** : he, it <il est en retard : he's late> <il se peut : it is possible> **2** (*as subject of an impersonal verb*) : it <il pleut : it's raining> **3 ils** *pron pl* : they **4 il y a** : there is, there are
île [il] *nf* : island, isle
illégal, -gale [ilegal] *adj, mpl* **-gaux** [-go] : illegal, unlawful — **illégalement** [-galmɑ̃] *adv*
illégalité [ilegalite] *nf* : illegality
illégitime [ileʒitim] *adj* **1** : illegitimate **2** : unwarranted, unjustified — **illégitimement** [-timmɑ̃] *adv*
illégitimité [ileʒitimite] *nf* : illegitimacy
illettré, -trée [iletre] *adj & n* ANALPHABÈTE : illiterate
illettrisme [iletrism] *nm* ANALPHABÉTISME : illiteracy
illicite [ilisit] *adj* : illicit — **illicitement** [-sitmɑ̃] *adv*
illico [iliko] *adv fam* : pronto, immediately
illimité, -tée [ilimite] *adj* **1** : unlimited, boundless **2** : indefinite
illisible [ilizibl] *adj* **1** : illegible **2** : unreadable
illisiblement [iliziblǝmɑ̃] *adv* : illegibly
illogique [ilɔʒik] *adj* : illogical — **illogiquement** [-ʒikmɑ̃] *adv*
illumination [ilyminasjɔ̃] *nf* **1** : illumination, lighting **2** : inspiration **3 illuminations** *nfpl* : lights
illuminer [ilymine] *vt* ÉCLAIRER : to illuminate
illusion [ilyzjɔ̃] *nf* **1** : illusion <illusion d'optique : optical illusion> **2** : deception, delusion <se faire des illusions : to delude oneself>
illusionner [ilyzjɔne] *vt* : to delude, to deceive — **s'illusionner** *vr*
illusionniste [ilyzjɔnist] *nmf* : conjurer
illusoire [ilyzwar] *adj* : illusory
illustrateur, -trice [ilystratœr, -tris] *n* : illustrator
illustratif, -tive [ilystratif, -tiv] *adj* : illustrative
illustration [ilystrasjɔ̃] *nf* : illustration
illustre [ilystr] *adj* : illustrious, renowned
illustré[1], **-trée** [ilystre] *adj* : illustrated
illustré[2] *nm* : illustrated magazine
illustrer [ilystre] *vt* : to illustrate — **s'illustrer** *vr* : to distinguish oneself
îlot [ilo] *nm* **1** : small island **2** : block (of houses) **3** : pocket (of resistance, etc.)
ils [il] → **il**
image [imaʒ] *nf* **1** : image **2** DESSIN : picture **3 images** *nfpl* : imagery
imagé, -gée [imaʒe] *adj* : full of imagery, colorful

imagerie [imaʒri] *nf* **1** : images *pl* **2** : imaging
imaginable [imaʒinabl] *adj* : imaginable
imaginaire[1] [imaʒinɛr] *adj* : imaginary
imaginaire[2] *nm* : (world of the) imagination
imaginatif, -tive [imaʒinatif, -tiv] *adj* : imaginative
imagination [imaʒinasjɔ̃] *nf* : imagination
imaginer [imaʒine] *vt* **1** : to imagine, to suppose **2** : to devise, to think up — **s'imaginer** *vr* **1** : to imagine, to picture **2** : to picture oneself **3** : to believe, to delude oneself
imbattable [ɛ̃batabl] *adj* : invincible, unbeatable
imbécile[1] [ɛ̃besil] *adj* : stupid, idiotic
imbécile[2] *nmf* **1** : imbecile **2** : fool, idiot <faire l'imbécile : to goof off, to play the fool>
imbécillité [ɛ̃besilite] *nf* **1** : idiocy, stupidity **2** : stupid act or remark, nonsense
imbiber [ɛ̃bibe] *vt* TREMPER : to soak — **s'imbiber** *vr* **1** : to soak up, to get soaked **2** *fam* : to get drunk
imbrication [ɛ̃brikasjɔ̃] *nf* **1** : overlapping **2** : interweaving, interlocking
imbriquer [ɛ̃brike] *vt* **1** : to overlap **2** : to interweave — **s'imbriquer** *vr*
imbroglio [ɛ̃brɔljo] *nm* : imbroglio
imbu, -bue [ɛ̃by] *adj* ~ **de** : imbued with, full of
imbuvable [ɛ̃byvabl] *adj* **1** : undrinkable **2** *fam* : insufferable
imitateur[1], **-trice** [imitatœr, -tris] *adj* : imitative
imitateur[2], **-trice** *n* **1** : imitator **2** : mimic, impersonator
imitatif, -tive [imitatif, -tiv] *adj* : imitative
imitation [imitasjɔ̃] *nf* **1** : imitation, copy <imitation cuir : simulated leather> **2** : impersonation, mimicry
imiter [imite] *vt* **1** : to imitate **2** : to mimic **3** : to copy, to forge
immaculé, -lée [imakyle] *adj* : immaculate
immanent, -nente [imanɑ̃, -nɑ̃t] *adj* : immanent
immangeable [ɛ̃mɑ̃ʒabl] *adj* : inedible
immanquable [ɛ̃mɑ̃kabl] *adj* **1** INÉVITABLE : inevitable **2** : impossible to miss
immanquablement [ɛ̃mɑ̃kabləmɑ̃] *adv* : without fail, inevitably
immatériel, -rielle [imaterjel] *adj* **1** : immaterial **2** : intangible
immatriculation [imatrikylasjɔ̃] *nf* **1** : registration **2 plaque d'immatriculation** : license plate
immatriculer [imatrikyle] *vt* : to register (a motor vehicle)
immature [imatyr] *adj* : immature
immaturité [imatyrite] *nf* : immaturity
immédiat[1], **-diate** [imedja, -djat] *adj* : immediate — **immédiatement** [-djatmɑ̃] *adv*
immédiat[2] *nm* **dans l'immédiat** : for the time being
immémorial, -riale [imemɔrjal] *adj, mpl* **-riaux** [-rjo] : immemorial, ancient
immense [imɑ̃s] *adj* : immense — **immensément** [imɑ̃semɑ̃] *adv*
immensité [imɑ̃site] *nf* : immensity
immerger [imɛrʒe] {17} *vt* : to submerge, to immerse — **s'immerger** *vr* : to dive, to submerge oneself
immérité, -tée [imerite] *adj* : undeserved
immersion [imɛrsjɔ̃] *nf* : immersion
immeuble[1] [imœbl] *adj* **biens immeubles** : real estate
immeuble[2] *nm* : building, apartment building, office building
immigrant, -grante [imigrɑ̃, -grɑ̃t] *adj & n* : immigrant
immigration [imigrasjɔ̃] *nf* : immigration
immigré, -grée [imigre] *n* : immigrant
immigrer [imigre] *vi* : to immigrate
imminence [iminɑ̃s] *nf* : imminence
imminent, -nente [iminɑ̃, -nɑ̃t] *adj* : impending, imminent
immiscer [imise] {6} *v* **s'immiscer** *vr* ~ **dans** : to interfere with, to meddle in
immixtion [imiksjɔ̃] *nf* : interference
immobile [imɔbil] *adj* **1** : motionless, still **2** : fixed, unchanging
immobilier, -lière [imɔbilje, -jɛr] *adj* : real estate, property <agent immobilier : real estate agent>
immobilisation [imɔbilizasjɔ̃] *nf* **1** : immobilization **2 immobilisations** *nfpl* : fixed assets
immobiliser [imɔbilize] *vt* **1** : to immobilize **2** : to bring to a halt — **s'immobiliser** *vr* : to come to a halt
immobilisme [imɔbilism] *nm* : opposition to change, conservatism
immobilité [imɔbilite] *nf* : immobility, stillness
immodéré, -rée [imɔdere] *adj* : immoderate, excessive — **immodérément** [-remɑ̃] *adv*
immodeste [imɔdɛst] *adj* : immodest
immoler [imɔle] *vt* SACRIFIER : to immolate, to sacrifice
immonde [imɔ̃d] *adj* **1** : foul, filthy **2** : vile, sordid, revolting
immondices [imɔ̃dis] *nfpl* : waste, refuse
immoral, -rale [imɔral] *adj, mpl* **-raux** [-ro] : immoral — **immoralement** [-ralmɑ̃] *adv*
immoralité [imɔralite] *nf* : immorality
immortaliser [imɔrtalize] *vt* : to immortalize
immortalité [imɔrtalite] *nf* : immortality
immortel[1], **-telle** [imɔrtel] *adj* : immortal

immortel[2], **-telle** *n* : immortal
immuable [imɥabl] *adj* : immutable, unchanging — **immuablement** [imɥablǝmɑ̃] *adv*
immuniser [imynize] *vt* : to immunize — **immunisation** [-nizasjɔ̃] *nf*
immunitaire [imyniter] *adj* : immune <système immunitaire : immune system>
immunité [imynite] *nf* : immunity
immunologie [imynɔlɔʒi] *nf* : immunology
impact [ɛ̃pakt] *nm* : impact
impair[1], **-paire** [ɛ̃per] *adj* : odd <nombres impairs : odd numbers>
impair[2] *nm* : blunder, faux pas
impala [impala] *nm* : impala
imparable [ɛ̃parabl] *adj* : unstoppable
impardonnable [ɛ̃pardɔnabl] *adj* : unforgivable, unpardonable
imparfait[1], **-faite** [ɛ̃parfɛ, -fɛt] *adj* **1** : imperfect **2** : incomplete, unfinished — **imparfaitement** [-fɛtmɑ̃] *adv*
imparfait[2] *nm* : imperfect (tense)
impartial, -tiale [ɛ̃parsjal] *adj, mpl* **-tiaux** [-sjo] : unbiased, impartial — **impartialement** [-sjalmɑ̃] *adv*
impartialité [ɛ̃parsjalite] *nf* : impartiality
impartir [ɛ̃partir] *vt* : to grant, to bestow
impasse [ɛ̃pas] *nf* **1** : impasse, deadlock **2** CUL-DE-SAC : dead end
impassible [ɛ̃pasibl] *adj* : impassive — **impassiblement** [-sibləmɑ̃] *adv*
impatiemment [ɛ̃pasjamɑ̃] *adv* : impatiently
impatient, -tiente [ɛ̃pasjɑ̃, -sjɑ̃t] *adj* : impatient — **impatience** [-sjɑ̃s] *nf*
impatienter [ɛ̃pasjɑ̃te] *vt* : to irritate, to annoy — **s'impatienter** *vr* : to lose patience
impayable [ɛ̃pɛjabl] *adj fam* : priceless
impayé, -payée [ɛ̃peje] *adj* : unpaid, outstanding
impeccable [ɛ̃pekabl] *adj* : impeccable — **impeccablement** [-kabləmɑ̃] *adv*
impécunieux, -nieuse [ɛ̃pekynjø, -njøz] *adj* : impecunious
impénétrable [ɛ̃penetrabl] *adj* **1** : impenetrable **2** : inscrutable
impénitent, -tente [ɛ̃penitɑ̃, -tɑ̃t] *adj* : unrepentant
impensable [ɛ̃pɑ̃sabl] *adj* : unthinkable, inconceivable
imper [ɛ̃per] *nm fam* → **imperméable**
impératif[1], **-tive** [ɛ̃peratif, -tiv] *adj* : imperative — **impérativement** [-tivmɑ̃] *adv*
impératif[2] *nm* **1** : requirement, necessity **2** : imperative (case)
impératrice [ɛ̃peratris] *nf* : empress
imperceptible [ɛ̃pɛ̃rsɛptibl] *adj* : imperceptible — **imperceptiblement** [-tibləmɑ̃] *adv*
imperfection [ɛ̃pɛrfɛksjɔ̃] *nf* : imperfection
impérial, -riale [ɛ̃perjal] *adj, mpl* **-riaux** [-rjo] : imperial
impérialisme [ɛ̃perjalism] *nm* : imperialism
impérialiste[1] [ɛ̃perjalist] *adj* : imperialist, imperialistic
impérialiste[2] *nmf* : imperialist
impérieusement [ɛ̃perjøzmɑ̃] *adv* **1** : imperiously **2** : urgently, absolutely
impérieux, -rieuse [ɛ̃perjø, -jøz] *adj* **1** : imperious **2** : pressing, urgent
impérissable [ɛ̃perisabl] *adj* : imperishable, undying
imperméabilisation [ɛ̃pɛrmeabilizasjɔ̃] *nf* : waterproofing
imperméabiliser [ɛ̃pɛrmeabilize] *vt* : to waterproof
imperméable[1] [ɛ̃pɛrmeabl] *adj* **1** : waterproof **2** ~ **à** : impervious to
imperméable[2] *nm* : raincoat
impersonnel, -nelle [ɛ̃pɛrsɔnɛl] *adj* : impersonal — **impersonnellement** [-nɛlmɑ̃] *adv*
impertinent, -nente [ɛ̃pɛrtinɑ̃, -nɑ̃t] *adj* : impertinent — **impertinence** [-tinɑ̃s] *nf*
imperturbable [ɛ̃pɛrtyrbabl] *adj* : imperturbable, unflappable
impétueux, -tueuse, [ɛ̃petɥø, -tɥøz] *adj* **1** : impetuous, rash **2** : raging, wild — **impétueusement** [-tɥøzmɑ̃] *adv*
impétuosité [ɛ̃petɥozite] *nf* : impetuosity
impie [ɛ̃pi] *adj* : impious, godless
impiété [ɛ̃pjete] *nf* : impiety
impitoyable [ɛ̃pitwajabl] *adj* : merciless, pitiless — **impitoyablement** [-jabləmɑ̃] *adv*
implacable [ɛ̃plakabl] *adj* **1** : implacable **2** : relentless — **implacablement** [-kabləmɑ̃] *adv*
implant [ɛ̃plɑ̃] *nm* : implant (in medicine)
implantation [ɛ̃plɑ̃tasjɔ̃] *nf* **1** : establishment, installation, setting up **2** : implantation
implanter [ɛ̃plɑ̃te] *vt* **1** : to establish, to set up **2** : to implant — **s'implanter** *vr* **1** : to be set up **2** : to settle (of persons)
implication [ɛ̃plikasjɔ̃] *nf* : implication
implicite [ɛ̃plisit] *adj* : implicit — **implicitement** [-sitmɑ̃] *adv*
impliquer [ɛ̃plike] *vt* **1** : to implicate, to involve **2** : to imply, to mean — **s'impliquer** *vr* : to become involved
implorer [ɛ̃plɔre] *vt* : to implore
imploser [ɛ̃ploze] *vi* : to implode — **implosion** [ɛ̃plozjɔ̃] *nf*
impoli, -lie [ɛ̃pɔli] *adj* : impolite, rude — **impoliment** [-limɑ̃] *adv*
impolitesse [ɛ̃pɔlitɛs] *nf* : impoliteness, rudeness
impondérable [ɛ̃pɔ̃derabl] *adj* : imponderable
impopulaire [ɛ̃pɔpylɛr] *adj* : unpopular — **impopularité** [-pylarite] *nf*

importance [ɛ̃pɔrtɑ̃s] *nf* **1** : importance **2** : size, extent, amount **3 d'importance** : important, considerable
important¹, -tante [ɛ̃pɔrtɑ̃, -tɑ̃t] *adj* **1** : important, significant **2** LARGE : considerable, sizable
important² *nm* : important point, main thing
importateur, -trice [ɛ̃pɔrtatœr, -tris] *n* : importer
importation [ɛ̃pɔrtasjɔ̃] *nf* **1** : importation **2** : import
importer [ɛ̃pɔrte] *vt* : to import — *vi* **1** : to matter, to be important <peu importe : no matter> **2 n'importe** : I don't mind, it doesn't matter **3 n'importe où** : anywhere **4 n'importe quand** : anytime **5 n'importe qui** : anyone, anybody **6 n'importe quoi** : anything
import–export [ɛ̃pɔrɛkspɔr] *nms & pl* : import-export (business)
importun¹, -tune [ɛ̃pɔrtœ̃, -tyn] *adj* **1** : troublesome, bothersome **2** : inopportune, untimely
importun², -tune *n* : nuisance, pest
importuner [ɛ̃pɔrtyne] *vt* : to pester, to annoy
imposable [ɛ̃pozabl] *adj* : taxable
imposant, -sante [ɛ̃pozɑ̃, -zɑ̃t] *adj* : imposing
imposé, -sée [ɛ̃poze] *adj* **1** : prescribed, compulsory (in sports) **2** : fixed (of prices, etc.)
imposer [ɛ̃poze] *vt* **1** : to impose **2** : to command (respect, etc.) **3** : to tax — **s'imposer** *vr* **1** : to be essential **2** : to impose (something) on oneself, to make it a rule **3** : to become known, to stand out **4 ~ à** : to impose (oneself) on
imposition [ɛ̃pozisjɔ̃] *nf* : taxation, tax <taux d'imposition : tax rate>
impossibilité [ɛ̃posibilite] *nf* : impossibility
impossible¹ [ɛ̃posibl] *adj* : impossible
impossible² *nm* **l'impossible** : the impossible <faire l'impossible : to do one's utmost>
imposte [ɛ̃post] *nf* : fanlight
imposteur [ɛ̃postœr] *nm* : impostor
imposture [ɛ̃postyr] *nf* : imposture, deception
impôt [ɛ̃po] *nm* : tax, duty <impôt sur le revenu : income tax>
impotence [ɛ̃potɑ̃s] *nf* : infirmity, disability
impotent, -tente [ɛ̃potɑ̃, -tɑ̃t] *adj* INFIRME : infirm, disabled
impraticable [ɛ̃pratikabl] *adj* **1** IRRÉALISABLE : impracticable, unworkable **2** : impassable
imprécis, -cise [ɛ̃presi, -siz] *adj* : imprecise, vague
imprécision [ɛ̃presizjɔ̃] *nf* : imprecision, vagueness
imprégner [ɛ̃preɲe] {87} *vt* **1** PÉNÉTRER : to impregnate, to soak **2** : to fill, to pervade — **s'imprégner** *vr* **~ de** : to immerse oneself in
imprenable [ɛ̃prənabl] *adj* : impregnable
imprégnation [ɛ̃preɲasjɔ̃] *nf* : impregnation, saturation
imprésario [ɛ̃presarjo] *nm* : impresario
impression [ɛ̃presjɔ̃] *nf* **1** : impression <faire bonne impression : to make a good impression> **2** : mark, imprint **3** : printing <envoyer à l'impression : to send to the press>
impressionnable [ɛ̃presjɔnabl] *adj* : impressionable
impressionnant, -nante [ɛ̃presjɔnɑ̃, -nɑ̃t] *adj* **1** : impressive, imposing **2** : disturbing, upsetting
impressionner [ɛ̃presjɔne] *vt* **1** : to impress **2** : to disturb, to upset **3** : to expose (film)
impressionnisme [ɛ̃presjɔnism] *nm* : impressionism
impressionniste¹ [ɛ̃presjɔnist] *adj* : impressionistic
impressionniste² *nmf* : impressionist
imprévisible [ɛ̃previzibl] *adj* : unforeseeable, unpredictable
imprévoyance [ɛ̃prevwajɑ̃s] *nf* : lack of foresight, improvidence
imprévoyant, -voyante [ɛ̃prevwajɑ̃, -vwajɑ̃t] *adj* : improvident
imprévu, -vue [ɛ̃prevy] *adj* : unforeseen, unexpected
imprimante [ɛ̃primɑ̃t] *nf* : printer <imprimante à laser : laser printer>
imprimé¹, -mée [ɛ̃prime] *adj* : printed
imprimé² *nm* **1** : print, printed fabric **2** FORMULAIRE : form **3** : printed matter
imprimer [ɛ̃prime] *vt* **1** : to print, to stamp **2** : to imprint **3** : to publish **4** : to impart, to transmit
imprimerie [ɛ̃primri] *nf* **1** : printing **2** : print shop, printer's
imprimeur, -meuse [ɛ̃primœr, -møz] *n* : printer
improbable [ɛ̃prɔbabl] *adj* : improbable — **improbabilité** [-babilite] *nf*
improductif, -tive [ɛ̃prɔdyktif, -tiv] *adj* : unproductive
impromptu, -tue [ɛ̃prɔ̃pty] *adj* : impromptu
impropre [ɛ̃prɔpr] *adj* **1** : inappropriate, incorrect (of words, etc.) **2 ~ à** : unsuited to, unfit for
improvisation [ɛ̃prɔvizasjɔ̃] *nf* : improvisation
improvisé, -sée [ɛ̃prɔvize] *adj* : improvised, makeshift
improviser [ɛ̃prɔvize] *v* : to improvise — **s'improviser** *vr* **1** : to be improvised **2** : to act as
improviste [ɛ̃prɔvist] **à l'improviste** : unexpectedly
imprudemment [ɛ̃prydamɑ̃] *adv* : carelessly, recklessly
imprudence [ɛ̃prydɑ̃s] *nf* : imprudence, carelessness

imprudent, -dente [ɛ̃prydɑ̃, -dɑ̃t] *adj* **1** : unwise, imprudent **2** : rash, foolhardy
impudence [ɛ̃pydɑ̃s] *nf* : impudence
impudent, -dente [ɛ̃pydɑ̃, -dɑ̃t] *adj* : impudent
impudeur [ɛ̃pydœr] *nf* : shamelessness, immodesty
impudique [ɛ̃pydik] *adj* : immodest, indecent — **impudiquement** [-dikmɑ̃] *adv*
impuissance [ɛ̃pɥisɑ̃s] *nf* **1** : helplessness, powerlessness **2** : (sexual) impotence
impuissant, -sante [ɛ̃pɥisɑ̃, -sɑ̃t] *adj* **1** : helpless, powerless **2** : impotent
impulsif, -sive [ɛ̃pylsif, -siv] *adj* : impulsive — **impulsivement** [-sivmɑ̃] *adv*
impulsion [ɛ̃pylsjɔ̃] *nf* **1** : impulse **2** : impetus
impulsivité [ɛ̃pylsivite] *nf* : impulsiveness
impunément [ɛ̃pynemɑ̃] *adv* : with impunity
impuni, -nie [ɛ̃pyni] *adj* : unpunished
impunité [ɛ̃pynite] *nf* : impunity
impur, -pure [ɛ̃pyr] *adj* : impure
impureté [ɛ̃pyrte] *nf* : impurity
imputable [ɛ̃pytabl] *adj* **1** : imputable, attributable **2** ~ **sur** : chargeable to (an account, etc.)
imputer [ɛ̃pyte] *vt* **1** : to impute, to attribute **2** : to charge
inabordable [inabɔrdabl] *adj* **1** : unapproachable, inaccessible **2** : prohibitive (in price)
inacceptable [inakseptabl] *adj* : unacceptable
inaccessibilité [inaksesibilite] *nf* : inaccessibility
inaccessible [inaksesibl] *adj* **1** : inaccessible, unattainable **2** ~ **à** : impervious to
inaccoutumé, -mée [inakutyme] *adj* : unaccustomed
inachevé, -vée [inaʃve] *adj* : unfinished
inactif, -tive [inaktif, -tiv] *adj* : inactive
inaction [inaksjɔ̃] *nf* : inaction, idleness
inactivité [inaktivite] *nf* : inactivity
inadaptation [inadaptasjɔ̃] *nf* **1** : maladjustment **2** : inappropriateness
inadapté¹, -tée [inadapte] *adj* **1** : maladjusted **2** INAPPROPRIÉ : unsuited, inappropriate
inadapté², -tée *n* : social misfit, maladjusted person
inadéquat, -quate [inadekwa, -kwat] *adj* : inadequate
inadéquation [inadekwasjɔ̃] *nf* : inadequacy
inadmissible [inadmisibl] *adj* : inadmissible, unacceptable
inadvertance [inadvɛrtɑ̃s] *nf* **par** ~ : inadvertently
inaliénable [inaljenabl] *adj* : inalienable
inaltérable [inalterabl] *adj* **1** : stable, unchanging <inaltérable à : unaffected by> **2** : constant, unfailing
inamical, -cale [inamikal] *adj, mpl* **-caux** [-ko] : inimical, unfriendly
inamovible [inamɔvibl] *adj* : fixed, permanent
inanimé, -mée [inanime] *adj* **1** : inanimate **2** : unconscious, senseless
inanité [inanite] *nf* : futility, pointlessness
inanition [inanisjɔ̃] *nf* : starvation <tomber d'inanition : to faint with hunger>
inaperçu, -çue [inapɛrsy] *adj* : unseen, unnoticed <passer inaperçu : to go unnoticed>
inapplicable [inaplikabl] *adj* : inapplicable
inappliqué, -quée [inaplike] *adj* **1** : lacking in application **2** : not applied, unenforced
inappréciable [inapresjabl] *adj* **1** : invaluable **2** : inappreciable, imperceptible
inapproprié, -priée [inapropɛrprije] *adj* : inappropriate
inapte [inapt] *adj* **1** : inept **2** : unfit, unsuited
inaptitude [inaptityd] *nf* : unfitness
inarticulé, -lée [inartikyle] *adj* : inarticulate
inassouvi, -vie [inasuvi] *adj* **1** : unsatisfied, unfulfilled **2** : insatiable
inattaquable [inatakabl] *adj* **1** IRRÉPROCHABLE : irreproachable **2** IRRÉFUTABLE : irrefutable **3** IMPRENABLE : impregnable
inattendu, -due [inatɑ̃dy] *adj* : unexpected
inattentif, -tive [inatɑ̃tif, -tiv] *adj* : inattentive, distracted <inattentif à l'avertissement : heedless of the warning>
inattention [inatɑ̃sjɔ̃] *nf* : inattention <faute d'inattention : careless mistake>
inaudible [inodibl] *adj* : inaudible
inaugural, -rale [inogyral] *adj, mpl* **-raux** [-ro] : inaugural <séance inaugurale : opening session>
inauguration [inogyrasjɔ̃] *nf* : inauguration
inaugurer [inogyre] *vt* **1** : to unveil, to open **2** : to inaugurate
inavouable [inavwabl] *adj* : shameful, unmentionable
inavoué, -vouée [inavwe] *adj* : unacknowledged, unavowed
incalculable [ɛ̃kalkylabl] *adj* : incalculable, countless
incandescent, -cente [ɛ̃kɑ̃desɑ̃, -sɑ̃t] *adj* : incandescent — **incandescence** [-desɑ̃s] *nf*
incantation [ɛ̃kɑ̃tasjɔ̃] *nf* : incantation
incapable [ɛ̃kapabl] *adj* : incapable, unable <incapable de chanter : unable to sing>

incapacité [ɛ̃kapasite] *nf* **1** : incapacity, inability <être dans l'incapacité de faire qqch : to be unable to do sth> **2** : incompetence **3** : (physical) disability
incarcérer [ɛ̃karsere] {87} *vt* : to incarcerate — **incarcération** [-serasjɔ̃] *nf*
incarnation [ɛ̃karnasjɔ̃] *nf* : incarnation
incarné, -née [ɛ̃karne] *adj* **1** : incarnate **2 ongle incarné** : ingrown toenail
incarner [ɛ̃karne] *vt* **1** : to incarnate, to embody **2** : to personify, to play
incartade [ɛ̃kartad] *nf* : escapade, prank
incassable [ɛ̃kasabl] *adj* : unbreakable
incendiaire[1] [ɛ̃sɑ̃djɛr] *adj* **1** : incendiary **2** : inflammatory
incendiaire[2] *nmf* : arsonist
incendie [ɛ̃sɑ̃di] *nm* **1** : fire **2 incendie criminel** : arson
incendier [ɛ̃sɑ̃dje] {96} *vt* **1** : to set on fire, to burn down **2** : to burn <ces piments incendient la gorge : these peppers burn my throat> **3** : to light up **4** : to stir up, to inflame
incertain, -taine [ɛ̃sɛrtɛ̃, -tɛn] *adj* **1** : uncertain, doubtful **2** : indistinct, blurred
incertitude [ɛ̃sɛrtityd] *nf* : uncertainty
incessant, -sante [ɛ̃sesɑ̃, -sɑ̃t] *adj* : incessant — **incessamment** [ɛ̃sesamɑ̃] *adv*
inceste [ɛ̃sest] *nm* : incest — **incestueux, -tueuse** [ɛ̃sestɥø, -tɥøz] *adj*
inchangé, -gée [ɛ̃ʃɑ̃ʒe] *adj* : unchanged
incidemment [ɛ̃sidamɑ̃] *adv* **1** : incidentally, in passing **2** : by chance
incidence [ɛ̃sidɑ̃s] *nf* **1** : effect, impact **2** : incidence (in physics)
incident[1], **-dente** [ɛ̃sidɑ̃, -dɑ̃t] *adj* : incidental
incident[2] *nm* **1** : incident, event **2** *or* **incident de parcours** : hitch, setback
incinérateur [ɛ̃sineratœr] *nm* : incinerator
incinération [ɛ̃sinerasjɔ̃] *nf* **1** : incineration **2** : cremation
incinérer [ɛ̃sinere] {87} *vt* **1** : to incinerate **2** : to cremate
inciser [ɛ̃size] *vt* **1** : to make an incision in, to incise **2** : to lance
incisif, -sive [ɛ̃sizif, -ziv] *adj* : incisive, cutting
incision [ɛ̃sizjɔ̃] *nf* : incision
incisive *nf* : incisor
incitatif, -tive [ɛ̃sitatif, -tiv] *adj* : motivating <mesure incitative : motivating factor, incentive>
incitation [ɛ̃sitasjɔ̃] *nf* **1** : incitement **2** : incentive
inciter [ɛ̃site] *vt* **1** : to incite (a riot, etc.) **2** : to encourage, to prompt
incivil, -vile [ɛ̃sivil] *adj* : uncivil, rude
inclassable [ɛ̃klasabl] *adj* : unclassifiable
inclinable [ɛ̃klinabl] *adj* : reclining, adjustable <fauteuil inclinable : recliner>
inclinaison [ɛ̃klinɛzɔ̃] *nf* : incline, slope, angle
inclination [ɛ̃klinasjɔ̃] *nf* **1** TENDANCE : inclination, tendency **2** : nod, bowing (of the head)
incliner [ɛ̃kline] *vt* **1** PENCHER : to tilt, to bend **2** : to incline, to prompt (s.o. to do sth) — *vi* **~ à** : to be inclined to, to tend toward — **s'incliner** *vr* **1** : to tilt, to lean **2 ~ devant** : to give in to **3 ~ devant** : to bow down before
inclure [ɛ̃klyr] {39} *vt* **1** : to include **2** : to enclose
inclus, -cluse [ɛ̃kly, -klyz] *adj* **1** COMPRIS : inclusive, including <de lundi à jeudi inclus : from Monday to Thursday inclusive> <samedi inclus : including Saturdays> **2** : impacted <dent incluse : impacted tooth> **3** → **ci-inclus**
inclusion [ɛ̃klyzjɔ̃] *nf* : inclusion
inclusivement [ɛ̃klyzivmɑ̃] *adv* : inclusive, inclusively
incognito [ɛ̃kɔgnito] *adv* & *adj* : incognito
incohérence [ɛ̃kɔerɑ̃s] *nf* **1** : incoherence **2** : inconsistency, discrepancy
incohérent, -rente [ɛ̃kɔerɑ̃, -rɑ̃t] *adj* **1** : incoherent **2** : inconsistent
incolore [ɛ̃kɔlɔr] *adj* : colorless
incomber [ɛ̃kɔ̃be] *vi* **~ à** : to be incumbent upon, to be the responsibility of
incombustible [ɛ̃kɔ̃bystibl] *adj* : incombustible
incommensurable [ɛ̃kɔmɑ̃syrabl] *adj* : immeasurable — **incommensurablement** [-rabləmɑ̃] *adv*
incommodant, -dante [ɛ̃kɔmɔdɑ̃, -dɑ̃t] *adj* **1** : unpleasant **2** : annoying
incommode [ɛ̃kɔmɔd] *adj* **1** : inconvenient **2** : uncomfortable, awkward — **incommodément** [-demɑ̃] *adv*
incommoder [ɛ̃kɔmɔde] *vt* : to bother, to inconvenience
incommodité [ɛ̃kɔmɔdite] *nf* **1** : inconvenience **2** : discomfort
incomparable [ɛ̃kɔ̃parabl] *adj* : incomparable — **incomparablement** [-rabləmɑ̃] *adv*
incompatible [ɛ̃kɔ̃patibl] *adj* : incompatible — **incompatibilité** [-tibilite] *nf*
incompétence [ɛ̃kɔ̃petɑ̃s] *nf* **1** : incompetence **2** : lack of knowledge, ignorance
incompétent, -tente [ɛ̃kɔ̃petɑ̃, -tɑ̃t] *adj* **1** : incompetent **2** : ignorant
incomplet, -plète [ɛ̃kɔ̃plɛ, -plɛt] *adj* : incomplete — **incomplètement** [-plɛtmɑ̃] *adv*
incompréhensible [ɛ̃kɔ̃preɑ̃sibl] *adj* : incomprehensible

incompréhensif, -sive [ɛ̃kɔ̃preɑ̃sif, -siv] *adj* : unsympathetic
incompréhension [ɛ̃kɔ̃preɑ̃sjɔ̃] *nf* : lack of understanding
incompris, -prise [ɛ̃kɔ̃pri, -priz] *adj* : misunderstood
inconcevable [ɛ̃kɔ̃svabl] *adj* : inconceivable, unimaginable
inconciliable [ɛ̃kɔ̃siljabl] *adj* : irreconcilable
inconditionnel[1], **-nelle** [ɛ̃kɔ̃disjɔnɛl] *adj* : unconditional — **inconditionnellement** [-nɛlmɑ̃] *adv*
inconditionnel[2], **-nelle** *n* : enthusiast <un inconditionnel du jazz : a jazz enthusiast>
inconduite [ɛ̃kɔ̃dɥit] *nf* : misconduct
inconfort [ɛ̃kɔ̃fɔr] *nm* : discomfort
inconfortable [ɛ̃kɔ̃fɔrtabl] *adj* : uncomfortable — **inconfortablement** [-tabləmɑ̃] *adv*
incongru, -grue [ɛ̃kɔ̃gry] *adj* **1** : incongruous **2** : unseemly, inappropriate
incongruité [ɛ̃kɔ̃gryite] *nf* **1** : incongruity **2** : unseemly remark
inconnu[1], **-nue** [ɛ̃kɔny] *adj* : unknown
inconnu[2], **-nue** *n* **1** : unknown (person) **2** : stranger
inconnue *nf* : unknown (in mathematics, etc.)
inconsciemment [ɛ̃kɔ̃sjamɑ̃] *adv* **1** : unconsciously **2** : thoughtlessly
inconscience [ɛ̃kɔ̃sjɑ̃s] *nf* **1** : unconsciousness **2** : thoughtlessness
inconscient[1], **-ciente** [ɛ̃kɔ̃sjɑ̃, -sjɑ̃t] *adj* **1** : unaware, oblivious **2** : unconscious
inconscient[2] *nm* **l'inconscient** : the unconscious
inconséquence [ɛ̃kɔ̃sekɑ̃s] *nf* **1** : inconsistency **2** : thoughtlessness
inconséquent, -quente [ɛ̃kɔ̃sekɑ̃, -kɑ̃t] *adj* **1** : inconsistent **2** : thoughtless
inconsidéré, -rée [ɛ̃kɔ̃sidere] *adj* : rash, thoughtless — **inconsidérément** [-remɑ̃] *adv*
inconsistant, -tante [ɛ̃kɔ̃sistɑ̃, -tɑ̃t] *adj* **1** : flimsy, weak **2** : watery, runny
inconsolable [ɛ̃kɔ̃sɔlabl] *adj* : inconsolable
inconstance [ɛ̃kɔ̃stɑ̃s] *nf* : inconstancy, fickleness
inconstant, -stante [ɛ̃kɔ̃stɑ̃, -stɑ̃t] *adj* : inconstant, fickle
inconstitutionnel, -nelle [ɛ̃kɔ̃stitysjɔnɛl] *adj* : unconstitutional
incontestable [ɛ̃kɔ̃tɛstabl] *adj* : unquestionable, indisputable — **incontestablement** [-stabləmɑ̃] *adv*
incontesté, -tée [ɛ̃kɔ̃tɛste] *adj* : uncontested, undisputed
incontinent, -nente [ɛ̃kɔ̃tinɑ̃, -nɑ̃t] *adj* : incontinent — **incontinence** [-tinɑ̃s] *nf*
incontournable [ɛ̃kɔ̃turnabl] *adj* : essential, that cannot be ignored
incontrôlable [ɛ̃kɔ̃trolabl] *adj* **1** : unverifiable **2** : uncontrollable
incontrôlé, -lée [ɛ̃kɔ̃trole] *adj* **1** : unchecked, unverified **2** : uncontrolled
inconvenance [ɛ̃kɔ̃vnɑ̃s] *nf* : impropriety, indecorousness
inconvenant, -nante [ɛ̃kɔ̃vnɑ̃, -nɑ̃t] *adj* INCONGRU : improper, indecorous, unseemly
inconvénient [ɛ̃kɔ̃venjɑ̃] *nm* : disadvantage, drawback
incorporation [ɛ̃kɔrpɔrasjɔ̃] *nf* **1** : incorporating, blending, mixing **2** : induction (into the military) **3** *Can* : incorporation (of a company)
incorporer [ɛ̃kɔrpɔre] *vt* **1** : to incorporate, to blend, to mix **2** : to induct (into the military) **3** *Can* : to incorporate (a company)
incorrect, -recte [ɛ̃kɔrɛkt] *adj* **1** IMPROPRE : incorrect **2** INCONVENANT : improper, unsuitable **3** DÉLOYAL : unfair, underhanded
incorrectement [ɛ̃kɔrɛktəmɑ̃] *adv* : incorrectly, wrongly
incorrigible [ɛ̃kɔriʒibl] *adj* : incorrigible
incorruptible [ɛ̃kɔryptibl] *adj* : incorruptible
incrédule [ɛ̃kredyl] *adj* : incredulous
incrédulité [ɛ̃kredylite] *nf* : incredulity
increvable [ɛ̃krəvabl] *adj* **1** : puncture-proof (of a tire) **2** *fam* : tireless
incriminer [ɛ̃krimine] *vt* : to incriminate — **incrimination** [ɛ̃kriminasjɔ̃] *nf*
incroyable [ɛ̃krwajabl] *adj* : unbelievable, incredible — **incroyablement** [-jabləmɑ̃] *adv*
incroyant, -croyante [ɛ̃krwajɑ̃, -jɑ̃t] *n* : unbeliever
incrustation [ɛ̃krystasjɔ̃] *nf* **1** : inlaying, inlay **2** : incrustation (in geology)
incruster [ɛ̃kryste] *vt* **1** : to encrust **2** : to inlay — **s'incruster** *vr* : to become embedded
incubateur [ɛ̃kybatœr] *nm* : incubator
incubation [ɛ̃kybasjɔ̃] *nf* : incubation
incuber [ɛ̃kybe] *vt* : to incubate
inculpation [ɛ̃kylpasjɔ̃] *nf* : indictment, charge
inculpé, -pée [ɛ̃kylpe] *n* : accused, defendant
inculper [ɛ̃kylpe] *vt* : to indict, to charge
inculquer [ɛ̃kylke] *vt* : to inculcate, to instill
inculte [ɛ̃kylt] *adj* **1** : uncultivated, wild **2** : unkempt **3** : uneducated, ignorant
inculture [ɛ̃kylтyr] *nf* : lack of culture
incurable [ɛ̃kyrabl] *adj* : incurable
incurie [ɛ̃kyri] *nf* NÉGLIGENCE : carelessness, negligence
incursion [ɛ̃kyrsjɔ̃] *nf* : foray, incursion, inroad
incurver [ɛ̃kyrve] *vt* : to bend, to curve — **s'incurver** *vr*
indécence [ɛ̃desɑ̃s] *nf* **1** : indecency **2** : indecent act or remark

indécent, -cente [ɛ̃desɑ̃, -sɑ̃t] *adj* : indecent — **indécemment** [-samɑ̃] *adv*
indéchiffrable [ɛ̃deʃifrabl] *adj* **1** : indecipherable **2** : incomprehensible
indécis, -cise [ɛ̃desi, -siz] *adj* **1** : indecisive **2** : undecided
indécision [ɛ̃desizjɔ̃] *nf* **1** : indecisiveness **2** : indecision
indécrottable [ɛ̃dekrɔtabl] *adj fam* : incorrigible
indéfectible [ɛ̃defɛktibl] *adj* : enduring, unfailing
indéfendable [ɛ̃defɑ̃dabl] *adj* : indefensible, untenable
indéfini, -nie [ɛ̃defini] *adj* **1** : indefinite **2** : undefined
indéfiniment [ɛ̃definimɑ̃] *adv* : indefinitely
indéfinissable [ɛ̃definisabl] *adj* : indefinable
indélébile [ɛ̃delebil] *adj* : indelible
indélicat, -cate [ɛ̃delika, -kat] *adj* **1** : coarse, indelicate **2** MALHONNÊTE : dishonest
indélicatesse [ɛ̃delikates] *nf* : indelicacy
indemne [ɛ̃dɛmn] *adj* : undamaged, unharmed
indemnisation [ɛ̃dɛmnizasjɔ̃] *nf* : compensation, indemnity
indemniser [ɛ̃dɛmnize] *vt* **1** : to indemnify, to compensate **2** : to reimburse (for expenses)
indemnité [ɛ̃dɛmnite] *nf* **1** COMPENSATION : indemnity, compensation **2** ALLOCATION : allowance <indemnité de logement : housing allowance>
indéniable [ɛ̃denjabl] *adj* : undeniable — **indéniablement** [-njabləmɑ̃] *adv*
indépendamment [ɛ̃depɑ̃damɑ̃] *adv* **1** : independently **2 ~ de** : regardless of, apart from **3 ~ de** : in addition to
indépendant, -dante [ɛ̃depɑ̃dɑ̃, -dɑ̃t] *adj* : independent — **indépendance** [-pɑ̃dɑ̃s] *nf*
indescriptible [ɛ̃dɛskriptibl] *adj* : indescribable
indésirable [ɛ̃dezirabl] *adj* : undesirable
indestructible [ɛ̃dɛstryktibl] *adj* : indestructible — **indestructibilité** [-tibilite] *nf*
indéterminé, -née [ɛ̃determinе] *adj* : indeterminate, unspecified
index [ɛ̃dɛks] *nm* **1** : index **2** : forefinger, index finger
indexation [ɛ̃dɛksasjɔ̃] *nf* **1** : indexing **2** : indexation (in economics)
indexer [ɛ̃dɛkse] *vt* : to index
indicateur[1], **-trice** [ɛ̃dikatœr, -tris] *adj* → **panneau, poteau**
indicateur[2] *nm* **1** INFORMATEUR : (police) informer **2** GUIDE : guide, directory **3** : gauge, meter <indicateur de vitesse : speedometer> **4** : economic indicator
indicatif[1], **-tive** [ɛ̃dikatif, -tiv] *adj* : indicative
indicatif[2] *nm* **1** : indicative (in grammar) **2** : theme (of a radio or television program) **3 indicatif de zone** : area code
indication [ɛ̃dikasjɔ̃] *nf* **1** APERÇU, SIGNE : indication **2** RENSEIGNEMENT : information **3 indications** *nfpl* : instructions, directions
indice [ɛ̃dis] *nm* **1** SIGNE : sign, indication **2** : clue, lead **3** : index <indice du coût de la vie : cost of living index> **4** : rating <indice d'écoute : audience ratings>
indicible [ɛ̃disibl] *adj* : unspeakable, inexpressible
indien, -dienne [ɛ̃djɛ̃, -djɛn] *adj* : Indian
Indien, -dienne *n* : Indian
indifféremment [ɛ̃diferamɑ̃] *adv* : indiscriminately, equally
indifférence [ɛ̃diferɑ̃s] *nf* : indifference
indifférent, -rente [ɛ̃diferɑ̃, -rɑ̃t] *adj* **1** : indifferent **2** : irrelevant, immaterial
indifférer [ɛ̃difere] {87} *vi* **~ à** : to be of no importance to <cela m'indiffère : it's all the same to me>
indigence [ɛ̃diʒɑ̃s] *nf* : indigence
indigène[1] [ɛ̃diʒɛn] *adj* : indigenous, native
indigène[2] *nmf* : native (of a country or region)
indigent[1], **-gente** [ɛ̃diʒɑ̃, -ʒɑ̃t] *adj* : indigent, destitute
indigent[2], **-gente** *n* **1** : pauper **2 les indigents** : the poor
indigeste [ɛ̃diʒɛst] *adj* : indigestible
indigestion [ɛ̃diʒɛstjɔ̃] *nf* : indigestion
indignation [ɛ̃diɲasjɔ̃] *nf* : indignation <avec indignation : indignantly>
indigne [ɛ̃diɲ] *adj* **1** : unworthy, undeserving **2** MÉPRISABLE : disgraceful
indigné, -gnée [ɛ̃diɲe] *adj* : indignant
indignement [ɛ̃diɲəmɑ̃] *adv* : disgracefully
indigner [ɛ̃diɲe] *vt* : to outrage — **s'indigner** *vr* : to be indignant
indignité [ɛ̃diɲite] *nf* **1** : unworthiness **2** : indignity, shameful act
indigo [ɛ̃digo] *adj & nm* : indigo
indiqué, -quée [ɛ̃dike] *adj* **1** : advisable, expedient **2** : appropriate
indiquer [ɛ̃dike] *vt* **1** : to indicate, to point out <ils m'ont indiqué le chemin : they showed me the way> **2** : to give, to name, to tell <indiquer l'heure : to give the time>
indirect, -recte [ɛ̃direkt] *adj* : indirect — **indirectement** [-rɛktəmɑ̃] *adv*
indiscernable [ɛ̃disɛrnabl] *adj* : indiscernible
indiscipline [ɛ̃disiplin] *nf* : lack of discipline
indisciplné, -née [ɛ̃disipline] *adj* : undisciplined, unruly
indiscret, -crète [ɛ̃diskrɛ, -krɛt] *adj* : indiscreet — **indiscrètement** [-krɛtmɑ̃] *adv*

indiscrétion [ɛ̃diskresjɔ̃] *nf* : indiscretion
indiscutable [ɛ̃diskytabl] *adj* : indisputable, unquestionable — **indiscutablement** [-tabləmɑ̃] *adv*
indispensable [ɛ̃dispɑ̃sabl] *adj* : indispensable, essential
indisponible [ɛ̃dispɔnibl] *adj* : unavailable
indisposé, -sée [ɛ̃dispoze] *adj* : unwell, indisposed
indisposer [ɛ̃dispoze] *vt* **1** : to annoy, to irritate **2** : to upset, to make ill
indisposition [ɛ̃dispozisjɔ̃] *nf* : disposition, illness
indissociable [ɛ̃disɔsjabl] *adj* : inseparable
indistinct, -tincte [ɛ̃distɛ̃kt, -tɛ̃kt] *adj* : indistinct
indistinctement [ɛ̃distɛ̃ktəmɑ̃] *adv* **1** : indistinctly **2** : indiscriminately
individu [ɛ̃dividy] *nm* : individual
individualiser [ɛ̃dividɥalize] *vt* : to individualize
individualisme [ɛ̃dividɥalism] *nm* : individualism
individualiste[1] [ɛ̃dividɥalist] *adj* : individualistic
individualiste[2] *nmf* : individualist
individualité [ɛ̃dividɥalite] *nf* : individuality
individuel, -duelle [ɛ̃dividɥɛl] *adj* **1** : individual, particular **2** : personal, private
individuellement [ɛ̃dividɥɛlmɑ̃] *adv* : individually
indivis, -vise [ɛ̃divi, -viz] *adj* **1** : undivided **2 par ~** : jointly, in common
indivisible [ɛ̃divizibl] *adj* : indivisible
indolence [ɛ̃dɔlɑ̃s] *nf* **1** : indolence, laziness **2** : apathy
indolent, -lente [ɛ̃dɔlɑ̃, -lɑ̃t] *adj* **1** : indolent, lazy **2** : apathetic
indolore [ɛ̃dɔlɔr] *adj* : painless
indomptable [ɛ̃dɔ̃tabl] *adj* **1** : indomitable, invincible **2** : untamable
indonésien[1], **-sienne** [ɛ̃dɔnezjɛ̃, -zjɛn] *adj* : Indonesian
indonésien[2] *nm* : Indonesian (language)
Indonésien, -sienne *n* : Indonesian
indu, -due [ɛ̃dy] *adj* **1** : unseemly, ungodly <à des heures indues : at this ungodly hour> **2** : unwarranted, unjustified
indubitable [ɛ̃dybitabl] *adj* : indubitable — **indubitablement** [-tabləmɑ̃] *adv*
induction [ɛ̃dyksjɔ̃] *nf* : induction
inductif, -tive [ɛ̃dyktif, -tiv] *adj* : inductive
induire [ɛ̃duir] {49} *vt* **1** INCITER : to induce, to incite <induire en erreur : to mislead> **2** CONCLURE : to infer, to conclude
indulgence [ɛ̃dylʒɑ̃s] *nf* **1** : indulgence, leniency **2** : indulgence (in religion)
indulgent, -gente [ɛ̃dylʒɑ, -ʒɑ̃t] *adj* : indulgent, lenient
indûment [ɛ̃dymɑ̃] *adv* : unduly, unjustifiably
industrialiser [ɛ̃dystrijalize] *vt* : to industrialize — **industrialisation** [-lizasjɔ̃] *nf*
industrie [ɛ̃dystri] *nf* : industry
industriel[1], **-trielle** [ɛ̃dystrijɛl] *adj* : industrial
industriel[2], **-trielle** *n* : manufacturer, industrialist
industrieux, -trieuse [ɛ̃dystrijø, -trijøz] *adj* TRAVAILLEUR : industrious
inébranlable [inebrɑ̃labl] *adj* : unwavering, unshakeable
inédit, -dite [inedi, -dit] *adj* **1** : unpublished **2** ORIGINAL : novel, original
ineffable [inefabl] *adj* : ineffable, inexpressible — **ineffablement** [-fabləmɑ̃] *adv*
ineffaçable [inefasabl] *adj* : indelible
inefficace [inefikas] *adj* **1** : inefficient **2** : ineffective
inefficacité [inefikasite] *nf* **1** : inefficiency **2** : ineffectiveness
inégal, -gale [inegal] *adj, mpl* **-gaux** [-go] **1** : unequal **2** IRRÉGULIER : irregular, uneven — **inégalement** [-galmɑ̃] *adv*
inégalé, -lée [inegale] *adj* : unequaled
inégalité [inegalite] *nf* **1** : inequality **2** IRRÉGULARITÉ : unevenness, irregularity
inélégant, -gante [inelegɑ̃, -gɑ̃t] *adj* **1** : inelegant **2** : discourteous — **inélégance** [-gɑ̃s] *nf*
inéligible [ineliʒibl] *adj* : ineligible — **inéligibilité** [-ʒibilite] *nf*
inéluctable [inelyktabl] *adj* : inescapable — **inéluctablement** [-tabləmɑ̃] *adv*
inemployé, -ployée [inɑ̃plwaje] *adj* : unused
inénarrable [inenarabl] *adj* : hilarious, beyond words
inepte [inɛpt] *adj* : inept
ineptie [inɛpsi] *nf* **1** : ineptitude **2** : stupid action or remark
inépuisable [inepɥizabl] *adj* : inexhaustible
inéquitable [inekitabl] *adj* : inequitable
inerte [inɛrt] *adj* **1** : lifeless **2** : passive, apathetic **3** : inert
inertie [inɛrsi] *nf* : inertia
inespéré, -rée [inɛspere] *adj* : unhoped for, unexpected
inestimable [inɛstimabl] *adj* : inestimable, priceless
inévitable [inevitabl] *adj* : inevitable, unavoidable — **inévitablement** [-tabləmɑ̃] *adv*
inexact, inexacte [inɛgza(kt), -ɛgzakt] *adj* **1** : inaccurate **2** : unpunctual, late
inexactement [inɛgzaktəmɑ̃] *adv* : inaccurately, wrong
inexactitude [inɛgzaktityd] *nf* **1** : inaccuracy **2** : lateness, unpunctuality

inexcusable [inɛkskyzabl] *adj* : inexcusable
inexécutable [inɛgzekytabl] *adj* : impracticable, unworkable
inexercé, -cée [inɛgzɛrse] *adj* : untrained, inexperienced
inexistant, -tante [inɛgzistɑ̃, -tɑ̃t] *adj* : nonexistent — **inexistence** [-zistɑ̃s] *nf*
inexorable [inɛgzɔrabl] *adj* : inexorable — **inexorablement** [-rablǝmɑ̃] *adv*
inexpérience [inɛksperjɑ̃s] *nf* : inexperience
inexpérimenté, -tée [inɛksperimɑ̃te] *adj* **1** : inexperienced **2** : untried, untested
inexplicable [inɛksplikabl] *adj* : inexplicable — **inexplicablement** [-kabləmɑ̃] *adv*
inexpliqué, -quée [inɛksplike] *adj* : unexplained
inexploité, -tée [inɛksplwate] *adj* : untapped, unexploited
inexpressif, -sive [inɛkspresif, -siv] *adj* : inexpressive, expressionless
inexprimable [inɛksprimabl] *adj* : inexpressible
inexprimé, -mée [inɛksprime] *adj* : unexpressed, unspoken
inextinguible [inɛkstɛ̃gibl] *adj* **1** : inextinguishable, unquenchable **2** : uncontrollable
in extremis [inɛkstremis] *adv* : at the last minute
inextricable [inɛkstrikabl] *adj* : inextricable — **inextricablement** [-kabləmɑ̃] *adv*
infaillibilité [ɛ̃fajibilite] *nf* : infallibility
infaillible [ɛ̃fajibl] *adj* **1** : infallible **2** : certain, reliable
infailliblement [ɛ̃fajibləmɑ̃] *adv* : without fail
infamant, -mante [ɛ̃famɑ̃, -mɑ̃t] *adj* **1** : defamatory **2** : dishonorable
infâme [ɛ̃fam] *adj* : vile, despicable
infamie [ɛ̃fami] *nf* **1** : infamy **2** CALOMNIE : calumny, slander
infanterie [ɛ̃fɑ̃tri] *nf* : infantry
infantile [ɛ̃fɑ̃til] *adj* : infantile, childish
infarctus [ɛ̃farktys] *nm or* **infarctus myocarde** : heart attack
infatigable [ɛ̃fatigabl] *adj* : indefatigable, tireless — **infatigablement** [-bləmɑ̃] *adv*
infatuation [ɛ̃fatɥasjɔ̃] *nf* : self-importance, conceit
infatué, -tuée [ɛ̃fatɥe] *adj* : conceited, self-important
infect, -fecte [ɛ̃fɛkt] *adj* **1** : foul, stinking **2** : horrible, vile
infecter [ɛ̃fɛkte] *vt* **1** : to infect **2** : to contaminate, to pollute, to poison — **s'infecter** *vr* : to become infected
infectieux, -tieuse [ɛ̃fɛksjø, -tjøz] *adj* : infectious
infection [ɛ̃fɛksjɔ̃] *nf* **1** : infection **2** PUANTEUR : stench
inférer [ɛ̃fere] {87} *vt* : to infer — **inférence** [ɛ̃ferɑ̃s] *nf*
inférieur[1], **-rieure** [ɛ̃ferjœr] *adj* **1** : inferior **2** : lower <lèvre inférieure : lower lip> **3** ~ **à** : less than
inférieur[2], **-rieure** *n* : inferior
infériorité [ɛ̃ferjɔrite] *nf* : inferiority
infernal, -nale [ɛ̃fernal] *adj, mpl* **-naux** [-no] **1** : infernal **2** : fiendish, diabolical
infertile [ɛ̃fertil] *adj* : infertile — **infertilité** [-tilite] *nf*
infester [ɛ̃feste] *vt* : to infest
infidèle[1] [ɛ̃fidɛl] *adj* **1** : unfaithful, disloyal **2** : inaccurate
infidèle[2] *nmf* **1** : infidel, unbeliever **2** : unfaithful spouse or lover
infidélité [ɛ̃fidelite] *nf* **1** : infidelity **2** : unfaithfulness, inaccuracy
infiltration [ɛ̃filtrasjɔ̃] *nf* : infiltration
infiltrer [ɛ̃filtre] *vt* : to infiltrate — **s'infiltrer** *vr* ~ **dans** : to penetrate, to seep into, to filter through
infime [ɛ̃fim] *adj* : minute, negligible
infini[1], **-nie** [ɛ̃fini] *adj* : infinite — **infiniment** [-nimɑ̃] *adv*
infini[2] *nm* **1** : infinity (in mathematics, etc.) **2 à l'infini** : endlessly, ad infinitum
infinité [ɛ̃finite] *nf* **1** : infinite number, lot **2** : infinity
infinitésimal, -male [ɛ̃finitezimal] *adj, mpl* **-maux** [-mo] : infinitesimal
infinitif [ɛ̃finitif] *nm* : infinitive
infirme[1] [ɛ̃firm] *adj* : disabled, infirm
infirme[2] *nmf* : disabled person, invalid
infirmer [ɛ̃firme] *vt* ANNULER : to invalidate, to annul
infirmerie [ɛ̃firmǝri] *nf* : infirmary
infirmier[1], **-mière** [ɛ̃firmje, -mjɛr] *adj* : nursing <personnel infirmier : nursing staff>
infirmier[2], **-mière** *n* GARDE-MALADE : nurse
infirmité [ɛ̃firmite] *nf* : disability, infirmity
inflammable [ɛ̃flamabl] *adj* : inflammable, flammable
inflammation [ɛ̃flamasjɔ̃] *nf* : inflammation
inflammatoire [ɛ̃flamatwar] *adj* : inflammatory
inflation [ɛ̃flasjɔ̃] *nf* : inflation
inflationniste [ɛ̃flasjɔnist] *adj* : inflationary
infléchir [ɛ̃fleʃir] *vt* **1** : to bend, to inflect **2** : to modify, to influence — **s'infléchir** *vr* **1** : to curve **2** : to deviate, to change course
inflexibilité [ɛ̃fleksibilite] *nf* : inflexibility
inflexible [ɛ̃fleksibl] *adj* : inflexible — **inflexiblement** [-sibləmɑ̃] *adv*
inflexion [ɛ̃fleksjɔ̃] *nf* **1** CHANGEMENT : change, shift **2** COURBE : bend <inflexion de la tête : brief nod> **3** : inflection (of the voice)

infliger [ɛ̃fliʒe] {17} *vt* **1** : to inflict **2** : to impose (a penalty, etc.)
influence [ɛ̃flyɑ̃s] *nf* : influence
influencer [ɛ̃flyɑ̃se] {6} *vt* : to influence
influent, -fluente [ɛ̃flyɑ̃, -flyɑ̃t] *adj* : influential
influer [ɛ̃flye] *vi* ~ **sur** : to have an influence on, to affect
infographie [ɛ̃fografi] *nf* : computer graphics *pl*
informateur, -trice [ɛ̃fɔrmatœr, -tris] *n* INDICATEUR : informant, informer
informaticien, -cienne [ɛ̃fɔrmatisjɛ̃, -sjɛn] *n* : computer programmer
informatif, -tive [ɛ̃fɔrmatif, -tiv] *adj* : informative
information [ɛ̃fɔrmasjɔ̃] *nf* **1** : information **2** : news item **3** *France* : (judicial) inquiry
informatique[1] [ɛ̃fɔrmatik] *adj* : computer <analyste informatique : computer analyst>
informatique[2] *nf* **1** : computer science, information technology **2** : data processing
informatiser [ɛ̃fɔrmatizé] *vt* : to computerize — **informatisation** [-tizasjɔ̃] *nf*
informe [ɛ̃fɔrm] *adj* : formless, shapeless
informel, -melle [ɛ̃fɔrmɛl] *adj* : informal
informer [ɛ̃fɔrme] *vt* : to inform — **s'informer** *vr* **1** : to inquire **2** : to inform oneself, to find out
infortune [ɛ̃fɔrtyn] *nf* : misfortune
infortuné, -née [ɛ̃fɔrtyne] *adj* : unfortunate, luckless
infraction [ɛ̃fraksjɔ̃] *nf* : infraction <infraction à la loi : breach of the law>
infranchissable [ɛ̃frɑ̃ʃisabl] *adj* **1** : insurmountable **2** : impassable
infrarouge [ɛ̃fraruʒ] *adj & nm* : infrared
infrastructure [ɛ̃frastryktyr] *nf* : infrastructure
infructueux, -tueuse [ɛ̃fryktɥø, -tɥøz] *adj* : fruitless
infus, -fuse [ɛ̃fy, -fyz] *adj* : innate <avoir la science infuse : to know a lot without studying>
infuser [ɛ̃fyze] *v* **1** : to infuse **2** : to brew, to steep
infusion [ɛ̃fyzjɔ̃] *nf* : infusion
ingénier [ɛ̃ʒenje] {96} *v* **s'ingénier** *vr* : to strive, to do one's utmost
ingénierie [ɛ̃ʒeniri] *nf* : engineering
ingénieur, -nieure [ɛ̃ʒenjœr] *n* : engineer
ingénieux, -nieuse [ɛ̃ʒenjø, -njøz] *adj* : ingenious — **ingénieusement** [-njøzmɑ̃] *adv*
ingéniosité [ɛ̃ʒenjɔzite] *nf* : ingenuity
ingénu, -nue [ɛ̃ʒeny] *adj* : ingenuous, naive — **ingénuement** *adv*
ingénue *nf* : ingenue
ingénuité [ɛ̃ʒenɥite] *nf* : ingenuousness, naïveté
ingérence [ɛ̃ʒerɑ̃s] *nf* : interference
ingérer [ɛ̃ʒere] {87} *vt* : to ingest — **s'ingérer** *vr* : to interfere, to meddle
ingouvernable [ɛ̃guvernabl] *adj* : ungovernable
ingrat[1], **-grate** [ɛ̃gra, -grat] *adj* **1** : ungrateful **2** : thankless, unrewarding **3** : barren **4** : unattractive
ingrat[2], **-grate** *n* : ingrate
ingratitude [ɛ̃gratityd] *nf* : ingratitude
ingrédient [ɛ̃gredjɑ̃] *nm* : ingredient
inguérissable [ɛ̃gerisabl] *adj* : incurable
ingurgiter [ɛ̃gyrʒite] *vt* **1** ENGLOUTIR : to gulp down **2** : to take in, to absorb (knowledge, etc.)
inhabile [inabil] *adj* : inept, clumsy
inhabitable [inabitabl] *adj* : uninhabitable
inhabité, -tée [inabite] *adj* : uninhabited
inhabituel, -tuelle [inabituɛl] *adj* : unusual
inhalant [inalɑ̃] *nm* : inhalant
inhalateur [inalatœr] *nm* : inhaler
inhaler [inale] *vt* : to inhale — **inhalation** [-alasjɔ̃] *nf*
inhérent, -rente [inerɑ̃, -rɑ̃t] *adj* : inherent
inhiber [inibe] *vt* : to inhibit
inhibition [inibisjɔ̃] *nf* : inhibition
inhospitalier, -lière [inɔspitalje, -ljɛr] *adj* : inhospitable
inhumain, -maine [inymɛ̃, -mɛn] *adj* : inhuman
inhumanité [inymanite] *nf* : inhumanity
inhumation [inymasjɔ̃] *nf* : burial, interment
inhumer [inyme] *vt* : to bury, to inter
ininflammable [inɛ̃flamabl] *adj* : nonflammable
inimaginable [inimaʒinabl] *adj* : unimaginable, incredible
inimitable [inimitabl] *adj* : inimitable
inimitié [inimitje] *nf* HOSTILITÉ : enmity, hostility
intelligent, -gente [inɛ̃teliʒɑ̃, -ʒɑ̃t] *adj* : unintelligent
intelligible [inɛ̃teliʒibl] *adj* : unintelligible
intéressant, -sante [inɛ̃teresɑ̃, -sɑ̃t] *adj* : uninteresting
ininterrompu, -pue [inɛ̃terɔ̃py] *adj* **1** : uninterrupted, non-stop **2** : unbroken **3** : continuous, unremitting
inique [inik] *adj* : iniquitous
iniquité [inikite] *nf* : iniquity
initial, -tiale [inisjal] *adj, mpl* **-tiaux** [-sjo] : initial — **initialement** [-sjalmɑ̃] *adv*
initiale *nf* : initial
initiateur, -trice [inisjatœr, -tris] *n* **1** : initiator **2** NOVATEUR : innovator, pioneer
initiation [inisjasjɔ̃] *nf* : initiation
initiatique [inisjatik] *adj* : initiatory

initiative [inisjativ] *nf* : initiative <prendre l'initiative : to take the initiative>
initié, -tiée [inisje] *n* : initiate, insider
initier [inisje] {96} *vt* **1 ~ à** : to initiate, to start **2 ~ à** : to introduce to — **s'initier** *vr* **~ à** : to learn
injecté, -tée [ɛ̃ʒɛkte] *adj* **yeux injectés (de sang)** : bloodshot eyes
injecter [ɛ̃ʒɛkte] *vt* : to inject
injection [ɛ̃ʒɛksjɔ̃] *nf* : injection
injonction [ɛ̃ʒɔ̃ksjɔ̃] *nf* : order, injunction
injure [ɛ̃ʒyr] *nf* : insult, abuse <faire injure à qqn : to insult s.o.>
injurier [ɛ̃ʒyrje] {96} *vt* : to insult
injurieux, -rieuse [ɛ̃ʒyrjø, -rjøz] *adj* : insulting, abusive
injuste [ɛ̃ʒyst] *adj* : unjust, unfair — **injustement** [ɛ̃ʒystəmɑ̃] *adv*
injustice [ɛ̃ʒystis] *nf* : injustice
injustifiable [ɛ̃ʒystifjabl] *adj* : unjustifiable, indefensible
injustifié, -fiée [ɛ̃ʒystifje] *adj* : unjustified
inlassable [ɛ̃lasabl] *adj* : tireless — **inlassablement** [-sabləmɑ̃] *adv*
inné, -née [ine] *adj* : innate, inborn
innocemment [inɔsamɑ̃] *adv* : innocently
innocence [inɔsɑ̃s] *nf* : innocence
innocent, -cente [inɔsɑ̃, -sɑ̃t] *adj & n* : innocent
innocenter [inɔsɑ̃te] *vt* **1** DISCULPER : to exonerate, to clear **2** EXCUSER : to excuse, to justify
innocuité [inɔkɥite] *nf* : innocuousness
innombrable [inɔ̃brabl] *adj* : innumerable
innommable [inɔmabl] *adj* : unspeakable, foul
innovateur[1], **-trice** [inɔvatœr, -tris] *adj* : innovative
innovateur[2], **-trice** *n* : innovator
innover [inɔve] *v* : to innovate — **innovation** [inɔvasjɔ̃] *nf*
inoccupation [inɔkypasjɔ̃] *nf* : inactivity
inoccupé, -pée [inɔkype] *adj* **1** : idle **2** : unoccupied, vacant
inoculer [inɔkyle] *vt* : to inoculate — **inoculation** [-kylasjɔ̃] *nf*
inodore [inɔdɔr] *adj* : odorless
inoffensif, -sive [inɔfɑ̃sif, -siv] *adj* : inoffensive, harmless
inondation [inɔ̃dasjɔ̃] *nf* : flood, inundation
inonder [inɔ̃de] *vt* **1** : to flood **2** : to inundate, to overrun
inopérable [inɔperabl] *adj* : inoperable
inopérant, -rante [inɔperɑ̃, -rɑ̃t] *adj* : ineffective, inoperative
inopiné, -née [inɔpine] *adj* : unexpected — **inopinément** [-nemɑ̃] *adv*
inopportun, -tune [inɔpɔrtœ̃, -tyn] *adj* INTEMPESTIF : inopportune, untimely — **inopportunément** [-tynemɑ̃] *adv*
inorganique [inɔrganik] *adj* : inorganic
inorganisé, -sée [inɔrganize] *adj* **1** : disorganized **2** : unorganized
inoubliable [inublijabl] *adj* : unforgettable — **inoubliablement** [inublijablemɑ̃]
inouï, inouïe [inwi] *adj* : incredible, unheard of
inoxydable[1] [inɔksidabl] *adj* **1** : rustproof **2 acier inoxydable** : stainless steel
inoxydable[2] *nm* : stainless steel
inqualifiable [ɛ̃kalifjabl] *adj* : unspeakable
inquiet, -quiète [ɛ̃kjɛ, -kjɛt] *adj* **1** ANXIEUX : worried, anxious **2** AGITÉ : restless
inquiétant, -tante [ɛ̃kjetɑ̃, -tɑ̃t] *adj* : worrisome, ominous
inquiéter [ɛ̃kjete] {87} *vt* **1** : to worry **2** : to bother, to disturb — **s'inquiéter** *vr* **1** : to be worried **2 ~ de** : to bother about, to inquire about
inquiétude [ɛ̃kjetyd] *nf* : worry, anxiety, concern
inquisiteur, -trice [ɛ̃kizitœr, -tris] *adj* : inquisitive
inquisition [ɛ̃kizisjɔ̃] *nf* : inquisition
insaisissable [ɛ̃sezisabl] *adj* **1** FUYANT : elusive **2** IMPERCEPTIBLE : imperceptible
insalubre [ɛ̃salybr] *adj* : unhealthy, insalubrious
insanité [ɛ̃sanite] *nf* **1** : insanity **2** : nonsense, rubbish
insatiable [ɛ̃sasjabl] *adj* : insatiable
insatisfaction [ɛ̃satisfaksjɔ̃] *nf* : dissatisfaction
insatisfait, -faite [ɛ̃satisfɛ, -fɛt] *adj* **1** : unsatisfied **2** MÉCONTENT : dissatisfied
inscription [ɛ̃skripsjɔ̃] *nf* **1** : inscription **2** : registration, enrollment
inscrire [ɛ̃skrir] {33} *vt* **1** : to inscribe **2** : to register, to enroll **3** : to write, to note down — **s'inscrire** *vr* **1** : to register, to enroll **2 s'inscrire en faux contre** : to deny strongly
inscrivait [ɛ̃skrive], **inscrivions** [ɛ̃skrivjɔ̃], *etc.* → **inscrire**
inscrive [ɛ̃skriv] *etc.* → **inscrire**
insecte [ɛ̃sɛkt] *nm* : insect
insecticide [ɛ̃sɛktisid] *nm* : insecticide
insectifuge [ɛ̃sɛktifyʒ] *nm* : insect repellent
insécurité [ɛ̃sekyrite] *nf* : insecurity
insémination [ɛ̃seminasjɔ̃] *nf* : insemination <insémination artificielle : artificial insemination>
inséminer [ɛ̃semine] *vt* : to inseminate
insensé, -sée [ɛ̃sɑ̃se] *adj* **1** : crazy, foolish, nonsensical **2** : considerable, phenomenal
insensibiliser [ɛ̃sɑ̃sibilize] *vt* ANESTHÉSIER : to anesthetize
insensibilité [ɛ̃sɑ̃sibilite] *nf* **1** : insensibility, numbness **2** : insensitivity, indifference

insensible [ɛ̃sɑ̃sibl] *adj* **1** : insensible, numb **2** : insensitive **3** : imperceptible
insensiblement [ɛ̃sɑ̃sibləmɑ̃] *adv* : gradually, imperceptibly
inséparable [ɛ̃separabl] *adj* : inseparable
insérer [ɛ̃sere] {87} *vt* INTRODUIRE : to insert — **s'insérer** *vr* **1 ~ dans** : to be part of, to be integrated into **2 ~ sur** : to be attached to (in anatomy)
insertion [ɛ̃sersjɔ̃] *nf* **1** INTRODUCTION : insertion **2** : integration
insidieux, -dieuse [ɛ̃sidjø, -djøz] *adj* : insidious — **insidieusement** [-djøzmɑ̃] *adv*
insigne[1] [ɛ̃siɲ] *adj* : great, distinguished <insigne honneur : great honor>
insigne[2] *nm* **1** : badge, emblem **2** *or* **insignes** *nmpl* : insignia
insignifiant, -fiante [ɛ̃siɲifjɑ̃, -fjɑt] *adj* **1** : insignificant, trivial **2** : meager, trifling — **insignifiance** [-nifjɑ̃s] *nf*
insinuant, -nuante [ɛ̃sinɥwɑ̃] *adj* : ingratiating
insinuation [ɛ̃sinɥasjɔ̃] *nf* : insinuation, innuendo
insinuer [ɛ̃sinɥe] *vt* : to insinuate, to imply — **s'insinuer** *vr* **1** : to insinuate oneself **2 s'insinuer dans les bonnes grâces de** : to ingratiate oneself with
insipide [ɛ̃sipid] *adj* : insipid
insistant, -tante [ɛ̃sistɑ̃, -tɑt] *adj* : insistent — **insistance** [ɛ̃sistɑ̃s] *nf*
insister [ɛ̃siste] *vi* **1** : to insist **2 ~ sur** : to stress, to emphasize — *vt* : to insist
insociable [ɛ̃sɔsjabl] *adj* : unsociable
insolation [ɛ̃sɔlasjɔ̃] *nf* : sunstroke
insolence [ɛ̃sɔlɑ̃s] *nf* : insolence <avec insolence : insolently>
insolent, -lente [ɛ̃sɔlɑ̃, -lɑt] *adj* **1** : insolent **2** : arrogant **3** : unabashed, outrageous
insolite [ɛ̃sɔlit] *adj* : unusual, bizarre
insoluble [ɛ̃sɔlybl] *adj* : insoluble
insolvabilité [ɛ̃sɔlvabilite] *nf* : insolvency
insolvable [ɛ̃sɔlvabl] *adj* : insolvent
insomniaque [ɛ̃sɔmnjak] *nmf* : insomniac
insomnie [ɛ̃sɔmni] *nf* : insomnia
insondable [ɛ̃sɔ̃dabl] *adj* : unfathomable
insonore [ɛ̃sɔnɔr] *adj* : soundproof
insonoriser [ɛ̃sɔnɔrize] *vt* : to soundproof
insouciance [ɛ̃susjɑ̃s] *nf* : insouciance, carefree attitude
insouciant, -ciante [ɛ̃susjɑ̃, -sjɑt] *adj* **1** : carefree, happy-go-lucky **2 ~ de** : unconcerned about, heedless of
insoumis[1], **-mise** [ɛ̃sumi, -miz] *adj* **1** : rebellious, unsubdued **2 soldat insoumis** : deserter, draft dodger
insoumis[2] *nm* : deserter, draft dodger
insoumission [ɛ̃sumisjɔ̃] *nf* **1** : rebelliousness **2** : desertion (of one's military post)
insoutenable [ɛ̃sutnabl] *adj* **1** INDÉFENDABLE : untenable **2** INSUPPORTABLE : unbearable
inspecter [ɛ̃spɛkte] *vt* : to inspect
inspecteur, -trice [ɛ̃spɛktœr, -tris] *n* : inspector
inspection [ɛ̃spɛksjɔ̃] *nf* : inspection
inspirant, -rante [ɛ̃spirɑ̃, -rɑt] *adj* : inspirational
inspiration [ɛ̃spirasjɔ̃] *nf* **1** : inspiration **2** : inhalation
inspiré, -rée [ɛ̃spire] *adj* **1** : inspired **2 bien inspiré** : well-advised **3 mal inspiré** : ill-advised
inspirer [ɛ̃spire] *vt* **1** : to inspire **2** : to breathe in, to inhale — *vi* : to inhale — **s'inspirer** *vr* **~ de** : to be inspired by
instabilité [ɛ̃stabilite] *nf* : instability
instable [ɛ̃stabl] *adj* **1** BRANLANT : unsteady, wobbly **2** : unsettled, unstable
installation [ɛ̃stalasjɔ̃] *nf* **1** : installation **2 installations** *nfpl* : installations, facilities, fittings <installations nucléaires : nuclear sites>
installer [ɛ̃stale] *vt* : to install, to put in, to set up — **s'installer** *vr* : to become established, to settle <ils se sont installés dans la maison : they have settled into the house>
instamment [ɛ̃stamɑ̃] *adv* : insistently
instance [ɛ̃stɑ̃s] *nf* **1** INSISTANCE : insistence, entreaty **2** AUTORITÉ : authority **3** : legal proceedings *pl*, lawsuit **4 en ~** : pending
instant[1], **-tante** [ɛ̃stɑ̃, -tɑt] *adj* : urgent, pressing
instant[2] *nm* : instant, moment <à l'instant : just this minute, a moment ago> <dans un instant : in a minute, soon> <en un instant : in no time at all> <par instants : at times>
instantané[1], **-née** [ɛ̃stɑ̃tane] *adj* **1** : instantaneous **2** : instant <café instantané : instant coffee> **3** : candid <photo instantané : candid photo> — **instantanément** [-nemɑ̃] *adv*
instantané[2] *nm* : snapshot
instar [ɛ̃star] **à l'instar de** : following the example of, like
instauration [ɛ̃storasjɔ̃] *nf* : institution, establishing
instaurer [ɛ̃store] *vt* **1** : to establish, to institute **2** : to instill
instigateur, -trice [ɛ̃stigatœr, -tris] *n* : instigator
instigation [ɛ̃stigasjɔ̃] *nf* : instigation
instiller [ɛ̃stile] *vt* **1** : to apply drop by drop (as eyedrops) **2** : to instill
instinct [ɛ̃stɛ̃] *nm* : instinct <d'instinct : instinctively>
instinctif, -tive [ɛ̃stɛ̃ktif, -tiv] *adj* : instinctive, instinctual — **instinctivement** [-tivmɑ̃] *adv*

instituer [ɛ̃stitɥe] *vt* **1** : to institute **2** : to appoint (in law)
institut [ɛ̃stity] *nm* **1** : institute **2 institut de beauté** : beauty salon
instituteur, -trice [ɛ̃stitytœr, -tris] *n* : schoolteacher
institution [ɛ̃stitysjɔ̃] *nf* **1** : instituting, establishment **2** : institution <institution dotée : endowment, foundation>
institutionnaliser [ɛ̃stitysjɔnalize] *vt* : to institutionalize
institutionnel, -nelle [ɛ̃stitysjɔnɛl] *adj* : institutional
instructeur, -trice [ɛ̃stryktœr, -tris] *n* : instructor
instructif, -tive [ɛ̃stryktif, -tiv] *adj* : instructive
instruction [ɛ̃stryksjɔ̃] *nf* **1** FORMATION : training, instruction **2** : education <sans instruction : uneducated> **3** DIRECTIVE : order, directive **4 instructions** *nfpl* : instructions, directions
instruire [ɛ̃strɥir] {49} *vt* **1** ÉDUQUER, FORMER : to teach, to train, to instruct **2** : to inform <ils m'ont instruit des règlements : they informed me of the rules> **3 instruire une affaire** *France* : to prepare a case (in law) — **s'instruire** *vr* **1** : to educate oneself, to learn **2 ~ de** : to find out about
instruisait [ɛ̃strɥizɛ], **instruisions** [ɛ̃strɥizjɔ̃], *etc.* → **instruire**
instruit, -truite [ɛ̃strɥi, -trɥit] *adj* : learned, educated
instrument [ɛ̃strymɑ̃] *nm* **1** : instrument, tool **2 instrument de musique** : musical instrument
instrumental, -tale [ɛ̃strymɑ̃tal] *adj, mpl* **-taux** [-to] : instrumental
instrumentation [ɛ̃strymɑ̃tasjɔ̃] *nf* : instrumentation
instrumentiste [ɛ̃strymɑ̃tist] *nmf* : instrumentalist
insu [ɛ̃sy] **à l'insu de** : without the knowledge of, unknown to
insubmersible [ɛ̃sybmɛrsibl] *adj* : unsinkable
insubordination [ɛ̃sybɔrdinasjɔ̃] *nf* : insubordination
insubordonné, -née [ɛ̃sybɔrdɔne] *adj* : insubordinate
insuccès [ɛ̃sykse] *nm* : failure
insuffisance [ɛ̃syfizɑ̃s] *nf* **1** : insufficiency, lack **2** : insufficiency (in medicine) **3 insuffisances** *nfpl* : shortcomings, weaknesses
insuffisant, -sante [ɛ̃syfizɑ̃, -zɑ̃t] *adj* **1** : insufficient **2** : inadequate, unsatisfactory — **insuffisamment** [-zamɑ̃] *adv*
insuffler [ɛ̃syfle] *vt* : to instill, to infuse <insuffler une nouvelle énergie à : to infuse new energy into>
insulaire[1] [ɛ̃sylɛr] *adj* **1** : island <la population insulaire : the island population> **2** : insular
insulaire[2] *nmf* : islander
insularité [ɛ̃sylarite] *nf* : insularity
insuline [ɛ̃sylin] *nf* : insulin
insultant, -tante [ɛ̃syltɑ̃, -tɑ̃t] *adj* : insulting
insulte [ɛ̃sylt] *nf* : insult
insulter [ɛ̃sylte] *vt* : to insult
insupportable [ɛ̃sypɔrtabl] *adj* : unbearable — **insupportablement** [-bləmɑ̃] *adv*
insurgé[1], **-gée** [ɛ̃syrʒe] *adj* : insurgent
insurgé[2], **-gée** *n* : insurgent, rebel
insurger [ɛ̃syrʒe] {17} *v* **s'insurger** *vr* : to rebel, to rise up
insurmontable [ɛ̃syrmɔ̃tabl] *adj* **1** : insurmountable **2** : invincible, unconquerable
insurrection [ɛ̃syrɛksjɔ̃] *nf* : insurrection
intact, -tacte [ɛ̃takt] *adj* : intact
intangible [ɛ̃tɑ̃ʒibl] *adj* **1** : intangible **2** : inviolable
intarissable [ɛ̃tarisabl] *adj* : inexhaustible
intégral, -grale [ɛ̃tegral] *adj, mpl* **-graux** [-gro] **1** : complete <remboursement intégral : repayment in full> **2** : uncut, unabridged
intégrale [ɛ̃tegral] *nf* **1** : integral **2** : complete works <l'intégrale des symphonies de Brahms : the complete symphonies of Brahms>
intégralement [ɛ̃tegralmɑ̃] *adv* : completely, in full
intégralité [ɛ̃tegralite] *nf* : entirety, whole
intégrant, -grante [ɛ̃tegrɑ̃, -grɑ̃t] *adj* **partie intégrante** : integral part
intégration [ɛ̃tegrasjɔ̃] *nf* : integration
intègre [ɛ̃tegr] *adj* HONNÊTE : honest
intégrer [ɛ̃tegre] {87} *vt* **1** : to insert, to include **2** : to integrate, to assimilate — **s'intégrer** *vr* **1** : to become integrated, to fit in **2** : to fit together
intégrisme [ɛ̃tegrism] *nm* : fundamentalism
intégriste [ɛ̃tegrist] *adj & nmf* : fundamentalist
intégrité [ɛ̃tegrite] *nf* : integrity
intellect [ɛ̃telɛkt] *nm* : intellect
intellectualisme [ɛ̃telɛktɥalism] *nm* : intellectualism
intellectuel, -tuelle [ɛ̃telɛktɥɛl] *adj & n* : intellectual — **intellectuellement** [-tɥɛlmɑ̃] *adv*
intelligemment [ɛ̃teliʒamɑ̃] *adv* : intelligently
intelligence [ɛ̃teliʒɑ̃s] *nf* **1** : intelligence **2** COMPRÉHENSION : understanding <avoir l'intelligence de : to have a (good) grasp of> **3** : (secret) agreement <agir d'intelligence avec : to have an understanding with> **4 : intelligences** *nfpl* : collusion, (secret) dealings <elle a des intelligences dans l'industrie : she has contacts in industry>
intelligent, -gente [ɛ̃teliʒɑ̃, -ʒɑ̃t] *adj* : intelligent

intelligentsia [ɛ̃teliʒɑ̃sja] *nf* : intelligentsia
intelligibilité [ɛ̃teliʒibilite] *nf* : intelligibility
intelligible [ɛ̃teliʒibl] *adj* : intelligible — **intelligiblement** [-ʒiblǝmɑ̃] *adv*
intempérant, -rante [ɛ̃tɑ̃perɑ̃, -rɑ̃t] *adj* : intemperate — **intempérance** [-perɑ̃s] *nf*
intempéries [ɛ̃tɑ̃peri] *nfpl* : bad weather
intempestif, -tive [ɛ̃tɑ̃pɛstif, -tiv] *adj* : untimely, inopportune
intemporel, -relle [ɛ̃tɑ̃pǝrɛl] *adj* : timeless
intenable [ɛ̃tǝnabl] *adj* **1** : unbearable **2** : untenable, indefensible
intendant, -dante [ɛ̃tɑ̃dɑ̃, -dɑ̃t] *n* **1** : steward **2** : quartermaster **3** : bursar
intense [ɛ̃tɑ̃s] *adj* : intense
intensément [ɛ̃tɑ̃semɑ̃] *adv* : intensely
intensif, -sive [ɛ̃tɑ̃sif, -siv] *adj* : intensive
intensification [ɛ̃tɑ̃sifikasjɔ̃] *nf* : intensification
intensifier [ɛ̃tɑ̃sifje] {96} *vt* : to intensify — **s'intensifier** *vr*
intensité [ɛ̃tɑ̃site] *nf* : intensity
intenter [ɛ̃tɑ̃te] *vt* : to initiate, to pursue (legal action) <intenter un procès contre : to sue>
intention [ɛ̃tɑ̃sjɔ̃] *nf* : intention, intent <avoir l'intention de : to intend to> <à l'intention de : aimed at, for> <sans intention : unintentionally>
intentionné, -née [ɛ̃tɑ̃sjǝne] *adj* **1 bien intentionné** : well-meaning **2 mal intentionné** : ill-disposed
intentionnel, -nelle [ɛ̃tɑ̃sjǝnɛl] *adj* : intentional, deliberate — **intentionnellement** [-nɛlmɑ̃] *adv*
interactif, -tive [ɛ̃teraktif, -tiv] *adj* : interactive
interaction [ɛ̃teraksjɔ̃] *nf* : interaction
intercalaire[1] [ɛ̃terkalɛr] *adj* **1 feuillet intercalaire** : insert **2 fiche intercalaire** : divider
intercalaire[2] *nm* : insert, inset, divider
intercaler [ɛ̃terkale] *vt* INSÉRER : to insert
intercéder [ɛ̃tersede] {87} *vi* : to intercede
intercepter [ɛ̃tersɛpte] *vt* : to intercept
interception [ɛ̃tersɛpsjɔ̃] *nf* : interception
intercession [ɛ̃tersesjɔ̃] *nf* : intercession
interchangeable [ɛ̃terʃɑ̃ʒabl] *adj* : interchangeable
interconfessionnel, -nelle [ɛ̃terkɔ̃fesjǝnɛl] *adj* : interdenominational
interconnexion [ɛ̃terkǝnɛksjɔ̃] *nf* : (electronic) networking
intercontinental, -tale [ɛ̃terkɔ̃tinɑ̃tal] *adj, mpl* **-taux** [-to] : intercontinental
interdépartemental, -tale [ɛ̃terdepartǝmɑ̃tal] *adj, mpl* **-taux** [-to] : interdepartmental
interdépendant, -dante [ɛ̃terdepɑ̃dɑ̃, -dɑ̃t] *adj* : interdependent — **interdépendance** [-dɑ̃s] *nf*
interdiction [ɛ̃terdiksjɔ̃] *nf* : ban, prohibition
interdire [ɛ̃terdir] {29} *vt* **1** : to ban, to prohibit **2** : to prevent, to block — **s'interdire** *vr* : to refrain from <je m'interdis d'y penser : I don't let myself think about it>
interdisciplinaire [ɛ̃terdisiplinɛr] *adj* : interdisciplinary
interdit, -dite [ɛ̃terdi, -dit] *adj* **1** : forbidden, prohibited **2** STUPÉFAIT : taken aback, dumbfounded
intéressant[1], **-sante** [ɛ̃teresɑ̃, -sɑ̃t] *adj* **1** : interesting **2** AVANTAGEUX : attractive, worthwhile
intéressant[2], **-sante** *n* **faire l'intéressant** : to call attention to oneself, to show off
intéressé[1], **-sée** *adj* **1** : interested, attentive **2** : concerned, involved **3** : self-interested, self-involved
intéressé[2], **-sée** [ɛ̃terese] *n* : person involved <les intéressés : the interested parties>
intéresser [ɛ̃terese] *vt* **1** : to interest **2** CONCERNER : to concern, to affect **3 être intéressé dans** : to have a (financial) stake in — **s'intéresser** *vr* ~ **à** : to take an interest in, to be interested in
intérêt [ɛ̃tere] *nm* **1** : interest <avoir de l'intérêt pour : to be interested in> <porter un intérêt à : to take an interest in> <elle a intérêt à refuser : she's well-advised to refuse> **2** : interest (in finance) <sans intérêt : interest-free> <intérêts composés : compound interest>
interface [ɛ̃terfas] *nf* : interface (in computer science)
interférence [ɛ̃terferɑ̃s] *nf* : interference
interférer [ɛ̃terfere] {87} *vi* : to interfere
intergalactique [ɛ̃tergalaktik] *adj* : intergalactic
intergouvernemental, -tale [ɛ̃tergu-vɛrnǝmɑ̃tal] *adj, mpl* **-taux** [-to] : intergovernmental
intérieur[1], **-rieure** [ɛ̃terjœr] *adj* **1** : interior, inner, inside **2** : internal, domestic
intérieur[2] *nm* **1** : inside <à l'intérieur : inside, indoors, within> <d'intérieur : indoor> **2** : interior (of a country, etc.)
intérieurement [ɛ̃terjœrmɑ̃] *adv* : inwardly, internally
intérim [ɛ̃terim] *nm* **1** : interim (period) **2** : temporary activity <faire des intérims : to work as a temp>

intérimaire[1] [ɛ̃terimɛr] *adj* : interim, temporary, acting
intérimaire[2] *nmf* : temporary employee, temp
interjection [ɛ̃terʒɛksjɔ̃] *nf* : interjection
interjeter [ɛ̃terʒəte] {8} *vt* **interjeter appel** : to file an appeal
interlocuteur, -trice [ɛ̃terlɔkytœr, -tris] *n* **1** : speaker <mon interlocuteur : the person I am speaking to> **2** : representative, negotiator
interlope [ɛ̃terlɔp] *adj* **1** LOUCHE : shady **2** ILLÉGAL : illegal
interloquer [ɛ̃terlɔke] *vt* DÉCONTENANCER : to disconcert, to take aback
interlude [ɛ̃terlyd] *nm* : (short) musical interlude
intermède [ɛ̃termɛd] *nm* : interlude
intermédiaire[1] [ɛ̃termedjɛr] *adj* : intermediate, intermediary
intermédiaire[2] *nmf* : intermediary, go-between, middleman
intermédiaire[3] *nm* : means, agency <sans intermédiaire : directly> <par l'intermédiaire de : by means of, through>
interminable [ɛ̃terminabl] *adj* : interminable — **interminablement** [-nabləmɑ̃] *adv*
intermittence [ɛ̃termitɑ̃s] *nf* **par ~** : intermittently, off and on
intermittent, -tente [ɛ̃termitɑ̃, -tɑ̃t] *adj* : intermittent, sporadic
international, -nale [ɛ̃ternasjɔnal] *adj, mpl* **-naux** [-no] : international — **internationalement** [-mɑ̃] *adv*
internaute [ɛ̃ternot] *nmf* : Internet user
interne[1] [ɛ̃tern] *adj* : internal, inner
interne[2] *nmf* **1** : boarder (at a school) **2** : intern
interné, -née [ɛ̃terne] *n* : internee
internement [ɛ̃ternəmɑ̃] *nm* **1** : (political) internment **2** : confinement (to a mental hospital, etc.)
interner [ɛ̃terne] *vt* **1** : to intern **2** : to confine (to an institution)
Internet [ɛ̃ternet] *nm* : Internet
internist [ɛ̃ternist] *nmf* : internist
interpellation [ɛ̃terpelasjɔ̃] *nf* **1** : shouting out **2** : questioning
interpeller [ɛ̃terpəle] *vt* **1** APOSTROPHER : to shout at, to call out to **2** INTERROGER : to question
interpersonnel, -nelle [ɛ̃terpɛrsɔnɛl] *adj* : interpersonal
interphone [ɛ̃terfɔn] *nm* : intercom
interplanétaire [ɛ̃terplaneter] *adj* : interplanetary
interpoler [ɛ̃terpɔle] *vt* : to interpolate
interposer [ɛ̃terpoze] *vt* : to interpose — **s'interposer** *vr* : to intervene, to interpose
interprétation [ɛ̃terpretasjɔ̃] *nf* : interpretation
interprète [ɛ̃terpret] *nmf* **1** : interpreter **2** : spokesperson **3** : performer
interpréter [ɛ̃terprete] {87} *vt* **1** : to interpret <mal interpreter : to misinterpret> **2** : to perform, to play (a role)
interprétif, -tive [ɛ̃terpretif, -tiv] *adj* : interpretive, interpretative
interracial, -ciale [ɛ̃terrasjal] *adj* : interracial
interrelation [ɛ̃terəlasjɔ̃] *nf* : interrelationship
interrogateur[1], **-trice** [ɛ̃terɔgatœr, -tris] *adj* : inquiring, questioning
interrogateur[2], **-trice** *n* : examiner, questioner
interrogatif[1], **-tive** [ɛ̃terɔgatif, -tiv] *adj* : interrogative
interrogatif[2] *nm* : interrogative (in grammar)
interrogation [ɛ̃terɔgasjɔ̃] *nf* **1** : questioning, interrogation **2** : test (in school) **3** : question <interrogation indirect : indirect question> **4** → **point**
interrogatoire [ɛ̃terɔgatwar] *nm* : interrogation, questioning, cross-examination
interroger [ɛ̃terɔʒe] {17} *vt* : to interrogate, to question — **s'interroger** *vr* **~ sur** : to wonder about
interrompre [ɛ̃terɔ̃pr] {77} *v* : to interrupt — **s'interrompre** *vr* : to break off, to come to a halt
interrupteur [ɛ̃teryptœr] *nm* : switch
interruption [ɛ̃terypsjɔ̃] *nf* **1** : interruption **2** : break <sans interruption : continuously>
intersection [ɛ̃terseksjɔ̃] *nf* : intersection (in geometry)
interstellaire [ɛ̃tersteler] *adj* : interstellar
interstice [ɛ̃terstis] *nm* : chink, crack
interuniversitaire [ɛ̃teryniversiter] *adj* : intercollegiate
interurbain[1], **-baine** [ɛ̃teryrbɛ̃, -bɛn] *adj* **1** : intercity **2** : long-distance
interurbain[2] *nm* **l'interurbain** : long-distance telephone service
intervalle [ɛ̃terval] *nm* **1** : space, gap **2** : interval, period of time <dans l'intervalle : in the meantime>
intervenir [ɛ̃tervənir] {92} *vi* **1** : to intervene **2** : to take place, to occur **3** OPÉRER : to operate (in medicine)
intervention [ɛ̃tervɑ̃sjɔ̃] *nf* **1** : intervention **2** DISCOURS : speech **3** OPÉRATION : (medical) operation
interversion [ɛ̃terverzjɔ̃] *nf* INVERSION : inversion
intervertir [ɛ̃tervertir] *vt* INVERSER : to invert, to reverse
interview [ɛ̃tervju] *nf* : interview
interviewer [ɛ̃tervjuve] *vt* : to interview
intervieweur, -vieweuse [ɛ̃tervjuvœr, -vjuvøz] *n* : interviewer
intestat [ɛ̃testa] *adj* : intestate
intestin [ɛ̃testɛ̃] *nm* **1** : intestine <gros intestin : large intestine> <intestin

grêle : small intestine> **2 intestins** *nmpl* : intestines, bowels
intestinal, -nale [ɛ̃tɛstinal] *adj, mpl* **-naux** [-no] : intestinal
intime[1] [ɛ̃tim] *adj* **1** : intimate, close **2** : private **3** : personal <hygiène intime : personal hygiene> **4** : innermost, profound <ma conviction intime : my deep conviction>
intime[2] *nmf* : close friend
intimement [ɛ̃timmɑ̃] *adv* : intimately
intimer [ɛ̃time] *vt* **1** : to tell, to instruct <intimer l'ordre : to order> **2** : to summon (to court)
intimidant, -dante [ɛ̃timidɑ̃, -dɑ̃t] *adj* : intimidating
intimider [ɛ̃timide] *vt* : to intimidate — **intimidation** [-midasjɔ̃] *nf*
intimité [ɛ̃timite] *nf* **1** : intimacy **2** : privacy <dans l'intimité : in private> **3** : depths *pl* <dans l'intimité de son âme : in the depths of one's soul>
intitulé [ɛ̃tityle] *nm* : title, heading
intituler [ɛ̃tityle] *vt* : to call, to title — **s'intituler** *vr* **1** : to be called, to be titled **2** : to call oneself
intolérable [ɛ̃tɔlerabl] *adj* : intolerable — **intolérablement** [-rabləmɑ̃] *adv*
intolérant, -rante [ɛ̃tɔlerɑ̃, -rɑ̃t] *adj* : intolerant — **intolérance** [-rɑ̃s] *nf*
intonation [ɛ̃tɔnasjɔ̃] *nf* : intonation
intouchable [ɛ̃tuʃabl] *adj & nmf* : untouchable
intoxication [ɛ̃tɔksikasjɔ̃] *nf* **1** EMPOISONNEMENT : poisoning <intoxication alimentaire : food poisoning> **2** : brainwashing
intoxiquer [ɛ̃tɔksike] *vt* **1** EMPOISONNER : to poison **2** : to brainwash
intraduisible [ɛ̃tradɥizibl] *adj* **1** : untranslatable **2** : inexpressible
intraitable [ɛ̃tretabl] *adj* : uncompromising, inflexible, intractable
intransigeance [ɛ̃trɑ̃ziʒɑs] *nf* : intransigence
intransigeant, -geante [ɛ̃trɑ̃ziʒɑ, -ʒɑ̃t] *adj* : intransigent, uncompromising
intransitif, -tive [ɛ̃trɑ̃zitif, -tiv] *adj* : intransitive
intraveineux, -neuse [ɛ̃travenø, -nøz] *adj* : intravenous
intrépide [ɛ̃trepid] *adj* : intrepid, fearless
intrépidité [ɛ̃trepidite] *nf* : fearlessness, boldness
intrigant[1], **-gante** [ɛ̃trigɑ̃, -gɑ̃t] *adj* : scheming, conniving
intrigant[2], **-gante** *n* : schemer
intrigue [ɛ̃trig] *nf* **1** : intrigue **2** : plot (of a story)
intriguer [ɛ̃trige] *vt* : to intrigue, to puzzle — *vi* : to plot, to scheme
intrinsèque [ɛ̃trɛ̃sɛk] *adj* : intrinsic — **intrinsèquement** [-sɛkmɑ̃] *adv*
introduction [ɛ̃trɔdyksjɔ̃] *nf* **1** : introduction <lettre d'introduction : letter of introduction> **2** : introduction, adoption (of customs, products, etc.) **3** INSERTION : insertion
introduire [ɛ̃trɔdɥir] {49} *vt* **1** : to introduce **2** : to show in, to usher into **3** INSÉRER : to insert **4** : to enter, to input (data in a computer) — **s'introduire** *vr* **1** : to be introduced **2** : to penetrate, to get in
introniser [ɛ̃trɔnize] *vt* **1** : to enthrone **2** : to establish, to set up
introspectif, -tive [ɛ̃trɔspɛktif, -tiv] *adj* : introspective — **introspectivement** [-tivmɑ̃] *adv*
introspection [ɛ̃trɔspɛksjɔ̃] *nf* : introspection
introuvable [ɛ̃truvabl] *adj* : unobtainable, nowhere to be found
introverti[1], **-tie** [ɛ̃trɔverti] *adj* : introverted
introverti[2], **-tie** *n* : introvert
intrus, -truse [ɛ̃try, -tryz] *n* : intruder
intrusion [ɛ̃tryzjɔ̃] *nf* : intrusion
intuitif, -tive [ɛ̃tɥitif, -tiv] *adj* : intuitive — **intuitivement** [-tivmɑ̃] *adv*
intuition [ɛ̃tɥisjɔ̃] *nf* : intuition <avoir l'intuition de : to have a feeling about>
inuit, inuite [inɥi, inɥit] *adj* : Inuit
Inuit, Inuite *n* : Inuit
inusable [inyzabl] *adj* : durable
inusité, -tée [inyzite] *adj* INHABITUEL : unusual, uncommon
inutile [inytil] *adj* **1** : useless **2** : pointless, unnecessary
inutilement [inytilmɑ̃] *adv* : needlessly, unnecessarily
inutilisable [inytilizabl] *adj* : unusable
inutilisé, -sée [inytilize] *adj* : unused
inutilité [inytilite] *nf* : uselessness
invaincu, -cue [ɛ̃vɛ̃ky] *adj* **1** : unbeaten, undefeated **2** : unconquered
invalide[1] [ɛ̃valid] *adj* **1** : disabled **2** : invalid
invalide[2] *nmf* : disabled person <les invalides : the disabled>
invalider [ɛ̃valide] *vt* : to invalidate
invalidité [ɛ̃validite] *nf* **1** : invalidity **2** : disability
invariable [ɛ̃varjabl] *adj* : invariable — **invariablement** [-bləmɑ̃] *adv*
invasif, -sive [ɛ̃vazif, -ziv] *adj* : invasive
invasion [ɛ̃vazjɔ̃] *nf* : invasion
invective [ɛ̃vɛktiv] *nf* : invective
invectiver [ɛ̃vɛktive] *vt* : to abuse verbally — *vi* ~ **contre** : to inveigh against
inventaire [ɛ̃vɑ̃tɛr] *nm* : inventory <faire l'inventaire de : to take an inventory of>
inventer [ɛ̃vɑ̃te] *vt* **1** : to invent **2** : to make up (excuses, etc.)
inventeur, -trice [ɛ̃vɑ̃tœr, -tris] *n* : inventor
inventif, -tive [ɛ̃vɑ̃tif, -tiv] *adj* : inventive
invention [ɛ̃vɑ̃sjɔ̃] *nf* **1** : invention **2** CRÉATIVITÉ : inventiveness **3** MENSONGE : fabrication, lie

inventivité [ɛ̃vɑ̃tivite] *nf* : inventiveness
inventorier [ɛ̃vɑ̃tɔrje] {96} *vt* : to inventory
inverse[1] [ɛ̃vɛrs] *adj* **1** : inverse <rapport inverse : inverse relationship> **2** : opposite, reverse <en sens inverse : in the opposite direction>
inverse[2] *nm* **1 l'inverse** : the reverse, the opposite **2 à l'inverse** : conversely
inversement [ɛ̃vɛrsəmɑ̃] *adv* **1** : conversely <et inversement : and vice versa> **2** : inversely (in mathematics)
inverser [ɛ̃vɛrse] *vt* : to reverse, to invert
inversion [ɛ̃vɛrsjɔ̃] *nf* : inversion, reversal
invertébré, -brée [ɛ̃vɛrtebre] *adj & nm* : invertebrate
investigateur, -trice [ɛ̃vɛstigatœr, -tris] *n* : investigator, inquirer
investigation [ɛ̃vɛstigasjɔ̃] *nf* : investigation, inquiry
investir [ɛ̃vɛstir] *vt* **1** : to invest **2** : to induct, to inaugurate — *vi* : to invest (in stocks, etc.) — **s'investir** *vr* ~ **dans** : to become involved in
investissement [ɛ̃vɛstismɑ̃] *nm* : investment
investisseur, -seuse [ɛ̃vɛstisœr, -søz] *n* : investor
investiture [ɛ̃vɛstityr] *nf* **1** : investiture, inauguration **2** : nomination
invétéré, -rée [ɛ̃vetere] *adj* : inveterate
invincibilité [ɛ̃vɛ̃sibilite] *nf* : invincibility
invincible [ɛ̃vɛ̃sibl] *adj* **1** : invincible, unbeatable **2** : insurmountable **3** : irresistible
inviolé, -lée [ɛ̃vjɔle] *adj* : inviolate
invisibilité [ɛ̃vizibilite] *nf* : invisibility
invisible [ɛ̃vizibl] *adj* **1** : invisible **2** : unseen <rester invisible : to stay out of sight>
invisiblement [ɛ̃vizibləmɑ̃] *adv* : invisibly
invitant, -tante [ɛ̃vitɑ̃, -tɑ̃t] *adj* : welcoming, hospitable
invitation [ɛ̃vitasjɔ̃] *nf* : invitation
invite [ɛ̃vit] *nf* : invitation, request
invité, -tée [ɛ̃vite] *n* : guest
inviter [ɛ̃vite] *vt* : to invite, to ask
invivable [ɛ̃vivabl] *adj* : unbearable
invocation [ɛ̃vɔkasjɔ̃] *nf* : invocation
involontaire [ɛ̃vɔlɔ̃tɛr] *adj* **1** : involuntary **2** : unintentional **3** : reluctant, unwilling
involontairement [ɛ̃vɔlɔ̃tɛrmɑ̃] *adv* : unintentionally, involuntarily
invoquer [ɛ̃vɔke] *vt* : to invoke
invraisemblable [ɛ̃vrɛsɑ̃blabl] *adj* **1** : improbable, unlikely **2** : incredible, fantastic, bizarre
invraisemblance [ɛ̃vrɛsɑ̃blɑ̃s] *nf* : improbability, unlikelihood
invulnérable [ɛ̃vylnerabl] *adj* : invulnerable
iode [jɔd] *nm* : iodine
iodé, -dée [jɔde] *adj* : iodized
iodler [jɔdle] *vi* : to yodel
iodure [jɔdyr] *nm* : iodide
ion [jɔ̃] *nm* : ion
ioniser [jɔnize] *vt* : to ionize
ionosphère [jɔnɔsfɛr] *nf* : ionosphere
iota [jɔta] *nm* : iota
ira [ira], *etc.* → **aller**
irakien, -kienne [irakjɛ̃, -kjɛn] *adj* : Iraqi
Irakien, -kienne *n* : Iraqi
iranien, -nienne [iranjɛ̃, -njɛn] *adj* : Iranian
Iranien, -nienne *n* : Iranian
iraquien, Iraquien [irakjɛ̃] → **irakien, Irakien**
irascible [irasibl] *adj* : irascible
iris [iris] *nm* **1** : iris (of the eye) **2** : iris (plant)
irisation [irizasjɔ̃] *nf* : iridescence
irisé, -sée [irize] *adj* : iridescent
irlandais[1], **-daise** [irlɑ̃dɛ, -dɛz] *adj* : Irish
irlandais[2] *nm* : Irish (language)
Irlandais, -daise *n* : Irishman *m*, Irishwoman *f*
ironie [irɔni] *nf* : irony
ironique [irɔnik] *adj* : ironic, ironical — **ironiquement** [-mɑ̃] *adv*
ironiser [irɔnize] *vi* : to speak ironically, to be ironic
irradiation [iradjasjɔ̃] *nf* **1** : radiation **2** : irradiation
irradier [iradje] {96} *vt* : to irradiate — *vi* : to radiate
irraisonné, -née [irɛzɔne] *adj* : unreasoning
irrationalité [irasjɔnalite] *nf* : irrationality
irrationnel, -nelle [irasjɔnɛl] *adj* : irrational — **irrationnellement** [-nɛlmɑ̃] *adv*
irréalisable [irealizabl] *adj* IMPRATICABLE : impracticable, unworkable
irréaliste [irealist] *adj* : unrealistic
irréalité [irealite] *nf* : unreality
irrecevable [irəsəvabl] *adj* : inadmissible
irréconciliable [irekɔ̃siljabl] *adj* : irreconcilable
irrécupérable [irekyperabl] **1** : irretrievable **2** : beyond repair **3** : irredeemable, beyond hope
irréductible [iredyktibl] *adj* **1** : irreducible **2** INDOMPTABLE : indomitable
irréel, -réelle [ireɛl] *adj* : unreal
irréfléchi, -chie [irefleʃi] *adj* : thoughtless, rash
irréfutable [irefytabl] *adj* : irrefutable — **irréfutablement** [-tablɑmɑ̃] *adv*
irrégularité [iregylarite] *nf* : irregularity
irrégulier, -lière [iregylje, -ljɛr] *adj* **1** : irregular, uneven **2** : erratic **3** : unauthorized, illegal
irrégulièrement [iregyljɛrmɑ̃] *adv* : irregularly

irréligieux, -gieuse [ireliʒjø, -ʒjøz] *adj* : irreligious
irrémédiable [iremedjabl] *adj* **1** : irreparable **2** : incurable — **irrémédiablement** [-djabləmɑ̃] *adv*
irremplaçable [irɑ̃plasabl] *adj* : irreplaceable
irréparable [ireparabl] *adj* : irreparable, beyond repair
irrépressible [irepresibl] *adj* : irrepressible
irréprochable [ireprɔʃabl] *adj* : irreproachable, beyond reproach
irrésistible [irezistibl] *adj* **1** : irresistible **2** : comical <elle est irrésistible : she's hilarious!>
irrésistiblement [irezistibləmɑ̃] *adv* : irresistibly
irrésolu, -lue [irezɔly] *adj* **1** : irresolute **2** : unresolved
irrespect [irespɛ] *nm* : disrespect
irrespectueux, -tueuse [irɛspɛktyø, -tyøz] *adj* : disrespectful
irrespirable [irɛspirabl] *adj* **1** : unbreathable **2** : stifling, oppressive
irresponsabilité [irɛspɔ̃sabilite] *nf* : irresponsibility
irresponsable [irɛspɔ̃sabl] *adj* : irresponsible
irrévérence [ireverɑ̃s] *nf* : irreverence
irrévérencieux, -cieuse [ireverɑ̃sjø, -sjøz] *adj* : irreverent
irréversible [ireversibl] *adj* : irreversible — **irréversibilité** [-sibilite] *nf*
irrévocabilité [irevɔkabilite] *nf* : irrevocability, finality
irrévocable [irevɔkabl] *adj* : irrevocable — **irrévocablement** [-kabləmɑ̃] *adv*
irrigation [irigasjɔ̃] *nf* : irrigation
irriguer [irige] *vt* : to irrigate
irritable [iritabl] *adj* : irritable — **irritabilité** [-tabilite] *nf*
irritant¹, -tante [ritɑ̃, -tɑ̃t] *adj* **1** : irritating, annoying **2** : irritant (in medicine)
irritant² *nm* : irritant (substance)
irritation [iritasjɔ̃] *nf* : irritation
irriter [irite] *vt* : to irritate — **s'irriter** *vr* : to get irritated
irruption [irypsjɔ̃] *nf* **1** : irruption **2** : inrush <faire irruption dans : to burst into>
islam [islam] *nm* : Islam
islamique [islamik] *adj* : Islamic
islandais¹, -daise [islɑ̃dɛ, -dɛz] *adj* : Icelandic
islandais² *nm* : Icelandic (language)
Islandais, -daise *n* : Icelander
isocèle [izɔsɛl] *adj* : isosceles
isolant¹, -lante [izɔlɑ̃, -lɑ̃t] *adj* : insulating
isolant² *nm* : insulating material, insulation
isolateur [izɔlatœr] *nm* : insulator
isolation [izɔlasjɔ̃] *nf* : insulation <isolation thermique : thermal insulation>
isolé, -lée [izɔle] *adj* **1** : isolated, separated **2** : remote, secluded
isolement [izɔlmɑ̃] *nm* **1** : isolation **2** ISOLATION : insulation
isolément [izɔlemɑ̃] *adv* : separately, individually
isoler [izɔle] *vt* **1** : to isolate **2** : to insulate — **s'isoler** *vr* : to isolate oneself, to withdraw
isoloir [izɔlwar] *nm* : voting booth
isométrique [izɔmetrik] *adj* : isometric
isotope [izɔtɔp] *nm* : isotope
israélien, -lienne [israeljɛ̃, -ljɛn] *adj* : Israeli
Israélien, -lienne *n* : Israeli
israélite [israelit] *adj* : Jewish
Israélite *nmf* **1** : Jew **2** : Israelite, Hebrew
issu, -sue [isy] *adj* **~ de 1** : descended from **2** : resulting from
issue *nf* **1** SORTIE : exit <rue sans issue : dead-end street> **2** SOLUTION : way out, solution **3** FIN : ending, outcome <à l'issue de : at the end of>
isthme [ism] *nm* : isthmus
italien¹, -lienne [italjɛ̃, -ljɛn] *adj* : Italian
italien² *nm* : Italian (language)
Italien, -lienne *n* : Italian
italique¹ [italik] *adj* : italic
italique² *nm* : italics *pl*
itinéraire [itinerɛr] *nm* : itinerary, route
itinérant¹, -rante [itinerɑ̃, -rɑ̃t] *adj* : itinerant, traveling
itinérant², -rante *n Can* : vagabond, tramp
ivoire [ivwar] *adj & nm* : ivory
ivoirien, -rienne [ivwarjɛ̃, -rjɛn] *adj* : of the Ivory Coast, Ivorian
Ivoirien, -rienne *n* : native or inhabitant of the Ivory Coast, Ivorian
ivre [ivr] *adj* **1** : drunk, intoxicated **2** **~ de** : drunk with <ivre de joie : delirious with joy>
ivresse [ivrɛs] *nf* : drunkenness, intoxication
ivrogne, ivrognesse [ivrɔɲ, -ɲɛs] *n* : drunkard

J

j [ʒi] *nm* : j, the 10th letter of the alphabet
jabot [ʒabo] *nm* **1** : crop (of a bird) **2** : jabot, ruffle
jacasser [ʒakase] *vi* BAVARDER : to chatter, to jabber
jachère [ʒaʃɛr] *nf* : fallow land <rester en jachère : to lie fallow>
jacinthe [ʒasɛ̃t] *nf* **1** : hyacinth **2 jacinthe des bois** : bluebell
jack [dʒak] *nm* : jack, (telephone) socket
jackpot *or* **jack pot** [dʒakpɔt] *nm* : jackpot
jade [ʒad] *nm* : jade
jadis[1] [ʒadis] *adv* AUTREFOIS : in times past, formerly
jadis[2] *adj* : former, olden <au temps jadis : in days of old>
jaguar [ʒaɡwar] *nm* : jaguar
jaillir [ʒajir] *vi* **1** : to spurt out, to gush (out) **2** : to spring up, to shoot out, to burst out **3** : to arise, to emerge
jaillissement [ʒajismɑ̃] *nm* JET : spurt, gush
jais [ʒɛ] *nms & pl* **1** : jet (stone) **2 de jais** *or* **d'un noir de jais** : jet-black
jalon [ʒalɔ̃] *nm* **1** : marker, milestone **2 poser les (premiers) jalons** : to pave the way
jalonner [ʒalɔne] *vt* **1** : to mark out (a route, etc.) **2** LONGER : to line, to border **3** MARQUER : to mark, to punctuate <une histoire jalonnée de tragédie : a story marked by tragedy>
jalouser [ʒaluze] *vt* : to be jealous of
jalousie [ʒaluzi] *nf* **1** : jealousy **2** : slatted blind, venetian blind
jaloux, -louse [ʒalu, -luz] *adj* : jealous **— jalousement** [-luzmɑ̃] *adv*
jamaïquain, -quaine [ʒamaikɛ̃, -kɛn] *adj* : Jamaican
Jamaïquain, -quaine *n* : Jamaican
jamais [ʒamɛ] *adv* **1** : never <il ne pense jamais aux autres : he never thinks of others> **2** : ever <c'est pire que jamais : it's worse than ever> **3 à (tout) jamais** *or* **pour ~** : forever
jambage [ʒɑ̃baʒ] *nm* **1** : downstroke (of a letter) **2** : jamb
jambe [ʒɑ̃b] *nf* **1** : leg **2 à toutes jambes** : as fast as one's legs can carry one **3 dans les jambes** *fam* : in the way, underfoot
jambon [ʒɑ̃bɔ̃] *nm* : ham
jamboree [ʒɑ̃bori] *nm* : jamboree
jante [ʒɑ̃t] *nf* : rim (of a wheel)
janvier [ʒɑ̃vje] *nm* : January
japonais[1], **-naise** [ʒapɔne, -nɛz] *adj* : Japanese
japonais[2] *nm* : Japanese (language)
Japonais, -naise *n* : Japanese
jappement [ʒapmɑ̃] *nm* : yap, yelp
japper [ʒape] *vi* : to yap, to yelp
jaquette [ʒakɛt] *nf* **1** : dust jacket **2** : morning coat (for men), jacket (for women)
jardin [ʒardɛ̃] *nm* **1** : garden **2** : yard **3 jardin d'enfants** *France* : kindergarten **4 jardin zoologique** : zoo
jardinage [ʒardinaʒ] *nm* : gardening
jardiner [ʒardine] *vi* : to garden
jardinier[1], **-nière** [ʒardinje, -njɛr] *adj* : garden <plantes jardinières : garden plants>
jardinier[2], **-nière** *n* : gardener
jardinière *nf* **1** : window box **2** : mixed vegetables
jargon [ʒargɔ̃] *nm* **1** : jargon **2** : gibberish
jarre [ʒar] *nf* : (earthenware) jar
jarret [ʒare] *nm* **1** : back of the knee, hamstring **2** : hock (of an animal) **3** : shank (in cooking)
jarretelle [ʒartɛl] *nf* : garter belt
jarretière [ʒartjɛr] *nf* : garter
jars [ʒar] *nms & pl* : gander (animal)
jaser [ʒaze] *vi* **1** BAVARDER : to chatter **2** MÉDIRE : to gossip
jasette [ʒazɛt] *or* **jase** [ʒaz] *nf* **avoir de la jasette** *Can fam* : to talk a mile a minute
jasmin [ʒasmɛ̃] *nm* : jasmine
jaspe [ʒasp] *nm* : jasper
jaspé, -pée [ʒaspe] *adj* : mottled, marbled
jatte [ʒat] *nf* : bowl, basin
jauge [ʒoʒ] *nf* **1** : capacity **2** : gauge <jauge d'essence : gas gauge> <jauge de niveau d'huile : dipstick>
jauger [ʒoʒe] {17} *vt* **1** : to gauge, to measure the capacity of **2** : to take the measure of, to size up
jaunâtre [ʒonatr] *adj* **1** : yellowish **2 teint jaunâtre** : sallow complexion
jaune[1] [ʒon] *adv* **rire jaune** : to force a laugh
jaune[2] *adj* : yellow
jaune[3] *nm* **1** : yellow **2** *or* **jaune d'œuf** : egg yolk
jaune[4] *nmf* : strikebreaker
jaunir [ʒonir] *v* : to turn yellow
jaunisse [ʒonis] *nf* : jaundice
javanais[1], **-naise** [ʒavanɛ, -nɛz] *adj* : Javanese
javanais[2], **-naise** *n* : Javanese (language)
Javanais, -naise *n* : Javanese
Javel [ʒavɛl] *nf* **eau de Javel** : bleach
javelliser [ʒavelize] *vt* : to chlorinate **— javellisation** [ʒavelizasjɔ̃] *nf*
javelot [ʒavlo] *nm* : javelin
jazz [dʒaz] *nm* : jazz
je [ʒə] (**j'** *before vowel or mute h*) *pron* : I
jean [dʒin] *nm* **1** : denim **2 jeans** *nmpl* : jeans, blue jeans
jeep [dʒip] *nf* : jeep
Jéhovah [ʒeɔva] *nm* : Jehovah

je–ne–sais–quoi [ʒənsekwa] *nms & pl* **un je–ne–sais–quoi** : a certain something
jérémiades [ʒeremjad] *nfpl fam* : whining, complaining
jersey [ʒɛrzɛ] *nm* : jersey (fabric)
je–sais–tout [ʒəsetu] *nmfs & pl* : know-it-all
Jésus [ʒezy] *nm* : Jesus
jet [ʒɛ] *nm* **1** : jet, spurt, flash (of light) <jet d'eau : fountain> **2** : throw, throwing <à un jet de pierre : a stone's throw away> **3** : jet (airplane) **4** : shoot (of a plant) **5 d'un seul jet** : in one try, at one go
jetable [ʒətabl] *adj* : disposable <rasoirs jetables : disposable razors>
jetée [ʒəte] *nm* **1** : pier, jetty **2** : breakwater
jeter [ʒəte] {8} *vt* **1** : to throw **2** : to throw away **3** ÉMETTRE : to cast, to give off, to let out <jeter un coup d'œil : to take a look> **4 jeter l'éponge** : to throw in the towel **5 jeter un sort** : to cast a spell **— se jeter** *vr* **1** : to throw oneself <se jeter sur : to pounce on> **2** : to be disposable **3** : to be discarded, to be disposed of **4 ~ dans** : to flow into
jeton [ʒətɔ̃] *nm* : token, counter
jette [ʒɛt], **jettera** [ʒɛra], *etc.* → **jeter**
jeu [ʒø] *nm, pl* **jeux 1** : play, playing <jeu d'enfant : child's play> <le jeu : gambling> <jeux de mains : horseplay> **2** : game <jeu d'equipe : team sport> **3** : hand (of playing cards) **4** : set <jeu d'échecs : chess set> <jeu de cartes : deck of cards> **5 en ~** : at stake **6 jeu de jambes** : footwork (in sports) **7 jeu de mots** : pun **8 jeu de société** : board game
jeudi [ʒødi] *nm* : Thursday
jeun [ʒœ̃] *adv* **à ~** : on an empty stomach
jeune[1] [ʒœn] *adv* : youthfully <s'habiller jeune : to dress young>
jeune[2] *adj* **1** : young, youthful <jeune homme : young man> <jeunes gens : young people> <jeune fille : girl> **2** CADET : younger <ma jeune sœur : my younger sister> **3** : new, recent <jeunes mariés : newlyweds>
jeune[3] *nmf* : young person <les jeunes : young people>
jeûne [ʒøn] *nm* : fast <rompre le jeûne : to break one's fast>
jeûner [ʒøne] *vi* : to fast
jeunesse [ʒœnɛs] *nf* **1** : youth **2** : youthfulness **3** : young people
joaillerie [ʒɔajri] *nf* **1** : jewelry making, jewel trade **2** : jeweler's shop **3** : jewelry
joaillier, -lière [ʒɔaje, -jɛr] *n* BIJOUTIER : jeweler
job [dʒɔb] *nm fam* : job
jockey [ʒɔkɛ] *nm* : jockey
jodhpurs [ʒɔdpyr] *nmpl* : jodhpurs
jodler [jɔdle] → **iodler**
joggeur, -guese [dʒɔgœr, -gøz] *n* : jogger
jogging [dʒɔgiŋ] *nm* **1** : jogging **2** : sweatsuit
joie [ʒwa] *nf* **1** : joy <joie de vivre : joie de vivre, enjoyment of life> **2** PLAISIR : pleasure, delight <avec joie : with pleasure>
joignait [ʒwɛ̃ɲɛ], **joignions** [ʒwɛ̃ɲɔ̃], *etc.* → **joindre**
joigne [ʒwɛ̃ɲ], *etc.* → **joindre**
joindre [ʒwɛ̃dr] {50} *vt* **1** : to join, to link, to combine **2** : to enclose, to attach **3** : to reach, to get in touch with <joindre qqn par téléphone : to reach s.o. by phone> **— se joindre** *vr* **1** : to join together (of hands, etc.) **2 ~ à** : to join in with, to become a part of
joint[1], **jointe** [ʒwɛ̃, ʒwɛ̃t] *adj* **1** : joined <à mains jointes : with clasped hands> **2 ~ à** : attached to, enclosed with
joint[2] *nm* **1** : joint <joint universel : universal joint> **2** : seal, gasket <joint de robinet : washer (for a faucet)>
jointure [ʒwɛ̃tyr] *nf* : joint (in anatomy or technology)
joker [ʒɔkɛr] *nm* : joker (in playing cards)
joli, -lie [ʒɔli] *adj* **1** : pretty, attractive **2** : nice <une jolie somme d'argent : a nice sum of money>
joliment [ʒɔlimɑ̃] *adv* **1** : nicely, prettily **2** *fam* : really, awfully
jonc [ʒɔ̃] *nm* **1** : rush, bullrush **2** : plain band, ring <jonc de mariage : wedding band>
joncher [ʒɔ̃ʃe] *vt* : to strew, to litter
jonction [ʒɔ̃ksjɔ̃] *nf* : junction
jongler [ʒɔ̃gle] *vi* : to juggle
jongleur, -gleuse [ʒɔ̃glœr, -gløz] *n* : juggler
jonque [ʒɔ̃k] *nf* : junk (boat)
jonquille [ʒɔ̃kij] *nf* : daffodil, jonquil
jordanien, -nienne [ʒɔrdanjɛ̃, -njɛn] *adj* : Jordanian
Jordanien, -nienne *n* : Jordanian
jouable [ʒwabl] *adj* : playable
joue [ʒu] *nf* **1** : cheek **2 mettre en joue** : to take aim at
jouer [ʒwe] *vi* **1** S'AMUSER : to play <jouer avec des poupées : to play with dolls> <jouer aux cartes : to play cards> <jouer du piano : to play the piano> **2** : to play, to perform <elle a joué dans les plus grands théâtres : she played the leading theaters> **3** : to gamble, to speculate <il jouait aux courses : he was playing the horses> <jouer à la Bourse : to play the stock market> **4** : to come into play, to apply <la question d'argent ne joue pas entre nous : money is not an issue between us> **5 jouer sur les mots** : to play with words **— *vt* 1** : to play (a card, etc.) **2** : to bet, to wager **3** : to perform <il jouera une sonate de

Mozart : he will play a Mozart sonata> <jouer la comédie : to put on an act> **4** : to feign, to affect <jouer les victimes : to play the victim> — **se jouer** *vr* **1** : to be played **2** : to be at stake **3 ~ de** : to make light work of **4 ~ de** : to defy

jouet [ʒwɛ] *nm* : toy, plaything

joueur, joueuse [ʒwœr, ʒwøz] *n* **1** : player <un beau joueur : a good sport> **2** : gambler

jouffl u, -flue [ʒufly] *adj* : chubby-cheeked

joug [ʒu] *nm* : yoke

jouir [ʒwir] *vi* **1** : to have an orgasm **2 ~ de** : to enjoy, to make good use of, to benefit from

jouissance [ʒwisɑ̃s] *nf* **1** PLAISIR : pleasure, enjoyment **2** : orgasm, climax **3** : use, (legal) possession

jour [ʒur] *nm* **1** : day <tous les jours : every day> <huit jours : a week> <de nos jours : nowadays> <de jour en jour : day by day> <jour de l'An : New Year's Day> <jour férié : public holiday> **2** : daylight, daytime <il fait jour : it's (day)light> **3** : aspect <sous un jour favorable : in a favorable light> **4 donner le jour à** : to bring into the world, to give birth to **5 mettre à jour** : to bring up to date, to update

journal [ʒurnal] *nm, pl* **journaux 1** : diary, journal **2** : newspaper **3 journal télévisé** : television news

journalier[1], **-lière** [ʒurnalje, -ljɛr] *adj* : daily

journalier[2], **-lière** *n* : day worker, laborer

journalisme [ʒurnalism] *nm* : journalism

journaliste [ʒurnalist] *nmf* : journalist — **journalistique** [-listik] *adj*

journée [ʒurne] *nf* **1** : day <toute la journée : all day long> **2** : workday <journée de repos : day off>

joute [ʒut] *nf* **1** : joust **2** : sparring match, battle (of wits, etc.)

jouter [ʒute] *vi* : to joust

jovial, -viale [ʒɔvjal] *adj, mpl* **jovials** *or* **joviaux** [-vjo] : jovial, jolly — **jovialement** [-vjalmɑ̃] *adv*

jovialité [ʒɔvjalite] *nf* : cheerfulness, joviality

joyau [ʒwajo] *nm, pl* **joyaux** : jewel, gem

joyeux, joyeuse [ʒwajø, -jøz] *adj* : joyful, happy <Joyeux Noël! : Merry Christmas!> — **joyeusement** [-jøzmɑ̃] *adv*

jubilation [ʒybilasjɔ̃] *nf* : jubilation

jubilé [ʒybile] *nm* : jubilee

jubiler [ʒybile] *vi* : to rejoice, to exult

jucher [ʒyʃe] *vt* : to perch <elle a juché le bébé sur sa chaise : she perched the baby on his chair> — **se jucher** *vr* **~ sur** : to perch on

judaïque [ʒydaik] *adj* : Judaic

judaïsme [ʒydaism] *nm* : Judaism

judiciaire [ʒydisjɛr] *adj* : judicial — **judiciairement** [-sjɛrmɑ̃] *adv*

judicieux, -cieuse [ʒydisjø, -sjøz] *adj* : judicious — **judicieusement** [-sjøzmɑ̃] *adv*

judo [ʒydo] *nm* : judo

juge [ʒyʒ] *nm* **1** : judge <juge de paix : justice of the peace> <tu es seul juge : only you can judge> **2** *or* **juge-arbitre** : referee <juge de touche : linesman>

jugement [ʒyʒmɑ̃] *nm* **1** : decision, verdict, sentence **2** : judgment, opinion

jugeote [ʒyʒɔt] *nf fam* : common sense

juger [ʒyʒe] {17} *vt* **1** ÉVALUER : to judge, to form an opinion about **2** : to judge, to try **3** : to think, to consider **4 ~ de** : to assess, to judge <c'est vrai, autant que je puisse en juger : it's true, as far as I can tell> — **se juger** *vr* S'ESTIMER : to consider oneself

jugulaire [ʒygylɛr] *nf* : jugular vein

juguler [ʒygyle] *vt* **1** ENRAYER : to halt, to check, to curb **2** : to suppress, to put down

juif, juive [ʒɥif, ʒɥiv] *adj* : Jewish

Juif, Juive *n* : Jew

juillet [ʒɥijɛ] *nm* : July

juin [ʒɥɛ̃] *nm* : June

juke-box [dʒukbɔks] *nm, pl* **juke-box** *or* **juke-boxes** : jukebox

jumeau, -melle [ʒymo, -mɛl] *adj & n, mpl* **jumeaux** : twin

jumeler [ʒymle] {8} *vt* : to twin, to couple

jumelles [ʒymɛl] *nfpl* : binoculars, field glasses

jument [ʒymɑ̃] *nf* : mare

jungle [ʒœgl] *nf* : jungle

junior [ʒynjɔr] *adj & nmf* : junior

junte [ʒœt] *nf* : junta

jupe [ʒyp] *nf* : skirt

Jupiter [ʒypiter] *nf* : Jupiter (planet)

jupon [ʒypɔ̃] *nm* : slip, petticoat

juré, -rée [ʒyre] *n* : juror

jurer [ʒyre] *vt* : to swear, to vow — *vi* **1** SACRER : to swear, to curse **2 ~ avec** : to clash with **3 ~ de** : to swear to <j'en jurerais : I would swear to it, I'm sure of it>

juridiction [ʒyridiksjɔ̃] *nf* : jurisdiction — **juridictionel, -nelle** [-diksjɔnɛl] *adj*

juridique [ʒyridik] *adj* LÉGAL : legal — **juridiquement** [-dikmɑ̃] *adv*

jurisprudence [ʒyrisprydɑ̃s] *nf* **1** : jurisprudence **2 faire jurisprudence** : to set a precedent

juriste [ʒyrist] *nmf* : jurist, legal expert

juron [ʒyrɔ̃] *nm* : curse, oath, expletive

jury [ʒyri] *nm* : jury

jus [ʒy] *nms & pl* **1** : juice **2** : gravy **3** *fam* : juice, electricity

jusqu'au-boutiste [ʒyskobutist] *nmf fam, pl* **jusqu'au-boutistes** : hard-liner, extremist

jusque [ʒyskə] (**jusqu'** [ʒysk] *before a vowel*) *prep* **1** *or* **jusqu'à** : up to, as far as <jusque chez moi : all the way to my house> <avoir de la boue jusqu'aux genoux : to be knee-deep in mud> <jusqu'à présent : up to now> **2** : even, as far as <des délits jusque dans les banlieues : crime even in the suburbs> **3 jusqu'à** : until, till <jusqu'à dix-sept heures : until five o'clock> **4 jusqu'à** : up to, as much as <jusqu'à 50 kilogrammes : not exceeding 50 kilograms> **5 jusqu'à** : up to, to the point of <méticuleux jusqu'au perfectionnisme : careful to the point of perfectionism> **6 jusqu'à ce que** *or* **jusqu'au moment où** : until

jusque–là [ʒyskəla] *adv* **1** : up to here, up to there **2** : up until then

justaucorps [ʒystokɔr] *nms & pl* : leotard

juste[1] [ʒyst] *adv* **1** : just, exactly <c'est juste le contraire : it's just the opposite> **2** : in tune, on key <chanter juste : to sing in tune> **3** : only, just <après juste un an : after only a year> **4** *or* **tout juste** : only just <arriver tout juste à temps : to arrive barely on time>

juste[2] *adj* **1** ÉQUITABLE : just, fair **2** EXACT : correct, accurate <l'heure juste : the exact time> **3** SERRÉ : tight **4 à juste titre** : justly, rightly **5 au juste** : exactly, precisely

justement [ʒystəmɑ̃] *adv* **1** EXACTEMENT : exactly, precisely **2** : correctly **3** : justifiably, justly **4** : just <il est justement parti : he just left>

justesse [ʒystɛs] *nf* **1** : accuracy **2** : aptness, soundness <avec justesse : aptly> **3 de ~** : just barely

justice [ʒystis] *nf* **1** : fairness, justice **2** : law, justice <être traduit en justice : to be brought before the courts> **3 se faire justice** : to take the law into one's own hands **4 se faire justice** : to commit suicide

justiciable [ʒystisjabl] *adj* **~ de** : subject to, answerable to

justifiable [ʒystifjabl] *adj* DÉFENDABLE : justifiable

justificatif[1], **-tive** [ʒystifikatif, -tiv] *adj* : supporting

justificatif[2] *nm* : supporting evidence

justification [ʒustifikasjɔ̃] *nf* **1** : justification, explanation **2** : proof

justifier [ʒystifje] {96} *vt* **1** : to justify **2** : to prove **— *vi* ~ de** : to give proof of **— se justifier** *vr* : to justify oneself <se justifier d'une accusation : to clear one's name>

jute [ʒyt] *nm* : jute

juteux, -teuse [ʒytø, -tøz] *adj* : juicy

juvénile [ʒyvenil] *adj* : juvenile, youthful

juxtaposer [ʒykstapoze] *vt* : to juxtapose **— juxtaposition** [-pozisjɔ̃] *nf*

K

k [ka] *nm* : the 11th letter of the alphabet

kaki[1] [kaki] *adj* : khaki

kaki[2] *nm* **1** : khaki **2** : persimmon

kaléidoscope [kaleidɔskɔp] *nm* : kaleidoscope

kangourou [kɑ̃guru] *nm* : kangaroo

kaolin [kaɔlɛ̃] *nm* : kaolin

karaté [karate] *nm* : karate

kascher [kaʃɛr] *adj* : kosher

kayak *or* **kayac** [kajak] *nm* : kayak

kenyan, kenyane [kenjɑ̃, -jan] *adj* : Kenyan

Kenyan, Kenyane *n* : Kenyan

kermesse [kɛrmɛs] *nf* : fair, bazaar

kérosène [kerɔzɛn] *nm* : kerosene

ketchup [kɛtʃœp] *nm* : ketchup

khan [kɑ̃] *nm* : khan

kibboutz [kibuts] *nm* : kibbutz

kidnapper [kidnape] *vt* : to kidnap

kidnappeur, -peuse [kidnapœr, -pøz] *n* : kidnapper

kif–kif [kifkif] *adj fam* **c'est kif–kif** : it's all the same

kilo [kilo] *nm* : kilo

kilogramme [kilɔgram] *nm* : kilogram

kilohertz [kilɔɛrts] *nms & pl* : kilohertz

kilométrage [kilɔmetraʒ] *nm* : distance in kilometers, mileage

kilomètre [kilɔmɛtr] *nm* : kilometer

kilo–octet [kilɔɔktɛ] *nm, pl* **kilo–octets** : kilobyte

kilowatt [kilɔwat] *nm* : kilowatt

kilt [kilt] *nm* : kilt

kimono [kimɔno] *nm* : kimono

kinésithérapeute [kinesiterapœt] *nmf* : physiotherapist, physical therapist

kinésithérapie [kineziterapi] *nf* : physical therapy

kiosque [kjɔsk] *nm* **1** : (garden) pavilion **2** : kiosk, stall <kiosque à journaux : newsstand> **3 kiosque à musique** : bandstand

kipper [kipœr] *nm* : kipper

kirsch [kirʃ] *nm* : kirsch

kiwi [kiwi] *nm* : kiwi

klaxon [klaksɔn] *nm* : horn

klaxonner [klaksɔne] *vt* : to honk, to toot **— *vi*** : to honk one's horn

kleptomane [kleptɔman] *nmf* : kleptomaniac

kleptomanie [kleptɔmani] *nf* : kleptomania

knickers [knikərs] *nmpl* : knickers

koala [kɔala] *nm* : koala
koweïtien, -tienne *adj* [kɔwɛjtjɛ̃, -tjɛn] : Kuwaiti
Koweïtien, -tienne *n* : Kuwaiti
krach [krak] *nm* : crash <krach boursier : stock-market crash>
kraft [kraft] *nm or* **papier kraft** : brown (wrapping) paper
krypton [kriptɔ̃] *nm* : krypton
kumquat [kumkwat] *nm* : kumquat
kung-fu [kuŋfu] *nm* : kung fu
kurde[1] [kyrd] *adj* : Kurdish
kurde[2] *nm* : Kurdish (language)
Kurde *nmf* : Kurd
kyrielle [kirjɛl] *nf* : whole series, long list <une kyrielle de plaintes : a string of complaints>
kyste [kist] *nm* : cyst

L

l [ɛl] *nm* : l, the 12th letter of the alphabet
l' *pron & art* → **le**
la *pron & art* → **le**
là [la] *adv* **1** (*indicating a place*) : there, here <c'est là : there it is> <je suis là : I'm here> **2** : then <à partir de là : after that, from then on> **3** (*indicating a situation or a certain point*) <c'est bien là où je voulais en venir : that's just it, that's the point> <c'est là que j'ai compris : that's when I understood> **4** (*referring to a specified person or thing*) <cette femme-là : that woman (over there)> **5 de ~** : from there, hence **6 ~ où** : where **7 par ~** : over here, this way **8 tout est là** : that's most important <la santé, tout est là : health is everything>
là-bas [laba] *adv* : over there
label [labɛl] *nm* **1** : label, mark **2** : seal, stamp <label de qualité : stamp of quality>
labeur [labœr] *nm* : toil, work
labial, -biale [labjal] *adj, mpl* **labiaux** [labjo] : labial
laboratoire [labɔratwar] *nm* : laboratory
laborieusement [labɔrjøzmɑ̃] *adv* : laboriously
laborieux, -rieuse [labɔrjø, -rjøz] *adj* **1** PÉNIBLE : laborious, arduous **2** TRAVAILLEUR : hardworking, industrious <les classes laborieuses : the working classes> **3** : labored (in style)
labour [labur] *nm* **1** : plowing **2** : plowed field
labourage [laburaʒ] *nm* : plowing
labourer [labure] *vt* **1** : to plow **2** CREUSER : to furrow, to churn up **3** LACÉRER : to dig into, to lacerate
labyrinthe [labirɛ̃t] *nm* DÉDALE : labyrinth, maze
lac [lak] *nm* : lake
lacer [lase] {6} *vt* : to lace up, to tie
lacération [laserasjɔ̃] *nf* **1** : ripping, tearing up **2** : laceration
lacérer [lasere] {87} *vt* **1** DÉCHIRER : to tear up **2** : to lacerate
lacet [lasɛ] *nm* **1** : shoelace **2** : sharp bend, curve <une route en lacets : a winding road>
lâche[1] [laʃ] *adj* **1** : loose, slack **2** : lax, slipshod **3** : cowardly
lâche[2] *nmf* POLTRON : coward
lâchement [laʃmɑ̃] *adv* **1** : loosely **2** : in a cowardly way
lâcher [laʃe] *vt* **1** RELÂCHER : to slacken, to loosen **2** : to let go <lâche-moi! : let me go!> **3** : to let out, to come out with **4** *fam* : to drop out of (school) **5** *fam* : to leave, to drop (someone) — *vi* **1** : to give way **2** : to fail (of brakes)
lâcheté [laʃte] *nf* **1** COUARDISE : cowardice **2** BASSESSE : baseness **3** : cowardly act
lâcheur, -cheuse [laʃœr, -ʃøz] *n fam* : quitter, unreliable person
lacis [lasi] *nms & pl* **1** : maze, tangle **2** : network (of veins, etc.)
laconique [lakɔnik] *adj* : laconic, terse — **laconiquement** [-nikmɑ̃] *adv*
lacrymogène [lakrimɔʒɛn] *adj* : tear-inducing <gaz lacrymogène : tear gas>
lactation [laktasjɔ̃] *nf* : lactation
lacté, -tée [lakte] *adj* **1** : milk, milky **2** → **voie**
lactique [laktik] *adj* : lactic
lacune [lakyn] *nf* : lacuna, gap
lacustre [lakystr] *adj* : lake, lakeside
là-dedans [laddɑ̃] *adv* : in here, in there
là-dessous [ladsu] *adv* : under here, under there
là-dessus [ladsy] *adv* **1** : on here, on there **2** : about it, on it <il n'y a aucun doute là-dessus : there's no doubt about it> **3** : with that, at that point <il est parti là-dessus : with that, he left>
ladite [ladit] → **ledit**
ladre [ladr] *adj* : stingy, miserly
ladrerie [ladrəri] *nf* : miserliness, avarice
lagon [lagɔ̃] *nm* : (coral reef) lagoon
lagune [lagyn] *nf* : lagoon
là-haut [lao] *adv* **1** : up there **2** : upstairs
lai [lɛ] *nm* : lay, ballad
laïc [laik] *nm* **les laïcs** : the laity
laîche [lɛʃ] *nf* : sedge
laid, laide [lɛ, lɛd] *adj* **1** : ugly **2** : mean, rude

laideron [lɛdrɔ̃] *nm* : ugly girl
laideur [lɛdœr] *nf* **1** : ugliness **2** : meanness
lainage [lɛnaʒ] *nm* **1** : woolen fabric **2** : woolen garment
laine [lɛn] *nf* **1** : wool <laine peignée : worsted wool> **2 laine d'acier** *Can* : scouring pad, steel wool
laineux, -neuse [lɛnø, -nøz] *adj* : woolly
laïque[1] [laik] *adj* : lay, secular
laïque[2] *nmf* : layman, laywoman
laisse [lɛs] *nf* : lead, leash
laissé–pour–compte, laissée–pour–compte [lɛsepurkɔ̃t] *adj, pl* **laissés–pour–compte, laissées–pour–compte 1** : returned unsold **2** : rejected (of a person)
laisser [lɛse] *vt* **1** : to leave <laisser un pourboire : to leave a tip> <laissez la porte ouverte : leave the door open> **2** OUBLIER : to leave, to forget <j'ai laissé mes gants au bureau : I left my gloves at the office> **3** QUITTER : to leave, to abandon <elle a laissé son mari : she left her husband> **4** ACCORDER : to give <laisse-lui du temps : give him some time> — *v aux* **1** : to let, to allow <ne laissez rien voir : let nothing show> **2 laisse faire!** : never mind!, let it go! — **se laisser** *vr* **1** : to let oneself <il ne se laisse pas faire : he won't be pushed around> **2 se laisser aller** : to let oneself go
laisser–aller [lɛseale] *nms & pl* : carelessness, sloppiness
laisser–faire [lɛsefɛr] *nms & pl* : laissez-faire, noninterference
laissez–passer [lɛsepase] *nms & pl* : pass, permit
lait [lɛ] *nm* **1** : milk <lait concentré *or* lait condensé : condensed milk> <lait entier : whole milk> <lait écrémé : skim milk> <lait demi-écrémé : low-fat milk> **2 lait de poule** : eggnog
laiterie [lɛtri] *nf* **1** : dairy industry **2** : dairy
laiteux, -teuse [lɛtø, -tøz] *adj* : milky <peau laiteuse : milky skin>
laitier[1], **-tière** [lɛtje, -tjɛr] *adj* : dairy
laitier[2], **-tière** *n* **1** : milkman **2** : dairyman, dairymaid *f*
laiton [lɛtɔ̃] *nm* : brass
laitue [lɛty] *nf* : lettuce
laïus [lajys] *nms & pl fam* : spiel, speech
lama [lama] *nm* **1** : lama <le Grand Lama : the Dalai Lama> **2** : llama
lambeau [lɑ̃bo] *nm, pl* **lambeaux 1** GUENILLE : rag, scrap, shred <tomber en lambeaux : to fall to pieces> **2** : bit, fragment
lambiner [lɑ̃bine] *vi fam* : to dawdle
lambineux, -neuse [lɑ̃binœr, -nøz] *n Can fam* : slowpoke
lambrequin [lɑ̃brəkɛ̃] *nm* : valance (of a bed)
lambris [lɑ̃bri] *nms & pl* : paneling, wainscoting
lambrisser [lɑ̃brise] *vt* : to panel
lame [lam] *nf* **1** : strip, slat, lath **2** : blade <lame de rasoir : razor blade> **3** : sword **4** : wave <lame de fond : groundswell>
lamé [lame] *nm* : lamé
lamelle [lamɛl] *nf* **1** : small strip, sliver **2** : gill (of a mushroom) **3** : flake (of rock, etc.) **4** : slide (for a microscope)
lamentable [lamɑ̃tabl] *adj* **1** DÉPLORABLE : deplorable, lamentable **2** PITOYABLE : pitiful, pathetic — **lamentablement** [-tabləmɑ̃] *adv*
lamentation [lamɑ̃tasjɔ̃] *nf* **1** : lamentation, wailing **2** : whining, complaining
lamenter [lamɑ̃te] *v* **se lamenter** *vr* : to lament, to moan
laminer [lamine] *vt* **1** : to laminate **2** : to wipe out, to decimate
lampadaire [lɑ̃padɛr] *nm* **1** : floor lamp **2** : streetlight
lampe [lɑ̃p] *nf* **1** : lamp **2 lampe à souder** : blowtorch **3 lampe de poche** : flashlight
lampée [lɑ̃pe] *nf fam* : swig, gulp
lamper [lɑ̃pe] *vt* : to gulp down
lampion [lɑ̃pjɔ̃] *nm* : Chinese lantern
lamproie [lɑ̃prwa] *nf* : lamprey
lance [lɑ̃s] *nf* **1** : spear, lance **2** *or* **lance à eau** : hose <lance d'incendie : fire hose>
lancée [lɑ̃se] *nf* : momentum <continuer sur sa lancée : to keep on going, to forge ahead>
lance–flammes [lɑ̃sflam] *nms & pl* : flamethrower
lancement [lɑ̃smɑ̃] *nm* **1** : throwing **2** : launching, liftoff <base de lancement : launching site>
lance–missiles [lɑ̃smisil] *nms & pl* : missile launcher
lance–pierres [lɑ̃spjɛr] *nms & pl* : slingshot
lancer[1] [lɑ̃se] {6} *vt* **1** : to throw, to hurl **2** : to launch **3** : to issue, to put out <lancer un appel au calme : to issue an appeal for calm> **4** : to start up, to get going — **se lancer** *vr* **1** : to throw oneself, to jump **2** : to hurl at each other, to exchange (insults, etc.) **3 ~ dans** : to take up, to embark on
lancer[2] *nm* **1** : throw, toss <lancer de poids : shotput> **2** : casting, rod-and-reel fishing
lancette [lɑ̃set] *nf* : lancet
lanceur, -ceuse [lɑ̃sœr, -søz] *n* **1** : thrower, pitcher (in baseball) **2** : promoter
lancinant, -nante [lɑ̃sinɑ̃, -nɑ̃t] *adj* **1** : shooting, throbbing **2** : haunting **3** : insistent, nagging
lanciner [lɑ̃sine] *vi* : to throb — *vt* **1** OBSÉDER : to haunt, to obsess **2** TOURMENTER : to torment
landau [lɑ̃do] *nm France* : baby carriage
lande [lɑ̃d] *nf* : moor

langage [lɑ̃gaʒ] *nm* : language <le langage des signes : sign language> <langage machine : machine language>
langagier, -gière [lɑ̃gaʒje, -ʒjɛr] *adj* LINGUISTIQUE : linguistic
lange [lɑ̃ʒ] *nm* **1** : baby blanket **2 être dans les langes** : to be in (its) infancy
langoureux, -reuse [lɑ̃gurø, -røz] *adj* : languorous **— langoureusement** [-røzmɑ̃] *adv*
langouste [lɑ̃gust] *nf* : crayfish, spiny lobster
langoustine [lɑ̃gustin] *nf* : langoustine, prawn
langue [lɑ̃g] *nf* **1** : tongue <tirer la langue : to stick out one's tongue> <donner sa langue au chat : to give up (guessing)> **2** : language <langue maternelle : native language, mother tongue> <de langue française : French-speaking> <langue vivante : modern language>
languette [lɑ̃get] *nf* **1** : tongue (of a shoe) **2** : strip
langueur [lɑ̃gœr] *nf* : languor, languidness
languir [lɑ̃gir] *vi* **1** : to languish, to pine **2** : to flag, to wilt
languissant, -sante [lɑ̃gisɑ̃, -sɑ̃t] *adj* **1** : languid, listless **2** : dull, tiresome **3** : lovesick
lanière [lanjɛr] *nf* : strap, lash, thong
lanoline [lanɔlin] *nf* : lanolin
lanterne [lɑ̃tɛrn] *nf* **1** : lantern **2** : parking light **3 lanterne magique** : magic lantern
laotien, -tienne [laosjɛ̃, -sjɛn] *adj* : Laotian
Laotien, -tienne *n* : Laotian
laper [lape] *vt* : to lap up
lapidaire [lapidɛr] *adj* **1** : lapidary **2** : terse, pithy
lapider [lapide] *vt* : to stone
lapin, -pine [lapɛ̃, -pin] *n* **1** : rabbit **2 poser un lapin à qqn** : to stand s.o. up
lapon[1], **-pone** *or* **-ponne** [lapɔ̃, -pɔn] *adj* : Lappish
lapon[2] *nm* : Lapp, Lappish (language)
Lapon, -pone *or* **-ponne** *n* : Lapp
laps [laps] *nms & pl* : lapse (of time)
lapsus [lapsys] *nms & pl* : slip, error
laquais [lakɛ] *nms & pl* : lackey, footman
laque[1] [lak] *nm* : lacquer, lacquerware
laque[2] *nf* **1** VERNIS : lacquer, shellac **2** : hair spray
laquelle → lequel
laquer [lake] *vt* : to lacquer, to shellac
larbin [larbɛ̃] *nm fam* : flunkey, toady
larcin [larsɛ̃] *nm* **1** : petty theft **2** : booty, spoils *pl*
lard [lar] *nm* **1** : fat, lard **2** : bacon **3 faire du lard** *fam* : to put on weight
large[1] [larʒ] *adv* : on a large scale, generously <prévoir large : to allow a bit extra>
large[2] *adj* **1** : wide, broad **2** : considerable, extensive <dans une large mesure : to a large extent> **3** : loose-fitting **4** : generous **5 être large d'idées** : to be broad-minded
large[3] *nm* **1** LARGEUR : width, breadth <10 mètres de large : 10 meters wide> **2 le large** : the open sea
largement [larʒəmɑ̃] *adv* **1** : widely **2** : greatly, by far **3** : generously, lavishly **4** : easily, at least
largesse [larʒɛs] *nf* **1** GÉNÉROSITÉ : generosity **2 largesses** *nfpl* : gifts
largeur [larʒœr] *nf* **1** : width, breadth **2** OUVERTURE : openness <largeur d'esprit : broad-mindedness>
larguer [large] *vt* **1** : to release, to drop **2** *fam* PLAQUER : to ditch, to get rid of
larme [larm] *nf* **1** : tear <elle pleurait à chaudes larmes : she was crying her eyes out> **2** *fam* : small quantity, drop <une larme de vin : a drop of wine>
larmoyant, -moyante [larmwajɑ̃, -mwajɑ̃t] *adj* : tearful
larmoyer [larmwaje] {58} *vi* **1** : to water (of eyes) **2** : to whine, to whimper
larron [larɔ̃] *nm* : bandit, thief
larvaire [larvɛr] *adj* : larval
larve [larv] *nf* **1** : larva **2** *fam* : wimp, lazybones
larvé, -vée [larve] *adj* : latent
laryngite [larɛ̃ʒit] *nf* : laryngitis
larynx [larɛ̃ks] *nms & pl* : larynx
las, lasse [la, las] *adj* **1** FATIGUÉ : weary, tired **2 ~ de** : sick and tired of
lasagne [lazaɲ] *nf* : lasagna
lascif, -cive [lasif, -siv] *adj* : lascivious **— lascivement** [-sivmɑ̃] *adv*
lascivité [lasivite] *nf* : lasciviousness, lechery
laser [lazɛr] *nm* **1** : laser **2 disque laser** : laser disc, optical disc
lassant, -sante [lasɑ̃, -sɑ̃t] *adj* : wearisome, tiresome, tedious
lasser [lase] *vt* **1** : to weary, to tire out **2** ENNUYER : to bore, to try the patience of **— se lasser** *vr* **~ de** : to grow weary of
lassitude [lasityd] *nf* : weariness, lassitude
lasso [laso] *nm* : lasso, lariat
latence [latɔ̃s] *nf* : latency
latent, -tente [latɑ̃, -tɑ̃t] *adj* : latent
latéral, -rale [lateral] *adj, mpl* **-raux** [-ro] : side, lateral
latéralement [lateralmɑ̃] *adv* : laterally, sideways
latex [lateks] *nms & pl* : latex
latin[1], **-tine** [latɛ̃, -tin] *adj* : Latin
latin[2] *nm* : Latin (language)
latino–américain, -caine [latinoamerikɛ̃, -kɛn] *adj* : Latin-American
Latino–Américain, -caine *n* : Latin American
latitude [latityd] *nf* **1** : latitude **2** : scope, freedom <je lui laissais toute latitude : I gave him all the room he needed>
latrines [latrin] *nfpl* : latrine

latte [lat] *nf* **1** : lath **2** : floorboard
lauréat, -réate [lɔrea, -reat] *n* : prize-winner
laurier [lɔrje] *nm* **1** : laurel <feuille de laurier : bay leaf> **2 lauriers** *nmpl* : laurels <reposer sur ses lauriers : to rest on one's laurels>
laurier–rose [lɔrjeroz] *nm, pl* **lauriers–roses** : oleander
lavable [lavabl] *adj* : washable
lavabo [lavabo] *nm* **1** : washbowl, (bathroom) sink **2 lavabos** *nmpl France* : toilets, washroom
lavage [lavaʒ] *nm* **1** : washing **2** : wash <mets tes chaussettes au lavage : put your socks in the wash> **3 lavage de cerveau** : brainwashing
lavande [lavɑ̃d] *nf* : lavender
lave [lav] *nf* : lava
lave–auto [lavɔto] *nm Can, pl* **lave–autos** : car wash
lave–glace [lavglas] *nm, pl* **lave–glaces** : windshield washer
lave–linge [lavlɛ̃ʒ] *nms & pl France* : washing machine
lavement [lavmɑ̃] *nm* : enema
laver [lave] *vt* **1** : to wash <laver la vaisselle : to do the dishes> <machine à laver : washing machine> **2** : to clear (one's conscience, someone's name, etc.) — **se laver** *vr* **1** : to wash oneself <se laver les mains : to wash one's hands> **2** SE DISCULPER : to vindicate oneself
laverie [lavri] *nf* : self-service laundry
lavette [lavɛt] *nf* **1** : dishcloth **2** *Can* : small mop or brush for washing dishes **3** *fam* : wimp, drip
laveur, -veuse [lavœr, -vøz] *n* : washer, cleaner <laveur de vitres : window washer>
laveuse *nf Can* : washing machine
lave–vaisselle [lavvesɛl] *nms & pl* : dishwasher
lavoir [lavwar] *nm Can* : self-service laundry
laxatif [laksatif] *nm* : laxative
laxisme [laksism] *nm* : laxity
le[1], la [lə, la] (**l'** [l] *before a vowel or mute h*) *pron, pl* **les** [le] **1** (*used as a direct object*) : him, her, it, them <je ne la connais pas : I don't know her> <il le mérite : he deserves it> <les voilà! : there they are!> **2** (*indicating a state or condition*) <elles le lui avaient bien dit : they told him so> <hier il n'était pas content, maintenant il l'est : he wasn't satisfied yesterday, (but) now he is>
le[2], la (**l'** *before a vowel or mute h*) *art, pl* **les 1** : the <le gateau est sur la table : the cake is on the table> <les enfants : the children> **2** (*used with abstract nouns and geographical names*) <la liberté : freedom> <le Canada : Canada> **3** (*used with parts of the body*) <avec un chapeau sur la tête : with a hat on his/her head> <se laver les dents : to brush one's teeth> **4** (*used with expressions of time*) <le 19 juin : June 19th> <je travaille le matin : I work mornings> **5** : a, an, per <trois fois la semaine : three times a week> <20 dollars l'once : 20 dollars an ounce> **6** (*used in exclamations*) <la belle fête! : (what) a lovely party!>
leader [lidœr] *nm* : leader
lécher [leʃe] {87} *vt* **1** : to lick **2** : to lap up **3** : to lick at, to wash up against **4** *fam* : to polish up (a text, etc.) — **se lécher** *vr* : to lick (one's fingers, etc.)
lèche–vitrines [lɛʃvitrin] *nms & pl* : window-shopping <faire du lèche-vitrines : to window-shop>
leçon [ləsɔ̃] *nf* **1** : schoolwork **2** COURS : lesson, class <prendre des leçons de piano : to take piano lessons> **3** ENSEIGNEMENT : lesson, lecture <il m'a fait la leçon : he gave me a lecture> <j'en ai tiré une leçon : I learned a lesson from it>
lecteur[1], -trice [lɛktœr, -tris] *n* : reader
lecteur[2] *nm* **1** : player <lecteur de CD : CD player> **2** : drive <lecteur de disquettes : disk drive> **3** : reader <lecteur de microfiches : microfiche reader>
lectorat [lɛktɔra] *nm* : readership
lecture [lɛktyr] *nf* **1** : reading **2 lecture sur les lèvres** : lipreading
ledit, ladite [lədi, ladit] *adj, pl* **lesdits, lesdites** [ledi, ledit] : the aforementioned, the aforesaid
légal, -gale [legal] *adj, mpl* **légaux** [lego] : legal, lawful — **légalement** [-galmɑ̃] *adv*
légaliser [legalize] *vt* **1** : to legalize **2** : to authenticate — **légalisation** [-lizasjɔ̃] *nf*
légalité [legalite] *nf* : legality, lawfulness
légat [lega] *nm* : legate
légation [legasjɔ̃] *nf* : legation
légendaire [leʒɑ̃dɛr] *adj* : legendary
légende [leʒɑ̃d] *nf* **1** : legend, story **2** : caption (of an illustration) **3** : key, legend (of a map, etc.)
léger, -gère [leʒe, -ʒɛr] *adj* **1** : light <légère comme une plume : light as a feather> <d'un cœur léger : with a light heart> <un repas léger : a light meal> **2** : slight, faint, weak <une légère augmentation : a slight increase> **3** : flimsy, superficial, frivolous <parler à la légère : to speak thoughtlessly> **4** : loose, lax, flighty <une femme légère : a loose woman>
légèrement [leʒɛrmɑ̃] *adv* **1** : lightly **2** : slightly **3** : thoughtlessly, rashly
légèreté [leʒɛrte] *nf* **1** : lightness **2** DÉSINVOLTURE : thoughtlessness, casualness
légiférer [leʒifere] {87} *vi* : to legislate
légion [leʒjɔ̃] *nf* : legion

légionnaire [leʒjɔnɛr] *nm* : legionary, legionnaire
législateur, -trice [leʒislatœr, -tris] *n* : legislator, lawmaker
législatif[1], **-tive** [leʒislatif, -tiv] *adj* : legislative
législatif[2] *nm* : legislature, legislative body
législation [leʒislasjɔ̃] *nf* : legislation
législature [leʒislatyr] *nf* **1** : term (of office) **2** : legislature
légiste[1] [leʒist] *adj* → **médecin**
légiste[2] *nm* : jurist
légitime [leʒitim] *adj* **1** LÉGAL : lawful **2** : legitimate, justifiable **3** : just, fair **4 légitime défense** : self-defense
légitimement [leʒitimmɑ̃] *adv* : legitimately
légitimer [leʒitime] *vt* **1** : to legitimize **2** JUSTIFIER : to justify
légitimité [leʒitimite] *nf* **1** : legitimacy **2** : fairness
legs [leɡ] *nms & pl* : legacy, bequest
léguer [lege] {87} *vt* **1** : to bequeath **2** TRANSMETTRE : to pass on
légume[1] [legym] *nm* : vegetable <légumes verts : green vegetables>
légume[2] *nf fam* **grosse légume** : bigwig
légumier [legymje] *nm* : vegetable dish
légumineuse [legyminøz] *nf* : legume, leguminous plant
lemming [lɛmiŋ] *nm* : lemming
lendemain [lɑ̃dmɛ̃] *nm* **1** : next day <le lendemain matin : the next morning> **2 au lendemain de** : just after, following **3 du jour au lendemain** : in a very short time, overnight **4 le lendemain** : the future <des lendemains heureux : happy days ahead> <sans lendemain : short-lived> **5 lendemains** *nmpl* : consequences, outcome
lénifiant, -fiante [lenifjɑ̃, -fjɑ̃t] *adj* : soothing
lent, lente [lɑ̃, lɑ̃t] *adj* : slow — **lentement** [lɑ̃tmɑ̃] *adv*
lente [lɑ̃t] *nm* : nit
lenteur [lɑ̃tœr] *nf* : slowness <avec lenteur : slowly> <lenteurs bureaucratiques : bureaucratic delays>
lentille [lɑ̃tij] *nf* **1** : lentil **2** : lens <lentilles cornéennes : contact lenses>
léonin, -nine [leɔnɛ̃, -nin] *adj* **1** : leonine **2** : one-sided, unfair, inequitable
léopard [leɔpar] *nm* : leopard
lèpre [lɛpr] *nf* : leprosy
lépreux[1], **-preuse** [leprø, -prøz] *adj* **1** : leprous **2** : flaking, peeling
lépreux[2], **-preuse** *n* : leper
lequel, laquelle [ləkɛl, lakɛl] *pron, pl* **lesquels, lesquelles** [lekɛl] (*with* **à** *and* **de** *contracted to* **auquel, auxquels, auxquelles; duquel, desquels, desquelles**) **1** : which <la réunion à laquelle il était convié : the meeting to which he was invited > <le compromis auquel il est parvenu : the compromise he reached> **2** : which one <lequel préférez-vous? : which one do you prefer?> **3** : who, whom <un de ses amis avec lequel il joue au tennis : one of his friends with whom he plays tennis>
les → **le**
lesbianisme [lɛsbjanism] *nm* : lesbianism
lesbienne [lɛsbjɛn] *nf* : lesbian
lesdits, lesdites → **ledit**
léser [leze] {87} *vt* **1** : to wrong **2** BLESSER : to injure
lésiner [lezine] *vi* ~ **sur** : to skimp on, to be stingy with
lésion [lezjɔ̃] *nf* : lesion
lesquels, lesquelles → **lequel**
lessivage [lɛsivaʒ] *nm* : washing
lessive [lɛsiv] *nf* **1** LAVAGE : washing, wash <faire la lessive : to do the wash> **2** DÉTERGENT : detergent **3** : lye
lessiver [lɛsive] *vt* **1** : to wash, to scrub **2** : to leach **3 être lessivé** *fam* : to be washed out, to be exhausted **4 se faire lessiver** *fam* : to be cleaned out (in a card game, etc.)
lest [lɛst] *nm* **1** : ballast **2 lâcher du lest** : to make concessions
leste [lɛst] *adj* **1** AGILE : nimble, agile **2** : coarse, risqué
lestement [lɛstəmɑ̃] *adv* : nimbly, agilely
lester [lɛste] *vt* **1** : to ballast, to weight **2** *fam* : to stuff, to cram
létal, -tale [letal] *adj, mpl* **létaux** [-to] : lethal
léthargie [letarʒi] *nf* : lethargy <tomber en léthargie : to become lethargic>
léthargique [letarʒik] *adj* : sluggish, lethargic
letton[1], **-tonne** [lɛtɔ̃, -tɔn] *adj* : Latvian
letton[2] *nm* : Latvian (language)
Letton, -tonne *n* : Latvian
lettre [lɛtr] *nf* **1** : letter (of the alphabet) <en toutes lettres : in words, written out> **2** : letter <lettre d'amour : love letter> **3 lettres** *nfpl* : arts, humanities **4 à la lettre** : to the letter, exactly
lettré, -trée [lɛtre] *adj* : well-read
leucémie [løsemi] *nf* : leukemia
leur[1] [lœr] *adj, pl* **leurs** : their <leur mère et leur père : their mother and father>
leur[2] *pron, pl* **leurs 1** : to them <nous leur donnerons le livre : we will give them the book> **2 le leur, la leur, les leurs** : theirs
leurre [lœr] *nm* **1** APPÂT : lure, bait **2** ILLUSION, TROMPERIE : deception, delusion
leurrer [lœre] *vt* TROMPER : to deceive, to delude — **se leurrer** *vr*
levain [ləvɛ̃] *nm* : leaven <sans levain : unleavened>

levant [ləvɑ̃] *adj m* **au soleil levant** : at sunrise
levé, -vée [ləve] *adj* **1** : up <voilà trois heures que je suis levé : I've been up for three hours> **2** : raised <voter à main levée : to vote by a show of hands>
levée [ləve] *nf* **1** : lifting, suspension **2** : collection <levée du courrier : mail pickup> **3** : levying (of troops or taxes) **4** : levee
lever[1] [ləve] {52} *vt* **1** : to raise <lever la main : to put up one's hand> **2** : to lift, to raise (an object) <lever les fenêtres : to raise the windows> <lever les filets : to haul up nets> **3** : to suspend, to end <lever une interdiction : to lift a ban> <elle a levé la séance : she closed the meeting> **4** : to levy (taxes), to raise (funds) **5** : to get (someone) out of bed **6** : to flush (game) **7** : to levy (troops) — *vi* **1** : to come up (of plants) **2** : to rise (in cooking) — **se lever** *vr* **1** : to get up <se lever tôt : to get up early> **2** : to stand up **3** : to rise (of the sun), to become light <le soleil se lève : the sun is rising> <le jour se lève : day is breaking> **4** : to clear up <l'orage s'est levé : the storm lifted>
lever[2] [ləve] *nm* **1** : rising, rise <le lever du jour : daybreak> <au lever du soleil : at sunrise> **2** (*referring to persons*) <au lever : on getting up (from bed)> **3 lever de rideau** : curtain, curtain-raising (in theater)
levier [ləvje] *nm* **1** : lever **2 levier de vitesse** : gearshift
lèvre [lɛvr] *nf* **1** : lip <du bout des lèvres : reluctantly, half-heartedly> <être suspendu aux lèvres de qqn : to hang on s.o.'s every word> **2** : edge, rim, lip (in geology)
lévrier [levrije] *nm* : greyhound
levure [ləvyr] *nf* **1** : yeast **2 levure chimique** : baking powder
lexicographe [lɛksikɔgraf] *nmf* : lexicographer
lexicographie [lɛksikɔgrafi] *nf* : lexicography — **lexicographique** [-grafik] *adj*
lexique [lɛksik] *nm* **1** : vocabulary, glossary **2** : lexicon
lézard [lezar] *nm* : lizard
lézarde [lezard] *nf* FISSURE : crack
lézarder [lezarde] *vt* : to crack — *vi fam* : to bask in the sun — **se lézarder** *vr* : to crack
liaison [ljezɔ̃] *nf* **1** : (logical) connection **2** : link <liaison satellite : satellite link> **3** : contact <établir une liaison : to establish contact> **4** AVENTURE : love affair **5** : liaison (in linguistics)
liant, liante [ljɑ̃, ljɑ̃t] *adj* AFFABLE : sociable
liard [ljar] *nm Can* : cottonwood (tree)
liasse [ljas] *nf* : bundle, wad <liasse d'argent : roll of bills>
libanais, -naise [libanɛ, -nɛz] *adj* : Lebanese
Libanais, -naise *n* : Lebanese
libelle [libɛl] *nm* : lampoon
libellé [libele] *nm* : wording (of a document)
libeller [libele] *vt* **1** : to word **2** : to draw up **3** : to make out (a check or money order)
libellule [libelyl] *nf* : dragonfly
libéral, -rale [liberal] *adj & n, mpl* **-raux** [-ro] : liberal — **libéralement** [-ralmɑ̃] *adv*
libéraliser [liberalize] *vt* : to liberalize — **libéralisation** [-lizasjɔ̃] *nf*
libéralisme [liberalism] *nm* : liberalism
libéralité [liberalite] *nf* : liberality, generosity
libérateur[1], **-trice** [liberatœr, -tris] *adj* : liberating
libérateur[2], **-trice** *n* : liberator
libération [liberasjɔ̃] *nf* **1** : freeing, releasing <libération conditionnelle : release on parole> **2** : liberation <libération de la femme : women's liberation>
libéré, -rée [libere] *adj* **1** : liberated **2 ~ de** : free from
libérer [libere] {87} *vt* **1** : to free, to release **2** : to liberate (a country, etc.) **3** : to relieve **4** : to deregulate
libérien, -rienne [liberjɛ̃, -rjen] *adj* : Liberian
Libérien, -rienne *n* : Liberian
liberté [libɛrte] *nf* **1** : freedom, liberty <liberté de la presse : freedom of the press> <en liberté conditionnelle : on probation> <mettre en liberté : to set free> **2 libertés** *nfpl* : liberties <prendre des libertés : to take liberties>
libertin[1], **-tine** [libɛrtɛ̃, -tin] *adj* : dissolute, licentious
libertin[2], **-tine** *n* : libertine
libidineux, -neuse [libidinø, -nøz] *adj* : lustful, lewd
libido [libido] *nf* : libido
libraire [librɛr] *nmf* : bookseller
librairie [librɛri] *nf* : bookstore
libre [libr] *adj* **1** : free <un pays libre : a free country> <libre de soucis : free from care> **2** : free (and easy), open <une manière libre : an easygoing manner> **3** DISPONIBLE : available, unoccupied <il y a deux chambres libres : there are two rooms available> <avoir du temps libre : to have some spare time> **4** DÉGAGÉ : clear, free <avoir les mains libres : to have one's hands free> <la voie est libre : the coast is clear> **5 libre arbitre** : free will
libre–échange [libreʃɑ̃ʒ] *nm, pl* **libres–échanges** [librəzeʃɑ̃ʒ] : free trade
librement [librəmɑ̃] *adv* : freely

libre–service [librəservis] *nm, pl* **libres–services 1** : self-service **2** : self-service store or restaurant
libyen, libyenne [libjɛ̃, libjɛn] *adj* : Libyan
Libyen, Libyenne *n* : Libyan
lice [lis] *nf* **entrer en lice** : to join in the fray, to be in the running
licence [lisɑ̃s] *nf* **1** : degree <licence ès lettres : bachelor of arts degree> **2** : license, permit **3** : license, freedom <licence poétique : poetic license>
licencié, -ciée [lisɑ̃sje] *n* **1** : (university) graduate <licencié de sciences : bachelor of science> **2** : permit holder, licensed vendor
licenciement [lisɑ̃simɑ̃] *nm* RENVOI : layoff, dismissal
licencier [lisɑ̃sje] {96} *vt* CONGÉDIER : to lay off, to dismiss
licencieux, -cieuse [lisɑ̃sjø, -sjøz] *adj* : licentious — **licencieusement** [-sjøzmɑ̃] *adv*
lichen [likɛn] *nm* : lichen
lichette [liʃɛt] *nf fam* : sliver, smidgin
licite [lisit] *adj* : lawful, licit
licorne [likɔrn] *nf* : unicorn
licou [liku] *nm* : halter (for an animal)
lie [li] *nf* **1** : sediment, lees *pl* **2 la lie de la société** : the dregs of society
lie–de–vin [lidvɛ̃] *adj s & pl* : wine-colored
liège [ljɛʒ] *nm* : cork (substance)
lien [ljɛ̃] *nm* **1** ATTACHE : bond, attachment **2** RAPPORT : link, connection **3** RELATION : tie, relationship <liens de parenté : family ties> <les liens d'amitié : the bonds of friendship>
lier [lje] {96} *vt* **1** : to bind, to tie up **2** RELIER : to link up, to join up **3** : to strike up (a friendship, etc.) **4** : to thicken (in cooking) — **se lier** *vr* ~ **avec** : to become friends with
lierre [ljɛr] *nm* : ivy
liesse [ljɛs] *nf* : jubilation <être en liesse : to be jubilant>
lieu [ljø] *nm, pl* **lieux 1** ENDROIT : place <lieu de naissance : birthplace> **2 au lieu de** : instead of **3 avoir lieu** : to take place <le spectacle aura lieu ce soir : the show is tonight> **4 avoir lieu de** : to have grounds to, to have every reason to **5 en premier lieu** : in the first place **6 lieu commun** : commonplace **7 tenir lieu de** : to serve as **8 lieux** *nmpl* : premises
lieu–dit *or* **lieudit** [ljødi] *nm, pl* **lieux–dits** *or* **lieudits** : locality
lieue [ljø] *nf* : league (measure of distance)
lieutenant [ljøtnɑ̃] *nm* : lieutenant
lieutenant–colonel [ljøtnɑ̃kɔlɔnɛl] *nm, pl* **lieutenants–colonels** : lieutenant colonel
lièvre [ljɛvr] *nm* : hare
lift [lift] *nm Can fam* : lift, ride
lifting [liftiŋ] *nm* : face-lift
ligament [ligamɑ̃] *nm* : ligament
ligature [ligatyr] *nf* : ligature
ligne [liɲ] *nf* **1** : line <ligne pointillée : dotted line> <en ligne droite : in a straight line> **2** : line, route <ligne de métro : subway line> <ligne d'autobus : bus route> **3** : telephone line, electric line, cable <la ligne est occupée : the line is busy> **4** : range, row <se mettre en ligne : to get into line, to line up> **5** : figure, shape <elle surveille sa ligne : she watches her weight> **6** : line, orientation <ligne de conduite : line of conduct> <grandes lignes : broad outlines> **7** : line (of products) **8 en** ~ : online (in computers) **9 lignes** *nfpl Can* : border (between the United States and Canada)
lignée [liɲe] *nf* **1** POSTÉRITÉ : descendants *pl* **2** : line, lineage **3** : tradition
ligneux, -neuse [liɲø, -ɲøz] *adj* : woody (of plants)
lignite [liɲit] *nm* : lignite
ligoter [ligɔte] *vt* GARROTTER : to tie up
ligue [liɡ] *nf* : league, alliance
liguer [liɡe] *v* **se liguer** *vr* **1** : to join forces **2** ~ **contre** : to conspire against, to gang up on
lilas [lila] *nms & pl* : lilac
limace [limas] *nf* : slug (mollusk)
limbes [lɛ̃b] *nmpl* **1** : limbo **2** : uncertainty <tout était dans les limbes : everything was up in the air>
lime [lim] *nf* : file <lime à ongles : nail file>
limer [lime] *vt* : to file — **se limer** *vr* **se limer les ongles** : to file one's nails
limier [limje] *nm* **1** : bloodhound **2** *or* **fin limier** *fam* : sleuth
limitatif, -tive [limitatif, -tiv] *adj* : restrictive, limiting
limitation [limitasjɔ̃] *nf* : limitation, restriction <limitation de temps : time limit> <limitation des naissances : birth control>
limite[1] [limit] *adj* **1 cas limite** : borderline case **2 date limite** : deadline **3 vitesse limite** : speed limit
limite[2] *nf* **1** : border, boundary **2** : limit <limite d'âge : age limit> <sans limites : limitless, boundless> <à la limite de : on the verge of> <dans les limites de : within the limits of> **3 limites** *nfpl* : limitations
limité, -tée [limite] *adj* : limited
limiter [limite] *vt* **1** BORNER : to bound **2** RESTREINDRE : to limit, to restrict — **se limiter** *vr* **1** : to limit oneself **2** ~ **à** : to be limited to, to be restricted to
limitrophe [limitrɔf] *adj* : bordering, adjoining
limogeage [limɔʒaʒ] *nm* : dismissal
limoger [limɔʒe] {17} *vt* : to dismiss
limon [limɔ̃] *nm* : silt
limonade [limɔnad] *nf* : lemonade
limousine [limuzin] *nf* : limousine
limpide [lɛ̃pid] *adj* **1** : limpid **2** : lucid, clear

limpidité [lɛ̃pidite] *nf* **1** : limpidity **2** : lucidity, clearness
lin [lɛ̃] *nm* **1** : flax <huile de lin : linseed oil> **2** : linen
linceul [lɛ̃sœl] *nm* : shroud
linéaire [lineɛr] *adj* : linear
linéaments [lineamɑ̃] *nmpl* : lineaments
linge [lɛ̃ʒ] *nm* **1** : linen <linge de maison : household linen(s)> **2** : wash, washing **3** : cloth <un linge doux : a soft cloth> <linge à vaisselle *Can* : dishcloth> **4** : underwear **5** *Can fam* : clothes *pl*, clothing
lingerie [lɛ̃ʒri] *nf* **1** : lingerie **2** *Can* : linen closet
lingot [lɛ̃go] *nm* : ingot
linguiste [lɛ̃gɥist] *nmf* : linguist
linguistique[1] [lɛ̃gɥistik] *adj* : linguistic
linguistique[2] *nf* : linguistics
liniment [linimɑ̃] *nm* : liniment
linoléum [linɔleɔm] *nm* : linoleum
linteau [lɛ̃to] *nm, pl* **linteaux** : lintel
lion, lionne [ljɔ̃, ljɔn] *n* : lion, lioness *f*
Lion *nm* : Leo
lionceau [ljɔ̃so] *nm, pl* **lionceaux** : lion cub
lippu, -pue [lipy] *adj* : thick-lipped
liquéfier [likefje] {96} *vt* : to liquefy — **se liquéfier** *vr*
liqueur [likœr] *nf* **1** : liqueur **2** *Can* : soft drink, soda
liquidation [likidasjɔ̃] *nf* **1** : liquidation **2** : clearance sale **3** : settlement, payment
liquide[1] [likid] *adj* : liquid
liquide[2] *nm* **1** : liquid **2** ESPÈCES : cash
liquider [likide] *vt* **1** : to liquidate, to settle **2** : to sell off, to clear (an inventory)
liquidité [likidite] *nf* **1** : liquidity **2 liquidités** *nfpl* : liquid assets
liquoreux, -reuse [likɔrø, -røz] *adj* : syrupy (of wine)
lire [lir] {51} *vt* **1** : to read <lire à haute voix : to read aloud> **2** : to discern, to see <elle lisait la peur dans mes yeux : she saw the fear in my eyes> **3 lire les lignes de la main** : to read one's palm
lis *or* **lys** [lis] *nms & pl* **1** : lily **2** → **fleur**
lisait [lizɛ], **lisions** [lizjɔ̃], *etc.* → **lire**
lise [liz], *etc.* → **lire**
lisible [lizibl] *adj* **1** : legible **2** : readable (of a novel, etc.) — **lisibilité** [-zibilite] *nf*
lisiblement [lizibləmɑ̃] *adv* : legibly
lisière [lizjɛr] *nf* **1** : selvage **2** : edge, outskirts *pl*
lisse [lis] *adj* : smooth, sleek
lisser [lise] *vt* **1** : to smooth out **2** : to preen (feathers)
liste [list] *nf* : list <liste d'attente : waiting list> <liste noire : blacklist> <liste électorale : electoral roll>
lit [li] *nm* **1** : bed <lit d'enfant : crib> <lit de mort : deathbed> <lits superposés : bunk (bed)> **2** : riverbed **3** : marriage <enfants du premier lit : children from the first marriage>
litanie [litani] *nf* : litany
literie [litri] *nf* : bedding
lithium [litjɔm] *nm* : lithium
lithographie [litɔgrafi] *nf* **1** : lithography **2** : lithograph
litière [litjɛr] *nf* **1** : litter, bedding (in a stable, etc.) **2 litière de chat** : kitty litter
litige [litiʒ] *nm* **1** : dispute <objet de litige : object of contention> **2** : litigation <parties en litige : litigants>
litigieux, -gieuse [litiʒjø, -ʒjøz] *adj* CONTENTIEUX : litigious, contentious
litote [litɔt] *nf* : understatement
litre [litr] *nm* : liter
littéraire [literɛr] *adj* : literary
littéral, -rale [literal] *adj, mpl* **-raux** [-ro] : literal — **littéralement** [-ralmɑ̃] *adv*
littérature [literatyr] *nf* : literature
littoral[1], **-rale** [litɔral] *adj, mpl* **-raux** [-ro] : littoral, coastal
littoral[2] *nm* : coast, coastline
lituanien[1], **-nienne** [lituanjɛ̃, -njɛn] *adj* : Lithuanian
lituanien[2] *nm* : Lithuanian (language)
Lituanien, -nienne *n* : Lithuanian
liturgie [lityrʒi] *nf* : liturgy
liturgique [lityrʒik] *adj* : liturgical
livide [livid] *adj* **1** BLÊME : pallid, pale **2** BLEUÂTRE : livid, bluish
livraison [livrezɔ̃] *nf* : delivery <livraison à domicile : home delivery>
livre[1] [livr] *nm* **1** : book <livre de poche : paperback> <livre de recettes : cookbook> <grand livre : ledger> **2 le livre** : the book trade **3 livres de comptes** : accounts, (account) books
livre[2] *nf* **1** : pound <une livre de beurre : a pound of butter> **2** *or* **livre sterling** : pound (monetary unit)
livrée [livre] *nf* **1** : livery **2 en livrée** : liveried
livrer [livre] *vt* **1** : to deliver **2** : to hand over, to surrender **3 livré à soi-même** : left to one's own devices — **se livrer** *vr* ~ **à 1** : to engage in, to devote oneself to **2** : to indulge in, to surrender to **3** : to confide in
livresque [livresk] *adj* : derived from books <savoir livresque : book learning>
livret [livre] *nm* **1** : booklet <livret de banque : bankbook> **2** : libretto
livreur, -vreuse [livrœr, -vrøz] *n* : deliveryman *m*, delivery woman *f*
lob [lɔb] *nm* : lob (in sports)
lobe [lɔb] *nm* : lobe <lobe de l'oreille : earlobe>
lober [lɔbe] *v* : to lob
lobotomie [lɔbɔtɔmi] *nf* : lobotomy
local[1], **-cale** [lɔkal] *adj, mpl* **locaux** [lɔko] : local — **localement** [-kalmɑ̃] *adv*

local[2] *nm, pl* **locaux** : place, premises *pl* <locaux commerciaux : office space>
localisation [lɔkalizasjɔ̃] *nf* **1** : localizing, confining **2** : location, locating
localiser [lɔkalize] *vt* **1** SITUER : to locate **2** CIRCONSCRIRE : to localize, to confine
localité [lɔkalite] *nf* **1** : locality **2** : village, small town
locataire [lɔkatɛr] *nmf* : tenant
location [lɔkasjɔ̃] *nf* **1** : renting, leasing **2** : rental <contrat de location : rental agreement>
lock-out [lɔkaut] *nms & pl* : lockout
locomoteur, -trice [lɔkɔmɔtœr, -tris] *adj* : locomotive
locomotion [lɔkɔmɔsjɔ̃] *nf* : locomotion
locomotive [lɔkɔmɔtiv] *nf* **1** : locomotive, engine **2** *fam* : driving force, pacesetter
locuteur, -trice [lɔkytœr, -tris] *n* : speaker <locuteur natif : native speaker>
locution [lɔkysjɔ̃] *nf* : phrase, locution <locution figée : set phrase>
logarithme [lɔgaritm] *nm* : logarithm
loge [lɔʒ] *nf* **1** : dressing room **2** : box (at the theater) <être aux premières loges : to have a ringside seat> **3** : lodge
logement [lɔʒmɑ̃] *nm* **1** APPARTEMENT : apartment, accommodations *pl* **2** : housing
loger [lɔʒe] {17} *vt* **1** : to put up, to house **2** : to accommodate <une salle qui loge 700 personnes : a room which accommodates 700 people> **3** : to put, to lodge — *vi* : to lodge, to stay (at a hotel) — **se loger** *vr* **1** : to find accommodations **2** : to lodge <la balle s'est logée dans son bras : the bullet lodged itself in his arm>
logiciel [lɔʒisjɛl] *nm* : software
logique[1] [lɔʒik] *adj* : logical — **logiquement** [-ʒikmɑ̃] *adv*
logique[2] *nf* : logic
logis [lɔʒi] *nms & pl* : dwelling, abode
logistique[1] [lɔʒistik] *adj* : logistic
logistique[2] *nf* : logistics
logo [logo] *nm* : logo
loi [lwa] *nf* **1** : law <voter une loi : to pass a law> <faire la loi : to lay down the law> <loi de la gravitation : law of gravity> **2** : rule, convention <les lois de la mode : the dictates of fashion> <loi du silence : code of silence>
loin[1] [lwɛ̃] *adv* **1** : far, a long way (off) **2** : a long time ago **3 ~ de** : far from, distant from **4 d'aussi loin que** : as far back as **5 plus loin** : farther, further
loin[2] *n* **1 au ~** : in the distance, afar **2 de ~** : from a distance **3 de ~** : by far, far and away **4 de loin en loin** : here and there, from time to time
lointain[1], **-taine** [lwɛ̃tɛ̃, -tɛn] *adj* **1** ÉLOIGNÉ : distant, far-off **2** : remote, distant (in time)
lointain[2] *nm* : distance (in space or time) <dans le lointain : in the distance>
loir [lwar] *nm* : dormouse
loisible [lwazibl] *adj* : permissible, allowable <il est loisible de nager ici : you're allowed to swim here>
loisir [lwazir] *nm* **1** : leisure <heures de loisir : leisure time, spare time> **2** : time, opportunity **3 loisirs** *nmpl* : leisure activities, recreation
lombago [lɔ̃bago] → **lumbago**
lombes [lɔ̃b] *nmpl* : loins
lombric [lɔ̃brik] *nm France* : earthworm
long[1] [lɔ̃] *adv* **1** BEAUCOUP : much, a lot <il en disait trop long : he revealed too much> **2 s'habiller long** : to wear long skirts
long[2], **longue** [lɔ̃, lɔ̃g] *adj* **1** : long (in space) <une jupe longue : a long skirt> <long de six mètres : six meters long> **2** : long (in time) <un long silence : a lengthy silence> <une longue amitié : a long-standing friendship> <être long à faire : to be slow to do> **3 de long en large** : up and down, to and fro
long[3] *nm* **1** : length (of space) <deux pouces de long : two inches long> <tomber de tout son long : to fall flat> **2** : length (of time) <tout au long de la nuit : throughout the night> **3 le long de** : along <le long de la route : along the road>
longanimité [lɔ̃ganimite] *nf* : forbearance
longe [lɔ̃ʒ] *nf* **1** : tether **2** : loin (in cooking)
longer [lɔ̃ʒe] {17} *vt* **1** : to go along, to follow **2** : to run alongside, to border
longévité [lɔ̃ʒevite] *nf* : longevity
longhorn [lɔ̃gɔrn] *nmf* : longhorn
longitude [lɔ̃ʒityd] *nf* : longitude
longitudinal, -nale [lɔ̃ʒitydinal] *adj, mpl* **-naux** [-no] : longitudinal — **longitudinalement** [-nalmɑ̃] *adv*
longtemps [lɔ̃tɑ̃] *adv* : a long time <il y a longtemps qu'il n'a pas joué : he hasn't gambled in a long time> <je n'en ai pas pour longtemps : I won't be long>
longue[1] → **long**[2]
longue[2] [lɔ̃g] *nf* **à la longue** : in the long run
longuement [lɔ̃gmɑ̃] *adv* **1** : for a long time **2** : at length, in detail
longueur [lɔ̃gœr] *nf* **1** : length <à longueur de journée : all day long> <sur une longueur de deux mètres : over two meters long> <longueur d'onde : wavelength> **2 longueurs** *nfpl* : tedious parts (of a film, etc.)
longue-vue [lɔ̃gvy] *nf, pl* **longues-vues** : telescope

look [luk] *nm* : look, image <un nouveau look : a new look>
lopin [lɔpɛ̃] *nm* **lopin de terre** : plot of land
loquace [lɔkas] *adj* BAVARD : talkative, loquacious
loquacité [lɔkasite] *nf* : loquacity, garrulousness
loque [lɔk] *nf* **1** : wreck (person) **2 loques** *nfpl* : rags
loquet [lɔkɛ] *nm* : latch
loqueteux, -teuse [lɔktø] *adj* : in rags, in tatters
lord [lɔr(d)] *nm* : lord (in Great Britain) <la Chambre de lords : the House of Lords>
lorgner [lɔrɲe] *vt* : to eye, to ogle, to leer at
lorgnette [lɔrɲɛt] *nf* : opera glasses *pl*
loriot [lɔrjo] *nm* : oriole
lors [lɔr] *adv* **1 ~ de** : at the time of **2 ~ de** : during **3 lors même que** : even though
lorsque [lɔrskə] **(lorsqu'** [lɔrsk] *before a vowel or mute h*) *conj* : when
losange [lɔzɑ̃ʒ] *nm* **1** : lozenge, diamond <en losange : diamond-shaped> **2** *Can* : baseball diamond
lot [lo] *nm* **1** SORT : fate, lot **2** : prize (in a lottery) **3** PART : share **4** : lot, plot (of land)
loterie [lɔtri] *nf* : lottery
loti, -tie [lɔti] *adj* **bien loti** : well-off
lotion [losjɔ̃] *nf* : lotion
lotir [lɔtir] *vt* : to divide into plots
lotissement [lɔtismɑ̃] *nm* **1** : housing development **2** : division (into plots)
lotus [lɔtys] *nm* : lotus
louable [lwabl] *adj* **1** : praiseworthy, commendable **2** : rentable
louage [lwaʒ] *nm* : renting <voiture de louage : rental car>
louange [lwɑ̃ʒ] *nf* : praise <à la louange de : in praise of> <chanter ses louanges : to sing one's praises>
louche[1] [luʃ] *adj* SUSPECT : shady, suspicious
louche[2] *nf* : ladle
loucher [luʃe] *vi* : to squint, to be cross-eyed
louer [lwe] *vt* **1** : to praise <Dieu soit loué! : praise be to God!> **2** : to rent (a car, etc.) **3** *or* **louer à bail** : to rent out, to lease (property) **— se louer** *vr* **1** : to be for rent **2** : to congratulate oneself
loufoque [lufɔk] *adj fam* : crazy, zany
loup [lu] *nm* **1** : wolf **2** *or* **loup de mer** : sea bass **3** : (eye) mask, domino
loup-cervier [luservje] *nm, pl* **loups-cerviers** : lynx
loupe [lup] *nf* : magnifying glass
louper [lupe] *vt fam* **1** : to bungle, to mess up **2** : to miss (a train, etc.)
loup-garou [lugaru] *nm, pl* **loups-garous** : werewolf
loup-marin [lumarɛ̃] *nm Can, pl* **loups-marins** : seal (animal)
lourd[1] [lur] *adv* **1 peser lourd** : to carry a lot of weight, to count heavily **2 il fait lourd** : it's hot and sticky (outside)
lourd[2], **lourde** [lur, lurd] *adj* **1** : heavy **2** : sultry, oppressive (of the weather) **3** : clumsy, ungainly **4** : weighty, serious **5** : dull, heavy-handed **6 ~ de** : fraught with
lourdaud[1], **-daude** [lurdo, -dod] *adj* : oafish
lourdaud[2], **-daude** *n* : oaf, clod
lourdement [lurdəmɑ̃] *adv* **1** PESAMMENT : heavily **2** MALADROITEMENT : clumsily **3** : GROSSIÈREMENT : greatly, grossly
lourdeur [lurdœr] *nf* **1** : heaviness <avoir des lourdeurs d'estomac : to feel bloated> **2** : clumsiness
lousse [lus] *adj Can fam* : loose, slack
loutre [lutr] *nf* : otter
louve [luv] *nf* : she-wolf
louveteau [luvto] *nm, pl* **louveteaux 1** : wolf cub **2** : Cub Scout
louvoyer [luvwaje] {58} *vi* **1** : to tack (in navigation) **2** : to hedge, to beat around the bush
lover [lɔve] *v* **se lover** *vr* : to coil up
loyal, loyale [lwajal] *adj, mpl* **loyaux** [lwajo] **1** FIDÈLE : loyal, faithful **2** HONNÊTE : honest, fair **— loyalement** [-jalmɑ̃] *adv*
loyauté [lwajote] *nf* **1** FIDÉLITÉ : loyalty, faithfulness **2** HONNÊTETÉ : honesty, fairness
loyer [lwaje] *nm* **1** : rent **2 loyer de l'argent** : interest rate
LSD [ɛlɛsde] *nm* : LSD
lu [ly] *pp* → **lire**
lubie [lybi] *nf* CAPRICE : whim, craze
lubricité [lybrisite] *nf* : lechery, lewdness
lubrifiant[1], **-fiante** [lybrifjɑ̃, -fjɑ̃t] *adj* : lubricating
lubrifiant[2] *nm* : lubricant
lubrifier [lybrifje] {96} *vt* : to lubricate **— lubrification** [lybrifikasjɔ̃] *nf*
lubrique [lybrik] *adj* **1** : lustful, lecherous **2** : lewd
lucarne [lykarn] *nf* **1** : skylight **2** : dormer window
lucide [lysid] *adj* **1** : lucid, clear-sighted **2** CONSCIENT : conscious, aware
lucidement [lysidmɑ̃] *adv* : clearly, lucidly
lucidité [lysidite] *nf* : lucidity, clear-sightedness
luciole [lysjɔl] *nf* : firefly
lucratif, -tive [lykratif, -tiv] *adj* : lucrative, profitable <organisation à but non lucratif : nonprofit organization>
ludique [lydik] *adj* : play, playing
luette [lyɛt] *nf* : uvula
lueur [lyœr] *nf* **1** : faint light **2** : glimmer, gleam <une lueur de colère dans les yeux : a gleam of anger in one's eyes> **3** : glow (of a fire, etc.)

luge [lyʒ] *nf* : sled

lugubre [lygybr] *adj* : gloomy, dismal — **lugubrement** [-gybrəmɑ̃] *adv*

lui [lɥi] *pron* **1** (*used as indirect object*) : (to) him, (to) her, (to) it <je le lui ai remis : I gave it back to her> **2** (*used as subject or for emphasis*) : he <elle va au théâtre, lui reste ici : she's going to the theater, he's staying here> **3** (*used as object of a preposition*) : him, it <ils vont chez lui : they're going to his house> <cette plume est à lui : this pen belongs to him> **4** (*used as a reflexive pronoun*) : himself <il ne pense qu'à lui : he only thinks of himself> **5 c'est tout lui!** : that's just like him!

lui-même [lɥimɛm] *pron* : himself, itself <c'est lui-même qui l'a dit : he said it himself>

luire [lɥir] {49} *vi* **1** : to shine, to gleam, to glisten **2** : to glow, to glimmer <l'espoir luit : there's a glimmer of hope>

luisant[1], **-sante** [lɥizɑ̃, -zɑ̃t] *adj* : shining, gleaming

luisant[2] *nm* : sheen

lumbago [lɛ̃bago, lœ̃-, lɔ̃-] *nm* : lumbago

lumière [lymjɛr] *nf* **1** : light <lumière du jour : daylight> <lumière du soleil : sunlight> <lumière des étoiles : starlight> <allumer la lumière : to turn on the light> **2** ÉCLAIRCISSEMENT : light, clarification <à la lumière de : in (the) light of> <mettre en lumière : to bring to light, to shed light on> **3** GÉNIE : luminary, shining light <elle n'est pas une lumière : she's hardly a genius> **4 lumières** *nfpl* : insight, understanding

luminaire [lyminɛr] *nm* : lamp, light

luminescent, -cente [lyminesɑ̃, -sɑ̃t] *adj* : luminescent — **luminescence** [-nesɑ̃s] *nf*

lumineusement [lyminøzmɑ̃] *adv* **1** : luminously **2** : clearly, lucidly

lumineux, -neuse [lyminø, -nøz] *adj* **1** : luminous, of light **2** : radiant <son sourire lumineux : her radiant smile> **3** : bright, intense <un jaune lumineux : bright yellow> **4** : clear, lucid <une idée lumineuse : a brilliant idea>

luminosité [lyminozite] *nf* : luminosity, radiance

lunaire [lynɛr] *adj* : lunar, moon

lunatique [lynatik] *adj* CAPRICIEUX : whimsical, temperamental

lunch [lœ̃ʃ] *nm, pl* **lunchs** *or* **lunches** **1** BUFFET : buffet **2** *Can* : lunch

lundi [lœ̃di] *nm* : Monday

lune [lyn] *nf* **1** : moon <pleine lune : full moon> **2 être dans la lune** : to have one's head in the clouds **3 lune de miel** : honeymoon <passer la lune de miel : to honeymoon>

luné, -née [lyne] *adj* **être bien (mal) luné** : to be in a good (bad) mood

lunette [lynɛt] *nf* **1** : opening, (round) window <lunette arrière : rear window (of an automobile)> **2** : toilet seat **3** : telescope <lunette d'approche : astronomical telescope> **4 lunettes** *nfpl* : glasses, spectacles, goggles <lunettes de soleil : sunglasses> <lunettes de ski : ski goggles>

lurette [lyrɛt] *nf* **belle lurette** : ages, a long time <il y a belle lurette : a long time ago> <ça fait belle lurette que : it's been ages since>

lustre [lystr] *nm* **1** : chandelier **2** : lustre, sheen **3 lustres** *nmpl* : ages <il y a des lustres : ages ago>

lustré, -trée [lystre] *adj* : shiny, glossy

lustrer [lystre] *vt* : to polish, to make shiny

luth [lyt] *nm* : lute

lutin [lytɛ̃] *nm* : imp, goblin, pixie

lutjanidé [lytjanide] *nm* : snapper

lutrin [lytrɛ̃] *nm* : lectern

lutte [lyt] *nf* **1** : fight, conflict <une lutte armée : an armed conflict> **2** : struggle, fight <la lutte contre la drogue : the fight against drugs> <lutte pour la vie : struggle for life> **3** : wrestling

lutter [lyte] *vi* **1** SE BATTRE : to fight, to contend **2** : to struggle **3** : to wrestle

lutteur, -teuse [lytœr, -tøz] *n* **1** : fighter **2** : wrestler

luxation [lyksasjɔ̃] *nf* : dislocation (of a joint)

luxe [lyks] *nm* : luxury <hôtel de luxe : luxury hotel>

luxembourgeois, -geoise [lyksɑ̃burʒwa, -ʒwaz] *adj* : Luxembourgian

Luxembourgeois, -geoise *n* : Luxembourger

luxer [lykse] *vt* : to dislocate (a joint) — **se luxer** *vr* : to dislocate <je me suis luxé l'épaule : I dislocated my shoulder>

luxueux, -xueuse [lyksɥø, -sɥøz] *adj* : luxurious — **luxueusement** [lyksɥøzmɑ̃] *adv*

luxure [lyksyr] *nf* : lust

luxuriant, -riante [lyksyrjɑ̃, -rjɑ̃t] *adj* : luxuriant, lush

luxurieux, -rieuse [lyksyrjø, -rjøz] *adj* : lascivious, lewd

luzerne [lyzɛrn] *nf* : alfalfa

lycée [lise] *nm France* : high school

lycéen, -céenne [liseɛ̃, -seɛn] *n France* : high school student

lymphatique [lɛ̃fatik] *adj* **1** : lymphatic **2** : lethargic, sluggish

lymphe [lɛ̃f] *nf* : lymph

lyncher [lɛ̃ʃe] *vt* : to lynch

lynx [lɛ̃ks] *nm* : lynx

lyophilisé, -sée [ljɔfilize] *adj* : freeze-dried

lyophiliser [ljɔfilize] *vt* : to freeze-dry

lyre [lir] *nf* : lyre
lyrique [lirik] *adj* **1** : lyrical **2** : lyric <poésie lyrique : lyric poetry> **3** : operatic, opera <chanteur lyrique : opera singer> <comédie lyrique : comic opera>
lyrisme [lirism] *nm* : lyricism
lys → lis

M

m [ɛm] *nm* : m, the 13th letter of the alphabet
ma → mon
maboul, -boule [mabul] *adj fam* CINGLÉ : loony, crazy
macabre [makabr] *adj* : macabre, gruesome
macadam [makadam] *nm* **1** : macadam **2** : (macadam) road
macareux [makarø] *nms & pl* : puffin
macaron [makarɔ̃] *nm* **1** : macaroon **2** : coil (of hair) **3** : (round) badge, sticker
macaronis [makarɔni] *nmpl* : macaroni <macaronis au gratin : macaroni and cheese>
macédoine [masedwan] *nf* : mixture (of fruits or vegetables) <macédoine de fruits : fruit salad> <macédoine de légumes : mixed vegetables>
macédonien, -nienne [masedɔnjɛ̃, -njɛn] *adj* : Macedonian
Macédonien, -nienne *n* : Macedonian
macérer [masere] {87} *vt* : to steep, to soak — *vi* : to soak <macérer dans une marinade : to marinate>
mâchefer [maʃfɛr] *nm* : clinker, slag
mâcher [maʃe] *vt* **1** MASTIQUER : to chew **2 ne pas mâcher ses mots** : not to mince one's words
machette [maʃɛt] *nf* : machete
machin [maʃɛ̃] *nm fam* : thingamajig, thing
Machin, -chine [maʃɛ̃, -ʃin] *n fam* : what's-his-name *m*, what's-her-name *f*
machinal, -nale [maʃinal] *adj, mpl* **-naux** [-no] AUTOMATIQUE : mechanical, automatic <une réaction machinale : an automatic reaction> — **machinalement** [-nalmɑ̃] *adv*
machination [maʃinasjɔ̃] *nf* COMPLOT : machination, plot
machine [maʃin] *nf* **1** : machine <machine à coudre : sewing machine> <machine à écrire : typewriter> <machine à laver : washing machine> **2** : engine <machine à vapeur : steam engine> **3** SYSTÈME : system, process <la machine administrative : bureaucratic machinery>
machine–outil [maʃinuti] *nf, pl* **machines–outils** : machine tool
machinerie [maʃinri] *nf* **1** : machinery, physical plant **2** : engine room
machinisme [maʃinism] *nm* : mechanization
machisme [matʃism] *nm* : machismo, male chauvinism
macho [matʃo] *adj fam* : macho
mâchoire [maʃwar] *nf* **1** : jaw <mâchoire supérieure : upper jaw> **2 mâchoire de frein** : brake shoe
mâchonner [maʃɔne] *vt* **1** : to chew **2** MARMONNER : to mumble
mâchouiller [maʃuje] *vt* : to chew (on), to nibble (at)
macis [masi] *nm* : mace (spice)
maçon [masɔ̃] *nm* **1** : bricklayer, mason **2** : builder
maçonner [masɔne] *vt* **1** : to construct (with masonry) **2** : to face (with stone), to brick up
maçonnerie [masɔnri] *nf* **1** : building, bricklaying **2** : masonry, stonework **3** : Freemasonry
maçonnique [masɔnik] *adj* : masonic
macramé [makrame] *nm* : macramé
macrocosme [makrɔkɔsm] *nm* : macrocosm
maculer [makyle] *vt* : to stain
madame [madam] *nf, pl* **mesdames** [medam] **1** : Mrs., Ms., Madam <bonjour, madame Dupont : good morning, Mrs. Dupont> **2** (*used as a polite form of address*) : lady <bonjour, mesdames : good morning, ladies> **3** (*used as a salutation*) <Madame : Dear Madam> <Mesdames, Mesdemoiselles, Messieurs! : Ladies and Gentlemen!>
mademoiselle [madmwazɛl] *nf, pl* **mesdemoiselles** [medmwazɛl] **1** : Miss, Ms. <bonjour, mademoiselle Dupont : good morning, Miss Dupont> **2** (*used as a polite form of address*) : Miss, Madam <merci, mademoiselle : thank you, Miss> **3** (*used as a salutation*) <Mademoiselle : Dear Madam> <Mesdames, Mesdemoiselles, Messieurs! : Ladies and Gentlemen!>
madère [madɛr] *nm* : Madeira (wine)
madone [madɔn] *nf* : Madonna
madrier [madrije] *nm* : beam (of wood)
madrigal [madrigal] *nm, pl* **-gaux** [-go] : madrigal
maelström [maɛlstrɔm] *nm* : maelstrom
maestria [maɛstrija] *nf* : mastery, skill, brilliance
mafia *or* **maffia** [mafja] *nf* : Mafia

magané, -née [magane] *adj Can fam* **1** : run-down, shabby **2** : weakened, tired
maganer [magane] *vt Can fam* : to ruin, to damage — **se maganer** *vr Can fam* : to tire out
magasin [magazɛ̃] *nm* **1** : shop, store <en magasin : in stock> <grand magasin : department store> **2** ENTREPÔT : warehouse **3** : magazine (of a gun or camera)
magasinage [magazinaʒ] *nm Can* : shopping
magasiner [magazine] *vi Can* : to shop, to go shopping
magazine [magazin] *nm* **1** REVUE : magazine **2** : program <un magazine d'actualités quotidiennes : a daily news program>
magenta [maʒẽta] *nm* : magenta
magicien, -cienne [maʒisjɛ̃, -sjɛn] *n* : magician
magie [maʒi] *nf* : magic
magique [maʒik] *adj* : magic, magical — **magiquement** [-ʒikmɑ̃] *adv*
magistral, -trale [maʒistral] *adj, mpl* **-traux** [-tro] **1** : brilliant, masterly **2** : authoritative **3 cours magistral** : lecture
magistralement [maʒistralmɑ̃] *adv* : masterfully
magistrat [maʒistra] *nm* : magistrate
magistrature [maʒistratyr] *nf* : magistracy
magma [magma] *nm* **1** : magma **2** : jumble
magnanime [maɲanim] *adj* : magnanimous
magnanimité [maɲanimite] *nf* : magnanimity
magnat [maɲa] *nm* : magnate, tycoon
magnésie [maɲezi] *nf* : magnesia
magnésium [maɲezjɔm] *nm* : magnesium
magnétique [maɲetik] *adj* : magnetic — **magnétiquement** [-tikmɑ̃] *adv*
magnétiser [maɲetize] *vt* : to magnetize — **magnétisme** [maɲetism] *nm*
magnétite [maɲetit] *nf* : magnetite, lodestone
magnétophone [maɲetɔfɔn] *nm* : tape recorder
magnétoscope [maɲetɔskɔp] *nm* : videocassette recorder, VCR
magnétoscoper [maɲetɔskɔpe] *vt* : to videotape
magnificence [maɲifisɑ̃s] *nf* **1** SPLENDEUR : magnificence, splendor **2** PRODIGALITÉ : lavishness, extravagance
magnifier [maɲifje] {96} *nf* **1** : to idealize **2** : to glorify
magnifique [maɲifik] *adj* SPLENDIDE : magnificent — **magnifiquement** [-fikmɑ̃] *adv*
magnitude [maɲityd] *nf* : magnitude
magnolia [maɲɔlja] *nm* : magnolia
magot [mago] *nm fam* : stash (of money), nest egg
magouille [maguj] *nf fam* : scheming, skulduggery
magouiller [maguje] *vi fam* : to scheme, to intrigue
mai [mɛ] *nm* : May
maigre[1] [mɛgr] *adj* **1** : thin, skinny **2** : meager, scanty **3** : lean, low-fat
maigre[2] *nm* **1** : lean (meat) **2 faire maigre** : to abstain from meat
maigrement [mɛgrəmɑ̃] *adv* : meagerly, poorly
maigreur [mɛgrœr] *nf* **1** : thinness **2** : scantiness, meagerness
maigrichon, -chonne [mɛgriʃɔ̃, -ʃɔn] *adj* : skinny, scrawny
maigrir [mɛgrir] *vt* : to thin, to make look thinner — *vi* : to lose weight, to reduce
mail [maj] *nm* : mall, promenade
maille [maj] *nf* **1** : stitch (in knitting) **2** : mesh **3** : link (in a chain) **4 → cotte**
maillet [maje] *nm* : mallet
maillon [majɔ̃] *nm* : link (in a chain)
maillot [majo] *nm* **1** : jersey, shirt (in sports) **2 maillot de bain** : bathing suit **3 maillot de corps** : undershirt
main [mɛ̃] *nf* **1** : hand <main droite : right hand> <la main dans la main : hand in hand> <serrer la main à : to shake hands with> <se tenir la main : to hold hands> **2** : skill <avoir la main : to have the knack> <se faire la main : to practice> **3** : style, touch <je reconnais la main d'un maître : I recognize the hand of a master> **4** : hand, deal (in card games) **5 de première main** : firsthand **6 de seconde main** : secondhand, used **7 donner un coup de main à** : to lend a helping hand to, to help **8 en mains propres** : in person **9 fait à la main** : handmade **10 main courante** : handrail **11 sous la main** : at hand, handy
main–d'œuvre [mɛ̃dœvr] *nf* : manpower, workforce
main–forte [mɛ̃fɔrt] *nf* : help, assistance <il m'a prêté main-forte : he came to my assistance>
mainmise [mɛ̃miz] *nf* : seizure, takeover
maint, mainte [mɛ̃, mɛ̃t] *adj* **1** : many a **2 maintes et maintes fois** : time and time again
maintenance [mɛ̃tnɑ̃s] *nf* : maintenance
maintenant [mɛ̃tnɑ̃] *adv* **1** : now <à partir de maintenant : from now on> **2** : nowadays
maintenir [mɛ̃tnir] {92} *vt* **1** ENTRETENIR : to maintain, to keep (up) **2** SOUTENIR : to hold up, to support **3** : to stand by (a decision, etc.) — **se maintenir** *vr* : to remain steady, to persist, to hold
maintien [mɛ̃tjɛ̃] *nm* **1** : maintaining, upholding <le maintien de l'ordre

: the maintenance of law and order> **2** : bearing, carriage

maire, mairesse [mɛr, mɛrɛs] *n* : mayor

mairie [meri] *nf* **1** : town hall, city hall **2** : town or city council

mais¹ [mɛ] *adv* **1** (*used to reinforce an interjection*) <mais bien sûr! : but of course!, certainly!> <mais non! : of course not!> **2 n'en pouvoir mais** : to be able to do nothing, to be helpless

mais² *conj* : but <elle est petite mais forte : she is small but strong> <mais ce n'est pas vrai : but that's not true> <non seulement délicieux mais encore salutaire : not only tasty but healthful>

maïs [mais] *nm* **1** : Indian corn, maize **2 maïs explosé** : popcorn

maison¹ [mɛzɔ̃] *adj* **1** : homemade <spécialité maison : specialty of the house> **2** : in-house **3** *fam* : first-rate

maison² *nf* **1** : house, home <maison de campagne : country house> <rester à la maison : to stay home> **2** : institution, home <maison de retraite : retirement home> **3** FIRME : firm, company <maison d'édition : publishing company> **4 maison close** : brothel **5 maison de correction** : reformatory **6 maison des jeunes** : youth center **7 maison mobile** *Can* : mobile home

maisonnée [mɛzɔne] *nf* : household

maisonnette [mɛzɔnɛt] *nf* : small house

maître¹, -tresse [mɛtr, -trɛs] *adj* **1** : main, key <l'idée maîtresse : the main idea> **2** : master, expert <maître boulanger : master baker>

maître², -tresse *n* **1** : master, mistress <maître de maison : host> <maîtresse de maison : lady of the house, hostess> **2** : owner (of a pet) **3 être maître de soi** : to have self-control <elle est maîtresse de soi : she's her own woman>

maître³ *nm* **1** : expert, master <être maître passé de : to be a past master at> **2** : master (of a pet) **3** : master (in the arts, etc.) <les vieux maîtres : the old masters> **4** (*used as a title for attorneys and other professionals*) : Mr., Mrs., Ms. **5 maître d'équipage** : boatswain **6 maître d'hôtel** : maître d'hôtel, headwaiter, butler

maître–chanteur [mɛtrəʃɑ̃tœr] *nm, pl* **maîtres–chanteurs** : blackmailer

maîtresse *nf* AMANTE : mistress

maîtrisable [metrizabl] *adj* : controllable

maîtrise [metriz] *nf* **1** : skill, mastery **2** : control <maîtrise de soi : self-control> **3** : master's degree

maîtriser [metrize] *vt* **1** : to master **2** : to control, to restrain — **se maîtriser** *vr*

majesté [maʒeste] *nf* : majesty

majestueux, -tueuse [maʒestɥø, -tɥøz] *adj* : majestic — **majestueusement** [-tɥøzmɑ̃] *adv*

majeur¹, -jeure [maʒœr] *adj* **1** IMPORTANT : major, main <en majeure partie : for the most part> **2** : of age **3** : major (in music)

majeur² *nm* : middle finger

majoration [maʒɔrasjɔ̃] *nf* : increase

majorer [maʒɔre] *vt* : to increase

majoritaire [maʒɔriter] *adj* : majority <le parti majoritaire : the majority party>

majorité [maʒɔrite] *nf* : majority <en majorité : in the majority>

majuscule¹ [maʒyskyl] *adj* : capital, uppercase

majuscule² *nf* : capital letter

mal¹ [mal] *adv* **1** : poorly, badly <j'ai mal dormi : I didn't sleep well> <mal tourner : to turn out badly> **2** : with difficulty <il respire mal : it's hard for him to breathe> **3** : in poor health <se porter mal : to be unwell> **4** : wrongly <mal comprendre : to misunderstand> **5 mal à l'aise** : ill at ease **6 pas mal** : not bad(ly) **7 pas mal** : quite, quite a few <elle est pas mal sympathique : she's quite nice> <pas mal d'enfants : quite a lot of children>

mal² *adj* **1** : wrong <c'est mal de voler : it's wrong to steal> **2** : bad <pas mal du tout : not bad at all> **3** : sick, ill <se sentir mal : to feel sick>

mal³ *nm, pl* **maux** [mo] **1** DOULEUR : pain <avoir mal à la gorge : to have a sore throat> **2** MALADIE : sickness <mal de mer : seasickness> **3** DOMMAGE : harm, hurt <le mal est fait : the damage is done> **4** : evil, ill <le bien et le mal : good and evil> **5** PEINE : trouble, difficulty <sans mal : easily>

malade¹ [malad] *adj* **1** : sick, ill <tomber malade : to get sick> <malade d'inquiétude : sick with worry> **2** : diseased (of an organ or a plant) **3** *fam* : crazy **4** : in a bad way <une économie malade : an ailing economy>

malade² *nmf* : sick person, patient

maladie [maladi] *nf* **1** : illness, disease <maladie mentale : mental illness> <maladie sexuellement transmissible : sexually transmitted disease> <maladie de Carré : distemper> **2** MANIE : mania, obsession

maladif, -dive [maladif, -div] *adj* **1** : sickly **2** MORBIDE : pathological <une jalousie maladive : pathological jealousy>

maladresse [maladrɛs] *nf* **1** : clumsiness, awkwardness **2** BÉVUE : blunder

maladroit, -droite [maladrwa, -drwat] *adj* MALHABILE : clumsy, awkward — **maladroitement** [-drwatmɑ̃] *adv*

malais[1], **-laise** [malɛ, -lɛz] *adj* : Malay, Malayan
malais[2] *nm* : Malay (language)
Malais, -laise *n* : Malay, Malayan
malaise [malɛz] *nm* **1** : faintness, dizziness <j'éprouvais un léger malaise : I was feeling faint> **2** : uneasiness, malaise
malaisé, -sée [maleze] *adj* PÉNIBLE : difficult
malaisément [malezemɑ̃] *adv* : with difficulty
malaisien, -sienne [malɛzjɛ̃, -zjɛn] *adj* : Malaysian
Malaisien, -sienne *n* : Malaysian
malard *or* **malart** [malar] *nm* **1** : drake **2** *Can* : mallard
malavenant, -nante [malavnɑ̃, -nɑ̃t] *adj Can* : disagreeable, unpleasant
malavisé, -sée [malvize] *adj* : ill-advised, unwise
malawien, -wienne [malawjɛ̃, -wjɛn] *adj* : Malawian
Malawien, -wienne *n* : Malawian
malaxer [malakse] *vt* : to blend, to mix
malaxeur [malaksœr] *nm* **1** : (cement) mixer **2** *Can* : (electric) beater, mixer **3** *Can* MÉLANGEUR : blender
malchance [malʃɑ̃s] *nf* : bad luck, misfortune
malchanceux, -ceuse [malʃɑ̃sø, -søz] *adj* : unlucky
malcommode [malkɔmɔd] *adj* **1** : impractical, uncomfortable, inconvenient **2** *Can* : ornery, cantankerous <un malade malcommode : a difficult patient>
mâle[1] [mal] *adj* **1** : male **2** : manly
mâle[2] *nm* : male
malédiction [malediksjɔ̃] *nf* : curse, malediction
maléfice [malefis] *nm* SORTILÈGE : evil spell
maléfique [malefik] *adj* : evil
malencontreusement [malɑ̃kɔ̃trøzmɑ̃] *adv* : inappropriately, ill-advisedly
malencontreux, -treuse [malɑ̃kɔ̃trø, -trøz] *adj* : unfortunate, untoward, inopportune
malendurant, -rante [malɑ̃dyrɑ̃, -rɑ̃t] *adj Can* : gruff, rough
malentendant[1], **-dante** [malɑ̃tɑ̃dɑ̃, -dɑ̃t] *adj* : hard of hearing
malentendant[2], **-dante** *n* **les malentendants** : the hearing impaired
malentendu [malɑ̃tɑ̃dy] *nm* : misunderstanding
mal-en-train [malɑ̃trɛ̃] *adj Can* : unwell, out of sorts
malfaçon [malfasɔ̃] *nf* DÉFAUT : fault, defect
malfaisant, -sante [malfəzɑ̃, -zɑ̃t] *adj* **1** NUISIBLE : harmful **2** : evil, wicked
malfaiteur [malfɛtœr] *nm* CRIMINEL : criminal, malefactor
malfamé, -mée [malfame] → **famé**
malformation [malfɔrmasjɔ̃] *nf* : malformation
malgache[1] [malgaʃ] *adj* : Madagascan, Malagasy
malgache[2] *nm* : Malagasy (language)
Malgache *nmf* : Madagascan, Malagasy
malgré [malgre] *prep* : in spite of, despite <malgré tout : in spite of everything, even so>
malhabile [malabil] *adj* MALADROIT : clumsy
malheur [malœr] *nm* **1** : misfortune, bad luck **2** CATASTROPHE : tragedy, calamity **3 faire un malheur** *fam* : to be very successful <le spectacle a fait un malheur : the show was a big hit>
malheureusement [malœrøzmɑ̃] *adv* : unfortunately
malheureux[1], **-reuse** [malœrø, -røz] *adj* **1** : unhappy, miserable **2** FÂCHEUX : unfortunate, regrettable <des suites malheureuses : unfortunate consequences> <c'est malheureux! : what a shame!>
malheureux[2], **-reuse** *n* **1** : unfortunate person, poor wretch **2** : poor person <les malheureux : the needy>
malhonnête [malɔnɛt] *adj* : dishonest — **malhonnêtement** [-nɛtmɑ̃] *adv*
malhonnêteté [malɔnɛtte] *nf* : dishonesty, uncleanliness
malice [malis] *nf* **1** : mischief, mischievousness <avec malice : mischievously> **2 sans ~** : innocent, guileless
malicieux, -cieuse [malisjø, -sjøz] *adj* ESPIÈGLE : mischievous — **malicieusement** [malisjøzmɑ̃] *adv*
malien, -lienne [maljɛ̃, -ljɛn] *adj* : Malian
Malien, -lienne *n* : Malian
malignité [malipite] *nf* **1** : malice, spite **2** : malignancy
malin, -ligne [malɛ̃, -liɲ] *adj* **1** FUTÉ : shrewd, clever **2** *fam* : tricky, difficult **3** : malicious **4** : malignant
malingre [malɛ̃gr] *adj* : puny
malintentionné, -née [malɛ̃tɑ̃sjɔne] *adj* : malicious, spiteful
malle [mal] *nf* **1** : trunk <faire ses malles : to pack one's bags> **2** *or* **malle arrière** : trunk (of a car)
malléable [maleabl] *adj* : malleable — **malléabilité** [-leabilite] *nf*
mallette [malɛt] *nf* **1** ATTACHÉ-CASE : attaché case, briefcase **2** : small suitcase, valise
malmener [malməne] {52} *vt* **1** MALTRAITER : to manhandle, to mistreat **2** : to give a rough time to
malnutrition [malnytrisjɔ̃] *nf* : malnutrition
malodorant, -rante [malɔdɔrɑ̃, -rɑ̃t] *adj* : foul-smelling, smelly
malotru, -true [malɔtry] *n* : boor
malpoli, -lie [malpɔli] *adj fam* : rude, impolite
malpropre [malprɔpr] *adj* **1** SALE : dirty, grubby **2** GROSSIER : vulgar,

smutty **3** MALHONNÊTE : dishonest, unsavory

malpropreté [malprɔprəte] *nf* : dirtiness

malsain, -saine [malsɛ̃, -sɛn] *adj* : unhealthy

malséant, -séante [malseɑ̃, -seɑ̃t] *adj* : unseemly, unbecoming

malsonnant, -nante [malsɔnɑ̃, -nɑ̃t] *adj* : offensive

malt [malt] *nm* : malt

maltais, -taise [maltɛ, -tɛz] *adj* : Maltese

Maltais, -taise *n* : Maltese

maltraiter [maltrete] *vt* **1** : to mistreat **2** : to criticize, to pan

malveillance [malvɛjɑ̃s] *nf* : spite, malevolence

malveillant, -lante [malvɛjɑ̃, -jɑ̃t] *adj* : spiteful, malicious

malvenu, -venue [malvəny] *adj* DÉPLACÉ : out of place <je suis malvenu de le critiquer : I'm in no position to criticize him>

malversation [malversasjɔ̃] *nf* : embezzlement

maman [mamɑ̃] *nf* : mom, mommy

mamelle [mamɛl] *nf* **1** : teat **2** PIS : udder

mamelon [mamɛlɔ̃] *nm* **1** : nipple **2** : hillock

mamie [mami] *nf France fam* : grandma, granny

mammaire [mamɛr] *adj* : mammary

mammifère [mamifɛr] *nm* : mammal

mammographie [mamɔgrafi] *nf* : mammogram

mammouth [mamut] *nm* : mammoth

management [manaʒmɑ̃, manadʒment] *nm* : management

manager [manadʒœr] *nm* : manager

manant [manɑ̃] *nm* : yokel, boor

manche[1] [mɑ̃ʃ] *nf* **1** : sleeve <sans manche : sleeveless> **2** : round, game, set **3** *Can* : inning (in baseball) **4** channel, strait(s)

manche[2] *nm* **1** : handle <manche à balai : broomstick> **2** : neck (of a musical instrument)

manchette [mɑ̃ʃɛt] *nf* **1** : cuff (of a shirt, etc.) **2** : headline

manchon [mɑ̃ʃɔ̃] *nm* : muff

manchot[1], **-chote** [mɑ̃ʃo, -ʃɔt] *adj* **1** : one-armed, one-handed **2** : armless, handless

manchot[2] *nm* : penguin

mandarin [mɑ̃darɛ̃] *nm* **1** : mandarin **2** : Mandarin (language)

mandarine [mɑ̃darin] *nf* : tangerine, mandarin orange

mandat [mɑ̃da] *nm* **1** : mandate **2** : term of office **3** : warrant <mandat d'arrêt : warrant for arrest> <mandat de perquisition : search warrant> **4** *or* **mandat postal** *or* **mandat–poste** : money order

mandataire [mɑ̃datɛr] *nmf* **1** REPRÉSENTANT : representative, agent **2** : proxy

mandater [mɑ̃date] *vt* : to appoint, to commission

mandibule [mɑ̃dibyl] *nf* : mandible

mandoline [mɑ̃dɔlin] *nf* : mandolin

manège [manɛʒ] *nm* **1** : riding school **2** : game, scheme, ploy **3** : merry-go-round, ride (in an amusement park)

manette [manɛt] *nf* : lever

manganèse [mɑ̃ganɛz] *nm* : manganese

mangeable [mɑ̃ʒabl] *adj* : edible

mangeoire [mɑ̃ʒwar] *nf* : feeding trough, manger

manger[1] [mɑ̃ʒe] {17} *vt* **1** : to eat **2** : to eat away, to devour **3** : to fill up, to cover up, to hide **4** : to consume, to use up **5 manger ses mots** : to mumble — *vi* : to eat

manger[2] *nm* : food <le boire et le manger : food and drink>

mange–tout [mɑ̃ʒtu] *nms & pl or* **pois mange–tout** : snow pea

mangeur, -geuse [mɑ̃ʒœr, -ʒøz] *n* : eater

manglier [mɑ̃glije] *nm* : mangrove

mangouste [mɑ̃gust] *nf* : mongoose

mangue [mɑ̃g] *nf* : mango

maniabilité [manjabilite] *nf* : maneuverability

maniable [manjabl] *adj* **1** COMMODE : handy **2** : easy to handle, maneuverable **3** : easily influenced

maniaque[1] [manjak] *adj* **1** : fussy, finicky **2** : maniacal

maniaque[2] *nmf* **1** : crank, fanatic **2** : maniac

manie [mani] *nf* **1** : quirk, odd habit **2** OBSESSION : mania, obsession

maniement [manimɑ̃] *nm* : handling, use, operation <maniement d'une langue : command of a language>

manier [manje] {96} *vt* **1** : to handle, to deal with **2** : to use, to operate — **se manier** *vr fam* : to get a move on

manière [manjɛr] *nf* **1** : manner, way <d'une certaine manière : in a way> <en aucune manière : in no way, under no circumstances> <de manière à : so as to> <de toute manière : in any case, anyway> **2** : way, personal style <sa manière de parler : his way of speaking> **3** : style <dans la manière romantique : in the romantic style> **4 manières** *nfpl* : manners

maniéré, -rée [manjere] *adj* : affected, mannered

manifestant, -tante [manifestɑ̃, -tɑ̃t] *n* : demonstrator, protestor

manifestation [manifestasjɔ̃] *nf* **1** : (political) demonstration, protest **2** : expression (of emotions) **3** : event <une manifestation sportive : a sporting event> **4** : symptom, sign

manifeste[1] [manifest] *adj* ÉVIDENT : manifest, obvious — **manifestement** [-festmɑ̃] *adj*

manifeste[2] *nm* : manifesto

manifester [manifɛste] *vt* **1** : to express, to indicate **2** RÉVÉLER : to reveal, to show — *vi* : to demonstrate, to hold a demonstration — **se manifester** *vr* **1** : to manifest itself **2** : to appear
manigance [manigɑ̃s] *nf* : scheme, intrigue, trick
manigancer [manigɑ̃se] {6} *vt* : to plot, to scheme
manipulateur, -trice [manipylatœr, -tris] *n* **1** : technician **2** : conjurer **3** : manipulator
manipulation [manipylasjɔ̃] *n* **1** MANIEMENT : handling **2** : manipulation
manipuler [manipyle] *vt* **1** : to handle **2** : to manipulate
manivelle [manivɛl] *nf* : crank
manne [man] *nf* **1** : manna **2** : godsend
mannequin [mankɛ̃] *nm* **1** : dummy, mannequin **2** : model
manœuvrable [manœvrabl] *adj* : maneuverable
manœuvre [manœvr] *nf* **1** : maneuver **2 fausse manœuvre** : wrong move, error
manœuvrer [manœvre] *vt* **1** : to maneuver **2** : to work, to operate **3** MANIPULER : to manipulate — *vi* : to maneuver
manoir [manwar] *nm* : country estate, manor
manque [mɑ̃k] *nm* **1** INSUFFISANCE : lack, shortage <par manque d'imagination : for want of imagination> <manque de rapport : irrelevance> **2** LACUNE : gap <manque de crédit : credibility gap> **3 être en manque** : to be in withdrawal (from alcohol or drugs) **4 manque à gagner** : loss of earnings, shortfall
manqué, -quée [mɑ̃ke] *adj* **1** : failed <poète manqué : failed poet> **2** : missed <occasion manquée : missed opportunity **3** → **garçon**
manquement [mɑ̃kmɑ̃] *nm* : breach, lapse
manquer [mɑ̃ke] *vt* **1** : to miss <manquer une bonne occasion : to miss a good opportunity> **2** FAILLIR : to fall short of, to just miss <elle a manqué (de) tomber : she nearly fell> — *vi* **1** : to be lacking, to be missing <ce n'est pas l'envie qui me manque : it's not that I don't want to> <il manque deux tasses : two cups are missing> **2** ÉCHOUER : to fail <j'ai manqué à mon devoir : I failed to do my duty> **3** : to be absent <elle n'a jamais manqué : she's never been absent> **4 ~ de** : to be short of, to lack <il manque d'argent : he has no money>
mansarde [mɑ̃sard] *nf* : attic room, garret
mansuétude [mɑ̃syetyd] *nf* : leniency
mante [mɑ̃t] *nf or* **mante religieuse** : praying mantis
manteau [mɑ̃to] *nm, pl* **manteaux** [-to] **1** : coat **2** : blanket (of fog), mantle (of snow, etc.) **3 manteau de cheminée** : mantelpiece **4 sous le manteau** : undercover, clandestinely
manucure[1] [manykyr] *nmf* : manicurist
manucure[2] *nf* : manicure
manucurer [manykyre] *vt* : to manicure
manuel[1], **-elle** [manyɛl] *adj* : manual — **manuellement** [-nyɛlmɑ̃] *adv*
manuel[2] *nm* **1** : manual, handbook **2** *or* **manuel scolaire** : textbook
manuel[3], **-nuelle** *n* : manual worker
manufacture [manyfaktyr] *nf* **1** USINE : factory **2** : manufacture
manufacturer [manyfaktyre] *vt* : to manufacture
manufacturier, -rière [manyfaktyrje, -rjɛr] *n* : manufacturer, factory owner
manuscrit[1], **-scrite** [manyskri, -skrit] *adj* : handwritten
manuscrit[2] *nm* : manuscript
manutention [manytɑ̃sjɔ̃] *nf* **1** : handling <frais de manutention : handling charges> **2** ENTREPÔT : storehouse, warehouse
mappemonde [mapmɔ̃d] *nf* : map of the world
maquereau [makro] *nm, pl* **-reaux** [-ro] : mackerel
maquette [makɛt] *nf* : scale model
maquignon [makiɲɔ̃] *nm* **1** : horse dealer, cattle trader **2** *France* : shady operator
maquillage [makijaʒ] *nm* **1** : makeup **2** : doctoring, faking
maquiller [makije] *vt* **1** : to make up (one's face) **2** FALSIFIER : to falsify, to fake **3** DÉGUISER : to disguise, to hide <maquiller la vérité : to hide the truth> — **se maquiller** *vr* : to put on makeup
maquilleur, -leuse [makijœr, -jøz] *n* : makeup artist
maquis [maki] *nm* **1** *France* : scrubland, brush **2** : tangle, labyrinth
maraîcher[1], **-chère** [mareʃe, -ʃɛr] *adj* : farming <culture maraîchère : truck farming>
maraîcher[2], **-chère** *n* : truck farmer
marais [marɛ] *nm* : marsh, swamp
marasme [marasm] *nm* **1** ACCABLEMENT : dejection, depression **2** : stagnation <marasme économique : economic stagnation>
marasquin [maraskɛ̃] *nm* : maraschino
marathon [maratɔ̃] *nm* : marathon
marâtre [maratr] *nf* : cruel mother
maraudage [marodaʒ] → **maraude**
maraude [marod] *nf* **1** : pilfering, thieving **2 en ~** : cruising <taxi en maraude : cruising taxi>
marauder [marode] *vi* **1** : to pilfer, to thieve **2** : to cruise (of a taxi), to prowl about

maraudeur, -deuse [marodœr, -døz] *n* **1** : prowler, pilferer **2** : marauder
marbre [marbr] *nm* **1** : marble **2** *Can* : home plate (in baseball) **3 rester de marbre** : to remain impassive, to be unmoved
marbrer [marbre] *vt* **1** : to marble <gateau marbré : marble cake> **2** : to mottle, to blotch
marbrure [marbryr] *nf* **1** : marbling (of paper, etc.) **2** : mottling, blotchiness
marc [mar] *nm* : (coffee) grounds
marchand[1], **-chande** [marʃɑ̃, -ʃɑ̃d] *adj* **1** : market, commercial <valeur marchande : market value> **2** → **marine**
marchand[2], **-chande** *n* **1** COMMERÇANT : storekeeper, merchant, dealer <marchand de vins : wine merchant> **2 marchand ambulant** : hawker, peddler **3 marchand en gros** GROSSISTE : wholesaler
marchandage [marʃɑ̃daʒ] *nm* : bargaining, haggling
marchander [marʃɑ̃de] *vt* **1** : to bargain over, to haggle over **2** : to spare <il n'a pas marchandé ses éloges : he wasn't sparing in his praise> — *vi* : to haggle, to bargain, to dicker
marchandeur, -deuse [marʃɑ̃dœr, -døz] *n* : haggler
marchandises [marʃɑ̃diz] *nfpl* : goods, merchandise
marche [marʃ] *nf* **1** : step, stair <attention à la marche : watch for the step!> **2** : walk, walking <faire une marche : to take a walk> **3** : moving, running <un véhicule en marche : a moving vehicle> <la marche du temps : the march of time> **4** : working, operating <en bon état de marche : in good working order> **5** : march, marching <marche de protestation : protest march> **6** : march (in music) <marche nuptiale : wedding march>
marché [marʃe] *nm* **1** : market <faire son marché : to do one's (grocery) shopping> <marché aux puces : flea market> **2** : market (in economics and finance) <le marché du travail : the labor market> <marché noir : black market> <étude de marché : market survey> **3** : deal <conclure un marché : to strike a deal> **4 bon marché** : cheap <à bon marché : at a good price, cheaply> **5 par-dessus le marché** : to top it all off
marchepied [marʃəpje] *nm* **1** : step, steps *pl* (of a vehicle) **2** : steppingstone
marcher [marʃe] *vi* **1** : to walk **2** : to step, to tread **3** FONCTIONNER : to work, to go, to run <ma montre ne marche pas : my watch isn't running> <cette auto marche trop vite : that car's going too fast> **4** : to be working, to be going well <si ça marche : if it works out> **5 faire marcher qqn** *fam* : to pull s.o.'s leg **6 marcher au pas** : to march
marchette [marʃɛt] *nf Can* : walker (for babies)
marcheur, -cheuse [marʃœr, -ʃøz] *n* : walker
mardi [mardi] *nm* **1** : Tuesday **2 mardi gras** : Mardi Gras
mare [mar] *nf* **1** : pond **2** : pool <une mare de sang : a pool of blood>
marécage [mareka3] *nm* : marsh, swamp
marécageux, -geuse [mareka3ø, -3øz] *adj* : marshy, swampy
maréchal [mareʃal] *nm, pl* **-chaux** [-ʃo] : marshal
maréchal-ferrant [mareʃalferɑ̃] *nm, pl* **maréchaux-ferrants** [mareʃoferɑ̃] : blacksmith
marée [mare] *nf* **1** : tide <à marée haute : at high tide> <marée descendante : ebb tide> **2** : flood, surge (of emotions, etc.) **3 marée noire** : oil slick
marelle [marɛl] *nf* : hopscotch
marémoteur, -trice [maremɔtœr, -tris] *adj* : tidal
margarine [margarin] *nf* : margarine
marge [marʒ] *nf* **1** : margin **2** : leeway, room <marge de manœuvre : room to maneuver> **3** *or* **marge bénéficiaire** : profit margin, markup **4 en marge de** : on the fringes of, outside <vivre en marge de la société : to live on the fringes of society> <en marge de la loi : outside the law>
marginal[1], **-nale** [marʒinal] *adj, mpl* **-naux** [-no] : marginal — **marginalement** [-nalmɑ̃] *adv*
marginal[2], **-nale** *n, mpl* **-naux** : dropout
marguerite [margərit] *nf* : daisy
mari [mari] *nm* : husband
mariage [marja3] *nm* **1** : marriage <mariage mixte : intermarriage, mixed marriage> **2** : wedding **3** : blend, merger, alliance
marié[1], **-riée** [marje] *adj* : married
marié[2], **-riée** *n* **1** : groom *m*, bride *f* **2 les mariés** : the newlyweds
marier [marje] {96} *vt* **1** : to marry, to unite in marriage <le curé les a mariés : the priest married them> **2** *Can* ÉPOUSER : to marry, to get married to <il voulait la marier : he wanted to marry her> **3** : to combine, to blend — **se marier** *vr* **1** : to get married <se marier avec : to get married to> **2** : to go well together
marieur, -rieuse [marjœr, -jøz] *n* : matchmaker
marijuana [marirwana] *nf* : marijuana
marin[1], **-rine** [marɛ̃, -rin] *adj* **1** : sea, marine <paysage marin : seascape> **2** : offshore
marin[2] *nm* : sailor, mariner
marina [marina] *nf* : marina
marine[1] [marin] *adj or* **bleu marine** : navy blue

marine[2] *nf* **1** : navy <officier de marine : naval officer> **2 marine marchande** : merchant marine
marine[3] *nm* : navy blue
mariner [marine] *v* : to marinate
maringouin [marɛ̃gwɛ̃] *nm Can* : mosquito
marinière [marinjɛr] *nf* : smock
marionnette [marjɔnɛt] *nf* **1** : puppet **2 marionnette à fils** : marionette
marionnettiste [marjɔnetist] *nmf* : puppeteer
marital, -tale [marital] *adj, mpl* **-taux** [-to] : marital
maritime [maritim] *adj* **1** : maritime, coastal, seaboard **2** : naval, nautical **3** : shipping
marjolaine [marʒɔlɛn] *nf* : marjoram
marketing [marketiŋ] *nm* : marketing
marmaille [marmaj] *nf fam* : brats *pl*, noisy kids *pl*
marmelade [marmɔlad] *nf* **1** COMPOTE : stewed fruit **2** : marmalade
marmite [marmit] *nf* : cooking pot
marmonnement [marmɔnmɑ̃] *nm* : mumble, mutter
marmonner [marmɔne] *v* : to mutter, to mumble
marmot [marmo] *nm fam* : kid, brat
marmotte [marmɔt] *nf* **1** : marmot **2 marmotte d'Amérique** : groundhog, woodchuck
marmotter [marmɔte] *v* MARMONNER : to mutter, to mumble
marocain, -caine [marɔkɛ̃, -kɛn] *adj* : Moroccan
Marocain, -caine *nmf* : Moroccan
marotte [marɔt] *nf* : craze, fad
marquant, -quante [markɑ̃, -kɑ̃t] *adj* MÉMORABLE : memorable, outstanding
marque [mark] *nf* **1** : mark, trace, sign <marques de doigts : finger marks> <marques d'usure : signs of wear> **2** : brand, make <marque déposée : registered trademark> **3** : eminence, prominence <personnalité de marque : prominent figure> **4** : hallmark, stamp **5** : proof, sign <une marque de confiance : a sign of confidence> **6** : score (in sports, in games) **7 à vos marques! prêts! partez!** : on your marks! get set! go!
marqué, -quée [marke] *adj* **1** : marked **2** NET : distinct, decided
marquer [marke] *vt* **1** : to mark **2** INDIQUER : to show, to indicate **3** : to brand **4** : to score (in sports) **5** : to write down, to note **6 marquer le pas** : to mark time — *vi* **1** : to leave a mark **2** : to be significant, to stand out
marqueur[1], **-queuse** [markœr, -køz] *n* : scorekeeper
marqueur[2] *nm* : marker (pen), highlighter
marquis, -quise [marki, -kiz] *n* : marquess *m*, marquis *m*, marchioness *f*, marquise *f*
marquise *nf* **1** : canopy, marquee **2** AUVENT : awning
marraine [marɛn] *nf* : godmother
marrant, -rante [marɑ̃, -rɑ̃t] *adj fam* : amusing, funny
marre [mar] *adv fam* : enough <j'en ai marre : I'm fed up>
marron[1], **-ronne** [marɔ̃, -rɔn] *adj* **1** MALHONNÊTE : crooked, bogus <médecin marron : quack> **2** : brown
marron[2] *nm* **1** : chestnut **2** : brown
marronnier [marɔnje] *nm* : chestnut tree
mars [mars] *nm* : March
Mars *nf* : Mars (planet)
marsouin [marswɛ̃] *nm* : porpoise
marsupial, -piale [marsypjal] *adj & nm, pl* **-piaux** [-pjo] : marsupial
marteau [marto] *nm, pl* **marteaux** [marto] **1** : hammer **2** : gavel **3** : knocker **4 marteau pneumatique** : pneumatic drill
marteau–piqueur [martopikœr] *nm, pl* **marteaux–piqueurs** : jackhammer
martèlement [martɛlmɑ̃] *nm* : hammering
marteler [martəle] {20} *vt* **1** : to hammer, to pound **2** : to hammer out (words)
martial, -tiale [marsjal] *adj, mpl* **-tiaux** [-sjo] : martial
martinet [martinɛ] *nm* **1** : small whip **2** : swift, martin
martin–pêcheur [martɛ̃pɛʃœr] *nm, pl* **martins–pêcheurs** : kingfisher
martre [martr] *nf* **1** : marten **2** : sable (fur)
martyr[1], **-tyre** [martir] *adj* **1** : martyred **2 enfant martyr** : battered child
martyr[2], **-tyre** *n* : martyr
martyre *nm* **1** : martyrdom **2** : agony, torture <souffrir le martyre : to be in agony>
martyriser [martirize] *vt* **1** : to martyr **2** : to torment, to maltreat
marxisme [marksism] *nm* : Marxism — **marxiste** [marksist] *adj & nmf*
mascara [maskara] *nm* : mascara
mascarade [maskarad] *nf* : masquerade
mascotte [maskɔt] *nf* : mascot
masculin[1], **-line** [maskylɛ̃, -lin] *adj* **1** : male **2** : men's **3** : masculine, manly
masculin[2] *nm* : masculine (in grammar)
masculinité [maskylinite] *nf* : masculinity
maskinongé [maskinɔ̃ʒe] *nm* : muskellunge
masochisme [mazɔʃism] *nm* : masochism
masochiste[1] [mazɔʃist] *adj* : masochistic
masochiste[2] *nmf* : masochist

masque [mask] *nm* : mask <masque à gaz : gas mask> <masque de plongée : diving mask>
masqué, -quée [maske] *adj* **1** : masked **2** : concealed, disguised
masquer [maske] *vt* DISSIMULER : to mask, to conceal, to block from view
massacrant, -crante [masakrɑ̃, -krɑ̃t] *adj* **humeur massacrante** : foul mood
massacre [masakr] *nm* : massacre
massacrer [masakre] *vt* **1** : to massacre, to butcher **2** *fam* BOUSILLER : to botch
massage [masaʒ] *nm* : massage
masse [mas] *nf* **1** : mass, body <masse d'air froide : mass of cold air> <masse d'eau : body of water> **2** : great quantity <la (grande) masse : the majority> <une masse de renseignements : a mass of information> <en masse : en masse, in a body, in bulk> **3** : common people <l'art de masse : popular art> <les masses : the masses, the people> **4** : (electrical) ground <mettre à la masse : to ground> **5** : sledgehammer **6** : mass (in science) **7** *or* **masse d'armes** : mace
massepain [maspɛ̃] *nm* : marzipan
masser [mase] *vt* **1** : to massage **2** : to mass, to gather — **se masser** *vr* : to assemble, to gather together
massette [masɛt] *nf* : cattail
masseur, -seuse [masœr, -søz] *n* : massage therapist, masseur *m*, masseuse *f*
massif[1], **-sive** [masif, -siv] *adj* **1** : massive, solid, heavy <bois massif : solid wood> **2** : mass <migrations massives : mass migrations>
massif[2] *nm* **1** : clump, cluster <un massif d'arbres : a clump of trees> **2** : massif
massivement [masivmɑ̃] *adv* : massively
mass media [masmedja] *nmpl* : mass media
massue [masy] *nf* **1** : club, bludgeon **2** **coup de massue** : staggering blow
mastic [mastik] *nm* **1** : mastic **2** : putty, caulk
mastication [mastikasjɔ̃] *nf* : chewing, mastication
mastiff [mastif] *nm* : mastiff
mastiquer [mastike] *vt* **1** : to chew, to masticate **2** : to fill in, to putty
mastoc [mastɔk] *adj* : hefty
mastodonte [mastɔdɔ̃t] *nm* **1** : mastodon **2** : huge person, hulk
mastoïde [mastɔid] *nf* : mastoid
masturbation [mastyrbasjɔ̃] *nf* : masturbation
masturber [mastyrbe] *v* **se masturber** *vr* : to masturbate
m'as-tu-vu [matyvy] *nmfs & pl* : show-off
masure [mazyr] *nf* : hovel
mat, mate [mat] *adj* **1** : dull, unpolished, matte **2** : checkmated
mât [ma] *nm* **1** : mast **2** POTEAU : pole, post **3** *or* **mât de drapeau** : flagpole
matador [matadɔr] *nm* : matador, bullfighter
matamore [matamɔr] *nm* : braggart
match [matʃ] *nm* **1** : match, game **2** **match nul** : tie, draw
matelas [matla] *nm* : mattress <matelas pneumatique : air mattress> <matelas d'eau : waterbed>
matelasser [matlase] *vt* **1** : to pad **2** : to quilt
matelot [matlo] *nm* MARIN : sailor, seaman
mater [mate] *vt* **1** DOMPTER : to subdue, to curb **2** : to checkmate
matérialiser [materjalize] *vt* CONCRÉTISER : to realize, to make happen — **se matérialiser** *vr* : to materialize
matérialisme [materjalism] *nm* : materialism
matérialiste[1] [materjalist] *adj* : materialistic, materialist
matérialiste[2] *nmf* : materialist
matériau [materjo] *nm, pl* **-riaux** [-rjo] **1** : material, substance **2** **matériaux** *nmpl* : materials (for construction, etc.) **3** **matériaux** *nmpl* : material, documentation
matériel[1], **-rielle** [materjel] *adj* **1** : material, physical **2** : materialistic — **matériellement** [-rjelmɑ̃] *adv*
matériel[2] *nm* **1** : equipment, material(s) <matériel de pêche : fishing gear> **2** : computer hardware
maternel, -nelle [maternel] *adj* **1** : maternal, motherly **2** **langue maternelle** : mother tongue — **maternellement** [-nɛlmɑ̃] *adv*
maternelle *nf or* **école maternelle** [ekɔlmaternɛl] : nursery school
materner [materne] *vt* : to mother
maternité [maternite] *nf* **1** : maternity, motherhood **2** GROSSESSE : pregnancy **3** : maternity hospital
mathématicien, -cienne [matematisjɛ̃, -sjɛn] *n* : mathematician
mathématique [matematik] *adj* : mathematical — **mathématiquement** [-tikmɑ̃] *adv*
mathématiques [matematik] *nfpl* : mathematics
maths *or* **math** [mat] *nfpl fam* : math
matière [matjɛr] *nf* **1** : matter, substance <matière organique : organic matter> **2** : subject, subject matter <ma meilleure matière : my best subject> <matière à discussion : matter for discussion> **3** : material <matières premières : raw materials> **4** **donner matière à** : to give cause for **5** **en matière de** : as far as
matin[1] [matɛ̃] *adv* : early in the morning <elle déjeune très matin : she has breakfast very early>
matin[2] *nm* : morning <le matin : in the morning> <du matin au soir : from dawn to dusk>

matinal, -nale [matinal] *adj, mpl* **-naux** [-no] **1** : morning **2 être matinal** : to be up early, to be an early riser
matinée [matine] *nf* **1** : morning **2** : matinee
matois, -toise [matwa, -twaz] *adj* RUSÉ : sly, crafty
matou [matu] *nm* : tomcat
matraque [matrak] *nf* : (billy) club, nightstick
matraquer [matrake] *vt* **1** : to club, to bludgeon **2** : to plug (a product), to hype **3** *fam* : to rip off
matriarcal, -cale [matrijarkal] *adj, mpl* **-caux** [-ko] : matriarchal
matriarcat [matrijarka] *nm* : matriarchy
matrice [matris] *nf* **1** : womb **2** : matrix, mold
matricide [matrisid] *nm* : matricide
matricule[1] [matrikyl] *nm* : serial number
matricule[2] *nf* : register
matrimonial, -niale [matrimɔnjal] *adj, mpl* **-niaux** [-njo] : matrimonial, marriage
matrone [matrɔn] *nf* **1** : matron, matriarch **2** *Can* : female warden
maturation [matyrasjɔ̃] *nf* : maturing, maturation
mature [matyr] *adj* : mature
mâture [matyr] *nf* : masts *pl*
maturité [matyrite] *nf* : maturity
maudire [modir] *vt* : to curse, to damn
maudit, -dite [modi, -dit] *adj* : damned <cette maudite pluie! : this damned rain!>
maugréer [mogree] {89} *vi* GROGNER : to grumble
mauricien, -cienne [morisjɛ̃, -sjɛn] *adj* : Mauritian
Mauricien, -cienne *n* : Mauritian
mauritanien, -nienne [moritanjɛ̃, -njɛn] *adj* : Mauritanian
Mauritanien, -nienne *n* : Mauritanian
mausolée [mozɔle] *nm* : mausoleum
maussade [mosad] *adj* **1** MOROSE : sullen, morose **2** : dismal, gloomy
maussaderie [mosadri] *nf* : sullenness, moroseness
mauvais[1] [movɛ] *adv* : bad, poorly <il fait mauvais : the weather is bad>
mauvais[2], **-vaise** [movɛ, -vɛz] *adj* **1** : bad <ses mauvaises notes : his bad grades> **2** : wrong <un mauvais numéro : a wrong number> **3** : nasty, unpleasant **4** : rough <la mer est mauvaise : the sea is rough> **5 → herbe 6**
mauvaises rencontres : bad company
mauve [mov] *adj & nm* : mauve
mauviette [movjet] *nf* : weakling
maxillaire [maksiler] *nm* : jawbone
maximal, -male [maksimal] *adj, mpl* **-maux** [-mo] : maximal, maximum
maxime [maksim] *nf* ADAGE : maxim, proverb
maximiser [maksimize] *vt* : to maximize
maximum[1] [maksimɔm] *adj, pl* **-mums** [-mɔm] *or* **-ma** [-ma] : maximum
maximum[2] *nm, pl* **-mums** *or* **-ma 1** : maximum **2 au ~** : as much as possible, at the very most
maya[1] [maja] *adj* : Mayan
maya[2] *nm* : Mayan (language)
Maya *nmf* : Maya
mayonnaise [majɔnɛz] *nf* : mayonnaise
mazout [mazut] *nm* : heating oil
me [mə] *pron* **1 (m'** [m] *before a vowel or mute h*) : me, to me <elles m'ont aidé : they helped me> <il m'apparaît : it seems to me> **2** : myself, to myself <je me disais : I said to myself>
méandres [meɑ̃dr] *nmpl* : meandering, rambling
mec [mɛk] *nm fam* : guy
mécanicien, -cienne [mekanisjɛ̃, -sjɛn] *n* **1** : mechanic **2** : engineer (of a locomotive), flight engineer
mécanique[1] [mekanik] *adj* : mechanical **— mécaniquement** [-nikmɑ̃] *adv*
mécanique[2] *nf* **1** : mechanics **2** : mechanical engineering **3** : machine, mechanism
mécanisation [mekanizasjɔ̃] *nf* : mechanization
mécaniser [mekanize] *vt* : to mechanize
mécanisme [mekanism] *nm* : mechanism
mécano [mekano] *nm fam* : mechanic
mécénat [mesena] *nm* : patronage, sponsorship
mécène [mesɛn] *nm* : patron, sponsor
méchamment [meʃamɑ̃] *adv* : nastily, maliciously
méchanceté [meʃɑ̃ste] *nf* : nastiness, meanness, badness, malice
méchant[1], **-chante** [meʃɑ̃, -ʃɑ̃t] *adj* **1** : nasty, malicious **2** : naughty, bad **3** : vicious <attention chien méchant! : beware of the dog!> **4** : mediocre, second-rate **5** : bad, serious <ce n'est pas bien méchant : that's not too serious> **6** *fam* : remarkable, terrific <quelle méchante idée! : what a fantastic idea!>
méchant[2], **-chante** *n* : villain (in a book or film)
mèche [mɛʃ] *nf* **1** : wick **2** : fuse (of an explosive) **3** : lock (of hair) <mèche rebelle : cowlick> **4** : bit (of a drill)
mécompte [mekɔ̃t] *nm* DÉCEPTION : letdown, disappointment
méconnaissable [mekɔnesabl] *adj* : unrecognizable
méconnaissance [mekɔnesɑ̃s] *nf* : ignorance, lack of understanding
méconnaître [mekɔnɛtr] {7} *vt* **1** IGNORER : to be unaware of **2** MÉJUGER : to misjudge, to underestimate **3** : to disregard (rules, duties, etc.)

méconnu, -nue [mekɔny] *adj* : unrecognized
mécontent, -tente [mekɔ̃tɑ̃, -tɑ̃t] *adj* INSATISFAIT : discontented, dissatisfied
mécontentement [mekɔ̃tɑ̃tmɑ̃] *nm* INSATISFACTION : discontent, dissatisfaction
mécontenter [mekɔ̃tɑ̃te] *vt* : to annoy, to displease
mécréant[1], **-créante** [mekreɑ̃,-kreɑ̃t] *adj* : skeptical, unbelieving
mécréant[2], **-créante** *n* INFIDÈLE : unbeliever
médaille [medaj] *nf* : medal
médaillé, -lée [medaje] *n* : medalist
médaillon [medajɔ̃] *nm* **1** : medallion **2** : locket
médecin [medsɛ̃] *nm* : doctor, physician <médecin généraliste : general practitioner> <médecin légiste : medical examiner>
médecine [medsin] *nf* : medicine <médecine légale : forensic medicine>
média [medja] *nm* : medium <les médias : the (mass) media>
médian, -diane [medjɑ̃, -djan] *adj* : median
médiane *nf* : median (in mathematics)
médiateur, -trice [medjatœr, -tris] *n* : mediator, arbitrator, ombudsman
médiathèque [medjatɛk] *nf* : multimedia library
médiation [medjasjɔ̃] *nf* : mediation, arbitration
médiatique [medjatik] *adj* : media, newsworthy <geste médiatique : publicity stunt>
médiatisation [medjatizasjɔ̃] *nf* : media coverage
médiatiser [medjatize] *vt* : to cover in the media
médical, -cale [medikal] *adj, mpl* **-caux** [-ko] : medical — **médicalement** [-kalmɑ̃] *adv*
médicament [medikamɑ̃] *nm* : medicine, drug
médicamenteux, -teuse [medikamɑ̃tø, -tøz] *adj* : medicinal
médication [medikasjɔ̃] *nf* : medication, treatment
médicinal, -nale [medisinal] *adj, mpl* **-naux** [-no] : medicinal
médico-légal, -gale [medikɔlegal] *adj, mpl* **-gaux** [-go] : forensic
médiéval, -vale [medjeval] *adj, mpl* **-vaux** [-vo] : medieval
médiocre [medjɔkr] *adj* : mediocre, second-rate, ordinary
médiocrité [medjɔkrite] *nf* : mediocrity
médire [medir] {29} *vi* **~ de** : to speak ill of
médisance [medizɑ̃s] *nf* : malicious gossip
médisant, -sante [medizɑ̃, -zɑ̃t] *adj* : slanderous, malicious
méditatif, -tive [meditatif, -tiv] *adj* PENSIF : meditative, thoughtful
méditation [meditasjɔ̃] *nf* : meditation
méditer [medite] *vt* **1** : to reflect on, to think over **2** : to have in mind <méditer un projet : to plan a project> — *vi* : to meditate
médium [medjɔm] *nm* : medium, psychic, spiritualist
méduse [medyz] *nf* : jellyfish
méduser [medyze] *vt* : to dumbfound
meeting [mitiŋ] *nm* **1** : meeting, rally **2** : meet (in sports)
méfait [mefɛ] *nm* **1** : misdeed, misdemeanour **2 méfaits** *nmpl* : ravages (of time, etc.)
méfiance [mefjɑ̃s] *nf* : distrust, suspicion
méfiant, -fiante [mefjɑ̃, -fjɑ̃t] *adj* : distrustful, suspicious
méfier [mefje] {96} *v* **se méfier** *vr* **1** : to be careful, to beware <méfiez-vous dans cette rue : be careful on this street> **2 ~ de** : to distrust, to be wary of
mégahertz [megaɛrts] *nm* : megahertz
mégaoctet [megaɔktɛ] *nm* : megabyte
mégaphone [megafɔn] *nm* PORTE-VOIX : megaphone
mégarde [megard] *nf* **par ~** : inadvertently
mégot [mego] *nm* : cigarette butt
meilleur[1] [mejœr] *adv* : better <il fait meilleur cet hiver : the weather is better this winter>
meilleur[2], **-leure** *adj* **1** (*comparative of* **bon**) : better <le meilleur des deux : the better of the two> **2** (*superlative of* **bon**) : best <le meilleur choix : the best choice> <meilleurs vœux : best wishes> **3 meilleur marché** : cheaper
meilleur[3], **-leure** *n* : best person <que le meilleur gagne : may the best man win>
meilleur[4] *nm* : better part, best bit <pour le meilleur et pour le pire : for better or for worse>
méjuger [meʒyʒe] {17} *vt* : to misjudge — *vi* **~ de** : to underestimate — **se méjuger** *vr* : to underestimate oneself
mél [mel] *nm Bel, France* : e-mail, electronic mail
mélancolie [melɑ̃kɔli] *nf* : melancholy, gloom
mélancolique [melɑ̃kɔlik] *adj* : melancholy, gloomy
mélange [melɑ̃ʒ] *nm* **1** : mixing, blending **2** : mixture, blend
mélanger [melɑ̃ʒe] {17} *vt* **1** : to mix, to blend **2** : to mix up, to confuse — **se mélanger** *vr* : to mix, to intermingle
mélangeur [melɑ̃ʒœr] *nm Can* : blender
mélant, -lante [melɑ̃, -lɑ̃t] *adj Can* : complicated, difficult to understand
mélasse [melas] *nf* : molasses

melé, -lée [mele] *adj Can* **1** : mixed <des sentiments melés : mixed feelings> **2** *Can* : mixed-up, confused
mêlée [mele] *nf* **1** : battle, conflict, fray **2** : commotion, confusion <mêlée générale : free-for-all>
mêler [mele] *vt* : to mix — **se mêler** *vr* **1** : to mix, to mingle **2** : to meddle <mêlez-vous de vos affaires : mind your own business>
mélèze [melɛz] *nm* : larch
méli–mélo [melimelo] *nm, pl* **mélis–mélos** : hodgepodge, muddle
mélodie [melɔdi] *nf* : melody
mélodieux, -dieuse [melɔdjø, -djøz] *adj* : melodious — **mélodieusement** [-djøzmɑ̃] *adv*
mélodique [melɔdik] *adj* : melodic — **mélodiquement** [-dikmɑ̃] *adv*
mélodrame [melɔdram] *nm* : melodrama — **mélodramatique** [-dramatik] *adj*
mélomane [melɔman] *nmf* : music lover
melon [melɔ̃] *nm* **1** : melon <melon d'eau : watermelon> **2** *or* **chapeau melon** : derby (hat)
membrane [mɑ̃bran] *nf* : membrane
membre [mɑ̃br] *nm* **1** : limb, member **2** : member (of a group)
mémé [meme] *nf France fam* : grandma, granny
même[1] [mɛm] *adv* **1** : even <personne n'y va, pas même Robert : nobody's going, not even Robert> <même si : even if, even though> **2 à ~** : directly on, straight from, right against <à même la bouteille : straight from the bottle> **3 de ~** : likewise, the same **4 de même que** : just as **5 tout de même** : even so, nonetheless
même[2] *adj* **1** : same, identical <le même jour : the same day> <en même temps : at the same time> **2** (*used as an intensifier*) : very, actual <ce sont ses paroles mêmes : those were his very words> **3 → elle–même, lui–même, eux–mêmes**
même[3] *pron* **le même, la même, les mêmes** : the same (one, ones)
mémérage [memeraʒ] *nm Can* : gossip
mémère [memɛr] *nf* **1** *fam* : grandma **2** *Can fam* : gossip
mémérer [memere] *vi Can fam* : to gossip
mémoire[1] [memwar] *nm* **1** : dissertation, thesis **2 mémoires** *nmpl* : memoirs
mémoire[2] *nf* **1** : memory <avoir de la mémoire : to have a good memory> <de mémoire : from memory> **2 mémoire vive** : random-access memory, RAM
mémorable [memɔrabl] *adj* : memorable — **mémorablement** [-rabləmɑ̃] *adv*
mémorandum [memɔrɑ̃dɔm] *nm* **1** : (diplomatic) memorandum **2** : note, memo
mémorial [memɔrjal] *nm, pl* **-riaux** [-rjo] : memorial
mémoriser [memɔrize] *vt* **1** : to memorize **2** : to store (data)
menaçant, -çante [mənasɑ̃, -sɑ̃t] *adj* : threatening, menacing, ominous
menace [mənas] *nf* : threat <menaces en l'air : idle threats>
menacer [mənase] {6} *vt* **1** : to threaten **2** : to pose a threat to <être menacé : to be at risk> — *vi* : to threaten <la pluie menace : it looks like rain>
ménage [menaʒ] *nm* **1** : household, family <un ménage de quatre personnes : a household of four people> **2** : married couple <heureux en ménage : happily married> **3** : housework, housekeeping <faire le ménage : to do the housework> **4 faire bon ménage avec** : to get along well with
ménagement [menaʒmɑ̃] *nm* : consideration, thoughtfulness <avec ménagement : gently, tactfully> <sans ménagement : bluntly>
ménager[1] [menaʒe] {17} *vt* **1** ÉPARGNER : to save <ménager son argent : to save one's money> **2** : to use carefully, to handle with care **3** : to treat considerately **4** : to arrange, to organize — **se ménager** *vr* : to take it easy
ménager[2], **-gère** [menaʒe, -ʒɛr] *adj* : household, domestic <travaux ménagers : housework>
ménagère [menaʒɛr] *nf* : housewife
ménagerie [menaʒri] *nf* : menagerie
mendiant, -diante [mɑ̃djɑ̃, -djɑ̃t] *n* : beggar, mendicant
mendicité [mɑ̃disite] *nf* : begging
mendier [mɑ̃dje] {96} *v* : to beg
mené [məne] *nm Can* : minnow
menées [məne] *nfpl* : scheming, intrigues
mener [məne] {52} *vt* **1** EMMENER : to take, to bring <mener promener un chien : to take a dog for a walk> **2** : to lead, to be at the head of **3** DIRIGER : to conduct, to run **4** : to carry out <mener à bien : to complete successfully, to see (something) through>
ménestrel [menɛstrɛl] *nm* : minstrel
meneur, -neuse [mənœr, -nøz] *n* **1** : leader <un meneur d'hommes : a born leader> **2** : ringleader **3 meneuse de claque** *Can* : cheerleader
méninges [menɛ̃ʒ] *nfpl fam* : brains <se creuser les méninges : to rack one's brains>
méningite [menɛ̃ʒit] *nf* : meningitis
ménopause [menɔpoz] *nf* : menopause
menotte [mənɔt] *nf* **1** : little hand **2 menottes** *nfpl* : handcuffs <passer les menottes à qqn : to handcuff s.o.>

mensonge [mɑ̃sɔ̃ʒ] *nm* **1** : lie **2 le mensonge** : lying
mensonger, -gère [mɑ̃sɔ̃ʒe, -ʒɛr] *adj* **1** FAUX : false **2** TROMPEUR : misleading
menstruation [mɑ̃stryasjɔ̃] *nf* RÈGLES : menstruation, period
menstruel, -struelle [mɑ̃stryɛl] *adj* : menstrual
mensualité [mɑ̃sɥalite] *nf* : monthly payment
mensuel[1], **-suelle** [mɑ̃sɥɛl] *adj* : monthly — **mensuellement** [-sɥɛlmɑ] *adv*
mensuel[2] *nm* : monthly (magazine)
mensurations [mɑ̃syrasjɔ̃] *nfpl* : measurements
mental, -tale [mɑ̃tal] *adj, mpl* **mentaux** [-to] : mental — **mentalement** [-talmɑ̃] *adv*
mentalité [mɑ̃talite] *nf* : mentality
menterie [mɑ̃tri] *nf Can fam* : lie, fib
menteur[1], **-teuse** [mɑ̃tœr, -tøz] *adj* : untruthful, false
menteur[2], **-teuse** *n* : liar
menthe [mɑ̃t] *nf* **1** : mint **2 menthe poivrée** : peppermint **3 menthe verte** : spearmint
menthol [mɑ̃tɔl] *nm* : menthol
mentholé, -lée [mɑ̃tɔle] *adj* : mentholated
mention [mɑ̃sjɔ̃] *nf* **1** : mention <faire mention de : to mention> **2** : note, comment <porter la mention «secret» : to be labeled "secret">
mentionner [mɑ̃sjɔne] *vt* : to mention
mentir [mɑ̃tir] {82} *vi* : to lie
menton [mɑ̃tɔ̃] *nm* : chin
menu[1] [məny] *adv* : finely, small <oignons coupés menu : finely chopped onions>
menu[2], **-nue** *adj* **1** PETIT : small, tiny, slender **2** : minor, trifling
menu[3] [məny] *nm* **1** : menu **2 par le menu** : in minute detail
menuet [mənɥɛ] *nm* : minuet
menuiserie [mənɥizri] *nf* : woodworking, carpentry
menuisier [mənɥizje] *nm* : woodworker, carpenter
méprendre [meprɑ̃dr] {70} *v* **se méprendre** *vr* ~ **sur** : to be mistaken about
mépris [mepri] *nm* **1** DÉDAIN : contempt, scorn **2 au mépris de** : regardless of, in defiance of
méprisable [meprizabl] *adj* VIL : despicable, contemptible
méprisant, -sante [meprizɑ̃, -zɑ̃t] *adj* : contemptuous, scornful
méprise [mepriz] *nf* **1** ERREUR : mistake, error **2** MALENTENDU : misunderstanding
mépriser [meprize] *vt* : to despise, to scorn
mer [mɛr] *nf* **1** : sea <en mer : at sea> <niveau de la mer : sea level> <prendre la mer : to put to sea> **2** MARÉE : tide <mer haute : high tide> <mer basse : low tide>
mercantile [mɛrkɑ̃til] *adj* **1** : mercenary, greedy **2** : mercantile, commercial
mercenaire [mɛrsənɛr] *adj & nmf* : mercenary
mercerie [mɛrsəri] *nf* **1** : notions *pl* **2** : notions store
merci[1] [mɛrsi] *nm* : thank-you <mille mercis : thank you so much>
merci[2] *nf* **1** : mercy <à la merci de : at the mercy of> **2 sans** ~ : merciless
merci[3] *interj* : thank you!, thanks! <merci beaucoup! *or* merci bien! : thank you very much!>
mercredi [mɛrkrədi] *nm* **1** : Wednesday **2 le mercredi des Cendres** : Ash Wednesday
mercure [mɛrkyr] *nm* : mercury
Mercure *nf* : Mercury (planet)
mère [mɛr] *nf* **1** : mother <mère célibataire : single mother> **2** : Mother (in religion)
méridien [meridjɛ̃] *nm* : meridian
méridional, -nale [meridjɔnal] *adj, mpl* **-naux** [-no] : southern
meringue [mərɛ̃g] *nf* : meringue
mérinos [merinos] *nm* : merino
merise [məriz] *nf* : wild cherry
méritant, -tante [meritɑ̃, -tɑ̃t] *adj* : deserving, meritorious
mérite [merit] *nm* **1** : merit, credit <le mérite lui revient : the credit goes to him> **2** VALEUR : merit, quality <ce film a ses mérites : this film has its merits>
mériter [merite] *vt* : to deserve, to merit
méritoire [meritwar] *adj* : commendable, praiseworthy
merlan [mɛrlɑ̃] *nm* : whiting
merle [mɛrl] *nm* : blackbird
merlu *or* **merlus** [mɛrly] *nm* : hake
mérou [meru] *nm* : grouper (fish)
merveille [mɛrvɛj] *nf* **1** : wonder, marvel **2 à** ~ : wonderfully, excellently
merveilleux, -leuse [mɛrvɛjø, -jøz] *adj* : wonderful, marvelous — **merveilleusement** [-jøzmɑ̃] *adv*
mes → mon
mésange [mezɑ̃ʒ] *nf* : titmouse
mésaventure [mezavɑ̃tyr] *nf* : misfortune, mishap
mesdames → madame
mesdemoiselles → mademoiselle
mésentente [mezɑ̃tɑ̃t] *nf* DÉSACCORD : misunderstanding, disagreement
mésestimer [mezestime] *vt* SOUS-ESTIMER : to underestimate, to underrate
mesquin, -quine [mɛskɛ̃, -kin] *adj* **1** : mean, petty **2** : cheap, stingy — **mesquinement** [-kinmɑ̃] *adv*
mesquinerie [mɛskinri] *nf* **1** PETITESSE : pettiness **2** AVARICE : meanness, stinginess
mess [mɛs] *nm* : mess

message [mɛsaʒ] *nm* **1** : message **2 message publicitaire** : commercial
messager, -gère [mɛsaʒe, -ʒɛr] *n* : messenger
messagerie [mɛsaʒri] *nf* **1** : parcel delivery service **2 messagerie électronique** : electronic mail
messe [mɛs] *nf* : Mass (in religion)
messeigneurs [mɛseɲœr] → **monseigneur**
messie [mɛsi] *nm* **le Messie** : the Messiah
messieurs → **monsieur**
mesurable [məzyrabl] *adj* : measurable
mesurage [məzyraʒ] *nm* : measuring, measurement
mesure [məzyr] *nf* **1** : measurement, measuring **2** : measure <unité de mesure : unit of measure> <pour faire bonne mesure : for good measure> **3** : measure, step <mesures draconiennes : drastic measures> **4** RETENUE : moderation, restraint **5** : degree, limit <dans la mesure où : insofar as> **6 à la mesure de** : worthy of **7 à mesure que** : as **8 outre ~** : excessively **9 sur ~** : made-to-order
mesuré, -rée [məzyre] *adj* : measured, restrained
mesurer [məzyre] *vt* **1** : to measure, to take measurements of **2** : to weigh, to assess <mesurer ses paroles : to measure one's words> **3** : to limit <le temps lui est mesuré : his time is limited> **4** : to adapt, to gear **— se mesurer** *vr* **1** : to be measurable **2 ~ avec** : to pit oneself against
métabolique [metabɔlik] *adj* : metabolic
métabolíser [metabɔlize] *vt* : to metabolize
métabolisme [metabɔlism] *nm* : metabolism
métal [metal] *nm, pl* **métaux** [meto] : metal
métallique [metalik] *adj* : metallic
métallurgie [metalyrʒi] *nf* : metallurgy
métallurgique [metalyrʒik] *adj* : metallurgical
métallurgiste [metalyrʒist] *nm* : metallurgist, metalworker
métamorphose [metamɔrfoz] *nf* : metamorphosis
métaphore [metafɔr] *nf* : metaphor
métaphorique [metafɔrik] *adj* : metaphoric, metaphorical **— métaphoriquement** [-rikmɑ̃] *adv*
métaphysique[1] [metafizik] *adj* : metaphysical
métaphysique[2] *nf* : metaphysics
métayer, -tayère [meteje, -tejɛr] *n* : sharecropper
météo [meteo] *nf* : weather forecast
météore [meteɔr] *nm* : meteor
météorique [meteɔrik] *adj* : meteoric
météorite [meteɔrit] *nmf* : meteorite
météorologie [meteɔrɔlɔʒi] *nf* : meteorology
météorologique [meteɔrɔlɔʒik] *adj* : meteorological, weather <prévisions météorologiques : weather forecast>
météorologiste [meteɔrɔlɔʒist] *nmf* : meteorologist
méthane [metan] *nm* : methane
méthode [metɔd] *nf* **1** : method, system, way <avec méthode : methodically> **2** : manual, primer
méthodique [metɔdik] *adj* : methodical **— méthodiquement** [-dikmɑ̃] *adv*
méticuleux, -leuse [metikylø, -løz] *adj* : meticulous **— méticuleusement** [-løzmɑ̃] *adv*
métier [metje] *nm* **1** : job, profession, occupation <gens du métier : professionals, experts> **2** : experience, skill <manquer de métier : to lack experience> **3** *or* **métier à tisser** : loom
métis, -tisse [metis] *adj & n* : half-breed, half-caste
métrage [metraʒ] *nm* **1** : length (of an object) **2** : footage, length (of a film) <court métrage : short film> <long métrage : feature film>
mètre [mɛtr] *nm* **1** : meter <mètre carré : square meter> **2** : metric ruler <mètre ruban : tape measure>
métrer [metre] {87} *vt* : to measure (in meters)
métrique [metrik] *adj* : metric
métro [metro] *nm* : subway, metro
métronome [metrɔnɔm] *nm* : metronome
métropole [metrɔpɔl] *nf* : city, metropolis
métropolitain, -taine [metrɔpɔlitɛ̃, -tɛn] *adj* : metropolitan
mets [mɛ] *nm* PLAT : dish <c'est mon mets préféré : it's my favorite dish>
mettable [metabl] *adj* PORTABLE : wearable
metteur [metœr] *nm* **metteur en scène** : producer, director
mettre [mɛtr] {53} *vt* **1** PLACER : to put, to place <mets la plante par terre : put the plant on the floor> **2** : to put on, to wear <mets tes chaussures : put your shoes on> <elle met des jupes longues : she wears long skirts> **3** AJOUTER : to add (in), to put in **4** ÉCRIRE : to put down, to put in writing **5** INSTALLER : to put in, to install **6** : to prepare, to arrange <mettre la table : to set the table> **7** : to take (time) <elle a mis trois heures à le considérer : she took three hours to consider it> **8** : to turn on, to switch on **9** *fam* : to suppose <mettons qu'il n'était pas content : let's say he wasn't very happy> **10 mettre à la poste** : to mail **11 mettre au monde** : to give birth to **12 mettre au point** : to develop **— se mettre** *vr* **1** : to become, to get <il s'est mis en colère : he got angry> **2** : to put on, to wear <je n'ai

rien à me mettre : I have nothing to wear> **3 ~ à** : to start (doing something) <se mettre au travail : to get to work> **4 se mettre à table** : to sit down at the table

meuble[1] [mœbl] *adj* **1** : easily worked, friable **2 biens meubles** : movable goods, personal assets

meuble[2] *nm* **1** : piece of furniture **2 meubles** *nmpl* : furniture <meubles de bureau : office furniture>

meublé, -blée [mœble] *adj* : furnished

meubler [mœble] *vt* **1** : to furnish **2** REMPLIR : to occupy, to fill up <il meuble bien son temps : he fills up his time well> **— se meubler** *vr* : to acquire furniture, to furnish one's home

meuglement [møgləmɑ̃] *nm* : mooing, lowing

meugler [møgle] *vi* : to moo, to low

meule [møl] *nf* **1** : millstone, grindstone **2** : round (of cheese) **3 meule de foin** : haystack

meuler [møle] *vt* : to grind down

meunier, -nière [mønje, -njɛr] *n* : miller

meure [mœr], **meurt** [mœr], *etc.* → **mourir**

meurtre [mœrtr] *nm* : murder

meurtrier[1], **-trière** [mœrtrije, -trijɛr] *adj* **1** : deadly, lethal **2** : murderous, dangerous

meurtrier[2], **-trière** *n* ASSASSIN : murderer, murderess *f*

meurtrir [mœrtrir] *vt* **1** : to bruise **2** BLESSER : to wound, to hurt (one's feelings, etc.)

meurtrissure [mœrtrisyr] *nf* : bruise

meut [mœ], **meuve** [møv], *etc.* → **mouvoir**

meute [møt] *nf* **1** : pack (of hounds) **2** : horde, crowd

mévente [mevɑ̃t] *nf* : slump, drop (in sales)

mexicain, -caine [meksikɛ̃, -kɛn] *adj* : Mexican

Mexicain, -caine *n* : Mexican

mezzanine [mɛdzanin] *nf* : mezzanine

miaou [mjau] *nm* : meow

miasme [mjasm] *nm* : miasma

miauler [mjole] *vi* : to meow

mi–bas [miba] *nms & pl* : kneesock

mica [mika] *nm* : mica

miche [miʃ] *nf* : round loaf of bread

mi–chemin [miʃmɛ̃] *adv* **à ~** : halfway, midway

mi–clos, -close [miklo, -kloz] *adj* : half-closed

mi–côte [mikot] *adv* **à ~** : halfway up (or down)

micro [mikro] *nm* : mike, microphone

microbe [mikrɔb] *nm* : germ, microbe

microbiologie [mikrɔbjɔlɔʒi] *nf* : microbiology

microcosme [mikrɔkɔsm] *nm* : microcosm

microfiche [mikrɔfiʃ] *nf* : microfiche

microfilm [mikrɔfilm] *nm* : microfilm

micromètre [mikrɔmɛtr] *nm* : micrometer

micro–onde [mikrɔɔ̃d] *nf* : microwave

micro–ondes [mikrɔɔ̃d] *nms & pl* : microwave oven

micro–ordinateur [mikrɔɔrdinatœr] *nm* : microcomputer

micro–organisme [mikrɔɔrganism] *nm* : microorganism

microphone [mikrɔfɔn] *nm* : microphone

microprocesseur [mikrɔprɔsesœr] *nm* : microprocessor

microscope [mikrɔskɔp] *nm* : microscope

microscopie [mikrɔskɔpi] *nf* : microscopy

microscopique [mikrɔskɔpik] *adj* : microscopic

microsillon [mikrɔsijɔ̃] *nm* : long-playing record, LP

midi [midi] *nm* **1** : midday, noon **2** : lunchtime **3** : south

mie [mi] *nf* : inside, soft part (of a loaf of bread)

miel [mjɛl] *nm* : honey

mielleux, -leuse [mjelø, -løz] *adj* DOUCEREUX : sugary, saccharine

mien,[1] **mienne** [mjɛ̃, mjɛn] *adj* : mine, my own <cette devise, que j'ai faite mienne : this motto that I have adopted> <une mienne amie : a friend of mine>

mien,[2] **mienne** *pron* **1 le mien, la mienne, les miens, les miennes** : mine <ce n'est pas le mien : it's not mine> **2 les miens** : my family

miette [mjɛt] *nf* **1** : crumb **2** : bit, scrap <en miettes : in pieces>

mieux[1] [mjø] *adv* **1** (*comparative of* **bien**) : better <il va mieux : he's feeling better> **2 le mieux, la mieux, les mieux** (*superlative of* **bien**) : the best <le mieux payé : the best paid> <c'est ici que je travaille le mieux : here's where I work best> **3 être mieux de** *Can* : to be better off to <vous seriez mieux de partir : it would be in your best interest to leave>

mieux[2] *adj* **1** (*comparative of* **bien**) : better <ses notes sont mieux cette année : her grades are better this year> **2 le mieux, la mieux, les mieux** (*superlative of* **bien**) : the best <le mieux de la ville : the best in town>

mieux[3] *nm* **1** : best <faire de son mieux : to do one's best> <pour le mieux : for the best> **2** : improvement <il y a du mieux : there's some improvement>

mieux–être [mjøzɛtr] *nm* : improved state, better quality of life

mièvre [mjɛvr] *adj* **1** : insipid **2** : mawkish, soppy

mièvrerie [mjɛvrəri] *nf* : sentimentality, mush

mignon, -gnonne [miɲɔ̃, -ɲɔn] *adj* **1** : sweet, cute **2** GENTIL : nice, kind

migraine [migrɛn] *nf* : headache, migraine
migrant, -grante [migrɑ̃, -grɑ̃t] *adj & n* : migrant
migrateur, -trice [migratœr, -tris] *adj* : migratory <oiseaux migrateurs : migratory birds>
migration [migrasjɔ̃] *nf* : migration
migrer [migre] *vi* : to migrate
mijoter [miʒɔte] *vt* **1** : to simmer **2** MANIGANCER : to plot, to cook up — *vi* : to simmer, to stew
mil [mil] → **mille**
milan [milɑ̃] *nm* : kite (bird)
mildiou [mildju] *nm* : mildew
mile [majl] *nm* MILLE : mile
milice [milis] *nf* : militia
milicien, -cienne [milisjɛ̃, -sjɛn] *n* : militiaman *m*, member of a militia
milieu [miljø] *nm, pl* **milieux** **1** : middle <au beau milieu de la table : right in the middle of the table> <le milieu du jour : midday, noon> **2** : middle ground <un juste milieu : a happy medium> **3** : milieu, environment **4** **au milieu de** : among, in the midst of **5** **le milieu** : the underworld
militaire[1] [militɛr] *adj* : military — **militairement** [-tɛrmɑ̃] *adv*
militaire[2] *nm* SOLDAT : soldier, serviceman
militant,[1] **-tante** [militɑ̃, -tɑ̃t] *adj* : militant
militant,[2] **-tante** *n* : militant, activist
militarisme [militarism] *nm* : militarism
militariste [militarist] *adj* : militaristic
millage [milaʒ] *nm Can* : mileage (of a motor vehicle)
mille[1] [mil] *adj* : a thousand, one thousand <mille lumières : a thousand lights>
mille[2] *nm* **1** : mile **2** **mille marin** : (nautical) knot
mille[3] *nms & pl* **1** : a thousand, one thousand **2** : bull's eye <taper dans le mille : to hit the bull's eye>
millénaire[1] [milenɛr] *adj* **1** : thousand-year-old **2** : age-old, ancient
millénaire[2] *nm* : millennium
mille-pattes [milpat] *nms & pl* **1** : centipede **2** : millipede
millésime [milezim] *nm* **1** : year of manufacture **2** : vintage year
millésimé, -mée [milezime] *adj* : vintage
millet [mijɛ] *nm* : millet
milliard [miljar] *nm* : billion
milliardaire [miljardɛr] *nmf* : billionaire
millième [miljɛm] *adj & nmf & nm* : thousandth
millier [milje] *nm* : thousand <par milliers : by the thousands>
milligramme [miligram] *nm* : milligram
millilitre [mililitr] *nm* : milliliter
millimètre [milimɛtr] *nm* : millimeter
million [miljɔ̃] *nm* : million
millionième [miljɔnjɛm] *adj & nmf & nm* : millionth
millionnaire [miljɔnɛr] *nmf* : millionaire
mime[1] [mim] *nmf* : mime (performer)
mime[2] *nm* : mime, miming
mimer [mime] *vt* **1** : to mime **2** : to mimic
mimétisme [mimetism] *nm* : mimicry (in biology)
mimique [mimik] *nf* **1** GRIMACE : facial expression, (funny) face **2** : gesticulations *pl*, sign language
minable [minabl] *adj* **1** MISÉRABLE : shabby, miserable **2** *fam* : pitiful, pathetic, measly <un film minable : a third-rate movie>
minaret [minarɛ] *nm* : minaret
minauder [minode] *vi* : to simper, to mince
mince [mɛ̃s] *adj* **1** : thin **2** : slim, slender **3** NÉGLIGEABLE : meager, scanty
minceur [mɛ̃sœr] *nf* : thinness, slenderness
mine [min] *nf* **1** : expression, appearance, demeanor <il avait bonne mine : he looked well> <je faisais mine de rien : I was acting as if nothing had happened> **2** : mine <mine de houille : coal mine> **3** : lead, graphite
miner [mine] *vt* **1** : to mine, to set mines in **2** : to erode, to eat away at **3** : to undermine
minerai [minrɛ] *nm* : ore
minéral[1], **-rale** [mineral] *adj, mpl* **-raux** [-ro] : mineral
minéral[2] *nm* : mineral
minéralogie [mineralɔʒi] *nf* : mineralogy — **minéralogiste** [-lɔʒist] *nmf*
minéralogique [mineralɔʒik] *adj* : mineralogical
minet, -nette [minɛ, -nɛt] *n* : kitty, pussy
mineur[1], **-neure** [minœr] *adj* : minor
mineur[2], **-neure** *nmf* : minor, underage person
mineur[3] *nm* : miner
miniature [minjatyr] *adj & nf* : miniature
minibus [minibys] *nm* : minibus
minier, -nière [minje, -njɛr] *adj* : mining
minijupe [miniʒyp] *nf* : miniskirt
minimal, -male [minimal] *adj, mpl* **-maux** [-mo] : minimal, minimum
minime [minim] *adj* : minimal, negligible, trifling
minimiser [minimize] *vt* : to minimize, to play down
minimum[1] [minimɔm] *adj, pl* **-mums** [-mɔm] *or* **-ma** [-ma] : minimum
minimum[2] *nm, pl* **-mums** *or* **-ma** **1** : minimum <au minimum : at the least> **2** **minimum vital** : living wage
mini-ordinateur [miniɔrdinatœr] *nm* : minicomputer

ministère [ministɛr] *nm* **1** : ministry, department (of government) <ministère des Relations extérieures : State Department> **2** : government, cabinet
ministériel, -rielle [ministerjɛl] *adj* : ministerial, governmental
ministre [ministr] *nm* : minister, secretary <premier ministre : prime minister> <le ministre du Commerce : the Secretary of Commerce>
minois [minwa] *nms & pl* : sweet little face
minoritaire [minɔriter] *adj* : minority
minorité [minɔrite] *nf* : minority
minoterie [minɔtri] *nf* : flour mill
minotier [minɔtje] *nm* MEUNIER : miller
minou [minu] *nm fam* **1** : kitty, pussy **2** : honey, sweetie
minoucher [minuʃe] *vt Can fam* : to caress, to pat
minoune [minun] *nf Can fam* **1** : (female) kitty **2** : honey, sweetie
minuit [minɥi] *nm* : midnight
minuscule[1] [minyskyl] *adj* : minute, tiny
minuscule[2] *nf* : small (lowercase) letter
minutage [minytaʒ] *nm* : timing
minute [minyt] *nf* **1** : minute **2 minute!** *fam* : just a minute!, hang on!
minuter [minyte] *vt* : to time
minuteur [minytœr] *nm* : timer
minuterie [minytri] *nf* : timer
minutie [minysi] *nf* : meticulousness <avec minutie : meticulously>
minutieux, -tieuse [minysjø, -sjøz] *adj* **1** MÉTICULEUX : meticulous **2** : detailed <travail minutieux : detailed work> **— minutieusement** [-sjøzmɑ̃] *adv*
miracle [mirakl] *nm* : miracle <par miracle : miraculously>
miraculeux, -leuse [mirakylø, -løz] *adj* : miraculous **— miraculeusement** [-løzmɑ̃] *adv*
mirador [miradɔr] *nm* : watchtower
mirage [miraʒ] *nm* : mirage
mire [mir] *nf* **1** : sight <ligne de mire : line of sight> **2 point de mire** : target, focal point <être le point de mire : to be the focus of attention>
mirifique [mirifik] *adj* : amazing, fabulous
mirobolant, -lante [mirɔbɔlɑ̃, -lɑ̃t] *adj fam* : fabulous, fantastic
miroir [mirwar] *nm* : mirror
miroitement [mirwatmɑ̃] *nm* : sparkling, shimmering
miroiter [mirwate] *vi* **1** BRILLER : to sparkle, to shimmer, to glint **2 faire miroiter** : to paint in glowing colors
mis[1] [mi] *pp* → **mettre**
mis[2], **mise** [mi, miz] *adj* : clad <bien mis : well dressed>
misanthrope[1] [mizɑ̃trɔp] *adj* : misanthropic
misanthrope[2] *nmf* : misanthrope
misanthropie [mizɑ̃trɔpi] *nf* : misanthropy
mise [miz] *nf* **1** : putting, placing <mise en marche : starting up> <mise en scène : production (in theater)> <mise à jour : updating> **2** : stake (in games of chance) **3** : dress, attire **4 mise de fonds** : investment
miser [mize] *vt* : to bet **— *vi* 1 ~ sur** : to bet on **2 ~ sur** : to count on
misérable[1] [mizerabl] *adj* **1** PITOYABLE : wretched, pitiful **2** INSIGNIFIANT : meager, paltry **3** PAUVRE : poverty-stricken
misérable[2] *nmf* **1** : wretch, pauper **2** : scoundrel
misérablement [mizerabləmɑ̃] *adv* **1** : miserably, wretchedly **2** : in poverty
misère [mizɛr] *nf* **1** : poverty, destitution **2** : misery, misfortune **3** : pittance, paltry sum
miséreux, -reuse [mizerø, -røz] *adj* : destitute, poverty-stricken
miséricorde [mizerikɔrd] *nf* : mercy, forgiveness
miséricordieux, -dieuse [mizerikɔrdjø, -djøz] *adj* : merciful, forgiving
misogyne [mizɔʒin] *nmf* : misogynist
missel [misɛl] *nm* : missal
missile [misil] *nm* : missile
mission [misjɔ̃] *nf* : mission
missionnaire [misjɔnɛr] *adj & nmf* : missionary
missive [misiv] *nf* : missive, letter
mitaine [mitɛn] *nf Can, Swiss* : mitten
mite [mit] *nf* : clothes moth
mi–temps[1] [mitɑ̃] *nms & pl* : part-time job <travailler à mi-temps : to work part-time>
mi–temps[2] *nfs & pl* : halftime (in sports)
miteux, -teuse [mitø, -tøz] *adj* : seedy, dingy, shabby
mitigation [mitigasjɔ̃] *nf* : mitigation
mitigé, -gée [mitiʒe] *adj* **1** : lukewarm, reserved **2** : mixed <sentiments mitigés : mixed feelings>
mitonner [mitɔne] *vt* **1** : to cook slowly, to simmer **2** : to prepare lovingly **— se mitonner** *vr* : to cook up for oneself
mitose [mitoz] *nf* : mitosis
mitoyen, mitoyenne [mitwajɛ̃, -jɛn] *adj* : common, dividing <mur mitoyen : dividing wall>
mitraille [mitraj] *nf* : hail of bullets
mitrailler [mitraje] *vt* : to machine-gun
mitraillette [mitrajɛt] *nf* : submachine gun
mitrailleuse [mitrajøz] *nf* : machine gun
mitre [mitr] *nf* : miter
mi–voix [mivwa] *nf* **à ~** : in a low voice
mixage [miksaʒ] *nm* : sound mixing
mixer [miksɛr] *or* **mixeur** [miksœr] *nm* : (food) mixer

mixette [miksɛt] *nf Can* : (small) mixer
mixité [miksite] *nf* : coeducation
mixte [mikst] *adj* **1** : mixed, joint **2** : coeducational
mixture [mikstyr] *nf* **1** : mixture **2** : concoction
mnémotechnique [mnemɔtɛknik] *adj* : mnemonic
mobile[1] [mɔbil] *adj* **1** : movable, removable <feuilles mobiles : loose-leaf paper> **2** : changeable <échelle mobile : sliding scale> **3** : mobile, moving (of populations, etc.) **4** : mobile, changing <un visage mobile : mobile features>
mobile[2] *nm* **1** : motive **2** : mobile
mobilier[1], **-lière** [mɔbilje, -ljɛr] *adj* **1** : movable <biens mobiliers : movable property> **2 valeurs mobilières** : securities, stocks and bonds
mobilier[2] *nm* MEUBLES : furniture
mobilisation [mɔbilizasjɔ̃] *nf* : mobilization
mobiliser [mɔbilize] *vt* : to mobilize
mobilité [mɔbilite] *nf* : mobility
mocassin [mɔkasɛ̃] *nm* : moccasin
moche [mɔʃ] *adj fam* **1** : ugly, awful **2** : rotten, despicable
modalité [mɔdalite] *nf* : form, mode <modalités de paiement : terms of payment>
mode[1] [mɔd] *nm* **1** : way, mode, method <mode de vie : way of life> <mode d'emploi : directions for use> **2** : mood (in grammar) **3** : mode (in computer science, music, philosophy)
mode[2] [mɔd] *nf* **1** : fashion <jupe à la mode : fashionable skirt> **2** : fashion industry
modèle[1] [mɔdɛl] *adj* : model, exemplary
modèle[2] *nm* **1** : model, pattern, example <prendre modèle sur : to take as a model> <servir de modèle : to serve as an example> <un modèle du bon élève : a model student> **2** : model, prototype <modèle réduit : small-scale model> **3** : (artist's) model, subject, sitter **4** : model, mannequin (in fashion) **5** : model (in commerce) <le dernier modèle : the latest model>
modeler [mɔdle] {20} *vt* **1** : to mold **2** : to model, to shape — **se modeler** *vr* **~ sur** : to model oneself on
modéliste [mɔdelist] *nmf* **1** : (clothing) designer **2** : model maker
modem [mɔdɛm] *nm* : modem
modérateur[1], **-trice** [mɔderatœr, -tris] *adj* : moderating, restraining
modérateur[2], **-trice** *n* : moderator, mediator
modération [mɔderasjɔ̃] *nf* MESURE : moderation, restraint
modéré, -rée [mɔdere] *adj* : moderate — **modérément** [-remɑ̃] *adv*
modérer [mɔdere] {87} *vt* : to moderate, to restrain, to curb — **se modérer** *vr* : to restrain oneself
moderne[1] [mɔdɛrn] *adj* : modern
moderne[2] *nm* : modern style
moderniser [mɔdernize] *vt* : to modernize — **modernisation** [-nizasjɔ̃] *nf*
modernité [mɔdernite] *nf* : modernity
modeste [mɔdɛst] *adj* **1** HUMBLE : modest, humble, simple <d'origine modeste : of humble origin> **2** MODIQUE : modest, small <un modeste salaire : a modest salary> **3** : modest, unpretentious, unassuming — **modestement** [-dɛstəmɑ̃] *adv*
modestie [mɔdɛsti] *nf* : modesty
modificateur [mɔdifikatœr, -tris] *nm* : modifier
modification [mɔdifikasjɔ̃] *nf* : modification
modifier [mɔdifje] {96} *vt* **1** : to modify, to alter **2** : to modify (in grammar) — **se modifier** *vr* : to change
modique [mɔdik] *adj* : modest <une somme modique : a modest sum> — **modiquement** [-dikmɑ̃] *adv*
modiste [mɔdist] *nmf* : milliner
modulaire [mɔdylɛr] *adj* : modular
modulation [mɔdylasjɔ̃] *nf* : modulation <modulation de fréquence : frequency modulation, FM>
module [mɔdyl] *nm* : module
moduler [mɔdyle] *vt* : to modulate
moelle [mwal] *nf* **1** : marrow (of bone), pith (of plants) **2 jusqu'à la moelle** : to the core **3 moelle épinière** : spinal cord
moelleux[1], **-leuse** [mwalø, -løz] *adj* **1** DOUX : soft <coussins moelleux : soft cushions> **2** : moist <gateau moelleux : moist cake> **3** : mellow, smooth
moelleux[2] *nm* : softness, mellowness
mœurs [mœr(s)] *nfpl* **1** CONDUITE : manners, morals **2** USAGES : customs, habits <c'est entré dans les mœurs : it's common practice> **3** : behavior (in zoology)
mohair [mɔɛr] *nm* : mohair
moi[1] [mwa] *nm* **le moi** : the self, the ego
moi[2] *pron* **1** : I <elle a depensé plus que moi : she spent more than I did> **2** : me <aide-moi : help me> <plus jeune que moi : younger than me> <moi, j'aime les chats : as for me, I like cats> **3 à ~** : mine <c'est à moi : it's mine> <c'est à moi de jouer : it's my turn to play>
moignon [mwaɲɔ̃] *nm* : stump (of a limb)
moi-même [mwamɛm] *pron* : myself
moindre [mwɛ̃dr] *adj* **1** : lesser, smaller, lower <à un moindre degré : to a lesser degree> **2 le moindre, la moindre** : the lesser, the least, the slightest <le moindre de deux maux : the lesser of two evils> <sans la moindre

hésitation : without a moment's hesitation>

moindrement [mwɛ̃drəmɑ̃] *adv Can* : <s'ils sont le moindrement intéressés : if they are the least bit interested>

moine [mwan] *nm* : monk

moineau [mwano] *nm, pl* **moineaux** : sparrow

moins[1] [mwɛ̃] *adv* **1** : less <moins grand que son frère : less tall than his brother> <moins je travaille, moins j'ai envie de travailler : the less I work, the less I feel like working> <de moins en moins : less and less> **2 le moins** : least, the least <le moins souvent : least often> <il est le moins fort : he's the least strong, he's the weakest (one)> **3 ~ de** : less than, fewer <moins de gens : fewer people> <pas moins de : no less than> **4 à moins de** : short of, barring **5 à moins que** : unless **6 en ~** : missing <une dent en moins : a missing tooth>

moins[2] *nm* **1** : minus (sign) **2 au ~** *or* **du ~** : at (the) least **3 pour le moins** *or* **tout le moins** : at (the very) least

moins[3] *prep* **1** : minus <sept moins deux font cinq : seven minus two equals five> **2** (*in expressions of time*) : to, of <il est cinq heures moins dix : it's ten to five> **3** (*in expressions of temperature*) : below <il fait moins cinq : it's five below zero, it's minus five>

mois [mwa] *nm* **1** : month **2** *France* : monthly salary **3** *Can* : monthly payment

moisi[1], **-sie** [mwazi] *adj* : moldy

moisi[2] *nm* : mold, mildew

moisir [mwazir] *vi* **1** : to become moldy, to mildew **2** *fam* : to stagnate, to rot <moisir en prison : to rot in jail>

moisissure [mwazisyr] *nf* : mold, mildew

moisson [mwasɔ̃] *nf* **1** : harvest, crop **2** : abundance <une moisson de renseignements : a wealth of information>

moissonner [mwasɔne] *vt* : to harvest, to reap

moissonneuse [mwasɔnøz] *nf* : harvester (machine)

moissonneuse–batteuse [mwasɔnøzbatøz] *nf, pl* **moissonneuses–batteuses** : combine (harvester)

moite [mwat] *adj* **1** : sweaty, sticky **2** : muggy

moitié [mwatje] *nf* **1** : half <la moitié du temps : half the time> <réduire de moitié : to reduce by half> **2 à ~** : half <à moitié rempli : half full> <faire à moitié : to do half-heartedly>

moitié–moitié *adv* : fifty-fifty

moka [moka] *nm* : mocha

molaire [mɔlɛr] *nf* : molar

moldave [mɔldav] *adj* : Moldavian

Moldave *nmf* : Moldavian

moléculaire [mɔlekylɛr] *adj* : molecular

molécule [mɔlekyl] *nf* : molecule

molester [mɔlɛste] *vt* : to maul, to manhandle

mollasse [mɔlas] *adj* **1** APATHIQUE : apathetic, lethargic **2** FLASQUE : soft, flabby

mollasson [mɔlasɔ̃] *adj fam* : sluggish

molle → mou

mollement [mɔlmɑ̃] *adv* **1** DOUCEMENT : softly, gently **2** : weakly, feebly **3** : halfheartedly

mollesse [mɔlɛs] *adj* **1** : softness **2** : limpness, flabbiness **3** INDOLENCE : indolence, apathy

mollet [mɔlɛ] *nm* : calf (of the leg)

molleton [mɔltɔ̃] *nm* : fleece, flannel

mollir [mɔlir] *vi* **1** : to soften, to go soft **2** : to die down, to abate (of wind, etc.) **3** : to weaken, to give way **4** : to flag, to wane

mollusque [mɔlysk] *nm* : mollusk

môme [mom] *nmf France fam* GOSSE : kid, youngster

moment [mɔmɑ̃] *nm* **1** : moment, while <prendre un moment : to take (quite) a while> <pour un bon moment : for a good while> **2** INSTANT : minute, instant <attends un moment! : just wait a minute!> **3** : moment, time, occasion <à tout moment : at any time> <au moment de sortir : just as she was leaving> <à ce moment : at this moment, now> **4** : present (time) <sujets du moment : issues of the day> **5 du moment que** PUISQUE : since **6 par moments** : at times, now and again

momentané, -née [mɔmɑ̃tane] *adj* : momentary, temporary — **momentanément** [-nemɑ̃] *adv*

momie [mɔmi] *nf* : mummy

mon [mɔ̃] , **ma** [ma] (**mon** *before feminine nouns or adjectives beginning with a vowel or mute h*) *adj, pl* **mes** [me] : my

monarchie [mɔnarʃi] *nf* : monarchy — **monarchiste** [mɔnarʃist] *nmf*

monarque [mɔnark] *nm* : monarch

monastère [mɔnaster] *nm* : monastery

monastique [mɔnastik] *adj* : monastic

monceau [mɔ̃so] *nm, pl* **monceaux** [mɔ̃so] : heap, pile

mondain, -daine [mɔ̃dɛ̃, -dɛn] *adj* **1** : society, social <soirées mondaines : social gatherings> **2** : fashionable, refined **3** : wordly, mundane

mondanités [mɔ̃danite] *nfpl* **1** : social events **2** : small talk

monde [mɔ̃d] *nm* **1** TERRE : world, earth <au monde : in the world, on earth> **2** SOCIÉTÉ : world, society <le monde est petit : it's a small world> <le tiers monde : the third world> **3** COMMUNAUTÉ, DOMAINE : world, community <le monde des affaires : the business world> <le monde

végétal : the vegetable kingdom> **4** GENS : people *pl* <il y avait du monde partout : there were people everywhere> **5 comme du monde** *Can* : properly **6 tout le monde** : everyone **7 venir au monde** NAÎTRE : to be born

mondial, -diale [mɔ̃djal] *adj, mpl* **-diaux** [-djo] **1** : world <record mondial : world record> **2** : worldwide, global

mondialement [mɔ̃djalmɑ̃] *adv* : throughout the world, globally

monétaire [mɔnetɛr] *adj* : monetary

mongol[1], **-gole** [mɔ̃gɔl] *adj* : Mongolian, Mongol

mongol[2] *nm* : Mongolian (language)

Mongol, -gole *n* : Mongolian

moniteur[1], **-trice** [mɔnitœr, -tris] *n* **1** : instructor, coach **2** : counselor (in a camp)

moniteur[2] *nm* : monitor, screen

monitorat [mɔnitɔra] *nm* : instructorship

monnaie [mɔnɛ] *nf* **1** : money, currency <fausse monnaie : counterfeit money> **2** APPOINT : change <petite monnaie : small change> **3** PIÈCE : coin <monnaies d'or : gold coins> **4 monnaie courante** : commonplace

monnayer [mɔnɛje] {11} *vt* **1** : to convert into cash **2** : to capitalize on (experience, etc.)

monnayeur [mɔnɛjœr] *nm* → **faux-monnayeur**

monochrome [mɔnɔkrom] *adj* & *nm* : monochrome

monocle [mɔnɔkl] *nm* : monocle

monocorde [mɔnɔkɔrd] *adj* : droning, monotonous

monogame [mɔnɔgam] *adj* : monogamous

monogamie [mɔnɔgami] *nf* : monogamy

monogramme [mɔnɔgram] *nm* : monogram

monographie [mɔnɔgrafi] *nf* : monograph

monolingue [mɔnɔlɛ̃g] *adj* : monolingual

monolithe[1] [mɔnɔlit] *adj* : monolithic

monolithe[2] *nm* : monolith

monolithique [mɔnɔlitik] *adj* : monolithic

monologue [mɔnɔlɔg] *nm* : monologue, soliloquy

monopole [mɔnɔpɔl] *nm* : monopoly

monopoliser [mɔnɔpɔlize] *vt* : to monopolize — **monopolisation** [-lizasjɔ̃] *nf*

monopolistique [mɔnɔpɔlistik] *adj* : monopolistic

monosyllabe [mɔnɔsilab] *nm* : monosyllable

monosyllabique [mɔnɔsilabik] *adj* : monosyllabic

monothéisme [mɔnɔteism] *nm* : monotheism

monothéiste [mɔnɔteist] *adj* : monotheistic

monotone [mɔnɔtɔn] *adj* : monotonous, dull

monotonie [mɔnɔtɔni] *nf* : monotony, dullness

monseigneur [mɔ̃seɲœr] *nm, pl* **messeigneurs** [meseɲœr] **1** (*form of address*) : Your Royal Highness (for a prince), Your Eminence (for a cardinal) **2** (*title*) : His Grace (for a duke, an archbishop, etc.)

monsieur [məsjø] *nm, pl* **messieurs** [mesjø] **1** (*form of address*) : Mr., Sir <bonjour, monsieur : good morning, Sir; good morning, Mr. X> **2** (*used in correspondence*) <Monsieur : Dear Sir> **3** : man, gentleman <c'est un grand monsieur : he's a great man>

monstre[1] [mɔ̃str] *adj* : huge, colossal

monstre[2] *nm* : monster

monstrueusement [mɔ̃strypzmɑ̃] *adv* : monstruously, hideously

monstrueux, -trueuse [mɔ̃strypø, -trypøz] *adj* **1** : monstrous **2** : hideous, ugly **3** : terrible <une monstrueuse erreur : an awful mistake>

monstruosité [mɔ̃stryozite] *nf* : monstrosity

mont [mɔ̃] *nm* : mount, mountain

montage [mɔ̃taʒ] *nm* **1** : assembly <chaîne de montage : assembly line> **2** : mounting, setting (of jewelry) **3** : editing (of a film)

montagnard[1], **-gnarde** [mɔ̃taɲar, -ɲard] *adj* : mountain

montagnard[2], **-gnarde** *n* : mountain dweller

montagne [mɔ̃taɲ] *nf* **1** : mountain **2 la montagne** : the mountains **3 montagnes russes** : roller coaster

montagneux, -gneuse [mɔ̃taɲø, -ɲøz] *adj* : mountainous, hilly

montant[1], **-tante** [mɔ̃tɑ̃, -tɑ̃t] *adj* : uphill, rising <chemin montant : uphill road>

montant[2] *nm* **1** : upright, post **2** SOMME : total, sum

mont-de-piété [mɔ̃dpjete] *nm, pl* **monts-de-piété** *France* : pawnshop

monte-charge [mɔ̃tʃarʒ] *nms & pl* : freight elevator

montée [mɔ̃te] *nf* **1** : rise, rising **2** : ascent, climb **3** PENTE : slope, upgrade

monter [mɔ̃te] *vi* **1** : to go up, to come up, to climb up <elle est montée : she went upstairs> **2** : to go uphill, to slope upward **3** : to rise (of rivers, temperature, prices, etc.) **4** : to well up <les larmes lui sont montées aux yeux : his eyes filled with tears> **5 ~ à** : to ride <monter à bicyclette : to ride a bicycle> **6 ~ dans** : to get into (a car or train), to board (a ship or plane) **7 ~ sur** : to get on (a horse) — *vt* (*with auxiliary verb* **avoir**) **1** : to take up, to bring up **2** : to put up, to raise (a curtain, etc.) **3** : to go up, to climb (up) **4** : to raise, to turn up (volume, etc.) **5** : to ride (a horse) **6** : to put together, to assemble (a machine, etc.), to edit (a film) **7** : to mount (an attack), to set up (a scheme, etc.), to put on (a show) — **se monter** *vr* **1** ~ **à** : to amount to **2** ~ **en** : to equip oneself with

monteur, -teuse [mɔ̃tœr, -tøz] *n* : film editor

montgolfière [mɔ̃gɔlfjɛr] *nf* : hot-air balloon

monticule [mɔ̃tikyl] *nm* **1** : hillock, mound **2** *Can* : pitcher's mound (in baseball)

montre [mɔ̃tr] *nf* **1** : watch <montre à quartz : quartz watch> **2** : show, display <en montre : on display> <faire montre de : to show, to display>

montréalais, -laise [mɔrealɛ, -lɛz] *adj* : of or from Montreal

Montréalais, -laise *n* : Montrealer

montre–bracelet [mɔ̃trəbrasle] *nf, pl* **montres–bracelets** : wristwatch

montrer [mɔ̃tre] *vt* **1** : to show **2** : to reveal, to display **3** : to point at, to point out <montrer qqn du doigt : to point the finger at s.o.> — **se montrer** *vr* **1** : to show oneself, to be seen **2** : to prove to be **3** : to appear, to come out

monture [mɔ̃tyr] *nf* **1** : mount (animal) **2** : setting (for jewelry) **3** : frames *pl* (for eyeglasses)

monument [mɔnymɑ̃] *nm* **1** : monument, memorial <monument aux morts : war memorial> **2** : (historic) building

monumental, -tale [mɔnymɑ̃tal] *adj, mpl* **-taux** [-to] : monumental

moquer [mɔke] *v* **se moquer** ~ **de** *vr* **1** : to make fun of, to mock <on se moque de toi : people are laughing at you> **2** : to be indifferent about <je m'en moque : I couldn't care less>

moquerie [mɔkri] *nf* : mockery

moquette [mɔket] *nf* : wall-to-wall carpeting

moqueur[1], **-queuse** [mɔkœr, -køz] *adj* : mocking — **moqueusement** [-køzmɑ̃] *adv*

moqueur[2] *nm* : mockingbird

moraillon [mɔrɑjɔ̃] *nm* : hasp (for a door)

moraine [mɔren] *nf* : moraine

moral[1], **-rale** [mɔral] *adj, mpl* **moraux** [mɔro] **1** : moral, ethical <sens moral : sense of right and wrong> **2** : mental <une victoire morale : a moral victory>

moral[2] *nm* : morale, spirits *pl* <je lui ai remonté le moral : I cheered him up>

morale *nf* **1** ÉTHIQUE : morals *pl*, ethics *pl* **2** : moral (of a story) **3 faire la morale à** SERMONNER : to lecture

moralement [mɔralmɑ̃] *adv* : morally, ethically

moralisateur, -trice [mɔralizatœr, -tris] *adj* : moralizing, sanctimonious

moraliser [mɔralize] *vi* : to moralize — *vt* SERMONNER : to lecture, to preach to

moraliste[1] [mɔralist] *adj* : moralistic

moraliste[2] *nmf* : moralist

moralité [mɔralite] *nf* **1** : morals *pl* **2** : morality **3** : moral, lesson

moratoire [mɔratwar] *nm* : moratorium

morbide [mɔrbid] *adj* : morbid — **morbidité** [-bidite] *nf*

morceau [mɔrso] *nm, pl* **morceaux 1** : piece, bit <couper en morceaux : to cut into pieces> <manger un morceau : to have a bite to eat> **2** : extract, passage (of a text) **3** : piece (of music)

morceler [mɔrsəle] {8} *vt* : to break up, to divide

mordant[1], **-dante** [mɔrdɑ̃, -dɑ̃t] *adj* : biting, cutting, scathing

mordant[2] *nm* : keenness, bite, punch

mordicus [mɔrdikys] *adv fam* : obstinately, stubbornly

mordillement [mɔrdijmɑ̃] *nm* : nibbling

mordiller [mɔrdije] *vt* : to nibble at, to chew at

mordoré, -rée [mɔrdɔre] *adj* : bronze-colored

mordre [mɔrdr] {63} *vt* **1** : to bite **2** : to eat into (of acid, etc.) — *vi* **1** : to bite <ça mord : the fish are biting> **2** ~ **dans** : to bite into, to take a bite out of **3** ~ **sur** : to cross over (a line) — **se mordre** *vr* **1 se mordre la langue** : to bite one's tongue **2 se mordre les doigts** : to have bitter regrets

mordu[1] [mɔrdy] *pp* → **mordre**

mordu[2], **-due** *adj* : smitten (with love)

mordu[3], **-due** *n fam* : fan, buff <un mordu de sport : a sports buff>

morelle [mɔrel] *nf* : nightshade

morfondre [mɔrfɔ̃dr] {63} *v* **se morfondre** *vr* : to hang around, to mope <se morfondre à attendre : to wait around dejectedly> **2** *Can* : to exhaust oneself, to wear oneself out

morgue [mɔrg] *nf* **1** : morgue, mortuary **2** ARROGANCE : haughtiness, arrogance

moribond[1], **-bonde** [mɔribɔ̃, -bɔ̃d] *adj* : moribund, dying

moribond[2], **-bonde** *n* : dying person

morille [mɔrij] *nf* : morel

morne [mɔrn] *adj* **1** SOMBRE : dismal, gloomy **2** : glum, sullen

morose [mɔroz] *adj* : morose, sullen

morosité [mɔrozite] *nf* : moroseness, sullenness

morphine [mɔrfin] *nf* : morphine

mors [mɔr] *nm* : bit (of a bridle)

morse [mɔrs] *nm* **1** : walrus **2** : Morse code

morsure [mɔrsyr] *nf* : bite (of a dog, etc.)

mort¹ [mɔr] *pp* → **mourir**
mort², morte [mɔr, mɔrt] *adj* **1** : dead **2** : dying <être mort de faim : to be starving, to be dying of hunger> **3** : lifeless, stagnant <un temps mort : a slack period>
mort³ *nf* **1** : death <mettre à mort : to put to death> <peine de mort : death penalty> <jusqu'à la mort : to the death, to the bitter end> **2** : great sorrow, agony <avoir la mort dans l'âme : to have a heavy heart>
mort⁴, morte *n* **1** : dead person, corpse **2** VICTIME : fatality, casualty
mortalité [mɔrtalite] *nf* : mortality <taux de mortalité : death rate>
mortel¹, -telle [mɔrtɛl] *adj* **1** : mortal **2** FATAL : fatal, deadly, lethal <maladie mortelle : fatal disease>
mortel², -telle *n* : mortal
mortellement [mɔrtɛlmɑ̃] *adv* **1** : mortally, fatally **2** : deadly <mortellement ennuyeux : deadly boring>
mortier [mɔrtje] *nm* : mortar
mortifier [mɔrtifje] {96} *vt* : to mortify
— mortification [-tifikasjɔ̃] *nf*
mort–né, -née [mɔrne] *adj, pl* **mort–nés, mort–nées** : stillborn
mortuaire [mɔrtɥɛr] *adj* **1** FUNÈBRE : funeral **2 salon mortuaire** *Can* : funeral home
morue [mɔry] *nf* : cod
morve [mɔrv] *nf* : nasal mucus
morveux, -veuse [mɔrvø, -vøz] *adj* : runny-nosed
mosaïque [mɔzaik] *adj & nf* : mosaic
mosquée [mɔske] *nf* : mosque
mot [mo] *nm* **1** : word (in language) <mot à mot : word for word> <peser ses mots : to weigh one's words> **2** PAROLE : word <avoir le dernier mot : to have the last word> <sans mot dire : without saying a word> **3** : note, line <écrire un mot à qqn : to drop a line to s.o.> **4 mot de passe** : password **5 mot d'ordre** : watchword, catchword **6 mots croisés** : crossword puzzle
motard [mɔtar] *nm* : motorcycle policeman
motel [mɔtɛl] *nm* : motel
moteur¹, -trice [mɔtœr, -tris] *adj* **1** : motor **2** : driving <force motrice : driving force> **3 à quatre roues motrices** : four-wheel drive
moteur² *nm* **1** : engine, motor **2 moteur à vapeur** : steam engine **3 moteur à combustion interne** *or* **moteur à explosion** : internal combustion engine **4 moteur à réaction** : jet engine
motif [mɔtif] *nm* **1** RAISON : motive, reason, grounds *pl* **2** DESSIN : pattern, design <nappe à motifs floraux : floral-design tablecloth> **3** : motif (in music)
motion [mɔsjɔ̃] *nf* **1** : motion <voter une motion : to pass a motion> **2 motion de censure** : vote of no confidence
motivant, -vante [mɔtivɑ̃, -vɑ̃t] *adj* : motivating
motivation [mɔtivasjɔ̃] *nf* : motivation
motivé, -vée [mɔtive] *adj* **1** : motivated <être peu motivé : to lack motivation> **2** : reasoned, justified
motiver [mɔtive] *vt* **1** : to motivate, to impel **2** : to justify, to explain
moto [mɔto] *nf* : motorbike
motocyclette [mɔtɔsiklɛt] *nf* : motorcycle
motocycliste [mɔtɔsiklist] *nmf* : motorcyclist
motoneige [mɔtɔnɛʒ] *nf* : snowmobile
motoriser [mɔtɔrize] *vt* : to motorize, to mechanize
motte [mɔt] *nf* : clod, lump (of earth, etc.), slab (of butter)
motton [mɔtɔ̃] *nm Can* : lump (of earth, of ice, etc.)
mou¹ [mu] (**mol** [mɔl] *before vowel or mute h*), **molle** [mɔl] *adj* **1** : soft **2** : weak, feeble <avoir les jambes molles : to be weak in the knees> **3** : limp, lifeless <une poignée de main molle : a limp handshake> **4** : sluggish, listless **5** : indulgent, lax
mou² *nm* : looseness, slack <donner du mou à : to loosen, to give some leeway to>
mouchard, -charde [muʃar, -ʃard] *n fam* : informer, stool pigeon
moucharder [muʃarde] *vt fam* : to spy on, to squeal on
mouche [muʃ] *nf* **1** : fly <mouche domestique : housefly> <mouche à miel : honeybee> **2** *or* **mouche artificielle** : fly (in fishing) **3** : beauty spot **4 faire mouche** : to hit the bull's eye
moucher [muʃe] *vt* **1** : to wipe the nose of (a child, etc.) **2** : to snuff out (a candle) **— se moucher** *vr* : to blow one's nose
moucheron [muʃrɔ̃] *nm* : gnat, midge
moucheter [muʃte] {8} *vt* TACHETER : to fleck, to speckle, to mottle
moucheture [muʃtyr] *nf* : spot, speck, speckle
mouchoir [muʃwar] *nm* **1** : handkerchief **2 mouchoir en papier** : tissue
moudre [mudr] {54} *vt* : to grind
moue [mu] *nf* **1** : pout **2 faire la moue** : to pout
mouette [mwɛt] *nf* : gull, seagull
mouffette *or* **moufette** [mufɛt] *nf* : skunk
moufle [mufl] *nf* : mitten
mouillage [mujaʒ] *nm* **1** : anchoring **2** : anchorage, moorings *pl*
mouillé, -lée [muje] *adj* : wet
mouiller [muje] *vt* **1** : to wet, to moisten **2** : to add liquid to, to dilute **3 mouiller l'ancre** : to drop anchor **— se mouiller** *vr* **1** : to get wet **2** *fam* : to become involved

moulage [mulaʒ] *nm* **1** : molding, casting **2** : cast
moulait [mulɛ], **moulions** [muljɔ̃], *etc.* → **moudre**
moulant, -lante [mulɑ̃, -lɑ̃t] *adj* : tight-fitting
moule[1] [mul], *etc.* → **moudre**
moule[2] [mul] *nm* **1** MATRICE : mold, matrix **2** : mold (in cooking) <moule à gâteau : cake pan>
moule[3] [mul] *nf* : mussel
mouler [mule] *vt* **1** : to mold **2** : to cast <moulé en bronze : cast in bronze> **3** : to hug (the body), to fit tightly
moulin [mulɛ̃] *nm* **1** : mill **2 moulin à café** : coffee grinder **3 moulin à paroles** *fam* : chatterbox **4 moulin à vent** : windmill
moulinet [mulinɛ] *nm* **1** : reel, winch **2** : waving (about)
moulu[1] [muly] *pp* → **moudre**
moulu[2], **-lue** *adj* **1** : ground <café moulu : ground coffee> **2** *fam* : worn-out, all in
moulure [mulyr] *nf* : molding
moumoute [mumut] *nf fam* : wig, toupee
mourant[1], **-rante** [murɑ̃, -rɑ̃t] *adj* : dying
mourant[2], **-rante** *n* : dying person
mourir [murir] {55} *vi* **1** : to die **2** : to die out, to die away **3 ~ de** : to be dying of <mourir d'ennui : to be bored to death> <mourir de faim : to be dying of hunger> <il l'aimait à en mourir : he was desperately in love with her>
mourra [mura], *etc.* → **mourir**
mousquet [muskɛ] *nm* : musket
mousquetaire [muskətɛr] *nm* : musketeer
mousqueton [muskətɔ̃] *nm* : carbine
moussant, -sante [musɑ̃, -sɑ̃t] *adj* **1** : foaming, lathering **2 bain moussant** : bubble bath
mousse [mus] *nf* **1** : moss **2** : froth, foam, lather **3** : mousse <mousse au chocolat : chocolate mousse> **4** *or* **caoutchouc mousse** : foam rubber
mousseline [muslin] *nf* **1** : muslin, chiffon **2 pommes mousseline** : pureed potatoes
mousser [muse] *vi* **1** : to foam, to froth, to lather **2 faire mousser** *fam* : to sing the praises of
mousseux[1], **-seuse** [musø, -søz] *adj* **1** : foaming, frothy **2 vin mousseux** : sparkling wine
mousseux[2] *nm* : sparkling wine
mousson [musɔ̃] *nf* : monsoon
moussu, -sue [musy] *adj* : mossy
moustache [mustaʃ] *nf* **1** : mustache **2 moustaches** *nfpl* : whiskers (of an animal)
moustachu, -chue [mustaʃy] *adj* : wearing a mustache
moustiquaire [mustikɛr] *nf* **1** : mosquito net **2** : screen (on windows and doors)
moustique [mustik] *nm* : mosquito
moutarde [mutard] *nf* : mustard
mouton [mutɔ̃] *nm* **1** : sheep, sheepskin **2** : mutton **3 moutons** *nmpl* : small fluffy clouds **4 moutons** *nmpl* : whitecaps
mouvement [muvmɑ̃] *nm* **1** : bodily movement, gesture **2** : movement, motion <mouvement perpétuel : perpetual motion> **3** : impulse, reaction **4** : activity, bustle **5** : trend, evolution <mouvement en hausse : upward trend> **6** : movement (in politics, etc.)
mouvementé, -tée [muvmɑ̃te] *adj* **1** VIVANT : animated, lively, hectic **2** ACCIDENTÉ : rough, uneven <terrain mouvementé : rough terrain>
mouvoir [muvwar] {56} *vt* **1** POUSSER : to move, to prompt **2** ACTIONNER : to drive <machine mue par l'électricité : electric-powered machine> **— se mouvoir** *vr* : to move
moyac [mɔjak] *nm Can* : eider (duck)
moyen[1], **-yenne** [mwajɛ̃, -jɛn] *adj* **1** : medium, medium-sized **2** : average, mean **3 la classe moyenne** : the middle class
moyen[2] *nm* **1** : way, means *pl* <par quel moyen? : how?> **2** : possibility <y a-t-il moyen de le voir? : is it possible to see him?> **3 moyens** *nmpl* : means, resources **4 au moyen de** : with, by means of
Moyen Âge [mwajɛnaʒ] *nm* : Middle Ages
moyennant [mwajɛnɑ̃] *prep* : for, in return for
moyenne [mwajɛn] *nf* : average <en moyenne : on an average>
moyennement [mwajɛnmɑ̃] *adv* MODÉRÉMENT : fairly, moderately
moyeu [mwajø] *nm, pl* **moyeux** : hub
mozambicain, -caine [mɔzɑ̃bikɛ̃, -kɛn] *adj* : Mozambican
Mozambicain, -caine *n* : Mozambican
mû [my] *pp* → **mouvoir**
mucilage [mysilaʒ] *nm* : mucilage
mucosité [mykozite] *nf* : mucus
mucus [mykys] *nm* : mucus
mue [my] *nf* : molting, shedding, sloughing
muer [mɥe] *vi* **1** : to molt, to shed, to slough **2** : to change, to break <sa voix mue : his voice is changing> **— se muer** *vr* : to transform oneself
muet[1], **muette** [mɥɛ, mɥɛt] *adj* **1** : dumb <sourd et muet : deaf and dumb> **2** : speechless, dumbfounded **3** SILENCIEUX : silent
muet[2], **-ette** *n* : mute, dumb person
muffin [mɔfœn] *nm Can* : muffin
mufle [myfl] *nm* **1** : muzzle **2** *fam* : boor, lout
muge [myʒ] *nm* : gray mullet

mugir [myʒir] *vi* **1** BEUGLER : to low, to moo, to bellow **2** : to howl, to wail, to roar
mugissement [myʒismɑ̃] *nm* **1** : lowing, bellowing, mooing **2** : howling (of the wind), roar (of the sea)
muguet [mygɛ] *nm* : lily of the valley
mulâtre, -tresse [mylatr, -trɛs] *n* : mulatto
mule [myl] *nf* **1** : female mule **2** PANTOUFLE : mule
mulet [mylɛ] *nm* **1** : male mule **2** : gray mullet
mulot [mylo] *nm* : field mouse
multicolore [myltikɔlɔr] *adj* : multicolored
multiculturel, -relle [myltikyltyrɛl] *adj* : multicultural
multiforme [myltifɔrm] *adj* : multiform, many-sided
multilatéral, -rale [myltilateral] *adj, mpl* **-raux** [-ro] : multilateral
multilingue [myltilɛ̃g] *adj* : multilingual — **multilinguisme** [-lɛ̃gɥism] *nm*
multimédia [myltimedja] *adj* : multimedia
multimillionnaire [myltimiljɔnɛr] *nmf* : multimillionaire
multinational, -nale [myltinasjɔnal] *adj, mpl* **-naux** [-no] : multinational
multiple[1] [myltipl] *adj* **1** NOMBREUX : multiple, numerous **2** DIVERS : many, various, diverse
multiple[2] *nm* : multiple
multiplication [myltiplikasjɔ̃] *nf* : multiplication
multiplicité [myltiplisite] *nf* : multiplicity
multiplier [myltiplije] {96} *vt* **1** ACCROÎTRE : to multiply, to increase **2** : to multiply (in mathematics) — **se multiplier** *vr* PROLIFÉRER : to increase, to proliferate
multitude [myltityd] *nf* : multitude, mass <une multitude de gens : a vast number of people>
municipal, -pale [mynisipal] *adj, mpl* **-paux** [-po] : municipal, local, town
municipalité [mynisipalite] *nf* **1** : municipality, town **2** : town council
munificent, -cente [mynifisɑ̃, -sɑ̃t] *adj* : munificent — **munificence** [-fisɑ̃s] *adj*
munir [mynir] *vt* : to equip, to provide <munir d'armes : to supply with arms> — **se munir** *vr* ~ **de** : to equip oneself with
munitions [mynisjɔ̃] *nfpl* : ammunition, munitions
muqueuse *nf* : mucous membrane
muqueux, -queuse [mykø, -køz] *adj* : mucous
mur [myr] *nm* **1** : wall **2** OBSTACLE : obstacle, brick wall **3 mur du son** : sound barrier
mûr, mûre [myr] *adj* **1** : ripe **2** : mature <l'âge mûr : middle age> **3** : ready, prepared <mûr pour des responsabilités accrues : ready for increased responsibility>
muraille [myraj] *nf* : (high) wall
mural, -rale [myral] *adj, mpl* **muraux** [myro] : wall, mural
murale [myral] *nf* : mural
mûre [myr] *nf* **1** : blackberry **2** : mulberry
mûrement [myrmɑ̃] *adv* : carefully, with thought <ayant mûrement réfléchi : after much thought>
murène [myrɛn] *nf* : moray eel
murer [myre] *vt* : to wall in, to wall up — **se murer** *vr* : to shut oneself away
mûrier [myrje] *nm* : mulberry (tree)
mûrir [myrir] *vi* **1** : to ripen **2** : to mature, to develop — *vt* **1** : to ripen **2** : to develop, to nurture (a project, etc.)
murmure [myrmyr] *nm* **1** CHUCHOTEMENT : murmur **2 murmures** *nmpl* : mutterings, murmurings
murmurer [myrmyre] *vi* **1** CHUCHOTER : to murmur **2** SE PLAINDRE : to mutter, to complain — *vt* : to murmur
musaraigne [myzarɛɲ] *nf* : shrew
musarder [myzarde] *vi* FLÂNER : to idle around, to dawdle about
musc [mysk] *nm* : musk
muscade [myskad] *nf or* **noix muscade** : nutmeg
muscat [myska] *nm* : muscatel
muscle [myskl] *nm* : muscle
musclé, -clée [myskle] *adj* **1** : muscular **2** *fam* : powerful, strong <une politique musclée : a forceful stand>
musculaire [myskylɛr] *adj* : muscular
musculation [myskylasjɔ̃] *nf* : bodybuilding
musculature [mysklatyr] *nf* : musculature, muscles *pl*
muse [myz] *nf* : muse
museau [myzo] *nm, pl* **museaux** : muzzle, snout
musée [myze] *nm* : museum
museler [myzle] {8} *vt* : to muzzle
muselière [myzəljɛr] *nf* : muzzle (for a dog, etc.)
musette [myzɛt] *nf* : satchel, haversack
muséum [myzeɔm] *nm* : museum of natural history
musical, -cale [myzikal] *adj* **-caux** [-ko] : musical — **musicalement** [-kalmɑ̃] *adv*
musicien[1], **-cienne** [myzisjɛ̃, -sjɛn] *adj* : musical
musicien[2], **-cienne** *n* : musician
musique [myzik] *nf* **1** : music <musique d'ambiance : background music> <musique de chambre : chamber music> **2** : piece of music **3** : band <musique militaire : military band>
musqué, -quée [myske] *adj* **1** : musky **2 bœuf musqué** : musk ox **3 rat musqué** ONDATRA : muskrat
musulman, -mane [myzylmɑ̃, -man] *adj & n* : Muslim
mutable [mytabl] *adj* : mutable, changeable — **mutabilité** [-tabilite] *nf*

mutant¹, -tante [mytɑ̃, -tɑ̃t] *adj* : mutant
mutant², -tante *n* : mutant
mutation [mytasjɔ̃] *nf* **1** : transformation, change **2** : transfer (of an employee) **3** : mutation
muter [myte] *vt* : to transfer, to move — *vi* : to mutate
mutilation [mytilasjɔ̃] *nf* : mutilation
mutiler [mytile] *vt* : to mutilate, to maim
mutin¹, -tine [mytɛ̃, -tin] *adj* ESPIÈGLE : mischievous
mutin² *nm* : mutineer
mutiné¹, -née [mytine] *adj* : mutinous, rebellious
mutiné², -née *n* : mutineer
mutiner [mytine] *v* **se mutiner** *vr* : to mutiny, to rebel
mutinerie [mytinri] *nf* RÉBELLION : mutiny, rebellion
mutisme [mytism] *nm* **1** : dumbness, muteness **2** : silence
mutuel, -elle [mytɥɛl] *adj* : mutual — **mutuellement** [-tɥɛlmɑ̃] *adv*
myope [mjɔp] *adj* : shortsighted, nearsighted
myopie [mjɔpi] *nf* : myopia, shortsightedness, nearsightedness
myosotis [mjozɔtis] *nm* : forget-me-not
myriade [mirjad] *nf* : myriad
myrrhe [mir] *nf* : myrrh
myrte [mirt] *nf* : myrtle
myrtille [mirtil] *nf France* : blueberry
mystère [mister] *nm* : mystery
mystérieux, -rieuse [misterjø, -rjøz] *adj* : mysterious — **mystérieusement** [-rjøzmɑ̃] *adv*
mysticisme [mistisism] *nm* : mysticism
mystification [mistifikasjɔ̃] *nf* **1** : hoax, practical joke **2** : myth, unfounded idea
mystifier [mistifje] {96} *vt* DUPER : to deceive, to dupe
mystique¹ [mistik] *adj* : mystical, mystic
mystique² *nmf* : mystic
mystique³ *nf* **1** : mysticism **2** : mystique
mythe [mit] *nm* : myth
mythique [mitik] *adj* : mythical
mythologie [mitɔlɔʒi] *nf* : mythology
mythologique [mitɔlɔʒik] *adj* : mythological

N

n [ɛn] *nm* : n, the 14th letter of the alphabet
nacre [nakr] *nf* : mother-of-pearl
nacré, -crée [nakre] *adj* : pearly
nadir [nadir] *nm* : nadir
nage [naʒ] *nf* **1** : swimming **2** : stroke (in swimming) <nage libre : freestyle> **3 en ~** : dripping with sweat
nageoire [naʒwar] *nf* **1** : fin (of a fish) **2** : flipper
nager [naʒe] {17} *vi* **1** : to swim **2 ~ dans** : to be filled with <il nageait dans l'amour : he was brimming with love> — *vt* : to swim
nageur, -geuse [naʒœr, -ʒøz] *n* : swimmer
naguère [nagɛr] *adv* **1** RÉCEMMENT : recently, a short time ago **2** AUTREFOIS : formerly
naïade [najad] *nf* : naiad
naïf, naïve [naif, -iv] *adj* **1** INGÉNU : ingenuous, naive **2** CRÉDULE : credulous, gullible — **naïvement** [naivmɑ̃] *adv*
nain¹, naine [nɛ̃, nɛn] *adj* : dwarf, miniature <rosier nain : miniature rosebush>
nain², naine *n* : dwarf, midget
naissait [nɛsɛ], **naissions** [nɛsjɔ̃], *etc.* → **naître**
naissance [nɛsɑ̃s] *nf* **1** : birth **2** DÉBUT : origin, beginning <prendre naissance : to arise, to originate>
naissant, -sante [nɛsɑ̃, -sɑ̃t] *adj* : incipient
naisse [nɛs], *etc.* → **naisse**
naître [nɛtr] {57} *vi* **1** : to be born <il est né en 1970 : he was born in 1970> **2** : to rise, to originate <faire naître : to give rise to>
naïveté [naivte] *nf* : naïveté
namibien, -bienne [namibjɛ̃, -bjɛn] *adj* : Namibian
Namibien, -bienne *n* : Namibian
nanti, -tie [nɑ̃ti] *adj* : affluent, well-to-do
nantir [nɑ̃tir] *vt* **~ de** : to provide with
nantissement [nɑ̃tismɑ̃] *nm* : collateral
naphtaline [naftalin] *nf or* **boules de naphtaline** : mothballs *pl*
naphte [naft] *nm* : naphtha
nappe [nap] *nf* **1** : tablecloth **2** : layer, sheet <nappe de brouillard : blanket of fog> <nappe d'eau : sheet of water> <nappe de mazout : oil slick>
napper [nape] *vt* : to coat, to cover <napper de sauce : to cover with sauce>
napperon [naprɔ̃] *nm* : mat, doily
narcisse [narsis] *nm* **1** : narcissus **2** : narcissist
narcissique [narsisik] *adj* : narcissistic — **narcissisme** [-sisism] *nm*
narcotique [narkɔtik] *adj & nm* : narcotic
narguer [narge] *vt* **1** : to mock, to taunt **2** : to flout (danger, etc.)
narine [narin] *nf* : nostril
narquois, -quoise [narkwa, -kwaz] *adj* RAILLEUR : sneering, derisive

narrateur, -trice [naratœr, -tris] *n* : narrator
narratif, -tive [naratif, -tiv] *adj* : narrative
narration [narasjɔ̃] *nf* : narration, narrative
narrer [nare] *vt* : to tell (a story), to relate (events, etc.)
narval [narval] *nm* : narwhal
nasal, -sale [nazal] *adj, mpl* **nasaux** [nazo] : nasal
naseau [nazo] *nm, pl* **naseaux** : nostril (of an animal)
nasillard, -larde [nazijar, -jard] *adj* : nasal <voix nasillarde : nasal voice>
nasiller [nazije] *vi* : to speak through one's nose, to have a nasal twang
natal, -tale [natal] *adj, mpl* **natals** : native, natal
natalité [natalite] *nf* : birthrate
natation [natasjɔ̃] *nf* : swimming
natif¹, -tive [natif, -tiv] *adj* : native
natif², -tive *n* : native
nation [nasjɔ̃] *nf* : nation
national, -nale [nasjɔnal] *adj, mpl* **-naux** [-no] : national — **nationalement** [-nalmɑ̃] *adv*
nationale *nf France* : highway
nationaliser [nasjɔnalize] *vt* : to nationalize — **nationalisation** [-lizasjɔ̃] *nf*
nationalisme [nasjɔnalism] *nm* : nationalism — **nationaliste** [-nalist] *adj & nmf*
nationalité [nasjɔnalite] *nf* : nationality
nativité [nativite] *nf* : nativity
natte [nat] *nf* **1** : mat **2** : braid, plait, pigtail
natter [nate] *vt* : to braid, to plait
naturaliser [natyralize] *vt* : to naturalize — **naturalisation** [-lizasjɔ̃] *nf*
naturalisme [natyralism] *nm* : naturalism
naturaliste¹ [natyralist] *adj* : naturalistic
naturaliste² *nmf* : naturalist
nature¹ [natyr] *nf* **1** : nature <les beautés de la nature : the beauties of nature> **2** CARACTÈRE : character, nature <une nature passive : a passive nature> **3 nature humaine** : human nature **4 nature morte** : still life
nature² *adj* : plain <yaourt nature : plain yogurt>
naturel¹, -relle [natyrɛl] *adj* : natural
naturel² *nm* **1** : nature, disposition **2** : naturalness **3 au naturel** : plain, unprocessed **4 au naturel** : in reality
naturellement [natyrɛlmɑ̃] *adv* **1** : naturally, by nature **2** : naturally, of course
naturisme [natyrism] *nm* : nudism — **naturiste** [-tyrist] *adj & nmf*
naufrage [nofraʒ] *nm* : shipwreck
naufragé, -gée [nofraʒe] *adj & n* : castaway
nauséabond, -bonde [nozeabɔ̃, -bɔnd] *adj* **1** : nauseating, revolting **2** : foul-smelling
nausée [noze] *nf* **1** : nausea **2 avoir la nausée** *or* **avoir des nausées** : to get sick to one's stomach
nautile [notil] *nm* : nautilus
nautique [notik] *adj* : nautical <ski nautique : water skiing>
nautisme [notism] *nm* : water sports
naval, -vale [naval] *adj, mpl* **navals** : naval
navet [navɛ] *nm* **1** : turnip **2** *fam* : third-rate film, novel, etc.
navette [navet] *nf* **1** : shuttle <navette spatiale : space shuttle> **2 faire la navette** : to commute
navigable [navigabl] *adj* : navigable — **navigabilité** [-gabilite] *nf*
navigant, -gante [navigɑ̃, -gɑ̃t] *adj* **1** : flying <personnel navigant : flight personnel, crew> **2** : seafaring
navigateur, -trice [navigatœr, -tris] *n* **1** : navigator **2** : sailor, seafarer **3** : browser (in computers)
navigation [navigasjɔ̃] *nf* **1** : navigation **2** : shipping
naviguer [navige] *vi* **1** : to sail **2** : to navigate **3** *fam* : to travel
navire [navir] *nm* **1** : ship, vessel **2 navire de guerre** : warship, man-of-war
navire–citerne [navirsitɛrn] *nm, pl* **navires–citernes** : tanker
navrant, -vrante [navrɑ̃, -vrɑ̃t] *adj* **1** : upsetting, distressing **2** : annoying
navrer [navre] *vt* **1** : to upset, to distress **2 être navré de** : to be sorry about
nazi, -zie [nazi] *adj & nmf* : Nazi — **nazisme** [nazism] *nm*
ne [nə] (**n'** *before a vowel or mute h*) *adv* **1** (*used with a negative word*) <il n'y a plus aucun espoir : there's no longer any hope> <elle ne sait pas : she doesn't know> <je ne lui parle guère : I almost never speak to him> **2** (*used with que*) : only, all that, not just <il n'y a pas que vous : you're not the only one> <il ne fait que se plaindre : all (that) he does is complain> **3** (*used alone*) <j'ai peur qu'elle n'oublie : I'm afraid she'll forget> <à moins qu'on ne t'appelle : unless they call you> <n'ayez crainte : don't worry, never fear>
né¹ [ne] *pp* → **naître**
né², née *adj* : born <un chanteur né : a born singer>
néanmoins [neɑ̃mwɛ̃] *adv* : nevertheless, yet
néant [neɑ̃] *nm* **1** : worthlessness, emptiness **2 le néant** : nothingness
nébuleuse [nebyløz] *nf* : nebula
nébuleux, -leuse [nebylø, -løz] *adj* **1** : cloudy <ciel nébuleux : cloudy sky> **2** : nebulous
nécessaire¹ [neseser] *adj* : necessary
nécessaire² *nm* **1** : necessity <le strict nécessaire : the bare essentials> **2** : need <je ferai le nécessaire : I'll do

what's needed> **3** : bag, kit <nécessaire de toilette : toilet kit>

nécessairement [nesesɛrmɑ̃] *adv* **1** : necessarily **2** INÉVITABLEMENT : inevitably

nécessité [nesesite] *nf* **1** : necessity **2** : need <être dans la nécessité : to be in need>

nécessiter [nesesite] *vt* EXIGER : to require, to call for

nécessiteux, -teuse [nesesitø, -tøz] *adj* : needy

nécrologie [nekrɔlɔʒi] *nf* : obituary

nécromancie [nekrɔmɑ̃si] *nf* : necromancy

nectar [nɛktar] *nm* : nectar

nectarine [nɛktarin] *nf* : nectarine

néerlandais[1], **-daise** [neɛrlɑ̃dɛ, -dɛz] *adj* : Dutch

néerlandais[2] *nm* : Dutch (language)

Néerlandais, -daise *n* **1** : Dutch person, Dutchman *m* **2 les Néerlandais** : the Dutch

nef [nɛf] *nf* : nave

néfaste [nefast] *adj* **1** NUISIBLE : harmful **2** : ill-fated, unlucky

négatif[1], **-tive** [negatif, -tiv] *adj* : negative — **négativement** [-tivmɑ̃] *adv*

négatif[2] *nm* : negative (of a photograph)

négation [negasjɔ̃] *nf* **1** : denial, negation **2** : negative (in grammar)

négative *nf* : negative <répondre par la négative : to reply in the negative>

négativement [negativmɑ̃] *adv* : negatively

négligé[1], **-gée** [negliʒe] *adj* **1** : neglected **2** : slovenly, untidy

négligé[2] *nm* **1** LAISSER-ALLER : slovenliness **2** DÉSHABILLÉ : negligee

négligeable [negliʒabl] *adj* INSIGNIFIANT : negligible, insignificant

négligemment [negliʒamɑ̃] *adv* : negligently, carelessly

négligence [negliʒɑ̃s] *nf* : negligence, carelessness

négligent, -gente [negliʒɑ̃, -ʒɑ̃t] *adj* : negligent, neglectful

négliger [negliʒe] {17} *vt* **1** : to neglect **2** : to disregard, to ignore **3** OMETTRE : to omit, to forget <il a négligé de m'avertir : he forgot to let me know> — **se négliger** *vr* : to neglect oneself

négoce [negɔs] *nm* : business, trade

négociable [negɔsjabl] *adj* : negotiable

négociant, -ciante [negɔsjɑ̃, -sjɑ̃t] *n* : merchant

négociateur, -trice [negɔsjatœr, -tris] *n* : negotiator

négociation [negɔsjasjɔ̃] *nf* : negotiation

négocier [negɔsje] {96} *v* : to negotiate — **négociable** [negɔsjabl] *adj*

nègre, négresse [nɛgr, negres] *adj & n sometimes offensive* : Negro

neige [nɛʒ] *nf* **1** : snow **2 neige carbonique** : dry ice **3 neige fondue** : slush

neiger [neʒe] {17} *v impers* : to snow <il neige : it's snowing>

neigeux, -geuse [nɛʒø, -ʒøz] *adj* : snowy

nénuphar [nenyfar] *nm* : water lily

néologisme [neɔlɔʒism] *nm* : neologism

néon [neɔ̃] *nm* : neon <éclairage au néon : neon lighting>

néophyte [neɔfit] *nmf* : neophyte, beginner

Néo–Zéalandais, -daise [neɔzelɑ̃dɛ, -dɛz] *n* : New Zealander

népalais[1], **-laise** [nepalɛ, -lɛz] *adj* : Nepali

népalais[2] *nm* : Nepali (language)

Népalais, -laise *n* : Nepali

népotisme [nepɔtism] *nm* : nepotism

Neptune [nɛptyn] *nf* : Neptune (planet)

nerf [nɛr] *nm* **1** : nerve **2** VIGUEUR : vigor, spirit **3 nerfs** *nmpl* : nerves <avoir les nerfs à vif : to be a bundle of nerves>

nerveux, -veuse [nɛrvø, -vøz] *adj* : nervous, tense — **nerveusement** [-vøzmɑ̃] *adv*

nervosité [nɛrvozite] *nf* : nervousness

nervure [nɛrvyr] *nf* **1** : vein (of a leaf, an insect's wing, etc.) **2** : rib (in architecture)

n'est–ce pas [nɛspa] *adv* : no?, isn't that right?, isn't it?, aren't you? <c'est bien ça, n'est-ce pas? : that's right, isn't it?> <tu viens, n'est-ce pas? : you're coming, aren't you?>

net[1] [nɛt] *adv* : plainly, flatly <j'ai refusé net : I flatly refused>

net[2], **nette** *adj* **1** PROPRE : clean, tidy **2** : net <salaire net : net earnings> **3** : clear <une nette amélioration : a clear improvement> **4** MARQUÉ : marked, distinct

nettement [nɛtmɑ̃] *adv* **1** : flatly, bluntly **2** DISTINCTEMENT : clearly, distinctly **3** : definitely

netteté [nɛtte] *nf* **1** : cleanness **2** : clearness, sharpness

nettoie [nɛtwa], **nettoiera** [nɛtwara], *etc.* → **nettoyer**

nettoyage [netwajaʒ] *nm* : cleaning

nettoyant [netwajɑ̃] *nm* : cleaning agent

nettoyer [nɛtwaje] {58} *vt* **1** : to clean, to clean off, to clean up **2** *fam* : to clean out, to rob

neuf[1] [nœf] *adj* **1** : nine **2** : ninth <le neuf juin : June ninth>

neuf[2] *nms & pl* : nine

neuf[3], **neuve** [nœf, nœv] *adj* : new <tout neuf : brand new>

neuf[4] *nm* : new thing <quoi de neuf? : what's new?>

neurologie [nørɔlɔʒi] *nf* : neurology

neurologique [nørɔlɔʒik] *adj* : neurological, neurologic

neurologue [nørɔlɔg] *nmf* : neurologist

neutraliser [nøtralize] *vt* : to neutralize — **neutralisation** [-lizasjɔ̃] *nf*

neutralité [nøtralite] *nf* : neutrality
neutre[1] [nøtr] *adj* **1** : neuter **2** : neutral
neutre[2] *nm* **1** : neuter (in grammar) **2** *Can* : neutral (gear position)
neutron [nøtrɔ̃] *nm* : neutron
neuvième [nœvjem] *adj & nmf & nm* : ninth
neveu [nəvø] *nm* : nephew
névralgie [nevralʒi] *nf* : neuralgia
névralgique [nevralʒik] *adj* **1** : neuralgic **2 point névralgique** : sensitive area, key point
névrite [nevrit] *nf* : neuritis
névrose [nevroz] *nf* : neurosis
névrosé, -sée [nevroze] *adj & n* : neurotic
névrotique [nevrɔtik] *adj* : neurotic
nez [ne] *nm* **1** : nose **2** : flair, good judgement **3 nez à nez** : face to face
ni [ni] *conj* **1 ni . . . ni** : neither . . . nor <ni l'un ni l'autre : neither one nor the other> **2 ni plus ni moins** : no more, no less
niais[1], **niaise** [nje, njez] *adj* : simple, foolish — **niaisement** [njezmɑ̃] *adv*
niais[2], **niaise** *n* : fool, simpleton
niaiser [njeze] *vi Can fam* **1** : to dillydally, to waste time **2 faire niaiser qqn** : to make s.o. wait — *vt Can fam* : to make (someone) look stupid
niaiserie [njezri] *nf* SOTTISE : silliness, foolishness, stupid remark <dire des niaiseries : to talk nonsense>
niaiseux, -seuse [njezø, -zøz] *n Can fam* : silly person, fool
nicaraguayen, -guayenne [nikaragwejɛ̃, -jen] *adj* : Nicaraguan
Nicaraguayen, -guayenne *n* : Nicaraguan
niche [niʃ] *nf* **1** : niche, recess **2** : kennel, doghouse
nicher [niʃe] *vi* : to nest, to brood — **se nicher** *vr* **1** : to nest **2** : to nestle **3** : to hide away
nickel [nikɛl] *nm* : nickel
nicotine [nikɔtin] *nf* : nicotine
nid [ni] *nm* **1** : nest **2** : den, lair <nid de brigands : den of thieves>
nid-de-poule *nm, pl* **nids-de-poule** : pothole
nièce [njes] *nf* : niece
nier [nje] {96} *vt* : to deny
nigaud, -gaude [nigo, nigod] *n* : simpleton, fool
nigérian, -rianne [niʒerjɑ̃, -rjan] *adj* : Nigerian
Nigérian, -rianne *n* : Nigerian
n'importe → importer
nirvana [nirvana] *nm* : nirvana
nitrate [nitrat] *nm* : nitrate
nitrique [nitrik] *adj* **acide nitrique** : nitric acid
nitrite [nitrik] *nm* : nitrite
nitroglycérine [nitrɔglisərin] *nf* : nitroglycerin, nitroglycerine
niveau [nivo] *nm, pl* **niveaux** [nivo] **1** : level <niveau de la mer : sea level> **2** : story <un bâtiment à trois niveaux : a three-story building> **3** : level, standard <niveau de vie : standard of living> **4** : stage, level, degree <négociations au plus haut niveau : top-level negotiations>
niveler [nivle] {8} *vt* : to level (off), to even out
nivellement [nivɛlmɑ̃] *nm* : leveling
noble[1] [nɔbl] *adj* **1** : noble **2 métaux nobles** : precious metals
noble[2] *nmf* : noble, nobleman *m*, noblewoman *f*
noblesse [nɔbles] *nf* : nobility
noce [nɔs] *nf* **1** : wedding, wedding party **2 noces** *nfpl* : wedding <noces d'or : golden wedding anniversary>
nocif, -cive [nɔsif, -siv] *adj* : noxious, harmful
noctambule [nɔktɑ̃byl] *nmf* : night owl
nocturne[1] [nɔktyrn] *adj* : nocturnal, night
nocturne[2] *nm* **1** : nocturne **2** : night hunter (bird)
nodule [nɔdyl] *nm* : nodule
Noël [nɔel] *nm* **1** : Christmas <joyeux Noël : Merry Christmas> **2 père Noël** : Santa Claus
noeud [nø] *nm* **1** : knot <noeud coulant : noose> **2** : bow <noeud papillon : bow tie> **3** : crux **4** : node **5** : knot (nautical speed)
noie [nwa], **noiera** [nwara], *etc.* → **noyer**
noir[1], **noire** [nwar] *adj* **1** : black **2** SALE : dirty, grimy **3** : dark <il fait noir : it's dark>
noir[2] *nm* **1** : black (color) **2** : darkness <peur du noir : fear of the dark> **3 au noir** : on the black market, on the side <travailler au noir : to moonlight> **4 noir à chaussures** *Can* : (black) shoe polish
Noir, Noire *n* : black man, black woman
noirâtre [nwaratr] *adj* : blackish
noirceur [nwarsœr] *nf* **1** : blackness **2** *Can* : darkness
noircir [nwarsir] *vi* : to darken, to turn black — *vt* : to black, to blacken <une réputation noircie : a tarnished reputation>
noircissure [nwarsisyr] *nf* : black mark
noise [nwaz] *nf* **chercher noise à qqn** : to pick a fight with s.o.
noisetier [nwaztje] *nm* : hazel (tree)
noisette [nwazɛt] *nf* **1** : hazelnut **2** : hazel (color)
noix [nwa] *nfs & pl* **1** : nut, walnut **2** : piece, lump <noix de beurre : round lump of butter> **3 → cajou, coco, muscade**
noliser [nɔlize] *vt* : to charter, to rent out
nom [nɔ̃] *nm* **1** : name <nom de plume : pen name> <nom de famille : surname> <nom de jeune fille : maiden name> **2** : noun **3 au nom de** : in the name of, on behalf of

nomade[1] [nɔmad] *adj* : nomadic
nomade[2] *nmf* : nomad
nombre [nɔ̃br] *nm* **1** : number <nombre entier : whole number, integer> <nombre impair : odd number> **2** QUANTITÉ : quantity, number <un grand nombre de : a lot of, many> <sans nombre : countless> **3** MASSE : numbers *pl* <la loi du nombre : the sheer weight of numbers> **4 au nombre de** : among
nombreux, -breuse [nɔ̃brø, -brøz] *adj* **1** : large <une famille nombreuse : a large family> **2** : many, numerous
nombril [nɔ̃bril] *nm* : navel
nombrilisme [nɔ̃brilism] *nm fam* : self-centeredness
nomenclature [nɔmɑ̃klatyr] *nf* **1** : nomenclature **2** : word list
nominal, -nale [nɔminal] *adj, mpl* **-naux** [-no] : nominal <valeur nominale : face value> **— nominalement** [-nalmɑ̃] *adv*
nominatif [nɔminatif] *nm* : nominative
nomination [nɔminasjɔ̃] *nf* : appointment, nomination
nommément [nɔmemɑ̃] *adv* : by name, namely
nommer [nɔme] *vt* **1** PRÉNOMMER : to name, to call **2** : to appoint, to nominate **3** CITER : to name, to mention **— se nommer** *vr* **1** S'APPELER : to be named <elle se nomme Julie : her name is Julie> **2** : to introduce oneself
non[1] [nɔ̃] *adv* **1** : no <mais non! : no!, of course not!> **2** (*used to replace a clause*) <je pense que non : I don't think so> <c'est à ton goût, non? : you like it, don't you?> <moi non plus : me neither, neither do I, neither am I> **3** (*used to modify an adjective or adverb*) <non loin d'ici : not far from here> <non moins : no less> **4 non seulement . . . mais (encore)** : not only . . . but (also)
non[2] *nm* : no
non-aligné, -née [nɔnaliɲe] *adj* : nonaligned
nonante[1] [nɔnɑ̃t] *adj* : *Belg, Switz* : ninety
nonante[2] *n* : *Belg, Switz* : ninety
nonchalamment [nɔ̃ʃalamɑ̃] *adv* : nonchalantly
nonchalance [nɔ̃ʃalɑ̃s] *nf* : nonchalance, casualness
nonchalant, -lante [nɔ̃ʃalɑ̃, -lɑ̃t] *adj* : nonchalant, casual
non-combattant, -tante [nɔ̃kɔ̃batɑ̃, -tɑ̃t] *n* : noncombatant
non-conformité [nɔ̃kɔ̃fɔrmite] *nf* : nonconformity **— non-conformiste** [-fɔrmist] *nmf*
non-croyant, -croyante [nɔ̃krwajɑ̃, -jɑ̃t] *n* : nonbeliever
non-existence [nɔnɛgzistɑ̃s] *nf* : nonexistence **— non-existent** [nɔnɛgzistɑ̃] *adj*
non-fumeur, -meuse [nɔ̃fymœr, -møz] *n* : nonsmoker
nono, nonote [nɔno] *n Can fam* : fool, idiot
nonobstant [nɔnɔpstɑ̃] *adv & prep* : notwithstanding
nonoune [nɔnun] *adj Can fam* : stupid, thick
non-paiement [nɔ̃pɛmɑ̃] *nm* : nonpayment
non-prolifération [nɔ̃prɔliferasjɔ̃] *nf* : nonproliferation
non-sens [nɔsɑ̃s] *nms & pl* **1** ABSURDITÉ : absurdity, nonsense **2** : meaningless word or phrase
non-violence [nɔ̃vjɔlɑ̃s] *nf* : nonviolence
non-violent, -lente [nɔ̃vjɔlɑ̃, -lɑ̃t] *adj* : nonviolent
non-voyant, -voyante [nɔ̃vwajɑ̃, -jɑ̃t] *n* : blind person
nord[1] [nɔr] *adj* : north, northern
nord[2] *nm* **1** : north <exposé au nord : with a northerly aspect> <vent du nord : north wind> **2 le Nord** : the North **3 perdre le nord** *fam* : to become disoriented
nord-américain, -caine [nɔramerikɛ̃, -kɛn] *adj* : North American
Nord-Américain, -caine *n* : North American
nord-coréen, -réenne [nɔrkɔreɛ̃, -ɛn] *adj* : North Korean
Nord-Coréen, -réenne *n* : North Korean
nord-est[1] [nɔrɛst] *adj s & pl* **1** : northeast, northeastern **2** : northeasterly
nord-est[2] *nm* : northeast
nordique[1] [nɔrdik] *adj* : Nordic, Scandinavian
nordique[2] *nm* : Norse (language)
Nordique *nmf* : Scandinavian
nord-ouest[1] [nɔrwɛst] *adj s & pl* **1** : northwest, northwestern **2** : northwesterly
nord-ouest[2] *nm* : northwest
normal, -male [nɔrmal] *adj, mpl* **normaux** [nɔrmo] **1** : normal, standard, usual **2** : normal, natural <c'est bien normal : it's only natural>
normale *nf* **1** : average, normal <au-dessous de la normale : below normal> **2** NORME : norm, standard
normalement [nɔrmalmɑ̃] *adv* : normally, usually
normaliser [nɔrmalize] *vt* : to normalize, to standardize **— normalisation** [-lizasjɔ̃] *nf*
normalité [nɔrmalite] *nf* : normality, normalcy
norme [nɔrm] *nf* : norm, standard
norvégien[1], **-gienne** [nɔrveʒjɛ̃, -ʒjɛn] *adj* : Norwegian
norvégien[2] *nm* : Norwegian (language)

Norvégien, -gienne *n* : Norwegian
nos → notre
nostalgie [nɔstalʒi] *nf* : nostalgia — **nostalgique** [nɔstalʒik] *adj*
notable[1] [nɔtabl] *adj* : notable, noteworthy
notable[2] *nm* : notable
notablement [nɔtabləmɑ̃] *adv* : notably, considerably
notaire [nɔtɛr] *nm* : notary public
notamment [nɔtamɑ̃] *adv* PARTICULIÈREMENT : especially, particularly
notation [nɔtasjɔ̃] *nf* : notation
note [nɔt] *nf* **1** : note <prendre des notes : to take notes> **2** ADDITION : bill, check **3** : mark, grade (in school) **4** : note (in music) **5** : touch, hint <une note de tristesse : a note of sadness> **6 note de service** : memorandum **7 note en bas de la page** : footnote
noter [nɔte] *vt* **1** REMARQUER : to note, to take notice of **2** MARQUER : to mark <noter un passage important : to mark an important passage> **3** : to mark, to grade **4** INSCRIRE : to write, to note down
notice [nɔtis] *nf* **1** : note <notice bibliographique : bibliographical note> **2** : instructions *pl*
notifier [nɔtifje] {96} *vt* : to notify — **notification** [-tifikasjɔ̃] *nf*
notion [nɔsjɔ̃] *nf* **1** : notion, idea **2 notions** *nfpl* : rudiments, basic knowledge
notoire [nɔtwar] *adj* **1** CONNU : well-known **2** : notorious
notoirement [nɔtwarmɑ̃] *adv* : notoriously
notoriété [nɔtɔrjete] *nf* **1** : fame, renown **2** : celebrity (person) **3 de notoriété publique** : common knowledge
notre [nɔtr] *adj, pl* **nos** [no] : our
nôtre[1] [notr] *adj* : our own <nous avons fait nôtres ces idées : we have made these ideas ours>
nôtre[2] *pron* **le nôtre, la nôtre, les nôtres** : ours <nous avons les nôtres : we have ours>
nouer [nwe] *vt* **1** : to tie, to knot, to fasten **2** : to start up, to establish <nouer des relations avec : to begin a relationship with> **3 avoir la gorge nouée** : to have a lump in one's throat
noueux, noueuse [nwø, -øz] *adj* : knotty, knobby, gnarled
nougat [nuga] *nm* : nougat
nouille [nuj] *nf* **1** *fam* : nitwit, idiot **2 nouilles** *nfpl* : noodles, pasta
nourri, -rie [nuri] *adj* **1** : heavy (of gunfire) **2** : sustained, prolonged
nourrice [nuris] *nf* : wet nurse
nourrir [nurir] *vt* **1** ALIMENTER : to feed, to nourish **2** ALLAITER : to breast-feed **3** : to provide for (a family, etc.) **4** : to nurse, to harbor <nourrir des doutes : to entertain doubts> — **se nourrir** *vr* **1** : to eat **2 ~ de** : to feed on
nourrissant, -sante [nurisɑ̃, -sɑ̃t] *adj* : nourishing, nutritious
nourrisson [nurisɔ̃] *nm* : infant
nourriture [nurityr] *nf* **1** : food **2** : diet **3** : (intellectual) nourishment
nous [nu] *pron* **1** : we **2** : us <il nous a dit de partir : he told us to go> **3** : ourselves <nous nous amusons : we're enjoying ourselves> **4 nous autres** *Can fam* : we <ils ne travaillent pas comme nous autres : they don't work as hard as we do>
nous-mêmes [numɛm] *pron* : ourselves
nouveau[1] [nuvo] (**-vel** [-vɛl] *before a vowel or mute h*), **-velle** [-vɛl] *adj, mpl* **nouveaux 1** : new **2** : novel, fresh <une nouvelle idée : an original idea> **3 de ~** *or* **à ~** : again, once again **4 nouveau venu** : newcomer
nouveau[2] *nm* **1 du nouveau** : something new **2 le nouveau** : the new
nouveau-né, -née [nuvone] *adj & n, mpl* **nouveau-nés** : newborn
nouveauté [nuvote] *nf* **1** : newness, novelty **2** : innovation
nouvelle [nuvɛl] *nf* **1** : piece of news <c'est une bonne nouvelle : that's good news> **2** : short story **3 nouvelles** *nfpl* : news <les nouvelles vont vite : news travels fast> <regarder les nouvelles : to watch the news>
nouvellement [nuvɛlmɑ̃] *adv* : newly, recently
novateur[1], **-trice** [nɔvatœr, -tris] *adj* : innovative
novateur[2], **-trice** *n* : innovator
novembre [nɔvɑ̃br] *nm* : November
novice[1] [nɔvis] *adj* : inexperienced
novice[2] *nmf* : novice, beginner
noviciat [nɔvisja] *nm* : novitiate
noyade [nwajad] *nf* : drowning
noyau [nwajo] *nm, pl* **noyaux 1** : pit, stone (of a fruit) **2** : nucleus, core (in science) **3** : group, core <un noyau de résistance : a pocket of resistance>
noyautage [nwajotaʒ] *nm* : infiltration
noyauter [nwajote] *vt* : to infiltrate
noyé[1], **noyée** [nwaje] *adj* **1** PERDU : lost, out of one's depth **2** : flooded <des yeux noyés de larmes : eyes brimming with tears>
noyé[2], **noyée** *n* : drowning victim
noyer[1] [nwaje] {58} *vt* **1** : to drown **2** : to flood <noyer le moteur : to flood the engine> **3** : to shroud, to blur, to drown out — **se noyer** *vr* **1** : to drown **2** : to be swamped, to be drowned (out) **3 ~ dans** : to get bogged down in
noyer[2] *nm* **1** : walnut tree **2 noyer blanc d'Amérique** : hickory (tree)
nu[1], **nue** [ny] *adj* **1** : naked, nude **2** : uncovered <être pieds nus : to be barefoot(ed)> <à main nue : bare-handed> **3** : bare, plain, unadorned

nu[2] *nm* **1** : nude (in art) **2 à ~** : bare, exposed <mettre à nu : to expose, to lay bare>
nuage [nɥaʒ] *nm* **1** : cloud <sans nuages : cloudless, unclouded> <être dans les nuages : to have one's head in the clouds> **2** : cloud, mass (of dust, smoke, etc.) <un nuage de lait : a dash of milk>
nuageux, -geuse [nɥaʒø, -ʒøz] *adj* **1** COUVERT : cloudy, overcast **2** : hazy, obscure
nuance [nɥɑ̃s] *nf* **1** TON : hue, shade <nuance de vert : shade of green> **2** : subtlety, nuance **3 une nuance de** : a touch of, a trace of
nuancer [nɥɑ̃se] {6} *vt* : to qualify (thoughts, opinions, etc.)
nubile [nybil] *adj* : nubile
nucléaire[1] [nykleɛr] *adj* : nuclear
nucléaire[2] *nm* : nuclear energy
nudisme [nydism] *nm* : nudism — **nudiste** [nydist] *adj & nmf*
nudité [nydite] *nf* **1** : nudity, nakedness **2** : bareness
nuée [nɥe] *nf* : cloud, swarm
nues [ny] *nfpl* **1 porter qqn aux nues** : to praise s.o. to the skies **2 tomber des nues** : to be taken aback
nuire [nɥir] {49} *vi* **~ à** : to harm, to injure — **se nuire** *vr*
nuisait [nɥizɛ], **nuisions** [nɥizjɔ̃], *etc.* → **nuire**
nuisance [nɥizɑ̃s] *nf* : pollution <nuisance sonore : noise pollution>
nuise [nɥiz], *etc.* → **nuire**
nuisible [nɥizibl] *adj* : harmful, injurious
nuit [nɥi] *nf* **1** : night, nighttime **2** : darkness <il fait nuit : it's dark out> **3 de ~** : nocturnal, at night, by night
nul[1], **nulle** [nyl] *adj* **1** : no <je n'ai nul besoin de sortir : I have no need to go out> <sans nul doute : without a doubt, undoubtedly> <nulle part : nowhere> **2** : nil, nonexistent **3** : invalid, null and void **4** : hopeless, useless, worthless <il est nul en biologie : he is hopeless in biology>
nul[2] *pron* : no one, nobody
nullement [nylmɑ̃] *adv* : by no means
nullité [nylite] *nf* **1** : incompetence, worthlessness **2** : nonentity **3** : nullity (of a contract, etc.)
numéraire [nymerer] *nm* : cash
numéral[1], **-rale** [nymeral] *adj, mpl* **-raux** : numeral
numéral[2] *nm, pl* **-raux** : numeral
numérateur [nymeratœr] *nm* : numerator
numération [nymerasjɔ̃] *nf* **1** : notation <numération décimale : decimal notation> **2 numération globulaire** : blood count
numérique [nymerik] *adj* **1** : numerical **2** : digital — **numériquement** *adv*
numéro [nymero] *nm* **1** : number <le numéro deux : number two> <numéro de téléphone : telephone number> **2** : issue (of a periodical) **3 quel numéro!** *fam* : what a character!
numéroter [nymerɔte] *vt* : to number
numismate [nymismat] *nmf* : numismatist, coin collector
numismatique [nymismatik] *nf* : numismatics
nu–pieds [nypje] *adj* : barefoot(ed)
nuptial, -tiale [nypsjal] *adj, mpl* **-tiaux** [-sjo] : nuptial, wedding
nuque [nyk] *nf* : nape of the neck
nutritif, -tive [nytritif, -tiv] *adj* **1** : nourishing, nutritious **2** : nutritional
nutrition [nytrisjɔ̃] *nf* : nutrition — **nutritionnel, -nelle** [-sjɔnɛl] *adj*
nylon [nilɔ̃] *nm* **1** : nylon **2 bas de nylon** : nylon stockings, panty hose
nymphe [nɛ̃f] *nf* : nymph

O

o [o] *nm* : o, the 15th letter of the alphabet
oasis [ɔazis] *nf* : oasis
obédience [ɔbedjɑ̃s] *nf* : allegiance, persuasion <pays d'obédience communiste : Communist countries>
obéir [ɔbeir] *vi* **~ à 1** : to obey **2** SE CONFORMER : to follow, to comply with **3** : to respond to <les freins obéissent à la pression : the brakes respond to pressure>
obéissance [ɔbeisɑ̃s] *nf* : obedience
obéissant, -sante [ɔbeisɑ̃, -sɑ̃t] *adj* : obedient
obélisque [ɔbelisk] *nm* : obelisk
obèse [ɔbɛz] *adj* : obese
obésité [ɔbezite] *nf* : obesity
objecter [ɔbʒɛkte] *vt* **1** : to raise as an objection <il m'objecta que . . . : he objected (to me) that . . .> **2** PRÉTEXTER : to plead <objecter la fatigue : to plead tiredness>
objecteur [ɔbʒɛktœr] *nm* : objector <objecteur de conscience : conscientious objector>
objectif[1], **-tive** [ɔbʒɛktif, -tiv] *adj* : objective — **objectivement** [-tivmɑ̃] *adv*
objectif[2] *nm* **1** BUT : objective, goal **2** : lens (of an optical instrument)
objection [ɔbʒɛksjɔ̃] *nf* : objection
objectivité [ɔbʒɛktivite] *nf* : objectivity
objet [ɔbʒɛ] *nm* **1** : object, thing **2** : subject, topic **3** BUT : goal, purpose <sans objet : pointless, aimless> **4** : object (in grammar) **5 bureau des objets**

trouvés : lost-and-found department **6 objet de famille** : heirloom
obligation [ɔbligasjɔ̃] *nf* **1** : obligation, duty **2** : bond, debenture
obligatoire [ɔbligatwar] *adj* **1** : compulsory, obligatory, mandatory **2** *fam* : inevitable
obligatoirement [ɔbligatwarmɑ̃] *adv* **1** : necessarily, imperatively **2** *fam* : inevitably
obligé, -gée [ɔbliʒe] *adj* **1 être obligé à** : to be indebted to **2 c'est obligé** *fam* : it's bound to happen, it's inevitable
obligeamment [ɔbliʒamɑ̃] *adv* : obligingly
obligeance [ɔbliʒɑ̃s] *nf* AMABILITÉ : kindness, helpfulness
obligeant, -geante [ɔbliʒɑ̃, -ʒɑ̃t] *adj* COMPLAISANT : obliging, kind
obliger [ɔbliʒe] {17} *vt* **1** CONTRAINDRE : to force, to compel **2** : to oblige <vous m'obligez beaucoup : I am much obliged to you>
oblique [ɔblik] *adj* **1** : oblique **2 en ~** : crosswise, diagonally — **obliquement** [ɔblikmɑ̃] *adv*
obliquer [ɔblike] *vi* : to bear, to turn (off) <obliquer à droite : to turn right>
oblitérer [ɔblitere] {87} *vt* : to cancel (a stamp) — **oblitération** [-terasjɔ̃] *nf*
oblong, oblongue [ɔblɔ̃, ɔblɔ̃g] *adj* : oblong
obnubiler [ɔbnybile] *vt* **1** OBSCURCIR : to cloud, to obscure **2** OBSÉDER : to obsess
obole [ɔbɔl] *nf* : small contribution
obscène [ɔpsɛn] *adj* : obscene
obscénité [ɔpsenite] *nf* : obscenity
obscur, -cure [ɔpskyr] *adj* **1** SOMBRE : dark **2** : obscure, vague **3** : abstruse, recondite — **obscurément** [-skyremɑ̃] *adv*
obscurcir [ɔpskyrsir] *vt* **1** ASSOMBRIR : to darken **2** : to obscure, to blur **3** : to make obscure, to confuse — **s'obscurcir** *vr* **1** : to become dark **2** : to become confused
obscurité [ɔpskyrite] *nf* **1** : darkness **2** ANONYMAT : obscurity
obsédant, -dante [ɔpsedɑ̃, -dɑ̃t] *adj* : obsessive, haunting
obsédé, -dée [ɔpsede] *n* : obsessive, fanatic
obséder [ɔpsede] {87} *vt* : to obsess, to haunt
obsèques [ɔpsɛk] *nfpl* : funeral
obséquieux, -quieuse [ɔpsekjø, -kjøz] *adj* : obsequious — **obséquieusement** [-kjøzmɑ̃] *adv*
obséquiosité [ɔpsekjozite] *nf* : obsequiousness
observance [ɔpsɛrvɑ̃s] *nf* : observance
observateur[1], **-trice** [ɔpsɛrvatœr, -tris] *adj* : observant, perceptive
observateur[2], **-trice** *n* : observer
observation [ɔpsɛrvasjɔ̃] *nf* **1** : observance **2** : observing, observation **3** REMARQUE : observation, remark
observatoire [ɔpsɛrvatwar] *nm* **1** : observatory **2** : observation post, vantage point
observer [ɔpsɛrve] *vt* **1** : to observe, to watch **2** : to note, to notice **3** : to keep, to maintain <observer sa position : to maintain one's position> <observer le silence : to keep quiet> — **s'observer** *vr*
obsession [ɔpsesjɔ̃] *nf* : obsession
obsessionnel, -nelle [ɔpsesjɔnɛl] *adj* : obsessive
obsolescent, -cente [ɔpsɔlesɑ̃, -sɑ̃t] *adj* : obsolescent — **obsolescence** [-lesɑ̃s] *nf*
obsolète [ɔpsɔlɛt] *adj* : obsolete
obstacle [ɔpstakl] *nm* **1** : obstacle <faire obstacle : to obstruct> **2** : fence, hurdle (in horseback riding)
obstétrical, -cale [ɔpstetrikal] *adj, mpl* **-caux** [-ko] : obstetric, obstetrical
obstétricien, -cienne [ɔpstetrisjɛ̃, -sjɛn] *n* : obstetrician
obstétrique [ɔpstetrik] *nf* : obstetrics
obstination [ɔpstinasjɔ̃] *nf* : obstinacy, stubbornness
obstiné, -née [ɔpstine] *adj* ENTÊTÉ : obstinate, stubborn — **obstinément** [-nemɑ̃] *adv*
obstiner [ɔpstine] *v* **s'obstiner** *vr* **1 s'obstiner à faire** : to insist on doing **2 ~ dans** : to persist in, to cling to
obstruction [ɔpstryksjɔ̃] *nf* **1** : obstruction, blockage <faire de l'obstruction : to obstruct, to be obstructive> **2** : filibuster <faire de l'obstruction parlementaire : to filibuster>
obstructionniste [ɔpstryksjɔnist] *adj* : obstructive
obstruer [ɔpstrye] *vt* : to obstruct, to block — **s'obstruer** *vr*
obtempérer [ɔptɑ̃pere] {87} *vi* **~ à** : to obey, to comply with
obtenir [ɔptənir] {92} *vt* : to obtain, to get, to secure — **s'obtenir** *vr*
obtention [ɔptɑ̃sjɔ̃] *nf* : obtaining
obtient [ɔptjɛ̃] *pp* → **obtenir**
obturateur [ɔptyratœr] *nm* : shutter (of a camera)
obturation [ɔptyrasjɔ̃] *nf* **1** : closing up, sealing **2** *or* **obturation dentaire** : filling
obturer [ɔptyre] *vt* **1** : to seal, to stop up **2** : to fill (a tooth)
obtus, -tuse [ɔpty, -tyz] *adj* **1** : obtuse (of an angle) **2** : slow-witted, dull
obus [ɔby] *nm* **1** : shell <obus de mortier : mortar shell> **2 éclats d'obus** : shrapnel
obusier [ɔbyzje] *nm* : howitzer
obvier [ɔbvje] {96} *vi* **~ à** : to guard against, to obviate
occasion [ɔkazjɔ̃] *nf* **1** : opportunity, chance **2** : occasion <les grandes occasions : special occasions> **3** : bar-

gain **4 d'~** : secondhand <vêtements d'occasion : secondhand clothing>
occasionnel[1], **-nelle** [ɔkazjɔnɛl] *adj* **1** : occasional **2** FORTUIT : chance, fortuitous
occasionnel[2], **-nelle** *n Can* : temp, temporary employee
occasionnellement [ɔkazjɔnɛlmɑ̃] *adv* : occasionally
occasionner [ɔkazjɔne] *vt* CAUSER : to cause, to bring about
occident [ɔksidɑ̃] *nm* **1** : west **2 l'Occident** : the West
occidental, -tale [ɔksidɑ̃tal] *adj, mpl* **-taux** [-to] : western, Western
Occidental, -tale *n, mpl* **-taux** [-to] : Westerner
occidentaliser [ɔsidɑ̃talize] *vt* : to westernize
occulte [ɔkylt] *adj* : supernatural, occult
occulter [ɔkylte] *vt* **1** : to overshadow **2** : to cover up, to conceal
occupant[1], **-pante** [ɔkypɑ̃,-pɑ̃t] *adj* : occupying
occupant[2], **-pante** *n* : occupant, occupier
occupation [ɔkypasjɔ̃] *nf* **1** : occupation, job **2** : occupancy **3** : (military) occupation
occupé, -pée [ɔkype] *adj* **1** : busy **2** : taken, in use <cette place est occupée : this seat is taken> <la ligne est occupée : the line is busy> **3** : occupied <zone occupée : occupied zone>
occuper [ɔkype] *vt* **1** : to occupy, to hold **2** : to employ, to keep busy **3** REMPLIR : to take up, to fill **4** : to inhabit — **s'occuper** *vr* **1** : to keep busy **2 ~ de** : to handle, to deal with, to take care of
occurrence [ɔkyrɑ̃s] *nf* : instance, case <en l'occurrence : in this case>
océan [ɔseɑ̃] *nm* : ocean
océanien, -nienne [ɔseanjɛ̃, -njɛn] *adj* : Oceanian
Océanien, -nienne *n* : Oceanian
océanique [ɔseanik] *adj* : oceanic, ocean
océanographie [ɔseanɔgrafi] *nf* : oceanography — **océanographique** [-grafik] *adj*
ocelot [ɔslo] *nm* : ocelot
ocre [ɔkr] *nmf* : ocher
octave [ɔktav] *nf* : octave
octet [ɔkte] *nm* : byte
octobre [ɔktɔbr] *nm* : October
octogone [ɔktɔgɔn] *nm* : octagon — **octogonal, -nale** [-gɔnal] *adj*
octroi [ɔktrwa] *nm* : granting
octroyer [ɔktrwaje] {58} *vt* : to grant, to bestow
oculaire[1] [ɔkylɛr] *adj* : ocular, eye
oculaire[2] *nm* : eyepiece
oculiste [ɔkylist] *nmf* : oculist
ode [ɔd] *nf* : ode
odeur [ɔdœr] *nf* : odor, smell, scent
odieux, -dieuse [ɔdjø, -djøz] *adj* EXÉCRABLE : odious, hateful — **odieusement** [-djøzmɑ̃] *adv*
odorant, -rante [ɔdɔrɑ̃, -rɑ̃t] *adj* PARFUMÉ : fragrant, sweet-smelling, odorous
odorat [ɔdɔra] *nm* : sense of smell
odoriférant, -rante [ɔdɔriferɑ̃, -rɑ̃t] *adj* : fragrant
odyssée [ɔdise] *nf* : odyssey
œcuménique [ekymenik] *adj* : ecumenical, nondenominational
œdème [edɛm] *nm* : edema
œil [œj] *nm, pl* **yeux** [jø] **1** : eye <yeux verts : green eyes> <avoir à l'œil : to keep an eye on> <coup d'œil : glance> **2** : look, view <jeter un œil à : to have a quick look at> <d'un œil jaloux : jealously> <voir d'un mauvais œil : to take a dim view of> **3** : eye (of a needle, potato, storm, etc.) **4 → clin**
œillade [œjad] *nf* **1** : wink, glance **2 faire des œillades à** : to make eyes at
œillères [œjɛr] *nfpl* **1** : blinders, blinkers **2 avoir des œillères** : to be narrow-minded
œillet [œjɛ] *nm* **1** : eyelet, grommet **2** : carnation, pink
œsophage [ezɔfaʒ] *nm* : esophagus
œstrogène [estrɔʒɛn] *nm* : estrogen
œuf [œf] *nm, pl* **œufs** [ø] **1** : egg <œufs pochés : poached eggs> **2 étouffer dans l'œuf** : to nip in the bud
œuvre[1] [œvr] *nm* : body of work <l'œuvre peint de Monet : Monet's paintings>
œuvre[2] *nf* **1** : work <œuvre d'art : work of art> **2** : undertaking, task, work <se mettre à l'œuvre : to get down to work> <mise en œuvre : implementation> **3** : effect, work <le médicament a fait son œuvre : the medicine has done its work> **4** *or* **œuvre de bienfaisance** : charitable organization
œuvrer [œvre] *vi* : to work
offensant, -sante [ɔfɑ̃sɑ̃, -sɑ̃t] *adj* INJURIEUX : offensive, insulting
offense [ɔfɑ̃s] *nf* **1** : offense, insult **2** : trespass, sin
offenser [ɔfɑ̃se] *vt* : to offend, to hurt — **s'offenser** *vr* : to take offense
offensif, -sive [ɔfɑ̃sif, -siv] *adj* : offensive, attacking — **offensivement** [-sivmɑ̃] *adv*
offensive *nf* **1** : offensive <passer à l'offensive : to go on the offensive> **2** : onset, onslaught
offert [ɔfɛr] *pp* → **offrir**
offertoire [ɔfertwar] *nm* : offertory
office [ɔfis] *nm* **1** : bureau, agency **2** : office, service (in religion) **3** : office, function <faire office de : to act as> **4 d'~** : automatically, as a matter of course <rejeter d'office : to dismiss out of hand>

officialiser [ɔfisjalize] *vt* : to make official
officiel¹, -cielle [ɔfisjɛl] *adj* : official — **officiellement** [-sjɛlmɑ̃] *adv*
officiel², -cielle *n* : official
officier¹ [ɔfisje] {96} *vi* : to officiate
officier² *nm* : officer
officieux, -cieuse [ɔfisjø, -sjøz] *adj* : unofficial, informal — **officieusement** [-sjøzmɑ̃] *adv*
officinal, -nale [ɔfisinal] *adj, mpl* **-naux** [-no] : medicinal <plantes officinales : medicinal plants>
officine [ɔfisin] *nf* **1** : pharmacy **2** : group, den (of conspirators, etc.)
offrande [ɔfrɑ̃d] *nf* : offering
offrant [ɔfrɑ̃] *nm* **vendre au plus offrant** : to sell to the highest bidder
offre [ɔfr] *nf* **1** : offer, bid <offre d'emploi : job opening> **2 l'offre et la demande** : supply and demand
offrir [ɔfrir] {83} *vt* : to give, to offer — **s'offrir** *vr* **1** : to offer oneself, to volunteer **2** : to treat oneself to <je me suis offerte des vacances : I gave myself a vacation> **3** SE PRÉSENTER : to present itself
offusquer [ɔfyske] *vt* : to offend — **s'offusquer** *vr* : to take offense
ogive [ɔʒiv] *nf* **1** : rib (in architecture) **2** : warhead <ogive nucléaire : nuclear warhead>
ogre, ogresse [ɔgr, ɔgrɛs] *n* **1** : ogre **2 manger comme un ogre** : to eat like a horse
oh¹ [o] *nm* **pousser des oh et des ah** : to ooh and ah
oh² *interj* : oh!
ohé [ɔe] *interj* **1** : hey there! **2 ohé du navire!** : ship ahoy!
ohm [om] *nm* : ohm
oie [wa] *nf* : goose
oignon [ɔɲɔ̃] *nm* **1** : onion **2** : bulb (of a flower) **3** : bunion **4 occupe-toi de tes oignons** *fam* : mind your own business
oindre [wɛ̃dr] {59} *vt* : to anoint
oiseau [wazo] *nm, pl* **oiseaux 1** : bird <oiseau chanteur : songbird> <oiseau de proie : bird of prey> <oiseau marin : seabird> **2** : hod (for bricks, etc.) **3** *fam* : character, oddball
oiseau-mouche [wazomuʃ] *nm, pl* **oiseaux-mouches** : hummingbird
oiseux, -seuse [wazø, -zøz] *adj* INUTILE : pointless, idle
oisif¹, -sive [wazif, -ziv] *adj* : idle — **oisivement** [-zivmɑ̃] *adv*
oisif², -sive *n* : idler
oisillon [wazijɔ̃] *nm* : fledgling
oisiveté [wazivte] *nf* : idleness
oison [wazɔ̃] *nm* : gosling
oléoduc [ɔleɔdyk] *nm* : (oil) pipeline
olfactif, -tive [ɔlfaktif, -tiv] *adj* : olfactory
oligarchie [ɔligarʃi] *nf* : oligarchy
olive¹ [ɔliv] *adj* : olive green
olive² *nf* : olive
olivier [ɔlivje] *nm* **1** : olive tree **2** : olive wood
olympiade [ɔlɛ̃pjad] *nf or* **olympiades** [-pjad] *nfpl* : Olympic Games, Olympics
olympique [ɔlɛ̃pik] *adj* : Olympic <les Jeux olympiques : the Olympic Games>
omanais, -naise [ɔmanɛ, -nɛz] *adj* : Omani
Omanais, -naise *n* : Omani
ombilical, -cale [ɔ̃bilikal] *adj, mpl* **-caux** [-ko] : umbilical
ombrage [ɔ̃braʒ] *nm* **1** : shade **2 porter ombrage à** : to offend **3 prendre ombrage de** : to take umbrage at
ombragé, -gée [ɔ̃braʒe] *adj* : shady, shaded
ombrager [ɔ̃braʒe] {17} *vt* : to shade, to darken
ombrageux, -geuse [ɔ̃braʒø, -ʒøz] *adj* **1** : skittish (of a horse) **2** : touchy, easily offended
ombre [ɔ̃br] *nf* **1** : shade <20 degrés à l'ombre : 20 degrees in the shade> **2** : shadow **3** : obscurity <sortir de l'ombre : to come out into the open> **4** : hint, trace <sans l'ombre d'un doute : without a shadow of a doubt> **5 ombre à paupières** : eyeshadow
ombrelle [ɔ̃brɛl] *nf* : parasol, sunshade
ombrer [ɔ̃bre] *vt* : to shade
omelette [ɔmlɛt] *nf* : omelet
omettre [ɔmɛtr] {53} *vt* : to omit, to leave out
omission [ɔmisjɔ̃] *nf* : omission
omnibus [ɔmnibys] *nm* : local train
omnipotent, -tente [ɔmnipotɑ̃, -tɑ̃t] *adj* : omnipotent — **omnipotence** [-tɑ̃s] *nf*
omniprésent, -sente [ɔmniprezɑ̃, -zɑ̃t] *adj* : omnipresent, ubiquitous
omniscient, -ciente [ɔmnisjɑ̃, -sjɑ̃t] *adj* : omniscient
omnivore [ɔmnivɔr] *adj* : omnivorous
omoplate [ɔmɔplat] *nf* : shoulder blade, scapula
on [ɔ̃] *pron* **1** : one, they, someone, you, we, people <on ne sait jamais : one never knows, you never know> <mon frère et moi, on va à Québec : my brother and I are going to Quebec> <on vous a appelé : someone called you> <comme on dit : as they say> <on jasait : people were talking> <ici on parle français : French is spoken here> **2** *fam* : we, you <alors, on est prêt? : well, are you (finally) ready?> <assez! on s'en va! : that's enough! we're leaving!>
once [ɔ̃s] *nf* : ounce
oncle [ɔ̃kl] *nm* : uncle
onction [ɔ̃ksjɔ̃] → **extrême-onction**
onctueux, -tueuse [ɔ̃ktɥø, -tɥøz] *adj* **1** : smooth, creamy **2** : unctuous
ondatra [ɔ̃datra] *nm* : muskrat

onde [ɔ̃d] *nf* **1** : wave <onde sonore : sound wave> <onde de choc : shock wave> <ondes courtes : shortwave> **2 sur les ondes** : on the radio, on the air
ondée [ɔ̃de] *nf* : (rain) shower
on–dit [ɔ̃di] *nms & pl* : rumor <ce ne sont que des on-dit : that's just hearsay>
ondoyer [ɔ̃dwaje] {58} *vi* : to ripple, to wave
ondulation [ɔ̃dylasjɔ̃] *nf* : undulation, wave
ondulé, -lée [ɔ̃dyle] *adj* **1** : wavy <cheveux ondulés : wavy hair> **2** : corrugated
onduler [ɔ̃dyle] *vi* **1** : to undulate, to wave **2 se faire onduler les cheveux** : to have one's hair waved, to get a permanent
onduleux, -leuse [ɔ̃dylø, -løz] *adj* : undulating, wavy
onéreux, -reuse [ɔnerø, -røz] *adj* COÛTEUX : costly **— onéreusement** [-røzmɑ̃] *adv*
ongle [ɔ̃gl] *nm* **1** : nail <ongles des mains : fingernails> <ongles des pieds : toenails> **2** : claw, talon
onglet [ɔ̃glɛ] *nm* **1** : thumbnail groove (on a knife, etc.) <assemblage à onglet : miter joint> **2** : thumb index
onguent [ɔ̃gɑ̃] *nm* : ointment
onirique [ɔnirik] *adj* : dreamlike, dreamy
onyx [ɔniks] *nm* : onyx
onze[1] [ɔ̃z] *adj* **1** : eleven **2** : eleventh <le onze mai : May eleventh>
onze[2] *nms & pl* : eleven
onzième [ɔ̃zjɛm] *adj & nmf & nm* : eleventh
opacité [ɔpasite] *nf* : opacity
opale [ɔpal] *nf* : opal
opaque [ɔpak] *adj* : opaque
opéra [ɔpera] *nm* **1** : opera <opéra bouffe : comic opera> **2** : opera house
opéra–comique [ɔperakɔmik] *nm, pl* **opéras–comiques** [-kɔmik] : light opera
opérateur, -trice [ɔperatœr, -tris] *n* **1** : operator (of a machine) **2 opérateur de saisie** : computer operator, keyboarder
opération [ɔperasjɔ̃] *nf* **1** : operation, process **2** : operation, surgery <salle d'opération : operating room> **3** CALCUL : calculation, (mathematical) operation **4** : transaction, dealing <opérations de bourse : stock transactions>
opérationnel, -nelle [ɔperasjɔnɛl] *adj* : operational
opératoire [ɔperatwar] *adj* **1** : operating, surgical **2** : operative
opérer [ɔpere] {87} *vt* **1** : to produce, to bring about **2** : to operate on **3** : to carry out, to implement **—** *vi* **1** : to take effect, to work **2** : to proceed, to operate **— s'opérer** *vr* SE PRODUIRE : to occur, to take place
opérette [ɔperɛt] *nf* : operetta, light opera
ophtalmologie [ɔftalmɔlɔʒi] *nf* : ophthalmology **— ophtalmologiste** [-lɔʒist] *or* **ophtalmologue** [-lɔg] *nmf*
opiacé [ɔpjase] *nm* : opiate
opiner [ɔpine] *vi* **1 ~ à** : to consent to **2 opiner du bonnet** : to nod in agreement
opiniâtre [ɔpinjatr] *adj* **1** OBSTINÉ : obstinate, stubborn **2** : dogged, persistent **— opiniâtrement** [-jatrəmɑ̃] *adv*
opiniâtreté [ɔpinjatrəte] *nf* **1** OBSTINATION : obstinacy, stubbornness **2** : doggedness, tenacity
opinion [ɔpinjɔ̃] *nf* : opinion, belief
opium [ɔpjɔm] *nm* : opium
opossum [ɔpɔsɔm] *nm* : opossum
opportun, -tune [ɔpɔrtœ̃, -tyn] *adj* : opportune, timely
opportunément [ɔpɔrtynemɑ̃] *adv* : at the right time, opportunely
opportunisme [ɔpɔrtynism] *nm* : opportunism
opportuniste[1] [ɔpɔrtynist] *adj* : opportunist, opportunistic
opportuniste[2] *nmf* : opportunist
opportunité [ɔpɔrtynite] *nf* : timeliness, appropriateness
opposant[1], **-sante** [ɔpozɑ̃, -zɑ̃t] *adj* : opposing
opposant[2], **-sante** *n* ADVERSAIRE : opponent
opposé[1], **-sée** [ɔpoze] *adj* **1** : opposing, conflicting <points de vues opposés : opposing views> **2** : opposite <le côté opposé : the opposite side> **3 ~ à** : opposed to
opposé[2] *nm* **1** : opposite **2 à l'opposé** : on the other hand **3 à l'opposé de** : contrary to
opposer [ɔpoze] *vt* **1** : to put forth (an objection, etc.) <il n'y a rien à opposer à celà : there's nothing to object to in that> **2** : to put up against <opposer nos troupes à l'ennemi : to pit our forces against the enemy> **3** : to set in opposition, to contrast (ideas, etc.) **4** : to divide, to bring into conflict **— s'opposer** *vr* **1** : to clash, to conflict, to be the opposite **2 ~ à** : to be opposed to
opposition [ɔpozisjɔ̃] *nf* **1** : opposition <en opposition avec : contrary to, against> <par opposition à : in contrast to> **2** : objection (in law, etc.) <faire opposition à un chèque : to stop a check>
oppressant, -sante [ɔpresɑ̃, -sɑ̃t] *adj* : oppressive
oppresser [ɔprese] *vt* : to oppress, to burden
oppresseur [ɔpresœr] *nm* : oppressor
oppressif, -sive [ɔpresif, -siv] *adj* : oppressive

oppression [ɔpresjɔ̃] *nf* **1** : oppression **2** : feeling of suffocation
opprimé, -mée [ɔprime] *n* : oppressed person, underdog
opprimer [ɔprime] *vt* **1** : to oppress **2** : to suppress, to stifle
opprobre [ɔprɔbr] *nm* : opprobrium, disgrace
opter [ɔpte] *vi* ~ **pour** : to opt for, to choose
opticien, -cienne [ɔptisjɛ̃, -sjɛn] *n* : optician
optimal, -male [ɔptimal] *adj, mpl* **-maux** [-mo] : optimal, optimum
optimisme [ɔptimism] *nm* : optimism
optimiste[1] [ɔptimist] *adj* : optimistic
optimiste[2] *nmf* : optimist
optimum [ɔptimɔm] *adj & nm* : optimum
option [ɔpsjɔ̃] *nf* : option, choice
optionnel, -nelle [ɔpsjɔnɛl] *adj* FACULTATIF : optional
optique[1] [ɔptik] *adj* : optic, optical
optique[2] *nf* **1** : optics **2** : perspective, viewpoint
optométrie [ɔptɔmetri] *nf* : optometry — **optométriste** [-metrist] *nmf*
opulent, -lente [ɔpylɑ̃, -lɑ̃t] *adj* : opulent — **opulence** [-lɑ̃s] *nf*
opus [ɔpys] *nm* : opus
or[1] [ɔr] *nm* : gold
or[2] *conj* **1** : but, yet **2** : now
oracle [ɔrakl] *nm* : oracle
orage [ɔraʒ] *nm* **1** : storm, thunderstorm **2** : turmoil
orageux, -geuse [ɔraʒø, -ʒøz] *adj* : stormy
oraison [ɔrɛzɔ̃] *nf* **1** PRIÈRE : prayer **2** **oraison funèbre** : funeral oration
oral, -rale [ɔral] *adj, mpl* **oraux** [ɔro] : oral — **oralement** [ɔralmɑ̃] *adv*
orange[1] [ɔrɑ̃ʒ] *adj* : orange
orange[2] *nf* : orange (fruit)
orange[3] *nm* : orange (color)
orangeade [ɔrɑ̃ʒad] *nf* : orangeade
oranger [ɔrɑ̃ʒe] *nm* : orange tree
orang-outan [ɔrɑutɑ̃] *nm, pl* **orangs-outans** [-utɑ̃] : orangutan
orateur, -trice [ɔratœr, -tris] *n* : orator, speaker
oratoire[1] [ɔratwar] *adj* **1** : oratorical **2** **l'art oratoire** : oratory, eloquence
oratoire[2] *nm* : chapel, oratory
oratorio [ɔratɔrjo] *nm* : oratorio
orbe [ɔrb] *nm* : orb
orbital, -tale [ɔrbital] *adj* **1** : orbital **2** : orbiting <station orbitale : space station>
orbite [ɔrbit] *nf* **1** : orbit <graviter dans l'orbite de : to orbit> **2** : eye socket
orchestre [ɔrkɛstr] *nm* : orchestra — **orchestral, -trale** [-kɛstral] *adj*
orchestrer [ɔrkɛstre] *vt* : to orchestrate — **orchestration** [-kɛstrasjɔ̃] *nf*
orchidée [ɔrkide] *nf* : orchid
ordinaire[1] [ɔrdinɛr] *adj* **1** : ordinary, common, standard **2** HABITUEL : habitual, usual — **ordinairement** [-nɛrmɑ̃] *adv*
ordinaire[2] *nm* **1** : ordinary <hors de l'ordinaire : out of the ordinary> **2** : regular (gas) **3** **comme à l'ordinaire** : as usual **4** **d'ordinaire** : usually, as a rule
ordinal[1], **-nale** [ɔrdinal] *adj, mpl* **-naux** [-no] : ordinal
ordinal[2] *nm* : ordinal number
ordinateur [ɔrdinatœr] *nm* **1** : computer **2** **ordinateur personnel** *or* **ordinateur individuel** : personal computer, PC
ordination [ɔrdinasjɔ̃] *nf* : ordination
ordonnance [ɔrdɔnɑ̃s] *nf* **1** : order, organization **2** : ordinance, ruling **3** : (medical) prescription
ordonnateur, -trice [ɔrdɔnatœr, -tris] *n* **1** : organizer **2** **ordonnateur des pompes funèbres** : funeral director
ordonné, -née [ɔrdɔne] *adj* : tidy, orderly
ordonner [ɔrdɔne] *vt* **1** ARRANGER : to put in order, to arrange **2** COMMANDER : to order, to decree **3** : to ordain (in religion)
ordre [ɔrdr] *nm* **1** : order <ordre alphabétique : alphabetical order> **2** : orderliness, tidiness **3** : order, command <à l'ordre de : payable to> **4** NATURE : nature, sort <d'ordre personnel : of a personal nature> **5** : order (in biology and architecture) **6** : order, society <l'ordre jésuite : the Jesuit order> **7** : (social) order <l'ordre publique : law and order> **8** **ordre du jour** : agenda
ordure [ɔrdyr] *nf* **1** : filth **2** **ordures** *nfpl* : trash, garbage
ordurier, -rière [ɔrdyrje] *adj* : filthy
oreille [ɔrɛj] *nf* **1** : ear <l'oreille interne : inner ear> <prêter l'oreille : to lend an ear, to listen> **2** OUÏE : hearing <avoir l'oreille fine : to have a keen sense of hearing> <dur d'oreille : hard of hearing> **3** : handle (of a bowl, etc.), wing (of furniture)
oreiller [ɔrɛje] *nm* : pillow
oreillette [ɔrɛjɛt] *nf* : auricle (of the heart)
oreillons [ɔrɛjɔ̃] *nmpl* : mumps
ores [ɔr] *adv* **d'ores et déjà** : already
orfèvre [ɔrfɛvr] *nm* : goldsmith
organe [ɔrgan] *nm* **1** : organ <organes génitaux : genitals> <organes des sens : sense organs> **2** : vehicle, instrument **3** VOIX : voice
organigramme [ɔrganigram] *nm* **1** : organizational chart **2** : diagram, flowchart
organique [ɔrganik] *adj* : organic — **organiquement** [-nikmɑ̃] *adv*
organisateur, -trice [ɔrganizatœr, -tris] *n* : organizer
organisation [ɔrganizasjɔ̃] *nf* : organization, organizing

organisationnel, -nelle [ɔrganizasjɔnɛl] *adj* : organizational
organisé, -sée [ɔrganize] *adj* : orderly, organized
organiser [ɔrganize] *vt* : to organize, to arrange, to structure — **s'organiser** *vr* : to get organized
organisme [ɔrganism] *nm* **1** : organism **2** : organization, body
organiste [ɔrganist] *nmf* : organist
orgasme [ɔrgasm] *nm* : orgasm, climax
orge[1] [ɔrʒ] *nm* : barley (grain)
orge[2] *nf* : barley (plant)
orgelet [ɔrʒəlɛ] *nm* : sty, stye (in the eye)
orgie [ɔrʒi] *nf* : orgy
orgue [ɔrg] *nm* : organ (musical instrument)
orgueil [ɔrgœj] *nm* : pride
orgueilleux, -leuse [ɔrgœjø, -jøz] *adj* : proud, haughty — **orgueilleusement** [-jøzmɑ̃] *adv*
orient [ɔrjɑ̃] *nm* **1** : east **2 l'Orient** : the Orient, the East
oriental, -tale [ɔrjɑ̃tal] *adj, mpl* **-taux** [-to] **1** : eastern **2** : oriental
Oriental, -tale *n, mpl* **-taux** : Oriental
orientation [ɔrjɑ̃tasjɔ̃] *nf* **1** POSITION : positioning, aspect (of a house, etc.) **2** : leanings*pl*, tendencies*pl* <orientation sexuelle : sexual orientation> **3** : guidance, counseling **4** : orientation, direction <sens de l'orientation : sense of direction>
orienter [ɔrjɑ̃te] *vt* **1** : to position, to orient **2** GUIDER : to guide, to direct — **s'orienter** *vr* : to find one's bearings
orifice [ɔrifis] *nm* : opening, orifice
oriflamme [ɔriflam] *nf* : banner
origan [ɔrigɑ̃] *nm* : oregano
originaire [ɔriʒinɛr] *adj* **être originaire de** : to be a native of
original[1], **-nale** [ɔriʒinal, -nal] *adj, mpl* **-naux** [-no] **1** : original **2** : eccentric
original[2], **-nale** *n, mpl* **-naux** : character, eccentric
original[3] *nm, pl* **-naux** : original (of a document, painting, etc.)
originalité [ɔriʒinalite] *nf* **1** : originality **2** : eccentricity
origine [ɔriʒin] *nf* **1** : origin **2 à l'origine** : originally
originel, -nelle [ɔriʒinɛl] *adj* : original <péché originel : original sin>
originellement [ɔriʒinɛlmɑ̃] *adv* **1** : originally **2** : from the beginning
orignal [ɔrinal] *nm, pl* **-naux** [-no] : moose
oripeaux [ɔripo] *nmpl* GUENILLES : rags, cheap finery
orme [ɔrm] *nm* : elm
ormeau [ɔrmo] *nm, pl* **ormeaux** [-mo] : abalone
orné, -née [ɔrne] *adj* : ornate, flowery
ornement [ɔrnəmɑ̃] *nm* **1** : ornament, adornment **2 ornements sacerdotaux** : (liturgical) vestments
ornemental, -tale [ɔrnəmɑ̃tal] *adj, mpl* **-taux** [-to] : ornamental
ornementation [ɔrnəmɑ̃tasjɔ̃] *nf* : ornamentation
orner [ɔrne] *vt* **1** DÉCORER : to decorate, to adorn **2** EMBELLIR : to embellish
ornière [ɔrnjɛr] *nf* **1** : rut (in a road) **2 sortir de l'ornière** : to get out of a rut, to get out of trouble
ornithologie [ɔrnitɔlɔʒi] *nf* : ornithology
ornithologiste [ɔrnitɔlɔʒist] *or* **ornithologue** [-tɔlɔg] *nmf* : ornithologist
ornithorynque [ɔrnitɔrɛ̃k] *nm* : platypus
orphelin, -line [ɔrfəlɛ̃, -lin] *n* : orphan
orphelinat [ɔrfəlina] *nm* : orphanage
orteil [ɔrtɛj] *nm* : toe <gros orteil : big toe>
orthodontie [ɔrtɔdɔ̃si] *nf* : orthodontics — **orthodondiste** [-dɔ̃tist] *nmf*
orthodoxe [ɔrtɔdɔks] *adj* : orthodox
orthodoxie [ɔrtɔdɔksi] *nf* : orthodoxy
orthographe [ɔrtɔgraf] *nf* : spelling, orthography
orthographier [ɔrtɔgrafje] {96} *vt* **1** : to spell **2 mal orthographier** : to misspell
orthographique [ɔrtɔgrafik] *adj* : orthographic
orthopédie [ɔrtɔpedi] *nf* : orthopedics — **orthopédiste** [-pedist] *nmf*
orthopédique [ɔrtɔpedi] *adj* : orthopedic
orthophonie [ɔrtɔfɔni] *nf* : speech therapy — **orthophoniste** [-fɔnist] *nmf*
ortie [ɔrti] *nf* : nettle
oryctérope [ɔrikterɔp] *nm* : aardvark
os [ɔs] *nm* **1** : bone **2 en chair et en os** : in the flesh, in person **3 jusqu'à l'os** *or* **jusqu'aux os** : to the core, completely <il était mouillé jusqu'aux os : he was soaked to the bone>
oscillation [ɔsilasjɔ̃] *nf* **1** : oscillation **2** VARIATION : fluctuation, variation **3** : rocking, swaying
osciller [ɔsile] *vi* **1** : to oscillate **2** HÉSITER : to vacillate, to waver **3** : to rock, to sway
osé, -sée [ɔze, -ze] *adj* **1** : daring, bold **2** : risqué
oseille [ɔzɛj] *nf* : sorrel (plant)
oser [ɔze] *vt* **1** : to dare **2 si j'ose dire** : if I may say so
osier [ɔzje] *nm* **1** : willow **2** : wicker <chaise en osier : wickerwork chair>
osmose [ɔsmɔz] *nf* : osmosis
ossature [ɔsatyr] *nf* **1** : skeleton, bone structure **2** : framework
osselets [ɔslɛ] *nmpl* : jacks (game)
ossements [ɔsmɑ̃] *nmpl* : remains, bones
osseux, -seuse [ɔsø, -søz] *adj* : bony <tissu osseux : bone tissue>
ostensible [ɔstɑ̃sibl] *adj* : conspicuous, open — **ostensiblement** [-sibləmɑ̃] *adv*

ostentation [ɔstɑ̃tasjɔ̃] *nf* : ostentation, display
ostentatoire [ɔstɑ̃tatwar] *adj* : ostentatious, showy
ostéopathie [ɔsteɔpati] *nf* : osteopathy — **ostéopathe** [-pat] *nmf*
ostéoporose [ɔsteɔpɔrɔz] *nf* : osteoporosis
ostracisme [ɔstrasism] *nm* : ostracism
otage [ɔtaʒ] *nm* : hostage
otarie [ɔtari] *nf* : sea lion
ôter [ote] *vt* **1** RETIRER : to remove, to take away **2** : to take off <ôte tes bottes : take off your boots> **3** SOUSTRAIRE : to subtract <3 ôté de 10 égale 7 : 3 (subtracted) from 10 equals 7> — **s'ôter** *vr fam* **ôte–toi de là!** : get out of the way!
otite [ɔtit] *nf* : ear infection
oto–rhino–laryngologiste [ɔtɔrinɔlarɛ̃gɔlɔʒist] *nmf* : ear, nose, and throat specialist
ottomane [ɔtɔman] *nf* CANAPÉ : ottoman, sofa
ou [u] *conj* **1** : or **2 ou . . . ou . . .** : either . . . or . . . <ou bien en Grèce ou bien en Inde : either in Greece or India>
où[1] [u] *adv* **1** : where, wherever <où étiez-vous? : where were you?> <où que tu ailles : wherever you go> <par où passer? : which way should we go?> **2 d'~** : from which, from where, therefore
où[2] *pron* : where, that, in which, on which, to which <la ville où je suis né : the town where I was born> <le jour où il est parti : the day that he left>
ouailles [waj] *nfpl* : flock (in religion)
ouais [wɛ] *interj fam* : yeah!, oh sure!
ouate [wat] *nf* **1** : absorbent cotton **2** BOURRE : padding, wadding
ouaté, -tée [wate] *adj* : padded, quilted
oubli [ubli] *nm* **1** : forgetfulness **2** : omission, oversight **3 tomber dans l'oubli** : to sink into oblivion
oublier [ublije] {96} *vt* **1** : to forget, to forget about **2** OMETTRE : to leave out, to omit **3** NÉGLIGER : to forget, to neglect — **s'oublier** *vr* **1** : to be forgotten **2** : to forget oneself
oubliettes [ublijɛt] *nfpl* **1** : dungeon **2 jeter aux oubliettes** : to put completely out of mind
oublieux, -lieuse [ublijø, -jøz] *adj* : forgetful
ouest[1] [wɛst] *adj* : west, western
ouest[2] *nm* **1** : west <un vent d'ouest : west wind> <vers l'ouest : westward> **2 l'Ouest** : the West
ougandais, -daise [ugɑ̃de, -dɛz] *adj* : Ugandan
Ougandais, -daise *n* : Ugandan
oui[1] [wi] *adv* : yes <mais oui! : yes!> <je pense que oui : I think so> <faut-il le prévenir, oui ou non? : do we have to warn him or not?> <tu viens, oui? : are you (really) coming?>
oui[2] *nms & pl* **1** : yes **2 pour un oui ou pour un non** : at the drop of a hat, for no apparent reason
oui–dire [widir] *nms & pl* : hearsay
ouïe [wi] *nf* **1** : sense of hearing **2 ouïes** *nfpl* : gills (of a fish)
ouïr [wir] {60} *vt* : to hear
ouistiti [wistiti] *nm* : marmoset
ouragan [uragɑ̃] *nm* **1** : hurricane **2** : storm, tumult
ourdir [urdir] *vt* : to hatch (a plot, etc.)
ourler [urle] *vt* : to hem
ourlet [urlɛ] *nm* : hem
ours [urs] *nm* **1** : bear **2 ours polaire** : polar bear
ourse [urs] *nf* **1** : she-bear **2 la Grande Ourse** : the Big Dipper, Ursa Major **3 la Petite Ourse** : the Little Dipper, Ursa Minor
oursin [ursɛ̃] *nm* : sea urchin
ourson [ursɔ̃] *nm* : bear cub
ouste *or* **oust** [ust] *interj fam* : out!
outarde [utard] *nf Can* : Canada goose
outil [uti] *nm* : tool
outillage [utijaʒ] *nm* **1** : set of tools **2** : equipment <outillage agricole : agricultural equipment>
outiller [utije] *vt* ÉQUIPER : to equip — **s'outiller** *vr*
outrage [utraʒ] *nm* **1** : insult **2 outrage à la pudeur** : indecent behavior **3 outrage à magistrat** *France* : contempt of court **4 outrage au tribunal** *Can* : contempt of court
outragé, -gée [utraʒe] *adj* : gravely offended, outraged
outrageant, -geante [utraʒɑ̃, -ʒɑ̃t] *adj* INJURIEUX : insulting, abusive
outrager [utraʒe] {17} *vt* INSULTER : to offend, to insult
outrageusement [utraʒøzmɑ̃] *adv* : outrageously, excessively
outrance [utrɑ̃s] *nf* : excess <boire à outrance : to drink to excess>
outrancier, -cière [utrɑ̃sje, -sjɛr] *adj* : excessive, extreme
outre[1] [utr] *adv* **1 en ~** : in addition, besides **2 outre mesure** : overly, unduly **3 passer outre à** : to pay no heed to, to disregard
outre[2] *prep* : besides, in addition to <outre cela : in addition to that, furthermore>
outré, -trée [utre] *adj* **1** EXAGÉRÉ : exaggerated, excessive **2** INDIGNÉ : indignant, outraged
outre–Atlantique [utratlɑ̃tik] *adv* : across the Atlantic
outrecuidance [utrəkɥidɑ̃s] *nf* : presumptuousness
outrecuidant, -dante [utrəkɥidɑ̃, -dɑ̃t] *adj* : presumptuous, arrogant
outre–mer [utrɔmɛr] *adv* : overseas
outrepasser [utrəpase] *vt* : to exceed, to overstep

outrer [utre] *vt* **1** EXAGÉRER : to exaggerate **2** INDIGNER : to outrage
ouvert[1] [uvɛr] *pp* → **ouvrir**
ouvert[2], **-verte** [uvɛr, -vɛrt] *adj* **1** : open <ouvert au public : open to the public> <grand ouvert : wide open> <à bras ouverts : with open arms> **2** : frank, open **3** : on, running <laissez la lumière ouverte : leave the light on>
ouvertement [uvɛrtəmɑ̃] *adv* : openly
ouverture [uvɛrtyr] *nf* **1** : opening, aperture **2** : openness <ouverture d'esprit : open-mindedness> **3** : overture (in music)
ouvrable [uvrabl] *adj* **1 jour ouvrable** : weekday, working day **2 heures ouvrables** : business hours
ouvrage [uvraʒ] *nm* **1** : work, working <se mettre à l'ouvrage : to get down to work> **2** : book **3** : piece of work <ouvrage d'art : construction work>
ouvragé, -gée [uvraʒe] *adj* : finely worked, elaborate
ouvrant, -vrante [uvrɑ̃, -vrɑ̃t] *adj* **toit ouvrant** : sunroof
ouvré, -vrée [uvre] *adj* : elaborate, finely worked
ouvre-boîtes [uvrəbwat] *nms & pl* : can opener
ouvre-bouteilles [uvrəbutɛj] *nms & pl* : bottle opener
ouvreur, -vreuse [uvrœr, -vrøz] *n* **1** : usher, usherette *f* (in a theater) **2** : opener (in games)
ouvrier[1], **-vrière** [uvrije, -vrijɛr] *adj* : working-class <la class ouvrière : the working class>
ouvrier[2], **-vrière** *n* : worker
ouvrir [uvrir] {83} *vt* **1** : to open **2** : to unlock, to undo **3** : to turn on (a light, radio, etc.) **4** : to start up, to begin <ouvrir le feu : to open fire> — *vi* : to open — **s'ouvrir** *vr* **1** : to open, to come open **2** : to open up, to confide **3** : to cut <s'ouvrir la main : to cut one's hand> **4** ~ **à** : to become open to (opportunities, etc.)
ouzbek [uzbɛk] *adj* : Uzbek
Ouzbek *nmf* : Uzbek
ovaire [ɔvɛr] *nm* : ovary — **ovarien, -rienne** [ɔvarjɛ̃, -rjɛn] *adj*
ovale [ɔval] *adj & nm* : oval
ovation [ɔvasjɔ̃] *nf* : ovation
ovationner [ɔvasjɔne] *vt* : to applaud, to give an ovation to
overdose [ɔvœrdoz] *nf* SURDOSE : overdose
ovuler [ɔvyle] *vi* : to ovulate
ovulation [ɔvylasjɔ̃] *nf* : ovulation
ovule [ɔvyl] *nm* : ovum
oxydable [ɔksidabl] *adj* : liable to rust
oxyde [ɔksid] *nm* **1** : oxide **2 oxyde de carbone** : carbon monoxide
oxyder [ɔkside] *vt* : to oxidize — **oxydation** [-sidasjɔ̃] *nf*
oxygène [ɔksiʒɛn] *nm* : oxygen
oxyure [ɔksyr] *nm* : pinworm
ozone [ozɔn] *nm* : ozone <couche d'ozone : ozone layer>

P

p [pe] *nm* : p, the 16th letter of the alphabet
pacage [pakaʒ] *nm* **1** : grazing **2** : pasture
pacane [pakan] *nf Can or* **noix de pacane** : pecan
pacemaker [pɛsmekœr] *nm* : pacemaker
pachyderme [paʃidɛrm] *nm* : pachyderm, elephant
pacificateur[1], **-trice** [pasifikatœr, -tris] *adj* : pacifying, peacemaking
pacificateur[2], **-trice** *n* : peacemaker
pacification [pasifikasjɔ̃] *nf* : pacification
pacifier [pasifje] {96} *vt* APAISER : to pacify, to calm
pacifique [pasifik] *adj* **1** PAISIBLE : peaceful, pacific **2 l'océan Pacifique** : the Pacific Ocean — **pacifiquement** [-fikmɑ̃] *adv*
pacifisme [pasifism] *nm* : pacificism
pacifiste[1] [pasifist] *adj* : pacifist, pacifistic
pacifiste[2] *nmf* : pacifist
pack [pak] *nm* : pack
pacotille [pakɔtij] *nf* : shoddy goods <bijoux de pacotille : cheap jewelry>
pacte [pakt] *nm* ACCORD : pact, agreement
pactiser [paktize] *vi* : to come to an agreement, to come to terms
pactole [paktɔl] *nm* : gold mine, bonanza
paddock [padɔk] *nm* : paddock
pagaie [pagɛ] *nf* : paddle
pagaille *or* **pagaïe** [pagaj] *nf fam* **1** : mess, chaos **2 il y en a en pagaille** : there are loads of them
paganisme [paganism] *nm* : paganism
pagayer [pagaje] {11} *vi* : to paddle
page [paʒ] *nf* **1** : page <page blanche : blank page> **2** : passage (in a book or piece of music)
pagination [paʒinasjɔ̃] *nf* : pagination
paginer [paʒine] *vt* : to paginate
pagne [paɲ] *nm* : loincloth
pagode [pagɔd] *nf* : pagoda
paie[1] [pɛ], **paiera** [pɛra], *etc.* → **payer**
paie[2] [pɛ] *nf* : pay, wages *pl*
paiement [pɛmɑ̃] *nm* : payment
païen, païenne [pajɛ̃, -jɛn] *adj & n* : pagan, heathen

paillard, -larde [pajar, -jard] *adj* : bawdy
paillardise [pajardiz] *nf* : bawdiness
paillasse[1] [pajas] *nf* : straw mattress
paillasse[2] *nm* : clown
paillasson [pajasɔ̃] *nm* : doormat
paille [paj] *nf* **1** : straw, piece of straw <être sur la paille : to be penniless> **2** : (drinking) straw **3 paille de fer** : steel wool
pailler [paje] *vt* : to mulch
paillette [pajɛt] *nf* **1** : sequin <robe à paillettes : sequined dress> **2** : speck, flake <savon en paillettes : soap flakes>
paillis [paji] *nms & pl* : mulch
pain [pɛ̃] *nm* **1** : bread <pain grillé : toast> <pain d'épice : gingerbread> <pain doré *Can* : French toast> **2** : loaf **3** : cake, bar <pain de savon : bar of soap>
pair[1], **paire** [pɛr] *adj* : even <nombre pair : even number>
pair[2] *nm* **1** NOBLE : peer **2** ÉGAL : peer, equal <aller de pair : to go hand in hand> <hors pair : without equal, unrivaled> **3** : par (in finance) **4 travailler au pair** : to work as an au pair
paire [pɛr] *nf* : pair
paisible [pezibl] *adj* : peaceful, quiet **— paisiblement** [-ziblə̃mɑ̃] *adv*
paître [pɛtr] {61} *vi* : to graze
paix [pɛ] *nf* **1** : peace <la paix mondiale : world peace> **2** CALME, TRANQUILLITÉ : peace, calm, tranquility
pakistanais, -naise [pakistanɛ, -nɛz] *adj* : Pakistani
Pakistanais, -naise *n* : Pakistani
palabrer [palabre] *vi* : to discuss endlessly
palabres [palabr] *nfpl* : endless discussions, palaver
palace [palas] *nm* : luxury hotel
palais [palɛ] *nms & pl* **1** : palace **2** : palate **3 palais de justice** : courthouse, courts of law
palan [palɑ̃] *nm* : hoist
pale [pal] *nf* **1** : blade (of a propeller, etc.) **2** : paddle
pâle [pal] *adj* **1** BLÊME : pale, pallid **2** CLAIR : light, pale <jaune pâle : pale yellow>
palefrenier, -nière [palfrənje] *n* : groom (in a stable)
paléontologie [paleɔ̃tɔlɔʒi] *nf* : paleontology **— paléontologiste** [-lɔʒist] *nmf*
paleron [palrɔ̃] *nm* : chuck (steak)
palestinien, -nienne [palestinjɛ̃, -njɛn] *adj* : Palestinian
Palestinien, -nienne *n* : Palestinian
palet [palɛ] *nm* : puck (in ice hockey)
paletot [palto] *nm* : short coat
palette [palɛt] *nf* **1** *Can* : wooden spatula (used in making maple products) **2** : palette **3** : shoulder <palette de porc : shoulder of pork> **4** : pallet, loading platform **5** : range (of colors, ideas, etc.)
palétuvier [paletyvje] *nm* : mangrove
pâleur [palœr] *nf* : paleness, pallor
palier [palje] *nm* **1** : landing (of a staircase), floor **2** NIVEAU : level, stage <par paliers : by stages>
pâlir [palir] *vi* **1** : to turn pale **2** : to fade, to dim
palissade [palisad] *nf* : fence, palisade
palissandre [palisɑ̃dr] *nm* : rosewood
palliatif[1], **-tive** [paljatif, -tiv] *adj* : palliative
palliatif[2] [paljatif] *nm* **1** : palliative **2** : stopgap, expedient
pallier [palje] {96} *vt* : to compensate for, to mitigate
palmarès [palmarɛs] *nms & pl* **1** : list of winners **2** : record of achievements
palme [palm] *nf* **1** : palm leaf **2** : palm, distinction <remporter la palme : to be victorious> **3** : flipper
palmé, -mée [palme] *adj* : webbed <patte palmée : webbed foot>
palmier [palmje] *nm* : palm tree
palmure [palmyr] *nf* : web (of a bird's foot)
pâlot, -lotte [palo, -lɔt] *adj* : pale, peaked
palourde [palurd] *nf* : clam
palpable [palpabl] *adj* : palpable, tangible
palper [palpe] *vt* **1** : to palpate (in medicine) **2** : to feel, to finger
palpitant, -tante [palpitɑ̃, -tɑ̃t] *adj* : thrilling, exciting
palpitation [palpitasjɔ̃] *nf* : palpitation
palpiter [palpite] *vi* **1** : to palpitate, to throb **2** : to quiver, to flutter
paludisme [palydism] *nm* : malaria
pâmer [pame] *v* **se pâmer** *vr* **1** : to be ecstatic, to swoon **2 ~ de** : to be overcome with
pâmoison [pamwazɔ̃] *nf* **tomber en pâmoison** : to swoon
pampa [pɑ̃pa] *nf* : pampas *pl*
pamphlet [pɑ̃flɛ] *nm* : lampoon
pamplemousse [pɑ̃pləmus] *nmf* : grapefruit
pan [pɑ̃] *nm* **1** : section, piece **2** : side, face **3** : tail (of a garment) <pan de chemise : shirttail>
panacée [panase] *nf* : panacea, nostrum
panache [panaʃ] *nm* **1** : plume <panache de fumée : trail of smoke> **2** : panache, verve
panaché, -chée [panaʃe] *adj* **1** : variegated, multicolored **2** : mixed <salade panachée : mixed salad>
panais [panɛ] *nms & pl* : parsnip
panaméen, -méenne [panameɛ̃, -meɛn] *adj* : Panamanian
Panaméen, -méenne *n* : Panamanian
pancarte [pɑ̃kart] *nf* **1** : sign, notice **2** : placard
pancréas [pɑ̃kreas] *nm* : pancreas **— pancréatique** [-kreatik] *adj*

panda [pãda] *nm* : panda
panégyrique [paneʒirik] *nm* : panegyric
paner [pane] *vt* : to coat with breadcrumbs, to bread
panier [panje] *nm* **1** : basket <panier à provisions : shopping basket> <panier de pêche : creel> **2 panier à salade** : lettuce spinner **3 panier percé** *fam* : spendthrift
panique[1] [panik] *adj* : panic <peur panique : terror>
panique[2] *nf* : panic <pris de panique : panic-stricken>
paniquer [panike] *vi fam* : to panic — *vt fam* : to throw into a panic
panne [pan] *nf* **1** : breakdown, failure <panne d'électricité : power failure, blackout> **2 en panne de** : out of <en panne d'essence : out of gas>
panneau [pano] *nm, pl* **panneaux 1** : panel **2** : sign, notice **3 panneau de signalisation** : road sign **4 panneau fibreux** : fiberboard **5 panneau indicateur** : signpost **6 panneau publicitaire** : billboard
panonceau [panɔ̃so] *nm, pl* **-ceaux 1** : plaque (at a professional office, etc.) **2** PANCARTE : sign
panoplie [panɔpli] *nf* **1** : display of arms **2** : array, range **3** : outfit, costume (for children)
panorama [panɔrama] *nm* **1** : panorama **2** : overview
panoramique [panɔramik] *adj* : panoramic
panse [pãs] *nf fam* : paunch, belly
pansement [pãsmã] *nm* : dressing, bandage
panser [pãse] *vt* **1** : to groom (a horse) **2** : to dress, to bandage
pansu, -sue [pãsy] *adj* : potbellied
pantalon [pãtalɔ̃] *nm* : pants *pl*, trousers *pl*
pantelant, -lante [pãtlã, -lãt] *adj* : panting, gasping for breath
panthère [pãtɛr] *nf* : panther
pantin [pãtɛ̃] *nm* **1** : jumping jack (toy) **2** FANTOCHE : puppet (person)
pantois, -toise [pãtwa, -twaz] *adj* : flabbergasted
pantomime [pãtɔmim] *nf* **1** : mime **2** : pantomime show **3** : scene, fuss
pantouflard, -flarde [pãtuflar, -flard] *n fam* : homebody
pantoufle [pãtufl] *nf* : slipper
pantoute [pãtut] *adv Can fam* : no, not at all
panure [panyr] *nf* CHAPELURE : bread crumbs *pl*
paon [pã] *nm* : peacock
papa [papa] *nm fam* : dad, daddy
papal, -pale [papal] *adj, mpl* **papaux** [papo] : papal
papauté [papote] *nf* : papacy
papaye [papaj] *nf* : papaya
pape [pap] *nm* : pope
paperasserie [paprasri] *nf* : paperwork, red tape
papeterie [papetri] *nf* : stationery
papier [papje] *nm* **1** : paper **2** : document, paper **3** : article, review **4 papier d'aluminium** : aluminum foil, tinfoil **5 papier de verre** *France* : sandpaper **6 papier hygiénique** : toilet paper **7 papier journal** : newsprint **8 papier mouchoir** *Can* : tissue **9 papier peint** : wallpaper **10 papier sablé** *Can* : sandpaper **11 papier tue–mouches** : flypaper **12 papiers** *nmpl* : (identification) papers
papier–monnaie [papjemɔne] *nm, pl* **papiers–monnaies** : paper money
papille [papij] *nf* **papilles gustatives** : taste buds
papillon [papijɔ̃] *nm* **1** : butterfly **2 papillon de nuit** : moth
papillonner [papijɔne] *vi* : to flit about, to flutter around
papillote [papijɔt] *nf* : aluminum foil, foil wrapping
papilloter [papijɔte] *vi* **1** : to flicker, to twinkle **2** : to blink, to flutter (of eyelids)
papotage [papɔtaʒ] *nm* : gabbing, chattering
papoter [papɔte] *vi* : to gab, to chatter
paprika [paprika] *nm* : paprika
papyrus [papirys] *nm* : papyrus
Pâque [pak] *nf* : Passover
paquebot [pakbo] *nm* : liner, ship
pâquerette [pakrɛt] *nf* : daisy
Pâques[1] [pak] *nm* : Easter <la semaine de Pâques : Easter week>
Pâques[2] *nfpl* : Easter <joyeuses Pâques! : Happy Easter!>
paquet [pakɛ] *nm* **1** : package, bundle **2** : packet, pack (of cigarettes, etc.) **3** : heap, pile, mass **4 mettre le paquet** *fam* : to go all out
paqueter [pakte] *vt Can fam* **1** : to pack (a suitcase) **2** : to pack, to fill to capacity
par [par] *prep* **1** : through <par la porte : through the door> **2** : by, by means of <par avion : by airmail> **3** : as, for <par exemple : for example> **4** : per <dix dollars par personne : ten dollars per person> **5** : around, near <il habite par ici : he lives around here> **6** : at, during <par moments : at times> **7** : from, out of, for the sake of <par amour : out of love> **8** : according to, by <classé par âge : ranked by age> **9 de ~** : throughout <de par le monde : all over the world> **10 de ~** : by virtue of **11** : **par–ci par–là** : here and there **12** : **par trop** : excessively
parabole [parabɔl] *nf* **1** : parable **2** : parabola
parabolique [parabɔlik] *adj* : parabolic
parachever [paraʃve] {52} *vt* PARFAIRE : to complete, to perfect

parachute [paraʃyt] *nm* : parachute — **parachuter** [-ʃyte] *vt*
parachutiste [paraʃytist] *nmf* **1** : parachutist **2** : paratrooper
parade [parad] *nf* **1** DÉFILÉ : parade **2** : parry (in sports) **3 de ~** : outward, superficial **4 faire parade de** : to display, to make a show of
parader [parade] *vi* : to strut about, to show off
paradigme [paradim] *nm* : paradigm
paradis [paradi] *nm* : paradise, heaven
paradisiaque [paradizjak] *adj* : heavenly
paradoxal, -xale [paradɔksal] *adj, mpl* **-xaux** [-kso] : paradoxical — **paradoxalement** [-ksalmɑ̃] *adv*
paradoxe [paradɔks] *nm* : paradox
parafe, parafer [paraf, parafe] → **paraphe, parapher**
paraffine [parafin] *nf* : paraffin
parafoudre [parafudr] *nm* : lightning rod
parages [paraʒ] *nmpl* **1** : waters <parages étrangers : foreign waters> **2 dans les parages** : in the vicinity, around
paragraphe [paragraf] *nm* : paragraph
paraguayen, -guayenne [paragwejɛ̃, -gwejɛn] *adj* : Paraguayan
Paraguayen, -guayenne *n* : Paraguayan
paraissait [parɛsɛ], *etc.* → **paraître**
paraisse [parɛs], *etc.* → **paraître**
paraître [paretr] {7} *vi* **1** : to appear <paraître en public : to appear in public> **2** : to be published <à paraître : forthcoming> **3** : to show, to be visible **4** SEMBLER : to seem, to look — *v impers* **1** : to seem, to appear <il paraît que tout s'est arrangé : everything seems to be all right> **2 paraît–il** *or* **à ce qu'il paraît** : apparently
parallèle[1] [paralɛl] *adj* **1** : parallel **2** SEMBLABLE : similar **3** : unofficial, alternative
parallèle[2] *nm* **1** : parallel **2** : comparison <mettre en parallèle : to compare>
parallèle[3] *nf* : parallel line
parallèlement [paralɛlmɑ̃] *adv* : at the same time, concurrently
parallélogramme [paralelɔgram] *nm* : parallelogram
paralyser [paralyze] *vt* **1** : to paralyze **2** : to bring to a standstill
paralysie [paralizi] *nf* **1** : paralysis **2 paralysie cérébrale** : cerebral palsy
paralytique [paralitik] *adj* : paralytic
paramètre [parametr] *nm* : parameter
parangon [paraɡɔ̃] *nm* MODÈLE : paragon
paranoïa [paranɔja] *nf* : paranoia
paranoïaque [paranɔjak] *adj & nmf* : paranoiac, paranoid
paranormal, -male [paranormal] *adj, mpl* **-maux** [-mo] : paranormal
parapet [parapɛ] *nm* : parapet
paraphe [paraf] *nm* **1** : initials *pl* **2** : signature **3** : flourish, ornamental stroke (on a signature)
parapher [parafe] *vt* **1** : to initial **2** : to sign **3** : to add a flourish to (a signature)
paraphrase [parafraz] *nf* : paraphrase
paraphraser [parafraze] *vt* : to paraphrase
paraplégique [parapleʒik] *adj & nmf* : paraplegic
parapluie [paraplɥi] *nm* : umbrella
parascolaire [paraskɔlɛr] *adj* : extracurricular
parasitaire [parazitɛr] *adj* : parasitic
parasite[1] [parazit] *adj* : parasitic
parasite[2] *nm* **1** : parasite **2 parasites** *nmpl* : interference, static
parasol [parasɔl] *nm* : parasol, sunshade
paratonnerre [paratɔnɛr] *nm* : lightning rod
paravent [paravɑ̃] *nm* : screen, partition
parc [park] *nm* **1** : park <parc d'attractions : amusement park> <parc zoologique : zoological gardens> **2** : grounds *pl* **3** ENCLOS : playpen, pen, enclosure <parc à huîtres : oyster bed> <parc à moutons : sheepfold> <parc de stationnement : parking lot> **4** : total number, stock <parc de voitures : fleet of automobiles>
parcelle [parsɛl] *nf* **1** : fragment **2** : plot, parcel <parcelle de terre : plot of land>
parcelliser [parselize] *vt* : to divide, to split up
parce que [parskə] *conj* : because
parchemin [parʃəmɛ̃] *nm* : parchment
parcimonie [parsimɔni] *nf* : parsimony <avec parcimonie : sparingly>
parcimonieux, -nieuse [parsimɔnjø, -njøz] *adj* : parsimonious, sparing — **parcimonieusement** [-njøzmɑ̃] *adv*
par–ci, par–là [parsiparla] → **par**
parcmètre [parkmetr] *nm France* : parking meter
parcomètre [parkɔmetr] *nm Can* : parking meter
parcourir [parkurir] {23} *vt* **1** : to cover (a distance), to travel through **2** : to leaf through, to skim (a text)
parcours [parkur] *nm* **1** : course (of a river), route (of a bus, etc.) **2** : course (in sports) **3** : career, (professional) development
par–delà *or* **par delà** [pardəla] *prep* : beyond, across <par-delà les mers : beyond the seas> <par-delà les siècles : across the centuries>
par–dessous [pardəsu] *adv & prep* : underneath
pardessus [pardəsy] *nm* **1** : overcoat **2** *Can* CLAQUES : rubbers *pl*
par–dessus[1] [pardəsy] *adv* : over, above, on top <sauter par-dessus : to

jump over (it)> <mets-le par-dessus : put it up top>

par–dessus[2] *prep* **1** : over, above <par-dessus le mur : above the wall> <jeter qqch par-dessus bord : to throw sth overboard> **2 par–dessus tout** : above all

par–devant[1] [pardəvɑ̃] *adv* : in front, at the front

par–devant[2] *prep* : in front of, in the presence of

pardon [pardɔ̃] *nm* **1** : forgiveness, pardon **2 pardon?** : pardon?, what did you say? **3 pardon!** : pardon me!, sorry!

pardonnable [pardɔnabl] *adj* : forgivable, pardonable, excusable

pardonner [pardɔne] *vt* **1** : to forgive, to pardon **2 pardonnez–moi!** : excuse me! — *vi* **ne pas pardonner** : to be fatal <une maladie qui ne pardonne pas : a fatal illness>

paré, -rée [pare] *adj* : ready, prepared <vous voilà paré! : you're all set!>

pare–balles [parbal] *adj s & pl* : bullet-proof

pare–brise [parbriz] *nms & pl* : windshield

pare–chocs [parʃɔk] *nms & pl* : bumper

pare–feu [parfø] *nms & pl* : firebreak

parégorique [paregɔrik] *nm or* **élixir parégorique** : paregoric

pareil[1] [parɛj] *adv fam* **1** : the same, in the same way <faire pareil : to do the same (thing)> **2** *Can fam* : all the same, anyhow <viens nous voir pareil : come see us anyway>

pareil[2], **-reille** [parɛj] *adj* **1** SEMBLABLE : similar, alike **2** TEL : such <une pareille maison : such a house, a house like this>

pareil[3], **-reille** *n* **1** : equal <il n'a pas son pareil : he's second to none> <son talent est sans pareil : her talent is unequaled> <une vue sans pareille : a view beyond compare> **2 ses pareils** : one's peers, one's fellows

pareil[4] *nm fam* **c'est du pareil au même** : it's all the same, six of one and a half dozen of the other

pareillement [parɛjmɑ̃] *adv* **1** ÉGALEMENT : in the same way <s'habiller pareillement : to dress alike> **2** AUSSI : also, too <et à vous pareillement : to you, too>

parement [parmɑ̃] *nm* : facing

parent[1], **-rente** [parɑ̃, -rɑ̃t] *adj* **1** : similar, related **2** ~ **à** *or* ~ **avec** : related to, kin to

parent[2], **-rente** *n* **1** : relative, relation **2 parent par alliance** : in-law

parental, -tale [parɑ̃tal] *adj, mpl* **-taux** [-to] : parental

parenté [parɑ̃te] *nf* **1** : relationship, kinship **2** : family, relations *pl*

parenthèse [parɑ̃tɛz] *nf* **1** : parenthesis, bracket **2** : digression <entre parenthèses *or* par parenthèse : incidentally, by the way>

parents [parɑ̃] *nmpl* **1** : parents **2** ANCÊTRES : ancestors, forebears

parer [pare] *vt* **1** : to adorn **2** : to dress, to trim (in cooking) **3** : to ward off, to parry — *vi* ~ **à** : to guard against, to be prepared for, to deal with — **se parer** *vr* **1** : to dress oneself up **2** ~ **contre** : to prepare oneself for

pare–soleil [parsɔlɛj] *nms & pl* : sun visor

paresse [parɛs] *nf* : laziness, idleness

paresser [parɛse] *vi* FAINÉANTER : to laze around

paresseux[1], **-seuse** [parɛsø, -søz] *adj* : lazy — **paresseusement** [-søzmɑ̃] *adv*

paresseux[2] *nm* : sloth (animal)

parfaire [parfɛr] {62} *vt* PEAUFINER : to perfect, to complete, to refine (style, etc.)

parfait[1], **-faite** [parfɛ, -fɛt] *adj* **1** : perfect **2** : absolute, complete — **parfaitement** [-fɛtmɑ̃] *adv*

parfait[2] *nm* **1** : perfect (tense) **2** : parfait (dessert)

parfois [parfwa] *adv* QUELQUEFOIS : sometimes

parfum [parfœ̃] *nm* **1** : scent, fragrance **2** : flavor (of ice cream, tea, etc.) **3** : perfume

parfumé, -mée [parfyme] *adj* **1** ODORANT : fragrant, scented, sweet-smelling **2** : flavored <parfumé au citron : lemon-flavored>

parfumer [parfyme] *vt* **1** : to scent, to perfume **2** : to flavor — **se parfumer** *vr* : to wear perfume

parfumerie [parfymri] *nf* **1** : perfume shop **2** : perfume industry **3** : perfumes *pl*

pari [pari] *nm* : bet, wager

paria [parja] *nm* : pariah, outcast

parier [parje] {96} *vt* : to bet, to wager

parieur, -rieuse [parjœr, -rjøz] *n* : bettor, better

parisien, -sienne [parizjɛ̃, -zjɛn] *adj* : Parisian

Parisien, -sienne *n* : Parisian

paritaire [paritɛr] *adj* : joint <commission paritaire : joint commission>

parité [parite] *nf* : parity, equality

parjure[1] [parʒyr] *adj* : disloyal, faithless

parjure[2] *nm* : betrayal

parjure[3] *nmf* : traitor

parjurer [parʒyre] *v* **se parjurer** *vr* : to perjure oneself

parka [parka] *nm* : parka

parking [parkiŋ] *nm* **1** STATIONNEMENT : parking **2** : parking lot

parlant, -lante [parlɑ̃, -lɑ̃t] *adj* **1** : talking (of movies, etc.) **2** : vivid, eloquent, graphic **3** : talkative

parlement [parləmɑ̃] *nm* : parliament

parlementaire[1] [parləmɑ̃tɛr] *adj* : parliamentary

parlementaire[2] *nmf* : parliamentarian
parlementer [parlɔmɑ̃te] *vi* NÉGOCIER : to negotiate, to parley
parler[1] [parle] *vt* : to talk, to speak <parler (le) français : to speak French> <parler affaires : to talk business> — *vi* **1** : to talk, to speak **2 ~ à** : to talk to (someone) **3 ~ de** : to mention, to refer to <sans parler de son accent : not to mention his accent> **4 n'en parlons plus** : let's forget about it — **se parler** *vr* **1** : to speak to each other **2** : to be on speaking terms **3** : to be spoken
parler[2] *nm* **1** : speech, way of speaking **2** : dialect
parleur, -leuse [parlœr, -løz] *n* : talker, speaker <beau parleur : smooth talker>
parloir [parlwar] *nm* : parlor
parlote *or* **parlotte** [parlɔt] *nf fam* CAUSETTE : chat, chitchat
parmesan [parməzɑ̃] *nm* : Parmesan
parmi [parmi] *prep* **1** : among <une possibilité parmi d'autres : one possibility among others> **2** : in the midst of, with
parodie [parɔdi] *nf* : parody
parodier [parɔdje] {96} *vt* : to parody, to mimic
paroi [parwa] *nf* **1** CLOISON : partition **2** : wall (in anatomy and biology) **3** : inner surface, face <paroi rocheuse : rock face>
paroisse [parwas] *nf* : parish
paroissial, -siale [parwasjal] *adj, mpl* **-siaux** [-sjo] : parish, parochial
paroissien, -sienne [parwasjɛ̃, -sjɛn] *n* : parishioner
parole [parɔl] *nf* **1** : (spoken) word <prendre la parole : to speak> **2** PROMESSE : word, promise <parole d'honneur : word of honor> **3** : speech <elle a retrouvé la parole : she regained the power of speech> **4 paroles** *nfpl* : lyrics
paroxysme [parɔksism] *nm* : height, climax (of pain, enthusiasm, etc.)
parquer [parke] *vt* **1** : to pen <bétail parqué : penned cattle> **2** ENTASSER : to herd together **3** GARER : to park
parquet [parkɛ] *nm* **1** : parquet (floor) **2** *France* : public prosecutor's office **3 parquet de la bourse** : floor of the stock exchange
parrain [parɛ̃] *nm* **1** : godfather **2** : sponsor, patron
parrainage [parɛnaʒ] *nm* : sponsorship
parrainer [parɛne] *vt* : to sponsor
parsemer [parsəme] {52} *vt* **1** : to sprinkle **2 ~ de** : to scatter with, to strew with, to intersperse with
part [par] *nf* **1** : portion, share, piece **2** : proportion, element <une part de chance : an element of chance> **3** : part, share <faire sa part : to do one's share> <prendre part à : to take part in> **4** : side, position <de toutes parts : from all sides> <d'une part . . . : on (the) one hand . . .> <de la part de : on behalf of> **5 à ~** : apart from <à part ça : besides that> **6 à ~** : to one side, separate(ly) **7 à ~** : apart, unique <un cas à part : a special case> **8 → autre, nul, quelque**
partage [partaʒ] *nm* **1** : sharing, dividing <sans partage : total, undivided> **2** : share, lot
partagé, -gée [partaʒe] *adj* **1** : divided <opinions partagées : divided opinions> **2** : shared, mutual
partager [partaʒe] {17} *vt* **1** DIVISER : to divide up **2** : to share — **se partager** *vr*
partance [partɑ̃s] *nf* **1 en ~** : outbound, ready to depart **2 en partance pour** : bound for
partant[1] [partɑ̃] *adj* **être partant pour** : to be ready for, to be up to
partant[2], **-tante** [partɑ̃, -tɑ̃t] *n* : runner, starter (in sports)
partenaire [partənɛr] *nmf* : partner
partenariat [partənarja] *nm* : partnership
parterre [parter] *nm* **1** : flower bed **2** : orchestra section (in a theater)
parti[1], **-tie** [parti] *adj fam* : intoxicated, high
parti[2] *nm* **1** : group, camp, side **2** : political party **3** : course of action, option <prendre parti : to take a stand> <prendre son parti : to make up one's mind, to come to terms> **4** : advantage, profit <tirer parti de : to take advantage of> **5 parti pris** : bias
partial, -tiale [parsjal] *adj, mpl* **-tiaux** [-sjo] : biased, partial
partialement [parsjalmɑ̃] *adv* : in a biased manner
partialité [parsjalite] *nf* : bias, partiality
participant, -pante [partisipɑ̃, -pɑ̃t] *n* **1** : participant **2** : entrant (in a competition)
participation [partisipasjɔ̃] *nf* **1** : participation **2** : contribution **3** : share, interest (in a company, etc.)
participe [partisip] *nm* : participle
participer [partisipe] *vi* **~ à 1** : to participate in, to take part in **2** : to contribute to **3** : to share in
particulariser [partikylarize] *vt* : to distinguish, to characterize — **se particulariser** *vr*
particularité [partikylarite] *nf* : distinctive feature, characteristic, idiosyncrasy
particule [partikyl] *nf* : particle
particulier[1], **-lière** [partikylje, -ljɛr] *adj* **1** : particular, specific **2** : special, unique, idiosyncratic **3** SINGULIER : unusual **4** : private, personal <cours particuliers : private lessons> **5 en ~** : especially, in particular
particulier[2] *nm* : individual, private person

particulièrement [partikyljɛrmɑ̃] *adv* SPÉCIALEMENT : especially, particularly
partie [parti] *nf* **1** : part (of a whole) **2** : game, match **3** : party, participant **4** SORTIE : party, outing <partie de pêche : fishing party> **5** : field, line (of work) **6 en ~** : partly, in part **7 faire partie de** : to be a part of, to belong to
partiel, -tielle [parsjɛl] *adj* : partial — **partiellement** [-sjɛlmɑ̃] *adv*
partir [partir] {82} *vi* **1** : to leave, to depart **2** : to start up, to take off **3** COMMENCER : to start, to begin **4** S'ENLEVER : to come off, to come out (of a stain, etc.) **5 à partir de** : from <à partir de maintenant : from now on>
partisan[1], **-sane** [partizɑ̃, -zan] *adj* : partisan
partisan[2], **-sane** *n* : supporter, partisan
partition [partisjɔ̃] *nf* : score <partition de piano : piano score>
partout [partu] *adv* **1** : everywhere **2** : all (in sports) <trois partout : three all>
paru [pary] *pp* → **paraître**
parure [paryr] *nf* **1** : finery **2** ENSEMBLE : set (of jewelry, linens, etc.)
parution [parysjɔ̃] *nf* : publication, launch
parvenir [parvənir] {92} *vi* **1 ~ à** : to reach, to arrive at <elle est parvenue à une résolution : she arrived at a solution> **2 ~ à** : to manage to, to succeed in, to achieve
parvenu, -nue [parvəny] *n* : parvenu, upstart
parvis [parvi] *nm* : square (in front of a church)
party [parti] *nm Can fam* : party, gathering
pas[1] [pa] → **ne**
pas[2] *adv* (*without* **ne**) **1** : not <pas du tout : not at all> <pas vraiment : not really> <pas mal de : quite a lot of> <pas croyable! : incredible!> **2 pas un, pas une** : no one, none <il le fait comme pas un : he does it like nobody else>
pas[3] *nms & pl* **1** : step, footstep **2** : footprint **3** : pace, gait **4** : move, progression <un pas en avant : a step forward> <faire le premier pas : to make the first move> **5** : step (in dancing) **6 de ce pas** : right away
pascal, -cale [paskal] *adj, mpl* **pascaux** [pasko] : Easter <congé pascal : Easter holiday>
passable [pasabl] *adj* **1** : passable, fair **2** *Can* : passable, negotiable <chemins passables : passable roads>
passablement [pasabləmɑ̃] *adv* **1** : quite, rather **2** : reasonably well
passade [pasad] *nf* : passing fancy
passage [pasaʒ] *nm* **1** : passing (by), crossing (through), traffic <être de passage : to be passing through> <au passage : in passing> **2** TARIF : fare, ticket **3** : transition, passage **4** CHEMIN : route, way **5** CORRIDOR : corridor, passageway <passage pour piétons : pedestrian crossing> **6** : entry <passage interdit : do not enter> **7** : passage (in a text)
passager[1], **-gère** [pasaʒe, -ʒɛr] *adj* **1** : passing, temporary **2** : busy <rue passagère : busy street>
passager[2], **-gère** *n* **1** : passenger **2 passager clandestin** : stowaway
passagèrement [pasaʒɛrmɑ̃] *adv* : temporarily
passant[1], **-sante** [pasɑ̃, -sɑ̃t] *adj* : busy <rue passante : busy street>
passant[2], **-sante** *n* : passerby
passe [pas] *nf* **1** : pass (in sports) **2** : period, time <j'ai traversé une mauvaise passe : I went through a difficult time> **3** : channel (in navigation)
passé[1], **-sée** [pase] *adj* **1** : last, past <l'an passé : last year> **2** : after, past <il est midi passé : it's after twelve> **3** : faded
passé[2] *nm* **1** : past <par le passé : in the past> **2** : past tense <passé composé : perfect tense>
passé[3] *prep* : after, beyond <passé l'église il y a un parc : beyond the church is a park> <passé minuit : after midnight>
passe-droit [pasdrwa] *nm, pl* **passe-droits** : privilege, special treatment
passementerie [pasmɑ̃tri] *nf* : trimmings *pl* (for clothing, etc.)
passe-partout [paspartu] *nms & pl* : master key
passe-passe [paspas] *nms & pl* **tour de passe-passe** : conjuring trick, sleight of hand
passepoil [paspwal] *nm* : piping (in sewing)
passeport [paspɔr] *nm* : passport
passer [pase] *vi* **1** : to cross, to go over **2** : to pass, to go past **3** : to pass, to run <passer la main sur une surface : to pass one's hand over a surface> **4** : to pass, to hand over, to give <passer un ballon : to pass a ball> <passez-moi le poivre : pass me the pepper> <passer un rhume à qqn : to give s.o. a cold> **5** : to put through to (on the telephone) **6** : to take (an exam, etc.), to take on **7** : to spend (time) **8** : to excuse, to forgive **9** : to skip, to pass over **10** : to go over <passer l'aspirateur : to vacuum> **11** ENFILER : to slip on **12** : to show (a film), to play (a cassette, etc.) **13** : to shift into (a gear) — *vi* **1** : to pass, to go past, to run <le chemin passe devant ma maison : the road runs in front of my house> **2** : to drop by **3** : to go <où est-il passé? : where did he go?> **4** : to get through <laissez-moi passer : let me through> **5** : to be over, to pass, to go by **6** : to pass down, to be hand-

ed down **7 ~ par** : to go through <en passant par : including> **8 ~ pour** : to pass for, to appear to be **9 ~ sur** : to pass over, to overlook, to forget about **10 en passant** : incidentally **11 y passer** *fam* : to die **— se passer** *vr* **1** : to take place, to happen **2** : to go, to turn out **3** : to pass, to go by (of time) **4 ~ de** : to do without, to dispense with **5 se faire passer** : to masquerade, to disguise oneself

passereau [pasro] *nm, pl* **-reaux** : sparrow

passerelle [pasrɛl] *nf* **1** : footbridge **2** : gangplank, ramp (of an airplane) **3** : bridge (of a ship)

passe–temps [pastɑ̃] *nms & pl* : hobby, pastime

passeur, -seuse [pasœr, -søz] *n* : smuggler

passible [pasibl] *adj* **~ de** : liable to, punishable by <passible d'une amende : liable to a fine>

passif[1], **-sive** [pasif, -siv] *adj* : passive **— passivement** [-sivmɑ̃] *adv*

passif[2] *nm* **1** : passive case **2** : liabilities *pl*

passion [pasjɔ̃] *nf* : passion

passionnant, -nante [pasjɔnɑ̃, -nɑ̃t] *adj* CAPTIVANT : exciting, fascinating

passionné[1], **-née** [pasjɔne] *adj* : passionate, enthusiastic **— passionnément** [-nemɑ̃] *adv*

passionné[2], **-née** *n* : enthusiast

passionnel, -nelle [pasjɔnɛl] *adj* : passionate <crime passionnel : crime of passion>

passionner [pasjɔne] *vt* **1** CAPTIVER : to fascinate **2** : to impassion, to inflame **— se passionner** *vr* **~ pour** : to have a passion for

passivement [pasivmɑ̃] *adv* : passively

passivité [pasivite] *nf* : passivity

passoire [paswar] *nf* : sieve, strainer, colander

pastel [pastɛl] *adj & nm* : pastel

pastèque [pastɛk] *nf* : watermelon

pasteur [pastœr] *nm* : minister, pastor

pasteuriser [pastœrize] *vt* : to pasteurize **— pasteurisation** [-rizasjɔ̃] *nf*

pastiche [pastiʃ] *nm* : pastiche

pastille [pastij] *nf* : lozenge <pastilles contre la toux : cough drops>

pastoral, -rale [pastɔral] *adj, mpl* **-raux** [-ro] : pastoral

pastorat [pastɔra] *nm* : pastorate, (Protestant) ministry

pat [pat] *nm* : stalemate

patate [patat] *nf* **1** *fam* : potato **2** *fam* : blockhead **3** *or* **patate douce** : sweet potato

pataud, -taude [pato, -tod] *adj* : clumsy, lumbering

patauger [patoʒe] {17} *vi* **1** : to splash about, to paddle **2** S'EMBROUILLER : to flounder about, to get confused

patchwork [patʃwœrk] *nm* : patchwork

pâte [pat] *nf* **1** : dough, pastry, batter **2** : paste <pâte dentifrice : toothpaste> <pâte à modeler : modeling clay> **3** : pulp <pâte à papier : paper pulp> **4 être bonne pâte** : to be easygoing **5 pâtes** *nfpl* : pasta

pâté [pate] *nm* **1** : pâté **2** : inkblot **3** *or* **pâté de maisons** : block (of houses)

pâtée [pate] *nf* : mash, feed, slop

patelin [patlɛ̃] *nm fam* : little village

patent, -tente [patɑ̃, -tɑ̃t] *adj* : obvious, patent

patente [patɑ̃t] *nf Can fam* **1** : thing, thingamajig **2** : gadget, gizmo

patenté, -tée [patɑ̃te] *adj fam* : established, out-and-out

patère [patɛr] *nf* : peg, hook (for coats, etc.)

paternel, -nelle [paternɛl] *adj* : fatherly, paternal **— paternellement** [-nɛlmɑ̃] *adv*

paternité [paternite] *nf* **1** : fatherhood, paternity **2** : authorship

pâteux, -teuse [patø, -tøz] *adj* **1** : pasty, doughy **2** : thick <avoir la langue pâteuse : to have a coated tongue>

pathétique [patetik] *adj* : pathetic, moving **— pathétiquement** [-tikmɑ̃] *adv*

pathologie [patɔlɔʒi] *nf* : pathology

pathologique [patɔlɔʒik] *adj* : pathological

pathologiste [patɔlɔʒist] *nmf* : pathologist

pathos [patos] *nms & pl* : pathos

patibulaire [patibyler] *adj* : sinister-looking

patiemment [pasjamɑ̃] *adv* : patiently

patience [pasjɑ̃s] *nf* **1** : patience <j'ai perdu patience : I lost my patience> **2 jeu de patience** : solitaire

patient, -tiente [pasjɑ̃, -sjɑ̃t] *adj & n* : patient

patienter [pasjɑ̃te] *vi* : to wait

patin [patɛ̃] *nm* : skate <patins à glace : ice skates> <patins à roulettes : roller skates>

patinage [patinaʒ] *nm* : skating <patinage artistique : figure skating>

patine [patin] *nf* : patina

patiner [patine] *vi* **1** : to skate **2** : to spin, to slip (of wheels) **3** *Can* : to hedge, to shilly-shally

patinette [patinɛt] *nf* TROTTINETTE : scooter

patineur, -neuse [patinœr, -nøz] *n* : skater

patinoire [patinwar] *nf* : skating rink

patio [patjo, pasjo] *nm* : patio

pâtir [patir] *vi* **~ de** : to suffer because of

pâtisserie [patisri] *nf* **1** : cake, pastry **2** : pastry shop, bakery

pâtissier, -sière [patisje, -sjɛr] *n* : pastry chef

patois [patwa] *nms & pl* **1** : patois **2** *Can* : swearword, oath

patraque [patrak] *adj fam* : out of sorts

patriarcat [patrijarka] *nm* : patriarchy
patriarche [patrijarʃ] *nm* : patriarch — **patriarcal, -cale** [-jarkal] *adj*
patrie [patri] *nf* : mother country, homeland, fatherland
patrimoine [patrimwan] *nm* **1** : patrimony, legacy **2** HÉRITAGE : heritage
patriote[1] [patrijɔt] *adj* : patriotic
patriote[2] *nmf* : patriot — **patriotique** [patrijɔtik] *adj*
patriotisme [patrijɔtism] *nm* : patriotism
patron[1], **-tronne** [patrɔ̃, -trɔn] *n* **1** : patron saint **2** : owner **3** : boss, manager, employer
patron[2] *nm* : pattern (in sewing)
patronage [patrɔnaʒ] *nm* : patronage
patronal, -nale [patrɔnal] *adj, mpl* **-naux** [-no] : of employers <syndicat patronal : employers' union>
patronat [patrɔna] *nm* : management
patronner [patrɔne] *vt* : to support, to sponsor
patrouille [patruj] *nf* : patrol
patrouiller [patruje] *vi* : to patrol
patrouilleur[1], **-leuse** [patrujœr, -jøz] *n* **1** : soldier on patrol **2** *Can* : police officer (in a patrol car)
patrouilleur[2] *nm* : patrol boat, patrol plane
patte [pat] *nf* **1** : paw, hoof, foot (of a bird), leg (of an insect) <patte de devant : foreleg> **2** *fam* : leg, foot, hand <traîner la patte : to drag one's feet, to fall behind> **3** : tab, flap
pattes-d'oie [patdwa] *nfpl* : crow's feet
pâturage [patyraʒ] *nm* : pasture
pâture [patyr] *nf* **1** : feed, fodder **2** : pasture
paume [pom] *nf* : palm (of the hand)
paumer [pome] *v fam* : to lose — **se paumer** *vr fam* : to get lost
paupière [popjɛr] *nf* : eyelid
pause [poz] *nf* **1** : break <faire une pause : to pause, to take a break> **2** : pause **3** : rest (in music)
pauvre[1] [povr] *adj* **1** : poor, impoverished **2** : unfortunate **3** : poor, sparse
pauvre[2] *nm* : poor man, pauper <les pauvres : the poor>
pauvrement [povrəmɑ̃] *adv* : poorly
pauvreté [povrəte] *nf* : poverty
pavage [pavaʒ] *nm* : paving, cobblestones *pl*
pavaner [pavane] *v* **se pavaner** *vr* : to strut about
pavé [pave] *nm* **1** : pavement **2** : cobblestone, paving stone
paver [pave] *vt* : to pave
pavillon [pavijɔ̃] *nm* **1** : pavilion **2** *France* : (detached) house **3** : ward (in a hospital), (university) building **4** : auricle (of the ear) **5** : bell (of a wind instrument) **6** : flag (on a ship)
pavoiser [pavwaze] *vt* : to deck with flags — *vi* : to rejoice
pavot [pavo] *nm* : poppy
payable [pejabl] *adj* : payable
payant, payante [pejɑ̃, -jɑ̃t] *adj* **1** : paying **2** : for which one pays <télé payante : pay-TV>
paye [pej] → **paie**
payement [pɛmɑ̃] → **paiement**
payer [peje] {11} *vt* **1** : to pay, to pay for **2** *fam* : to buy <je lui ai payé un verre : I bought him a drink> **3** : to pay for, to suffer the consequences of **4** : to cover (one's expenses, etc.) — *vi* : to pay <un métier qui paie bien : a well-paying job> — **se payer** *vr* **1** : to have to be paid for **2** : to treat oneself
pays [pei] *nm* **1** : country **2** : region, area <du pays : local> **3** : village **4** : people (of a country) <s'adresser au pays : to address the nation>
paysage [peizaʒ] *nm* : scenery, landscape
paysagiste [peizaʒist] *nm* **1** : landscape painter **2** : landscape gardener
paysan[1], **-sanne** [peizɑ̃, -zan] *adj* **1** : agricultural, farming **2** : rural, rustic
paysan[2], **-sanne** *n* **1** : small farmer **2** : peasant
péage [peaʒ] *nm* **1** : toll **2** : tollbooth
peau [po] *nf, pl* **peaux** **1** : (human) skin <être bien dans sa peau : to be at peace with oneself> **2** : hide, pelt <peau de mouton : sheepskin> <peau de daim : buckskin> <gants de peau : leather gloves> **3** : peel, rind, skin (of fruits or vegetables)
peaufiner [pofine] *vt* : to put the finishing touches on, to perfect
pécan *or* **pecan** [pekɑ̃] *nm France or* **noix de pécan** : pecan
peccadille [pekadij] *nf* : peccadillo
pêche [pɛʃ] *nf* **1** : peach **2** : fishing **3** : catch <une bonne pêche : a good catch of fish>
péché [peʃe] *nm* : sin
pécher [peʃe] {87} *vi* : to sin
pêcher[1] [pɛʃe] *vt* **1** : to fish for **2** *fam* : to get, to unearth — *vi* : to fish <pêcher à la ligne : to angle>
pêcher[2] [pɛʃœr] *nm* : peach tree
pêcherie [pɛʃri] *nf* **1** : fishery, fishing ground **2** : fish processing factory
pêcheur, -cheresse [pɛʃœr, -ʃres] *n* : sinner
pêcheur, -cheuse [pɛʃœr, -ʃøz] *n* **1** : fisherman **2** **pêcheur à la ligne** : angler
pectine [pɛktin] *nf* : pectin
pectoral[1], **-rale** [pɛktɔral] *adj, mpl* **-raux** [-ro] **1** : pectoral **2** : cough <sirop pectoral : cough syrup>
pectoraux [pɛktɔro] *nmpl* : pectoral muscles
pécule [pekyl] *nm* ÉCONOMIES : savings *pl*
pécuniaire [pekynjɛr] *adj* FINANCIER : financial — **pécuniairement** [-njɛrmɑ̃] *adv*
pédagogie [pedagɔʒi] *nf* **1** : education, pedagogy **2** : teaching skill

pédagogique [pedagɔʒik] *adj* : educational, teaching <formation pédagogique : teacher training>
pédagogue [pedagɔg] *nmf* : educator, teacher
pédale [pedal] *nf* : pedal
pédaler [pedale] *vi* : to pedal
pédalier [pedalje] *nm* **1** : drive mechanism (of a bicycle) **2** : pedals *pl* (of an organ)
pédalo [pedalo] *nm* : pedal boat
pédant[1], **-dante** [pedɑ̃, -dɑ̃t] *adj* : pedantic
pédant[2], **-dante** *n* : pedant
pédantisme [pedɑ̃tism] *nm* : pedantry
pédestre [pedɛstr] *adj* : on foot <randonnée pédestre : hike>
pédiatre [pedjatr] *nmf* : pediatrician
pédiatrie [pedjatri] *nf* : pediatrics
pédiatrique [pedjatrik] *adj* : pediatric
pédicure [pedikyr] *nmf* : chiropodist
pedigree [pedigre] *nm* : pedigree
pègre [pɛgr] *nf* : (criminal) underworld
peignait [pɛɲe], **peignions** [pɛɲɔ̃], *etc.* → **peindre**
peigne[1] [pɛɲ], *etc.* → **peindre**
peigne[2] [pɛɲ] *nm* : comb
peigner [pɛɲe] *vt* **1** : to comb **2** : to card (fibers) — **se peigner** *vr* : to comb one's hair
peignoir [pɛɲwar] *nm* : bathrobe, dressing gown
peignure [pɛɲyr] *nf Can fam* : hairdo, hairstyle
peindre [pɛ̃dr] {37} *vt* **1** : to paint **2** : to depict, to portray — *vi* : to paint — **se peindre** *vr* : to show, to manifest itself
peine [pɛn] *nf* **1** : sorrow, sadness **2** : trouble, effort <se donner la peine de : to take the trouble to> <ce n'est pas la peine : it's not worth the effort, never mind, forget it> **3** : difficulty <sans peine : easily> **4** : punishment, penalty <peine capitale : capital punishment> **5 à ~** : hardly, just, barely
peiner [pene] *vt* ATTRISTER : to distress, to sadden — *vi* **1** : to have trouble, to struggle **2** : to strain, to labor (of an engine, etc.)
peintre [pɛ̃tr] *nm* : painter
peinture [pɛ̃tyr] *nf* **1** : paint **2** : painting, picture **3** : painting <elle fait de la peinture à l'huile : she paints in oil>
peinturer [pɛ̃tyre] *vt Can* : to paint <peinturer la maison : to paint the house>
peinturlurer [pɛ̃tyrlure] *vt* : to daub (with paint)
péjoratif, -tive [peʒɔratif, -tiv] *adj* : pejorative, derogatory — **péjorativement** [-tivmɑ̃] *adv*
pelage [pəlaʒ] *nm* : coat, fur (of an animal)
pelé, -lée [pəle] *adj* **1** : hairless, bald **2** : bare, barren
pêle–mêle [pɛlmɛl] *adv* : every which way, pell-mell
peler [pəle] {20} *v* : to peel
pèlerin, -rine [pɛlrɛ̃] *n* : pilgrim
pèlerinage [pɛlrinaʒ] *nm* : pilgrimage
pèlerine [pɛlrin] *nf* : cape
pélican [pelikɑ̃] *nm* : pelican
pellagre [pɛlagr] *nf* : pellagra
pelle [pɛl] *nf* **1** : shovel **2 pelle à poussière** : dustpan
pelletée [pɛlte] *nf* : shovelful
pelleter [pɛlte] {8} *vt* : to shovel
pelleteuse [pɛltøz] *nf* : power shovel, excavator
pellicule [pelikyl] *nf* **1** : (photographic) film **2** : thin layer, film **3 pellicules** *nfpl* : dandruff
pelote [pəlɔt] *nf* **1** : ball (of string, thread, yarn, etc.) **2** : pincushion **3 pelote de neige** *Can* : snowball
peloter [pəlɔte] *vt fam* : to grope, to paw, to fondle — *vi fam* : to neck
peloton [pəlɔtɔ̃] *nm* **1** : group <peloton de tête : front runners, leaders of the pack> **2** : squad, platoon <peloton d'exécution : firing squad>
pelotonner [pəlɔtɔne] *v* **se pelotonner** *vr* : to curl up (into a ball), to snuggle
pelouse [pəluz] *nf* **1** : lawn, grass **2** : field (in sports)
peluche [pəlyʃ] *nf* **1** : plush **2** : (piece of) fluff, lint **3** *or* **animal en peluche** : stuffed animal, soft toy
pelucheux, -cheuse [pəlyʃø, -ʃøz] *adj* : fluffy
pelure [pəlyr] *nf* : peel, skin (of an apple, etc.)
pelvien, -vienne [pɛlvjɛ̃, -vjɛn] *adj* : pelvic
pelvis [pɛlvis] *nm* : pelvis
pénal, -nale [penal] *adj, mpl* **pénaux** [peno] : penal
pénalisation [penalizasjɔ̃] *nf* : penalty (in sports)
pénaliser [penalize] *vt* : to penalize
pénalité [penalite] *nf* : penalty (in sports)
penaud, -naude [pəno, -nod] *adj* : sheepish
penchant [pɑ̃ʃɑ̃] *nm* : tendency, inclination
pencher [pɑ̃ʃe] *vt* INCLINER : to tilt, to tip — *vi* **1** : to slant, to lean **2 ~ pour** : to incline towards, to favor — **se pencher** *vr* **1** : to hunch over, to bend (down) **2 ~ sur** : to look into, to examine
pendaison [pɑ̃dɛzɔ̃] *nf* **1** : hanging **2 pendaison de crémaillère** : housewarming
pendant[1], **-dante** [pɑ̃dɑ̃, -dɑ̃t] *adj* **1** : hanging, dangling **2** : pending
pendant[2] *nm* **1** *or* **pendant d'oreille** : drop earring **2** : counterpart, matching piece
pendant[3] *prep* **1** : during, for <pendant l'été : during the summer> <tra-

vailler pendant des heures : to work for hours> **2 pendant que** : while <pendant que vous y êtes : while you're at it>

pendentif [pɑ̃dɑ̃tif] *nm* : pendant

penderie [pɑ̃dri] *nf* : closet, wardrobe

pendre [pɑ̃dr] {63} *vt* **1** SUSPENDRE : to hang, to suspend **2** : to hang (someone) — *vi* **1** : to hang **2** : to hang down, to sag — **se pendre** *vr* : to hang oneself

pendule[1] [pɑ̃dyl] *nm* : pendulum

pendule[2] *nf* : clock

pêne [pɛn] *nm* : bolt (of a lock)

pénétrant, -trante [penetrɑ̃, -trɑ̃t] *adj* **1** : penetrating, piercing **2** : shrewd, perceptive

pénétration [penetrasjɔ̃] *nf* **1** : penetration **2** : perception, insight

pénétré, -trée [penetre] *adj* : earnest, intense <être pénétré de son importance : to be full of one's own importance>

pénétrer [penetre] {87} *vt* **1** IMPRÉGNER : to penetrate, to soak into **2** COMPRENDRE : to fathom, to understand — *vi* **1** S'ENFONCER : to penetrate, to sink in **2** S'INTRODUIRE : to enter, to penetrate

pénible [penibl] *adj* **1** : painful, distressing **2** ARDU : difficult, arduous

péniblement [penibləmɑ̃] *adv* **1** : with difficulty, laboriously **2** : barely, just about

péniche [peniʃ] *nf* **1** : barge **2 péniche aménagée** : houseboat

pénicilline [penisilin] *nf* : penicillin

péninsule [penɛ̃syl] *nf* : peninsula — **péninsulaire** [-syler] *adj*

pénis [penis] *nm* : penis

pénitence [penitɑ̃s] *nf* **1** : penitence, repentance **2** : punishment

pénitencier [penitɑ̃sje] *nm* : penitentiary

pénitent[1], **-tente** [penitɑ̃, -tɑ̃t] *adj* : penitent, repentant

pénitent[2], **-tente** *n* : penitent

pénitentiaire [penitɑ̃sjɛr] *adj* : penal

penne [pɛn] *nf* : quill, quill pen

pénombre [penɔ̃br] *nf* : half-light

pense–bête [pɑ̃sbɛt] *nm, pl* **pense–bêtes** [-bɛt] : reminder

pensée [pɑ̃se] *nf* **1** : thought **2** : mind <en pensée : in one's mind> **3** : thinking <pensée claire : clear thinking> **4** : pansy

penser [pɑ̃se] *vt* **1** : to think <penser du bien de : to think well of> <qu'en pensez-vous? : what do you think about it?> **2** : to believe, to suppose <penser que oui : to think so> <je pense qu'elle a raison : I think she's right> **3** : to intend, to plan on <il pense sortir : he intends to go out> — *vi* **1** : to think **2 ~ à** : to think about <penser au passé : to think about the past>

penseur, -seuse [pɑ̃sœr, -søz] *n* : thinker

pensif, -sive [pɑ̃sif, -siv] *adj* MÉDITATIF : pensive, thoughtful

pension [pɑ̃sjɔ̃] *nf* **1** : pension <pension alimentaire : alimony> **2** : boarding-house **3** : room and board

pensionnaire [pɑ̃sjɔnɛr] *nmf* : boarder, roomer

pensionnat [pɑ̃sjɔna] *nm* : boarding school

pensivement [pɑ̃sivmɑ̃] *adv* : pensively, thoughtfully

pentagone [pɛ̃tagɔn] *nm* : pentagon — **pentagonal** [-gɔnal] *adj*

pente [pɑ̃t] *nf* **1** : slope **2 en ~** : sloping

Pentecôte [pɑ̃tkot] *nf* : Pentecost

pénurie [penyri] *nf* : shortage, scarcity

péon [peɔ̃] *nm* : peon

pépé [pepe] *nm France fam* : grandpa

pépère[1] [pepɛr] *adj fam* : quiet, easy

pépère[2] *nm fam* **1** : chubby boy **2** : old-timer **3** : grandpa

pépiement [pepimɑ̃] *nm* : peep, peeping

pépier [pepje] {96} *vi* : to chirp, to tweet, to peep

pépin [pepɛ̃] *nm* **1** : pip, seed **2** *fam* : snag, hitch

pépinière [pepinjɛr] *nf* **1** : (tree) nursery **2** : breeding ground

pépite [pepit] *nf* : nugget

péquenaud, -naude [pekno, -nod] *n France fam* : yokel, bumpkin

percale [pɛrkal] *nf* : percale

perçant, -çante [pɛrsɑ̃, -sɑ̃t] *adj* **1** : piercing, shrill **2** : sharp, keen <vue perçante : keen eyesight>

percée [pɛrse] *nf* **1** : opening, gap **2** : breakthrough, discovery

perce–neige [pɛrsəneʒ] *nmfs & pl* : snowdrop

perce–oreille [pɛrsɔrɛj] *nm, pl* **perce–oreilles** [-ɔrɛj] : earwig

percepteur [pɛrsɛptœr] *nm* : tax collector

perceptible [pɛrsɛptibl] *adj* : perceptible, noticeable

perception [pɛrsɛpsjɔ̃] *nf* **1** : perception **2** RECOUVREMENT : collection (of taxes)

percer [pɛrse] {6} *vt* **1** : to pierce **2** : to open up, to build (a road, etc.) **3** PÉNÉTRER : to fathom, to penetrate **4 percer ses dents** : to be teething — *vi* **1** : to break through (of the sun) **2** : to come through (of a tooth)

perceuse [pɛrsøz] *nf* : drill

percevable [pɛrsəvabl] *adj* : collectable, payable

percevoir [pɛrsəvwar] {26} *vt* **1** : to perceive, to sense **2** RECOUVRER : to receive (money, etc.), to collect (taxes)

perche [pɛrʃ] *nf* **1** : pole **2** : perch, bass (fish)

percher [pɛrʃe] *vi* : to perch — **se percher** *vr* : to roost

perchoir [perʃwar] *nm* : perch, roost
perclus, -cluse [perkly, -klyz] *adj* **~ de** : crippled with
perçoit [perswa], **perçoive** [perswav], *etc.* → **percevoir**
percolateur [perkɔlatœr] *nm* : percolator
perçu [persy] *pp* → **percevoir**
percussion [perkysjɔ̃] *nf* : percussion **— percussionniste** [-kysjɔnist] *nmf*
percutant, -tante [perkytɑ̃, -tɑ̃t] *adj* : forceful, striking
percuter [perkyte] *vt* : to strike, to crash into **— *vi* 1** : to explode **2 ~ contre** : to crash into
perdant[1], **-dante** [perdɑ̃, -dɑ̃t] *adj* : losing
perdant[2], **-dante** *n* : loser
perdition [perdisjɔ̃] *nf* **1** : perdition **2 en ~** : in distress
perdre [perdr] {63} *vt* **1** : to lose **2** : to waste <perdre son temps : to waste one's time> **3** MANQUER : to miss **4** : to ruin (one's reputation, etc.) **— *vi*** : to lose **— se perdre** *vr* **1** : to get lost, to disappear **2** : to get lost, to lose one's way
perdreau [perdro] *nm, pl* **perdreaux** : (young) partridge
perdrix [perdri] *nfs & pl* : partridge
perdu, -due [perdy] *adj* **1** : lost **2** : wasted **3** : ruined **4** : spare, free <à mes moments perdus : in my spare time> **5** : isolated, remote
père [per] *nm* **1** : father **2 pères** *nmpl* : ancestors, forefathers
pérégrinations [peregrinasjɔ̃] *nfpl* : travels
péremptoire [perɑ̃ptwar] *adj* : peremptory
péréquation [perekwasjɔ̃] *nf* : equalization, adjustment (in finance)
perfectible [perfektibl] *adj* : perfectible
perfection [perfeksjɔ̃] *nf* **1** : perfection **2 à la perfection** : to perfection, perfectly
perfectionné, -née [perfeksjɔne] *adj* : advanced, sophisticated
perfectionnement [perfeksjɔnmɑ̃] *nm* : perfecting, improvement
perfectionner [perfeksjɔne] *vt* : to perfect, to improve **— se perfectionner** *vr*
perfectionnisme [perfeksjɔnism] *nm* : perfectionism
perfectionniste[1] [perfeksjɔnist] *adj* : perfectionist, perfectionistic
perfectionniste[2] *nmf* : perfectionist
perfide [perfid] *adj* : treacherous, perfidious **— perfidement** [-fidmɑ̃] *adv*
perfidie [perfidi] *nf* : treachery
perforation [perfɔrasjɔ̃] *nf* : perforation
perforer [perfɔre] *vt* PERCER : to perforate, to pierce
performance [perfɔrmɑ̃s] *nf* **1** : performance **2** : achievement
performant, -mante [perfɔrmɑ̃, -mɑ̃t] *adj* **1** : high-performance (of machines, etc.) **2** : high-return (of investments)
péricliter [periklite] *vi* : to decline sharply
péril [peril] *nm* : peril, danger <au péril de sa vie : at the risk of one's life>
périlleux, -leuse [perijø, -jøz] *adj* : perilous **— périlleusement** [-jøzmɑ̃] *adv*
périmé, -mée [perime] *adj* **1** : outdated **2** : out-of-date, expired
périmètre [perimetr] *nm* : perimeter
période [perjɔd] *nf* **1** : period, time **2 par périodes** : periodically, from time to time
périodique[1] [perjɔdik] *adj* **1** : periodic (in science) **2** : periodical **3** : recurring
périodique[2] *nm* : periodical
périodiquement [perjɔdikmɑ̃] *adv* : periodically
péripétie [peripesi] *nf* : incident, event
périphérie [periferi] *nf* **1** : periphery, circumference **2** : outskirts *pl*
périphérique[1] [periferik] *adj* **1** : peripheral **2** : outlying
périphérique[2] *nm* : peripheral (in computer science)
périple [peripl] *nm* : journey
périr [perir] *vi* : to perish
périscope [periskɔp] *nm* : periscope
périssable [perisabl] *adj* : perishable
perle [perl] *nf* **1** : pearl, bead **2** : gem, treasure, paragon **3** : drop <perle de sang : drop of blood> **4** *fam* : howler, blunder
perlé, -lée [perle] *adj* **1** : pearly **2** : beaded
perler [perle] *vi* : to form in droplets
permanence [permanɑ̃s] *nf* **1** : permanence **2 en ~** : permanently, without interruption **3 être de permanence** : to be on duty
permanent[1], **-nente** [permanɑ̃, -nɑ̃t] *adj* **1** : permanent **2** : constant
permanent[2], **-nente** *n* : permanent employee or member
permanente *nf* : permanent, perm
perméable [permeabl] *adj* **1** : permeable **2 ~ à** : receptive to
permettre [permetr] {53} *vt* **1** : to allow, to permit **2** : to enable, to make possible **— se permettre** *vr* **1** : to allow oneself **2 ~ de** : to take the liberty of
permis [permi] *nm* LICENCE : license, permit <permis de conduire : driver's license>
permissif, -sive [permisif, -siv] *adj* : permissive
permission [permisjɔ̃] *nf* **1** : permission **2** : leave (in the military)
permissivité [permisivite] *nf* : permissiveness
permutation [permytasjɔ̃] *nf* **1** : permutation **2** : exchange (of jobs)
permuter [permyte] *vt* : to exchange, to switch around **— *vi*** : to switch places

pernicieux, -cieuse [pɛrnisjø, -sjøz] *adj* : pernicious — **pernicieusement** [-sjøzmɑ̃] *adv*
péroné [pɛrɔne] *nm* : fibula
pérorer [pɛrɔre] *vi* : to declaim, to hold forth
peroxyde [pɛrɔksid] *nm* : peroxide <peroxyde d'hydrogène : hydrogen peroxide>
perpendiculaire [pɛrpɑ̃dikylɛr] *adj* : perpendicular — **perpendiculairement** [-lɛrmɑ̃] *adv*
perpétration [pɛrpetrasjɔ̃] *nf* : perpetration (of a crime, etc.)
perpétrer [pɛrpetre] {87} *vt* : to perpetrate
perpétuel, -tuelle [pɛrpetɥɛl] *adj* **1** : perpetual **2** : permanent, for life
perpétuellement [pɛrpetɥɛlmɑ̃] *adv* : constantly, perpetually
perpétuer [pɛrpetɥe] *vt* ÉTERNISER : to perpetuate
perpétuité [pɛrpetɥite] *nf* **à ~** : for life
perplexe [pɛrpleks] *adj* : perplexed, puzzled
perplexité [pɛrpleksite] *nf* : perplexity, bafflement
perquisition [pɛrkizisjɔ̃] *nf* : (police) search
perquisitionner [pɛrkizisjɔne] *vi* : to carry out a search
perron [pɛrɔ̃] *nm* **1** : (front) steps **2** *Can* GALERIE : porch
perroquet [pɛrɔke] *nm* : parrot
perruche [pɛryʃ] *nf* : parakeet
perruque [pɛryk] *nf* : wig
pers [pɛr] *adj* : bluish green
persan[1], **-sane** [pɛrsɑ̃, -san] *adj* : Persian
persan[2] *nm* : Persian (language)
Persan, -sane *n* : Persian
persécuter [pɛrsekyte] *vt* **1** MARTYRISER : to persecute, to torment **2** HARCELER : to harass
persécuteur, -trice [pɛrsekytœr, -tris] *n* : persecutor, tormentor
persécution [pɛrsekysjɔ̃] *nf* : persecution
persévérance [pɛrseverɑ̃s] *nf* : perseverance
persévérant, -rante [pɛrseverɑ̃, -rɑ̃t] *adj* : persevering, persistent
persévérer [pɛrsevere] {87} *vi* : to persevere, to persist
persienne [pɛrsjɛn] *nf* : shutter
persiflage [pɛrsiflaʒ] *nm* : mockery
persil [pɛrsi] *nm* : parsley
persistance [pɛrsistɑ̃s] *nf* : persistence
persistant, -tante [pɛrsistɑ̃, -tɑ̃t] *adj* : persistent — **persistance** [-tɑ̃s] *nf*
persister [pɛrsiste] *vi* **1** PERSÉVÉRER : to persist, to persevere **2** : to continue, to last
personnage [pɛrsɔnaʒ] *nm* **1** : (fictional) character **2** : character, individual **3** : influential person, celebrity
personnaliser [pɛrsɔnalize] *vt* : to personalize
personnalité [pɛrsɔnalite] *nf* **1** : personality <une personnalité forte : a strong personality> **2** : celebrity
personne[1] [pɛrsɔn] *nf* **1** : person <quelques personnes : a few people> <la personne : the individual> **2** : self, (bodily) person <être bien de sa personne : to be good-looking> <content de sa (petite) personne : pleased with oneself> <en personne : in person> **3** : person (in grammar)
personne[2] *pron* **1** (*in negative constructions*) : no one, nobody <je n'ai vu personne : I didn't see anyone> <personne ne dit ça : nobody says that> **2** : anyone, anybody <mieux que personne : better than anybody> <presque personne : hardly anyone>
personnel[1], **-nelle** [pɛrsɔnɛl] *adj* **1** : personal, private **2** : selfish, self-centered **3** : personal (in grammar)
personnel[2] *nm* : personnel, staff
personnellement [pɛrsɔnɛlmɑ̃] *adv* : personally, in person
personne–ressource [pɛrsɔnrəsurs] *nf Can, pl* **personnes–ressources** : specialist, expert
personnifier [pɛrsɔnifje] {96} *vt* : to personify — **personnification** [-nifikasjɔ̃] *nf*
perspective [pɛrspektiv] *nf* **1** : perspective (in art) **2** : view **3** : point of view, viewpoint **4** : outlook, prospect <en perspective : in prospect, in the offing>
perspicace [pɛrspikas] *adj* : perspicacious, insightful, perceptive
perspicacité [pɛrspikasite] *nf* : insight, perspicacity
persuader [pɛrsɥade] *vt* CONVAINCRE : to persuade, to convince — **se persuader** *vr*
persuasif, -sive [pɛrswazif, -ziv] *adj* : persuasive
persuasion [pɛrsɥazjɔ̃] *nf* : persuasion
perte [pɛrt] *nf* **1** : loss **2** : waste **3** : disaster, ruin **4 à perte de vue** : as far as the eye can see **5 pertes** *nfpl* : losses
pertinemment [pɛrtinamɑ̃] *adv* : to the point <savoir pertinemment : to know full well>
pertinence [pɛrtinɑ̃s] *nf* : pertinence, relevance
pertinent, -nente [pɛrtinɑ̃, -nɑ̃t] *adj* : pertinent, relevant
perturbateur[1], **-trice** [pɛrtyrbatœr, -tris] *adj* : disruptive
perturbateur[2], **-trice** *n* : troublemaker
perturber [pɛrtyrbe] *vt* **1** : to disrupt **2** DÉRANGER : to disturb, to upset
péruvien, -vienne [peryvjɛ̃, -vjɛn] *adj* : Peruvian
Péruvien, -vienne *n* : Peruvian
pervenche [pɛrvɑ̃ʃ] *nf* : periwinkle (plant)

pervers[1], **-verse** [pɛrvɛr, -vɛrs] *adj* : perverted, depraved
pervers[2], **-verse** *n* : pervert
perversion [pɛrvɛrsjɔ̃] *nf* : perversion
perversité [pɛrvɛrsite] *nf* : perversity
pervertir [pɛrvɛrtir] *vt* CORROMPRE : to pervert, to corrupt
pesage [pəzaʒ] *nm* : weighing
pesamment [pəzamɑ̃] *adv* LOURDEMENT : heavily
pesant, -sante [pəzɑ̃, -zɑ̃t] *adj* **1** : heavy **2** : burdensome, oppressive **3** : unwieldy, ungainly
pesanteur [pəzɑ̃tœr] *nf* **1** : gravity **2** : heaviness, weight
pesée [pəze] *nf* **1** : weighing **2** : weight **3** : force
pèse–personne [pɛzpɛrsɔn] *nm, pl* **pèse–personnes** : (bathroom) scales *pl*
peser [pəze] {52} *vt* **1** : to weigh **2** EXAMINER : to consider — *vi* **1** : to weigh <combien pèses-tu? : how much do you weigh?> <peser lourd : to be heavy> **2** INFLUER : to carry weight, to have bearing **3** ~ **sur** : to press, to pressure, to weigh on
pessimisme [pesimism] *nm* : pessimism
pessimiste[1] [pesimist] *adj* : pessimistic
pessimiste[2] *nmf* : pessimist
peso [pezo, peso] *nm* : peso
peste [pɛst] *nf* **1** : plague, pestilence **2** : pest, nuisance
pester [pɛste] *vi* ~ **contre** : to curse
pesticide [pɛstisid] *nm* : pesticide
pestilence [pɛstilɑ̃s] *nf* : stench
pestilentiel, -tielle [pɛstilɑ̃sjɛl] *adj* FÉTIDE : foul, fetid
pétale [petal] *nm* : petal
pétanque [petɑ̃k] *nf* : petanque (game of bowls)
pétant, -tante [petɑ̃, -tɑ̃t] *adj fam* : sharp, on the dot <à neuf heures pétantes : at nine o'clock sharp>
pétarade [petarad] *nf* : backfiring
pétarader [petarade] *vi* : to backfire
pétard [petar] *nm* **1** : firecracker **2 être en pétard** *fam* : to be fuming
péter [pete] {87} *vi fam* **1** : to go off, to explode **2** : to bust, to break — *vt fam* **1** : to bust, to break **2 péter le feu** : to be full of energy
pétillant, -lante [petijɑ̃, -jɑ̃t] *adj* **1** : sparkling **2** : bubbly
pétillement [petijmɑ̃] *nm* **1** : fizziness, fizz **2** : crackling **3** : sparkle (of the eyes, etc.)
pétiller [petije] *vi* **1** : to sparkle **2** : to bubble, to fizz **3** : to crackle (of fire)
petit[1] [p(ə)ti] *adv* **1 tailler petit** : to run small **2 voir petit** : to underestimate **3 petit à petit** : gradually, little by little
petit[2], **-tite** [p(ə)ti, -tit] *adj* **1** : small, little **2** COURT : short **3** : young <ma petite sœur : my little sister> **4** (*used in terms of affection*) <mon petit chéri : my sweetie> **5** : minor, insignificant, slight **6 petit ami, petite amie** : boyfriend, girlfriend **7 petit déjeuner** : breakfast **8 petit doigt** : little finger **9 petite monnaie** : small change **10 petit pois** : (green) pea **11 petite vérole** : smallpox
petit[3], **-tite** *n* : child, little boy *m,* little girl *f*
petit[4] *nm* : cub (of an animal)
petitement [p(ə)titmɑ̃] *adv* **1** : poorly, humbly <petitement logé : living in cramped quarters> **2** : pettily
petitesse [p(ə)titɛs] *nf* **1** : smallness **2** MESQUINERIE : pettiness
petit–fils, petite–fille [p(ə)tifis, p(ə)titfij] *n* : grandson *m,* granddaughter *f*
pétition [petisjɔ̃] *nf* : petition
pétitionnaire [petisjɔnɛr] *nmf* : petitioner
pétitionner [petisjɔne] *vi* : to petition
petit–lait [p(ə)tilɛ] *nm, pl* **petits–laits** : whey
petits–enfants [p(ə)tizɑ̃fɑ̃] *nmpl* : grandchildren
pétrification [petrifikasjɔ̃] *nf* : petrification
pétrifier [petrifje] {96} *vt* : to petrify
pétrin [petrɛ̃] *nm fam* : fix, jam
pétrir [petrir] *vt* : to knead
pétrole [petrɔl] *nm* **1** : oil, petroleum **2** *or* **pétrole lampant** : kerosene
pétrolier[1], **-lière** [petrɔlje, -ljɛr] *adj* : oil, petroleum <industrie pétrolière : oil industry>
pétrolier[2] *nm* **1** : oil tanker **2** : oilman
pétulance [petylɑ̃s] *nf* EXUBÉRANCE : vivacity, exuberance
pétulant, -lante [petylɑ̃, -lɑ̃t] *adj* EXUBÉRANT : vivacious, exuberant
pétunia [petynja] *nm* : petunia
peu[1] [pø] *adv* **1** : little, not much <elle a dormi peu : she slept little> **2** : not very <peu connu : little known> **3** : shortly <peu après : not long after>
peu[2] *nm* **1** : lack <peu d'appétit : lack of appetite> **2** : little, bit <attends un peu : wait a little (longer)> <un peu moins de gens : somewhat fewer people> **3 le peu de** : the few, the little <le peu d'argent que j'ai mis de côté : the little money I've saved up> **4 peu à peu** : little by little **5 pour un peu** : almost, very nearly
peu[3] *pron* **1** : few (people) <peu lui font confiance : few trust him> **2** ~ **de** : few, little <peu de mots : few words> <c'est peu de chose : it's just a little, it's not much>
peuplade [pøplad] *nf* : (small) tribe
peuple [pœpl] *nm* **1** : people *pl,* nation <le peuple anglais : the English people> **2** : common people *pl,* masses *pl* <un homme du peuple : a man of the people> **3** FOULE : crowd, multitude
peuplé, -lée [pœple] *adj* : populated
peuplement [pœpləmɑ̃] *nm* **1** : populating **2** : population

peupler [pœple] *vt* **1** : to populate, to stock, to plant **2** HABITER : to inhabit **3** : to occupy, to fill — **se peupler** *vr* : to become populated
peuplier [pøplije] *nm* : poplar
peur [pœr] *nf* **1** : fear **2 de peur que** : lest **3 faire peur à** : to frighten
peureusement [pœrøzmɑ̃] *adv* : fearfully
peureux, -reuse [pœrø, -røz] *adj* CRAINTIF : fearful, afraid
peut [pø], *etc.* → **pouvoir**
peut–être [pøtɛtr] *adv* : perhaps, maybe
phalange [falɑ̃ʒ] *nf* : phalanx
phallique [falik] *adj* : phallic
phallus [falys] *nms & pl* : phallus
pharaon [faraɔ̃] *nm* : pharaoh
phare [far] *nm* **1** : lighthouse **2** : headlight **3** : beacon
pharmaceutique [farmasøtik] *adj* : pharmaceutical
pharmacie [farmasi] *nf* : pharmacy, drugstore
pharmacien, -cienne [farmasjɛ̃, -sjɛn] *n* : pharmacist
pharmacologie [farmakɔlɔʒi] *nf* : pharmacology
pharynx [farɛ̃ks] *nm* : pharynx
phase [faz] *nf* : phase, stage
phénix [feniks] *nm* **1** : phoenix **2** : paragon
phénoménal, -nale [fenɔmenal] *adj, mpl* **-naux** [-no] : phenomenal — **phénoménalement** [-nalmɑ̃] *adv*
phénomène [fenɔmɛn] *nm* **1** : phenomenon **2** : freak (in a circus, etc.)
philanthrope [filɑ̃trɔp] *nmf* : philanthropist
philanthropie [filɑ̃trɔpi] *nf* : philanthropy — **philanthropique** [-trɔpik] *adj*
philatélie [filateli] *nf* : stamp collecting, philately
philippin, -pine [filipɛ̃, -pin] *adj* : Filipino, Philippine
Philippin, -pine *n* : Filipino
philistin[1], **-tine** [filistɛ̃, -tin] *adj* : philistine
philistin[2] *nm* : philistine
philodendron [filɔdɛ̃drɔ̃] *nm* : philodendron
philosophe[1] [filɔzɔf] *adj* : philosophical
philosophe[2] *nmf* : philosopher
philosopher [filɔzɔfe] *vi* : to philosophize
philosophie [filɔzɔfi] *nf* : philosophy
philosophique [filɔzɔfik] *adj* : philosophical — **philosophiquement** [-fikmɑ̃] *adv*
phlébite [flebit] *nf* : phlebitis
phlox [flɔks] *nms & pl* : phlox
phobie [fɔbi] *nf* : phobia
phonème [fɔnɛm] *nm* : phoneme
phonétique[1] [fɔnetik] *adj* : phonetic
phonétique[2] *nf* : phonetics
phonograph [fɔnɔgraf] *nm* : phonograph
phoque [fɔk] *nm* **1** : seal **2** : sealskin
phosphate [fɔsfat] *nm* : phosphate
phosphore [fɔsfɔr] *nm* : phosphorous
phosphorescence [fɔsfɔresɑ̃s] *nf* : phosphorescence — **phosphorescent, -cente** [-resɑ̃, -sɑ̃t] *adj*
photo [fɔto] *nf* : photo <photo d'identité : passport photo>
photocopie [fɔtɔkɔpi] *nf* **1** : photocopy **2** : photocopying
photocopier [fɔtɔkɔpje] {96} *vt* : to photocopy
photocopieur [fɔtɔkɔpjœr] *nm* : photocopier
photocopieuse [fɔtɔkɔpjøz] *nf* → **photocopieur**
photoélectrique [fɔtɔelektrik] *adj* : photoelectric
photogénique [fɔtɔʒenik] *adj* : photogenic
photographe [fɔtɔgraf] *nmf* : photographer
photographie [fɔtɔgrafi] *nf* **1** : photography **2** : photograph
photographier [fɔtɔgrafje] {96} *vt* : to photograph
photographique [fɔtɔgrafik] *adj* : photographic — **photographiquement** [-fikmɑ̃] *adv*
photosynthèse [fɔtɔsɛ̃tɛz] *nf* : photosynthesis
phrase [fraz] *nf* **1** : sentence **2** : phrase
phraséologie [frazeɔlɔʒi] *nf* **1** : phraseology **2** : verbiage, verbosity
phylum [filɔm] *nm* : phylum
physicien, -cienne [fizisjɛ̃, -sjɛn] *n* : physicist
physiologie [fizjɔlɔʒi] *nf* : physiology
physiologique [fizjɔlɔʒik] *adj* : physiological, physiologic
physiologiste [fizjɔlɔʒist] *nmf* : physiologist
physionomie [fizjɔnɔmi] *nf* : physiognomy
physiothérapie [fizjɔterapi] *nf* : physiotherapy, physical therapy
physique[1] [fizik] *adj* : physical — **physiquement** [-zikmɑ̃] *adv*
physique[2] *nm* : physique
physique[3] *nf* : physics
pi [pi] *nm* : pi
piaffer [pjafe] *vi* : to stamp one's feet, to tap one's foot
piailler [pjaje] *vi* : to squawk, to chirp
pianiste [pjanist] *nmf* : pianist
piano [pjano] *nm* : piano <piano à queue : grand piano>
pianoter [pjanɔte] *vi* **1** : to tinkle away (at the piano) **2** : to tap, to drum (one's fingers)
piastre [pjastr] *nf Can fam* : dollar, buck
piaule [pjol] *nf fam* : room, pad
piaulement [pjolmɑ̃] *nm* : cheep, peep
piauler [pjole] *vi* **1** : to cheep, to peep **2** *fam* : to whimper, to whine

pic [pik] *nm* **1** : woodpecker **2** CIME : peak <à pic : straight down, vertically> **3** : pick, pickax <pic à glace : ice pick>
pic–bois [pikbwa] *nm Can, pl* **pic–bois** : woodpecker
piccolo *or* **picolo** [pikɔlo] *nm* : piccolo
pichet [piʃɛ] *nm* **1** : pitcher **2** : pitcherful
pichou [piʃu] *nm Can fam* : slipper, (baby's) bootee
pickpocket [pikpɔkɛt] *nm* : pickpocket
pick–up [pikœp] *nm* : pickup (truck)
picoler [pikɔle] *vi fam* : to tipple, to drink
picorer [pikɔre] *v* : to peck
picot [piko] *nm Can* : polka dot
picotement [pikɔtmɑ̃] *nm* : prickling, stinging, tingling
picoter [pikɔte] *vt* **1** PICORER : to peck **2** : to sting — *vi* : to prickle, to sting
picotin [pikɔtɛ̃] *nm* : peck
pictural, -rale [piktyral] *adj, mpl* **-raux** [-ro] : pictorial
pie[1] [pi] *adj* : piebald, pied
pie[2] [pi] *nf* **1** : magpie **2** *fam* : chatterbox
pièce [pjɛs] *nf* **1** : piece, bit <mettre en pièces : to smash to pieces> **2** : piece, item <la pièce : apiece> <pièce de collection : collector's item> <pièce à conviction : exhibit (in a court of law)> **3** : room, bedroom **4** : paper, document <pièce jointe : enclosure> **5** : piece (in music or theater) <pièce de théâtre : play> **6** *or* **pièce de monnaie** : coin
pied [pje] *nm* **1** : foot <coup de pied : kick> <à pied : on foot> <pied à pied : inch by inch> **2** : base, bottom, leg (of a table, etc.) **3** : foot (in measurement) **4** : stalk, bunch, head <pied de salade : head of lettuce> **5 mettre sur pied** : to set up, to get off the ground
piédestal [pjedɛstal] *nm, pl* **-taux** [-to] : pedestal
piège [pjɛʒ] *nm* **1** : trap, snare **2** : snag, pitfall **3 prendre au piège** : to entrap
piéger [pjeʒe] {64} *vt* **1** : to trap **2** : to booby-trap
pie–grièche [pigrijeʃ] *nf, pl* **pies–grièches** : shrike
pierre [pjɛr] *nf* **1** : stone **2 pierre à aiguiser** : whetstone **3 pierre angulaire** : cornerstone **4 pierre tombale** : tombstone, gravestone, headstone
pierreries [pjɛrri] *nfpl* : precious stones, gems
pierreux, -reuse [pjɛrø, -øz] *adj* : stony
piété [pjete] *nf* : piety
piétiner [pjetine] *vt* : to trample on, to crush underfoot — *vi* **1** : to stamp one's feet (with impatience, etc.) **2** STAGNER : to make no headway
piéton, -tonne [pjetɔ̃, -tɔn] *n* : pedestrian
piétonnier, -nière [pjetɔnje, -njɛr] *adj* : pedestrian
piètre [pjɛtr] *adj* : very poor, sorry <piètre consolation : cold comfort> <une piètre figure : a sorry figure>
pieu [pjø] *nm, pl* **pieux** : post, stake
pieuvre [pjøvr] *nf* POULPE : octopus
pieux, pieuse [pjø, pjøz] *adj* : pious — **pieusement** [pjøzmɑ̃] *adv*
pige [piʒ] *nf* **travailler à la pige** *or* **faire des piges** : to work freelance
pigeon [piʒɔ̃] *nm* : pigeon
pigeonneau [piʒɔno] *nm* : squab
pigeonnier [piʒɔnje] *nm* : pigeon house, dovecote
piger [piʒe] {17} *vt* **1** *fam* : to understand, to catch on to <tu piges? : get it?> **2** *Can* : to pick (a card, a number, etc.)
pigiste [piʒist] *nmf* : freelancer
pigment [pigmɑ̃] *nm* : pigment — **pigmentation** [-mɑ̃tasjɔ̃] *nf*
pignon [piɲɔ̃] *nm* **1** : gable **2** : cogwheel
pilaf [pilaf] *nm* : pilaf
pile[1] [pil] *adv fam* **1** : abruptly <arrêter pile : to stop dead> **2** : exactly <à dix heures pile : at ten o'clock sharp>
pile[2] *nf* **1** : pile, heap **2** : (storage) battery **3** : pier (of a bridge) **4** : reverse (of a coin) <pile ou face? : heads or tails?>
piler [pile] *vt* **1** BROYER : to crush, to pound **2** *fam* : to clobber, to defeat **3** *Can* : to mash (potatoes, etc.) — *vi* **1** *Can fam* : to walk, to step <j'ai pilé dans une flaque d'eau : I walked into a puddle> **2** *France fam* : to slam on the brakes
pilier [pilje] *nm* **1** : pillar, column **2** SOUTIEN : prop, mainstay
pillage [pijaʒ] *nm* : looting, pillaging
pillard, -larde [pijar, -jard] *n* : looter
piller [pije] *vt* : to loot, to pillage, to plunder
pilleur, -leuse [pilœr, -løz] *n* : pillager, looter
pilon [pilɔ̃] *nm* **1** : pestle **2** : wooden leg **3** : (chicken) drumstick
pilonner [pilɔne] *vt* **1** : to crush **2** : to bombard, to shell
pilori [pilɔri] *nm* : stocks *pl,* pillory
pilosité [pilozite] *nf* : hairiness
pilotage [pilɔtaʒ] *nm* : piloting, flying
pilote[1] [pilɔt] *adj* : pilot, test <projet pilote : pilot project>
pilote[2] *nm* **1** : pilot <pilote de ligne : airline pilot> **2** GUIDE : guide **3 pilote de course** : racing-car driver
piloter [pilɔte] *vt* **1** : to pilot, to fly, to drive **2** : to guide, to direct
pilotis [pilɔti] *nm* : stilts *pl,* piling
pilule [pilyl] *nf* : pill
piment [pimɑ̃] *nm* **1** : pepper <piment rouge : chili pepper> <piment de la Jamaïque : allspice> <piment doux : pimiento> **2** : piquancy, spice
pimenter [pimɑ̃te] *vt* **1** : to season with red pepper **2** : to spice up

pimpant, -pante [pɛ̃pɑ̃] *adj* : spruce, dapper
pin [pɛ̃] *nm* : pine (tree or wood)
pinacle [pinakl] *nm* **1** : pinnacle, summit **2 porter qqn au pinacle** : to praise s.o. to the skies
pinailler [pinaje] *vi fam* : to split hairs, to quibble
pinard [pinar] *nm fam* : (cheap) wine
pince [pɛ̃s] *nf* **1** : pliers *pl* **2** : tongs *pl* **3** : pincer, claw **4** : pleat, fold **5 pince à cheveux** : bobby pin **6 pince à épiler** : tweezers *pl* **7 pince à linge** : clothespin
pincé, -cée [pɛ̃se] *adj* : forced, stiff
pinceau [pɛ̃so] *nm, pl* **pinceaux** : paintbrush
pincée [pɛ̃se] *nf* : pinch <une pincée de sel : a pinch of salt>
pincement [pɛ̃smɑ̃] *nm* **1** : pinch **2** : twinge, pang
pince–monseigneur [pɛ̃smɔ̃sɛɲœr] *nf, pl* **pinces–monseigneur** : crowbar, jimmy
pincer [pɛ̃se] {6} *vt* **1** : to pinch **2** : to nip at, to sting (of wind, cold, etc.) **3** : to purse (one's lips) **4** : to pluck (a stringed instrument) **5** *fam* : to nab — *vi* : to be nippy (of weather) — **se pincer** *vr* **1** : to pinch oneself <se pincer le nez : to hold one's nose> **2** : to get caught, to be pinched <je me suis pincé le doigt dans la porte : I caught my finger in the door>
pince–sans–rire [pɛ̃ssɑ̃rir] *adj s & pl* : deadpan
pincettes [pɛ̃set] *nfpl* **1** : small tweezers **2** : (fire) tongs
pinçon [pɛ̃sɔ̃] *nm* : pinch mark
pinède [pinɛd] *nf* : pine forest
pingouin [pɛ̃gwɛ̃] *nm* : auk
pingre [pɛ̃gr] *adj* AVARE : niggardly, stingy
pingrerie [pɛ̃grəri] *nf* : meanness, stinginess
pinotte [pinɔt] *nf Can fam* : peanut
pintade [pɛ̃tad] *nf* : guinea fowl
pinte [pɛ̃t] *nf* : pint
pioche [pjɔʃ] *nf* : pickax, pick
piocher [pjɔʃe] *vt* **1** CREUSER : to dig (up) **2** : to draw (a card) **3** *fam* : to cram for (an exam)
piolet [pjɔle] *nm* : ice ax
pion[1], pionne [pjɔ̃, pjɔn] *n France fam* : student monitor
pion[2] *nm* **1** : pawn (in chess) **2** : piece (in checkers)
pionnier, -nière [pjɔnje, -njɛr] *n* : pioneer
pipe [pip] *nf* : pipe <fumer la pipe : to smoke a pipe>
pipeau [pipo] *nm, pl* **pipeaux** : (reed) pipe, flute
pipeline [pajplajn] *nm* : pipeline
piper [pipe] *vi* **ne pas piper (mot)** : to keep mum
piquant[1], -quante [pikɑ̃, -kɑ̃t] *adj* **1** : prickly, bristly **2** ÉPICÉ : hot, spicy **3** : sharp, biting **4** : racy, spicy
piquant[2] *nm* **1** : spiciness, piquancy **2** : prickle, thorn, barb **3** : spine, quill (of a porcupine, etc.)
pique[1] [pik] *nm* : spade (in playing cards)
pique[2] *nf* **1** : pike (weapon) **2** POINTE : cutting remark
piqué[1], -quée [pike] *adj* **1** : quilted **2** : sour, mildewed **3** : staccato (in music)
piqué[2] *nm* **1** : piqué (fabric) **2** : nosedive
pique–assiette [pikasjet] *nmfs & pl* : freeloader, sponger
pique–feu [pikfø] *nms & pl* TISONNIER : poker
pique–nique [piknik] *nm, pl* **pique–niques** : picnic
pique–niquer [piknike] *vi* : to have a picnic
piquer [pike] *vt* **1** : to prick, to puncture **2** : to give an injection to, to vaccinate **3** : to sting, to bite **4** : to stick (on), to pin (up) **5** : to make holes in **6** : to stitch **7** : to prickle, to tickle **8** : to needle, to irritate **9** ÉVEILLER : to arouse, to stimulate (interest, etc.) **10** *fam* : to pinch, to swipe **11** *fam* : to nab, to catch **12 piquer un somme** : to take a nap — *vi* **1** : to be prickly **2** : to sting, to burn **3** : to dive, to swoop down — **se piquer** *vr* **1** : to prick oneself, to inject oneself **2** : to get mildewed, to turn sour **3 ~ de** : to pride oneself on
piquet [pike] *nm* **1** : post, stake **2** : peg **3 piquet de grève** : picket line
piqueter [pikte] {8} *vt* **1** : to stake out **2** : to mark, to dot — *vi Can* : to picket
piqueteur, -teuse [piktœr, -tøz] *n Can* : picketer, striker
piquette [piket] *nf* : (cheap) wine
piqûre [pikyr] *nf* **1** : prick **2** : sting, bite **3** : injection, shot **4** : small hole, pitting **5** : stitch (in sewing)
piranha [pirana] *nm* : piranha
piratage [pirataʒ] *nm* : piracy (of software, etc.)
pirate [pirat] *nm* **1** : pirate **2** : crook, swindler **3 pirate de l'air** : hijacker
pirater [pirate] *vt* : to pirate
piraterie [piratri] *nf* **1** : piracy **2 piraterie aérienne** : hijacking
pire[1] [pir] *adj* **1** : worse <pire que jamais : worse than ever> **2 le pire, la pire, les pires** : the worst <le pire jour de ma vie : the worst day of my life> **3 pas tant pire** *Can* : not too bad, OK
pire[2] *nm* **1 le pire** : the worst **2 au pire** : at the worst
pirogue [pirɔg] *nf* : dugout (canoe)
pirouette [pirwet] *nf* : pirouette
pis[1] [pi] *adv* **1** : worse <de mal en pis : from bad to worse> **2 au pis aller**

: if worst comes to worst **3 tant pis** : too bad

pis[2] *adj* : worse

pis[3] *nms & pl* **1** : udder **2 le pis** : the worst

pis-aller [pizale] *nms & pl* : last resort, stopgap

piscine [pisin] *nf* : swimming pool

pissenlit [pisɑ̃li] *nm* : dandelion

pistache [pistaʃ] *nf* : pistachio

piste [pist] *nf* **1** TRACE : track, trail <sur la bonne piste : on the right track> **2** : trail, slope <piste de ski : ski slope> **3** : racetrack **4** INDICE : lead, clue **5** : path, route, course <piste cyclable : bike path> **6** *or* **piste d'atterrissage** : runway, airstrip **7 piste sonore** : soundtrack

pistil [pistil] *nm* : pistil

pistolet [pistɔlɛ] *nm* **1** : pistol, handgun **2** : spray gun

piston [pistɔ̃] *nm* **1** : piston **2** : valve (in a musical instrument)

pistonner [pistɔne] *vt fam* : to pull strings for

pitance [pitɑ̃s] *nf* : ration, sustenance

piteusement [pitøzmɑ̃] *adv* : pathetically, pitifully

piteux, -teuse [pitø, -tøz] *adj* : pitiful, miserable <un état piteux : a sorry state>

pitié [pitje] *nf* COMPASSION : pity, mercy

piton [pitɔ̃] *nm* **1** : hook **2** : piton **3** : peak (of a mountain) **4** *Can fam* : button, switch

pitonner [pitɔne] *vi Can fam* : to push a button, to flip a switch, to zap (with a remote control)

pitoyable [pitwajabl] *adj* : pitiful, pathetic — **pitoyablement** [-jablɔmɑ̃] *adv*

pitre [pitr] *nm* CLOWN : clown, buffoon

pittoresque [pitɔresk] *adj* : picturesque

pituitaire [pituiter] *adj* : pituitary <glande pituitaire : pituitary gland>

pivoine [pivwan] *nf* : peony

pivot [pivo] *nm* : pivot

pivoter [pivɔte] *vi* : to pivot, to revolve, to swivel

pizza [pidza] *nf* : pizza

pizzeria [pidzerja] *nf* : pizzeria

placage [plakaʒ] *nm* **1** : veneer **2** : (metal) plating **3** : tackle (in football)

placard [plakar] *nm* **1** : cupboard, closet **2** AFFICHE : poster, placard

placarder [plakarde] *vt* : to post, to put up (posters, notices, etc.)

place [plas] *nf* **1** : place, spot <chaque chose à sa place : everything in its place> <mets-les à leur place : put them where they belong> **2** : room, space <prendre de la place : to take up space> <il n'y a pas de place : there's no room> **3** : seat <louer des places au théâtre : to book seats at the theater> **4** : rank, position <prendre la première place : to take first place> **5** : placing, position, situation <à la place de : instead of, in place of> <se mettre en place : to be set up, to position oneself> **6** : (public) square **7** : job, position **8** : (financial) market **9 de place en place** : here and there

placebo [plasebo] *nm* : placebo

placement [plasmɑ̃] *nm* **1** : investment **2** : placement <bureau de placement : placement agency> **3** : field goal

placenta [plasɛ̃ta] *nm* : placenta

placer [plase] {6} *vt* **1** : to place, to set, to put **2** : to put in, to slip in, to interject <je n'ai pas pu placer un seul mot : I couldn't get a word in edgewise> **3** : to seat (someone) **4** : to sell, to place (a product) **5** : to invest **6** : to place, to find a job for — **se placer** *vr* **1** : to position oneself **2** : to rank **3** : to get a job

placeur, -ceuse [plasœr, -søz] *n* : usher (in a theater)

placide [plasid] *adj* : placid, calm — **placidement** [-sidmɑ̃] *adv*

placier, -cière [plasje, -sjɛr] *n* : traveling salesman

placoter [plakɔte] *vi Can fam* : to chat, to chitchat — *vt Can fam* : to divulge, to disclose

plafond [plafɔ̃] *nm* : ceiling

plafonner [plafɔne] *vt* : to put a ceiling in — *vi* : to reach a maximum

plafonnier [plafɔnje] *nm* : ceiling light

plage [plaʒ] *nf* **1** : beach, shore **2** : seaside resort **3 plage horaire** : time slot

plagiaire [plaʒjɛr] *nmf* : plagiarist

plagiat [plaʒja] *nm* : plagiarism

plagier [plaʒje] {96} *vt* : to plagiarize

plaider [plede] *vi* : to plead, to litigate — *vt* : to plead (a case)

plaideur, -deuse [pledœr, -døz] *n* : litigant

plaie [plɛ] *nf* **1** BLESSURE : wound, cut, sore **2** : scourge, plague **3** *fam* : pest

plaignait [plɛɲɛ], *etc.* → **plaindre**

plaignard, -gnarde [plɛɲar, -ɲard] *n Can* : complainer, grouch

plaignant, -gnante [plɛɲɑ̃, -ɲɑ̃t] *n* : plaintiff

plaigne [plɛɲ], *etc.* → **plaindre**

plain [plɛ̃] *nm* : high tide

plaindre [plɛ̃dr] {65} *vt* : to pity, to feel sorry for — **se plaindre** *vr* **1** : to complain, to moan **2** : to protest

plaine [plɛn] *nf* : plain, lowland

plain-pied [plɛ̃pje] *adj* **1 de ~** : on the same level <une maison de plain-pied : a single-story house> **2 être de plain-pied avec** : to be at ease with, to be on an equal footing with

plainte [plɛ̃t] *nf* **1** : complaint **2** : moan, groan

plaintif, -tive [plɛ̃tif, -tiv] *adj* : plaintive — **plaintivement** [-tivmɑ̃] *adv*

plaire [plɛr] {66} *vi* **1** : to be attractive, to be pleasing **2 ~ à** : to please, to suit — *v impers* : to please <ce qu'il

vous plaît : whatever you like> <s'il vous plaît : please> — **se plaire** *vr* **1** : to like oneself **2** : to like each other **3** ~ **à** : to enjoy

plaisait [plɛze], **plaisions** [plɛzjɔ̃], *etc.* → **plaire**

plaisamment [plɛzamɑ̃] *adv* **1** : pleasantly **2** DRÔLEMENT : amusingly

plaisance [plɛzɑ̃s] *nf or* **navigation de plaisance** : sailing, boating

plaisancier, -cière [plɛzɑ̃sje, -sjɛr] *n* : amateur sailor, boating enthusiast

plaisant[1], **-sante** [plɛzɑ̃, -zɑ̃t] *adj* **1** AGRÉABLE : pleasant **2** AMUSANT : amusing, funny

plaisant[2] *nm* **mauvais plaisant** : practical joker

plaisanter [plɛzɑ̃te] *vi* : to joke, to jest — *vt* : to tease, to make fun of

plaisanterie [plɛzɑ̃tri] *nf* **1** BLAGUE : joke, jest **2** FARCE : prank

plaisantin [plɛzɑ̃tɛ̃] *nm* FARCEUR : practical joker

plaise [plɛz], *etc.* → **plaire**

plaisir [plɛzir] *nm* **1** : pleasure <avec plaisir! : with pleasure> <faire plaisir à : to please> **2 au plaisir** : see you soon **3 avec plaisir**! : of course!

plan[1], **plane** [plɑ̃, plan] *adj* PLAT : flat, level, plane

plan[2] *nm* **1** : plane **2** : plan, strategy, program **3** : map, diagram, blueprint **4** : outline, synopsis **5 laisser en plan** : to leave in the lurch **6 premier plan** : foreground

planche[1] [plɑ̃ʃ] *adj Can* : flat, even

planche[2] *nf* **1** : board, plank <planche à repasser : ironing board> **2** : plate (in engraving) **3** : plate, illustration (in a book) **4 planche à roulettes** : skateboard **5 les planches** : the stage

plancher [plɑ̃ʃe] *nm* **1** : floor **2** : minimum, lower limit

plancton [plɑ̃ktɔ̃] *nm* : plankton

planer [plane] *vi* **1** : to glide, to soar, to hover **2** ~ **sur** : to hang over, to hover over **3 avoir l'air de planer** : to be above it all, to appear distracted

planétaire [planetɛr] *adj* **1** : planetary **2** MONDIAL : global, worldwide

planétarium [planetarjɔm] *nm* : planetarium

planète [planɛt] *nf* : planet

planification [planifikasjɔ̃] *nf* : planning

planifier [planifje] {96} *vt* : to plan

planning [planiŋ] *nm* : planning <planning familial : family planning>

planque [plɑ̃k] *nf fam* **1** : hideout **2** : easy job

planquer [plɑ̃ke] *vt fam* : to hide away, to stash

plant [plɑ̃] *nm* **1** : patch, bed **2** : seedling, young plant

plantain [plɑ̃tɛ̃] *nm* : plantain

plantation [plɑ̃tasjɔ̃] *nf* **1** : planting **2** : plantation

plante [plɑ̃t] *nf* **1** : sole (of the foot) **2** : plant <plante grimpante : climbing plant>

planté, -tée [plɑ̃te] *adj* **1** : positioned, placed <dents mal plantées : uneven teeth> **2** *fam* : standing, rooted (to the spot) **3 bien planté** : sturdy, robust (of a child)

planter [plɑ̃te] *vt* **1** : to plant **2** : to stick in, to drive in **3** : to set, to set up **4** *fam* : to ditch, to drop — **se planter** *vr* **1** : to become embedded **2** *fam* : to stand, to plant oneself **3** *fam* : to crash, to smash **4** *fam* : to get it wrong, to mess up

planteur, -teuse [plɑ̃tœr, -tøz] *n* : planter

planton [plɑ̃tɔ̃] *nm* : orderly (in the military)

plantureux, -reuse [plɑ̃tyrø, -røz] *adj* **1** : copious, lavish <un repas plantureux : a lavish repast> **2** : buxom

plaque [plak] *nf* **1** : plate, sheet <plaques de glace : patches of ice> **2** : plaque, nameplate, badge (of a policeman) **3** : patch (of ice, etc.) **4 plaque chauffante** : hotplate, griddle **5 plaque d'immatriculation** : license plate **6 plaque dentaire** : dental plaque

plaqué, -quée [plake] *adj* : plated <plaqué or : gold-plated>

plaquer [plake] *vt* **1** : to veneer, to plate **2** : to stick, to plaster, to pin down **3** : to tackle (in football) **4** *fam* : to ditch, to get rid of

plaquette [plaket] *nf* **1** : small sheet <plaquette de beurre : pat of butter> **2** : booklet

plasma [plasma] *nm* : plasma

plastique[1] [plastik] *adj* **1** : plastic, malleable **2 chirurgie plastique** : plastic surgery

plastique[2] *nm* : plastic

plastique[3] *nf* **1** : plastic arts *pl*, modeling, sculpture **2** : beauty of form

plat[1], **plate** [pla, plat] *adj* **1** : flat, level **2** : shallow **3** : dull, bland, insipid **4** : obsequious **5** : lank <cheveux plats : lank hair> **6** *Can* : boring, dull

plat[2] *nm* **1** : plate **2** : dish <un plat méditerranéen : a Mediterranean dish> **3** : course <plat de résistance : main course, entrée> **4** : flat (part) <plat de la main : flat of the hand> **5 à** ~ : flat (down) <tomber à plat : to fall flat> **6 à** ~ : dead (of a battery)

platane [platan] *nm* : plane tree

plat–bord [plabɔr] *nm, pl* **plats–bords** : gunwale

plateau [plato] *nm, pl* **plateaux 1** : tray, platter **2** : plateau <plateau continental : continental shelf> **3** : stage, set (in theater) **4** : pan (of a scale)

plate–bande [platbɑ̃d] *nf, pl* **plates–bandes** : flower bed

plate–forme [platfɔrm] *nf, pl* **plates–formes** : platform

platement [platmɑ̃] *adv* **1** : dully, uninterestingly **2** : abjectly
platine[1] [platin] *nm* : platinum
platine[2] *nf* **1** : turntable **2 platine cassette** : cassette deck **3 platine laser** : CD player
platitude [platityd] *nf* **1** BANALITÉ : banality, triteness **2** : platitude
platonique [platɔnik] *adj* : platonic
plâtre [platr] *nm* **1** : plaster **2** : plaster cast
plâtrer [platre] *vt* **1** : to plaster **2** : to put in a (plaster) cast
plâtrier [platrije] *nm* : plasterer
plausibilité [plozibilite] *nf* : plausibility
plausible [plozibl] *adj* VRAISEMBLABLE : plausible, likely
plèbe [plɛb] *nf* : common people *pl*, masses *pl*
plébéien, -béienne [plebejɛ̃, -bejɛn] *adj* : plebeian
plébiscite [plebisit] *nm* : plebiscite
plein[1], **pleine** [plɛ̃, plɛn] *adj* **1** REMPLI : full <une tasse pleine : a full cup> **2** : filled (up) <une salle pleine de monde : a roomful of people, a crowded room> <saisir à pleines mains : to grasp with both hands, to take a firm hold> <une journée pleine : a busy day> **3** : solid, rounded, full <la pleine lune : the full moon> **4** : pregnant (of an animal) **5** (*used as an intensifier*) <en pleine rue : in the middle of the street> <en plein jour : in broad daylight> **6 la pleine mer** : the open sea **7 le plein air** : the outdoors **8 plein d'entrain** : high-spirited **9 plein de soi-même** : conceited, self-centered
plein[2] *nm* **1** : fullest point, maximum <faire le plein de : to fill up on, to stock up with> <donner son plein : to give one's all> **2 à ~** *or* **en ~** : fully, totally, at full capacity
pleinement [plɛnmɑ̃] *adv* ENTIÈREMENT : fully, entirely
plénier, -nière [plenje, -njɛr] *adj* : plenary
plénipotentiaire [plenipɔtɑ̃sjɛr] *nmf* : plenipotentiary
plénitude [plenityd] *nf* **1** AMPLEUR : scale, extent **2** : fullness, peak
pléthore [pletɔr] *nf* : plethora, overabundance
pleumer [plə(œ)me] *vi Can fam* : to peel (of skin)
pleurer [plœre] *vt* **1** : to weep for, to lament **2** : to cry <pleurer des larmes de joie : to cry tears of joy> — *vi* **1** : to cry, to weep **2** : to water <il a les yeux qui pleurent : his eyes are watering> **3 ~ sur** : to shed tears over, to bemoan
pleurésie [plœrezi] *nf* : pleurisy
pleurnicher [plœrniʃe] *vi fam* : to whine, to snivel
pleurs [plœr] *nmpl* **être en pleurs** : to be in tears
pleut [plø] → **pleuvoir**
pleuvoir [pløvwar] {67} *v impers* : to rain <il pleut à verse : it's pouring> — *vi* : to rain down, to pour down <les invitations pleuvaient sur nous : invitations were pouring in on us>
pli [pli] *nm* **1** : fold, pleat **2** : crease **3** HABITUDE : habit <prendre un mauvais pli : to get into a bad habit> **4** : envelope, letter <sous ce pli : enclosed> **5** : trick (in card games)
pliable [plijabl] *adj* : pliable, flexible
pliant, pliante [plijɑ̃, plijɑ̃t] *adj* : folding <chaise pliante : folding chair>
plier [plije] {96} *vt* **1** : to fold, to fold up **2** : to bend **3 plié en deux** *fam* : doubled up with laughter — *vi* **1** : to bend, to sag **2** : to yield, to give in — **se plier** *vr* **1** : to bend over, to fold **2 ~ à** : to submit to
plinthe [plɛ̃t] *nf* **1** : plinth **2** : baseboard
plissé[1], **-sée** [plise] *adj* : pleated
plissé[2] *nm* : pleating, pleats *pl*
plisser [plise] *vt* **1** : to pleat, to fold **2** : to crease, to wrinkle (clothing) **3** FRONCER : to wrinkle (one's brow), to pucker (one's lips), to screw up (one's eyes) — **se plisser 1** : to get wrinkled **2** : to pucker up
pliure [plijyr] *nf* : fold, bend (of the arm or leg)
plomb [plɔ̃] *nm* **1** : lead <essence sans plomb : unleaded gas> **2** : shot, (lead) pellet **3** FUSIBLE : (electrical) fuse **4** : sinker (in fishing)
plombage [plɔ̃baʒ] *nm* : filling (of a tooth)
plomber [plɔ̃be] *vt* **1** : to weight with lead **2** : to fill (a tooth) **3** : to plumb
plomberie [plɔ̃bri] *nf* : plumbing
plombier [plɔ̃bje] *nm* : plumber
plonge [plɔ̃ʒ] *nf* **1** : dishwashing <faire la plonge : to wash dishes> **2 prendre une plonge** *Can fam* : to tumble down, to crash down
plongeant, -geante [plɔ̃ʒɑ̃, -ʒɑ̃t] *adj* **1** : plunging **2** : from above <vue plongeante : bird's-eye view>
plongée [plɔ̃ʒe] *nf* **1** : diving **2 plongée sous-marine** : skin diving, deep-sea diving
plongeoir [plɔ̃ʒwar] *nm* : diving board
plongeon [plɔ̃ʒɔ̃] *nm* **1** : dive **2** : loon (bird)
plonger [plɔ̃ʒe] {17} *vt* : to thrust, to plunge — *vi* **1** : to dive **2 ~ dans** : to plunge into — **se plonger** *vr* **~ dans** : to immerse oneself in, to sink into
plongeur, -geuse [plɔ̃ʒœr, -ʒøz] *n* **1** : diver **2** : dishwasher (person)
plot [plo] *nm* : (electrical) contact
plouc [pluk] *nm France fam* : bumpkin
plouf [pluf] *nm* : splash
ploutocratie [plutɔkrasi] *nf* : plutocracy
ployer [plwaje] {58} *vt* : to bow, to bend — *vi* **1** : to bend, to sag **2** CÉDER : to give in, to yield

plu¹ [ply] *pp* → **plaire**
plu² [ply] *pp* → **pleuvoir**
pluie [pluɥi] *nf* **1** : rain, rainfall **2** : shower, hail, stream <une pluie de compliments : a shower of compliments>
plumage [plymaʒ] *nm* : plumage, feathers *pl*
plume [plym] *nf* **1** : feather **2** : quill pen, pen nib
plumeau [plymo] *nm, pl* **plumeaux** [plymo] : feather duster
plumer [plyme] *vt* : to pluck
plumet [plyme] *nm* : plume
plumitif [plymitif] *nm* : pencil pusher, hack writer
plupart [plypar] *nf* **1 la plupart des** : most, the majority of <dans la plupart des cas : in most cases> **2 pour la plupart** : mostly, for the most part
pluralité [plyralite] *nf* : plurality
pluriel¹, -rielle [plyrjɛl] *adj* : plural
pluriel² *nm* : plural
plus¹ [ply(s)] *adv* **1** : more <peux-tu aller plus vite? : can you go faster?> <plus je dors, plus j'ai envie de dormir : the more I sleep, the more I want to sleep> <plus que tout : more than anything> **2** (*used in negation*) : no more, no longer <il ne les voit plus : he doesn't see them anymore> <je n'ai plus soif : I'm no longer thirsty> **3 ~ de** : more, more than <plus de café : more coffee> <avoir plus de 50 ans : to be over 50> **4 le plus** : most, the most <le plus souvent : most often, most of the time> <le plus d'argent : the most money> <au plus : at the most> **5 de ~** : in addition, furthermore **6 en ~** : as well, extra **7 non plus** : neither, either <moi non plus : me neither> **8 plus ou moins** : more or less, approximately
plus² *nm* **1** : plus (sign) **2** *fam* : plus, advantage <son expérience est un vrai plus : his experience is a real plus>
plus³ *conj* : plus <deux plus cinq font sept : two plus five equals seven>
plusieurs [plyzjœr] *adj & pron* : several
plutocracy [plytɔkrasi] *nf* : plutocracy
Pluton [plytɔ̃] *nf* : Pluto (planet)
plutonium [plytɔnjɔm] *nm* : plutonium
plutôt [plyto] *adv* : rather, instead <plutôt moins que trop : rather too little than too much> <plutôt du beurre que de l'huile : butter instead of oil> <plutôt que de les convaincre : rather than convincing them>
pluvial, -viale [plyvjal] *adj, mpl* **pluviaux** [plyvjo] : rain <eau pluviale : rainwater>
pluvier [plyvje] *nm* : plover
pluvieux, -vieuse [plyvjø, -vjøz] *adj* : rainy, wet
pneu [pnø] *nm, pl* **pneus** : tire
pneumatique [pnømatik] *adj* **1** : pneumatic **2** : inflatable <matelas pneumatique : inflatable mattress>
pneumonie [pnømɔni] *nf* : pneumonia
poche [pɔʃ] *nf* **1** : pocket (in clothing) **2** : pocket, cavity <une poche d'eau : a pocket of water> **3** SAC : bag, pouch **4 poches** *nfpl* CERNES : bags, circles <il a des poches sous les yeux : he has bags under his eyes>
pocher [pɔʃe] *vt* **1** : to poach (in cooking) **2 pocher l'œil à qqn** : to give s.o. a black eye — *vi* : to get baggy
pochette [pɔʃɛt] *nf* **1** : folder, case, (record) sleeve <pochette d'allumettes : book of matches> **2** : pocket handkerchief **3** : pouch, clutch bag
pochoir [pɔʃwar] *nm* : stencil
podium [pɔdjɔm] *nm* : podium
podologie [pɔdɔlɔʒi] *nf* : chiropody, podiatry
podologue [pɔdɔlɔg] *nmf* : podiatrist
poêle¹ [pwal] *nm* **1** FOURNEAU : stove <poêle à bois : wood-burning stove> **2** : pall, coffin cloth
poêle² *nf or* **poêle à frire** : frying pan
poêlon [pwalɔ̃] *nm* **1** : casserole dish **2** *Can* : frying pan
poème [pɔɛm] *nm* : poem
poésie [pɔezi] *nf* **1** : poetry **2** : poem
poète [pɔɛt] *nmf* : poet
poétique [pɔetik] *adj* : poetic
pogné, -gnée [pɔɲe] *adj Can fam* : uptight, tense
pogner [pɔɲe] *vt Can fam* **1** : to get, to catch <il l'a pognée à voler : he caught her stealing> **2 pogner les nerfs** : to have a fit — *vi Can fam* **1** : to be inhibited, to be hung up **2** : to be successful <artiste qui pogne : successful artist> — **se pogner** *vr Can fam* **~ avec** : to get into a fight with
pognon [pɔɲɔ̃] *nm France fam* : dough, money
pogrom [pɔgrɔm] *nm* : pogrom
poids [pwa] *nms & pl* **1** : weight, heaviness **2** FARDEAU : burden, responsibility **3** : weight <les poids et mesures : weights and mesures> <poids et haltères : weight lifting> **4** : meaning, importance <avoir du poids : to carry weight> **5 poids lourd** : heavyweight (in sports)
poignant, -gnante [pwaɲɑ̃, -ɲɑ̃t] *adj* ÉMOUVANT : moving, poignant
poignard [pwaɲar] *nm* : dagger
poignarder [pwaɲarde] *vt* : to stab
poigne [pwaɲ] *nf* **1** : grip, grasp **2 à ~** : firm, forceful
poignée [pwaɲe] *nf* **1** : handful **2** : handle **3 poignée de main** : handshake
poignet [pwaɲe] *nm* **1** : wrist **2** : cuff
poil [pwal] *nm* **1** : hair **2** : fur, coat <chat à poil long : long-haired cat> **3** : bristle (of a brush) **4** : nap (of fabric) **5 à ~** *fam* : stark naked
poilu, -lue [pwaly] *adj* : hairy

poinçon [pwɛ̃sɔ̃] *nm* **1** : awl, punch **2** MARQUE : hallmark, stamp
poinçonner [pwɛ̃sɔne] *vt* **1** : to hallmark, to stamp **2** : to punch, to perforate
poinçonneuse [pwɛ̃sɔnøz] *nf* : punch
poing [pwɛ̃] *nm* **1** : fist **2 coup de poing** : punch
point[1] [pwɛ̃] *adv* : not <je ne l'aime point : I do not like him> <point du tout : not at all>
point[2] *nm* **1** : point, position <point de départ : point of departure> <aller d'un point à un autre : to go from one place to the next> **2** DEGRÉ : degree, extent <à tel point que : to such an extent that, so much so that> **3** : period, dot (in punctuation) <point décimal : decimal point> <point d'exclamation : exclamation point> <point d'interrogation : question mark> <points de suspension : ellipsis> **4** QUESTION : question, matter, point <sur ce point, ils n'étaient pas d'accord : they couldn't agree on this matter> **5** : point (in sports) **6** : stitch (in sewing) **7 à ~** : just right <arriver à point : to arrive just in time> <faire cuire à point : to cook medium rare> **8 au point** : well designed, well done <mettre au point : to adjust, to perfect> **9 point culminant** : highlight **10 point de fusion** : melting point **11 point de vue** : point of view **12 point du jour** : daybreak **13 point mort** : blind spot (of an automobile) **14 point noir** : blackhead **15 points cardinaux** : points of the compass **16 → deux–points**
pointage [pwɛ̃taʒ] *nm* **1** : checking off, marking off (on a list) **2** : aiming (of a firearm) **3** *Can* : points *pl*, score (in sports)
pointe [pwɛ̃t] *nf* **1** : point, tip <en pointe : pointed> <sur la pointe des pieds : on tiptoe> **2** : point, headland **3** : high (level), peak <vitesse de pointe : top speed> <heures de pointe : rush hour> <technologie de pointe : state-of-the-art technology> **4** SOUPÇON : touch, hint **5** PIQUE : cutting remark, dig **6** CLOU : nail **7 pointes** *nfpl* : spiked shoes (in sports)
pointer [pwɛ̃te] *vt* **1** COCHER : to check, to mark off **2** : to aim, to point <pointer un doigt sur : to point a finger at> <pointer un fusil vers : to aim a rifle at> — *vi* **1** : to clock in **2** : to stick out, to rise up **3** : to break, to dawn, to come up — **se pointer** *vr fam* : to show up
pointeur, -teuse [pwɛ̃tœr, -tøz] *n* **1** : timekeeper **2** *Can* : scorekeeper
pointillé[1], **-lée** [pwɛ̃tije] *adj* : dotted, stippled
pointillé[2] *nm* : dotted line
pointilleux, -leuse [pwɛ̃tijø, -jøz] *adj* : finicky, fussy
pointu, -tue [pwɛ̃ty] *adj* **1** : pointed, sharp **2** : sharp, querulous **3** : shrill **4** : precise, specialized
pointure [pwɛ̃tyr] *nf* : size (of clothing)
point–virgule [pwɛ̃virgyl] *nm, pl* **points–virgules** : semicolon
poire [pwar] *nf* : pear
poireau [pwaro] *nm, pl* **poireaux** : leek
poireauter [pwarote] *vi fam* : to hang around
poirier [pwarje] *nm* : pear tree
pois [pwa] *nms & pl* **1** : pea <petit pois : green peas> <pois chiche : chickpea> **2** : dot <à pois : spotted, polka-dot>
poison [pwazɔ̃] *nm* : poison
poisse [pwas] *nf fam* : bad luck
poisser [pwase] *vt* : to make sticky — *vi* : to be sticky
poisseux, -seuse [pwasø, -søz] *adj* GLUANT : sticky
poisson [pwasɔ̃] *nm* **1** : fish <poisson rouge : goldfish> <poisson plat : flatfish> **2 poisson d'avril!** : April fool!
poisson–chat [pwasɔ̃ʃa] *nm, pl* **poissons–chats** : catfish
poissonnerie [pwasɔnri] *nf* : fish market
poissonnier, -nière [pwasɔnje, -njɛr] *n* : fish merchant, fishmonger
Poissons [pwasɔ̃] *nmpl* : Pisces
poitrine [pwatrin] *nf* **1** : chest **2** : breasts *pl*, bust, bosom **3** : breast (in cooking)
poivre [pwavr] *nm* **1** : pepper **2 poivre de cayenne** : cayenne pepper
poivré, -vrée [pwavre] *adj* : peppery
poivrer [pwavre] *vt* : to pepper
poivrier [pwavrije] *nm* **1** : pepper plant **2** : pepper shaker
poivrière [pwavrijɛr] *nf* : pepper shaker
poivron [pwavrɔ̃] *nm* : pepper <poivron vert : green pepper>
poix [pwa] *nm* : pitch, tar
poker [pɔkɛr] *nm* : poker <partie de poker : game of poker>
polaire [pɔlɛr] *adj* : polar
polarisation [pɔlarizasjɔ̃] *nf* : polarization
polariser [pɔlarize] *vt* **1** : to polarize **2** : to concentrate, to focus **3** ATTIRER : to attract — **se polariser** *vr*
pôle [pol] *nm* : pole <le pôle Nord : the North Pole>
polémique[1] [pɔlemik] *adj* : controversial, polemical
polémique[2] *nf* : debate, controversy, polemics
poli[1], **-lie** [pɔli] *adj* **1** COURTOIS : polite **2** LISSE : polished, smooth
poli[2] *nm* : polish, shine
police [pɔlis] *nf* **1** : police, police force **2** : law enforcement, policing **3** : font (in printing) **4 police d'assurance** : insurance policy

policier[1], **-cière** [pɔlisje, -sjɛr] *adj* **1** : police **2** : detective <roman policier : detective novel>
policier[2], **-cière** *n* : police officer
policlinique [pɔliklinik] *nf* : outpatient clinic
poliment [pɔlimɑ̃] *adv* : politely
poliomyélite [pɔljɔmjelit] *nf* : poliomyelitis
polir [pɔlir] *vt* **1** : to polish, to shine **2** PARFAIRE : to refine, to perfect (style, etc.)
polisson, -sonne [pɔlisɔ̃, -sɔn] *n* : scamp, naughty child, brat
politesse [pɔlitɛs] *nf* **1** COURTOISIE : politeness, courtesy **2** : polite remark, pleasantry <échanger des politesses : to exchange courtesies>
politicien, -cienne [pɔlitisjɛ̃, -sjɛn] *n* : politician
politique[1] [pɔlitik] *adj* : political — **politiquement** [-tikmɑ̃] *adv*
politique[2] *nf* **1** : politics **2** TACTIQUE : policy, procedure
politique[3] *nm* : politician
polka [pɔlka] *nf* : polka
pollen [pɔlɛn] *nm* : pollen
pollinisation [pɔlinizasjɔ̃] *nf* : pollination
polliniser [pɔlinize] *vt* : to pollinate
polluant[1], **-luante** [pɔlɥɑ̃, -lɥɑ̃t] *adj* : polluting
polluant[2] *nm* : pollutant
polluer [pɔlɥe] *vt* : to pollute — **pollution** [pɔlysjɔ̃] *nf*
polo [pɔlo] *nm* **1** : polo **2** : polo shirt
polonais[1], **-naise** [pɔlɔnɛ, -nɛz] *adj* : Polish
polonais[2] *nm* : Polish (language)
Polonais, -naise *n* : Pole
poltron,[1] **-tronne** [pɔltrɔ̃, -trɔn] *adj* : cowardly
poltron,[2] **-tronne** *n* : coward
polycopie [pɔlikɔpi] *nf* : mimeograph
polyester [pɔliɛstɛr] *nm* : polyester
polygame[1] [pɔligam] *adj* : polygamous
polygame[2] *nmf* : polygamist
polygamie [pɔligami] *nf* : polygamy
polygone [pɔligɔn] *nm* **1** : polygon **2** *or* **polygone de tir** : firing range
polymère [pɔlimɛr] *nm* : polymer
polynésien[1], **-sienne** [pɔlinezjɛ̃, -zjɛn] *adj* : Polynesian
polynésien[2] *nm* : Polynesian (language)
Polynésien, -sienne *n* : Polynesian
polype [pɔlip] *nm* : polyp
polythéisme [pɔliteism] *nm* : polytheism
polythéiste [pɔliteist] *adj* : polytheist, polytheistic
polyvalent, -lente [pɔlivalɑ̃, -lɑ̃t] *adj* **1** : polyvalent **2** : versatile, multipurpose, all-around
polyvalente [pɔlivalɑ̃, -lɑ̃t] *nf or* **école polyvalente** *Can* : general and vocational high school
pommade [pɔmad] *nf* : ointment
pomme [pɔm] *nf* **1** : apple **2 pomme d'Adam** : Adam's apple **3 pomme de discorde** : bone of contention **4 pomme de pin** : pinecone **5 pomme de terre** : potato **6 pommes frites** : French fries
pommeau [pɔmo] *nm* : knob, pommel
pommelé, -lée [pɔmle] *adj* : dappled, mottled
pommette [pɔmɛt] *nf* : cheekbone
pommier [pɔmje] *nm* : apple tree
pompe [pɔ̃p] *nf* **1** : pump <pompe à essence : gas pump> **2** : pomp, ceremony **3 pompes funèbres** : funeral home, funeral parlor
pomper [pɔ̃pe] *vt* **1** : to pump **2** : to soak up
pompette [pɔ̃pɛt] *adj fam* : tipsy
pompeux, -peuse [pɔ̃pø, -pøz] *adj* : pompous — **pompeusement** [-pøzmɑ̃] *adv*
pompier[1], **-pière** [pɔ̃pje, -pjɛr] *adj* : pompous, pretentious
pompier[2] *nm* : firefighter, fireman
pompiste [pɔ̃pist] *nmf* : service station attendant
pompon [pɔ̃pɔ̃] *nm* : pompom
pomponner [pɔ̃pɔne] *vt* : to dress up — **se pomponner** *vr* : to get all dressed up, to preen oneself, to primp (up)
ponce [pɔ̃s] *nf* **pierre ponce** : pumice stone
ponceau [pɔ̃so] *nm, pl* **ponceaux** : small bridge
poncer [pɔ̃se] {6} *vt* : to sand (down)
poncho [pɔ̃tʃo] *nm* : poncho
poncif [pɔ̃sif] *nm* BANALITÉ : cliché, platitude
ponction [pɔ̃ksjɔ̃] *nf* : puncture (in medicine)
ponctualité [pɔ̃ktɥalite] *nf* : punctuality
ponctuation [pɔ̃ktɥasjɔ̃] *nf* : punctuation
ponctuel, -elle [pɔ̃ktɥɛl] *adj* **1** : prompt, punctual **2** : limited, selective
ponctuellement [pɔ̃ktɥɛlmɑ̃] *adv* : punctually
ponctuer [pɔ̃ktɥe] *vt* : to punctuate
pondération [pɔ̃derasjɔ̃] *nf* **1** : balancing **2** MESURE : levelheadedness
pondéré, -rée [pɔ̃dere] *adj* : levelheaded, sensible
pondérer [pɔ̃dere] {87} *vt* : to balance
pondeuse [pɔ̃døz] *nf* : laying hen, layer
pondre [pɔ̃dr] {63} *vt* **1** : to lay (eggs) **2** *fam* : to crank out, to produce
poney [ponɛ] *nm* : pony
pont [pɔ̃] *nm* **1** : bridge <pont suspendu : suspension bridge> **2** : deck (of a ship) **3** : axle (of an automobile) **4 pont aérien** : airlift
ponte [pɔ̃t] *nf* : laying (of eggs)
pontife [pɔ̃tif] *nm* : pontiff
pontifical, -cale [pɔ̃tifikal] *adj* : pontifical

pontifier [pɔ̃tifje] {96} *vi* : to pontificate
pont–levis [pɔ̃ləvi] *nm, pl* **ponts–levis** : drawbridge
ponton [pɔ̃tɔ̃] *nm* : pontoon
pop [pɔp] *adj s & pl* **pop** : pop <musique pop : pop music>
pop–corn [pɔpkɔrn] *nms & pl* : popcorn
popeline [pɔplin] *nf* : poplin
popote [pɔpɔt] *nf* **1** : mess (in the military) **2 faire la popote** *fam* : to do the cooking
populace [pɔpylas] *nf* : rabble
populaire [pɔpylɛr] *adj* **1** : popular **2** : working-class **3** : colloquial, vernacular
populariser [pɔpylarize] *vt* : to popularize
popularité [pɔpylarite] *nf* : popularity
population [pɔpylasjɔ̃] *nf* : population
populeux, -leuse [pɔpylø, -løz] *adj* : densely populated
populiste [pɔpylist] *adj & nmf* : populist — **populisme** [-pylism] *nm*
poque [pɔk] *nf Can fam* : bump, bruise
poquer [pɔke] *vt Can fam* : to dent (a car)
porc [pɔr] *nm* **1** : pig, hog **2** : pork **3** : pigskin
porcelaine [pɔrsəlɛn] *nf* **1** : porcelain **2** : china, chinaware
porcelet [pɔrsəlɛ] *nm* : piglet
porc–épic [pɔrkepik] *nm, pl* **porcs–épics** : porcupine
porche [pɔrʃ] *nm* : porch
porcherie [pɔrʃəri] *nf* : pigpen, pigsty
porcin, -cine [pɔrsɛ̃, -sin] *adj* **1** : pig, porcine **2** : piglike, piggy
pore [pɔr] *nm* : pore
poreux, -reuse [pɔrø, -røz] *adj* : porous
pornographie [pɔrnɔgrafi] *nf* : pornography — **pornographique** [-grafik] *adj*
porridge [pɔridʒ] *nm* : porridge
port [pɔr] *nm* **1** : port, harbor **2** : port city **3** HAVRE : haven, refuge **4** : wearing, carrying (a weapon, etc.) **5** MAINTIEN : carriage, bearing **6** : postage <port payé : postpaid>
portable [pɔrtabl] *adj* **1** METTABLE : wearable **2** PORTATIF : portable, laptop
portage [pɔrtaʒ] *nm* **1** : carrying, porterage **2** : portage
portail [pɔrtaj] *nm* : portal, gate
portant, -tante [pɔrtɑ̃, -tɑ̃t] *adj* **1 bien portant** : in good health **2 mal portant** : in poor health, ailing
portatif, -tive [pɔrtatif, -tiv] *adj* **1** : portable **2 ordinateur portatif** : laptop computer
porte [pɔrt] *nf* **1** : door, doorway <porte d'entrée : front door> <porte de sortie : exit, way out> <de porte à porte : door-to-door> **2** : gate <porte d'embarquement : departure gate> **3** : gateway, opening <ouvrir la porte à : to pave the way for>
porte–à–faux [pɔrtafo] *nms & pl* **1** : overhang, cantilever **2 être en porte à faux** : to be in an awkward position
porte–avions [pɔrtavjɔ̃] *nms & pl* : aircraft carrier
porte–bagages [pɔrtbagaʒ] *nms & pl* : luggage rack, roof rack
porte–bébé [pɔrtbebe] *nm, pl* **porte–bébés** : baby carrier
porte–bonheur [pɔrtbɔnœr] *nms & pl* : lucky charm
porte–clés *or* **porte–clefs** [pɔrtəkle] *nms & pl* : key ring
porte–documents [pɔrtdɔkymɑ̃] *nms & pl* ATTACHÉ-CASE : attaché case, briefcase
porte–drapeau [pɔrtdrapo] *nm, pl* **porte–drapeaux** : standard-bearer
portée [pɔrte] *nf* **1** : range <à longue portée : long-range> <portée de voix : earshot> <d'une grande portée : far-reaching> <à la portée de la main : within arm's reach, handy> **2** : impact, significance **3** : litter (of kittens) **4** : staff (in music)
portefeuille [pɔrtəfœj] *nm* **1** : wallet, billfold **2** : portfolio (in politics or finance)
porte–jarretelles [pɔrtʒartɛl] *nms & pl* : garter belt
portemanteau [pɔrtmɑ̃to] *nm, pl* **-teaux** [-to] : coat rack
porte–monnaie [pɔrtmɔnɛ] *nms & pl* : change purse
porte–parole [pɔrtparɔl] *nms & pl* : spokesperson, spokesman *m*, spokeswoman *f*
porte–poussière [pɔrt(ə)pusjɛr] *nms & pl Can* : dustpan
porter [pɔrte] *vt* **1** TRANSPORTER : to carry, to bear **2** : to wear **3** APPORTER : to bring **4** : to hold, to keep, to use <elle porte son nom de fille : she uses her maiden name> **5 être porté à** : to be inclined to — *vi* **1** : to carry <une voix qui porte : a voice that carries> **2 ~ sur** : to be about — **se porter** *vr* **1** : to be worn **2** : to be (in a certain state) <il se porte bien : he is doing well> **3 ~ à** : to carry out, to indulge in **4 se porter garant de** : to vouch for **5 ~ sur** : to turn to, to spread to
porte–savon [pɔrtsavɔ̃] *nms & pl* : soap dish
porte–serviettes [pɔrtsɛrvjɛt] *nms & pl* : towel rack
porteur[1], **-teuse** [pɔrtœr, -tøz] *adj* **1** : load-bearing, carrier (in technology) **2** : flourishing, booming (in commerce) **3 ~ de** : bringing, expressing <être porteur de : to be the bearer of> <être porteur de sens : to have meaning>
porteur[2], **-teuse** *n* **1** : porter **2** : holder, bearer **3** : carrier (of disease)

porte–voix [pɔrtəvwa] *nms & pl* : megaphone
portier, -tière [pɔrtje, -tjɛr] *n* : doorman *m*, attendant (at an entrance)
portière *nf* : door (of an automobile)
portillon [pɔrtijɔ̃] *nm* : gate
portion [pɔrsjɔ̃] *nf* **1** : portion, share **2** : helping (of food) **3** : part, section (of a road, etc.)
portique [pɔrtik] *nm* **1** : portico **2** *Can fam* : hall, lobby
porto [pɔrto] *nm* : port wine
portoricain, -caine [pɔrtɔrikɛ̃, -kɛn] *adj* : Puerto Rican
Portoricain, -caine *n* : Puerto Rican
portrait [pɔrtre] *nm* **1** : portrait **2** : picture, description **3** : image, likeness <il est le portrait de son père : he looks just like his father>
portraitiste [pɔrtretist] *nmf* : portrait painter
portuaire [pɔrtɥɛr] *adj* : harbor, port
portugais[1], **-gaise** [pɔrtygɛ, -gɛz] *adj* : Portuguese
portugais[2] *nm* : Portuguese (language)
Portugais, -gaise *n* : Portuguese
pose [poz] *nf* **1** : installing, putting in, laying **2** : pose, posture <prendre la pose : to pose> **3** : pose, affectation **4** : exposure <film de 24 poses : 24-exposure film>
posé, -sée [poze] *adj* **1** : composed, calm **2** : steady, even
posément [pozemɑ̃] *adv* : calmly, coolly, thoughtfully
poser [poze] *vt* **1** : to put (down), to place **2** INSTALLER : to put up, to install **3** : to state, to assert **4** : to ask (a question) **5 poser sa candidature** : to apply for a job — *vi* **1** : to pose, to sit **2** : to put on airs — **se poser** *vr* **1** : to be installed <cette fenêtre se pose facilement : this window is easy to install> **2** : to land, to touch down, to alight **3** : to arise, to come up <la question ne se pose pas : it goes without saying> **4 ~ en** : to pose as, to claim to be
positif, -tive [pozitif, -tiv] *adj* : positive
position [pozisjɔ̃] *nf* **1** : position, place **2** : position, stance <prendre position : to take a stand> **3** SITUATION : position, situation <une position délicate : a difficult situation>
positionner [pozisjɔne] *vt* : to position, to place
positivement [pozitivmɑ̃] *adv* : positively
posologie [pozɔlɔʒi] *nf* : dosage
possédé, -dée [posede] *adj* : possessed
posséder [posede] {87} *vt* **1** AVOIR : to possess, to have **2** MAÎTRISER : to know thoroughly, to have mastered — **se posséder** *vr* : to control oneself
possesseur [posesœr] *nm* : owner, possessor
possessif, -sive [posesif, -siv] *adj* : possessive
possession [posesjɔ̃] *nf* : possession, ownership
possibilité [posibilite] *nf* **1** ÉVENTUALITÉ : possibility **2** OCCASION : opportunity, option **3 possibilités** *nfpl* : means, resources
possible[1] [posibl] *adj* **1** : possible, feasible <dès que possible : as soon as possible> **2** PROBABLE : possible, probable <il est possible qu'il pleuve : it's likely to rain>
possible[2] *nm* **1 dans la mesure du possible** : as far as possible **2 faire son possible** : to do one's utmost
possiblement [posibləmɑ̃] *adv Can* : possibly, perhaps
postal, -tale [postal] *adj, mpl* **postaux** [posto] : postal, mail
postdater [postdate] *vt* : to postdate
poste[1] [post] *nm* **1** : job, position **2** : post, station <poste d'essence : gas station, service station> <poste de travail : workstation> <poste de pilotage : cockpit> **3** : set <poste de télévision : television set> **4** : extension (of a phone system) **5 poste de pompiers** *Can* : fire station
poste[2] *nf* **1** : mail service <mettre à la poste : to put in the mail> **2** : post office
poster[1] [poste] *vt* **1** : to post, to station **2** : to mail
poster[2] [postɛr] *nm* : poster
postérieur[1], **-rieure** [posterjœr] *adj* **1** : later **2** : posterior, rear, back
postérieur[2] *nm fam* : bottom, buttocks *pl*
postérieurement [posterjœrmɑ̃] *adv* : subsequently, later
postérité [posterite] *nf* **1** : posterity **2** LIGNÉE : descendants *pl*
posthume [postym] *adj* : posthumous
postiche[1] [postiʃ] *adj* : false, fake
postiche[2] *nm* : hairpiece, toupee
postier, -tière [postje, -tjɛr] *n* : postal worker
postnatal, -tale [postnatal] *adj, mpl* **-tals** *or* **-taux** [-to] : postnatal
postopératoire [postɔperatwar] *adj* : postoperative
postscolaire [postskɔlɛr] *adj* **l'enseignement postscolaire** : continuing education
post–scriptum [postskriptɔm] *nms & pl* : postscript
postulant, -lante [postylɑ̃, -lɑ̃t] *n* **1** CANDIDAT : candidate, contestant **2** : postulant (in religion)
postulat [postyla] *nm* : postulate
postuler [postyle] *vt* **1** : to apply for **2** : to postulate
posture [postyr] *nf* **1** POSITION : posture, position **2** SITUATION : situation
pot [po] *nm* **1** : pot, jar, container <pot de fleurs : flowerpot> **2** : potful **3** *fam* : drink, glass **4 pot d'échappement** : muffler (of an automobile)

potable [pɔtabl] *adj* **1** BUVABLE : drinkable <eau potable : drinking water> **2** *fam* : fair, passable
potage [pɔtaʒ] *nm* : soup
potager[1], **-gère** [pɔtaʒe, -ʒɛr] *adj* : edible <plantes potagères : edible plants>
potager[2] *nm or* **jardin potager** : vegetable garden
potasse [pɔtas] *nf* : potash
potassium [pɔtasjɔm] *nm* : potassium
pot–au–feu [pɔtofø] *nms & pl* : beef stew
pot–de–vin [podvɛ̃] *nm, pl* **pots–de–vin** : bribe
pote [pɔt] *nm fam* : pal, buddy
poteau [pɔto] *nm, pl* **poteaux 1** : post, stake, pole <poteau de téléphone : telephone pole> **2** : goalpost **3 poteau indicateur** : signpost, guidepost
potelé, -lée [pɔtle] *adj* GRASSOUILLET : chubby, plump
potence [pɔtɑ̃s] *nf* : gallows
potentat [pɔtɑ̃ta] *nm* : potentate, ruler
potentiel[1], **-tielle** [pɔtɑ̃sjɛl] *adj* : potential — **potentiellement** [-sjɛlmɑ̃] *adv*
potentiel[2] *nm* : potential
poterie [pɔtri] *nf* : pottery
potiche [pɔtiʃ] *nf* **1** : large vase **2** : figurehead, puppet
potier, -tière [pɔtje, -tjɛr] *n* : potter
potin [pɔtɛ̃] *nm fam* **1** *France* : noise, racket **2 potins** *nmpl* : gossip
potion [pɔsjɔ̃] *nf* : potion
potiron [pɔtirɔ̃] *nm* : variety of large pumpkin
pot–pourri [popuri] *nm, pl* **pots–pourris** : potpourri
pou [pu] *nm, pl* **poux** : louse
poubelle [pubɛl] *nf* : garbage can, trash barrel
pouce [pus] *nm* **1** : thumb <se tourner les pouces : to twiddle one's thumbs> **2** : big toe **3** : inch **4 faire du pouce** *Can* : to hitchhike
pouding → **pudding**
poudre [pudr] *nf* **1** : powder <lait en poudre : powdered milk> **2** *or* **poudre à canon** : gunpowder **3** : face powder **4 poudre à pâte** *Can* : baking powder
poudrer [pudre] *vt* : to powder — *v impers Can* : to drift (of snow) — **se poudrer** *vr*
poudrerie [pudrəri] *nf Can* : (snow) flurries *pl*
poudreux, -dreuse [pudrø, -drøz] *adj* : powdery
poudrier [pudrije] *nm* : (face powder) compact
pouf [puf] *nm* : hassock
pouffer [pufe] *vi* **pouffer de rire** : to burst out laughing
pouilleux, -leuse [pujø, -jøz] *adj* **1** : lousy, flea-ridden **2** : seedy, shabby
pouillot [pujo] *nm* : warbler
poulailler [pulaje] *nm* : henhouse, chicken coop
poulain [pulɛ̃] *nm* **1** : colt, foal **2** PROTÉGÉ : protégé
poule [pul] *nf* **1** : hen **2** : (stewing) chicken **3 poule mouillée** *fam* : chicken, wimp
poulet [pulɛ] *nm* : chicken
poulette [pulɛt] *nf* : pullet, young hen
pouliche [puliʃ] *nf* : filly
poulie [puli] *nf* : pulley
pouliner [puline] *vi* : to foal
poulpe [pulp] *nm* PIEUVRE : octopus
pouls [pu] *nms & pl* : pulse
poumon [pumɔ̃] *nm* : lung
poupe [pup] *nf* : stern <en poupe : astern>
poupée [pupe] *nf* **1** : doll **2** : finger bandage
poupin, -pine [pupɛ̃, -pin] *adj* : chubby <visage poupin : baby face>
poupon [pupɔ̃] *nm* **1** : tiny baby **2** : baby doll
pouponner [pupɔne] *vi* : to dote (over a baby), to play mother
pouponnière [pupɔnjɛr] *nf* : nursery (for babies)
pour[1] [pur] *prep* **1** : for <en avance pour son âge : advanced for his age> <partir pour Québec : to leave for Quebec> **2** : to, in order to <on doit travailler dur pour réussir : you have to work hard to succeed> **3 pour cent** : percent **4 pour que** : in order that, so that
pour[2] *nm* **le pour et le contre** : the pros and cons
pourboire [purbwar] *nm* : tip
pourcentage [pursɑ̃taʒ] *nm* : percentage
pourchasser [purʃase] *vt* POURSUIVRE : to pursue, to hunt down
pourlécher [purleʃe] {87} *v* **se pourlécher** *vr* : to lick one's lips
pourparlers [purparle] *nmpl* : talks, negotiations, parley
pourpre[1] [purpr] *adj & nm* : crimson, reddish purple
pourpre[2] *nf* : purple (dye)
pourquoi[1] [purkwa] *adv & conj* : why
pourquoi[2] *nm* **1** : reason, cause **2 le pourquoi et le comment** : the whys and wherefores
pourra [pura], *etc.* → **pouvoir**
pourri, -rie [puri] *adj* **1** : rotten, decayed **2** : coddled, spoiled **3** CORROMPU : corrupt, rotten **4** *fam* DÉGUEULASSE : lousy, abominable (of weather, etc.)
pourrir [purir] *vi* **1** SE DÉCOMPOSER : to rot **2** : to spoil, to go bad **3** SE DÉTÉRIORER : to deteriorate — *vt* **1** : to rot, to decay **2** GÂTER : to spoil, to pamper
pourrissement [purismɑ̃] *nm* : deterioration

pourriture [purityr] *nf* **1** : rot, rottenness **2** : corruption, (moral) decay **3** *fam* : rotten person, swine
poursuite [pursɥit] *nf* **1** : pursuit, chase **2 poursuites** *nfpl* : legal proceedings, lawsuit
poursuivant, -vante [pursɥivɑ̃, -vɑ̃t] *n* **1** : pursuer **2** : plaintiff
poursuivre [pursɥivr] {88} *vt* **1** : to pursue, to chase **2** : to carry on with, to continue **3** : to sue, to prosecute **4** HARCELER : to pester, to hound — *vi* : to continue, to go on
pourtant [purtɑ̃] *adv* : however, yet, nevertheless
pourtour [purtur] *nm* **1** CIRCONFÉRENCE : perimeter, circumference **2** : periphery, surrounding area
pourvoi [purvwa] *nm* : appeal (in law)
pourvoir [purvwar] {68} *vt* **1** : to fill (a position, etc.) **2 ~ de** : to provide with, to equip with **3 ~ de** : to endow with <pourvu d'un remarquable talent : gifted with an extraordinary talent> — *vi* **~ à** : to provide for — **se pourvoir** *vr* **1** : to appeal (in law) **2 ~ de** : to provide oneself with
pourvoyeur, -voyeuse [purvwajœr, -vwajøz] *n* : provider, supplier, purveyor
pourvu [purvy] *conj* **~ que 1** : provided that **2** : let's hope (that) <pourvu qu'il fasse beau! : let's hope the weather is good!>
pousse [pus] *nf* **1** : growth, sprouting **2** : shoot, sprout
poussé, -sée [puse] *adj* : elaborate, extensive, exhaustive <un argument poussé : an elaborate argument> <études poussées : advanced studies>
poussée [puse] *nf* **1** : pressure **2** : push, shove **3** : rise, upsurge **4** ACCÈS : fit, attack (in medicine)
pousse–pousse [puspus] *nms & pl* : rickshaw
pousser [puse] *vt* **1** : to push, to shove **2** INCITER : to encourage, to urge **3** POURSUIVRE : to pursue, to continue **4** : to let out, to emit <il a poussé un cri : he let out a scream> <pousser un soupir : to heave a sigh> — *vi* **1** : to push **2** CROÎTRE : to grow — **se pousser** *vr* **1** : to move along, to get out of the way **2** *fam* : to push ahead, to make one's way
poussette [puset] *nf* : stroller
poussière [pusjer] *nf* : dust
poussiéreux, -reuse [pusjerø, -røz] *adj* : dusty
poussif, -sive [pusif, -siv] *adj* : wheezing, wheezy
poussin [pusɛ̃] *nm* : chick
poussoir [puswar] *nm* : push button
poutine [putin] *nf Can* : French fries served with cheese and gravy
poutre [putr] *nf* : beam, girder
pouvoir[1] [puvwar] {69} *v aux* **1** : to be able to, to have the capacity to <peux-tu m'aider? : can you help me?> <elle pourrait vous surprendre : she might surprise you> **2** : to be permitted to <est-ce que je peux m'en aller maintenant? : can I go now?> — *v impers* : to be possible <il pourrait y avoir un changement à l'horaire : there might be a change of plans> — *vt* **1** : to do something about, to cope with **2 je n'en peux plus!** : I can't take anymore! — **se pouvoir** *vr impers* : to be possible <ça ne se peut pas! : it can't be!>
pouvoir[2] *nm* **1** FACULTÉ : faculty, ability **2** : power, control **3** : authority
pragmatique [pragmatik] *adj* : pragmatic — **pragmatisme** [-matism] *nm*
praire [prɛr] *nf* : clam
prairie [preri] *nf* **1** PRÉ : meadow **2** *or* **prairies** *nfpl* : prairie, grassland, meadowland
praticable [pratikabl] *adj* **1** FAISABLE : practicable, feasible **2** ACCESSIBLE : accessible, passable (of roads, etc.)
praticien, -cienne [pratisjɛ̃, -sjɛn] *n* : practitioner
pratiquant[1], **-quante** [pratikɑ̃, -kɑ̃t] *adj* : practicing
pratiquant[2], **-quante** *n* : churchgoer, follower (of a religion)
pratique[1] [pratik] *adj* **1** : practical, useful **2** COMMODE : convenient, handy
pratique[2] *nf* **1** : practice <mettre en pratique : to put into practice> **2** : practicing, observance
pratiquer [pratike] *vt* **1** : to practice **2** : to play (a sport) **3** : to use, to apply **4** : to carry out, to execute — *vi* : to attend church regularly — **se pratiquer** *vr* : to be done, to be practiced
pré [pre] *nm* : meadow
préalable[1] [prealabl] *adj* **1** : preliminary **2** : previous, prior <sans avis préalable : without prior notice> **3 ~ à** : preceding
préalable[2] *nm* **1** : prerequisite, precondition **2 au préalable** : beforehand, in advance
préalablement [prealabləmɑ̃] *adv* **1** AUPARAVANT : beforehand **2 ~ à** : prior to
préambule [preɑ̃byl] *nm* **1** : preamble, prelude **2 sans ~** : without warning
préau [preo] *nm, pl* **préaux** [preo] : courtyard
préavis [preavi] *nm* : (prior) notice
précaire [preker] *adj* : precarious, fragile, insecure
précarité [prekarite] *nf* : precariousness
précaution [prekosjɔ̃] *nf* **1** : precaution **2** PRUDENCE : caution, care <avec précaution : cautiously> <prends des précautions : be careful>
précautionneux, -neuse [prekosjɔnø, -nøz] *adj* : cautious, careful —

précautionneusement [-sjɔnøzmɑ̃] *adv*
précédemment [presedamɑ̃] *adv* : previously, before
précédent¹, -dente [presedɑ̃, -dɑ̃t] *adj* ANTÉRIEUR : previous, prior
précédent² *nm* : precedent
précéder [presede] {87} *vt* **1** : to precede **2** : to get ahead of
précepte [presɛpt] *nm* : precept
précepteur, -trice [presɛptœr, -tris] *n* : (private) tutor
préchauffer [preʃofe] *vt* : to preheat
prêcher [preʃe] *v* : to preach
prêcheur¹, -cheuse [preʃœr, -ʃøz] *adj* : preachy, moralizing
prêcheur², -cheuse *n* : preacher
précieusement [presjøzmɑ̃] *adv* SOIGNEUSEMENT : carefully
précieux, -cieuse [presjø, -sjøz] *adj* **1** : precious, valuable **2** : valued, invaluable, useful **3** : affected
préciosité [presjozite] *nf* : affectation, preciosity
précipice [presipis] *nm* **1** GOUFFRE : abyss, chasm **2 au bord du précipice** : on the brink of collapse
précipitamment [presipitamɑ̃] *adv* : hurriedly, hastily
précipitation [presipitasjɔ̃] *nf* **1** : hurry, haste **2 précipitations** *nfpl* : precipitation, rain, snow
précipité, -tée [presipite] *adj* **1** : hurried, rapid **2** : hasty, rash
précipiter [presipite] *vt* **1** : to hurl, to throw **2** : to hasten, to speed up — **se précipiter** *vr* **1** : to rush **2** : to act rashly **3** : to throw oneself <je me suis précipitée dans ses bras : I threw myself into his arms>
précis¹, -cise [presi, -siz] *adj* **1** EXACT : precise, exact, accurate **2** : clear, specific **3** : particular, very <à ce moment précis : at that very moment>
précis² *nms & pl* **1** ABRÉGÉ : abstract, summary **2** : handbook
précisément [presizemɑ̃] *adv* EXACTEMENT : precisely, exactly
préciser [presize] *vt* **1** DÉTERMINER : to specify, to state exactly **2** : to clarify — **se préciser** *vr* : to take shape, to become clearer
précision [presizjɔ̃] *nf* **1** EXACTITUDE : precision, accuracy **2** CLARTÉ : clarity
précoce [prekɔs] *adj* **1** : early <dépistage précoce : early detection> **2** : precocious <enfant précoce : precocious child>
précocement [prekɔsmɑ̃] *adv* : precociously
précocité [prekɔsite] *nf* : precocity
préconçu, -çue [prekɔ̃sy] *adj* : preconceived
préconiser [prekɔnize] *vt* PRÔNER : to recommend, to advocate
précurseur¹ [prekyrsœr] *adj* : precursory
précurseur² *nm* : forerunner, precursor
prédateur¹, -trice [predatœr, -tris] *adj* : predatory
prédateur² *nm* : predator
prédécesseur [predesesœr] *nm* : predecessor
prédestiner [predestine] *vt* : to predestine — **prédestination** [-stinasjɔ̃] *nf*
prédéterminer [predeterminе] *vt* : to predetermine
prédicateur, -trice [predikatœr, -tris] *n* : preacher
prédiction [prediksjɔ̃] *nf* : prediction
prédilection [predilɛksjɔ̃] *nf* **1** : predilection, partiality **2 de ~** : favorite <c'est mon lieu de prédilection : it's my favorite place>
prédire [predir] {29} *vt* : to foretell, to predict
prédisposer [predispoze] *vt* : to predispose — **prédisposition** [-pozisjɔ̃] *nf*
prédominance [predɔminɑ̃s] *nf* : predominance, prevalence
prédominer [predɔmine] *vi* : to predominate, to prevail
prééminence [preeminɑ̃s] *nf* : preeminence — **prééminent, -nente** [-minɑ̃, -nɑ̃t] *adj*
préexister [preɛgziste] *vi* : to preexist
préfabriqué, -quée [prefabrike] *adj* : prefabricated
préface [prefas] *nf* : preface — **préfacer** [-fase] *vt*
préfecture [prefɛktyr] *nf* **préfecture de police** *France* : police headquarters
préférable [preferabl] *adj* : preferable — **préférablement** [-rabləmɑ̃] *adv*
préféré¹, -rée [prefere] *adj* : favorite
préféré², -rée *n* : favorite (personal thing)
préférence [preferɑ̃s] *nf* **1** : preference **2 de ~** : preferably
préférentiel, -tielle [preferɑ̃sjɛl] *adj* : preferential
préférer [prefere] {87} *vt* : to prefer
préfet [prefe] *nm* **préfet de police** *France* : police commissioner
préfigurer [prefigyre] *vt* : to prefigure
préfixe [prefiks] *nm* : prefix
préhensile [preɑ̃sil] *adj* : prehensile
préhistorique [preistɔrik] *adj* : prehistoric
préjudice [preʒydis] *nm* : harm, damage <porter préjudice à : to harm, to cause harm to> <au préjudice de : to the detriment of>
préjudiciable [preʒydisjabl] *adj* **~ à** : detrimental to, harmful to
préjugé [preʒyʒe] *nm* : prejudice, bias
préjuger [preʒyʒe] {17} *vt* : to prejudge
prélart [prelar] *nm Can* : linoleum
prélasser [prelase] *v* **se prélasser** *vr* : to lounge (around)
prélat [prela] *nm* : prelate
prélèvement [prelɛvmɑ̃] *nm* **1** : withdrawal, deduction **2** : sample

<prélèvement de sang : blood sample>

prélever [prelave] {52} *vt* **1** : to withdraw, to deduct, to debit **2** : to take (a sample of), to remove (an organ)

préliminaire [preliminɛr] *adj* : preliminary

préliminaires [preliminɛr] *nmpl* : preliminaries

prélude [prelyd] *nm* : prelude

prématuré, -rée [prematyre] *adj* : premature — **prématurément** [-tyremɑ̃] *adv*

préméditation [premeditasjɔ̃] *nf* **1** : premeditation **2 avec préméditation** : with malice aforethought

préméditer [premedite] *vt* : to premeditate

prémenstruel, -struelle [premɑ̃stryɛl] *adj* : premenstrual

premier[1], **-mière** [prəmje, -mjɛr] *adj* **1** : first <à première vue : at first sight> **2** : top, leading **3** : primary, principal **4** : initial, original **5 premier ministre** : prime minister

premier[2], **-mière** *n* : first (person or thing)

premier[3] *nm* **1** (*used in dates*) : first <le premier avril : the first of April> **2 en ~** : first of all, in the first place

première *nf* **1** : first class <billet de première : first-class ticket> **2** : premiere **3** : first gear, low gear

premièrement [prəmjɛrmɑ̃] *adv* : in the first place, firstly

prémisse [premis] *nf* : premise

prémolaire [premɔlɛr] *nf* : premolar, bicuspid

prémonition [premɔnisjɔ̃] *nf* : premonition

prémunir [premynir] *vt* **~ contre** : to protect (someone) against — **se prémunir** *vr* **~ contre** : to protect oneself against

prenait [prənɛ], *etc.* → **prendre**

prendre [prɑ̃dr] {70} *vt* **1** : to take <prendre en main : to take in hand> **2** : to bring (along) <prends ton chapeau : take your hat> **3** : to get, to take out, to pick up **4** : to have (food or drink), to take (medicine) **5** : to take (a break, holiday, etc.) **6** : to take up (space or time) **7** : to take on (an employee, etc.) **8** : to catch (a thief, etc.) <se faire prendre : to get caught> **9** : to get (a warning, etc.), to catch (a cold) **10** : to take (a train, a road, etc.) **11** : to take on (responsibility), to tackle (a problem) **12** : to take down (notes, etc.) **13** : to assume, to take over (control) **14** : to seize, to capture — *vi* **1** : to set, to thicken (of cement, gelatin, etc.) **2** : to take hold, to catch on **3** : to break out (of fire) **4** : to go, to turn, to follow <prendre à droite : to bear right> **5 prendre sur soi** : to take upon oneself, to take responsibility — **se prendre** *vr* **1** : to be taken <ce médicament se prend avant les repas : this medicine is taken before meals> **2** : to get caught **3** : to catch <se prendre les doigts dans la porte : to catch one's fingers in the door> **4 ~ à** : to get caught up in **5 ~ pour** : to consider oneself <il se prend pour un autre : he thinks he's better than anyone else> **6 s'y prendre** : to go about it, to act <il faut s'y prendre à l'avance : it must be done in advance>

preneur, -neuse [prənœr, -nøz] *n* : buyer, taker <je suis preneur : I'll take it>

prenne [prɛn], *etc.* → **prendre**

prénom [prenɔ̃] *nm* : given name, first name

prénommer [prenɔme] *vt* : to name — **se prénommer** *vr* : to be called <elle se prénomme Anne : her first name is Anne>

prénuptial, -tiale [prenypsjal] *adj, mpl* **-tiaux** [-sjo] : prenuptial

préoccupant, -pante [preɔkypɑ̃, -pɑ̃t] *adj* INQUIÉTANT : worrisome

préoccupation [preɔkypasjɔ̃] *nf* INQUIÉTUDE : worry, concern

préoccuper [preɔkype] *vt* **1** INQUIÉTER : to worry, to concern **2** : to preoccupy — **se préoccuper** *vr*

préparateur, -trice [preparatœr, -tris] *n* : (laboratory) assistant

préparatifs [preparatif] *nmpl* : preparations

préparation [preparasjɔ̃] *nf* : preparation

préparatoire [preparatwar] *adj* : preparatory

préparer [prepare] *vt* **1** : to prepare, to make ready <préparer un repas : to prepare a meal> <préparer une prescription : to dispense a prescription> **2** : to prepare for (an exam, etc.) **3** : to prepare, to train — **se préparer** *vr* **1** : to prepare, to get ready **2** : to be in the offing

prépondérance [prepɔ̃derɑ̃s] *nf* : predominance

prépondérant, -rante [prepɔ̃derɑ̃, -rɑ̃t] *adj* : predominant, dominating

préposé, -sée [prepoze] *n* **1** : official, clerk, attendant **2** *France* : mailman

préposer [prepoze] *vt* : to appoint <être préposé à : to be (put) in charge of>

préposition [prepozisjɔ̃] *nf* : preposition — **prépositionnel, -nelle** [prepozisjɔnɛl] *adj*

prérequis [prereki] *nms & pl Can* : prerequisite (in college)

prérogative [prerɔgativ] *nf* : prerogative

près [prɛ] *adv* **1** : close, near <c'est tout près : it's close by> **2** : near, soon <lundi, c'est trop près : Monday's too soon> <les vacances sont tout près maintenant : it's almost time for vacation> **3 à . . . près** : more or less, close enough to, within about <à un centimètre près : within about a centimeter> <à cela près : except for that> **4 à peu près** PRESQUE : almost, just about, approximately **5 de ~** : closely <regarder de près : to take a close look at> **6 ~ de** : near, close to <près de partir : about to leave> <près d'ici : nearby>

présage [prezaʒ] *nm* : omen, sign, augur

présager [prezaʒe] {17} *vt* **1** PRÉVOIR : to foresee, to predict **2** : to portend, to bode

presbyte [prɛsbit] *adj* HYPERMÉTROPE : farsighted

presbytère [prɛsbitɛr] *nm* : rectory

presbytie [prɛsbisi] *nf* HYPERMÉTROPIE : farsightedness

prescience [presjɑ̃s] *nf* : foresight, prescience

préscolaire [preskɔlɛr] *adj* : preschool

prescription [prɛskripsjɔ̃] *nf* **1** : prescription **2** : limitation (in law)

prescrire [prɛskrir] {33} *vt* **1** : to prescribe **2** : to stipulate, to lay down

prescrivait [prɛskrivɛ], **prescrivions** [prɛskrivjɔ̃], *etc.* → **prescrire**

prescrive [prɛskriv], *etc.* → **prescrire**

préséance [preseɑ̃s] *nf* : precedence

présence [prezɑ̃s] *nf* **1** : presence, attendance **2 en ~** : face to face **3 en présence de** : in the presence of, in front of **4 présence d'esprit** : presence of mind

présent[1], **-sente** [prezɑ̃, -zɑ̃t] *adj* **1** : present, in attendance **2** : existing, actual, current <le souvenir toujours présent : the ever-present memory> **3** : present, at hand <la présente lettre : the present letter, this letter>

présent[2] *nm* : present (time) <jusqu'à présent : until now>

présentateur, -trice [prezɑ̃tatœr, -tris] *n* : newscaster, anchor

présentation [prezɑ̃tasjɔ̃] *nf* **1** : presentation **2** ALLURE : appearance, look **3** : introduction <il a fait les présentations : he introduced us>

présente [prezɑ̃t] *nf* **1 par la présente** : hereby **2 des présentes** : hereof

présentement [prezɑ̃tmɑ̃] *adv* ACTUELLEMENT : at the moment, now

présenter [prezɑ̃te] *vt* **1** MONTRER : to present, to show, to display **2** : to introduce **3** : to offer, to give <présenter ses condoléances : to offer one's condolences> <présenter des excuses : to apologize> **4** : to submit (a proposal, etc.) **5** : to anchor (a television news program) — *vi* **présenter bien** : to have a pleasing appearance, to look well — **se présenter** *vr* **1** : to go, to come, to appear **2** : to introduce oneself **3 ~ à** : to run for (an office), to apply for (a job)

présentoir [prezɑ̃twar] *nm* : display shelf

préservatif [prezɛrvatif] *nm* CONDOM : condom

préservation [prezɛrvasjɔ̃] *nf* **1** : protection **2** CONSERVATION : preservation, conservation

préserver [prezɛrve] *vt* **1** : to protect **2** CONSERVER : to preserve, to conserve

présidence [prezidɑ̃s] *nf* **1** : presidency **2** : chairmanship

président, -dente [prezidɑ̃, -dɑ̃t] *n* **1** : president **2** : chair, chairperson **3 président de jury** : foreman (of a jury)

présidentiel, -tielle [prezidɑ̃sjɛl] *adj* : presidential

présidentielles [prezidɑ̃sjɛl] *nfpl France* : presidential election

présider [prezide] *vt* : to preside over, to chair — *vi* **~ à** : to rule over, to govern

présomption [prezɔ̃psjɔ̃] *nf* **1** : presumption, supposition **2** PRÉTENTION : pretentiousness

présomptueux, -tueuse [prezɔ̃ptɥø, -tɥøz] *adj* : presumptuous

presque [prɛsk] *adv* : almost, hardly, scarcely <presque jamais : hardly ever> <presque rien : next to nothing>

presqu'île [prɛskil] *nf* : peninsula

pressant, -sante [prɛsɑ̃, -sɑ̃t] *adj* : urgent, pressing

presse [prɛs] *nf* **1** : press (newspapers, magazines, etc.) <agence de presse : news agency> **2** : printing press **3 il n'y a pas de presse** *Can* : there's no hurry

pressé, -sée [prɛse] *adj* **1** : hurried **2** : urgent **3** : squeezed, pressed

presse-fruits [prɛsfrɥi] *nms & pl* : juicer

pressentiment [prɛsɑ̃timɑ̃] *nm* : premonition, hunch

pressentir [prɛsɑ̃tir] {82} *vt* **1** : to sense, to have a premonition about **2** : to contact, to approach

presse-papiers [prɛspapje] *nms & pl* : paperweight

presser [prɛse] *vt* **1** : to press, to squeeze **2** : to push **3** : to urge **4** : to hurry, to rush <presser le pas : to hurry up> **5 presser de questions** : to ply with questions — *vi* : to be pressing, to be urgent <le temps presse : time is running out> — **se presser** *vr* **1** : to crowd, to throng **2** SE HÂTER : to hurry up **3 ~ contre** *or* **~ sur** : to snuggle up against

pression [prɛsjɔ̃] *nf* **1** : pressure <pression artérielle : blood pressure> <faire pression sur : to put pressure on> **2** BOUTON-PRESSION : snap (fastener)

pressurer [presyre] *vt* : to press, to squeeze

pressuriser [presyrize] *vt* : to pressurize
prestance [prestãs] *nf* : (imposing) presence, bearing
prestataire [prestater] *nm* **1** : recipient **2 prestataire de bien–être social** *Can* : welfare recipient
prestation [prestasjõ] *nf* **1** : benefit, allowance **2** : performance **3 prestations d'assurance–chômage** *Can* : unemployment insurance benefits
preste [prest] *adj* : nimble — **prestement** [prestəmã] *adv*
prestidigitateur, -trice [prestidiʒitatœr, -tris] *n* : magician, conjurer
prestidigitation [prestidiʒitasjõ] *nf* : sleight of hand, conjuring
prestige [prestiʒ] *nm* : prestige
prestigieux, -gieuse [prestiʒjø, -ʒjøz] *adj* : prestigious
presto [presto] *interj* : presto!
présumément [prezymemã] *adv Can* : presumably, supposedly
présumer [prezyme] *vt* : to presume, to suppose — *vi* **~ de** : to overestimate, to overrate
présupposer [presypoze] *vt* : to presuppose — **présupposition** [-pozisjõ] *nf*
prêt¹, prête [prɛ, prɛt] *adj* **1** PRÉPARÉ : ready, prepared <tout est prêt : everything's ready> **2** DISPOSÉ : willing <être tout prêt à : to be ready and willing to>
prêt² *nm* EMPRUNT : loan
prêt–à–porter [prɛtapɔrte] *nm, pl* **prêts–à–porter** : ready-to-wear (clothing)
prétendant¹, -dante [pretãdã, -dãt] *n* : pretender (to a throne)
prétendant² *nm* : suitor
prétendre [pretãdr] {63} *vt* **1** AFFIRMER : to claim, to maintain **2** : to expect <il ne prétend pas être récompensé : he doesn't expect to be rewarded> — *vi* **~ à** : to lay claim to, to aspire to
prétendu, -due [pretãdy] *adj* SOI-DISANT : so-called, alleged
prétendument [pretãdymã] *adv* : allegedly, supposedly
prétentieux, -tieuse [pretãsjø, -sjøz] *adj* : pretentious — **prétentieusement** [-sjøzmã] *adv*
prétention [pretãsjõ] *nf* **1** : pretentiousness **2** AMBITION : claim, pretension, pretense
prêter [prete] *vt* **1** : to lend **2** ATTRIBUER : to attribute, to ascribe <prêter de l'importance à : to attach importance to> **3** ACCORDER : to offer, to give <prêter l'oreille : to listen, to lend an ear> <prêter attention : to pay attention> <prêter une main : to lend a hand> — *vi* **~ à** : to cause, to give rise to — **se prêter** *vr* **1 ~ à** : to lend oneself to **2 ~ à** : to be suitable for
prêteur, -teuse [pretœr, -tøz] *n* **1** : lender, moneylender **2 prêteur sur gages** : pawnbroker
prétexte [pretekst] *nm* : pretext, excuse
prétexter [pretekste] *vt* : to give as a pretext, to plead
prêtre [pretr] *nm* : priest
prêtresse [pretres] *nf* : priestess
prêtrise [pretriz] *nf* : priesthood
preuve [prœv] *nf* **1** : proof, evidence **2 faire preuve de** : to show
prévale [preval], *etc.* → **prévaloir**
prévaloir [prevalwar] {71} *vi* PRÉDOMINER : to prevail — **se prévaloir** *vr* **1 ~ de** : to take advantage of **2 ~ de** : to claim, to boast of
prévaudra [prevodra], *etc.* → **prévaloir**
prévaut [prevo], *etc.* → **prévaloir**
prévenance [prevnãs] *nf* : consideration, thoughtfulness
prévenant, -nante [prevnã, -nãt] *adj* ATTENTIONNÉ : considerate, thoughtful
prévenir [prevnir] {92} *vt* **1** ÉVITER : to prevent, to avoid **2** AVISER, INFORMER : to inform **3** AVERTIR : to warn **4** ANTICIPER : to anticipate **5 ~ contre** : to prejudice (someone) against
préventif, -tive [prevãtif, -tiv] *adj* : preventive
prévention [prevãsjõ] *nf* **1** : prevention <prévention routière : road safety> **2** : prejudice, bias
prévenu, -nue [prevny] *n* : defendant, accused
prévisible [previzibl] *adj* : predictable, foreseeable
prévision [previzjõ] *nf* **1** : prediction, expectation **2 prévisions** *nfpl* : forecast <prévisions météorologiques : weather forecast>
prévoir [prevwar] {99} *vt* **1** : to predict, to anticipate, to forecast **2** : to plan (on), to schedule **3** : to provide for, to allow (for)
prévoyance [prevwajãs] *nf* : foresight
prévoyant, -voyante [prevwajã, -vwajãt] *adj* : provident, farsighted
prier [prije] {96} *vi* : to pray — *vt* **1** : to beg, to implore **2** : to ask, to request <vous êtes prié d'assister : you are requested to attend> **3 je vous en prie** : please, don't mention it, you're welcome
prière [prijer] *nf* **1** : prayer **2** : request, entreaty, plea
primaire [primer] *adj* **1** : primary, elementary **2** : limited, simplistic
primate [primat] *nm* : primate (in zoology)
prime¹ [prim] *adj* **1** : first <de prime abord : at first> <prime enfance : early childhood> **2** : prime (in mathematics) **3** *Can* : temperamental, irascible
prime² *nf* **1** INDEMNITÉ : premium, allowance **2** : bonus, gift
primer [prime] *vt* **1** : to take precedence over, to prevail over **2** : to award a

prize to — *vi* : to dominate, to be of primary importance

primesautier, -tière [primsotje, -tjɛr] *adj* : impulsive

primeur [primœr] *nf* **1 avoir la primeur de** : to be the first with, to be the first to hear **2 primeurs** *nfpl* : early fruit and vegetables

primevère [primvɛr] *nf* : primrose

primitif, -tive [primitif, -tiv] *adj* **1** : primitive **2** INITIAL : original, initial

primo [primo] *adv* : firstly, first (of all)

primordial, -diale [primɔrdjal] *adj, mpl* **-diaux** [-djo] **1** : essential, vital **2** : primordial

prince [prɛ̃s] *nm* : prince

princesse [prɛ̃sɛs] *nf* : princess

princier, -cière [prɛ̃sje, -sjɛr] *adj* : princely

principal[1], **-pale** [prɛ̃sipal] *adj, mpl* **-paux** [-po] : main, principal <plat principal : main course> <un rôle principal : a leading role>

principal[2] *nm* **1** ESSENTIEL : main thing **2** CAPITAL : principal (in finance)

principalement [prɛ̃sipalmɑ̃] *adv* : primarily, mainly

principauté [prɛ̃sipote] *nf* : principality

principe [prɛ̃sip] *nm* **1** : principle, rule <en principe : in principle, as a rule> **2** : assumption <partir du principe que : to work on the assumption that> **3** : concept, guiding principle **4** : origin, prime mover

printanier, -nière [prɛ̃tanje, -njɛr] *adj* : spring, springlike

printemps [prɛ̃tɑ̃] *nms & pl* : spring

priorité [prijɔrite] *nf* **1** : priority <en priorité : first> **2** : right-of-way

pris[1] [pri] *pp* → **prendre**

pris[2], **prise** [pri, priz] *adj* **1** : taken, full, sold (out) **2** : stricken, afflicted <pris de peur : panic-stricken> **3** : occupied, busy

prise [priz] *nf* **1** : taking, capture, catch **2** : hold, grip **3** *Can* : strike (in baseball) **4** *or* **prise de médicament** : dose (of medicine) **5 prise de bec** : squabble, spat **6 prise de courant** : (electrical) outlet **7 prise de sang** : blood specimen **8 prise d'eau** : hydrant **9 prise directe** : high gear

priser [prize] *vt* **1** : to take, to snort (drugs, snuff) **2** : to prize, to value

prisme [prism] *nm* : prism

prison [prizɔ̃] *nf* **1** : prison **2** : imprisonment <faire de la prison : to serve time>

prisonnier[1], **-nière** [prizɔnje, -njɛr] *adj* : captive, imprisoned

prisonnier[2], **-nière** *n* : prisoner

privation [privasjɔ̃] *nf* **1** : deprivation, loss **2** : privation, want <une vie de privations : a life of hardships>

privatisation [privatizasjɔ̃] *nf* : privatization — **privatiser** [-tize] *vt*

privautés [privote] *nfpl* : liberties <se permettre des privautés avec : to take liberties with>

privé[1], **-vée** [prive] *adj* : private

privé[2] *nm* **1** : private life <en privé : in private> **2** : private sector

priver [prive] *vt* : to deprive — **se priver** *vr* **1 ~ de** : to go without, to do without **2 ne pas se priver de** : not to hesitate to

privilège [privilɛʒ] *nm* : privilege

privilégier [privileʒje] {96} *vt* FAVORISER : to privilege, to favor — **privilégié, -giée** [-leʒje] *adj*

prix [pri] *nms & pl* **1** : price, cost <hors de prix : exorbitantly expensive> <à tout prix : at all costs> <à prix coûtant : at cost> **2** : prize

probabilité [prɔbabilite] *nf* : probability, likelihood

probable [prɔbabl] *adj* : probable, likely <peu probable : unlikely>

probablement [prɔbabləmɑ̃] *adv* : probably

probant, -bante [prɔbɑ̃, -bɑ̃t] *adj* : convincing, conclusive

probité [prɔbite] *nf* : probity, integrity

problématique [prɔblematik] *adj* : problematic

problème [prɔblɛm] *nm* : problem

procédé [prɔsede] *nm* **1** : process, procedure **2** COMPORTEMENT : conduct, behavior

procéder [prɔsede] {87} *vi* **1** AVANCER : to proceed **2** : to act, to behave **3 ~ à** : to carry out, to proceed with

procédure [prɔsedyr] *nf* **1** : procedure **2** : (legal) proceedings *pl*

procès [prɔsɛ] *nms & pl* **1** : lawsuit **2** : trial

procession [prɔsesjɔ̃] *nf* : procession

processus [prɔsesys] *nms & pl* : process, system

procès–verbal [prɔseverbal] *nm, pl* **procès–verbaux** [-verbo] **1** : minutes *pl* (of a meeting) **2** : (judicial) record, (police) report **3** *France* : (parking) ticket

prochain[1], **-chaine** [prɔʃɛ̃, -ʃɛn] *adj* **1** SUIVANT : next, following **2** : imminent, forthcoming **3 à la prochaine!** *fam* : see you!, until next time!

prochain[2] *nm* : fellowman

prochainement [prɔʃɛnmɑ̃] *adv* BIENTÔT : soon, shortly

proche [prɔʃ] *adj* **1** : near, nearby <proche de : close to, neighboring on> **2** : near, imminent <l'avenir proche : the near future> **3** : closely related <le plus proche parent : the next of kin> **4 de proche en proche** : step by step, gradually

proches [prɔʃ] *nmpl* : close relatives

proclamation [prɔklamasjɔ̃] *nf* : proclamation

proclamer [prɔklame] *vt* **1** : to proclaim **2** : to announce, to declare

procréer [prɔkree] {89} *vt* : to procreate — **procréation** [-kreasjɔ̃] *nf*
procuration [prɔkyrasjɔ̃] *nf* **1** : proxy (in an election) **2** : power of attorney
procurer [prɔkyre] *vt* **1** : to provide, to give <procurer un emploi à qqn : to give s.o. a job> **2** OCCASIONNER : to provide, to cause <le plaisir procuré par la musique : the pleasure provided by music> — **se procurer** *vr* : to get, to obtain
procureur [prɔkyrœr] *nm* **1** *or* **procureur général** : prosecutor **2 procureur de la République** *France* : attorney general **3 procureur de la Couronne** *Can* : Crown attorney (attorney general)
prodigalité [prɔdigalite] *nf* : lavishness, extravagance
prodige [prɔdiʒ] *nm* **1** : prodigy **2** : marvel, wonder
prodigieux, -gieuse [prɔdiʒjø, -ʒjøz] *adj* EXTRAORDINAIRE : prodigious, extraordinary — **prodigieusement** [-ʒjøzmɑ̃] *adv*
prodigue [prɔdig] *adj* **1** DÉPENSIER : prodigal, extravagant **2** GÉNÉREUX : generous, lavish
prodiguer [prɔdige] *vt* : to lavish
producteur[1], **-trice** [prɔdyktœr, -tris] *adj* : producing
producteur[2] *nm* : producer
productif, -tive [prɔdyktif, -tiv] *adj* **1** : productive **2** RENTABLE : profitable
production [prɔdyksjɔ̃] *nf* **1** : production, output **2** : produce, products *pl*
productivité [prɔdyktivite] *nf* : productivity
produire [prɔduir] {49} *vt* **1** : to produce, to generate, to yield **2** : to cause, to bring about — **se produire** *vr* **1** : to occur, to happen **2** : to perform, to appear (on stage)
produisait [prɔduize], **produisions** [prɔduizjɔ̃], *etc.* → **produire**
produise [prɔduiz], *etc.* → **produire**
produit [prɔdui] *nm* **1** : product **2** : proceeds *pl*, yield
proéminence [prɔeminɑ̃s] *nf* : prominence, protuberance — **proéminent, -nente** [prɔeminɑ̃, -nɑ̃t] *adj*
profanation [prɔfanasjɔ̃] *nf* : desecration, defilement
profane[1] [prɔfan] *adj* **1** : secular **2** : ignorant, uninitiated
profane[2] *nmf* **1** : layperson **2** : beginner, tyro
profaner [prɔfane] *vt* : to defile, to desecrate
proférer [prɔfere] {87} *vt* : to utter <proférer des menaces : to make threats>
professer [prɔfese] *vt* : to profess, to declare
professeur [prɔfesœr] *nm* **1** : teacher, schoolteacher **2** : professor
profession [prɔfesjɔ̃] *nf* **1** OCCUPATION : occupation, trade **2** : profession, declaration
professionnel, -nelle [prɔfesjɔnɛl] *adj & n* : professional — **professionnellement** [-nɛlmɑ̃] *adv*
professoral, -rale [prɔfesɔral] *adj, mpl* **-raux** [-ro] : professorial
professorat [prɔfesɔra] *nm* : teaching
profil [prɔfil] *nm* **1** : profile **2 de ~** : in profile, from the side
profiler [prɔfile] *vt* : to profile, to outline — **se profiler** *vr* **1** : to emerge, to take shape **2** : to stand out
profit [prɔfi] *nm* **1** : profit **2** : benefit, advantage <tirer profit de : to benefit from, to take advantage of>
profitable [prɔfitabl] *adj* : profitable — **profitablement** [-tablemɑ̃] *adv*
profiter [prɔfite] *vi* **1 ~ à** : to be of benefit to **2 ~ de** : to take advantage of
profiteur, -teuse [prɔfitœr, -tøz] *n* : profiteer
profond[1] [prɔfɔ̃] *adv* : deeply
profond[2], **-fonde** [prɔfɔ̃, -fɔ̃d] *adj* **1** : deep <profond de deux mètres : two meters deep> <une voix profonde : a deep voice> <au plus profond de : in the depths of> **2** : deep-seated, underlying **3** : profound, penetrating
profondément [prɔfɔ̃demɑ̃] *adv* : deeply, profoundly
profondeur [prɔfɔ̃dœr] *nf* : depth, profundity
profusion [prɔfyzjɔ̃] *nf* : profusion <à profusion : in abundance>
profusément [prɔfyzemɑ̃] *adv* : profusely
progéniture [prɔʒenityr] *nf* : offspring, progeny
programmable [prɔgramabl] *adj* : programmable
programmation [prɔgramasjɔ̃] *nf* : programming
programme [prɔgram] *nm* **1** : program **2** : plan, schedule **3** : curriculum, syllabus
programmer [prɔgrame] *vt* **1** : to program (a computer) **2** : to plan, to schedule
programmeur, -meuse [prɔgramœr, -møz] *n* : (computer) programmer
progrès [prɔgrɛ] *nm* : progress <faire des progrès : to make progress>
progresser [prɔgrese] *vi* **1** : to progress, to advance **2** : to make progress, to improve
progressif, -sive [prɔgresif, -siv] *adj* : progressive — **progressivement** [-sivmɑ̃] *adv*
progression [prɔgresjɔ̃] *nf* **1** : progress, advance **2** : progression, spread, increase
prohiber [prɔibe] *vt* : to prohibit, to ban
prohibitif, -tive [prɔibitif, -tiv] *adj* : prohibitive
prohibition [prɔibisjɔ] *nf* : prohibition

proie [prwa] *nf* **1** : prey **2 en proie à** : prey to, beset with, suffering from
projecteur [prɔʒɛktœr] *nm* **1** : projector **2** : spotlight, floodlight
projectile [prɔʒɛktil] *nm* : missile, projectile
projection [prɔʒɛksjɔ̃] *nf* **1** : projection, showing <salle de projection : screening room> **2** : throwing (off), discharge, spattering **3** : projection (in mathematics or psychology)
projet [prɔʒɛ] *nm* **1** : plan, project **2** ÉBAUCHE : draft, outline
projeter [prɔʃte] {8} *vt* **1** LANCER : to throw **2** : to project, to show (a film, etc.) **3** : to cast, to project (light) **4** : to plan
prolétaire [prɔletɛr] *adj & nmf* : proletarian
prolétariat [prɔletarjat] *nm* : proletariat
prolétarien, -rienne [prɔletarjɛ̃, -rjɛn] *adj* : proletarian
proliférer [prɔlifere] {87} *vi* SE MULTIPLIER : to proliferate — **prolifération** [-ferasjɔ̃] *nf*
prolifique [prɔlifik] *adj* : prolific
prolixe [prɔliks] *adj* : verbose, wordy
prologue [prɔlɔg] *nm* : prologue
prolongation [prɔlɔ̃gasjɔ̃] *nf* **1** ALLONGEMENT : extension, prolongation **2** *or* **prolongations** *nfpl* : overtime (in sports)
prolongement [prɔlɔ̃ʒmɑ̃] *nm* **1** : extension (of a road, railway, etc.) **2** : outcome, consequence
prolonger [prɔlɔ̃ʒe] {17} *vt* : to prolong, to extend — **se prolonger** *vr* : to continue, to persist, to go on
promenade [prɔmnad] *nf* **1** : walk, stroll **2** : ride, trip **3** : walkway, promenade
promener [prɔmne] {52} *vt* **1** : to take (out) for a walk <promener son chien : to walk one's dog> **2** : to run over, to move across <promener son regard sur une foule : to cast one's eyes over a crowd> — **se promener** *vr* **1** SE BALADER : to go for a walk **2 ~ sur** : to wander over, to roam across (with one's eyes, fingers, etc.)
promeneur, -neuse [prɔmnœr, -nøz] *n* : walker, stroller
promesse [prɔmɛs] *nf* **1** : promise <manquer à sa promesse : to break one's word> **2** : (legal) commitment <promesse d'achat : commitment to buy> **3 être plein de promesses** : to be full of promise
prometteur, -teuse [prɔmetœr, -tøz] *adj* : promising
promettre [prɔmɛtr] {53} *vt* : to promise — *vi* : to promise, to show promise — **se promettre** *vr* **~ de** : to resolve to
promis, -mise [prɔmi, -miz] *adj* **1** : promised **2 ~ à** : destined for
promiscuité [prɔmiskɥite] *nf* : overcrowding, lack of privacy
promontoire [prɔmɔ̃twar] *nm* : promontory, headland
promoteur, -trice [prɔmɔtœr, -tris] *n* : promoter
promotion [prɔmɔsjɔ̃] *nf* **1** : promotion, advancement **2** : promotion, (special) offer (in advertising)
promotionnel, -nelle [prɔmɔsjɔnɛl] *adj* : promotional
promouvoir [prɔmuvwar] {56} *vt* : to promote
prompt, prompte [prɔ̃, prɔ̃t] *adj* : prompt, swift, rapid <être prompt à réagir : to be quick to react>
promptement [prɔ̃tmɑ̃] *adv* : promptly, swiftly
promptitude [prɔ̃tityd] *nf* : swiftness, rapidity
promulgation [prɔmylgasjɔ̃] *nf* : promulgation, enactment
promulguer [prɔmylge] *vt* : to promulgate
prôner [prone] *vt* : to extol, to advocate, to commend
pronom [prɔnɔ̃] *nm* : pronoun
pronominal, -nale [prɔnɔminal] *adj, mpl* **-naux** [-no] **1** : pronominal **2** : reflexive <verbe pronominal : reflexive verb>
prononcé, -cée [prɔnɔ̃se] *adj* : pronounced, marked
prononcer [prɔnɔ̃se] {6} *vt* **1** : to pronounce **2** : to state, to declare — *vi* : to hand down a decision (in law) — **se prononcer** *vr* **1** : to be pronounced **2** : to give one's opinion, to declare oneself
prononciation [prɔnɔ̃sjasjɔ̃] *nf* : pronunciation
pronostic [prɔnɔstik] *nm* **1** : prognosis **2** PRÉDICTION : forecast, prediction
pronostiquer [prɔnɔstike] *vt* : to forecast
propagande [prɔpagɑ̃d] *nf* : propaganda
propagation [prɔpagasjɔ̃] *nf* **1** : propagation **2** : spreading
propager [prɔpaʒe] {17} *vt* **1** : to propagate **2** : to spread — **se propager** *vr*
propane [prɔpan] *nm* : propane
propension [prɔpɑ̃sjɔ̃] *nf* TENDANCE : propensity
propergol [prɔpɛrgɔl] *nm* : (rocket) propellant
prophète, prophétesse [prɔfɛt, prɔfetɛs] *n* : prophet, prophetess *f*
prophétie [prɔfesi] *nf* : prophecy
prophétique [prɔfetik] *adj* : prophetic — **prophétiquement** [-tikmɑ̃] *adv*
prophétiser [prɔfetize] *vt* : to prophesy
propice [prɔpis] *adj* : favorable, propitious
proportion [prɔpɔrsjɔ̃] *nf* **1** : proportion, ratio, relation <hors de proportion : out of proportion> <une proportion de dix contre un : a ratio of ten to one> <à proportion de : proportional to> <en proportion

: proportionately> **2 proportions** *nfpl* : dimensions, size

proportionné, -née |prɔpɔrsjɔne| *adj* **1** : proportioned <bien proportionné : well-proportioned> **2 ~ à** : proportionate to

proportionnel, -nelle |prɔpɔrsjɔnɛl| *adj* : proportional — **proportionnellement** |-nɛlmɑ̃| *adv*

proportionner |prɔpɔrsjɔne| *vt* : to proportion

propos |prɔpo| *nms & pl* **1** : subject **2** : intention, point **3 propos** *nmpl* : comments, talk **4 à ~** : appropriate, apropos **5 à propos de** : regarding, about

proposer |prɔpoze| *vt* **1** : to suggest, to propose **2** : to offer **3** : to nominate — **se proposer** *vr* **~ de** : to intend to

proposition |prɔpozisjɔ̃| *nf* **1** : suggestion **2** : proposal, offer **3** : proposition (in logic) **4** : clause <proposition subordonnée : subordinate clause>

propre[1] |prɔpr| *adj* **1** NET : clean, neat **2** : toilet trained, housebroken **3** : own <par sa propre faute : through his own fault> **4** : correct, proper <le mot propre : the correct word> **5 ~ à** : likely to <propre à lui faire plaisir : likely to please her> **6 ~ à** : characteristic of **7 ~ à** : suitable for

propre[2] *nm* **1** : cleanliness, neatness <cette maison sent le propre : this house smells clean> **2** : distinctive feature <être le propre de : to be peculiar to> **3 au propre** : literally

proprement |prɔprəmɑ̃| *adv* **1** : cleanly, neatly **2** : properly, correctly **3** : strictly, precisely <à proprement parler : strictly speaking> **4 proprement dit** : actual, as such <le débat proprement dit : the debate itself>

propret, -prette |prɔpre, -prɛt| *adj* : clean and neat

propreté |prɔprəte| *nf* : cleanliness, neatness

propriétaire |prɔprijeter| *nmf* **1** : owner, proprietor **2** : landlord, landlady *f*

propriété |prɔprijete| *nf* **1** : property <propriété privée : private property> **2** : ownership **3** CARACTÉRISTIQUE : property, characteristic **4** : appropriateness, suitability

propulser |prɔpylse| *vt* **1** : to propel **2** : to hurl, to fling

propulsif, -sive |prɔpylsif, -siv| *adj* : propellant, propulsive

propulsion |prɔpylsjɔ̃| *nf* : propulsion

prorata |prɔrata| *nms & pl* **au prorata de** : in proportion to

prorogation |prɔrɔgasjɔ̃| *nf* **1** : extension, deferment **2** : adjournment

proroger |prɔrɔʒe| {17} *vt* **1** : to extend, to defer **2** : to adjourn

prosaïque |prɔzaik| *adj* : prosaic, mundane

proscription |prɔskripsjɔ̃| *nf* **1** : ban, prohibition **2** : banishment

proscrire |prɔskrir| {33} *vt* **1** INTERDIRE : to ban, to prohibit **2** BANNIR : to banish

proscrit, -scrite |prɔskri, -skrit| *n* : outcast

prose |prɔz| *nf* : prose

prospecter |prɔspɛkte| *vt* **1** : to prospect (for oil, etc.) **2** : to canvass

prospecteur, -trice |prɔspɛktœr, -tris| *n* **1** : prospector **2** : canvasser

prospectus |prɔspɛktys| *nms & pl* : prospectus, leaflet

prospère |prɔsper| *adj* **1** : prosperous **2** : thriving, flourishing

prospérer |prɔspere| {87} *vi* : to flourish, to thrive

prospérité |prɔsperite| *nf* : prosperity

prostate |prɔstat| *nf* : prostate (gland)

prosterner |prɔsterne| *v* **se prosterner** *vr* : to bow down, to prostrate oneself

prostituée |prɔstitɥe| *nf* : prostitute

prostituer |prɔstitɥe| *vi* : to prostitute — **se prostituer** *vr* : to prostitute oneself

prostitution |prɔstitysjɔ̃| *nf* : prostitution

prostration |prɔstrasjɔ̃| *nf* : prostration

prostré, -trée |prɔstre| *adj* : prostrate

protagoniste |prɔtagɔnist| *nmf* : protagonist

protecteur[1], **-trice** |prɔtɛktœr, -tris| *adj* : protective

protecteur[2], **-trice** *n* **1** : protector, guardian **2** : patron **3 protecteur du citoyen** *Can* : ombudsman

protection |prɔtɛksjɔ̃| *nf* **1** : protection **2** : patronage, support

protectorat |prɔtɛktɔra| *nm* : protectorate

protégé, -gée |prɔteʒe| *n* : protégé

protéger |prɔteʒe| {64} *vt* **1** : to protect, to defend **2** PATRONNER : to support, to encourage — **se protéger** *vr* **~ de** : to protect oneself from

protéine |prɔtein| *nf* : protein

protestant, -tante |prɔtestɑ̃, -tɑ̃t| *adj & n* : Protestant — **protestantisme** |-tɑ̃tism| *nm*

protestataire |prɔtestater| *nmf* : protester

protestation |prɔtestasjɔ̃| *nf* **1** : protest **2** : protestation, declaration

protester |prɔteste| *vi* **1** : to protest **2 ~ de** : to declare, to profess

prothèse |prɔtɛz| *nf* **1** : prosthesis **2 prothèse dentaire** : denture

protocolaire |prɔtɔkɔlɛr| *adj* : formal, conforming to protocol

protocole |prɔtɔkɔl| *nm* : protocol

proton |prɔtɔ̃| *nm* : proton

protoplasme |prɔtɔplasm| *nm* : protoplasm

prototype |prɔtɔtip| *nm* : prototype

protozoaire |prɔtɔzɔɛr| *nm* : protozoan

protubérance [prɔtyberɑ̃s] *nf* : protuberance
protubérant, -rante [prɔtyberɑ̃, -rɑ̃t] *adj* : protuberant, bulging, protruding
proue [pru] *nf* : prow, bow (of a ship)
prouesse [pruɛs] *nf* EXPLOIT : feat, exploit
prouver [pruve] *vt* **1** ÉTABLIR : to prove **2** MONTRER : to show, to demonstrate
provenance [prɔvnɑ̃s] *nf* **1** : source, origin **2 en provenance de** : from <train en provenance de Paris : train (arriving) from Paris>
provençal, -çale [prɔvɑ̃sal] *adj, mpl* **-çaux** [-so] : Provençal
Provençal, -çale *n* : Provençal
provenir [prɔvnir] {92} *vi* **1 ~ de** : to come from (a place) **2 ~ de** : to result from, to stem from
proverbe [prɔverb] *nm* : proverb
proverbial, -biale [prɔverbjal] *adj, mpl* **-biaux** [-bjo] : proverbial — **proverbialement** [-bjalmɑ̃] *adv*
providence [prɔvidɑ̃s] *nf* : providence — **providentiel, -tielle** [-dɑ̃sjɛl] *adj*
province [prɔvɛ̃s] *nf* : province — **provincial, -ciale** [-vɛ̃sjal] *adj, mpl* **-ciaux** [-sjo]
proviseur [prɔvizœr] *nm France* : principal (of a school)
provision [prɔvizjɔ̃] *nf* **1** : stock, supply <faire provision de : to stock up on> **2** : advance, retainer **3** : funds *pl* (in a bank) <un chèque sans provision : a bad check> **4 provisions** *nfpl* : provisions, food
provisoire [prɔvizwar] *adj* : provisional, temporary, interim — **provisoirement** [-zwarmɑ̃] *adv*
provocant, -cante [prɔvɔkɑ̃, -kɑ̃t] *adj* : provocative
provocateur[1], **-trice** [prɔvɔkatœr, -tris] *adj* : provocative, challenging
provocateur[2] *nm* : agitator, troublemaker
provocation [prɔvɔkasjɔ̃] *nf* : provocation
provoquer [prɔvɔke] *vt* **1** : to cause, to give rise to <provoquer des rires : to provoke laughter> **2** : to provoke, to stir up, to trigger
proximité [prɔksimite] *nf* : proximity, nearness, closeness
pruche [pryʃ] *nf Can* : hemlock (tree)
prude[1] [pryd] *adj* : prudish
prude[2] *nf* : prude
prudemment [prydamɑ̃] *adv* : carefully, cautiously
prudence [prydɑ̃s] *nf* **1** : care, caution **2 avec ~** : cautiously
prudent, -dente [prydɑ̃, -dɑ̃t] *adj* **1** AVISÉ : prudent, sensible **2** : careful, cautious <soyez prudents : be careful>
prune[1] [pryn] *adj* : plum-colored
prune[2] *nf* **1** : plum **2** *Can* : bruise
pruneau [pryno] *nm, pl* **pruneaux 1** : prune **2** *Can* : plum
prunelle [prynɛl] *nf* : pupil (of the eye)
prunier [prynje] *nm* : plum tree
psalmodie [psalmɔdi] *nf* : chanting, droning
psalmodier [psalmɔdje] {96} *v* **1** : to chant **2** : to drone
psaume [psom] *nm* : psalm
pseudonyme [psødɔnim] *nm* : pseudonym
psoriasis [psɔrjazis] *nm* : psoriasis
psychanalyse [psikanaliz] *nf* : psychoanalysis — **psychanalyste** [-list] *nmf*
psychanalyser [psikanalize] *vt* : to psychoanalyse
psychanalytique [psikanalitik] *adj* : psychoanalytic
psyché [psiʃe] *nf* : psyche
psychédélique [psikedelik] *adj* : psychedelic
psychiatre [psikjatr] *nmf* : psychiatrist
psychiatrie [psikjatri] *nf* : psychiatry
psychiatrique [psikjatrik] *adj* : psychiatric
psychique [psiʃik] *adj* : psychic, mental
psychisme [psiʃism] *nm* : psyche, mind
psychologie [psikɔlɔʒi] *nf* : psychology
psychologique [psikɔlɔʒik] *adj* : psychological — **psychologiquement** [-ʒikmɑ̃] *adv*
psychologue [psikɔlɔg] *nmf* : psychologist
psychopathe[1] [psikɔpat] *adj* : psychopathic
psychopathe[2] *nmf* : psychopath
psychose [psikoz] *nf* : psychosis
psychosomatique [psikɔsɔmatik] *adj* : psychosomatic
psychothérapeute [psikɔterapøt] *nmf* : psychotherapist
psychothérapie [psikɔterapi] *nf* : psychotherapy
psychotique [psikɔtik] *adj & nmf* : psychotic
pseudonyme[1] [psødɔnim] *adj* : pseudonymous
pseudonyme[2] *nm* : pseudonym
pu [py] *pp* → **pouvoir**
puant, puante [pɥɑ̃, -ɑ̃t] *adj* **1** : foul-smelling, stinking **2** *fam* : conceited, obnoxious
puanteur [pɥɑ̃tœr] *nf* : stink, stench
puberté [pyberte] *nf* : puberty
pubien, -bienne [pybjɛ̃, -bjɛn] *adj* : pubic
public[1], **-blique** [pyblik] *adj* : public
public[2] *nm* **1** : public <le grand public : the general public> **2** : audience, spectators *pl*
publication [pyblikasjɔ̃] *nf* : publication
publiciste [pyblisist] *nmf* : publicist, advertising executive
publicitaire [pyblisitɛr] *adj* : advertising, promotional

publicité [pyblisite] *nf* **1** : publicity **2** : advertisement, commercial
publier [pyblije] {96} *vt* : to publish
publiquement [pyblikmɑ̃] *adv* : publicly
puce [pys] *nf* **1** : flea **2** : computer chip
puceron [pysrɔ̃] *nm* : aphid
pudding *or* **pouding** [pudiŋ] *nm* : pudding
pudeur [pydœr] *nf* **1** : modesty, decency **2** : sense of propriety, tact
pudibond, -bonde [pydibɔ̃, -bɔ̃d] *adj* : prudish, prim
pudibonderie [pydibɔ̃dri] *nf* : prudishness
pudique [pydik] *adj* **1** : modest, decent **2** : restrained, discreet
pudiquement [pydikmɑ̃] *adv* **1** : modestly **2** : discreetly
puer [pɥe] *vi* : to smell, to stink — *vt* : to reek of
puéril, -rile [pɥeril] *adj* : childish, puerile
puérilité [pɥerilite] *nf* : childishness
pugilat [pyʒila] *nm* : fistfight
pugnace [pygnas] *adj* : pugnacious
puis [pɥi] *adv* **1** ENSUITE : then, afterwards, next **2 et puis** : and besides **3 et puis après?** *or* **et puis quoi?** *fam* : so?, so what?
puisard [pɥizar] *nm* : cesspool
puiser [pɥize] *vt* **~ dans** : to draw from, to dip into
puisque [pɥiskə] *conj* **1** : since, as, because <puisque vous insistez : since you insist> **2** (*used as an intensifier*) <puisque je te le dis! : because I'm telling you so!>
puissance [pɥisɑ̃s] *nf* : power
puissant, -sante [pɥisɑ̃, -sɑ̃t] *adj* : powerful
puisse [pɥis], *etc.* → **pouvoir**
puits [pɥi] *nms & pl* **1** : well <puits artésien : artesian well> <puits de pétrole : oil well> **2** : shaft <puits de mine : mine shaft> **3 puits de science** : font of knowledge, learned person
pull *or* **pull–over** [pyl, pylɔvɛr] *nm France* : pullover sweater
pullulement [pylylmɑ̃] *nm* : proliferation
pulluler [pylyle] *vi* **1** SE MULTIPLIER : to proliferate **2** GROUILLER : to swarm, to teem
pulmonaire [pylmɔnɛr] *adj* : pulmonary, lung
pulpe [pylp] *nf* : pulp
pulpeux, -peuse [pylpø, -pøz] *adj* : pulpy
pulsation [pylsasjɔ̃] *nf* **1** : beat, pulsation **2** POULS : pulse
pulsion [pylsjɔ̃] *nf* : drive, urge
pulvérisateur [pylverizatœr] *nm* VAPORISATEUR : spray, atomizer
pulvériser [pylverize] *vt* **1** : to pulverize **2** : to spray **3** : to demolish (an argument, etc.)
puma [pyma] *nm* : puma, cougar
punaise [pynɛz] *nf* **1** : bug <punaise de lit : bedbug> **2** : thumbtack
punch [pɔ̃ʃ] *nm* **1** : punch (drink) **2** [pœnʃ] : punch, blow (of a boxer, etc.) **3** : drive, energy
punir [pynir] *vt* **1** : to punish **2** *Can* : to penalize (in sports)
punissable [pynisabl] *adj* : punishable
punitif, -tive [pynitif, -tiv] *adj* : punitive
punition [pynisjɔ̃] *nf* **1** : punishment **2** *Can* : penalty (in sports)
pupe [pyp] *nf* : pupa
pupille[1] [pypij] *nmf* : ward (of the court), orphan
pupille[2] *nf* : pupil (of the eye)
pupitre [pypitr] *nm* **1** BUREAU : desk **2** LUTRIN : lectern **3** : console, keyboard, control panel **4** : music stand
pur, pure [pyr] *adj* : pure — **purement** [pyrmɑ̃] *adv*
purée [pyre] *nf* **1** : puree <purée de pommes de terre : mashed potatoes> **2 purée de pois** : thick fog, pea soup
pureté [pyrte] *nf* : purity
purgatif[1], **-tive** [pyrgatif, -tiv] *adj* : purgative
purgatif[2] *nm* : purgative, laxative
purgatoire [pyrgatwar] *nm* : purgatory
purge [pyrʒ] *nf* : purge, purging
purger [pyrʒe] {17} *vt* **1** : to drain (a radiator, etc.), to bleed (brakes) **2** : to rid of, to purge **3** : to purge, to give a laxative to **4** : to serve (a jail sentence)
purificateur [pyrifikatœr] *nm* : purifier <purificateur d'air : air purifier>
purification [pyrifikasjɔ̃] *nf* : purification
purifier [pyrifje] {96} *vt* : to purify — **se purifier** *vr*
purin [pyrɛ̃] *nm* : liquid manure
puritain[1], **-taine** [pyritɛ̃, -tɛn] *adj* : puritanical
puritain[2], **-taine** *n* : puritan
pur–sang [pyrsɑ̃] *nms & pl* : Thoroughbred
pus [py] *nm* : pus
pusillanime [pyzilanim] *adj* : pusillanimous
pustule [pystyl] *nf* : pustule
putain [pytɛ̃] *nf usu vulgar* : whore
putois [pytwa] *nms & pl* : polecat
putréfier [pytrefje] {96} *vt* : to putrefy — **se putréfier** *vr* : to putrefy, to rot
putride [pytrid] *adj* : putrid, rotten
puzzle [pœzl] *nm* : jigsaw puzzle
Pygmée [pigme] *nmf* : Pygmy
pyjama [piʒama] *nm* : pajamas *pl*
pylône [pilon] *nm* : pylon
pyramide [piramid] *nf* : pyramid
pyromane [pirɔman] *nmf* : pyromaniac
pyromanie [pirɔmani] *nf* : pyromania
pyrotechnie [pirɔtekni] *nf* : fireworks *pl*, pyrotechnics *pl*
python [pitɔ̃] *nm* : python

Q

q [ky] *nm* : q, the 17th letter of the alphabet
quadrant [kwadrɑ̃] *nm* : quadrant
quadrilatère [kwadrilatɛr] *nm* : quadrilateral, quadrangle (in geometry)
quadrillage [kadrijaʒ] *nm* : crisscross pattern, grid
quadrillé, -lée [kadrije] *adj* : squared <papier quadrillé : graph paper>
quadriller [kadrije] *vt* **1** : to mark into squares **2** : to surround, to control (an area)
quadrupède [kwadrypɛd] *nm* : quadruped
quadruple [k(w)adrypl] *adj* : quadruple
quadrupler [k(w)adryple] *v* : to quadruple
quadruplés, -plées [k(w)adryple] *npl* : quadruplets
quai [kɛ] *nm* **1** : quay, wharf **2** : platform (at a railway station)
qualification [kalifikasjɔ̃] *nf* : qualification
qualifié, -fiée [kalifje] *adj* : qualified, skilled
qualifier [kalifje] {96} *vt* **1** : to qualify **2** CARACTÉRISER : to describe, to call **— se qualifier** *vr*
qualité [kalite] *nf* **1** : quality, excellence **2** : quality, property, attribute **3** : capacity, role <en qualité d'observateur : in his role as an observer>
quand[1] [kɑ̃] *adv* : when <quand partez-vous? : when are you leaving?> <je sais quand ils arriveront : I know when they will arrive>
quand[2] *conj* **1** : when <quand je la verrai : when I see her> **2** (*used for emphasis*) <quand je vous le disais! : I told you so!> **3 quand même** : still, even so
quant [kɑ̃] **~ à** : as for, as to, regarding
quant-à-soi [kɑ̃taswa] *nm* : reserve, aloofness <rester sur son quant-à-soi : to keep one's distance>
quantifier [kɑ̃tifje] {96} *vt* : to quantify **— quantifiable** [-tifjabl] *adj*
quantitatif, -tive [kɑ̃titatif, -tiv] *adj* : quantitative **— quantitativement** [-tivmɑ̃] *adv*
quantité [kɑ̃tite] *nf* : quantity, amount, number <une quantité de : a lot of>
quantum [kwɑ̃tɔm] *nm, pl* **quanta** : quantum <théorie des quanta : quantum theory>
quarantaine [karɑ̃tɛn] *nf* **1** : quarantine **2 avoir la quarantaine** : to be in one's forties **3 une quarantaine de** : about forty
quarante [karɑ̃t] *adj & nms & pl* : forty
quarantième [karɑ̃tjɛm] *adj & nmf & nm* : fortieth
quart [kar] *nm* **1** : quarter, forth <un kilo et quart : a kilo and a quarter> **2** (*in expressions of time*) : quarter <deux heures et quart : a quarter after two> <un quart d'heure : fifteen minutes>
quarte-arrière [kartarjɛr] *nm Can* : quarterback (in football)
quartier [kartje] *nm* **1** : piece, segment, quarter <un quartier de pomme : a piece of apple> <quartier de devant : forequarter> **2** : area, district **3 quartier général** : headquarters (in the army, etc.)
quartz [kwarts] *nm* : quartz
quasi [kazi] *adv* : nearly, almost <quasi impossible : practically impossible>
quasiment [kazimɑ̃] *adv* : nearly, almost
quatorze[1] [katɔrz] *adj* **1** : fourteen **2** : fourteenth <le quatorze février : the fourteenth of February>
quatorze[2] *nms & pl* : fourteen
quatorzième [katɔrzjɛm] *adj & nmf & nm* : fourteenth
quatre[1] [katr] *adj* **1** : four **2** : fourth <le quatre avril : the fourth of April>
quatre[2] *nms & pl* **1** : four **2 à quatre pattes** : on all fours
quatre-vingt-dix [katrəvɛ̃dis] *adj & nms & pl* : ninety
quatre-vingt-dixième [katrəvɛ̃dizjɛm] *adj & nmf & nm* : ninetieth
quatre-vingtième [katrəvɛ̃tjɛm] *adj & nmf & nm* : eightieth
quatre-vingts [katrəvɛ̃] **(quatre-vingt** *with another numeral adjective*) *adj & nms & pl* : eighty <quatre-vingt-un : eighty-one> <quatre-vingts personnes : eighty people>
quatrième[1] [katrijɛm] *adj & nmf* **1** : fourth **2 en quatrième vitesse** : in a hurry
quatrième[2] *nmf* : fourth (in a series)
quatuor [kwatyɔr] *nm* : quartet
que[1] [kə] *adv* **1** : how <que c'est beau! : how beautiful!> **2** : why <que n'est-il venu? : why didn't he come?>
que[2] *conj* **1** : that <il a avoué qu'il avait tort : he admitted that he was wrong> **2** : than <travailler plus que nécessaire : to work harder than necessary> **3** (*used in a subjunctive clause expressing an order or desire*) <qu'elle vienne! : tell her to come!> **4** : whether <qu'il fasse soleil ou non : whether it's sunny or not> **5 → ne**
que[3] *pron* **1** : who, whom, that <l'homme que vous aimez : the man that you love> **2** : that, which <c'était la seule chose qu'il pouvait faire : it was the only thing that he could do> **3** : what <que faire? : what should we do?> <qu'est-ce que tu as? : what's wrong?> <qu'est-ce que c'est que ça? : what's that?>
québécois, -coise [kebekwa, -kwaz] *adj* : Quebec, from or of Quebec

Québécois, -coise *n* : Quebecer, person from Quebec
quel¹, quelle [kɛl] *adj* **1** : what, which <quelle heure est-il? : what time is it?> **2** (*used as an intensifier*) <quel dommage! : what a pity!> **3** : whatever, whichever, whoever <quelle que soit la raison : whatever the reason may be>
quel², quelle *pron* : who, which one <de quel s'agit-il? : which one are you talking about?>
quelconque [kɛlkɔ̃k] *adj* **1** : some sort of, any <une quelconque mesure : some sort of action> **2** : ordinary <un être quelconque : an ordinary person>
quelque¹ [kɛlkə̃] *adv* **1** : about, approximately <quelque 200 personnes : about 200 people> **2** : however <quelque important qu'il soit : however important he may be>
quelque² *adj* **1** : a few, several, some <il a dit quelques mots : he said a few words> **2 quelque chose** : something **3 quelque part** : somewhere **4 quelque peu** : somewhat <quelque peu déçu : somewhat disappointed>
quelquefois [kɛlkəfwa] *adv* : sometimes
quelques–uns, quelques–unes [kɛlkəzœ̃, kɛlkəzyn] *pron* : some, a few
quelqu'un [kɛlkœ̃] *pron* **1** : someone, somebody <quelqu'un d'autre : someone else> **2** : anyone, anybody <y a-t-il quelqu'un? : is anyone there?>
quémander [kemɑ̃de] *vt* : to beg for
qu'en–dira–t–on [kɑ̃diratɔ̃] *nms & pl* : gossip
quenouille [kənuj] *nf Can* : cattail (plant)
querelle [kərɛl] *nf* : quarrel
quereller [kərele] *v* **se quereller** *vr* : to quarrel
querelleur, -leuse [kərelœr, -løz] *adj* : quarrelsome
question [kɛstjɔ̃] *nf* **1** : question <poser une question : to ask a question> **2** : matter, issue
questionnaire [kɛstjɔnɛr] *nm* : questionnaire
questionner [kɛstjɔne] *vt* : to question **— se questionner** *vr*
quétaine [ketɛn] *adj Can fam* : hokey, corny
quête [kɛt] *nf* **1** : quest, search **2** : collection (of money)
quêter [kete] *vt* : to seek, to solicit (favors, money, etc.) **—** *vi* : to take a collection
quêteur, -teuse [kɛtœr, -tøz] *n* : collector
quêteux, -teuse [kɛtœ, -tøz] *n Can* : beggar
queue [kø] *nf* **1** : tail **2** : tail end, rear, bottom **3** : stem, stalk **4** : handle (of a pot) **5** : cue (in billiards) **6** : line <faire la queue : to stand in line> **7 queue d'aronde** : dovetail **8 queue de cheval** : ponytail
qui [ki] *pron* **1** : who, whom <qui est-ce? : who is it?> <à qui de droit : to whom it may concern> **2** : which, that <un livre qui est sur la table : a book which is on the table> **3 qui que** : whoever, whomever
quiconque [kikɔ̃k] *pron* **1** : whoever, whomever **2** : anyone, anybody
quiétude [kjetyd] *nf* : quiet, tranquility
quignon [kiɲɔ̃] *nm* : hunk, heel (of a loaf of bread)
quille [kij] *nf* **1** : keel **2 quilles** *nfpl or* **jeu de quilles** : ninepins
quincaillerie [kɛ̃kajri] *nf* **1** : hardware **2** : hardware store
quincaillier, -lière [kɛ̃kaje, -jɛr] *n* : hardware dealer
quinine [kinin] *nf* : quinine
quinquagénaire [kɛ̃kaʒenɛr] *nmf* : person in his or her fifties
quinquennal, -nale [kɛ̃kenal] *adj, mpl* **-naux** [-no] : five-year <plan quinquennal : five-year plan>
quintal [kɛ̃tal] *nm, pl* **quintaux** [kɛ̃to] : quintal
quinte [kɛ̃t] *nf or* **quinte de toux** : coughing fit
quintessence [kɛ̃tesɑ̃s] *nf* : quintessence **— quintessentiel, -tielle** [-sɑ̃sjɛl] *adv*
quintette [kɛ̃tɛt] *nm* : quintet
quintuple [kɛ̃typl] *adj* : quintuple, fivefold
quintupler [kɛ̃type] *vt* : to quintuple
quintuplés, -plées [kɛ̃type] *npl* : quintuplets
quinzaine [kɛ̃zɛn] *nf* **1 une quinzaine de** : about fifteen **2 une quinzaine de jours** : two weeks, a fortnight
quinze¹ [kɛ̃z] *adj* **1** : fifteen **2** : fifteenth <le quinze juin : June fifteenth>
quinze² *nms & pl* : fifteen
quinzième [kɛ̃zjem] *adj & nmf & nm* : fifteenth
quiproquo [kiprɔko] *nm* **1** : mistake, mistaken identity **2** MALENTENDU : misunderstanding
quiscale [kɥiskal] *nm* : grackle
quittance [kitɑ̃s] *nf* : receipt
quitte [kit] *adj* **1** : released from debt <être quitte envers : to be squared away with, to be quits with> <en être quitte pour : to get away with> **2 ~ à** : even if, at the risk of
quitter [kite] *vt* **1** : to leave, to abandon, to separate from **2** : to leave, to depart **3 ne quittez pas** : hold the (telephone) line **— se quitter** *vr* : to part, to separate
qui–vive [kiviv] *nms & pl* **être sur le qui–vive** : to be on the alert
quoi [kwa] *pron* **1** : what <à quoi bon? : what's the point?> <je sais à quoi tu penses : I know what you're thinking

about> **2** (*used as an interjection or interrogative)* : what!, what? **3 quoi que** : whatever <quoi qu'il arrive : whatever happens>

quoique [kwakə] *conj* : although, though, notwithstanding

quolibet [kɔlibɛ] *nm* : gibe, jeer

quorum [k(w)ɔrɔm] *nm* : quorum

quota [kɔta] *nm* **1** : quota **2 : avoir son quota** *Can fam* : to have had enough

quote–part [kɔtpar] *nf, pl* **quotes–parts** : share <payer sa quote-part : to pay one's share>

quotidien[1], **-dienne** [kɔtidjɛ̃, -djɛn] *adj* **1** : daily, every day **2** : everyday, routine

quotidien[2] *nm* **1** : daily (newspaper) <quotidien populaire : tabloid> **2 le quotidien** : everyday life

quotidiennement [kɔtidjɛnmɑ̃] *adv* : daily

quotient [kɔsjɑ̃] *nm* : quotient

R

r [ɛr] *nm* : r, the 18th letter of the alphabet

rabâcher [rabaʃe] *vt* : to repeat endlessly, to keep harping on — *vi* : to keep repeating oneself

rabais [rabɛ] *nms & pl* **1** RÉDUCTION : reduction, discount **2 au ~** : at a discount, cut-rate

rabaisser [rabɛse] *vt* **1** : to reduce, to lower, to lessen **2** DÉPRÉCIER : to belittle

rabat [raba] *nm* : flap

rabat–joie [rabaʒwa] *nmfs & pl* : killjoy, spoilsport

rabattre [rabatr] {12} *vt* **1** : to reduce, to diminish **2** : to bring down, to pull down **3** : to fold back — **se rabattre** *vr* **1** : to fold up, to go back (by itself) **2 ~ sur** : to fall back on, to make do with

rabbin [rabɛ̃] *nm* : rabbi

râblé, -blée [rable] *adj* : heavyset, stocky

rabot [rabo] *nm* : plane (tool)

raboter [rabɔte] *vt* : to plane (down)

raboteux, -teuse [rabɔtø, -tøz] *adj* INÉGAL : rough, uneven

rabougri, -grie [rabugri] *adj* **1** : stunted, puny **2** : wizened, shriveled (up)

rabrouer [rabrue] *vt* : to snub, to slight

racaille [rakaj] *nf* : riffraff, rabble

raccommoder [rakɔmɔde] *vt* RAPIÉCER : to mend, to patch up — **se raccommoder** *vr fam* : to make up (with someone)

raccompagner [rakɔ̃paɲe] *vt* : to take (someone) back, to see home

raccord [rakɔr] *nm* **1** : linkage, connection **2** : touch-up (in painting)

raccordement [rakɔrdəmɑ̃] *nm* : linking, connecting, joining (up)

raccorder [rakɔrde] *vt* : to connect, to link up — **se raccorder** *vr*

raccourci [rakursi] *nm* **1** : shortcut **2 en ~** : in short, briefly

raccourcir [rakursir] *vt* : to shorten — *vi* : to become shorter, to shrink

raccrocher [rakrɔʃe] *vt* **1** : to hang back up **2** : to rescue, to save at the last minute — *vi* : to hang up — **se raccrocher** *vr* : to hang on, to grab hold

race [ras] *nf* **1** : race <la race humaine : the human race> **2** : breed (of animals) **3** : line, descent **4 de ~** : Thoroughbred

racé, -cée [rase] *adj* **1** : Thoroughbred **2** DISTINGUÉ : distinguished

rachat [raʃa] *nm* **1** : repurchase **2** : atonement

racheter [raʃte] {20} *vt* **1** : to buy back **2** : to buy more of **3** : to redeem **4** : to atone for — **se racheter** *vr* : to redeem oneself

rachitisme [raʃitism] *nm* : rickets

racial, -ciale [rasjal] *adj, mpl* **raciaux** [rasjo] : racial, race — **racialement** [-sjalmɑ̃] *adv*

racine [rasin] *nf* **1** : root **2** : origin, source **3 racine carrée** : square root

racisme [rasism] *nm* : racism

raciste [rasist] *adj & nmf* : racist

racket [raket] *nm* : racket, racketeering

racketteur [raketœr] *nm* : racketeer

raclée [rakle] *nf fam* : beating, thrashing

racler [rakle] *vt* : to scrape (off), to scrape against

racloir [raklwar] *nm* GRATTOIR : scraper

racolage [rakɔlaʒ] *nm* : canvassing (in politics)

racoler [rakɔle] *vt* : to solicit (support, etc.), to canvass

racoleur, -leuse [rakɔlœr, -løz] *adj* : enticing, eye-catching

racontars [rakɔ̃tar] *nmpl* : gossip

raconter [rakɔ̃te] *vt* **1** CONTER : to tell, to relate **2** : to say, to talk about <qu'est-ce que tu racontes? : what are you talking about?>

raconteur, -teuse [rakɔ̃tœr, -tøz] *n* : raconteur, storyteller

racornir [rakɔrnir] *vt* : to toughen, to harden — **se racornir** *vr* **1** : to become hardened **2** SE RATATINER : to shrivel up

radar [radar] *nm* : radar

rade [rad] *nf* **1** : harbor **2 laisser en rade** : to leave stranded
radeau [rado] *nm, pl* **radeaux** : raft
radial, -diale [radjal] *adj, mpl* **radiaux** [radjo] : radial
radiant, -diante [radjɑ̃, -djɑ̃t] *adj* : radiant
radiateur [radjatœr] *nm* **1** : radiator **2** : heater <radiateur électrique : electric heater>
radiation [radjasjɔ̃] *nf* **1** : radiation **2** : crossing off (from a list)
radical[1], **-cale** [radikal] *adj, mpl* **-caux** [-ko] : radical — **radicalement** [-kalmɑ̃] *adv*
radical[2], **-cale** *n* : radical
radier [radje] {96} *vt* **1** : to radiate **2** RAYER : to cross off <radier un avocat : to disbar a lawyer>
radieux, -dieuse [radjø, -djøz] *adj* **1** : radiant, glowing (with joy, etc.) **2** : glorious, dazzling — **radieusement** [-djøzmɑ̃] *adv*
radin[1], **-dine** [radɛ̃, -din] *adj fam* : stingy
radin[2], **-dine** *n fam* : skinflint, cheapskate
radio[1] [radjo] *nf* **1** : radio **2** RADIOGRAPHIE : X ray
radio[2] *nm* : radio operator
radioactif, -tive [radjɔaktif, -tiv] *adj* : radioactive — **radioactivité** [-tivite] *nf*
radioamateur [radjɔamatœr] *nm* : ham (radio operator)
radiodiffuser [radjɔdifyze] *vt* : to broadcast
radiodiffusion [radjɔdifyzjɔ̃] *nf* : broadcasting
radiographie [radjɔgrafi] *nf* : radiography, X ray
radiographier [radjɔgrafje] {96} *vt* : to X-ray
radiologie [radjɔlɔʒi] *nf* : radiology
radiologique [radjɔlɔʒik] *adj* : radiological, radiologic
radiologiste [radjɔlɔʒist] *or* **radiologue** [radjɔlɔg] *nmf* : radiologist
radis [radi] *nm* : radish
radium [radjɔm] *nm* : radium
radja [radʒa] → **rajah**
radon [radɔ̃] *nm* : radon
radoter [radɔte] *vi* : to ramble on
radoucir [radusir] *vt* : to soften (up) — **se radoucir** *vr* **1** : to grow milder **2** : to calm down
rafale [rafal] *nf* **1** BOURRASQUE : gust (of wind, etc.) **2** : burst (of gunfire)
raffermir [rafɛrmir] *vt* **1** TONIFIER : to firm up, to tone up **2** : to strengthen, to reinforce
raffinage [rafinaʒ] *nm* : refining
raffiné, -née [rafine] *adj* : refined, sophisticated
raffinement [rafinmɑ̃] *nm* : refinement
raffiner [rafine] *vt* : to refine — *vi* ~ **sur** : to be meticulous about
raffinerie [rafinri] *nf* : refinery
raffoler [rafɔle] *vi* ~ **de** : to adore, to be crazy about
raffut [rafy] *nm fam* : din, racket
rafiot [rafjo] *nm fam* : old vessel, tub
rafistoler [rafistɔle] *vt fam* : to patch up, to fix up
rafle [rafl] *nf* DESCENTE : (police) raid
rafler [rafle] *vt fam* **1** : to swipe **2** : to walk off with <elle a raflé tous les prix : she walked off with all the prizes>
rafraîchir [rafrɛʃir] *vt* : to refresh, to cool, to chill — **se rafraîchir** *vr* **1** : to get cooler **2** : to freshen up **3 se rafraîchir la mémoire** : to refresh one's memory
rafraîchissant, -sante [rafrɛʃisɑ̃, -sɑ̃t] *adj* : refreshing
rafraîchissement [rafrɛʃismɑ̃] *nm* **1** : cooling **2 rafraîchissements** *nmpl* : cool drinks, refreshments
ragaillardir [ragajardir] *vt* REVIGORER : to perk up, to invigorate — **se ragaillardir** *vr* : to perk up
rage [raʒ] *nf* **1** : rage, fury <mettre en rage : to enrage> **2** : rabies **3 avoir la rage de** : to have a passion for **4 faire rage** : to rage (of storms, etc.)
rager [raʒe] {17} *vi* : to rage, to fume
rageur, -geuse [raʒœr, -ʒøz] *adj* **1** FURIEUX : furious **2** COLÉREUX : bad-tempered
rageusement [raʒøzmɑ̃] *adv* : furiously
ragot [rago] *nm fam* COMMÉRAGE : gossip, malicious rumor
ragoût [ragu] *nm* : ragout, stew
ragoûtant, -tante [ragutɑ̃, -tɑ̃t] *adj* **peu ragoûtant** : unappetizing, not very pleasant
ragtime [ragtajm] *nm* : ragtime
rai [rɛ] *nm* : ray, shaft (of light)
raid [rɛd] *nm* : raid <raid aérien : air raid>
raide[1] [rɛd] *adv* **1** : steeply **2 tomber raide** : to drop dead
raide[2] *adj* **1** : stiff, rigid **2** : taut, tight **3** : steep **4** : straight
raideur [rɛdœr] *nf* **1** : stiffness <avec raideur : stiffly> **2** : steepness
raidir [rɛdir] *vt* : to stiffen, to tighten, to tense (up) — **se raidir** *vr*
raie [rɛ] *nf* **1** : stripe **2** : part (in hair) **3** : ray, skate (fish)
raifort [rɛfɔr] *nm* : horseradish
rail [raj] *nm* **1** : rail, track **2 remettre sur les rails** : to put back on track
railler [raje] *vt* : to make fun of, to jeer at — **se railler** *vr* : to scoff
raillerie [rajri] *nf* : mockery
railleur, -leuse [rajœr, -jøz] *adj* MOQUEUR : mocking, derisive
rainer [rene] *vt* : to groove, to cut a groove in
rainure [renyr] *nf* : groove, slot
raisin [rɛzɛ̃] *nm* **1** : grape **2 raisin sec** : raisin **3 raisin de Corinthe** : currant

raison [rɛzɔ̃] *nf* **1** : reason, rationality, good sense <as-tu perdu la raison? : are you out of your mind?> <comme de raison : as one might expect> <à juste raison : justifiably> **2** MOTIF : reason, motive, grounds *pl* **3** : rate, ratio <à raison de deux par semaine : at the rate of two a week> **4 avoir raison** : to be right **5 en raison de** : due to, because of
raisonnable [rɛzɔnabl] *adj* **1** SENSÉ : sensible, reasonable **2** : moderate, fair <à des prix raisonnables : moderately priced>
raisonnablement [rɛzɔnabləmɑ̃] *adv* **1** : reasonably **2** : moderately, fairly
raisonné, -née [rɛzɔne] *adj* : well thought-out, reasoned
raisonnement [rɛzɔnmɑ̃] *nm* **1** : reasoning **2** ARGUMENTATION : argument, rationale
raisonner [rɛzɔne] *vi* **1** PENSER : to reason, to think **2** : to argue, to reason <raisonner sur : to argue about> — *vt* : to reason with — **se raisonner** *vr* : to try to be reasonable, to reason with oneself
raja *or* **rajah** [raʒa] *nm* : rajah
rajeunir [raʒœnir] *vt* **1** : to rejuvenate, to make (someone) look younger **2** : to modernize, to update — *vi* : to look younger — **se rajeunir** *vr*
rajeunissement [raʒœnismɑ̃] *nm* : rejuvenation
rajout [raʒu] *nm* : addition
rajouter [raʒute] *vt* **1** : to add **2 en ~** : to exaggerate
rajuster [raʒyste] *vt* **1** : to adjust, to straighten (clothing, etc.) **2** RÉAJUSTER : to readjust
râle [ral] *nm* **1** : groan **2 râle de la mort** : death rattle
ralenti[1], **-tie** [ralɑ̃ti] *adj* : slow, idling
ralenti[2] *nm* **1** : slow motion **2** : idling speed (of an automobile)
ralentir [ralɑ̃tir] *v* : to slow down, to decelerate
ralentissement [ralɑ̃tismɑ̃] *nm* : slowing down, slowdown
râler [rale] *vi* **1** : to groan **2** *fam* : to moan, to grumble
ralliement [ralimɑ̃] *nm* : rallying
rallier [ralje] {96} *vt* **1** : to rally (troops, etc.) **2** : to win over **3** : to rejoin — **se rallier** *vr* **~ à** : to rally to, to join up with
rallonge [ralɔ̃ʒ] *nf* **1** : extension **2** : extension cord **3** : leaf (of a table)
rallonger [ralɔ̃ʒe] {17} *vt* : to lengthen, to extend — *vi fam* : to get longer
rallumer [ralyme] *vt* **1** : to relight, to turn back on **2** : to rekindle, to revive
ramage [ramaʒ] *nm* **1** : song (of a bird) **2 ramages** *nmpl* : floral pattern (on cloth, etc.)
ramassage [ramasaʒ] *nm* **1** : collection **2** : picking, gathering **3 ramassage scolaire** *France* : school bus service
ramassé, -sée [ramase] *adj* **1** : squat, stocky **2** : compact (of style, etc.)
ramasser [ramase] *vt* **1** : to pick up, to collect **2** CUEILLIR : to pick, to gather <ramasser des framboises : to pick raspberries> — **se ramasser** *vr* SE PELOTONNER : to huddle up, to crouch
ramassis [ramasi] *nm* : bunch, pile, jumble
rambarde [rɑ̃bard] *nf* : guardrail
rame [ram] *nf* **1** AVIRON : oar **2** : train <rame de métro : subway train> **3** : ream (of paper)
rameau [ramo] *nm, pl* **rameaux 1** : branch, bough **2 dimanche des Rameaux** : Palm Sunday
ramener [ramne] {52} *vt* **1** : to bring back, to take back **2** : to restore <ramener la semaine de travail à 32 heures : to restore the work week to 32 hours> **3** RÉDUIRE : to reduce **4** : to draw up, to pull back — **se ramener** *vr* **~ à** : to come down to, to be nothing more than
ramer [rame] *vi* : to row
rameur, -meuse [ramœr, -møz] *n* : rower
rami [rami] *nm* : rummy (card game)
ramification [ramifikasjɔ̃] *nf* : ramification
ramifier [ramifje] {96} *v* **se ramifier** *vr* : to branch out, to ramify
ramolli, -lie [ramɔli] *adj* **1** : soft, softened **2** *fam* : soft in the head
ramollir [ramɔlir] *vt* : to soften — **se ramollir** *vr*
ramoner [ramɔne] *vt* : to sweep (a chimney), to clean out (pipes, etc.)
ramoneur [ramɔnœr] *nm* : chimney sweep
rampe [rɑ̃p] *nf* **1** : ramp **2** : banister, handrail **3** : footlights *pl* **4 rampe de lancement** : launching pad
ramper [rɑ̃pe] *vi* **1** : to crawl **2** : to creep (of a plant) **3** S'ABAISSER : to grovel, to lower oneself
ramure [ramyr] *nf* **1** : branches *pl* (of a tree) **2** : antlers *pl*
rancard [rɑ̃kar] *nm France fam* **1** : rendezvous, date **2** : lowdown, tip
rancart [rɑ̃kar] *nm* **mettre au rancart** *fam* : to discard, to scrap
rance [rɑ̃s] *adj* : rancid
ranch [rɑ̃tʃ] *nm* : ranch
rancir [rɑ̃sir] *vi* : to turn rancid
rancoeur [rɑ̃kœr] *nf* RESSENTIMENT : rancor, resentment
rançon [rɑ̃sɔ̃] *nf* : ransom
rançonner [rɑ̃sɔne] *vt* : to ransom
rancune [rɑ̃kyn] *nf* **1** : rancor, resentment **2** : grudge <garder rancune à : to hold a grudge against>
rancunier, -nière [rɑ̃kynje, -njɛr] *adj* : vindictive, spiteful

randonnée [rɑ̃dɔne] *nf* **1** : ride, trip **2** : walk, hike <faire de la randonnée : to backpack>
randonneur, -neuse [rɑ̃dɔnœr, -nøz] *n* : hiker, walker
rang [rɑ̃] *nm* **1** RANGÉE : row, line **2** : rank <de haut rang : high-ranking> **3** : standing, position (in society, etc.) **4** : ranks *pl* (in the military) <sortir du rang : to come up through the ranks>
rangé, -gée [rɑ̃ʒe] *adj* **1** : orderly, tidy **2** : well-behaved
rangée *nf* : row, line <une rangée d'arbres : a row of trees>
rangement [rɑ̃ʒmɑ̃] *nm* **1** : tidying up, putting away **2** AGENCEMENT : arrangement, layout **3** : storage space
ranger [rɑ̃ʒe] {17} *vt* **1** : to tidy up **2** : to put away, to store **3** CLASSER : to put in order — **se ranger** *vr* **1** : to line up **2** SE GARER : to pull over, to move aside **3** : to go along with, to side with **4** S'ASSAGIR : to settle down
ranimer [ranime] *vt* **1** : to revive, to resuscitate **2** : to renew, to rekindle — **se ranimer** *vr* **1** : to revive, to come to **2** : to flare up, to be rekindled
rapace[1] [rapas] *adj* : rapacious
rapace[2] *nm* : bird of prey
rapatriement [rapatrimɑ̃] *nm* : repatriation
rapatrier [rapatrije] {96} *vt* : to repatriate
râpe [rap] *nf* **1** : grater **2** : rasp
râpé, -pée [rape] *adj* **1** : grated **2** : threadbare
râper [rape] *vt* **1** : to grate **2** : to file down (with a rasp)
rapetasser [raptase] *vt fam* : to patch up
rapetisser [raptise] *vt* **1** : to shorten, to make smaller **2** : to belittle — *vi* **1** : to get shorter **2** : to shrink — **se rapetisser** *vr* : to get smaller, to shrink
râpeux, -peuse [rapø, -pøz] *adj* **1** : rough, harsh, grating **2** ÂPRE : bitter, harsh (of wine, etc.)
rapide[1] [rapid] *adj* **1** : quick, rapid **2** : steep
rapide[2] *nm* **1** : rapid **2** : express train
rapidement [rapidmɑ̃] *adv* : rapidly, quickly
rapidité [rapidite] *nf* : rapidity, speed
rapiécer [rapjese] {6} *vt* : to patch (up), to mend
rapière [rapjɛr] *nf* : rapier
rappel [rapɛl] *nm* **1** : reminder **2** : recall, return **3** : curtain call **4** ÉVOCATION : recall, remembrance **5** : repeat, repetition **6** : booster shot **7** **rappel à l'ordre** : call to order
rappeler [raple] {8} *vt* **1** : to remind **2** : to call back — **se rappeler** *vr* : to remember, to recall
rapport [rapɔr] *nm* **1** : report **2** : connection, association <sans rapport : irrelevant> **3** RENDEMENT : return, yield **4** : contact <en rapport avec : in touch with> **5** : ratio **6** **rapports** *nmpl* : dealings, affairs, relations <avoir de bons rapports avec : to have good relations with> <rapports avec l'étranger : foreign affairs> **7** **rapports** *nmpl* : sexual intercourse
rapporter [raporte] *vt* **1** : to bring back, to take back **2** : to yield (in finance) **3** RELATER : to tell, to report **4** : to add, to insert **5** : to relate to — *vi* **1** : to yield a profit **2** *fam* : to tell tales — **se rapporter** *vr* ~ **à** : to relate to
rapporteur[1], **-teuse** [raportœr, -tøz] *n* : tattletale
rapporteur[2] *nm* : protractor
rapproché, -chée [rɑ̃prɔʃe] *adj* **1** : close, nearby **2** frequent, at close intervals
rapprochement [raprɔʃmɑ̃] *nm* **1** : bringing together, coming together **2** : reconciliation **3** LIEN : link, connection
rapprocher [raprɔʃe] *vt* **1** : to bring closer, to move closer **2** COMPARER : to compare — **se rapprocher** *vr* **1** : to come closer **2** ~ **de** : to get closer to, to approximate **3** ~ **de** : to resemble
rapsodie [rapsɔdi] *nf* → **rhapsodie**
rapt [rapt] *nm* : abduction, kidnapping
raquette [raket] *nf* **1** : racket <raquette de tennis : tennis racket> **2** : snowshoe
rare [rar] *adj* **1** : rare, uncommon, unusual **2** : rare, infrequent **3** : few, sparse, thin
raréfaction [rarefaksjɔ̃] *nf* **1** : rarefaction **2** : scarcity
raréfier [rarefje] {96} *vt* **1** : to rarefy **2** : to make scarce — **se raréfier** *vr*
rarement [rarmɑ̃] *adv* : seldom, rarely
rareté [rarte] *nf* : rarity, scarcity
ras[1] [ra] *adv* : short <couper ras : to cut short>
ras[2], **rase** [ra, raz] *adj* **1** : close-cropped <à poil ras : short-haired> <pelouse rase : closely-mown grass> **2** : level <cuillerée rase : level spoonful> <à ras bord : to the brim> **3** **en rase campagne** : in open country
rasage [razaʒ] *nm* : shaving
rasant, -sante [razɑ̃, -zɑ̃t] *adj fam* : boring
raser [raze] {87} *vt* **1** : to shave **2** : to raze **3** FRÔLER : to graze, to skim — **se raser** *vr* : to shave
raseur, -seuse [razœr, -zøz] *n fam* : bore <quelle raseuse! : what a bore she is!>
rasoir [razwar] *nm* : razor <rasoir électrique : electric razor>
rassasier [rasazje] {96} *vt* : to satisfy, to satiate — **se rassasier** *vr*
rassemblement [rasɑ̃bləmɑ̃] *nm* : gathering, assembly
rassembler [rasɑ̃ble] *vt* **1** RÉUNIR : to gather, to collect **2** **rassembler en**

troupeau : to herd — **se rassembler** *vr* : to gather together, to assemble
rasseoir [raswar] {9} *v* **se rasseoir** *vr* : to sit down again
rassérener [raserene] {87} *vt* CALMER : to calm, to make serene — **se rassérener** *vr* : to calm down
rassir [rasir] {72} *vi* : to go stale — **se rassir** *vr*
rassis, -sise [rasi, -siz] *adj* : stale
rassurant, -rante [rasyrɑ̃, -rɑ̃t] *adj* : reassuring
rassurer [rasyre] *vt* : to reassure
rat [ra] *nm* **1** : rat **2 rat musqué** : muskrat
ratatiner [ratatine] *v* **se ratatiner** *vr* **1** : to dry up, to shrivel **2** : to become wizened
rate [rat] *nf* : spleen
raté[1], **-tée** [rate] *n* : failure
raté[2] *nm* : backfiring
râteau [rato] *nm, pl* **râteaux** : rake
râteler [ratle] {8} *vt* : to rake up
râtelier [ratəlje] *nm* **1** : hayrack **2 manger à tous les râteliers** : to have a finger in every pie
rater [rate] *vt* **1** MANQUER : to miss (a chance, a train, etc.) **2** : to fail at — *vi* **1** ÉCHOUER : to fail, to miss **2** : to misfire
ratifier [ratifje] {96} *vt* : to ratify — **ratification** [-tifikasjɔ̃] *nf*
ratine [ratin] *nf Can* : terry cloth
ratio [rasjo] *nm* : ratio
ration [rasjɔ̃] *nf* **1** PORTION : share, ration **2** : rations *pl* (in the military)
rationaliser [rasjɔnalize] *vt* : to rationalize — **rationalisation** [-lizasjɔ̃] *nf*
rationnel, -nelle [rasjɔnɛl] *adj* : rational — **rationnellement** [-nɛlmɑ̃] *adv*
rationner [rasjɔne] *vt* : to ration
ratisser [ratise] *vt* **1** : to rake **2** : to search, to comb
raton [ratɔ̃] *nm* **raton laveur** : raccoon
ratoureur[1], **-reuse** [raturœr, -røz] *adj Can* : crafty, sly
ratoureur[2], **-reuse** *n* : crafty person
rattacher [ratafe] *vt* **1** : to tie up again **2** RELIER : to link, to connect — **se rattacher** *vr* ~ **à** : to be connected with, to relate to
rattrapage [ratrapaʒ] *nm* **1** : adjustment (of salaries, etc.) **2 cours de rattrapage** : remedial class(es)
rattraper [ratrape] *vt* **1** : to recapture **2** : to catch up with **3** : to make up for
raturer [ratyre] *vt* BIFFER : to cross out
rauque [rok] *adj* **1** : hoarse **2** : raucous
ravager [ravaʒe] {17} *vt* : to ravage, to devastate
ravages [ravaʒ] *nmpl* **1** : ravages, devastation **2 faire des ravages** : to wreak havoc
ravalement [ravalmɑ̃] *nm* : refacing (of a building), restoration
ravaler [ravale] *vt* **1** : to clean, to restore (a building, etc.) **2** : to choke back, to stifle, to swallow <ravaler ses larmes : to hold back tears>
ravauder [ravode] *vt Can* : to make a racket
ravi, -vie [ravi] *adj* ENCHANTÉ : delighted
ravigoter [ravigɔte] *vt fam* : to perk up, to invigorate
ravin [ravɛ̃] *nm* : ravine, gulch
raviner [ravine] *vt* : to furrow
ravir [ravir] *vt* **1** ENCHANTER : to delight **2** ~ **à** : to rob of (a loved one, etc.) **3 à** ~ : delightfully, beautifully
raviser [ravise] *v* **se raviser** *vr* : to change one's mind
ravissant, -sante [ravisɑ̃, -sɑ̃t] *adj* : delightful, beautiful
ravissement [ravismɑ̃] *nm* : rapture
ravisseur, -seuse [ravisœr, -søz] *n* KIDNAPPEUR : kidnapper, abductor
ravitaillement [ravitajmɑ̃] *nm* **1** : provision, supplying **2** : refueling
ravitailler [ravitaje] *vt* **1** : to supply (with food, etc.) **2** : to refuel
raviver [ravive] *vt* **1** RANIMER : to rekindle **2** : to brighten up
ravoir [ravwar] {73} *vt* : to get back
rayé, -yée [reje] *adj* **1** : striped, lined **2** : scratched
rayer [reje] {11} *vt* **1** ÉRAFLER : to scratch **2** : to cross out, to delete, to erase
rayon [rejɔ̃] *nm* **1** : ray, beam <rayon de soleil : sunbeam> <rayon de lune : moonbeam> **2** : radius **3** : range, scope **4** ÉTAGÈRE : shelf, bookshelf **5** : department (in a store) **6** : domain, concern **7 rayon de miel** : honeycomb **8 rayons** *nmpl* : rays, radiation <rayons gamma : gamma rays> <rayons X : X rays>
rayonnant, -nante [rejɔnɑ̃, -nɑ̃t] *adj* RADIEUX : radiant
rayonne [rejɔn] *nf* : rayon
rayonnement [rejɔnmɑ̃] *nm* **1** : radiation **2** : radiance **3** : influence (of art, culture, etc.)
rayonner [rejɔne] *vi* **1** : to radiate **2** : to shine, to glow **3** : to exert influence **4** : to tour around
rayure [rejyr] *nf* **1** : stripe <chemise à rayures : striped shirt> **2** ÉRAFLURE : scratch
raz-de-marée [radmare] *nms & pl* : tidal wave
razzia [razja] *nf* : raid, foray
réabonner [reabɔne] *v* **se réabonner** *vr* : to renew one's subscription
réaccoutumer [reakutyme] *v* **se réaccoutumer** *vr* SE RÉHABITUER : to get reaccustomed to
réacteur [reaktœr] *nm* **1** : jet engine **2** : reactor <réacteur nucléaire : nuclear reactor>
réaction [reaksjɔ̃] *nf* **1** : reaction <réaction en chaîne : chain reaction> **2 à** ~ : jet-propelled **3** → **avion, moteur**

réactionnaire [reaksjɔnɛr] *adj & nmf* : reactionary
réactiver [reaktive] *vt* : to reactivate
réadaptation [readaptasjɔ̃] *nf* **1** : readjustment **2** : (physical) rehabilitation
réadapter [readapte] *v* **se réadapter** *vr* : to readjust
réaffirmer [reafirme] *vt* : to reaffirm
réagir [reaʒir] *vi* : to react
réajuster [reaʒyste] *vt* : to readjust, to adjust **— réajustement** [-ʒystəmã] *nm*
réalisable [realizabl] *adj* FAISABLE : feasible
réalisateur, -trice [realizatœr, -tris] *n* : director (in movies, television, theater)
réalisation [realizasjɔ̃] *nf* **1** ÉXÉCUTION : execution, carrying out **2** : directory, production (of a film) **3** : achievement, accomplishment
réaliser [realize] *vt* **1** : to carry out, to execute **2** : to produce, to direct (a film) **3** : to achieve, to accomplish **4** : to realize (a profit) **— se réaliser** *vr* **1** : to materialize, to come true **2** : to fulfill oneself
réalisme [realism] *nm* : realism
réaliste[1] [realist] *adj* : realistic
réaliste[2] *nmf* : realist
réalité [realite] *nf* **1** : reality **2 en ~** : in fact, actually
réaménager [reamenaʒe] {17} *vt* : to refurbish
réanimer [reanime] *vt* : to resuscitate **— réanimation** [-nimasjɔ̃] *nf*
réapparaître [reaparɛtr] {7} *vi* : to reappear, to come back, to recur
réapparition [reaparisjɔ̃] *nf* : reappearance
réarranger [rearãʒe] {17} *vt* : to rearrange
rebaptiser [rəbatize] *vt* : to rename
rébarbatif, -tive [rebarbatif, -tiv] *adj* **1** : forbidding, grim-looking **2** : daunting
rebattu, -tue [rəbaty] *adj* : hackneyed
rebelle[1] [rəbɛl] *adj* **1** : rebellious, unruly **2** : rebel <le camp rebelle : the rebel camp>
rebelle[2] *nmf* : rebel
rebeller [rəbɛle] *v* **se rebeller** *vr* : to rebel
rébellion [rebɛljɔ̃] *nf* : rebellion
rebiffer [rəbife] *v* **se rebiffer** *vr fam* : to rebel against, to strike back at
rebond [rəbɔ̃] *nm* : bounce, rebound
rebondi, -die [rəbɔ̃di] *adj* **1** : rounded **2** : plump, chubby
rebondir [rəbɔ̃dir] *vi* **1** : to bounce, to rebound **2** : to start (up) again
rebondissement [rəbɔ̃dismã] *nm* : new development
rebord [rəbɔr] *nm* : rim, edge, sill (of a window)
reboucher [rəbuʃe] *vt* **1** : to put the cork back in **2** : to plug, to stop up
rebours [rəbur] *nm* **1 à ~** : the wrong way **2 → compte**
rebrousse-poil [rəbruspwal] **à rebrousse-poil** : the wrong way, against the grain
rebrousser [rəbruse] *vt* **1** : to brush back **2 rebrousser chemin** : to turn back
rebuffade [rəbyfad] *nf* : rebuff, snub
rébus [rebys] *nm* : rebus, riddle
rebut [rəby] *nm* **1** : trash, waste, scrap **2 de ~** : rejected, unwanted **3 mettre au rebut** : to discard, to throw away
rebutant, -tante [rəbytã, -tãt] *adj* : repellent, disagreeable
rebuter [rəbyte] *vt* **1** DÉCOURAGER : to dishearten, to discourage, to put off **2** : to disgust, to repel
récalcitrant, -trante [rekalsitrã, -trãt] *adj* : recalcitrant
recaler [rəkale] *vt France fam* : to fail (a student)
récapitulatif, -tive [rekapitylatif, -tiv] *adj* : summary
récapituler [rekapityle] *vt* RÉSUMER : to recapitulate, to sum up **— récapitulation** [-tylasjɔ̃] *nf*
recel [rəsɛl] *nm* : possession of stolen goods
receler [rəsəle] {20} *vt* : to receive (stolen goods), to conceal (a criminal)
récemment [resamã] *adv* DERNIÈREMENT : recently
recensement [rəsãsmã] *nm* **1** : census (of populations) **2** : inventory
recenser [rəsãse] *vt* **1** : to take a census of **2** : to list, to inventory
récent, -cente [resã, -sãt] *adj* : recent
récépissé [resepise] *nm* : receipt
réceptacle [reseptakl] *nm* : container, receptacle
récepteur[1], **-trice** [reseptœr, -tris] *adj* : receiving
récepteur[2] *nm* : receiver <récepteur de téléphone : telephone receiver> <récepteur de radiomessagerie : beeper>
réceptif, -tive [reseptif, -tiv] *adj* : receptive **— réceptivité** [-tivite] *nf*
réception [resepsjɔ̃] *nf* **1** : receiving, receipt **2** ACCUEIL : reception, welcome **3** : admission (into an organization, etc.) **4** FÊTE : reception, party **5** : registration desk **6** : reception (of radio, television, etc.)
réceptionner [resepsjɔne] *vt* : to receive, to take delivery of
réceptionniste [resepsjɔnist] *nmf* : receptionist
récession [resesjɔ̃] *nf* : recession
recette [rəsɛt] *nf* **1** : recipe **2** : formula, prescription **3** : take, receipts *pl*
recevable [rəsəvabl] *adj* : admissible, acceptable
recevant, -vante [rəsəvã, -vãt] *adj Can* : welcoming, hospitable
receveur, -veuse [rəsəvœr, -vøz] *n* **1** : recipient (of blood, transplants, etc.) **2** *Can* : catcher (in sports) **3 receveur**

des contributions : tax collector **4 receveur des postes** : postmaster

recevoir [rəsəvwar] {26} *vt* **1** : to receive, to get **2** ACCUEILLIR : to welcome, to be host to **3** : to see, to receive (patients, etc.) **4** ADMETTRE : to admit, to accept (into a society, school, etc.) <être reçu à l'université : to be accepted at the university> **5** : to accommodate, to hold **6** : to receive (radio or television signals) — **se recevoir** *vr* : to land (in sports, dance, etc.)

rechange [rəʃɑ̃ʒ] *nm* **1 de ~** : spare, extra <vêtements de rechange : change of clothes> **2 de ~** : alternative

réchapper [reʃape] *vi* **~ de** : to come through, to pull through

recharge [rəʃarʒ] *nf* **1** : refill, reload(ing) **2** : recharging (of a battery, etc.)

rechargeable [rəʃarʒabl] *adj* : rechargeable, refillable

recharger [rəʃarʒe] {17} *vt* **1** : to refill, to reload **2** : to recharge

réchaud [reʃo] *nm* **1** : (portable) stove **2 réchaud de table** : chafing dish

réchauffer [reʃofe] *vt* : to reheat, to warm up — **se réchauffer** *vr* **1** : to warm up, to get warmer **2** : to warm oneself up

rêche [rɛʃ] *adj* : rough, prickly, scratchy

recherche [rəʃɛrʃ] *nf* **1** : search <à la recherche de : in search of> **2** : research **3** : meticulousness, refinement **4** : affectation, pretentiousness **5 recherches** *nfpl* : investigations

recherché, -chée [rəʃɛrʃe] *adj* **1** : sought-after, in demand **2** : refined, studied, meticulous **3** : affected, pretentious

rechercher [rəʃɛrʃe] *vt* **1** : to search for, to seek **2** : to look into, to investigate

rechigner [rəʃiɲe] *vi* **1** : to grumble **2 ~ à** : to balk at

rechute [rəʃyt] *nf* : relapse <faire une rechute : to have a relapse>

rechuter [rəʃyte] *vi* : to relapse

récidive [residiv] *nf* **1** : second (or subsequent) offense **2** : recurrence (of an illness)

récidiver [residive] *vi* **1** : to relapse into crime **2** : to recur (of an illness)

récif [resif] *nm* : reef

récipiendaire [resipjɑ̃dɛr] *nmf* : recipient (of a diploma, a nomination, etc.)

récipient [resipjɑ̃] *nm* : container

réciprocité [resiprɔsite] *nf* : reciprocity

réciproque [resiprɔk] *adj* : reciprocal, mutual — **réciproquement** [-prɔkmɑ̃] *adv*

récit [resi] *nm* : account, story

récital [resital] *nm, pl* **-tals** : recital

récitation [resitasjɔ̃] *nf* **1** : recitation **2 apprendre une récitation** : to learn a text by heart

réciter [resite] *vt* : to recite

réclamation [reklamasjɔ̃] *nf* **1** PLAINTE : complaint **2** : claim (in law)

réclame [reklam] *nf* **1** : advertisement **2** : advertising, publicity **3 en ~** : on special (offer), on sale

réclamer [reklame] *vt* **1** : to ask for, to claim **2** : to demand, to call for — *vi* : to complain — **se réclamer** *vr* **~ de** : to claim an association with (a person or an organization)

reclasser [rəklase] *vt* : to reclassify

reclus, -cluse [rəkly, -klyz] *n* : recluse

réclusion [reklyzjɔ̃] *nf* DÉTENTION : imprisonment

recoin [rəkwɛ̃] *nm* : nook, corner <tous les coins et les recoins : every nook and cranny>

reçoit [rəswa], **reçoive** [rəswav], *etc.* → **recevoir**

recoller [rəkɔle] *vt* : to stick back together

récolte [rekɔlt] *nf* **1** : harvesting, gathering **2** : harvest, crop

récolter [rekɔlte] *vt* **1** : to harvest **2** : to gather, to collect

recommandable [rəkɔmɑ̃dabl] *adj* : commendable

recommandation [rəkɔmɑ̃dasjɔ̃] *nf* : recommendation

recommander [rəkɔmɑ̃de] *vt* **1** : to recommend **2** : to advise **3** : to register (a letter, etc.)

recommencement [rəkɔmɑ̃smɑ̃] *nm* : new beginning

recommencer [rəkɔmɑ̃se] {6} *v* : to begin again, to start anew

récompense [rekɔ̃pɑ̃s] *nf* : reward

récompenser [rekɔ̃pɑ̃se] *vt* : to reward

réconciliation [rekɔ̃siljasjɔ̃] *nf* : reconciliation

réconcilier [rekɔ̃silje] {96} *vt* : to reconcile — **se réconcilier** *vr*

reconduction [rəkɔ̃dyksjɔ̃] *nf* : renewal (of a budget, contract, etc.)

reconduire [rəkɔ̃duir] {49} *vt* **1** RACCOMPAGNER : to take home **2** : to show to the door **3** : to renew, to extend <reconduire qqn dans ses fonctions : to reelect s.o.>

réconfort [rekɔ̃fɔr] *nm* : comfort

réconfortant, -tante [rekɔ̃fɔrtɑ̃, -tɑ̃t] *adj* **1** : comforting **2** : fortifying, invigorating

réconforter [rəkɔ̃fɔrte] *vt* **1** CONSOLER : to comfort **2** REVIGORER : to fortify, to invigorate

reconnaissable [rəkɔnɛsabl] *adj* : recognizable

reconnaissance [rekɔnɛsɑ̃s] *nf* **1** : recognition **2** GRATITUDE : gratitude **3** : admission, acknowledgment (of wrongs, debts, etc.) **4** : reconnaissance (in the military)

reconnaissant, -sante [rəkɔnesɑ̃, -sɑ̃t] *adj* : grateful
reconnaître [rəkɔnɛtr] {7} *vt* **1** : to recognize **2** : to admit, to acknowledge **3** : to reconnoiter — **se reconnaître** *vr* **1** : to see oneself (in someone) **2** : to recognize each other **3** : to be recognizable **4** : to orient oneself, to find one's way **5** S'AVOUER : to admit (to being), to own up
reconnu, -nue [rəkɔny] *adj* : recognized, well-known
reconquérir [rəkɔ̃kerir] {21} *vt* **1** : to reconquer **2** : to regain, to win back
reconsidérer [rəkɔ̃sidere] {87} *vt* : to reconsider
reconstituer [rəkɔ̃stituɛ] *vt* **1** : to piece together, to recreate, to rebuild **2** : to reconstruct (a crime)
reconstruction [rəkɔ̃stryksjɔ̃] *nf* : reconstruction, rebuilding
reconstruire [rəkɔ̃struir] {49} *vt* : to reconstruct, to rebuild
reconvertir [rəkɔ̃vɛrtir] *vt* **1** : to redeploy **2** : to convert, to restructure
recopier [rəkɔpje] {96} *vt* : to copy out (again), to transcribe
record [rəkɔr] *nm* : record
recoudre [rəkudr] {22} *vt* **1** : to sew back on **2** : to stitch up (in surgery)
recouper [rəkupe] *vt* **1** : to cut again **2** : to tally with — **se recouper** *vr* **1** : to tally, to add up **2** : to intersect
recourbé, -bée [rəkurbe] *adj* : curved, hooked <un nez recourbé : a hooked nose>
recourir [rəkurir] {23} *vi* **1** : to run again **2** : to appeal **3** ~ **à** : to resort to
recours [rəkur] *nm* **1** : recourse, resort <en dernier recours : as a last resort> <avoir recours à : to have recourse to, to fall back on> **2** : appeal (in law)
recouvert, -verte [rkuvɛr, -vɛrt] *adj* : overgrown
recouvrement [rəkuvrəmɑ̃] *nm* **1** : collection **2** : recovery **3** : covering, cover
recouvrer [rəkuvre] *vt* **1** : to recover, to regain **2** : to collect (taxes, etc.)
recouvrir [rəkuvrir] {83} *vt* **1** : to cover, to re-cover **2** MASQUER : to conceal, to hide — **se recouvrir** *vr* : to overlap
récréatif, -tive [rekreatif, -tiv] *adj* : recreational, entertaining
récréation [rekreasjɔ̃] *nf* **1** : recreation, entertainment **2** : recess, break
recréer [rəkree] {89} *vt* : to re-create
récrier [rekrije] {96} *v* **se récrier** *vr* : to exclaim
récrimination [rekriminasjɔ̃] *nf* : recrimination, reproach
récriminer [rekrimine] *vi* ~ **contre** : to recriminate against, to reproach
récrire [rekrir] {33} *vt* : to rewrite
recroqueviller [rəkrɔkvije] *v* **se recroqueviller** *vr* **1** : to huddle up, to curl up **2** : to shrivel up
recru, -crue [rəkry] *adj or* **recru de fatigue** : exhausted
recrudescence [rəkrydesɑ̃s] *nf* : new outbreak
recrue [rəkry] *nf* : recruit
recrutement [rəkrytmɑ̃] *nm* : recruitment
recruter [rəkryte] *vt* : to recruit, to appoint, to take on
rectal, -tale [rɛktal] *adj, mpl* **-taux** [-to] : rectal
rectangle [rɛktɑ̃gl] *nm* : rectangle — **rectangulaire** [-tɑ̃gylɛr] *adj*
recteur, -trice [rɛktœr, -tris] *nm* **1** *France* : superintendent (of schools) **2** : rector, administrator (of a university) **3** : rector (in religion)
rectificatif [rɛktifikatif] *nm* : correction <publier un rectificatif : to publish a correction>
rectification [rɛktifikasjɔ̃] *nf* : correcting, correction
rectifier [rɛktifje] {96} *vt* : to rectify, to correct
rectitude [rɛktityd] *nf* **1** : straightness (of a line) **2** DROITURE : uprightness, rectitude
recto [rɛkto] *nm* : recto
rectum [rɛktɔm] *nm* : rectum
reçu[1] [rəsy] *pp* → **recevoir**
reçu[2], **-cue** [rəsy] *adj* : accepted, approved
reçu[3] *nm* : receipt
recueil [rəkœj] *nm* : collection, compilation
recueillement [rəkœjmɑ̃] *nm* MÉDITATION : meditation, contemplation
recueillir [rəkœjir] {3} *vt* **1** : to collect, to gather **2** : to get, to obtain, to win **3** : to take in (a stray, etc.) — **se recueillir** *vr* **1** : to collect one's thoughts, to reflect **2** : to meditate
recuire [rəkuir] {49} *vt* : to anneal
recul [rəkyl] *nm* **1** : recoil (of a firearm) **2** : retreat, backward movement <prendre du recul : to stand back> **3** : detachment <avec le recul : in retrospect, with hindsight> **4** : decline, drop (in production, prices, etc.)
reculer [rəkyle] *vt* **1** REPOUSSER : to move back, to push back **2** : to defer, to postpone — *vi* **1** : to move back **2** : to back up **3** : to be on the decline **4** ~ **devant** : to shrink from, to balk at
reculons [rəkylɔ̃] **à** ~ : backwards
récupérable [rekyperabl] *adj* **1** : recoverable **2** : salvageable, reusable
récupération [rekyperasjɔ̃] *nf* **1** : recovery, recuperation **2** : salvage, recycling
récupérer [rekypere] {87} *vt* **1** : to recover, to get back **2** : to salvage, to recycle **3** : to make up <récupérer des heures de travail : to make up the hours (at work)> **4** : to take over, to appropriate — *vi* SE RÉTABLIR : to recover, to recuperate

récurer [rekyre] *vt* : to scour <poudre à récurer : scouring powder>
récurrent, -rente [rekyrɑ̃, -rɑ̃t] *adj* : recurrent, recurring
récuser [rekyze] *vt* : to challenge, to object to (in law)
recyclable [rəsiklabl] *adj* : recyclable
recyclage [rəsiklaʒ] *nm* **1** : retraining **2** : recycling
recycler [rəsikle] *vt* **1** : to retrain **2** : to recycle — **se recycler** *vr* **1** : to update one's skills, to retrain **2** : to change jobs
rédacteur, -trice [redaktœr, -tris] *n* : editor
rédaction [redaksjɔ̃] *nf* **1** : writing, editing **2** : editorial staff
rédactionnel, -nelle [redaksjɔnɛl] *adj* : editorial
reddition [redisjɔ̃] *nf* : surrender
redécouvrir [rədekuvrir] *vt* : to rediscover
redéfinir [rədefinir] *vt* : to redefine
rédempteur[1], -trice [redɑ̃ptœr, -tris] *adj* : redeeming
rédempteur[2] *nm* : redeemer
rédemption [redɑ̃psjɔ̃] *nf* : redemption
redescendre [rədesɑ̃dr] {63} *vt* **1** : to take down again **2** : to go down (stairs, a hill, etc.) again — *vi* : to go down again
redevable [rədəvabl] *adj* **être redevable à** : to be indebted to
redevance [rədəvɑ̃s] *nf* : payments *pl*, fees *pl* (for services)
rediffusion [rədifyzjɔ̃] *nf* : rerun, rebroadcast, repeat
rédiger [redize] {17} *vt* : to write, to draft
redire [rədir] {29} *vt* RÉPÉTER : to say again, to repeat
redistribuer [rədistribye] *vt* : to redistribute
redite [rədit] *nf* : (needless) repetition
redondant, -dante [rədɔ̃dɑ̃, -dɑ̃t] *adj* SUPERFLU : redundant — **redondance** [-dɔ̃dɑ̃s] *nf*
redonner [rədɔne] *vt* **1** RENDRE : to give back, to return **2** RÉTABLIR : to restore (confidence, etc.) **3** : to give again
redoubler [rəduble] *vt* **1** DOUBLER : to double **2** : to repeat (a class, etc.) **3** : to intensify <redoubler ses efforts : to redouble one's efforts> — *vi* **1** : to intensify **2 ~ de** : to increase in, to step up <redoubler de larmes : to cry even harder>
redoutable [rədutabl] *adj* : formidable, fearsome
redouter [rədute] *vt* : to fear, to dread
redressement [rədresmɑ̃] *nm* **1** : recovery, upturn (of the economy) **2 maison de redressement** : reformatory
redresser [rədrese] *vt* **1** : to set upright, to straighten up, to straighten out **2** : to turn around, to set back on its feet **3** : to rectify, to redress (errors, wrongs, etc.) — **se redresser** *vr* **1** : to stand up, to sit up (straight) **2** : to recover, to pick up again
réduction [redyksjɔ̃] *nf* **1** : discount, rebate **2** : decrease, cut, reduction
réduire [reduir] {49} *vt* **1** DIMINUER : to reduce, to decrease **2** : to scale down, to boil down **3** : to subdue (an enemy) **4 ~ à** : to reduce to, to constrain to <réduit au silence : reduced to silence> **5 ~ en** : to crush into <réduit en cendres : reduced to ashes>
réduit[1], -duite [reduɪ, -dɥit] *adj* **1** : reduced, smaller, lower **2** : small, limited
réduit[2] *nm* : recess, nook
réédition [reedisjɔ̃] *nf* : new edition
rééducation [reedykasjɔ̃] *nf* **1** : rehabilitation (of criminals, etc.) **2** : physical therapy, (medical) rehabilitation
rééduquer [reedyke] *vt* : to rehabilitate (in law or medicine)
réel[1], -elle [reɛl] *adj* **1** : real **2** VÉRITABLE : true
réel[2] *nm* : reality
réélire [reelir] {51} *vt* : to reelect — **réélection** [-eleksjɔ̃] *nf*
réellement [reɛlmɑ̃] *adv* : really, in fact
réemployer [reɑ̃plwaje] {58} *vt* **1** : to reuse **2** : to reinvest **3** : to reemploy, to take on again
rééquilibrer [reekilibre] *vt* : to readjust, to balance
réévaluer [reevalye] *vt* **1** : to revalue **2** : to reappraise, to reevaluate
réexamen [reɛgzamɛ̃] *nm* : reassessment, reconsideration
réexaminer [reɛgzamine] *vt* : to reexamine, to reassess
refaire [rəfɛr] {42} *vt* **1** : to do again **2** : to redo, to redecorate **3** : to change completely, to start all over again — **se refaire** *vr* **1** : to recoup one's losses **2** : to change (oneself) **3 se refaire une santé** : to regain one's health, to recuperate
réfection [refɛksjɔ̃] *nf* : repairing
référence [referɑ̃s] *nf* **1** : reference **2 faire référence à** : to refer to
référendum [referẽdɔm] *nm* : referendum
référer [refere] {87} *vi* **en référer à** : to consult, to refer (a matter) to — **se référer** *vr* **~ à** : to refer to
refermer [rəfɛrme] *vt* : to close again
refiler [rəfile] *vt fam* : to palm off, to foist
réfléchi, -chie [reflɛʃi] *adj* **1** : reflective, thoughtful **2** : reflexive <verbe réfléchi : reflexive verb>
réfléchir [reflɛʃir] *vt* : to reflect — *vi* **1** PENSER : to reflect, to think things over **2 ~ à** : to think about, to reflect on
réfléchissant, -sante [reflɛʃisɑ̃, -sɑ̃t] *adj* : reflective (in physics)
réflecteur [reflɛktœr] *nm* : reflector

reflet [rəflɛ] *nm* **1** : reflection, image **2** : sheen, highlight
refléter [rəflete] {87} *vt* : to reflect — **se refléter** *vr*
réflexe [refleks] *adj & nm* : reflex
réflexion [refleksjɔ̃] *nf* **1** : reflection (of light, waves, etc.) **2** : reflection, thought **3** : comment, remark
refluer [rəflye] *vi* **1** : to ebb, to flow back **2** : to surge back (of crowds, etc.)
reflux [rəfly] *nm* **1** : ebb, flowing back **2** : backward surge
refondre [rəfɔ̃dr] {63} *vt* **1** : to recast **2** : to rewrite, to rework (a text)
réformateur[1], **-trice** [reformatœr, -tris] *adj* : reforming
réformateur[2], **-trice** *n* : reformer
réforme [reform] *nf* **1** : reform **2 la Réforme** : the Reformation
reformer [rəforme] *vt* : re-form, to form again — **se reformer** *vr*
réformer [reforme] *vt* **1** AMÉLIORER : to reform, to improve <réformer les écoles : to reform the school system> **2** : to declare unfit for service, to discharge (a soldier) — **se réformer** *vr* : to reform, to turn over a new leaf
refoulement [rəfulmɑ̃] *nm* **1** : pushing back, holding back **2** : repression (in psychology)
refouler [rəfule] *vt* **1** : to drive back **2** : to hold back, to suppress **3** : to repress (in psychology)
réfractaire [refraktɛr] *adj* **1** : refractory **2** ~ **à** : resistant to
réfracter [refrakte] *vt* : to refract — **réfraction** [-fraksjɔ̃] *nf*
refrain [rəfrɛ̃] *nm* : refrain, chorus
refréner [rəfrene] *or* **réfréner** [refrene] {87} *vt* : to curb, to check
réfrigérant, -rante [refriʒerɑ̃, -rɑ̃t] *adj* : cooling, refrigerating
réfrigérateur [refriʒeratœr] *nm* : refrigerator
réfrigérer [refriʒere] {87} *vt* : to refrigerate — **réfrigération** [-ʒerasjɔ̃] *nf*
refroidir [rəfrwadir] *vt* **1** : to cool, to chill **2** : to cool down, to dampen — *vi* : to cool down, to get cold — **se refroidir** *vr*
refroidissement [rəfrwadismɑ̃] *nm* **1** : cooling **2** RHUME : cold, chill <prendre un refroidissement : to catch a cold>
refuge [rəfyʒ] *nm* : refuge, shelter, haven
réfugié, -giée [refyʒje] *n* : refugee
réfugier [rəfyʒje] {96} *v* **se réfugier** *vr* : to take refuge
refus [rəfy] *nm* : refusal
refuser [rəfyze] *vt* **1** : to refuse, to turn down **2** : to deny (access, etc.) **3** : to reject, to turn away — **se refuser** *vr* **1** : to deny oneself **2** ~ **à** : to refuse to
réfuter [refyte] *vt* : to refute — **réfutation** [-fytasjɔ̃] *nf*
regagner [rəgaɲe] *vt* **1** : to win back, to regain **2** : to return to
regain [rəgɛ̃] *nm* **1** : renewal, resurgence **2** : second crop (in agriculture)
régal [regal] *nm, pl* **régals** DÉLICE : delight, treat
régaler [regale] *vt* : to treat to a delicious meal — **se régaler** *vr* **1** : to eat something delicious **2** : to enjoy oneself thoroughly
regard [rəgar] *nm* **1** : look, glance, gaze **2** : look, expression **3 au regard de** : in regard to, concerning **4 en regard de** : in comparison with
regardant, -dante [rəgardɑ̃, -dɑ̃t] *adj* **1** : fussy, particular **2** AVARE : stingy
regarder [rəgarde] *vt* **1** : to look at, to watch **2** : to consider, to regard **3** : to concern, to involve <ça ne vous regarde pas : it's none of your business> — *vi* **1** : to look <regarder par la fenêtre : to look out the window> **2** ~ **à** : to think about, to take into account — **se regarder** *vr* : to look at oneself
régate [regat] *nf* : regatta
régénération [reʒenerasjɔ̃] *nf* : regeneration
régénérer [reʒenere] {87} *vt* : to regenerate — **se régénérer** *vr*
régent, -gente [reʒɑ̃, -ʒɑ̃t] *n* : regent
régenter [reʒɑ̃te] *vt* : to dictate, to rule over
régie [reʒi] *nf* **1** *France or* **régie d'État** : state-owned corporation **2** *Can* : provincially controlled public-service agency
régime [reʒim] *nm* **1** : regime, government **2** : scheme, system, regulations *pl* <régime pénitentiaire : prison system> **3** : diet, regimen <être au régime : to be on a diet> **4** : cluster, bunch <régime de bananes : bunch of bananas>
régiment [reʒimɑ̃] *nm* : regiment
région [reʒjɔ̃] *nf* : region, area
régional, -nale [reʒjɔnal] *adj, mpl* **-naux** [-no] : regional — **régionalement** [-nalmɑ̃] *adv*
régir [reʒir] *vt* : to control, to govern
régisseur [reʒisœr] *nm* **1** : steward, manager **2** : stage manager
registre [rəʒistr] *nm* **1** : register, record **2** : range (of a voice or instrument) **3** : damper (in a chimney)
réglable [reglabl] *adj* **1** : adjustable **2** : payable
réglage [reglaʒ] *nm* **1** : regulating, setting, tuning (of a motor) **2** : adjustment
règle [regl] *nf* **1** : ruler **2** : rule, regulation **3 règles** *nfpl* : menstrual period <avoir ses règles : to menstruate> **4 en** ~ : in order, valid **5 en règle générale** : generally, as a rule
réglé, -glée [regle] *adj* **1** ORGANISÉ : orderly, organized **2** : settled, decided

<tout est réglé : everything has been taken care of> **3** : ruled, lined

règlement [rɛgləmɑ̃] *nm* **1** : rules *pl*, regulations *pl* **2** : settlement, resolution **3** : payment

réglementaire [rɛgləmɑ̃tɛr] *adj* **1** : prescribed, regulation **2** : regulatory

réglementation [rɛgləmɑ̃tasjɔ̃] *nf* **1** : regulation, control **2** : rules *pl*

réglementer [rɛgləmɑ̃te] *vt* : to regulate, to control

régler [rɛgle] {87} *vt* **1** : to regulate, to adjust **2** : to resolve, to settle **3** : to rule (a page)

réglisse [rɛglis] *nf* : licorice

règne [rɛɲ] *nm* **1** : reign, rule **2** : kingdom <le règne animal : the animal kingdom>

régner [rɛɲe] {87} *vi* : to reign, to rule, to prevail

regorger [rəgɔrʒe] {17} *vi* ~ **de** : to overflow with, to abound with

régresser [rɛgrese] *vi* **1** : to diminish, to recede, to decline **2** : to regress

régressif, -sive [regresif, -siv] *adj* : regressive

régression [regresjɔ̃] *nf* **1** : decline **2** : regression

regret [rəgrɛ] *nm* : regret <avec regret : regretfully> — **regrettable** [-grɛtabl] *adj*

regretter [rəgrɛte] *vt* **1** : to regret, to be sorry about <je regrette de ne pas t'avoir écrit : I'm sorry I haven't written to you> **2** : to miss <nous la regrettons beaucoup : we miss her very much>

regroupement [rəgrupmɑ̃] *nm* **1** : grouping together **2** : merger **3** : rallying, rounding up

regrouper [rəgrupe] *vt* **1** : to group together, to pool **2** : to reassemble, to regroup

régulariser [regularize] *vt* **1** : to put in order, to sort out **2** : to regulate

régularité [regularite] *nf* : regularity

régulateur[1], **-trice** [regulatœr, -tris] *adj* : regulating

régulateur[2] *nm* : regulator, governor (of a machine)

régulation [regulasjɔ̃] *nf* : regulation

régulier, -lière [regulje, -ljɛr] *adj* **1** : regular, fixed, established <un programme régulier : a regular schedule> **2** : even, symmetrical <visage régulier : regular features> **3** : steady, consistent <à intervalles réguliers : with regularity, at regular intervals> **4** : legitimate, in order

régulièrement [reguljɛrmɑ̃] *adv* **1** : regularly **2** : evenly **3** : steadily

régurgiter [regyrʒite] *vt* : to regurgitate

réhabilitation [reabilitasjɔ̃] *nf* : rehabilitation

réhabiliter [reabilite] *vt* **1** : to rehabilitate **2** : to restore to favor **3** RÉNOVER : to renovate — **se réhabiliter** *vr* : to redeem oneself

réhabituer [reabitye] *vt* : to reaccustom — **se réhabituer** *vr* : to get reaccustomed to

rehausser [rəose] *vt* **1** SURÉLEVER : to heighten **2** : to set off, to enhance

réimpression [reɛ̃prɛsjɔ̃] *nf* **1** : reprinting **2** : reprint

réimprimer [reɛ̃prime] *vt* : to reprint

rein [rɛ̃] *nm* **1** : kidney **2 reins** *nmpl* : back <avoir mal aux reins : to have a backache>

réincarnation [reɛ̃karnasjɔ̃] *nf* : reincarnation

réincarner [reɛ̃karne] *vt* : to reincarnate

reine [rɛn] *nf* : queen

réinsérer [reɛ̃sere] {87} *vt* **1** : to reinsert **2** : to rehabilitate, to reintegrate (into society, etc.) — **réinsertion** [reɛ̃sɛrsjɔ̃] *nf*

réintégrer [reɛ̃tegre] {87} *vt* **1** : to return to (a place) **2** : to reinstate

réitérer [reitere] {87} *vt* : to reiterate, to repeat — **réitération** [-terasjɔ̃] *nf*

rejaillir [rəʒajir] *vi* **1** : to splash up **2** ~ **sur** : to reflect on, to fall upon (someone)

rejet [rəʒɛ] *nm* **1** : rejection **2** : discharge, disposal **3** : shoot (from a tree stump)

rejeter [rəʒte] {8} *vt* **1** RELANCER : to throw back **2** : to reject (in medicine), to throw up **3** : to discharge, to eject **4** REFUSER : to decline, to turn down **5 rejeter la faute** : to shift the blame

rejeton [rəʒtɔ̃] *nm* : offshoot (in botany)

rejoindre [rəʒwɛ̃dr] {50} *vt* **1** RENCONTRER : to meet, to join **2** RATTRAPER : to catch up with **3** REGAGNER : to return to, to get back to **4** : to agree with — **se rejoindre** *vr* **1** SE RENCONTRER : to meet **2** : to be in agreement

réjouir [reʒwir] *vt* : to gladden, to delight — **se réjouir** *vr* : to be delighted, to exult, to rejoice

réjouissance [reʒwisɑ̃s] *nf* **1** : rejoicing **2 réjouissances** *nfpl* : festivities, merrymaking

réjouissant, -sante [reʒwisɑ̃, -sɑ̃t] *adj* : cheering, delightful

relâche [rəlaʃ] *nf* **1** RÉPIT : break, respite **2** : closure <le lundi est notre jour de relâche : we're closed on Mondays>

relâché, -chée [rəlaʃe] *adj* : loose, lax

relâcher [rəlaʃe] *vt* **1** DESSERRER : to relax, to loosen up (restraints, muscles, etc.) **2** LIBÉRER : to release, to let go **3** : to relax, to slacken (efforts, discipline, etc.) — **se relâcher** *vr* **1** : to loosen, to go slack **2** : to become lax

relais [rəle] *nm* **1** : relay (in sports and telecommunications) <course de relais : relay race> <relais de télévision : television relay station> **2** : shift

<travailler par relais : to work shifts> **3 prendre le relais** : to take over

relance [rəlɑ̃s] *nf* : boost, revival, upsurge

relancer [rəlɑ̃se] {6} *vt* **1** REJETER : to throw back **2** : to restart (an engine) **3** : to revive, to boost

relater [rəlate] *vt* : to recount, to relate

relatif, -tive [rəlatif, -tiv] *adj* : relative — **relativement** [-tivmɑ̃] *adv*

relation [rəlasjɔ̃] *nf* **1** RAPPORT : relation, connection **2** : relationship <relations professionnelles : professional relationships> **3** CONNAISSANCE : acquaintance <avoir des relations : to have (personal) connections> **4 relations** *nfpl* : relations <relations extérieures : foreign relations> <relations sexuelles : sexual relations>

relativité [rəlativite] *nf* : relativity

relax, -laxe [rəlaks] *adj fam* : relaxed, easygoing

relaxation [rəlaksasjɔ̃] *nf* : relaxation

relaxer [rəlakse] *vt* **1** : to relax **2** : to release — **se relaxer** *vr*

relayer [rəleje] {11} *vt* **1** : to take over from, to relieve **2** : to relay (in telecommunications) — **se relayer** *vr* : to take turns

reléguer [rəlege] {87} *vt* : to relegate — **relégation** [-legasjɔ̃] *nf*

relent [rəlɑ̃] *nm* **1** : foul smell, stench **2** TRACE : hint, trace

relève [rəlɛv] *nf* **1** : relief, replacement **2 prendre la relève** : to take over

relevé[1], **-vée** [rəlɛve] *adj* **1** RETROUSSÉ : turned up, rolled up **2** : elevated, refined **3** : spicy, pungent

relevé[2] *nm* **1** : statement <relevé de compte : bank statement> **2** : reading (of electricity, gas, etc.)

relèvement [rəlɛvmɑ̃] *nm* **1** : rise, increase **2** : rebuilding, recovery (of the economy, etc.)

relever [rəlve] {52} *vt* **1** : to stand up again, to raise (up) **2** : to turn up, to roll up **3** AUGMENTER : to raise, to increase **4** : to rebuild **5** RAMASSER : to collect, to pick up **6** ASSAISONNER : to season, to spice up **7** : to relieve, to take over from **8** NOTER : to take notice of **9** : to enhance, to elevate — *vi* **1 ~ de** : to be a matter for, to concern **2 ~ de** : to recover from (an illness) — **se relever** *vr* **1** : to get up again **2 ~ de** : to get over (an illness)

relief [rəljef] *nm* **1** : relief (in art, geography, etc.) **2 mettre en relief** : to accentuate, to highlight

relier [rəlje] {96} *vt* **1** : to link, to join **2** : to bind (a book)

relieur, -lieuse [rəljœr, -ljøz] *n* : binder, bookbinder

religieusement [rəliʒjøzmɑ̃] *adv* : religiously, faithfully

religieux[1], **-gieuse** [rəliʒjø, -ʒjøz] *adj* **1** : religious **2** : reverent, conscientious

religieux[2], **-gieuse** *n* : monk *m*, friar *m*, nun *f*

religion [rəliʒjɔ̃] *nf* : religion

reliquat [rəlika] *nm* : remainder, balance

relique [rəlik] *nf* : relic

relire [rəlir] {51} *vt* : to reread

relish [rəliʃ] *nf Can* : relish (condiment)

reliure [rəljyr] *nf* : binding

reluire [rəlɥir] {49} *vi* BRILLER : to glisten, to gleam, to shine

reluisant, -sante [rəlɥizɑ̃, -zɑ̃t] *adj* **1** : gleaming **2 peu reluisant** : unpromising, far from brilliant

reluquer [rəlyke] *vt fam* : to ogle, to eye

remâcher [rəmaʃe] *vt* : to stew over, to brood about

remaniement [rəmanimɑ̃] *nm* : revision, modification

remanier [rəmanje] {96} *vt* : to revise, to redraft, to modify

remarier [rəmarje]{96} *v* **se remarier** *vr* : to remarry

remarquable [rəmarkabl] *adj* : remarkable — **remarquablement** [-kabləmɑ̃] *adv*

remarque [rəmark] *nf* : remark, comment

remarquer [rəmarke] *vt* **1** : to remark, to observe <faire remarquer : to point out> **2** : to notice **3 se faire remarquer** : to attract attention, to come to the fore

remballer [rɑ̃bale] *vt* : to repack, to pack up (again)

rembarrer [rɑ̃bare] *vt fam* : to rebuff, to put someone in his or her place

remblai [rɑ̃ble] *nm* : embankment

remblayer [rɑ̃bleje] {11} *vt* : to fill in, to bank up

rembobiner [rɑ̃bɔbine] *vt* : to rewind

rembourrage [rɑ̃buraʒ] *nm* : stuffing, padding

rembourrer [rɑ̃bure] *vt* : to stuff, to pad

remboursable [rɑ̃bursabl] *adj* : refundable

remboursement [rɑ̃bursəmɑ̃] *nm* : repayment, reimbursement

rembourser [rɑ̃burse] *vt* **1** : to repay **2** : to refund, to reimburse

rembrunir [rɑ̃brynir] *v* **se rembrunir** *vr* : to cloud over, to become gloomy

remède [rəmɛd] *nm* : remedy, cure

remédier [rəmedje] {96} *vi* **~ à** : to remedy, to cure, to put right

remémorer [rəmemɔre] *v* **se remémorer** *vr* SE RAPPELER : to remember, to recall

remerciement [rəmɛrsimɑ̃] *nm* **1** : thanking <lettre de remerciement : thank-you letter> **2 remerciements** *nmpl* : thanks

remercier [rəmɛrsje] {96} *vt* **1** : to thank **2** CONGÉDIER : to dismiss, to fire

remettre [rəmɛtr] {53} *vt* **1** REPLACER : to put back **2** : to put back on, to switch back on, to restart **3** RA-

JOUTER : to add, to put more in **4** REMPLACER : to replace (a button, etc.) **5** DONNER : to deliver, to hand over **6** REPORTER : to postpone, to put off **7** RECONNAÎTRE : to recognize, to place **8 : remettre à neuf** : to restore, to refurbish **— se remettre** *vr* **1** : to return, to get back **2** : to put on again **3** : to recover, to get better **4 ~ à** : to begin again <elle s'est remise à parler : she started to talk again> **5 ~ à** : to rely on **6 s'en remettre à** : to leave it up to, to defer to

réminiscence [reminisɑ̃s] *nf* : reminiscence

remise [rəmiz] *nf* **1** : putting off, postponement **2** LIVRAISON : handing over, delivery <remise des diplômes : commencement, graduation> **3** : remission (of a debt, etc.) **4** RABAIS : discount **5** : shed

remiser [rəmize] *vt* : to put away, to store

rémission [remisjɔ̃] *nf* : remission

remodeler [rəmɔdle] {20} *vt* **1** : to remodel **2** : to reorganize, to restructure

remontant [rəmɔ̃tɑ̃] *nm* TONIQUE : tonic

remontée [rəmɔ̃te] *nf* **1** : climb, ascent **2 remontée mécanique** : ski lift

remonte–pente [rəmɔ̃tpɑt] *nm, pl* **remonte–pentes** : ski lift

remonter [rəmɔ̃te] *vt* **1** : to take back up, to bring back up, to raise up (again) **2** : to go back up **3** : to cheer up, to invigorate — *vi* **1** : to rise (again) **2 ~ à** : to date back to **3 remonter dans le temps** : to go back in time

remontrance [rəmɔ̃trɑ̃s] *nf* REPROCHE : reproach, reprimand

remords [rəmɔr] *nm* : remorse

remorquage [rəmɔrkaʒ] *nm* : towing, tow

remorque [rəmɔrk] *nf* **1** : trailer **2 être en remorque** : to be in tow

remorquer [rəmɔrke] *vt* : to tow

remorqueur [rəmɔrkœr] *nm* : tugboat

remorqueuse [rəmɔrkøz] *nf Can* : tow truck

remous [rəmu] *nm* **1** : eddy **2** : backwash

rempart [rɑ̃par] *nm* : rampart

rempirer [rɑ̃pire] *vi Can fam* : to worsen, to become worse

remplaçable [rɑ̃plasabl] *adj* : replaceable

remplaçant, -çante [rɑ̃plasɑ̃, -sɑ̃t] *n* SUPPLÉANT : substitute, stand-in, alternate

remplacement [rɑ̃plasmɑ̃] *nm* : replacement

remplacer [rɑ̃plase] {6} *vt* **1** : to replace **2** : to substitute for, to stand in for

remplir [rɑ̃plir] *vt* **1** : to fill (up) **2** : to fill out (a form, etc.) **3** : to carry out, to fulfill

remplissage [rɑ̃plisaʒ] *nm* : filling, filler

remporter [rɑ̃pɔrte] *vt* **1** REPRENDRE : to take back, to take away (again) **2** : to win, to achieve

remuant, -ante [rəmɥɑ̃, -ɑ̃t] *adj* : restless, fidgety

remue–ménage [rəmymenaʒ] *nms & pl* : commotion, upheaval

remue–méninges [rəmymenɛ̃ʒ] *nms & pl* : brainstorming

remuer [rəmɥe] *vt* **1** : to move <remuer les lèvres : to move one's lips> <remuer la queue : to wag its tail> **2** : to stir, to mix **3** ÉMOUVOIR : to stir, to touch, to move — *vi* **1** : to move **2** : to fidget, to squirm **— se remuer** *vr* **1** : to move (about) **2** *fam* : to get a move on

rémunérateur, -trice [remyneratœr, -tris] *adj* LUCRATIF : lucrative

rémunération [remynerasjɔ̃] *nf* : remuneration

rémunérer [remynere] {87} *vt* : to remunerate

renâcler [rənakle] *vi* **1** : to snort (of an animal) **2 ~ à** : to be reluctant to, to grumble about

renaissance [rənɛsɑ̃s] *nf* **1** : rebirth, revival **2 la Renaissance** : the Renaissance

renaître [rənɛtr] {57} *vi* **1** : to be reborn, to come back to life **2** : to revive, to return

rénal, -nale [renal] *adj, mpl* **rénaux** [reno] : renal

renard [rənar] *nm* : fox

renarde [rənard] *nf* : vixen

renchérir [rɑ̃ʃerir] *vi* **1** : to become more expensive **2 ~ sur** : to go (one step) further than

renchérissement [rɑ̃ʃerismɑ̃] *nm* : rise, increase (in price)

rencontre [rɑ̃kɔ̃tr] *nf* **1** : meeting <rencontre au sommet : summit meeting> **2** : encounter **3** : junction, intersection **4** : (military) engagement **5** : match, game, meet (in sports)

rencontrer [rɑ̃kɔ̃tre] *vt* **1** : to meet **2** : to come across, to encounter **3** : to join, to intersect **4** HEURTER : to strike **5** : to oppose, to play against (in sports) **— se rencontrer** *vr* **1** : to meet, to come together **2** : to be found

rendement [rɑ̃dmɑ̃] *nm* **1** : output, production **2** : yield, return

rendez–vous [rɑ̃devu] *nms & pl* **1** : appointment, meeting **2** : meeting place, rendezvous

rendre [rɑ̃dr] {63} *vt* **1** : to give back, to return **2** : to give, to render <rendre grâce : to give thanks> <rendre service : to render aid> **3** : to yield **4** : to pronounce (a verdict or decree) **5** : to express, to convey **6 rendre les larmes** : to give up **7 rendre la monnaie** : to make change **— se rendre** *vr* **1** : to surrender, to give in **2 ~ à**

: to go to, to travel to 3 **se rendre compte de** : to realize, to be aware of
rêne [rɛn] *nf* : rein
renégat, -gate [rənega, -gat] *n* : renegade, turncoat
renégocier [rənegɔsje] {96} *vt* : to renegotiate
renfermé[1], **-mée** [rɑ̃ferme] *adj* : withdrawn
renfermé[2] *nm* : mustiness <sentir le renfermé : to smell musty>
renfermer [rɑ̃ferme] *vt* **1** : to contain, to hold **2** : to hold in, to hide — **se renfermer** *vr* : to withdraw (into oneself)
renflé, -flée [rɑ̃fle] *adj* : bulging, bulbous
renflement [rɑ̃fləmɑ̃] *nm* : bulge
renflouer [rɑ̃flue] *vt* **1** : to refloat **2** : to bail out (a person, business, etc.)
renfoncement [rɑ̃fɔ̃smɑ̃] *nm* : recess
renfoncer [rɑ̃fɔ̃se] {6} *vt* : to push further in
renforcement [rɑ̃fɔrsəmɑ̃] *nm* : reinforcement
renforcer [rɑ̃fɔrse] {6} *vt* : to reinforce, to strengthen — **se renforcer** *vr* : to increase, to become stronger
renfort [rɑ̃fɔr] *nm* **1** : reinforcement **2 à grand renfort de** : with a great deal of
renfrogné, -gnée [rɑ̃frɔɲe] *adj* : sullen, scowling
renfrogner [rɑ̃frɔɲe] *v* **se renfrogner** *vr* : to scowl
rengager [rɑ̃gaʒe] {17} *vt* : to rehire, to take on again — **se rengager** *vr* : to reenlist
rengaine [rɑ̃gɛn] *nf* : cliché, old story <c'est toujours la même rengaine : it's always the same old story>
rengainer [rɑ̃gene] *vt* : to sheathe, to put back in its holster
reniement [rənimɑ̃] *nm* : denial, disavowal
renier [rənje] {96} *vt* **1** : to deny, to disavow **2** : to renounce, to repudiate
reniflement [rənifləmɑ̃] *nm* : sniffing, sniffling, snorting
renifler [rənifle] *v* : to sniff, to sniffle, to snort
renne [rɛn] *nm* : reindeer
renom [rənɔ̃] *nm* **1** : renown, fame **2** : reputation
renommé, -mée [rənɔme] *adj* : famous, renowned
renommée *nf* : fame, renown
renoncement [rənɔ̃smɑ̃] *nm* : renouncing, renunciation
renoncer [rənɔ̃se] {6} *vi* ~ **à** : to renounce, to give up
renonciation [rənɔ̃sjasjɔ̃] *nf* : renunciation
renouer [rənwe] *vt* **1** : to retie **2** : to renew, to revive — **se renouer** *vr* : to get together again
renouveau [rənuvo] *nm, pl* **-veaux** : revival
renouvelable [rənuvlabl] *adj* : renewable
renouveler [rənuvle] {8} *vt* **1** : to renew, to revive **2** : to repeat — **se renouveler** *vr* : to recur, to be repeated
renouvellement [rənuvelmɑ̃] *nm* **1** : renewal **2** : recurrence, repetition
rénovation [renɔvasjɔ̃] *nf* : renovation
rénover [renɔve] *vt* **1** : to renovate, to restore **2** : to reform
renseignement [rɑ̃sɛɲəmɑ̃] *nm* **1** : information <bureau des renseignements : information center> **2** : intelligence <agent de renseignements : intelligence agent>
renseigner [rɑ̃seɲe] *vt* : to inform <mal renseigner : to misinform> <bien renseigné : well-informed> — **se renseigner** *vr* **1** : to ask, to make inquiries <renseignez-vous auprès de la réceptionniste : please ask the receptionist> **2** ~ **sur** : to inquire about
rentable [rɑ̃tabl] *adj* : profitable — **rentabilité** [-tabilite] *nf*
rente [rɑ̃t] *nf* **1** : annuity **2** : (private) income
rentrée [rɑ̃tre] *nf* **1** : start, beginning <la rentrée des classes : the start of the new school year> **2** : return **3** : comeback (in entertainment, politics, etc.) **4** : income, revenue
rentrer [rɑ̃tre] *vi* **1** : to go in, to get in **2** : to go back in **3** : to return <rentrer chez soi : to return home> **4** : to start (up) again, to reopen **5** : to come in <faire rentrer l'argent : to bring in money> **6** : to fit <rentrer dans la serrure : to fit into the lock> **7** ~ **dans** : to be a part of, to be included in — *vt* **1** : to bring in, to take in **2** : to put in **3** : to hold back, to suppress
renversant, -sante [rɑ̃versɑ̃, -sɑ̃t] *adj* AHURISSANT : astounding, amazing
renverse [rɑ̃vɛrs] *nf* **tomber à la renverse** : to fall over backward
renversement [rɑ̃vɛrsəmɑ̃] *nm* **1** INVERSION : reversal, inversion **2** : shift, change (of direction) **3** : overthrow **4** : spilling, spillage
renverser [rɑ̃verse] *vt* **1** : to knock down, to overturn **2** : to spill **3** : to turn over, to invert **4** : to reverse (sides, roles, etc.) **5** : to tilt (back) **6** : to overthrow **7** : to astound, to astonish — **se renverser** *vr* **1** : to fall over **2** : to bend over backwards
renvoi [rɑ̃vwa] *nm* **1** : return, sending back **2** : dismissal, discharge **3** : cross-reference **4** : postponement **5** : burp, belch <avoir des renvois : to burp>
renvoie [rɑ̃vwa], *etc.* → **renvoyer**
renvoyer [rɑ̃vwaje] {36} *vt* **1** : to send back, to throw back **2** CONGÉDIER : to dismiss, to expel **3** REMETTRE : to put back, to postpone **4** ~ **à** : to refer to, to relate back to **5** *Can fam* : to throw up

réorganiser [reɔrganize] *vt* : to reorganize — **réorganisation** [-nizasjɔ̃] *nf*
repaire [rəpɛr] *nm* : den, lair
répandre [repɑ̃dr] {63} *vt* **1** : to spread, to scatter, to spill **2** : to shed (blood, tears) **3** : to spread, to propagate (rumors, terror, etc.) **4** : to give off, to emit — **se répandre** *vr*
répandu, -due [repɑ̃dy] *adj* : widespread
réparable [reparabl] *adj* : reparable
reparaître [rəparetr] → **réapparaître**
réparation [reparasjɔ̃] *nf* **1** : repair, repairing **2** : **réparations** *nfpl* : reparations, damages
réparer [repare] *vt* **1** : to repair, to fix, to mend **2** : to make up for **3** : to restore (health, strength, etc.)
repartie [rəparti] *nf* : repartee, rejoinder
repartir [rəpartir] {82} *vt* : to retort — *vi* **1** : to leave again **2** : to start again <repartir à zero : to rebound>
répartir [repartir] *vt* **1** : to divide up, to distribute **2** : to spread (out) — **se répartir** *vr* : to divide, to split
répartition [repartisjɔ̃] *nf* : distribution, dividing up
repas [rəpa] *nm* **1** : meal **2 l'heure du repas** : mealtime
repassage [rəpasaʒ] *nm* : ironing
repasser [rəpase] *vt* **1** : to pass again, to take again, to show again **2** : to iron, to press **3** : to go (back) over <repasser ses leçons : to go over one's lessons> **4** : to hand over — *vi* : to pass by again, to come again
repentant, -tante [rəpɑ̃tɑ̃, -tɑ̃t] *adj* : repentant, penitent
repentir[1] [rəpɑ̃tir] {82} *v* **se repentir** *vr* **1** : to repent **2** : to regret
repentir[2] *nm* : repentance
répercussion [reperkysjɔ̃] *nf* : repercussion
répercuter [reperkyte] *vt* **1** : to reverberate, to echo **2** TRANSMETTRE : to reflect, to pass on — **se répercuter** *vr* **1** : to echo **2** ~ **sur** : to affect, to have an effect on
repère [rəpɛr] *nm* **1** : line, mark **2** : point of reference, landmark (in space or time)
repérer [rəpere] {87} *vt* **1** : to mark **2** : to locate, to pinpoint **3** : to spot, to catch sight of — **se repérer** *vr fam* : to get one's bearings, to find one's way
répertoire [repertwar] *nm* **1** : list, index **2** : notebook, directory <répertoire d'adresses : address book> **3** : repertory, repertoire
répertorier [repertɔrje] {96} *vt* : to index, to list
répéter [repete] {87} *vt* **1** : to repeat **2** : to tell, to relate **3** : to go over, to rehearse — **se répéter** *vr* **1** : to repeat oneself **2** : to recur
répétitif, -tive [repetitif, -tiv] *adj* : repetitive
répétition [repetisjɔ̃] *nf* **1** : repetition **2** : rehearsal
répit [repi] *nm* : respite, break
replacer [rəplase] {6} *vt* **1** : to replace, to put back **2** : to reassign (to a new job) — **se replacer** *vr* : to find a new job
replanter [rəplɑ̃te] *vt* **1** : to transplant **2** : to replant
replâtrer [rəplatre] *vt* **1** : to replaster **2** *fam* : to patch up, to paper over
replet, -plète [rəplɛ, -plɛt] *adj* GRASSOUILLET : plump, chubby
repli [rəpli] *nm* **1** : fold, crease **2** : withdrawal (of troops, etc.) **3 replis** *nmpl* : inner recesses <les replis de l'âme : the depths of the soul>
replier [rəplije] {96} *vt* **1** : to fold up, to fold over **2** : to withdraw, to pull back — **se replier** *vr* **1** : to fold up **2** : to withdraw **3 se replier sur soi-même** : to withdraw into oneself
réplique [replik] *nf* **1** RIPOSTE : retort, reply **2** : line (in a play) **3** : replica
répliquer [replike] *vt* RÉPONDRE : to reply, to retort — *vi* **1** : to respond, to answer back <répliquer à la critique : to respond to criticism> **2** : to retaliate
répondant, -dante [repɔ̃dɑ̃, -dɑ̃t] *n* : guarantor
répondeur [repɔ̃dœr] *nm* : answering machine
répondre [repɔ̃dr] {63} *vt* : to answer, to reply — *vi* **1** : to answer, to reply, to respond **2** : to meet, to fulfill <répondre aux critères : to meet the criteria> **3** RÉPLIQUER : to answer back **4** ~ **de** : to answer for, to vouch for
réponse [repɔ̃s] *nf* : answer, reply
report [rəpɔr] *nm* RENVOI : postponement
reportage [rəpɔrtaʒ] *nm* **1** : report **2** : reporting
reporter[1] [rəpɔrte] *vt* **1** : to take back **2** REMETTRE : to postpone, to put off **3** : to carry forward (a calculation, etc.), to transfer, to copy out **4** : to transfer, to shift <reporter ses affections : to shift one's affections>
reporter[2] [rəpɔrtɛr] *nm* : reporter
repos [rəpo] *nm* **1** : rest <jour de repos : day of rest> **2** TRANQUILLITÉ : peace, tranquillity <avoir l'esprit en repos : to put one's mind at rest> **3 à repos!** : at ease! **4 de tout repos** : safe, secure
reposant, -sante [rəpozɑ̃, -zɑ̃t] *nm* : restful, relaxing
reposé, -sée [rəpoze] *adj* : rested, refreshed
repose-pied [rəpozpje] *nm, pl* **repose-pieds** : footrest
reposer [rəpoze] *vt* **1** : to put (back) down, to put down again **2** : to ask

again **3** : to rest (one's body or mind) — *vi* **1** : to rest, to lie **2** : to sleep, to be at rest <qu'il repose en paix : may he rest in peace> **3** ~ **sur** : to be based on, to rest upon — **se reposer** *vr* **1** : to rest **2** ~ **sur** : to rely on

repoussant, -sante [rəpusã, -sãt] *adj* DÉGOÛTANT : repulsive

repousser [rəpuse] *vi* : to grow back — *vt* **1** : to push back **2** : to disgust, to repel **3** REJETER : to refuse, to turn down **4** REPORTER : to put off, to postpone

repoussoir [rəpuswar] *nm* : foil, complement <servir de repoussoir : to act as a foil>

répréhensible [repreẽsibl] *adj* : reprehensible

reprendre [rəprãdr] {70} *vt* **1** : to take (up) again **2** : to take back, to regain, to recapture **3** : to take over (a business, etc.) **4** : to take back (merchandise) <ça ne peut être ni repris ni échangé : it can't be returned or exchanged> **5** : to begin again, to continue <reprendre la parole : to resume speaking> **6** : to repair, to touch up, to correct — *vi* **1** : to pick up, to improve **2** RECOMMENCER : to start again — **se reprendre** *vr* **1** : to correct oneself **2** : to pull oneself together

représailles [rəprezaj] *nfpl* : reprisals, retaliation

représentant, -tante [rəprezãtã, -tãt] *n* **1** : representative **2** : salesman <représentant de commerce : traveling salesman>

représentatif, -tive [rəprezãtatif, -tiv] *adj* : representative

représentation [rəprezãtasjõ] *nf* **1** : representation **2** : performance (in theater)

représenter [rəprezãte] *vt* **1** : to represent, to act for **2** JOUER : to perform **3** : to depict, to show **4** : to symbolize, to stand for **5** : to signify, to mean — **se représenter** *vr* **1** : to imagine, to picture **2** : to come up again

répressif, -sive [represif, -siv] *adj* : repressive

répression [represjõ] *nf* : repression, suppression

réprimande [reprimãd] *nf* : reprimand

réprimander [reprimãde] *vt* : to reprimand, to scold

réprimé, -mée [reprime] *adj* : suppressed, held in

réprimer [reprime] *vt* : to repress, to suppress

reprise [rəpriz] *nf* **1** : recapture **2** : resumption **3** : rerun, repeat, revival (in movies, television, etc.) **4** : recovery <reprise économique : economic recovery> **5** : trade-in (of goods) **6** : round (in sports) **7** : acceleration (of an automobile) **8** : mend, darn (in sewing) **9 à maintes reprises** : on numerous occasions, repeatedly

repriser [rəprize] *vt* : to darn, to mend

réprobateur, -trice [reprɔbatœr, -tris] *adj* : reproving, reproachful

réprobation [reprɔbasjõ] *nf* : disapproval

reproche [rəprɔʃ] *nm* : reproach <faire des reproches à : to reproach, to blame> <sans reproche : beyond reproach>

reprocher [rəprɔʃe] *vt* ~ **à** : to reproach, to rebuke

reproducteur, -trice [rəprɔdyktœr, -tris] *adj* : reproductive

reproduction [rəprɔdyksjõ] *nf* : reproduction

reproduire [rəprɔduir] {49} *vt* **1** : to reproduce **2** : to make a copy of **3** : to breed — **se reproduire** *vr* **1** : to reproduce, to breed **2** SE RÉPÉTER : to recur

réprouver [repruve] *vt* : to reprove, to condemn

reptile [reptil] *nm* : reptile

reptilien, -lienne [reptiljẽ, -ljen] *adj* : reptilian

repu, -pue [rəpy] *adj* : satiated, full

républicain, -caine [repyblikẽ, -kɛn] *adj & n* : republican

république [repyblik] *nf* : republic

répudier [repydje] {96} *vt* : to repudiate — **répudiation** [repydjasjõ] *nf*

répugnance [repyɲãs] *nf* **1** : repugnance, aversion **2** : reluctance

répugnant, -nante [repyɲã, -ɲãt] *adj* : repugnant, disgusting

répugner [repyɲe] *vt* : to disgust, to be repugnant to — *vi* ~ **à** : to be averse to <je ne répugne pas au travail : I'm not averse to work>

répulsion [repylsjõ] *nf* : repulsion, repugnance

réputation [repytasjõ] *nf* : reputation

réputé, -tée [repyte] *adj* : renowned, famous

requérir [rəkerir] {21} *vt* **1** NÉCESSITER : to call for, to require **2** : to request, to summon

requête [rəkɛt] *nf* **1** : request **2** : petition (in law)

requiem [rekɥijɛm] *nms & pl* : requiem

requière [rəkjɛr], **requiert** [rəkjɛr], *etc.* → **requérir**

requin [rəkẽ] *nm* : shark

requinquer [rəkẽke] *vt fam* : to pep up

requis[1] [rəki] *pp* → **requérir**

requis[2], **-quise** [rəki, -kiz] *adj* : requisite, required

réquisition [rekizisjõ] *nf* : requisition

réquisitionner [rekizisjɔne] *vt* : to requisition

réquisitoire [rekizitwar] *nm* : indictment <un réquisitoire contre les moeurs contemporaines : an indictment against contemporary mores>

rescapé, -pée [rɛskape] *n* : survivor

rescousse [rɛskus] *nf* : rescue, aid <aller à la rescousse : to go to the rescue>
réseau [rezo] *nm, pl* **réseaux** : network
réservation [rezɛrvasjɔ̃] *nf* : reservation
réserve [rezɛrv] *nf* **1** : reserve, stock **2** RETENUE : reserve, restraint **3** : reservation <réserve indienne : Indian reservation> **4** : preserve, sanctuary **5** : storeroom **6** : reservation, hesitation <sous réserve de : subject to>
réservé, -vée [rezɛrve] *adj* **1** : private, reserved **2** : reserved, reticent
réserver [rezɛrve] *vt* **1** : to reserve, to book **2** : to reserve, to set aside — **se réserver** *vr* **1** : to save oneself **2** : to set aside for oneself
réservoir [rezɛrvwar] *nm* **1** : tank, cistern **2** : reservoir **3** : bulb (of a thermometer)
résidence [rezidɑ̃s] *nf* **1** : residence **2** **résidence universitaire** : dormitory
résident, -dente [rezidɑ̃, -dɑ̃t] *adj & n* : resident
résidentiel, -tielle [rezidɑ̃sjɛl] *adj* : residential
résider [rezide] *vi* **1** : to reside, to dwell **2** ~ **en** : to lie in, to consist of
résidu [rezidy] *nm* **1** : residue **2** RESTE : remainder **3** **résidus** *nmpl* : waste <résidus industriels : industrial waste>
résiduel, -duelle [reziduɛl] *adj* : residual
résignation [reziɲasjɔ̃] *nf* : resignation
résigner [reziɲe] *vt* : to relinquish, to resign — **se résigner** *vr* ~ **à** : to resign oneself to
résilier [rezilje] {96} *vt* : to terminate (a contract, etc.)
résille [rezij] *nf* : hair net
résine [rezin] *nf* : resin
résineux[1], **-neuse** [rezinø, -nøz] *adj* : resinous
résineux[2] *nmpl* : coniferous trees
résistance [rezistɑ̃s] *nf* **1** : resistance, opposition **2** : strength, endurance
résistant, -tante [rezistɑ̃, -tɑ̃t] *adj* **1** : resistant **2** : tough, hardy, durable
résister [reziste] *vi* **1** ~ **à** : to resist, to oppose **2** ~ **à** : to stand up to, to withstand **3** ~ **à** : to bear, to tolerate
résolu[1] [rezɔly] *pp* → **résoudre**
résolu[2], **-lue** [rezɔly] *adj* : resolute, determined
résolument [rezɔlymɑ̃] *adj* : resolutely, firmly, adamantly
résolution [rezɔlysjɔ̃] *nf* **1** : resolution, decision **2** : determination, resolve **3** : solution
résonance [rezɔnɑ̃s] *nf* **1** : resonance **2** : echo, overtone
résonnant, -nante [rezɔnɑ̃, -nɑ̃t] *adj* : resonant
résonner [rezɔne] *vi* : to resound, to ring out
résorber [rezɔrbe] *vt* : to absorb, to reduce — **se résorber** *vr*
résoudre [rezudr] {74} *vt* : to solve, to resolve — **se résoudre** *vr* **1** ~ **à** : to decide to **2** ~ **à** : to reconcile oneself to
respect [rɛspɛ] *nm* **1** : respect, consideration **2** **respects** *nmpl* : respects, regards
respectabilité [rɛspɛktabilite] *nf* : respectability
respectable [rɛspɛktabl] *adj* : respectable
respecter [rɛspɛkte] *vt* **1** : to respect **2** **faire respecter** : to enforce
respectif, -tive [rɛspɛktif, -tiv] *adj* : respective — **respectivement** [-tivmɑ̃] *adv*
respectueux, -euse [rɛspɛktɥø, -øz] *adj* : respectful — **respectueusement** [-tɥøzmɑ̃] *adv*
respirateur [rɛspiratœr] *nm* : respirator
respiration [rɛspirasjɔ̃] *nf* : breathing, respiration
respiratoire [rɛspiratwar] *adj* : respiratory
respirer [rɛspire] *vi* : to breathe — *vt* **1** : to breathe in, to inhale **2** : to exude
resplendir [rɛsplɑ̃dir] *vi* **1** : to shine **2** ~ **de** : to be radiant with (joy, etc.)
resplendissant, -sante [rɛsplɑ̃disɑ̃, -sɑ̃t] *adj* : radiant, resplendent
responsabilité [rɛspɔ̃sabilite] *nf* **1** : responsibility **2** : liability
responsable [rɛspɔ̃sabl] *adj* : responsible, answerable
resquiller [rɛskije] *vi fam* **1** : to sneak in without paying **2** : to cut in line
ressac [rəsak] *nm* : undertow, backwash
ressaisir [rəsezir] *v* **se ressaisir** *vr* : to pull oneself together, to rally
ressasser [rəsase] *vt* **1** RABÂCHER : to keep repeating **2** RUMINER : to brood over, to dwell on
ressemblance [rəsɑ̃blɑ̃s] *nf* **1** : resemblance, likeness <avoir une ressemblance avec qqn : to resemble s.o.> **2** : similarity
ressemblant, -blante [rəsɑ̃blɑ̃, -blɑ̃t] *adj* : lifelike
ressembler [rəsɑ̃ble] *vi* ~ **à** : to look like, to resemble — **se ressembler** *vr* **1** : to look alike **2** : to be alike
ressentiment [rəsɑ̃timɑ̃] *nm* : resentment
ressentir [rəsɑ̃tir] {82} *vt* : to feel — **se ressentir** *vr* ~ **de** : to feel the effects of
resserre [rəsɛr] *nf* REMISE : shed
resserrement [rəsɛrmɑ̃] *nm* **1** : tightening (up) **2** : narrowing, narrow part
resserrer [rəsɛre] *vt* **1** : to tighten **2** : to close up, to constrict — **se resserrer** *vr*
ressort [rəsɔr] *nm* **1** : spring (of a watch, mattress, etc.) **2** : impulse, drive, mo-

tivation **3** : recourse, appeal <en dernier ressort : as a last resort>
ressortir [rəsɔrtir] {82} *vt* **1** : to take out again, to bring out again **2** : to release again, to rerun — *vi* **1** : to go out again **2** : to stand out — *v impers* : to emerge, to be evident <il en ressort des faits intéressants : interesting facts are coming to light>
ressortissant, -sante [rəsɔrtisɑ̃, -sɑ̃t] *n* : national <ressortissants étrangers : foreign nationals>
ressource [rəsurs] *nf* **1** : recourse, option **2** : resourcefulness <avoir de la ressource : to be resourceful> **3 ressources** *nfpl* : resources, funds, reserves <ressources énergétiques : energy reserves> **4 ressources** *nfpl* : resources, possibilities <ressources de l'imaginaire : powers of the imagination>
ressusciter [resysite] *vt* **1** : to resuscitate, to bring back to life **2** : to revive, to rekindle — *vi* : to revive, to come back to life
restant[1], **-tante** [rɛstɑ̃, -tɑ̃t] *adj* : remaining
restant[2] *nm* : remainder, rest
restaurant [rɛstɔrɑ̃] *nm* : restaurant
restaurateur, -trice [rɛstɔrɑtœr, -tris] *n* **1** : restaurant owner **2** : restorer (of artwork, etc.)
restauration [rɛstɔrasjɔ̃] *nf* **1** : restoration **2** : catering, food service <la restauration rapide : the fast-food industry>
restaurer [rɛstɔre] *vt* : to restore — **se restaurer** *vr* : to have something to eat
reste [rɛst] *nm* **1** : remainder, rest **2 au ~** *or* **du ~** : besides, moreover **3 restes** *nmpl* : leftovers, leavings **4 restes** *nmpl* : (last) remains
rester [rɛste] *vi* **1** DEMEURER : to stay, to remain <rester éveillé : to stay awake> <il ne peut pas rester en place : he can't sit still> **2** : to be left, to remain <il ne nous reste plus d'argent : we have no money left> **3** DURER : to last, to live on — *v impers* : to remain <il reste à savoir : it remains to be seen>
restituer [rɛstitɥe] *vt* **1** : to restore, to return **2** : to reconstruct **3** : to reproduce (sound, etc.) **4** *Can fam* : to throw up
restitution [rɛstitysjɔ̃] *nf* **1** : restitution, restoration **2** : reproduction
restreindre [rɛstrɛ̃dr] {37} *vt* : to restrict, to limit, to constrain — **se restreindre** *vr* **1** : to cut back **2** : to narrow, to become more limited
restreint, -treinte [rɛstrɛ̃, -trɛt] *adj* : restricted, limited
restrictif, -tive [rɛstriktif, -tiv] *adj* : restrictive
restriction [rɛstriksjɔ̃] *nf* : restriction, limitation
restructuration [rəstryktyrasjɔ̃] *nf* : restructuring
restructurer [rəstryktyre] *vt* : to restructure
résultant, -tante [rezyltɑ̃, -tɑ̃t] *adj* : resultant
résultat [rezylta] *nm* **1** : result, outcome **2 résultats** *nmpl* : results (of an election, etc.), grades (of an exam) **3 résultats** *nmpl* : findings, results
résulter [rezylte] {75} *vi* **~ de** : to result from — *v impers* : to follow
résumé [rezyme] *nm* **1** : summary **2 en ~** : in short
résumer [rezyme] *vt* : to summarize, to sum up — **se résumer** *vr* **1** : to sum up **2 ~ à** : to come down to
résurgence [rezyrʒɑ̃s] *nf* : resurgence
résurrection [rezyrɛksjɔ̃] *nf* **1** : resurrection **2** : revival, rebirth
rétablir [retablir] *vt* **1** : to reestablish, to restore **2** : to reinstate (in a job, etc.) — **se rétablir** *vr* **1** : to get better, to recover **2** : to be restored, to return
rétablissement [retablismɑ̃] *nm* **1** : reestablishment, restoration **2** GUÉRISON : recovery
retaper [rətape] *vt* **1** : to retype **2** : to renovate **3** *fam* : to pep up — **se retaper** *vr fam* : to recover, to get back on one's feet
retard [rətar] *nm* **1** : lateness, delay <avoir du retard : to be late> <sans retard : without delay> <être en retard : to be behind schedule> <prendre du retard : to fall behind> **2** : backwardness <être en retard pour son âge : to be backward for one's age> <en retard sur son temps : behind the times>
retardataire[1] [rətardatɛr] *adj* **1** : late, delayed **2** : outdated
retardataire[2] *nmf* : latecomer
retardé, -dée [rətarde] *adj* : backward
retardement [rətardəmɑ̃] *nm* **1 à ~** : delayed-action **2 bombe à retardement** : time bomb
retarder [rətarde] *vt* **1** : to delay **2** : to put off, to postpone **3** : to set back (a clock, etc.) — *vi* **1** : to be slow, to lose time **2** : to be behind the times **3** *fam* : to be out of touch
retenir [rətənir] {92} *vt* **1** : to hold back, to stop, to check **2** : to keep, to detain **3** : to retain, to absorb **4** : to reserve, to book **5** : to remember **6** : to carry (in mathematics) — **se retenir** *vr* **1** : to restrain oneself **2 ~ à** : to hold onto, to grip
rétention [retɑ̃sjɔ̃] *nf* : retention, withholding
retentir [rətɑ̃tir] *vi* **1** : to ring, to resound, to boom **2 ~ sur** : to have an effect on
retentissant, -sante [rətɑ̃tisɑ̃, -sɑ̃t] *adj* : resounding <succès retentissant : resounding success>

retentissement [rətɑ̃tismɑ̃] *nm* **1** : resounding, ringing, booming **2** : effect, impact, repercussions *pl*
retenue [rətəny] *nf* **1** : deduction **2** : detention (in school) **3** RÉSERVE : reserve, self-restraint
réticent, -cente [retisɑ̃, -sɑ̃t] *adj* : reticent, reluctant — **réticence** [-tisɑ̃s] *nf*
rétif, -tive [retif, -tiv] *adj* **1** : restive **2** : rebellious
rétine [retin] *nf* : retina
retiré, -rée [rətire] *adj* **1** : remote, secluded **2** : isolated, withdrawn **3** : retired
retirer [rətire] *vt* **1** : to take off (clothing, etc.), to remove **2** : to withdraw, to move away **3** : to withdraw, to take back **4** : to collect (baggage, etc.), to withdraw (funds), to extract (minerals, etc.) **5** RECUEILLIR : to derive, to obtain <retirer un bénéfice : to make a profit> **6** *Can* : to retire, to put out (in baseball) — **se retirer** *vr* **1** : to withdraw, to retreat **2** : to retire
retombées [rətɔ̃be] *nfpl* **1** : repercussions, consequences **2 retombées radioactives** : radioactive fallout
retomber [rətɔ̃be] *vi* **1** : to come down, to land **2** : to fall again **3** : to subside, to die away **4** : to fall back, to relapse **5** : to fall, to go down (of temperature, value, etc.) **6 ~ sur** : to fall on <la responsabilité retombe toujours sur nous : the responsibility always falls on us>
rétorquer [retɔrke] *vt* : to retort
retors, -torse [rətɔr, -tɔrs] *adj* : wily, sly
rétorsion [retɔrsjɔ̃] *nf* : retaliation
retouche [rətuʃ] *nf* **1** : touching up **2** : alteration
retoucher [rətuʃe] *vt* **1** : to touch up **2** : to alter, to make alterations
retour [rətur] *nm* **1** : return <à mon retour : on my return> <être sur le chemin de retour : to be on the way back> <billet de retour : return ticket> **2 de ~** : back <de retour de la campagne : back (home) from the country> **3 retour de flamme** : backfire **4 retour en arrière** : flashback **5 sans ~** : irrevocably, forever
retournement [rəturnəmɑ̃] *nm* : reversal
retourner [rəturne] *vt* **1** : to turn over, to turn upside down, to turn around <retourner la situation : to reverse the situation> **2** : to turn inside out **3** : to return (a compliment, etc.) **4** : to return, to send back **5** *fam* : to shake up, to upset — *vi* REVENIR : to return, to go back — **se retourner** *vr* **1** : to turn around **2** : to turn over, to overturn **3** : to sort things out, to turn things around **4 ~ contre** : to turn against **5 s'en retourner** : to go back
retracer [rətrase] {6} *vt* **1** : to redraw, to trace over **2** : to recount (an event)
rétracter [retrakte] *v* **se rétracter** *vr* : to retract — **rétractable** [-traktabl] *adj* — **rétraction** [-traksjɔ̃] *nf*
retrait [rətrɛ] *nm* **1** : withdrawal (of funds, permission, etc.) **2 en ~** : set back <rester en retrait : to stand back, to stay in the background> **3** *Can* : out (in baseball) **4 retrait au bâton** : strikeout
retraite [rətrɛt] *nf* **1** : retreat (in religion, the military, etc.) **2** : pension <mettre à la retraite : to pension off> **3** : retirement <prendre sa retraite : to retire>
retraité[1], **-tée** [rətrɛte] *adj* : retired
retraité[2], **-tée** *n* : retiree
retrancher [rətrɑ̃ʃe] *vt* **1** ENLEVER : to take out, to remove **2** : to deduct **3** FORTIFIER : to entrench — **se retrancher** *vr* : to entrench oneself, to take refuge
retransmettre [rətrɑ̃smɛtr] {53} *vt* : to broadcast, to relay
retransmission [rətrɑ̃smisjɔ̃] *nf* : broadcast
rétrécir [retresir] *vt* **1** : to shrink **2** : to take in, to shorten (clothing) — *vi* : to shrink — **se rétrécir** *vr* **1** : to become narrower **2** : to contract, to shrink
rétrécissement [retresismɑ̃] *nm* **1** : narrowing (of a road, etc.) **2** : shrinkage (of clothing, etc.)
rétribuer [retribɥe] *vt* RÉMUNÉRER : to pay, to remunerate
rétribution [retribysjɔ̃] *nf* RÉMUNÉRATION : payment, remuneration
rétroactif, -tive [retrɔaktif, -tiv] *adj* : retroactive — **rétroactivement** [-tivmɑ̃] *adv*
rétrograde [retrɔgrad] *adj* **1** RÉACTIONNAIRE : reactionary, retrograde **2** : backward <un mouvement rétrograde : a backward movement>
rétrograder [retrɔgrade] *vt* : to demote — *vi* **1** : to regress **2** : to downshift
rétrospective [retrɔspektiv] *nf* : retrospective — **rétrospectif, -tive** [-tif, -tiv] *adj*
rétrospectivement [retrɔspektivmɑ̃] *adv* : retrospectively, in retrospect
retrousser [rətruse] *vt* : to turn up, to roll up <retrousser ses manches : to roll up one's sleeves>
retrouvailles [rətruvaj] *nfpl* : reunion
retrouver [rətruve] *vt* **1** : to find (again) **2** REDÉCOUVRIR : to rediscover **3** REVOIR : to see again, to be reunited with **4** SE RAPPELER : to recall, to remember **5** RECONNAÎTRE : to recognize — **se retrouver** *vr* **1** : to find oneself **2** : to meet again **3** : to find one's way
rétroviseur [retrɔvizœr] *nm* : rearview mirror
réunion [reynjɔ̃] *nf* **1** : meeting **2** : gathering, reunion **3** : uniting, merging
réunir [reynir] *vt* RASSEMBLER : to gather, to collect, to bring together

— **se réunir** *vr* : to meet, to get together

réussi, -sie [reysi] *adj* : successful

réussir [reysir] *vi* : to succeed — *vt* **1** : to make a success of, to bring off **2** : to pass (an exam)

réussite [reysit] *nf* : success

réutiliser [reytilize] *vt* : to reuse

revaloir [rəvalwar] {95} *vt* : to pay back <je te revaudrai cela! : I'll get even with you for that!>

revalorisation [rəvalɔrizasjɔ̃] *nf* : revaluation, raising (of salaries, fees, etc.)

revaloriser [rəvalɔrize] *vt* **1** : to revalue, to raise (salaries, etc.) **2** : to reassess, to upgrade

revanche [rəvɑ̃ʃ] *nf* **1** : revenge **2** : return match (in sports) **3 en ~** : on the other hand

rêvasser [rɛvase] *vi* : to daydream

rêve [rɛv] *nm* **1** : dream **2 de ~** *or* **de ses rêves** : ideal, of one's dreams <la maison de ses rêves : the house of his dreams> **3 rêve éveillé** : daydream

rêvé, -vée [rɛve] *adj* : ideal

revêche [rəveʃ] *adj* ACARIÂTRE : surly, crabby

réveil [revɛj] *nm* **1** : waking up **2** : awakening <un réveil brutal : a rude awakening> **3** : reawakening, recurrence **4** : alarm clock

réveille-matin [revɛjmatɛ̃] *nms & pl* : alarm clock

réveiller [reveje] *vt* **1** : to wake up **2** : to awaken, to revive, to arouse — **se réveiller** *vr*

réveillon [revɛjɔ̃] *nm* **1** : Christmas Eve supper or party **2** : New Year's Eve supper or party

réveillonner [revɛjɔne] *vi* : to celebrate Christmas Eve or New Year's Eve

révélateur, -trice [revelatœr, -tris] *adj* : revealing

révélation [revelasjɔ̃] *nf* : revelation

révéler [revele] {87} *vt* **1** DÉVOILER : to reveal, to disclose **2** INDIQUER : to show **3** : to develop (photographic film) — **se révéler** *vr* **1** : to show oneself as **2** : to turn out to be **3** : to be revealed

revenant, -nante [rəvnɑ̃, -nɑ̃t] *n* SPECTRE : ghost

revendeur, -deuse [rəvɑ̃dœr, -døz] *n* **1** DÉTAILLANT : retailer **2** : secondhand dealer

revendication [rəvɑ̃dikasjɔ̃] *nf* : claim, demand

revendiquer [rəvɑ̃dike] *vt* **1** : to claim **2** EXIGER : to demand

revendre [rəvɑ̃dr] {63} *vt* **1** : to sell (one's car, house, etc.) **2 à ~** : in abundance, to spare

revenir [rəvnir] {92} *vi* **1** : to come back, to return <je reviens tout de suite : I'll be right back> **2** : to recur, to reappear <un problème qui revient : a problem that comes up again> **3 ~ à** : to return to, to go back to <revenir à la barbarie : to revert to savagery> **4 ~ à** : to hark back to <ça me revient! : now it comes back to me!, now I remember!> **5 ~ à** : to come down to, to amount to **6 ~ de** : to get over (an illness, etc.), to abandon (ideas) **7 ~ sur** : to go back over, to review **8 faire revenir** : to brown (in cooking) **9 revenir à la vie** : to come back to life, to revive **10 revenir à soi** : to come to, to regain consciousness

revente [rəvɑ̃t] *nf* : resale

revenu [rəvəny] *nm* : revenue, income

rêver [rɛve] *vt* **1** : to dream **2** : to dream of, to imagine — *vi* **1** : to dream **2 ~ de** : to dream of, to aspire to

réverbération [reverberasjɔ̃] *nf* **1** : reflection **2** : reverberation

réverbère [reverbɛr] *nm* LAMPADAIRE : streetlight, streetlamp

réverbérer [reverbere] {87} *vt* : to reflect (light, heat, etc.) — **se réverbérer** *vr* **1** : to be reflected **2** : to reverberate

révérence [reverɑ̃s] *nf* **1** : reverence **2** : bow, curtsy <faire une révérence : to curtsy>

révérencieux, -cieuse [reverɑ̃sjø, -sjøz] *adj* : reverent

révérend, -rende [reverɑ̃, -rɑ̃d] *adj* : reverend <le Révérend Père Michel : Reverend Father Michel>

révérer [revere] {87} *vt* : to revere, to venerate

rêverie [rɛvri] *nf* : daydreaming, reverie

revers [rəver] *nm* **1** ENVERS : back, reverse (side) **2** : lapel, cuff **3** : backhand (in tennis) **4** ÉCHEC : setback

réversible [reversibl] *adj* : reversible

revêtement [rəvɛtmɑ̃] *nm* **1** : coating, covering, facing (in construction) **2** : surface (of a road)

revêtir [rəvetir] {97} *vt* **1** : to put on, to don **2** : to assume, to take on (an appearance, etc.) **3** : to coat, to cover, to surface — **se revêtir** *vr* **1 ~ de** : to dress up in **2 ~ de** : to be covered with

rêveur[1], **-veuse** [rɛvœr, -vøz] *adj* : dreamy

rêveur[2], **-veuse** *n* : dreamer

revigorant, -rante [rəvigɔrɑ̃, -rɑ̃t] *adj* : invigorating

revigoration [rəvigɔrasjɔ̃] *nf* : invigoration

revigorer [rəvigɔre] *vt* : to invigorate, to revive

revirement [rəvirmɑ̃] *nm* : reversal, turnabout

revirer [rəvire] *vi Can fam* **revirer à l'envers** : to turn upside down and inside out — **se revirer** *vr Can fam* : to turn one's back

réviser [revize] *vt* **1** : to review, to reexamine **2** : to overhaul (a vehicle, etc.) **3** : to revise

révision [revizjɔ̃] *nf* **1** : review, reappraisal **2** : checkup, service (of a vehicle) **3** : revision (of a text)
revitaliser [rəvitalize] *vt* : to revitalize
revivre [rəvivr] {98} *vt* : to relive — *vi* : to come to life again
révocation [revɔkasjɔ̃] *nf* **1** : dismissal **2** : revocation, repeal
revoir[1] [rəvwar] {99} *vt* **1** : to see again **2** : to review, to reexamine — **se revoir** *vr* : to meet (each other) again
revoir[2] *nm* **1** : meeting again **2 au revoir** : goodbye
revoler [rəvɔle] *vi Can fam* **1** : to be flung into the air **2** : to spurt, to squirt
révoltant, -tante [revɔltɑ̃, -tɑ̃t] *adj* : revolting, appalling
révolte [revɔlt] *nf* **1** : revolt, rebellion **2** : outrage
révolter [revɔlte] *vt* : to outrage, to revolt — **se révolter** *vr* : to rebel
révolu, -lue [revɔly] *adj* : past, completed, over <en des temps révolus : in days gone by>
révolution [revɔlysjɔ̃] *nf* : revolution
révolutionnaire [revɔlysjɔnɛr] *adj & nmf* : revolutionary
révolutionner [revɔlysjɔne] *vt* **1** : to revolutionize **2** : to agitate, to stir up
revolver [revɔlvɛr] *nm* : revolver
révoquer [revɔke] *vt* **1** : to dismiss **2** : to revoke, to rescind
revue [rəvy] *nf* **1** : magazine, journal **2** : review, inspection (of troops) **3** : review, examination <passer en revue : to have a look at, to go over> **4** : revue
révulser [revylse] *vt* **1** : to revolt, to appall **2** : to contort — **se révulser** *vr* **1** : to be contorted **2** : to roll upward (of eyes)
révulsion [revylsjɔ̃] *nf* : revulsion
rez-de-chaussée [redʃose] *nms & pl* : first floor, ground floor
rhabiller [rabije] *vt* : to dress again — **se rhabiller** *vr*
rhapsodie [rapsɔdi] *nf* : rhapsody
rhéostat [reɔsta] *nm* : dimmer (for lights)
rhétorique[1] [retɔrik] *adj* : rhetorical
rhétorique[2] *nf* : rhetoric
rhinocéros [rinɔseros] *nm* : rhinoceros
rhododendron [rɔdɔdẽdrɔ̃] *nm* : rhododendron
rhombe [rɔ̃b] *nm* : rhombus
rhubarbe [rybarb] *nf* : rhubarb
rhum [rɔm] *nm* : rum
rhumatismal, -male [rymatismal] *adj, mpl* **-maux** [-mo] : rheumatic
rhumatisme [rymatism] *nm* : rheumatism
rhume [rym] *nm* **1** : cold <rhume de cerveau : head cold> **2 rhume des foins** : hay fever
riant, riante [rijɑ̃, -jɑ̃t] *adj* **1** : smiling **2** : cheerful, pleasant
ribambelle [ribɑ̃bɛl] *nf* : flock, swarm, multitude
riboflavine [riboflavin] *nf* : riboflavin
ricanement [rikanmɑ̃] *nm* : snickering, sneering, giggling
ricaner [rikane] *vi* : to snicker, to giggle, to sneer
riche[1] [riʃ] *adj* **1** : rich, wealthy **2** : sumptuous, luxurious **3** : fertile (of soil), nutritious, rich (of foods) **4 ~ en** : rich in, full of
riche[2] *nmf* : rich person
richement [riʃmɑ̃] *adv* : richly
richesse [riʃɛs] *nf* **1** : wealth **2** : richness, luxuriousness **3 : richesses** *nfpl* : riches, wealth
ricin [risɛ̃] *nf* **huile de ricin** : castor oil
ricocher [rikɔʃe] *vi* : to ricochet, to rebound
ricochet [rikɔʃɛ] *nm* : ricochet, rebound
ride [rid] *nf* **1** : wrinkle **2** : ripple (on water)
rideau [rido] *nm, pl* **rideaux** : curtain <rideau de douche : shower curtain>
rider [ride] *vt* **1** : to wrinkle **2** : to ripple (water) — **se rider** *vr*
ridicule[1] [ridikyl] *adj* : ridiculous — **ridiculement** [-kylmɑ̃] *adv*
ridicule[2] *nm* **1** : ridicule **2** : ridiculousness, absurdity
ridiculiser [ridikylize] *vt* : to ridicule — **se ridiculiser** *vr* : to make a fool of oneself
rien[1] [rjɛ̃] *nm* : trifle, little thing <perdre son temps à des riens : to waste one's time on trivia> <en un rien de temps : in no time at all>
rien[2] *pron* **1** : nothing <rien de nouveau : nothing new> <il n'y a plus rien : there's nothing left> <ça ne fait rien : it doesn't matter> **2** : anything <avant de ne rien faire : before doing anything> <rien d'autre : nothing else> **3 de ~** : don't mention it, you're welcome **4 rien que** : only, just <rien que pour elle : only for her>
rieur, rieuse [rijœr, -jøz] *adj* : cheerful
rigide [riʒid] *adj* **1** : rigid **2** : strict — **rigidement** [-ʒidmɑ̃] *adv*
rigidité [riʒidite] *nf* : rigidity, stiffness
rigolade [rigɔlad] *nf fam* **1** : fun <quelle rigolade! : what fun!, what a laugh!> **2** : joke, farce <la vie n'est qu'une rigolade : life is just a joke>
rigole [rigɔl] *nf* : trench, channel
rigoler [rigɔle] *vi fam* **1** : to have fun **2** : to laugh, to joke
rigolo[1], **-lote** [rigɔlɔ, -lɔt] *adj fam* : funny, comical
rigolo[2], **-lote** *n fam* : joker, card
rigoureux, -reuse [rigurø, -røz] *adj* **1** : rigorous, strict **2** : harsh, severe — **rigoureusement** [-røzmɑ̃] *adv*
rigueur [rigœr] *nf* **1** : rigor, harshness **2** : precision, meticulousness **3 à la rigueur** : if absolutely necessary **4 à la rigueur** : at the most **5 de ~** : essential, obligatory **6 rigueurs** *nfpl* : rigors, hardships

rime [rim] *nf* : rhyme
rimer [rime] *vi* : to rhyme
rinçage [rɛ̃saʒ] *nm* : rinsing, rinse
rince–doigts [rɛ̃sdwa] *nms & pl* : finger bowl
rincer [rɛ̃se] {6} *vt* : to rinse — **se rincer** *vr*
ring [riŋ] *nm* : boxing ring
ringard, -garde [rɛ̃gar, -gard] *adj France fam* : old-fashioned, corny
ripaille [ripaj] *nf fam* **faire ripaille** : to have a feast
riposte [ripɔst] *nf* **1** RÉPLIQUE : retort **2** CONTRE-ATTAQUE : counterattack, reprisal
riposter [ripɔste] *v* : to retort
rire[1] [rir] {76} *vi* **1** : to laugh **2** : to joke around, to have fun **3** ~ **de** : to mock, to make fun of
rire[2] *nm* : laugh, laughter
risée [rize] *nf or* **objet de risée** : laughingstock
risible [rizibl] *adj* : ridiculous, laughable
risque [risk] *nm* **1** : risk **2 à vos risques et périls** : at your own risk
risqué, -quée [riske] *adj* **1** : risky **2** : risqué
risquer [riske] *vt* **1** : to risk **2** ~ **de** : to be liable to, to have a chance of <il risque de s'ennuyer : he might be bored> <ça risque d'arriver : it may very well happen> — **se risquer** *vr* : to venture, to take a chance
rissoler [risɔle] *v* : to brown (in cooking)
ristourne [risturn] *nf* REMISE : discount, rebate
rite [rit] *nm* : rite, ritual
rituel[1], **-tuelle** [rituɛl] *adj* : ritual
rituel[2] *nm* : rite, ritual
rituellement [rituɛlmɑ̃] *adj* **1** : ritually **2** : religiously, unfailingly
rivage [rivaʒ] *nm* : shore
rival, -vale [rival] *adj & n, mpl* **rivaux** [rivo] : rival
rivaliser [rivalize] *vi* ~ **avec** : to compete with, to rival
rivalité [rivalite] *nf* : rivalry
rive [riv] *nf* : bank (of a river)
river [rive] *vt* **1** : to rivet, to fasten **2** : to clinch (a nail)
riverain[1], **-raine** [rivrɛ̃, -rɛn] *adj* **1** : riverside, lakeside **2** : bordering the street, roadside
riverain[2], **-raine** *n* **1** : riverside or lakeside resident **2** : resident (along a street)
rivet [rivɛ] *nm* : rivet
riveter [rivte] {8} *vt* : to rivet
rivière [rivjɛr] *nf* : river
rixe [riks] *nf* BAGARRE : brawl, fight
riz [ri] *nm* : rice
rizière [rizjɛr] *nf* : (rice) paddy
robe [rɔb] *nf* **1** : dress, robe <robe de chambre : bathrobe> <robe d'intérieur : housecoat> <robe de mariée : wedding gown> **2** : gown (of a judge, etc.) **3** PELAGE : coat (of an animal) **4 robe de nuit** *Can* : nightgown
robinet [rɔbinɛ] *nm* : faucet
robot [rɔbo] *nm* **1** : robot **2 robot de cuisine** : food processor
robotique [rɔbɔtik] *nf* : robotics
robuste [rɔbyst] *adj* : robust, sturdy
robustesse [rɔbystɛs] *nf* : robustness, sturdiness
roc [rɔk] *nm* : rock
rocaille [rɔkaj] *nf* **1** : loose stones *pl* **2** : rock garden
rocailleux, -leuse [rɔkajø, -jøz] *adj* **1** : stony, rocky **2** : harsh, gravelly (of a voice)
rocambolesque [rɔkɑ̃bɔlɛsk] *adj* : incredible, extraordinary
roche [rɔʃ] *nf* : rock
rocher [rɔʃe] *nm* : rock
rochet [rɔʃɛ] *nm* : ratchet
rocheux, -cheuse [rɔʃø, -ʃøz] *adj* : rocky
rock [rɔk] *nm* : rock (music)
rodéo [rɔdeo] *nm* : rodeo
roder [rɔde] *vt* **1** : to break in (a vehicle) **2** *fam* : to polish up (a performance, etc.)
rôder [rode] *vi* **1** : to prowl **2** ERRER : to wander around, to roam about
rôdeur, -deuse [rodœr, -døz] *n* : prowler
rodomontades [rɔdɔmɔ̃tad] *nfpl* : bragging, boasting
rogne [rɔɲ] *nf fam* : anger, bad temper <être en rogne : to get mad, to see red>
rogner [rɔɲe] *vt* **1** : to trim, to clip **2** : to cut back on, to reduce (expenses, etc.)
rognon [rɔɲɔ̃] *nm* : kidney (in cooking)
rognures [rɔɲyr] *nfpl* **1** : trimmings, clippings **2** : scraps
rogue [rɔg] *adj* : arrogant, haughty
roi [rwa] *nm* : king
roitelet [rwatlɛ] *nm* : wren
rôle [rol] *nm* **1** : role, part **2** : list, roll **3 à tour de rôle** : one after the other, in turn
romain, -maine [rɔmɛ̃, -mɛn] *adj* : Roman
Romain, -maine *n* : Roman
romaine *nf* : romaine (lettuce)
roman[1], **-mane** [rɔmɑ̃, -man] *adj* **1** : Romance (in linguistics) **2** : Romanesque
roman[2] *nm* **1** : romance, chivalric tale **2** : novel
romance [rɔmɑ̃s] *nf* : ballad, love song
romancer [rɔmɑ̃se] {6} *vt* : to romanticize
romancier, -cière [rɔmɑ̃sje, -sjɛr] *n* : novelist
romanesque [rɔmanɛsk] *adj* **1** : fabulous, fantastic **2** : romantic **3** : fictional, novelistic
roman–feuilleton [rɔmɑ̃fœjtɔ̃] *nm, pl* **romans–feuilletons** → **feuilleton**

roman–savon [rɔmɑ̃savɔ̃] *nm Can, pl* **romans–savons** : soap opera
romantique [rɔmɑ̃tik] *adj* : romantic
romantisme [rɔmɑ̃tism] *nm* : romanticism
romarin [rɔmarɛ̃] *nm* : rosemary
rompre [rɔ̃pr] {77} *vt* **1** : to break (off) **2** : to break, to burst, to shatter **3** : to break (someone) in — *vi* : to break up
rompt [rɔ̃] → **rompre**
rompu, -pue [rɔ̃py] *adj* **1** FOURBU : worn-out, exhausted **2** ~ **à** : well accustomed to
romsteck [rɔmstɛk] *nm* : rump steak
ronce [rɔ̃s] *nf* : bramble (bush)
ronchonnement [rɔ̃ʃɔnmɑ̃] *nm fam* : griping, grousing
ronchonner [rɔ̃ʃɔne] *vi fam* ROUSPÉTER : to grumble, to grouse
rond[1] [rɔ̃] *adv* **tourner rond** : to run smoothly, to go well <ça ne tourne pas rond : something's not quite right>
rond[2], **ronde** [rɔ̃, rɔ̃d] *adj* : round
rond[3] *nm* **1** : circle <en rond : in a circle> **2** : ring <rond de serviette : napkin ring> **3** : round slice **4** *Can* : burner (of a stove)
ronde *nf* **1** : rounds *pl,* patrol <faire sa ronde : to be on patrol> **2** : round dance **3** : whole note **4 à la ronde** : around <à des milles à la ronde : for miles around>
rondelet, -lette [rɔ̃dlɛ, -lɛt] *adj fam* **1** : plump **2 une somme rondelette** : a tidy sum
rondelle [rɔ̃dɛl] *nf* **1** : washer **2** : (round) slice **3** *Can* : (hockey) puck
rondement [rɔ̃dmɑ̃] *adv* **1** : briskly, promptly **2** : frankly, straight out
rondeur [rɔ̃dœr] *nf* **1** : roundness, curve (of the body) **2** : frankness
rondin [rɔ̃dɛ̃] *nm* : log <cabane en rondins : log cabin>
rond–point [rɔ̃pwɛ̃] *nm, pl* **ronds–points** : traffic circle, rotary
ronéo [rɔneɔ] *nf* : mimeograph
ronflement [rɔ̃fləmɑ̃] *nm* **1** : snore, snoring **2** : humming, drone, roar (of a fire, etc.)
ronfler [rɔ̃fle] *vi* **1** : to snore **2** : to hum, to drone, to roar
ronger [rɔ̃ʒe] {17} *vt* **1** : to gnaw, to nibble **2** : to corrode **3** : to eat away at, to wear down <rongé par le chagrin : grief-stricken> — **se ronger** *vr* **se ronger les ongles** : to bite one's nails
rongeur [rɔ̃ʒœr] *nm* : rodent
ronronnement [rɔ̃rɔnmɑ̃] *nm* : purring, humming
ronronner [rɔ̃rɔne] *vi* **1** : to purr **2** : to hum (of an engine, etc.)
roquette[1] [rɔkɛt] *nf* : rocket
roquette[2] *nf* : arugula
rosaire [rɔzɛr] *nm* : rosary
rosbif [rɔzbif] *nm* : roast beef
rose[1] [rɔz] *adj & nm* : rose, pink
rose[2] *nf* **1** : rose (flower) **2 rose trémière** : hollyhock
rosé, -sée [rɔze] *adj* : rose, pinkish
roseau [rɔzo] *nm, pl* **roseaux** : reed
rosée [rɔze] *nf* : dew <goutte de rosée : dewdrop>
rosette [rɔzɛt] *nf* : rosette
rosier [rɔzje] *nm* : rosebush
rosir [rɔzir] *v* : to turn pink
rosse[1] [rɔs] *adj fam* : nasty, horrid, mean
rosse[2] *nf fam* : nasty person, beast
rosser [rɔse] *vt* : to beat, to thrash
rossignol [rɔsiɲɔl] *nm* : nightingale
rostre [rɔstr] *nm* : rostrum
rot [ro] *nm fam* : belch, burp
rotatif, -tive [rɔtatif, -tiv] *adj* : rotary
rotation [rɔtasjɔ̃] *nf* : rotation
roter [rɔte] *vi fam* : to burp, to belch
rôti [roti] *nm* : roast (meat)
rôtie [roti] *nf* : toasted bread, toast
rotin [rɔtɛ̃] *nm* : rattan
rôtir [rɔtir] *v* : to roast
rôtissoire [rɔtiswar] *nf* : rotisserie, spit
rotonde [rɔtɔ̃d] *nf* : rotunda
rotondité [rɔtɔ̃dite] *nf* : roundness
rotor [rɔtɔr] *nm* : rotor
rotule [rɔtyl] *nf* : kneecap, patella
roturier, -rière [rɔtyrje, -rjɛr] *n* : commoner
rouage [rwaʒ] *nm* **1** : cogwheel <les rouages d'une montre : the movement of a watch> **2 rouages** *nmpl* : workings <les rouages de l'État : the wheels of state>
rouan[1], **rouanne** [rwɑ̃, rwan] *adj* : roan
rouan[2], **rouanne** *n* : roan (horse)
roublard, -blarde [rublar, -blard] *adj fam* : crafty, sly
rouble [rubl] *nm* : ruble
roucoulement [rukulmɑ̃] *nm* **1** : cooing **2** *fam* : billing and cooing
roucouler [rukule] *vi* : to coo
roue [ru] *nf* **1** : wheel (of a vehicle) <roue de secours : spare tire> **2** : (mechanical) wheel <roue dentée : cogwheel> <grande roue : Ferris wheel> **3** : cartwheel (in gymnastics)
roué, rouée [rwe] *adj* FUTÉ : slick, cunning
rouer [rwe] *vt* **rouer de coups** : to thrash, to beat
rouerie [ruri] *nf* : slyness, cunning
rouet [rwɛ] *nm* : spinning wheel
rouge[1] [ruʒ] *adj* : red
rouge[2] *n* : red <rouge à lèvres : lipstick> <être dans le rouge : to be in the red>
rougeâtre [ruʒatr] *adj* : reddish
rougeaud, -geaude [ruʒo, -ʒod] *adj* : red-faced, ruddy, florid
rouge–gorge [ruʒgɔrʒ] *nm, pl* **rouges–gorges** : robin
rougeoiement [ruʒwamɑ̃] *nm* : reddish glow
rougeole [ruʒɔl] *nf* : measles
rougeoyant, -geoyante [ruʒwajɑ̃, -ʒwajɑ̃t] *adj* : red, glowing

rougeoyer [ruʒwaje] {58} *vi* : to turn red, to glow
rouget [ruʒɛ] *nm* : red mullet
rougeur [ruʒœr] *nf* **1** : redness **2** : flushing **3** : red blotch, eruption (in medicine)
rougir [ruʒir] *vt* **1** : to make red **2** : to make red-hot — *vi* **1** : to redden, to turn red **2** : to blush **3** : to glow red
rouille [ruj] *nf* : rust
rouillé, -lée [ruje] *adj* : rusty
rouiller [ruje] *v* : to rust — **se rouiller** *vr*
roulant, -lante [rulɑ̃, -lɑ̃t] *adj* **1** : rolling **2** : on wheels
rouleau [rulo] *nm, pl* **rouleaux 1** : roller <rouleau à pâtisserie : rolling pin> <rouleau compresseur : steamroller> **2** : roll, scroll <rouleau de papier : roll of paper> **3** : roller, curler **4** : breaker (wave)
roulement [rulmɑ̃] *nm* **1** : rolling <avoir un roulement d'yeux : to roll one's eyes> **2** : rumble, roll <roulement de tonnerre : rumble of thunder> <roulement de tambour : drum roll> **3** : circulation, turnover (in finance) **4** : rotation, shift(s) <travailler par roulement : to work (in) shifts> **5 roulement à billes** : ball bearing
rouler [rule] *vt* **1** : to roll, to move along, to wheel **2** : to roll up **3** : to roll, to sway, to swing <rouler les yeux : to roll one's eyes> <rouler les hanches : to swing one's hips> — *vi* **1** : to roll <rouler en bas de la colline : to roll down the hill> **2** : to go, to run, to drive <roule moins vite! : slow down!> <ça roule bien : traffic is moving along well> **3** : to take turns, to rotate **4** : to circulate (of funds) **5** : to rumble, to roll **6 ~ sur** : to turn on, to be centered upon
roulette [rulɛt] *nf* **1** : caster (on furniture, etc.) **2** : roulette **3** : (dentist's) drill
roulis [ruli] *nm* : rolling (of a ship)
roulotte [rulɔt] *nf Can* : trailer, camper
roumain[1], **-maine** [rumɛ̃, -mɛn] *adj* : Romanian
roumain[2] *nm* : Romanian (language)
Roumain, -maine *n* : Romanian
roupie [rupi] *nf* : roupee
roupiller [rupije] *vi fam* : to snooze, to sleep
rouquin[1], **-quine** [rukɛ̃, -kin] *adj fam* : red-haired
rouquin,[2] **-quine** *n fam* : redhead
rouspétance [ruspetɑ̃s] *nf fam* : complaint, gripe
rouspéter [ruspete] {87} *vi fam* RONCHONNER : to fuss, to grumble
rouspéteur, -teuse [ruspetœr, -tøz] *n fam* : grumbler, grouch, nag
roussâtre [rusatr] *adj* **1** : reddish **2** : reddish brown, russet
rousseler [rusle] *vt Can* : to freckle
rousseur [rusœr] *nf* **1** : redness, russet color **2 → tache**
roussir [rusir] *vt* **1** : to turn brown **2** : to scorch, to singe — *vi* **1** : to become brown **2 faire roussir** : to brown (in cooking)
route [rut] *nf* **1** : road <route de montagne : mountain road> <tenir la route : to hold the road> <par (la) route : by road> **2** : route, way, course <route aérienne : air route> <se mettre en route : to set out, to get going> <perdre sa route : to lose one's way> **3** : trip, journey <il y a deux heures de route : it's a two-hour journey> <bonne route! : have a good trip!>
routier[1], **-tière** [rutje, -tjɛr] *adj* : road <transport routier : road transportation>
routier[2] *nm* **1** : truck driver **2** : cyclist (in bicycle racing) **3** : truck stop
routine [rutin] *nf* : routine
routinier, -nière [rutinje, -njɛr] *adj* **1** : routine, humdrum **2** : set in one's ways
rouvrir [ruvrir] {83} *v* : to reopen, to open again — **se rouvrir** *vr*
roux[1], **rousse** [ru, rus] *adj* **1** : russet, red **2** : redheaded
roux[2], **rousse** *n* : redhead
royal, royale [rwajal] *adj, mpl* **royaux** [rwajo] : royal, regal — **royalement** [-jalmɑ̃] *adv*
royaume [rwajom] *nm* : kingdom, realm
royauté [rwajote] *nf* : royalty
ruade [ryad] *nf* : kick, bucking (of a horse)
ruban [rybɑ̃] *nm* **1** : ribbon **2 ruban adhésif** : adhesive tape
rubéole [rybeɔl] *nf* : German measles
rubicond, -conde [rybikɔ̃, -kɔ̃d] *adj* : ruddy, rosy-cheeked
rubis [rybi] *nms & pl* **1** : ruby **2** : jewel (of a watch)
rubrique [rybrik] *nf* **1** : column (in a newspaper) **2** : heading
ruche [ryʃ] *nf* : beehive
rucher [ryʃe] *nm* : apiary
rude [ryd] *adj* **1** : rough (to the touch) **2** PÉNIBLE : hard, tough, difficult **3** : harsh, severe <un rude hiver : a harsh winter>
rudement [rydmɑ̃] *adv* **1** : roughly, harshly **2** *fam* DRÔLEMENT : awfully, terribly
rudesse [rydɛs] *nf* **1** RUGOSITÉ : roughness **2** SÉVÉRITÉ : harshness, severity
rudimentaire [rydimɑ̃tɛr] *adj* ÉLÉMENTAIRE : rudimentary, basic
rudiments [rydimɑ̃] *nmpl* : rudiments
rudoyer [rydwaje] {58} *vt* : to treat harshly
rue [ry] *nf* : street <rue à sens unique : one-way street>
ruée [rye] *nf* : rush
ruelle [ryɛl] *nf* : alley(way)

ruer [rɥe] *v* **se ruer** *vr* **1 ~ sur** : to fling oneself at **2 ~ vers** : to rush toward
rugir [ryʒir] *vt* : to bellow out — *vi* **1** : to roar (of lions, etc.) **2** : to howl
rugissement [ryʒismɑ̃] *nm* **1** : roar **2** : howling <rugissement du vent : howling of the wind>
rugosité [rygozite] *nf* : roughness
rugueux, -gueuse [rygø, -gøz] *adj* : rough, rugged
ruine [rɥin] *nf* **1** : ruin **2** : destruction, collapse **3 ruines** *nfpl* : ruins
ruiner [rɥine] *vt* **1** : to ruin **2** : to destroy, to wreck — **se ruiner** *vr*
ruineux, -neuse [rɥinø, -nøz] *adj* : extravagantly expensive, exorbitant
ruisseau [rɥiso] *nm, pl* **ruisseaux 1** : stream, brook **2** : flood, stream (of tears, etc.) **3** : gutter
ruisseler [rɥisle] {8} *vi* **1** : to stream, to flood
ruisselet [rɥisle] *nm* : small brook, stream
ruissellement [rɥisɛlmɑ̃] *nm* : streaming <le ruissellement de l'eau sur la rue : water streaming down the street>
rumeur [rymœr] *nf* **1** : rumor **2** : murmur, hum, rumble
ruminant[1], **-nante** [ryminɑ̃, -nɑ̃t] *adj* : ruminant
ruminant[2] *nm* : ruminant
ruminer [rymine] *vt* : to ruminate over — *vi* **1** : to ruminate, to chew the cud **2** : to brood
rupture [ryptyr] *nf* **1** : break, breaking **2** : breakup (of a relationship) **3** : breach (of contract)
rural, -rale [ryral] *adj, mpl* **ruraux** [ryro] : rural, country
ruse [ryz] *nf* **1** : ruse, trick **2** : cunning, cleverness
rusé, -sée [ryze] *adj* FUTÉ, MALIN : cunning, sly
russe[1] [rys] *adj* : Russian
russe[2] *nm* : Russian (language)
Russe *nmf* : Russian
rustaud, -taude [rysto, -tod] *n* : bumpkin, hick
rustique [rystik] *adj* : rural, rustic
rustre [rystr] *nmf* : boor, oaf, clod, bumpkin
rut [ryt] **être en rut** : to be in rut, to be in heat
rutilant, -lante [rytilɑ̃, -lɑ̃t] *adj* : gleaming
rutiler [rytile] *vi* BRILLER : to gleam, to shine
rwandais, -daise [rwɑ̃dɛ, -dɛz] *adj* : Rwandan
Rwandais, -daise *n* : Rwandan
rythme [ritm] *nm* **1** : rhythm, beat **2** : rate, pace, tempo
rythmé, -mée [ritme] *adj* : rhythmic, rhythmical
rythmer [ritme] *vt* : to give rhythm to
rythmique [ritmik] *adj* : rhythmic, rhythmical — **rythmiquement** [-mikmɑ̃] *adv*

S

s [ɛs] *nm* : s, the 19th letter of the alphabet
sabbat [saba] *nm* : Sabbath
sabbatique [sabatik] *adj* **congé sabbatique** : sabbatical
sable [sabl] *nm* **1** : sand **2 sables mouvants** : quicksand
sablé[1], **-blée** [sable] *adj* **1** : sandy **2 → papier**
sablé[2] *nm* : shortbread (cookie)
sabler [sable] *vt* **1** : to sand **2 sabler le champagne** : to celebrate with champagne
sableux, -bleuse [sablø, -bløz] *adj* : sandy
sablier [sablije] *nm* : hourglass
sablonneux, -neuse [sablɔnø, -nøz] *adj* : sandy
saborder [sabɔrde] *vt* **1** : to scuttle (a ship) **2** : to put an end to, to scrap (a project, etc.)
sabot [sabo] *nm* **1** : clog, wooden shoe **2** : hoof **3 sabot de frein** : brake shoe **4 sabot de la Vierge** *or* **sabot de Vénus** : lady's slipper
sabotage [sabɔtaʒ] *nm* **1** : sabotage **2** : sabotaging, botching up
saboter [sabɔte] *vt* **1** : to sabotage **2** BÂCLER : to spoil, to botch up
saboteur, -teuse [sabɔtœr, -tøz] *n* : saboteur
sabre [sabr] *nm* : saber
sabrer [sabre] *vt* **1** : to cut down (an enemy) **2** : to cut, to slash <sabrer les dépenses : to cut spending> **3** *fam* : to tear to shreds, to pan
sac [sak] *nm* **1** : sack, bag <sac à dos : backpack, knapsack> <sac de couchage : sleeping bag> <sac à main : handbag, purse> <sac de voyage : traveling bag, valise> **2** : sac (in anatomy and botany) **3 mettre à sac** : to sack, to ransack
saccade [sakad] *nf* : jerk, jolt
saccadé, -dée [sakade] *adj* : jerky, abrupt
saccage [sakaʒ] *nm* : destruction, havoc
saccager [sakaʒe] {17} *vt* **1** PILLER : to sack, to pillage **2** DÉVASTER : to ravage, to vandalize, to wreck

saccharine [sakarin] *nf* : saccharin
saccharose [sakaroz] *nm* : sucrose
sacerdoce [saserdɔs] *nm* **1** PRÊTRISE : priesthood **2** VOCATION : vocation
sacerdotal, -tale [saserdɔtal] *adj, pl* **-taux** [-to] : sacerdotal, priestly
sache [saʃ], *etc.* → **savoir**
sachet [saʃɛ] *nm* **1** : packet, small bag <sachet de thé : tea bag> **2** : sachet
sacoche [sakɔʃ] *nf* **1** : bag, satchel **2** : saddlebag **3** *Bel, Can* : purse, pocketbook
sacramentel, -telle [sakramɑ̃tel] *adj* : sacramental
sacre [sakr] *nm* **1** COURONNEMENT : coronation **2** CONSÉCRATION : consecration
sacré, -crée [sakre] *adj* **1** : sacred, holy **2** *fam* : damned, hell of a <un sacré spectacle : a damned good show>
sacrement [sakrəmɑ̃] *nm* : sacrament
sacrer [sakre] *vt* **1** COURONNER : to crown **2** CONSACRER : to consecrate — *vi* : to swear
sacrifice [sakrifis] *nm* : sacrifice — **sacrificiel, -cielle** [-fisjel] *adj*
sacrifier [sakrifje] {96} *vt* : to sacrifice — *vi* ~ **à** : to conform to — **se sacrifier** *vr* : to sacrifice oneself
sacrilège[1] [sakrileʒ] *adj* : sacrilegious
sacrilège[2] *nm* : sacrilege
sacristain [sakristɛ̃] *nm* : sexton
sacristie [sakristi] *nf* : sacristy, vestry
sacro–saint, -sainte [sakrɔsɛ̃, sakrɔsɛ̃t] *adj* : sacrosanct
sadique[1] [sadik] *adj* : sadistic — **sadiquement** [-dikmɑ̃] *adv*
sadique[2] *nmf* : sadist
sadisme [sadism] *nm* : sadism
safari [safari] *nm* : safari
safran [safrɑ̃] *nm* : saffron
saga [saga] *nf* : saga
sagace [sagas] *adj* : shrewd, sagacious
sagacité [sagasite] *nf* : shrewdness, sagacity
sage[1] [saʒ] *adj* **1** SENSÉ : wise, sensible, sage **2** DOCILE : well-behaved, obedient **3** MODÉRÉ : moderate, restrained, sober
sage[2] *nm* : sage, wise person
sage–femme [saʒfam] *nf, pl* **sages–femmes** : midwife
sagement [saʒmɑ̃] *adv* **1** : wisely, sensibly **2** : quietly, properly
sagesse [saʒɛs] *nf* **1** : wisdom, good sense **2** : good behavior **3** MODÉRATION : moderation, restraint
Sagittaire [saʒiter] *nm* : Sagittarius
saignant, -gnante [sɛ̃ɲɑ̃, -ɲɑ̃t] *adj* **1** : bleeding **2** : rare, undercooked
saignée [seɲe] *nf* **1** : bleeding, bloodletting **2** *or* **saignée du bras** : bend of the arm **3** : drain (on finances) **4** : cut, groove, channel
saignement [seɲmɑ̃] *nm* **1** : bleeding **2** **saignement de nez** : nosebleed
saigner [seɲe] *v* : to bleed
saillant, -lante [sajɑ̃, -jɑ̃t] *adj* **1** : prominent, projecting **2** : salient, notable
saillie [saji] *nf* **1** : projection, protuberance, ledge <en saillie : projecting> **2** : sally, witticism
saillir [sajir] {78} *vi* : to jut out, to project
sain, saine [sɛ̃, sɛn] *adj* **1** : healthy, sound <sain et sauf : safe and sound> <sain d'esprit : sane> **2** : wholesome, salutary
saindoux [sɛ̃du] *nm* : lard
sainement [senmɑ̃] *adv* : healthily, soundly
saint[1], **sainte** [sɛ̃, sɛ̃t] *adj* **1** : holy <la Sainte Bible : the Holy Bible> **2** : godly, saintly **3** **la Sainte Vierge** : the Blessed Virgin
saint[2], **sainte** *n* : saint
Saint–Esprit [sɛ̃tɛspri] *nm* : Holy Spirit
sainteté [sɛ̃tte] *nf* : holiness, sanctity, saintliness
saisie [sezi] *nf* **1** : seizure (of property) **2** **saisie de données** : data entry
saisir [sezir] *vt* **1** : to seize, to grab, to impound **2** COMPRENDRE : to grasp, to understa: d **3** IMPRESSIONNER : to strike, to impress **4** : to keyboard, to enter (data) — **se saisir** *vr* ~ **de** : to take possession of, to capture
saisissant, -sante [sezisɑ̃, -sɑ̃t] *adj* **1** FRAPPANT : striking, gripping **2** : biting, piercing (of cold)
saison [sezɔ̃] *nf* : season
saisonnier, -nière [sezɔnje, -njer] *adj* : seasonal
salace [salas] *adj* : salacious
salade [salad] *nf* **1** : salad **2** LAITUE : lettuce **3** *fam* : muddle, mess **4** **salades** *nfpl fam* : stories, tall tales
saladier [saladje] *nm* : salad bowl
salaire [saler] *nm* **1** : salary, wages **2** : reward
salamandre [salamɑ̃dr] *nf* : salamander
salami [salami] *nm* : salami
salarial, -riale [salarjal] *adj, mpl* **-riaux** [-rjo] : wage, pay <hausse salariale : wage increase>
salarié, -riée [salarje] *n* : salaried employee, wage earner
salaud [salo] *nm usu vulgar* : bastard
sale [sal] *adj* **1** : dirty, dingy, grimy **2** : nasty, foul <un sale tour : a dirty trick> <sale temps : nasty weather>
salé, -lée [sale] *adj* **1** : salty **2** : salted **3** *fam* : steep, stiff <condamnation salée : stiff sentence> **4** *fam* : risqué, spicy
saler [sale] *vt* : to salt
saleté [salte] *nf* **1** : dirt, filth **2** : dirtiness, filthiness, mess **3** OBSCÉNITÉ : obscenity **4** *fam* : dirty trick
salière [saljer] *nf* : saltshaker
salin, -line [salɛ̃, -lin] *adj* : saline
salir [salir] *vt* : to soil, to dirty — **se salir** *vr* : to get dirty

salissant, -sante [salisã, -sãt] *adj* **1** : easily soiled **2** : dirty, messy <travail salissant : dirty work>
salivaire [saliver] *adj* : salivary
saliver [salive] *vi* : to salivate
salive [saliv] *nf* : saliva
salle [sal] *nf* **1** : room <salle d'attente : waiting room> <salle de bains : bathroom> <salle à manger : dining room> <salle de séjour : living room> **2** : auditorium, hall <salle de concert : concert hall> <salles obscures : movie theaters> **3** : audience, house <faire salle comble : to play to a full house>
salmigondis [salmigɔ̃di] *nms & pl* : hodgepodge
salon [salɔ̃] *nm* **1** : living room, parlor, lounge **2** : salon <salon de beauté : beauty salon, beauty parlor> **3** EXPOSITION : exhibition, show **4 salon de thé** : tearoom **5 salon funéraire** *or* **salon mortuaire** *Can* : funeral parlor
salopette [salɔpɛt] *nf* : overalls *pl*
salsepareille [salsəparɛj] *nf* : sarsaparilla
saltimbanque [saltɛ̃bãk] *nmf* : acrobat
salubre [salybr] *adj* : salubrious, healthy
salubrité [salybrite] *nf* **1** : healthiness **2 salubrité publique** : public health
saluer [salɥe] *vt* **1** : to greet **2** : to say goodbye to **3** : to salute
salut [saly] *nm* **1** : greeting, wave, nod <salut! : hello!, hi!, good-bye!> **2** : salute **3** SAUVEGARDE : safety, security **4** : salvation (in religion)
salutaire [salyter] *adj* : salutary, beneficial
salutation [salytasjɔ̃] *nf* **1** : salutation, greeting **2 veuillez agréer mes salutations distinguées** : yours truly, yours sincerely
salvadorien, -rienne [salvadɔrjɛ̃, -rjɛn] *adj* : El Salvadoran
Salvadorien, -rienne *n* : El Salvadoran
salve [salv] *nf* : salvo, volley
samedi [samdi] *nm* : Saturday
samoan, -moane [samoã, -moan] *adj* : Samoan
Samoan, -moane *n* : Samoan
sanatorium [sanatɔrjɔm] *nm* : sanitarium
sanctifier [sãktifje] {96} *vt* : to sanctify
sanction [sãksjɔ̃] *nf* **1** APPROBATION : sanction, approval **2** : sanction, penalty <prendre des sanctions contre : to take sanctions against>
sanctionner [sãksjɔne] *vt* **1** CONSACRER : to sanction, to approve **2** PUNIR : to penalize
sanctuaire [sãktyer] *nm* **1** : sanctuary (in a church) **2** : shrine
sandale [sãdal] *nf* : sandal
sandwich [sãdwitʃ] *nm, pl* **sandwiches** *or* **sandwichs** [-witʃ] : sandwich
sang [sã] *nm* : blood
sang-froid [sãfrwa] *nms & pl* **1** : composure, calm **2 de ~** : in cold blood
sanglant, -glante [sãglã, -glãt] *adj* **1** ENSANGLANTÉ : bloody **2** : cruel, savage <critique sanglante : scathing criticism>
sangle [sãgl] *nf* : strap, cinch
sangler [sãgle] *vt* : to girth, to cinch (a horse)
sanglier [sãglije] *nm* : wild boar
sanglot [sãglo] *nm* : sob
sangloter [sãglɔte] *vi* : to sob
sangsue [sãsy] *nf* : leech, bloodsucker
sanguin, -guine [sãgɛ̃, -gin] *adj* **1** : blood <groupe sanguin : blood type> **2** : sanguine
sanguinaire [sãginer] *adj* **1** : bloodthirsty **2** : bloody
sanguinolent, -lente [sãginɔlã, -lãt] *adj* : bloodstained
sanitaire [saniter] *adj* **1** : sanitary **2** : health, medical <risques sanitaires : health risks> **3 appareils sanitaires** : bathroom plumbing fixtures
sans[1] [sã] *adv* : without <je ferai sans : I'll do without>
sans[2] *prep* **1** : without <sans doute : doubtless, no doubt> <sans plus tarder : without further ado> **2 sans que** : without <sans que vous le sachiez : without your knowing it>
sans-abri [sãzabri] *nmfs & pl* : homeless person
sans-emploi [sãzɑ̃plwa] *nmfs & pl* : unemployed person
sans-gêne[1] [sãʒɛn] *adj* : inconsiderate
sans-gêne[2] *nm* : lack of consideration
santal [sãtal] *nm* : sandalwood
santé [sãte] *nf* **1** : health **2 à votre santé!** : to your health!, cheers!
saoudien, -dienne [saudjɛ̃, -djɛn] *adj* : Saudi, Saudi Arabian
Saoudien, -dienne *n* : Saudi, Saudi Arabian
saoul, saoule [su, sul] → **soûl**
saouler [sule] → **soûler**
saper [sape] *vt* MINER : to undermine
sapeur-pompier [sapœrpɔ̃pje] *nm, pl* **sapeurs-pompiers** *France* : firefighter
saphir [safir] *nm* **1** : sapphire **2** : needle (of a record player)
sapin [sapɛ̃] *nm* **1** : fir **2 sapin baumier** : balsam fir **3 sapin de Noël** : Christmas tree
sapinette [sapinet] *nf* : spruce
sarcasme [sarkasm] *nm* : sarcasm
sarcastique [sarkastik] *adj* : sarcastic — **sarcastiquement** [-tikmã] *adv*
sarcelle [sarsɛl] *nf* : teal (duck)
sarcler [sarkle] *vt* : to weed, to hoe
sarcophage [sarkɔfaʒ] *nm* : sarcophagus
sardine [sardin] *nf* : sardine
sardonique [sardɔnik] *adj* : sardonic — **sardoniquement** [-nikmã] *adv*
sari [sari] *nm* : sari

sarrasin [sarazɛ̃] *nm* : buckwheat
sarrau [saro] *nm, pl* **sarraus** : smock
sas [sas] *nm* **1** CRIBLE : sieve **2** : enclosure (in a canal lock) **3** : airlock
sassafras [sasafra] *nm* : sassafras
Satan [satɑ̃] *nm* : Satan
satanique [satanik] *adj* : satanic
satellite [satelit] *nm* : satellite
satiété [sasjete] *nf* : satiation, satiety <manger à satiété : to eat one's fill>
satin [satɛ̃] *nm* : satin
satire [satir] *nf* : satire
satirique [satirik] *adj* : satiric, satirical
satiriser [satirize] *vt* : to satirize
satisfaction [satisfaksjɔ̃] *nf* : satisfaction, gratification
satisfaire [satisfɛr] {42} *vt* CONTENTER : to satisfy — *vi* ~ **à** : to satisfy, to fulfill, to meet — **se satisfaire** *vr* ~ **de** : to be content with
satisfaisant, -sante [satisfəzɑ̃, -zɑ̃t] *adj* **1** : satisfactory, acceptable **2** : satisfying, pleasing
satisfait, -faite [satisfɛ, -fɛt] *adj* : satisfied, pleased
saturer [satyre] *vt* : to saturate — **saturation** [-tyrasjɔ̃] *nf*
Saturne [satyrn] *nf* : Saturn (planet)
satyre [satir] *nm* **1** : satyr **2** : lecher
sauce [sos] *nf* : sauce
saucisse [sosis] *nf* **1** : sausage (meat) **2** **saucisse de Francfort** *or* **saucisse à hot–dog** *Can* : frankfurter, hot dog
saucisson [sosisɔ̃] *nm* : sausage, bologna, cold cut
sauf[1], **sauve** [sof, sov] *adj* **1** : safe, unharmed **2** : intact, saved
sauf[2] *prep* **1** : except (for), apart from **2** **sauf si** : unless <sauf s'il neige : unless it snows>
sauge [soʒ] *nf* : sage (herb)
saugrenu, -nue [sogrəny] *adj* ABSURDE : preposterous, absurd
saule [sol] *nm* : willow <saule pleureur : weeping willow>
saumâtre [somatr] *adj* : brackish, briny
saumon[1] [somɔ̃] *adj* : salmon pink
saumon[2] *nm* : salmon
saumure [somyr] *nf* : brine
sauna [sona] *nm* : sauna
saupoudrer [sopudre] *vt* : to sprinkle
saura [sɔra], *etc.* → **savoir**
saut [so] *nm* **1** BOND : jump <saut en hauteur : high jump> <saut de main : handspring> <saut périlleux : somersault> <saut à skis : ski jump> **2** : leap, drop <faire le saut : to take the plunge> **3** **faire faire un saut à qqn** *Can* : to scare s.o., to make s.o. jump **4** **faire un saut chez qqn** : to drop in on s.o.
saute–mouton [sotmutɔ̃] *nms & pl* : leapfrog
sauter [sote] *vt* **1** FRANCHIR : to jump over, to clear **2** OMETTRE : to skip, to leave out — *vi* **1** BONDIR : to jump, to leap <sauter à cloche-pied : to hop> <sauter à la corde : to jump rope> **2** : to leap up, to jump <sauter aux yeux : to be glaringly obvious> **3** : to come off, to slip (of a gear, etc.) **4** EXPLOSER : to go off, to blow up **5** **faire sauter** : to sauté
sauterelle [sotrɛl] *nf* : grasshopper
sauteur, -teuse [sotœr, -tøz] *n* : jumper (in sports)
sautillement [sotijmɑ̃] *nm* : hop, skip
sautiller [sotije] *vi* **1** : to hop, to skip **2** : to flit about
sautoir [sotwar] *nm* : long necklace, chain
sauvage[1] [sovaʒ] *adj* **1** : savage **2** : wild **3** FAROUCHE : unsociable, shy
sauvage[2] *nmf* **1** : savage **2** : unsociable person
sauvagerie [sovaʒri] *nf* **1** : savagery **2** : shyness, unsociability
sauvagine [sovaʒin] *nf* : waterfowl
sauve → **sauf**[1]
sauvegarde [sovgard] *nf* **1** : safeguard **2** : safety, security **3** : backup (of a computer file)
sauvegarder [sovgarde] *vt* **1** : to safeguard **2** : to save (a computer file)
sauve–qui–peut [sovkipø] *nms & pl* : stampede, panic
sauver [sove] *vt* **1** : to save, to rescue **2** : to salvage **3** : to redeem — **se sauver** *vr* **1** : to escape **2** *fam* FILER : to leave, to split, to rush off
sauvetage [sovtaʒ] *nm* **1** : rescue, lifesaving **2** : salvage
sauveteur [sovtœr] *nm* : rescuer, lifesaver
sauvette [sovɛt] **à la sauvette** **1** : hastily, in a rush **2** : illegally, on the sly
sauveur [sovœr] *nm* : savior
savamment [savamɑ̃] *adv* **1** : learnedly **2** HABILEMENT : skillfully
savane [savan] *nf* **1** : savanna **2** *Can* : swamp
savant[1], **-vante** [savɑ̃, -vɑ̃t] *adj* **1** ÉRUDIT : learned, scholarly **2** HABILE : skillful, clever
savant[2], **-vante** *n* **1** ÉRUDIT : savant, scholar **2** SCIENTIFIQUE : scientist
saveur [savœr] *nf* GOÛT : flavor, savor
savoir[1] [savwar] {79} *vt* **1** : to know <savoir par coeur : to know by heart> <je le sais loyal : I know he's loyal> <en savoir long de : to know a great deal about> <sans le savoir : unknowingly> **2** POUVOIR : to know how to, to be able to <elle sait jouer du piano : she can play the piano> <je ne sais pas mentir : I cannot tell a lie> **3** **à** ~ : that is to say, namely — **se savoir** *vr* : to become known
savoir[2] *nm* : learning, knowledge
savoir–faire [savwarfɛr] *nms & pl* : know-how, expertise
savoir–vivre [savwarvivr] *nms & pl* : good manners *pl*, tact
savon [savɔ̃] *nm* **1** : soap **2** *fam* **passer un savon à** : to reprimand

savonner [savɔne] *vt* : to soap (up), to lather
savonnette [savɔnɛt] *nf* : bar of soap
savonneux, -neuse [savɔnø, -nøz] *adj* : soapy
savourer [savure] *vt* : to savor
savoureux, -reuse [savurø, -røz] *adj* **1** DÉLECTABLE : savory, tasty **2** PIQUANT : racy, juicy <anecdote savoureuse : racy anecdote>
saxophone [saksɔfɔn] *nm* : saxophone — **saxophoniste** [-fɔnist] *nmf*
scabreux, -breuse [skabrø, -brøz] *adj* **1** INDÉCENT : indecent, risqué **2** : risky, tricky
scalpel [skalpɛl] *nm* : scalpel
scalper [skalpe] *vt* : to scalp
scandale [skɑ̃dal] *nf* **1** : scandal <faire scandale : to cause a scandal> **2** ÉCLAT : scene, uproar
scandaleux, -leuse [skɑ̃dalø, -løz] *adj* : scandalous, disgraceful — **scandaleusement** [-løzmɑ̃] *adv*
scandaliser [skɑ̃dalize] *vt* : to scandalize
scander [skɑ̃de] *vt* **1** : to scan (poetry) **2** : to chant **3** : to accentuate, to stress
scandinave [skɑ̃dinav] *adj* : Scandinavian
Scandinave *nmf* : Scandinavian
scanner [skanɛr] *nm* : scanner
scansion [skɑ̃sjɔ̃] *nf* : scan, scanning (in literature)
scaphandre [skafɑ̃dr] *nm* **1** : diving suit **2** : space suit
scaphandrier [skafɑ̃drije] *nm* : deep-sea diver
scarabée [skarabe] *nm* **1** : beetle **2** : scarab
scarlatine [skarlatin] *nf* : scarlet fever
scarole [skarɔl] *nf* : endive, escarole
sceau [so] *nm* **1** : seal **2** : hallmark, stamp
scélérat[1], **-rate** [selera, -rat] *adj* : villainous
scélérat[2], **-rate** *n* : villain, rogue
scellé [sele] *nm* : seal
sceller [sele] *vt* **1** : to seal **2** : to attach securely, to fix
scénario [senarjo] *nm* **1** : scenario **2** : screenplay
scène [sɛn] *nf* **1** : scene (in theater) **2** : stage <être en scène : to be on stage> **3** : scene, row <faire une scène : to make a scene> **4** → **metteur, mise**
scénique [senik] *adj* : theatrical
scepticisme [sɛptisism] *nm* : skepticism
sceptique[1] [sɛptik] *adj* : skeptical
sceptique[2] *nmf* : skeptic
sceptre [sɛptr] *nm* : scepter
scheik [ʃɛk] *nm* → **cheik**
schéma [ʃema] *nm* **1** : diagram **2** ESQUISSE : sketch, outline
schématique [ʃematik] *adj* **1** : schematic **2** : (over)simplified
schisme [ʃism] *nm* : schism
schiste [ʃist] *nm* **schiste argileux** : shale
schizophrène [skizɔfrɛn] *adj & nmf* : schizophrenic
schizophrénie [skizɔfreni] *nf* : schizophrenia
schooner [ʃunœr] *nm* GOÉLETTE : schooner
scie [si] *nf* **1** : saw <scie à métaux : hacksaw> <scie sauteuse : jigsaw> <scie à chaîne : chainsaw> **2** : catchphrase **3** *fam* : drag, bore
sciemment [sjamɑ̃] *adv* : knowingly
science [sjɑ̃s] *nf* **1** : science **2** SAVOIR : knowledge, learning
science–fiction [sjɑ̃sfiksjɔ̃] *nf* : science fiction
scientifique[1] [sjɑ̃tifik] *adj* : scientific — **scientifiquement** [-fikmɑ̃] *adv*
scientifique[2] *nmf* : scientist
scier [sje] {96} *vt* : to saw
scierie [siri] *nf* : sawmill
scinder [sɛ̃de] *vt* DIVISER : to split, to divide — **se scinder** *vr* : to be divided, to split up
scintillant, -lante [sɛ̃tijɑ̃, -jɑ̃t] *adj* : sparkling, twinkling
scintillement [sɛ̃tijmɑ̃] *nm* : sparkling, twinkling
scintiller [sɛ̃tije] *vi* : to scintillate, to twinkle, to sparkle
scission [sisjɔ̃] *nf* **1** : schism, split <faire scission : to secede, to break away> **2** : fission (in biology and physics)
sciure [sjyr] *nf* : sawdust
scolaire [skɔlɛr] *adj* : school, scholastic <l'année scolaire : the school year>
scolarité [skɔlarite] *nf* : schooling
scooter [skutœr] *nm* : motor scooter
scorbut [skɔrbyt] *nm* : scurvy
score [skɔr] *nm* : score
scorie [skɔri] *nf* **1** : slag **2** : dross, dregs
scorpion [skɔrpjɔ̃] *nm* : scorpion
Scorpion *nm* : Scorpio
scotch [skɔtʃ] *nm* : Scotch whiskey
scout[1], **scoute** [skut] *adj* : scout <camp scout : scout camp>
scout[2], **scoute** *n* : Boy Scout *m*, Girl Scout *f*
scribe [skrib] *nm* : scribe
script [skript] *nm* **1** : printing, lettering **2** : script (in movies, television, etc.)
scrotum [skrɔtɔm] *nm* : scrotum
scrupule [skrypyl] *nm* : scruple, qualm, compunction
scrupuleux, -leuse [skrypylø, -løz] *adj* : scrupulous — **scrupuleusement** [-løzmɑ̃] *adv*
scruter [skryte] *vt* : to scrutinize
scrutin [skrytɛ̃] *nm* **1** : ballot, voting **2** : polling, polls *pl*
sculpter [skylte] *vt* : to sculpt, to sculpture, to carve
sculpteur [skyltœr] *nm* : sculptor <elle est sculpteur : she's a sculptor>
sculpture [skyltyr] *nf* : sculpture — **sculptural, -rale** [-tyral] *adj*
se [sə] (**s'** *before a vowel or mute h*) *pron* **1** (*used with reflexive verbs*) : oneself,

himself, herself, themselves, itself <elle se regarde : she looks at herself> **2** (*used to indicate reciprocity*) : each other, one another <ils se sont parlés : they spoke to each other> **3** (*used in passive constructions*) <ça ne se fait pas : that is not done> **4** (*used when referring to parts of the body*) <il se lave les dents : he brushes his teeth> **5** (*used with impersonal verbs*) <il se peut qu'elle arrive demain : she may arrive tomorrow>

séance [seɑ̃s] *nf* **1** : session, meeting **2** : showing, performance **3 séance de spiritisme** : séance **4 séance tenante** : immediately, without delay

seau [so] *nm, pl* **seaux** : bucket, pail

sec[1] [sɛk] *adv* **1** : hard <frapper sec : to strike hard> **2** BRUSQUEMENT : abruptly, sharply

sec[2], **sèche** [sɛk, sɛʃ] *adj* **1** : dry **2** : dried <abricots secs : dried apricots> **3** MAIGRE : lean, gaunt **4** DUR : hard, harsh, sharp <une voix sèche : a harsh voice> <avec un bruit sec : with a snap>

sec[3] *nm* **1** : dryness **2 être à sec** *fam* : to be dried up, to go broke

sécateur [sekatœr] *nm* : clippers *pl*, (garden) shears

sécession [sesesjɔ̃] *nf* : secession <faire sécession : to secede>

sèche–cheveux [sɛʃʃəvø] *nms & pl* : hairdryer

sèchement [sɛʃmɑ̃] *adv* : dryly, curtly

sécher [seʃe] {87} *vt* **1** : to dry **2** *France fam* : to skip, to cut (a class, etc.) — *vi* **1** : to dry, to dry up, to dry out **2** *fam* : to be stumped, to draw a blank

sécheresse [seʃres] *nf* **1** : drought **2** : dryness **3** : curtness

séchoir [seʃwar] *nm* : dryer

second[1], **-conde** [səgɔ̃, -gɔ̃d] *adj* **1** : second **2 de seconde main** : secondhand

second[2], **-conde** *nmf* : second

second[3] *nm* **1** : assistant, helper **2** : first mate **3** : second floor

secondaire [səgɔ̃dɛr] *adj* **1** : secondary **2 → école**

seconde [səgɔ̃d] *nf* **1** : second <attends une seconde! : wait a second!> **2** : second class <voyager en seconde : to travel second class>

seconder [səgɔ̃de] *vt* : to assist, to back up

secouer [sɔkwe] *vt* **1** : to shake <secouer la tête : to shake one's head> **2** : to shake off **3** *fam* : to shake up, to rouse — **se secouer** *vr* : to pull oneself together, to get going

secourable [sɔkurabl] *adj* : helpful

secourir [sɔkurir] {23} *vt* **1** AIDER : to help, to aid **2** : to rescue

secourisme [sɔkurism] *nm* : first aid

secouriste [sɔkurist] *nmf* : first aid worker

secours [sɔkur] *nms & pl* **1** : help, aid <au secours! : help!> **2 de ~** : for emergency <pneu de secours : spare tire> <sortie de secours : emergency exit> **3 secours** *nmpl* : rescuers, reinforcements

secousse [sɔkus] *nf* **1** CAHOT : jolt, jerk **2** CHOC : shock, upset **3** *Can* : period of time **4** : tremor

secret[1], **-crète** [sɔkrɛ, -krɛt] *adj* **1** : secret **2** : secretive, reserved

secret[2] *nm* **1** : secret **2** : secrecy

secrétaire[1] [sɔkretɛr] *nmf* : secretary

secrétaire[2] *nm* : secretary (desk)

secrétariat [sɔkretarjat] *nm* **1** : secretariat **2** : secretarial work

secrètement [sɔkrɛtmɑ̃] *adv* : secretly

sécréter [sekrete] {87} *vt* : to secrete <sécréter du lait : to lactate> — **sécrétion** [-resjɔ̃] *nf*

sectaire [sɛktɛr] *adj* : sectarian

secte [sɛkt] *nm* : sect

secteur [sɛktœr] *nm* : sector, area, zone <le secteur privé : the private sector>

section [sɛksjɔ̃] *nf* **1** : section **2** : department, branch

sectionner [sɛksjɔne] *vt* **1** DIVISER : to section, to divide **2** TRANCHER : to sever

séculaire [sekylɛr] *adj* **1** : ancient, age-old, a hundred years old **2** : secular

séculier, -lière [sekylje, -ljɛr] *adj* LAÏQUE : secular

secundo [səgɔ̃do] *adv* : second, secondly

sécuriser [sekyrize] *vt* **1** RASSURER : to reassure **2** : to make (someone) feel secure

sécurité [sekyrite] *nf* **1** : security <sentiment de sécurité : sense of security> **2** : safety <sécurité publique : public safety>

sédatif[1], **-tive** [sedatif, -tiv] *adj* : sedative

sédatif[2] *nm* : sedative

sédation [sedasjɔ̃] *nf* : sedation

sédentaire [sedɑ̃tɛr] *adj* : sedentary

sédiment [sedimɑ̃] *nm* : sediment — **sédimentaire** [-mɑ̃tɛr] *adj*

séditieux, -tieuse [sedisjø, -sjøz] *adj* : seditious

sédition [sedisjɔ̃] *nf* : insurrection, revolt

séducteur[1], **-trice** [sedyktœr, -tris] *adj* : seductive

séducteur[2], **-trice** *n* : seducer

séduction [sedyksjɔ̃] *nf* **1** : seduction **2** : charm, appeal

séduire [seduir] {49} *vt* **1** : to seduce **2** : to charm **3** : to appeal to

séduisant, -sante [seduizɑ̃, -zɑ̃t] *adj* : seductive, attractive

segment [segmɑ̃] *nm* : segment

segmentaire [segmɑ̃tɛr] *adj* : segmented

ségrégation [segregasjɔ̃] *nf* : segregation

seiche [seʃ] *nf* : cuttlefish

seigle [segl] *nm* : rye

seigneur [sɛɲœr] *nm* **1** : lord **2 le Seigneur** : the Lord
sein [sɛ̃] *nm* **1** : breast, bosom <donner le sein à : to breast-feed> **2** VENTRE : womb **3 au sein de** : within
séisme [seism] *nm* : earthquake
seize[1] [sɛz] *adj* **1** : sixteen **2** : sixteenth <le seize octobre : October sixteenth>
seize[2] *nms & pl* : sixteen
seizième [sɛzjɛm] *adj & nmf & nm* : sixteenth
séjour [seʒur] *nm* **1** : stay, sojourn **2 → salle**
séjourner [seʒurne] *vi* **1** : to stay (at a hotel, etc.) **2** RESTER : to lie, to remain (of water, fog, etc.)
sel [sɛl] *nm* **1** : salt <sel gemme : rock salt> **2** : piquancy, wit
sélect, -lecte [selɛkt] *adj fam* : select, exclusive, posh
sélectif, -tive [selɛktif, -tiv] *adj* : selective
sélection [selɛksjɔ̃] *nf* **1** : selection **2 sélection naturelle** : natural selection
sélectionner [selɛksjɔne] *vt* : to select, to choose
self-made-man [sɛlfmedman] *nm* : self-made man
self-service [sɛlfsɛrvis] *nm, pl* **self-services** : self-service store or restaurant
selle [sɛl] *nf* **1** : saddle **2 aller à la selle** : to have a bowel movement
seller [sele] *vt* : to saddle
sellette [selɛt] *nf* **être sur la sellette** : to be in the hot seat
selon [səlɔ̃] *prep* **1** : according to **2 ~ que** : depending on whether
semailles [səmaj] *nfpl* : sowing, seeding
semaine [səmɛn] *nf* **1** : week <une semaine de quarante heures : a forty-hour week> **2 vivre à la petite semaine** : to live day by day
sémantique[1] [semɑ̃tik] *adj* : semantic
sémantique[2] *nf* : semantics
sémaphore [semafɔr] *nm* : semaphore
semblable[1] [sɑ̃blabl] *adj* **1** : similar, like **2** TEL : such <il faut de semblables mesures : such measures are necessary>
semblable[2] *nmf* : fellow creature, like <vous et vos semblables : you and your kind>
semblant [sɑ̃blɑ̃] *nm* **1** : semblance, appearance **2 faire semblant** : to pretend
sembler [sɑ̃ble] *vi* : to seem <elle semble contente : she seems (to be) happy> **— *v impers* il semble que** : it seems that
semelle [səmɛl] *nf* **1** : sole **2** *or* **semelle intérieure** : insole
semence [səmɑ̃s] *nf* **1** GRAINE : seed **2** : tack, brad
semer [sɔme] {52} *vt* **1** : to sow, to seed **2** RÉPANDRE : to strew, to scatter **3** *fam* : to lose, to shake off (pursuers, etc.)
semestre [səmɛstr] *nm* : semester
semestriel, -trielle [səmɛstrijɛl] *adj* : biannual **— semestriellement** *adv*
semeur, -meuse [səmœr, -møz] *n* : sower
semi-circulaire [səmisirkylɛr] *adj* DEMI-CIRCULAIRE : semicircular
semi-conducteur [sɛmikɔ̃dyktœr] *nm, pl* **semi-conducteurs** : semiconductor
sémillant, -lante [semijɑ̃, -jɑ̃t] *adj* VIF : lively, spirited
séminaire [seminɛr] *nm* **1** : seminary **2** : seminar
séminal, -nale [seminal] *adj, mpl* **-naux** [-no] : seminal
semi-remorque [səmirəmɔrk] *nm, pl* **semi-remorques** : semitrailer
semis [səmi] *nm* **1** : seedling **2** : sowing **3** : seedbed **4** : small repeated pattern
semoir [səmwar] *nm* : drill (in agriculture)
semonce [səmɔ̃s] *nf* **1** RÉPRIMANDE : reprimand **2 coup de semonce** : warning shot
semoule [səmul] *nf* : semolina <semoule de maïs : cornflour>
sempiternel, -nelle [sɑ̃pitɛrnɛl] *adj* ÉTERNEL : eternal
sénat [sena] *nm* : senate
sénateur [senatœr] *nm* : senator
sénatrice [senatris] *nf Can* : (female) senator
sénégalais, -laise [senegalɛ, -lɛz] *adj* : Senegalese
Sénégalais, -laise *n* : Senegalese
sénile [senil] *adj* : senile
sénilité [senilite] *nf* : senility
sens [sɑ̃s] *nms & pl* **1** : sense (in physiology) <sens du toucher : sense of touch> **2** SIGNIFICATION : sense, meaning <dépourvu de sens : meaningless> **3** INSTINCT : sense, feeling <sens du rythme : sense of rhythm> **4** RAISON : sense <cela n'a pas de sens : that doesn't make any sense> **5** DIRECTION : direction, way <sens unique : one-way> **6** OPINION : opinion <à mon sens : in my opinion> **7 sens dessus dessous** : upside down
sensation [sɑ̃sasjɔ̃] *nf* **1** : sensation, feeling **2 faire sensation** : to cause a sensation
sensationnel, -nelle [sɑ̃sasjɔnɛl] *adj* : sensational
sensé, -sée [sɑ̃se] *adj* : sensible
sensibiliser [sɑ̃sibilize] *vt* : to sensitize
sensibilité [sɑ̃sibilite] *nf* : sensitivity, sensibility
sensible [sɑ̃sibl] *adj* **1** : sensitive **2** APPRÉCIABLE : appreciable, considerable **3** PERCEPTIBLE : perceptible

sensiblement [sɑ̃sibləmɑ̃] *adv* **1** : appreciably, noticeably **2** : roughly, approximately
sensiblerie [sɑ̃sibləri] *nf* : sentimentality
sensitif, -tive [sɑ̃sitif, -tiv] *adj* **1** : oversensitive **2** : sensory
sensoriel, -rielle [sɑ̃sɔrjɛl] *adj* : sensory
sensualité [sɑ̃sɥalite] *nf* : sensuality, sensuousness
sensuel, -suelle [sɑ̃sɥɛl] *adj* : sensual, sensuous — **sensuellement** [-sɥɛlmɑ̃] *adv*
sentence [sɑ̃tɑ̃s] *nf* **1** JUGEMENT : sentence **2** MAXIME : maxim, proverb
sentencieux, -cieuse [sɑ̃tɑ̃sjø, -sjøz] *adj* : sententious
senteur [sɑ̃tœr] *nf* : scent
senti, -tie [sɑ̃ti] *adj* **bien senti** : blunt, forthright <mots bien sentis : well-chosen words>
sentier [sɑ̃tje] *nm* : path <hors des sentiers battus : off the beaten track>
sentiment [sɑ̃timɑ̃] *nm* **1** : sentiment, feeling <avoir le sentiment de : to be aware of> <faire du sentiment : to be sentimental> **2** AVIS : opinion, feeling <c'est mon sentiment : that's my feeling, that's what I think> **3 recevez l'expression de mes sentiments respectueux** : yours truly
sentimental, -tale [sɑ̃timɑ̃tal] *adj, mpl* **-taux** [-to] : sentimental — **sentimentalité** [-talite] *nf*
sentinelle [sɑ̃tinɛl] *nf* : sentinel, sentry
sentir [sɑ̃tir] {82} *vt* **1** : to smell, to taste **2** : to smell like, to smell of <ça sent la rose : it smells like a rose> **3** : to feel <il n'a rien senti : he felt nothing> **4** : to have a feeling (for), to appreciate <je sens que c'est important : I have a feeling that it's important> <elle sent l'art moderne : she appreciates modern art> **5** : to smack of, to be indicative of — *vi* : to smell — **se sentir** *vr* **1** : to feel <il se sent malade : he feels sick> **2** : to be felt, to show
seoir [swar] {80} *vi* **~ à** : to suit, to be appropriate to — *v impers* **il sied** : it is fitting, it is appropriate
séparation [separasjɔ̃] *nf* : separation
séparé, -rée [separe] *adj* **1** : separate **2** : separated (from one's spouse)
séparément [separemɑ̃] *adv* : separately, apart
séparer [separe] *vt* **1** DÉTACHER : to separate, to detach **2** DISTINGUER : to distinguish (between) **3** : to divide — **se séparer** *vr* **1** : to separate, to part, to split up **2** : to divide **3 ~ de** : to part with, to be without
sépia [sepja] *nf* : sepia
sept[1] [sɛt] *adj* **1** : seven **2** : seventh <le sept mai : May seventh>
sept[2] *nms & pl* : seven
septante[1] [sɛptɑ̃t] *adj Bel, Switz* **1** : seventy **2** : seventieth
septante[2] *nms & pl Bel, Switz* : seventy
septembre [sɛptɑ̃br] *nm* : September
septentrional, -nale [sɛptɑ̃trijɔnal] *adj, mpl* **-naux** [-no] : northern
septième [sɛtjɛm] *adj & nmf & nm* : seventh
septique [sɛptik] *adj* **1** : septic **2 → fosse**
sépulcre [sepylkr] *nm* : sepulchre, tomb
sépulture [sepyltyr] *nf* **1** TOMBE : grave **2** ENTERREMENT : burial
séquelle [sekɛl] *nf* **1** CONSÉQUENCE : consequence **2 séquelles** *nfpl* : aftereffects
séquence [sekɑ̃s] *nf* SUITE : sequence
séquentiel, -tielle [sekɑ̃sjɛl] *adj* : sequential
séquestre [sekɛstr] *nm* : escrow <en séquestre : in escrow>
séquestrer [sekɛstre] *vt* : to sequester
séquoia [sekɔja] *nm* : sequoia
sera [sərɑ], *etc.* → **être**
sérail [seraj] *nm* : seraglio
séraphin, -phine [serafɛ̃, -fin] *adj Can fam* : stingy, miserly
serbe[1] [sɛrb] *adj* : Serb, Serbian
serbe[2] *nm* : Serbian (language)
Serbe *nmf* : Serb, Serbian
serein, -reine [sərɛ̃, -rɛn] *adj* **1** : clear, tranquil (of the sky, weather, etc.) **2** CALME : calm, serene — **sereinement** [-rɛnmɑ̃] *adv*
sérénade [serenad] *nf* : serenade
sérénité [serenite] *nf* : serenity
serf, serve [sɛrf, sɛrv] *n* : serf
serge [sɛrʒ] *nf* : serge
sergé [sɛrʒe] *nm* : twill
sergent [sɛrʒɑ̃] *nm* : sergeant
série [seri] *nf* **1** : series **2** : set, range, line **3 de ~** : mass-produced, standard, stock **4 fabrication en série** : mass production
sériel, -rielle [serjɛl] *adj* : serial
sérieusement [serjøzmɑ̃] *adv* : seriously
sérieux[1], **-rieuse** [serjø, -rjøz] *adj* **1** : serious, solemn **2** : important <une sérieuse argumentation : a weighty argument> **3** : reliable, dependable **4** : responsible, conscientious
sérieux[2] *nm* : seriousness, earnestness <se prendre au sérieux : to take oneself seriously>
serin [sərɛ̃] *nm* : canary
seringue [sərɛ̃g] *nf* : syringe
serment [sɛrmɑ̃] *nm* **1** : oath <prêter serment : to take the oath> **2** : vow, promise
sermon [sɛrmɔ̃] *nm* **1** : sermon **2** : lecture, talking-to
sermonner [sɛrmɔne] *vt* : to lecture
serpent [sɛrpɑ̃] *nm* **1** : snake, serpent **2 serpent à sonnettes** CROTALE : rattlesnake
serpenter [sɛrpɑ̃te] *vi* : to wind, to meander

serpentin [sɛrpɑ̃tɛ̃] *nm* : streamer
serrage [sɛraʒ] *nm* : tightening
serre [sɛr] *nf* **1** : greenhouse, hothouse <l'effet de serre : greenhouse effect> **2 serres** *nfpl* : claws, talons
serré, -rée [sɛre] *adj* **1** : tight **2** : thick, cramped, dense **3** : strict, tight,-close <surveillance serrée : close supervision>
serre–livres [sɛrlivr] *nms & pl* : bookend
serrement [sɛrmɑ̃] *nm* : pressing, squeezing, constriction <serrement de main : handshake> <serrement de coeur : pang (of sorrow)>
serrer [sɛre] *vt* **1** : to press, to squeeze, to grip <serrer les poings : to clench one's fists> **2** : to tighten **3** : to squeeze tightly <ces chaussures me serrent : these shoes are too tight> **4** : to stay close to <serrer le trottoir : to hug the curb> **5** : to push (close) together, to pack together **6** : to cut (expenses, etc.) **— se serrer** *vr* **1** : to huddle up (together) **2** : to tighten up **3 se serrer la main** : to shake hands
serre–tête [sɛrtɛt] *nm, pl* **serre–têtes** : headband
serrure [sɛryr] *nf* : lock
serrurier [sɛryrje] *nm* : locksmith
sert [sɛr], *etc.* → **servir**
sertir [sɛrtir] *vt* : to set, to mount (gems)
sérum [sɛrɔm] *nm* : serum
serveur[1], **-veuse** [sɛrvœr, -vøz] *n* : waiter *m*, waitress *f*
serveur[2] *nm* **1** : server (in sports) **2** : dealer (in card games) **3** : (computer) server
serviable [sɛrvjabl] *adj* OBLIGEANT : helpful, obliging
service [sɛrvis] *nm* **1** : service <mettre en service : to put in service, to set up> <hors service : out of order> <service de bus : bus service> **2** FAVEUR : favor <rendre un service à : to do a favor for> **3** : serving, course <repas à trois services : three-course meal> **4** : service, serving <être au service se son pays : to serve one's country> <à votre service! : not at all!, don't mention it!> <service militaire : military service> <faire le service : to serve a meal, to wait tables> **5** : department <service du personnel : personnel department> <services sociaux : social services> <service des urgences : emergency room> **6** : set <service de café : coffee service> **7** : service, serve (in sports)
serviette [sɛrvjɛt] *nf* **1** : napkin **2** : towel **3** : briefcase, portfolio **4 serviette hygiénique** : sanitary napkin
servile [sɛrvil] *adj* : servile **— servilité** [sɛrvilite] *nf*
servir [sɛrvir] {8I} *vt* **1** : to serve **2** AIDER : to help, to assist **3** : to deal (cards) **— *vi* 1** : to be useful <ça ne sert à rien : that is of no use> **2** : to serve (in the military) **3** : to deal (in card games) **4 ~ de** : to serve as **— se servir** *vr* **1** : to serve oneself, to help oneself **2 ~ de** : to make use of
serviteur [sɛrvitœr] *nm* : servant
servitude [sɛrvityd] *nf* **1** : servitude **2** : obligation, constraint
ses → son
sésame [sezam] *nm* : sesame (plant and seed)
session [sesjɔ̃] *nf* : session
set [sɛt] *nm* **1** : set (in tennis, etc.) **2** *or* **set de table** : placemat
seuil [sœj] *nm* **1** : threshold, doorstep **2 au seuil de** : on the threshold, on the brink of
seul[1], **seule** [sœl] *adv* **1** : alone, only <seule Marie répondit : only Marie replied> **2** : by oneself, singlehandedly <tout seul : all by oneself>
seul[2], **seule** *adj* **1** : alone <j'ai besoin d'être seul : I need to be alone> **2** : only, unique <le seul problème : the only problem> **3** SOLITAIRE : lonely, solitary
seul[3], **seule** *pron* : only one, single one <c'est le seul qui reste : it's the only one left>
seulement[1] [sœlmɑ̃] *adv* **1** : only <seulement trois fois : only three times> <pas seulement . . . , mais encore : not only . . . , but also> **2** MÊME : even <sans seulement dire un mot : without even saying a word>
seulement[2] *conj* CEPENDANT : however, but, only <je l'achèterais, seulement je n'ai pas d'argent : I'd buy it, only I don't have any money>
sève [sɛv] *nf* **1** : sap **2** VIGUEUR : vim, vigor
sévère [sevɛr] *adj* **1** : strict, severe, stern **2** : austere **— sévèrement** [-vɛrmɑ̃] *adv*
sévérité [severite] *nf* : severity
sévices [sevis] *nmpl* : cruelty, brutality, abuse
sévir [sevir] *vi* **1** : to clamp down, to impose restrictions <sévir contre la corruption : to clamp down on corruption> **2** : to be rampant, to rage
sevrage [sɔvraʒ] *nm* : weaning
sevrer [sɔvre] *vt* : to wean
sexe [sɛks] *nm* **1** : sex **2** : sex organs, genitals
sexisme [sɛksism] *nm* : sexism
sexiste [sɛksist] *adj & nmf* : sexist
sextant [sɛkstɑ̃] *nm* : sextant
sextuor [sɛkstɥɔr] *nm* : sextet
sexualité [sɛksɥalite] *nf* : sexuality
sexuel, sexuelle [sɛksɥɛl] *adj* : sexual **— sexuellement** [-sɥɛlmɑ̃] *adv*
sexy [sɛksi] *adj* : sexy
seyant, seyante [sejɑ̃, -jɑ̃t] *adj* : becoming, flattering
shampooing [ʃɑ̃pwɛ̃] *nm* : shampoo

shampouiner *or* **shampooiner** [ʃɑ̃pwine] *vt* : to shampoo
shérif [ʃerif] *nm* : sheriff
shopping [ʃɔpiŋ] *nm* : shopping <faire le shopping : to go shopping>
short [ʃɔrt] *nm* : shorts *pl*
si¹ [si] *adv* **1** TELLEMENT : so, such, as <elle est si intelligente : she is so intelligent> <un si grand pays : such a big country> <il n'est pas si célèbre que ça : he's not as famous as all that> **2** (*used to contradict a negative statement or question*) : yes <il n'est pas arrivé à l'heure? si : he didn't arrive on time? yes, he did> **3 si bien que** : with the result that, so **4 si . . . que** : however <si riche qu'elle soit : however wealthy she is>
si² *conj* : if, whether <si vous voulez : if you please> <je ne sais pas si elle vient ou pas : I don't know whether she's coming or not>
siamois, -moise [sjamwa, -waz] *adj* : Siamese
Siamois, -moise *n* : Siamese
sida [sida] *nm* : AIDS
sidérer [sidere] {87} *vt fam* : to stagger, to amaze
sidérurgie [sideryrʒi] *nf* : steel industry
sidérurgique [sideryrʒik] *adj* : steel <usine sidérurgique : ironworks, steelworks>
siècle [sjɛkl] *nm* : century
siège [sjɛʒ] *nm* **1** : seat <siège arrière : back seat (of an automobile)> **2** *or* **siège social** : headquarters **3** : siege
siéger [sjeʒe] {64} *vi* **1** : to sit, to serve <siéger à un comité : to sit on a committee> **2** : to be in session **3** : to be located, to have its headquarters
sien¹, sienne [sjɛ̃, sjɛn] *adj* : his, hers, its, one's
sien², sienne *pron* **le sien, la sienne, les siens, les siennes** : his, hers, its, one's, theirs
sieste [sjɛst] *nf* : siesta, nap
sifflement [sifləmɑ̃] *nm* **1** : whistle, whistling, hoot (of a train) **2** : hiss, hissing
siffler [sifle] *vt* **1** : to whistle **2** : to whistle for, to whistle at **3** : to boo **4** *fam* : to swill down, to swig — *vi* **1** : to whistle, to blow a whistle, to hoot (of a train) **2** : to hiss **3** : to wheeze
sifflet [siflɛ] *nm* **1** : whistle **2 sifflets** *nmpl* : boos, catcalls
siffloter [sifloʒte] *v* : to whistle
sigle [sigl] *nm* : acronym
signal [siɲal] *nm, pl* **signaux** [siɲo] **1** : sign, signal (gesture) <donner le signal : to give the signal> **2** : signal <signal d'alarme : alarm (signal)>
signalement [siɲalmɑ̃] *nm* : description
signaler [siɲale] *vt* **1** : to signal **2** : to point out, to indicate **3** : to report — **se signaler** *vr* : to distinguish oneself, to stand out
signalisation [siɲalizasjɔ̃] *nf* : signals *pl*, signs *pl* <signalisation routière : road signs>
signataire [siɲatɛr] *nmf* : signatory
signature [siɲatyr] *nf* **1** : signature **2** : signing
signe [siɲ] *nm* **1** : sign, gesture <en signe d'estime : as a sign of respect> <faire signe que oui : to nod in agreement> **2** : sign, indication <signes de vie : signs of life> **3** : mark, symbol <signe de ponctuation : punctuation mark> <signe du zodiaque : sign of the zodiac> **4 signe avant-coureur** : herald, precursor
signer [siɲe] *vt* : to sign (one's name) — **se signer** *vr* : to cross oneself
signet [siɲe] *nm* : bookmark
significatif, -tive [siɲifikatif, -tiv] *adj* : significant
signification [siɲifikasjɔ̃] *nf* : significance, meaning
signifier [siɲifje] {96} *vt* : to signify, to mean
silence [silɑ̃s] *nm* **1** : silence <silence absolu : dead silence> <garder le silence : to keep quiet> **2** : rest (in music)
silencieux¹, -cieuse [silɑ̃sjø, -sjøz] *adj* : silent, quiet — **silencieusement** [-sjøzmɑ̃] *adv*
silencieux² *nm* **1** : silencer (of a firearm) **2** : muffler
silex [silɛks] *nm* : flint
silhouette [silwɛt] *nf* : silhouette, outline
silice [silis] *nf* : silica
silicium [silisjɔm] *nm* : silicon
sillage [sijaʒ] *nm* : wake (of a ship)
sillon [sijɔ̃] *nm* **1** : furrow **2** : groove (of a disc, etc.)
sillonner [sijɔne] *vt* **1** CREUSER : to furrow **2** PARCOURIR : to go all over, to crisscross
silo [silo] *nm* : silo
simagrée [simagre] *nf* **faire des simagrées** : to put on airs
similaire [similɛr] *adj* : similar — **similarité** [similarite] *nf*
simili [simili] *nm* : imitation (of leather, gems, etc.)
similitude [similityd] *nf* : similarity, resemblance
simple¹ [sɛ̃pl] *adj* **1** : simple, straightforward <directions simples : easy instructions> **2** : mere <une simple formalité : a mere formality> **3** : simple, plain, unaffected **4** *or* **simple d'esprit** : simpleminded **5** : single <lit simple : single bed> <un aller simple : a one-way ticket>
simple² *nm* **1** : singles (in tennis) **2** *Can* : single (in baseball)
simplement [sɛ̃pləmɑ̃] *adv* **1** : simply, merely, just **2** : simply, plainly **3** : easily
simplet, -plette [sɛ̃plɛ, -plɛt] *adj* **1** : simpleminded **2** SIMPLISTE : simplistic

simplicité [sɛ̃plisite] *nf* **1** : simplicity, informality **2** : simpleness
simplifier [sɛ̃plifje] {96} *vt* : to simplify — **simplification** [sɛ̃plifikasjɔ̃] *nf*
simpliste [sɛ̃plist] *adj* : simplistic, oversimplified
simulacre [simylakr] *nm* : sham, pretense
simuler [simyle] *vt* : to simulate — **simulation** [simylasjɔ̃] *nf*
simultané, -née [simyltane] *adj* : simultaneous — **simultanément** [-nemɑ̃] *adv*
sincère [sɛ̃sɛr] *adj* : sincere — **sincèrement** [-sɛrmɑ̃] *adv*
sincérité [sɛ̃serite] *nf* : sincerity
singapourien, -rienne [sɛ̃gapurjɛ̃, -rjɛn] *adj* : Singaporean
Singapourien, -rienne *n* : Singaporean
singe [sɛ̃ʒ] *nm* **1** : monkey <les grands singes : the great apes> **2 faire le singe** : to monkey about, to clown around
singer [sɛ̃ʒe] {17} *vt* **1** IMITER : to ape, to mimic **2** : to feign
singeries [sɛ̃ʒri] *nfpl* : antics
singulariser [sɛ̃gylarize] *vt* : to draw attention to (someone) — **se singulariser** *vr* : to call attention to oneself
singularité [sɛ̃gylarite] *nf* **1** : peculiarity, strangeness **2** : uniqueness
singulier[1], **-lière** [sɛ̃gylje, -ljɛr] *adj* **1** : uncommon, strange, remarkable **2** : singular (in grammar)
singulier[2] *nm* : singular (in grammar)
singulièrement [sɛ̃gyljɛrmɑ̃] *nm* **1** BEAUCOUP : very much, extremely **2** BIZARREMENT : oddly, strangely **3** PARTICULIÈREMENT : particularly
sinistre[1] [sinistr] *adj* **1** : sinister, eerie **2** : dismal, gloomy
sinistre[2] *nm* **1** DÉSASTRE : disaster **2** DOMMAGE : damage
sinistré[1], **-trée** [sinistre] *adj* : damaged, stricken
sinistré[2], **-trée** *n* : disaster victim
sinon [sinɔ̃] *conj* **1** : or else **2** : if not **3 ~ que** : except that
sinueux, -nueuse [sinyø, -nyøz] *adj* : sinuous, winding, meandering
sinus [sinys] *nms & pl* **1** : sinus **2** : sine (in mathematics)
sionisme [sjɔnism] *nm* : Zionism
sioniste [sjɔnist] *adj & nmf* : Zionist
siphon [sifɔ̃] *nm* **1** : siphon **2** : trap (in plumbing)
siphonner [sifɔne] *vt* : to siphon
sire [sir] *nm* **1** SEIGNEUR : lord **2 triste sire** : unsavory individual
sirène [siren] *nf* **1** : siren, mermaid (in mythology) **2** : siren, alarm
sirop [siro] *nm* : syrup <sirop d'érable : maple syrup> <sirop contre la toux : cough syrup>
siroter [sirɔte] *vt fam* : to sip
sirupeux, -peuse [sirypø, -pøz] *adj* : syrupy
sis, sise [si, siz] *adj* : located (in law)
sisal [sizal] *nm* : sisal
sismique [sismik] *adj* : seismic
site [sit] *nm* **1** : site <site historique : historic site> <site Internet : Internet site> **2** : setting, locale
sitôt [sito] *adv* **1** (*used with a participle*) <sitôt arrivé : as soon as he arrives, immediately upon his arrival> <sitôt dit, sitôt fait : no sooner said than done> **2 sitôt après** : immediately after **3 sitôt que** : as soon as
sittelle [sitel] *nf* : nuthatch
situation [sityasjɔ̃] *nf* **1** : situation **2 situation de famille** : marital status
situer [situe] *vt* : to situate, to locate — **se situer** *vr*
six[1] [sis, *before consonant* si, *before vowel* siz] *adj* **1** : six **2** : sixth <le six décembre : December sixth>
six[2] *nms & pl* : six
sixième [sizjɛm] *adj & nmf & nm* : sixth
ski [ski] *nm* **1** : ski **2** : skiing **3 ski nautique** : waterskiing
skier [skje] {96} *vi* : to ski
skieur, skieuse [skjœr, skjøz] *n* : skier
slave [slav] *adj* : Slavic
Slave *nmf* : Slav
slip [slip] *nm* **1** : briefs *pl*, men's underpants *pl* **2** : panties *pl*
slogan [slɔgɑ̃] *nm* : slogan
slovaque[1] [slɔvak] *adj* : Slovak, Slovakian
slovaque[2] *nm* : Slovakian (language)
Slovaque *nmf* : Slovak
slovène[1] [slɔvɛn] *adj* : Slovene, Slovenian
slovène[2] *nm* : Slovene (language)
Slovène *nmf* : Slovene, Slovenian
smoking [smɔkiŋ] *nm* : tuxedo
snob[1] [snɔb] *adj* : snobbish
snob[2] *nmf* : snob
snober [snɔbe] *vt* : to snub
snobisme [snɔbism] *nm* : snobbery, snobbishness
sobre [sɔbr] *adj* **1** : sober, abstemious **2** : restrained — **sobrement** [-brəmɑ̃] *adv*
sobriété [sɔbrijete] *nf* : sobriety
sobriquet [sɔbrikɛ] *nm* : nickname
soc [sɔk] *nm* : plowshare
soccer [sɔkɛr] *nm Can* : soccer
sociable [sɔsjabl] *adj* : sociable — **sociabilité** [sɔsjabilite] *nf*
social, -ciale [sɔsjal] *adj, mpl* **-ciaux** [-sjo] : social — **socialement** [-sjalmɑ̃] *adv*
socialiser [sɔsjalize] *vt* : to socialize
socialisme [sɔsjalism] *nm* : socialism — **socialiste** [-sjalist] *adj & nmf*
sociétaire [sɔsjeter] *nmf* : member
société [sɔsjete] *nf* **1** : society <la haute société : high society> <la société de ses semblables : the society of one's peers> **2** : colony (of bees, etc.) **3** COMPAGNIE : company, firm **4**

ASSOCIATION : society, association, club

sociologie [sɔsjɔlɔʒi] *nf* : sociology

sociologique [sɔsjɔlɔʒik] *adj* : sociological

sociologue [sɔsjɔlɔg] *nmf* : sociologist

socle [sɔkl] *nm* BASE : base, pedestal

socque [sɔk] *nm* SABOT : clog, wooden shoe

soda [sɔda] *nm* **1** : soda, soft drink **2** : soda water

sodium [sɔdjɔm] *nm* : sodium

soeur [sœr] *nf* **1** : sister **2** : nun, sister

sofa [sɔfa] *nm* : sofa

soi [swa] *pron* : oneself, himself, herself, itself <chacun pour soi : every man for himself> <en soi : in itself> <cela va de soi : it goes without saying>

soi–disant[1] [swadizɑ̃] *adv* : supposedly

soi–disant[2] *adj* : so-called

soie [swa] *nf* **1** : silk **2** : bristle

soif [swaf] *nf* : thirst <avoir soif : to be thirsty>

soigné, -gnée [swaɲe] *adj* **1** : carefully done, meticulous **2** : well-groomed, neat

soigner [swaɲe] *vt* **1** : to treat, to nurse **2** : to look after, to take care of **3** : to do with care, to take trouble over — **se soigner** *vr* **1** : to treat oneself (for an illness, etc.) **2** : to be treated

soigneux, -gneuse [swaɲø, -ɲøz] *adj* **1** : careful, meticulous **2** : neat, tidy — **soigneusement** [swaɲøzmɑ̃] *adv*

soi–même [swamem] *pron* : oneself <par soi-même : (all) by oneself>

soin [swɛ̃] *nm* **1** ATTENTION : care, attention <prendre soin de : to take care of, to look after> **2** SOUCI : concern **3 soins** *nmpl* : (medical) attention, treatment <premiers soins : first aid> **4 soins** *nmpl* : care <confier aux bons soins de : to leave in the care of>

soir [swar] *nm* : evening, night <demain soir : tomorrow night>

soirée [sware] *nf* **1** : evening <pendant la soirée : during the evening> **2** FÊTE : party **3** : evening performance (of a show)

soit[1] [swa], *etc.* → **être**

soit[2] *adv* : so be it, very well

soit[3] *conj* **1** : that is, in other words, or <48 heures soit deux jours : 48 hours, that is, two days> **2** (*introducing an hypothesis*) <soit un triangle XYZ : let XYZ be a triangle> **3 soit . . . soit . . .** : either . . . or . . . <soit ceci soit cela : either this or that>

soixante[1] [swasɑ̃t] *adj* : sixty <les années soixantes : the sixties>

soixante[2] *nms & pl* : sixty

soixante–dix[1] [swasɑ̃tdis] *adj* : seventy

soixante–dix[2] *nms & pl* : seventy

soixante–dixième [swasɑ̃tdizjem] *adj & nmf & nm* : seventieth

soixantième [swasɑ̃tjem] *adj & nmf & nm* : sixtieth

soja [sɔʒa] *nm* : soybean <sauce de soja : soy sauce>

sol [sɔl] *nm* **1** : ground, floor, surface **2** PLANCHER : flooring **3** TERRE : soil (in agriculture, etc.) **4** TERRITOIRE : territory, soil <sol canadien : Canadian soil>

solage [sɔlaʒ] *nm Can* : foundation (of a house)

solaire [sɔlɛr] *adj* **1** : solar **2** : sun <crème solaire : suntan lotion>

soldat [sɔlda] *nm* : soldier

solde[1] [sɔld] *nf* : pay

solde[2] *nm* **1** : balance (in finance) **2** : sale <en solde : on sale> **3 soldes** *nmpl* : sale, bargains

solder [sɔlde] *vt* **1** : to settle (an account, etc.) **2** BRADER : to sell off, to put on sale — **se solder** *vr* **1 ~ par** : to end in **2 ~ par** : to show <se solder par un excédent : to show a surplus>

sole [sɔl] *nf* : sole (fish)

soleil [sɔlɛj] *nm* **1** : sun **2** : sunshine, sunlight **3** : sunflower

solennel, -nelle [sɔlanɛl] *adj* **1** : solemn **2** : formal — **solennellement** *adv*

solennité [sɔlanite] *nf* : solemnity

solfège [sɔlfɛʒ] *nm* : music theory

solidaire [sɔlidɛr] *adj* **1** : united, in solidarity <être solidaire de : to stand by, to back> **2** INTERDÉPENDANT : interdependent

solidariser [sɔlidarize] *v* **se solidariser avec** *vr* : to show solidarity with

solidarité [sɔlidarite] *nf* : solidarity

solide[1] [sɔlid] *adj & nm* **1** : solid **2** : sturdy, strong

solide[2] *nm* : solid

solidement [sɔlidmɑ̃] *adv* **1** : solidly **2** : firmly, securely

solidité [sɔlidite] *nf* : solidity

solidifier [sɔlidifje] {96} *vt* : to solidify — **se solidifier** *vr*

soliloque [sɔlilɔk] *nm* : soliloquy

soliste [sɔlist] *nmf* : soloist

solitaire[1] [sɔliter] *adj* **1** SEUL : solitary, lonely **2** ISOLÉ : isolated

solitaire[2] *nmf* : loner, recluse

solitaire[3] *nm* : solitaire

solitude [sɔlityd] *nf* **1** : solitude **2** : loneliness

solive [sɔliv] *nf* : joist

sollicitation [sɔlisitasjɔ̃] *nf* : appeal, entreaty

solliciter [sɔlisite] *vt* **1** : to solicit, to seek (a favor, etc.) **2** : to appeal to, to approach

solliciteur, -teuse [sɔlisitœr] *nm* **1** : supplicant **2 solliciteur général** *Can* : attorney general

sollicitude [sɔlisityd] *nf* : solicitude, concern

solo[1] [sɔlo] *adj* : solo

solo[2] [sɔlo] *nm, pl* **solos** *or* **soli** : solo

solstice [sɔlstis] *nm* : solstice <solstice d'été : summer solstice>

soluble [sɔlybl] *adj* **1** : soluble **2** : solvable
solution [sɔlysjɔ̃] *nf* : solution
solutionner [sɔlysjɔne] *vt* : to solve
solvabilité [sɔlvabilite] *nf* : solvency
solvable [sɔlvabl] *adj* : solvent
solvant [sɔlvɑ̃] *nm* : solvent
somali, -lie [sɔmali] *adj* : somali
Somali, -lie *n* : Somali
somalien, -lienne [sɔmaljɛ̃, -ljɛn] *adj* : Somalian
Somalien, -lienne *n* : Somalian, Somali
sombre [sɔ̃br] *adj* **1** OBSCUR : dark **2** TRISTE : somber, gloomy — **sombrement** [sɔ̃brəmɑ̃] *adv*
sombrer [sɔ̃bre] *vi* **1** COULER : to sink **2** : to decline, to collapse, to fail
sommaire[1] [sɔmɛr] *adj* **1** COURT : brief **2** EXPÉDITIF : summary **3** RUDIMENTAIRE : rudimentary, superficial
sommaire[2] *nm* : summary
sommation [sɔmasjɔ̃] *nf* **1** : notice, summons (in law) **2** : warning <tirer sans sommation : to shoot without warning>
somme[1] [sɔm] *nf* **1** : sum **2 en somme** : on the whole, all in all
somme[2] *nm* : short nap, catnap
sommeil [sɔmɛj] *nm* : sleep <avoir sommeil : to be sleepy>
sommeiller [sɔmɛje] *vi* **1** SOMNOLER : to doze **2** : to lie dormant
sommelier, -lière [sɔmɔlje, -ljɛr] *n* : wine steward
sommer [sɔme] *vt* **1** : to summon **2** ENJOINDRE : to enjoin, to order <il m'a sommé de répondre : he commanded me to answer>
sommet [sɔmɛ] *nm* **1** CIME : summit, top, apex **2** : vertex (in geometry)
sommier [sɔmje] *nm* **1** : bed springs *pl*, box spring **2** : lintel, crossbar **3** *France* : register, (police) records *pl*
sommité [sɔmite] *nf* : leading figure, authority
somnambule [sɔmnɑ̃byl] *nmf* : sleepwalker
somnambulisme [sɔmnɑ̃bylism] *nm* : sleepwalking
somnifère [sɔmnifɛr] *nm* : sleeping pill
somnolence [sɔmnɔlɑ̃s] *nf* **1** : somnolence, drowsiness **2** LÉTHARGIE : lethargy
somnolent, -lente [sɔmnɔlɑ̃, -lɑ̃t] *adj* **1** : drowsy **2** LÉTHARGIQUE : lethargic
somnoler [sɔmnɔle] *vi* : to doze
somptueux, -tueuse [sɔ̃ptɥø, -tɥøz] *adj* : sumptuous, lavish
son[1], **sa** [sɔ̃, sa] *adj, pl* **ses** [se] : his, her, its, one's
son[2] *nm* **1** : sound <au son de : to the sound of> **2** : volume <monter le son : to turn up the volume> **3** : bran
sonar [sɔnar] *nm* : sonar
sonate [sɔnat] *nf* : sonata
sondage [sɔ̃daʒ] *nm* **1** ENQUÊTE : poll, survey **2** : probing, sounding
sonde [sɔ̃d] *nf* **1** : probe <sonde spatiale : space probe> **2** : sounding line **3** : catheter, probe (in medicine) **4** : drill (in geology, etc.)
sonder [sɔ̃de] *vt* **1** : to sound out, to survey, to poll **2** : to sound, to probe **3** : to drill (in geology)
songe [sɔ̃ʒ] *nm* RÊVE : dream
songer [sɔ̃ʒe] {17} *vt* : to consider, to imagine <avez-vous songé aux frais? : have you considered the costs?> — *vi* **1** : to dream **2** ~ **à** : to think about, to contemplate, to consider
songeur, -geuse [sɔ̃ʒœr, -ʒøz] *adj* PENSIF : pensive
sonique [sɔnik] *adj* : sonic, sound
sonnant, -nante [sɔnɑ̃, -nɑ̃t] *adj* **à dix heures sonnantes** : at the stroke of ten
sonné, -née [sɔne] *adj* **1** : past <deux heures sonnées : past two o'clock> **2** *fam* : groggy **3** *fam* : crazy, nuts
sonner *v* **1** : to ring **2** : to strike, to sound
sonnerie [sɔnri] *nf* **1** : ringing, ring **2** : alarm (bell), chimes *pl* **3** : sounding, blare (of a trumpet, etc.)
sonnet [sɔnɛ] *nm* : sonnet
sonnette [sɔnɛt] *nf* : bell, doorbell, buzzer
sonore [sɔnɔr] *adj* **1** : sonorous, resonant **2** : sound <bande sonore : soundtrack> <effets sonores : sound effects> **3** : voiced (in linguistics)
sonorisation [sɔnɔrizasjɔ̃] *nf* : sound system, public address system
sonoriser [sɔnɔrize] *vt* **1** : to add sound to **2** : to install a sound system
sonorité [sɔnɔrite] *nf* **1** : sonority, tone **2** : resonance, acoustics
sophistication [sɔfistikasjɔ̃] *nf* : sophistication
sophistiqué, -quée [sɔfistike] *adj* : sophisticated
soporifique [sɔpɔrifik] *adj* : soporific
soprano [sɔprano] *nmf* : soprano
sorbet [sɔrbɛ] *nm* : sorbet, sherbet
sorcellerie [sɔrsɛlri] *nf* : sorcery, witchcraft
sorcier, -cière [sɔrsje, -sjɛr] *n* : sorcerer, wizard, witch
sordide [sɔrdid] *adj* **1** RÉPUGNANT : sordid **2** MISÉRABLE : squalid — **sordidement** [-didmɑ̃] *adv*
sorgho [sɔrgo] *nm* : sorghum
sornettes [sɔrnɛt] *nfpl* : nonsense
sort [sɔr] *nm* **1** : fate, lot, destiny **2** SORTILÈGE : spell, hex <jeter un sort à : to hex>
sortant, -tante [sɔrtɑ̃, -tɑ̃t] *adj* : outgoing, resigning <le président sortant : the outgoing president>
sorte [sɔrt] *nf* **1** ESPÈCE : sort, kind **2 de sorte à** : in order to **3 en aucune sorte** : not in the least **4 en quelque sorte** : somewhat, in a way
sortie [sɔrti] *nf* **1** : exit <sortie de secours : emergency exit> **2** DÉPART

: departure **3** : launch, release (of a film, book, etc.) **4** EXCURSION : outing **5** : sortie (of troops, etc.) **6** *fam* : quip, sally

sortilège [sɔrtilɛʒ] *nm* : spell, hex, enchantment

sortir[1] [sɔrtir] {82} *vt* **1** : to take out, to bring out **2** : to launch, to release, to issue — *vi* **1** : to go out, to come out, to open (of a film, etc.) **2** PARTIR : to leave, to exit **3** ~ **de** : to come from, to come out of — **se sortir** *vr* **1** ~ **de** : to get out of **2 s'en sortir** : to manage, to get by, to pull through (of an illness)

sortir[2] *nm* **au sortir de** : at the end of

sosie [sɔzi] *nm* : double

sot, sotte[1] [so, sɔt] *adj* RIDICULE : foolish, silly — **sottement** [sɔtmɑ̃] *adv*

sot, sotte[2] *n* : fool

sottise [sɔtiz] *nf* **1** : foolishness, stupidity **2** : foolish act or remark

sou [su] *nm* **1 sans le sou** : penniless **2 un sou de** : the least bit of <ils n'ont pas un sou de bon sens : they haven't an ounce of common sense>

soubassement [subasmɑ̃] *nm* : bedrock

soubresaut [subrəso] *nm* : jolt, start

souche [suʃ] *nf* **1** : stump (of a tree) **2** : stock, descent **3** : stub (of a check, etc.)

soucí [susi] *nm* **1** INQUIÉTUDE : worry, care, concern **2** : marigold

soucier [susje] {96} *v* **se soucier** *vr* : to worry, to care

soucieux, -cieuse [susjø, -sjøz] *adj* : worried, concerned

soucoupe [sukup] *nf* **1** : saucer **2 soucoupe volante** : flying saucer

soudain[1] [sudɛ̃] *adv* SOUDAINEMENT : suddenly

soudain[2], **-daine** [sudɛ̃, -dɛn] *adj* : sudden — **soudainement** [-dɛnmɑ̃] *adv*

soudaineté [sudɛnte] *nf* : suddenness

soudanais, -naise [sudane, -nɛz] *adj* : Sudanese

Soudanais, -naise *n* : Sudanese

soude [sud] *nf* : soda (in chemistry)

souder [sude] *vt* **1** : to weld, to solder **2** UNIR : to join, to bind

soudeur, -deuse [sudœr, -døz] *n* : welder

soudoyer [sudwaje] {58} *vt* : to bribe

soudure [sudyr] *nf* **1** : solder **2** : soldering, welding **3** : weld, joint

soue [su] *nf Can or* **soue à cochon** : sty, pigpen

souffert [sufɛr] *pp* → **souffrir**

souffle [sufl] *nm* **1** : breath <être à bout de souffle : to be out of breath> <second souffle : second wind> **2** RESPIRATION : breathing **3** : puff, gust, breath (of air) **4** INSPIRATION : inspiration

soufflé [sufle] *nm* : soufflé

souffler [sufle] *vt* **1** : to blow **2** : to blow out **3** CHUCHOTER : to whisper **4** : to blast, to blow down **5** *fam* : to take, to pinch **6 souffler son rôle à** : to prompt, to cue — *vi* **1** : to blow **2** : to pant, to puff

soufflet [sufle] *nm* **1** : bellows **2** GIFLE : slap **3** AFFRONT : insult, affront

souffleur, -fleuse [suflœr, -fløz] *n* **1** : glassblower **2** : prompter (in theater)

souffleuse *nf Can or* **souffleuse à neige** : snowblower

souffrance [sufrɑ̃s] *nf* **1** : suffering **2 en** ~ : pending, awaiting

souffrant, -frante [sufrɑ̃, -frɑ̃t] *adj* **1** INDISPOSÉ : unwell **2** : suffering, miserable

souffreteux, -teuse [sufrətø, -tøz] *adj* : sickly

souffrir [sufrir] {83} *vt* **1** SUPPORTER : to tolerate, to stand, to put up with **2** PERMETTRE : to allow, to permit — *vi* : to suffer

soufre [sufr] *nm* : sulfur, brimstone

souhait [swe] *nm* **1** VOEU : wish **2 à vos souhaits!** : bless you!

souhaitable [swetabl] *adj* : desirable

souhaiter [swete] *vt* : to wish, to wish for, to hope for <souhaiter la bonne année à qqn : to wish s.o. Happy New Year>

souiller [suje] *vt* **1** SALIR : to soil **2** : to sully, to defile

souillure [sujyr] *nf* : stain, taint, blemish

soûl, soûle [su, sul] *adj fam* : drunk

soulagement [sulaʒmɑ̃] *nm* : relief

soulager [sulaʒe] {17} *vt* : to relieve — **se soulager** *vr*

soûler [sule] *vt* ENIVRER : to make drunk, to intoxicate — **se soûler** *vr* **1** : to get drunk **2** ~ **de** : to be intoxicated with

soulèvement [sulɛvmɑ̃] *nm* **1** : uprising, upheaval (of the earth, etc.) **2** : insurrection, uprising

soulever [sulve] {52} *vt* **1** LEVER : to lift, to raise **2** PROVOQUER : to stir up, to arouse — **se soulever** *vr* **1** : to rise up **2** : to lift oneself up

soulier [sulje] *nm* : shoe

soulignement [suliɲmɑ̃] *nm* : underlining

souligner [suliɲe] *vt* **1** : to underline **2** : to emphasize

soumettre [sumetr] {53} *vt* **1** SUBJUGUER : to subjugate, to subdue **2** PRÉSENTER : to submit **3** ~ **à** : to subject to — **se soumettre** *vr* : to submit, to give in

soumis, -mise [sumi, -miz] *adj* : submissive

soumission [sumisjɔ̃] *nf* **1** : submission, subjection **2** : bid

soumissionner [sumisjɔne] *vt* : to bid for

soupape [supap] *nf* : valve

soupçon [supsɔ̃] *nm* **1** : suspicion <au dessus de tout soupçon : above sus-

picion> **2** : drop, touch <un soupçon d'ironie : a hint of irony>
soupçonner [supsɔne] *vt* : to suspect
soupçonneux, -neuse [supsɔnø, -nøz] *adj* : suspicious — **soupçonneusement** [supsɔnøzmɑ̃] *adv*
soupe [sup] *nf* : soup <soupe à l'oignon : onion soup>
soupente [supɑ̃t] *nf* **1** : attic, garret **2** : closet (under the stairs)
souper[1] [supe] *vi Bel, Switz, Can* : to have supper
souper[2] *nm Bel, Switz, Can* : supper
soupeser [supəze] {52} *vt* **1** : to feel the weight of, to heft **2** PESER : to weigh, to consider
soupière [supjɛr] *nf* : tureen
soupir [supir] *nm* **1** : sigh **2** : quarter rest (in music)
soupirant [supirɑ̃] *nm* : suitor
soupirer [supire] *vi* **1** : to sigh **2** ~ **après** *or* ~ **pour** : to yearn for, to pine for
souple [supl] *adj* **1** : supple, flexible **2** : smooth, flowing — **souplement** [suplɔmɑ̃] *adv*
souplesse [suplɛs] *nf* : suppleness, flexibility
source [surs] *nf* **1** : source <tenir de bonne source : to have on good authority> **2** : spring, source (of waters) **3** **sources** *nfpl* : headwaters
sourcil [sursi] *nm* **1** : eyebrow **2** **froncer les sourcils** : to frown
sourciller [sursije] *vi* : to raise one's eyebrows, to react <sans sourciller : without batting an eye>
sourcilleux, -leuse [sursijø, -jøz] *adj* **1** HAUTAIN : haughty, supercilious **2** POINTILLEUX : finicky, fussy
sourd[1], **sourde** [sur, surd] *adj* **1** : deaf **2** : dull, muffled **3** : secret, clandestine **4** : voiceless <consonnes sourdes : voiceless consonants>
sourd[2], **sourde** *n* : deaf person
sourdine [surdin] *nf* **1** : mute (in music) <en sourdine : muted, quietly> **2** **mettre une sourdine à** : to tone down
sourd-muet, sourde-muette [surmyɛ, surdmyɛt] *n* : deaf-mute
sourdre [surdr] {84} *vi* **1** : to rise, to seep up **2** MONTER : to well up
souriant, -riante [surjɑ̃, -rjɑ̃t] *adj* : smiling, cheerful
souricière [surisjɛr] *nf* : mousetrap
sourire[1] [surir] {76} *vi* **1** : to smile **2** ~ **à** : to smile on, to be favorable to **3** ~ **à** : to appeal to
sourire[2] *nm* : smile
souris [suri] *nf* : mouse
sournois[1], **-noise** [surnwa, -nwaz] *adj* **1** : sly, shifty **2** : underhanded, backhanded
sournois[2], **-noise** *n* : sly person, sneaky person
sournoisement [surnwazmɑ̃] *adv* : slyly, in an underhanded manner
sous [su] *prep* **1** : under, beneath **2** : within <sous huit jours : within a week> <sous peu : shortly> **3** : during <sous le règne de : during the reign of> **4** : under the effect of <sous anesthésie : under anesthesia> <sous la pression : under pressure>
sous-alimentation [suzalimɑ̃tasjɔ̃] *nf* : malnutrition
sous-alimenté, -tée [suzalimɑ̃te] *adj* : malnourished, undernourished
sous-bois [subwa] *nms & pl* : undergrowth, underbrush
sous-comité [sukɔmite] *nm, pl* **sous-comités** : subcommittee
souscripteur, -trice [suskriptœr] *n* : subscriber
souscription [suskripsjɔ̃] *nf* : subscription
souscrire [suskrir] {33} *vi* ~ **à** : to subscribe to
sous-développé, -pée [sudevlɔpe] *adj* : underdeveloped
sous-développement [sudevlɔpmɑ̃] *nm, pl* **sous-développements** : underdevelopment
sous-entendre [suzɑ̃tɑ̃dr] {63} *vt* : to imply, to infer
sous-entendu [suzɑ̃tɑ̃dy] *nm, pl* **sous-entendus** : insinuation, innuendo
sous-estimer [suzɛstime] *vt* : to underestimate
sous-évaluer [suzevalye] *vt* : undervalue
sous-exposer [suzɛkspoze] *vt* : to underexpose (a photograph)
sous-jacent, -cente [suʒasɑ̃, -sɑ̃t] *adj* : underlying
sous-lieutenant [suljøtnɑ̃] *nm, pl* **sous-lieutenants** : second lieutenant
sous-louer [sulwe] *vt* : to sublet
sous-marin[1], **-rine** [sumarɛ̃, -rin] *adj* : underwater, submarine
sous-marin[2] *nm, pl* **sous-marins** : submarine
sous-officier [suzɔfisje] *nm, pl* **sous-officiers** : noncommissioned officer
sous-produit [suprɔdɥi] *nm, pl* **sous-produits** : by-product
sous-secrétaire [susɔkretɛr] *nmf* : undersecretary
sous-sol [susɔl] *nm, pl* **sous-sols** : basement, cellar
sous-titre [sutitr] *nm, pl* **sous-titres** : subtitle
soustraction [sustraksjɔ̃] *nf* : subtraction
soustraire [sustrɛr] {40} *vt* **1** : to subtract **2** : to remove, to take away, to steal **3** : to shield, to hide (a person) — **se soustraire** *vr* ~ **à** : to escape from, to evade
sous-traîter [sutrete] *vt* : to subcontract
sous-verre [suvɛr] *nms & pl Can* : coaster

sous-vêtement [suvɛtmɑ̃] *nm* **1** : undergarment **2 sous-vêtements** *nmpl* : underwear, underclothes
soutane [sutan] *nf* : cassock
soute [sut] *nf* : hold (of a ship)
soutenable [sutnabl] *adj* **1** DÉFENDABLE : defensible, supportable (of an argument, etc.) **2** SUPPORTABLE : bearable
soutènement [sutɛnmɑ̃] *nm* **mur de soutènement** : retaining wall
souteneur [sutnœr] *nm* : pimp
soutenir [sutnir] {92} *vt* **1** MAINTENIR : to support, to hold up **2** : to support, to back, to stand by **3** : to defend, to uphold <soutenir que : to maintain that> **4** : to sustain, to keep up **5** : to withstand, to bear — **se soutenir** *vr* **1** : to support each other **2** : to be defensible **3** : to hold oneself up
soutenu, -nue [sutny] *adj* **1** ÉLEVÉ : elevated, formal **2** : sustained, steady **3** VIF : bold, vivid (of colors)
souterrain[1], **-raine** [sutɛrɛ̃, -rɛn] *adj* **1** : underground, subterranean **2** : secret, hidden
souterrain[2] *nm* : underground passage
soutien [sutjɛ̃] *nm* **1** : support **2 soutien de famille** : breadwinner
soutien-gorge [sutjɛ̃gɔrʒ] *nm, pl* **soutiens-gorge** : bra, brassiere
soutirer [sutire] *vt* **~ à** : to extract from, to squeeze out of
souvenir[1] [suvnir] {92} *v* **se souvenir** *vr* **1 ~ de** : to remember **2 ~ que** : to remember that — *v impers* **il me (lui,** etc.) **souvient** : I remember (he remembers, etc.)
souvenir[2] *nm* **1** : memory **2** : souvenir, memento **3** : regards, (good) wishes <mes meilleurs souvenirs à : my best regards to>
souvent [suvɑ̃] *adv* : often
souverain[1], **-raine** [suvrɛ̃, -rɛn] *adj* **1** SUPRÊME : supreme, superior <un remède souverain : an excellent remedy> **2** : sovereign <territoire souverain : sovereign territory>
souverain[2], **-raine** *n* : sovereign, monarch
souveraineté [suvrɛnte] *nf* : sovereignty
soviétique [sɔvjetik] *adj* : Soviet
soya [sɔja] → **soja**
soyeux, soyeuse [swajø, -jøz] *adj* : silky
spacieux, -cieuse [spasjø, -sjøz] *adj* : spacious
spaghetti [spagɛti] *nmpl* : spaghetti <boîte de spaghettis : box of spaghetti>
sparadrap [sparadra] *nm* : adhesive tape, adhesive bandage
spasme [spasm] *nm* : spasm — **spasmodique** [spasmɔdik] *adj*
spatial, -tiale [spasjal] *adj, mpl* **spatiaux 1** : spatial **2** : space <vaisseau spatial : spaceship>
spatule [spatyl] *nf* **1** : spatula **2** : tip (of a ski)
speaker[1], **-kerine** [spikœr, -krin] *n France* : announcer (on radio, TV, etc.)
speaker[2] *nm* **le Speaker** : the Speaker (of a legislative body)
spécial, -ciale [spesjal] *adj, mpl* **spéciaux** [-sjo] **1** : special **2** BIZARRE : odd, peculiar
spécialement [spesjalmɑ̃] *adv* **1** EXPRÈS : specially **2** TRÈS : especially, particularly
spécialiser [spesjalize] *v* **se spécialiser** *vr* : to specialize — **spécialisation** [-lizasjɔ̃] *nf*
spécialiste [spesjalist] *nmf* : specialist
spécialité [spesjalite] *nf* : specialty, field
spécieux, -cieuse [spesjø, -sjøz] *adj* : specious — **spécieusement** [-sjøzmɑ̃] *adv*
spécifier [spesifje] {96} *vt* : to specify — **spécification** [spesifikasjɔ̃] *nf*
spécifique [spesifik] *adj* : specific — **spécifiquement** [-fikmɑ̃] *adv*
spécimen [spesimɛn] *nm* **1** : specimen, example **2** : sample
spectacle [spɛktakl] *nm* **1** : spectacle, sight <se donner en spectacle : to make a spectacle of oneself> **2** REPRÉSENTATION : show, performance <spectacle somptueux : extravaganza> **3** : show businesss
spectaculaire [spɛktakylɛr] *adj* : spectacular
spectateur, -trice [spɛktatœr, -tris] *n* **1** : spectator, audience member **2** : observer, onlooker, bystander
spectre [spɛktr] *nm* **1** : specter, ghost **2** : spectrum
spéculateur, -trice [spekylatœr, -tris] *n* : speculator
spéculatif, -tive [spekylatif, -tiv] *adj* : speculative
spéculer [spekyle] *vi* : to speculate — **spéculation** [spekylasjɔ̃] *nf*
sperme [spɛrm] *nm* : sperm, semen
sphère [sfɛr] *nf* : sphere
sphérique [sferik] *adj* : spherical
spinal, -nale [spinal] *adj, mpl* **spinaux** [-no] : spinal
spiral, -rale [spiral] *adj, mpl* **spiraux** [-ro] : spiral
spirale *nf* : spiral
spire [spir] *nf* : whorl (of a shell)
spiritisme [spiritism] *nm* : spiritualism
spiritualité [spirituɥalite] *nf* : spirituality
spirituel, -tuelle [spirituɥɛl] *adj* **1** : spiritual **2** : witty — **spirituellement** [-tuɛlmɑ̃] *adv*
spiritueux [spirituø] *nms & pl* : spirit <vins et spiritueux : wines and spirits>
spleen [splin] *nm* : spleen, melancholy
splendeur [splɑ̃dœr] *nf* MAGNIFICENCE : splendor, magnificence, glory

splendide [splɔ̃did] *adj* MAGNIFIQUE : splendid, magnificent — **splendidement** [-didmɑ̃] *adv*
spolier [spɔlje] {96} *vt* : to despoil
spongieux, -gieuse [spɔ̃ʒjø, -ʒjøz] *adj* : spongy
sponsor [spɔ̃sɔr] *nm* : sponsor
sponsoriser [spɔ̃sɔrize] *vt* : to sponsor
spontané, -née [spɔ̃tane] *adj* : spontaneous — **spontanément** [-nemɑ̃] *adv*
spontanéité [spɔ̃taneite] *nf* : spontaneity
sporadique [spɔradik] *adj* : sporadic — **sporadiquement** [-dikmɑ̃] *adv*
spore [spɔr] *nf* : spore
sport[1] [spɔr] *adj* **1** : sport, sports <vêtements sport : sport clothes> **2** SPORTIF : sporting
sport[2] *nm* : sport <sports d'équipe : team sports>
sportif[1], **-tive** [spɔrtif, -tiv] *adj* **1** : sport, sports <chroniqueur sportif : sportscaster> **2** : sporting, sportsmanlike **3** : athletic, sporty
sportif[2], **-tive** *n* : sportsman *m*, sportswoman *f*
sportivité [spɔrtivite] *nf* : sportsmanship
spot [spɔt] *nm* **1** : spotlight **2** PUBLICITÉ : spot, commercial
sprint [sprint] *nm* : sprint
sprinter [sprinte] *vi* : to sprint
square [skwar] *nm France* : small public garden
squash [skwaʃ] *nm* : squash (sport)
squatter[1] [skwate] *vt* : to squat in (land, a property, etc.)
squatter[2] [skwatœr] *nm* : squatter
squelette [skəlet] *nm* **1** : skeleton **2** : outline **3** : framework, skeleton (of a ship, etc.)
squelettique [skəletik] *adj* **1** : skeletal, scrawny **2** : sketchy, skimpy
sri lankais, -kaise [srilɑ̃ke, -kɛz] *adj* : Sri Lankan
Sri Lankais, -kaise *n* : Sri Lankan
stabilisateur[1], **-trice** [stabilizatœr, -tris] *adj* : stabilizing
stabilisateur[2] *nm* : stabilizer
stabiliser [stabilize] *vt* : to stabilize — **se stabiliser** *vr* **1** : to become stable **2** : to settle down
stabilité [stabilite] *nf* : stability
stable [stabl] *adj* : stable, steady
stade [stad] *nm* **1** : stadium **2** ÉTAPE : stage, phase
stage [staʒ] *nm* : training period, internship <faire un stage : to intern>
stagiaire [staʒjɛr] *nmf* : trainee, intern
stagnant, -nante [stagnɑ̃, -nɑ̃t] *adj* : stagnant
stagner [stagne] *vi* : to stagnate — **stagnation** [-gnasjɔ̃] *nf*
stalactite [stalaktit] *nf* : stalactite
stalagmite [stalagmit] *nf* : stalagmite
stalle [stal] *nf* : stall
stand [stɑd] *nm* **1** : stand, stall **2 stand de tir** : shooting range
standard[1] [stɑ̃dar] *adj* : standard
standard[2] *nm* **1** : norm, standard **2** : (telephone) switchboard
standardiser [stɑ̃dardize] *vt* : to standardize
standardiste [stɑ̃dardist] *nmf* : switchboard operator, telephone operator
standing [stɑ̃diŋ] *nm* **1** : standing, status **2 de grand standing** : luxury
star [star] *nf* VEDETTE : star <star de cinéma : movie star>
starter [starter] *nm* **1** : choke (of an automobile) **2** : starter (in a race)
station [stasjɔ̃] *nf* **1** : station **2** : resort <station balnéaire : seaside resort> **3** : posture, position **4** : stop, pause
stationnaire [stasjɔner] *adj* **1** : stationary **2** : stable (in medicine)
stationnement [stasjɔnmɑ̃] *nm* : parking <stationnement interdit : no parking>
stationner [stasjɔne] *vi* : to park
station-service [stasjɔ̃servis] *nf, pl* **stations-service** : gas station, service station
statique [statik] *adj* : static
statisticien, -cienne [statistisjɛ̃, -sjɛn] *n* : statistician
statistique[1] [statistik] *adj* : statistical
statistique[2] *nf* **1** : statistic **2** : statistics (field)
statue [staty] *nf* : statue
statuer [statɥe] *vi* : to decree, to ordain
statuette [statɥet] *nf* : statuette
statu quo [statykwo] *nm* : status quo
stature [statyr] *nf* : stature
statut [staty] *nm* **1** : statute **2** : status
statutaire [statyter] *adj* : statutory
steak [stek] *nm* : steak <steak haché : ground beef>
stellaire [steler] *adj* : stellar
sténographe [stenɔgraf] *nmf* : stenographer
sténographie [stenɔgrafi] *nf* : stenography
steppe [step] *nf* : steppe
stéréo [stereo] *adj & nf* : stereo
stéréophonique [stereɔfɔnik] *adj* : stereophonic
stéréotype [stereɔtip] *nm* **1** : stereotype **2** : cliché
stéréotypé, -pée [stereɔtipe] *adj* : stereotyped, stereotypical
stérile [steril] *adj* : sterile
stériliser [sterilize] *vt* : to sterilize — **stérilisation** [-lizasjɔ̃] *nf*
stérilité [sterilite] *nf* : sterility
sterne [stern] *nf* : tern
sternum [sternɔm] *nm* : sternum, breastbone
stéthoscope [stetɔskɔp] *nm* : stethoscope
stigmate [stigmat] *nm* : stigma
stigmatiser [stigmatize] *vt* : to stigmatize — **stigmatisation** [-tizasjɔ̃] *nf*
stimulant[1], **-lante** [stimylɑ̃, -lɑ̃t] *adj* : stimulating

stimulant[2] *nm* **1** : stimulant **2** : stimulus
stimulateur [stimylatœr] *nm* : stimulator (in medicine) <stimulateur cardiaque : pacemaker>
stimuler [stimyle] *vt* : to stimulate — **stimulation** [-mylasjɔ̃] *nf*
stipuler [stipyle] *vt* : to stipulate — **stipulation** [-pylasjɔ̃] *nf*
stock [stɔk] *nm* : stock (of merchandise) <en stock : in stock>
stockage [stɔkaʒ] *nm* : storage (of data)
stocker [stɔke] *vt* : to stock, to store
stoïcisme [stɔisizm] *nm* : stoicism
stoïque[1] [stɔik] *adj* : stoic, stoical — **stoïquement** [-ikmɑ̃] *adv*
stoïque[2] *nmf* : stoic
stolon [stɔlɔ̃] *nm* : runner (of a plant)
stop[1] [stɔp] *nm* **1** : stop sign **2** : brake light
stop[2] *interj* : stop
stopper [stɔpe] *vt* **1** ARRÊTER : to stop, to halt **2** RÉPARER : to mend — *vi* : to stop
store [stɔr] *nm* **1** : awning **2** : blind, window shade <store vénitien : venetian blind>
strabisme [strabism] *nm* : squint
strangulation [strɑ̃gylasjɔ̃] *nf* : strangulation
strapontin [strapɔ̃tɛ̃] *nm* : folding seat, jump seat
stratagème [stratazɛm] *nm* : stratagem
strate [strat] *nf* : stratum
stratégie [stratezi] *nf* : strategy
stratégique [stratezik] *adj* : strategic — **stratégiquement** [-zikmɑ̃] *adv*
stratifié, -fiée [stratifje] *adj* : laminated, stratified
stratosphère [stratɔsfɛr] *nf* : stratosphere
stress [stres] *nms & pl* : stress
stressant, -sante [stresɑ̃, -sɑ̃t] *adj* : stressful
stresser [strese] *vt* : to put under stress
strict, stricte [strikt] *adj* **1** : strict **2** : austere, severe, plain — **strictement** [striktəmɑ̃] *adv*
strident, -dente [stridɑ̃, -dɑ̃t] *adj* : strident, shrill
strier [strije] {96} *vt* **1** : to streak **2** : to groove
strophe [strɔf] *nf* : stanza
structural, -rale [stryktyral] *adj, mpl* **-raux** [-ro] : structural — **structuralement** [-ralmɑ̃] *adv*
structure [stryktyr] *nf* : structure
structurer [stryktyre] *vt* : to structure, to organize — **se structurer** *vr* : to be structured, to take shape
stuc [styk] *nm* : stucco
studieux, -dieuse [stydjø, -djøz] *adj* : studious — **studieusement** [-djøzmɑ̃] *adv*
studio [stydjo] *nm* **1** : studio **2** : studio apartment
stupéfaction [stypefaksjɔ̃] *nf* ÉTONNEMENT : stupefaction, astonishment
stupéfaire [stypefɛr] {85} *vt* : to amaze, to astonish
stupéfait, -faite [stypefɛ, -fɛt] *adj* ÉTONNÉ : amazed, astounded
stupéfiant[1], **-fiante** [stypefjɑ̃, -fjɑ̃t] *adj* ÉTONNANT : amazing, astounding
stupéfiant[2] *nm* : drug, narcotic
stupéfié [stypefje] *pp* → **stupéfaire**
stupéfier [stypefje] {96} *vt* **1** : to astonish, to stun **2** : to stupefy (in medicine)
stupeur [stypœr] *nf* **1** ÉTONNEMENT : astonishment, amazement **2** HÉBÉTUDE : stupor
stupide [stypid] *adj* : stupid — **stupidement** [-pidmɑ̃] *adv*
stupidité [stypidite] *nf* : stupidity
style [stil] *nm* **1** : style <style de vie : lifestyle> <style gothique : Gothic style> **2** : speech form <style direct : direct speech> **3** : stylus
stylet [stilɛ] *nm* : stiletto
styliser [stilize] *vt* : to stylize
stylo [stilo] *nm* : pen <stylo à bille : ballpoint pen>
stylo–feutre [stilofœtr] *nm, pl* **stylos–feutres** : felt-tip pen, marker
su [sy] *pp* → **savoir**
suave [sɥav] *adj* **1** : sweet (of odors) **2** : smooth, mellow **3** : suave, sophisticated
suavement [sɥavmɑ̃] *adv* : sweetly
suavité [sɥavite] *nf* **1** : sweetness **2** : smoothness
subalterne [sybaltɛrn] *adj & nmf* : subordinate
subconscient[1], **-ciente** [sybkɔ̃sjɑ̃, -sjɑ̃t] *adj* : subconscious
subconscient[2] *nm* : subconscious
subdiviser [sybdivize] *vt* : to subdivide — **subdivision** [-vizjɔ̃] *nf*
subir [sybir] *vt* **1** : to undergo **2** : to suffer, to sustain <subir des pertes : to suffer losses> **3** : to be under, to come under <subir l'influence de : to come under the influence of> **4 faire subir à** : to inflict on
subit, -bite [sybi, -bit] *adj* : sudden — **subitement** [-bitmɑ̃] *adv*
subjectif, -tive [sybʒɛktif, -tiv] *adj* : subjective
subjectivité [sybʒɛktivite] *nf* : subjectivity
subjonctif [sybʒɔ̃ktif] *nm* : subjunctive
subjuguer [sybʒuge] *vt* **1** : to captivate **2** : to subjugate
sublime [syblim] *adj* : sublime
sublimer [syblime] *v* : to sublimate
submerger [sybmɛrʒe] {17} *vt* **1** : to submerge **2** : to overwhelm, to engulf, to swamp
submersible [sybmɛrsibl] *adj & nm* : submersible
submersion [sybmɛrsjɔ̃] *nf* : submersion

subordination [sybɔʀdinasjɔ̃] *nf* : subordination

subordonné, -née [sybɔʀdɔne] *adj & n* : subordinate

subordonner [sybɔʀdɔne] *vt* : to subordinate

suborner [syboʀne] *vt* : to bribe (a witness)

subreptice [sybʀɛptis] *adj* : surreptitious — **subrepticement** [-tismɑ̃] *adv*

subséquent, -quente [sybsekɑ̃, -kɑ̃t] *adj* : subsequent

subside [sypsid] *nm* : grant, subsidy

subsidiaire [sybzidjɛʀ] *adj* : subsidiary

subsistance [sybzistɑ̃s] *nf* : subsistence

subsister [sybziste] *vi* **1** SURVIVRE : to subsist, to survive (on) **2** RESTER : to remain

substance [sypstɑ̃s] *nf* : substance

substantiel, -tielle [sypstɑ̃sjɛl] *adj* : substantial

substantif [sypstɑ̃tif] *nm* : substantive, noun

substituer [sypstitɥe] *vt* : to substitute — **se substituer** *vr* ~ **à** : to substitute for

substitut [sypstity] *nm* : substitute

substitution [sypstitysjɔ̃] *nf* : substitution

subterfuge [sypteʀfyʒ] *nm* : subterfuge, ploy

subtil, -tile [syptil] *adj* : subtle — **subtilement** [-tilmɑ̃] *adv*

subtiliser [syptilize] *vt fam* : to steal, to pinch

subtilité [syptilite] *nf* : subtlety

subvenir [sybvənir] {92} *vi* ~ **à** : to provide for (a family), to meet (expenses, etc.)

subvention [sybvɑ̃sjɔ̃] *nf* SUBSIDE : subsidy

subventionner [sybvɑ̃sjɔne] *vt* : to subsidize

subversif, -sive [sybvɛʀsif, -siv] *adj* : subversive

subversion [sybvɛʀsjɔ̃] *nf* : subversion

suc [syk] *nm* **1** JUS : juice **2** SÈVE : sap **3** : pith, substance

succédané [syksedane] *nm* : substitute (for a medication, food product, etc.) <succédané de sucre : sugar substitute>

succéder [syksede] {87} *vi* ~ **à** : to succeed, to follow — **se succéder** *vr*

succès [syksɛ] *nm* : success <avoir du succès : to be successful>

successeur [syksesœʀ] *nm* : successor

successif, -sive [syksesif, -siv] *adj* : successive — **successivement** [-sivmɑ̃] *adv*

succession [syksesjɔ̃] *nf* : succession

succinct, -cincte [syksɛ̃, -sɛ̃t] *adj* : succinct — **succinctement** [-sɛ̃tmɑ̃] *adv*

succion [syksjɔ̃, sysjɔ̃] *nf* : suction, sucking

succomber [sykɔ̃be] *vi* **1** : to die **2** : to collapse, to give way **3** ~ **à** : to succumb to

succulent, -lente [sykylɑ̃, -lɑ̃t] *adj* : succulent

succursale [sykyrsal] *nf* : branch (of a bank, store, etc.)

sucer [syse] {6} *vt* : to suck

sucette [syset] *nf* **1** : lollipop **2** : pacifier

suçon [sysɔ̃] *nm Can* : lollipop

sucre [sykʀ] *nm* : sugar <sucre en poudre : powdered sugar> <sucre d'érable : maple sugar>

sucré, -crée [sykʀe] *adj* **1** : sweet, sweetened **2** : sugary, honeyed (of speech, etc.)

sucrer [sykʀe] *vt* : to sweeten, to add sugar to

sucrerie [sykʀəri] *nf* **1** : sugar refinery **2** *Can* : sugar-maple forest **3 sucreries** *nfpl* : sweets, candy

sucrier[1], **-crière** [sykʀije, -kʀijɛʀ] *adj* : sugar <la production sucrière : sugar production>

sucrier[2] *nm* : sugar bowl

sud[1] [syd] *adj* : south, southern, southerly

sud[2] *nm* **1** : south <au sud de Montréal : south of Montreal> <exposé au sud : with a southerly aspect> <vent du sud : south wind> **2 le Sud** : the South

sud-africain, -caine [sydafʀikɛ̃, -kɛn] *adj* : South African

Sud-Africain, -caine *n* : South African

sud-américain, -caine [sydameʀikɛ̃, -kɛn] *adj* : South American

Sud-Américain, -caine *n* : South American

sud-est[1] [sydɛst] *adj s & pl* : southeast, southeastern

sud-est[2] *nm* : southeast

sud-ouest[1] [sydwɛst] *adj s & pl* : southwest, southwestern

sud-ouest[2] *nm* : southwest

suède [sɥɛd] *nm* : suede

suédois[1], **-doise** [sɥedwa, -dwaz] *adj* : Swedish

suédois[2] *nm* : Swedish (language)

Suédois, -doise *n* : Swede

suer [sɥe] *vi* : to sweat — *vt* **1** : to sweat, to ooze **2** : to exude

sueur [sɥœʀ] *nf* : sweat

suffire [syfiʀ] {86} *vi* : to suffice, to be enough <ça suffit! : that's enough!> — **se suffire** *vr or* **se suffire à soi-même** : to be self-sufficient

suffisais [syfize], **suffisions** [syfizjɔ̃], *etc.* → **suffire**

suffisamment [syfizamɑ̃] *adv* : sufficiently, enough

suffisance [syfizɑ̃s] *nf* **1** : self-importance, conceit **2 en** ~ : sufficient

suffisant, -sante [syfizɑ̃, -zɑ̃t] *adj* **1** ADÉQUAT : sufficient, adequate **2** VANITEUX : self-important, conceited

suffise [syfiz], *etc.* → **suffire**

suffixe [syfiks] *nm* : suffix

suffocant, -cante [syfɔkɑ̃, -kɑ̃t] *adj* : suffocating
suffocation [syfɔkasjɔ̃] *nf* : suffocation
suffoquer [syfɔke] *vt* **1** ÉTOUFFER : to suffocate, to choke **2** : to stagger, to stun — *vi* S'ÉTOUFFER : to suffocate
suffrage [syfraʒ] *nm* : suffrage, vote
suggérer [sygʒere] {86} *vt* : to suggest
suggestible [sygʒɛstibl] *adj* : suggestible
suggestif, -tive [sygʒɛstif, -tiv] *adj* : suggestive
suggestion [sygʒɛstjɔ̃] *nf* : suggestion <faire une suggestion : to suggest>
suicidaire [sɥisidɛr] *adj* : suicidal
suicide [sɥisid] *nm* : suicide
suicidé, -dée [sɥiside] *n* : suicide
suicider *v* **se suicider** *vr* : to commit suicide
suie [sɥi] *nf* : soot
suif [sɥif] *nm* **1** : tallow **2** : suet
suintement [sɥɛ̃tma] *nm* : seepage
suinter [sɥɛ̃te] *vi* : to ooze, to seep
suisse[1] [sɥis] *adj* : Swiss
suisse[2] *nm Can* : chipmunk
Suisse *nmf* : Swiss
suit [sɥi], *etc.* → **suivre**
suite [sɥit] *nf* **1** : suite **2** CONTINUATION : continuation, rest <sans suite : disconnected, discontinuous> **3** SÉRIE : series, sequence <à la suite : one after another> **4** CONSÉQUENCE : consequence, result <donner suite à : to follow up> **5 par la suite** : later, afterwards **6 par ~** : therefore, consequently **7 par suite de** : due to, as a result of
suivant[1], **-vante** [sɥivɑ̃, -vɑ̃t] *adj* : following, next
suivant[2], **-vante** *n* : next one, following one <au suite! : next!>
suivant[3] *prep* **1** SELON : according to **2** : along, in the direction of **3** : depending on
suivi[1], **-vie** [sɥivi] *adj* **1** RÉGULIER : regular, steady **2** COHÉRENT : coherent
suivi[2] *nm* : follow-up
suivre [sɥivr] {88} *vt* **1** : to follow **2** : to take (a course) **3** : to keep up with — *vi* **1** : to follow **2** : to pay attention, to keep up **3 faire suivre** : to forward (mail) — **se suivre** *vr* **1** : to follow one another **2** : to be in (the right) order **3** : to be coherent
sujet[1], **-jette** [sɥʒɛ, -ʒɛt] *adj* **~ à** : subject to, prone to
sujet[2], **-jette** *n* : subject (of a state or country)
sujet[3] *nm* **1** : subject, topic **2** RAISON : cause
sujétion [sɥʒesjɔ̃] *nf* **1** SOUMISSION : subjection **2** CONTRAINTE : constraint
sulfureux, -reuse [sylfyrø, -røz] *adj* : sulfurous
sulfurique [sylfyrik] *adj* **acide sulfurique** : sulfuric acid
sultan [syltɑ̃] *nm* : sultan
sumac [symak] *nm* **1** : súmac **2 sumac vénéneux** : poison ivy
summum [sɔmɔm] *nm* : height, peak, acme
sundae [sɔnde] *nm Can* : sundae
super [sypɛr] *adj s & pl fam* EXTRA : super, great
superbe[1] [syperb] *adj* : superb — **superbement** [-perbəmɑ̃] *adv*
superbe[2] *nm* : arrogance, pride
supercherie [syperʃəri] *nf* : deception, fraud
superficialité [syperfisjalite] *nf* : superficiality
superficie [syperfisi] *nf* : area, surface
superficiel, -cielle [syperfisjɛl] *adj* : superficial
superflu[1], **-flue** [syperfly] *adj* : superfluous
superflu[2] *nm* : superfluity
supérieur[1], **-rieure** [syperjœr] *adj* **1** : superior **2** : upper <coin gauche supérieur : upper left-hand corner> **3** : higher <à un taux supérieur : at a higher rate>
supérieur[2], **-rieure** *n* : superior
supérieurement [syperjœrmɑ̃] *adv* : exceptionally
supériorité [syperjɔrite] *nf* : superiority
superlatif[1], **-tive** [syperlatif, -tiv] *adj* : superlative
superlatif[2] *nm* : superlative
supermarché [supermarʃe] *nm* : supermarket
superposer [syperpoze] *vt* **1** : to stack **2** : to superimpose
superpuissance [syperpɥisɑ̃s] *nf* : superpower
supersonique [supersɔnik] *adj* : supersonic
superstitieux, -tieuse [syperstisjø, -sjøz] *adj* : superstitious — **superstitieusement** [-sjøzmɑ̃] *adv*
superstition [syperstisjɔ̃] *nf* : superstition
superstructure [syperstryktyr] *nf* : superstructure
superviser [supervize] *vt* : to supervise — **supervision** [-vizjɔ̃] *nf*
superviseur [supervizœr] *nm* : supervisor
supplanter [sypläte] *vt* : to supplant
suppléant, -pléante [sypleɑ̃, -pleɑ̃t] *adj & n* : substitute, replacement, alternate
suppléer [syplee] {89} *vt* **1** REMPLACER : to replace, to fill in for **2** COMPENSER : to make up for, to compensate for — *vi* **~ à** : to make up for, to compensate for
supplément [syplemɑ̃] *nm* **1** : supplement **2** : extra charge, extra amount
supplémentaire [syplemɑ̃tɛr] *adj* **1** : additional, extra, supplementary **2** → **heure**
supplication [syplikasjɔ̃] *nf* : supplication, entreaty

supplice [syplis] *nm* **1** TORTURE : torture **2 être au supplice** : to be in agony
supplicier [syplisje] {96} *vt* TORTURER : to torture
supplier [syplije] {96} *vt* : to supplicate, to implore, to beg
support [sypɔr] *nm* **1** ÉTAI : support, stay, prop **2** : medium <support publicitaire : advertising medium>
supportable [sypɔrtabl] *adj* : bearable, tolerable
supporter[1] [sypɔrte] *vt* **1** SOUTENIR : to support, to hold up **2** ENDURER : to tolerate, to bear, to endure **3** : to stand up to, to withstand — **se supporter** *vr* **1** : to be bearable **2** : to stand each other
supporter[2] [sypɔrter] *nm* : supporter, fan (in sports, etc.)
supposer [sypoze] *vt* **1** IMAGINER : to suppose, to assume **2** IMPLIQUER : to imply, to presuppose
supposition [sypozisjɔ̃] *nf* : supposition, assumption
suppositoire [sypozitwar] *nm* : suppository
suppôt [sypo] *nm* : henchman <suppôt de Satan : fiend>
suppression [sypresjɔ̃] *nf* **1** : abolition, elimination, suppression **2** : deletion (from a text)
supprimer [syprime] *vt* **1** : to abolish, to eliminate, to suppress **2** : to take out, to delete
suppurer [sypyre] *vi* : to suppurate, to fester
supputer [sypyte] *vt* : to compute, to calculate — **supputation** [-pytasjɔ̃] *nf*
suprématie [sypremasi] *nf* : supremacy
suprême [syprɛm] *adj* : supreme — **suprêmement** [-prɛmmɑ̃] *adv*
sur[1] [syr] *prep* **1** : on, upon, in <sur la table : on the table> <sur la photo : in the photo> **2** : over, above <sur les montagnes : over the mountains> **3** : about, on <un essai sur l'histoire : an essay about history> **4** VERS : towards <sur mon quatre-vingtième an : towards my eightieth year> **5** PARMI : out of <quatre sur cinq : four out of five> **6** : by <cinq mètres sur trois : five by three meters> **7 sur ce** : whereupon, upon which, hereon
sur[2], **sure** [syr] *adj* : sour
sûr, sûre [syr] *adj* **1** CERTAIN : sure, certain **2** FIABLE : reliable, trustworthy **3** : safe, secure **4** : sound <jugement sûr : sound judgment> — **sûrement** [syrmɑ̃] *adv*
surabondant, -dante [syrabɔ̃dɑ̃, -dɑ̃t] *adj* : overabundant — **surabondance** [-bɔ̃dɑ̃s] *nf*
suralimenter [syralimɑ̃te] *vt* : to overfeed
suranné, -née [syrane] *adj* : outdated, old-fashioned
surcharge [syrʃarʒe] *nf* **1** : extra load, overload **2** : correction, alteration **3** : surcharge
surcharger [syrʃarʒe] {17} *vt* **1** : to overload, to overburden **2** : to correct, to alter **3** : to impose a surcharge
surchauffer [syrʃofe] *vt* : to overheat
surclasser [syrklase] *vt* : to outclass
surcroît [syrkrwa] *nm* **1** : increase <un surcroît de travail : extra work> **2 de ~** *or* **par ~** : in addition, moreover **3 en ~** : in addition
surdité [syrdite] *nf* : deafness
surdose [syrdoz] *nf* : overdose
surdoué, -douée [syrdwe] *adj* : extremely intelligent, gifted
sureau [syro] *nm, pl* **sureaux** : elder (tree)
surélever [syrelve] {52} *vt* : to raise, to heighten
surenchère [syrɑ̃ʃɛr] *nf* **1** : higher bid **2** : exaggeration, overstatement
surenchérir [syrɑ̃ʃerir] *vi* **1** : to bid higher **2 ~ sur** : to outbid, to go one better than
surestimer [syrɛstime] *vt* : to overestimate, to overrate
sûreté [syrte] *nf* **1** SÉCURITÉ : safety, security **2** : soundness, steadiness, reliability **3** : surety, guarantee (in law) **4** : safety catch, safety lock
surexcité, -tée [syrɛksite] *adj* : overexcited
surexposer [syrɛkspoze] *vt* : to overexpose
surf [sœrf] *nm* : surfing, surfboarding
surface [syrfas] *nf* **1** : surface <faire surface : to surface> <en surface : on the surface, aboveground> **2 de ~** : superficial
surfait, -faite [syrfɛ, -fɛt] *adj* : overrated
surgelé [syrʒəle] *nm* : frozen food
surgeler [syrʒəle] {20} *vt* : to quick-freeze
surgir [syrʒir] *vi* **1** : to appear suddenly, to loom up **2** : to come up, to arise
surhumain, -maine [syrymɛ̃, -mɛn] *adj* : superhuman
surinamien, -mienne [syrinamjɛ̃, -mjɛn] *adj* : Surinamese
Surinamien, -mienne *n* : Surinamese
sur-le-champ [syrləʃɑ̃] *adv* : immediately, at once
surlendemain [syrlɑ̃dmɛ̃] *nm* **le surlendemain** : two days later
surmener [syrməne] {52} *vt* : to overwork — **se surmener** *vr* : to overwork, to work too hard
surmonter [syrmɔ̃te] *vt* **1** : to overcome, to surmount **2** : to top, to crown (a building, etc.)
surnager [syrnaʒe] {17} *vi* **1** FLOTTER : to float **2** PERSISTER : to persist, to linger on
surnaturel[1], **-relle** [syrnatyrɛl] *adj* : supernatural

surnaturel[2] *nm* **le surnaturel** : the supernatural
surnom [syrnɔ̃] *nm* SOBRIQUET : nickname
surnombre [syrnɔ̃bʀ] *nm* **en ~** : excess, surplus <trois copies en surnombre : three too many copies>
surnommer [syrnɔme] *vt* : to nickname, to call
surpasser [syrpase] *vt* : to surpass, to outdo — **se surpasser** *vr*
surpeuplé, -plée [syrpœple] *adj* : overpopulated
surpeuplement [syrpœpləmɑ̃] *nm* : overpopulation
surplis [syrpli] *nm* : surplice
surplomb [syrplɔ̃] *nm* : overhang <en surplomb : overhanging>
surplomber [syrplɔ̃be] *v* : to overhang
surplus [syrply] *nm* **1** : surplus **2 au surplus** : moreover
surpopulation [syrpɔpylasjɔ̃] *nf* : overpopulation
surprenant, -nante [syrprənɑ̃, -nɑ̃t] *adj* : surprising, amazing
surprendre [syrprɑ̃dʀ] {70} *vt* **1** ÉTONNER : to surprise, to amaze **2** : to take by surprise, to catch in the act **3** : to overhear, to intercept
surprise [syrpriz] *nf* : surprise <avoir la bonne surprise : to be pleasantly surprised> <par surprise : by surprise>
surproduction [syrprɔdyksjɔ̃] *nf* : overproduction
surréalisme [syrrealism] *nm* : surrealism — **surréaliste** [-alist] *adj & nmf*
sursaut [syrso] *nm* **1** : start, jump <en sursaut : with a start> **2** : burst <un sursaut d'énergie : a burst of energy>
sursauter [syrsote] *vi* : to start, to jump
surseoir [syrswar] {90} *vi* **~ à** : to postpone, to defer
sursis[1] [syrsi] *pp* → **surseoir**
sursis[2] [syrsi] *nm* **1** : reprieve <condamné avec sursis : given a suspended sentence> **2** : respite, deferment, extension **3 être un mort en sursis** : to live on borrowed time
surtaxe [syrtaks] *nf* : surcharge
surtension [syrtɑ̃sjɔ̃] *nf* : surge (of electricity)
surtout[1] [syrtu] *adv* **1** : above all <surtout, pas de peur : above all, don't be afraid> **2** : especially, particularly <j'aime surtout la poésie : I especially like poetry>
surtout[2] *nm* : centerpiece
surveillance [syrvejɑ̃s] *nf* : surveillance, supervision <en surveillance médicale : under medical supervision>
surveillant, -lante [syrvɛjɑ̃, -jɑ̃t] *n* **1** : supervisor, overseer **2 surveillant de baignade** : lifeguard **3 surveillant de prison** : prison warden
surveiller [syrveje] *vt* **1** : to watch (over), to keep an eye on **2** : to supervise, to oversee
survenir [syrvənir] {92} *vi* **1** : to occur, to take place **2** : to arrive (unexpectedly)
survie [syrvi] *nf* **1** : survival (of a person) **2** : afterlife
survivance [syrvivɑ̃s] *nf* : survival
survivant, -vante [syrvivɑ̃, -vɑ̃t] *n* : survivor
survivre [syrvivʀ] {98} *vi* **1** : to survive **2 ~ à** : to survive, to outlive, to outlast
survol [syrvɔl] *nm* **1** : flying over **2** : quick look, overview
survoler [syrvɔle] *vi* **1** : to fly over **2** : to skim through
survolté, -tée [syrvɔlte] *adj* **1** : boosted (of an electronic circuit) **2** : overexcited
sus [sy(s)] *adv* **1 en ~** : extra **2 en sus de** : in addition to, on top of
susceptibilité [syseptibilite] *nf* : sensitivity, touchiness
susceptible [syseptibl] *adj* **1** : sensitive, touchy **2 ~ de** : likely to, capable of
susciter [sysite] *vt* **1** ÉVEILLER : to arouse (interest, feeling, etc.) **2** CRÉER : to create, to give rise to (problems, obstacles, etc.)
susmentionné, -née [sysmɑ̃sjɔne] *adj* : aforesaid, aforementioned
suspect[1], **-pecte** [syspɛ, -pɛkt] *adj* : suspicious, suspect
suspect[2], **-pecte** *n* : suspect
suspecter [syspɛkte] *vt* : to suspect
suspendre [syspɑ̃dʀ] {63} *vt* **1** : to suspend, to break off **2** PENDRE : to hang, to hang up — **se suspendre** *vr* **~ à** : to hang from
suspens [syspɑ̃] *nm* **1 en ~** : unresolved, uncertain **2 tenir en suspens** : to keep in suspense
suspense [syspɑ̃s] *nm* : suspense
suspension [syspɑ̃sjɔ̃] *nf* **1** : suspension **2 en ~** : suspended, hanging
suspicieux, -cieuse [syspisjø, -sjøz] *adj* : suspicious
suspicion [syspisjɔ̃] *nf* : suspicion
susurrer [sysyre] *v* CHUCHOTER : whisper
suture [sytyr] *nf* **1** : suture **2 point de suture** : stitch
suturer [sytyre] *vt* : to suture, to stitch
suzerain [syzʀɛ̃] *nm* : liege, (feudal) lord
svelte [zvelt] *adj* : slender, svelte
sycomore [sikɔmɔʀ] *nm* : sycamore
syllabe [silab] *nf* : syllable — **syllabique** [-labik] *adj*
sylvestre [silvɛstʀ] *adj* : sylvan, forest
sylviculture [silvikyltyr] *nf* : forestry
symbole [sɛ̃bɔl] *nm* **1** : symbol **2** : creed <le Symbole des Apôtres : the Apostle's Creed>
symbolique [sɛ̃bɔlik] *adj* : symbolic — **symboliquement** [-likmɑ̃] *adv*
symboliser [sɛ̃bɔlize] *vt* : to symbolize
symbolisme [sɛ̃bɔlism] *nm* : symbolism

symétrie [simetri] *nf* : symmetry
symétrique [simetrik] *adj* : symmetrical, symmetric — **symétriquement** [-trikmɑ̃] *adv*
sympa [sɛ̃pa] *adj fam* : friendly, nice
sympathie [sɛ̃pati] *nf* **1** : liking, affection, fellow feeling **2** CONDOLÉANCES : condolences, sympathy
sympathique [sɛ̃patik] *adj* **1** AIMABLE : nice, likeable, pleasant **2** : sympathetic (in medicine)
sympathisant, -sante [sɛ̃patizɑ̃, -zɑ̃t] *n* : sympathizer
sympathiser [sɛ̃patize] *vi* : to get along <sympathiser avec qqn : to get on well with s.o.>
symphonie [sɛ̃fɔni] *nf* : symphony
symphonique [sɛ̃fɔnik] *adj* : symphonic
symptomatique [sɛ̃ptɔmatik] *adj* : symptomatic
symptôme [sɛ̃ptom] *nm* : symptom
synagogue [sinagɔg] *nf* : synagogue
synchroniser [sɛ̃krɔnize] *vt* : to synchronize
syncope [sɛ̃kɔp] *nf* **1** : faint, blackout **2** : syncopation
syncopé, -pée [sɛ̃kɔpe] *adj* : syncopated
syndicaliser [sɛ̃dikalize] *vt* : to unionize — **se syndicaliser** *vr*
syndicat [sɛ̃dika] *nm* : union, labor union
syndiquer [sɛ̃dike] *vt* : to unionize — **se syndiquer** *vr* : to join a union
syndrome [sɛ̃drom] *nm* : syndrome
synonyme[1] [sinɔnim] *adj* : synonymous
synonyme[2] *nm* : synonym
synopsis [sinɔpsis] *nf* : synopsis
syntaxe [sɛ̃taks] *nf* : syntax
synthèse [sɛ̃tɛz] *nf* : synthesis
synthétique [sɛ̃tetik] *adj* : synthetic — **synthétiquement** [-tikmɑ̃] *adv*
synthétiser [sɛ̃tetize] *vt* : to synthesize
syphilis [sifilis] *nf* : syphilis
syrien, -rienne [sirjɛ̃, -rjɛn] *adj* : Syrian
Syrien, -rienne *n* : Syrian
systématique [sistematik] *adj* : systematic — **systématiquement** [-tikmɑ̃] *adv*
systématiser [sistematize] *vt* : to systematize
système [sistɛm] *nm* : system <système métrique : metric system> <système solaire : solar system>
systémique [sistemik] *adj* : systemic

T

t [te] *nm* : t, the 20th letter of the alphabet
tabac [taba] *nm* **1** : tobacco **2 tabac à priser** : snuff **3** *France* : tobacco shop **4 c'est toujours le même tabac** *fam* : it's always the same old thing
tabagie [tabaʒi] *nf* **1** smoke-filled place **2** : *Can* : tobacco shop
tabasser [tabase] *vt fam* : to beat up, to clobber
tabatière [tabatjɛr] *nf* **1** : snuffbox **2** : skylight
tabernacle [tabɛrnakl] *nm* : tabernacle
table [tabl] *nf* **1** : table <mettre la table : to set the table> <se mettre à table : to sit down to eat> **2** : table, list <table des matières : table of contents> <table de multiplication : multiplication table> **3 table basse** : coffee table **4 table de chevet** *or* **table de nuit** : bedside table, night table **5 table ronde** : round table, roundtable
tableau [tablo] *nm, pl* **tableaux 1** PEINTURE : painting **2** : picture, scene **3** : table, chart **4 tableau d'affichage** : bulletin board **5 tableau de bord** : dashboard **6** *or* **tableau noir** : blackboard
tabler [table] *vt* ~ **sur** : to count on, to rely on
tablette [tablɛt] *nf* **1** : shelf **2** : bar (of candy), stick (of gum) **3** : tablet (in pharmacy) **4** *Can* : notepad
tableur [tablœr] *nm* : spreadsheet
tablier [tablije] *nm* **1** : apron **2** : roadway, deck (on a bridge)
tabloïde *or* **tabloïd** [tablɔid] *nm* : tabloid
tabou[1], **-boue** [tabu] *adj* : taboo
tabou[2] *nm* : taboo
tabouret [taburɛ] *nm* : stool, footstool
tabulaire [tabylɛr] *adj* : tabular
tabulateur [tabylatœr] *nm* : tab, tabulator
tac [tak] *nm* **1** : tap, click **2 du tac au tac** : tit for tat
tache [taʃ] *nf* **1** : stain, spot **2 taches de rousseur** : freckles
tâche [taʃ] *nf* : task, job
tacher [taʃe] *vt* SALIR : to stain, to spot — **se tacher** *vr*
tâcher [taʃe] *vt* **tâcher que** : to try and be sure that <tâchez que ce soit correct : make sure that it's correct> — *vi* ~ **de** : to try to <tâcher de réussir : to try to succeed>
tâcheron [taʃrɔ̃] *nm* **1** : hard worker, drudge **2** : jobber
tacheter [taʃte] {8} *vt* : to spot, to speckle
tacite [tasit] *adj* : tacit — **tacitement** [tasitmɑ̃] *adv*

taciturne |tasityrn| *adj* : taciturn
tacot |tako| *nm fam* : jalopy
tact |takt| *nm* DÉLICATESSE : tact <avec tact : tactfully>
tactile |taktil| *adj* : tactile
tactique[1] |taktik| *adj* : tactical — **tactiquement** |-tikmɑ̃| *adv*
tactique[2] *nf* STRATÉGIE : tactics *pl*, strategy, procedure
taffetas |tafta| *nms & pl* : taffeta
tahitien[1], **-tienne** |taisjɛ̃, -sjɛn| *adj* : Tahitian
tahitien[2] *nm* : Tahitian (language)
Tahitien, -tienne *n* : Tahitian
taie |tɛ| *nf or* **taie d'oreiller** : pillowcase
taillader |tajade| *vt* : to slash, to gash, to hack
taille |taj| *nf* **1** : cutting, pruning **2** : size <de taille moyenne : medium-sized> <de taille : sizable> **3** : height <une femme de haute taille : a tall woman> **4** : waist, waistline
taille-crayon |tajkrɛjɔ̃| *nm, pl* **taille-crayons** : pencil sharpener
tailler |taje| *vt* **1** : to cut, to prune, to trim **2** : to sharpen (a pencil) — *vi* **1** ~ **dans** : to cut into **2 tailler grand/petit** : to run large/small (of clothes) — **se tailler** *vr* : to carve out (a way, a success, etc.) for oneself
tailleur |tajœr| *nm* **1** : woman's suit **2** : tailor
taillis |taji| *nms & pl* : coppice, copse
taire |tɛr| {91} *vt* : to hush up, to keep secret — **se taire** *vr* **1** : to be quiet <tais-toi! : be quiet!> **2** : to fall silent
taisait |tɛzɛ|, **taisions** |tɛzjɔ̃|, *etc.* → **taire**
taise |tɛz|, *etc.* → **taire**
taiwanais, -naise |tajwanɛ, -nɛz| *adj* : Taiwanese
Taiwanais, -naise *n* : Taiwanese
talc |talk| *nm* : talc, talcum powder
talent |talɑ̃| *nm* : talent, gift <avoir du talent : to be talented>
talentueux, -tueuse |talɑ̃tɥø, -tɥøz| *adj* : talented
taler |tale| *vt* : to bruise (fruit)
talion |taljɔ̃| *nm* **la loi du talion** : an eye for an eye
talisman |talismɑ̃| *nm* : talisman
taloche |taloʃ| *nf fam* : slap, blow
talon |talɔ̃| *nm* **1** : heel **2** : stub (of a check)
talonner |talɔne| *vt* **1** : to follow closely **2** : to hound, to harass
talus |taly| *nms & pl* : embankment, slope
tambour |tɑ̃bur| *nm* **1** : drum **2** : drummer **3 sans tambour ni trompette** : without fanfare **4 tambour battant** : briskly
tambourin |tɑ̃burɛ̃| *nm* : tambourine
tambouriner |tɑ̃burine| *vt* : to drum, to tap (one's fingers, one's feet, etc.)
tamia |tamja| *nm* : chipmunk
tamis |tami| *nms & pl* : sieve, sifter
tamiser |tamize| *vt* **1** : to sift **2** : to filter <lumière tamisée : subdued lighting>
tampon |tɑ̃pɔ̃| *nm* **1** BOUCHON : plug, stopper **2** : pad <tampon à récurer : scouring pad> <tampon encreur : stamp pad, ink pad> **3** : buffer **4** : rubber stamp **5 tampon hygiénique** : tampon
tamponner |tɑ̃pɔne| *vt* **1** : to dab, to swab **2** HEURTER : to crash into, to collide with **3** : to stamp, to validate
tam-tam |tamtam| *nm, pl* **tam-tams** : tom-tom
tancer |tɑ̃se| {6} *vt* : to reprimand
tandem |tɑ̃dɛm| *nm* **1** : tandem (bicycle) **2 travailler en tandem** : to work in tandem
tandis |tɑ̃di| **tandis que 1** : while **2** : whereas
tangent, -gente |tɑ̃ʒɑ̃, -ʒɑ̃t| *adj* : tangential
tangente |tɑ̃ʒɑ̃t| *nf* : tangent
tangible |tɑ̃ʒibl| *adj* : tangible — **tangiblement** |-ʒibləmɑ̃| *adv*
tango |tɑ̃go| *nm* : tango
tanguer |tɑ̃ge| *vi* : to pitch, to toss about
tanière |tanjɛr| *nf* : lair, den
tanin |tanɛ̃| *nm* : tannin
tank |tɑ̃k| *nm* : tank
tanker |tɑ̃kœr| *nm* : tanker
tanné, -née |tane| *adj* : weathered, leathery (of skin)
tanner |tane| *vt* **1** : to tan (leather, skin) **2** *fam* : to pester, to annoy
tannerie |tanri| *nf* : tannery
tanneur, -neuse |tanœr, -nøz| *n* : tanner
tant |tɑ̃| *adv* **1** : so much, so many <tant de bruit : so much noise> <comme tant d'autres : like so many others> <il y a tant à faire : there's so much to do> **2** : so <tant il est déterminé : (since) he is so determined> **3 en tant que** : as, in so far as **4 en tant que tel** : as such **5 tant mieux!** : so much the better! **6 tant pis!** : too bad! **7 tant que** : as much as, so much as **8 tant que** : as long as
tante |tɑ̃t| *nf* : aunt
tantinet |tɑ̃tine| *nm* : little bit
tantôt |tɑ̃to| *adv* **1** : sometimes <tantôt à bicyclette, tantôt à pied : sometimes by bicycle, sometimes on foot> **2** *Can* : later **3** *France* : this afternoon
tanzanien, -nienne |tɑ̃zanjɛ̃, -njɛn| *adj* : Tanzanian
Tanzanien, -nienne *n* : Tanzanian
taon |tɑ̃| *nm* : horsefly
tapage |tapaʒ| *nm* **1** VACARME : racket, uproar, din **2** SCANDALE : furor, scandal
tapageur, -geuse |tapaʒœr, -ʒøz| *adj* **1** : noisy, rowdy **2** VOYANT : flashy, ostentatious, garish

tapant, -pante [tapɑ̃, -pɑ̃t] *adj* : sharp, on the dot <à midi tapant : at twelve o'clock sharp>
tape [tap] *nf* : slap, tap, pat
tape-à-l'oeil[1] [tapalœj] *adj* : flashy, showy, gaudy
tape-à-l'oeil[2] *nms & pl* : flashiness, show
taper [tape] *vt* **1** : to hit, to slap, to beat **2** : to type **3 taper qqn de qqch** : to bum sth from s.o. — *vi* **1** : to hit, to knock, to bang <taper sur un clou : to hit (on) a nail> <taper à la porte : to knock on the door> **2** : to beat down (of the sun) **3** *or* **taper à la machine** : to type **4 taper des mains** : to clap one's hands **5 taper des pieds** : to stamp one's feet — **se taper** *vr* **1** *fam* : to knock each other down **2** *fam* : to put away, to eat, to drink **3** *fam* : to get stuck with (a chore)
tapette [tapɛt] *nf* **1** : light tap, pat **2 tapette à mouches** : flyswatter
tapinois [tapɛnwa] **en ~** : furtively
tapioca [tapjɔka] *nm* : tapioca
tapir [tapir] *v* **se tapir** *vr* **1** : to crouch (down) **2** : to hide away, to retreat
tapis [tapi] *nms & pl* **1** : carpet **2 tapis roulant** : moving walkway, (baggage) carousel, conveyor belt
tapisser [tapise] *vt* **1** : to wallpaper **2** : to upholster **3** : to cover, to carpet
tapisserie [tapisri] *nf* **1** : tapestry **2** : wallpaper **3 faire tapisserie** : to be a wallflower
taponner [tapɔne] *vt Can fam* : to touch, to handle <arrête de taponner mes choses : stop playing with my things>
tapotement [tapɔtmɑ̃] *nm* : tap, pat
tapoter [tapɔte] *vt* : to tap, to pat
taquin[1], **-quine** [takɛ̃, -kin] *adj* : teasing
taquin[2], **-quine** *n* : tease
taquiner [takine] *vt* : to tease
taquinerie [takinri] *nf* : teasing
tarabiscoté, -cotée [tarabiskɔte] *adj* : fussy, overelaborate
tarabuster [tarabyste] *vt* **1** : to pester **2** : to worry, to bother <ça me tarabuste : that's getting me down>
tard [tar] *adv* : late <plus tard : later> <au plus tard : at the latest>
tarder [tarde] *vi* **1** : to delay, to be a long time coming <ça ne devrait pas tarder : it shouldn't take long> **2 sans ~** : without delay
tardif, -dive [tardif, -div] *adj* : late <repas tardif : late meal>
tardivement [tardivmɑ̃] *adv* : late, belatedly
tare [tar] *nf* DÉFAUT : defect, flaw
tarentule [tarɑ̃tyl] *nf* : tarantula
targette [tarʒɛt] *nf* : bolt (on a door, etc.)
targuer [targe] *v* **se targuer** *vr* **~ de** : to boast about
tarif [tarif] *nm* **1** : rate, fare <payer plein tarif : to pay full fare> **2** : price, schedule of prices <tarif horaire : price per hour> **3 tarif douanier** : tariff, customs duty
tarir [tarir] *vt* : to dry up — *vi* **1** : to run dry, to dry up **2 ne pas tarir d'éloges** : to be full of praise
tartan [tartɑ̃] *nm* : tartan
tarte[1] [tart] *adj fam* : stupid, ridiculous
tarte[2] *nf* : pie
tartelette [tartəlɛt] *nf* : tart
tartine [tartin] *nf or* **tartine beurrée** : slice of bread and butter
tartiner [tartine] *vt* : to spread (with butter, etc.) <fromage à tartiner : cheese spread>
tartre [tartr] *nm* : tartar
tas [ta] *nms & pl* **1** : heap, pile **2 des tas de** : a lot of, piles of **3 formation sur le tas** : on-the-job training
tasse [tas] *nf* : cup <tasse à thé : teacup>
tasseau [taso] *nm, pl* **tasseaux** : brace, bracket
tasser [tase] *vt* **1** : to pack down **2** ENTASSER : to pack together, to cram **3** *Can* : to move over, to move aside — **se tasser** *vr* **1** : to shrink **2** : to squeeze together, to cram <elles sont tassées dans la voiture : they are crammed into the car>
tâter [tate] *vt* **1** PALPER : to feel **2** : to sound out <tâter le terrain : to check out the lay of the land> — *vi* **~ de** : to try one's hand at
tatillon[1], **-lonne** [tatijɔ̃, -jɔn] *adj* POINTILLEUX : fussy, finicky
tatillon[2], **-lonne** *n* : fussy person, fuss-budget
tâtonner [tatɔne] *vi* : to grope one's way, to feel around
tâtons [tatɔ̃] **avancer à tâtons** : to feel one's way (along)
tatou [tatu] *nm* : armadillo
tatouage [tatwaʒ] *nm* **1** : tattoo **2** : tattooing
tatouer [tatwe] *vt* : to tattoo
taudis [todi] *nms & pl* : hovel, slum
taule [tol] *nf fam* : prison <faire de la taule : to do time>
taupe [top] *nf* **1** : mole **2 myope comme une taupe** : blind as a bat
taupinière [topinjɛr] *nf* : molehill
taureau [tɔro] *nm, pl* **taureaux** : bull
Taureau *nm* : Taurus
tauromachie [tɔrɔmaʃi] *nf* : bullfighting
taux [to] *nms & pl* **1** : rate <taux de change : exchange rate> <taux de natalité : birthrate> **2** : level <taux de cholestérol : cholesterol level>
tavelé, -lée [tavle] *adj* : marked, spotted
taverne [tavɛrn] *nf* : inn, tavern
taxe [taks] *nf* : tax — **taxation** [taksasjɔ̃] *nf*

taxer [takse] *vt* **1** IMPOSER : to tax **2** ACCUSER : to accuse <il m'a taxé de paresse : he accused me of laziness>
taxi [taksi] *nm* : taxi, taxicab
taxidermie [taksidɛrmi] *nf* : taxidermy — **taxidermiste** [-dɛrmist] *nmf*
tchadien, -dienne [tʃadjɛ̃, -djɛn] *adj* : Chadian
Tchadien, -dienne *n* : Chadian
tchécoslovaque [tʃekɔslɔvak] *adj* : Czechoslovak, Czechoslovakian
Tchécoslovaque *nmf* : Czechoslovak, Czechoslovakian
tchèque[1] [tʃɛk] *adj* : Czech
tchèque[2] *nm* : Czech (language)
Tchèque *nmf* : Czech
te [tə] (**t'** *before a vowel or mute h*) *pron* **1** : you, to you <je t'aime : I love you> <je te le donne : I'm giving it to you> **2** : yourself <tu vas te couper : you're going to cut yourself>
technicien, -cienne [tɛknisjɛ̃, -sjɛn] *n* : technician
technique[1] [tɛknik] *adj* : technical — **techniquement** [-nikmɑ̃] *adv*
technique[2] *nf* : technique
technologie [tɛknɔlɔʒi] *nf* : technology
technologique [tɛknɔlɔʒik] *adj* : technological
technologue [tɛknɔlɔg] *nmf* : technologist
teck [tɛk] *nm* : teak
teckel [tɛkɛl] *nm* : dachshund
tee-shirt [tiʃœrt] *nm, pl* **tee-shirts** : T-shirt
teigne [tɛɲ] *nf* **1** : ringworm **2** : moth **3** *fam* : nasty person, louse
teindre [tɛ̃dr] {37} *vt* : to dye — **se teindre** *vr* **se teindre les cheveux** : to dye one's hair
teint [tɛ̃] *nm* **1** : complexion, coloring **2 grand teint** *or* **bon teint** : colorfast
teinte [tɛ̃t] *nf* **1** TON : shade, hue **2** : tinge, hint
teinter [tɛ̃te] *vt* **1** : to tint, to stain **2 ~ de** : to tinge with <tristesse teintée de soulagement : sorrow tinged with relief>
teinture [tɛ̃tyr] *nf* **1** : dye **2** : dyeing **3** : tincture <teinture d'iode : tincture of iodine>
teinturerie [tɛ̃tyrri] *nf* : dry cleaner (shop)
teinturier, -rière [tɛ̃tyrje, -rjɛ] *n* : dry cleaner
tel[1], **telle** [tɛl] *adj* **1** : such <une telle femme : such a woman, a woman like that> <un tel bonheur! : such happiness!> <de telle manière que : in such a way that> **2** : such and such, a certain <je viens tel jour : I'm coming on such and such a day> **3 tel que** : such as, like <des livres tels que les dictionnaires : books such as dictionaries> **4 tel quel** : as (it) is <laissez-les tels quels : leave them as they are>
tel[2], **telle** *pron* **1** : a certain one, someone **2 un tel, une telle** : so-and-so, what's-his-name, what's-her-name
télé [tele] *nf fam* : TV
téléavertisseur [teleavɛrtisœr] *nm Can* : beeper
téléchargement [teleʃarʒmɑ̃] *nm* : download, downloading
télécharger [teleʃarʒe] {17} *vt* : to download (a computer file)
télécommande [telekɔmɑ̃d] *nf* : remote control
télécommunication [telekɔmynikasjɔ̃] *nf* : telecommunication
télécopie [telekɔpi] *nf* : fax, facsimile
télécopieur [telekɔpjœr] *nm* : fax machine
télédiffuser [teledifyze] *vt* : to broadcast (on television), to televise
téléfilm [telefilm] *nm* : film made for TV
télégramme [telegram] *nm* : telegram
télégraphe [telegraf] *nm* : telegraph — **télégraphique** [-grafik] *adj*
télégraphier [telegrafje] {96} *v* : to telegraph
télépathie [telepati] *nf* : telepathy
télépathique [telepatik] *adj* : telepathic
téléphone [telefɔn] *nm* : telephone, phone <donner un coup de téléphone : to make a phone call> <être au téléphone : to be (talking) on the telephone> <téléphone portable : cell phone *US*, mobile phone *Brit*>
téléphoner [telefɔne] *vt* **1** : to telephone, to call **2 téléphoner en PVC** *France* : to call collect **3 téléphoner à frais vivés** *Can* : to call collect
téléphonique [telefɔnik] *adj* : telephone <cabine téléphonique : telephone booth>
téléphoniste [telefɔnist] *nmf* : telephone operator
télescope [teleskɔp] *nm* : telescope
télescoper [teleskɔpe] *vt* : to crash into, to collide with (a vehicle) — **se télescoper** *vr* **1** : to collide with each other **2** : to overlap, to intermingle (of ideas, etc.)
télescopique [teleskɔpik] *adj* : telescopic
télésiège [telesjɛʒ] *nm* : chairlift
téléski [teleski] *nm* : ski lift
téléspectateur, -trice [telespɛktatœr, -tris] *n* : television viewer
téléviser [televize] *vt* : to televise
téléviseur [televizœr] *nm* : television set
télévision [televizjɔ̃] *nf* **1** : television <à la télévision : on television> **2** TÉLÉVISEUR : television set
tellement [tɛlmɑ̃] *adv* **1** : so, so much <tellement vite : so fast> <c'est tellement mieux : it's so much better> **2 ~ de** : so many, so much <tellement de travail : so much work> **3 pas tellement** : not much, not really <il

n'a pas tellement changé : he hasn't really changed>

téméraire [temerɛr] *adj* : rash, reckless

témérité [temerite] *nf* : rashness, recklessness

témoignage [temwaɲaʒ] *nm* **1** RÉCIT : account, story **2** : testimony (in court) **3** PREUVE : evidence, sign <témoignage d'affection : token of affection>

témoigner [temwaɲe] *vt* **1** : to testify, to attest **2** MONTRER : to show, to evince — *vi* **1** : to testify, to give evidence **2** ~ **de** : to show, to give evidence of

témoin [temwɛ̃] *nm* **1** : witness <témoin oculaire : eyewitness> **2** PREUVE : evidence, mark **3** : baton (in a relay)

tempe [tɑ̃p] *nf* : temple <tempes grisonnantes : graying temples>

tempérament [tɑ̃peramɑ̃] *nm* CARACTÈRE : temperament, disposition

tempérance [tɑ̃perɑ̃s] *nf* : temperance

tempérant, -rante [tɑ̃perɑ̃, -rɑ̃t] *adj* : temperate, sober

température [tɑ̃peratyr] *nf* : temperature

tempéré, -rée [tɑ̃pere] *adj* : temperate

tempérer [tɑ̃pere] {87} *vt* : to temper, to ease, to moderate

tempête [tɑ̃pɛt] *nf* : storm <tempête de neige : snowstorm, blizzard>

tempêter [tɑ̃pete] *vi* FULMINER : to rage, to rant

temple [tɑ̃pl] *nm* **1** : temple **2** : (protestant) church, meetinghouse

tempo [tempo] *nm* : tempo

temporaire [tɑ̃porɛr] *adj* : temporary — **temporairement** [-rɛrmɑ̃] *adv*

temporel, -relle [tɑ̃porɛl] *adj* : temporal

temporiser [tɑ̃porize] *vi* : to stall, to play for time

temps [tɑ̃] *nms & pl* **1** : time <à temps : in time, on time> <de temps à autre : from time to time> <pendant ce temps : meanwhile, in the meantime> <travailler à plein temps : to work full-time> <les temps ont changé : times have changed> **2** : weather <un temps pluvieux : rainy weather> <quel temps fait-il? : what's the weather like?, what's it like outside?> **3** : tense (in grammar)

tenable [tənabl] *adj* SUPPORTABLE : bearable <ce n'était pas tenable : it was unbearable>

tenace [tənas] *adj* : tenacious, persistent

tenacité [tənasite] *nf* : tenacity

tenailler [tenaje] *vt* TOURMENTER : to torture, to torment

tenailles [tənaj] *nfpl* **1** : pincers, nippers **2** : tongs

tenancier, -cière [tənɑ̃sje, -sjɛr] *n* : manager (of a hotel, etc.)

tenant, -nante [tənɑ̃, -nɑ̃t] *n* **1** PARTISAN : supporter **2 tenant d'un titre** : titleholder (in sports) **3 les tenants et les aboutissants** : the ins and outs

tendance [tɑ̃dɑ̃s] *nf* **1** : tendency **2** COURANT : trend

tendineux, -neuse [tɑ̃dinø, -nøz] *adj* **1** : tendinous, sinewy **2** : stringy (of meat)

tendon [tɑ̃dɔ̃] *nm* : tendon, sinew, hamstring

tendre[1] [tɑ̃dr] {63} *vt* **1** : to tense, to stretch (out), to draw tight **2** : to put up, to set up <tendre un piège à : to set a trap for> **3** : to spread out (cloth, etc.) **4** : to hold out, to extend <tendre la main : to hold out one's hand> <tendre le cou : to crane one's neck> <tendre l'oreille : to prick up one's ears> — *vi* **1** ~ **à** : to tend to **2** ~ **vers** : to strive for — **se tendre** *vr* **1** : to tighten, to become taut **2** : to become strained

tendre[2] *adj* **1** : tender, soft **2** : loving <un regard tendre : a tender glance>

tendrement [tɑ̃drəmɑ̃] *adv* : lovingly, tenderly

tendresse [tɑ̃drɛs] *nf* : tenderness, affection

tendu, -due [tɑ̃dy] *adj* **1** : tight, taut **2** : tense, strained

ténèbres [tenɛbr] *nfpl* : darkness

ténébreux, -breuse [tenebrø, -brøz] *adj* **1** OBSCUR : dark, gloomy **2** MYSTÉRIEUX : mysterious, obscure

teneur [tənœr] *nf* : content <teneur en gras : fat content>

ténia [tenja] *nm* : tapeworm

tenir [tənir] {92} *vt* **1** : to hold, to keep <tenir en position : to hold in place> <tenez la porte fermée : keep the door shut> **2** : to have, to catch <je te tiens! : I've got you!> <tenir les voleurs : to catch the thieves> **3** : to take hold of, to control <tenir les enfants : to keep the children under control> **4** : to run, to manage (a hotel, store, etc.) **5** : to hold down, to hold up, to keep up **6** : to hold (a quantity), to take up (a space) **7** : to regard, to consider <il me tient responsable : he holds me responsible> — *vi* **1** : to hold, to stay in place **2** : to hold up, to last **3** : to fit (into a space) **4** *or* **tenir bon** : to hang on, to hold out **5** ~ **à** : to be fond of, to like **6** ~ **à** : to be due to **7** ~ **à** : to want to, to be anxious to **8** ~ **de** : to be like (someone), to take after **9** ~ **de** : to border on — *v impers* : to depend <il ne tient qu'à toi : it's up to you> — **se tenir** *vr* **1** : to hold, to hold up, to hold onto <se tenir par la main : to hold hands> **2** : to remain, to stay <se tenir prêt : to be ready> <se tenir debout : to stand still> **3** : to behave (oneself) **4** : to hold up, to make sense **5** : to consider oneself **6** : to hold to, to stand by <s'en tenir à : to confine oneself to>

tennis [tenis] *nm* **1** : tennis <tennis de table : table tennis> **2 tennis** *nmpl France* : sneakers
ténor [tenɔr] *nm* : tenor
tension [tɑ̃sjɔ̃] *nf* **1** : tension **2** *or* **tension artérielle** : blood pressure
tentacule [tɑ̃takyl] *nm* : tentacle
tentant, -tante [tɑ̃tɑ̃, -tɑ̃t] *adj* : tempting, tantalizing
tentateur, -trice [tɑ̃tatœr, -tris] *n* : tempter
tentation [tɑ̃tasjɔ̃] *nf* : temptation
tentative [tɑ̃tativ] *nf* : attempt <tentative d'homicide : attempted murder>
tente [tɑ̃t] *nf* : tent
tenter [tɑ̃te] *vt* **1** : to tempt <tenter le diable : to tempt fate> **2** ESSAYER : to attempt, to try <tenter la chance : to try one's luck>
tenture [tɑ̃tyr] *nf* : hanging, wall covering
tenu[1] [təny] *pp* → **tenir**
tenu[2], **-nue** [təny] *adj* **1** : obliged, bound **2** : controlled, kept in check **3 bien tenu** : well kept, tidy
ténu, -nue [teny] *adj* **1** : fine, slender **2** : thin (of voices, air, etc.) **3** : tenuous, subtle
tenue *nf* **1** : holding, running (of a meeting, etc.) **2** : organizing, keeping <tenue de livres : bookkeeping> **3** : conduct, manners *pl* **4** MAINTIEN : bearing, posture **5** : clothes *pl*, dress, outfit <tenue d'hiver : winter clothing> <tenue militaire : military dress, uniform> <tenue de soirée : formal dress>
térébenthine [terebɑ̃tin] *nf* : turpentine
tergiverser [tɛrʒiverse] *vi* : to shillyshally, to beat around the bush
terme [tɛrm] *nm* **1** : term, word <en d'autres termes : in other words> **2** : end, termination <mettre un terme à : to put an end to> **3** ÉCHÉANCE : due date, deadline (for payment) **4 termes** *nmpl* : terms (of a contract) **5 termes** *nmpl* : relations <être en bons termes avec : to be on good terms with>
terminaison [terminɛzɔ̃] *nf* : termination, ending
terminal[1], **-nale** [terminal] *adj, mpl* **-naux** [-no] **1** : final, last **2** : terminal (in medicine)
terminal[2] *nm, pl* **-naux 1** : station, terminal **2** : computer terminal
terminer [termine] *v* FINIR : to end, to finish **— se terminer** *vr* : to end, to finish up
terminologie [terminɔlɔʒi] *nf* : terminology
terminus [terminys] *nms & pl* : terminus, end of the line (of a train, bus, etc.)
termite [termit] *nm* : termite
terne [tɛrn] *adj* **1** FADE : colorless, drab **2** ENNUYEUX : dull, dreary
ternir [ternir] *vt* **1** : to tarnish, to dull **2** : to stain, to tarnish (one's reputation, etc.)
ternissure [ternisyr] *nf* : tarnish
terrain [terɛ̃] *nm* **1** : ground, soil **2** PARCELLE : plot (of land) **3** : land, terrain **4** : field <terrain de football : football field> <terrain de jeu : playground> <terrain de camping : campsite> <terrain d'aviation : airfield> **5** : field, sphere (of activity) <le terrain juridique : the field of law> **6** : area, ground, territory <perdre du terrain : to lose ground> <terrain d'entente : common ground> <être en terrain connu : to be on familiar territory>
terrasse [teras] *nf* : terrace
terrassement [terasmɑ̃] *nm* : excavation
terrasser [terase] *vt* **1** : to knock down, to floor **2** : to strike down <terrassé par une maladie : struck down by sickness>
terre [tɛr] *nf* **1** : ground <par terre : on the ground, on the floor> <sous terre : underground> **2** TERRAIN : land <basse terre : lowland> **3** : (dry) land <aller à terre : to go ashore> **4** : dirt, soil <chemin de terre : dirt road> **5** : earth, world <sur la terre : on earth, in the world> **6** : clay (for pottery), earthenware **7 terre à terre** : down-to-earth, matter-of-fact **8 terre cuite** : terra-cotta
Terre *nf* : Earth (planet)
terreau [tero] *nm, pl* **terreaux** : loam, compost
terre-plein [terplɛ̃] *nm, pl* **terre-pleins** : median strip
terrer [tere] *v* **se terrer** *vr* : to hide, to go underground
terrestre [terestr] *adj* **1** : earth, terrestrial **2** : earthly, worldly
terreur [terœr] *nf* : terror
terreux, -reuse [terø, -røz] *adj* **1** : muddy **2** BLAFARD : sallow, pallid **3** : earthy
terrible [teribl] *adj* **1** : terrible, dreadful **2** : intense, excessive **3** *fam* FORMIDABLE : terrific, great
terrien, -rienne [terjɛ̃, -rjen] *adj* **propriétaire terrien** : landowner
terrier [terje] *nm* **1** : hole, burrow **2** : terrier
terrifiant, -fiante [terifjɑ̃, -fjɑ̃t] *adj* : terrifying
terrifier [terifje] {96} *vt* ÉPOUVANTER : to terrify
territoire [teritwar] *nm* : territory
territorial, -riale [teritɔrjal] *adj, mpl* **-riaux** [-rjo] : territorial
terroir [terwar] *nm* **1** : region, locality **2** : country, rural region
terroriser [terɔrize] *vt* : to terrorize
terrorisme [terɔrism] *nm* : terrorism **— terroriste** [-rɔrist] *adj & nmf*
tertiaire [tɛrsjɛr] *adj* : tertiary

tertre [tɛrtr] *nm* MONTICULE : hillock, mound
tes → ton[1]
tesson [tesɔ̃] *nm* : piece, fragment, shard <tesson de bouteille : piece of broken glass>
test [tɛst] *nm* : test
testament [tɛstamɑ̃] *nm* **1** : will, last will and testament **2** : legacy **3 Testament** *m* : Testament <Ancien Testament : Old Testament> <Nouveau Testament : New Testament>
tester [tɛste] *vt* : to test — *vi* : to make a will
testicule [tɛstikyl] *nm* : testicle
tétanos [tetanos] *nms & pl* : tetanus, lockjaw
têtard [tɛtar] *nm* : tadpole
tête [tɛt] *nf* **1** : head <être tête nue : to be bareheaded> <la tête haute : with head held high> **2** : (head of) hair <se laver la tête : to wash one's hair> **3** : face <faire la tête : to make a face, to sulk> **4** : mind, head <passer par la tête : to cross one's mind> <garder sa tête : to keep one's head> **5** : neck, life <risquer sa tête : to risk one's neck> **6** : head, leader **7** : head (of cattle, etc.) **8** : top, lead, head <tête d'un arbre : treetop> <à la tête de la classe : at the head of the class> **9** : header (in soccer) **10 tenir tête à** : to stand up to **11 tête brulée** : hothead **12 tête de mort** : skull **13 tête de pont** : beachhead
tête-à-queue [tɛtakø] *nms & pl* : spin (of an automobile)
tête-à-tête [tɛtatɛt] *nms & pl* **1** : tête-à-tête **2 être en tête-à-tête** : to be alone together
tétée [tete] *nf* : nursing, feeding (at the breast)
téter [tete] {87} *vt* : to suck at (the breast) — *vi* : to suckle, to nurse
tétine [tetin] *nf* **1** : teat **2** : nipple (of a baby bottle) **3** : pacifier
téton [tetɔ̃] *nm fam* : breast
têtu, -tue [tety] *adj* : stubborn
texte [tɛkst] *nm* : text
textile [tɛkstil] *nm* : textile
textuel, -elle [tɛkstɥɛl] *adj* : literal, word for word
textuellement [tɛkstɥɛlmɑ̃] *adv* : literally, verbatim
texture [tɛkstyr] *nf* : texture
thaï [taj] *nm* : Thai (language)
thaïlandais, -daise [tajlɑ̃de, -dɛz] *adj* : Thai
Thaïlandais, -daise *n* : Thai
thé [te] *nm* : tea
théâtral, -trale [teatral] *adj, mpl* **-traux** [-tro] : theatrical
théâtre [teatr] *nm* **1** : theater (building, area) **2** : drama, theater **3 faire du théâtre** : to be an actor
thélère [tejɛr] *nf* : teapot
théisme [teism] *nm* : theism
thème [tɛm] *nm* : theme
théologie [teɔlɔʒi] *nf* : theology
théologique [teɔlɔʒik] *adj* : theological
théologien, -gienne [teɔlɔʒjɛ̃, -ʒjɛn] *n* : theologian
théorème [teɔrɛm] *nm* : theorem
théorie [teɔri] *nf* : theory
théorique [teɔrik] *adj* : theoretical — **théoriquement** [-rikmɑ̃] *adv*
théoriser [teɔrize] *vi* : to theorize
thérapeute [terapøt] *nmf* : therapist
thérapeutique[1] [terapøtik] *adj* : therapeutic
thérapeutique[2] *nf* : therapy, treatment
thérapie [terapi] *nf* : therapy
thermal, -male [tɛrmal] *adj, mpl* **thermaux** [tɛrmo] : thermal <station thermale : spa>
thermique [tɛrmik] *adj* : thermal <centrale thermique : thermal power station>
thermodynamique [tɛrmɔdinamik] *nf* : thermodynamics
thermomètre [tɛrmɔmɛtr] *nm* : thermometer
thermos [tɛrmos] *nmfs & pl* : thermos
thermostat [tɛrmɔsta] *nm* : thermostat
thésauriser [tezɔrize] *vt* : to hoard — *vi* : to hoard money
thèse [tɛz] *nf* : thesis
thiamine [tjamin] *nf* : thiamine
thon [tɔ̃] *nm* : tuna
thorax [tɔraks] *nm* : thorax
thym [tɛ̃] *nm* : thyme
thyroïde [tirɔid] *nf* : thyroid (gland)
tiare [tjar] *nf* : tiara
tibétain[1], **-taine** [tibetɛ̃, -ten] *adj* : Tibetan
tibétain[2] *nm* : Tibetan (language)
Tibétain, -taine *n* : Tibetan
tibia [tibja] *nm* **1** : tibia, shinbone **2** : shin
tic [tik] *nm* **1** : tic, twitch **2** : mannerism
ticket [tikɛ] *nm* BILLET : ticket
tic-tac [tiktak] *nms & pl* : tick, ticking
tiède [tjɛd] *adj* **1** : lukewarm, tepid **2** : warm, mild (of weather, etc.)
tièdement [tjɛdmɑ̃] *adv* : halfheartedly
tiédir [tjedir] *vi* : to warm up, to cool down
tien[1], **tienne** [tjɛ̃, tjɛn] *adj* : yours, of yours <une tienne amie : a friend of yours> <je suis tien : I'm yours>
tien[2], **tienne** *pron* **le tien, la tienne, les tiens, les tiennes** : yours <le tien est plus joli : yours is prettier>
tiendra [tjɛ̃dra], *etc.* → **tenir**
tienne [tjɛn], *etc.* → **tenir**
tient [tjɛ̃], *etc.* → **tenir**
tiers[1], **tierce** [tjɛr, tjɛrs] *adj* : third <tierce personne : third person>
tiers[2] *nm* **1** : third <un tiers du livre : a third of the book> **2** : third party
tiers-monde [tjɛrmɔ̃d] *nm, pl* **tiers-mondes** : Third World
tige [tiʒ] *nf* **1** : stem, stalk **2** : (metal) rod
tignasse [tiɲas] *nf* : mop, shock (of hair)
tigre [tigr] *nm* : tiger

tigré, -grée [tigre] *adj* : striped
tigresse [tigrɛs] *nf* : tigress
tilleul [tijœl] *nm* : linden (tree)
timbale [tɛ̃bal] *nf* **1** : kettledrum **2 timbales** *nfpl* : timpani
timbre [tɛ̃br] *nm* **1** : (postage) stamp **2** : official stamp, postmark **3** SONNETTE : bell **4** TON : timbre, tone
timbré, -brée [tɛ̃bre] *adj* **1** : rich, mellow (of the voice) **2** *fam* : crazy, nuts
timbre–poste [tɛ̃brɔpɔst] *nm, pl* **timbres–poste** : (postage) stamp
timbrer [tɛ̃bre] *vt* : to stamp, to postmark
timide [timid] *adj* : timid, shy — **timidement** [-midmɑ̃] *adv*
timidité [timidite] *nf* : timidity, shyness
timoré, -rée [timɔre] *adj* : timorous
tintamarre [tɛ̃tamar] *nm* : din, racket
tintement [tɛ̃tmɑ̃] *nm* : ringing, chiming, tinkling, clinking
tinter [tɛ̃te] *vt* : to ring, to toll — *vi* **1** : to ring, to chime **2** : to tinkle, to jingle, to clink **3** : to ring, to buzz (of ears)
tipi [tipi] *nm* : tepee
tique [tik] *nf* : tick (insect)
tiquer [tike] *vi* : to wince, to flinch
tir [tir] *nm* **1** : shooting, gunnery **2** : firing <déclencher le tir : to open fire> **3 tir à l'arc** : archery **4 tir antiaérien** : flak
tirade [tirad] *nf* : tirade
tirage [tiraʒ] *nm* **1** IMPRESSION : printing **2** : impression, run <second tirage : second printing> **3** : circulation (of a newspaper, etc.) **4** : (computer) printout **5** *or* **tirage au sort** : drawing (in a lottery) **6** : draft (of a chimney, etc.) **7** : pulling, hauling
tiraillement [tirajmɑ̃] *nm* **1** : tugging, pulling **2** : cramp, pang **3** : conflict <tiraillements internes : internal conflicts>
tirailler [tiraje] *vt* : to pull at, to tug at <être tiraillé entre le bien et le mal : to be torn between right and wrong>
tirant [tirɑ̃] *nm* **tirant d'eau** : draft (of a ship)
tire [tir] *nf Can* **1** : taffy **2** *or* **tire d'érable** : maple-sugar candy
tiré, -rée [tire] *adj* : drawn, haggard
tire–bouchon [tirbuʃɔ̃] *nm, pl* **tire–bouchons** : corkscrew
tire–d'aile [tirdɛl] **à ~** : in a flurry, hurriedly
tirelire [tirlir] *nf* : piggy bank
tirer [tire] *vt* **1** : to pull, to pull up, to pull back **2** : to draw (a curtain), to pull down (a blind, etc.) **3** : to fire, to shoot **4** : to take (in sports) <tirer un coup franc : to take a free kick> **5** : to draw (a card, a ticket, etc.) **6** : to withdraw **7** : to draw away, to pull out **8** : to derive (information) — *vi* **1** : to pull **2** : to fire, to shoot **3** : to take a shot (in sports) **4** *or* **tirer au sort** : to draw lots **5** : to draw (of a chimney) **6 ~ sur** : to draw from (an account, etc.) — **se tirer** *vr* **1 ~ de** : to get through, to extricate oneself from **2 se tirer une balle** : to shoot oneself **3 s'en tirer** *fam* : to cope, to pull through
tiret [tirɛ] *nm* **1** : dash **2** : hyphen
tireur, -reuse [tirœr, -røz] *n* **1** : gunman, marksman, markswoman *f* <tireur d'élite : sharpshooter> **2 tireur de cartes** : fortune-teller>
tiroir [tirwar] *nm* : drawer
tiroir–caisse [tirwarkɛs] *nm, pl* **tiroirs–caisses** : cash register, till
tisane [tizan] *nf* : herbal tea
tisonnier [tizɔnje] *nm* : poker
tissage [tisaʒ] *nm* **1** : weaving **2** : weave
tisser [tise] *vt* : to weave
tisserand, -rande [tisrɑ̃, -rɑ̃d] *n* : weaver
tissu [tisy] *nm* **1** : material, fabric **2** : tissue <tissu conjonctif : connective tissue> **3** : web, string (of lies, etc.) **4** : makeup, fabric <tissu social : social fabric>
titane [titan] *nm* : titanium
titanesque [titanɛsk] *adj* GIGANTESQUE : titanic, gigantic
titiller [titije] *vt* **1** : to titillate **2** : to tickle
titre [titr] *nm* **1** : title (of a book, song, etc.) **2** : title, rank, qualification <titre mondial : world title> **3** *or* **gros titre** : headline **4** : basis, respect, capacity <à titre d'exemple : as an example, for example> <à titre d'information : for your information> **5** : security (in the stock market) **6** : deed, title
titrer [titre] *vt* **1** : to run as a headline **2** : to subtitle (in movies) **3** : to titrate, to assay (in chemistry)
titubant, -bante [titybɑ̃, -bɑ̃t] *adj* : reeling, unsteady
tituber [titybe] *vi* : to reel, to stagger
titulaire[1] [tityler] *adj* : tenured, permanent
titulaire[2] *nmf* : officeholder, incumbent
titularisation [titylarizasjɔ̃] *nf* : tenure
toast [tost] *nm* **1** : toast <un toast aux nouveaux mariés : a toast to the newlyweds> **2** : (slice of) toast
toaster [tɔste] *vt Can* : to toast (bread)
toboggan [tɔbɔgɑ̃] *nm* : toboggan
toc[1] [tɔk] *adj fam* : trashy, tacky
toc[2] *nm* **en ~** : imitation, fake
tocsin [tɔksɛ̃] *nm* : alarm <sonner le tocsin : to sound the alarm>
toge [tɔʒ] *nf* **1** : gown, robe (of a judge, etc.) **2** : toga
togolais, -laise [tɔgɔlɛ, -lɛz] *adj* : Togolese
Togolais, -laise *n* : Togolese
tohu–bohu [tɔybɔy] *nms & pl* : noisy confusion, hubbub
toi [twa] *pron* **1** : you <je crois en toi : I believe in you> <occupe-toi! : keep

busy!> <toi, tu t'imagines des choses : you're imagining things> **2** TOI-MÊME : yourself <prends soin de toi : take care of yourself>

toile [twal] *nf* **1** : cloth, fabric <de la grosse toile : canvas> <toile à sac : burlap> <toile cirée : oilcloth> <toile goudronnée : tarpaulin> **2** TABLEAU : canvas, painting **3** WEB : Web **4 toile d'araignée** : spider's web **5 toile de fond** : backdrop

toilette [twalɛt] *nf* **1** : washing up, grooming <faire sa toilette : to get washed up> <produits de toilette : toiletries> **2** : grooming (of animals) **3** TENUE : clothing, outfit **4** *Can* : toilet, bathroom **5 toilettes** *nfpl* : toilet, bathroom <aller aux toilettes : to go to the bathroom>

toi–même [twamɛm] *pron* : yourself <tu l'as fait toi-même : you did it yourself>

toiser [twaze] *vt* : to look (a person) up and down

toison [twazɔ̃] *nf* **1** : fleece **2** : mane, mop (of hair)

toit [twa] *nm* : roof

toiture [twatyr] *nf* : roofing

tôle [tol] *nf* **1** : sheet metal **2 tôle ondulée** : corrugated iron

tolérable [tɔlerabl] *adj* : tolerable

tolérance [tɔlerɑ̃s] *nf* : tolerance — **tolérant, -rante** [tɔlerɑ̃, -rɑ̃t] *adj*

tolérer [tɔlere] {87} *vt* : to tolerate

tolet [tɔlɛ] *nm* : oarlock

tollé [tɔle] *nm* : outcry

tomate [tɔmat] *nf* : tomato

tombant, -bante [tɔ̃bɑ̃, -bɑ̃t] *adj* : sloping, drooping

tombe [tɔ̃b] *nf* **1** SÉPULTURE : grave, tomb **2** : gravestone, tombstone

tombeau [tɔ̃bo] *nm, pl* **tombeaux** : tomb, mausoleum

tombée [tɔ̃be] *nf* **à la tombée du jour** *or* **à la tombée de la nuit** : at nightfall, at the close of day

tomber [tɔ̃be] *vi* **1** : to fall (down), to fall off, to drop **2** : to come down, to fall <la pluie tombait : rain was falling> **3** : to go down (of prices, etc.), to die down, to subside **4** : to droop, to sag, to slope **5** : to hang, to fall (of hair, clothing, etc.) **6** : to come, to fall <tomber dans la désuétude : to fall into disuse> <tomber aux mains de : to fall into the hands of> **7** : to become <tomber amoureux : to fall in love> <elle est tombée malade : she fell ill> **8 ~ sur** : to run into, to come across **9 faire tomber** : to bring down, to break down **10 laisser tomber** : to give up, to drop (plans, etc.)

tombola [tɔ̃bɔla] *nf* : raffle

tome [tɔm] *nm* : volume (of a book)

ton[1] [tɔ̃ [tɔn] *before a vowel or mute h*)], **ta** [ta] *adj, pl* **tes** [te] : your

ton[2] *nm* **1** : tone, pitch **2** : hue, shade **3 de bon ton** : in good taste, appropriate

tonalité [tɔnalite] *nf* **1** : tone (of voice, etc.) **2** : tonality, key (in music) **3** : dial tone

tondeuse [tɔ̃døz] *nf* **1** *or* **tondeuse à gazon** : lawn mower **2** : clippers *pl*, shears *pl*

tondre [tɔ̃dr] {63} *vt* **1** : to mow **2** : to clip, to shear

tongane, -ganne [tɔ̃gan] *adj* : Tongan

Tongane, -ganne *n* : Tongan

tonifiant, -fiante [tɔnifjɑ̃, -fjɑ̃t] *adj* : invigorating, bracing

tonifier [tɔnifje] {96} *vt* **1** REVIGORER : to invigorate **2** RAFFERMIR : to tone <muscles bien tonifiés : well-toned muscles>

tonique[1] [tɔnik] *adj* : fortifying, stimulating

tonique[2] *nm* : tonic (in medicine)

tonique[3] *nf* : tonic (in music)

tonitruant, -truante [tɔnitryɑ̃, -tryɑ̃t] *adj* : thundering, booming

tonnage [tɔnaʒ] *nm* : tonnage

tonne [tɔn] *nf* : ton

tonneau [tɔno] *nm, pl* **tonneaux 1** BARRIQUE : barrel, cask **2** : rollover (of a motor vehicle)

tonnelet [tɔnlɛ] *nm* : keg

tonnelle [tɔnɛl] *nf* : arbor

tonner [tɔne] *vi* : to thunder

tonnerre [tɔner] *nm* **1** : thunder <coup de tonnerre : thunderbolt> **2** : tumult, thundering <un tonnerre d'applaudissements : thundering applause> **3 du tonnerre** *fam* : great, terrific

tonte [tɔ̃t] *nf* : shearing

tonton [tɔ̃tɔ̃] *nm fam* : uncle

tonus [tɔnys] *nms & pl* **1** : tone <tonus musculaire : muscular tone> **2** : energy, vigor

topaze [tɔpaz] *nf* : topaze

topo [tɔpo] *nm fam* : spiel, story <c'est toujours le même topo : it's always the same old story>

topographie [tɔpɔgrafi] *nf* : topography

topographique [tɔpɔgrafik] *adj* : topographical, topographic

toquade [tɔkad] *nf fam* **1** : craze, fad **2** : crush, infatuation

toque [tɔk] *nf* : brimless hat <toque de fourrure : fur hat> <toque de cuisinier : toque, chef's hat>

toqué, -quée [tɔke] *adj fam* : crazy, touched

toquer [tɔke] *vi fam* : to rap, to knock <toquer à la porte : to knock on the door>

torche [tɔrʃ] *nf* : torch

torcher [tɔrʃe] *vt fam* : to wipe

torchon [tɔrʃɔ̃] *nm* CHIFFON : piece of cloth, rag

tordant, -dante [tɔrdɑ̃, -dɑ̃t] *adj fam* MARRANT : very funny, hilarious

tordre [tɔrdr] {63} *vt* : to twist, to wring — **se tordre** *vr* **1** : to twist <se tordre la cheville : to twist one's ankle> **2** : to writhe, to double up (with pain, laughter, etc.)
tordu, -due [tɔrdy] *adj* : twisted, warped
torero [tɔrero] *nm* : bullfighter, matador
tornade [tɔrnad] *nf* : tornado
toron [tɔrɔ̃] *nm* : strand (of rope)
torpeur [tɔrpœr] *nf* : torpor
torpide [tɔrpid] *adj* : torpid
torpille [tɔrpij] *nf* : torpedo
torréfier [tɔrefje] {96} *vt* : to roast (coffee, etc.)
torrent [tɔrɑ̃] *nm* **1** : torrent <pleuvoir à torrents : to be pouring> **2 un torrent de** : a flood of
torrentiel, -tielle [tɔrɑ̃sjɛl] *adj* : torrential
torride [tɔrid] *adj* : torrid, scorching hot
tors, torse [tɔr, tɔrs] *adj* **1** : twisted **2** : crooked, bent
torsade [tɔrsad] *nf* : twist, coil
torsader [tɔrsade] *vt* : to twist
torse [tɔrs] *nm* : torso, chest
torsion [tɔrsjɔ̃] *nf* **1** : twisting **2** : torsion
tort [tɔr] *nm* **1** : fault <reconnaître ses torts : to admit one's faults> **2** DÉFAUT : error, mistake **3** DOMMAGE : wrong, harm <faire du tort à qqn : to do harm to s.o.> **4 avoir tort** : to be wrong **5 à ~** : wrongly, unjustly **6 à tort et à travers** : senselessly
torticolis [tɔrtikɔli] *nms & pl* : stiff neck, crick in the neck
tortillement [tɔrtijmɑ̃] *nm* : wiggling, twisting
tortiller [tɔrtije] *vt* : to twist — *vi* : to wriggle — **se tortiller** *vr* : to squirm
tortillon [tɔrtijɔ̃] *nm* : twist
tortionnaire [tɔrsjɔnɛr] *nmf* : torturer
tortue [tɔrty] *nf* : turtle, tortoise
tortueux, -euse [tɔrtyø, -øz] *adj* **1** : winding **2** : convoluted, tortuous
torture [tɔrtyr] *nf* : torture
torturer [tɔrtyre] *vt* : to torture
tôt [to] *adv* **1** : soon <le plus tôt possible : as soon as possible> **2** : early <se coucher tôt : to go to bed early> **3 tôt ou tard** : sooner or later
total[1], -tale [tɔtal] *adj, mpl* **totaux** [tɔto] : total — **totalement** [tɔtalmɑ̃] *adv*
total[2] *nm, mpl* **totaux** [tɔto] : total
totaliser [tɔtalize] *vt* : to total
totalitaire [tɔtaliter] *adj* : totalitarian
totalitarisme [tɔtalitarism] *nm* : totalitarianism
totalité [tɔtalite] *nf* **1** : total amount, totality **2 en ~** : completely, entirely
totem [tɔtem] *nm* : totem
touchant, -chante [tuʃɑ̃, -ʃɑ̃t] *adj* ÉMOUVANT : touching, moving
touche [tuʃ] *nf* **1** : key (on a keyboard), button **2** : stroke, touch (in art) **3** : trace, hint, touch **4** : touchline (in sports) **5** : bite (in fishing)
touché [tuʃe] *nm* : touchdown (in football)
toucher[1] [tuʃe] *vt* **1** : to touch, to handle **2** : to be in contact with, to hit **3** : to touch (in sports) **4** : to affect, to concern **5** ÉMOUVOIR : to move, to touch <toucher son coeur : to touch one's heart> **6** : to receive, to earn <toucher un bon salaire : to earn a good salary> **7** : to touch on, to be adjacent to — *vi* **1 ~ à** : to touch upon, to get into, to bring up **2 ~ à** : to relate to, to concern **3 ~ à** : to infringe on — **se toucher** *vr* : to touch, to be in contact
toucher[2] *nm* **1** : sense of touch **2** : feel
touffe [tuf] *nf* : tuft, clump
touffu, -fue [tufy] *adj* **1** : thick, dense, bushy <forêt touffue : dense forest> **2** : complex, dense (of style)
toujours [tuʒur] *adv* **1** : always, forever **2** ENCORE : still **3** : anyway, in any case
toundra [tundra] *nf* : tundra
toupet [tupɛ] *nm* **1** : forelock **2** *fam* : nerve, cheek
toupie [tupi] *nf* : top (toy)
tour[1] [tur] *nm* **1** : tour, circuit <faire le tour du monde : to go around the world> **2** : walk, ride <faire un tour : to go for a stroll> **3** : turn, revolution, rotation **4** : circumference, measurement (around) <tour de faille : girth (of a person)> **5** : turn, move <attendre son tour : to wait one's turn> **6** : trick <jouer un tour à qqn : to play a trick on s.o.> **7** : direction, aspect <prendre un mauvais tour : to take a bad turn, to go wrong> **8** : lathe **9 avoir le tour** *Can* : to be clever, to be skillful **10 tour de scrutin** : ballot, round of voting
tour[2] *nf* **1** : tower **2** : high-rise building **3** : castle (in chess)
tourbe [turb] *nf* : peat
tourbière [turbjɛr] *nf* : peat bog, peat marsh
tourbillon [turbijɔ̃] *nm* **1** : whirlwind, whirlpool **2** : whirl, bustle
tourbillonner [turbijɔne] *vi* : to whirl, to swirl (around)
tourelle [turɛl] *nf* : turret
tourisme [turism] *nm* : tourism
touriste [turist] *nmf* : tourist
touristique [turistik] *adj* : tourist <la saison touristique : the tourist season>
tourment [turmɑ̃] *nm* : torment
tourmente [turmɑ̃t] *nf* **1** : tempest, storm **2** : turmoil
tourmenter [turmɑ̃te] *vt* : to torment — **se tourmenter** *vr* S'INQUIÉTER : to worry
tournant[1], -nante [turnɑ̃, -nɑ̃t] *adj* : turning, revolving

tournant[2] *nm* **1** : bend (in a road, etc.) **2** : turning point
tourne–disque [turnədisk] *nm, pl* **tourne–disques** : record player
tournée [turne] *nf* **1** : tour **2** *fam* : round (of drinks)
tourner [turne] *vt* **1** : to turn, to rotate **2** : to stir, to toss **3** : to shoot (a film, scene, etc.) **4** : to get around, to circumvent **5** : to phrase, to present <une lettre bien tournée : a nicely phrased letter> **6 tourner en dérision** : to ridicule — *vi* **1** : to turn, to revolve, to spin <tourner autour de : to revolve around> <tourner en rond : to go around in circles> **2** : to turn, to change direction <tournez à droite : turn right> **3** : to run (of an engine, etc.) <tourner rond : to run smoothly> **4** : to turn out <bien tourner : to turn out well, to go well> **5** : to film, to make a film **6** : to go bad, to sour — **se tourner** *vr* : to turn around
tournesol [turnəsɔl] *nm* **1** : sunflower **2** : litmus <papier de tournesol : litmus paper>
tournevis [turnəvis] *nms & pl* : screwdriver
tourniquet [turnikɛ] *nm* **1** : turnstile **2** : tourniquet **3** : sprinkler
tournoi [turnwa] *nm* : tournament
tournoiement [turnwamɑ̃] *nm* : spinning, whirling
tournoyer [turnwaje] {58} *vi* **1** : to whirl, to spin, to gyrate **2** : to swirl around
tournure [turnyr] *nf* **1** : turn <tournure des événements : turn of events> **2** : turn of phrase, expression
tourte [turt] *nf France* : (meat or fish) pie
tourtereaux [turtəro] *nmpl* : lovebirds
tourterelle [turtərɛl] *nf* : turtledove
tourtière [turtjɛr] *nf* **1** *France* : pie pan **2** *Can* : meat pie
tousser [tuse] *vi* : to cough
tout[1] [tu] **(toute(s)** [tut] *before feminine adjectives beginning with a consonant or an aspirate h*) *adv* **1** COMPLÈTEMENT : completely <tout neuf : completely new> **2** : quite, very, all <tout dernièrement : very recently> <elle sont toutes seules : they are all alone> **3** : while <tout en travaillant : while working> **4** : already <tout prêt : ready-made> **5 tout à coup** : suddenly **6 tout à fait** : completely, entirely **7 tout de suite** : immediately, right away
tout[2], **toute** *adj, pl* **tous, toutes 1** : all <tout le monde : everyone, everybody> <tous les dix : all ten of them> <en toute franchise : in all honesty> **2** : each, every <toutes les fois : every time> <tous les jours : every day> <tous les trois ans : every three years> **3** : any <toute autre solution : any other solution> <à tout âge : at any age> **4** : utmost, full <à toute vitesse : at full speed>
tout[3] *nm* **1 le tout** : the main thing, the whole **2 du tout au tout** : completely, entirely **3 du tout** *or* **pas du tout** : not at all
tout[4] *pron, pl* **tous, toutes 1** : all, everything <tout change : everything changes> <nous sommes tous coupables : we are all guilty> **2** : anyone, everyone <oublié de tous : forgotten by everyone> **3 tout compte fait** : all in all
toutefois [tutfwa] *adv* : however
toute–puissance [tutpɥisɑ̃s] *nf, pl* **toutes–puissances** : omnipotence
tout–puissant, toute–puissante [tutpɥisɑ̃,-sɑ̃t] *adj, pl* **tout–puissants, toutes–puissantes** : all-powerful
toutou [tutu] *nm* **1** *fam* : doggie **2** *Can fam* : stuffed animal
toux [tu] *nfs & pl* : cough
toxicité [tɔksisite] *nf* : toxicity
toxicomane [tɔksikɔman] *nmf* : drug addict
toxicomanie [tɔksikɔmani] *nf* : drug addiction
toxine [tɔksin] *nf* : toxin
toxique [tɔksik] *adj* : toxic, poisonous
trac [trak] *nm* : stage fright, jitters *pl*
tracas [traka] *nms & pl* **1** : worry **2 tracas** *nmpl* ENNUIS : troubles, problems
tracasser [trakase] *vt* : to worry, to bother — **se tracasser** *vr*
trace [tras] *nf* **1** : track, trail <traces d'ours : bear tracks> <traces de pas : footprints> <suivre les traces de qqn : to follow in s.o.'s footsteps> **2** : mark <traces de doigts : finger marks> **3** : trace, vestige, sign <traces d'une ville disparue : traces of a lost city>
tracé [trase] *nm* **1** PLAN : plan, layout **2** : course (of a river, road, etc.) **3** : line, contour
tracer [trase] {6} *vt* **1** : to trace, to lay out **2** DESSINER : to draw <tracer une ligne : to draw a line> **3** : to map out, to plot <tracer le chemin : to pave the way>
trachée [traʃe] *nf* : trachea, windpipe
tract [trakt] *nm* : leaflet
tractations [traktasjɔ̃] *nfpl* : negotiations
tracter [trakte] *vt* : to tow
tracteur [traktœr] *nm* : tractor
traction [traksjɔ̃] *nf* **1** : traction **2** : pulling, haulage **3** : push-up, chin-up **4 traction avant** : front-wheel drive
tradition [tradisjɔ̃] *nf* : tradition
traditionnel, -nelle [tradisjɔnɛl] *adj* : traditional — **traditionnellement** [-nɛlmɑ̃] *adv*
traducteur, -trice [tradyktœr, -tris] *n* : translator
traduction [tradyksjɔ̃] *nf* : translation

traduire [tradɥir] {49} *vt* **1** : to translate **2 traduire en justice** : to arraign — **se traduire** *vr* **1** : to be translated **2** ~ **par** : to result in
traduisait [tradɥizɛ], **traduisions** [tradɥizjɔ̃], *etc.* → **traduire**
traduise [tradɥiz], *etc.* → **traduire**
trafic [trafik] *nm* **1** : traffic **2** : trafficking <trafic de drogue : drug trafficking>
trafiquant, -quante [trafikɑ̃, -kɑ̃t] *n* : dealer, trafficker <trafiquant de drogue : drug dealer>
trafiquer [trafike] *vt* : to doctor, to tamper with — *vi* : to traffic, to trade (in the black market)
tragédie [traʒedi] *nf* : tragedy
tragique [traʒik] *adj* : tragic — **tragiquement** [-ʒikmɑ̃] *adv*
trahir [trair] *vt* **1** : to betray **2** RÉVÉLER : to reveal, to divulge **3** : to go against, to break <trahir sa promesse : to break one's word>
trahison [traizɔ̃] *nf* : betrayal
train [trɛ̃] *nm* **1** : train <train de voyageurs : passenger train> **2** : pace, rate <au train où vont les choses : at the rate things are going> **3** : series, set <train de réformes : series of reforms> **4 en train de** : in the process of **5 train de vie** : lifestyle
traînant, -nante [trɛnɑ̃, -nɑ̃t] *adj* : drawling <parler d'une voix traînante : to drawl>
traînard, -narde [trɛnar, -nard] *n* : slowpoke, laggard, straggler
traîne [trɛn] *nf* **1** : train (of a dress) **2** : dragnet, seine **3** *Can* : toboggan, sled **4 rester à la traîne** : to lag behind
traîneau [trɛno] *nm, pl* **traîneaux 1** : sled, sleigh **2** : dragnet
traînée [trɛne] *nf* **1** : streak (of blood, paint, etc.) **2** : trail (of light, of a comet, etc.) **3** : drag (of an airplane, etc.)
traîner [trɛne] *vt* **1** : to pull, to drag **2 traîner les pieds** : to drag one's feet — *vi* **1** : to drag along, to trail (on the ground) **2** : to dawdle, to lag behind **3** : to linger, to drag on **4** : to be lying around <elle laisse traîner son linge : she doesn't pick up after herself> **5** : to speak slowly, to drawl **6** : to wander about <traîner dans les rues : to roam the streets> — **se traîner** *vr* **1** : to drag oneself, to crawl (along) **2** : to drag on
train-train [trɛ̃trɛ̃] *nms & pl* ROUTINE : routine
traire [trɛr] {40} *vt* : to milk (an animal)
trait [trɛ] *nm* **1** : trait <trait de caractère : character trait> **2** : stroke <d'un trait de plume : with a stroke of the pen> **3 avoir trait à** : to relate to, to concern **4 tout d'un trait** : in one breath, in one gulp **5 trait d'esprit** : witticism, quip **6 trait d'union** : hyphen **7 traits** *nmpl* : features <traits fins : delicate features>
traitant, -tante [trɛtɑ̃, -tɑ̃t] *adj* **médecin traitant** : family doctor
traite [trɛt] *nf* **1** : trade (in human beings) <la traite des Noirs : the slave trade> **2** : milking **3 d'une traite** : in one go, without stopping **4 traite bancaire** : bank draft
traité [trete] *nm* **1** : treaty **2** : treatise
traitement [trɛtmɑ̃] *nm* **1** : treatment **2** : stipend, salary **3 traitement des données** *or* **traitement de l'information** : data processing **4 traitement de texte** : word processing
traiter [trete] *vt* **1** : to treat **2** : to process (data) **3** : to characterize as, to call <je l'ai traité d'imbécile : I called him a fool> **4** : to deal with, to handle — *vi* ~ **de** : to deal with, to be concerned with
traiteur [trɛtœr] *nm* : caterer
traître[1], **-tresse** [trɛtr, -trɛs] *adj* **1** : treacherous, betraying **2 pas un traître mot** : not a single word
traître[2], **-tresse** *n* **1** : traitor **2 en** ~ : in an underhanded way, treacherously
traîtreusement [trɛtrøzmɑ̃] *adv* : treacherously
traîtrise [trɛtriz] *nf* : treachery, betrayal
trajectoire [traʒɛktwar] *nf* : path, trajectory
trajet [traʒɛ] *nm* **1** CHEMIN : path, way, route <le trajet le plus direct : the quickest route> **2** : journey, trip
tralala [tralala] *nm fam* : fuss
trame [tram] *nf* **1** : weft (of fabric) **2** : framework
tramer [trame] *vt* **1** : to plot **2** : to weave
trampoline [trampolin] *nm* : trampoline
tramway [tramwɛ] *nm* : streetcar, trolley
tranchant[1], **-chante** [trɑ̃ʃɑ̃, -ʃɑ̃t] *adj* **1** : sharp, keen-edged **2** COUPANT : curt, sharp <une remarque tranchante : a cutting remark>
tranchant[2] *nm* **1** : cutting edge, sharpness **2 à double tranchant** : double-edged
tranche [trɑ̃ʃ] *nf* **1** : slice **2** : period, phase, stage <tranche horaire : time slot> <tranche d'âge : age bracket> **3** : edge (of a book, coin, etc.)
tranché, -chée [trɑ̃ʃe] *adj* **1** : sliced **2** : distinct, contrasting **3** : clear-cut, marked
tranchée *nf* : trench
trancher [trɑ̃ʃe] *vt* **1** COUPER : to cut (through), to slice, to sever **2** : to settle, to resolve **3** : to cut short — *vi* **1** : to contrast, to stand out **2** : to come to a decision
tranquille [trɑ̃kil] *adj* **1** : calm, quiet <tiens-toi tranquille! : sit still!> **2** : untroubled, assured <avoir la con-

science tranquille : to have a clear conscience> <soyez tranquille! : don't worry!>

tranquillement [trɑ̃kilmɑ̃] *adv* **1** CALMEMENT : quietly, calmly **2** LENTEMENT : unhurriedly, at a leisurely pace

tranquillisant[1], -sante [trɑ̃kilizɑ̃, -zɑ̃t] *adj* RASSURANT : reassuring

tranquillisant[2] *nm* : tranquilizer

tranquilliser [trɑ̃kilize] *vt* RASSURER : to reassure

tranquillité [trɑ̃kilite] *nf* **1** CALME : peacefulness, tranquillity **2 tranquillité d'esprit** : peace of mind

transaction [trɑ̃zaksjɔ̃] *nf* : transaction <transactions financières : financial transactions>

transatlantique [trɑ̃zatlɑ̃tik] *adj* : transatlantic

transcendant, -dante [trɑ̃sɑ̃dɑ̃, -dɑ̃t] *adj* **1** SUBLIME : sublime, transcendent **2** : transcendental

transcender [trɑ̃sɑ̃de] *vt* : to transcend **— se transcender** *vr* : to surpass oneself

transcontinental, -tale [trɑ̃skɔ̃tinɑ̃tal] *adj, mpl* **-taux** [-to] : transcontinental

transcription [trɑ̃skripsjɔ̃] *nf* : transcription, transcript

transcrire [trɑ̃skrir] {33} *vt* : to transcribe

transe [trɑ̃s] *nf* **1** : trance <entrer en transe : to go into a trance> **2 transes** *nfpl* : anxiety, upset <être dans les transes : to get all worked up>

transférer [trɑ̃sfere] *vt* : to transfer **— transférable** [trɑ̃sferabl] *adj*

transfert [trɑ̃sfɛr] *nm* : transfer <transfert de fonds : transfer of funds>

transfigurer [trɑ̃sfigyre] *vt* : to transfigure **— transfiguration** [-gyrasjɔ̃] *nf*

transformateur [trɑ̃sfɔrmatœr] *nm* : transformer

transformation [trɑ̃sfɔrmasjɔ̃] *nf* **1** : transformation **2** : conversion (in sports)

transformer [trɑ̃sfɔrme] *vt* **1** : to transform, to change, to alter **2** : to convert (in sports) **3 ~ en** : to convert (a building, etc.) into **— se transformer** *vr* **1** : to change, to be transformed **2 ~ en** : to turn into

transfuge [trɑ̃sfyʒ] *nmf* **1** : renegade, defector **2** : deserter (in the military)

transfuser [trɑ̃sfyze] *vt* : to transfuse

transfusion [trɑ̃sfyzjɔ̃] *nf* : transfusion

transgresser [trɑ̃sgrese] *vt* ENFREINDRE : to infringe, to violate, to disobey

transgression [trɑ̃sgresjɔ̃] *nf* : infringement, transgression

transi, -sie [trɑ̃zi] *adj* **1** : numb (with cold) **2** : paralyzed (with fear)

transiger [trɑ̃ziʒe] {17} *vi* : to compromise

transir [trɑ̃zir] *vt* : to numb (with cold)

transistor [trɑ̃zistɔr] *nm* : transistor

transit [trɑ̃zit] *nm* : transit <en transit : in transit>

transitif, -tive [trɑ̃zitif, -tiv] *adj* : transitive

transition [trɑ̃zisjɔ̃] *nf* : transition

transitoire [trɑ̃zitwar] *adj* **1** : transitory, transient **2** : transitional

translucide [trɑ̃slysid] *adj* : translucent

transmetteur [trɑ̃smetœr] *nm* : transmitter

transmettre [trɑ̃smetr] {53} *vt* **1** : to transmit (signals, data, etc.) **2** : to pass on, to convey **3** : to broadcast **4** : to transfer (power, etc.) **5** : to transmit (a disease)

transmissible [trɑ̃smisibl] *adj* : transmittable, communicable

transmission [trɑ̃smisjɔ̃] *nf* : transmission

transparaître [trɑ̃sparetr] {7} *vi* **1** : to show through **2 laisser transparaître** : to manifest, to let show (of emotions, etc.)

transparence [trɑ̃sparɑ̃s] *nf* : transparency

transparent, -rente [trɑ̃sparɑ̃, -rɑ̃t] *adj* : transparent

transpercer [trɑ̃sperse] {6} *vt* : to go through, to pierce <la douleur me transperçait le dos : pain was shooting through my back>

transpiration [trɑ̃spirasjɔ̃] *nf* **1** SUEUR : perspiration, sweat **2** : transpiration (in botany)

transpirer [trɑ̃spire] *vt* **1** SUER : to perspire, to sweat **2** : to transpire (in botany) **3** : to come to light

transplantation [trɑ̃splɑ̃tasjɔ̃] *nm* : transplant

transplanter [trɑ̃splɑ̃te] *vt* : to transplant

transport [trɑ̃spɔr] *nm* **1** : transport (of goods, etc.) <transport aérien : air transport> **2 transports** *nmpl* : (system of) transportation <transports en commun : public transportation> **3 transports** *nmpl* : transports, strong emotions

transporter [trɑ̃spɔrte] *vt* **1** : to carry, to bear **2** : to transport, to convey (goods, etc.) **3** : to transport, to carry away <être transporté de joie : to be overjoyed>

transporteur [trɑ̃spɔrtœr] *nm* **1** : carrier, transporter (company) **2** : conveyor (machine)

transposer [trɑ̃spoze] *vt* : to transpose **— transposition** [-pozisjɔ̃] *nf*

transvaser [trɑ̃svaze] *vt* : to decant (a liquid)

transversal, -sale [trɑ̃sversal] *adj, mpl* **-saux** [-so] : transverse, cross(ing) <coupe transversale : cross section> <rues transversales : cross streets>

transversalement [trɑ̃sversalmɑ̃] *adv* : crosswise

trapèze [trapɛz] *nm* **1** : trapezoid **2** : trapeze
trappe [trap] *nf* **1** PIÈGE : trap, snare **2** : trapdoor
trappeur [trapœr] *nm* : trapper
trapu, -pue [trapy] *adj* : stocky, squat
traquenard [traknar] *nm* : trap
traquer [trake] *vt* POURSUIVRE : to pursue, to chase, to track down
traumatisant, -sante [tromatizɑ̃, -zɑ̃t] *adj* : traumatic
traumatiser [tromatize] *vt* : to traumatize
traumatisme [tromatism] *nm* : trauma
travail [travaj] *nm, pl* **travaux** [travo] **1** : work <travail scolaire : schoolwork> <se mettre au travail : to get down to work> **2** TÂCHE : task, job, work <avoir du travail : to have work to do> **3** EMPLOI : work, employment <travail à plein temps : full-time work> <sans travail : unemployed> <vivre de son travail : to work for one's living> **4** : labor <division de travail : division of labor> **5** : working, fashioning <travail du bois : woodworking> **6** : work (of art, literature, etc.) **7** : labor (in giving birth) **8 travaux** *nmpl* : works <travaux publics : public works> **9 travaux** *nmpl* : work, operations <travaux d'aiguille : needlework> <travaux de la ferme : farmwork>
travaillant, -lante [travajɑ̃, -jɑt] *adj Can* : hardworking, industrious
travaillé, -lée [travaje] *adj* : elaborate, finely made
travailler [travaje] *vt* **1** : to work, to treat <travailler la terre : to work the land> **2** : to mix together (in cooking) **3** : to work on, to practice, to polish up **4** : to bother, to worry <ça me travaille : it's preying on my mind> — *vi* **1** : to work <travailler beaucoup trop : to work too hard> **2** : to work (at a job) <travailler en indépendent : to be self-employed> <travailler au noir : to moonlight> **3** : to train, to work out **4 ~ à** : to work toward, to endeavor to
travailleur[1], **-leuse** [travajœr, -jøz] *adj* : hardworking, industrious
travailleur[2], **-leuse** *n* : worker
travée [trave] *nf* **1** : row (of seats) **2** : span (of a bridge)
travers [traver] *nms & pl* **1** : fault, failing **2 à ~** : across, through <à travers la chambre : across the room> <à travers les siècles : down through the centuries> **3 au travers** : through <passer au travers : to escape> **4 au travers de** : by means of **5 de ~** : askew, crooked, wrongly <comprendre de travers : to misunderstand> **6 en ~** : crosswise, sideways
traverse [travers] *nf* **1** : railroad tie **2** : transom
traversée [traverse] *nf* : crossing
traverser [traverse] *vt* **1** : to cross <traverser la rue : to cross the road> **2** : to run through, to pass through, to flow through **3** : to penetrate, to soak through **4** : to go through, to experience (a crisis, etc.) **5 traverser l'esprit de qqn** : to cross s.o.'s mind
traversier [traversje] *nm Can* : ferryboat
traversin [traversɛ̃] *nm* : bolster
trayait [trɛje], **trayions** [trɛjɔ̃], *etc.* → **traire**
trébuchement [trebyʃmɑ̃] *nm* : stumble, stumbling
trébucher [trebyʃe] *vi* : to stumble
trèfle [trɛfl] *nm* **1** : clover, shamrock **2** : clubs *pl* (in playing cards)
treillage [trejaʒ] *nm* : trellis, lattice
treille [trɛj] *nf* : climbing vine
treillis [trɛji] *nms & pl* : trellis, lattice
treize[1] [trɛz] *adj* **1** : thirteen **2** : thirteenth <le treize janvier : January thirteenth>
treize[2] *nms & pl* : thirteen
treizième [trɛzjɛm] *adj & nmf & nm* : thirteenth
tremblant, -blante [trɑ̃blɑ̃, -blɑ̃t] *adj* : shaking, trembling
tremble [trɑ̃bl] *nm* : aspen
tremblement [trɑ̃bləmɑ̃] *nm* **1** : shaking, trembling **2** : quavering, shakiness (of the voice, etc.) **3** : fluttering, flickering **4 tremblement de terre** : earthquake
trembler [trɑ̃ble] *vi* **1** : to shake, to tremble **2** : to quiver, to quaver **3** : to flutter, to flicker
trembloter [trɑ̃blɔte] *vi* : to tremble, to quiver, to shiver
trémie [tremi] *nf* : hopper
trémousser [tremuse] *v* **se trémousser** *vr* : to wriggle around
trempage [trɑ̃paʒ] *nm* : soak, soaking
trempe [trɑ̃p] *nf* **1** : temper (of metals) **2** : caliber, quality <un homme de sa trempe : a man of his caliber>
trempé, -pée [trɑ̃pe] *adj* **1** : soaked, drenched **2 acier trempé** : tempered steel
tremper [trɑ̃pe] *vt* **1** : to soak **2** : to dip, to dunk **3** : to temper (steel, etc.)
trempette [trɑ̃pet] *nf* **1** : dip (in swimming) <faire trempette : to take a quick dip> **2** *Can* : dip <trempette aux légumes : vegetable dip>
tremplin [trɑ̃plɛ̃] *nm* **1** : springboard **2** : stepping stone (in a career, etc.) **3** *or* **tremplin à ski** : ski jump
trémulation [tremylasjɔ̃] *nf* : tremor
trente[1] [trɑ̃t] *adj* **1** : thirty **2** : thirtieth <le trente septembre : September thirtieth>
trente[2] *nms & pl* : thirty
trente–sous [trɑ̃tsu] *nms & pl Can fam* : quarter (unit of currency)
trentième [trɑ̃tjɛm] *adj & nmf & nm* : thirtieth

trépasser [trepase] *vi* DÉCÉDER : to pass away
trépidant, -dante [trepidɑ̃, -dɑ̃t] *adj* **1** : vibrating **2** : hectic, frantic
trépidation [trepidasjɔ̃] *nf* **1** : vibration **2** : flurry, bustle
trépider [trepide] *vi* : to vibrate
trépied [trepje] *nm* : tripod
trépigner [trepiɲe] *vi* : to stamp one's feet
très [trɛ] *adv* : very <très heureux : very happy> <très bien : very well> <très à la mode : very fashionable> <elle a très soif : she's very thirsty>
trésor [trezɔr] *nm* **1** : treasure **2 le Trésor (public)** : public revenue **3 mon trésor** : my darling
trésorerie [trezɔrri] *nf* **1** : funds *pl*, accounts *pl* **2** : public revenue office
trésorier, -rière [trezɔrje, -rjɛr] *n* : treasurer
tressaillement [tresajmɑ̃] *nm* : wincing, flinching
tressaillir [tresajir] {93}*vi* **1** : to start, to flinch, to wince **2** : to quiver, to vibrate
tressauter [tresote] *vi* SURSAUTER : to start, to jump
tresse [tres] *nf* : braid, plait
tresser [trese] *vt* **1** : to braid, to plait **2** : to weave (a basket, etc.)
tréteau [treto] *nm, pl* **tréteaux** : trestle
treuil [trœj] *nm* : winch, windlass
trêve [trɛv] *nf* **1** : truce **2** : respite
tri [tri] *nm* : sorting (out)
triade [triad] *nf* : triad
triangle [trijɑ̃gl] *nm* : triangle
triangulaire [trijɑ̃gylɛr] *adj* : triangular
tribal, -bale [tribal] *adj, mpl* **tribaux** [tribo] : tribal
tribord [tribɔr] *nm* : starboard
tribu [triby] *nf* : tribe
tribulations [tribylasjɔ̃] *nfpl* : tribulations
tribunal [tribynal] *nm, pl* **-naux** [-no] **1** : courthouse, court <porter une affaire devant le tribunal : to take a matter to court> **2** : judgment, justice <le tribunal de l'histoire : the judgment of history>
tribune [tribyn] *nf* **1** : gallery, grandstand **2** : rostrum, platform **3** DÉBAT : forum
tribut [triby] *nm* : tribute
tributaire [tribytɛr] *adj* **être tributaire de** : to be dependent on
tricher [triʃe] *vi* **1** : to cheat **2** ~ **sur** : to lie about
tricherie [triʃri] *nf* : cheating
tricheur, -cheuse [triʃœr, -ʃøz] *n* : cheat
tricolore [trikɔlɔr] *adj* : tricolor
tricot [triko] *nm* **1** : knitting **2** : knitted fabric **3** CHANDAIL : sweater, jersey
tricoter [trikɔte] *v* : to knit
tricoteur, -teuse [trikɔtœr, -tøz] *n* : knitter
trictrac [triktrak] *nm France* : backgammon
tricycle [trisikl] *nm* : tricycle
trident [tridɑ̃] *nm* : trident
tridimensionnel, -nelle [tridimɑ̃sjɔnɛl] *adj* : three-dimensional
triennal, -nale [trijenal] *adj, mpl* **-naux** [-no] : triennial
trier [trije] {96} *vt* **1** CLASSER : to sort (out) **2** : to pick out, to select
trigonométrie [trigɔnɔmetri] *nf* : trigonometry
trille [trij] *nf* : trill
triller [trije] *v* : to trill
trilogie [trilɔʒi] *nf* : trilogy
trimbaler *or* **trimballer** [trɛ̃bale] *vt fam* : to cart around, to drag along
trimer [trime] *vi fam* : to slave away
trimestre [trimɛstr] *nm* **1** : quarter (in economics, etc.) **2** : term (in school)
trimestriel, -trielle [trimɛstrijɛl] *adj* : quarterly
trimestriellement [trimɛstrijɛlmɑ̃] *adv* : quarterly
tringle [trɛ̃gl] *nf* : rod
trinidadien, -dienne [trinidadjɛ̃, -djɛn] *adj* : Trinidadian
Trinidadien, -dienne *n* : Trinidadian
trinité [trinite] *nf* **1** : trinity **2 la Trinité** : the (Holy) Trinity
trinquer [trɛ̃ke] *vi* **1** : to clink glasses, to toast **2** *fam* : to pay the price, to take the rap
trio [trijo] *nm* : trio
triomphal, -phale [trijɔ̃fal] *adj, mpl* **triomphaux** [-fo] : triumphal, triumphant
triomphalement [trijɔ̃falmɑ̃] *adv* : triumphantly
triomphant, -phante [trijɔ̃fɑ̃, -fɑ̃t] *adj* : triumphant
triomphateur, -trice [trijɔ̃fatœr, -tris] *n* : victor
triomphe [trijɔ̃f] *nm* : triumph, success
triompher [trijɔ̃fe] *vi* : to triumph, to prevail
tripartite [tripartit] *adj* : tripartite
tripe [trip] *nf* **1 tripes** *nfpl* : tripe **2 tripes** *nfpl fam* : guts <rendre tripes et boyaux : to vomit, to be sick as a dog>
triple [tripl] *adj & nm* : triple, treble
triplement [triplɔmɑ̃] *adv* : triply, three times over
tripler [triple] *v* : to triple
triplés, -plées [triple] *npl* : triplets
tripoter [tripɔte] *vt* **1** : to fiddle with, to play around with **2** : to handle, to paw — *vi* **1** : to rummage about **2** : to dabble (in shady activities)
trique [trik] *nf* : cudgel
trisannuel, -nuelle [trizanɥɛl] *adj* : triennial
triste [trist] *adj* **1** : sad, sorrowful **2** : dismal, dreary <un paysage triste : a bleak landscape> **3** LAMENTABLE : deplorable, sorry <en un triste état : in a sorry state>

tristement [tristəmɑ̃] *adv* **1** : sadly, sorrowfully **2** : regrettably <c'est tristement vrai : it's all too true>
tristesse [tristɛs] *nf* : sadness, sorrow
triton [tritɔ̃] *nm* : newt
triturer [trityre] *vt* **1** BROYER : to grind **2** PÉTRIR : to knead **3** MANIPULER : to manipulate
trivial, -viale [trivjal] *adj, mpl* **triviaux** [-vjo] **1** GROSSIER : coarse, crude **2** BANAL : mundane, trivial
trivialité [trivjalite] *nf* **1** : coarseness, crudeness **2** : banality, triteness
troc [trɔk] *nm* **1** ÉCHANGE : exchange, swap **2** : barter
troène [trɔɛn] *nm* : privet (hedge)
trognon [trɔɲɔ̃] *nm* : core (of an apple, etc.), stalk (of cabbage, etc.)
trois[1] [trwa] *adj* **1** : three **2** : third <le trois juin : June third>
trois[2] *nms & pl* : three
troisième[1] [trwazjɛm] *adj & nmf* : third
troisième[2] *nm* : third floor
troisièmement [trwazjɛmmɑ̃] *adv* : thirdly
trolley [trɔlɛ] *nm* : trolley
trombe [trɔ̃b] *nf* **1** : waterspout **2** : whirlwind <en trombe : in a flurry> **3 trombes d'eau** : downpour, cloudburst
tromblon [trɔ̃blɔ̃] *nm* : blunderbuss
trombone [trɔ̃bɔn] *nm* **1** : trombone **2** : paper clip
tromboniste [trɔ̃bɔnist] *nmf* : trombonist
trompe [trɔ̃p] *nf* **1** : horn **2** : trunk, proboscis
trompe-l'oeil [trɔ̃plœj] *nms & pl* : trompe l'oeil
tromper [trɔ̃pe] *vt* **1** DUPER : to deceive, to mislead **2** : to be unfaithful to **3** : to elude, to outwit **4** : to fool, to trick <c'est ce qui m'a trompé : that's what fooled me> **5** : to stave off — **se tromper** *vr* : to make a mistake <se tromper de route : to take the wrong road>
tromperie [trɔ̃pri] *nf* : deception, deceit
trompette [trɔ̃pet] *nf* : trumpet
trompettiste [trɔ̃petist] *nmf* : trumpet player
trompeur[1], **-peuse** [trɔ̃pœr, -pøz] *adj* **1** : deceitful **2** : deceptive, misleading
trompeur[2], **-peuse** *n* : deceiver
trompeusement [trɔ̃pøzmɑ̃] *adv* : deceitfully, deceptively
tronc [trɔ̃] *nm* **1** : trunk (of a tree) **2** : collection box (in a church) **3** TORSE : torso **4 tronc commun** : common origin
tronçon [trɔ̃sɔ̃] *nm* : section
tronçonner [trɔ̃sɔne] *vt* : to cut into sections, to saw up
tronçonneuse [trɔ̃sɔnøz] *nf* : chain saw
trône [tron] *nm* : throne
trôner [trone] *vi* : to have the place of honor
tronquer [trɔ̃ke] *vt* **1** : to truncate **2** : to curtail, to shorten
trop [tro] *adv* **1** : too <trop difficile : too hard> <j'ai beaucoup trop dit : I've said far too much> **2 ~ de** : too many, too much <trop de livres : too many books> <il a bu trop de café : he's had too much coffee> **3 de ~** *or* **en ~** : too many, extra <une personne de trop : one person too many>
trophée [trɔfe] *nm* : trophy
tropical, -cale [trɔpikal] *adj, mpl* **-caux** [-ko] : tropical
tropique [trɔpik] *nm* **1** : tropic <tropique du Cancer : tropic of Cancer> **2 tropiques** *nmpl* : tropics
trop-plein [trɔplɛ̃] *nm, pl* **trop-pleins** **1** : overflow **2** SURPLUS : excess, surplus
troquer [trɔke] *vt* : to swap, to trade
trot [tro] *nm* : trot
trotte [trɔt] *nf fam* : good distance <ça fait une trotte : it's a good walk>
trotter [trɔte] *vi* **1** : to trot **2** : to scamper, to run along **3 trotter dans la tête** : to keep running through one's mind
trotteuse [trɔtøz] *nf* : second hand (of a watch)
trottiner [trɔtine] *vi* : to scurry along
trottinette [trɔtinet] *nf* PATINETTE : scooter
trottoir [trɔtwar] *nm* **1** : sidewalk **2 trottoir roulant** : moving walkway
trou [tru] *nm* **1** : hole **2** TERRIER : burrow **3** : eye (of a needle) **4** DÉCHIRURE : tear, rip, hole **5** : gap (of time) <avoir une heure de trou : to have an hour's free time> <trou de mémoire : blank, memory lapse> **6** *fam* : little place, hole-in-the-wall **7 trou d'homme** : manhole **8 trou noir** : black hole **9 trou de serrure** : keyhole
troubadour [trubadur] *nm* : troubadour
troublant, -blante [trublɑ̃, -blɑ̃t] *adj* : disturbing, unsettling
trouble[1] [trubl] *adj* **1** : cloudy, dim **2** FLOU : blurred **3** : confused, unclear
trouble[2] *nm* **1** : distress, confusion, embarrassment **2** : trouble, discord <semer le trouble : to sow discord> **3** : disorder (in medicine) <trouble respiratoire : respiratory disorder> **4 troubles** *nmpl* : unrest <troubles politiques : political unrest>
troubler [truble] *vt* **1** : to disturb, to trouble **2** : to disrupt **3** BROUILLER : to blur, to cloud **4** : to confuse, to disconcert — **se troubler** *vr* **1** : to become cloudy **2** : to get confused
trouée [true] *nf* : gap, breach
trouer [true] *vt* : to make a hole in, to pierce
trouillard, -larde [trujar, -jard] *n fam* : chicken, coward

trouille [truj] *nf fam* : fear, fright <avoir la trouille : to be scared stiff>
troupe [trup] *nf* **1** : troop **2** : troupe **3** : herd (of horses, elephants, etc.) **4 la troupe** : the army
troupeau [trupo] *nm, pl* **troupeaux** : herd, flock
trousse [trus] *nf* **1** : kit, case <trousse de secours : first-aid kit> **2 aux trousses de** : on the heels of <la police est à mes trousses : the police are after me>
trousseau [truso] *nm, pl* **trousseaux 1** : trousseau **2 trousseau de clefs** : bunch of keys
trousser [truse] *vt* : to truss (a fowl)
trouvaille [truvaj] *nf* **1** DÉCOUVERTE : find **2** : inspiration, brainstorm
trouver [truve] *vt* **1** DÉCOUVRIR : to find, to discover **2** SE PROCURER : to find, to obtain, to get **3** IMAGINER : to find, to think up **4** ESTIMER : to think, to consider <je trouve que c'est incroyable : I think it's incredible> — **se trouver** *vr* **1** : to be (found) <ça se trouve un peu partout : it's found almost anywhere> **2** : to find oneself <je me suis trouvé incapable de répondre : I found myself unable to answer> **3** : to feel <il se trouve mieux : he feels better> — *v impers* **il se trouve que** : it turns out that
truand [tryã] *nm* : gangster, crook
truc [tryk] *nm* **1** ASTUCE : trick <trucs du métier : tricks of the trade> **2** *fam* MACHIN : thingamajig, contraption, thing
trucage [trykaʒ] *nm* : special effect (in movies)
truchement [tryʃmã] *nm* **par le truchement de** : through, with the help of, by means of
truculent, -lente [trykylã, -lãt] *adj* : earthy, racy, colorful
truelle [tryɛl] *nf* : trowel
truffe [tryf] *nf* **1** : truffle **2** : nose (of a dog)
truffer [tryfe] *vt* : to fill with, to pepper with, to riddle with
truie [trɥi] *nf* : sow (pig)
truisme [tryism] *nm* : truism
truite [trɥit] *nf* : trout
truquage [trykaʒ] *nm* → **trucage**
truquer [tryke] *vt* **1** : to fix, to rig (an election, etc.) **2** : to use special effects in
trust [trœst] *nm* : trust, cartel
tsar [tsar, dzar] *nm* : czar
tsarine [tsarin, dzarin] *nf* : czarina
t-shirt [tiʃœrt] *nm* → **tee-shirt**
tu[1] [ty] *pp* → **taire**
tu[2] [ty] *pron* : you
tuant, tuante [tɥã, tɥãt] *adj fam* **1** : exhausting **2** : exasperating
tuba [tyba] *nm* **1** : tuba **2** : snorkel
tube [tyb] *nm* **1** : tube, pipe **2** : tube (of toothpaste, etc.) **3 tube digestif** : digestive tract, alimentary canal
tubercule [tybɛrkyl] *nm* : tuber
tuberculeux, -leuse [tybɛrkylø, -løz] *adj* : tubercular, tuberculous
tuberculose [tybɛrkyloz] *nf* : tuberculosis
tubulaire [tybylɛr] *adj* : tubular
tubulure [tybylyr] *nf* : manifold (of an automobile)
tue-mouches[1] [tymuʃ] *adj* **papier tue-mouches** : flypaper
tue-mouches[2] *nms & pl Can* : fly-swatter
tuer [tɥe] *vt* **1** : to kill **2** ÉPUISER : to wear out, to exhaust **3 tuer le temps** : to kill time — **se tuer** *vr* **1** : to be killed, to die **2** : to kill oneself
tuerie [tyri] *nf* CARNAGE : slaughter, carnage
tue-tête [tytɛt] **à ~** : at the top of one's lungs
tueur, tueuse [tɥœr, tɥøz] *n* MEURTRIER : killer, murderer
tuile [tɥil] *nf* **1** : tile **2** *fam* : bad luck
tulipe [tylip] *nf* : tulip
tuméfié, -fiée [tymefje] *adj* : swollen, puffed-up
tumeur [tymœr] *nf* : tumor, growth
tumulte [tymylt] *nm* **1** BROUHAHA : tumult, commotion, hubbub **2** : (emotional) turmoil
tumultueux, -tueuse [tymyltɥø, -tɥøz] *adj* : stormy, turbulent — **tumultueusement** [-tɥøzmã] *adv*
tungstène [tœ̃ksten] *nm* : tungsten
tunique [tynik] *nf* : tunic
tunisien, -sienne [tynizjɛ̃, -zjɛn] *adj* : Tunisian
Tunisien, -sienne *n* : Tunisian
tunnel [tynɛl] *nm* : tunnel
tuque [tyk] *nf Can* : stocking cap, tuque
turban [tyrbã] *nm* : turban
turbide [tyrbid] *adj* : turbid
turbine [tyrbin] *nf* : turbine
turbopropulseur [tyrbɔpropylsœr] *nm* : turboprop
turboréacteur [tyrbɔreaktœr] *nm* : turbojet
turbulence [tyrbylãs] *nf* : turbulence
turbulent, -lente [tyrbylã, -lãt] *adj* **1** : boisterous, unruly **2** : turbulent
turc[1], **turque** [tyrk] *adj* : Turkish
turc[2] *nm* : Turkish (language)
Turc, Turque *n* : Turk
turf [tœrf] *nm* **1** : racetrack **2** : horse racing
turquoise[1] [tyrkwaz] *adj* : turquoise
turquoise[2] *nf* : turquoise (stone)
turquoise[3] *nm* : turquoise (color)
tutelle [tytɛl] *nf* **1** : guardianship **2** : trusteeship **3** : care, protection (of the law, etc.)
tuteur[1], **-trice** [tytœr, -tris] *n* **1** : guardian **2** : tutor
tuteur[2] *nm* : stake, prop (for plants)
tutoiement [tytwamã] *nm* : use of the familiar "tu" form

tutoyer [tytwaje] {58} *vt* : to address someone as "tu"
tuyau [tɥijo] *nm, pl* **tuyaux 1** : pipe, tube, conduit <tuyau d'échappement : exhaust pipe> <tuyau d'arrosage : garden hose> **2** : quill **3** *fam* : tip, inside information
tuyauter [tɥijote] *vt* **1** : to flute, to pleat **2** *fam* : to give someone a tip
tuyauterie [tɥijotri] *nf* : piping, pipes *pl*, plumbing
tuyère [tɥjɛr] *nf* : nozzle
TV [teve] *nf* : TV
tweed [twid] *nm* : tweed
tympan [tɛ̃pɑ̃] *nm* : eardrum
type [tip] *nm* **1** : type, kind **2** : example, model **3** : (physical) type **4** *fam* : guy, fellow
typé, -pée [tipe] *adj* : typical, distinctive (of features)
typhoïde [tifɔid] *adj & nf* : typhoid
typhon [tifɔ̃] *nm* : typhoon
typhus [tifys] *nms & pl* : typhus
typique [tipik] *adj* : typical — **typiquement** [-pikmɑ̃] *adv*
typographie [tipɔgrafi] *nf* : typography
typographique [tipɔgrafik] *adj* : typographic, typographical — **typographiquement** [-fikmɑ̃] *adv*
tyran [tirɑ̃] *nm* : tyrant
tyrannie [tirani] *nf* : tyranny
tyrannique [tiranik] *adj* : tyrannical — **tyranniquement** [-nikmɑ̃] *adv*
tyranniser [tiranize] *vt* : to tyrannize
tzar [tsar, dzar] → **tsar**
tzigane [dzigan] *adj & nmf* : gypsy

U

u [y] *nm* : u, the 21st letter of the alphabet
ubiquité [ybikɥite] *nf* : ubiquity
ukrainien[1], **-nienne** [ykrɛnjɛ̃, -njɛn] *adj* : Ukrainian
ukrainien[2] *nm* : Ukrainian (language)
Ukrainien, -nienne *n* : Ukrainian
ulcération [ylserasjɔ̃] *nf* : ulceration
ulcère [ylsɛr] *nm* : ulcer <ulcère à l'estomac : stomach ulcer>
ulcérer [ylsere] {87} *vt* **1** : to ulcerate **2** RÉVOLTER : to revolt, to appall
ulcéreux, -reuse [ylserø, -røz] *adj* **1** : ulcerous **2** : ulcerated
ultérieur, -rieure [ylterjœr] *adj* : later, subsequent
ultérieurement [ylterjœrmɑ̃] *adv* : at a later time, subsequently
ultimatum [yltimatɔm] *nm* : ultimatum
ultime [yltim] *adj* : ultimate, final
ultraviolet, -lette [yltravjole, -lɛt] *adj* : ultraviolet
ululement, uluer [ylylmɑ̃] → **ululement, hululer**
un[1], **une** [œ̃ (œn *before a vowel or mute h*), yn] *adj* : a, an, one <rester une semaine : to stay a week, to stay one week> <il y a un seul problème : there's just one problem>
un[2], **une** *n* : one <les filles marchent une par une : the girls are walking one by one> <la page une : page one>
un[3] *nm* : (number) one <huit et un font neuf : eight and one are nine>
un[4], **une** *pron, pl* **uns, unes** : one <un de ces jours : one of these days> <l'une de mes amies : one of my friends>
un[5], **une** *art, pl* **des 1** (*used in the singular*) : a, an <un exemple : an example> <une nouvelle maison : a new house> **2** (*used in the plural*) : some <voici des bonbons : here are some candies> <des gens sont déjà arrivés : some people have already arrived> **3** (*used for emphasis*) <il a attendu des heures : he waited for hours> <il y a une pluie! : there's so much rain!>
unanime [ynanim] *adj* : unanimous — **unanimement** [-nimmɑ̃] *adv*
unanimité [ynanimite] *nf* : unanimity
une [yn] *nf* **faire la une** : to be on the front page
uni, -nie [yni] *adj* **1** : united <les États-Unis : the United States> **2** LISSE : smooth, even **3** : plain-colored, solid **4** : close-knit
unième [ynjɛm] *adj* : first <trente et unième : thirty-first>
unificateur, -trice [ynifikatœr, -tris] *adj* : unifying
unification [ynifikasjɔ̃] *nf* : unification
unifier [ynifje] {96} *vt* **1** UNIR : to unite, to unify **2** NORMALISER : to standardize — **s'unifier** *vr* : to unite
uniforme[1] [ynifɔrm] *adj* **1** RÉGULIER : uniform, even **2** : unchanging
uniforme[2] *nm* : uniform
uniformément [ynifɔrmemɑ̃] *adv* : uniformly
uniformiser *vt* **1** : to make uniform **2** STANDARDISER : to standardize
uniformité [ynifɔrmite] *nf* : uniformity, evenness
unilatéral, -rale [ynilateral] *adj, pl* **-raux** [-ro] : unilateral — **unilatéralement** [-ralmɑ̃] *adv*
unilingue [ynilɛ̃g] *adj* : monolingual
union [ynjɔ̃] *nf* **1** : union <union conjugale : marriage> <Union soviétique : Soviet Union> **2** ASSOCIATION : association
unique [ynik] *adj* **1** SEUL : only <mon unique espoir : my only hope> **2** EXCEPTIONNEL : unique, exceptional **3** → **enfant**

uniquement [ynikmɑ̃] *adv* **1** EXCLUSIVEMENT : exclusively **2** SEULEMENT : only, solely
unir [ynir] *vt* **1** : to unite, to bring together **2** : to combine — **s'unir** *vr* **1** : to unite **2** : to be joined in marriage
unisson [ynisɔ̃] *nm* : unison
unitaire [ynitɛr] *adj* **1** : unitary **2 prix unitaire** : unit price
unité [ynite] *nf* **1** : unity **2** : unit
univers [ynivɛr] *nm* : universe
universel, -selle [ynivɛrsɛl] *adj* : universal — **universellement** [-selmɑ̃] *adv*
universitaire[1] [ynivɛrsitɛr] *adj* : university, academic
universitaire[2] *nmf* : academic
université [ynivɛrsite] *nf* : university
univoque [ynivɔk] *adj* : unambiguous, certain
uranium [yranjɔm] *nm* : uranium
Uranus [yranys] *nm* : Uranus
urbain, -baine [yrbɛ̃, -bɛn] *adj* : urban, city
urbanisme [yrbanism] *nm* : city planning
urbanité [yrbanite] *nf* : urbanity
urètre [yrɛtr] *nm* : urethra
urgence [yrʒɑ̃s] *nf* **1** : urgency **2** : emergency **3 d'urgence** : immediately, without delay
urgent, -gente [yrʒɑ̃, -ʒɑ̃t] *adj* : urgent
urinaire [yrinɛr] *adj* : urinary
urinal [yrinal] *nm, pl* **-naux** [-no] : urinal, bedpan
urine [yrin] *nf* : urine
uriner [yrine] *vi* : to urinate — **urination** [yrinasjɔ̃] *nf*
urinoir [yrinwar] *nm* : (public) urinal
urne [yrn] *nf* **1** : urn **2** : ballot box
urticaire [yrtikɛr] *nf* : hives
uruguayen, -guayenne [yrygwejɛ̃, -jɛn] *adj* : Uruguayan
Uruguayen, -guayenne *n* : Uruguayan
us [ys] *nmpl* **les us et coutumes** : habits and customs
usage [yzaʒ] *nm* **1** : use <à usage thérapeutique : for therapeutic use> <perdre l'usage d'un bras : to lose the use of an arm> **2** : usage (of a word or expression) **3** COUTUME : usage, custom <c'est l'usage : it's customary> **4** POLITESSE : (good) manners
usagé, -gée [yzaʒe] *adj* **1** : worn **2** : used, secondhand
usager [yzaʒe] *nm* : user
usé, -sée [yze] *adj* **1** : worn (down), worn-out **2** : hackneyed, trite
user [yze] *vt* **1** CONSOMMER : to use, to consume **2** : to wear out, to use up — *vi* **1 ~ de** : to exercise (one's rights) **2 ~ de** : to make use of — **s'user** *vr* **1** : to wear out, to get used up **2** : to wear oneself out
usine [yzin] *nf* : factory
usiner [yzine] *vt* **1** : to machine **2** : to manufacture
usité, -tée [yzite] *adj* : common, commonly used <prénom peu usité : uncommon name>
ustensile [ystɑ̃sil] *nm* : utensil, implement
usuel, -suelle [yzɥɛl] *adj* **1** : common, everyday **2** : usual <dans l'ordre usuel : in the usual order>
usuellement [yzɥɛlmɑ̃] *adv* : usually, ordinarily
usure [yzyr] *nf* **1** : wear (and tear) **2** : wearing down, erosion **3** : usury
usurpateur, -trice [yzyrpatœr, -tris] *n* : usurper
usurper [yzyrpe] *vt* : to usurp
utérin, -rine [yterɛ̃, -rin] *adj* : uterine
utérus [yterus] *nms & pl* : uterus
utile [ytil] *adj* : useful — **utilement** [ytilmɑ̃] *adv*
utilisable [ytilizabl] *adj* : usable
utilisateur, -trice [ytilizatœr, -tris] *n* : user
utilisation [ytilizasjɔ̃] *nf* : utilization, use
utiliser [ytilize] *vt* : to utilize, to use
utilitaire [ytilitɛr] *adj* : utilitarian
utilité [ytilite] *nf* : utility, usefulness
utopie [ytɔpi] *nf* : utopia
utopique [ytɔpik] *adj* : utopian

V

v [ve] *nm* : v, the 22d letter of the alphabet
va [va], *etc.* → **aller**
vacance [vakɑ̃s] *nf* **1** : vacancy, opening **2 vacances** *nfpl* : vacation, holiday *Brit* <en vacances : on vacation>
vacancier, -cière [vakɑ̃sje, -sjɛr] *n* : vacationer
vacant, -cante [vakɑ̃, -kɑ̃t] *adj* : vacant <poste vacant : vacant position>
vacarme [vakarm] *nm* : racket, din
vacataire [vakatɛr] *nmf France* : temporary worker, substitute
vaccin [vaksɛ̃] *nm* : vaccine
vacciner [vaksine] *vt* : to vaccinate — **vaccination** [vaksinasjɔ̃] *nf*
vache[1] [vaʃ] *adj fam* : mean, nasty
vache[2] *nf* **1** : cow <vache laitière : dairy cow> **2** : cowhide **3** *fam* : nasty person, swine
vachement [vaʃmɑ̃] *adv fam* JOLIMENT : really, very <cela m'aide vachement! : that's a big help!>
vacher, -chère [vaʃe, -ʃɛr] *n* : cowherd, cowboy *m*, cowgirl *f*

vacherie [vaʃri] *nf fam* **1** : nastiness, meanness **2** : dirty trick
vacillant, -lante [vasijɑ̃, -jɑ̃t] *adj* **1** : unsteady, shaky **2** : flickering **3** : failing, faltering (of memory, etc.)
vacillement [vasijmɑ̃] *nm* **1** : flickering **2** : wavering, faltering
vaciller [vasije] *vi* **1** : to stagger, to totter **2** : to flicker, to wobble, to sway **3** : to waver, to falter, to be failing
vacuité [vakɥite] *nf* : vacuity, emptiness
vadrouille [vadruj] *nf* **1** *Can* : long-handled mop for cleaning or dusting floors **2 en ~** *fam* : wandering
vadrouiller [vadruje] *vi fam* : to wander about, to ramble
va-et-vient [vaevjɛ̃] *nms & pl* **1** : comings and goings **2** : to-and-fro motion **3** : two-way switch
vagabond[1], **-bonde** [vagabɔ̃, -bɔ̃d] *adj* : wandering, roving
vagabond[2], **-bonde** *n* : vagrant, tramp, vagabond
vagabondage [vagabɔ̃daʒ] *nm* **1** : vagrancy **2** : wandering <vagabondage de l'esprit : wandering(s) of the mind>
vagabonder [vagabɔ̃de] *vi* **1** : to wander **2** : to stray (of thoughts, etc.)
vagin [vaʒɛ̃] *nm* : vagina
vaginal, -nale [vaʒinal] *adj, mpl* **-naux** [-no] : vaginal
vague[1] [vag] *adj* **1** IMPRÉCIS : vague **2** : vacant, abstracted **3** : loose-fitting, ample
vague[2] *nf* : wave
vague[3] *nm* **1** : vagueness <rester dans le vague : to remain vague> **2 regarder dans le vague** : to stare into space
vaguement [vagmɑ̃] *adv* : vaguely
vaillamment [vajamɑ̃] *adv* : bravely, courageously
vaillance [vajɑ̃s] *nf* : valor, courage
vaillant, -lante [vajɑ̃, -jɑ̃t] *adj* **1** COURAGEUX : valiant, courageous **2** : strong, robust
vaille [vaj], *etc.* → **valoir**
vain, vaine [vɛ̃, vɛn] *adj* **1** FUTILE : vain, futile <en vain : in vain> **2** VANITEUX : vain **— vainement** [vɛnmɑ̃] *adv*
vaincre [vɛ̃kr] {94} *vt* **1** BATTRE : to defeat **2** SURMONTER : to overcome, to master
vaincu[1], **-cue** [vɛ̃ky] *adj* : defeated
vaincu[2], **-cue** *n* : loser
vainquais [vɛ̃kɛ], **vainquions** [vɛ̃kjɔ̃], *etc.* → **vaincre**
vainque [vɛ̃k], *etc.* → **vaincre**
vainqueur [vɛ̃kœr] *nm* : victor, winner
vairon [vɛrɔ̃] *nm* : minnow
vaisseau [vɛso] *nm, pl* **vaisseaux 1** : vessel <vaisseau sanguin : blood vessel> **2** : vessel, ship <vaisseau spatial : spaceship> **3** : nave
vaisselle [vɛsɛl] *nf* : crockery, dishes *pl*
val [val] *nm, pl* **vals** *or* **vaux** : valley
valable [valabl] *adj* **1** VALIDE : valid **2** BON : good, worthwhile
valablement [valabləmɑ̃] *adv* : validly, legitimately
valentin [valɑ̃tɛ̃] *nm Can* : valentine
valet [valɛ] *nm* **1** : valet, manservant <valet de pied : footman> **2** : jack (in playing cards)
valeur [valœr] *nf* **1** : value, worth, merit <objets de valeur : valuables> <valeur nominale : face value> **2** VALIDITÉ : validity **3** : (moral) value <valeurs familiales : family values> **4 valeurs** *nfpl* : stocks, securities **5 c'est de valeur** *Can fam* : that's a pity, that's too bad **6 mettre en valeur** : to develop (land)
valeureux, -reuse [valœrø, -røz] *adj* : courageous, valiant
valide [valid] *adj* **1** : valid **2** : fit, able-bodied
valider [valide] *vt* : to validate
validité [validite] *nf* : validity
valise [valiz] *nf* : suitcase <faire ses valises : to pack one's bags>
vallée [vale] *nf* : valley
vallon [valɔ̃] *nm* : small valley, dale
vallonné, -née [valɔne] *adj* : undulating, hilly
valoir [valwar] {95} *vi* **1** : to have a (certain) cost <valoir très cher : to be very expensive> **2** : to have value <il sait ce qu'il vaut : he knows what he's worth> <valoir rien : to be worthless> **3** : to apply, to be valid <cela vaut pour tous les employés : that holds for all employees> **4 faire valoir** : to put forth, to point out, to assert <faire valoir ses droits : to assert one's rights> **—** *vt* **1** PROCURER : to provide, to bring (to) **2** : to be equivalent to <un dollar vaut 100 cents : one dollar equals 100 cents> **3** : to be worth <valoir la peine : to be worth the trouble> **—** *v impers* **valoir mieux** : to be better <il vaut mieux rester ici : it would be better to stay here> **— se valoir** *vr* : to be the same (thing)
valoriser [valɔrize] *vt* : to increase the value of, to develop, to enhance
valse [vals] *nf* : waltz
valser [valse] *vi* : to waltz
valve [valv] *nf* : valve
vampire [vɑ̃pir] *nm* : vampire
vandale [vɑ̃dal] *nmf* : vandal
vandalisme [vɑ̃dalism] *nm* : vandalism
vanille [vanij] *nf* : vanilla
vanité [vanite] *nf* : vanity
vaniteux, -teuse [vanitø, -tøz] *adj* : vain, conceited **— vaniteusement** [-tøzmɑ̃] *adv*
vanne [van] *nf* **1** : sluice, sluiceway **2** *fam* : dig, gibe
vanner [vane] *vt* : to winnow, to husk

vannerie [vanri] *nf* : wickerwork
vantail [vɑ̃taj] *nm, pl* **-taux** [-to] : leaf, casement <portes à deux vantaux : double doors>
vantard¹, -tarde [vɑ̃tar, -tard] *adj* : boastful, bragging
vantard², -tarde *n* : braggart
vantardise [vɑ̃tardiz] *nf* **1** : boastfulness **2** : boast, brag
vanter [vɑ̃te] *vt* : to vaunt **— se vanter** *vr* **1** : to boast, to brag **2 ~ de** : to pride oneself on
va-nu-pieds [vanypje] *nmfs & pl* : beggar, tramp, ragamuffin
vapeur¹ [vapœr] *nf* **1** : steam **2** : vapor, fume <vapeurs d'essence : gas fumes>
vapeur² *nm* : steamship, steamboat
vaporeux, -reuse [vapɔrø, -røz] *adj* **1** : misty, hazy **2** : filmy, diaphanous
vaporisateur [vaporizatœr] *nm* ATOMISEUR : spray, atomizer
vaporiser [vaporize] *vt* **1** : to spray **2** : to vaporize
vaquer [vake] *vi* **~ à** : to attend to, to see to
varappe [varap] *nf* : rock climbing
varech [varek] *nm* : kelp, seaweed
vareuse [varøz] *nf* **1** : loose-fitting jacket, tunic **2** : pea jacket
variable¹ [varjabl] *adj* CHANGEANT : variable, changeable
variable² *nf* : variable
variante [varjɑ̃t] *nf* : variant
variation [varjasjɔ̃] *nf* : variation
varice [varis] *nf* : varicose vein
varicelle [varisel] *nf* : chicken pox
varié, -riée [varje] *adj* **1** : varied, varying **2** : various
varier [varje] {96} *v* : to vary
variété [varjete] *nf* : variety
variole [varjol] *nf* : smallpox
vasculaire [vaskyler] *adj* : vascular
vase¹ [vaz] *nf* BOUE : mud, silt
vase² *nm* **1** : vase (for flowers) **2** : vessel, container <vase à bec : beaker>
vaseux, -seuse [vazø, -zøz] *adj* **1** BOUEUX : muddy **2** *fam* : sickly, under the weather **3** : hazy, woolly (of thinking, etc.)
vasistas [vazistas] *nms & pl* : fanlight, transom
vasque [vask] *nf* **1** : basin (of a fountain) **2** : bowl **3 vasque pour les oiseaux** : birdbath
vaste [vast] *adj* **1** IMMENSE : huge, immense **2** ÉTENDU : extensive, wide
va-tout [vatu] *nms & pl* **jouer son va-tout** : to risk one's all
vaudeville [vodvil] *nm* : vaudeville
vaudou [vodu] *nm* : voodoo
vaudra [vodra], *etc.* → **valoir**
vau-l'eau [volo] *adv* **aller à vau-l'eau** : to be ruined, to be going down the drain
vaurien, -rienne [vorjɛ̃, -rjen] *n* : good-for-nothing, scoundrel, rogue
vaut [vo], *etc.* → **valoir**
vautour [votur] *nm* : vulture
vautrer [votre] *v* **se vautrer** *vr* **1** : to sprawl **2** : to wallow
va-vite [vavit] **à la va-vite** : quickly, hurriedly
veau [vo] *nm, pl* **veaux 1** : calf **2** : veal **3** : calfskin
vecteur [vɛktœr] *nm* **1** : vector **2** : carrier (of disease)
vécu¹ [veky] *pp* → **vivre**
vécu², -cue [veky] *adj* : real, real-life
vedette [vədɛt] *nf* **1** STAR : star (in movies, etc.), celebrity <avoir la vedette : to be in the limelight> <mettre en vedette : to put the spotlight on> **2** : patrol boat, launch
végétal¹, -tale [veʒetal] *adj, mpl* **-taux** : vegetable, plant <le règne végétal : the plant kingdom>
végétal² *nm* : vegetable, plant
végétarien, -rienne [veʒetarjɛ̃, -rjen] *adj & n* : vegetarian
végétarisme [veʒetarism] *nm* : vegetarianism
végétatif, -tive [veʒetatif, -tiv] *adj* : vegetative
végétation [veʒetasjɔ̃] *nf* **1** : vegetation **2 végétations** *nfpl* : adenoids
végéter [veʒete] {87} *vi* : to vegetate
véhémence [veemɑ̃s] *nf* : vehemence <avec véhémence : vehemently>
véhément, -mente [veemɑ̃, -mɑ̃t] *adj* : vehement
véhicule [veikyl] *nm* **1** : vehicle **2 véhicule utilitaire sport** *Can* : sport-utility vehicle
véhiculer [veikyle] *vt* : to convey
veille [vɛj] *nf* **1** : day before, eve <la veille de Noël : Christmas Eve> **2** : watch, vigil **3** : wakefulness
veillée [veje] *nf* **1** SOIRÉE : evening **2 veillée funèbre** : wake
veiller [veje] *vt* : to sit up with, to watch over **— *vi* 1** : to stay awake **2** : to keep watch **3** : to be vigilant **4 ~ à** : to watch over, to look after
veilleur, -leuse [vejœr, -jøz] *n* **1** : lookout, sentry **2 veilleur de nuit** : night watchman
veilleuse *nf* **1** : night-light **2** : pilot light **3 mettre en veilleuse** : to put on hold, to set aside **4 mettre en veilleuse** : to dim (a light)
veine [vɛn] *nf* **1** : vein (in anatomy and botany) **2** : vein, lode (of a mineral) **3** : (artistic) inspiration **4** *fam* : luck <coup de veine : fluke> **5 en veine de** : in the mood for
veiné, -née [vene] *adj* : veined, grained
velléitaire [veleiter] *adj* : indecisive
velléité [veleite] *nf* : vague impulse, whim
vélo [velo] *nm* : bike, bicycle <faire du vélo : to ride a bike>
véloce [velɔs] *adj* : swift
vélocité [velɔsite] *nf* **1** : swiftness **2** : velocity

velours [vəlur] *nm* **1** : velvet, velour **2 velours côtelé** : corduroy
velouté[1], **-tée** [vəlute] *adj* : velvety, smooth
velouté[2] *nm* : softness, smoothness
velu, -lue [vəly] *adj* POILU : hairy
venaison [vənezɔ̃] *nf* : venison
vénal, -nale [venal] *adj* : venal
vendable [vɑ̃dabl] *adj* : marketable
vendange [vɑ̃dɑ̃ʒ] *nf* : grape harvest
vendanger [vɑ̃dɑ̃ʒe] {17} *vi* : to harvest (the) grapes — *vt* : to harvest (grapes)
vendetta [vɑ̃deta] *nf* : vendetta
vendeur, -deuse [vɑ̃dœr, -døz] *n* **1** : salesperson, salesman *m*, saleswoman *f* **2** : seller, vendor
vendre [vɑ̃dr] {63} *vt* **1** : to sell **2 à ~** : for sale — **se vendre** *vr* **1** : to be sold **2** : to sell <ça se vend bien : it's selling well>
vendredi [vɑ̃drədi] *nm* : Friday <vendredi saint : Good Friday>
vénéneux, -neuse [venenø, -nøz] *adj* : poisonous
vénérable [venerabl] *adj* : venerable, revered
vénérer [venere] {87} *vt* RÉVÉRER : to venerate — **vénération** [-rasjɔ̃] *nf*
vénérien, -rienne [venerjɛ̃, -rjɛn] *adj* : venereal <maladie vénérienne : venereal disease>
vénézuélien, -lienne [venezɥeljɛ̃, -ljɛn] *adj* : Venezuelan
Vénézuélien, -lienne *n* : Venezuelan
vengeance [vɑ̃ʒɑ̃s] *nf* : vengeance, revenge
venger [vɑ̃ʒe] {17} *vt* : to avenge — **se venger** *vr* : to take revenge, to avenge oneself
vengeur[1], **-geresse** [vɑ̃ʒœr, -ʒres] *adj* : vengeful
vengeur[2], **-geresse** *n* : avenger
véniel, -nielle [venjɛl] *adj* : venial
venimeux, -meuse [vənimø, -møz] *adj* **1** : venomous, poisonous **2** : spiteful
venin [vənɛ̃] *nm* **1** : venom, poison **2** : ill will, malice
venir [vənir] {92} *vi* **1** : to come **2 en venir à** : to come to <en venir aux coups : to come to blows> <j'en suis venu à une conclusion : I've reached a conclusion> **3 faire venir** : to send for **4 ~ de** : to come from — *v aux* **1** : to come and, to come to <viens la voir : come and see her> **2 ~ de** : to have just <je viens de nager : I've just been swimming>
vent [vɑ̃] *nm* **1** : wind <il y a du vent : it's windy> <le vent du changement : the winds of change> **2 avoir vent de** : to get wind of
vente [vɑ̃t] *nf* : sale, selling <en vente : for sale>
venteux, -teuse [vɑ̃tø, -tøz] *adj* : windy
ventilateur [vɑ̃tilatœr] *nm* : (electric) fan, ventilator
ventilation [vɑ̃tilasjɔ̃] *nf* **1** : ventilation **2** : breakdown (in finance)
ventiler [vɑ̃tile] *vt* **1** AÉRER : to ventilate **2** : to break down <ventiler les dépenses : to break down expenses>
ventouse [vɑ̃tuz] *nf* **1** : suction cup **2** : plunger **3** : sucker (in zoology)
ventre [vɑ̃tr] *nm* **1** : stomach, belly <avoir mal au ventre : to have a stomachache> **2** : womb **3 avoir qqch dans le ventre** *fam* : to have guts
ventricule [vɑ̃trikyl] *nm* : ventricle
ventriloque [vɑ̃trilɔk] *nmf* : ventriloquist
ventriloquie [vɑ̃trilɔki] *nf* : ventriloquism
ventru, -true [vɑ̃try] *adj* **1** PANSU : potbellied **2** RENFLÉ : bulging, swelling
venu[1] [vəny] *pp* → **venir**
venu[2], **-nue** [vəny] *adj* **1 bien venu** : timely, welcome **2 mal venu** : ill-advised, unwelcome **3 nouveau venu** : newcomer **4 premier venu** : just anyone
venue *nf* AVÈNEMENT : coming, advent
Vénus [venys] *nf* : Venus (planet)
vêpres [vɛpr] *nfpl* : vespers
ver [vɛr] *nm* : worm <vers blanc : grub> <ver luisant : glowworm> <ver à soie : silkworm> <ver de terre : earthworm> <ver solitaire : tapeworm>
véracité [verasite] *nf* : veracity, truthfulness
véranda [verɑ̃da] *nf* : veranda, porch
verbal, -bale [vɛrbal] *adj, mpl* **verbaux** [-bo] : verbal — **verbalement** [-balmɑ̃] *adv*
verbaliser [vɛrbalize] *vt* : to verbalize
verbe [vɛrb] *nm* **1** : verb <verbe pronominal : reflexive verb> **2** : language, words <la magie du verbe : the magic of words> **3** : tone of voice
verbeux, -beuse [vɛrbø, -bøz] *adj* : wordy, verbose
verbiage [vɛrbjaʒ] *nm* : verbiage
verdâtre [vɛrdatr] *adj* : greenish
verdeur [vɛrdœr] *nf* **1** ACIDITÉ : tartness, acidity **2** VIGUEUR : vigor, vitality **3** GROSSIÈRETÉ : crudeness
verdict [vɛrdikt] *nm* : verdict
verdir [vɛrdir] *v* : to turn green
verdoyant, verdoyante [vɛrdwajɑ̃, -jɑ̃t] *adj* : green, verdant
véreux, -reuse [verø, -røz] *adj* **1** : wormy **2** LOUCHE : shady, suspect
verge [vɛrʒ] *nf* **1** BAGUETTE : rod, stick **2** *Can* : yard (measure) **3** PÉNIS : penis **4 verge d'or** : goldenrod
verger [vɛrʒe] *nm* : orchard
verglacé, -cée [vɛrglase] *adj* : icy
verglas [vɛrgla] *nm* : black ice
vergogne [vɛrgɔɲ] *nf* **sans ~** : shamelessly
vergue [vɛrg] *nf* : yard (of a ship)
véridique [veridik] *adj* : truthful
vérifiable [verifjabl] *adj* : verifiable

vérificateur, -trice [verifikatœr, -tris] *n* **1** : controller, inspector **2 vérificateur de comptes** : (financial) auditor
vérification [verifikasjɔ̃] *nf* : check, verification
vérifier [verifje] {96} *vt* CONFIRMER : to verify, to check
vérin [verɛ̃] *nm* : jack <vérin hydraulique : hydraulic jack>
véritable [veritabl] *adj* **1** RÉEL : true, actual, real <mon véritable nom : my real name> **2** AUTHENTIQUE : genuine, authentic **3** (*used as an intensive*) : real <c'est un véritable cauchemar! : it's a real nightmare!>
véritablement [-tabləmɑ̃] *adv* **1** : actually, really **2** (*used as an intensive*) : absolutely
vérité [verite] *nf* **1** : truth <dire la vérité : to tell the truth> **2** : fact, truth <une vérité éternelle : an eternal truth> **3** : sincerity, truthfulness
vermeil, -meille [vermɛj] *adj* : vermilion
vermicelle [vermisɛl] *nm* : vermicelli
vermine [vermin] *nf* : vermin
vermoulu, -lue [vermuly] *adj* : worm-eaten, dilapidated
vermouth *or* **vermout** [vermut] *nm* : vermouth
vernir [vernir] *vt* : to varnish
vernis [verni] *nms & pl* **1** LAQUE : varnish, lacquer **2** APPARENCE : veneer, facade **3 vernis à ongles** : nail polish
vernissage [vernisaʒ] *nm* **1** : varnishing **2** : opening (of an art exhibition)
vernisser [vernise] *vt* : to glaze
vérole [verɔl] *nf* **1** *fam* : syphilis **2** → **petit²**
verra [vera], *etc.* → **voir**
verrat [vera] *nm* : male pig, boar
verre [ver] *nm* **1** : glass **2** : (drinking) glass <verre à vin : wineglass> <verre à pied : goblet> **3** : glassful <prendre un verre : to have a drink> **4 verres** *nmpl* : eyeglasses, lenses <verres de contact : contact lenses> <verres à double foyer : bifocals>
verrerie [verri] *nf* **1** : glassware **2** : glass-making **3** : glass factory
verrière [verjer] *nf* **1** : glass roof **2** : stained-glass window
verrou [veru] *nm* : bolt <sous les verrous : locked up>
verrouiller [veruje] *vt* : to bolt, to lock
verrue [very] *nf* : wart
vers¹ [ver] *nms & pl* **1** : line, verse (of poetry) **2** : verse <vers libre : free verse>
vers² *prep* **1** : toward, towards <vers le nord : toward the north> **2** : about, around, near <vers treize heures : around one o'clock>
versant [versɑ̃] *nm* : slope, side (of a hill, etc.)
versatile [versatil] *adj* : fickle
verse [vers] *nf* **pleuvoir à verse** : to pour (rain)
versé, -sée [verse] *adj* ~ **dans** : (well) versed in
Verseau [verso] *nm* : Aquarius
versement [versəmɑ̃] *nm* **1** : payment **2** : installing, installment
verser [verse] *vt* **1** : to pour **2** PAYER : to pay **3** RÉPANDRE : to shed (tears, blood etc.) — *vi* **1** : to overturn **2** ~ **dans** : to lapse into
verset [verse] *nm* : verse (of the Bible, etc.)
version [versjɔ̃] *nf* **1** : version **2** : translation (into one's native language)
verso [verso] *nm* : verso, back (of a page)
vert¹, verte [ver, vert] *adj* **1** : green **2** : unripe, sour **3** GAILLARD : vigorous, sprightly **4** CRU : crude, forthright **5** SÉVÈRE : harsh, severe
vert² *nm* : green
vertébral, -brale [vertebral] *adj, mpl* **-braux** [-bro] : vertebral, back
vertèbre [vertɛbr] *nf* : vertebra
vertébré¹, -brée [vertebre] *adj* : vertebrate
vertébré² *nm* : vertebrate
vertement [vertəmɑ̃] *adv* : sharply, severely
vertical, -cale [vertikal] *adj, mpl* **-caux** [-ko] : vertical — **verticalement** [-kalmɑ̃] *adv*
verticale *nf* : vertical
verticille [vertisil] *nf* : whorl (of petals, leaves etc.)
vertige [vertiʒ] *nm* : vertigo, dizziness
vertigineux, -neuse [vertiʒinø, -nøz] *adj* **1** : dizzy, giddy <hauteurs vertigineuses : dizzying heights> **2** : breathtaking
vertu [verty] *nf* **1** : virtue **2** : power, property **3 en vertu de** : by virtue of, according to
vertueux, -tueuse [vertɥø, -tɥøz] *adj* : virtuous — **vertueusement** [-tɥøzmɑ̃] *adv*
verve [verv] *nf* BRIO : verve, panache
vésicule [vezikyl] *nf* **1** : vesicle **2 vésicule biliaire** : gallbladder
vessie [vesi] *nf* : bladder
veste [vest] *nf* **1** : jacket **2** *Can* : vest
vestiaire [vestjɛr] *nm* **1** : cloakroom **2** : locker room **3** : locker
vestibule [vestibyl] *nm* : vestibule, hall
vestige [vestiʒ] *nm* **1** RESTE : vestige, trace **2** : relic, remains *pl*
vestimentaire [vestimɑ̃tɛr] *adj* : clothing, sartorial
veston [vestɔ̃] *nm* : (man's) jacket
vêtement [vetmɑ̃] *nm* **1** : garment, article of clothing **2 vêtements** *nmpl* : clothes, clothing **3 vêtement sacerdotal** : vestment (in religion)
vétéran [veterɑ̃] *nm* : veteran
vétérinaire¹ [veterinɛr] *adj* : veterinary
vétérinaire² *nmf* : veterinarian
vétille [vetij] *nf* BAGATELLE : trifle

vêtir |vetir| {97} *vt* HABILLER : to dress — **se vêtir** *vr*
veto |veto| *nms & pl* : veto
vêtu, -tue |vɛty| *adj* : dressed <bien vêtu : well-dressed>
vétuste |vetyst| *adj* : dilapidated
veuf[1], **veuve** |vœf, vœv| *adj* : widowed
veuf[2], **veuve** *n* : widower *m*, widow *f*
veuille |vœj|, *etc.* → **vouloir**
veule |vœl| *adj* : weak, spineless
veut |vœ|, *etc.* → **vouloir**
veuvage |vœvaʒ| *nm* : widowhood
veuve → **veuf**
vexant, vexante |vɛksɑ̃, -ksɑ̃t| *adj* **1** : hurtful (of a remark, etc.) **2** : vexing, annoying
vexation |vɛksasjɔ̃| *nf* : humiliation
vexer |vɛkse| *vt* : to vex, to upset — **se vexer** *vr* : to be upset, to take offense
via |vja| *prep* : via
viabilité |vjabilite| *nf* **1** : viability **2** : practicality
viable |vjabl| *adj* **1** : viable **2** : practical, feasible
viaduc |vjadyk| *nm* : viaduct
viager, -gère |vjaʒe, -ʒɛr| *adj or* **rente viagère** : life annuity
viande |vjɑ̃d| *nf* : meat <viande de bœuf : beef> <viande hachée : hamburger>
vibrant, -brante |vibrɑ̃, -brɑ̃t| *adj* **1** : vibrating **2** : vibrant, stirring
vibration |vibrasjɔ̃| *nf* : vibration
vibrer |vibre| *vi* **1** : to vibrate **2** : to stir, to thrill
vicaire |vikɛr| *nm* : vicar, curate
vice |vis| *nm* **1** DÉBAUCHE : vice **2** DÉFAUT : defect, fault, flaw
vice–amiral |visamiral| *nm, pl* **-raux** [-ro] : vice admiral
vice–président, -dente |visprezidɑ̃, -dɑ̃t| *n, pl* **-dents, -dentes** : vice president
vice–roi |visrwa| *nm, pl* **vice–rois** : viceroy
vice versa *or* **vice–versa** |vis(e)vɛrsa| *adv* : vice versa
vichy |viʃi| *nm* **1** : gingham **2** : Vichy water
vicier |visje| {96} *vt* **1** : to pollute, to taint **2** : to invalidate (in law)
vicieusement |visjøzmɑ̃| *nm* : viciously
vicieux, -cieuse |visjø, -sjøz| *adj* **1** : vicious (of an animal) **2** : devious, sly **3** PERVERS : perverse, depraved **4** FAUTIF : incorrect, faulty **5 cercle vicieux** : vicious circle
vicissitudes |visisityd| *nfpl* : vicissitudes, trials and tribulations
vicomte |vikɔ̃t| *nm* : viscount
vicomtesse |vikɔ̃tɛs| *nf* : viscountess
victime |viktim| *nf* : victim
victoire |viktwar| *nf* : victory
victorien, -rienne |viktɔrjɛ̃, -rjɛn| *adj* : Victorian
victorieux, -rieuse |viktɔrjø, -rjøz| *adj* : victorious <l'équipe victorieuse : the winning team> — **victorieusement** |-rjøzmɑ̃| *adv*
victuailles |viktɥaj| *nfpl* : victuals, provisions
vidange |vidɑ̃ʒ| *nf* **1** : emptying, draining **2** : oil change <faire la vidange : to change the oil> **3 vidanges** *nfpl* : sewage **4 vidanges** *nfpl Can* : garbage collection
vidanger |vidɑ̃ʒe| {17} *vt* : to empty, to drain
vide[1] |vid| *adj* **1** : empty <les mains vides : empty-handed> **2** : blank
vide[2] *nm* **1** : emptiness, void, space **2** : vacuum **3** : gap <combler le vide : to fill the gap>
vidéo[1] |video| *adj s & pl* : video
vidéo[2] *nf* : video
vidéocassette |videɔkasɛt| *nf* : videocassette, videotape
vider |vide| *vt* **1** : to empty **2** : to empty out (a place) **3** VIDANGER : to drain **4** : to core (fruit), to clean (a fowl), to gut (a fish) **5** *fam* : to kick out, to throw out
vie |vi| *nf* **1** : life <être en vie : to be alive> **2** : lifetime, life <à vie : for life> <jamais de la vie! : never!> **3** : living, livelihood
vieil → **vieux**
vieillard |vjɛjar| *nm* : old man
vieille → **vieux**
vieillesse |vjɛjɛs| *nf* : old age
vieilli, -lie |vjeji| *adj* **1** : aged, old-looking **2** DÉMODÉ : old-fashioned, dated
vieillir |vjejir| *vt* : to make (someone) look older — *vi* **1** : to grow old, to age **2** : to become outdated — **se vieillir** *vr* : to make oneself seem older
vieillissant, -sante |vjejisɑ̃, -sɑ̃t| *adj* : aging, ageing
vieillissement |vjejismɑ̃| *nm* : aging, growing old
vieillot, -lotte |vjejo, -jɔt| *adj* : quaint, antiquated
viendra |vjɛ̃dra|, *etc.* → **venir**
vienne |vjɛn|, *etc.* → **venir**
vient |vjɛ̃|, *etc.* → **venir**
vierge[1] |vjɛrʒ| *adj* **1** : virgin **2** : blank, empty <cassette vierge : blank tape> **3** : fresh, unspoiled
vierge[2] *nf* : virgin <la Sainte Vierge : the Blessed Virgin>
Vierge *nf* : Virgo
vietnamien[1], **-mienne** |vjɛtnamjɛ̃, -mjɛn| *adj* : Vietnamese
vietnamien[2] *nm* : Vietnamese (language)
Vietnamien, -mienne *n* : Vietnamese
vieux[1] |vjø| (**vieil** |vjɛj| *before a vowel or mute h*), **vieille** |vjɛj| *adj, mpl* **vieux** **1** : old **2 vieille fille** : old maid **3 vieux jeu** : old-fashioned, old hat
vieux[2], **vieille** *n* : old man *m*, old woman *f*
vif[1], **vive** |vif, viv| *adj* **1** VIVANT : living, live <de vive voix : in person> **2**

ANIMÉ : lively, vivacious **3** AIGU : sharp, keen **4** EMPORTÉ : brusque, quick-tempered **5** : bright, vivid **6** : brisk, bracing **7** → **mémoire**

vif² *nm* **1 à ~** : open, raw, exposed **2 entrer dans le vif du sujet** : to get to the heart of the matter **3 piqué au vif** : cut to the quick **4 sur le vif** : on the spot, live

vif–argent [vifarʒɑ̃] *nm, pl* **vifs–argents** : quicksilver

vigie [viʒi] *nf* **1** : lookout **2** : crow's nest, lookout (post)

vigilant, -lante [viʒilɑ̃, -lɑ̃t] *adj* : vigilant — **vigilance** [viʒilɑ̃s] *nf*

vigile¹ [viʒil] *nf* : vigil (in religion)

vigile² *nm* : security guard

vigne [viɲ] *nf* **1** : grapevine **2** VIGNOBLE : vineyard

vigneron, -ronne [viɲrɔ̃, -rɔn] *n* : winegrower

vignette [viɲɛt] *nf* **1** : label **2** : vignette

vignoble [viɲɔbl] *nm* : vineyard

vigoureux, -reuse [viguʀø, -ʀøz] *adj* **1** : vigorous, sturdy **2** : lively, energetic — **vigoureusement** [-ʀøzmɑ̃] *adv*

vigueur [vigœʀ] *nf* **1** : vigor **2 en ~** : in force, in effect

VIH [veiaʃ] *nm* : HIV

Viking [vikiŋ] *nmf* : Viking

vil, vile [vil] *adj* **1** MÉPRISABLE : vile, despicable **2 à vil prix** : very cheap

vilain, -laine [vilɛ̃, -lɛn] *adj* **1** MÉCHANT : naughty **2** LAID : ugly **3** : nasty, disagreeable

vilebrequin [vilbʀəkɛ̃] *nm* **1** : brace (for a bit) **2** : crankshaft

vilement [vilmɑ̃] *adv* : vilely, basely

vilenie [vilɛni] *nf* **1** : vileness, baseness **2** : base deed

vilipender [vilipɑ̃de] *vt* : to revile

villa [vila] *nf* : villa

village [vilaʒ] *nm* : village

villageois, -geoise [vilaʒwa, -ʒwaz] *n* : villager

ville [vil] *nf* : city, town <aller en ville : to go into town, to go downtown>

villégiature [vileʒjatyʀ] *nf* **1** : vacation **2** *or* **lieu de villégiature** : resort

vin [vɛ̃] *nm* : wine

vinaigre [vinɛgʀ] *nm* : vinegar <vinaigre balsamique : balsamic vinegar>

vinaigrette [vinɛgʀɛt] *nf* : vinaigrette

vinaigrier [vinɛgʀije] *nm* : vinegar cruet

vindicatif, -tive [vɛ̃dikatif, -tiv] *adj* : vindictive

vingt¹ [vɛ̃ (vɛ̃t *before a vowel, mute h, and the numbers 22-29*)] *adj* **1** : twenty **2** : twentieth <le vingt avril : April twentieth>

vingt² *nms & pl* : twenty

vingtaine [vɛ̃tɛn] *nf* : about twenty, group of twenty

vingtième [vɛ̃tjɛm] *adj & nmf & nm* : twentieth

vinicole [vinikɔl] *adj* VITICOLE : wine, wine-growing

vinyle [vinil] *nm* : vinyl

viol [vjɔl] *nm* **1** : rape **2** PROFANATION : violation, desecration

violacé, -cée [vjɔlase] *adj* : purplish

violateur, -trice [vjɔlatœʀ] *n* : violator

violation [vjɔlasjɔ̃] *nf* : violation

violemment [vjɔlamɑ̃] *adv* : violently

violent, -lente [vjɔlɑ̃, -lɑ̃t] *adj* : violent — **violence** [vjɔlɑ̃s] *nf*

violenter [vjɔlɑ̃te] *vt* **1** : to do violence to **2** VIOLER : to rape

violer [vjɔle] *vt* **1** : to rape **2** : to desecrate **3** : to violate, to break (a law, promise, etc.)

violet¹, -lette [vjɔlɛ, -lɛt] *adj* : purple, violet

violet² *nm* : purple, violet

violette *nf* : violet (flower)

violeur [vjɔlœʀ] *nm* : rapist

violon [vjɔlɔ̃] *nm* : violin, fiddle

violoncelle [vjɔlɔ̃sɛl] *nm* : cello

violoncelliste [vjɔlɔ̃selist] *nmf* : cellist

violoniste [vjɔlɔnist] *nmf* : violinist, fiddler

vipère [vipɛʀ] *nf* : adder, viper

virage [viraʒ] *nm* **1** COURBE : bend, turn, curve **2** : change, shift (in orientation) **3** : change in color

viral, -rale [viral] *adj, mpl* **viraux** [viʀo] : viral <infection virale : viral infection>

virée [vire] *nf fam* : outing, trip <faire une virée : to go for a spin>

virement [virmɑ̃] *nm* : transfer (in finance) <virement bancaire : bank transfer>

virer [vire] *vt* **1** : to transfer (funds) **2** : to tone (a photograph) **3** *fam* : to fire, to expel, to throw out — *vi* **1** : to veer, to turn **2** : to change color **3 ~ à** : to turn (to), to change to <virer au vert : to turn green>.

virevolte [virvɔlt] *nf* **1** : twirl **2** VOLTE-FACE : about-face

virevolter [virvɔlte] *vi* : to twirl

virginité [viʀʒinite] *nf* : virginity

virgule [virgyl] *nf* **1** : comma **2** : point, decimal point <5 virgule 7 milliards : 5 point 7 billion>

viril, -rile [viril] *adj* : virile, manly

virilité [virilite] *nf* : virility, manliness

virtuel, -tuelle [virtɥɛl] *adj* **1** : virtual (in science) **2** POTENTIEL : potential

virtuose [virtɥoz] *nmf* : virtuoso

virtuosité [virtɥozite] *nf* : virtuosity

virulent, -lente [virylɑ̃, -lɑ̃t] *adj* : virulent — **virulence** [virylɑ̃s] *nf*

virus [virys] *nms & pl* : virus

vis [vi] *nfs & pl* : screw

visa [viza] *nm* **1** : visa **2** : stamp, seal

visage [vizaʒ] *nm* **1** : face <un visage familier : a familiar face> <à visage découvert : openly> **2** : aspect, nature

visagiste [vizaʒist] *nmf* ESTHÉTICIEN : beautician

vis-à-vis[1] [vizavi] *adv* **1 ~ de** : opposite, facing **2 ~ de** : towards, with respect to
vis-à-vis[2] *nms & pl* **1** : person opposite **2** : building opposite
viscéral, -rale [viseral] *adj, mpl* **-raux** [-ro] : visceral
viscères [viser] *nmpl* : viscera, innards
viscosité [viskozite] *nf* : viscosity
visée [vize] *nf* **1** : aim, design **2** : sighting, aiming
viser [vize] *vt* **1** : to aim for, to aim at **2** : to stamp (a document) — *vi* **1** : to aim, to take aim **2 ~ à** : to aim at, to intend
viseur [vizœr] *nm* **1** : viewfinder **2** : sight (of a firearm)
visibilité [vizibilite] *nf* : visibility
visible [vizibl] *adj* **1** : visible **2** : obvious — **visiblement** [-zibləmɑ̃] *adv*
visière [vizjɛr] *nf* : visor (of a cap, etc.)
vision [vizjɔ̃] *nf* **1** : vision, eyesight **2** : view, outlook **3** : vision, apparition
visionnaire [vizjɔnɛr] *adj & nmf* : visionary
visionner [vizjɔne] *vt* : to view
visionneuse [vizjɔnøz] *nf* : viewer (for slides)
visite [vizit] *nf* **1** : visit <rendre visite à : to visit> <heures de visite : visiting hours> **2** VISITEUR : visitor <avoir une visite : to have a visitor> **3** : examination, inspection <visite de douane : customs inspection>
visiter [vizite] *vt* **1** : to visit **2** EXAMINER : to inspect, to examine
visiteur, -teuse [vizitœr, -tøz] *n* **1** : visitor **2** : inspector
vison [vizɔ̃] *nm* : mink
visqueux, -queuse [viskø, -køz] *adj* **1** : viscous **2** : slimy, gooey
visser [vise] *vt* : to screw, to screw on — **se visser** *vr* : to screw together
visualiser [vizualize] *vt* : to visualize — **visualisation** [-zualizasjɔ̃] *nf*
visuel, -suelle [vizuɛl] *adj* : visual — **visuellement** [-zuɛlmɑ̃] *adv*
vital, -tale [vital] *adj, mpl* **vitaux** [vito] : vital
vitalité [vitalite] *nf* : vitality
vitamine [vitamin] *nf* : vitamin
vite [vit] *adv* **1** RAPIDEMENT : fast, quickly <fais vite! : hurry up!> **2** TÔT : soon <au plus vite : as soon as possible>
vitesse [vitɛs] *nf* **1** : speed <à toute vitesse : at full speed> **2** : gear <en première vitesse : in first gear> **3 boîte de vitesses** : transmission **4 → limite**
viticole [vitikɔl] *adj* VINICOLE : wine, wine-growing
viticulture [vitikyltyr] *nf* : wine growing
vitrail [vitraj] *nm, pl* **vitraux** [vitro] : stained-glass window
vitre [vitr] *nf* **1** : pane, windowpane **2** : window (of a car, train, etc.) <vitre arrière : rear window>
vitré, -trée [vitre] *adj* **1** : glass, glazed **2 → baie**
vitreux, -treuse [vitrø, -trøz] *adj* **1** : vitreous **2** : glassy <les yeux vitreux : glassy eyes>
vitrier [vitrije] *nm* : glazier
vitrine [vitrin] *nf* **1** : shop window **2** : showcase, display case
vitupération [vityperasjɔ̃] *nf* : vituperation
vitupérer [vitypere] {87} *vt* : to vituperate, to berate — *vi* **~ contre** : to rant and rave against
vivable [vivabl] *adj* SUPPORTABLE : bearable
vivace [vivas] *adj* **1** : hardy <plante vivace : perennial plant> **2** DURABLE : enduring
vivacité [vivasite] *nf* **1** : vivacity, liveliness **2** : brusqueness, quickness **3** : vividness, intensity
vivant[1], **-vante** [vivɑ̃, -vɑ̃t] *adj* **1** VIF : living, live **2** ANIMÉ : lively, vivacious, peppy **3 → langue**
vivant[2] *nm* **1** : living being **2 du vivant de** : during the lifetime of
vivats [viva] *nmpl* : cheers
vive [viva] *interj* : long live, three cheers for <vive le roi! : long live the king!>
vivement [vivmɑ̃] *adv* **1** RAPIDEMENT : quickly **2** FORTEMENT : strongly, sharply, hotly
vivier [vivje] *nm* **1** : fishpond, fish tank **2** : breeding ground
vivifiant, -fiante [vivifjɑ̃, -fjɑ̃t] *adj* : bracing, invigorating
vivifier [vivifje] {96} *vt* REVIGORER : to invigorate
vivisection [viviseksjɔ̃] *nf* : vivisection
vivoter [vivɔte] *vi* : to get by, to subsist
vivre [vivr] {98} *vt* : to live through, to experience — *vi* **1** : to live **2 faire vivre** : to support **3 ~ de** : to live on, to live by
vivres [vivr] *nmpl* PROVISIONS : food, provisions
vocable [vɔkabl] *nm* MOT : term, word
vocabulaire [vɔkabylɛr] *nm* : vocabulary
vocal, -cale [vɔkal] *adj, mpl* **vocaux** [vɔko] : vocal — **vocalement** [-kalmɑ̃] *adv*
vocaliser [vɔkalize] *v* : to vocalize
vocation [vɔkasjɔ̃] *nf* : vocation, calling
vociférer [vɔsifere] {87} *v* : to shout, to scream
vodka [vɔdka] *nf* : vodka
vœu [vø] *nm, pl* **vœux 1** SOUHAIT : wish <faire un vœu : to make a wish> <mes meilleurs vœux : my best wishes> **2** SERMENT : vow
vogue [vɔg] *nf* : vogue, fashion

voguer [vɔge] *vi* : to sail, to navigate
voici [vwasi] *prep* **1** : here is, here are <me voici : here I am> <la voici qui vient : here she comes> **2** : this is, these are <voici pourquoi : this is why> **3** (*indicating a period of time*) <il est parti voici trois jours : he left three days ago> <voici un mois que je ne les vois plus : it's a month since I've seen them>
voie [vwa] *nf* **1** : road, route, way <voie express : expressway> <voie à sens unique : one-way street> <voie navigable : waterway> **2** : lane <route à deux voies : two-lane road> **3** *or* **voie ferrée** : railroad track **4** : way, course <montrer la voie : to show the way> <une voie médiane : a middle course> **5** : means *pl*, channels *pl* **6** : passage, duct (in physiology) **7 en voie de** : on the way to, in the process of **8 voie d'eau** : leak (of a boat) **9 la Voie lactée** : the Milky Way
voilà [vwala] *prep* **1** : there is, there are <les voilà! : there they are!> **2** : that is, those are <voilà tout! : that's all!> **3** VOICI : here is, here are **4** (*indicating a period of time*) <voilà un an : a year ago> <voilà quatre jours qu'il neige : it's been snowing for four days>
voile[1] [vwal] *nf* **1** : sail **2** : sailing
voile[2] *nm* **1** : veil **2** : voile (fabric) **3** : veil, covering <lever le voile : to reveal, to bring to the open> **4** : mist (of tears, fog, etc.)
voiler [vwale] *vt* **1** : to veil, to cover **2** : to conceal **3** : to mist (up), to cloud **4** : to warp — **se voiler** *vr*
voilier [vwalje] *nm* : sailboat
voilure [vwalyr] *nf* : sails *pl*
voir [vwar] {99} *v* **1** : to see **2** : to view, to imagine **3** : to look at, to consider **4** : to discover <c'est à voir : that remains to be seen> **5** : to visit, to call on **6 faire voir** *or* **laisser voir** : to show **7 n'avoir rien à voir avec** : to have nothing to do with — *vi* **1** : to see <voir double : to see double> **2** : to find out, to understand <il faut voir : we must wait and see> **3** : to take a look <voyons : well, let's see> **4 ~ à** : to see to, to make sure that <voyez à la prévenir : be sure to warn her> — **se voir** *vr* **1** : to see oneself **2** : to see each other **3** : to be visible, to show <ça se voit : that's obvious, it shows>
voire [vwar] *adv* : indeed, or even
voirie [vwari] *nf* **1** : highway department **2** *France* : garbage collection
voisin[1], **-sine** [vwazɛ̃, -zin] *adj* **1** : adjoining, neighboring **2** : similar, closely related <voisin de : akin to, resembling>
voisin[2], **-sine** *n* : neighbor
voisinage [vwazinaʒ] *nm* **1** : neighborhood **2** : proximity, closeness **3** : neighbors *pl*
voisiner [vwazine] *vi* **1** : to visit one's neighbors **2 ~ avec** : to be side by side with
voiture [vwatyr] *nf* **1** AUTOMOBILE : car, automobile <voiture de course : racing car> **2** WAGON : (railroad) car, coach **3** : carriage, cart <voiture d'enfant : baby carriage>
voix [vwa] *nfs & pl* **1** : voice <à haute voix : out loud, aloud> <voix traînante : drawl> **2** : voice, counsel <la voix de la raison : the voice of reason> **3** VOTE : vote <mettre aux voix : to put to the vote>
vol [vɔl] *nm* **1** : flight <prendre son vol : to take flight> <vols internationaux : international flights> **2** : theft, robbery <vol à main armée : armed robbery> <vol à la tire : pickpocketing> **3** VOLÉE : flock **4 au vol** : in midair
volage [vɔlaʒ] *adj* INCONSTANT : fickle, flighty
volaille [vɔlaj] *nf* **1** : poultry **2** : fowl, bird
volant[1], **-lante** [vɔlɑ̃, -lɑ̃t] *adj* : flying
volant[2] *nm* **1** : steering wheel **2** : shuttlecock **3** : flounce (of a skirt, etc.)
volatil, -tile [vɔlatil] *adj* : volatile
volatile *nm* : fowl, chicken, bird
volatiliser [vɔlatilize] *v* **se volatiliser** *vr* **1** : to volatilize **2** : to disappear, to vanish into thin air
volcan [vɔlkɑ̃] *nm* **1** : volcano **2** : hothead
volcanique [vɔlkanik] *adj* : volcanic
volée [vɔle] *nf* **1** : volley **2** VOL : flock, flight
voler [vɔle] *vt* **1** : to steal **2** : to rob, to cheat **3 voler à l'étalage** : to shoplift — *vi* **1** : to fly **2 voler en éclats** : to smash to bits, to shatter
volet [vɔlɛ] *nm* **1** : shutter **2** : flap (of an airplane, etc.) **3** : section (of a document) **4** : constituent, part, facet
voleter [vɔlte] {8} *vi* : to flutter, to flit
voleur[1], **-leuse** [vɔlœr, -løz] *adj* : thieving, dishonest
voleur[2], **-leuse** *n* **1** : thief, robber **2 voleur à la tire** : pickpocket **3 voleur à l'étalage** : shoplifter
volière [vɔljɛr] *nf* : aviary
volley [vɔlɛ] *or* **volley–ball** [vɔlɛbol] *nm* : volleyball
volontaire[1] [vɔlɔ̃tɛr] *adj* **1** : voluntary **2** : willful, deliberate **3** : headstrong
volontaire[2] *nmf* : volunteer
volontairement [vɔlɔ̃tɛrmɑ̃] *adv* : voluntarily, deliberately
volonté [vɔlɔ̃te] *nf* **1** : will <bonne volonté : willingness, goodwill> **2** : willpower **3 à ~** : at will
volontiers [vɔlɔ̃tje] *adv* : willingly, gladly
volt [vɔlt] *nm* : volt
voltage [vɔltaʒ] *nm* : voltage

volte–face [vɔltəfas] *nfs & pl* : about-face
voltige [vɔltiʒ] *nf* : acrobatics
voltiger [vɔltiʒe] {17} *vi* **1** : to do acrobatics **2** : to flutter about, to flit
voltigeur, -geuse [vɔltiʒœr, -ʒøz] *n Can* : outfielder
volubile [vɔlybil] *adj* : voluble
volume [vɔlym] *nm* : volume
volumineux, -neuse [vɔlyminø, -nøz] *adj* : voluminous
volupté [vɔlypte] *nf* : sensual pleasure, voluptuousness
voluptueux, -tueuse [vɔlyptɥø, -tɥøz] *adj* : voluptuous — **voluptueusement** [-tɥøzmɑ̃] *adv*
volute [vɔlyt] *nf* : curl, coil (of smoke, etc.)
vomi [vɔmi] *nm* : vomit
vomir [vɔmir] *vt* **1** : to vomit, to bring up **2** : to spew out — *vi* : to vomit
vomissement [vɔmismɑ̃] *nm* : vomiting
vorace [vɔras] *adj* : voracious — **voracement** [-rasmɑ̃] *adv*
voracité [vɔrasite] *nf* : voracity
votant, -tante [vɔtɑ̃, -tɑ̃t] *n* : voter
vote [vɔt] *nm* : vote
voter [vɔte] *vi* : to vote — *vt* : to vote for
votre [vɔtr] *adj, pl* **vos** [vo] : your
vôtre[1] [votr] *adj* : yours <ce livre est vôtre : this book is yours>
vôtre[2] *pron* **le vôtre, la vôtre, les vôtres** : yours, your own <c'est le vôtre : it's yours> <mes amitiés à vous et les vôtres : my regards to you and yours>
voudra [vudra], *etc.* → **vouloir**
vouer [vwe] *vt* **1** PROMETTRE : to vow, to pledge **2** CONSACRER : to dedicate, to consecrate <vouer sa vie : to devote one's life> **3** DESTINER : to destine, to doom <voué à l'échec : doomed to failure>
voulait [vulɛ], **voulions** [vuljɔ̃], *etc.* → **vouloir**
vouloir[1] [vulwar] {100} *vt* **1** : to want, to wish for <veux-tu du vin? : do you want some wine?> <je voudrais y aller : I would like to go> **2** ACCEPTER : to agree to, to be willing to <veuillez patienter : please wait> <voudriez-vous ouvrir la porte? : would you mind opening the door?> **3** : to expect, to intend <je ne leur veux aucun mal : I mean them no harm> <sans le vouloir : unintentionally> **4 en vouloir à** : to bear a grudge against **5 vouloir dire** : to mean <qu'est-ce que ça veut dire? : what does that mean?> — **se vouloir** *vr* **1** : to think of oneself as **2** : to try to be **3 s'en vouloir** : to be annoyed with oneself
vouloir[2] *nm* : will <bon vouloir : good-will>
voulu, -lue [vuly] *adj* **1** DÉLIBÉRÉ : intentional, deliberate **2** REQUIS : required
vous [vu] *pron* **1** (*as subject or direct object*) : you <vous êtes mon ami : you're my friend> <elle vous aime : she loves you> **2** (*as indirect object*) : you, to you <il vous a écrit une lettre : he wrote you a letter> **3** : yourself <servez-vous : help yourself> <pensez à vous : think about yourselves> **4 à ~** : yours <est-ce que cette maison est à vous? : is this house yours?, is this your house?>
vous–même [vumɛm], *pl* **vous–mêmes** *pron* : yourself
voûte [vut] *nf* **1** : vault, arch **2 voûte du palais** : roof of the mouth
voûter [vute] *vt* : to vault, to arch — **se voûter** *vr* : to become stooped
vouvoyer [vuvwaje] {58} *vt* : to address as *vous*
voyage [vwajaʒ] *nm* **1** : voyage, trip **2 avoir son voyage** *Can fam* : to be fed up
voyager [vwajaʒe] {17} *vi* : to travel
voyageur, -geuse [vwajaʒœr, -ʒøz] *n* **1** : traveler **2** PASSAGER : passenger
voyait [vwaje], **voyions** [vwajɔ̃], *etc.* → **voir**
voyance [vwajɑ̃s] *nf* : clairvoyance
voyant[1], **voyante** [vwajɑ̃, -jɑ̃t] *adj* : loud, gaudy, garish
voyant[2], **voyante** *n* : seer, clairvoyant
voyant[3] *nm* : warning light, indicator light
voyelle [vwajɛl] *nf* : vowel
voyeur, voyeuse [vwajœr, -jøz] *n* : voyeur
voyou [vwaju] *nm* : thug, hoodlum
vrac [vrak] *adv* **1 en ~** : loose, in bulk **2 en ~** : jumbled, disorganized
vrai[1], **vraie** [vrɛ] *adj* **1** : true **2** : real
vrai[2] *nm* : truth <à vrai dire : to tell the truth>
vraiment [vrɛmɑ̃] *adv* : really
vraisemblable [vrɛzɑ̃blabl] *adj* : likely, probable — **vraisemblablement** [-blabləmɑ̃] *adv*
vraisemblance [vrɛzɑ̃blɑ̃s] *nf* **1** : likelihood, probability **2** : verisimilitude
vrille [vrij] *nf* **1** : gimlet (tool), auger **2** : spiral, tailspin **3** : tendril
vriller [vrije] *vt* : to bore into, to pierce
vrombir [vrɔ̃bir] *vi* **1** : to hum, to buzz **2** : to roar (of an engine)
vrombissement [vrɔ̃bismɑ̃] *nm* : humming, buzzing, roaring
vu[1] [vy] *pp* → **voir**
vu[2], **vue** [vy] *adj* : seen, regarded <bien vu : well thought of>
vu[3] *prep* : in view of, considering <vu sa timidité, c'est un homme brave : considering his timidity, he's a brave man>
vue *nf* **1** : sight <à première vue : at first sight> **2** : eyesight **3** : view, vista <vue d'ensemble : overall view> **4** : opinion, view **5 vues** *nfpl* : plans, designs **6 vues** *nfpl Can* : <aller aux vues : to go to the movies>

vulcaniser [vylkanize] *vt* : to vulcanize
vulgaire [vylɡɛr] *adj* **1** GROSSIER : vulgar, coarse **2** ORDINAIRE : common, ordinary
vulgairement [vylɡɛrmɑ̃] *adv* : vulgarly
vulgariser [vylɡarize] *vt* : to popularize — **vulgarisation** [vylɡarizasjɔ̃] *nf*
vulgarité [vylɡarite] *nf* : vulgarity
vulnérabilité [vylnerabilite] *nf* : vulnerability
vulnérable [vylnerabl] *adj* : vulnerable
vulve [vylv] *nf* : vulva

W

w [dubləve] *nm* : w, the 23rd letter of the alphabet
wagon [vaɡɔ̃] *nm* **1** : car (of a train) **2** : carload, truckload, wagonload
wagon–citerne [vaɡɔ̃sitɛrn] *nm, pl* **wagons–citernes** : tanker
wagon–lit [vaɡɔ̃li] *nm, pl* **wagons–lits** : sleeping car, Pullman
wagonnet [vaɡɔnɛ] *nm* : small transport car (on a train)
wagon–restaurant [vaɡɔ̃rɛstɔrɑ̃] *nm, pl* **wagons–restaurants** : dining car
wallaby [walabi] *nm, pl* **wallabies** : wallaby
wallon[1], **-lonne** [walɔ̃, -lɔn] *adj* : Walloon
wallon[2] *nm* : Walloon (language)
Wallon, -lonne *n* : Walloon
wampum [wampum] *nm* : wampum
wapiti [wapiti] *nm* : wapiti
water–polo [watɛrpɔlo] *nm* : water polo
watt [wat] *nm* : watt
Web [web] *nm* TOILE : World Wide Web, Web
week–end [wikɛnd] *nm, pl* **week–ends** : weekend
western [wɛstɛrn] *nm* : western (movie)
wharf [warf] *nm* : wharf
whippet [wipɛt] *nm* : whippet
whisky [wiski] *nm, pl* **whiskies** : whiskey
wigwam [wiɡwam] *nm* : wigwam
wolfram [vɔlfram] *nm* : wolfram

X

x [iks] *nm* : x, the 24th letter of the alphabet
X [iks] *nm* (*used to designate an unknown*) <monsieur X : Mr. X>
xénon [ɡzenɔ̃] *nm* : xenon
xénophile [ɡzenɔfil] *adj & nmf* : xenophile
xénophobe[1] [ɡzenɔfɔb] *adj* : xenophobic
xénophobe[2] *nmf* : xenophobe
xénophobie [ɡzenɔfɔbi] *nf* : xenophobia
xérès [ɡzeres, kseres] *nm* : sherry
xylophone [ksilɔfɔn] *nm* : xylophone

Y

y [iɡrɛk] *nm* : y, the 25th letter of the alphabet
y[1] [i] *adv* **1** : there <il n'y était pas : he was not there> **2 ça y est !** : finally!, there you have it!
y[2] *pron* : it, for it, about it <nous n'y pouvons rien : we can't do anything about it> <pensons-y : let's think about it> <j'y suis! : I've got it!>
yacht [jɔt] *nm* : yacht
yachting [jɔtiŋ] *nm* : yachting
yack *or* **yak** [jak] *nm* : yak
yankee[1] [jɑ̃ki] *adj* : yankee
Yankee[2] *nmf* : Yankee
yaourt [jaurt] *nm* : yogurt
yéménite [jemenit] *adj* : Yemeni
Yéménite *nmf* : Yemeni
yeux [jø] → **œil**
yoga [jɔɡa] *nm* : yoga
yogourt *or* **yoghourt** [jɔɡurt] → **yaourt**
Yom Kippour [jɔmkipur] *nm* : Yom Kippur
yougoslave [juɡɔslav] *adj* : Yugoslav, Yugoslavian
Yougoslave *nmf* : Yugoslav, Yugoslavian
yo–yo *or* **yoyo** [jojo] *nm* : yo-yo
yucca [juka] *nm* : yucca

Z

z [zɛd] *nm* : z, the 26th letter of the alphabet
zaïrois, -roise [zairwa, -rwaz] *adj* : Zairian
Zaïrois, -roise *n* : Zairian
zambien, -bienne [zɑ̃bjɛ̃, -bjɛn] *adj* : Zambian
Zambien, -bienne *n* : Zambian
zèbre [zɛbr] *nm* : zebra
zébré, -brée [zebre] *adj* RAYÉ : striped, streaked
zébrure [zebryr] *nf* **1** RAYURE : stripe **2** : wheal, welt (on the skin) **3** : streak (of lightning)
zélateur, -trice [zelatœr, -tris] *n* : zealot, partisan
zèle [zɛl] *nm* : zeal
zélé, -lée [zele] *adj* : zealous
zénith [zenit] *nm* : zenith
zéphyr [zefir] *nm* : zephyr
zeppelin [zɛplɛ̃] *nm* : zeppelin
zéro[1] [zero] *adj* **1** : zero **2** : nil, worthless
zéro[2] *nm* : zero, nought
zeste [zɛst] *nm* : zest, peel (of a lemon, etc.)
zézaiement [zezemɑ̃] *nm* : lisp
zézayer [zezeje] {11} *vi* : to lisp
zibeline [ziblin] *nf* : sable
zieuter [zjøte] *vt fam* RELUQUER : to ogle, to eye
zig *or* **zigue** [zig] *nm fam* : guy, fellow
zigzag [zigzag] *nm* : zigzag
zigzaguer [zigzage] *vi* : to zigzag
zimbabwéen, -wéenne [zimbabweẽ, -weɛn] *adj* : Zimbabwean
Zimbabwéen, -wéenne *n* : Zimbabwean
zinc [zɛ̃g] *nm* : zinc
zinnia [zinja] *nm* : zinnia
zip [zip] *nm* : zipper
zipper [zipe] *vt* : to zip (up)
zircon [zirkɔ̃] *nm* : zircon
zirconium [zirkɔnjɔm] *nm* : zirconium
zizanie [zizani] *nf* DISCORDE : discord, conflict
zodiaque [zɔdjak] *nm* : zodiac
zombie [zɔ̃bi] *nm* : zombie
zona [zona] *nm* : shingles
zonage [zonaʒ] *nm* : zoning
zone [zon] *nf* : zone, area
zoo [zo(o)] *nm* : zoo
zoologie [zɔɔlɔʒi] *nf* : zoology
zoologique [zɔɔlɔʒik] *adj* : zoological
zoologiste [zɔɔlɔʒist] *nmf* : zoologist
zoom [zum] *nm* **1** : zoom lens **2 faire un zoom** : to zoom in (in photography)
zozo [zozo] *nm fam* : nitwit
zozoter [zɔzɔte] *vi* : to lisp
zut [zyt] *interj fam* : darn!, damn it!
zygote [zigɔt] *nm* : zygote

English–French Dictionary

A

a[1] [ˈeɪ] *n, pl* **a's** or **as** [ˈeɪz] : a *m*, première lettre de l'alphabet

a[2] [ə, ˈeɪ] *art* **(an** [ən, ˈæn] *before a vowel or silent h*) **1** : un *m*, une *f* <a book : un livre> <half an hour : une demi-heure> **2** PER : par <twice a month : deux fois par mois>

aardvark [ˈɑrdˌvɑrk] *n* : oryctérope *m*

aback [əˈbæk] *adv* **taken aback** : déconcerté, décontenancé

abacus [ˈæbəkəs] *n, pl* **abaci** [ˈæbəˌsɑɪ, -kɪː] or **abacuses** : boulier *m*

abaft [əˈbæft] *adv* : en poupe, sur l'arrière

abalone [ˌæbəˈloːni] *n* : ormeau *m*

abandon[1] [əˈbændən] *vt* **1** DESERT, FORSAKE : abandonner, délaisser **2** LEAVE : abandonner, quitter (un lieu) <abandon ship! : abandonnez le navire!> **3** GIVE UP, SUSPEND : renoncer à, laisser tomber <she abandoned her studies : elle a laissé tomber ses études> **4 to abandon oneself to** : se livrer à, s'abandonner à

abandon[2] *n* : abandon *m*, désinvolture *m*

abandoned [əˈbændənd] *adj* **1** DESERTED : abandonné, délaissé **2** UNRESTRAINED : sans retenue

abandonment [əˈbændənmənt] *n* : abandon *m*

abase [əˈbeɪs] *vt* **abased; abasing** : abaisser, humilier

abasement [əˈbeɪsmənt] *n* : abaissement *f*, humiliation *f*

abash [əˈbæʃ] *vt* : décontenancer, confondre

abashed [əˈbæʃt] *adj* : décontenancé, confondu

abate [əˈbeɪt] *v* **abated; abating** *vt* REDUCE : baisser, réduire, diminuer — *vi* DECREASE : s'apaiser, se calmer, diminuer <the fever abated : la fièvre s'est calmée>

abatement [əˈbeɪtmənt] *n* : apaisement *m*, diminution *f*

abattoir [ˈæbəˌtwɑr] *n* : abattoir *m*

abbess [ˈæbɪs, -ˌbɛs, -bəs] *n* : abbesse *f*

abbey [ˈæbi] *n, pl* **-beys** : abbaye *f*

abbot [ˈæbət] *n* : abbé *m*

abbreviate [əˈbriːviˌeɪt] *vt* **-ated; -ating** : abréger

abbreviation [əˌbriːviˈeɪʃən] *n* : abréviation *f*

abdicate [ˈæbdɪˌkeɪt] *v* **-cated; -cating** : abdiquer

abdication [ˌæbdɪˈkeɪʃən] *n* : abdication *f*

abdomen [ˈæbdəmən, æbˈdoːmən] *n* : abdomen *m*

abdominal [æbˈdɑmənəl] *adj* : abdominal

abduct [æbˈdʌkt] *vt* : enlever

abduction [æbˈdʌkʃən] *n* : enlèvement *m*

abductor [æbˈdʌktər] *n* : ravisseur *m*, -seuse *f*

abed [əˈbɛd] *adv & adj* : au lit, dans le lit

aberrant [æˈbɛrənt, ˈæbərənt] *adj* : aberrant

aberration [ˌæbəˈreɪʃən] *n* : aberration *f*

abet [əˈbɛt] *vt* **abetted; abetting 1** ENCOURAGE : encourager, soutenir **2 to aid and abet** : être complice de

abettor *or* **abetter** [əˈbɛtər] *n* : complice *mf*

abeyance [əˈbeɪənʌs] *n* **1** SUSPENSION : suspension *f*, interruption *f* **2 in ~** : en suspens

abhor [əbˈhɔr, æb-] *vt* **-horred; -horring** : abhorrer, détester

abhorrence [əbˈhɔrənʌs, æb-] *n* : horreur *f*

abhorrent [əbˈhɔrənt, æb-] *adj* : odieux, détestable

abide [əˈbɑɪd] *v* **abode** [əˈboːd] *or* **abided; abiding** *vt* STAND, TOLERATE : endurer, supporter — *vi* **1** LAST : continuer, durer **2** RESIDE : demeurer, habiter **3 to abide by** : respecter, se conformer à

ability [əˈbɪləti] *n, pl* **-ties 1** CAPABILITY : capacité *f*, aptitude *f* **2** SKILL : habileté *f*, talent *m*

abject [ˈæbˌdʒɛkt, æbˈ-] *adj* **1** WRETCHED : abject, misérable **2** SERVILE : servile, obséquieux — **abjectly** *adv*

ablaze [əˈbleɪz] *adj* **1** BURNING : en flammes, en feu **2** RADIANT : brillant, resplendissant

able [ˈeɪbəl] *adj* **abler; ablest 1** CAPABLE : capable **2** SKILLED : compétent, habile

able–bodied [ˌeɪbəlˈbɑdɪd] *n* : robuste, vigoureux

ably [ˈeɪbəli] *adv* : habilement

abnormal [æbˈnɔrməl] *adj* : anormal — **abnormally** *adv*

abnormality [ˌæbnɔrˈmæləti, -nɔr-] *n, pl* **-ties** : anormalité *f* (état), anomalie *f* (trait)

aboard[1] [əˈbɔrd] *adv* : à bord

aboard[2] *prep* : à bord de, dans <aboard the train : dans le train>

abode [əˈboːd] *n* : demeure *f*, domicile *m*

abolish [əˈbɑlɪʃ] *vt* : supprimer, abolir

abolition [ˌæbəˈlɪʃən] *n* : abolition *f*, suppression *f*

abominable [əˈbɑmənəbəl] *adj* : abominable

abominate [əˈbɑmənˌeɪʃən] *vt* **-nated; -nating** : abhorrer, abominer

abomination [əˈbɑmənˌeɪt] *n* : abomination *f*

aboriginal [ˌæbəˈrɪdʒənəl] *adj* : aborigène, indigène

aborigine [ˌæbəˈrɪdʒəni] *n* : aborigène *mf*

abort [əˈbɔrt] *vt* **1** TERMINATE : faire avorter **2** SUSPEND : abandonner, interrompre — *vi* : avorter
abortion [əˈbɔrʃən] *n* : avortement *m*
abortive [əˈbɔrtɪv] *adj* **1** : avorté, manqué <abortive efforts : efforts avortés> **2** : abortif <abortive agent : agent abortif>
abound [əˈbaʊnd] *vi* : abonder
about[1] [əˈbaʊt] *adv* **1** APPROXIMATELY : vers, environ, à peu près **2** AROUND : autour, à la ronde <he looked all about : il regardait tout autour> **3** NEARBY : près, par ici, par là **4** : de tous côtés, ça et là, ici et là <books lying all about : des livres de tous côtés> **5** ALMOST : tout juste, à peu près, presque **6 to be about to** : être sur le point de
about[2] *prep* **1** AROUND : autour de, par, dans <to walk about the city : se promener dans la ville> **2** CONCERNING : sur, de, concernant <a book about jazz : un livre sur le jazz> <he's talking about me : il parle de moi> <what's it about? : de quoi s'agit-il?>
above[1] [əˈbʌv] *adv* **1** OVERHEAD : au-dessus, en haut **2** : ci-dessus, plus haut <as mentioned above : comme cité ci-dessus>
above[2] *prep* **1** OVER : au-dessus de, en haut de **2** EXCEEDING : plus de, au-dessus de <above one hundred applicants : plus de cent candidats> **3** BEYOND : au-delà de <above the call of duty : au-delà du strict devoir>
aboveboard[1] [əˈbʌvˌbɔrd, -ˌbɔrd] *adv* : ouvertement, franchement
aboveboard[2] *adj* : ouvert, franc
abrade [əˈbreɪd] *vt* **abraded; abrading** **1** SCRAPE : érafler (la peau), user en frottant **2** IRRITATE : agacer, irriter
abrasion [əˈbreɪʒən] *n* **1** ABRADING : abrasion *f* **2** SCRATCH : écorchure *f*, éraflure *f*
abrasive[1] [əˈbreɪsɪv] *adj* : abrasif
abrasive[2] *n* : abrasif *m*
abreast [əˈbrɛst] *adv* **1** : de front, côte à côte <two abreast : à deux de front> **2 to keep abreast of** : se tenir au courant de
abridge [əˈbrɪdʒ] *vt* **abridged; abridging** : abréger
abridgment *or* **abridgement** [əˈbrɪdʒmənt] *n* **1** ABRIDGING : abrégement *m* **2** SUMMARY : abrégé *m*, résumé *m*
abroad [əˈbrɔd] *adv* **1** WIDELY : au loin, de tous côtés <to spread abroad : circuler de tous côtés> **2** OVERSEAS : à l'étranger
abrupt [əˈbrʌpt] *adj* **1** SUDDEN : soudain, précipité **2** CURT : abrupt, brusque **3** STEEP : escarpé, abrupt
abruptly [əˈbrʌptlɪ] *adv* : brusquement, tout d'un coup
abscess [ˈæbˌsɛs] *n* : abcès *m*
abscond [æbˈskɑnd] *vi* : s'enfuir
absence [ˈæbsənʦ] *n* **1** : absence *f* (d'une personne) **2** LACK : manque *m*
absent[1] [æbˈsɛnt] *vt* **to absent oneself** : s'absenter
absent[2] [ˈæbsənt] *adj* : absent
absentee [ˌæbsənˈtiː] *n* : absent *m*, -sente *f*
absentminded [ˌæbsənˈtmaɪndəd] *adj* : distrait, préoccupé
absentmindedly [ˌæbsənˈtmaɪndədlɪ] *adv* : d'un air distrait, distraitement
absentmindedness [ˌæbsənˈtmaɪndədnəs] *n* : distraction *f*
absolute [ˈæbsəˌluːt, ˌæbsəˈluːt] *adj* **1** COMPLETE, PERFECT : absolu, total, parfait **2** UNCONDITIONAL : absolu, inconditionnel **3** DEFINITE : formel, définitif
absolutely [ˈæbsəˌluːtlɪ, ˌæbsəˈluːtlɪ] *adv* **1** : absolument, tout à fait **2 absolutely not** : pas du tout
absolution [ˌæbsəˈluːʃən] *n* : absolution *f*
absolve [əbˈzɑlv, æb-, -ˈsɑlv] *vt* **-solved; -solving** : absoudre
absorb [əbˈzɔrb, æb-, -ˈsɔrb] *vt* **1** : absorber (des liquides), amortir (des chocs, des sons, etc.), assimiler (personnes) **2 to become absorbed in** : s'absorber dans
absorbency [əbˈzɔrbənʦi, æb-, -ˈsɔr-] *n, pl* **-cies** : pouvoir *m* absorbant
absorbent [əbˈzɔrbənt, æb-, -ˈsɔr-] *adj* : absorbant
absorbing [əbˈzɔrbɪŋ, æb-, -ˈsɔr-] *adj* : absorbant, fascinant
absorption [əbˈzɔrpʃən, æb-, -ˈsɔrp-] *n* **1** : absorption *f* (des liquides), amortissement *m* (d'un choc, etc.) **2** CONCENTRATION : concentration *f* (d'esprit)
abstain [əbˈstɛɪn, æb-] *vi* : s'abstenir
abstemious [æbˈstiːmiəs] *adj* : sobre, frugal — **abstemiously** *adv*
abstemiousness [æbˈstiːmiəsnəs] *n* : sobriété *f*, tempérence *f*
abstention [əbˈstɛnʃən, æb-] *n* : abstention *f*
abstinence [ˈæbstənənʦ] *n* : abstinence *f*
abstinent [ˈæbstənənt] *adj* : sobre, frugal, modéré
abstract[1] [æbˈstrækt, ˈæbˌ-] *vt* **1** REMOVE : extraire, retirer **2** SUMMARIZE : résumer
abstract[2] *adj* : abstrait — **abstractly** [æbˈstræktlɪ, ˈæbˌ-] *adv*
abstract[3] [ˈæbˌstrækt] *n* **1** SUMMARY : résumé *m* **2** : abstrait *m* <in the abstract : dans l'abstrait>
abstraction [æbˈstrækʃən] *n* **1** : abstraction *f*, idée *f* abstraite **2** REMOVAL : extraction *f* **3** PREOCCUPATION : préoccupation *f*, distraction *f*
abstruse [əbˈstruːs, æb-] *adj* : abstrus
absurd [əbˈsɔrd, -ˈzɔrd] *adj* : absurde, ridicule, insensé

absurdity [əb'sərdəti, -'zər-] *n, pl* **-ties** : absurdité *f*, ridicule *m*
absurdly [əb'sərdli, -'zərd-] *adv* : ridiculement, de manière insensée
abundance [ə'bʌndənʌs] *n* : abondance *f*, profusion *f*
abundant [ə'bʌndənt] *adj* : abondant
abundantly [ə'bʌndəntli] *adv* : abondamment, en profusion
abuse[1] [ə'bju:z] *vt* **abused; abusing 1** MISUSE : abuser de **2** MISTREAT : maltraiter **3** INSULT : injurier, insulter
abuse[2] [ə'bju:s] *n* **1** MISUSE : abus *m* **2** MISTREATMENT : abus *m*, mauvais traitement *m* **3** INSULTS : insultes *fpl*, injures *fpl*
abusive [ə'bju:sɪv] *adj* **1** IMPROPER : abusif **2** HURTFUL : injurieux, brutal **3** OFFENSIVE : grossier — **abusively** *adv*
abut [ə'bʌt] *v* **abutted; abutting** *vt* : juxtaposer — *vi* **to abut on** : être contigu à
abutment [ə'bʌtmənt] *n* : contrefort *m*, butée *f*
abysmal [ə'bɪzməl] *adj* **1** DEEP : abyssal, insondable **2** WRETCHED : épouvantable
abysmally [ə'bɪzməli] *adv* : atrocement, abominablement
abyss [ə'bɪs, 'æbɪs] *n* : abîme *m*, gouffre *m*
acacia [ə'keɪʃə] *n* : acacia *m*
academic[1] [ˌækə'demɪk] *adj* **1** SCHOLASTIC : académique, scolaire <the academic year : l'année scolaire> **2** THEORETICAL : théorique
academic[2] *n* : universitaire *mf*
academically [ˌækə'demɪkli] *adv* : sur le plan intellectuel, intellectuellement
academy [ə'kædəmi] *n, pl* **-mies 1** SCHOOL : école *f*, collège *m* **2** SOCIETY : académie *f*, société *f* <the French Academy : l'Académie française>
acanthus [ə'kænθəs] *ns & pl* : acanthe *f*
accede [æk'si:d] *vi* **-ceded; -ceding 1** : monter <to accede to the throne : monter sur le trône> **2 to accede to** : agréer, accepter <she acceded to his request : elle a agréé sa demande>
accelerate [ɪk'seləˌreɪt, æk-] *v* **-ated; -ating** : accélérer
acceleration [ɪkˌselə'reɪʃən, æk-] *n* : accélération *f*
accelerator [ɪk'seləˌreɪtər, æk-] *n* : accélérateur *m*
accent[1] ['ækˌsent, æk'sent] *vt* : accentuer
accent[2] ['ækˌsent, -sənt] *n* : accent *m* <a Russian accent : un accent russe> <to put the accent on : mettre l'accent sur>
accentuate [ɪk'sentʃuˌeɪt, æk-] *vt* **-ated; -ating** : accentuer, souligner
accept [ɪk'sept, æk-] *vt* **1** : accepter <to accept a present : accepter un cadeau> **2** ACKNOWLEDGE : accepter, admettre
acceptability [ɪkˌseptə'bɪləti, æk-] *n* : acceptabilité *f*
acceptable [ɪk'septəbəl, æk-] *adj* : acceptable
acceptably [ɪk'septəbli] *adv* : passablement, suffisamment
acceptance [ɪk'septənʌs, æk-] *n* **1** ACCEPTING : acceptation *f* **2** APPROVAL : approbation *f*
access[1] ['ækˌses] *vt* : accéder à
access[2] *n* : accès *m* <no access : accès interdit>
accessibility [ɪkˌsesə'bɪləti] *n* : accessibilité *f*
accessible [ɪk'sesəbəl, æk-] *adj* : accessible
accession [ɪk'seʃən, æk-] *n* **1** : accession *f* <accession to the throne : accession au trône> **2** INCREASE : augmentation *f* **3** ACQUISITION : acquisition *f*
accessory[1] [ɪk'sesəri, æk-] *adj* : accessoire, auxiliaire
accessory[2] *n, pl* **-ries 1** ACCOMPLICE : complice *mf* **2** ADJUNCT : accessoire *m*
accident ['æksədənt] *n* **1** MISHAP : accident *m* **2** CHANCE : hasard *m*, chance *f* <by accident : par hasard>
accidental [ˌæksə'dentəl] *adj* : accidentel, fortuit
accidentally [ˌæksə'dentəli, -'dentli] *adv* : accidentellement, par hasard
acclaim[1] [ə'kleɪm] *vt* **1** PRAISE : acclamer **2** DECLARE, PROCLAIM : proclamer
acclaim[2] *n* : acclamation *f*, louange *f*
acclamation [ˌæklə'meɪʃən] *n* : acclamation *f* <elected by acclamation : élu par acclamation>
acclimate ['ækləˌmeɪt, ə'klaɪmət] → **acclimatize**
acclimatize [ə'klaɪməˌtaɪz] *vt* **-tized; -tizing 1** : acclimater **2 to acclimatize oneself** : s'acclimater
accolade ['ækəˌleɪd, -ˌlɑd] *n* : acclamation *f*, accolade *f*
accommodate [ə'kɑməˌdeɪt] *vt* **-dated; -dating 1** ADAPT : accommoder, adapter **2** RECONCILE : concilier **3** SATISFY : satisfaire, répondre aux besoins de **4** HOLD : contenir, avoir une capacité de
accommodation [əˌkɑmə'deɪʃən] *n* **1** ADJUSTMENT : accommodation *f*, adaptation *f* **2 accomodations** *npl* LODGING : logement *m*, hébergement *m*
accompaniment [ə'kʌmpənəmənt, -'kʌm-] *n* : accompagnement *m*
accompanist [ə'kʌmpənɪst, -'kʌm-] *n* : accompagnateur *m*, -trice *f*
accompany [ə'kʌmpəni, -'kʌm-] *vt* **-nied; -nying** : accompagner
accomplice [ə'kʌmpləs, -'kʌm-] *n* : complice *mf*

accomplish [ə'kɑmplɪʃ, -'kʌm-] *vt* : accomplir, réaliser
accomplished [ə'kɑmplɪʃt, -'kʌm-] *adj* : accompli <an accomplished pianist : un pianiste accompli>
accomplishment [ə'kɑmplɪʃmənt, -'kʌm-] *n* **1** COMPLETION : réalisation *f*, accomplissement *m* **2** ACHIEVEMENT : œuvre *f* accomplie, réussite *f* **3** SKILL : talent *m*
accord[1] [ə'kɔrd] *vt* CONCEDE, GRANT : accorder, concéder — *vi* AGREE : s'accorder, concorder
accord[2] *n* **1** AGREEMENT : accord *m* **2 of one's own accord** : de son plein gré, de soi-même
accordance [ə'kɔrdənts] *n* **1** ACCORD : accord *m*, conformité *f* **2 in accordance with** : conformément à, suivant
accordingly [ə'kɔrdɪŋli] *adv* **1** CORRESPONDINGLY : en conséquence <to act accordingly : agir en conséquence> **2** CONSEQUENTLY, THEREFORE : donc, par conséquent
according to [ə'kɔrdɪŋ] *prep* **1** : conformément à, selon, suivant <according to plan : conformément au plan prévu> **2** : selon, d'après <according to them : d'après eux>
accordion [ə'kɔrdiən] *n* : accordéon *m*
accordionist [ə'kɔrdiənɪst] *n* : accordéoniste *mf*
accost [ə'kɔst] *vt* : accoster, aborder
account[1] [ə'kaʊnt] *vt* CONSIDER : estimer, juger — *vi* **1 to account for** EXPLAIN : justifier, expliquer **2 to account for** REPRESENT : représenter
account[2] *n* **1** : compte *m* <bank account : compte bancaire> **2** REPORT : compte *m* rendu, exposé *m* **3** WORTH : importance *f* <to be of little account : avoir peu d'importance> **4 on account of** BECAUSE OF : à cause de **5 on no account** : en aucun cas, sous aucun prétexte **6 on one's account** : à cause de soi, à son sujet <don't worry on my account : ne t'inquiète pas à mon sujet> **7 to take into account** : tenir compte de
accountability [əˌkaʊntə'bɪləti] *n* : responsabilité *f*
accountable [ə'kaʊntəbəl] *adj* : responsable
accountant [ə'kaʊntənt] *n* : comptable *mf*
accounting [ə'kaʊntɪŋ] *n* : comptabilité *f*
accoutrements *or* **accouterments** [ə'ku:trəmənts, -'ku:tər-] *npl* **1** EQUIPMENT : équipement *m* **2** ACCESSORIES : accessoires *mpl* **3** TRAPPINGS : attributs *mpl* (du pouvoir, etc.)
accredit [ə'krɛdət] *vt* : accréditer
accreditation [əˌkrɛdə'teɪʃən] *n* : accréditation *f*
accrual [ə'kru:əl] *n* : accumulation *f*
accrue [ə'kru:] *vi* **-crued; -cruing 1** : s'accumuler **2 to accrue to** : revenir à
accumulate [ə'kju:mjəˌleɪt] *v* **-lated; -lating** *vt* : accumuler — *vi* s'accumuler
accumulation [əˌkju:mjə'leɪʃən] *n* : accumulation *f*
accuracy ['ækjərəsi] *n, pl* **-cies** : exactitude *f*, précision *f*
accurate ['ækjərət] *adj* : exact, précis, juste — **accurately** *adv*
accusation [ˌækjə'zeɪʃən] *n* : accusation *f*
accuse [ə'kju:z] *vt* **-cused; -cusing** : accuser
accused [ə'kju:zd] *ns & pl* : accusé *m*, -sée *f*; inculpé *m*, -pée *f*
accuser [ə'kju:zər] *n* : accusateur *m*, -trice *f*
accustom [ə'kʌstəm] *vt* **1** : habituer, accoutumer **2 to get accustomed to** : s'habituer à, s'accoutumer à
accustomed [ə'kʌstəmd] *adj* **1** USED : habitué, accoutumé **2** USUAL : habituel, familier
ace ['eɪs] *n* : as *m*
acerbic [ə'sərbɪk, æ-] *adj* : acerbe
acetate ['æsəˌteɪt] *n* : acétate *m*
acetylene [ə'setələn, -ˌtəˌli:n] *n* : acétylène *m*
ache[1] [eɪk] *vi* **ached; aching 1** HURT : avoir mal, faire mal <he aches all over : il a mal partout> <my leg aches : ma jambe me fait mal> **2 to ache for** : avoir très envie de
ache[2] *n* : douleur *f*, mal *m*
achieve [ə'tʃi:v] *vt* **achieved; achieving** : accomplir, atteindre
achievement [ə'tʃi:vmənt] *n* : accomplissement *m*, réussite *f*
acid[1] ['æsəd] *adj* : acide
acid[2] *n* : acide *m*
acidic [ə'sɪdɪk, æ-] *adj* : acide
acidity [ə'sɪdəti, æ-] *n, pl* **-ties** : acidité *f*
acknowledge [ɪk'nɑlɪdʒ, æk-] *vt* **-edged; -edging 1** ADMIT : admettre, reconnaître **2** RECOGNIZE : reconnaître **3** : remercier de, manifester sa gratitude pour **4 to acknowledge receipt of** : accuser réception de
acknowledgment [ɪk'nɑlɪdʒmənt, æk-] *n* **1** RECOGNITION : reconnaissance *f* **2** THANKS : remerciement *m* **3 acknowledgment of receipt** : accusé *m* de réception
acme ['ækmi] *n* : point *m* culminant, apogée *m*
acne ['ækni] *n* : acné *f*
acorn ['eɪˌkɔrn, -kərn] *n* : gland *m*
acoustic [ə'ku:stɪk] *or* **acoustical** [ə'ku:stɪkəl] *adj* : acoustique — **acoustically** *adv*
acoustics [ə'ku:stɪks] *ns & pl* : acoustique *f*
acquaint [ə'kweɪnt] *vt* **1** INFORM : informer, aviser, renseigner **2 to be ac-**

quainted with : connaître (une personne, un lieu, etc.), être au courant de (un fait, une situation, etc.)
acquaintance [ə'kweɪntəns] *n* **1** KNOWLEDGE : connaissance *f* **2** : relation *f*, connaissance *f* <friends and acquaintances : amis et relations>
acquiesce [ˌækwi'ɛs] *vi* **-esced; -escing** : acquiescer
acquiescence [ˌækwi'ɛsənts] *n* : acquiescement *m*
acquire [ə'kwaɪr] *vt* **-quired; -quiring** : acquérir
acquisition [ˌækwə'zɪʃən] *n* : acquisition *f*
acquisitive [ə'kwɪzəṭɪv] *adj* : âpre au gain, avide
acquit [ə'kwɪt] *vt* **-quitted; -quitting 1** : acquitter <to be acquitted of a crime : être disculpé d'un délit> **2 to acquit oneself** : se conduire, s'en tirer
acquittal [ə'kwɪṭəl] *n* : acquittement *m*
acre ['eɪkər] *n* : acre *m*
acreage ['eɪkərɪdʒ] *n* : superficie *f*
acrid ['ækrəd] *adj* **1** PUNGENT : âcre **2** CAUSTIC : caustique, acerbe
acrimonious [ˌækrə'moːniəs] *adj* : acrimonieux **— acrimoniously** *adv*
acrimony ['ækrəˌmoːni] *n, pl* **-nies** : acrimonie *f*
acrobat ['ækrəˌbæt] *n* : acrobate *mf* **— acrobatic** [ˌækrə'bæṭɪk] *adj*
acrobatics [ˌækrə'bæṭɪks] *ns & pl* : acrobatie *f*
across[1] [ə'krɔs] *adv* **1** : de large <40 feet across : 40 pieds de large> **2 ~ from** : en face de **3 to get one's point across** : se faire comprendre
across[2] *prep* **1** : de l'autre côté de <the house across the street : la maison de l'autre côté de la rue> <to go across the mountain : traverser la montagne> **2** : en travers de <a tree (lying) across the stream : un arbre en travers du ruisseau>
acrylic [ə'krɪlɪk] *n* : acrylique *m*
act[1] ['ækt] *vt* PERFORM : jouer (un rôle) **—** *vi* **1** : agir <we must act quickly : il faut agir rapidement> **2** PERFORM : jouer, faire du théâtre **3** BEHAVE : agir, se comporter **4** : agir (en médecine) **5 to act as** : servir de, faire office de **6 to act on** : suivre (de l'avis, etc.)
act[2] *n* **1** DEED : action *f*, acte *m* **2** DECREE : loi *f* **3** : acte *m* <a three-act play : une pièce en trois actes> **4** PRETENSE : comédie *f* <to put on an act : jouer la comédie>
action ['ækʃən] *n* **1** ACT, DEED : action *f*, acte *m*, fait *m* **2** LAWSUIT : procès *m*, action *f* <to take legal action : poursuivre en justice> **3** COMBAT : combat *m* **4** PLOT : intrigue *f* **5** MOVEMENT : mouvement *m* **6** MECHANISM : mécanisme *m* **7 actions** *npl* CONDUCT : conduite *f*, actes *mpl*
activate ['æktəˌveɪt] *vt* **-vated; -vating** : activer
active ['æktɪv] *adj* : actif
actively ['æktɪvlɪ] *adv* : activement
activity [æk'tɪvəṭɪ] *n, pl* **-ties** : activité *f*
actor ['æktər] *n* : acteur *m*, -trice *f*; comédien *m*, -dienne *f*
actress ['æktrəs] *n* : actrice *f*, comédienne *f*
actual ['æktʃʊəl] *adj* **1** REAL : réel, véritable **2** VERY : même <the actual house where he was born : la maison même où il est né>
actuality [ˌæktʃʊ'æləṭɪ] *n, pl* **-ties** : réalité *f*
actually ['æktʃʊəli, -ʃəli] *adv* : vraiment, en fait, en réalité
actuary ['æktʃʊˌɛri] *n, pl* **-aries** : actuaire *mf*
acumen [ə'kjuːmən] *n* : perspicacité *f*, finesse *f* <business acumen : sens des affaires>
acupuncture ['ækjʊˌpʌŋktʃər] *n* : acupuncture *f*
acute [ə'kjuːt] *adj* **acuter; acutest 1** KEEN : fin <an acute sense of hearing : une ouïe fine> **2** PERCEPTIVE : perspicace, pénétrant **3** SEVERE : aigu, grave <an acute illness : une maladie grave> **4 acute accent** : accent *m* aigu **5 acute angle** : angle *m* aigu
acuteness [ə'kjuːtnəs] *n* **1** SEVERITY : violence *f* (d'une maladie) **2** : finesse *f* (d'un sens) **3** PERSPICACITY : perspicacité *f*, finesse *f*
ad ['æd] *n* **1 → advertisement 2 classified ad** *or* **want ad** : petite annonce *f*
adage ['ædɪdʒ] *n* : adage *m*
adamant ['ædəmənt, -ˌmænt] *adj* : inflexible, résolu **— adamantly** *adv*
adapt [ə'dæpt] *vt* : adapter **—** *vi* : s'adapter
adaptability [əˌdæptə'bɪləṭɪ] *n* : adaptabilité *f*
adaptable [əˌdæptəbəl] *adj* : adaptable
adaptation [ˌæˌdæp'teɪʃən, -dəp-] *n* : adaptation *f*
adapter [ə'dæptər] *n* : adapteur *m*
add ['æd] *vt* **1** : ajouter <I have nothing to add : je n'ai rien à ajouter> **2 to add up** TOTAL : additionner, totaliser **—** *vi* **1** : faire des additions **2 that doesn't add up** : cela ne s'accorde pas
adder ['ædər] *n* : vipère *f*
addict[1] [ə'dɪkt] *vt* **to be addicted to** : s'adonner à, avoir une dépendance à
addict[2] ['ædɪkt] *n* **1** DEVOTEE : fanatique *mf* **2** *or* **drug addict** : toxicomane *mf*; drogué *m*, -guée *f*
addiction [ə'dɪkʃən] *n* **1** : dépendance *f* **2 drug addiction** : toxicomanie *f*
addictive [ə'dɪktɪv] *adj* : qui crée une dépendance
addition [ə'dɪʃən] *n* **1** : ajout *m*, adjonction *f* (à une maison, une liste,

etc.) **2** : addition *f* (en mathématiques) **3 in ~** : en plus

additional [ə'dɪʃənəl] *adj* : additionnel, supplémentaire

additionally [ə'dɪʃənəli] *adv* : en plus, en outre

additive ['ædətɪv] *n* : additif *m*

addle ['ædəl] *vt* **-dled; -dling** : embrouiller

address[1] [ə'dres] *vt* **1** : adresser, mettre l'adresse sur (une lettre, etc.) **2** : s'adresser à <to address the chair : s'adresser au président> **3** TACKLE : aborder (un problème, etc.)

address[2] [ə'dres, 'æˌdres] *n* **1** : adresse *f* <change of address : changement d'adresse> **2** SPEECH : discours *m*

addressee [ˌæˌdre'si, əˌdre'si] *n* : destinataire *mf*

adduce [ə'du:s, -'dju:s] *vt* **-duced; -ducing** : citer, alléguer

adenoids ['ædˌnɔɪdz, -dənˌɔɪdz] *npl* : végétations *fpl* (adénoïdes)

adept [ə'dɛpt] *adj* : expert, adroit, habile — **adeptly** *adv*

adequate ['ædɪkwət] *adj* : adéquat, suffisant

adequately ['ædɪkwətli] *adv* : suffisamment

adhere [æd'hir, əd-] *vi* **-hered; -hering 1** STICK : adhérer, coller **2 to adhere to** : adhérer à (un conviction, etc.), observer (une règle, etc.)

adherence [æd'hɪrənts, əd-] *n* : adhésion *f*

adherent [æd'hɪrənt, əd-] *n* FOLLOWER : partisan *m*, -sane *f*; adhérent *m*, -rente *f*

adhesion [æd'hiʒən, əd-] *n* : adhésion *f*, adhérence *f*

adhesive[1] [æd'hi:sɪv, əd-, -zɪv] *adj* : adhésif

adhesive[2] *n* : adhésif *m*

adjacent [ə'dʒeɪsənt] *adj* : contigu, voisin, adjacent

adjectival [ˌædʒɪk'taɪvəl] *adj* : adjectif, adjectival

adjective ['ædʒɪktɪv] *n* : adjectif *m*

adjoin [ə'dʒɔɪn] *vt* : avoisiner, être contigu à, toucher à — *vi* : être contigu, se toucher

adjoining [ə'dʒɔɪnɪŋ] *adj* : attenant, contigu

adjourn [ə'dʒərn] *vt* SUSPEND : ajourner, lever <to adjourn the meeting : lever la séance> — *vi* **1** : suspendre la séance, lever la séance **2** : se retirer, passer <they adjourned to another room : ils sont passés dans une autre pièce>

adjournment [ə'dʒərnmənt] *n* : ajournement *m*, suspension *f*

adjudicate [ə'dʒu:dɪˌkeɪt] *vt* **-cated; -cating** : juger, décider, régler

adjunct ['æˌdʒʌŋkt] *n* **1** ASSISTANT : adjoint *m*, -jointe *f* **2** ACCESSORY : accessoire *m*

adjust [ə'dʒʌst] *vt* : régler, ajuster — *vi* ADAPT : s'adapter

adjustable [ə'dʒʌstəbəl] *adj* : réglable, ajustable

adjustment [ə'dʒʌstmənt] *n* : ajustement *m*, réglage *m*

adjutant ['ædʒətənt] *n* : adjudant *m* (dans les forces armées)

ad-lib[1] ['æd'lɪb] *vt* **ad-libbed; ad-libbing** : improviser

ad-lib[2] *adj* : improvisé, spontané

ad-lib[3] *n* : improvisation *f*

administer [æd'mɪnəstər, əd-] *vt* : administrer, diriger, gérer

administration [æd,mɪnə'streɪʃən, əd-] *n* **1** MANAGING : administration *f*, gestion *f* **2** GOVERNMENT, MANAGEMENT : gouvernement *m*, direction *f*

administrative [æd'mɪnəˌstreɪtɪv, əd-] *adj* : administratif — **administratively** *adv*

administrator [æd'mɪnəˌstreɪtər, əd-] *n* : administrateur *m*, -trice *f*

admirable ['ædmərəbəl] *adj* : admirable — **admirably** *adv*

admiral ['ædmərəl] *n* : amiral *m*

admiration [ˌædmə'reɪʃən] *n* : admiration *f*

admire [æd'maɪr] *vt* **-mired; -miring** : admirer

admirer [æd'maɪrər] *n* : admirateur *m*, -trice *f*

admiring [æd'maɪrɪŋ] *adj* : admiratif

admiringly [æd'maɪrɪŋli] *adv* : avec admiration, admirativement

admissible [æd'mɪsəbəl] *adj* : admissible

admission [æd'mɪʃən] *n* **1** ADMITTANCE : admission *f*, entrée *f*, accès *m* <no admission : accès interdit> <admission is free : l'entrée est gratuite> **2** CONFESSION : aveu *m* <by her own admission : de son propre aveu>

admit [æd'mɪt, əd-] *vt* **-mitted; -mitting 1** ACKNOWLEDGE : admettre, reconnaître, avouer <he admits his guilt : il reconnaît sa culpabilité> **2** : laisser entrer, laisser passer, admettre <to admit light : laisser entrer la lumière> <admitted to the hospital : admis à l'hôpital> <the ticket admits one : le billet est valable pour une personne>

admittance [æd'mɪtənts, əd-] *n* : entrée *f*, admission *f*, accès *m*

admittedly [æd'mɪtədli, əd-] *adv* : il faut en convenir, c'est vrai

admonish [æd'mɑnɪʃ, əd-] *vt* **1** REPRIMAND : admonester, réprimander **2** ADVISE, EXHORT : conseiller, exhorter

admonition [ˌædmə'nɪʃən] *n* **1** REPROOF : réprimande *f*, admonition *f* **2** WARNING : avertissement *m*

ado [ə'du:] *n* **1** FUSS : agitation *f* **2 without further ado** : sans plus de cérémonie

adobe [ə'do:bi] *n* : adobe *m*

adolescence [ˌædəlˈɛsənts] *n* : adolescence *f*
adolescent[1] [ˌædəlˈɛsənt] *adj* : adolescent, de l'adolescence
adolescent[2] *n* : adolescent *m*, -cente *f*
adopt [əˈdɑpt] *vt* : adopter
adoption [əˈdɑpʃən] *n* : adoption *f*
adorable [əˈdɔrəbəl] *adj* : adorable — **adorably** [-rəbli] *adv*
adoration [ˌædəˈreɪʃən] *n* : adoration *f*
adore [əˈdɔr] *vt* **adored; adoring** : adorer
adorn [əˈdɔrn] *vt* **1** DECORATE : orner, parer **2 to adorn oneself** : se parer
adornment [əˈdɔrnmənt] *n* : ornement *m*, décoration *f*
adrift [əˈdrɪft] *adv & adj* : à la dérive
adroit [əˈdrɔɪt] *adj* : adroit, habile — **adroitly** *adv*
adroitness [əˈdrɔɪtnəs] *n* : adresse *f*, habileté *f*
adult[1] [əˈdʌlt, ˈædʌlt] *adj* : adulte
adult[2] *n* : adulte *mf*
adulterate [əˈdʌltəˌreɪt] *vt* **-ated; -ating** : frelater, falsifier
adulterer [əˈdʌltərər] *n* : adultère *m*
adulteress [əˈdʌltərəs] *n* : adultère *f*
adulterous [əˈdʌltərəs] *adj* : adultère
adultery [əˈdʌltəri] *n, pl* **-teries** : adultère *m*
adulthood [əˈdʌltˌhʊd] *n* : âge *m* adulte
advance[1] [ædˈvænts, əd-] *v* **-vanced; -vancing** *vt* **1** : avancer, faire avancer <to advance the troops : avancer les troupes> **2** PROMOTE : promouvoir, servir (une cause, etc.) **3** PROPOSE : avancer (une théorie, etc.) **4** : avancer, faire une avance de (une somme d'argent) — *vi* **1** PROCEED : avancer **2** PROGRESS : progresser
advance[2] *adj* : fait à l'avance
advance[3] *n* **1** PROGRESSION : avance *f* **2** PROGRESS : progrès *m* <advances in medicine : des progrès en médecine> **3** INCREASE : hausse *f*, augmentation *f* **4 in ~** : à l'avance, d'avance **5 in advance of** : avant, en avance sur
advanced [ædˈvænst, əd-] *adj* **1** : avancé <the advanced stages : les étapes avancées> **2** SUPERIOR : supérieur, avancé <advanced technology : technologie de pointe>
advancement [ædˈvænsmənt, əd-] *n* : avancement *m*
advantage [ədˈvæntɪdʒ, æd-] *n* **1** : avantage *m* **2 to take advantage of** : profiter de
advantageous [ˌæd,vænˈteɪdʒəs, -vən-] *adj* : avantageux — **advantageously** *adv*
advent [ˈæd,vɛnt] *n* **1** : avènement *m*, venue *f*, arrivée *f* <the advent of spring : la venue du printemps> **2 Advent** : l'avent *m*
adventure [ædˈvɛntʃər, əd-] *n* : aventure *f*
adventurer [ædˈvɛntʃərər, əd-] *n* : aventurier *m*, -rière *f*
adventuresome [ædˈvɛntʃərsəm, əd-] *adj* : téméraire, aventureux
adventurous [ædˈvɛntʃərəs, əd-] *adj* **1** : aventureux <adventurous explorers : explorateurs aventureux> **2** RISKY : hasardeux, dangereux <an adventurous voyage : un voyage hasardeux>
adverb [ˈæd,vərb] *n* : adverbe *m* — **adverbial** [ædˈvərbiəl] *adj*
adversary [ˈædvərˌsɛri] *n, pl* **-saries** : adversaire *mf*
adverse [ædˈvɛrs, ˈæd,-] *adj* : adverse, défavorable <in adverse circumstances : dans l'adversité>
adversity [ædˈvərsəti, əd-] *n, pl* **-ties** : adversité *f*
advertise [ˈædvərˌtaɪz] *v* **-tised; -tising** *vt* **1** : faire de la publicité pour (un produit) **2** : mettre une annonce pour (un poste, etc.) **3** PUBLICIZE : afficher, signaler — *vi* **1** : faire de la publicité (en commerce) **2** : passer une annonce <to advertise on television : passer une annonce à la télévision>
advertisement [ˈædvərˌtaɪzmənt; ædˈvərtəzmənt] *n* **1** : publicité *f*, annonce *f* (publicitaire), réclame *f* **2 →ad**
advertiser [ˈædvərˌtaɪzɛr] *n* : annonceur *m* (publicitaire)
advertising [ˈædvərˌtaɪzɪŋ] *n* : publicité *f*, réclame *f*
advice [ædˈvaɪs] *n* **1** COUNSEL : conseils *mpl*, avis *m* **2** NOTICE : avis *m*, annonce *f*
advisability [ædˌvaɪzəˈbɪləti, əd-] *n* : opportunité *f*
advisable [ædˈvaɪzəbəl, əd-] *adj* : recommandé, prudent
advise [ædˈvaɪz, əd-] *v* **-vised; -vising** *vt* **1** COUNSEL : conseiller, donner des conseils à **2** RECOMMEND : recommander <they advised caution : ils ont recommandé la prudence> **3** INFORM : aviser — *vi* **to advise on** : conseiller sur
adviser [ædˈvaɪzər, əd-] *or* **advisor** *n* : conseiller *m*, -lère *f*
advisory [ædˈvaɪzəri, əd-] *adj* : consultatif <in an advisory capacity : à titre consultatif>
advocate[1] [ˈædvəˌkeɪt] *vt* **-cated; -cating** : recommander, préconiser
advocate[2] [ˈædvəkət] *n* **1** SUPPORTER : défenseur *m*; avocat *m*, -cate *f*; partisan *m*, -sane *f* **2** ATTORNEY : avocat *m*, -cate *f*
adze [ˈædz] *n* : herminette *f*
aegis [ˈiːdʒəs] *n* : égide *f*
aeon [ˈiːən, ˈiːˌɑn] *n* : éternité *f*
aerate [ˈæreɪt] *vt* **-ated; -ating** : aérer
aeration [ˌærˈeɪʃən] *n* : aération *f*
aerial[1] [ˈæriəl] *adj* : aérien
aerial[2] *n* : antenne *f*
aerie [ˈæri, ˈɪri, ˈeɪəri] *n* : aire *f* (d'aigle)

aerobic |ˌæˈroːbɪk| *adj* : aérobie, aérobique *Can*
aerobics |ˌæˈroːbɪks| *ns & pl* : aérobic *m*
aerodynamic |ˌæroːdaɪˈnæmɪk| *adj* : aérodynamique — **aerodynamically** *adv*
aerodynamics |ˌæroːdaɪˈnæmɪks| *ns & pl* : aérodynamique *f*
aeronautical |ˌærəˈnɔtɪkəl| *adj* : aéronautique
aeronautics |ˌærəˈnɔtɪks| *n* : aéronautique *f*
aerosol |ˈærəˌsɔl| *n* : aérosol *m*
aerospace |ˈæroˌspeɪs| *adj* : aérospatial <the aerospace industry : l'industrie aérospatiale>
aesthetic |esˈθetɪk| *adj* : esthétique — **aesthetically** |-tɪkli| *adv*
aesthetics |esˈθetɪks| *ns & pl* : esthétique *f*
afar |əˈfɑr| *adv* **1** : au loin, à distance **2 from ~** : de loin
affability |ˌæfəˈbɪləti| *n* : affabilité *f*
affable |ˈæfəbəl| *adj* : affable — **affably** *adv*
affair |əˈfær| *n* **1** : affaire *f* <their affairs are in order : leurs affaires sont réglées> <a grand affair : une affaire prestigieuse> **2** *or* **love affair** : liaison *f*, affaire *f* de cœur
affect |əˈfekt, æ-| *vt* **1** INFLUENCE : affecter, influencer **2** FEIGN : affecter, feindre **3** MOVE : émouvoir, toucher
affectation |ˌæfekˈteɪʃən| *n* : affectation *f*
affected |əˈfektəd, æ-| *adj* **1** MANNERED : affecté, maniéré **2** MOVED : ému, touché
affectedly |əˈfektədli| *adv* : avec affectation
affecting |əˈfektɪŋ, æ-| *adj* MOVING : touchant, émouvant
affection |əˈfekʃən| *n* : affection *f*
affectionate |əˈfekʃənət| *adj* : affectueux — **affectionately** *adv*
affidavit |ˌæfəˈdeɪvət, ˈæfəˌ-| *n* : déclaration *f* (écrite) sous serment
affiliate[1] |əˈfɪliˌeɪt| *vt* **-ated; -ating** : affilier
affiliate[2] |əˈfɪliət| *n* : filiale *f* (organisation); affilié *m*, -liée *f* (personne)
affiliation |əˌfɪliˈeɪʃən| *n* : affiliation *f*
affinity |əˈfɪnəti| *n, pl* **-ties** : affinité *f*
affirm |əˈfərm| *vt* : affirmer, soutenir
affirmation |ˌæfərˈmeɪʃən| *n* : affirmation *f*
affirmative[1] |əˈfərmətɪv| *adj* : affirmatif — **affirmatively** *adv*
affirmative[2] *n* **1** : affirmatif *m* (en grammaire) **2** : affirmative *f* <to answer in the affirmative : répondre par l'affirmative, répondre affirmativement>
affix |əˈfɪks| *vt* : apposer (une signature), coller (un timbre)
afflict |əˈflɪkt| *vt* **1** : affliger **2 to be afflicted with** : souffrir de, être touché de
affliction |əˈflɪkʃən| *n* : affliction *f*
affluence |ˈæˌfluːənts; æˈfluː-, ə-| *n* **1** WEALTH : richesse *f* **2** PROFUSION : abondance *f*
affluent |ˈæˌfluːənt; æˈfluː-, ə-| *adj* **1** WEALTHY : riche, aisé **2** ABUNDANT, PROFUSE : abondant
afford |əˈfɔrd| *vt* **1** : avoir les moyens de <he can't afford to buy a car : il n'a pas les moyens d'acheter une voiture> **2** PROVIDE : fournir, offrir **3** : se permettre <I can't afford to wait : je ne peux pas me permettre d'attendre>
affront[1] |əˈfrʌnt| *vt* : offenser, insulter
affront[2] *n* : affront *m*, insulte *f*
afghan |ˈæfˌgæn, -gən| *n* : couverture *f* en lainage
Afghan[1] *adj* : afghan
Afghan[2] *n* : Afghan *m*, -ghane *f*
afire[1] |əˈfaɪr| *adv* **1** : en feu **2 to set afire** : mettre le feu à, embraser
afire[2] *adj* : en feu, embrasé
aflame |əˈfleɪm| *adj & adv* : en flammes
afloat |əˈfloːt| *adj & adv* : à flot
afoot |əˈfʊt| *adv & adj* **1** WALKING : à pied **2** UNDER WAY : en train
aforesaid |əˈfɔrˌsɛd| *adj* : susmentionné
afraid |əˈfreɪd| *adj* **1 to be afraid of** FEAR : avoir peur de, craindre <he's afraid of falling : il a peur de tomber> **2** (*indicating regret*) <I'm afraid I can't come : je regrette de ne pas pouvoir venir> <I'm afraid not : hélas, non>
afresh |əˈfrɛʃ| *adv* **1** ANEW : de nouveau **2 to start afresh** : recommencer
African[1] |ˈæfrɪkən| *adj* : africain
African[2] *n* : Africain *m*, -caine *f*
aft |ˈæft| **adv** : l'arrière
after[1] |ˈæftər| *adv* **1** AFTERWARD : après, ensuite **2** BEHIND : en arrière
after[2] *adj* (*indicating a later time*) <in after years : plus tard dans la vie>
after[3] *conj* : après que <after he leaves : après qu'il part>
after[4] *prep* **1** FOLLOWING : après <after lunch : après le déjeuner> <day after day : tous les jours> <after four o'clock : après quatre heures> **2** BEHIND : derrière, après <close the door after me : fermez la porte derrière moi> **3** (*indicating pursuit*) <he was running after the cat : il courait après le chat> <the police are after me : je suis recherché par la police> **4 after all** : après tout
aftereffect |ˈæftərɪˌfɛkt| *n* : répercussion *f*, séquelle *f* (en médecine)
afterlife |ˈæftərˌlaɪf| *n* : vie *f* future, vie *f* après la mort
aftermath |ˈæftərˌmæθ| *n* CONSEQUENCES : suites *fpl*

afternoon [ˌæftərˈnuːn] *n* : après-midi *mf*
afterthought ['æftərˌθɔt] *n* : pensée *f* après coup
afterward ['æftərwərd] *or* **afterwards** [-wərdz] *adv* : après, ensuite <soon afterward : peu après>
again [əˈgɛn, -gɪn] *adv* **1** : encore (une fois), de nouveau <say it again : dites-le encore> <again and again : maintes et maintes fois> **2** BESIDES : en plus, d'ailleurs **3 then again** : d'autre part
against [əˈgɛnʃt, -ˈgɪnʃt] *prep* **1** : contre <against the wall : contre le mur> <a war against drugs : une guerre contre les drogues> **2** : sur <red flowers against the blue sky : des fleurs rouges sur un ciel bleu> **3 to go against** : aller à l'encontre
agape [əˈgeɪp] *adj* : bouche bée
agate ['ægət] *n* : agate *f*
age[1] ['eɪdʒ] *v* : vieillir
age[2] *n* **1** : âge *m* <what age is she? : quel âge a-t-elle?> <she's 16 years of age : elle a 16 ans> **2** ERA : ère *f*, époque *f* **3 for ages** : depuis longtemps **4 to come of age** : atteindre la majorité **5 old age** : vieillesse *f*
aged ['eɪdʒəd, 'eɪdʒd] *adj* **1** : âgé de <a man aged 40 years : un homme âgé de 40 ans> **2** : âgé, vieux (se dit du vin, du fromage, etc.) **3** ['eɪdʒd] OLD : vieux, âgé <my aged mother : ma vieille mère>
ageless ['eɪdʒləs] *adj* **1** : sans âge, toujours jeune **2** TIMELESS : éternel
agency ['eɪdʒənʃɪ] *n, pl* **-cies 1** : agence *f*, bureau *m* <travel agency : agence de voyages> **2 through the agency of** : par l'entremise de
agenda [əˈdʒɛndə] *n* : ordre *m* du jour, programme *m*
agent ['eɪdʒənt] *n* : agent *m*
aggravate ['ægrəˌveɪt] *vt* **-vated; -vating 1** WORSEN : aggraver, empirer **2** IRRITATE : agacer, énerver
aggravation [ˌægrəˈveɪʃən] *n* **1** WORSENING : aggravation *f* **2** IRRITATION : agacement *m*, irritation *f*
aggregate[1] ['ægrɪˌgeɪt] *vt* **-gated; -gating** : agréger, rassembler — *vi* : s'agréger
aggregate[2] ['ægrɪgət] *adj* : total, global
aggregate[3] ['ægrɪgət] *n* **1** TOTAL : ensemble *m*, total *m* **2** MASS : agrégat *m* (en géologie, etc.)
aggression [əˈgrɛʃən] *n* : agression *f*
aggressive [əˈgrɛsɪv] *adj* : agressif — **aggressively** *adv*
aggressiveness [əˈgrɛsɪvnəs] *n* : agressivité *f*
aggressor [əˈgrɛsər] *n* : agresseur *m*
aggrieved [əˈgriːvd] *adj* **1** DISTRESSED : affligé, peiné **2 the aggrieved party** : la partie lésée
aghast [əˈgæst] *adj* : horrifié, atterré
agile ['ædʒəl] *adj* : agile, leste
agility [əˈdʒɪləṭi] *n, pl* **-ties** : agilité *f*
agitate ['ædʒəˌteɪt] *v* **-tated; -tating** *vt* **1** SHAKE : agiter, secouer **2** TROUBLE : agiter, troubler — *vi* **to agitate against** : faire campagne contre
agitation [ˌædʒəˈteɪʃən] *n* : agitation *f*
agnostic[1] [ˈægˈnɑstɪk] *adj* : agnostique
agnostic[2] *n* : agnostique *mf*
ago [əˈgoː] *adv* : il y a <a week ago : il y a une semaine> <not long ago : il y a peu de temps>
agog [əˈgɑg] *adj* : en émoi
agonize [ˈægəˌnaɪz] *vi* **-nized; -nizing** : se tourmenter
agonizing ['ægəˌnaɪzɪŋ] *adj* PAINFUL : douloureux, déchirant
agony ['ægəni] *n, pl* **-nies 1** : angoisse *f*, douleur *f* atroce **2 death agony** : agonie *f*
agrarian [əˈgrɛriən] *adj* : agraire
agree [əˈgriː] *v* **agreed; agreeing** *vt* **1** ACKNOWLEDGE, ADMIT : convenir, reconnaître <I agree that you should go : je reconnais que vous devriez y aller> **2** CONSENT : accepter, consentir — *vi* **1** CONCUR : être d'accord **2** CONSENT : consentir **3** CORRESPOND, TALLY : correspondre, concorder **4 to agree with** : réussir à, convenir (bien) à <spicy food doesn't agree with me : la nourriture épicée ne me réussit pas>
agreeable [əˈgriːəbəl] *adj* **1** PLEASING : agréable **2** WILLING : consentant <to be agreeable to : être d'accord pour> **3** ACCEPTABLE : acceptable, satisfaisant
agreeably [əˈgriːəbli] *adv* : agréablement
agreement [əˈgriːmənt] *n* : accord *m* <to be in agreement : être d'accord> <international agreement : accord international>
agricultural [ˌægrɪˈkʌlṭʃərəl] *adj* : agricole
agriculture ['ægrɪˌkʌlṭʃər] *n* : agriculture *f*
aground[1] [əˈgraʊnd] *adv* **to run aground** : s'échouer
aground[2] *adj* : échoué
ahead [əˈhɛd] *adv* **1** FORWARD : en avant, devant <he walked ahead : il marchait en avant> **2** BEFOREHAND : à l'avance **3** LEADING : de tête, en avance **4 go ahead!** : allez-y! **5 to get ahead** : prendre de l'avance
ahead of *prep* **1** : devant, d'avance sur <go ahead of me : mettez-vous devant moi> **2** : avant, en avance sur <to be ahead of one's time : être en avance sur son temps>
ahoy [əˈhɔɪ] *interj* **ship ahoy!** : ohé du navire!
aid[1] ['eɪd] *vt* **1** HELP : aider **2 to aid and abet** : être complice de
aid[2] *n* **1** HELP : aide *f*, secours *m* **2** ASSISTANT : aide *mf*; assistant *m*, -tante *f* **3** DEVICE : appareil *m* <hearing aid : appareil auditif>

aide [ˈeɪd] *n* : aide *mf;* assistant *m,* -tante *f*
AIDS [ˈeɪdz] *n* : sida *m,* SIDA *m*
ail [ˈeɪl] *vt* TROUBLE : affliger <what ails you? : qu'avez-vous?> — *vi* : être souffrant
aileron [ˈeɪləˌrɑn] *n* : aileron *m*
ailment [ˈeɪlmənt] *n* : maladie *f,* affection *f*
aim[1] [ˈeɪm] *vt* **1** : braquer (une arme à feu), diriger (une remarque, etc.) **2** INTEND : avoir l'intention de — *vi* **to aim at** *or* **to aim for** : viser
aim[2] *n* **1** GOAL : but *m,* objectif *m* **2 to take aim at** : viser
aimless [ˈeɪmləs] *adj* : sans but, sans objet
aimlessly [ˈeɪmləsli] *adv* : sans but
air[1] [ˈær] *vt* **1** VENTILATE : aérer, ventiler **2** EXPRESS : exprimer, faire connaître **3** BROADCAST : diffuser
air[2] *n* **1** : air *m* **2** MELODY : air *m* **3** APPEARANCE : air *m,* aspect *m* <an air of mystery : un air mystérieux> **4 to be on the air** : être à l'antenne **5 to go by air** : voyager par avion **6 to put on airs** : se donner de grands airs
airborne [ˈærˌborn] *adj* **1** : aéroporté (se dit des troupes, etc.) **2 to become airborne** : décoller
air–conditioned [ˌærkənˈdɪʃənd] *adj* : climatisé
air conditioner [ˌærkənˈdɪʃənər] *n* : climatiseur *m*
air–conditioning [ˌærkənˈdɪʃəniŋ] *n* : climatisation *f*
aircraft [ˈærˌkræft] *ns & pl* : avion *m,* aéronef *m*
aircraft carrier *n* : porte-avions *m*
airfield [ˈærˌfiːld] *n* : aérodrome *m,* terrain *m* d'aviation
air force *n* : armée *f* de l'air
airlift [ˈærˌlɪft] *n* : pont *m* aérien
airline [ˈærˌlaɪn] *n* : ligne *f* (aérienne), compagnie *f* d'aviation
airliner [ˈærˌlaɪnər] *n* : avion *m* de ligne
airmail [ˈærˌmeɪl] *n* **1** : poste *f* aérienne **2 by ~** : par avion
airman [ˈærmən] *n, pl* **-men** [-mən, -ˌmɛn] **1** AVIATOR : aviateur *m* **2** : soldat *m* de l'armée de l'air
airplane [ˈærˌpleɪn] *n* : avion *m*
airport [ˈærˌpɔrt] *n* : aéroport *m*
airship [ˈærˌʃɪp] *n* : dirigeable *m*
airstrip [ˈærˌstrɪp] *n* : piste *f* (d'atterrissage)
airtight [ˈærˈtaɪt] *adj* : hermétique, étanche (à l'air)
airwaves [ˈærˌweɪvz] *npl* : ondes *fpl*
airy [ˈæri] *adj* **airier; -est 1** VENTILATED : aéré **2** DELICATE, LIGHT : léger **3** LOFTY : en l'air
aisle [ˈaɪl] *n* : nef *f* latérale (d'une église), allée *f* (d'un théâtre ou d'un magasin), couloir *m* (d'un avion, d'un train, etc.)
ajar [əˈdʒɑr] *adj & adv* : entrouvert
akimbo [əˈkɪmbo] *adj & adv* **with arms akimbo** : les poings sur les hanches
akin [əˈkɪn] *adj* **1** RELATED : apparenté **2 ~ to** : semblable à, qui ressemble à
alabaster [ˈæləˌbæstər] *n* : albâtre *m*
alacrity [əˈlækrəti] *n* : empressement *m*
alarm[1] [əˈlɑrm] *vt* **1** WARN : alerter **2** FRIGHTEN : alarmer, faire peur à
alarm[2] *n* **1** WARNING : alarme *f,* alerte *f* **2** FEAR : inquiétude *f,* alarme *f*
alarm clock *n* : réveil *m,* réveille-matin *m,* cadran *m Can fam*
alas [əˈlæs] *interj* : hélas!
Albanian[1] [ælˈbeɪniən] *adj* : albanais
Albanian[2] *n* **1** : Albanais *m,* -naise *f*
albatross [ˈælbəˌtrɔs] *n, pl* **-tross** *or* **-trosses** : albatros *m*
albeit [ɔlˈbiːət, æl-] *conj* : bien que, quoique
albino [ælˈbaɪno] *n, pl* **-nos** : albinos *mf*
album [ˈælbəm] *n* : album *m*
albumen [ælˈbjuːmən] *n* **1** : albumen *m,* blanc *m* d'œuf **2** → **albumin**
albumin [ælˈbjuːmən] *n* : albumine *f*
alchemy [ˈælkəmi] *n* : alchimie *f*
alcohol [ˈælkəˌhɔl] *n* **1** : alcool *m* **2** DRINK : boisson *f* alcoolisée, verre *m*
alcoholic[1] [ˌælkəˈhɔlɪk] *adj* : alcoolisé, alcoolique
alcoholic[2] *n* : alcoolique *mf*
alcoholism [ˈælkəhɔˌlɪzəm] *n* : alcoolisme *m*
alcove [ˈælˌkoːv] *n* **1** : alcôve *f* (d'une salle) **2** RECESS : renfoncement *m,* niche *f*
alderman [ˈɔldərmən] *n, pl* **-men** [-mən, -ˌmɛn] : conseiller *m* municipal, conseillère *f* municipale
ale [ˈeɪl] *n* : bière *f*
alert[1] [əˈlɜrt] *vt* : alerter, donner l'alerte à
alert[2] *adj* **1** WATCHFUL : vigilant **2** LIVELY : alerte, vif, éveillé
alert[3] *n* : alerte *f* <on the alert : en état d'alerte>
alertness [əˈlɜrtnəs] *n* **1** VIGILANCE : vigilance *f* **2** LIVELINESS : vivacité *f*
alfalfa [ælˈfælfə] *n* : luzerne *f*
alga [ˈælgə] *n, pl* **-gae** [ˈælˌdʒiː] : algue *f*
algebra [ˈældʒəbrə] *n* : algèbre *f*
algebraic [ˌældʒəˈbreɪɪk] *adj* : algébrique — **algebraically** *adv*
Algerian[1] [ælˈdʒɪriən] *adj* : algérien
Algerian[2] *n* : Algérien *m,* -rienne *f*
alias[1] [ˈeɪliəs] *adv* : alias
alias[2] *n* : nom *m* d'emprunt, faux nom *m*
alibi [ˈæləˌbaɪ] *n* : alibi *m*
alien[1] [ˈeɪliən] *adj* **1** FOREIGN : étranger **2** EXTRATERRESTRIAL : extraterrestre
alien[2] *n* **1** FOREIGNER : étranger *m,* -gère *f* **2** EXTRATERRESTRIAL : extraterrestre *mf*
alienate [ˈeɪliəˌneɪt] *vt* **-ated; -ating** : aliéner
alienation [ˌeɪliəˈneɪʃən] *n* : aliénation *f*

alight [ə'laɪt] *vi* **1** : descendre (se dit des personnes), se poser (se dit des oiseaux)
align [ə'laɪn] *vt* : aligner
alignment [ə'laɪnmənt] *n* **1** : alignement *m* <to be out of alignment : être désaligné> **2** *or* **wheel alignment** : parallélisme *m* des roues
alike[1] [ə'laɪk] *adv* : de la même façon
alike[2] *adj* **1** : semblable, pareil **2 to be alike** : se ressembler
alimentary [ˌælə'mentəri] *adj* **1** : alimentaire **2 alimentary canal** : tube *m* digestif
alimony ['ælˌmoːni] *n, pl* **-nies** : pension *f* alimentaire
alive [ə'laɪv] *adj* **1** LIVING : vivant, en vie **2** LIVELY : vif, animé **3** AWARE : conscient, sensible <they are alive to the danger : ils sont conscients du danger>
alkali ['ælkəlaɪ] *n, pl* **-lies** *or* **-lis** : alcali *m*
alkaline ['ælkələn, -ˌlaɪn] *adj* : alcalin
all[1] ['ɔl] *adv* **1** COMPLETELY : tout, complètement <all alone : tout seul> **2** : partout <the score is six all : le score est de six partout> **3 all at once** : tout d'un coup **4 all the better** : tant mieux
all[2] *adj* : tout <in all probability : en toute probabilité> <all those people : tous ces gens>
all[3] *pron* **1** EVERYTHING : tout <is that all? : c'est tout?> **2** EVERYONE : tous, toutes <all have left the premises : tous sont partis des lieux> <they've all left : elles sont toutes parties> **3 all in all** : tout compte fait
Allah ['ɑlɑ, ɑ'lɑ] *n* : Allah *m*
all-around [ˌɔlə'raʊnd] *adj* **1** GENERAL : général **2** VERSATILE : complet, polyvalent <an all-around athlete : un athlète polyvalent>
allay [ə'leɪ] *vt* : soulager, apaiser
allegation [ˌælɪ'geɪʃən] *n* : allégation *f*
allege [ə'ledʒ] *vt* **-leged; -leging** : alléguer, prétendre
alleged [ə'ledʒd, ə'ledʒəd] *adj* : présumé, prétendu, allégué
allegedly [ə'ledʒədli] *adv* : prétendument
allegiance [ə'liːdʒənts] *n* : allégeance *f*
allegorical [ˌælə'gɔrɪkəl] *adj* : allégorique
allegory ['æləˌgori] *n, pl* **-ries** : allégorie *f*
alleluia [ˌɑlə'luːjə, ˌæ-] → **hallelujah**
allergic [ə'lərdʒɪk] *adj* : allergique
allergy ['ælərdʒi] *n, pl* **-gies** : allergie *f*
alleviate [ə'liːviˌeɪt] *vt* **-ated; -ating** : soulager, alléger, apaiser
alleviation [əˌliːvi'eɪʃən] *n* : soulagement *m*, allègement *m*
alley ['æli] *n, pl* **-leys 1** : ruelle *f*, allée *f* (dans un jardin, etc.) **2 bowling alley** : bowling *m*
alliance [ə'laɪənts] *n* : alliance *f*
alligator ['æləˌgeɪtər] *n* : alligator *m*
alliteration [əˌlɪtə'reɪʃən] *n* : allitération *f*
allocate ['æləˌkeɪt] *vt* **-cated; -cating** : allouer, assigner
allocation ['æləˌkeɪʃən] *n* : allocation *f*, affectation *f*
allot [ə'lɑt] *vt* **allotted; allotting 1** ASSIGN : attribuer, assigner **2** DISTRIBUTE : répartir, distribuer
allotment [ə'lɑtmənt] *n* : répartition *f*, allocation *f*
allow [ə'laʊ] *vt* **1** PERMIT : permettre **2** CONCEDE : admettre, reconnaître **3** GRANT : accorder, allouer — *vi* **to allow for** : tenir compte de
allowable [ə'laʊəbəl] *adj* **1** PERMISSIBLE : permis, admissible **2** DEDUCTIBLE : déductible
allowance [ə'laʊənts] *n* **1** : allocation *f* (pour les dépenses), argent *m* de poche (pour les enfants) **2 to make allowances for** : tenir compte de
alloy ['æˌlɔɪ] *n* : alliage *m*
all right[1] *adv* **1** YES : d'accord **2** WELL : bien <she's doing all right : elle va bien> **3** CERTAINLY : bien, sans doute <it's hot all right : il fait bien chaud>
all right[2] *adj* : pas mal, bien <I'm all right, thanks : je vais bien, merci>
all-round [ˌɔl'raʊnd] → **all-around**
allspice ['ɔlˌspaɪs] *n* : piment *m* de la Jamaïque
allude [ə'luːd] *vi* **-luded; -luding** : faire allusion (à)
allure[1] [ə'lʊr] *vt* **-lured; -luring** : séduire, attirer
allure[2] *n* : attrait *m*, charme *m*
allusion [ə'luːʒən] *n* : allusion *f*
ally[1] [ə'laɪ, 'æˌlaɪ] *vt* **-lied; -lying 1** : allier **2 to ally oneself with** : s'allier avec
ally[2] ['æˌlaɪ, ə'laɪ] *n, pl* **allies** : allié *m*, -liée *f*
almanac ['ɔlməˌnæk, 'æl-] *n* : almanach *m*
almighty [ɔl'maɪti] *adj* : tout puissant, formidable
almond ['ɑmənd, 'ɑl-, 'æ-, 'æl-] *n* : amande *f*
almost ['ɔlˌmoːst, ɔl'moːst] *adv* : presque <almost everyone : presque tout le monde> <she almost died : elle a failli mourir>
alms ['ɑmz, 'ɑlmz, 'ælmz] *ns & pl* : aumône *f*
aloft [ə'lɔft] *adv* : en haut, en l'air
alone[1] [ə'loːn] *adv* **1** : seul <il travaille seul : he works alone> <she alone can do it : elle seule peut le faire> **2 to leave alone** : laisser tranquille, laisser en paix
alone[2] *adj* : seul <I'm all alone : je suis tout seul>
along[1] [ə'lɔŋ] *adv* **1** FORWARD : en avant <to step along : faire un pas en avant, avancer> <further along : plus avancé> **2** (*often not translated*) <to

bring along : apporter> <to run along : courir> <to pull along : tirer avec soi> **3 ~ with** : avec, accompagné de

along[2] *prep* **1** : le long de <along the coast : le long de la côte> **2** ON : sur <along the way : sur le chemin>

alongside[1] [ə,lɔŋ'saɪd] *adv* **1** : à côté **2 to come alongside** : accoster

alongside[2] *or* **alongside of** *prep* BESIDE : à côté de

aloof [ə'lu:f] *adj* : distant <to stand aloof from : se tenir à l'écart de>

aloofness [ə'lu:fnəs] *n* : réserve *f*

aloud [ə'laʊd] *adv* : à haute voix

alpaca [æl'pækə] *n* : alpaga *m*

alphabet ['ælfə,bet] *n* : alphabet *m*

alphabetic [,ælfə'betɪk] *or* **alphabetical** [-tɪkəl] *adj* : alphabétique — **alphabetically** [-tɪkli] *adv*

alphabetize ['ælfəbə,taɪz] *vt* **-ized; -izing** : alphabétiser, classer par ordre alphabétique

already [ɔl'redi] *adv* : déjà

also ['ɔl,so:] *adv* **1** TOO : aussi, également **2** FURTHERMORE : de plus, en outre

altar ['ɔltər] *n* : autel *m*

alter ['ɔltər] *vt* **1** CHANGE : changer, modifier **2** : retoucher (un vêtement)

alteration [,ɔltə'reɪʃən] *n* **1** : changement *m*, modification *f* **2 alterations** *npl* : retouches *fpl*

altercation [,ɔltər'keɪʃən] *n* : altercation *f*

alternate[1] ['ɔltər,neɪt] *v* **-nated; -nating** *vt* : faire alterner — *vi* : alterner, se relayer

alternate[2] ['ɔltərnət] *adj* : alternatif — **alternately** *adv*

alternate[3] ['ɔltərnət] *n* : remplaçant *m*, -çante *f*

alternating current ['ɔltər,neɪtɪŋ] *n* : courant *m* alternatif

alternation [,ɔltər'neɪʃən] *n* : alternance *f*

alternative[1] [ɔl'tərnəṭɪv] *adj* : alternatif

alternative[2] *n* **1** : alternative *f* **2 to have no alternative** : ne pas avoir le choix

alternator ['ɔltər,neɪṭər] *n* : alternateur *m*

although [ɔl'ðo:] *conj* : bien que, quoique

altitude ['ælṭə,tu:d, -,tju:d] *n* : altitude *f*

alto ['æl,to:] *n, pl* **-tos** : contralto *m* (voix), alto *m* (instrument)

altogether [,ɔltə'geðər] *adv* **1** COMPLETELY : complètement, tout à fait **2** ON THE WHOLE : dans l'ensemble **3** : en tout <how much altogether? : combien en tout?>

altruism ['æltru,ɪzəm] *n* : altruisme *m*

altruist ['æltruɪst] *n* : altruiste *mf*

altruistic [,æltru'ɪstɪk] *adj* : altruiste

alum ['æləm] *n* : alun *m*

aluminum [ə'lu:mənəm] *n* : aluminium *m*

alumna [ə'lʌmnə] *n, pl* **-nae** [-,ni:] : ancienne élève *f*

alumnus [ə'lʌmnəs] *n, pl* **-ni** [-,naɪ] : ancien élève *m*

always ['ɔlwiz, -,weɪz] *adv* **1** INVARIABLY : toujours **2** FOREVER : pour toujours

am → **be**

amalgam [ə'mælgəm] *n* : amalgame *m*

amalgamate [ə'mælgə,meɪt] *v* **-ated; -ating** *vt* : amalgamer, fusionner — *vi* : s'amalgamer, fusionner

amalgamation [ə'mælgə,meɪʃən] *n* : fusion *f*, amalgamation *f*

amaryllis [,æmə'rɪləs] *n* : amaryllis *f*

amass [ə'mæs] *vt* : amasser, accumuler

amateur[1] ['æmətʃər, -tər, -,tʊr, -,tjʊr] *adj* : amateur

amateur[2] *n* : amateur *m*

amateurish ['æmə,tʃərɪʃ, -,tər-, -,tʊr-, -,tjʊr-] *adj* : d'amateur

amaze [ə'meɪz] *vt* **amazed; amazing** : étonner, stupéfier

amazement [ə'meɪzmənt] *n* : stupéfaction *f*, étonnement *m*

amazing [ə'meɪzɪŋ] *adj* : étonnant, stupéfiant

amazingly [ə'meɪzɪŋli] *adv* : étonnamment, incroyablement

ambassador [æm'bæsə,dər] *n* : ambassadeur *m*, -drice *f*

amber ['æmbər] *n* : ambre *m*

ambergris ['æmbər,gris, -gri:s] *n* : ambre *m* gris

ambidextrous [,æmbɪ'dekstrəs] *adj* : ambidextre

ambience *or* **ambiance** ['æmbiənts, 'ɑmbi,ɑnts] *n* : ambiance *f*

ambiguity [,æmbə'gju:əṭi] *n, pl* **-ties** : ambiguïté *f*

ambiguous [æm'bɪgjʊəs] *adj* : ambigu

ambition [æm'bɪʃən] *n* : ambition *f*

ambitious [æm'bɪʃəs] *adj* : ambitieux — **ambitiously** *adv*

ambivalence [æm'bɪvələnts] *n* : ambivalence *f*

ambivalent [æm'bɪvələnt] *adj* : ambivalent

amble[1] ['æmbəl] *vi* **-bled; -bling** : marcher d'un pas tranquille, aller l'amble (se dit d'un cheval)

amble[2] *n* : pas *m* tranquille, amble *m* (de cheval)

ambulance ['æmbjələnts] *n* : ambulance *f*

ambulatory ['æmbjələ,to:ri] *adj* : ambulatoire

ambush[1] ['æmbʊʃ] *vt* **1** : tendre une embuscade à **2** WAYLAY : attirer dans une embuscade

ambush[2] *n* : embuscade *f*

ameba, amebic → **amoeba, amoebic**

ameliorate [ə'mi:ljə,reɪt] *v* **-rated; -rating** *vt* : améliorer — *vi* : s'améliorer

amelioration [ə,mi:ljə'reɪʃən] *n* : amélioration *f*

amen ['eɪ'men, 'ɑ-] *interj* : amen, ainsi soit-il

amenable [əˈmiːnəbəl, -ˈmɛ-] *adj* : accommodant <to be amenable to : être disposé à>
amend [əˈmɛnd] *vt* : amender
amendment [əˈmɛndmənt] *n* : amendement *m*
amends [əˈmɛndz] *ns & pl* **1 to make amends** : se racheter, réparer ses torts **2 to make amends for** : dédommager de, réparer
amenity [əˈmɛnəti, -ˈmiː-] *n, pl* **-ties 1** PLEASANTNESS : agrément *m* **2 amenities** *npl* : équipements *mpl*, aménagements *mpl*
American[1] [əˈmɛrɪkən] *adj* : américain
American[2] *n* : Américain *m*, -caine *f*
American Indian *n* : indien *m*, -dienne *f* d'Amérique
amethyst [ˈæməθəst] *n* : améthyste *f*
amiability [ˌeɪmiːəˈbɪləti] *n* : amabilité *f*
amiable [ˈeɪmiːəbəl] *adj* : aimable — **amiably** *adv*
amicable [ˈæmɪkəbəl] *adj* : amical — **amicably** *adv*
amid [əˈmɪd] *or* **amidst** [əˈmɪdst] *prep* : au milieu de, parmi
amino acid [əˈmiːno] *n* : acide *m* aminé
amiss[1] [əˈmɪs] *adv* **1** WRONGLY : incorrectement, mal **2 to take sth amiss** : prendre qqch de travers
amiss[2] *adj* **1** WRONG : incorrect, mal à propos **2 something is amiss** : quelque chose ne va pas
ammeter [ˈæˌmiːtər] *n* : ampèremètre *m*
ammonia [əˈmoːnjə] *n* **1** : ammoniac *m* (gaz) **2** : ammoniaque *f* (liquide)
ammunition [ˌæmjəˈnɪʃən] *n* : munitions *fpl*
amnesia [æmˈniːʒə] *n* : amnésie *f*
amnesiac[1] [æmˈniːʒiˌæk, -zi-] *or* **amnesic** [æmˈniːʒɪk, -sɪk] *adj* : amnésique
amnesiac[2] *or* **amnesic** *n* : amnésique *mf*
amnesty [ˈæmnəsti] *n, pl* **-ties** : amnistie *f*
amoeba [əˈmiːbə] *n, pl* **-bas** *or* **-bae** [-biː] : amibe *f*
amoebic [əˈmiːbɪk] *adj* : amibien
amok [əˈmʌk, -ˈmɑk] *adv* **to run amok** : être pris d'un accès de folie furieuse
among [eˈmʌŋ] *prep* : parmi, entre <among others : entre autres> <among young people : chez les jeunes>
amoral [eɪˈmɔrəl] *adj* : amoral
amorous [ˈæmərəs] *adj* : amoureux — **amorously** *adv*
amorphous [əˈmɔrfəs] *adj* : informe, amorphe (en science)
amortize [ˈæmərˌtaɪz, əˈmɔr-] *vt* **-tized; -tizing** : amortir
amount[1] [əˈmaʊnt] *vi* **to amount to 1** TOTAL : se monter à, s'élever à **2** : équivaloir à, revenir à <that amounts to the same thing : cela revient au même>
amount[2] *n* **1** QUANTITY : quantité *f* **2** SUM : somme *f*, montant *m*
ampere [ˈæmˌpɪr] *n* : ampère *m*
ampersand [ˈæmpərˌsænd] *n* : esperluette *f*
amphibian [æmˈfɪbiən] *n* : amphibien *m*
amphibious [æmˈfɪbiəs] *adj* : amphibie
amphitheater [ˈæmfəˌθiːəʧər] *n* : amphithéâtre *m*
ample [ˈæmpəl] *adj* **-pler; -plest 1** LARGE, SPACIOUS : ample, grand, vaste **2** PLENTIFUL : largement suffisant, abondant
amplification [ˌæmpləfəˈkeɪʃən] *n* : amplification *f*
amplifier [ˈæmpləˌfaɪər] *n* : amplificateur *m*
amplify [ˈæmpləˌfaɪ] *vt* **-fied; -fying** : amplifier
amply [ˈæmpli] *adv* : largement, amplement
amputate [ˈæmpjəˌteɪt] *v* **-tated; -tating** : amputer
amputation [ˌæmpjəˈteɪʃən] *n* : amputation *f*
amuck [əˈmʌk] → **amok**
amulet [ˈæmjələt] *n* : amulette *f*
amuse [əˈmjuːz] *vt* **amused; amusing 1** ENTERTAIN : distraire, divertir **2** : amuser, faire rire <the joke amused me : la plaisanterie m'a fait rire>
amusement [əˈmjuːzmənt] *n* **1** ENTERTAINMENT : distraction *f*, divertissement *m* **2** ENJOYMENT, MIRTH : amusement *m*
an → **a**[2]
anachronism [əˈnækrəˌnɪzəm] *n* : anachronisme *m*
anachronistic [əˌnækrəˈnɪstɪk] *adj* : anachronique
anaconda [ˌænəˈkɑndə] *n* : anaconda *m*
anagram [ˈænəˌgræm] *n* : anagramme *f*
anal [ˈeɪnəl] *adj* : anal
analgesic[1] [ˌænəlˈdʒiːzɪk, -sɪk] *adj* : analgésique
analgesic[2] *n* : analgésique *m*
analog [ˈænəˌlɔg, -ˌlɑg] *adj* : analogique
analogous [əˈnæləgəs] *adj* : analogue
analogy [əˈnælədʒi] *n, pl* **-gies** : analogie *f*
analyse *Brit* → **analyze**
analysis [əˈnæləsəs] *n, pl* **-yses** [-ˌsiːz] **1** : analyse *f* **2** → **psychoanalysis**
analyst [ˈænəlɪst] *n* **1** : analyste *mf* **2** → **psychoanalyst**
analytic [ˌænəˈlɪtɪk] *or* **analytical** [-ʧɪkəl] *adj* : analytique — **analytically** [-ʧɪkli] *adv*
analyze *or Brit* **analyse** [ˈænəˌlaɪz] *vt* **-lyzed** *or Brit* **-lysed; -lyzing** *or Brit* **-lysing** : analyser
anarchist [ˈænərkɪst, -ˌnɑr-] *n* : anarchiste *mf*
anarchy [ˈænərki, -ˌnɑr-] *n* : anarchie *f*
anathema [əˈnæθəmə] *n* : anathème *m*
anatomic [ˌænəˈtɑmɪk] *or* **anatomical** [-mɪkəl] *adj* : anatomique — **anatomically** [-mɪkli] *adv*

anatomy [ə'nætəmi] *n, pl* **-mies** : anatomie *f*
ancestor ['æn,sestər] *n* : ancêtre *mf*
ancestral [æn'sestrəl] *adj* : ancestral
ancestry ['æn,sestri] *n* **1** LINEAGE : ascendance *f* **2** ANCESTORS : ancêtres *mpl*
anchor[1] ['æŋkər] *vt* **1** MOOR : ancrer, mettre à l'ancre **2** SECURE : fixer, ancrer **3** : présenter (un programme de télévision) — *vi* : jeter l'ancre, mouiller l'ancre
anchor[2] *n* **1** : ancre *f* **2** : présentateur *m*, -trice *f* (à la télévision)
anchorage ['æŋkərɪdʒ] *n* : mouillage *m*
anchovy ['æn,tʃo:vi, æn'tʃo:-] *n, pl* **-vies** *or* **-vy** : anchois *m*
ancient ['eɪnʃənt] *adj* **1** : ancien <ancient history : histoire ancienne> **2** OLD : très vieux
ancients ['eɪnʃənts] *npl* : les anciens
and ['ænd] *conj* **1** : et **2** (*used with numbers*) <three hundred and two : trois cent deux> **3** (*used between two verbs*) <come and see : venez voir> **4** (*used between two adjectives*) <better and better : de mieux en mieux> <more and more : de plus en plus>
andiron ['æn,deɪərn] *n* : chenet *m*
Andorran[1] [æn'dɔrən] *adj* : andorran
Andorran[2] *n* : Andorran *m*, -rane *f*
androgynous [æn'drɑdʒənəs] *adj* : androgyne
anecdotal [,ænɪk'do:ṭəl] *adj* : anecdotique
anecdote ['ænɪk,do:ṭ] *n* : anecdote *f*
anemia [ə'ni:miə] *n* : anémie *f*
anemic [ə'ni:mɪk] *adj* **1** : anémique **2** INSIPID : fade
anemone [ə'nɛməni] *n* : anémone *f*
anesthesia [,ænəs'θi:zə] *n* : anesthésie *f*
anesthetic[1] ['ænəs'θeṭɪk] *adj* : anesthésique
anesthetic[2] *n* : anesthésique *m*
anesthetist [ə'nɛsθətɪst] *n* : anesthésiste *mf*
anesthetize [ə'nɛsθətaɪz] *vt* **-tized; -tizing** : anesthésier
anew [ə'nu:, -'nju:] *adv* : encore, de nouveau
angel ['eɪndʒəl] *n* : ange *m*
angelic [æn'dʒɛlɪk] *or* **angelical** [-lɪkəl] *adj* : angélique — **angelically** [-lɪkli] *adv*
anger[1] ['æŋgər] *vt* : fâcher, mettre en colère — *vi* : se fâcher, se mettre en colère
anger[2] *n* : colère *f*
angina [æn'dʒaɪnə] *n or* **angina pectoris** : angine *f* de poitrine
angle[1] ['æŋgəl] *v* **-gled; -gling** *vt* : orienter, incliner — *vi* FISH : pêcher à la ligne
angle[2] *n* **1** : angle *m* <at an angle : de biais> **2** POINT OF VIEW : point *m* de vue
angler ['æŋglər] *n* : pêcheur *m*, -cheuse *f* à la ligne
angling ['æŋglɪŋ] *n* : pêche *f* (à la ligne)
Anglo-Saxon[1] [,aŋglo'sæksən] *adj* : anglo-saxon
Anglo-Saxon[2] *n* **1** : Anglo-Saxon *m*, -Saxonne *f* (personne) **2** : anglo-saxon *m* (langue)
Angolan[1] [æŋ'go:lən, æn-] *adj* : angolais
Angolan[2] *n* : Angolais *m*, -laise *f*
angora [æŋ'gorə, æn-] *n* : angora *m*
angrily ['æŋgrəli] *adv* : avec colère
angry ['æŋgri] *adj* **-grier; -est** : fâché, en colère, furieux
anguish ['æŋgwɪʃ] *n* : angoisse *f*, douleur *f*
anguished ['æŋgwɪʃt] *adj* : angoissé, tourmenté
angular ['æŋgjələr] *adj* : anguleux (se dit du visage), angulaire (se dit des objets)
animal ['ænəməl] *n* : animal *m*
animate[1] ['ænə,meɪt] *vt* **-mated; -mating** : animer, stimuler
animate[2] ['ænəmət] *adj* **1** ALIVE : vivant **2** ANIMATED : animé
animated ['ænə,meɪṭəd] *adj* **1** LIVELY : animé **2 animated cartoon** : dessin *m* animé
animation [,ænə'meɪʃən] *n* : animation *f*
animosity [,ænə'mɑsəṭi] *n, pl* **-ties** : animosité *f*
anise ['ænəs] *n* : anis *m*
ankle ['æŋkəl] *n* : cheville *f*
annals ['ænəlz] *npl* : annales *fpl*
anneal [ə'ni:l] *vt* : recuire
annex[1] [ə'nɛks, 'æ,nɛks] *vt* : annexer
annex[2] ['æ,nɛks, -nɪks] *n* : annexe *f*
annexation [,æ,nɛk'seɪʃən] *n* : annexion *f*
annihilate [ə'naɪə,leɪt] *vt* **-lated; -lating** : anéantir, annihiler
annihilation [ə,naɪə'leɪʃən] *n* : anéantissement *m*
anniversary [,ænə'vərsəri] *n, pl* **-ries** : anniversaire *m*
annotate ['ænə,teɪt] *vt* **-tated; -tating** : annoter
annotation [,ænə'teɪʃən] *n* : annotation *f*
announce [ə'naʊnts] *vt* **-nounced; -nouncing** : annoncer
announcement [ə'naʊntsmənt] *n* **1** DECLARATION : annonce *f* **2** NOTIFICATION : avis *m*, faire-part *m*
announcer [ə'naʊntsər] *n* : présentateur *m*, -trice *f*; annonceur *m*, -ceuse *f*; speaker *m*, -kerine *f France*
annoy [ə'nɔɪ] *vt* : agacer, gêner, ennuyer, achaler *Can fam*
annoyance [ə'nɔɪənts] *n* : agacement *m*, contrariété *f*
annoying [ə'nɔɪɪŋ] *adj* : agaçant, gênant, ennuyant *Can*
annual[1] ['ænjʊəl] *adj* : annuel — **annually** *adv*

annual[2] *n* **1** YEARBOOK : annuaire *m* **2** *or* **annual plant** : plante *f* annuelle
annuity [ə'nu:ətɪ] *n, pl* **-ties** : rente *f*
annul [ə'nʌl] *vt* **anulled; anulling** : annuler
annulment [ə'nʌlmənt] *n* : annulation *f*
anode ['æˌno:d] *n* : anode *f*
anoint [ə'nuɪnt] *vt* : oindre
anomalous [ə'nɑmələs] *adj* ABNORMAL : anormal
anomaly [ə'nɑməlɪ] *n, pl* **-lies** : anomalie *f*
anonymity [ˌænə'nɪmətɪ] *n* : anonymat *m*
anonymous [ə'nɑnəməs] *adj* : anonyme — **anonymously** *adv*
anorexia [ˌænə'rɛksiə] *n* : anorexie *f* — **anorexic** *adj*
another[1] [ə'nʌðər] *adj* : un autre, encore un <another girl : une autre fille> <another beer : encore une bière> <without another word : sans rien dire de plus> <in another three years : dans trois ans>
another[2] *pron* **1** : un autre *m*, une autre *f* **2 many another** : beaucoup d'autres **3 one after another** : l'un après l'autre
answer[1] ['ænʃər] *vt* **1** : répondre à **2 to answer the door** : aller ouvrir la porte — *vi* **1** : répondre, donner une réponse **2 to answer for** : répondre de
answer[2] *n* **1** REPLY : réponse *f* <in answer to : en réponse à> **2** SOLUTION : solution *f*
answerable ['ænʃərəbəl] *adj* : responsable
ant ['ænt] *n* : fourmi *f*
antagonism [æn'tægəˌnɪzəm] *n* : antagonisme *m*
antagonist [æn'tægənɪst] *n* : antagoniste *mf*
antagonistic [ænˌtægə'nɪstɪk] *adj* : antagoniste
antagonize [æn'tægəˌnɑɪz] *vt* **-nized; -nizing** : éveiller l'hostilité de, contrarier
antarctic [ænt'ɑrktɪk, -'ɑrtɪk] *adj* : antarctique <antarctic circle : cercle polaire antarctique>
anteater ['æntˌiːtər] *n* : fourmilier *m*
antecedent[1] [ˌæntə'si:dənt] *adj* : antérieur, précédent
antecedent[2] *n* : antécédent *m*
antelope ['æntəlˌo:p] *n, pl* **-lope** *or* **-lopes** : antilope *f*
antenna [æn'tɛnə] *n, pl* **-nae** *or* **-nas** : antenne *f*
anterior [æn'tɪrɪər] *adj* : antérieur
anteroom ['æntiˌru:m] *n* : antichambre *f*
anthem ['ænθəm] *n* : hymne *m* <national anthem : hymne national>
anther ['ænθər] *n* : anthère *f*
anthill ['æntˌhɪl] *n* : fourmilière *f*
anthology [æn'θɑlədʒɪ] *n, pl* **-gies** : anthologie *f*
anthracite ['ænθrəˌsɑɪt] *n* : anthracite *m*
anthropoid[1] ['ænθrəˌpɔɪd] *adj* : anthropoïde
anthropoid[2] *n* : anthropoïde *m*
anthropological [ˌænθrəpə'lɑdʒɪkəl] *adj* : anthropologique
anthropologist [ˌænθrə'pɑlədʒɪst] *n* : anthropologue *mf*, anthropologiste *mf*
anthropology [ˌænθrə'pɑlədʒɪ] *n* : anthropologie *f*
antiaircraft [ˌæntɪ'ærˌkræft, ˌæn,taɪ-] *adj* : antiaérien
antibiotic[1] [ˌæntɪbaɪ'ɑtɪk, ˌæn,taɪ-, -bi-] *adj* : antibiotique
antibiotic[2] *n* : antibiotique *m*
antibody ['æntiˌbɑdi] *n, pl* **-bodies** : anticorps *m*
anticipate [æn'tɪsəˌpeɪt] *vt* **-pated; -pating 1** FORESEE : anticiper, prévoir **2** EXPECT : s'attendre à **3** FORESTALL : devancer
anticipation [ænˌtɪsə'peɪʃən] *n* : anticipation *f*
anticipatory [æn'tɪsəpəˌtori] *adj* : d'anticipation
anticlerical [ˌæntɪ'klɛrɪkəl, ˌæn,taɪ-] *adj* : anticlérical
anticlimax [ˌæntɪ'klɑɪˌmæks] *n* : déception *f*
anticommunist[1] [ˌæntɪ'kɑmjənɪst, ˌæn-,taɪ-] *adj* : anticommuniste
anticommunist[2] *n* : anticommuniste *mf*
antics ['æntɪks] *npl* : bouffonnerie *f*
anticyclone [ˌæntɪ'sɑɪˌklon] *n* : anticyclone *m*
antidemocratic [ˌæntɪ'dɛmə'krætɪk, ˌæn-,taɪ-] *adj* : antidémocratique
antidepressant[1] [ˌæntɪdɪ'prɛsənt, ˌæn,taɪ] *adj* : antidépresseur
antidepressant[2] *n* : antidépresseur *m*
antidote ['æntɪˌdo:t] *n* : antidote *m*
antifreeze ['æntɪˌfri:z] *n* : antigel *m*
antihistamine [ˌæntɪ'hɪstəˌmin, ˌæn,taɪ-, -mən] *n* : antihistaminique *m*
anti–inflammatory [ˌæntɪn'flæməˌtori] *adj* : anti-inflammatoire
antilock ['æntiˌlɑk, 'æn,taɪ-] *adj* **antilock brakes** : freins *mpl* antiblocage
antimony ['æntəˌmo:ni] *n* : antimoine *m*
antioxidant[1] [ˌæntɪ'ɑksədənt, ˌæn,taɪ-] *adj* : antioxydant
antioxidant[2] *n* : antioxydant *m*
antipathy [æn'tɪpəθi] *n, pl* **-thies** : antipathie *f*
antiperspirant [ˌæntɪ'pərspərənt, ˌæn,taɪ-] *n* : déodorant *m*
antiquated ['æntəˌkweɪtəd] *adj* **1** OUTMODED : vieillot, dépassé **2** ANCIENT : très vieux
antique[1] [æn'ti:k] *adj* : ancien, antique
antique[2] *n* : objet *m* ancien, antiquité *f*
antiquity [æn'tɪkwətɪ] *n, pl* **-ties** : antiquité *f*
anti–Semitic [ˌæntɪsə'mɪtɪk, ˌæn,taɪ-] *adj* : antisémite
anti–Semitism [ˌæntɪ'sɛməˌtɪzəm, ˌæn-,taɪ-] *n* : antisémitisme *m*

antiseptic[1] [ˌæntəˈsɛptɪk] *adj* : antiseptique
antiseptic[2] *n* : antiseptique *m*
antismoking [ˌæntiˈsmoːkɪŋ, ˌæn,taɪ-] *n* : antitabac
antisocial [ˌæntiˈsoːʃəl, ˌæn,taɪ-] *adj* **1** : antisocial <antisocial behavior : comportement antisocial> **2** UNSOCIABLE : peu sociable
antitheft [ˌæntiˈθɛft, ˌæn,taɪ-] *adj* : antivol
antithesis [æn'tɪθəsɪs] *n, pl* **-eses** [-ˌsiːz] : antithèse *f*
antitoxin [ˌæntiˈtɑksən, ˌæn,taɪ-] *n* : antitoxine *f*
antitrust [ˌæntiˈtrʌst, ˌæn,taɪ-] *adj* : antitrust
antlers [ˈæntlərz] *npl* : bois *mpl*, ramure *f*
antonym [ˈæntəˌnɪm] *n* : antonyme *m*
anus [ˈeɪnəs] *n* : anus *m*
anvil [ˈænvəl, -vɪl] *n* : enclume *f*
anxiety [æŋˈzaɪəti] *n, pl* **-ties 1** APPREHENSION, UNEASINESS : anxiété *f*, appréhension *f* **2** CONCERN : souci *m* <he's a great anxiety to me : il me donne énormément de soucis> **3** EAGERNESS : désir *m* ardent
anxious [ˈæŋkʃəs] *adj* **1** WORRIED : inquiet, anxieux **2** EAGER : impatient, anxieux
anxiously [ˈæŋkʃəsli] *adv* **1** UNEASILY : avec inquiétude, anxieusement **2** EAGERLY : avec impatience
any[1] [ˈɛni] *adv* **1** (*used in questions and conditional clauses*) : un peu <can they work any faster? : peuvent-ils travailler un peu plus vite?> <do you want any more coffee? : voulez-vous encore du café?> **2** (*used in negative constructions*) <I don't smoke any longer : je ne fume plus> <she doesn't know any more than that : c'est tout ce qu'elle sait> **3** AT ALL : du tout <that didn't help any : cela n'a pas aidé du tout>
any[2] *adj* **1** (*used in questions*) : de, de la, du, des <do you have any advice? : avez-vous des conseils?> **2** (*used in negative constructions*) <we don't have any money : nous n'avons pas d'argent> <without any problem : sans le moindre problème> <he hasn't any idea : il n'a aucune idée> **3** WHICHEVER : quelconque, n'importe quel, tout <take any book : prenez n'importe quel livre> <at any moment : à tout moment>
any[3] *pron* **1** : en <if you have any : si tu en as> <I don't like any of them : je n'en aime aucun d'entre eux> **2** : n'importe lequel <take any you want : prenez n'importe lequel>
anybody [ˈɛniˌbɑdi, -ˌbɑ-] → **anyone**
anyhow [ˈɛniˌhaʊ] *adv* **1** IN ANY CASE : de toute façon, en tout cas **2** HAPHAZARDLY : n'importe comment
anymore [ˌɛniˈmor] *adv* : plus <I don't dance anymore : je ne danse plus>
anyone [ˈɛniˌwʌn] *pron* **1** (*in questions or conditional clauses*) : quelqu'un <is anyone home? : est-ce qu'il y a quelqu'un à la maison?> **2** (*in negative constructions*) : personne <you didn't see anyone? : tu n'as vu personne?> **3** : tout le monde <anyone can play : tout le monde peut jouer>
anyplace [ˈɛniˌpleɪs] → **anywhere**
anything [ˈɛniˌθɪŋ] *pron* **1** : tout, n'importe quoi <he eats anything : il mange n'importe quoi> **2** SOMETHING : quelque chose <can anything be done? : peut-on faire quelque chose?> **3** : rien <hardly anything : presque rien> **4 anything but** : tout sauf
anytime [ˈɛniˌtaɪm] *adv* : n'importe quand <call me anytime : appelez-moi n'importe quand>
anyway [ˈɛniˌweɪ] → **anyhow**
anywhere [ˈɛniˌhwɛr] *adv* **1** : n'importe où, partout <sit down anywhere : asseyez-vous n'importe où> <anywhere else : partout ailleurs> **2** (*in questions*) : quelque part <do you have some glue anywhere? : avez-vous de la colle quelque part?> **3** (*in negative constructions*) : nulle part <she doesn't go anywhere : elle ne va nulle part>
aorta [eɪˈɔrtə] *n, pl* **-tas** *or* **-tae** : aorte *f*
apart [əˈpɑrt] *adv* **1** : l'un de l'autre, d'intervalle <far apart : éloigné l'un de l'autre> <shots five minutes apart : des coups de feu à cinq minutes d'intervalle> **2** ASIDE : à part, à l'écart <apart from : en dehors de> **3** SEPARATELY : séparément **4 to fall apart** : s'en aller en morceaux, se défaire **5 to take apart** : démonter **6 to tell apart** : distinguer
apartheid [əˈpɑrˌteɪt, -ˌtaɪt] *n* : apartheid *m*
apartment [əˈpɑrtmənt] *n* **1** : appartement *m* **2** *or* **apartment house** : immeuble *m*
apathetic [ˌæpəˈθɛt̬ɪk] *adj* : apathique
apathetically [ˌæpəˈθɛt̬ɪkli] *adv* : avec apathie
apathy [ˈæpəθi] *n* : apathie *f*
ape[1] [ˈeɪp] *vt* **aped; aping** : singer
ape[2] *n* : grand singe *m*
aperture [ˈæpərtʃər, -ˌtʃʊr] *n* : ouverture *f*
apex [ˈeɪˌpɛks] *n, pl* **apexes** *or* **apices** [ˈeɪpəˌsiːz, ˈæ-] : sommet *m*, point *m* culminant
aphid [ˈeɪfɪd, ˈæ-] *n* : puceron *m*
aphorism [ˈæfəˌrɪzəm] *n* : aphorisme *m*
aphrodisiac [ˌæfrəˈdiːziˌæk, -ˈdɪ-] *n* : aphrodisiaque *m*
apiary [ˈeɪpiˌɛri] *n, pl* **-aries** : rucher *m*
apiece [əˈpiːs] *adv* **1** : par personne, chacun <two candies apiece : deux bon-

bons par personne> **2** : la pièce, chacun <they cost two dollars apiece : ils coûtent deux dollars la pièce>

aplenty [ə'plɛnti] *adv* : en abondance

aplomb [ə'plɑm, -'plʌm] *n* : aplomb *m*

apocalypse [ə'pɑkəˌlɪps] *n* : apocalypse *f*

apocalyptic [əˌpɑkə'lɪptɪk] *adj* : apocalyptique

apocrypha [ə'pɑkrəfə] *n* **the Apocrypha** : les Apocryphes

apologetic [ə'pɑlə'dʒɛtɪk] *adj* **1** : d'excuse <in an apologetic tone : d'un ton contrit> **2 to be apologetic** : s'excuser

apologetically [ə'pɑlə'dʒɛtɪkli] *adv* : en s'excusant, d'un air contrit

apologize [ə'pɑləˌdʒaɪz] *vi* **-gized; -gizing** : s'excuser, faire des excuses

apology [ə'pɑlədʒi] *n, pl* **-gies** : excuses *fpl*

apoplectic [ˌæpə'plɛktɪk] *adj* : apoplectique

apoplexy ['æpəˌplɛksi] *n* : apoplexie *f*

apostle [ə'pɑsəl] *n* : apôtre *m*

apostolic [ˌæpə'stɑlɪk] *adj* : apostolique

apostrophe [ə'pɑstrəˌfi:] *n* : apostrophe *f*

apothecary [ə'pɑθəˌkɛri] *n, pl* **-caries** : pharmacien *m*, -cienne *f*

appall *or Brit* **appal** [ə'pɔl] *vt* **-palled; -palling** : épouvanter, horrifier

appalling [ə'pɔlɪŋ] *adj* : épouvantable, effroyable <appalling ignorance : ignorance consternante>

apparatus [ˌæpə'ræt̬əs, -'reɪ-] *n, pl* **-tuses** *or* **-tus** : appareil *m*, équipement *m*, agrès *mpl* (de gymnastique)

apparel [ə'pærəl] *n* : habillement *m*, vêtements *mpl*

apparent [ə'pærənt] *adj* **1** VISIBLE : visible **2** OBVIOUS : évident **3** SEEMING : apparent

apparently [ə'pærəntli] *adv* : apparemment

apparition [ˌæpə'rɪʃən] *n* : apparition *f*

appeal[1] [ə'pi:l] *vt* : faire appel contre, en appeler de (un jugement) — *vi* **1** : interjeter appel (en droit) **2 to appeal for** : lancer un appel à **3 to appeal to** ATTRACT : attirer, plaire **4 to appeal to** INVOKE : faire appel à

appeal[2] *n* **1** CALL : appel *m* **2** ENTREATY : supplication *f* **3** ATTRACTION : attrait *m*

appear [ə'pɪr] *vi* **1** : apparaître, arriver <to appear on the scene : arriver sur place> **2** SEEM : sembler, paraître **3** COME OUT : sortir, paraître, être publié **4 to appear in court** : comparaître (devant le tribunal)

appearance [ə'pɪrənts] *n* **1** APPEARING : apparition *f*, arrivée *f*, comparution *f* (devant le tribunal) **2** LOOK : apparence *f*, semblant *m* **3 appearances** *npl* : apparences *fpl* <to keep up appearances : sauver les apparences>

appease [ə'pi:z] *vt* **-peased; -peasing** : apaiser

appeasement [ə'pi:zmənt] *n* : apaisement *m*

append [ə'pɛnd] *vt* : ajouter

appendage [ə'pɛndɪdʒ] *n* : appendice *m*

appendectomy [ˌæpən'dɛktəmi] *n, pl* **-mies** : appendicectomie *f*

appendicitis [əˌpɛndə'saɪt̬əs] *n* : appendicite *f*

appendix [ə'pɛndɪks] *n, pl* **-dixes** *or* **-dices** [-dəˌsi:z] : appendice *m*

appetite ['æpəˌtaɪt] *n* : appétit *m*

appetizer ['æpəˌtaɪzər] *n* : amuse-gueule *m*

appetizing ['æpəˌtaɪzɪŋ] *adj* : appétissant

applaud [ə'plɔd] *v* : applaudir

applause [ə'plɔz] *n* : applaudissements *mpl*

apple ['æpəl] *n* : pomme *f*

appliance [ə'plaɪənts] *n* : appareil *m*

applicable ['æplɪkəbəl, ə'plɪkə-] *adj* : applicable

applicant ['æplɪkənt] *n* : candidat *m*, -date *f*

application [ˌæplə'keɪʃən] *n* **1** USE : application *f* **2** REQUEST : demande *f* <application form : formulaire de demande> **3** DILIGENCE : assiduité *f*, zèle *m*

applicator ['æpləˌkeɪt̬ər] *n* : applicateur *m*

appliqué[1] [ˌæplə'keɪ] *vt* **-quéd; -quéing** : orner d'appliques

appliqué[2] *n* : applique *f*

apply [ə'plaɪ] *v* **-plied; -plying** *vt* **1** : appliquer, mettre <to apply varnish : appliquer du vernis> **2** EXERT : exercer <apply pressure : exercez une pression> **3 to apply oneself** : s'appliquer — *vi* **1** : s'appliquer <the law applies to everyone : la loi s'applique à tous> **2 to apply for** : poser sa candidature pour, faire une demande de

appoint [ə'pɔɪnt] *vt* **1** DESIGNATE, SET : désigner, fixer **2** NAME : nommer **3** EQUIP : équiper <a well-appointed office : un bureau bien aménagé>

appointee [əˌpɔɪn'ti:, æ-] *n* : candidat *m* retenu, candidate *f* retenue

appointment [ə'pɔɪntmənt] *n* **1** NOMINATION : nomination *f*, désignation *f* **2** MEETING : rendez-vous *m* **3** POSITION : poste *m*

apportion [ə'porʃən] *vt* ALLOT : répartir, distribuer

apportionment [ə'porʃənmənt] *n* : répartition *f*

apposite ['æpəzət] *adj* PERTINENT : pertinent, juste

appraisal [ə'preɪzəl] *n* : évaluation *f*, appréciation *f*

appraise [ə'preɪz] *vt* **-praised; -praising** : évaluer, estimer, apprécier

appreciable [ə'pri:ʃəbəl, -'prɪʃiə-] *adj* : appréciable, sensible

appreciably [ə'pri:ʃəbli, -'prɪʃiə-] *adv* : sensiblement

appreciate [ə'pri:ʃi,eɪt, -'prɪ-] *v* **-ated; -ating** *vt* **1** VALUE : apprécier **2** REALIZE, UNDERSTAND : comprendre, se rendre compte de **3** : être sensible à, être reconnaissant de <I appreciate your kindness : je vous suis reconnaissant de votre gentillesse> — *vi* : s'apprécier

appreciation [ə,pri:ʃi'eɪʃən, -,prɪ-] *n* **1** EVALUATION : appréciation *f*, estimation *f* **2** GRATITUDE : reconnaissance *f* **3** UNDERSTANDING : compréhension *f* **4** INCREASE : hausse *f* (de valeur)

appreciative [ə'pri:ʃətɪv, -'prɪ-; ə'pri:ʃi,eɪ-] *adj* **1** GRATEFUL : reconnaissant **2** ADMIRING : admiratif, élogieux

apprehend [,æprɪ'hend] *vt* **1** ARREST : arrêter, appréhender **2** UNDERSTAND : comprendre **3** DREAD : appréhender, redouter

apprehensive [,æprɪ'hentsɪv] *adj* : inquiet

apprehensively [,æprɪ'hentsɪvli] *adv* : avec inquiétude

apprentice[1] [ə'prentɪs] *vt* **-ticed; -ticing** : mettre en apprentissage

apprentice[2] *n* : apprenti *m*, -tie *f*

apprenticeship [ə'prentɪsʃɪp] *n* : apprentissage *m*

apprise [ə'praɪz] *vt* **-prised; -prising** : informer, prévenir

approach[1] [ə'pro:tʃ] *vt* **1** NEAR : s'approcher de, s'avancer vers **2** : s'adresser à, aborder <he approached me : il m'a abordé> **3** CONSIDER : aborder (un problème, etc.) — *vi* NEAR : s'approcher

approach[2] *n* **1** NEARING : approche *f*, arrivée *f* <the approach of winter : la venue de l'hiver> **2** HANDLING : façon *f* (de faire), approche *f* **3** ACCESS : accès *m*, voie *f* d'accès

approachable [ə'pro:tʃəbəl] *adj* : abordable, d'un abord facile, accessible

approbation [,æprə'beɪʃən] *n* : approbation *f*

appropriate[1] [ə'pro:pri,eɪt] *vt* **-ated; -ating 1** SEIZE, TAKE : s'approprier **2** ALLOCATE, ASSIGN : affecter, consacrer

appropriate[2] [ə'pro:priət] *adj* : approprié, convenable, qui convient

appropriately [ə'pro:priətli] *adv* : convenablement, avec à-propos

appropriateness [ə'pro:priətnəs] *n* : convenance *f*, à-propos *m*

appropriation [ə,pro:pri'eɪʃən] *n* **1** SEIZURE : appropriation *f* **2** ALLOCATION : affectation *f*, allocation *f*

approval [ə'pru:vəl] *n* **1** : approbation *f* **2 on ~** : à l'essai

approve [ə'pru:v] *v* **-proved; -proving** *vt* : approuver — *vi* **to approve of** : apprécier, être d'accord avec

approximate[1] [ə'prɑksə,meɪt] *vt* **-mated; -mating** : se rapprocher de

approximate[2] [ə'prɑksəmət] *adj* : approximatif

approximately [ə'prɑksəmətli] *adv* : à peu près, environ

approximation [ə,prɑksə'meɪʃən] *n* : approximation *f*

appurtenance [ə'pərtənənts] *n* : accessoire *m*

apricot ['æprə,kɑt, 'eɪ-] *n* : abricot *m*

April ['eɪprəl] *n* : avril *m*

apron ['eɪprən] *n* : tablier *m*

apropos[1] [,æprə'po:, 'æprə,po:] *adv* : à propos

apropos[2] *adj* : opportun, à propos

apropos of *prep* CONCERNING : quant à, à propos de

apt ['æpt] *adj* **1** SUITABLE : convenable, approprié **2** CLEVER : doué **3 to be apt to** : avoir tendance à <she's apt to forget : elle oublie facilement>

aptitude ['æptə,tu:d, -,tju:d] *n* : aptitude *f*

aptly ['æptli] *adv* : avec justesse, bien <aptly chosen : bien choisi>

aqua ['ækwə, 'ɑ-] *adj* : bleu-vert

aquarium [ə'kwæriəm] *n, pl* **-iums** *or* **-ia** [-iə] : aquarium *m*

Aquarius [ə'kwæriəm] *n* : Verseau *m*

aquatic [ə'kwɑtɪk, -'kwæ-] *adj* : aquatique (se dit des plantes et des animaux), nautique (se dit des sports)

aqueduct ['ækwə,dʌkt] *n* : aqueduc *m*

aquiline ['ækwə,laɪn, -lən] *adj* : aquilin

Arab[1] ['ærəb] *adj* : arabe

Arab[2] *n* : Arabe *mf*

arabesque [,ærə'bɛsk] *n* : arabesque *f*

Arabian[1] [ə'reɪbiən] *adj* : arabe

Arabian[2] *n* → **Arab**[2]

Arabic[1] ['ærəbɪk] *adj* : arabe

Arabic[2] *n* : arabe *m* (langue)

arable ['ærəbəl] *adj* : arable

arbiter ['ɑrbətər] *n* : arbitre *m*

arbitrary ['ɑrbə,treri] *adj* : arbitraire — **arbitrarily** [,ɑrbə'trerəli] *adv*

arbitrate ['ɑrbə,treɪt] *v* **-trated; -trating** *vt* : arbitrer, juger — *vi* : arbitrer

arbitration [,ɑrbə'treɪʃən] *n* : arbitrage *m*

arbitrator ['ɑrbə,treɪtər] *n* : médiateur *m*, -trice *f*; arbitre *m*

arbor *or Brit* **arbour** ['ɑrbər] *n* : tonnelle *f*

arboreal [ɑr'boriəl] *adj* : arboricole

arbour *Brit* → **arbor**

arc[1] ['ɑrk] *vi* **arced; arcing** : décrire un arc

arc[2] *n* : arc *m*

arcade [ɑr'keɪd] *n* **1** ARCHES : arcade *f* **2 shopping arcade** : galerie *f* marchande

arcane [ɑr'keɪn] *adj* : mystérieux, obscur

arch[1] ['ɑrtʃ] *vt* **1** BEND : arquer, courber **2** VAULT : voûter — *vi* : former une voûte

arch[2] *adj* **1** CHIEF : principal <your arch opponent : ton principal adversaire> **2** MISCHIEVOUS : espiègle, malicieux
arch[3] *n* **1** : voûte *f*, arc *m*, arche *f* **2** ARCHING : courbe *f* (des sourcils, etc.)
archaeological [ˌɑrkiəˈlɑdʒɪkəl] *adj* : archéologique
archaeologist [ˌɑrkiˈɑlədʒɪst] *n* : archéologue *mf*
archaeology *or* **archeology** [ˌɑrkiˈɑlədʒi] *n* : archéologie *f*
archaic [ɑrˈkeɪɪk] *adj* : archaïque
archangel [ˈɑrkˌeɪndʒəl] *n* : archange *m*
archbishop [ˌɑrtʃˈbɪʃəp] *n* : archevêque *m*
archdiocese [ˌɑrtʃˈdaɪəsəs, -ˌsiːz, -ˌsiːs] *n* : archidiocèse *m*
archer [ˈɑrtʃər] *n* : archer *m*
archery [ˈɑrtʃəri] *n* : tir *m* à l'arc
archetype [ˈɑrkiˌtaɪp] *n* : archétype *m*
archipelago [ˌɑrkəˈpeləˌgoː, ˌɑrtʃə-] *n, pl* **-goes** *or* **-gos** [-goːz] : archipel *m*
architect [ˈɑrkəˌtɛkt] *n* : architecte *mf*
architectural [ˌɑrkəˈtɛktʃərəl] *adj* : architectural
architecturally [ˌɑrkəˈtɛktʃərəli] *adv* : du point de vue architectural
architecture [ˈɑrkəˌtɛktʃər] *n* : architecture *f*
archives [ˈɑrˌkaɪvz] *npl* : archives *fpl*
archivist [ˈɑrkəvɪst, -ˌkaɪ-] *n* : archiviste *mf*
archway [ˈɑrtʃˌweɪ] *n* : voûte *f*, arcade *f*
arctic [ˈɑrktɪk, ˈɑrt-] *adj* **1** : arctique **2** FRIGID : glacial
arctic circle *n* : cercle *m* polaire arctique
ardent [ˈɑrdənt] *adj* : ardent
ardently [ˈɑrdəntli] *adv* : ardemment, passionnément
ardor *or Brit* **ardour** [ˈɑrdər] *n* : ardeur *f*
arduous [ˈɑrdʒʊəs] *adj* : ardu, pénible
arduously [ˈɑrdʒʊəsli] *adv* : péniblement
arduousness [ˈɑrdʒʊəsnəs] *n* : difficulté *f*, dureté *f*
area [ˈæriə] *n* **1** REGION : région *f*, zone *f*, quartier *m* **2** SURFACE : aire *f*, superficie *f* <the area of a circle : l'aire d'un cercle> **3** FIELD : domaine *m* <area of expertise : domaine d'expertise>
area code *n* : indicatif *m* de zone, indicatif *m* régional *Can*
arena [əˈriːnə] *n* : arène *f*, aréna *m Can*
aren't [ˈɑrnt, ˈɑrənt] (*contraction of* **are** *and* **not**) → **be**
Aries [ˈɛriːz, -iˌiːz] *n* : Bélier *m*
Argentine[1] [ˈɑrdʒənˌtaɪn, -ˌtiːn] *or* **Argentinean** *or* **Argentinian** [ˌɑrdʒənˈtɪniən] *adj* : argentin
Argentine[2] *or* **Argentinean** *or* **Argentinian** *n* : Argentin *m*, -tine *f*
argon [ˈɑrˌɡɑn] *n* : argon *m*
argot [ˈɑrɡət, -ˌɡoː] *n* : argot *m*
arguable [ˈɑrɡjʊəbəl] *adj* : discutable
argue [ˈɑrˌɡjuː] *v* **-gued**; **-guing** *vt* **1** DEBATE, DISCUSS : discuter **2** PLEAD : plaider <to argue a case : plaider une cause> **3** MAINTAIN : soutenir **4** PERSUADE : persuader — *vi* **1** QUARREL : se disputer **2** DEBATE : argumenter
argument [ˈɑrɡjəmənt] *n* **1** QUARREL : dispute *f* **2** DEBATE : discussion *f*, débat *m* **3** REASONING : argument *m*, raisonnement *m* <his argument is that : il soutient que>
argumentative [ˌɑrɡjəˈmɛntəˌtɪv] *adj* : querelleur, ergoteur
argyle [ˈɑrˌɡaɪl] *adj* : à motifs de losanges
aria [ˈɑriə] *n* : aria *f*
arid [ˈærəd] *adj* : aride
aridity [əˈrɪdəˌti, æ-] *n* : aridité *f*
arise [əˈraɪz] *vi* **arose** [əˈroːz]; **arisen** [əˈrɪzən]; **arising 1** RISE : se lever **2** APPEAR, OCCUR : se présenter, survenir <if the occasion arises : si l'occasion se présente> **3 to arise from** : provenir de, résulter de
aristocracy [ˌærəˈstɑkrəsi] *n, pl* **-cies** : aristocratie *f*
aristocrat [əˈrɪstəˌkræt] *n* : aristocrate *mf*
aristocratic [əˌrɪstəˈkræˌtɪk] *adj* : aristocratique
arithmetic[1] [ˌærɪθˈmɛˌtɪk] *or* **arithmetical** [-ˌtɪkəl] *adj* : arithmétique
arithmetic[2] [əˈrɪθməˌtɪk] *n* : arithmétique *f*
ark [ˈɑrk] *n* : arche *f*
arm[1] [ˈɑrm] *vt* : armer
arm[2] *n* **1** : bras *m* (du corps ou d'une machine), accoudoir *m* (d'une chaise), manche *f* (d'un vêtement) **2** WEAPON : arme *f* <to take up arms : prendre les armes> **3** BRANCH : branche *f*, section *f* **4** → **coat of arms**
armada [ɑrˈmɑdə, -ˈmeɪ-] *n* : armada *f*
armadillo [ˌɑrməˈdɪlo] *n, pl* **-los** : tatou *m*
armament [ˈɑrməmənt] *n* : armement *m*
armchair [ˈɑrmˌtʃɛr] *n* : fauteuil *m*
armed [ˈɑrmd] *adj* : armé <armed robbery : vol à main armée>
armed forces *npl* : forces *fpl* armées
Armenian[1] [ɑrˈmiːniən] *adj* : arménien
Armenian[2] *n* **1** : Arménien *m*, -nienne *f* **2** : arménien *m* (langue)
armistice [ˈɑrməstɪs] *n* : armistice *m*
armor *or Brit* **armour** [ˈɑrmər] *n* **1** : armure *f* <a suit of armor : une armure complète> **2** *or* **armor plating** : blindage *m*
armored *or Brit* **armoured** [ˈɑrmərd] *adj* : blindé
armory *or Brit* **armoury** [ˈɑrməri] *n, pl* **-mories** *or Brit* **-mouries** : arsenal *m* (dépôt d'armes), fabrique *f* d'armes
armpit [ˈɑrmˌpɪt] *n* : aisselle *f*

army ['ɑrmi] *n, pl* **-mies** : armée *f*
aroma [ə'roːmə] *n* : arôme *m*
aromatic [ˌærə'mætɪk] *adj* : aromatique
around[1] [ə'raʊnd] *adv* **1** : de circonférence <a tree two meters around : un arbre deux mètres de circonférence> **2** : autour, de tous côtés <all around : tout autour> <for miles around : sur un rayon de plusieurs milles> **3** NEARBY : pas loin, là, dans les parages <will he be around tonight? : il sera là ce soir?> **4** APPROXIMATELY : environ, à peu près <it costs around five dollars : ça coûte environ cinq dollars>
around[2] *prep* **1** SURROUNDING : autour de <the trees around the house : les arbres autour de la maison> **2** THROUGHOUT : à travers de <she traveled around the country : elle a voyagé partout dans le pays> <somewhere around the house : quelque part dans la maison> **3** AT : vers <come around noon : viens vers midi> **4 around here** : par ici **5 to go around the corner** : tourner le coin
arousal [ə'raʊzəl] *n* : excitation *f*
arouse [ə'raʊz] *vt* **aroused; arousing 1** AWAKEN : réveiller **2** STIMULATE : exciter, éveiller
arraign [ə'reɪn] *vt* : accuser, traduire en justice
arraignment [ə'reɪnmənt] *n* : lecture *f* de l'acte d'accusation
arrange [ə'reɪndʒ] *v* **-ranged; -ranging** *vt* : arranger — *vi* **to arrange for** : s'arranger pour, prendre des dispositions pour
arrangement [ə'reɪndʒmənt] *n* **1** LAYOUT : arrangement *m*, disposition *f* **2** AGREEMENT : arrangement *m*, accord *m* <under the present arrangement : selon l'accord actuel> **3 arrangements** *npl* PLANS : mesures *fpl*, dispositions *fpl*
array[1] [ə'reɪ] *vt* **1** ARRANGE : arranger, disposer, déployer (des troupes) **2** ADORN : parer <to array oneself : se parer>
array[2] *n* **1** ARRANGEMENT : arrangement *m*, ordre *m*, déploiement *m* (de troupes) **2** FINERY : parure *f*, habits *mpl* d'apparat **3** RANGE, SELECTION : panoplie *f*, sélection *f*
arrears [ə'rɪrz] *npl* **1** : arriéré *m* <rent arrears : arriéré de loyer> **2 to be in arrears** : avoir du retard
arrest[1] [ə'rɛst] *vt* : arrêter
arrest[2] *n* **1** : arrêt *m* <cardiac arrest : arrêt du cœur> **2** : arrestation *f* <under arrest : en état d'arrestation>
arrival [ə'raɪvəl] *n* : arrivée *f* (de personnes, d'avions, etc.), arrivage *m* (de marchandises)
arrive [ə'raɪv] *vi* **-rived; -riving 1** : arriver **2 to arrive at** : parvenir à (une résolution, etc.), atteindre (un état)
arrogance ['ærəgənʦ] *n* : arrogance *f*
arrogant ['ærəgənt] *adj* : arrogant, insolent
arrogantly ['ærəgəntli] *adv* : avec arrogance
arrow ['æro] *n* : flèche *f*
arrowhead ['æroˌhɛd] *n* : pointe *f* de flèche
arsenal ['ɑrsənəl] *n* : arsenal *m*
arsenic ['ɑrsənɪk] *n* : arsenic *m*
arson ['ɑrsən] *n* : incendie *m* criminel
arsonist ['ɑrsənɪst] *n* : incendiaire *mf*
art ['ɑrt] *n* **1** : art *m* **2** SKILL : art *m*, habileté *f*
artefact *Brit* → **artifact**
arterial [ɑr'tɪriəl] *adj* : artériel
arteriosclerosis [ɑrˌtɪrioskləˈroːsɪs] *n* : artériosclérose *f*
artery ['ɑrtəri] *n, pl* **-teries** : artère *f*
artful ['ɑrtfəl] *adj* **1** CLEVER, INGENIOUS : astucieux, ingénieux **2** CRAFTY : rusé, malin
arthritic [ɑr'θrɪtɪk] *adj* : arthritique
arthritis [ɑr'θraɪtəs] *n, pl* **-thritides** [-'θrɪtəˌdiːz] : arthrite *f*
arthropod ['ɑrθrəˌpɑd] *n* : arthropode *m*
artichoke ['ɑrtəˌʧoːk] *n* : artichaut *m*
article ['ɑrtɪkəl] *n* **1** THING : objet *m* <articles of clothing : vêtements> **2** : article *m* (dans une publication ou dans un acte judiciaire) **3** : article *m* <definite article : article défini>
articulate[1] [ɑr'tɪkjəˌleɪt] *vt* **-lated; -lating** : articuler
articulate[2] [ɑr'tɪkjələt] *adj* **1** INTELLIGIBLE : distinct, intelligible **2** WELL-SPOKEN : qui s'exprime bien **3** JOINTED : articulé
articulately [ɑr'tɪkjələtli] *adv* : clairement, distinctement
articulation [ɑrˌtɪkjə'leɪʃən] *n* : articulation *f*
artifact *or Brit* **artefact** ['ɑrtəˌfækt] *n* : objet *m* fabriqué
artifice ['ɑrtəfəs] *n* : artifice *m*
artificial [ˌɑrtə'fɪʃəl] *adj* : artificiel — **artificially** *adv*
artificial respiration *n* : respiration *f* artificielle
artillery [ɑr'tɪləri] *n, pl* **-leries** : artillerie *f*
artisan ['ɑrtəzən, -sən] *n* : artisan *m*, -sane *f*
artist ['ɑrtɪst] *n* : artiste *mf*
artistic [ɑr'tɪstɪk] *adj* : artistique — **artistically** [-tɪkli] *adv*
artistry ['ɑrtəstri] *n* : art *m*
artless ['ɑrtləs] *adj* **1** NATURAL : naturel **2** NAIVE : naïf, ingénu
arty ['ɑrti] *adj* **artier; -est** : prétentieusement artistique
arugula [ə'ruːgələ] *n* : roquette *f*
as[1] ['æz] *adv* **1** EQUALLY : aussi <as green as grass : aussi vert que l'herbe> **2** : par exemple <some trees, as oak or pine : des arbres, par exemple le chêne ou le pin>
as[2] *conj* **1** LIKE : comme <white as snow : blanc comme la neige> **2**

WHEN, WHILE : tandis que, alors que, comme <he spoke to me as I was leaving : il m'a parlé tandis que je partais> **3** SINCE : puisque, comme <she stayed home as she has no car : elle est restée chez elle puisqu'elle n'a pas de voiture> **4** : que <so guilty as to leave no doubt : si coupable qu'il n'y a aucun doute> **5 as is** : tel quel

as[3] *prep* **1** LIKE : comme <to behave as a child : se comporter comme un enfant> **2** : en tant que <she works as an editor : elle travaille en tant qu'éditeur> **3** : en <he dressed as a clown : il s'est habillé en clown>

as[4] *pron* **1** : que <the same price as before : le même prix qu'avant> **2** : comme <she's rich, as you know : elle est riche, comme vous savez>

asbestos [æz'bɛstəs, æs-] *n* : amiante *m*

ascend [ə'sɛnd] *vt* : monter, monter à, gravir <to ascend the staircase : monter l'escalier> <to ascend to the throne : monter sur le trône> — *vi* : monter

ascendancy [ə'sɛndənʃsi] *n* : ascendant *m*

ascendant[1] [ə'sɛndənt] *adj* : dominant

ascendant[2] *n* **to be in the ascendant** : être à l'ascendant

ascension [ə'sɛnʃən] *n* : ascension *f*

ascent [ə'sɛnt] *n* **1** RISING : ascension *f* **2** INCLINE : montée *f*, pente *f*

ascertain [ˌæsər'teɪn] *vt* : vérifier, établir, constater

ascertainable [ˌæsər'teɪnəbəl] *adj* : vérifiable

ascetic[1] [ə'sɛʧɪk] *adj* : ascétique

ascetic[2] *n* : ascète *mf*

asceticism [ə'sɛʧəˌsɪzəm] *n* : ascétisme *m*

ascribable [ə'skraɪbəbəl] *adj* : attribuable

ascribe [ə'skraɪb] *vt* **-cribed; -cribing** : attribuer

aseptic [eɪ'sɛptɪk] *adj* : aseptique

as for *prep* CONCERNING : quant à

ash ['æʃ] *n* **1** : cendre *f* <to reduce to ashes : réduire en cendres> **2** : frêne *m* (arbre)

ashamed [ə'ʃeɪmd] *adj* **1** : honteux **2 to be ashamed** : avoir honte

ashen ['æʃən] *adj* : cendreux, blême

ashore [ə'ʃɔr] *adv* **1** : à terre **2 to go ashore** : débarquer

ashtray ['æʃˌtreɪ] *n* : cendrier *m*

Asian[1] ['eɪʒən, -ʃən] *adj* : asiatique

Asian[2] *n* : Asiatique *mf*

aside[1] [ə'saɪd] *adv* **1** : de côté <let's put it aside : mettons-le de côté> **2** APART : à part, à l'écart

aside[2] *n* : aparté *m*

aside from *prep* **1** BESIDES : à part, en plus de **2** EXCEPT : sauf

as if *conj* : comme si

asinine ['æsənˌaɪn] *adj* : sot

ask ['æsk] *vt* **1** : poser, demander <to ask a question : poser une question> <to ask directions : demander son chemin> **2** REQUEST : demander <that's asking a lot! : c'est beaucoup en demander!> **3** INVITE : inviter <to ask s.o. in : inviter qqn à entrer> **4 to ask oneself** : se demander — *vi* : demander

askance [ə'skænʧ] *adv* **to look askance at** : regarder de travers, regarder d'un air méfiant

askew [ə'skjuː] *adv & adj* : de travers

asleep [ə'sliːp] *adj* **1** : endormi **2 to fall asleep** : s'endormir

as of *prep* : dès, à partir de

asparagus [ə'spærəgəs] *ns & pl* : asperge *f* <do you have any asparagus? : avez-vous des asperges?>

aspect ['æˌspɛkt] *n* **1** SIDE : aspect *m* <to study the question from every aspect : étudier la question sous tous ses aspects> **2** ORIENTATION : orientation *f*, exposition *f* **3** APPEARANCE : aspect *m*, air *m*, mine *f*

aspen ['æspən] *n* : tremble *m*

asperity [æ'spɛrəʧi, ə-] *n, pl* **-ties** : aspérité *f*

aspersion [ə'spərʒən] *n* **1** : calomnie *f* **2 to cast aspersions on** : dénigrer

asphalt ['æsˌfɔlt] *n* : asphalte *m*

asphyxiate [æ'sfɪksiˌeɪt] *vt* **-ated; -ating** : asphyxier

asphyxiation [æˌsfɪksi'eɪʃən] *n* : asphyxie *f*

aspic ['æspɪk] *n* : aspic *m*

aspirant ['æspərənt, ə'spaɪrənt] *n* : aspirant *m*, -rante *f*

aspiration [ˌæspə'reɪʃən] *n* : aspiration *f*

aspire [ə'spaɪr] *vi* **-pired; -piring** : aspirer

aspirin ['æsprən, 'æspə-] *n, pl* **aspirin** *or* **aspirins** : aspirine *f*

ass ['æs] *n* **1** : âne *m* **2** FOOL : idiot *m*, -diote *f*

assail [ə'seɪl] *vt* : assaillir, attaquer

assailant [ə'seɪlənt] *n* : agresseur *m*; assaillant *m*, -lante *f*

assassin [ə'sæsən] *n* : assassin *m*

assassinate [ə'sæsənˌeɪt] *vt* **-nated; -nating** : assassiner

assassination [əˌsæsən'eɪʃən] *n* : assassinat *m*

assault[1] [ə'sɔlt] *vt* : agresser, attaquer

assault[2] *n* : agression *f*, assaut *m* (militaire) <sexual assault : agression sexuelle> <assault and battery : coups et blessures>

assay[1] [æ'seɪ, 'æˌseɪ] *vt* : essayer

assay[2] ['æˌseɪ, æ'seɪ] *n* ANALYSIS : analyse *f*

assemble [ə'sɛmbəl] *v* **-bled; -bling** *vt* **1** CONSTRUCT : assembler **2** GATHER : rassembler — *vi* CONVENE : se rassembler, se réunir

assembly [ə'sɛmbli] *n, pl* **-blies 1** MEETING : assemblée *f*, réunion *f* **2** ASSEMBLING : assemblage *m*, montage *m* <assembly line : chaîne de montage>

assent[1] [ə'sɛnt] *vi* : consentir, donner son assentiment
assent[2] *n* : assentiment *m*
assert [ə'sərt] *vt* **1** DECLARE : affirmer, déclarer **2** DEMAND : revendiquer (ses droits, etc.) **3 to assert oneself** : s'affirmer, s'imposer
assertion [ə'sərʃən] *n* **1** DECLARATION : affirmation *f*, assertion *f* **2** CLAIM : revendication *f*
assertive [ə'sərtɪv] *adj* : assuré
assertiveness [ə'sərtɪvnəs] *n* : manière *f* assurée
assess [ə'sɛs] *vt* **1** EVALUATE : évaluer, estimer **2** IMPOSE : imposer (un impôt, etc.)
assessment [ə'sɛsmənt] *n* : évaluation *f*, estimation *f*
assessor [ə'sɛsər] *n* : expert *m*; contrôleur *m*, -leuse *f* (des impôts)
asset ['æˌsɛt] *n* **1** ADVANTAGE : avantage *m*, atout *m* **2 assets** *npl* : biens *mpl*, actif *m*, capital *m* <assets and liabilities : l'actif et le passif>
assiduity [ˌæsə'duːəti, -'djuː-] *n, pl* **-ities** : assiduité *f*
assiduous [ə'sɪdʒʊəs] *adj* : assidu
assiduously [ə'sɪdʒʊəsli] *adv* : assidûment
assign [ə'saɪn] *vt* **1** ALLOT : assigner **2** FIX, SPECIFY : fixer **3** APPOINT : nommer **4** ATTRIBUTE : attribuer
assignment [ə'saɪnmənt] *n* **1** TASK : tâche *f*, mission *f* **2** HOMEWORK : devoir *m* **3** ALLOCATION : allocation *f*, affectation *f*
assimilate [ə'sɪməˌleɪt] *v* **-lated; -lating** *vt* : assimiler — *vi* : s'assimiler
assimilation [əˌsɪmə'leɪʃən] *n* : assimilation *f*
assist [ə'sɪst] *vt* : aider, assister
assistance [ə'sɪstənts] *n* : aide *f*, assistance *f*
assistant [ə'sɪstənt] *n* : assistant *m*, -tante *f*; adjoint *m*, -jointe *f*
associate[1] [ə'soːʃiˌeɪt, -siˌ] *v* **-ated; -ating** *vt* **1** : associer **2 to be associated with** : être associé à, faire partie de — *vi* **to associate with** : fréquenter
associate[2] [ə'soːʃiət, -siət] *n* : associé *m*, -ciée *f*
association [əˌsoːʃi'eɪʃən, -si-] *n* : association *f*
as soon as *conj* : aussitôt que
assorted [ə'sɔrtəd] *adj* : assorti
assortment [ə'sɔrtmənt] *n* : assortiment *m*
assuage [ə'sweɪdʒ] *vt* **-suaged; -suaging** **1** CALM, EASE : apaiser, calmer **2** SATISFY : assouvir (la faim, etc.)
assume [ə'suːm] *vt* **-sumed; -suming** **1** TAKE ON : prendre, assumer **2** ADOPT, FEIGN : adopter, affecter **3** SUPPOSE : supposer, présumer
assumption [ə'sʌmpʃən] *n* **1** SUPPOSITION : supposition *f* **2** APPROPRIATION : appropriation *f*, prise *f* (de pouvoir, etc.)
assurance [ə'ʃʊrənts] *n* : assurance *f*
assure [ə'ʃʊr] *vt* **-sured; -suring** : assurer
assured [ə'ʃʊrd] *adj* **1** CERTAIN : assuré **2** CONFIDENT : assuré, plein d'assurance
assuredly [ə'ʃʊrədli] *adv* : assurément
aster ['æstər] *n* : aster *m*
asterisk ['æstəˌrɪsk] *n* : astérisque *m*
astern [ə'stərn] *adv* : à l'arrière
asteroid ['æstəˌrɔɪd] *n* : astéroïde *m*
asthma ['æzmə] *n* : asthme *m*
asthmatic [æz'mæt̬ɪk] *adj* : asthmatique
as though → as if
astigmatism [ə'stɪgməˌtɪzəm] *n* : astigmatisme *m*
astir [ə'stər] *adj* **1** UP : debout **2** ACTIVE, MOVING : en mouvement, animé
as to *prep* **1** ABOUT : sur, concernant **2 → according to**
astonish [ə'stɑnɪʃ] *vt* : étonner, ahurir
astonishing [ə'stɑnɪʃɪŋ] *adj* : étonnant
astonishingly [ə'stɑnɪʃɪŋli] *adv* : incroyablement
astonishment [ə'stɑnɪʃmənt] *n* : étonnement *m*, stupéfaction *f*
astound [ə'staʊnd] *vt* : stupéfier
astounding [ə'staʊndɪŋ] *adj* : stupéfiant, ahurissant
astraddle [ə'strædəl] → **astride**
astral ['æstrəl] *adj* : astral
astray [ə'streɪ] *adv* **1 to go astray** : s'égarer **2 to lead s.o. astray** : égarer qqn, détourner qqn du droit chemin
astride [ə'straɪd] *adv* : à califourchon
astringent [ə'strɪndʒənt] *adj* : astringent
astrologer [ə'strɑlədʒər] *n* : astrologue *mf*
astrological [ˌæstrə'lɑdʒɪkəl] *adj* : astrologique
astrology [ə'strɑlədʒi] *n* : astrologie *f*
astronaut ['æstrəˌnɔt] *n* : astronaute *mf*
astronautics [ˌæstrə'nɔt̬ɪks] *ns & pl* : astronautique *f*
astronomer [ə'strɑnəmər] *n* : astronome *mf*
astronomical [ˌæstrə'nɑmɪkəl] *adj* : astronomique
astronomy [ə'strɑnəmi] *n, pl* **-mies** : astronomie *f*
astute [ə'stuːt, -'stjuːt] *adj* : astucieux — **astutely** *adv*
astuteness [ə'stuːtnəs, -'stjuːt-] *n* : astuce *f*
asunder [ə'sʌndər] *adv* : en morceaux
as well as[1] *conj* AND : en plus de
as well as[2] *prep* : ainsi que, à part
asylum [ə'saɪləm] *n* : asile *m*
asymmetrical [ˌeɪsə'metrɪkəl] *or* **asymmetric** [ˌeɪsə'metrɪk] *adj* : asymétrique
asymmetry [ˌeɪ'sɪmətri] *n* : asymétrie *f*
asymptomatic [ˌeɪˌsɪmptə'mæt̬ɪk] *adj* : asymptomatique
at ['æt] *prep* **1** : à <at the end : à la fin> <be here at 3 o'clock : soyez là à trois

heures> <at his age : à son âge> **2** : chez <at the dentist's : chez le dentiste> **3** : en <at war : en guerre> <to be good at : être bon en> **4** : de <to laugh at : rire de> **5** : sur <to shoot at : tirer sur> **6** : contre <to be angry at : être fâché contre>

at all *adv* : du tout

ate [ˈeɪt] → **eat**

atheism [ˈeɪθiˌɪzəm] *n* : athéisme *m*

atheist [ˈeɪθiɪst] *n* : athée *mf*

atheistic [ˌeɪθiˈɪstɪk] *adj* : athée

athlete [ˈæθˌliːt] *n* : athlète *mf*

athletic [æθˈleṭɪk] *adj* : athlétique

athletics [æθˈleṭɪks] *ns & pl* : athlétisme *m*

atlas [ˈætləs] *n* : atlas *m*

atmosphere [ˈætməˌsfɪr] *n* : atmosphère *f*

atmospheric [ˌætməˈsfɪrɪk, -ˈsfɛr-] *adj* : atmosphérique

atoll [ˈæˌtɔl, ˈeɪ-, -ˌtɑl] *n* : atoll *m*

atom [ˈætəm] *n* : atome *m*

atomic [əˈtɑmɪk] *adj* : atomique

atomic bomb *n* : bombe *f* atomique

atomizer [ˈæṭəˌmaɪzər] *n* : atomiseur *m*

atone [əˈtoːn] *v* **atoned; atoning** *vt* EXPIATE : expier — *vi* **to atone for** : expier

atonement [əˈtoːnmənt] *n* : expiation *f*

atop[1] [əˈtɑp] *adv & adj* : en haut

atop[2] *prep* : sur, en haut de

atrocious [əˈtroːʃəs] *adj* : atroce — **atrociously** *adv*

atrocity [əˈtrɑsəṭi] *n, pl* **-ties** : atrocité *f*

atrophy[1] [ˈætrəfi] *v* **-phied; phying** *vt* : atrophier — *vi* : s'atrophier

atrophy[2] *n, pl* **-phies** : atrophie *f*

attach [əˈtæṭʃ] *vt* **1** FASTEN, JOIN : attacher, fixer, joindre **2** ATTRIBUTE : attribuer, attacher <she attached little importance to the message : elle a attaché peu d'importance au message> **3** SEIZE : saisir (des biens) **4 to become attached to** : s'attacher à — *vi* ADHERE : s'attacher

attaché [ˌæṭəˈʃeɪ, ˌæˌtæ-, əˌtæ-] *n* : attaché *m*, -chée *f*

attaché case *n* : attaché-case *m*

attachment [əˈtæṭʃmənt] *n* **1** AFFECTION, CLOSENESS : attachement *m*, affection *f* **2** ACCESSORY : accessoire *m* **3** SEIZURE : saisie *f* (de biens) **4** FASTENING : fixation *f*

attack[1] [əˈtæk] *vt* **1** ASSAULT : attaquer, agresser **2** TACKLE : s'attaquer à <he attacked the problem aggressively : il s'est attaqué au problème agressivement>

attack[2] *n* **1** ASSAULT : attaque *f*, assaut *m* **2** : crise *f*, accès *m* <heart attack : crise cardiaque> <an attack of fever : un accès de fièvre>

attain [əˈteɪn] *vt* : atteindre

attainable [əˈteɪnəbəl] *adj* : réalisable

attainment [əˈteɪnmənt] *n* **1** ACHIEVING : réalisation *f* **2** ACCOMPLISHMENT : réussite *f*, résultat *m* obtenu

attempt[1] [əˈtempt] *vt* : tenter

attempt[2] *n* : tentative *f*, effort *m*, essai *m*

attend [əˈtɛnd] *vt* **1** : assister à (une réunion, etc.), aller à (l'église, etc.) **2** LOOK AFTER : soigner, servir **3** ACCOMPANY : accompagner — *vi* **1 to attend to** : s'occuper de (affaires, etc.), s'appliquer à (travaux) **2 to attend to** HEED : prêter attention à

attendance [əˈtɛndənʌs] *n* **1** PRESENCE : présence *f* **2** TURNOUT : assistance *f*

attendant[1] [əˈtɛndənt] *adj* : concomitant

attendant[2] *n* **1** : gardien *m*, -dienne *f* (à un musée, etc.) **2 service station attendant** : pompiste *mf*

attention [əˈtɛnṭʃən] *n* **1** : attention *f* **2 to stand at attention** : se mettre au garde-à-vous **3** → **pay**

attentive [əˈtɛnṭɪv] *adj* : attentif — **attentively** *adv*

attentiveness [əˈtɛnṭɪvnəs] *n* **1** CONCENTRATION : attention *f* **2** SOLICITUDE : prévenance *f*, égard *m*

attenuate [əˈtɛnjəˌweɪt] *vt* **-ated; -ating** : atténuer

attest [əˈtɛst] *vt* **1** AFFIRM : attester **2** PROVE, SHOW : démontrer, témoigner de — *vi* TESTIFY : témoigner

attestation [ˌæˌtɛsˈteɪʃən] *n* : attestation *f*

attic [ˈætɪk] *n* : grenier *m*

attire[1] [əˈtaɪr] *vt* **-tired; -tiring** : vêtir

attire[2] *n* : vêtements *mpl*

attitude [ˈæṭəˌtuːd, -ˌtjuːd] *n* **1** : attitude *f* <a negative attitude : une attitude négative> **2** POSTURE : position *f*, attitude *f* <to strike an attitude : prendre une pose affectée>

attorney [əˈtɔrni] *n, pl* **-neys** : avocat *m*, -cate *f*

attract [əˈtrækt] *vt* : attirer

attraction [əˈtrækʃən] *n* : attraction *f*

attractive [əˈtræktɪv] *adj* : séduisant, attrayant, attirant

attractively [əˈtræktɪvli] *adv* : de manière attrayante

attractiveness [əˈtræktɪvnəs] *n* : attrait *m*, charme *m*

attributable [əˈtrɪbjuṭəbəl] *adj* : attribuable

attribute[1] [əˈtrɪˌbjuːṭ] *vt* **-uted; -uting** : attribuer

attribute[2] [ˈætrəˌbjuːṭ] *n* : attribut *m*

attribution [ˌætrəˈbjuːʃən] *n* : attribution *f*

attune [əˈtuːn, -ˈtjuːn] *vt* : accorder <to be attuned to : être en accord avec>

auburn [ˈɔbərn] *adj* : auburn

auction[1] [ˈɔkʃən] *vt* : vendre aux enchères, encanter *Can*

auction[2] *n* : vente *f* aux enchères

auctioneer [ˌɔkʃəˈnɪr] *n* : commissaire-priseur *m*, encanteur *m Can*
audacious [ɔˈdeɪʃəs] *adj* : audacieux — **audaciously** *adv*
audacity [ɔˈdæsəṭi] *n, pl* **-ties** : audace *f*
audible [ˈɔdəbəl] *adj* : audible
audibly [ˈɔdəbli] *adv* : distinctement
audience [ˈɔdiənṭs] *n* **1** PUBLIC : assistance *f*, public *m* **2** HEARING, INTERVIEW : audience *f*
audio[1] [ˈɔdiˌoː] *adj* : audio
audio[2] *n* : son *m*, acoustique *f*
audiovisual [ˌɔdioˈvɪʒʊəl] *adj* : audiovisuel
audit[1] [ˈɔdət] *vt* **1** : vérifier (des comptes, etc.) **2 to audit a course** : suivre un cours en auditeur libre
audit[2] *n* : audit *m*
audition[1] [ɔˈdɪʃən] *v* : auditionner
audition[2] *n* : audition *f*
auditor [ˈɔdəṭər] *n* **1** : vérificateur *m*, -trice *f* (de comptes) **2** : auditeur *m*, -trice *f* (d'un cours)
auditorium [ˌɔdəˈtoriəm] *n, pl* **-riums** *or* **-ria** [-riə] : salle *f*, amphithéâtre *m*
auditory [ˈɔdəˌtori] *adj* : auditif
auger [ˈɔgər] *n* : vrille *f*
augment [ɔgˈment] *vt* : augmenter
augmentation [ˌɔgmənˈteɪʃən] *n* : augmentation *f*
augur[1] [ˈɔgər] *vt* : présager — *vi* **to augur well** : être de bon augure
augur[2] *n* : augure *m*
augury [ˈɔgjʊri, -gər-] *n, pl* **-ries** : augure *m*, présage *m*
august [ɔˈgʌst] *adj* : auguste
August [ˈɔgəst] *n* : août *m*
auk [ˈɔk] *n* **great auk** : grand pingouin *m*
aunt [ˈænt, ˈant] *n* : tante *f*
aura [ˈɔrə] *n* : aura *f*, atmosphère *f*
aural [ˈɔrəl] *adj* : auditif
auricle [ˈɔrɪkəl] *n* : oreillette *f* (du cœur)
aurora borealis [əˈrorəˌborɪˈæləs] *n* : aurore *f* boréale
auspices [ˈɔspəsəz, -ˌsiːz] *npl* : auspices *mpl*
auspicious [ɔˈspɪʃəs] *adj* : favorable, propice, prometteur
austere [ɔˈstɪr] *adj* : austère — **austerely** *adv*
austerity [ɔˈstɛrəṭi] *n, pl* **-ties** : austérité *f*
Australian[1] [ɔˈstreɪljən] *adj* : australien
Australian[2] *n* : Australien *m*, -lienne *f*
Austrian[1] [ˈɔstriən] *adj* : autrichien
Austrian[2] *n* : Autrichien *m*, -chienne *f*
authentic [əˈθɛnṭɪk, ɔ-] *adj* : authentique — **authentically** [-tɪkli] *adv*
authenticate [əˈθɛnṭiˌkeɪt, ɔ-] *vt* **-cated; -cating** : authentifier
authenticity [ˌɔθɛnˈtɪsəṭi] *n* : authenticité *f*
author [ˈɔθər] *n* : auteur *m*, auteure *f Can*
authoritarian [ɔˌθɔrəˈteriən, ə-] *adj* : autoritaire
authoritative [əˈθɔrəˌteiṭɪv, ɔ-] *adj* **1** DICTATORIAL : autoritaire **2** DEFINITIVE : qui fait autorité
authoritatively [əˈθɔrəˌteiṭɪvli, ɔ-] *adv* : de manière autoritaire, avec autorité
authority [əˈθɔrəṭi, ɔ-] *n, pl* **-ties 1** AUTHORIZATION : autorisation *f*, droit *m* **2** POWER : autorité *f*, pouvoir *m* **3** FORCEFULNESS : autorité *f*, assurance *f* <to speak with authority : parler avec autorité> **4 authorities** *npl* : autorités *fpl*, administration *f*
authorization [ˌɔθərəˈzeɪʃən] *n* : autorisation *f*
authorize [ˈɔθəˌraɪz] *vt* **-rized; -rizing** : autoriser
authorship [ˈɔθərˌʃɪp] *n* : paternité *f*
auto [ˈɔto] *n, pl* **autos** : auto *f*, voiture *f*
autobiographical [ˌɔṭobaɪəˈgræfɪkəl] *adj* : autobiographique
autobiography [ˌɔṭobaɪˈɑgrəfi] *n, pl* **-phies** : autobiographie *f*
autocracy [ɔˈtɑkrəsi] *n, pl* **-cies** : autocratie *f*
autocrat [ˈɔtoˌkræt] *n* : autocrate *mf*
autocratic [ˌɔtəˈkræṭɪk] *adj* : autocratique
autograph[1] [ˈɔtəˌgræf] *vt* : dédicacer (un livre, etc.), signer
autograph[2] *n* : autographe *m*
automate [ˈɔtəˌmeɪt] *v* **-mated; -mating** : automatiser
automatic [ˌɔtəˈmæṭɪk] *adj* : automatique — **automatically** [-ṭɪkli] *adv*
automation [ˌɔṭəˈmeɪʃən] *n* : automatisation *f*
automaton [ɔˈtɑməˌtɑn] *n, pl* **-atons** *or* **-ata** [-ṭə, -tɑ] : automate *m*
automobile [ˌɔṭəmoˈbiːl, -ˈmoːˌbiːl] *n* : automobile *f*, voiture *f*
automotive [ˌɔṭəˈmoːṭɪv] *adj* : automobile
autonomous [ɔˈtɑnəməs] *adj* : autonome
autonomy [ɔˈtɑnəmi] *n, pl* **-mies** : autonomie *f*
autopsy [ˈɔˌtɑpsi, -təp-] *n, pl* **-sies** : autopsie *f*
autumn [ˈɔṭəm] *n* : automne *m*
autumnal [ɔˈtʌmnəl] *adj* : automnal, d'automne
auxiliary[1] [ɔgˈzɪljəri, -ˈzɪləri] *adj* : auxiliaire
auxiliary[2] *n, pl* **-ries 1** : auxiliaire *mf* **2** *or* **auxiliary verb** : auxiliaire *m*
avail[1] [əˈveɪl] *vt* **to avail oneself of** : profiter de, se servir de
avail[2] *n* **1 to be of no avail** : être inutile, n'avoir aucun effet **2 to no avail** : en vain, sans résultat
availability [əˌveɪləˈbɪləṭi] *n, pl* **-ties** : disponibilité *f*

available [əˈveɪləbəl] *adj* : disponible
avalanche [ˈævəˌlænt͡ʃ] *n* : avalanche *f*
avarice [ˈævərəs] *n* : avarice *f*, avidité *f*, cupidité *f*
avaricious [ˌævəˈrɪʃəs] *adj* : avare, cupide, pingre
avenge [əˈvɛnd͡ʒ] *vt* **avenged; avenging** : venger
avenger [əˈvɛnd͡ʒər] *n* : vengeur *m*, -geresse *f*
avenue [ˈæv(ə)ˌnuː, -ˌnjuː] *n* **1** STREET : avenue *f* **2** MEANS, WAY : voie *f*, route *f*
average[1] [ˈæv(ə)rɪd͡ʒ, ˈæv(ə)-] *vt* **-aged; -aging 1** : faire en moyenne <she averaged two goals per game : elle a fait en moyenne deux buts par jeu> **2** : faire la moyenne de (en mathématiques)
average[2] *adj* : moyen
average[3] *n* : moyenne *f*
averse [əˈvərs] *adj* **1** : opposé **2 to be averse to** : répugner à
aversion [əˈvər͡ʒən] *n* : aversion *f*
avert [əˈvərt] *vt* **1** : détourner <to avert one's eyes : détourner les yeux> **2** AVOID : éviter, prévenir
aviary [ˈeɪviˌɛri] *n, pl* **-aries** : volière *f*
aviation [ˌeɪviˈeɪʃən] *n* : aviation *f*
aviator [ˈeɪviˌeɪtər] *n* : aviateur *m*, -trice *f*
avid [ˈæv(ɪ)d] *adj* **1** GREEDY : avide <to be avid for : être avide de> **2** ENTHUSIASTIC : passionné, fervent
avidly [ˈæv(ɪ)dɪli] *adv* : avidement, avec ferveur
avocado [ˌæv(ə)ˈkɑdo, ˌɑv(ə)-] *n, pl* **-dos** : avocat *m*
avocation [ˌæv(ə)ˈkeɪʃən] *n* HOBBY : passe-temps *m*
avoid [əˈvɔɪd] *vt* : éviter, prévenir
avoidable [əˈvɔɪdəbəl] *adj* : évitable
avoidance [əˈvɔɪdən͡ʃs] *n* : action *f* d'éviter
avoirdupois [ˌæv(ə)rdəˈpɔɪz] *n* : avoirdupois *m*
avow [əˈvaʊ] *vt* **1** DECLARE : affirmer, déclarer **2** ADMIT : avouer, reconnaître
avowal [əˈvaʊəl] *n* **1** DECLARATION : affirmation *f* **2** ADMISSION : aveu *m*
await [əˈweɪt] *vt* : attendre
awake[1] [əˈweɪk] *v* **awoke** [əˈwoːk]; **awoken** [əˈwoːkən] *or* **awaked** [əˈweɪkt]; **awaking** *vt* AROUSE : réveiller, éveiller — *vi* WAKE UP : se réveiller, s'éveiller
awake[2] *adj* : éveillé, réveillé
awaken [əˈweɪkən] **awakened; awakening** → **awake**[1]
award[1] [əˈwɔrd] *vt* **1** GRANT : accorder **2** CONFER : décerner
award[2] *n* **1** PRIZE : prix *m*, distinction *f* honorifique **2** GRANT : bourse *f*
aware [əˈwær] *adj* **1** CONSCIOUS : conscient **2** INFORMED : au courant
awareness [əˈwærnəs] *n* : conscience *f*
awash [əˈwɔʃ] *adj* : inondé
away[1] [əˈweɪ] *adv* **1** (*indicating movement*) <to get away early : partir en avance> <go away! : hors d'ici!, allez-vous en!> **2** (*indicating the opposite direction*) <to look away : détourner les yeux> **3** (*indicating an ending*) <the wind died away : le vent s'est arrêté> **4** (*indicating the end of possession*) <she gave away her money : elle a donné son argent> **5** NONSTOP : sans arrêt <to chatter away : bavarder sans arrêt> **6** (*indicating distance in space or time*) <away back in 1850 : en 1850>
away[2] *adj* **1** ABSENT : absent **2** : de distance <10 kilometers away : à 10 kilomètres de distance> **3** : à l'extérieur (aux sports) <an away game : un match à l'extérieur>
awe[1] [ˈɔ] *vt* **awed; awing** : impressionner, intimider
awe[2] *n* : crainte *f* mêlée de respect, crainte *f* révérentielle
awesome [ˈɔsəm] *adj* : impressionnant, imposant
awestruck [ˈɔˌstrʌk] *adj* : impressionné
awful [ˈɔfəl] *adj* **1** TERRIBLE : affreux, terrible **2 an awful lot of** : énormément de
awfully [ˈɔfəli] *adv* EXTREMELY : extrêmement, terriblement, très
awhile [əˈ*h*waɪl] *adv* : un moment
awkward [ˈɔkwərd] *adj* **1** CLUMSY : gauche, maladroit **2** EMBARRASSING : embarrassant, gênant **3** DIFFICULT : difficile, incommode
awkwardly [ˈɔkwərdli] *adv* **1** CLUMSILY : maladroitement, avec maladresse **2** EMBARRASSEDLY : d'un ton embarrassé **3** INCONVENIENTLY : de façon malcommode
awkwardness [ˈɔkwərdnəs] *n* **1** CLUMSINESS : gaucherie *f*, maladresse *f* **2** EMBARRASSMENT : embarras *m*, gêne *f*
awl [ˈɔl] *n* : poinçon *m*, alène *f* (pour le cuir)
awning [ˈɔnɪŋ] *n* : auvent *m*
awoke, awoken → **awake**[1]
awry [əˈraɪ] *adv & adj* **1** : de travers **2 to go awry** : mal tourner
ax *or* **axe** [ˈæks] *n* : hache *f*
axiom [ˈæksiəm] *n* : axiome *m*
axiomatic [ˈæksiəmæt͡ɪk] *adj* : axiomatique
axis [ˈæksɪs] *n, pl* **axes** [-siːz] : axe *m*
axle [ˈæksəl] *n* : essieu *m*
aye[1] [ˈaɪ] *adv* : oui <to vote aye : voter oui>
aye[2] *n* : oui *m*
azalea [əˈzeɪljə] *n* : azalée *f*
azimuth [ˈæzəməθ] *n* : azimut *m*
azure[1] [ˈæʒər] *adj* : d'azur
azure[2] *n* : azur *m*

B

b [ˈbiː] *n, pl* **b's** *or* **bs** biːz] : b *m*, deuxième lettre de l'alphabet

babble[1] [ˈbæbəl] *v* **-bled; -bling** *vt* : bafouiller <babbling an excuse : bafouillant une excuse> — *vi* **1** PRATTLE : babiller **2** CHATTER : bavarder **3** : gazouiller <a babbling brook : un ruisseau gazouillant>

babble[2] *n* : babillage *m* (d'un enfant), bavardage *m* (d'un adulte), rumeur *f* (de voix), gazouillement *m* (d'un ruisseau, etc.)

babe [ˈbeɪb] → **baby**[2]

babel [ˈbeɪbəl, ˈbæ-] *n* HUBBUB : brouhaha *m*

baboon [bæˈbuːn] *n* : babouin *m*

baby[1] [ˈbeɪbi] *vt* **-bied; -bying** : dorloter

baby[2] *n, pl* **-bies** : bébé *m*

baby carriage *n* : voiture *f* d'enfant, landau *m France*

babyhood [ˈbeɪbiˌhʊd] *n* : petite enfance *f*

babyish [ˈbeɪbiɪʃ] *adj* : enfantin, puéril

baby–sit [ˈbeɪbiˌsɪt] *vi* **-sat** [-ˌsæt]; **-sitting** : garder des enfants, faire du baby-sitting *France*

baby–sitter [ˈbeɪbiˌsɪtər] *n* : gardienne *f* d'enfants, baby-sitter *mf France*

baccalaureate [ˈbækəˈlɔriət] *n* : licence *f*

bachelor [ˈbætʃələr] *n* **1** : célibataire *m* **2** GRADUATE : licencié *m*, -ciée *f* <bachelor of science : licencié de sciences>

bacillus [bəˈsɪləs] *n, pl* **-li** [-ˌlaɪ] : bacille *m*

back[1] [ˈbæk] *vt* **1** *or* **to back up** SUPPORT : soutenir, appuyer **2** FINANCE : financer **3** *or* **to back up** : reculer (un véhicule), mettre en marche arrière — *vi* **1 to back up** : reculer, faire marche arrière **2 to back out of** : se soustraire à, se dégager de **3 to back down** : céder, se résigner

back[2] *adv* **1** BACKWARD : en arrière, vers l'arrière **2** AGO : antérieurement **3 to come back** : être de retour **4 to give back** : rendre **5 to go back** : retourner **6 to walk back and forth** : marcher de long en large

back[3] *adj* **1** REAR : arrière, de derrière <the back door : la porte arrière> **2** OVERDUE : arriéré, impayé <back pay : rappel de salaire> **3 back street** : petite rue *f*

back[4] *n* **1** : dos *m* (du corps) <back to back : dos à dos> **2** REAR : derrière *m*, arrière *m*, fond *m* **3** : dossier *m* (d'un siège) **4** : arrière *m* (aux sports)

backache [ˈbækˌeɪk] *n* : mal *m* de dos

backbite [ˈbækˌbaɪt] *vt* **-bit** [-ˌbɪt]; **-bitten** [-ˌbɪtən]; **-biting** : médire de, dénigrer

backbone [ˈbækˌboːn] *n* **1** : colonne *f* vertébrale **2** FORTITUDE : fermeté *f*, caractère *m*

backdrop [ˈbækˌdrɑp] *n* : toile *f* de fond

backer [ˈbækər] *n* SUPPORTER : partisan *m*, -sane *f*; allié *m*, -liée *f*

backfire[1] [ˈbækˌfaɪr] *vi* **-fired; -firing 1** : pétarader (se dit d'une voiture) **2** FAIL : échouer, tourner mal

backfire[2] *n* : pétarade *f* (d'une voiture)

background [ˈbækˌgraʊnd] *n* **1** : arrière-plan *m*, fond *m* (d'un tableau) **2** EXPERIENCE, EDUCATION : expérience *f*, formation *f*

backhand[1] [ˈbækˌhænd] *adj* & *adv* : en revers

backhand[2] *n* : revers *m* (au tennis)

backhanded [ˈbækˌhændəd] *adj* **1** : en revers, de revers **2** INDIRECT, DEVIOUS : équivoque, sournois

backing [ˈbækɪŋ] *n* **1** SUPPORT : soutien *m*, appui *m* **2** REINFORCEMENT : renfort *m*, renforcement *m*

backlash [ˈbækˌlæʃ] *n* : contrecoup *m*, répercussion *f*

backlog [ˈbækˌlɔg] *n* : arriéré *m*, accumulation *f*

backpack[1] [ˈbækˌpæk] *vi* : faire de la randonnée

backpack[2] *n* : sac *m* à dos

backrest [ˈbækˌrɛst] *n* : dossier *m*

backslide [ˈbækˌslaɪd] *vi* **-slid** [-ˌslɪd]; **-slid** *or* **-slidden** [-ˌslɪdən]; **-sliding** : retomber, récidiver

backstage [ˌbækˈstɛɪdʒ, ˈbæk,-] *adv* : dans les coulisses, derrière la scène

backtrack [ˈbækˌtræk] *vi* **1** : revenir sur ses pas **2** : faire marche arrière, revenir <she backtracked on her commitment : elle est revenue sur son engagement>

backup [ˈbækˌʌp] *n* **1** SUPPORT : soutien *m*, appui *m* **2** SUBSTITUTE : réserve *f*, remplaçant *m* **3** : sauvegarde *f* (en informatique)

backward[1] [ˈbækwərd] *or* **backwards** [-wərdz] *adv* **1** BACK : en arrière **2** : à la renverse <to fall over backward : tomber à la renverse> **3** : à l'envers <say it backwards : dis-le à l'envers>

backward[2] *adj* **1** : en arrière, rétrograde <a backward glance : un regard en arrière> <backward motion : mouvement rétrograde> **2** RETARDED, SLOW : arriéré, peu avancé **3** UNDERDEVELOPED : sous-développé, arriéré <backward countries : pays arriérés> **4** BASHFUL, HESITANT : timide, peu disposé

backwardness [ˈbækwərdnəs] *n* **1** : retard *m* mental (d'une personne), sous-développement *m* (d'un pays) **2** BASHFULNESS : timidité *f*

backwoods [ˌbækˈwʊdz] *ns & pl* : région *f* forestière peu peuplée, forêts *fpl* de l'intérieur

bacon |beɪkən| *n* : lard *m*, bacon *m*
bacterial |bækˈtɪrɪəl| *adj* : bactérien
bacteriologist |bækˌtɪriˈɑlədʒɪst| *n* : bactériologiste *mf*
bacteriology |bækˌtɪriˈɑlədʒi| *n* : bactériologie *f*
bacterium |bækˈtɪriəm| *n, pl* **-ria** |-riə| : bactérie *f*
bad[1] |ˈbæd| *adv* → **badly**
bad[2] *adj* **worse; worst 1** POOR : mauvais <bad weather : mauvais temps> <bad breath : mauvaise haleine> **2** ROTTEN : pourri **3** SERIOUS, SEVERE : grave (se dit d'un accident, etc.), aigu (se dit d'une douleur) **4** DEFECTIVE : défectueux, de mauvaise qualité **5** WICKED : méchant, mauvais **6** UNWELL : malade, mal <to feel bad : se sentir mal> **7** HARMFUL : néfaste, nuisible **8** : sans provision <a bad check : un chèque sans provision> **9** NAUGHTY : méchant **10 from bad to worse** : de mal en pis
bad[3] *n* : mauvais *m* <to take the good with the bad : prendre le bon avec le mauvais>
bade → **bid**
badge |ˈbædʒ| *n* : insigne *m*, plaque *f* (d'un agent de police)
badger[1] |ˈbædʒər| *vt* : harceler, importuner
badger[2] *n* : blaireau *m*
badly |ˈbædli| *adv* **1** : mal <badly dressed : mal habillé> **2** SEVERELY : gravement, grièvement <badly injured : grièvement blessé> **3** URGENTLY : énormément, avec grand besoin <to want sth badly : avoir très envie de qqch>
badminton |ˈbædˌmɪntən, -ˌmɪt-| *n* : badminton *m*
badness |ˈbædnəs| *n* : méchanceté *f*
baffle |ˈbæfəl| *vt* **-fled; -fling** : déconcerter, confondre
bafflement |ˈbæfəlmənt| *n* : confusion *f*, perplexité *f*
bag[1] |ˈbæg| *v* **bagged; bagging** *vt* **1** : mettre en sac, ensacher (des marchandises) **2** KILL : tuer (du gibier) — *vi* SAG : pocher, faire des poches
bag[2] *n* **1** : sac *m* <plastic bag : sac en plastique> **2** POCKETBOOK : sac *m* à main **3** SUITCASE : valise *f*, mallette *f*
bagatelle |ˌbægəˈtɛl| *n* : bagatelle *f*
bagel |ˈbeɪgəl| *n* : petit pain *m* en couronne, bagel *m Can*
baggage |ˈbægɪdʒ| *n* : bagages *mpl*
baggy |ˈbægi| *adj* **baggier; -est** : ample, qui fait des poches
bagpipes |ˈbægˌpaɪps| *npl* : cornemuse *f*
Bahamian[1] |bəˈheɪmiən, -ˈhɔ-| *adj* : des Bahamas
Bahamian[2] *n* : habitant *m*, -tante *f* des Bahamas
Bahraini[1] |bɑːˈreɪni| *adj* : bahreïni
Bahraini[2] *n* : Bahreïni *m*, -nie *f*
bail[1] |ˌbeɪl| *vt* **1** : vider (l'eau d'un bateau), écoper (un bateau) **2 to bail out** RELEASE : mettre en liberté sous caution **3 to bail out** EXTRICATE : tirer d'affaire — *vi* **to bail out** : sauter en parachute
bail[2] *n* **1** SECURITY : caution *f* **2 to release on bail** : mettre en liberté sous caution
bailiff |ˈbeɪlɪf| *n* : huissier *m*
bailiwick |ˈbeɪliˌwɪk| *n* : domaine *m*
bait[1] |ˈbeɪt| *vt* **1** : appâter, amorcer (un hameçon, etc.) **2** HARASS : harceler, tourmenter
bait[2] *n* : appât *m*, amorce *f*
bake |ˈbeɪk| *v* **baked; baking** *vt* : faire cuire au four — *vi* : cuire au four
baker |ˈbeɪkər| *n* : boulanger *m*, -gère *f*
bakery |ˈbeɪkəri| *n, pl* **-ries** : boulangerie *f*
bakeshop |ˈbeɪkˌʃɑp| → **bakery**
baking powder *n* : levure *f* chimique, poudre *f* à pâte *Can*
baking soda *n* : bicarbonate *m* de soude
balance[1] |ˈbæləns| *v* **-anced; -ancing** *vt* **1** ADJUST : équilibrer (un budget, des roues, etc.) **2** WEIGH : peser <to balance the pros and cons : peser le pour et le contre> **3** : mettre en équilibre, poser en équilibre <he balanced the book on his head : il a posé le livre en équilibre sur sa tête> **4** OFFSET : compenser, contrebalancer — *vi* : être en équilibre, s'équilibrer
balance[2] *n* **1** SCALES : balance *f* <to hang in the balance : être en jeu> **2** EQUILIBRIUM : équilibre *m* **3** REMAINDER : solde *m* (en finances), restant *m* **4** COUNTERBALANCE, WEIGHT : contrepoids *m*
balcony |ˈbælkəni| *n, pl* **-nies** : balcon *m*
bald |ˈbɔld| *adj* **1** HAIRLESS : chauve **2** BARREN : pelé <a bald mountain : une montagne pelée> **3** PLAIN : pur, simple <the bald truth : la vérité pure et simple>
bald eagle *n* : aigle *m* d'Amérique, aigle *m* à tête blanche
balding |ˈbɔldɪŋ| *adj* : qui devient chauve
baldly |ˈbɔldli| *adv* : franchement, sans détours
baldness |ˈbɔldnəs| *n* : calvitie *f*
bale[1] |ˈbeɪl| *vt* **baled; baling** : mettre en balles, emballer
bale[2] *n* : balle *f*
baleful |ˈbeɪlfəl| *adj* OMINOUS : menaçant, sinistre
balk[1] |ˈbɔk| *vt* THWART : contrecarrer, frustrer — *vi* **to balk at** : reculer devant, rechigner à
balk[2] *n* HINDRANCE : obstacle *m*
balky |ˈbɔki| **balkier; -est** *adj* : contrariant, entêté

ball[1] ['bɔl] *vt* : mettre en boule, pelotonner — *vi or* **to ball up** : s'agglomérer
ball[2] *n* **1** : balle *f*, ballon *m*, boule *f* <to play ball : jouer au ballon> **2** : pelote *f* (de ficelle, etc.) **3** DANCE : bal *m* **4 ball of the foot** : plante *f* du pied
ballad ['bæləd] *n* **1** : ballade *f*
ballast[1] ['bæləst] *vt* : lester
ballast[2] *n* : lest *m*, ballast *m*
ball bearing *n* : roulement *m* à billes
ballerina [ˌbælə'riːnə] *n* : ballerine *f*
ballet [bæ'leɪ, 'bæˌleɪ] *n* : ballet *m*
ballistic [bə'lɪstɪk] *adj* : balistique <ballistic missile : engin balistique>
ballistics [bə'lɪstɪks] *ns & pl* : balistique *f*
balloon[1] [bə'luːn] *vi* **1** : faire une ascension en ballon **2** SWELL : gonfler **3** INCREASE : augmenter (rapidement)
balloon[2] *n* **1** : ballon *m*, balloune *f Can* **2** *or* **hot–air balloon** : montgolfière *f*
ballot[1] ['bælət] *vt* : sonder par vote — *vi* : voter au scrutin
ballot[2] *n* **1** VOTE : vote *m* **2** VOTING : scrutin *m*
ballroom ['bɔlˌruːm, -ˌrʊm] *n* : salle *f* de danse, salle *f* de bal
balm ['bɑm, 'bɑlm] *n* : baume *m*
balmy ['bɑmi, 'bɑl-] *adj* **balmier; -est 1** MILD : doux <a balmy climate : un climat doux> **2** CRAZY : toqué *fam*, timbré *fam*
baloney [bə'loːni] *n* NONSENSE : balivernes *fpl*
balsa ['bɔlsə] *n* : balsa *m*
balsam ['bɔlsəm] *n* **1** : baume *m* **2** *or* **balsam fir** : balsamine *f*
balsamic vinegar [bɔl'sæmɪk-] *n* : vinaigre *m* balsamique
baluster ['bæləstər] *n* : balustre *m*
balustrade ['bæləˌstreɪd] *n* : balustrade *f*
bamboo [bæm'buː] *n, pl* **-boos** : bambou *m*
bamboozle [bæm'buːzəl] *vt* **-zled; -zling** : embobiner *fam*, faire emplir *Can*
ban[1] ['bæn] *vt* **banned; banning** : interdire, défendre
ban[2] *n* : interdiction *f*
banal [bə'nɑl, -'næl, 'beɪnəl] *adj* : banal
banality [bə'nælətɪ] *n* : banalité *f*
banana [bə'nænə] *n* : banane *f*
band[1] ['bænd] *vt* **1** BIND : lier, attacher **2** *or* **to band together** UNITE : unir, réunir — *vi* **to band together** : se réunir, se grouper
band[2] *n* **1** STRIP : bande *f*, bandelette *f* **2** GROUP : groupe *m*, troupe *f* **3** : ruban *m* (d'un chapeau) **4** : bande *f* (de transmission) **5** : orchestre *m* **6** → **rubber band**
bandage[1] ['bændɪdʒ] *vt* : bander, mettre un pansement sur
bandage[2] *n* : pansement *m*, bandage *m*
bandanna *or* **bandana** [bæn'dænə] *n* : foulard *m*
bandit ['bændət] *n* : bandit *m*
banditry ['bændətri] *n* : banditisme *m*
bandstand ['bænd,stænd] *n* : kiosque *m* à musique
bandwagon ['bænd,wægən] *n* **to jump on the bandwagon** : suivre le mouvement, prendre le train en marche
bandy[1] ['bændi] *vt* **-died; -dying 1** EXCHANGE : échanger **2 to bandy about** : faire circuler, avancer (des idées)
bandy[2] *adj* : arqué <bandy legs : jambes arquées>
bane [beɪn] *n* **1** POISON : poison *m* **2** : fléau *m* <the bane of one's existence : le fléau de son existence>
bang[1] ['bæŋ] *vt* **1** SLAM : claquer **2** HIT, STRIKE : se cogner, se frapper <to bang one's head : se cogner la tête> <he banged his fists on the table : il a frappé ses poings sur la table>
bang[2] *adv* : exactement, en plein <bang in the middle : en plein milieu>
bang[3] *n* **1** : claquement *m* (d'une porte, etc.) **2** : détonation *f* (d'un fusil) **3** BLOW : coup *m* **4 bangs** *npl* : frange *f* (de cheveux)
Bangladeshi[1] [ˌbɑŋglə'deʃi, ˌbæŋ-, ˌbʌŋ-, -deɪ-] *adj* : bangladais
Bangladeshi[2] *n* : Bangladais *m*, -daise *f*
bangle ['bæŋgəl] *n* : bracelet *m*
banish ['bænɪʃ] *vt* **1** EXILE : exiler, bannir **2** EXPEL : expulser
banishment ['bænɪʃmənt] *n* **1** EXILE : exile *m*, bannissement *m* **2** EXPULSION : expulsion *f*
banister ['bænəstər] *n* **1** BALUSTER : balustre *m* **2** HANDRAIL : rampe *f* (d'escalier)
banjo ['bænˌdʒoː] *n, pl* **-jos** : banjo *m*
bank[1] ['bæŋk] *vt* **1** : déposer (de l'argent, des chèques) à la banque **2** *or* **to bank up** : relever (un virage) **3** : couvrir (un feu) — *vi* **1** : avoir un compte en banque **2** PILE UP : s'entasser, s'amonceler **3** TILT : s'incliner sur l'aile (se dit d'un avion) **4 to bank on** : compter sur
bank[2] *n* **1** EMBANKMENT : talus *m* **2** : bord *m*, rive *f* <left bank : rive gauche> <the bank of a road : le bord d'une rue> **3** SHOAL : banc *m* <sand bank : banc de sable> **4** : banque *f*, institution *f* bancaire **5 data bank** : banque *f* de données
bankbook ['bæŋkˌbʊk] *n* : carnet *m* de banque, livret *m* bancaire
banker ['bæŋkər] *n* : banquier *m*
banking ['bæŋkɪŋ] *n* **1** : opérations *fpl* bancaires **2** : profession *f* de banquier
banknote ['bæŋkˌnoːt] *n* : billet *m* (de banque)
bankrupt[1] ['bæŋkrʌpt] *vt* : mettre en faillite, ruiner

bankrupt[2] *adj* **1** : failli **2** LACKING : dépourvu, dénué <bankrupt of ideas : dénué d'idées>
bankrupt[3] *n* : failli *m*, -lie *f*
bankruptcy ['bæŋ,krʌpʧi] *n, pl* **-cies** : faillite *f*
banner[1] ['bænər] *adj* : record, excellent <a banner year : une année record>
banner[2] *n* : bannière *f*, étendard *m*
banns ['bænz] *npl* : bans *mpl* (de mariage)
banquet ['bæŋkwət] *n* : banquet *m*, festin *m*
bantam ['bæntəm] *n* : coq *m* nain, poule *f* naine
banter[1] ['bæntər] *vi* : badiner, plaisanter
banter[2] *n* : badinage *m*, plaisanterie *f*
baptism ['bæp,tɪzəm] *n* : baptême *m*
baptismal [bæp'tɪzməl] *adj* : de baptême, baptismal
baptize [bæp'taɪz, 'bæp,taɪz] *vt* **-tized; -tizing** : baptiser
bar[1] ['bɑr] *vt* **barred; barring 1** OBSTRUCT : barrer, bloquer **2** EXCLUDE : exclure **3** BAN, PROHIBIT : défendre, interdire **4** : mettre la barre à (une porte, etc.)
bar[2] *n* **1** ROD, STRIP : barre *f* (de métal), barreau *m* (d'une fenêtre) **2** : barre *f*, tablette *f* (de chocolat, etc.) **3** OBSTRUCTION : obstacle *m*, barrière *f* **4** : barreau *m* <to be admitted to the bar : s'inscrire au barreau> **5** BAND, STREAK : raie *f* (de lumière), bande *f* (de couleur) **6** COUNTER : comptoir *m* **7** CAFÉ, TAVERN : bar *m*, café *m* **8 behind bars** : sous les verrous
bar[3] *prep* **1** : excepté, sauf **2 bar none** : sans exception
barb ['bɑrb] *n* **1** POINT : ardillon *m* (d'hameçon), barbe *f* (d'une plume) **2** GIBE : moquerie *f*, raillerie *f*
barbarian[1] [bɑr'bæriən] *adj* : barbare, de barbare
barbarian[2] *n* : barbare *mf*
barbaric [bɑr'bærɪk] *adj* : barbare
barbarism ['bɑrbə,rɪzəm] *n* : barbarie *f*
barbarity [bɑr'bærəṭi] *n, pl* **-ties** : barbarie *f*, cruauté *f*
barbarous ['bɑrbərəs] *adj* : barbare, cruel
barbarously ['bɑrbərəsli] *adv* : d'une façon barbare, cruellement
barbecue[1] ['bɑrbɪ,kju:] *vt* **-cued; -cuing** : griller au charbon de bois
barbecue[2] *n* : barbecue *m*
barbed [bɑrbd] *adj* : barbelé <a barbed-wire fence : une haie barbelée>
barber ['bɑrbər] *n* : coiffeur *m*, -feuse *f*; barbier *m*
barbiturate [bɑr'bɪtʃərət] *n* : barbiturique *m*
bard ['bɑrd] *n* : barde *m*, poète *m*
bare[1] ['bær] *vt* **bared; baring 1** UNCOVER : mettre à nu, se découvrir (la tête) **2 to bare one's teeth** : montrer les dents
bare[2] *adj* **barer; barest 1** NAKED : nu **2** EXPOSED : découvert, nu **3** EMPTY : vide <the cupboard was bare : l'armoire était vide> **4** PLAIN, STRICT : strict <the bare minimum : le strict minimum> **5** MERE : simple <the bare statement of facts : le simple énoncé des faits>
bareback ['bær,bæk] *or* **barebacked** [-,bækt] *adv & adj* : à cru
barefaced ['bær,feɪst] *adj* : éhonté <barefaced lie : mensonge éhonté>
barefoot[1] ['bær,fʊt] *or* **barefooted** [-,fʊtəd] *adv* : nu-pieds, pieds nus
barefoot[2] *or* **barefooted** *adj* : aux pieds nus, nu-pieds
bareheaded[1] ['bær,hedəd] *adv* : nu-tête, (la) tête nue
bareheaded[2] *adj* : à la tête nue
barely ['bærli] *adv* : à peine, tout juste
bareness ['bærnəs] *n* **1** NUDITY : nudité *f* **2** AUSTERITY : dépouillement *m*
bargain[1] ['bɑrgən] *vi* **1** NEGOTIATE : négocier **2** HAGGLE : marchander
bargain[2] *n* **1** : occasion *f*, (bonne) affaire *f* <that's a real bargain : c'est une véritable occasion> **2** AGREEMENT : marché *m* <to strike a bargain : conclure un marché>
barge[1] ['bɑrdʒ] *vi* **barged; barging 1** : se bousculer <they were barging through the crowd : ils se bousculaient à travers la foule> **2 to barge into** : faire irruption dans (une pièce, etc.), interrompre (une conversation)
barge[2] *n* : chaland *m*, péniche *f*
bar graph *n* : histogramme *m*
baritone ['bærə,to:n] *n* : baryton *m*
barium ['bæriəm] *n* : baryum *m*
bark[1] ['bɑrk] *vi* **1** : aboyer (se dit d'un chien) **2** SHOUT : crier, gueuler *fam* — *vt or* **to bark out** : aboyer
bark[2] *n* **1** : écorce *f* (d'un arbre) **2** : aboiement *m* (d'un chien) **3** BOAT : barque *f*
barker ['bɑrkər] *n* : bonimenteur *m* (à une foire)
barley ['bɑrli] *n* : orge *f* (plante), orge *m* (grain)
barn ['bɑrn] *n* : grange *f*, écurie *f* (de chevaux), étable *f* (de bovins)
barnacle ['bɑrnɪkəl] *n* : anatife *m*
barnyard ['bɑrn,jɑrd] *n* : basse-cour *f*
barometer [bə'rɑməṭər] *n* : baromètre *m*
barometric ['bærə'metrɪk] *adj* : barométrique
baron ['bærən] *n* : baron *m*
baroness ['bærənɪs, -nəs, -nes] *n* : baronne *f*
baronet [,bærə'net, 'bærənət] *n* : baronnet *m*
baronial [bə'ro:niəl] *adj* **1** : de baron **2** STATELY : imposant

baroque [bə'roːk, -'rɑk] *adj* : baroque
barracks ['bærəks] *ns & pl* : caserne *f*
barracuda [ˌbærə'kuːdə] *n, pl* **-da** *or* **-das** : barracuda *m*
barrage [bə'rɑʒ, -'rɑdʒ] *n* **1** : tir *m* de barrage (en artillerie) **2** DELUGE : pluie *f*, déluge *m* (de questions, etc.)
barrel[1] ['bærəl] *v* **-reled** *or* **-relled; -reling** *or* **-relling** *vt* : mettre en tonneau — *vi or* **to barrel along** : foncer *fam*
barrel[2] *n* **1** : tonneau *m*, fût *m*, baril *m* **2** : canon *m* (d'une arme à feu)
barren ['bærən] *adj* **1** STERILE : stérile, infertile <barren plants : plantes stériles> **2** BARE, DESOLATE : désertique, aride **3** UNPRODUCTIVE : aride, stérile
barrenness ['bærənnəs] *n* : aridité *f*, stérilité *f*
barrette [bə'rɛt, bə-] *n* : barrette *f*
barricade[1] *vt* ['bærəˌkeɪd, ˌbærə'-] **-caded; -cading** : barricader
barricade[2] *n* : barricade *f*
barrier ['bæriər] *n* : barrière *f*
barring ['bɑrɪŋ] *prep* : excepté, sauf, à moins de
barroom ['bɑrˌruːm, -rʊm] *n* : bar *m*
barrow ['bærˌoː] → **wheelbarrow**
bartender ['bɑrˌtendər] *n* : barman *m*
barter[1] ['bɑrtər] *vt* : échanger, troquer — *vi* : faire un échange, faire un troc
barter[2] *n* : échange *m*, troc *m*
basalt [bə'sɔlt, 'beɪˌ-] *n* : basalte *m*
base[1] ['beɪs] *vt* **based; basing 1** FOUND : baser, fonder (une opinion, un calcul, etc.) **2** LOCATE : baser
base[2] *adj* **baser; basest 1** CONTEMPTIBLE : bas, vil **2 base metal** : métal *m* non précieux
base[3] *n, pl* **bases 1** BOTTOM : base *f*, pied *m* **2** BASIS : fondement *m*, base *f*, point *m* de départ **3** *or* **army base** : base *f* militaire **4** : but *m Can* (au baseball)
baseness ['beɪsnəs] *n* : bassesse *f*, vilenie *f*
baseball ['beɪsˌbɔl] *n* : baseball *m*, baseball *m*
baseless ['beɪsləs] *adj* : sans fondement
basely ['beɪsli] *adv* : bassement, vilement
basement ['beɪsmənt] *n* : sous-sol *m*
bash[1] ['bæʃ] *vt* **1** HIT : cogner, frapper **2 to bash in** SMASH : enfoncer, défoncer
bash[2] *n* **1** BLOW : coup *m* **2** PARTY : fête *f*
bashful ['bæʃfəl] *adj* SHY : timide, gêné *Can*
bashfulness ['bæʃfəlnəs] *n* : timidité *f*
basic ['beɪsɪk] *adj* **1** : fondamental, de base <basic principle : principe fondamental> **2** : basique <basic salt : sel basique>
basically ['beɪsɪklɪ] *adv* : au fond, fondamentalement
basil ['beɪzel, 'bæzəl] *n* : basilic *m*
basilica [bə'sɪlɪkə] *n* : basilique *f*
basin ['beɪsən] *n* **1** WASHBOWL : cuvette *f*, lavabo *m* **2** : bassin *m* (d'un fleuve)
basis ['beɪsəs] *n, pl* **bases 1** BASE : base *f*, fondement *m* **2** PRINCIPLE : condition *f*, terme *m* <on that basis : dans ces conditions> **3 on a weekly basis** : à la semaine
bask ['bæsk] *vi* **1** : se prélasser (au soleil, etc.) **2** REVEL : se délecter
basket ['bæskət] *n* : corbeille *f*, panier *m*
basketball ['bæskətˌbɔl] *n* **1** : basket *m*, basket-ball *m*, basketball *m*, ballon-panier *m Can* (jeu) **2** : ballon *m* de basket <lancer un ballon de basket : to throw a basketball>
bas-relief [ˌbɑrɪ'liːf] *n* : bas-relief *m*
bass[1] ['bæs] *n, pl* **bass** *or* **basses 1** : perche *f*, bar *m* (pêche) **2** *or* **black bass** : achigan *m Can*
bass[2] ['beɪs] *n* : basse *f* (voix, instrument)
basset hound ['bæsətˌhaʊnd] *n* : basset *m*
bassinet [ˌbæsə'nɛt] *n* : berceau *m*, bercelonnette *f*
bassoon [bə'suːn, bæ-] *n* : basson *m*
bastard[1] ['bæstərd] *adj* : bâtard
bastard[2] *n* **1** : bâtard *m*, -tarde *f* **2** JERK : salaud *m*
bastardize ['bæstərˌdaɪz] *vt* **-ized; -izing** DEBASE : corrompre, abâtardir
baste ['beɪst] *vt* **basted; basting 1** : faufiler, bâtir (en couture) **2** : arroser (un rôti, etc.)
bastion ['bæstʃən] *n* : bastion *m*
bat[1] ['bæt] *v* **batted; batting** *vt* **1** HIT : frapper (une balle) **2 without batting an eye** : sans sourciller — *vi* : manier la batte (au cricket)
bat[2] *n* **1** : batte *f*, bâton *m Can* <baseball bat : batte de baseball> **2** STROKE : coup *m* (au cricket) **3** : chauve-souris *f* (animal)
batch ['bætʃ] *n* **1** : fournée *f* <a batch of bread : une fournée de pain> **2** QUANTITY : liasse *f* (de papiers, etc.), lot *m* (de marchandises)
bate ['beɪt] *vt* **bated; bating 1** REDUCE : réduire, diminuer **2 with bated breath** : en retenant son souffle
bath ['bæθ, 'baθ] *n, pl* **baths 1** : bain *m* <to take a bath : prendre un bain> **2** BATHROOM : salle *f* de bains **3** LOSS : perte *f* <he took a bath in the market : il a subi des pertes sur le marché>
bathe ['beɪð] *v* **bathed; bathing** *vt* : baigner, laver — *vi* : se baigner, prendre un bain
bather ['beɪðər] *n* : baigneur *m*, -gneuse *f*
bathrobe ['bæθˌroːb] *n* : peignoir *m* (de bain), robe *f* de chambre

bathroom [ˈbæθˌru:m, -ˌrʊm] *n* **1** : salle *f* de bains **2 to go to the bathroom** : aller aux toilettes
bathtub [ˈbæθˌtʌb] *n* : baignoire *f*
batiste [bəˈti:st] *n* : batiste *f*
baton [bəˈtɑn] *n* : bâton *m*
battalion [bəˈtæljən] *n* : bataillon *m*
batten [ˈbætən] *vt* **to batten down the hatches** : fermer les écoutilles
batter[1] [ˈbæt̬ər] *vt* BEAT : battre, frapper
batter[2] *n* **1** : pâte *f* <pancake batter : pâte à crêpes> **2** : batteur *m* (au baseball)
battered [ˈbæt̬ərd] *adj* : cabossé <a battered old hat : un vieux chapeau cabossé>
battering ram *n* : bélier *m*
battery [ˈbæt̬əri] *n, pl* **-teries 1** : pile *f* (d'une radio, etc.), batterie *f* (d'un véhicule) **2** : batterie *f* (d'artillerie) **3** SERIES : série *f*, batterie *f* <a battery of tests : une batterie d'examens> **4** → **assault**
batting [ˈbæt̬ɪŋ] *n* **1** *or* **cotton batting** : ouate *f*, bourre *f* **2** : maniement *m* de la batte (aux sports)
battle[1] [ˈbæt̬əl] *v* **-tled; -tling** *vi* : lutter, se battre — *vt* : lutter contre
battle[2] *n* **1** FIGHT : bataille *f*, combat *m* **2** STRUGGLE : lutte *f*
battle-ax [ˈbæt̬əlˌæks] *n* : hache *f* d'armes
battlefield [ˈbæt̬əlˌfi:ld] *n* : champ *m* de bataille
battlement [ˈbæt̬əlmənt] *n* : rempart *m*, créneau *m*
battleship [ˈbæt̬əlˌʃɪp] *n* : cuirassé *m*
batty [ˈbæt̬i] *adj* **battier; battiest** : toqué *fam*, fou
bauble [ˈbɔbəl] *n* : babiole *f*
bawdiness [ˈbɔdinəs] *n* : paillardise *f*
bawdy [ˈbɔdi] *adj* **bawdier; -est** : paillard, grivois
bawl [ˈbɔl] *vi* : brailler *fam*
bawl out *vt* : engueuler *fam*
bay[1] [ˈbeɪ] *vi* : aboyer
bay[2] *adj* : bai (se dit d'un cheval)
bay[3] *n* **1** INLET : baie *f*, golfe *m* **2** *or* **bay horse** : cheval *m* bai **3** LAUREL : laurier *m* **4** BAYING : aboiement *m* (d'un chien, etc.) **5** AREA : aire *f* <cargo bay : aire de chargement> **6 to be at bay** : être aux abois
bayberry [ˈbeɪˌberi] *n, pl* **-ries** : baie *f* de laurier
bayonet[1] [ˌbeɪəˈnet, ˈbeɪəˌnet] *vt* **-neted; -neting** : passer à la baïonnette
bayonet[2] *n* : baïonnette *f*
bayou [ˈbaɪˌu:, -ˌo] *n* : bayou *m*
bay window *n* : fenêtre *m* en saillie
bazaar [bəˈzɑr] *n* **1** : bazar *m* **2** SALE : vente *f* (de charité)
bazooka [bəˈzu:kə] *n* : bazooka *m*
BB [ˈbi:bi:] *n* **1** : plomb *m* **2 BB gun** : carabine *f* à air comprimé
be [ˈbi:] *v* **was** [ˈwəz, ˈwɑz], **were** [ˈwər]; **been** [ˈbɪn]; **being; am** [ˈæm], **is** [ˈɪz], **are** [ˈɑr] *vi* **1** (*expressing an attribute*) : être <the sky is blue : le ciel est bleu> **2** (*expressing a state*) : être, avoir <he is healthy : il est en bonne santé> <I'm hot : j'ai chaud> **3** (*expressing age*) : avoir <how old is he? : quel âge a-t-il?> **4** (*expressing origin*) : être <she is from Canada : elle est canadienne> **5** LIVE : être, exister <I think, therefore I am : je pense, donc je suis> **6** (*expressing location*) : être, se trouver <the cottage is on a lake : la villa se trouve au bord d'un lac> **7** (*expressing equality*) : faire, égaler <two and two are four : deux et deux font quatre> **8** (*expressing health or well-being*) : aller, se porter <how are you? : comment allez-vous?> **9** (*expressing cost*) : coûter <meat is very expensive : la viande coûte très cher> — *v aux* **1** : être en train de <he is reading : il lit, il est en train de lire> **2** (*indicating obligation*) : devoir <you are to come when called : tu dois venir quand on t'appelle> **3** (*used in passive constructions*) : être <the doors had been locked : les portes avaient été barrées> — *v impers* **1** (*indicating weather*) : faire <it's nice out : il fait beau> **2** (*indicating time*) : être <it's ten o'clock : il est dix heures> <it's late : il est tard>
beach[1] [ˈbi:tʃ] *vt* : échouer (un bateau)
beach[2] *n* : plage *f*, grève *f*
beachhead [ˈbi:tʃˌhed] *n* : tête *f* de pont
beacon [ˈbi:kən] *n* : phare *m*, signal *m* lumineux
bead[1] [ˈbi:d] *vt* STRING : enfiler — *vi* : perler (se dit d'un liquide)
bead[2] *n* **1** : perle *f*, grain *m* <rosary beads : grains d'un chapelet> **2** DROP : goutte *f*, perle *f* **3 beads** *npl* NECKLACE : collier *m*
beady [ˈbi:di] *adj* **beadier; -est** : perçant, brillant
beagle [ˈbi:gəl] *n* : beagle *m*
beak [ˈbi:k] *n* : bec *m*
beaker [ˈbi:kər] *n* **1** CUP : gobelet *m* **2** : vase *f* à bec (en chimie)
beam[1] [ˈbi:m] *vt* : transmettre, diffuser (une émission) — *vi* **1** SHINE : rayonner **2** SMILE : sourire d'un air radieux
beam[2] *n* **1** : poutre *f* (de bois) **2** RAY : rayon *m* **3** *or* **radio beam** : faisceau *m* de guidage **4** SMILE : grand sourire *m*
bean [ˈbi:n] *n* **1** : haricot *m* <green bean : haricot vert> **2** : grain *m* (de café) **3** → **broad bean**
bear[1] [ˈbær] *v* **bore** [ˈbɔr]; **borne** [ˈbɔrn]; **bearing** *vt* **1** CARRY : porter, transporter **2** PRODUCE : produire, porter <a fruit-bearing tree : un arbre qui

produit des fruits> **3** : donner naissance *f* à (un enfant) **4** ENDURE : supporter, tolérer <he doesn't bear pain well : il ne supporte pas bien la douleur> — *vi* **1** : diriger, prendre <bear right : prenez à droite> **2 to bear down on** : exercer une pression sur **3 to bear with** : patienter **4 to bear in mind** : ne pas oublier

bear[2] *n, pl* **bears** *or* **bear** : ours *m*, ourse *f*

bearable ['bærəbəl] *adj* : supportable, tolérable

beard[1] ['bɪrd] *vt* DEFY : affronter, braver

beard[2] *n* **1** : barbe *f* (d'un homme), barbiche *f* (d'une chèvre) **2** TUFT : barbe *f* (d'une plante)

bearded ['bɪrdəd] *adj* : barbu, à barbe

bearer ['bærər] *n* **1** : porteur *m*, -teuse *f* **2** : titulaire *mf* (d'un passeport)

bearing ['bærɪŋ] *n* **1** MANNER : allure *f*, maintien *m* **2** SIGNIFICANCE : relation *f*, rapport *m* <to have no bearing : n'avoir aucun rapport> **3** COURSE, DIRECTION : orientation *f*, direction *f* <I've lost my bearings : je suis désorienté> **4 → ball bearing**

bearish ['bærɪʃ] *adj* : rude, bourru

beast ['bi:st] *n* **1** : bête *f*, animal *m* **2** BRUTE : brute *f* (personne)

beastly ['bi:stli] *adj* **beastlier; -est 1** BRUTAL : bestial, brutal **2** NASTY : sale <what beastly weather! : quel sale temps!>

beat[1] ['bi:t] *v* **beat; beaten** ['bi:tən] *or* **beat; beating** *vt* **1** STRIKE : battre, frapper **2** DEFEAT : vaincre, battre <to beat one's competitors : devancer la compétition> <to beat s.o. up the hill : arriver au sommet avant qqn> <it beats me! : ça me dépasse!> **3** AVOID : éviter <to beat the crowds : éviter la foule> **4** MASH, WHIP : battre (des œufs, des pommes de terre, etc.) — *vi* THROB : battre, palpiter <with beating heart : le cœur battant>

beat[2] *adj* EXHAUSTED : éreinté, crevé *fam*

beat[3] *n* **1** BEATING : battement *m* <the beat of a drum : le battement d'un tambour> **2** RHYTHM : rythme *m*, temps *m*

beater ['bi:tər] **→ eggbeater**

beatific [ˌbiəˈtɪfɪk] *adj* : béatifique

beating ['bi:tɪŋ] *n* **1** : battement *m* (de cœur, d'un tambour, etc.) **2** THRASHING : correction *f*, raclée *f fam* **3** DEFEAT : défaite *f*

beatitude [bi'æt̬ə,tu:d] *n* **1** : béatitude *f* **2 the Beatitudes** : les béatitudes

beau [bo] *n, pl* **beaux** *or* **beaus** : galant *m*

beauteous ['bju:t̬iəs] **→ beautiful**

beautician [bju:'tɪʃən] *n* : esthéticien *m*, -cienne *f*

beautiful ['bju:t̬ɪfəl] *adj* **1** : beau <a beautiful woman : une belle femme> **2** SPLENDID : magnifique, merveilleux

beautifully ['bju:t̬ɪfəli] *adv* **1** ATTRACTIVELY : admirablement, à la perfection **2** SPLENDIDLY : parfaitement, merveilleusement <that will do beautifully : cela convient parfaitement>

beautify ['bju:t̬ɪˌfaɪ] *vt* **-fied; -fying** : embellir, orner

beauty ['bju:t̬i] *n, pl* **-ties** : beauté *f*

beauty shop *n or* **beauty salon** : salon *m* de beauté

beaver ['bi:vər] *n* : castor *m*

because [bi'kʌz, -'kɔz] *conj* : parce que

because of *prep* : à cause de

beck ['bɛk] *n* **to be at the beck and call of** : obéir au doigt et à l'œil à

beckon ['bɛkən] *vt* : faire signe à, attirer — *vi* : faire signe

become [bi'kʌm] *v* **-came** [-'keɪm]; **-come; -coming** *vt* SUIT : aller à, convenir à <the moustache doesn't become him : la moustache ne lui va pas> — *vi* : devenir <what's become of him? : qu'est-ce qu'il est devenu?> <they became friends : elles sont devenues amies>

becoming [bi'kʌmɪŋ] *adj* **1** SUITABLE : convenable, correct <becoming modesty : modestie convenable> **2** FLATTERING : seyant <a becoming hat : un chapeau seyant>

bed[1] ['bɛd] *vt* **bedded; bedding 1** : coucher **2** *or* **to bed out** : repiquer (des plantes)

bed[2] *n* **1** : lit *m* <to go to bed : se coucher, se mettre au lit> <to get out of bed : se lever> **2** LAYER : couche *f*, gisement *m* **3** BOTTOM : fond *m* (de la mer), lit *m* (d'un fleuve)

bedbug ['bɛdˌbʌg] *n* : punaise *f* de lit

bedclothes ['bɛdˌkloːðz, -ˌkloːz] *npl* : draps *mpl* et couvertures *fpl*

bedding ['bɛdɪŋ] *n* **1 → bedclothes 2** : litière *f* (pour les animaux)

bedeck [bɪ'dɛk] *vt* : parer, orner

bedevil [bɪ'dɛvəl] *vt* **-iled or -illed; -iling or -illing 1** PLAGUE : tourmenter, harceler **2** BEWILDER : déconcerter, embrouiller

bedlam ['bɛdləm] *n* UPROAR : chahut *m*, charivari *m*

bedraggled [bɪ'drægəld] *adj* : débraillé, désordonné

bedridden ['bɛdˌrɪdən] *adj* : alité, cloué au lit

bedrock ['bɛdˌrɑk] *n* **1** : soubassement *m* (en géologie) **2** BASIS : base *f*, fondation *f*

bedroom ['bɛdˌruːm, -ˌrʊm] *n* : chambre *f* (à coucher)

bedsheet → sheet

bedspread ['bɛdˌsprɛd] *n* : couvre-lit *m*

bee ['bi:] *n* **1** : abeille *f* **2** GATHERING : groupe *m*, club *m* <sewing bee : groupe de couture>

beech [ˈbiːtʃ] *n, pl* **beeches** *or* **beech** : hêtre *m*
beechnut [ˈbiːtʃˌnʌt] *n* : faine *f*
beef[1] [ˈbiːf] *vt or* **to beef up** : renforcer, étoffer (un discours, etc.) — *vi* COMPLAIN : se plaindre, rouspéter *fam*
beef[2] *n* **1** : bœuf *m* <roast beef : rôti de bœuf> **2** *pl* **beefs** [ˈbiːfs] *or* **beeves** [ˈbiːvz] STEER : bœuf *m*
beefsteak [ˈbifˌsteɪk] *n* : bifteck *m*
beehive [ˈbiːˌhaɪv] *n* : ruche *f*
beekeeper [ˈbiːˌkiːpər] *n* : apiculteur *m*, -trice *f*
beeline [ˈbiːˌlaɪn] *n* : ligne *f* droite <to make a beeline for : se diriger tout droit vers>
been → **be**
beep[1] [ˈbiːp] *vi* : klaxonner (se dit d'une voiture), faire bip (se dit d'un appareil électronique)
beep[2] *n* : coup *m* de klaxon, bip *m*
beeper [ˈbiːpər] *n* : récepteur *m* de radiomessagerie *f*, téléavertisseur *m Can*
beer [ˈbɪr] *n* : bière *f*
beeswax [ˈbiːzˌwæks] *n* : cire *f* d'abeille
beet [ˈbiːt] *n* : betterave *f*
beetle [ˈbiːtəl] *n* : scarabée *m*
befall [bɪˈfɔl] *v* **-fell** [-ˈfɛl] ; **-fallen** [-ˈfɔlən] *vt* : arriver à <a misfortune befell her : il lui arriva un malheur> — *vi* HAPPEN : arriver, advenir
befit [bɪˈfɪt] *vt* **-fitted; -fitting** : convenir à
before[1] [bɪˈfɔr] *adv* **1** AHEAD : devant, en avant <marching on before : marchant devant> **2** PREVIOUSLY : avant <before and after : avant et après> <long before : bien avant> **3** EARLIER : en avance, avant <come at six o'clock, not before : viens à six heures, pas avant>
before[2] *prep* **1** : devant, en présence de <before the court : devant le tribunal> **2** : avant <before long : avant longtemps> **3** ABOVE : avant, plutôt que <he puts quantity before quality : il préfère la quantité plutôt que la qualité> **4 before my eyes** : sous mes yeux
before[3] *conj* **1** : avant de, avant que <before going : avant de partir> <before you go : avant que tu partes> **2** : plutôt que de <he would die before surrendering : il mourrait plutôt que de se rendre>
beforehand [bɪˈfɔrˌhænd] *adv* : d'avance, à l'avance, au préalable
befriend [bɪˈfrɛnd] *vt* : se lier d'amitié avec
befuddle [bɪˈfʌdəl] *vt* **-dled; -dling** : brouiller les idées de, embrouiller
beg [ˈbɛg] *v* **begged; begging** *vt* **1** : mendier (la charité, la nourriture) **2** REQUEST, SOLICIT : demander, solliciter **3** ENTREAT : supplier, prier <I beg your mercy : je vous prie grâce> — *vi* **1** : mendier **2** : faire le beau (se dit d'un chien)
beget [bɪˈgɛt] *vt* **-got** [-gɑt]; **-gotten** [-gɑtən] *or* **-got; -getting** : engendrer
beggar [ˈbɛgər] *n* : mendiant *m*, -diante *f*; quêteux *m*, -teuse *f*
begin [bɪˈgɪn] *v* **-gan** [-ˈgæn]; **-gun** [-ˈgʌn]; **-ginning** *vt* **1** START : commencer, débuter **2** FOUND : inaugurer, fonder — *vi* **1** START : commencer **2** ORIGINATE : débuter, être fondé **3 to begin with** FIRST : d'abord
beginner [bɪˈgɪnər] *n* : débutant *m*, -tante *f*
beginning [bɪˈgɪnɪŋ] *n* : début *m*, commencement *m*
begone [biˈgɔn] *interj* : va-t-en!
begonia [biˈgoːnjə] *n* : bégonia *m*
begrudge [bɪˈgrʌdʒ] *vt* **-grudged; -grudging 1** : en vouloir à, accorder à regret **2** ENVY : envier
beguile [bɪˈgaɪl] *vt* **-guiled; -guiling 1** DECEIVE : tromper, duper **2** CHARM : séduire **3 to beguile (away) the time** : faire passer le temps agréablement
behalf [bɪˈhæf, -haf] *n* **1** INTEREST : défense *f*, sujet *m* <he argued in our behalf : il a argumenté pour notre défense> <in my behalf : à mon sujet> **2 on behalf of** : de la part de, au nom de
behave [bɪˈheɪv] *vi* **-haved; -having** : se conduire, se comporter
behavior *or Brit* **behaviour** [bɪˈheɪvjər] *n* : conduite *f*, comportement *m*
behead [bɪˈhɛd] *vt* : décapiter
behest [bɪˈhɛst] *n* **1** : demande *f*, instance *f* **2 at the behest of** : sur l'ordre de
behind[1] [bɪˈhaɪnd] *adv* **1** BACK : derrière, en arrière <I looked behind : j'ai regardé en arrière> <from behind : par derrière> **2** LATE : en retard <she's behind in her work : elle est en retard dans son travail>
behind[2] *prep* **1** : derrière, en arrière de <behind the building : derrière l'édifice> **2** : en retard sur <behind the times : en retard sur son temps> **3** SUPPORTING : soutenant <to be behind s.o. : soutenir qqn>
behold [bɪˈhoːld] *vt* **-held; -holding** : voir, apercevoir
beholder [bɪˈhoːldər] *n* : spectateur *m*, -trice *f*
behoove [bɪˈhuːv] *vt* **-hooved; -hooving** : incomber à, être de l'intérêt de
beige[1] [ˈbeɪʒ] *adj* : beige
beige[2] *n* : beige *m*
being [ˈbiːɪŋ] *n* **1** : être *m*, créature *f* **2** EXISTENCE : existence *f*
belabor *or Brit* **belabour** [bɪˈleɪbər] *vt* **to belabor the point** : insister sur le point
belated [bɪˈleɪtəd] *adj* : tardif
belch[1] [ˈbɛltʃ] *vi* BURP : faire un renvoi, roter *fam* — *vt* : vomir, cracher <to

belch (out) smoke : cracher de la fumée>

belch[2] *n* : renvoi *m*, rot *m fam*

beleaguer [bɪ'li:gər] *vt* **1** BESIEGE : assiéger **2** HARASS : harceler, assaillir

belfry ['bɛlfri] *n, pl* **-fries** : beffroi *m*, clocher *m*

Belgian[1] [bɛldʒən] *adj* : belge

Belgian[2] *n* : Belge *mf*

belie [bɪ'laɪ] *vt* **-lied; -lying 1** MISREPRESENT : donner une fausse idée de **2** CONTRADICT : démentir, contredire

belief [bə'li:f] *n* **1** OPINION : croyance *f*, conviction *f* **2** TRUST : confiance *f* **3** FAITH : foi *f*, confession *f*

believe [bə'li:v] *v* **-lieved; -lieving** *vt* **1** : croire <she believes the reports : elle croit les reportages> **2** SUPPOSE : croire, estimer, penser <I believe it will rain : je crois qu'il va pleuvoir> — *vi* : croire <he believes in God : il croit en Dieu>

believable [bə'li:vəbəl] *adj* : croyable, crédible

believer [bə'li:vər] *n* **1** : croyant *m*, croyante *f* (en religion) **2** SUPPORTER : partisan *m*, -sane *f*; adepte *mf*

belittle [bɪ'lɪṭəl] *vt* **-littled; -littling** : déprécier, rabaisser

Belizean[1] [bə'li:ziən] *adj* : bélizien

Belizean[2] *n* : Bélizien *m*, -zienne *f*

bell [bɛl] *n* **1** : cloche *f*, clochette *f* **2** : sonnette *f* (d'une porte, etc.)

belladonna [ˌbɛlə'dɑnə] *n* : belladone *f*

belle ['bɛl] *n* : beauté *f*, belle *f* <the belle of the ball : la reine du bal>

bellhop ['bɛlˌhɑp] *n* : chasseur *m*

bellicose ['bɛlɪˌkoːs] *adj* : belliqueux, guerrier

belligerence [bə'lɪdʒərənʦ] *or* **belligerency** [bə'lɪdʒərənʦi] *n* : belligérance *f*

belligerent [bə'lɪdʒərənt] *adj* : belligérant

bellow[1] ['bɛˌloː] *vt* : brailler *fam* — *vi* **1** : beugler, mugir **2** HOWL, SHOUT : brailler *fam*, hurler

bellow[2] *n* **1** : beuglement *m*, mugissement *m* **2** HOWL : hurlement *m*

bellows ['bɛˌloːz] *ns & pl* : soufflet *m*

bellwether ['bɛlˌwɛðər] *n* LEADER : dirigeant *m*, -geante *f*; chef *m*

belly[1] ['bɛli] *vi* **-lied; -lying** SWELL, BULGE : se gonfler, bomber

belly[2] *n, pl* **-lies** : ventre *m*

belong [bɪ'lɔŋ] *vi* **1 to belong to** : appartenir à, être à <it belongs to me : c'est à moi> **2** : être à sa place, aller <put it back where it belongs : remets-le à sa place> <where does it belong? : où va-t-il?> **3** : être membre, faire partie <he belongs to the athletic club : il fait partie du cercle sportif>

belongings [bɪ'lɔŋɪŋz] *npl* : affaires *fpl*, possessions *fpl*, effets *mpl* <personal belongings : effets personnels>

beloved[1] [bɪ'lʌvəd, -'lʌvd] *adj* : bien-aimé, chéri

beloved[2] *n* : bien-aimé *m*, -mée *f*; chéri *m*, -rie *f*

below[1] [bɪ'loː] *adv* : en dessous, en bas, plus bas

below[2] *prep* **1** : sous, au-dessous de, en dessous de <below the surface : sous la surface> <below average : au-dessous de la moyenne> **2** : au-dessous de, inférieur à <temperatures below normal : températures inférieures à la normale>

belt[1] ['bɛlt] *vt* **1** : mettre une ceinture à (des pantalons, etc.) **2** THRASH : donner un coup à

belt[2] *n* **1** : ceinture *f* <safety belt : ceinture de sécurité> **2** : courroie *f* (d'une machine) <courroie de ventilateur : fan belt> **3** AREA : zone *f*, région *f*

bemoan [bɪ'moːn] *vt* : déplorer, se lamenter sur

bemuse [bɪ'mjuːz] *vt* **-mused; -musing 1** BEWILDER : déconcerter, rendre perplexe **2** ENGROSS : absorber

bench ['bɛnʧ] *n* **1** : banc *m*, banquette *f* **2** : cour *f*, tribunal *m* <to appear before the bench : comparaître devant le tribunal> **3** → **workbench**

bend[1] ['bɛnd] *v* **bent** ['bɛnt]; **bending** *vt* **1** : plier, courber, fléchir <to bend one's arm : plier le bras> <bend your head : baissez ta tête> **2** DIRECT : diriger <to bend one's step toward : se diriger vers> **3** DISTORT, TWIST : tordre, crochir *Can*, travestir (la vérité) <to bend the rules : contourner les règlements> — *vi* **1** : se courber, se pencher, plier **2** TURN : tourner, faire un coude

bend[2] *n* **1** BENDING : pli *m*, flexion *f* **2** CURVE, TURN : tournant *m*, virage *m*, coude *m* **3 bends** *npl* : maladie *f* des caissons

beneath[1] [bɪ'niːθ] *adv* : au-dessous, dessous, en bas

beneath[2] *prep* **1** UNDER : sous, en dessous de <beneath the bed : sous le lit> **2** : indigne de <the work is beneath him : le travail est indigne de lui>

benediction [ˌbɛnə'dɪkʃən] *n* : bénédiction *f*

benefactor ['bɛnəˌfæktər] *n* : bienfaiteur *m*, -trice *f*

beneficence [bə'nɛfəsənʦ] *n* : bienfaisance *f*

beneficent [bə'nɛfəsənt] *adj* : bienfaisant, généreux

beneficial [ˌbɛnə'fɪʃəl] *adj* : avantageux, salutaire, favorable

beneficially [ˌbɛnə'fɪʃəli] *adv* : avantageusement

beneficiary [ˌbɛnə'fɪʃiˌɛri, -'fɪʃəri] *n, pl* **-ries** : bénéficiaire *mf*

benefit[1] ['bɛnəfɪt] *vt* : faire du bien à, profiter à, être avantageux pour — *vi* : profiter, faire du bien, tirer avantage

benefit[2] *n* **1** : avantage *m* <it's to your benefit : c'est à votre avantage> <fringe benefits : avantages sociaux> **2** : allocation *f* <unemployment benefit : allocation de chômage>

benevolence [bə'nɛvələnʦ] *n* : bienveillance *f*, charité *f*

benevolent [bə'nɛvələnt] *adj* : bienveillant

benevolently [bə'nɛvələntli] *adv* : avec bienveillance

Bengali[1] [bɛn'gɔli, bɛŋ-] *adj* : bengali

Bengali[2] *n* **1** : bengali *m* (langue) **2** : Bengali *mf*

benign [bi'naɪn] *adj* **1** KINDLY : bienveillant, affable, gentil **2** : bénin (en médecine) **3** MILD : doux

Beninese[1] [bə,ni'ni:z, -,ni:-, -'ni:s; ,bɛni'-] *adj* : béninois

Beninese[2] *n* : Béninois *m*, -noise *f*

bent[1] ['bɛnt] *adj* **1** CURVED : tordu, courbé **2 to be bent on doing** : être décidé à faire

bent[2] *n* : aptitude *f*, dispositions *fpl*, penchant *m*

benumb [bi'nʌm] *vt* : engourdir, endormir

benzene ['bɛnˌzi:n] *n* : benzène *m*

bequeath [bi'kwi:θ, -kwi:ð] *vt* : léguer

bequest [bi'kwɛst] *n* : legs *m*

berate [bi'reɪt] *vt* **-rated; -rating** : réprimander

bereaved[1] [bi'ri:vd] *adj* : endeuillé, attristé

bereaved[2] *ns & pl* **the bereaved** : la famille du défunt

bereavement [bi'ri:vmənt] *n* : deuil *m*

bereft [bi'reft] *adj* : privé, dénué <bereft of hope : désespérée>

beret [bə'reɪ] *n* : béret *m*

beriberi [ˌberi'berɪ] *n* : béribéri *m*

berry ['berɪ] *n, pl* **-ries** : baie *f*

berserk [bər'sərk, -'zərk] *adj* **1** : fou, enragé **2 to go berserk** : être pris de folie furieuse

berth[1] ['berθ] *vt* : amarrer, donner un poste d'amarrage à — *vi* : mouiller l'ancre, s'amarrer

berth[2] *n* **1** ANCHORAGE : mouillage *m*, poste *m* d'amarrage **2** BUNK : couchette *f* **3 to give s.o. a wide berth** : éviter qqn

beryl ['berəl] *n* : béryl *m*

beseech [bi'si:tʃ] *vt* **-seeched** *or* **-sought** [-'sɔt]; **-seeching** : supplier, implorer

beset [bi'sɛt] *vt* **-set; -setting 1** ASSAIL, HARASS : assaillir, harceler <beset with doubts : assailli de doutes> **2** SURROUND : encercler

beside [bi'saɪd] *prep* **1** : à côté de, près de **2 to be beside oneself** : être hors de soi

besides[1] [bi'saɪdz] *adv* **1** : de plus, en outre <nothing besides : rien de plus> **2** MOREOVER : d'ailleurs, du reste <besides, I like him : d'ailleurs, je l'aime>

besides[2] *prep* **1** : en plus de, outre <besides being rich, he's handsome : outre qu'il est riche, il est beau> **2** EXCEPT : sauf, hormis <no one besides me : personne hormis moi>

besiege [bi'si:dʒ] *vt* **-sieged; -sieging** : assiéger, encercler

besmirch [bi'smərtʃ] *vt* : souiller, entacher

besought → **beseech**

best[1] ['bɛst] *vt* OUTDO : l'emporter sur, vaincre

best[2] *adv* (*superlative of* **well**) : le mieux, le plus <the best dressed man : l'homme le mieux habillé> <the best known actress : l'actrice la plus connue>

best[3] *adj* (*superlative of* **good**) **1** : meilleur <the best student : le meilleur élève> **2** : plus beau <her best dress : sa plus belle robe>

best[4] *n* **1** : meilleur *m*, -leure *f* <she's the best : elle est la meilleure> **2** : mieux *m* <all for the best : tout pour le mieux> **3 to do one's best** : faire tout son possible

bestial ['bɛstʃəl, 'bi:s-] *adj* : bestial

bestir [bi'stər] *vt* **-stirred; -stirring 1** : activer, pousser à agir **2 to bestir oneself** : s'activer, s'agiter

best man *n* : garçon *m* d'honneur, témoin *m*

bestow [bi'sto:] *vt* : accorder, conférer

bet[1] ['bɛt] *v* **bet; betting** *vt* : parier, miser, gager *Can* — *vi* **to bet on** : parier sur

bet[2] *n* : pari *m*, gageure *f Can*

betoken [bi'to:kən] *vt* : présager, annoncer, être l'indice de

betray [bi'treɪ] *vt* **1** DECEIVE : trahir, tromper **2** REVEAL : révéler, laisser voir, divulguer (un secret, etc.)

betrayal [bi'treɪəl] *n* **1** : trahison *f* **2 betrayal of trust** : abus *m* de confiance

betrothal [bi'tro:ðəl, -'trɔ-] *n* : fiançailles *fpl*

betrothed [bi'tro:ðd, -trɔθt] *n* : fiancé *m*, -cée *f*

better[1] ['bɛtər] *vt* **1** IMPROVE : améliorer <to better oneself : améliorer sa condition> **2** SURPASS : dépasser, surpasser

better[2] *adv* (*comparative of* **well**) **1** : mieux <he plays better than you : il joue mieux que toi> **2 all the better** : tant mieux

better[3] *adj* (*comparative of* **good**) **1** : meilleur <this store is better than that one : ce magasin est meilleur que celui-là> **2** MORE : plus <better than nine miles : plus de neuf milles> **3 to get better** : s'améliorer, se remettre

better[4] *n* **1** : meilleur *m* <the better of the two : le meilleur des deux> **2 change for the better** : amélioration *f*, changement *m* en mieux **3 to get the better of** : l'emporter sur

betterment [ˈbɛʧərmənt] *n* : amélioration *f*
bettor *or* **better** [ˈbɛʧər] *n* : parieur *m*, -rieuse *f*
between[1] [bɪˈtwiːn] *adv* **1** : au milieu, dans l'intervalle **2 in ~** : entre les deux
between[2] *prep* : entre <between five and ten : entre cinq et dix> <between you and me : entre nous>
bevel[1] [ˈbɛvəl] *vt* **-eled** *or* **-elled; -eling** *or* **-elling** : biseauter, tailler en biseau
bevel[2] *n* **1** : surface *f* oblique **2** *or* **bevel edge** : biseau *m*
beverage [ˈbɛvrɪʤ, ˈbɛvə-] *n* : boisson *f*
bevy [ˈbɛvi] *n, pl* **bevies** : groupe *m* (de personnes), volée *f* (d'oiseaux)
bewail [bɪˈweɪl] *vt* : se lamenter sur, pleurer
beware [bɪˈwær] *vi* **to beware of** : se méfier de, prendre garde à
bewilder [bɪˈwɪldər] *vt* : dérouter, rendre perplexe, déconcerter
bewilderment [bɪˈwɪldərmənt] *n* : perplexité *f*, confusion *f*
bewitch [bɪˈwɪʧ] *vt* **1** : ensorceler **2** CHARM : enchanter, captiver
beyond[1] [biˈjɑnd] *adv* : au-delà, plus loin, au loin <the mountains beyond : les montagnes au loin> <2000 and beyond : 2000 et au-delà>
beyond[2] *prep* **1** : au-delà de <beyond the sea : au-delà de la mer> **2** : au-dessus de, hors de <beyond doubt : hors de doute> **3** : plus de <he won't stay beyond a week : il ne restera pas plus d'une semaine> **4 it's beyond me** : ça me dépasse
biannual [ˌbaɪˈænjʊəl] *adj* : bisannuel, semestriel **— biannually** *adv*
bias[1] [ˈbaɪəs] *vt* **-ased** *or* **-assed; -asing** *or* **-assing** : influencer, prévenir (contre)
bias[2] *n* **1** : biais *m* <cut on the bias : coupé en biais> **2** PREJUDICE : préjugé *m*, parti *m* pris **3** TENDENCY : penchant *m*, tendance *f*
biased [ˈbaɪəst] *adj* : partial
bib [ˈbɪb] *n* : bavoir *m* (d'un bébé), bavette *f* (sur un vêtement)
Bible [ˈbaɪbəl] *n* : Bible *f*
biblical [ˈbɪblɪkəl] *adj* : biblique
bibliographer [ˌbɪbliˈɑgrəfər] *n* : bibliographe *mf*
bibliography [ˌbɪbliˈɑgrəfi] *n, pl* **-phies** : bibliographie *f* **— bibliographic** [-bliəˈgræfɪk] *adj*
bicameral [ˌbaɪˈkæmərəl] *adj* : bicaméral
bicarbonate [ˌbaɪˈkɑrbənət, -ˌneɪt] *n* : bicarbonate *m*
bicentennial [ˌbaɪsɛnˈtɛniəl] *n* : bicentenaire *m*
biceps [ˈbaɪˌsɛps] *ns & pl* : biceps *m*
bicker [ˈbɪkər] *vi* : se chamailler
bicuspid [baɪˈkʌspɪd] *n* : prémolaire *f*
bicycle[1] [ˈbaɪsɪkəl, -ˌsɪ-] *vi* **-cled; -cling** : faire de la bicyclette, faire du vélo
bicycle[2] *n* : bicyclette *f*, vélo *m*
bicyclist [ˈbaɪsɪkəlɪst] *n* : cycliste *mf*
bid[1] [ˈbɪd] *v* **bade** [ˈbæd, ˈbeɪd] *or* **bid** [ˈbɪd]; **bidden** [ˈbɪdən] *or* **bid; bidding** *vt* **1** ORDER : demander, ordonner **2** SAY : dire, souhaiter <to bid s.o. goodbye : dire au revoir à qqn> **3** INVITE : inviter <I bid him to come in : je l'ai invité à rentrer> **4** OFFER : offrir, faire une offre de <she bid five dollars : elle a fait une offre de cinq dollars> **—** *vi* : offrir, faire une offre
bid[2] *n* **1** OFFER : offre *f*, enchère *f* **2** INVITATION : invitation *f* **3** ATTEMPT : essai *m*, tentative *f*
bidder [ˈbɪdər] *n* : offrant *m*; enchérisseur *m*, -seuse *f* <to the highest bidder : au plus offrant>
bide [ˈbaɪd] *vt* **bode** [ˈboːd] *or* **bided; bided; biding** : attendre <to bide one's time : attendre le bon moment>
biennial [baɪˈɛniəl] *adj* : biennal **— biennially** *adv*
bier [ˈbɪr] *n* **1** STAND : catafalque *m* **2** COFFIN : bière *f*
bifocals [baɪˌfoːkəlz] *npl* : lunettes *fpl* bifocales, verres *mpl* à double foyer
big [ˈbɪg] *adj* **bigger; biggest 1** LARGE : grand, gros **2** OLDER : grand, aîné <his big brother : son frère aîné> **3** IMPORTANT : important, grand <a big difference : une grande différence> <a big mistake : une grave erreur> **4** POPULAR : à la mode **5 to have a big heart** : avoir grand cœur
bigamist [ˈbɪgəmɪst] *n* : bigame *mf*
bigamous [ˈbɪgəməs] *adj* : bigame
bigamy [ˈbɪgəmi] *n* : bigamie *f*
Big Dipper → dipper
bighorn sheep [ˈbɪgˌhɔrn] *n* : mouton *m* sauvage à grandes cornes
bight [ˈbaɪt] *n* **1** COIL, LOOP : boucle *f* **2** BAY : baie *f*, anse *f*
bigot [ˈbɪgət] *n* : fanatique *mf*; bigot *m*, -gote *f* (en religion)
bigoted [ˈbɪgəʧəd] *adj* : fanatique, intolérant
bigotry [ˈbɪgətri] *n, pl* **-tries** : fanatisme *m*, intolérance *f*
big shot *n* : grosse légume *f fam*, gros bonnet *m fam*
bigwig [ˈbɪgˌwɪg] **→ big shot**
bike [ˈbaɪk] *n* **1** : vélo *m* **2** MOTORBIKE, MOTORCYCLE : moto *f*, motocyclette *f*
bikini [bəˈkiːni] *n* : bikini *m*
bilateral [baɪˈlæʧərəl] *adj* : bilatéral **— bilaterally** *adv*
bile [ˈbaɪl] *n* **1** : bile *f* **2** IRRITABILITY : mauvaise humeur *f*
bilingual [baɪˈlɪŋgwəl] *adj* : bilingue
bilious [ˈbɪliəs] *adj* : bilieux
bilk [ˈbɪlk] *vt* : escroquer, frauder
bill[1] [ˈbɪl] *vt* **1** : facturer, envoyer la facture à **2** ADVERTISE : annoncer, mettre à l'affiche **—** *vi* **to bill and coo** : roucouler

bill[2] *n* **1** : bec *m* (d'un oiseau) **2** INVOICE : facture *f*, note *f*, addition *f* (au restaurant) **3** : projet *m* de loi <to pass a bill : voter un projet de loi> **4** POSTER : affiche *f* **5** BANKNOTE : billet *m* (de banque)

billboard ['bɪl,bɔrd] *n* : panneau *m* publicitaire

billet[1] ['bɪlət] *vt* : cantonner, loger

billet[2] *n* : cantonnement *m*

billfold ['bɪl,fo:ld] *n* : portefeuille *m*

billiards ['bɪljərdz] *n* : billard *m*

billion ['bɪljən] *n* : milliard *m*

billow[1] ['bɪlo] *vi* **1** RISE, ROLL : se soulever (se dit de la mer) **2** SWELL : se gonfler (se dit d'une voile), onduler (se dit d'un drapeau)

billow[2] *n* **1** WAVE : vague *f* **2** CLOUD : nuage *m* <a billow of smoke : un nuage de fumée>

billowy ['bɪlowi] *adj* : houleux (se dit de la mer), ondoyant (se dit des nuages, de la fumée, etc.)

billy goat ['bɪli,go:t] *n* : bouc *m*

bin ['bɪn] *n* : coffre *m*, boîte *f*

binary ['baɪnəri, -,neri] *adj* : binaire

bind ['baɪnd] *vt* **bound** ['baʊnd]; **binding** **1** TIE : lier, attacher, ligoter **2** OBLIGATE : obliger, contraindre **3** ENCIRCLE, GIRD : entourer, ceindre **4** BANDAGE : bander, panser (une blessure) **5** : relier (un livre)

binder ['baɪndər] *n* **1** : relieur *m*, -lieuse *f* (de livres) **2** FOLDER : classeur *m*

binding ['baɪndɪŋ] *n* : reliure *f* (d'un livre)

binge ['bɪndʒ] *n* : bringue *f fam* <to go on a binge : faire la bringue>

bingo ['bɪŋ,go:] *n, pl* **-gos** : bingo *m*

binocular [bə'nɑkjələr, bə-] *adj* : binoculaire

binoculars [bə'nɑkjələrz, baɪ-] *npl* : jumelles *fpl*

biochemical [baɪo'kɛmɪkəl] *adj* : biochimique

biochemist [,baɪo'kɛmɪst] *n* : biochimiste *mf*

biochemistry [,baɪo'kɛməstri] *n* : biochimie *f*

biodegradable [,baɪodɪ'greɪdəbəl] *adj* : biodégradable

biographer [bar'ɑgrəfər] *n* : biographe *mf*

biographical [,baɪə'græfɪkəl] *adj* : biographique

biography [bar'ɑgrəfi, bi:-] *n, pl* **-phies** : biographie *f*

biological [-dʒɪkəl] *adj* : biologique

biologist [bar'ɑlədʒɪst] *n* : biologiste *mf*

biology [bar'ɑlədʒi] *n* : biologie *f*

biophysicist [,baɪo'fɪzəsɪst] *n* : biophysicien *m*, -cienne *f*

biophysics [,baɪo'fɪzɪks] *ns & pl* : biophysique *f*

biopsy ['baɪ,ɑpsi] *n, pl* **-sies** : biopsie *f*

biotechnology [,baɪotɛk'nɑlədʒi] *n* : biotechnologie *f*

bipartisan [baɪ'pɑrtəzən, -sən] *adj* : bipartite

biped ['baɪ,ped] *n* : bipède *m*

birch ['bərtʃ] *n* : bouleau *m*

bird ['bərd] *n* **1** : oiseau *m* **2** FOWL : volaille *f*

birdbath ['bərd,bæθ, -baθ] *n* : vasque *f* pour les oiseaux

bird dog *n* : chien *m* d'arrêt

birdhouse ['bərd,haʊs] *n* : volière *f*

bird of prey *n* : oiseau *m* de proie, rapace *m*

birdseed ['bərd,si:d] *n* : graines *fpl* pour les oiseaux

bird's–eye view ['bərdz,aɪ] *n* : vue *f* panoramique, vue *f* d'ensemble

birth ['bərθ] *n* **1** : naissance *f*, accouchement *m* <to give birth : accoucher> **2** ORIGIN : naissance *f*, début *m* **3** LINEAGE : descendance *f*, lignée *f*

birthday ['bərθ,deɪ] *n* : anniversaire *m* <happy birthday! : joyeux anniversaire!>

birthmark ['bərθ,mɑrk] *n* : tache *f* de vin

birthplace ['bərθ,pleɪs] *n* : lieu *m* de naissance

birthrate ['bərθ,reɪt] *n* : natalité *f*

birthright ['bərθ,raɪt] *n* : droit *m* (acquis à la naissance)

biscuit ['bɪskət] *n* : petit pain *m* au lait

bisect ['baɪ,sekt, ,baɪ'-] *vt* : couper en deux, diviser — *vi* INTERSECT : se couper, se croiser

bisexual [,baɪ'sɛkʃəwəl, -'sɛkʃəl] *adj* : bisexuel

bishop ['bɪʃəp] *n* **1** : évêque *m* **2** : fou *m* (aux échecs)

bishopric ['bɪʃə,prɪk] *n* : évêché *m*

bismuth ['bɪzməθ] *n* : bismuth *m*

bison [baɪzən, -sən] *ns & pl* **-son** : bison *m*

bistro ['bi:stro, 'bɪs-] *n, pl* **-tros** : bistro *m*, bistrot *m*

bit ['bɪt] *n* **1** : mors *m* (d'un cheval) **2** PIECE : morceau *m*, bout *m*, petit peu *m* <a bit of paper : un bout de papier> **3** : bit *m* (en informatique) **4 a bit** RATHER, SOMEWHAT : un peu *m*, un petit peu *m*

bitch[1] ['bɪtʃ] *vi* COMPLAIN : râler *fam*, rouspéter *fam*

bitch[2] *n* : chienne *f*

bite[1] ['baɪt] *v* **bit** ['bɪt]; **bitten** ['bɪtən]; **biting** *vt* **1** : mordre **2** STING : piquer — *vi* : mordre

bite[2] *n* **1** : morsure *f* (de chien, etc.) **2** STING : piqûre *f* **3** MOUTHFUL : bouchée *f* **4** SNACK : morceau *m* <let's grab a bite : mangeons un morceau> **5** : touche *f* (de pêche)

biting *adj* **1** PENETRATING : pénétrant, cinglant **2** CAUSTIC : mordant, caustique

bitter ['bɪtər] *adj* **1** ACRID : amer, âpre <a bitter taste : un goût amer> **2** PENETRATING : pénétrant, cinglant <bitter cold : froid glacial> **3** HARSH : acerbe, dur <to the bitter end

: jusqu'au bout> **4** FIERCE, RELENTLESS : acharné, féroce, violent <a bitter hatred : une haine profonde>

bitterly ['bɪtərlɪ] *adv* : amèrement

bittern ['bɪtərn] *n* : butor *m*

bitterness [ˈbɪtərnəs] *n* : amertume *f*, âpreté *f*

bituminous [bəˈtuːmənəs, -ˈtjuː-] *adj* **1** : bitumineux **2 bituminous coal** : huile *f* grasse

bivalve ['baɪˌvælv] *n* : bivalve *m*

bivouac[1] ['bɪvəˌwæk, 'bɪvˌwæk] *vi* **-ouacked; -ouacking** : bivouaquer

bivouac[2] *n* : bivouac *m*

bizarre [bəˈzɑr] *adj* : bizarre — **bizarrely** *adv*

blab ['blæb] *vi* **blabbed; blabbing** CHATTER : jaser, jacasser, babiller

black[1] ['blæk] *vt* : noircir

black[2] *adj* **1** : noir (se dit de la couleur ou de la race) **2** DARK : obscur, sans lumière **3** WICKED : noir, mauvais **4** DIRTY : sale, noir **5** GLOOMY : noir, sombre

black[3] *n* **1** : noir *m* (couleur) **2** : Noir *m*, Noire *f* (personne) **3** DARKNESS : obscurité *f*, ténèbres *fpl* **4 to be in the black** : être créditeur

black–and–blue [ˌblækənˈbluː] *adj* : couvert de bleus

blackball[1] ['blækˌbɔl] *vt* : blackbouler *fam*

blackball[2] *n* : vote *m* contraire

blackberry ['blækˌbɛrɪ] *n, pl* **-ries** : mûre *f*

blackbird ['blækˌbərd] *n* : merle *m*

blackboard ['blækˌbɔrd] *n* : tableau *m* (noir)

blacken ['blækən] *vt* **1** BLACK : noircir **2** DEFAME : ternir, souiller, noircir

blackhead ['blækˌhɛd] *n* : point *m* noir

black hole *n* : trou *m* noir

blackish [ˈblækɪʃ] *adj* : noirâtre

blackjack ['blækˌjæk] *n* **1** : assommoir *m* (arme) **2** : vingt-et-un *m* (jeu de cartes)

blacklist[1] ['blækˌlɪst] *vt* : mettre sur la liste noire

blacklist[2] *n* : liste *f* noire

blackmail[1] ['blækˌmeɪl] *vi* : faire chanter

blackmail[2] *n* : chantage *m*

blackmailer ['blækˌmeɪlər] *n* : maître-chanteur *m*

blackness ['blækˌnəs] *n* **1** : noirceur *f* **2** DARKNESS : obscurité *f*

blackout ['blækˌaʊt] *n* **1** : panne *f* d'électricité **2** FAINT : évanouissement *m*

black out *vi* **1** : avoir une panne d'électricité **2** FAINT : s'évanouir

blacksmith ['blækˌsmɪθ] *n* : forgeron *m*

blacktop ['blækˌtɑp] *n* : asphalte *m*

bladder ['blædər] *n* : vessie *f*

blade ['bleɪd] *n* **1** : brin *m* (d'herbe) **2** : lame *f* (de couteau) **3** : pale *f* (d'hélice, de rame, etc.)

blame[1] ['bleɪm] *vt* **blamed; blaming** : blâmer, reprocher

blame[2] *n* **1** CONDEMNATION : blâme *m*, reproches *mpl* **2** RESPONSIBILITY : faute *f*, responsabilité *f*

blameless ['bleɪmləs] *adj* : irréprochable

blameworthy ['bleɪmˌwərðɪ] *adj* : blâmable, coupable

blanch ['blænt∫] *vt* WHITEN : blanchir — *vi* PALE : pâlir

bland ['blænd] *adj* **1** SUAVE : affable, aimable **2** SOOTHING : apaisant, calmant **3** DULL, INSIPID : fade, insipide

blandly ['blændlɪ] *adv* : avec affabilité, affablement

blandness ['blændnəs] *n* **1** SUAVENESS : affabilité *f* **2** TASTELESSNESS : fadeur *f*

blandishment ['blændɪ∫mənt] *n* : flatterie *f*, cajoleries *fpl*

blank[1] ['blæŋk] *adj* **1** EXPRESSIONLESS : sans expression **2** DAZED, DISCONCERTED : déconcerté, dérouté **3** : blanc, vierge <a blank sheet : une feuille blanche> **4** EMPTY : vide <a blank wall : un mur vide> **5** DOWNRIGHT : catégorique, absolu <a blank refusal : un refus catégorique>

blank[2] *n* **1** GAP, SPACE : blanc *m*, vide *m*, trou *m* (de mémoire, etc.) **2** FORM : formulaire *m* à remplir, fiche *f* vierge **3** CARTRIDGE : cartouche *f* à blanc

blanket[1] ['blæŋkət] *vt* : couvrir, recouvrir

blanket[2] *adj* : général, global <blanket agreement : accord général>

blanket[3] *n* **1** : couverture *f* (d'un lit) **2** : couche *f*, manteau *f* <a blanket of snow : une couche de neige>

blankly ['blæŋklɪ] *adv* : sans expression, d'un air ébahi

blare[1] ['blær] *vi* **blared; blaring** : beugler, jouer à plein volume

blare[2] *n* : beuglement *m* (d'une radio, etc.), sonnerie *f* (d'une trompette)

blarney ['blɑrnɪ] *n* : boniment *m*, baratin *m*

blasé [blɑˈzeɪ] *adj* : blasé

blaspheme [blæsˈfiːm, ˈblæsˌ-] *v* **-phemed; -pheming** : blasphémer

blasphemous [ˈblæsfəməs] *adj* : blasphématoire

blasphemy ['blæsfəmɪ] *n, pl* **-mies** : blasphème *m*

blast[1] ['blæst] *vt* **1** BLOW UP : faire sauter, dynamiter **2** ATTACK, CRITICIZE : attaquer violemment **3** BLIGHT : flétrir, détruire (des cultures) — *vi* **1** BLARE : beugler, retentir **2 to blast off** : décoller

blast[2] *n* **1** GUST : coup *m* de vent, rafale *f* **2** EXPLOSION : explosion *f* **3 at full blast** : à plein volume

blatant ['bleɪtənt] *adj* : flagrant, criant

blatantly ['bleɪtəntlɪ] *adv* : d'une manière flagrante

blaze[1] ['bleɪz] *v* **blazed; blazing** *vt* MARK : griffer, marquer (un arbre), frayer <to blaze a trail : frayer un chemin> — *vi* **1** BURN, FLAME : flamber **2** SHINE : flamboyer, resplendir <the blazing sun : le soleil flamboyant>

blaze[2] *n* **1** : marque *f*, encoche *f* (sur un arbre) **2** FLAME : flamme *f*, feu *m* **3** BURST : éclat *m* (de couleur), torrent *m* (de lumière), explosion *f* (de colère)

blazer ['bleɪzər] *n* : blazer *m*

bleach[1] ['bli:tʃ] *vt* : blanchir, décolorer

bleach[2] *n* : décolorant *m*, eau *f* de Javel

bleachers ['bli:tʃərz] *npl* : gradins *mpl*

bleak ['bli:k] *adj* **1** GLOOMY : sombre, morne, lugubre <bleak thoughts : de sombres réflections> **2** DESOLATE : désolé <a bleak landscape : un terrain désolé>

bleakly ['bli:kli] *adv* : sombrement, lugubrement

bleakness ['bli:knəs] *n* **1** GLOOMINESS : caractère *m* sombre, monotonie *f* **2** BARRENNESS : désolation *f* (d'un paysage)

bleary ['blɪri] *adj* : trouble, voilé <bleary-eyed : aux yeux troubles>

bleat[1] ['bli:t] *vi* : bêler

bleat[2] *n* : bêlement *m*

bleed ['bli:d] *v* **bled** ['bled]; **bleeding** *vt* **1** : saigner **2** DRAIN : purger (des freins, etc.) **3 to bleed s.o. dry** : tirer de l'argent à qqn — *vi* **1** : saigner, perdre du sang **2 my heart bleeds for you** : tu me fends le cœur

blemish[1] ['blemɪʃ] *vt* : tacher, ternir

blemish[2] *n* : tache *f*, défaut *m*, imperfection *f*

blend[1] ['blend] *vt* : mélanger, mêler, marier (des couleurs) — *vi* : se mélanger, se mêler

blend[2] *n* : mélange *m*, alliance *f*

blender ['blendər] *n* : mixer *m*, mélangeur *m Can*

bless ['bles] *vt* **blessed** ['blest]; **blessing** **1** GLORIFY : bénir, glorifier <bless the Lord : béni soit le Seigneur> **2** CONSECRATE : bénir, sanctifier **3** ENDOW : doter <to be blessed with : avoir le bonheur de, être doué de> **4 bless you!** : à vos souhaits! (lorsqu'on éternue) **5 to bless oneself** : se signer

blessed ['blesəd] *or* **blest** ['blest] *adj* **1** HOLY : bénit, saint **2** HAPPY : bienheureux, heureux

blessing ['blesɪŋ] *n* **1** : bénédiction *f* (en religion) **2** BENEFIT : avantage *m*, bienfait *m* <a blessing in disguise : un bienfait inattendu> **3** APPROVAL : bénédiction *f*, approbation *f*

blew → **blow**

blight[1] ['blaɪt] *vt* : détruire, flétrir

blight[2] *n* **1** : rouille *f* (des plantes) **2** SCOURGE : fléau *m* <urban blight : dégradation urbaine>

blimp ['blɪmp] *n* : dirigeable *m*

blind[1] ['blaɪnd] *adv* : sans visibilité <to fly blind : voler aux instruments>

blind[2] *vt* **1** : aveugler, rendre aveugle **2** DAZZLE : éblouir

blind[3] *adj* **1** SIGHTLESS : aveugle **2** UNQUESTIONING : aveugle, absolu, ignorant <blind faith : foi absolue> **3** CLOSED : sans issue <a blind alley : une voie sans issue>

blind[4] *n* **1** : store *m* <venetian blind : store vénitien> **2** COVER : affût *m* (en chasse) **3 the blind** : les non-voyants

blindfold[1] ['blaɪnd,fo:ld] *vt* : bander les yeux à

blindfold[2] *n* : bandeau *m*

blindly ['blaɪndli] *adv* : aveuglément, à l'aveuglette

blindness ['blaɪndnəs] *n* **1** : cécité *f* <snow blindness : cécité des neiges> **2** : aveuglement *m* <blindness to the truth : aveuglement devant la vérité>

blink[1] ['blɪŋk] *vt* : cligner (des yeux) — *vi* **1** : cligner des yeux **2** FLICKER : clignoter, vaciller

blink[2] *n* : battement *m* des paupières

blinker ['blɪŋkər] *n* : clignotant *m*

bliss ['blɪs] *n* **1** HAPPINESS : félicité *f*, bonheur *m* absolu **2** HEAVEN : paradis *m*

blissful ['blɪsfəl] *adj* : heureux, bienheureux — **blissfully** *adv*

blister[1] ['blɪstər] *vi* **1** : se couvrir d'ampoules, cloquer (se dit de la peau) **2** : se boursoufler (se dit de la peinture, etc.)

blister[2] *n* **1** : ampoule *f*, cloque *f* (sur la peau) **2** : boursouflure *f* (sur une surface peinte)

blithe ['blaɪθ, 'blaɪð] *adj* **blither; blithest** CHEERFUL : joyeux, gai — **blithely** *adv*

blitz[1] ['blɪts] *vt* : bombarder

blitz[2] *n* : bombardement *m*, raid *m* aérien

blizzard ['blɪzərd] *n* : tempête *f* de neige

bloat ['blo:t] *vi* SWELL : se gonfler, enfler

bloated ['blo:təd] *adj* : boursouflé, gonflé

blob ['blab] *n* : tache *f*, (grosse) goutte *f*

bloc ['blak] *n* : bloc *m*

block[1] ['blak] *vt* **1** OBSTRUCT : bloquer, barrer **2** IMPEDE : bloquer, gêner, faire opposition à (un adversaire, un projet de loi, etc.) **3 to block out** HIDE : cacher, empêcher d'entrer **4 to block out** OUTLINE : ébaucher

block[2] *n* **1** : bloc *m*, billot *m* <a block of ice : un bloc de glace> <butcher's block : billot de boucherie> **2** OBSTRUCTION : obstacle *m*, obstruction *f* **3** : pâté *m* de maisons, bloc *m Can* <to walk around the block : faire le tour du pâté de maisons> <two blocks away : à deux rues d'ici> **4**

BUILDING : immeuble *m* <office block : immeuble de bureaux> **5** GROUP : groupe *m*, série *f* (de billets, etc.) **6 block and tackle** HOIST : palan *m*

blockade[1] [blɑ'keɪd] *vt* **-aded; -ading 1** OBSTRUCT : bloquer **2** : faire le blocus de (un port)

blockade[2] *n* : blocus *m*

blockage ['blɑkɪdʒ] *n* : obstruction *f*, blocage *m*

blockhead ['blɑk,hed] *n* : imbécile *mf fam*

bloke ['blo:k] *n Brit* : type *m*

blond[1] *or* **blonde** ['blɑnd] *adj* : blond

blond[2] *or* **blonde** *n* : blond *m*, blonde *f*

blood ['blʌd] *n* **1** : sang *m* **2** LINEAGE : lignée *f*, descendance *f*

blood bank *n* : banque *f* du sang

bloodcurdling ['blʌd,kərdəlɪŋ] *adj* : à vous figer le sang

bloodhound ['blʌd,haʊnd] *n* : limier *m*

bloodless ['blʌdləs] *adj* **1** : sans effusion de sang **2** SPIRITLESS : apathique, sans vie

bloodmobile ['blʌdmo,bi:l] *n* : centre *m* mobile de collecte du sang

blood pressure *n* : tension *f* artérielle

bloodshed ['blʌd,ʃed] *n* : effusion *f* de sang, carnage *m*

bloodshot ['blʌd,ʃɑt] *adj* : injecté de sang

bloodstain ['blʌd,steɪn] *n* : tache *f* de sang

bloodstream ['blʌd,stri:m] *n* : sang *m*, système *m* sanguin

bloodsucker ['blʌd,sʌkər] *n* : sangsue *f*

bloodthirsty ['blʌd,θərsti] *adj* : sanguinaire, assoiffé de sang

blood vessel *n* : vaisseau *m* sanguin

bloody ['blʌdi] *adj* **bloodier; -est 1** : sanglant <a bloody battle : un combat sanglant> **2** : ensanglanté <bloody hands : mains ensanglantées>

bloom[1] ['blu:m] *vi* **1** FLOWER : fleurir, éclore **2** FLOURISH : s'épanouir

bloom[2] *n* **1** FLOWER : fleur *f* **2** BLOOMING : floraison *f*, épanouissement *m* **3 in bloom** *or* **in full bloom** : en fleurs, en pleine floraison

blooper ['blu:pər] *n* : gaffe *f fam*

blossom[1] ['blɑsəm] *vi* **1** : fleurir, être en fleurs **2** MATURE : s'épanouir, se développer **3 to blossom into** : devenir

blossom[2] *n* : fleur *f*

blot[1] ['blɑt] *vt* **blotted; blotting 1** STAIN : tacher, souiller **2** DRY : sécher (encre, etc.) **3 to blot out** : rayer, effacer

blot[2] *n* **1** SPOT : tache *f* **2** *or* **inkblot** : pâté *m* **3** BLEMISH : souillure *f*, tare *f*

blotch[1] ['blɑtʃ] *vt* : tacher, marbrer

blotch[2] *n* : tache *f*, marbrure *f* (sur la peau)

blotchy ['blɑtʃi] *adj* **blotchier; -est 1** : couvert de taches, marbré <blotchy complexion : teint marbré> **2** SMEARED : barbouillé <blotchy drawing : dessin barbouillé>

blotter ['blɑtər] *n* : buvard *m*

blouse ['blaʊs, 'blaʊz] *n* : chemisier *m*, corsage *m*

blow[1] [blo:] *v* **blew** ['blu:]; **blown** ['blo:n]; **blowing** *vt* **1** : souffler, pousser (un navire), chasser (des feuilles, etc.) <to blow sth away : faire voler qqch> <to blow one's nose : se moucher> **2** SOUND : jouer de (une trompette, etc.), donner (un coup de sifflet) **3** SHAPE : souffler, donner une forme à (le verre) **4** BUNGLE : rater, manquer <I blew it! : j'ai tout raté!> **5 to blow out** : souffler sur (une chandelle, etc.) — *vi* **1** : souffler **2** *or* **to blow away** : s'envoler **3** SOUND : sonner (se dit d'une trompette, etc.) **4 to blow down** FALL : se renverser, tomber **5 to blow out** : éclater (se dit d'un pneu), s'éteindre (se dit d'une bougie)

blow[2] *n* **1** GALE : coup *m* de vent **2** HIT, STROKE : coup *m*, coup *m* de poing **3** MISFORTUNE : coup *m*, malheur *m* **4 to come to blows** : en venir aux mains

blowout ['blo:,aʊt] *n* : éclatement *m* (d'un pneu)

blowtorch ['blo,tɔrtʃ] *n* : lampe *f* à souder, chalumeau *m*

blow up *vt* **1** EXPLODE : faire sauter, faire exploser **2** INFLATE : gonfler — *vi* : exploser, sauter

blubber[1] ['blʌbər] *vi* : pleurer (comme un veau)

blubber[2] *n* : graisse *f* de baleine

bludgeon[1] ['blʌdʒən] *vt* : matraquer

bludgeon[2] *n* : gourdin *m*, matraque *f*

blue[1] ['blu:] *adj* **bluer; bluest 1** : bleu <blue with cold : bleu de froid> **2** MELANCHOLY : triste

blue[2] *n* **1** : bleu *m*, azur *m* **2 out of the blue** : de façon imprévue

bluebell ['blu:,bel] *n* : jacinthe *f* des bois

blueberry ['blu:,beri] *n, pl* **-ries** : myrtille *f France*, bleuet *m Can*

bluebird ['blu:,bərd] *n* : oiseau *m* bleu

blue cheese *n* : (fromage *m*) bleu *m*

bluefish ['blu:,fɪʃ] *n, pl* **-fish** *or* **-fishes** : poisson *m* bleu de la côte atlantique

blue jay *n* : geai *m* bleu

blueprint ['blu:,prɪnt] *n* **1** : bleu *m* **2** PROGRAM : plan *m* (de travail), projet *m*

blues ['blu:z] *npl* **1** DEPRESSION : cafard *m*, mélancolie *f* **2** : blues *m* (en musique)

bluff[1] ['blʌf] *v* : bluffer

bluff[2] *adj* **1** STEEP : escarpé, à pic **2** FRANK : carré, direct

bluff[3] *n* **1** CLIFF : falaise *f*, escarpement *m* **2** DECEPTION, RUSE : bluff *m*

bluing *or* **blueing** ['blu:ɪŋ] *n* : produit *m* blanchissant

blunder[1] ['blʌndər] *vi* **1** *or* **to blunder along** : avancer à l'aveuglette, avancer à tâtons **2** ERR : faire une bévue, faire une gaffe
blunder[2] *n* MISTAKE : bévue *f*, gaffe *f fam*, impair *m*
blunderbuss ['blʌndərˌbʌs] *n* : tromblon *m*
blunt[1] ['blʌnt] *vt* : émousser (des couteaux, des ciseaux, etc.), épointer (des crayons), couper (l'appétit)
blunt[2] *adj* **1** DULL : émoussé, épointé **2** ABRUPT, DIRECT : brusque, abrupt, carré
bluntly ['blʌntli] *adv* : franchement, carrément
bluntness *n* **1** DULLNESS : manque *m* de tranchant **2** ABRUPTNESS, FRANKNESS : brusquerie *f*, franc-parler *m*
blur[1] ['blər] *v* **blurred; blurring** *vt* : troubler, brouiller, rendre flou <eyes blurred with tears : yeux brouillés de larmes> — *vi* : se brouiller
blur[2] *n* **1** : image *f* floue, contour *m* imprécis **2** SMEAR : tache *f*
blurb ['blərb] *n* : notice *f* publicitaire
blurry ['blərɪ] *adj* **blurrier; -est** : flou, troublé <blurry vision : vision troublée>
blurt ['blərt] *vt or* **to blurt out** : laisser échapper
blush[1] ['blʌʃ] *vi* : rougir
blush[2] *n* : rougeur *f*
bluster[1] ['blʌstər] *vi* **1** BLOW, STORM : souffler violemment **2** BOAST : fanfaronner
bluster[2] *n* **1** : hurlement *m* (du vent) **2** BOASTING : fanfaronnade *f*
blustery ['blʌstərɪ] *adj* : violent, orageux
boa ['boːə] *n* : boa *m*
boar ['bor] *n* **1** PIG : verrat *m* **2** → **wild boar**
board[1] ['bord] *vt* **1** : monter à bord de (un avion, un navire), monter dans (un train) **2** LODGE : prendre en pension **3 to board up** : couvrir de planches
board[2] *n* **1** PLANK : planche *f* **2** : pension *f* <room and board : pension complète> **3** COMMITTEE, COUNCIL : conseil *m*, commission *f* <board meeting : réunion du conseil> **4** : tableau *m* (d'un jeu) **5 to go on board** : monter à bord
boarder ['bordər] *n* : pensionnaire *mf*
boardinghouse ['bordɪŋˌhaʊs] *n* : pension *f*
boarding school *n* : pensionnat *m*
boardwalk ['bordˌwɔk] *n* : promenade *f* (en planches)
boast[1] ['boːst] *vt* : se glorifier de, être fier de posséder <the town boasts five churches : la ville est fière de posséder cinq églises> — *vi* : se vanter, fanfaronner
boast[2] *n* : vantardise *f*, fanfaronnade *f*
boaster ['boːstər] *n* : vantard *m*, -tarde *f*; fanfaron *m*, -ronne *f*
boastful ['boːstfəl] *adj* : vantard, fanfaron
boastfully ['boːstfəlɪ] *adv* : en se vantant, en fanfaronnant
boat[1] ['boːt] *vt* : transporter en bateau — *vi* : aller en bateau
boat[2] *n* **1** : bateau *m* <to go by boat : prendre le bateau> <to be in the same boat : être tous dans la même galère> **2** → **rowboat, ship, sailboat**
boatswain ['boːsən] *n* : maître *m* d'équipage
bob[1] ['bab] *v* **bobbed; bobbing** *vt* : couper court (les cheveux) — *vi* **1** : monter et descendre <to bob in the water : danser sur l'eau> **2 to bob up** APPEAR : apparaître, surgir
bob[2] *n* **1** : coupe *f* au carré (des cheveux) **2** FLOAT : bouchon *m* (de pêche) **3** NOD : hochement *m* de tête
bobbin ['babən] *n* : bobine *f*
bobby pin ['babiˌpɪn] *n* : pince *f* à cheveux
bobcat ['babˌkæt] *n* : lynx *m* (roux)
bobolink ['babəˌlɪŋk] *n* : oiseau *m* chanteur de l'Amérique du Nord, goglu *m Can*
bobsled ['babˌslɛd] *n* : bob *m*, bobsleigh *m*
bobwhite ['babˈhwaɪt] *n* : caille *f* de l'Amérique du Nord
bode[1] [boːd] *vt* **boded; boding** : présager, augurer <to bode well for : être de bon augure pour>
bode[2] → **bide**
bodice ['badəs] *n* : corsage *m* (d'une robe)
bodily[1] ['badəlɪ] *adv* **1** PHYSICALLY : physiquement, à bras-le-corps **2** ENTIRELY : tout entier
bodily[2] *adj* PHYSICAL : physique, corporel <bodily contact : contact physique>
body ['badɪ] *n, pl* **bodies 1** : corps *m* **2** CORPSE : cadavre *m* **3** PERSON : personne *f*, être *m* humain **4** COLLECTION, MASS : masse *f*, ensemble *m* <in a body : en masse> <a body of evidence : un ensemble de preuves> **5** SUBSTANCE : corps *m*, fond *m* <the body of a letter : le corps d'une lettre> **6** : carrosserie *f* (d'une voiture), fuselage *m* (d'un avion)
bodyguard ['badiˌgard] *n* : garde *m* du corps
bog[1] ['bag, 'bɔg] *vi* **bogged; bogging** *or* **to bog down** : s'embourber, s'enliser, s'empêtrer (dans un discours)
bog[2] *n* **1** MARSH : marais *m*, marécage *m* **2** *or* **peat bog** : tourbière *f*
bogey [ˌbogi, 'boː-] *n, pl* **-geys 1** GHOST : fantôme *m*, spectre *m* **2** *or* **bogeyman** : croque-mitaine *m*, épouvantail *m*
boggle ['bagəl] *v* **-gled; -gling** *vt* **to boggle the mind** : dépasser l'imagination

— *vi* **the mind boggles** : ça laisse perplexe, on a du mal à imaginer ça
boggy [ˈbɑgi, ˈbɔ-] *adj* **boggier; -est** : marécageux
bogus [ˈboːgəs] *adj* SHAM : faux, bidon *fam*
bohemian[1] [boːˈhiːmiən] *adj* : bohème
bohemian[2] *n* : bohème *mf*
boil[1] [ˈbɔil] *vt* : faire bouillir — *vi* **1** : bouillir **2** SEETHE : bouillir, bouillonner
boil[2] *n* **1** : ébullition *f* <to bring to a boil : amener à ébullition> **2** : furoncle *m* (en médecine)
boiler [ˈbɔilər] *n* : chaudière *f*
boisterous [ˈbɔistərəs] *adj* **1** NOISY, ROWDY : bruyant, tapageur **2** STORMY : houleux, tumultueux
boisterously [ˈbɔistərəsli] *adv* : bruyamment, tumultueusement
bold [boːld] *adj* **1** COURAGEOUS, DARING : hardi, audacieux **2** IMPUDENT : insolent, effronté — **boldly** *adv*
boldface [boːldˌfeɪs] *n or* **boldface type** : caractères *mpl* gras
boldness [ˈboːldnəs] *n* : hardiesse *f*, audace *f*
bolero [bəˈlɛro] *n, pl* **-ros** : boléro *m*
Bolivian[1] [bəˈlɪviən] *adj* : bolivien
Bolivian[2] *n* : Bolivien *m*, -vienne *f*
boll weevil [ˈboːlˌwiːvəl] *n* : charançon *m* (du cotonnier)
bologna [bəˈloːni] *n* : gros saucisson *m*
bolster[1] [ˈboːlstər] *vt* **-stered; -stering** : soutenir, renforcer <to bolster morale : remonter le moral>
bolster[2] *n* : traversin *m*
bolt[1] [ˈboːlt] *vt* **1** LOCK : verrouiller, fermer au verrou **2** *or* **to bolt down** : engloutir (de la nourriture) — *vi* **1** : s'emballer (se dit d'un cheval) **2** DASH : se précipiter, se lancer
bolt[2] *n* **1** THUNDERBOLT : éclair *m*, coup *m* de foudre **2** LOCK : verrou *m* **3** : rouleau *m* (de tissu) **4** : boulon *m* <nuts and bolts : écrous et boulons>
bomb[1] [ˈbɑm] *vt* : bombarder
bomb[2] *n* : bombe *f*
bombard [bɑmˈbɑrd, bəm-] *vt* : bombarder
bombardier [ˌbɑmbəˈdɪr] *n* : bombardier *m*
bombardment [bɑmˈbɑrdmənt] *n* : bombardement *m*
bombast [ˈbɑmˌbæst] *n* : grandiloquence *f*
bombastic [bɑmˈbæstɪk] *adj* : grandiloquent, ampoulé
bomber [ˈbɑmər] *n* : bombardier *m* (avion)
bombshell [ˈbɑmˌʃɛl] *n* : bombe *f*
bona fide [ˈboːnəˌfaɪd, ˈbɑ-; ˌboːnəˈfaɪdi] *adj* **1** : de bonne foi **2** GENUINE : authentique, véritable
bonanza [bəˈnænzə] *n* : filon *m*, aubaine *f*
bonbon [ˈbɑnˌbɑn] *n* : bonbon *m*
bond[1] [ˈbɑnd] *vt* **1** : entreposer (des marchandises) **2** *or* **to bond together** STICK : coller, faire adhérer — *vi* **1** STICK : adhérer **2 to bond with** : s'attacher à
bond[2] *n* **1** TIE : lien *m*, attache *f* <the bonds of marriage : les liens conjugaux> **2** AGREEMENT : contrat *m*, engagement *m*, caution *f* (en droit) **3** ADHESION : adhérence *f* **4** SECURITY : bon *m* <savings bond : bon d'épargne> **5 bonds** *npl* FETTERS : fers *mpl*, chaînes *fpl*
bondage [ˈbɑndɪdʒ] *n* : esclavage *m*
bondholder [ˈbɑndˌhoːldər] *n* : porteur *m* de bons
bondsman [ˈbɑndzmən] *n* **1** SLAVE : esclave *m*, serf *m* **2** SURETY : garant *m*, -rante *f*
bone[1] [ˈboːn] *vt* **boned; boning** : désosser (de la viande), ôter les arêtes de (un poisson)
bone[2] *n* : os *m*, arête *f* (de poisson)
boneless [ˈboːnləs] *adj* : sans os, sans arêtes
boner [ˈboːnər] *n* BLUNDER : gaffe *f*, bourde *f*
bonfire [ˈbɑnˌfaɪr] *n* : feu *m* de joie
bonito [bəˈniːto] *n, pl* **-tos** *or* **-to** : bonite *f*
bonnet [ˈbɑnət] *n* : bonnet *m*, chapeau *m*
bonny [ˈbɑni] *adj* **bonnier; -est** *Brit* : joli, beau
bonus [ˈboːnəs] *n* : gratification *f*, prime *f*
boo[1] [ˈbuː] *vt* : huer, siffler
boo[2] *n, pl* **boos** : huée *f*
booby [ˈbuːbi] *n, pl* **-bies** DOPE : nigaud *m*, -gaude *f*
book[1] [ˈbʊk] *vt* : réserver, retenir <to book a room : réserver une chambre>
book[2] *n* **1** : livre *m*, bouquin *m fam* **2** : carnet *m*, pochette *f* <a book of stamps : un carnet de timbres> <a book of matches : une pochette d'allumettes> **3** STANDARD : règlement *m* <to go by the book : suivre le règlement> **4** LIBRETTO : livret *m* **5 books** *npl* RECORDS : registre *m* **6 books** *npl* ACCOUNTS : comptes *mpl*
bookcase [ˈbʊkˌkeɪs] *n* : bibliothèque *f*
bookend [ˈbʊkˌend] *n* : serre-livres *m*, appui-livres *m Can*
bookie [ˈbʊki] → **bookmaker**
bookish [ˈbʊkɪʃ] *adj* : studieux
bookkeeper [ˈbʊkˌkiːpər] *n* : comptable *mf*
bookkeeping [ˈbʊkˌkiːpɪŋ] *n* : comptabilité *f*
booklet [ˈbʊklət] *n* : brochure *f*
bookmaker [ˈbʊkˌmeɪkər] *n* : bookmaker *m*
bookmark [ˈbʊkˌmɑrk] *n* : signet *m*
bookseller [ˈbʊkˌsɛlər] *n* : libraire *mf*
bookshelf [ˈbʊkˌʃɛlf] *n, pl* **-shelves** : rayon *m*, étagère *f*

bookstore ['bʊkˌstɔr] *n* : librairie *f*
bookworm ['bʊkˌwərm] *n* : rat *m* de bibliothèque
boom¹ ['bu:m] *vi* **1** RESOUND : gronder, mugir (se dit de la mer), retentir (se dit de la voix) **2** FLOURISH, PROSPER : être en expansion, être en plein essor
boom² *n* **1** BOOMING : grondement *m*, mugissement *m*, retentissement *m* **2** : gui *m* (d'un bateau) **3** FLOURISHING : essor *m*, boom *m* (en commerce)
boomerang ['bu:məˌræŋ] *n* : boomerang *m*
boon¹ ['bu:n] *adj* **boon companion** : gai compagnon *m*, bon compère *m*
boon² *n* : bienfait *m*, bénédiction *f*, aubaine *f*
boondocks ['bu:nˌdɑks] *npl* : bled *m fam*
boor ['bʊr] *n* : rustre *m*; malotru *m*, -true *f*
boorish ['bʊrɪʃ] *adj* : rustre, grossier
boost¹ ['bu:st] *vt* **1** : soulever (une personne) **2** INCREASE, RAISE : augmenter, faire monter (des prix, etc.) <to boost morale : remonter le moral> **3** : survolter (un circuit électrique)
boost² *n* **1** INCREASE : hausse *f*, augmentation *f* **2** STIMULATION : encouragement *m*, stimulation *f* **3 to give s.o. a boost** : soulever qqn
booster ['bu:stər] *n* **1** SUPPORTER : partisan *m*, -sane *f*; supporter *m* **2** : survolteur *m* (en électricité) **3** *or* **booster rocket** : fusée *f* d'appoint **4** *or* **booster shot** : vaccin *m* de rappel
boot¹ ['bu:t] *vt* **1** KICK : donner un coup de pied à **2** : amorcer (en informatique) **3 to boot out** FIRE : mettre à la porte, congédier
boot² *n* **1** : botte *f*, bottine *f* **2** KICK : coup *m* de pied
bootee *or* **bootie** ['bu:ti] *n* : petit chausson *m* (de bébé), pichou *m Can fam*
booth ['bu:θ] *n, pl* **booths** ['bu:ðz, 'bu:θs] : baraque *f* (d'un marché), cabine *f* (téléphonique), guichet *m* (pour acheter des billets)
booty ['bu:ti] *n, pl* **-ties** : butin *m*
booze ['bu:z] *n* : alcool *m*, boissons *fpl* alcoolisées
borax ['bɔrˌæks] *n* : borax *m*
border¹ ['bɔrˌdər] *vt* **1** EDGE, SURROUND : border, entourer <bordered with flowers : entouré de fleurs> **2** BOUND : toucher, avoir une frontière commune avec — *vi* **to border on** : friser, frôler <it borders on insanity : cela frôle la folie>
border² *n* **1** EDGE : bord *m*, lisière *f* <the border of a lake : le bord d'un lac> **2** BOUNDARY : frontière *f* (d'un pays, etc.) **3** EDGING, STRIP : bordure *f* <a cement border : une bordure en ciment>
bore¹ ['bɔr] *vt* **bored; boring 1** DRILL, PIERCE : percer, creuser (un trou), forer (un puits) **2** TIRE : ennuyer, embêter
bore² *n* **1** DIAMETER : calibre *m* (d'un fusil) **2** : barbe *f fam*, corvée *f* <what a bore! : quelle barbe!> **3** : raseur *m*, -seuse *f fam*; casse-pieds *mf fam* (personne)
bore³ → **bear¹**
boredom ['bɔrdəm] *n* : ennui *m*
boring ['bɔrɪŋ] *adj* : ennuyeux, sans intérêt, ennuyant *Can*, plat *Can*
born ['bɔrn] *adj* **1** : né <born in Paris : né à Paris> **2** INNATE : né, parfait <he's a born dancer : il est né danseur> <a born fool : un parfait idiot>
borne → **bear¹**
boron ['bɔrˌɑn] *n* : bore *m*
borough ['bərə] *n* : arrondissement *m* urbain
borrow ['bɑroˌ] *vt* : emprunter, s'approprier <I borrowed his pen : j'ai emprunté son stylo> <to borrow an idea : s'approprier une idée>
Bosnian¹ ['bɑznɪən, bɔz-] *adj* : bosniaque
Bosnian² *n* : Bosniaque *mf*
bosom¹ ['bʊzəm, 'bu:-] *adj* : intime <bosom friend : ami intime>
bosom² *n* **1** CHEST : poitrine *f* **2** BREASTS : seins *mpl*, poitrine *f* <a big bosom : une grosse poitrine> **3** : sein *m*, milieu *m* <in the bosom of her family : au sein de sa famille>
boss¹ ['bɔs] *vt* **1** SUPERVISE : diriger **2 to boss around** : mener à la baguette
boss² *n* : patron *m*, -tronne *f*; chef *m*
bossy ['bɔsi] *adj* **bossier; -est** : autoritaire, dictatorial
botanical [bəˈtænɪkəl] *adj* : botanique
botanist ['bɑtənɪst] *n* : botaniste *mf*
botany ['bɑtəni] *n* : botanique *f*
botch ['bɑtʃ] *vt* : bousiller *fam*, saboter, estropier
both¹ ['bo:θ] *adj* : les deux <I like both dresses : j'aime les deux robes>
both² *conj* : et . . . et, à la fois <both his brother and his sister : et son frère et sa sœur> <she's both beautiful and intelligent : elle est à la fois belle et intelligente>
both³ *pron* : tous les deux, l'un et l'autre <they were both there : elles étaient là toutes les deux>
bother¹ ['bɑðər] *vt* **1** ANNOY, IRK : agacer, ennuyer, embêter **2** PESTER : harceler **3** WORRY : inquiéter, préoccuper — *vi* : s'en faire, se déranger <don't bother : ne te dérange pas>
bother² *n* **1** ANNOYANCE : ennui *m* <what a bother! : quel ennui!> **2** TROUBLE : peine *f* <it's not worth the bother : ça ne vaut pas la peine>
bothersome ['bɑðərsəm] *adj* : ennuyeux, gênant
bottle¹ ['bɑtəl] *vt* **bottled; bottling** : mettre en bouteille

bottle[2] *n* **1** : bouteille *f* **2** : biberon *m* (d'un bébé) **3** FLASK : flacon *m* <a bottle of perfume : un flacon de parfum> **4 bottle opener** : ouvre-bouteilles *m*

bottleneck ['bɒtəl,nek] *n* **1** NARROWING : rétrécissement *m* (de la chaussée) **2** CONGESTION : embouteillage *m* (de la circulation) **3** HOLDUP : goulot *m* d'étranglement

bottom[1] ['bɒtəm] *adj* **1** : du bas, inférieur <bottom lip : lèvre inférieure> **2** : premier <the bottom step : la première marche>

bottom[2] *n* **1** : bas *m*, pied *m* (d'un escalier, d'une page, etc.), fond *m* (de la mer) **2** : dernière place *f*; bas *m* <at the bottom of her class : dernière de classe> **3** ORIGIN, ROOT : origine *f*, fond *m* <to get to the bottom of sth : découvrir le fin fond de qqch> **4** BUTTOCKS : fesses *fpl*, derrière *m fam*

bottomless ['bɒtəmləs] *adj* : sans fond, insondable

botulism ['bɒtʃə,lɪzəm] *n* : botulisme *m*

bough ['baʊ] *n* : branche *f*, rameau *m*

bought → **buy**[1]

bouillon ['bu:,jɑn; 'bʊl,jɑn, -jən] *n* : bouillon *m*

boulder ['bo:ldər] *n* : rocher *m*

boulevard ['bʊlə,vɑrd, 'bu:-] *n* : boulevard *m*

bounce[1] ['baʊnʃ] *v* **bounced; bouncing** *vt* : faire rebondir (une balle) — *vi* **1** : rebondir, faire des bonds <the ball bounced into the air : la balle a rebondi dans l'espace> **2** : être sans provision (se dit d'un chèque)

bounce[2] *n* **1** : bond *m* (d'une balle) **2** LIVELINESS : vitalité *f*

bound[1] ['baʊnd] *vt* CONFINE : limiter, borner — *vi* LEAP : bondir, sauter

bound[2] *adj* **1** TIED : lié, attaché <bound hand and foot : pieds et poings liés> **2** OBLIGED : obligé, tenu **3** CERTAIN : sûr, certain <it's bound to rain : il est sûr de pleuvoir> **4** : relié (se dit d'un livre) **5 bound for** : à destination de, en route pour

bound[3] *n* **1** LEAP : bond *m*, saut *m* **2 bounds** *npl* LIMIT : limite *f*, bornes *fpl*

boundary ['baʊndri, -dəri] *n, pl* **-aries 1** : limite *f*, frontière *f* **2** *or* **boundary line** : limites *fpl* du terrain

boundless ['baʊndləs] *adj* : sans limites, sans bornes

bounteous ['baʊntiəs] *adj* **1** GENEROUS : généreux **2** ABUNDANT : abondant <a bounteous harvest : une bonne récolte>

bountiful ['baʊntɪfəl] *adj* **1** GENEROUS : généreux, libéral **2** PLENTIFUL : abondant, copieux

bounty ['baʊnti] *n, pl* **-ties 1** : générosité *f*, libéralité *f* **2** REWARD : prime *f*

bouquet [bo:'keɪ, bu:-] *n* **1** : bouquet *m* (de fleurs) **2** : arôme *m*, bouquet *m* (de vin, etc.)

bourbon ['bərbən, 'bʊr-] *n* : bourbon *m*

bourgeois[1] ['bʊrʒ,wɑ, bʊrʒ'wɑ] *adj* : bourgeois

bourgeois[2] *n* : bourgeois *m*, -geoise *f*

bourgeoisie [,bʊrʒ,wɑ'zi] *n* : bourgeoisie *f*

bout ['baʊt] *n* **1** CONTEST : combat *m*, match *m* **2** ATTACK : accès *m*, crise *f* <a bout of fever : un accès de fièvre> **3** PERIOD : période *f* (de travail, etc.) <a drinking bout : une beuverie>

boutique [bu:'ti:k] *n* : boutique *f*

bovine ['bo:,vaɪn, -,vi:n] *adj* : bovin

bow[1] ['baʊ] *vi* **1** : s'incliner, saluer de la tête <to bow to the audience : saluer le public> **2** BEND : se courber **3** YIELD : s'incliner, se soumettre — *vt* : incliner, courber <to bow one's head : baisser la tête>

bow[2] ['baʊ:] *n* **1** BOWING : révérence *f*, salut *m* **2** : proue *f*, avant *m* (d'un navire)

bow[3] ['bo:] *n* **1** ARCH, BEND : arche *f*, arc *m*, courbe *f* **2** : arc *m* <bows and arrows : des arcs et des flèches> **3** : nœud *m* <bow tie : nœud papillon> **4** : archet *m* (de violon)

bowels ['baʊəlz] *npl* **1** INTESTINES : intestins *mpl* **2** DEPTHS : entrailles *fpl*, profondeurs *fpl* <the bowels of the earth : les entrailles de la terre>

bower ['baʊər] *n* : tonnelle *f*, berceau *m* de verdure

bowl[1] ['bo:l] *vt* **1** : faire rouler (une boule) **2 to bowl over** OVERWHELM : bouleverser, renverser — *vi* : jouer au bowling

bowl[2] *n* : bol *m*, bassin *m*, cuvette *f*

bowling ['bo:lɪŋ] *n* : bowling *m*

bowling alley *n* : bowling *m*, allée *f* de quilles *Can*

box[1] ['bɑks] *vt* **1** : mettre en boîte **2** SLAP : gifler, claquer (les oreilles, etc.) — *vi* : boxer, faire de la boxe

box[2] *n* **1** : boîte *f*, caisse *f*, coffre *m* <a box of chocolates : une boîte de chocolats> **2** : loge *f* (de théâtre), barre *f* (de témoin) **3** SLAP : gifle *f*, claque *f* **4** *pl* **box** *or* **boxes** : buis *m* (plante)

boxcar ['bɑks,kɑr] *n* : wagon *m* de marchandises

boxer ['bɑksər] *n* **1** FIGHTER : boxeur *m* **2** : boxer *m* (chien)

boxing ['bɑksɪŋ] *n* : boxe *f*

box office *n* : guichet *m*, billetterie *f*

boxwood ['bɑks,wʊd] *n* : buis *m*

boy ['bɔɪ] *n* : garçon *m*

boycott[1] ['bɔɪ,kɑt] *vt* : boycotter

boycott[2] *n* : boycott *m*, boycottage *m*

boyfriend ['bɔɪ,frend] *n* : petit ami *m*, chum *m Can fam*

boyhood ['bɔɪ,hʊd] *n* : enfance *f*

boyish ['bɔɪɪʃ] *adj* : de garçon, d'enfant

bra ['brɑ] → **brassiere**

brace[1] ['breɪs] *vt* **braced; bracing 1** STRENGTHEN : soutenir, renforcer **2**

INVIGORATE : revigorer **3 to brace oneself** : rassembler ses forces

brace[2] *n* **1** PAIR : paire *f* <a brace of quail : une paire de cailles> **2** SUPPORT : attache *f*, support *m* **3** *or* **brace and bit** : vilbrequin *m* **4** : appareil *m* orthopédique, appareil *m* orthodontique (en médecine) **5** BRACKET : accolade *f*

bracelet ['breɪslət] *n* : bracelet *m*

bracken ['brækən] *n* : fougère *f*

bracket[1] ['brækət] *vt* **1** : mettre entre parenthèses, mettre entre crochets **2** GROUP : regrouper, mettre dans le même groupe

bracket[2] *n* **1** SUPPORT : support *m*, tasseau *m* **2** : parenthèse *f*, crochet *m* <in square brackets : entre crochets> **3** CATEGORY : catégorie *f*, tranche *f* <the lower income bracket : la tranche des petits revenus>

brackish ['brækɪʃ] *adj* : saumâtre

brad ['bræd] *n* : semence *f*, clou *m* (sans tête)

brag[1] ['bræg] *vi* **bragged; bragging** : se vanter

brag[2] *n* : vantardise *f*, fanfaronnades *fpl*

braggart ['brægərt] *n* : vantard *m*, -tarde *f*

braid[1] ['breɪd] *vt* **1** INTERWEAVE : entrelacer **2** : tresser (les cheveux)

braid[2] *n* **1** TRIMMING : galon *m*, ganse *f* **2** : tresse *f*, natte *f* (de cheveux)

braille ['breɪl] *n* : braille *m*

brain[1] ['breɪn] *vt* KNOCK OUT : assommer

brain[2] *n* **1** : cerveau *m*, cervelle *f* **2** : intelligence *f* <to have brains : être intelligent>

brainless ['breɪnləs] *adj* : stupide, idiot

brainstorm ['breɪnˌstɔrm] *n* : idée *f* de génie, inspiration *f*

brainy ['breɪnɪ] *adj* **brainier; -est** : intelligent, calé *fam*

braise ['breɪz] *vt* **braised; braising** : braiser

brake[1] ['breɪk] *vi* **braked; braking** : freiner

brake[2] *n* : frein *m*

bramble ['bræmbəl] *n* : ronce *f*

bran ['bræn] *n* : son *m*

branch[1] ['brænt∫] *vi* **1** : se ramifier (se dit d'une plante) **2** *or* **to branch off** DIVERGE : bifurquer

branch[2] *n* **1** : branche *f* (d'une plante) **2** : embranchement *m* (d'une route) **3** DIVISION : succursale *f*, agence *f*, section *f* <branch manager : directeur de succursale>

brand[1] ['brænd] *vt* **1** : marquer (au fer rouge) **2** LABEL, STIGMATIZE : flétrir, étiqueter, stigmatiser

brand[2] *n* **1** : marque *f* (sur des animaux) **2** STIGMA : marque *f*, stigmate *m* **3** MAKE : marque *f* (de fabrique)

brandish ['brændɪ∫] *vt* : brandir

brand–new ['brænd'nu:, -'nju:] *adj* : tout neuf

brandy ['brændɪ] *n, pl* **-dies** : cognac *m*, eau-de-vie *f*

brash ['bræ∫] *adj* **1** IMPULSIVE, RASH : impétueux, irréfléchi **2** IMPUDENT : impertinent, effronté

brass ['bræs] *n* **1** : cuivre *m* (jaune), laiton *m* **2** : cuivres *mpl* (d'un orchestre) **3** GALL, NERVE : impudence *f*, toupet *m fam* **4** OFFICERS : officiers *mpl* (militaires)

brassiere [brə'zɪr, brɑ-] *n* : soutien-gorge *m*, brassière *f Can*

brassy ['bræsɪ] *adj* **brassier; -est 1** : cuivré **2** IMPUDENT : effronté, impertinent

brat ['bræt] *n* : môme *mf France fam;* gosse *mf France fam;* polisson *m*, -sonne *f*

bravado [brə'vɑdo] *n, pl* **-does** *or* **-dos** : bravade *f*

brave[1] ['breɪv] *vt* **braved; braving** : braver, défier

brave[2] *adj* **braver; bravest** : courageux, brave — **bravely** *adv*

brave[3] *n* : guerrier *m* indien

bravery ['breɪvərɪ] *n, pl* **-eries** : courage *m*, bravoure *f*

bravo ['brɑˌvo:] *n, pl* **-vos** : bravo *m*

brawl[1] ['brɔl] *vi* : se bagarrer

brawl[2] *n* : bagarre *f*, rixe *f*

brawn ['brɔn] *n* : muscles *mpl*

brawny ['brɔnɪ] *adj* **brawnier; -est** : musclé

bray[1] ['breɪ] *vi* : braire

bray[2] *n* : braiment *m*

brazen ['breɪzən] *adj* **1** COPPER : de cuivre **2** IMPUDENT : effronté, impudent <a brazen lie : un mensonge effronté>

brazenly ['breɪzənlɪ] *adv* : effrontément

brazier ['breɪʒər] *n* : brasero *m*

Brazilian[1] [brə'zɪljən] *adj* : brésilien

Brazilian[2] *n* : Brésilien *m*, -lienne *f*

breach[1] [bri:t∫] *vt* **1** BREAK, VIOLATE : enfreindre, transgresser **2** PENETRATE : ouvrir une brèche dans (un mur, etc.)

breach[2] *n* **1** VIOLATION : infraction *f*, violation *f* **2** : abus *m* <breach of faith : abus de confiance> **3** : rupture *f*, annulation *f* <breach of contract : rupture de contrat> **4** GAP : brèche *f*, ouverture *f*

bread[1] ['bred] *vt* : paner, couvrir de chapelure

bread[2] *n* : pain *m*

breadth ['bretθ] *n* : largeur *f*

breadwinner ['bredˌwɪnər] *n* : soutien *m* de famille

break[1] ['breɪk] *v* **broke** ['bro:k]; **broken** ['bro:kən]; **breaking** *vt* **1** : casser, briser **2** VIOLATE : violer, transgresser **3** TELL : annoncer, faire part de <to break the news : annoncer la nouvelle> **4** SOFTEN : amortir, adoucir (une chute) **5** INTERRUPT : interrompre <to break the silence : percer le silence> **6** SURPASS : battre (un record, etc.) **7 to break down** : abattre, enfoncer <she broke down the door : elle a enfoncé la porte> — *vi* **1** : se casser, se briser **2** : se lever, se montrer <day is breaking : le jour se lève> **3** *or* **to break out** ESCAPE : s'évader, se libérer **4** HALT : prendre une pause, arrêter **5 to break down** FAIL : tomber en panne **6 to break down** COLLAPSE : s'effondrer, s'écrouler **7 to break in** : entrer par effraction (dans une maison) **8 to break up** SEPARATE : rompre, se quitter

break² *n* **1** : cassure *f*, rupture *f* **2** GAP : trouée *f*, brèche *f* **3** REST : pause *f*, récréation *f*, break *m Can* <to take a break : faire une pause> **4** CHANCE : chance *f*, veine *f fam* <I had a lucky break : j'ai eu de la chance> **5** : interruption *f* (d'une émission)

breakage [ˈbreɪkɪdʒ] *n* : casse *f*, bris *m*

breakdown [ˈbreɪkˌdaʊn] *n* **1** : rupture *f* <breakdown in negotiations : rupture des négociations> **2** FAILURE : panne *f* (d'une machine) **3** *or* **nervous breakdown** : dépression *f* nerveuse

breaker [ˈbreɪkər] *n* **1** WAVE : brisant *m* **2 → circuit breaker**

breakfast [ˈbrɛkfəst] *n* : petit déjeuner *m France*, déjeuner *m Can*

breakwater [ˈbrekˌwɔt̬ər, -ˌwɑ-] *n* : jetée *f*, brise-lames *m*

breast [ˈbrɛst] *n* **1** : sein *m* (d'une femme) **2** CHEST : poitrine *f*

breastbone [ˈbrɛstˌboːn] *n* : sternum *m*

breast–feed [ˈbrɛstˌfiːd] *vt* **-fed** [-ˌfɛd]; **-feeding** : allaiter

breath [ˈbrɛθ] *n* **1** : souffle *m*, haleine *f* <out of breath : à bout de souffle> <bad breath : mauvaise haleine> **2** GUST : souffle *m* <a breath of air : un souffle d'air>

breathe [ˈbriːð] *v* **breathed; breathing** *vt* **1** : respirer **2** : pousser, laisser échapper <I breathed a sigh of relief : j'ai poussé un soupir de soulagement> **3** UTTER : souffler <don't breathe a word about it : n'en souffle pas mot> — *vi* **1** : respirer **2** LIVE : vivre, être en vie

breathless [ˈbrɛθləs] *adj* : à bout de souffle, haletant

breathlessly [ˈbrɛθləsli] *adv* : en haletant

breathtaking [ˈbrɛθˌteɪkɪŋ] *adj* : à vous couper le souffle, stupéfiant

breeches [ˈbrɪtʃəz, briː-] *npl* PANTS : culotte *f*, pantalon *m*

breed¹ [ˈbriːd] *v* **bred** [ˈbrɛd]; **breeding** *vt* **1** RAISE : élever, faire l'élevage de **2** CAUSE, PRODUCE : faire naître, engendrer — *vi* : se reproduire, se multiplier

breed² *n* **1** : race *f*, espèce *f* **2** KIND : espèce *f*, sorte *f*

breeze¹ [ˈbriːz] *vi* **breezed; breezing 1** : aller vite <to breeze in : entrer en coup de vent> **2 to breeze through** : réussir facilement (un examen, etc.)

breeze² *n* **1** : brise *f* **2 it's a breeze!** : c'est du gâteau!, c'est facile comme tout!

breezy [ˈbriːzi] *adj* **breezier; -est 1** AIRY, WINDY : venteux, éventé **2** NONCHALANT : désinvolte, léger

brevity [ˈbrɛvət̬i] *n, pl* **-ties** : brièveté *f*

brew¹ [ˈbruː] *vt* **1** : brasser (de la bière) **2** : préparer, faire infuser (du thé) — *vi* **1** : fermenter (se dit de la bière), infuser (se dit du thé, etc.) **2** : se préparer <there's a storm brewing : un orage se prépare, il y a de l'orage dans l'air>

brew² *n* **1** BEER : bière *f* **2** INFUSION : infusion *f* (de thé, etc.)

brewery [ˈbruːəri, ˈbrʊri] *n, pl* **-ries** : brasserie *f*

briar → brier

bribe¹ [ˈbraɪb] *vt* **bribed; bribing** : soudoyer, acheter, suborner (un témoin)

bribe² *n* : pot-de-vin *m*

bribery [ˈbraɪbəri] *n, pl* **-eries** : corruption *f*

bric–a–brac [ˈbrɪkəˌbræk] *ns & pl* : bric-à-brac *m*

brick¹ [ˈbrɪk] *vt* **to brick up** : murer

brick² *n* : brique *f*

bricklayer [ˈbrɪkˌleɪər] *n* : maçon *m*

bricklaying [ˈbrɪkˌleɪɪŋ] *n* : maçonnerie *f*

bridal [ˈbraɪdəl] *adj* : nuptial, de mariée, de noce

bride [ˈbraɪd] *n* : mariée *f*

bridegroom [ˈbraɪdˌgruːm] *n* : marié *m*

bridesmaid [ˈbraɪdzˌmeɪd] *n* : demoiselle *f* d'honneur

bridge¹ [ˈbrɪdʒ] *vt* **1** : construire un pont sur **2 to bridge a gap** : combler une lacune, établir un rapprochement

bridge² *n* **1** : pont *m* **2** : arête *f* (du nez) **3** : passerelle *f* (d'un navire) **4** DENTURE : bridge *m* (dentaire) **5** : bridge *m* (jeu de cartes)

bridle¹ [ˈbraɪdəl] *v* **-dled; -dling** *vt* **1** : brider (un cheval) **2** RESTRAIN : refréner, brider <to bridle one's tongue : tenir sa langue> — *vi* **to bridle at** : se cabrer contre

bridle² *n* : bride *f* (d'un cheval)

brief¹ [ˈbriːf] *vt* : donner des instructions à, mettre au courant

brief² *adj* : bref, court, concis

brief³ *n* **1** SYNOPSIS : résumé *m* **2** : cause *f* à plaider, dossier *m* (en droit) **3 briefs** *npl* UNDERPANTS : slip *m*

briefcase [ˈbriːfˌkeɪs] *n* : serviette *f*, porte-documents *m*

briefly [ˈbriːfli] *adv* **1** CONCISELY : brièvement, de façon concise **2** IN SHORT : en bref

brier [ˈbraɪər] *n* **1** BRAMBLE : ronce *f* **2** HEATH : bruyère *f*

brig [ˈbrɪg] *n* **1** : brick *m* (navire) **2** : cellule *f* à bord d'un navire
brigade [brɪˈgeɪd] *n* : brigade *f*
brigadier general [ˌbrɪgəˈdɪr] *n* : général *m* de brigade
brigand [ˈbrɪgənd] *n* : brigand *m*, bandit *m*
bright [ˈbraɪt] *adj* **1** BRILLIANT, SHINING : brillant, éclatant **2** CLEVER : intelligent **3** VIVID : vif <bright colors : couleurs vives> **4** CHEERFUL : joyeux, animé, gai
brighten [ˈbraɪtən] *vt* **1** : faire briller **2** ENLIVEN : égayer, animer — *vi* : s'éclaircir (se dit du temps)
brightly [ˈbraɪtli] *adv* **1** INTENSELY : brillamment, intensément **2** CHEERFULLY : joyeusement, gaiement
brilliance [ˈbrɪljənts] *n* **1** RADIANCE : éclat *m* (d'une lumière) **2** SPLENDOR : splendeur *f*, éclat *m* **3** : grande intelligence *f*
brilliant [ˈbrɪljənt] *adj* **1** BRIGHT : éclatant **2** SPLENDID : brillant, génial <a brilliant idea : une idée géniale> **3** GIFTED : très intelligent, doué
brilliantly [ˈbrɪljəntli] *adv* **1** RADIANTLY : avec éclat **2** EXCELLENTLY : brillamment **3** PARTICULARLY : extrêmement
brim[1] [ˈbrɪm] *vi* **brimmed; brimming 1** *or* **to brim over** : être plein jusqu'à déborder **2 to brim with tears** : se remplir de larmes
brim[2] *n* : bord *m* <full to the brim : plein à ras bord>
brimful [ˈbrɪmˈfʊl] *adj* : plein à déborder
brimstone [ˈbrɪmˌstoːn] *n* : soufre *m*
brindled [ˈbrɪndəld] *adj* : moucheté, tacheté
brine [ˈbraɪn] *n* **1** : eau *f* salée, saumure *f* **2** OCEAN : mer *f*, océan *m*
bring [ˈbrɪŋ] *vt* **brought** [ˈbrɔt]; **bringing 1** CARRY, CONVEY : amener (une personne ou un animal), apporter (une chose) **2** *or* **to bring about** PRODUCE : provoquer, causer, entraîner **3** INDUCE, PERSUADE : amener, pousser, persuader **4** LEAD : amener, mener, conduire **5** YIELD : rapporter (en finance) **6 to bring to light** : mettre en lumière **7 to bring sth to an end** : mettre fin à qqch
bring around *vt* **1** PERSUADE : convaincre, convertir **2** → **bring to**
bring out *vt* : sortir (un produit, un livre, etc.)
bring to *vt* REVIVE : ranimer
bring up *vt* **1** REAR : élever **2** MENTION : mentionner, signaler, aborder
brink [ˈbrɪŋk] *n* : bord *m* <on the brink of war : au bord de la guerre> <on the brink of doing : sur le point de faire>
briny [ˈbraɪni] *adj* **brinier; -est** : saumâtre, salé
brisk [ˈbrɪsk] *adj* **1** LIVELY : vif, animé **2** INVIGORATING : vivifiant, frais **3** QUICK : vif, rapide
bristle[1] [ˈbrɪsəl] *vi* **-tled; -tling 1** : se hérisser (se dit des cheveux, etc.) **2** : s'irriter, se hérisser <she's bristling with anger : elle se hérisse de colère>
bristle[2] *n* **1** : soie *f* (d'un animal) **2** : poil *m* (d'une brosse)
bristly [ˈbrɪsəli] *adj* **bristlier; -est 1** PRICKLY : qui pique **2** : hérissé (se dit des cheveux, etc.)
British[1] [ˈbrɪtɪʃ] *adj* : britannique
British[2] *npl* **the British** : les Britanniques
brittle [ˈbrɪtəl] *adj* **-tler; -tlest** : fragile, cassant
broach [ˈbroːtʃ] *vt* BRING UP : aborder, entamer <to broach a subject : aborder un sujet>
broad [ˈbrɔd] *adj* **1** WIDE : large **2** SPACIOUS : vaste, immense **3** GENERAL : grand, général <broad outlines : grandes lignes> **4** OBVIOUS : transparent <a broad hint : une allusion transparente> **5** LIBERAL : large, libéral <broad ideas : idées larges> **6** CRUDE : gros, vulgaire **7 in broad daylight** : en plein jour
broad bean *n* : fève *f*
broadcast[1] [ˈbrɔdˌkæst] *v* **-cast; -casting** *vt* **1** SCATTER : semer (des graines, etc.) **2** TRANSMIT : diffuser, téléviser **3** SPREAD : répandre — *vi* : émettre, faire des émissions
broadcast[2] *n* **1** BROADCASTING : transmission *f*, diffusion *f* **2** PROGRAM : émission *f* <news broadcast : bulletin d'informations>
broadcaster [ˈbrɔdˌkæstər] *n* : personnalité *f*, journaliste *mf* (de la radio, de la télévision)
broadcloth [ˈbrɔdkləθ] *n* : drap *m* fin
broaden [ˈbrɔdən] *vt* : élargir <to broaden one's outlook : élargir ses horizons> — *vi* EXPAND, WIDEN : s'élargir
broadloom [ˈbrɔdˌluːm] *adj* : en grande largeur
broadly [ˈbrɔdli] *adv* **1** WIDELY : largement **2** GENERALLY : en gros, en général
broad-minded [ˈbrɔdˈmaɪndəd] *adj* : tolérant, large d'esprit
broad-mindedness [brɔdˈmaɪndədnəs] *n* : largeur *f* d'esprit
broadside[1] [ˈbrɔdˌsaɪd] *adv* : par le travers
broadside[2] *n* **1** VOLLEY : bordée *f* **2** TIRADE : invective *f*, attaque *f* cinglante
brocade [broˈkeɪd] *n* : brocart *m*
broccoli [ˈbrɑkəli] *n* : brocoli *m*
brochure [broˈʃʊr] *n* : brochure *f*, dépliant *m*
brogue [ˈbroːg] *n* : accent *m* irlandais
broil [ˈbrɔɪl] *v* : griller
broiler [ˈbrɔɪlər] *n* **1** GRILL : gril *m* **2** : poulet *m* à rôtir

broke[1] ['bro:k] → **break**[1]

broke[2] *adj* : fauché *fam,* à sec *fam,* cassé *Can fam* <to go broke : faire faillite>

broken ['bro:kən] *adj* **1** DAMAGED, SHATTERED : cassé; brisé **2** IRREGULAR, UNEVEN : brisé, découpé, accidenté <a broken line : une ligne brisée> <broken coastlines : littoraux découpés> **3** VIOLATED : rompu, manqué <a broken promise : une promesse manquée> **4** IMPERFECT : mauvais, imparfait <in broken French : en mauvais français> **5** CRUSHED : brisé, abattu <he's a broken man : il a le cœur brisé>

brokenhearted [ˌbro:kən'hɑrt̬əd] *adj* : au cœur brisé

broker ['bro:kər] *n* **1** : courtier *m,* -tière *f;* agent *m* **2** → **stockbroker**

brokerage ['bro:kərɪdʒ] *n* : courtage *m*

bromine ['bro:ˌmi:n] *n* : brome *m*

bronchial tubes ['brɑnkiəl] *npl* : bronches *fpl*

bronchitis [brɑŋ'kaɪt̬əs, brɑn-] *n* : bronchite *f*

bronze[1] ['brɑnz] *vt* **bronzed; bronzing** : bronzer

bronze[2] *n* : bronze *m*

brooch ['bro:tʃ, 'bru:tʃ] *n* : broche *f,* épinglette *f Can*

brood[1] ['bru:d] *vi* **1** : couver (se dit d'un oiseau) **2** PONDER : broyer du noir, ruminer

brood[2] *n* : couvée *f,* nichée *f*

brook[1] ['brʊk] *vt* TOLERATE : accepter, tolérer

brook[2] *n* : ruisseau *m*

broom ['bru:m, 'brʊm] *n* **1** : genêt *m* (plante) **2** : balai *m* (pour balayer)

broomstick ['bru:mˌstɪk, 'brʊm-] *n* : manche *m* à balai

broth ['brɔθ] *n, pl* **broths** ['brɔθs, 'brɔðz] : bouillon *m*

brothel ['brɑθəl, 'brɔ-] *n* : maison *f* close, bordel *m fam*

brother ['brʌðər] *n* : frère *m*

brotherhood ['brʌðərˌhʊd] *n* **1** : fraternité *f* **2** ASSOCIATION : confrérie *f*

brother–in–law ['brʌðərɪnˌlɔ] *n, pl* **brothers–in–law** : beau-frère *m*

brotherly ['brʌðərli] *adj* : fraternel <brotherly love : amour fraternel>

brought → **bring**

brow ['braʊ] *n* **1** EYEBROW : sourcil *m* **2** FOREHEAD : front *m* **3** : sommet *m* <the brow of a hill : le sommet d'une colline>

browbeat ['braʊˌbi:t] *vt* **-beat; -beaten** [-ˌbi:t̬ən] *or* **-beat; -beating** : intimider

brown[1] [ˌbraʊn] *vt* **1** : faire dorer (en cuisine) **2** TAN : bronzer, brunir — *vi* : dorer (en cuisine)

brown[2] *adj* **1** : brun, marron **2** TANNED : bronzé, bruni

brown[3] *n* : brun *m,* marron *m*

brownish [ˌbraʊnɪʃ] *adj* : brunâtre

browse ['braʊz] *vi* **browsed; browsing** **1** GRAZE : brouter, paître **2** LOOK : regarder

browser ['braʊzər] *n* : navigateur *m* (en informatique)

bruin ['bru:ɪn] *n* BEAR : ours *m*

bruise[1] ['bru:z] *v* **bruised; bruising** *vt* **1** : faire un bleu à, contusionner **2** : taler (un fruit) — *vi* : se faire des bleus (se dit d'une personne), se taler (se dit d'un fruit)

bruise[2] *n* : bleu *m,* contusion *f,* meurtrissure *f,* prune *f Can*

brunch ['brʌntʃ] *n* : brunch *m*

brunet[1] [bru:'net] *or* **brunette** *adj* : châtain, brun (se dit des cheveux)

brunet[2] *or* **brunette** *n* : brun *m,* brune *f*

brunt ['brʌnt] *n* BURDEN : poids *m* <to bear the brunt of : subir tout le poids de, porter le plus gros de>

brush[1] ['brʌʃ] *vt* **1** : brosser, se brosser <I brushed my hair : je me suis brossé les cheveux> **2** GRAZE : frôler, effleurer **3** *or* **to brush up** SWEEP : balayer, ramasser **4 to brush off** DISMISS : écarter, repousser — *vi* **to brush up on** : se remettre à, réviser

brush[2] *n* **1** : brosse *f* (à cheveux), pinceau *m* (de peintre) **2** SCRUB, UNDERBRUSH : brousse *f,* broussailles *fpl,* fardoches *fpl Can* **3** TOUCH : effleurement *m* **4** SKIRMISH : accrochage *m,* escarmouche *f* <to have a brush with the law : avoir des démêlés avec la justice>

brush–off ['brʌʃˌɔf] *n* **to give s.o. the brush–off** : envoyer promener qqn

brusque ['brʌsk] *adj* : brusque

brusquely ['brʌskli] *adv* : brusquement, avec brusquerie

brutal ['bru:t̬əl] *adj* : brutal, cruel — **brutally** *adv*

brutality [bru:'tæləɾi] *n, pl* **-ties** : brutalité *f*

brutalize ['bru:t̬əlˌaɪz] *vt* **-ized; -izing** : brutaliser

brute[1] ['bru:t] *adj* **1** : bestial, animal **2** SHEER : brutal, vif, simple <brute force : force brutale>

brute[2] *n* **1** BEAST : brute *f,* bête *f* **2** : brute *f* (personne)

brutish ['bru:tɪʃ] *adj* **1** : de brute, bestial **2** CRUEL : brutal, cruel **3** STUPID : bête, stupide

bubble[1] ['bʌbəl] *vi* **-bled; -bling** **1** : bouillonner, pétiller **2 to bubble over** : déborder

bubble[2] *n* : bulle *f*

bubbly ['bʌbəli] *adj* **bubblier; -est** **1** BUBBLING : plein de bulles, pétillant **2** LIVELY : plein d'entrain

bubonic plague [bu:'bɑnɪk, 'bju:-] *n* : peste *f* bubonique

buccaneer [ˌbʌkə'nɪr] *n* : boucanier *m*

buck[1] ['bʌk] *vi* **1** : lancer une ruade (se dit d'un cheval) **2 to buck up** : se secouer — *vt* OPPOSE : résister, s'op-

poser à <to buck the system : lutter contre le système>
buck[2] *n, pl* **bucks 1** *or pl* **buck** : mâle *m* (d'un animal) **2** DOLLAR : dollar *m*, piastre *f Can fam* **3** MONEY : fric *m fam* <to make a buck : se faire du fric> **4 to pass the buck** : refiler la responsabilité aux autres
bucket ['bʌkət] *n* : seau *m*
buckle[1] ['bʌkəl] *v* **-led; -ling** *vt* **1** FASTEN : boucler **2** DISTORT, WARP : gauchir, déformer — *vi* **1** BEND, WARP : se courber, se voiler **2 to buckle down** : s'atteler, s'appliquer
buckle[2] *n* **1** CLASP : boucle *f* **2** WARPING : gauchissement *m*
buckshot ['bʌkˌʃɑt] *n* : chevrotine *f*
buckskin ['bʌkˌskɪn] *n* : peau *f* de daim
bucktooth ['bʌkˌtu:θ] *n, pl* **-teeth** : dent *f* saillante <to have buckteeth : avoir des dents de lapin>
buckwheat ['bʌkˌhwi:t] *n* : sarrasin *m*, blé *m* noir
bucolic [ˌbju:'kɑlɪk] *adj* : bucolique
bud[1] ['bʌd] *vi* **budded; budding** : bourgeonner, former des boutons
bud[2] *n* : bourgeon *m* (d'une feuille), bouton *m* (d'une fleur)
Buddhism ['bu:ˌdɪzəm, 'bʊ-] *n* : bouddhisme *m*
Buddhist[1] ['bu:ˌdɪst, 'bʊ-] *adj* : bouddhiste
Buddhist[2] *n* : bouddhiste *mf*
buddy ['bʌdi] *n, pl* **-dies** : copain *m*, -pine *f*
budge ['bʌdʒ] *vi* **budged; budging 1** MOVE : bouger, se déplacer **2** YIELD : changer d'avis, céder
budget[1] ['bʌdʒət] *vt* : budgétiser — *vi* : dresser un budget
budget[2] *n* : budget *m*
budgetary ['bʌdʒəˌteri] *adj* : budgétaire
buff[1] ['bʌf] *vt* POLISH : polir, lustrer
buff[2] *adj* : chamois, beige
buff[3] *n* **1** : chamois *m* (couleur) **2** ENTHUSIAST : mordu *m*, -due *f fam;* fanatique *mf*
buffalo ['bʌfəˌlo:] *n, pl* **-lo** *or* **-loes** : buffle *m*, bison *m* (d'Amérique)
buffer ['bʌfər] *n* **1** : tampon *m* <buffer zone : région tampon> **2 nail buffer** : polissoir à ongles
buffet[1] ['bʌfət] *vt* BATTER : frapper, battre
buffet[2] *n* BLOW : coup *m*
buffet[3] [ˌbʌ'feɪ, ˌbu:-] *n* **1** : buffet *m* (repas) **2** SIDEBOARD : buffet *m*
buffoon [ˌbʌ'fu:n] *n* : bouffon *m*, clown *m*
buffoonery [ˌbʌ'fu:nəri] *n, pl* **-eries** : bouffonnerie *f*
bug[1] ['bʌg] *vt* **bugged; bugging 1** : installer un microphone dans **2** BOTHER : embêter
bug[2] *n* **1** INSECT : insecte *m*, bestiole *f*, bébite *f Can fam* **2** FLAW : défaut *m*, erreur *f* (en informatique, etc.) **3** GERM : microbe *m*, virus *m* **4** MICROPHONE : microphone *m*
bugaboo ['bʌgəˌbu:] *n, pl* **-boos** → **bugbear**
bugbear ['bʌgˌbær] *n* BOGEY : épouvantail *m*, croque-mitaine *m*
buggy ['bʌgi] *n, pl* **-gies 1** CARRIAGE : buggy *m*, boghei *m*, calèche *f* **2** BABY CARRIAGE : voiture *f* d'enfant, landau *m France*
bugle ['bju:gəl] *n* : clairon *m*
bugler ['bju:gələr] *n* : clairon *m*
build[1] ['bɪld] *v* **built** ['bɪlt]; **building** *vt* **1** CONSTRUCT : construire, bâtir **2** DEVELOP, ESTABLISH : bâtir, établir, fonder **3** INCREASE : augmenter — *vi* INTENSIFY : augmenter
build[2] *n* PHYSIQUE : carrure *f*, charpente *f*
building ['bɪldɪŋ] *n* **1** EDIFICE : bâtiment *m*, immeuble *m* **2** CONSTRUCTION : construction *f*
built-in ['bɪltˈɪn] *adj* : encastré
bulb ['bʌlb] *n* **1** : bulbe *m* (d'une plante), réservoir *m* (d'un thermomètre) **2** LIGHTBULB : ampoule *f*
bulbous ['bʌlbəs] *adj* : bulbeux
Bulgarian[1] [bʌl'gæriən, bʊl-] *adj* : bulgare
Bulgarian[2] *n* **1** : Bulgare *mf* **2** : bulgare *m* (langue)
bulge[1] ['bʌldʒ] *vi* **bulged; bulging 1** SWELL : bomber, être gonflé **2** : sortir de la tête (se dit des yeux)
bulge[2] *n* : renflement *m*
bulk ['bʌlk] *n* **1** MAGNITUDE : masse *f*, volume *m* **2** FIBER : fibre *m* (alimentaire) **3 in ~** : en gros **4 the bulk of** : la majeure partie de, le plus gros de
bulkhead ['bʌlkˌhɛd] *n* : cloison *f*
bulky ['bʌlki] *adj* **bulkier; -est** : volumineux, encombrant
bull ['bʊl] *n* **1** : taureau *m* **2** MALE : mâle *m* (de l'orignal, de la baleine, etc.) **3** *or* **papal bull** : bulle *f* (papale) **4** DECREE : décret *m*, règlement *m*
bulldog ['bʊlˌdɔg] *n* : bouledogue *m*
bulldoze ['bʊlˌdo:z] *vt* **-dozed; -dozing 1** : démolir au bulldozer, raser au bulldozer **2** FORCE : forcer <to bulldoze one's way : se frayer un chemin>
bulldozer ['bʊlˌdo:zər] *n* : bulldozer *m*
bullet ['bʊlət] *n* : balle *f* (d'un fusil)
bulletin ['bʊlətən, -ləˌtən] *n* **1** NOTICE : bulletin *m*, communiqué *m* <news bulletin : bulletin d'informations> **2** NEWSLETTER : bulletin *m*
bulletin board *n* : tableau *m* d'affichage, babillard *m Can*
bulletproof ['bʊlətˌpru:f] *adj* : pare-balles (se dit des vêtements), blindé (se dit d'une voiture)
bullfight ['bʊlˌfaɪt] *n* : corrida *f*
bullfighter ['bʊlˌfaɪtər] *n* : matador *m*, torero *m*
bullfrog ['bʊlˌfrɔg] *n* : grenouille *f* taureau

bullheaded ['bʊlˌhɛdəd] *adj* : entêté, têtu
bullion ['bʊljən] *n* : or *m* en lingots, argent *m* en lingots
bullock ['bʊlək] *n* **1** : bouvillon *m* **2** STEER : bœuf *m*
bull's–eye ['bʊlzˌaɪ] *n, pl* **bull's–eyes** : centre *m* (de la cible), mille *m*
bully[1] ['bʊli] *vt* **-lied; -lying** : intimider, malmener, tyranniser
bully[2] *n, pl* **-lies** : tyran *m*, petite brute *f*
bulrush ['bʊlˌrʌʃ] *n* : jonc *m*
bulwark ['bʊlˌwərk, -ˌwɔrk; 'bʌlˌwərk] *n* : rempart *m*, fortification *f*
bum[1] ['bʌm] *v* **bummed; bumming** *vt* : taper qqn de *fam*, quémander <to bum money : quémander de l'argent> — *vi* **to bum around** LOAF : fainéanter, paresser
bum[2] *adj* BAD : minable, faux, mauvais <a bum rap : une accusation mensongère>
bum[3] *n* **1** HOBO, TRAMP : clochard *m*, -charde *f* **2** LOAFER : fainéant *m*, fainéante *f*
bumblebee ['bʌmbəlˌbiː] *n* : bourdon *m*
bump[1] ['bʌmp] *vt* HIT : heurter, cogner <to bump one's head : se cogner la tête> — *vi* **to bump into** MEET : tomber sur, rencontrer par hasard
bump[2] *n* **1** JOLT : secousse *f* **2** COLLISION, IMPACT : choc *m*, heurt *m* **3** LUMP : bosse *f*, poque *f Can fam*
bumper[1] ['bʌmpər] *adj* : exceptionnel, record
bumper[2] *n* : pare-chocs *m*
bumpkin ['bʌmpkən] *n* : péquenaud *m*, -naude *f France fam;* rustre *mf*
bumpy ['bʌmpi] *adj* **bumpier; -est 1** ROUGH, UNEVEN : cahoteux, bosselé **2** : agité <a bumpy crossing : une traversée agitée>
bun ['bʌn] *n* : petit pain *m* (au lait)
bunch[1] ['bʌntʃ] *vt* : mettre ensemble, mettre en bottes — *vi* **to bunch up** : se serrer (se dit des personnes), être retroussé (se dit des vêtements)
bunch[2] *n* **1** : bouquet *m* (de fleurs), grappe *f* (de raisins), botte *f* (de légumes, etc.) **2** GROUP : groupe *m*
bundle[1] ['bʌndəl] *v* **-dled; -dling** *vt* **1** PACKAGE : mettre en paquet, empaqueter **2 to bundle up** : emmitoufler (un enfant, etc.) — *vi* **to bundle up** : s'emmitoufler
bundle[2] *n* **1** PACKAGE : paquet *m*, ballot *m* **2** : liasse *f* (de papiers, etc.), botte *f* (de foin, de légumes) **3** LOT : grande quantité *f*, tas *m* (d'argent, etc.)
bungalow ['bʌŋgəˌloː] *n* : maison *f* sans étage
bungle ['bʌŋgəl] *vt* **-gled; -gling** BOTCH : gâcher, bousiller *fam*
bungler ['bʌŋgələr] *n* : bousilleur *m*, -leuse *f*
bunion ['bʌnjən] *n* : oignon *m*
bunk[1] ['bʌŋk] *vi* : coucher
bunk[2] *n* **1** BERTH : couchette *f* **2** NONSENSE : balivernes *fpl*, sottises *fpl* **3** *or* **bunk bed** : lits *mpl* superposés
bunker ['bʌŋkər] *n* **1** : coffre *m*, soute *f* (d'un navire) <coal bunker : soute à charbon> **2** : blockhaus *m* (militaire)
bunny ['bʌni] *n, pl* **-nies → rabbit**
bunt ['bʌnt] *n* : amorti *m Can* (au baseball)
bunting ['bʌntɪŋ] *n* **1** : bruant *m* (oiseau) **2** : étamine *f*, étoffe *f* (pour les drapeaux)
buoy[1] ['buːi, 'bɔi] *vt* **1** : faire flotter **2** *or* **to buoy up** CHEER, HEARTEN : revigorer, soutenir
buoy[2] *n* : bouée *f*, balise *f* (flottante)
buoyancy ['bɔiənsi, 'buːjən-] *n* : flottabilité *f*
buoyant ['bɔiənt, 'buːjənt] *adj* **1** : flottable **2** LIGHTHEARTED : gai, enjoué
bur *or* **burr** ['bər] *n* : bardane *f*
burden[1] ['bərdən] *vt* : charger, accabler
burden[2] *n* : charge *f*, fardeau *m*
burdensome ['bərdənsəm] *adj* : lourd, pesant
burdock ['bərˌdɑk] *n* : bardane *f*
bureau ['bjʊroˌ] *n* **1** CHEST OF DRAWERS : commode *f* **2** DEPARTMENT : service *m* (gouvernemental) **3** AGENCY : agence *f*, bureau *m* <credit bureau : agence de recouvrement>
bureaucracy [bjʊ'rɑkrəsi] *n, pl* **-cies** : bureaucratie *f*
bureaucrat ['bjʊrəˌkræt] *n* : bureaucrate *mf* — **bureaucratic** [ˌbjʊrə'krætɪk] *adj*
burgeon ['bərdʒən] *vi* **1** BLOOM : éclore, bourgeonner **2** FLOURISH : fleurir, croître
burglar ['bərglər] *n* : cambrioleur *m*, -leuse *f*
burglarize ['bərgləˌraɪz] *vt* **-ized; -izing** : cambrioler, dévaliser
burglary ['bərgləri] *n, pl* **-glaries** : cambriolage *m*
burgundy ['bərgəndi] *n, pl* **-dies** : bourgogne *m* (vin)
burial ['beriəl] *n* : enterrement *m*, inhumation *f*
burlap ['bərˌlæp] *n* : toile *f* à sac
burlesque[1] [bər'lesk] *vt* **-lesqued; -lesquing** : tourner en ridicule, parodier
burlesque[2] *n* **1** PARODY : burlesque *m*, parodie *f* **2** *or* **burlesqe show** : revue *f* déshabillée
burly ['bərli] *adj* **burlier; -est** : de forte carrure, costaud *fam*
burn[1] ['bərn] *v* **burned** ['bərnd, 'bərnt] *or* **burnt** ['bərnt]; **burning** *vi* **1** : brûler <to burn down : brûler complètement> <burning with desire : brûlant de désir> <she burns easily : elle brûle facilement> **2** : être allumé (se dit d'une lumière) — *vt* **1** : brûler, incendier **2** CONSUME : consommer, brûler (de l'essence, des calories, etc.)

burn² *n* : brûlure *f*
burner [ˈbərnər] *n* : brûleur *m* (d'une cuisinière), rond *m Can*
burnish [ˈbərnɪʃ] *vt* : brunir, polir
burp¹ [ˈbərp] *vi* : avoir des renvois, roter *fam*
burp² *n* : renvoi *m*, rot *m fam*
burro [ˈbərə, ˈbʊr-] *n, pl* **burros** : (petit) âne *m*
burrow¹ [ˈbərə] *vt* : creuser — *vi* **1** : creuser un terrier **2 to burrow into** SEARCH : fouiller dans
burrow² *n* : terrier *m*
bursar [ˈbərsər] *n* : économe *m/f*
burst¹ [ˈbərst] *v* **burst** *or* **bursted; bursting** *vt* : crever, faire éclater — *vi* **1** : crever, éclater (se dit d'un obus, d'une bombe, etc.) **2** OVERFLOW : déborder, être rempli <bursting with energy : débordant d'énergie> **3 to burst in** : entrer en coup de vent **4 to burst into tears** : fondre en larmes **5 to burst out laughing** : éclater de rire
burst² *n* **1** EXPLOSION : éclatement *m*, explosion *f* **2** OUTBURST : élan *m* (d'enthousiasme), éclat *m* (de rire)
Burundian¹ [bʊˈruːndiən, -ˈrʊn-] *adj* : burundais
Burundian² *n* : Burundais *m*, -daise *f*
bury [ˈberi] *vt* **buried; burying 1** INTER : enterrer, ensevelir **2** CONCEAL : enfouir, cacher **3** IMMERSE : plonger, immerger
bus¹ [ˈbʌs] *v* **bused** *or* **bussed** [ˈbʌst]; **busing** *or* **bussing** [ˈbʌsɪŋ] *vt* : transporter en autobus — *vi* : voyager en autobus
bus² *n, pl* **buses** *or* **busses** : bus *m*, autobus *m*
bush [ˈbʊʃ] *n* **1** SHRUB : buisson *m*, arbuste *m* **2** THICKET : fourré *m* **3 the bush** WILDERNESS : la brousse
bushel [ˈbʊʃəl] *n* : boisseau *m*
bushy [ˈbʊʃi] *adj* **bushier; -est** : touffu, broussailleux
busily [ˈbɪzəli] *adv* : activement
business [ˈbɪznəs, -nəz] *n* **1** OCCUPATION : occupation *f*, profession *f* <he's in the restaurant business : il est restaurateur de profession> **2** COMMERCE, TRADE : affaires *fpl*, commerce *m* **3** FIRM : entreprise *f*, firme *f*, affaire *f* **4** AFFAIR, CONCERN : affaire *f*, question *f* <that's none of your business : ce n'est pas de vos affaires>
businessman [ˈbɪznəsˌmæn, -nəz-] *n, pl* **-men** : homme *m* d'affaires
businesswoman [ˈbɪznəsˌwʊmən, -nəz-] *n, pl* **-women** : femme *f* d'affaires
bust¹ [ˈbʌst] *vt* **1** BREAK, SMASH : casser, briser **2** TAME : dresser (un cheval sauvage, etc.)
bust² *n* **1** : buste *m* (en sculpture) **2** BREASTS : seins *mpl*, poitrine *f*
bustle¹ [ˈbʌsəl] *vi* **-tled; -tling** : s'affairer, s'agiter
bustle² *n or* **hustle and bustle** : agitation *f*, activité *f*
busy¹ [ˈbɪzi] *vt* **busied; busying 1** : occuper **2 to busy oneself** : s'occuper
busy² *adj* **busier; -est 1** : occupé, affairé <to look busy : avoir l'air occupé> **2** : occupé, engagé *Can fam* (se dit d'une ligne téléphonique) **3** BUSTLING : animé, actif (se dit d'une rue, d'une ville, etc.)
busybody [ˈbɪziˌbɑdi] *n* **to be a busybody** : faire la mouche du coche
but¹ [ˈbʌt] *conj* **1** EXCEPT : mais <I would like to stay but I can't : j'aimerais rester mais je ne peux pas> **2** THAT : que <there is no doubt but he will win : il n'y a pas de doute qu'il gagnera> **3** YET : mais <poor but proud : pauvre mais fière>
but² *prep* EXCEPT : sauf, excepté <everyone but Anne : tout le monde sauf Anne> <it's nothing but an insult : ça n'est qu'une insulte>
butcher¹ [ˈbʊtʃər] *vt* **1** SLAUGHTER : abattre, tuer (un animal) **2** KILL : massacrer (une personne) **3** BOTCH : bousiller *fam*
butcher² *n* : boucher *m*, -chère *f*
butler [ˈbʌtlər] *n* : maître *m* d'hôtel
butt¹ [ˈbʌt] *vt* **1** : donner un coup de tête à, donner un coup de corne à **2** ABUT : être contigu à — *vi* **to butt in** : interrompre, se mêler
butt² *n* **1** BUTTING : coup *m* de tête, coup *m* de corne **2** TARGET : cible *f*, victime *f* <the butt of a practical joke : la victime d'une farce> **3** END : crosse *f* (d'un rifle), mégot *m fam* (de cigarette)
butte [ˈbjuːt] *n* : butte *f*, tertre *m*
butter¹ [ˈbʌtər] *vt* : beurrer
butter² *n* : beurre *m*
buttercup [ˈbʌtərˌkʌp] *n* : bouton-d'or *m*
butterfat [ˈbʌtərˌfæt] *n* : matière *f* grasse
butterfly [ˈbʌtərˌflaɪ] *n, pl* **-flies** : papillon *m*
buttermilk [ˈbʌtərˌmɪlk] *n* : babeurre *m*
butterscotch [ˈbʌtərˌskɑtʃ] *n* : caramel *m* dur au beurre
buttocks [ˈbʌtəks, -ˌtɑks] *npl* : fesses *fpl*
button¹ [ˈbʌtən] *vt* : boutonner (une blouse, etc.) — *vi* : se boutonner
button² *n* **1** : bouton *m* (de vêtements) **2** SWITCH : bouton *m*, piton *m Can fam*
buttonhole¹ [ˈbʌtənˌhoːl] *vt* **-holed; -holing** : accrocher, retenir (une personne)
buttonhole² *n* : boutonnière *f*
buttress¹ [ˈbʌtrəs] *vt* : étayer
buttress² *n* **1** : contrefort *m* (en architecture) **2** SUPPORT : pilier *m*, soutien *m*
buxom [ˈbʌksəm] *adj* : plantureux, bien en chair
buy¹ [ˈbaɪ] *vt* **bought** [ˈbɔt]; **buying** : acheter

buy[2] *n* **1** BARGAIN : affaire *f* <a good buy : une bonne affaire> **2** PURCHASE : acquisition *f*
buyer ['bʌɪər] *n* : acheteur *m*, -teuse *f*
buzz[1] ['bʌz] *vi* : bourdonner, vrombrir
buzz[2] *n* **1** : bourdonnement *m* (des insectes) **2** MURMUR : brouhaha *m* (de voix), murmure *m* **3** : coup *m* de fil *fam* <I gave him a buzz : je lui ai passé un coup de fil>
buzzard ['bʌzərd] *n* : buse *f*
buzzer ['bʌzər] *n* : sonnette *f*
buzzword ['bʌzˌwərd] *n* : mot *m* à la mode
by[1] ['bʌɪ] *adv* **1** NEAR : près <close by : tout près> **2 to go by** : passer <he walked straight by : il est passé tout droit> <in times gone by : il y a bien longtemps> **3 to stop by** : s'arrêter en passant
by[2] *prep* **1** NEAR : près de, à côté de <he's sitting by the window : il est assis près de la fenêtre> **2** VIA : par, en <by car : en voiture> <by airmail : par avion> **3** PAST : devant, à côté de <she went by the house : elle est passée devant la maison> **4** DURING : pendant <he studied by night : il étudiait pendant la nuit> **5** BEFORE : avant, pas plus tard que <he'll be home by ten : il sera rentré avant dix heures> **6** ACCORDING TO : d'après, selon <by what she says : d'après ce qu'elle dit> **7** (*indicating cause or agent*) : par <she was sent by me : elle était envoyée par moi> <to divide by 4 : diviser par 4>
by and by *adv* : bientôt
by and large *adv* : en général
bygone[1] ['bʌɪˌgɔn] *adj* : passé, d'autrefois <in bygone days : jadis>
bygone[2] *n* **let bygones be bygones** : oublions le passé
bylaw *or* **byelaw** ['bʌɪˌlɔ] *n* : statut *m* (d'une organisation), arrêté *m* (municipal)
by–line ['bʌɪˌlʌɪn] *n* : signature *f* de journaliste
bypass[1] ['bʌɪˌpæs] *vt* CIRCUMVENT : contourner, éviter
bypass[2] *n* **1** : route *f* de contournement, déviation *f* **2** : pontage *m* (en médecine)
by–product ['bʌɪˌprɑdəkt] *n* : sous-produit *m*, dérivé *m*
bystander ['bʌɪˌstændər] *n* : spectateur *m*, -trice *f*
byway ['bʌɪˌweɪ] *n* : route *f* secondaire
byword ['bʌɪˌwərd] *n* : proverbe *m*

C

c ['si:] *n*, *pl* **c's** *or* **cs** : c *m*, troisième lettre de l'alphabet
cab ['kæb] *n* **1** TAXICAB : taxi *m* **2** : cabine *f* (d'un camion, d'une locomotive, etc.) **3** CARRIAGE : fiacre *m*
cabal [kə'bɑl, -'bæl] *n* : cabale *f*
cabana [kə'bænjə, -'bænə] *n* : cabine *f* de plage, tente *f* de plage
cabaret [ˌkæbə'reɪ] *n* : cabaret *m*
cabbage ['kæbɪdʒ] *n* : chou *m*
cabdriver ['kæbˌdrʌɪvər] *n* : chauffeur *m* de taxi
cabin ['kæbən] *n* **1** : cabine *f* (d'un navire, d'un avion, etc.) **2** HUT : cabane *f*
cabinet ['kæbnət, 'kæbə-] *n* **1** : meuble *m* de rangement, vitrine *f* **2** : cabinet *m* (du gouvernement) **3** *or* **filing cabinet** : classeur *m* **4** *or* **medicine cabinet** : armoire *f* à pharmacie
cabinetmaker ['kæbnətˌmeɪkər 'kæbə-] *n* : ébéniste *mf*
cabinetmaking ['kæbnətˌmeɪkɪŋ 'kæbə-] *n* : ébénisterie *f*
cable[1] ['keɪbəl] *vt* **-bled; -bling** : câbler
cable[2] *n* **1** ROPE, WIRE : câble *m* **2** → **cablegram**
cablegram ['keɪbəlˌgræm] *n* : câblogramme *m*, câble *m*
caboose [kəˌbu:s] *n* : fourgon *m* de queue
cabstand ['kæbˌstænd] *n* : station *f* de taxis
cacao [kə'kaʊ, -'keɪo] *n*, *pl* **cacaos** : cacao *m*
cache ['kæʃ] *n* : cache *f* (de provisions), cachette *f*
cachet [kæ'ʃeɪ] *n* : cachet *m*
cackle[1] ['kækəl] *vi* **-led; -ling** : caqueter, glousser
cackle[2] *n* : caquet *m*, gloussement *m*
cacophony [kə'kɑfəni, -kɔ-] *n*, *pl* **-nies** : cacophonie *f*
cactus ['kæktəs] *n*, *pl* **cacti** [-ˌtʌɪ] *or* **-tuses** : cactus *m*
cadaver [kə'dævər] *n* : cadavre *m*
caddie *or* **caddy** ['kædi] *n*, *pl* **-dies** : caddie *m*
caddy ['kædi] *n*, *pl* **-dies** : boîte *f* à thé
cadence ['keɪdənʦ] *n* : cadence *f*, rythme *m*
cadet [kə'dɛt] *n* : élève *mf* officier, élève *mf* agent de police
cadge ['kædʒ] *vt* **cadged; cadging** : quémander, se procurer en quémandant
cadmium ['kædmiəm] *n* : cadmium *m*
cadre ['kæˌdreɪ, 'kɑ-, -dri:] *n* : cadre *m*
caesarean [sɪ'zæriən, -zɛr-] → **cesarean**
caesium *Brit* → **cesium**
café [kæ'feɪ] *n* : café *m*
cafeteria [ˌkæfə'tɪriə] *n* : cafétéria *f*, restaurant *m* libre-service, cantine *f* (dans une école)
caffeine [kæ'fi:n, kə-] *n* : caféine *f*
cage[1] ['keɪdʒ] *vt* **caged; caging** : mettre en cage

cage² *n* : cage *f*
cagey ['keɪdʒi] *adj* **cagier; -est 1** CAUTIOUS : prudent, réticent **2** SHREWD : perspicace, astucieux
caisson ['keɪˌsɑn, -sən] *n* : caisson *m*
cajole [kə'dʒo:l] *vt* **-joled; -joling** : cajoler, enjôler
Cajun¹ ['keɪdʒən] *adj* : acadien, cajun
Cajun² *n* : Acadien *m*, -dienne *f*; Cajun *mf*
cake¹ ['keɪk] *v* **caked; caking** *vt* ENCRUST : former une croûte sur <caked with mud : couvert de boue séchée> — *vi* HARDEN : durcir, faire croûte
cake² *n* **1** : gâteau *m* **2** BAR : pain *m* (de savon)
calabash ['kælə,bæʃ] *n* : calebasse *f*
calamine ['kælə,maɪn] *n* : calamine *f*
calamitous [kə'læmətəs] *adj* : catastrophique, désastreux — **calamitously** *adv*
calamity [kə'læmət̬i] *n, pl* **-ties** : calamité *f*
calcium ['kælsiəm] *n* : calcium *m*
calculate ['kælkjə,leɪt] *v* **-lated; -lating** *vt* **1** COMPUTE : calculer **2** ESTIMATE : calculer, évaluer, estimer — *vi* **1** : calculer, faire des calculs **2** COUNT, RELY : compter <he had calculated on winning : il avait compté sur une victoire>
calculating ['kælkjə,leɪt̬ɪŋ] *adj* : calculateur, astucieux
calculation [ˌkælkjə'leɪʃən] *n* : calcul *m*
calculator ['kælkjə,leɪt̬ər] *n* : calculatrice *f*
calculus ['kælkjələs] *n, pl* **-li** [-ˌlaɪ] : calcul *m*
caldron ['kɔldrən] → **cauldron**
calendar ['kæləndər] *n* **1** : calendrier *m* **2** SCHEDULE : programme *m*, agenda *m*
calf ['kæf, 'kaf] *n, pl* **calves** ['kævz, 'kavz] **1** : veau *m* (de bovin) **2** : mollet *m* (de la jambe)
calfskin ['kæfskɪn] *n* : veau *m*
caliber *or* **calibre** ['kæləbər] *n* **1** : calibre *m* <a .38 caliber revolver : un revolver de calibre 38> **2** QUALITY, STATURE : qualité *f*, calibre *m*
calibrate ['kæləbreɪt] *vt* **-brated; -brating** : calibrer (une arme, etc.), étalonner (une balance)
calibration ['kælə,breɪʃən] *n* : calibrage *m*, étalonnage *m*
calico ['kælɪˌko:] *n, pl* **-coes** *or* **-cos 1** : calicot *m* **2** *or* **calico cat** : chat *m* tigré
calipers *or Brit* **callipers** ['kæləpərz] *n* : compas *m* (à calibrer)
caliph *or* **calif** ['keɪləf, 'kæ-] *n* : calife *m*
calisthenics [ˌkæləs'θeɪnɪks] *ns & pl* : gymnastique *f* suédoise
calk ['kɔk] → **caulk**
call¹ ['kɔl] *vi* **1** CRY, SHOUT : crier **2 to call for** REQUIRE : exiger, demander **3** VISIT : rendre visite, passer — *vt* **1** *or* **to call out** : appeler (un nom, etc.), crier (un ordre), annoncer (des résultats) **2** SUMMON : appeler, faire venir, convoquer **3** TELEPHONE : téléphoner à, appeler (au téléphone) **4** NAME : appeler, nommer **5** WAKEN : réveiller **6 to call back** : rappeler **7 to call off** CANCEL : annuler
call² *n* **1** CRY, SHOUT : appel *m*, cri *m* (d'un animal) **2** *or* **telephone call** : appel *m* <to give a call to : appeler, téléphoner à> **3** SUMMONS : appel *m* **4** DEMAND, NEED : demande *f* <a call for improvement : une demande d'amélioration> <there's no call to worry : il n'y a aucune raison de s'inquiéter> **5** VISIT : visite *f* <to pay a call : rendre visite>
caller ['kɔlər] *n* **1** VISITOR : visiteur *m*, -teuse *f* **2** : personne *f* qui appelle (au téléphone)
calling ['kɔlɪŋ] *n* : vocation *f*, profession *f*
calliope [kə'laɪəˌpi:, 'kæliˌo:p] *n* : orgue *m* à vapeur
callipers *Brit* → **calipers**
callous¹ ['kæləs] *vt* : rendre calleux
callous² *adj* **1** : calleux <callous skin : peau calleuse> **2** UNFEELING : insensible, sans cœur
callously ['kæləsli] *adv* : insensiblement, impitoyablement
callousness ['kæləsnəs] *n* : insensibilité *f*, dureté *f*
callow ['kælo] *adj* : sans expérience, gauche
callus ['kæləs] *n* : cal *m*
calm¹ ['kɑm, 'kɑlm] *v* **calmed; calming** *vt* : calmer, apaiser — *vi* : se calmer <calm down! : calmez-vous!>
calm² *adj* : calme, tranquille — **calmly** *adv*
calm³ *n* **1** QUIETNESS : calme *m*, tranquillité *f* **2** COMPOSURE : sang-froid *m*
caloric [kə'lɔrɪk] *adj* : calorique
calorie ['kæləri] *n* : calorie *f*
calve ['kæv, 'kav] *vi* **calved; calving** : vêler (se dit de la vache)
calves → **calf**
calypso [kə'lɪpˌso:] *n, pl* **-sos** : calypso *m*
calyx ['keɪlɪks, 'kæ-] *n, pl* **-lyxes** *or* **-lyces** [-ləˌsi:z] : calice *m*
cam ['kæm] *n* : came *f*
camaraderie [ˌkɑmə'rɑdəri, ˌkæm-; ˌkɑmə'rɑ-] *n* : camaraderie *f*
Cambodian¹ [kæm'bo:diən] *adj* : cambodgien
Cambodian² *n* : Cambodgien *m*, -gienne *f*
came → **come**
camel ['kæməl] *n* : chameau *m*
camellia [kə'mi:ljə] *n* : camélia *f*
cameo ['kæmiˌo:] *n, pl* **-eos** : camée
camera ['kæmrə, 'kæmərə] *n* : appareil *m* photo, caméra *f*

Cameroonian[1] [ˌkæmə'ru:niən] *adj* : camerounais
Cameroonian[2] *n* : Camerounais *m*, -naise *f*
camouflage[1] ['kæmə,flɑʒ, -,flɑdʒ] *vt* **-flaged; -flaging** : camoufler
camouflage[2] *n* : camouflage *m*
camp[1] ['kæmp] *vi* : camper, faire du camping
camp[2] *n* **1** : camp *m* <to pitch camp : planter son camp> **2** FACTION, GROUP : camp *m*, parti *m* <in the same camp : du même côté>
campaign[1] [kæm'peɪn] *vi* : faire campagne
campaign[2] *n* : campagne *f*
campground ['kæmp,graʊnd] *n* : camping *m*, terrain *m* de camping
camphor ['kæmpfər] *n* : camphre *m*
campus ['kæmpəs] *n* : campus *m*, cité *f* universitaire *Can*
can[1] ['kæn] *v aux, past* **could** ['kʊd]; *present s & pl* **can 1** (*expressing possibility*) : pouvoir <he couldn't go : il ne pouvait pas aller> <how can we know? : comment peut-on savoir?> **2** (*expressing knowledge or ability*) : savoir <I can speak three languages : je sais parler trois langues> <her son can't drive : son fils ne sait pas conduire> **3** (*expressing permission*) <can they stay? : peuvent-ils rester?> <you can't smoke here : vous n'avez pas le droit de fumer ici> **4** (*with verbs of sense perception*) <he can see the mountain : il voit la montagne> <I can taste garlic : je goûte l'ail> **5** (*in emphatic expressions*) <that cannot be! : cela n'est pas possible!>
can[2] *vt* **canned; canning** : mettre en boîte, conserver, canner *Can*
can[3] *n* : boîte *f* (d'aliments), canette *f* (de boissons), bidon *m* (d'essence, etc.)
Canada goose *n* : outarde *f Can*
Canadian[1] [kə'neɪdiən] *adj* : canadien
Canadian[2] *n* : Canadien *m*, -dienne *f*
canal [kə'næl] *n* **1** : canal *m* <Panama Canal : Canal de Panama> **2** : conduit *m*, canal *m* (en anatomie)
canapé ['kænəpi, -ˌpeɪ] *n* : canapé *m*
canary [kə'nɛri] *n, pl* **-naries** : canari *m*, serin *m*
cancel ['kænt͡səl] *vt* **-celed** *or* **-celled; -celing** *or* **-celling** : annuler
cancellation [ˌkænt͡sə'leɪʃən] *n* : annulation *f*
cancer ['kænt͡sər] *n* : cancer *m* — **cancerous** *adj*
Cancer *n* : Cancer *m*
cancerous ['kænt͡sərəs] *adj* : cancéreux
candelabra [ˌkændə'lɑbrə, -læ-] *n* : candélabre *m*
candelabrum [ˌkændə'lɑbrəm, -læ-] *n, pl* **-bra → candelabra**
candid ['kændɪd] *adj* **1** : franc, sincère **2** : instantané (se dit d'une photo)
candidacy ['kændədəsi] *n, pl* **-cies** : candidature *f*
candidate ['kændə,deɪt, -dət] *n* : candidat *m*, -date *f*
candidly ['kændɪdli] *adv* : franchement, sincèrement
candidness ['kændɪdnəs] *n* : franchise *f*
candle ['kændəl] *n* : bougie *f*, chandelle *f*, cierge *m* (à l'église)
candlestick ['kændəl,stɪk] *n* : chandelier *m*, bougeoir *m*
candor *or Brit* **candour** ['kændər] *n* : franchise *f*
candy[1] ['kændi] *vt* **-died; -dying** : confire
candy[2] *n, pl* **-dies 1** : bonbon *m* **2 candies** *pl* : confiserie *f*
cane[1] ['keɪn] *vt* **caned; caning 1** FLOG : donner des coups de badine à (un élève, etc.) **2** : canner (une chaise, etc.)
cane[2] *n* **1** : canne *f* (d'une plante) **2** STICK : canne *f* (pour marcher), badine *f* (pour punir) **3** RATTAN, RUSH : rotin *m*, jonc *m*
canine[1] ['keɪ,naɪn] *adj* : canin
canine[2] *n* **1** *or* **canine tooth** : canine *f* **2** DOG : canidé *m*
canister ['kænəstər] *n* : boîte *f* (métallique)
canker ['kæŋkər] *n* : ulcère *f* buccale
cannery ['kænəri] *n, pl* **-ries** : conserverie *f*
cannibal ['kænəbəl] *n* : cannibale *mf*, anthropophage *mf*
cannibalism ['kænəbə,lɪzəm] *n* : cannibalisme *m*, anthropophagie *f*
cannon [kænən] *n, pl* **-nons** *or* **-non** : canon *m*
cannonball ['kænən,bɔl] *n* : boulet *m* de canon
cannot (can not) ['kæn,ɑt, kə'nɑt] → **can**[1]
canny ['kæni] *adj* **cannier; -est** SHREWD : prudent, astucieux
canoe [kə'nu:] *n* : canoë *m*, canot *m Can*
canon ['kænən] *n* **1** : canon *m* <canon law : droit canon> **2** WORKS : œuvres *fpl* (littéraires) **3** RULE : canon *m*, règle *f* <the canons of good taste : les règles du bon goût> **4** : chanoine *m* (ecclésiastique)
canonize ['kænə,naɪz] *vt* **-ized; -izing** : canoniser
canopy ['kænəpi] *n, pl* **-pies** : auvent *m*, baldaquin *m*
cant[1] ['kænt] *v* **canted; canting** *vt* TILT : incliner, pencher — *vi* LEAN, TIP : s'incliner, se pencher
cant[2] *n* **1** SLANT : pente *f*, inclinaison *f* **2** JARGON : jargon *m* **3** : paroles *fpl* hypocrites
can't ['kænt, 'kant] (*contraction of* **can not**) → **can**[1]
cantaloupe ['kæntəl,o:p] *n* : cantaloup *m*
cantankerous [kæn'tæŋkərəs] *adj* : acariâtre, grincheux, malcommode *Can*

cantata [kən'tɑtə] *n* : cantate *f*
canteen [kæn'ti:n] *n* **1** CAFETERIA : cantine *f* **2** FLASK : flasque *f*, gourde *f*
canter[1] ['kæntər] *vi* : aller au petit galop
canter[2] *n* : petit galop *m*
cantilever[1] ['kæntəˌli:vər, -ˌlɛvər] *adj* : cantilever <cantilever bridge : pont cantilever>
cantilever[2] *n* : cantilever *m*
canto ['kænˌto:] *n, pl* **-tos** : chant *m* (d'un poème)
cantor ['kæntər] *n* : chantre *m*
canvas ['kænvəs] *n* **1** : toile *f*, canevas *m* **2** SAIL : voile *f* **3** PAINTING : toile *f*
canvass[1] ['kænvəs] *vt* **-vassed; -vassing 1** POLL : sonder (des opinions) **2** SOLICIT : faire du démarchage électoral auprès
canvass[2] *n* **1** SURVEY : sondage *m* **2** : démarchage *m* électoral
canyon ['kænjən] *n* : canyon *m*
cap[1] ['kæp] *vt* **capped; capping 1** COVER : couvrir **2** CROWN : couronner (une dent) **3** OUTDO : surpasser **4** LIMIT : restreindre, limiter
cap[2] *n* **1** : casquette *f*, bonnet *m*, calotte *f* *Can* <baseball cap : casquette de baseball> **2** COVER, TOP : capsule *f* (d'une bouteille), capuchon *m* (d'un stylo), couronne *f* (d'une dent) **3** LIMIT : plafond *m*, limite *f*
capability [ˌkeɪpə'bɪlətˌi] *n, pl* **-ties** : aptitude *f*, capacité *f*
capable ['keɪpəbəl] *adj* : compétent, capable
capably ['keɪpəbli] *adv* : avec compétence
capacious [kə'peɪʃəs] *adj* : de grande capacité
capacity[1] [kə'pæsəˌti] *adj* FILLED, PACKED : comble
capacity[2] *n, pl* **-ties 1** ROOM, SPACE : capacité *f*, contenance *f* **2** ABILITY : aptitude *f*, capacité *f* **3** FUNCTION, ROLE : qualité *f*, fonction *f* <in his capacity as supervisor : en qualité de superviseur>
cape ['keɪp] *n* **1** CLOAK : cape *f*, pèlerine *f* **2** : cap *m* <Cape of Good Hope : le cap de Bonne Espérance>
caper[1] ['keɪpər] *vi* GAMBOL : gambader, cabrioler
caper[2] *n* **1** : câpre *f* (assaisonnement) **2** LEAP : gambade *f*, cabriole *f* **3** PRANK : farce *f*
Cape Verdean[1] ['keɪp'vərdiən] *adj* : capverdien
Cape Verdean[2] *n* : Cap-Verdien *m*, -dienne *f*
capillary[1] ['kæpəˌleri] *adj* : capillaire
capillary[2] *n, pl* **-laries** : capillaire *m*
capital[1] ['kæpətˌəl] *adj* **1** : capital <capital punishment : peine capitale> **2** UPPERCASE : majuscule <capital A : A majuscule> **3** : de capital, des capitaux <capital gain : revenu des capitaux> **4** FIRST-RATE : excellent <a capital idea : une idée excellente>
capital[2] *n* **1** *or* **capital letter** : majuscule *f* **2** *or* **capital city** : capitale *f* **3** WEALTH : capital *m*, fonds *mpl* **4** : chapiteau *m* (d'une colonne)
capitalism ['kæpətˌəlˌɪzəm] *n* : capitalisme *m*
capitalist[1] ['kæpətˌəlɪst] *or* **capitalistic** ['kæpətˌəlˌɪstɪk] *adj* : capitaliste
capitalist[2] *n* : capitaliste *mf*
capitalization [ˌkæpətˌələ'zeɪʃən] *n* **1** : capitalisation *f* (en finance) **2** : emploi *m* de lettres majuscules
capitalize ['kæpətˌəlˌaɪz] *v* **-ized; -izing** *vt* **1** : capitaliser (en finance) **2** : écrire en majuscules — *vi* **to capitalize on** : tirer profit de, tirer parti de
capitol ['kæpətˌəl] *n* : capitole *m*
capitulate [kə'pɪtʃəˌleɪt] *vi* **-lated; -lating** : capituler
capitulation [kəˌpɪtʃə'leɪʃən] *n* : capitulation *f*
capon ['keɪˌpɑn, -pən] *n* : chapon *m*
caprice [kə'pri:s] *n* : caprice *m*
capricious [kə'prɪʃəs, -'pri:-] *adj* : capricieux — **capriciously** *adv*
Capricorn ['kæprɪˌkɔrn] *n* : Capricorne *m*
capsize ['kæpˌsaɪz, kæp'saɪz] *v* **-sized; -sizing** *vt* : faire chavirer — *vi* : chavirer
capstan ['kæpstən, -ˌstæn] *n* : cabestan *m*
capsule ['kæpsəl, -ˌsu:l] *n* : capsule *f*
captain[1] ['kæptən] *vt* : être le capitaine de
captain[2] *n* : capitaine *m*
caption[1] ['kæpʃən] *vt* : mettre une légende à (une illustration), sous-titrer (un film)
caption[2] *n* **1** HEADING, TITLE : titre *m* **2** : légende *f* (d'une illustration) **3** SUBTITLE : sous-titre *m*
captivate ['kæptəˌveɪt] *vt* **-vated; -vating** : captiver, fasciner
captive[1] ['kæptɪv] *adj* : captif
captive[2] *n* : captif *m*, -tive *f*
captivity [kæp'tɪvəˌti] *n* : captivité *f*
captor ['kæptər] *n* : personne *f* qui capture
capture[1] ['kæpʃər] *vt* **-tured; -turing 1** SEIZE : capturer, prendre **2** : rendre (une ressemblance), gagner (l'intérêt), captiver (l'imagination)
capture[2] *n* : capture *f*, prise *f*
car ['kɑr] *n* **1** AUTOMOBILE : voiture *f*, automobile *f* **2** *or* **railroad car** : wagon *m* **3** *or* **elevator car** : cabine *f* (d'ascenseur)
carafe [kə'ræf, -'rɑf] *n* : carafe *f*
caramel ['kɑrməl; 'kærəməl, -ˌmɛl] *n* : caramel *m*
carat ['kærət] *n* : carat *m*
caravan ['kærəˌvæn] *n* : caravane *f*
caraway ['kæraˌweɪ] *n* : carvi *m*
carbine ['kɑrˌbaɪn, -ˌbi:n] *n* : carabine *f*

carbohydrate [ˌkɑrbo'haɪdreɪt, -drət] *n* : hydrate *m* de carbone
carbon [ˈkɑrbən] *n* : carbone *m*
carbonated [ˈkɑrbəˌneɪṭəd] *adj* : gazéifié
carbon copy *n* **1** : copie *f* carbone **2** REPLICA : réplique *f*
carbon paper *n* : carbone *m*, papier *m* carbone
carbuncle [ˈkɑrˌbʌŋkəl] *n* : furoncle *m*
carburetor [ˈkɑrbəˌreɪṭər, -bjə-] *n* : carburateur *m*
carcass [ˈkɑrkəs] *n* : carcasse *f*
carcinogen [kɑrˈsɪnədʒən, ˈkɑrsənəˌdʒɛn] *n* : carcinogène *m*, cancérogène *m*
carcinogenic [ˌkɑrsənoˈdʒɛnɪk] *adj* : carcinogène, cancérogène
card[1] [ˈkɑrd] *vt* **carded; carding** : carder (des fibres textiles)
card[2] *n* **1** : carte *f* <library card : carte de bibliothèque> <Christmas card : carte de Noël> **2** : carde *f* (pour carder fibres) **3 → playing card**
cardboard [ˈkɑrdˌbɔrd] *n* : carton *m*
cardiac [ˈkɑrdiˌæk] *adj* : cardiaque
cardigan [ˈkɑrdɪgən] *n* : cardigan *m*
cardinal[1] [ˈkɑrdənəl] *adj* CHIEF : cardinal
cardinal[2] *n* : cardinal *m*
cardinal number *n* : nombre *m* cardinal
cardinal point *n* : point *m* cardinal
cardiologist [ˌkɑrdiˈɑlədʒɪst] *n* : cardiologue *mf*
cardiology [ˌkɑrdiˈɑlədʒi] *n* : cardiologie *f*
cardiovascular [ˌkɑrdioˈvæskjələr] *adj* : cardio-vasculaire
care[1] [ˈkær] *v* **cared; caring** *vi* **1** : se soucier, s'intéresser <she cares about the poor : elle se soucie des pauvres> <I don't care : ça m'est égal> **2 to care for** LIKE : aimer **3 to care for** LOOK AFTER : s'occuper de, soigner <to care for the sick : soigner les malades> — *vt* WISH : vouloir, désirer <would you care to come in? : voulez-vous entrer?>
care[2] *n* **1** ANXIETY : souci *m*, ennui *m* **2** TREATMENT : soins *mpl*, traitement *m* <medical care : soins médicaux> **3** MAINTENANCE, UPKEEP : entretien *m* **4** ATTENTION : soin *m*, attention *f* <take care not to fall : faites attention de ne pas tomber>
careen [kəˈriːn] *vi* **-reened; -reening 1** LURCH : tanguer **2 → career**[1]
career[1] [kəˈrɪr] *vi* : aller à toute vitesse
career[2] *n* : carrière *f*, profession *f*
carefree [ˈkærˌfriː, ˌkærˈ-] *adj* : insouciant
careful [ˈkærfəl] *adj* **1** CAUTIOUS : prudent <be careful! : soyez prudent!> <be careful of the ice : fais attention à la glace> **2** THOROUGH : soigneux, approfondi
carefully [ˈkærfəli] *adv* : prudemment, avec soin
careless [ˈkærləs] *adj* : négligent
carelessly [ˈkærləsli] *adv* : négligemment, sans faire attention
carelessness [ˈkærləsnəs] *n* : négligence *f*, étourderie *f*, inattention *f*
caress[1] [kəˈrɛs] *vt* : caresser, minoucher *Can fam*
caress[2] *n* : caresse *f*
caret [ˈkærət] *n* : signe *m* d'insertion
caretaker [ˈkɛrˌteɪkər] *n* : gardien *m*, -dienne *f*; concierge *mf* (d'un immeuble, etc.)
cargo [ˈkɑrˌgoː] *n, pl* **-goes** *or* **-gos** : chargement *m*, cargaison *f*
caribou [ˈkærəˌbuː] *n, pl* **-bou** *or* **-bous** : caribou *m*
caricature[1] [ˈkærɪkəˌtʃʊr] *vt* **-tured; -turing** : caricaturer
caricature[2] *n* : caricature *f*
caricaturist [ˈkærɪkəˌtʃʊrɪst] *n* : caricaturiste *mf*
caries [ˈkæriːz] *ns & pl* : carie *f*
carillon [ˈkærəˌlɑn] *n* : carillon *m*
carmine [ˈkɑrmən, -ˌmaɪn] *n* : carmin *m*
carnage [ˈkɑrnɪdʒ] *n* : carnage *m*, boucherie *f*
carnal [ˈkɑrnəl] *adj* : charnel
carnation [kɑrˈneɪʃən] *n* : œillet *m*
carnival [ˈkɑrnəvəl] *n* : carnaval *m*, fête *f* foraine
carnivore [ˈkɑrnəˌvor] *n* : carnivore *m*, carnassier *m*
carnivorous [kɑrˈnɪvərəs] *adj* : carnivore, carnassier
carol[1] [ˈkærəl] *vi* **-oled** *or* **-olled; -oling** *or* **-olling** : chanter des chants de Noël
carol[2] *n* : chant *m* de Noël
carom[1] [ˈkærəm] *vi* **1** : caramboler (au billiard) **2** REBOUND : rebondir
carom[2] *n* : carambolage *m*
carouse [kəˈraʊz] *vi* **-roused; -rousing** : faire la bombe *fam*
carousel [ˌkærəˈsɛl, ˈkærəˌ-] *n* **1** MERRY-GO-ROUND : manège *m* **2** : carrousel *m* (pour les bagages, les diapositives, etc.)
carp[1] [ˈkɑrp] *vi* **1** COMPLAIN : se plaindre **2 to carp at** : critiquer
carp[2] *n, pl* **carp** *or* **carps** : carpe *f*
carpel [ˈkɑrpəl] *n* : carpelle *m*
carpenter [ˈkɑrpəntər] *n* : charpentier *m*, menuisier *m*
carpentry [ˈkɑrpəntri] *n* : charpenterie *f*, menuiserie *f*
carpet[1] [ˈkɑrpəṭ] *vt* **1** : recouvrir d'un tapis, recouvrir d'une moquette **2** COVER : tapisser <carpeted with leaves : tapissé de feuilles>
carpet[2] *n* : tapis *m*, moquette *f*
carpeting [ˈkɑrpəṭɪŋ] *n* : moquette *f*
carport [ˈkɑrˌpɔrt] *n* : abri *m* d'auto, auvent *m* pour voiture
carriage [ˈkærɪdʒ] *n* **1** TRANSPORT : transport *m* **2** BEARING : maintien *m*, port *m* **3** *or* **horse-drawn carriage** : calèche *f*, fiacre *m*, carrosse *m* **4 → baby carriage**

carrier ['kæriər] *n* **1** TRANSPORTER : transporteur *m* **2** : porteur *m*, -teuse *f* (d'une maladie) **3** → **aircraft carrier**

carrion ['kærien] *n* : charogne *f*

carrot ['kærət] *n* : carotte *f*

carrousel → **carousel**

carry ['kæri] *v* **-ried; -rying** *vt* **1** TRANSPORT : transporter, porter, emporter **2** BEAR : porter, supporter **3** STOCK : vendre, tenir en magasin **4** WIN : remporter, emporter, gagner <the motion was carried by 10 votes : la motion l'a emporté par 10 votes> **5** ENTAIL : comporter, entraîner **6 to carry oneself** : se présenter, se comporter — *vi* : porter <her voice carries well : sa voix porte bien>

carryall ['kæri,ɔl] *n* : fourre-tout *m*

carry away *vt* **to get carried away** : se laisser emporter, s'emballer

carry on *vt* CONDUCT : conduire (des affaires), entretenir (une correspondence, etc.) — *vi* **1** : se conduire, faire des histoires <he's always carrying on over nothing : il fait toujours des histoires pour des riens> **2** CONTINUE : continuer

carry out *vt* ACCOMPLISH, EXECUTE : réaliser, effectuer, accomplir, mettre à l'exécution

cart[1] ['kɑrt] *vt* **1** CONVEY : charrier **2** HAUL : trimbaler *fam*

cart[2] *n* : charette *f* (de foin, etc.), chariot *m* <shopping cart : chariot de supermarché>

cartel [kɑr'tel] *n* : cartel *m*

cartilage ['kɑrtəlɪdʒ] *n* : cartilage *m*

cartilaginous [,kɑrtə'lædʒənəs] *adj* : cartilagineux

cartographer [kɑr'tɑgrəfər] *n* : cartographe *mf*

cartography [kɑr'tɑgrəfi] *n* : cartographie *f*

carton ['kɑrtən] *n* **1** : carton *m*, boîte *f* de carton **2** : cartouche *f* (de cigarettes)

cartoon [kɑr'tu:n] *n* **1** : dessin *m* humoristique, caricature *f* **2** COMIC STRIP : bande *f* dessinée **3** *or* **animated cartoon** : dessin *m* animé

cartoonist [kɑr'tu:nɪst] *n* : dessinateur *m*, -trice *f* (humoristique); caricaturiste *mf*

cartridge ['kɑrtrɪdʒ] *n* : cartouche *f*

carve ['kɑrv] *vt* **carved; carving 1** : tailler (la pierre, le bois, etc.) **2** INSCRIBE : graver **3** SLICE : couper <to carve a turkey : couper une dinde>

cascade[1] [kæs'keɪd] *vi* **-caded; -cading** : tomber en cascade

cascade[2] *n* : cascade *f*

case[1] ['keɪs] *vt* **cased; casing 1** BOX, PACK : emballer, empaqueter **2** INSPECT : surveiller (un lieu)

case[2] *n* **1** BOX, CRATE : boîte *f*, caisse *f* **2** CONTAINER : étui *m* (à lunettes, etc.), écrin *m*, coffre *m*, boîte *f* <a display case : une vitrine> **3** INSTANCE : cas *m*, exemple *m* <a case of the flu : un cas de grippe> **4** : cas *m* (en grammaire) **5** : affaire *f*, procès *m* (en droit) **6 in any case** : en tout cas **7 in case** : au cas où **8 in case of** : en cas de

casement ['keɪsmənt] *n or* **casement window** : fenêtre *f* à battants

cash[1] ['kæʃ] *vt* **1** : encaisser (un chèque) **2 to cash in** : se faire rembourser, réaliser (un bon, etc.)

cash[2] *n* : espèces *fpl*, argent *m* liquide

cashew ['kæ,ʃu:, kə'ʃu:] *n or* **cashew nut** : noix *f* de cajou

cashier[1] [kæ'ʃɪr] *vt* DISMISS : renvoyer, congédier

cashier[2] *n* : caissier *m*, -sière *f*

cashmere ['kæʒ,mɪr, 'kæʃ-] *n* : cachemire *m*

cash register *n* : caisse *f* (enregistreuse)

casino [kə'si:,no:] *n*, *pl* **-nos** : casino *m*

cask ['kæsk] *n* : fût *m*, tonneau *f*

casket ['kæskət] *n* : cercueil *m*

casserole ['kæsə,ro:l] *n* **1** *or* **casserole dish** : cocotte *f*, marmite *f* **2** : ragoût *m* (cuit au four)

cassette [kə'set, kæ-] *n* : cassette *f*

cassock ['kæsək] *n* : soutane *f*

cast[1] ['kæst] *vt* **cast; casting 1** THROW : jeter, lancer <to cast dice : jeter les dés> <to cast an eye on : jeter un coup d'œil sur> <to cast aside : mettre de côté> **2** : déposer (un vote) <to cast a vote for : voter pour> **3** : distribuer les rôles de (une pièce de théâtre, un film, etc.) <he was cast in the leading role : on lui a donné le rôle principal> **4** MOLD : mouler, couler, fondre <to cast metal : faire fondre du métal>

cast[2] *n* **1** : lancer *m* (d'une ligne de pêche) **2** : distribution *f* (d'acteurs) **3** MOLD : moulage *m* **4** *or* **plaster cast** : plâtre *m* **5** APPEARANCE : aspect *f*, forme *f* <the delicate cast of her features : la finesse de ses traits>

castanets [,kæstə'nets] *npl* : castagnettes *fpl*

castaway[1] ['kæstə,weɪ] *adj* : naufragé

castaway[2] *n* : naufragé *m*, -gée *f*

caste ['kæst] *n* : caste *f*

caster ['kæstər] *n* : roulette *f* (d'un meuble)

castigate ['kæstə,geɪt] *vt* **-gated; -gating 1** PUNISH : punir, châtier **2** CRITICIZE : critiquer sévèrement

castigation ['kæstə,geɪʃən] *n* **1** PUNISHMENT : punition *f*, châtiment *m* **2** CRITICISM : critique *f* sévère, condamnation *f*

cast iron *n* : fonte *f*

castle ['kæsəl] *n* **1** : château *m* **2** : tour *f* (aux échecs)

cast–off ['kæst,ɔf] *adj* : dont on ne veut, mis au rebut

castoff ['kæst,ɔf] *n*, *pl* **castoffs** : vêtement *m* dont on ne veut

castrate ['kæs,treɪt] *vt* **-trated; -trating** : castrer, châtrer
castration [kæ'streɪʃən] *n* : castration *f*
casual ['kæʒʊəl] *adj* **1** CHANCE : fortuit, de hasard **2** OCCASIONAL : intermittent, de passage **3** NONCHALANT : désinvolte, nonchalant **4** INFORMAL : simple, détendu <casual clothes : vêtements sport>
casually ['kæʒʊəli, 'kæʒəli] *adv* **1** FORTUITOUSLY : par hasard, accidentellement **2** NONCHALANTLY : nonchalamment **3** INFORMALLY : simplement
casualty ['kæʒʊəlti, 'kæʒəl-] *n, pl* **-ties 1** ACCIDENT : accident *m* grave, désastre *m* **2** VICTIM : blessé *m*, -sée *f*; accidenté *m*, -tée *f*; mort *m*, morte *f* <casualties of battle : pertes de bataille>
cat ['kæt] *n* **1** : chat *m*, chatte *f* **2** FELINE : félin *m* <the big cats : les grands félins>
cataclysm ['kæṭəˌklɪzəm] *n* : cataclysme *m*
catacombs ['kæṭəˌko:mz] *npl* : catacombes *fpl*
catalog[1] *or* **catalogue** ['kæṭəˌlɔg] *vt* **-loged** *or* **-logued; -loging** *or* **-loguing** : cataloguer, dresser un catalogue de
catalog[2] *or* **catalogue** *n* : catalogue *m*
catalpa [kə'tælpə, -'tɔl-] *n* : catalpa *m*
catalyst ['kætələst] *n* : catalyseur *m*
catalytic [ˌkæṭəl'ɪṭɪk] *adj* : catalytique
catamaran [ˌkæṭəmə'ræn, 'kæṭəmə,ræn] *n* : catamaran *m*
catapult[1] ['kæṭəˌpʌlt, -ˌpʊlt] *vt* : catapulter
catapult[2] *n* : catapulte *f*
cataract ['kæṭəˌrækt] *n* : cataracte *f*
catarrh [kə'tɑr] *n* : catarrhe *m*
catastrophe [kə'tæstrəˌfi:] *n* : catastrophe *f* — **catastrophic** [ˌkæṭə'strɑfɪk] *adj* : catastrophique
catcalls ['kætˌkɔlz] *npl* : huées *fpl*, sifflets *mpl*
catch[1] ['kætʃ, 'kɛtʃ] *v* **caught** ['kɔt]; **catching** *vi* **1** CAPTURE, TRAP : attraper, piéger **2** CONTRACT : attraper, prendre <to catch a cold : attraper un rhume> **3** SURPRISE : surprendre, prendre <I caught him red-handed : je l'ai pris en flagrant délit> **4** GRASP, SEIZE : attraper, saisir **5** SNAG : accrocher **6** PERCEIVE : discerner, remarquer (une expression, une odeur, etc.) <to catch sight of : apercevoir> **7** : attraper, prendre (un train, etc.) **8 to catch one's breath** : reprendre son souffle — *vi* **1** START : démarrer (se dit d'un moteur), prendre (se dit du feu) **2** HOOK, SNAG : s'accrocher, se prendre <her fingers caught in a drawer : ses doigts se sont pris dans un tiroir>
catch[2] *n* **1** CATCHING : prise *f* **2** : prise *f*, pêche *f* (de poissons) **3** LATCH : loquet *m* **4** PITFALL, SNAG : piège *f*
catcher ['kætʃər, 'kɛ-] *n* : receveur *m* *Can* (au baseball)
catching ['kætʃɪŋ, 'kɛ-] *adj* : contagieux
catch on *vi* **1** UNDERSTAND : comprendre, saisir **2** : devenir populaire, devenir célèbre <the song caught on : la chanson est devenue populaire>
catchup ['kætʃəp, 'kɛ-] → **ketchup**
catch up *vi* **to catch up with** : rattraper
catchword ['kætʃˌwərd, 'kɛtʃ-] *n* : slogan *m*, mot *m* d'ordre
catchy ['kætʃi, 'kɛ-] *adj* **catchier; -est** : entraînant <a catchy tune : un air entraînant>
catechism ['kæṭəˌkɪzəm] *n* : catéchisme *m*
categorical [ˌkæṭə'gɔrɪkəl] *adj* : catégorique, absolu, indiscutable — **categorically** [-rəkli] *adv*
categorize ['kæṭɪgəraɪz] *vt* **-ized; -izing** : classer (par catégories)
category ['kæṭəˌgori] *n, pl* **-ries** : catégorie *f*, classe *f*
cater ['keɪṭər] *vi* **1** : fournir des repas (pour les fêtes, les noces, etc.) **2 to cater to** : pourvoir à <she caters to his every need : elle pourvoit à tous ses besoins>
catercorner[1] ['kæṭiˌkɔrnər, 'kæṭə-, 'kɪṭi-] *adv* : diagonalement
catercorner[2] *adj* : diagonal
caterer ['keɪṭərər] *n* : traiteur *m*
caterpillar ['kæṭərˌpɪlər] *n* : chenille *f*
catfish ['kætˌfɪʃ] *n* : poisson-chat *m*
catgut ['kætˌgʌt] *n* : boyau *m* (de chat)
catharsis [kə'θɑrsɪs] *n, pl* **catharses** [-ˌsi:z] : catharsis *f*
cathartic [kə'θɑrṭɪk] *adj* : cathartique
cathedral [kə'θi:drəl] *n* : cathédrale *f*
catheter ['kæθəṭər] *n* : cathéter *m*, sonde *f*
cathode ['kæˌθo:d] *n* : cathode *f*
catholic ['kæθəlɪk] *adj* UNIVERSAL : universel
Catholic[1] *adj* : catholique <the Catholic Church : l'Église catholique>
Catholic[2] *n* : catholique *mf*
Catholicism [kə'θɑləˌsɪzəm] *n* : catholicisme *m*
catkin ['kætkɪn] *n* : chaton *m*
catnap[1] ['kætˌnæp] *vi* **-napped; -napping** : faire un somme
catnap[2] *n* : somme *m*
catnip ['kætˌnɪp] *n* : herbe *f* aux chats
catsup ['kɛtʃəp, 'kætsəp] → **ketchup**
cattail ['kætˌteɪl] *n* : massette *f*, quenouille *f* *Can*
cattiness ['kæṭiməs] *n* : méchanceté *f*, malveillance *f*
cattle ['kæṭəl] *npl* : bétail *m*, bovins *mpl*
cattleman ['kæṭəlmən, -ˌmæn] *n* : bouvier *m*, -vière *f*; vacher *m*, -chère *f*
catty ['kæṭi] *adj* **cattier; -est** : méchant, malveillant
catwalk ['kætˌwɔk] *n* : passerelle *f*
Caucasian[1] [kɔ'keɪʒən] *adj* : caucasien
Caucasian[2] *n* : Caucasien *m*, -sienne *f*

caucus ['kɔkəs] *n* : comité *m* électoral
caught → **catch**[1]
cauldron ['kɔldrən] *n* : chaudron *m*
cauliflower ['kɑlɪˌflaʊər, 'kɔ-] *n* : choufleur *m*
caulk[1] ['kɔk] *vt* : calfater (un bateau), mastiquer (une fenêtre, etc.)
caulk[2] *n* : mastic *m*
causal ['kɔzəl] *adj* : causal
cause[1] ['kɔz] *vt* **caused; causing** : causer, occasionner
cause[2] *n* **1** ORIGIN : cause *f* **2** MOTIVE, REASON : raison *f*, motif *m* <with good cause : à juste titre> **3** GROUNDS : cause *f* (en droit) **4** MOVEMENT : cause *f*, mouvement *m*
causeway ['kɔzˌweɪ] *n* : chaussée *f*
caustic ['kɔstɪk] *adj* **1** CORROSIVE : caustique, corrosif **2** BITING : mordant, sarcastique
cauterize ['kɔṭəˌraɪz] *vt* **-ized; -izing** : cautériser
caution[1] ['kɔʃən] *vt* WARN : avertir, mettre en garde
caution[2] *n* **1** WARNING : avertissement *m* **2** CARE : prudence *f*, précaution *f*
cautious ['kɔʃəs] *adj* : prudent, avisé, circonspect
cautiously ['kɔʃəsli] *adv* : prudemment, avec prudence
cavalcade [ˌkævəl'keɪd, 'kævəl-] *n* **1** : cavalcade *f* **2** SERIES : série *f*
cavalier[1] ['kævə'lɪr] *adj* OFFHAND : cavalier, désinvolte
cavalier[2] *n* : cavalier *m*
cavalierly [ˌkævə'lɪrli] *adv* : de façon cavalière
cavalry ['kævəlri] *n, pl* **-ries** : cavalerie *f*
cavalryman ['kævəlrimən] *n, pl* **-men** [-mən, -ˌmɛn] : cavalier *m*
cave[1] ['keɪv] *vi* **caved; caving** *or* **to cave in** : s'affaisser, s'effondrer
cave[2] *n* : grotte *f*, caverne *f*
cavern ['kævərn] *n* : caverne *f*
cavernous ['kævərnəs] *adj* : caverneux
caviar *or* **caviare** ['kæviˌɑr, 'kɑ-] *n* : caviar *m*
cavity ['kæviṭi] *n, pl* **-ties 1** HOLE : cavité *f* **2** CARIES : carie *f* (dentaire), cavité *f*
cavort [kə'vɔrt] *vi* CAPER : gambader, faire des cabrioles
caw[1] ['kɔ] *vi* : croasser
caw[2] *n* : croassement *m*
cayenne pepper [ˌkaɪ'en, ˌkeɪ-] *n* : poivre *m* de cayenne
CD [ˌsi'di:] *n* : CD *m*, disque *m* compact
cease ['si:s] *v* **ceased; ceasing** : cesser
ceaseless ['si:sləs] *adj* : incessant, continuel
cedar ['si:dər] *n* : cèdre *m*
cede ['si:d] *vt* **ceded; ceding** : céder
cedilla [sɪ'dɪlə] *n* : cédille *nf*
ceiling ['si:lɪŋ] *n* **1** : plafond *m* **2** LIMIT : plafond *m*, limite *f*
celebrate ['sɛləˌbreɪt] *vt* **-brated; -brating** *vt* **1** FETE : fêter, célébrer **2** : célébrer <to celebrate Mass : célébrer la messe> **3** EXTOL : louer, glorifier
celebration [ˌsɛlə'breɪʃən] *n* **1** : célébration *f*, fête *f* **2** PRAISE : louange *f*
celebrated ['sɛləˌbreɪṭəd] *adj* FAMOUS : célèbre, réputé
celebrity [sə'lɛbrəṭi] *n, pl* **-ties 1** FAME : célébrité *f*, renommée *f* **2** PERSONALITY : célébrité *f*, vedette *f*
celery ['sɛləri] *n, pl* **-eries** : céleri *m*
celestial [sə'lestʃəl, -'lestiəl] *adj* : céleste
celibacy ['sɛləbəsi] *n* : célibat *m*
celibate[1] ['sɛləbəṭ] *adj* **1** CHASTE : chaste **2** UNMARRIED : célibataire
celibate[2] *n* : célibataire *mf*
cell ['sɛl] *n* **1** : cellule *f* (d'un organisme, d'une prison, etc.) **2** : élément *m* (d'une pile)
cellar ['sɛlər] *n* : cave *f* <wine cellar : cave à vin>
cellist ['ʧelɪst] *n* : violoncelliste *mf*
cello ['ʧeˌloː] *n, pl* **-los** : violoncelle *m*
cellophane ['sɛləˌfeɪn] *n* : cellophane *f*
cell phone *n US* : téléphone *m* portable, portable *m*
cellular ['sɛljələr] *adj* : cellulaire
cellulose ['sɛljəˌloːs] *n* : cellulose *f*
Celsius ['sɛlsiəs] *adj* : Celsius, centigrade
Celt ['kɛlt, 'sɛlt] *n* : Celte *mf*
Celtic ['kɛltɪk, 'sɛl-] *adj* : celte, celtique
cement[1] [sɪ'ment] *vt* : cimenter
cement[2] *n* **1** : ciment *m* **2** GLUE : colle *f*
cemetery ['sɛməˌṭeri] *n, pl* **-teries** : cimetière *m*
censer ['sɛnʦər] *n* : encensoir *m*
censor[1] ['sɛnʦər] *vt* : censurer
censor[2] *n* : censeur *m*
censorship ['sɛnʦərˌʃɪp] *n* : censure *f*
censure[1] ['sɛnʦər] *vt* **-sured; -suring** : critiquer, blâmer
censure[2] *n* : censure *f*
census ['sɛnʦəs] *n* : recensement *m*
cent ['sɛnt] *n* : cent *m*
centaur ['sɛnˌṭɔr] *n* : centaure *m*
centennial [sɛn'teniəl] *n* : centenaire *m*
center[1] *or Brit* **centre** ['sɛntər] *vt* **centered** *or Brit* **centred; centering** *or Brit* **centring 1** : centrer **2** CONCENTRATE, FOCUS : concentrer, fixer — *vi* **to center around** : se concentrer sur, tourner autour de
center[2] *or Brit* **centre** *n* **1** : centre *m* <center of attention : centre d'attention> **2** SEAT : siège (du gouvernement, etc.) **3** : centre *m* (aux sports)
centigrade ['sɛntəˌgreɪd, 'sɑn-] *adj* : centigrade
centigram ['sɛntəˌgræm, 'sɑn-] *n* : centigramme *m*
centimeter ['sɛntəˌmiːṭər, 'sɑn-] *n* : centimètre *m*
centipede ['sɛntəˌpiːd] *n* : mille-pattes *m*
central ['sɛntrəl] *adj* **1** : central <in a central location : au centre-ville> **2**

MAIN, PRINCIPAL : fundamental, principal

Central American[1] *adj* : centraméricain

Central American[2] *n* : Centraméricain *m*, -caine *f*

centralization [ˌsɛntrələˈzeɪʃən] *n* : centralisation *f*

centralize [ˈsɛntrəˌlaɪz] *vt* **-ized; -izing** : centraliser

central nervous system *n* : système *m* nerveux central

centre [ˈsɛntər] *Brit* → **center**

centrifugal force [sɛnˈtrɪfjəgəl, -ˈtrɪfɪgəl] *n* : force *f* centrifuge

century [ˈsɛntʃəri] *n, pl* **-ries** : siècle *m*

ceramic [səˈræmɪk] *adj* : céramique <ceramic tiles : carreaux en céramique>

ceramics [səˈræmɪks] *npl* : céramique *f*

cereal[1] [ˈsɪriəl] *adj* : céréalier

cereal[2] *n* : céréale *f*

cerebellum [ˌsɛrəˈbɛləm] *n, pl* **-bellums** *or* **-bella** [-ˈbɛlə] : cervelet *m*

cerebral [səˈriːbrəl, ˈsɛrə-] *adj* : cérébral

cerebral palsy *n* : paralysie *f* cérébrale

cerebrum [səˈriːbrəm, ˈsɛrə-] *n, pl* **-brums** *or* **-bra** [-brə] : cerveau *m*

ceremonial[1] [ˌsɛrəˈmoːniəl] *adj* : cérémoniel, de cérémonie

ceremonial[2] *n* : cérémonial *m*

ceremonious [ˌsɛrəˈmoːniəs] *adj* **1** FORMAL : cérémonieux **2** CEREMONIAL : cérémonial

ceremony [ˈsɛrəˌmoːni] *n, pl* **-nies** : cérémonie *f*

cerise [səˈriːs] *n* : cerise *f*

certain[1] [ˈsərtən] *adj* **1** FIXED : certain, déterminé <a certain percentage : un pourcentage déterminé> **2** SURE : certain, convaincu <I'm certain that he got lost : je suis convaincu qu'il s'est perdu> **3** : certain, quelconque <a certain charm : un certain charme> **4** : sûr, assuré <she is certain to win : elle est assurée de gagner> **5** INEVITABLE : certain <a certain death : une mort certaine>

certain[2] *pron* : certains, certaines *pl* <certain of my friends : certains de mes amis>

certainly [ˈsərtənli] *adv* **1** DEFINITELY : certainement, assurément **2** OF COURSE : bien sûr

certainty [ˈsərtənti] *n, pl* **-ties** : certitude *f*

certificate [sərˈtɪfɪkət] *n* : certificat *m*, acte *m*, extrait *m* <birth certificate : extrait de naissance>

certification [ˌsərṭəfəˈkeɪʃən] *n* : certification *f*, attestation *f*

certify [ˈsərṭəˌfaɪ] *vt* **-fied; -fying 1** CONFIRM : certifier **2** GUARANTEE : certifier (un chèque), garantir (des marchandises, etc.)

certitude [ˈsərṭəˌtuːd, -ˌtjuːd] *n* : certitude *f*

cervical [ˈsərvɪkəl] *adj* : cervical

cervix [ˈsərvɪks] *n, pl* **-vices** [-vəˌsiːz] *or* **-vixes** : col *m* de l'utérus

cesarean section [sɪˈzæriən] *n* : césarienne *f*

cesium *or Brit* **caesium** [ˈsiːziəm] *n* : césium *m*

cessation [seˈseɪʃən] *n* : cessation *f*

cesspool [ˈsɛsˌpuːl] *n* : fosse *f* d'aisances

Chadian[1] [ˈtʃædiən] *adj* : tchadien

Chadian[2] *n* : Tchadien *m*, **-dienne** *f*

chafe [ˈtʃeɪf] *v* **chafed; chafing** *vt* IRRITATE : irriter — *vi* **1** RUB : frotter **2** : s'irriter, s'impatienter <to chafe at : s'irriter de>

chaff [ˈtʃæf] *n* : balle *f* (en agriculture)

chafing dish [ˈtʃeɪfɪŋˌdɪʃ] *n* : réchaud *m* de table

chagrin[1] [ʃəˈgrɪn] *vt* VEX : contrarier, décevoir

chagrin[2] *n* : dépit *m*, déception *f*

chain[1] [ˈtʃeɪn] *vt* : enchaîner

chain[2] *n* **1** : chaîne *f* **2** SEQUENCE, SERIES : série *f*, suite *f* <a chain of events : une série d'événements> **3 chains** *npl* FETTERS : entraves *fpl*

chair[1] [ˈtʃɛr] *vt* : présider

chair[2] *n* **1** : chaise *f* **2** : chaire *f* (dans une université) **3** CHAIRMAN, CHAIRWOMAN : président *m*, -dente *f*

chairman [ˈtʃɛrmən] *n, pl* **-men** [-mən, -ˌmɛn] : président *m*

chairmanship [ˈtʃɛrmənˌʃɪp] : présidence *f*

chairwoman [ˈtʃɛrˌwʊmən] *n, pl* **-women** [-ˌwɪmən] : présidente *f*

chaise longue [ˈʃeɪzˈlɔŋ] *n, pl* **chaise longues** [-ˈlɔn, -ˈlɔnz] : chaise *f* longue

chalet [ʃæˈleɪ] *n* : chalet *m*

chalice [ˈtʃælɪs] *n* : calice *m*

chalk[1] [ˈtʃɔk] *vt* **1** : écrire avec de la craie **2 to chalk up** CREDIT : attribuer, mettre <chalk it up to experience : mets-le au compte de l'expérience> **3 to chalk up** ACHIEVE, ATTAIN : marquer (des points), remporter (une victoire)

chalk[2] *n* **1** LIMESTONE : calcaire *m* **2** : craie *f* (pour écrire)

chalkboard [ˈtʃɔkˌbɔrd] → **blackboard**

chalky [ˈtʃɔki] *adj* **chalkier; -est** : calcaire (se dit de l'eau, du sol, etc.), couvert de craie (se dit des mains), crayeux (se dit du teint)

challenge[1] [ˈtʃælɪndʒ] *vt* **-lenged; -lenging 1** DISPUTE : contester, remettre en question **2** DARE, DEFY : défier

challenge[2] *n* : défi *m* <to meet the challenge : relever le défi>

challenger [ˈtʃælɪndʒər] *n* : challenger *m* (aux sports, en politique)

challenging [ˈtʃælɪndʒɪŋ] *adj* : stimulant, provocateur

chamber [ˈtʃeɪmbər] *n* **1** ROOM : chambre *f*, salle *f* **2** BODY : chambre *f* <chamber of commerce : chambre de commerce> **3** : chambre *f* (d'une arme à feu) **4** CAVITY : cavité *f* (du cœur) **5 chambers** *npl* : cabinet *m* (d'un juge)

chambermaid [ˈtʃeɪmbərˌmeɪd] *n* : femme *f* de chambre

chamber music *n* : musique *f* de chambre

chameleon [kəˈmiːljən, -liən] *n* : caméléon *m*

chamois [ˈʃæmi] *n, pl* **chamois** [-mi, -miz] : chamois *m*

champ[1] [ˈtʃæmp, ˈtʃɑmp] *vi* **1** CHEW : mâchonner **2 to champ at the bit** : ronger son frein

champ[2] [ˈtʃæmp] → **champion**[1]

champagne [ʃæmˈpeɪn] *n* : champagne *m*

champion[1] [ˈtʃæmpiən] *vt* : défendre, soutenir <to champion a cause : se faire le champion d'un mouvement>

champion[2] *n* : champion *m*, -pionne *f*

championship [ˈtʃæmpiənˌʃɪp] *n* : championnat *m*

chance[1] [ˈtʃæns] *v* **chanced; chancing** *vi* **1** HAPPEN : arriver (par hasard) **2 to chance upon** : rencontrer par hasard — *vt* RISK : hasarder, courir le risque de

chance[2] *adj* : fortuit, accidentel

chance[3] *n* **1** LUCK : hasard *m* **2** OPPORTUNITY : occasion *f* **3** PROBABILITY : chances *fpl* **4** RISK : risque *m* **5** : billet *m* (de loterie) **6 by chance** : par hasard

chancellor [ˈtʃænsələr] *n* **1** : chancelier *m* **2** : président *m*, -dente *f* (d'une université)

chancre [ˈʃæŋkər] *n* : chancre *m*

chandelier [ˌʃændəˈlɪr] *n* : lustre *m*

change[1] [ˈtʃeɪndʒ] *v* **changed; changing** *vt* **1** ALTER : changer, modifier **2** EXCHANGE : changer de <to change places : changer de place> — *vi* **1** : changer <times change : les temps changent> **2** *or* **to change clothes** : se changer **3** : muer (se dit de la voix)

change[2] *n* **1** : changement *m*, modification *f* **2** COINS : monnaie *f*

changeable [ˈtʃeɪndʒəbəl] *adj* : changeant, variable

changeless [ˈtʃeɪndʒləs] *adj* UNCHANGING : inaltérable, immuable

channel[1] [ˈtʃænəl] *vt* **-neled** *or* **-nelled; -neling** *or* **-nelling** : canaliser, creuser

channel[2] *n* **1** PASSAGE : voie *f*, canal *m* **2** : chenal *m* (dans un fleuve, un port, etc.) **3** STRAIT : détroit *m* **4** : chaîne *f* (de télévision)

chant[1] [ˈtʃænt] *vt* **1** : psalmodier, chanter **2** : scander (un slogan, etc.) — *vi* : psalmodier

chant[2] *n* : chant *m*, psalmodie *f* (en religion), chant *m* scandé (d'un slogan, etc.)

chantey *or* **chanty** [ˈʃænti, ˈtʃæn-] *n, pl* **-teys** *or* **-ties** : chanson *f* de marin

Chanukah [ˈxɑnəkə, ˈhɑ-] → **Hanukkah**

chaos [ˈkeɪˌɑs] *n* : chaos *m*

chaotic [keɪˈɑṭɪk] *adj* : chaotique

chap[1] [ˈtʃæp] *v* **chapped; chapping** *vt* : gercer — *vi* : se gercer

chap[2] *n* : type *m fam*, bonhomme *m fam*

chapel [ˈtʃæpəl] *n* : chapelle *f*

chaperon[1] *or* **chaperone** [ˈʃæpəˌroːn] *vt* **-oned; -oning** : chaperonner

chaperon[2] *or* **chaperone** *n* : chaperon *m*

chaplain [ˈtʃæplɪn] *n* : aumônier *m*

chapter [ˈtʃæptər] *n* **1** : châpitre *m* (d'un livre, etc.) **2** BRANCH : section *f*, division *f* (d'un groupe)

char [ˈtʃɑr] *vt* **charred; charring 1** BURN : carboniser, réduire en charbon **2** SCORCH : brûler légèrement

character [ˈkæriktər] *n* **1** LETTER, SYMBOL : caractère *m* **2** CHARACTERISTIC : caractère *m* **3** NATURE, PERSONALITY : caractère *m*, personnalité *f* **4** PERSON : individu *m* <he's quite a character : c'est un drôle de type> **5** : personnage *m* (d'un roman, d'un film, etc.)

characteristic[1] [ˌkæriktəˈrɪstɪk] *adj* : caractéristique, distinctif

characteristic[2] *n* : caractéristique *f*

characteristically [ˌkæriktəˈrɪstɪkli] *adv* : typiquement, comme d'habitude

characterization [ˌkæriktərəˈzeɪʃən] *n* : caractérisation *f*

characterize [ˈkæriktəˌraɪz] *vt* : caractériser

charade [ʃəˈreɪd] *n* **1** PRETENSE : feinte *f*, comédie **2 charades** *npl* : charades *fpl* (jeu)

charcoal [ˈtʃɑrˌkoːl] *n* **1** : charbon *m* de bois **2** : fusain *m* <charcoal drawing : portrait au fusain>

chard [ˈtʃɑrd] → **Swiss chard**

charge[1] [ˈtʃɑrdʒ] *v* **charged; charging** *vt* **1** : charger <to charge a battery : charger une batterie> **2** ENTRUST : charger, confier **3** COMMAND : ordonner **4** ACCUSE : inculper **5** ATTACK : donner l'assaut à, charger **6** : porter à un compte, payer par carte de crédit — *vi* **1** ATTACK : charger, donner l'assaut **2** RUSH : se précipiter, foncer, se précipiter **3** ASK : demander, faire payer <they charge too much : ils font payer de trop>

charge[2] *n* **1** : charge *f* (éléctrique) **2** RESPONSIBILITY : charge *f*, responsabilité *f* <to be in charge : être responsable> **3** COST : frais *mpl*, charge *f* <free of charge : gratuit> **4** ACCUSATION : inculpation *f*, accusation *f* **5** ATTACK : charge *f*, attaque *f* <charge! : à l'assaut!>

charge card → **credit card**

charger [ˈtʃɑrdʒər] *n* : cheval *m* de bataille

chariot [ˈtʃæriət] *n* : char *m*

charisma [kəˈrɪzmə] *n* : charisme *m*

charismatic [ˌkærəzˈmæṭɪk] *adj* : charismatique

charitable [ˈtʃærəɪ̯təbəl] *adj* : charitable, caritatif <a charitable organization : une organisation caritative>
charitably [ˈtʃærəɪ̯təbli] *adv* : charitablement
charity [ˈtʃærəɪ̯ti] *n, pl* **-ties 1** GOODWILL : charité *f* **2** GENEROSITY : charité *f*, générosité *f* **3** ALMS : aumônes *fpl* **4** : organisation *f* caritative
charlatan [ˈʃɑrlətən] *n* : charlatan *m*
charley horse [ˈtʃɑrliˌhɔrs] *n* : courbature *f* (de jambe)
charm[1] [ˈtʃɑrm] *vt* : charmer, enchanter
charm[2] *n* **1** SPELL : charme *m*, sortilège *m* **2** AMULET : amulette *f* <a lucky charm : un porte-bonheur> **3** APPEAL : charme *m* **4** : breloque *f* <a charm bracelet : un bracelet à breloques>
charming [ˈtʃɑrmɪŋ] *adj* : charmant, engageant
charmingly [ˈtʃɑrmɪŋli] *adv* : de façon charmante
chart[1] [ˈtʃɑrt] *vt* **1** MAP : porter (une route) sur la carte **2** GRAPH : faire la courbe de **3** *or* **to chart out** : tracer (un plan, etc.)
chart[2] *n* **1** MAP : carte *f* (marine) **2** GRAPH, DIAGRAM : courbe *f*, graphique *m*, tableau *m*
charter[1] [ˈtʃɑrtər] *vt* **1** : accorder une charte à (une organisation) **2** HIRE : affréter, noliser <chartered flights : vols affrétés>
charter[2] *n* **1** STATUTES : charte *f*, statuts *mpl* **2** LEASE : affrètement *m*
chartreuse [ʃɑrˈtrɜːz, -ˈtruːs] *n* : couleur *f* vert-jaune intense
chary [ˈtʃæri] *adj* **charier; -est** : prudent, méfiant, circonspect
chase[1] [ˈtʃeɪs] *v* **chased; chasing** *vt* **1** PURSUE : poursuivre, courir après **2** *or* **to chase away** : chasser <he chased the dog from the garden : il a chassé le chien du jardin> **3** : ciseler (des métaux)
chase[2] *n* **1** PURSUIT : poursuite *f* **2 the chase** HUNTING : la chasse
chasm [ˈkæzəm] *n* : gouffre *m*, abîme *m*
chassis [ˈtʃæsi, ˈʃæsi] *ns & pl* : châssis *m*
chaste [ˈtʃeɪst] *adj* **chaster; chastest 1** MODEST : chaste, pure **2** AUSTERE : austère, sévère
chastely [ˈtʃeɪstli] *adv* : chastement
chasten [ˈtʃeɪsən] *vt* DISCIPLINE : châtier
chastise [ˈtʃæsˌtaɪz, tʃæsˈ-] *vt* **-tised; -tising 1** PUNISH : châtier, punir **2** CASTIGATE : fustiger, critiquer
chastisement [ˈtʃæsˌtaɪzmənt, tʃæsˈtaɪz-, ˈtʃæstəz-] *n* : châtiment *m*, admonition *f*
chastity [ˈtʃæstəɪ̯ti] *n* : chasteté *f*
chat[1] [ˈtʃæt] *vi* **chatted; chatting** : bavarder, causer, placoter *Can fam*
chat[2] *n* : causerie *f*, causette *f fam*
château [ʃæˈtoː] *n, pl* **-teaus** [-ˈtoːz] *or* **-teaux** [-ˈtoːˌ -ˈtoːz] : château *m*
chattel [ˈtʃætəl] *n* : bien *m* meuble <goods and chattels : biens et effets>
chatter[1] [ˈtʃætər] *vi* **1** : claquer (se dit des dents) **2** GAB : bavarder, papoter, jacasser
chatter[2] *n* **1** : claquement *m* (de dents) **2** GABBING : bavardage *m*, papotage *m*
chatterbox [ˈtʃætərˌbɑks] *n* : moulin *m* à paroles *fam*
chatterer [ˈtʃæɪ̯tərər] *n* : bavard *m*, -varde *f*
chatty [ˈtʃæɪ̯ti] *adj* **chattier; -est** : bavard
chauffeur[1] [ˈʃoːfər, ʃoˈfər] *vi* : travailler comme chauffeur — *vt* : conduire
chauffeur[2] *n* : chauffeur *m*
chauvinism [ˈʃoːvəˌnɪzəm] *n* : chauvinisme *m*
chauvinist[1] [ˈʃoːvənɪst] *or* **chauvinistic** [ˌʃoːvəˈnɪstɪk] *adj* : chauvin
chauvinist[2] *n* : chauvin *m*, -vine *f*
cheap[1] [ˈtʃiːp] *adv* : à bon marché, au rabais
cheap[2] *adj* **1** INEXPENSIVE : bon marché **2** SHODDY : de mauvaise qualité **3** STINGY : mesquin
cheapen [ˈtʃiːpən] *vt* **1** : baisser le prix de **2** DEGRADE, LOWER : rabaisser, abaisser
cheaply [ˈtʃiːpli] *adv* : à bon marché, à bon compte
cheapskate [ˈtʃiːpˌskeɪt] *n* : radin *m*, -dine *f fam*
cheat[1] [ˈtʃiːt] *vt* : frauder, tromper, duper — *vi* **to cheat on** : tricher à (un examen, etc.), tromper (un époux)
cheat[2] *n* **1** DECEPTION : déception *f*, fraude *f* **2** → **cheater**
cheater [ˈtʃiːɪ̯tər] *n* : tricheur *m*, -cheuse *f*; fraudeur *m*, -deuse *f*
check[1] [ˈtʃɛk] *vt* **1** HALT : freiner, arrêter **2** RESTRAIN : retenir, contenir **3** VERIFY : vérifier **4** INSPECT : inspecter, contrôler **5** MARK : cocher **6** : enregistrer (ses bagages), mettre au vestiaire (un manteau, un chapeau) **7** CHECKER : faire des carreaux — *vi* **1** STOP : s'arrêter **2** CONFIRM : vérifier
check[2] *n* **1** HALT : arrêt *m*, pause *f* **2** RESTRAINT : limite *f*, frein *m* **3** INSPECTION : contrôle *m*, vérification *f* **4** *or Brit* **cheque** : chèque *m* <to pay by check : payer par chèque> **5** : ticket *m* <baggage check : ticket de bagages> **6** BILL : addition *f*, note *f* **7** SQUARE : carreau *m* **8** MARK, TICK : croix *f* **9** : échec *m* au roi (aux échecs)
checker[1] [ˈtʃɛkər] *vt* : marquer avec des carreaux
checker[2] *n* **1** : pièce *f* (de jeu de dames) **2** CASHIER : caissier *m*, -sière *f* **3** SQUARE : carreau *m* **4** : personne *f* qui vérifie qqch

checkerboard [ˈtʃɛkərˌbɔrd] *n* : damier *m*
checkers [ˈtʃɛkərz] *n* : jeu *m* de dames
check in *vi* : s'inscrire (à l'hôtel), enregistrer
checkmate[1] [ˈtʃɛkˌmeɪt] *vt* **1** THWART : contrecarrer **2** : faire échec et mat à (aux échecs)
checkmate[2] *n* : échec *m* et mat
check out *vt* INVESTIGATE : enquêter sur, vérifier — *vi* : régler sa note (à l'hôtel)
checkpoint [ˈtʃɛkˌpɔɪnt] *n* : poste *m* de contrôle
checkup [ˈtʃɛkˌʌp] *n* : examen *m* médical, bilan *m* de santé
cheddar [ˈtʃɛdər] *n* : cheddar *m*
cheek [ˈtʃik] *n* **1** : joue *f* **2** IMPUDENCE : culot *m fam*, toupet *m fam*
cheeky [ˈtʃiːki] *adj* **cheekier; -est** : effronté, culotté *fam*
cheep[1] [ˈtʃiːp] *vi* : piauler
cheep[2] *n* : piaulement *m*
cheer[1] [ˈtʃɪr] *vt* **1** COMFORT : encourager, réconforter <his card cheered me up : sa carte m'a remonté le moral> **2** GLADDEN : réjouir **3** ACCLAIM : applaudir, acclamer
cheer[2] *n* **1** GLADNESS : bonne humeur *f*, gaieté *f* **2** APPLAUSE : acclamation *f*, bravos *mpl* **3 cheers!** : à votre santé!, à la vôtre!
cheerful [ˈtʃɪrfəl] *adj* : de bonne humeur, joyeux, gaie
cheerfully [ˈtʃɪrfəli] *adv* : joyeusement, gaiement
cheerfulness [ˈtʃɪrfəlnəs] *n* : gaieté *f*
cheerily [ˈtʃɪrəli] *adv* : joyeusement
cheerleader [ˈtʃɪrˌliːdər] *n* : meneuse *f* de claque *Can*
cheerless [ˈtʃɪrləs] *adj* : sombre, triste, morne
cheery [ˈtʃɪri] *adj* **cheerier; -est** : gai, joyeux
cheese [ˈtʃiːz] *n* : fromage *m*
cheesecloth [ˈtʃiːzˌklɔθ] *n* : étamine *f*
cheesy [ˈtʃiːzi] *adj* **cheesier; -est 1** : qui a le goût de fromage, qui sent le fromage **2** CHEAP, TACKY : de mauvaise qualité, minable
cheetah [ˈtʃiːtə] *n* : guépard *m*
chef [ˈʃɛf] *n* : cuisinier *m*, -nière *f*; chef *m* cuisinier
chemical[1] [ˈkɛmɪkəl] *adj* : chimique — **chemically** [-mɪkli] *adv*
chemical[2] *n* : produit *m* chimique
chemise [ʃəˈmiːz] *n* **1** : chemise *f* (de femme) **2** *or* **chemise dress** : robe-chemisier *f*
chemist [ˈkɛmɪst] *n* : chimiste *mf*
chemistry [ˈkɛmɪstri] *n, pl* **-tries** : chimie *f*
chemotherapy [ˌkiːmoˈθɛrəpi, ˌkɛmo-] *n, pl* **-pies** : chimiothérapie *f*
chenille [ʃəˈniːl] *n* : chenille *f*
cheque *Brit* → **check**[2] **4**
cherish [ˈtʃɛrɪʃ] *vt* **1** LOVE : chérir, aimer **2** HARBOR, ENTERTAIN : caresser, tenir à (des espoirs, etc.)
cherry [ˈtʃɛri] *n, pl* **cherries** : cerise *f* (fruit), cerisier *m* (arbre)
cherub [ˈtʃɛrəb] *n* **1** *pl* **cherubim** [ˈtʃɛrəˌbɪm, ˈtʃɛrjə-] ANGEL : chérubin *m*, ange *m* **2** *pl* **cherubs** : angelot *m*, enfant *m* au visage angélique
cherubic [tʃɛˈruːbɪk] *adj* : de chérubin, angélique
chess [ˈtʃɛs] *n* : échecs *mpl*
chest [ˈtʃɛst] *n* **1** BOX : coffre *m*, caisse *f* **2** : poitrine *f* <chest pain : douleur à la poitrine>
chestnut[1] [ˈtʃɛstˌnʌt] *adj* : châtain (couleur)
chestnut[2] *n* **1** : marron *m*, châtaigne *f* (fruit) **2** : marronier *m*, châtaignier *m* (arbre)
chest of drawers *n* : commode *f*
chevron [ˈʃɛvrən] *n* : chevron *m*
chew[1] [ˈtʃuː] *vt* **1** : mâcher, mastiquer **2** : chiquer (du tabac)
chew[2] *n* : chique *f* (de tabac)
chewing gum *n* : chewing-gum *m France*, gomme *f* à mâcher
chic[1] [ˈʃiːk] *adj* : chic, élégant, à la mode
chic[2] *n* : chic *m*, élégance *f*
chick [ˈtʃɪk] *n* **1** : poussin *m* (de poulet) **2** FLEDGLING : oisillon *m*
chickadee [ˈtʃɪkədi] *n* : mésange *f* à tête noire
chicken [ˈtʃɪkən] *n* **1** : poulet *m* **2** COWARD : poltron *m*, -tronne *f*; poule *f* mouillée *fam*
chickenhearted [ˈtʃɪkənˌhɑrtəd] *adj* : poltron, peureux
chicken pox *n* : varicelle *f*
chicle [ˈtʃɪkəl] *n* : chiclé *m*
chicory [ˈtʃɪkəri] *n, pl* **-ries 1** : endive *f* (pour les salades) **2** : chicorée *f* (additif de café)
chide [ˈtʃaɪd] *vt* **chid** [ˈtʃɪd] *or* **chided; chid** *or* **chidden** [ˈtʃɪdən] *or* **chided; chiding** [ˈtʃaɪdɪŋ] : gronder, réprimander
chief[1] [ˈtʃiːf] *adj* : principal, en chef <chief editor : rédacteur en chef>
chief[2] *n* : chef *m*
chiefly [ˈtʃiːfli] *adv* : principalement, surtout
chieftain [ˈtʃiːftən] *n* : chef *m* (d'une tribu)
chiffon [ʃɪˈfɑn, ˈʃɪˌ-] *n* : mousseline *f* (de soie)
chigger [ˈtʃɪgər] *n* : aoûtat *m*
chignon [ˈʃiːnˌjɑn, -jən] *n* : chignon *m*
chilblain [ˈtʃɪlˌbleɪn] *n* : engelure *f*
child [ˈtʃaɪld] *n, pl* **children** [ˈtʃɪldrən] **1** YOUNGSTER : enfant *mf* **2** OFFSPRING : fils *m*, fille *f*
childbirth [ˈtʃaɪldˌbərθ] *n* : accouchement *m*
childhood [ˈtʃaɪldˌhʊd] *n* : enfance *f*
childish [ˈtʃaɪldɪʃ] *adj* : puéril, enfantin
childishly [ˈtʃaɪldɪʃli] *adv* : puérilement

childishness ['tʃaɪldɪʃnəs] *n* : puérilité *f*, enfantillage *m*
childless ['tʃaɪldləs] *adj* : sans enfants
childlike ['tʃaɪldˌlaɪk] *adj* : enfantin, d'enfant <a childlike voice : une voix d'enfant>
childproof ['tʃaɪldˌpruːf] *adj* : de sécurité pour enfants
Chilean[1] ['tʃɪliən, tʃɪ'leɪən] *adj* : chilien
Chiliean[2] *n* : Chilien *m*, -lienne *f*
chili *or* **chile** *or* **chilli** ['tʃɪli] *n, pl* **chilies** *or* **chiles** *or* **chillies 1** *or* **chili pepper** : piment *m* fort **2** : chili *m* con carne
chill[1] ['tʃɪl] *vt* : refroidir, réfrigérer, mettre au frais — *vi* : se refroidir
chill[2] *adj* : frais <a chill wind : un vent frais>
chill[3] *n* **1** CHILLINESS : fraîcheur *f*, froideur *f* **2** SHIVER : frisson *m* <it sent a chill down my spine : ça m'a donné des frissons> **3 to catch a chill** : attraper un coup de froid
chilliness ['tʃɪlinəs] *n* : fraîcheur *f*, froideur *f*
chilly ['tʃɪli] *adj* **chillier; -est** : frais, froid
chime[1] ['tʃaɪm] *v* **chimed; chiming** *vt* : sonner <to chime the hour : sonner l'heure> — *vi* : carillonner, sonner
chime[2] *n* : carillon *m*
chime in *vi* : interrompre
chimera *or* **chimaera** [kaɪ'mɪrə, kə-] *n* : chimère *f*
chimney ['tʃɪmni] *n, pl* **-neys 1** : cheminée *f* **2** : verre *m* (d'une lampe)
chimney sweep *n* : ramoneur *m*
chimp ['tʃɪmp, 'ʃɪmp] → **chimpanzee**
chimpanzee ['tʃɪmˌpænˈziː, ˌʃɪm-; tʃɪmˈpænzi, ʃɪm-] *n* : chimpanzé *m*
chin *n* : menton *m*
china ['tʃaɪnə] *n* **1** PORCELAIN : porcelaine *f* **2** TABLEWARE : vaisselle *f*
chinchilla [tʃɪnˈtʃɪlə] *n* : chinchilla *m*
Chinese[1] ['tʃaɪˈniːz, -niːs] *adj* : chinois
Chinese[2] *n* **1** : Chinois *m*, -noise *f* **2** : chinois *m* (langue)
chink ['tʃɪŋk] *n* : fente *f*, fissure *f*
chintz ['tʃɪnts] *n* : chintz *m*
chip[1] ['tʃɪp] *v* **chipped; chipping** *vt* : ébrécher, éborgner *Can* (de la vaisselle, etc.), écorner (des meubles), écailler (de la peinture) — *vi* **1** : s'ébrécher, s'écorner, s'écailler **2 to chip in** CONTRIBUTE : contribuer
chip[2] *n* **1** PIECE : éclat *m* (de verre, etc.), copeau *m* (de bois ou de métal), fragment *m* <he's a chip off the old block : il est bien le fils de son père> **2** COUNTER : jeton *m* (de poker, etc.) **3** NICK : ébréchure *f* **4** *or* **computer chip** : puce *f* **5 → potato chips**
chipmunk ['tʃɪpˌmʌŋk] *n* : tamia *m*, suisse *m Can*
chipper ['tʃɪpər] *adj* : vif, en pleine forme
chiropodist [kəˈrɑpədɪst, ʃə-] *n* PODIATRIST : pédicure *mf*, podologue *mf*
chiropody [kəˈrɑpədi, ʃe-] *n* PODIATRY : podologie *f*
chiropractic ['kaɪrəˌpræktɪk] *n* : chiropraxie *f*, chiropractie *f*, chiropractique *f Can*
chiropractor ['kaɪrəˌpræktər] *n* : chiropraticien *m*, -cienne *f*
chirp[1] ['tʃərp] *vi* : pépier (se dit des oiseaux), chanter (se dit des insectes)
chirp[2] *n* : pépiement *m*, chant *m*
chisel[1] ['tʃɪzəl] *vt* **-eled** *or* **-elled; -eling** *or* **-elling 1** : ciseler, tailler au ciseau **2** CHEAT : carotter *fam*
chisel[2] *n* : ciseau *m*
chit ['tʃɪt] *n* VOUCHER : bon *m*, note *f*
chitchat ['tʃɪtˌtʃæt] *n* : bavardage *m*
chivalric [ʃəˈvælrɪk] → **chivalrous**
chivalrous ['ʃɪvəlrəs] *adj* **1** KNIGHTLY : chevaleresque **2** GENTLEMANLY : galant, courtois
chivalry ['ʃɪvəlri] *n, pl* **-ries 1** : chevalerie *f* **2** COURTESY : courtoisie *f*, galanterie *f*
chive ['tʃaɪv] *n* : ciboulette *f*
chloride ['kloˌraɪd] *n* : chlorure *m*
chlorinate ['klorəˌneɪt] *vt* **-nated; -nating** : javelliser
chlorination [ˌklorəˈneɪʃən] *n* : javellisation *f*
chlorine ['kloriˌiːn] *n* : chlore *m*
chloroform[1] ['klorəˌfɔrm] *vt* : chloroformer
chloroform[2] *n* : chloroforme *m*
chlorophyll ['klorəˌfɪl] *n* : chlorophylle *f*
chock-full ['tʃɑkˈfʊl, 'tʃʌk-] *adj* : bondé, plein à craquer
chocolate ['tʃɑkələt, 'tʃɔk-] *n* : chocolat *m*
choice[1] ['tʃɔɪs] *adj* **choicer; choicest** EXCELLENT, SELECT : de choix, de première qualité
choice[2] *n* : choix *m*
choir ['kwaɪr] *n* : chœur *m*
choke[1] ['tʃoːk] *v* **choked; choking** *vt* **1** STRANGLE : étrangler, asphyxier, étouffer **2** BLOCK : boucher, embouteiller, obstruer — *vi* : s'étouffer, s'étrangler <to choke to death : mourir étouffé>
choke[2] *n* **1** CHOKING : étouffement *m* **2** : starter *m* (d'une voiture)
choker ['tʃoːkər] *n* : collier *m* court
cholera ['kɑlərə] *n* : choléra *m*
cholesterol [kəˈlestəˌrɔl] *n* : cholestérol *m*
choose ['tʃuːz] *v* **chose** ['tʃoːz]; **chosen** ['tʃoːzən]; **choosing** *vt* **1** SELECT : choisir, élire <to choose sides : choisir son camp> **2** DECIDE : décider **3** PREFER : préférer, aimer mieux — *vi* : choisir
choosy *or* **choosey** ['tʃuːzi] *adj* **choosier; -est** : difficile, exigeant
chop[1] ['tʃɑp] *vt* **chopped; chopping 1** : couper <to chop wood : couper du bois> **2** MINCE : hacher (des légumes,

etc.) **3 to chop down** : abattre **4 to chop off** : trancher, couper

chop[2] *n* **1** BLOW, CUT : coup *m* **2** : côtelette *f* <pork chops : côtelettes de porc> **3 chops** *npl* : joue *f* (d'une personne), bajoues *fpl* (d'un animal) <to lick one's chops : se lécher les babines>

chopper ['tʃɑpər] → **helicopter**

choppy ['tʃɑpi] *adj* **choppier; -est 1** : agité <a choppy sea : une mer agitée> **2** DISCONNECTED, JERKY : saccadé, discontinu, irrégulier

chopsticks ['tʃɑpˌstɪks] *npl* : baguettes *fpl*

choral ['kɔrəl] *adj* : choral

chorale [kə'ræl, -'ral] *n* **1** : choral *m*, chant *m* religieux **2** CHOIR, CHORUS : chorale *f*

chord ['kɔrd] *n* **1** : accord *m* (en musique) **2** : corde *f* (géométrique)

chore ['tʃɔr] *n* **1** TASK : besogne *f*, travail *m* de routine <household chores : travaux ménagers> **2** BURDEN : corvée *f*

choreograph ['koriəˌgræf] *vt* : chorégraphier

choreographer [ˌkori'ɑgrəfər] *n* : chorégraphe *mf*

choreography [ˌkori'ɑgrəfi] *n, pl* **-phies** : chorégraphie *f* — **choreographic** [-ə'græfɪk] *adj*

chorister ['kɔrɪstər] *n* : choriste *mf*

chortle[1] ['tʃɔrtəl] *vi* **-tled; -tling** : glousser

chortle[2] *n* : gloussement *m*, petit rire *m*

chorus[1] ['kɔrəs] *vt* : chanter en chœur

chorus[2] *n* **1** : chœur *m* (de chanteurs), troupe *f* (de danseurs) **2** REFRAIN : refrain *m* **3** SONG : chœur *m*, choral *m* **4** : concert *m* <a chorus of cries : un concert de cris>

chose → **choose**

chosen ['tʃoːzən] *adj* : choisi, privilégié <the chosen few : les privilégiés>

chow ['tʃaʊ] *n* **1** FOOD, GRUB : bouffe *f fam* **2** → **chow chow**

chow chow ['tʃaʊˌtʃaʊ] *n* : chow-chow *m* (chien)

chowder ['tʃaʊdər] *n* : soupe *f* au poisson, soupe *f* aux fruits de mer

christen ['krɪsən] *vt* **1** BAPTIZE : baptiser **2** NAME : appeler, nommer

Christendom ['krɪsəndəm] *n* : chrétienté *f*

christening ['krɪsənɪŋ] *n* : baptême *m*

Christian[1] ['krɪstʃən] *adj* : chrétien

Christian[2] *n* : chrétien *m*, -tienne *f*

Christianity [ˌkrɪstʃi'ænəˌti, ˌkrɪs'tʃæ-] *n* : christianisme *m*

Christian name *n* : nom *m* de baptême, prénom *m*

Christmas ['krɪsməs] *n* : Noël *m* <the Christmas season : la période de Noël>

chromatic [kroː'mæˌtɪk] *adj* : chromatique

chrome ['kroːm] *n* : chrome *m*

chromium ['kroːmiəm] *n* : chrome *m*

chromosome ['kroːməˌsoːm, -ˌzoːm] *n* : chromosome *m*

chronic ['krɑnɪk] *adj* : chronique — **chronically** [-nɪkli] *adv*

chronicle[1] ['krɑnɪkəl] *vt* **-cled; -cling** : faire la chronique de, écrire une chronique de

chronicle[2] *n* : chronique *f*

chronicler ['krɑnɪklər] *n* : chroniqueur *m*, -queuse *f*

chronological [ˌkrɑnəl'ɑdʒɪkəl] *adj* : chronologique — **chronologically** [-kli] *adv*

chronology [krə'nɑlədʒi] *n, pl* **-gies** : chronologie *f*

chronometer [krə'nɑməˌtər] *n* : chronomètre *m*

chrysalis ['krɪsələs] *n, pl* **chrysalides** [krɪ'sæləˌdiːz] *or* **chrysalises:** chrysalide *f*

chrysanthemum [krɪ'sænɪθəməm] *n* : chrysanthème *m*

chubby ['tʃʌbi] *adj* **chubbier; -est** : dodu, potelé, grassouillet

chuck[1] ['tʃʌk] *vt* **1** PAT, TAP : tapoter <to chuck s.o. under the chin : tapoter le menton de qqn> **2** TOSS : tirer, lancer **3** GIVE UP : renoncer à, laisser tomber (une activité)

chuck[2] *n* **1** PAT, TAP : tapotement *m* **2** TOSS : lancer *m* **3** *or* **chuck steak** : paleron *m* de bœuf

chuckle[1] ['tʃʌkəl] *vi* **-led; -ling** : glousser, rire tout bas

chuckle[2] *n* : gloussement *m*, petit rire *m*

chug ['tʃʌg] *vi* **chugged; chugging** PUFF : haleter (se dit d'un moteur)

chum[1] ['tʃʌm] *vi* **chummed; chumming** : être copain, être copine <to chum around with : être copain avec>

chum[2] *n* : copain *m*, -pine *f*; camarade *mf*

chummy ['tʃʌmi] **chummier; -est** : familier, amical, sociable

chump ['tʃʌmp] *n* : gourde *f fam*; idiot *m*, -diote *f*

chunk ['tʃʌŋk] *n* **1** PIECE : morceau *m* **2** : grande quantité *f* (d'argent, etc.)

chunky ['tʃʌŋki] *adj* **chunkier; -est 1** STOCKY : trapu **2** : qui contient des morceaux

church ['tʃərtʃ] *n* **1** : église *f* **2** : Église *f* <Church and State : l'Église et l'État> **3** DENOMINATION : culte *m*, confession *f* **4** CONGREGATION : assemblée *f* de fidèles

churchgoer ['tʃərtʃˌgoːər] *n* : pratiquant *m*, -quante *f*

churchyard ['tʃərtʃˌjɑrd] *n* : cimetière *m* (autour d'une église)

churn[1] ['tʃərn] *vt* **1** : battre (du beurre), baratter (de la crème) **2** STIR : agiter, remuer — *vi* : bouillonner

churn[2] *n* : baratte *f*

chute ['ʃuːt] *n* **1** : glissière *f* (de paquets, etc.) **2** : piste *f* de toboggan (aux sports) **3** → **parachute**
chutney ['tʃʌtni] *n, pl* **-neys** : chutney *m*
chutzpah ['hʊtspə, 'xʊt-, -,spɑ] *n* GALL, NERVE : culot *m fam*, toupet *m fam*
cicada [sə'keɪdə, -'kɑ-] *n* : cigale *f*
cider ['saɪdər] *n* : cidre *m*
cigar [sɪ'gɑr] *n* : cigare *m*
cigarette [ˌsɪgə'ret, 'sɪgəˌret] *n* : cigarette *f*
cinch[1] ['sɪntʃ] *vt* **1** : sangler (un cheval) **2** : attacher (une selle) par une sangle
cinch[2] *n* **1** : sangle *f* (de selle) **2** : quelque chose facile ou sûr <it's a cinch : c'est du gateau>
cincture ['sɪŋktʃər] *n* : ceinture *f* (d'un religieux)
cinder ['sɪndər] *n* **1** EMBER : morceau *m* de braise **2 cinders** *npl* ASHES : cendres *fpl*
cinema ['sɪnəmə] *n* : cinéma *m*
cinematic [ˌsɪnə'mætɪk] *adj* : cinématographique
cinnamon ['sɪnəmən] *n* : cannelle *f*
cipher ['saɪfər] *n* **1** ZERO : zéro *m* **2** CODE : chiffre *m*, code *m* secret
circa ['sərkə] *prep* : environ, vers <born circa 1700 : né au début du 18e siècle>
circle[1] ['sərkəl] *v* **-cled; -cling** *vt* **1** SURROUND : entourer, encercler **2** : tourner autour de, faire le tour de <the earth circles the sun : la terre tourne autour du soleil> — *vi* : faire des cercles
circle[2] *n* **1** : cercle *m* **2** CYCLE : cycle *m* <to come full circle : boucler la boucle> **3** GROUP : cercle *m*, milieu *m* (social)
circuit ['sərkət] *n* **1** BOUNDARY : limite *f*, frontière *f* **2** TOUR : circuit *m*, tour *m* **3** : circuit *m* (électrique)
circuit breaker *n* : disjoncteur *m*
circuitous [ˌsərˈkjuːətəs] *adj* **1** : détourné, indirect <a circuitous route : un chemin détourné> **2** : contourné, compliqué <circuitous reasoning : raisonnement contourné>
circuitry ['sərkətri] *n, pl* **-ries** : système *m* de circuits
circular[1] ['sərkjələr] *adj* ROUND : circulaire, rond
circular[2] *n* **1** LEAFLET : circulaire *f* **2** ADVERTISEMENT : prospectus *m*
circulate ['sərkjəˌleɪt] *v* **-lated; -lating** *vt* : faire circuler, propager <to circulate a rumor : propager une rumeur> — *vi* : circuler
circulation [ˌsərkjə'leɪʃən] *n* **1** FLOW : circulation *f* **2** : tirage *m* (d'un journal)
circulatory ['sərkjələˌtori] *adj* : circulatoire
circumcise ['sərkəmˌsaɪz] *vt* **-cised; -cising** : circoncire
circumcision [ˌsərkəm'sɪʒən, 'sərkəmˌ-] *n* : circoncision *f*
circumference [sərˈkʌmfrənts] *n* : circonférence *f*
circumflex ['sərkəmˌfleks] *n* : accent *m* circonflexe
circumlocution [ˌsərkəmlo'kjuːʃən] *n* : circonlocution *f*
circumnavigate [ˌsərkəm'nævəˌgeɪt] *vt* **-gated; -gating** : faire le tour de, contourner
circumscribe ['sərkəmˌskraɪb] *vt* **1** : circonscrire (en géométrie) **2** LIMIT : circonscrire, limiter
circumspect ['sərkəmˌspekt] *adj* : circonspect, prudent
circumspection [ˌsərkəm'spekʃən] *n* : circonspection *f*, prudence *f*
circumstance ['sərkəmˌstænts] *n* **1** EVENT, FACT : circonstance *f*, événement *m* **2 circonstances** *npl* CONDITIONS : circonstances *fpl*, situation *f* <financial circumstances : situation financière> <under no circumstances : en aucun cas>
circumstantial [ˌsərkəm'stænt̬ʃəl] *adj* **1** INCIDENTAL : accidentel, fortuit <circumstantial evidence : preuves indirectes> **2** DETAILED : détaillé, circonstancié
circumvent [ˌsərkəm'vent] *vt* : contourner, circonvenir <to circumvent the law : contourner la loi>
circus ['sərkəs] *n* : cirque *m*
cirrhosis [sə'roːsɪs] *n, pl* **-rhoses** [-ˌsiːz] : cirrhose *f*
cirrus ['sɪrəs] *n, pl* **-ri** ['sɪrˌaɪ] : cirrus *m*
cistern ['sɪstərn] *n* TANK : citerne *f*
citadel ['sɪt̬ədəl, -ˌdel] *n* : citadelle *f*
citation [saɪ'teɪʃən] *n* : citation *f*
cite ['saɪt] *vt* **cited; citing 1** SUMMON : citer, appeler (en justice) **2** QUOTE : citer **3** COMMEND : citer
citizen ['sɪt̬əzən] *n* : citoyen *m*, -toyenne *f*
citizenry ['sɪt̬əzənri] *n, pl* **-ries** : ensemble *m* des citoyens
citizenship ['sɪt̬əzənˌʃɪp] *n* : citoyenneté *f*
citron ['sɪtrən] *n* : cédrat *m*
citrus ['sɪtrəs] *n, pl* **citrus** *or* **citruses** *or* **citrus fruit** : agrume *m*
city ['sɪt̬i] *n, pl* **cities** : ville *f*
city hall *n* : hôtel *m* de ville
civic ['sɪvɪk] *adj* : civique
civics ['sɪvɪks] *ns & pl* : instruction *f* civique
civil ['sɪvəl] *adj* **1** : civil <civil engineering : génie civil> **2** POLITE : courtois, civil
civilian [sə'vɪljən] *n* : civil *m*, -vile *f*
civility [sə'vɪlət̬i] *n, pl* **-ties** POLITENESS : civilité *f*, courtoisie *f*
civilization [ˌsɪvələ'zeɪʃən] *n* : civilisation *f*
civilize ['sɪvəˌlaɪz] *vt* **-lized; -lizing** : civiliser

civilly ['sɪvəli] *adj* : poliment
civil rights *npl* : droits *mpl* civiques, droits *mpl* civils
civil service *n* : fonction *f* publique
civil war *n* : guerre *f* civile
clack[1] ['klæk] *vi* : cliqueter
clack[2] *n* : cliquetis *m*
clad ['klæd] *adj* **1** CLOTHED : vêtu, habillé **2** COVERED : couvert
claim[1] ['kleɪm] *vt* **1** DEMAND : revendiquer, réclamer <to claim one's rights : réclamer ses droits> **2** MAINTAIN : déclarer, prétendre <he claims to know you : il prétend vous connaître> **3 to claim a life** : faire un mort, faire une victime
claim[2] *n* **1** DEMAND : revendication *f*, demande *f* **2** ASSERTION : déclaration *f*, affirmation *f* **3** *or* **land claim** : concession *f* (de terrain)
clairvoyance [klærˈvɔɪənʦ] *n* : voyance *f*, don *m* de seconde vue
clairvoyant[1] [klærˈvɔɪənt] *adj* : doué de seconde vue
clairvoyant[2] *n* : voyant *m*, -voyante *f*
clam ['klæm] *n* : palourde *f*
clamber ['klæmbər] *vi* : grimper, se hisser (avec difficulté)
clammy ['klæmi] *adj* **clammier; -est** : moite, humide et froid
clamor[1] *or Brit* **clamour** ['klæmər] *vi* **1** : vociférer, crier **2 to clamor for** : demander, réclamer
clamor[2] *or Brit* **clamour** *n* **1** UPROAR : clameur *f*, vociférations *fpl* **2** DEMAND : réclamations *fpl* **3** PROTEST : protestation *f*
clamorous ['klæmərəs] *adj* : bruyant, vociférant
clamour *Brit* → **clamor**
clamp[1] ['klæmp] *vt* **1** CLENCH : serrer <she clamped her mouth shut : elle serrait les mâchoires> **2** ATTACH : cramponner, fixer
clamp[2] *n* : crampon *m*, pince *f*
clan ['klæn] *n* : clan *m*
clandestine [klænˈdɛstɪn] *adj* : clandestin, secret
clang[1] ['klæŋ] *vi* : résonner, retentir
clang[2] *n* : bruit *m* métallique
clangor *or Brit* **clangour** ['klæŋər, -gər] *n* : suite *f* de bruits métalliques
clank[1] ['klæŋk] *vi* : résonner, cliqueter
clank[2] *n* : cliquetis *m*
clannish ['klænɪʃ] *adj* : exclusif, fermé
clap[1] ['klæp] *vt* **clapped; clapping 1** STRIKE : frapper bruyamment **2** APPLAUD : applaudir — *vi* APPLAUD : applaudir
clap[2] *n* **1** NOISE : retentissement *m*, coup *m* <a clap of thunder : un grondement de tonnerre> **2** PAT, SLAP : claque *f*, petite tape *f* **3** APPLAUDING : applaudissement *m*
clapboard ['klæbərd, 'klæpˌbɔrd] *n* : bardeau *m* (en bois)
clapper ['klæpər] *n* : battant *m* (d'une cloche)
claret ['klærət] *n* : bordeaux *m* (vin)
clarification [ˌklærəfəˈkeɪʃən] *n* : clarification *f*
clarify ['klærəˌfaɪ] *vt* **-fied; -fying** : clarifier, éclaircir
clarinet [ˌklærəˈnɛt] *n* : clarinette *f*
clarinetist *or* **clarinettist** [ˌklærəˈnɛʧɪst] *n* : clarinettiste *mf*
clarion ['klæriən] *adj* : claironnant, sonore
clarity ['klærəʧi] *n* : clarté *f*
clash[1] ['klæʃ] *vi* **1** : produire un bruit métallique, résonner **2** CONFLICT, COLLIDE : s'opposer, se heurter
clash[2] *n* **1** : bruit *m* métallique, retentissement *m* **2** CONFLICT : conflit *m*, incompatibilité *f* **3** : discordance *f* (se dit des couleurs)
clasp[1] ['klæsp] *vt* **1** FASTEN : attacher **2** EMBRACE, GRASP : étreindre, embrasser, serrer
clasp[2] *n* **1** FASTENER : attache *f*, fermoir *m* **2** EMBRACE, HOLD : étreinte *f*, prise *f*
class[1] ['klæs] *vt* : classer, classifier
class[2] *n* **1** TYPE, KIND : classe *f*, division *f*, catégorie *f* **2** *or* **social class** : classe *f*, rang *m* social **3** COURSE : cours *m* <night classes : cours du soir> **4** : classe *f* (d'élèves)
classic[1] ['klæsɪk] *adj* : classique
classic[2] *n* : classique *m*
classical ['klæsɪkəl] *adj* : classique
classically ['klæsɪkli] *adv* : de façon classique, dans un style classique
classicism ['klæsəˌsɪzəm] *n* : classicisme *m*
classification [ˌklæsəfəˈkeɪʃən] *n* : classification *f*
classified ['klæsəˌfaɪd] *adj* **1** : classifié <classified ads : des petites annonces> **2** SECRET : secret, confidentiel
classify ['klæsəˌfaɪ] *vt* **-fied; -fying** : classer, classifier
classmate ['klæsˌmeɪt] *n* : compagnon *m* de classe, compagne *f* de classe
classroom ['klæsˌru:m] *n* : salle *f* de classe
clatter[1] ['klæʧər] *vi* : faire du bruit, s'entrechoquer
clatter[2] *n* : bruit *m*, cliquetis *m*
clause ['klɔz] *n* **1** : clause *f* (dans les actes judiciaires, etc.) **2** : proposition *f* (en grammaire)
claustrophobia [ˌklɔstrəˈfo:biə] *n* : claustrophobie *f* — **claustrophobic** [-ˈfo:bɪk] *adj*
clavicle ['klæˌvɪkəl] *n* : clavicule *f*
claw[1] ['klɔ] *vt* : griffer
claw[2] *n* : griffe *f* (d'un chat, etc.), pince *f* (des crustacés)
clay ['kleɪ] *n* : argile *f*
clayey ['kleɪi] *adj* : argileux
clean[1] ['kli:n] *vt* : nettoyer, laver
clean[2] *adv* **1** FAIRLY, PROPERLY : de façon propre, sans faute (en sports) **2** COMPLETELY : complètement **3 to**

come clean about : tout dire sur, révéler
clean[3] *adj* **1** : propre **2** UNADULTERATED : pur **3** DECENT, UNSULLIED : honorable, sans tache **4** COMPLETE : définitif
cleanliness ['klɛnlinəs] *n* : propreté *f*
cleanly[1] ['kli:nli] *adv* : proprement, nettement
cleanly[2] ['klɛnli] *adj* **cleanlier; -est** : propre
cleanness ['kli:nnəs] *n* : propreté *f*
cleanse ['klɛnz] *vt* **cleansed; cleansing** : nettoyer, purifier
clear[1] ['kli:r] *vt* **1** CLARIFY : clarifier **2** *or* **to clear away** : débarrasser, déblayer, déboucher (un tuyau, etc.), dégager (une voie) <to clear the table : débarrasser la table> **3** VINDICATE : innocenter, disculper <to clear one's name : blanchir son nom, se disculper> **4** LIQUIDATE : liquider (un compte, etc.) **5** NET : réaliser, rapporter <to clear a profit : réaliser un profit> **6** : franchir, éviter <to clear a hurdle : franchir une haie> **7 to clear up** RESOLVE : résoudre (un problème) — *vi* **1** *or* **to clear up** : s'éclaircir, se lever (se dit du temps) **2** *or* **to clear up** VANISH : disparaître <the symptoms cleared up : les symptômes ont disparu> **3** : être compensé (se dit d'un chèque)
clear[2] *adv* **1** DISTINCTLY : distinctement, nettement **2** COMPLETELY : complètement **3 to get clear of** : se débarrasser de
clear[3] *adj* **1** BRIGHT : éclatant, lumineux **2** FAIR : clair, beau (se dit du temps) <a clear sky : un ciel sans nuages> **3** TRANSPARENT : transparent, clair, limpide **4** EXPLICIT, STRAIGHTFORWARD : clair, explicite, intelligible **5** FREE, UNBLOCKED : libre, dégagé
clear[4] *n* **in the clear** : libre de tout soupçon
clearance ['klɪrənʦ] *n* **1** : déblaiement *m*, dégagement *m* **2** SPACE : espace *m* libre **3** AUTHORIZATION : autorisation *f* (d'une chèque)
clearing ['klɪrɪŋ] *n* : clairière *f* (dans un bois)
clearly ['klɪrli] *adv* **1** DISTINCTLY : clairement, distinctement **2** EVIDENTLY : évidemment, manifestement
cleat ['kli:t] *n* **1** : taquet *m* (d'un navire) **2 cleats** *mpl* : chaussures *fpl* à crampons
cleavage ['kli:vɪdʒ] *n* **1** CLEAVING, SPLIT : clivage *m* **2** : décolleté *m* <a dress showing cleavage : une robe décolletée>
cleave[1] ['kli:v] *vi* **cleaved** ['kli:vd] *or* **clove** ['klo:v]; **cleaving** CLING : adhérer, coller
cleave[2] *vt* **cleaved; cleaving** SPLIT : diviser, fendre
cleaver ['kli:vər] *n* : couperet *m*
clef ['klɛf] *n* : clé *f*, clef *f* (en musique)
cleft ['klɛft] *n* : crevasse *f*, fissure *f*
clemency ['klɛmənʦi] *n, pl* **-cies** : clémence *f*
clement ['klɛmənt] *adj* **1** LENIENT, MERCIFUL : clément, indulgent **2** MILD : doux, clément (se dit de la température)
clench ['klɛnʧ] *vt* : serrer <to clench one's fist : serrer le poing> <to clench one's teeth : serrer les dents>
clergy ['klərdʒi] *n, pl* **-gies** : clergé *m*
clergyman ['klərdʒimən] *n, pl* **-men** [-mən, -ˌmen] : ecclésiastique *m*
cleric ['klɛrɪk] *n* : ecclésiastique *m*
clerical ['klɛrɪkəl] *adj* **1** : clérical, du clergé **2** : de bureau <clerical work : travail de bureau>
clerk ['klərk, *Brit* 'klɑrk] *n* **1** : commis *mf* (de bureau); employé *m*, -ployée *f* de bureau **2** SALESPERSON : vendeur *m*, -deuse *f*
clever ['klɛvər] *adj* **1** SKILLFUL : habile, adroit **2** WITTY : ingénieux, astucieux
cleverly ['klɛvərli] *adv* **1** SKILLFULLY : habilement **2** INTELLIGENTLY : astucieusement, intelligemment
cleverness ['klɛvərnəs] *n* **1** SKILL : habileté *f* **2** INTELLIGENCE : intelligence *f*
clew ['klu:] → **clue**
cliché [kli'ʃeɪ] *n* : cliché *m*
click[1] ['klɪk] *vt* : faire claquer — *vi* **1** : faire un déclic **2** AGREE, GET ALONG : bien fonctionner ensemble, bien s'entendre **3** SUCCEED : bien marcher **4** : cliquer (en informatique)
click[2] *n* : clic *m*, déclic *m*
client ['klaɪənt] *n* : client *m*, cliente *f*
clientele [ˌklaɪən'tel, ˌkli:-] *n* : clientèle *f*
cliff ['klɪf] *n* : falaise *f*, escarpement *m*
climate ['klaɪmət] *n* : climat *m*
climax[1] ['klaɪˌmæks] *vi* : atteindre un point culminant
climax[2] *n* : point *m* culminant, apogée *m*
climb[1] ['klaɪm] *vt* : monter, gravir, escalader <to climb a mountain : gravir une montagne> — *vi* RISE, ASCEND : monter, augmenter <prices are climbing : les prix augmentent>
climb[2] *n* : montée *f*, ascension *f*
clinch[1] ['klɪnʧ] *vt* **1** FASTEN, SECURE : river (un clou), attacher **2** SETTLE : résoudre, conclure <to clinch the deal : conclure l'affaire>
clinch[2] *n* EMBRACE : étreinte *f*, corps à corps *m* (en boxe)
cling ['klɪŋ] *vi* **clung** ['klʌŋ]; **clinging 1** STICK : adhérer, coller **2** : se cramponner, s'agripper <he was clinging to the railing : il se cramponnait à la balustrade>

clinic ['klɪnɪk] *n* : clinique *f*
clinical ['klɪnɪkəl] *adj* : clinique **— clinically** [-kli] *adv*
clink[1] ['klɪŋk] *vi* : tinter
clink[2] *n* : tintement *m*
clinker ['klɪŋkər] *n* : mâchefer *m*, scories *fpl*
clip[1] ['klɪp] *vt* **clipped; clipping 1** CUT : couper, tailler **2** HIT : frapper, donner un coup de poing à **3** FASTEN : attacher (avec un trombone)
clip[2] *n* **1 → clippers 2** BLOW : coup *m*, taloche *f fam* **3** PACE : pas *m* rapide <at a good clip : à vive allure> **4** FASTENER : attache *f*, pince *f* **5 → paper clip**
clipper ['klɪpər] *n* **1** *or* **clipper ship** : clipper *m* **2 clippers** *npl or* **nail clippers** : coupe-ongles *m* **3 clippers** *npl* SHEARS : tondeuse *f*
clique ['kli:k, 'klɪk] *n* : clique *m*, coterie *f*
clitoris ['klɪtərəs, klɪ'tɔrəs] *n, pl* **clitorides** [-'tɔrə,di:z] : clitoris *m*
cloak[1] ['klo:k] *vt* : cacher, camoufler <cloaked in secrecy : empreint de secret>
cloak[2] *n* **1** CAPE : cape *f* **2** PRETENSE, DISGUISE : masque *m*, voile *m*
clobber ['klɑbər] *vt* : tabasser *fam*
clock[1] ['klɑk] *vi* : chronométrer (un coureur, etc.)
clock[2] *n* **1** : horloge *f*, chronomètre *m* (aux sports) **2 to work around the clock** : travailler 24 heures d'affilée
clockwise ['klɑkwaɪz] *adv & adj* : dans le sens des aiguilles d'une montre
clod ['klɑd] *n* **1** : motte *f* (de terre) **2** OAF : rustre *m*; lourdaud *m*, -daude *f*
clog[1] ['klɑg] *v* **clogged; clogging** *vt* **1** HINDER : entraver, gêner **2** OBSTRUCT : boucher, bloquer, obstruer **—** *vi or* **to clog up** : se boucher
clog[2] *n* **1** HINDRANCE : entrave *f* **2** : sabot *m* (chaussure)
cloister[1] ['klɔɪstər] *vt* : cloîtrer
cloister[2] *n* : cloître *m*
clone ['klo:n] *n* : clone *m*
close[1] ['klo:z] *v* **closed; closing** *vt* **1** SHUT : fermer **2** STOP, END : terminer, clore, conclure **3** REDUCE : réduire, diminuer <to close a gap : réduire un espace> **—** *vi* **1** : fermer, se fermer **2** TERMINATE : prendre fin, se terminer **3 to close in** APPROACH : se rapprocher
close[2] ['klo:s] *adv* **1** NEARBY : tout près **2** SOON : dans peu de temps **3 to hold s.o. close** : serrer qqn dans ses bras
close[3] *adj* **closer; closest 1** CONFINING : étroit, limité <to live in close quarters : vivre à l'étroit> **2** SECRETIVE : peu communicatif, réservé **3** STRICT : rigoureux, étroit <a close watch : une surveillance étroite> **4** STUFFY : mal aéré (se dit d'une salle, etc.), lourd (se dit du temps) **5** TIGHT : serré <it's a close fit : il est très serré> **6** INTIMATE : intime, proche <close friends : amies intimes> **7** ACCURATE : précis, exact <a close translation : une traduction très exacte> **8** : serré (se dit d'une concurrence) <a close contest : une lutte serrée>
close[4] ['klo:z] *n* CONCLUSION, END : fin *f*, conclusion *f*
closely ['klo:sli] *adv* **1** NEAR : de près **2** ATTENTIVELY : attentivement
closeness ['klo:snəs] *n* : proximité *f*
closet[1] ['klɑzət] *vt* : enfermer <to be closeted with s.o. : être tête à tête avec qqn>
closet[2] *n* : placard *m*, garde-robe *f*, penderie *f*
closure ['klo:ʒər] *n* : fermeture *f*, clôture *f*
clot[1] ['klɑt] *vi* **clotted; clotting** : former des caillots, se coaguler
clot[2] *n* : caillot *m*
cloth ['klɔθ] *n, pl* **cloths** ['klɔðz, 'klɔθs] **1** FABRIC : tissu *m*, étoffe *f* **2** RAG : chiffon *m* **3** TABLECLOTH : nappe *f*
clothe ['klo:ð] *vt* **clothed** *or* **clad** ['klæd]; **clothing** : habiller, vêtir
clothes ['klo:z, 'klo:ðz] *npl* **1 → clothing 2 → bedclothes**
clothespin ['klo:z,pɪn, 'klo:ðz-] *n*: pince *f* (à linge)
clothier ['klo:ðjər, 'klo:ðiər] *n* : marchand *m* de vêtements
clothing ['klo:ðɪŋ] *n* : vêtements *mpl*
cloud[1] ['klaʊd] *vt* : embuer, obscurcir **—** *vi or* **to cloud over** : se couvrir de nuages
cloud[2] *n* **1** : nuage *m* **2** SWARM : essaim *m*, nuée *f* (d'insectes)
cloudburst ['klaʊd,bərst] *n* : trombes *fpl* d'eau, grosse averse *f*
cloudy ['klaʊdi] *adj* **cloudier; -est** : nuageux, couvert
clout[1] ['klaʊt] *vt* : donner un coup (de poing) à
clout[2] *n* **1** BLOW : coup *m*, taloche *f fam* **2** INFLUENCE, PULL : influence *m*, pouvoir *m*
clove[1] ['klo:v] *n* **1** : clou *m* de girofle **2** *or* **garlic clove** : gousse *f* d'ail
clove[2] **→ cleave**
clover ['klo:vər] *n* : trèfle *m*
cloverleaf ['klo:vər,li:f] *n, pl* **-leafs** *or* **-leaves** [-,li:vz] : croisement *m* en trèfle
clown[1] ['klaʊn] *vi or* **to clown around** : faire le clown
clown[2] *n* : clown *m*
cloying ['klɔɪɪŋ] *adj* **1** DISGUSTING : écœurant **2** MAWKISH : mièvre
club[1] ['klʌb] *vt* **clubbed; clubbing** : frapper
club[2] *n* **1** BLUDGEON : massue *f*, matraque *f* **2** : club *m* (aux sports) **3** : trèfle *m* (aux cartes) **4** ASSOCIATION : club *m*, groupe *m*, association *f*
clubfoot ['klʌb,fʊt] *n, pl* **-feet** : pied *m* bot

clubhouse ['klʌbˌhaʊs] *n* : club *m*, maison *f* de club
cluck[1] ['klʌk] *vi* : glousser
cluck[2] *n* : gloussement *m*
clue[1] ['klu:] *vt* **clued; clueing** *or* **cluing** INFORM : mettre au courant, informer
clue[2] *n* : indice *m*, indication *f* <I haven't got a clue : je n'ai aucune idée>
clump[1] ['klʌmp] *vi* : marcher lourdement
clump[2] *n* **1** : massif *m* (d'arbres), touffe *f* (d'herbe) **2** : pas *m* lourd
clumsiness ['klʌmzinəs] *n* **1** AWKWARDNESS : gaucherie *f* **2** TACTLESSNESS : manque *m* de tact
clumsy ['klʌmzi] *adj* **clumsier; -est 1** AWKWARD : maladroit, gauche **2** TACTLESS : sans tact, malhabile, gauche — **clumsily** *adv*
clung → **cling**
cluster[1] ['klʌstər] *vt* : rassembler — *vi* : se rassembler, se grouper
cluster[2] *n* : groupe *m* (de personnes), grappe *f* (de raisins, etc.), ensemble *m* (de maisons, d'idées, etc.)
clutch[1] ['klʌtʃ] *vt* GRASP : saisir, étreindre — *vi* **to clutch at** : s'agripper à, se cramponner à
clutch[2] *n* **1** GRASP, GRIP : prise *f*, étreinte *f* <to fall into s.o.'s clutches : tomber dans les griffes de qqn> **2** : embrayage *m* (d'une voiture) **3** *or* **clutch pedal** : pédale *f* d'embrayage
clutter[1] ['klʌtər] *vt* : encombrer, mettre en désordre
clutter[2] *n* : désordre *m*, fouillis *m*
coach[1] ['ko:tʃ] *vt* **1** : entraîner (une équipe sportive) **2** TUTOR : donner des leçons à
coach[2] *n* **1** CARRIAGE : carrosse *m* **2** : voiture *f*, wagon *m* (d'un train) **3** BUS : autocar *m*, autobus *m* **4** : deuxième classe *f* (en avion) **5** TRAINER : entraîneur *m*, -neuse *f*
coagulate [ko'ægjəˌleɪt] *v* **-lated; -lating** *vt* CLOT : coaguler — *vi* : se coaguler
coagulation [koˌægjə'leɪʃən] *n* : coagulation *f*
coal ['ko:l] *n* **1** : charbon *m*, houille *f* **2 coals** *npl* : EMBERS : braise *f*
coalesce [ˌko:ə'les] *vi* **-alesced; -alescing** : s'unir
coalition [ˌko:ə'lɪʃən] *n* : coalition *f*
coarse [ˌkors] *adj* **coarser; coarsest 1** : gros (se dit du sable, du sel, etc.), grossier (se dit des textiles), épais (se dit des cheveux, etc.) **2** CRUDE : grossier, vulgaire
coarsely [ˌkorsli] *adv* : grossièrement
coarsen ['korsən] *vt* : rendre rude, rendre grossier — *vi* : devenir rude, devenir grossier
coarseness ['korsnəs] *n* **1** ROUGHNESS : rudesse *f* **2** CRUDENESS : grossièreté *f*, vulgarité *f*
coast[1] ['ko:st] *vi* : avancer en roue libre
coast[2] *n* : côte *f*, littoral *m*
coastal ['ko:stəl] *adj* : côtier, littoral
coaster ['ko:stər] *n* : dessous-de-verre *m*, sous-verre *m Can*
coast guard *n* : gendarmerie *f* maritime *France*, garde *f* côtière *Can*
coastline ['ko:stˌlaɪn] *n* : littoral *m*
coat[1] ['ko:t] *vt* : couvrir (d'une couche), enduire
coat[2] *n* **1** : manteau *m* (vêtement) **2** FUR : fourrure *f*, pelage *m*, poil *m* **3** LAYER : couche *f* <a coat of paint : une couche de peinture>
coat hanger → **hanger**
coating ['ko:tɪŋ] *n* : couche *f*, revêtement *m*
coat of arms *n* : blason *m*, armoiries *fpl*
coatrack ['ko:tˌræk] *n* : portemanteau *m*
coax ['ko:ks] *vt* : amadouer, cajoler, enjoler
cob ['kɑb] → **corncob**
cobalt ['ko:ˌbɔlt] *n* : cobalt *m*
cobble ['kɑbəl] *vt* **-bled; -bling** *or* **to cobble together** : concocter (à la hâte), bricoler
cobbled ['kɑbəld] *adj* : pavé
cobbler ['kɑblər] *n* **1** SHOEMAKER : cordonnier *m*, -nière *f* **2** *or* **fruit cobbler** : tarte *f* aux fruits
cobblestone ['kɑbəlˌsto:n] *n* : pavé *m*
cobra ['ko:brə] *n* : cobra *m*
cobweb ['kɑbˌwɛb] *n* : toile *f* d'araignée
cocaine [ko'keɪn, 'ko:ˌkeɪn] *n* : cocaïne *f*
cock[1] ['kɑk] *vt* **1** : armer (un fusil) **2** TILT : pencher (la tête, etc.) **3 to cock one's ears** : dresser les oreilles
cock[2] *n* **1** ROOSTER : coq *m* **2** FAUCET : robinet *m* **3** : chien *m* (de fusil)
cockatoo ['kɑkəˌtu:] *n, pl* **-toos** : cacatoès *m*
cockeyed ['kɑkˌaɪd] *adj* **1** ASKEW : de travers **2** ABSURD : absurde, insensé
cockiness ['kɑkɪnəs] *n* : impertinence *f*, impudence *f*
cockle ['kɑkəl] *n* : coque *f*
cockpit ['kɑkˌpɪt] *n* : cockpit *m*, poste *m* de pilotage
cockroach ['kɑkˌro:tʃ] *n* : cafard *m*, blatte *f France*, coquerelle *f Can*
cocktail ['kɑkˌteɪl] *n* : cocktail *m*
cocky ['kɑki] *adj* **cockier; -est** : impudent, suffisant
cocoa ['ko:ˌko:] *n* : cacao *m*
coconut ['ko:kəˌnʌt] *n* : noix *f* de coco
coconut palm *n* : cocotier *m*
cocoon [kə'ku:n] *n* : cocon *m*
cod ['kɑd] *ns & pl* : morue *f*
coddle ['kɑdəl] *vt* **-dled; -dling** : dorloter
code ['ko:d] *n* **1** CIPHER : code *m*, chiffre *m* **2** RULES : code *m*, règlement *m* <penal code : code pénal>
codeine ['ko:ˌdi:n] *n* : codéine *f*
codger ['kɑdʒər] *n* : vieux bonhomme *m*, vieillard *m*

codicil ['kɑdəsəl, -ˌsɪl] *n* : codicille *m*
codify ['kɑdəˌfaɪ, 'koː-] *vt* **-fied; -fying** : codifier
coeducation [ˌkoːˌɛdʒə'keɪʃən] *n* : éducation *f* mixte
coeducational [ˌkoːˌɛdʒə'keɪʃənəl] *adj* : mixte
coefficient [ˌkoːə'fɪʃənt] *n* : coefficient *m*
coerce [ko'ərs] *vt* **-erced; -ercing** : obliger, contraindre
coercion [ko'ərʒən, -ʃən] *n* : contrainte *f*, coercition *f*
coercive [ko'ərsɪv] *adj* : coercitif
coexist [ˌkoːɪg'zɪst] *vi* : coexister
coexistence [ˌkoːɪg'zɪstəntˢ] *n* : coexistence *f*
coffee ['kɔfi] *n* : café *m*
coffeepot ['kɔfiˌpɑt] *n* : cafetière *f*
coffer ['kɔfər] *n* : coffre *m*, caisse *f*
coffin ['kɔfən] *n* : cercueil *m*, bière *f*
cog ['kɑg] *n* : dent *f* (d'une roue)
cogent ['koːdʒənt] *adj* : convaincant, persuasif
cogitate ['kɑdʒəˌteɪt] *vi* **-tated; -tating** : réfléchir, méditer
cogitation [ˌkɑdʒə'teɪʃən] *n* : réflexion *f*, méditation *f*
cognac ['koːnˌjæk] *n* : cognac *m*
cognate[1] ['kɑgˌneɪt] *adj* : apparenté
cognate[2] *n* : mot *m* apparenté
cognizant ['kɑgnəzənt] *adj* : conscient
cogwheel ['kɑgˌhwiːl] *n* : roue *f* dentée, pignon *m*
cohabit [ˌkoː'hæbət] *vi* : cohabiter
cohere [ko'hɪr] *vi* **-hered; -hering 1** ADHERE : adhérer **2** : être cohérent, être logique
coherence [ko'hɪrənt̬ˢ] *n* : cohérence *f*
coherent [ko'hɪrənt] *adj* : cohérent, logique — **coherently** *adv*
cohesion [ko'hiːʒən] *n* : cohésion *f*
cohort ['koːˌhɔrt] *n* **1** : cohorte *f* (militaire) **2** COMPANION : compagnon *m*, compagne *f*, collègue *mf*
coiffure [kwɑ'fjʊr] *n* : coiffure *f*
coil[1] ['kɔɪl] *vt* : enrouler — *vi* : s'enrouler
coil[2] *n* : rouleau *m*, bobine *f*, boucle *f* (de cheveux), volute *f* (de fumée)
coin[1] ['kɔɪn] *vt* **1** MINT : frapper (de la monnaie) **2** INVENT : forger, inventer (un mot, un terme) <to coin a phrase : comme on dit>
coin[2] *n* : pièce *f* de monnaie
coincide [ˌkoːɪn'saɪd, 'koːɪnˌsaɪd] *vi* **-cided; -ciding** : coïncider
coincidence [ko'ɪnt̬ˢədənt̬ˢ] *n* : coïncidence *f*
coincidental [koˌɪnt̬ˢə'dɛntəl] *adj* : fortuit, de coïncidence
coincidentally [koˌɪnt̬ˢə'dɛntəli] *adv* : par hasard
coitus ['koːətəs] *n* : coït *m*
coke ['koːk] *n* : coke *m* <coke stove : four à coke>
colander ['kɑləndər, 'kʌ-] *n* : passoire *f*
cold[1] ['koːld] *adj* : froid <it's cold out : il fait froid> <my feet are cold : j'ai froid aux pieds> <to be cold toward s.o. : être froid avec qqn> <a cold heart : un cœur de pierre>
cold[2] *n* **1** : froid *m* **2** : rhume *m* (en médecine) <to have a cold : être enrhumé>
cold-blooded ['koːld'blʌdəd] *adj* **1** : à sang froid (se dit des animaux) **2** CRUEL : cruel, sans pitié
coldly ['koːldli] *adv* : avec froideur, froidement
coldness ['koːldnəs] *n* : froideur *f*
coleslaw ['koːlˌslɔ] *n* : salade *f* de chou cru
colic ['kɑlɪk] *n* : coliques *fpl*
coliseum [ˌkɑlə'siːəm] *n* : stade *m*, arène *f*
collaborate [kə'læbəˌreɪt] *vi* **-rated; -rating** : collaborer, coopérer
collaboration [kəˌlæbə'reɪʃən] *n* : collaboration *f*
collaborator [kə'læbəˌreɪtər] *n* : collaborateur *m*, -trice *f*
collapse[1] [kə'læps] *vi* **-lapsed; -lapsing 1** : s'effondrer, s'écrouler **2** FOLD : se plier
collapse[2] *n* : effondrement *m*, écroulement *m*
collapsible [kə'læpsəbəl] *adj* : pliant <collapsible chair : chaise pliante>
collar[1] ['kɑlər] *vt* : saisir au collet, arrêter (un criminel)
collar[2] *n* : col *m*
collarbone ['kɑlərˌboːn] *n* : clavicule *f*
collate [kə'leɪt; 'kɑˌleɪt; 'koː-] *vt* **-lated; -lating 1** COMPARE : comparer **2** ASSEMBLE : collationner (les feuilles d'un livre)
collateral[1] [kə'læt̬ˢərəl] *adj* **1** SECONDARY : secondaire, subsidiaire **2** PARALLEL : parallèle, concomitant
collateral[2] *n* : nantissement *m*
colleague ['kɑˌliːg] *n* : confrère *m*, consœur *f*, collègue *mf*
collect[1] [kə'lɛkt] *vt* **1** GATHER : ramasser, recueillir **2** : percevoir, encaisser (une somme d'argent) **3** : collectionner (des objets) — *vi* **1** CONGREGATE : se regrouper, se rejoindre **2** ACCUMULATE : s'accumuler
collect[2] *adv* **to call collect** : téléphoner en PCV *France*, téléphoner à frais virés *Can*
collection [kə'lɛkʃən] *n* **1** COLLECTING : ramassage *m* (d'objets), recouvrement *m* (de dettes, etc.), rassemblement *m* (d'information), accumulation *f* (de richesses) **2** : collection *f* <book collection : collection de livres>
collective[1] [kə'lɛktɪv] *adj* : collectif
collective[2] *n* : coopérative *f*, entreprise *f* collective
college ['kɑlɪdʒ] *n* **1** : établissement *m* d'enseignement supérieur **2** GROUP

: association *f* (de professionels, etc.), collège *m* (électoral)
collegiate [kə'li:dʒət] *adj* : universitaire
collide [kə'laɪd] *vi* **-lided; -liding** : se heurter, entrer en collision
collie ['kɑli] *n* : colley *m*
collision [kə'lɪʒən] *n* : collision *f*
colloquial [kə'lo:kwiəl] *adj* : familier
colloquialism [kə'lo:kwiə,lɪzəm] *n* : expression *f* familière
collusion [kə'lu:ʒən] *n* : collusion *f*
cologne [kə'lo:n] *n* : eau *f* de Cologne
Colombian[1] [kə'lʌmbiən] *adj* : colombien
Colombian[2] *n* : Colombien *m*, -bienne *f*
colon[1] ['ko:lən] *n, pl* **colons** *or* **cola** [-lə] : côlon *m* (en anatomie)
colon[2] *n, pl* **colons** : deux-points *m* (signe orthographique)
colonel ['kərnəl] *n* : colonel *m*
colonial[1] [kə'lo:niəl] *adj* : colonial
colonial[2] *n* : colonial *m*, -niale *f*
colonist ['kɑlənɪst] *n* : colon *m*
colonization [,kɑlənə'zeɪʃən] *n* : colonisation *f*
colonize ['kɑlə,naɪz] *vt* **-nized; -nizing** : établir une colonie en, coloniser
colonnade [,kɑlə'neɪd] *n* : colonnade *f*
colony ['kɑlənɪ] *n, pl* **-nies** : colonie *f*
color[1] *or Brit* **colour** ['kʌlər] *vt* **1** : colorer **2** INFLUENCE : influer sur, influencer — *vi* BLUSH : rougir
color[2] *or Brit* **colour** *n* **1** : couleur *f* <bright colors : couleurs vives> **2** INTEREST, VIVIDNESS : couleur *f* <local color : couleur locale> **3 colors** *npl* FLAG : couleurs *fpl*
color-blind *or Brit* **colour-blind** ['kʌlər,blaɪnd] *adj* : daltonien
colored *or Brit* **coloured** ['kʌlərd] *adj* **1** : coloré **2** : de couleur (se dit des personnes)
colorfast *or Brit* **colourfast** ['kʌlər,fæst] *adj* : grand teint, bon teint
colorful *or Brit* **colourful** ['kʌlərfəl] *adj* **1** : coloré **2** PICTURESQUE, STRIKING : pittoresque, frappant, original
colorless *or Brit* **colourless** ['kʌlərləs] *adj* **1** : incolore **2** DULL : terne, fade
colossal [kə'lɑsəl] *adj* : colossal
colossus [kə'lɑsəs] *n, pl* **-si** [-,saɪ] : colosse *m*
colour *Brit* → **color**
colt ['ko:lt] *n* : poulain *m*
column ['kɑləm] *n* **1** : colonne *f* (en architecture) **2** : colonne *f* (en imprimerie), rubrique *f* (dans la presse), chronique *f* (dans un journal)
columnist ['kɑləmnɪst, -ləmɪst] *n* : chroniqueur *m*, -queuse *f*
coma ['ko:mə] *n* : coma *m*
comatose ['ko:mə,to:s, 'kɑ-] *adj* : comateux, dans le coma
comb[1] ['ko:m] *vt* **1** : peigner <to comb one's hair : se peigner> **2** *or* **to comb out** : démêler (les cheveux) **3** SEARCH : ratisser, passer (un lieu) au peigne fin
comb[2] *n* **1** : peigne *m* **2** : crête *f* (d'un coq)
combat[1] [kəm'bæt, 'kɑm,bæt] *vt* **-bated** *or* **-batted; -bating** *or* **-batting** : combattre, lutter contre
combat[2] ['kɑm,bæt] *n* : combat *m*
combatant [kəm'bætənt] *n* : combattant *m*, -tante *f*
combative [kəm'bæṭɪv] *adj* : combatif, belliqueux
combination [,kɑmbə'neɪʃən] *n* : combinaison *f*
combine[1] [kəm'baɪn] *v* **-bined; -bining** *vt* : combiner, joindre, unir — *vi* : se combiner, s'associer, s'unir
combine[2] ['kɑm,baɪn] *n* **1** ASSOCIATION : association *f*, cartel *m* (en finances) **2** HARVESTER : moissonneuse-batteuse *f*
combustible [kəm'bʌstəbəl] *adj* : combustible, inflammable
combustion [kəm'bʌstʃən] *n* : combustion *f*
come ['kʌm] *vi* **came; come; coming 1** APPROACH : venir, s'approcher <come here! : viens ici!> <he came running : il est venu en courant> **2** ARRIVE : arriver <they came last night : ils sont arrivés hier soir> **3** ORIGINATE : venir, provenir <this cheese comes from Provence : ce fromage provient de Provence> **4** AMOUNT : monter, s'élever <the charge comes to $200 : les frais s'élèvent à $200> **5 to come clean** : décharger sa conscience **6 to come into** GAIN : acquérir, gagner <to come into a fortune : hériter d'une fortune> **7 to come off** SUCCEED : réussir **8 to come out** : paraître, sortir (se dit d'une publication, d'un produit commercial, etc.) **9 to come to** REVIVE : revenir à soi, reprendre conscience **10 to come to pass** HAPPEN : arriver, se produire <how come? : comment ça se fait?> **11 to come to terms** : parvenir à une entente
comeback ['kʌm,bæk] *n* **1** RETORT : réplique *f* **2** RETURN : retour *f*, rentrée *f* <to make a comeback : faire une rentrée>
come back *vi* **1** RETORT : répliquer, rétorquer **2** RETURN : revenir <I came back with him : je suis revenu avec lui> <this hairdo is coming back : cette coiffure revient à la mode>
comedian [kə'mi:diən] *n* : comédien *m*, -dienne *f*; comique *mf*
comedienne [kə,mi:di'en] *n* : comédienne *f*
comedy ['kɑmədi] *n, pl* **-dies** : comédie *f*
comely ['kʌmli] *adj* **comelier; -est** : beau, gracieux
comet ['kɑmət] *n* : comète *f*

comfort[1] [ˈkʌmpfərt] *vt* **1** CONSOLE : console **2** CHEER : encourager, réconforter

comfort[2] *n* **1** SOLACE : consolation *f* **2** WELL-BEING : confort *m*, bien-être *m* **3** CONVENIENCE : commodité *f*, confort *m* <the comforts of home : le confort du foyer>

comfortable [ˈkʌmpfərtəbəl, ˈkʌmpftə-] *adj* : confortable, agréable — **comfortably** *adv*

comforter [ˈkʌmpfərtər] *n* **1** : consolateur *m*, -trice *f* **2** QUILT : édredon *m*, douillette *f Can*

comic[1] [ˈkɑmɪk] *adj* **1** : comique, qui appartient à la comédie **2** COMICAL : drôle, amusant

comic[2] *n* **1** COMEDIAN : comédien *m*, -dienne *f*; comique *mf* *2 or* **comic book** : magazine *m* de bandes dessinées

comical [ˈkɑmɪkəl] *adj* : drôle, amusant

comic strip *n* : bande *f* dessinée

coming [ˈkʌmɪŋ] *adj* : suivante <during the coming week : pendant la semaine suivante>

comma [ˈkɑmə] *n* : virgule *f*

command[1] [kəˈmænd] *vt* **1** ORDER : ordonner, mandater **2** CONTROL : diriger, commander **3** DEMAND : demander, exiger <he commands a high price : il exige un prix élevé> — *vi* **1** ORDER : donner des ordres **2** GOVERN : diriger, gouverner

command[2] *n* **1** ORDER : ordre *m*, commande *f* (en informatique) **2** : commandement *m* (dans les forces armées) **3** MASTERY : maîtrise *f*

commandant [ˈkɑmənˌdɑnt, -ˌdænt] *n* : commandant *m*

commandeer [ˌkɑmənˈdɪr] *vt* : réquisitionner

commander [kəˈmændər] *n* : commandant *m*

commandment [kəˈmændmənt] *n* : commandement *m* <the Ten Commandments : les dix commandements>

commemorate [kəˈmɛməˌreɪt] *vt* **-rated; -rating** : commémorer

commemoration [kəˌmɛməˈreɪʃən] *n* : commémoration *f*

commemorative [kəˈmɛmrətɪv, -ˈmɛməˌreɪtɪv] *adj* : commémoratif

commence [kəˈmɛnts] *v* **-menced; -mencing** *vt* : commencer <to commence working : commencer à travailler> — *vi* : commencer

commencement [kəˈmɛntsmənt] *n* **1** BEGINNING : commencement *m*, début *m* **2** : remise *f* des diplômes

commend [kəˈmɛnd] *vt* **1** ENTRUST : confier **2** RECOMMEND : recommander, préconiser **3** PRAISE : louer

commendable [kəˈmɛndəbəl] *adj* : louable

commendation [ˌkɑmənˈdeɪʃən] *n* : louange *f*, éloge *m*

commensurate [kəˈmɛnʃərət, -ˈmɛntʃərət] *adj* **to be commensurate with** : être proportionné à

comment[1] [ˈkɑˌmɛnt] *vi* : faire des commentaires, faire une remarque

comment[2] *n* : commentaire *m*, remarque *f*

commentary [ˈkɑmənˌtɛri] *n, pl* **-taries** : commentaire *m*

commentator [ˈkɑmənˌteɪtər] *n* : commentateur *m*, -trice *f*

commerce [ˈkɑmərs] *n* : commerce *m*

commercial[1] [kəˈmərʃəl] *adj* : commercial

commercial[2] *n* : annonce *f* publicitaire

commercialize [kəˈmərʃəˌlaɪz] *vt* **-ized; -izing** : commercialiser

commiserate [kəˈmɪzəˌreɪt] *vi* **-ated; -ating** : éprouver de la sympathie, compatir

commiseration [kəˌmɪzəˈreɪʃən] *n* : commisération *f*

commission[1] [kəˈmɪʃən] *vt* **1** APPOINT : nommer (un officier) **2** : commander <to commission a portrait : commander un portrait>

commission[2] *n* **1** : brevet *m* (militaire) **2** COMMITTEE : commission *f*, comité *m* **3** COMMITTING : perpétration *f*, commission *f* **4** FEE, PERCENTAGE : commission *f*

commissioned officer *n* : officier *m*

commissioner [kəˈmɪʃənər] *n* : commissaire *m*

commit [kəˈmɪt] *vt* **committed; committing 1** ENTRUST : confier **2** CONFINE : interner (dans un hôpital) **3** PERPETRATE : commettre <to commit a crime : commettre un crime> **4 to commit oneself** : s'engager

commitment [kəˈmɪtmənt] *n* **1** ENGAGEMENT, PROMISE : engagement *m* **2** OBLIGATION : obligation *f*, responsabilité *f*

committee [kəˈmɪti] *n* : comité *m*

commodious [kəˈmoːdiəs] *adj* : spacieux, ample, vaste

commodity [kəˈmɑdəti] *n, pl* **-ties** : produit *m*, denrée *f* (alimentaire), marchandise *f*

commodore [ˈkɑməˌdɔr] *n* : commodore *m*

common[1] [ˈkɑmən] *adj* **1** PUBLIC : commun, public <for the common good : pour le bien commun> **2** GENERAL : universel, général, public <it's common knowledge : c'est de notoriété publique> **3** ORDINARY : commun, ordinaire <the common man : l'homme du peuple> **4** SHARED : commun, semblable <common tastes : goûts semblables>

common[2] *n* **1** : terre *f* commune **2 in common** : en commun

common cold *n* : rhume *m*

common denominator *n* : dénominateur *m* commun

commoner ['kɑmənər] *n* : roturier *m*, -rière *f*
commonly ['kɑmənli] *adv* : communément, généralement
commonplace[1] ['kɑmən,pleɪs] *adj* : commun, banal, ordinaire
commonplace[2] *n* : lieu *m* commun, banalité *f*
common sense *n* : bon sens *m*, sens *m* commun
commonwealth ['kɑmən,wɛlθ] *n* : corps *m* politique <the British Commonwealth : le Commonwealth>
commotion [kə'mo:ʃən] *n* **1** AGITATION : agitation *f*, émoi *m* **2** RUCKUS, TUMULT : vacarme *m*, brouhaha *m*
communal [kə'mju:nəl] *adj* : communautaire
commune[1] [kə'mju:n] *vi* **-muned; -muning** : communier <to commune with nature : communier avec la nature>
commune[2] ['kɑ,mju:n, kə'mju:n] *n* : communauté *f*
communicable [kə'mju:nɪkəbəl] *adj* CONTAGIOUS : contagieux, transmissible
communicate [kə'mju:nə,keɪt] *v* **-cated; -cating** *vt* **1** CONVEY : communiquer, transmettre **2** TRANSMIT : transmettre (une maladie) — *vi* : communiquer
communication [kə,mju:nə'keɪʃən] *n* : communication *f*
communicative [kə'mju:nɪ,keɪṭɪv, -kəṭɪv] *adj* : communicatif
communion [kə'mju:njən] *n* **1** SHARING : communion *f* **2 Communion** : Communion *f*
communiqué [kə'mju:nə,keɪ, -,mju:nə'keɪ] *n* : communiqué *m*
communism *or* **Communism** ['kɑmjə-,nɪzəm] *n* : communisme *m*
communist[1] *or* **Communist** ['kɑmjə-,nɪst] *adj* : communiste
communist[2] *or* **Communist** *n* : communiste *mf*
communistic *or* **Communistic** *adj* : communiste
community [kə'mju:nəṭi] *n, pl* **-ties** : communauté *f*
commute[1] [kə'mju:t] *v* **-muted; -muting** *vt* REDUCE : commuer (une peine) — *vi* : faire la navette, faire un trajet journalier (à son travail)
commute[2] *n* : trajet *m* journalier
compact[1] [kəm'pækt, 'kɑm,pækt] *vt* PACK : comprimer, tasser
compact[2] [kəm'pækt, 'kɑm,pækt] *adj* **1** DENSE, SOLID : compact, dense **2** CONCISE : concis, bref
compact[3] ['kɑm,pækt] *n* **1** AGREEMENT : entente *f*, accord *m* **2** *or* **powder compact** : poudrier *m* **3** *or* **compact car** : voiture *f* compacte
compact disc ['kɑm,pækt'dɪsk] *n* : disque *m* compact, compact *m*
companion [kəm'pænjən] *n* **1** FRIEND : compagnon *m*, compagne *f* **2** COUNTERPART : pendant *m*
companionable [kəm'pænjənəbəl] *adj* : sociable
companionship [kəm'pænjən,ʃɪp] *n* : compagnie *f*
company ['kʌmpəni] *n, pl* **-nies 1** FIRM : compagnie *f*, société *f* **2** GROUP : compagnie *f* (militaire), troupe *f* (de théâtre) **3** VISITORS : invités *mpl*
comparable ['kɑmpərəbəl] *adj* : comparable
comparative[1] [kəm'pærəṭɪv] *adj* : comparatif — **comparatively** *adv*
comparative[2] *n* : comparatif *m*
compare [kəm'pær] *v* **-pared; -paring** *vt* : comparer — *vi* : être comparable
comparison [kəm'pærəsən] *n* : comparaison *f*
compartment [kəm'pɑrtmənt] *n* : compartiment *m*
compass ['kʌmpəs, 'kɑm-] *n* **1** : boussole *f* <the points of the compass : les points cardinaux> **2** : compas *m* (en géométrie) **3** RANGE, SCOPE : étendue *f*, portée *f*
compassion [kəm'pæʃən] *n* : compassion *f*, sympathie *f*
compassionate [kəm'pæʃənət] *adj* : compatissant
compatibility [kəm,pæṭə'bɪləṭi] *n* : compatibilité *f*
compatible [kəm'pæṭəbəl] *adj* : compatible
compatriot [kəm'peɪtriət, -'pæ-] *n* : compatriote *mf*
compel [kəm'pɛl] *vt* **-pelled; -pelling** : contraindre, obliger
compelling [kəm'pɛlɪŋ] *adj* : irrésistible, convaincant
compendium [kəm'pɛndiəm] *n, pl* **-diums** *or* **-dia** [-diə] : abrégé *m*
compensate ['kɑmpən,seɪt] *v* **-sated; -sating** *vt* : compenser, indemniser — *vi* **to compensate for** : compenser
compensation [,kɑmpən'seɪʃən] *n* : compensation *f*, indemnisation *f*
compensatory [kəm'pɛnsə,tori] *adj* : compensatoire
compete [kəm'pi:t] *vi* **-peted; -peting** : faire concurrence, rivaliser
competence ['kɑmpəṭənṭs] *n* : compétence *f*, capacité *f*, aptitude *f*
competency ['kɑmpəṭənṭsi] *n, pl* **-cies** → **competence**
competent ['kɑmpəṭənt] *adj* : compétent, qualifié, capable
competition [,kɑmpə'tɪʃən] *n* : compétition *f*, concurrence *f*
competitive [kəm'peṭəṭɪv] *adj* : compétitif, concurrentiel
competitiveness [kəm'peṭəṭɪvnəs] *n* : compétitivité *f*
competitor [kəm'peṭəṭər] *n* : concurrent *m*, -rente *f*
compilation ['kɑmpɪ'leɪʃən] *n* : compilation *f*

compile [kəm'paɪl] *vt* **-piled; -piling** : compiler, dresser (une liste, etc.)
compiler [kəm'paɪlər] *n* : compilateur *m*, -trice *f*
complacency [kəm'pleɪsənt͡si] *n, pl* **-cies** : satisfaction *f* de soi, suffisance *f*
complacent [kəm'pleɪsənt] *adj* : satisfait de soi, suffisant
complain [kəm'pleɪn] *vi* **1** GRIPE, GRUMBLE : se plaindre **2** PROTEST : faire une réclamation, se plaindre
complaint [kəm'pleɪnt] *n* **1** GRIPE : plainte *f* **2** AILMENT : maladie *f*, affection *f* **3** ACCUSATION, PROTEST : réclamation *f* <to lodge a complaint : se plaindre>
complement[1] ['kɑmpləˌmɛnt] *vt* : compléter
complement[2] ['kɑmpləmənt] *n* **1** : complément *m* (en mathématiques, en grammaire, etc.) **2** QUOTA : effectif *m* (complet)
complementary [ˌkɑmplə'mɛntəri] *adj* : complémentaire
complete[1] [kəm'pliːt] *vt* **-pleted; -pleting 1** FINISH : terminer, achever **2** : compléter <this piece completes the puzzle : cette pièce complète le puzzle>
complete[2] *adj* **-pleter; -est 1** WHOLE : complet, intégral <a complete set : un jeu complet> **2** FINISHED : terminé, achevé **3** THOROUGH : complet, total, absolu
completely [kəm'pliːtli] *adv* : complètement, totalement
completion [kəm'pliːʃən] *n* : achèvement *m*
complex[1] [kɑm'plɛks, kəm-; 'kɑmˌplɛks] *adj* INTRICATE : complexe
complex[2] ['kɑmˌplɛks] *n* **1** : complexe *m* (psychologique) **2** GROUP : complexe *m*, ensemble *m* <housing complex : complexe résidentiel
complexion [kəm'plɛkʃən] *n* : teint *m* <a fair complexion : un teint clair>
complexity [kəm'plɛksəṭi, kɑm-] *n, pl* **-ties** : complexité *f*
compliance [kəm'plaɪənt͡s] *n* **1** : conformité *f* **2 in compliance with** : conformément à
compliant [kəm'plaɪənt] *n* : docile, accommodant
complicate ['kɑmpləˌkeɪt] *vt* **-cated; -cating** : compliquer
complicated ['kɑmpləˌkeɪṭəd] *adj* : compliqué, complexe
complication [ˌkɑmplə'keɪʃən] *n* : complication *f*, difficulté *f*
complicity [kəm'plɪsəṭi] *n, pl* **-ties** : complicité *f*
compliment[1] ['kɑmpləˌmɛnt] *vt* : complimenter
compliment[2] ['kɑmpləmənt] *n* **1** : compliment *m* **2 compliments** *npl* : compliments *mpl*, respects *mpl* <to pay one's compliments to s.o. : faire ses compliments à qqn>
complimentary [ˌkɑmplə'mɛntəri] *adj* **1** FLATTERING : flatteur **2** FREE : gratuit, (à titre) gracieux <complimentary ticket : billet de faveur>
comply [kəm'plaɪ] *vi* **-plied; -plying 1** : se soumettre, obéir **2 to comply with** : respecter, observer
component[1] [kəm'poːnənt, 'kɑmˌpoː-] *adj* : composant, constituant
component[2] *n* : composant *m*, composante *f* (en mathématiques), pièce *f*
compose [kəm'poːz] *vt* **-posed; -posing 1** FORM : former, composer **2** : composer (un texte, une chanson, etc.) **3 to compose oneself** : retrouver son calme
composer [kəm'poːzər] *n* : compositeur *m*, -trice *f*
composite[1] [kɑm'pɑzət, kəm-; 'kɑmpəzət] *adj* : composite
composite[2] *n* : composite *m*
composition [ˌkɑmpə'zɪʃən] *n* **1** CREATION : composition *f*, création *f* **2** WORK : œuvre *m*, composition *f*, dissertation *f* (à l'école)
compost ['kɑmˌpoːst] *n* : compost *m*
composure [kəm'poːʒər] *n* : calme *m*, sang-froid *m*, sérénité *f*
compound[1] [kɑm'paʊnd, kəm-; 'kɑmˌpaʊnd] *vt* **1** COMBINE : combiner, mélanger **2** AUGMENT : augmenter, aggraver <to compound a problem : aggraver un problème>
compound[2] ['kɑmˌpaʊnd; kɑm'paʊnd, kəm-] *adj* : composé <compound interest : intérêt composé>
compound[3] ['kɑmˌpaʊnd] *n* **1** *or* **compound word** : mot *m* composé **2** ENCLOSURE : enceinte *f*, enclos *m* **3** : composé *m* (en chimie)
comprehend [ˌkɑmpri'hɛnd] *vt* **1** UNDERSTAND : comprendre, saisir **2** INCLUDE : comprendre, comporter
comprehensible [ˌkɑmpri'hɛnt͡sɪbəl] *adj* : compréhensible, clair
comprehension [ˌkɑmpri'hɛnt͡ʃən] *n* : compréhension *f*
comprehensive [ˌkɑmpri'hɛnt͡sɪv] *adj* : compréhensif, complet, détaillé
compress[1] [kəm'prɛs] *vt* : comprimer
compress[2] ['kɑmˌprɛs] *n* : compresse *f*
compression [kəm'prɛʃən] *n* : compression *f*
comprise [kəm'praɪz] *vt* **-prised; -prising 1** INCLUDE : comprendre, inclure, consister en **2** MAKE UP : constituer, composer <girls comprise half of the students : les filles constituent une moitié des étudiants>
compromise[1] ['kɑmprəˌmaɪz] *v* **-mised; -mising** *vi* : faire un compromis — *vt* JEOPARDIZE : compromettre, mettre en péril
compromise[2] *n* : compromis *m*
comptroller [kən'troːlər, 'kɑmpˌtroː-] *n* : contrôleur *m*, -leuse *f* (de finances)

compulsion [kəm'pʌlʃən] *n* **1** COERCION : coercition *f*, contrainte *f* **2** IMPULSE : compulsion *f* (en psychologie)
compulsive [kəm'pʌlsɪv] *adj* : compulsif
compulsory [kəm'pʌlsəri] *adj* : obligatoire
compunction [kəm'pʌŋkʃən] *n* **1** QUALM : scruple *m* **2** REMORSE : remords *m*
computation [kɑmpjʊ'teɪʃən] *n* : calcul *m*
compute [kəm'pju:t] *vt* **-puted; -puting** : calculer
computer [kəm'pju:ṭər] *n* : ordinateur *m*
computerize [kəm'pju:ṭəˌraɪz] *vt* **-ized; -izing** : informatiser, mettre sur ordinateur
comrade ['kɑmˌræd] *n* : camarade *mf*, compagnon *m*, compagne *f*
comradeship ['kɑmræd,ʃɪp] *n* : camaraderie *f*
con[1] ['kɑn] *vt* **conned; conning** SWINDLE : duper, escroquer
con[2] *adv* : contre
con[3] *n* **1** DISADVANTAGE : désavantage *m*, inconvénient *m* <the pros and cons : le pour et le contre> **2** SWINDLE : escroquerie *f*
concave [kɑn'keɪv, 'kɑnˌkeɪv] *adj* : concave
conceal [kən'si:l] *vt* : dissimuler, cacher
concealment [kən'si:lmənt] *n* : dissimulation *f*
concede [kən'si:d] *v* **-ceded; -ceding** *vt* GRANT : accorder, concéder — *vi* YIELD : céder
conceit [kən'si:t] *n* : suffisance *f*, vanité *f*
conceited [kən'si:təd] *adj* : suffisant, vaniteux
conceive [kən'si:v] *v* **-ceived; -ceiving** *vt* **1** : concevoir (un enfant) **2** IMAGINE : imaginer, concevoir — *vi* **1** : devenir enceinte **2 to conceive of** : concevoir
concentrate[1] ['kɑnṭsənˌtreɪt] *v* **-trated; -trating** *vt* : concentrer — *vi* : se concentrer
concentrate[2] *n* : concentré *m* <orange juice concentrate : concentré du jus d'orange>
concentration [ˌkɑnṭsən'treɪʃən] *n* : concentration *f*
concentric [kən'sentrɪk] *adj* : concentrique
concept ['kɑnˌsɛpt] *n* : concept *m*
conception [kən'sɛpʃən] *n* **1** : conception *f* (en médecine) **2** IDEA : idée *f*, concept *m*
concern[1] [kən'sərn] *vt* **1** AFFECT : concerner, intéresser **2** INVOLVE : concerner <as far as I'm concerned : en ce qui me concerne> **3** : traiter de, parler de <the novel concerns the war : le roman traite de la guerre> **4** WORRY : inquiéter <that concerns me very much : ça m'inquiète beaucoup>
concern[2] *n* **1** AFFAIR : affaire *f* <it's not my concern : ce n'est pas de mes affaires> **2** WORRY : inquiétude *f* **3** BUSINESS : firme *f*, société *f* <a banking concern : une firme bancaire>
concerned [kən'sərnd] *adj* **1** ANXIOUS : préoccupé, inquiet **2** INTERESTED : intéressé **3** IMPLICATED : impliqué
concerning [kən'sərnɪŋ] *prep* REGARDING : concernant, touchant
concert ['kɑnˌsərt] *n* **1** : concert *m*, récital *m* (musical) **2** AGREEMENT, UNISON : concert *m* <to work in concert : travailler de concert>
concerted [kən'sərṭəd] *adj* : concerté
concertina [ˌkɑnṭsər'ti:nə] *n* : concertina *m*
concerto [kən'tʃɛrṭo:] *n, pl* **-ti** [-ṭi, -ṭi:] *or* **-tos** : concerto *m* <piano concerto : concerto pour piano>
concession [kən'seʃən] *n* : concession *f*
conch ['kɑŋk, 'kɑntʃ] *n, pl* **conchs** ['kɑŋks] *or* **conches** ['kɑntʃəz] : conque *f*
conciliatory [kən'sɪliəˌtori] *adj* : conciliateur, conciliant
concise [kən'saɪs] *adj* : concis, bref, succinct
concisely [kən'saɪsli] *adv* : avec concision
conciseness [kən'saɪsnəs] *n* : concision *f*
conclave ['kɑnˌkleɪv] *n* : conclave *m*
conclude [kən'klu:d] *v* **-cluded; -cluding** *vt* **1** END : terminer, conclure **2** DECIDE : décider **3** INFER : inférer, déduire — *vi* END : s'achever, se terminer
conclusion [kən'klu:ʒən] *n* : conclusion *f*
conclusive [kən'klu:sɪv] *adj* : concluant, définitif
conclusively [kən'klu:sɪvli] *adv* : définitivement, de façon concluant
concoct [kən'kɑkt, kɑn-] *vt* **1** PREPARE : préparer, confectionner **2** DEVISE : fabriquer, concocter (une excuse, etc.)
concoction [kən'kɑkʃən] *n* **1** PREPARATION : élaboration *f* **2** MIXTURE : mélange *m*
concord ['kɑnˌkɔrd, 'kɑŋ-] *n* : concorde *f*, harmonie *f*
concordance [kən'kɔrdənṭs] *n* **1** AGREEMENT : accord *m* **2** INDEX : concordance *f*, index *f*
concourse ['kɔnˌkɔrs] *n* **1** GATHERING : rassemblement *m*, assemblée *f* **2** HALL : hall *m*, lieu *m* de rassemblement
concrete[1] [kɑn'kri:t, 'kɑnˌkri:t] *adj* **1** REAL : concret, réel **2** : de béton <concrete walls : murs de béton>
concrete[2] ['kɑnˌkri:t, kɑn'kri:t] *n* : béton *m*
concur [kən'kər] *vi* **-curred, -curring 1** AGREE : être d'accord **2** TALLY : coïncider, concorder
concurrent [kən'kərənt] *adj* : simultané, concomitant

concussion [kən'kʌʃən] *n* : commotion *f* cérébrale
condemn [kən'dɛm] *vt* **1** CENSURE : condamner, censurer **2** CONVICT : condamner <condemned to death : condamné à mort> **3** : déclarer inhabitable (se dit d'un bâtiment)
condemnation [ˌkɑnˌdɛm'neɪʃən] *n* : condamnation *f*
condensation [ˌkɑnˌdɛn'seɪʃən] *n* : condensation *f*
condense [kən'dɛnts] *vt* **-densed; -densing 1** COMPRESS : condenser, comprimer **2** ABRIDGE : abréger, condenser
condescend [ˌkɑndɪ'sɛnd] *vt* **1 to condescend to do** : daigner faire, condescendre à faire **2 to condescend to s.o.** : être condescendant envers qqn
condescension [ˌkɑndɪ'sɛnʃən] *n* : condescendance *f*
condiment ['kɑndəmənt] *n* : condiment *m*
condition[1] [kən'dɪʃən] *vt* **1** TRAIN : conditionner **2** : mettre en forme (le corps, etc.), traiter (les cheveux)
condition[2] *n* **1** STIPULATION : condition *f*, stipulation *f* <on the condition that : à condition que> **2** STATE : état *m*, condition *f* **3 conditions** *npl* : circonstances *fpl*, conditions *fpl* <living conditions : conditions de vie>
conditional [kən'dɪʃənəl] *adj* : conditionnel — **conditionally** *adv*
condolence [kən'do:lənts] *n* : condoléance *f*
condom ['kɑndəm] *n* : condom *m*, préservatif *m*
condominium [ˌkɑndə'mɪniəm] *n, pl* **-ums** : condominium *m*
condone [kən'do:n] *vt* **-doned; -doning** : fermer les yeux sur, pardonner
condor ['kɑndər, -ˌdɔr] *n* : condor *m*
conducive [kən'du:sɪv, -'dju:-] *adj* : favorable
conduct[1] [kən'dʌkt] *vt* **1** GUIDE : conduire, guider <a conducted tour : une visite guidée> **2** DIRECT : diriger (un orchestre) **3** CARRY ON : mener, conduire <to conduct an investigation : conduire une enquête> **4** TRANSMIT : conduire (l'électricité, etc.) **5 to conduct oneself** : se comporter
conduct[2] ['kɑnˌdʌkt] *n* **1** BEHAVIOR : comportement *m*, conduite *f* **2** MANAGEMENT : conduite *f* (des affaires, etc.)
conduction [kən'dʌkʃən] *n* : conduction *f*
conductivity [ˌkɑnˌdʌk'tɪvəṭi] *n, pl* **-ties** : conductivité *f*
conductor [kən'dʌktər] *n* **1** : conducteur *m* (d'électricité) **2** : chef *m* d'orchestre **3** : contrôleur *m* (de train)
conduit ['kɑnˌdu:ət, -dju:-] *n* : conduit *m*, tuyau *m*
cone ['ko:n] *n* **1** : cône *m* (fruit du pin) **2** : cône *m* (en géométrie) **3** *or* **ice-cream cone** : cornet *m* (de crème glacée)
confection [kən'fɛkʃən] *n* : confiserie *f*, friandise *f*, bonbon *m*
confectioner [kən'fɛkʃənər] *n* : confiseur *m*, -seuse *f*
confederacy [kən'fɛdərəsi] *n, pl* **-cies** : confédération *f*
confederate[1] [kən'fɛdəˌreɪt] *v* **-ated; -ating** *vt* : confédérer — *vi* : se confédérer
confederate[2] [kən'fɛdə,rət] *adj* : confédéré
confederate[3] *n* : allié *m*, -liée *f*; complice *mf*
confederation [kənˌfɛdə'reɪʃən] *n* : confédération *f*
confer [kən'fɛr] *v* **-ferred; -ferring** *vt* BESTOW : conférer, accorder — *vi* CONSULT : conférer, parler
conference ['kɑnfrənts, -fərənts] *n* : conférence *f*
confess [kən'fɛs] *vt* : confesser, avouer — *vi* **1** : avouer, faire des aveux <the prisoner confessed : le prisonnier a fait des aveux> **2** : se confesser (en religion)
confession [kən'fɛʃən] *n* : confession *f*
confessional [kən'fɛʃənəl] *n* : confessionnal *m*
confetti [kən'fɛṭi] *n* : confettis *mpl*
confidant ['kɑnfəˌdɑnt, -ˌdænt] *n* : confident *m*
confidante ['kɑnfəˌdɑnt, -ˌdænt] *n* : confidente *f*
confide [kən'faɪd] *v* **-fided; -fiding** *vt* ENTRUST : confier — *vi* : se confier <to confide in s.o. : se confier à qqn>
confidence ['kɑnfədənts] *n* **1** TRUST : confiance *f* **2** SELF-CONFIDENCE : confiance *f*, assurance *f* **3** SECRET : confidence *f*
confident ['kɑnfədənt] *adj* **1** TRUSTFUL : confiant, ouvert **2** SELF-CONFIDENT : confiant, sûr de soi
confidential [ˌkɑnfə'dɛnʃəl] *adj* : confidentiel — **confidentially** *adv*
configuration [kənˌfɪgjə'reɪʃən] *n* : configuration *f*
configure [kən'fɪgjər] *vt* : configurer
confine [kən'faɪn] *vt* **-fined; -fining 1** LIMIT : confiner, limiter **2** IMPRISON : emprisonner, enfermer
confines ['kɑnˌfaɪnz] *npl* BOUNDS : confins *mpl*, limites *fpl*
confirm [kən'fərm] *vt* **1** : confirmer, fortifier <to confirm one's faith : confirmer sa foi> **2** RATIFY : approuver, sanctionner **3** VERIFY : démontrer, corroborer **4** : confirmer (en religion)
confirmation [ˌkɑnfər'meɪʃən] *n* : confirmation *f*
confiscate ['kɑnfəˌskeɪt] *vt* **-cated; -cating** : confisquer
confiscation [ˌkɑnfə'skeɪʃən] *n* : confiscation *f*

conflagration [ˌkɑnfləˈgreɪʃən] *n* : conflagration *f*, incendie *f*
conflict[1] [kənˈflɪkt] *vi* : être en conflit, s'opposer
conflict[2] [ˈkɑnˌflɪkt] *n* : conflit *m*
conform [kənˈfɔrm] *vi* **to conform with** : se conformer à, être conforme à
conformity [kənˈfɔrmət̬i] *n, pl* **-ties** : conformité *f*
confound [kənˈfaʊnd, kɑn-] *vt* : confondre, déconcerter
confront [kənˈfrʌnt] *vt* : confronter, affronter, faire face à
confrontation [ˌkɑnfrənˈteɪʃən] *n* : confrontation *f*
confuse [kənˈfjuːz] *vt* **-fused; -fusing 1** PERPLEX : confondre, déconcerter **2** JUMBLE : embrouiller, brouiller
confusing [kənˈfjuːzɪŋ] *adj* : déroutant, embrouillé, mêlant *Can*
confusion [kənˈfjuːʒən] *n* **1** PERPLEXITY : confusion *f*, embarras *m* **2** MESS, TURMOIL : désordre *m*, confusion *f*
congeal [kənˈdʒiːl] *vt* **1** FREEZE : congeler **2** COAGULATE : figer, coaguler — *vi* : se figer, se coaguler
congenial [kənˈdʒiːniəl] *adj* : agréable, sympathique
congenital [kənˈdʒɛnət̬əl] *adj* : congénital
congest [kənˈdʒɛst] *vt* **1** : congestionner (en médecine) **2** CLOG, OBSTRUCT : embouteiller, encombrer
congestion [kənˈdʒɛstʃən] *n* : congestion *f*
conglomerate[1] [kənˈglɑmərət] *adj* : conglomeré
conglomerate[2] *n* : conglomérat *m*
conglomeration [kənˌglɑməˈreɪʃən] *n* : conglomérat *m*, agglomération *f*
Congolese[1] [ˌkɑŋgəˈliːz, -ˈliːs] *adj* : congolais
Congolese[2] *n* : Congolais *m*, -laise *f*
congratulate [kənˈgrædʒəˌleɪt, -ˈgrætʃə-] *vt* **-lated; -lating** : féliciter
congratulations [kənˌgrædʒəˈleɪʃənz, -ˌgrætʃə-] *npl* : félicitations *fpl*
congregate [ˈkɑŋgrəˌgeɪt] *v* **-gated; -gating** *vt* ASSEMBLE : rassembler, réunir — *vi* GATHER : se réunir
congregation [ˌkɑŋgrəˈgeɪʃən] *n* **1** GATHERING : assemblée *f*, rassemblement *m* **2** CHURCHGOERS : assemblée *f* des fidèles
congress [ˈkɑŋgrəs] *n* : congrès *m*
congressional [kənˈgreʃənəl, kɑn-] *adj* : d'un congrès
congressman [ˈkɑŋgrəsmən] *n, pl* **-men** [-mən, -men] : membre *m* du Congrès
congresswoman [ˈkɑŋgrəsˌwʊmən] *n, pl* **-women** [-ˌwɪmən] : membre *m* du Congrès
congruent [kənˈgruːənt, ˈkɑŋgruənt] *adj* : congru <congruent triangles : triangles congrus>
conic [ˈkɑnɪk] → **conical**
conical [ˈkɑnɪkəl] *adj* : conique
conifer [ˈkɑnəfər, ˈkoː-] *n* : conifère *m*
coniferous [koːˈnɪfərəs, kə-] *adj* : conifère
conjecture[1] [kənˈdʒɛktʃər] *vt* : conjecturer, présumer
conjecture[2] *n* : conjecture *f*, supposition *f*
conjugal [ˈkɑndʒɪgəl, kənˈdʒuː-] *adj* : conjugal
conjugate [ˈkɑndʒəˌgeɪt] *vt* **-gated; -gating** : conjuguer
conjugation [ˌkɑndʒəˈgeɪʃən] *n* : conjugaison *f*
conjunction [kənˈdʒʌŋkʃən] *n* **1** UNION : conjonction *f*, union *f* **2** : conjonction *f* (en astronomie, en grammaire) **3 in conjunction with** : conjointement avec
conjure [ˈkɑndʒər, ˈkʌn-] *v* **-jured; -juring** *vt* **1** ENTREAT : implorer, supplier **2 to conjure up** : invoquer (des esprits), évoquer (une image) — *vi* : faire des tours de magie
connect [kəˈnɛkt] *vt* **1** JOIN, LINK : joindre, relier **2** ASSOCIATE : associer, lier — *vi* : assurer la correspondance (se dit des trains, des avions, etc.)
connection [kəˈnɛkʃən] *n* **1** LINK : lien *m*, rapport *m* **2** RELATIONSHIP : lien *m*, relation *f* <business connections : relations d'affaires> **3** : correspondance *f* <train connection : correspondance de train>
connective [kəˈnɛktɪv] *adj* : conjonctif <connective tissue : tissu conjonctif>
connivance [kəˈnaɪvənt̬s] *n* : connivence *f*, complicité *f*
connive [kəˈnaɪv] *vi* **-nived; -niving** : être de connivence
connoisseur [ˌkɑnəˈsər] *n* : connaisseur *m*, -seuse *f*
connotation [ˌkɑnəˈteɪʃən] *n* : connotation *f*
connote [kəˈnoːt] *vt* **-noted; -noting 1** CONVEY : évoquer **2** IMPLY : indiquer
conquer [ˈkɑŋkər] *vt* : conquérir, vaincre
conqueror [ˈkɑŋkərər] *n* : conquérant *m*, -rante *f*
conquest [ˈkɑnˌkwɛst, ˈkɑŋ-] *n* : conquête *f*
conscience [ˈkɑnt̬ʃənt̬s] *n* : conscience *f* <to have a clear conscience : avoir la conscience tranquille>
conscientious [ˌkɑnt̬ʃiˈɛnt̬əs] *adj* : consciencieux — **conscientiously** *adv*
conscious [ˈkɑnt̬əs] *adj* **1** AWARE : conscient <to become conscious of : prendre conscience de> **2** ALERT, AWAKE : conscient, lucide **3** INTENTIONAL : délibéré, intentionnel
consciously [ˈkɑnt̬əsli] *adv* : consciemment
consciousness [ˈkɑnt̬ʃəsnəs] *n* **1** AWARENESS : conscience *f* **2** : connaissance *f* <to lose consciousness : perdre connaissance>
conscription [kənˈskrɪpʃən] *n* : conscription *f*

consecrate ['kɑnʦəˌkreɪt] *vt* **-crated; -crating** : consacrer
consecration [ˌkɑnʦə'kreɪʃən] *n* : consécration *f*
consecutive [kən'sɛkjʊɪv] *adj* : consécutif — **consecutively** *adv*
consensus [kən'sɛnʦəs] *n* : consensus *m*
consent¹ [kən'sɛnt] *vi* : consentir
consent² *n* : consentement *m*, accord *m*
consequence ['kɑnʦəˌkwɛnʦ, -kwənʦ] *n* **1** RESULT : conséquence *f*, effet *m*, suite *f* **2** IMPORTANCE : importance *f*, conséquence *f* <a person of consequence : une personne importante>
consequential [ˌkɑnʦə'kwɛnʃəl] *adj* : important, conséquent
consequently ['kɑnʦəkwəntli, -ˌkwɛnt-] *adv* : par conséquent
conservation [ˌkɑnʦər'veɪʃən] *n* : conservation *f*, préservation *f*
conservatism [kən'sərvəˌtɪzəm] *n* : conservatisme *m*
conservative¹ [kən'sərvəṭɪv] *adj* **1** : conservateur **2** CAUTIOUS : prudent, modéré <a conservative estimate : une estimation prudente>
conservative² *n* : conservateur *m*, -trice *f*
conservatory [kən'sərvəˌtori] *n, pl* **-ries** : conservatoire *m*
conserve¹ [kən'sərv] *vt* **-served; -serving** : conserver, préserver
conserve² *n* PRESERVE : confiture *f*
consider [kən'sɪdər] *vt* **1** STUDY, WEIGH : considérer, étudier **2** REGARD : tenir compte de <he doesn't consider my feelings : il ne tient pas compte de mes sentiments> **3** BELIEVE : croire, penser, considérer <he considers this essential : il considère que c'est essentiel>
considerable [kən'sɪdərəbəl] *adj* : considérable — **considerably** *adv*
considerate [kən'sɪdərət] *adj* THOUGHTFUL : attentionné, prévenant
consideration [kənˌsɪdə'reɪʃən] *n* **1** DELIBERATION : considération *f*, réflexion *f* **2** THOUGHTFULNESS : attention *f*, considération *f* **3** PAYMENT : rémunération *f*, paiement *m*
considering [kən'sɪdərɪŋ] *prep* : étant donné, vu <considering the circumstances, it's better to stay here : vu les circonstances, il vaut mieux rester ici>
consign [kən'saɪn] *vt* **1** ENTRUST : confier **2** SEND : expédier, envoyer (des marchandises)
consignment [kən'saɪnmənt] *n* : expédition *f*, envoi *m*
consist [kən'sɪst] *vi* **1** LIE, RESIDE : consister <charity consists in good deeds : la charité consiste à faire de bonnes actions> **2 to consist of** : se composer de, consister en
consistency [kən'sɪstənʦi] *n, pl* **-cies 1** TEXTURE : consistance *f* **2** UNIFORMITY : cohérence *f*, uniformité *f*
consistent [kən'sɪstənt] *adj* **1** REGULAR, STEADY : constant, régulier <consistent behavior : comportement constant> **2 consistent with** : selon <consistent with our records : selon nos dossiers>
consistently [kən'sɪstəntli] *adv* : constamment, régulièrement
consolation [ˌkɑnʦə'leɪʃən] *n* : consolation *f*
console¹ [kən'soːl] *vt* **-soled; -soling** : consoler, réconforter
console² ['kɑnˌsoːl] *n* : console *f*
consolidate [kən'sɑləˌdeɪt] *vt* **-dated; -dating** : consolider
consolidation [kənˌsɑlə'deɪʃən] *n* : consolidation *f*
consommé [ˌkɑnʦə'meɪ] *n* : consommé *m*
consonant ['kɑnʦənənt] *n* : consonne *f*
consort¹ [kən'sɔrt] *vi* **to consort with** : fréquenter
consort² ['kɑnˌsɔrt] *n* : époux *m*, épouse *f* (d'un roi ou d'une reine)
conspicuous [kən'spɪkjʊəs] *adj* **1** OBVIOUS : évident, visible **2** STRIKING : remarquable, voyant
conspicuously [kən'spɪkjʊəsli] *adv* **1** NOTICEABLY : bien en évidence **2** STRIKINGLY : de façon voyante, remarquablement
conspiracy [kən'spɪrəsi] *n, pl* **-cies** : conspiration *f*, complot *m*
conspirator [kən'spɪrəṭər] *n* : conspirateur *m*, -trice *f*
conspire [kən'spaɪr] *vi* **-spired; -spiring** : conspirer, comploter — **conspiratorial** [kənˌspɪrə'toriel] *adj*
constable ['kɑnʦtəbəl] *n* : gendarme *m*, agent *m* de police
constancy ['kɑnʦtənʦi] *n, pl* **-cies 1** STEADFASTNESS : constance *f* **2** LOYALTY : fidélité *f*, loyauté *f*
constant¹ ['kɑnʦtənt] *adj* **1** STEADFAST : constant **2** UNCHANGING : constant, régulier **3** CONTINUAL : continuel, constant
constant² *n* : constante *f*
constantly ['kɑnʦtəntli] *adv* : constamment, continuellement
constellation [ˌkɑnʦtə'leɪʃən] *n* : constellation *f*
consternation [ˌkɑnʦtər'neɪʃən] *n* : consternation *f*
constipate ['kɑnʦtəˌpeɪt] *vt* **-pated; -pating** : constiper
constipation [ˌkɑnʦtə'peɪʃən] *n* : constipation *f*
constituent¹ [kən'stɪtʃʊənt] *adj* **1** COMPONENT : composant, constituant **2** : constituant, constitutif <constituent assembly : assemblée constituante>

constituent[2] *n* **1** ELEMENT : élément *m* constitutif, composant *m* **2** VOTER : électeur *m* , -trice *f*

constitute [ˈkɑnɪstəˌtuːt, -tjuːt] *vt* **-tuted; -tuting 1** ESTABLISH : constituer, créer **2** FORM : composer, former

constitution [ˌkɑnɪstəˈtuːʃən, -ˈtjuː-] *n* **1** COMPOSITION : constitution *f*, composition *f* **2** : constitution *f* (d'un pays)

constitutional[1] [ˌkɑnɪstəˈtuːʃənəl, -ˈtjuː-] *adj* : constitutionnel

constitutional[2] *n* WALK : promenade *f*, petit tour *m*

constrain [kənˈstreɪn] *vt* **1** COMPEL, FORCE : contraindre, obliger **2** CONFINE : restreindre, limiter

constraint [kənˈstreɪnt] *n* : contrainte *f*

constrict [kənˈstrɪkt] *vt* : resserrer, serrer

constriction [kənˈstrɪkʃən] *n* : constriction *f*, resserrement *m*

construct [kənˈstrʌkt] *vt* : construire, bâtir

construction [kənˈstrʌkʃən] *n* : construction *f*

constructive [kənˈstrʌktɪv] *adj* : constructif

construe [kənˈstruː] *vt* **-strued; -struing** : interpréter, expliquer

consul [ˈkɑnsəl] *n* : consul *m* — **consular** [ˈkɑnsələr] *adj*

consulate [ˈkɑnsələt] *n* : consulat *m*

consult [kənˈsʌlt] *vt* : consulter — *vi* : se consulter <to consult with : entrer en consultation avec>

consultant [kənˈsʌltənt] *n* : consultant *m*, -tante *f*

consultation [ˌkɑnsəlˈteɪʃən] *n* : consultation *f*

consume [kənˈsuːm] *vt* **-sumed; -suming 1** DESTROY : détruire <consumed by fire : détruit par le feu> **2** USE UP : utiliser, consommer **3** INGEST : consommer (de la nourriture ou de la boisson)

consumer [kənˈsuːmər] *n* : consommateur *m*, -trice *f*

consummate[1] [ˈkɑnsəˌmeɪt] *vt* **-mated; -mating** : consommer (un mariage, etc.)

consummate[2] [kənˈsʌmət, ˈkɑnsəmət] *adj* : consommé, accompli, parfait <a consummate liar : un menteur accompli>

consummation [ˌkɑnsəˈmeɪʃən] *n* : consommation *f*

consumption [kənˈsʌmpʃən] *n* **1** : consommation *f* <oil consumption : consommation d'huile> **2** TUBERCULOSIS : tuberculose *f*

contact[1] [ˈkɑnˌtækt, kənˈ-] *vt* : contacter, se mettre en contact avec

contact[2] [ˈkɑnˌtækt] *n* **1** TOUCHING : contact *m* **2** CONNECTION : contact *m* <business contacts : contacts professionnels> **3** COMMUNICATION : contact *m*, communication *f* <to be in contact with : être en rapport avec>

contact lens [ˈkɑnˌtæktˈlenz] *n* : verre *m* de contact, lentille *f* de contact

contagion [kənˈteɪdʒən] *n* : contagion *f*

contagious [kənˈteɪdʒəs] *adj* : contagieux

contain [kənˈteɪn] *vt* **1** HOLD : contenir, renfermer **2** INCLUDE : contenir, inclure **3** RESTRAIN : contenir, maîtriser <to contain oneself : se contenir>

container [kənˈteɪnər] *n* : récipient *m*, conteneur *m* (de transport)

contaminate [kənˈtæməˌneɪt] *vt* **-nated; -nating** : contaminer

contamination [kənˌtæməˈneɪʃən] *n* : contamination *f*

contemplate [ˈkɑntəmˌpleɪt] *vt* **-plated; -plating 1** VIEW : contempler **2** PONDER : réfléchir sur **3** CONSIDER, PLAN : envisager, considérer

contemplation [ˌkɑntəmˈpleɪʃən] *n* : contemplation *f*, réflexion *f*

contemplative [kənˈtemplətɪv, ˈkɑntəmˌpleɪtɪv] *adj* : contemplatif

contemporaneous [kənˌtempəˈreɪniəs] *adj* → **contemporary**[1]

contemporary[1] [kənˈtempəˌreri] *adj* : contemporain, moderne

contemporary[2] *n* : contemporain *m*, -raine *f*

contempt [kənˈtempt] *n* **1** SCORN : mépris, dédain **2** *or* **contempt of court** : outrage *m* à magistrat *France*, outrage *m* au tribunal *Can*

contemptible [kənˈtemptəbəl] *adj* DESPICABLE : méprisable

contemptuous [kənˈtemptʃuəs] *adj* : méprisant — **contemptuously** *adv*

contend [kənˈtend] *vt* ARGUE, MAINTAIN : soutenir, maintenir — *vi* **1** COMPETE : rivaliser <to contend for first prize : rivaliser pour le premier prix> **2 to contend with** : affronter, faire face à <problems to contend with : problèmes à affronter>

contender [kənˈtendər] *n* : concurrent *m*, -rente *f* (aux sports); candidat *m*, -date *f* (en politique)

content[1] [kənˈtent] *vt* : contenter, satisfaire

content[2] *adj* : content, satisfait

content[3] *n* → **contentment**

content[4] [ˈkɑnˌtent] *n* **1** GIST : contenu *m*, signification *f* **2** : teneur *f* <high fiber content : haute teneur en fibres> **3 contents** *npl* : contenu *m* **4 table of contents** : table *f* des matières

contented [kənˈtentəd] *adj* : satisfait, content

contention [kənˈtenʃən] *n* **1** ARGUMENT : dispute *f*, discussion *f* **2** RIVALRY : compétition *f*, rivalité *f* **3** OPINION : assertion *f*, affirmation *f*

contentious [kənˈtenʃəs] *adj* **1** : litigieux **2** BELLIGERENT : belliqueux, combatif — **contentiously** *adv*

contentment [kən'tentmənt] *n* : contentement *m*, satisfaction *f*

contest[1] [kən'test] *vt* : contester, disputer

contest[2] ['kɑn,test] *n* **1** STRUGGLE : lutte *f* **2** GAME : concours *m*, compétition *f*

contestant [kən'testənt] *n* : concurrent *m*, -rente *f*; adversaire *mf*

context ['kɑn,tekst] *n* : contexte *m*

contiguous [kən'tɪgjʊəs] *adj* : contigu

continence ['kɑntənənʦ] *n* : continence *f*

continent[1] ['kɑntənənt] *adj* : continent

continent[2] *n* : continent *m* — **continental** [,kɑntən'entəl] *adj*

contingency [kən'tɪndʒənʦi] *n, pl* **-cies** : éventualité *f*, contingence *f*

contingent[1] [kən'tɪndʒənt] *adj* **1** : contingent **2 to be contingent on** : dépendre de

contingent[2] *n* : contingent *m*

continual [kə'tɪnjʊəl] *adj* : continuel — **continually** [-'tɪnjʊəli, -'tɪnjəli] *adv*

continuance [kə'tɪnjʊənʦ] *n* **1** CONTINUATION : continuation *f* **2** DURATION : durée *f* **3** : ajournement *m* (d'un procès)

continuation [kən,tɪnjʊ'eɪʃən] *n* : continuation *f*

continue [kən'tɪnju:] *v* **-tinued; -tinuing** *vt* **1** KEEP UP : continuer <to continue writing : continuer à écrire> **2** RESUME : continuer, reprendre **3** EXTEND : continuer, prolonger — *vi* **1** CARRY ON : continuer **2** LAST : durer, se perpétuer <his good luck seems to continue : sa bonne fortune semble durer>

continuity [,kɑntən'u:ət̬i, -'ju:-] *n, pl* **-ties** : continuité *f*

continuous [kən'tɪnjʊəs] *adj* : continu

continuously [kən'tɪnjʊəsli] *adv* : continuellement, constamment

contort [kən'tɔrt] *vt* : tordre

contortion [kən'tɔrʃən] *n* : contorsion *f*

contour ['kɑn,tʊr] *n* **1** OUTLINE : contour *m* **2 contours** *npl* SHAPE : contours *fpl*, forme *f*

contraband ['kɑntrə,bænd] *n* : contrebande *f*

contraception [,kɑntrə'sɛpʃən] *n* : contraception *f*

contraceptive[1] [,kɑntrə'sɛptɪv] *adj* : contraceptif

contraceptive[2] *n* : contraceptif *m*

contract[1] [kən'trækt, *vt and vi usu* 'kɑn,trækt] *vt* **1** INCUR : contracter (des dettes, etc.) **2** ARRANGE : contracter (un mariage, etc.) **3** CATCH : contracter, attraper (un virus) **4** TIGHTEN : contracter (un muscle) **5** SHORTEN : contracter (un mot) — *vi* : se contracter

contract[2] ['kɑn,trækt] *n* AGREEMENT : contrat *m*

contraction [kən'trækʃən] *n* : contraction *f*

contractor ['kɑn,trækt̬ər, kən'trækt̬-] *n* : entrepreneur *m*, -neuse *f*; contracteur *m*, -teuse *f Can*

contractual [kən'trækt̬ʃʊəl] *adj* : contractuel — **contractually** *adv*

contradict [,kɑntrə'dɪkt] *vt* : contredire

contradiction [,kɑntrə'dɪkʃən] *n* : contradiction *f*

contradictory [,kɑntrə'dɪkt̬əri] *adj* : contradictoire

contralto [kən'trælˌto:] *n, pl* **-tos** : contralto *m* (voix), contralto *mf* (chanteur)

contraption [kən'træpʃən] *n* : truc *m fam*, machin *m fam*

contrary[1] ['kɑn,treri *often* kən'treri] *adj* **1** OPPOSITE : contraire **2** CONFLICTING : contradictoire <contrary evidence : preuves contradictoires> **3** BALKY, STUBBORN : têtu, opiniâtre **4 contrary to** : contrairement à

contrary[2] *n, pl* **-traries** : contraire *m* <on the contrary : au contraire>

contrast[1] [kən'træst] *vt* : mettre en contraste — *vi* : contraster

contrast[2] *n* : contraste *m*

contribute [kən'trɪbjət] *v* **-uted; -uting** *vi* : contribuer — *vt* GIVE, SUPPLY : donner, apporter

contribution [,kɑntrə'bju:ʃən] *n* : contribution *f*

contrite ['kɑn,traɪt, kən'traɪt] *adj* : contrit, pénitent

contrition [kən'trɪʃən] *n* : contrition *f*, pénitence *f*

contrivance [kən'traɪvənʦ] *n* **1** DEVICE : appareil *m*, dispositif *m* **2** SCHEME : machination *f*, manigance *f*

contrive [kən'traɪv] *v* **-trived; -triving** *vt* DEVISE : concevoir, inventer — *vi* **to contrive to** : parvenir à, réussir à, trouver le moyen de <she contrived to extricate herself from the situation : elle a trouvé le moyen de s'en sortir>

control[1] [kən'tro:l] *vt* **-trolled; -trolling** **1** REGULATE : contrôler **2** RULE : diriger, dominer **3** RESTRAIN : maîtriser (des émotions, etc.)

control[2] *n* **1** AUTHORITY : contrôle *m*, autorité *f* **2** RESTRAINT : maîtrise *f* **3** REGULATION : régulation *f*, contrôle *m* <price control : régulation des prix> **4** DEVICE : bouton *m*, commande *f* <remote control : commande à distance>

controller [kən'tro:lər, 'kɑn,-] *n* : contrôleur *m*, -leuse *f* <air traffic controller : contrôleur du trafic aérien>

controversial [,kɑntrə'vərʃəl, -siəl] *adj* : controversé, contesté

controversy ['kɑntrə,vərsi] *n, pl* **-sies** : controverse *f*

contusion [kən'tu:ʒən, -tju:-] *n* : contusion *f*, ecchymose *f*

conundrum [kəˈnʌndrəm] *n* : énigme *f*
convalesce [ˌkɑnvəˈlɛs] *vi* **-lesced; -lescing** : se remettre, être en convalescence
convalescence [ˌkɑnvəˈlɛsənʦ] *n* : convalescence *f*
convalescent[1] [ˌkɑnvəˈlɛsənt] *adj* : convalescent
convalescent[2] *n* : convalescent *m*, -cente *f*
convection [kənˈvɛkʃən] *n* : convection *f*
convene [kənˈviːn] *v* **-vened; -vening** *vt* : convoquer — *vi* MEET : se réunir, s'assembler
convenience [kənˈviːnjənʦ] *n* **1** AMENITY : commodité *f*, confort *m* <modern conveniences : commodités modernes> **2 at your convenience** : quand cela vous conviendra **3 at your earliest convenience** : dans les meilleurs délais, dès que cela vous sera possible
convenient [kənˈviːnjənt] *adj* : commode, qui convient
conveniently [kənˈviːnjəntli] *adv* : commodément
convent [ˈkɑnvənt, -ˌvɛnt] *n* : couvent *m*
convention [kənˈvɛnʧən] *n* **1** AGREEMENT : convention *f* **2** ASSEMBLY, MEETING : conférence *f*, congrès *m* **3** CUSTOM : convention *f*, usage *m*
conventional [kənˈvɛnʧənəl] *adj* : conventionnel — **conventionally** *adv*
converge [kənˈvərdʒ] *vi* **-verged; -verging** : converger
conversant [kənˈvərsənt] *adj* **to be conversant with** : connaître, être versé dans
conversation [ˌkɑnvərˈseɪʃən] *n* : conversation *f*
conversational [ˌkɑnvərˈseɪʃənəl] *adj* : familier <conversational style : style familier>
converse[1] [kənˈvɛrs] *vi* **-versed; -versing** : converser
converse[2] [kənˈvərs, ˈkɑnˌvɛrs] *adj* : contraire, inverse (en mathématiques, etc.)
conversely [kənˈvərsli, ˈkɑnˌvɛrs-] *adv* : inversement
conversion [kənˈvərʒən] *n* **1** : conversion *f* (en religion) **2** CHANGE : transformation *f*, changement *m*
convert[1] [kənˈvərt] *vt* **1** : convertir (en religion) **2** CHANGE : transformer, changer — *vi* : se convertir
convert[2] [ˈkɑnˌvərt] *n* : converti *m*, -tie *f*
converter *or* **convertor** [kənˈvərʧər] *n* : convertisseur *m*
convertible[1] [kənˈvərʧəbəl] *adj* : convertible
convertible[2] *n* : décapotable *f* (voiture)
convex [kɑnˈvɛks, ˈkɑnˌ-, kən-] *adj* : convexe
convey [kənˈveɪ] *vt* **-veyed; -veying 1** TRANSPORT : transporter **2** COMMUNICATE, TRANSMIT : transmettre, exprimer, communiquer
conveyance [kənˈveɪənʦ] *n* **1** TRANSPORT : transport *m* **2** COMMUNICATION : transmission *f*, communication *f*
convict[1] [kənˈvɪkt] *vt* : déclarer coupable, condamner
convict[2] [ˈkɑnˌvɪkt] *n* : détenu *m*, -nue *f*
conviction [kənˈvɪkʃən] *n* **1** : condamnation *f* (en droit) **2** BELIEF : conviction *f*, certitude *f* <personal convictions : convictions personnelles>
convince [kənˈvɪnʦ] *vt* **-vinced; -vincing** : convaincre, persuader
convincing [kənˈvɪnʦɪŋ] *adj* : convaincant, persuasif
convivial [kənˈvɪvjəl, -ˈvɪviəl] *adj* : convivial, jovial
conviviality [kənˌvɪviˈæləʧi] *n, pl* **-ties** : convivialité *f*, gaieté *f*
convocation [ˌkɑnvəˈkeɪʃən] *n* : convocation *f*
convoke [kənˈvoːk] *vt* **-voked; -voking** : convoquer
convoluted [ˈkɑnvəˌluːʧəd] *adj* **1** TWISTED : convoluté **2** INTRICATE : alambiqué, compliqué <convoluted reasoning : raisonnement alambiqué>
convoy [ˈkɑnˌvɔɪ] *n* : convoi *m*
convulse [kənˈvʌls] *v* **-vulsed; -vulsing** *vt* : convulser <convulsed with pain : convulsé par la douleur> <to be convulsed with laughter : se tordre de rire> — *vi* : se convulser, souffrir de convulsions
convulsion [kənˈvʌlʃən] *n* : convulsion *f*
convulsive [kənˈvʌlʃɪv] *adj* : convulsif
coo[1] [ˈkuː] *vi* : roucouler
coo[2] *n* : roucoulement *m*
cook[1] [ˈkʊk] *vi* **1** : cuire (se dit des aliments) **2**: cuisiner, faire la cuisine (se dit d'une personne) — *vt* **1** : cuisiner, cuire **2** *or* **to cook up** CONCOCT : inventer, mijoter
cook[2] *n* : cuisinier *m*, -nière *f*
cookbook [ˈkʊkˌbʊk] *n* : livre *m* de recettes, livre *m* de cuisine
cookery [ˈkʊkəri] *n, pl* **-eries** : cuisine *f*
cookie *or* **cooky** [ˈkʊki] *n, pl* **-ies** : biscuit *m*, gâteau *m* sec
cool[1] [ˈkuːl] *vt* : refroidir — *vi* **1** *or* **to cool down** : se refroidir **2** : se dissiper <his anger cooled : sa colère s'est dissipée>
cool[2] *adj* **1** : frais <a cool breeze : une brise fraîche> **2** CALM : calme **3** UNFRIENDLY : indifférent, froid
cool[3] *n* **1** COOLNESS : fraîcheur *m* **2** COMPOSURE : calme *m*, sang-froid *m* <to lose one's cool : perdre son sang-froid>
coolant [ˈkuːlənt] *n* : liquide *m* de refroidissement
cooler [ˈkuːlər] *n* : glacière *f*
coolie [ˈkuːli] *n* : coolie *m*

coolly ['kuːli] *adv* : froidement
coolness ['kuːlnəs] *n* **1** : fraîcheur *f* <the coolness of the evening : la fraîcheur du soir> **2** COLDNESS, INDIFFERENCE : froideur *m*, indifférence *f* **3** COMPOSURE : calme *m*, sang-froid *m*
coop[1] ['kuːp, 'kʊp] *vt or* **to coop up** : enfermer <cooped up in his apartment : enfermé dans son appartement>
coop[2] *n* : poulailler *m*
co–op ['koʊˌɑp] → **cooperative**[2]
cooperate [koʊ'ɑpəˌreɪt] *vi* **-ated; -ating** : coopérer, collaborer
cooperation [koʊˌɑpə'reɪʃən] *n* : coopération *f*, collaboration *f*
cooperative[1] [koʊ'ɑpərəˌtɪv] *adj* : coopératif
cooperative[2] *n* : coopérative *f*
co–opt [koʊ'ɑpt] *vt* : coopter
coordinate[1] [koʊ'ɔrdənˌeɪt] *v* **-nated; -nating** *vt* : coordonner — *vi* : agir en coordination
coordinate[2] [koʊ'ɔrdənət] *adj* : coordonné <coordinate clause : proposition coordonnée>
coordinate[3] [koʊ'ɔrdənət] *n* : coordonnée *f*
coordination [koʊˌɔrdən'eɪʃən] *n* : coordination *f*
coordinator [koʊ'ɔrdənˌeɪṭər] *n* : coordinateur *m*, -trice *f*
cop ['kɑp] *n* : flic *m fam*
cope ['koːp] *vi* **coped; coping 1** MANAGE : se débrouiller, s'en sortir **2 to cope with** DEAL, FACE : faire face à, affronter <I can't cope with all that : je ne peux pas supporter tout cela>
copier ['kɑpiər] *n* **1** : copieur *m*, -pieuse *f* (personne) **2** PHOTOCOPIER : photocopieur *m*, machine à photocopier
copilot ['koːˌpaɪlət] *n* : copilote *mf*
copious ['koːpiəs] *adj* : copieux, abondant
copiously ['koːpiəsli] *adv* : copieusement, abondamment
copper ['kɑpər] *n* : cuivre *m*
copperhead ['kɑpərˌhɛd] *n* : vipère *f* cuivrée
coppery ['kɑpəri] *adj* : cuivré
coppice ['kɑpəs] *n* THICKET : taillis *m*
copra ['koːprə, 'kɑ-] *n* : copra *m*
copse ['kɑps] → **coppice**
copulate ['kɑpjəˌleɪt] *vi* **-lated; -lating** : copuler
copulation [ˌkɑpjə'leɪʃən] *n* : copulation *f*
copy[1] ['kɑpi] *v* **copied; copying** : copier
copy[2] *n, pl* **copies 1** IMITATION, REPRODUCTION : copie *f*, reproduction *f* **2** : exemplaire *m* (d'un livre, etc.), numéro *m* (d'une revue)
copyright[1] ['kɑpiˌraɪt] *vt* : protéger les droits d'auteur de
copyright[2] *n* : droits *mpl* d'auteur, copyright *m*
coquette [koː'kɛt] *n* : coquette *f*
coral ['kɔrəl] *n* **1** : corail *m* <coral reef : récif de corail> **2** : couleur *f* de corail
coral snake *n* : serpent *m* corail
cord ['kɔrd] *n* **1** ROPE, STRING : corde *f*, cordon *m* **2** : cordon *m* (ombilical) **3** *or* **electrical cord** : fil *m* (électrique) **4** : corde *f* (de bois)
cordial[1] ['kɔrdʒəl] *adj* : cordial, amical — **cordially** *adv*
cordial[2] *n* LIQUEUR : cordial *m*
cordon ['kɔrdən] *n* : cordon *m* (d'agents de police)
corduroy ['kɔrdəˌrɔɪ] *n* **1** : velours *m* côtelé **2 corduroys** *npl* : pantalon *m* en velours côtelé
core[1] ['kɔr] *vt* **cored; coring** : enlever le cœur de (un fruit)
core[2] *n* **1** : cœur *m*, trognon *m* (d'un fruit) **2** CENTER : cœur *m*, noyau *m* <the core of the problem : le cœur du problème> **3 to the core** : jusqu'à l'os <honest to the core : honnête jusqu'à l'os>
cork[1] ['kɔrk] *vt* : boucher (avec un bouchon)
cork[2] *n* **1** : liège *m* **2** : bouchon *m* (d'une bouteille)
corkscrew ['kɔrkˌskruː] *n* : tire-bouchon *m*
cormorant ['kɔrmərənt, -ˌrænt] *n* : cormoran *m*
corn ['kɔrn] *n* **1** GRAIN : grain *m* (de blé, etc.) **2** → **Indian corn 3** : cor *m* (sur le pied)
corncob ['kɔrnˌkɑb] *n* : épi *m* de maïs
cornea ['kɔrniə] *n* : cornée *f*
corned beef *n* : corned-beef *m*
corner[1] ['kɔrnər] *vt* **1** TRAP : acculer (un animal, etc.) **2** MONOPOLIZE : accaparer <to corner the market : accaparer le marché> — *vi* TURN : prendre un virage (se dit d'une voiture)
corner[2] *n* **1** : coin *m*, angle *m*, encoignure *f* <the corner of a room : le coin d'une chambre> **2** INTERSECTION : coin *m*, intersection *f* <to turn the corner : tourner au coin de la rue> <around the corner : à deux pas d'ici> **3** PLACE : coin *m*, endroit *m* <a quiet corner : un endroit tranquille> **4** MONOPOLY : monopole *m*
cornerstone ['kɔrnərˌstoːn] *n* : pierre *f* angulaire
cornet [kɔr'nɛt] *n* : cornet *m* à pistons
cornice ['kɔrnɪs] *n* : corniche *f*
cornmeal ['kɔrnˌmiːl] *n* : farine *f* de maïs
cornstalk ['kɔrnˌstɔk] *n* : tige *f* de maïs
cornstarch ['kɔrnˌstɑrtʃ] *n* : fécule *f* de maïs
cornucopia [ˌkɔrnə'koːpiə, -njə-] *n* : corne *f* d'abondance
corny ['kɔrni] *adj* **cornier; -est** : bateau, banal, quétaine *Can fam* <corny novels : des romans à l'eau de rose>
corolla [kə'rɑlə] *n* : corolle *f*

corollary ['kɔrəˌleri] *n, pl* **-laries** : corollaire *m*
corona ['kəˈroːnə] *n* : couronne *f* (en astronomie)
coronary[1] ['kɔrəˌneri] *adj* : coronaire
coronary[2] *n, pl* **-naries** HEART ATTACK : infarctus *m* myocarde, crise *f* cardiaque
coronation [ˌkɔrəˈneɪʃən] *n* : couronnement *m*
coroner ['kɔrənər] *n* : coroner *m*
corporal[1] ['kɔrpərəl] *adj* : corporel <corporal punishment : châtiment corporel>
corporal[2] *n* : caporal-chef *m*
corporate ['kɔrpərət] *adj* **1** : de la société, d'entreprise **2** COLLECTIVE : collectif, commun
corporation [ˌkɔrpəˈreɪʃən] *n* : compagnie *f* commerciale, société *f*
corporeal [kɔrˈporiəl] *adj* **1** PHYSICAL : physique, corporel **2** MATERIAL : matériel
corps ['kɔr] *ns & pl* **1** : corps *m* (militaire) **2** BODY, GROUP : corps *m* <diplomatic corps : corps diplomatique>
corpse ['kɔrps] *n* : cadavre *m*
corpulence ['kɔrpjələnʦ] *n* : corpulence *f*, embonpoint *m*
corpulent ['kɔrpjələnt] *adj* : corpulent, gras
corpus ['kɔrpəs] *n, pl* **-pora** [-pərə] : recueil *m* (d'œuvres écrits)
corpuscle ['kɔrˌpʌsəl] *n* **1** : corpuscule *m* (en physiologie) **2 red blood corpuscles** : globules *m* rouges
corral[1] [kəˈræl] *vt* **-ralled; -ralling** : enfermer dans un corral (se dit du bétail)
corral[2] *n* : corral *m*
correct[1] [kəˈrɛkt] *vt* **1** RECTIFY : corriger (un texte, etc.), rectifier (une situation, etc.) **2** : corriger (un examen, une erreur), reprendre (à une personne) <to correct s.o.'s French : corriger le français de qqn>
correct[2] *adj* **1** RIGHT : exact, correct, juste <that's correct : c'est exact> **2** APPROPRIATE : correct, convenable
correction [kəˈrɛkʃən] *n* : correction *f*
corrective [kəˈrɛktɪv] *adj* : correctif
correctly [kəˈrɛktli] *adv* : correctement
correlate ['kɔrəˌleɪt] *vt* **-lated; -lating** : mettre en corrélation
correlation [ˌkɔrəˈleɪʃən] *n* : corrélation *f*
correspond [ˌkɔrəˈspɑnd] *vi* **1** MATCH, TALLY : correspondre, concorder **2** WRITE : correspondre, s'écrire
correspondence [ˌkɔrəˈspɑndənʦ] *n* : correspondance *f*
correspondent [ˌkɔrəˈspɑndənt] *n* **1** : correspondant *m*, -dante *f* **2** REPORTER : journaliste *mf;* correspondant *m*, -dante *f*
corridor ['kɔrədər, -ˌdɔr] *n* : corridor *m*, passage *m*, couloir *m*
corroborate [kəˈrɑbəˌreɪt] *vt* **-rated; -rating** : corroborer, confirmer
corroboration [kəˌrɑbəˈreɪʃən] *n* : confirmation *f*, corroboration *f*
corrode [kəˈroːd] *v* **-roded; -roding** *vt* : corroder — *vi* : se corroder
corrosion [kəˈroːʒən] *n* : corrosion *f*
corrosive [kəˈroːsɪv] *adj* : corrosif
corrugated ['kɔrəˌgeɪʧəd] *adj* : ondulé <corrugated cardboard : carton ondulé>
corrupt[1] [kəˈrʌpt] *vt* **1** DEBASE, PERVERT : corrompre, pervertir **2** BRIBE : corrompre, soudoyer **3** ALTER : altérer (un texte)
corrupt[2] *adj* **1** IMMORAL : corrumpu, dépravé **2** ALTERED : altéré
corruption [kəˈrʌpʃən] *n* : corruption *f*
corsage [kɔrˈsɑʒ, -ˈsɑʤ] *n* : petit bouquet *m* de fleurs (porté au corsage d'une robe, etc.)
corset ['kɔrsət] *n* : corset *m*
Corsican[1] ['kɔrsɪkən] *adj* : corse
Corsican[2] *n* : Corse *mf*
cortege [kɔrˈteʒ] *n* : cortège *m*
cortex ['kɔrˌteks] *n, pl* **-tices** ['kɔrʧəˌsiːz] *or* **-texes** : cortex *m*
cortisone ['kɔrʧəˌsoːn, -zoːn] *n* : cortisone *f*
cosmetic[1] [kɑzˈmeʧɪk] *adj* : cosmétique, esthétique <cosmetic surgery : chirurgie esthétique>
cosmetic[2] *n* : cosmétique *f*
cosmic ['kɑzmɪk] *adj* **1** : cosmique <cosmic ray : rayon cosmique> **2** VAST : vaste, gigantesque
cosmonaut ['kɑzməˌnɔt] *n* : cosmonaute *mf*
cosmopolitan [ˌkɑzməˈpɑlətən] *adj* : cosmopolite
cosmos ['kɑzməs, -ˌmoːs, -ˌmɑs] *n* : cosmos *m*, univers *m*
cost[1] ['kɔst] *v* **cost; costing** *vt* : coûter <how much does it cost? : combien ça coûte?> <it cost him his job : ça lui a coûté son emploi> — *vi* : coûter <this one costs less : celui-ci coûte moins cher>
cost[2] *n* **1** PRICE : coût *m*, prix *m* <the cost of living : le coût de la vie> <victory at any cost : la victoire à tout prix> <at cost : à prix coûtant> **2 costs** *npl* : frais *mpl*, dépenses *fpl* <traveling costs : frais de voyage-ment>
Costa Rican[1] [ˌkɔstəˈriːkən] *adj* : costaricain
Costa Rican[2] *n* : Costaricain *m*, -caine *f*
costly ['kɔstli] *adj* **costlier; -est** : coûteux, cher
costume ['kɑsˌtuːm, -ˌtjuːm] *n* **1** : costume *m* <national costume : costume national> <Halloween costume : costume d'Halloween> **2** OUTFIT : costume *m* (d'une femme)
cosy ['koːzi] → **cozy**
cot ['kɑt] *n* : lit *m* de camp

cottage ['kɑtɪʤ] *n* : petite maison *f*, chalet *m Can*
cottage cheese *n* : fromage *m* blanc, fromage *m* cottage
cotton ['kɑtən] *n* : coton *m*
cottonwood ['kɑtən,wʊd] *n* : liard *m Can*
couch[1] ['kaʊtʃ] *vt* : formuler, exprimer <couched in diplomatic language : formulé en langage diplomatique>
couch[2] *n* SOFA : canapé *m*, sofa *m*, divan *m*
cougar ['ku:gər] *n* : puma *m*, couguar *m*
cough[1] ['kɔf] *vi* : tousser
cough[2] *n* : toux *f*
could ['kʊd] → **can**[1]
council ['kaʊnʧəl] *n* : conseil *m*, assemblée *f* <city council : conseil municipal>
councillor *or* **councilor** ['kaʊnʧələr] *n* : conseiller *m*, -lère *f*
counsel[1] ['kaʊnʧəl] *v* **-seled** *or* **-selled; -seling** *or* **-selling** *vt* ADVISE : conseiller, guider — *vi* CONSULT : consulter
counsel[2] *n* **1** ADVICE : conseil *m* **2** CONSULTATION : consultation *f*, délibération *f* **3** LAWYER : avocat *m*, -cate *f*
counselor *or* **counsellor** ['kaʊnʧələr] *n* **1** : conseiller *m*, -lère *f* <guidance counselor : conseiller d'orientation> **2** LAWYER : avocat *m*, -cate *f* **3** *or* **camp counselor** : moniteur *m*, -trice *f*
count[1] ['kaʊnt] *vt* ENUMERATE : dénombrer, compter — *vi* **1** : compter <to count to ten : compter jusqu'à dix> **2** MATTER : compter, importer **3 to count on** : compter sur
count[2] *n* **1** COMPUTATION : compte *m*, décompte *m* **2** CHARGE : chef *m* d'accusation <convicted on two counts : condamné pour deux chefs d'accusation> **3** : comte *m* (noble)
countable ['kaʊntəbəl] *adj* : nombrable, dénombrable
countenance[1] ['kaʊntənənʦ] *vt* **-nanced; -nancing** : approuver, sanctionner
countenance[2] *n* FACE : visage *m*, expression *f*
counter[1] ['kaʊntər] *vt* OPPOSE : s'opposer à, contrecarrer — *vi* RETALIATE : contre-attaquer, riposter
counter[2] *adv* **counter to** : à l'encontre de <to act counter to his advice : agir à l'encontre de ses conseils>
counter[3] *adj* : contraire, opposé
counter[4] *n* **1** PIECE : jeton *m* (d'un jeu de société) **2** : comptoir *m*, guichet *m* <post office counter : guichet de la poste> **3** : compteur *m* (dispositif) <Geiger counter : compteur Geiger>
counteract [,kaʊntər'ækt] *vt* : contrebalancer, neutraliser
counterattack[1] ['kaʊntərə,tæk] *vi* : contre-attaquer
counterattack[2] *n* : contre-attaque *f*
counterbalance[1] [,kaʊntər'bælənʦ] *vt* : contrebalancer, faire contrepoids à
counterbalance[2] *n* : contrepoids *m*
counterclockwise [,kaʊntər'klɑk,waɪz] *adv & adj* : dans le sens contraire des aiguilles d'une montre
counterfeit[1] ['kaʊntər,fɪt] *vt* **1** : contrefaire, falsifier (une monnaie, etc.) **2** FEIGN : feindre (une émotion)
counterfeit[2] *adj* : faux <counterfeit money : fausse monnaie>
counterfeit[3] *n* : contrefaçon *f*, faux *m*
counterfeiter ['kaʊntər,fɪʧər] *n* : faussaire *mf*, faux-monnayeur *m*
countermand ['kaʊntər,mænd] *vt* : annuler (un ordre)
counterpart ['kaʊntər,pɑrt] *n* : homologue *mf* (d'une personne), équivalent *m* (d'une chose)
counterpoint ['kaʊntər,pɔɪnt] *n* : contrepoint *m*
counterrevolution [,kaʊntər,revə'lu:ʃən] *n* : contre-révolution *f*
counterrevolutionary[1] [,kaʊntər,revə'lu:ʃən,eri] *adj* : contre-révolutionnaire
counterrevolutionary[2] *n, pl* **-aries** : contre-révolutionnaire *mf*
countersign ['kaʊntər,saɪn] *vt* : contresigner
countess ['kaʊntɪs] *n* : comtesse *f*
countless ['kaʊntləs] *adj* : innombrable, incalculable
country[1] ['kʌntri] *adj* RURAL : champêtre, rural
country[2] *n, pl* **-tries 1** NATION : pays *m*, patrie *f*, nation *f* <neighboring countries : pays voisins> <love of one's country : amour de la patrie> **2** : campagne *f* <she lives in the country : elle demeure à la campagne>
countryman ['kʌntrimən] *n, pl* **-men** [-mən, -,mɛn] **1** COMPATRIOT : compatriote *mf* **2** RUSTIC : campagnard *m*, -gnarde *f*; habitant *m*, -tante *f* de la campagne
countryside ['kʌntri,saɪd] *n* : campagne *f*
county ['kaʊnti] *n, pl* **-ties** : comté *m*
coup ['ku:] *n, pl* **coups 1** ACT, FEAT : (beau) coup *m* **2** *or* **coup d'état** : coup *m* d'état
coupé [ku:'peɪ] *or* **coupe** ['ku:p] *n* : coupé *m*
couple[1] ['kʌpəl] *v* **-pled; -pling** *vt* : accoupler — *vi* : s'accoupler
couple[2] *n* **1** : couple *m* <a happy couple : un couple heureux> **2 a couple of** : deux <a couple of days ago : il y a deux ou trois jours>
coupling ['kʌplɪŋ] *n* : couplage *m* (en électricité, etc.)
coupon ['ku:,pɑn, 'kju:-] *n* : coupon *m*
courage ['kərɪʤ] *n* : courage *m*
courageous [kə'reɪʤəs] *adj* : courageux — **courageously** *adv*
courier ['kʊriər, 'kərɪər] *n* MESSENGER : messager *m*, -gère *f*

course[1] ['kɔrs] *vi* **coursed; coursing** FLOW : couler, ruisseler <blood was coursing through his veins : le sang coulait dans ses veines>
course[2] *n* **1** PROGRESS : cours *m* <in the course of : au cours de> **2** DIRECTION, PATH : cours *m* (d'un fleuve, etc.), direction *f*, ligne *f* <to change course : changer de direction> <course of action : ligne de conduite> **3** : parcours *m*, terrain *m* (aux sports) <golf course : terrain de golf> **4** : service *m*, plat *m* <seven-course meal : repas de sept services> **5** : cours *m* (universitaire) **6 of course** : évidemment, bien sûr
court[1] ['kɔrt] *vt* : courtiser, faire la cour à
court[2] *n* **1** : cour *f* (d'un souverain) **2** COURTYARD : cour *f* **3** : court *m*, terrain *m* (aux sports) **4** TRIBUNAL : cour *f*, tribunal *m* <to appear in court : comparaître au tribunal>
courteous ['kərtiəs] *adj* : courtois, poli **— courteously** *adv*
courtesan ['kərtəzən, 'kər-] *n* : courtisane *f*
courtesy ['kərtəsi] *n, pl* **-sies** : courtoisie *f*
courthouse ['kɔrtˌhaʊs] *n* : palais *m* de justice
courtier ['kɔrtiər, 'kɔrtjər] *n* : courtisan *m*
courtly ['kɔrtli] *adj* **courtlier; -est** : poli, élégant
court–martial ['kɔrtˌmɑrʃəl] *n, pl* **courts–martial** ['kɔrtsˌmɑrʃəl] : cour *f* martiale
courtroom ['kɔrtˌru:m] *n* : salle *f* d'audience
courtship ['kɔrtˌʃɪp] *n* : cour *f*
courtyard ['kɔrtˌjɑrd] *n* : cour *f*, patio *m*
cousin ['kʌzən] *n* : cousin *m*, -sine *f*
cove ['ko:v] *n* : anse *f*, crique *f*
coven ['kəvən, 'ko:-] *n* : groupe *m* de sorcières
covenant ['kʌvənənt] *n* : contrat *m*, pacte *m*
cover[1] ['kʌvər] *vt* **1** : couvrir, recouvrir **2** PROTECT : couvrir, protéger **3** HIDE : cacher, dissimuler **4** INCLUDE, TREAT : inclure, comprendre **5** : faire un reportage sur <she covered the story : elle a fait un reportage sur l'affaire> **6** INSURE : assurer, couvrir
cover[2] *n* **1** SHELTER : abri *m*, refuge *m* <to take cover : se mettre à l'abri> **2** LID : couvercle *m* **3** : couverture *f* (d'un livre), pochette *f* (d'un disque) **4 → slipcover 5 covers** *npl* BEDCLOTHES : couvertures *fpl*
coverage ['kʌvərɪdʒ] *n* **1** COVERING : couverture *f* **2** REPORTING : reportage *m*, couverture *f* **3** *or* **insurance coverage** : couverture *f* d'assurance
coverlet ['kʌvərlət] *n* BEDSPREAD : couvre-lit *m*
covert[1] ['ko:ˌvərt, 'kʌvərt] *adj* : voilé, secret
covert[2] ['kʌvərt, 'ko:-] *n* THICKET : fourré *m*
cover-up ['kʌvərˌʌp] *n* : opération *f* de camouflage
covet ['kʌvət] *vt* : convoiter
covetous ['kʌvətəs] *adj* : avide, cupide
covey ['kʌvi] *n, pl* **-eys 1** : compagnie *f* (d'oiseaux) **2** GROUP : groupe *m*
cow[1] ['kaʊ] *vt* : intimider, effrayer
cow[2] *n* : vache *f*
coward ['kaʊərd] *n* : lâche *mf;* poltron *m*, -tronne *f*
cowardice ['kaʊərdɪs] *n* : lâcheté *f*
cowardly ['kaʊərdli] *adj* : lâche
cowboy ['kaʊˌbɔɪ] *n* : cow-boy *m*, vacher *m*
cower ['kaʊər] *vi* : se tapir (se dit d'un animal), trembler (de peur)
cowgirl ['kaʊˌgərl] *n* : vachère *f*
cowhide ['kaʊˌhaɪd] *n* : peau *f* de vache
cowl ['kaʊl] *n* : capuchon *m*
cowlick ['kaʊˌlɪk] *n* : mèche *f* rebelle
cowpuncher ['kaʊˌpʌntʃər] **→ cowboy**
cowslip ['kaʊˌslɪp] *n* : primevère *f* sauvage, coucou *m*
coxswain ['kɑksən, -ˌsweɪn] *n* : patron *m* (d'un bateau)
coy ['kɔɪ] *adj* **1** SHY : (faussement) timide **2** COQUETTISH : coquet
coyote [kaɪ'o:ti, 'kaɪˌo:t] *n, pl* **coyotes** *or* **coyote** : coyote *m*
cozen ['kʌzən] *vt* : décevoir
cozy ['ko:zi] *adj* **cozier; -est** : douillet, confortable
crab ['kræb] *n* : crabe *m*
crabby ['kræbi] *adj* **crabbier; -est** : revêche, acariâtre, grognon
crack[1] ['kræk] *vt* **1** SPLIT : fêler, fendre **2** BREAK : casser (un œuf, etc.) **3** : faire claquer (un fouet), faire craquer (les jointures) **4 to crack jokes** : faire des blagues **—** *vi* **1** SPLIT : se fêler, se fendre **2** : craquer, claquer <the whip cracked : le fouet a claqué> **3** BREAK : se casser, muer (se dit de la voix) **4** : craquer, s'effondrer <he cracked under the strain : il s'est effondré faute d'un trop grand effort>
crack[2] *adj* FIRST-RATE : de première classe, d'élite
crack[3] *n* **1** SNAP : craquement *m*, bruit *m* sec **2** SPLIT : crevasse *f*, fissure *f*, craque *f Can* **3** JOKE : plaisanterie *f*, blague *f* **4** ATTEMPT : essai *m*, tentative *f* <to have a crack at : essayer (un coup)>
crackdown ['kræk,daʊn] *n* : mesures *fpl* énergiques
crack down *vi* : prendre des mesures énergiques
cracker ['krækər] *n* : biscuit *m* salé
crackle[1] ['krækəl] *vi* **-led; -ling** : crépiter, pétiller <a crackling fire : un feu qui crépite>
crackle[2] *n* : crépitement *m*

crackpot ['kræk,pɑt] *n* : excentrique *mf*, personne *f* originale
crack-up ['kræk,ʌp] *n* **1** CRASH : accident *m*, collision *f* **2** BREAKDOWN : dépression *f* nerveuse
crack up *vi* **1** CRASH : s'écraser **2** LAUGH : rire **3** BREAK DOWN : s'effondrer
cradle[1] ['kreɪdəl] *vt* **-dled; -dling** : tenir délicatement, bercer (un enfant)
cradle[2] *n* : berceau *m*
craft ['kræft] *n* **1** SKILL, TRADE : métier *m*, art *m* **2** CRAFTINESS : astuce *f*, ruse *f* **3** *pl usu* **craft** BOAT : bateau *m*, embarcation *f* **4** *pl usu* **craft** AIRCRAFT : avion *m*, aéronef *m*
craftiness ['kræftinəs] *n* : astuce *f*, ruse *f*
craftsman ['kræftsmən] *n, pl* **-men** [-mən, -,men] : artisan *m*, -sane *f*
crafty ['kræfti] *adj* **craftier; -est** : astucieux, rusé, ratourneur *Can*
crag ['kræg] *n* : rocher *m* escarpé
craggy ['krægi] *adj* **craggier; -est** : escarpé et rocheux
cram ['kræm] *v* **crammed; cramming** *vt* JAM, PACK : fourrer, bourrer, entasser — *vi* : étudier (à la dernière minute)
cramp[1] ['kræmp] *vt* HAMPER : entraver, gêner <to cramp s.o.'s style : priver qqn de ses moyens> — *vi* : avoir une crampe
cramp[2] *n* : crampe *f* (musculaire)
cranberry ['kræn,beri] *n, pl* **-berries** : canneberge *f*, atoca(s) *m Can*
crane[1] ['kreɪn] *vt* **craned; craning** STRETCH : tendre <to crane one's neck : tendre le cou>
crane[2] *n* : grue *f* (oiseau ou machine)
cranial ['kreɪniəl] *adj* : crânien
cranium ['kreɪniəm] *n, pl* **-niums** *or* **-nia** : crâne *m*, boîte *f* crânienne
crank[1] ['kræŋk] *vt or* **to crank up** : démarrer (un moteur) à la manivelle
crank[2] *n* **1** : manivelle *f* **2** ECCENTRIC : excentrique *mf*
cranky ['kræŋki] *adj* **crankier; -est** : de mauvaise humeur, irritable
cranny ['kræni] *n, pl* **-nies 1** CREVICE : (petite) fente *f* **2** NOOK : coin *m*, recoin *m* <every nook and cranny : tous les coins et recoins>
crash[1] ['kræʃ] *vt* **to crash one's car** : avoir un accident de voiture — *vi* **1** SMASH : se fracasser, s'écraser <to crash to the ground : s'écraser au sol> **2** RESOUND : retentir **3** : faire faillite (se dit des banques, etc.), s'effondrer (se dit des prix à la Bourse)
crash[2] *n* **1** DIN : fracas *m*, bruit *m* sourd <a crash of thunder : un coup de tonnerre> **2** COLLISION : accident *m*, collision *f* **3** FAILURE : effondrement *m*, krach *m* (boursier)
crass ['kræs] *adj* : crasse, grossier
crate[1] ['kreɪt] *vt* **crated; crating** : mettre en cageot, mettre en caisse
crate[2] *n* : cageot *m*, caisse *f*
crater ['kreɪtər] *n* : cratère *m*
cravat [krə'væt] *n* **1** SCARF : foulard *m* **2** NECKTIE : cravate *f*
crave ['kreɪv] *vt* **craved; craving** : désirer, avoir très envie de
craven ['kreɪvən] *adj* : lâche, poltron
craving ['kreɪvɪŋ] *n* : envie *f* (incontrôlable), soif *f*
crawfish ['krɔ,fɪʃ] → **crayfish**
crawl[1] ['krɔl] *vi* **1** : ramper, se traîner, marcher à quatre pattes (se dit d'un bébé) **2** SWARM : fourmiller, grouiller <to be crawling with : grouiller de>
crawl[2] *n* **1** : pas *m* de tortue <to move at a crawl : avancer à un pas de tortue> **2** : crawl *m* (en natation)
crayfish ['kreɪ,fɪʃ] *n* **1** : écrevisse *f* (d'eau douce) **2** : langouste *f* (de mer)
crayon ['kreɪ,ɑn, -ən] *n* : crayon *m* de cire
craze ['kreɪz] *n* FAD : mode *f*, vogue *f*
crazily ['kreɪzəli] *adv* : comme un fou, d'une manière insensée
craziness ['kreɪzinəs] *n* : folie *f*
crazy ['kreɪzi] *adj* **crazier; -est 1** INSANE : fou, dément **2** FOOLISH : fou, insensé **3 to be crazy about** : être fou de
creak[1] ['kri:k] *vi* : grincer, craquer
creak[2] *n* : grincement *m*, craquement *m*
creaky ['kri:ki] *adj* **creakier; -est** : grinçant, qui craque
cream[1] ['kri:m] *vt* **1** BEAT, BLEND : battre en crème, travailler <to cream butter and sugar together : travailler le beurre et le sucre> **2** : préparer (des légumes, etc.) à la béchamel
cream[2] *n* **1** : crème *f* (de lait) **2** LOTION : crème *f*, lotion *f* **3** ELITE : crème *f*, élite *f* <the cream of society : la crème de la société>
creamery ['kri:məri] *n, pl* **-eries** DAIRY : laiterie *f*
creamy ['kri:mi] *adj* **creamier; -est 1** : crémeux **2** : laiteux <creamy skin : peau laiteuse>
crease[1] ['kri:s] *v* **creased; creasing** *vt* **1** : faire les plis de (pantalons, etc.) **2** CRUMPLE : froisser — *vi* : se froisser
crease[2] *n* : pli *m*, faux pli *m*
create [kri'eɪt] *vt* **-ated; -ating 1** MAKE : créer, faire **2** CAUSE : créer, provoquer
creation [kri'eɪʃən] *n* : création *f*
creative [kri'eɪtɪv] *adj* : créatif, créateur
creatively [kri'eɪtɪvli] *adv* : de manière créative
creativity [,kri:eɪ'tɪvəti] *n* : créativité *f*
creator [kri'eɪtər] *n* **1** : créateur *m*, -trice *f* **2 the Creator** : le Créateur
creature ['kri:tʃər] *n* **1** : créature *f* **2** ANIMAL : animal *m*, bête *f*
credence ['kri:dənʃs] *n* : crédit *m*
credentials [krɪ'dentʃəlz] *n* : références *fpl*, lettres *fpl* de créance

credibility [ˌkrɛdəˈbɪləṭi] *n* : crédibilité *f*
credible [ˈkrɛdəbəl] *adj* : credible
credit[1] [ˈkrɛdɪt] *vt* **1** BELIEVE : croire, ajouter foi à (une histoire, etc.) **2** ATTRIBUTE : attribuer <they credit him with the new idea : on lui attribue la nouvelle idée> **3** : créditer (un compte de banque)
credit[2] *n* **1** *or* **credit balance** : solde *m* créditeur (d'un compte) **2** : crédit *m* <to buy on credit : acheter à crédit> **3** CREDENCE : crédit *m*, croyance *f* <to lose credit in s.o.'s eyes : perdre de son crédit aux yeux de qqn> **4** HONOR : honneur *m*, mérite *m* <it's to his credit : c'est à son honneur> <to be a credit to : faire honneur à>
creditable [ˈkrɛdɪṭəbəl] *adj* : honorable <a creditable attempt : une tentative honorable> — **creditably** [-bli] *adv*
credit card *n* : carte *f* de crédit
creditor [ˈkrɛdɪṭər] *n* : créancier *m*, -cière *f*
credulity [krɪˈduːləṭi, -ˈdjuː-] *n* : crédulité *f*
credulous [ˈkrɛdʒələs] *adj* : crédule
creed [ˈkriːd] *n* : crédo *m*, croyance *f*
creek [ˈkriːk, ˈkrɪk] *n* **1** STREAM : ruisseau *m*, crique *m* *Can* **2** *Brit* COVE, INLET : crique *f*, anse *f*
creel [ˈkriːl] *n* : panier *m* de pêche
creep[1] [ˈkriːp] *vi* **crept; creeping 1** CRAWL : ramper, se glisser, marcher à quatre pattes (se dit des enfants) **2** : avancer lentement, marcher sans bruit <to creep out of the house : partir de la maison sans aucun bruit> **3** SPREAD : ramper, grimper (se dit des plantes) **4 to creep up on** : s'approcher furtivement
creep[2] *n* **1** CRAWL : pas *m* de tortue, ralenti *m* <traffic's moving at a creep : la circulation avance au ralenti> **2 creeps** *npl* : frissons *mpl* <to give s.o. the creeps : donner froid dans le dos à qqn>
cremate [ˈkriːˌmeɪt] *vt* **-mated; -mating** : incinérer
cremation [krɪˈmeɪʃən] *n* : incinération *f*
creole [ˈkriːˌoːl] *adj* : créole
Creole *n* **1** : créole *m* (langue) **2** : Créole *mf* (personne)
creosote [ˈkriːəˌsoːt] *n* : créosote *f*
crepe *or* **crêpe** [ˈkreɪp] *n* **1** : crêpe *m* (tissu) **2** PANCAKE : crêpe *f*
crescendo [krɪˈʃɛnˌdoː] *n, pl* **-dos** *or* **-does** : crescendo *m*
crescent [ˈkrɛsənt] *n* : croissant *m*
cress [ˈkrɛs] *n* : cresson *m*
crest [ˈkrɛst] *n* **1** : crête *f* (d'un oiseau) **2** PEAK : crête *f*, sommet *m* (d'une montagne) **3** COAT OF ARMS : armoiries *fpl* **4** : timbre *m* (au-dessus des armoiries)
crestfallen [ˈkrɛstˌfɔlən] *adj* : déconfit, abattu
cretin [ˈkriːtən] *n* : crétin *m*, -tine *f*
crevasse [krɪˈvæs] *n* : crevasse *f*
crevice [ˈkrɛvəs] *n* : fissure *f*, fente *f*
crew[1] *Brit* → **crow**[1]
crew[2] [ˈkruː] *n* **1** : équipage *m* (d'un navire) **2** TEAM : équipe *f* (d'ouvriers ou d'athlètes)
crib [ˈkrɪb] *n* **1** MANGER : mangeoire *f* **2** : lit *m* d'enfant
crick [ˈkrɪk] *n* SPASM : crampe *f* <to have a crick in one's neck : avoir un torticolis>
cricket [ˈkrɪkəṭ] *n* **1** : grillon *m* (insecte), criquet *m* *Can* **2** : cricket *m* (jeu)
crier [ˈkraɪər] *n* : crieur *m* <the town crier : le crieur public>
crime [ˈkraɪm] *n* : crime *m*, délit *m*
criminal[1] [ˈkrɪmənəl] *adj* : criminel
criminal[2] *n* : criminel *m*, -nelle *f*
crimp [ˈkrɪmp] *vt* : onduler, friser <to crimp one's hair : friser ses cheveux>
crimson [ˈkrɪmzən] *n* : cramoisi *m*
cringe [ˈkrɪndʒ] *vi* **cringed; cringing** : avoir un mouvement de recul
crinkle [ˈkrɪŋkəl] *v* **-kled; -kling** *vt* : froisser, gaufrer, chiffonner — *vi* : se froisser, se chiffonner
crinkly [ˈkrɪŋkəli] *adj* **crinklier; -est** : gaufré
cripple[1] [ˈkrɪpəl] *vt* **-pled; -pling 1** DISABLE : estropier **2** INCAPACITATE : mettre hors d'usage, paralyser <crippled by fear : paralysé par la peur>
cripple[2] *n, sometimes taken to be offensive* : infirme *mf*; handicapé *m*, -pée *f*
crisis [ˈkraɪsɪs] *n, pl* **crises** [-ˌsiːz] : crise *f*
crisp [ˈkrɪsp] *adj* **1** CRUNCHY : croustillant, croquant <crisp cereal : céréale croustillante> <crisp celery : céleri croquant> **2** SHARP : sec, brusque <a crisp comment : un commentaire sec> **3** INVIGORATING : frais, rafraîchissant <the air was crisp : l'air était rafraîchissant> **4** CLEAR : net, clair <a crisp illustration : une illustration nette>
crisply [ˈkrɪspli] *adv* SHARPLY : d'un ton acerbe, brusquement
crispy [ˈkrɪspi] *adj* **crispier; -est** : croustillant, croquant
crisscross [ˈkrɪsˌkrɔs] *vt* : entrecroiser
criterion [kraɪˈtɪriən] *n, pl* **-ria** [-riə] : critère *m*
critic [ˈkrɪṭɪk] *n* **1** : critique *mf* <movie critic : critique de cinéma> **2** FAULTFINDER : critiqueur *m*, -queuse *f*; détracteur *m*, -trice *f*
critical [ˈkrɪṭɪkəl] *adj* **1** DISAPPROVING : critique **2** ANALYTICAL : critique <critical analysis : analyse critique> **3** CRUCIAL : critique, décisif <critical stage : étape critique>
criticism [ˈkrɪṭəˌsɪzəm] *n* : critique *f*
criticize [ˈkrɪṭəˌsaɪz] *vt* **-cized; -cizing** : critiquer

critique [krɪˈtiːk] *n* : critique *f*
croak[1] [ˈkroːk] *vi* : coasser (se dit d'une grenouille)
croak[2] *n* : coassement *m*
Croatian[1] [kroˈeɪʃən] *adj* : croate
Croatian[2] *n or* **Croat** [ˈkroˌæt] : Croate *mf*
crochet[1] [kroːˈʃeɪ] *vt* : faire (qqch) au crochet — *vi* : faire du crochet
crochet[2] *n* : crochet *m*
crock [ˈkrɑk] *n* : pot *m* (en terre cuite)
crockery [ˈkrɑkəri] *n* EARTHENWARE : faïence *f*
crocodile [ˈkrɑkəˌdaɪl] *n* : crocodile *m*
crocus [ˈkroːkəs] *n, pl* **-cuses** : crocus *m*
crone [ˈkroːn] *n* : vieille *f* bique, vieille *f* taupe
crony [ˈkroːni] *n, pl* **-nies** : copain *m*, -pine *f*
crook[1] [ˈkrʊk] *vt* : recourber (le doigt), plier (le coude)
crook[2] *n* **1** : houlette *f* (d'un berger), crosse *f* (d'un évêque) **2** CRIMINEL : escroc *m* **3** BEND, CURVE : courbe *f*, coude *m*
crooked [ˈkrʊkəd] *adj* **1** BENT : crochu, croche *Can* <nez crochu : crooked nose> **2** DISHONEST : malhonnête
croon [ˈkruːn] *v* : chantonner, chanter doucement
crop[1] [ˈkrɑp] *v* **cropped; cropping** *vt* TRIM : tailler, couper court — *vi* **to crop up** : surgir, se présenter
crop[2] *n* **1** : jabot *m* (d'un oiseau) **2** WHIP : cravache *f* **3** PRODUCE : culture *f* <food crops : cultures vivières> **4** : HARVEST : récolte *f*, moisson *f*
croquet [ˌkroːˈkeɪ] *n* : croquet *m*
croquette [ˌkroːˈkɛt] *n* : croquette *f*
crosier [ˈkroːʒər] *n* : crosse *f* (d'évêque)
cross[1] [ˈkrɔs] *vt* **1** TRAVERSE : traverser <to cross the road : traverser la rue> **2** *or* **to cross out** CANCEL : rayer, biffer <to cross out a word : rayer un mot> **3** CROSSBREED : croiser (deux espèces) **4** OPPOSE : aller à l'encontre de **5** : se croiser (les bras, les jambes, etc.) — *vi* INTERSECT : se croiser
cross[2] *adj* **1** : transversal <cross street : rue transversale> **2** CONTRARY : contraire, opposé <at cross purposes : ayant des buts contraires> **3** ANGRY : fâché, contrarié
cross[3] *n* **1** : croix *f* **2** HYBRID : croisement *m*, hybride *m*
crossbones [ˈkrɔsˌboːnz] *npl* **1** : os *mpl* en croix **2** → **skull**
crossbow [ˈkrɔsˌboː] *n* : arbalète *f*
crossbreed [ˈkrɔsˌbriːd] *vt* **-bred** [-ˌbrɛd, -ˈbrɛd]; **-breeding** : croiser (deux espèces)
cross–examination [ˌkrɔsɪgˌzæməˈneɪʃən] *nm* : contre-interrogatoire *m*
cross–examine [ˌkrɔsɪgˈzæmən] *vt* **-ined; -ining** : faire subir un contre-interrogatoire à, interroger
cross–eyed [ˈkrɔsˌaɪd] *adj* : qui louche, coq-d'œil *Can*
crossing [ˈkrɔsɪŋ] *n* **1** INTERSECTION : croisement *m* **2** VOYAGE : traversée *f* (de la mer) **3** → **crosswalk**
cross–reference [ˌkrɔsˈrɛfrənts, -ˈrɛfərənts] *n* : renvoi *m*
crossroads [ˈkrɔsˌroːdz] *ns & pl* : carrefour *m*
cross section *n* **1** SECTION : coupe *f* transversale **2** SAMPLE : échantillon *m* <a cross section of the population : un échantillon de la population>
crosswalk [ˈkrɔsˌwɔk] *n* : passage *m* pour piétons
crossways [ˈkrɔsˌweɪz] → **crosswise**
crosswise[1] [ˈkrɔsˌwaɪz] *adv* : transversalement
crosswise[2] *adj* : en travers
crossword puzzle [ˈkrɔsˌwərd] *n* : mots *mpl* croisés
crotch [ˈkrɑtʃ] *n* : entre-jambes *m* (d'un vêtement), fourche *f* (d'un arbre)
crotchety [ˈkrɑtʃəti] *adj* : grincheux, grognon
crouch [ˈkraʊtʃ] *vi* : s'accroupir
croup [ˈkruːp] *n* : croup *m*
crouton [ˈkruːˌtɑn] *n* : croûton *m*
crow[1] [ˈkroː] *vi* **crowed** *or in sense 1 Brit* **crew; crowing 1** : chanter (se dit du coq) **2** EXULT : exulter **3** BOAST : se vanter
crow[2] *n* **1** : corbeau *m* (oiseau) **2** : chant *m* (du coq)
crowbar [ˈkroːˌbɑr] *n* : (pince à) levier *m*
crowd[1] [ˈkraʊd] *vt* CRAM, PACK : entasser, serrer — *vi* : se presser, s'entasser
crowd[2] *n* **1** THRONG : foule *f* **2** GROUP : bande *f* <to stand out from the crowd : se distinguer de la masse>
crown[1] [ˈkraʊn] *vt* : couronner
crown[2] *n* **1** : couronne *f* **2** SUMMIT : sommet *m*, cime *f* **3** : fond *m* (d'une casquette)
crow's nest *n* : nid *m* de pie
crucial [ˈkruːʃəl] *adj* : crucial
crucible [ˈkruːsəbəl] *n* : creuset *m*
crucifix [ˈkruːsəˌfɪks] *n* : crucifix *m*
crucifixion [ˌkruːsəˈfɪkʃən] *n* : crucifixion *f*
crucify [ˈkruːsəˌfaɪ] *vt* **-fied; -fying** : crucifier
crude [ˈkruːd] *adj* **cruder; -est 1** RAW, UNREFINED : brut <crude sugar : sucre brut> **2** VULGAR : grossier, fruste **3** ROUGH : grossier, rudimentaire <a crude shelter : un abri rudimentaire>
crudely [ˈkruːdli] *adv* : grossièrement
cruel [ˈkruːəl] *adj* **-eler** *or* **-eller; -elest** *or* **-ellest** : cruel — **cruelly** *adv*
cruelty [ˈkruːəlti] *n, pl* **-ties** : cruauté *f*
cruet [ˈkruːɪt] *n* **1** : burette *f* (en religion) **2** : huilier *m*, vinaigrier *m* (pour la table)
cruise[1] [ˈkruːz] *vi* **cruised; cruising 1** : faire une croisière, croiser (se dit

d'un bateau) **2** : rouler à sa vitesse de croisière (se dit d'une voiture), voler à sa vitesse de croisière (se dit d'un avion)

cruise² *n* : croisière *f*

cruiser [ˈkruːzər] *n* **1** WARSHIP : croiseur *m* **2** *or* **police cruiser** : véhicule *m* de police

crumb [ˈkrʌm] *n* : miette *f*

crumble [ˈkrʌmbəl] *v* **-bled; -bling** *vt* : émietter — *vi* : s'émietter, s'effriter

crumbly [ˈkrʌmbli] *adj* **crumblier; -est** : friable

crumple [ˈkrʌmpəl] *v* **-pled; -pling** *vt* : froisser, chiffonner — *vi* **1** *or* **to crumple up** : se froisser **2** COLLAPSE : s'effondrer

crunch¹ [ˈkrʌntʃ] *vt* **1** CHEW : croquer **2** CRUSH : faire crisser — *vi* : craquer, crisser <the snow was crunching underfoot : la neige craquait sous nos pas>

crunch² *n* : craquement *m*, crissement *m*

crunchy [ˈkrʌntʃi] *adj* **crunchier; -est** : croquant

crusade [kruːˈseɪd], *n* **1** CAMPAIGN : croisade *f*, campagne *f* **2 the Crusades** : les croisades *f*

crusader [kruːˈseɪdər] *n* **1** : croisé *m* (militaire) **2** ACTIVIST : militant *m*, -tante *f*

crush¹ [ˈkrʌʃ] *vt* **1** SQUASH : écraser, aplatir, écrapoutir *Can* **2** GRIND : broyer, concasser **3** OVERWHELM : écraser

crush² *n* **1** CROWD, MOB : bousculade *f*, cohue *f* **2** INFATUATION : tocade *f* *fam*, béguin *m*

crust [ˈkrʌst] *n* **1** : croûte *f* (de pain) **2** LAYER : couche *f* <a crust of snow : une couche de neige>

crustacean [ˌkrʌsˈteɪʃən] *n* : crustacé *m*

crusty [ˈkrʌsti] *adj* **crustier; -est 1** : croustillant **2** CROSS, GRUMPY : grincheux, hargneux <a crusty reply : une brusque réplique>

crutch [ˈkrʌtʃ] *n* : béquille *f*

crux [ˈkrʌks, kruːks] *n, pl* **cruxes** : point *m* crucial, cœur *m*, noyau *m* <the crux of the matter : le cœur de l'affaire>

cry¹ [ˈkraɪ] *v* **cried; crying** *vi* **1** SHOUT : crier, pousser un cri **2** WEEP : pleurer — *vt* SHOUT : crier

cry² *n, pl* **cries** : cri *m*

crypt [ˈkrɪpt] *n* : crypte *f*

cryptic [ˈkrɪptɪk] *adj* : énigmatique, secret

crystal [ˈkrɪstəl] *n* : cristal *m*

crystalline [ˈkrɪstəlɪn] *adj* : cristallin

crystallize [ˈkrɪstəˌlaɪz] *v* **-lized; -lizing** *vt* : cristalliser — *vi* : se cristalliser

cub [ˈkʌb] *n* : petit *m* (d'un animal)

Cuban¹ [ˈkjuːbən] *adj* : cubain

Cuban² *n* : Cubain *m*, -baine *f*

cubbyhole [ˈkʌbiˌhoːl] *n* : réduit *m*

cube¹ [ˈkjuːb] *vt* **cubed; cubing 1** : élever (un nombre) au cube **2** DICE : couper en cubes

cube² *n* : cube *m*

cubic [ˈkjuːbɪk] *adj* : cubique

cubicle [ˈkjuːbɪkəl] *n* : box *m*

Cub Scout *n* : louveteau *m*

cuckoo¹ [ˈkuːˌkuː, ˈkʊ-] *adj* : toqué *fam*, cinglé *fam*

cuckoo² *n, pl* **-oos** : coucou *m* (oiseau)

cucumber [ˈkjuːˌkʌmbər] *n* : concombre *m*

cud [ˈkʌd] *n* **to chew the cud** : ruminer

cuddle [ˈkʌdəl] *v* **-dled; -dling** *vt* : caresser, câliner — *vi* : se câliner

cudgel¹ [ˈkʌdʒəl] *vt* **-geled** *or* **-gelled; -geling** *or* **-gelling** : battre (à coups de gourdin), matraquer

cudgel² *n* : gourdin *m*, trique *f*

cue [ˈkjuː] *n* **1** SIGNAL : signal *m*, réplique *f* (au théâtre) **2** *or* **cue stick** : queue *f* de billard

cuff¹ [ˈkʌf] *vt* SLAP : gifler, claquer

cuff² *n* **1** : poignet *m* (de chemise), revers *m* (de pantalon) **2** SLAP : gifle *f*, claque *f* **3 cuffs** *npl* → **handcuffs**

cuisine [kwɪˈziːn] *n* : cuisine *f*

culinary [ˈkʌləˌnɛri, ˈkjuːlə-] *adj* : culinaire

cull [ˈkʌl] *vt* CHOOSE : choisir, sélectionner

culminate [ˈkʌlmənˌeɪt] *vi* **-nated; -nating** : culminer, plafonner

culmination [ˌkʌlmənˈeɪʃən] *n* : point *m* culminant

culpable [ˈkʌlpəbəl] *adj* BLAMEWORTHY : répréhensible, condamnable

culprit [ˈkʌlprɪt] *n* : coupable *mf*

cult [ˈkʌlt] *n* : culte *m*

cultivate [ˈkʌltəˌveɪt] *vt* **-vated; -vating 1** : cultiver (la terre) **2** FOSTER : promouvoir, encourager **3** IMPROVE, REFINE : cultiver, perfectionner <to cultivate one's mind : se cultiver l'esprit>

cultivation [ˌkʌltəˈveɪʃən] *n* **1** : culture *f* <under cultivation : en culture> **2** REFINEMENT : raffinement *m*, perfectionnement *m*

cultural [ˈkʌltʃərəl] *adj* : culturel — **culturally** *adv*

culture [ˈkʌltʃər] *n* **1** CULTIVATION : culture *f* **2** REFINEMENT : culture *f*, savoir *m* **3** CIVILIZATION : culture *f*, civilisation *f*

culvert [ˈkʌlvərt] *n* : passage *m* hydraulique

cumbersome [ˈkʌmbərsəm] *adj* : encombrant, embarrassant, lourd

cumulative [ˈkjuːmjələˌtɪv, -ˌleɪtɪv] *adj* : cumulatif

cumulus [ˈkjuːmjələs] *n, pl* **-li** [-laɪ, -liː] : cumulus

cunning¹ [ˈkʌnɪŋ] *adj* **1** CRAFTY : astucieux **2** CLEVER : ingénieux, habile **3**

CUTE : joli, mignon <a cunning baby : un joli petit bébé>

cunning[2] *n* **1** CRAFTINESS : astuce *f*, ruse *f* **2** SKILL : ingéniosité *f*, habileté *f*

cup[1] ['kʌp] *vt* **cupped; cupping** : faire prendre la forme d'une tasse <to cup one's hands around sth : mettre les mains autour de qqch>

cup[2] *n* **1** : tasse *f* <a cup of tea : une tasse de thé> <a cup of flour : une tasse *f* de farine> **2** TROPHY : coupe *f*

cupboard ['kʌbərd] *n* : placard *m*, armoire *f*

cupcake ['kʌpˌkeɪk] *n* : petit gateau *m*

cupful ['kʌpˌfʊl] *n* : tasse *f*

cupidity [kjuːˈpɪdətɪ] *n, pl* **-ties** GREED : cupidité *f*

cupola ['kjuːpələ, -ˌloː] *n* : coupole *f*

cur ['kər] *n* : chien *m* métis, sale chien *m*

curate ['kjʊrət] *n* : vicaire *m*

curator ['kjʊrˌeɪtər, kjʊˈreɪtər] *n* : conservateur *m*, -trice *f* (d'un musée)

curb[1] ['kərb] *vt* : refréner, mettre un frein à

curb[2] *n* **1** CHECK : contrainte *f*, frein *m* **2** : bord *m* du trottoir <to step off the curb : descendre du trottoir>

curdle ['kərdəl] *v* **-dled; -dling** *vt* : cailler — *vi* : se cailler, se figer

curds ['kərdz] *npl* : lait *m* caillé

cure[1] ['kjʊr] *vt* **cured; curing 1** HEAL, REMEDY : guérir **2** : fumer, saler <to cure meat : fumer de la viande>

cure[2] *n* **1** RECOVERY : rétablissement *m*, guérison *f* **2** REMEDY : remède *m*

curfew ['kərˌfjuː] *n* : couvre-feu *m*

curio ['kjʊriˌoː] *n, pl* **-rios** : curiosité *f*, babiole *f*

curiosity [ˌkjʊriˈɑsəṭi] *n, pl* **-ties 1** INQUISITIVENESS : curiosité *f* **2** → **curio**

curious ['kjʊriəs] *adj* **1** INQUISITIVE : curieux **2** ODD : étrange, curieux

curl[1] ['kərl] *vt* **1** : friser (les cheveux) **2** COIL : enrouler **3 to curl one's lip** : faire une moue (de mépris) — *vi* : se friser, boucler

curl[2] *n* **1** RINGLET : boucle *f* (de cheveux) **2** SPIRAL : spirale *f* <curl of smoke : spirale de fumée>

curler ['kərlər] *n* : bigoudi *m*, rouleau *m*

curlew ['kərˌluː, 'kərlˌjuː] *n, pl* **-lews** *or* **-lew** : courlis *m*

curly ['kərli] *adj* **curlier; -est** : frisé

currant ['kərənt] *n* **1** : groseille *f*, gadelle *f* *Can* **2** RAISIN : raisin *m* de Corinthe

currency ['kərənṭsi] *n, pl* **-cies 1** MONEY : monnaie *f*, devise *f* <foreign currency : devises étrangères> **2** PREVALENCE : cours *m*, acceptation *f*

current[1] ['kərənt] *adj* **1** PRESENT : actuel, en cours <the current week : la semaine en cours> **2** PREVALENT : courant, commun <current customs : coutumes usuelles>

current[2] *n* **1** FLOW : courant *m*, cours *m* <the current of a river : le cours d'un fleuve> **2** TREND : tendance *f*, penchant *m* **3** : courant *m* (électrique)

curriculum [kəˈrɪkjələm] *n, pl* **-la** [-lə] : programme *m* (scolaire)

curry[1] ['kəri] *vt* **-ried; -rying 1** : étriller (un cheval) **2** : faire un curry de (en cuisine) **3 to curry favor with** : chercher à gagner la faveur de

curry[2] *n, pl* **-ries** : curry *m*

curse[1] ['kərs] *v* **cursed; cursing** *vt* **1** : maudire <the gods cursed him : les dieux l'ont maudit> **2** AFFLICT : affliger — *vi* SWEAR : sacrer, jurer

curse[2] *n* **1** : malédiction *f* <to put a curse on : appeler une malédiction sur> **2** CALAMITY : fléau *m*, calamité *f* **3** OATH, SWEARWORD : juron *m*

cursor ['kərsər] *n* : curseur *m* (en informatique)

cursory ['kərsəri] *adj* : superficiel, hâtif

curt ['kərt] *adj* : brusque, sec

curtail [kərˈteɪl] *vt* : réduire, diminuer <to curtail expenses : réduire les dépenses>

curtailment [kərˈteɪlmənt] *n* : réduction *f*, diminution *f*

curtain ['kərtən] *n* : rideau *m*

curtly ['kərtli] *adv* : brusquement, sèchement

curtsy[1] *or* **curtsey** ['kərtsi] *vi* **-sied** *or* **-seyed; -sying** *or* **-seying** : faire une révérence

curtsy[2] *or* **curtsey** *n, pl* **-sies** *or* **-seys** : révérence *f*

curvature ['kərvəˌtʃʊr] *n* : courbure *f*

curve[1] ['kərv] *v* **curved; curving** *vt* : courber — *vi* : se courber

curve[2] *n* : courbe *f*

cushion[1] ['kʊʃən] *vt* **1** : mettre des coussins à **2** LESSEN : amortir, réduire <to cushion the blow : amortir le choc>

cushion[2] *n* : coussin *m*

cusp ['kʌsp] *n* : cuspide *f* (d'une dent, etc.)

cuspid ['kʌspɪd] *n* : canine *f* (dent)

custard ['kʌstərd] *n* : flan *m*

custody ['kʌstədi] *n, pl* **-dies 1** CARE : garde *f* <in the custody of : sous la garde de> **2** DETENTION : détention *f*, emprisonnement *m*

custom[1] ['kʌstəm] *adj* : fait sur commande

custom[2] *n* **1** CONVENTION, TRADITION : coutume *f*, tradition *f*, usage *m* **2 customs** *npl* : douane *f*

customarily [ˌkʌstəˈmerəli] *adv* : habituellement, normalement

customary ['kʌstəˌmeri] *adj* : habituel, coutumier

customer ['kʌstəmər] *n* : client *m*, cliente *f*

cut¹ ['kʌt] *v* **cut; cutting** *vt* **1** : couper <to cut paper : couper du papier> **2** SLICE : découper (du gâteau, des viandes, etc.) **3** SLASH : se couper <I cut my finger : je me suis coupé le doigt> **4** TRIM : couper (les ongles), tailler (une barbe, des cheveux, etc.) **5** INTERSECT : croiser **6** SHORTEN : couper (un texte, etc.) **7** REDUCE : réduire, diminuer <to cut costs : réduire les coûts> **8 to cut a tooth** : faire une dent — *vi* **1** : couper **2 to cut in** : interrompre, s'interposer, s'immiscer

cut² *n* **1** : coupure *f* **2** REDUCTION : réduction *f*, diminution *f* <a cut in pay : une réduction de salaire>

cute ['kju:t] *adj* **cuter; -est** : mignon, joli

cuticle ['kju:tɪkəl] *n* : petites peaux *fpl* (de l'ongle)

cutlass ['kʌtləs] *n* : coutelas *m*

cutlery ['kʌtləri] *n* **1** KNIVES : coutellerie *f* **2** FLATWARE : couverts *mpl*

cutlet ['kʌtlət] *n* : escalope *f*

cutter ['kʌt̬ər] *n* **1** : coupoir *m* (outil) **2** : cotre *m* (bateau)

cutthroat¹ ['kʌtˌθro:t] *adj* : acharné, féroce <cutthroat competition : compétition acharnée>

cutthroat² *n* : meurtrier *m*, -trière *f*; assassin *m*

cutting ['kʌt̬ɪŋ] *adj* **1** SHARP : aigu, cinglant <a cutting wind : un vent cinglant> **2** CURT, SCATHING : mordant, tranchant

cyanide ['saɪəˌnaɪd, -nɪd] *n* : cyanure *m*

cyberspace ['saɪbərˌspeɪs] *n* : cyberespace *m*

cycle¹ ['saɪkəl] *vi* **-cled; -cling** : faire de la bicyclette

cycle² *n* **1** : cycle *m* <life cycle : cycle de vie> **2** BICYCLE : bicyclette *f*, vélo *m* **3** MOTORCYCLE : motocyclette *f*

cyclic ['saɪklɪk, sɪ-] *or* **cyclical** [-klɪkəl] *adj* : cyclique, périodique

cyclist ['saɪklɪst] *n* : cycliste *mf*

cyclone ['saɪˌklo:n] *n* **1** : cyclône *m* **2** TORNADO : tornade *f*

cyclopedia *or* **cyclopaedia** [ˌsaɪklə'pi:diə] → **encyclopedia**

cylinder ['sɪləndər] *n* : cylindre *m*

cylindrical [sə'lɪndrɪkəl] *adj* : cylindrique

cymbal ['sɪmbəl] *n* : cymbale *f*

cynic ['sɪnɪk] *n* : cynique *mf*

cynical ['sɪnɪkəl] *adj* : cynique

cynicism ['sɪnəsɪzəm] *n* : cynisme *m*

cypress ['saɪprəs] *n* : cyprès *m*

Cypriot¹ *or* **Cypriote** ['sɪpriət, -ˌɑt] *adj* : chypriote, cypriote

Cypriot² *or* **Cypriote** *n* : Chypriote *mf*, Cypriote *mf*

cyst ['sɪst] *n* : kyste *m*

cytoplasm ['saɪt̬oˌplæzəm] *n* : cytoplasme *m*

czar ['zɑr, 'sɑr] *n* : tsar *m*

czarina [zɑ'ri:nə, sɑ-] *n* : tsarine *f*

Czech¹ ['tʃɛk] *adj* : tchèque

Czech² *n* **1** : Tchèque *mf* **2** : tchèque *m* (langue)

Czechoslovak¹ [ˌtʃɛko'slo:ˌvɑk, -ˌvæk] *or* **Czechoslovakian** [-slo'vɑkiən, -'væ-] *adj* : tchécoslovaque

Czechoslovak² *or* **Czechoslovakian** *n* : Tchécoslovaque *mf*

D

d ['di:] *n, pl* **d's** *or* **ds** ['di:z] : d *m*, quatrième lettre de l'alphabet

dab¹ ['dæb] *vt* **dabbed; dabbing 1** PAT : tamponner **2** APPLY : appliquer (par petites touches)

dab² *n* BIT, TOUCH : touche *f*, petite quantité *f*

dabble ['dæbəl] *v* **-bled; -bling** *vt* SPATTER : éclabousser — *vi* **1** SPLASH : faire des éclaboussures (dans l'eau) **2** : s'intéresser brièvement <to dabble in art : faire un peu d'art>

dabbler ['dæbələr] *n* : dilettante *mf*, amateur *m*

dachshund ['dɑksˌhʊnd, -hʊnd; 'dɑksənt, -sənd] *n* : teckel *m*

dad ['dæd] *n* : papa *m fam*

daddy ['dædi] *n, pl* **-dies** : papa *m fam*

daffodil ['dæfəˌdɪl] *n* : jonquille *f*

daft ['dæft] *adj* : idiot, bête

dagger ['dægər] *n* : dague *f*, poignard *m*

dahlia ['dæljə, 'dɑl-, 'deɪl-] *n* : dahlia *m*

daily¹ ['deɪli] *adv* : quotidiennement

daily² *adj* : quotidien, journalier

daily³ *n, pl* **-lies** *or* **daily newspaper** : quotidien *m*

daintily ['deɪntəli] *adv* : délicatement

daintiness ['deɪntinəs] *n* : délicatesse *f*

dainty¹ ['deɪnti] *adj* **daintier; -est 1** DELICATE : délicat, mignon **2** TASTY : de choix <dainty food : nourriture de choix> **3** FINICKY : difficile (sur la nourriture)

dainty² *n, pl* **-ties** DELICACY : mets *m* délicat

dairy ['dæri] *n, pl* **-ies** : laiterie *f*, crémerie *f France*

dairymaid ['dæriˌmeɪd] *n* : fille *f* de laiterie

dairyman ['dærimən, -mæn] *n, pl* **-men** [-mən, -ˌmɛn] : employé *m* de laiterie

dais ['deɪəs] *n* : estrade *f*

daisy ['deɪzi] *n, pl* **-sies** : marguerite *f*

dale ['deɪl] *n* : vallée *f*, val *m*

dally ['dæli] *vi* **-lied; -lying 1** TRIFLE : jouer, badiner **2** DAWDLE : traîner, lambiner *fam*

dalmatian [dælˈmeɪʃən, dəl-] *n* : dalmatien *m*
dam¹ ['dæm] *vt* **dammed; damming** : construire un barrage sur
dam² *n* **1** : barrage *m* **2** : mère *f* (d'un animal domestique)
damage¹ ['dæmɪdʒ] *vt* **-aged; -aging** : endommager (des objets), abîmer (sa santé), nuire à (une réputation, etc.)
damage² *n* **1** : dégâts *mpl* **2 damages** *npl* : dommages *mpl* et intérêts *mpl*
damask ['dæməsk] *n* : damas *m*
dame ['deɪm] *n* LADY : dame *f*
damn¹ ['dæm] *vt* **1** CONDEMN : condamner **2** CURSE : maudire
damn² *n* **1 not to give a damn** : s'en ficher *fam* **2 it's not worth a damn** : ça ne vaut pas un clou
damnable ['dæmnəbəl] *adj* **1** REPREHENSIBLE : condamnable **2** DETESTABLE : fichu *fam* <this damnable weather! : ce fichu temps!>
damnation [dæmˈneɪʃən] *n* : damnation *f*
damned ['dæmd] *adj* DAMNABLE : sacré *fam*, fichu *fam*
damp¹ ['dæmp] → **dampen**
damp² *adj* : humide, moite
damp³ *n* : humidité *f*
dampen ['dæmpən] *vt* **1** MOISTEN : humecter **2** COOL, DEADEN : refroidir <to dampen s.o.'s spirits : décourager qqn>
damper ['dæmpər] *n* **1** : registre *m* (d'une cheminée) **2 to put a damper on** : jeter un froid sur, décourager
dampness ['dæmpnəs] *n* : humidité *f*
damsel ['dæmzəl] *n* : demoiselle *f*
dance¹ ['dænʦ] *v* **danced; dancing** : danser
dance² *n* **1** : danse *f* **2** : soirée *f* dansante
dancer ['dænʦər] *n* : danseur *m*, -seuse *f*
dandelion ['dændəˌlaɪən] *n* : pissenlit *m*
dander ['dændər] *n* TEMPER : colère *f*, rogne *f* <don't get your dander up : ne te mets pas en colère>
dandruff ['dændrəf] *n* : pellicules *fpl*
dandy¹ ['dændi] *adj* **dandier; -est** : chouette *fam*, épatant *fam*
dandy² *n, pl* **-dies** : dandy *m*
Dane ['deɪn] *n* : danois *m*, -noise *f*
danger ['deɪndʒər] *n* : danger *m*
dangerous ['deɪndʒərəs] *adj* : dangereux
dangle ['dæŋgəl] *v* **-gled; -gling** *vi* HANG : se balancer, pendre — *vt* **1** SWING : balancer, laisser pendre **2** : faire miroiter <they dangled the prospect of a promotion before him : on lui a fait miroiter une promotion>
Danish¹ ['deɪnɪʃ] *adj* : danois
Danish² *nm* **1** : danois *m* (langue) **2 the Danish** : les Danois *mpl*
Danish³ *n* **the Danish** : les Danois
dank ['dæŋk] *adj* : froid et humide
dapper ['dæpər] *adj* : soigné
dappled ['dæpəld] *adj* : tacheté, pommelé
dare¹ ['dær] *v* **dared; daring** *vt* CHALLENGE : lancer un défi à, défier — *vi* VENTURE : oser
dare² *n* CHALLENGE : défi *m*
daredevil ['dærˌdevəl] *n* : casse-cou *mf*
daring¹ ['deɪrɪŋ] *adj* BOLD : audacieux, hardi
daring² *n* : audace *f*, hardiesse *f*
dark¹ ['dɑrk] *adj* **1** : noir, sombre, foncé <dark clothes : vêtements foncés> <to get dark : faire nuit> **2** GLOOMY : lugubre, sombre
dark² *n* **1** NIGHT : tombée *f* du jour **2** DARKNESS : noir *m*, obscurité *f*
darken ['dɑrkən] *vt* : obscurcir, assombrir — *vi* : s'obscurcir, s'assombrir
darkly ['dɑrkli] *adv* **1** DIMLY : sombrement **2** GLOOMILY : d'un air lugubre **3** MYSTERIOUSLY : énigmatiquement, mystérieusement
darkness ['dɑrknəs] *n* : obscurité *f*, ténèbres *fpl*, noirceur *f Can*
darling¹ ['dɑrlɪŋ] *adj* **1** BELOVED : bien-aimé, chéri **2** CHARMING : adorable <a darling puppy : un chiot adorable>
darling² *n* **1** BELOVED : chéri *m*, -rie *f* **2** FAVORITE : chouchou *m*, -choute *f fam*; coqueluche *f fam*
darn¹ ['dɑrn] *vt* : repriser (en couture)
darn² *n* **1** : reprise *f* **2** → **damn²**
dart¹ ['dɑrt] *vi* : se précipiter, s'élancer <he darted out : il est sorti comme une flèche>
dart² *n* **1** : flèche *f* (courte), fléchette *f*, dard *m Can* **2 darts** *npl* : fléchettes *fpl* (jeu) **3** : pince *f* (en couture)
dash¹ ['dæʃ] *vt* **1** SMASH : briser, fracasser **2** HURL : lancer violemment **3** SPLASH : éclabousser **4** RUIN : détruire, anéantir <to dash s.o.'s hopes : anéantir les espoirs de qqn> **5** *or* **to dash off** : terminer à la hâte — *vi* : se précipiter, se ruer
dash² *n* **1** BURST, SPLASH : éclat *m*, plouf *m* **2** : tiret *m* (signe de ponctuation) **3** DROP, PINCH : pincée *f*, soupçon *m* <a dash of pepper : une pincée de poivre> **4** VERVE : brio *m*, panache *m* **5** RUSH : mouvement *m* précipité, course *f* folle **6** : sprint *m* (aux sports) **7** → **dashboard**
dashboard ['dæʃˌbɔrd] *n* : tableau *m* de bord
dashing ['dæʃɪŋ] *adj* : fringant, élégant
data ['deɪtə, 'dæ-, 'dɑ-] *ns & pl* : données *fpl*
database ['deɪtəˌbeɪs, 'dæ-, 'dɑ-] *n* : base *f* de données
date¹ ['deɪt] *v* **dated; dating** *vt* **1** : dater (un chèque, un objet, etc.) **2** : sortir avec — *vi* **1** : sortir avec quelqu'un, se fréquenter **2** ORIGINATE : remonter <a friendship dating from high school : une amitié qui remonte au lycée>

date² *n* **1** : date *f* <date of birth : date de naissance> **2** PERIOD : date *f*, période *f* (historique) **3** APPOINTMENT : rendez-vous *m* **4** : datte *f* (fruit) **5 to ~** : à ce jour, jusqu'à maintenant

dated ['deɪtəd] *adj* OLD-FASHIONED : vieilli, démodé

datum ['deɪtəm, 'dæ-, 'dɑ-] *n, pl* **-ta** [-tə] *or* **-tums** : donnée *f*

daub¹ ['dɔb] *vt* **1** COVER : couvrir <daubed with mud : couvert de boue> **2** SMEAR : barbouiller

daub² *n* : barbouillage *m*

daughter ['dɔtər] *n* : fille *f*

daughter–in–law ['dɔtərɪnˌlɔ] *n, pl* **daughters–in–law** : belle-fille *f*, bru *f*

daunt ['dɔnt] *vt* : décourager, intimider

dauntless ['dɔntləs] *adj* : intrépide, hardi

davenport ['dævənˌport] *n* : canapé *m*

dawdle ['dɔdəl] *vi* **-dled; -dling 1** DALLY : traîner, lambiner *fam*, farfiner *Can fam* **2** LOITER : flâner

dawn¹ ['dɔn] *vi* **1** : se lever (se dit du jour) **2 to dawn on** : venir à <it dawned on him that it was late : il s'est aperçu qu'il était tard>

dawn² *n* **1** : aube *f* **2** BEGINNING : aube *f*, début *m* <the dawn of the space age : le début de l'ère spatiale>

day ['deɪ] *n* **1** : jour *m* <every day : tous les jours> <day by day : jour après jour> **2** : journée *f* <have a good day! : bonne journée!> <an eight-hour day : une journée de huit heures> **3** AGE, TIME : époque *f*, temps *m* <in my day : à mon époque> <in this day and age : par les temps qui courent> **4 → weekday, workday**

daybreak ['deɪˌbreɪk] *n* : aube *f*, point *m* du jour, lever *m* du jour

day care *n* : service *m* de garderie

daydream¹ ['deɪˌdriːm] *vi* : rêver, rêvasser

daydream² *n* : rêve *m*, rêverie *f*

daylight ['deɪˌlaɪt] *n* **1** : lumière *f* du jour <in broad daylight : en plein jour> **2 → daybreak 3 → daytime**

daylight saving time *n* : heure *f* d'été, heure *f* avancée (de l'Est) *Can*

daytime ['deɪˌtaɪm] *n* : jour *m*, journée *f* <in the daytime : pendant le jour>

daze¹ ['deɪz] *vt* **dazed; dazing 1** STUN : étourdir, abasourdir **2** DAZZLE : éblouir

daze² *n* : ahurissement *m*, étourdissement *m*

dazzle ['dæzəl] *vt* **-zled; -zling 1** BLIND : éblouir, aveugler **2** IMPRESS : impressionner, épater *fam*

DDT [ˌdiːˌdiːˈtiː] *n* : DDT *m*

deacon ['diːkən] *n* : diacre *m*

dead¹ ['ded] *adv* **1** ABSOLUTELY : absolument <dead certain : absolument sûr> **2** SUDDENLY : soudainement <to stop dead : s'arrêter net> **3** DIRECTLY : directement, droit <dead ahead : droit devant, tout droit>

dead² *adj* **1** LIFELESS : mort **2** NUMB : engourdi **3** EXTINCT, INACTIVE : inactif, éteint, mort **4** : coupé (se dit d'une ligne téléphonique), à plat (se dit d'une batterie) **5** EXHAUSTED : éreinté, crevé *fam* **6** OBSOLETE : mort, désuet <dead language : langue morte> **7** EXACT : exact, précis <at the dead center : exactement au centre> **8** COMPLETE : absolu, total <dead silence : silence absolu>

dead³ *ns & pl* **1** DEPTHS : milieu *m*, profondeur *f* <in the dead of night : au plus profond de la nuit> <in the dead of winter : en plein hiver> **2 the dead** : les morts

deadbeat ['dedˌbiːt] *n* : bon à rien *m*, bonne à rien *f*

deaden ['dedən] *vt* **1** ALLAY : calmer, endormir (des douleurs) **2** CUSHION, SOFTEN : assourdir (des sons), amortir (un coup, etc.)

dead–end ['dedˈend] *adj* : sans issue (se dit d'une rue), sans perspectives (se dit d'un travail)

dead end *n* : cul-de-sac *m*, impasse *f*

dead heat *n* TIE : match *m* nul

deadline *n* ['dedˌlaɪn] : date *f* limite, délai *m*

deadlock¹ ['dedˌlɑk] *vt* : mettre dans une impasse

deadlock² *n* : impasse *f*

deadly¹ ['dedli] *adv* : extrêmement, très <deadly serious : très sérieux>

deadly² *adj* **deadlier; -est 1** LETHAL : mortel **2** ACCURATE : précis, juste <deadly accuracy : une extrême précision> **3** : capital <the seven deadly sins : les sept péchés capitaux> **4** EXTREME : extrême, absolu

deadpan ['dedˌpæn] *adj* : impassible, pince-sans-rire

deaf ['def] *adj* : sourd

deafen ['defən] *vt* : assourdir

deaf–mute ['defˈmjuːt] *n* : sourd-muet *m*, sourde-muette *f*

deafness ['defnəs] *n* : surdité *f*

deal¹ ['diːl] *v* **dealt; dealing** *vt* **1** APPORTION : rendre <to deal (out) justice : rendre la justice> **2** DISTRIBUTE : donner, distribuer (des cartes à jouer) **3** DELIVER : administrer, assener (un coup) **4** SELL : revendre (des drogues) — *vi* **1** : distribuer les cartes **2 to deal in** SELL : être dans le commerce de **3 to deal with** CONCERN, TREAT : traiter de **4 to deal with** FACE : accepter, faire face à

deal² *n* **1** : donne *f* (aux cartes) **2** AGREEMENT, TRANSACTION : accord *m*, affaire *f*, marché *m* **3** TREATMENT : traitement *m* <to get a bad deal : être mal traité> **4** BARGAIN : bonne affaire *f* **5 a good deal** LOTS : beaucoup

dealer ['di:lər] *n* : marchand *m*, -chande *f*; négociant *m*, -ciante *f*
dealings ['di:lɪŋz] *npl* **1** : relations *fpl* (personnelles) **2** TRANSACTIONS : transactions *fpl*, affaires *fpl*
dean ['di:n] *n* : doyen *m*, doyenne *f*
dear[1] ['dɪr] *adj* **1** ESTEEMED, LOVED : cher <a dear friend : un ami très cher> **2** (*used in correspondence*) : cher <Dear Anne : Chère Anne> **3** COSTLY : cher, coûteux **4** EARNEST : cher, sincère <my dearest wish : mon vœu le plus cher>
dear[2] *n* : chéri *m*, -rie *f*
dearly ['dɪrli] *adv* **1 to love dearly** : aimer tendrement, aimer beaucoup **2 to pay dearly** : payer cher
dearness ['dɪrnəs] *n* **1** FONDNESS : affection *f*, amitié *f* **2** COSTLINESS : cherté *f*
dearth ['dərθ] *n* : pénurie *f*, manque *m*
death ['deθ] *n* **1** : mort *f*, décès *m* **2** DESTRUCTION, END : disparition *f* <the death of all hope : la disparition de tout espoir> <he'll be the death of me : il me fera mourir>
deathless ['deθləs] *adj* : immortel
deathly[1] ['deθli] *adv* : de mort, comme la mort <deathly pale : pâle comme la mort>
deathly[2] *adj* **1** FATAL : mortel **2** : cadavérique <deathly pallor : pâleur cadavérique>
debacle [dɪ'bɑkəl, -'bæ-] *n* : débâcle *f*, désastre *m*, fiasco *m*
debar [di'bɑr] *vt* **-barred; -barring** : exclure, interdire à
debark [di'bɑrk] → **disembark**
debase [di'beɪs] *vt* **-based; -basing** : avilir, abaisser, dégrader
debasement [di'beɪsmənt] *n* : avilissement *m*, abaissement *m*, dégradation *f*
debatable [dɪ'beɪṭəbəl] *adj* : discutable
debate[1] [dɪ'beɪt] *v* **-bated; -bating** *vt* : débattre, discuter — *vi* : discuter
debate[2] *n* : débat *m*, discussion *f*
debauch [dɪ'bɔtʃ] *vt* : débaucher
debauchery [dɪ'bɔtʃəri] *n, pl* **-eries** : débauche *f*
debilitate [dɪ'bɪlə,teɪt] *vt* **-tated; -tating** : débiliter, affaiblir
debility [dɪ'bɪləṭi] *n, pl* **-ties** : débilité *f*
debit[1] ['debɪt] *vt* : débiter (un compte bancaire, etc.)
debit[2] *n* : débit
debonair [,debə'nær] *adj* : élégant, raffiné
debris [də'bri:, deɪ-; 'deɪ,bri:] *n, pl* **-bris** [-'bri:z, -,bri:z] **1** RUBBLE : décombres *mpl*, débris *mpl* **2** RUBBISH : déchets *mpl*
debt ['det] *n* : dette *f*, créance *f*
debtor ['detər] *n* : débiteur *m*, -trice *f*
debug [di'bʌg] *vt* **-bugged; -bugging** : déboguer
debunk [di'bʌŋk] *vt* : discréditer, démentir
debut[1] [deɪ'bju:, 'deɪ,bju:] *vi* : débuter
debut[2] *n* **1** : débuts *mpl* <my acting debut : mes débuts sur la scène> **2** : entrée *f* dans le monde
debutante ['debjuˌtɑnt] *n* : débutante *f*
decade ['de,keɪd, de'keɪd] *n* : décennie *f*
decadence ['dekədənʦ] *n* : décadence *f*
decadent ['dekədənt] *adj* : décadent
decal ['di:,kæl, di'kæl] *n* : décalcomanie *f*
decamp [di'kæmp] *vi* : décamper, déguerpir
decant [di'kænt] *vt* : transvaser (un liquide), décanter (du vin)
decanter [di'kæntər] *n* : carafe *f*
decapitate [di'kæpə,teɪt] *vt* **-tated; -tating** : décapiter
decay[1] [di'keɪ] *vi* **1** DETERIORATE : se détériorer, se délabrer (se dit d'un édifice) **2** DECOMPOSE, ROT : se décomposer, se putréfier **3** : se carier (se dit d'une dent)
decay[2] *n* **1** DETERIORATION : délabrement *f*, pourrissement *m* **2** DECOMPOSITION, ROTTING : décomposition *f* **3** *or* **tooth decay** : carie *f* (dentaire)
decease[1] [di'si:s] *vi* **-ceased; -ceasing** : décéder
decease[2] *n* DEATH : décès *m*
deceit [dɪ'si:t] *n* **1** DUPLICITY : duplicité *f*, fausseté *f* **2** TRICK : tromperie *f*
deceitful [dɪ'si:tfəl] *adj* **1** MISLEADING : trompeur **2** DISHONEST : malhonnête
deceitfully [dɪ'si:tfəli] *adv* : de façon malhonnête, trompeusement
deceive [dɪ'si:v] *v* **-ceived; -ceiving** *vt* : tromper, leurrer — *vi* : donner une fausse impression
deceiver [dɪ'si:vər] *n* : trompeur *m*, -peuse *f*
decelerate [di'selə,reɪt] *v* **-ated; -ating** : ralentir
December [di'sembər] *n* : décembre *m*
decency ['disənʦi] *n, pl* **-cies** : décence *f*, bienséance *f*
decent ['di:sənt] *adj* **1** PROPER, SUITABLE : décent, convenable, approprié **2** CLOTHED : habillé **3** ADEQUATE : acceptable, suffisant **4** KIND : gentil, sympathique
decently ['di:səntli] *adv* **1** PROPERLY : décemment, convenablement **2** ADEQUATELY : acceptablement
deception [dɪ'sɛpʃən] *n* **1** : tromperie *f*, duperie *f* **2** FRAUD : fraude *f*
deceptive [dɪ'sɛptɪv] *adj* : trompeur
deceptively [dɪ'sɛptɪvli] *adv* : trompeusement <it's deceptively small : c'est plus grand qu'il n'y paraît>
decibel ['desəbəl, -,bɛl] *n* : décibel *m*
decide [dɪ'saɪd] *v* **-cided; -ciding** *vt* **1** : décider <I decided to buy a hat : j'ai décidé d'acheter un chapeau> **2** DETERMINE, SETTLE : décider de, trancher **3** PERSUADE : décider — *vi* : se décider

decided [dɪ'saɪdəd] *adj* **1** RESOLUTE : décidé, ferme **2** UNQUESTIONABLE : incontestable, certain
decidedly [dɪ'saɪdədlɪ] *adv* **1** RESOLUTELY : résolument **2** UNQUESTIONABLY : vraiment, décidément
deciduous [dɪ'sɪdʒʊəs] *adj* : caduc <deciduous tree : arbre à feuilles caduques>
decimal[1] ['dɛsəməl] *adj* : décimal
decimal[2] *n* : décimale *f*
decimal point *n* : virgule *f*
decipher [dɪ'saɪfər] *vt* : déchiffrer
decision [dɪ'sɪʒən] *n* : décision *f*
decisive [dɪ'saɪsɪv] *adj* **1** DECIDING : décisif <the decisive vote : le vote décisif> **2** RESOLUTE : résolu, déterminé **3** CONCLUSIVE : définitif, décisif
deck[1] ['dɛk] *vt* **1** FLOOR : envoyer par terre **2 to deck out** : orner, décorer, parer (une personne)
deck[2] *n* **1** : pont *m* (d'un navire) **2** *or* **deck of cards** : jeu *m* de cartes **3** TERRACE : terrasse *f* (d'une maison, etc.)
declaim [dɪ'kleɪm] *v* : déclamer
declaration [ˌdɛklə'reɪʃən] *n* : déclaration *f*
declarative [dɪ'klærətɪv, -klɛr-] *adj* : déclaratif
declare [dɪ'klɛr] *vt* **-clared; -claring 1** ANNOUNCE : déclarer, annoncer <to declare war : déclarer la guerre> **2** AFFIRM : déclarer, maintenir
declension [dɪ'klɛnʃən] *n* : déclinaison *f* (en grammaire)
decline[1] [dɪ'klaɪn] *v* **-clined; -clining** *vt* **1** REFUSE : décliner, refuser **2** : décliner (un nom) — *vi* **1** DESCEND, DROP : descendre, baisser **2** WANE : être sur le déclin **3** DETERIORATE, WEAKEN : s'affaiblir, dépérir **4** REFUSE : refuser
decline[2] *n* **1** DETERIORATION : déclin *m* **2** LOWERING : baisse *f*, chute *f* (des prix) **3** SLOPE : pente *f*, descente *f*
decode [dɪ'koːd] *vt* **-coded; -coding** : décoder, déchiffrer
decompose [ˌdiːkəm'poːz] *vt* **-posed; -posing** : décomposer — *vi* : se décomposer
decomposition [ˌdiːˌkɑmpə'zɪʃən] *n* : décomposition *f*
decongestant [ˌdiːkən'dʒɛstənt] *n* : décongestif *m*, décongestionnant *m*
decor *or* **décor** [deɪ'kɔr, 'deɪˌkɔr] *n* : décor *m*
decorate ['dɛkəˌreɪt] *vt* **-rated; -rating 1** ADORN : décorer, embellir **2** : décorer <decorated for bravery : décoré pour son courage>
decoration [ˌdɛkə'reɪʃən] *n* : décoration *f*
decorative ['dɛkərətɪv, -ˌreɪ-] *adj* : décoratif, ornemental
decorator ['dɛkəˌreɪtər] *n* : décorateur *m*, -trice *f*
decorum [dɪ'koːrəm, -kɔr-] *n* : bienséance *f*, décorum *m*
decoy[1] ['diˌkɔɪ] *vt* : attirer avec un appeau
decoy[2] *n* : appeau *m*, leurre *m*
decrease[1] [dɪ'kriːs] *v* **-creased; -creasing** *vi* : diminuer, décroître — *vt* REDUCE : diminuer, réduire
decrease[2] ['diˌkris, dɪ'-] *n* : diminution *f*, baisse *f*
decree[1] [dɪ'kriː] *vt* **-creed; -creeing** : décréter
decree[2] *n* : décret *m*
decrepit [dɪ'krɛpɪt] *adj* **1** FEEBLE : décrépit **2** DILAPIDATED : délabré, en ruine
decry [dɪ'kraɪ] *vt* **-cried; -crying** : décrier, dénigrer
dedicate ['dɛdɪˌkeɪt] *vt* **-cated; -cating 1** DEVOTE : dédier, consacrer **2** : dédier <she dedicated the book to her daughter : elle a dédié le livre à sa fille>
dedication [dɛdɪ'keɪʃən] *n* **1** DEVOTION : dévouement *m* **2** INSCRIPTION : dédicace *f* **3** CONSECRATION : consécration *f* (d'une église, etc.)
deduce [dɪ'duːs, -'djuːs] *vt* **-duced; -ducing** : déduire, inférer
deduct [dɪ'dʌkt] *vt* : déduire, prélever
deductible [dɪ'dʌktəbəl] *adj* : déductible
deduction [dɪ'dʌkʃən] *n* **1** SUBTRACTION : déduction *f* **2** CONCLUSION : déduction *f*, raisonnement *m* déductif
deed[1] ['diːd] *vt* : transférer (par acte notarié)
deed[2] *n* **1** ACT : action *f* **2** FEAT : exploit *m* **3** : acte *m* notarié, titre *m* de propriété
deem ['diːm] *vt* CONSIDER : juger, estimer, considérer
deep[1] ['diːp] *adj* **1** : profond <a deep well : un puits profond> **2** WIDE : large, profond **3** ENGROSSED : préoccupé, absorbé <deep in thought : préoccupé par ses pensées> **4** LOW : grave, profond <a deep voice : une voix profonde> **5** DARK : intense <a deep blue : un bleu intense> **6** INTENSE, PROFOUND : profond <a deep insight : un aperçu profond>
deep[2] *n* **1** : cœur *m*, profondeur *f* <in the deep of winter : au plus profond de l'hiver, au cœur de l'hiver> **2 the deep** : l'océan *m*
deepen ['diːpən] *vt* **1** : approfondir **2** INTENSIFY : intensifier, augmenter — *vi* **1** : devenir plus profond **2** INTENSIFY : augmenter, s'intensifier
deeply ['diːplɪ] *adv* : profondément
deep–seated ['diːp'siːtəd] *adj* : fermement établi, profondément enraciné
deer ['dɪr] *ns & pl* : cerf *m*, chevreuil *m*, biche *f*
deerskin ['dɪrˌskɪn] *n* : peau *f* de daim
deface [dɪ'feɪs] *vt* **-faced; -facing** : abîmer, dégrader, défigurer

defamation |ˌdɛfəˈmeɪʃən| *n* : diffamation *f*
defamatory |dɪˈfæməˌtori| *adj* : diffamatoire
defame |dɪˈfeɪm| *vt* **-famed; -faming** : diffamer
default[1] |dɪˈfɔlt, ˈdiːˌfɔlt| *vi* **1** : ne pas s'acquitter (se dit d'une dette), ne pas régler (se dit d'un compte) **2** : manquer de comparaître (devant le tribunal)
default[2] *n* **1** : non-paiement *m* (d'une dette) **2** : non-comparution *f* (en cour) **3 by ~** : par forfait
defeat[1] |dɪˈfiːt| *vt* **1** BEAT : battre, vaincre **2** FRUSTRATE : faire échouer, mettre fin à (un plan, une ambition)
defeat[2] *n* : défaite *f*, échec *m*
defecate |ˈdɛfiˌkeɪt| *vi* **-cated; -cating** : déféquer
defect[1] |dɪˈfɛkt| *vi* : faire défection, s'enfuir
defect[2] |ˈdiːˌfɛkt, dɪˈfɛkt| *n* : défaut *m*
defection |dɪˈfɛkʃən| *n* : défection *f*
defective |dɪˈfɛktɪv| *adj* **1** FAULTY : défectueux **2** DEFICIENT : déficient <defective eyesight : yeux déficients>
defector |dɪˈfɛktər| *n* : transfuge *mf*
defence *Brit* → **defense**
defend |dɪˈfɛnd| *vt* : défendre
defendant |dɪˈfɛndənt| *n* : défendeur *m*, -deresse *f*; intimé *m*, -mée *f* (en appel)
defender |dɪˈfɛndər| *n* **1** ADVOCATE : défenseur *m*, avocat *m* **2** : défenseur *m* (aux sports)
defense *or Brit* **defence** |dɪˈfɛnts, ˈdiːˌfɛnts| *n* : défense *f*
defenseless *or Brit* **defenceless** |dɪˈfɛntsləs| *adj* : sans défense
defensive[1] |dɪˈfɛntsɪv| *adj* : défensif
defensive[2] *n* : défensive *f* <to be on the defensive : se tenir sur la défensive>
defer |dɪˈfər| *v* **-ferred; -ferring** *vt* POSTPONE : remettre, reporter — *vi* **to defer to** : s'en remettre à, déférer à
deference |ˈdɛfərənts| *n* : déférence *f*, égard *m* <in deference to his family : par égard pour sa famille>
deferential |ˌdɛfəˈrɛntʃəl| *adj* : déférent, respectueux
deferment |dɪˈfərmənt| *n* : report *m*, renvoi *m*
defiance |dɪˈfaɪənts| *n* **1** : défi *m* **2 in defiance of** : au mépris de
defiant |dɪˈfaɪənt| *adj* : provocant, de défi
deficiency |dɪˈfɪʃəntsi| *n, pl* **-cies 1** INADEQUACY : manque *m*, insuffisance *f* **2** FLAW : faille *f*, faiblesse *f*
deficient |dɪˈfɪʃənt| *adj* **1** INADEQUATE : insuffisant **2** FAULTY : défectueux
deficit |ˈdɛfəsɪt| *n* : déficit *m*
defile |dɪˈfaɪl| *vt* **-filed; -filing 1** SULLY : souiller **2** PROFANE : profaner, déshonorer
defilement |dɪˈfaɪlmənt| *n* **1** DEBASEMENT : souillure *f* **2** DESECRATION : profanation *f*
define |dɪˈfaɪn| *vt* **-fined; -fining 1** BOUND : définir, délimiter **2** CLARIFY : clarifier, définir <the issues are not well defined : les problèmes ne sont pas clairs> **3** : définir (un mot)
definite |ˈdɛfənɪt| *adj* **1** CLEAR, DISTINCT : précis, déterminé, net **2** CERTAIN : certain, sûr <is that definite? : c'est sûr?> **3** : défini (en grammaire) <definite article : article défini>
definitely |ˈdɛfənɪtli| *adv* **1** CERTAINLY : certainement, sans aucun doute **2** APPRECIABLY : sensiblement, nettement **3** CATEGORICALLY : absolument, catégoriquement <definitely! : bien sûr!>
definition |ˌdɛfəˈnɪʃən| *n* : définition *f*
definitive |dəˈfɪnətɪv| *adj* **1** CONCLUSIVE : définitif, décisif **2** AUTHORITATIVE : qui fait autorité
deflate |dɪˈfleɪt| *v* **-flated; -flating** *vt* **1** : dégonfler (un ballon, etc.) **2** REDUCE : saper, miner (l'égo, la confiance) — *vi* : se dégonfler
deflation |dɪˈfleɪʃən| *n* **1** : dégonflement *m* (d'un ballon, etc.) **2** : déflation *f* (économique)
deflect |dɪˈflɛkt| *vt* : faire dévier, détourner — *vi* DEVIATE : dévier
deforest |diˈfɔrəst| *vt* : déboiser
deform |diˈfɔrm| *vt* : déformer
deformity |diˈfɔrməti| *n, pl* **-ties** : difformité *f*
defraud |diˈfrɔd| *vt* : frauder, escroquer
defray |diˈfreɪ| *vt* : rembourser, couvrir (des coûts)
defrost |diˈfrɔst| *vt* **1** THAW : décongeler (des aliments) **2** : dégivrer (un réfrigérateur, etc.)
deft |ˈdɛft| *adj* : adroit, habile — **deftly** *adv*
defunct |dɪˈfʌŋkt| *adj* : défunt
defy |dɪˈfaɪ| *vt* **-fied; -fying 1** CHALLENGE : défier, braver **2** RESIST : résister à, s'opposer à <to defy all one's efforts : résister à tous les efforts>
degenerate[1] |dɪˈdʒɛnəˌreɪt| *vi* **-ated; -ating** : dégénérer, s'abâtardir
degenerate[2] |dɪˈdʒɛnərət| *adj* : dégénéré
degeneration |didʒɛnəˈreɪʃən| *n* : dégénérescence *f*
degradation |ˌdɛgrəˈdeɪʃən| *n* : dégradation *f*
degrade |dɪˈgreɪd| *vt* **-graded; -grading 1** : dégrader **2 to degrade oneself** : s'abaisser
degree |dɪˈgriː| *n* **1** AMOUNT, EXTENT : degré *m*, point *m*, mesure *f* <to a certain degree : à un certain degré, jusqu'à un certain point> **2** : diplôme *m* <college degree : diplôme universitaire> **3** : degré *m* (en physique, en mathématiques, etc.) **4 by degrees** : par degrés, petit à petit

dehydrate [di'haɪˌdreɪt] *v* **-drated; -drating** *vt* : déshydrater — *vi* : se déshydrater
dehydration [ˌdiːhaɪ'dreɪʃən] *n* : déshydratation *f*
deice [ˌdiː'aɪs] *vt* **-iced; -icing** : dégivrer
deify ['diːəˌfaɪ, 'deɪ-] *vt* **-fied; -fying** : déifier
deign ['deɪn] *vt* : daigner, condescendre à
deity ['diːət̬i, 'deɪ-] *n, pl* **-ties 1** GOD, GODDESS : dieu *m*, déesse *f* **2 the Deity** : Dieu *m*
dejected [dɪ'dʒɛktəd] *adj* : découragé, abattu
dejection [dɪ'dʒɛkʃən] *n* : découragement *m*, abattement *m*
delay¹ [dɪ'leɪ] *vt* **1** POSTPONE : reporter, différer **2** HOLD UP : retarder, retenir <he delayed me for no reason : il m'a retenu sans raison>
delay² *n* 1 POSTPONEMENT : report *m* **2** HOLDUP : délai *m* <without further delay : sans plus tarder>
delectable [dɪ'lɛktəbəl] *adj* : délicieux
delegate¹ ['dɛlɪˌgeɪt] *vt* **-gated; -gating** : déléguer
delegate² ['dɛlɪgət, -ˌgeɪt] *n* : délégué *m*, -guée *f*
delegation [ˌdɛlə'geɪʃən] *n* : délégation *f*
delete [dɪ'liːt] *vt* **-leted; -leting** : supprimer, effacer
deletion [dɪ'liːʃən] *n* : suppression *f*
deliberate¹ [dɪ'lɪbəˌreɪt] *v* **-ated; -ating** *vt* : délibérer sur, réfléchir sur — *vi* : délibérer, considérer
deliberate² [dɪ'lɪbərət] *adj* **1** CONSIDERED : délibéré, réfléchi **2** INTENTIONAL : délibéré, intentionnel **3** UNHURRIED : mesuré, posé
deliberately [dɪ'lɪbərət̬li] *adv* **1** INTENTIONALLY : délibérément, à dessein, exprès **2** STEADILY : de façon mesurée
deliberation [dɪˌlɪbə'reɪʃən] *n* **1** CONSIDERATION : délibération *f*, réflexion *f* **2** DISCUSSION : délibérations *fpl*, débats *mpl* **3** RESTRAINT : mesure *f*, manière *f* posée
delicacy ['dɛlɪkəsi] *n, pl* **-cies 1** : mets *m* délicat **2** FINENESS : délicatesse *f*, finesse *f* **3** FRAILTY : délicatesse *f*, fragilité *f*
delicate ['dɛlɪkət] *adj* **1** SUBTLE : délicat <a delicate fragrance : un parfum délicat> **2** DAINTY, FINE : délicat, fin **3** FRAGILE : fragile **4** SENSITIVE : délicat, sensible <a delicate situation : une question délicate>
delicately ['dɛlɪkət̬li] *adv* : délicatement, avec délicatesse
delicatessen [ˌdɛlɪkə'tɛsən] *n* : charcuterie *f*
delicious [dɪ'lɪʃəs] *adj* : délicieux
delight¹ [dɪ'laɪt] *vt* : réjouir, enchanter — *vi* **to delight in** : prendre plaisir à
delight² *n* 1 PLEASURE : plaisir *m*, joie *f* **2** : délice *m*, merveille *f* <my new car is a delight : ma nouvelle voiture est une merveille>
delightful [dɪ'laɪtfəl] *adj* : charmant, merveilleux, ravissant
delightfully [dɪ'laɪtfəli] *adv* : de façon charmante, merveilleusement
delineate [dɪ'lɪniˌeɪt] *vt* **-eated; -eating 1** SKETCH : tracer **2** PORTRAY : décrire, dépeindre
delinquency [dɪ'lɪŋkwənt̬si] *n, pl* **-cies** : délinquance *f*
delinquent¹ [dɪ'lɪŋkwənt] *adj* **1** : délinquant <delinquent children : enfants délinquants> **2** OVERDUE : arriéré
delinquent² *n* : délinquant *m*, -quante *f*
delirious [dɪ'lɪriəs] *adj* : délirant, en délire
delirium [dɪ'lɪriəm] *n* : délire *m*
deliver [dɪ'lɪvər] *vt* **1** FREE : délivrer <deliver us from evil : délivre-nous de tout mal> **2** DISTRIBUTE : livrer **3** : mettre au monde (un enfant) **4** : faire, prononcer <to deliver a speech : prononcer un discours> **5** DEAL : porter, assener <to deliver a blow : porter un coup>
deliverance [dɪ'lɪvərənt̬s] *n* : délivrance *f*
delivery [dɪ'lɪvəri] *n, pl* **-eries 1** LIBERATION : délivrance *f* **2** DISTRIBUTION : livraison *f*, distribution *f* **3** CHILDBIRTH : accouchement *m* **4** SPEECH : élocution *f*, débit *m*
dell ['dɛl] *n* : vallon *m* (boisé)
delta ['dɛltə] *n* : delta *m*
delude [dɪ'luːd] *vt* **-luded; -luding 1** : tromper, duper **2 to delude oneself** : se leurrer, se faire des illusions
deluge¹ ['dɛljuːdʒ, -juːʒ] *vt* **-uged; -uging 1** FLOOD : inonder **2** SWAMP : inonder, submerger <deluged with calls : inondé d'appels>
deluge² *n* : inondation *f*, déluge *m*
delusion [dɪ'luːʒən] *n* **1** : illusion *f* **2 delusions of grandeur** : la folie des grandeurs
deluxe [dɪ'lʌks, -lʊks] *adj* : de luxe, luxueux
delve ['dɛlv] *vi* **delved; delving 1** DIG : creuser **2 to delve into** : fouiller dans
demand¹ [dɪ'mænd] *vt* : exiger, réclamer
demand² *n* 1 REQUIREMENT : exigence *f* **2** CLAIM : réclamation *f*, revendication *f* **3** : demande *f* (en commerce) **4 → supply**
demarcation [ˌdiːˌmɑr'keɪʃən] *n* : démarcation *f*
demean [dɪ'miːn] *vt* **1** : abaisser, rabaisser **2 to demean oneself** : s'abaisser
demeanor *or Brit* **demeanour** [dɪ'miːnər] *n* **1** BEHAVIOR : comportement *m* **2** MANNER : air *m*, allure *f*, mine *f*

demented [dɪ'mentəd] *adj* : dément, fou
demerit [dɪ'merət] *n* : démérite *m*
demigod ['demiˌgɑd, -ˌgɔd] *n* : demi-dieu *m*
demise [dɪ'maɪz] *n* **1** DEATH : mort *f*, décès *m* **2** END : fin *f*, mort *f* (d'une institution, etc.)
demitasse ['demiˌtæs, -ˌtɑs] *n* : tasse *f* de café noir
demobilize [di'mo:bəˌlaɪz-] *vt* **-lized; -lizing** : démobiliser
democracy [dɪ'mɑkrəsi] *n, pl* **-cies** : démocratie *f*
democrat ['deməˌkræt] *n* : démocrate *mf*
democratic [ˌdeməˈkræt̬ɪk] *adj* : démocratique — **democratically** *adv*
demolish [di'mɑlɪʃ] *vt* **1** RAZE : démolir, raser **2** DESTROY : détruire, démolir (une théorie, etc.)
demolition [ˌdeməˈlɪʃən, ˌdi:-] *n* : démolition *f*
demon ['di:mən] *n* : démon *m*
demonic [dɪ'mɑnɪk, di-] *adj* : diabolique
demonstrably [dəˈmɑnɪstrəbli] *adv* : manifestement
demonstrate ['demənˌstreɪt] *v* **-strated; -strating** *vt* **1** SHOW : manifester, démontrer **2** EXPLAIN, PROVE : démontrer, établir **3** : faire une démonstration de — *vi* **1** : faire une démonstration **2** PROTEST : manifester, protester
demonstration [deməˈnstreɪʃən] *n* **1** : démonstration *f* **2** PROTEST : manifestation *f*
demonstrative [dɪ'mɑnstrət̬ɪv] *adj* : démonstratif
demonstrator ['deməˌnstreɪt̬ər] *n* **1** : démonstrateur *m*, -trice *f* **2** PROTESTOR : manifestant *m*, -tante *f*
demoralize [dɪ'mɔrəˌlaɪz] *vt* **-ized; -izing** : démoraliser
demote [di'mo:t] *vt* **-moted; -moting** : rétrograder
demur [dɪ'mər] *vi* **-murred; -murring** : élever des objections, s'opposer
demure [dɪ'mjʊr] *adj* : modeste, réservé
den ['den] *n* **1** LAIR : antre *m*, tanière *f* **2** HIDEOUT : repaire *m* <a den of iniquity : un lieu de perdition> **3** STUDY : petit salon *m*, petit bureau *m* de travail
denature [di'neɪtʃər] *vt* **-tured; -turing** : dénaturer
denial [di'naɪəl] *n* **1** DENYING : démenti *m*, dénégation *f* **2** REFUSAL : refus *m*, rejet *m* **3** DISAVOWAL : reniement *m*
denigrate ['denɪˌgreɪt] *vt* **-grated; -grating** : dénigrer
denim ['denəm] *n* **1** : jean *m* **2 denims** *npl* JEANS : jean *m*, blue-jean *m*
denizen ['denəzən] *n* : habitant *m*, -tante *f*
denomination [dɪˌnɑmə'neɪʃən] *n* **1** : confession *f* (religieuse) **2** DESIGNATION : dénomination *f* **3** VALUE : valeur *f* (de monnaie)
denominator [dɪ'nɑməˌneɪt̬ər] *n* : dénominateur *m*
denote [di'no:t] *vt* **-noted; -noting 1** INDICATE : dénoter **2** MEAN : signifier
denouement [ˌdeɪˌnu:'mɑ:] *n* : dénouement *m*
denounce [dɪ'naʊnts] *vt* **-nounced; -nouncing 1** CENSURE : dénoncer **2** ACCUSE : accuser
dense ['dents] *adj* **denser; -est 1** THICK : dense **2** STUPID : bête, obtus
densely ['dentsli] *adv* : densément
density ['dentsət̬i] *n, pl* **-ties** : densité *f*
dent[1] ['dent] *vt* : bosseler, poquer *Can fam* (une voiture), cabosser (un chapeau, etc.)
dent[2] *n* : bosse *f* (en métal), creux *m*
dental ['dentəl] *adj* : dentaire
dental floss *n* : fil *m* dentaire
dentifrice ['dentəfrɪs] *n* : dentifrice *m*, pâte *f* dentifrice
dentist ['dentɪst] *n* : dentiste *mf*
dentistry ['dentɪstri] *n* : dentisterie *f*
dentures ['dentʃərz] *npl* : dentier *m*
denude [di'nu:d, -'nju:d] *vt* **-nuded; -nuding** : dénuder
denunciation [dɪˌnʌntsi'eɪʃən] *n* : dénonciation *f*
deny [dɪ'naɪ] *vt* **-nied; -nying 1** REFUTE : démentir, nier <he denied the charges : il a démenti les accusations> **2** REPUDIATE : renier <to deny one's religion : renier sa religion> **3** REFUSE : refuser **4 to deny oneself** : se priver
deodorant [di'o:dərənt] *n* **1** : déodorant *m* **2** *or* **room deodorant** : désodorisant *m*
deodorize [di'o:dəˌraɪz] *vt* **-ized; -izing** : désodoriser
depart [dɪ'pɑrt] *vt* : quitter <to depart this life : quitter ce monde> — *vi* LEAVE : partir
department [dɪ'pɑrtmənt] *n* **1** DIVISION : ministère *m* (gouvernemental), service *m* (d'un hôpital, etc.), rayon *m* (d'un magasin) **2** FIELD : champ *m*, domaine *m* <it's not my department : ce n'est pas mon champ d'expertise>
departmental [dɪˌpɑrt'mentəl, ˌdi:-] *adj* : de service, de département
department store *n* : grand magasin *m*
departure [dɪ'pɑrtʃər] *n* **1** LEAVING : départ *m* **2** DEVIATION : écart *m*, déviation *f*, entorse *f* <a departure from procedure : un écart à la procédure>
depend [dɪ'pend] *vi* **1** RELY : compter, se fier <depend on me! : comptez sur moi!> **2 to depend on** : dépendre de <success depends on hard work : le succès est le résultat d'un travail acharné> **3 depending on** : selon, dépendamment de *Can* <depending

on what happens : selon ce qui se passera>

dependable [dɪˈpendəbəl] *adj* : fiable, sûr

dependent[1] [dɪˈpendənt] *adj* : dépendant

dependent[2] *n* : personne *f* à charge

depict [dɪˈpɪkt] *vt* : dépeindre, décrire

deplete [dɪˈpliːt] *vt* **-pleted; -pleting** : épuiser, réduire

depletion [dɪˈpliːʃən] *n* : diminution *f*, réduction *f*

deplorable [dɪˈplorəbəl] *adj* : déplorable, lamentable

deplore [dɪˈplor] *vt* **-plored; -ploring** : déplorer, regretter

deploy [dɪˈplɔɪ] *vt* : déployer

deployment [dɪˈplɔɪmənt] *n* : déploiement *m*

deport [dɪˈport] *vt* **1** EXPEL : déporter, expulser (d'un pays) **2 to deport oneself** BEHAVE : se comporter

deportment [dɪˈportmənt] *n* BEHAVIOR : comportement *m*

depose [dɪˈpoːz] *vt* **-posed; -posing** : déposer (un souverain, etc.)

deposit[1] [dɪˈpɑzət] *vt* **-ited; -iting** : déposer

deposit[2] *n* **1** : dépôt *m* <a $500 deposit : un dépôt de 500$> **2** DOWN PAYMENT : acompte *m*, arrhes *fpl France* **3** : dépôt *m* (en géologie)

depositor [dɪˈpɑzət̬ər] *n* : déposant *m*, -sante *f*

depository [dɪˈpɑzə̯tori] *n, pl* **-ries** : dépôt *m*, lieu *m* sûr

depot [*1 usu* ˈdeˌpoː, *2 usu* ˈdiː-] *n* **1** WAREHOUSE : dépôt *m*, entrepôt *m* **2** STATION : gare *f* (ferroviaire), gare *f* d'autobus

deprave [dɪˈpreɪv] *vt* **-praved; -praving** : dépraver, corrompre

depravity [dɪˈprævə̯ti] *n, pl* **-ties** : dépravation *f*

depreciate [dɪˈpriːʃi̯ˌeɪt] *v* **-ated; -ating** *vt* **1** DEVALUE : dévaluer **2** DISPARAGE : déprécier, dénigrer — *vi* : se déprécier (se dit d'une valeur)

depreciation [dɪˌpriʃiˈeɪʃən] *n* : dépréciation *f*

depress [dɪˈpres] *vt* **1** PRESS : appuyer sur **2** REDUCE : réduire, faire baisser (les ventes, les prix, etc.) **3** DISCOURAGE, SADDEN : déprimer, attrister **4** DEVALUE : dévaluer

depressant [dɪˈpresənt] *n* : dépresseur *m*

depressed [dɪˈprest] *adj* : déprimé, abattu

depressing [dɪˈpresɪŋ] *adj* : déprimant, décourageant

depression [dɪˈpreʃən] *n* **1** : dépression *f* (en médecine) **2** : récession *f*, crise *f* <economic depression : crise économique> **3** HOLLOW : creux *m*, dépression *f*

deprivation [ˌdeprəˈveɪʃən] *n* : privation *f*

deprive [dɪˈpraɪv] *vt* **-prived; -priving** : priver

depth [ˈdepθ] *n, pl* **depths 1** : profondeur *f* <the depth of a cupboard : la profondeur d'une armoire> **2** EXTENT : étendue *f* <the depth of his knowledge : l'étendue de ses connaissances> **3** INTENSITY : intensité *f* (de couleurs) **4 in the depths of** : au milieu de, au cœur de

deputize [ˈdepjə̯ˌtaɪz] *vt* **-tized; -tizing** : députer

deputy [ˈdepjə̯ti] *n, pl* **-ties** : député *m*, -tée *f*

derail [diˈreɪl] *vt* : faire dérailler — *vi* : dérailler

derailment [diˈreɪlmənt] *n* : déraillement *m*

derange [dɪˈreɪndʒ] *vt* **-ranged; -ranging 1** DISARRANGE : déranger, déplacer **2** CRAZE : rendre fou

derangement [dɪˈreɪndʒmənt] *n* **1** DISARRAY : confusion *f*, désordre *m* **2** INSANITY : aliénation *f* mentale

derby [ˈdərbi] *n, pl* **-bies 1** : derby *m* (course de chevaux) **2** *or* **derby hat** : chapeau *m* melon

deregulate [diˈregjə̯ˌleɪt] *vt* **-lated; -lating** : déréglementer

deregulation [diˌregjə̯ˈleɪʃən] *n* : déréglementation *f*

derelict[1] [ˈderəˌlɪkt] *adj* **1** ABANDONED : abandonné **2** NEGLIGENT : négligent, insouciant

derelict[2] *n* **1** : propriété *f* abandonnée, navire *m* abandonné **2** VAGRANT : vagabond *m*, -bonde *f*; clochard *m*, -charde *f*

deride [dɪˈraɪd] *vt* **-rided; -riding** : railler, tourner en dérision

derision [dɪˈrɪʒən] *n* : dérision *f*

derisive [dɪˈraɪsɪv] *adj* : moqueur, railleur

derivation [ˌderəˈveɪʃən] *n* : dérivation *f*

derivative[1] [dɪˈrɪvə̯t̬ɪv] *adj* : dérivé

derivative[2] *n* : dérivé *m*

derive [dɪˈraɪv] *v* **-rived; -riving** *vt* **1** OBTAIN : tirer, trouver **2** DEDUCE : déduire, dériver de — *vi* **to derive from** : découler de, provenir de

dermatologist [ˌdərməˈtɑlədʒɪst] *n* : dermatologue *mf*

dermatology [ˌdərməˈtɑlədʒi] *n* : dermatologie *f*

derogatory [dɪˈrɑgə̯ˌtori] *adj* : désobligeant

derrick [ˈderɪk] *n* **1** CRANE : grue *f* **2** : tour *f* de forage (pour le pétrole)

descend [dɪˈsend] *vt* : descendre — *vi* **1** : descendre <she descended from the train : elle est descendue du train> **2** DERIVE : dériver, provenir <to be descended from : descendre de> **3** INCLINE : descendre **4** STOOP : s'abaisser, descendre (au niveau de qqn) **5 to descend upon** : se précipiter sur, s'élancer vers

descendant[1] *or* **descendent** [dɪˈsɛndənt] *adj* : descendant
descendant[2] *or* **descendent** *n* : descendant *m*, -dante *f*
descent [dɪˈsɛnt] *n* **1** : descente *f* <the descent of the airplane : la descente de l'avion> **2** LINEAGE : origine *f*, descendance *f* **3** DECLINE, SLOPE : descente *f* **4** ATTACK, INRUSH : descente *f*, irruption *f*
describe [dɪˈskraɪb] *vt* **-scribed; -scribing** : décrire
description [dɪˈskrɪpʃən] *n* : description *f*
descriptive [dɪˈskrɪptɪv] *adj* : descriptif
desecrate [ˈdɛsɪˌkreɪt] *vt* **-crated; -crating** : profaner
desecration [ˌdɛsɪˈkreɪʃən] *n* : profanation *f*
desegregate [diˈsɛgrəˌgeɪt] *vt* **-gated; -gating** : éliminer la ségrégation raciale dans
desegregation [diˌsɛgrəˈgeɪʃən] *n* : déségrégation *f*
desert[1] [ˈdɛzərt] *vt* : abandonner (une personne ou un lieu), déserter (une cause) — *vi* : déserter
desert[2] [ˈdɛzərt] *adj* : désert <a desert isle : une île déserte>
desert[3] *n* **1** [ˈdɛzərt] : désert *m* **2** [diˈzərt] → **deserts**
deserter [dɪˈzərtər] *n* : déserteur *m*
desertion [dɪˈzərʃən] *n* : désertion *f*
deserts [dɪˈzərts] *npl* **to get one's just deserts** : avoir ce que l'on mérite
deserve [dɪˈzərv] *vt* **-served; -serving** : mériter
desiccate [ˈdɛsɪˌkeɪt] *vt* **-cated; -cating** : sécher, dessécher
design[1] [dɪˈzaɪn] *vt* **1** DEVISE : concevoir, élaborer **2** DRAW, SKETCH : dessiner **3** INTEND : concevoir, destiner <a book designed for students : un livre destiné pour les étudiants>
design[2] *n* **1** CONCEPTION : conception *f*, élaboration *f* **2** PLAN : plan *m*, projet *m* **3** PURPOSE : dessein *m*, intention *f* <by design : à dessein, exprès> **4** SKETCH : dessin *m*, croquis *m* **5** PATTERN : motif *m*
designate [ˈdɛzɪgˌneɪt] *vt* **-nated; -nating 1** INDICATE : indiquer, montrer **2** APPOINT : nommer, désigner
designation [ˌdɛzɪgˈneɪʃən] *n* **1** APPOINTMENT : nomination *f*, désignation *f* **2** NAME : désignation *f*, dénomination *f*
designer [dəˈzaɪnər] *n* **1** : concepteur *m*, -trice *f*; dessinateur *m*, -trice *f* **2** *or* **fashion designer** : designer *m*, couturier *m*
desirable [dɪˈzaɪrəbəl] *adj* **1** ATTRACTIVE : désirable, enviable **2** ADVISABLE : désirable, souhaitable
desire[1] [dɪˈzaɪr] *vt* **-sired; -siring 1** WANT : désirer, avoir envie de **2** REQUEST : demander
desire[2] *n* **1** LONGING : désir *m*, envie *f* **2** REQUEST : demande *f*, requête *f*
desist [dɪˈsɪst] *vi* : cesser, s'arrêter
desk [ˈdɛsk] *n* : bureau *m*, pupitre *m* (d'un élève)
desolate[1] [ˈdɛsəˌleɪt, -zə-] *vt* **-lated; -lating** RAVAGE : dévaster, ravager
desolate[2] [ˈdɛsələt, -zə-] *adj* **1** BARREN : désolé, désert <a desolate landscape : un paysage désert> **2** GLOOMY : morne, sombre
desolation [ˈdɛsəˈleɪʃən, -zə-] *n* **1** BARRENNESS : désolation *f* **2** GRIEF : affliction *f*, chagrin *m*
despair[1] [dɪˈspɛr] *vi* : désespérer, perdre espoir
despair[2] *n* : désespoir *m*
desperate [ˈdɛspərət] *adj* : désespéré — **desperately** *adv*
desperation [ˌdɛspəˈreɪʃən] *n* : désespoir *m*
despicable [dɪˈspɪkəbəl, ˈdɛspɪ-] *adj* : ignoble, méprisable
despise [dɪˈspaɪz] *vt* **-spised; -spising** : mépriser, détester
despite [dəˈspaɪt] *prep* : malgré, en dépit de
despoil [dəˈspɔɪl] *vt* : dépouiller, spolier
despondency [dɪˈspɑndənt͡si] *n* : abattement *m*, découragement *m*
despondent [dɪˈspɑndənt] *adj* : abattu, découragé
despot [ˈdɛspət, -ˌpɑt] *n* : despote *m*
despotic [dəsˈpɑtɪk] *adj* : despotique, tyrannique
despotism [ˈdɛspəˈtɪzəm] *n* : despotisme *m*
dessert [dɪˈzərt] *n* : dessert *m*
destination [ˌdɛstɪˈneɪʃən] *n* : destination *f*
destined [ˈdɛstənd] *adj* **1** FATED : prédestiné **2** BOUND : destiné, en route <destined for Quebec : à destination de Québec>
destiny [ˈdɛstəni] *n, pl* **-nies** : destin *m*, destinée *f*
destitute [ˈdɛstəˌtuːt] *adj* **1** LACKING : dépourvu, dénué <a lake destitute of fish : un lac dépourvu de poissons> **2** POOR : sans ressources, indigent
destitution [ˈdɛstəˈtuːʃən, -ˈtjuː-] *n* : misère *f*, indigence *f*
destroy [dɪˈstrɔɪ] *vt* **1** RUIN : détruire **2** KILL : détruire, anéantir
destroyer [dɪˈstrɔɪər] *n* **1** : destructeur *m*, -trice *f* **2** WARSHIP : contre-torpilleur *m*
destructible [dɪˈstrʌktəbəl] *adj* : destructible
destruction [dɪˈstrʌkʃən] *n* : destruction *f*
destructive [dɪˈstrʌktɪv] *adj* : destructeur, destructif
desultory [ˈdɛsəlˌtori] *adj* : décousu, sans suite

detach [dɪ'tætʃ] *vt* **1** SEPARATE : détacher, séparer **2 to detach oneself** : se détacher

detached [dɪ'tætʃt] *adj* **1** SEPARATE : détaché, séparé **2** ALOOF : distant, indifférent **3** IMPARTIAL : objectif, désintéressé

detachment [dɪ'tætʃmənt] *n* **1** SEPARATION : séparation *f* **2** ALOOFNESS : détachement *m*, indifférence *f* **3** IMPARTIALITY : impartialité *f* **4** : détachement *m* (militaire)

detail[1] [dɪ'teɪl, 'di:,teɪl] *vt* : détailler, énumérer

detail[2] *n* **1** : détail *m* <to go into details : rentrer dans les détails> **2** : détachement *m* (militaire)

detain [dɪ'teɪn] *vt* **1** : détenir (un prisonnier) **2** DELAY : retenir, retarder

detect [dɪ'tɛkt] *vt* : détecter, déceler, découvrir

detection [dɪ'tɛkʃən] *n* : détection *f*, découverte *f*

detective [dɪ'tɛktɪv] *n* : détective *mf* <private detective : détective privé>

detector [dɪ'tɛktər] *n* : détecteur *m*

detention [dɪ'tɛntʃən] *n* : détention *f*

deter [dɪ'tər] *vt* **-terred; -terring** : dissuader, décourager

detergent [dɪ'tərdʒənt] *n* : détergent *m*

deteriorate [dɪ'tɪriə,reɪt] *vi* **-rated; -rating** : se détériorer, se dégrader

deterioration [dɪ,tɪriə'reɪʃən] *n* : détérioration *f*

determination [dɪ,tərmə'neɪʃən] *n* **1** DECISION : décision *f*, jugement *m* **2** RESOLVE : détermination *f*, résolution *f*

determine [dɪ'tərmən] *vt* **-mined; -mining 1** FIND OUT : déterminer, découvrir **2** FIX, SETTLE : fixer, déterminer **3** RESOLVE : décider **4** CAUSE, GOVERN : décider de, déterminer

determined [dɪ'tərmənd] *adj* RESOLUTE : déterminé, résolu

deterrence [dɪ'tərənts, -'tɛr-] *n* : dissuasion *f*

deterrent[1] [dɪ'tərənt] *adj* : dissuasif

deterrent[2] *n* : moyen *m* de dissuasion

detest [dɪ'tɛst] *vt* : détester, haïr

detestable [dɪ'tɛstəbəl] *adj* : détestable

dethrone [di'θro:n] *vt* **-throned; -throning** : détrôner

detonate ['dɛtən,eɪt] *v* **-nated; -nating** *vt* : faire détoner — *vi* EXPLODE : détoner

detonation [,dɛtən'eɪʃən, 'dɛtən-] *n* : détonation *f*, explosion *f*

detour[1] ['di:,tʊr, di'tʊr] *vt* DIVERT : détourner, dévier — *vi* : faire un détour

detour[2] *n* : détour *m*

detract [dɪ'trækt] *vt* : détourner <to detract attention : détourner l'attention> — *vi* **to detract from** : diminuer, porter atteinte à

detriment ['dɛtrəmənt] *n* : détriment *m*, préjudice *m*

detrimental [,dɛtrə'mɛntəl] *adj* : nuisible, préjudiciable

devaluation [di,vælju'eɪʃən] *n* : dévaluation *f*

devalue [di'vælju:] *vt* : dévaluer

devastate ['dɛvə,steɪt] *vt* **-tated; -tating** : dévaster, ravager

devastation [,dɛvə'steɪʃən] *n* : dévastation *f*

develop [dɪ'vɛləp] *vt* **1** FOSTER, PERFECT : mettre au point, développer, cultiver **2** EXPLOIT : développer, exploiter, mettre en valeur (des terres, etc.) **3** : développer (un film) **4** CONTRACT : contracter (une maladie) **5** ACQUIRE : développer, acquérir <he acquired a taste for olives : il a développé un goût pour les olives> — *vi* **1** GROW : se développer, grandir **2** HAPPEN : se produire, se manifester **3** UNFOLD : se développer, se dérouler

developing [dɪ'vɛləpɪŋ] *adj* : en expansion <developing countries : pays en expansion>

development [dɪ'vɛləpmənt] *n* **1** FORMATION, GROWTH : développement *m*, formation *f*, expansion *f* **2** : exploitation *f*, mise *f* en valeur (de ressources) **3** INCIDENT : événement *m*, fait *m* nouveau **4** *or* **housing development** : ensemble *m* résidentiel

deviant ['di:viənt] *adj* : déviant

deviate ['di:vi,eɪt] *vi* **-ated; -ating** : dévier, s'écarter

deviation [,di:vi'eɪʃən] *n* : déviation *f*

device [dɪ'vaɪs] *n* **1** MECHANISM : appareil *m*, dispositif *m*, mécanisme *m* **2** SCHEME : ruse *f*, stratagème *m* **3 to leave s.o. to their own devices** : laisser qqn se débrouiller tout seul

devil[1] ['dɛvəl] *vt* **-iled** *or* **-illed; -iling** *or* **-illing 1** : assaisonner avec des épices fortes <deviled eggs : œufs à la diable> **2** PESTER : ennuyer, agacer

devil[2] *n* **1** DEMON : diable *m*, démon *m* **2 the Devil** : le Démon *m*, Satan *m* **3** : monstre *m*, démon *m* <what a little devil! : quel petit monstre!>

devilish ['dɛvəlɪʃ] *adj* : diabolique

devious ['di:viəs] *adj* **1** CUNNING : sournois, astucieux **2** WINDING : tortueux, sinueux

devise [dɪ'vaɪz] *vt* **-vised; -vising 1** INVENT : inventer, concevoir **2** PLOT : manigancer

devoid [dɪ'vɔɪd] *adj* ~ **of** : dépourvu de, dénué de

devote [dɪ'vo:t] *vt* **-voted; -voting 1** DEDICATE : consacrer, vouer **2 to devote oneself to** : se consacrer à

devoted [dɪ'vo:təd] *adj* **1** FAITHFUL : dévoué, fidèle **2 to be devoted to** : être très attaché à

devotee [,dɛvə'ti:, -'teɪ] *n* **1** ENTHUSIAST : passionné *m*, -née *f* (d'un sport, etc.) **2** FOLLOWER : adepte *mf*; partisan *m*, -sane *f*

devotion [dɪ'voʊʃən] *n* **1** DEDICATION : dévouement *m* **2** PIETY : dévotion *f*, piété *f* **3 devotions** *npl* PRAYER : dévotions *fpl*, prières *fpl*
devour [dɪ'vaʊər] *vt* : dévorer
devout [dɪ'vaʊt] *adj* **1** PIOUS : dévot, pieux **2** EARNEST : fervent, ardent
devoutness [dɪ'vaʊtnəs] *n* : dévotion *f*, piété *f*
dew ['du:, 'dju:] *n* : rosée *f*
dewdrop ['du:,drɑp, 'dju:-] *n* : goutte *f* de rosée
dewlap ['du,læp, 'dju-] *n* : fanon *m*
dexterity [dɛk'stɛrəṭi] *n, pl* **-ties** : dextérité *f*, adresse *f*
dexterous ['dɛkstrəs] *adj* : adroit, habile, agile
dextrose ['dɛk,stro:s] *n* : dextrose *m*
diabetes [,daɪə'bi:ṭi:z] *n* : diabète *m*
diabetic[1] [,daɪə'bɛṭɪk] *adj* : diabétique
diabetic[2] *n* : diabétique *mf*
diabolic [,daɪə'bɑlɪk] *or* **diabolical** [-lɪkəl] *adj* : diabolique
diacritic [,daɪə'krɪṭɪk] *n or* **diacritical mark** [,daɪə'krɪṭɪkəl] : signe *m* diacritique
diadem ['daɪə,dɛm, -dəm] *n* : diadème *m*
diagnose ['daɪəg,no:s, ,daɪəg'no:s] *vt* **-nosed; -nosing** : diagnostiquer
diagnosis [,daɪəg'no:sɪs] *n, pl* **-noses** [-'no:si:z] : diagnostic *m*
diagnostic [,daɪəg'nɑstɪk] *adj* : diagnostique
diagonal[1] [daɪ'ægənəl] *adj* : diagonal
diagonal[2] *n* : diagonale *f*
diagram[1] ['daɪə,græm] *vt* **-grammed** *or* **-gramed; -gramming** *or* **-graming** : donner une représentation graphique de
diagram[2] *n* : diagramme *m*, schéma *m*
dial[1] ['daɪl] *vt* **-aled** *or* **-alled; -aling** *or* **-alling** : faire, composer (un numéro de téléphone)
dial[2] *n* : cadran *m* (d'une horloge, d'un téléphone), bouton *m* (d'une radio, etc.)
dialect ['daɪə,lɛkt] *n* : dialecte *m*
dialogue ['daɪə,lɔg] *n* : dialogue *m*
diameter [daɪ'æmə̱ṭər] *n* : diamètre *m*
diametric [,daɪə'mɛtrɪk] *or* **diametrical** [-trɪkəl] *adj* : diamétral — **diametrically** [-trɪkəli] *adv*
diamond ['daɪmənd, 'daɪə-] *n* **1** : diamant *m* (pierre précieuse) **2** : losange *m* (forme géométrique) **3** : carreau *m* (aux cartes) **4** INFIELD : terrain *m* de baseball, losange *m Can*
diaper ['daɪpər, 'daɪə-] *n* : couche *f* (de bébé)
diaphragm ['daɪə,fræm] *n* : diaphragme *m*
diarrhea *or Brit* **diarrhoea** [,daɪə'riə] *n* : diarrhée *f*
diary ['daɪəri:] *n, pl* **-ries** : journal *m* intime
diatribe ['daɪə,traɪb] *n* : diatribe *f*
dice[1] ['daɪs] *vt* **diced; dicing** CUBE : couper en dés
dice[2] *ns & pl* **1** → **die**[2] **2** : dé *m* (jeu) <to play dice : jouer aux dés>
dicker ['dɪkər] *vi* : marchander
dictate[1] ['dɪk,teɪt] *vt* **-tated; -tating** : dicter
dictate[2] *n* : précepte *m*, ordre *m* <the dictates of conscience : la voix de la conscience>
dictation [dɪk'teɪʃən] *n* : dictée *f*
dictator ['dɪk,teɪṭər] *n* : dictateur *m*
dictatorship [dɪk'teɪṭər,ʃɪp, 'dɪk,-] *n* : dictature *f*
diction ['dɪkʃən] *n* **1** WORDING : langage *m*, style *m* **2** ENUNCIATION : diction *f*, élocution *f*
dictionary ['dɪkʃə,nɛri] *n, pl* **-naries** : dictionnaire *m*
did → **do**
didactic [daɪ'dæktɪk] *adj* : didactique
die[1] ['daɪ] *vi* **died** ['daɪd]; **dying** ['daɪɪŋ] **1** : mourir, décéder **2** *or* **to die down** SUBSIDE : tomber (se dit du vent, de la colère, etc.) **3** STOP : s'arrêter <the motor died : le moteur s'est arrêté> **4** LONG : mourir d'envie <I'm dying to go : je meurs d'envie d'y aller>
die[2] ['daɪ] *n, pl* **dice** ['daɪs] : dé *m* (à jouer)
die[3] *n, pl* **dies** ['daɪz] MOLD, STAMP : étampe *f*, matrice *f*
diesel ['di:zəl, -səl] *n* : diesel *m*
diet[1] ['daɪət] *vi* : suivre un régime
diet[2] *n* **1** NOURISHMENT : alimentation *f*, nourriture *f* <a balanced diet : une alimentation équilibrée> **2** : régime *m* <to be on a diet : être au régime>
dietary ['daɪə,ṭɛri] *adj* : alimentaire, diététique
dietitian *or* **dietician** [daɪə'tɪʃən] *n* : diététicien *m*, -cienne *f*
differ ['dɪfər] *vi* **1** : différer, être différent **2** VARY : varier **3** DISAGREE : être en désaccord
difference ['dɪfrənts, 'dɪfərənts] *n* : différence *f*
different ['dɪfrənt, 'dɪfərənt] *adj* **1** DISSIMILAR : différent **2** OTHER : autre <that's different : c'est autre chose> **3** VARIOUS : divers, différent, plusieurs
differentiate [dɪfə'rɛnt,ʃi,eɪt] *v* **-ated; -ating** *vt* : différencier, distinguer — *vi* **to differentiate between** : faire la différence entre
differently ['dɪfrəntli, 'dɪfərəntli] *adv* : différemment, autrement
difficult ['dɪfɪ,kʌlt] *adj* : difficile
difficulty ['dɪfɪ,kʌlti] *n, pl* **-ties** : difficulté *f*
diffidence ['dɪfədənts] *n* **1** SHYNESS : timidité *f*, manque *m* d'assurance **2** RETICENCE : réserve *f*, réticence *f*
diffident ['dɪfədənt] *adj* **1** SHY : qui manque d'assurance, timide **2** RESERVED : réservé
diffuse[1] [dɪ'fju:z] *v* **-fused; -fusing** *vt* : diffuser — *vi* : se diffuser

diffuse[2] [dɪˈfjuːs] *adj* **1** WORDY : verbeux, diffus **2** : diffus, non concentré (se dit de la lumière, etc.)
diffusion [dɪˈfjuːʒən] *n* : diffusion *f*
dig[1] [ˈdɪg] *v* **dug** [ˈdʌg]; **digging** *vt* **1** : creuser (un trou), bêcher (la terre) **2** *or* **to dig up** EXTRACT : arracher, extraire **3** POKE, THRUST : enfoncer <to dig s.o. in the ribs : donner un coup de coude dans les côtes de qqn> **4 to dig up** UNEARTH : déterrer — *vi* **1** EXCAVATE : creuser **2 to dig in** : se retrancher
dig[2] *n* **1** POKE : coup *m* de coude **2** GIBE : pointe *f*, remarque *f* blessante
digest[1] [daɪˈdʒest, dɪ-] *vt* **1** : digérer (de la nourriture) **2** ASSIMILATE : assimiler, digérer **3** SUMMARIZE : résumer
digest[2] [ˈdaɪˌdʒest] *n* : résumé *m*
digestible [daɪˈdʒestəbəl, dɪ-] *adj* : digestible
digestion [daɪˈdʒestʃən] *n* : digestion *f*
digestive [daɪˈdʒestʃən, dɪ-] *adj* : digestif <the digestive system : l'appareil digestif>
digit [ˈdɪdʒət] *n* **1** NUMERAL : chiffre *m* **2** FINGER : doigt *m* **3** TOE : orteil *m*
digital [ˈdɪdʒət̬əl] *adj* : digital
dignified [ˈdɪgnəˌfaɪd] *adj* : digne, plein de dignité
dignify [ˈdɪgnəˌfaɪ] *vt* **-fied; -fying** : donner de la dignité à
dignitary [ˈdɪgnət̬eri] *n, pl* **-taries** : dignitaire *m*
dignity [ˈdɪgnət̬i] *n, pl* **-ties** : dignité *f*
digress [daɪˈgres, də-] *vi* : faire une digression, s'écarter
digression [daɪˈgreʃən, də-] *n* : digression *f*
dike [ˈdaɪk] *n* : digue *f*
dilapidated [dəˈlæpəˌdeɪt̬əd] *adj* : délabré
dilapidation [dəˌlæpəˈdeɪʃən] *n* : délabrement *m*
dilate [daɪˈleɪt, ˈdaɪˌleɪt] *v* **-lated; -lating** *vt* : dilater — *vi* : se dilater
dilemma [dɪˈlemə] *n* : dilemme *m*
dilettante [ˈdɪlə̯ˌtɑnt, -ˌtænt] *n, pl* **-tantes** *or* **-tanti** [-tɑntɪ, -tænts] : dilettante *mf*
diligence [ˈdɪlədʒənts] *n* : assiduité *f*, application *f*
diligent [ˈdɪlədʒənt] *adj* : assidu, appliqué
diligently [ˈdɪlədʒəntli] *adv* : assidûment, avec zèle
dill [ˈdɪl] *n* : aneth *m*
dillydally [ˈdɪliˌdæli] *vi* **-lied; -lying** : traîner, lambiner *fam*, farfiner *Can fam*, niaiser *Can fam*
dilute [daɪˈluːt, də-] *vt* **-luted; -luting** : diluer
dilution [daɪˈluːʃən, də-] *n* : dilution *f*
dim[1] [ˈdɪm] *v* **dimmed; dimming** *vt* : baisser (les lumières), ternir (des couleurs, etc.), affaiblir (des sons), effacer (des souvenirs) — *vi* : baisser, se ternir, s'effacer, s'affaiblir
dim[2] *adj* **dimmer; dimmest 1** DARK : sombre **2** FAINT : faible (se dit de la lumière), terne (se dit des couleurs, etc.), vague (se dit des sons, des formes, de la mémoire)
dime [ˈdaɪm] *n* : pièce *f* de dix cents
dimension [dəˈmenʃən, daɪ-] *n* **1** : dimension *f* **2 dimensions** *npl* SCOPE : étendue *f*, ampleur *f*
diminish [dəˈmɪnɪʃ] *vt* REDUCE : diminuer, réduire, amoindrir — *vi* DWINDLE : diminuer, se réduire
diminutive [dəˈmɪnjət̬ɪv] *adj* : minuscule
dimly [ˈdɪmli] *adv* **1** : sombrement <dimly lit : sombrement éclairé> **2** FAINTLY : vaguement, indistinctement
dimmer [ˈdɪmər] *n* : rhéostat *m* (d'une lumière)
dimple [ˈdɪmpəl] *n* : fossette *f*
din [ˈdɪn] *n* : vacarme *m*, tapage *m*
dine [ˈdaɪn] *vi* **dined; dining** : dîner
diner [ˈdaɪnər] *n* **1** : dîneur *m*, -neuse *f* **2** : wagon-restaurant *m* (d'un train) **3** : petit restaurant *m*
dinghy [ˈdɪŋi, ˈdɪŋgi, ˈdɪŋki] *n, pl* **-ghies** : petit canot *m*
dingy [ˈdɪndʒi] *adj* **dingier; -est 1** DIRTY : malpropre, sale **2** SHABBY : minable, miteux
dinner [ˈdɪnər] *n* : dîner *m*
dinosaur [ˈdaɪnəˌsɔr] *n* : dinosaure *m*
dint [ˈdɪnt] *n* **by dint of** : à force de
diocese [ˈdaɪəsəs, -ˌsiːz, -ˌsiːs] *n, pl* **-ceses** [ˈdaɪəsəsəz] : diocèse *m*
dip[1] [ˈdɪp] *v* **dipped; dipping** *vt* **1** PLUNGE : plonger, tremper **2** LADLE : servir avec une louche — *vi* **1** DESCEND, DROP : baisser, diminuer <prices dipped : les prix ont baissé> <to dip below the horizon : disparaître derrière l'horizon> **2** INCLINE : descendre, s'incliner
dip[2] *n* **1** SWIM : petite baignade *f* <to go for a dip : aller faire trempette> **2** DROP : baisse *f*, diminution *f* **3** INCLINE : inclinaison *f*, pente *f* **4** SAUCE : trempette *f Can*, sauce *f*
diphtheria [dɪfˈθɪriə] *n* : diphtérie *f*
diphthong [ˈdɪfˌθɔŋ] *n* : diphtongue *f*
diploma [dəˈploːmə] *n* : diplôme *m*
diplomacy [dəˈploːməsi] *n* : diplomatie *f*
diplomat [ˈdɪpləˌmæt] *n* : diplomate *mf*
diplomatic [ˌdɪpləˈmæt̬ɪk] *adj* **1** : diplomatique <diplomatic relations : relations diplomatiques> **2** TACTFUL : diplomate, plein de tact
dipper [ˈdɪpər] *n* **1** LADLE : louche *f* **2 Big Dipper** : Grande Ourse *f* **3 Little Dipper** : Petite Ourse *f*
dire [ˈdaɪr] *adj* **direr; -est 1** HORRIBLE : affreux, terrible **2** EXTREME : extrême, absolu <dire poverty : misère noire> <dire necessity : nécessité absolue>

direct[1] |dəˈrɛkt, daɪ-| *vt* **1** ADDRESS : adresser, diriger **2** AIM : destiner <directed to the public : destiné au grand public> **3** GUIDE : diriger, indiquer le chemin à **4** CONTROL : diriger, gérer, être en charge de **5** ORDER : ordonner

direct[2] *adv* : directement

direct[3] *adj* **1** : direct <a direct flight : un vol direct> **2** FRANK : direct, franc

direct current *n* : courant *m* continu

direction |dəˈrɛkʃən, daɪ-| *n* **1** SUPERVISION : direction *f* **2** ORDER : instruction *f*, ordre *m* **3** COURSE : direction *f*, sens *m* <in the right direction : dans le bon sens> **4** TENDENCY, TREND : direction *f*, tendence *f* **5 directions** *npl* INSTRUCTIONS : indications *fpl*

directly |dəˈrɛktli, daɪ-| *adv* **1** STRAIGHT : directement **2** FRANKLY : franchement **3** EXACTLY : juste, exactement <directly opposite my house : juste en face de ma maison> **4** IMMEDIATELY : immédiatement, tout de suite

directness |dəˈrɛktnəs, daɪ-| *n* FRANKNESS : franchise *f*

director |dəˈrɛktər, daɪ-| *n* **1** HEAD, MANAGER : directeur *m*, -trice *f* **2** : réalisateur *m*, -trice *f* (d'un film ou d'une pièce de théatre); metteur *m* en scène (d'une pièce de théâtre)

directory |dəˈrɛktəri, daɪ-| *n, pl* **-ries** : répertoire *m* (d'adresses), annuaire *m* (téléphonique)

dirge |ˈdərdʒ| *n* : hymne *m* funèbre

dirigible |ˈdɪrədʒəbəl, dəˈrɪdʒə-| *n* : dirigeable *m*

dirt |ˈdərt| *n* **1** FILTH : saleté *f*, crasse *f* **2** SOIL : terre *f*

dirtiness |ˈdərṭinəs| *n* : saleté *f*

dirty[1] |ˈdərṭi| *vt* **dirtied; dirtying** : salir

dirty[2] *adj* **dirtier; -est 1** SOILED : sale, malpropre **2** DISHONEST, UNFAIR : sale, malhonnête <a dirty trick : un sale tour> **3** INDECENT : obscène, cochon *fam*

disability |ˌdɪsəˈbɪləṭi| *n, pl* **-ties** : infirmité *f*, incapacité *f*, handicap *m*

disable |dɪsˈeɪbəl| *vt* **-abled; -abling 1** : rendre infirme, handicaper (une personne) **2** : immobiliser (une machine), mettre hors d'action (un navire, etc.)

disabled |dɪsˈeɪbəld| *adj* : handicapé

disabuse |ˌdɪsəˈbjuːz| *vt* **-bused; -busing** : détromper

disadvantage |ˌdɪsədˈvæntɪdʒ| *n* : désavantage *m*

disadvantageous |ˌdɪsˌæd,vænˈteɪdʒəs| *adj* : défavorable, désavantageux

disagree |ˌdɪsəˈgriː| *vi* **1** DIFFER : ne pas concorder, différer **2** DISSENT : être en désaccord, s'opposer **3** : ne pas convenir <fried foods disagree with me : les aliments frits ne me conviennent pas>

disagreeable |ˌdɪsəˈgriːəbəl| *adj* : désagréable, déplaisant, malavenant *Can*

disagreement |ˌdɪsəˈgriːmənt| *n* **1** DISAGREEING : désaccord *m* **2** DISCREPANCY : différence *f* **3** ARGUMENT : différend *m*

disappear |ˌdɪsəˈpɪr| *vi* : disparaître

disappearance |ˌdɪsəˈpiːrənʌs| *n* : disparition *f*

disappoint |ˌdɪsəˈpɔɪnt| *vt* : désappointer, décevoir

disappointment |ˌdɪsəˈpɔɪntmənt| *n* : désappointement *m*, déception *f*

disapproval |ˌdɪsəˈpruːvəl| *n* : désapprobation *f*

disapprove |ˌdɪsəˈpruːv| *vi* **-proved; -proving 1** : ne pas être d'accord **2 to disapprove of** : désapprouver

disarm |dɪsˈɑrm| *v* : désarmer

disarmament |dɪsˈɑrməmənt| *n* : désarmement *m*

disarming |dɪsˈɑrmɪŋ| *adj* : désarmant

disarrange |ˌdɪsəˈreɪndʒ| *vt* **-ranged; -ranging** : mettre en désordre, déranger

disarray |dɪsəˈreɪ| *n* **1** DISORDER, MESS : désordre *m* **2** CONFUSION : désarroi *m*, confusion *f*

disassemble |dɪsəˈsɛmbəl| *vt* **-bled; -bling** : démonter

disaster |dɪˈzæstər| *n* : désastre *m*, catastrophe *f*

disastrous |dɪˈzæstrəs| *adj* : désastreux

disband |dɪsˈbænd| *vi* DISPERSE : se disperser — *vt* DISSOLVE : dissoudre

disbar |dɪsˈbɑr| *vt* **-barred; -barring** : radier (un avocat)

disbelief |ˌdɪsbɪˈliːf| *n* : incrédulité *f*

disbelieve |ˌdɪsbɪˈliːv| *vt* **-lieved; -lieving** : ne pas croire

disburse |dɪsˈbərs| *vt* **-bursed; -bursing** : débourser

disbursement |dɪsˈbərsmənt| *n* : débours *m*

disc |ˈdɪsk| → **disk**

discard |dɪsˈkɑrd, ˈdɪsˌkɑrd| *vt* **1** THROW AWAY : se débarrasser de, jeter **2** : se défausser de (une carte à jouer)

discern |dɪˈsərn, -ˈzərn| *vt* : discerner, percevoir

discernible |dɪˈsərnəbəl, -ˈzərn-| *adj* : perceptible, visible

discernment |dɪˈsərnmənt, -zərn-| *n* : discernement *m*

discharge[1] |dɪsˈtʃɑrdʒ, ˈdɪs-| *vt* **-charged; -charging 1** UNLOAD : décharger (un chargement), débarquer (des passagers) **2** SHOOT : décharger (un fusil) **3** DISMISS : renvoyer (un salarié) **4** RELEASE : décharger, libérer (un soldat) **5** EMIT : émettre (un gaz, un courant d'électricité) **6** PERFORM : remplir, s'acquitter de (un devoir)

discharge[2] |ˈdɪsˌtʃɑrdʒ, dɪsˈ-| *n* **1** FIRING : décharge *f* (d'un fusil) **2** FLOW : écoulement *m* <discharge of blood : écoulement de sang> **3** DISMISSAL

: renvoi *m* **4** RELEASE : libération *f* (d'un soldat)

disciple [dɪ'saɪpəl] *n* : disciple *mf*

disciplinary [ˈdɪsəpəˌnɛri] *adj* : disciplinaire

discipline[1] [ˈdɪsəplən] *vt* **-plined; -plining 1** PUNISH : punir **2** CONTROL, TRAIN : discipliner, former **3 to discipline oneself** : se discipliner

discipline[2] *n* **1** FIELD : discipline *f*, matière *f* **2** TRAINING : discipline *f* **3** PUNISHMENT : punition *f* **4** CONTROL : discipline *f*, maîtrise *f*

disc jockey *n* : disc-jockey *mf*

disclaim [dɪs'kleɪm] *vt* DENY : démentir, nier

disclose [dɪs'kloːz] *vt* **-closed; -closing** : divulguer, révéler

disclosure [dɪs'kloːʒər] *n* : divulgation *f*, révélation *f*

discolor [dɪs'kʌlər] *vt* **1** FADE : décolorer **2** YELLOW : jaunir — *vi* : se décolorer

discoloration [dɪsˌkʌlə'reɪʃən] *n* : décoloration *f*

discomfit [dɪs'kəmfət] *vt* : déconcerter

discomfort [dɪs'kʌmfərt] *n* : malaise *m*

disconcert [ˌdɪskən'sərt] *vt* : déconcerter, dérouter

disconnect [ˌdɪskə'nɛkt] *vt* : débrancher (un appareil électrique), couper (l'électricité, etc.)

disconsolate [dɪs'kɑntsələt] *adj* : inconsolable, triste

discontent [ˌdɪskən'tɛnt] *n* : mécontentement *m*

discontented [ˌdɪskən'tɛntəd] *adj* : mécontent

discontinue [ˌdɪskən'tɪnˌjuː] *vt* **-tinued; -tinuing** : cesser, interrompre

discord [ˈdɪsˌkɔrd] *n* **1** STRIFE : discorde *m*, dissensions *fpl* **2** : dissonance *f* (en musique)

discordant [dɪs'kɔrdənt] *adj* : discordant

discount[1] [ˈdɪsˌkaʊnt, dɪs'-] *vt* **1** : faire une remise de, escompter (de l'argent) **2** DISREGARD : ne pas tenir compte de

discount[2] [ˈdɪsˌkaʊnt] *n* : rabais *m*, remise *f*

discourage [dɪs'kərɪdʒ] *vt* **-aged; -aging 1** DISHEARTEN : décourager, abattre **2** DISSUADE : décourager, détourner, dissuader

discouragement [dɪs'kərɪdʒmənt] *n* : découragement *m*

discourse[1] [dɪs'kɔrs] *vi* **-coursed; -coursing** : discourir

discourse[2] [ˈdɪsˌkɔrs] *n* **1** CONVERSATION : conversation *f* **2** SPEECH : discours *m*

discourteous [dɪs'kərt̬iəs] *adj* : impoli, peu courtois

discourtesy [dɪs'kərt̬əsi] *n, pl* **-sies** : manque *m* de courtoisie

discover [dɪs'kʌvər] *vt* : découvrir

discoverer *n* [dɪs'kʌvərər] : découvreur *m* (d'une terre), personne *f* qui a découvert qqch

discovery [dɪs'kʌvəri] *n, pl* **-eries** : découverte *f*

discredit[1] [dɪs'krɛdət] *vt* **1** DISBELIEVE : ne pas croire **2** QUESTION : discréditer, mettre en doute

discredit[2] *n* : discrédit *m*

discreet [dɪ'skriːt] *adj* : discret

discreetly [dɪs'kriːtli] *adv* : discrètement

discrepancy [dɪs'krɛpənt̬si] *n, pl* **-cies** : divergence *f*, désaccord *m*

discrete [dɪs'kriːt] *adj* : distinct

discretion [dɪs'krɛʃən] *n* : discrétion *f*

discriminate [dɪs'krɪməˌneɪt] *v* **-nated; -nating** *vt* DIFFERENTIATE : distinguer, différencier — *vi* **1** DISTINGUISH : distinguer, faire une distinction **2 to discriminate against** : établir une discrimination contre

discrimination [dɪsˌkrɪmə'neɪʃən] *n* **1** DISCERNMENT : discernement *m* **2** PREJUDICE : discrimination *f*, préjugés *mpl*

discriminatory [dɪs'krɪmənəˌtori] *adj* : discriminatoire

discus [ˈdɪskəs] *n, pl* **-cuses** [-kəsəz] : disque *m* <discus thrower : lanceur de disque>

discuss [dɪs'kʌs] *vt* : discuter de, parler de

discussion [dɪs'kʌʃən] *n* : discussion *f*, conversation *f*, débat *m*

disdain[1] [dɪs'deɪn] *vt* : dédaigner <he disdained to answer : il a dédaigné de répondre>

disdain[2] *n* : dédain *m*

disdainful [dɪs'deɪnfəl] *adj* : dédaigneux — **disdainfully** *adv*

disease [dɪ'ziːz] *n* : maladie *f*

diseased [dɪ'ziːzd] *adj* : malade

disembark [ˌdɪsɪm'bɑrk] *v* : débarquer

disembarkation [dɪsˌɛmˌbɑr'keɪʃən] *n* : débarquement *m*

disembodied [ˌdɪsɪm'bɑdɪd] *adj* : désincarné

disenchant [ˌdɪsɪn'tʃænt] *vt* : désenchanter

disenchantment [ˌdɪsɪn'tʃæntmənt] *n* : désenchantement *m*

disengage [ˌdɪsɪn'geɪdʒ] *vt* **-gaged; -gaging 1** RELEASE : dégager **2 to disengage the clutch** : débrayer

disentangle [ˌdɪsɪn'tæŋgəl] *vt* **-gled; -gling** : démêler

disfavor [dɪs'feɪvər] *n* : défaveur *f*, désapprobation *f*

disfigure [dɪs'fɪgjər] *vt* **-ured; -uring** : défigurer

disfigurement [dɪs'fɪgjərmənt] *n* : défigurement *m*

disfranchise [dɪs'frænˌtʃaɪz] *vt* **-chised; -chising** : priver du droit électoral

disgrace[1] [dɪ'skreɪs] *vt* **-graced; -gracing** : déshonorer, faire honte à

disgrace² *n* **1** DISFAVOR : disgrâce *f*, défaveur *f* <fallen into disgrace : tombé en disgrâce> **2** SHAME : honte *f*, déshonneur *f*
disgraceful [dɪˈskreɪsfəl] *adj* : honteux, scandaleux — **disgracefully** *adv*
disgruntled [dɪsˈgrʌntəld] *adj* : mécontent
disguise¹ [dɪˈskaɪz] *vt* **-guised; -guising** **1** : déguiser <to be disguised as : être déguisé en> **2** CONCEAL : camoufler, dissimuler
disguise² *n* : déguisement *m*
disgust¹ [dɪˈskʌst] *vt* : dégoûter, écœurer
disgust² *n* : dégoût *m*, aversion *f*, répugnance *f*
disgusting [dɪˈskʌstɪŋ] *adj* : dégoûtant
dish¹ [ˈdɪʃ] *vt or* **to dish up** : servir (de la nourriture)
dish² *n* **1** PLATE : assiette *f* **2** : mets *m*, plat *m* <a Mexican dish : un mets mexicain> **3** SERVING : plat *m* <a dish of strawberries : un plat de fraises> **4 dishes** *npl* : vaisselle *f* <to wash the dishes : faire la vaisselle>
dishcloth [ˈdɪʃˌklɔθ] *n* : torchon *m* (à vaisselle), linge à vaisselle
dishearten [dɪsˈhɑrtən] *vt* : décourager, abattre
disheveled *or* **dishevelled** [dɪˈʃɛvəld] *adj* : en désordre (se dit des vêtements, etc.), échevelé (se dit des cheveux)
dishonest [dɪˈsɑnəst] *adj* : malhonnête — **dishonestly** *adv*
dishonesty [dɪˈsɑnəsti] *n* : malhonnêteté *f*
dishonor¹ [dɪˈsɑnər] *vt* : déshonorer
dishonor² *n* : déshonneur *m*
dishonorable [dɪˈsɑnərəbəl] *adj* : déshonorant
dishonorably [dɪˈsɑnərəbli] *adv* : de façon déshonorante
dishrag [ˈdɪʃˌræg] → **dishcloth**
dishwasher [ˈdɪʃˌwɔʃər] *n* : lave-vaisselle *m*
disillusion [dɪsəˈluːʒən] *vt* : désillusionner
disillusionment [ˌdɪsəˈluːʒənmənt] *n* : désillusion *f*
disinclination [ˌdɪsɪnkləˈneɪʃən, -ɪŋ-] *n* : manque *m* d'enthousiasme
disinclined [ˌdɪsɪnˈklaɪnd] *adj* : peu disposé
disinfect [ˌdɪsɪnˈfɛkt] *vt* : désinfecter
disinfectant¹ [ˌdɪsɪnˈfɛktənt] *adj* : désinfectant
disinfectant² *n* : désinfectant *m*
disinherit [ˌdɪsɪnˈhɛrət] *vt* : déshériter
disintegrate [dɪsˈɪntəˌgreɪt] *v* **-grated; -grating** *vt* : désintégrer, désagréger — *vi* : se désintégrer, se désagréger
disintegration [dɪsˌɪntəˈgreɪʃən] *n* : désintégration *f*, désagrégation *f*
disinterested [dɪsˈɪntərəstəd, -ˌrɛs-] *adj* **1** INDIFFERENT : indifférent **2** UNBIASED : désintéressé
disjointed [dɪsˈdʒɔɪntəd] *adj* : décousu, incohérent <disjointed speech : discours décousu>
disk *or* **disc** [ˈdɪsk] *n* : disque *m*
diskette [ˌdɪsˈkɛt] → **floppy disk**
dislike¹ [dɪsˈlaɪk] *vt* **-liked; -liking** : ne pas aimer
dislike² *n* : aversion *f*, antipathie *f*
dislocate [ˈdɪsləˌkeɪt, dɪsˈloː-] *vt* **-cated; -cating** : luxer, déboîter, démettre <to dislocate one's knee : se luxer le genou>
dislocation [ˌdɪsloˈkeɪʃən] *n* : luxation *f*, déboîtement *m*
dislodge [dɪsˈlɑdʒ] *vt* **-lodged; -lodging** : déplacer, dégager, déloger
disloyal [dɪsˈlɔɪəl] *adj* : déloyal
disloyalty [dɪsˈlɔɪəlti] *n* : déloyauté *f*
dismal [ˈdɪzməl] *adj* : sombre, lugubre, triste
dismantle [dɪsˈmæntəl] *vt* **-tled; -tling** : démanteler, démonter
dismay¹ [dɪsˈmeɪ] *vt* : consterner
dismay² *n* : consternation *f*, désarroi *m*
dismember [dɪsˈmɛmbər] *vt* : démembrer
dismiss [dɪsˈmɪs] *vt* **1** : laisser sortir <class dismissed! : vous pouvez sortir!> **2** DISCHARGE : démettre (de ses fonctions), renvoyer, congédier **3** REJECT : ne pas tenir compte de, écarter
dismissal [dɪsˈmɪsəl] *n* **1** : permission *f* de partir **2** DISCHARGE, LAYOFF : licenciement *m*, renvoi *m* **3** : rejet *m* (devant les tribunaux)
dismount [dɪsˈmaʊnt] *vt* DISASSEMBLE : démonter — *vi* **to dismount from** : descendre de
disobedience [ˌdɪsəˈbiːdiəns] *n* : désobéissance *f*
disobedient [dɪsəˈbiːdiənt] *adj* : désobéissant
disobey [ˌdɪsəˈbeɪ] *vt* : désobéir à — *vi* : désobéir
disorder¹ [dɪsˈɔrdər] *vt* : mettre en désordre
disorder² *n* **1** UNTIDINESS : désordre *m*, fouillis *m* **2** CONFUSION : désordre *m*, confusion *f* **3** RIOTING, UNREST : troubles *mpl*, émeutes *fpl* **4** AILMENT : troubles *mpl*, maladie *f* <digestive disorder : troubles digestifs>
disorderly [dɪsˈɔrdərli] *adj* **1** UNTIDY : désordonné **2** UNRULY : turbulent, incontrôlé, désordonné <disorderly conduct : conduite désordonnée>
disorganization [dɪsˌɔrgənəˈzeɪʃən] *n* : désorganisation *f*
disorganize [dɪsˈɔrgəˌnaɪz] *vt* **-nized; -nizing** : désorganiser
disown [dɪsˈoːn] *vt* : désavouer, renier
disparage [dɪsˈpærɪdʒ] *vt* **-aged; -aging** : dénigrer, déprécier
disparagement [dɪsˈpærɪdʒmənt] *n* : dénigrement *m*

disparate [ˈdɪspərət, dɪsˈpærət] *adj* : disparate
disparity [dɪsˈpærəṭi] *n, pl* **-ties** : disparité *f*
dispassionate [dɪsˈpæʃənət] *adj* : impartial, objectif
dispatch[1] [dɪsˈpætʃ] *vt* **1** SEND : envoyer, expédier **2** KILL : tuer **3** HANDLE : expédier (une tâche, etc.)
dispatch[2] *n* **1** SHIPMENT : envoi *m*, expédition *f* **2** PROMPTNESS : promptitude *f* **3** *or* **news dispatch** : dépêche *f*
dispel [dɪsˈpel] *vt* **-pelled; -pelling** : chasser, dissiper
dispensation [ˌdɪspenˈseɪʃən] *n* : dispense *f*
dispense [dɪsˈpenʦ] *v* **-pensed; -pensing** *vt* **1** DISTRIBUTE : dispenser, distribuer **2** ADMINISTER : exercer, administrer (la justice, etc.) **3** : préparer (une prescription) — *vi* **to dispense with** : se passer de
dispenser [dɪsˈpenʦər] *n* : distributeur *m*
dispersal [dɪsˈpərsəl] *n* : dispersion *f*
disperse [dɪsˈpərs] *v* **-persed; -persing** *vt* **1** SCATTER : disperser, disséminer **2** DISSIPATE : disperser, dissiper — *vi* : se disperser
displace [dɪsˈpleɪs] *vt* **-placed; -placing** **1** EXPEL : expulser, déplacer <displaced persons : personnes déplacées> **2** REPLACE : supplanter, remplacer **3** : déplacer (un liquide, etc.)
displacement [dɪsˈpleɪsmənt] *n* : déplacement *m*, remplacement *m*
display[1] [dɪsˈpleɪ] *vt* **1** PRESENT : exposer, étaler **2** SHOW : faire preuve de, montrer <he displayed great talent : il a montré beaucoup de talent>
display[2] *n* **1** PRESENTATION : exposition *f*, étalage *m* **2** MANIFESTATION : démonstration *f*, manifestation *f*
displease [dɪsˈpliːz] *vt* **-pleased; -pleasing** : déplaire à, mécontenter
displeasure [dɪsˈpleʒər] *n* : déplaisir *m*, mécontentement *m*
disposable [dɪsˈpoːzəbəl] *adj* **1** : jetable <disposable diapers : couches jetables> **2** AVAILABLE : disponible <disposable income : revenu disponible>
disposal [dɪsˈpoːzəl] *n* **1** ARRANGEMENT : disposition *f*, ordre *m* **2** AVAILABILITY : disposition *f* <to have at one's disposal : avoir à sa disposition> **3** : élimination *f* (des déchets)
dispose [dɪsˈpoːz] *v* **-posed; -posing** *vt* **1** ARRANGE : disposer, arranger **2** INCLINE : disposer <disposed to help : prêt à aider> — *vi* **1 to dispose of** HANDLE : expédier **2 to dispose of** DISCARD : se débarrasser de
disposition [ˌdɪspəˈzɪʃən] *n* **1** ARRANGEMENT : disposition *f*, arrangement *m* **2** TEMPERAMENT : tempérament *m*, caractère *m* **3** TENDENCY : inclination *f*, penchant *m*
dispossess [ˌdɪspəˈzɛs] *vt* : déposséder, dépouiller
disproportion [ˌdɪsprəˈporʃən] *n* : disproportion *f*
disproportionate [ˌdɪsprəˈporʃənət] *adj* : disproportionné
disprove [dɪsˈpruːv] *vt* **-proved; -proving** : réfuter
disputable [dɪsˈpjuːṭəbəl, ˈdɪspjuṭəbəl] *adj* : discutable, contestable
dispute[1] [dɪsˈpjuːt] *v* **-puted; -puting** *vt* **1** QUESTION : contester, mettre en doute **2** CONTEST : disputer — *vi* ARGUE, DEBATE : se disputer, débattre
dispute[2] *n* **1** DEBATE : débat *m* <beyond dispute : incontestable> **2** QUARREL : dispute *f*, conflit *m*
disqualification [dɪsˌkwɑləfəˈkeɪʃən] *n* : exclusion *f*, disqualification *f*
disqualify [dɪsˈkwɑləˌfaɪ] *vt* **-fied; -fying** : disqualifier
disquiet[1] [dɪsˈkwaɪəṭ] *vt* : inquiéter, troubler
disquiet[2] *n* ANXIETY : inquiétude *f*
disregard[1] [ˌdɪsrɪˈgɑrd] *vt* : ne tenir aucun compte de, ne pas s'occuper de
disregard[2] *n* : indifférence *f*, négligence *f*, mépris *m* (du danger)
disrepair [ˌdɪsrɪˈpær] *n* : délabrement *m*
disreputable [dɪsˈrɛpjuṭəbəl] *adj* : peu recommandable, mal famé
disrepute [ˌdɪsrɪˈpjuːt] *n* : discrédit *m*, déconsidération *f*
disrespect [ˌdɪsrɪˈspɛkt] *n* : irrespect *m*, manque *m* de respect
disrespectful [ˌdɪsrɪˈspɛktfəl] *adj* : irrespectueux
disrobe [dɪsˈroːb] *vi* **-robed; -robing** UNDRESS : se déshabiller
disrupt [dɪsˈrʌpt] *vt* : perturber, déranger
disruption [dɪsˈrʌpʃən] *n* : perturbation *f*, bouleversement *m*
disruptive [dɪsˈrʌptɪv] *adj* : perturbateur
dissatisfaction [dɪsˌsæṭəsˈfækʃən] *n* : insatisfaction *f*, mécontentement *m*
dissatisfied [dɪsˈsæṭəsˌfaɪd] *adj* : mécontent
dissatisfy [dɪsˈsæṭəsˌfaɪ] *vt* **-fied; -fying** : ne pas satisfaire
dissect [dɪˈsɛkt] *vt* : disséquer
dissection [dɪˈsɛkʃən] *n* : dissection *f*
dissemble [dɪˈsɛmbəl] *v* **-bled; -bling** : dissimuler
disseminate [dɪˈsɛməˌneɪt] *vt* **-nated; -nating** : disséminer, propager
dissemination [dɪˌsɛməˈneɪʃən] *n* : dissémination *f*
dissension [dɪˈsɛnʃən] *n* : dissension *f*
dissent[1] [dɪˈsɛnt] *vi* : différer, être en désaccord
dissent[2] *n* : dissentiment *m*
dissertation [ˌdɪsərˈteɪʃən] *n* **1** TREATISE : traité *m* **2** THESIS : thèse *f*

disservice [dɪs'sərvɪs] *n* : mauvais service *m*
dissident[1] ['dɪsədənt] *adj* : dissident
dissident[2] *n* : dissident *m*, -dente *f*
dissimilar [dɪ'sɪmələr] *adj* : dissemblable, différent
dissimilarity [dɪˌsɪmə'lærəṭi] *n, pl* **-ties** : dissemblance *f*
dissipate ['dɪsəˌpeɪt] *v* **-pated; -pating** *vt* **1** DISPERSE : dissiper, disperser **2** SQUANDER : gaspiller — *vi* : se dissiper
dissipation [ˌdɪsə'peɪʃən] *n* : dissipation *f*
dissolute ['dɪsəˌluːt] *adj* : dissolu, corrompu
dissolution [ˌdɪsə'luːʃən] *n* : dissolution *f*
dissolve [dɪ'zɑlv] *v* **-solved; -solving** *vt* : dissoudre — *vi* : se dissoudre <to dissolve into tears : fondre en larmes>
dissonance ['dɪsənənʌs] *n* : dissonance *f*
dissonant ['dɪsənənt] *adj* : dissonant
dissuade [dɪ'sweɪd] *vt* **-suaded; -suading** : dissuader
distance ['dɪstənʌs] *n* **1** : distance *f* <at a distance of nine miles : à une distance de neuf milles> <in the distance : au loin> **2** RESERVE : distance *f*, réserve *f* <to keep one's distance : garder ses distances>
distant ['dɪstənt] *adj* **1** (*indicating separation*) <five miles distant from here : à cinq milles d'ici> **2** FARAWAY, REMOTE : lointain, éloigné **3** COLD : distant, réservé
distantly ['dɪstəntli] *adv* **1** : vaguement, un peu <distantly related : d'une parenté éloignée> **2** COLDLY : froidement, d'un air distant
distaste [dɪs'teɪst] *n* : aversion *f*, répugnance *f*
distasteful [dɪs'teɪstfəl] *adj* : déplaisant, répugnant
distemper [dɪs'tempər] *n* : maladie *f* de Carré
distend [dɪs'tend] *vt* : gonfler — *vi* : se gonfler, se distendre
distill *or Brit* **distil** [dɪ'stɪl] *vt* **-tilled; -tilling** : distiller
distillation [ˌdɪstə'leɪʃən] *n* : distillation *f*
distillery [dɪ'stɪləri, -'stɪlri] *n, pl* **-ries** : distillerie *f*
distinct [dɪ'stɪŋkt] *adj* **1** DIFFERENT : distinct, différent **2** CLEAR : distinct, net <a distinct impression : une nette impression>
distinction [dɪ'stɪŋkʃən] *n* : distinction *f*
distinctive [dɪ'stɪŋktɪv] *adj* : distinctif
distinctively [dɪ'stɪŋktɪvli] *adv* : de manière distinctive
distinctly [dɪ'stɪŋktli] *adv* : distinctement, clairement
distinguish [dɪ'stɪŋgwɪʃ] *vt* **1** DIFFERENTIATE : distinguer, différencier **2** DISCERN : distinguer, discerner **3 to distinguish oneself** : se distinguer, s'illustrer — *vi* DISCRIMINATE : faire une distinction
distinguished [dɪ'stɪŋgwɪʃt] *adj* : distingué <distinguished-looking : à l'allure distinguée>
distort [dɪ'stɔrt] *vt* **1** DEFORM : déformer, distordre <a face distorted by pain : un visage déformé par la douleur> **2** MISREPRESENT : déformer, dénaturer
distortion [dɪ'stɔrʃən] *n* : déformation *f*
distract [dɪ'strækt] *vt* : distraire <to distract s.o.'s attention : détourner l'attention de qqn>
distraction [dɪ'strækʃən] *n* **1** INTERRUPTION : distraction *f*, interruption *f* **2** INATTENTION : inattention *f* **3** CONFUSION, MADNESS : folie *f* <to drive to distraction : rendre fou> **4** AMUSEMENT : distraction *f*, divertissement *m*
distraught [dɪ'strɔt] *adj* : bouleversé, éperdu
distress[1] [dɪ'stres] *vt* : affliger, peiner
distress[2] *n* **1** SUFFERING : douleur *f*, souffrance *f*, affliction *f* **2** MISFORTUNE : détresse *f*, adversité *f* **3** DANGER : détresse *f* <a ship in distress : un navire en détresse>
distressful [dɪ'stresfəl] *adj* : pénible, affligeant
distribute [dɪ'strɪˌbjuːt, -bjʊt] *vt* **-uted; -uting** : distribuer, répartir
distribution [ˌdɪstrə'bjuːʃən] *n* : distribution *f*, répartition *f*
distributor [dɪ'strɪbjʊṭər] *n* **1** : distributeur *m*, -trice *f* (personne) **2** : distributeur *m* (d'une voiture)
district ['dɪsˌtrɪkt] *n* **1** AREA : région *f* **2** : quartier *m* <residential district : quartier résidentiel> **3** : district *m* (administratif), circonscription *f* (électorale)
distrust[1] [dɪs'trʌst] *vt* : se méfier de
distrust[2] *n* : méfiance *f*
distrustful [dɪs'trʌstfəl] *adj* : méfiant
disturb [dɪ'stərb] *vt* **1** BOTHER : déranger, interrompre **2** DISARRANGE : déplacer, déranger **3** WORRY : troubler, inquiéter **4 to disturb the peace** : troubler l'ordre public
disturbance [dɪ'stərbənʌs] *n* **1** INTERRUPTION : dérangement *m*, interruption *f* **2** COMMOTION : troubles *mpl*, émeute *f*, tapage *m* <to cause a disturbance : faire du tapage>
disuse [dɪs'juːs] *n* : désuétude *f*
ditch[1] [dɪtʃ] *vt* **1** : creuser un fossé dans **2** DISCARD : se débarrasser de
ditch[2] *n* : fossé *m*
dither ['dɪðər] *n* **to be in a dither** : être dans tous ses états
ditto ['dɪṭoː] *adv* : idem
ditty ['dɪṭi] *n, pl* **-ties** : chansonnette *f*

diurnal [daɪˈərnəl] *adj* **1** DAILY : quotidien **2** : diurne (se dit des animaux et des plantes)
divan [ˈdaɪˌvæn, dɪ-] *n* : divan *m*
dive¹ [ˈdaɪv] *vi* **dived** *or* **dove** [ˈdo:v]; **dived; diving 1** : plonger <to dive into the water : plonger dans l'eau> **2** SUBMERGE : s'immerger **3** DESCEND : descendre en piqué, piquer (se dit d'un avion, etc.)
dive² *n* **1** : plongeon *m* (dans l'eau) **2** DESCENT, NOSEDIVE : piqué *m*
diver [ˈdaɪvər] *n* : plongeur *m*, -geuse *f*
diverge [dəˈvərdʒ, daɪ-] *vi* **-verged; -verging 1** SEPARATE : diverger, s'écarter **2** DIFFER : diverger, différer
divergence [dəˈvərdʒənts, daɪ-] *n* : divergence *f* — **divergent** [-dʒənt] *adj*
diverse [daɪˈvərs, də-, ˈdaɪˌvərs] *adj* : divers, varié
diversification [dəˌvərsəfəˈkeɪʃən] *n* : diversification *f*
diversify [daɪˈvərsəˌfaɪ, də-] *v* **-fied; -fying** *vt* : diversifier — *vi* : se diversifier
diversion [daɪˈvərʒən, də-] *n* **1** DEVIATION : déviation *f* **2** AMUSEMENT : distraction *f*, divertissement *m*
diversity [daɪˈvərsəṭi, də-] *n, pl* **-ties** : diversité *f*
divert [dəˈvərt, daɪ-] *vt* **1** DEFLECT : détourner, dévier **2** DISTRACT : distraire **3** AMUSE : divertir
divest [daɪˈvest, də-] *vt* **1** DISPOSSESS : dépouiller **2 to divest oneself of** : se débarrasser de, se défaire de
divide [dəˈvaɪd] *v* **-vided; -viding** *vt* **1** SEPARATE : diviser, séparer, désunir **2** SHARE : diviser, partager **3** : diviser <twelve divided by three is four : douze divisé par trois égale quatre> — *vi* : se diviser, se séparer
dividend [ˈdɪvɪˌdend, -dənd] *n* **1** : dividende *m* (en finance et en mathématiques) **2** BONUS : prime *f*
divider [dɪˈvaɪdər] *n* **1** *or* **file divider** : intercalaire *m*, fiche *f* intercalaire **2** *or* **room divider** : cloison *f*, meuble *m* de séparation
divine¹ [dəˈvaɪn] *adj* **diviner; -est 1** : divin **2** SUPERB : divin, sublime
divine² *n* CLERGYMAN : ecclésiastique *m*
divinely [dəˈvaɪnli] *adv* : divinement
divinity [dəˈvɪnəṭi] *n, pl* **-ties** : divinité *f*
divisible [dɪˈvɪzəbəl] *adj* : divisible
division [dɪˈvɪʒən] *n* : division *f*
divisor [dɪˈvaɪzər] *n* : diviseur *m*
divorce¹ [dəˈvors] *v* **-vorced; -vorcing** *vi* : divorcer — *vt* : divorcer de, divorcer avec
divorce² *n* : divorce *m*
divorcé [dɪˌvorˈseɪ, -si:; -ˈvorˌ-] *n* : divorcé *m*
divorcée [dɪˌvorˈseɪ, -si:; -ˈvorˌ-] *n* : divorcée *f*
divulge [dəˈvʌldʒ, daɪ-] *vt* **-vulged; -vulging** : divulguer, révéler, placoter *Can fam*
dizziness *n* [ˈdɪzɪnəs] : vertige *m*, étourdissement *m*
dizzy [ˈdɪzi] *adj* **dizzier; -est 1** GIDDY, UNSTEADY : pris de vertiges **2** : vertigineux <dizzy heights : des hauteurs vertigineuses>
DNA [ˌdi:ˌenˈeɪ] *n* : ADN *m*
do [ˈdu:]; **did** [ˈdɪd]; **done** [ˈdʌn]; **doing; does** [ˈdʌz] *vt* **1** CARRY OUT, PERFORM : faire, accomplir (une action, une tâche) <do your best : fais de ton mieux> **2** PRACTICE : faire, entreprendre <what does he do for a living? : que fait-il comme métier?> **3** ARRANGE : arranger <to do one's hair : se coiffer> **4** PREPARE : faire, préparer <do your homework : fais tes devoirs> — *vi* **1** ACT, BEHAVE : faire <do as I say : faites ce que je dis> **2** FARE : réussir <he does well in school : il réussit bien à l'école> **3** SUFFICE : suffire, faire l'affaire <that will do : ça suffit> **4 to do away with** DESTROY, KILL : tuer, détruire **5 to do away with** ELIMINATE : éliminer, abolir — *v aux* **1** (*in interrogative sentences*) <does he work? : travaille-t-il?> **2** (*in negative sentences*) <I don't know : je ne sais pas> <don't go : n'y va pas> **3** (*for emphasis*) <do be careful : fais attention, je t'en prie> **4** (*as a substitute for a preceding predicate*) <he succeeds better than I do : il réussit mieux que moi>
docile [ˈdɑsəl] *adj* : docile
dock¹ [ˈdɑk] *vt* **1** SHORTEN : couper la queue à (un chien) **2** DEDUCT : faire une retenue sur <they docked $10 from his paycheck : ils ont retenu 10 $ sur son chèque de paie> — *vi* : se mettre à quai (se dit d'un bateau)
dock² *n* **1** BERTH : dock *m* **2** WHARF : embarcadère *m*, quai *m* **3** : banc *m* des accusés (dans un tribunal)
doctor¹ [ˈdɑktər] *vt* **1** TREAT : soigner (un patient) **2** ALTER : altérer, falsifier
doctor² *n* **1** : docteur *m* <Doctor of Law : docteur en droit> **2** PHYSICIAN : médecin *m*; docteur *m*
doctrine [ˈdɑktrɪn] *n* : doctrine *f*
document¹ [ˈdɑkjəˌment] *vt* : documenter
document² [ˈdɑkjəmənt] *n* : document *m*
documentary¹ [ˌdɑkjəˈmentəri] *adj* : documentaire
documentary² *n, pl* **-ries** : documentaire *m*
documentation [ˌdɑkjəmənˈteɪʃən] *n* : documentation *f*
dodge¹ [ˈdɑdʒ] *v* **dodged; dodging** *vt* : esquiver, éviter, échapper à — *vi* : faire un saut de côté, faire une esquive

dodge[2] *n* **1** : mouvement *m* de côté, esquive *f* (aux sports) **2** RUSE, TRICK : ruse *f*, truc *m*
dodo ['dˌdo:] *n, pl* **-does** *or* **-dos** : dodo *m*
doe ['do:] *n, pl* **does** *or* **doe** : biche *f*
doer ['du:ər] *n* : personne *f* qui préfère l'action, personne *f* efficace
does → **do**
doff ['dɑf, 'dɔf] *vt* : ôter, enlever (son chapeau, etc.)
dog[1] ['dɔg, 'dɑg] *vt* **dogged; dogging 1** FOLLOW : talonner, suivre de près <he's dogging my footsteps : il marche sur mes talons> **2** HOUND : poursuivre, être en proie à <dogged by financial worries : en proie à des difficultés financières>
dog[2] *n* : chien *m*
dog–eared ['dɔgˌɪrd] *adj* : écorné
dogged ['dɔgəd] *adj* : tenace, persévérant
doghouse ['dɔgˌhaʊs] *n* : niche *f* (à chien)
dogma ['dɔgmə] *n* : dogme *m*
dogmatic [dɔg'mæt̬ɪk] *adj* : dogmatique
dogmatism ['dɔgmə'tɪzəm] *n* : dogmatisme *m*
dogwood ['dɔgˌwʊd] *n* : cornouiller *m*
doily ['dɔɪli] *n, pl* **-lies** : napperon *m*
doings ['du:ɪŋz] *npl* GOINGS-ON : événements *mpl*, faits *mpl* et gestes *mpl*
doldrums ['do:ldrəmz, 'dɑl-] *npl* **1** : zone *f* des calmes (équatoriaux) **2** BLUES : cafard *m*, mélancolie *f* **3** STAGNATION : marasme *m* <economic doldrums : marasme économique>
dole ['do:l] *n* : allocation *f* de chômage, indemnité *f* de chômage
doleful ['do:lfəl] *adj* : dolent, triste
dolefully ['do:lfəli] *adv* : d'un air triste
dole out *vt* **doled out; doling out** : distribuer, donner
doll ['dɑl, 'dɔl] *n* : poupée *f*
dollar ['dɑlər] *n* : dollar *m*, piastre *f Can fam*
dolly ['dɑli] *n, pl* **-lies 1** → **doll 2** CART, PLATFORM : chariot *m*, plate-forme *f*
dolphin ['dɑlfən, 'dɔl-] *n* : dauphin *m*
dolt ['do:lt] *n* : balourd *m*, -lourde *f*
domain [do'meɪn, də-] *n* **1** TERRITORY : domaine *m*, territoire *m* **2** SPHERE : domaine *m* <the domain of art : le domaine de l'art>
dome ['do:m] *n* : dôme *m*, coupole *f*
domestic[1] [də'mestɪk] *adj* **1** HOUSEHOLD : domestique **2** : intérieur, national <domestic affairs : affaires intérieures> **3** TAME : domestique
domestic[2] *n* SERVANT : domestique *mf*
domesticate [də'mestɪˌkeɪt] *vt* **-cated; -cating** : domestiquer, apprivoiser
domicile ['dɑməˌsaɪl, 'do:-; 'dɑməsɪl] *n* : domicile *m*
dominance ['dɑmənənʧs] *n* : dominance *f*, prédominance *f*
dominant ['dɑmənənt] *adj* : dominant
dominate ['dɑməˌneɪt] *v* **-nated; -nating** : dominer
domination [ˌdɑmə'neɪʃən] *n* : domination *f*
domineer [ˌdɑmə'nɪr] *vi* : agir en maître, se montrer autoritaire
Dominican[1] [də'mɪnɪkən] *adj* : dominicain
Dominican[2] *n* : Dominicain *m*, -caine *f*
dominion [də'mɪnjən] *n* **1** SUPREMACY : domination *f* **2** TERRITORY : territoire *m*, domaine *m*
domino ['dɑməˌno:] *n, pl* **-noes** *or* **-nos** : domino *m*
don ['dɑn] *vt* **donned; donning** : mettre (des vêtements)
donate ['do:ˌneɪt, do:'-] *v* **-nated; -nating** *vt* : faire (un) don de — *vi* : faire un don
donation [do:'neɪʃən] *n* : don *m*, donation *f*
done[1] ['dʌn] → **do**
done[2] *adj* **1** FINISHED : fini, terminé **2** WELL-DONE : bien cuit
donkey ['dɑŋki, 'dʌŋ] *n, pl* **-keys** : âne *m*
donor ['do:nər] *n* : donateur *m*, -trice *f*; donneur *m*, -neuse *f* <blood donor : donneur de sang>
doodle[1] ['du:dəl] *v* **-dled; -dling** : gribouiller
doodle[2] *n* : gribouillage *m*
doom[1] ['du:m] *vt* **1** CONDEMN : condamner **2** DESTINE : vouer <doomed to failure : voué à l'échec>
doom[2] *n* **1** JUDGMENT : jugement *m*, sentence *f* **2** DESTINY : destin *m*, sort *m* **3** RUIN : perte *f*, ruine *f*
door ['dɔr] *n* **1** : porte *f*, portière *f* (d'une voiture) **2** ENTRANCE : entrée *f* <pay at the door : payez à l'entrée>
doorbell ['dɔrˌbel] *n* : sonnette *f*
doorknob ['dɔrˌnɑb] *n* : poignée *f* de porte, bouton *m* de porte
doorman ['dɔrmən] *n, pl* **-men** : portier *m*
doormat ['dɔrˌmæt] *n* : paillasson *m*
doorstep ['dɔrˌstep] *n* : seuil *m* (de porte), pas *m* de la porte
doorway ['dɔrˌweɪ] *n* : embrasure *f* (de la porte)
dope[1] ['do:p] *vt* **doped; doping** : droguer (une personne), doper (un animal, un athlète)
dope[2] *n* **1** DRUG : narcotique *m*, stupéfiant *m* **2** IDIOT : cornichon *m fam*, imbécile *mf* **3** INFORMATION, TIP : tuyau *m fam*, renseignement *m*
dormant ['dɔrmənt] *adj* : qui sommeille, latent, dormant (en botanique)
dormer ['dɔrmər] *n* : lucarne *f*
dormitory ['dɔrməˌtori] *n, pl* **-ries** : dortoir *m*, résidence *f* universitaire
dormouse ['dɔrˌmaʊs] *n, pl* **-mice** : loir *m*

dorsal ['dɔrsəl] *adj* : dorsal
dory ['dori] *n, pl* **-ries** : doris *m*
dosage ['do:sɪdʒ] *n* : posologie *f*
dose¹ ['do:s] *vt* **dosed; dosing** : doser, administrer un médicament à
dose² *n* : dose *f*
dot¹ ['dɑt] *vt* **dotted; dotting** : mettre un point sur (un *i*, etc.)
dot² *n* **1** POINT, SPECK : point *m* **2 on the dot** : à l'heure pile *fam*
dote ['do:t] *vi* **doted; doting** : raffoler, adorer <to dote on s.o. : aimer qqn à la folie, raffoler de qqn>
double¹ ['dʌbəl] *v* **-bled; -bling** *vt* **1** : doubler (une quantité) **2** BEND, FOLD : plier (en deux) **3 to double one's fists** : serrer les poings — *vi* **1** : doubler **2 to double up in pain** : se plier en deux par la douleur
double² *adv* **1** TWICE : deux fois <she's double your age : elle est deux fois plus âgé que toi> **2** : double <to see double : voir double>
double³ *adj* : double
double⁴ *n* : double *m*
double bass *n* : contrebasse *f*
double–cross [ˌdʌbəl'krɔs] *vt* : trahir, doubler *fam*
double–jointed [ˌdʌbəl'dʒɔɪntəd] *adj* : désarticulé
double–talk ['dʌbəlˌtɔk] *n* : paroles *fpl* trompeuses, paroles *fpl* ambiguës
doubly ['dʌbli] *adv* : doublement, deux fois plus
doubt¹ ['daʊt] *vt* **1** : douter <I doubt that he'll accept : je doute qu'il accepte> **2** DISTRUST : douter de <I doubt it very much : j'en doute beaucoup>
doubt² *n* **1** UNCERTAINTY : doute *m*, incertitude *f* **2** DISTRUST : doute *m*, méfiance *f* **3** SKEPTICISM : doute *m*, scepticisme *m*
doubtful ['daʊtfəl] *adj* **1** UNCERTAIN : douteux, incertain **2** QUESTIONABLE : douteux, discutable
doubtless ['daʊtləs] *adv* : sans aucun doute, sûrement
douche ['du:ʃ] *n* : douche *f* (en médecine)
dough ['do:] *n* : pâte *f* (en cuisine)
doughnut ['do:ˌnʌt] *n* : beignet *m*, beigne *m Can*
doughty ['daʊti] *adj* **doughtier; -est** : vaillant
dour ['daʊər, 'dʊr] *adj* **1** STERN : austère, dur **2** SULLEN : maussade, renfrogné
douse ['daʊs, 'daʊz] *vt* **doused; dousing** **1** DRENCH : inonder, tremper **2** EXTINGUISH : éteindre
dove¹ ['do:v] → **dive¹**
dove² ['dʌv] *n* : colombe *f*
dovetail ['dʌvˌteɪl] *vt* **1** : assembler à queue d'aronde (en charpenterie) **2** : faire concorder (des plans, etc.) — *vi* AGREE : concorder, bien cadrer
dowdy ['daʊdi] *adj* **dowdier; -est** : sans chic
dowel ['daʊəl] *n* : goujon *m*
down¹ ['daʊn] *vt* **1** KNOCK DOWN : terrasser, abattre **2** DEFEAT : vaincre
down² *adv* **1** DOWNWARD : en bas, vers le bas **2 down to** : jusqu'à <down to the present : jusqu'à nos jours> **3 to lie down** : se coucher, s'allonger **4 to put down** PAY : payer, verser **5 to put down** WRITE : écrire **6 to sit down** : s'asseoir
down³ *adj* **1** : qui descend <the down escalator : l'escalier mécanique qui descend> **2** LOWER : qui diminue, qui baisse <sales were down : les ventes avaient diminué> **3** DOWNCAST : déprimé, abattu
down⁴ *n* : duvet *m*
down⁵ *prep* **1** : en bas de, dans <he fell down the stairs : il est tombé dans l'escalier> **2** ALONG : le long de <to walk down the road : marcher le long de la rue> **3** THROUGH : au cours de, à travers de <down through the ages : à travers les siècles>
downcast ['daʊnˌkæst] *adj* **1** SAD : abattu, découragé **2** LOWERED : baissé <with a downcast glance : avec les yeux baissés>
downfall ['daʊnˌfɔl] *n* : chute *f*, renversement *m*
downgrade¹ ['daʊnˌgreɪd] *vt* **-graded; -grading** : déclasser (un poste, etc.), rétrograder (une personne)
downgrade² *n* : descente *f*, pente *f*
downhearted ['daʊn'hɑrtəd] *adj* : abattu, découragé
downhill¹ ['daʊn'hɪl] *adv* **to go downhill** : descendre
downhill² *adj* : en pente, qui descend
download¹ ['daʊnˌlo:d] *vt* : télécharger (en informatique)
download² *n* : téléchargement *m*
down payment *n* : acompte *m*, arrhes *fpl France*
downpour ['daʊnˌpor] *n* : déluge *m*, averse *f*
downright¹ ['daʊnˌraɪt] *adv* THOROUGHLY : carrément, tout à fait
downright² *adj* ABSOLUTE : véritable, catégorique
downstairs¹ [*adv* 'daʊn'stærz, *adj* 'daʊnˌstærz] *adv & adj* : en bas
downstairs² ['daʊn'stærz, -ˌstærz] *n* : rez-de-chaussé *m*
downstream ['daʊn'stri:m] *adv* : en aval
down–to–earth [ˌdaʊntu'ərθ] *adj* : terre à terre, avec les pieds sur terre
downtown¹ [ˌdaʊn'taʊn] *adv* : en ville
downtown² *adj* : du centre-ville
downtown³ [ˌdaʊn'taʊn, 'daʊnˌtaʊn] *n* : centre-ville *m*
downtrodden ['daʊnˌtrɑdən] *adj* : opprimé
downward¹ ['daʊnwərd] *or* **downwards** [-wərdz] *adv* : en bas, vers le bas <to look downward : regarder en bas> <the prophets from Elijah downward : les prophètes depuis Élie>

downward[2] *adj* : vers le bas <a downward movement : un mouvement vers le bas> <a downward trend : une tendence à la baisse>
downwind ['daʊn'wɪnd] *adv & adj* : dans le sens du vent
downy ['daʊni] *adj* **downier; -est** : duveteux
dowry ['daʊri] *n, pl* **-ries** : dot *f*
doze[1] ['doːz] *vi* **dozed; dozing** : sommeiller, somnoler
doze[2] *n* : somme *m*, sieste *f*
dozen ['dʌzən] *n, pl* **-ens** *or* **-en** : douzaine *f*
drab ['dræb] *adj* **drabber; drabbest** : terne, fade
draft[1] ['dræft, 'drɑft] *vt* **1** : appeler (des soldats) sous les drapeaux **2** OUTLINE : faire le brouillon de **3** COMPOSE : rédiger
draft[2] *adj* : en fût, à la pression <draft beer : bière en fût>
draft[3] *n* **1** HAULAGE : tirage *m*, traction *f* **2** DRINK, GULP : trait *m*, gorgée *f* **3** OUTLINE : brouillon *m*, avant-projet *m* **4** CONSCRIPTION : service *m* militaire, conscription *f* **5** : courant *m* d'air **6** *or* **bank draft** : traite *f* bancaire
draftsman ['dræftsmən] *n, pl* **-men** [-mən, -ˌmɛn] : dessinateur *m*, -trice *f*
drafty ['dræfti] *adj* **draftier; -est** : plein de courants d'air
drag[1] ['dræg] *v* **dragged; dragging** *vt* **1** HAUL : tirer, traîner **2** TRAIL : traîner <to drag one's feet : traîner les pieds> **3** DREDGE : draguer **4** : glisser (en informatique) — *vi* TRAIL : traîner
drag[2] *n* **1** RESISTANCE : résistance *f*, traînée *f* **2** DREDGE : drague *f* **3** SLEDGE : traîneau *m* **4** : barbe *f fam* <what a drag! : quelle barbe!> **5** PUFF : bouffée *f* (de cigarette)
dragnet ['dræɡˌnɛt] *n* **1** TRAWL : drège *f* **2** : rafle *f*, descente *f* (policière)
dragon ['drægən] *n* : dragon *m*
dragonfly ['drægənˌflaɪ] *n, pl* **-flies** : libellule *f*
drain[1] ['dreɪn] *vt* **1** EMPTY : vider, drainer **2** DEPLETE, EXHAUST : fatiguer, épuiser — *vi* : s'écouler (se dit d'un cours d'eau), s'égoutter (se dit de la vaisselle)
drain[2] *n* **1** : tuyau *m* d'écoulement **2** SEWER : égout *m* **3** DEPLETION : épuisement *m*, perte *f*
drainage ['dreɪnɪdʒ] *n* : drainage *m*
drainpipe ['dreɪnˌpaɪp] *n* : tuyau *m* d'évacuation, drain *m*
drake ['dreɪk] *n* : canard *m* (mâle)
drama ['drɑmə, 'dræ-] *n* **1** : art *m* dramatique, théâtre *m* **2** PLAY : drame *m*, pièce *f* de théâtre
dramatic [drə'mætɪk] *adj* : dramatique
dramatically [drə'mætɪkli] *adv* : d'une manière dramatique
dramatist ['dræmətɪst, 'drɑ-] *n* : dramaturge *mf*
dramatization [ˌdræmətə'zeɪʃən] *n* **1** : adaptation *f* pour la scène **2** DRAMATIZING : dramatisation *f*
dramatize ['dræməˌtaɪz, 'drɑ-] *vt* **-tized; -tizing** : dramatiser
drank → **drink**[1]
drape[1] ['dreɪp] *v* **draped; draping** *vt* : draper — *vi* : tomber <silk drapes beautifully : la soie tombe à merveille>
drape[2] *n* **1** HANG : drapé *m* (d'une étoffe) **2** **drapes** *npl* CURTAINS : rideaux *mpl*
drapery ['dreɪpəri] *n, pl* **-eries 1** HANGINGS : tentures *fpl* **2** CURTAINS : rideaux *mpl*
drastic ['dræstɪk] *adj* **1** : drastique <a drastic purgative : un purgatif drastique> **2** SEVERE : rigoureux, énergique <drastic measures : mesures énergiques>
draught ['dræft, 'draft] → **draft**[3]
draughty ['drafti] → **drafty**
draw[1] ['drɔ] *v* **drew** ['druː]; **drawn** ['draʊn]; **drawing** ['drɔɪŋ] *vt* **1** PULL : tirer **2** ATTRACT : attirer **3** PROVOKE : provoquer, susciter **4** INHALE : aspirer, respirer **5** EXTRACT : extraire, retirer **6** TAKE : prendre <to draw a number : prendre un numéro> **7** COLLECT : toucher (un salaire) **8** BEND : bander <to draw a bow : bander un arc> **9** TIE : faire match de (aux sports) **10** SKETCH : dessiner, tracer **11** MAKE : faire (une distinction, une comparaison, etc.) **12** *or* **to draw up** DRAFT, FORMULATE : dresser (une liste, etc.), rédiger (un plan) — *vi* **1** SKETCH : dessiner **2** (*indicating movement*) <to draw near : approcher> <to draw to an end : tirer à sa fin> **3** : tirer (se dit d'une cheminée, d'une pipe, etc.)
draw[2] *n* **1** DRAWING : tirage *m* (au sort) **2** TIE : match *m* nul (aux sports) **3** ATTRACTION : attraction *f* **4** PUFF : bouffée *f* (de cigarette, etc.)
drawback ['drɔˌbæk] *n* : désavantage *m*, inconvénient *m*
drawbridge ['drɔˌbrɪdʒ] *n* : pont-levis *m*
drawer ['drɔr, 'drɔər] *n* **1** ILLUSTRATOR : dessinateur *m*, -trice *f* **2** : tiroir *m* (d'un meuble) **3** **drawers** *npl* UNDERPANTS : caleçon *m* (d'homme), culotte *f* (de femme)
drawing ['drɔɪŋ] *n* **1** LOTTERY : tirage *m* (au sort), loterie *f* **2** SKETCH : dessin *m*
drawl[1] ['drɔl] *vt* : dire d'une voix traînante — *vi* : parler d'une voix traînante
drawl[2] *n* : voix *f* traînante
draw out *vt* : faire parler (une personne)
draw up *vt* **1** FORMULATE : dresser, rédiger **2** APPROACH : approcher **3** *or* **to draw oneself up** : se redresser — *vi* STOP : s'arrêter

dread[1] ['drɛd] *vt* : redouter, craindre
dread[2] *adj* : redoutable, terrible
dread[3] *n* : crainte *f*, terreur *f*
dreadful ['drɛdfəl] *adj* **1** HORRIBLE : affreux, épouvantable **2** TERRIBLE, UNPLEASANT : terrible <a dreadful cold : un rhume terrible>
dream[1] ['dri:m] *v* **dreamed** ['drɛmpt, 'dri:md] *or* **dreamt** ['drɛmpt]; **dreaming** *vi* **1** : rêver <to dream about : rêver de> **2** DAYDREAM : rêvasser, songer — *vt* **1** : rêver <to dream a dream : faire un rêve> **2** IMAGINE : imaginer, penser, songer
dream[2] *n* **1** : rêve *m* **2** DAYDREAM : rêverie *f* **3** : merveille *f*, bijou *m* <my new car is a dream : ma nouvelle voiture est une merveille> **4** IDEAL : idéal *m*
dreamer ['dri:mər] **1** : rêveur *m*, -veuse *f* **2** IDEALIST : idéaliste *mf*
dreamless ['dri:mləs] *adj* : sans rêves
dreamlike ['dri:m,laɪk] *adj* : irréel
dreamy ['dri:mi] *adj* **dreamier; -est 1** : rêveur <a dreamy child : un enfant rêveur> **2** SOOTHING : apaisant, reposant **3** DELIGHTFUL : ravissant, superbe
drearily ['drɪrəli] *adv* : tristement, sombrement
dreary ['drɪri] *adj* **drearier; -est** : morne, sombre
dredge[1] ['drɛdʒ] *vt* **dredged; dredging 1** : draguer **2** COAT : saupoudrer, paner (en cuisine)
dredge[2] *n* : drague *f*
dregs ['drɛgz] *npl* : lie *f* <the dregs of society : la lie de la société>
drench ['drɛntʃ] *vt* : tremper, mouiller
dress[1] ['drɛs] *vt* **1** CLOTHE : habiller, vêtir **2** DECORATE : décorer <to dress a shop window : faire une vitrine> **3** : préparer, parer (une dinde, etc.), assaisonner (une salade) **4** BANDAGE : panser (une blessure) **5** FERTILIZE : fertiliser (la terre) — *vi* **1** : s'habiller **2** *or* **to dress up** : se mettre en grande toilette
dress[2] *n* **1** CLOTHING : habillement *m*, tenue *f* **2** : robe *f* (de femme) <a silk dress : une robe de soie>
dresser ['drɛsər] *n* : commode *f* à miroir
dressing ['drɛsɪŋ] *n* **1** CLOTHING : habillement *m* **2** SAUCE : sauce *f*, vinaigrette *f* **3** BANDAGE : pansement *m* **4** FERTILIZER : engrais *m*
dressmaker ['drɛs,meɪkər] *n* : couturière *f*
dressmaking ['drɛs,meɪkɪŋ] *n* : couture *f*
dressy ['drɛsi] *adj* **dressier; -est** : habillé, élégant
drew → **draw**[1]
dribble[1] ['drɪbəl] *vi* **-bled; -bling 1** TRICKLE : dégoutter, tomber goutte à goutte **2** DROOL : baver **3** : dribbler (au basketball)
dribble[2] *n* **1** TRICKLE : filet *m* (d'eau) **2** DROOL : bave *f* **3** : dribble *m* (au basketball)
drier, driest → **dry**[2]
drift[1] ['drɪft] *vi* **1** : dériver (sur l'eau), être emporté (par le vent) **2** ACCUMULATE : s'amonceler, former des bancs *Can*, poudrer *Can* (se dit de la neige) **3 to drift along** : flâner, errer <she drifted through life : elle a passé sa vie à errer> **4 to drift away** : s'éloigner
drift[2] *n* **1** COURSE : mouvement *m*, courant *m* **2** HEAP, MASS : amoncellement *m*, entassement *m*, banc *m* (de neige) *Can* **3** MEANING : sens *m*, portée *f*
drill[1] ['drɪl] *vt* **1** BORE : percer, forer **2** TRAIN : faire faire des exercices à, entraîner — *vi* **1** BORE : forer, percer un trou **2** PRACTICE, TRAIN : faire de l'exercice
drill[2] *n* **1** : perceuse *f* (outil) **2** EXERCISE, PRACTICE : exercice *m* **3** : semoir *m* (en agriculture)
drily → **dryly**
drink[1] ['drɪŋk] *v* **drank** ['dræŋk]; **drunk** ['drʌŋk] *or* **drank; drinking** *vt* **1** : boire **2 to drink up** ABSORB : boire, s'imbiber — *vi* : boire
drink[2] *n* **1** BEVERAGE : boisson *f* **2** : boisson *f* alcoolisée
drip[1] ['drɪp] *v* **dripped; dripping** *vt* : laisser tomber goutte à goutte — *vi* : tomber goutte à goutte, dégoutter
drip[2] *n* **1** DROP : goutte *f* **2** : bruit *m* de goutte
drive[1] ['draɪv] *v* **drove** ['dro:v]; **driven** ['drɪvən]; **driving** *vt* **1** : mener, conduire (un troupeau) **2** : conduire, piloter (un véhicule) **3** COMPEL : inciter **4** PUSH : conduire, amener <hunger drove him to steal : la faim l'a amené à voler> **5** PROPEL : envoyer (une balle) — *vi* : conduire, rouler <I was driving at 65 mph : je roulais à 65 milles à l'heure>
drive[2] *n* **1** : promenade *f* (en voiture) **2** CAMPAIGN : campagne *f* **3** VIGOR : énergie *f*, initiative *f* **4** NEED : besoin *m* fondamental
drivel ['drɪvəl] *n* : bêtises *fpl*
driver ['draɪvər] *n* **1** : conducteur *m*, -trice *f* **2** CHAUFFEUR : chauffeur *m*
driveway ['draɪv,weɪ] *n* : allée *f*, entrée *f* (de garage)
drizzle[1] ['drɪzəl] *vi* **-zled; -zling** : bruiner, crachiner
drizzle[2] *n* : bruine *f*, crachin *m*
droll ['dro:l] *adj* **1** COMICAL : drôle, comique **2** ODD : curieux, bizarre
dromedary ['drɑmə,dɛri] *n, pl* **-daries** : dromadaire *m*
drone[1] ['dro:n] *vi* **droned; droning 1** BUZZ, HUM : bourdonner (se dit d'un insecte), ronronner (se dit d'un moteur) **2** *or* **to drone on** : parler d'un ton monotone

drone² *n* **1** BEE : abeille *f* mâle **2** HUM : bourdonnement *m* (d'un insecte), ronronnement *m* (d'un moteur)
drool¹ ['dru:l] *vi* : baver
drool² *n* : bave *f*
droop¹ ['dru:p] *vi* **1** HANG, SAG : pencher (se dit de la tête), tomber (se dit des épaules ou des paupières), se faner (se dit des fleurs) **2** FLAG : baisser <her spirits were drooping : elle était démoralisée>
droop² *n* : abaissement *m*, affaissement *m*, attitude *f* penchée
drop¹ ['drɑp] *v* **dropped; dropping** *vt* **1** : laisser tomber <he dropped the book : il a laissé tomber le livre> **2** LOWER : baisser <to drop one's voice : baisser la voix> **3** SEND : envoyer <drop me a line : écris-moi un mot> **4** ABANDON : abandonner (une conversation, une matière, etc.) **5** OMIT : omettre, supprimer **6 to drop a hint about** : faire allusion à, suggérer **7 to drop off** LEAVE : déposer, laisser — *vi* **1** DRIP : tomber goutte à goutte **2** FALL : tomber **3** DECREASE : se calmer (se dit du vent), baisser (se dit des prix) **4 to drop back** *or* **to drop behind** : rester en arrière, prendre du retard **5 to drop by** VISIT : passer, entrer en passant
drop² *n* **1** : goutte *f* (de liquide) **2** DECLINE, FALL : réduction *f*, diminution *f* **3** DESCENT : hauteur *f* de chute, descente *f* <a 10-foot drop : une hauteur de 10 pieds> **4** : pastille *f*, bonbon *f* <cough drops : pastilles contre la toux>
droplet ['drɑplət] *n* : gouttelette *f*
dropper ['drɑpər] *n* : compte-gouttes *m*
dross ['drɑs, 'drɔs] *n* **1** : crasse *f*, scories *fpl* (de métaux) **2** WASTE : déchets *mpl*
drought ['draʊt] *n* : sécheresse *f*
drove¹ ['dro:v] → **drive¹**
drove² *n* **1** HERD : troupeau *m* **2** CROWD : foule *f* <people came in droves : il y avait une foule de gens>
drown ['draʊn] *vt* **1** : noyer **2** *or* **to drown out** : noyer, couvrir (un son, une voix) — *vi* : se noyer
drowse¹ ['draʊz] *vi* **drowsed; drowsing** : somnoler, sommeiller
drowse² *n* DOZE : somme *m*, sieste *f*
drowsiness ['draʊzinəs] *n* : somnolence *f*
drowsy ['draʊzi] *adj* **drowsier; -est** : somnolent, qui a envie de dormir
drub ['drʌb] *vt* **drubbed; drubbing 1** BEAT : battre, maltraiter **2** DEFEAT : vaincre
drudge¹ ['drʌdʒ] *vi* **drudged; drudging** : besogner, trimer *fam*
drudge² *n* : bête *f* de somme, gratte-papier *m*
drudgery ['drʌdʒəri] *n, pl* **-eries** : corvée *f*, (grosse) besogne *f*
drug¹ ['drʌg] *vt* **drugged; drugging** : droguer
drug² *n* **1** MEDICATION : médicament *m* **2** NARCOTIC : drogue *f*, stupéfiant *m*
druggist ['drʌgɪst] *n* : pharmacien *m*, -cienne *f*
drugstore ['drʌg,stɔr] *n* : pharmacie *f*
drum¹ ['drʌm] *v* **drummed; drumming** *vi* : jouer du tambour — *vt* **1** TAP : tambouriner (les doigts, les pieds, etc.) **2** DRIVE, PUSH : enfoncer, fourrer <he drummed it into my head : il me l'a enfoncé dans la tête>
drum² *n* **1** : tambour *m* **2** *or* **oil drum** : bidon *m*
drumbeat ['drʌm,bi:t] *n* : roulement *m* de tambour
drumstick ['drʌm,stɪk] *n* **1** : baguette *f* de tambour **2** : cuisse *f* (de poulet)
drunk¹ → **drink¹**
drunk² ['drʌŋk] *adj* : ivre, soûl *fam*, en boisson *Can* <drunk driving : conduite en état d'ébriété>
drunk³ *n* : ivrogne *m*, ivrognesse *f*
drunkard ['drʌŋkərd] *n* : ivrogne *m*, ivrognesse *f*
drunken ['drʌŋkən] *adj* : ivre, en état d'ébriété
drunkenly ['drʌŋkənli] *adv* : comme un ivrogne
drunkenness ['drʌŋkənli] *n* : ivresse *f*, ébriété
dry¹ ['draɪ] *v* **dried; drying** *vt* **1** : sécher **2** WIPE : essuyer — *vi* : sécher
dry² *adj* **drier; driest 1** : sec <a dry climate : un climat sec> **2** THIRSTY : assoiffé **3** : qui interdit la vente d'alcool <a dry town : une ville où on ne vend pas d'alcool> **4** UNINTERESTING : plate, aride **5** BITING, KEEN : mordant, caustique <to have a dry wit : être pince-sans-rire> **6** : sec (se dit du vin), brut (se dit du champagne) **7 on dry land** : sur la terre ferme
dry–clean ['draɪ,kli:n] *vt* : nettoyer à sec
dry cleaner *n* : teinturerie *f* (service)
dry cleaning *n* : nettoyage *m* à sec
dryer ['draɪər] *n* : séchoir *m*
dry goods *npl* : tissus *mpl*, étoffes *fpl*
dry ice *n* : neige *f* carbonique
dryly ['draɪli] *adv* : sèchement
dryness ['draɪnəs] *n* : sécheresse *f*
dual ['du:əl, 'dju:-] *adj* : double
dub ['dʌb] *vt* **dubbed; dubbing 1** NAME, NICKNAME : surnommer **2** : doubler (un film, etc.)
dubious ['du:biəs, 'dju:-] *adj* **1** DOUBTFUL : dubitatif **2** QUESTIONABLE : louche, suspect
dubiously ['du:biəsli, 'dju:-] *adv* : d'un air incertain, avec doute
duchess ['dʌtʃəs] *n* : duchesse *f*
duck¹ ['dʌk] *vt* **1** PLUNGE : plonger (dans l'eau) **2** LOWER : baisser <to duck one's head : baisser la tête> **3** AVOID, DODGE : éviter, esquiver — *vi* : se baisser vivement, esquiver un coup (en boxe)
duck² *n, pl* **ducks** *or* **duck** : canard *m*

duckling ['dʌklɪŋ] *n* : caneton *m*, canette *f*
duct ['dʌkt] *n* **1** PIPE : conduite *f* (d'eau, etc.) **2** CHANNEL, TUBE : conduit *m*, canal *m* <tear duct : canal lacrymal>
dude ['du:d, 'dju:d] *n* **1** DANDY : dandy *m* **2** GUY : gars *m fam*, mec *m fam*
due[1] ['du:, 'dju:] *adv* DIRECTLY : plein, droit vers <due north : plein nord>
due[2] *adj* **1** OWING : dû, payable **2** APPROPRIATE : qui convient, dû <after due consideration : après mûre réflexion> **3** EXPECTED : attendu <the plane is due at midnight : l'avion doit arriver à minuit>
due[3] *n* **1 to give s.o. his (her) due** : rendre justice à qqn **2 dues** *npl* FEE : cotisation *f*
duel[1] ['du:əl, 'dju:-] *vi* **duelled; duelling** : se battre en duel
duel[2] *n* : duel *m*
duet [du'ɛt, dju:-] *n* : duo *m*
due to *prep* : en raison de, à cause de
dug → dig[1]
dugout ['dʌg,aʊt] *n* **1** CANOE : pirogue *f* **2** SHELTER : tranchée-abri *f*
duke ['du:k, 'dju:k] *n* : duc *m*
dull[1] ['dʌl] *vt* **1** BLUNT : émousser, épointer **2** DIM, TARNISH : ternir (des couleurs, des métaux, etc.)
dull[2] *adj* **1** STUPID : stupide, lent **2** BLUNT : émoussé <a dull knife : un couteau émoussé> **3** BORING : ennuyeux, ennuyant *Can* **4** LACKLUSTER : terne, fade <a dull red : un rouge fade>
dullness ['dʌlnəs] *n* **1** STUPIDITY : stupidité *f*, lenteur *f* **2** BLUNTNESS : manque *m* de tranchant **3** TEDIUM : monotonie *f*
duly ['du:li] *adv* **1** PROPERLY : dûment, de façon convenable <duly recorded : dûment enregistré> **2** EXPECTEDLY : comme prévu
dumb ['dʌm] *adj* **1** MUTE : muet **2** STUPID : bête
dumbbell ['dʌm,bɛl] *n* **1** WEIGHT : haltère *m* **2** DOPE : idiot *m*, -diote *f*; gourde *f fam*
dumbfound *or* **dumfound** [,dʌm'faʊnd] *vt* AMAZE : abasourdir, sidérer *fam*
dummy ['dʌmi] *n, pl* **-mies 1** DOPE, FOOL : imbécile *mf*, ballot *m fam* **2** MANNEQUIN : mannequin *m*
dump[1] ['dʌmp] *vt* : déposer, jeter, déverser
dump[2] *n* **1** : tas *m* d'ordures **2 to be down in the dumps** : avoir le cafard
dumpling ['dʌmplɪŋ] *n* : boulette *f* de pâte
dumpy ['dʌmpi] *adj* **dumpier; -est** CHUBBY : boulot, rondelet *fam*
dun[1] ['dʌn] *vt* **dunned; dunning** : harceler (afin d'obtenir un paiement)
dun[2] *adj* : brun gris
dunce [dʌnʦ] *n* : cancre *m fam*
dune ['du:n, 'dju:n] *n* : dune *f*
dung ['dʌŋ] *n* : excréments *mpl*, fumier *m*, bouse *f* (de vache), crottin *m* (de cheval)
dungaree [,dʌŋgə'ri:] *n* **1** DENIM : jean *m* **2 dungarees** *npl* JEANS : jean *m*, blue-jean *m*
dungeon ['dʌndʒən] *n* : cachot *m* (souterrain)
dunghill ['dʌŋ,hɪl] *n* : tas *m* de fumier
dunk ['dʌŋk] *vt* : tremper
duo ['du:o:, 'dju:-] *n, pl* **duos** : duo *m*
dupe[1] ['du:p, 'dju:p] *vt* **duped; duping** : duper, tromper
dupe[2] *n* : dupe *f*
duplex[1] ['du:,pleks, 'dju:-] *adj* : double
duplex[2] *n* : duplex *m*, maison *f* jumelée
duplicate[1] ['du:plɪ,keɪt, 'dju:-] *vt* **-cated; -cating 1** COPY : faire un double de, copier **2** REPEAT : répéter, refaire
duplicate[2]**-** ['du:plɪkət, 'dju:-] *adj* : en double
duplicate[3] ['du:plɪkət, 'dju:-] *n* : double *m*, copie *f* exacte
duplication [,du:plɪ'keɪʃən, ,dju:-] *n* **1** DUPLICATING : action *f* de copier, reproduction *f* **2** REPETITION : répétition *f*
duplicity [du'plɪsəṭi, ,dju:-] *n, pl* **-ties** : duplicité *f*
durability [,durə'bɪləṭi, ,djur-] *n* : durabilité *f*, résistance *f*
durable ['durəbəl, 'djur-] *adj* : durable, résistant
duration [du'reɪʃən, djʊ-] *n* : durée *f*
duress [du'rɛs, djʊ-] *n* : contrainte *f*
during ['durɪŋ, 'djur-] *prep* : durant, pendant
dusk ['dʌsk] *n* : crépuscule *m*, nuit *f* tombante, brunante *f Can*
dusky ['dʌski] *adj* **duskier; -est** : sombre, obscur (se dit des couleurs)
dust[1] ['dʌst] *vt* **1** : épousseter **2** SPRINKLE : saupoudrer
dust[2] *n* : poussière *f*
duster ['dʌstər] *n* **1** *or* **dust cloth** : chiffon *m* à poussière **2** *or* **feather duster** : plumeau *m* **3** HOUSECOAT : blouse *f*, sarrau *m*
dustpan ['dʌst,pæn] *n* : pelle *f* à poussière, porte-poussière *m Can*
dusty ['dʌsti] *adj* **dustier; -est** : poussiéreux
Dutch[1] ['dʌtʃ] *adj* : néerlandais, hollandais
Dutch[2] *n* **1** : néerlandais *m*, hollandais *m* (langue) **2 the Dutch** *npl* : les Néerlandais, les Hollandais
Dutch treat *n* : sortie *f* où chacun paie sa part
dutiful ['du:ṭɪfəl, 'dju:-] *adj* : obéissant, respectueux, consciencieux
duty ['du:ṭi, ,dju:-] *n, pl* **-ties 1** TASK : fonction *f* <to perform one's duties : remplir ses fonctions> **2** OBLIGATION : devoir *m* **3** TAX : taxe *f*, droit *m* **4 to be on duty** : être de garde
DVD [,di:,vi:'di:] *n* : DVD *m*
dwarf[1] ['dwɔrf] *vt* **1** STUNT : rabougrir (un arbre) **2** : faire paraître tout petit

dwarf[2] *n* : nain *m*, naine *f*
dwell [ˈdwɛl] *vi* **dwelled** *or* **dwelt** [ˈdwɛlt]; **dwelling 1** RESIDE : résider, demeurer **2 to dwell on** : penser sans cesse à, ruminer
dweller [ˈdwɛlər] *n* : habitant *m*, -tante *f*
dwelling [ˈdwɛlɪŋ] *n* : demeure *f*, résidence *f*
dwindle [ˈdwɪndəl] *vi* **-dled; -dling** : diminuer
dye[1] [ˈdaɪ] *vt* **dyed; dyeing** : teindre <to dye one's hair : se teindre les cheveux>
dye[2] *n* : teinture *f*
dying → die[1]
dyke → dike
dynamic [daɪˈnæmɪk] *adj* : dynamique
dynamite[1] [ˈdaɪnəˌmaɪt] *vt* **-mited; -miting** : dynamiter
dynamite[2] *n* : dynamite *f*
dynamo [ˈdaɪnəˌmoː] *n, pl* **-mos** : dynamo *f*
dynasty [ˈdaɪnəsti, -næs-] *n, pl* **-ties** : dynastie *f*
dysentery [ˈdɪsənˌtɛri] *n, pl* **-teries** : dysenterie *f*
dyslexia [dɪsˈlɛksiə] *n* : dyslexie *f* — **dyslexic** [-ˈlɛksɪk] *adj*
dystrophy [ˈdɪstrəfi] *n, pl* **-phies 1** : dystrophie *f* **2 → muscular dystrophy**

E

e [ˈiː] *n, pl* **e's** *or* **es** [ˈiːz] : e *m*, cinquième lettre de l'alphabet
each[1] [ˈiːtʃ] *adv* APIECE : chacun, la pièce <one dollar each : un dollar la pièce>
each[2] *adj* : chaque <each week : chaque semaine>
each[3] *pron* **1** : chacun *m*, -cune *f* <each of the girls : chacune des filles> <each and every one : chacun sans exception> **2 each other** : l'un l'autre <they love each other : ils s'aiment (l'un l'autre)> **3 to each his own** : chacun son goût
eager [ˈiːgər] *adj* **1** ENTHUSIASTIC : désireux, avide **2** ANXIOUS, IMPATIENT : impatient, pressé
eagerly [ˈiːgərli] *adv* : avidement, avec empressement
eagerness [ˈiːgərnəs] *n* : avidité *f*, empressement *m*
eagle [ˈiːgəl] *n* : aigle *m*
ear [ˈɪr] *n* **1** : oreille *f* (en anatomie) **2** : épi *m* (de maïs, etc.)
earache [ˈɪrˌeɪk] *n* : mal *m* d'oreille
eardrum [ˈɪrˌdrʌm] *n* : tympan *m*
earl [ˈərl] *n* : comte *m*
earlobe [ˈɪrˌloːb] *n* : lobe *m* de l'oreille
early[1] [ˈərli] *adv* **earlier; -est 1** : tôt, de bonne heure <to go to bed early : se coucher de bonne heure> <as early as possible : le plus tôt possible> **2** : en avance <five minutes early : en avance de cinq minutes>
early[2] *adj* **earlier; -est 1** FIRST : premier <his early novels : ses premiers romans> **2** (*referring to a designated time*) <to be early : arriver de bonne heure> <early fruits : fruits précoces> <an early death : une mort prématurée> **3** (*referring to a beginning*) <in the early afternoon : au commencement de l'après-midi> <in early December : début décembre> **4** ANCIENT : ancien, primitif <early man : l'homme primitif>
earmark [ˈɪrˌmɑrk] *vt* : réserver, désigner
earn [ˈərn] *vt* **1** : gagner <to earn one's living : gagner sa vie> **2** DESERVE : mériter
earnest[1] [ˈərnəst] *adj* **1** SERIOUS : sérieux **2** SINCERE : sincère — **earnestly** *adv*
earnest[2] *n* **in ~** : sérieusement
earnestness [ˈərnəstnəs] *n* : sérieux *m*, gravité *f*
earnings [ˈərnɪŋz] *npl* **1** WAGES : salaire *m* **2** PROFITS : bénéfices *mpl*, profits *mpl*
earphone [ˈɪrˌfoːn] *n* : écouteur *m*
earring [ˈɪrˌrɪŋ] *n* : boucle *f* d'oreille
earshot [ˈɪrˌʃɑt] *n* : portée *f* de voix
earth [ˈərθ] *n* **1** GROUND, SOIL : terre *f*, sol *m* **2 the Earth** : la Terre
earthen [ˈərθən, -ðən] *adj* : en terre
earthenware [ˈərθənˌwær, -ðən-] *n* : faïence *f*
earthly [ˈərθli] *adj* **1** : terrestre <earthly pleasures : joies terrestres> **2** (*indicating possibility*) <of no earthly use : d'aucune utilité>
earthquake [ˈərθˌkweɪk] *n* : tremblement *m* de terre
earthworm [ˈərθˌwərm] *n* : ver *m* de terre, lombric *m France*
earthy [ˈərθi] *adj* **earthier; -est 1** : terreux <earthy colors : couleurs de terre> **2** DOWN-TO-EARTH : pratique, terre à terre **3** COARSE, CRUDE : truculent, grossier
earwax [ˈɪrˌwæks] *n* : cérumen *m*
earwig [ˈɪrˌwɪg] *n* : perce-oreille *m*
ease[1] [ˈiːz] *v* **eased; easing** *vt* **1** FACILITATE : faciliter **2** ALLEVIATE, LESSEN : soulager, atténuer, calmer (l'inquiétude) **3 to ease oneself into** : se laisser glisser dans — *vi or* **to ease up** : s'atténuer, se détendre
ease[2] *n* **1** : aise *f* <to put s.o. at ease : mettre qqn à son aise> **2** FACILITY : facilité *f* **3** COMFORT : bien-être *m*,

tranquillité *f* **4** AFFLUENCE : aisance *f* **5 at ease!** : repos! **6 with ~** : aisément, facilement

easel [ˈiːzəl] *n* : chevalet *m*

easily [ˈiːzəli] *adv* **1** : facilement, aisément **2** UNQUESTIONABLY : sans doute, de loin

easiness [ˈiːzinəs] *n* : facilité *f*

east[1] [ˈiːst] *adv* : vers l'est, à l'est

east[2] *adj* : est <the east coast : la côte est> <the east wind : le vent d'est>

east[3] *n* **1** : est *m* **2 the East** : l'Est *m*, l'Orient *m*

Easter [ˈiːstər] *n* : Pâques *m*, Pâques *fpl*

easterly[1] [ˈiːstərli] *adv* : vers l'est

easterly[2] *adj* : d'est, de l'est <in an easterly direction : en direction de l'est>

eastern [ˈiːstərn] *adj* **1** : est, de l'est **2 Eastern** : de l'Est, d'Orient

easy[1] [ˈiːzi] *adv* **easier; -est** : doucement <to go easy on : aller doucement avec> <easy does it! : doucement!>

easy[2] *adj* **easier; -est 1** : facile, aisé **2** RELAXED : décontracté <an easy manner : une attitude pleine d'aisance> **3** LENIENT : indulgent, clément

easygoing [ˌiːziˈgoːɪŋ] *adj* : accommodant, complaisant

eat [ˈiːt] *v* **ate** [ˈeɪt]; **eaten** [ˈiːtən]; **eating** *vt* **1** : manger, prendre (un repas) **2** CONSUME : manger, consommer (des ressources, des bénéfices, etc.) **3** CORRODE : ronger, corroder — *vi* : manger

eatable [ˈiːtəbəl] *adj* : mangeable, bon à manger

eaves [ˈiːvz] *npl* : avant-toit *m*

eavesdrop [ˈiːvzˌdrɑp] *vi* **-dropped; -dropping** : écouter aux portes

ebb[1] [ˈɛb] *vi* **1** : refluer, descendre (se dit de la mer) **2** DECLINE : décliner, baisser

ebb[2] *n* **1** : reflux *m* (de la mer) **2** DECLIN : déclin *m*, baisse *f*

ebony[1] [ˈɛbəni] *adj* **1** : d'ébène **2** BLACK : d'un noir d'ébène

ebony[2] *n, pl* **-nies** : ébène *f*

ebullience [ɪˈbʊljənts, -ˈbʌl-] *n* : exubérance *f*

ebullient [ɪˈbʊljənt, -ˈbʌl-] *adj* : exubérant

eccentric[1] [ɪkˈsɛntrɪk] *adj* : excentrique — **eccentrically** [-trɪkli] *adv*

eccentric[2] *n* : excentrique *mf*

eccentricity [ˌɛkˌsɛnˈtrɪsəṭi] *n, pl* **-ties** : excentricité *f*

ecclesiastic [ɪˌkliːziˈæstɪk] *n* : ecclésiastique *mf*

ecclesiastical [ɪˌkliːziˈæstɪkəl] *or* **ecclesiastic** *adj* : ecclésiastique

echelon [ˈɛʃəˌlɑn] *n* : échelon *m*

echo[1] [ˈɛˌkoː] *v* **echoed; echoing** *vt* : répercuter (un son), répéter (des mots) — *vi* : se répercuter, résonner

echo[2] *n, pl* **echoes** : écho *m*

éclair [eɪˈklær, i-] *n* : éclair *m*

eclectic [eˈklɛktɪk, ɪ-] *adj* : éclectique

eclipse[1] [ɪˈklɪps] *vt* **eclipsed; eclipsing** : éclipser

eclipse[2] *n* : éclipse *f*

ecological [ˌiːkəˈlɑdʒɪkəl, ˌɛkə-] *adj* : écologique — **ecologically** *adv*

ecologist [iˈkɑlədʒɪst, ɛ-] *n* : écologiste *mf*

ecology [iˈkɑlədʒi, ɛ-] *n, pl* **-gies** : écologie *f*

economic [ˌiːkəˈnɑmɪk, ˌɛkə-] *adj* : économique

economical [ˌiːkəˈnɑmɪkəl, ˌɛkə-] *adj* THRIFTY : économe

economically [ˌiːkəˈnɑmɪkli, ˌɛkə-] *adv* : économiquement, de façon économique

economics [ˌiːkəˈnɑmɪks, ˌɛkə-] *ns & pl* : sciences *fpl* économiques, économie *f*

economist [iˈkɑnəmɪst] *n* : économiste *mf*

economize [iˈkɑnəˌmaɪz] *v* **-mized; -mizing** : économiser

economy [iˈkɑnəmi] *n, pl* **-mies** : économie *f*

ecosystem [ˈiːkoˌsɪstəm] *n* : écosystème *m*

ecru [ˈɛˌkruː, ˈeɪ-] *n* : écru *m*

ecstasy [ˈɛkstəsi] *n, pl* **-sies** : extase *f*

ecstatic [ɛkˈstæṭɪk, ɪk-] *adj* : extatique, ravi, en extase

ecstatically [ɛkˈstæṭɪkli, ɪk-] *adv* : avec extase

Ecuadoran[1] [ˌɛkwəˈdorən] *or* **Ecuadorean** *or* **Ecuadorian** [-ˈdoriən] *adj* : équatorien

Ecuadoran[2] *or* **Ecuadorean** *or* **Ecuadorian** *n* : Equatorien *m*, -rienne *f*

ecumenical [ˌɛkjuˈmɛnɪkəl] *adj* : œcuménique

eczema [ɪgˈziːmə, ˈɛgzəmə, ˈɛksə-] *n* : eczéma *m*

eddy[1] [ˈɛdi] *vi* **eddied; eddying** : tourbillonner

eddy[2] *n, pl* **-dies** : tourbillon *m*

edema [ɪˈdiːmə] *n* : œdème *m*

edge[1] [ˈɛdʒ] *vt* **edged; edging 1** BORDER : border **2** SHARPEN : aiguiser, affiler **3 to edge one's way** : avancer lentement **4 to edge out** : pousser (qqn) doucement vers la sortie, évincer en douceur — *vi* ADVANCE : avancer (doucement)

edge[2] *n* **1** BORDER, MARGIN : bord *m* **2** : tranchant *m*, fil *m* (d'un couteau, etc.) **3** ADVANTAGE : avantage *m*

edgewise [ˈɛdʒˌwaɪz] *adv* **1 → sideways 2 to get a word in edgewise** : placer un mot

edginess [ˈɛdʒinəs] *n* : nervosité *f*

edging [ˈɛdʒɪŋ] *n* : bordure *f*

edgy [ˈɛdʒi] *adj* **edgier; -est** : énervé

edible [ˈɛdəbəl] *adj* : comestible

edict [ˈiːˌdɪkt] *n* : édit *m*, décret *m*

edification [ˌɛdəfəˈkeɪʃən] *n* : édification *f*

edifice [ˈɛdəˈfɪs] *n* : édifice *m*
edify [ˈɛdəˈfaɪ] *vt* **-fied; -fying** : édifier
edit [ˈɛdɪt] *vt* **1** : réviser, corriger, diriger la rédaction de **2 to edit out** : couper, supprimer
edition [ɪˈdɪʃən] *n* : édition *f* <limited edition : édition à tirage limité>
editor [ˈɛdɪtər] *n* : rédacteur *m*, -trice *f* (d'un journal); éditeur *m*, -trice *f* (d'un livre); monteur *m*, -teuse *f* (d'un film)
editorial[1] [ˌɛdɪˈtoriəl] *adj* **1** : de la rédaction <editorial staff : personnel de rédaction> **2** : éditorial <an editorial comment : un commentaire éditorial>
editorial[2] *n* : éditorial *m*
educate [ˈɛdʒəˌkeɪt] *vt* **-cated; -cating 1** INSTRUCT, TEACH : instruire, donner l'instruction à (des élèves) **2** DEVELOP, REFINE : éduquer <to educate s.o.'s taste : éduquer le goût de qqn>
education [ˌɛdʒəˈkeɪʃən] *n* **1** : éducation *f*, études *fpl* <university education : études supérieures> **2** TEACHING : enseignement *m*, instruction *f*
educational [ˌɛdʒəˈkeɪʃənəl] *adj* **1** INSTRUCTIVE : éducatif **2** TEACHING : d'enseignement, pédagogique
educator [ˈɛdʒəˌkeɪtər] *n* : éducateur *m*, -trice *f*
eel [ˈiːl] *n* : anguille *f*
eerie [ˈɪri] *adj* **eerier; -est** : sinistre, étrange
eerily [ˈɪrəli] *adv* : d'une manière sinistre
efface [ɪˈfeɪs, ɛ-] *vt* **-faced; -facing** : effacer
effect[1] [ɪˈfɛkt] *vt* : effectuer, réaliser
effect[2] *n* **1** RESULT : effet *m*, conséquence *f* **2** MEANING : sens *m* <something to that effect : quelque chose dans ce sens> **3** EFFECTIVENESS : efficacité *f* <to little effect : sans grand résultat> **4 effects** *npl* BELONGINGS : effets *mpl* (personnels) **5 to go into effect** : entrer en vigueur **6 in ~** REALLY : en fait, en réalité
effective [ɪˈfɛktɪv] *adj* **1** EFFECTUAL : efficace **2** ACTUAL : effectif **3** OPERATIVE : en vigueur
effectively [ɪˈfɛktɪvli] *adv* **1** EFFICIENTLY : efficacement **2** ACTUALLY, REALLY : effectivement
effectiveness [ɪˈfɛktɪvnəs] *n* : efficacité *f*
effectual [ɪˈfɛktʃʊəl] *adj* : efficace — **effectually** *adv*
effeminate [əˈfɛmənət] *adj* : efféminé
effervesce [ˌɛfərˈvɛs] *vi* **-vesced; -vescing 1** FIZZ : pétiller **2** : être exubérant (se dit des personnes)
effervescence [ˌɛfərˈvesənts] *n* : effervescence *f*
effervescent [ˌɛfərˈvesənt] *adj* : effervescent
effete [ɛˈfiːt, ɪ-] *adj* **1** DECADENT, WEAKENED : veule, affaibli, décadent **2** EFFEMINATE : efféminé
efficacious [ˌɛfəˈkeɪʃəs] *adj* : efficace
efficacy [ˈɛfɪkəsi] *n, pl* **-cies** : efficacité *f*
efficiency [ˈɪfɪʃəntsi] *n pl* **-cies** : efficacité *f*, efficience *f*
efficient [ɪˈfɪʃənt] *adj* : efficace, efficient
efficiently [ɪˈfɪʃəntli] *adv* : efficacement <to work efficiently : fonctionner à bon rendement>
effigy [ˈɛfədʒi] *n, pl* **-gies** : effigie *f*
effort [ˈɛfərt] *n* **1** EXERTION : effort *m* <to be worth the effort : en valoir la peine> **2** ATTEMPT : essai *m*, tentative *f*
effortless [ˈɛfərtləs] *adj* : facile, aisé — **effortlessly** *adv*
effrontery [ɪˈfrʌntəri] *n, pl* **-teries** : effronterie *f*
effusion [ɪˈfjuːʒən, ɛ-] *n* : effusion *f*
effusive [ɪˈfjuːsɪv, ɛ-] *adj* : expansif, démonstratif <an effusive welcome : un accueil chaleureux>
effusively [ɪˈfjuːsɪvli, ɛ-] *adv* : avec effusion
egg[1] [ˈɛg] *vt* **to egg on** : inciter, pousser
egg[2] *n* : œuf *m*
eggbeater [ˈɛgˌbiːtər] *n* : batteur *m* (à œufs)
eggnog [ˈɛgˌnɑg] *n* : lait *m* de poule
eggplant [ˈɛgˌplænt] *n* : aubergine *f*
eggshell [ˈɛgˌʃɛl] *n* : coquille *f* d'œuf
ego [ˈiːgoː] *n, pl* **egos 1** SELF : ego *m*, moi *m* **2** SELF-ESTEEM : amour-propre *m*
egocentric [iːgoˈsɛntrɪk] *adj* : égocentrique
egoism [ˈiːgoˌwɪzəm] *m* : égoïsme *m*
egoist [ˈiːgowɪst] *n* : égoïste *mf*
egoistic [ˌiːgoˈwɪstɪk] *adj* : égoïste
egotism [ˈiːgəˈtɪzəm] *n* : égotisme *m*
egotist [ˈiːgətɪst] *n* : égotiste *mf*
egotistic [ˌiːgəˈtɪstɪk] *or* **egotistical** [-ˈtɪstɪkəl] *adj* : égotiste
egregious [ɪˈgriːdʒəs] *adj* : flagrant <an egregious error : une erreur énorme>
egress [ˈiːˌgrɛs] *n* : sortie *f*, issue *f*
egret [ˈiːgrət, -ˌgrɛt] *n* : aigrette *f*
Egyptian[1] [iˈdʒɪpʃən] *adj* : égyptien
Egyptian[2] *n* : Égyptien *m*, -tienne *f*
eider [ˈaɪdər] *n* : eider *m*, moyac *m* Can
eiderdown [ˈaɪdərˌdaʊn] *n* **1** DOWN : duvet *m* **2** COMFORTER : édredon *m*
eight[1] [ˈeɪt] *adj* : huit
eight[2] *n* : huit *m*
eighteen[1] [eɪˈtiːn] *adj* : dix-huit
eighteen[2] *n* : dix-huit *m*
eighteenth[1] [eɪˈtiːnθ] *adj* : dix-huitième
eighteenth[2] *n* **1** : dix-huitième *mf* (dans une série) **2** : dix-huitième *m* (en mathématiques) **3** (*used for dates*) <the eighteenth of May : le dix-huit mai>

eighth[1] ['eɪtθ] *adj* : huitième
eighth[2] *n* **1** : huitième *mf* (dans une série) **2** : huitième *m* (en mathématiques) **3** (*used in dates*) <the eighth of June : le huit juin>
eightieth[1] [eɪtiəθ] *adj* : quatre-vingtième
eightieth[2] *n* **1** : quatre-vingtième *mf* (dans une série) **2** : quatre-vingtième *m* (en mathématiques)
eighty[1] [eɪti] *adj* : quatre-vingts
eighty[2] *n, pl* **eighties** : quatre-vingts *m* <in the late eighties : vers la fin des années quatre-vingts>
either[1] ['iːðər, 'aɪ-] *adj* **1** EACH : chaque <there are trees on either side : il y a des arbres de chaque côté> **2** (*referring to one or the other*) <take either road : prenez l'une ou l'autre des deux routes> <he doesn't like either restaurant : il n'aime ni l'un ni l'autre de ces restaurants> <give me either book : donnez-moi n'importe quel livre>
either[2] *pron* : l'un ou l'autre, n'importe lequel <take either one : prenez l'un ou l'autre> <I don't believe either of them : je ne les crois ni l'un ni l'autre>
either[3] *conj* **either . . . or** : ou . . . ou, ou bien . . . ou bien, soit . . . soit <you either love him or hate him : soit on l'adore, soit on le déteste>
ejaculate [i'dʒækjəˌleɪt] *vi* **-lated; -lating 1** : éjaculer (en physiologie) **2** EXCLAIM : s'exclamer, s'écrier
ejaculation [iˌdʒækjə'leɪʃən] *n* **1** : éjaculation *f* (en physiologie) **2** EXCLAMATION : exclamation *f*, cri *m*
eject [i'dʒekt] *vt* : éjecter, expulser
ejection [i'dʒekʃən] *n* : éjection *f*, expulsion *f*
eke [iːk] *vt* **eked; eking** *or* **to eke out 1** SUPPLEMENT : augmenter **2** : gagner difficilement <she eked out a living : elle a gagné tout juste sa vie>
elaborate[1] [i'læbəˌreɪt] *v* **-rated; -rating** *vt* : élaborer (un plan, etc.) — *vi* **to elaborate on** : donner des détails sur, développer
elaborate[2] [i'læbərət] *adj* **1** DETAILED : minutieux **2** ORNATE : orné, travaillé **3** COMPLEX : compliqué, complexe
elapse [i'læps] *vi* **elapsed; elapsing** : s'écouler, passer
elastic[1] [i'læstɪk] *adj* : élastique
elastic[2] *n* : élastique *m*
elasticity [iˌlæs'tɪsəṭi, ˌiːˌlæs-] *n, pl* **-ties** : élasticité *f*
elate [i'leɪt] *vt* **elated; elating** : ravir, transporter de joie
elation [i'leɪʃən] *n* : exultation *f*, joie *f*
elbow[1] ['elˌboː] *vt* : donner un coup de coude à
elbow[2] *n* : coude *m* <to be at s.o.'s elbow : être à portée de main>
elder[1] ['eldər] *adj* : aîné, plus âgé <an elder sister : une sœur aînée>
elder[2] *n* **1** : aîné *m*, aînée *f* **2** : ancien *m* (d'une église ou d'un village)
elderberry ['eldərˌbɛri] *n, pl* **-ries 1** : sureau *m* (arbre) **2** : baie *f* de sureau (fruit)
elderly ['eldərli] *adj* : âgé
eldest ['eldəst] *adj* : aîné <his eldest son : son fils aîné>
elect[1] [i'lekt] *vt* : élire, choisir
elect[2] *adj* : élu, futur <the president elect : le futur president>
elect[3] *npl* **the elect** : les élus
election [i'lekʃən] *n* : élection *f*
elective[1] [i'lektɪv] *adj* **1** : électif **2** OPTIONAL : facultatif
elective[2] *n* : cours *m* facultatif
electoral [i'lektərəl] *adj* : électoral
electorate [i'lektərət] *n* : électorat *m*
electric [i'lektrɪk] *or* **electrical** [-trɪkəl] *adj* : électrique — **electrically** [-trɪkəli] *adv*
electrician [iˌlek'trɪʃən] *n* : électricien *m*, -cienne *f*
electricity [iˌlek'trɪsəṭi] *n, pl* **-ties 1** : électricité *f* **2** CURRENT : courant *m* électrique
electrification [iˌlektrəfə'keɪʃən] *n* : électrification *f*
electrify [i'lektrəˌfaɪ] *vt* **-fied; -fying 1** : électrifier, électriser **2** THRILL : électriser
electrocardiogram [iˌlektro'kɑrdiəˌgræm] *n* : électrocardiogramme *m*
electrocardiograph [iˌlektro'kɑrdiəˌgræf] *n* : électrocardiographe *m*
electrocute [i'lektrəˌkjuːṭ] *vt* **-cuted; -cuting** : électrocuter
electrocution [iˌlektrə'kjuːʃən] *n* : électrocution *f*
electrode [i'lekˌtroːd] *n* : électrode *f*
electrolysis [iˌlek'trɑləsɪs] *n* : électrolyse *f*
electrolyte [i'lektrəˌlaɪt] *n* : électrolyte *m*
electromagnet [iˌlektro'mægnət] *n* : électroaimant *m*
electromagnetic [iˌlektromæg'neṭɪk] *adj* : électromagnétique
electromagnetism [iˌlektro'mægnəṭɪˌzəm] *n* : électromagnétisme *m*
electron [i'lekˌtrɑn] *n* : électron *m*
electronic [iˌlek'trɑnɪk] *adj* : électronique — **electronically** [-nɪkli] *adv*
electronic mail → e-mail
electronics [iˌlek'trɑnɪks] *n* : électronique *f*
elegance ['eliɡənts] *n* : élégance *f*
elegant ['eliɡənt] *adj* : élégant
elegantly ['eliɡəntli] *adv* : élégamment
elegiac [ˌeləˌdʒaɪək] *adj* : élégiaque
elegy ['eləˌdʒi] *n, pl* **-gies** : élégie *f*
element ['eləˌmənt] *n* **1** : élément *m* (en science) **2** COMPONENT : élément *m*, part *f*, facteur *m* <an element of truth : une part de vérité> <the element of chance : le facteur chance> **3 elements** *npl* RUDIMENTS : éléments

mpl, rudiments *mpl* **4 the elements** WEATHER : les éléments
elemental [ˌɛləˈmɛntəl] *adj* : élémentaire
elementary [ˌɛləˈmɛntri] *adj* **1** SIMPLE : élémentaire **2** : de l'enseignement primaire
elementary school *n* : école *f* primaire
elephant [ˈɛləfənt] *n* : éléphant *m*
elevate [ˈɛləˌveɪt] *vt* **-vated; -vating** : élever
elevation [ˌɛləˈveɪʃən] *n* **1** ELEVATING : élévation *f* **2** ALTITUDE : altitude *f*, hauteur *f*
elevator [ˈɛləˌveɪtər] *n* **1** : ascenseur *m* (dans un bâtiment) **2** *or* **grain elevator** : élévateur *m*
eleven[1] [ɪˈlɛvən] *adj* : onze
eleven[2] *n* : onze *m*
eleventh[1] [ɪˈlɛvənɪθ] *adj* : onzième
eleventh[2] *n* **1** : onzième *mf* (dans une série) **2** : onzième *m* (en mathématiques) **3** (*used in dates*) <the eleventh of February : le onze février>
elf [ˈɛlf] *n, pl* **elves** [ˈɛlvz] : elfe *m*, lutin *m*
elfin [ˈɛlfən] *adj* **1** : d'elfe, de lutin **2** ENCHANTING, MAGICAL : féerique
elicit [ɪˈlɪsət] *vt* : tirer, arracher, provoquer
eligibility [ˌɛlədʒəˈbɪləṭi] *n, pl* **-ties** : éligibilité *f*, admissibilité *f*
eligible [ˈɛlədʒəbəl] *adj* : éligible, admissible <eligible for a job : admissible à un poste> <to be eligible for a pension : avoir droit à une retraite>
eliminate [ɪˈlɪməˌneɪt] *vt* **-nated; -nating** : éliminer
elimination [ɪˌlɪməˈneɪʃən] *n* : élimination *f* <by process of elimination : en procédant par élimination>
elite [eɪˈliːt, i-] *n* : élite *f*
elixir [iˈlɪksər] *n* : élixir *m*
elk [ˈɛlk] *n* : élan *m* (d'Europe), wapiti *m* (d'Amérique)
ellipse [iˈlɪps, ɛ-] *n* : ellipse *f*
ellipsis [iˈlɪpsəs, ɛ-] *n, pl* **-lipses 1** : ellipse *f* **2** : points *mpl* de suspension (en ponctuation)
elliptical [iˈlɪptɪkəl, ɛ-] *or* **elliptic** [-tɪk] *adj* : elliptique
elm [ˈɛlm] *n* : orme *m*
elocution [ˌɛləˈkjuːʃən] *n* : élocution *f*
elongate [iˈlɔŋˌgeɪt] *vt* **-gated; -gating** : allonger
elongation [ˌiːˌlɔŋˈgeɪʃən] *n* : allongement *m*
elope [iˈloːp] *vi* **eloped; eloping** : s'enfuir (pour se marier)
elopement [iˈloːpmənt] *n* : fugue *f* amoureuse
eloquence [ˈɛləˌkwənts] *n* : éloquence *f*
eloquent [ˈɛləˌkwənt] *adj* : éloquent
eloquently [ˈɛləˌkwəntli] *adv* : éloquemment
El Salvadoran[1] [ɛlˌsælvəˈdɔrən] *adj* : salvadorien
El Salvadoran[2] *n* : Salvadorien *m*, -rienne *f*
else[1] [ˈɛls] *adv* **1** DIFFERENTLY : d'autre, de plus <what else could I do? : que pouvais-je faire d'autre?> **2** ELSEWHERE : ailleurs, autre part <everywhere else : partout ailleurs> **3 or else** : autrement, sinon, ou bien <leave now or else you'll be late : partez vite, autrement vous serez en retard>
else[2] *adj* **1** OTHER : d'autre <somebody else : quelqu'un d'autre> <everyone else : tous les autres> **2** MORE : de plus, d'autre <nothing else : rien d'autre> <what else? : quoi d'autre?> <what else did he say? : que disait-il de plus?>
elsewhere [ˈɛls,ʰwɛr] *adv* : ailleurs, autre part <my thoughts were elsewhere : j'avais l'esprit ailleurs>
elucidate [iˈluːsəˌdeɪt] *vt* **-dated; -dating** : élucider, expliquer
elucidation [iˌluːsəˈdeɪʃən] *n* : élucidation *f*, explication *f*
elude [iˈluːd] *vt* **eluded; eluding** : éluder, échapper à
elusive [iˈluːsɪv] *adj* : élusif, évasif, insaisissable
elusively [iˈluːsɪvli] *adv* : de façon élusive
elves → elf
emaciated [iˈmeɪʃiˌeɪṭəd] *adj* : émacié, décharné
emaciation [iˈmeɪsiˌeɪʃən, -ʃi-] *n* : émaciation *f*, amaigrissement *m*
e-mail [ˈiːˌmeɪl] *n* : e-mail *m*, courriel *m*, courrier *m* électronique, mél *m*
emanate [ˈɛməˌneɪt] *v* **-nated; -nating** *vi* : émaner — *vt* : exsuder, rayonner de
emanation [ˌɛməˈneɪʃən] *n* : émanation *f*
emancipate [iˈmænts̩əˌpeɪt] *vt* **-pated; -pating** : émanciper, affranchir (un esclave)
emancipation [iˌmænts̩əˈpeɪʃən] *n* : émancipation *f*, affranchissement *m* (d'un esclave)
emasculate [iˌmæskjəˈleɪt] *vt* **-lated; -lating** : émasculer
embalm [ɪmˈbɑm, ɛm-, -bɑlm] *vt* : embaumer
embankment [ɪmˈbæŋkmənt, ɛm-] *n* **1** : digue *f* (d'une rivière) **2** : remblai *m*, talus *m* (d'une route)
embargo[1] [ɪmˈbɑrgo, ɛm-] *vt* **-goed; -going** : mettre l'embargo sur
embargo[2] *n, pl* **-goes** : embargo *m*
embark [ɪmˈbɑrk, ɛm-] *vt* : embarquer — *vi* **1** : s'embarquer **2 to embark upon** : entreprendre, s'embarquer dans
embarkation [ˌɛmˌbɑrˈkeɪʃən] *n* : embarquement *m*
embarrass [ɪmˈbærəs, ɛm-] *vt* : gêner, embarrasser
embarrassment [ɪmˈbærəsmənt, ɛm-] *n* : gêne *f*, embarras *m*

embassy [ˈɛmbəsi] *n, pl* **-sies** : ambassade *f*
embed [ɪmˈbɛd, ɛm-] *vt* **-bedded; -bedding** : enfoncer, enchâsser <embedded in one's memory : gravé dans sa mémoire>
embellish [ɪmˈbɛlɪʃ, ɛm-] *vt* : embellir, orner, décorer
embellishment [ɪmˈbɛlɪʃmənt, ɛm-] *n* : embellissement *m*, ornement *m*
ember [ˈɛmbər] *n* **1** : charbon *m* ardent, morceau *m* de braise **2 embers** *npl* : braise *f*
embezzle [ɪmˈbɛzəl, ɛm-] *vt* **-zled; -zling** : détourner
embezzlement [ɪmˈbɛzəlmənt, ɛm-] *n* : détournement *m* de fonds
embitter [ɪmˈbɪtər, ɛm-] *vt* : aigrir, remplir d'amertume
emblem [ˈɛmbləm] *n* : emblème *m*
emblematic [ˌɛmbləˈmætɪk] *adj* : emblématique
embodiment [ɪmˈbɑdɪmənt, ɛm-] *n* : incarnation *f*, personnification *f*
embody [ɪmˈbɑdi, ɛm-] *vt* **-bodied; -bodying 1** INCARNATE : incarner, personnifier **2** INCLUDE : incorporer, inclure
emboss [ɪmˈbɑs, ɛm-, -ˈbɔs] *vt* : emboutir, estamper (un métal), gaufrer (des étoffes, du cuir, du papier)
embrace[1] [ɪmˈbreɪs, ɛm-] *vt* **-braced; -bracing 1** HUG : embrasser, étreindre **2** ADOPT, TAKE ON : embrasser, adopter, épouser **3** INCLUDE : comprendre, inclure
embrace[2] *n* : étreinte *f*, enlacement *m*
embroider [ɪmˈbrɔɪdər, ɛm-] *vt* : broder
embroidery [ɪmˈbrɔɪdəri, ɛm-] *n, pl* **-deries** : broderie *f*
embroil [ɪmˈbrɔɪl, ɛm-] *vt* : entraîner, mêler <to become embroiled in : se laisser entraîner dans>
embryo [ˈɛmbriˌo:] *n* : embryon *m*
embryonic [ˌɛmbriˈɑnɪk] *adj* : embryonnaire
emend [iˈmɛnd] *vt* : corriger
emendation [ˌi:mɛnˈdeɪʃən] *n* : correction *f*
emerald[1] [ˈɛmrəld, ˈɛmə-] *adj* : émeraude, en émeraude
emerald[2] *n* : émeraude *f* (pierre précieuse), émeraude *m* (couleur)
emerge [iˈmərdʒ] *vi* **emerged; emerging 1** APPEAR : apparaître, surgir **2 to emerge from** : émerger de
emergence [iˈmərdʒənts] *n* : apparition *f*, émergence *f*
emergency [iˈmərdʒənsi] *n, pl* **-cies 1** : cas *m* d'urgence *f* <in case of emergency : en cas d'urgence> **2 emergency exit** : sortie *f* de secours **3 emergency room** : salle *f* des urgences **4 state of emergency** : état *m* d'urgence
emergent [iˈmərdʒənt] *adj* : qui émerge, naissant <emergent nations : pays en voie de développement>
emery [ˈɛməri] *n, pl* **-eries** : émeri *m*
emery board *n* : lime *f* à ongles
emetic[1] [iˈmɛtɪk] *adj* : émétique
emetic[2] *n* : émétique *m*
emigrant [ˈɛmɪgrənt] *n* : émigrant *m*, -grante *f*
emigrate [ˈɛməˌgreɪt] *vi* **-grated; -grating** : émigrer
emigration [ˌɛməˈgreɪʃən] *n* : émigration *f*
eminence [ˈɛmənənts] *n* **1** DISTINCTION, PROMINENCE : distinction *f*, rang *m* éminent **2** ELEVATION : éminence *f*, hauteur *f* **3 Your Eminence** : Votre Éminence
eminent [ˈɛmənənt] *adj* : éminent
eminently [ˈɛmənəntli] *adv* : éminemment, hautement
emissary [ˈɛməˌsɛri] *n, pl* **-saries** : émissaire *m*
emission [iˈmɪʃən] *n* : émission *f*
emit [iˈmɪt] *vt* **emitted; emitting** : émettre, dégager
emote [iˈmo:t] *vi* **emoted; emoting** : donner dans les émotions (exalté)
emotion [iˈmo:ʃən] *n* : émotion *f*
emotional [iˈmo:ʃənəl] *adj* **1** : émotionnel, émotif <emotional reactions : réactions émotives> **2** MOVING : émouvant
emotionally [iˈmo:ʃənəli] *adv* : avec émotion <to be emotionally disturbed : avoir des troubles émotifs>
emperor [ˈɛmpərər] *n* : empereur *m*
emphasis [ˈɛmfəsɪs] *n, pl* **-phases** [-ˌsi:z] : accent *m*
emphasize [ˈɛmfəˌsaɪz] *vt* **-sized; -sizing** : insister sur, mettre l'accent sur
emphatic [ɪmˈfætɪk, ɛm-] *adj* : énergique, catégorique <an emphatic refusal : un refus catégorique> **— emphatically** [-ɪkli] *adv*
empire [ˈɛmˌpaɪr] *n* : empire *m*
empirical [ɪmˈpɪrɪkəl, ɛm-] *adj* : empirique **— empirically** [-ɪkli] *adv*
employ[1] [ɪmˈplɔɪ, ɛm-] *vt* : employer
employ[2] [ɪmˈplɔɪ, ɛm-; ˈɪmˌ-, ˈɛmˌ-] *n* **to be in the employ of** : être employé par
employee *or* **employe** [ɪmˌplɔɪˈi:, ɛm-, -ˈplɔɪˌi:] *n* : employé *m*, -ployée *f*; salarié *m*, -riée *f*
employer [ɪmˈplɔɪər, ɛm-] *n* : employeur *m*, -ployeuse *f*
employment [ɪmˈplɔɪmənt, ɛm-] *n* : emploi *m*, travail *m*
empower [ɪmˈpaʊər, ɛm-] *vt* : autoriser, habiliter
empowerment [ɪmˈpaʊərmənt, ɛm-] *n* : autorisation *f*
empress [ˈɛmprəs] *n* : impératrice *f*
emptiness [ˈɛmptɪnəs] *n* : vide *m*
empty[1] [ˈɛmpti] *v* **-tied; -tying** *vt* : vider **—** *vi* **1** : se vider **2** : se jeter <the river empties into the ocean : la rivière se jette dans l'océan>
empty[2] *adj* **emptier; -est 1** : vide **2** VACANT : inocupé, vacant, désert **3**

MEANINGLESS : creux (se dit d'un discours), vain (se dit d'une menace, d'une promesse, etc.)

empty–handed [ˌɛmptiˈhændəd] *adj* : les mains vides

empty–headed [ˌɛmptiˈhɛdəd] *adj* : écervelé

emu [ˈiːˌmjuː] *n* : émeu *m*

emulate [ˈɛmjəˌleɪt] *vt* **-lated; -lating** : imiter

emulation [ˌɛmjəˈleɪʃən] *n* : émulation *f*, imitation *f*

emulsify [ɪˈmʌlsəˌfaɪ] *vt* **-fied; -fying** : émulsionner

emulsion [ɪˈmʌlʃən] *n* : émulsion *f*

enable [ɪˈneɪbəl, ɛ-] *vt* **-abled; -abling 1** EMPOWER : habiliter **2** PERMIT : permettre <it enabled him to swim : ça lui permettait de nager>

enact [ɪˈnækt, ɛ-] *vt* **1** : promulguer (une loi, etc.) **2** PERFORM : jouer, représenter (une scène, un rôle, etc.)

enactment [ɪˈnæktmənt, ɛ-] *n* **1** : promulgation *f* (d'une loi) **2** PERFORMANCE : représentation *f*

enamel[1] [ɪˈnæməl] *vt* **-eled** *or* **-elled; -eling** *or* **-elling** : émailler

enamel[2] *n* : émail *m*

enamor *or Brit* **enamour** [ɪˈnæmər] *vt* **to be enamored of** : être épris de (une personne), être enchanté de (une chose)

encamp [ɪnˈkæmp, ɛn-] *vi* : camper

encampment [ɪnˈkæmpmənt, ɛn-] *n* : campement *m*

encase [ɪnˈkeɪs, ɛn-] *vt* **-cased; -casing 1** CONTAIN : enfermer **2** COVER : recouvrir, entourer

enchant [ɪnˈtʃænt, ɛn-] *vt* : enchanter

enchanting [ɪnˈtʃæntɪŋ, ɛn-] *adj* : charmant, enchanteur, ravissant

enchantment [ɪnˈtʃæntmənt, ɛn-] *n* : enchantement *m*

enchantress [ɪnˈtʃæntrəs, ɛn-] *n* : enchanteresse *f*

encircle [ɪnˈsərkəl, ɛn-] *vt* **-cled; -cling** : entourer, encercler

enclose [ɪnˈkloːz, ɛn-] *vt* **-closed; -closing 1** SURROUND : entourer, clôturer **2** INCLUDE : joindre (à une lettre) <enclosed please find : veuillez trouver ci-joint>

enclosure [ɪnˈkloːʒər, ɛn-] *n* **1** ENCLOSING : clôture *f* **2** AREA, SPACE : enclos *m*, enceinte *f* **3** : pièce *f* jointe (à une lettre)

encompass [ɪnˈkʌmpəs, ɛn-, -ˈkʌm-] *vt* **1** ENCIRCLE : entourer **2** INCLUDE : inclure, comprendre

encore [ˈɑnˌkor] *n* **1** : bis *m* **2 to call for an encore** : bisser

encounter[1] [ɪnˈkaʊntər, ɛn-] *vt* : rencontrer

encounter[2] *n* : rencontre *f*

encourage [ɪnˈkərɪdʒ, ɛn-] *vt* **-aged; -aging 1** HEARTEN : encourager **2** FOSTER, STIMULATE : stimuler, favoriser

encouragement [ɪnˈkərɪdʒmənt, ɛn-] *n* : encouragement *m*

encroach [ɪnˈkroːtʃ, ɛn-] *vi* **to encroach upon** : empiéter sur

encrust [ɪnˈkrʌst, ɛn-] *vt* : incruster

encumber [ɪnˈkʌmbər, ɛn-] *vt* : encombrer, grever <encumbered by debts : grevé de dettes>

encumbrance [ɪnˈkʌmbrəns, ɛn-] *n* **1** BURDEN : charge *f*, fardeau *m* **2** HINDRANCE : gêne *f*, entrave *f*

encyclopedia [ɪnˌsaɪkləˈpiːdiə, ɛn-] *n* : encyclopédie *f* — **encyclopedic** [-dɪk] *adj*

end[1] [ˈɛnd] *vt* **1** STOP : finir, achever, terminer **2** CONCLUDE : conclure — *vi* **1** : finir, s'achever, se terminer **2 to end up** : finir **3 to end up with** : finir par

end[2] *n* **1** : fin *f* **2** EXTREMITY : bout *m*, extrémité *f* **3** PURPOSE : but *m*, fin *f*, dessein *m* <to this end : dans ce but>

endanger [ɪnˈdeɪndʒər, ɛn-] *vt* : mettre en danger

endear [ɪnˈdɪr, ɛn-] *vt* : faire aimer <to endear oneself to s.o. : se faire aimer de qqn>

endearment [ɪnˈdɪrmənt, ɛn-] *n* : tendresse *f* <terms of endearment : mots tendres>

endeavor[1] *or Brit* **endeavour** [ɪnˈdɛvər, ɛn-] *vt* : s'efforcer, essayer <to endeavor to understand : s'efforcer de comprendre>

endeavor[2] *or Brit* **endeavour** *n* : effort *m*, tentative *f*

ending [ˈɛndɪŋ] *n* **1** CONCLUSION : fin *f*, dénouement *m* <a happy ending : un dénouement heureux> **2** SUFFIX : terminaison *f*

endive [ˈɛnˌdaɪv, ˌanˈdiːv] *n* : endive *f*

endless [ˈɛndləs] *adj* **1** INTERMINABLE : sans fin, interminable **2** INNUMERABLE : innombrable, sans nombre **3** INEXHAUSTIBLE : inépuisable, infini

endlessly [ˈɛndləsli] *adv* : interminablement, continuellement, sans fin

endocrine [ˈɛndəkrən, -ˌkraɪn, -ˌkriːn] *adj* : endocrine

endorse [ɪnˈdɔrs, ɛn-] *vt* **-dorsed; -dorsing 1** SIGN : endosser **2** SUPPORT : avaliser **3** APPROVE : approuver

endorsement [ɪnˈdɔrsmənt, ɛn-] *n* **1** SIGNATURE : endossement *m* **2** SUPPORT : aval *m* **3** APPROVAL : approbation *f*

endow [ɪnˈdaʊ, ɛn-] *vt* : doter

endowment [ɪnˈdaʊmənt, ɛn-] *n* : dotation *f*

endurable [ɪnˈdʊrəbəl, ɛn-, -ˈdjʊr-] *adj* : supportable, endurable

endurance [ɪnˈdʊrəns, ɛn-, -ˈdjʊr-] *n* : endurance *f*

endure [ɪnˈdʊr, ɛn-, -ˈdjʊr-] *v* **-dured; -during** *vt* BEAR, TOLERATE : supporter, endurer — *vi* LAST : durer

enema [ˈɛnəmə] *n* : lavement *m*

enemy [ˈɛnəmi] *n, pl* **-mies** : ennemi *m*, -mie *f*
energetic [ˌɛnərˈdʒɛtɪk] *adj* : énergique **— energetically** [-tɪkli] *adv*
energize [ˈɛnərˌdʒaɪz] *vt* **-gized; -gizing** : donner de l'énergie à, stimuler
energy [ˈɛnərdʒi] *n, pl* **-gies** : énergie *f*
enervate [ˈɛnərˌveɪt] *vt* **-vated; -vating** : affaiblir, débiliter
enfold [ɪnˈfoːld, ɛn-] *vt* : envelopper, étreindre
enforce [ɪnˈfors, ɛn-] *vt* **-forced; -forcing** : appliquer, imposer (la discipline, etc.), faire respecter (une loi) <to enforce obedience : se faire obéir>
enforcement [ɪnˈforsmənt, ɛn-] *n* : exécution *f*, application *f*
enfranchise [ɪnˈfræn,tʃaɪz, ɛn-] *vt* **-chised; -chising** : accorder le droit de vote à
enfranchisement [ɪnˈfræn,tʃaɪzmənt, ɛn-] *n* : admission *f* au suffrage
engage [ɪnˈgeɪdʒ, ɛn-] *v* **-gaged; -gaging** *vt* **1** INVOLVE : engager <to engage s.o. in conversation : engager la conversation avec qqn> **2** EMPLOY : embaucher, engager **3** ATTRACT, DRAW : attirer, éveiller <to engage s.o.'s attention : éveiller l'attention de qqn> **4 to engage the clutch** : embrayer **—** *vi* **1 to engage in** : se lancer dans, prendre part à **2 to engage in combat** : engager l'ennemi
engaged [ɪnˈgeɪdʒd, ɛn-] *adj* : fiancé <to get engaged to : se fiancer à>
engagement [ɪnˈgeɪdʒmənt, ɛn-] *n* **1** APPOINTMENT : rendez-vous *m* **2** : engagement *m* (d'un acteur, etc.) **3** BETROTHAL : fiançailles *fpl*
engaging [ɪnˈgeɪdʒɪŋ, ɛn-] *adj* : engageant, attirant
engender [ɪnˈdʒɛndər, ɛn-] *vt* **-dered; -dering** : engendrer
engine [ˈɛndʒən] *n* **1** MOTOR : moteur *m* (d'une voiture) **2** LOCOMOTIVE : locomotive *f*
engineer[1] [ˌɛndʒəˈnɪr] *vt* **1** CONSTRUCT : construire **2** CONTRIVE, PLOT : manigancer
engineer[2] *n* **1** : ingénieur *m*, -nieure *f* <civil engineer : ingénieur civil> **2** : mécanicien *m*, -cienne *f* (d'une locomotive)
engineering [ˌɛndʒəˈnɪrɪŋ] *n* : ingénierie *f*, génie *m* <chemical engineering : génie chimique>
English[1] [ˈɪŋglɪʃ, ˈɪŋlɪʃ] *adj* : anglais
English[2] *n* **1** : anglais *m* (langue) **2 the English** : les Anglais
Englishman [ˈɪŋglɪʃmən, ˈɪŋlɪʃ-] *n* : Anglais *m*
Englishwoman [ˈɪŋglɪʃˌwʊmən, ˈɪŋlɪʃ-] *n* : Anglaise *f*
engrave [ɪnˈgreɪv, ɛn-] *vt* **-graved; -graving** : graver
engraver [ɪnˈgreɪvər, ɛn-] *n* : graveur *m*, -veuse *f*
engraving [ɪnˈgreɪvɪŋ, ɛn-] *n* : gravure *f*
engross [ɪnˈgroːs, ɛn-] *vt* : absorber, occuper
engulf [ɪnˈgʌlf, ɛn-] *vt* : engouffrer, engloutir
enhance [ɪnˈhænʃ, ɛn-] *vt* **-hanced; -hancing** : améliorer, augmenter, rehausser
enhancement [ɪnˈhænʃmənt, ɛn-] *n* : amélioration *f*, augmentation *f*, majoration *f*
enigma [ɪˈnɪgmə] *n* : énigme *f*
enigmatic [ˌɛnɪgˈmæt̬ɪk, ˌiːnɪg-] *adj* : énigmatique **— enigmatically** [-t̬ɪkli] *adv*
enjoin [ɪnˈdʒɔɪn, ɛn-] *vt* **1** COMMAND : enjoindre, ordonner **2** FORBID : interdire
enjoy [ɪnˈdʒɔɪ, ɛn-] *vt* **1** : aimer, prendre plaisir à <I enjoy reading : je prends plaisir à lire> **2** : jouir de <she enjoys good health : elle jouit d'une bonne santé> **3 to enjoy oneself** : s'amuser
enjoyable [ɪnˈdʒɔɪəbəl, ɛn-] *adj* : agréable
enjoyment [ɪnˈdʒɔɪmənt, ɛn-] *n* : plaisir *m*, jouissance *f*
enlarge [ɪnˈlɑrdʒ, ɛn-] *v* **-larged; -larging** *vt* : agrandir, élargir **—** *vi* **1** : s'agrandir **2 to enlarge upon** : s'étendre sur, développer
enlargement [ɪnˈlɑrdʒmənt, ɛn-] *n* : agrandissement *m*, élargissement *m*
enlighten [ɪnˈlaɪtən, ɛn-] *vt* : éclairer
enlightenment [ɪnˈlaɪtənmənt, ɛn-] *n* **1** CLARIFICATION : éclaircissements *mpl* **2** EDIFICATION : édification *f*, instruction *f* **3 the Enlightenment** : le Siècle des lumières
enlist [ɪnˈlɪst, ɛn-] *vt* **1** ENROLL : enrôler, recruter **2** OBTAIN : obtenir, mobiliser (du soutien, etc.) **—** *vi* : s'engager, s'enrôler <he enlisted in the army : il s'est engagé dans l'armée>
enlistment [ɪnˈlɪstmənt, ɛn-] *n* : engagement *m*, recrutement *m*, enrôlement *m*
enliven [ɪnˈlaɪvən, ɛn-] *vt* : animer, égayer
enmity [ˈɛnməd̬i] *n, pl* **-ties** : inimitié *f*, hostilité *f*
ennoble [ɪˈnoːbəl, ɛ-] *vt* **-bled; -bling** : ennoblir, élever
ennui [ˌɑnˈwiː] *n* : ennui *m*
enormity [ɪˈnɔrmət̬i] *n, pl* **-ties 1** ATROCITY : atrocité *f* **2** IMMENSITY : énormité *f*
enormous [ɪˈnɔrməs] *adj* : énorme, immense
enormously [ɪˈnɔrməsli] *adv* EXTREMELY : énormément, extrêmement
enough[1] [iˈnʌf] *adv* : assez, suffisamment <he's old enough : il est suffisamment grand> <she writes well enough : elle écrit assez bien>
enough[2] *adj* **1** : assez de, suffisant **2 more than enough** : plus qu'il n'en faut

enough[3] *pron* (*representing a sufficient number, quantity, or amount*) <to have eaten enough : avoir assez mangé> <I've had enough of his foolishness : j'en ai assez de ses bêtises>
enquire [ɪnˈkwaɪr, ɛn-], **enquiry** [ˈɪn,kwaɪri, ˈɛn-, -kwər-; ɪnˈkwaɪri, ɛn-] → **inquire, inquiry**
enrage [ɪnˈreɪdʒ, ɛn-] *vt* **-raged; -raging** : rendre furieux, mettre en rage
enrich [ɪnˈrɪtʃ, ɛn-] *vt* : enrichir
enrichment [ɪnˈrɪtʃmənt, ɛn-] *n* : enrichissement *m*
enroll *or* **enrol** [ɪnˈroːl, ɛn-] *v* **-rolled; -rolling** *vt* **1** : inscrire (à l'école, etc.) **2** ENLIST : enrôler — *vi* : s'inscrire, s'enrôler
enrollment [ɪnˈroːlmənt, ɛn-] *n* **1** REGISTRATION : inscription *f* **2** ENLISTMENT : enrôlement *m*
en route [ɑnˈruːt, ɛnˈraʊt] *adv* : en route
ensconce [ɪnˈskɑnts, ɛn-] *vt* **-sconced; -sconcing 1** INSTALL, SETTLE : installer, placer **2 to ensconce oneself** : bien s'installer
ensemble [ɑnˈsɑmbəl] *n* : ensemble *m*
enshrine [ɪnˈʃraɪn, ɛn-] *vt* **-shrined; -shrining** : conserver pieusement
ensign [ˈɛnsən, ˈɛn,saɪn] *n* **1** FLAG : drapeau *m*, pavillon *m* **2** : enseigne *m* (de vaisseau)
enslave [ɪnˈsleɪv, ɛn-] *vt* **-slaved; -slaving** : asservir
ensnare [ɪnˈsnær, ɛn-] *vt* **-snared; -snaring** : prendre au piège, attraper
ensue [ɪnˈsuː, ɛn-] *vi* **-sued; -suing** : s'ensuivre
ensure [ɪnˈʃʊr, ɛn-] *vt* **-sured; -suring** : assurer, garantir
entail [ɪnˈteɪl, ɛn-] *vt* : entraîner, occasionner
entangle [ɪnˈtæŋgəl, ɛn-] *vt* **-gled; -gling** : emmêler, enchevêtrer
entanglement [ɪnˈtæŋgəlmənt, ɛn-] *n* : enchevêtrement *m*
enter [ˈɛntər] *vt* **1** : entrer dans, entrer à **2** RECORD : inscrire, noter **3** INSERT : entrer des données (en informatique) **4** BEGIN : entrer dans, entamer **5 to enter one's mind** : venir à l'esprit — *vi* **1** : entrer **2 to enter into** : entamer, entrer en
enterprise [ˈɛntər,praɪz] *n* **1** UNDERTAKING : entreprise *f* **2** BUSINESS : affaire *f* commerciale **3** INITIATIVE : initiative *f*
enterprising [ˈɛntər,praɪzɪŋ] *adj* : entreprenant
entertain [ˌɛntərˈteɪn] *vt* **1** AMUSE : amuser, divertir **2** : recevoir <to entertain guests : recevoir des invités> **3** CONSIDER : penser à, considérer (une idée, etc.)
entertainment [ˌɛntərˈteɪnmənt] *n* **1** AMUSEMENT : amusement *m*, divertissement *m* **2** PERFORMANCE : spectacle *m*
enthrall *or* **enthral** [ɪnˈθrɔl, ɛn-] *vt* **-thralled; -thralling** : captiver, passionner
enthusiasm [ɪnˈθuːziˌæzəm, ɛn-, -ˈθjuː-] *n* : enthousiasme *m*
enthusiast [ɪnˈθuːziˌæst, ɛn-, -ˈθjuː-, -əst] *n* : enthousiaste *mf*; passionné *m*, -née *f* <a soccer enthusiast : un passionné de football>
enthusiastic [ɪnˌθuːziˈæstɪk, ɛn-, -ˈθjuː-] *adj* : enthousiaste
enthusiastically [ɪnˌθuːziˈæstɪkli, ɛn-, -ˈθjuː-] *adv* : avec enthousiasme
entice [ɪnˈtaɪs, ɛn-] *vt* **-ticed; -ticing** : attirer, allécher <to entice s.o. away from : entraîner qqn à l'écart de>
enticement [ɪnˈtaɪsmənt, ɛn-] *n* : attrait *m*
entire [ɪnˈtaɪr, ɛn-] *adj* : entier, complet <my entire life : toute ma vie>
entirely [ɪnˈtaɪrli, ɛn-] *adv* : entièrement, totalement
entirety [ɪnˈtaɪrti, ɛn-, -taɪrəti] *n, pl* **-ties 1** : totalité *f* **2 in its entirety** : en son entier, dans son ensemble
entitle [ɪnˈtaɪtəl, ɛn-] *vt* **-tled; -tling 1** NAME : intituler **2** AUTHORIZE : autoriser, donner droit à **3 to be entitled to** : avoir le droit de
entitlement [ɪnˈtaɪtəlmənt, ɛn-] *n* : droit *m*
entity [ˈɛntəti] *n, pl* **-ties** : entité *f*
entomologist [ˌɛntəˈmɑlədʒɪst] *n* : entomologiste *mf*
entomology [ˌɛntəˈmɑlədʒi] *n* : entomologie *f*
entourage [ˌɑnto͞ˈrɑʒ] *n* : entourage *m*
entrails [ˈɛn,treɪlz, -trəlz] *npl* : entrailles *fpl*
entrance[1] [ɪnˈtrænts, ɛn-] *vt* **-tranced; -trancing** : transporter, ravir
entrance[2] [ˈɛntrənts] *n* : entrée *f* <main entrance : entrée principale> <to make an entrance : faire son entrée>
entrant [ˈɛntrənt] *n* : concurrent *m*, -rente *f* (dans une course); candidat *m*, -date *f*; participant *m*, -pante *f*
entrap [ɪnˈtræp, ɛn-] *vt* **-trapped; -trapping** : prendre au piège
entreat [ɪnˈtriːt, ɛn-] *vt* : implorer, supplier
entreaty [ɪnˈtriːti, ɛn-] *n, pl* **-ties** : supplication *f*, prière *f*
entrée *or* **entree** [ˈɑnˌtreɪ, ˌɑnˈ-] *n* : entrée *f*, plat *m* principal
entrench [ɪnˈtrɛntʃ, ɛn-] *vt* : retrancher
entrenched [ɪnˈtrɛntʃt, ɛn-] *adj* **1** UNWAVERING : inébranlable, ferme **2** ESTABLISHED : implanté, bien établi
entrepreneur [ˌɑntrəprəˈnər, -ˈnjʊr] *n* : entrepreneur *m*, -neuse *f*
entrust [ɪnˈtrʌst, ɛn-] *vt* : confier <to entrust s.o. with a mission : confier une mission à qqn>
entry [ˈɛntri] *n, pl* **-tries 1** ENTRANCE : entrée *f* **2** : inscription *f* (sur une liste), entrée *f*

entwine [ɪn'twaɪn, ɛn-] *vt* **-twined; -twining** : entrelacer, enlacer
enumerate [ɪ'nu:mə,reɪt, ɛ-, -'nju:-] *vt* **-ated; -ating 1** LIST : énumérer **2** COUNT : dénombrer
enumeration [ɪ,nu:mə'reɪʃən, ɛ-, -,nju:-] *n* : énumération *f*, dénombrement *m*
enunciate [ɪ'nʌnsi,eɪt, ɛ-] *vt* **-ated; -ating 1** STATE : énoncer, exprimer **2** PRONOUNCE : articuler, prononcer
enunciation [ɪ,nʌnʃsi'eɪʃən, ɛ-] *n* **1** STATEMENT : énonciation *f*, exposition *f* **2** PRONUNCIATION : articulation *f*
envelop [ɪn'vɛləp, ɛn-] *vt* : envelopper
envelope ['ɛnvə,lo:p, 'ɑn-] *n* : enveloppe *f*
enviable ['ɛnviəbəl] *adj* : enviable
envious ['ɛnviəs] *adj* : envieux, jaloux
enviously ['ɛnviəsli] *adv* : avec envie
environment [ɪn'vaɪrənmənt, ɛn-, -vaɪərn-] *n* : environnement *m*, milieu *m*
environmental [ɪn,vaɪrən'mɛntəl, ɛn-, -,vaɪərn-] *adj* : du milieu, écologique <environmental studies : études de l'environnement>
environmentalist [ɪn,vaɪrən'mɛntəlɪst, ɛn-, -,vaɪərn] *n* : écologiste *mf*
environs [ɪn'vaɪrənz, ɛn-, -'vaɪərnz] *npl* : environs *mpl*, alentours *mpl*
envisage [ɪn'vɪzɪʤ, ɛn-] *vt* **-aged; -aging 1** IMAGINE : envisager **2** FORESEE : prévoir
envision [ɪn'vɪʒən, ɛn-] *vt* : envisager
envoy ['ɛn,vɔɪ, 'ɑn-] *n* : envoyé *m*, -voyée *f*
envy¹ ['ɛnvi] *vt* **-vied; -vying** : envier
envy² *n* : envie *f*, jalousie *f*
enzyme ['ɛn,zaɪm] *n* : enzyme *f*
eon ['i:ən, i:,ɑn] → **aeon**
epaulet [,ɛpə'lɛt] *n* : épaulette *f*
ephemeral [ɪ'fɛmərəl, -'fi:-] *adj* : éphémère
epic¹ ['ɛpɪk] *adj* : épique
epic² *n* : épopée *f*
epicure ['ɛpɪ,kjʊr] *n* : gourmet *m*, gastronome *mf*
epicurean [,ɛpɪkjʊ'ri:ən, -'kjʊriən] *adj* : épicurien
epidemic¹ [,ɛpə'dɛmɪk] *adj* : épidémique
epidemic² *n* : épidémie *f*
epidermis [,ɛpə'dərməs] *n* : épiderme *m*
epigram ['ɛpə,græm] *n* : épigramme *f*
epilepsy ['ɛpə,lɛpsi] *n, pl* **-sies** : épilepsie *f*
epileptic¹ [,ɛpə'lɛptɪk] *adj* : épileptique <epileptic fit : crise d'épilepsie>
epileptic² *n* : épileptique *mf*
episcopal [ɪ'pɪskəpəl] *adj* : épiscopal <the Episcopal Church : l'Église épiscopale>
episode ['ɛpə,so:d] *n* : épisode *m*
episodic [,ɛpə'sɑdɪk] *adj* : épisodique
epistle [ɪ'pɪsəl] *n* : épître *f*
epitaph ['ɛpə,tæf] *n* : épitaphe *f*
epithet ['ɛpə,θɛt, -θət] *n* : épithète *f*
epitome [ɪ'pɪtəmi] *n* **1** SUMMARY : abrégé *m*, résumé *m* **2** EMBODIMENT : exemple *m* même, modèle *m*
epitomize [ɪ'pɪtə,maɪz] *vt* **-mized; -mizing 1** SUMMARIZE : abréger **2** EMBODY : incarner, personnifier
epoch ['ɛpɑk, 'ɛ,pɑk, 'i:,pɑk] *n* : époque *f*
equable ['ɛkwəbəl, 'i:-] *adj* : égal, constant (se dit du climat), placide (se dit des personnes)
equal¹ ['i:kwəl] *vt* **equaled** *or* **equalled; equaling** *or* **equalling** : égaler
equal² *adj* **1** SAME : égal, même <equal pay : salaire égal> <of equal value : de même valeur> **2 to be equal to** : être à la hauteur de <I didn't feel equal to going : je ne me sentais pas capable de sortir>
equal³ *n* : égal *m*, -gale *f*
equality [ɪ'kwɑləti] *n, pl* **-ties** : égalité *f*
equalize ['i:kwə,laɪz] *vt* **-ized; -izing** : égaliser
equally ['i:kwəli] *adv* : également <to divide sth equally : diviser qqch en parts égales>
equanimity [,i:kwə'nɪməti, ,ɛ-] *n, pl* **-ties** : égalité *f* d'humeur, sérénité *f*, équanimité *f*
equate [ɪ'kweɪt] *vt* **equated; equating 1** LIKEN, COMPARE : mettre sur le même pied, assimiler **2** EQUALIZE : égaliser **3 to equate with** : mettre en équation avec (en mathématiques)
equation [ɪ'kweɪʒən] *n* : équation *f*
equator [ɪ'kweɪtər] *n* : équateur *m*
equatorial [,i:kwə'toriəl, ,ɛ-] *adj* : équatorial
equestrian¹ [ɪ'kwɛstriən, ɛ-] *adj* : équestre
equestrian² *n* : cavalier *m*, -lière *f*
equilateral [,i:kwə'læṭərəl, ,ɛ-] *adj* : équilatéral
equilibrium [,i:kwə'lɪbriəm, ,ɛ-] *n, pl* **-riums** *or* **-ria** : équilibre *m*
equine ['i:,kwaɪn, 'ɛ-] *adj* : chevalin
equinox ['i:kwə,nɑks, 'ɛ-] *n* : équinoxe *m*
equip [ɪ'kwɪp] *vt* **equipped; equipping 1** FURNISH, SUPPLY : équiper, outiller, munir **2** PREPARE : préparer
equipment [ɪ'kwɪpmənt] *n* : équipement *m*, matériel *m*
equitable ['ɛkwəṭəbəl] *adj* : équitable, juste
equity ['ɛkwəṭi] *n, pl* **-ties 1** FAIRNESS : équité *f* **2 equities** *npl* SECURITIES : actions *fpl* ordinaires
equivalence [ɪ'kwɪvələnʃs] *n* : équivalence *f*
equivalent¹ [ɪ'kwɪvələnt] *adj* : équivalent
equivalent² *n* : équivalent *m*
equivocal [ɪ'kwɪvəkəl] *adj* : équivoque
equivocate [ɪ'kwɪvə,keɪt] *vi* **-cated; -cating** : user d'équivoques
equivocation [ɪ,kwɪvə'keɪʃən] *n* : paroles *fpl* équivoques

era [ˈɪrə, ˈerə, ˈiːrə] *n* : ère *f*, époque *f*
eradicate [ɪˈrædəˌkeɪt] *vt* **-cated; -cating** : éradiquer
erase [ɪˈreɪs] *vt* **erased; erasing** : effacer, gommer
eraser [ɪˈreɪsər] *n* : gomme *f*, efface *f* *Can*
erasure [ɪˈreɪʃər] *n* : effacement *m*
ere[1] [ˈer] *conj* : avant que
ere[2] *prep* **1** BEFORE : avant **2 ere long** : sous peu, bientôt
erect[1] [ɪˈrɛkt] *vt* **1** BUILD : bâtir, construire **2** RAISE : ériger, élever (une statue, un édifice, etc.) **3** ESTABLISH : ériger, établir
erect[2] *adj* : droit <to stand erect : se tenir droit>
erection [ɪˈrɛkʃən] *n* **1** CONSTRUCTION : construction *f* **2** : érection *f* (en physiologie)
ergonomic [ˌərgəˈnamɪk] *adj* : ergonomique
Eritrean[1] [ˌerəˈtriːən, -ˈtreɪən] *adj* : erythréen
Eritrean[2] *n* : Erythréen *m*, -thréenne *f*
ermine [ˈərmən] *n* : hermine *f*
erode [ɪˈroːd] *v* **eroded; eroding** *vt* : éroder, ronger — *vi* : s'éroder
erosion [ɪˈroːʒən] *n* : érosion *f*
erotic [ɪˈrɑtɪk] *adj* : érotique — **erotically** [-ɪkli] *adv*
eroticism [ɪˈrɑtəˌsɪzəm] *n* : érotisme *m*
err [ˈer, ˈər] *vi* : se tromper <to err on the side of caution : pécher par excès de prudence>
errand [ˈerənd] *n* : course *f*, commission *f*
errant [ˈerənt] *adj* **1** WANDERING : errant **2** MISBEHAVING : dévoyé
erratic [ɪˈræt̬ɪk] *adj* **1** IRREGULAR, UNPREDICTABLE : irrégulier, imprévisible **2** : erratique (en géologie, en médecine)
erratically [ɪˈræt̬ɪkli] *adv* : irregulièrement, de manière capricieuse
erroneous [ɪˈroːniəs, ɛ-] *adj* : erroné, faux
erroneously [ɪˈroːniəsli, ɛ-] *adv* : à tort, erronément
error [ˈɛrər] *n* : erreur *f*, faute *f* <to see the error of one's ways : revenir de ses erreurs>
erstwhile [ˈərstˌhwaɪl] *adj* FORMER : d'autrefois, ancien
erudite [ˈɛrəˌdaɪt, ˈɛrjʊ-] *adj* : érudit, savant
erudition [ˌɛrəˈdɪʃən, ˌɛrjʊ-] *n* : érudition *f*
erupt [ɪˈrʌpt] *vi* **1** : entrer en éruption (se dit d'un volcan) **2** : éclater (se dit de la guerre, d'un rire, etc.)
eruption [ɪˈrʌpʃən] *n* : éruption *f*
escalate [ˈɛskəˌleɪt] *v* **-lated; -lating** *vt* **1** INTENSIFY : intensifier, aggraver **2** INCREASE : augmenter — *vi* **1** INTENSIFY : s'intensifier, s'aggraver **2** INCREASE : monter en flèche (se dit des prix, etc.)
escalation [ˌɛskəˈleɪʃən] *n* **1** INTENSIFICATION : intensification *f* **2** INCREASE : montée *f* en flèche
escalator [ˈɛskəˌleɪtər] *n* : escalier *m* mécanique
escapade [ˈɛskəˌpeɪd] *n* : équipée *f*, frasque *f*
escape[1] [ɪˈskeɪp, ɛ-] *v* **-caped; -caping** *vt* **1** AVOID : échapper à, éviter **2** ELUDE : échapper à <his name escapes me : son nom m'échappe> **3 to escape notice** : passer inaperçu — *vi* **1** : s'échapper, s'évader **2 to escape from reality** : fuir la réalité
escape[2] *n* **1** FLIGHT : fuite *f*, évasion *f* **2** LEAKAGE : fuite *f* (d'un liquide ou d'un gaz), échappement *m* (de vapeurs)
escapee [ɪˌskeɪˈpiː, ˌɛ-] *n* : évadé *m*, -dée *f*
escarole [ˈɛskəˌroːl] *n* : scarole *f*
escarpment [ɪsˈkɑrpmənt, ɛs-] *n* : escarpement *m*
eschew [ɛˈtʃuː, ɪsˈtʃuː] *vt* : éviter, s'abstenir de
escort[1] [ɪˈskɔrt, ɛ-] *vt* : escorter, accompagner
escort[2] [ˈɛsˌkɔrt] *n* **1** : escorte *f* <under police escort : sous escorte policière> **2** COMPANION : compagnon *m*, compagne *f*
escrow [ˈɛsˌkroː] *n* : séquestre *m* <in escrow : en séquestre>
esophagus [ɪˈsɑfəgəs, iː-] *n, pl* **-gi** [-ˌgaɪ, -ˌdʒaɪ] : œsophage *m*
esoteric [ˌɛsəˈtɛrɪk] *adj* : ésotérique
especially [ɪˈspɛʃəli] *adv* **1** PARTICULARLY : particulièrement, surtout **2** EXPRESSLY : exprès <he came especially to see you : il est venu exprès pour vous voir> **3 especially as** : d'autant plus que
espionage [ˈɛspiəˌnɑʒ, -ˌnɑdʒ] *n* : espionnage *m*
espouse [ɪˈspaʊz, ɛ-] *vt* **espoused; espousing** : épouser
espresso [ɛˈspreˌsoː] *n, pl* **-sos** : express *m*, café *m* express
essay[1] [ɛˈseɪ, ˈɛˌseɪ] *vt* ATTEMPT : essayer, tenter
essay[2] [ˈɛˌseɪ] *n* **1** ATTEMPT : essai *m*, tentative *f* **2** COMPOSITION : essai *m* (littéraire), dissertation *f* académique
essayist [ˈɛˌseɪɪst] *n* : essayiste *mf*
essence [ˈɛsənts] *n* **1** CORE : essence *f* <in essence : par essence, essentiellement> **2** EXTRACT : essence *f*, extrait *m* <essence of violets : essence de violette> <essence of vanilla : extrait de vanille>
essential[1] [ɪˈsɛnt̬ʃəl] *adj* : essentiel — **essentially** *adv*
essential[2] *n* **1** : objet *m* essentiel **2 the essentials** : l'essentiel *m*
establish [ɪˈstæblɪʃ, ɛ-] *vt* **1** PROVE : établir, démontrer **2** FOUND : établir, fonder, créer

establishment [ɪˈstæblɪʃmənt, ɛ-] *n* **1** ESTABLISHING : fondation *f*, création *f*, établissement *m* **2** INSTITUTION : établissement *m* **3 the Establishment** : les pouvoirs établis
estate [ɪˈsteɪt, ɛ-] *n* **1** POSSESSIONS : biens *mpl*, fortune *f* **2** LAND, PROPERTY : propriété *f*, domaine *m*
esteem[1] [ɪˈstiːm, ɛ-] *vt* : estimer
esteem[2] *n* : estime *f* <in high esteem : en haute estime>
ester [ˈɛstər] *n* : ester *m*
esthetic [ɛsˈθɛt̬ɪk] → **aesthetic**
estimable [ˈɛstəməbəl] *adj* : estimable
estimate[1] [ˈɛstəˌmeɪt] *vt* **-mated; -mating** : estimer, évaluer
estimate[2] [ˈɛstəmət] *n* : estimation *f*, évaluation *f*, devis *m*
estimation [ˌɛstəˈmeɪʃən] *n* **1** JUDGMENT : jugement *m* <in my estimation : à mon avis> **2** ESTIMATE : estimation *f* **3** ESTEEM : estime *f*, considération *f*
Estonian[1] [eˈstoːniən] *adj* : estonien
Estonian[2] *n* **1** : Estonien *m*, -nienne *f* **2** : estonien *m* (langue)
estrange [ɪˈstreɪndʒ, ɛ-] *vt* **-tranged; -tranging** : brouiller, éloigner
estrangement [ɪˈstreɪndʒmənt, ɛ-] *n* : éloignement *m*, brouille *f* (avec un ami), séparation *f* (d'un époux)
estrogen [ˈɛstrədʒən] *n* : estrogène *m*
estuary [ˈɛstʃuˌweri] *n, pl* **-aries** : estuaire *m*
et cetera [ɛtˈseɪ̯tərə, -ˈsɛtrə] : et cætera, et cetera
etch [ˈɛtʃ] *vt* : graver à l'eau-forte <etched in her memory : gravé dans sa mémoire>
etching [ˈɛtʃɪŋ] *n* : eau-forte *f* (dessin), gravure *f* à l'eau-forte (technique)
eternal [ɪˈtərnəl, iː-] *adj* : éternel — **eternally** *adv*
eternity [ɪˈtərnə̯ti, iː-] *n, pl* **-ties** : éternité *f*
ethane [ˈɛˌθeɪn] *n* : éthane *m*
ether [ˈiːθər] *n* : éther *m*
ethereal [ɪˈθɪriəl, iː-] *adj* : éthéré
ethical [ˈɛθɪkəl] *adj* : éthique, moral
ethically [ˈɛθɪkəli] *adv* : moralement
ethics [ˈɛθɪks] *ns & pl* : éthique *f*, morale *f*
Ethiopian[1] [ˌiːθiˈoːpiən] *adj* : éthiopien
Ethiopian[2] *n* : Éthiopien *m*, -pienne *f*
ethnic [ˈɛθnɪk] *adj* : ethnique
ethnologist [ɛθˈnɑlədʒɪst] *n* : ethnologue *mf*
ethnology [ɛθˈnɑlədʒi] *n* : ethnologie *f*
etiquette [ˈɛt̬ɪkət, -ˌkɛt] *n* : étiquette *f*, convenances *fpl*, bienséance *f*
etymological [ˌɛt̬əməˈlɑdʒɪkəl] *adj* : étymologique
etymology [ˌɛt̬əˈmɑlədʒi] *n, pl* **-gies** : étymologie *f*
eucalyptus [ˌjuːkəˈlɪptəs] *n, pl* **-ti** [-ˌtaɪ] *or* **-tuses** [-təsəz] : eucalyptus *m*
Eucharist [ˈjuːkərɪst] *n* : Eucharistie *f*
eulogize [ˈjuːləˌdʒaɪz] *vt* **-gized; -gizing** : faire l'éloge de, faire le panégyrique de
eulogy [ˈjuːlədʒi] *n, pl* **-gies** : éloge *m*, panégyrique *m*
eunuch [ˈjuːnək] *n* : eunuque *m*
euphemism [ˈjuːfəˌmɪzəm] *n* : euphémisme *m*
euphemistic [ˌjuːfəˈmɪstɪk] *adj* : euphémique
euphony [ˈjuːfəni] *n, pl* **-nies** : euphonie *f*
euphoria [joˈforiə] *n* : euphorie *f*
euphoric [joˈforɪk] *adj* : euphorique
European[1] [ˌjuːrəˈpiːən, -piːn] *adj* : européen
European[2] *n* : Européen *m*, -péenne *f*
euthanasia [ˌjuːθəˈneɪʒə, -ʒiə] *n* : euthanasie *f*
evacuate [ɪˈvækjuˌeɪt] *vt* **-ated; -ating** : évacuer
evacuation [ɪˌvækjoˈeɪʃən] *n* : évacuation *f*
evade [ɪˈveɪd] *vt* **evaded; evading** : éviter, esquiver, échapper à
evaluate [ɪˈvæljuˌeɪt] *vt* **-ated; -ating** : évaluer
evaluation [ɪˈvæljoˈeɪʃən] *n* : évaluation *f*
evangelical [ˌiːˌvænˈdʒɛlɪkəl, ˌɛvən-] *adj* : évangélique
evangelist [ɪˈvændʒəlɪst] *n* : évangéliste *m*
evaporate [ɪˈvæpəˌreɪt] *v* **-rated; -rating** *vi* **1** VAPORIZE : s'évaporer **2** DISAPPEAR : s'envoler, s'évaporer *fam* — *vt* : faire évaporer
evaporation [ɪˌvæpəˈreɪʃən] *n* : évaporation *f*
evasion [ɪˈveɪʒən] *n* : évasion *f*
evasive [ɪˈveɪsɪv] *adj* : évasif
eve [ˈiːv] *n* : veille *f* <Christmas Eve : la veille de Noël>
even[1] [ˈiːvən] *vt* : égaliser — *vi or* **to even out** : s'égaliser
even[2] *adv* **1** : même <even a child can do it : même un enfant peut le faire> <he didn't even try : il n'a même pas essayé> **2** (*in comparisons*) : encore <even better : encore mieux> **3 even as** : au moment même où **4 even if** : même si **5 even so** : quand même **6 even then** : même alors
even[3] *adj* **1** REGULAR, STEADY : régulier, égal, constant <an even temperature : une température constante> **2** FLAT, SMOOTH : uni, plat **3** EQUAL : égal, équitable <an even trade : un échange équitable> <to get even : se venger> <we're even! : nous sommes quittes!> **4** : pair <an even number : un nombre pair>
evening [ˈiːvnɪŋ] *n* **1** : soir *m* <he's going out this evening : il sort ce soir> <good evening! : bon soir!> <every evening : tous les soirs> **2** (*emphasizing duration*) : soirée *f* <the whole

evening : toute la soirée> <have a nice evening! : bonne soirée!>

event [ɪ'vɛnt] *n* **1** OCCURRENCE : événement *m* **2** CONTINGENCY : cas *m* <in any event : en tout cas> <in the event that : au cas où> **3** : épreuve *f* (aux sports)

eventful [ɪ'vɛntfəl] *adj* **1** : mouvementé <an eventful week : une semaine mouvementée> **2** MOMENTOUS : mémorable

eventual [ɪ'vɛntʃʊəl] *adj* : final, qui s'ensuit <his eventual ruin : sa ruine finale>

eventuality [ɪˌvɛntʃʊ'ælətɪ] *n, pl* **-ties** : éventualité *f*

eventually [ɪ'vɛntʃʊəlɪ] *adv* : finalement

ever ['ɛvər] *adv* **1** ALWAYS : toujours <he's the same as ever : il est toujours le même> **2** : jamais <more beautiful than ever : plus belle que jamais> <nothing ever happens : il ne se passe jamais rien> **3 ever since** : depuis (lors)

evergreen[1] ['ɛvərˌgriːn] *adj* : à feuilles persistantes

evergreen[2] *n* : plante *f* à feuilles persistantes

everlasting [ˌɛvər'læstɪŋ] *adj* : éternel

every ['ɛvrɪ] *adj* **1** EACH : chaque, tout, tous les <every morning : chaque matin> <every moment : à tout moment> <every store in town : tous les magasins de la ville> **2** ALL : tous <every kind of : toutes sortes de> **3** COMPLETE : plein, entier <to have every confidence in : avoir pleine confiance en> **4 every other** : tous les deux <every other day : tous les deux jours>

everybody ['ɛvrɪˌbʌdɪ, -ˌbɑ-] *pron* : tout le monde, chacun

everyday [ˌɛvrɪ'deɪ, 'ɛvrɪˌ-] *adj* : quotidien, de tous les jours <everyday clothes : vêtements de tous les jours> <in everyday use : d'usage courant>

everyone ['ɛvrɪˌwʌn] → **everybody**

everything ['ɛvrɪˌθɪŋ] *pron* : tout

everywhere ['ɛvrɪˌhwɛr] *adv* : partout <everywhere in the world : partout dans le monde>

evict [ɪ'vɪkt] *vt* : expulser

eviction [ɪ'vɪkʃən] *n* : expulsion *f*

evidence ['ɛvədənʦ] *n* **1** INDICATION : signe *m*, marque *f* <to be in evidence : être (très) en vue> **2** PROOF : témoignage *m*, évidence *f* **3** TESTIMONY : témoignage *m*, déposition *f* <to give evidence : témoigner>

evident ['ɛvɪdənt] *adj* : évident, manifeste

evidently ['ɛvɪdəntlɪ, ˌɛvɪ'dentlɪ] *adv* **1** OBVIOUSLY : évidemment, manifestement **2** APPARENTLY : apparemment

evil[1] ['iːvəl, -vɪl] *adj* **eviler** *or* **eviller; evilest** *or* **evillest** : mauvais, méchant

evil[2] *n* : mal *m* <good and evil : le bien et le mal>

evildoer [ˌiːvəl'duːər, ˌiːvɪl-] *n* : malfaiteur *m*; scélérat *m*, -rate *f*

evince [ɪ'vɪnʦ] *vt* **evinced; evincing** : manifester, faire preuve de

eviscerate [ɪ'vɪsəˌreɪt] *vt* **-ated; -ating** : éventrer, étriper

evocation [ˌiːvo'keɪʃən, ˌɛ-] *n* : évocation *f*

evocative [ɪ'vɑkəɾɪv] *adj* : évocateur

evoke [ɪ'voːk] *vt* **evoked; evoking** : évoquer

evolution [ˌɛvə'luːʃən, ˌiː-] *n* : évolution *f*

evolve [ɪ'vɑlv] *v* **evolved; evolving** *vt* : développer, élaborer — *vi* : évoluer

ewe ['juː] *n* : brebis *f*

exact[1] [ɪg'zækt, ɛ-] *vt* : exiger

exact[2] *adj* : exact, précis, juste <to have the exact time : avoir l'heure juste> <can you be more exact? : pouvez-vous préciser un peu?>

exacting [ɪ'zæktɪŋ, ɛg-] *adj* : exigeant, astreignant

exactitude [ɪg'zæktəˌtuːd, ɛg-, -ˌtjuːd] *n* : exactitude *f*

exactly [ɪg'zæktlɪ, ɛg-] *adv* : exactement, juste <that's exactly what I thought : c'est exactement ce que je pensais> <it's exactly four o'clock : il est quatre heures juste>

exaggerate [ɪg'zædʒəˌreɪt, ɛg-] *v* **-ated; -ating** : exagérer

exaggeration [ɪgˌzædʒə'reɪʃən, ɛg-] *n* : exagération *f*

exalt [ɪg'zɔlt, ɛg-] *vt* : exalter, glorifier

exaltation [ˌɛgˌzɔl'teɪʃən, ɛkˌsɔl-] *n* : exaltation *f*

exam [ɪg'zæm, ɛg-] → **examination**

examination [ɪgˌzæmə'neɪʃən, ɛg-] *n* **1** TEST : examen *m* **2** INSPECTION : inspection *f*, examen *m* **3** INTERROGATION : interrogatoire *m*

examine [ɪg'zæmən, ɛg-] *vt* **-ined; -ining 1** TEST : examiner **2** INSPECT : examiner, inspecter, étudier **3** QUESTION : interroger <to examine a witness : interroger un témoin>

example [ɪg'zæmpəl, ɛg-] *n* : exemple *m* <for example : par exemple> <to set an example : donner l'exemple>

exasperate [ɪg'zæspəˌreɪt, ɛg-] *vt* **-ated; -ating 1** : exaspérer **2 to become exasperated** : s'exaspérer

exasperation [ɪgˌzæspə'reɪʃən, ɛg-] *n* : exaspération *f*

excavate ['ɛkskəˌveɪt] *v* **-vated; -vating** *vt* **1** DIG : creuser, excaver **2** UNEARTH : fouiller, déterrer — *vi* : faire des fouilles (en archéologie)

excavation [ˌɛkskə'veɪʃən] *n* **1** DIGGING : excavation *f*, creusement *m* **2** : fouilles *nfpl* (en archéologie)

exceed [ɪk'siːd, ɛk-] *vt* **1** SURPASS : excéder, dépasser **2** OVERSTEP : excéder, outrepasser <to exceed one's authority : outrepasser ses pouvoirs>

exceedingly [ɪk'si:dɪŋli, ɛk-] *adv* : extrêmement

excel [ɪk'sɛl, ɛk-] *v* **-celled; -celling** *vt* : surpasser — *vi* : exceller

excellence ['ɛksə,lənʦ] *n* : excellence *f*

excellency ['ɛksələnʦi] *n, pl* **-cies** : excellence *f* <Your Excellency : Votre Excellence>

excellent ['ɛksə,lənt] *adj* : excellent

excellently *adv* : admirablement, de façon excellente

except[1] [ɪk'sɛpt] *vt* : excepter, exclure

except[2] *conj* : sauf que, mais <I'd go except it's too far : j'irais mais c'est trop loin>

except[3] *prep* **1** : sauf, excepté <everyone except me : tout le monde sauf moi> **2** (*in questions and negative constructions*) : sinon, sauf <what can one do except wait? : que peut-on faire sinon attendre?> **3 except for** : à part, à l'exception de

exception [ɪk'sɛpʃən] *n* **1** : exception *f* <to make an exception for : faire une exception pour> **2 to take exception to** : s'offenser de

exceptional [ɪk'sɛpʃənəl] *adj* : exceptionnel — **exceptionally** *adv*

excerpt[1] [ɛk'sərpt, ɛg'zərpt, 'ɛk,-, 'ɛg,-] *vt* : extraire

excerpt[2] [ɛk'sərpt, 'ɛg,zərpt] *n* : extrait *m*

excess[1] ['ɛk,sɛs, ɪk'sɛs] *adj* : excédentaire, en trop <excess baggage : un excédent de bagages>

excess[2] [ɪk'sɛs, 'ɛk,sɛs] *n* **1** : excès *m* <to drink to excess : boire à l'excès> **2** SURPLUS : surplus *m*, excédent *m* **3 in excess of** : en plus de, dépassant

excessive [ɪk'sɛsɪv, ɛk-] *adj* : excessif — **excessively** *adv*

exchange[1] [ɪks'ʧeɪnʤ, ɛks-; 'ɛks,ʧeɪnʤ] *vt* **-changed; -changing** : échanger

exchange[2] *n* **1** : échange *m* <in exchange for : en échange de> <exchange of ideas : échange d'idées> **2** : change *m* (en finances) <rate of exchange : taux de change>

excise[1] [ɪk'saɪz, ɛk-] *vt* **-cised; -cising** : exciser

excise[2] ['ɛksaɪz] *n or* **excise tax** : taxe *f*

excision [ɪk'sɪʒən, ɛk-] *n* : excision *f*

excitable [ɪk'saɪʧəbəl, ɛk-] *adj* : excitable, nerveux (se dit d'une personne)

excite [ɪk'saɪt, ɛk-] *vt* **-cited; -citing 1** STIMULATE : exciter <to excite enthusiasm : enthousiasmer> **2** AROUSE : exciter, éveiller, piquer (l'intérêt, la curiosité, etc.)

excited [ɪk'saɪʧəd, ɛk-] *adj* **1** : excité, énervé, agité **2 to get excited** : s'exciter

excitedly [ɪk'saɪʧədli, ɛk-] *adv* : avec agitation <to speak excitedly : parler sur un ton animé>

excitement [ɪk'saɪtmənt, ɛk-] *n* : excitation *f*, agitation *f*

exciting [ɪk'saɪtɪŋ, ɛk-] *adj* : passionnant, excitant

exclaim [ɪks'kleɪm, ɛk-] *vt* : s'écrier — *vi* : s'exclamer

exclamation [,ɛksklə'meɪʃən] *n* : exclamation *f*

exclamation point *n* : point *m* d'exclamation

exclamatory [ɪks'klæmə,tori, ɛks-] *adj* : exclamatif

exclude [ɪks'klu:d, ɛks-] *vt* **-cluded; -cluding** : exclure

excluding [ɪks'klu:dɪŋ, ɛks-] *prep* : à part, à l'exclusion de

exclusion [ɪks'klu:ʒən, ɛks-] *n* : exclusion *f*

exclusive [ɪks'klu:sɪv, ɛks-] *adj* : exclusif — **exclusively** *adv*

excommunicate [ɛkskə'mju:nə,keɪt] *vt* **-cated; -cating** : excommunier

excommunication [,ɛkskə,mju:nə'keɪʃən] *n* : excommunication *f*

excrement ['ɛkskrəmənt] *n* : excréments *mpl*

excrete [ɪk'skri:t, ɛk-] *vt* **-creted; -creting** : excréter

excretion [ɪk'skri:ʃən, ɛk-] *n* : excrétion *f*

excruciating [ɪk'skru:ʃi,eɪtɪŋ, ɛk-] *adj* : atroce, insupportable — **excruciatingly** *adv*

exculpate ['ɛkskəl,peɪt] *vt* **-pated; -pating** : disculper

excursion [ɪk'skərʒən, ɛk-] *n* **1** OUTING : excursion *f*, sortie *f* **2** DIGRESSION : digression *f*

excuse[1] [ɪk'skju:z, ɛk-] *vt* **-cused; -cusing 1** PARDON : excuser, pardonner **2** EXEMPT : exempter, dispenser **3** JUSTIFY : excuser, justifier **4 to excuse oneself** : s'excuser (de la table, etc.)

excuse[2] [ɪk'skju:s, ɛk-] *n* **1** JUSTIFICATION : excuse *f* **2** PRETEXT : prétexte *m*, excuse *f* **3 to make one's excuses** : présenter ses excuses

execute ['ɛksɪ,kju:t] *vt* **-cuted; -cuting** : exécuter

execution [,ɛksɪ'kju:ʃən] *n* : exécution *f*

executioner [,ɛksɪ'kju:ʃənər] *n* : bourreau *m*

executive[1] [ɪg'zɛkjəʧɪv, ɛg-] *adj* : exécutif

executive[2] *n* **1** MANAGER : cadre *m*, dirigeant *m*, -geante *f* **2** *or* **executive branch** : pouvoir *m* exécutif

executor [ɪg'zɛkjəʧər, ɛg-] *n* : exécuteur *m* testamentaire

executrix [ɪg'zɛkjə,trɪks, ɛg-] *n, pl* **executrices** [-zɛkjə'traɪsi:z] *or* **executrixes** [-'zɛkjə,trɪksəz] : exécutrice *f* testamentaire

exemplary [ɪg'zɛmpləri, ɛg-] *adj* : exemplaire

exemplify [ɪg'zɛmplə,faɪ, ɛg-] *vt* **-fied; -fying** : exemplifier, illustrer

exempt[1] [ɪg'zɛmpt, ɛg-] *vt* : exempter, dispenser
exempt[2] *adj* : exempt
exemption [ɪg'zɛmpʃən, ɛg-] *n* : exemption *f*
exercise[1] ['ɛksər,saɪz] *v* **-cised; -cising** *vt* **1** : exercer (le corps) **2** APPLY : exercer, user de, faire valoir — *vi* : faire de l'exercice
exercise[2] *n* **1** : exercice *m* **2 exercises** *npl* CEREMONY : cérémonie *f*
exert [ɪg'zərt, ɛg-] *vt* **1** APPLY, WIELD : exercer, employer **2 to exert oneself** : se dépenser, s'appliquer, se donner de la peine
exertion [ɪg'zərʃən, ɛg-] *n* **1** EFFORT : effort *m* **2** USE : exercice *m*, emploi *m* (de la force, etc.)
exhalation [,ɛksə'leɪʃən, ,ɛkshə-] *n* : expiration *f*, exhalation *f*
exhale [ɛks'heɪl] *v* **-haled; -haling** *vt* **1** : expirer, exhaler **2** EMIT : exhaler (une odeur) — *vi* : expirer
exhaust[1] [ɪg'zɔst, ɛg-] *vt* **1** : épuiser **2 to exhaust oneself** : s'épuiser, se morfondre *Can*
exhaust[2] *n* **1** *or* **exhaust fumes** : gaz *m* d'échappement **2** *or* **exhaust pipe** : tuyau *m* d'échappement
exhaustion [ɪg'zɔstʃən, ɛg-] *n* : épuisement *m*
exhaustive [ɪg'zɔstɪv, ɛg-] *adj* : exhaustif
exhibit[1] [ɪg'zɪbət, ɛg-] *vt* **1** DISPLAY : exposer (des œuvres d'art, etc.), étaler (des marchandises) **2** PRESENT : montrer, présenter (un document, etc.) **3** MANIFEST : manifester, montrer
exhibit[2] *n* **1** : objet *m* exposé, œuvre *f* exposée **2** EXHIBITION : exposition *f* **3** : pièce *f* à conviction (dans les poursuites judiciaires)
exhibition [,ɛksə'bɪʃən] *n* **1** EXHIBIT : exposition *f* **2 to make an exhibition of oneself** : se donner en spectacle
exhibitor [ɪg'zɪbət̬ər] *n* : exposant *m*, -sante *f*
exhilarate [ɪg'zɪlə,reɪt, ɛg-] *vt* **-rated; -rating** : griser, vivifier
exhilaration [ɪg'zɪlə'reɪʃən, ɛg-] *n* : joie *f*, griserie *f*
exhort [ɪg'zɔrt, ɛg-] *vt* : exhorter
exhortation [,ɛksɔr'teɪʃən, -sər-; ,ɛg-,zɔr-] *n* : exhortation *f*
exhume [ɪg'zu:m, -'zju:m; ɪks'ju:m, -'hju:m] *vt* **-humed; -huming** : exhumer
exigencies ['ɛksɪdʒənt̬siz, ɪg'zɪdʒənt̬si:z] *npl* : exigences *fpl*
exile[1] ['ɛg,zaɪl, 'ɛk,saɪl] *vt* **exiled; exiling** : exiler
exile[2] *n* **1** BANISHMENT : exil *m* **2** OUTCAST : exilé *m*, -lée *f*
exist [ɪg'zɪst, ɛg-] *vi* **1** BE : exister **2** LIVE, SURVIVE : vivre, survivre
existence [ɪg'zɪstən̬ts, ɛg-] *n* : existence *f*
exit[1] ['ɛgzət, 'ɛksət] *vi* : sortir — *vt* LEAVE : sortir de, quitter
exit[2] *n* : sortie *f*
exodus ['ɛksədəs] *n* : exode *m*
exonerate [ɪg'zɑnə,reɪt, ɛg-] *vt* **-ated; -ating** : disculper, innocenter
exoneration [ɪg,zɑnə'reɪʃən, ɛg-] *n* : disculpation *f*
exorbitant [ɪg'zɔrbət̬ənt, ɛg-] *adj* : exorbitant, excessif
exorcise ['ɛk,sɔr,saɪz, -sər-] *vt* **-cised; -cising** : exorciser
exorcism ['ɛksər,sɪzəm] *n* : exorcisme *m*
exotic [ɪg'zɑtɪk, ɛg-] *adj* : exotique
expand [ɪk'spænd, ɛk-] *vt* **1** ENLARGE, EXTEND : étendre, élargir **2** DEVELOP : développer — *vi* **1** GROW, SPREAD : s'étendre, s'agrandir, se dilater (se dit des métaux) **2** DEVELOP : se développer
expanse [ɪk'spænt̬s, ɛk-] *n* : étendue *f*
expansion [ɪk'spænt̬ʃən, ɛk-] *n* : expansion *f*, élargissement *m*, développement *m*
expansive [ɪk'spænt̬sɪv, ɛk-] *adj* **1** OUTGOING : expansif, démonstratif **2** AMPLE : large, vaste
expansively [ɪk'spænt̬sɪvli, ɛk-] *adv* : de manière expansive
expansiveness [ɪk'spænt̬sɪvnəs, ɛk-] *n* : expansivité *f*
expatriate[1] [,ɛks'peɪtri,eɪt] *vt* **-ated; -ating** : expatrier
expatriate[2] [ɛks'peɪtriət, -,eɪt] *adj* : expatrié
expatriate[3] [ɛks'peɪtriət, -,eɪt] *n* : expatrié *m*, -triée *f*
expect [ɪk'spɛkt, ɛk-] *vt* **1** ANTICIPATE : s'attendre à <expect the worst : attendez-vous au pire> **2** AWAIT : attendre **3** REQUIRE : exiger, demander — *vi* **to be expecting** : attendre un bébé, être enceinte
expectancy [ɪk'spɛkt̬ən̬si, ɛk-] *n, pl* **-cies** : attente *f*, espérance *f* <life expectancy : espérance de vie>
expectant [ɪk'spɛkt̬ənt, ɛk-] *adj* **1** ANTICIPATING : qui attend **2** EXPECTING : futur <an expectant mother : une future mère>
expectation [,ɛk,spɛk'teɪʃən] *n* : attente *f*
expedient[1] [ɪk'spi:diənt] *adj* : opportun, indiqué, convenable
expedient[2] *n* : expédient *m*
expedite ['ɛkspə,daɪt] *vt* **-dited; -diting** : expédier, accélerer, hâter
expedition [,ɛkspə'dɪʃən] *n* : expédition *f*
expeditious [,ɛkspə'dɪʃəs] *adj* : expéditif, rapide
expel [ɪk'spɛl, ɛk-] *vt* **-pelled; -pelling** : expulser, renvoyer (un élève)
expend [ɪk'spɛnd, ɛk-] *vt* **1** SPEND : dépenser (de l'argent) **2** UTILIZE : utiliser, employer, consacrer (de l'énergie, du temps, etc.) **3** EXHAUST : épuiser

expendable [ɪk'spɛndəbəl, ɛk-] *adj* : remplaçable
expenditure [ɪk'spɛndɪtʃər, ɛk-, -ˌtʃʊr] *n* : dépense *f*
expense [ɪk'spɛnt͵s, ɛk-] *n* **1** COST : coût *m*, dépense *f* **2 expenses** *npl* : frais *mpl* **3 at the expense of** : aux dépens de
expensive [ɪk'spɛnt͵sɪv, ɛk-] *adj* : cher, coûteux
expensively [ɪk'spɛnt͵sɪvli, ɛk-] *adv*-: à grands frais
experience[1] [ɪk'spɪrɪənt͵s, ɛk-] *vt* **-enced; -encing** : éprouver, faire l'expérience de, connaître <to experience difficulties : rencontrer des difficultés>
experience[2] *n* : expérience *f*
experienced [ɪk'spɪrɪənt͵st, ɛk-] *adj* : expérimenté
experiment[1] [ɪk'spɛrəmənt, ɛk-, -'spɪr-] *vi* : expérimenter, faire des expériences
experiment[2] *n* : expérience *f*
experimental [ɪkˌspɛrə'mɛntəl, ɛk-, -ˌspɪr-] *adj* : expérimental
experimentation [ɪkˌspɛrəmən'teɪʃən, ɛk-, -ˌspɪr-] *n* : expérimentation *f*
expert[1] ['ɛkˌspərt, ɪk'spərt] *adj* : expert <expert testimony : témoignage d'expert>
expert[2] ['ɛkˌspərt] *n* : expert *m*, -perte *f*; spécialiste *mf*
expertise [ˌɛkspər'ti:z] *n* : compétence *f*, expertise *f*
expertly ['ɛkˌspərtli] *adv* : de manière experte
expiate ['ɛkspiˌeɪt] *vt* **-ated; -ating** : expier
expiation [ˌɛkspi'eɪʃən] *n* : expiation *f*
expiration [ˌɛkspə'reɪʃən] *n* : expiration *f*
expire [ɪk'spaɪr, ɛk-] *vi* **-pired; -piring 1** EXHALE : expirer **2** END : expirer, arriver à terme **3** DIE : mourir
explain [ɪk'spleɪn, ɛk-] *vt* **1** : expliquer **2 to explain oneself** : s'expliquer
explanation [ˌɛksplə'neɪʃən] *n* : explication *f*
explanatory [ɪk'splænə͵tori, ɛk-] *adj* : explicatif
expletive ['ɛksplə͵tɪv] *n* SWEARWORD : juron *m*
explicable [ɛk'splɪkəbəl, 'ɛksplɪ-] *adj* : explicable
explicit [ɪk'splɪsət, ɛk-] *adj* : explicite — **explicitly** *adv*
explode [ɪk'sploːd, ɛk-] *v* **-ploded; -ploding** *vt* **1** BURST : faire exploser **2** DISCREDIT : discréditer — *vi* **1** : exploser **2 to explode with laughter** : éclater de rire
exploit[1] [ɪk'splɔɪt, ɛk-] *vt* : exploiter
exploit[2] ['ɛkˌsplɔɪt] *n* : exploit *m*
exploitation [ˌɛkˌsplɔɪ'teɪʃən] *n* : exploitation *f*
exploration [ˌɛksplə'reɪʃən] *n* : exploration *f*
exploratory [ɪk'sploraˌtori, ɛk-] *adj* : exploratoire
explore [ɪk'splor, ɛk-] *v* **-plored; -ploring** : explorer
explorer [ɪk'splorər, ɛk-] *n* : explorateur *m*, -trice *f*
explosion [ɪk'sploːʒən, ɛk-] *n* : explosion *f*
explosive[1] [ɪk'sploːsɪv, ɛk-] *adj* : explosif
explosive[2] *n* : explosif *m*
exponent [ɪk'spoːnənt, 'ɛkˌspoː-] *n* **1** : exposant *m* (en mathématiques) **2** ADVOCATE : partisan *m*, -sane *f*; avocat *m*, -cate *f*
export[1] [ɛk'sport, 'ɛkˌsport] *v* : exporter
export[2] ['ɛkˌsport] *n* : exportation *f*
expose [ɪk'spoːz, ɛk-] *vt* **-posed; -posing 1** DISPLAY : exposer **2** DISCLOSE : révéler, démasquer **3 to expose oneself to** : s'exposer à
exposé [ˌɛkspo'zeɪ] *n* : exposé *m*, révélation *f*
exposition [ˌɛkspə'zɪʃən] *n* : exposition *f*
exposure [ɪk'spoːʒər, ɛk-] *n* **1** : exposition *f* (au danger, etc.) <to die of exposure : mourir de froid> **2** DISCLOSURE : révélation *f*, divulgation *f* **3** : pose *f* (en photographie) **4** ORIENTATION : exposition *f* <to have a southern exposure : être exposé au sud>
expound [ɪk'spaʊnd, ɛk-] *vt* : exposer, expliquer — *vi* **to expound on** : disserter sur
express[1] [ɪk'sprɛs, ɛk-] *vt* **1** CONVEY : exprimer, énoncer **2** SQUEEZE : exprimer, extraire (du jus, etc.)
express[2] *adv* : en exprès <to send express : envoyer en exprès>
express[3] *adj* **1** EXPLICIT, SPECIFIC : exprès, explicite, formel <with the express purpose of : dans le seul but de> **2** FAST : rapide, express <an express bus : un autobus express>
express[4] *n* **1** *or* **express train** : rapide *m*, express *m* **2 to send by express** : envoyer par transport rapide
expression [ɪk'sprɛʃən, ɛk-] *n* : expression *f*
expressionless [ɪk'sprɛʃənləs, ɛk-] *adj* : inexpressif, sans expression
expressive [ɪk'sprɛsɪv, ɛk-] *adj* : expressif
expressiveness [ɪk'sprɛsɪvnəs, ɛk-] *n* : expressivité *f*
expressly [ɪk'sprɛsli, ɛk-] *adv* : expressément
expressway [ɪk'sprɛs͵weɪ, ɛk-] *n* : autoroute *f*
expulsion [ɪk'spʌlʃən, ɛk-] *n* : expulsion *f*, renvoi *m* (d'un élève)
expurgate ['ɛkspər͵geɪt] *vt* **-gated; -gating** : expurger
exquisite [ɛk'skwɪzət, 'ɛkˌskwɪ-] *adj* **1** FINE : exquis, raffiné **2** INTENSE : vif (se dit des plaisirs, etc.), aigu (se dit d'une douleur)
extant ['ɛkstənt, ɛk'stænt] *adj* : existant

extemporaneous [ɛkˌstɛmpə'reɪmiəs] *adj* : improvisé, impromptu
extend [ɪk'stɛnd, ɛk-] *vt* **1** STRETCH : étendre **2** PROLONG : prolonger **3** ENLARGE : agrandir **4 to extend one's hand** : tendre la main — *vi* **1** STRETCH : s'étendre **2** LAST : se prolonger
extension [ɪk'stɛnʃən, ɛk-] *n* **1** EXTENDING : extension *f* **2** PROLONGATION : prolongation *f*, délai *m* **3** ADDITION, ANNEX : agrandissement *m* (d'une maison), prolongement *m* (d'une route, etc.) **4** : poste *m* (de téléphone) **5 extension cord** : rallonge *f*
extensive [ɪk'stɛntsɪv, ɛk-] *adj* : étendu, vaste
extensively [ɪk'stɛntsɪvli, ɛk-] *adv* : considérablement, abondamment
extent [ɪk'stɛnt, ɛk-] *n* **1** SIZE : étendue *f* **2** SCOPE : importance *f*, ampleur *f* **3** DEGREE : mesure *f*, degré *m* <to a certain extent : dans une certaine mesure, jusqu'à un certain point>
extenuating [ɪk'stɛnjəˌweɪtɪŋ, ɛk-] *adj* : atténuant
exterior[1] [ɛk'stɪriər] *adj* : extérieur
exterior[2] *n* : extérieur *m*
exterminate [ɪk'stərməˌneɪt, ɛk-] *vt* **-nated; -nating** : exterminer
extermination [ɪkˌstərmə'neɪʃən, ɛk-] *n* : extermination *f*
external [ɪk'stərnəl, ɛk-] *adj* : externe <for external use only : à usage externe>
externally [ɪk'stərnəli, ɛk-] *adv* : extérieurement
extinct [ɪk'stɪŋkt, ɛk-] *adj* : éteint (se dit d'un volcan, d'un feu, etc.), disparu (se dit d'une espèce)
extinction [ɪk'stɪŋkʃən, ɛk-] *n* : extinction *f*, disparition *f*
extinguish [ɪk'stɪŋgwɪʃ, ɛk-] *vt* : éteindre
extinguisher [ɪk'stɪŋgwɪʃər, ɛk-] *n* : extincteur *m*
extirpate ['ɛkstərˌpeɪt] *vt* **-pated; -pating** : extirper
extol [ɪk'stoːl, ɛk-] *vt* **-tolled; -tolling** : louer
extort [ɪk'stɔrt, ɛk-] *vt* : extorquer
extortion [ɪk'stɔrʃən, ɛk-] *n* : extorsion *f*
extra[1] ['ɛkstrə] *adv* **1** ESPECIALLY : plus que d'habitude, particulièrement <extra nice : plus gentil que d'habitude> **2 to pay extra** : payer un supplément **3 to cost extra** : coûter plus cher
extra[2] *adj* **1** ADDITIONAL : supplémentaire, en supplément <extra hours : heures supplémentaires> <the wine is extra : le vin est en plus> **2** SPARE : en trop, de trop <an extra chair : une chaise en trop> **3** SUPERIOR : supérieur <extra quality : de qualité supérieure>
extra[3] *n* **1** ADDITION : supplément *m* **2** : édition *f* spéciale (d'un journal) **3** : figurant *m*, -rante *f* (au cinéma)
extract[1] [ɪk'strækt, ɛk-] *vt* : extraire, arracher (une dent, un aveu, etc.)
extract[2] ['ɛkˌstrækt] *n* : extrait *m*
extraction [ɪk'strækʃən, ɛk-] *n* **1** REMOVAL : extraction *f* **2** ORIGIN : origine *f* <of French extraction : d'origine française>
extracurricular [ˌɛkstrəkə'rɪkjələr] *adj* : parascolaire
extradite ['ɛkstrəˌdaɪt] *vt* **-dited; -diting** : extrader
extradition [ˌɛkstrə'dɪʃən] *n* : extradition *f*
extramarital [ˌɛkstrə'mærəɡəl] *adj* : extraconjugal
extraneous [ɛk'streɪniəs] *adj* **1** OUTSIDE : extérieur, étranger **2** SUPERFLUOUS : superflu
extraordinary [ɪk'strɔrdənˌɛri, ˌɛkstrə'ɔrd-] *adj* : extraordinaire — **extraordinarily** [ɪkˌstrɔrdən'ɛrəli, ˌɛkstrəˌɔrd-] *adv*
extrasensory [ˌɛkstrə'sɛntsəri] *adj* : extrasensoriel
extraterrestrial[1] [ˌɛkstrətə'rɛstriəl] *adj* : extraterrestre
extraterrestrial[2] *n* : extraterrestre *mf*
extravagance [ɪk'strævɪɡənts, ɛk-] *n* **1** EXCESS : extravagance *f* **2** WASTEFULNESS : prodigalité *f* **3** LUXURY : luxe *m*
extravagant [ɪk'strævɪɡənt, ɛk-] *adj* **1** EXCESSIVE : extravagant, excessif **2** WASTEFUL : prodigue **3** LUXURIOUS : luxueux
extravagantly [ɪk'strævɪɡəntli, ɛk-] *adv* **1** LAVISHLY : avec prodigalité, luxueusement **2** EXCESSIVELY : d'une manière extravagante, à outrance
extravaganza [ɪkˌstrævə'ɡænzə, ɛk-] *n* : œuvre *f* à grand spectacle, spectacle *m* somptueux
extreme[1] [ɪk'striːm, ɛk-] *adj* : extrême — **extremely** *adv*
extreme[2] *n* **1** : extrême *m* **2 to go to extremes** : pousser (les choses) à l'extrême
extremity [ɪk'strɛmətɪ, ɛk-] *n, pl* **-ties** : extrémité *f*
extricate ['ɛkstrəˌkeɪt] *vt* **-cated; -cating 1** : dégager, extirper **2 to extricate oneself from** : se dégager de, se sortir de
extrovert ['ɛkstrəˌvərt] *n* : extraverti *m*, -tie *f*
extroverted ['ɛkstrəˌvərtəd] *adj* : extraverti
extrude [ɪk'struːd, ɛk-] *vt* **-truded; -truding** : extruder, faire sortir
exuberance [ɪɡ'zuːbərənts, ɛɡ-] *n* : exubérance *f*
exuberant [ɪɡ'zuːbərənt, ɛɡ-] *adj* : exubérant
exuberantly [ɪɡ'zuːbərəntli, ɛɡ-] *adv* : avec exubérance

exude [ɪg'zu:d, ɛg-] *v* **-uded; -uding** *vt* **1** : exsuder (un liquide) **2 to exude confidence** : respirer la confiance en soi — *vi* : exsuder
exult [ɪg'zʌlt, ɛg-] *vi* : exulter, se réjouir
exultant [ɪg'zʌltənt, ɛg-] *adj* : triomphant, jubilant
exultation [ˌɛksəl'teɪʃən, ˌɛgzəl-] *n* : exultation *f*
eye¹ ['aɪ] *vt* **eyed; eyeing** *or* **eying** : regarder, lorgner
eye² *n* **1** : œil *m* <to have brown eyes : avoir les yeux bruns> <the eye of the storm : l'œil de la tempête> **2** VISION : vision *f* **3** GLANCE : regard *m* <her eyes fell on the letter : son regard est tombé sur la lettre> **4** POINT OF VIEW : point *m* de vue <in the eyes of the law : selon la loi> **5 eye of a needle** : chas *m*
eyeball ['aɪˌbɔl] *n* : globe *m* oculaire
eyebrow ['aɪˌbraʊ] *n* : sourcil *m*
eyedropper ['aɪˌdrɑpər] → **dropper**
eyeglasses ['aɪˌglæsəz] *npl* : lunettes *fpl*
eyelash ['aɪˌlæʃ] *n* : cil *m*
eyelet ['aɪlət] *n* : œillet *m*
eyelid [aɪˌlɪd] *n* : paupière *f*
eye–opener ['aɪˌo:pənər] *n* : révélation *f*
eyepiece ['aɪˌpiːs] *n* : oculaire *m*
eyesight ['aɪˌsaɪt] *n* : vue *f*, vision *f* <to lose one's eyesight : perdre la vue>
eyesore ['aɪˌsor] *n* : horreur *f* <to be an eyesore : choquer la vue>
eyestrain ['aɪˌstreɪn] *n* : fatigue *f* des yeux
eyetooth ['aɪˌtu:θ] *n, pl* **-teeth** [-ˌti:θ] : dent *f* canine
eyewitness ['aɪˌwɪtnəs] *n* : témoin *m* oculaire
eyrie ['aɪri] → **aerie**

F

f ['ɛf] *n, pl* **f's** *or* **fs** ['ɛfs] : f *m*, sixième lettre de l'alphabet
fable ['feɪbəl] *n* : fable *f*, légende *f*
fabled ['feɪbəld] *adj* : légendaire, fabuleux
fabric ['fæbrɪk] *n* **1** CLOTH : tissu *m*, étoffe *f* **2** STRUCTURE : structure *f* <the fabric of society : la structure de la société>
fabricate ['fæbrɪˌkeɪt] *vt* **-cated; -cating** **1** CONSTRUCT : fabriquer (un objet) **2** INVENT : fabriquer, inventer (une histoire, etc.)
fabrication [ˌfæbrɪ'keɪʃən] *n* **1** CONSTRUCTION : fabrication *f* **2** FALSEHOOD : mensonge *m*
fabulous ['fæbjələs] *adj* **1** LEGENDARY : fabuleux, légendaire **2** INCREDIBLE : incroyable **3** MARVELOUS : fabuleux, formidable
fabulously ['fæbjələsli] *adv* : fabuleusement
facade [fə'sɑd] *n* : façade *f*
face¹ ['feɪs] *vt* **faced; facing** **1** CONFRONT : faire face à, affronter <to be faced with : se trouver confronté à> **2** COVER : revêtir (un mur, etc.) **3** : faire face à <to face the sun : faire face au soleil> **4** FRONT, OVERLOOK : être en face de, donner sur
face² *n* **1** : visage *m*, figure *f* **2** EXPRESSION : mine *f*, air *m* <he put on a sad face : il faisait triste mine> **3** : grimace *f* <to make a face : faire la grimace> **4** APPEARANCE : aspect *m*, visage *m*, apparence *f* (de la société, etc.) **5** PRESENCE : présence *f* <in the face of the enemy : face à l'ennemi> **6** SURFACE : face *f* (d'une monnaie), façade *f* (d'un bâtiment) **7** DIGNITY : face *f* <to lose face : perdre la face> **8 in the face of** DESPITE : en dépit de
facedown ['feɪsˌdaʊn] *adv* : face contre terre <to lie facedown : être étendu à plat ventre>
faceless ['feɪsləs] *adj* ANONYMOUS : anonyme
face–lift ['feɪsˌlɪft] *n* **1** : lifting *m* **2** RENOVATION : ravalement *m* (d'une façade), restauration *f*
facet ['fæsət] *n* **1** : facette *f* (d'une pierre précieuse) **2** ASPECT : aspect *m*, facette *f*
facetious [fə'si:jəs] *adj* : facétieux — **facetiously** *adv*
facetiousness [fə'si:jəsnəs] *n* : caractère *m* facétieux
face–to–face *adv* : face à face, en personne
faceup ['feɪs'ʌp] *adv* : face en dessus <to lie faceup : être étendu sur le dos>
face value *n* : valeur *f* nominale
facial¹ ['feɪʃəl] *adj* : facial, du visage
facial² *n* : soin *m* du visage
facile ['fæsəl] *adj* **1** EASY : facile **2** SUPERFICIAL : superficiel, creux **3** FLUENT : coulant, aisé
facilitate [fə'sɪləˌteɪt] *vt* **-tated; -tating** : faciliter
facility [fə'sɪləṭi] *n, pl* **-ties** **1** EASE : facilité *f*, aisance *f* **2** APTITUDE : facilité *f*, aptitude *f* **3** CENTER, COMPLEX : complexe *m* <hospital facility : complexe hospitalier> **4 facilities** *npl* : installations *fpl*, équipements *mpl* <sports facilities : équipements sportifs>
facing ['feɪsɪŋ] *n* **1** : revers *m* (en couture) **2** : revêtement *m* (d'un bâtiment)
facsimile [fæk'sɪməli] *n* **1** REPRODUCTION : fac-similé *m* **2** FAX : fac-similé *m*, télécopie *f*

fact |ˈfækt| *n* **1** DATA, INFORMATION : fait *m* **2** REALITY : faits *mpl*, réalité *f* **3 in ~** : en fait, effectivement
faction |ˈfækʃən| *n* : faction *f*
factitious |fækˈtɪʃəs| *adj* : factice, artificiel
factor |ˈfæktər| *n* : facteur *m*
factory |ˈfæktəri| *n, pl* **-ries** : usine *f*, fabrique *f*
factual |ˈfæktʃʊəl| *adj* : factuel, basé sur les faits
factually |ˈfæktʃʊəli| *adv* : en se tenant aux faits
faculty |ˈfækəlti| *n, pl* **-ties 1** : faculté *f* <the faculty of hearing : la faculté de l'ouïe> **2** APTITUDE : aptitude *f*, faculté *f* **3** TEACHERS : faculté *f* (dans une université), corps *m* enseignant
fad |ˈfæd| *n* : mode *f* passagère, marotte *f*
fade |ˈfeɪd| *v* **faded; fading** *vt* : décolorer — *vi* **1** WITHER : se flétrir, se faner **2** DISCOLOR : se décolorer **3** DIM : s'affaiblir, diminuer (se dit de la lumière) **4** VANISH : disparaître <to fade from sight : disparaître aux regards>
faded |ˈfeɪdəd| *adj* : décoloré, délavé
fag |ˈfæg| *vt* **fagged; fagging** EXHAUST : épuiser, fatiguer
fagot *or* **faggot** |ˈfægət| *n* : fagot *m*
Fahrenheit |ˈfærənˌhaɪt| *adj* : Fahrenheit
fail[1] |ˈfeɪl| *vi* **1** WEAKEN : faiblir, baisser <my eyes are failing : ma vue faiblit> **2** BREAK DOWN : tomber en panne, lâcher (se dit des freins) <her heart failed : son cœur s'est arrêté> **3** (*indicating a lack of success*) : échouer, ne pas réussir, faire faillite <the business is failing : l'entreprise fait faillite> **4 to fail in** : manquer à, faire défaut à <I failed in my duty : j'ai manqué à mon devoir> — *vt* **1** DISAPPOINT, LET DOWN : décevoir, laisser tomber, faire défaut **2** NEGLECT : manquer à, négliger <to fail to keep one's word : manquer à sa parole> **3** : échouer à, ne pas réussir à <to fail an exam : échouer à un examen>
fail[2] *n* **1** FAILURE : échec *m* **2 without ~** : à coup sûr, sans faute
failing[1] |ˈfeɪlɪŋ| *n* : défaut *m*
failing[2] *prep* : à défaut de
failure |ˈfeɪljər| *n* **1** : échec *m*, insuccès *m*, faillite *f* (en finances) <a complete failure : un échec total> **2** LACK, OMISSION : manque *m*, manquement *m*, défaut *m* **3** BREAKDOWN, LOSS : panne *f*, défaillance *f* (en médecine) <power failure : panne de courant> <crop failure : perte des récoltes> **4 to be a failure** : être nul, ne pas être doué
faint[1] |ˈfeɪnt| *vi* : s'évanouir
faint[2] *adj* **1** COWARDLY : lâche, peureux **2** WEAK : défaillant, faible <to feel faint : se sentir mal> **3** FEEBLE, SLIGHT : faible, léger **4** INDISTINCT : vague, flou
faint[3] *n* : évanouissement *m*
fainthearted |ˈfeɪntˈhɑrtəd| *adj* : timide, timoré
faintly |ˈfeɪntli| *adv* **1** SLIGHTLY : faiblement **2** INDISTINCTLY : vaguement
faintness |ˈfeɪntnəs| *n* **1** INDISTINCTNESS : faiblesse *f*, légèreté *f* **2** DIZZINESS : vertige *m*
fair[1] |ˈfær| *adv* → **fairly**
fair[2] *adj* **1** BEAUTIFUL : beau **2** FINE : beau (se dit du temps), favorable (se dit du vent) **3** HONEST, JUST : juste, équitable <it's not fair : ce n'est pas juste> <fair play : franc jeu> **4** BLOND, LIGHT : blond (se dit des cheveux), clair (se dit de la peau) **5** ADEQUATE : assez bon, passable **6** LARGE : considérable, important
fair[3] *n* : foire *f*, fête *f* foraine
fairground |ˈfærˌgraʊnd| *n* : champ *m* de foire
fairly |ˈfærli| *adv* **1** HONESTLY, JUSTLY : équitablement, impartialement, honnêtement **2** QUITE, RATHER : assez, passablement **3** POSITIVELY : vraiment <fairly bursting with pride : vraiment fier de soi>
fairness |ˈfærnəs| *n* **1** IMPARTIALITY : équité *f*, impartialité *f*, justice *f* <in all fairness : en toute justice> **2** LIGHTNESS : blondeur *f* (des cheveux), blancheur *f* (de la peau)
fairy |ˈfæri| *n, pl* **fairies** : fée *f*
fairyland |ˈfæriˌlænd| *n* : royaume *m* des fées, féerie *f*
fairy tale *n* : conte *m* de fées
faith |ˈfeɪθ| *n, pl* **faiths** |ˈfeɪθs, ˈfeɪðz| **1** LOYALTY : loyauté *f*, foi *f* **2** BELIEF : foi *f*, croyance *f* (en Dieu) **3** CONFIDENCE, TRUST : confiance *f*, foi *f* <to have faith in : avoir confiance en> <in good faith : en toute bonne foi> **4** RELIGION : foi *f*, religion *f*
faithful |ˈfeɪθfəl| *adj* **1** RELIABLE : fidèle, loyal **2** ACCURATE : fidèle, exact — **faithfully** *adv*
faithfulness |ˈfeɪθfəlnəs| *n* : fidélité *f*
faithless |ˈfeɪθləs| *adj* : déloyal, infidèle — **faithlessly** *adv*
faithlessness |ˈfeɪθləsnəs| *n* : déloyauté *f*, infidélité *f*
fake[1] |ˈfeɪk| *v* **faked; faking** *vt* **1** COUNTERFEIT, FALSIFY : falsifier, contrefaire **2** FEIGN : simuler, feindre — *vi* **1** PRETEND : faire semblant **2** : feinter (aux sports)
fake[2] *adj* : faux, falsifié
fake[3] *n* **1** : article *m* truqué, faux *m* (œuvre d'art) **2** : imposteur *m* (personne) **3** : feinte *f* (aux sports)
fakir |fəˈkɪr, ˈfeɪkər| *n* : fakir *m*
falcon |ˈfælkən, ˈfɔl-| *n* : faucon *m*
falconry |ˈfælkənri, ˈfɔl-| *n* : fauconnerie *f*

fall[1] ['fɔl] *vi* **fell** ['fɛl]; **fallen** ['fɔlən]; **falling 1** : tomber <to fall off a roof : tomber d'un toit> <the snow was falling : la neige tombait> **2** DROP : baisser, tomber, diminuer **3** HANG : tomber (se dit des cheveux), descendre (se dit des rideaux, etc.) **4** : tomber, être renversé <the government has fallen : le gouvernement a été renversé> **5** SIN : tomber, pécher **6** OCCUR : tomber, arriver <Christmas falls on a Wednesday : Noël tombe un mercredi> **7 to fall asleep** : s'endormir **8 to fall behind** : prendre du retard **9 to fall in love** : tomber amoureux

fall[2] *n* **1** : chute *f* <to have a fall : faire une chute, tomber> <a heavy fall of snow : une forte chute de neige> **2** DECREASE : baisse *f*, chute *f* (des prix, de la température, etc.), dépréciation *f* (de la monnaie) **3** COLLAPSE : effondrement *m* (d'un édifice), chute *f*, renversement *m* (d'un régime, etc.) **4** AUTUMN : automne *m* **5 falls → waterfall**

fallacious [fə'leɪʃəs] *adj* : fallacieux

fallacy ['fæləsi] *n, pl* **-cies** : erreur *f*, faux raisonnement *m*

fall back *vi* **1** RETREAT : reculer, se retirer **2 to fall back on** : avoir recours à

fallible ['fæləbəl] *adj* : faillible

fallout ['fɔl,aʊt] *n* **1** : retombées *fpl* (radioactives) **2** CONSEQUENCES : répercussions *fpl*

fall out *vi* QUARREL : se disputer, se quereller

fallow[1] ['fælo] *vt* : labourer une terre en vue des récoltes à venir

fallow[2] *adj* **1** : en jachère (se dit d'une terre) **2** DORMANT : inactif

false ['fɔls] *adj* **falser; falsest 1** UNTRUE : faux, erroné **2** FAKE : faux, artificiel **3** DECEPTIVE : faux, mensonger **4** DISLOYAL : faux, déloyal

falsehood ['fɔls,hʊd] *n* **1** LIE : mensonge *m* **2** LYING : fausseté *f*

falsely ['fɔlsli] *adv* : faussement

falseness ['fɔlsnəs] *n* : fausseté *f*

falsetto [fɔl'seṭo:] *n, pl* **-tos** : fausset *m*

falsification [,fɔlsəfə'keɪʃən] *n* : falsification *f*

falsify ['fɔlsə,faɪ] *vt* **-fied; -fying** : falsifier

falsity ['fɔlsəṭi] *n, pl* **-ties** : fausseté *f*

falter ['fɔltər] *vi* **1** STUMBLE : chanceler, trébucher **2** STAMMER : bredouiller **3** WAVER : hésiter, vaciller, chanceler

fame ['feɪm] *n* : célébrité *f*, renommée *f*

famed ['feɪmd] *adj* : célèbre, renommé

familial [fə'mɪljəl, -liəl] *adj* : familial

familiar [fə'mɪljər] *adj* **1** KNOWN : familier, (bien) connu <to be on familiar ground : être en terrain connu> <to be familiar with sth : bien connaître qqch> **2** INFORMAL, INTIMATE : familier, intime **3** FORWARD : entreprenant, effronté

familiarity [fə,mɪli'ærəṭi, -,mɪl'jær-] *n, pl* **-ties 1** ACQUAINTANCE, KNOWLEDGE : connaissance *f*, caractère *m* familier **2** INFORMALITY, INTIMACY : familiarité *f*, intimité *f* **3** FORWARDNESS : familiarités *fpl*, privautés *fpl*

familiarize [fə'mɪljə,raɪz] *vt* **-ized; -izing 1** : familiariser **2 to familiarize oneself with** : se familiariser avec

family ['fæmli, 'fæmə-] *n, pl* **-lies** : famille *f*

family name → surname

family tree *n* : arbre *m* généalogique

famine ['fæmən] *n* : famine *f*

famished ['fæmɪʃt] *adj* : affamé <I'm famished! : je meurs de faim!>

famous ['feɪməs] *adj* : célèbre, renommé

famously ['feɪməsli] *adv* : à merveille, rudement bien *fam*

fan[1] ['fæn] *vt* **fanned; fanning 1** : éventer (le visage, etc.), attiser (un feu) **2** STIMULATE : attiser, aviver

fan[2] *n* **1** : éventail *m*, ventilateur *m* (électrique) **2** ADMIRER, ENTHUSIAST : admirateur *m*, -trice *f*; enthousiaste *mf*; fan *mf* (d'une vedette)

fanatic[1] [fə'nætɪk] *or* **fanatical** [-ṭɪkəl] *adj* : fanatique

fanatic[2] *n* : fanatique *mf*

fanaticism [fə'næṭə,sɪzəm] *n* : fanatisme *m*

fanciful ['fænsɪfəl] *adj* **1** IMAGINATIVE : imaginatif **2** CAPRICIOUS, WHIMSICAL : fantasque, bizarre, capricieux

fancy[1] ['fænsi] *vt* **-cied; -cying 1** IMAGINE : s'imaginer, se figurer, croire **2** LIKE, WANT : avoir envie de, aimer

fancy[2] *adj* **fancier; -est 1** ELABORATE : élaboré, extravagant **2** LUXURIOUS : de luxe

fancy[3] *n, pl* **-cies 1** LIKING : goût *m*, envie *f* <to take a fancy to s.o. : se prendre d'affection pour qqn> **2** WHIM : caprice *m*, fantaisie *f* **3** IMAGINATION : imagination *f*, fantaisie *f*

fanfare ['fæn,fær] *n* : fanfare *f*

fang ['fæŋ] *n* : croc *m* (d'un animal), crochet *m* (d'un serpent)

fanlight ['fæn,laɪt] *n* : imposte *f*

fantasia [fæn'teɪʒə, -ziə; ,fæntə'ziːə] *n* : fantaisie *f*

fantasize ['fæntə,saɪz] *vi* **-sized; -sizing** : fantasmer

fantastic [fæn'tæstɪk] *adj* **1** FANCIFUL, STRANGE : fantasque, bizarre **2** INCREDIBLE : incroyable, fabuleux, inouï **3** WONDERFUL : superbe, sensationnel

fantastically [fæn'tæstɪkli] *adv* : fantastiquement, incroyablement

fantasy ['fæntəsi] *n, pl* **-sies 1** IMAGINATION : imagination *f*, fantaisie *f* **2** FANTASIZING : fantasme *m*, rêverie *f*

far[1] [ˈfɑr] *adv* **farther** [ˈfɑrðər] *or* **further** [ˈfər-]; **farthest** *or* **furthest** [-ðəst] **1** : loin <is it far? : est-ce loin?> <far away : au loin, dans le lointain> <far and wide : de tous côtés> **2** MUCH : beaucoup, bien <far worse : bien pire> <far too short : beaucoup trop court> **3** (*expressing degree or extent*) <as far as possible : autant que possible> <as far as the city : jusqu'à la ville> <as far as that goes : pour ce qui est de cela> **4** (*expressing progress*) : loin <she'll go far : elle ira loin> **5 by ~** : de loin **6 far from it!** : pas du tout! **7 so far** : jusqu'ici, jusqu'à maintenant

far[2] *adj* **farther** *or* **further**; **farthest** *or* **furthest 1** REMOTE : éloigné, lointain <a far country : un pays lointain> **2** LONG : long <a far journey : un long voyage> **3** OTHER : autre <the far side of the lake : l'autre côté du lac> **4** EXTREME : extrême <the far right : l'extrême droite>

faraway [ˈfɑrəˌweɪ] *adj* : éloigné, lointain

farce [ˈfɑrs] *n* : farce *f*

farcical [ˈfɑrsɪkəl] *adj* : risible, grotesque

fare[1] [ˈfær] *vi* **fared; faring** : aller, se passer

fare[2] *n* **1** : tarif *m*, prix *m* du billet <full fare : plein tarif> **2** FOOD : nourriture *f*

farewell[1] [færˈwel] *adj* : d'adieu <a farewell speech : un discours d'adieu>

farewell[2] *n* : adieu *m* <to say one's farewells : faire ses adieux>

far–fetched [ˈfɑrˈfɛtʃt] *adj* : improbable, bizarre

farm[1] [ˈfɑrm] *vt* : cultiver, exploiter (une terre) — *vi* : être fermier

farm[2] *n* : ferme *f*, exploitation *f* agricole

farmer [ˈfɑrmər] *n* : fermier *m*, -mière *f*; agriculteur *m*, -trice *f*; habitant *m* *Can*

farmhand [ˈfɑrmˌhænd] *n* : ouvrier *m*, -vrière *f* agricole

farmhouse [ˈfɑrmˌhaʊs] *n* : ferme *f*

farming [ˈfɑrmɪŋ] *n* : agriculture *f*, élevage *m* (de bovins, etc.)

farmland [ˈfɑrmˌlænd] *n* : terres *fpl* arables, terres *fpl* cultivées

farmyard [ˈfɑrmˌjɑrd] *n* : cour *f* de ferme

far–off [ˈfɑrˌɔf, -ˈɔf] *adj* : lointain

far–reaching [ˈfɑrˈriːtʃɪŋ] *adj* : considérable, d'une grande portée

farsighted [ˈfɑrˌsaɪtəd] *adj* **1** : hypermétrope, presbyte **2** SHREWD : clairvoyant, perspicace

farsightedness [ˈfɑrˌsaɪtədnəs] *n* **1** : hypermétropie *f*, presbytie *f* **2** SHREWDNESS : clairvoyance *f*, perspicacité *f*

farther[1] [ˈfɑrðər] *adv* **1** : plus loin <nothing could be farther from the truth : rien n'est plus loin de la vérité> <farther ahead : loin devant> **2** MORE : encore plus, davantage

farther[2] *adj* : plus éloigné, plus lointain <the farther side of the house : l'autre côté de la maison>

farthest[1] [ˈfɑrðəst] *adv* **1** : le plus loin **2** MOST : le plus

farthest[2] *adj* : le plus éloigné, le plus lointain

fascicle [ˈfæsɪkəl] *n* : fascicule *m*

fascinate [ˈfæsənˌeɪt] *vt* **-nated; -nating** : fasciner, captiver

fascination [ˌfæsənˈeɪʃən] *n* : fascination *f*

fascism [ˈfæʃˌɪzəm] *n* : fascisme *m*

fascist[1] [ˈfæʃɪst] *adj* : fasciste

fascist[2] *n* : fasciste *mf*

fashion[1] [ˈfæʃən] *vt* : façonner, fabriquer

fashion[2] *n* **1** MANNER : façon *f*, manière *f* **2** STYLE : mode *f*, vogue *f* <the latest fashion : la dernière mode> <to be out of fashion : être démodé>

fashionable [ˈfæʃənəbəl] *adj* : à la mode, en vogue

fashionably [ˈfæʃənəbli] *adv* : à la mode, élégamment

fast[1] [ˈfæst] *vi* : jeûner

fast[2] *adv* **1** SECURELY : solidement, ferme **2** DEEPLY : profondément <fast asleep : profondément endormi> **3** SWIFTLY : rapidement, vite

fast[3] *adj* **1** SECURE : solide, ferme <to make fast : amarrer (un bateau)> **2** LOYAL : fidèle, sûr <fast friends : amis fidèles> **3** SWIFT : rapide, vite **4** DEEP : profond <a fast sleep : un sommeil profond> **5** COLORFAST : grand teint **6** : en avance (se dit d'une montre) <my watch is fast : ma montre avance>

fast[4] *n* : jeûne *m*

fasten [ˈfæsən] *vt* **1** ATTACH, SECURE : attacher, fermer **2** FIX, FOCUS : fixer — *vi* : s'attacher, se fermer

fastener [ˈfæsənər] *n* **1** HOOK, SNAP : attache *f*, bouton-pression *m* **2** LATCH : fermeture *f* (d'une porte) **3** CLASP : fermoir *m* (d'un bracelet, d'un sac, etc.)

fastening [ˈfæsənɪŋ] → **fastener**

fastidious [fæsˈtɪdiəs] *adj* **1** FUSSY : exigeant, difficile à contenter **2** METICULOUS : méticuleux

fastidiously [fæsˈtɪdiəsli] *n* : méticuleusement

fat[1] [ˈfæt] *adj* **fatter; fattest 1** OBESE : gros, gras, corpulent **2** THICK : gros, épais **3** PROFITABLE : gros, lucratif <a fat contract : un gros contrat>

fat[2] *n* **1** : gras *m* (de la viande), graisse *f* (du corps) **2** : matières *fpl* grasses <fat content : teneur en matières grasses>

fatal [ˈfeɪtəl] *adj* **1** DEADLY : mortel **2** FATEFUL : fatidique **3** DISASTROUS : fatal
fatalism [ˈfeɪtəˌlɪzəm] *n* : fatalisme *m*
fatalist [ˈfeɪtəlɪst] *n* : fataliste *mf*
fatalistic [ˌfeɪtəlˈɪstɪk] *adj* : fataliste
fatality [feɪˈtæləṭi, fə-] *n, pl* **-ties** : accident *m* mortel, mort *m*
fatally [ˈfeɪtəli] *adv* : mortellement
fate [ˈfeɪt] *n* **1** DESTINY : destin *m*, sort *m* **2** OUTCOME : sort *m* <a fate worse than death : un sort pire que la mort>
fated [ˈfeɪṭəd] *adj* : destiné
fateful [ˈfeɪtfəl] *adj* : fatidique
father[1] [ˈfɑðər] *vt* **1** BEGET : engendrer **2** : créer, inventer (un projet, etc.)
father[2] *n* **1** PARENT : père *m* **2** ANCESTOR : père *m*, ancêtre *m* **3** FOUNDER : père *m*, fondateur *m* **4** PRIEST : père *m* <Father Brown : le père Brown> **5 Father** GOD : Père *m*, Dieu *m*
fatherhood [ˈfɑðərˌhʊd] *n* : paternité *f*
father–in–law [ˈfɑðərɪnˌlɔ] *n, pl* **fathers–in–law** : beau-père *m*
fatherland [ˈfɑðərˌlænd] *n* : patrie *f*
fatherless [ˈfɑðərləs] *adj* : sans père
fatherly [ˈfɑðərli] *adj* : paternel
fathom[1] [ˈfæðəm] *vt* **1** SOUND : sonder **2** PENETRATE, UNDERSTAND : sonder, pénétrer, comprendre
fathom[2] *n* : brasse *f*
fatigue[1] [fəˈtiːg] *vt* **-tigued; -tiguing** : fatiguer, épuiser
fatigue[2] *n* : fatigue *f*, épuisement *m*
fatness [ˈfætnəs] *n* : corpulence *f*, embonpoint *m*
fatten [ˈfætən] *vt* : engraisser (un animal)
fatty [ˈfæti] *adj* **fattier; -est** : gras (se dit de la viande, etc.), graisseux (se dit d'un tissu)
fatuous [ˈfætʃʊəs] *adj* : imbécile, stupide, niais
fatuously [ˈfætʃʊəsli] *adv* : niaisement, bêtement
faucet [ˈfɔsət] *n* : robinet *m*, champlure *f Can*
fault[1] [ˈfɔlt] *vt* : trouver des défauts à, critiquer
fault[2] *n* **1** FLAW : défaut *m*, imperfection *f* **2** SHORTCOMING : défaut *m*, faiblesse *f* **3** RESPONSIBILITY : faute *f* <it's my fault : c'est de ma faute> **4** MISTAKE : erreur *f* **5** : faille *f* (géologique)
faultfinder [ˈfɔltˌfaɪndər] *n* : critiqueur *m*, -queuse *f*
faultfinding [ˈfɔltˌfaɪndɪŋ] *n* : critiques *fpl*
faultless [ˈfɔltləs] *adj* : irréprochable, impeccable
faultlessly [ˈfɔltləsli] *adv* : parfaitement, impeccablement
faulty [ˈfɔlti] *adj* **faultier; -est** : fautif, défectueux
fauna [ˈfɔnə] *n* : faune *f*
faux pas [ˌfoːˈpɑ] *ns & pl* : faux pas *m*, gaffe *f*
favor[1] *or Brit* **favour** [ˈfeɪvər] *vt* **1** SUPPORT : favoriser, être partisan de, appuyer **2** OBLIGE : rendre un service à **3** PREFER : favoriser, préférer **4** RESEMBLE : ressembler à
favor[2] *or Brit* **favour** *n* **1** APPROVAL : faveur *f*, approbation *f* **2** PARTIALITY : faveur *f*, partialité *f* **3** : service *m*, faveur *f* <can you do me a favor? : peux-tu me rendre un service?> **4 to be in favor of** : être pour
favorable *or Brit* **favourable** [ˈfeɪvərəbəl] *adj* : favorable **— favorably** *or Brit* **favourably** [-rəbli] *adv*
favorite[1] *or Brit* **favourite** [ˈfeɪvərət] *adj* : favori, préféré
favorite[2] *or Brit* **favourite** *n* : favori *m*, -rite *f*; préféré *m*, -rée *f*
favoritism *or Brit* **favouritism** [ˈfeɪvərəˌtɪzəm] *n* : favoritisme *m*
favour *Brit* → **favor**
favourite *Brit* → **favorite**
fawn[1] [ˈfɔn] *vi* **to fawn upon** : flatter servilement, faire fête à (se dit d'un chien)
fawn[2] *n* : faon *m*
fax[1] [ˈfæks] *vt* : faxer, envoyer par télécopie
fax[2] *n* : fax *m*, télécopie *f*
faze [ˈfeɪz] *vt* **fazed; fazing** : déconcerter
fear[1] [ˈfɪr] *vt* : craindre, avoir peur de <I fear he won't come : j'ai peur qu'il ne vienne pas> **— *vi* 1** : avoir peur **2 to fear for** : craindre pour
fear[2] *n* : crainte *f*, peur *f*
fearful [ˈfɪrfəl] *adj* **1** DREADFUL : affreux **2** AFRAID : craintif, peureux
fearfully [ˈfɪrfəli] *adv* : craintivement, peureusement
fearless [ˈfɪrləs] *adj* : intrépide, sans peur
fearlessly [ˈfɪrləsli] *adv* : avec intrépidité
fearlessness [ˈfɪrləsnəs] *n* : intrépidité *f*
fearsome [ˈfɪrsəm] *adj* **1** FRIGHTENING : effrayant **2** FORMIDABLE : redoutable
feasibility [ˈfiːzəˈbɪləṭi] *n* : faisabilité *f*, possibilité *f*
feasible [ˌfiːzəbəl] *adj* : faisable, possible, réalisable
feast[1] [ˈfiːst] *vt* **1** : donner un banquet en l'honneur de **2 to feast one's eyes on** : se délecter à regarder **— *vi* 1** : festoyer **2 to feast on** : se régaler de
feast[2] *n* **1** BANQUET : banquet *m*, festin *m* **2** FESTIVAL : fête *f* religieuse
feat [ˈfiːt] *n* : exploit *m*, prouesse *f*
feather[1] [ˈfeðər] *vt* **1** : empenner, couvrir de plumes **2 to feather one's nest** : s'enrichir
feather[2] *n* : plume *f* (d'oiseau), penne *f* (de flèche)
feathered [ˈfeðərd] *adj* : à plumes

feathery ['feðəri] *adj* : duveteux, doux et léger comme la plume
feature[1] ['fi:tʃər] *vt* : mettre en vedette (une personne), faire figurer (des nouvelles, etc.) — *vi* : figurer
feature[2] *n* **1** : trait *m* (du visage) **2** CHARACTERISTIC : caractéristique *f*, trait *m*, particularité *f* **3** : article *m* de fond (en journalisme) **4** *or* **feature film** : long métrage *m*
February ['febjuˌeri, 'febə-, 'febrə-] *n* : février *m*
fecal ['fi:kəl] *adj* : fécal
feces ['fi:ˌsi:z] *npl* : fèces *fpl*
feckless ['fekləs] *adj* **1** IRRESPONSIBLE : irresponsable **2** INEFFECTUAL : inepte, incapable
fecund ['fekənd, 'fi:-] *adj* : fécond
fecundity [fi'kʌndəṭi, fe-] *n* : fécondité *f*
federal ['fedrəl, -dərəl] *adj* : fédéral
federalism ['fedrəˌlɪzəm, -dərə-] *n* : fédéralisme *m*
federalist[1] ['fedrəlɪst, -dərə-] *adj* : fédéraliste
federalist[2] *n* : fédéraliste *mf*
federate ['fedəˌreiṭ] *vt* **-ated; -ating** : fédérer
federation [ˌfedə'reiʃən] *n* : fédération *f*
fed up *adj* **to be fed up** : en avoir assez, en avoir marre *fam*
fee ['fi:] *n* **1** : frais *mpl* (de scolarité), honoraires *mpl* (médicaux), cachet *m* (d'un artiste, etc.) **2** *or* **entrance fee** : droit *m* d'entrée
feeble ['fi:bəl] *adj* **-bler; -blest 1** FRAIL : faible, frêle **2** INADEQUATE, POOR : pauvre, piètre <a feeble excuse : une piètre excuse>
feebleminded [ˌfi:bəl'maɪndəd] *adj* : faible d'esprit
feeblemindedness [ˌfi:bəl'maɪndədnəs] *n* : faiblesse *f* d'esprit
feebleness ['fi:bəlnəs] *n* : faiblesse *f*
feebly ['fi:bli] *adv* **1** WEAKLY : faiblement **2** : sans grande conviction
feed[1] ['fi:d] *v* **fed** ['fed]; **feeding** *vt* **1** : nourrir, donner à manger à <to feed a child : nourrir un enfant> **2** : alimenter (une machine, un feu, etc.) — *vi* EAT : manger, se nourrir
feed[2] *n* **1** NOURISHMENT : nourriture *f* **2** FODDER : fourrage *m*
feel[1] ['fi:l] *v* **felt** ['felt]; **feeling** *vt* **1** TOUCH : toucher, tâter, palper **2** SENSE : sentir **3** EXPERIENCE : éprouver, ressentir (un sentiment) **4** BELIEVE : avoir l'impression que, estimer que **5 to feel out** : sonder (une personne) — *vi* **1** : se sentir <I feel much better : je me sens beaucoup mieux> **2** SEEM : sembler, donner l'impression **3 to feel like** : avoir envie de
feel[2] *n* **1** TOUCH : toucher *m* <soft to the feel : doux au toucher> **2** FEELING, SENSATION : sensation *f* **3** KNACK : facilité *f* <a feel for learning : une facilité d'apprentissage>
feeler ['fi:lər] *n* : antenne *f* (d'un insecte)
feeling ['fi:lɪŋ] *n* **1** TOUCH : toucher *m* **2** SENSATION : sensation *f* **3** SENSE : sentiment *m*, impression *f* **4** BELIEF : opinion *f*, sentiment *m* **5 feelings** *npl* : sentiments *mpl*, sensibilité *f* <to hurt s.o.'s feelings : blesser qqn, faire de la peine à qqn>
feet → foot
feign ['feɪn] *vt* : feindre, simuler
feint[1] ['feɪnt] *vi* : feinter
feint[2] *n* : feinte *f*
felicitate [fi'lɪsəˌteɪt] *vt* **-tated; -tating** : féliciter, congratuler
felicitation [fiˌlɪsə'teɪʃən] *n* : félicitation *f*
felicitous [fi'lɪsəṭəs] *adj* : heureux
felicity [fi'lɪsəṭi] *n, pl* **-ties 1** HAPPINESS : félicité *f* **2** APPROPRIATENESS : justesse *f* (d'une expression, etc.)
feline[1] ['fi:ˌlaɪn] *adj* : félin
feline[2] *n* : félin *m*
fell[1] ['fel] *vt* **1** : abattre, bûcher *Can* (des arbres) **2** : assommer (des personnes)
fell[2] **→ fall**[1]
fellow ['feˌlo:] *n* **1** COMPANION : camarade *mf*; compagnon *m*, compagne *f* **2** EQUAL, PEER : semblable *m*, pair *m* **3** COLLEAGUE : confrère *m* **4** BOY, MAN : gars *m fam*, type *m fam*
fellowman [ˌfelo'mæn] *n, pl* **-men** [-mən, -men] : prochain *m*
fellowship ['felo,ʃɪp] *n* **1** COMPANIONSHIP : camaraderie *f* **2** ASSOCIATION : association *f* **3** GRANT : bourse *f* universitaire
felon ['felən] *n* : criminel *m*, -nelle *f*
felonious [fə'lo:niəs] *adj* : criminel
felony ['felənɪ] *n, pl* **-nies** : crime *m*
felt[1] ['felt] *n* : feutre *m*
felt[2] **→ feel**[1]
female[1] ['fi:ˌmeɪl] *adj* : femelle (se dit des animaux et des plantes), féminin (se dit des personnes)
female[2] *n* **1** : femelle *f* (animal ou plante) **2** GIRL, WOMAN : femme *f*, fille *f*
feminine ['femənən] *adj* : féminin
femininity [ˌfemə'nɪnəṭi] *n* : féminité *f*
feminism ['femə,nɪzəm] *n* : féminisme *m*
feminist[1] ['femənɪst] *adj* : féministe
feminist[2] *n* : féministe *mf*
femoral ['femərəl] *adj* : fémoral
femur ['fi:mər] *n, pl* **femurs** *or* **femora** ['femərə] : fémur *m*
fence[1] ['fens] *v* **fenced; fencing** *vt* ENCLOSE : clôturer, entourer d'une clôture — *vi* : faire de l'escrime (aux sports)
fence[2] *n* : clôture *f*, barrière *f*
fencer ['fensər] *n* : escrimeur *m*, -meuse *f*

fencing [ˈfenʧɪŋ] *n* **1** : escrime *f* (sport) **2** : matériaux *mpl* pour clôture **3** FENCES : clôture *f*, barrière *f*
fend [ˈfend] *vt or* **to fend off** : parer (un coup), détourner (une attaque), éluder (une question) — *vi* **to fend for oneself** : se débrouiller tout seul
fender [ˈfendər] *n* : aile *f* (d'une voiture)
fennel [ˈfenəl] *n* : fenouil *m*
ferment[1] [fərˈment] *vi* : fermenter
ferment[2] [ˈfər,ment] *n* **1** : ferment *m* (en chimie) **2** TURMOIL : agitation *f*, effervescence *f*
fermentation [,fərmənˈteɪʃən, -,mɛn-] *n* : fermentation *f*
fern [ˈfərn] *n* : fougère *f*
ferocious [fəˈroːʃəs] *adj* : féroce — **ferociously** *adv*
ferociousness [fəˈroːʃəsnəs] *n* : férocité *f*
ferocity [fəˈrɑsəṭi] *n* : férocité *f*
ferret[1] [ˈferət] *vi* **to ferret out** : découvrir, dénicher — *vi* DELVE, RUMMAGE : fureter, fouiller
ferret[2] *n* : furet *m*
ferric [ˈferɪk] *or* **ferrous** [ˈferəs] *adj* : ferrique, ferreux
Ferris wheel [ˈferɪs] *n* : grande roue *f*
ferry[1] [ˈferi] *vt* **-ried; -rying** : transporter, faire passer (en bac, par avion, etc.)
ferry[2] *n, pl* **-ries** : bac *m*, ferry-boat *m*, traversier *m Can*
ferryboat [ˈferi,boːt] → **ferry**[2]
fertile [ˈfərṭəl] *adj* : fertile, fécond
fertility [fərˈtɪləṭi] *n* : fertilité *f*, fécondité *f*
fertilization [,fərṭələˈzeɪʃən] *n* : fertilisation *f*, fécondation *f*
fertilize [ˈfərṭəl,aɪz] *vt* **-ized; -izing** : fertiliser (une terre), féconder (un œuf, etc.)
fertilizer [ˈfərṭəl,aɪzər] *n* : engrais *m*
fervent [ˈfərvənt] *adj* : fervent, ardent
fervently [ˈfərvəntli] *adv* : avec ferveur
fervid [ˈfərvɪd] *adj* IMPASSIONED : passionné
fervor *or Brit* **fervour** [ˈfərvər] *n* : ferveur *f*, ardeur *f*
fester [ˈfestər] *vi* : suppurer
festival [ˈfestəvəl] *n* **1** FEAST : fête *f* (religieuse) **2** : festival *m* <a dance festival : un festival de danse>
festive [ˈfestɪv] *adj* : joyeux, de fête
festivity [fesˈtɪvəṭi] *n, pl* **-ties 1** MERRIMENT : réjouissance *f* **2 festivities** *npl* : réjouissances *fpl*, festivités *fpl*
festoon[1] [fesˈtuːn] *vt* : festonner, orner de festons
festoon[2] *n* : feston *m*, guirlande *f*
fetal [ˈfiːṭəl] *adj* : fœtal
fetch [ˈfeʧ] *vt* **1** BRING : aller chercher, apporter **2** REALIZE : rapporter (de l'argent), atteindre (un prix)
fetching [ˈfeʧɪŋ] *adj* : attrayant, charmant
fete[1] *or* **fête** [ˈfeɪt, ˈfet] *vt* **feted** *or* **fêted; feting** *or* **fêting** : fêter
fete[2] *or* **fête** *n* : fête *f*
fetid [ˈfeṭəd] *adj* : fétide
fetish [ˈfeṭɪʃ] *n* : fétiche *m*
fetlock [ˈfeṭ,lɑk] *n* : boulet *m* (d'un cheval)
fetter [ˈfeṭər] *vt* **1** SHACKLE : enchaîner, entraver (un animal) **2** HAMPER : entraver
fetters [ˈfeṭərz] *npl* : fers *mpl*, chaînes *fpl*, entraves *fpl* (d'un animal)
fettle [ˈfeṭəl] *n* **in fine fettle** : en pleine forme, en bonne condition
fetus [ˈfiːṭəs] *n* : fœtus *m*
feud[1] [ˈfjuːd] *vi* : se quereller, se disputer
feud[2] *n* : querelle *f*, vendetta *f* <a family feud : une querelle familiale>
feudal [ˈfjuːdəl] *adj* : féodal
feudalism [ˈfjuːdəl,ɪzəm] *n* : féodalisme *m*
fever [ˈfiːvər] *n* : fièvre *f*, température *f*
feverish [ˈfiːvərɪʃ] *adj* : fiévreux, fébrile — **feverishly** *adv*
few[1] [ˈfjuː] *adj* **1** : peu de <we have few friends : nous avons peu d'amis> **2 a few** : quelques <in a few minutes : dans quelques minutes>
few[2] *pron* : peu, quelques-uns, quelques-unes <few remember him : peu se souviennent de lui> <a few of them : quelques-unes d'entre elles> <quite a few : un assez grand nombre de>
fewer[1] [ˈfjuːər] *adj* : moins de <no fewer than : pas moins de>
fewer[2] *pron* : moins <the fewer the better : le moins possible>
fez [ˈfɛz] *n, pl* **fezzes** : fez *m*
fiancé [,fiːˌɑnˈseɪ, ,fiːˌɑnˌseɪ] *n* : fiancé *m*
fiancée [,fiːˌɑnˈseɪ, ,fiːˌɑnˌseɪ] *n* : fiancée *f*
fiasco [fiˈæs,koː] *n, pl* **-coes** : fiasco *m*
fiat [ˈfiːˌɑt, -ˌæt, -ˌɔt; ˈfaɪət, -ˌæt] *n* : décret *m*
fib[1] [ˈfɪb] *vi* **fibbed; fibbing** : blaguer *fam*, raconter des histoires
fib[2] *n* : blague *f fam*; bobard *m fam*, menterie *f Can fam*
fibber [ˈfɪbər] *n* : blagueur *m*, -gueuse *f fam*
fiber *or* **fibre** [ˈfaɪbər] *n* : fibre *f*
fiberboard [ˈfaɪbər,bɔrd] *n* : panneau *m* fibreux
fiberglass [ˈfaɪbər,glæs] *n* : fibre *f* de verre
fibrillation [,fɪbrəˈleɪʃən] *n* : fibrillation *f*
fibrous [ˈfaɪbrəs] *adj* : fibreux
fibula [ˈfɪbjələ] *n, pl* **-lae** [-,liː, -,laɪ] *or* **-las** : péroné *m*
fickle [ˈfɪkəl] *adj* : volage, inconstant
fickleness [ˈfɪkəlnəs] *n* : inconstance *f*
fiction [ˈfɪkʃən] *n* **1** : fiction *f*, invention *f* <truth is stranger than fiction : la réalité dépasse la fiction> **2** *or* **works of fiction** : romans *mpl*, œuvres *fpl* de fiction
fictional [ˈfɪkʃənəl] *adj* : fictif — **fictionally** *adv*

fictitious [fɪkˈtɪʃəs] *adj* : fictif, imaginaire
fiddle[1] [ˈfɪdəl] *vi* **-dled; -dling 1** : jouer du violon **2 to fiddle with** : tripoter, bricoler, jouer avec
fiddle[2] *n* : violon *m*
fiddler [ˈfɪdlər, ˈfɪdələr] *n* : joueur *m* de violon, joueuse *f* de violon
fiddlesticks [ˈfɪdəlˌstɪks] *interj* : flûte alors!, quelle blague!
fidelity [fəˈdɛləṭi, faɪ-] *n, pl* **-ties 1** LOYALTY : fidélité *f*, loyauté *f* **2** ACCURACY : exactitude *f*, fidélité *f*
fidget[1] [ˈfɪdʒət] *vi* : remuer, s'agiter, gigoter *fam*
fidget[2] *n* **to have the fidgets** : ne pas tenir en place
fidgety [ˈfɪdʒəṭi] *adj* : remuant, agité
fiduciary[1] [fəˈduːʃiˌɛri, -ˈdjuː-, -ʃəri] *adj* : fiduciaire
fiduciary[2] *n, pl* **-ries** : fiduciaire *mf*
field[1] [ˈfiːld] *vt* **1** : attraper (une balle), faire jouer (une équipe) **2** : répondre à (des questions, etc.)
field[2] *adj* : de campagne <field artillery : artillerie de campagne>
field[3] [ˈfiːld] *n* **1** : champ *m* (de cultures, de bataille) **2** : domaine *m*, sphère *f* <the field of science : le domaine de la science> **3** : terrain *m* (de sport) **4** : champ *m* <magnetic field : champ magnétique> <field of vision : champ de vision>
field day *n* **1** : grande occasion *f* **2 to have a field day** : s'en donner à cœur joie
fielder [ˈfiːldər] *n* : joueur *m* de champ (au baseball)
field glasses *npl* : jumelles *fpl*
field goal *n* : placement *m*
field hockey *n* : hockey *m* sur gazon
field test : essai *m* sur le terrain
field trip : sortie *f* éducative
fiend [ˈfiːnd] *n* **1** DEMON, DEVIL : diable *m*, démon *m* **2** EVILDOER : monstre *m* **3** FANATIC : mordu *m*, -due *f fam* **4** ADDICT : toxicomane *mf*
fiendish [ˈfiːndɪʃ] *adj* : diabolique — **fiendishly** *adv*
fierce [ˈfɪrs] *adj* **fiercer; -est 1** FEROCIOUS : féroce, sauvage **2** HEATED : virulent **3** INTENSE : intense, acharné, violent
fiercely [ˈfɪrsli] *adv* : férocement, violemment, avec acharnement
fierceness [ˈfɪrsnəs] *n* **1** : férocité *f* (d'un animal) **2** INTENSITY : fureur *f* (d'un orage), violence *f* (d'un combat, etc.)
fieriness [ˈfaɪərinəs] *n* : ardeur *f*, fougue *f*
fiery [ˈfaɪəri] *adj* **fierier; -est 1** BURNING : brûlant, ardent **2** RED : rougeoyant **3** ARDENT, SPIRITED : fougueux, ardent
fiesta [fiˈestə] *n* : fête *f*
fife [ˈfaɪf] *n* : fifre *m*
fifteen[1] [fɪfˈtiːn] *adj* : quinze
fifteen[2] *n* : quinze *m*
fifteenth[1] [fɪfˈtiːnθ] *adj* : quinzième
fifteenth[2] *n* **1** : quinzième *mf* (dans une série) **2** : quinzième *m* (en mathématiques) **3** (*used in dates*) <the fifteenth of August : le quinze août>
fifth[1] [ˈfɪfθ] *adj* : cinquième
fifth[2] *n* **1** : cinquième *mf* (dans une série) **2** : cinquième *m* (en mathématiques) **3** (*used in dates*) <the fifth of September : le cinq septembre>
fiftieth[1] [ˈfɪfṭiəθ] *adj* : cinquantième
fiftieth[2] *n* **1** : cinquantième *mf* (dans une série) **2** : cinquantième *m* (en mathématiques)
fifty[1] [ˈfɪfṭi] *adj* : cinquante
fifty[2] *n, pl* **-ties 1** : cinquante *m* **2 fifties** *npl* : cinquantaine *f* <she's in her fifties : elle est dans la cinquantaine>
fifty–fifty[1] [ˌfɪfṭiˈfɪfṭi] *adv* : moitié-moitié <to go fifty-fifty : faire moitié-moitié>
fifty–fifty[2] *adj* **to have a fifty–fifty chance** : avoir une chance sur deux
fig [ˈfɪg] *n* : figue *f*
fight[1] [ˈfaɪt] *v* **fought** [ˈfɔṭ]; **fighting** *vt* **1** : se battre avec, combattre (un ennemi) **2** : lutter contre, combattre (une maladie, un incendie, etc.) — *vi* **1** : combattre **2** QUARREL : se quereller, se disputer
fight[2] *n* **1** BATTLE, BRAWL : combat *m*, bataille *f*, bagarre *f* **2** MATCH : combat *m* (de boxe) **3** STRUGGLE : lutte *f* <the fight against cancer : la lutte contre le cancer> **4** QUARREL : querelle *f*, dispute *f* <to pick a fight with : chercher querelle à>
fighter [ˈfaɪṭər] *n* **1** COMBATANT : combattant *m*, -tante *f*; lutteur *m*, -teuse *f* **2** BOXER : boxeur *m* **3** *or* **fighter plane** : avion *m* de chasse
figment [ˈfɪgmənṭ] *n* **figment of the imagination** : produit *m* de l'imagination
figurative [ˈfɪgjərəṭɪv, -gə-] *adj* : figuré, métaphorique
figuratively [ˈfɪgjərəṭɪvli, -gə-] *adv* : au sens figuré
figure[1] [ˈfɪgjər, -gər] *v* **-ured; -uring** *vt* **1** REPRESENT : représenter, illustrer **2** CONCLUDE, THINK : penser, supposer **3** CALCULATE, COMPUTE : calculer — *vi* **1** APPEAR : figurer **2 that figures!** : ça se comprend!, ça se tient!
figure[2] *n* **1** NUMERAL : chiffre *m* **2** PRICE : prix *m* **3** FORM, OUTLINE : forme *f*, silhouette *f* **4** : ligne *f* <to watch one's figure : surveiller sa ligne> **5** ILLUSTRATION : figure *f*, image *f* **6** PATTERN : motif *m* **7** PERSONAGE : figure *f*, personnage *m* **8 figures** *npl* : calcul *m* <he's good at figures : il est bon en calcul>
figurehead [ˈfɪgjərˌhɛd, -gər-] *n* **1** : homme *m* de paille **2** : figure *f* de proue (d'un navire)

figure of speech *n* : figure *f* de rhétorique, façon *f* de parler
figure out *vt* **1** UNDERSTAND : arriver à comprendre **2** SOLVE : calculer (une somme), résoudre (un problème)
figurine [ˌfɪgjəˈriːn] *n* : figurine *f*
Fijian[1] [ˈfiːdʒiən, fiˈjiːən] *adj* : fidjien
Fijian[2] *n* **1** : Fidjien *m*, -jienne *f* **2** : fidjien *m* (langue)
filament [ˈfɪləmənt] *n* : filament *m*
filbert [ˈfɪlbərt] *n* : aveline *f*
filch [ˈfɪltʃ] *vt* : chiper *fam*, piquer *fam*, voler
file[1] [ˈfaɪl] *v* **filed; filing** *vt* **1** CLASSIFY : classer, ranger **2** : déposer (une plainte), intenter (un procès) **3** : limer (ses ongles, etc.) — *vi* **1** : marcher en file <to file past : défiler devant> **2 to file for** : demander (un divorce, etc.)
file[2] *n* **1** : lime *f* (outil) **2** FOLDER : dossier *m* **3** *or* **file cabinet** : classeur *m* **4** RECORD : dossier *m* **5** : fichier *m* (en informatique) **6** LINE : file *f* <in single file : en file>
filial [ˈfɪliəl, ˈfɪljəl] *adj* : filial
filibuster[1] [ˈfɪləˌbʌstər] *vi* : faire de l'obstruction parlementaire
filibuster[2] *n* : obstruction *f* parlementaire
filigree [ˈfɪləˌgriː] *n* : filigrane *m*
Filipino[1] [ˌfɪləˈpiːnoː] *adj* : philippin
Filipino[2] *n* : Philippin *m*, -pine *f*
fill[1] [ˈfɪl] *vt* **1** : remplir <to fill a cup : remplir une tasse> <tears filled her eyes : ses yeux se remplissaient de larmes> **2** PLUG : boucher (un trou), plomber (une dent) **3** SATIATE : rassasier **4** *or* **to fill out** COMPLETE : remplir <to fill out a form : remplir un formulaire> **5** HOLD : prendre, occuper (un poste) **6** SATISFY : remplir, pourvoir à — *vi* : se remplir
fill[2] *n* **1** FILLING : remplissage *m* **2 to eat one's fill** : se rassasier **3 to have had one's fill of** : en avoir assez de
filler [ˈfɪlər] *n* : remplissage *m*
fillet[1] [fɪˈleɪ, ˈfɪˌleɪ, ˈfɪlət] *vt* : découper en filets
fillet[2] *n* : filet *m*
fill in *vt* INFORM : mettre au courant — *vi* **to fill in for** : remplacer
filling [ˈfɪlɪŋ] *n* **1** : plombage *m* (d'une dent), obturation *f* dentaire **2** : garniture *f* (d'une tarte, etc.)
filling station → **service station**
filly [ˈfɪli] *n, pl* **-lies** : pouliche *f*
film[1] [ˈfɪlm] *vt* : filmer, tourner (une scène) — *vi* **1** FILM : tourner **2** *or* **to film over** : s'embuer, se voiler
film[2] *n* **1** : pellicule *f* (en photographie) **2** COATING : couche *f*, pellicule *f* **3** MOTION PICTURE : film *m*
filmstrip [ˈfɪlmˌstrɪp] *n* : film *m* fixe
filmy [ˈfɪlmi] *adj* **filmier; -est 1** HAZY : embué, voilé **2** GAUZY : léger, transparent
filter[1] [ˈfɪltər] *v* : filtrer
filter[2] *n* : filtre *m*
filth [ˈfɪlθ] *n* **1** DIRT : saleté *f*, crasse *f* **2** OBSCENITY : obscénités *fpl*
filthiness [ˈfɪlθinəs] *n* : saleté *f*
filthy [ˈfɪlθi] *adj* **filthier; -est 1** DIRTY : sale, crasseux **2** VILE : dégoûtant **3** OBSCENE : obscène, ordurier
filtration [fɪlˈtreɪʃən] *n* : filtration *f*
fin [ˈfɪn] *n* **1** : nageoire *f* (d'un poisson), aileron *m* (d'un requin) **2** : aileron *m*, empennage *m* (d'un avion)
finagle [fəˈneɪgəl] *vt* **-gled; -gling** : obtenir par des moyens subreptices, se débrouiller pour obtenir
final[1] [ˈfaɪnəl] *adj* **1** CONCLUSIVE : définitif, irrévocable **2** LAST : dernier **3** ULTIMATE : ultime, final <our final goal : notre but ultime>
final[2] *n* **1** : finale *f* (d'une compétition) **2 finals** *npl* : examens *mpl* de fin de semestre
finale [fɪˈnæli, -ˈnɑ-] *n* **1** : finale *m* **2 grand finale** : apothéose *f*
finalist [ˈfaɪnəlɪst] *n* : finaliste *mf*
finality [faɪˈnæləti, fə-] *n, pl* **-ties** : irrévocabilité *f*
finalize [ˈfaɪnəlˌaɪz] *vt* **-ized; -izing** : mettre au point
finally [ˈfaɪnəli] *adv* : enfin, finalement
finance[1] [fəˈnænts, ˈfaɪˌnænts] *vt* **-nanced; -nancing** : financer
finance[2] *n* **1** : finance *f* <high finance : la haute finance> **2 finances** *npl* RESOURCES : finances *fpl*
financial [fəˈnænʃəl, faɪ-] *adj* : financier
financially [fəˈnænʃəli, faɪ-] *adv* : financièrement
financier [ˌfɪnənˈsɪr, ˌfaɪˌnæn-] *n* : financier *m*
finch [ˈfɪntʃ] *n* : fringillidé *m*
find[1] [ˈfaɪnd] *v* **found** [ˈfaʊnd]; **finding** *vt* **1** LOCATE : trouver, rencontrer, retrouver <I can't find it : je ne peux pas le trouver> <to find one's voice : retrouver sa voix> <to find its mark : atteindre sa cible> **2** DISCOVER, REALIZE : trouver, découvrir, s'apercevoir <I find it difficult : je trouve que c'est difficile> **3** DECLARE : déclarer, prononcer <to find s.o. guilty : prononcer qqn coupable> — *vi* : prononcer <to find for the accused : prononcer en faveur de l'accusé>
find[2] *n* : découverte *f*, trouvaille *f*
finder [ˈfaɪndər] *n* **1** : celui *m*, celle *f* qui trouve **2** : chercheur *m* (de télescope, etc.)
finding [ˈfaɪndɪŋ] *n* **1** FIND : découverte *f* **2** VERDICT : verdict *m* (en droit) **3 findings** *npl* : conclusions *fpl*
find out *vt* DISCOVER : découvrir — *vi* **to find out about** : se renseigner sur
fine[1] [ˈfaɪn] *vt* **fined; fining** : infliger une amende à, condamner à une amende

fine[2] *adv* **1** ALL RIGHT : très bien <I'm doing fine : je vais très bien> **2** FINELY : fin

fine[3] *adj* **finer; -est 1** PURE : pur (se dit de l'or, etc.) **2** DELICATE, THIN : fin <fine hair : cheveux fins> **3** : fin <fine sand : sable fin> **4** SUBTLE : subtil, sensible **5** EXCELLENT : beau, excellent <she did a fine job : elle a fait un beau travail> **6** FAIR : beau <the weather is fine : il fait beau> **7 to be fine** : aller bien <everyone's fine : tout le monde va bien> <that's fine with me : ça me va>

fine[4] *n* : amende *f*, contravention *f*

fine art *n* : beaux-arts *mpl*

finely ['faɪnli] *adv* **1** : finement, fin <to chop finely : hacher finement, hacher menu> **2** EXCELLENTLY : admirablement **3** PRECISELY : avec précision **4** ELEGANTLY : élégamment

fineness ['faɪnnəs] *n* **1** DELICACY : finesse *f* (d'un tissu, etc.) **2** EXCELLENCE : pureté *f* (d'un métal), excellence *f* **3** SUBTLETY : subtilité *f*, délicatesse *f*

finery ['faɪnəri] *n, pl* **-eries** : parure *f*

finesse[1] [fə'nɛs] *vt* **-nessed; -nessing** : manipuler adroitement

finesse[2] *n* : finesse *f*

finger[1] ['fɪŋgər] *vt* HANDLE : toucher, palper, tâter

finger[2] *n* : doigt *m*

fingerling ['fɪŋgərlɪŋ] *n* : petit poisson *m*

fingernail ['fɪŋgər,neɪl] *n* : ongle *m*

fingerprint[1] ['fɪŋgər,prɪnt] *vt* : prendre les empreintes digitales de

fingerprint[2] *n* : empreinte *f* digitale

fingertip ['fɪŋgər,tɪp] *n* : bout *m* du doigt

finicky ['fɪnɪki] *adj* : tatillon, pointilleux

finish[1] ['fɪnɪʃ] *vt* **1** COMPLETE, TERMINATE : terminer, finir, achever **2** : mettre une finition sur (un meuble, un parquet, etc.) — *vi* : finir, se terminer

finish[2] *n* **1** END : fin *f* **2** *or* **finish line** : arrivée *f* **3** : finition *f*, fini *m Can* <a glossy finish : une finition brillante>

finite ['faɪ,naɪt] *adj* : fini, limité

Finn ['fɪn] *n* : Finlandais *m*, -daise *f*

Finnish[1] ['fɪnɪʃ] *adj* : finlandais

Finnish[2] *n* : finnois *m* (langue)

fiord [fi'ɔrd] → **fjord**

fir ['fər] *n* : sapin *m*

fire[1] ['faɪr] *vt* **fired; firing 1** IGNITE : incendier **2** STIR : exciter, enflammer (l'imagination) **3** DISMISS : renvoyer, congédier (un employé) **4** SHOOT : tirer, décharger <to fire a gun : tirer un coup de fusil> **5** : cuire (de la poterie)

fire[2] *n* **1** : feu *m* **2** BURNING : feu *m*, incendie *m* <forest fire : incendie de forêt> **3** ENTHUSIASM : enthousiasme *m*, ardeur *f* **4** SHOOTING : feu *m*, tir *m* <to open fire : ouvrir le feu>

fire alarm *n* : avertisseur *m* d'incendie

firearm ['faɪr,ɑrm] *n* : arme *f* à feu

fireball ['faɪr,bɔl] *n* **1** : boule *f* de feu **2** METEORITE : bolide *m*

firebreak ['faɪr,breɪk] *n* : pare-feu *m*, coupe-feu *m*

firebug ['faɪr,bʌg] *n* : incendiaire *mf*, pyromane *mf*

firecracker ['faɪr,krækər] *n* : pétard *m*

fire escape *n* : escalier *m* de secours

fire extinguisher *n* : extincteur *m*

firefighter ['faɪr,faɪtər] *n* : pompier *m*, sapeur-pompier *m France*

firefly ['faɪr,flaɪ] *n, pl* **-flies** : luciole *f*

fire hall *Brit* → **fire station**

fireman ['faɪrmən] *n, pl* **-men** [-mən, -,men] **1** → **firefighter 2** STOKER : chauffeur *m*

fireplace ['faɪr,pleɪs] *n* : cheminée *f*, foyer *m*

fireplug ['faɪr,plʌg] → **hydrant**

fireproof[1] ['faɪr,pru:f] *vt* : ignifuger

fireproof[2] *adj* : ignifuge, à l'épreuve du feu

fireside[1] ['faɪr,saɪd] *adj* : familier, informel

fireside[2] *n* : coin *m* du feu

fire station *n* : caserne *f* de pompiers *France*, poste *m* de pompiers *Can*

firewood ['faɪr,wʊd] *n* : bois *m* de chauffage

fireworks ['faɪr,wərk] *n* : feux *mpl* d'artifice

firm[1] ['fərm] *vt or* **to firm up** : raffermir (des muscles), confirmer (des plans, etc.)

firm[2] *adj* **1** STRONG : ferme <to have a firm grip on : tenir fermement> **2** HARD, SOLID : ferme <on firm ground : sur la terre ferme> **3** STEADY : solide, stable **4** DEFINITE : solide, déterminé **5** RESOLUTE : ferme, résolu **6** STEADFAST : solide, ferme <a firm friendship : une amitié solide>

firm[3] *n* : entreprise *f*, firme *f*

firmament ['fərməmənt] *n* : firmament *m*

firmly ['fərmli] *adv* : fermement

firmness ['fərmnəs] *n* : fermeté *f*, solidité *f*

first[1] ['fərst] *adv* **1** : en premier, d'abord <first of all : tout d'abord> **2** : pour la première fois <when I first visited France : la première fois que je suis allé en France> **3** RATHER : plutôt <I'd die first : plutôt mourir>

first[2] *adj* : premier <at first sight : à première vue> <I don't know the first thing about physics : je ne connais absolument rien à la physique>

first[3] *n* **1** : premier *m*, -mière *f* (dans une série) **2** (*used in dates*) : premier *m* <the first of July : le premier juillet> **3** *or* **first gear** : première *f* **4 at ~** : au début

first aid *n* : premiers secours *mpl*, premiers soins *mpl*
first–class[1] ['fərst'klæs] *adv* : en première <to travel first-class : voyager en première>
first–class[2] *adj* **1** EXCELLENT : excellent, de première qualité **2** : de première classe (se dit d'une place dans un avion, etc.), à tarif normal (se dit d'une lettre, etc.)
first class *n* : première classe *f*
first lieutenant *n* : lieutenant *m*
firstly ['fərstli] *adv* : premièrement
first–rate[1] ['fərst'reɪt] *adv* : très bien
first–rate[2] *adj* : excellent, de premier ordre
fiscal ['fɪskəl] *adj* : fiscal — **fiscally** *adv*
fish[1] ['fɪʃ] *vi* **1** : pêcher **2 to fish for** SEEK : chercher
fish[2] *n, pl* **fish** *or* **fishes** : poisson *m*
fisherman ['fɪʃərmən] *n, pl* **-men** [-mən, -men] : pêcheur *m*, -cheuse *f*
fishery ['fɪʃəri] *n, pl* **-eries 1 → fishing 2** : pêcherie *f*, zone *f* de pêche
fishhook ['fɪʃˌhʊk] *n* : hameçon *m*
fishing ['fɪʃɪŋ] *n* : pêche *f*
fishy ['fɪʃi] *adj* **fishier; -est 1** : de poisson <a fishy taste : un goût de poisson> **2** QUESTIONABLE : douteux, louche
fission ['fɪʃən, -ʒən] *n* : fission *f*
fissure ['fɪʃər] *n* : fissure *f*
fist [fɪst] *n* : poing *m* <to clench one's fists : serrer les poings>
fistfight ['fɪstˌfaɪt] *n* : coups *mpl* de poing, bagarre *f*
fit[1] ['fɪt] *v* **fitted; fitting** *vt* **1** : aller à <this suit fits you well : ce complet vous va bien> **2** MATCH : répondre à, correspondre à <to fit one's mood : correspondre à son humeur> **3** INSTALL : installer, mettre en place **4** EQUIP : équiper **5 to fit s.o. for** : prendre les mesures de qqn pour (un vêtement) — *vi* **1** : aller, être de la bonne taille <this dress doesn't fit : cette robe n'est pas à ma taille> **2** *or* **to fit in** BELONG : s'intégrer
fit[2] *adj* **fitter; fittest 1** APPROPRIATE, SUITED : convenable, qui convient <to see fit to : trouver bon de> **2** COMPETENT, QUALIFIED : capable, digne **3** HEALTHY : en bonne santé, en (pleine) forme
fit[3] *n* **1** : coupe *f* (d'un vêtement) <it's a tight fit : c'est trop juste> **2** : crise *f*, accès *m* <a fit of anger : un accès de colère>
fitful ['fɪtfəl] *adj* : agité, intermittent
fitfully ['fɪtfəli] *adv* : de manière intermittente
fitness ['fɪtnəs] *n* **1** HEALTH : santé *f*, forme *f* physique **2** SUITABILITY : aptitude *f*, compétences *fpl* (d'une personne), justesse *f* (d'une remarque)
fitting[1] ['fɪtɪŋ] *adj* SUITABLE : approprié, convenable
fitting[2] *n* **1** : essayage *m* (de vêtements) **2** : installation *f* (électrique)
five[1] ['faɪv] *adj* : cinq
five[2] *n* : cinq *m*
fix[1] ['fɪks] *vt* **1** ATTACH, SECURE : fixer, attacher **2** ESTABLISH : fixer <to fix a date : fixer un rendez-vous> **3** FOCUS : fixer **4** REPAIR : réparer **5** PREPARE : préparer **6** : truquer, arranger <to fix a race : truquer une course>
fix[2] *n* **1** PREDICAMENT : pétrin *m fam* **2** : position *f* <to get a fix on : déterminer la position de>
fixate ['fɪkˌseɪt] *vi* **-ated; -ating** : faire une fixation <to be fixated on : être fixé sur>
fixation [fɪk'seɪʃən] *n* : fixation *f*
fixed ['fɪkst] *adj* **1** STATIONARY : fixe, immobile **2** INTENT : fixe <a fixed stare : un regard fixe> **3** SET : constant, fixe <fixed income : revenu fixe> <a fixed idea : une idée arrêtée>
fixedly ['fɪksədli] *adv* : fixement
fixture ['fɪkstʃər] *n* : installation *f* <bathroom fixtures : installations sanitaires>
fizz[1] ['fɪz] *vi* EFFERVESCE : pétiller
fizz[2] *n* : pétillement *m*
fizzle[1] ['fɪzəl] *vi* **-zled; -zling 1** FIZZ : pétiller **2** *or* **to fizzle out** FAIL : échouer, ne rien donner
fizzle[2] *n* FAILURE : échec *m*, fiasco *m*
fjord [fi'ɔrd] *n* : fjord *m*
flabbergast ['flæbərˌgæst] *vt* : sidérer *fam*, stupéfier
flabbiness ['flæbinəs] *n* : flaccidité *f*
flabby ['flæbi] *adj* **flabbier; -est** : flasque
flaccid ['flæksəd, 'flæsəd] *adj* : flasque, mou
flag[1] ['flæg] *v* **flagged; flagging** *vt* SIGNAL : faire signe à (un taxi, etc.) — *vi* DECLINE, WEAKEN : dépérir, languir, faiblir
flag[2] *n* **1** : drapeau *m*, pavillon *m* (d'un navire) **2** *or* **flagstone** : dalle *f*
flagon ['flægən] *n* : cruche *f*, grosse bouteille *f*
flagpole [ˌflægˌpoːl] *n* : mât *m* (de drapeau)
flagrant ['fleɪgrənt] *adj* : flagrant
flagrantly ['fleɪgrəntli] *adv* : d'une manière flagrante
flagship ['flægˌʃɪp] *n* : navire *m* amiral
flagstaff ['flægˌstæf] → **flagpole**
flagstone ['flægˌstoːn] → **flag**[2]
flail[1] ['fleɪl] *vt* **1** : battre (des grains) au fléau **2** : agiter (les bras, etc.)
flail[2] *n* : fléau *m*
flair ['flær] *n* **1** TALENT : aptitude *f*, don *m* **2** STYLE : classe *f*, style *m*
flak ['flæk] *ns & pl* **1** : tir *m* antiaérien **2** CRITICISM : critiques *fpl*
flake[1] ['fleɪk] *v* **flaked; flaking** *vi or* **to flake off** : s'écailler, s'effriter — *vt* : émietter (un poisson, etc.)

flake[2] *n* : flocon *m* (de neige), paillette *f* (de métal, de savon, etc.), écaille *f* (de peinture)
flamboyance [flæm'bɔɪənʦ] *n* : extravagance *f*
flamboyant [flæm'bɔɪənt] *adj* : extravagant, éclatant
flame[1] ['fleɪm] *vi* **flamed; flaming 1** BURN : flamber, brûler **2** BLAZE, GLOW : flamboyer
flame[2] *n* **1** : flamme *f* <to burst into flames : s'embraser> <to go up in flames : s'enflammer> **2** ARDOR : flamme *f*, feu *m*
flamethrower ['fleɪmˌθroːər] *n* : lance-flammes *m*
flaming ['fleɪmɪŋ] *adj* **1** : flamboyant <flaming red hair : cheveux rouges flamboyants> **2** PASSIONATE : ardent
flamingo [flə'mɪŋgoˌ] *n, pl* **-gos** : flamant *m*
flammable ['flæməbəl] *adj* : inflammable
flange ['flændʒ] *n* : bride *f* (d'une pipe), boudin *m* (d'une roue)
flank[1] ['flæŋk] *vt* **1** : flanquer (dans l'armée) **2** BORDER : border, entourer
flank[2] *n* : flanc *m*
flannel ['flænəl] *n* : flanelle *f*
flap[1] ['flæp] *v* **flapped; flapping** *vt* : battre (des ailes) — *vi* : battre, claquer <to flap in the wind : battre au vent>
flap[2] *n* **1** : battement *m* (d'ailes), claquement *m* (d'une voile) **2** : rabat *m* (d'une enveloppe, d'un vêtement, etc.), abattant *m* (d'une table)
flapjack ['flæpˌdʒæk] → **pancake**
flare[1] ['flær] *vi* **flared; flaring 1** FLAME : flamboyer, s'enflammer **2** WIDEN : s'évaser **3 to flare up** : s'emporter, fulminer (contre une personne) **4 to flare up** BREAK OUT, INTENSIFY : s'intensifier, éclater
flare[2] *n* **1** BLAZE : flamboiement *m* **2** SIGNAL : signal *m* lumineux **3** ROCKET : fusée *f* éclairante
flash[1] ['flæʃ] *vt* **1** PROJECT : projeter, diriger <he flashed the light in my eyes : il a dirigé la lumière dans mes yeux> **2** TRANSMIT : transmettre (un message, etc.) **3** SHOW : faire apparaître soudainement **4** : lancer (un sourire), jeter (un regard) — *vi* **1** GLEAM, SPARKLE : étinceler, briller **2** BLINK : clignoter (se dit d'une lumière, d'un signal lumineux) **3 to flash past** : passer comme un éclair
flash[2] *adj* : subit <flash flood : crue subite>
flash[3] *n* **1** : éclair *m* (de génie), éclat *m* (d'un diamant), lueur *f* (d'espoir) **2** INSTANT : minute *f*, instant *m* <I'll be back in a flash : je serai de retour dans un instant> **3** : flash *m* (d'un appareil photographique) **4 flash of lightning** : éclair *m*
flashiness ['flæʃɪnəs] *n* : tape-à-l'œil *m*
flashlight ['flæʃˌlaɪt] *n* : lampe *f* de poche
flashy ['flæʃi] *adj* **flashier; -est** : tape-à-l'œil, tapageur, criard
flask ['flæsk] *n* : flacon *m*, flasque *f*
flat[1] ['flæt] *adv* **1** : à plat, planche *Can* <to lay (down) flat : mettre à plat> <to fall flat : tomber de tout son long> **2** EXACTLY : pile *fam* <in one hour flat : dans une heure pile> **3** : faux, en dessous du ton (en musique) **4 to be flat broke** : être complètement fauché
flat[2] *adj* **flatter; flattest 1** : plat (se dit d'une surface) **2** DOWNRIGHT : net, catégorique <a flat refusal : un refus catégorique> **3** FIXED : fixe <a flat rate : un taux fixe> **4** MONOTONOUS : plat, monotone **5** : éventé (se dit des boissons gazeuses) **6** DEFLATED : crevé, dégonflé **7** : faux (se dit d'une voix), bémol (se dit d'une note)
flat[3] *n* **1** PLAIN : plaine *f* **2** : plat *m* (de la main) **3** : bémol *m* (en musique) **4** *Brit* APARTMENT : appartement *m* **5** *or* **flat tire** : crevaison *f*
flatcar ['flætˌkɑr] *n* : wagon *m* plat
flatfish ['flætˌfɪʃ] *n* : poisson *m* plat
flatly ['flætli] *adv* CATEGORICALLY : carrément, catégoriquement
flatness ['flætnəs] *n* **1** EVENNESS : égalité *f* **2** DULLNESS : monotonie *f*
flat–out ['flætˈaʊt] *adj* OUT-AND-OUT : complet, total, absolu
flatten ['flæt̬ən] *vt* : aplatir, aplanir — *vi or* **to flatten out** : s'aplanir
flatter ['flæt̬ər] *vt* **1** PRAISE : flatter, louer **2** : flatter, avantager <this portrait flatters me : ce portrait me flatte>
flatterer ['flæt̬ərər] *n* : flatteur *m*, -teuse *f*
flattering ['flæt̬ərɪŋ] *adj* : flatteur
flattery ['flæt̬əri] *n, pl* **-ries** : flatterie *f*
flatulence ['flæt̬ʃələnʦ] *n* : flatulence *f*
flatulent ['flæt̬ʃələnt] *adj* : flatulent
flatware ['flætˌwær] *n* : couverts *mpl*
flaunt ['flɔnt] *vt* : faire étalage de, étaler
flavor[1] *or Brit* **flavour** ['fleɪvər] *vt* : assaisonner, relever le goût de
flavor[2] *or Brit* **flavour** *n* **1** : saveur *f*, goût *m* **2** FLAVORING : assaisonnement *m*, arôme *m*, parfum *m* <artificial flavors : arômes artificiels>
flavorful *or Brit* **flavourful** ['fleɪvərfəl] *adj* : savoureux, délectable
flavoring *or Brit* **flavouring** ['fleɪvərɪŋ] *n* : assaisonnement *m*, arôme *m*, parfum *m*
flavorless *or Brit* **flavourless** ['fleɪvərləs] *adj* : sans saveur
flavour *Brit* → **flavor**
flaw ['flɔ] *n* : défaut *m*, imperfection *f*
flawless ['flɔləs] *adj* : sans défaut, parfait
flawlessly ['flɔləsli] *adv* : parfaitement
flax ['flæks] *n* : lin *m*

flaxen ['flæksən] *adj* : de lin
flay ['fleɪ] *vt* **1** SKIN : écorcher (un animal) **2** CRITICIZE : éreinter
flea ['fli:] *n* : puce *f*
fleck[1] ['flek] *vt* : tacheter, moucheter
fleck[2] *n* : petite tache *f*, moucheture *f*
fledgling ['fledʒlɪŋ] *n* : oisillon *m*
flee ['fli:] *v* **fled** ['fled]; **fleeing** *vt* : s'enfuir de, fuir — *vi* : s'enfuir, fuir
fleece[1] ['fli:s] *vt* **fleeced; fleecing 1** SHEAR : tondre **2** SWINDLE : escroquer
fleece[2] *n* : toison *f*
fleecy ['fli:si] *adj* **fleecier; -est** : laineux (se dit d'un tissu), cotonneux (se dit des nuages, etc.)
fleet[1] ['fli:t] *vi* : s'enfuir
fleet[2] *adj* : rapide
fleet[3] *n* : flotte *f* (de navires), parc *m* (de taxis, etc.)
fleet admiral *n* : amiral *m*
fleeting ['fli:tɪŋ] *adj* : bref, éphémère, fugace
Flemish[1] ['flemɪʃ] *adj* : flamand
Flemish[2] *n* **1** : flamand *m* (langue) **2 the Flemish** : les Flamands
flesh ['fleʃ] *n* **1** : chair *f* (d'un animal) **2** : chair *f*, pulpe *f* (d'un fruit)
flesh out *vt* : étoffer, enrichir
fleshly ['fleʃli] *adj* **1** BODILY : corporel **2** CARNAL : charnel, sensuel
fleshy ['fleʃi] *adj* **fleshier; -est** : charnu (se dit des fruits, etc.), bien en chair (se dit des personnes)
flew → **fly**[1]
flex ['fleks] *vt* : faire jouer (des muscles), fléchir (un bras, une jambe, etc.)
flexibility ['fleksə'bɪləti] *n* : flexibilité *f*
flexible ['fleksəbəl] *adj* : flexible, souple — **flexibly** [-bli] *adv*
flick[1] ['flɪk] *vt* **1** STRIKE : donner un petit coup à, donner une chiquenaude à **2 to flick a switch** : appuyer sur un bouton — *vi* **to flick through** : feuilleter (un livre, etc.)
flick[2] *n* : petit coup *m*, chiquenaude *f*
flicker[1] ['flɪkər] *vi* **1** FLUTTER : cligner, battre **2** : vaciller, trembloter <a flickering flame : une flamme qui vacille>
flicker[2] *n* **1** : clignement *m*, battement *m* (d'une paupière) **2** GLIMMER : lueur *f* <a flicker of hope : une lueur d'espoir> **3** : vacillement *m* (d'une flamme)
flier ['flaɪər] *n* **1** PILOT : aviateur *m*, -trice *f* **2** *or* **flyer** LEAFLET : prospectus *m*
flight ['flaɪt] *n* **1** FLYING : vol *m* (d'un oiseau, d'un avion), trajectoire *f* (d'un projectile) **2** GROUP : volée *f* (d'oiseaux), escadrille *f* (d'avions) **3** ESCAPE : fuite *f* **4 flight of fancy** : élan *m* de l'imagination **5 flight of stairs** : escalier *m*
flightless ['flaɪtləs] *adj* : coureur <flightless birds : oiseaux coureux>
flighty ['flaɪti] *adj* **flightier; -est** : volage, inconstant
flimsiness ['flɪmzinəs] *n* : fragilité *f*, construction *f* peu solide
flimsy ['flɪmzi] *adj* **flimsier; -est 1** LIGHT, THIN : fin, léger **2** WEAK : fragile, peu solide **3** IMPLAUSIBLE : pauvre, mince <a flimsy excuse : une pauvre excuse>
flinch ['flɪntʃ] *vi* **1** WINCE : tressaillir **2** RECOIL : reculer, fuir
fling[1] ['flɪŋ] *vt* **flung** ['flʌŋ]; **flinging 1** THROW : jeter, lancer, flanquer *fam* **2 to fling oneself** : se lancer, se jeter
fling[2] *n* **1** THROW : jet *m*, lancer *m* **2** ATTEMPT : essai *m* <to have a fling at sth : essayer de faire qqch> **3** AFFAIR : aventure *f*
flint ['flɪnt] *n* : silex *m*
flinty ['flɪnti] *adj* **flintier; -est 1** : à silex **2** STERN, UNYIELDING : dur, de pierre
flip[1] ['flɪp] *v* **flipped; flipping** *vt* **1** TOSS : lancer **2** FLICK : appuyer sur (un bouton) **3 to flip a coin** : jouer à pile ou face — *vi* **1** *or* **to flip over** : se retourner **2 to flip through** : feuilleter (un livre, etc.)
flip[2] *adj* : désinvolte, impertinent
flip[3] *n* **1** FLICK : petit coup *m* **2** SOMERSAULT : saut *m* périlleux
flippancy ['flɪpənʧsi] *n, pl* **-cies** : désinvolture *f*, impertinence *f*
flippant ['flɪpənt] *adj* : désinvolte
flipper ['flɪpər] *n* : nageoire *f*
flirt[1] ['flərt] *vi* : flirter
flirt[2] *n* : charmeur *m*, -meuse *f*; personne *f* qui flirte
flirtation [,flər'teɪʃən] *n* : flirt *m*
flirtatious [,flər'teɪʃəs] *adj* : charmeur, séducteur
flit ['flɪt] *vi* **flitted; flitting 1** : voleter, voltiger **2 to flit about** : passer rapidement
float[1] ['flo:t] *vt* **1** : faire flotter **2** ISSUE : émettre, lancer (en finances) <to float a loan : émettre un emprunt> — *vi* : flotter
float[2] *n* **1** RAFT : radeau *m* **2** CORK : flotteur *m*, bouchon *m* **3** : char *m* (de carnaval)
flock[1] ['flak] *vi* : affluer, se rassembler
flock[2] *n* **1** : volée *f* (d'oiseaux), troupeau *m* (de moutons) **2** CROWD : foule *f* **3** : ouailles *fpl* (en religion)
floe ['flo:] *n or* **ice floe** : banquise *f*
flog ['flag] *vt* **flogged; flogging** : flageller, fouetter
flood[1] ['flʌd] *vt* : inonder, noyer — *vi* : déborder (se dit d'une rivière)
flood[2] *n* **1** : inondation *f*, crue *f* <spring flood : crue du printemps> **2** TORRENT : déluge *m*, torrent *m* <a flood of words : un déluge de paroles>
floodlight ['flʌd,laɪt] *n* : projecteur *m*
floodwaters ['flʌd,wɔʧərz] *npl* : eaux *fpl* de crue

floor¹ ['flor] *vt* **1** : faire le sol de, parqueter (une maison, une salle) **2** KNOCK DOWN : terrasser (un adversaire) **3** NONPLUS : dérouter

floor² *n* **1** : plancher *m*, parquet *m* (d'une salle, etc.) <dance floor : piste de danse> **2** BOTTOM, GROUND : sol *m*, fond *m* (de la mer) **3** STORY : étage *m* <a 10-floor building : un édifice de 10 étages> <on the ground floor : au rez-de-chaussée>

floorboard ['flor,bord] *n* : planche *f*, latte *f*

flooring ['florɪŋ] *n* **1** : revêtement *m* de sol **2** FLOOR : plancher *m*, parquet *m*

flop¹ ['flɑp] *vi* **flopped; flopping 1** FLAP : s'agiter mollement **2** *or* **to flop down** : s'affaler **3** FAIL : échouer, faire un four *fam*

flop² *n* FAILURE : fiasco *m*, four *m fam*

floppy ['flɑpi] *adj* **floppier; -est** : mou, pendant

floppy disk *n* : disquette *f*

flora ['florə] *n* : flore *f*

floral ['florəl] *adj* : floral

florid ['florɪd] *adj* **1** ORNATE : fleuri **2** RUDDY : rougeaud

florist ['florɪst] *n* : fleuriste *mf*

floss¹ ['flɔs] *vt* : utiliser du fil dentaire

floss² *n* **1** *or* **embroidery floss** : soie *f* à broder **2** → **dental floss**

flotation [flo'teɪʃən] *n* : mise *f* à flot

flotilla [flo'tɪlə] *n* : flottille *f*

flotsam ['flɑtsəm] *n* : épave *f* flottante

flounce¹ ['flaʊnʦ] *vi* **flounced; flouncing** : passer brusquement <to flounce in : entrer dans un mouvement d'humeur>

flounce² *n* : volant *m* (d'une jupe, etc.)

flounder¹ ['flaʊndər] *vi* **1** THRASH : patauger, se débattre **2** BOG DOWN, FALTER : s'empêtrer (dans un discours), piétiner (dans une carrière)

flounder² *n, pl* **flounder** *or* **flounders** : flet *m*, poisson *m* plat

flour¹ ['flaʊər] *vt* : fariner, enrober de farine

flour² *n* : farine *f*

flourish¹ ['flərɪʃ] *vt* BRANDISH : brandir — *vi* **1** PROSPER : prospérer **2** THRIVE : fleurir, s'épanouir

flourish² *n* **1** : fioriture *f* (en musique), paraphe *f* (d'une signature) **2** FANFARE : fanfare *f* **3** WAVING : grand geste *m* (de la main), moulinet *m* (d'une épée, etc.)

flourishing ['flərɪʃɪŋ] *adj* : florissant, prospère

flout ['flaʊt] *vt* : se moquer de, passer outre à

flow¹ ['flo:] *vi* **1** COURSE, RUN : couler, s'écouler <to flow past : passer devant> **2** CIRCULATE : circuler (se dit du sang, du trafic, etc.) **3** BILLOW, HANG : flotter, onduler

flow² *n* **1** STREAM : écoulement *m* **2** CIRCULATION : circulation *f* <blood flow : circulation du sang>

flower¹ ['flaʊər] *vi* **1** : fleurir **2** DEVELOP, FLOURISH : s'épanouir, se développer

flower² *n* **1** : fleur *f* **2** BLOOM : épanouissement *m* <in full flower : en plein épanouissement>

floweriness ['flaʊərɪnəs] *n* : ornementation *f*, fioritures *fpl*

flowering ['flaʊərɪŋ] *n* : floraison *f*

flowerpot ['flaʊər,pɑt] *n* : pot *m* de fleurs

flowery ['flaʊəri] *adj* : fleuri

flown → **fly¹**

flu ['flu:] *n* : grippe *f*

flub ['flʌb] *vt* **flubbed; flubbing** : louper *fam*, rater

fluctuate ['flʌktʃʊ,eɪt] *vi* **-ated; -ating** : fluctuer

fluctuation [,flʌktʃʊ'eɪʃən] *n* : fluctuation *f*

flue ['flu:] *n* : conduit *m* (de cheminée)

fluency ['flu:ənʦi] *n* : aisance *f*, facilité *f*

fluent ['flu:ənt] *adj* : coulant, aisé <she speaks fluent French : elle parle couramment le français>

fluently ['flu:əntli] *adv* : couramment

fluff¹ ['flʌf] *vt* **1** *or* **to fluff up** : faire bouffer **2** BOTCH : louper *fam*, rater

fluff² *n* **1** DOWN : duvet *m* **2** FUZZ : peluches *fpl*

fluffy ['flʌfi] *adj* **fluffier; -est 1** DOWNY, FUZZY : duveteux, pelucheux **2** LIGHT : léger, moelleux

fluid¹ ['flu:ɪd] *adj* : fluide

fluid² *n* : fluide *m*, liquide *m*

fluidity [flu:'ɪdəti] *n* : fluidité *f*

fluid ounce *n* : once *f* liquide

fluke ['flu:k] *n* : coup *m* de chance, coup *m* de veine *fam*

flung → **fling¹**

flunk ['flʌŋk] *vt* FAIL : rater

fluorescence [,flor'esənʦ, ,flɔr-] *n* : fluorescence *f*

fluorescent [,flor'esənt, ,flɔr-] *adj* : fluorescent

fluoridate ['flɔrə,deɪt, 'flor-] *vt* **-dated; -dating** : ajouter du fluor à

fluoridation [,flɔrə'deɪʃən, ,flor-] *n* : traitement *m* au fluor, fluoration *f*

fluoride ['flɔr,aɪd, 'flor-] *n* : fluorure *m*

fluorine ['flɔr,i:n] *n* : fluor *m*

flurry¹ ['flər̩i] *vt* **flurried; flurrying** FLUSTER : agiter, énerver

flurry² *n, pl* **-ries 1** GUST : rafale *f*, poudrerie *f Can* <snow flurries : rafales de neige> **2** BUSTLE : tourbillon *m* **3** BARRAGE : déluge *m* (de questions, etc.)

flush¹ ['flʌʃ] *vt* **1** REDDEN : empourprer, rougir (les joues) **2** *or* **to flush out** : lever, faire s'envoler (du gibier) **3 to flush the toilet** : tirer la chasse d'eau — *vi* BLUSH : rougir

flush² *adv* : de niveau, à ras

flush³ *adj* **1** FILLED : plein à déborder **2** RUDDY : rouge, coloré **3** LEVEL : au même niveau **4** AFFLUENT : en fonds

flush[4] *n* **1** FLUSHING : chasse *f* (d'eau) **2** SURGE : élan *m*, accès *m* <a flush of anger : un accès de colère> **3** BLUSH : rougeur *f*

fluster[1] ['flʌstər] *vt* : énerver, troubler

fluster[2] *n* : trouble *m*, agitation *f*

flute ['flu:t] *n* : flûte *f*

fluted ['flu:ṭəd] *adj* GROOVED : cannelé

flutist ['flu:ṭɪst] *n* : flûtiste *mf*

flutter[1] ['flʌṭər] *vi* **1** FLAP : battre (se dit des ailes) **2** BEAT : palpiter (se dit du cœur) **3** DRIFT, FLY : flotter <a sail fluttering in the wind : une voile qui flotte au vent> **4 to flutter about** : s'agiter, s'affairer

flutter[2] *n* **1** FLAPPING : battement *m* (d'ailes) **2** STIR : agitation *f*, émoi *m*

flux ['flʌks] *n* **1** : flux *m* (en médecine et en physique) **2** CHANGE : changement *m* <in a state of flux : dans un état de perpétuel changement>

fly[1] ['flaɪ] *v* **flew** ['flu:]; **flown** ['flo:n]; **flying** *vt* : faire voler — *vi* **1** : voler (se dit d'un oiseau, d'un avion, etc.) **2** TRAVEL : prendre l'avion **3** FLOAT : flotter, onduler **4** FLEE : fuir, s'enfuir **5** PASS : passer vite, filer *fam* <time was flying by : le temps filait>

fly[2] *n, pl* **flies 1** : mouche *f* (insecte) **2** : braguette *f* (d'un pantalon)

flyer → **flier**

flying saucer *n* : soucoupe *f* volante

flypaper ['flaɪˌpeɪpər] *n* : papier *m* tue-mouches

flyspeck ['flaɪˌspɛk] *n* **1** : chiure *f* de mouche **2** SPECK : petite tache *f*

flyswatter ['flaɪˌswaṭər] *n* : tapette *f* à mouches, tue-mouches *m Can*

foal[1] ['fo:l] *vi* : pouliner, mettre bas

foal[2] *n* : poulain *m*

foam[1] ['fo:m] *vi* : mousser, écumer

foam[2] *n* : mousse *f*, écume *f*

foamy ['fo:mi] *adj* **foamier; -est** : mousseux, écumeux

focal ['fo:kəl] *adj* : focal

fo'c'sle ['fo:kəl] → **forecastle**

focus[1] ['fo:kəs] *vt* **1** : mettre au point (un instrument), fixer (les yeux) **2** CONCENTRATE : concentrer, faire converger — *vi* : converger, se concentrer

focus[2] *n, pl* **foci** ['fo:ˌsaɪ, -ˌkaɪ] **1** : foyer *m* <to be in focus : être au point> <to bring into focus : mettre au point> **2** CENTER : centre *m* <the focus of attention : le centre d'attention, le point de mire>

fodder ['fɑdər] *n* : fourrage *m*

foe ['fo:] *n* : ennemi *m*, -mie *f*; adversaire *mf*

fog[1] ['fɔg, 'fɑg] *v* **fogged; fogging** *vt* : embuer, brouiller — *vi or* **to fog up** : s'embuer, se couvrir de buée

fog[2] *n* **1** : brouillard *m*, brume *f* **2** CONFUSION : brouillard *m*, confusion *f*

foggy ['fɔgi, 'fɑ-] *adj* **foggier; -est 1** : brumeux <a foggy night : une nuit brumeuse> **2** CONFUSED : confus <I haven't the foggiest notion : je n'en ai pas la moindre idée>

foghorn ['fɔgˌhɔrn, 'fɑg-] *n* : corne *f* de brume

fogy ['fo:gi] *n, pl* **-gies** : vieille baderne *f fam*

foible ['fɔɪbəl] *n* : petit défaut *m*, petite manie *f*

foil[1] ['fɔɪl] *vt* THWART : déjouer, contrecarrer

foil[2] *n* **1** SWORD : fleuret *m* **2** : feuille *f* <aluminum foil : feuille d'aluminium> **3** COMPLEMENT, CONTRAST : repoussoir *m*

foist ['fɔɪst] *vt* **1 to foist sth off on** : refiler qqch à **2 to foist oneself on** : s'imposer à

fold[1] ['fo:ld] *vt* **1** : plier <to fold a blanket : plier une couverture> **2** CLASP : croiser (les bras), joindre (les mains) **3** EMBRACE : serrer, enlacer — *vi* FAIL : échouer, s'écrouler

fold[2] *n* **1** CREASE, PLEAT : pli *m* **2** SHEEPFOLD : parc *m* à moutons **3** GROUP : bercail *m*, sein *m* <to return to the fold : rentrer au bercail>

folder ['fo:ldər] *n* **1** FILE : chemise *f*, dossier *m* **2** CIRCULAR : dépliant *m*

foliage ['fo:liɪdʒ, -lɪdʒ] *n* : feuillage *m*

folio ['fo:liˌo:] *n, pl* **-lios** : folio *m*

folk[1] ['fo:k] *adj* : populaire, folklorique

folk[2] *n, pl* **folk** *or* **folks 1** PEOPLE : gens *mfpl* <plain folks : des gens ordinaires> **2 folks** *npl* PARENTS : famille *f*, parents *mpl*

folklore ['fo:kˌlor] *n* : folklore *m*

folk music *n* : musique *f* folklorique, folk *m*

folksy ['fo:ksi] *adj* **folksier; -est** : populaire, sympa *fam*

follicle ['fɑlɪkəl] *n* : follicule *m*

follow ['fɑlo] *vt* **1** : suivre <follow the guide : suivez le guide> <they followed the road : ils ont longé la route> **2** PURSUE : exercer, poursuivre (une carrière, etc.) **3** OBEY : suivre, se soumettre à, se conformer à **4** UNDERSTAND : suivre, comprendre — *vi* **1** : suivre <in the days that followed : dans les jours qui ont suivi> **2** ENSUE : s'ensuivre, résulter **3** UNDERSTAND : suivre

follower ['fɑloər] *n* : partisan *m*, -sane *f*; disciple *mf*

following[1] ['fɑloɪŋ] *adj* : suivant

following[2] *n* : partisans *mpl*

following[3] *prep* : après

follow through *vi* **to follow through on** : suivre (jusqu'au bout)

follow up *vt* : donner suite à, confirmer

folly ['fɑli] *n, pl* **-lies** : folie *f*, absurdité *f*

foment [fo'mɛnt] *vt* : fomenter

fond ['fɑnd] *adj* **1** LOVING : affectueux, tendre **2** FERVENT : cher, fervent <my fondest hope : mon espoir le plus cher> **3 to be fond of** : aimer beaucoup

fondle [ˈfɑndəl] *vt* **-dled; -dling** : caresser

fondly [ˈfɑndli] *adv* **1** AFFECTIONATELY : affectueusement **2** DEARLY : chèrement

fondness [ˈfɑndnəs] *n* **1** AFFECTION : affection *f*, tendresse *f* **2** PARTIALITY : prédilection *f*, penchant *m*

fondue [fɑnˈduː, -ˈdjuː] *n* : fondue *f*

font [ˈfɑnt] *n* **1** *or* **baptismal font** : fonts *mpl* baptismaux **2** SOURCE : source *f*, fontaine *f* **3** : police *f* (de caractères typographiques)

food [ˈfuːd] *n* **1** : nourriture *f*, aliments *mpl* **2** : cuisine *f*, mets *m* <Chinese food : mets chinois> **3 food for thought** : matière *f* à réflexion

food chain *n* : chaîne *f* alimentaire

food poisoning : intoxication *f* alimentaire

foodstuffs [ˈfuːdˌstʌfs] *npl* : aliments *mpl*, denrées *fpl* alimentaires

fool[1] [ˈfuːl] *vt* DECEIVE : duper, berner — *vi* **1** JOKE : plaisanter <I was just fooling : je plaisantais> **2 to fool around** : perdre son temps **3 to fool with** : jouer avec

fool[2] *n* **1** : imbécile *mf*; idiot *m*, -diote *f*; nono *m*, -note *f Can fam* <don't be a fool! : ne fais pas l'idiot!> **2** JESTER : fou *m*

foolhardiness [ˈfuːlˌhɑrdinəs] *n* : témérité *f*

foolhardy [ˈfuːlˌhɑrdi] *adj* RASH : téméraire

foolish [ˈfuːlɪʃ] *adj* **1** STUPID : bête, idiot **2** RIDICULOUS : absurde, ridicule

foolishly [ˈfuːlɪʃli] *adv* : bêtement, sottement

foolishness [ˈfuːlɪʃnəs] *n* **1** STUPIDITY : bêtise *f*, sottise *f* **2** FOLLY : folie *f*, absurdité *f*

foolproof [ˈfuːlˌpruːf] *adj* : infaillible

foot [ˈfʊt] *n, pl* **feet** [ˈfiːt] **1** : pied *m* **2** : bas *m* <at the foot of the page : au bas de la page>

footage [ˈfʊtɪdʒ] *n* **1** : longueur *f* en pieds **2** : métrage *m* (d'un film)

football [ˈfʊtˌbɔl] *n* : football *m* américain, football *m Can*

footbridge [ˈfʊtˌbrɪdʒ] *n* : passerelle *f*

foothills [ˈfʊtˌhɪlz] *npl* : contreforts *mpl*

foothold [ˈfʊtˌhoːld] *n* **1** : prise *f* de pied **2 to gain a foothold in** : prendre pied sur

footing [ˈfʊtɪŋ] *n* **1** FOOTHOLD : prise *f* de pied <to keep one's footing : conserver l'équilibre> **2** STATUS : position *f*, niveau *m* <on the same footing : sur le même pied d'égalité>

footlights [ˈfʊtˌlaɪts] *npl* : rampe *f*

footloose [ˈfʊtˌluːs] *adj* : libre de toute attache

footman [ˈfʊtmən] *n, pl* **-men** [-mən, -ˌmɛn] : valet *m* de pied

footnote [ˈfʊtˌnoːt] *n* : note *f* en bas de la page

footpath [ˈfʊtˌpæθ] *n* : sentier *m*

footprint [ˈfʊtˌprɪnt] *n* : empreinte *f* (de pied), trace *f* (de pas)

footrest [ˈfʊtˌrɛst] *n* : repose-pied *m*

footstep [ˈfʊtˌstɛp] *n* : pas *m*

footstool [ˈfʊtˌstuːl] *n* : tabouret *m*

footwear [ˈfʊtˌwɛr] *n* : chaussures *fpl*

footwork [ˈfʊtˌwɜrk] *n* : jeu *m* de jambes

fop [ˈfɑp] *n* : dandy *m*

for[1] [ˈfɔr] *conj* BECAUSE : car

for[2] *prep* **1** (*indicating a purpose*) : pour <to get ready for a trip : se préparer pour un voyage> <what's it for? : c'est pour quoi faire?> **2** BECAUSE OF : de, à cause de <to cry for joy : pleurer de joie> **3** (*indicating a recipient*) : pour <gifts for her sister : des cadeaux pour sa sœur> **4** (*indicating support*) : pour <to fight for one's country : se battre pour sa patrie> <he speaks for the poor : il parle au nom des pauvres> **5** (*indicating a goal or remedy*) : contre, pour <a cure for cancer : un remède contre le cancer> <it's for your own good : c'est pour ton bien> **6** (*indicating equivalence or exchange*) : pour <I bought it for $10 : je l'ai acheté pour 10 $> **7** (*indicating duration*) : pour, pendant, depuis <he's here for three days : il est là pour trois jours> <we talked for hours : on a parlé pendant des heures> <I've lived here for two years : j'habite ici depuis deux ans> **8** (*indicating destination*) : pour, à destination de <to leave for New York : partir pour New York> <a train for Paris : un train à destination de Paris> **9 → as for**

forage[1] [ˈfɔrɪdʒ] *vi* **-aged; -aging** : fourrager, fouiller

forage[2] *n* : fourrage *m*

foray [ˈfɔrˌeɪ] *n* : incursion *f*

forbear[1] [fɔrˈbɛr] *vi* **-bore** [-ˈbɔr]; **-borne** [-ˈbɔrn]; **-bearing 1** ABSTAIN : s'abstenir **2** : être patient

forbear[2] → **forebear**

forbearance [fɔrˈbɛrəns] *n* **1** RESTRAINT : abstention *f* **2** PATIENCE : patience *f*

forbid [fərˈbɪd] *vt* **-bade** [-ˈbæd, -ˈbeɪd] *or* **-bad** [-ˈbæd]; **-bidden** [-ˈbɪdən]; **-bidding 1** PROHIBIT : interdire, défendre **2** PREVENT : empêcher

forbidding [fərˈbɪdɪŋ] *adj* **1** DISAGREEABLE : rebutant, déplaisant **2** MENACING : menaçant

force[1] [ˈfɔrs] *vt* **forced; forcing 1** COMPEL : forcer, contraindre, obliger **2** *or* **to force open** : forcer **3** PRESS, PUSH : forcer <I forced my way through : je me suis frayé un passage> **4 to force a smile** : se forcer à sourire

force[2] *n* **1** POWER, STRENGTH : force *f* **2** *or* **forces** *npl* : forces *fpl*, troupes *fpl* <ground forces : forces terrestres> <the police force : les forces de po-

lice> **3** : force *f* (en physique) <the force of gravity : la pesanteur> **4 in ~** : en grand nombre, en force **5 in ~** : en vigueur (se dit d'une loi, etc.)

forceful |ˈfɔrsfəl| *adj* : puissant, énergique, vigoureux

forcefully |ˈfɔrsfəli| *adv* : avec force, avec vigueur

forceps |ˈfɔrsəps, -ˌsɛps| *ns & pl* : forceps *m*

forcible |ˈfɔrsəbəl| *adj* **1** FORCED : de force **2** POWERFUL : énergique, vigoureux

forcibly |ˈfɔrsəbli| *adv* **1** : de force **2** VIGOROUSLY : avec vigueur, énergiquement

ford¹ |ˈford| *vt* : passer à gué

ford² *n* : gué *m*

fore¹ |ˈfɔr| *adv* : à l'avant

fore² *adj* : à l'avant, antérieur

fore³ *n* **1** : avant *m* (d'un navire) **2 to come to the fore** : se faire remarquer, se mettre en évidence

fore–and–aft |ˈfɔrənˈæft, -ənd-| *adj* : aurique <fore-and-aft sail : voile aurique>

forearm |ˈfɔrˌɑrm| *n* : avant-bras *m*

forebear |ˈfɔrˌbɛr| *n* : ancêtre *mf*

foreboding |fɔrˈboːdɪŋ| *n* : (mauvais) pressentiment *m*, prémonition *f*

forecast¹ |ˈfɔrˌkæst| *vt* **-cast; -casting** : prévoir

forecast² *n* **1** PREDICTION : prévision *f* **2** *or* **weather forecast** : prévisions *fpl* météorologiques, météo *f Can fam*

forecastle |ˈfoːksəl| *n* : gaillard *m* d'avant

foreclose |fɔrˈkloːz| *vt* **-closed; -closing** : saisir (un bien hypothéqué)

foreclosure |fɔrˈkloːʒər| *n* : forclusion *f*

forefathers |ˈfɔrˌfɑðərz| *npl* : ancêtres *mfpl*, aïeux *mpl*

forefinger |ˈfɔrˌfɪŋgər| *n* : index *m*

forefoot |ˈfɔrˌfʊt| *n, pl* **-feet** |ˌfiːt| : pied *m* antérieur

forefront |ˈfɔrˌfrʌnt| *n* : premier rang *m*

forego¹ |fɔrˈgoː| *vt* **-went; -gone; -going** PRECEDE : précéder

forego² → **forgo**

foregoing |fɔrˈgoːɪŋ| *adj* : précédent

foregone |fɔrˈgɔn| *adj* **it's a foregone conclusion** : c'est gagné d'avance

foreground |ˈfɔrˌgraʊnd| *n* : premier plan *m*

forehand¹ |ˈfɔrˌhænd| *adj* : de coup droit

forehand² *n* : coup *m* droit

forehead |ˈfɔrəd, ˈfɔrˌhɛd| *n* : front *m*

foreign |ˈfɔrən| *adj* **1** : étranger <a foreign language : une langue étrangère> **2** : extérieur <foreign trade : commerce extérieur> **3** ALIEN : étranger <foreign bodies : corps étrangers>

foreigner |ˈfɔrənər| *n* : étranger *m*, -gère *f*

foreknowledge |fɔrˈnɑlɪdʒ| *n* : connaissance *f* anticipée, prescience *f*

foreleg |ˈfɔrˌlɛg| *n* : jambe *f* antérieure, patte *f* de devant

foreman |ˈfɔrmən| *n, pl* **-men** |-mən, -ˌmɛn| **1** : président *m* du jury **2** SUPERVISOR : contremaître *m*

foremost¹ |ˈfɔrˌmoːst| *adv* **first and foremost** : tout d'abord, avant tout

foremost² *adj* : principal, le plus en vue

forenoon |ˈfɔrˌnuːn| *n* : matinée *f*

forensic |fəˈrɛnsɪk| *adj* : légal, médico-légal

foreordain |ˌfɔrərˈdeɪn| *vt* : prédestiner, prédéterminer

forequarter |ˈfɔrˌkwɔrtər| *n* : quartier *m* de devant

forerunner |ˈfɔrˌrʌnər| *n* : précurseur *m*

foresee |fɔrˈsiː| *vt* **-saw; -seen; -seeing** : prévoir, anticiper

foreseeable |fɔrˈsiːəbəl| *adj* : prévisible

foreshadow |fɔrˈʃædoː| *vt* : présager, annoncer

foresight |ˈfɔrˌsaɪt| *n* **1** PRESCIENCE : prévision *f* **2** PRUDENCE : prévoyance *f*, prudence *f*

foresighted |ˈfɔrˌsaɪtəd| *adj* : prévoyant, prudent

forest |ˈfɔrəst| *n* : forêt *f*

forestall |fɔrˈstɔl| *vt* **1** PREVENT : empêcher, prévenir **2** ANTICIPATE : anticiper, devancer

forested |ˈfɔrəstəd| *adj* : boisé, forestier

forester |ˈfɔrəstər| *n* : forestier *m*, -tière *f*

forestry |ˈfɔrəstri| *n* : sylviculture *f*, foresterie *f*

foreswear → **forswear**

foretaste |ˈfɔrˌteɪst| *n* : avant-goût *m*

foretell |fɔrˈtɛl| *vt* **-told; -telling** : prédire

forethought |ˈfɔrˌθɔt| *n* **1** PREMEDITATION : préméditation *f* **2** FORESIGHT : prévoyance *f*

forever |fɔrˈɛvər| *adv* **1** ETERNALLY : toujours, éternellement **2** CONTINUALLY : toujours, sans cesse

forevermore |fɔrˌɛvərˈmor| *adv* : (pour) toujours

forewarn |fɔrˈwɔrn| *vt* : avertir, prévenir

foreword |ˈfɔrwərd| *n* : avant-propos *m*

forfeit¹ |ˈfɔrfət| *vt* : perdre, renoncer à (ses droits, etc.)

forfeit² *n* **1** PENALTY : prix *m*, peine *f* **2** : gage *m* <to pay a forfeit : avoir un gage>

forge¹ |ˈfɔrdʒ| *v* **forged; forging** *vt* **1** : forger (un métal, un plan, etc.) **2** COUNTERFEIT : contrefaire, falsifier — *vi* **to forge ahead** : prendre de l'avance, avancer

forge² *n* : forge *f*

forger |ˈfɔrdʒər| *n* : faussaire *mf*, faux-monnayeur *m*

forgery |ˈfɔrdʒəri| *n, pl* **-eries** : contrefaçon *f*, falsification *f*

forget [fərˈgɛt] *v* **-got** [-ˈgɑt]; **-gotten** [-ˈgɑtən] *or* **-got; -getting** *vt* **1** : oublier <I've forgotten your name : j'ai oublié votre nom> **2** NEGLECT : négliger, oublier **3 forget it!** : n'en parlons plus! — *vi* : oublier

forgetful [fərˈgɛtfəl] *adj* **1** ABSENTMINDED : distrait **2** NEGLECTFUL : oublieux, négligent

forgetfulness [fərˈgɛtfəlnəs] *n* **1** ABSENTMINDEDNESS : distraction *f* **2** CARELESSNESS : étourderie *f*, négligence *f*

forget–me–not [fərˈgɛtmiˌnɑt] *n* : myosotis *m*

forgettable [fərˈgɛtəbəl] *adj* : peu mémorable

forgivable [fərˈgɪvəbəl] *adj* : pardonnable

forgive [fərˈgɪv] *vt* **-gave** [-ˈgeɪv]; **-given** [-ˈgɪvən]; **-giving** : pardonner

forgiveness [fərˈgɪvnəs] *n* : pardon *m*, indulgence *f*

forgiving [fərˈgɪvɪŋ] *adj* : indulgent, clément

forgo *or* **forego** [fərˈgoː] *vt* **-went; -gone; -going** : renoncer à, se priver de

fork[1] [ˈfɔrk] *vt* **1** : fourcher <to fork (up) the earth : fourcher la terre> **2** *or* **to fork over** : allonger *fam* — *vi* : bifurquer, fourcher <the road forks : la route bifurque>

fork[2] *n* **1** : fourchette *f* <dessert fork : fourchette à dessert> **2** PITCHFORK : fourche *f* (à foin) **3** JUNCTION : bifurcation *f* (d'une route), embranchement *m* (d'une voie ferrée)

forked [ˈfɔrkt, ˈfɔrkəd] *adj* : fourchu

forklift [ˈfɔrkˌlɪft] *n* : chariot *m* élévateur

forlorn [fərˈlɔrn] *adj* **1** DESOLATE : abandonné, désolé **2** SAD : triste, misérable **3** DESPERATE : désespéré

forlornly [fərˈlɔrnli] *adv* : d'un air triste

form[1] [ˈfɔrm] *vt* **1** FASHION, SHAPE : former, façonner **2** ARRANGE : se mettre en <to form a line : se mettre en ligne> **3** ACQUIRE, DEVELOP : se former, se faire (une idée, etc.), contracter (une habitude) **4** INSTRUCT, TRAIN : former **5** CONSTITUTE : constituer, former — *vi* : se former, prendre forme

form[2] *n* **1** SHAPE : forme *f* **2** FIGURE : forme *f*, corps *m* <the human form : la forme humaine> **3** DOCUMENT : formulaire *m* <to fill out a form : remplir un formulaire> **4** KIND : forme *f*, genre *m* **5** CONDITION : forme *f*, condition *f* <to be in good form : être en pleine forme>

formal[1] [ˈfɔrməl] *adj* **1** : officiel <a formal reception : une réception officielle> <a formal contract : un contrat en bonne et due forme> **2** ELEVATED : soigné, soutenu <formal language : langage soutenu>

formal[2] *n* **1** *or* **formal dance** : bal *m* **2** *or* **formal dress** : tenue *f* de soirée

formaldehyde [fɔrˈmældəˌhaɪd] *n* : formaldéhyde *m*

formality [fɔrˈmæləṭi] *n, pl* **-ties** : formalité *f*

formalize [ˈfɔrməˌlaɪz] *vt* **-ized; -izing** : formaliser

formally [ˈfɔrməli] *adv* **1** OFFICIALLY : officiellement **2** CEREMONIOUSLY : cérémonieusement, solennellement

format[1] [ˈfɔrˌmæt] *vt* **-matted; -matting** **1** : concevoir le format de **2** : formater (une diskette)

format[2] *n* : format *m*

formation [fɔrˈmeɪʃən] *n* **1** FORMING : formation *f*, établissement *m* **2** ARRANGEMENT, SHAPE : formation *f*

formative [ˈfɔrməṭɪv] *adj* : formateur

former [ˈfɔrmər] *adj* **1** PREVIOUS : ancien, précédent <a former president : un ancien président> **2** : premier (de deux choses)

formerly [ˈfɔrmərli] *adv* : autrefois, jadis

formidable [ˈfɔrmədəbəl, fərˈmɪdə-] *adj* **1** : redoutable, terrible <a formidable foe : un ennemi redoutable> **2** OUTSTANDING : impressionnant, remarquable

formless [ˈfɔrmləs] *adj* : informe

formula [ˈfɔrmjələ] *n, pl* **-las** or **-lae** [-ˌliː, -ˌlaɪ] **1** : formule *f* **2** *or* **baby formula** : lait *m* en poudre (pour biberon)

formulate [ˈfɔrmjəˌleɪt] *vt* **-lated; -lating** : formuler

formulation [ˌfɔrmjəˈleɪʃən] *n* : formulation *f*

fornicate [ˈfɔrnəˌkeɪt] *vi* **-cated; -cating** : forniquer

fornication [ˌfɔrnəˈkeɪʃən] *n* : fornication *f*

forsake [fərˈseɪk] *vt* **-sook** [-ˈsʊk]; **-saken** [-ˈseɪkən]; **-saking** : abandonner, délaisser

forswear [fɔrˈswær] *v* **-swore; -sworn; -swearing** *vt* RENOUNCE : abjurer, renoncer à — *vi* : commettre un parjure

forsythia [fərˈsɪθiə] *n* : forsythia *m*

fort [ˈfɔrt] *n* : fort *m*

forte [ˈfɔrt, ˈfɔrˌteɪ] *n* : fort *m*

forth [ˈforθ] *adv* **1** FORWARD : en avant <from this day forth : dorénavant, à partir d'aujourd'hui> **2 and so forth** : et ainsi de suite

forthcoming [forθˈkʌmɪŋ, ˈforθ-] *adj* **1** COMING : prochain, à venir, à paraître **2** COMMUNICATIVE, OPEN : ouvert, communicatif

forthright [ˈforθˌraɪt] *adj* : franc, direct

forthrightly [ˈforθˌraɪtli] *adv* : franchement, directement

forthrightness [ˈforθˌraɪtnəs] *n* : franchise *f*

forthwith [forθˈwɪθ, -ˈwɪð] *adv* : sur-le-champ, aussitôt

fortieth[1] |ˈfɔrtiəθ| *adj* : quarantième
fortieth[2] *n* **1** : quarantième *mf* (dans une série) **2** : quarantième *m* (en mathématiques)
fortification |ˌfɔrtəfəˈkeɪʃən| *n* : fortification *f*
fortify |ˈfɔrtəˌfaɪ| *vt* **-fied; -fying 1** STRENGTHEN, SECURE : fortifier (une ville, etc.) **2** ENCOURAGE, INVIGORATE : remonter, réconforter
fortitude |ˈfɔrtəˌtu:d, -ˌtju:d| *n* : force *f* d'âme, courage *m*
fortnight |ˈfɔrtˌnaɪt| *n* : quinzaine *f*, quinze jours *mpl*
fortnightly[1] |ˈfɔrtˌnaɪtli| *adv* : tous les quinze jours
fortnightly[2] *adj* : bimensuel
fortress |ˈfɔrtrəs| *n* : forteresse *f*
fortuitous |fɔrˈtu:ətəs, -ˈtju:-| *adj* : fortuit, imprévu
fortunate |ˈfɔrtʃənət| *adj* **1** AUSPICIOUS : propice, prometteur **2** LUCKY : heureux, chanceux
fortunately |ˈfɔrtʃənətli| *adv* : heureusement
fortune |ˈfɔrtʃən| *n* **1** CHANCE, LUCK : chance *f*, fortune *f*, hasard *m* **2** DESTINY : destin *m*, sort *m* **3** WEALTH : fortune *f* <to make a fortune : faire fortune>
fortune–teller |ˈfɔrtʃənˌtelər| *n* : diseur *m*, -seuse *f* de bonne aventure; voyant *m*, voyante *f*
fortune–telling |ˈfɔrtʃənˌtelɪŋ| *n* : pratique *f* de dire la bonne aventure, divination *f*
forty[1] |ˈfɔrti| *adj* : quarante
forty[2] *n, pl* **forties** : quarante *m*
forum |ˈfɔrəm| *n, pl* **-rums** : forum *m*
forward[1] |ˈfɔrwərd| *vt* **1** PROMOTE : avancer, favoriser **2** SEND : expédier (des marchandises), faire suivre (du courrier)
forward[2] *adv* **1** : en avant, vers l'avant **2 from that day forward** : à partir de ce jour-là
forward[3] *adj* **1** : avant, en avant **2** BRASH : effronté, impertinent
forward[4] *n* : avant *m* (aux sports)
forwarder |ˈfɔrwərdər| *n* : expéditeur *m*, -trice *f*
forwardness |ˈfɔrwərdnəs| *n* : effronterie *f*, impertinence *f*
forwards |ˈfɔrwərdz| → **forward**[2]
fossil[1] |ˈfɑsəl| *adj* : fossile
fossil[2] *n* : fossile *m*
fossilize |ˈfɑsəˌlaɪz| *v* **-ized; -izing** *vt* : fossiliser — *vi* : se fossiliser
foster[1] |ˈfɔstər| *vt* **1** NURTURE : élever, placer (un enfant) **2** CHERISH : entretenir, nourrir (un espoir, etc.) **3** ENCOURAGE : favoriser, encourager
foster[2] *adj* : adoptif, d'accueil <foster parents : parents adoptifs> <foster home : famille d'accueil>
fought → **fight**[1]
foul[1] |ˈfɑʊl| *vt* **1** DIRTY, POLLUTE : salir, souiller, polluer **2** CLOG : encrasser, obstruer **3** TANGLE : emmêler
foul[2] *adj* **1** REPULSIVE : infect, fétide **2** POLLUTED : pollué, vicié **3** DETESTABLE : horrible, atroce **4** OBSCENE : grossier, ordurier **5** NASTY : sale, infect <what foul weather! : quel sale temps!> **6** : déloyal, irrégulier (aux sports) <a foul play : un jeu irrégulier>
foul[3] *n* : coup *m* irrégulier, faute *f* (aux sports)
foully |ˈfɑʊli| *adv* : de façon grossière
foulmouthed |ˈfɑʊlˌmæu:ðd, -ˌmæʊθt| *adj* : grossier
foulness |ˈfɑʊlnəs| *n* : grossièreté *f*
foul play *n* : violence *f*, meurtre *m*
foul–up |ˈfɑʊlˌʌp| *n* : cafouillage *m fam*, confusion *f*
foul up *vt* **1** CONTAMINATE : polluer **2** CLOG : obstruer
found[1] → **find**[1]
found[2] |ˈfɑʊnd| *vt* **1** ESTABLISH : fonder, établir **2** BASE : fonder, baser <founded on facts : basé sur des faits>
foundation |fɑʊnˈdeɪʃən| *n* **1** FOUNDING : fondation *f*, établissement *m* **2** BASIS : base *f*, fondement *m* **3** ENDOWMENT : fondation *f*, institution *f* dotée **4** : fondations *fpl* (d'un édifice), solage *m Can*
founder[1] |ˈfɑʊndər| *vi* COLLAPSE, SINK : sombrer, s'effondrer
founder[2] *n* : fondateur *m*, -trice *f*
foundling |ˈfɑʊndlɪŋ| *n* : enfant *m* trouvé, enfant *f* trouvée
foundry |ˈfɑʊndri| *n, pl* **-dries** : fonderie *f*
fount |ˈfɑʊnt| *n* : source *f*
fountain |ˈfɑʊntən| *n* **1** : fontaine *f*, jet *m* d'eau <drinking fountain : jet d'eau potable> **2** SOURCE : fontaine *f*, source *f* **3** SPRING : source *f*
four[1] |ˈfɔr| *adj* : quatre
four[2] *n* : quatre *m*
fourfold |ˈfɔrˌfo:ld, -ˈfo:ld| *adj* : quadruple
fourscore |ˈfɔrˈskɔr| *adj* EIGHTY : quatre-vingts
fourteen[1] |fɔrˈti:n| *adj* : quatorze
fourteen[2] *n* : quatorze *m*
fourteenth[1] |fɔrˈti:nθ| *adj* : quatorzième
fourteenth[2] *n* **1** : quatorzième *mf* (dans une série) **2** : quatorzième *m* (en mathématiques) **3** (*used in dates*) <the fourteenth of June : le quatorze juin>
fourth[1] |ˈfɔrθ| *adj* : quatrième
fourth[2] *n* **1** : quatrième *mf* (dans une série) **2** : quart *m* (en mathématiques) **3** (*used in dates*) <the Fourth of July : le quatre juillet>
fowl |ˈfɑʊl| *n, pl* **fowl** *or* **fowls 1** BIRD : oiseau *m* **2** CHICKEN : poulet *m* **3** POULTRY : volaille *f*

fox¹ ['fɑks] *vt* TRICK : tromper, berner
fox² *n, pl* **foxes** : renard *m*
foxglove ['fɑksˌglʌv] *n* : digitale *f* (pourprée)
foxhole ['fɑksˌhoːl] *n* : gourbi *m*
foxy ['fɑksi] *adj* **foxier; -est** SLY : rusé, malin
foyer ['fɔɪər, 'fɔɪˌjeɪ] *n* : vestibule *m*, entrée *f*
fracas ['freɪkəs, 'fræ-] *n, pl* **-cases** [-kəsəz] : bagarre *f*, rixe *f*
fraction ['frækʃən] *n* **1** : fraction *f* (en mathématiques) **2** PORTION : fraction *f*, (petite) partie *f*
fractional ['frækʃənəl] *adj* **1** : fractionnaire **2** INCONSIDERABLE : infime, tout petit
fractious ['frækʃəs] adj **1** UNRULY : indiscipliné, difficile **2** IRRITABLE : revêche
fracture¹ ['frækʃər] *vt* **-tured; -turing** : fracturer
fracture² *n* : fracture *f*
fragile ['frædʒəl, -ˌdʒaɪl] *adj* : fragile
fragility [frə'dʒɪləṭi] *n* : fragilité *f*
fragment¹ ['frægˌmənt] *vt* : fragmenter
fragment² ['frægmənt] *n* : fragment *m*, morceau *m*
fragmentary ['frægmənˌtɛri] *adj* : fragmentaire
fragmentation [ˌfrægmən'teɪʃən, -ˌmɛn-] *n* : fragmentation *f*
fragrance ['freɪgrənʃs] *n* : parfum *m*, fragrance *f*
fragrant ['freɪgrənt] *adj* : parfumé, odorant
frail ['freɪl] *adj* : frêle, fragile
frailty ['freɪlti] *n, pl* **-ties** : fragilité *f*
frame¹ ['freɪm] *vt* **framed; framing 1** FORMULATE : formuler, élaborer **2** BORDER, ENCLOSE : encadrer **3** INCRIMINATE : monter un coup contre
frame² *n* **1** PHYSIQUE : charpente *f*, ossature *f* **2** STRUCTURE : charpente *f* (d'un édifice), châssis *m* (d'une voiture), cadre *m* (d'une bicyclette, etc.) **3** BORDER : cadre *m* (d'un tableau, d'une fenêtre, etc.) **4 frames** *npl* : monture *f* (de lunettes) **5 frame of mind** : état *m* d'esprit
framework ['freɪmˌwərk] *n* **1** STRUCTURE : charpente *f*, squelette *f* **2** BASIS : cadre *m*
franc ['frænk] *n* : franc *m*
franchise ['frænˌtʃaɪz] *n* **1** : franchise *f* (en commerce) **2** SUFFRAGE : droit *m* de vote, suffrage *m*
frank¹ ['frænk] *vt* POSTMARK : affranchir
frank² *adj* CANDID : franc
frankfurter ['frænkfərṭər, -ˌfər-] *or* **frankfurt** [-fərt] *n* : saucisse *f* de Francfort, saucisse *f* à hot-dog *Can*
frankincense ['frænkənˌsɛnʃs] *n* : encens *m*
frankly ['frænkli] *adv* : franchement
frankness ['frænknəs] *n* : franchise *f*
frantic ['fræntɪk] *adj* : frénétique, effréné
frantically ['fræntɪkli] *adv* : frénétiquement
fraternal [frə'tərnəl] *adj* : fraternel — **fraternally** *adv*
fraternity [frə'tərnəṭi] *n, pl* **-ties 1** BROTHERHOOD : fraternité *f* **2** : confrérie *f* d'étudiants <fraternity pin : insigne de confrérie>
fraternization [ˌfræṭənə'zeɪʃən] *n* : fraternisation *f*
fraternize ['fræṭəˌnaɪz] *vi* **-nized; -nizing** : fraterniser
fratricide ['frætrəˌsaɪd] *n* : fratricide *m*
fraud ['frɔd] *n* **1** DECEPTION, SWINDLE : fraude *f*, tromperie *f* **2** IMPOSTOR : imposteur *m*
fraudulent ['frɔdʒələnt] *adj* : frauduleux — **fraudulently** *adv*
fraught ['frɔt] *adj* : rempli, plein, chargé <fraught with danger : rempli de dangers>
fray¹ ['freɪ] *vt* **1** : effilocher, effiler (des tissus, etc.) **2** IRRITATE : mettre (les nerfs) à vif — *vi* : s'effilocher
fray² *n* BRAWL, FIGHT : bagarre *f*, rixe *f* <to join the fray : se jeter dans la mêlée>
frazzle¹ ['fræzəl] *vt* **-zled; -zling 1** FRAY : effiler, effranger **2** EXHAUST : épuiser, éreinter
frazzle² *n* **worn to a frazzle** : éreinté, crevé *fam*
freak ['friːk] *n* **1** ODDITY : phénomène *m*, monstre *m* <a freak of nature : un caprice de la nature> **2** ENTHUSIAST : fana *mf fam*
freakish ['friːkɪʃ] *adj* : anormal, bizarre
freckle¹ ['frɛkəl] *vi* **-led; -ling** : se couvrir de taches de rousseur, rousseler *Can*
freckle² *n* : tache *f* de rousseur
free¹ ['friː] *vt* **freed; freeing 1** LIBERATE : libérer, relâcher **2** RELIEVE, RID : libérer, dégager **3** RELEASE, UNTIE : détacher, dégager **4** CLEAR, UNBLOCK : déboucher
free² *adv* **1** FREELY : en toute liberté, librement **2** : gratuitement <children admitted free : entrée gratuite pour les enfants>
free³ *adj* **freer; freest 1** : libre <a free country : un pays libre> **2** : exempt <free from taxes : exempt d'impôt> **3** : gratuit <free admission : entrée gratuite> **4** VACANT : libre <is this seat free? : est-ce que la place est libre?> **5** OPEN : ouvert, franc **6** CLEAR : libre, dégagé
freebooter ['friːˌbuːṭər] *n* : pirate *m*
freeborn ['friːˈbɔrn] *adj* : né libre
freedom ['friːdəm] *n* : liberté *f*
free–for–all ['friːfərˌɔl] *n* : mêlée *f* générale
freelance ['friːˌlænʃs] *adj* : indépendant

freelancer ['fri:,lænʧər] *n* : travailleur *m* indépendant, travailleuse *f* indépendante; pigiste *mf*
freeload ['fri:,lo:d] *vi* : vivre en pique-assiette
freeloader ['fri:,lo:dər] *n* : pique-assiette *mf*
freely ['fri:li] *adv* **1** FRANKLY, OPENLY : librement **2** LAVISHLY : largement
Freemason ['fri:'meɪsən] *n* : franc-maçon *m*
Freemasonry ['fri:'meɪsənri] *n* : franc-maçonnerie *f*
freestanding ['fri:'stændɪŋ] *adj* : non-encastré, sur pied
freeway ['fri:,weɪ] *n* : autoroute *f*
freewill ['fri:,wɪl] *adj* : volontaire
free will *n* : libre arbitre *m*
freeze[1] ['fri:z] *v* **froze** ['fro:z]; **frozen** ['fro:zən]; **freezing** *vt* **1** : geler (de l'eau), congeler (de l'eau, des aliments, etc.) **2** : geler, bloquer (des prix, etc.) — *vi* **1** : geler <the lake has frozen over : le lac a gelé> **2** : se congeler, se surgeler <bread freezes well : le pain se congèle bien> **3 to be frozen in one's tracks** : rester cloué sur place **4 it's freezing!** : on caille! *France fam*, on gèle **5 to freeze to death** : mourir de froid
freeze[2] *n* **1** FREEZING, FROST : gel *m* **2** : gel *m*, blocage *m* <salary freeze : gel des salaires>
freeze–dry ['fri:z'draɪ] *vt* **-dried; -drying** : lyophiliser
freezer ['fri:zər] *n* : congélateur *m*
freezing point *n* : point *m* de congélation
freight[1] ['freɪt] *vt* : transporter (des marchandises)
freight[2] *n* **1** SHIPPING : transport *m* **2** GOODS : fret *m*, marchandises *fpl*
freighter ['freɪtər] *n* : cargo *m* (navire), avion-cargo *m*
French[1] ['frenʧ] *adj* : français
French[2] *n* **1** : français *m* (langue) **2 the French** : les Français
French Canadian[1] *adj* : canadien français
French Canadian[2] *n* : Canadien *m* français, Canadienne *f* française
french fries ['frenʧ,fraɪz] *npl* : frites *fpl*
Frenchman ['frenʧmən] *n, pl* **-men** [-mən, -,men] : Français *m*
Frenchwoman ['frenʧ,wʊmən] *n, pl* **-women** [-,wɪmən] : Française *f*
frenetic [fri'netɪk] *adj* : frénétique — **frenetically** [-ṭɪkli] *adv*
frenzied ['frenzid] *adj* : frénétique, agité
frenzy ['frenzi] *n, pl* **-zies** : frénésie *f*
frequency ['fri:kwənsi] *n, pl* **-cies** : fréquence *f*
frequent[1] [fri'kwent, 'fri:kwənt] *vt* : fréquenter
frequent[2] ['fri:kwənt] *adj* : fréquent
frequently ['fri:kwəntli] *adv* : fréquemment
fresco ['freskoʊ] *n, pl* **-coes** : fresque *f*
fresh ['freʃ] *adj* **1** : frais <fresh bread : du pain frais> **2** : frais, récent <fresh paint : peinture fraîche> **3** : doux <fresh water : eau douce> **4** PURE : frais, pur <fresh air : air pur> **5** NEW : nouveau <a fresh start : un nouveau départ> **6** BRISK : frais <a fresh wind : un vent frais> **7** IMPUDENT : insolent
freshen ['freʃən] *vt* : se rafraîchir (la mémoire) — *vi* **1** : fraîchir <the wind has freshened : le vent a fraîchi> **2 to freshen up** : se rafraîchir
freshet ['freʃət] *n* : crue *f* soudaine
freshly ['freʃli] *adv* RECENTLY : fraîchement, récemment
freshman ['freʃmən] *n, pl* **-men** [-mən, -,men] : étudiant *m*, -diante *f* de première année (à l'université)
freshness ['freʃnəs] *n* : fraîcheur *f*
freshwater ['freʃ,wɔṭər] *adj* : d'eau douce
fret[1] ['fret] *vi* **fretted; fretting** : se tracasser, s'en faire
fret[2] *n* **1** IRRITATION, WORRY : irritation *f*, inquiétude *f* **2** : frette *f* (d'une guitare)
fretful ['fretfəl] *adj* : irritable, agité, énervé
fretfully ['fretfəli] *adj* : avec inquiétude, avec énervement
friar ['fraɪər] *n* : frère *m*, moine *m*
fricassee[1] ['frɪkə,si:, ,frɪkə'si:] *vt* **-seed; -seeing** : fricasser
fricassee[2] *n* : fricassée *f*
friction ['frɪkʃən] *n* **1** RUBBING : friction *f*, frottement *m* **2** DISAGREEMENT : friction *f*, désaccord *m*
Friday ['fraɪdeɪ, -di] *n* : vendredi *m*
friend ['frend] *n* : ami *m*, amie *f*
friendless ['frendləs] *adj* : sans amis
friendliness ['frendlinəs] *n* : gentillesse *f*, attitude *f* amicale
friendly ['frendli] *adj* **friendlier; -est** : gentil, amical
friendship ['frend,ʃɪp] *n* : amitié *f*
frieze ['fri:z] *n* : frise *f*
frigate ['frɪgət] *n* : frégate *f*
fright ['fraɪt] *n* : peur *f*, frayeur *f*
frighten ['fraɪtən] *vt* : faire peur à, effrayer
frightful ['fraɪtfəl] *adj* **1** TERRIFYING : terrible, épouvantable **2** SHOCKING, STARTLING : effrayant, effarant <frightful costs : coûts effarants> **3** EXTREME : terrible <a frightful thirst : une soif terrible>
frightfully ['fraɪtfəli] *adv* : terriblement, affreusement
frightfulness ['fraɪtfəlnəs] *n* : horreur *f*
frigid ['frɪdʒɪd] *adj* : glacial
frigidity [fri'dʒɪdəṭi] *n* **1** : frigidité *f* (en médecine) **2** COLDNESS : froideur *f*
frill ['frɪl] *n* **1** RUFFLE : jabot *m* (d'une chemise), volant *m* (d'une jupe) **2** EMBELLISHMENT : fioriture *f*

frilly [ˈfrɪli] *adj* **frillier; -est 1** : à jabot, à volant **2** : à fioritures (se dit du style, etc.)
fringe[1] [ˈfrɪndʒ] *vt* **fringed; fringing** : franger, border
fringe[2] *n* **1** : frange *f* **2** EDGE : bordure *f*, bord *m* **3 fringe benefits** : avantages *mpl* sociaux, avantages *mpl* en nature
frisk [ˈfrɪsk] *vt* SEARCH : fouiller (un suspect) — *vi* FROLIC : gambader, folâtrer
friskiness [ˈfrɪskinəs] *n* : vivacité *f*
frisky [ˈfrɪski] *adj* **friskier; -est 1** SPIRITED : fringant (se dit d'un cheval) **2** PLAYFUL : vif, folâtre
fritter[1] [ˈfrɪtər] *vt or* **to fritter away** : gaspiller
fritter[2] *n* : beignet *m*
frivolity [frɪˈvɑləṭi] *n, pl* **-ties** : frivolité *f*
frivolous [ˈfrɪvələs] *adj* : frivole — **frivolously** *adv*
frizz[1] [ˈfrɪz] *vt* : friser (ses cheveux)
frizz[2] *n* : cheveux *mpl* frisés
frizzy [ˈfrɪzi] *adj* **frizzier; -est** : frisé, bouclé
fro [ˈfroː] *adv* **to and fro** : de long en large
frock [ˈfrɑk] *n* DRESS : robe *f*
frog [ˈfrɔg, ˈfrɑg] *n* **1** : grenouille *f* **2** LOOP : brandebourg *m* **3 to have a frog in one's throat** : avoir un chat dans la gorge
frogman [ˈfrɔgˌmæn, ˈfrɑg-, -mən] *n, pl* **-men** [-mən, -ˌmɛn] : homme-grenouille *m*
frolic[1] [ˈfrɑlɪk] *vi* **-icked; -icking** : gambader, folâtrer
frolic[2] *n* : gambades *fpl*, ébats *mpl*
frolicsome [ˈfrɑlɪksəm] *adj* : folâtre
from [ˈfrʌm, ˈfrəm] *prep* **1** (*indicating a starting point*) : de, à partir de <they're coming from Boston : ils arrivent de Boston> <from that day on : à partir de ce jour-là> **2** (*indicating removal or separation*) : contre <protection from the sun : protection contre le soleil> **3** (*indicating a source or cause*) : de, par, à <he's suffering from a cold : il souffre d'un rhume> <to work from necessity : travailler par nécessité> <to borrow money from a friend : emprunter de l'argent à un ami>
frond [ˈfrɑnd] *n* : fronde *f* (d'une fougère), feuille *f* (d'un palmier)
front[1] [ˈfrʌnt] *vi* **1** FACE : faire face <the building fronts south : l'édifice fait face au sud> **2 to front for** : servir de couverture à (qqn) **3 to front on** : donner sur — *vt* FACE : donner sur
front[2] *adj* : de devant, premier, (en) avant <the front row : le premier rang>
front[3] *n* **1** : avant *m*, devant *m* (d'une voiture, etc.), façade *f* (d'un bâtiment) **2** APPEARANCE : air *m*, contenance *f* <a bold front : une contenance assurée> **3** : front *m* (en météorologie) **4** VANGUARD : front *m* <the western front : le front ouest>
frontage [ˈfrʌntɪdʒ] *n* : façade *f*, devanture *f*
frontal [ˈfrʌntəl] *adj* : frontal, de front
frontier [ˌfrʌnˈtɪr] *n* : frontière *f*
frontiersman [ˌfrʌnˈtɪrzmən] *n, pl* **-men** [-mən, -ˌmɛn] : homme *m* de la frontière
frontispiece [ˈfrʌntəsˌpiːs] *n* : frontispice *m*
frost[1] [ˈfrɔst] *vt* **1** FREEZE : geler, givrer **2** ICE : glacer (un gâteau)
frost[2] *n* **1** : givre *m* **2** FREEZING : gel *m*, gelée *f*
frostbite [ˈfrɔstˌbaɪt] *n* : gelure *f*
frostbitten [ˈfrɔstˌbɪtən] *adj* : gelé
frosting [ˈfrɔstɪŋ] *n* ICING : glaçage *m* (d'un gâteau)
frosty [ˈfrɔsti] *adj* **frostier; -est 1** : givré, couvert de givre <frosty windows : vitres givrées> **2** FRIGID : glacial
froth [ˈfrɔθ] *n, pl* **froths** [ˈfrɔθs, ˈfrɔðz] : écume *f*, mousse *f*, broue *f Can*
frothy [ˈfrɔθi, -ði] *adj* **frothier; -est** : écumeux, mousseux
frown[1] [ˈfraʊn] *vi* : froncer les sourcils
frown[2] *n* : froncement *m* de sourcils
frowsy *or* **frowzy** [ˈfraʊzi] *adj* **frowsier** *or* **frowzier; -est** : négligé, peu soigné
froze, frozen → **freeze**[1]
frugal [ˈfruːgəl] *adj* : économe, frugal
frugality [fruːˈgæləṭi] *n* : frugalité *f*
frugally [ˈfruːgəli] *adv* : simplement, frugalement
fruit[1] [ˈfruːt] *vi* : donner des fruits
fruit[2] *n* **1** : fruit *m* **2 fruits** *npl* RESULTS : fruits *mpl* <the fruits of one's labors : les fruits de son travail>
fruitcake [ˈfruːtˌkeɪk] *n* : cake *m*
fruitful [ˈfruːtfəl] *adj* : fécond, fructueux
fruitfulness [ˈfruːtfəlnəs] *n* : fécondité *f*
fruition [fruːˈɪʃən] *n* : réalisation *f* <to come to fruition : se réaliser>
fruitless [ˈfruːtləs] *adj* : stérile <a fruitless discussion : une discussion sans résultat>
fruitlessly [ˈfruːtləsli] *adv* : en vain
fruity [ˈfruːṭi] *adj* **fruitier; -est** : fruité, de fruit
frumpy [ˈfrʌmpi] *adj* **frumpier; -est** : mal fagoté
frustrate [ˈfrʌsˌtreɪt] *vt* **-trated; -trating 1** DISAPPOINT, DISCOURAGE : frustrer, décevoir **2** THWART : contrecarrer, faire échouer
frustrating [ˈfrʌsˌtreɪṭɪŋ] *adj* : frustrant
frustration [ˌfrʌsˈtreɪʃən] *n* : frustration *f*
fry[1] [ˈfraɪ] *v* **fried; frying** : frire
fry[2] *n, pl* **fries 1** FRYING : friture *f* **2 fries** *npl* FRENCH FRIES : frites *fpl* **3** *pl* **fry** : fretin *m* (poisson) **4 small fry** : menu fretin *m*
frying pan *n* : poêle *f*, poêlon *m Can*

fuddle [ˈfʌdəl] *vt* **-dled; -dling** : brouiller, embrouiller
fudge[1] [ˈfʌdʒ] *v* **fudged; fudging** *vt* **1** FALSIFY : truquer **2** DODGE : esquiver — *vi* HEDGE : esquiver le problème
fudge[2] *n* : caramel *m* mou
fuel[1] [ˈfjuːəl] *vt* **-eled** *or* **-elled; -eling** *or* **-elling 1** : alimenter en combustible (un fourneau), ravitailler en carburant (un navire, etc.) **2** STIMULATE : aviver (des soupçons, etc.)
fuel[2] *n* : combustible *m*, carburant *m*
fugitive[1] [ˈfjuːdʒətɪv] *adj* **1** RUNAWAY : fugitif **2** ELUSIVE : fugace, éphémère
fugitive[2] *n* : fugitif *m*, -tive *f*
fulcrum [ˈfʊlkrəm, ˈfʌl-] *n, pl* **-crums** *or* **-cra** [-krə] : point *m* d'appui
fulfill *or* **fulfil** [fʊlˈfɪl] *vt* **-filled; -filling 1** EXECUTE : accomplir, réaliser **2** FILL, MEET : remplir, satisfaire à, répondre à
fulfillment [fʊlˈfɪlmənt] *n* **1** ACCOMPLISHMENT : accomplissement *m*, réalisation *f* **2** SATISFACTION : satisfaction *f*, contentement *m*
full[1] [ˈfʊl, ˈfʌl] *adv* **1** VERY : très, fort <you knew full well : tu le savais très bien> **2** ENTIRELY : entièrement <to turn full around : faire volte-face> **3** DIRECTLY : carrément <he hit me full in the face : il m'a frappé en plein visage>
full[2] *adj* **1** FILLED : plein, rempli, complet <the hotel is full : l'hôtel est complet> **2** COMPLETE, ENTIRE : entier, total <a full year : une année entière> **3** PLUMP : plein, rond <a full face : un visage rond> **4** AMPLE : ample **5** SATIATED : repu, rassasié <I'm full : j'ai assez mangé>
full[3] *n* **1 in ~** : en détail, intégralement **2 to the full** : au plus haut degré
full-fledged [ˈfʊlˈflɛdʒd] *adj* : à part entière
fullness [ˈfʊlnəs] *n* **1** ABUNDANCE : abondance *f* **2** : rondeur *f* (d'une silhouette), ampleur *f* (d'un vêtement)
fully [ˈfʊli] *adv* **1** COMPLETELY : tout à fait, complètement **2** : au moins <fully nine tenths of us : au moins neuf dixièmes d'entre nous>
fulsome [ˈfʊlsəm] *adj* : excessif, exagéré
fumble[1] [ˈfʌmbəl] *v* **-bled; -bling** *vt* : manier maladroitement, mal attraper (aux sports) — *vi* : tâtonner, fouiller
fumble[2] *n* : tâtonnement *m*
fume[1] [ˈfjuːm] *vi* **fumed; fuming 1** SMOKE : émettre des vapeurs, fumer **2** RAGE : fulminer, bouillonner
fume[2] *n* : émanation *f*, gaz *m* d'échappement (d'une voiture)
fumigate [ˈfjuːməˌgeɪt] *vt* **-gated; -gating** : désinfecter par fumigation
fumigation [ˌfjuːməˈgeɪʃən] *n* : fumigation *f*
fun[1] [ˈfʌn] *adj* : amusant, marrant *fam*
fun[2] *n* **1** ENJOYMENT : amusement *m*, plaisir *m*, fun *m Can fam* <to have fun : s'amuser> **2 for ~** : pour rire **3 to make fun of** : se moquer de
function[1] [ˈfʌŋkʃən] *vi* **1** WORK : fonctionner, marcher **2 to function as** : faire fonction de, servir de
function[2] *n* **1** OCCUPATION : fonction *f*, charge *f* **2** PURPOSE : fonction *f*, rôle *m* **3** CEREMONY : réception *f*, cérémonie *f*
functional [ˈfʌŋkʃənəl] *adj* : fonctionnel — **functionally** *adv*
functionary [ˈfʌŋkʃəˌnɛri] *n, pl* **-aries** : fonctionnaire *mf*
fund[1] [ˈfʌnd] *vt* : financer, fournir des fonds à
fund[2] *n* **1** SUPPLY : fond *m*, réserve *f* <a fund of jokes : un répertoire de plaisanteries> **2** : caisse *f*, fonds *mpl* <relief fund : caisse de secours> **3 funds** *npl* RESOURCES : fonds *mpl*, capitaux *mpl*
fundamental[1] [ˌfʌndəˈmɛntəl] *adj* **1** BASIC : fondamental, essentiel **2** PRINCIPAL : principal — **fundamentally** *adv*
fundamental[2] *n* : principe *m* essentiel
funeral[1] [ˈfjuːnərəl] *adj* : funèbre, funéraire
funeral[2] *n* : enterrement *m*, funérailles *fpl*
funeral home *or* **funeral parlor** *n* : entreprise *f* de pompes funèbres, salon *m* funéraire *Can*, salon *m* mortuaire *Can*
funereal [fjuːˈnɪriəl] *adj* : funèbre
fungal [ˈfʌŋgəl] *adj* : fongique
fungicide [ˈfʌndʒəˌsaɪd, ˈfʌŋgə-] *n* : fongicide *m*
fungicidal [ˌfʌndʒəˈsaɪdəl, ˌfʌŋgə-] *adj* : fongicide
fungous [ˈfʌŋgəs] → **fungal**
fungus [ˈfʌŋgəs] *n, pl* **fungi** [ˈfʌnˌdʒaɪ, ˈfʌŋˌgaɪ] **1** MUSHROOM : champignon *m* **2** MOLD : moisissure *f*
funnel[1] [ˈfʌnəl] *vt* **-neled; -neling 1** : faire passer dans un entonnoir **2** CHANNEL : canaliser
funnel[2] *n* **1** : entonnoir *m* **2** SMOKESTACK : cheminée *f*
funnies [ˈfʌniz] *npl* : bandes *fpl* dessinées
funny [ˈfʌni] *adj* **funnier; -est 1** AMUSING : drôle, amusant, rigolo *fam* **2** PECULIAR : bizarre, curieux, drôle
fur[1] [ˈfər] *adj* : de fourrure
fur[2] *n* **1** : fourrure *f*, pelage *m* (d'un animal) **2** : fourrure *f* <fake fur : fausse fourrure>
furbish [ˈfərbɪʃ] *vt* **1** POLISH : fourbir, polir **2** RENOVATE : remettre à neuf
furious [ˈfjʊriəs] *adj* **1** ANGRY : furieux **2** FIERCE, VIOLENT : acharné, déchaîné <a furious storm : un orage déchaîné>

furiously ['fjʊriəsli] *adv* **1** ANGRILY : furieusement **2** FRANTICALLY : frénétiquement
furlong ['fər,lɔŋ] *n* : furlong *m* (201,17 mètres)
furlough[1] ['fər,lo:] *vt* : accorder une permission à
furlough[2] *n* : congé *m*, permission *f*
furnace ['fərnəs] *n* : fourneau *m*, fournaise *f Can*
furnish ['fərnɪʃ] *vt* **1** SUPPLY : fournir, donner **2** : meubler <a furnished apartment : un appartement meublé>
furnishings ['fərnɪʃɪŋz] *npl* : ameublement *m*, meubles *mpl*
furniture ['fərnɪtʃər] *n* : meubles *mpl*
furor ['fjʊr,ɔr, -ər] *n* **1** RAGE : fureur *f* **2** UPROAR : scandale *m*, tumulte *m*
furrier ['fəriər] *n* : fourreur *m*, -reuse *f*
furrow[1] ['fəro:] *vt* **1** : sillonner (la terre) **2 to furrow one's brow** : plisser son front
furrow[2] *n* **1** : sillon *m* **2** WRINKLE : ride *f*
furry ['fəri] *adj* **furrier; -est** : au poil touffu (se dit d'un animal), en peluche (se dit d'un jouet, etc.)
further[1] ['fərðər] *vt* PROMOTE : promouvoir, avancer
further[2] *adv* **1** FARTHER : plus loin **2** MORE : davantage, plus **3** MOREOVER : en outre
further[3] *adj* **1** FARTHER : plus éloigné **2** ADDITIONAL : nouveau, supplémentaire <until further notice : jusqu'à nouvel ordre>
furtherance ['fərðərənʦ] *n* : avancement *m*
furthermore ['fərðər,mor] *adv* : en outre, de plus
furthermost ['fərðər,mo:st] *adj* : le plus lointain
furthest ['fərðəst] *adv & adj* → **farthest**
furtive ['fərṭɪv] *adj* : furtif **— furtively** *adv*
furtiveness ['fərṭɪvnəs] *n* : caractère *m* furtif
fury ['fjʊri] *n, pl* **-ries 1** RAGE : furie *f*, fureur *f* **2** VIOLENCE : fureur *f*, violence *f* **3** FRENZY : frénésie *f*
fuse[1] *or* **fuze** ['fju:z] *vt* **fused** *or* **fuzed; fusing** *or* **fuzing** : munir d'un fusible
fuse[2] *v* **fused; fusing** *vt* **1** MELT : fondre (des métaux) **2** BLEND, UNITE : fusionner, unifier **—** *vi* : fusionner
fuse[3] *n* **1** : mèche *f* (d'un explosif) **2** : fusible *m*, plomb *m* <to blow a fuse : faire sauter un plomb> **3** *usu* **fuze** : détonateur *m*
fuselage ['fju:sə,lɑʒ, -zə-] *n* : fuselage *m*
fusillade ['fju:sə,lɑd, -,leɪd, ,fju:sə'-, -zə-] *n* : fusillade *f*
fusion ['fju:ʒən] *n* : fusion *f*
fuss[1] ['fʌs] *vi* **1** : s'affairer <fussing over the children : s'affairant autour des enfants> **2** WORRY : s'inquiéter, se tracasser
fuss[2] *n* **1** AGITATION, COMMOTION : agitation *f*, remue-ménage *m* **2** PROTEST : histoires *fpl* <to make a fuss : faire des histoires>
fussbudget ['fʌs,bʌdʒət] *n* : tatillon *m*, -lonne *f*
fussiness ['fʌsinəs] *n* : façon *f* tatillonne
fussy ['fʌsi] *adj* **fussier; -est 1** IRRITABLE : irritable **2** FINICKY : tatillon, pointilleux, difficile <he's a fussy eater : il est difficile pour la nourriture> **3** OVERELABORATE : tarabiscoté
futile ['fju:ṭəl, 'fju:,taɪl] *adj* : futile, vain
futility [fju:'tɪləṭi] *n* : futilité *f*
future[1] ['fju:tʃər] *adj* : futur
future[2] *n* **1** : avenir *m*, futur *m* <in the near future : dans un proche avenir> **2** *or* **future tense** : futur *m*
futuristic [,fju:tʃə'rɪstɪk] *adj* : futuriste
fuze → **fuse**
fuzz ['fʌz] *n* **1** DOWN : duvet *m* **2** FLUFF : peluches *fpl*
fuzziness ['fʌzinəs] *n* **1** : caractère *m* duveteux **2** : flou *m* (en photographie)
fuzzy ['fʌzi] *adj* **fuzzier; -est 1** DOWNY : duveteux **2** INDISTINCT : flou

G

g ['dʒi:] *n, pl* **g's** *or* **gs** ['dʒi:z] : g *m*, septième lettre de l'alphabet
gab[1] ['gæb] *vi* **gabbed; gabbing** : bavarder, jacasser, papoter
gab[2] *n* CHATTER : bavardage *m*, papotage *m*
gabardine ['gæbər,di:n] *n* : gabardine *f*
gabby ['gæbi] *adj* **gabbier; -est** : bavard
gable ['geɪbəl] *n* : pignon *m*
Gabonese[1] [,gæbə'ni:z] *adj* : gabonais
Gabonese[2] *n* : Gabonais *m*, -naise *f*
gad ['gæd] *vi* **gadded; gadding** *or* **to gad about** : se balader, vadrouiller *fam*
gadfly ['gæd,flaɪ] *n, pl* **-flies 1** : taon *m* (insecte) **2** FAULTFINDER : critiqueur *m*, -queuse *f*; casse-pieds *mf fam*
gadget ['gædʒəṭ] *n* : gadget *m*, bebelle *f Can fam*
gadgetry ['gædʒətri] *n* : gadgets *mpl*
gaff ['gæf] *n* HOOK : gaffe *f*
gaffe ['gæf] *n* : gaffe *f*
gag[1] ['gæg] *v* **gagged; gagging** *vt* : bâillonner **—** *vi* **1** CHOKE : s'étrangler **2** RETCH : avoir des haut-le-coeur
gag[2] *n* **1** : bâillon *m* **2** JOKE : blague *f*
gage → **gauge**

gaggle ['gægəl] *n* : troupeau *m* (d'oies, etc.)
gaiety ['geɪəṭi] *n, pl* **-eties** : gaieté *f*
gaily ['geɪli] *adv* : gaiement, de bonne humeur
gain[1] ['geɪn] *vt* **1** ACQUIRE : acquérir, gagner, obtenir <to gain ground : gagner du terrain> <to gain experience : acquérir de l'expérience> **2** REACH : arriver, atteindre <to gain the shore : atteindre la rive> **3** INCREASE : prendre <to gain weight : prendre du poids> — *vi* **1** PROFIT : gagner, profiter **2** ADVANCE : avancer (se dit d'une horloge) **3 to gain on** : rattraper
gain[2] *n* **1** PROFIT : profit *m*, bénéfice *m* <gains and losses : profits et pertes> **2** INCREASE : augmentation *f*
gainful ['geɪnfəl] *adj* : rémunéré
gait ['geɪt] *n* : démarche *f*
gal ['gæl] *n* : jeune fille *f*
gala[1] ['geɪlə, 'gæ-, 'gɑ-] *adj* : de gala
gala[2] *n* : gala *m*
galactic [gə'læktɪk] *adj* : galactique
galaxy ['gæləksi] *n, pl* **-axies** : galaxie *f*
galé ['geɪl] *n* **1** WIND : vent *m* fort **2** OUTBURST : éclat *m* <gales of laughter : éclats de rire>
gall[1] ['gɔl] *vt* **1** CHAFE : écorcher, excorier **2** IRRITATE : irriter, exaspérer
gall[2] *n* **1** BILE : bile *f* **2** IMPUDENCE : impudence *f* **3** SORE : écorchure *f* **4** : galle *f* (d'une plante)
gallant ['gælənt] *adj* **1** BRAVE : vaillant, courageux **2** CHIVALROUS : galant, courtois
gallantly ['gæləntli] *adv* **1** BRAVELY : vaillamment **2** CHIVALROUSLY : galamment
gallantry ['gæləntri] *n, pl* **-ries** : galanterie *f*
gallbladder ['gɔlˌblædər] *n* : vesicule *f* biliaire
galleon ['gæljən] *n* : galion *m*
gallery ['gæləri] *n, pl* **-leries 1** BALCONY : galerie *f*, tribune *f* <press gallery : tribune de la presse> **2** ARCADE, CORRIDOR : galerie *f* **3** *or* **art gallery** : musée *m* des beaux-arts, galerie *f*
galley ['gæli] *n, pl* **-leys 1** SHIP : galère *f* **2** KITCHEN : coquerie *f* (d'un navire)
gallium ['gæliəm] *n* : gallium *m*
gallivant ['gælə,vænt] *vi* : se balader, courir la galipote *Can*
gallon ['gælən] *n* : gallon *m*
gallop[1] ['gæləp] *vi* : galoper
gallop[2] *n* : galop *m*
gallows ['gæˌloːz] *n, pl* **-lows** *or* **-lowses** [-ˌloːzəz] : gibet *m*, potence *f*
gallstone ['gɔlˌstoːn] *n* : calcul *m* biliaire
galore [gə'lor] *adj* : en abondance
galoshes [gə'lɑʃəz] *npl* : caoutchoucs *mpl*, claques *fpl Can*
galvanize ['gælvəˌnaɪz] *vt* **-nized; -nizing** : galvaniser
Gambian[1] ['gæmbiən] *adj* : gambien
Gambian[2] *n* : Gambien *m*, -bienne *f*
gambit ['gæmbɪt] *n* **1** : gambit *m* (aux échecs) **2** STRATAGEM : stratagème *m*, manœuvre *f*
gamble[1] ['gæmbəl] *v* **-bled; -bling** *vi* : jouer — *vt* WAGER : parier
gamble[2] *n* **1** BET : pari *m* **2** RISK : entreprise *f* risquée
gambler ['gæmbələr] *n* : joueur *m*, joueuse *f*
gambol ['gæmbəl] *vi* **-boled** *or* **-bolled; -boling** *or* **-bolling** : gambader
game[1] ['geɪm] *adj* **1** PLUCKY : courageux **2** READY : partant <to be game for anything : être toujours partant> **3** LAME : estropié
game[2] *n* **1** : jeu *m* <game of chance : jeu de hasard> **2** MATCH : match *m*, partie *f* **3** : gibier *m* <big game : gros gibier>
gamekeeper ['geɪmˌkiːpər] *n* : garde-chasse *m*
gamely ['geɪmli] *adv* : courageusement
gamete ['gæˌmiːt, gə'miːt] *n* : gamète *m*
gamma ray ['gæmə] *n* : rayon *m* gamma
gamut ['gæmət] *n* : gamme *f* <the whole gamut : toute la gamme>
gamy *or* **gamey** ['geɪmi] *adj* **gamier; -est** : faisandé
gander ['gændər] *n* **1** : jars *m* (oiseau) **2** GLANCE : coup *m* d'oeil
gang[1] ['gæŋ] *vi* **to gang up on** : se liguer contre
gang[2] *n* : bande *f*, gang *f Can fam*, gang *m France* (de criminels)
gangling ['gæŋglɪŋ] *adj* LANKY : dégingandé
ganglion ['gæŋgliən] *n, pl* **-glia** /-gliə/ : ganglion *m*
gangplank ['gæŋˌplæŋk] *n* : passerelle *f*
gangrene ['gæŋˌgriːn, 'gæn-; gæŋ'-, gæn'-] *n* : gangrène *f*
gangrenous ['gæŋgrənəs] *adj* : gangreneux
gangster ['gæŋstər] *n* : gangster *m*
gangway ['gæŋˌweɪ] *n* **1** PASSAGEWAY : passage *m* **2** GANGPLANK : passerelle *f* **3 gangway!** : dégagez le passage!
gannet ['gænət] *n* : fou *m* de Bassan
gap ['gæp] *n* **1** OPENING : trou *m*, vide *m*, brèche *f* **2** INTERVAL : intervalle *m*, période *f* **3** DISPARITY : gouffre *m*, écart *m* **4** LACUNA : lacune *f* <a gap in one's knowledge : une lacune dans sa connaissance> **5** GORGE : gorge *f*, col *m*
gape[1] ['geɪp] *vi* **gaped; gaping 1** OPEN : bâiller, s'ouvrir **2** STARE : rester bouche bée
gape[2] *n* **1** CHASM, OPENING : trou *m* béant **2** STARE : regard *m* ébahi, regard *m* bouche bée
garage[1] [gə'rɑʒ, -'rɑdʒ] *vt* **-raged; -raging** : mettre au garage
garage[2] *n* : garage *m*

garb[1] ['gɑrb] *vt* : vêtir
garb[2] *n* : costume *m*, mise *f*
garbage ['gɑrbɪdʒ] *n* : ordures *fpl*
garbage can *n* : poubelle *f*
garbageman ['gɑrbɪdʒˌmən] *n, pl* **-men** [-ˌmɛn, -ˌmen] : éboueur *m*
garble ['gɑrbəl] *vt* **-bled; -bling** : raconter de travers, déformer, embrouiller
garbled ['gɑrbəld] *adj* : confus, embrouillé, déformé
garden[1] ['gɑrdən] *vi* : jardiner
garden[2] *n* : jardin *m*
gardener ['gɑrdənər] *n* : jardinier *m*, -nière *f*
gardenia [gɑr'diːnjə] *n* : gardénia *m*
gargantuan [gɑr'gæntʃʊən] *adj* : gargantuesque
gargle[1] ['gɑrgəl] *vi* **-gled; -gling** : se gargariser
gargle[2] *n* : gargarisme *m* (acte et produit)
gargoyle ['gɑrˌgɔɪl] *n* : gargouille *f*
garish ['gærɪʃ] *adj* : criard, voyant
garland[1] ['gɑrlənd] *vt* : enguirlander (de fleurs, etc.)
garland[2] *n* : guirlande *f*
garlic ['gɑrlɪk] *n* : ail *m*
garment ['gɑrmənt] *n* : vêtement *m*
garner ['gɑrnər] *vt* : accumuler, recueillir, engranger (des récoltes)
garnet ['gɑrnət] *n* : grenat *m*
garnish[1] ['gɑrnɪʃ] *vt* : garnir
garnish[2] *n* : garniture *f*
garret ['gærət] *n* : mansarde *f*
garrison[1] ['gærəsən] *vt* **1** QUARTER : mettre (des troupes) en garnison **2** OCCUPY : placer une garnison dans (une ville, etc.)
garrison[2] *n* : garnison *f*
garrulous ['gærələs] *adj* : loquace, bavard
garrulousness ['gærələsnəs] *n* : loquacité *f*
garter ['gɑrtər] *n* : jarretière *f*
gas[1] ['gæs] *v* **gassed; gassing** *vt* : gazer — *vi* **to gas up** : faire le plein d'essence
gas[2] *n, pl* **gases 1** : gaz *m* <to cook with gas : cuisiner au gaz> **2** GASOLINE : essence *f*
gaseous ['gæʃəs, 'gæsiəs] *adj* : gazeux
gash[1] ['gæʃ] *vt* : entailler
gash[2] *n* : entaille *f*
gasket ['gæskət] *n* : joint *m*
gasoline ['gæsəˌliːn, ˌgæsə'-] *n* : essence *f*, gaz *m* *Can fam*
gasp[1] ['gæsp] *vi* **1** : avoir le souffle coupé (par la surprise, etc.) **2** PANT : haleter — *vt* : dire en haletant
gasp[2] *n* : halètement *m* <to the last gasp : jusqu'au dernier souffle>
gastric ['gæstrɪk] *adj* : gastrique
gastronomy [gæs'trɑnəmi] *n* : gastronomie *f* — **gastronomic** [ˌgæstrə'nɑmɪk] *adj*
gate ['geɪt] *n* **1** DOOR : porte *f* **2** BARRIER : barrière *f*, grille *f*
gatekeeper ['geɪtˌkiːpər] *n* : gardien *m*, -dienne *f*; portier *m*, -tière *f*
gateway ['geɪtˌweɪ] *n* : porte *f*, portail *m*
gather[1] ['gæðər] *vt* **1** ASSEMBLE : rassembler **2** COLLECT : recueillir, ramasser **3** DEDUCE : déduire **4** : froncer (une étoffe) **5 to gather speed** : prendre de la vitesse — *vi* ASSEMBLE : se rassembler, se réunir
gather[2] *n* : fronce *f* (d'une étoffe)
gathering ['gæðərɪŋ] *n* : rassemblement *m*
gauche ['goːʃ] *adj* : gauche
gaudy ['gɔdi] *adj* **gaudier; -est** : criard, tape-à-l'oeil
gauge[1] ['geɪdʒ] *vt* **gauged; gauging 1** MEASURE : jauger, mesurer **2** ESTIMATE : évaluer, calculer
gauge[2] *n* **1** INDICATOR : jauge *f*, indicateur *m* **2** CALIBER : calibre *m* **3** INDICATION : moyen *m* de jauger, test *m* (de caractère, etc.)
gaunt ['gɔnt] *adj* : décharné, émacié
gauntlet ['gɔntlət] *n* : gant *m* (à crispin) <to throw down the gauntlet : jeter le gant>
gauze ['gɔz] *n* : gaze *f*
gauzy ['gɔzi] *adj* **gauzier; -est** : transparent, diaphane
gave → **give**[1]
gavel ['gævəl] *n* : marteau *m* (de magistrat, etc.)
gawk ['gɔk] *vi* **to gawk at** : regarder bouche bée, être bouche bée devant
gawky ['gɔki] *adj* **gawkier; -est** : gauche, malhabile, emprunté
gay ['geɪ] *adj* **1** MERRY : gai, joyeux **2** BRIGHT, COLORFUL : vif, éclatant **3** HOMOSEXUAL : gai, gay
gaze[1] ['geɪz] *vi* **gazed; gazing** : regarder (fixement)
gaze[2] *n* : regard *m*
gazelle [gə'zɛl] *n* : gazelle *f*
gazette [gə'zɛt] *n* **1** NEWSPAPER : journal *m* **2** : journal *m* officiel
gazetteer [ˌgæzə'tɪr] *n* : dictionnaire *m* géographique, index *m* géographique
gear[1] ['gɪr] *vt* ADAPT, ORIENT : adapter <a book geared to children : un livre adapté aux enfants> — *vi* **to gear up** : se préparer, être fin prêt
gear[2] *n* **1** EQUIPMENT : équipement *m*, matériel *m* <fishing gear : matériel de pêche> **2** BELONGINGS : effets *mpl* personnels **3** SPEED : vitesse *f* <to change gear : changer de vitesse> <to be in first gear : être en première> **4** COGWHEEL : roue *f* dentée, pignon *m*
gearshift ['gɪrˌʃɪft] *n* : levier *m* de vitesses
geese → **goose**
Geiger counter ['gaɪgərˌkaʊntər] *n* : compteur *m* Geiger
gelatin ['dʒɛlətən] *n* : gélatine *f*
gem ['dʒɛm] *n* **1** : pierre *f* précieuse, gemme *f* **2** JEWEL : joyau *m* <the gem

of my collection : le joyau de ma collection>

Gemini ['dʒɛmə,naɪ] *n* : Gémeaux *mpl*

gemstone ['dʒɛm,stoːn] *n* : pierre *f* précieuse

gender ['dʒɛndər] *n* **1** : genre *m* (en grammaire) **2** SEX : sexe *m*

gene ['dʒiːn] *n* : gène *m*

genealogical [,dʒiːniə'lɑdʒɪkəl] *adj* : généalogique

genealogy [,dʒiːni'ɑlədʒi, ,dʒɛ-, -'æ-] *n, pl* **-gies** : généalogie *f*

genera → **genus**

general[1] ['dʒɛnrəl, 'dʒɛnə-] *adj* : général <as a general rule : en règle générale>

general[2] *n* **1** : général *m* (militaire) **2 in ~** : en général

generality [,dʒɛnə'rælət̬i] *n, pl* **-ties** : généralité *f*

generalization [,dʒɛnrələ'zeɪʃən, ,dʒɛnərə-] *n* : généralisation *f*

generalize ['dʒɛnrə,laɪz, 'dʒɛnərə-] *vi* **-ized; -izing** : généraliser

generally ['dʒɛnrəli, 'dʒɛnərə-] *adv* **1** USUALLY : généralement, en général **2** OVERALL, WIDELY : dans l'ensemble, en général

generate ['dʒɛnə,reɪt] *vt* **-ated; -ating** : générer

generation [,dʒɛnə'reɪʃən] *n* : génération *f*

generator ['dʒɛnə,reɪt̬ər] *n* **1** PRODUCER : générateur *m* **2** : génératrice *f* (d'énergie électrique)

generic [dʒə'nɛrɪk] *adj* : générique

generosity [,dʒɛnə'rɑsət̬i] *n, pl* **-ties** : générosité *f*

generous ['dʒɛnərəs] *adj* **1** OPEN-HANDED : généreux **2** ABUNDANT, COPIOUS : abondant, copieux — **generously** *adv*

genetic [dʒə'nɛt̬ɪk] *adj* : génétique — **genetically** *adv*

geneticist [dʒə'nɛt̬ɪsəst] *n* : généticien *m*, -cienne *f*

genetics [dʒə'nɛt̬ɪks] *n* : génétique *f*

genial ['dʒiːniəl] *adj* : affable, cordial, aimable — **genially** *adv*

geniality [,dʒiːni'æləṭi] *n* : cordialité *f*

genie ['dʒiːni] *n* : génie *m*

genital ['dʒɛnət̬əl] *adj* : génital

genitals ['dʒɛnət̬əlz] *npl* : organes *mpl* génitaux

genius ['dʒiːnjəs] *n* : génie *m*

genocide ['dʒɛnə,saɪd] *n* : génocide *m*

genre ['ʒɑnrə, 'ʒɑr] *n* : genre *m*

genteel [dʒɛn'tiːl] *adj* : distingué

gentile ['dʒɛn,taɪl] *n* : gentil *m*

gentility [,dʒɛn'tɪləṭi] *n, pl* **-ties 1** GENTRY : petite noblesse *f* **2** COURTESY : politesse *f*

gentle ['dʒɛntəl] *adj* **-tler; -tlest 1** NOBLE : noble, de bonne famille **2** DOCILE, MILD : doux **3** LIGHT : léger <a gentle blow : un coup bien léger> **4** GRADUAL : doux, sans heurts <a gentle slope : une pente douce> <to come to a gentle stop : s'arrêter doucement>

gentleman ['dʒɛntəlmən] *n, pl* **-men** [-mən, -,mɛn] **1** MAN : monsieur *m* **2** : gentleman *m* <to act like a gentleman : agir en gentleman>

gentlemanly ['dʒɛntəlmənli] *adj* : courtois, distingué

gentleness ['dʒɛntəlnəs] *n* : douceur *f*

gentlewoman ['dʒɛntəl,wʊmən] *n, pl* **-women** [-,wɪmən] : dame *f* (bien née)

gentry ['dʒɛntri] *n, pl* **-tries** : petite noblesse *f*

genuflect ['dʒɛnjʊ,flɛkt] *vi* : faire une génuflexion

genuflection [,dʒɛnjʊ'flɛkʃən] *n* : génuflexion *f*

genuine [,dʒɛnjʊwən] *adj* **1** AUTHENTIC, REAL : authentique, vrai, véritable **2** SINCERE : sincère — **genuinely** *adv*

genus ['dʒiːnəs] *n, pl* **genera** ['dʒɛnərə] : genre *m*

geochemistry [,dʒiːo'kɛməstri] *n* : géochimie *f*

geodesic [,dʒiːə'dɛsɪk, -'diː-, -zɪk] *adj* : géodésique

geographer [dʒi'ɑgrəfər] *n* : géographe *mf*

geographic [,dʒiːə'græfɪk] *or* **geographical** [-fɪkəl] *adj* : géographique — **geographically** [-fɪkli] *adv*

geography [dʒi'ɑgrəfi] *n, pl* **-phies** : géographie *f*

geologic [,dʒiːə'lɑdʒɪk] *or* **geological** [-dʒɪkəl] *adj* : géologique — **geologically** [-dʒɪkli] *adv*

geologist [dʒi'ɑlədʒɪst] *n* : géologue *mf*

geology [dʒi'ɑlədʒi] *n, pl* **-gies** : géologie *f*

geomagnetic [dʒiːomæg'nɛt̬ɪk] *adj* : géomagnétique

geometric [,dʒiːə'mɛtrɪk] *or* **geometrical** [-'mɛtrɪkəl] *adj* : géométrique

geometry [dʒi'ɑmətri] *n, pl* **-tries** : géométrie *f*

geranium [dʒə'reɪniəm] *n* : géranium *m*

gerbil ['dʒərbəl] *n* : gerbille *f*

geriatric [,dʒeri'ætrɪk] *adj* : gériatrique

geriatrics [,dʒeri'ætrɪks] *n* : gériatrie *f*

germ ['dʒərm] *n* **1** MICROBE : microbe *m*, germe *m* **2** : germe *m* (en biologie) **3** RUDIMENTS : germe *m* (d'une idée, etc.)

German[1] ['dʒərmən] *adj* : allemand

German[2] *n* **1** : Allemand *m*, -mande *f* **2** : allemand *m* (langue)

germane [dʒər'meɪn] *adj* : pertinent

germanium [dʒər'meɪniəm] *n* : germanium *m*

German measles *n* : rubéole *f*

German shepherd *n* : berger *m* allemand

germ cell *n* : gamète *m*, cellule *f* germinale

germicide ['dʒərmə,saɪd] *n* : germicide *m*

germinate [ˈdʒərmə,neɪt] *v* **-nated; -nating** *vi* : germer — *vt* : faire germer
germination [,dʒərmə'neɪʃən] *n* : germination *f*
gerund [ˈdʒerənd] *n* : gérondif *m*
gestation [dʒɛ'steɪʃən] *n* : gestation *f*
gesture[1] [ˈdʒɛstʃər] *vi* **-tured; -turing 1** : gesticuler, faire des gestes **2 to gesture to** : faire signe à
gesture[2] *n* : geste *m*
get [ˈgɛt] *v* **got** [ˈgɑt]; **got** *or* **gotten** [ˈgɑtən]; **getting** *vt* **1** OBTAIN : obtenir, trouver, se procurer **2** RECEIVE : recevoir, avoir <the garden gets a lot of sun : le jardin reçoit beaucoup de soleil> **3** EARN : gagner, mériter **4** FETCH : chercher (un objet), aller chercher (une personne) **5** CATCH : prendre (un train, etc.), attraper (une balle, un rhume), saisir (une personne) **6** PUT, TAKE : faire parvenir <to get sth to s.o. : faire parvenir qqch à qqn> <we can get the car through here : nous pouvons faire passer la voiture par ici> **7** UNDERSTAND : comprendre, piger *fam* <now I get it! : je pige!> **8** PREPARE : préparer <to get dinner : préparer le dîner> **9** PERSUADE : persuader, convaincre <I got her to agree : j'ai réussi à obtenir son accord> **10** (*to cause to be*) <to get one's hair cut : se faire couper les cheveux> **11 to have got** : avoir <I've got a headache : j'ai mal à la tête> **12 to have got to** : devoir — *vi* **1** BECOME : devenir <she's getting impatient : elle devient impatiente> <it's getting late : il se fait tard> **2** GO, MOVE : aller, arriver, se rendre <to get to the top of : arriver au sommet> <where did he get to? : où en est-il allé?> **3** PROGRESS : avancer <she got to be a director : elle a avancé à la position de directeur> **4 to get ahead** : progresser, prendre de l'avance **5 to get around** EVADE : contourner **6 to get at** REACH : atteindre **7 to get at** INSINUATE, MEAN : vouloir dire <what are you getting at? : où voulez-vous en venir?> **8 to get at** ASCERTAIN : découvrir, parvenir à **9 to get away with** : échapper à, s'en tirer à **10 to get back at** : se venger de **11 to get over** : se remettre de (une maladie, etc.) **12 to get together** MEET : se réunir
get along *vi* **1** PROGRESS : avancer, progresser **2** MANAGE : aller <how are you getting along? : comment vas-tu?> **3 to get along with** : bien s'entendre avec
getaway [ˈgɛtə,weɪ] *n* : fuite *f* <to make one's getaway : s'enfuir>
get off *vi* **1** START : partir **2** : tirer d'affaire, s'en tirer <to get off lightly : s'en tirer à bon compte>
get out *vi* **1** ESCAPE : sortir **2** : être révélé <our secret got out : notre secret est révélé>
get-together [ˈgɛttə,geðər] *n* : réunion *f*, petite fête *f*
get up *vi* ARISE : se lever — *vt* **1** PREPARE, ORGANIZE : former, organiser **2** DRESS : habiller
geyser [ˈgaɪzər] *n* : geyser *m*
Ghanian[1] [ˈgɑnian, ˈgæ-] *adj* : ghanéen
Ghanian[2] *n* : Ghanéen *m*, -néenne *f*
ghastly [ˈgæstli] *adj* **ghastlier; -est 1** HORRIBLE : horrible, épouvantable **2** PALE : blème, blafard
gherkin [ˈgərkən] *n* : cornichon *m*
ghetto [ˈgɛto:] *n, pl* **-tos** *or* **-toes** : ghetto *m*
ghost [ˈgo:st] *n* : fantôme *m*, spectre *m*
ghostly [ˈgo:stli] *adj* **ghostlier; -est** : spectral
ghost town *n* : ville *f* morte
ghoul [ˈgu:l] *n* : goule *f*
ghoulish [ˈgu:lɪʃ] *adj* : macabre
GI [,dʒi:ˈaɪ] *n, pl* **GI's** *or* **GIs** : soldat *m* américain
giant[1] [ˈdʒaɪənt] *adj* : géant, gigantesque
giant[2] *n* : géant *m*, géante *f*
gibberish [ˈdʒɪbərɪʃ] *n* : charabia *m fam*, baragouin *m*
gibbon [ˈgɪbən] *n* : gibbon *m*
gibe[1] [ˈdʒaɪb] *vi* **gibed; gibing** : se moquer <to gibe at s.o. : railler qqn, se moquer de qqn>
gibe[2] *n* : raillerie *f*, moquerie *f*
giblets [ˈdʒɪbləts] *npl* : abats *mpl* (de volaille)
giddiness [ˈgɪdinəs] *n* **1** DIZZINESS : vertiges *mpl*, étourdissements *mpl* **2** SILLINESS : légèreté *f*, étourderie *f*
giddy [ˈgɪdi] *adj* **giddier; -est 1** DIZZY : vertigineux **2** FRIVOLOUS, SILLY : frivole, écervelé, étourdi
gift [ˈgɪft] *n* **1** PRESENT : cadeau *m* **2** TALENT : don *m*
gifted [ˈgɪftəd] *adj* TALENTED : doué
gigantic [dʒaɪˈgæntɪk] *adj* : gigantesque
giggle[1] [ˈgɪgəl] *vi* **-gled; -gling** : rire bêtement
giggle[2] *n* : fou rire *m*, petit rire *m* sot
Gila monster [ˈhi:lə] *n* : monstre *m* de Gila
gild [ˈgɪld] *vt* **gilded** [ˈgɪldəd] *or* **gilt** [ˈgɪlt]; **gilding** : dorer
gill [ˈgɪl] *n* : branchie *f*, ouïe *f*
gilt[1] [ˈgɪlt] *adj* : doré
gilt[2] *n* : dorure *f*
gimlet [ˈgɪmlət] *n* : vrille *f* (outil)
gimmick [ˈgɪmɪk] *n* : truc *m*, gadget *m* <publicity gimmick : truc publicitaire>
gin [ˈdʒɪn] *n* **1** *or* **cotton gin** : égreneuse *f* (de coton) **2** : gin *m* (boisson)
ginger [ˈdʒɪndʒər] *n* : gingembre *m*
ginger ale *n* : boisson *f* gazeuse au gingembre
gingerbread [ˈdʒɪndʒər,brɛd] *n* : pain *m* d'épice

gingerly ['dʒɪndʒərli] *adv* : précautionneusement, avec circonspection
gingham ['gɪŋəm] *n* : vichy *m*
ginseng ['dʒɪnˌsɪŋ] *n* : ginseng *m*
giraffe [dʒə'ræf] *n* : girafe *f*
gird ['gərd] *vt* **girded** ['gərdəd] *or* **girt** ['gərt]; **girding 1** PUT ON : ceindre **2 to gird oneself** : se préparer
girder ['gərdər] *n* : poutre *f*
girdle[1] ['gərdəl] *vt* **-dled; -dling** : encercler
girdle[2] *n* CORSET : gaine *f*
girl ['gərl] *n* **1** : fille *f*, jeune fille *f* **2** SWEETHEART : petite amie *f* **3** DAUGHTER : fille *f*
girlfriend ['gərlˌfrend] *n* : copine *f*, petite amie *f*, blonde *f Can fam*
girlhood ['gərlˌhʊd] *n* : jeunesse *f*
girlish ['gərlɪʃ] *adj* : de jeune fille
girth ['gərθ] *n* **1** CIRCUMFERENCE : circonférence *f* (d'un arbre, etc.), tour *m* de taille (d'une personne) **2** : sangle *f* (d'une selle de cheval)
gist ['dʒɪst] *n* : essentiel *m*
give[1] ['gɪv] *v* **gave** ['geɪv]; **given** ['gɪvən]; **giving** *vt* **1** : donner, faire don à, conférer (un honneur, etc.) **2** PAY : payer **3** CAUSE : faire, causer <to give s.o. to understand : faire entendre à qqn> — *vi* **1** : donner **2** YIELD : céder **3 to give in** *or* **to give up** : se rendre **4 to give out** DISTRIBUTE : distribuer **5 to give out** COLLAPSE : s'épuiser
give[2] *n* : élasticité *f*, souplesse *f*
giveaway ['gɪvəˌweɪ] *n* **1** : révélation *f* (involontaire) **2** GIFT : prime *f*, cadeau *m*
given ['gɪvən] *adj* **1** SPECIFIED : donné, déterminé **2** INCLINED : enclin <given to violence : enclin à la violence>
given name *n* : prénom *m*
gizzard ['gɪzərd] *n* : gésier *m*
glacial ['gleɪʃəl] *adj* **1** FRIGID : glacial **2** : glaciaire (en géologie)
glacier ['gleɪʃər] *n* : glacier *m*
glad ['glæd] *adj* **gladder; gladdest 1** HAPPY, PLEASED : content, heureux **2** JOYFUL, PLEASANT : joyeux, heureux <glad tidings : bonnes nouvelles> **3 to be glad to** : être heureux de <I'll be glad to do it! : avec plaisir!>
gladden ['glædən] *vt* : réjouir
glade ['gleɪd] *n* : clairière *f*
gladiator ['glædiˌeɪtər] *n* : gladiateur *m*
gladiolus [ˌglædiˈoːləs] *n, pl* **-li** [-li, -ˌlaɪ] : glaïeul *m*
gladly ['glædli] *adv* : avec plaisir, de bon coeur, volontiers
gladness ['glædnəs] *n* : joie *f*, contentement *m*
glamor *or* **glamour** ['glæmər] *n* **1** ALLURE : fascination *f*, charme *m* **2** ELEGANCE : élégance *f*, chic *m*
glamorize ['glæməˌraɪz] *vt* **-ized; -izing** : idéaliser, présenter sous des couleurs séduisantes
glamorous ['glæmərəs] *adj* **1** ALLURING : séduisant, fascinant **2** ELEGANT, EXCITING : élégant, brillant
glance[1] ['glænʃs] *vi* **glanced; glancing 1 to glance at** : jeter un coup d'œil à **2 to glance off** : ricocher sur (un mur, etc.)
glance[2] *n* : coup *m* d'œil
gland ['glænd] *n* : glande *f*
glandular ['glændʒʊlər] *adj* : glandulaire
glare[1] ['glær] *vi* **glared; glaring 1** SHINE : briller d'un éclat éblouissant **2 to glare at** : lancer un regard furieux à, regarder avec colère
glare[2] *n* **1** BRIGHTNESS : lumière *f* éblouissante **2** STARE : regard *m* furieux
glaring ['glæriŋ] *adj* **1** BRIGHT : éblouissant **2** FLAGRANT : flagrant, qui saute aux yeux **3** FIERCE : furieux
glass[1] ['glæs] *vt or* **to glass in** : vitrer
glass[2] *adj* : en verre
glass[3] *n* **1** : verre *m* <broken glass : éclats de verre> <a glass of wine : un verre de vin> **2 glasses** *npl* SPECTACLES : lunettes *fpl*
glassblowing ['glæsˌbloːɪŋ] *n* : soufflage *m* du verre
glassful ['glæsˌfʊl] *n* : verre *m*
glassware ['glæsˌwær] *n* : verrerie *f*
glassy ['glæsi] *adj* **glassier; -est 1** VITREOUS : vitreux **2** SMOOTH : lisse **3 glassy eyes** : yeux *mpl* vitreux
glaucoma [glaʊˈkoːmə, glɔ-] *n* : glaucome *m*
glaze[1] ['gleɪz] *vt* **glazed; glazing 1** : vitrer (une fenêtre, etc.) **2** : vernisser (des céramiques), vitrifier (des carreaux, etc.) **3** ICE : glacer (des pâtisseries)
glaze[2] *n* **1** GLAZING : glaçage *m* **2** : vernis *m* (de céramiques), glacé *m* (d'étoffes, de photos, etc.)
glazier ['gleɪʒər] *n* : vitrier *m*
gleam[1] ['gliːm] *vi* : luire, reluire
gleam[2] *n* : lueur *f* <the first gleam of dawn : les premières lueurs de l'aube> <a gleam of hope : une lueur d'espoir>
glean ['gliːn] *vt* : glaner
glee ['gliː] *n* : joie *f*, allégresse *f*
gleeful ['gliːfəl] *adj* : joyeux — **gleefully** *adv*
glen ['glen] *n* : vallon *m*, vallée *f* encaissée
glib ['glɪb] *adj* **glibber; glibbest** : facile, désinvolte
glibly ['glɪbli] *adv*: avec désinvolture
glide[1] ['glaɪd] *vi* **glided; gliding** : glisser (sur une surface), planer (en l'air)
glide[2] *n* : glissement *m*
glider ['glaɪdər] *n* **1** : planeur *m* (en aéronautique) **2** SWING : balançoire *f*
glimmer[1] ['glɪmər] *vi* : jeter une faible lueur
glimmer[2] *n* GLEAM : lueur *f*

glimpse[1] ['glɪmps] *vt* **glimpsed; glimpsing** : entrevoir
glimpse[2] *n* : aperçu *m*
glint[1] ['glɪnt] *vi* : étinceler, miroiter (sur l'eau, etc.)
glint[2] *n* : reflet *m*, miroitement *m*
glisten ['glɪsən] *vi* : briller, miroiter, luire
glitter[1] ['glɪtər] *vi* : scintiller, étinceler
glitter[2] *n* : scintillement *m*
gloat ['glo:t] *vi* : jubiler <to gloat over : se réjouir de>
glob ['glɑb] *n* : globule *m*, petite boule *f*
global ['glo:bəl] *adj* : mondial — **globally** *adv*
globe ['glo:b] *n* : globe *m*
globe-trotter ['glo:bˌtrɑtər] *n* : globe-trotter *m*
globular ['glɑbjʊlər] *adj* : globulaire
globule ['glɑbju:l] *n* : gouttelette *f*
glockenspiel ['glɑkənˌspi:l, -ʃpi:l] *n* : glockenspiel *m*
gloom ['glu:m] *n* **1** DARKNESS : obscurité *f*, ténèbres *fpl* **2** SADNESS : tristesse *f*, mélancolie *f*
gloomily ['glu:məli] *adv* : sombrement, tristement
gloomy ['glu:mi] *adj* **gloomier; -est 1** DARK : obscur, sombre **2** MELANCHOLY : mélancolique, lugubre **3** PESSIMISTIC : sombre, triste **4** DEPRESSING : déprimant, morne
glorification [ˌglorəfə'keɪʃən] *n* : glorification *f*
glorify ['glorəˌfaɪ] *vt* **-fied; -fying** : glorifier
glorious ['glori:əs] *adj* : glorieux — **gloriously** *adv*
glory[1] ['glori] *vi* **-ried; -rying** : se glorifier <to glory in : se glorifier de>
glory[2] *n, pl* **-ries 1** : gloire *f* **2 in all one's glory** : dans toute sa splendeur
gloss[1] ['glɑs, 'glɔs] *vt* **1** EXPLAIN, DEFINE : gloser **2** POLISH : faire briller, lustrer **3 to gloss over** : glisser sur, atténuer, dissimuler (la vérité, etc.)
gloss[2] *n* **1** SHINE : brillant *m*, lustre *m* **2** EXPLANATION : glose *f*
glossary ['glɑsəri, 'glɑ-] *n, pl* **-ries** : glossaire *m*
glossy ['glɑsi, 'glɑ-] *adj* **glossier; -est** : brillant, luisant, glacé (se dit du papier)
glove ['glʌv] *n* : gant *m*
glow[1] ['glo:] *vi* **1** SHINE : rougeoyer, luire **2** : rayonner <to glow with health : rayonner de santé>
glow[2] *n* : rougeoiement *m*, lueur *f*
glower ['glɑʊər] *vi* : lancer des regards furieux
glowworm ['glo:ˌwərm] *n* : ver *m* luisant
glucose ['glu:ˌko:s] *n* : glucose *m*
glue[1] ['glu:] *vt* **glued; gluing 1** : coller **2 to glue one's eyes on** : garder les yeux rivés sur
glue[2] *n* : colle *f*
gluey ['glu:i] *adj* **gluier; -est** : gluant, collant
glum ['glʌm] *adj* **glummer; glummest** : morne, triste, morose
glut[1] ['glʌt] *vt* **glutted; glutting** SATURATE : inonder, saturer
glut[2] *n* : surabondance *f*, excès *m*
glutinous ['glu:tənəs] *adj* : gluant
glutton ['glʌtən] *n* : glouton *m*, -tonne *f*; gourmand *m*, -mande *f*
gluttonous ['glʌtənəs] *adj* : glouton
gluttony ['glʌtəni] *n, pl* **-tonies** : gloutonnerie *f*
gnarled ['nɑrld] *adj* : noueux
gnash ['næʃ] *vt* **to gnash one's teeth** : grincer des dents
gnat ['næt] *n* : moucheron *m*, brulôt *m Can*
gnaw ['nɔ] *vt* : ronger
gnome ['no:m] *n* : gnome *m*
gnu ['nu:, 'nju:] *n, pl* **gnu** *or* **gnus** : gnou *m*
go[1] ['go:] *v* **went** ['wɛnt]; **gone** ['gɔn]; **going** ['go:ɪŋ]; **goes** ['go:z] *vi* **1** : aller **2** LEAVE : partir, s'en aller <I have to go : il faut que je m'en aille> **3** EXTEND : s'étendre <this road goes to the river : cette rue s'étend jusqu'au fleuve> **4** SELL : se vendre <it goes for $15 : cela se vend pour 15 $> **5** BECOME : devenir <he's going crazy : il devient fou> **6** FUNCTION : marcher <to get it going : le mettre en marche> **7** DISAPPEAR : disparaître <my pen is gone! : mon stylo a disparu!> **8 to go back on** BETRAY : trahir **9 to go for** FAVOR : aimer **10 to go off** EXPLODE : exploser **11 to go off** RING : sonner **12 to go out** LEAVE : sortir **13 to go out** : s'éteindre <the fire went out : le feu s'est éteint> **14 to go over** CHECK : vérifier — *vt* **to go it alone** : le faire tout seul — *v aux* **to be going to** : aller <I'm going to talk to you (about it) : je vais t'en parler>
go[2] *n, pl* **goes 1** ATTEMPT : essai *m*, tentative *f* <to have a go at sth : essayer de faire qqch> **2** SUCCESS : réussite *f* <to make a go of sth : réussir qqch> **3 to be always on the go** : ne s'arrêter jamais
goad[1] ['go:d] *vt* : aiguillonner (un animal), provoquer (une personne)
goad[2] *n* : aiguillon *m*
goal ['go:l] *n* : but *m*
goalie ['go:li] → **goalkeeper**
goalkeeper ['go:lˌki:pər] *n* : gardien *m* de but, cerbère *m Can*
goat ['go:t] *n* **1** : chèvre *f* **2** *or* **billie goat** : bouc *m*
goatee [go:'ti:] *n* : barbiche *f*
goatskin ['go:tˌskɪn] *n* : cuir *m* de chèvre
gob ['gɑb] *n* **1** LUMP : boule *f* **2 gobs of** : beaucoup de
gobble ['gɑbəl] *v* **-bled; -bling** *vt or* **to gobble up** DEVOUR : engloutir — *vi* : glouglouter (se dit d'un dindon)

gobbledygook ['gɑbəldiˌgʊk, -ˌgu:k] *n* : charabia *m fam*

go–between ['go:bɪˌtwi:n] *n* : intermédiaire *mf*

goblet ['gɑblət] *n* : verre *m* à pied

goblin ['gɑblən] *n* : lutin *m*

god ['gɑd, 'gɔd] *n* **1** : dieu *m* **2 God** : Dieu *m*

godchild ['gɑdˌtʃaɪld, 'gɔd-] *n, pl* **-children** : filleul *m*, -leule *f*

goddess ['gɑdəs, 'gɔ-] *n* : déesse *f*

godfather ['gɑdˌfɑðər, 'gɔd-] *n* : parrain *m*

godless ['gɑdləs, 'gɔd-] *adj* : impie

godlike ['gɑdˌlaɪk, 'gɔd-] *adj* : divin

godly ['gɑdli, 'gɔd-] *adj* **godlier; est 1** DIVINE : divin **2** DEVOUT, PIOUS : dévot, pieux

godmother ['gɑdˌmʌðər, 'gɔd-] *n* : marraine *f*

godparent ['gɑdˌpærənt, 'gɔd-] *n* : parrain *m*, marraine *f*

godsend ['gɑdˌsɛnd, 'gɔd-] *n* : aubaine *f*, bénédiction *f*, don *m* (du ciel)

goes → go¹

go–getter ['go:ˌgɛtər] *n* : battant *m*, -tante *f*; fonceur *m*, -ceuse *f fam*

goggle ['gɑgəl] *vi* **-gled; -gling** : ouvrir de grands yeux, regarder avec des yeux ronds

goggles ['gɑgəlz] *npl* : lunettes *fpl* (protectrices)

goings–on [ˌgo:ɪŋˈzɑn, -ˈɔn] *npl* : événements *mpl*, activités *fpl*, conduite *f*

goiter *or Brit* **goitre** ['gɔɪtər] *n* : goitre *m*

gold ['go:ld] *n* : or *m*

golden ['go:ldən] *adj* **1** : en or, d'or **2** : doré, (couleur) d'or <golden hair : cheveux dorés> **3** FAVORABLE : idyllique, en or <a golden opportunity : une occasion magnifique, une occasion en or>

golden mean *n* : juste milieu *m*

goldenrod ['go:ldənˌrɑd] *n* : verge *f* d'or

golden rule *n* : règle *f* d'or

goldfinch ['go:ldˌfɪntʃ] *n* : chardonneret *m*

goldfish ['go:ldˌfɪʃ] *ns & pl* : poisson *m* rouge

goldsmith ['go:ldˌsmɪθ] *n* : orfèvre *m*

golf¹ ['gɑlf, 'gɔlf] *vi* : jouer au golf

golf² *n* : golf *m*

golfer ['gɑlfər, 'gɔl-] *n* : golfeur *m*, -feuse *f*; joueur *m*, joueuse *f* de golf

gondola ['gɑndələ, gɑnˈdo:lə] *n* : gondole *f*

gone ['gɔn] *adj* **1** LOST : perdu **2** PAST : passé <gone is the time when . . . : le temps n'est plus où . . . > **3** DEAD : mort **4** WORN : usé **5 to be far gone** : être bien faible

goner ['gɔnər] *n* **to be a goner** : être fichu *fam*

gong ['gɔŋ, 'gɑŋ] *n* : gong *m*

gonorrhea [ˌgɑnəˈri:ə] *n* : blennorragie *f*

good¹ ['gʊd] *adv* **1** (*used as an intensifier*) : bien, bon <a good strong rope : une corde bien forte> <a good long walk : une bonne promenade> **2 to make good** : réussir

good² *adj* **better** ['bɛtər]; **best** ['bɛst] **1** : bon <good news : bonnes nouvelles> <a good salary : un bon salaire> <good evening : bonsoir> <good morning : bonjour> **2** KIND : bon, aimable <a good deed : une bonne action> **3** FULL : bon <she waited for a good hour : elle attendu pendant une bonne heure> **4** SKILLED : bon, habile <to be good at : être bon en (des études), être bon à (un jeu)> **5** OBEDIENT : sage <be good! : sois sage!> **6** : beau <good weather : beau temps>

good³ *n* **1** RIGHT : bien *m* <good and evil : le bien et le mal> **2** GOODNESS : bonté *f* **3** BENEFIT : bien *m* <for your own good : pour votre bien> **4 goods** *npl* PROPERTY : biens *mpl* **5 goods** *npl* WARES : marchandises *fpl* **6 for ~** : pour de bon **7 the good** : les bons *mpl*

good–bye *or* **good–by** [gʊdˈbaɪ] *n* : au revoir *m*

good–for–nothing ['gʊdfərˌnʌθɪŋ] *adj* : bon à rien

Good Friday *n* : le Vendredi saint

good–hearted ['gʊdˈhɑrtəd] *adj* : généreux, qui a bon coeur

good–looking ['gʊdˈlʊkɪŋ] *adj* : beau

goodly ['gʊdli] *adj* **goodlier; -est** : grand, ample <a goodly sum : une somme considérable>

good–natured ['gʊdˈneɪtʃərd] *adj* : aimable, qui a un bon naturel

goodness ['gʊdnəs] *n* **1** : bonté *f* **2 goodness me!** *or* **my goodness!** : mon Dieu!

good–tempered ['gʊdˈtɛmpərd] *adj* : de bon caractère

goodwill [ˌgʊdˈwɪl] *n* : bienveillance *f*

goody ['gʊdi] *n, pl* **goodies 1** : bon *m* **2 goody!** : chouette! *f fam* **3 goodies** *npl* : friandises *fpl*

gooey ['gu:i] *adj* **gooier; gooiest** : gluant

goof¹ ['gu:f] *vi* **1** *or* **to goof up** : gaffer *fam*, faire une gaffe **2 to goof around** : faire l'imbécile

goof² *n* : gaffe *f fam*

goofy ['gu:fi] *adj* **goofier; -est** : dingue *fam*

goose ['gu:s] *n, pl* **geese** ['gi:s] : oie *f*

gooseberry ['gu:sˌberi:, 'gu:z-] *n, pl* **-berries** : groseille *f* à maquereau

goose bumps *npl* : chair *f* de poule

gooseflesh ['gu:sˌflɛʃ] → **goose bumps**

goose pimples → goose bumps

gopher ['go:fər] *n* : gaufre *m Can*

gore¹ ['gor] *vt* **gored; goring** : encorner

gore² *n* BLOOD : sang *m*

gorge[1] ['gɔrdʒ] *vt* **gorged; gorging 1** SATIATE : rassasier **2 to gorge oneself** : se gorger
gorge[2] *n* RAVINE : gorge *f*, défilé *m*
gorgeous ['gɔrdʒəs] *adj* : magnifique, splendide
gorilla [gə'rɪlə] *n* : gorille *m*
gory ['gori] *adj* **gorier; -est** : sanglant
gosling ['gɑzlɪŋ, 'gɔz-] *n* : oison *m*
gospel ['gɑspəl] *n* **1 the Gospel** : l'Évangile *m* **2 the gospel truth** : la vérité vraie
gossamer ['gɑsəmər, 'gɑzə-] *n* **1** COBWEB : fils *mpl* de la Vierge **2** : étoffe *f* très légère
gossip[1] ['gɑsɪp] *vi* : bavarder, faire des commérages, mémérer *Can fam*
gossip[2] *n* **1** : commère *f fam* (personne) **2** RUMOR : racontars *mpl*, commérages *mpl fam*, cancans *mpl*, ragots *mpl fam*, mémérage *m Can*
gossipy ['gɑsɪpi] *adj* : bavard, cancanier
got → get
Gothic ['gɑθɪk] *adj* : gothique
gotten → get
gouge[1] ['gaʊdʒ] *vt* **gouged; gouging 1** : creuser, tailler à la gouge **2** SWINDLE : estamper
gouge[2] *n* **1** CHISEL : gouge *f* **2** GROOVE : rainure *f*
goulash ['guːˌlɑʃ, -ˌlæʃ] *n* : goulasch *mf*, goulache *mf*
gourd ['gɔrd, 'gʊrd] *n* : gourde *f*
gourmand ['gʊrˌmɑnd] *n* : gourmand *m*, -mande *f*
gourmet ['gʊrˌmeɪ, gʊr'meɪ] *n* : gourmet *m*
gout ['gaʊt] *n* : goutte *f*
govern ['gʌvərn] *vt* **1** RULE : gouverner **2** CONTROL, DETERMINE : régir **3** RESTRAIN : maîtriser, dominer (les émotions, etc.) — *vi* : gouverner
governess ['gʌvərnəs] *n* : gouvernante *f*
government ['gʌvərmənt] *n* : gouvernement *m* — **governmental** [ˌgʌvər'mɛntəl] *adj*
governor ['gʌvənər, 'gʌvərnər] *n* **1** : gouverneur *m* **2** : régulateur *m* (d'une machine)
governorship ['gʌvənərˌʃɪp, 'gʌvərnər-] *n* : fonctions *fpl* de gouverneur
gown ['gaʊn] *n* **1** : robe *f* <evening gown : robe du soir> **2** : toge *f* (de juge, etc.)
grab[1] ['græb] *v* **grabbed; grabbing** *vt* SEIZE : saisir, empoigner — *vi* CLING : s'agripper
grab[2] *n* **1 to make a grab for** : essayer d'attraper **2 to be up for grabs** : être disponible, être à prendre
grace[1] ['greɪs] *vt* **graced; gracing 1** HONOR : honorer **2** ADORN : orner, embellir
grace[2] *n* **1** : grâce *f* <by the grace of God : par la grâce de Dieu> **2** PRAYER : bénédicité *m* <to say grace : dire le bénédicité> **3** RESPITE : grâce *f*, répit *m* <a grace period : un délai> **4** GRACIOUSNESS : bienveillance *f*, gentillesse *f* **5** ELEGANCE : élégance *f*, charme *m*, grâce *f* **6 to be in the good graces of** : être dans les bonnes grâces de
graceful ['greɪsfəl] *adj* : gracieux — **gracefully** *adv*
gracefulness ['greɪsfəlnəs] *n* : grâce *f*
graceless ['greɪsləs] *adj* : inélégant, gauche
grace note *n* : note *f* d'agrément
gracious ['greɪʃəs] *adj* : courtois, gracieux — **graciously** *adv*
graciousness ['greɪʃəsnəs] *n* : bienveillance *f*, gentillesse *f*, courtoisie *f*
grackle ['grækəl] *n* : quiscale *m*
gradation [greɪ'deɪʃən, grə-] *n* : gradation *f*
grade[1] ['greɪd] *vt* **graded; grading 1** CLASSIFY : classer **2** LEVEL : niveler **3** MARK : noter (à l'école)
grade[2] *n* **1** CLASS, QUALITY : catégorie *f*, calibre *m*, qualité *f* **2** RANK : rang *m*, grade *m* **3** YEAR : classe *f* (à l'école) **4** MARK : note *f* **5** SLOPE : pente *f*
grade school → elementary school
gradual ['grædʒʊəl] *adj* : graduel, progressif — **gradually** *adv*
graduate[1] ['grædʒʊˌeɪt] *v* **-ated; -ating** *vi* : recevoir son diplôme — *vt* : graduer <a graduated thermometer : un thermomètre gradué>
graduate[2] ['grædʒʊət] *n* : diplômé *m*, -mée *f*
graduation [ˌgrædʒʊ'eɪʃən] *n* **1** : remise *f* des diplômes (à l'université) **2** CALIBRATION : graduation *f*
graffiti [grə'fiːtiˌ, græ-] *npl* : graffiti *mpl*
graft[1] ['græft] *vt* : greffer
graft[2] *n* **1** : greffe *f* **2** CORRUPTION : magouille *f*
grain ['greɪn] *n* **1** : grain *m* <a grain of sand : un grain de sable> **2** CEREALS : céréales *fpl* **3** : fibre *f* (de bois, de cuir, etc.), fil *m* (de fibres) **4 to go against one's grain** : n'être pas dans sa nature
gram ['græm] *n* : gramme *m* (unité de mesure et de masse)
grammar ['græmər] *n* : grammaire *f*
grammar school → elementary school
grammatical [grə'mætɪkəl] *adj* : grammatical — **grammatically** [-kli] *adv*
granary ['greɪnəri, 'græ-] *n, pl* **-ries** : grenier *m* à blé
grand ['grænd] *adj* **1** FOREMOST : plus grand, principal <the grand prize : le grand prix> **2** IMPRESSIVE : grand, magnifique, grandiose <in a grand manner : dans un style de grand seigneur> **3** DIGNIFIED, MAJESTIC : digne, majestueux **4** PRETENTIOUS : prétentieux, suffisant **5** GREAT, WONDERFUL : formidable *fam* **6**

grand total : somme *f* globale, résultat *m* final

grandaunt ['græn'dænt, -'dant] *n* : grand-tante *f*

grandchild ['grænd,tʃaɪld] *n, pl* **-children** [-,tʃɪldrən] : petit-fils *m*, petite-fille *f*

granddaughter ['grænd,dɔtər] *n* : petite-fille *f*

grandeur ['grændʒər] *n* : grandeur *f*, splendeur *f*, magnificence *f*

grandfather ['grænd,fɑðər] *n* : grand-père *m*

grandiose ['grændi,oːs, ,grændi'-] *adj* : grandiose

grandma ['grænd,ma, -mɔ] *n* : mémé *f* *France fam*, mémère *f fam*

grandmother ['grænd,mʌðər] *n* : grand-mère *f*

grandparents ['grænd,pærənts] *npl* : grands-parents *mpl*

grand piano *n* : piano *m* à queue

grandson ['grænd,sʌn] *n* : petit-fils *m*

grandstand ['grænd,stænd] *n* : tribune *f*

granduncle ['græn'dəŋkəl] *n* : grand-oncle *m*

granite ['grænɪt] *n* : granit *m*, granite *m*

grant[1] ['grænt] *vt* **1** ALLOW, BESTOW : accorder, octroyer **2** ADMIT : admettre, reconnaître **3 to take for granted** : prendre pour acquis

grant[2] *n* **1** CONCESSION : concession *f* **2** SUBSIDY : subvention *f* **3** SCHOLARSHIP : bourse *f*

granular ['grænjulər] *adj* : granuleux

grape ['greɪp] *n* : raisin *m* <a bunch of grapes : une grappe de raisins>

grapefruit ['greɪp,fruːt] *n* : pamplemousse *mf*

grapevine ['greɪp,vaɪn] *n* **1** : vigne *f* **2 to hear through the grapevine** : entendre dire, apprendre à travers les branches

graph ['græf] *n* : graphique *m*

graphic ['græfɪk] *adj* **1** : graphique <graphic art : l'art graphique> **2** VIVID : vivant — **graphically** [-ɪkli] *adv*

graphite ['græ,faɪt] *n* : graphite *m*

grapnel ['græpnəl] *n* : grappin *m*

grapple ['græpəl] *v* **-pled; -pling** *vt* : saisir avec un grappin — *vi* STRUGGLE : lutter, se colleter

grasp[1] ['græsp] *vt* **1** GRIP, SEIZE : saisir **2** UNDERSTAND : comprendre, saisir

grasp[2] *n* **1** GRIP : prise *f*, poigne *f* **2** COMPREHENSION : compréhension *f* **3** REACH : portée *f* <within the grasp of : à la portée de>

grass ['græs] *n* **1** : herbe *f* (plante) **2** LAWN : gazon *m*, pelouse *f*

grasshopper ['græs,hɑpər] *n* : sauterelle *f*

grassland ['græs,lænd] *n* : prairie *f*

grassy ['græsi] *adj* **grassier; -est** : herbeux

grate[1] ['greɪt] *v* **grated; -ing** *vt* **1** : râper <to grate cheese : râper du fromage> **2 to grate one's teeth** : grincer des dents — *vi* **1** CREAK, RASP : grincer **2** IRRITATE : agacer <to grate on the nerves of : taper sur les nerfs de>

grate[2] *n* **1** : grille *f* de foyer (de cuisine) **2** GRATING : grille *f*

grateful ['greɪtfəl] *adj* : reconnaissant

gratefully ['greɪtfəli] *adv* : avec reconnaissance

gratefulness ['greɪtfəlnəs] *n* : gratitude *f*, reconnaissance *f*

grater ['greɪtər] *n* : râpe *f*

gratification [,græt̬əfə'keɪʃən] *n* : satisfaction *f*, plaisir *m*

gratify ['græt̬ə,faɪ] *vt* **-fied; -fying 1** PLEASE : faire plaisir à **2** SATISFY : satisfaire

grating ['greɪt̬ɪŋ] *n* : grille *f*

gratis[1] ['græt̬əs, 'greɪ-] *adv* : gratis, gratuitement

gratis[2] *adj* : gratis, gratuit

gratitude ['græt̬ə,tuːd, -,tjuːd] *n* : gratitude *f*, reconnaissance *f*

gratuitous [grə'tuːət̬əs] *adj* : gratuit

gratuity [grə'tuːət̬i] *n, pl* **-ities** TIP : pourboire *m*

grave[1] ['greɪv] *adj* **graver; -est** : grave

grave[2] *n* : tombe *f*

gravel ['grævəl] *n* : gravier *m*, gravillon *m*

gravelly ['grævəli] *adj* **1** : graveleux **2** HARSH, GRATING : râpeux <a gravelly voice : une voix râpeuse>

gravely ['greɪvli] *adv* : gravement

gravestone ['greɪv,stoːn] *n* : pierre *f* tombale

graveyard ['greɪv,jɑrd] *n* : cimetière *m*

gravitate ['grævə,teɪt] *vi* **-tated; -tating** : graviter

gravitation [,grævə'teɪʃən] *n* : gravitation *f*

gravity ['grævət̬i] *n, pl* **-ties 1** SERIOUSNESS : gravité *f* **2** GRAVITATION : gravitation *f*, pesanteur *f* <the law of gravity : la loi de la pesanteur>

gravy ['greɪvi] *n, pl* **-vies** : sauce *f* (au jus de viande)

gray[1] ['greɪ] *vi or* **to turn gray** : grisonner

gray[2] *adj* **1** : gris <gray hair : cheveux gris> **2** GLOOMY : morne **3** DREARY, DULL : terne

gray[3] *n* : gris *m*

grayish ['greɪɪʃ] *adj* : grisâtre

graze ['greɪz] *v* **grazed; grazing** *vi* : paître, brouter — *vt* **1** PASTURE : faire paître (des animaux) **2** SCRAPE : écorcher, érafler **3** BRUSH, TOUCH : frôler

grease[1] ['griːs] *vt* **greased; greasing** : graisser, lubrifier (une voiture)

grease[2] *n* : graisse *f*, lubrifiant *m* (pour une voiture)

greasy ['griːsi] *adj* **greasier; -est 1** : graisseux **2** OILY : gras

great ['greɪt] *adj* **1** LARGE : grand <a great mountain : une grande montagne> **2** INTENSE : grand <to be in great pain : souffrir beaucoup> **3** EMINENT : grand, éminent <a great man : un grand homme> **4** FANTASTIC : génial *fam*, formidable *fam* <to have a great time : s'amuser follement>
great–aunt [ˌgreɪtˈænt, -ˈant] → **grand-aunt**
great–grandchild [ˌgreɪtˈgrænd,tʃaɪld] *n, pl* **-children** [-ˌtʃɪldrən] : arrière-petit-enfant *m*, arrière-petite-enfant *f*
great–grandfather [ˌgreɪtˈgrænd,fɑðər] *n* : arrière-grand-père *m*
great–grandmother [ˌgreɪtˈgrænd,mʌðər] *n* : arrière-grand-mère *f*
greatly ['greɪtli] *adv* **1** MUCH : beaucoup <greatly improved : beaucoup amélioré> **2** VERY : très, énormément <greatly surprised : très surpris>
greatness ['greɪtnəs] *n* : grandeur *f*
great–uncle [ˌgreɪtˈʌŋkəl] → **grand-uncle**
grebe ['gri:b] *n* : grèbe *m*
greed ['gri:d] *n* **1** AVARICE : avidité *f*, cupidité *f*, avarice *f* **2** GLUTTONY : gloutonnerie *f*
greedily ['gri:dəli] *adv* : avidement
greediness ['gri:dinəs] → **greed**
greedy ['gri:di] *adj* **greedier; -est 1** AVARICIOUS : avare, cupide, pingre **2** GLUTTONOUS : glouton
Greek[1] ['gri:k] *adj* : grec
Greek[2] *n* **1** : Grec *m*, Grecque *f* **2** : grec *m* (langue)
green[1] ['gri:n] *adj* **1** : vert **2** INEXPERIENCED : inexpérimenté, naïf
green[2] *n* **1** : vert *m* (couleur) **2 greens** *npl.* : légumes *mpl* verts
greenery ['gri:nəri] *n, pl* **-eries** : verdure *f*
greenhorn ['gri:nˌhɔrn] *n* : novice *mf*
greenhouse ['gri:nˌhaʊs] *n* : serre *f*
greenhouse effect *n* : effet *m* de serre
greenish ['gri:nɪʃ] *adj* : verdâtre
green onion → chive, scallion
green pepper *n* : poivron *m* vert
green thumb *n* **to have a green thumb** : avoir la main verte
greet ['gri:t] *vt* **1** WELCOME : saluer, accueillir **2 to be greeted with** : provoquer <to greet with laughter : provoquer des rires>
greeting ['gri:tɪŋ] *n* **1** : salutation *f* **2 greetings** *npl* REGARDS : voeux *mpl* <Christmas greetings : voeux de Noël>
gregarious [grɪˈgæriəs] *adj* : grégaire (se dit des animaux), sociable (se dit des personnes)
gregariousness [grɪˈgæriəsnəs] *n* : sociabilité *f*
gremlin ['grɛmlən] *n* : lutin *m*, diablotin *m*
grenade [grəˈneɪd] *n* : grenade *f*
Grenadian[1] [grəˈneɪdiən] *adj* : grenadin
Grenadian[2] *n* : Grenadin *m*, -dine *f*
grew → grow
grey → gray
greyhound ['greɪˌhaʊnd] *n* : lévrier *m*
grid [grɪd] *n* **1** GRATING : grille *f* **2** NETWORK : réseau *m* (électrique) **3** : quadrillage *m* (d'une carte routière)
griddle ['grɪdəl] *n* : plaque *f* chauffante
griddle cake → pancake
gridiron ['grɪdˌaɪərn] *n* **1** GRILL : gril *m* **2** : terrain *m* de football américain
grief ['gri:f] *n* **1** SORROW : chagrin *m*, douleur *f* **2 to come to grief** : avoir des ennuis **3 good grief!** : mon Dieu!
grievance ['gri:vənʃs] *n* : grief *m*
grieve ['gri:v] *v* **grieved; grieving** *vt* DISTRESS : peiner, chagriner, affliger — *vi* **1** : avoir de la peine, s'affliger **2 to grieve for** : pleurer
grievous ['gri:vəs] *adj* **1** GRAVE, SERIOUS : grave, sérieux <a grievous injury : une blessure sérieuse> **2** CRUEL, ONEROUS : cruel, atroce <a grievous offense : un délit atroce>
grill[1] ['grɪl] *vt* **1** : griller, faire griller (en cuisine) **2** INTERROGATE : cuisiner *fam*
grill[2] *n* **1** : gril *m* (de cuisine) **2** RESTAURANT : grill *m*
grille *or* **grill** ['grɪl] *n* GRATING : grille *f*
grim ['grɪm] *adj* **grimmer; grimmest 1** STERN : sévère <with grim determination : avec une volonté inflexible> **2** GLOOMY : lugubre, sinistre **3** UNPLEASANT : désagréable, (très) mauvais, pas bien
grimace[1] ['grɪməs, grɪˈmeɪs] *vi* **-maced; -macing** : grimacer
grimace[2] *n* : grimace *f*
grime ['graɪm] *n* : saleté *f*, crasse *f*
grimly ['grɪmli] *adv* **1** SEVERELY : sévèrement, durement **2** RESOLUTELY : d'un air résolu, fermement
grimy ['graɪmi] *adj* **grimier; -est** : sale, crasseux
grin[1] ['grɪn] *vi* **grinned; grinning** : sourire
grin[2] *n* : (grand) sourire *m*
grind[1] ['graɪnd] *v* **ground** [graʊnd]; **grinding** *vt* **1** CRUSH : moudre, pulvériser **2** POLISH, SHARPEN : aiguiser, affûter, polir **3 to grind down** OPPRESS : opprimer **4 to grind one's teeth** : grincer des dents, gricher des dents *Can* — *vi* : grincer
grind[2] *n* CHORE : corvée *f*
grinder ['graɪndər] *n* : moulin *m* <coffee grinder : moulin à café>
grindstone ['graɪndˌstoːn] *n* : meule *f*
grip[1] ['grɪp] *vt* **gripped; gripping 1** SEIZE : serrer **2** CAPTIVATE : empoigner, captiver **3 to grip the road** : adhérer à la route
grip[2] *n* **1** GRASP : étreinte *f*, prise *f* **2** CONTROL : contrôle *m* <to get a grip on oneself : se ressaisir> **3** UNDERSTANDING : compréhension *f* **4** TRAC-

TION : adhérence *f* **5** HANDLE : poignée *f*

gripe[1] ['graɪp] *vi* **griped; griping** : rouspéter *fam*, ronchonner *fam*

gripe[2] *n* : plainte *f*, rouspétance *f fam*

grippe ['grɪp] *n* : grippe *f*

grisly ['grɪzli] *adj* **grislier; -est** : horrible, macabre

grist ['grɪst] *n* **1** : blé *m* (à moudre) **2 it's all grist for his mill** : ça apporte de l'eau à son moulin

gristle ['grɪsəl] *n* : cartilage *m*

gristly ['grɪsli] *adj* **gristlier; -est** : cartilagineux

grit[1] ['grɪt] *vt* **gritted; gritting** : serrer <to grit one's teeth : serrer les dents>

grit[2] *n* **1** GRAVEL, SAND : sable *m*, gravillon *m* **2** PLUCK : cran *m fam*, courage *m* **3 grits** *npl* : gruau *m* de maïs

gritty ['grɪti] *adj* **grittier; -est 1** : sablonneux, graveleux **2** PLUCKY : courageux

grizzled ['grɪzəld] *adj* : grisonnant

groan[1] ['groːn] *vi* : gémir

groan[2] *n* : gémissement *m*

grocer ['groːsər] *n* : épicier *m*, -cière *f*

grocery ['groːsəri, -ʃəri] *n, pl* **-ceries 1** *or* **grocery store** : épicerie *f* **2 groceries** *npl* : épiceries *fpl*, provisions *fpl*

groggy ['grɑgi] *adj* **groggier; -est** : chancelant, sonné *fam*

groin ['grɔɪn] *n* : aine *f*

grommet ['grɑmət, 'grʌ-] *n* : œillet *m*

groom[1] ['groːm, 'grʊm] *vt* **1** : panser (un animal) **2** PREPARE : préparer, former

groom[2] *n* **1** : palefrenier *m*, -nière *f* **2** BRIDEGROOM : marié *m*

groove[1] ['groːv] *vt* **grooved; grooving** : rainer, canneler

groove[2] *n* **1** FURROW, SLOT : rainure *f*, sillon *m* **2** ROUTINE, RUT : routine *f*

grope ['groːp] *v* **groped; groping** *vi* **1** : tâtonner **2 to grope for** : chercher à tâtons — *vt* **1** PAW : peloter **2 to grope one's way** : avancer à tâtons

gross[1] ['groːs] *vt* : gagner brut, produire brut

gross[2] *adj* **1** FLAGRANT : flagrant, crasse **2** OBESE : gros, obèse **3** TOTAL : brut <gross domestic product : produit intérieur brut> **4** VULGAR : grossier

gross[3] *n* **1** *pl* **gross** : grosse *f* (12 douzaines) **2** *or* **gross income** : recettes *fpl* brutes

grossly ['groːsli] *adv* **1** EXTREMELY : extrêmement **2** CRUDELY : grossièrement

grotesque [groːˈtɛsk] *adj* : grotesque

grotesquely [groːˈtɛskli] *adv* : de façon grotesque

grotto ['grɑtoː] *n, pl* **-toes** : grotte *f*

grouch[1] ['graʊtʃ] *vi* : grogner, rouspéter *fam*, ronchonner *fam*

grouch[2] *n* **1** GRUMBLER : rouspéteur *m*, -teuse *f fam*; plaignard *m*, -gnarde *f Can* **2** COMPLAINT : grognement *m*

grouchy ['graʊtʃi] *adj* **grouchier; -est** : grognon, grincheux

ground[1] ['graʊnd] *vt* **1** BASE : baser, fonder **2** INSTRUCT : former <to be well grounded in : avoir une bonne formation en> **3** : mettre à la terre (un appareil électrique) **4** : faire échouer (un navire) **5** : interdire de voler à (un avion ou un pilote)

ground[2] *n* **1** EARTH, SOIL : sol *m*, terre *f* <on the ground : par terre> **2** LAND, TERRAIN : terrain *m* <on hilly ground : sur un terrain vallonné> **3** BASIS, REASON : motif *m*, raison *f* <grounds for complaint : motifs de se plaindre> **4** : terre *f* (pour l'électricité) **5 grounds** *npl* PREMISES : parc *m* **6 grounds** *npl* : marc *m* (de café)

ground[3] → **grind**[1]

groundhog ['graʊnd,hɔg] *n* : marmotte *f* d'Amérique

groundless ['graʊndləs] *adj* : sans fondement

groundwork ['graʊnd,wərk] *n* : travail *m* préparatoire

group[1] ['gruːp] *vt* : grouper, réunir — *vi* **to group together** : se grouper

group[2] *n* : groupe *m*

grouper ['gruːpər] *n* : mérou *m*

grouse[1] ['graʊs] *vi* **groused; grousing** COMPLAIN : rouspéter *fam*, râler *fam*

grouse[2] *n, pl* **grouse** *or* **grouses** : grouse *f*

grove ['groːv] *n* : bosquet *m*

grovel ['grɑvəl, 'grʌ-] *vi* **-eled** *or* **-elled; -eling** *or* **-elling** : ramper

grow ['groː] *v* **grew** ['gruː]; **grown** ['groːn]; **growing** *vi* **1** : pousser (se dit des plantes, des cheveux, etc.), grandir (se dit des personnes) **2** INCREASE : croître, augmenter **3** BECOME : devenir <she's growing old : elle devient vieille> — *vt* **1** CULTIVATE : cultiver, faire pousser **2** : laisser pousser <he grew a beard : il a laissé pousser la barbe>

grower ['groːər] *n* : cultivateur *m*, -trice *f*

growl[1] ['graʊl] *vi* : grogner, gronder

growl[2] *n* : grognement *m*, grondement *m*

grown-up[1] ['groːnəp] *adj* : adulte

grown-up[2] *n* : adulte *mf*, grande personne *f*

growth ['groːθ] *n* **1** : croissance *f*, développement *m* <to stunt one's growth : retarder sa croissance> **2** INCREASE : croissance *f*, augmentation *f* **3** GROWING : pousse *f* (des plantes) **4** LUMP, TUMOR : grosseur *f*, tumeur *f*

grub[1] ['grʌb] *vi* **grubbed; grubbing 1** DIG : fouir **2** RUMMAGE : fouiller **3** DRUDGE : besogner

grub[2] *n* **1** LARVA : larve *f* **2** FOOD : bouffe *f fam*

grubby ['grʌbi] *adj* **grubbier; -est** : sale

grudge[1] ['grʌdʒ] *vt* **grudged; grudging** : donner à contrecœur <to grudge s.o. their success : en vouloir à qqn de sa réussite>
grudge[2] *n* : rancune *f* <to hold a grudge against : garder rancune à, avoir de la rancune contre>
gruel ['gru:əl] *n* : bouillie *f* (d'avoine)
grueling *or* **gruelling** ['gru:lɪŋ, gruə-] *adj* : exténuant, épuisant <a grueling experience : une expérience très dure>
gruesome ['gru:səm] *adj* : horrible, épouvantable
gruff ['grʌf] *adj* : bourru, brusque, malendurant *Can*
gruffly ['grʌfli] *adv* : d'un ton bourru, avec brusquerie
grumble[1] ['grʌmbəl] *vi* **-bled; -bling 1** COMPLAIN, GROUSE : grommeler, ronchonner *fam* **2** RUMBLE : gronder
grumble[2] *n* **1** GROUSING : ronchonnement *m fam* **2** RUMBLE : grondement *m*
grumpy ['grʌmpi] *adj* **grumpier; -est** : grincheux, grognon
grunt[1] ['grʌnt] *vi* : grogner
grunt[2] *n* : grognement *m*
guarantee[1] [ˌgærən'ti:] *vt* **-teed; -teeing** : garantir
guarantee[2] *n* : garantie *f*
guarantor [ˌgærən'tɔr] *n* : garant *m*, -rante *f*
guaranty [ˌgærən'ti:] → **guarantee**
guard[1] ['gɑrd] *vt* **1** DEFEND : garder, défendre **2** WATCH : surveiller, garder — *vi* **to guard against** : se garder de
guard[2] *n* **1** SENTRY, WARDEN : garde *m* **2** GUARDIAN, OVERSEER : gardien *m*, -dienne *f*; surveillant *m*, -lante *f* **3** PROTECTION : garde *f*, protection *f* **4** READINESS : garde *f* <to be on one's guard : être sur ses gardes> **5** SAFEGUARD : sauvegarde *f*, dispositif *m* de sûreté
guardhouse ['gɑrdˌhaʊs] *n* **1** : guérite *f* (pour des sentinelles) **2** PRISON : salle *f* de garde (militaire)
guardian ['gɑrdiən] *n* : gardien *m*, -dienne *f*
guardianship ['gɑrdiənˌʃɪp] *n* : tutelle *f*
Guatemalan[1] [ˌgwɑtəˈmɑlən] *adj* : guatémaltèque
Guatemalan[2] *n* : Guatémaltèque *mf*
guava ['gwɑvə] *n* : goyave *f*
gubernatorial [ˌgu:bənəˈtori:əl, ˌgju:-] *adj* : du gouverneur
guerrilla *or* **guerilla** [gəˈrɪlə] *n* **1** : guérillero *m* **2 guerrillas** *npl* : guérilla *f* (combattants) **3 guerrilla warfare** : guérilla *f*
guess[1] ['gɛs] *vt* **1** CONJECTURE : deviner <guess who! : devine qui c'est!> <to guess s.o.'s age : deviner l'âge de qqn> **2** SUPPOSE : penser, croire <I guess so : je pense que oui> — *vi* : deviner
guess[2] *n* : conjecture *f*, supposition *f* <he made a good guess : il a deviné juste>
guesswork ['gɛsˌwərk] *n* : hypothèse *f*, supposition *f*
guest ['gɛst] *n* **1** VISITOR : invité *m*, -tée *f*; hôte *mf* **2** PATRON : client *m*, cliente *f*; hôte *mf* (d'un hôtel, etc.)
guffaw[1] [gəˈfɔ] *vi* : s'esclaffer
guffaw[2] [gəˈfɔ, ˈgʌˌfɔ] *n* : gros éclat *m* de rire
guidance ['gaɪdənʌs] *n* : conseils *mpl*, direction *f*
guide[1] ['gaɪd] *vt* **guided; guiding 1** DIRECT : guider, diriger **2** ADVISE, COUNSEL : conseiller, guider
guide[2] *n* : guide *m*
guidebook ['gaɪdˌbʊk] *n* : guide *m*
guideline ['gaɪdˌlaɪn] *n* : ligne *f* directrice
guidepost ['gaɪdˌpo:st] *n* : poteau *m* indicateur
guild ['gɪld] *n* : association *f*
guile ['gaɪl] *n* : ruse *f*, astuce *f*
guileful ['gaɪlfəl] *adj* : rusé
guileless ['gaɪlləs] *adj* : candide, sans astuce
guillotine[1] ['gɪləˌti:n, ˌgi:jə-] *vt* **-tined; -tining** : guillotiner
guillotine[2] *n* : guillotine *f*
guilt ['gɪlt] *n* : culpabilité *f*
guilty ['gɪlti] *adj* **guiltier; -est** : coupable
guinea fowl ['gɪni] *n* : pintade *f*
guinea pig *n* : cobaye *m*
Guinean[1] ['gɪniən] *adj* : guinéen
Guinean[2] *n* : Guinéen *m*, -néenne *f*
guise ['gaɪz] *n* : apparence *f* <under the guise of : sous l'apparence de>
guitar [gəˈtɑr, gɪ-] *n* : guitare *f*
gulch ['gʌltʃ] *n* : ravin *m*
gulf ['gʌlf] *n* **1** : golfe *m* <the gulf of California : le golfe de la Californie> **2** ABYSS : gouffre *m*, abîme *m*
gull ['gʌl] *n* : mouette *f*
gullet ['gʌlət] *n* **1** THROAT : gosier *m* **2** ESOPHAGUS : œsophage *m*
gullible ['gʌlɪbəl] *adj* : crédule
gully ['gʌli] *n, pl* **-lies 1** GULCH : ravin *m* **2** TRENCH : rigole *f*
gulp[1] ['gʌlp] *vt or* **to gulp down 1** SWALLOW : avaler (à grosses bouchées), caler *Can* **2** SUPPRESS : ravaler <to gulp down tears : ravaler des larmes> — *vi* : avoir la gorge serrée
gulp[2] *n* : gorgée *f*, bouchée *f*
gum ['gʌm] *n* **1** CHEWING GUM : chewing-gum *m France*, gomme *f* à mâcher **2 gums** *npl* : gencives *fpl*
gumbo ['gʌmˌbo:] *n* : gombo *m*
gumdrop ['gʌmˌdrɑp] *n* : boule *f* de gomme
gummy ['gʌmi] *adj* **gummier; -est** : gluant
gumption ['gʌmpʃən] *n* : initiative *f*, cran *m fam*

gun¹ [ˈgʌn] *vt* **gunned; gunning 1** *or* **to gun down** : abattre **2 to gun the engine** : accélérer le moteur
gun² *n* **1** FIREARM : arme *f* à feu, fusil *m* **2** CANNON : canon *m* **3 → spray gun 4 to jump the gun** : brûler le feu
gunboat [ˈgʌnˌboːt] *n* : canonnière *f*
gunfight [ˈgʌnˌfaɪt] *n* : combat *m* avec armes à feu
gunfire [ˈgʌnˌfaɪr] *n* : fusillade *f*, coups *mpl* de feu
gunman [ˈgʌnmən] *n, pl* **-men** [-mən, -ˌmɛn] : bandit *m* armé
gunner [ˈgʌnər] *n* : artilleur *m*
gunnery [ˈgʌnəri] *n* : artillerie *f*
gunpowder [ˈgʌnˌpaʊdər] *n* : poudre *f* (à canon)
gunshot [ˈgʌnˌʃɑt] *n* : coup *m* de feu
gunwale [ˈgʌnəl] *n* : plat-bord *m*
guppy [ˈgʌpi] *n, pl* **-pies** : guppy *m*
gurgle¹ [ˈgərgəl] *vi* **-gled; -gling 1** : murmurer, glouglouter *fam* <a gurgling stream : un ruisseau murmurant> **2** : gazouiller (se dit d'un bébé)
gurgle² *n* **1** : glouglou *m fam* (d'un liquide) **2** : gazouillement *m* (d'un enfant)
gush [ˈgʌʃ] *vi* **1** SPOUT : jaillir **2 to gush over** : s'extasier devant
gust [ˈgʌst] *n* : rafale *f*, bourrasque *f* <a gust of wind : un coup de vent>
gusto [ˈgʌsˌtoː] *n, pl* **-toes** : enthousiasme *m*, entrain *m*
gusty [ˈgʌsti] *adj* **gustier; -est** : venteux <gusty wind : rafales de vent>
gut¹ [ˈgʌt] *vt* **gutted; gutting 1** EVISCERATE : vider **2** DESTROY : ravager
gut² *n* **1** INTESTINE : intestin *m*, boyau *m* **2 guts** *npl* INNARDS : entrailles *fpl*, tripes *fpl fam* **3 guts** *npl* COURAGE : cran *m fam*
gutter [ˈgʌtər] *n* **1** : gouttière *f* (d'un toit) **2** : caniveau *m* (de la rue)
guttural [ˈgʌtərəl] *adj* : guttural
guy [ˈgaɪ] *n* **1** *or* **guyline** : corde *f* de tente **2** FELLOW : type *m fam*, mec *m fam*, gars *m fam*
Guyanese¹ [ˌgaɪəˈniːz] *adj* : guyanais
Guyanese² *n* : Guyanais *m*, -naise *f*
guzzle [ˈgʌzəl] *vt* **-zled; -zling** : bâfrer *fam*, engloutir
gym [ˈdʒɪm] → **gymnasium**
gymnasium [dʒɪmˈneɪziəm, -ʒəm] *n, pl* **-siums** *or* **-sia** [-ziːə, -ʒə] : gymnase *m*
gymnast [ˈdʒɪmnəst, -ˌnæst] *n* : gymnaste *mf*
gymnastic [dʒɪmˈnæstɪk] *adj* : gymnastique
gymnastics [dʒɪmˈnæstɪks] *n* : gymnastique *f*
gynecologic [ˌgaɪnɪkəˈlɑdʒɪk] *or* **gynecological** [-ˈlɑdʒɪkəl] *adj* : gynécologique
gynecologist [ˌgaɪnəˈkɑlədʒɪst] *n* : gynécologue *mf*
gynecology [ˌgaɪnəˈkɑlədʒi] *n* : gynécologie *f*
gyp¹ [ˈdʒɪp] *vt* **gypped; gypping** : escroquer, arnaquer *fam*
gyp² *n* **1** CHEAT, SWINDLER : escroc *m*; arnaqueur *m*, -queuse *f fam* **2** FRAUD, SWINDLE : escroquerie *f*, arnaque *f fam*
gypsum [ˈdʒɪpsəm] *n* : gypse *m*
Gypsy [ˈdʒɪpsi] *n, pl* **-sies** : gitan *m*, -tane *f*
gyrate [ˈdʒaɪˌreɪt] *vi* **-rated; -rating** : tournoyer
gyroscope [ˈdʒaɪrəˌskoːp] *n* : gyroscope *m*

H

h [ˈeɪtʃ] *n, pl* **h's** *or* **hs** [ˈeɪtʃəz] : h *m*, huitième lettre de l'alphabet
haberdashery [ˈhæbərˌdæʃəri] *n, pl* **-eries** : magasin *m* de vêtements pour hommes
habit [ˈhæbɪt] *n* **1** : habit *m* (religieux) **2** CUSTOM : habitude *f*, coutume *f* **3** ADDICTION : accoutumance *f*, dépendance *f*
habitable [ˈhæbɪtəbəl] *adj* : habitable
habitat [ˈhæbɪˌtæt] *n* : habitat *m*
habitation [ˌhæbɪˈteɪʃən] *n* **1** OCCUPANCY : habitation *f* **2** RESIDENCE : habitation *f*, domicile *m*, résidence *f*
habit–forming [ˈhæbɪtˌfɔrmɪŋ] *adj* ADDICTIVE : qui crée une accoutumance
habitual [həˈbɪtʃʊəl] *adj* **1** CUSTOMARY : habituel **2** INVETERATE : invétéré <a habitual drunkard : un ivrogne invétéré>
habitually [həˈbɪtʃʊəli] *adv* : habituellement
habituate [həˈbɪtʃʊˌeɪt] *vt* **-ated; -ating 1** : habituer **2 to habituate oneself to** : s'habituer à, s'accoutumer à
hack¹ [ˈhæk] *vt* : tailler, taillader <to hack one's way through sth : tailler un passage à travers qqch> — *vi* **1** CHOP : donner des coups de couteau **2** COUGH : tousser (d'une toux sèche) **3 to hack into** : s'introduire dans, entrer dans (en informatique)
hack² *n* **1** : entaille *f* **2** BLOW : coup *m* violent **3** HORSE : cheval *m* de louage **4** *or* **hack writer** : écrivaillon *m*, plumitif *m* **5** COUGH : toux *f* sèche
hackle [ˈhækəl] *n* **1** : plume *f* du cou (d'un oiseau) **2 hackles** *npl* : poils *mpl* hérissés (d'un chien, etc.) <don't get your hackles up : ne t'énerve pas>
hackney [ˈhækni] *n, pl* **-neys** : fiacre *m*

hackneyed [ˈhæknid] *adj* TRITE : banal, rebattu
hacksaw [ˈhæk,sɔ] *n* : scie *f* à métaux
had → have
haddock [ˈhædək] *ns & pl* : églefin *m*
hadn't [ˈhædənt] (*contraction of* **had not**) **→ have**
haft [ˈhæft] *n* : manche *m* (d'un outil), poignée *f* (d'une dague)
hag [ˈhæg] *n* **1** WITCH : sorcière *f* **2** CRONE : vieille *f* bique, grébiche *f Can*
haggard [ˈhægərd] *adj* : hâve, exténué
haggle [ˈhægəl] *vi* **-gled; -gling** : marchander
ha–ha [ˌhɑˈhɑ, ˈhɑˈhɑ] *interj* : ha ha
hail¹ [ˈheɪl] *vi* : grêler (en météorologie) — *vt* **1** GREET : saluer, acclamer **2** : héler (un taxi)
hail² *n* **1** : grêle *f* (en météorologie) **2** GREETING : salutation *f*
hailstone [ˈheɪl,stoːn] *n* : grêlon *m*
hailstorm [ˈheɪl,stɔrm] *n* : averse *f* de grêle
hair [ˈhær] *n* **1** : cheveux *mpl* <to have short hair : avoir les cheveux courts> **2** : poil *m* <to have hair on one's legs : avoir du poil sur les jambes> <dog hair : poils de chien>
hairbreadth [ˈhær,brɛdθ] *or* **hairsbreadth** [ˈhærz-] *n* **by a hairbreadth** : d'un poil, de justesse
hairbrush [ˈhær,brʌʃ] *n* : brosse *f* à cheveux
haircut [ˈhær,kʌt] *n* : coupe *f* de cheveux
hairdo [ˈhær,duː] *n, pl* **-dos** : coiffure *f*, peignure *f Can fam*
hairdresser [ˈhær,drɛsər] *n* : coiffeur *m*, -feuse *f*
hairiness [ˈhærinəs] *n* : pilosité *f*
hairless [ˈhærləs] *adj* : sans cheveux, glabre (se dit du corps), sans poils (se dit des animaux)
hairline [ˈhær,laɪn] *n* **1** : ligne *f* très mince **2** : naissance *f* des cheveux <to have a receding hairline : avoir un front qui se dégarnit>
hairpin [ˈhær,pɪn] *n* : épingle *f* à cheveux
hair–raising [ˈhær,reɪzɪŋ] *adj* : à faire dresser les cheveux sur la tête, horrifique
hairy [ˈhæri] *adj* **hairier; -est** : poilu, velu
Haitian¹ [ˈheɪʃən, ˈheɪtiən] *adj* : haïtien
Haitian² *n* : Haïtien *m*, -tienne *f*
hake [ˈheɪk] *n* : merlu *m* (vivant), colin *m* (en cuisine)
hale¹ [ˈheɪl] *vt* **haled; haling** HAUL : haler, tirer <to hale into court : traîner devant le tribunal>
hale² *adj* : vigoureux <hale and hearty : en pleine forme>
half¹ [ˈhæf, ˈhaf] *adv* : à demi, à moitié <to be half full : être à demi rempli>
half² *adj* **1** : demi <a half sheet of paper : une demi-feuille de papier> <two hours and a half : deux heures et demie> **2** PARTIAL : demi <a half smile : un demi sourire>
half³ *n, pl* **halves** [ˈhævz, ˈhavz] **1** : demi *m* <two halves : deux demis> **2** : moitié *f* <half of the profits : la moitié des profits> **3** *or* **halftime** : mi-temps *f* (aux sports)
half brother *n* : demi-frère *m*
halfhearted [ˈhæfˈhɑrtəd] *adj* : qui manque d'enthousiasme
halfheartedly [ˈhæfˈhɑrtədli] *adv* : sans enthousiasme, sans conviction
half–life [ˈhæf,laɪf] *n* : demi-vie *f*
half sister *n* : demi-soeur *f*
halfway [ˈhæfˈweɪ] *adv & adj* : à mi-chemin
half–wit [ˈhæf,wɪt] *n* : imbécile *mf*; idiot *m*, idiote *f*
half–witted [ˈhæf,wɪtəd] *adj* : bête, stupide
halibut [ˈhælɪbət] *ns & pl* : flétan *m*
halitosis [ˌhæləˈtoʊsəs] *n* : mauvaise haleine *f*
hall [ˈhɔl] *n* **1** AUDITORIUM : salle *f* (de concert, etc.) **2** LOBBY : entrée *f*, vestibule *m*, hall *m* (d'entrée), portique *m Can fam* **3** DORMITORY : résidence *f* universitaire **4 → city hall**
hallelujah [ˌhæləˈluːjə, ˌhɑˌloːd] *interj* : alléluia
hallmark [ˈhɔl,mɑrk] *n* : caractéristique *f*, sceau *m*
hallow [ˈhæˌloː] *vt* : sanctifier, consacrer
hallowed [ˈhæˌloːd, ˈhæˌloːəd, ˈhɑ-] *adj* : sanctifié, saint
Halloween [ˌhæləˈwiːn, ˌhɑ-] *n* : Halloween *f*
hallucinate [həˈluːsənˌeɪt] *vi* **-nated; -nating** : avoir des hallucinations
hallucination [həˌluːsənˈeɪʃən] *n* : hallucination *f*
hallucinogen [həˈluːsənədʒən] *n* : hallucinogène *m*
hallucinogenic [həˌluːsənəˈdʒɛnɪk] *adj* : hallucinogène
hallway [ˈhɔlˌweɪ] *n* **1** ENTRANCE : entrée *f*, vestibule *m* **2** CORRIDOR : corridor *m*, couloir *m*
halo [ˈheɪˌloː] *n, pl* **-los** *or* **-loes** : auréole *f*
halt¹ [ˈhɔlt] *vi* : s'arrêter — *vt* **1** STOP : arrêter (une personne) **2** : interrompre <the strike halted buses : la grève a interrompu le service d'autobus>
halt² *n* : halte *f*, arrêt *m* <to come to a halt : s'interrompre>
halter [ˈhɔltər] *n* **1** : licou *m* (d'un animal) **2** *or* **halter top** : chemisier *m* à dos nu
halting [ˈhɔltɪŋ] *adj* HESITANT : hésitant
halve [ˈhæv, ˈhav] *vt* **halved; halving 1** DIVIDE : couper en deux **2** REDUCE : réduire de moitié
halves → half³
ham [ˈhæm] *n* **1** : jambon *m* **2** *or* **ham actor** : cabotin *m*, -tine *f* **3 hams** *npl*

BUTTOCKS, THIGHS : cuisses *fpl*, fesses *fpl* 4 *or* **ham radio operator** : radioamateur *m*

hamburger [ˈhæmˌbərgər] *or* **hamburg** [-ˌbərg] *n* **1** : hamburger *m* (cuit) **2** : viande *f* hachée <a pound of hamburger : une livre de viande hachée>

hamlet [ˈhæmlət] *n* : hameau *m*

hammer[1] [ˈhæmər] *vt* : marteler, enfoncer (à coups de marteau) — *vi* : frapper à coups de marteau

hammer[2] *n* **1** : marteau *m* **2** : chien *m* (d'une arme à feu)

hammock [ˈhæmək] *n* : hamac *m*

hamper[1] [ˈhæmpər] *vt* : entraver, gêner

hamper[2] *n* : panier *m* <clothes hamper : panier à linge sale>

hamster [ˈhæmpstər] *n* : hamster *m*

hamstring[1] [ˈhæmˌstrɪŋ] *vt* **-strung** [-ˈstrʌŋ]; **-stringing** [-ˈstrɪŋɪŋ] **1** : couper le jarret à (un animal) **2** INCAPACITATE : paralyser <hamstrung by guilt : paralysé par les remords>

hamstring[2] *n* : jarret *m* (d'un animal), tendon *m* (d'une personne)

hand[1] [ˈhænd] *vt* : donner, passer

hand[2] *n* **1** : main *f* <good with one's hands : adroit de ses mains> <to lend a hand : prêter une main> **2** POINTER : aiguille *f* (d'une montre, etc.) **3** SIDE : côté *m* <on the other hand : par contre, d'un autre côté> **4** HANDWRITING : écriture *f* **5** HELP : aide *f* <to give s.o. a hand : donner un coup de main à qqn> **6** APPLAUSE : applaudissements *mpl* **7** : main *f*, jeu *m* (aux cartes) **8** WORKER : ouvrier *m*, -vrière *f* **9 to ask for s.o.'s hand (in marriage)** : demander qqn en mariage **10 to try one's hand at** : s'essayer à

handbag [ˈhænd,bæg] *n* : sac *m* à main

handball [ˈhænd,bɔl] *n* : handball *m*

handbill [ˈhænd,bɪl] *n* : prospectus *m*

handbook [ˈhænd,bʊk] *n* : manuel *m*, guide *m*

handcuff [ˈhænd,kʌf] *vt* : passer les menottes à

handcuffs [ˈhænd,kʌfs] *npl* : menottes *fpl*

handful [ˈhænd,fʊl] *n* : poignée *f*

handgun [ˈhænd,gʌn] *n* : pistolet *m*, revolver *m*

handicap[1] [ˈhændi,kæp] *vt* **-capped; -capping** : handicaper

handicap[2] *n* **1** DISABILITY : handicap *m* **2** DISADVANTAGE : désavantage *m*, handicap *m*

handicapped [ˈhændi,kæpt] *adj* : handicapé

handicraft [ˈhændi,kræft] *n* **1** : travail *m* artisanal **2 handicrafts** *npl* : objets *mpl* artisanaux

handily [ˈhændəli] *adv* EASILY : haut la main

handiwork [ˈhændi,wərk] *n* **1** WORK : travail *m* manuel **2** ARTICLES, CRAFTS : objets *mpl* artisanaux

handkerchief [ˈhæŋkərtʃəf, -ˌtʃiːf] *n, pl* **-chiefs** : mouchoir *m*

handle[1] [ˈhændəl] *vt* **-dled; -dling 1** TOUCH : toucher à, manipuler **2** STAND : supporter <I can't handle the heat : je ne peux pas supporter la chaleur> **3** MANAGE : manier, gérer

handle[2] *n* : manche *m* (d'un ustensile), poignée *f* (de porte), anse *f* (de panier)

handlebars [ˈhændəlˌbɑrz] *npl* : guidon *m*

handmade [ˈhænd,meɪd] *adj* : fait à la main

hand–me–downs [ˈhændmiˌdaʊnz] *npl* : vêtements *mpl* de seconde main

handout [ˈhænd,aʊt] *n* **1** CHARITY : aumône *f*, don *m* **2** LEAFLET : prospectus *m*

handpick [ˈhænd,pɪk] *vt* : sélectionner avec soin

handrail [ˈhænd,reɪl] *n* **1** : rampe *f*, main *f* courante (d'un escalier) **2** : garde-fou *m* (d'un pont)

handsaw [ˈhænd,sɔ] *n* : scie *f* à main

hands down *adv* EASILY, UNQUESTIONABLY : sans aucun doute

handshake [ˈhænd,ʃeɪk] *n* : poignée *f* de main

handsome [ˈhænt͡səm] *adj* **handsomer; -est 1** CONSIDERABLE : important, considérable **2** GENEROUS : généreux **3** GOOD-LOOKING : beau

handsomely [ˈhænt͡səmli] *adv* **1** ELEGANTLY : élégamment **2** GENEROUSLY : avec générosité

handspring [ˈhænd,sprɪŋ] *n* : saut *m* de mains

handstand [ˈhænd,stænd] *n* : équilibre *m* sur les mains

hand–to–hand [ˈhænd͡tə,hænd] *adj* : (au) corps à corps

handwriting [ˈhænd,raɪtɪŋ] *n* : écriture *f*

handwritten [ˈhænd,rɪtən] *adj* : écrit à la main

handy [ˈhændi] *adj* **handier; -est 1** NEARBY : à portée de la main, proche **2** CONVENIENT, USEFUL : utile, pratique **3** CLEVER : adroit, habile

handyman [ˈhændimən] *n, pl* **-men** [-mən, -ˌmɛn] : bricoleur *m*, homme *m* à tout faire

hang[1] [ˈhæŋ] *v* **hung** [ˈhʌŋ]; **hanging** *vt* **1** SUSPEND : suspendre, accrocher **2** (*past tense often* **hanged**) : pendre (un criminel) **3** : poser (une porte, etc.) **4 to hang one's head** : baisser la tête de honte — *vi* **1** DANGLE : être accroché, être suspendu **2** FALL : être accroché, être suspendu (se dit des vêtements, des rideaux, etc.) **3** HOVER : flotter, être suspendu (en l'air) **4** DROOP : pencher, tomber

hang[2] *n* **1** : drapé *m* (d'un rideau, etc.) **2 to get the hang of doing sth** : prendre le coup pour faire qqch <I can't get the hang of it! : je ne pige pas!>

hangar [ˈhæŋər, ˈhæŋgər] *n* : hangar *m*

hanger [ˈhæŋər] *n or* **coat hanger** : cintre *m*

hangman [ˈhæŋmən] *n, pl* **-men** [-mən, -ˈmɛn] : bourreau *m*

hangnail [ˈhæŋˌneɪl] *n* : envie *f*

hangout [ˈhæŋˌɑʊt] *n* : endroit *m* préféré (pour flâner)

hangover [ˈhæŋˌoːvər] *n* : gueule *f* de bois

hank [ˈhæŋk] *n* : écheveau *m*

hanker [ˈhæŋkər] *vi* **to hanker for** : désirer, avoir envie de

hankering [ˈhæŋkərɪŋ] *n* : désir *m*, envie *f*

hansom [ˈhænt͡səm] *n* : cabriolet *m*

Hanukkah [ˈxɑnəkə, ˈhɑ-] *n* : Hanukkah *m*

haphazard [hæpˈhæzərd] *adj* : fortuit, mal organisé <in a haphazard way : de façon peu méthodique>

haphazardly [hæpˈhæzərdli] *adv* : n'importe comment, sans organisation

hapless [ˈhæpləs] *adj* : infortuné, malchanceux

happen [ˈhæpən] *vi* **1** OCCUR : arriver, se passer <what's happening? : qu'est-ce qui se passe?> **2** CHANCE : arriver par hasard <I happened to overhear her plans : j'ai entendu ses plans par hasard> **3** : se trouver <it so happens that I was right : il se trouve que j'avais raison> **4** BEFALL : arriver <what happened to you? : qu'est-ce qui t'est arrivé?>

happening [ˈhæpənɪŋ] *n* : incident *m*, événement *m*

happily [ˈhæpəli] *adv* : heureusement

happiness [ˈhæpɪnəs] *n* : bonheur *m*

happy [ˈhæpi] *adj* **happier; -est 1** FORTUNATE : heureux, favorable **2** CHEERFUL : heureux **3** PLEASED : content, satisfait **4** (*expressing willingness*) <to be happy to do sth : être heureux de faire qqch> <I'm happy to help you : je suis ravi de vous aider>

happy–go–lucky [ˈhæpigoːˈlʌki] *adj* : insouciant

harangue[1] [həˈræŋ] *vt* **-rangued; -ranguing** : haranguer

harangue[2] *n* : harangue *f*

harass [həˈræs, ˈhærəs] *vt* **1** TORMENT, WORRY : tourmenter, harceler **2** ANNOY, PESTER : harceler

harassment [həˈræsmənt, ˈhærəsmənt] *n* : harcèlement *m*

harbinger [ˈhɑrbɪnd͡ʒər] *n* **1** PRECURSOR : signe *m* avant-coureur, précurseur *m* **2** OMEN : présage *m* <a harbinger of doom : un mauvais présage>

harbor[1] *or Brit* **harbour** [ˈhɑrbər] *vt* **1** SHELTER : héberger (une personne), receler (un criminel) **2** HOLD, KEEP : nourrir (un espoir, etc.), entretenir (de doutes)

harbor[2] *or Brit* **harbour** *n* PORT : port *m*

hard[1] [ˈhɑrd] *adv* **1** FORCEFULLY, STRENUOUSLY : dur, fort <to work hard : travailler dur> <to snow hard : neiger fort> **2 to take sth hard** : mal prendre qqch

hard[2] *adj* **1** FIRM : dur, solide **2** : calcaire <hard water : eau calcaire> **3** DEFINITE : définitif **4** SEARCHING : pénétrant <a hard look : un regard pénétrant> **5** UNFEELING : dur, insensible **6** TROUBLESOME : difficile, pénible **7** INTENSE : dur, ferme <hard blows : coups durs> **8** DILIGENT : consciencieux

harden [ˈhɑrdən] *vt* : durcir, endurcir <to harden one's heart : endurcir son coeur> — *vi* : s'endurcir

hardheaded [ˈhɑrdˈhɛdəd] *adj* **1** STUBBORN : têtu, obstiné **2** REALISTIC : réaliste, pratique

hard–hearted [ˈhɑrdˈhɑrt͡ʃəd] *adj* : dur, insensible

hardly [ˈhɑrdli] *adv* **1** BARELY : à peine, ne ... guère **2** NOT : ne ... pas, presque jamais <it's hardly surprising : ce n'est pas surprenant>

hardness [ˈhɑrdnəs] *n* **1** FIRMNESS : dureté *f* **2** DIFFICULTY : difficulté *f*, dureté *f* **3** SEVERITY : sévérité *f*, dureté *f*

hardship [ˈhɑrdˌʃɪp] *n* **1** DIFFICULTY : détresse *f* **2** DISTRESS, SUFFERING : épreuves *fpl*, privations *fpl*

hardware [ˈhɑrdˌwɛr] *n* **1** : quincaillerie *f* **2** : matériel *m* (en informatique)

hardwood [ˈhɑrdˌwʊd] *n* : bois *m* dur, bois *m* franc *Can*

hardworking [ˈhɑrdˈwərkɪŋ] *adj* : travailleur, travaillant *Can*

hardy [ˈhɑrdi] *adj* **hardier; -est 1** BOLD : hardi, intrépide **2** ROBUST : résistant, robuste

hare [ˈhɛr] *n, pl* **hare** *or* **hares** : lièvre *m*

harebrained [ˈhɛrˌbreɪnd] *adj* : écervelé, insensé

harelip [ˈhɛrˈlɪp] *n* : bec-de-lièvre *m*

harem [ˈhɛrəm] *n* : harem *m*

hark [ˈhɑrk] *vi* **1** LISTEN : prêter l'oreille, ouïr **2 to hark back to** : revenir à

harlequin [ˈhɑrlɪkən, -kwən] *n* : arlequin *m*

harm[1] [ˈhɑrm] *vt* : faire du mal à, nuire à

harm[2] *n* : mal *m*, dommage *m*, tort *m*

harmful [ˈhɑrmfəl] *adj* : nuisible, nocif

harmfully [ˈhɑrmfəli] *adv* : de façon nuisible

harmless [ˈhɑrmləs] *adj* : inoffensif, anodin

harmlessly [ˈhɑrmləsli] *adv* : sans faire de mal

harmonic [hɑrˈmɑnɪk] *adj* : harmonique — **harmonically** [-nɪkli] *adv*

harmonica [hɑrˈmɑnɪkə] *n* : harmonica *m*

harmonious [hɑrˈmoːniəs] *adj* : harmonieux — **harmoniously** *adv*

harmonize [ˈhɑrmə,naɪz] *v* **-nized; -nizing** *vt* : harmoniser — *vi* : s'harmoniser
harmony [ˈhɑrməni] *n, pl* **-nies** : harmonie *f*
harness[1] [ˈhɑrnəs] *vt* **1** : harnacher (un cheval) **2** UTILIZE : exploiter (de l'énergie, etc.)
harness[2] *n* : harnais *m,* harnachement *m*
harp[1] [ˈhɑrp] *vi* **to harp on** : rabâcher, répéter continuellement
harp[2] *n* : harpe *f*
harpist [ˈhɑrpɪst] *n* : harpiste *mf*
harpoon[1] [hɑrˈpuːn] *vt* : harponner
harpoon[2] *n* : harpon *m*
harpsichord [ˈhɑrpsɪˌkɔrd] *n* : clavecin *m*
harrow[1] [ˈhæro:] *vt* **1** : herser (la terre) **2** TORMENT, VEX : torturer, tourmenter
harrow[2] *n* : herse *f*
harry [ˈhæri] *vt* **-ried; -rying** HARASS : harceler
harsh [ˈhɑrʃ] *adj* **1** ROUGH : rude <a harsh surface : une surface rude> **2** SEVERE : dur, sévère **3** DIFFICULT, RIGOROUS : rigoureux
harshly [ˈhɑrʃli] *adv* : sévèrement, durement
harshness [ˈhɑrʃnəs] *n* : sévérité *f*
hart [ˈhɑrt] *n Brit* STAG : cerf *m*
harvest[1] [ˈhɑrvəst] *vt* : moissonner, récolter
harvest[2] *n* : moisson *f,* récolte *f*
harvester [ˈhɑrvəstər] *n* **1** : moissonneur *m,* -neuse *f* (personne) **2** : moissonneuse *f* (machine)
has → **have**
hash[1] [ˈhæʃ] *vt* **1** CHOP : hacher **2 to hash over** DISCUSS : parler de, discuter
hash[2] *n* **1** : hachis *m* **2** JUMBLE, MESS : gâchis *m*
hasn't [ˈhæzənt] (*contraction of* **has not**) → **have**
hasp [ˈhæsp] *n* : moraillon *m,* loquet *m*
hassle[1] [ˈhæsəl] *v* **-sled; -sling** *vi* ARGUE : se chamailler, se disputer — *vt* ANNOY, HARASS : tracasser, harceler
hassle[2] *n* **1** QUARREL : chicane *f,* dispute *f* **2** BOTHER, TROUBLE : embêtements *mpl,* ennuis *mpl*
hassock [ˈhæsək] *n* **1** CUSHION : coussin *m* (d'agenouilloir) **2** FOOTSTOOL : pouf *m,* tabouret *m*
haste [ˈheɪst] *n* : hâte *f,* précipitation *f* <to make haste : se hâter>
hasten [ˈheɪsən] *vt* : hâter, précipiter — *vi* HURRY : se hâter, se dépêcher
hastily [ˈheɪstəli] *adv* : à la hâte
hasty [ˈheɪsti] *adj* **hastier; -est 1** HURRIED : précipité, à la hâte **2** RASH : hâtif, irréfléchi
hat [ˈhæt] *n* : chapeau *m*
hatch[1] [ˈhætʃ] *vt* **1** INCUBATE : couver, faire éclore **2** CONCOCT : ourdir (un complot) — *vi* : éclore
hatch[2] *n* **1** : écoutille *f* (d'un navire) **2** BROOD : couvée *f,* éclosion *f*
hatchery [ˈhætʃəri] *n, pl* **-ries 1** : couvoir *m* (de poules) **2** *or* **fish hatchery** : station *f* d'alevinage
hatchet [ˈhætʃət] *n* : hachette *f*
hatchway [ˈhætʃˌweɪ] *n* HATCH : écoutille *f* (d'un navire)
hate[1] [ˈheɪt] *vt* **hated; hating** : détester, haïr, avoir horreur de
hate[2] *n* : haine *f*
hateful [ˈheɪtfəl] *adj* : odieux, détestable — **hatefully** *adv*
hatred [ˈheɪtrəd] *n* : haine *f*
hatter [ˈhætər] *n* : chapelier *m,* -lière *f*
haughtily [ˈhɔtəli] *adv* : de façon hautaine
haughty [ˈhɔti] *adj* **haughtier; -est** : hautain, arrogant
haul[1] [ˈhɔl] *vt* **1** DRAG, PULL : tirer **2** TRANSPORT : transporter, camionner
haul[2] *n* **1** PULL, TUG : coup *m* **2** CATCH : prise *f* (de poissons) **3** LOOT : butin *m* **4** JOURNEY : chemin *m,* route *f,* voyage *m* <it's a long haul : la route est longue>
hauler [ˈhɔlər] *n* DRIVER, TRUCKER : routier *m;* camionneur *m,* -neuse *f*
haunch [ˈhɔntʃ] *n* **1** HIP : hanche *f* **2 haunches** *npl* HINDQUARTERS : arrière-train *m,* derrière *m* (d'un animal)
haunt[1] [ˈhɔnt] *vt* **1** : hanter <a haunted house : une maison hantée> **2** PREOCCUPY : hanter, obséder **3** FREQUENT : fréquenter, hanter
haunt[2] *n* : lieu *m* fréquenté
haunting [ˈhɔntɪŋ] *adj* : obsédant
have [ˈhæv, *in senses 3 and 4 as an auxiliary verb usu* ˈhəf] *v* **had** [ˈhæd]; **having; has** [ˈhæz, *in senses 3 and 4 as an auxiliary verb usu* ˈhəz] *vt* **1** POSSESS : avoir <do you have change? : avez-vous de la monnaie?> <April has 30 days : il y a 30 jours en avril> **2** EXPERIENCE, UNDERGO : avoir <I have a cold : j'ai un rhume> **3** (*indicating consumption*) <to have a sandwich : manger un sandwich> <to have a cigarette : fumer une cigarette> **4** RECEIVE : recevoir, avoir <to have permission : avoir la permission> <I have a letter from Anne : j'ai reçu une lettre d'Anne> **5** WANT : vouloir, prendre <I'll have coffee : je voudrais du café> **6** ALLOW : permettre, tolérer <I won't have it! : je ne le tolérerai pas!> **7** HOLD : tenir, faire <he had me by the arm : il me tenait par le bras> <to have a party : faire une fête> **8** BEAR : avoir (un enfant) **9** (*indicating causation*) <she had a dress made : elle s'est fait faire une robe> — *v aux* **1** : avoir, être <he had seen me : il m'avait vu> <she has left : elle est partie> **2** (*used in tags*) <you have finished, haven't you? : vous avez fini, n'est-ce pas?> **3 to have to**

: devoir <we have to meet the deadline : nous devons rencontrer la date d'échéance> **4 to have to do with** : concerner

haven ['heɪvən] *n* : refuge *m*, havre *m*

havoc ['hævək] *n* **1** DEVASTATION : destruction *f*, dévastation *f* **2** CHAOS : désordre *m*, chaos *m*

Hawaiian[1] [hə'waɪən] *adj* : hawaïen

Hawaiian[2] *n* **1** : Hawaïen *m*, -waïenne *f* **2** : hawaïen *m* (langue)

hawk[1] ['hɔk] *vt* : colporter, vendre (à la criée)

hawk[2] *n* : faucon *m* (oiseau)

hawker ['hɔkər] *n* PEDDLER : colporteur *m*, -teuse *f*

hawthorn ['hɔˌθɔrn] *n* : aubépine *f*, cenellier *m Can*

hay ['heɪ] *n* : foin *m*

hay fever *n* : rhume *m* des foins

hayloft ['heɪˌlɔft] *n* : grenier *m* à foin

haystack ['heɪˌstæk] *n* : meule *f* de foin

haywire ['heɪˌwaɪr] *adj* : détraqué <to go haywire : se détraquer>

hazard[1] ['hæzərd] *vt* : hasarder, risquer

hazard[2] *n* **1** PERIL : danger *m*, risque *m* **2** CHANCE : chance *f*, hasard *m*

hazardous ['hæzərdəs] *adj* : dangereux, risqué

haze[1] ['heɪz] *vi* **hazed; hazing** *or* **to haze over** : devenir brumeux

haze[2] *n* : brume *f*

hazel ['heɪzəl] *n* **1** : noisetier *m* (arbre) **2** : noisette *f* (couleur)

hazelnut ['heɪzəlˌnʌt] *n* : noisette *f*

haziness ['heɪzinəs] *n* **1** MISTINESS : état *m* brumeux **2** VAGUENESS : flou *m*

hazy ['heɪzi] *adj* **hazier; -est 1** : brumeux <hazy sky : ciel brumeux> **2** VAGUE : vague, flou

he ['hi:] *pron* **1** : il <he spoke to me : il m'a parlé> **2** : lui <she's younger than he (is) : elle est plus jeune que lui>

head[1] ['hed] *vt* **1** LEAD : être en tête de **2** DIRECT : diriger **3** TITLE : intituler — *vi* **1** : former une tête (se dit d'un chou, etc.) **2** : se diriger, aller <where are you headed? : où vas-tu?>

head[2] *adj* CHIEF : en chef

head[3] *n* **1** : tête *f* <from head to toe : de la tête aux pieds> **2** MIND : tête *f*, esprit *m* **3** END : bout *m* (d'une table), chevet *m* (d'un lit) **4** DIRECTOR : chef *m*; directeur *m*, -trice *f* **5** : personne *f* <$8.00 per head : 8,00 $ par personne> **6 at the head of** : à la tête de (une classe, etc.) **7 to come to a head** : arriver au point critique

headache ['hedˌeɪk] *n* : mal *m* de tête

headband ['hedˌbænd] *n* : bandeau *m*

headdress ['hedˌdrɛs] *n* : coiffe *f*

headfirst ['hedˈfərst] *adv* : la tête la première

headgear ['hedˌgɪr] *n* : couvre-chef *m*, coiffure *f*

heading ['hedɪŋ] *n* **1** DIRECTION : cap *m* (d'un navire) **2** : titre *m* (d'un article), rubrique *f* (d'un sujet) **3** LETTERHEAD : en-tête *m*

headland ['hedlənd, -ˌlænd] *n* : promontoire *m*

headlight ['hedˌlaɪt] *n* : phare *m*

headline ['hedˌlaɪn] *n* : manchette *f*, (gros) titre *m*

headlong[1] ['hedˈlɔŋ] *adv* **1** HEADFIRST : la tête la première **2** HASTILY, RECKLESSLY : à toute allure, à toute vitesse

headlong[2] ['hedˌlɔŋ] *adj* : précipité

headmaster ['hedˌmæstər] *n* : directeur *m* (d'école)

headmistress ['hedˌmɪstrəs, -ˈmɪs-] *n* : directrice *f* (d'école)

head–on ['hedˈɑn, -ˈɔn] *adv & adj* : de front, face-à-face

headphones ['hedˌfoʊnz] *npl* : écouteurs *mpl*, casque *m*

headquarters ['hedˌkwɔrtərz] *ns & pl* **1** : siège *m* social (d'une compagnie) **2** : quartier *m* général (dans l'armée, etc.)

headrest ['hedˌrest] *n* : appui-tête *m*

head start *n* : avance *f*, longueur *f* d'avance

headstone ['hedˌstoʊn] *n* : pierre *f* tombale

headstrong ['hedˌstrɔŋ] *adj* : têtu, obstiné

headwaiter ['hedˈweɪtər] *n* : maître *m* d'hôtel

headwaters ['hedˌwɔtərz, -ˌwɑ-] *npl* : sources *fpl*

headway ['hedˌweɪ] *n* **1** PROGRESS : progrès *m* **2 to make headway** : avancer, progresser

heady ['hedi] *adj* **headier; -est 1** INTOXICATING : qui monte à la tête **2** EXCITING, STIMULATING : passionnant, excitant

heal ['hi:l] *vt* : guérir, cicatriser — *vi* : guérir, se cicatriser

healer ['hi:lər] *n* : guérisseur *m*, -seuse *f*

health ['helθ] *n* : santé *f*

healthful ['helθfəl] *adj* : bon pour la santé, sain

healthily ['helθəli] *adv* : sainement

health maintenance organization → **HMO**

healthy ['helθi] *adj* **healthier; -est 1** WELL : en bonne santé **2** PROSPEROUS : prospère, florissant

heap[1] ['hi:p] *vt* : entasser, amasser

heap[2] *n* PILE : amas *m*, tas *m*

hear ['hɪr] *v* **heard** ['hərd]; **hearing** *vt* **1** : entendre <I can't hear you : je ne t'entends pas> **2** HEED : écouter **3** LEARN : apprendre, entendre <I heard the news : j'ai appris la nouvelle> — *vi* **1** : entendre <she doesn't hear very well : elle n'entends pas très bien> **2 to hear from** : avoir des nouvelles de

hearing ['hɪrɪŋ] *n* **1** : ouïe *f*, audition *f* **2** : audience *f* (d'un tribunal) **3 within hearing** : à portée de voix

hearing aid *n* : appareil *m* auditif
hearken ['hɑrkən] *vi* **to hearken to** : écouter
hearsay ['hɪr,seɪ] *n* : ouï-dire *m*, rumeur *f*
hearse ['hərs] *n* : corbillard *m*
heart ['hɑrt] *n* **1** : cœur *m* **2** AFFECTION, LOVE : cœur *m*, amour *m* **3** COURAGE : courage *m*, ardeur *f* <to lose heart : perdre courage> **4** CENTER : cœur *m*, centre *m* <the heart of the matter : le fond du problème> **5** : cœur *m* (aux cartes) **6 at ~** : au fond **7 by ~** : par cœur
heartache ['hɑrt,eɪk] *n* : chagrin *m*, peine *f*
heart attack *n* : crise *f* cardiaque
heartbeat ['hɑrt,bi:t] *n* : battement *m* de cœur
heartbreak ['hɑrt,breɪk] *n* : déchirement *m*, douleur *f*, chagrin *m*
heartbreaking ['hɑrt,breɪkɪŋ] *adj* : déchirant, qui fend le cœur
heartbroken ['hɑrt,bro:kən] *adj* **to be heartbroken** : avoir le cœur brisé
heartburn ['hɑrt,bərn] *n* : brûlures *fpl* d'estomac
hearten ['hɑrtən] *vt* : encourager
hearth ['hɑrθ] *n* : foyer *m*, âtre *m*
heartily ['hɑrt,əli] *adv* **1** ENTHUSIASTICALLY : de tout son cœur <to laugh heartily : rire de bon cœur> **2** TOTALLY : tout à fait <I agree heartily : je suis tout à fait d'accord>
heartless ['hɑrtləs] *adj* : sans cœur, cruel
heartsick ['hɑrt,sɪk] *adj* : déprimé <to be heartsick : avoir la mort dans l'âme>
heartstrings ['hɑrt,strɪŋz] *npl* : corde *f* sensible
heartwarming ['hɑrt,wərmɪŋ] *adj* CHEERING : réconfortant
heartwood ['hɑrt,wʊd] *n* : cœur *m* du bois
hearty ['hɑrti] *adj* **heartier; -est 1** JOVIAL : jovial, enjoué **2** VIGOROUS : vigoureux, robuste **3** CORDIAL, WARM : cordial, chaleureux **4** AMPLE : copieux
heat[1] ['hi:t] *v* : chauffer
heat[2] *n* **1** WARMTH : chaleur *f* **2** TEMPERATURE : température *f*, chaleur *f* **3** HEATING : chauffage *m* **4** PASSION : feu *m*, intensité *f* <in the heat of the moment : dans l'excitation du moment>
heated ['hi:ṭəd] *adj* **1** WARMED : chauffé **2** IMPASSIONED : animé, passionné
heatedly ['hi:ṭədli] *adv* : avec fougue
heater ['hi:ṭər] *n* : radiateur *m*, appareil *m* de chauffage
heath ['hi:θ] *n* **1** HEATHER : bruyère *f* **2** MOOR : lande *f*
heathen[1] [hi:ðən] *adj* : païen
heathen[2] *n, pl* **-thens** *or* **-then** : païen *m*, païenne *f*
heather ['heðər] *n* : bruyère *f*
heave[1] ['hi:v] *v* **heaved** *or* **hove** ['ho:v]; **heaving** *vt* **1** LIFT : lever, soulever (avec effort) **2** HURL : lancer, jeter **3 to heave a sigh** : pousser un soupir — *vi* **1** : se soulever et s'abaisser (se dit de la poitrine) **2 to heave up** RISE : se soulever
heave[2] *n* **1** EFFORT : effort *m* **2** THROW : lancement *m* (avec force)
heaven ['hevən] *n* **1** : ciel *m* <heaven and hell : le ciel et l'enfer> <for heaven's sake! : pour l'amour du ciel!> **2 heavens** *npl* SKY : ciel *m*
heavenly ['hevənli] *adj* : céleste, divin
heavily ['hevəli] *adv* **1** : lourdement, pesamment <to walk heavily : marcher lourdement> **2** LABORIOUSLY : péniblement **3** MUCH : beaucoup
heaviness ['hevinəs] *n* : lourdeur *f*, pesanteur *f*
heavy ['hevi] *adj* **heavier; -est 1** WEIGHTY : lourd, pesant **2** BURDENSOME : lourd, gros <a heavy sorrow : un lourd chagrin> **3** DENSE, THICK : dense, abondant **4** DEEP : profond <heavy sleep : sommeil profond> **5** STOUT : gros, corpulent **6** IMMODERATE : gros <a heavy smoker : un gros fumeur>
heavy–duty ['hevi'du:ṭi, -'dju:-] *adj* : à haute résistance, à usage industriel
heavyweight ['hevi,weɪt] *n* : poids *m* lourd (aux sports)
Hebrew[1] ['hi:,bru:] *adj* : hébreu, hébraïque
Hebrew[2] *n* **1** : Hébreu *m*, Israélite *mf* **2** : hébreu *m* (langue)
heckle ['hekəl] *vt* **-led; -ling** : interrompre bruyamment
hectic ['hekṭɪk] *adj* : mouvementé, agité
hedge[1] ['hedʒ] *v* **hedged; hedging** *vt* **1** *or* **to hedge in** ENCIRCLE : entourer, encercler **2 to hedge one's bets** : se couvrir — *vi* : chercher des échappatoires, patiner *Can*
hedge[2] *n* **1** : haie *f* **2** SAFEGUARD : sauvegarde *f*, protection *f*
hedgehog ['hedʒ,hɔg, -,hɑg] *n* : hérisson *m*
heed[1] ['hi:d] *vt* : faire attention à, écouter
heed[2] *n* : attention *f* <to take heed of : tenir compte de>
heedful ['hi:dfəl] *adj* : attentif — **heedfully** *adv*
heedless ['hi:dləs] *adj* : sans prêter attention, irréfléchi, insouciant
heedlessly ['hi:dləsli] *adv* : avec insouciance
heel[1] ['hi:l] *vi* : gîter (se dit d'un bateau)
heel[2] *n* : talon *m*
heft ['heft] *vt* : hisser, soulever
hefty ['hefti] *adj* **heftier; -est** : pesant, lourd
heifer ['hefər] *n* : génisse *f*
height ['haɪt] *n* **1** PEAK : comble *m*, point *m* culminant **2** TALLNESS : taille

f, hauteur *f* <what is your height? : combien mesures-tu?> **3** ALTITUDE : altitude *f*, élévation *f*

heighten [ˈhaɪtən] *vt* **1** RAISE : rehausser, élever **2** INTENSIFY : augmenter, intensifier

heinous [ˈheɪnəs] *adj* : odieux, exécrable, atroce

heir [ˈær] *n* : héritier *m*, -tière *f*

heiress [ˈærəs] *n* : héritière *f*

heirloom [ˈærˌluːm] *n* : objet *m* de famille

held → hold[1]

helicopter [ˈheləˌkɑptər] *n* : hélicoptère *m*

helium [ˈhiːliəm] *n* : hélium *m*

helix [ˈhiːlɪks] *n, pl* **-lices** [-ləˌsiːz] : hélice *f*

hell [ˈhel] *n* : enfer *m*

he'll [ˈhiːl] (*contraction of* **he shall** *or* **he will**) → **shall, will**

hellish [ˈhelɪʃ] *adj* : infernal, diabolique

hello [həˈloː, hɛ-] *or Brit* **hullo** [hʌˈleʊ] *interj* : bonjour!, allô! (au téléphone)

helm [ˈhelm] *n* : barre *f*, gouvernail *m* <to take the helm : prendre la barre>

helmet [ˈhelmət] *n* : casque *m*

help[1] [ˈhelp] *vt* **1** AID, ASSIST : aider, venir à l'aide de **2** ALLEVIATE : aider, améliorer **3** PREVENT : empêcher <they couldn't help the accident : ils n'ont pas pu empêcher l'accident> **4** SERVE : se servir <help yourself! : servez-vous!>

help[2] *n* **1** ASSISTANCE : aide *f*, secours *m* **2** STAFF : personnel *m*; employés *mpl*, -ployées *fpl*

helper [ˈhelpər] *n* : aide *mf*; assistant *m*, -tante *f*

helpful [ˈhelpfəl] *adj* **1** USEFUL : utile **2** OBLIGING : serviable, obligeant

helpfully [ˈhelpfəli] *adv* : avec obligeance

helpfulness [ˈhelpfəlnəs] *n* **1** KINDNESS : obligeance *f* **2** USEFULNESS : utilité *f*

helping [ˈhelpɪŋ] *n* SERVING : portion *f*

helpless [ˈhelpləs] *adj* **1** DEFENSELESS : sans défense, désarmé **2** POWERLESS : impuissant

helplessly [ˈhelpləsli] *adv* : en vain, désespérément

helplessness [ˈhelpləsnəs] *n* : impuissance *f*, impotence *f*

helter-skelter [ˌheltərˈskeltər] *adv* : à la débandade

hem[1] [ˈhem] *vt* **hemmed; hemming 1** : ourler, faire un ourlet à (une jupe, etc.) **2 to hem in** SURROUND : entourer

hem[2] *n* : ourlet *m*

hemisphere [ˈheməˌsfɪr] *n* : hémisphère *m*

hemispheric [ˌheməˈsfɪrɪk, -ˈsfɛr-] *or* **hemispherical** [-ɪkəl] *adj* : hémisphérique

hemlock [ˈhemˌlɑk] *n* **1** : ciguë *f* (plante) **2** : tsuga *m* du Canada, pruche *f Can* (arbre)

hemoglobin [ˈhiːməˌgloːbən] *n* : hémoglobine *f*

hemophilia [ˌhiːməˈfɪliə] *n* : hémophilie *f*

hemophiliac[1] [ˌhiːməˈfɪliˌæk] *adj* : hémophile

hemophiliac[2] *n* : hémophile *mf*

hemorrhage[1] [ˈhemərɪdʒ] *vi* **-rhaged; -rhaging** : faire une hémorragie

hemorrhage[2] *n* : hémorragie *f*

hemorrhoids [ˈheməˌrɔɪdz, ˈhemˌrɔɪdz] *npl* : hémorroïdes *fpl*

hemp [ˈhemp] *n* : chanvre *m*

hen [ˈhen] *n* : poule *f*

hence [ˈhents] *adv* **1** THEREFORE : d'où, donc **2** : d'ici <ten years hence : d'ici dix ans>

henceforth [ˈhentsˌforθ, ˌhentsˈ-] *adv* : dorénavant, désormais

henchman [ˈhentʃmən] *n, pl* **-men** [-mən, -ˌmen] : partisan *m*, adepte *m*

henna [ˈhenə] *n* : henné *m*

henpeck [ˈhenˌpek] *vt* : mener par le bout du nez

hepatitis [ˌhepəˈtaɪtəs] *n, pl* **-titides** [-ˈtɪtəˌdiːz] : hépatite *f*

her[1] [ˈhər] *adj* : son, sa, ses

her[2] [ˈhər, ər] *pron* **1** (*used as a direct object*) : la, l' <I can see her : je la vois> **2** (*used as an indirect object*) : lui <tell her that I want to go home : dis-lui que je veux rentrer> **3** (*used as an object of a preposition*) : elle <he's thinking of her : il pense à elle>

herald[1] [ˈherəld] *vt* ANNOUNCE : annoncer, proclamer

herald[2] *n* **1** MESSENGER : héraut *m* **2** HARBINGER : signe *m* avant-coureur

heraldic [heˈrældɪk, hə-] *adj* : héraldique

heraldry [ˈherəldri] *n, pl* **-ries** : héraldique *f*

herb [ˈərb, ˈhərb] *n* : herbe *f*

herbicide [ˈərbəˌsaɪd, ˈhər-] *n* : herbicide *m*

herbivore [ˈərbəˌvor, ˈhər-] *n* : herbivore *m*

herbivorous [ˌərˈbɪvərəs, ˌhər-] *adj* : herbivore

herculean [ˌhərkjəˈliːən, ˌhərˈkjuːliən] *adj* : herculéen

herd[1] [ˈhərd] *vt* : rassembler en troupeau — *vi or* **to herd together** : s'assembler

herd[2] *n* : troupeau *m* (de bétail), troupe *f* (de chevaux, d'éléphants, etc.)

herder [ˈhərdər] → **herdsman**

herdsman [ˈhərdzmən] *n, pl* **-men** [-mən, -ˌmen] : gardien *m* de troupeau

here [ˈhɪr] *adv* **1** : ici, là <turn here : tournez ici> <he's not here today : il n'est pas là aujourd'hui> **2** NOW : alors, à ce moment-là **3 here!** : tenez!, écoutez!

hereabouts [ˈhɪrəˌbaʊts] *or* **hereabout** [-ˌbaʊt] *adv* : par ici, près d'ici, dans les environs
hereafter[1] [hɪrˈæftər] *adv* **1** HENCEFORTH : désormais, à l'avenir **2** : ci-après (en droit)
hereafter[2] *n* **the hereafter** : l'au-delà *m*
hereby [hɪrˈbaɪ] *adv* : par la présente
hereditary [həˈrɛdəˌtɛri] *adj* : héréditaire
heredity [həˈrɛdətɪ] *n* : hérédité *f*
herein [hɪrˈɪn] *adv* : ci-après
hereof [hɪrˈʌv] *adv* : des présentes (en droit)
hereon [hɪrˈɑn, -ˈɔn] *adv* : sur ce
heresy [ˈhɛrəsi] *n, pl* **-sies** : hérésie *f*
heretic [ˈhɛrəˌtɪk] *n* : hérétique *mf*
heretical [həˈrɛtɪkəl] *adj* : hérétique
hereto [hɪrˈtuː] *adv* : à ceci, à cela
heretofore [ˈhɪrtəˌfɔr] *adv* : jusqu'ici
hereunder [hɪrˈʌndər] *adv* : ci-après
hereupon [ˈhɪrəˌpɑn, -ˌpɔn] *adv* : sur ce, à ce moment
herewith [hɪrˈwɪθ] *adv* **1** : ci-joint **2** HEREBY : par la présente
heritage [ˈhɛrətɪdʒ] *n* : héritage *m*, patrimoine *m*
hermaphrodite [hərˈmæfrəˌdaɪt] *n* : hermaphrodite *mf*
hermetic [hərˈmɛtɪk] *adj* : hermétique — **hermetically** [-ɪkli] *adv*
hermit [ˈhərmət] *n* : ermite *m*
hernia [ˈhərniə] *n, pl* **-nias** *or* **-niae** [-niˌiː, -niˌaɪ] : hernie *f*
hero [ˈhiːroː, ˈhɪroː] *n, pl* **-roes** : héros *m*
heroic [hɪˈroːɪk] *adj* : héroïque — **heroically** [-ɪkli] *adv*
heroics [hɪˈroːɪks] *npl* : mélodrame *m*
heroin [ˈhɛroən] *n* : héroïne *f*
heroine [ˈhɛroən] *n* : héroïne *f*
heroism [ˈhɛroˌɪzəm] *n* : héroïsme *m*
heron [ˈhɛrən] *n* : héron *m*
herpes [ˈhərˌpiːz] *n* : herpès *m*
herring [ˈhɛrɪŋ] *n, pl* **-ring** *or* **-rings** : hareng *m*
hers [ˈhərz] *pron* **1** : le sien, la sienne, les siens, les siennes <my suggestion is good, but hers is better : ma suggestion est bonne, mais la sienne est meilleure> **2** (*used after a preposition*) <some friends of hers : des amis à elle>
herself [hərˈsɛlf] *pron* **1** (*used reflexively*) : se, s' <she hurt herself : elle s'est blessée> **2** (*used emphatically*) <she did it herself : elle l'a fait elle-même>
hertz [ˈhərts, ˈhɛrts] *ns & pl* : hertz *m*
he's [ˈhiːz] (*contraction of* **he is** *or* **he has**) → **be, have**
hesitancy [ˈhɛzətənsi] *n, pl* **-cies** : hésitation *f*, indécision *f*
hesitant [ˈhɛzətənt] *adj* : hésitant, indécis
hesitantly [ˈhɛzətəntli] *adv* : avec hésitation
hesitate [ˈhɛzəˌteɪt] *vi* **-tated; -tating 1** : hésiter **2** PAUSE : faire une pause
hesitation [ˌhɛzəˈteɪʃən] *n* : hésitation *f*
heterogeneous [ˌhɛtərəˈdʒiːniəs, -njəs] *adj* : hétérogène
heterosexual[1] [ˌhɛtəroˈsɛkʃʊəl] *adj* : hétérosexuel
heterosexual[2] *n* : hétérosexuel *m*, -sexuelle *f*
heterosexuality [ˌhɛtərəˌsɛkʃʊˈæləti] *n* : hétérosexualité *f*
hew [ˈhjuː] *v* **hewed; hewed** *or* **hewn** [ˈhjuːn]; **hewing** *vt* **1** CUT, SHAPE : tailler, couper **2** FELL : abattre (un arbre) — *vi* ADHERE : se conformer
hex[1] [ˈhɛks] *vt* : jeter un sort à
hex[2] *n* : sort *m*, sortilège *m*
hexagon [ˈhɛksəˌgɑn] *n* : hexagone *m* — **hexagonal** [hɛkˈsægənəl] *adj*
hey [ˈheɪ] *interj* : hé!, ohé!
heyday [ˈheɪˌdeɪ] *n* : sommet *m*, apogée *f* <in the heyday of his power : au sommet de son pouvoir>
hi [ˈhaɪ] *interj* : hé!, ohé!, salut!
hiatus [haɪˈeɪtəs] *n* **1** GAP : hiatus *m*, lacune *f* **2** PAUSE : pause *f*
hibernate [ˈhaɪbərˌneɪt] *vi* **-nated; -nating** : hiberner
hibernation [ˌhaɪbərˈneɪʃən] *n* : hibernation *f*
hiccup[1] [ˈhɪkəp] *vi* **-cuped; -cuping** : hoqueter
hiccup[2] *n* : hoquet *m* <to have the hiccups : avoir le hoquet>
hick [ˈhɪk] *n* BUMPKIN : rustre *mf*, plouc *mf France fam*
hickory [ˈhɪkəri] *n, pl* **-ries** : hickory *m*, noyer *m* blanc d'Amérique
hide[1] [ˈhaɪd] *v* **hid** [ˈhɪd]; **hidden** [ˈhɪdən] *or* **hid; hiding** *vt* **1** CONCEAL : cacher **2** : dissimuler, occulter <to hide one's motives : occulter ses motifs> **3** SHIELD : voiler <the clouds were hiding the sun : les nuages voilaient le soleil> — *vi* : se cacher
hide[2] *n* : peau *f* d'animal
hide–and–seek [ˈhaɪdənd͡ˌsiːk] *n* : cache-cache *m*, cachette *f Can*
hidebound [ˈhaɪdˌbaʊnd] *adj* : à l'esprit étroit, borné
hideous [ˈhɪdiəs] *adj* : hideux, affreux — **hideously** *adv*
hideout [ˈhadˌaʊt] *n* : cachette *f*
hierarchical [ˌhaɪəˈrɑrkɪkəl] *adj* : hiérarchique
hierarchy [ˈhaɪəˌrɑrki] *n, pl* **-chies** : hiérarchie *f*
hieroglyphic [ˌhaɪərəˈglɪfɪk] *n* : hiéroglyphe *m*
high[1] [ˈhaɪ] *adv* : haut
high[2] *adj* **1** TALL : haut <how high is the table? : quelle est la hauteur de la table?> **2** : haut, élevé <high prices : prix élevés> **3** : aigu, haut (en musique) **4** GREAT, IMPORTANT : haut, éminent <high society : haute société> **5** INTOXICATED : parti *fam*, drogué

high[3] *n* **1** RECORD : record *m*, niveau *m* élevé <to reach an all-time high : réaliser un niveau élevé> **2** : zone *f* de haute pression (en météorologie) **3** *or* **high gear** : quatrième vitesse *f* **4 on ~** : dans le ciel

highbrow [ˈhaɪˌbraʊ] *n* : intellectuel *m*, -tuelle *f*

higher [ˈhaɪər] *adj* **1** : plus haut **2** ADVANCED : supérieur

high fidelity *n* : haute-fidélité *f*

high–flown [ˈhaɪˈflo:n] *adj* : ampoulé

high–handed [ˈhaɪˈhændəd] *adj* : despotique, autoritaire

highland [ˈhaɪlənd] *n* : région *f* montagneuse

highlander [ˈhaɪləndər] *n* : montagnard *m*, -narde *f*

highlight[1] [ˈhaɪˌlaɪt] *vt* **1** EMPHASIZE : souligner **2** : être le point culminant de (une cérémonie, etc.) **3** : rehausser (en photographie, etc.)

highlight[2] *n* : clou *m*, point *m* culminant

highly [ˈhaɪli] *adv* **1** VERY : très, extrêmement **2** FAVORABLY : bien <to think very highly of : penser beaucoup de bien de>

highness [ˈhaɪnəs] *n* **1** HEIGHT : hauteur *f* **2** (*used as a title*) <His/Her Highness : son Altesse>

high–rise [ˈhaɪˌraɪz] *adj* : dans une tour

high school *n* : lycée *m France*, école *f* secondaire *Can*, polyvalente *f Can*

high seas *npl* : haute mer *f*

high–spirited [ˈhaɪˈspɪrəˌtəd] *adj* : plein d'entrain

high–strung [ˈhaɪˈstrʌŋ] *adj* : nerveux, très tendu

highway [ˈhaɪˌweɪ] *n* **1** : route *f* **2** → **interstate**

highwayman [ˈhaɪˌweɪmən] *n, pl* **-men** [-mən, -ˌmen] : bandit *m* de grand chemin

hijack [ˈhaɪˌdʒæk] *vt* : détourner (un avion), saisir de force (une voiture)

hijacker [ˈhaɪˌdʒækər] *n* : pirate *m* de l'air

hike[1] [ˈhaɪk] *v* **hiked; hiking** *vi* : faire une randonnée — *vt or* **to hike up** RAISE : augmenter

hike[2] *n* **1** WALK : randonnée *f* **2** INCREASE : hausse *f*

hiker [ˈhaɪkər] *n* : randonneur *m*, -neuse *f*

hilarious [hɪˈlæriəs, haɪ-] *adj* : désopilant, hilarant

hilarity [hɪˈlærəti, haɪ-] *n* : hilarité *f*

hill [ˈhɪl] *n* : colline *f*

hillbilly [ˈhɪlˌbɪli] *n, pl* **-lies** : montagnard *m*, -narde *f*

hillock [ˈhɪlək] *n* : petite colline *f*, butte *f*

hillside [ˈhɪlˌsaɪd] *n* : coteau *m*

hilltop [ˈhɪlˌtɑp] *n* : sommet *m* d'une colline

hilly [ˈhɪli] *adj* **hillier; -est** : vallonné, côteux *Can*

hilt [ˈhɪlt] *n* : poignée *f* (d'une épée), manche *m* (d'un poignard)

him [ˈhɪm, əm] *pron* **1** (*used as a direct object*) : le, l' <I met him at the restaurant : je l'ai rencontré au restaurant> **2** (*used as an indirect object*) : lui <tell him that I am delighted : dis-lui que je suis ravi> **3** (*used as object of a preposition*) : lui <richer than him : plus riche que lui>

himself [hɪmˈself] *pron* **1** (*used reflexively*) : se, s' <he washed himself : il s'est lavé> **2** (*used emphatically*) : lui-même <he did it himself : il l'a fait lui-même> **3** (*used after a preposition*) : lui, lui-même <by himself : par lui-même, tout seul>

hind[1] [ˈhaɪnd] *adj* REAR : de derrière

hind[2] *n* : biche *f*

hinder [ˈhɪndər] *vt* : empêcher, entraver

hindquarters [ˈhaɪndˌkwɔrtərz] *npl* : arrière-train *m*

hindrance [ˈhɪndrəns] *n* : entrave *f*, obstacle *m*

hindsight [ˈhaɪndˌsaɪt] *n* **in ~** : avec du recul

Hindu[1] [ˈhɪnˌdu:] *adj* : hindou

Hindu[2] *n* : Hindou *m*, -doue *f*

Hinduism [ˈhɪndu:ˌɪzəm] *n* : hindouisme *m*

hinge[1] [ˈhɪndʒ] *v* **hinged; hinging** *vi* **to hinge on** : dépendre de — *vt* : mettre une charnière à

hinge[2] *n* : charnière *f*, gond *m*

hint[1] [ˈhɪnt] *vt* : insinuer — *vi* **to hint at** : faire une allusion à

hint[2] *n* **1** SUGGESTION : allusion *f*, insinuation *f* **2** CLUE : indice *m*, idée *f* **3** TRACE : soupçon *m*, trace *f* <a hint of perfume : un soupçon de parfum>

hinterland [ˈhɪntərˌlænd, -lənd] *n* : arrière-pays *m*

hip [ˈhɪp] *n* : hanche *f*

hippie *or* **hippy** [ˈhɪpi] *n, pl* **hippies** : hippie *mf*, hippy *mf*

hippopotamus [ˌhɪpəˈpɑtəməs] *n, pl* **-muses** *or* **-mi** [-ˌmaɪ] : hippopotame *m*

hire[1] [ˈhaɪr] *vt* **hired; hiring 1** EMPLOY : engager, embaucher **2** RENT : louer

hire[2] *n* **1** WAGES : gages *mpl* **2** RENTAL : location *f* <for hire : à louer> **3** EMPLOYEE : employé *m*, -ployée *f*

his[1] [ˈhɪz, ɪz] *adj* : son, sa, ses <his house : sa maison> <it's his : c'est à lui>

his[2] *pron* **1** : le sien, la sienne, les siens, les siennes **2** (*used after a preposition*) <a friend of his : un ami à lui, un de ses amis>

Hispanic[1] [hɪˈspænɪk] *adj* : hispanique

Hispanic[2] *n* : Hispano-Américain *m*, Hispano-Américaine *f*

hiss[1] [ˈhɪs] *vi* : siffler, chuinter

hiss[2] *n* : sifflement *m*

historian [hɪˈstɔriən] *n* : historien *m*, -rienne *f*

historic [hɪˈstɔrɪk] *or* **historical** [-ɪkəl] *adj* : historique — **historically** [-ɪkli] *adv*

history [ˈhɪstəri] *n, pl* **-ries 1** : histoire *f* **2** RECORD : antécédents *mpl* <medical history : antécédents médicaux>

histrionics [ˌhɪstriˈɑnɪks] *ns & pl* : airs *mpl* dramatiques

hit[1] [ˈhɪt] *v* **hit; hitting** *vt* **1** STRIKE : frapper **2** : heurter, percuter <the car hit a tree : la voiture a heurté un arbre> **3** AFFECT : affecter, toucher <the loss hit him hard : la perte l'a beaucoup affecté> **4** REACH : atteindre, arriver à — *vi* **1** : frapper, cogner **2** OCCUR : arriver, se produire <the storm hit without warning : la tempête est arrivée par surprise>

hit[2] *n* **1** BLOW : coup *m* **2** SUCCESS : succès *m*

hitch[1] [ˈhɪtʃ] *vt* **1** FASTEN, HARNESS : accrocher, atteler **2** → **hitchhike 3 to hitch up** : remonter (ses pantalons, etc.)

hitch[2] *n* **1** JERK : saccade *f*, secousse *f* **2** OBSTACLE : problème *m*, pépin *m*

hitchhike [ˈhɪtʃˌhaɪk] *vi* **-hiked; -hiking** : faire de l'auto-stop, faire du pouce *Can*

hitchhiker [ˈhɪtʃˌhaɪkər] *n* : auto-stoppeur *m*, -peuse *f*

hither [ˈhɪðər] *adv* : ici <come hither : venez çà>

hitherto [ˈhɪðərˌtuː, ˌhɪðərˈ-] *adv* : jusqu'ici, jusqu'à présent

hitter [ˈhɪtər] *n* BATTER : batteur *m*

HIV [ˌeɪtʃˌaɪˈviː] *n* : VIH *m*

hive [ˈhaɪv] *n* **1** *or* **beehive** : ruche *f* **2** SWARM : essaim *m* **3 a hive of activity** : une vraie ruche

hives [ˈhaɪvz] *ns & pl* : urticaire *f*

HMO [ˌeɪtʃˌemˈoː] *n* : centre *m* de santé financé par sa clientèle

hoard[1] [ˈhɔrd] *vt* : accumuler, amasser, faire des réserves de — *vi* : faire des réserves

hoard[2] *n* : réserve *f*, provisions *fpl*

hoarfrost [ˈhɔrˌfrɔst] *n* : gelée *f* blanche, givre *m*

hoarse [ˈhɔrs] *adj* **hoarser; -est 1** GRATING : discordant **2** : rauque, enroué <a hoarse cough : une toux rauque>

hoarsely [ˈhɔrsli] *adv* : d'une voix rauque

hoary [ˈhɔri] *adj* **hoarier; -est** : aux cheveux blancs, chenu

hoax[1] [ˈhoːks] *vt* : faire un canular à

hoax[2] *n* : canular *m*, farce *f*

hobble[1] [ˈhɑbəl] *v* **-bled; -bling** *vi* LIMP : boitiller — *vt* FETTER : entraver (un animal)

hobble[2] *n* **1** LIMP : boitillement *m* **2** : entrave *f* (d'un animal)

hobby [ˈhɑbi] *n, pl* **-bies** : passe-temps *m*

hobgoblin [ˈhɑbˌgɑblən] *n* **1** GOBLIN : lutin *m* **2** BOGEY : épouvantail *m*

hobnail [ˈhɑbˌneɪl] *n* : caboche *f*

hobnailed [ˈhɑbˌneɪld] *adj* : ferré

hobnob [ˈhɑbˌnɑb] *vi* **-nobbed; -nobbing** : frayer <to hobnob with : fréquenter, frayer avec>

hobo [ˈhoːˌboː] *n, pl* **-boes** : vagabond *m*, -bonde *f*; clochard *m*, -charde *f*

hock[1] [ˈhɑk] *vt* : mettre au clou, mettre en gage

hock[2] *n* **in ~** : au clou

hockey [ˈhɑki] *n* : hockey *m*

hod [ˈhɑd] *n* : oiseau *m*, auge *f* (de maçon)

hodgepodge [ˈhɑdʒˌpɑdʒ] *n* JUMBLE : méli-mélo *m*, salmigondis *m*

hoe[1] [ˈhoː] *vi* **hoed; hoeing** : sarcler, biner

hoe[2] *n* : houe *f*, binette *f*

hog[1] [ˈhɔg, ˈhɑg] *vt* **hogged; hogging** : monopoliser

hog[2] *n* **1** : porc *m*, cochon *m* **2** GLUTTON : glouton *m*, -tonne *f*

hoggish [ˈhɔgɪʃ, ˈhɑg-] *adj* : glouton, goulu

hogshead [ˈhɔgzˌhed, ˈhɑgz-] *n* CASK : barrique *f*

hoist[1] [ˈhɔɪst] *vt* : hisser

hoist[2] *n* : palan *m*, monte-charge *m*

hold[1] [ˈhoːld] *v* **held** [ˈhɛld]; **holding** *vt* **1** POSSESS : posséder **2** RESTRAIN : tenir <hold the dog! : tiens le chien!> **3** GRASP : tenir **4** SUPPORT : soutenir, supporter (un poids) **5** CONTAIN : contenir **6** REGARD : avoir, tenir <I hold him in high esteem : j'ai beaucoup d'estime pour lui> **7** CONDUCT : organiser (un colloque, etc.) **8** : avoir, occuper (un poste) **9** : détenir (un prisonnier) **10** : avoir, maintenir (une opinion) — *vi* **1** LAST : durer, continuer **2** APPLY : tenir, être en vigueur <the rule still holds : le règlement est encore en vigueur> **3 to hold forth** : pérorer **4 to hold to** : s'en tenir à **5 to hold with** : être d'accord avec

hold[2] *n* **1** GRIP : prise *f* **2** INFLUENCE : emprise *f* **3** : cale *f* (d'un navire)

holder [ˈhoːldər] *n* : détenteur *m*, -trice *f*; titulaire *mf*

holdings [ˈhoːldɪŋz] *npl* PROPERTY : propriétés *fpl*

holdup [ˈhoːldˌʌp] *n* **1** ROBBERY : vol *m* à main armée **2** DELAY : retard *m*

hold up *vt* **1** ROB : faire un vol à main armée **2** DELAY : retarder

hole [ˈhoːl] *n* : trou *m*

holiday [ˈhɑləˌdeɪ] *n* **1** : jour *m* férié **2** *Brit* VACATION : vacances *fpl*

holiness [ˈhoːlinəs] *n* **1** : sainteté *f* **2** (*used as a title*) <His Holiness : Sa Sainteté>

holistic [hoːˈlɪstɪk] *adj* : holistique

holler[1] [ˈhɑlər] *vi* : gueuler *fam*, hurler

holler[2] *n* : hurlement *m*

hollow[1] [-ˈhɑloː] *vt or* **to hollow out** : creuser

hollow[2] *adj* **hollower; -est 1** : creux **2** MUFFLED : caverneux <a hollow laugh : un rire forcé> **3** MEANING-

LESS : faux <hollow promises : fausses promesses>
hollow[3] *n* **1** CAVITY : creux *m*, dépression *f*, cavité *f* **2** VALLEY : vallon *m*
hollowness [ˈhɑˌloːnəs] *n* **1** HOLLOW : creux *m*, cavité *f* **2** FALSENESS : fausseté *f* **3** EMPTINESS : vide *m*
holly [ˈhɑli] *n, pl* **-lies** : houx *m*
hollyhock [ˈhɑliˌhɑk] *n* : rose *f* trémière
holocaust [ˈhɑləˌkɔst, ˈhoː-, ˈhɔ-] *n* : holocauste *m*
holster [ˈhoːlstər] *n* : étui *m* de revolver
holy [ˈhoːli] *adj* **holier; -est 1** SAINTLY : saint **2** SACRED : bénit <holy water : eau bénite>
Holy Ghost → Holy Spirit
Holy Spirit *n* : Saint-Esprit *m*
homage [ˈɑmɪdʒ, ˈhɑ-] *n* : hommage *m*
home[1] [ˈhoːm] *adv* **1** : à la maison, chez soi **2** DEEPLY : à fond <to hammer a nail home : enfoncer un clou jusqu'au bout>
home[2] *n* **1** RESIDENCE : maison *f* **2** : foyer *m*, chez-soi *m* <home is where the heart is : où le coeur aime, là est le foyer> **3** HABITAT : habitat *m* **4 → funeral home, nursing home**
homecoming [ˈhoːmˌkʌmɪŋ] *n* : retour *m* au foyer
homegrown [ˈhoːmˈgroːn] *adj* : du pays, du jardin
homeland [ˈhoːmˌlænd] *n* : pays *m* natal, patrie *f*
homeless [ˈhoːmləs] *adj* : sans foyer
homely [ˈhoːmli] *adj* **homelier; -est 1** SIMPLE : simple, sans prétentions **2** UNATTRACTIVE : sans attraits
homemade [ˈhoːmˈmeɪd] *adj* : fait à la maison <homemade cookies : biscuits maison>
homemaker [ˈhoːmˌmeɪkər] *n* : femme *f* au foyer
home run *n* : coup *m* de circuit *Can*
homesick [ˈhoːmˌsɪk] *adj* : nostalgique <to be homesick : avoir le mal du pays>
homesickness [ˈhoːmˌsɪknəs] *n* : nostalgie *f*, mal *m* du pays
homespun [ˈhoːmˌspʌn] *adj* : simple, naturel
homestead [ˈhoːmˌsted] *n* : propriété *f*, terres *fpl*
homeward[1] [ˈhoːmwərd] *or* **homewards** [-wərdz] *adv* : vers la maison, vers la patrie <homeward bound : sur le chemin du retour>
homeward[2] *adj* : de retour
homework [ˈhoːmˌwərk] *n* : devoirs *mpl*
homey [ˈhoːmi] *adj* **homier; -est** : accueillant
homicidal [ˌhɑməˈsaɪdəl, ˌhoː-] *adj* : homicide
homicide [ˈhɑməˌsaɪd, ˈhoː-] *n* : homicide *m*
hominy [ˈhɑməni] *n* : bouillie *f* de semoule de maïs
homogeneity [ˌhoːmədʒəˈniːəti, -ˈneɪ-] *n* : homogénéité *f*
homogeneous [ˌhoːməˈdʒiːniəs, -njəs] *adj* : homogène
homogenize [hoːˈmɑdʒəˌnaɪz, hə-] *vt* **-nized; -nizing** : homogénéiser
homograph [ˈhɑməˌgræf, ˈhoː-] *n* : homographe *m*
homonym [ˈhɑməˌnɪm, ˈhoː-] *n* : homonyme *m*
homophone [ˈhɑməˌfoːn, ˈhoː-] *n* : homophone *m*
homosexual[1] [ˌhoːməˈsɛkʃʊəl] *adj* : homosexuel
homosexual[2] *n* : homosexuel *m*, -sexuelle *f*
homosexuality [ˌhoːməˌsɛkʃʊˈæləṭi] *n* : homosexualité *f*
Honduran[1] [hɑnˈdʊrən, -ˈdjʊr-] *adj* : hondurien
Honduran[2] *n* : Hondurien *m* -rienne *f*
hone [ˈhoːn] *vt* **honed; honing** : aiguiser, affûter
honest [ˈɑnəst] *adj* **1** STRAIGHTFORWARD, TRUTHFUL : honnête, franc **2** CREDITABLE : bon, honorable <an honest day's work : une bonne journée de travail>
honestly [ˈɑnəstli] *adv* : honnêtement
honesty [ˈɑnəsti] *n* : honnêteté *f*
honey [ˈhʌni] *n, pl* **-eys** : miel *m*
honeybee [ˈhʌniˌbiː] *n* : abeille *f*
honeycomb[1] [ˈhʌniˌkoːm] *vi* : cribler (de petits trous)
honeycomb[2] *n* : rayon *m* de miel
honeymoon[1] [ˈhʌniˌmuːn] *vi* : passer sa lune de miel
honeymoon[2] *n* : lune *f* de miel
honeysuckle [ˈhʌniˌsʌkəl] *n* : chèvrefeuille *m*
honk[1] [ˈhɑŋk, ˈhɔŋk] *vi* : cacarder (se dit d'une oie), klaxonner (se dit d'une voiture)
honk[2] *n* : cri *m* (de l'oie), coup *m* de klaxon (d'une voiture)
honor[1] *or Brit* **honour** [ˈɑnər] *vt* **1** : honorer <honor your parents : honore tes parents> **2** : honorer (un chèque, etc.), remplir (un engagement)
honor[2] *or Brit* **honour** *n* **1** RECOGNITION, RESPECT : honneur *m* <in honor of : en l'honneur de> **2 honors** *npl* AWARDS : distinctions *fpl* honorifiques **3 Your Honor** : Votre Honneur
honorable *or Brit* **honourable** [ˈɑnərəbəl] *adj* : honorable **— honorably** *or Brit* **honourably** [-bli] *adv*
honorary [ˈɑnəˌrɛri] *adj* : honoraire, honorifique <an honorary member : un membre honoraire> <an honorary title : un titre honorifique>
honour *Brit* **→ honor**
hood [ˈhʊd] *n* **1** : capuchon *m* (d'un vêtement) **2** : capot *m* (d'une voiture)
hooded [ˈhʊdəd] *adj* : à capuchon
hoodlum [ˈhʊdləm, ˈhuːd-] *n* : voyou *m*, truand *m*
hoodwink [ˈhʊdˌwɪŋk] *vt* : tromper, duper

hoof [ˈhʊf, ˈhu:f] *n, pl* **hooves** [ˈhʊvz, ˈhu:vz] *or* **hoofs** : sabot *m* (d'un animal)
hoofed [ˈhʊft, ˈhu:ft] *adj* : à sabots
hook[1] [ˈhʊk] *vt* : accrocher
hook[2] *n* **1** : crochet *m* **2** FASTENER : agrafe *f* **3** → **fishhook**
hookworm [ˈhʊkˌwɔrm] *n* : ankylostome *m*
hooligan [ˈhu:lɪgən] *n* : vandale *m*, voyou *m*
hoop [ˈhu:p] *n* : cerceau *m*
hoorah [hʊˈra] **, hooray** [hʊˈreɪ] → **hurrah**
hoot[1] [ˈhu:t] *vi* **1** SHOUT : huer, hurler <to hoot with laughter : pouffer de rire> **2** : hululer (se dit d'un hibou), siffler (se dit d'un train), klaxonner (se dit d'une voiture)
hoot[2] *n* **1** : hululement *m* (d'un hibou), sifflement *m* (d'un train) **2 hoots** *npl* BOOS : huées *fpl* **3 I don't give a hoot** : je m'en fiche
hop[1] [hɑp] *v* **hopped; hopping** *vi* : sauter, sautiller — *vt or* **to hop over** : sauter, franchir
hop[2] *n* **1** LEAP : saut *m*, sautillement *m* **2** : houblon *m* (plante) **3** FLIGHT : court vol *m* en avion
hope[1] [ˈho:p] *v* **hoped; hoping** : espérer
hope[2] *n* : espoir *m*, espérance *f*
hopeful [ˈho:pfəl] *adj* **1** : plein d'espoir, optimiste **2** PROMISING : prometteur
hopefully [ˈho:pfəli] *adv* **1** OPTIMISTICALLY : avec optimisme, avec espoir **2** : avec un peu de chance <hopefully, he will come : on espère qu'il viendra>
hopefulness [ˈho:pfəlnəs] *n* : espoir *m*
hopeless [ˈho:pləs] *adj* : désespéré
hopelessly [ˈho:pləsli] *adv* : éperdument
hopelessness [ˈho:pləsnəs] *n* : désespoir *m*
hopper [ˈhɑpər] *n* : trémie *f*
hopscotch [ˈhɑpˌskɑtʃ] *n* : marelle *f*
horde [ˈhɔrd] *n* : horde *f*, foule *f*, essaim *m*
horizon [həˈraɪzən] *n* : horizon *m*
horizontal [ˌhɔrəˈzɑntəl] *adj* : horizontal — **horizontally** *adv*
hormone [ˈhɔrˌmo:n] *n* : hormone *f* — **hormonal** [hɔrˈmo:nəl] *adj*
horn [ˈhɔrn] *n* **1** : corne *f* (d'un animal) **2** : cor *m* (instrument de musique) **3** : klaxon *m* (d'un véhicule)
horned [ˈhɔrnd] *adj* : cornu
hornless [ˈhɔrnləs] *adj* : sans cornes
hornet [ˈhɔrnət] *n* : frelon *m*
horn of plenty → **cornucopia**
horny [ˈhɔrni] *adj* **hornier; -est** : calleux
horoscope [ˈhɔrəˌsko:p] *n* : horoscope *m*
horrendous [hɔˈrendəs] *adj* : épouvantable, effroyable
horrible [ˈhɔrəbəl] *adj* : horrible, affreux, détestable — **horribly** [-bli] *adv*
horrid [ˈhɔrɪd] *adj* **1** HIDEOUS : horrible, hideux **2** DISGUSTING : repoussant
horrify [ˈhɔrəˌfaɪ] *vt* **-fied; -fying** : horrifier, remplir d'horreur
horror [ˈhɔrər] *n* : horreur *f*
hors d'oeuvre [ɔrˈdərv] *n, pl* **hors d'oeuvres** [-ˈdərvz] : hors-d'œuvre *m*
horse [ˈhɔrs] *n* : cheval *m*
horseback [ˈhɔrsˌbæk] *n* **on ~** : à cheval
horse chestnut *n* : marronnier *m* (arbre), marron *m* (noix)
horsefly [ˈhɔrsˌflaɪ] *n, pl* **-flies** : taon *m*
horsehair [ˈhɔrsˌhær] *n* : crin *m* (de cheval)
horseman [ˈhɔrsmən] *n, pl* **-men** [-mən, -ˌmɛn] : cavalier *m*
horsemanship [ˈhɔrsmənˌʃɪp] *n* : équitation *f*
horseplay [ˈhɔrsˌpleɪ] *n* : jeux *mpl* de mains
horsepower [ˈhɔrsˌpaʊər] *n* : cheval-vapeur *m*
horseradish [ˈhɔrsˌrædɪʃ] *n* : raifort *m*
horseshoe [ˈhɔrsˌʃu:] *n* : fer *m* à cheval
horsewhip [ˈhɔrsˌhwɪp] *vt* **-whipped; -whipping** : cravacher
horsewoman [ˈhɔrsˌwʊmən] *n, pl* **-women** [-ˌwɪmən] : cavalière *f*
horsey *or* **horsy** [ˈhɔrsi] *adj* **horsier; -est** : chevalin
horticultural [ˌhɔrtəˈkʌltʃərəl] *adj* : horticole
horticulture [ˈhɔrtəˌkʌltʃər] *n* : horticulture *f*
hosanna [ho:ˈzænə, -za-] *interj* : hosanna!
hose[1] [ˈho:z] *vt* **hosed; hosing** : arroser
hose[2] *n* **1** *pl* **hoses** : tuyau *m* <garden hose : tuyau d'arrosage> <fire hose : tuyau d'incendie> **2** *pl* **hose** STOCKINGS : bas *mpl*, collants *mpl*
hosiery [ˈho:ʒərɪ; ˈho:zə-] *n* : bas *mpl*, collants *mpl*
hospice [ˈhɑspəs] *n* : hospice *m*
hospitable [hɑsˈpɪtəbəl, ˈhɑˌspɪ-] *adj* : hospitalier, accueillant, invitant *Can*, recevant *Can*
hospitably [hɑsˈpɪtəbli, ˈhɑˌspɪ-] *adv* : avec hospitalité
hospital [ˈhɑsˌpɪtəl] *n* : hôpital *m*
hospitality [ˌhɑspəˈtæləti] *n, pl* **-ties** : hospitalité *f*
hospitalization [ˌhɑsˌpɪtələˈzeɪʃən] *n* : hospitalisation *f*
hospitalize [ˈhɑsˌpɪtəˌlaɪz] *vt* **-ized; -izing** : hospitaliser
host[1] [ˈho:st] *vt* **1** : être l'hôte de <to host a dinner : recevoir à dîner> **2** : animer (une émission de télévision, etc.)
host[2] *n* **1** ARMY : armée *f* **2** MULTITUDE : foule *f* **3** : hôte *mf* (à la maison, etc.) **4** EUCHARIST : hostie *f*, Eucharistie *f* **5** : animateur *m*, -trice *f* <radio host : animateur de radio> **6** : hôte *m* (en biologie)
hostage [ˈhɑstɪdʒ] *n* : otage *m*

hostel [ˈhɑstəl] *n* : auberge *f* <youth hostel : auberge de jeunesse>
hostess [ˈhoːstəs] *n* : hôtesse *f*
hostile [ˈhɑstəl, -ˌtaɪl] *adj* : hostile — **hostilely** *adv*
hostility [hɑsˈtɪləṭi] *n, pl* **-ties** : hostilité *f*
hot [ˈhɑt] *adj* **hotter; hottest 1** : chaud <a hot stove : une cuisinière chaude> <it's hot today : il fait chaud aujourd'hui> **2** ARDENT, FIERY : coléreux <to have a hot temper : s'emporter facilement> **3** SPICY : fort, épicé **4** EAGER : empressé, passionné **5** LATEST : dernier <hot news : les dernières nouvelles> **6** RADIOACTIVE : radioactif **7** STOLEN : volé
hot air *n* : paroles *fpl* en l'air
hotbed [ˈhɑtˌbɛd] *n* **1** : couche *f* chaude, pépinière *f* (en botanique) **2** CENTER, SOURCE : foyer *m* <a hotbed of dissent : un foyer de conflit>
hot dog *n* : hot-dog *m*
hotel [hoːˈtɛl] *n* : hôtel *m*
hothead [ˈhɑtˌhɛd] *n* : tête *f* brûlée
hotheaded [ˈhɑtˈhɛdəd] *adj* : impétueux, exalté
hothouse [ˈhɑtˌhaʊs] *n* : serre *f*
hotly [ˈhɑtli] *adv* : vivement, passionnément
hound[1] [ˈhaʊnd] *vt* : traquer, poursuivre
hound[2] *n* : chien *m* de meute
hour [ˈaʊər] *n* : heure *f*
hourglass [ˈaʊərˌglæs] *n* : sablier *m*
hourly [ˈaʊərli] *adv & adj* : toutes les heures
house[1] [ˈhaʊz] *vt* **housed; housing** : loger, héberger
house[2] [ˈhaʊs] *n, pl* **houses** [ˈhaʊzəz, -səz] **1** HOME, RESIDENCE : maison *f* **2** : chambre *f* (en politique) **3** COMPANY, FIRM : maison *f*, compagnie *f* **4** AUDIENCE : assistance *f*, auditoire *m*
houseboat [ˈhaʊsˌboːt] *n* : péniche *f* aménagée
housebroken [ˈhaʊsˌbroːkən] *adj* : propre
housefly [ˈhaʊsˌflaɪ] *n, pl* **-flies** : mouche *f*
household[1] [ˈhaʊsˌhoːld] *adj* **1** DOMESTIC : ménager **2** COMMON, FAMILIAR : commun
household[2] *n* : maison *f*, ménage *m*
householder [ˈhaʊsˌhoːldər] *n* : propriétaire *mf*, chef *m* de famille
housekeeper [ˈhaʊsˌkiːpər] *n* : ménagère *f*, gouvernante *f*
housekeeping [ˈhaʊsˌkiːpɪŋ] *n* : ménage *m*
housemaid [ˈhaʊsˌmeɪd] *n* : bonne *f*, femme *f* de chambre
housewarming [ˈhaʊsˌwɔrmɪŋ] *n* : pendaison *f* de crémaillère
housewife [ˈhaʊsˌwaɪf] *n, pl* **-wives** : femme *f* au foyer, ménagère *f*
housework [ˈhaʊsˌwərk] *n* : travaux *mpl* ménagers
housing [ˈhaʊzɪŋ] *n* **1** LODGING : logement *m* **2** CASING : boîtier *m*
hove → heave[1]
hovel [ˈhʌvəl, ˈhɑ-] *n* : bicoque *f*, baraque *f*, masure *f*, taudis *m*
hover [ˈhʌvər] *vi* **1** : planer, voltiger **2** *or* **to hover about** : rôder
how[1] [ˈhaʊ] *adv* **1** : comment <how are you? : comment allez-vous?> <how do you spell it? : comment ça s'écrit?> <I know how to do it : je sais comment faire> **2** (*referring to degree or extent*) <how old are you? : quel âge as-tu?> <how tall is he? : combien mesure-t-il?> **3** (*used in exclamations*) : comme, que <how beautiful it is! : comme c'est beau!> **4 how about . . .** ? : que dirais-tu de . . . ? **5 how come** WHY : comment, pourquoi
how[2] *conj* : comment <I asked them how they were : je leur ai demandé comment ils allaient>
however[1] [haʊˈɛvər] *adv* **1** : cependant, toutefois, pourtant **2** : comme <however you want : comme tu veux> **3** : si . . . que, quelque . . . que <however important it is : si important que ce soit>
however[2] *conj* : de quelque manière que <I will help you however I can : je vais t'aider de quelque manière que ce soit>
howl[1] [ˈhaʊl] *vi* : hurler
howl[2] *n* : hurlement *m*
hub [ˈhʌb] *n* **1** CENTER : centre *m*, pivot *m* **2** : moyeu *m* (d'une roue)
hubbub [ˈhʌˌbʌb] *n* : vacarme *m*, brouhaha *m*
hubcap [ˈhʌbˌkæp] *n* : enjoliveur *m*
huckleberry [ˈhʌkəlˈbɛri] *n, pl* **-ries** : myrtille *f France*, bleuet *m Can*
huckster [ˈhʌkstər] *n* PEDDLER : camelot *m*; colporteur *m*, -teuse *f*
huddle[1] [ˈhʌdəl] *vi* **-dled; -dling 1** : se blottir **2** *or* **to huddle together** : se serrer, se blottir les uns contre les autres
huddle[2] *n* : (petit) groupe *m* <to go into a huddle : se réunir en petit comité>
hue [ˈhjuː] *n* : couleur *f*, teinte *f*
huff [ˈhʌf] *n* **to be in a huff** : être fâché, être vexé
huffy [ˈhʌfi] *adj* **huffier; -est 1** IRRITATED : fâché, vexé **2** TOUCHY : susceptible
hug[1] [ˈhʌg] *vt* **hugged; hugging 1** EMBRACE : serrer dans ses bras, étreindre **2** : serrer, longer <the ship was hugging the coast : le navire serrait la côte>
hug[2] *n* : étreinte *f*
huge [ˈhjuːdʒ] *adj* **huger; hugest** : énorme, immense — **hugely** *adv*
hulk [ˈhʌlk] *n* **1** : mastodonte *m* (homme) **2** : épave *f* (d'un navire)

hulking [ˈhʌlkɪŋ] *adj* : énorme, massif
hull[1] [ˈhʌl] *vt* SHELL, SHUCK : écosser (des pois), écaler (des noix), décortiquer (du grain, des noix, etc.)
hull[2] *n* **1** : cosse *f* (de pois), écale *f* (d'une noix) **2** : coque *f* (d'un navire ou d'un avion)
hullabaloo [ˈhʌləbəˌluː] *n, pl* **-loos** : raffut *m fam*, boucan *m fam*
hullo *Brit* → **hello**
hum[1] [ˈhʌm] *v* **hummed; humming** *vi* **1** BUZZ, DRONE : bourdonner **2** BUSTLE : grouiller — *vt* : fredonner, chantonner
hum[2] *n* : bourdonnement *m*
human[1] [ˈhjuːmən, ˈjuː-] *adj* **1** : humain <the human race : le genre humain> **2** : de la personne <human rights : droits de la personne>
human[2] *n* : humain *m*, être *m* humain
humane [hjuːˈmeɪn, juː-] *adj* : humain — **humanely** *adv*
humanism [ˈhjuːməˌnɪzəm, ˈjuː-] *n* : humanisme *m*
humanist[1] [ˈhjuːmənɪst, ˈjuː-] *or* **humanistic** [ˌhjuːməˈnɪstɪk, ˈjuː-] *adj* : humaniste
humanist[2] *n* : humaniste *mf*
humanitarian[1] [hjuːˌmænəˈtɛriən, juː-] *adj* : humanitaire
humanitarian[2] *n* : humaniste *m*
humanity [hjuːˈmænəti, juː-] *n, pl* **-ties** : humanité *f*
humankind [ˈhjuːmənˈkaɪnd, ˈjuː-] *n* : humanité *f*, le genre humain
humanly [ˈhjuːmənli, ˈjuː-] *adv* : humainement
humble[1] [ˈhʌmbəl] *vt* **-bled; -bling 1** : humilier **2 to humble oneself** : s'humilier
humble[2] *adj* **humbler; -blest** : humble, modeste <of humble origin : d'origine modeste> — **humbly** [ˈhʌmbli] *adv*
humbug [ˈhʌmˌbʌg] *n* **1** : charlatan *m* (personne) **2** NONSENSE : balivernes *fpl*
humdrum [ˈhʌmˌdrʌm] *adj* : monotone, banal
humid [ˈhjuːməd, ˈjuː-] *adj* : humide
humidifier [hjuːˈmɪdəˌfaɪər, juː-] *n* : humidificateur *m*
humidify [hjuːˈmɪdəˌfaɪ, juː-] *vt* **-fied; -fying** : humidifier
humidity [hjuːˈmɪdəti, juː-] *n, pl* **-ties** : humidité *f*
humiliate [hjuːˈmɪliˌeɪt, juː-] *vt* **-ated; -ating** : humilier
humiliating [hjuːˈmɪliˌeɪtɪŋ, juː-] *adj* : humiliant
humiliation [hjuːˌmɪliˈeɪʃən, juː-] *n* : humiliation *f*
humility [hjuːˈmɪləti, juː-] *n* : humilité *f*
hummingbird [ˈhʌmɪŋˌbərd] *n* : oiseau-mouche *m*
hummock [ˈhʌmək] *n* : monticule *m*
humor[1] *or Brit* **humour** [ˈhjuːmər, ˈjuː-] *vt* : faire plaisir à, ménager
humor[2] *or Brit* **humour** *n* **1** MOOD : humeur *f* **2** WIT : humour *m*
humorist [ˈhjuːmərɪst, ˈjuː-] *n* : humoriste *mf*
humorless *or Brit* **humourless** [ˈhjuːmərləs, ˈjuː-] *adj* : qui manque d'humour
humorous [ˈhjuːmərəs, ˈjuː-] *adj* : plein d'humour, drôle
humorously [ˈhjuːmərəsli, ˈjuː-] *adv* : avec humour
humour *Brit* → **humor**
hump [ˈhʌmp] *n* : bosse *f*
humpback [ˈhʌmpˌbæk] *n* : bosse *f*
humpbacked [ˈhʌmpˌbækt] *adj* : bossu
humus [ˈhjuːməs, ˈjuː-] *n* : humus *m*
hunch[1] [ˈhʌntʃ] *vt* **to hunch one's shoulders** : rentrer les épaules — *vi or* **to hunch over** : se pencher
hunch[2] *n* : pressentiment *m*, intuition *f*
hunchback [ˈhʌntʃˌbæk] *n* **1** : bosse *f* (sur le dos d'une personne) **2** : bossu *m*, -sue *f* (personne)
hunchbacked [ˈhʌntʃˌbækt] *adj* : bossu
hundred[1] [ˈhʌndrəd] *adj* : cent
hundred[2] *n, pl* **-dreds** *or* **-dred** : cent *m*
hundredth[1] [ˈhʌndrədθ] *adj* : centième
hundredth[2] *n* **1** : centième *mf* (dans une série) **2** : centième *m* (en mathématiques)
hung → **hang**[1]
Hungarian[1] [hʌŋˈgæriən] *adj* : hongrois
Hungarian[2] *n* **1** : Hongrois *m*, -groise *f* **2** : hongrois *m* (langue)
hunger[1] [ˈhʌŋgər] *vi* : avoir faim <to hunger for : avoir faim de, avoir envie de>
hunger[2] *n* **1** : faim *f* **2** CRAVING : désir *m*, envie *f*
hungrily [ˈhʌŋgrəli] *adv* : avidement, voracement
hungry [ˈhʌŋgri] *adj* **hungrier; -est 1** : avide <hungry for affection : avide d'affection> **2 to be hungry** : avoir faim
hunk [ˈhʌŋk] *n* : gros morceau *m*
hunt[1] [ˈhʌnt] *vt* **1** : chasser <to hunt buffalo : chasser le bison> **2** *or* **to hunt for** PURSUE, SEEK : rechercher, chercher, poursuivre
hunt[2] *n* **1** : chasse *f* (sport) **2** SEARCH : recherche *f*
hunter [ˈhʌntər] *n* : chasseur *m*, -seuse *f*
hurdle[1] [ˈhərdəl] *vt* **-dled; -dling** : franchir, sauter
hurdle[2] *n* **1** : haie *f* (aux sports) **2** OBSTACLE : obstacle *m*
hurl [ˈhərl] *vt* : lancer, jeter
hurrah [hʊˈrɑ, -ˈrɔ] *interj* : hourra!
hurricane [ˈhərəˌkeɪn] *n* : ouragan *m*
hurriedly [ˈhərədli] *adv* : à la hâte, précipitamment
hurry[1] [ˈhəri] *v* **-ried; -rying** *vt* : presser, bousculer, brusquer — *vi* : se presser, se dépêcher, se hâter <hurry up! : dépêche-toi!>

hurry[2] *n* : hâte *f*, empressement *m*
hurt[1] ['hərt] *v* **hurt; hurting** *vt* **1** INJURE : faire mal à, blesser <I hurt my thumb : je me suis fait mal au pouce> **2** OFFEND : blesser, offenser — *vi* : faire mal <my foot hurts : mon pied me fait mal> <my throat hurts : j'ai mal à la gorge>
hurt[2] *n* **1** INJURY, PAIN : blessure *f*, mal *m* **2** DISTRESS : peine *f*
hurtful ['hərtfəl] *adj* : blessant, pénible
hurtle ['hərtəl] *vi* **-tled; -tling** : aller à toute vitesse
husband[1] ['hʌzbənd] *vt* : ménager, économiser
husband[2] *n* : mari *m*, époux *m*
husbandry ['hʌzbəndri] *n* **1** THRIFT : économie *f* **2** AGRICULTURE : agriculture *f* <animal husbandry : l'élevage>
hush[1] ['hʌʃ] *vt* **1** *or* **to hush up** : faire taire **2** CALM, SOOTHE : calmer, appaiser <to hush a baby : appaiser un bébé> — *vi* **1** : se taire **2 hush!** : chut!
hush[2] *n* SILENCE : silence *m*
husk[1] ['hʌsk] *vt* : écaler (des noix), éplucher (des légumes), vanner (du blé)
husk[2] *n* : écale *f* (de noix), cosse *f* (de pois, etc.), enveloppe *f* (de maïs)
huskily ['hʌskəli] *adv* : d'une voix enrouée
husky[1] ['hʌski] *adj* **huskier; -est 1** HOARSE : enroué **2** BURLY : costaud *fam*
husky[2] *n, pl* **-kies** : chien *m* esquimau
hustle[1] ['hʌsəl] *v* **-tled; -tling** *vt* : presser, pousser, bousculer — *vi* HURRY : se dépêcher, se presser
hustle[2] *n* BUSTLE : grande activité *f*
hut ['hʌt] *n* : hutte *f*, cabane *f*, bicoque *f*
hutch ['hʌtʃ] *n* **1** CUPBOARD : dressoir *m* **2** : cage *f* <rabbit hutch : cage à lapin>
hyacinth ['haɪəˌsɪnθ] *n* : jacinthe *f*
hybrid[1] ['haɪbrɪd] *adj* : hybride
hybrid[2] *n* : hybride *m*
hydrant ['haɪdrənt] *n* **1** : prise *f* d'eau **2** *or* **fire hydrant** : bouche *f* d'incendie, borne-fontaine *f Can*
hydraulic [haɪ'drɔlɪk] *adj* : hydraulique — **hydraulically** [-lɪkli] *adv*
hydrocarbon [ˌhaɪdrɔ'kɑrbən] *n* : hydrocarbure *m*
hydrochloric acid [ˌhaɪdrɔ'klɔrɪk] *n* : acide *m* chlorhydrique
hydroelectric [ˌhaɪdroɪ'lektrɪk] *adj* : hydroélectrique
hydrogen ['haɪdrədʒən] *n* : hydrogène *m*
hydrogen bomb *n* : bombe *f* à hydrogène
hydrogen peroxide *n* : eau *f* oxygénée
hydrophobia [ˌhaɪdrə'fo:biə] *n* : hydrophobie *f*
hydroplane ['haɪdrəˌpleɪn] *n* : hydroglisseur *m*
hyena [haɪ'i:nə] *n* : hyène *f*
hygiene ['haɪˌdʒi:n] *n* : hygiène *f*
hygienic [haɪ'dʒenɪk, -'dʒi:-; ˌhaɪdʒi:'enɪk] *adj* : hygiénique — **hygienically** [-nɪkli] *adv*
hygienist [haɪ'dʒi:nɪst, -'dʒe:-, 'haɪˌdʒi:-] *n* : hygiéniste *mf*
hygrometer [haɪ'grɑmətər] *n* : hygromètre *m*
hymn ['hɪm] *n* : hymne *m*, cantique *m*
hymnal ['hɪmnəl] *n* : livre *m* d'hymnes
hype ['haɪp] *n* : battage *m* publicitaire
hyperactive [ˌhaɪpər'æktɪv] *adj* : hyperactif
hyperbole [haɪ'pərbəli] *n* : hyperbole *f*
hypercritical [ˌhaɪpər'krɪtəkəl] *adj* : excessivement critique
hypersensitive [ˌhaɪpər'sentsətɪv] *adj* : hypersensible
hypertension [ˌhaɪpər'tentʃən] *n* : hypertension *f*
hypertext ['haɪpərˌtɛkst] *n* : hypertexte *m*
hyphen ['haɪfən] *n* : trait *m* d'union
hyphenate ['haɪfənˌeɪt] *vt* **-ated; -ating** : mettre un trait d'union à
hypnosis [hɪp'no:sɪs] *n, pl* **-noses** [-ˌsi:z] : hypnose *f*
hypnotic [hɪp'nɑtɪk] *adj* : hypnotique
hypnotism ['hɪpnəˌtɪzəm] *n* : hypnotisme *m*
hypnotize ['hɪpnəˌtaɪz] *vt* **-tized; -tizing** : hypnotiser
hypochondria [ˌhaɪpə'kɑndriə] *n* : hypocondrie *f*
hypochondriac [ˌhaɪpə'kɑndriˌæk] *n* : hypocondriaque *mf*
hypocrisy [hɪ'pɑkrəsi] *n, pl* **-sies** : hypocrisie *f*
hypocrite ['hɪpəˌkrɪt] *n* : hypocrite *mf*
hypocritical [ˌhɪpə'krɪtɪkəl] *adj* : hypocrite — **hypocritically** [-ɪkli] *adv*
hypodermic[1] [ˌhaɪpə'dərmɪk] *adj* : hypodermique
hypodermic[2] *n* : piqûre *f* hypodermique
hypotenuse [haɪ'pɑtəˌnu:s, -ˌu:z, -ˌju:s, -ˌju:z] *n* : hypoténuse *f*
hypothesis [haɪ'pɑθəsɪs] *n, pl* **-eses** [-ˌsi:z] : hypothèse *f*
hypothetical [ˌhaɪpə'θetɪkəl] *adj* : hypothétique — **hypothetically** [-ɪkli] *adv*
hysterectomy [ˌhɪstə'rektəmi] *n, pl* **-mies** : hystérectomie *f*
hysteria [hɪs'teriə, -'tɪr-] *n* : hystérie *f*
hysterical [hɪs'terɪkəl] *adj* : hystérique — **hysterically** [-ɪkli] *adv*
hysterics [hɪs'terɪks] *ns & pl* : crise *f* (de nerfs, de rire, etc.)

I

i [ˈaɪ] *n, pl* **i's** *or* **is** [ˈaɪz] : i *m*, neuvième lettre de l'alphabet
I [ˈaɪ] *pron* : je
ibis [ˈaɪbəs] *n, pl* **ibis** *or* **ibises** : ibis *m*
ice[1] [ˈaɪs] *v* **iced; icing** *vt* **1** FREEZE : glacer **2** CHILL : rafraîchir **3** FROST : glacer (un gâteau, etc.) — *vi or* **to ice up** : se givrer
ice[2] *n* **1** : glace *f* **2** SHERBET : sorbet *m*
ice age *n* : période *f* glacière
iceberg [ˈaɪsˌbərg] *n* : iceberg *m*
icebox [ˈaɪsˌbɑks] → **refrigerator**
icebreaker [ˈaɪsˌbreɪkər] *n* : brise-glace *m*
ice cap *n* : calotte *f* glacière
ice-cold [ˈaɪsˈkoːld] *adj* : glacé
ice cream *n* : glace *f France*, crème *f* glacée *Can*
ice floe → **floe**
Icelander [ˈaɪsˌlændər, -lən-] *n* : Islandais *m*, -daise *f*
Icelandic[1] [aɪsˈlændɪk] *adj* : islandais
Icelandic[2] *n* : islandais *m* (langue)
ice–skate [ˈaɪsˌskeɪt] *vi* **-skated; -skating** : patiner
ice skater *n* : patineur *m*, -neuse *f*
ichthyology [ˌɪkθiˈɑlədʒi] *n* : ichtyologie *f*
icicle [ˈaɪˌsɪkəl] *n* : glaçon *m*
icily [ˈaɪsəli] *adv* : d'un ton glacial, d'un air glacial
icing [ˈaɪsɪŋ] *n* : glaçage *m*, crémage *m Can*
icon [ˈaɪˌkɑn, -kən] *n* : icône *f*
iconoclasm [aɪˈkɑnəˌklæzəm] *n* : iconoclasme *m*
iconoclast [aɪˈkɑnəˌklæst] *n* : iconoclaste *mf*
icy [ˈaɪsi] *adj* **icier; -est 1** FREEZING : glacial, glacé **2** : verglacé <an icy road : une route verglacée> **3** FROSTY : glacial <an icy smile : un sourire glacial>
id [ˈɪd] *n* : ça *m*
I'd [ˈaɪd] (*contraction of* **I should** *or* **I would**) → **should, would**
idea [aɪˈdiːə] *n* : idée *f*
ideal[1] [aɪˈdiːəl] *adj* : idéal
ideal[2] *n* : idéal *m*
idealism [aɪˈdiːəˌlɪzəm] *n* : idéalisme *m*
idealist [aɪˈdiːəˌlɪst] *n* : idéaliste *mf*
idealistic [aɪˌdiːəˈlɪstɪk] *adj* : idéaliste
idealization [aɪˌdiːələˈzeɪʃən] *n* : idéalisation *f*
idealize [aɪˈdiːəˌlaɪz] *vt* **-ized; -izing** : idéaliser
ideally [aɪˈdiːəli] *adv* : idéalement
identical [aɪˈdɛntɪkəl] *adj* : identique — **identically** [-tɪkli] *adv*
identifiable [aɪˌdɛntəˈfaɪəbəl] *adj* : identifiable
identification [aɪˌdɛntəfəˈkeɪʃən] *n* **1** : identification *f* **2** *or* **identification card** : carte *f* d'identité
identify [aɪˈdɛntəˌfaɪ] *v* **-fied; -fying** *vt* : identifier — *vi* **to identify with** : s'identifier à
identity [aɪˈdɛntəti] *n, pl* **-ties** : identité *f*
ideological [ˌaɪdiəˈlɑdʒɪkəl, ˌɪ-] *adj* : idéologique
ideologically [ˌaɪdiəˈlɑdʒɪkli, ˌɪ-] *adv* : du point de vue idéologique
ideology [ˌaɪdiˈɑlədʒi, ˌɪ-] *n, pl* **-gies** : idéologie *f*
idiocy [ˈɪdiəsi] *n, pl* **-cies 1** : idiotie *f* (en médecine) **2** NONSENSE : idiotie *f*, stupidité *f*
idiom [ˈɪdiəm] *n* **1** LANGUAGE : idiome *m*, langue *f* **2** EXPRESSION : idiotisme *m*, expression *f* idiomatique
idiomatic [ˌɪdiəˈmæt̬ɪk] *adj* : idiomatique
idiosyncrasy [ˌɪdioˈsɪŋkrəsi] *n, pl* **-sies** : particularité *f*, idiosyncrasie *f*
idiosyncratic [ˌɪdiosɪnˈkræt̬ɪk] *adj* : particulier, caractéristique
idiot [ˈɪdiət] *n* : idiot *m*, -diote *f*
idiotic [ˌɪdiˈɑt̬ɪk] *adj* : idiot — **idiotically** [-t̬ɪkli] *adv*
idle[1] [ˈaɪdəl] *v* **idled; idling** *vi* **1** *or* **to idle about** : fainéanter, traîner **2** : tourner au ralenti (se dit d'un moteur) — *vt or* **to idle away** : gaspiller (son temps)
idle[2] *adj* **idler; idlest 1** VAIN : vain, inutile <idle curiosity : pure curiosité> **2** INACTIVE : oisif, désœuvré **3** LAZY : paresseux
idleness [ˈaɪdəlnəs] *n* : oisiveté *f*, désœuvrement *m*
idler [ˈaɪdələr] *n* : paresseux *m*, -seuse *f*
idly [ˈadəli] *adv* **1** LAZILY : paresseusement **2** ABSENTMINDEDLY : d'un air distrait
idol [ˈaɪdəl] *n* : idole *f*
idolatry [aɪˈdɑlətri] *n, pl* **-tries** : idolâtrie *f*
idolization [ˌaɪdələˈzeɪʃən] *n* : idolâtrie *f*
idolize [ˈaɪdəlˌaɪz] *vt* **-ized; izing** : idolâtrer
idyll [ˈaɪdəl] *n* : idylle *f*
idyllic [aɪˈdɪlɪk] *adj* : idyllique
if [ˈɪf] *conj* **1** : si <I would do it if I could : je le ferais si je pouvais> <as if : comme si> <if I were you : si j'étais vous> **2** WHETHER : si <do you know if they are here? : savez-vous s'ils sont ici?> **3** THOUGH : bien que, même que <it's pretty, if somewhat old-fashioned : c'est joli, bien qu'un peu démodé>
igloo [ˈɪˌgluː] *n, pl* **-loos** : igloo *m*
ignite [ɪgˈnaɪt] *v* **-nited; -niting** *vt* : mettre le feu à, enflammer — *vi* : prendre feu, s'enflammer
ignition [ɪgˈnɪʃən] *n* **1** : allumage *m* **2** *or* **ignition switch** : contact *m*

ignoble [ɪg'no:bəl] *adj* : infâme
ignominious [ˌɪgnə'mɪnɪəs] *adj* : ignominieux — **ignominiously** *adv*
ignominy ['ɪgnəˌmɪnɪ] *n, pl* **-nies** : ignominie *f*
ignoramus [ˌɪgnə'reɪməs] *n* : ignare *mf*
ignorance ['ɪgnərənʦ] *n* : ignorance *f*
ignorant ['ɪgnərənt] *adj* : ignorant
ignorantly ['ɪgnərəntlɪ] *adv* : d'une manière grossière <to speak ignorantly : parler par ignorance>
ignore [ɪg'nor] *vt* **-nored; -noring** : ignorer, ne pas tenir compte de, ne pas faire attention à
iguana [ɪ'gwɑnə] *n* : iguane *m*
ilk ['ɪlk] *n* : espèce *f*, acabit *m*
ill[1] ['ɪl] *adv* **worse** ['wərs]; **worst** ['wərst] : mal <ill prepared : mal préparé> <to speak ill of : dire du mal de>
ill[2] *adj* **worse; worst 1** SICK : malade <to be taken ill : tomber malade> **2** BAD : mauvais <ill humor : mauvaise humeur>
ill[3] *n* : mal *m*
I'll ['aɪl] (*contraction of* **I shall** *or* **I will**) → **shall, will**
illegal [ɪl'li:gəl] *adj* : illégal — **illegally** *adv*
illegality [ɪliˈgæləʦɪ] *n* : illégalité *f*
illegible [ɪl'ledʒəbəl] *adj* : illisible — **illegibly** [-bli] *adv*
illegitimacy [ˌɪlɪ'dʒɪʦəməsɪ] *n* : illégitimité *f*
illegitimate [ˌɪlɪ'dʒɪʦəmət] *adj* : illégitime — **illegitimately** *adv*
illicit [ɪl'lɪsət] *adj* : illicite — **illicitly** *adv*
illimitable [ɪl'lɪməʦəbəl] *adj* : illimité
illiteracy [ɪl'lɪʦərəsɪ] *n, pl* **-cies** : analphabétisme *m*
illiterate[1] [ɪl'lɪʦərət] *adj* **1** : analphabète, illettré **2** IGNORANT : ignorant, sans éducation
illiterate[2] *n* : analphabète *mf*
ill-mannered [ˌɪl'mænərd] *adj* : impoli, grossier
ill-natured [ˌɪl'neɪʧərd] *adj* : désagréable — **ill-naturedly** *adv*
illness ['ɪlnəs] *n* : maladie *f*
illogical [ɪl'lɑdʒɪkəl] *adj* : illogique — **illogically** [-kli] *adv*
ill-tempered [ˌɪl'tempərd] → **ill-natured**
ill-treat [ˌɪl'tri:t] *vt* : maltraiter
ill-treatment [ˌɪl'tri:tmənt] *n* : mauvais traitement *m*
illuminate [ɪ'lu:məˌneɪt] *vt* **-nated; -nating** : éclairer, illuminer
illumination [ɪˌlu:məˈneɪʃən] *n* : éclairage *m*, illumination *f*
ill-use ['ɪl'ju:z] → **ill-treat**
illusion [ɪ'luʒən] *n* : illusion *f*
illusory [ɪ'lu:sərɪ, -zərɪ] *adj* : illusoire
illustrate ['ɪləsˌtreɪt] *v* **-trated; -trating** : illustrer
illustration [ˌɪləs'treɪʃən] *n* : illustration *f*
illustrative [ɪ'lʌstrəʦɪv, 'ɪləˌstreɪʦɪv] *adj* : explicatif
illustrator ['ɪləˌstreɪʦər] *n* : illustrateur *m*, -trice *f*
illustrious [ɪ'lʌstrɪəs] *adj* RENOWNED : illustre
illustriousness [ɪ'lʌstrɪəsnəs] *n* RENOWN : renommée *f*
ill will *n* : malveillance *f*, rancune *f*
I'm ['aɪm] (*contraction of* **I am**) → **be**
image ['ɪmɪdʒ] *n* : image *f*
imagery ['ɪmɪdʒrɪ] *n, pl* **-eries 1** : images *fpl* (en litérature, etc.) **2** PICTURES : imagerie *f*
imaginable [ɪ'mædʒənəbəl] *adj* : imaginable
imaginary [ɪ'mædʒəˌnerɪ] *adj* : imaginaire
imagination [ɪ'mædʒəˈneɪʃən] *n* : imagination *f*
imaginative [ɪ'mædʒɪnəʦɪv] *adj* : imaginatif, plein d'imagination
imaginatively [ɪ'mædʒɪnəʦɪvlɪ] *adv* : avec imagination
imagine [ɪ'mædʒən] *vt* **-ined; -ining 1** : imaginer, se représenter (une scène, etc.) **2** SUPPOSE : s'imaginer, supposer
imbalance [ɪm'bælənʦ] *n* : déséquilibre *m*
imbecile[1] ['ɪmbəsəl, -ˌsɪl] *or* **imbecilic** [ˌɪmbə'sɪlɪk] *adj* : imbécile
imbecile[2] *n* : imbécile *mf*
imbecility [ˌɪmbə'sɪləʦɪ] *n, pl* **-ties** : imbécillité *f*
imbibe [ɪm'baɪb] *v* **-bibed; -bibing** *vt* ABSORB : assimiler, absorber — *vi* DRINK : boire
imbue [ɪm'bju:] *vt* **-bued; -buing 1** : imprégner **2 to be imbued with** : être imbu de
imitate ['ɪməˌteɪʦ] *vt* **-tated; -tating** : imiter
imitation[1] [ˌɪmə'teɪʃən] *adj* : artificiel, faux
imitation[2] *n* : imitation *f*
imitative ['ɪməˌteɪʦɪv] *adj* : imitatif, imitateur
imitator ['ɪməˌteɪʦər] *n* : imitateur *m*, -trice *f*
immaculate [ɪ'mækjələʦ] *adj* **1** PURE : immaculé **2** CLEAN, IMPECCABLE : impeccable
immaculately [ɪ'mækjələʦlɪ] *adv* : impeccablement
immaterial [ˌɪmə'ʦɪrɪəl] *adj* : sans importance
immature [ˌɪmə'ʦʃʊr, -'tjʊr, -'ʦʊr] *adj* : immature
immaturity [ˌɪmə'ʦʃʊrəʦɪ, -'tjʊr-, -'ʦʊr-] *n, pl* **-ties** : immaturité *f*
immeasurable [ɪ'meʒərəbəl] *adj* : incommensurable — **immeasurably** [-bli] *adv*
immediate [ɪ'mi:dɪət] *adj* **1** INSTANT, URGENT : immédiat, urgent **2** NEARBY : proche, immédiat <our immediate neighbors : nos voisins

immédiats> **3** DIRECT : direct, immédiat <the immediate cause of her death : la cause immédiate de sa mort>

immediately [ɪ'mi:diətlɪ] *adv* **1** INSTANTLY : immédiatement **2** DIRECTLY, JUST : juste <immediately after : juste après>

immemorial [ˌɪmə'moriəl] *adj* : immémorial

immense [ɪ'mens] *adj* : immense

immensely [ɪ'mensəlɪ] *adv* : immensément, énormément

immensity [ɪ'mensəṭi] *n, pl* **-ties** : immensité *f*

immerse [ɪ'mərs] *vt* **-mersed; -mersing 1** : plonger, immerger **2 to immerse oneself in** : se plonger dans

immersion [ɪ'mərʒən] *n* : immersion *f*

immigrant [ˈɪmɪgrənt] *n* : immigrant *m*, -grante *f*

immigrate [ˈɪmə,greɪt] *vi* **-grated; -grating** : immigrer

immigration [ˌɪmə'greɪʃən] *n* : immigration *f*

imminence [ˈɪmənənts] *n* : imminence *f*

imminent [ˈɪmənənt] *adj* : imminent

immobile [ɪ'mo:bəl] *adj* **1** FIXED, IMMOVABLE : fixe, impossible à déplacer **2** MOTIONLESS : immobile

immobility [ˌɪmo'bɪləṭi] *n* : immobilité *f*

immobilize [ɪ'mo:bə,laɪz] *vt* **-ized; -izing** : immobiliser

immoderate [ɪ'mɑdərət] *adj* : immodéré, excessif — **immoderately** *adv*

immodest [ɪ'mɑdəst] *adj* **1** VAIN : vaniteux **2** INDECENT : impudique, indécent

immodestly [ɪ'mɑdəstlɪ] *adv* : sans modestie, impudiquement

immodesty [ɪ'mɑdəstɪ] *n* **1** VANITY : vanité *f* **2** INDECENCY : indécence *f*, impudeur *f*

immoral [ɪ'mɔrəl] *adj* : immoral — **immorally** *adv*

immorality [ˌɪmɔ'ræləṭi, ˌɪmə-] *n* : immoralité *f*

immortal[1] [ɪ'mɔrṭəl] *adj* : immortel

immortal[2] *n* : immortel *m*, -telle *f*

immortality [ˌɪˌmɔr'tæləṭi] *n* : immortalité *f*

immortalize [ɪ'mɔrṭəˌlaɪz] *vt* **-ized; -izing** : immortaliser

immovable [ɪ'mu:vəbəl] *adj* **1** STATIONARY : fixe **2** UNYIELDING : inébranlable

immune [ɪ'mju:n] *adj* **1** : immunisé <immune against measles : immunisé contre la rougeole> **2** EXEMPT : exempt

immune system *n* : système *m* immunitaire

immunity [ɪ'mju:nəṭi] *n, pl* **-ties** : immunité *f*

immunization [ˌɪmjʊnə'zeɪʃən] *n* : immunisation *f*

immunize [ˈɪmjʊˌnaɪz] *vt* **-nized; -nizing** : immuniser

immunology [ˌɪmjʊ'nɑlədʒi] *n* : immunologie *f*

immutable [ɪ'mju:ṭəbəl] *adj* : immuable — **immutably** [-bli] *adv*

imp [ˈɪmp] *n* **1** DEMON : lutin *m*, diablotin *m* **2** RASCAL : polisson *m*, -sonne *f*

impact[1] [ɪm'pækt] *vt* **1** STRIKE : frapper, percuter **2** AFFECT : avoir un impact sur, affecter — *vi* **to impact on** : avoir un impact sur

impact[2] [ˈɪmˌpækt] *n* : impact *m*

impacted [ɪm'pæktəd] *adj* : inclus <impacted tooth : dent incluse>

impair [ɪm'pær] *vt* **1** DIMINISH, WEAKEN : diminuer, affaiblir, affecter **2** DAMAGE : détériorer (la santé, etc.)

impairment [ɪm'pærmənt] *n* : affaiblissement *m*, diminution *f* <visual impairment : troubles visuels>

impala [ɪm'pɑlə, -'pæ-] *n, pl* **impalas** *or* **impala** : impala *m*

impale [ɪm'peɪl] *vt* **-paled; -paling** : empaler

impanel [ɪm'pænəl] *vt* **-eled** *or* **-elled; -eling** *or* **-elling** : constituer (un jury, etc.)

impart [ɪm'pɑrt] *vt* **1** COMMUNICATE : communiquer **2** BESTOW, CONVEY : donner, transmettre

impartial [ɪm'pɑrʃəl] *adj* : impartial — **impartially** *adv*

impartiality [ɪmˌpɑrʃɪ'æləṭi] *n* : impartialité *f*

impassable [ɪm'pæsəbəl] *adj* : impraticable, infranchissable

impasse [ˈɪmˌpæs] *n* : impasse *f*

impassioned [ɪm'pæʃənd] *adj* : passionné

impassive [ɪm'pæsɪv] *adj* : impassible — **impassively** *adv*

impatience [ɪm'peɪʃənts] *n* : impatience *f*

impatient [ɪm'peɪʃənt] *adj* : impatient

impatiently [ɪm'peɪʃəntlɪ] *adv* : impatiemment

impeach [ɪm'pi:tʃ] *vt* : destituer (un fonctionnaire du gouvernement)

impeachment [ɪm'pi:tʃmənt] *n* : destitution *f* (d'un fonctionnaire du gouvernement)

impeccable [ɪm'pekəbəl] *adj* : impeccable — **impeccably** [-bli] *adv*

impecunious [ˌɪmpɪ'kju:niəs] *adj* : impécunieux

impede [ɪm'pi:d] *vt* **-peded; -peding** : entraver, gêner

impediment [ɪm'pedəmənt] *n* **1** HINDRANCE : entrave *f*, obstacle *m* **2** *or* **speech impediment** : défaut *m* de l'élocution

impel [ɪm'pel] *vt* **-pelled; -pelling 1** URGE : inciter **2** DRIVE : pousser

impend [ɪm'pend] *vi* : être imminent

impending [ɪm'pendɪŋ] *adj* : imminent

impenetrable [ɪmˈpɛnətrəbəl] *adj* : impénétrable
impenitent [ɪmˈpɛnətənt] *adj* : impénitent
imperative[1] [ɪmˈpɛrətɪv] *adj* **1** AUTHORITATIVE : autoritaire **2** URGENT : impérieux, urgent — **imperatively** *adv*
imperative[2] *n* : impératif *m*
imperceptible [ˌɪmpərˈsɛptəbəl] *adj* : imperceptible — **imperceptibly** [-bli] *adv*
imperfect[1] [ɪmˈpərfɪkt] *adj* : imparfait — **imperfectly** *adv*
imperfect[2] *n or* **imperfect tense** : imparfait *m*
imperfection [ɪmˈpərˈfɛkʃən] *n* : imperfection *f*
imperial [ɪmˈpɪriəl] *adj* **1** SOVEREIGN : impérial **2** IMPERIOUS : impérieux
imperialism [ɪmˈpɪriəˌlɪzəm] *n* : impérialisme *m*
imperialist[1] [ɪmˈpɪriəlɪst] *or* **imperialistic** [ɪmˌpɪriəˈlɪstɪk] *adj* : impérialiste
imperialist[2] *n* : impérialiste *mf*
imperil [ɪmˈpɛrəl] *vt* **-iled** *or* **-illed; -iling** *or* **-illing** : mettre en péril
imperious [ɪmˈpɪriəs] *adj* : impérieux — **imperiously** *adv*
imperishable [ɪmˈpɛrɪʃəbəl] *adj* : impérissable
impermanent [ɪmˈpərmənənt] *adj* : éphémère, fugace
impermeable [ɪmˈpərmiəbəl] *adj* : imperméable
impersonal [ɪmˈpərsənəl] *adj* : impersonnel — **impersonally** *adv*
impersonate [ɪmˈpərsənˌeɪt] *vt* **-ated; -ating** : se faire passer pour
impersonation [ɪmˌpərsənˈeɪʃən] *n* : imitation *f*
impersonator [ɪmˈpərsənˌeɪtər] *n* : imitateur *m*, -trice *f*
impertinence [ɪmˈpərtənənts] *n* : impertinence *f*
impertinent [ɪmˈpərtənənt] *adj* : impertinent
impertinently [ɪmˈpərtənəntli] *adv* : avec impertinence
imperturbable [ˌɪmpərˈtərbəbəl] *adj* : imperturbable
impervious [ɪmˈpərviəs] *adj* **1** IMPENETRABLE : imperméable **2** UNAFFECTED : indifférent
impetuosity [ɪmˌpɛtʃuˈɑsəti] *n, pl* **-ties** : impétuosité *f*
impetuous [ɪmˈpɛtʃuəs] *adj* : impétueux — **impetuously** *adv*
impetus [ˈɪmpətəs] *n* : impulsion *f*
impiety [ɪmˈpaɪəti] *n, pl* **-ties** : impiété *f*
impinge [ɪmˈpɪndʒ] *vi* **-pinged; -pinging 1 to impinge on** AFFECT : affecter **2 to impinge on** VIOLATE : empiéter sur
impious [ˈɪmpiəs, ɪmˈpaɪəs] *adj* : impie
impish [ˈɪmpɪʃ] *adj* : espiègle
impishly [ˈɪmpɪʃli] *adv* : en espiègle
impishness [ˈɪmpɪʃnəs] *n* : espièglerie *f*
implacable [ɪmˈplækəbəl] *adj* : implacable — **implacably** [-bli] *adv*
implant[1] [ɪmˈplænt] *vt* **1** INSERT : implanter **2** INSTILL : inculquer
implant[2] [ˈɪmˌplænt] *n* : implant *m*
implantation [ˌɪmˌplænˈteɪʃən] *n* : implantation *f*
implausibility [ɪmˌplɔzəˈbɪləti] *n, pl* **-ties** : invraisemblance *f*
implausible [ɪmˈplɔzəbəl] *adj* : peu plausible, invraisemblable
implement[1] [ˈɪmpləˌmɛnt] *vt* : mettre en œuvre, exécuter
implement[2] [ˈɪmpləmənt] *n* : outil *m*, instrument *m*
implementation [ˌɪmpləmənˈteɪʃən] *n* : mise *f* en œuvre, exécution *f*
implicate [ˈɪmpləˌkeɪt] *vt* **-cated; -cating** : impliquer
implication [ˌɪmpləˈkeɪʃən] *n* **1** CONSEQUENCE : implication *f* **2** INFERENCE : insinuation *f*
implicit [ɪmˈplɪsət] *adj* **1** IMPLIED, POTENTIAL : implicite **2** UNQUESTIONING : absolu, total
implicitly [ɪmˈplɪsətli] *adv* **1** TACITLY : implicitement **2** ABSOLUTELY : absolument
implode [ɪmˈploːd] *vi* **-ploded; -ploding** : imploser
implosion [ɪmˈploːʒən] *n* : implosion *f*
implore [ɪmˈplor] *vt* **-plored; -ploring** : implorer, supplier
imply [ɪmˈplaɪ] *vt* **-plied; -plying 1** MEAN : impliquer, laisser entendre **2** INDICATE : suggérer, impliquer <her answer implies a true understanding : sa réponse suggère une vraie compréhension>
impolite [ˌɪmpəˈlaɪt] *adj* : impoli — **impolitely** *adv*
impoliteness [ˌɪmpəˈlaɪtnəs] *n* : impolitesse *f*
impolitic [ɪmˈpɑləˌtɪk] *adj* : peu politique, mal avisé
imponderable [ɪmˈpɑndərəbəl] *adj* : impondérable
import[1] [ɪmˈport] *vt* **1** : importer (des marchandises) **2** SIGNIFY : signifier
import[2] [ˈɪmˌport] *n* **1** IMPORTANCE, MEANING : signification *f*, importance *f* **2** IMPORTATION : importation *f*
importance [ɪmˈpɔrtənts] *n* : importance *f*
important [ɪmˈpɔrtənt] *adj* : important
importantly [ɪmˈpɔrtəntli] *adv* **1** : avec importance **2 more importantly** : ce qui est plus important
importation [ˌɪmˌpɔrˈteɪʃən] *n* : importation *f*
importer [ɪmˈpɔrtər] *n* : importateur *m*, -trice *f*
importunate [ɪmˈpɔrtʃənət] *adj* : importun
importune [ˌɪmpərˈtuːn, -ˈtjuːn; ɪmˈpɔrtʃən] *vt* **-tuned; -tuning** : importuner, harceler

impose [ɪmˈpoːz] *v* **-posed; -posing** *vt* : imposer, infliger <to impose a penalty : infliger une peine> — *vi* : s'imposer
imposing [ɪmˈpoːzɪŋ] *adj* : imposant, impressionnant
imposition [ˌɪmpəˈzɪʃən] *n* : imposition *f*
impossibility [ɪmˌpɑsəˈbɪləṭi] *n, pl* **-ties** : impossibilité *f*
impossible [ɪmˈpɑsəbəl] *adj* : impossible
impossibly [ɪmˈpɑsəbli] *adv* **1** : de façon impossible **2** UNBELIEVABLY : incroyablement, extrêmement
impostor *or* **imposter** [ɪmˈpɑstər] *n* : imposteur *m*
imposture [ɪmˈpɑstʃər] *n* : imposture *f*
impotence [ˈɪmpətənʦ] *n* : impuissance *f*
impotency [ˈɪmpətənʦi] → **impotence**
impotent [ˈɪmpətənt] *adj* : impuissant
impound [ɪmˈpɑʊnd] *vt* : saisir, confisquer
impoverish [ɪmˈpɑvərɪʃ] *vt* : appauvrir
impoverishment [ɪmˈpɑvərɪʃmənt] *n* : appauvrissement *m*
impracticable [ɪmˈpræktɪkəbəl] *adj* : impraticable, irréalisable
impractical [ɪmˈpræktɪkəl] *adj* : peu pratique, peu réaliste
imprecise [ˌɪmprɪˈsaɪs] *adj* : imprécis
imprecisely [ˌɪmprɪˈsaɪsli] *adv* : de manière imprécise
imprecision [ˌɪmprɪˈsɪʒən] *n* : imprécision *f*
impregnable [ɪmˈpregnəbəl] *adj* : imprenable
impregnate [ɪmˈpreg,neɪt] *vt* **-nated; -nating 1** FERTILIZE : féconder **2** SATURATE : imprégner
impregnation [ˌɪmˌpreg'neɪʃən] *n* **1** FERTILIZATION : fécondation *f* **2** SATURATION : imprégnation *f*
impresario [ˌɪmprəˈsɑriˌo, -ˈsær-] *n, pl* **-rios** : impresario *m*
impress [ɪmˈpres] *vt* **1** IMPRINT : imprimer **2** AFFECT, INFLUENCE : faire impression sur, impressionner <he didn't impress me : il ne m'a pas impressionné> **3 to impress upon s.o.** : faire bien comprendre à qqn
impression [ɪmˈpreʃən] *n* **1** IMPRINT : marque *f*, empreinte *f*, impression *f* **2** IDEA, NOTION : idée *f*, impression *f* **3** PRINTING : tirage *m*
impressionable [ɪmˈpreʃənəbəl] *adj* : impressionnable
impressive [ɪmˈpresɪv] *adj* : impressionnant
impressively [ɪmˈpresɪvli] *adv* : remarquablement, de manière impressionnante
imprint[1] [ɪmˈprɪnt, ˈɪmˌ-] *vt* : imprimer
imprint[2] [ˈɪmˌprɪnt] *n* : empreinte *f*, marque *f*
imprison [ɪmˈprɪzən] *vt* : emprisonner, mettre en prison
imprisonment [ɪmˈprɪzənmənt] *n* : emprisonnement *m*
improbability [ɪmˌprɑbəˈbɪləṭi] *n, pl* **-ties** : improbabilité *f*, invraisemblance *f*
improbable [ɪmˈprɑbəbəl] *adj* : improbable, invraisemblable
impromptu[1] [ɪmˈprɑmpˌtuː, -ˌtjuː] *adv* : à l'impromptu
impromptu[2] *adj* : impromptu
improper [ɪmˈprɑpər] *adj* **1** UNSEEMLY : malséant, inconvenant **2** INCORRECT : incorrect, erroné **3** INDECENT : indécent
improperly [ɪmˈprɑpərli] *adv* **1** INCORRECTLY : incorrectement **2** INDECENTLY : indécemment
impropriety [ˌɪmprəˈpraɪəṭi] *n, pl* **-ties** : inconvenance *f*
improve [ɪmˈpruːv] *v* **-proved; -proving** *vt* : améliorer, perfectionner — *vi* : s'améliorer, se perfectionner
improvement [ɪmˈpruːvmənt] *n* : amélioration *f*
improvidence [ɪmˈprɑvədənʦ] *n* : imprévoyance *f*
improvident [ɪmˈprɑvədənt] *adj* : imprévoyant
improvisation [ɪmˌprɑvəˈzeɪʃən, ˌɪmprə-və-] *n* : improvisation *f*
improvise [ˈɪmprəˌvaɪz] *v* **-vised; -vising** : improviser
imprudence [ɪmˈpruːdənʦ] *n* : imprudence *f*
imprudent [ɪmˈpruːdənt] *adj* : imprudent
impudence [ˈɪmpjədənʦ] *n* : impudence *f*, insolence *f*, effronterie *f*
impudent [ˈɪmpjədənt] *adj* : insolent, impudent
impugn [ɪmˈpjuːn] *vt* : contester
impulse [ˈɪmˌpʌls] *n* **1** : impulsion *f* **2 on ~** : sans réfléchir
impulsive [ɪmˈpʌlsɪv] *adj* : impulsif — **impulsively** *adv*
impulsiveness [ɪmˈpʌlsɪvnəs] *n* : impulsivité *f*
impunity [ɪmˈpjuːnəṭi] *n* **1** : impunité *f* **2 with ~** : impunément
impure [ɪmˈpjʊr] *adj* : impur
impurity [ɪmˈpjʊrəṭi] *n, pl* **-ties** : impureté *f*
impute [ɪmˈpjuːt] *vt* **-puted; -puting** ATTRIBUTE : imputer, attribuer
in[1] [ˈɪn] *adv* **1** INSIDE : dedans, à l'intérieur <to come in : entrer> **2 to be in** : être là, être chez soi <is she in today? : est-elle là aujourd'hui?> **3 to be in** : être au pouvoir <the democrats are in : les démocrates sont au pouvoir> **4 to be in for** : aller avoir **5 to be in on** : être dans le coup
in[2] *adj* **1** INSIDE : intérieur <the in part : la partie intérieure> **2** FASHIONABLE : à la mode
in[3] *prep* **1** (*indicating location or position*) <in France : en France> <in Canada : au Canada> <in Montreal : à Montréal> <in the hospital : à

l'hôpital> <in my house : chez moi> **2** (*indicating time or season*) <in 1938 : en 1938> <in the spring : au printemps> <in the summer : en été> <in the past : dans le passé> **3** (*indicating manner*) <in French : en français> <written in pencil : écrit en crayon> <in this way : de cette manière> **4** (*indicating states or circumstances*) <to be in luck : avoir de la chance> <to be in love : être amoureux> <to be in a hurry : être pressé> **5** (*indicating purpose*) <in response : en réponse> **6** INSIDE, WITHIN : dans <in this book : dans ce livre> <I'll be back in a week : je serai de retour dans une semaine> **7** INTO : dans, en <she went in the house : elle est entrée dans la maison> <he broke it in pieces : il l'a cassé en morceaux> **8** DURING : pendant, dans <in the afternoon : pendant l'après-midi, dans l'après-midi>

inability [ˌɪnəˈbɪləṭi] *n, pl* **-ties** : incapacité *f*

inaccessibility [ˌɪnɪkˌsɛsəˈbɪləṭi] *n, pl* **-ties** : inaccessibilité *f*

inaccessible [ˌɪnɪkˈsɛsəbəl] *adj* : inaccessible

inaccuracy [ɪnˈækjərəsi] *n, pl* **-cies** : inexactitude *f*

inaccurate [ɪnˈækjərət] *adj* : inexact — **inaccurately** *adv*

inaction [ɪnˈækʃən] *n* : inaction *f*

inactive [ɪnˈæktɪv] *adj* : inactif

inactivity [ˌɪnˌækˈtɪvəṭi] *n, pl* **-ties** : inactivité *f*, inaction *f*

inadequacy [ɪˈnædɪkwəsi] *n, pl* **-cies 1** INSUFFICIENCY : insuffisance *f* **2** DEFICIENCY : défauts *mpl*, incompétence *f*

inadequate [ɪˈnædɪkwət] *adj* : insuffisant

inadmissible [ˌɪnəd'mɪsəbəl] *adj* : inadmissible

inadvertence [ˌɪnəd'vərtənʦ] *n* : inadvertance *f*

inadvertent [ˌɪnəd'vərtənt] *adj* : commis par inadvertance, involontaire

inadvertently [ˌɪnəd'vərtəntli] *adv* : par inadvertance

inadvisable [ˌɪnəd'vaɪzəbəl] *adj* : déconseillé

inalienable [ɪnˈeɪljənəbəl, -ˈeɪliən-] *adj* : inaliénable

inane [ɪˈneɪn] *adj* **inaner; -est** : inepte, stupide

inanimate [ɪˈnænəmət] *adj* : inanimé

inanity [ɪˈnænəṭi] *n, pl* **-ties 1** STUPIDITY : stupidité *f* **2** NONSENSE : ineptie *f*

inapplicable [ɪˈnæplɪkəbəl, ˌɪnəˈplɪkəbəl] *adj* : inapplicable

inappreciable [ˌɪnəˈpriːʃəbəl] *adj* : inappréciable, imperceptible

inappropriate [ˌɪnəˈpro:priət] *adj* : inapproprié, inopportun

inappropriately [ˌɪnəˈpro:priətli] *adv* : mal à propos, inopportunément

inapt [ɪnˈæpt] *adj* : inapte

inarticulate [ˌɪnɑrˈtɪkjələt] *adj* **1** INCOHERENT : incohérent, incapable de s'exprimer **2** INEXPRESSIBLE : inexprimable **3** : inarticulé (en physiologie)

inasmuch as [ɪnˌæzˈmʌtʃæz] *conj* : attendu que, vu que, dans la mesure où

inattention [ˌɪnəˈtɛnʃən] *n* : inattention *f*

inattentive [ˌɪnəˈtɛntɪv] *adj* : inattentif

inattentively [ˌɪnəˈtɛntɪvli] *adv* : distraitement, sans prêter attention

inaudible [ɪnˈɔdəbəl] *adj* : inaudible

inaudibly [ɪnˈɔdəbli] *adv* : de manière inaudible, indistinctement

inaugural[1] [ɪˈnɔgjərəl, -gərəl] *adj* : inaugural

inaugural[2] *n* **1** *or* **inaugural address** : discours *m* d'inauguration **2** INAUGURATION : investiture *f*, installation *f*

inaugurate [ɪˈnɔgjəˌreɪt, -gə-] *vt* **-rated; -rating 1** BEGIN : inaugurer **2** INDUCT : investir, installer

inauguration [ɪˌnɔgjəˈreɪʃən, -gə-] *n* **1** BEGINNING : inauguration *f* **2** INDUCTION : investiture *f*, installation *f*

inauspicious [ˌɪnɔˈspɪʃəs] *adj* : peu propice, défavorable

inborn [ˈɪnˌbɔrn] *adj* : inné, congénital

inbred [ˈɪnˌbrɛd] *adj* **1** : consanguin **2** INNATE : inné

inbreed [ˈɪnˌbriːd] *vt* **-bred; -breeding** : croiser (des animaux de même souche)

incalculable [ɪnˈkælkjələbəl] *adj* : incalculable

incandescence [ˌɪnkənˈdɛsənʦ] *n* : incandescence *f*

incandescent [ˌɪnkənˈdɛsənt] *adj* : incandescent

incantation [ˌɪnˌkænˈteɪʃən] *n* : incantation *f*

incapable [ɪnˈkeɪpəbəl] *adj* : incapable

incapacitate [ˌɪnkəˈpæsəˌteɪt] *vt* **-tated; -tating** : rendre incapable

incapacity [ˌɪnkəˈpæsəṭi] *n, pl* **-ties** : incapacité *f*

incarcerate [ɪnˈkɑrsəˌreɪt] *vt* **-ated; -ating** : incarcérer

incarceration [ɪnˌkɑrsəˈreɪʃən] *n* : incarcération *f*

incarnate[1] [ɪnˈkɑrˌneɪt] *vt* **-ated; -ating** : incarner

incarnate[2] [ɪnˈkɑrnət, -ˌneɪt] *adj* : incarné

incarnation [ˌɪnˌkɑrˈneɪʃən] *n* : incarnation *f*

incendiary[1] [ɪnˈsɛndiˌɛri] *adj* : incendiaire

incendiary[2] *n, pl* **-aries** ARSONIST : incendiaire *mf*

incense[1] [ɪnˈsɛnʦ] *vt* **-censed; -censing** : mettre en colère, rendre furieux

incense[2] ['ɪnsɛnts] *n* : encens *m*
incentive [ɪn'sɛntɪv] *n* : motivation *f*
inception [ɪn'sɛpʃən] *n* : début *m*, commencement *m*
incessant [ɪn'sɛsənt] *adj* : incessant — **incessantly** *adv*
incest ['ɪnˌsɛst] *n* : inceste *m*
incestuous [ɪn'sɛstʃʊəs] *adj* : incestueux
inch[1] ['ɪntʃ] *v* : avancer petit à petit
inch[2] *n* : pouce *m*
incidence ['ɪntsədənts] *n* : fréquence *f*, taux *m*
incident ['ɪntsədənt] *n* : incident *m*
incidental[1] [ˌɪntsə'dɛntəl] *adj* **1** ACCESSORY : secondaire, accessoire **2** FORTUITOUS : fortuit
incidental[2] *n* **1** : détail *m* secondaire **2 incidentals** *npl* EXPENSES : (faux) frais *mpl*
incidentally [ˌɪntsə'dɛntəli, -'dɛntli] *adv* : à propos
incinerate [ɪn'sɪnəˌreɪt] *vt* **-ated; -ating** : incinérer
incinerator [ɪn'sɪnəˌreɪtər] *n* : incinérateur *m*
incipient [ɪn'sɪpiənt] *adj* : naissant
incise [ɪn'saɪz] *vt* **-cised; -cising 1** CUT : inciser **2** ENGRAVE : graver
incision [ɪn'sɪʒən] *n* : incision *f*
incisive [ɪn'saɪsɪv] *adj* : incisif
incisively [ɪn'saɪsɪvli] *adv* : d'une manière incisive
incisor [ɪn'saɪzər] *n* : incisive *f*
incite [ɪn'saɪt] *vt* **-cited; -citing** : inciter
incitement [ɪn'saɪtmənt] *n* : incitation *f*
inclemency [ɪn'klɛmənts] *n* : inclémence *f* (du temps)
inclement [ɪn'klɛmənt] *adj* : inclément
inclination [ˌɪnklə'neɪʃən] *n* **1** PROPENSITY : tendance *f* **2** DESIRE : envie *f*, désir *m* **3** BOW, NOD : inclination *f*
incline[1] [ɪn'klaɪn] *v* **-clined; -clining** *vi* **1** SLOPE : s'incliner **2** TEND : avoir tendance, tendre — *vt* **1** DISPOSE, PROMPT : incliner, disposer **2** BEND : pencher, incliner
incline[2] ['ɪnˌklaɪn] *n* : inclinaison *f*
inclined *adj* **1** SLOPING : incliné **2 to be inclined to** : avoir tendance à
inclose, inclosure → **enclose, enclosure**
include [ɪn'klu:d] *vt* **-cluded; -cluding** : inclure, comprendre
inclusion [ɪn'klu:ʒən] *n* : inclusion *f*
inclusive [ɪn'klu:sɪv] *adj* : inclus, compris
incognito [ˌɪnˌkɑg'ni:ˌto, ɪn'kɑgnəˌto:] *adv & adj* : incognito
incoherence [ˌɪnko'hɪrənts, -'hɛr-] *n* : incohérence *f*
incoherent [ˌɪnko'hɪrənt, -'hɛr-] *adj* : incohérent
incoherently [ˌɪnko'hɪrəntli, -'hɛr-] *adv* : de manière incohérente
incombustible [ˌɪnkəm'bʌstəbəl] *adj* : incombustible
income ['ɪnˌkʌm] *n* : revenu *m*
income tax *n* : impôt *m* sur le revenu
incoming ['ɪnˌkʌmɪŋ] *adj* **1** ARRIVING : entrant, qui arrive **2** NEW : nouveau
incommunicado [ˌɪnkəˌmju:nə'kɑdo] *adj* : tenu au secret, sans contact avec l'extérieur
incomparable [ɪn'kɑmpərəbəl] *adj* : incomparable — **incomparably** [-bli] *adv*
incompatibility [ˌɪnkəmˌpæɾə'bɪləɾi] *n* : incompatibilité *f*
incompatible [ˌɪnkəm'pæɾəbəl] *adj* : incompatible
incompetence [ɪn'kɑmpəɾənts] *n* : incompétence *f*
incompetent [ɪn'kɑmpəɾənt] *adj* : incompétent
incomplete [ˌɪnkəm'pli:t] *adj* : incomplet, inachevé
incompletely [ˌɪnkəm'pli:tli] *adv* : incomplètement
incomprehensible [ˌɪnˌkɑmpri'hɛntsəbəl] *adj* : incompréhensible
inconceivable [ˌɪnkən'si:vəbəl] *adj* : inconcevable
inconceivably [ˌɪnkən'si:vəbli] *adv* : incroyablement
inconclusive [ˌɪnkən'klu:sɪv] *adj* : peu concluant
incongruity [ˌɪnkən'gru:əɾi, -ˌkɑn-] *n, pl* **-ties** : incongruité *f*
incongruous [ɪn'kɑŋgrʊəs] *adj* : incongru, déplacé
incongruously [ɪn'kɑŋgrʊəsli] *adv* : de façon incongrue
inconsequential [ˌɪnˌkɑnsə'kwɛnʃəl] *adj* : sans importance
inconsiderable [ˌɪnkən'sɪdərəbəl] *adj* : insignifiant, négligeable
inconsiderate [ˌɪnkən'sɪdərət] *adj* : qui manque de considération, irréfléchi
inconsiderately [ˌɪnkən'sɪdərətli] *adv* : sans aucune considération
inconsistency [ˌɪnkən'sɪstənsi] *n, pl* **-cies** : incohérence *f*, contradiction *f*
inconsistent [ˌɪnkən'sɪstənt] *adj* **1** CHANGEABLE, ERRATIC : inégal, changeant **2** CONTRADICTORY : contradictoire
inconsolable [ˌɪnkən'so:ləbəl] *adj* : inconsolable
inconsolably [ˌɪnkən'so:ləbli] *adv* : de façon inconsolable
inconspicuous [ˌɪnkən'spɪkjʊəs] *adj* : peu apparent, qui passe inaperçu
inconspicuously [ˌɪnkən'spɪkjʊəsli] *adv* : discrètement
incontestable [ˌɪnkən'tɛstəbəl] *adj* : incontestable — **incontestably** [-bli] *adv*
incontinent [ɪn'kɑntənənt] *adj* : incontinent
inconvenience[1] [ˌɪnkən'vi:njənts] *vt* **-nienced; -niencing** : déranger
inconvenience[2] *n* **1** BOTHER : dérangement *m* **2** DISADVANTAGE : inconvénient *m*

inconvenient [ˌɪnkənˈviːnjənt] *adj* : incommode, inopportun

inconveniently [ˌɪnkənˈviːnjəntli] *adv* **1** INOPPORTUNELY : inopportunément **2** : de façon peu practique <inconveniently located : mal placé>

incorporate [ɪnˈkɔrpəˌreɪt] *v* **-rated; -rating** *vt* INCLUDE : incorporer — *vi* : se constituer en société commerciale

incorporated [ɪnˈkɔrpəˌreɪtəd] *adj* : constitué en société commerciale

incorporation [ɪnˌkɔrpəˈreɪʃən] *n* **1** INCLUSION, INTEGRATION : incorporation *f*, intégration *f* **2** *Can* : incorporation *f* (d'une société)

incorporeal [ˌɪnˌkɔrˈpɔriəl] *adj* : incorporel

incorrect [ˌɪnkəˈrɛkt] *adj* **1** WRONG : erroné **2** IMPROPER : incorrect

incorrectly [ˌɪnkəˈrɛktli] *adv* : inexactement, incorrectement

incorrigible [ɪnˈkɔrədʒəbəl] *adj* : incorrigible

incorruptible [ɪnkəˈrʌptəbəl] *adj* : incorruptible

increase[1] [ɪnˈkriːs, ˈɪnˌkriːs] *v* **-creased; -creasing** : augmenter

increase[2] [ˈɪnˌkriːs, ɪnˈkriːs] *n* **1** : augmentation *f* **2 on the increase** : en hausse, à la hausse

increasingly [ɪnˈkriːsɪŋli] *adv* : de plus en plus

incredible [ɪnˈkrɛdəbəl] *adj* : incroyable — **incredibly** [-bli] *adv*

incredulity [ˌɪnkrɪˈduːləti, -ˈdjuː-] *n* : incrédulité *f*

incredulous [ɪnˈkrɛdʒələs] *adj* : incrédule

incredulously [ɪnˈkrɛdʒələsli] *adv* : avec incrédulité

increment [ˈɪnkrəmənt, ˈɪn-] *n* : augmentation *f*

incremental [ˌɪnkrəˈməntəl, ˈɪn-] *adj* : progressif, par augmentation

incriminate [ɪnˈkrɪməˌneɪt] *vt* **-nated; -nating** : incriminer

incrimination [ɪnˌkrɪməˈneɪʃən] *n* : incrimination *f*

incriminatory [ɪnˈkrɪmənəˌtɔri] *adj* : compromettant

incubate [ˈɪŋkjəˌbeɪt, ˈɪn-] *v* **-bated; -bating** *vt* : incuber — *vi* : être en incubation

incubation [ˌɪŋkjəˈbeɪʃən, ˌɪn-] *n* : incubation *f*

incubator [ˈɪŋkjəˌbeɪtər, -ˈɪn-] *n* : incubateur *m*, couveuse *f* (pour enfants)

inculcate [ɪnˈkʌlˌkeɪt, ˈɪnˌkʌl-] *vt* **-cated; -cating** : inculquer

incumbency [ɪnˈkʌmbənsi] *n, pl* **-cies** : office *m*, période *f* de fonction

incumbent[1] [ɪnˈkʌmbənt] *adj* : obligatoire <to be incumbent upon : incomber à>

incumbent[2] *n* OFFICEHOLDER : titulaire *mf*

incur [ɪnˈkər] *vt* **-curred; -curring** : encourir <to incur expenses : encourir des dépenses>

incurable [ɪnˈkjʊrəbəl] *adj* : incurable

incursion [ɪnˈkərʒən] *n* : incursion *f*

indebted [ɪnˈdɛtəd] *adj* **1** : endetté **2 to be indebted to** : être redevable à

indebtedness [ɪnˈdɛtədnəs] *n* : dette *f*, endettement *m*

indecency [ɪnˈdiːsənsi] *n, pl* **-cies** : indécence *f*

indecent [ɪnˈdiːsənt] *adj* : indécent

indecently [ɪnˈdiːsəntli] *adv* : indécemment

indecipherable [ˌɪndɪˈsaɪfərəbəl] *adj* : indéchiffrable

indecision [ˌɪndɪˈsɪʒən] *n* : indécision *f*

indecisive [ˌɪndɪˈsaɪsɪv] *adj* : indécis

indecisively [ˌɪndɪˈsaɪsɪvli] *adv* : de manière indécise

indecorous [ɪnˈdɛkərəs, ˌɪndɪˈkorəsli] *adj* : inconvenant

indecorously [ɪnˈdɛkərəsli] *adv* : de manière inconvenante

indecorousness [ɪnˈdɛkərəsnəs, ˌɪndɪˈkorəs-] *n* : inconvenance *f*

indeed [ɪnˈdiːd] *adv* **1** TRULY : vraiment, en effet, comme de fait *Can* **2** (*used as an intensifier*) <it's very big indeed : c'est vraiment très grand> **3** OF COURSE : bien sûr

indefatigable [ˌɪndɪˈfæt̬ɪgəbəl] *adj* : infatigable, inlassable

indefensible [ˌɪndɪˈfɛnt̬səbəl] *adj* : inexcusable, injustifiable

indefinable [ˌɪndɪˈfaɪnəbəl] *adj* : indéfinissable

indefinite [ɪnˈdɛfənət] *adj* **1** : indéfini <an indefinite period : une période indéfinie> **2** VAGUE : imprécis

indefinite article *n* : article *m* indéfini

indefinitely [ɪnˈdɛfənətli] *adv* : indéfiniment

indelible [ɪnˈdɛləbəl] *adj* : indélébile

indelibly [ɪnˈdɛləbli] *adv* : de manière indélébile

indelicacy [ɪnˈdɛləkəsi] *n* : indélicatesse *f*

indelicate [ɪnˈdɛlɪkət] *adj* : indélicat

indemnify [ɪnˈdɛmnəˌfaɪ] *vt* **-fied; -fying** **1** INSURE : assurer **2** COMPENSATE : indemniser

indemnity [ɪnˈdɛmnət̬i] *n, pl* **-ties** : indemnité *f*

indent [ɪnˈdɛnt] *vt* **1** : renfoncer, mettre en alinéa <indent 4 spaces : renfoncez de 4 espaces> **2** DENT : bosseler

indentation [ˌɪnˌdɛnˈteɪʃən] *n* **1** DENT : creux *m*, bosse *f* **2** SPACE : alinéa *m* (en typographie)

indenture[1] [ɪnˈdɛntʃər] *vt* **-tured; -turing** : engager sous contrat

indenture[2] *n* : contrat *m* d'apprentissage

independence [ˌɪndəˈpɛndənts] *n* : indépendance *f*

Independence Day *n* : fête *f* de l'Indépendance américaine (le 4 juillet)
independent[1] [ˌɪndə'pendənt] *adj* : indépendant
independent[2] *n* : indépendant *m*, -dante *f*
independently [ˌɪndə'pendəntli] *adv* : de façon indépendante, indépendamment
indescribable [ˌɪndɪ'skraɪbəbəl] *adj* : indescriptible
indescribably [ˌɪndɪ'skraɪbəbli] *adv* : incroyablement
indestructibility [ˌɪndɪˌstrʌktə'bɪləṭi] *n* : indestructibilité *f*
indestructible [ˌɪndɪ'strʌktəbəl] *adj* : indestructible
indeterminate [ˌɪndɪ'tərmənət] *adj* : déterminé
index[1] ['ɪnˌdeks] *vt* **1** : mettre un index à (un livre, etc.) **2** CATALOG : classer, cataloguer
index[2] *n, pl* **-dexes** *or* **-dices** ['ɪndəˌsi:z] **1** LIST : index *m* **2** INDICATION : indice *m* <cost of living index : indice du coût de la vie>
index finger *n* : index *m*
Indian[1] ['ɪndiən] *adj* : indien
Indian[2] *n* : Indien *m*, -dienne *f*
Indian corn *n* : maïs *m*, blé *m* d'Inde *Can*
indicate ['ɪndəˌkeɪt] *vt* **-cated; -cating** : indiquer
indication [ˌɪndə'keɪʃən] *n* : indice *m*, indication *f*
indicative [ɪn'dɪkəṭɪv] *adj* : indicatif
indicator ['ɪndəˌkeɪṭər] *n* : indicateur *m*
indict [ɪn'daɪt] *vt* : inculper
indictment [ɪn'daɪtmənt] *n* : inculpation *f*
indifference [ɪn'dɪfrənʧ, -'dɪfə-] *n* : indifférence *f*
indifferent [ɪn'dɪfrənt, -'dɪfə-] *adj* **1** UNCONCERNED : indifférent **2** MEDIOCRE : médiocre, quelconque
indifferently [ɪn'dɪfrəntli, -'dɪfə-] *adv* **1** UNCONCERNEDLY : avec indifférence **2** SO-SO : médiocrement
indigence ['ɪndɪdʒənʧ] *n* : indigence *f*
indigenous [ɪn'dɪdʒənəs] *adj* : indigène
indigent ['ɪndɪdʒənt] *adj* : indigent
indigestible [ˌɪndaɪ'dʒestəbəl, -dɪ-] *adj* : indigeste
indigestion [ˌɪndaɪ'dʒestʃən, -dɪ-] *n* : indigestion *f*
indignant [ɪn'dɪgnənt] *adj* : indigné, outré
indignantly [ɪn'dɪgnəntli] *adv* : avec indignation
indignation [ˌɪndɪg'neɪʃən] *n* : indignation *f*
indignity [ɪn'dɪgnəṭi] *n, pl* **-ties** : indignité *f*
indigo ['ɪndɪˌgo:] *n, pl* **-gos** *or* **-goes** : indigo *m*
indirect [ˌɪndə'rɛkt, -daɪ-] *adj* : indirect — **indirectly** *adv*
indiscernible [ˌɪndɪ'sərnəbəl, -'zər-] *adj* : indiscernable, imperceptible
indiscreet [ˌɪndɪ'skri:t] *adj* : indiscret
indiscreetly [ˌɪndɪ'skri:tli] *adv* : indiscrètement
indiscretion [ˌɪndɪ'skrɛʃən] *n* : indiscrétion *f*
indiscriminate [ˌɪndɪ'skrɪmənət] *adj* **1** : qui manque de discernement **2** HAPHAZARD : fait au hasard
indiscriminately [ˌɪndɪ'skrɪmənətli] *adv* **1** : sans discernement **2** RANDOMLY : au hasard
indispensable [ˌɪndɪ'spenʧəbəl] *adj* : indispensable
indisposed [ˌɪndɪ'spo:zd] *adj* **1** ILL : indisposé **2** DISINCLINED : peu disposé, peu enclin
indisposition [ˌɪnˌdɪspə'zɪʃən] *n* : indisposition *f*
indisputable [ˌɪndɪ'spju:ṭəbəl] *adj* : incontestable — **indisputably** [-bli] *adv*
indistinct [ˌɪndɪ'stɪŋkt] *adj* : indistinct — **indistinctly** *adv*
individual[1] [ˌɪndə'vɪdʒʊəl] *adj* **1** SEPARATE : individuel **2** DISTINCTIVE, PERSONAL : particulier, personnel, original
individual[2] *n* : individu *m*
individualist [ˌɪndə'vɪdʒʊəlɪst] *n* : individualiste *mf*
individuality [ˌɪndəˌvɪdʒʊ'æləṭi] *n, pl* **-ties** : individualité *f*
individually [ˌɪndə'vɪdʒʊəli, -dʒəli] *adv* **1** SEPARATELY : individuellement **2** DISTINCTIVELY : de façon distinctive
indivisible [ˌɪndɪ'vɪzəbəl] *adj* : indivisible
indoctrinate [ɪn'dɑktrəˌneɪt] *vt* **-nated; -nating** : endoctriner
indoctrination [ɪnˌdɑktrə'neɪʃən] *n* : endoctrinement *m*
indolence ['ɪndələnʧ] *n* : indolence *f*
indolent ['ɪndələnt] *adj* : indolent
indomitable [ɪn'dɑməṭəbəl] *adj* : indomptable, invincible, irréductible
indomitably [ɪn'dɑməṭəbli] *adv* : de façon indomptable
Indonesian[1] [ˌɪndə'ni:ʒən, -ʃən] *adj* : indonésien
Indonesian[2] *n* **1** : Indonésien *m*, -sienne *f* **2** : indonésien *m* (langue)
indoor ['ɪn'dor] *adj* **1** : d'intérieur, à l'intérieur **2** : couvert <indoor swimming pool : piscine couverte>
indoors ['ɪn'dorz] *adv* : à l'intérieur
indubitable [ɪn'du:bəṭəbəl, -'dju:-] *adj* : indubitable — **indubitably** [-bli] *adv*
induce [ɪn'du:s, -'dju:s] *vt* **-duced; -ducing** **1** PERSUADE : persuader **2** CAUSE : provoquer, déclencher <to induce labor : déclencher l'accouchement>
inducement [ɪn'du:smənt, -'dju:s-] *n* **1** INCENTIVE : motivation *f* **2** REWARD : récompense *f*
induct [ɪn'dʌkt] *vt* **1** INSTALL : installer (qqn dans ses fonctions) **2** DRAFT, RECRUIT : incorporer

inductee [ˌɪnˌdʌkˈtiː] *n* DRAFTEE : appelé *m*, conscrit *m*
induction [ɪnˈdʌkʃən] *n* **1** INSTALLATION : installation *f*, incorporation *f* **2** : induction *f* (en logique, en électricité)
inductive [ɪnˈdʌktɪv] *adj* : inductif
indulge [ɪnˈdʌldʒ] *v* **-dulged; -dulging** *vt* **1** GRATIFY : céder à, satisfaire **2** PAMPER, SPOIL : gâter — *vi* **to indulge in** : se livrer à, se permettre
indulgence [ɪnˈdʌldʒənts] *n* **1** TOLERANCE : complaisance *f*, indulgence *f* **2** GRATIFICATION : satisfaction *f*, gratification *f* **3** : indulgence *f* (en religion)
indulgent [ɪnˈdʌldʒənt] *adj* : indulgent
indulgently [ɪnˈdʌldʒəntlɪ] *adv* : avec indulgence
industrial [ɪnˈdʌstrɪəl] *adj* : industriel
industrialist [ɪnˈdʌstrɪəlɪst] *n* : industriel *m*, -trielle *f*
industrialization [ɪnˌdʌstrɪələˈzeɪʃən] *n* : industrialisation *f*
industrialize [ɪnˈdʌstrɪəˌlaɪz] *vt* **-ized; -izing** : industrialiser
industrious [ɪnˈdʌstrɪəs] *adj* : industrieux, travailleur, travaillant *Can*
industriously [ɪnˈdʌstrɪəslɪ] *adv* : avec diligence
industriousness [ɪnˈdʌstrɪəsnəs] *n* : assiduité *f*, application *f*
industry [ˈɪndəstrɪ] *n, pl* **-tries 1** : industrie *f* <the steel industry : l'industrie sidérurgique> **2** DILIGENCE : assiduité *f*
inebriated [ɪˈniːbrɪˌeɪtəd] *adj* : ivre
inebriation [ɪˌniːbrɪˈeɪʃən] *n* : ivresse *f*
inedible [ɪˈnɛdəbəl] *adj* : non comestible (se dit d'une plante, etc.), immangeable (se dit d'un plat)
ineffable [ɪnˈɛfəbəl] *adj* : ineffable — **ineffably** [-blɪ] *adv*
ineffective [ˌɪnɪˈfɛktɪv] *adj* **1** INEFFECTUAL : inefficace **2** INCAPABLE : incapable
ineffectively [ˌɪnɪˈfɛktɪvlɪ] *adv* : sans effet, en vain
ineffectual [ˌɪnɪˈfɛktʃʊəl], **ineffectually** [ˌɪnɪˈfɛktʃʊəlɪ] → **ineffective, ineffectively**
inefficiency [ˌɪnɪˈfɪʃəntsɪ] *n, pl* **-cies** : inefficacité *f*
inefficient [ˌɪnɪˈfɪʃənt] *adj* **1** : inefficace (se dit d'une machine, etc.) **2** INCOMPETENT : incompétent, mal organisé
inefficiently [ˌɪnɪˈfɪʃəntlɪ] *adv* : inefficacement
inelegance [ɪnˈɛləgənts] *n* : inélégance *f*
inelegant [ɪnˈɛləgənt] *adj* : inélégant
ineligibility [ɪnˌɛlədʒəˈbɪlətɪ] *n* : inéligibilité *f*
ineligible [ɪnˈɛlədʒəbəl] *adj* : inéligible
inept [ɪˈnɛpt] *adj* **1** INCOMPETENT : inepte **2** INAPPROPRIATE : inapproprié
ineptitude [ɪnˈnɛptəˌtuːd, -ˌtjuːd] *n* : ineptie *f*
inequality [ˌɪnɪˈkwɑlətɪ] *n, pl* **-ties** : inégalité *f*
inert [ɪˈnərt] *adj* : inerte
inertia [ɪˈnərʃə] *n* : inertie *f*
inescapable [ˌɪnɪˈskeɪpəbəl] *adj* : inéluctable, indéniable — **inescapably** [-blɪ] *adv*
inessential [ˌɪnɪˈsɛnʃəl] *adj* : non essentiel, superflu
inestimable [ɪnˈɛstəməbəl] *adj* : inestimable
inevitability [ɪnˌɛvətəˈbɪlətɪ] *n, pl* **-ties** : inévitabilité *f*
inevitable [ɪnˈɛvətəbəl] *adj* : inévitable — **inevitably** [-blɪ] *adv*
inexact [ˌɪnɪgˈzækt] *adj* : inexact
inexactly [ˌɪnɪgˈzæktlɪ] *adv* : inexactement, incorrectement
inexcusable [ˌɪnɪkˈskjuːzəbəl] *adj* : inexcusable
inexcusably [ˌɪnɪkˈskjuːzəblɪ] *adv* : de façon inexcusable
inexhaustible [ˌɪnɪgˈzɔstəbəl] *adj* **1** LIMITLESS : inépuisable **2** INDEFATIGABLE : infatigable
inexorable [ɪnˈɛksərəbəl] *adj* : inexorable — **inexorably** [-blɪ] *adv*
inexpedient [ˌɪnɪkˈspiːdiənt] *adj* : inopportun, malavisé
inexpensive [ˌɪnɪkˈspɛntsɪv] *adj* : pas cher, bon marché
inexperience [ˌɪnɪkˈspɪrɪənts] *n* : inexpérience *f*
inexperienced [ˌɪnɪkˈspɪrɪəntst] *adj* : inexpérimenté
inexplicable [ˌɪnɪkˈsplɪkəbəl] *adj* : inexplicable — **inexplicably** [-blɪ] *adv*
inexpressible [ˌɪnɪkˈsprɛsəbəl] *adj* : inexprimable
inextricable [ˌɪnɪkˈstrɪkəbəl, ɪnˈɛkˌstrɪ-] *adj* : inextricable — **inextricably** [-blɪ] *adv*
infallibility [ɪnˌfæləˈbɪlətɪ] *n* : infaillibilité *f*
infallible [ɪnˈfæləbəl] *adj* : infaillible — **infallibly** [-blɪ] *adv*
infamous [ˈɪnfəməs] *adj* : infâme, notoire
infamy [ˈɪnfəmɪ] *n, pl* **-mies** : infamie *f*
infancy [ˈɪnfəntsɪ] *n, pl* **-cies 1** : petite enfance *f* **2 in its infancy** : à ses débuts
infant [ˈɪnfənt] *n* : petit enfant *m*, petite enfant *f*; bébé *m*; nourrisson *m*
infantile [ˈɪnfənˌtaɪl, -təl, -ˌtiːl] *adj* : infantile
infantile paralysis → poliomyelitis
infantry [ˈɪnfəntrɪ] *n, pl* **-tries** : infanterie *f*
infatuated [ɪnˈfætʃʊˌeɪtəd] *adj* **to be infatuated with** : être entiché de
infatuation [ɪnˌfætʃʊˈeɪʃən] *n* : engouement *m*
infect [ɪnˈfɛkt] *vt* : infecter
infection [ɪnˈfɛkʃən] *n* : infection *f*
infectious [ɪnˈfɛkʃəs] *adj* **1** : infectieux, contagieux <une maladie infectieuse : an infectious disease> **2** : con-

tagieux, communicatif <rythme communicatif : infectious rhythm>
infer [ɪn'fər] *vt* **-ferred; -ferring** : déduire, inférer
inference ['ɪnfərəns] *n* : déduction *f*, inférence *f*
inferior[1] [ɪn'fɪrɪər] *adj* : inférieur
inferior[2] *n* : inférieur *m*, -rieure *f*
inferiority [ɪnˌfɪrɪ'ɔrəṭi] *n, pl* **-ties** : infériorité *f*
infernal [ɪn'fərnəl] *adj* : infernal
infernally [ɪn'fərnəli] *adv* TERRIBLY : terriblement, abominablement
inferno [ɪn'fərˌno:] *n, pl* **-nos 1** BLAZE, FIRE : brasier *m* **2** HELL : enfer *m*
infertile [ɪn'fərṭəl, -ˌtaɪl] *adj* : infertile, stérile
infertility [ˌɪnfərˈtɪləṭi] *n* : infertilité *f*
infest [ɪn'fɛst] *vt* : infester
infidel ['ɪnfədəl, -ˌdɛl] *n* : infidèle *mf*
infidelity [ˌɪnfə'dɛləṭi, -faɪ-] *n, pl* **-ties** : infidélité *f*
infield ['ɪnˌfi:ld] *n* : petit champ *m*
infiltrate [ɪn'fɪlˌtreɪt, 'ɪnfɪl-] *v* **-trated; -trating** *vt* : infiltrer — *vi* : s'infiltrer
infiltration [ˌɪnfɪl'treɪʃən] *n* : infiltration *f*
infinite ['ɪnfənət] *adj* **1** LIMITLESS : infini **2** VAST : sans bornes, incalculable, infini
infinitely ['ɪnfənətli] *adv* : infiniment
infinitesimal [ˌɪnfənə'tɛsəməl] *adj* : infinitésimal — **infinitesimally** *adv*
infinitive [ɪn'fɪnəṭɪv] *n* : infinitif *m*
infinity [ɪn'fɪnəṭi] *n, pl* **-ties 1** : infinité *f* **2** : infini *m* (en mathématiques)
infirm [ɪn'fərm] *adj* : infirme
infirmary [ɪn'fərməri] *n, pl* **-ries** : infirmerie *f*
infirmity [ɪn'fərməṭi] *n, pl* **-ties** : infirmité *f*
inflame [ɪn'fleɪm] *v* **-flamed; -flaming** *vt* **1** IGNITE : enflammer, mettre le feu à **2** : enflammer (en médecine) **3** EXCITE, STIR UP : exciter, enflammer — *vi* : s'enflammer
inflammable [ɪn'flæməbəl] *adj* : inflammable, flammable
inflammation [ˌɪnfləˈmeɪʃən] *n* : inflammation *f*
inflammatory [ɪn'flæməˌtori] *adj* **1** : incendiaire <inflammatory remarks : propos incendiaires> **2** : inflammatoire (en médecine)
inflatable [ɪn'fleɪṭəbəl] *adj* : gonflable
inflate [ɪn'fleɪt] *v* **-flated; -flating** *vt* : gonfler — *vi* : se gonfler
inflation [ɪn'fleɪʃən] *n* : inflation *f*
inflationary [ɪn'fleɪʃəˌnɛri] *adj* : inflationniste
inflect [ɪn'flɛkt] *vt* **1** CURVE : infléchir **2** MODULATE : moduler (la voix) **3** CONJUGATE : conjuger (un verbe) **4** DECLINE : décliner (un adjectif, etc.)
inflection [ɪnˌflɛkʃən] *n* **1** : inflexion *f*, modulation *f* (de la voix) **2** : flexion *f* (en linguistique) **3** : inflexion *f* (en mathématiques)
inflexibility [ɪnˌflɛksəˈbɪləṭi] *n, pl* **-ties** : inflexibilité *f*
inflexible [ɪn'flɛksɪbəl] *adj* : inflexible
inflict [ɪn'flɪkt] *vt* : infliger
influence[1] ['ɪnˌflu:əns, ɪnˈflu:əns] *vt* **-enced; -encing** : influencer, influer sur
influence[2] *n* **1** : influence *f* **2 under the influence of** : sous l'effet de
influential [ˌɪnflu'ɛnʃəl] *adj* : influent
influenza [ˌɪnflu'ɛnzə] *n* : grippe *f*
influx ['ɪnˌflʌks] *n* : afflux *m*
inform [ɪn'fɔrm] *vt* : informer, renseigner — *vi* **to inform on** : dénoncer
informal [ɪn'fɔrməl] *adj* **1** UNCEREMONIOUS : sans cérémonie **2** CASUAL : familier (se dit du langage) **3** UNOFFICIAL : officieux, non officiel
informality [ˌɪnfɔr'mæləṭi, -fər-] *n* **1** : simplicité *f*, absence *f* de cérémonie **2** : style *m* familier (de langage)
informally [ɪn'fɔrməli] *adv* **1** CASUALLY : sans cérémonie, simplement **2** UNOFFICIALLY : officieusement **3** COLLOQUIALLY : familièrement
informant [ɪn'fɔrmənt] *n* : informateur *m*, -trice *f*
information [ˌɪnfərˈmeɪʃən] *n* **1** : renseignements *mpl*, information *f* **2 for your information** : à titre d'information
informative [ɪn'fɔrməṭɪv] *adj* : informatif
informer [ɪn'fɔrmər] *n* : informateur *m*, -trice *f*
infraction [ɪn'frækʃən] *n* : infraction *f*
infrared [ˌɪnfrə'rɛd] *adj* : infrarouge
infrastructure ['ɪnfrəˌstrʌktʃər] *n* : infrastructure *f*
infrequent [ɪn'fri:kwənt] *adj* : rare, peu fréquent
infrequently [ɪn'fri:kwəntli] *adv* : rarement
infringe [ɪn'frɪndʒ] *v* **-fringed; -fringing** *vt* : enfreindre — *vi* **to infringe on** : empiéter sur
infringement [ɪn'frɪndʒmənt] *n* : infraction *f* (à la loi)
infuriate [ɪn'fjʊriˌeɪt] *vt* **-ated; -ating** : rendre furieux
infuse [ɪn'fju:z] *vt* **-fused; -fusing 1** IMBUE, INSPIRE : insuffler, inspirer **2** STEEP : infuser
infusion [ɪn'fju:ʒən] *n* : infusion *f*
ingenious [ɪn'dʒi:njəs] *adj* : ingénieux — **ingeniously** *adv*
ingenue *or* **ingénue** ['ɑnˌdʒɛnˌnu:, 'æn-; 'æʒə-, 'ɑ-] *n* : ingénue *f*
ingenuity [ˌɪndʒə'nu:əṭi, -'nju:-] *n, pl* **-ties** : ingéniosité *f*
ingenuous [ɪn'dʒɛnjʊəs] *adj* **1** FRANK : candide, franc **2** NAIVE : naïf — **ingenuously** *adv*
ingenuousness [ɪn'dʒɛnjʊəsnəs] *n* **1** FRANKNESS : franchise *f* **2** NAÏVETÉ : naïveté *f*

ingest [ɪn'dʒɛst] *vt* : ingérer
ingot ['ɪŋgət] *n* : lingot *m*
ingrained [ɪn'greɪnd] *adj* : enraciné, invétéré
ingrate ['ɪn,greɪt] *n* : ingrat *m*, -grate *f*
ingratiate [ɪn'greɪʃi,eɪt] *vt* **-ated; -ating** : trouver grâce aux yeux de (qqn) <to ingratiate oneself with : s'insinuer dans les bonnes grâces de>
ingratiating [ɪn'greɪʃi,eɪtɪŋ] *adj* : insinuant
ingratitude [ɪn'græt̬ə'tu:d, -'tju:d] *n* : ingratitude *f*
ingredient [ɪn'gri:diənt] *n* : ingrédient *m*
ingrown ['ɪn,gro:n] *adj* : incarné <ingrown nail : ongle incarné>
inhabit [ɪn'hæbət] *vt* : habiter
inhabitable [ɪn'hæbət̬əbəl] *adj* : habitable
inhabitant [ɪn'hæbət̬ənt] *n* : habitant *m*, -tante *f*
inhalant [ɪn'heɪlənt] *n* : inhalant *m*
inhale [ɪn'heɪl] *v* **-haled; -haling** *vt* : inhaler, aspirer — *vi* : inspirer
inhaler [ɪn'heɪlər] *n* : inhalateur *m*
inhere [ɪn'hɪr] *vi* **-hered; -hering** : être inhérent
inherent [ɪn'hɪrənt, -'hɛr-] *adj* : inhérent
inherently [ɪn'hɪrəntli, -'hɛr-] *adv* : fondamentalement, naturellement
inherit [ɪn'hɛrət] *v* : hériter
inheritance [ɪn'hɛrət̬ənʦ] *n* : héritage *m*
inheritor [ɪn'hɛrət̬ər] *n* : héritier *m*, -tière *f*
inhibit [ɪn'hɪbət] *vt* INPEDE : entraver, gêner
inhibition [,ɪnhə'bɪʃən, ,ɪnə-] *n* : inhibition *f*
inhuman [ɪn'hju:mən, -'ju:-] *adj* : inhumain — **inhumanly** *adv*
inhumane [,ɪnhju'meɪn, -ju-] *adj* : inhumain, cruel
inhumanity [,ɪnhju'mænət̬i, -ju-] *n, pl* **-ties** : inhumanité *f*
inimical [ɪ'nɪmɪkəl] *adj* **1** UNFAVORABLE : peu favorable **2** HOSTILE : inamical, hostile
inimitable [ɪ'nɪmət̬əbəl] *adj* : inimitable
iniquitous [ɪ'nɪkwət̬əs] *adj* : inique
iniquity [ɪ'nɪkwət̬i] *n, pl* **-ties** : iniquité *f*
initial[1] [ɪ'nɪʃəl] *vt* **-tialed** *or* **-tialled; -tialing** *or* **-tialling** : parapher
initial[2] *adj* **1** INCIPIENT : initial **2** FIRST : premier
initially [ɪ'nɪʃəli] *adv* : à l'origine, au départ
initial[3] *n* : initiale *f*
initiate[1] [ɪ'nɪʃi,eɪt] *vt* **-ated; -ating 1** BEGIN : commencer, entreprendre **2** INDUCT : initier, admettre (à un club, etc.) **3** INTRODUCE : initier (qqn au rudiments de qqch)
initiate[2] [ɪ'nɪʃiət] *n* : initié *m*, -tiée *f*
initiation [ɪ,nɪʃi'eɪʃən] *n* : initiation *f*
initiative [ɪ'nɪʃət̬ɪv] *n* : initiative *f*
inject [ɪn'dʒɛkt] *vt* : injecter
injection [ɪn'dʒɛkʃən] *n* : injection *f*
injudicious [,ɪndʒu'dɪʃəs] *adj* : peu judicieux
injunction [ɪn'dʒʌŋkʃən] *n* : injonction *f*
injure ['ɪndʒər] *vt* **-jured; -juring 1** WOUND : blesser **2** HARM : nuire à, faire du tort à **3 to injure oneself** : se blesser
injurious [ɪn'dʒʊriəs] *adj* : nuisible, préjudiciable <injurious to one's health : nuisible à la santé>
injury ['ɪndʒəri] *n, pl* **-ries 1** WOUND : blessure *f* **2** WRONG : tort *m*, dommage *m*
injustice [ɪn'dʒʌsʧəs] *n* : injustice *f*
ink[1] ['ɪŋk] *vt* : encrer
ink[2] *n* : encre *f*
inkling ['ɪŋklɪŋ] *n* : petite idée *f*
inkwell ['ɪŋk,wɛl] *n* : encrier *m*
inky ['ɪŋki] *adj* **inkier; -est 1** : tâché d'encre **2** DARK : noir comme de l'encre
inland[1] ['ɪn,lænd, -lənd] *adv* : à l'intérieur, vers l'intérieur
inland[2] *adj* : intérieur
inland[3] *n* : intérieur *m*
in–law ['ɪn,lɔ] *n* **1** : parent *m* par alliance **2 in–laws** *npl* : beaux-parents *mpl*
inlay[1] [ɪn'leɪ, 'ɪn,leɪ] *vt* **-laid** [-'leɪd, -,leɪd]; **-laying** : incruster
inlay[2] ['ɪn,leɪ] *n* : incrustation *f*
inlet ['ɪn,let, -lət] *n* : crique *f*, bras *m* de mer
inmate ['ɪn,meɪt] *n* **1** PRISONER : détenu *m*, -nue *f* **2** PATIENT : malade *mf*
in memoriam [,ɪnmə'moriəm] *prep* : en mémoire de
inmost ['ɪn,mo:st] *adj* INNERMOST : le plus profond, le plus intime
inn ['ɪn] *n* **1** HOTEL : auberge *f* **2** TAVERN : taverne *f*
innards ['ɪnərdz] *npl* : entrailles *fpl*
innate [ɪ'neɪt] *adj* **1** INBORN : inné **2** INHERENT : inhérent
inner ['ɪnər] *adj* : intérieur, interne
innermost ['ɪnər,mo:st] *adj* INMOST : le plus profond, le plus intime
innersole ['ɪnər'so:l] → **insole**
inning ['ɪnɪŋ] *n* : tour *m* de batte, manche *f* *Can* (au baseball)
innkeeper ['ɪn,ki:pər] *n* : aubergiste *mf*
innocence ['ɪnəsənʦ] *n* : innocence *f*
innocent[1] ['ɪnəsənt] *adj* : innocent
innocent[2] *n* : innocent *m*, -cente *f*
innocently ['ɪnəsəntli] *adv* : innocemment
innocuous [ɪ'nɑkjəwəs] *adj* : inoffensif
innovate ['ɪnə,veɪt] *v* **-vated; -vating** : innover
innovation [,ɪnə'veɪʃən] *n* : innovation *f*
innovative ['ɪnə,veɪt̬ɪv] *adj* : innovateur, novateur
innovator ['ɪnə,veɪt̬ər] *n* : innovateur *m*, -trice *f*; novateur *m*, -trice *f*

innuendo [ˌɪnjuˈɛndoʊ] *n, pl* **-dos** *or* **-does** : insinuation *f*, allusion *f* (malveillante)
innumerable [ɪˈnuːmərəbəl, -ˈnjuː-] *adj* : innombrable, sans nombre
inoculate [ɪˈnɑkjəˌleɪt] *vt* **-lated; -lating** : inoculer, vacciner
inoculation [ɪˌnɑkjəˈleɪʃən] *n* : inoculation *f*
inoffensive [ˌɪnəˈfɛntsɪv] *adj* : inoffensif
inoperable [ɪnˈɑpərəbəl] *adj* : inopérable
inoperative [ɪnˈɑpərəṭɪv, -ˌreɪ-] *adj* : inopérant
inopportune [ɪnˌɑpərˈtuːn, -ˈtjuːn] *adj* : inopportun
inopportunely [ɪnˌɑpərˈtuːnli, -ˈtjuːn-] *adv* : inopportunément
inordinate [ɪnˈɔrdənət] *adj* : excessif, démesuré — **inordinately** *adv*
inorganic [ˌɪnɔrˈgænɪk] *adj* : inorganique
inpatient [ˈɪnˌpeɪʃənt] *n* : malade *m* hospitalisé, malade *f* hospitalisée
input[1] [ˈɪnˌpʊt] *vt* **inputted** *or* **input; inputting** : entrer (des données)
input[2] *n* **1** CONTRIBUTION : contribution *f*, concours *m* **2** ENTRY : entrée *f* (de données) **3** ADVICE, OPINION : conseils *mpl*
inquest [ˈɪnˌkwɛst] *n* : enquête *f*
inquire [ɪnˈkwaɪr] *v* **-quired; -quiring** *vt* : demander — *vi* **1 to inquire about** : se renseigner sur, s'informer de **2 to inquire into** INVESTIGATE : enquêter sur
inquirer [ɪnˈkwaɪrər] *n* : investigateur *m*, -trice *f*
inquiringly [ɪnˈkwaɪrɪŋli] *adv* : d'un air interrogateur
inquiry [ɪnˈkwaɪri, ˈɪnˌkwaɪri, ˈɪnkwəri] *n, pl* **-ries 1** QUESTION : demande *f* **2** INVESTIGATION : enquête *f*
inquisition [ˌɪnkwəˈzɪʃən, ˌɪŋ-] *n* **1** : inquisition *f* **2 the Inquisition** : l'Inquisition *f*
inquisitive [ɪnˈkwɪzəṭɪv] *adj* : inquisiteur, curieux
inquisitively [ɪnˈkwɪzəṭɪvli] *adv* : avec curiosité
inquisitiveness [ɪnˈkwɪzəṭɪvnəs] *n* : curiosité *f*
inroad [ˈɪnˌroːd] *n* **1** ENCROACHMENT : incursion *f* **2 to make inroads into** : entamer
inrush [ˈɪnˌrʌʃ] *n* : irruption *f*
insane [ɪnˈseɪn] *adj* **1** MAD : fou **2** ABSURD : insensé, démentiel
insanely [ɪnˈseɪnli] *adv* : follement, comme un fou
insanity [ɪnˈsænəṭi] *n, pl* **-ties** : folie *f*, démence *f*
insatiable [ɪnˈseɪʃəbəl] *adj* : insatiable
inscribe [ɪnˈskraɪb] *vt* **-scribed; -scribing 1** ENGRAVE : graver **2** ENROLL : inscrire **3** DEDICATE : dédicacer (un livre, etc.)
inscription [ɪnˈskrɪpʃən] *n* : inscription *f*
inscrutable [ɪnˈskruːṭəbəl] *adj* : impénétrable, énigmatique
inseam [ˈɪnˌsiːm] *n* : longueur *f* d'un pantalon
insect [ˈɪnˌsɛkt] *n* : insecte *m*
insecticide [ɪnˈsɛktəˌsaɪd] *n* : insecticide *m*
insecure [ˌɪnsɪˈkjʊr] *adj* **1** UNCERTAIN : incertain **2** UNSAFE : peu sûr **3** FEARFUL : anxieux
insecurity [ˌɪnsɪˈkjʊrəṭi] *n, pl* **-ties** : insécurité *f*, manque *m* d'assurance
inseminate [ɪnˈsɛməˌneɪt] *vt* **-nated; -nating** : inséminer
insemination [ɪnˌsɛməˈneɪʃən] *n* : insémination *f*
insensibility [ɪnˌsɛntsəˈbɪləṭi] *n, pl* **-ties** : insensibilité *f*
insensible [ɪnˈsɛntsəbəl] *adj* **1** NUMB : insensible **2** UNCONSCIOUS : inconscient **3** UNAWARE : inconscient
insensitive [ɪnˈsɛntsəṭɪv] *adj* : insensible
insensitivity [ɪnˌsɛntsəˈtɪvəṭi] *n* : insensibilité *f*
inseparable [ɪnˈsɛpərəbəl] *adj* : inséparable
insert[1] [ɪnˈsɛrt] *vt* : insérer, introduire
insert[2] [ˈɪnˌsərt] *n* : insertion *f*, encart *m* (dans un texte)
insertion [ɪnˈsərʃən] *n* : insertion *f*
inset [ˈɪnˌsɛt] *n* **1** INSERTION : insertion *f* **2** : encart *m* (dans un livre), entre-deux *m* (dans un vêtement), insert *m* (dans une carte)
inshore[1] [ˈɪnˈʃor] *adv* : vers la côte, près de la côte
inshore[2] *adj* : côtier
inside[1] [ɪnˈsaɪd, ˈɪnˌsaɪd] *adv* : à l'intérieur
inside[2] *adj* : intérieur <the inside pages : les pages intérieures> <to get inside information : obtenir des renseignements à la source>
inside[3] *n* **1** : intérieur *m* **2 insides** *npl* GUTS : entrailles *fpl*, tripes *fpl fam*
inside[4] *prep* : à l'intérieur de
inside of *prep* INSIDE : à l'intérieur de, dans
inside out *adv* : à l'envers
insider [ɪnˈsaɪdər] *n* : initié *m*, -tiée *f*
insidious [ɪnˈsɪdiəs] *adj* : insidieux — **insidiously** *adv*
insight [ˈɪnˌsaɪt] *n* **1** PERSPICACITY : perspicacité *f* **2** UNDERSTANDING : aperçu *m*
insightful [ˈɪnsaɪtfəl] *adj* : perspicace
insignia [ɪnˈsɪgniə] *or* **insigne** [-ˌniː] *n, pl* **-nia** *or* **-nias** : insigne *m*
insignificance [ˌɪnsɪgˈnɪfɪkənts] *n* : insignifiance *f*
insignificant [ˌɪnsɪgˈnɪfɪkənt] *adj* : insignifiant
insincere [ˌɪnsɪnˈsɪr] *adj* : pas sincère
insincerely [ˌɪnsɪnˈsɪrli] *adv* : de manière peu sincère

insincerity [ˌɪnsɪnˈsɛrəṭi, -ˈsɪr-] *n, pl* **-ties** : manque *m* de sincérité
insinuate [ɪnˈsɪnjuˌeɪt] *vt* **-ated; -ating** : insinuer
insinuation [ɪnˌsɪnjuˈeɪʃən] *n* : insinuation *f*
insipid [ɪnˈsɪpəd] *adj* : fade, insipide
insist [ɪnˈsɪst] *vi* : insister — *vt* AFFIRM, MAINTAIN : affirmer, insister
insistence [ɪnˈsɪstənṭs] *n* : insistance *f*
insistent [ɪnˈsɪstənṭ] *adj* PERSISTENT : insistant **2** COMPELLING : pressant
insistently [ɪnˈsɪstəntli] *adv* : avec insistance
insofar as [ˌɪnsoˈfɑræz] *conj* : dans la mesure où
insole [ˈɪnˌso:l] *n* : semelle *f* (intérieure)
insolence [ˈɪnṭsələnṭs] *n* : insolence *f*
insolent [ˈɪnṭsələnṭ] *adj* : insolent
insolubility [ɪnˌsɑljuˈbɪləṭi] *n* : insolubilité *f*
insoluble [ɪnˈsɑljuḃəl] *adj* : insoluble
insolvency [ɪnˈsɑlvənṭsi] *n, pl* **-cies** : insolvabilité *f*
insolvent [ɪnˈsɑlvənṭ] *adj* : insolvable
insomnia [ɪnˈsɑmniə] *n* : insomnie *f*
insomuch as [ˌɪnsoˈmʌtʃæz] → **inasmuch as**
insomuch that *conj* SO : à tel point que
inspect [ɪnˈspɛkt] *vt* **1** EXAMINE : examiner, inspecter **2** REVIEW : passer en revue (des troupes)
inspection [ɪnˈspɛkʃən] *n* **1** : inspection *f* **2** : revue *f* (des troupes)
inspector [ɪnˈspɛktər] *n* : inspecteur *m*, -trice *f*
inspiration [ˌɪnṭspəˈreɪʃən] *n* : inspiration *f*
inspirational [ˌɪnṭspəˈreɪʃənəl] *adj* : inspirant
inspire [ɪnˈspaɪr] *v* **-spired; -spiring** *vt* **1** INHALE : inspirer, aspirer **2** INCITE : stimuler, inciter **3** IMPEL, MOTIVATE : inspirer, motiver — *vi* INHALE : inspirer
instability [ˌɪnṭstəˈbɪləṭi] *n* : instabilité *f*
install [ɪnˈstɔl] *vt* **-stalled; -stalling 1** : installer <to install a fan : installer un ventilateur> <to install a new president : installer un nouveau président> **2 to install oneself** SETTLE : s'installer
installation [ˌɪnṭstəˈleɪʃən] *n* : installation *f*
installment [ɪnˈstɔlmənt] *n* **1** PAYMENT : versement *m*, acompte *m* **2** CHAPTER, EPISODE : épisode *m*
instance [ˈɪnṭstənṭs] *n* **1** CIRCUMSTANCE : cas *m*, circonstance *f* <in the first instance : en premier lieu> **2** EXAMPLE : exemple *m* <for instance : par exemple>
instant[1] [ˈɪnṭstənṭ] *adj* **1** IMMEDIATE : instantané, immédiat **2** : instantané, soluble <instant coffee : café instantané>
instant[2] *n* MOMENT : instant *m*, moment *m*
instantaneous [ˌɪnṭstənˈteɪniəs] *adj* : instantané — **instantaneously** *adv*
instantly [ˈɪnṭstəntli] *adv* : instantanément, immédiatement, sur-le-champ
instead [ɪnˈstɛd] *adv* : plutôt, au lieu de cela <she couldn't go, so I went instead : elle n'a pas pu y aller, donc j'y suis allé à sa place>
instead of *prep* : au lieu de, à la place de
instep [ˈɪnˌstɛp] *n* : cou-de-pied *m*
instigate [ˈɪnṭstəˌgeɪt] *vt* **-gated; -gating** : inciter, engager
instigation [ˌɪnṭstəˈgeɪʃən] *n* : instigation *f*, incitation *f*
instigator [ˈɪnṭstəˌgeɪṭər] *n* : instigateur *m*, -trice *f*
instill *or Brit* **instil** [ɪnˈstɪl] *vt* **-stilled; -stilling** : instiller, inculquer
instinct [ˈɪnˌstɪŋkt] *n* : instinct *m*
instinctive [ɪnˈstɪŋktɪv] *adj* : instinctif — **instinctively** *adv*
instinctual [ɪnˈstɪŋktʃʊəl] *adj* : instinctif
institute[1] [ˈɪnstəˌtu:t, -ˌtju:t] *vt* **-tuted; -tuting** : instituer
institute[2] *n* : institut *m*
institution [ˌɪnstəˈtu:ʃən, -ˈtju:-] *n* : institution *f*, établissement *m*
institutional [ˌɪnstəˈtu:ʃənəl, -ˈtju:-] *adj* : institutionnel
institutionalize [ˌɪnstəˈtu:ʃənəˌlaɪz, -ˈtju:-] *vt* **-ized; -izing 1** ESTABLISH : institutionnaliser **2** INTERN : interner, placer dans un établissement spécialisé
instruct [ɪnˈstrʌkt] *vt* **1** TEACH : instruire, former, enseigner **2** COMMAND : charger
instruction [ɪnˈstrʌkʃən] *n* : instruction *f*
instructional [ɪnˈstrʌkʃənəl] *adj* : instructif, éducatif
instructive [ɪnˈstrʌktɪv] *adj* : instructif
instructor [ɪnˈstrʌktər] *n* : instructeur *m*, -trice *f*; éducateur *m*, -trice *f*
instrument [ˈɪnṭstrəmənt] *n* : instrument *m*
instrumental [ˌɪnṭstrəˈmentəl] *adj* **1** : instrumental **2 to be instrumental in** : contribuer à
instrumentalist [ˌɪnṭstrəˈmentəlɪst] *n* : instrumentaliste *mf*
insubordinate [ˌɪnsəˈbɔrdənət] *adj* : insubordonné
insubordination [ˌɪnsəˌbɔrdənˈeɪʃən] *n* : insubordination *f*
insubstantial [ˌɪnsəbˈstænʃəl] *adj* **1** : peu substantiel, peu solide **2** IMAGINARY : imaginaire, irréel
insufferable [ɪnˈsʌfərəḃəl] *adj* : intolérable, insupportable — **insufferably** [-bli] *adv*
insufficiency [ˌɪnsəˈfɪʃənṭsi] *n, pl* **-cies** : insuffisance *f*
insufficient [ˌɪnsəˈfɪʃənṭ] *adj* : insuffisant — **insufficiently** *adv*

insular [ˈɪnʃʊlər, -sjʊ-] *adj* **1** : insulaire **2** NARROW-MINDED : borné, étroit d'esprit
insularity [ˌɪnʃʊˈlærəṭi, -sjʊ-] *n* : insularité *f*
insulate [ˈɪnsəˌleɪt] *vt* **-lated; -lating** : isoler
insulation [ˌɪnsəˈleɪʃən] *n* **1** : isolation *f* <thermal insulation : isolation thermique> **2** (*referring to material*) : isolant *m* <fiberglass insulation : isolant en fibre de verre>
insulator [ˈɪnsəˌleɪṭər] *n* : isolateur *m*
insulin [ˈɪnsələn] *n* : insuline *f*
insult[1] [ɪnˈsʌlt] *vt* : insulter, injurier
insult[2] [ˈɪnˌsʌlt] *n* : insulte *f*, injure *f*
insulting [ɪnˈsʌltɪŋ] *adj* : insultant, injurieux
insultingly [ɪnˈsʌltɪŋli] *adv* : de façon insultante
insurance [ɪnˈʃʊrənʦ] *n* : assurance *f* <fire insurance : assurance contre l'incendie>
insure [ɪnˈʃʊr] *vt* **-sured; -suring 1** UNDERWRITE : assurer **2** ENSURE : assurer, garantir
insured [ɪnˈʃʊrd] *n* : assuré *m*, -rée *f*
insurer [ɪnˈʃʊrər] *n* : assureur *m*
insurgence [ɪnˈsərdʒənʦ] *n* : insurrection *f*
insurgency [ɪnˈsərdʒənʦi] *n, pl* **-cies** → **insurgence**
insurgent[1] [ɪnˈsərdʒənt] *adj* : insurgé
insurgent[2] *n* : insurgé *m*, -gée *f*
insurmountable [ˌɪnsərˈmaʊntəbəl] *adj* : insurmontable
insurrection [ˌɪnsəˈrɛkʃən] *n* : insurrection *f*
intact [ɪnˈtækt] *adj* : intact
intake [ˈɪnˌteɪk] *n* **1** OPENING : prise *f*, arrivée *f* <intake valve : soupape d'admission> **2** ADMISSION : admission *f* **3** CONSUMPTION : consommation *f*
intangible [ɪnˈtændʒəbəl] *adj* : intangible
integer [ˈɪntɪdʒər] *n* : nombre *m* entier
integral [ˈɪntɪgrəl] *adj* **1** ENTIRE, WHOLE : intégral, complet **2** CONSTITUENT : intégrant <to be an integral part of : faire partie intégrante de>
integrate [ˈɪntəˌgreɪt] *v* **-grated; -grating** *vt* : intégrer — *vi* : s'intégrer
integration [ˌɪntəˈgreɪʃən] *n* : intégration *f*
integrity [ɪnˈtɛgrəṭi] *n* : intégrité *f*
intellect [ˈɪntəˌlɛkt] *n* : intelligence *f*, esprit *m*
intellectual[1] [ˌɪntəˈlɛktʃʊəl] *adj* : intellectuel — **intellectually** *adv*
intellectual[2] *n* : intellectuel *m*, -tuelle *f*
intellectualism [ˌɪntəˈlɛktʃʊəˌlɪzəm] *n* : intellectualisme *m*
intelligence [ɪnˈtɛlədʒənʦ] *n* **1** : intelligence *f* **2** INFORMATION : renseignements *mpl*
intelligent [ɪnˈtɛlədʒənt] *adj* : intelligent
intelligently [ɪnˈtɛlədʒəntli] *adv* : intelligemment
intelligibility [ɪnˌtɛlədʒəˈbɪləṭi] *n* : intelligibilité *f*
intelligible [ɪnˈtɛlədʒəbəl] *adj* : intelligible — **intelligibly** [-bli] *adv*
intemperance [ɪnˈtɛmpərənʦ] *n* : intempérance *f*, manque *m* de modération
intemperate [ɪnˈtɛmpərət] *adj* : intempérant, incontrôlé
intend [ɪnˈtɛnd] *vt* **1** DESTINE : destiner <a movie intended for children : un film destiné aux enfants> **2 to intend to** : avoir en tête de, avoir l'intention de <I intend to go : j'ai l'intention d'y aller, je pense y aller>
intended[1] [ɪnˈtɛndəd] *adj* **1** PLANNED : projeté, voulu **2** INTENTIONAL : intentionnel
intended[2] *n* BETROTHED : fiancé *m*, -cée *f*
intense [ɪnˈtɛnʦ] *adj* : intense, vif <intense pain : douleur intense>
intensely [ɪnˈtɛnʦli] *adv* **1** : intensément, avec intensité **2** EXTREMELY : extrêmement, profondément
intensification [ɪnˌtɛnʦəfəˈkeɪʃən] *n* : intensification *f*
intensify [ɪnˈtɛnʦəˌfaɪ] *v* **-fied; -fying** *vt* : intensifier, renforcer — *vi* : s'intensifier
intensity [ɪnˈtɛnʦəṭi] *n, pl* **-ties** : intensité *f*
intensive [ɪnˈtɛnʦɪv] *adj* : intensif — **intensively** [ɪnˈtɛnʦɪvli] *adv*
intent[1] [ɪnˈtɛnt] *adj* **1** CONCENTRATED : absorbé, fixe <an intent stare : un regard fixe> **2 intent on** *or* **intent upon** : résolu à
intent[2] *n* **1** PURPOSE : intention *f* **2 for all intents and purposes** : à toutes fins utiles
intention [ɪnˈtɛnʃən] *n* : intention *f*
intentional [ɪnˈtɛnʃənəl] *adj* : intentionnel, voulu
intentionally [ɪnˈtɛnʃənəli] *adv* : intentionnellement
intently [ɪnˈtɛntli] *adv* : attentivement
inter [ɪnˈtər] *vt* **-terred; -terring** : enterrer
interact [ˌɪntərˈækt] *vi* **1** : agir l'un sur l'autre <we interact well : le courant passe bien entre nous> **2** (*referring to chemical reactions*) : agir réciproquement
interaction [ˌɪntərˈækʃən] *n* : interaction *f*
interactive [ˌɪntərˈækṭɪv] *adj* : interactif
interbreed [ˌɪntərˈbriːd] *v* **-bred** [-ˈbrɛd]; **-breeding** *vt* : croiser — *vi* : se croiser
intercede [ˌɪntərˈsiːd] *vi* **-ceded; -ceding** : intercéder
intercept [ˌɪntərˈsɛpt] *vt* : intercepter

interception [ˌɪntərˈsɛpʃən] *n* : interception *f*
intercession [ˌɪntərˈsɛʃən] *n* : intercession *f*
interchange[1] [ˌɪntərˈtʃeɪndʒ] *vt* **-changed; -changing** EXCHANGE : échanger
interchange[2] *n* ['ɪntərˌtʃeɪndʒ] **1** EXCHANGE : échange *m* **2** JUNCTION : échangeur *m*
interchangeable [ˌɪntərˈtʃeɪndʒəbəl] *adj* : interchangeable
intercity ['ɪntərˈsɪti] *adj* : interurbain
intercollegiate [ˌɪntərkəˈliːdʒət, -dʒiət] *adj* : interuniversitaire
intercontinental [ˌɪntərˌkɑntənˈɛntəl] *adj* : intercontinental
intercourse ['ɪntərˌkɔrs] *n* **1** RELATIONS : relations *fpl*, rapports *mpl* **2** COPULATION : rapports *mpl* sexuels
interdenominational [ˌɪntərdɪˌnɑmə'neɪʃənəl] *adj* : interconfessionnel
interdepartmental [ˌɪntərdɪˌpɑrtˈmɛntəl, -ˌdiː-] *adj* : interdépartemental
interdependence [ˌɪntərdɪˈpɛndənts] *n* : interdépendance *f*
interdependent [ˌɪntərdɪˈpɛndənt] *adj* : interdépendant
interdict [ˌɪntərˈdɪkt] *vt* PROHIBIT : interdire
interest[1] ['ɪntrəst, -təˌrɛst] *vt* : intéresser
interest[2] *n* **1** CURIOSITY : intérêt *m* **2** BENEFIT : avantage *m*, intérêt *m* <the public interest : l'intérêt public> **3** CHARGE : intérêt *m*, intérêts *mpl* <compound interest : intérêts composés> <interest rate : taux d'intérêt> **4** SHARE, STAKE : intérêts *mpl* **5** PURSUIT : centre *m* d'intérêt
interesting ['ɪntrəstɪŋli, -təˌrɛstɪŋli] *adj* : intéressant
interestingly ['ɪntrəstɪŋ, -təˌrɛstɪŋ] *adv* : de façon intéressante
interface ['ɪntərˌfeɪs] *n* : interface *f*
interfere [ˌɪntərˈfɪr] *vi* **-fered; -fering 1** INTERVENE : intervenir, s'interposer **2** MEDDLE : s'immiscer, s'ingérer **3 to interfere with** DISRUPT : perturber, déranger **4 to interfere with** TOUCH : toucher à <who interfered with my work? : qui est-ce qui a touché à mon travail?>
interference [ˌɪntərˈfɪrənts] *n* **1** INTERVENTION : intervention *f*, ingérence *f* **2** : interférence *f* (en physique, de radio, etc.)
intergalactic [ˌɪntərgəˈlæktɪk] *adj* : intergalactique
intergovernmental [ˌɪntərˌgʌvərˈmɛntəl, -vərn-] *adj* : intergouvernemental
interim[1] [ˌɪntərəm] *adj* : provisoire, intérimaire <interim government : gouvernement provisoire>
interim[2] *n* **1** : intérim *m* **2 in the interim** : entre-temps
interior[1] [ɪnˈtɪriər] *adj* : intérieur
interior[2] *n* : intérieur *m*
interject [ˌɪntərˈdʒɛkt] *vt* : placer, lancer (un mot)
interjection [ˌɪntərˈdʒɛkʃən] *n* **1** : interjection *f* (en linguistique) **2** INTERRUPTION : interruption *f*
interlace [ˌɪntərˈleɪs] *vt* **-laced; -lacing** : entrelacer, entrecroiser
interlock [ˌɪntərˈlɑk] *vt* **1** INTERTWINE : entrelacer **2** ENGAGE, MESH : enclencher — *vi* : s'enclencher
interloper [ˌɪntərˈloːpər] *n* INTRUDER : intrus *m*, -truse *f*
interlude ['ɪntərˌluːd] *n* **1** INTERVAL : intervalle *m* **2** : intermède *m* (au théâtre) **3** : interlude *m* (en musique)
intermarriage [ˌɪntərˈmærɪdʒ] *n* : mariage *m* mixte
intermarry [ˌɪntərˈmæri] *vi* **-married; -marrying 1** : se marier (entre membres d'autres groupes) **2** : se marier entre soi (entre membres du même groupe)
intermediary[1] [ˌɪntərˈmiːdiˌɛri] *adj* : intermédiaire
intermediary[2] *n, pl* **-aries** : intermédiaire *mf*
intermediate[1] [ˌɪntərˈmiːdiət] *adj* : intermédiaire
intermediate[2] *n* : intermédiaire *mf*
interment [ɪnˈtərmənt] *n* : enterrement *m*, inhumation *f*
interminable [ɪnˈtərmənəbəl] *adj* : interminable — **interminably** [-bli] *adv*
intermingle [ˌɪntərˈmɪŋgəl] *v* **-mingled; -mingling** *vt* : entremêler — *vi* : se mélanger, s'entremêler
intermission [ˌɪntərˈmɪʃən] *n* **1** BREAK, PAUSE : interruption *f*, pause *f* **2** : entracte *m* (au théâtre)
intermittent [ˌɪntərˈmɪtənt] *adj* : intermittent
intermittently [ˌɪntərˈmɪtəntli] *adv* : par intermittence
intern[1] ['ɪnˌtərn, ɪnˈtərn] *vt* : interner — *vi* : faire un stage, faire son internat (en médecine)
intern[2] ['ɪnˌtərn] *n* **1** : interne *mf* (à l'hôpital) **2** : stagiaire *mf* (en entreprise)
internal [ɪnˈtərnəl] *adj* **1** : interne <internal investigation : enquête interne> <internal bleeding : hémorragie interne> <internal combustion engine : moteur à combustion interne> **2** : intérieur <internal affairs : affaires intérieures>
internally [ɪnˈtərnəli] *adv* : intérieurement
international [ˌɪntərˈnæʃənəl] *adj* : international — **internationally** *adv*
internationalize [ˌɪntərˈnæʃənəˌlaɪz] *vt* **-ized; -izing** : internationaliser
internee [ˌɪnˌtərˈniː] *n* : interné *m*, -née *f*
Internet ['ɪntərˌnɛt] *n* : Internet *m*
internist ['ɪnˌtərnɪst] *n* : interniste *mf*
internment [ɪnˈtərnmənt, 'ɪn-] *n* : internement *m*

internship [ˈɪnˌtɛrnˌʃɪp] *n* : stage *m* (en entreprise), internat *m* (en médecine)
interpersonal [ˌɪntərˈpərsənəl] *adj* : interpersonnel
interplay [ˈɪntərˌpleɪ] *n* : interaction *f*
interpolate [ɪnˈtərpəˌleɪt] *vt* **-lated; -lating** : interpoler
interpose [ˌɪntərˈpoːz] *v* **-posed; -posing** *vt* : interposer — *vi* : s'interposer, intervenir
interposition [ˌɪntərpəˈzɪʃən] *n* : interposition *f*
interpret [ɪnˈtərprət] *vt* : interpréter
interpretation [ɪnˌtərprəˈteɪʃən] *n* : interprétation *f*
interpretative [ɪnˈtərprəˌteɪtɪv] *adj* : interprétatif
interpreter [ɪnˈtərprət̬ər] *n* : interprète *mf*
interpretive [ɪnˈtərprət̬ɪv] → **interpretative**
interracial [ˌɪntərˈreɪʃəl] *adj* : interracial
interrelate [ˌɪntərɪˈleɪt] *v* **-lated; -lating** *vt* : mettre en corrélation — *vi* : être en corrélation
interrelationship [ˌɪntərɪˈleɪʃənˌʃɪp] *n* : interrelation *f*, corrélation *f*
interrogate [ɪnˈterəˌgeɪt] *vt* **-gated; -gating** : interroger
interrogation [ɪnˌterəˈgeɪʃən] *n* : interrogation *f*
interrogative[1] [ˌɪntəˈrɑgət̬ɪv] *adj* : interrogatif, interrogateur
interrogative[2] *n* : interrogatif *m* (en linguistique)
interrogator [ɪnˈterəˌgeɪt̬ər] *n* : interrogateur *m*, -trice *f*
interrogatory [ˌɪntəˈrɑgəˌtɔri] → **interrogative**[1]
interrupt [ˌɪntəˈrʌpt] *v* : interrompre
interruption [ˌɪntəˈrʌpʃən] *n* : interruption *f*
intersect [ˌɪntərˈsɛkt] *vt* : croiser, couper — *vi* : se croiser, se couper
intersection [ˌɪntərˈsɛkʃən] *n* **1** JUNCTION : croisement *m*, carrefour *m* **2** : intersection *f* (en géométrie)
intersperse [ˌɪntərˈspɛrs] *vt* **-spersed; -spersing** : parsemer, entremêler
interstate [ˈɪntərˌsteɪt] *n or* **interstate highway** : autoroute *f*
interstellar [ˌɪntərˈstɛlər] *adj* : interstellaire
interstice [ɪnˈtərstəs] *n, pl* **-stices** [-stəˌsiːz, -stəsəz] : interstice *m*
intertwine [ˌɪntərˈtwaɪn] *v* **-twined; -twining** *vt* : entrelacer — *vi* : s'entrelacer
interval [ˈɪntərvəl] *n* : intervalle *m*
intervene [ˌɪntərˈviːn] *vi* **-vened; -vening** **1** ELAPSE : s'écouler **2** INTERCEDE : intervenir, s'interposer
intervention [ˌɪntərˈvɛnʃən] *n* : intervention *f*
interview[1] [ˈɪntərˌvjuː] *vt* **1** : faire passer un entretien, faire passer une entrevue **2** : interviewer (à la télévision, etc.)
interview[2] *n* **1** : entretien *m*, entrevue *f* **2** : interview *f* (à la télévision, etc.)
interviewer [ˈɪntərˌvjuːər] *n* **1** : personne *f* qui fait passer des entretiens **2** : intervieweur *m*, -vieweuse *f* (à la télévision)
interweave [ˌɪntərˈwiːv] *v* **-wove** [-ˈwoːv]; **-woven** [-ˈwoːvən]; **-weaving** *vt* : entremêler, entrelacer — *vi* : s'entremêler, s'entrelacer
intestate [ɪnˈtɛsˌteɪt, -t̬ət] *adj* : intestat
intestinal [ɪnˈtɛstənəl] *adj* : intestinal
intestine [ɪnˈtɛstən] *n* : intestin *m* <large intestine : gros intestin> <small intestine : intestin grêle>
intimacy [ˈɪntəməsi] *n, pl* **-cies** : intimité *f*
intimate[1] [ˈɪntəˌmeɪt] *vt* **-mated; -mating** : laisser entendre, insinuer
intimate[2] [ˈɪntəmət] *adj* : intime — **intimately** *adv*
intimate[3] *n* : intime *mf*
intimation [ˌɪntəˈmeɪʃən] *n* : indication *f*, pressentiment *m*
intimidate [ɪnˈtɪməˌdeɪt] *vt* **-dated; -dating** : intimider
intimidation [ɪnˌtɪməˈdeɪʃən] *n* : intimidation *f*
into [ˈɪnˌtuː] *prep* **1** (*indicating motion*) : dans, en <to go into the house : entrer dans la maison> <to go into town : aller en ville> <to put into a drawer : mettre dans un tiroir> **2** (*indicating state or condition*) : en <to burst into tears : fondre en larmes> <to translate into English : traduire en anglais> **3** AGAINST : contre <to crash into a wall : s'écraser contre un mur> **4** (*used in mathematics*) <3 into 12 is 4 : 12 divisé par 3 fait 4>
intolerable [ɪnˈtɑlərəbəl] *adj* : intolérable — **intolerably** [-bli] *adv*
intolerance [ɪnˈtɑlərənt̬s] *n* : intolérance *f*
intolerant [ɪnˈtɑlərənt] *adj* : intolérant
intonation [ˌɪntəˈneɪʃən] *n* : intonation *f*
intoxicate [ɪnˈtɑksəˌkeɪt] *vt* **-cated; -cating** : enivrer
intoxicated [ɪnˈtɑksəˌkeɪt̬əd] *adj* : ivre
intoxicating [ɪnˈtɑksəˌkeɪt̬ɪŋ] *adj* : enivrant, excitant
intoxication [ɪnˌtɑksəˈkeɪʃən] *n* : ivresse *f*
intractable [ɪnˈtræktəbəl] *adj* : intraitable, inflexible
intramural [ˌɪntrəˈmjʊrəl] *adj* : interne, entre élèves de la même université
intransigence [ɪnˈtrænsəd̬ʒənt̬s, -ˈtrænzə-] *n* : intransigeance *f*
intransigent [ɪnˈtrænsəd̬ʒənt, -ˈtrænzə-] *adj* : intransigeant
intravenous [ˌɪntrəˈviːnəs] *adj* : intraveineux
intrepid [ɪnˈtrɛpəd] *adj* : intrépide
intricacy [ˈɪntrɪkəsi] *n, pl* **-cies** : complexité *f*
intricate [ˈɪntrɪkət] *adj* : compliqué, complexe

intricately [ˈɪntrɪkətlɪ] *adv* : de façon complexe
intrigue[1] [ɪnˈtriːg] *v* **-trigued; -triguing** : intriguer
intrigue[2] [ˈɪnˌtriːg, ɪnˈtriːg] *n* : intrigue *f*
intriguing [ɪnˈtriːgɪŋ] *adj* : fascinant
intrinsic [ɪnˈtrɪnzɪk, -ˈtrɪnʃɪk] *adj* : intrinsèque — **intrinsically** [-zɪkli, -sɪ-] *adv*
introduce [ˌɪntrəˈduːs, -ˈdjuːs] *vt* **-duced; -ducing 1** : introduire (une idée, un nouveau produit, etc.) **2** PRESENT : présenter <let me introduce my father : permettez-moi de présenter mon père>
introduction [ˌɪntrəˈdʌkʃən] *n* **1** : introduction *f* (d'une idée, d'un produit, etc.) **2** PRESENTATION : présentation *f*
introductory [ˌɪntrəˈdʌktərɪ] *adj* : d'introduction, préliminaire
introspection [ˌɪntrəˈspɛkʃən] *n* : introspection *f*
introspective [ˌɪntrəˈspɛktɪv] *adj* : introspectif — **introspectively** *adv*
introvert [ˈɪntrəˌvərt] *n* : introverti *m*, -tie *f*
introverted [ˈɪntrəˌvərṭəd] *adj* : introverti
intrude [ɪnˈtruːd] *vi* **-truded; -truding 1** INTERRUPT : s'imposer <I don't wish to intrude : je ne veux pas vous déranger> **2** INTERFERE : s'ingérer, s'immiscer <to intrude on s.o.'s private life : s'immiscer dans la vie privée de qqn>
intruder [ɪnˈtruːdər] *n* : intrus *m*, -truse *f*
intrusion [ɪnˈtruːʒən] *n* : intrusion *f*
intrusive [ɪnˈtruːsɪv] *adj* : importun, gênant
intuit [ɪnˈtuːɪt, -ˈtjuː-] *vt* : savoir intuitivement
intuition [ˌɪntuˈɪʃən, -tjuː-] *n* : intuition *f*
intuitive [ɪnˈtuːəṭɪv, -ˈtjuː-] *adj* : intuitif — **intuitively** *adv*
Inuit[1] [ˈɪnuwət, -njuː-] *adj* : inuit
Inuit[2] *n* : Inuit *m*, Inuite *f*
inundate [ˈɪnənˌdeɪt] *vt* **-dated; -dating** : inonder
inundation [ˌɪnənˈdeɪʃən] *n* : inondation *f*
inure [ɪˈnʊr, -ˈnjʊr] *vt* **-ured; -uring** : endurcir <to be inured to hardship : être habitué aux épreuves>
invade [ɪnˈveɪd] *vt* **-vaded; -vading** : envahir
invader [ɪnˈveɪdər] *n* : envahisseur *m*, -seuse *f*
invalid[1] [ɪnˈvæləd] *adj* NULL : invalide
invalid[2] [ˈɪnvələd] *adj* ILL : malade, infirme
invalid[3] [ˈɪnvələd] *n* : invalide *mf*
invalidate [ɪnˈvæləˌdeɪt] *vt* **-dated; -dating** : invalider
invalidity [ˌɪnvəˈlɪdəṭɪ] *n, pl* **-ties** : invalidité *f*
invaluable [ɪnˈvæljəbəl, -ˈvæljʊə-] *adj* : inestimable, précieux
invariable [ɪnˈværiəbəl] *adj* : invariable — **invariably** [-bli] *adv*
invasion [ɪnˈveɪʒən] *n* : invasion *f*
invasive [ɪnˈveɪsɪv] *adj* : invasif
invective [ɪnˈvɛktɪv] *n* : invective *f*
inveigh [ɪnˈveɪ] *vi* **to inveigh against** : invectiver contre
inveigle [ɪnˈveɪgəl, -ˈviː-] *vt* **-gled; -gling** : enjôler, manipuler
invent [ɪnˈvɛnt] *vt* : inventer
invention [ɪnˈvɛnṭʃən] *n* : invention *f*
inventive [ɪnˈvɛnṭɪv] *adj* : inventif
inventiveness [ɪnˈvɛnṭɪvnəs] *n* : esprit *m* d'invention
inventor [ɪnˈvɛnṭər] *n* : inventeur *m*, -trice *f*
inventory[1] [ˈɪnvənˌṭɔrɪ] *vt* **-ried; -rying** : inventorier
inventory[2] *n, pl* **-ries 1** LIST : inventaire *m* **2** STOCK : stock *m*
inverse[1] [ɪnˈvərs, ˈɪnˌvərs] *adj* : inverse — **inversely** *adv*
inverse[2] *n* : inverse *m*
inversion [ɪnˈvərʒən] *n* : inversion *f*
invert [ɪnˈvərt] *vt* : inverser, renverser
invertebrate[1] [ɪnˈvərṭəbrət, -ˌbreɪt] *adj* : invertébré
invertebrate[2] *n* : invertébré *m*
invest [ɪnˈvɛst] *vt* **1** AUTHORIZE, EMPOWER : investir **2** CONFER, ENDOW : investir, revêtir **3** : investir (de l'argent, du temps, etc.) — *vi* : investir <to invest in stocks : investir en actions>
investigate [ɪnˈvɛstəˌgeɪt] *v* **-gated; -gating** *vt* : enquêter sur, examiner — *vi* : enquêter
investigation [ɪnˌvɛstəˈgeɪʃən] *n* : investigation *f*, enquête *f*
investigative [ɪnˈvɛstəˌgeɪṭɪv] *adj* : d'investigation <investigative reporter : journaliste d'investigation>
investigator [ɪnˈvɛstəˌgeɪṭər] *n* : investigateur *m*, -trice *f*
investiture [ɪnˈvɛstəˌṭʃʊr, -ṭʃər] *n* : investiture *f*
investment [ɪnˈvɛstmənt] *n* : investissement *m*, placement *m*
investor [ɪnˈvɛstər] *n* : investisseur *m*, -seuse *f*; actionnaire *mf*
inveterate [ɪnˈveṭərət] *adj* : invétéré
invidious [ɪnˈvɪdiəs] *adj* **1** OBNOXIOUS : odieux **2** UNJUST : injuste
invigorate [ɪnˈvɪgəˌreɪt] *vt* **-rated; -rating** : revigorer
invigorating [ɪnˈvɪgəˌreɪṭɪŋ] *adj* : revigorant
invigoration [ɪnˌvɪgəˈreɪʃən] *n* : revigoration *f*
invincibility [ɪnˌvɪnṭsəˈbɪləṭɪ] *n* : invincibilité *f*
invincible [ɪnˈvɪnṭsəbəl] *adj* : invincible
inviolable [ɪnˈvaɪələbəl] *adj* : inviolable
inviolate [ɪnˈvaɪələṭ] *adj* : inviolé
invisibility [ɪnˌvɪzəˈbɪləṭɪ] *n* : invisibilité *f*

invisible [ɪnˈvɪzəbəl] *adj* : invisible — **invisibly** [-bli] *adv*
invitation [ˌɪnvəˈteɪʃən] *n* : invitation *f*
invite [ɪnˈvaɪt] *vt* **-vited; -viting 1** ASK : inviter <we invited them for dinner : nous les avons invités à dîner> **2** PROVOKE : provoquer, chercher <to invite trouble : chercher des ennuis> **3** REQUEST, SOLICIT : solliciter (des questions, des observations, etc.)
inviting [ɪnˈvaɪtɪŋ] *adj* : attrayant, engageant
invocation [ˌɪnvəˈkeɪʃən] *n* : invocation *f*
invoice[1] [ˈɪnˌvɔɪs] *vt* **-voiced; -voicing** : facturer
invoice[2] *n* : facture *f*
invoke [ɪnˈvoːk] *vt* **-voked; -voking 1** : invoquer, demander (de l'aide, etc.) **2** CITE : invoquer **3** CONJURE UP : évoquer, invoquer (des esprits, etc.)
involuntary [ɪnˈvɑlənˌtɛri] *adj* : involontaire — **involuntarily** [ɪnˌvɑlənˈtɛrəli] *adv*
involve [ɪnˈvɑlv] *vt* **-volved; -volving 1** ENGAGE : engager **2** IMPLICATE : impliquer <to be involved in a crime : être impliqué dans un crime> **3** ENTAIL : entraîner, impliquer, occasionner
involved [ɪnˈvɑlvd] *adj* INTRICATE : compliqué
involvement [ɪnˈvɑlvmənt] *n* **1** PARTICIPATION : participation *f* **2** RELATIONSHIP : relation *f*, rapport *m*
invulnerable [ɪnˈvʌlnərəbəl] *adj* : invulnérable
inward[1] [ˈɪnwərd] *or* **inwards** [ˈɪnwərdz] *adv* : vers l'intérieur
inward[2] *adj* INSIDE : intérieur
inwardly [ˈɪnwərdli] *adv* **1** INTERNALLY : intérieurement **2** PRIVATELY : secrètement, en son for intérieur
iodide [ˈaɪəˌdaɪd] *n* : iodure *m*
iodine [ˈaɪəˌdaɪn] *n* : iode *m*, teinture *f* d'iode
iodized [ˈaɪəˌdaɪzd] *adj* : iodé
ion [ˈaɪən, ˈaɪˌɑn] *n* : ion *m*
ionize [ˈaɪəˌnaɪz] *v* **-ized; -izing** : ioniser
ionosphere [aɪˈɑnəˌsfɪr] *n* : ionosphère *f*
iota [aɪˈoːtə] *n* : iota *m*, brin *m*
IOU [ˌaɪˌoˈjuː] *n* : reconnaissance *f* de dette
Iranian[1] [ɪˈreɪnɪən, -ˈræ-, -ˈrɑ-; aɪ-] *adj* : iranien
Iranian[2] *n* : Iranien *m*, -nienne *f*
Iraqi[1] [ɪˈraki, -ˈræ-] *adj* : irakien
Iraqi[2] *n* : Irakien *m*, -kienne *f*
irascible [aɪˈræsəbəl] *adj* : irascible
irate [aɪˈreɪt] *adj* : furieux — **irately** *adv*
ire [ˈaɪr] *n* : courroux *m*, colère *f*
iridescence [ˌɪrəˈdesənts] *n* : irisation *f*
iridescent [ˌɪrəˈdesənt] *adj* : irisé
iris [ˈaɪrəs] *n*, *pl* **irises** *or* **irides** [ˈaɪrəˌdiːz, ˈɪr-] **1** : iris *m* (de l'œil) **2** *pl* **irises** : iris *m* (plante)
Irish[1] [ˈaɪrɪʃ] *adj* : irlandais
Irish[2] *n* **1** : irlandais *m* (langue) **2 the Irish** : les Irlandais
Irishman [ˈaɪrɪʃmən] *n* : Irlandais *m*
Irishwoman [ˈaɪrɪʃˌwʊmən] *n* : Irlandaise *f*
irk [ˈərk] *vt* : ennuyer, irriter, agacer
irksome [ˈərksəm] *adj* : ennuyeux, irritant, agaçant
iron[1] [ˈaɪərn] *vt* **1** : repasser (des vêtements) **2 to iron out** : aplanir (un problème) — *vi* : se repasser
iron[2] *n* **1** : fer *m* (métal) **2** : fer *m* à repasser
ironclad [ˈaɪərnˈklæd] *adj* **1** : cuirassé (se dit d'un navire) **2** STRICT : rigoureux, strict
ironic [aɪˈrɑnɪk] *or* **ironical** [-nɪkəl] *adj* : ironique — **ironically** [-kli] *adv*
ironing [ˈaɪərnɪŋ] *n* : repassage *m*
ironwork [ˈaɪərnˌwərk] *n* **1** : ferronnerie *f* **2 ironworks** *npl* : usine *f* sidérurgique
irony [ˈaɪrəni] *n*, *pl* **-nies** : ironie *f*
irradiate [ɪˈreɪdiˌeɪt] *vt* **-ated; -ating** : irradier
irradiation [ɪˌreɪdiˈeɪʃən] *n* : irradiation *f*
irrational [ɪˈræʃənəl] *adj* : irrationnel — **irrationally** *adv*
irrationality [ɪˌræʃəˈnæləti] *n* : irrationalité *f*
irreconcilable [ɪˌrɛkənˈsaɪləbəl] *adj* : irréconciliable, inconciliable
irrecoverable [ˌɪrɪˈkʌvərəbəl] *adj* : irrécupérable
irredeemable [ˌɪrɪˈdiːməbəl] *adj* **1** HOPELESS : irrémédiable **2** : non remboursable (se dit d'un bon, etc.)
irreducible [ˌɪrɪˈduːsəbəl, -ˈdjuː-] *adj* : irréductible — **irreducibly** [-bli] *adv*
irrefutable [ˌɪrɪˈfjuːtəbəl, ɪrˈrɛfjə-] *adj* : irréfutable — **irrefutably** [-bli] *adv*
irregular [ɪˈrɛgjələr] *adj* : irrégulier
irregularity [ɪˌrɛgjəˈlærəti] *n*, *pl* **-ties** : irrégularité *f*
irregularly [ɪˈrɛgjələrli] *adv* : irrégulièrement
irrelevance [ɪˈrɛləvənts] *n* : manque *m* de rapport
irrelevant [ɪˈrɛləvənt] *adj* : sans rapport, non pertinent
irreligious [ˌɪrɪˈlɪdʒəs] *adj* : irréligieux
irreparable [ɪˈrɛpərəbəl] *adj* : irréparable
irreplaceable [ˌɪrɪˈpleɪsəbəl] *adj* : irremplaçable
irrepressible [ˌɪrɪˈprɛsəbəl] *adj* : irrépressible
irreproachable [ˌɪrɪˈproːtʃəbəl] *adj* : irréprochable
irresistible [ˌɪrɪˈzɪstəbəl] *adj* : irrésistible — **irresistibly** [-bli] *adv*
irresolute [ɪˈrɛzəˌluːt] *adj* : irrésolu, indécis
irresolutely [ɪˈrɛzəˌluːtli, -ˌrɛzəˈluːt-] *adv* : d'un air indécis

irrespective of [ˌɪrɪˈspɛktɪvəv] *prep* : sans tenir compte de
irresponsibility [ˌɪrɪˌspɑnt͡səˈbɪləɾi] *n* : irresponsabilité *f*
irresponsible [ˌɪrɪˈspɑnt͡səbəl] *adj* : irresponsable
irresponsibly [ˌɪrɪˈspɑnt͡səbli] *adv* : de façon irresponsable
irretrievable [ˌɪrɪˈtriːvəbəl] *adj* **1** LOST : introuvable **2** IRREPARABLE : irréparable, irrémédiable
irreverence [ɪˈrɛvərənt͡s] *n* : irrévérence
irreverent [ɪˈrɛvərənt] *adj* : irrévérencieux
irreversible [ˌɪrɪˈvərsəbəl] *adj* : irréversible
irrevocable [ɪˈrɛvəkəbəl] *adj* : irrévocable — **irrevocably** [-bli] *adv*
irrigate [ˈɪrəˌɡeɪt] *vt* **-gated; -gating** : irriguer
irrigation [ˌɪrəˈɡeɪʃən] *n* : irrigation *f*
irritability [ˌɪrəɾəˈbɪləɾi] *n* : irritabilité *f*
irritable [ˈɪrəɾəbəl] *adj* : irritable
irritably [ˈɪrəɾəbli] *adv* : avec irritation
irritant[1] [ˈɪrətənt] *adj* : irritant
irritant[2] *n* : irritant *m*
irritate [ˈɪrəˌteɪt] *vt* **-tated; -tating 1** ANNOY : irriter, agacer **2** INFLAME : irriter
irritating [ˈɪrəˌteɪɾɪŋ] *adj* : irritant, agaçant
irritatingly [ˈɪrəˌteɪɾɪŋli] *adv* : de façon irritante
irritation [ˌɪrəˈteɪʃən] *n* : irritation *f*
is → be
Islam [ɪsˈlɑm, ɪz-, -ˈlæm; ˈɪsˌlɑm] *n* : islam *m* — **Islamic** [-mɪk] *adj*
island [ˈaɪlənd] *n* : île *f*
islander [ˈaɪləndər] *n* : insulaire *mf*
isle [ˈaɪl] *n* : île *f*, îlot *m*
islet [ˈaɪlət] *n* : îlot *m*
isolate [ˈaɪsəˌleɪt] *vt* **-lated; -lating** : isoler
isolation [ˌaɪsəˈleɪʃən] *n* : isolement *m* <to be in isolation : être isolé>
isometric [ˌaɪsəˈmɛtrɪk] *adj* : isométrique
isometrics [ˌaɪsəˈmɛtrɪks] *ns & pl* : exercices *mpl* isométriques
isosceles [aɪˈsɑsəˌliːz] *adj* : isocèle
isotope [ˈaɪsəˌtoːp] *n* : isotope *m*
Israeli[1] [ɪzˈreɪli] *adj* : israélien
Israeli[2] *n* : Israélien *m*, -lienne *f*
issue[1] [ˈiˌʃuː] *v* **-sued; -suing** *vi* **1** EMERGE : s'écouler, sortir, déboucher **2** EMANATE, RESULT : provenir, résulter — *vt* **1** EMIT : émaner, émettre **2** DISTRIBUTE : distribuer **3** PUBLISH : publier, sortir **4** GIVE : donner, émettre <to issue orders : donner des ordres> <to issue a permit : émettre un permis>
issue[2] *n* **1** EGRESS : sortie *f*, issue *f* **2** OFFSPRING : descendance *f*, progéniture *f* **3** RESULT : résultat *m* **4** MATTER, QUESTION : question *f*, problème *m* **5** PUBLICATION : publication *f*, émission *f* **6** : numéro *m* <the latest issue of the magazine : le dernier numéro de la revue>
isthmus [ˈɪsməs] *n* : isthme *m*
it [ˈɪt] *pron* **1** (*as subject*) : il, elle **2** (*as direct object*) : le, la l' <give it to me : donne-le moi> **3** (*as indirect object*) : lui <I'll give it some water : je lui donnerai de l'eau> **4** (*as a nonspecific subject*) : ce, cela, ça <it's me : c'est moi> <what does it mean? : qu'est-ce que cela veut dire?> <that's it : c'est ça> **5** (*as subject of an impersonal verb*) <it's snowing : il neige> <it doesn't matter : cela ne fait rien>
Italian[1] [ɪˈtæliən, aɪ-] *adj* : italien
Italian[2] *n* **1** : Italien *m*, -lienne *f* **2** : italien *m* (langue)
italic[1] [ɪˈtælɪk, aɪ-] *adj* : italique
italic[2] *n* : italique *m* <in italics : en italique>
italicize [ɪˈtæləˌsaɪz, aɪ-] *vt* **-cized; -cizing** : mettre en italique
itch[1] [ˈɪt͡ʃ] *vi* **1** : avoir des démangeaisons **2** DESIRE : avoir très envie
itch[2] *n* **1** IRRITATION : démangeaison *f* **2** URGE : envie *f*, démangeaison *f*
itchy [ˈɪt͡ʃi] *adj* **itchier; -est** : qui démange
item [ˈaɪɾəm] *n* **1** OBJECT : article *m* **2** POINT, ISSUE : point *m* **3** *or* **news item** ARTICLE : article *m*
itemize [ˈaɪɾəˌmaɪz] *vt* **-ized; -izing** : détailler
itinerant [aɪˈtɪnərənt] *adj* : itinérant, ambulant
itinerary [aɪˈtɪnəˌrɛri] *n, pl* **-aries** : itinéraire *m*
its ["Its] *adj* : son, sa, ses <she liked its smell : elle aimait son odeur>
it's ["Its] (*contraction of* **it is** *or* **it has**) **→ be, have**
itself [ɪtˌsɛlf] *pron* **1** (*used reflexively*) : se <the cat hurt itself : le chat s'est fait mal> **2** (*for emphasis*) : lui-même, elle-même, soi-même <the car itself was not damaged : la voiture elle-même n'était pas endommagée>
I've [ˈaɪv] (*contraction of* **I have**) **→ have**
ivory [ˈaɪvəri] *n, pl* **-ries** : ivoire *m*
ivy [ˈaɪvi] *n, pl* **ivies 1** : lierre *m* **2 → poison ivy**

J

j ['dʒeɪ] *n, pl* **j's** *or* **js** ['dʒeɪz] : j *m*, dixième lettre de l'alphabet

jab[1] ['dʒæb] *v* **jabbed; jabbing** *vt* **1** PIERCE : piquer **2** THRUST : enfoncer, planter — *vi* **to jab at** : donner un coup à, envoyer un direct à (un boxeur)

jab[2] *n* : petit coup *m*, direct *m* (en boxe)

jabber[1] ['dʒæbər] *vi* : jacasser, bavarder

jabber[2] *n* **1** CHATTER : bavardage *m*, papotage *m* **2** GIBBERISH : baragouin *m*

jack[1] ['dʒæk] *vt or* **to jack up 1** : soulever avec un cric **2** INCREASE : faire monter (des prix, etc.)

jack[2] *n* **1** : cric *m*, vérin *m* <hydraulic jack : vérin hydraulique> **2** FLAG : pavillon *m* **3** SOCKET : jack *m* **4** : valet *m* (aux cartes) **5 jacks** *npl* : osselets *mpl* (jeu)

jackal ['dʒækəl] *n* : chacal *m*

jackass ['dʒæk,æs] *n* **1** DONKEY : âne *m*, baudet *m fam* **2** FOOL : idiot *m*, -diote *f*

jacket ['dʒækət] *n* **1** : veste *f*, veston *m* **2** : jaquette *f* (d'un livre), pochette *f* (d'un disque)

jackhammer ['dʒæk,hæmər] *n* : marteau-piqueur *m*

jack–in–the–box ['dʒækɪnðə,bɑks] *n, pl* **jack–in–the–boxes** *or* **jacks–in–the–box** : diable *m* à ressort

jackknife[1] ['dʒæk,naɪf] *vi* **-knifed; -knifing** : se mettre en travers de la route (se dit d'un camion)

jackknife[2] *n, pl* **-knives:** couteau *m* de poche

jack–of–all–trades *n, pl* **jacks–of–all–trades** : homme *m* à tout faire

jack–o'–lantern ['dʒækə,læntərn] *n* : citrouille *f* taillée en forme de visage

jackpot ['dʒæk,pɑt] *n* : gros lot *m*

jackrabbit ['dʒæk,ræbət] *n* : gros lièvre *m* d'Amérique

jade ['dʒeɪd] *n* : jade *m*

jaded ['dʒeɪdəd] *adj* **1** EXHAUSTED : fatigué **2** BORED : blasé

jagged ['dʒægəd] *adj* : dentelé, irrégulier

jaguar ['dʒæg,wɑr, 'dʒægjʊ,wɑr] *n* : jaguar *m*

jail[1] ['dʒeɪl] *vt* : emprisonner, incarcérer

jail[2] *n* : prison *f*

jailbreak ['dʒeɪl,breɪk] *n* : évasion *f* de prison

jailer *or* **jailor** ['dʒeɪlər] *n* : geôlier *m*, -lière *f*

jalopy [dʒə'lɑpi] *n, pl* **-lopies** : tacot *m fam*, guimbarde *f fam*, bazou *m Can fam*

jam[1] ['dʒæm] *v* **jammed; jamming** *vt* **1** CRAM : entasser **2** : bloquer, coincer <the computer keys are jammed : les touches de l'ordinateur sont coincées> **3** CONGEST, OBSTRUCT : bloquer, boucher — *vi* **1** : se bloquer, se coincer **2** PACK : s'entasser, s'empiler

jam[2] *n* **1** CONGESTION : encombrement *m*, embouteillage *m* **2** PRESERVE : confiture *f* **3** FIX, PREDICAMENT : pétrin *m fam*

Jamaican[1] [dʒə'meɪkən] *adj* : jamaïquain

Jamaican[2] *n* : Jamaïquain *m*, -quaine *f*

jamb ['dʒæm] *n* : jambage *m*

jamboree [,dʒæmbə'ri:] *n* : grande fête *f*

jangle[1] ['dʒæŋgəl] *v* **-gled; -gling** *vi* : cliqueter — *vt* : faire cliqueter

jangle[2] *n* : cliquetis *m*

janitor ['dʒænətər] *n* : gardien *m*, -dienne *f*; concierge *mf*

January ['dʒænjʊ,ɛri] *n* : janvier *m*

Japanese[1] [,dʒæpə'ni:z, -'ni:s] *adj* : japonais

Japanese[2] *n* **1** : Japonais *m*, -naise *f* **2** : japonais *m* (langue)

jar[1] ['dʒɑr] *v* **jarred; jarring** *vi* **1** GRATE : grincer, crisser **2** CLASH : jurer **3 to jar on** : heurter <to jar on s.o.'s feelings : heurter la sensibilité de qqn> — *vt* **1** UNSETTLE : perturber **2** JOLT, SHAKE : ébranler, secouer

jar[2] *n* **1** JOLT, SHOCK : secousse *f*, choc *m* **2** : bocal *m*, pot *m* <a jar of honey : un bocal de miel>

jargon ['dʒɑrgən] *n* : jargon *m*

jasmine ['dʒæzmən] *n* : jasmin *m*

jasper ['dʒæspər] *n* : jaspe *m*

jaundice ['dʒɔndɪs] *n* : jaunisse *f*

jaundiced ['dʒɔndɪst] *adj* **1** : qui a la jaunisse **2** EMBITTERED : aigri, cynique, négatif <with a jaundiced eye : d'un mauvais œil>

jaunt ['dʒɔnt] *n* : balade *f*, excursion *f*

jauntily ['dʒɔntəli] *adv* : d'un air vif, joyeusement

jauntiness ['dʒɔntinəs] *n* : vivacité *f*, animation *f*

jaunty ['dʒɔnti] *adj* **jauntier; -est** : joyeux, guilleret

Javanese[1] [,dʒævə'ni:z, ,dʒavə-; -'ni:s] *adj* : javanais

Javanese[2] *n* : Javanais *m*, -naise *f*

javelin ['dʒævələn] *n* : javelot *m*

jaw[1] ['dʒɔ] *vi* GAB : papoter, bavarder

jaw[2] *n* **1** : mâchoire *f* (d'un animal, d'un outil) **2 the jaws of death** : les griffes de la mort

jawbone ['dʒɔ,boːn] *n* : maxillaire *m*

jay ['dʒeɪ] *n* : geai *m*

jaybird ['dʒeɪ,bərd] → **jay**

jaywalk ['dʒeɪ,wɔk] *vi* : traverser la rue en dehors des passages pour piétons

jaywalker ['dʒeɪ,wɔkər] *n* : piéton *m* qui traverse la rue en dehors des passages pour piétons

jazz[1] ['dʒæz] *vt or* **to jazz up** ENLIVEN : égayer, animer

jazz[2] *n* : jazz *m*
jazzy [ˈdʒæzi] *adj* **jazzier; -est 1** : de jazz **2** FLASHY, SHOWY : tapageur, voyant
jealous [ˈdʒɛləs] *adj* : jaloux — **jealously** *adv*
jealousy [ˈdʒɛləsi] *n, pl* **-sies** : jalousie *f*
jeans [ˈdʒiːnz] *npl* : jean *m*, blue-jean *m*
jeep [ˈdʒiːp] *n* : jeep *f*
jeer[1] [ˈdʒɪr] *vi* SCOFF : se moquer, se railler — *vt* **1** BOO : huer **2** TAUNT : railler
jeer[2] *n* TAUNT : raillerie *f*
Jehovah [dʒɪˈhoːvə] *n* : Jéhovah *m*
jell [ˈdʒɛl] *vi* **1** CONGEAL, SET : prendre (en gelée), se gélifier **2** CRYSTALLIZE : prendre forme
jelly[1] [ˈdʒɛli] *v* **jellied; jellying** *vi* JELL : se gélifier — *vt* : gélifier
jelly[2] *n, pl* **-lies** : gelée *f*
jellyfish [ˈdʒɛliˌfɪʃ] *n* : méduse *f*
jeopardize [ˈdʒɛpərˌdaɪz] *vt* **-dized; -dizing** : mettre en danger, compromettre
jeopardy [ˈdʒɛpərdi] *n* : danger *m*, péril *m*
jerk[1] [ˈdʒərk] *vt* **1** TUG, YANK : tirer brusquement **2** JOLT : secouer — *vi* *or* **to jerk about** : cahoter
jerk[2] *n* **1** JOLT : saccade *f*, secousse *f* **2** : mouvement *m* brusque <he got up with a jerk : il s'est levé brusquement> **3** FOOL : idiot *m*, -diote *f*
jerkily [ˈdʒərkəli] *adv* : d'une manière saccadée, par à-coups
jerkin [ˈdʒərkən] *n* : gilet *m*
jerky [ˈdʒərki] *adj* **jerkier; -est** : saccadé
jerry-built [ˈdʒɛriˌbɪlt] *adj* : peu solide, construit en carton-pâte
jersey [ˈdʒərzi] *n, pl* **-seys 1** : jersey *m* (tissu) **2** : tricot *m* (vêtement)
jest[1] [ˈdʒɛst] *vi* : plaisanter
jest[2] *n* : plaisanterie *f*
jester [ˈdʒɛstər] *n* : bouffon *m*
Jesus [ˈdʒiːzəs, -zəz] *n* : Jésus *m*
jet[1] [dʒɛt] *vi* **jetted; jetting 1** SPURT : gicler, jaillir **2** : voyager en avion
jet[2] *n* **1** : jais *m* (minéral) **2** SPURT : jet *m* **3** *or* **jet airplane** : jet *m*, avion *m* à réaction
jet engine *n* : moteur *m* à réaction, réacteur *m*
jet-propelled *adj* : à réaction
jetsam [ˈdʒɛtsəm] *n* : épave *f* flottante <flotsam and jetsam : épaves flottantes>
jettison [ˈdʒɛtəsən] *vt* **1** : jeter par-dessus bord **2** DISCARD : se débarrasser de
jetty [ˈdʒɛti] *n, pl* **-ties 1** PIER, WHARF : embarcadère *m* **2** BREAKWATER : jetée *f*, brise-lames *m*
Jew [ˈdʒuː] *n* : Juif *m*, Juive *f*
jewel [ˈdʒuːəl] *n* **1** : bijou *m* **2** GEM : pierre *f* précieuse **3** : rubis *m* (d'une montre) **4** TREASURE : perle *f* (personne)
jeweler *or* **jeweller** [ˈdʒuːələr] *n* : bijoutier *m*, -tière *f*; joaillier *m*, -lière *f*
jewelry *or Brit* **jewellery** [ˈdʒuːəlri] *n* : bijoux *mpl*
Jewish [ˈdʒuːɪʃ] *adj* : juif
jib [ˈdʒɪb] *n* : foc *m*
jibe [dʒaɪb] *vi* **jibed; jibing** AGREE : concorder
jiffy [ˈdʒɪfi] *n, pl* **-fies** : seconde *f*, instant *m* <in a jiffy : en un rien de temps>
jig[1] [ˈdʒɪg] *vi* **jigged; jigging** : danser la gigue
jig[2] *n* : gigue *f* (danse)
jigger [ˈdʒɪgər] *n* : mesure *f* qui contient une ou deux onces
jiggle[1] [ˈdʒɪgəl] *v* **-gled; -gling** *vt* : secouer, agiter — *vi* : se trémousser
jiggle[2] *n* : secousse *f*
jigsaw [ˈdʒɪgˌsɔ] *n* : scie *f* sauteuse
jigsaw puzzle *n* : puzzle *m*
jilt [ˈdʒɪlt] *vt* : abandonner, plaquer *fam*
jimmy[1] [ˈdʒɪmi] *vt* **-mied; -mying** : forcer à la pince-monseigneur
jimmy[2] *n, pl* **-mies** : pince-monseigneur *m*
jingle[1] [ˈdʒɪŋgəl] *v* **-gled; -gling** *vt* : faire tinter — *vi* : tinter
jingle[2] *n* **1** TINKLE : tintement *m* **2** : jingle *m*, refrain *m* publicitaire
jinx[1] [ˈdʒɪŋks] *vt* : porter la poisse à *fam*, porter la guigne à *fam*
jinx[2] *n* : guigne *f fam*, poisse *f fam*
jitters [ˈdʒɪtərz] *npl* : frousse *f* <to have the jitters : être nerveux>
jittery [ˈdʒɪtəri] *adj* : nerveux
job [ˈdʒɑb] *n* **1** EMPLOYMENT : emploi *m*, travail *m* <to have a good job : avoir une belle situation> **2** TASK, WORK : travail *m*, tâche *f*
jobber [ˈdʒɑbər] *n* : grossiste *mf*
jobless [ˈdʒɑbləs] *adj* : sans emploi
jockey[1] [ˈdʒɑki] *v* **-eyed; -eying** *vt* MANIPULATE : manoeuvrer, manipuler — *vi* **to jockey for position** : essayer de se placer
jockey[2] *n, pl* **-eys** : jockey *m*
jocose [dʒoˈkoːs] *adj* **1** MERRY : jovial, joyeux **2** HUMOROUS : facétieux
jocular [ˈdʒɑkjʊlər] *adj* : badin, jovial
jocularity [ˌdʒɑkjʊˈlærəti] *n* : jovialité *f*
jocularly [ˈdʒɑkjʊlərli] *adv* : joviale-ment
jodhpurs [ˈdʒɑdpərz] *npl* : jodhpurs *mpl*
jog[1] [ˈdʒɑg] *v* **jogged; jogging** *vt* **1** NUDGE : donner un petit coup à **2 to jog s.o.'s memory** : rafraîchir la mémoire à qqn — *vi* : faire du jogging
jog[2] *n* **1** PUSH, SHAKE : coup *m*, petite secousse *f* **2** : jogging *m* (aux sports), petit trot *m* (d'un cheval) **3** BEND : coude *m*, tournant *m* (d'une route)
jogger [ˈdʒɑgər] *n* : joggeur *m*, -geuse *f*
join [ˈdʒɔɪn] *vt* **1** UNITE : relier, unir <to be joined in marriage : être uni par les liens du mariage> **2** ADJOIN : avoisiner, être contigu à **3** MEET : rejoindre, retrouver **4** : se joindre à, de-

venir membre (d'un club, etc.) — *vi* **1** MEET : se rejoindre **2** : devenir membre (d'un club, etc.) **3 to join together** : s'unir, se rejoindre

joiner ['dʒɔɪnər] *n* CARPENTER : menuisier *m*

joint[1] [dʒɔɪnt] *adj* : commun, conjugué

joint[2] *n* **1** : articulation *f* <knee joint : articulation du genou> <to put one's shoulder out of joint : se déboîter l'épaule> **2** JUNCTURE : joint *m*, raccord *m* (en menuiserie)

jointed [dʒɔɪntəd] *adj* : articulé

jointly ['dʒɔɪntlɪ] *adv* : conjointement

joist ['dʒɔɪst] *n* : solive *f*

joke[1] ['dʒo:k] *vi* **joked; joking** : plaisanter

joke[2] *n* : plaisanterie *f*, blague *f*

joker ['dʒo:kər] *n* **1** WAG : farceur *m*, -ceuse *f*; blagueur *m*, -gueuse *f* **2** : joker *m* (aux cartes)

jokingly ['dʒo:kɪŋlɪ] *adv* : en plaisantant

jollity ['dʒɑlət̬ɪ] *n*, *pl* **-ties** : gaieté *f*

jolly ['dʒɑlɪ] *adj* **jollier; -est** : joyeux, gai

jolt[1] ['dʒo:lt] *vt* : secouer — *vi or* **to jolt along** : cahoter

jolt[2] *n* **1** BLOW, JAR : secousse *f*, coup *m* **2** SHOCK : choc *m* <the defeat was quite a jolt : la défaite nous a fait tout un choc>

jonquil ['dʒɑnkwɪl] *n* : jonquille *f*

Jordanian[1] [dʒɔr'deɪniən] *adj* : jordanien

Jordanian[2] *n* : Jordanien *m*, -nienne *f*

josh ['dʒɑʃ] *vt* TEASE : taquiner — *vi* JOKE : blaguer

jostle ['dʒɑsəl] *v* **-tled; -tling** *vt* : bousculer — *vi* : se bousculer

jot[1] ['dʒɑt] *vt* **jotted; jotting** : prendre note de <jot this down : prends ça en note>

jot[2] *n* BIT : iota *m* <it doesn't matter a jot : ça n'a pas la moindre importance>

jounce[1] ['dʒæonʦ] *vt* **jounced; jouncing** : secouer

jounce[2] *n* JOLT : secousse *f*

journal ['dʒərnəl] *n* **1** DIARY : journal *m* intime **2** PERIODICAL : revue *f* **3** NEWSPAPER : journal *m*, quotidien *m*

journalism ['dʒərnəl,ɪzəm] *n* : journalisme *m*

journalist ["dʒ^{ə}rn^{ə}lIst] *n* : journaliste *mf*

journalistic [,dʒərnə'ɪstɪk] *adj* : journalistique

journey[1] ['dʒərni] *vi* **-neyed; -neying** TRAVEL : voyager

journey[2] *n*, *pl* **-neys** : voyage *m*

journeyman ['dʒərnimən] *n*, *pl* **-men** [-mən, -,men] : compagnon *m*

joust[1] ['dʒɑʊst] *vi* : jouter

joust[2] *n* : joute *f*

jovial ['dʒo:viəl] *adj* : jovial — **jovially** *adv*

joviality [,dʒo:vi'ælət̬ɪ] *n* : jovialité *f*

jowl ['dʒæʊl] *n* **1** JAW : mâchoire *f* **2** CHEEK : bajoue *f*

joy ['dʒɔɪ] *n* **1** HAPPINESS : joie *f*, allégresse *f* **2** PLEASURE : joie *f*, plaisir *m* <she's the joy of my life : elle est la joie de ma vie>

joyful ['dʒɔɪfəl] *adj* : joyeux — **joyfully** *adv*

joyless ['dʒɔɪləs] *adj* : sans joie, triste

joyous ['dʒɔɪəs] *adj* JOYFUL : joyeux — **joyously** *adv*

joyride ['dʒɔɪ,raɪd] *n* : virée *f* dans une voiture volée

jubilant ['dʒu:bələnt] *adj* : exultant, débordant de joie

jubilation [,dʒu:bə'leɪʃən] *n* : jubilation *f*

jubilee ['dʒu:bə,li:] *n* : jubilé *m*

Judaic [dʒu:'deɪɪk] *adj* : judaïque

Judaism ['dʒu:də,ɪzəm, 'dʒu:di-, 'dʒu:,deɪ-] *n* : judaïsme *m*

judge[1] ['dʒʌdʒ] *vt* **judged; judging 1** ASSESS : juger, évaluer **2** TRY : juger (une cause) **3** CONSIDER, DEEM : juger, estimer

judge[2] *n* **1** : juge *m* **2 to be a good judge of** : savoir juger de, être un bon juge en

judgment *or* **judgement** ['dʒʌdʒmənt] *n* **1** RULING : jugement *m*, verdict *m* **2** OPINION : avis *m*, opinion *f* **3** DISCERNMENT : jugement *m*, discernement *m*

judgmental [,dʒʌdʒ'mentəl] *adj* : enclin à juger <to be judgmental : s'ériger toujours en juge>

judicature ['dʒu:dɪkə,t̬ʃʊr] *n* : justice *f*

judicial [dʒʊ'dɪʃəl] *adj* : judiciaire — **judicially** *adv*

judiciary[1] [dʒʊ'dɪʃi,eri, -'dɪʃəri] *adj* : judiciaire

judiciary[2] *n* **1 → judicature 2** : système *m* judiciaire

judicious [dʒʊ'dɪʃəs] *adj* : judicieux — **judiciously** *adv*

judo ['dʒu:,do:] *n* : judo *m*

jug ['dʒʌg] *n* : cruche *f*, pichet *m*, carafe *f*

juggernaut ['dʒʌgər,nɔt] *n* : force *f* irrésistible

juggle ['dʒʌgəl] *vi* **-gled; -gling 1** : jongler **2 to juggle with** MANIPULATE : jongler avec

juggler ['dʒʌgələr] *n* : jongleur *m*, -gleuse *f*

jugular vein ['dʒʌgjʊlər] *n* : jugulaire *f*

juice ['dʒu:s] *n* **1** : jus *m* <orange juice : jus d'orange> **2** ELECTRICITY : jus *m fam*, électricité *f*

juicer ['dʒu:sər] *n* : presse-fruits *m*

juiciness ['dʒu:sinəs] *n* : teneur *f* en jus

juicy ['dʒu:si] *adj* **juicier; -est 1** : juteux <a juicy fruit : un fruit juteux> **2** RACY : savoureux

jukebox ['dʒu:k,bɑks] *n* : juke-box *m*

julep ['dʒu:ləp] *n* : cocktail *m* à la menthe

July [dʒʊˈlaɪ] *n* : juillet *m*
jumble[1] [ˈdʒʌmbəl] *vt* **-bled; -bling** : brouiller, mélanger
jumble[2] *n* : fouillis *m*, désordre *m*
jumbo[1] [ˈdʒʌmˌboː] *adj* : énorme, géant
jumbo[2] *n, pl* **-bos** : quelque chose de très grand en son genre
jump[1] [ˈdʒʌmp] *vi* **1** LEAP : sauter, bondir **2** START : sursauter **3** MOVE : passer <she jumped from job to job : elle a passé d'un emploi à un autre> **4** RISE : monter en flèche (se dit des prix, etc) **5 to jump at** : saisir (une occasion, etc.) — *vt* : sauter, franchir <to jump a hurdle : franchir une haie>
jump[2] *n* **1** LEAP : saut *m*, bond *m* **2** INCREASE : bond *m*, hausse *f* **3** ADVANTAGE : avantage *m* <to get the jump on s.o. : devancer qqn>
jumper [ˈdʒʌmpər] *n* **1** : sauteur *m*, -teuse *f* (aux sports) **2** : robe-chasuble *f* (vêtement)
jumpy [ˈdʒʌmpi] *adj* **jumpier; -est** : nerveux
junction [ˈdʒʌŋkʃən] *n* **1** JOINING : jonction *f* **2** : carrefour *m*, embranchement *m* (de deux routes)
juncture [ˈdʒʌŋktʃər] *n* **1** JOINT : joint *m*, jointure *f* **2** POINT, SITUATION : conjoncture *f* <at this juncture : dans la conjoncture actuelle>
June [ˈdʒuːn] *n* : juin *m*
jungle [ˈdʒʌŋgəl] *n* : jungle *f*
junior[1] [ˈdʒuːnjər] *adj* **1** YOUNGER : cadet, plus jeune **2** SUBORDINATE : subalterne
junior[2] *n* **1** : cadet *m*, -dette *f* <a man six years my junior : un homme de six ans mon cadet> **2** SUBORDINATE : subalterne *mf* **3** : élève *mf* de troisième année; étudiant *m*, -diante *f* de troisième année
juniper [ˈdʒuːnəpər] *n* : genévrier *m*
junk[1] [ˈdʒʌŋk] *vt* SCRAP : balancer *fam*, mettre au rancart *fam*
junk[2] *n* **1** RUBBISH : camelote *f fam*, pacotille *f* **2** STUFF : choses *fpl*, trucs *mpl fam* **3** : jonque *f* (bateau)
junket [ˈdʒʌŋkət] *n* : voyage *m* (aux frais de l'État)
junta [ˈhʊntə, ˈdʒʌn-, ˈhʌn-] *n* : junte *f*
Jupiter [ˈdʒuːpətər] *n* : Jupiter *f* (planète)
jurisdiction [ˌdʒʊrəsˈdɪkʃən] *n* : juridiction *f*
jurisprudence [ˌdʒʊrəsˈpruːdəns] *n* : jurisprudence *f*
jurist [ˈdʒʊrɪst] *n* : juriste *mf*
juror [ˈdʒʊrər] *n* : juré *m*, -rée *f*
jury [ˈˈdʒʊri] *n, pl* **-ries** : jury *m*
just[1] [ˈdʒʌst] *adv* **1** EXACTLY : exactement <it's just right : c'est parfait> **2** : tout juste <the bell just rang : la cloche vient tout juste de sonner> **3** BARELY : à peine <he just made it : il est à peine arrivé à temps> **4** SIMPLY : simplement <just be yourself : sois toi-même, tout simplement> **5** QUITE : vraiment <just wonderful : vraiment merveilleux> **6** POSSIBLY : peut-être <it just might work : ça peut peut-être marcher> **7 just about** ALMOST : presque
just[2] *adj* **1** FAIR : juste, équitable **2** DESERVED : mérité
justice [ˈdʒʌstɪs] *n* **1** : justice *f*, équité *f* **2** JUDGE : juge *m*
justifiable [ˌdʒʌstəˈfaɪəbəl] *adj* : justifiable
justification [ˌdʒʌstəfəˈkeɪʃən] *n* : justification *f*
justify [ˈdʒʌstəˌfaɪ] *vt* **-fied; -fying** : justifier
justly [ˈdʒʌstli] *adv* : avec justice, justement
jut [ˈdʒʌt] *vi* **jutted; jutting** *or* **to jut out** : dépasser, s'avancer en saillie
jute [ˈdʒuːt] *n* : jute *m*
juvenile[1] [ˈdʒuːvəˌnaɪl, -vənəl] *adj* **1** YOUNG : jeune <juvenile delinquent : jeune délinquant> **2** CHILDISH : puéril
juvenile[2] *n* : mineur *m*, -neure *f*; jeune *mf*
juxtapose [ˈdʒʌkstəˌpoːz] *vt* **-posed; -posing** : juxtaposer
juxtaposition [ˌdʒʌkstəpəˈzɪʃən] *n* : juxtaposition *f*

K

k [ˈkeɪ] *n, pl* **k's** *or* **ks** [ˈkeɪz] : k *m*, onzième lettre de l'alphabet
kale [ˈkeɪl] *n* : chou *m* frisé
kaleidoscope [kəˈlaɪdəˌskoːp] *n* : kaléidoscope *m*
kangaroo [ˌkæŋgəˈruː] *n, pl* **-roos** : kangourou *m*
kaolin [ˈkeɪələn] *n* : kaolin *m*
karat [ˈkærət] *n* : carat *m*
karate [kəˈrɑṭi] *n* : karaté *m*
katydid [ˈkeɪṭiˌdɪd] *n* : sauterelle *f* d'Amérique du Nord
kayak [ˈkaɪˌæk] *n* : kayak *m*, kayac *m*
keel[1] [ˈkiːl] *vi* **to keel over** : chavirer (se dit d'un bateau), s'évanouir, tomber dans les pommes *fam* (se dit des personnes)
keel[2] *n* : quille *f*
keen [ˈkiːn] *adj* **1** SHARP : aiguisé, affilé **2** PENETRATING : vif, pénétrant **3** EA-

GER, ENTHUSIASTIC : enthousiaste **4** ACUTE : perçant <keen eyesight : vue perçante>

keenly ['kiːnli] *adv* : vivement, profondément

keep¹ ['kiːp] *v* **kept** [kɛpt]; **keeping** *vt* **1** FULFILL : tenir (une promesse, etc.) **2** PROTECT : garder **3** MAINTAIN : tenir, garder <to keep a diary : tenir un journal> **4** DETAIN, RETAIN : garder, retenir **5** PRESERVE : garder (un secret) **6 to keep out** : empêcher d'entrer **7 to keep up** : continuer, maintenir — *vi* **1** : garder <keep to the right : gardez la droite> **2** REFRAIN : s'empêcher **3** : se conserver <food that keeps well : des aliments qui se conservent bien> **4 to keep on** : continuer <she kept on trying : elle continuait à essayer>

keep² *n* **1** : donjon *m* (d'un château fort) **2 to earn one's keep** : gagner de quoi vivre **3 for keeps** : pour de bon

keeper ['kiːpər] *n* : gardien *m*, -dienne *f*

keeping ['kiːpɪŋ] *n* **1** CARE : garde *f* <in the keeping of : à la garde de> **2 in keeping with** : en accord avec, conformément à

keepsake ['kiːpˌseɪk] *n* : souvenir *m*

keg ['kɛg] *n* : baril *m*, tonnelet *m*

kelp ['kɛlp] *n* : varech *m*

ken ['kɛn] *n* **1** SIGHT : vision *f* **2** UNDERSTANDING : entendement *m* <it's beyond my ken : ça dépasse mon entendement>

kennel ['kɛnəl] *n* : chenil *m*

Kenyan¹ ['kɛnjən, 'kiːn-] *adj* : kenyan

Kenyan² *n* : Kenyan *m*, Kenyane *f*

kept → **keep**

kerchief ['kərtʃəf, -ˌtʃiːf] *n* : fichu *m*

kernel ['kərnəl] *n* **1** : amande *f* (d'un fruit ou d'une noix) **2** SEED : graine *f* (d'une céréale) **3** CORE : noyau *m*, cœur *m* <a kernel of truth : un fond de vérité>

kerosene *or* **kerosine** ['kɛrəˌsiːn, ˌkɛrə'-] *n* : kérosène *m*, pétrole *m* lampant

ketchup ['kɛtʃəp, 'kæ-] *n* : ketchup *m*

kettle ['kɛtəl] *n* : bouilloire *f*

kettledrum ['kɛtəlˌdrʌm] *n* : timbale *f*

key¹ ['kiː] *vt* **1** ATTUNE : accorder **2 to be keyed up** : être tendu, être surexcité

key² *adj* : fondamental, clé, crucial

key³ *n* **1** : clé *f*, clef *f* <car key : clé de voiture> **2** MEANS, SOLUTION : clé *f*, clef *f* **3** : légende *f* (sur une carte) **4** : touche *f* (d'un clavier) **5** PITCH : ton *m* <in a major key : en majeur> **6** REEF : récif *m*

keyboard¹ ['kiːˌbɔrd] *vt* : saisir

keyboard² *n* : clavier *m*

keyhole ['kiːˌhoːl] *n* : trou *m* de serrure

keynote ['kiːˌnoːt] *n* **1** : tonique *f* (en musique) **2** : thème *m* principal, point *m* capital

keystone ['kiːˌstoːn] *n* : clé *f* de voûte

khaki ['kæki, 'kɑ-] *n* : kaki *m*

khan ['kɑn, 'kæn] *n* : khan *m*

kibbutz [kəˈbʊts, -ˈbuːts] *n, pl* **-butzim** [-ˌbʊtˈsiːm, -ˌbuːt-] : kibboutz *m*

kibitz ['kɪbɪts] *vi* : se mêler des affaires d'autrui

kibitzer ['kɪbɪtsər, kɪˈbɪt-] *n* : personne *f* qui se mêle des affaires d'autrui

kick¹ ['kɪk] *vt* : donner un coup de pied à — *vi* **1** PROTEST : se plaindre **2** RECOIL : reculer (se dit d'un fusil)

kick² *n* **1** : coup *m* de pied **2** RECOIL : recul *m* (d'un fusil) **3** PLEASURE, THRILL : plaisir *m* <to get a kick out of : prendre plaisir à>

kicker ['kɪkər] *n* : botteur *m*, -teuse *f* (aux sports)

kid¹ ['kɪd] *v* **kidded; kidding** *vi* : blaguer, plaisanter <no kidding! : sans blague!> — *vt* TEASE : taquiner

kid² *n* **1** GOAT : chevreau *m*, -vrette *f* **2** CHILD : gosse *mf France fam;* gamin *m*, -mine *f fam;* flot *m Can*

kidder ['kɪdər] *n* : blagueur *m*, -gueuse *f fam*

kidnap ['kɪdˌnæp] *vt* **-napped** *or* **-naped** [-ˌnæpt]; **-napping** *or* **-naping** [-ˌnæpɪŋ] : kidnapper, enlever

kidnapper *or* **kidnaper** ['kɪdˌnæpər] *n* : ravisseur *m*, -seuse *f;* kidnappeur *m*, -peuse *f*

kidney ['kɪdˌni] *n, pl* **-neys** : rein *m*

kidney bean *n* : haricot *m* rouge

kill¹ ['kɪl] *vt* **1** : tuer **2** DEFEAT : mettre son véto à (une loi, etc.) **3 to kill time** : tuer le temps — *vi* : tuer

kill² *n* **1** KILLING : mise *f* à mort **2** PREY : proie *f*

killer ['kɪlər] *n* : meurtrier *m*, -trière *f;* tueur *m*, tueuse *f*

killjoy ['kɪlˌdʒɔɪ] *n* : rabat-joie *mf*

kiln ['kɪl, 'kɪln] *n* : four *m* (à céramique)

kilo ['kiːˌloː] *n, pl* **-los** : kilo *m*

kilogram ['kɪləˌgræm, 'kiː-] *n* : kilogramme *m*

kilohertz ['kɪləˌhərts] *ns & pl* : kilohertz *m*

kilometer [kɪˈlɑmət̬ər] *n* : kilomètre *m*

kilowatt ['kɪləˌwɑt] *n* : kilowatt *m*

kilt ['kɪlt] *n* : kilt *m*

kilter ['kɪltər] *n* **out of kilter** : en panne, détraqué, en dérangement

kimono [kəˈmoːno, -nə] *n, pl* **-nos** : kimono *m*

kin ['kɪn] *n* : parents *mpl*, famille *f*

kind¹ ['kaɪnd] *adj* : gentil, bienveillant, aimable

kind² *n* **1** ESSENCE : nature *f*, essence *f* <in degree, not in kind : en degré, pas en nature> **2** TYPE : genre *m*, sorte *f*, type *m* **3** CATEGORY : classe *f*

kindergarten ['kɪndərˌgɑrtən, -dən] *n* : jardin *m* d'enfants *France*, maternelle *f*, école *f* maternelle

kindhearted ['kaɪndˈhɑrt̬əd] *adj* : bon, qui a bon cœur

kindle [ˈkɪndəl] *vt* **-dled; -dling 1** LIGHT : allumer, enflammer **2** AROUSE : susciter, éveiller — *vi* : s'enflammer
kindliness [ˈkaɪndlinəs] *n* : gentillesse *f*, amabilité *f*
kindling [ˈkɪndlɪŋ, kɪndlən] *n* : petit bois *m*
kindly[1] [ˈkaɪndli] *adv* **1** AMIABLY, WARMLY : chaleureusement, affablement **2** COURTEOUSLY : gentiment, aimablement **3** PLEASE : s'il vous plaît <would you kindly pass the salad : pouvez-vous me passer la salade, s'il vous plaît> **4 to look kindly on sth** : voir qqch d'un bon œil
kindly[2] *adj* **kindlier; -est** : aimable, bienveillant
kindness [ˈkaɪndnəs] *n* : gentillesse *f*, bonté *f*
kind of *adv* SOMEWHAT : quelque peu
kindred[1] [ˈkɪndrəd] *adj* : apparenté, semblable <kindred spirits : âmes sœurs>
kindred[2] *n* : parents *mpl*, famille *f*
kinfolk [ˈkɪnˌfoːk] *or* **kinfolks** *npl* → **kin**
king [ˈkɪŋ] *n* : roi *m*
kingdom [ˈkɪŋdəm] *n* : royaume *m*
kingfisher [ˈkɪŋˌfɪʃər] *n* : martin-pêcheur *m*
kingly [ˈkɪŋli] *adj* : royal, majestueux
king–size [ˈkɪŋˌsaɪz] *or* **king–sized** [-ˌsaɪzd] *adj* : (très) grand, géant
kink[1] [ˈkɪŋk] *vt* : entortiller — *vi* : s'entortiller
kink[2] *n* **1** TWIST : nœud *m* **2** CRAMP : crampe *f* <a kink in one's back : une crampe dans le dos> **3** IMPERFECTION : défaut *m*
kinky [ˈkɪŋki] *adj* **kinkier; -est** : excentrique, bizarre
kinship [ˈkɪnˌʃɪp] *n* : parenté *f*
kinsman [ˈkɪnzmən] *n, pl* **-men** [-mən, -ˌmɛn] : parent *m*
kinswoman [ˈkɪnzˌwʊmən] *n, pl* **-women** [-ˌwɪmən] : parente *f*
kipper [ˈkɪpər] *n* : kipper *m*, hareng *m* saur
kiss[1] [ˈkɪs] *vt* : embrasser, donner un baiser à — *vi* : s'embrasser
kiss[2] *n* : baiser *m*, bec *m Can fam*
kit [ˈkɪt] *n* **1** : trousse *f* <first-aid kit : trousse de secours> **2 the whole kit and caboodle** : tout le bataclan *fam*
kitchen [ˈkɪtʃən] *n* : cuisine *f*
kite [ˈkaɪt] *n* **1** : milan *m* (oiseau) **2** : cerf-volant *m* <to fly a kite : faire voler un cerf-volant>
kith [ˈkɪθ] *n* **kith and kin** : amis *mpl* et parents *mpl*
kitten [ˈkɪtən] *n* : chaton *m*
kitty [ˈkɪti] *n, pl* **-ties 1** KITTEN : chaton *m* **2** FUND : cagnotte *f*
kitty–corner [ˈkɪtiˌkɔrnər] *or* **kitty–cornered** [-nərd] → **catercorner**
kiwi [ˈkiːˌwiː] *n* : kiwi *m*
kleptomania [ˌklɛptəˈmeɪniə] *n* : kleptomanie *f*
kleptomaniac [ˌklɛptəˈmeɪniˌæk] *n* : kleptomane *mf*
knack [ˈnæk] *n* : don *m* <to have a knack for : avoir le don de>
knapsack [ˈnæpˌsæk] *n* : sac *m* à dos
knave [ˈneɪv] *n* **1** → **rascal 2** JACK : valet *m* (aux cartes)
knead [ˈniːd] *vt* **1** : pétrir (de la pâte) **2** MASSAGE : masser
knee [ˈniː] *n* : genou *m*
kneecap [ˈniːˌkæp] *n* : rotule *f*
kneel [ˈniːl] *vi* **knelt** [ˈnɛlt] *or* **kneeled** [ˈniːld]; **kneeling** : s'agenouiller
knell [ˈnɛl] *n* : glas *m*
knew → **know**
knickers [ˈnɪkərz] *npl* : knickers *mpl*, pantalons *mpl* de golf
knickknack [ˈnɪkˌnæk] *n* : bibelot *m*, babiole *f*
knife[1] [ˈnaɪf] *vt* **knifed** [ˈnaɪft]; **knifing** : donner un coup de couteau à
knife[2] *n, pl* **knives** [ˈnaɪvz] : couteau *m*
knight[1] [ˈnaɪt] *vt* : faire chevalier
knight[2] *n* **1** : chevalier *m* **2** : cavalier *m* (aux échecs)
knighthood [ˈnaɪtˌhʊd] *n* : chevalerie *f*
knightly [ˈnaɪtli] *adv* : chevaleresque
knit[1] [ˈnɪt] *v* **knit** *or* **knitted; knitting** *vt* **1** UNITE : joindre **2** : tricoter <to knit a sweater : tricoter un chandail> **3 to knit one's brows** : froncer les sourcils — *vi* : tricoter
knit[2] *n* : tricot *m*
knitter [ˈnɪtər] *n* : tricoteur *m*, -teuse *f*
knob [ˈnɑb] *n* : poignée *f*, bouton *m*
knobby [ˈnɑbi] *adj* **knobbier; -est** : noueux
knock[1] [ˈnɑk] *vt* **1** HIT : cogner, frapper **2** DRIVE : enfoncer (un clou) **3** CRITICIZE : critiquer, dénigrer <don't knock it! : arrête de critiquer!> **4 to knock out** : assommer <the drug knocked him out : le médicament l'a assommé> **5 to knock out** DESTROY : mettre hors service — *vi* **1** : cogner <the engine is knocking : le moteur cogne> **2** COLLIDE : heurter
knock[2] *n* : coup *m*
knock down *vt* : renverser, envoyer par terre
knocker [ˈnɑkər] *n* : heurtoir *m* (d'une porte)
knock–kneed [ˈnɑkˈniːd] *adj* : cagneux
knoll [ˈnoːl] *n* : butte *f*, tertre *m*
knot[1] [ˈnɑt] *v* **knotted; knotting** *vt* : nouer, faire un nœud dans (une cravate, etc.) — *vi* : se nouer
knot[2] *n* **1** : nœud *m* (dans une corde, dans un tronc d'arbre) **2** CLUSTER : petit groupe *m* **3** : nœud *m*, mille *m* marin (en navigation) **4 to tie the knot** : se marier
knotty [ˈnɑti] *adj* **knottier; -est 1** GNARLED : noueux **2** INTRICATE : compliqué, complexe
know [ˈnoː] *v* **knew** [ˈnuː, ˈnjuː]; **known** [ˈnoːn]; **knowing** *vt* **1** : connaître (une personne, un lieu) <he knows me well

: il me connaît bien> <to be known to : être connu de> **2** : savoir <she knows everything : elle sait tout> <he knows how to write : il sait écrire> **3** UNDERSTAND : comprendre <they know English : ils comprennent l'anglais> **4** RECOGNIZE : reconnaître **5** DISCERN, DISTINGUISH : discerner, distinguer **6 to know how to** : savoir <I don't know how to swim : je ne sais pas nager> — *vi* **1** : savoir <not that I know : pas que je sache> **2 to know about** : être au courant de (des nouvelles, etc.), s'y connaître en (un sujet)

knowable [ˈnoːəbəl] *adj* : connaissable

knowing [ˈnoːɪŋ] *adj* : entendu <a knowing look : un regard entendu>

knowingly [ˈnoːɪŋli] *adv* : d'un air entendu

know–it–all [ˈnoːɪtˌɔl] *n* : je-sais-tout *mf*

knowledge [ˈnɑlɪdʒ] *n* **1** LEARNING : connaissances *fpl*, savoir *m* **2** UNDERSTANDING : connaissance *f* <to the best of my knowledge : au meilleur de ma connaissance>

knowledgeable [ˈnɑlɪdʒəbəl] *adj* : bien informé

knuckle [ˈnʌkəl] *n* : jointure *f* du doigt, articulation *f* du doigt

koala [koˈwɑlə] *n* : koala *m*

kohlrabi [ˌkoːlˈrɑbi, -ˈræ-] *n, pl* **-bies** : chou-rave *m*

Koran [kəˈrɑn, -ˈræn] *n* **the Koran** : le Coran

Korean[1] [kəˈriːən] *adj* : coréen

Korean[2] *n* **1** : Coréen *m*, -réenne *f* **2** : coréen *m* (langue)

kosher [ˈkoːʃər] *adj* : kascher, casher

kowtow [ˌkɑʊˈtɑʊ, ˈkɑʊˌtɑʊ] *vi* **to kowtow to** : faire des courbettes à

krypton [ˈkrɪpˌtɑn] *n* : krypton *m*

kudos [ˈkjuːˌdɑs, ˈkuː-, -ˌdoːz] *n* : prestige *m*

kumquat [ˈkʌmˌkwɑt] *n* : kumquat *m*

Kuwaiti[1] [koˈweɪti] *adj* : koweïtien

Kuwaiti[2] *n* : Koweïtien *m*, -tienne *f*

L

l [ˈɛl] *n, pl* **l's** *or* **ls** [ˈɛlz] : l *m*, douzième lettre de l'alphabet

lab [ˈlæb] → **laboratory**

label[1] [ˈleɪbəl] *vt* **-beled** *or* **-belled; -beling** *or* **-belling 1** : étiqueter <to label a jar : étiqueter un bocal> **2** BRAND, CATEGORIZE : classer, étiqueter

label[2] *n* **1** TAG : étiquette *f* **2** BRAND : marque *f*

labial [ˈleɪbiəl] *adj* : labial

labor[1] *or Brit* **labour** [ˈleɪbər] *vi* **1** TOIL : travailler **2** STRUGGLE : gravir, aller péniblement <the truck was laboring up the hill : le camion montait péniblement la côte> — *vt* BELABOR : insister sur (un point)

labor[2] *or Brit* **labour** *n* **1** WORK : travail *m*, labeur *m* **2** : travail *m*, accouchement *m* (en médecine) <to be in labor : être en travail> **3** TASK : tâche *f* **4** WORKERS : main-d'œuvre *f*

laboratory [ˈlæbrəˌtori, ləˈbɔrə-] *n, pl* **-ries** : laboratoire *m*

Labor Day *or Brit* **Labour Day** *n* : fête *f* du Travail

laborer *or Brit* **labourer** [ˈleɪbərər] *n* : ouvrier *m*, -vrière *f*

laborious [ləˈboriəs] *adj* : laborieux, pénible — **laboriously** [-riəsli] *adv*

labor union *or Brit* **labour union** → **union**

labyrinth [ˈlæbəˌrɪnθ] *n* : labyrinthe *m*

lace[1] [ˈleɪs] *vt* **laced; lacing 1** TIE : lacer (ses souliers) **2** : orner (une robe, etc.) de dentelle **3 to be laced with** : être mêlé de

lace[2] *n* **1** SHOELACE : lacet *m* **2** : dentelle *f* <lace doilies : napperons en dentelle>

lacerate [ˈlæsəˌreɪt] *vt* **-ated; -ating** : lacérer

laceration [ˌlæsəˈreɪʃən] *n* : lacération *f*

lack[1] [ˈlæk] *vt* : manquer de <he lacks strength : il manque de force> — *vi* *or* **to be lacking** : manquer

lack[2] *n* : manque *m*, faute *f*

lackadaisical [ˌlækəˈdeɪzɪkəl] *adj* : apathique, amorphe, indolent

lackey [ˈlæki] *n, pl* **-eys 1** SERVANT : laquais *m* **2** TOADY : larbin *m fam*

lackluster [ˈlækˌlʌstər] *adj* : terne

laconic [ləˈkɑnɪk] *adj* : laconique — **laconically** [-nɪkli] *adv*

lacquer[1] [ˈlækər] *vt* : laquer, vernir

lacquer[2] *n* : laque *m*

lacrosse [ləˈkrɔs] *n* : crosse *f*

lactate [ˈlækˌteɪt] *vi* **-tated; -tating** : sécréter du lait

lactation [lækˈteɪʃən] *n* : lactation *f*

lactic [ˈlæktɪk] *adj* : lactique

lacuna [ləˈkuːnə, -ˈkjuː-] *n, pl* **-nae** [-ˌniː, -ˌnaɪ] *or* **-nas** : lacune *f*

lacy [ˈleɪsi] *adj* **lacier; -est** : de dentelle

lad [ˈlæd] *n* : garçon *m*

ladder [ˈlædər] *n* : échelle *f*

laden [ˈleɪdən] *adj* : chargé

ladle[1] [ˈleɪdəl] *vt* **-dled; -dling** : servir à la louche

ladle[2] *n* : louche *f*

lady [ˈleɪdi] *n, pl* **-dies 1** WOMAN : dame *f* **2** : madame *f* <ladies and gentlemen : mesdames et messieurs>

ladybird [ˈleɪdiˌbərd] → **ladybug**

ladybug [ˈleɪdiˌbʌg] *n* : coccinelle *f*

lag[1] ['læg] *vi* **lagged; lagging** : traîner, rester en arrière <to lag behind : prendre du retard>
lag[2] *n* **1** DELAY : retard *m* **2** INTERVAL : intervalle *m*, décalage *m*
lager ['lɑgər] *n* : bière *f* blonde
laggard[1] ['lægərd] *adj* : tardif
laggard[2] *n* : traînard *m*, -narde *f fam*
lagoon [lə'gu:n] *n* : lagune *f*
laid → **lay**[1]
lain → **lie**[1]
lair ['lær] *n* : tanière *f*, repaire *m*
laissez–faire *or Brit* **laisser–faire** [ˌleˌser'fær, ˌleɪˌzeɪ-] *n* : laisser-faire *m*
laity ['leɪəṭi] *n* : laïcs *mpl*
lake ['leɪk] *n* : lac *m*
lama ['lɑmə] *n* : lama *m*
lamb ['læm] *n* : agneau *m*
lambaste [læm'beɪst] *or* **lambast** [-'bæst] *vt* **-basted; -basting 1** BEAT, THRASH : battre, rosser **2** CENSURE : critiquer, réprimander
lame[1] ['leɪm] *vt* **lamed; laming** : estropier
lame[2] *adj* **lamer; lamest 1** : boiteux **2** WEAK : pauvre, piètre <a lame excuse : une piètre excuse>
lamé [lɑ'meɪ, læ-] *n* : lamé *m*
lamely ['leɪmli] *adv* : de façon peu convaincante
lameness ['leɪmnəs] *n* **1** : claudication (en médecine) **2** : faiblesse *f* (d'une excuse, etc.)
lament[1] [lə'mɛnt] *vt* **1** MOURN : pleurer **2** DEPLORE : déplorer, regretter
lament[2] *n* : lamentation *f*
lamentable ['læmənṭəbəl, lə'mɛnṭə-] *adj* : lamentable, déplorable — **lamentably** [-bli] *adv*
lamentation [ˌlæmən'teɪʃən] *n* : lamentation *f*
laminate ['læməˌneɪṭ] *vt* **-nated; -nating** : laminer
laminated ['læməˌneɪṭəd] *adj* : stratifié (se dit du bois), feuilleté (se dit du verre)
lamp ['læmp] *n* : lampe *f*
lampoon[1] [læm'pu:n] *vt* : railler, ridiculiser
lampoon[2] *n* : satire *f*
lamprey ['læmpri] *n, pl* **-preys** : lamproie *f*
lance[1] ['lænṭs] *vt* **lanced; lancing** : inciser, percer (en médecine)
lance[2] *n* SPEAR : lance *f*
lance corporal *n* : soldat *m* de première classe
lancet ['lænṭsəṭ] *n* : lancette *f*, bistouri *m*
land[1] ['lænd] *vt* **1** DISEMBARK : débarquer (des passagers) **2** CATCH : attraper (un poisson) **3** GAIN, SECURE : décrocher (un emploi, etc.) **4** : flanquer *fam* <to land a punch : flanquer un coup de poing> — *vi* **1** : atterrir (se dit d'un avion), accoster (se dit d'un navire) **2** ALIGHT : tomber, retomber <to land on one's feet : retomber sur ses pieds> **3** END UP : finir, atterir <he landed in jail : il s'est retrouvé en prison>
land[2] *n* **1** : terre *f* <on dry land : sur la terre ferme> **2** COUNTRY : pays *m* **3** PROPERTY : terrain *m* <land for sale : terrain à vendre>
landfill ['lænd,fɪl] *n* : enfouissement *m* de déchets
landing ['lændɪŋ] *n* **1** : atterrissage *m* (d'un avion) **2** : débarquement *m* (d'un navire) **3** : palier *m* (d'un escalier)
landing strip → **airstrip**
landlady ['lænd,leɪdi] *n, pl* **-dies** : propriétaire *f*
landless ['lændləs] *adj* : sans terre
landlocked ['lænd,lɑkṭ] *adj* : sans accès à la mer
landlord ['lænd,lɔrd] *n* : propriétaire *m*
landlubber ['lænd,lʌbər] *n* : marin *m* d'eau douce
landmark ['lænd,mɑrk] *n* **1** : point *m* de repère **2** MILESTONE : étape *f* décisive, étape *f* importante (dans la vie de qqn) **3** MONUMENT : monument *m* (historique)
landowner ['lænd,o:nər] *n* : propriétaire *m* foncier, propriétaire *f* foncière
landscape[1] ['lænd,skeɪp] *vt* **-scaped; -scaping** : aménager (un terrain)
landscape[2] *n* : paysage *m*
landslide ['lænd,slaɪd] *n* **1** : glissement *m* de terrain **2** *or* **landslide victory** : victoire *f* écrasante
landward ['lændwərd] *adv & adj* : vers la terre, en direction de la terre
lane ['leɪn] *n* : voie *f* (d'une autoroute), chemin *m* (de campagne)
language ['læŋgwɪdʒ] *n* **1** : langue *f* <she speaks three languages : elle parle trois langues> **2** : langage *m* <computer language : langage informatique>
languid ['læŋgwɪd] *adj* : languissant
languidly ['læŋgwɪdli] *adv* : langoureusement
languish ['læŋgwɪʃ] *vi* **1** WEAKEN, WITHER : dépérir **2** PINE : croupir
languor ['læŋgər] *n* : langueur *f*
languorous ['læŋgərəs] *adj* : langoureux — **languorously** *adv*
lank ['læŋk] *adj* **1** THIN : maigre **2** LIMP : plat
lanky ['læŋki] *adj* **lankier; -est** : grand et maigre, dégingandé
lanolin ['lænəlɪn] *n* : lanoline *f*
lantern ['læntərn] *n* : lanterne *f*
Laotian[1] ['leɪo:ʃən, 'lɑoʊʃən] *adj* : laotien
Laotian[2] *n* : Laotien *m*, -tienne *f*
lap[1] ['læp] *v* **lapped; lapping** *vt* **1** *or* **to lap up** : laper (du lait, etc.) **2** SWALLOW : gober *fam*, avaler <the crowd lapped up every word he said : la foule gobait tout ce qu'il disait> **3** OVERLAP : chevaucher — *vi* SPLASH : clapoter (se dit des vagues)

lap² *n* **1** : genoux *mpl*, giron *m* <to sit on s.o.'s lap : s'asseoir sur les genoux de qqn> **2** : tour *m* de piste, tour *m* de circuit (aux sports) **3** : étape *f* (d'un voyage)

lapdog ['læpˌdɔg] *n* : chien *m* de manchon, petit chien *m* d'appartement

lapel [lə'pel] *n* : revers *m*

Lapp ['læp] *n* **1** : Lapon *m*, -ponne *f* **2** : lapon *m* (langue)

Lappish¹ ['læpɪʃ] *adj* : lapon

Lappish² *n* : lapon *m* (langue)

lapse¹ ['læps] *vi* **lapsed; lapsing 1** CEASE, EXPIRE : expirer, cesser d'être en vigueur **2** ELAPSE : s'écouler, passer **3 to lapse into** : tomber dans <they lapsed into silence : ils se sont tus> <to lapse into unconsciousness : perdre connaissance>

lapse² *n* **1** : trou *m* (de mémoire, etc.) **2** EXPIRATION : expiration *f*, échéance *f* **3** INTERVAL : intervalle *m*, laps *m* (de temps)

laptop ['læpˌtɑp] *adj* : portable <laptop computer : ordinateur portable>

larboard ['lɑrbərd] *n* : bâbord *m*

larceny ['lɑrsəni] *n, pl* **-nies** : vol *m*

larch ['lɑrtʃ] *n* : mélèze *m*

lard ['lɑrd] *n* : saindoux *m*

larder ['lɑrdər] *n* PANTRY : garde-manger *m*

large ['lɑrdʒ] *adj* **larger; largest 1** BIG : grand, gros **2 at ~** FREE : en liberté **3 at ~** : en général <the public at large : le grand public>

largely ['lɑrdʒli] *adv* **1** : en grande partie, en grande mesure **2** MOSTLY : principalement

largeness ['lɑrdʒnəs] *n* : grandeur *f*

largesse *or* **largess** [lɑr'ʒes, -'dʒes] *n* : largesse *f*, générosité *f*

lariat ['lærɪət] *n* : lasso *m*

lark ['lɑrk] *n* **1** : alouette *f* (oiseau) **2** JOKE, PRANK : rigolade *f*

larva ['lɑrvə] *n, pl* **-vae** [-ˌvi:, -ˌvaɪ] : larve *f*

larval ['lɑrvəl] *adj* : larvaire

laryngitis [ˌlærən'dʒaɪtəs] *n* : laryngite *f*

larynx ['lærɪŋks] *n, pl* **-rynges** [lə'rɪnˌdʒi:z] *or* **-ynxes** ['lærɪŋksəz] : larynx *m*

lasagna [lə'zɑnjə] *n* : lasagnes *fpl*

lascivious [lə'sɪviəs] *adj* : lascif

lasciviousness [lə'sɪviəsnəs] *n* : lascivité *f*

laser ['leɪzər] *n* : laser *m*

lash¹ ['læʃ] *vt* **1** WHIP : fouetter **2** BIND : attacher, lier — *vi* **1** BEAT : battre <the rain lashed at the windowpanes : la pluie battait contre les vitres> **2 to lash out at** : invectiver contre

lash² *n* **1** WHIP : fouet *m* **2** BLOW, STRIKE : coup *m* de fouet **3** EYELASH : cil *m*

lass ['læs] *or* **lassie** ['læsi] *n* : fille *f*

lassitude ['læsəˌtu:d, -ˌtju:d] *n* : lassitude *f*

lasso¹ ['læˌso:, læ'su:] *vt* : prendre au lasso

lasso² *n, pl* **-sos** *or* **-soes** : lasso *m*

last¹ ['læst] *vi* **1** CONTINUE, ENDURE : durer **2** : se conserver (se dit des aliments), faire de l'usage (se dit des tissus), durer — *vt* **1** : faire <it lasted me three days : ça m'a fait trois jours> <they will last you a lifetime : vous en aurez pour la vie> **2 to last out** : tenir jusqu'à la fin de

last² *adv* **1** : en dernier <he came last : il est arrivé en dernier> **2** RECENTLY : dernièrement **3** FINALLY : enfin, en conclusion

last³ *adj* : dernier

last⁴ *n* **1** : dernier *m*, -nière *f* **2** : forme *f* (pour les souliers) **3 at ~** FINALLY : enfin, finalement

lastly ['læstli] *adv* : enfin, en dernier lieu

latch¹ ['lætʃ] *vt* : fermer au loquet, clencher *Can* — *vi* **to latch onto** : s'accrocher à

latch² *n* : loquet *m*

late¹ ['leɪt] *adv* **later; latest** : en retard

late² *adj* **later; latest 1** : en retard <he's always late : il est toujours en retard> **2** : tardif <a late spring : un printemps tardif> **3** DECEASED : défunt, feu <his late son : son défunt fils> <the late queen : feu la reine> **4** RECENT : dernier, récent

latecomer ['leɪtˌkʌmər] *n* : retardataire *mf*

lately ['leɪtli] *adv* : récemment, dernièrement

lateness ['leɪtnəs] *n* : retard *m*

latent ['leɪtənt] *adj* : latent

later ['leɪtər] *adv* : plus tard, tantôt *Can*

lateral ['lætərəl] *adj* : latéral — **laterally** *adv*

latex ['leɪˌteks] *n, pl* **-tices** ['leɪtəˌsi:z, 'lætə-] *or* **-texes** : latex *m*

lath ['læθ, 'læð] *n, pl* **laths** *or* **lath** : latte *f*

lathe ['leɪð] *n* : tour *m*

lather¹ ['læðər] *vt* : savonner — *vi* : mousser

lather² *n* : mousse *f* (à savon), écume *f* (sur un cheval)

Latin¹ ['lætən] *adj* : latin

Latin² *n* **1** : latin *m* (langue) **2 → Latin American**

Latin–American ['lætənə'merɪkən] *adj* : latino-américain

Latin American *n* : Latino-américain *m*, -caine *f*

latitude ['læt̬əˌtu:d, -ˌtju:d] *n* : latitude *f*

latrine [lə'tri:n] *n* : latrines *fpl*, toilette *f*

latter¹ ['læt̬ər] *adj* LAST, SECOND : dernier, second

latter² *pron* **the latter** : le dernier, le second

lattice ['læt̬əs] *n* : treillis *m*, treillage *m*

Latvian¹ ['lætviən] *adj* : letton

Latvian² *n* **1** : Letton *m*, -tonne *f* **2** : letton *m* (langue)

laud[1] ['lɔd] *vt* : louer
laud[2] *n* : louanges *fpl*
laugh[1] ['læf] *vi* : rire
laugh[2] *n* : rire *m*
laughable ['læfəbəl] *adj* : risible
laughingly ['læfɪŋli] *adv* : en riant
laughingstock ['læfɪŋˌstɑk] *n* : risée *f*, objet *m* de risée
laughter ['læftər] *n* : rire *m*, rires *mpl*
launch[1] ['lɔnʃ] *vt* **1** HURL : lancer **2** : mettre à l'eau (un bateau) **3** START : lancer (un programme, une campagne, etc.)
launch[2] *n* : vedette *f*, bateau *m* de plaisance
launder ['lɔndər] *vt* : laver (du linge)
launderer ['lɔndərər] *n* : blanchisseur *m*, -seuse *f*; buandier *m*, -dière *f Can*
laundress ['lɔndrəs] *n* : blanchisseuse *f*, buandière *f Can*
laundry ['lɔndri] *n, pl* **-dries 1** : lavage *m*, linge *m* <to do the laundry : faire la lessive> **2** : blanchisserie *f* (commerciale)
laureate ['lɔriət] *n* : lauréat *m*, -réate *f*
laurel ['lɔrəl] *n* **1** : laurier *m* (arbre) **2 laurels** *npl* : lauriers *mpl* <to rest on one's laurels : reposer sur ses lauriers>
lava ['lɑvə, 'læ-] *n* : lave *f*
lavatory ['lævəˌtori] *n, pl* **-ries** : toilettes *fpl*
lavender ['lævəndər] *n* : lavande *f*
lavish[1] ['lævɪʃ] *vt* : prodiguer
lavish[2] *adj* **1** EXTRAVAGANT : prodigue **2** ABUNDANT : abondant, copieux **3** LUXURIOUS : somptueux, fastueux
lavishly ['lævɪʃli] *adv* : généreusement, luxueusement
law ['lɔ] *n* **1** : loi *f* <to break the law : enfreindre la loi> **2** : droit *m* <to study law : faire son droit> <civil law : droit civil> **3** LEGISLATION : loi *f*, législation *f* <the law of the land : la législation du pays> **4** PRINCIPLE : loi *f*, principe *m* <the law of gravity : la loi de la pesanteur>
law-abiding ['lɔəˌbaɪdɪŋ] *adj* : respectueux des lois
lawbreaker ['lɔˌbreɪkər] *n* : personne *f* qui enfreint la loi
lawful ['lɔfəl] *adj* : légal, légitime — **lawfully** *adv*
lawgiver ['lɔˌgɪvər] → **legislator**
lawless ['lɔləs] *adj* : anarchique <a lawless person : une personne sans foi ni loi>
lawmaker ['lɔˌmeɪkər] *n* : législateur *m*, -trice *f*
lawman ['lɔmən] *n, pl* **-men** [-mən, -ˌmen] : policier *m*
lawn ['lɔn] *n* : pelouse *f*
lawn mower *n* : tondeuse *f*
lawsuit ['lɔˌsuːt] *n* : procès *m*
lawyer ['lɔɪər, 'lɔjər] *n* : avocat *m*, -cate *f*
lax ['læks] *adj* **1** LOOSE, SLACK : lâche, relâché **2** NEGLIGENT : négligent
laxative ['læksətɪv] *n* : laxatif *m*
laxity ['læksəti] *n* : laxisme *m*
lay[1] ['leɪ] *vt* **laid** ['leɪd]; **laying 1** PLACE : mettre, poser, déposer **2** : pondre (des œufs) **3** IMPOSE : imposer (une taxe) **4 to lay a bet** : parier **5 to lay out** ARRANGE, DISPLAY : étaler, disposer **6 to lay out** DESIGN : concevoir
lay[2] → **lie**[1]
lay[3] *adj* **1** SECULAR : laïc **2** NONPROFESSIONAL : profane
lay[4] *n* **1** : emplacement *m*, position *f* <the lay of the land : l'emplacement du terrain> **2** BALLAD : lai *m*
layer ['leɪər] *n* **1** : pondeuse *f* (poule) **2** : couche *f* (de peinture), strate *f* (en géologie)
layman ['leɪmən] *n, pl* **-men** [-mən, -ˌmen] : profane *mf*, laïque *mf* (en religion)
layoff ['leɪˌɔf] *n* : licenciement *m*, renvoi *m*
lay off *vt* : licencier, congédier (un employé)
layout ['leɪˌaʊt] *n* **1** ARRANGEMENT : disposition *f*, arrangement *m* **2** : mise *f* en page (en informatique), plan *m* (d'une ville)
layperson ['leɪˌpərsən] *n* : profane *mf*
lay up *vt* **1** STORE : mettre de côté **2 to be laid up** : être alité
laywoman ['leɪˌwʊmən] *n, pl* **-women** [-ˌwɪmən] : laïque *f*
lazily ['leɪzəli] *adv* : paresseusement
laziness ['leɪzɪnəs] *n* : paresse *f*
lazy ['leɪzi] *adj* **lazier; -est** : paresseux
leach ['liːtʃ] *vt* : lessiver
lead[1] ['liːd] *v* **led** ['led]; **leading** *vt* **1** GUIDE : mener, conduire **2** DIRECT : diriger (un orchestre, etc.) **3** HEAD : être à la tête de **4** CONDUCT : mener <he leads a quiet life : il mène une vie tranquille> — *vi* : mener
lead[2] *n* INITIATIVE : initiative *f*
lead[3] ['led] *n* **1** : plomb *m* (métal) **2** GRAPHITE : mine *f* <pencil lead : mine de crayon>
leaden ['ledən] *adj* **1** : de plomb **2** HEAVY : lourd <with leaden steps : d'un pas lourd>
leader ['liːdər] *n* : chef *m*; dirigeant *m*, -geante *f*
leadership ['liːdərˌʃɪp] *n* : direction *f*
leaf[1] ['liːf] *vi* **1** : se feuiller (se dit d'un arbre) **2 to leaf through** : feuilleter (un livre, etc.)
leaf[2] *n, pl* **leaves** ['liːvz] **1** : feuille *f* <maple leaves : feuilles d'érable> **2** : page *f* (d'un livre) **3** : rallonge *f* (de table)
leafless ['liːfləs] *adj* : sans feuilles
leaflet ['liːflət] *n* : dépliant *m*, prospectus *m*
leafy ['liːfi] *adj* **leafier; -est** : feuillu
league[1] ['liːg] *v* **leagued; leaguing** *vt* : allier — *vi* : se liguer
league[2] *n* **1** : lieue *f* <three leagues from here : à trois lieues d'ici> **2** ASSOCIA-

TION : ligue *f* **3** CLASS : classe *f*, niveau *m*

leak[2] ['li:k] *vt* **1** : faire couler (un liquide) **2** : répandre (une nouvelle), divulguer (un secret) — *vi* **1** : fuir (se dit d'un liquide ou d'un gaz) **2** : faire eau (se dit d'un bateau) **3** *or* **to leak out** : filtrer, être divulgué (se dit de l'information)

leak[2] *n* : fuite *f*, voie *f* d'eau

leakage ['li:kɪdʒ] *n* : fuite *f* (d'eau)

leaky ['li:ki] *adj* **leakier; -est** : qui prend l'eau

lean[1] ['li:n] *v* **leaned** *or Brit* **leant** ['lɛnt]; **leaning** *vi* **1** BEND : se pencher, s'incliner **2** RECLINE : s'appuyer **3** TILT : pencher **4 to lean on** DEPEND ON : se fier sur, compter sur, dépendre de **5 to lean toward** : pencher pour, pencher vers — *vt* **1** PROP, REST : appuyer **2** INCLINE : incliner, pencher

lean[2] *adj* **1** THIN : mince, maigre **2** : maigre <lean meat : viande maigre> **3** : difficile <lean years : années difficiles>

leaning ['li:nɪŋ] *n* INCLINATION : tendance *f*

leanness ['li:nnəs] *n* : minceur *f*, maigreur *f*

leant *Brit* → **lean**[1]

leap[1] ['li:p] *vi* **leaped** *or* **leapt** ['li:pt, 'lɛpt]; **leaping** : sauter, bondir

leap[2] *n* : saut *m*, bond *m*

leap year *n* : année *f* bissextile

learn ['lərn] *v* **learned** ['lərnd, 'lərnt] *or Brit* **learnt** ['lərnt]; **learning** *vt* **1** : apprendre <to learn a language : apprendre une langue> **2** MEMORIZE : mémoriser **3** HEAR : apprendre <I just learned the news : je viens d'apprendre la nouvelle> — *vi* : apprendre

learned ['lərnəd] *adj* : savant, érudit

learner ['lərnər] *n* : débutant *m*, -tante *f*

learning ['lərnɪŋ] *n* **1** KNOWLEDGE : savoir *m*, érudition *f* **2** : apprentissage *m* <the learning of a trade : l'apprentissage d'un métier>

learnt *Brit* → **learn**

lease[1] ['li:s] *vt* **leased; leasing** : louer à bail

lease[2] *n* : bail *m*

leash[1] ['li:ʃ] *vt* : tenir (un animal) en laisse

leash[2] *n* : laisse *f* (d'un animal)

least[1] ['li:st] *adv* : (le) moins <to be least interesting : être le moins intéressant>

least[2] *adj* **1** : moins <the least money : le moins d'argent> **2** SLIGHTEST : moindre <the least noise startles her : le moindre bruit la surprend>

least[3] *n* **1** : moins *m* <you have the least : c'est vous qui en avez le moins> **2 at ~** : au moins **3 to say the least** : c'est le moins qu'on puisse dire

leather ['lɛðər] *n* : cuir *m*

leathery ['lɛðəri] *adj* : tanné

leave[1] ['li:v] *v* **left** ['lɛft]; **leaving** *vt* **1** BEQUEATH : léguer **2** : partir de, quitter <to leave the house : partir de la maison> <she left her husband : elle a quitté son mari> **3** FORGET : laisser <I left my books at home : j'ai laissé mes livres à la maison> **4** EQUAL : égaler <4 from 7 leaves 3 : 7 moins 4 égale 3> **5** LET : laisser <leave her alone : laisse-la tranquille> <leave the door open : laissez la porte ouverte> **6 to be left** : rester <there's no money left : il ne reste plus d'argent> **7 to leave out** : omettre — *vi* DEPART : partir

leave[2] *n* **1** PERMISSION : permission *f* **2** *or* **leave of absence** : congé *m* **3 to take one's leave** : prendre son congé

leaved ['li:vd] *adj* : qui a des feuilles

leaven ['lɛvən] *n* : levain *m*

leaves → **leaf**

leavings ['li:vɪŋz] *npl* : restes *mpl*

Lebanese[1] [,lɛbə'ni:z, -'ni:s] *adj* : libanais

Lebanese[2] *n* : Libanais *m*, -naise *f*

lecherous ['lɛtʃərəs] *adj* : lubrique, lascif

lechery ['lɛtʃəri] *n* : lubricité *f*, lascivité *f*

lecture[1] ['lɛktʃər] *v* **-tured; -turing** *vt* : faire la morale à, sermonner — *vi* : faire une conférence

lecture[2] *n* **1** TALK : conférence *f* **2** : cours *m* magistral (à l'université) **3** REPRIMAND : sermon *m*

lecturer ['lɛktʃərər] *n* : conférencier *m*, -cière *f*

led → **lead**[1]

ledge ['lɛdʒ] *n* : rebord *m* (d'une fenêtre, etc.), saillie *f* (d'une montagne)

ledger ['lɛdʒər] *n* : grand livre *m* (en comptabilité)

lee[1] ['li:] *adj* : sous le vent

lee[2] *n* : côté *m* sous le vent

leech ['li:tʃ] *n* : sangsue *f*

leek ['li:k] *n* : poireau *m*

leer[1] ['lɪr] *vi* **to leer at** : lorgner

leer[2] *n* : regard *m* malveillant, regard *m* lubrique

leery ['lɪri] *adj* : méfiant, soupçonneux <to be leery of : se méfier de>

lees ['li:z] *npl* DREGS : lie *f*

leeward[1] ['li:wərd, 'lu:ərd] *adj* : sous le vent

leeward[2] *n* : côté *m* sous le vent

leeway ['li:ˌwei] *n* : marge *f* de manœuvre

left[1] → **leave**[1]

left[2] ['lɛft] *adv* : à gauche

left[3] *adj* : gauche

left[4] *n* : gauche *f* <it's on your left : c'est à votre gauche>

leg ['lɛg] *n* **1** : patte *f* (d'un animal), jambe *f* (d'une personne ou d'un pantalon) **2** : pied *m* (d'une table, etc.) **3** STAGE : étape *f* (d'un voyage)

legacy ['lɛgəsi] *n, pl* **-cies** : legs *m*, héritage *m*

legal ['li:gəl] *adj* **1** LAWFUL : légal, légitime **2** JUDICIAL : juridique, judiciaire <legal adviser : conseiller juridique> <legal aid : aide judiciaire>
legality [li'gæləti] *n, pl* **-ties** : légalité *f*
legalize ['li:gə,laɪz] *vt* **-ized; -izing** : légaliser
legally ['li:gəli] *adv* : légalement
legate ['legət] *n* : légat *m*
legation [li'geɪʃən] *n* : légation *f*
legend ['ledʒənd] *n* : légende *f*
legendary ['ledʒən,deri] *adj* : légendaire
legerdemain [,ledʒərdə'meɪn] → **sleight of hand**
leggings ['legɪnz, 'legənz] *npl* : caleçon *m* (porté comme pantalon)
legibility [,ledʒə'bɪləti] *n* : lisibilité *f*
legible ['ledʒəbəl] *adj* : lisible — **legibly** [-bli] *adv*
legion ['li:dʒən] *n* : légion *f*
legionary ['li:dʒənəri] → **legionnaire**
legionnaire [,li:dʒə'nær] *n* : légionnaire *m*
legislate ['ledʒəs,leɪt] *vi* **-lated; -lating** : légiférer
legislation [,ledʒəs'leɪʃən] *n* : législation *f*
legislative ['ledʒəs,leɪtɪv] *adj* : législatif
legislator ['ledʒəs,leɪtər] *n* : législateur *m*, -trice *f*
legislature ['ledʒəs,leɪtʃər] *n* : législatif *m*, corps *m* législatif
legitimacy [lɪ'dʒɪtəməsi] *n* : légitimité *f*
legitimate [lɪ'dʒɪtəmət] *adj* **1** LAWFUL : légitime **2** VALID : légitime, admissible
legitimately [lɪ'dʒɪtəmətli] *adv* : légitimement
legitimize [lɪ'dʒɪtə,maɪz] *vt* **-mized; -mizing** : légitimer
legless ['legləs] *adj* : sans jambes
legume ['leˌgju:m, lɪ'gju:m] *n* : légumineuse *f*
leisure ['li:ʒər, 'lɛ-] *n* **1** : loisir *m* <leisure time : les loisirs> **2 at your leisure** : à votre convenance
leisurely[1] ['li:ʒərli, 'lɛ-] *adv* : sans hâte, sans se presser
leisurely[2] *adj* : tranquille, paisible <a leisurely stroll : une balade faite sans se presser>
lemming ['lemɪŋ] *n* : lemming *m*
lemon ['lemən] *n* : citron *m*
lemonade [,lemə'neɪd] *n* : limonade *f*
lemony ['leməni] *adj* : citronné
lend ['lend] *vt* **lent** ['lent]; **lending 1** : prêter <to lend money : prêter de l'argent> **2** GIVE, SUPPORT : conférer, apporter <to lend a hand : prêter une main> **3 to lend itself to** : se prêter à
lender ['lendər] *n* : prêteur *m*, -teuse *f*
length ['leŋkθ] *n* **1** : longueur *f* <10 meters in length : 10 mètres de longueur> **2** DURATION : durée *f* **3** PIECE, SECTION : bout *m*, morceau *m* <a length of pipe : un bout de tuyau> **4 at ~** : longuement, en détail **5 to go to great lengths** : se donner beaucoup de mal
lengthen ['leŋkθən] *vt* **1** : rallonger (une jupe, etc.) **2** PROLONG : prolonger — *vi* : s'allonger, se prolonger
lengthways ['leŋkθ,weɪz] → **lengthwise**
lengthwise ['leŋkθ,waɪz] *adv & adj* : dans le sens de la longueur
lengthy ['leŋkθi] *adj* **lengthier; -est** : long, interminable
leniency ['li:niənt̬si] *n* : indulgence *f*, clémence *f*
lenient ['li:niənt] *adj* : indulgent, clément
leniently ['li:niəntli] *adv* : avec indulgence, avec clémence
lens ['lenz] *n* **1** : lentille *f*, objectif *m* (d'un instrument) **2** : cristallin *m* (de l'œil) **3** : verre *m* (d'une paire de lunettes) **4 → contact lens**
Lent ['lent] *n* : carême *m*
Lenten ['lentən] *adj* : de carême
lentil ['lentəl] *n* : lentille *f*
Leo ['li:o:] *n* : Lion *m*
leopard ['lepərd] *n* : léopard *m*
leotard ['li:ə,tɑrd] *n* : justaucorps *m*
leper ['lepər] *n* : lépreux *m*, -preuse *f*
leprechaun ['leprə,kɑn] *n* : lutin *m*
leprosy ['leprəsi] *n* : lèpre *f*
lesbian[1] ['lezbiən] *adj* : lesbien
lesbian[2] *n* : lesbienne *f*
lesbianism ['lezbiə,nɪzəm] *n* : lesbianisme *m*
lesion ['li:ʒən] *n* : lésion *f*
less[1] ['les] (*comparative of* **little**[1]) *adv* **1** : moins <much less important : beaucoup moins important> **2 less and less** : de moins en moins
less[2] (*comparative of* **little**[2]) *adj* **1** : moins <less money : moins d'argent> **2** : moindre <of less importance : de moindre importance>
less[3] *prep* MINUS : moins <the regular price less a discount : le prix régulier moins un escompte>
less[4] *pron* : moins <I cannot do less : je ne peux pas en faire moins>
lessen ['lesən] *vi* DECREASE : diminuer — *vt* REDUCE : amoindrir, diminuer
lesser[1] ['lesər] *adv* LESS : moins <lesser-known writers : des écrivains moins connus>
lesser[2] *adj* : moindre <to a lesser degree : à un moindre degré>
lesson ['lesən] *n* : leçon *f*
lest ['lest] *conj* : de peur que, de crainte que
let ['let] *vt* **let; letting 1** MAKE : laisser <let me know : laisse-moi savoir> **2** RENT : louer <rooms to let : chambres à louer> **3** ALLOW, PERMIT : laisser <let them through : laissez-les passer> **4** (*used in commands*) <let him try : qu'il essaie> **5 to let go** RELEASE : lâcher
letdown ['let,daʊn] *n* DISAPPOINTMENT : déception *f*
let down *vt* DISAPPOINT : décevoir

lethal [ˈliːθəl] *adj* : mortel, létal
lethargic [lɪˈθɑrdʒɪk] *adj* : léthargique
lethargy [ˈlɛθərdʒi] *n* : léthargie *f*
let on *vi* ADMIT : admettre, révéler
let's [ˈlɛts] (*contraction of* **let us**) → **let**
letter[1] [ˈlɛtər] *vt* : inscrire des lettres sur
letter[2] *n* **1** : lettre *f* (de l'alphabet) **2** : lettre *f* <a letter to my mother : une lettre à ma mère> **3 letters** *npl* CORRESPONDENCE : courrier *m* <letters to the editor : courrier des lecteurs> **4 letters** *npl* : belles-lettres *fpl*, littérature *f* **5 the letter of the law** : la lettre de la loi
letterhead [ˈlɛtərˌhɛd] *n* : en-tête *m*
lettuce [ˈlɛtəs] *n* : laitue *f*
let up *vi* ABATE : diminuer, se calmer
leukemia [luːˈkiːmiə] *n* : leucémie *f*
levee [ˈlɛvi] *n* : digue *f*
level[1] [ˈlɛvəl] *vt* **-eled** *or* **-elled; -eling** *or* **-elling 1** FLATTEN : niveler, aplanir **2** AIM, DIRECT : lancer (une accusation), braquer (une arme) **3** RAZE : raser (un immeuble)
level[2] *adj* **1** FLAT : plat **2** HORIZONTAL : horizontal <in a level position : à l'horizontale> **3** EVEN : à égalité <to draw level : se trouver à égalité> **4** CALM, STEADY : calme, mesuré <to keep a level head : garder son sang-froid>
level[3] *n* : niveau *m*
levelheaded [ˈlɛvəlˈhɛdəd] *adj* : pondéré, équilibré
lever [ˈlɛvər, ˈliː-] *n* : levier *m*
leverage [ˈlɛvərɪdʒ, ˈliː-] *n* **1** : force *f* de levier (en physique) **2** INFLUENCE : influence *f*, moyen *m* de pression
leviathan [lɪˈvaɪəθən] *n* : chose *f* énorme et redoutable
levity [ˈlɛvəṭi] *n* : légèreté *f*, manque *m* de sérieux
levy[1] [ˈlɛvi] *vt* **levied; levying 1** IMPOSE : imposer, prélever (des impôts) **2** COLLECT : lever, percevoir (des impôts) **3** ENLIST : lever (des troupes)
levy[2] *n, pl* **levies 1** : impôt *m*, taxe *f* **2** : levée *f* (militaire)
lewd [ˈluːd] *adj* : luxurieux, lubrique
lewdly [ˈluːdli] *adv* : de façon obscène
lewdness [ˈluːdnəs] *n* : lubricité *f*
lexicographer [ˌlɛksəˈkɑgrəfər] *n* : lexicographe *mf*
lexicographical [ˌlɛksəkoˈgræfɪkəl] *or* **lexicographic** [-ˈgræfɪk] *adj* : lexicographique
lexicography [ˌlɛksəˈkɑgrəfi] *n* : lexicographie *f*
lexicon [ˈlɛksɪˌkɑn] *n, pl* **-ica** [-kə] *or* **-icons** : lexique *m*
liability [ˌlaɪəˈbɪləṭi] *n, pl* **-ties 1** RESPONSIBILITY : responsabilité *f* **2** DRAWBACK : désavantage *m*, handicap *m* **3 liabilities** *npl* : passif *m*, dettes *fpl* <assets and liabilities : l'actif et le passif>
liable [ˈlaɪəbəl] *adj* **1** : responsable <liable for damages : responsable pour les dommages> **2** LIKELY : probable <it's liable to rain : il se peut qu'il pleuve> **3** SUSCEPTIBLE : sujet, susceptible <he's liable to fall : il est sujet aux chutes>
liaison [ˈliːəˌzɑn, liˈeɪ-] *n* : liaison *f*
liar [ˈlaɪər] *n* : menteur *m*, -teuse *f*
libel[1] [ˈlaɪbəl] *vt* **-beled** *or* **-belled; -beling** *or* **-belling** : diffamer, calomnier
libel[2] *n* : diffamation *f*, calomnie *f*
libelous *or* **libellous** [ˈlɪbləbləs] *adj* : diffamatoire
liberal[1] [ˈlɪbrəl, ˈlɪbərəl] *adj* **1** ABUNDANT, GENEROUS : libéral, prodigue **2** TOLERANT : libéral, tolérant
liberal[2] *n* : libéral *m*, -rale *f*
liberal arts *n* : arts *mpl* et sciences *fpl* humaines
liberalism [ˈlɪbrəˌlɪzəm, ˈlɪbərə-] *n* : libéralisme *m*
liberality [ˌlɪbəˈræləṭi] *n, pl* **-ties** : libéralité *f*
liberalize [ˈlɪbrəˌlaɪz, ˈlɪbərə-] *vt* **-ized; -izing** : libéraliser
liberally [ˈlɪbrəli, ˈlɪbərə-] *adv* : libéralement
liberate [ˈlɪbəˌreɪt] *vt* **-ated; -ating** : libérer
liberation [ˌlɪbəˈreɪʃən] *n* : libération *f*
liberator [ˈlɪbəˌreɪṭər] *n* : libérateur *m*, -trice *f*
Liberian[1] [laɪˈbɪriən] *adj* : libérien
Liberian[2] *n* : Libérien *m*, -rienne *f*
libertine [ˈlɪbərˌtiːn] *n* : libertin *m*, -tine *f*
liberty [ˈlɪbərṭi] *n, pl* **-ties 1** FREEDOM : liberté *f* **2** CHANCE, RISK : risque *m* <he's taking liberties with his health : il prend des risques avec sa santé> **3 liberties** *npl* FAMILIARITY : libertés *fpl*
libido [ləˈbiːdoː, -ˈbaɪ-] *n, pl* **-dos** : libido *f*
Libra [ˈliːbrə] *n* : Balance *f*
librarian [laɪˈbrɛriən] *n* : bibliothécaire *mf*
library [ˈlaɪˌbrɛri] *n, pl* **-braries** : bibliothèque *f*
libretto [lɪˈbrɛṭo] *n, pl* **-tos** *or* **-ti** [-ṭiː] : livret *m*
Libyan[1] [ˈlɪbiən] *adj* : libyen
Libyan[2] *n* : Libyen *m*, Libyenne *f*
lice → louse
license[1] [ˈlaɪsənʦ] *vt* **-censed; -censing 1** : accorder une licence à **2** AUTHORIZE : autoriser
license[2] *or* **licence** *n* **1** PERMIT : permis *m*, licence *f* <driver's license : permis de conduire> **2** FREEDOM : licence *f*, liberté *f* **3** AUTHORIZATION : licence *f*, autorisation *f*
licentious [laɪˈsɛnʃəs] *adj* : licencieux **— licentiously** *adv*
lichen [ˈlaɪkən] *n* : lichen *m*
licit [ˈlɪsəṭ] *adj* LAWFUL : licite
lick[1] [ˈlɪk] *vt* **1** : lécher **2** BEAT : battre à plate couture, écraser

lick[2] *n* **1** : coup *m* de langue **2** BIT : brin *m* <a lick and a promise : un brin de toilette>
licorice *or Brit* **liquorice** ['lɪkərɪʃ, -rəs] *n* : réglisse *f*
lid ['lɪd] *n* **1** COVER : couvercle *m* **2** EYELID : paupière *f*
lie[1] ['laɪ] *vi* **lay** ['leɪ]; **lain** ['leɪn]; **lying** ['laɪɪŋ] **1** *or* **to lie down** : se coucher, s'allonger <to lie on the grass : s'allonger sur l'herbe> <to lie motionless : rester immobile> **2** : se trouver, être <the book is lying on the table : le livre se trouve sur la table> **3** EXTEND, STRETCH : s'étendre <the route lay to the west : la route s'étendait vers l'ouest> **4** REMAIN : être, rester <to lie idle : être arrêté> **5 to lie in** : résider en
lie[2] *vi* **lied; lying** ['laɪɪŋ] : mentir
lie[3] *n* **1** : mensonge *m* **2** : position *f* (au golf), configuration *f* (de la terre)
liege ['liːdʒ] *n* : suzerain *m*, seigneur *m*
lien ['liːn] *n* : droit *m* de rétention
lieutenant [luːˈtenənt] *n* : lieutenant *m*
lieutenant colonel *n* : lieutenant-colonel *m*
lieutenant commander *n* : capitaine *m* de corvette
lieutenant general *n* : général *m* de corps d'armée
life ['laɪf] *n, pl* **lives** ['laɪvz] **1** EXISTENCE : vie *f*, existence *f* **2** : vie *f* <his adult life : sa vie adulte> <plant life : la flore> <way of life : mode de vie> **3** BIOGRAPHY : biographie *f* **4** DURATION : durée *f* (d'une machine, etc.) **5** LIVELINESS : vie *f*, animation *f*
lifeblood ['laɪfˌblʌd] *n* : force *f* vitale
lifeboat ['laɪfˌboːt] *n* : canot *m* de sauvetage
lifeguard ['laɪfˌgɑrd] *n* : surveillant *m*, -lante *f* de baignade
lifeless ['laɪfləs] *adj* : inanimé, sans vie
lifelike ['laɪfˌlaɪk] *adj* : ressemblant
lifelong ['laɪfˈlɔŋ] *adj* : de toute la vie
life preserver *n* : gilet *m* de sauvetage
lifesaver ['laɪfˌseɪvər] *n* **1** → **lifeguard 2 to be a lifesaver** : sauver la vie à qqn
lifesaving ['laɪfˌseɪvɪŋ] *n* : sauvetage *m*
lifestyle ['laɪfˌstaɪl] *n* : mode *m* de vie
lifetime ['laɪfˌtaɪm] *n* : vie *f* <a lifetime of regrets : toute une vie de regrets>
lift[1] ['lɪft] *vt* **1** RAISE : lever, soulever **2** END : lever <to lift a ban : lever une interdiction> **3** BOOST : remonter — *vi* **1** CLEAR UP : se dissiper <the fog has lifted : la brume s'est dissipée> **2** *or* **to lift off** : décoller (se dit d'un avion, etc.)
lift[2] *n* **1** LIFTING : soulèvement *m* **2** BOOST : encouragement *m*, stimulation *f* <to give s.o.'s spirits a lift : remonter le moral à qqn> **3** *Brit* → **elevator 4 to give s.o. a lift** : emmener qqn en voiture
liftoff ['lɪftˌɔf] *n* : lancement *m* (en aéronautique)
ligament ['lɪgəmənt] *n* : ligament *m*
ligature ['lɪgəˌtʃʊr, -tʃər] *n* : ligature *f*
light[1] ['laɪt] *v* **lit** ['lɪt] *or* **lighted; lighting** *vt* **1** : allumer (un feu) **2** GUIDE : éclairer, illuminer <to light the way : éclairer le chemin> — *vi* **1** BRIGHTEN : s'éclairer, s'illuminer **2** ALIGHT : se poser **3** DISMOUNT : descendre
light[2] *adv* : légèrement <to travel light : voyager avec peu de bagages>
light[3] *adj* **1** BRIGHT : clair **2** PALE : pâle <light blue : bleu pâle> **3** LIGHTWEIGHT : léger **4** GENTLE : léger <a light breeze : une brise légère> <a light rain : une pluie fine> **5** EASY : léger, facile <light reading : quelque chose de facile à lire> <light work : des travaux peu fatigants>
light[4] *n* **1** : lumière *f* <ray of light : rayon de lumière> **2** DAYLIGHT : lumière *f* du jour **3** LAMP : lumière *f* **4** ASPECT : jour *m*, lumière *f* <in a different light : sous un autre jour> <in the light of recent developments : à la lumière des derniers événements> **5** FLAME : feu *m* <do you have a light? : as-tu du feu?> **6** → **traffic light 7 lights** *npl* : phares *mpl* (d'une voiture)
lightbulb ['laɪtˌbʌlb] *n* : ampoule *f*
lighten ['laɪtən] *vt* **1** BRIGHTEN : éclairer (les esprits, une salle, les cheveux) **2** ALLEVIATE, RELIEVE : alléger, soulager — *vi* : s'éclairer
lighter ['laɪtər] *n* : briquet *m*
lighthearted ['laɪtˌhɑrtəd] *adj* : allègre, joyeux — **lightheartedly** *adv*
lighthouse ['laɪtˌhaʊs] *n* : phare *m*
lightly ['laɪtli] *adv* **1** GENTLY : légèrement **2** FRIVOLOUSLY : à la légère, légèrement **3 to get off lightly** : s'en tirer à bon compte
lightness ['laɪtnəs] *n* **1** : légèreté *f* **2** BRIGHTNESS : clarté *f*
lightning ['laɪtnɪŋ] *n* : éclairs *mpl*, foudre *f*
lightning bug → **firefly**
lightproof ['laɪtˌpruːf] *adj* : à l'épreuve de la lumière
lightweight ['laɪtˌweɪt] *adj* : léger <lightweight fabric : tissu léger>
light–year ['laɪtˌjɪr] *n* : année-lumière *f*
lignite ['lɪgˌnaɪt] *n* : lignite *m*
likable *or* **likeable** ['laɪkəbəl] *adj* : agréable, sympathique
like[1] ['laɪk] *v* **liked; liking** *vt* **1** ENJOY : aimer <he likes tennis : il aime le tennis> **2** WANT : aimer, vouloir <I would like a drink of water : j'aimerais un verre d'eau> — *vi* CHOOSE, PREFER : vouloir, plaire <if you like : si vous voulez>
like[2] *adj* SIMILAR : pareil, semblable
like[3] *n* **1** LIKING, PREFERENCE : goût *m* <our likes and dislikes : ce que nous aimons et ce que nous n'aimons pas> **2 the like** : une chose pareille <I've never seen the like : je n'ai jamais rien vu de pareil> <cats, dogs,

and the like : des chats, des chiens et d'autres animaux de ce genre>

like[4] *conj* **1** AS : comme <she talks exactly like I do : elle parle exactement comme moi> **2** AS IF : comme si <he acted like he was cold : il s'est conduit comme s'il avait froid> <it looks like it might rain : on dirait qu'il va pleuvoir>

like[5] *prep* **1** : comme <you're not like the rest of them : tu n'es pas comme les autres> <it's just like her to be late : c'est bien son genre d'être en retard> **2** SUCH AS : comme, tel que <a city like Chicago : une ville telle que Chicago>

likelihood ['laɪkli,hʊd] *n* : probabilité *f*

likely[1] ['laɪkli] *adv* : probablement <most likely : très probablement>

likely[2] *adj* **likelier; -est 1** PROBABLE : probable **2** BELIEVABLE : plausible, vraisemblable <a likely excuse! : une belle excuse!> **3** PROMISING : prometteur

liken ['laɪkən] *vt* : comparer

likeness ['laɪknəs] *n* **1** SIMILARITY : ressemblance *f* **2** PORTRAIT : portrait *m*

likewise ['laɪk,waɪz] *adv* **1** SIMILARLY : de même <do likewise : fais de même> **2** ALSO : de plus, aussi

liking ['laɪkɪŋ] *n* **1** LEANING, TASTE : goût *m*, penchant *m* **2** FONDNESS : affection *f* <to take a liking to : se prendre d'affection pour>

lilac ['laɪlək, -læk, -lɑk] *n* : lilas *m*

lilt ['lɪlt] *n* : rythme *m*, cadence *f* (en musique), intonation *f* (de la voix)

lily ['lɪli] *n, pl* **lilies** : lis *m*, lys *m*

lima bean ['laɪmə] *n* : haricot *m* de Lima

limb ['lɪm] *n* **1** : membre *m* (en anatomie) **2** BRANCH : branche *f* (d'un arbre)

limber[1] ['lɪmbər] *vt or* **to limber up** : assouplir — *vi* **to limber up** : s'échauffer

limber[2] *adj* : souple, agile

limbo ['lɪm,boː] *n, pl* **-bos 1** : limbes *mpl* (en religion) **2** UNCERTAINTY : incertitude *f*, état *m* d'incertitude

lime ['laɪm] *n* **1** : chaux *m* (en agriculture) **2** : citron *m* vert (fruit)

limelight ['laɪm,laɪt] *n* **to be in the limelight** : être en vedette, avoir la vedette

limerick ['lɪmərɪk] *n* : petit poème *m* humoristique

limestone ['laɪm,stoːn] *n* : calcaire *m*

limit[1] ['lɪmət] *vt* : limiter

limit[2] *n* **1** BOUNDARY : limite *f* **2** RESTRICTION : limitation *f*

limitation [,lɪmə'teɪʃən] *n* : limitation *f*, restriction *f*

limitless ['lɪmətləs] *adj* : illimité

limousine ['lɪmə,ziːn, ,lɪmə'-] *n* : limousine *f*

limp[1] ['lɪmp] *vi* : boiter

limp[2] *adj* : mou, flasque

limp[3] *n* : boiterie *f*, claudication *f*

limpid ['lɪmpəd] *adj* : limpide, transparent

limply ['lɪmpli] *adv* : mollement

limpness ['lɪmpnəs] *n* : mollesse *f*

linden ['lɪndən] *n* : tilleul *m*

line[1] ['laɪn] *v* **lined; lining** *vt* **1** : ligner <lined paper : papier ligné> **2** BORDER : border <lined with trees : bordé d'arbres> **3** : doubler (un vêtement) **4** ALIGN : aligner, mettre en ligne — *vi* **to line up** : se mettre en ligne, faire la queue

line[2] *n* **1** ROPE : cordage *m*, corde *f* **2** CABLE, WIRE : ligne *f* <power line : ligne à haute tension> **3** *or* **telephone line** : ligne *f* de téléphone <the line has gone dead : il n'y a plus de tonalité> **4** ROW : rangée *f* **5** QUEUE : file *f*, queue *f*, filée *f Can fam* **6** NOTE : mot *m* <drop me a line : écris-moi un mot> **7** ORIENTATION, OUTLOOK : ligne *f* **8** AGREEMENT : accord *m* <to be in line with s.o. : être conforme à qqn> **9** JOB, OCCUPATION : métier *m* **10** LINEAGE : lignée *f*, descendance *f* **11** ROUTE : ligne *f* <bus line : ligne d'autobus> **12** WRINKLE : ride *f* **13** RANGE : gamme *f* (de produits) **14** MARK : ligne *f* <dotted line : ligne pointillée> **15** *or* **dividing line** LIMIT : limite *f* **16** → **online**

lineage ['lɪnɪɪdʒ] *n* : lignée *f*, descendance *f*

lineal ['lɪniəl] *adj* : en ligne directe

lineaments ['lɪniəmənts] *npl* : linéaments *mpl*, traits *mpl*

linear ['lɪniər] *adj* : linéaire

linen ['lɪnən] *n* : lin *m*

liner ['laɪnər] *n* **1** LINING : doublure *f* **2** : paquebot *m* (navire), gros-porteur *m* (avion)

lineup ['laɪn,əp] *n* **1** : séance *f* d'identification de suspects **2** : équipe *f* (aux sports) **3** : composition *f* (d'un programme, etc.)

linger ['lɪŋgər] *vi* **1** TARRY : s'attarder **2** PERSIST : persister, persévérer

lingerie [,lɑnʤə'reɪ, ,lænʒə'riː] *n* : lingerie *f*

lingo ['lɪŋgo] *n, pl* **-goes 1** LANGUAGE : langue *f* (du pays) **2** JARGON : jargon *m*

linguist ['lɪŋgwɪst] *n* : linguiste *mf*

linguistic [lɪŋ'gwɪstɪk] *adj* : linguistique

linguistics [lɪŋ'gwɪstɪks] *n* : linguistique *f*

liniment ['lɪnəmənt] *n* : liniment *m*, onguent *m*

lining ['laɪnɪŋ] *n* : doublure *f*

link[1] ['lɪŋk] *vt* : relier, lier — *vi or* **to link up** : s'associer, se rejoindre

link[2] *n* **1** : maillon *m* (d'une chaîne) **2** BOND : lien *m*, rapport *m* **3** : liaison *f* <satellite link : liaison satellite>

linkage ['lɪŋkɪdʒ] *n* LINK : lien *m*, rapport *m*
linoleum [lə'no:liəm] *n* : linoléum *m*, prélart *m Can*
linseed oil ['lɪnˌsi:d] *n* : huile *f* de lin
lint ['lɪnt] *n* : peluches *fpl*
lintel ['lɪntəl] *n* : linteau *m*
lion ['laɪən] *n* : lion *m*
lioness ['laɪənɪs] *n* : lionne *f*
lionize ['laɪəˌnaɪz] *vt* **-ized; -izing** : aduler, fêter comme une célébrité
lip ['lɪp] *n* **1** : lèvre *f* <the upper lip : la lèvre supérieure> **2** EDGE, RIM : bord *m*, rebord *m*
lipreading ['lɪpˌri:dɪŋ] *n* : lecture *f* sur les lèvres
lipstick ['lɪpˌstɪk] *n* : rouge *m* à lèvres
liquefy ['lɪkwəˌfaɪ] *v* **-fied; -fying** *vt* : liquéfier — *vi* : se liquéfier
liqueur [lɪ'kər, -'kʊr, -'kjʊr] *n* : liqueur *f*
liquid[1] ['lɪkwəd] *adj* : liquide
liquid[2] *n* : liquide *m*
liquidate ['lɪkwəˌdeɪt] *vt* **-dated; -dating** : liquider
liquidation [ˌlɪkwə'deɪʃən] *n* : liquidation *f*
liquidity [lɪk'wɪdəti] *n* : liquidité *f*
liquor ['lɪkər] *n* : alcool *m*, boissons *fpl* alcoolisées
liquorice *Brit* → **licorice**
lisp[1] ['lɪsp] *vi* : zézayer
lisp[2] *n* : zézaiement *m*
lissome ['lɪsəm] *adj* : souple, agile
list[1] ['lɪst] *vt* **1** ENUMERATE : énumérer **2** : mettre sur une liste — *vi* TILT : donner de la bande, gîter (se dit d'un bateau)
list[2] *n* **1** : liste *f* **2** SLANT : gîte *f*, bande *f* (d'un bateau)
listen ['lɪsən] *vi* **1 to listen to** HEAR : écouter <listen to the rain : écoutez la pluie> **2 to listen to** HEED : tenir compte de, écouter
listener ['lɪsənər] *n* : personne *f* qui écoute <he's a good listener : il sait écouter les autres>
listless ['lɪstləs] *adj* : apathique, amorphe
listlessly ['lɪstləsli] *adv* : avec apathie, sans énergie
listlessness ['lɪstləsnəs] *n* : apathie *f*, manque *m* d'énergie
lit ['lɪt] → **light**[1]
litany ['lɪtəni] *n, pl* **-nies** : litanie *f*
liter ['li:tər] *n* : litre *m*
literacy ['lɪtərəsi] *n* **1** : capacité *f* de lire et d'écrire **2 literacy campaign** : campagne *f* d'alphabétisation
literal ['lɪtərəl] *adj* : littéral — **literally** *adv*
literary ['lɪtəˌrɛri] *adj* : littéraire
literate ['lɪtərət] *adj* : qui sait lire et écrire
literature ['lɪtərəˌtʃʊr, -tʃər] *n* : littérature *f*
lithe ['laɪð, 'laɪθ] *adj* : souple, agile
lithesome ['laɪðsəm, 'laɪθ-] → **lissome**
lithium ['lɪθiəm] *n* : lithium *m*
lithograph ['lɪθəˌgræf] *n* : lithographie *f*
lithographer [lɪ'θɑgrəfər, 'lɪθəˌgræfər] *n* : lithographe *mf*
lithography [lɪ'θɑgrəfi] *n* : lithographie *f* — **lithographic** [ˌlɪθə'græfɪk] *adj*
Lithuanian[1] [ˌlɪθə'weɪniən, -njən] *adj* : lituanien
Lithuanian[2] *n* **1** : Lituanien *m*, -nienne *f* **2** : lituanien *m* (langue)
litigant ['lɪtɪgənt] *n* : plaideur *m*, -deuse *f*
litigate ['lɪtəˌgeɪt] *v* **-gated; -gating** *vi* : plaider — *vt* : mettre en litige
litigation [ˌlɪtə'geɪʃən] *n* : litige *m*
litmus paper ['lɪtməs] *n* : papier *m* de tournesol
litre → **liter**
litter[1] ['lɪtər] *vt* : mettre du désordre dans, laisser des détritus dans
litter[2] *n* **1** : portée *f* <a litter of puppies : une portée de chiots> **2** STRETCHER : brancard *m*, civière *f* **3** RUBBISH : détritus *mpl* **4** *or* **kitty litter** : litière *f* (de chat)
little[1] ['lɪtəl] *adv* **less** ['lɛs]; **least** ['li:st] **1** RARELY : peu <she sings very little these days : elle chante tres peu ces temps-ci> **2 little did I think that** . . . : jamais j'aurais cru que . . . **3 as little as possible** : le moins possible
little[2] *adj* **littler** *or* **less** ['lɛs] *or* **lesser** ['lɛsər]; **littlest** *or* **least** ['li:st] **1** SMALL : petit <little feet : petits pieds> **2** : peu de <very little money : bien peu d'argent> <little time : peu de temps> **3** YOUNG : petit, jeune <my little brother : mon petit frère> **4** TRIVIAL : insignifiant, sans importance
little[3] *n* **1** : peu *m* <I'm happy with little : je me contente de peu> **2 a little** SOMEWHAT : un peu
Little Dipper → **dipper**
liturgical [lə'tərdʒɪkəl] *adj* : liturgique
liturgy ['lɪtərdʒi] *n, pl* **-gies** : liturgie *f*
livable ['lɪvəbəl] *adj* **1** INHABITABLE : habitable **2** ENDURABLE : supportable
live[1] ['lɪv] *v* **lived; living** *vi* **1** : être vivant, vivre **2** DWELL : demeurer, habiter **3 to live on** : vivre de, se nourrir de **4 to live for** : vivre pour — *vt* : vivre <to live one's life : vivre sa vie>
live[2] ['laɪv] *adj* **1** LIVING : vivant **2** BURNING : ardent <live coals : charbons ardents> **3** : sous tension <live circuits : circuits sous tension> **4** : non explosé <a live bomb : une bombe non explosée> **5** : d'actualité <live issues : sujets d'actualité> **6** : en direct <a live interview : une entrevue en direct>
livelihood ['laɪvliˌhʊd] *n* : moyens *mpl* de subsistance
liveliness ['laɪvlinəs] *n* : vivacité *f*, entrain *m*
livelong ['lɪv'lɔŋ] *adj* **all the livelong day** : tout au long de la journée

lively ['laɪvli] *adj* **livelier; -est** : vif, vivant, entraînant, enlevant *Can*
liven ['laɪvən] *vt* ENLIVEN : animer, égayer — *vi* : s'animer, s'égayer
liver ['lɪvər] *n* : foie *m*
liveried ['lɪvərɪd, 'lɪvrɪd] *adj* : en livrée
livery ['lɪvərɪ] *n, pl* **-eries 1** UNIFORM : livrée *f* **2** : pension *f* (pour un cheval)
lives → **life**
livestock ['laɪvˌstɑk] *n* : bétail *m*
livid ['lɪvəd] *adj* **1** BLACK-AND-BLUE : couvert de bleus **2** PALE : livide, blême **3** ENRAGED : furibond, en rage
living¹ ['lɪvɪŋ] *adj* : vivant
living² *n* **to earn one's living** : gagner sa vie
living room *n* : salle *f* de séjour, salon *m*
lizard ['lɪzərd] *n* : lézard *m*
llama ['lɑmə, ˈjɑ-] *n* : lama *m*
load¹ ['loːd] *vt* **1** : charger <to load a truck : charger un camion> **2** : charger (un fusil, un appareil photo, etc.) **3 to be loaded (down) with** : être chargé de, être plein de
load² *n* **1** CARGO : chargement *m*, cargaison *f* **2** WEIGHT : charge *f* **3** BURDEN : fardeau *m*, poids *m* **4 loads of** : beaucoup <loads of work : beaucoup de travail>
loaf¹ ['loːf] *vi* : fainéanter, paresser
loaf² *n, pl* **loaves** ['loːvz] : pain *m* <a loaf of bread : un pain>
loafer ['loːfər] *n* : fainéant *m*, fainéante *f*
loam ['loːm] *n* : terreau *m*
loan¹ ['loːn] *vt* : prêter
loan² *n* : emprunt *m*, prêt *m*
loath ['loːθ, 'loːð] *adj* : peu enclin, peu disposé
loathe ['loːð] *vt* **loathed; loathing** : détester, haïr
loathing ['loːðɪŋ] *n* : aversion *f*, répugnance *f*
loathsome ['loːθsəm, 'loːð-] *adj* : répugnant, dégoûtant
lob¹ ['lɑb] *v* **lobbed; lobbing** : lober (aux sports)
lob² *n* : lob *m*
lobby¹ ['lɑbi] *v* **-bied; -bying** *vt* : faire des pressions sur (en politique) — *vi* : faire pression
lobby² *n, pl* **-bies 1** : hall *m*, vestibule *m* <hotel lobby : hall d'hôtel> **2** LOBBYISTS : groupe *m* de pression
lobbyist ['lɑbɪɪst] *n* : membre *m* d'un groupe de pression
lobe ['loːb] *n* : lobe *m*
lobster ['lɑbstər] *n* : homard *m*
local¹ ['loːkəl] *adj* : local — **locally** *adv*
local² *n* **1** : omnibus *m* local, train *m* local **2 locals** *npl* : gens *mpl* du pays, personnes *fpl* du coin
locale [loˈkæl] *n* **1** PLACE : endroit *m*, lieu *m* **2** SETTING : scène *f*
locality [loˈkælət̬i] *n, pl* **-ties** : localité *f*
localization [ˌloːkələˈzeɪʃən] *n* : localisation *f*
localize ['loːkəˌlaɪz] *vt* **-ized; -izing** : localiser
locate ['loːˌkeɪt] *v* **-cated; -cating** *vi* SETTLE : s'établir — *vt* **1** POSITION, SITUATE : situer **2** FIND : trouver, localiser
location [loˈkeɪʃən] *n* **1** POSITION : emplacement *m*, site *m* **2** PLACE : endroit *m* **3 on ~** : en extérieur <filmed on location : tourné en extérieur>
lock¹ ['lɑk] *vt* **1** : fermer à clé, verrouiller, barrer *Can* <lock the door : verrouillez la porte> **2** CONFINE : enfermer **3** GRIP : bloquer (un mécanisme) **4** HOLD : serrer <to be locked in an embrace : être enlacé> — *vi* **1** : se fermer à clé **2** : se bloquer (se dit des freins, etc.)
lock² *n* **1** : mèche *f*, boucle *f* <a lock of hair : une mèche de cheveux> **2** : serrure *f* (d'une porte, etc.) **3** : écluse *f* (dans un canal)
locker ['lɑkər] *n* : vestiaire *m*
locket ['lɑkət] *n* : médaillon *m* (bijou)
lockjaw ['lɑkˌjɔ] *n* : tétanos *m*
lockout ['lɑkˌaʊt] *n* : lock-out *m*
locksmith ['lɑkˌsmɪθ] *n* : serrurier *m*
locomotion [ˌloːkəˈmoːʃən] *n* : locomotion *f*
locomotive¹ [ˌloːkəˈmoːt̬ɪv] *adj* : locomoteur
locomotive² *n* : locomotive *f*
locust ['loːkəst] *n* **1** : criquet *m* migrateur (insecte) **2** *or* **locust tree** : caroubier *m*
locution [loˈkjuːʃən] *n* : locution *f*
lode ['loːd] *n* : veine *f*, filon *m*
lodestone ['loːdˌstoːn] *n* : magnétite *f*
lodge¹ ['lɑdʒ] *v* **lodged; lodging** *vt* **1** HOUSE : loger, héberger **2** FILE : déposer <to lodge a complaint : porter plainte> — *vi* : se loger <the bullet was lodged in a tree : la balle s'est logée dans un arbre>
lodge² *n* **1** : pavillon *m* <hunting lodge : pavillon de chasse> **2** : abri *m* (d'un animal) **3** : loge *f* (de francs-maçons)
lodger ['lɑdʒər] *n* : locataire *mf*, pensionnaire *mf*
lodging ['lɑdʒɪŋ] *n* **1** : hébergement *m* **2 lodgings** *npl* : logement *m*
loft [lɔft] *n* **1** ATTIC : grenier *m* **2** *or* **hayloft** : grenier *m* à foin **3** GALLERY : tribune *f* <choir loft : tribune de la chorale>
lofty ['lɔfti] *adj* **loftier; -est 1** NOBLE : noble **2** HAUGHTY : fier, hautain **3** HIGH : haut, élevé
log¹ ['lɔg, 'lɑg] *vt* **logged; logging 1** : abattre, tronçonner (des arbres) **2** RECORD : noter, consigner (des renseignements)
log² *n* **1** : rondin *m*, bûche *f*, billot *m* *Can* **2** RECORD : journal *m* de bord (d'un avion, d'un navire)
logarithm ['lɔgəˌrɪðəm, 'lɑ-] *n* : logarithme *m*

logger [ˈlɔgər, ˈlɑ-] *n* : bûcheron *m*, -ronne *f*

loggerhead [ˈlɔgərˌhɛd, ˈlɑ-] *n* **to be at loggerheads** : être en désaccord

logic [ˈlɑdʒɪk] *n* : logique *f*

logical [ˈlɑdʒɪkəl] *adj* : logique — **logically** [-kli] *adv*

logician [loˈdʒɪʃən] *n* : logicien *m*, -cienne *f*

logistic [ləˈdʒɪstɪk, lo-] *adj* : logistique

logistics [ləˈdʒɪstɪks, lo-] *ns & pl* : logistique *f*

logo [ˈloːˌgoː] *n, pl* **logos** [-ˌgoːz] : logo *m*

loin [ˈlɔɪn] *n* **1** : longe *f* (de porc, etc.) **2 loins** *npl* : reins *mpl* (en anatomie)

loiter [ˈlɔɪtər] *vi* : traîner, lambiner *fam*

loiterer [ˈlɔɪtərər] *n* : flâneur *m*, -neuse *f*

loll [ˈlɑl] *vi* LOUNGE : se prélasser

lollipop *or* **lollypop** [ˈlɑliˌpɑp] *n* : sucette *f France*, suçon *m Can*

lone [ˈloːn] *adj* **1** SOLITARY : seul, solitaire **2** SOLE : seul, unique

loneliness [ˈloːnlinəs] *n* : solitude *f*

lonely [ˈloːnli] *adj* **lonelier; -est 1** SOLITARY : solitaire, isolé **2** LONESOME : seul

loner [ˈloːnər] *n* : solitaire *mf*

lonesome [ˈloːnsəm] *adj* : seul

long[1] [ˈlɔŋ] *vi* **to long for** : désirer, avoir envie de

long[2] *adv* **1** : longtemps <long ago : il y a longtemps> **2 all day long** : toute la journée **3 as long as** *or* **so long as** : aussi longtemps que **4 so long!** : à bientôt!

long[3] *adj* **longer** [ˈlɔŋgər]; **longest** [ˈlɔŋgəst] **1** (*indicating length*) : long <a long road : une route longue> <10 feet long : 10 pieds de long> **2** (*indicating time*) : long <a long silence : un long silence> <how long is the trip? : combien de temps durera le voyage?> **3 to be long on** : avoir beaucoup de

long[4] *n* **1 before long** : dans peu de temps **2 the long and short** : l'essentiel *m*

longevity [lɑnˈdʒɛvəṭi] *n* : longévité *f*

longhand [ˈlɔŋˌhænd] *n* : écriture *f* normale <written in longhand : écrit à la main>

longhorn [ˈlɔŋˌhɔrn] *n* : longhorn *mf*

longing [ˈlɔŋɪŋ] *n* : désir *m*, envie *f*

longingly [ˈlɔŋɪŋli] *adj* : avec désir, avec envie

longitude [ˈlɑndʒəˌtuːd, -ˌtjuːd] *n* : longitude *f*

longitudinal [ˌlɑndʒəˈtuːdənəl, -ˌtjuːd-] *adj* : longitudinal — **longitudinally** *adv*

longshoreman [ˈlɔŋˈʃormən] *n, pl* **-men** [-mən, -ˌmɛn] : débardeur *m*, docker *m*

look[1] [ˈlʊk] *vi* **1** SEE : regarder <look, here he comes! : regarde, le voici!> **2** SEEM : sembler <it looks unlikely : cela semble peu probable> **3** FACE : être exposé, être orienté <the house looks east : la maison est exposée à l'est> **4 to look after** : prendre soin de **5 to look for** EXPECT : attendre **6 to look for** SEEK : chercher **7 to look upon** CONSIDER : considérer, regarder — *vt* : regarder <to look s.o. in the eye : regarder qqn dans les yeux>

look[2] *n* **1** : coup *m* d'œil <to take a look around : jeter un coup d'œil> **2** EXPRESSION : apparence *f*, mine *f* **3** ASPECT : aspect *m*, air *m*

lookout [ˈlʊkˌɑʊt] *n* **1** WATCHMAN : guetteur *m*, sentinelle *f* **2** WATCH : guet *m* <to be on the lookout : faire le guet>

loom[1] [ˈluːm] *vi* **1** APPEAR : surgir **2** APPROACH : être imminent **3 to loom large** : menacer

loom[2] *n* : métier *m* à tisser

loon [ˈluːn] *n* : plongeon *m*, huard *m Can*

loony *or* **looney** [ˈluːni] *adj* **loonier; -est** : dingue *fam*, fou

loop[1] [ˈluːp] *vt* : boucler — *vi* : faire une boucle

loop[2] *n* : boucle *f*

loophole [ˈluːpˌhoːl] *n* : échappatoire *m*, lacune *f*

loose[1] [ˈluːs] *v* **loosed; loosing** *vt* **1** RELEASE : libérer **2** UNTIE : défaire **3** UNLEASH : déchaîner (la colère, etc.)

loose[2] *adj* **looser; -est 1** : qui bouge, mal fixé <a loose tooth : une dent qui bouge> <a loose board : une planche mal fixée> **2** SLACK : lâche, mou, lousse *Can fam* **3** ROOMY : ample, flottant **4** APPROXIMATE : libre, peu exact **5** FREE : échappé, évadé <the horse is loose : le cheval s'est échappé> **6** FRIABLE : meuble <loose soil : terre meuble> **7** : mobile, volant <loose sheets of paper : feuilles mobiles> **8** : dissolu <loose conduct : conduite dissolue>

loosely [ˈluːsli] *adv* **1** : sans serrer **2** APPROXIMATELY : approximativement

loosen [ˈluːsən] *vt* : desserrer, relâcher

looseness [ˈluːsnəs] *n* : relâchement *m* (d'une corde), ampleur *f* (d'un vêtement)

loot[1] [ˈluːt] *vi* : piller

loot[2] *n* : butin *m*

looter [ˈluːṭər] *n* : pillard *m*, -larde *f*

lop [ˈlɑp] *vt* **lopped; lopping** PRUNE : élaguer, tailler

lope[1] [ˈloːp] *vi* **loped; loping 1** : courir en bondissant (se dit d'un animal) **2 to lope away** : partir à grandes foulées

lope[2] *n* : course *f* (d'un animal), pas *m* de course (d'une personne)

lopsided [ˈlɑpˌsaɪdəd] *adj* **1** CROOKED : de travers **2** ASYMMETRICAL : asymétrique

loquacious [loˈkweɪʃəs] *adj* : loquace, bavard

loquacity [lo'kwæsəti] *n* : loquacité *f*
lord ['lɔrd] *n* **1** : seigneur *m* <his lord and master : son seigneur et maître> **2** : lord *m* <Lord Carrington : Lord Carrington> **3 the Lord** : le Seigneur
lordly ['lɔrdli] *adj* **lordlier; -est** : hautain, altier
lordship ['lɔrdʃɪp] *n* **Your Lordship** : Monsieur le comte, Monsieur le juge, etc.
Lord's Supper *n* : Eucharistie *f*
lore ['lɔr] *n* : traditions *fpl*, coutumes *fpl*
lose ['lu:z] *v* **lost** ['lɔst]; **losing** ['lu:zɪŋ] *vt* **1** : perdre <I've lost my keys : j'ai perdu mes clés> <to lose weight : perdre du poids> <to lose one's way : perdre son chemin> **2** : faire perdre <the errors lost him his job : les erreurs lui ont fait perdre son emploi> **3** : retarder de <my watch loses three minutes a day : ma montre retarde de trois minutes par jour> — *vi* **1** : perdre **2** : retarder (se dit des horloges, etc.)
loser ['lu:zər] *n* : perdant *m*, -dante *f*
loss ['lɔs] *n* **1** : perte *f* <loss of sight : perte de vue> <it's no great loss : ce n'est pas une grosse perte> **2** : déperdition *f*, perte *f* <loss of heat : déperdition de chaleur> **3 losses** *npl* : pertes *fpl*, victimes *fpl* (de la guerre) **4 to be at a loss for words** : ne pas savoir quoi dire
lost ['lɔst] *adj* **1** MISSED : perdu, manqué <a lost opportunity : une occasion manquée> **2** : perdu, égaré <a lost child : un enfant perdu> <to get lost : se perdre> **3** BEWILDERED : perdu, désorienté **4 to be lost in thought** : être absorbé par ses pensées, être plongé dans la réflexion
lot ['lɑt] *n* **1** : tirage *m* <to draw lots : tirer au sort> **2** SHARE : part *m*, partage *m* **3** FATE : lot *m*, destin *m*, sort *m* **4** PLOT : lot *m*, parcelle *f* (de terrain) **5 a lot** : beaucoup <a lot of money : beaucoup d'argent> **6 a lot** OFTEN : souvent
loth ['lo:θ, 'loːð] → **loath**
lotion ['lo:ʃən] *n* : lotion *f*
lottery ['lɑtəri] *n, pl* **-teries** : loterie *f*
lotus ['lo:təs] *n* : lotus *m*
loud[1] ['laʊd] *adv* : fort <to think out loud : penser tout haut>
loud[2] *adj* **1** : fort, grand <loud music : musique forte> <a loud cry : un grand cri> **2** FLASHY : criard, voyant
loudly ['laʊdli] *adv* : bruyamment
loudness ['laʊdnəs] *n* : force *f*, intensité *f*
loudspeaker ['laʊd,spi:kər] *n* : haut-parleur *m*
lounge[1] ['laʊndʒ] *vi* **lounged; lounging** : flâner, paresser
lounge[2] *n* : salon *m*
louse ['laʊs] *n, pl* **lice** ['laɪs] : pou *m*
lousy ['laʊzi] *adj* **lousier; -est 1** : pouilleux, couvert de poux **2** POOR, SORRY : piètre, mauvais <lousy results : de piètres résultats>
lout ['laʊt] *n* : rustre *m*
louver *or* **louvre** ['lu:vər] *n* **1** SLAT : lame *f* **2** *or* **louver window** : persienne *f*, jalousie *f*
lovable ['lʌvəbəl] *adj* : adorable, charmant
love[1] ['lʌv] *v* **loved; loving** *vt* **1** CHERISH : aimer **2** LIKE : aimer, adorer *fam* <he loved to play the violin : il adorait jouer du violon> — *vi* : aimer
love[2] *n* **1** : amour *m* <to fall in love : être amoureux> **2** ENTHUSIASM, INTEREST : amour *m*, passion *f* **3** BELOVED : amour *m*
loveless ['lʌvləs] *adj* : sans amour
loveliness ['lʌvlinəs] *n* : beauté *f*, charme *f*
lovelorn ['lʌv,lɔrn] *adj* : malheureux en amour, privé d'amour
lovely ['lʌvli] *adj* **lovelier; -est 1** ATTRACTIVE : beau, joli **2** ENJOYABLE : agréable <we had a lovely time : ce fut très agréable>
lover ['lʌvər] *n* : amant *m*, -mante *f*
lovingly ['lʌvɪŋli] *adv* : affectueusement, tendrement
low[1] ['lo:] *vi* : meugler
low[2] *adv* : bas <aim low : visez bas>
low[3] *adj* **lower; lowest 1** : bas <a low wall : un mur bas> <low prices : des bas prix> **2** HUMBLE : modeste <of low birth : d'origine modeste> **3** DEPRESSED : démoralisé, déprimé **4** POOR, INFERIOR : faible <low income : faible revenu> **5** UNFAVORABLE : piètre
low[4] *n* **1** : bas *m* <to reach a low : atteindre un bas> **2** *or* **low gear** : première *f* **3** MOO : meuglement *m*
lowbrow ['lo:,braʊ] *n* : personne *f* peu intellectuelle
lower[1] ['laʊər, 'lo:ər] *vi* **1** SCOWL : se renfrogner **2** DARKEN : s'assombrir
lower[2] ['lo:ər] *vt* **1** : baisser <to lower one's eyes : baisser les yeux> **2** REDUCE : baisser, diminuer **3 to lower oneself** : s'abaisser, s'humilier — *vi* DROP, DIMINISH : baisser
lower[3] *adj* : inférieur, bas
lowland ['lo:lənd, -,lænd] *n* : plaine *f*, basse terre *f*
lowly ['lo:li] *adj* **lowlier; -est** : humble, modeste
loyal ['lɔiəl] *adj* : loyal, fidèle — **loyally** *adv*
loyalist ['lɔiəlɪst] *n* : loyaliste *mf*
loyalty ['lɔiəlti] *n, pl* **-ties** : loyauté *f*
lozenge ['lɑzəndʒ] *n* : pastille *f*
LSD [,ɛl,ɛs'di:] *n* : LSD *m*
lubricant ['lu:brɪkənt] *n* : lubrifiant *m*
lubricate ['lu:brə,keɪt] *vt* **-cated; -cating** : lubrifier
lubrication [,lu:brə'keɪʃən] *n* : lubrification *f*

lucid ['lu:səd] *adj* : lucide, clair — **lucidly** *adv*

lucidity [lu:'sɪdəṭi] *n* : lucidité *f*

luck ['lʌk] *n* **1** FORTUNE : chance *f*, fortune *f* <good luck! : bonne chance!> **2** CHANCE, OPPORTUNITY : hasard *m*, chance *f* <a stroke of luck : un heureux hasard> <as luck would have it : par hasard> <to be out of luck : ne pas avoir de chance>

luckily ['lʌkəli] *adv* : heureusement, par bonheur

luckless ['lʌkləs] *adj* : malchanceux

lucky ['lʌki] *adj* **luckier; -est 1** FORTUNATE : chanceux **2** FORTUITOUS : heureux, fortuné **3** : de chance, porte-bonheur <my lucky day : mon jour de chance>

lucrative ['lu:krəṭɪv] *adj* : lucratif

ludicrous ['lu:dəkrəs] *adj* : ridicule, insensé — **ludicrously** *adv*

lug ['lʌg] *vt* **lugged; lugging** : traîner, trimbaler *fam*

luggage ['lʌgɪdʒ] *n* : bagages *mpl*

lugubrious [lo'gu:briəs] *adj* : lugubre — **lugubriously** *adv*

lukewarm ['lu:k'wɔrm] *adj* **1** TEPID : tiède **2** HALFHEARTED : tiède, indifférent

lull[1] ['lʌl] *vt* **1** CALM : apaiser, calmer **2 to lull to sleep** : endormir

lull[2] *n* : accalmie *f*

lullaby ['lʌləˌbaɪ] *n, pl* **-bies** : berceuse *f*

lumbago [lʌm'beɪgo] *n* : lumbago *m*

lumber[1] ['lʌmbər] *vt* : abattre les arbres — *vi* : marcher pesamment, avancer d'un pas lourd

lumber[2] *n* : bois *m*

lumberjack ['lʌmbərˌdʒæk] *n* : bûcheron *m*, -ronne *f*

lumberyard ['lʌmbərˌjɑrd] *n* : dépôt *m* de bois

luminary ['lu:məˌnɛri] *n, pl* **-naries** : lumière *f*, sommité *f*

luminescence [ˌlu:mə'nɛsənʦ] *n* : luminescence *f*

luminescent [lu:mə'nɛsənt] *adj* : luminescent

luminosity [ˌlu:mə'nɑsəṭi] *n, pl* **-ties** : luminosité *f*

luminous ['lu:mənəs] *adj* : lumineux — **luminously** *adv*

lump[1] ['lʌmp] *vt or* **to lump together** : regrouper, rassembler

lump[2] *n* **1** CHUNK, PIECE : morceau *m*, motton *m Can* <a lump of butter : un morceau de beurre> **2** SWELLING : bosse *f*, grosseur *f* **3** : grumeau *m* (dans la sauce, etc.) **4 to have a lump in one's throat** : avoir la gorge serrée

lumpy ['lʌmpi] *adj* **lumpier; -est** : grumeleux (se dit d'une sauce), plein de bosses (se dit d'un matelas)

lunacy ['lu:nəsi] *n, pl* **-cies** : folie *f*, démence *f*

lunar ['lu:nər] *adj* : lunaire

lunatic[1] ['lu:nəˌṭɪk] *adj* : fou, dément

lunatic[2] *n* : fou *m*, folle *f*; dément *m*, -mente *f*

lunch[1] ['lʌnʧ] *vi* : déjeuner, dîner *Can*

lunch[2] *n* : déjeuner *m*, dîner *m Can*, lunch *m Can*

luncheon ['lʌnʧən] *n* : déjeuner *m*

lung ['lʌŋ] *n* : poumon *m*

lunge[1] ['lʌnʤ] *vi* **lunged; lunging 1** : se jeter en avant **2 to lunge at** : porter une botte à (en escrime)

lunge[2] *n* **1 THRUST** : botte *f*, coup *m* **2 to lunge forward** : faire un mouvement vers l'avant

lurch[1] ['lərʧ] *vi* **1** STAGGER : vaciller, tituber **2** : faire une embardée (se dit d'une voiture)

lurch[2] *n* : embardée *f* (d'une voiture), écart *m* (d'une personne)

lure[1] ['lʊr] *vt* **lured; luring** : attirer

lure[2] *n* **1** BAIT : leurre *m*, amorce *f* **2** ATTRACTION : attrait *m*

lurid ['lʊrəd] *adj* **1** GRUESOME : affreux, horrible **2** SENSATIONAL : à sensation **3** GAUDY : criard, voyant

lurk ['lərk] *vi* : se cacher, se tapir

luscious ['lʌʃəs] *adj* **1** DELICIOUS, DELIGHTFUL : succulent, délicieux **2** SEDUCTIVE : séduisant

lush ['lʌʃ] *adj* : luxuriant, riche

lust[1] ['lʌst] *vi* **to lust after** : désirer (une personne), convoiter (des richesses, etc.)

lust[2] *n* **1** DESIRE : désir *m* (charnel) **2** CRAVING : soif *f*, convoitise *f*

luster *or* **lustre** ['lʌstər] *n* **1** SHEEN : lustre *m* **2** SPLENDOR : éclat *m*

lusterless ['lʌstərləs] *adj* : sans éclat

lustful ['lʌstfəl] *adj* : concupiscent

lustily ['lʌstəli] *adv* : avec vigueur

lustrous ['lʌstrəs] *adj* : lustré, brillant

lusty ['lʌsti] *adj* **lustier; -est** : robuste, vigoureux

lute ['lu:ṭ] *n* : luth *m*

Luxembourger ['lʌksəmbərgər] *n* : Luxembourgeois *m*, -geoise *f*

Luxembourgian [ˌlʌksəm'bərgiən] *adj* : luxembourgeois

luxuriance [ˌlʌg'ʒʊriənʦ, ˌlʌk'fʊr-] *n* : luxuriance *f*

luxuriant [ˌlʌg'ʒʊriənt, ˌlʌk'fʊr-] *adj* : luxuriant, abondant

luxuriate [ˌlʌg'ʒʊriˌeɪṭ, ˌlʌk'fʊr-] *vi* **-ated; -ating 1** FLOURISH : pousser, proliférer **2 to luxuriate in** : prendre plaisir à, s'abandonner à

luxurious [ˌlʌg'ʒʊriəs, ˌlʌk'fʊr-] *adj* : luxueux — **luxuriously** *adv*

luxury ['lʌkʃəri, 'lʌgʒə-] *n, pl* **-ries** : luxe *m*

lye ['laɪ] *n* : lessive *f*

lying → **lie**[1], **lie**[2]

lymph ['lɪmpf] *n* : lymphe *f*

lymphatic [lɪm'fæṭɪk] *adj* : lymphatique

lynch ['lɪntʃ] *vt* : lyncher
lynx ['lɪŋks] *n, pl* **lynx** *or* **lynxes** : lynx *m*, loup-cervier *m*
lyre ['laɪr] *n* : lyre *f*
lyric¹ ['lɪrɪk] *adj* : lyrique
lyric² *n* 1 : poème *m* lyrique **2 lyrics** *npl* : paroles *fpl* (d'une chanson)
lyrical ['lɪrɪkəl] → **lyric¹**

M

m ['ɛm] *n, pl* **m's** *or* **ms** ['ɛmz] : m *m*, treizième lettre de l'alphabet
ma'am ['mæm] → **madam**
macabre [mə'kɑb, -'kɑbər, -'kɑbrə] *adj* : macabre
macadam [mə'kædəm] *n* : macadam *m*
macaroni [ˌmækə'roːni] *n* : macaronis *mpl*
macaroon [ˌmækə'ruːn] *n* : macaron *m*
macaw [mə'kɔ] *n* : ara *m*
mace ['meɪs] *n* **1** : masse *f* (arme ou symbole) **2** : macis *m* (épice)
Macedonian¹ [ˌmæsə'doːnjən, -niən] *adj* : macédonien
Macedonian² *n* : Macédonien *m*, -nienne *f*
machete [mə'ʃeɪi] *n* : machette *f*
machination [ˌmækə'neɪʃən, ˌmæʃə-] *n* : machination *f*, complot *m*
machine¹ [mə'ʃiːn] *vt* **-chined; -chining** : fabriquer (à la machine), usiner
machine² *n* 1 VEHICLE : véhicule *m* **2** : machine *f* <sewing machine : machine à coudre>
machine gun *n* : mitrailleuse *f*
machine language *n* : langage *m* machine
machine–readable *adj* : exploitable par (une) machine
machinery [mə'ʃiːnəri] *n, pl* **-eries 1** MACHINES : machines *fpl* **2** MECHANISM : mécanisme *m* **3** SYSTEM : rouages *mpl* <the machinery of state : les rouages de l'état>
machinist [mə'ʃiːnɪst] *n* : opérateur *m*, -trice *f* (sur machine)
mackerel ['mækərəl] *n, pl* **-el** *or* **-els** : maquereau *m*
mackinaw ['mækəˌnɔ] *n* : grosse veste *f* de laine
mackintosh ['mækənˌtɑʃ] *n Brit* RAINCOAT : imperméable *m*
macramé ['mækrəˌmeɪ] *n* : macramé *m*
mad ['mæd] *adj* **madder; maddest 1** INSANE : fou **2** FOOLISH : insensé **3** ANGRY : furieux **4** ENTHUSIASTIC, CRAZY : fou <mad about her : fou d'elle> **5** RABID : enragé
Madagascan¹ [ˌmædə'gæskən] *adj* : malgache
Madagascan² *n* : Malgache *mf*
madam ['mædəm] *n, pl* **mesdames** [meɪ'dɑm, -'dæm] : madame *f*
madcap¹ ['mædˌkæp] *adj* : fou, écervelé, étourdi
madcap² *n* : fou *m*, folle *f*
madden ['mædən] *vt* **1** CRAZE : rendre fou, exaspérer **2** ENRAGE : mettre en rage, rendre furieux
maddeningly ['mædənɪŋli] *adv* : de façon exaspérante <maddeningly slow : d'une lenteur exaspérante>
made → **make¹**
madhouse ['mædˌhaʊs] *n* : maison *f* de fous
madly ['mædli] *adv* : follement <to love s.o. madly : aimer qqn à la folie>
madman ['mædˌmæn, -mən] *n, pl* **-men** [-mən, -ˌmɛn] : fou *m*, aliéné *m*
madness ['mædnəs] *n* : folie *f*, démence *f*
madwoman ['mædˌwʊmən] *n, pl* **-women** [-ˌwɪmən] : folle *f*, aliénée *f*
maelstrom ['meɪlstrəm] *n* : maelström *m*
maestro ['maɪˌstroː] *n, pl* **-stros** *or* **-stri** [-ˌstriː] : maestro *m*
Mafia ['mɑfiə] *n* : mafia *f*
magazine ['mægəˌziːn] *n* **1** STOREHOUSE : magasin *m* **2** PERIODICAL : magazine *m*, revue *f* **3** : chargeur *m* (d'une arme à feu)
magenta [mə'dʒɛntə] *n* : magenta *m*
maggot ['mægət] *n* : ver *m*, asticot *m*
magic¹ ['mædʒɪk] *or* **magical** ['mædʒɪkəl] *adj* : magique
magic² *n* : magie *f* <as if by magic : comme par enchantement>
magically ['mædʒɪkli] *adv* : magiquement, par magie
magician [mə'dʒɪʃən] *n* : magicien *m*, -cienne *f*
magistrate ['mædʒəˌstreɪt] *n* : magistrat *m*
magma ['mægmə] *n* : magma *m*
magnanimity [ˌmægnə'nɪmətɪ] *n, pl* **-ties** : magnanimité *f*
magnanimous [mæg'nænəməs] *adj* : magnanime
magnanimously [mæg'nænəməsli] *adv* : avec magnanimité
magnesium [mæg'niːziəm, -ʒəm] *n* : magnésium *m*
magnet ['mægnət] *n* : aimant *m*
magnetic [mæg'nɛtɪk] *adj* : magnétique **— magnetically** [-tɪkli] *adv*
magnetic field *n* : champ *m* magnétique
magnetic tape *n* : bande *f* magnétique
magnetism ['mægnəˌtɪzəm] *n* : magnétisme *m*
magnetize ['mægnəˌtaɪz] *vt* **-tized; -tizing 1** : aimanter **2** ATTRACT : magnétiser

magnification [ˌmægnəfəˈkeɪʃən] *n* : grossissement *m*
magnificence [mægˈnɪfəsənts] *n* : magnificence *f*
magnificent [mægˈnɪfəsənt] *adj* : magnifique — **magnificently** *adv*
magnify [ˈmægnəˌfaɪ] *vt* **-fied; -fying 1** ENLARGE : grossir **2** EXAGGERATE : exagérer
magnifying glass *n* : loupe *f*
magnitude [ˈmægnəˌtuːd, -ˌtjuːd] *n* **1** GREATNESS : ampleur *f*, grandeur *f* **2** QUANTITY : quantité *f* **3** IMPORTANCE : importance *f*, magnitude *f*
magnolia [mægˈnoːljə] *n* : magnolia *m*
magpie [ˈmægˌpaɪ] *n* : pie *f*
mahogany [məˈhɑgəni] *n, pl* **-nies** : acajou *m*
maid [ˈmeɪd] *n* **1** MAIDEN : demoiselle *f*, vierge *f* **2** *or* **maidservant** : bonne *f*, domestique *f*, femme *f* de chambre
maiden[1] [ˈmeɪdən] *adj* **1** UNMARRIED : célibataire **2** FIRST : premier, inaugural <maiden voyage : voyage inaugural>
maiden[2] *n* : demoiselle *f*, vierge *f*
maidenhood [ˈmeɪdənˌhʊd] *n* : virginité *f*
maiden name *n* : nom *m* de jeune fille
mail[1] [ˈmeɪl] *vt* : envoyer par la poste
mail[2] *n* **1** : poste *f* <to put in the mail : mettre à la poste> **2** LETTERS : courrier *m* **3** : mailles *fpl* <coat of mail : cotte de mailles>
mailbox [ˈmeɪlˌbɑks] *n* : boîte *f* aux lettres
mailman [ˈmeɪlˌmæn, -mən] *n, pl* **-men** [-mən, -ˌmɛn] : facteur *m*
maim [ˈmeɪm] *vt* : estropier, mutiler
main[1] [ˈmeɪn] *adj* : principal <the main course : le plat principal>
main[2] *n* **1** : canalisation *f* principale (d'eau, de gaz), conduite *f* principale (d'électricité) **2** HIGH SEAS : large *m*, haute mer *f*
mainframe [ˈmeɪnˌfreɪm] *n* : ordinateur *m* central
mainland [ˈmeɪnˌlænd, -lənd] *n* : continent *m*
mainly [ˈmeɪnli] *adv* : principalement, surtout
mainstay [ˈmeɪnˌsteɪ] *n* : pilier *m*, soutien *m* (principal)
mainstream[1] [ˈmeɪnˌstriːm] *adj* : dominant, traditionnel
mainstream[2] *n* : courant *m* dominant
maintain [meɪnˈteɪn] *vt* **1** SERVICE : entretenir (un véhicule, une route, etc.) **2** PRESERVE : maintenir <to maintain silence : garder le silence> **3** SUPPORT : soutenir **4** ASSERT : affirmer
maintenance [ˈmeɪntənənts] *n* **1** UPKEEP : entretien *m* **2** UPHOLDING : maintien *m*
maize [ˈmeɪz] → **indian corn**
majestic [məˈdʒɛstɪk] *adj* : majestueux — **majestically** [-tɪkli] *adv*
majesty [ˈmædʒəsti] *n, pl* **-ties 1** : majesté *f* <Your Majesty : Votre Majesté> **2** GRANDEUR : grandeur *f*, majesté *f*
major[1] [ˈmeɪdʒər] *vi* **-jored; -joring** : se spécialiser
major[2] *adj* **1** MAIN : principal <the major part : la plus grande partie> **2** NOTEWORTHY : majeur, notable **3** SERIOUS : majeur <major surgery : une grosse opération> **4** : majeur (en musique)
major[3] *n* **1** : commandant *m* (de l'armée) **2** FIELD : spécialité *f* (universitaire)
major general *n* : général *m* de division
majority [məˈdʒɔrəti] *n, pl* **-ties** : majorité *f*
make[1] [ˈmeɪk] *v* **made** [ˈmeɪd]; **making** *vt* **1** CREATE : faire, créer <to make noise : faire du bruit> **2** MANUFACTURE : fabriquer, faire **3** CONSTITUTE : constituer <made of gold : en or> **4** PREPARE : préparer <to make a meal : préparer un repas> **5** RENDER : rendre <to make sick : rendre malade> **6** FORM : faire, former **7** COMPEL : faire, obliger <you make me laugh : tu me fais rire> **8** EARN : gagner <to make a living : gagner sa vie> **9** ATTAIN : atteindre, arriver jusqu'à (une position, etc.) — *vi* **1** HEAD : se diriger <she made for home : elle s'est dirigée vers la maison> **2 to make do** : se débrouiller **3 to make good** SUCCEED : réussir **4 to make of** : comprendre à **5 to make off with** : partir avec
make[2] *n* BRAND : marque *f*
make–believe[1] [ˌmeɪkbəˈliːv] *adj* : imaginaire
make–believe[2] *n* : fantaisie *f* <a world of make-believe : un monde d'illusions>
make out *vt* **1** WRITE : faire, écrire <to make out a cheque : faire un chèque> **2** DISCERN : discerner, distinguer **3** UNDERSTAND : comprendre — *vi* FARE : se débrouiller <how did you make out? : comment ça s'est passé?>
maker [ˈmeɪkər] *n* MANUFACTURER : fabricant *m*, -cante *f*
makeshift [ˈmeɪkˌʃɪft] *adj* : improvisé
makeup [ˈmeɪkˌʌp] *n* **1** COMPOSITION : composition *f* **2** COSMETICS : maquillage **3** CHARACTER : caractère *m*, nature *f*
make up *vt* **1** INVENT : inventer **2** : rattraper <to make up the time : rattraper le temps> — *vi* RECONCILE : se réconcilier
maladjusted [ˌmæləˈdʒʌstəd] *adj* : inadapté
maladjustment [ˌmæləˈdʒʌstmənt] *n* : inadaptation *f*

maladroit [ˌmælə'drɔɪt] *adj* : maladroit
malady ['mælədi] *n, pl* **-dies** : maladie *f*, mal *m*
Malagasy[1] [ˌmælə'gæsi; ˌmɑlə'gɑsi, -ʃi] *adj* : malgache
Malagasy[2] *n* **1** : Malgache *mf* **2** : malgache *m* (langue)
malaise [mɑ'leɪz] *n* : malaise *m*
malamute ['mælaˌmjuːt, -ˌmuːt] *n* : malamute *m*, chien *m* malamute
malapropism ['mælaˌprɑpɪzəm] *n* : impropriété *f* de langage
malaria [mɑ'lɛriə] *n* : paludisme *m*
malarkey [mɑ'lɑrki] *n* : balivernes *fpl*, sottises *fpl*
Malawian[1] [mɑ'lɑwiən] *adj* : malawien
Malawian[2] *n* : Malawien *m*, -wienne *f*
Malay[1] [mɑ'leɪ, 'meɪˌleɪ] *or* **Malayan** [mə'leɪən, meɪ-; 'meɪˌleɪən] *adj* : malais
Malay[2] *n* **1** *or* **Malayan** : Malais *m*, -laise *f* **2** : malais *m* (langue)
Malaysian[1] [mə'leɪʒən] *adj* : malaisien
Malaysian[2] *n* : Malaisien *m*, -sienne *f*
male[1] ['meɪl] *adj* **1** : mâle **2** MASCULINE : masculin
male[2] *n* **1** : mâle *m* (en botanique ou en zoologie) **2** MAN : homme *m*
malefactor ['mæləˌfæktər] *n* : malfaiteur *m*, -trice *f*
maleness ['meɪlnəs] *n* : masculinité *f*
malevolence [mə'levələnts] *n* : malveillance *f*
malevolent [mə'levələnt] *adj* : malveillant
malformation [ˌmælfɔr'meɪʃən] *n* : malformation *f*
malformed ['mælˌfɔrmd] *adj* : difforme
malfunction[1] ['mæl'fʌŋkʃən] *vi* : mal fonctionner
malfunction[2] *n* : défaillance *f*, mauvais fonctionnement *m*
Malian[1] ['maliən] *adj* : malien
Malian[2] *n* : Malien *m*, -lienne *f*
malice ['mælɪs] *n* **1** : malveillance *f*, méchanceté *f* **2 with malice aforethought** : avec préméditation
malicious [mə'lɪʃəs] *adj* : malveillant, méchant
maliciously [mə'lɪʃəsli] *adv* : méchamment, avec méchanceté
malign[1] [mə'laɪn] *vt* : calomnier, diffamer
malign[2] *adj* : nuisible, pernicieux
malignancy [mə'lɪgnənsi] *n, pl* **-cies** : malignité *f*
malignant [mə'lɪgnənt] *adj* : malin
malinger [mə'lɪŋgər] *vi* : faire le malade
mall [mɔl] *n* **1** PROMENADE : mail *m*, allée *f* **2** *or* **shopping mall** : centre *m* commercial
mallard ['mælərd] *n, pl* **-lard** *or* **-lards** : colvert *m*, malard *m Can*
malleable ['mæliəbəl] *adj* : malléable
mallet ['mælət] *n* : maillet *m*
malnourished [mæl'nərɪʃt] *adj* : sous-alimenté
malnutrition [ˌmælnu'trɪʃən, -nju-] *n* : sous-alimentation *f*, malnutrition *f*
malodorous [mæl'oːdərəs] *adj* : malodorant
malpractice [ˌmæl'præktəs] *n* : faute *f* professionnelle
malt ['mɔlt] *n* : malt *m*
Maltese[1] [mɔl'tiːz, -'tiːs] *adj* : maltais
Maltese[2] *n* : Maltais *m*, -taise *f*
maltreat [mæl'triːt] *vt* : maltraiter
mama *or* **mamma** ['mɑmə] *n* : maman *f*
mammal ['mæməl] *n* : mammifère *m*
mammary gland ['mæməri] *n* : glande *f* mammaire
mammogram ['mæməˌgræm] *n* : mammographie *f*
mammoth[1] ['mæmə θ] *adj* : colossal, énorme
mammoth[2] *n* : mammouth *m*
man[1] ['mæn] *vt* **manned; manning** : équiper en personnel, assurer une permanence à
man[2] *n, pl* **men** ['mɛn] **1** PERSON : homme *m*, personne *f* **2** MALE : homme *m* **3** MANKIND : humanité *f*
manacles ['mænɪkəlz] *npl* **1** SHACKLES : chaînes *fpl* **2** HANDCUFFS : menottes *fpl*
manage ['mænɪdʒ] *v* **-aged; -aging** *vt* **1** HANDLE : manier **2** DIRECT : gérer, diriger **3** CONTRIVE : réussir, arriver — *vi* COPE : se débrouiller
manageable ['mænɪdʒəbəl] *adj* : maniable
management ['mænɪdʒmənt] *n* **1** DIRECTION : gestion *f*, direction *f* **2** MANAGERS : direction *f*
manager ['mænɪdʒər] *n* : directeur *m*, -trice *f*; gérant *m*, -rante *f*; manager *m* (aux sports)
managerial [ˌmænə'dʒɪriəl] *adj* : directorial
mandarin ['mændərən] *n* **1** : mandarin *m* **2** *or* **mandarin orange** : mandarine *f*
mandate ['mænˌdeɪt] *n* : mandat *m*
mandatory ['mændəˌtɔri] *adj* : obligatoire
mandible ['mændəbəl] *n* **1** JAW : mâchoire *f* inférieure **2** : mandibule *f* (d'un oiseau ou d'un insecte)
mandolin [ˌmændə'lɪn, 'mændələn] *n* : mandoline *f*
mane ['meɪn] *n* : crinière *f*
maneuver[1] *or Brit* **manoeuvre** [mə'nuːvər, -'nju:-] *v* **-vered** *or Brit* **-vred; -vering** *or Brit* **-vring** : manœuvrer
maneuver[2] *or Brit* **manoeuvre** *n* : manœuvre *f*
maneuverable [mə'nuːvərəbəl, -'nju:-] *adj* : manœuvrable
manfully ['mænfəli] *adv* : courageusement, vaillamment
manganese ['mæŋgəˌniːz, -ˌniːs] *n* : manganèse *m*
mange ['meɪndʒ] *n* : gale *f*
manger ['meɪndʒər] *n* : mangeoire *f*

mangle ['mæŋgəl] *vt* **-gled; -gling 1** MUTILATE : mutiler, déchirer **2** BOTCH : estropier (un texte, un discours, etc.)
mango ['mæŋ,go:] *n, pl* **-goes** : mangue *f*
mangrove ['mæn,gro:v, 'mæŋ-] *n* : manglier *m*
mangy ['meɪndʒi] *adj* **mangier; -est 1** : galeux **2** SHABBY : minable, miteux, élimé
manhandle ['mæn,hændəl] *vt* **-dled; -dling** : malmener, maltraiter
manhole ['mæn,ho:l] *n* : trou *m* d'homme, bouche *f* d'égout
manhood ['mæn,hʊd] *n* **1** COURAGE, MANLINESS : courage *m*, virilité *f* **2** ADULTHOOD : âge *m* d'homme **3** MEN : hommes *mpl*
manhunt ['mæn,hʌnt] *n* : chasse *f* à l'homme
mania ['meɪniə, -njə] *n* : manie *f*
maniac ['meɪni,æk] *n* : fou *m*, folle *f*; maniaque *mf*
maniacal [mə'naɪəkəl] *adj* : maniaque
manicure¹ ['mænə,kjʊr] *vt* **-cured; -curing 1** : manucurer, faire les ongles de **2** CUT, TRIM : tondre <a manicured lawn : une pelouse impeccable>
manicure² *n* : manucure *f*
manicurist ['mænə,kjʊrɪst] *n* : manucure *mf*
manifest¹ ['mænə,fest] *vt* : manifester
manifest² *adj* : manifeste, évident — **manifestly** *adv*
manifestation [,mænəfə'steɪʃən] *n* : manifestation *f*
manifesto [,mænə'fes,to:] *n, pl* **-tos** *or* **-toes** : manifeste *m*
manifold¹ ['mænə,fo:ld] *adj* : multiple, nombreux
manifold² *n* : collecteur *m* (d'échappement), tubulure *f* (d'admission)
manipulate [mə'nɪpjə,leɪt] *vt* **-lated; -lating** : manipuler
manipulation [mə,nɪpjə'leɪʃən] *n* : manipulation *f*
mankind ['mæn'kaɪnd, -,kaɪnd] *n* : humanité *f*, le genre humain
manliness ['mænlinəs] *n* : virilité *f*
manly ['mænli] *adj* **manlier; -est** : viril
manna ['mænə] *n* : manne *f*
mannequin ['mænɪkən] *n* : mannequin *m*
manner ['mænər] *n* **1** KIND : sorte *f* **2** WAY, METHOD : manière *f*, façon *f* <a manner of speaking : une façon de parler> **3** BEARING : attitude *f*, maintien *m* **4 manners** *npl* ETIQUETTE : manières *fpl* **5 manners** *npl* CUSTOMS : mœurs *fpl*, usages *mpl*
mannered ['mænərd] *adj* **1** AFFECTED : maniéré, affecté **2 well-mannered** : bien élevé
mannerism ['mænə,rɪzəm] *n* **1** HABIT : particularité *f*, manie *f*, tic *m* **2** AFFECTATION : maniérisme *m*
mannerly ['mænərli] *adj* : poli, bien élevé
mannish ['mænɪʃ] *adj* : masculin, hommasse
manoeuvre *Brit* → **maneuver**
man–of–war [,mænə'wɔr, -ə'vʊr] *n, pl* **men–of–war** [,men-] : bâtiment *m* de guerre, navire *m* de guerre
manor ['mænər] *n* : manoir *m*
manpower ['mæn,paʊər] *n* : main-d'œuvre *f*
mansion ['mænʃən] *n* : château *m*, manoir *m*, hôtel *m* particulier
manslaughter ['mæn,slɔ,tər] *n* : homicide *m* involontaire
mantel ['mæntəl] *or* **mantelpiece** ['mæntəl,pi:s] *n* : cheminée *f*
mantis ['mæntɪs] *n, pl* **-tises** *or* **-tes** ['mæn,ti:z] : mante *f*
mantle ['mæntəl] *n* **1** CLOAK : manteau *m*, cape *f* **2** BLANKET, COVERING : manteau *f*, couche *f* <a mantle of fog : un manteau de brume>
manual¹ ['mænjʊəl] *adj* : manuel — **manually** *adv*
manual² *n* : manuel *m*
manufacture¹ [,mænjə'fæktʃər] *vt* **-tured; -turing** : fabriquer, manufacturer, confectionner (des vêtements)
manufacture² *n* : fabrication *f*
manufacturer [,mænjə'fæktʃərər] *n* : fabricant *m*, -cante *f*
manure [mə'nʊr, -'njʊr] *n* **1** : fumier *m* (des animaux) **2** FERTILIZER : engrais *m*
manuscript ['mænjə,skrɪpt] *n* : manuscrit *m*
many¹ ['meni] *adj* **more** ['mor]; **most** ['mo:st] **1** : beaucoup de, un grand nombre de **2 as many** : autant de **3 many a time** : maintes fois **4 so many** : tant de **5 too many** : trop de
many² *pron* : beaucoup, un grand nombre
map¹ ['mæp] *vt* **mapped; mapping 1** : faire la carte de **2** *or* **to map out** PLAN : tracer, organiser
map² *n* : carte *f*
maple ['meɪpəl] *n* **1** : érable *m* **2 maple syrup** : sirop *m* d'érable
mar ['mɑr] *vt* **marred; marring** : gâter, gâcher
maraschino [,mærə'ski:no:, -'ʃi:-] *n, pl* **-nos** : marasquin *m*
marathon ['mærə,θɑn] *n* : marathon *m*
maraud [mə'rɔd] *vi* : marauder
marauder [mə'rɔdər] *n* : maradeur *m*, -deuse *f*
marble ['mɑrbəl] *n* **1** : marbre *m* **2** : bille *f* <to play marbles : jouer aux billes>
marbling ['mɑrblɪŋ] *n* : marbrure *f*
march¹ ['mɑrtʃ] *vi* **1** : marcher (au pas) **2** DEMONSTRATE : manifester (en signe de protestation) **3 to march (right) up to** : s'approcher (de qqn) d'un air décidé
march² *n* **1** MARCHING : marche *f* **2** DEMONSTRATION : manifestation *f* **3**

PROGRESS : avancée *f* <the march of time : la marche du temps> **4** : marche *f* (en musique)
March *n* : mars *m*
marchioness [ˈmɑrʃənɪs] *n* : marquise *f*
Mardi Gras [ˈmɑrdiˌgrɑ] *n* : mardi *m* gras
mare [ˈmær] *n* : jument *f*
margarine [ˈmɑrdʒərən] *n* : margarine *f*
margin [ˈmɑrdʒən] *n* **1** : marge *f* (du papier, etc.) **2** EDGE : bord *m*
marginal [ˈmɑrdʒənəl] *adj* : marginal
marigold [ˈmærəˌgoːld] *n* : souci *m*
marijuana [ˌmærəˈhwɑnə] *n* : marijuana *f*
marina [məˈriːnə] *n* : marina *f*
marinate [ˈmærəˌneɪt] *v* **-nated; -nating** : mariner
marine[1] [məˈriːn] *adj* **1** UNDERWATER : marin <marine biology : biologie marine> **2** NAUTICAL : maritime <marine law : droit maritime>
marine[2] *n* **1** : fusilier *m* marin **2 merchant marine** : marine *f* marchande
mariner [ˈmærɪnər] *n* : marin *m*
marionette [ˌmæriəˈnɛt] *n* : marionnette *f* (à fils)
marital [ˈmærəɾəl] *adj* **1** : matrimonial, conjugal **2 marital status** : état *m* civil, situation *f* de famille
maritime [ˈmærəˌtaɪm] *adj* : maritime
marjoram [ˈmɑrdʒərəm] *n* : marjolaine *f*
mark[1] [ˈmɑrk] *vt* **1** : marquer **2** STAIN : tacher, marquer **3** CHARACTERIZE : caractériser **4** INDICATE : marquer, indiquer **5** GRADE : corriger (des examens, etc.) **6** : faire attention à <mark my words! : notez bien ce que je vous dis!> **7 to mark down** : noter, inscrire **8 to mark off** : délimiter
mark[2] *n* **1** TARGET : cible *f* **2** SIGN, SYMBOL : marque *f*, signe *m* **3** GRADE : note *f* **4** IMPRINT : empreinte *f*, marque *f* **5** BLEMISH : tache *f*, marque *f*
marked [ˈmɑrkɪt] *adj* NOTICEABLE : marqué
markedly [ˈmɑrkədli] *adv* : sensiblement, d'une façon marquée
marker [ˈmɑrkər] *n* **1** SIGN : marque *f*, repère *m* **2** *or* **marker pen** : marqueur *m*
market[1] [ˈmɑrkət] *vt* : vendre, commercialiser
market[2] *n* **1** MARKETPLACE : marché *m* <the black market : le marché noir> <wholesale market : marché en gros> **2** DEMAND : demande *f*, marché *m* **3** *or* **food market** : marché *m* (de vivres) <fish market : marché aux poissons> **4 → stock market**
marketable [ˈmɑrkəɾəbəl] *adj* : vendable
marketplace [ˈmɑrkəɾˌpleɪs] *n* : marché *m*
marksman [ˈmɑrksmən] *n, pl* **-men** [-mən, -ˌmɛn] : tireur *m*, -reuse *f* d'élite
marksmanship [ˈmɑrksmənˌʃɪp] *n* : adresse *f* au tir, habileté *f* au tir
marlin [ˈmɑrlɪn] *n* : marlin *m*
marmalade [ˈmɑrməˌleɪd] *n* : marmelade *f*
marmoset [ˈmɑrməˌsɛt] *n* : ouistiti *m*
marmot [ˈmɑrmət] *n* : marmotte *f*
maroon[1] [məˈruːn] *vt* : abandonner
maroon[2] *n* : bordeaux *m* (couleur)
marquee [mɑrˈkiː] *n* **1** CANOPY : marquise *f* **2** *Brit* TENT : grande tente *f*
marquess [ˈmɑrkwɪs] *or* **marquis** [ˈmɑrkwɪs, mɑrˈkiː] *n, pl* **-quesses** *or* **-quises** [-ˈkiːz, -ˈkiːzəz] *or* **-quis** [-ˈkiː, -ˈkiːz] : marquis *m*
marquise [mɑrˈkiːz] *nf* → **marchioness**
marriage [ˈmærɪdʒ] *n* **1** : mariage *m* <aunt by marriage : tante par alliance> **2** WEDDING : mariage *m*, noces *fpl*
marriageable [ˈmærɪdʒəbəl] *adj* : mariable <of marriageable age : en âge de se marier>
married [ˈmærɪd] *adj* **1** : marié <a married couple : un couple marié> <married life : la vie conjugale> **2 to get married** : se marier
marrow [ˈmæroː] *n* : moelle *f*
marry [ˈmæri] *v* **-ried; -rying** *vt* **1** WED : se marier avec, épouser, marier *Can* **2** : marier <the priest married them : le prêtre les a mariés> — *vi* : se marier
Mars [ˈmɑrz] *n* : Mars *f* (planète)
marsh [ˈmɑrʃ] *n* : marais *m*, marécage *m*
marshal[1] [ˈmɑrʃəl] *vt* **-shaled** *or* **-shalled; -shaling** *or* **-shalling 1** ARRANGE, ASSEMBLE : assembler **2** USHER : conduire
marshal[2] *n* **1** : commisaire *m*, capitaine *m* <fire marshall : capitaine des pompiers> **2** : maréchal *m* (militaire) **3** : membre *m* du service d'ordre (d'un défilé, d'une cérémonie, etc.)
marshmallow [ˈmɑrʃˌmɛloː, -ˌmælo:] *n* : guimauve *f*
marshy [ˈmɑrʃi] *adj* **marshier; -est** : marécageux
marsupial [mɑrˈsuːpiəl] *n* : marsupial *m*
mart [ˈmɑrt] *n* MARKET : marché *m*
marten [ˈmɑrtən] *n, pl* **-ten** *or* **-tens** : martre *f*
martial [ˈmɑrʃəl] *adj* : martial <martial law : la loi martiale>
martin [ˈmɑrtən] *n* : martinet *m* (oiseau)
martyr[1] [ˈmɑrtər] *vt* : martyriser
martyr[2] *n* : martyr *m*, -tyre *f*
martyrdom [ˈmɑrtərdəm] *n* : martyre *m*
marvel[1] [ˈmɑrvəl] *vi* **-veled** *or* **-velled; -veling** *or* **-velling** : s'émerveiller
marvel[2] *n* : merveille *f*, miracle *m*
marvelous [ˈmɑrvələs] *or* **marvellous** *adj* : merveilleux — **marvelously** *adv*
Marxism [ˈmɑrkˌsɪzəm] *n* : marxisme *m*
Marxist[1] [ˈmɑrksɪst] *adj* : marxiste
Marxist[2] *n* : marxiste *mf*

mascara [mæs'kærə] *n* : mascara *m*
mascot ['mæs,kɑt, -kət] *n* : mascotte *f*
masculine ['mæskjələn] *adj* : masculin
masculinity [,mæskjə'lɪnəṭi] *n* : masculinité *f*
mash[1] ['mæʃ] *vt* **1** CRUSH : écraser **2** PUREE : faire une purée de, piler *Can*
mash[2] *n* **1** PUREE : purée *f* **2** FEED : pâtée *f* **3** MALT : moût *m*
mask[1] ['mæsk] *vt* **1** DISGUISE : masquer **2** COVER, HIDE : cacher (des émotions, etc.)
mask[2] *n* : masque *m*
masochism ['mæsə,kɪzəm, 'mæzə-] *n* : masochisme *m*
masochist ['mæsə,kɪst, 'mæzə-] *n* : masochiste *mf*
masochistic [,mæsə'kɪstɪk] *adj* : masochiste
mason ['meɪsən] *n* **1** : maçon *m* **2** → **Freemason**
masonry ['meɪsənri] *n, pl* **-ries 1** : maçonnerie *f* **2** → **Freemasonry**
masquerade[1] [,mæskə'reɪd] *vi* **-aded; -ading** : se déguiser, se faire passer
masquerade[2] *n* : mascarade *f*
mass[1] ['mæs] *vi* : se masser
mass[2] *n* **1** : masse *f* (en physique) **2** CLUSTER : masse *f*, ensemble *m* <a mass of houses : un ensemble de maisons> **3** QUANTITY : quantité *f*, masse *f* **4 the masses** : les masses *fpl*
Mass *n* : messe *f*
massacre[1] ['mæsɪkər] *vt* **-cred; -cring** : massacrer
massacre[2] *n* : massacre *m*
massage[1] [mə'sɑʒ] *vt* **-saged; -saging** : masser
massage[2] *n* : massage *m*
masseur [mæ'sər] *n* : masseur *m*
masseuse [mæ'søz, -'suːz] *n* : masseuse *f*
massive ['mæsɪv] *adj* **1** BULKY : massif **2** HUGE : énorme — **massively** *adv*
mass media → **media**
mast ['mæst] *n* **1** : mât *m* (d'un navire) **2** POLE, POST : pylône *m*
master[1] ['mæstər] *vt* **1** CONTROL, SUBDUE : dominer, dompter, maîtriser **2** LEARN : maîtriser
master[2] *n* **1** : maître *m* **2** *or* **master copy** : original *m* **3 master's degree** : maîtrise *f*
masterful ['mæstərfəl] *adj* **1** IMPERIOUS : autoritaire, impérieux, dominateur **2** SKILLFUL : magistral
masterfully ['mæstərfəli] *adv* : magistralement
masterly ['mæstərli] *adj* : magistral
masterpiece ['mæstər,piːs] *n* : chef *m* d'œuvre
masterwork ['mæstər,wərk] → **masterpiece**
mastery ['mæstəri] *n* **1** CONTROL : domination *f*, maîtrise *f* **2** KNOWLEDGE, SKILL : maîtrise *f*
masticate ['mæstə,keɪt] *vt* **-cated; -cating** : mastiquer
mastiff ['mæstɪf] *n* : mastiff *m*
mastodon ['mæstə,dɑn] *n* : mastodonte *m*
masturbate ['mæstər,beɪt] *vi* **-bated; -bating** : se masturber
masturbation [,mæstər'beɪʃən] *n* : masturbation *f*
mat[1] ['mæt] *v* **matted; matting** *vt* TANGLE : emmêler — *vi* : s'emmêler
mat[2] *n* **1** DOORMAT : paillasson *m* **2** RUG : natte *f*, tapis *m* **3** TANGLE : enchevêtrement *m* **4** *or* **exercise mat** : tapis *m* (d'exercice) **5** *or* **matt** *or* **matte** FRAME : bord *m*, cadre *m*
mat[3] → **matte**
matador ['mætə,dɔr] *n* : matador *m*
match[1] ['mætʃ] *vt* **1** OPPOSE, PIT : opposer, rivaliser avec **2** EQUAL : égaler **3** : s'accorder avec, aller avec <her shoes match her dress : ses chaussures vont avec sa robe> — *vi* CORRESPOND : correspondre
match[2] *n* **1** EQUAL : égal *m*, égale *f* <to meet one's match : trouver à qui parler (avec qqn)> **2** : allumette *f* <to strike a match : gratter une allumette> **3** FIGHT, GAME : match *m* **4** MARRIAGE : mariage *m* <they're a good match : ils vont bien ensemble>
matchless ['mætʃləs] *adj* : sans pareil, incomparable
matchmaker ['mætʃ,meɪkər] *n* : marieur *m*, -rieuse *f*
mate[1] ['meɪt] *v* **mated; mating** *vi* **1** FIT : s'emboîter **2** COUPLE : s'accoupler **3** : s'accoupler (se dit des animaux) — *vt* : accoupler (des animaux)
mate[2] *n* **1** COMPANION : camarade *mf*; compagnon *m*, compagne *f* **2** : mâle *m*, femelle *f* (d'animaux) **3** *or* **first mate** : second *m*
material[1] [mə'tɪriəl] *adj* **1** PHYSICAL : matériel <the material world : le monde matériel> <material goods : biens matériels> **2** IMPORTANT : important, pertinent **3 material evidence** : preuve *f* matérielle
material[2] *n* **1** : matière *f*, substance *f* <raw materials : matières premières> **2** FABRIC : tissu *m*, étoffe *f*
materialism [mə'tɪriə,lɪzəm] *n* : matérialisme *m*
materialist [mə'tɪriəlɪst] *n* : matérialiste *mf*
materialistic [mə,tɪriə'lɪstɪk] *adj* : matérialiste
materialize [mə'tɪriə,laɪz] *v* **-ized; -izing** *vt* : matérialiser — *vi* : se matérialiser, se réaliser, prendre forme
materially [mə'tɪriəli] *adv* : matériellement
maternal [mə'tərnəl] *adj* : maternel — **maternally** *adv*
maternity[1] [mə'tərnəṭi] *adj* : de maternité <maternity leave : congé de maternité>
maternity[2] *n, pl* **-ties** : maternité *f*

math [ˈmæθ] → **mathematics**

mathematical [ˌmæθəˈmæt͡ɪkəl] *adj* : mathématique — **mathematically** *adv*

mathematician [ˌmæθəməˈt͡ɪʃən] *n* : mathématicien *m*, -cienne *f*

mathematics [ˌmæθəˈmæt͡ɪks] *ns & pl* : mathématiques *fpl*

matinee *or* **matinée** [ˌmætənˈeɪ] *n* : matinée *f*

matriarch [ˈmeɪtriˌɑrk] *n* : matrone *f*, femme *f* chef de famille

matriarchy [ˈmeɪtriˌɑrki] *n, pl* **-chies** : matriarcat *m*

matriculate [məˈtrɪkjəˌleɪt] *vi* **-lated; -lating** ENROLL : s'inscrire

matriculation [məˌtrɪkjəˈleɪʃən] *n* : inscription *f*, immatriculation *f*

matrimonial [ˌmætrəˈmoːniəl] *adj* : matrimonial, conjugal

matrimony [ˈmætrəˌmoːni] *n* : mariage *m*

matrix [ˈmeɪtrɪks] *n, pl* **-trices** [ˈmeɪtrəˌsiːz, ˈmæ-] *or* **-trixes** [ˈmeɪtrɪksəz] : matrice *f*

matron [ˈmeɪtrən] *n* : matrone *f*

matronly [ˈmeɪtrənli] *adj* : de matrone

matte [ˈmæt] *adj* : mat <a photo with a matte finish : une photo mate>

matter[1] [ˈmæt͡ər] *vi* : importer, avoir de l'importance <it doesn't matter : cela ne fait rien, peu importe>

matter[2] *n* **1** SUBSTANCE : matière *f* **2** QUESTION : question *f* <a matter of taste : une question de goût> **3** AFFAIR : affaire *f*, cas *m*, sujet *m* **4** (*indicating a problem or trouble*) <what's the matter? : qu'est-ce qui se passe?> <what's the matter with your leg? : qu'est-ce que vous avez à la jambe?> **5 matters** *npl* CIRCUMSTANCES : choses *fpl*, circonstances *fpl* <to make matters worse : pour ne rien arranger> **6 as a matter of fact** : à vrai dire, en fait **7 for that matter** : d'ailleurs **8 no matter how** : peu importe comment **9 no matter when** : quelle que soit l'heure

mattress [ˈmætrəs] *n* : matelas *m*

mature[1] [məˈt͡ʊr, -ˈt͡jʊr, -ˈt͡ʃʊr] *vi* **-tured; -turing 1** : mûrir (se dit d'une personne) **2** : arriver à maturité (se dit du vin), se faire (se dit du fromage) **3** : échoir, arriver à échéance (se dit d'une dette, etc.)

mature[2] *adj* **-turer; -est 1** : mûr **2** DUE : échu

maturity [məˈt͡ʊrət͡i, -ˈt͡jʊr-, -ˈt͡ʃʊr-] *n* : maturité *f*

maudlin [ˈmɔdlɪn] *adj* : larmoyant

maul[1] [ˈmɔl] *vt* **1** MANGLE, MUTILATE : mutiler **2** MANHANDLE : malmener

maul[2] *n* MALLET : maillet *m*

Mauritanian[1] [ˌmɔrəˈteɪniən] *adj* : mauritanien

Mauritanian[2] *n* : Mauritanien *m*, -nienne *f*

Mauritian[1] [mɔˈriːʃən] *adj* : mauricien

Mauritian[2] *n* : Mauricien *m*, -cienne *f*

mausoleum [ˌmɔsəˈliːəm, ˌmɔzə-] *n, pl* **-leums** *or* **-lea** [-ˈliːə] : mausolée *m*

mauve [ˈmoːv, ˈmɔv] *n* : mauve *m*

maven *or* **mavin** [ˈmeɪvən] *n* EXPERT : expert *m*, -perte *f*

maverick [ˈmævrɪk, ˈmævə-] *n* **1** : veau *m* non marqué **2** NONCONFORMIST : non-conformiste *mf*

mawkish [ˈmɔkɪʃ] *adj* : mièvre

maxim [ˈmæksəm] *n* : maxime *f*, adage *m*

maximize [ˈmæksəˌmaɪz] *vt* **-mized; -mizing** : maximiser, porter au maximum

maximum[1] [ˈmæksəməm] *adj* : maximum

maximum[2] *n, pl* **-ma** [ˈmæksəmə] *or* **-mums** : maximum *m*

may [ˈmeɪ] *v aux, past* **might** [ˈmaɪt]; *present s & pl* **may 1** (*expressing permission*) : pouvoir <you may leave : vous pouvez partir> <may I? : puis-je?> **2** (*expressing possibility or probability*) : pouvoir <it may fall : il peut tomber> <you may be right : tu as peut-être raison> <it may rain : il se peut qu'il pleuve> **3** (*expressing desires, intentions, or contingencies*) <come what may : quoiqu'il arrive> <may the best man win! : que le meilleur gagne!>

May [ˈmeɪ] *n* : mai *m*

maybe [ˈmeɪbi] *adv* PERHAPS : peut-être

mayfly [ˈmeɪˌflaɪ] *n, pl* **-flies** : éphémère *m*

mayhem [ˈmeɪˌhɛm, ˈmeɪəm] *n* **1** MUTILATION : mutilation *f* **2** HAVOC : destruction *f*, désordre *m*

mayonnaise [ˈmeɪəˌneɪz] *n* : mayonnaise *f*

mayor [ˈmeɪər, ˈmɛr] *n* : maire *m*, mairesse *f*

mayoral [ˈmeɪərəl, ˈmɛrəl] *adj* : de maire

maze [ˈmeɪz] *n* : dédale *m*, labyrinthe *m*

me [ˈmiː] *pron* **1** : moi <give me the book : donne-moi le livre> <for me : pour moi> <it's me : c'est moi> <as big as me : aussi grand que moi> **2** : me, m' <she told me : elle m'a dit> <he's looking at me : il me regarde>

meadow [ˈmɛdoː] *n* : pré *m*, prairie *f*

meadowland [ˈmɛdoˌlænd] *n* : prairies *fpl*

meager *or* **meagre** [ˈmiːgər] *adj* : maigre — **meagerly** *adv*

meagerness [ˈmiːgərnəs] *n* : maigreur *f*

meal [ˈmiːl] *n* **1** : repas *m* <to have a meal : prendre un repas> **2** : farine *f* (de maïs, etc.)

mealtime [ˈmiːlˌt͡aɪm] *n* : heure *f* de repas

mealy [ˈmiːli] *adj* **mealier; -est** : farineux

mean[1] [ˈmiːn] *vt* **meant** [ˈmɛnt]; **meaning 1** INTEND : avoir l'intention de <I

mean to go : j'ai l'intention d'aller> <to be meant for : être destiné à> **2** SIGNIFY : signifier, vouloir dire <what do you mean? : qu'est-ce que tu veux dire?> **3** MATTER : compter, importer <it means a lot to me : ça compte beaucoup pour moi>

mean³ *adj* **1** LOWLY : pauvre, misérable **2** AVERAGE : moyen **3** STINGY : avare, mesquin **4** MALICIOUS : méchant **5 that's no mean feat** : ce n'est pas un mince exploit

mean³ *n* **1** MIDPOINT : milieu *m* **2** AVERAGE : moyenne *f* **3 means** *npl* WAY : moyen *m* **4 means** *npl* RESOURCES : ressources *fpl*, moyens *mpl*

meander [mi'ændər] *vi* **1** WIND : serpenter, faire des méandres **2** WANDER : errer

meaning ['mi:nɪŋ] *n* **1** : sens *m*, signification *f* <double meaning : double sens> **2** INTENT : intention *f*

meaningful ['mi:nɪŋfəl] *adj* : significatif

meaningfully ['mi:nɪŋfəli] *adv* : de façon significative

meaningless ['mi:nɪŋləs] *adj* : sans signification, dénué de sens

meanness ['mi:nnəs] *n* **1** NASTINESS : méchanceté *f* **2** STINGINESS : avarice *f*

meantime¹ ['mi:n,taɪm] *adv* → **meanwhile¹**

meantime² *n* **1** : intervalle *m* **2 in the meantime** : en attendant, entretemps

meanwhile¹ ['mi:n,ˌhwaɪl] *adv* : entretemps

meanwhile² *n* → **meantime²**

measles ['mi:zəlz] *npl* : rougeole *f*

measly ['mi:zli] *adj* **measlier; -est** : misérable, minable *fam*

measurable ['meʒərəbəl, 'meɪ-] *adj* : mesurable

measure¹ ['meʒər, 'meɪ-] *v* **-sured; -suring** : mesurer

measure² *n* **1** AMOUNT : mesure *f*, dose *f* <in large measure : dans une large mesure> <a measure of success : un certain succès> **2** DIMENSIONS : mesure *f* **3** RULER : règle *f* **4 measures** *npl* : mesures *fpl* <security measures : mesures de sécurité>

measureless ['meʒərləs, 'meɪ-] *adj* : infini, incommensurable

measurement ['meʒərmənt, 'meɪ-] *n* **1** MEASURING : mesurage *m* **2** DIMENSION : dimension *f*, mesure *f*

measure up *vi* **to measure up to** : être à la hauteur de

meat ['mi:t] *n* **1** : viande *f* **2** FOOD : aliments *mpl*, nourriture *f* **3** SUBSTANCE : substance *f*

meatball ['mi:t,bɔl] *n* : boulette *f* de viande

meaty ['mi:ti] *adj* **meatier; -est 1** : de viande **2** SUBSTANTIAL : substantiel

mechanic [mɪ'kænɪk] *n* : mécanicien *m*, -cienne *f*

mechanical [mɪ'kænɪkəl] *adj* **1** : mécanique **2** AUTOMATIC : machinal, automatique **— mechanically** *adv*

mechanics [mɪ'kænɪks] *ns & pl* **1** : mécanique *f* **2** MECHANISMS, WORKINGS : mécanismes *mpl*

mechanism ['mekə,nɪzəm] *n* : mécanisme *m*

mechanization [,mekənə'zeɪʃən] *n* : mécanisation *f*

mechanize ['mekə,naɪz] *vt* **-nized; -nizing** : mécaniser

medal ['medəl] *n* : médaille *f*

medalist *or* **medallist** ['medəlɪst] *n* : médaillé *m*, -lée *f*

medallion [mə'dæljən] *n* : médaillon *m*

meddle ['medəl] *vi* **-dled; -dling** : se mêler

meddlesome ['medəlsəm] *adj* : qui se mêle de tout, indiscret

media ['mi:diə] *ns & pl* **the media** : les médias *mpl*

median¹ ['mi:diən] *adj* : médian

median² *n* : médiane *f* (en mathématiques)

mediate ['mi:di,eɪt] *vi* **-ated; -ating** : servir de médiateur, arbitrer

mediation [,mi:di'eɪʃən] *n* : médiation *f*

mediator ['mi:di,eɪtər] *n* : médiateur *m*, -trice *f*

medical ['medɪkəl] *adj* : médical **— medically** [-kli] *adv*

medicated ['medə,keɪtəd] *adj* : médical, traitant

medication [,medə'keɪʃən] *n* **1** TREATMENT : médication *f*, soins *mpl* **2** MEDICINE : médicament *m*

medicinal [mə'dɪsənəl] *adj* : médicinal

medicine ['medəsən] *n* **1** : médecine *f* <she's studying medicine : elle étudie la médecine> **2** MEDICATION : médicament *m*

medicine man *n* : sorcier *m*

medieval *or* **mediaeval** [mɪ'di:vəl, ,mi:-, ,me-, -di'i:vəl] *adj* : médiéval

mediocre [,mi:di'o:kər] *adj* : médiocre

mediocrity [,mi:di'ɑkrəti] *n, pl* **-ties** : médiocrité *f*

meditate ['medə,teɪt] *vi* **-tated; -tating** : méditer

meditation [,medə'teɪʃən] *n* : méditation *f*

meditative ['medə,teɪtɪv] *adj* : méditatif

medium¹ ['mi:diəm] *adj* : moyen <of medium height : de taille moyenne>

medium² *n, pl* **-diums** *or* **-dia** ['mi:diə] **1** MEAN : milieu *m* <the happy medium : le juste milieu> **2** MEANS : moyen *m* (de communication) **3** SUBSTANCE : milieu *m*, véhicule *m* (en biologique ou en physique) **4** : moyen *m* (artistique) **5** *pl* **mediums** SPIRITUALIST : médium *m*

medley ['medli] *n, pl* **-leys 1** MIXTURE : mélange *m* **2** : pot-pourri *m* (de chansons)

meek ['mi:k] *adj* : doux, docile

meekly ['mi:kli] *adv* : doucement

meekness ['mi:knəs] *n* : douceur *f*
meet[1] ['mi:t] *v* **met** ['mɛt]; **meeting** *vt* **1** ENCOUNTER : rencontrer **2** : faire la connaissance de <I've never met her : je n'ai pas fait sa connaissance> **3** JOIN : rejoindre **4** CONFRONT : affronter <to meet the enemy : affronter l'ennemi> **5** SATISFY : satisfaire **6** AWAIT : attendre <I'll meet you at the station : je t'attendrai à la gare> — *vi* **1** : se rencontrer **2** : ASSEMBLE : se réunir
meet[2] *n* : rencontre *f* (aux sports)
meeting ['mi:ɾɪŋ] *n* : réunion *f*
meetinghouse ['mi:ɾɪŋˌhaʊs] *n* : temple *m*
megabyte ['mɛgəˌbaɪt] *n* : mégaoctet *m*
megahertz ['mɛgəˌhɚts, -ˌhɛrts] *ns & pl* : mégahertz *m*
megaphone ['mɛgəˌfo:n] *n* : porte-voix *m*, mégaphone *m*
melancholy[1] ['mɛlənˌkɑli] *adj* : mélancolique
melancholy[2] *n, pl* **-cholies** : mélancolie *f*
melanoma [ˌmɛlə'no:mə] *n, pl* **-mas** : mélanome *m*
melee ['meɪˌleɪ, meɪ'leɪ] *n* : mêlée *f*
meliorate ['mi:ljəˌreɪt, 'mi:liə-] → **ameliorate**
mellow[1] ['mɛlo:] *vt* : adoucir — *vi* **1** : s'adoucir **2** AGE : mûrir
mellow[2] *adj* **1** MILD : doux, moelleux **2** RIPE : mûr **3** RELAXED : détendu
mellowness ['mɛlonəs] *n* : douceur *f*, moelleux *m*
melodic [mə'lɑdɪk] *adj* : mélodique — **melodically** [-dɪkli] *adv*
melodious [mə'lo:diəs] *adj* : mélodieux — **melodiously** *adv*
melodrama ['mɛləˌdrɑmə, -ˌdræ-] *n* : mélodrame *m*
melodramatic [ˌmɛlədrə'mæɾɪk] *adj* : mélodramatique
melodramatically [ˌmɛlədrə'mæɾɪkli] *adv* : de façon mélodramatique
melody ['mɛlədi] *n, pl* **-dies** : mélodie *f*
melon ['mɛlən] *n* : melon *m*
melt ['mɛlt] *vi* **1** : fondre **2** SOFTEN : s'attendrir — *vt* **1** : fondre, faire fondre **2** SOFTEN : attendrir <to melt s.o.'s heart : attendrir le cœur de qqn>
melting point *n* : point *m* de fusion
member ['mɛmbɚ] *n* **1** : membre *m;* adhérent *m*, -rente *f* **2** LIMB : membre *m*
membership ['mɛmbɚˌʃɪp] *n* **1** : adhésion *f* **2** MEMBERS : membres *mpl;* adhérents *mpl*, -rentes *fpl*
membrane ['mɛmˌbreɪn] *n* : membrane *f* — **membranous** [mɛmbrənəs] *adj*
memento [mɪ'mɛnˌto:] *n, pl* **-tos** *or* **-toes** : souvenir *m*
memo ['mɛmo:] *n, pl* **memos** : mémorandum *m*
memoirs ['mɛmˌwɑrz] *npl* : mémoires *mpl*
memorabilia [ˌmɛmərə'biliə, -'bɪljə] *npl* : souvenirs *mpl*
memorable ['mɛmərəbəl] *adj* : mémorable
memorably ['mɛmərəbli] *adv* : de façon mémorable
memorandum [ˌmɛmə'rændəm] *n, pl* **-dums** *or* **-da** [-də] : mémorandum *m*
memorial[1] [mə'moriəl] *adj* : commémoratif
memorial[2] *n* : mémorial *m*, monument *m* (commémoratif)
Memorial Day *n* : le dernier lundi du mois de mai (férié aux États-Unis en commémoration des soldats morts à la guerre)
memorialize [mə'moriəˌlaɪz] *vt* **-ized; -izing** COMMEMORATE : commémorer
memorize ['mɛməˌraɪz] *vt* **-rized; -rizing** : mémoriser
memory ['mɛmri, 'mɛmə-] *n, pl* **-ries 1** : mémoire *f* <to have a good memory : avoir une bonne mémoire> **2** RECOLLECTION : souvenir *m*
men → man[2]
menace[1] ['mɛnəs] *vt* **-aced; -acing** : menacer
menace[2] *n* **1** THREAT : menace *f* **2** DANGER : danger *m*
menacing ['mɛnəsɪŋ] *adj* : menaçant
menagerie [mə'nædʒəri, -'næʒəri] *n* : ménagerie *f*
mend[1] ['mɛnd] *vt* **1** IMPROVE : améliorer **2** REPAIR : réparer **3** DARN, SEW : repriser, raccommoder — *vi* HEAL : s'améliorer
mend[2] *n* : reprise *f*
mendicant ['mɛndɪkənt] *n* BEGGAR : mendiant *m*, -diante *f*
menial[1] ['mi:niəl] *adj* : servile <a menial position : un poste subalterne>
menial[2] *n* : domestique *mf*
meningitis [ˌmɛnən'dʒaɪɾəs] *n, pl* **-gitides** [-'dʒɪɾəˌdi:z] : méningite *f*
menopause ['mɛnəˌpɔz] *n* : ménopause *f*
menorah [mə'nɔrə] *n* : candélabre *m* (employé dans des cérémonies religieuses juives)
menstrual ['mɛnɾstruəl] *adj* : menstruel
menstruate ['mɛnɾstruˌeɪt] *vi* **-ated; -ating** : avoir ses règles
menstruation [ˌmɛnɾstru'eɪʃən] *n* : menstruation *f*, règles *fpl*
mental ['mɛntəl] *adj* : mental — **mentally** *adv*
mentality [mɛn'tæləɾi] *n, pl* **-ties** : mentalité *f*
menthol ['mɛnˌθɔl, -ˌθo:l] *n* : menthol *m*
mentholated ['mɛnθəˌleɪɾəd] *adj* : mentholé
mention[1] ['mɛnɾʃən] *vt* **1** : mentionner **2 don't mention it!** : il n'y a pas de quoi! **3 not to mention** : sans parler de
mention[2] *n* : mention *f*

mentor [ˈmɛnˌtɔr, ˈmɛntər] *n* : mentor *m*
menu [ˈmɛnˌju:] *n* : menu *m*
meow[1] [mi:ˈaʊ] *vi* : miauler
meow[2] *n* : miaou *m*
mercantile [ˈmɛrkənˌti:l, -ˌtaɪl] *adj* : mercantile, commercial
mercenary[1] [ˈmərsənˌɛri] *adj* : mercenaire
mercenary[2] *n, pl* **-naries** : mercenaire *mf*
merchandise [ˈmərtʃənˌdaɪz, -ˌdaɪs] *n* : marchandises *fpl*
merchant [ˈmərtʃənt] *n* : marchand *m*, -chande *f*; commerçant *m*, -çante *f*; négociant *m*, -ciante *f*
merchant marine *n* : marine *f* marchande
merciful [ˈmərsɪfəl] *adj* : miséricordieux
mercifully [ˈmərsɪfli] *adv* **1** COMPASSIONATELY : avec clémence **2** FORTUNATELY : par bonheur, heureusement
merciless [ˈmərsɪləs] *adj* : impitoyable — **mercilessly** *adv*
mercurial [mərˈkjʊriəl] *adj* TEMPERAMENTAL : inconstant, d'humeur inégale
mercury [ˈmərkjəri] *n* : mercure *m*
Mercury [ˈmərkjəri] *n* : Mercure *f* (planète)
mercy [ˈmərsi] *n, pl* **-cies 1** CLEMENCY : clémence *f*, miséricorde *f* (en religion) **2** BLESSING, FORTUNE : chance *f*, bonheur *m*
mere [ˈmɪr] *adj, superlative* **merest** : simple, pur, seul <the mere sight of him : sa seule vue> <a mere ten percent : dix pour cent seulement>
merely [ˈmɪrli] *adv* : simplement, seulement
merge [ˈmərdʒ] *v* **merged; merging** *vi* **1** BLEND, COMBINE : se mêler, se joindre, se fondre **2** : fusionner (se dit des affaires) — *vt* : fusionner, joindre
merger [ˈmərdʒər] *n* : fusion *f*
meridian [məˈrɪdiən] *n* : méridien *m*
meringue [məˈræŋ] *n* : meringue *f*
merino [məˈri:noˌ] *n, pl* **-nos** : mérinos *m*
merit[1] [ˈmɛrət] *vt* : mériter
merit[2] *n* : mérite *m*
meritorious [ˌmɛrəˈtoriəs] *adj* : méritoire (se dit d'une action, etc.), méritant (se dit d'une personne)
mermaid [ˈmərˌmeɪd] *n* : sirène *f*
merriment [ˈmɛrɪmənt] *n* : gaieté *f*, hilarité *f*
merry [ˈmɛri] *adj* **merrier; -est** : joyeux, gai <Merry Christmas! : Joyeux Noël!> — **merrily** *adv*
merry-go-round [ˈmɛrigoˌraʊnd] *n* : manège *m* (de chevaux de bois)
merrymaker [ˈmɛriˌmeɪkər] *n* : fêtard *m*, -tarde *f*
merrymaking [ˈmɛriˌmeɪkɪŋ] *n* : réjouissances *fpl*
mesa [ˈmeɪsə] *n* : mesa *f*
mesdames → madam, Mrs.
mesh[1] [ˈmɛʃ] *vi* **1** ENGAGE : s'engrener (en méchanique) **2** TANGLE : s'enchevêtrer **3** COINCIDE, TALLY : cadrer, concorder
mesh[2] *n* **1** NET : maille *f* **2** NETWORK : réseau *m* **3** MESHING : engrenure *f* (en technologie)
mesmerize [ˈmɛzməˌraɪz] *vt* **-ized; -izing 1** HYPNOTIZE : hypnotiser **2** FASCINATE : fasciner, captiver
mess[1] [ˈmɛs] *vt* **1** SOIL : salir **2 to mess up** DISARRANGE : mettre en désordre **3 to mess up** BUNGLE : gâcher — *vi* **1 to mess around** PUTTER : bricoler **2 to mess with** INTERFERE : s'immiscer
mess[2] *n* **1** : mess *m* <officer's mess : mess des officiers> **2** DISORDER : désordre *m*, gâchis *m* <your room is a mess : ta chambre est un désastre>
message [ˈmɛsɪdʒ] *n* : message *m*
messenger [ˈmɛsəndʒər] *n* : messager *m*, -gère *f*
Messiah [məˈsaɪə] *n* **the Messiah** : le Messie *m*
Messrs. → Mr.
messy [ˈmɛsi] *adj* **messier; -est 1** DIRTY : sale **2** UNTIDY : désordonné, en désordre **3** AWKWARD, DIFFICULT : embrouillé, difficile
met → meet[1]
metabolic [ˌmɛtəˈbɑlɪk] *adj* : métabolique
metabolism [məˈtæbəˌlɪzəm] *n* : métabolisme *m*
metabolize [məˈtæbəˌlaɪz] *vt* **-lized; -lizing** : métaboliser
metal [ˈmɛtəl] *n* : métal *m*
metallic [məˈtælɪk] *adj* : métallique
metallurgy [ˈmɛtəlˌərdʒi] *n* : métallurgie *f*
metalwork [ˈmɛtəlˌwərk] *n* : ferronnerie *f*
metamorphosis [ˌmɛtəˈmɔrfəsɪs] *n, pl* **-phoses** [-ˈsi:z] : métamorphose *f*
metaphor [ˈmɛtəˌfɔr, -fər] *n* : métaphore *f*
metaphoric [ˌmɛtəˈfɔrɪk] *or* **metaphorical** [-ɪkəl] *adj* : métaphorique
metaphysical [ˌmɛtəˈfɪzɪkəl] *adj* : métaphysique
metaphysics [ˌmɛtəˈfɪzɪks] *n* : métaphysique *f*
mete [ˈmi:t] *vt* **meted; meting** : infliger, rendre <to mete out punishment : infliger un châtiment>
meteor [ˈmi:tiər, -ˌti,ər] *n* : météore *m*
meteoric [ˌmi:tiˈɔrɪk] *adj* : météorique
meteorite [ˈmi:tiəˌraɪt] *n* : météorite *mf*
meteorologic [ˌmi:tiərəˈlɑdʒɪk] *or* **meteorological** [-ˈlɑdʒɪkəl] *adj* : météorologique
meteorologist [ˌmi:tiəˈrɑlədʒɪst] *n* : météorologue *mf*, météorologiste *mf*
meteorology [ˌmi:tiəˈrɑlədʒi] *n* : météorologie *f*

meter *or Brit* **metre** ['mi:tər] *n* **1** : mètre *m* <two meters high : deux mètres de hauteur> **2** : compteur *m* (d'électricité, etc.) **3** : mesure *f* (en poésie, en musique, etc.) **4** *or* **parking meter** : parcmètre *m France*, parcomètre *m Can*
methane ['meˌθeɪn] *n* : méthane *m*
method ['meθəd] *n* : méthode *f*
methodical [mə'θɑdɪkəl] *adj* : méthodique **— methodically** *adv*
meticulous [mə'tɪkjələs] *adj* : méticuleux **— meticulously** *adv*
metre *Brit* → **meter**
metric ['metrɪk] *or* **metrical** [-trɪkəl] *adj* : métrique
metric system *n* : système *m* métrique
metronome ['metrəˌno:m] *n* : métronome *m*
metropolis [mə'trɑpələs] *n* : métropole *f*
metropolitan [ˌmetrə'pɑlətən] *adj* : métropolitain
mettle ['metəl] *n* : courage *m*, ardeur *f* <to show one's mettle : montrer de quoi on est capable>
Mexican[1] ['meksɪkən] *adj* : mexicain
Mexican[2] *n* : Mexicain *m*, -caine *f*
mezzanine ['mezəˌni:n, ˌmezə'ni:n] *n* : mezzanine *f*
miasma [maɪ'æzmə] *n* : miasme *m*
mica ['maɪkə] *n* : mica *m*
mice → **mouse**
microbe ['maɪˌkro:b] *n* : microbe *m*
microbiology [ˌmaɪkrobaɪ'ɑlədʒi] *n* : microbiologie *f*
microcomputer ['maɪkrokəmˌpju:ṭər] *n* : micro-ordinateur *m*
microcosm ['maɪkroˌkɑzəm] *n* : microcosme *m*
microfilm ['maɪkroˌfɪlm] *n* : microfilm *m*
micrometer *or Brit* **micrometre** ['maɪkroˌmi:tər] *n* : micromètre *m* (unité de mesure)
micron ['maɪˌkrɑn] → **micrometer**
microorganism [ˌmaɪkro'ɔrgəˌnɪzəm] *n* : micro-organisme *m*
microphone ['maɪkrəˌfo:n] *n* : microphone *m*
microprocessor [ˌmaɪkro'prɑˌsɛsər] *n* : microprocesseur *m*
microscope ['maɪkrəˌsko:p] *n* : microscope *m*
microscopic [ˌmaɪkrə'skɑpɪk] *adj* : microscopique
microscopy [maɪ'krɑskəpi] *n* : microscopie *f*
microwave ['maɪkrəˌweɪv] *n* **1** : microonde *f* **2** *or* **microwave oven** : four *m* à micro-ondes, micro-ondes *m*
mid ['mɪd] *adj* : mi <since mid-June : dès la mi-juin> <in the mid nineteenth century : au milieu du dix-neuvième siècle> <she's in her mid thirties : elle a dans les 35 ans>
midair ['mɪd'ær] *n* **in ~** : en plein ciel
midday ['mɪd'deɪ] *n* NOON : midi *m*
middle[1] ['mɪdəl] *adj* **1** CENTRAL : du milieu, central **2** INTERMEDIATE : moyen
middle[2] *n* **1** CENTER : centre *m*, milieu *m* **2 in the middle of** : au milieu de
middle age *n* : la cinquantaine, l'âge *m* mûr
Middle Ages *npl* : Moyen Âge *m*
middle class *n* : classe *f* moyenne
middleman ['mɪdəlˌmæn] *n, pl* **-men** [-mən, -ˌmɛn] : intermédiaire *mf*
middling ['mɪdlɪŋ, -lən] *adj* **1** AVERAGE : moyen **2** MEDIOCRE : médiocre
midge ['mɪdʒ] *n* : moucheron *m*
midget ['mɪdʒət] *n* : nain *m*, naine *f*
midland ['mɪdlənd, -ˌlænd] *n* : région *f* centrale (d'un pays)
midnight ['mɪdˌnaɪt] *n* : minuit *m*
midpoint ['mɪdˌpɔɪnt] *n* : milieu *m*
midriff ['mɪdˌrɪf] *n* : ventre *m*
midshipman ['mɪdˌʃɪpmən, ˌmɪd'ʃɪp-] *n, pl* **-men** [-mən, -ˌmɛn] : aspirant *m*
midst[1] ['mɪdst] *n* : milieu *m* <in the midst of : en plein milieu de> <in our midst : parmi nous>
midst[2] *prep* : parmi
midstream ['mɪd'stri:m, -ˌstri:m] *n* **in ~** : au milieu du courant
midsummer ['mɪd'sʌmər, -ˌsʌ-] *n* : milieu *m* de l'été
midway ['mɪdˌweɪ] *adv* : à mi-chemin
midweek ['mɪdˌwi:k] *n* : milieu *m* de la semaine
midwife ['mɪdˌwaɪf] *n, pl* **-wives** [-ˌwaɪvz] : sage-femme *f*
midwinter ['mɪd'wɪntər, -ˌwɪn-] *n* : milieu *m* de l'hiver
midyear ['mɪdˌjɪr] *n* : milieu *m* de l'année
mien ['mi:n] *n* DEMEANOR : mine *f*
miff ['mɪf] *vt* : vexer
might[1] ['maɪt] (*used to express permission or possibility or as a polite alternative to* **may**) → **may** <it might be true : il se peut que cela soit vrai> <might I speak with her? : puis-je lui parler?>
might[2] *n* **1** STRENGTH : force *f* **2** POWER : puissance *f*, pouvoir *m*
mightily ['maɪṭəli] *adv* **1** EXTREMELY : extrêmement **2** VIGOROUSLY : vigoureusement
mighty[1] ['maɪṭi] *adv* : très, rudement *fam* <that's mighty nice : c'est rudement gentil>
mighty[2] *adj* **mightier; -est 1** STRONG : puissant **2** GREAT : imposant, grand
migraine ['maɪˌgreɪn] *n* : migraine *f*
migrant ['maɪgrənt] *n* : migrant *m*, -grante *f*
migrate ['maɪˌgreɪt] *vi* **-grated; -grating** : migrer
migration [maɪ'greɪʃən] *n* : migration *f*
migratory ['maɪgrəˌtori] *adj* : migrateur <migratory birds : oiseaux migrateurs>
mild ['maɪld] *adj* **1** GENTLE : doux **2** LIGHT : léger **3** TEMPERATE : tempéré

<a mild climate : un climat tempéré> <it's a mild day : il fait doux>

mildew[1] ['mɪl,du:, -,dju:] *vi* : moisir

mildew[2] *n* : moisissure *f*

mildly ['maɪldlɪ] *adv* **1** GENTLY : doucement, avec douceur **2** LIGHTLY, MODERATELY : légèrement, modérément

mildness ['maɪldnəs] *n* : douceur *f*

mile ['maɪl] *n* : mille *m*, mile *m*

mileage ['maɪlɪdʒ] *n* **1** *or* **mileage allowance** : indemnité *f* **2** CONSUMPTION : consommation *f* (de l'essence) <the car gets better mileage : la voiture consomme moins> **3** DISTANCE : distance *f*, nombre *m* de milles, millage *m Can*

milestone ['maɪl,stoːn] *n* **1** LANDMARK : borne *f* milliaire **2** : étape *f* importante, jalon *m* <an important milestone in science : un jalon important dans la science>

milieu [miːl'juː, -'jø] *n, pl* **-lieus** *or* **-lieux** [-'juːz, -'jø] SURROUNDINGS : milieu *m*

militant[1] ['mɪlətənt] *adj* : militant

militant[2] *n* : militant *m*, -tante *f*

militarism ['mɪlətə,rɪzəm] *n* : militarisme *m*

militaristic [,mɪlətə'rɪstɪk] *adj* : militariste

military[1] ['mɪlə,tɛri] *adj* : militaire

military[2] *n* **the military** *n* : l'armée *f*

militia [mə'lɪʃə] *n* : milice *f*

milk[1] ['mɪlk] *vt* **1** : traire (une vache, etc.) **2** EXPLOIT : exploiter

milk[2] *n* : lait *m*

milkman ['mɪlk,mæn, -mən] *n, pl* **-men** [-mən, -,mɛn] : laitier *m*

milk shake *n* : milk-shake *m*

milkweed ['mɪlk,wiːd] *n* : laiteron *m*

milky ['mɪlkɪ] *adj* **milkier; -est** : laiteux

Milky Way : la Voie lactée

mill[1] ['mɪl] *vt* **1** GRIND : moudre **2** GROOVE : créneler — *vi or* **to mill about** SWARM : fourmiller

mill[2] *n* **1** : moulin *m* **2** FACTORY : usine *f*, fabrique *f*

millennium [mə'lɛniəm] *n, pl* **-nia** [-niə] *or* **-niums** : millénaire *m*

miller ['mɪlər] *n* : meunier *m*, -nière *f*

millet ['mɪlət] *n* : millet *m*

milligram ['mɪlə,græm] *n* : milligramme *m*

milliliter ['mɪlə,liːtər] *n* : millilitre *m*

millimeter *or Brit* **millimetre** ['mɪlə,miːtər] *n* : millimètre *m*

milliner ['mɪlənər] *n* : modiste *mf*

million[1] ['mɪljən] *adj* **a million** : un million de

million[2] *n, pl* **millions** *or* **million 1** : million *m* **2 millions** *npl* MASSES : masses *fpl*

millionaire [,mɪljə'nær, 'mɪljə,nær] *n* : millionnaire *mf*

millionth[1] ['mɪljənθ] *adj* : millionième

millionth[2] *n* **1** : millionième *mf* (dans une série) **2** : millionième *m* (en mathématiques)

millipede ['mɪlə,piːd] *n* : mille-pattes *m*

millstone ['mɪl,stoːn] *n* : meule *f*

mime[1] ['maɪm] *v* **mimed; miming** *vt* : mimer — *vi* : faire du mime

mime[2] *n* : mime *mf*

mimeograph[1] ['mɪmiə,græf] *vt* : polycopier

mimeograph[2] *n* : polycopie *f*

mimic[1] ['mɪmɪk] *vt* **-icked; -icking 1** IMITATE : imiter, mimer **2** APE : singer, parodier

mimic[2] *n* : imitateur *m*, -trice *f*

mimicry ['mɪmɪkrɪ] *n, pl* **-ries** : imitation *f*

minaret [,mɪnə'rɛt] *n* : minaret *m*

mince ['mɪnts] *v* **minced; mincing** *vt* **1** CHOP : hacher **2 not to mince one's words** : ne pas mâcher ses mots — *vi* : marcher d'un air affecté

mind[1] ['maɪnd] *vt* **1** TEND : garder, surveiller **2** OBEY : obéir à **3** WATCH : faire attention à <mind your language! : surveille ton langage!> <mind the step! : attention à la marche!> **4** (*indicating dislike*) <I don't mind going : ça ne me dérange pas d'aller> <I wouldn't mind a drink : j'aimerais bien un verre> — *vi* **1** OBEY : obéir **2** (*indicating an objection*) <I don't mind : ça m'est égal> <do you mind if I take the car? : est-ce que cela vous ennuie que je prenne la voiture?>

mind[2] *n* **1** : esprit *m* <state of mind : état d'esprit> <it never entered my mind : cela ne m'est jamais venu à l'esprit> <mind over matter : l'esprit sur la matière> **2** INTELLIGENCE : intelligence *f* **3** OPINION : avis *m* <to change one's mind : changer d'avis> **4** MEMORY : mémoire *f* <to call to mind : se rappeler> **5** REASON : raison *f* <he's out of his mind : il est fou>

minded ['maɪndəd] *adj* **1** INCLINED : disposé **2** (*used in combination*) <narrow-minded : étroit d'esprit> <health-minded : soucieux de la santé>

mindful ['maɪndfəl] *adj* AWARE : attentif — **mindfully** *adv*

mindless ['maɪndləs] *adj* **1** SENSELESS : insensé, stupide **2** HEEDLESS : insouciant **3** BORING : machinal, ennuyeux <a mindless task : un travail machinal>

mindlessly ['maɪndləslɪ] *adv* **1** SENSELESSLY : stupidement **2** HEEDLESSLY : avec insouciance **3** AUTOMATICALLY : machinalement

mine[1] ['maɪn] *vt* **mined; mining 1** : extraire (du charbon, etc.) **2** : miner (avec des explosifs)

mine[2] *n* : mine *f*

mine[3] *pron* : le mien *m*, la mienne *f*, les miens *mpl*, les miennes *fpl* <not your car but mine : pas ta voiture mais la mienne> <her French is better than mine : son français est

supérieur au mien> <a friend of mine : un ami à moi>

minefield [ˈmaɪnˌfiːld] *n* : champ *m* de mines

miner [ˈmaɪnər] *n* : mineur *m*

mineral [ˈmɪnərəl] *n* : minéral *m* — **mineral** *adj*

mineralogical [ˌmɪnərəˈlɑdʒɪkəl] *adj* : minéralogique

mineralogy [ˌmɪnəˈrɑlədʒi] *n* : minéralogie *f*

mingle [ˈmɪŋgəl] *v* **-gled; -gling** *vt* : mêler, mélanger — *vi* : se mêler, se mélanger

miniature[1] [ˈmɪniəˌtʃʊr, ˈmɪnɪˌtʃʊr, -tʃər] *adj* : en miniature

miniature[2] *n* : miniature *f*

minibus [ˈmɪniˌbʌs] *n* : minibus *m*

minicomputer [ˈmɪnikəmˌpjuːtər] *n* : mini-ordinateur *m*

minimal [ˈmɪnəməl] *adj* : minimal

minimally [ˈmɪnəmli] *adv* : à peine, très légèrement

minimize [ˈmɪnəˌmaɪz] *vt* **-mized; -mizing** : minimiser

minimum[1] [ˈmɪnəmem] *adj* : minimum, minimal

minimum[2] *n, pl* **-ma** [ˈmɪnəme] *or* **-mums** : minimum *m*

miniscule → **minuscule**

miniskirt [ˈmɪniˌskərt] *n* : minijupe *f*

minister[1] [ˈmɪnəstər] *vi* **to minister to** : pourvoir à, donner des soins à

minister[2] *n* **1** : ministre *m* (en politique) **2** : pasteur *m* (d'une église)

ministerial [ˌmɪnəˈstɪriəl] *adj* : ministériel

ministry [ˈmɪnəstri] *n, pl* **-tries** : ministère *m*

minivan [ˈmɪniˌvæn] *n* : fourgonnette *f*

mink [ˈmɪŋk] *n, pl* **mink** *or* **minks** : vison *m*

minnow [ˈmɪnoː] *n* : vairon *m*, mené *m Can*

minor[1] [ˈmaɪnər] *adj* **1** UNIMPORTANT : mineur **2** SECONDARY : secondaire <minor role : rôle secondaire>

minor[2] *n* : mineur *m*, -neure *f*

minority [məˈnɔrəṭi, maɪ-] *n, pl* **-ties** : minorité *f*

minstrel [ˈmɪnɪstrəl] *n* : ménestrel *m*

mint[1] [ˈmɪnt] *vt* : frapper

mint[2] *adj* **in mint condition** : à l'état neuf

mint[3] *n* **1** : menthe *f* (herbe) **2** : bonbon *m* à la menthe **3 the Mint** : l'Hôtel *m* de la Monnaie, la Monnaie **4 to be worth a mint** : valoir une fortune

minuet [ˌmɪnjoˈɛt] *n* : menuet *m*

minus[1] [ˈmaɪnəs] *n* **1** : quantité *f* négative **2** *or* **minus sign** : moins *m*

minus[2] *prep* **1** : moins <four minus two : quatre moins deux> **2** WITHOUT : sans <minus her gloves : sans ses gants>

minuscule *or* **miniscule** [ˈmɪnəsˌkjuːl, mɪˈnʌs-] *adj* : minuscule

minute[1] [maɪˈnuːt, mɪ-, -ˈnjuːt] *adj* **minuter; -est 1** TINY : minuscule **2** DETAILED : minutieux

minute[2] [ˈmɪnət] *n* **1** : minute *f* <in ten minutes : dans dix minutes> **2** MOMENT : moment *m* **3 minutes** *npl* : procès-verbal *m* (d'une réunion)

minutely [maɪˈnuːtli, mɪ-, -ˈnjuːt-] *adv* : minutieusement

miracle [ˈmɪrɪkəl] *n* : miracle *m*

miraculous [məˈrækjələs] *adj* : miraculeux — **miraculously** *adv*

mirage [mɪˈrɑʒ, *chiefly Brit* ˈmɪrˌɑʒ] *n* : mirage *m*

mire[1] [ˈmaɪr] *vt* **mired; miring** STICK : embourber <to get mired down in : s'embourber dans>

mire[2] *n* : boue *f*, fange *f*

mirror[1] [ˈmɪrər] *vt* : refléter, réfléchir

mirror[2] *n* : miroir *m*, glace *f*

mirth [ˈmərθ] *n* : gaité *f*, hilarité *f*

mirthful [ˈmərθfəl] *adj* : gai, joyeux

misanthrope [ˈmɪsənˌθroːp] *n* : misanthrope *mf*

misanthropic [ˌmɪsənˈθrɑpɪk] *adj* : misanthrope

misanthropy [mɪˈsænθrəpi] *n* : misanthropie *f*

misapprehend [ˌmɪsˌæprəˈhɛnd] *vt* : mal comprendre

misapprehension [ˌmɪsˌæprəˈhɛnʃən] *n* : malentendu *m*, méprise *f*

misappropriate [ˌmɪsəˈproːpriˌeɪt] *vt* **-ated; -ating** : détourner

misbegotten [ˌmɪsbiˈgɑtən] *adj* **1** ILLEGITIMATE : illégitime **2** : mal conçu (se dit des plans, des lois, etc.)

misbehave [ˌmɪsbiˈheɪv] *vi* **-haved; -having** : se conduire mal

misbehavior [ˌmɪsbiˈheɪvjər] *n* : mauvaise conduite *f*

miscalculate [mɪsˈkælkjəˌleɪt] *v* **-lated; -lating** *vt* : mal calculer — *vi* : se tromper

miscalculation [mɪsˌkælkjəˈleɪʃən] *n* : erreur *f* de calcul, mauvais calcul *m*

miscarriage [ˌmɪsˈkæriʤ, ˈmɪsˌkæriʤ] *n* **1** : fausse couche *f* **2** FAILURE : échec *m* <miscarriage of justice : erreur judiciaire>

miscarry [ˌmɪsˈkæri, ˈmɪsˌkæri] *vi* **-ried; -rying 1** ABORT : faire une fausse couche **2** FAIL : échouer

miscellaneous [mɪsəˈleɪniəs] *adj* : divers, varié

miscellany [ˈmɪsəˌleɪni] *n, pl* **-nies** : mélange *m*, collection *f* disparate

mischance [mɪsˈtʃæns] *n* : malchance *f*

mischief [ˈmɪstʃəf] *n* : espièglerie *f*, malice *f*

mischievous [ˈmɪstʃəvəs] *adj* : espiègle, malicieux

mischievously [ˈmɪstʃəvəsli] *adv* : malicieusement

misconception [ˌmɪskənˈsɛpʃən] *n* : idée *f* fausse

misconduct [mɪsˈkɑndəkt] *n* : inconduite *f*, mauvaise conduite *f*

misconstrue [ˌmɪskənˈstruː] *vt* **-strued; -struing** : mal interpréter
miscreant [ˈmɪskriənt] *n* VILLAIN : scélérat *m*, -rate *f*
misdeed [mɪsˈdiːd] *n* : méfait *m*
misdemeanor [ˌmɪsdɪˈmiːnər] *n* : méfait *m*, délit *m* (judiciaire)
miser [ˈmaɪzər] *n* : avare *m*
miserable [ˈmɪzərəbəl] *adj* **1** UNHAPPY : triste, malheureux **2** WRETCHED : misérable, minable **3** AWFUL : affreux
miserably [ˈmɪzərəbli] *adv* **1** SADLY : tristement **2** WRETCHEDLY : misérablement, lamentablement
miserly [ˈmaɪzərli] *adj* : avare, séraphin *Can*
misery [ˈmɪzəri] *n, pl* **-eries** : tristesse *f*, misère *f*
misfire [mɪsˈfaɪr] *vi* **-fired; -firing** : rater <the engine is misfiring : le moteur a des ratés> <the gun misfired : l'arme a fait long feu>
misfit [ˈmɪsˌfɪt] *n* : inadapté *m*, -tée *f*
misfortune [mɪsˈfɔrtʃən] *n* : malchance *f*, infortune *f*
misgiving [mɪsˈgɪvɪŋ] *n* : doute *m*, crainte *f*
misguided [mɪsˈgaɪdəd] *adj* : malencontreux, fourvoyé, peu judicieux
mishap [ˈmɪsˌhæp] *n* : mésaventure *f*
misinform [ˌmɪsɪnˈfɔrm] *vt* : mal renseigner
misinterpret [ˌmɪsɪnˈtərprət] *vt* : mal interpréter
misinterpretation [ˌmɪsɪnˌtərprəˈteɪʃən] *n* : interprétation *f* erronée
misjudge [mɪsˈdʒʌdʒ] *vt* **-judged; -judging** : mal juger
mislay [mɪsˈleɪ] *vt* **-laid** [-ˈleɪd]; **-laying** : égarer
mislead [mɪsˈliːd] *vt* **-led** [-ˈlɛd]; **-leading** : tromper, induire en erreur
misleading [mɪsˈliːdɪŋ] *adj* : trompeur
mismanage [mɪsˈmænɪdʒ] *vt* **-aged; -aging** : mal gérer, mal administrer
mismanagement [mɪsˈmænɪdʒmənt] *n* : mauvaise gestion *f*
misnomer [mɪsˈnoːmər] *n* : nom *m* inapproprié
misogynist [mɪˈsɑdʒənɪst] *n* : misogyne *mf*
misplace [mɪsˈpleɪs] *vt* **-placed; -placing** : mal placer, égarer
misprint [ˈmɪsˌprɪnt, mɪsˈ-] *n* : faute *f* typographique, coquille *f*
mispronounce [ˌmɪsprəˈnaʊnts] *vt* **-nounced; -nouncing** : mal prononcer
mispronunciation [ˌmɪsprəˌnʌnʧiˈeɪʃən] *n* : faute *f* de prononciation
misquote [mɪsˈkwoːt] *vt* **-quoted; -quoting** : citer inexactement
misread [mɪsˈriːd] *vt* **-read** [-ˈrɛd]; **-reading 1** : mal lire **2** MISUNDERSTAND : mal interpréter
misrepresent [ˌmɪsˌrɛprɪˈzɛnt] *vt* : dénaturer , déformer
misrule[1] [mɪsˈruːl] *vt* **-ruled; -ruling** : mal gouverner
misrule[2] *n* : mauvais gouvernement *m*
miss[1] [ˈmɪs] *vt* **1** : rater, manquer <to miss the target : manquer le but> <he missed his plane : il a raté son avion> **2** : regretter l'absence de <she misses her brother : son frère lui manque> **3** AVOID, ESCAPE : éviter, échapper <he just missed being caught : il a failli être pris> **4** OMIT : omettre, sauter — *vi* : rater son coup (aux sports)
miss[2] *n* **1** : coup *m* manqué **2** FAILURE : échec *m* **3** : mademoiselle *f* <Miss Jones : Mademoiselle Jones> <excuse me, miss : pardonnez-moi, mademoiselle>
missal [ˈmɪsəl] *n* : missel *m*
misshapen [mɪˈʃeɪpən] *adj* : difforme (se dit d'une personne), déformé (se dit d'une chose)
missile [ˈmɪsəl] *n* **1** : missile *m* <guided missile : missile téléguidé> **2** PROJECTILE : projectile *m*
missing [ˈmɪsɪŋ] *adj* **1** ABSENT : absent **2** LOST : égaré, disparu <missing person : personne disparue>
mission [ˈmɪʃən] *n* : mission *f*
missionary[1] [ˈmɪʃəˌnɛri] *adj* : missionnaire
missionary[2] *n, pl* **-aries** : missionnaire *mf*
missive [ˈmɪsɪv] *n* : missive *f*
misspell [mɪsˈspɛl] *vt* : mal orthographier, mal écrire
misspelling [mɪsˈspɛlɪŋ] *n* : faute *f* d'orthographe
misstep [ˈmɪsˌstɛp] *n* : faux pas *m*
mist [ˈmɪst] *n* **1** FOG : brume *f* **2** CONDENSATION : buée *f*
mistake[1] [mɪˈsteɪk] *vt* **-took** [-ˈstʊk]; **-taken** [-ˈsteɪkən]; **-taking 1** MISINTERPRET : mal comprendre **2** CONFUSE : confondre <he mistook her for Nicole : il l'a prise pour Nicole>
mistake[2] *n* **1** ERROR : faute *f*, erreur *f* <by mistake : par erreur> <to make a mistake : se tromper> **2** MISUNDERSTANDING : méprise *f*, malentendu *m*
mistaken [mɪˈsteɪkən] *adj* WRONG : erroné
mistakenly [mɪˈsteɪkənli] *adv* : à tort, par erreur
mister [ˈmɪstər] *n* : monsieur *m* <watch out, mister! : attention, monsieur!>
mistletoe [ˈmɪsəlˌtoː] *n* : gui *m*
mistreat [mɪsˈtriːt] *vt* : maltraiter
mistreatment [mɪsˈtriːtmənt] *n* : mauvais traitement *m*
mistress [ˈmɪstrəs] *n* : maîtresse *f*
mistrust[1] [mɪsˈtrʌst] *vt* : se méfier de, douter de
mistrust[2] *n* : méfiance *f*
mistrustful [mɪsˈtrʌstfəl] *adj* : méfiant
misty [ˈmɪsti] *adj* **mistier; -est 1** FOGGY : brumeux, embrumé **2** TEARFUL : embué

misunderstand [ˌmɪsʌndərˈstænd] *vt* **-stood** [-ˈstʊd]; **-standing** : mal comprendre
misunderstanding [ˌmɪsʌndərˈstændɪŋ] *n* : malentendu *m*
misuse[1] [mɪsˈju:z] *vt* **-used; -using 1** : faire mauvais usage de **2** MISTREAT : maltraiter
misuse[2] [mɪsˈju:s] *n* : abus *m*, mauvais usage *m*
mite [ˈmaɪt] *n* **1** : mite *f* (insecte) **2** BIT : brin *m*, grain *m*
miter *or* **mitre** [ˈmaɪtər] *n* **1** : mitre *f* (d'un évêque, etc.) **2** *or* **miter joint** : assemblage *m* à onglet
mitigate [ˈmɪtəˌgeɪt] *vt* **-gated; -gating** : atténuer, réduire, adoucir
mitigation [ˌmɪtəˈgeɪʃən] *n* : atténuation *f*, adoucissement *m*
mitosis [maɪˈto:sɪs] *n, pl* **-toses** [-ˌsi:z] : mitose *f*
mitt [ˈmɪt] *n* **1** → **mitten 2** : gant *m* (de baseball)
mitten [ˈmɪtən] *n* : moufle *f*, mitaine *f* *Can*
mix[1] [ˈmɪks] *vt* **1** COMBINE : mélanger, combiner **2** STIR : malaxer **3 to mix up** CONFUSE : confondre — *vi* : se mélanger, se mêler
mix[2] *n* : mélange *m*
mixer [ˈmɪksər] *n* **1** *or* **cake mixer** : batteur *m* (électrique), mixer *m*, malaxeur *m* *Can* **2** : malaxeur *m* (de ciment, etc.)
mixture [ˈmɪkstʃər] *n* : mélange *m*
mix-up [ˈmɪksʌp] *n* CONFUSION : confusion *f*
mnemonic [nɪˈmɑnɪk] *adj* : mnémotechnique
moan[1] [ˈmo:n] *vi* : gémir
moan[2] *n* : gémissement *m*
moat [ˈmo:t] *n* : douve *f*
mob[1] [ˈmɑb] *vt* **mobbed; mobbing 1** ATTACK : assaillir **2** CROWD : entourer
mob[2] *n* **1** THRONG : foule *f* **2** GANG : bande *f*
mobile[1] [ˈmo:bəl, -ˌbi:l, -ˌbaɪl] *adj* : mobile
mobile[2] [ˈmo:ˌbi:l] *n* : mobile *m*
mobility [moˈbɪləṭi] *n* : mobilité *f*
mobilization [ˌmobələˈzeɪʃən] *n* : mobilisation *f*
mobilize [ˈmo:bəˌlaɪz] *vt* **-lized; -lizing** : mobiliser
moccasin [ˈmɑkəsən] *n* **1** : mocassin *m* **2** *or* **water moccasin** : serpent *m* venimeux de l'Amérique du nord
mocha [ˈmo:kə] *n* : moka *m*
mock[1] [ˈmɑk, ˈmɔk] *vt* **1** RIDICULE : se moquer de **2** MIMIC : singer, parodier
mock[2] *adj* **1** SIMULATED : simulé **2** PHONY : faux
mockery [ˈmɑkəri, ˈmɔ-] *n, pl* **-eries** : moquerie *f*
mockingbird [ˈmɑkɪŋˌbərd, ˈmɔ-] *n* : oiseau *m* moqueur
mode [ˈmo:d] *n* **1** MANNER : mode *m*, manière *f*, façon *f* **2** FASHION : mode *m*
model[1] [ˈmɑdəl] *v* **-eled** *or* **-elled; -eling** *or* **-elling** *vt* **1** SHAPE : modeler **2** : présenter <to model a dress : présenter une robe> — *vi* : travailler comme mannequin
model[2] *adj* **1** EXEMPLARY : modèle <a model student : un élève modèle> **2** MINIATURE : en miniature
model[3] *n* **1** PATTERN : modèle *m* **2** MINIATURE : maquette *f*, modèle *m* réduit **3** MANNEQUIN : mannequin *m*
modem [ˈmo:dəm, -ˌdɛm] *n* : modem *m*
moderate[1] [ˈmɑdəˌreɪt] *v* **-ated; -ating** *vt* : modérer, tempérer — *vi* **1** CALM : se modérer **2** PRESIDE : présider
moderate[2] [ˈmɑdərəṭ] *adj* : modéré, modique
moderate[3] *n* : modéré *m*, -rée *f*
moderately [ˈmɑdərəṭli] *adv* **1** FAIRLY : moyennement **2** REASONABLY : modérément, avec modération <moderately priced : d'un prix raisonnable>
moderation [ˌmɑdəˈreɪʃən] *n* : modération *f*
moderator [ˈmɑdəˌreɪṭər] *n* : animateur *m*, -trice *f*; président *m*, -dente *f*
modern [ˈmɑdərn] *adj* : moderne
modernity [moˈdərnəṭi] *n* : modernité *f*
modernization [ˌmɑdərnəˈzeɪʃən] *n* : modernisation *f*
modernize [ˈmɑdərˌnaɪz] *vt* **-nized; -nizing** : moderniser
modest [ˈmɑdəst] *adj* **1** HUMBLE : modeste **2** DEMURE : pudique, modeste **3** MODERATE : modique <a modest sum : une somme modique>
modestly [ˈmɑdəstli] *adv* **1** : modestement, avec modestie **2** DEMURELY : décemment, avec pudeur **3** SIMPLY : simplement, sans prétensions
modesty [ˈmɑdəsti] *n* : modestie *f*
modicum [ˈmɑdɪkəm] *n* : petite quantité *f*
modification [ˌmɑdəfəˈkeɪʃən] *n* : modification *f*
modifier [ˈmɑdəˌfaɪər] *n* : modificateur *m*
modify [ˈmɑdəˌfaɪ] *vt* **-fied; -fying** : modifier
modish [ˈmɑdɪʃ] *adj* STYLISH : à la mode
modular [ˈmɑdʒələr] *adj* : modulaire
modulate [ˈmɑdʒəˌleɪt] *vt* **-lated; -lating** : moduler
modulation [ˌmɑdʒəˈleɪʃən] *n* : modulation *f*
module [ˈmɑˌdʒu:l] *n* : module *m*
mogul [ˈmo:gəl] *n* : magnat *m*
mohair [ˈmo:ˌhær] *n* : mohair *m*
moist [ˈmɔɪst] *adj* **1** DAMP : humide **2** : moelleux <gâteau moelleux : moist cake>
moisten [ˈmɔɪsən] *vt* : humecter
moistness [ˈmɔɪstnəs] *n* : humidité *f*, moiteur *f*

moisture [ˈmɔɪstʃər] *n* : humidité *f*
moisturize [ˈmɔɪstʃəˌraɪz] *vt* **-ized; -izing** : hydrater
moisturizer [ˈmɔɪstʃəˌraɪzər] *n* : crème *f* hydratante
molar [ˈmoːlər] *n* : molaire *f*
molasses [məˈlæsəz] *n* : mélasse *f*
mold[1] [ˈmoːld] *vt* **1** SHAPE : mouler, modeler **2** FASHION : façonner, former — *vi* : moisir <the bread will mold : le pain moisira>
mold[2] *n* **1** FORM : moule *m* **2** FUNGUS : moisissure *f*
Moldavian[1] [molˈdeɪviən] *adj* : moldave
Moldavian[2] *n* : Moldave *mf*
molder [ˈmoːldər] *vi* CRUMBLE : tomber en poussière, émietter
molding [ˈmoːldɪŋ] *n* : moulure *f* (en architecture)
moldy [ˈmoːldi] *adj* **moldier; -est** : moisi
mole [ˈmoːl] *n* **1** : grain *m* de beauté (sur la peau) **2** : taupe *f* (animal)
molecular [məˈlɛkjələr] *adj* : moléculaire
molecule [ˈmɑlɪˌkjuːl] *n* : molécule *f*
molehill [ˈmoːlˌhɪl] *n* : taupinière *f*
molest [məˈlɛst] *vt* : molester
mollify [ˈmɑləˌfaɪ] *vt* **-fied; -fying** : apaiser
mollusk *or* **mollusc** [ˈmɑləsk] *n* : mollusque *m*
mollycoddle [ˈmɑliˌkɑdəl] *vt* **-dled; -dling** PAMPER : dorloter
molt [ˈmoːlt] *vi* : muer
molten [ˈmoːltən] *adj* : en fusion
mom [ˈmɑm] *n* : maman *f*
moment [ˈmoːmənt] *n* **1** INSTANT : instant *m*, moment *m* <a moment ago : il y a un instant> **2** TIME : moment *m* <at the moment : en ce moment> **3** IMPORTANCE : importance *f* <to be of great moment : être de grande importance>
momentarily [ˌmoːmənˈterəli] *adv* **1** : momentanément **2** SOON : dans un instant, immédiatement
momentary [ˈmoːmənˌteri] *adj* : momentané
momentous [moˈmɛntəs] *adj* : important, capital
momentum [moˈmɛntəm] *n, pl* **-ta** [-tə] *or* **-tums 1** : moment *m* (en physique) **2** IMPETUS : élan *m*, vitesse *f*
monarch [ˈmɑˌnɑrk, -nərk] *n* : monarque *m*
monarchism [ˈmɑˌnɑrˌkɪzəm, -nər-] *n* : monarchisme *m*
monarchist [ˈmɑˌnɑrkɪst, -nər-] *n* : monarchiste *mf*
monarchy [ˈmɑˌnɑrki, -nər-] *n, pl* **-chies** : monarchie *f*
monastery [ˈmɑnəˌsteri] *n, pl* **-teries** : monastère *m*
monastic [məˈnæstɪk] *adj* : monastique
Monday [ˈmʌnˌdeɪ, -di] *n* : lundi *m*
monetary [ˈmɑnəˌteri, ˈmʌnə-] *adj* : monétaire
money [ˈmʌni] *n, pl* **-eys** *or* **-ies** [ˈmʌniz] : argent *m*
moneyed [ˈmʌnid] *adj* : nanti, riche
moneylender [ˈmʌniˌlɛndər] *n* : prêteur *m*, -teuse *f*
money order *n* : mandat-poste *m*, mandat *m* postal
Mongolian[1] [mɑnˈgoːliən, mɑŋ-] *adj* : mongol
Mongolian[2] *n* **1** : Mongol *m*, -gole *f* **2** : mongol *m* (langue)
mongoose [ˈmɑnˌguːs, ˈmɑŋ-] *n, pl* **-gooses** : mangouste *f*
mongrel [ˈmɑŋgrəl, ˈmʌŋ-] *n* : chien *m* bâtard
monitor[1] [ˈmɑnəˌtər] *vt* : surveiller
monitor[2] *n* : moniteur *m*
monk [ˈmʌŋk] *n* : moine *m*
monkey[1] [ˈmʌŋki] *vi* **-keyed; -keying 1 to monkey around** : s'amuser **2 to monkey with** : tripoter
monkey[2] *n, pl* **-keys** : singe *m*
monkey wrench *n* : clé *f* à molette
monkshood [ˈmʌŋksˌhʊd] *n* : aconit *m*
monocle [ˈmɑnɪkəl] *n* : monocle *m*
monogamous [məˈnɑgəməs] *adj* : monogame
monogamy [məˈnɑgəmi] *n* : monogamie *f*
monogram[1] [ˈmɑnəˌgræm] *vt* **-grammed; -gramming** : marquer d'un monogramme
monogram[2] *n* : monogramme *m*
monograph [ˈmɑnəˌgræf] *n* : monographie *f*
monolingual [ˌmɑnəˈlɪŋgwəl] *adj* : monolingue
monolith [ˈmɑnəˌlɪθ] *n* : monolithe *m* — **monolithic** [ˌmɑnəˈlɪθɪk] *adj*
monologue [ˈmɑnəˌlɔg] *n* : monologue *m*
monoplane [ˈmɑnəˌpleɪn] *n* : monoplan *m*
monopolize [məˈnɑpəˌlaɪz] *vt* **-lized; -lizing** : monopoliser
monopoly [məˈnɑpəli] *n, pl* **-lies** : monopole *m*
monosyllabic [ˌmɑnəsəˈlæbɪk] *adj* : monosyllabique
monosyllable [ˈmɑnəˌsɪləbəl] *n* : monosyllabe *m*
monotheism [ˈmɑnəθiːˌɪzəm] *n* : monothéisme *m*
monotheistic [ˌmɑnəθiːˈɪstɪk] *adj* : monothéiste
monotone [ˈmɑnəˌtoːn] *n* : voix *f* monotone
monotonous [məˈnɑtənəs] *adj* : monotone
monotonously [məˈnɑtənəsli] *adv* : de façon monotone
monotony [məˈnɑtəni] *n* : monotonie *f*
monoxide [məˈnɑkˌsaɪd] *n* : monoxyde *m*
monsoon [mɑnˈsuːn] *n* : mousson *f*
monster [ˈmɑnˌstər] *n* : monstre *m*
monstrosity [mɑnˈstrɑsəti] *n, pl* **-ties** : monstruosité *f*

monstrous ['mɑnʌstrəs] *adj* : monstrueux — **monstrously** *adv*
montage [mɑn'tɑʒ] *n* : montage *m*
month ['mʌnθ] *n* : mois *m*
monthly[1] ['mʌnθli] *adv* : mensuellement
monthly[2] *adj* : mensuel
monthly[3] *n, pl* **-lies** : mensuel *m*, publication *f* mensuelle
monument ['mɑnjəmənt] *n* : monument *m*
monumental [ˌmɑnjə'mɛntəl] *adj* : monumental
moo[1] ['mu:] *vi* : meugler
moo[2] *n* : meuglement *m*
mood ['mu:d] *n* **1** : humeur *f* <to be in a good mood : être de bonne humeur> <I'm not in the mood : ça ne me dit rien> **2** ATMOSPHERE : ambiance *f*
moodily ['mu:dəli] *adv* : d'un air morose
moodiness ['mu:dinəs] *n* : humeur *f* changeante
moody ['mu:di] *adj* **moodier; -est 1** SAD : de mauvaise humeur **2** TEMPERAMENTAL : lunatique, d'humeur changeante
moon ['mu:n] *n* : lune *f*
moonbeam ['mu:nˌbi:m] *n* : rayon *m* de lune
moonlight[1] ['mu:nˌlaɪt] *vi* **-ed; -ing** : travailler au noir
moonlight[2] *n* : clair *m* de lune
moonlit ['mu:nˌlɪt] *adj* : éclairé par la lune
moonshine ['mu:nˌʃaɪn] *n* **1** MOONLIGHT : claire *m* de lune **2** NONSENSE : balivernes *fpl* **3** *or* **moonshine liquor** : alcool *m* de contrebande
moor[1] ['mʊr] *vt* : amarrer
moor[2] *n* : lande *f*
mooring ['mʊrɪŋ] *n* : mouillage *m*
moose ['mu:s] *ns & pl* : orignal *m*
moot ['mu:t] *adj* DEBATABLE : discutable
mop[1] ['mɑp] *vt* **mopped; mopping** : laver (à grande eau)
mop[2] *n* : balai *m* à franges, balai *m* éponge
mope ['mo:p] *vi* **moped; moping** : broyer du noir
moped ['mo:ˌpɛd] *n* : cyclomoteur *m*
moral[1] ['mɔrəl] *adj* : moral <moral support : soutien moral> — **morally** *adv*
moral[2] *n* **1** LESSON : morale *f* **2 morals** *npl* : mœurs *fpl*
morale [mə'ræl] *n* SPIRITS : moral *m*
morality [mə'rælətɪ] *n, pl* **-ties** : moralité *f*
morass [mə'ræs] *n* **1** SWAMP : marais *m* **2** CONFUSION, MESS : fatras *m*, bourbier *m*
moratorium [ˌmɔrə'toriəm] *n, pl* **-riums** *or* **-ria** [-iə] : moratoire *m*
moray ['mɔrˌeɪ, mə'reɪ] *n or* **moray eel** : murène *f*
morbid ['mɔrbɪd] *adj* : morbide
morbidity [ˌmɔr'bɪdətɪ] *n* : morbidité *f*
more[1] ['mɔr] *adv* : plus, davantage <more important : plus important> <the more you eat, the more you want : plus on mange, plus on veut> <once more : une fois de plus> <I don't remember more : je ne me souviens pas davantage>
more[2] *adj* : plus de <more work : plus de travail>
more and more *adv* : de plus en plus
morel [mə'rɛl, mɔ-] *n* : morille *f*
moreover [mɔr'o:vər] *adv* : de plus
mores ['mɔrˌeɪz, -i:z] *npl* CUSTOMS : mœurs *fpl*
morgue ['mɔrg] *n* : morgue *f*
moribund ['mɔrəˌbʌnd] *adj* : moribond
morning ['mɔrnɪŋ] *n* **1** : matin *m*, avant-midi *f Can* <tomorrow morning : demain matin> **2** (*indicating duration*) : matinée *f* <all morning long : pendant toute la matinée>
Moroccan[1] [mə'rɑkən] *adj* : marocain
Moroccan[2] *n* : Marocain *m*, -caine *f*
moron ['mɔrˌɑn] *n* : crétin *m*, -tine *f*
morose [mə'ro:s] *adj* : morose
morosely [mə'ro:sli] *adv* : avec morosité
moroseness [mə'ro:snəs] *n* : morosité *f*
morphine ['mɔrˌfi:n] *n* : morphine *f*
morrow ['mɑro:] *n* : lendemain *m*
Morse code ['mɔrs] *n* : morse *m*
morsel ['mɔrsəl] *n* : morceau *m*, bouchée *f*
mortal[1] ['mɔrtəl] *adj* : mortel — **mortally** *adv*
mortal[2] *n* : mortel *m*, -telle *f*
mortality [mɔr'tælətɪ] *n* : mortalité *f*
mortar ['mɔrtər] *n* : mortier *m*
mortgage[1] ['mɔrgɪdʒ] *vt* **-gaged; -gaging** : hypothéquer
mortgage[2] *n* : hypothèque *f*
mortification [ˌmɔrtəfə'keɪʃən] *n* : mortification *f*
mortify ['mɔrtəˌfaɪ] *vt* **-fied; -fying 1** : mortifier (en religion) **2** HUMILIATE : humilier
mortuary ['mɔrtʃəˌwɛri] *n, pl* **-aries** : morgue *f*
mosaic [mo'zeɪɪk] *n* : mosaïque *f*
Moslem ['mɑzləm] → **Muslim**
mosque [mɑsk] *n* : mosquée *f*
mosquito [mə'ski:ˌto] *n, pl* **-toes** : moustique *m*, cousin *m*, maringouin *m Can*
moss ['mɔs] *n* : mousse *f*
mossy ['mɔsi] *adj* **-mossier; -iest** : moussu
most[1] ['mo:st] *adv* : très, bien, fort <it's most interesting : c'est fort intéressant> <the most beautiful girl : la plus belle fille>
most[2] *adj* **1** : la plupart de <most people believe it : la plupart des gens y croient> **2** GREATEST : le plus de <the most money : le plus d'argent>

most[3] *n* : plus *m* <three weeks at the most : trois semaines au plus> <she had the most : elle en avait le plus>
most[4] *pron* : la plupart <most are discouraged : la plupart sont découragés>
mostly ['mo:stli] *adv* **1** MAINLY : principalement, surtout **2** USUALLY : la plupart du temps
mote ['mo:t] *n* SPECK : grain *m*
motel [mo'tel] *n* : motel *m*
moth ['mɔθ] *n* **1** : papillon *m* de nuit **2** : mite *f* (qui détruit des vêtements)
mother[1] ['mʌðər] *vt* **1** BEAR : donner naissance à **2** PAMPER, PROTECT : dorloter
mother[2] *n* : mère *f*
motherhood ['mʌðər,hʊd] *n* : maternité *f*
mother–in–law ['mʌðərɪn,lɔ] *n, pl* **mothers–in–law** : belle-mère *f*
motherland ['mʌðər,lænd] *n* : patrie *f*
motherly ['mʌðərli] *adj* : maternel
motif [mo'ti:f] *n* : motif *m*
motion[1] ['mo:ʃən] *vi* **to motion to** : faire signe à
motion[2] *n* **1** MOVEMENT : mouvement *m* <to set in motion : mettre en mouvement> **2** PROPOSAL : motion *f* <to second the motion : appuyer la motion>
motionless ['mo:ʃənləs] *adj* : immobile
motion picture *n* MOVIE : film *m*
motivate ['mo:tə,veɪt] *vt* **-vated; -vating** : motiver
motivation [,mo:tə'veɪʃən] *n* : motivation *f*
motive[1] ['mo:tɪv] *adj* : moteur <motive power : force motrice>
motive[2] *n* : motif *m*
motley ['mɑtli] *adj* **1** DIVERSE : divers, hétéroclite **2** MULTICOLORED : bigarré, bariolé
motor[1] ['mo:tər] *vi* : voyager en voiture
motor[2] *n* : moteur *m*
motorbike ['mo:tər,baɪk] *n* : moto *f*
motorboat ['mo:tər,bo:t] *n* : canot *m* automobile
motorcar ['mo:tər,kɑr] *n* : automobile *m*, voiture *f*
motorcycle ['mo:tər,saɪkəl] *n* : motocyclette *f*
motorcyclist ['mo:tər,saɪkəlɪst] *n* : motocycliste *mf*
motorist ['mo:tərɪst] *n* : automobiliste *mf*
mottle ['mɑtəl] *vt* **-tled; -tling** : tacheter, moucheter
motto ['mɑto:] *n, pl* **-toes** : devise *f*
mould ['mo:ld] → **mold**
mound ['maʊnd] *n* **1** PILE : monceau *m*, tas *m* **2** HILL : monticule *m*, tertre *m*
mount[1] ['maʊnt] *vt* : monter — *vi* INCREASE : augmenter, monter
mount[2] *n* **1** SUPPORT : support *m* **2** HORSE : monture *f* **3** MOUNTAIN : mont *m*
mountain ['maʊntən] *n* : montagne *f*
mountaineer [,maʊntən'ɪr] *n* : alpiniste *mf*
mountain goat *n* : chamois *m*
mountain lion → **cougar**
mountaintop ['maʊntən,tɑp] *n* : cime *f*, sommet *m*
mounting ['maʊntɪŋ] *n* SUPPORT : support *m*
mourn ['morn] *v* : pleurer
mournful ['mornfəl] *adj* : triste, lugubre — **mournfully** *adv*
mourning ['mornɪŋ] *n* : deuil *m* <to be in mourning : porter le deuil>
mouse ['maʊs] *n, pl* **mice** ['maɪs] : souris *f*
mousetrap ['maʊs,træp] *n* : souricière *f*
mousse ['mu:s] *n* : mousse *f*
moustache ['mʌ,stæʃ, mə'stæʃ] → **mustache**
mouth[1] ['maʊθ] *vt* **1** : débiter, dire sans conviction <to mouth platitudes : débiter des lieux communs> **2** : articuler silencieusement
mouth[2] ['maʊθ] *n* : bouche *f*
mouthful ['maʊθ,fʊl] *n* : bouchée *f*
mouthpiece ['maʊθ,pi:s] *n* : embouchure *f*, bec *m*
movable *or* **moveable** ['mu:vəbəl] *adj* : mobile
move[1] ['mu:v] *v* **moved; moving** *vi* **1** : bouger <don't move! : ne bougez pas!> **2** PROCEED : avancer **3** RELOCATE : déménager **4** ACT : agir **5** : jouer (aux échecs, etc.) **6** PROPOSE : proposer — *vt* **1** SHIFT : déplacer, bouger **2** PERSUADE : inciter, pousser **3** : émouvoir, toucher <she moved him to tears : elle l'a ému jusqu'aux larmes>
move[2] *n* **1** MOVEMENT : mouvement *m* **2** RELOCATION : déménagement *m* **3** STEP : coup *m*, tour *m* <his next move : son prochain coup> <it's her move : c'est à elle de jouer>
movement ['mu:vmənt] *n* : mouvement *m*
mover ['mu:vər] *n* : déménageur *m*, -geuse *f*
movie ['mu:vi] *n* **1** : film *m* **2 movies** *npl* : cinéma *m*, vues *fpl Can*
mow[1] ['mo:] *vt* **mowed; mowed** *or* **mown** ['mo:n]; **mowing** : tondre
mow[2] ['maʊ] *n* : meule *f*
mower ['mo:ər] → **lawn mower**
Mozambican[1] [,mo:zəm'bi:kən, -zam-] *adj* : mozambicain
Mozambican[2] *n* : Mozambicain *m*, -caine *f*
Mr. ['mɪstər] *n, pl* **Messrs.** ['mɛsərz] : Monsieur *m*
Mrs. ['mɪsəz, -səs, *esp South* 'mɪzəz, -zəs] *n, pl* **Mesdames** [meɪ'dɑm, -'dæm] : Madame *f*
Ms. ['mɪz] *n, pl* **Mss.** *or* **Mses.** ['mɪzəz] : Madame *f*, Mademoiselle *f*

much[1] ['mʌtʃ] *adv* **more** ['mor]; **most** ['mo:st] **1** : beaucoup <much better : beaucoup mieux> **2 as much** : autant

much[2] *adj* **more; most** : beaucoup de <I don't have much money : je n'ai pas beaucoup d'argent>

much[3] *pron* : beaucoup <there is much to do : il y a beaucoup à faire>

mucilage ['mju:səlɪdʒ] *n* : mucilage *m*

muck ['mʌk] *n* **1** MANURE : fumier *m* **2** DIRT, FILTH : saleté *f* **3** MIRE, MUD : boue *f*, fange *f*

mucous ['mju:kəs] *adj* : muqueux

mucus ['mju:kəs] *n* : mucus *m*

mud ['mʌd] *n* : boue *f*, bouette *f Can fam*

muddle[1] ['mʌdəl] *v* **muddled; muddling** *vt* : confondre, embrouiller — *vi* **to muddle through** : se tirer d'affaire

muddle[2] *n* : désordre *m*, fouillis *m*

muddleheaded [,mʌdəl'hedəd, 'mʌdəl,-] *adj* : désordonné, confus

muddy[1] ['mʌdi] *vt* **muddied; muddying** : salir, couvrir de boue

muddy[2] *adj* **muddier; -est** : boueux

muff[1] ['mʌf] *vt* BUNGLE : rater, gâcher, louper *fam*

muff[2] *n* : manchon *m*

muffin ['mʌfən] *n* : muffin *m Can*

muffle ['mʌfəl] *vt* **muffled; muffling 1** ENVELOP : envelopper **2** DEADEN : étouffer, assourdir (des sons)

muffler ['mʌflər] *n* **1** SCARF : écharpe *f*, cache-nez *m* **2** : silencieux *m* (d'un véhicule)

mug[1] ['mʌg] *v* **mugged; mugging** *vi* : faire des grimaces — *vt* ASSAULT : agresser

mug[2] *n* : tasse *f* (pour le café), chope *f* (pour la bière)

mugger ['mʌgər] *n* : agresseur *m*

muggy ['mʌgi] *adj* **muggier; -est** : lourd et humide

mulatto [mu'laṭo, -'læ-] *n, pl* **-toes** *or* **-tos** : mulâtre *m*, -tresse *f*

mulberry ['mʌl,beri] *n, pl* **-ries** : mûrier *m* (arbre), mûre *f* (fruit)

mulch[1] ['mʌltʃ] *vt* : pailler

mulch[2] *n* : paillis *m*

mule ['mju:l] *n* : mule *f*, mulet *m*

mulish ['mju:lɪʃ] *adj* : entêté, têtu

mull ['mʌl] *vt or* **to mull over** : ruminer, réfléchir sur

mullet ['mʌlət] *n, pl* **-let** *or* **-lets** : muge *m*, rouget *m*

multicolored ['mʌlti,kʌlərd, 'mʌl,taɪ-] *adj* : multicolore, bigarré, bariolé

multifaceted [,mʌlti'fæsəṭəd, ,mʌl,taɪ-] *adj* : à multiples facettes

multifamily ['mʌlti,fæmli, ,mʌl,taɪ-] *adj* : pour plusieurs familles

multifarious [,mʌltə'færiəs] *adj* : divers, très varié

multilateral [,mʌlti'læṭərəl, ,mʌl,taɪ-] *adj* : multilatéral

multimedia [,mʌlti'mi:diə, ,mʌl,taɪ-] *adj* : multimédia

multimillionaire [,mʌlti,mɪljə'nær, ,mʌl-,taɪ-, -'mɪljə,nær] *n* : multimillionaire *mf*

multinational [,mʌlti'næʃənəl, ,mʌl,taɪ-] *adj* : multinational

multiple[1] ['mʌltəpəl] *adj* : multiple

multiple[2] *n* : multiple *m*

multiple sclerosis [sklə'ro:sɪs] *n* : sclérose *f* en plaques

multiplication [,mʌltəplə'keɪʃən] *n* : multiplication *f*

multiplicity [,mʌltə'plɪsəṭi] *n, pl* **-ties** : multiplicité *f*

multiply ['mʌltəplaɪ] *v* **-plied; -plying** *vt* : multiplier — *vi* : se multiplier

multipurpose [,mʌlti'pərpəs, ,mʌltaɪ-] *adj* : polyvalent, aux usages multiples

multitude ['mʌltə,tu:d, -,tju:d] *n* : multitude *f*

multitudinous [,mʌltə'tu:dnəs, -'tju:d-, -'tu:dənəs, -'tju:-] *adj* : innombrable

mum[1] ['mʌm] *adj* SILENT : silencieux <to keep mum : garder le silence>

mum[2] *n* **1** → **chrysanthemum 2** *Brit* → **mom**

mumble[1] ['mʌmbəl] *v* **-bled; -bling** : marmonner

mumble[2] *n* : marmonnement *m*

mummy ['mʌmi] *n, pl* **-mies** : momie *f*

mumps ['mʌmps] *ns & pl* : oreillons *mpl*

munch ['mʌntʃ] *v* : croquer

mundane [,mʌn'deɪn, 'mʌn,-] *adj* **1** EARTHLY, WORLDLY : de ce monde, terrestre **2** COMMONPLACE : banal, ordinaire

municipal [mju'nɪsəpəl] *adj* : municipal

municipality [mju,nɪsə'pæləṭi] *n, pl* **-ties** : municipalité *f*

munificent [mju'nɪfəsənt] *adj* : munificent

munitions [mju'nɪʃənz] *npl* : munitions *fpl*

mural[1] ['mjʊrəl] *adj* : mural

mural[2] *n* : peinture *f* murale, murale *f*

murder[1] ['mərdər] *vt* : assassiner

murder[2] *n* : meurtre *m*

murderer ['mərdərər] *n* : meurtrier *m*, -trière *f*; assassin *m*

murderess ['mərdərɪs, -də,rɛs, -dərəs] *n* : meurtrière *f*

murderous ['mərdərəs] *adj* : meurtrier

murk ['mərk] *n* DARKNESS : obscurité *f*

murkiness ['mərkinəs] *n* : obscurité *f*

murky ['mərki] *adj* **murkier; -est** : obscur, sombre

murmur[1] ['mərmər] *v* : murmurer

murmur[2] *n* : murmure *m*

muscatel [,məskə'tel] *n* : muscat *m*

muscle[1] ['mʌsəl] *vi* **-cled; -cling** *or* **to muscle in** INTERVENE : intervenir

muscle[2] *n* **1** : muscle *m* **2** BRAWN : force *f*, muscle *m* **3** POWER : puissance *f*, poids *m*

muscular ['mʌskjələr] *adj* **1** : musculaire <muscular tissue : tissu musculaire> **2** STRONG : musclé

muscular dystrophy *n* : dystrophie *f* musculaire
musculature [ˈmʌskjələˌtʃʊr, -tʃər] *n* : musculature *f*
muse[1] [ˈmjuːz] *vi* **mused; musing** PONDER : méditer
muse[2] *n* : muse *f*
museum [mjuˈziːəm] *n* : musée *m*
mush [ˈmʌʃ] *n* **1** : bouillie *f* **2** SENTIMENTALITY : mièverie *f*
mushroom[1] [ˈmʌʃˌruːm, -ˌrʊm] *vi* GROW, MULTIPLY : proliférer, se multiplier
mushroom[2] *n* : champignon *m*
mushy [ˈmʌʃi] *adj* **mushier; -est 1** SOFT : en bouillie (se dit de la nourriture), bourbeux (se dit de la terre) **2** MAWKISH : mièvre
music [ˈmjuːzɪk] *n* : musique *f*
musical[1] [ˈmjuːzɪkəl] *adj* : musical <musical instruments : instruments de musique> **— musically** *adv*
musical[2] *n* : comédie *f* musicale
musician [mjuˈzɪʃən] *n* : musicien *m*, -cienne *f*
musk [ˈmʌsk] *n* : musc *m*
musket [ˈmʌskət] *n* : mousquet *m*
musketeer [ˌmʌskəˈtɪr] *n* : mousquetaire *m*
muskrat [ˈmʌskˌræt] *n, pl* **-rat** *or* **-rats** : rat *m* musqué
Muslim[1] [ˈmʌzləm, ˈmʊs-, ˈmʊz-] *adj* : musulman
Muslim[2] *n* : Musulman *m*, -mane *f*
muslin [ˈmʌzlən] *n* : mousseline *f*
muss [ˈmʌs] *vt* : chiffonner, froisser, décoiffer (les cheveux de qqn)
mussel [ˈmʌsəl] *n* : moule *f*
must[1] [ˈmʌst] *v aux* **1** (*expressing obligation or necessity*) : falloir, devoir <you must go : il faut que tu y ailles> <we must obey : nous devons obéir> **2** (*expressing probability*) : devoir <you must be tired : vous devez être fatigué> <it must be late : il doit être tard>
must[2] *n* : nécessité *f* <exercise is a must : l'exercice est indispensable>
mustache [ˈmʌˌstæʃ, mʌˈstæʃ] *n* : moustache *f*
mustang [ˈmʌˌstæŋ] *n* : mustang *m*
mustard [ˈmʌstərd] *n* : moutarde *f*
muster[1] [ˈmʌstər] *vt* : rassembler, réunir
muster[2] *n* **1** : rassemblement *m* **2 to pass muster** : être acceptable
mustiness [ˈmʌstinəs] *n* : odeur *f* de moisi, odeur *f* de renfermé
musty [ˈmʌsti] *adj* **mustier; -est** : de moisi, de renfermé
mutable [ˈmjuːtəbəl] *adj* : mutable
mutant[1] [ˈmjuːtənt] *adj* : mutant
mutant[2] *n* : mutant *m*, -tante *f*
mutate [ˈmjuːˌteɪt] *vi* **-tated; -tating** : muter
mutation [mjuˈteɪʃən] *n* : mutation *f*
mute[1] [ˈmjuːt] *vt* **muted; muting** MUFFLE : étouffer, assourdir
mute[2] *adj* **muter; mutest** : muet
mute[3] *n* : muet *m*, muette *f*
mutilate [ˈmjuːtəˌleɪt] *vt* **-lated; -lating** : mutiler
mutilation [ˌmjuːtəˈleɪʃən] *n* : mutilation *f*
mutineer [ˌmjuːtənˈɪr] *n* : mutiné *m*, -née *f*
mutinous [ˈmjuːtənəs] *adj* : mutiné
mutiny[1] [ˈmjuːtəni] *vi* **-nied; -nying** : se mutiner
mutiny[2] *n, pl* **-nies** : mutinerie *f*
mutt [ˈmʌt] *n* MONGREL : chien *m* bâtard
mutter [ˈmʌtər] *vi* **1** MUMBLE : marmonner **2** GRUMBLE : grommeler
mutton [ˈmʌtən] *n* : mouton *m*
mutual [ˈmjuːtʃʊəl] *adj* **1** : mutuel, réciproque **2** COMMON : commun <a mutual friend : un ami commun>
mutually [ˈmjuːtʃʊəli, -tʃəli] *adv* **1** : mutuellement, réciproquement **2** JOINTLY : conjointement
muzzle[1] [ˈmʌzəl] *vt* **-zled; -zling** : museler
muzzle[2] *n* **1** SNOUT : museau *m* **2** : muselière *f* (pour un chien, etc.) **3** : canon *m* (d'une arme à feu)
my[1] [ˈmaɪ] *adj* : mon, ma, mes <my parents : mes parents> <in my opinion : à mon avis>
my[2] *interj* **oh, my!** : eh, bien!, oh là là!, mon Dieu!
myopia [maɪˈoːpiə] *n* : myopie *f*
myopic [maɪˈoːpɪk, -ˈɑ-] *adj* : myope
myriad[1] [ˈmɪriəd] *adj* : innombrable
myriad[2] *n* : myriade *f*
myrrh [ˈmər] *n* : myrrhe *f*
myrtle [ˈmərtəl] *n* : myrte *m*
myself [maɪˈsɛlf] *pron* **1** (*used reflexively*) : me <I hurt myself : je me suis fait mal> **2** (*used for emphasis*) : moi-même <I tried it myself : je l'ai essayé moi-même> **3 all by myself** : tout seul
mysterious [mɪˈstɪriəs] *adj* : mystérieux **— mysteriously** *adv*
mysteriousness [mɪˈstɪriəsnəs] *n* : mystère *m*, caractère *m* mystérieux
mystery [ˈmɪstəri] *n, pl* **-teries** : mystère *m*
mystic[1] [ˈmɪstɪk] *adj or* **mystical** [ˈmɪstɪkəl] : mystique **— mystically** [-kli] *adv*
mystic[2] *n* : mystique *mf*
mysticism [ˈmɪstəˌsɪzəm] *n* : mysticisme *m*
mystify [ˈmɪstəˌfaɪ] *vt* **-fied; -fying 1** PUZZLE : déconcerter **2** DECEIVE, DUPE : mystifier
mystique [mɪˈstiːk] *n* : mystique *f*
myth [ˈmɪθ] *n* : mythe *m*
mythical [ˈmɪθɪkəl] *adj* : mythique
mythological [ˌmɪθəˈlɑdʒɪkəl] *adj* : mythologique
mythology [mɪˈθɑlədʒi] *n, pl* **-gies** : mythologie *f*

N

n ['ɛn] *n, pl* **n's** *or* **ns** ['ɛnz] : n *m*, quatorzième lettre de l'alphabet
nab ['næb] *vt* **nabbed; nabbing 1** APPREHEND : arrêter, pincer *fam* **2** STEAL : piquer *fam*, voler
nadir ['neɪˌdɪr, 'neɪdər] *n* : nadir *m*, point *m* le plus bas
nag¹ ['næg] *v* **nagged; nagging** *vi* **1** COMPLAIN : se plaindre, maugréer **2** PERSIST : persister <a nagging toothache : un mal de dents qui persiste> — *vt* SCOLD : critiquer, enquiniquer *fam*
nag² *n* **1** HORSE : canasson *m fam* **2** GROUCH : rouspéteur *m*, -teuse *f fam*
naiad ['neɪəd, 'naɪ-, -ˌæd] *n, pl* **-iads** *or* **-iades** [-əˌdiz] : naïade *f*
nail¹ ['neɪl] *vt* : clouer
nail² *n* **1** FINGERNAIL : ongle *m* <to bite one's nails : se ronger les ongles> **2** : clou *m* (en technologie) <to hit the nail on the head : mettre le doigt dessus>
naïve *or* **naïve** [nɑ'i:v] *adj* **-iver; -est** : naïf
naïveté [ˌnɑˌi:və'teɪ, nɑ'i:vəˌ-] *n* : naïveté *f*
naked ['neɪkəd] *adj* **1** NUDE : nu **2** UNADORNED : tout nu, brut <the naked truth : la vérité pure et simple> **3 to the naked eye** : à l'œil nu
nakedness ['neɪkədnəs] *n* : nudité *f*
name¹ ['neɪm] *vt* **named; naming 1** CALL : nommer, appeler <I named him "John" : je l'ai nommé «John»> **2** CITE : nommer, citer **3** APPOINT : nommer **4** SPECIFY : choisir, fixer <to name the date : choisir la date> <to name a price : fixer un prix>
name² *adj* : de marque <name brand : produit de marque>
name³ *n* **1** : nom *m* <what is your name? : comment t'appelles-tu?, quel est ton nom?> **2** REPUTATION : nom *m*, réputation *f* <to make a name for oneself : se faire un nom> **3 to call someone names** : traiter quelqu'un de tous les noms
nameless ['neɪmləs] *adj* **1** : sans nom <a nameless grave : une tombe sans nom> **2** UNKNOWN : anonyme **3** INDEFINABLE : indéfinissable, inexplicable
namely ['neɪmli] *adv* : notamment, c'est-à-dire
namesake ['neɪmˌseɪk] *n* : homonyme *m*
Namibian¹ [nə'mɪbiən] *adj* : namibien
Namibian² *n* : Namibien *m*, -bienne *f*
nap¹ ['næp] *vi* **napped; napping** : faire un somme, faire une sieste
nap² *n* **1** SNOOZE : somme *m*, sieste *f* **2** : poil *m* (d'un tissu)
nape ['neɪp, 'næp] *n* : nuque *f*
naphtha ['næfθə] *n* : naphte *m*
napkin ['næpkən] *n* **1** : serviette *f* (de table) **2** → **sanitary**
narcissism ['nɑrsəˌsɪzəm] *n* : narcissisme *m*
narcissist ['nɑrsəsɪst] *n* : narcisse *m*
narcissistic [ˌnɑrsə'sɪstɪk] *adj* : narcissique
narcissus [nɑr'sɪsəs] *n, pl* **-cissi** *or* **-cissuses** *or* **-cissus** [-'sɪˌsaɪ, -ˌsi:] : narcisse *m* (fleur)
narcotic¹ [nɑr'kɑtˌɪk] *adj* : narcotique
narcotic² *n* **1** : narcotique *m* (en pharmacie) **2** DRUG : stupéfiant *m*
narrate ['nærˌeɪt] *vt* **narrated; narrating** : raconter, narrer
narration [næ'reɪʃən] *n* : narration *f*, récit *m*
narrative¹ ['nærətɪv] *adj* : narratif
narrative² *n* : récit *m*, histoire *f*, narration *f*
narrator ['nærˌeɪtər] *n* : narrateur *m*, -trice *f*
narrow¹ ['nærˌo:] *vt* **1** LIMIT : limiter **2** REDUCE : réduire — *vi* : se rétrécir <the road narrows : la route se rétrécit>
narrow² *adj* **1** : étroit <a narrow passage : un passage étroit> **2** LIMITED : limité, restreint **3** BIGOTED : étroit, borné **4 by a narrow margin** : de justesse
narrowly ['næroli] *adv* : de justesse, de peu
narrow–minded [ˌnæro'maɪndəd] *adj* : étroit d'esprit
narrowness ['næronəs] *n* : étroitesse *f*
narrows ['nærozˌ] *npl* STRAIT : passages *mpl* étroits
narwhal ['nɑrˌhwɑl, 'nɑrwəl] *n* : narval *m*
nasal ['neɪzəl] *adj* : nasal
nasally ['neɪzəli] *adv* : d'une voix nasale
nastily ['næstəli] *adv* : méchamment
nastiness ['næstinəs] *n* : méchanceté *f*
nasturtium [nə'stərʃəm, næ-] *n* : capucine *f*
nasty ['næsti] *adj* **nastier; -est 1** FILTHY : sale, crasseux **2** INDECENT : obscène **3** MALICIOUS : méchant <a nasty disposition : un air méchant> **4** UNPLEASANT : sale, vilain <nasty weather : sale temps> <a nasty trick : un vilain tour>
natal ['neɪtəl] *adj* : natal
nation ['neɪʃən] *n* : pays *m*, nation *f*
national¹ ['næʃənəl] *adj* : national — **nationally** *adv*
national² *n* : ressortissant *m*, -sante *f*
nationalism ['næʃənəˌlɪzəm] *n* : nationalisme *m*
nationalist ['næʃənəlɪst] *n* : nationaliste *mf*
nationalistic [ˌnæʃənə'lɪstɪk] *adj* : nationaliste
nationality [ˌnæʃə'nælətˌi] *n, pl* **-ties** : nationalité *f*
nationalization [ˌnæʃənələ'zeɪʃən] *n* : nationalisation *f*

nationalize [ˈnæʃənəˌlaɪz] *vt* **-ized; -izing** : nationaliser
nationwide [ˈneɪʃənˈwaɪd] *adj* : dans tout le pays
native[1] [ˈneɪṭɪv] *adj* **1** NATURAL : inné **2** : natal <in his native country : dans son pays natal> **3** : maternel <her native language : sa langue maternelle>
native[2] *n* **to be a native of** : être originaire de, être natif de
Native American → American Indian
nativity [nəˈtɪvəṭi, neɪ-] *n, pl* **-ties 1** : Nativité *f* (en religion) **2** BIRTH : naissance *f*
natty [ˈnæṭi] *adj* **nattier; -est** : coquet, élégant
natural[1] [ˈnætʃərəl] *adj* **1** : à l'état naturel <natural woodlands : forêt à l'état naturel> **2** : naturel <natural causes : causes naturelles> **3** INBORN : né, inné <natural abilities : talents innés> **4** SIMPLE : naturel, simple
natural[2] *n* : quelqu'un qui a un talent inné
naturalism [ˈnætʃərəˌlɪzəm] *n* : naturalisme *m*
naturalist [ˈnætʃərəlɪst] *n* : naturaliste *mf*
naturalistic [ˌnæchərəˈlɪstɪk] *adj* : naturaliste
naturalization [ˌnætʃərələˈzeɪʃən] *n* : naturalisation *f*
naturalize [ˈnætʃərəˌlaɪz] *vt* **-ized; -izing** : naturaliser
naturally [ˈnætʃərəli] *adv* **1** : naturellement <naturally blonde : naturellement blonde> **2** OF COURSE : bien sûr, bien entendu, évidemment
naturalness [ˈnætʃərəlnəs] *n* : naturel *m*
nature [ˈneɪṭʃər] *n* **1** ESSENCE : nature *f*, essence *f* **2** KIND : espèce *f*, genre *m* **3** DISPOSITION : nature *f*, tempérament *m* <a generous nature : une nature généreuse> **4** : nature *f* <the beauties of nature : les beautés de la nature>
naught [ˈnɔt] *n* **1** NOTHING : rien *m* <to come to naught : ne mener à rien> **2** ZERO : zéro *m*
naughtiness [ˈnɔṭɪnəs] *n* : désobéissance *f*, mauvaise conduite *f*
naughty [ˈnɔti] *adj* **naughtier; -est 1** DISOBEDIENT, MISCHIEVOUS : méchant, vilain **2** RISQUÉ : osé, risqué
nausea [ˈnɔzə, ˈnɔʃə] *n* **1** : nausée *f* **2** DISGUST : nausée *f*, écœurement *m*
nauseate [ˈnɔziˌeɪt, -ʒi-, -si-, -ʃi-] *v* **-ated; -ating** *vi* : avoir la nausée — *vt* : donner la nausée à
nauseating [ˈnɔziˌeɪṭɪŋ] *adj* : écœurant
nauseatingly [ˈnɔziˌeɪṭɪŋli, -ʒi-, -si-, -ʃi-] *adv* : au point d'écœurer <nauseatingly sweet : d'une douceur écœurante>
nauseous [ˈnɔʃəs, -ziəs] *adj* **1** SICK : écœuré **2** REVOLTING : nauséabond
nautical [ˈnɔṭɪkəl] *adj* : nautique
nautilus [ˈnɔṭələs] *n, pl* **-luses** *or* **-li** [-ˌlaɪ, -ˌli:] : nautile *m*
naval [ˈneɪvəl] *adj* : naval
nave [ˈneɪv] *n* : nef *f* (d'une église)
navel [ˈneɪvəl] *n* : nombril *m*
navigable [ˈnævɪgəbəl] *adj* : navigable
navigability [ˌnævɪgəˈbɪləṭi] *n* : navigabilité *f*
navigate [ˈnæveˌgeɪt] *v* **-gated; -gating** *vi* SAIL : naviguer, voguer — *vt* **1** SAIL : naviguer sur, traverser **2** STEER : diriger, gouverner (un bateau)
navigation [ˌnæveˈgeɪʃən] *n* : navigation *f*
navigator [ˈnæveˌgeɪṭər] *n* : navigateur *m*, -trice *f*
navy [ˈneɪvi] *n, pl* **-vies 1** FLEET : flotte *f* **2** : marine *f* (nationale) <the United States Navy : la Marine américaine> **3** *or* **navy blue** : marine *m*
nay[1] [ˈneɪ] *adv* EVEN : que dis-je, voire <a huge, nay, monstrous animal : un animal énorme, que dis-je, monstrueux>
nay[2] *n* : non *m*, vote *m* négatif <the nays outnumbered the ayes : les non l'ont emporté sur les oui>
Nazi[1] [ˈnɑtsi, ˈnæt-] *adj* : nazi
Nazi[2] *n* : nazi *m*, -zie *f*
Nazism [ˈnɑtˌsɪzəm, ˈnæt-] *or* **Naziism** [ˈnɑtsiˌɪzəm, ˈnæt-] *n* : nazisme *m*
near[1] [ˈnɪr] *vt* : approcher — *vi* : s'approcher
near[2] *adv* **1** : près <she lives very near : elle habite tout près> <to draw near : approcher> **2** ALMOST, NEARLY : presque <near dead : presque mort>
near[3] *adj* : proche <in the near future : dans un proche avenir> <to the nearest dollar : à un dollar près> <the nearest route : le chemin le plus court>
near[4] *prep* : à côté de, près de <the table near the window : la table à côté de la fenêtre>
nearby[1] [ˌnɪrˈbaɪ, ˈnirˌbaɪ] *adv* CLOSE : tout près, à proximité
nearby[2] *adj* : voisin, proche <a nearby house : une maison voisine>
nearly [ˈnɪrli] *adv* : presque
nearness [ˈnɪrnəs] *n* : proximité *f*
nearsighted [ˈnɪrˌsaɪṭəd] *adj* : myope
nearsightedness [ˈnɪrˌsaɪṭədnəs] *n* : myopie *f*
neat [ˈni:t] *adj* **1** UNDILUTED : sec, pur **2** PRETTY, SMART : joli, coquet **3** CLEAN, ORDERLY : propre, soigné **4** SKILLFUL : habile <a neat trick : un truc habile>
neatly [ˈni:tli] *adv* **1** TIDILY : proprement, soigneusement **2** CLEVERLY : habilement
neatness [ˈni:tnəs] *n* : ordre *m*, propreté *f*
nebula [ˈnɛbjʊlə] *n, pl* **-lae** [-ˌli:, -ˌlaɪ] : nébuleuse *f*

nebulous [ˈnɛbjʊləs] *adj* : nébuleux
necessarily [ˌnɛsəˈserəli] *adv* : nécessairement, forcément
necessary[1] [ˈnɛsəˌseri] *adj* **1** INEVITABLE : inévitable **2** COMPULSORY : obligatoire **3** ESSENTIAL : indispensable
necessary[2] *n, pl* **-saries** : nécessaire *m*
necessitate [nɪˈsɛsəˌteɪt] *vt* **-tated; -tating** : nécessiter, exiger
necessity [nɪˈsɛsəṭi] *n, pl* **-ties 1** NEED : nécessité *f*, besoin *m* **2** : quelque chose d'indispensable <eating is a necessity : il est indispensable de manger> **3** POVERTY : pauvreté *f* **4 necessities** *npl* : le nécessaire, les choses essentielles
neck[1] [ˈnɛk] *vi* : se peloter *fam*
neck[2] *n* **1** : cou *m* **2** COLLAR : col *m*, encolure *f* <a high neck : un col montant> **3** : col *m*, goulot *m* (d'une bouteille)
neckerchief [ˈnɛkərtʃəf, -ˌtʃiːf] *n, pl* **-chiefs** [-tʃəfs, -ˌtʃiːfs] : foulard *m*
necklace [ˈnɛkləs] *n* : collier *m*
necktie [ˈnɛkˌtaɪ] *n* : cravate *f*
nectar [ˈnɛktər] *n* : nectar *m*
nectarine [ˌnɛktəˈriːn] *n* : nectarine *f*
née *or* **nee** [ˈneɪ] *adj* : né
need[1] [ˈniːd] *vi* : avoir besoin, être dans le besoin — *vt* **1** : avoir besoin de <he needs a car : il a besoin d'une voiture> **2 to need to** : devoir <something needs to be done : on doit faire quelque chose> — *v aux* : avoir besoin de, devoir, être obligé de <you need not answer : vous n'êtes pas obligé de répondre> <need we go? : est-ce que nous devons vraiment y aller?>
need[2] *n* **1** OBLIGATION : besoin *m*, nécessité *f* **2** DISTRESS : difficulté *f* <in times of need : pendant les moments difficiles> **3** WANT : besoin *m* <to be in need : être dans le besoin> **4 if need be** : si nécessaire, s'il le faut
needful [ˈniːdfəl] *adj* : nécessaire
needle[1] [ˈniːdəl] *vt* **-dled; -dling** TEASE : taquiner
needle[2] *n* : aiguille *f*
needlepoint [ˈniːdəlˌpɔɪnt] *n* **1** LACE : dentelle *f* à l'aiguille **2** EMBROIDERY : tapisserie *f* à l'aiguille
needless [ˈniːdləs] *adj* **1** UNNECESSARY : inutile **2 needless to say** : il va sans dire
needlessly [ˈniːdləsli] *adv* : inutilement
needlework [ˈniːdəlˌwərk] *n* : travaux *mpl* d'aiguille
needy [ˈniːdiː] *adj* **needier; -est** : dans le besoin
nefarious [nɪˈfæriəs] *adj* : infâme, odieux
negate [nɪˈgeɪt] *vt* **-gated; -gating 1** DENY : nier, contredire **2** NULLIFY : abroger
negation [nɪˈgeɪʃən] *n* : négation *f*
negative[1] [ˈnɛgəṭɪv] *adj* : négatif
negative[2] *n* **1** *or* **negative number** : nombre *m* négatif **2** : négatif *m* (en photographie) **3** : négation *f* (en grammaire) **4 to answer in the negative** : répondre par la négative
negatively [ˈnɛgəṭɪvli] *adv* : négativement
negativity [ˌnɛgəˈtɪvəṭi] *n* : négativité *f*
neglect[1] [nɪˈglɛkt] *vt* **1** DISREGARD : négliger **2** : manquer à (son devoir, une promesse, etc.)
neglect[2] *n* **1** : négligence *f* <due to neglect : dû à la négligence> **2** : manque *m* de soins (envers une personne), manque *m* d'entretien (d'un bâtiment, etc.)
neglectful [nɪˈglɛktfəl] *adj* : négligent
negligee [ˌnɛgləˈʒeɪ] *n* : négligé *m*, déshabillé *m*
negligence [ˈnɛglɪdʒənṭs] *n* : négligence *f* <criminal negligence : négligence criminelle>
negligent [ˈnɛglɪdʒənt] *adj* : négligent — **negligently** *adv*
negligible [ˈnɛglɪdʒəbəl] *adj* : négligeable
negotiable [nɪˈgoːʃəbəl, -ʃiə-] *adj* : négociable
negotiate [nɪˈgoːʃiˌeɪt] *v* **-ated; -ating** *vi* : négocier — *vt* **1** : négocier (une entente, etc.) **2** : franchir, surmonter (une difficulté)
negotiation [nɪˌgoʃiˈeɪshən, -siˈeɪ-] *n* : négociation *f*
negotiator [nɪˈgoːʃiˌeɪṭər, -siˌeɪ-] *n* : négociateur *m*, -trice *f*
Negro[1] [ˈniːˌgroː] *adj* : noir, nègre
Negro[2] *n, pl* **-groes** *sometimes offensive* : nègre *m sometimes offensive*, négresse *f sometimes offensive*
neigh[1] [ˈneɪ] *vi* : hennir
neigh[2] *n* : hennissement *m*
neighbor[1] *or Brit* **neighbour** [ˈneɪbər] *vt* : avoisiner — *vi* **to neighbor on** : être voisin de
neighbor[2] *or Brit* **neighbour** *n* **1** : voisin *m*, -sine *f* **2** FELLOWMAN : prochain *m* <love thy neighbor : aime ton prochain>
neighborhood *or Brit* **neighbourhood** [ˈneɪbərˌhʊd] *n* **1** : voisinage *m* **2 in the neighborhood of** APPROXIMATELY : au voisinage de, environ
neighborly *or Brit* **neighbourly** [ˈneɪbərli] *adj* : amical, de bon voisin
neighbour *Brit* → **neighbor**
neither[1] [ˈniːðər, ˈnaɪ-] *adj* : aucun (des deux) <neither girl : aucune des deux filles>
neither[2] *conj* **1** : non plus <he doesn't want to go, and neither do I : il ne veut pas y aller, et moi non plus> **2 neither . . . nor** : ni . . . ni <neither good nor bad : ni bon ni mauvais>
neither[3] *pron* : aucun <neither of the bottles is full : aucune des deux bouteilles n'est pleine>

nemesis [ˈneməsɪs] *n, pl* **-eses** [-ˌsiːz] **1** RIVAL : vieux rival *m* **2** RETRIBUTION : juste punition *f*
neologism [niˈɑləˌdʒɪzəm] *n* : néologisme *m*
neon [ˈniːˌɑn] *n* : néon *m* <neon lighting : éclairage au néon>
neophyte [ˈniːəˌfaɪt] *n* : néophyte *mf*
Nepali[1] [nəˈpɔliː, -ˈpɑ-, -ˈpæ-] *adj* : népalais
Nepali[2] *n* **1** : Népalais *m*, -laise *f* **2** : népalais *m* (langue)
nephew [ˈneˌfjuː, *chiefly Brit* ˈneˌvjuː] *n* : neveu *m*
nepotism [ˈnepəˌtɪzəm] *n* : népotisme *m*
Neptune [ˈneptˌtuːn, -ˌtjuːn] *n* : Neptune *f* (planète)
nerd [ˈnərd] *n* : crétin *m*, -tine *f fam*
nerve [ˈnərv] *n* **1** : nerf *m* <sensory nerve : nerf sensoriel> **2** AUDACITY : culot *m fam*, toupet *m fam* <to have a lot of nerve : avoir du culot> **3** FORTITUDE : confiance *f*, assurance *f* **4 nerves** *npl* JITTERS : nerfs *mpl* <to be all nerves : être sur les nerfs>
nervous [ˈnərvəs] *adj* **1** : nerveux <nervous system : système nerveux> **2** ANXIOUS : appréhensif, anxieux **3** TIMID : timide <a nervous smile : un sourire timide>
nervously [ˈnərvəsli] *adv* : nerveusement, avec inquiétude
nervousness [ˈnərvəsnəs] *n* : nervosité *f*
nervy [ˈnərvi] *adj* **nervier; -est 1** BOLD : audacieux **2** INSOLENT : culotté *fam*, effronté **3** NERVOUS : nerveux
nest[1] [ˈnɛst] *vi* : se nicher, faire son nid
nest[2] *n* **1** : nid *m* **2** SET : ensemble *m* (de tables, etc.)
nestle [ˈnɛsəl] *vi* **-tled; -tling** : se blottir
net[1] [ˈnɛt] *vt* **netted; netting 1** CATCH : prendre au filet (des poissons) **2** YIELD : rapporter (en finance)
net[2] *adj* : net <net salary : salaire net>
net[3] *n* : filet *m*
nether [ˈneðər] *adj* **1** LOWER : inférieur, bas **2 the nether regions** : les enfers
nettle[1] [ˈnɛtəl] *vt* **-tled; -tling** : piquer au vif, irriter
nettle[2] *n* : ortie *f*
network [ˈnɛtˌwərk] *n* : réseau *m*
neural [ˈnʊrəl, ˈnjʊr-] *adj* : neural
neuralgia [nʊˈrældʒə, njʊ-] *n* : névralgie *f*
neuralgic [nʊˈrældʒɪk] *adj* : névralgique
neuritis [nʊˈraɪtəs, njʊ-] *n, pl* **-ritides** [-ˈrɪtəˌdiːz] *or* **-ritises** : névrite *f*
neurological [ˌnʊrəˈlɑdʒɪkəl, ˌnjʊr-] *or* **neurologic** [ˌnʊrəˈlɑdʒɪk, ˌnjʊ-] *adj* : neurologique
neurologist [nʊˈrɑlədʒɪst, njʊ-] *n* : neurologue *mf*
neurology [nʊˈrɑlədʒi, njʊ-] *n* : neurologie *f*
neurosis [nʊˈroːsɪs, njʊ-] *n, pl* **-roses** [-ˌsiːz] : névrose *f*
neurotic[1] [nʊˈrɑtɪk, njʊ-] *adj* : névrosé
neurotic[2] *n* : névrosé *m*, -sée *f*
neuter[1] [ˈnuːtər, ˈnjuː-] *vt* : châtrer
neuter[2] *adj* : neutre (en grammaire)
neutral[1] [ˈnuːtrəl, ˈnjuː-] *adj* **1** : neutre <neutral territory : territoire neutre> **2** IMPARTIAL : neutre, objectif **3** : neutre (se dit d'une couleur, d'une charge électrique)
neutral[2] *n or* **neutral gear** : point *m* mort, neutre *m Can*
neutralization [ˌnuːtrələˈzeɪʃən, ˌnjuː-] *n* : neutralisation *f*
neutralize [ˈnuːtrəˌlaɪz, ˈnjuː-] *vt* **-ized; -izing** : neutraliser
neutrality [nuːˈtræləṭi, njuː-] *n* : neutralité *f*
neutron [ˈnuːˌtrɑn, ˈnjuː-] *n* : neutron *m*
never [ˈnɛvər] *adv* **1** : jamais <I never saw her : je ne l'ai jamais vue> **2** (*used for emphasis*) <never fear : ne crains pas> <I never said a word : je n'ai rien dit>
nevermore [ˌnɛvərˈmor] *adv* : plus jamais, jamais plus
nevertheless [ˌnɛvərðəˈlɛs] *adv* : néanmoins
new[1] [ˈnuː, ˈnjuː] *adv* NEWLY : fraîchement <a new-mown lawn : une pelouse fraîchement tondue>
new[2] *adj* **1** RECENT : nouveau, moderne <a new arrival : un nouveau arrivé> <what's new? : quoi de neuf?> **2** : neuf <we bought a new house : nous avons acheté une maison neuve> **3** DIFFERENT, NOVEL : nouveau, original <a new idea : une nouvelle idée> **4 like new** : comme neuf
newborn[1] [ˈnuːˌbɔrn, ˈnjuː-] *adj* : nouveau-né
newborn[2] *n, pl* **-born** *or* **-borns** : nouveau-né *m*, nouveau-née *f*
newly [ˈnuːli, ˈnjuː-] *adv* : récemment, nouvellement <newly furnished : nouvellement meublé> <newly painted : fraîchement peint>
new moon *n* : nouvelle lune *f*
newness [ˈnuːnəs, ˈnjuː-] *n* : nouveauté *f*
news [ˈnuːz, ˈnjuːz] *n* : nouvelles *fpl*
newscast [ˈnuːzˌkæst, ˈnjuːz-] *n* : journal *m* télévisé
newscaster [ˈnuːzˌkæstər, ˈnjuːz-] *n* : présentateur *m*, -trice *f* (d'un journal télévisé)
newsgroup [ˈnuːzˌgruːp] *n* : forum *m*
newsletter [ˈnuːzˌleṭər, ˈnjuːz-] *n* : bulletin *m*
newsman [ˈnuːzmən, ˈnjuːz-, -ˌmæn] *n, pl* **-men** [-mən, -ˌmɛn] : journaliste *m*
newspaper [ˈnuːzˌpeɪpər, ˈnjuːz-] *n* : journal *m*
newspaperman [ˈnuːzˌpeɪpərˌmæn, ˈnjuːz-] *n, pl* **-men** [-mən, -ˌmɛn] : journaliste *m*
newsprint [ˈnuːzˌprɪnt, ˈnjuːz-] *n* : papier *m* journal
newsstand [ˈnuːzˌstænd, ˈnjuːz-] *n* : kiosque *m* à journaux

newswoman ['nu:zˌwʊmən, 'nju:z-] *n, pl* **-women** [-ˌwɪmən] : journaliste *f*
newsworthy ['nu:zˌwərði, 'nju:z-] *adj* : médiatique
newsy ['nu:zi:, 'nju:-] *adj* **newsier; -est** : plein de nouvelles
newt ['nu:t, 'nju:t] *n* : triton *m*
New Testament *n* : Nouveau Testament *m*
New Year *n* : Nouvel An *m*
New Year's Day *n* : jour *m* de l'An
New Zealander [nu:'zi:lən̩dər, nju:-] *n* : Néo-Zélandais *m*, -daise *f*
next[1] ['nɛkst] *adv* **1** AFTERWARD : ensuite, après <what happened next? : que s'est-il passé ensuite?> **2** NOW : maintenant <what is she doing next? : qu'est-ce qu'elle fait maintenant?> **3** : la prochaine fois <when next we meet : quand nous nous rencontrerons la prochaine fois>
next[2] *adj* **1** : prochain <the next time : la prochaine fois> **2** FOLLOWING : suivant <the next page : la page suivante>
next door *adv* : à côté (de chez nous)
next–door ['nɛkst'dor] *adj* : voisin, d'à côté
next to *prep* **1** : à côté de <next to the bank : à côté de la banque> **2** : à comparer à <next to you I'm wealthy : à comparer à toi je suis riche>
nib ['nɪb] *n* : bec *m* (d'un stylo)
nibble[1] ['nɪbəl] *v* **-bled; -bling** *vt* : grignoter, mordiller — *vi* : grignoter
nibble[2] *n* **1** NIBBLING : mordillement *m* **2** SNACK : collation *f*
Nicaraguan[1] [ˌnɪkə'rɑgwən] *adj* : nicaraguayen
Nicaraguan[2] *n* : Nicaraguayen *m*, -guayenne *f*
nice ['naɪs] *adj* **nicer; nicest 1** FINICKY : particulier <too nice a palate : un palais trop particulier> **2** PRECISE : subtil, fin **3** PLEASANT : bon <we had a nice time : nous avons eu du bon temps> **4** AGREEABLE : gentil, aimable **5** WELL-BRED : respectable
nicely ['naɪsli] *adv* **1** WELL : bien <he is doing nicely : il se porte bien> **2** KINDLY, POLITELY : gentiment **3** PRECISELY : avec précision
niceness ['naɪsnəs] *n* : gentillesse *f*
nicety ['naɪsəṭi] *n, pl* **-ties 1** SUBTLETY : subtilité *f* **2 niceties** *npl* : raffinements *mpl*
niche ['nɪtʃ] *n* **1** RECESS : niche *f* **2** PLACE : place *f*, voie *f* <she found her niche : elle a trouvé sa place>
nick[1] ['nɪk] *vt* : faire une entaille dans, faire une encoche sur
nick[2] *n* **1** NOTCH : entaille *f*, encoche *f* **2 in the nick of time** : juste à temps
nickel ['nɪkəl] *n* **1** : nickel *m* (métal) **2** : pièce *f* de cinq cents
nickname[1] ['nɪkˌneɪm] *vt* : surnommer
nickname[2] *n* : surnom *m*
nicotine ['nɪkəˌtiːn] *n* : nicotine *f*
niece ['niːs] *n* : nièce *f*
Nigerian[1] [naɪ'dʒɪriən] *adj* : nigérian
Nigerian[2] *n* : Nigérian *m*, -rianne *f*
niggardly ['nɪgərdli] *adj* : avare, mesquin
niggling ['nɪgəlɪŋ] *adj* **1** PETTY : insignifiant <niggling details : détails insignifiants> **2** PERSISTENT : persistant <a niggling doubt : un doute persistant>
nigh[1] ['naɪ] *adv* **1** NEARLY : presque **2 to draw nigh** : se rapprocher
nigh[2] *adj* CLOSE, NEAR : proche <the end is nigh : la fin est proche>
night[1] ['naɪt] *adj* : de nuit <night shift : équipe de nuit>
night[2] *n* **1** EVENING : nuit *f*, soir *m* <at night : le soir> <last night : hier soir> <night and day : nuit et jour> **2** : soir *m* <it's his night off : ce soir il est libre> **3** DARKNESS : nuit *f*
nightclothes ['naɪtˌkloːðz, -ˌkloːz] *npl* : vêtements *mpl* de nuit
nightclub ['naɪtˌklʌb] *n* : boîte *f* de nuit
night crawler *n* → **earthworm**
nightfall ['naɪtˌfɔl] *n* : tombée *f* de la nuit
nightgown ['naɪtˌgaʊn] *n* : chemise *f* de nuit, robe *f* de nuit *Can*
nightingale ['naɪtən̩ˌgeɪl, 'naɪtɪŋ-] *n* : rossignol *m*
nightly[1] ['naɪtli] *adv* : tous les soirs
nightly[2] *adj* : de tous les soirs
nightmare ['naɪtˌmɛr] *n* : cauchemar *m*
nightmarish ['naɪtˌmɛrɪʃ] *adj* : cauchemardesque
nightshade ['naɪtˌʃeɪd] *n* : morelle *f*
nighttime ['naɪtˌtaɪm] *n* : nuit *f*
nil[1] ['nɪl] *adj* : nul <visibility is nil : la visibilité est nulle>
nil[2] *n* NOTHING, ZERO : zéro *m*
nimble ['nɪmbəl] *adj* **-bler; -blest 1** AGILE : agile, leste **2** CLEVER : vif, alerte
nimbleness ['nɪmbəlnəs] *n* : agilité *f*
nimbly ['nɪmbli] *adv* : agilement
nincompoop ['nɪnkəmˌpuːp, 'nɪŋ-] *n* FOOL : imbécile *mf*; idiot *m*, -diote *f*
nine[1] ['naɪn] *adj* : neuf
nine[2] *n* : neuf *m*
ninepins ['naɪnˌpɪnz] *n* : quilles *fpl*
nineteen[1] [naɪn'tiːn] *adj* : dix-neuf
nineteen[2] *n* : dix-neuf *m*
nineteenth[1] [naɪn'tiːnθ] *adj* : dix-neuvième
nineteenth[2] *n* **1** : dix-neuvième *mf* (dans une série) **2** : dix-neuvième *m* (en mathématiques) **3** (*used in dates*) <the nineteenth of May : le dix-neuf mai>
ninetieth[1] ['naɪnṭiəθ] *adj* : quatre-vingt-dixième
ninetieth[2] *n* **1** : quatre-vingt-dixième *mf* (dans une série) **2** : quatre-vingt-dixième *m* (en mathématiques)
ninety[1] ['naɪnṭi] *adj* : quatre-vingt-dix, nonante *Bel, Switz*

ninety[2] *n, pl* **-ties** : quatre-vingt-dix *m*, nonante *mf Bel, Switz*
ninny ['nɪni] *n, pl* **ninnies** NITWIT : cruche *f fam*, imbécile *mf*
ninth[1] ['naɪnθ] *adj* : neuvième
ninth[2] *n* **1** : neuvième *mf* (dans une série) **2** : neuvième *m* (en mathématiques) **3** (*used in dates*) <the ninth of September : le neuf septembre>
nip[1] ['nɪp] *vt* **nipped; nipping 1** BITE : mordre **2** PINCH : pincer **3 to nip in the bud** : tuer dans l'œuf
nip[2] *n* **1** BITE : morsure *f* (d'un animal) **2** PINCH : pincement *m* **3** TANG : piquant *m* **4** SWALLOW : goutte *f* (d'alcool, etc.) **5 there's a nip in the air** : il fait frisquet
nipple ['nɪpəl] *n* : mamelon *m*
nippy ['nɪpi] *adj* **nippier; -est 1** PUNGENT : piquant, fort **2** CHILLY : frisquet
nit ['nɪt] *n* : lente *f*
nitrate ['naɪˌtreɪt] *n* : nitrate *m*
nitric acid ['naɪtrɪk] *n* : acide *m* nitrique
nitrite ['naɪˌtraɪt] *n* : nitrite *m*
nitrogen ['naɪtrədʒən] *n* : azote *m*
nitroglycerin *or* **nitroglycerine** [ˌnaɪtroˈglɪsərən] *n* : nitroglycérine *f*
nitwit ['nɪtˌwɪt] *n* : andouille *f fam*, imbécile *mf*
no[1] ['no:] *adv* **1** (*used to express the negative of an alternative choice*) : non <shall we go out or no? : allons-nous sortir ou non?> **2** : pas <he is no better than the others : il n'est pas mieux que les autres> **3** (*used to express negation, dissent, denial or refusal*) : non <no, I'm not going : non, je n'y vais pas> **4** (*used as an interjection of surprise or doubt*) : mais <no, you don't say! : mais, ce n'est pas possible!> **5** : plus <we can no longer pretend : nous ne pouvons plus faire semblant>
no[2] *adj* **1** : pas de, point de <he has no money : il n'a pas d'argent> **2** (*used to express an order or command*) <no parking : stationnement interdit> **3 to be no** : ne pas être <I'm no liar : je ne suis pas menteur>
no[3] *n, pl* **noes** *or* **nos** ['no:z] **1** REFUSAL : non *m* **2** : non *m*, vote *m* négatif <ayes and noes : les oui et les non>
nobility [noˈbɪləṭi] *n* : noblesse *f*
noble ['nobəl] *adj* **-bler; -blest 1** EMINENT : noble, distingué **2** ARISTOCRATIC : noble, aristocratique **3** STATELY : majestueux <a noble building : un édifice majestueux>
nobleman ['no:bəlmən] *n* : noble *m*, aristocrate *m*
nobleness ['no:bəlnəs] *n* : noblesse *f*
noblewoman ['no:bəlˌwʊmən] *n, pl* **-women** [-ˌwɪmən] : noble *f*, aristocrate *f*
nobody[1] ['no:bədi, -ˌbɑdi] *n, pl* **-bodies** : moins que rien *mf*, zéro *m* <he's a nobody : il est complètement insignifiant>
nobody[2] *pron* : personne <nobody waited for me : personne ne m'a attendu>
nocturnal [nɑkˈtərnəl] *adj* : nocturne
nocturne ['nɑkˌtərn] *n* : nocturne *m*
nod[1] ['nɑd] *v* **nodded; nodding** *vt* : incliner (la tête), faire un signe de la tête <we nodded in agreement : nous avons fait un signe d'assentiment> — *vi* **to nod off** : s'endormir
nod[2] *n* : signe *m* de la tête, hochement *m* de la tête
node ['no:d] *n* : nœud *m* (d'une plante)
nodule ['nɑˌdʒu:l] *n* : nodule *m*
noel [noˈɛl] *n* **1** CAROL : chant *m* de Noël **2 Noel** CHRISTMAS : Noël *m*
noes → **no**
noise[1] ['nɔɪz] *vt* **noised; noising** : ébruiter
noise[2] *n* : bruit *m*, son *m*
noiseless ['nɔɪzləs] *adj* : silencieux — **noiselessly** *adv*
noisemaker ['nɔɪzˌmeɪkər] *n* : crécelle *f*
noisily ['nɔɪzəli] *adv* : bruyamment
noisiness ['nɔɪzinəs] *n* : bruit *m*
noisome ['nɔɪsiəm] *adj* **1** NOXIOUS : nocif **2** OFFENSIVE : nauséabond <a noisome stench : une odeur nauséabonde>
noisy ['nɔɪzi] *adj* **noisier; -est** : bruyant
nomad[1] ['no:ˌmæd] *adj* → **nomadic**
nomad[2] *n* : nomade *mf*
nomadic [noˈmædɪk] *adj* : nomade
nomenclature ['no:mənˌkleɪtʃər] *n* : nomenclature *f*
nominal ['nɑmənəl] *adj* **1** : de nom <the nominal president : président que de nom> **2** TRIFLING : insignifiant
nominally ['nɑmənəli] *adv* : nominalement
nominate ['nɑməˌneɪt] *vt* **-nated; -nating 1** PROPOSE : proposer (comme candidat) **2** APPOINT : nommer, désigner
nomination [ˌnɑməˈneɪʃən] *n* : nomination *f*
nominative[1] ['nɑmənəṭɪv] *adj* : nominatif
nominative[2] *n or* **nominative case** : nominatif *m*
nominee [ˌnɑməˈni:] *n* : candidat *m*, -date *f*
nonaddictive [ˌnɑnəˈdɪktɪv] *adj* : qui ne crée pas de dépendance
nonalcoholic [ˌnɑnˌælkəˈhɔlɪk] *adj* : non alcoolisé
nonaligned [ˌnɑnəˈlaɪnd] *adj* : non aligné
nonbeliever [ˌnɑnbəˈli:vər] *n* : noncroyant *m*, -croyante *f*
nonbreakable [ˌnɑnˈbreɪkəbəl] *adj* : incassable
nonce ['nɑnʃs] *n* **for the nonce** : pour l'instant
nonchalance [ˌnɑnʃəˈlɑnʃs] *n* : nonchalance *f*

nonchalant [ˌnɑnʃə'lɑnt] *adj* : nonchalant
nonchalantly [ˌnɑnʃə'lɑntli] *adv* : nonchalamment
noncombatant *n* : non-combattant *m*, -tante *f*
noncombustible *adj* : incombustible
noncommissioned officer [ˌnɑnkə'mɪʃənd] *n* : sous-officier *m*
noncommittal [ˌnɑnkə'mɪtəl] *adj* : évasif
nonconductor [ˌnɑnkən'dʌktər] *n* : mauvais conducteur *m*
nonconformist [ˌnɑnkən'fɔrmɪst] *n* : non-conformiste *mf*
nonconformity [ˌnɑnkən'fɔrmətɪ] *n* : non-conformité *f*
nondenominational [ˌnɑndɪˌnɑmə'neɪʃənəl] *adj* : œcuménique
nondescript [ˌnɑndɪ'skrɪpt] *adj* : indéfinissable, quelconque
none[1] ['nʌn] *adv* **1 none too** : loin de <it's none too clear : c'est loin d'être clair> <they arrived none too soon : ils sont arrivés juste à temps> **2 to be none the worse** : n'en être pas plus mal
none[2] *pron* : aucun, aucune <none of them went : aucun d'entre eux n'y est allé>
nonentity [ˌnɑn'ɛntətɪ] *n, pl* **-ties** : être *m* insignifiant, nullité *f*
nonessential [ˌnɑnɪ'sɛnʃəl] *adj* : accessoire, non essentiel
nonetheless [ˌnʌnðə'lɛs] *adv* NEVERTHELESS : néanmoins
nonexistence [ˌnɑnɪg'zɪstənts] *n* : non-existence *f* — **nonexistent** [-stənt] *adj*
nonfat [ˌnɑn'fæt] *adj* : sans matières grasses
nonfiction [ˌnɑn'fɪkʃən] *n* : œuvres *fpl* non fictionnelles
nonflammable [ˌnɑn'flæməbəl] *adj* : inflammable
nonpareil[1] [ˌnɑnpə'rɛl] *adj* : inégalé, sans égal
nonpareil[2] *n* **1** : personne *f* sans égale **2** : petit disque *m* en chocolat recouvert de sucre
nonpartisan [ˌnɑn'pɑrtəzən, -sən] *adj* : impartial, neutre
nonperson [ˌnɑn'pərsən] *n* : personne *f* non reconnue
nonplus [ˌnɑn'plʌs] *vt* **-plussed; -plussing** DISCONCERT : déconcerter, dérouter
nonproductive [ˌnɑnprə'dʌktɪv] *adj* : improductif
nonprofit [ˌnɑn'prɑfət] *adj* : à but non lucratif
nonproliferation [ˌnɑnprəˌlɪfə'reɪʃən] *n* : non-prolifération *f*
nonrefundable [ˌnɑnri'fəndəbəl] *adj* : non remboursable
nonrenewable [ˌnɑnri'nu:əbəl, -'nju:-] *adj* : non renouvelable
nonresident [ˌnɑn'rɛzədənt, -ˌdɛnt] *n* : non-résident *m*, -dente *f*
nonscheduled [ˌnɑn'skɛˌdʒu:ld] *adj* : irrégulier <nonscheduled flights : vols irréguliers>
nonsectarian [ˌnɑnˌsɛk'tæriən] *adj* : non sectaire
nonsense ['nɑnˌsɛnts, -sənts] *n* : absurdités *fpl*, sottises *fpl*
nonsensical [nɑn'sɛntsɪkəl] *adj* : absurde, insensé — **nonsensically** [-kli] *adv*
nonsmoker [ˌnɑn'smo:kər] *n* : non-fumeur *m*, -meuse *f*
nonstandard [ˌnɑn'stændərd] *adj* : non standard
nonstick [ˌnɑn'stɪk] *adj* : antiadhésif <nonstick pan : poêle antiadhésive>
nonstop [ˌnɑn'stɑp] *adj* **1** : sans arrêt <to drive nonstop : rouler sans arrêt> **2** : direct, sans escale <nonstop flight : vol direct>
nonsupport [ˌnɑnsə'pɔrt] *n* : défaut *m* de versement de pension alimentaire
nontaxable [ˌnɑn'tæksəbəl] *adj* : non imposable
nonviolence [ˌnɑn'vaɪlənts, -'vaɪə-] *n* : non-violence *f*
nonviolent [ˌnɑn'vaɪlənt, -'vaɪə-] *adj* : non violent
noodle ['nu:dəl] *n* : nouille *f*
nook ['nʊk] *n* : coin *m*, recoin *m* <every nook and cranny : tous les coins et les recoins>
noon[1] ['nu:n] *adj* : de midi
noon[2] *n* : midi *m*
noonday ['nu:nˌdeɪ] → **midday, noon**
no one *pron* : personne *f*
noontime ['nu:nˌtaɪm] → **noon**
noose ['nu:s] *n* : nœud *m* coulant
nor ['nɔr] *conj* : ni <neither young nor old : ni jeune ni vieux> <he can't swim, nor can I : il ne sait pas nager, moi non plus>
norm ['nɔrm] *n* : norme *f*
normal ['nɔrməl] *adj* : normal — **normally** *adv*
normalcy ['nɔrməlsɪ] → **normality**
normality [nɔr'mæləti] *n* : normalité *f*
normalization [ˌnɔrmələ'zeʃən] *n* : normalisation *f*
normalize ['nɔrməˌlaɪz] *vt* **-ized; -izing** : normaliser
north[1] ['nɔrθ] *adv* : au nord, vers le nord
north[2] *adj* : nord <the north coast : la côte nord>
north[3] *n* **1** : nord *m* **2 the North** : le Nord
North American[1] *adj* : nord-américain
North American[2] *n* : Nord-Américain *m*, -caine *f*
northbound ['nɔrθˌbaʊnd] *adj* : en direction du nord
northeast[1] [nɔrθ'i:st] *adv* : au nord-est, vers le nord-est
northeast[2] *adj* : de nord-est <northeast winds : vents de nord-est>
northeast[3] *n* : nord-est *m*

northeasterly[1] [nɔrθˈiːstərli] *adv* : vers le nord-est
northeasterly[2] *adj* : du nord-est
northeastern [nɔrθˈiːstərn] *adj* : nord-est, du nord-est
northerly[1] [ˈnɔrðərli] *adv* : vers le nord
northerly[2] *adj* : du nord
northern [ˈnɔrðərn] *adj* : nord, du nord <northern Canada : le nord du Canada>
Northerner [ˈnɔrðərnər] *n* : natif *m* du Nord, native *f* du Nord
northern lights → aurora borealis
North Pole *n* : pôle *m* Nord
North Star *n* : étoile *f* polaire
northward[1] [ˈnɔrθwərd] *adv* : vers le nord
northward[2] *adj* : du côté nord
northwest[1] [nɔrθˈwɛst] *adv* : au nord-ouest, vers le nord-ouest
northwest[2] *adj* : de nord-ouest <northwest winds : vents de nord-ouest>
northwest[3] *n* : nord-ouest *m*
northwesterly[1] [nɔrθˈwɛstərli] *adv* : vers le nord-ouest
northwesterly[2] *adj* : du nord-ouest
northwestern [nɔrθˈwɛstərn] *adj* : nord-ouest, du nord-ouest
Norwegian[1] [nɔrˈwiːdʒən] *adj* : norvégien
Norwegian[2] *n* **1** : Norvégien *m*, -gienne *f* **2** : norvégien *m* (langue)
nose[1] [ˈnoːz] *v* **nosed; nosing** *vt* **1** SMELL : flairer, sentir **2** : pousser avec le museau <the dog nosed the door open : le chien a ouvert la porte avec son museau> **3 to nose in** : avancer avec précaution <the ship nosed into its berth : le bateau avançait prudemment dans son emplacement> — *vi* PRY : fouiner *fam* <stop nosing in my business! : arrête de fouiner dans mes affaires!>
nose[2] *n* **1** : nez *m* (d'une personne), museau *m* (d'un animal) **2** : flair *m*, odorat *m* <a dog with a good nose : un chien avec du flair> **3** FRONT : devant *m*, nez *m* (d'un avion, etc.) **4** INSTINCT : flair *m*, instinct *m* <to have a keen nose for politics : avoir du flair politique> **5 to blow one's nose** : se moucher
nosebleed [ˈnoːzˌbliːd] *n* : saignement *m* de nez
nosedive [ˈnoːzˌdaɪv] *n* **1** : piqué *m* (d'un avion) **2** DROP : chute *f* (des prix, etc.)
nose–dive *vi* **-dived; -diving 1** : piquer (se dit d'un avion) **2** : chuter *fam* (se dit des prix, etc.)
nostalgia [nɑˈstɛldʒə, nə-] *n* : nostalgie *f* — **nostalgic** [-dʒɪk] *adj*
nostril [ˈnɑstrəl] *n* : narine *f* (d'une personne), naseau *m* (d'un animal)
nostrum [ˈnɑstrəm] *n* : panacée *f*
nosy *or* **nosey** [ˈnoːzi] *adj* **nosier; -est** : fureteur
not [ˈnɑt] *adv* **1** (*used to form a negative*) : ne . . . pas <the boys are not here : les garçons ne sont pas ici> **2** (*used to replace a negative clause*) : pas <I don't see why not : je ne vois pas pourquoi> **3** : non <I hope not : j'espère que non>
notable[1] [ˈnoːtəbəl] *adj* **1** NOTEWORTHY : notable, remarquable **2** PROMINENT : notable, important
notable[2] *n* : notable *m*
notably [ˈnoːtəbli] *adv* **1** VERY : très <notably impressed : très impressionné> **2** ESPECIALLY : notamment
notarize [ˈnoːtəˌraɪz] *vt* **-rized; -rizing** : certifier
notary public [ˈnoːtəri] *n, pl* **notaries public** *or* **notary publics** : notaire *m*
notation [noˈteɪʃən] *n* **1** NOTE : note *f*, notation *f* **2** : notation *f* (en musique)
notch[1] [ˈnɑtʃ] *vt* : entailler, encocher
notch[2] *n* : entaille *f*, encoche *f*, coche *f*
note[1] [ˈnoːt] *vt* **noted; noting 1** NOTICE : noter, remarquer, observer **2** *or* **to note down** : noter, inscrire
note[2] *n* **1** : note *f* (de musique) **2** REMINDER : note *f*, avis *m* **3** LETTER : billet *m*, mot *m* **4** DISTINCTION : renom *m* <an artist of note : un artiste de renom> **5 to take note of** : prendre note de
notebook [ˈnoːtˌbʊk] *n* : carnet *m*, calepin *m*
noted [ˈnoːtəd] *adj* FAMOUS : éminent, célèbre
notepad [ˈnoːtˌpæd] *n* : bloc-notes *m*, tablette *f Can*
noteworthy [ˈnoːtˌwərði] *adj* : notable, remarquable
nothing[1] [ˈnʌθɪŋ] *adv* **1 nothing daunted** : pas le moindrement découragé **2 nothing like** : pas du tout
nothing[2] *n* **1** TRIFLE : rien *m* **2** ZERO : zéro *m* **3** : nullité *f*, zéro *m* <he feels like a nothing : il se sent comme un zéro> **4** NOTHINGNESS : néant *m*
nothing[3] *pron* : rien <there's nothing in the box : il n'y a rien dans la boîte> <it means nothing to me : ça m'est égal>
nothingness [ˈnʌθɪŋnəs] *n* : néant *m*
notice[1] *vt* **-ticed; -ticing 1** OBSERVE : s'apercevoir de, remarquer **2 to take notice of** : faire attention à
notice[2] [ˈnoːtɪs] *n* **1** ANNOUNCEMENT : avis *m*, annonce *f* **2** DISMISSAL : congé *m* **3** RESIGNATION : démission *f* **4 to give notice** : donner un préavis
noticeable [ˈnoːtɪsəbəl] *adj* : visible, perceptible
notification [ˌnoːtəfəˈkeɪʃən] *n* : avis *m*, notification *f*
notify [ˈnoːtəˌfaɪ] *vt* **-fied; -fying** : notifier, aviser, avertir
notion [ˈnoːʃən] *n* **1** IDEA : notion *f*, concept *m* **2** WHIM : envie *f*, idée *f* <a sudden notion : une envie soudaine> **3 notions** *npl* : mercerie *f*
notoriety [ˌnoːtəˈraɪəti] *n, pl* **-ties** : notoriété *f*

notorious [noˈtoːriəs] *adj* : notoire — **notoriously** *adv*
notwithstanding[1] [ˌnɑtwɪθˈstændɪŋ, -wɪð-] *adv* NEVERTHELESS : nonobstant, néanmoins
notwithstanding[2] *conj* : quoique
notwithstanding[3] *prep* : en dépit de, malgré
nougat [ˈnuːgət] *n* : nougat *m*
nought [ˈnɔt, ˈnɑt] → **naught**
noun [ˈnɑʊn] *n* : nom *m*, substantif *m*
nourish [ˈnərɪʃ] *vt* : nourrir
nourishing [ˈnərɪʃɪŋ] *adj* : nourrissant
nourishment [ˈnərɪʃmənt] *n* : nourriture *f*, alimentation *f*
novel[1] [ˈnɑvəl] *adj* : nouveau, original
novel[2] *n* : roman *m*
novelist [ˈnɑvəlɪst] *n* : romancier *m*, -cière *f*
novelty [ˈnɑvəlti] *n, pl* **-ties 1** : nouveauté *f* **2 novelties** *npl* TRINKETS : bibelots *mpl*, babioles *fpl*
November [noˈvembər] *n* : novembre *m*
novice [ˈnɑvɪs] *n* : novice *mf*; débutant *m*, -tante *f*
now[1] [ˈnɑʊ] *adv* **1** : maintenant, à présent <now what are we going to do? : qu'allons-nous faire maintenant?> **2** PRESENTLY : en ce moment, présentement <he is busy now : il est occupé en ce moment> **3** FORTHWITH : maintenant <you can come in now : vous pouvez rentrer maintenant> **4** (*used to express a command, a request, or an admonition*) <now, hear this : écoutez bien> **5** (*used to indicate a transition*) : or <now, his point of view seems illogical : or, son point de vue semble illogique> **6** SOMETIMES : tantôt <now one and now another : tantôt l'un et tantôt l'autre> **7 now and then** : de temps en temps
now[2] *n* **1** (*indicating the present time*) <up until now : jusqu'à maintenant, jusqu'à présent> **2 the now** : le présent
now[3] *conj* **now that** : maintenant que <now that you're here we can begin : maintenant que tu es ici, nous pouvons commencer>
nowadays [ˈnɑʊəˌdeɪz] *adv* : de nos jours
nowhere [ˈnoːˌhwɛr] *adv* : nulle part
noxious [ˈnɑkʃəs] *adj* : nocif
nozzle [ˈnɑzəl] *n* : ajutage *m* (d'un tuyau d'arrosage), lance *f* (à eau)
nuance [ˈnuːˌɑnʌs, ˈnjuː-] *n* : nuance *f*
nub [ˈnʌb] *n* **1** KNOB, LUMP : protubérance *f* **2** GIST : cœur *m*, fond *m*
nubile [ˈnuːˌbaɪl, ˈnjuː-, -bəl] *adj* : nubile
nuclear [ˈnuːkliər, ˈnjuː-] *adj* : nucléaire
nucleus [ˈnuːkliəs, ˈnjuː-] *n, pl* **-clei** [-kliˌaɪ] : noyau *m*
nude[1] [ˈnuːd, ˈnjuːd] *adj* **nuder; nudest** NAKED : nu
nude[2] *n* : nu *m*
nudge[1] [ˈnʌdʒ] *vt* **nudged; nudging** : donner un coup de coude à
nudge[2] *n* : coup *m* de coude
nudism [ˈnuːˌdɪzəm, ˈnjuː-] *n* : nudisme *m*
nudist [ˈnuːdɪst, ˈnjuː-] *n* : nudiste *mf*
nudity [ˈnuːdəti, ˈnjuː-] *n* : nudité *f*
nugget [ˈnʌgət] *n* : pépite *f* (d'or, etc.)
nuisance [ˈnuːsənʌs, ˈnjuː-] *n* **1** ANNOYANCE : embêtement *m*, désagrément *m* **2** : casse-pieds *mf fam*, peste *f* <he's a real nuisance : il est vraiment casse-pieds>
null [ˈnʌl] *adj* : nul <null and void : nul et non avenu>
nullify [ˈnʌləˌfaɪ] *vt* **-fied; -fying** : annuler, invalider
numb[1] [ˈnʌm] *vt* : engourdir, transir (par le froid)
numb[2] *adj* : engourdi, transi, paralysé <numb with cold : transi par le froid> <numb with fear : paralysé par la peur>
number[1] [ˈnʌmbər] *vt* **1** COUNT : compter, énumérer **2** : numéroter (des pages) **3** TOTAL : compter **4 to number among** INCLUDE : compter parmi
number[2] *n* **1** : nombre *m*, numéro *m* <the number 35 : le nombre 35> **2** : chiffre *m* <add the numbers : additionne les chiffres> **3 a number of** : un certain nombre de, plusieurs, divers
numberless [ˈnʌmbərləs] *adj* : innombrable
numbness [ˈnʌmnəs] *n* : engourdissement *m*
numeral [ˈnuːmərəl, ˈnjuː-] *n* : nombre *m*, chiffre *m* <Roman numeral : chiffre romain>
numerator [ˈnuməˌreɪtər, ˈnjuː-] *n* : numérateur *m*
numerical [noˈmerɪkəl, nyo-] *or* **numeric** [-ˈmerɪk] *adj* : numérique — **numerically** [-kli] *adv*
numerous [ˈnuːmərəs, ˈnjuː-] *adj* : nombreux
numismatics [ˌnuːməzˈmætɪks, ˌnjuː-] *n* : numismatique *f*
numskull [ˈnʌmˌskʌl] *n* : cruche *f fam*, imbécile *mf*
nun [ˈnʌn] *n* : religieuse *f*
nuptial [ˈnʌpʃəl] *adj* : nuptial
nuptials [ˈnʌpʃəlz] *npl* WEDDING : noces *fpl*
nurse[1] [ˈnərs] *v* **nursed; nursing** *vt* **1** BREAST-FEED : allaiter **2** : soigner (un malade) **3 to nurse a grudge** : entretenir une rancune — *vi* SUCKLE : téter
nurse[2] *n* : infirmier *m*, -mière *f*; garde-malade *mf*
nursery [ˈnərsəri] *n, pl* **-eries 1** : crèche *f France*, garderie *f Can* **2** : pépinière *f* (pour les plantes)
nursing home *n* : maison *f* de retraite, centre *m* d'accueil *Can*

nurture[1] ['nərtʃər] *vt* **-tured; -turing 1** FEED : nourrir **2** EDUCATE : élever, éduquer **3** FOSTER : nourrir, entretenir (des espoirs, des plans, etc.)
nurture[2] *n* **1** UPBRINGING : éducation *f* **2** NOURISHMENT : nourriture *f*
nut ['nʌt] *n* **1** : noix *f* <Brazil nut : noix du Brésil> **2** : écrou *m* <nuts and bolts : des écrous et des boulons> **3** LUNATIC : fou *m*, folle *f*; cinglé *mf fam* **4** ENTHUSIAST : mordu *m*, -due *f fam*; passionné *m*, -née *f* <a golf nut : un mordu du golf>
nutcracker ['nʌtˌkrækər] *n* : casse-noix *m*, casse-noisettes *m*
nuthatch ['nʌtˌhætʃ] *n* : sittelle *f*
nutmeg ['nʌtˌmɛg] *n* : muscade *f*
nutrient ['nu:triənt, 'nju:-] *n* : substance *f* nutritive
nutriment ['nu:trəmənt, 'nju:-] *n* : nourriture *f*
nutrition [nʊ'trɪʃən, njʊ-] *n* : nutrition *f*, alimentation *f*
nutritional [nʊ'trɪʃənəl, njʊ-] *adj* : nutritif
nutritious [nʊ'trɪʃəs, njʊ-] *adj* : nourrissant, nutritif
nuts ['nʌts] *adj* **1** FANATICAL : fanatique **2** CRAZY : fou, cinglé *fam*
nutshell ['nʌtˌʃɛl] *n* : coquille *f* de noix
nutty ['nʌti] *adj* **nuttier; -est** : timbré *fam*, toqué *fam*
nuzzle ['nʌzəl] *v* **-zled; -zling** *vt* : frotter son nez contre — *vi* NESTLE : se blottir
nylon ['naɪˌlɑn] *n* **1** : nylon *m* **2 nylons** *npl* : bas *mpl* de nylon
nymph ['nɪmpf] *n* : nymphe *f*

O

o ['o:] *n, pl* **o's** *or* **os** ['o:z] **1** : o *m*, quinzième lettre de l'alphabet **2** ZERO : zéro *m*
O ['o:] → **oh**
oaf ['o:f] *n* : balourd *m*, -lourde *f*
oafish ['o:fɪʃ] *adj* : balourd, lourdaud
oak ['o:k] *n, pl* **oaks** *or* **oak** : chêne *m*
oaken ['o:kən] *adj* : de chêne, en chêne
oar ['or] *n* : rame *f*, aviron *m*
oarlock ['or,lɑk] *n* : tolet *m*
oasis [o'eɪsɪs] *n, pl* **oases** [-ˌsi:z] : oasis *f*
oat ['o:t] *n* : avoine *f*
oath ['o:θ] *n, pl* **oaths** ['o:ðz, 'o:θs] **1** : serment *m* <to take the oath : prêter serment> **2** SWEARWORD : juron *m*
oatmeal ['o:tˌmi:l] *n* : farine *f* d'avoine, gruau *m Can*
obdurate ['abdʊrət, -djʊ-] *adj* : opiniâtre
obedience [o'bi:diənʃ] *n* : obéissance *f*
obedient [o'bi:diənt] *adj* : obéissant
obediently [o'bi:diəntli] *adv* : avec obéissance, docilement
obelisk ['abəˌlɪsk] *n* : obélisque *m*
obese [o'bi:s] *adj* : obèse
obesity [o'bi:sətˌi] *n* : obésité *f*
obey [o'beɪ] *v* **obeyed; obeying** *vt* : obéir à <to obey the law : obéir à la loi> — *vi* : obéir
obfuscate ['abfəˌskeɪt] *vt* **-cated; -cating** : obscurcir
obituary [ə'bɪtʃʊˌɛri] *n, pl* **-aries** : nécrologie *f*
object[1] [əb'dʒɛkt] *vt* : objecter — *vi* : protester, s'opposer, soulever des objections
object[2] ['abdʒɪkt] *n* **1** : objet *m* **2** OBJECTIVE, PURPOSE : objectif *m*, but *m* **3** : complément *m* d'objet (en grammaire) <direct object : complément d'objet direct>
objection [əb'dʒɛkʃən] *n* : objection *f*
objectionable [əb'dʒɛkʃənəbəl] *adj* : désagréable, offensif — **objectionably** [-bli] *adv*
objective[1] [əb'dʒɛktɪv] *adj* : objectif
objective[2] *n* **1** AIM : objectif *m*, but *m* **2** *or* **objective case** : accusatif *m*
objectively [əb'dʒɛktɪvli] *adv* : objectivement
objectivity [ˌab,dʒɛk'tɪvətˌi] *n, pl* **-ties** : objectivité *f*
obligate ['abləˌgeɪt] *vt* **-gated; -gating** : contraindre, obliger
obligation [ˌablə'geɪʃən] *n* : obligation *f*
obligatory [ə'blɪgəˌtori] *adj* : obligatoire
oblige [ə'blaɪdʒ] *vt* **obliged; obliging 1** COMPEL : obliger **2 to oblige s.o.** : rendre service à qqn **3 to be obliged to s.o.** : savoir gré à qqn
obliging [ə'blaɪdʒɪŋ] *adj* : obligeant — **obligingly** *adv*
oblique [o'bli:k] *adj* **1** SLANTING : oblique **2** INDIRECT : indirect — **obliquely** *adv*
obliterate [ə'blɪtəˌreɪt] *vt* **-ated; -ating** : effacer, détruire
obliteration [əˌblɪtə'reɪʃən] *n* : effacement *m*
oblivion [ə'blɪviən] *n* : oubli *m*
oblivious [ə'blɪviəs] *adj* : inconscient — **obliviously** *adv*
oblong[1] ['aˌblɔŋ] *adj* : oblong
oblong[2] *n* : rectangle *m*
obnoxious [əb'nɑkʃəs, əb-] *adj* : odieux, exécrable — **obnoxiously** *adv*
oboe ['oˌbo:] *n* : hautbois *m*
oboist ['oˌboɪst] *n* : hautboïste *mf*
obscene [əb'si:n, əb-] *adj* : obscène
obscenely [əb'si:nli, əb-] *adv* : d'une manière obscène
obscenity [əb'sɛnətˌi, əb-] *n, pl* **-ties** : obscénité *f*

obscure[1] [əbˈskjʊr, əb-] *vt* **-scured; -scuring 1** CLOUD, DIM : obscurcir **2** HIDE : cacher
obscure[2] *adj* **1** DIM : obscur **2** UNKNOWN : inconnu **3** VAGUE : vague
obscurely [əbˈskjʊrli, əb-] *adv* : obscurément
obscurity [əbˈskjʊrəṭi, əb-] *n, pl* **-ties** : obscurité *f*
obsequious [əbˈsiːkwiəs] *adj* : obséquieux — **obsequiously** *adv*
observable [əbˈzərvəbəl] *adj* : visible, perceptible
observance [əbˈzərvənts] *n* **1** OBSERVATION : observance *f*, observation *f* **2** PRACTICE : observance *f* (en religion, etc.)
observant [əbˈzərvənt] *adj* : observateur
observation [ˌɑbsərˈveɪʃən, -zər-] *n* : observation *f*
observatory [əbˈzərvəˌtori] *n, pl* **-ries** : observatoire *m*
observe [əbˈzərv] *v* **-served; -serving** *vt* **1** OBEY : respecter, observer <observe the rules : observez les règles> **2** CELEBRATE : observer <to observe the sabbath : observer le sabbat> **3** NOTICE : observer, remarquer **4** REMARK : dire, faire remarquer — *vi* LOOK : regarder
obsess [əbˈsɛs] *vt* : obséder
obsession [əbˈsɛʃən, əb-] *n* : obsession *f*
obsessive [əbˈsɛsɪv, əb-] *adj* **1** : obsessionnel <obsessive-compulsive disorder : trouble obsessionnel compulsif> **2** HAUNTING : obsédant
obsessively [əbˈsɛsɪvli, əb-] *adv* : d'une manière obsessionnelle
obsolescence [ˌɑbsəˈlɛsənts] *n* : obsolescence *f* — **obsolescent** [-ˈlɛsənt] *adj*
obsolete [ˌɑbsəˈliːt, ˈɑbsəˌ-] *adj* : obsolète, démodé
obstacle [ˈɑbstɪkəl] *n* : obstacle *m*
obstetric [əbˈstɛtrɪk] *or* **obstetrical** [-trɪkəl] *adj* : obstétrical
obstetrician [ˌɑbstəˈtrɪʃən] *n* : obstétricien *m*, -cienne *f*
obstetrics [əbˈstɛtrɪks] *ns & pl* : obstétrique *f*
obstinacy [ˈɑbstənəsi] *n, pl* **-cies** : obstination *f*, entêtement *m*
obstinate [ˈɑbstənət] *adj* : obstiné, entêté
obstinately [ˈɑbstənətli] *adv* : obstinément, avec acharnement
obstreperous [əbˈstrɛpərəs] *adj* : tapageur, turbulent
obstruct [əbˈstrʌkt] *vt* : obstruer, bloquer
obstruction [əbˈstrʌkʃən] *n* : obstruction *f*, obstacle *m*
obstructive [əbˈstrəktɪv] *adj* : obstructionniste
obtain [əbˈteɪn] *vt* : obtenir, se procurer — *vi* PREVAIL : régner, avoir cours
obtainable [əbˈteɪnəbəl] *adj* : qu'on peut obtenir, disponible
obtrude [əbˈtruːd] *v* **-truded; -truding** *vt* **1** EXTRUDE : extruder, faire sortir **2** IMPOSE : imposer — *vi* INTRUDE : s'imposer
obtrusive [əbˈtruːsɪv] *adj* **1** BOTHERSOME, MEDDLESOME : importun **2** PROTRUDING : protubérant
obtuse [əbˈtuːs, əb-, -ˈtjuːs] *adj* **1** DULL, STUPID : obtus **2** INDISTINCT : vague, indistinct **3 obtuse angle** : angle *m* obtus
obviate [ˈɑbviˌeɪt] *vt* **-ated; -ating** : obvier à, éviter
obvious [ˈɑbviəs] *adj* : évident
obviously [ˈɑbviəsli] *adv* **1** CLEARLY : manifestement **2** OF COURSE : évidemment, bien sûr
occasion[1] [əˈkeɪʒən] *vt* : occasionner, provoquer, entraîner
occasion[2] *n* **1** INSTANCE : occasion *f* <on one occasion : une fois> **2** OPPORTUNITY : occasion *f* <should the occasion arise : si l'occasion se présente> **3** CAUSE : raison *f*, motif *m* **4** EVENT : événement *m* **5 on ~** : de temps en temps
occasional [əˈkeɪʒənəl] *adj* : occasionnel — **occasionally** *adv*
occidental [ˌɑksəˈdɛntəl] *adj* : occidental
occult[1] [əˈkʌlt, ˈɑˌkʌlt] *adj* : occulte
occult[2] *n* : sciences *fpl* occultes
occupancy [ˈɑkjəpənṭsi] *n, pl* **-cies** : occupation *f*
occupant [ˈɑkjəpənt] *n* **1** : occupant *m*, -pante *f*; habitant *m*, -tante *f* **2** TENANT : locataire *mf*
occupation [ˌɑkjəˈpeɪʃən] *n* **1** OCCUPYING : occupation *f* **2** VOCATION : profession *f*, métier *m*
occupational [ˌɑkjəˈpeɪʃənəl] *adj* : professionnel, du métier <occupational hazard : risque du métier>
occupy [ˈɑkjəˌpaɪ] *vt* **-pied; -pying 1** : occuper **2 to occupy oneself with** : s'occuper de
occur [əˈkər] *vi* **occurred; occurring 1** HAPPEN : avoir lieu, se produire, arriver **2** APPEAR, EXIST : se trouver, se présenter **3** : venir à l'esprit <it occurred to him that . . . : il lui est venu à l'esprit que . . . >
occurrence [əˈkərənts] *n* **1** EVENT : événement *m*, occurrence *f* **2** INSTANCE, PRESENCE : cas *m*, apparition *f* (d'une maladie, etc.)
ocean [ˈoːʃən] *n* : océan *m*
oceanic [ˌoːʃiˈænɪk] *adj* : océanique
oceanography [ˌoːʃəˈnɑgrəfi] *n* : océanographie *f* — **oceanographic** [-nəˈgræfɪk] *adj*
ocelot [ˈɑsəˌlɑt, ˈoː-] *n* : ocelot *m*
ocher *or* **ochre** [ˈoːkər] *n* : ocre *mf*
o'clock [əˈklɑk] *adv* (*used in telling time*) <it's ten o'clock : il est dix heures> <at six o'clock : à six heures>

octagon [ˈɑktəˌɡɑn] *n* : octogone *m* — **octagonal** [ɑkˈtæɡənəl] *adj*
octave [ˈɑktɪv] *n* : octave *f*
October [ɑkˈtoːbər] *n* : octobre *m*
octopus [ˈɑktəˌpʊs, -pəs] *n, pl* **-puses** *or* **-pi** [-ˌpaɪ] : pieuvre *f*, poulpe *m*
ocular [ˈɑkjələr] *adj* : oculaire
oculist [ˈɑkjəlɪst] *n* **1** OPHTHALMOLOGIST : ophtalmologiste *mf*, oculiste *mf* **2** OPTOMETRIST : optométriste *mf*
odd [ˈɑd] *adj* **1** : seul, dépareillé <an odd sock : une chaussette dépareillée> **2** UNEVEN : impair <odd numbers : nombres impairs> **3** : et quelques <a hundred odd dollars : cent dollars et quelques> <forty odd years ago : il y a une quarantaine d'années> **4** STRANGE : étrange, bizarre **5** OCCASIONAL : divers <odd jobs : petits boulots>
oddity [ˈɑdəṭi] *n, pl* **-ties** : étrangeté *f*, bizarrerie *f*
oddly [ˈɑdli] *adv* : étrangement
oddness [ˈɑdnəs] *n* : étrangeté *f*
odds [ˈɑdz] *npl* **1** CHANCES : chances *fpl* **2** RATIO : cote *f* <the odds are eight to five against : la cote est de huit contre cinq> **3 to be at odds** : être en conflit
ode [ˈoːd] *n* : ode *f*
odious [ˈoːdiəs] *adj* : odieux — **odiously** *adv*
odor *or Brit* **odour** [ˈoːdər] *n* : odeur *f*
odorless *or Brit* **odourless** [ˈoːdərləs] *adj* : inodore
odorous [ˈoːdərəs] *adj* : odorant
odour *Brit* → **odor**
odyssey [ˈɑdəsi] *n, pl* **-seys** : odyssée *f*
o'er [ˈor] → **over**
of [ˈʌv, ˈəv] *prep* **1** FROM : de <a man of the city : un homme de la ville> **2** (*indicating a characteristic quality or possession*) : de <a woman of great ability : une femme de grand talent> **3** (*indicating cause*) : de <he died of the flu : il est mort de la grippe> **4** BY : de <the works of Shakespeare : les œuvres de Shakespeare> **5** (*indicating parts, contents, or material*) : de, en <a glass of water : un verre d'eau> <a house of wood : une maison en bois> **6** (*indicating quantity or amount*) : de <thousands of dollars : des milliers de dollars> **7** (*indicating belonging or connection*) : de <the front of the house : le devant de la maison> **8** ABOUT : sur, de <tales of the West : contes de l'Ouest> **9** (*indicating a particular example*) : de <the city of Chicago : la ville de Chicago> **10** FOR : pour, de <love of country : amour de la patrie> **11** (*indicating time or date*) <five minutes of ten : dix heures moins cinq> <the eighth of April : le huit avril>
off[1] [ˈɔf] *adv* **1** (*indicating change of position or state*) <to march off : s'en aller> <he dozed off : il s'est endormi> **2** (*indicating distance in space or time*) <far off : éloigné> <some miles off : à quelques kilomètres de distance> <the holiday is three weeks off : la fête est en trois semaines> **3** (*indicating removal*) <this paint comes off : cette peinture s'enlève> <to cut off : couper> **4** (*indicating termination*) <to finish off : terminer> <shut the television off : éteins la télévision> <shut the engine off : coupez le contact> **5** (*indicating suspension of work*) <to take a day off : prendre un jour de congé> **6 off and on** : par périodes, par intervalles
off[2] *adj* **1** OUT : éteint, fermé <the light is off : la lumière est éteinte> **2** STARTED : démarré <to be off on a spree : démarrer une partie de plaisir> **3** FREE : libre, de congé <his day off : son jour de congé> **4** CANCELED : annulé **5** DOWN : en baisse <stocks were off : les actions étaient en baisse> **6 on an off chance** : pour le cas où cela pourrait servir
off[3] *prep* **1** (*indicating physical separation*) : de <she took it off the table : elle l'a pris de la table> <a shop off the main street : un magasin prêt de la rue principale> **2** : aux frais de <he lives off his sister : il vit aux frais de sa sœur> **3** (*indicating the suspension of an activity*) <to be off duty : être libre> <she's off meat : elle ne mange plus de viande> **4 to be off one's game, to be off one's stride** : ne pas être à son meilleur
offal [ˈɔfəl] *n* : abats *mpl*
offend [əˈfɛnd] *vt* **1** HURT : offenser, blesser <to be easily offended : être très susceptible> **2** OUTRAGE, SHOCK : choquer, outrager
offender [əˈfɛndər] *n* : délinquant *m*, -quante *f*; contrevenant *m*, -nante *f*
offense *or* **offence** [əˈfɛnʦ, ˈɔˌfɛnʦ] *n* **1** INSULT : offense *f* <to take offense : s'offenser> **2** CRIME : délit *m*, infraction *f* **3** : attaque *f* (aux sports)
offensive[1] [əˈfɛnʦɪv, ˈɔˌfɛnʦ-] *adj* : offensif — **offensively** *adv*
offensive[2] *n* : offensive *f*, attaque *f* <to go on the offensive : passer à l'offensive>
offer[1] [ˈɔfər] *vt* **1** : offrir, présenter <they offered him the job : ils lui ont offert le poste> **2** PROPOSE : proposer, suggérer **3** PROVIDE : donner, offrir <to offer no resistance : ne donner aucune résistance>
offer[2] *n* : proposition *f*, offre *f*
offering [ˈɔfərɪŋ] *n* : offre *f*, offrande *f* (en réligion)
offhand[1] [ˈɔfˈhænd] *adv* : spontanément, sur-le-champ
offhand[2] *adj* : désinvolte, impromptu
office [ˈɔfəs] *n* **1** : bureau *m*, cabinet *m* (d'un médecin, d'un avocat) **2** POSITION : fonction *f*, charge *f*, poste *m*

<a person in high office : une personne haut placée>
officeholder ['ɔfəs,ho:ldər] *n* : fonctionnaire *mf*
officer ['ɔfəsər] *n* **1** *or* **police officer** : policier *m*, -cière *f*; agent *m* de police **2** OFFICIAL : fonctionnaire *mf* **3** → **commissioned officer**
official[1] [ə'fɪʃəl] *adj* : officiel — **officially** *adv*
official[2] *n* : officiel *m*, -cielle *f*
officiate [ə'fɪʃi,eɪt] *vi* **-ated; -ating 1** PRESIDE : officier, présider **2** : arbitrer (aux sports)
officious [ə'fɪʃəs] *adj* : importun, trop empressé
offing ['ɔfɪŋ] *n* **in the offing** : en perspective, en vue
offset ['ɔf,sɛt] *vt* **-set; -setting** : compenser, contrebalancer
offshoot ['ɔf,ʃu:t] *n* **1** : ramification *f*, conséquence *f* (d'une idée, etc.) **2** : rejeton *m* (en botanie)
offshore[1] ['ɔf'ʃɔr] *adv* : en mer
offshore[2] *adj* : côtier, marin <offshore drilling : forage marin>
offspring ['ɔf,sprɪŋ] *ns & pl* PROGENY : progéniture *f*
often ['ɔfən, 'ɔftən] *adv* : souvent, fréquemment
oftentimes ['ɔfən,taɪmz, 'ɔftən-] *or* **oftimes** [ɔft,taɪmz] → **often**
ogle ['o:gəl] *vt* **ogled; ogling** : lorgner, reluquer *fam*
ogre ['o:gər] *n* : ogre *m*, ogresse *f*
oh ['o:] *interj* : oh! <oh, really? : vraiment?> <oh dear! : oh la la!>
ohm ['o:m] *n* : ohm *m*
oil[1] ['ɔɪl] *vt* : huiler, lubrifier, graisser
oil[2] *n* **1** : huile *f* <oil painting : peinture à l'huile> <olive oil : huile d'olive> **2** PETROLEUM : pétrole *m* **3** *or* **heating oil** : mazout *m*
oilcloth ['ɔɪl,klɔθ] *n* : toile *f* cirée
oiliness ['ɔɪlinəs] *n* : nature *f* huileuse
oilskin ['ɔɪl,skɪn] *n* **1** OILCLOTH : toile *f* cirée **2** *or* **oilskins** *npl* : ciré *m*
oily ['ɔɪli] **oilier; -est** *adj* : huileux
ointment ['ɔɪntmənt] *n* : pommade *f*
OK[1] *or* **okay** [,o:'keɪ] *vt* **OK'd** *or* **okayed; OK'ing** *or* **okaying** APPROVE, AUTHORIZE : approuver
OK[2] *or* **okay** *adv* **1** WELL : bien <everything's going OK : tout va bien> **2** YES : oui
OK[3] *adj* : bien <I'm OK : je vais bien> <it's OK with me : je suis d'accord>
OK[4] *n* APPROVAL *n* : accord *m*, approbation *f*
okra ['o:krə, *south also* -kri] *n* : gombo *m*
old[1] ['o:ld] *adj* **1** : vieux <an old man : un vieil homme> **2** ANCIENT : ancien, antique **3** (*indicating a certain age*) <he's ten years old : il a dix ans> <she's not old enough : elle n'est pas encore en âge> **4** FORMER : ancien <her old neighborhood : son ancien voisinage> **5** WORN-OUT : usé **6 any old** : n'importe quel **7 old age** : vieillesse *f*
old[2] *n* **1 the old** : les vieux **2 in the days of old** : d'antan, d'autrefois
olden ['o:ldən] *adj* : vieux, d'autrefois, d'antan <in olden days : autrefois, jadis>
old-fashioned ['o:ld'fæʃənd] *adj* : démodé, suranné <old-fashioned charm : charme suranné>
old maid *n* **1** SPINSTER : vieille fille *f* **2** FUSSBUDGET : tatillon *m*, -lonne *f*
Old Testament *n* : Ancien Testament *m*
old-timer ['o:ld'taɪmər] *n* : vieillard *m*; ancien *m*, -cienne *f*
old-world ['o:ld'wərld] *adj* : d'autrefois, pittoresque
oleander ['o:li,ændər] *n* : laurier-rose *m*
oleomargarine [,o:lio'mardʒərən] → **margarine**
olfactory [ɑl'fæktəri, ol-] *adj* : olfactif
oligarchy ['ɑlə,gɑrki, 'o:lə-] *n, pl* **-chies** : oligarchie *f*
olive ['ɑlɪv, -ləv] *n* **1** : olive *f* (fruit) **2** : olivier *m* (arbre) **3** *or* **olive green** : vert *m* olive
Olympic Games [o'lɪmpɪk] *or* **Olympics** [-pɪks] *npl* : jeux *mpl* Olympiques
Omani[1] [o'mani] *adj* : omanais
Omani[2] *n* : Omanais *m*, -naise *f*
ombudsman ['ɑm,bʊdzmən, ɑm'bʊdz-] *n, pl* **-men** [-mən, -,mɛn] : médiateur *m*, -trice *f France;* protecteur *m* du citoyen *Can*
omelet *or* **omelette** ['ɑmlət, 'ɑmə-] *n* : omelette *f*
omen ['o:mən] *n* : augure *m*, présage *m*
ominous ['ɑmənəs] *adj* : inquiétant, menaçant
ominously ['ɑmənəsli] *adv* : de manière inquiétante
omission [o'mɪʃən] *n* : omission *f*
omit [o'mɪt] *vt* **omitted; omitting** : omettre <to omit to do sth : omettre de faire qqch>
omnipotence [ɑm'nɪpət̬ənts] *n* : omnipotence *f* — **omnipotent** [-t̬ənt] *adj*
omnipresent [,ɑmnɪ'prɛzənt] *adj* : omniprésent
omniscient [ɑm'nɪʃənt] *adj* : omniscient
omnivorous [ɑm'nɪvərəs] *adj* **1** : omnivore **2** AVID : avide
on[1] ['ɑn, 'ɔn] *adv* **1** (*indicating contact with a surface*) <put the top on : mets le couvercle> <he has a hat on : il porte un chapeau> **2** (*indicating forward movement*) <from that moment on : à partir de ce moment-là> <farther on : un peu plus loin> **3** (*indicating operation or operating position*) <turn the light on : allumez la lumière>
on[2] *adj* **1** (*being in operation*) <the radio is on : la radio est allumée> <the faucet is on : le robinet est ouvert> <the engine is on : le moteur est en

marche> **2** (*taking place*) <the game is on : le match aura lieu> **3 to be on** : être mis <the lid is on : le couvercle est mis>

on³ *prep* **1** (*indicating position*) : sur, à, de <on the table : sur la table> <on horseback : à cheval> <on page two : à la page deux> **2** AT, TO : à <on the right : à droite> **3** ABOARD, IN : en, dans <on the plane : dans l'avion> **4** (*indicating time*) <she worked on Saturdays : elle travaillait le samedi> <every hour on the hour : à toutes les heures justes> <on Tuesday : mardi> **5** (*indicating means or agency*) <to talk on the telephone : parler au téléphone> <he cut himself on a tin can : il s'est coupé avec une boîte de conserve> **6** (*indicating a state or process*) : en, à <on fire : en feu> <to be on the increase : aller en augmentant> <on foot : à pied> <on a diet : au régime> **7** (*indicating connection or membership*) <she's on a committee : elle fait partie d'un comité> **8** (*indicating an activity*) <on vacation : en vacances> **9** ABOUT, CONCERNING : sur <a book on insects : un livre sur les insectes> <reflect on that : réfléchissez-y>

once¹ ['wʌnts] *adv* **1** : une fois <once a month : une fois par mois> <once and for all : une fois pour toutes> **2** EVER : jamais <if you hesitate once, all will be lost : si jamais tu hésites, tout sera perdu> **3** FORMERLY : autrefois

once² *adj* FORMER : ancien, précédent

once³ *n* **1** : une fois <for once : pour une fois> **2 at ~** SIMULTANEOUSLY : en même temps, simultanément **3 at ~** IMMEDIATELY : tout de suite, immédiatement

once⁴ *conj* : dès que, une fois que

once–over [ˌwʌnts'oːvər, 'wʌnts,-] *n* : coup *m* d'œil <to give something the once-over : jeter un coup d'œil sur>

oncoming ['ɑnˌkʌmɪŋ, 'ɔn-] *adj* : approchant, qui approche <oncoming traffic : circulation venant en sens inverse>

one¹ ['wʌn] *adj* **1** (*being a single unit*) : un, une <the only wants one apple : il ne veut qu'une pomme> <with one motion : d'un seul mouvement> **2** (*being a particular one*) : un, une <he arrived early one morning : il est arrivé tôt un matin> **3** (*being the same*) : même <one and the same thing : la même chose> **4** SOME : un, une <one day we'll come : un jour nous viendrons> **5** ONLY : seul, unique <her one day off : son unique jour de congé>

one² *n* **1** : un *m* (numéro) **2** (*indicating the first of a set or series*) <from day one : depuis le premier jour> <one o'clock : une heure> **3** (*indicating a single person or thing*) <the one (girl) on the left : celle à gauche> <you can't have one without the other : l'un ne va pas sans l'autre>

one³ *pron* **1** : un, une <one of his friends : un de ses amis> <one never knows : l'on ne sait jamais> **2 one and all** : tous, tout le monde **3 one another** : l'un l'autre **4 this one, that one** : celui-là, celle-là **5 which one?** : lequel?, laquelle?

oneness ['wʌnnəs] *n* **1** SINGLENESS : unité *f* **2** AGREEMENT : accord *m* **3** SAMENESS : identité *f*

onerous ['ɑnərəs, 'oːnə-] *adj* : pénible

oneself [ˌwən'self] *pron* **1** (*used reflexively*) : se <to control oneself : se contrôler> **2** (*used for emphasis*) : soi-même <to do it oneself : le faire soi-même> **3** (*used after prepositions*) : soi <sure of oneself : sûr de soi> **4 by ~** : seul

one–sided ['wʌn'saɪdəd] *adj* **1** UNEQUAL : inégal **2** PARTIAL : partial **3** UNILATERAL : unilatéral

onetime ['wʌn'taɪm] *adj* FORMER : ancien

one–way ['wʌn'weɪ] *adj* **1** : à sens unique (se dit d'une route) **2** : simple <a one-way ticket : un aller simple, un billet simple>

ongoing ['ɑnˌgoːɪŋ] *adj* : continu, en cours

onion ['ʌnjən] *n* : oignon *m*

online ['ɑnˈlaɪn, 'ɔn-] *adj* : en ligne

only¹ ['oːnli] *adv* **1** MERELY : seulement, ne...que <he's only five : il n'a que cinq ans> <this will only take a moment : ceci ne prendra qu'un moment> <only once : seulement une fois> **2** EXCLUSIVELY : seulement, uniquement <only in the morning : le matin seulement> <I'll tell it only to you : je le dirai seulement à toi> <only he knows it : lui seul le sait> **3** (*indicating a result*) <you know only too well : vous ne savez que trop bien> **4 if only** : si, si seulement <if he could only dance : si seulement il pouvait danser>

only² *adj* : seul, unique <an only child : un enfant unique> <the only chance : la seule chance> <we're the only ones : nous sommes les seuls>

only³ *conj* BUT : mais <I would go, only I'm sick : j'irais mais je suis malade>

onset ['ɑnˌset] *n* : début *m*, commencement *m*

onslaught ['ɑnˌslɔt, 'ɔn-] *n* : assaut *m*, attaque *f*

onto ['ɑnˌtuː, 'ɔn-] *prep* : sur

onus ['oːnəs] *n* : responsabilité *f*, charge *f*

onward¹ ['ɑnwərd, 'ɔn-] *adv* **1** FORWARD : en avant <to go onward : avancer> **2** (*used to express continuance from a point*) <from today onward : à partir d'aujourd'hui>

onward[2] *adj* : progressif <the onward march of time : la fuite du temps>
onyx [ˈɑnɪks] *n* : onyx *m*
ooze[1] [ˈuːz] *v* **oozed; oozing** *vi* : suinter — *vt* EXUDE : respirer <to ooze confidence : respirer la confiance>
ooze[2] *n* SLIME : vase *f*, boue *f*
opacity [oˈpæsəɾi] *n, pl* **-ties** : opacité *f*
opal [ˈoːpəl] *n* : opale *f*
opaque [oˈpeɪk] *adj* : opaque
open[1] [ˈoːpən] *vt* **1** : ouvrir **2** START : commencer, entamer (une négociation, etc.) **3** INAUGURATE : inaugurer, ouvrir (une entreprise, etc.) **4** CLEAR : ouvrir, dégager (la voie) — *vi* **1** : s'ouvrir **2** BEGIN : débuter, sortir <the film opens tomorrow : le film sort demain> **3 to open on to** : donner sur
open[2] *adj* **1** : ouvert <an open window : une fenêtre ouverte> <the store is open : le magasin est ouvert> **2** FRANK : franc **3** CLEAR : dégagé **4** DEBATABLE : discutable **5** VACANT : vacant **6** UNCOVERED : découvert
open[3] *n* **in the open 1** OUTDOORS : à la belle étoile, au grand air **2** KNOWN : connu
open–air [ˈoːpənˈær] *adj* OUTDOOR : en plein air
open–and–shut [ˈoːpənənd͡ˈʃʌt] *adj* : clair, évident
opener [ˈoːpənər] *n* **1** : ouvreur *m*, -vreuse *f* (aux jeux, etc.) **2** : outil *m* servant à ouvrir <a can opener : un ouvre-boîtes>
openhanded [ˌoːpənˈhændəd] *adj* GENEROUS : généreux
openhearted [ˌoːpənˈhɑrɾəd] *adj* **1** FRANK : franc, sincère **2** GENEROUS, KIND : généreux, qui a bon cœur
opening [ˈoːpənɪŋ] *n* **1** BEGINNING : commencement *m* **2** APERTURE : ouverture *f* **3** OPPORTUNITY : occasion *f*, chance *f* **4** : vernissage *m* (d'une exposition)
opera[1] → **opus**
opera[2] [ˈɑprə, ˈɑpərə] *n* : opéra *m*
opera glasses *n* : jumelles *fpl* de théâtre
operate [ˈɑpəˌreɪt] *v* **-ated; -ating** *vi* **1** FUNCTION : fonctionner, marcher **2 to operate on s.o.** : opérer qqn — *vt* **1** WORK : faire fonctionner **2** MANAGE : effectuer, gérer
operatic [ˌɑpəˈræɾɪk] *adj* : d'opéra
operation [ˌɑpəˈreɪʃən] *n* **1** FUNCTIONING : fonctionnement *m* **2** SURGERY : opération *f*, intervention *f* chirurgicale <to have an operation : se faire opérer> **3** DEALING, TRANSACTION : opération *f*
operational [ˌɑpəˈreɪʃənəl] *adj* : opérationnel
operative [ˈɑpərəɾɪv, -ˌreɪ-] *adj* **1** OPERATING : en vigueur **2** OPERATIONAL, WORKING : opérationnel **3** SURGICAL : opératoire
operator [ˈɑpəˌreɪɾər] *n* **1** : opérateur *m*, -trice *f* (d'une machine, etc.) **2** *or* **switchboard operator** : standardiste *mf*
operetta [ˌɑpəˈreɾə] *n* : opérette *f*
ophthalmologist [ˌɑf,θælˈmɑlədʒɪst, -θəˈmɑ-] *n* : ophtalmologiste *mf*
ophthalmology [ˌɑf,θælˈmɑlədʒi, -θəˈmɑ-] *n* : ophtalmologie *f*
opiate [ˈoːpiət, -piˌeɪt] *n* : opiacé *m*
opinion [əˈpɪnjən] *n* : opinion *f*, avis *m*
opinionated [əˈpɪnjəˌneɪɾəd] *adj* : opiniâtre
opium [ˈoːpiəm] *n* : opium *m*
opossum [əˈpɑsəm] *n* : opossum *m*
opponent [əˈpoːnənt] *n* : adversaire *mf*
opportune [ˌɑpərˈtuːn, -ˈtjuːn] *adj* : opportun — **opportunely** *adv*
opportunism [ˌɑpərˈtuːˌnɪzəm, -ˈtjuː-] *n* : opportunisme *m*
opportunist [ˌɑpərˈtuːnɪst, -ˈtjuː-] *n* : opportuniste *mf*
opportunistic [ˌɑpərtuːˈnɪstɪk, -tjuː-] *adj* : opportuniste
opportunity [ˌɑpərˈtuːnəɾi, -ˈtjuː-] *n, pl* **-ties** : occasion *f*
oppose [əˈpoːz] *vt* **-posed; -posing 1** CONTRAST : opposer **2** RESIST : s'opposer à, combattre
opposite[1] [ˈɑpəzət] *adv* : en face
opposite[2] *adj* **1** FACING : d'en face <the opposite side : le côté d'en face> **2** CONTRARY : opposé, inverse, contraire <in the opposite direction : en sens inverse> <the opposite sex : le sexe opposé>
opposite[3] *n* : contraire *m*
opposite[4] *prep* : en face de
opposition [ˌɑpəˈzɪʃən] *n* : opposition *f*, résistance *f*
oppress [əˈprɛs] *vt* **1** PERSECUTE : opprimer **2** BURDEN : oppresser
oppression [əˈpreʃən] *n* : oppression *f*
oppressive [əˈprɛsɪv] *adj* : oppressif
oppressor [əˈprɛsər] *n* : oppresseur *m*
opprobrium [əˈproːbriəm] *n* : opprobre *m*
opt [ˈɑpt] *vi* : opter
optic [ˈɑptɪk] *adj* : optique <the optic nerve : le nerf optique>
optical [ˈɑptɪkəl] → **optic**
optician [ɑpˈtɪʃən] *n* : opticien *m*, -cienne *f*
optics [ˈɑptɪks] *n* : optique *f*
optimal [ˈɑptəməl] *adj* : optimal
optimism [ˈɑptəˌmɪzəm] *n* : optimisme *m*
optimist [ˈɑptəmɪst] *n* : optimiste *mf*
optimistic [ˌɑptəˈmɪstɪk] *adj* : optimiste
optimistically [ˌɑptəˈmɪstɪkli] *adv* : avec optimisme
optimum[1] [ˈɑptəməm] *adj* : optimum
optimum[2] *n, pl* **-ma** [ˈɑptəmə] : optimum *m*
option [ˈɑpʃən] *n* : option *f*
optional [ˈɑpʃənəl] *adj* : facultatif, optionnel

optometrist [ɑp'tɑmətrɪst] *n* : optométriste *mf*
optometry [ɑp'tɑmətri] *n* : optométrie *f*
opulence ['ɑpjələnʦ] *n* : opulence *f* — **opulent** [-lənt] *adj*
opus ['o:pəs] *n, pl* **opera** ['o:pərə, 'ɑpə-] : opus *m*
or ['ɔr] *conj* **1** (*indicating an alternative*) : ou <one or the other : l'un ou l'autre> **2** (*following a negative*) : ni <he didn't have his keys or his wallet : il n'avait eu ni ses clés ni son portefeuille> **3** OTHERWISE : sinon <do what I tell you, or you'll be sorry : faites ce que je dis, sinon vous le regretterez>
oracle ['ɔrəkəl] *n* : oracle *m*
oral ['ɔrəl] *adj* : oral — **orally** *adv*
orange ['ɔrɪnʤ] *n* **1** : orange *f* (fruit) **2** : orange *m* (couleur)
orangeade [ˌɔrɪnʤ'eɪd] *n* : orangeade *f*
orangutan [ə'rænˌʤˌtæŋ, -'ræŋgə-, -ˌtæn] *n* : orang-outan *m*
oration [ə'reɪʃən] *n* : discours *m* (solennel), allocution *f*
orator ['ɔrətər] *n* : orateur *m*, -trice *f*
oratorical [ˌɔrə'tɔrɪkəl] *adj* : oratoire
oratorio [ˌɔrə'tori,o:] *n, pl* **-rios** : oratorio *m*
oratory ['ɔrəˌtori] *n, pl* **-ries** : éloquence *f*, art *m* oratoire
orb ['ɔrb] *n* : orbe *m*
orbit[1] ['ɔrbət] *vt* : graviter autour de — *vi* : décrire une orbite
orbit[2] *n* : orbite *f*
orbital ['ɔrbətəl] *adj* : orbital
orchard ['ɔrtʃərd] *n* : verger *m*
orchestra ['ɔrkəstrə] *n* : orchestre *m* — **orchestral** [ɔr'kestrəl] *adj*
orchestrate ['ɔrkəˌstreɪt] *vt* **-trated; -trating** : orchestrer
orchestration [ˌɔrkə'streɪʃən] *n* : orchestration *f*
orchid ['ɔrkɪd] *n* : orchidée *f*
ordain [ɔr'deɪn] *vt* **1** : ordonner (en religion) **2** DECREE : décréter, ordonner
ordeal [ɔr'di:l, 'ɔrˌdi:l] *n* : épreuve *f*, calvaire *m*
order[1] ['ɔrdər] *vt* **1** ORGANIZE : arranger, ranger **2** COMMAND : ordonner **3** REQUEST : commander (un repas, etc.) — *vi* : commander
order[2] *n* **1** : ordre *m* <religious order : ordre religieux> **2** COMMAND : commande *f*, ordre *m* <to give orders : donner des ordres> **3** REQUEST : commande *f*, bon *m* <purchase order : bon de commande> **4** DISCIPLINE : ordre *m* <law and order : l'ordre public> **5** CONDITION : état *m* <in working order : en bon état> **6** ARRANGEMENT : ordre *m* <in alphabetical order : en ordre alphabétique> **7 in order to** : afin de **8 orders** *npl or* **holy orders** : ordres *mpl* **9 out of order** : en panne
orderliness ['ɔrdərlinəs] *n* : ordre *m*
orderly[1] ['ɔrdərli] *adj* **1** TIDY : en ordre, ordonné **2** DISCIPLINED : discipliné, réglé
orderly[2] *n, pl* **-lies 1** : planton *m* (dans l'armée) **2** : aide-infirmier *m* (dans un hôpital)
ordinal ['ɔrdənəl] *n or* **ordinal number** : ordinal *m*
ordinance ['ɔrdənənʦ] *n* : ordonnance *f*
ordinarily [ˌɔrdən'erəli] *adv* : d'ordinaire, d'habitude
ordinary ['ɔrdənˌeri] *adj* **1** NORMAL, USUAL : normal, habituel **2** AVERAGE : ordinaire **3** COMMONPLACE : quelconque
ordination [ˌɔrdən'eɪʃən] *n* : ordination *f*
ordnance ['ɔrdnənʦ] *n* **1** SUPPLIES : équipement *m* militaire **2** ARTILLERY : artillerie *f*
ore ['ɔr] *n* : minerai *m*
oregano [ə'regəˌno:] *n* : origan *m*
organ ['ɔrgən] *n* **1** : orgue *m* (instrument de musique) **2** : organe *m* (du corps) **3** PERIODICAL : périodique *m*
organic [ɔr'gænɪk] *adj* : organique — **organically** *adv*
organism ['ɔrgəˌnɪzəm] *n* : organisme *m*
organist ['ɔrgənɪst] *n* : organiste *mf*
organization [ˌɔrgənə'zeɪʃən] *n* **1** ORGANIZING : organisation *f* **2** BODY : organisme *m*
organizational [ˌɔrgənə'zeɪʃənəl] *adj* : organisationnel, d'organisation
organize ['ɔrgəˌnaɪz] *vt* **-nized; -nizing 1** : organiser, mettre à l'ordre **2 to get organized** : s'organiser
organizer ['ɔrgəˌnaɪzər] *n* : organisateur *m*, -trice *f*
orgasm ['ɔrˌgæzəm] *n* : orgasme *m*
orgy ['ɔrʤi] *n, pl* **-gies** : orgie *f*
orient ['oriˌent] *vt* : orienter
Orient *n* **the Orient** : l'Orient *m*
oriental [ˌori'entəl] *adj* : oriental, d'Orient
Oriental *n* : Oriental *m*, -tale *f*
orientation [ˌoriən'teɪʃən] *n* : orientation *f*
orifice ['ɔrəfəs] *n* : orifice *m*
origin ['ɔrəʤən] *n* **1** ANCESTRY : origine *f* <of Canadian origin : d'origine canadienne> **2** SOURCE : source *f*, provenance *f*
original[1] [ə'rɪʤənəl] *adj* : original
original[2] *n* : original *m*
originality [əˌrɪʤə'nælətˌi] *n* : originalité *f*
originally [ə'rɪʤənəli] *adv* **1** AT FIRST : à l'origine, initialement, au début **2** INVENTIVELY : originalement, d'une manière originale
originate [ə'rɪʤəˌneɪt] *v* **-nated; -nating** *vt* : créer, donner naissance à — *vi* : provenir, prendre naissance <the

fire originated in the basement : le feu a pris naissance au sous-sol>

originator [ə'rɪdʒəˌneɪtər] *n* : créateur *m*, -trice *f*; auteur *m*

oriole ['ori,o:l, -iəl] *n* : loriot *m*

ornament[1] ['ɔrnəmənt] *vt* : orner

ornament[2] *n* : ornement *m* — **ornamental** [ˌɔrnə'mentəl] *adj*

ornamentation [ˌɔrnəmən'teɪʃən] *n* : ornementation *f*

ornate [ɔr'neɪt] *adj* : orné

ornery ['ɔrnəri, 'ornəri] *adj* **ornerier; -est** : méchant, acariâtre, malcommode *Can*

ornithologist [ˌɔrnə'θɑlədʒɪst] *n* : ornithologiste *mf*, ornithologue *mf*

ornithology [ˌɔrnə'θɑlədʒi] *n, pl* **-gies** : ornithologie *f*

orphan[1] ['ɔrfən] *vt* : rendre orphelin

orphan[2] *n* : orphelin *m*, -line *f*

orphanage ['ɔrfənɪdʒ] *n* : orphelinat *m*

orthodontics [ˌɔrθə'dɑntɪks] *n* : orthodontie *f*

orthodontist [ˌɔrθə'dɑntɪst] *n* : orthodontiste *mf*

orthodox ['ɔrθəˌdɑks] *adj* : orthodoxe

orthodoxy ['ɔrθəˌdɑksi] *n, pl* **-doxies** : orthodoxie *f*

orthographic [ˌɔrθə'græfɪk] *adj* : orthographique

orthography [ɔr'θɑgrəfi] *n* : orthographie *f*

orthopedic [ˌɔrθə'pi:dɪk] *adj* : orthopédique

orthopedics [ˌɔrθə'pi:dɪks] *ns & pl* : orthopédie *f*

orthopedist [ˌɔrθə'pi:dɪst] *n* : orthopédiste *mf*

oscillate ['ɑsəˌleɪt] *vi* **-lated; -lating** : osciller

oscillation [ˌɑsə'leɪʃən] *n* : oscillation *f*

osmosis [ɑz'mo:səs, ɑs-] *n* : osmose *f*

osprey ['ɑspri, -ˌpreɪ] *n, pl* **-preys** : balbuzard *m* (pêcheur)

ostensible [ɑ'stentəsəbəl] *adj* : ostensible — **ostensibly** [-bli] *adv*

ostentation [ˌɑstən'teɪʃən] *n* : ostentation *f*

ostentatious [ˌɑstən'teɪʃəs] *adj* : ostentatoire — **ostentatiously** *adv*

osteopath ['ɑstiəˌpæθ] *n* : ostéopathe *mf*

osteopathy [ˌɑsti'ɑpəθi] *n* : ostéopathie *f*

osteoporosis [ˌɑstiopə'rosɪs] *n, pl* **-roses** [-ˌsi:z] : ostéoporose *f*

ostracism ['ɑstrəˌsɪzəm] *n* : ostracisme *m*

ostracize ['ɑstrəˌsaɪz] *vt* **-cized; -cizing** : frapper d'ostracisme, mettre au ban de la société

ostrich ['ɑstrɪtʃ, 'ɔs-] *n* : autruche *f*

other[1] ['ʌðər] *adv* **other than** : autrement que, à part

other[2] *adj* : autre <the other boys : les autres garçons> <on the other hand : d'autre part, par contre> <every other day : tous les deux jours>

other[3] *pron* : autre <one in front of the other : l'un devant l'autre>

otherwise[1] ['ʌðərˌwaɪz] *adv* **1** DIFFERENTLY : autrement <he could not act otherwise : il n'a pas pu agir autrement> **2** : à part cela <I'm dizzy, but otherwise I'm fine : j'ai la tête qui tourne, mais à part cela je vais bien> **3** OR ELSE : sinon <do what I tell you, otherwise you'll be sorry : fais comme je dis, sinon tu le regretteras>

otherwise[2] *adj* : autre <the facts are otherwise : les faits sont autres>

otter ['ɑtər] *n* : loutre *f*

ouch ['aʊtʃ] *interj* : aïe!, ayoye! *Can*

ought ['ɔt] *v aux* : devoir <you ought to take care of the children : vous devriez vous occuper des enfants>

oughtn't ['ɔtənt] (*contraction of* **ought not**) → **ought**

ounce ['aʊnts] *n* : once *f*

our ['ɑr, 'aʊr] *adj* : notre, nos <our house : notre maison> <our children : nos enfants>

ours ['aʊrz, 'ɑrz] *pron* : le nôtre, la nôtre <the car is ours : la voiture est la nôtre> <a cousin of ours : un de nos cousins> <that's ours : c'est à nous>

ourselves [ɑr'selvz, aʊr-] *pron* **1** (*used reflexively*) : nous <we amused ourselves : nous nous sommes divertis> **2** (*used for emphasis*) : nous-mêmes <we did it ourselves : nous l'avons fait nous-mêmes>

oust ['aʊst] *vt* : évincer

ouster ['aʊstər] *n* : expulsion *f* (d'un pays, etc.), renvoi *m* (d'un poste)

out[1] ['aʊt] *vi* : se savoir <the truth will out : la vérité se saura>

out[2] *adv* **1** (*indicating direction or movement*) : dehors, à l'extérieur <let's go out tonight : sortons ce soir> <she opened the door and looked out : elle a ouvert la porte et regardait à l'extérieur> **2** (*indicating a location away from home or work*) <to eat out : aller au restaurant, dîner en ville> **3** (*indicating completion or discontinuance*) <his money ran out : il s'est trouvé à court d'argent> <to turn out the light : éteindre la lumière> **4** (*indicating possession or control*) <to lend out money : prêter de l'argent> <they let the secret out : ils ont laissé échapper le secret> **5** OUTSIDE : dehors <put the cat out : mettez le chat dehors> <the sun came out : il faisait soleil>

out[3] *adj* **1** OUTER : extérieur **2** ABSENT : absent **3** UNFASHIONABLE : démodé **4** EXTINGUISHED : éteint

out[4] *prep* **1** (*used to indicate an outward movement*) : par <I looked out the window : je regardais par la fenêtre> **2** → **out of**

out-and-out ['aʊtən'aʊt] *adj* UTTER : total, absolu

outboard motor ['aʊtˌbɔrd] *n* : horsbord *m*
outbound ['aʊtˌbaʊnd] *adj* : en partance
outbreak ['aʊtˌbreɪk] *n* : début *m*, déclenchement *m* (de la guerre, etc.), éruption *f* (de violence, d'une maladie, etc.)
outbuilding ['aʊtˌbɪldɪŋ] *n* : dépendance *f*
outburst ['aʊtˌbərst] *n* : accès *m* (de colère, etc.), explosion *f*
outcast ['aʊtˌkæst] *n* : proscrit *m*, -crite *f*; banni *m*, -nie *f*
outcome ['aʊtˌkʌm] *n* : résultat *m*
outcrop ['aʊtˌkrɑp] *n* : affleurement *m*
outcry ['aʊtˌkraɪ] *n, pl* **-cries** : tollé *m*
outdated [ˌaʊt'deɪtəd] *adj* : démodé
outdistance [ˌaʊt'dɪstənʦ] *vt* **-tanced; -tancing** : distancer
outdo [ˌaʊt'du:] *vt* **-did** [-'dɪd]; **-done** [-'dʌn]; **-doing** [-'du:ɪŋ]; **-does** [-'dʌz] : surpasser
outdoor ['aʊtˌdɔr] *adj* : en plein air, de plein air, d'extérieur <outdoor activities : activités en plein air> <outdoor sports : sports de plein air> <outdoor clothes : vêtements d'extérieur>
outdoors[1] ['aʊtˌdɔrz] *adv* : à la belle étoile, au grand air, en plein air
outdoors[2] *n* **the great outdoors** : les grands espaces naturels, la pleine nature
outer ['aʊtər] *adj* : externe, extérieur
outermost ['aʊtərˌmo:st] *adj* : le plus extérieur
outer space *n* : espace *m* intersidéral
outfield ['aʊtˌfi:ld] *n* : champ *m* extérieur
outfielder ['aʊtˌfi:ldər] *n Can* : voltigeur *m*, -geuse *f*
outfit[1] ['aʊtˌfɪt] *vt* **-fitted; -fitting** EQUIP : équiper
outfit[2] *n* **1** EQUIPMENT : équipement *m*, attirail *m* **2** COSTUME : tenue *f* **3** GROUP : équipe *f*, bande *f*
outgoing ['aʊtˌgo:ɪŋ] *adj* **1** OUTBOUND : en partance **2** DEPARTING : sortant <the outgoing president : le président sortant> **3** EXTROVERTED : extraverti
outgrow [ˌaʊt'gro:] *vt* **-grew** [-'gru:]; **-grown** [-'gro:n]; **-growing** : devenir trop grand pour
outgrowth ['aʊtˌgro:θ] *n* : excroissance *f*
outing ['aʊtɪŋ] *n* : excursion *f*, sortie *f*
outlandish [aʊt'lændɪʃ] *adj* : bizarre, excentrique
outlast [ˌaʊt'læst] *vt* : durer plus longtemps que
outlaw[1] ['aʊtˌlɔ] *vt* : proscrire, rendre illégal
outlaw[2] *n* : hors-la-loi *m*
outlay ['aʊtˌleɪ] *n* : débours *m*, dépense *f*, mise *f* de fonds
outlet ['aʊtˌlet, -lət] *n* **1** EXIT : sortie *f*, issue *f* **2** RELEASE : exutoire *m* **3** MARKET : débouché *m*, point *m* de vente **4** *or* **electrical outlet** : prise *f* de courant
outline[1] ['aʊtˌlaɪn] *vt* **-lined; -lining 1** SKETCH : esquisser, tracer **2** SUMMARIZE : résumer
outline[2] *n* **1** CONTOUR : contour *m* **2** SKETCH : ébauche *f* **3** SUMMARY : esquisse *f*
outlive [ˌaʊt'lɪv] *vt* **-lived; -living** : survivre à
outlook ['aʊtˌlʊk] *n* **1** VIEW : vue *f* **2** POINT OF VIEW : perspective *f* **3** PROSPECTS : perspectives *fpl*
out loud *adv* ALOUD : à haute voix
outlying ['aʊtˌlaɪɪŋ] *adj* : isolé, périphérique <outlying areas : régions périphériques>
outmoded [ˌaʊt'mo:dəd] *adj* : démodé
outnumber [ˌaʊt'nʌmbər] *vt* : être plus nombreux que, surpasser en nombre
out of *prep* **1** (*indicating direction or movement from within*) : de, par <to look out of the window : regarder par la fenêtre> <we ran out of the house : nous sommes sortis de la maison en courant> **2** (*being beyond the limits of*) <out of control : hors de contrôle> **3** OF : sur <one out of four : un sur quatre> **4** (*indicating absence or loss*) : sans <out of money : sans argent> <we're out of matches : nous n'avons plus d'allumettes> **5** BECAUSE OF : par <out of curiosity : par curiosité> **6** FROM : en <made out of plastic : fait en plastique>
out-of-date [ˌaʊtəv'deɪt] *adj* **1** OUTMODED : démodé **2** EXPIRED : périmé
out-of-door [ˌaʊtəv'dor] *or* **out-of-doors** [-'dorz] → **outdoor**
out-of-doors → **outdoors**
outpatient ['aʊtˌpeɪʃənt] *n* : malade *mf* en consultation externe
outpost ['aʊtˌpo:st] *n* : avant-poste *m*
output[1] ['aʊtˌpʊt] *vt* **-putted** *or* **-put; -putting** : sortir (en informatique)
output[2] *n* : rendement *m*, production *f*, productivité *f*
outrage[1] ['aʊtˌreɪʤ] *vt* **-raged; -raging** : outrager
outrage[2] *n* **1** AFFRONT, SCANDAL : outrage *m*, affront *m*, scandale *m* **2** ATROCITY : atrocité *f* **3** ANGER : indignation *f*
outrageous [ˌaʊt'reɪʤəs] *adj* **1** SCANDALOUS : scandaleux **2** BIZARRE, UNCONVENTIONAL : extravagant, bizarre
outright[1] ['aʊtˌraɪt] *adv* **1** COMPLETELY : complètement **2** INSTANTLY : sur le coup **3** FRANKLY : franchement, carrément
outright[2] *adj* **1** COMPLETE, UTTER : total, absolu <an outright lie : un mensonge absolu> **2** : sans réserve <an outright gift : un cadeau pur et simple, un cadeau sans réserve>
outset ['aʊtˌsɛt] *n* : début *m*, commencement *m*

outshine [ˌaʊtˈʃaɪn] *vt* **-shone** [-ˈʃoːn, -ˈʃɒn] *or* **-shined; shining** : éclipser, surpasser
outside[1] [ˌaʊtˈsaɪd, ˈaʊt,-] *adv* : à l'extérieur, dehors
outside[2] *adj* **1** OUTER : extérieur <the outside edge : le bord extérieur> **2** OUTDOOR : extérieur, à l'extérieur **3** POOR, REMOTE : faible <an outside chance : une faible chance>
outside[3] *n* **1** EXTERIOR : extérieur *m*, dehors *m* **2** MOST : maximum *m*, plus *m* <three weeks at the outside : trois semaines au plus>
outside[4] *prep* : en dehors de, à l'extérieur de
outside of *prep* **1** → **outside**[4] **2** → **besides**[2]
outsider [ˌaʊtˈsaɪdər] *n* : étranger *m*, -gère *f*
outskirts [ˈaʊtˌskərts] *npl* : banlieue *f*, périphérie *f*
outsmart [ˌaʊtˈsmɑrt] → **outwit**
outspoken [ˌaʊtˈspoːkən] *adj* : franc, carré
outstanding [ˌaʊtˈstændɪŋ] *adj* **1** UNPAID : impayé, dû **2** NOTABLE : exceptionnel
outstandingly [ˌaʊtˈstændɪŋli] *adv* : exceptionnellement
outstrip [ˌaʊtˈstrɪp] *vt* **-stripped; -stripping 1** PASS : dépasser, devancer **2** SURPASS : surpasser
outward[1] [ˈaʊtwərd] *or* **outwards** [-wərdz] *adv* : au dehors <outward bound : en partance>
outward[2] *adj* **1** : vers l'extérieur <an outward flow : un écoulement vers l'extérieur> **2** EXTERIOR : extérieur, externe <an outward calm : un calme apparent>
outwardly [ˈaʊtwərdli] *adv* **1** EXTERNALLY : à l'extérieur **2** APPARENTLY : en apparence
outwit [ˌaʊtˈwɪt] *vt* **-witted; -witting** : se montrer plus futé que, duper
ova → **ovum**
oval[1] [ˈoːvəl] *adj* : ovale
oval[2] *n* : ovale *m*
ovary [ˈoːvəri] *n, pl* **-ries** : ovaire *m*
ovation [oˈveɪʃən] *n* : ovation *f*
oven [ˈʌvən] *n* : four *m*
over[1] [ˈoːvər] *adv* **1** (*indicating movement across*) <he flew over to London : il est venu à Londres en avion> <come on over! : venez donc!> **2** (*indicating an additional amount*) <the show ran 10 minutes over : le spectacle a duré 10 minutes de trop> <over twenty dollars : plus de vingt dollars> **3** ABOVE, OVERHEAD : au-dessus **4** AGAIN : encore, de nouveau <over and over : à plusieurs reprises> <to start over : commencer de nouveau> **5 all over** EVERYWHERE : partout
over[2] *adj* **1** HIGHER, UPPER : supérieur **2** REMAINING : en plus **3** ENDED : terminé, fini <the job is finally over : enfin le travail est fini>
over[3] *prep* **1** ABOVE : au-dessus de, par-dessus <over the fireplace : au-dessus de la cheminée> <the hawk flew over the hills : le faucon a volé par-dessus les collines> **2** : plus de <over $50 : plus de 50 $> **3** ALONG : sur <to glide over the ice : glisser sur la glace> **4** (*indicating movement across*) <he jumped over the ditch : il a franchi le fossé d'un bond> **5** DURING : pendant, au cours de <over the last few years : au cours des dernières années> **6** (*referring to a means of communication*) <to speak over the telephone : parler au téléphone> **7** BECAUSE OF : à cause de, au sujet de
overabundance [ˌoːvərəˈbʌndənʦ] *n* : surabondance *f* — **overabundant** [-dənt] *adj*
overactive [ˌoːvərˈæktɪv] *adj* : trop actif
overall[1] [ˌoːvərˈɔl] *adv* **1** : d'un bout à l'autre, en tout **2** GENERALLY : en général
overall[2] *adj* : d'ensemble, total, global <an overall view : une vue d'ensemble>
overalls [ˈoːvərˌɔlz] *npl* : salopette *f*
overawe [ˌoːvərˈɔ] *vt* **-awed; -awing** : impressionner, intimider
overbearing [ˌoːvərˈbærɪŋ] *adj* : impérieux, autoritaire
overboard [ˈoːvərˌbɔrd] *adv* : par-dessus bord
overburden [ˌoːvərˈbərdən] *vt* : surcharger
overcast [ˈoːvərˌkæst] *adj* CLOUDY : couvert
overcharge [ˌoːvərˈtʃɑrdʒ] *v* **-charged; -charging** *vt* : faire payer trop cher à — *vi* : demander un prix excessif
overcoat [ˈoːvərˌkoːt] *n* : pardessus *m*
overcome [ˌoːvərˈkʌm] *v* **-came** [-ˈkeɪm]; **-come; -coming** *vt* **1** CONQUER : vaincre, surmonter **2** OVERWHELM : accabler, écraser — *vi* : vaincre
overconfidence [ˌoːvərˈkɑnfədənʦ] *n* : confiance *f* excessive
overconfident [ˌoːvərˈkɑnfədənt] *adj* : trop confiant
overcook [ˌoːvərˈkʊk] *vt* : faire trop cuire
overdo [ˌoːvərˈduː] *vt* **-did** [-ˈdɪd]; **-done** [-ˈdʌn]; **-doing; -does** [-ˈdʌz] **1** : exagérer **2** → **overcook**
overdose [ˈoːvərˌdoːs] *n* : overdose *f*, surdose *f*
overdraft [ˈoːvərˌdræft] *n* : découvert *m*
overdraw [ˌoːvərˈdrɔ] *vt* **-drew** [-ˈdruː]; **-drawn** [-ˈdrɔn]; **-drawing** : mettre à découvert
overdue [ˌoːvərˈduː] *adj* **1** UNPAID : arriéré **2** TARDY : en retard
overeat [ˌoːvərˈiːt] *vt* **-ate** [-ˈeɪt]; **-eating** : trop manger
overelaborate [ˌoːvərrˈlæbərət] *adj* : trop recherché

overestimate [ˌo:vərˈestəˌmeɪt] *vt* **-mated; -mating** : surestimer
overexcited [ˌo:vərɪkˈsaɪtəd] *adj* : surexcité
overexpose [ˌo:vərɪkˈspo:z] *vt* **-posed; posing** : surexposer
overfeed [ˌo:vərˈfi:d] *vt* **-fed** [-ˈfɛd]; **-feeding** : suralimenter
overflow[1] [ˌo:vərˈflo:] *v* : déborder
overflow[2] [ˈo:vərˌflo:] *n* **1** : trop-plein *m*, débordement *m* (d'une rivière, etc.) **2** SURPLUS : surplus *m*, excédent *m*
overfly [ˌo:vərˈflaɪ] *vt* **-flew** [-ˈflu:]; **-flown** [-ˈflo:n]; **-flying** : survoler
overgrown [ˌo:vərˈgro:n] *adj* **1** EXCESSIVE, HUGE : démesuré **2** : couvert, envahi <overgrown with weeds : couvert de mauvaises herbes>
overhand[1] [ˈo:vərˌhænd] *adv* : pardessus la tête
overhand[2] *adj* : par le haut
overhang[1] [ˌo:vərˈhæŋ] *vt* **-hung** [-ˈhʌŋ]; **-hanging** : surplomber
overhang[2] [ˈo:vərˌhæŋ] *n* : surplomb *m*
overhaul [ˌo:vərˈhɔl] *vt* **1** : réviser (un moteur, etc.) **2** OVERTAKE : dépasser
overhead[1] [ˌo:vərˈhɛd] *adv* : au-dessus
overhead[2] [ˈo:vərˌhɛd] *adj* : au-dessus de la tête, aérien <overhead lighting : éclairage au plafond>
overhead[3] [ˈo:vərˌhɛd] *n or* **overhead expenses** : frais *mpl* généraux
overhear [ˌo:vərˈhɪr] *vt* **-heard** [-ˈhərd]; **-hearing** : entendre par hasard
overheat [ˌo:vərˈhi:t] *vt* : surchauffer
overjoyed [ˌo:vərˈdʒɔɪd] *adj* : ravi, rempli de joie
overkill [ˈo:vərˌkɪl] *n* : excès *m*
overland[1] [ˈo:vərˌlænd, -lənd] *adv* : par voie de terre
overland[2] *adj* : par (la) route
overlap[1] [ˌo:vərˈlæp] *v* **-lapped; -lapping** *vt* : chevaucher — *vi* : chevaucher, se recouvrir
overlap[2] [ˈo:vərˌlæp] *n* : chevauchement *m*
overlay[1] [ˌo:vərˈleɪ] *vt* **-laid** [-ˈleɪd]; **-laying** : recouvrir
overlay[2] [ˈo:vərˌleɪ] *n* : revêtement *m*, recouvrement *m*
overload [ˌo:vərˈlo:d] *vt* : surcharger
overlong [ˌo:vərˈlɔŋ] *adj* : trop long
overlook [ˌo:vərˈlʊk] *vt* **1** INSPECT : inspecter **2** : donner sur <the house overlooks the beach : la maison donne sur la plage> **3** MISS : manquer **4** IGNORE : laisser passer **5** SUPERVISE : surveiller
overly [ˈo:vərli] *adv* : trop
overnight[1] [ˌo:vərˈnaɪt] *adv* **1** : pendant la nuit **2** SUDDENLY : du jour au lendemain
overnight[2] [ˈo:vərˌnaɪt] *adj* **1** : de nuit, d'une nuit <an overnight stay : une visite d'une nuit> **2** SUDDEN : soudain, subit
overpass [ˈo:vərˌpæs] *n* : voie *f* surélevée
overpopulated [ˌo:vərˈpɑpjəˌleɪtəd] *adj* : surpeuplé
overpower [ˌo:vərˈpaʊər] *vt* **1** CONQUER : vaincre **2** OVERWHELM : accabler
overrate [ˌo:vərˈreɪt] *vt* **-rated; -rating** : surestimer
override [ˌo:vərˈraɪd] *vt* **-rode** [-ˈro:d]; **-ridden** [-ˈrɪdən]; **-riding** : passer outre à, outrepasser
overrule [ˌo:vərˈru:l] *vt* **-ruled; -ruling** : rejeter
overrun [ˌo:vərˈrʌn] *v* **-ran** [-ˈræn]; **-running** *vt* **1** INVADE : envahir **2** INFEST : infester **3** EXCEED : dépasser — *vi* : dépasser le temps prévu
overseas[1] [ˌo:vərˈsi:z] *adv* : à l'étranger, outre-mer
overseas[2] [ˈo:vərˌsi:z] *adj* : à l'étranger, extérieur, d'outre-mer
oversee [ˌo:vərˈsi:] *vt* **-saw** [-ˈsɔ] ; **-seen** [-ˈsi:n]; **-seeing** SUPERVISE : surveiller
overseer [ˈo:vərˌsi:ər] *n* : surveillant *m*, -lante *f*; contremaître *m*, -tresse *f*
overshadow [ˌo:vərˈʃæˌdo:] *vt* **1** DARKEN : ombrager **2** ECLIPSE, OUTSHINE : éclipser, surpasser
overshoe [ˈo:vərˌʃu:] *n* **1** : galoche *f* **2** **overshoes** *npl* GALOSHES : caoutchoucs *mpl*, bottes *fpl* de caoutchouc
overshoot [ˌo:vərˈʃu:t] *vt* **-shot** [-ˈʃɑt]; **-shooting** : dépasser
oversight [ˈo:vərˌsaɪt] *n* **1** ERROR, OMISSION : oubli *m*, omission *f* **2** SUPERVISION : surveillance *f*
oversleep [ˌo:vərˈsli:p] *vi* **-slept** [-ˈslɛpt]; **-sleeping** : dormir trop longtemps
overstate [ˌo:vərˈsteɪt] *vt* **-stated; -stating** EXAGGERATE : exagérer
overstatement [ˌo:vərˈsteɪtmənt] *n* : exagération *f*
overstep [ˌo:vərˈstɛp] *vt* **-stepped; -stepping** : dépasser, outrepasser
overt [oˈvərt, ˈo:ˌvərt] *adj* : évident, manifeste
overtake [ˌo:vərˈteɪk] *vt* **-took** [-ˈtʊk]; **-taken** [-ˈteɪkən]; **-taking** : dépasser, doubler, devancer
overthrow[1] [ˌo:vərˈθro:] *vt* **-threw** [-ˈθru:]; **-thrown** [-ˈθro:n]; **-throwing** **1** OVERTURN : renverser **2** DEFEAT : vaincre
overthrow[2] [ˈo:vərˌθro:] *n* : renversement *m*, défaite *f*
overtime [ˈo:vərˌtaɪm] *n* **1** : heures *fpl* supplémentaires (de travail) **2** : prolongations *fpl* (aux sports)
overtone [ˈo:vərˌto:n] *n* : son *m* harmonique
overture [ˈo:vərˌtʃʊr, -tʃər] *n* **1** : ouverture *f* (en musique) **2** PROPOSAL : proposition *f*
overturn [ˌo:vərˈtərn] *vt* **1** : renverser **2** NULLIFY : annuler — *vi* : se renverser
overuse [ˌo:vərˈju:z] *vt* **-used; -using** : abuser de, trop employer
overview [ˈo:vərˌvju:] *n* : vue *f* d'ensemble

overweening [ˌoːvərˈwiːnɪŋ] *adj* **1** ARROGANT : outrecuidant, arrogant **2** EXCESSIVE : démesuré
overweight [ˌoːvərˈweɪt] *adj* : trop gros, obèse
overwhelm [ˌoːvərˈhwɛlm] *vt* : écraser, accabler
overwhelmingly [ˌoːvərˈhwɛlmɪŋ] *adj* : accablant, écrasant
overwork [ˌoːvərˈwɛrk] *vt* **1** : surmener (une personne) **2** OVERUSE : abuser de — *vi* : se surmener
overwrought [ˌoːvərˈrɔt] *adj* : à bout de nerfs
ovoid [ˈoˌvɔɪd] *or* **ovoidal** [oːˈvɔɪdəl] *adj* : ovoïde
ovulate [ˈɑvjəˌleɪt, ˈoː-] *vi* **-lated; -lating** : ovuler
ovulation [ˌɑvjəˈleɪʃən, ˌoː-] *n* : ovulation *f*
ovum [ˈoːvəm] *n, pl* **ova** [-və] : ovule *m*
owe [ˈoː] *vt* **owed; owing** : devoir <you owe me $10 : tu me dois 10 $> <he owes his wealth to his father : il doit sa fortune à son père>
owing to *prep* : pour cause de
owl [ˈaʊl] *n* : hibou *m*
own¹ [ˈoːn] *vt* **1** POSSESS : posséder **2** ADMIT : reconnaître, admettre — *vi* **to own up** : avouer
own² *adj* : propre <his own car : sa propre voiture>
own³ *pron* **my (your, his/her, our, their) own** : le mien, la mienne; le tien, la tienne; le vôtre, la vôtre; le sien, la sienne; le nôtre, la nôtre; le leur, la leur <it's my own : c'est le mien> <to each his own : chacun son goût> <to be on one's own : être tout seul>
owner [ˈoːnər] *n* : propriétaire *mf*
ownership [ˈoːnərˌʃɪp] *n* : possession *f*
ox [ˈɑks] *n, pl* **oxen** [ˈɑksən] : bœuf *m*
oxide [ˈɑkˌsaɪd] *n* : oxyde *m*
oxidize [ˈɑksəˌdaɪz] *vt* **-dized; -dizing** : oxyder
oxygen [ˈɑksɪdʒən] *n* : oxygène *m*
oyster [ˈɔɪstər] *n* : huître *f*
ozone [ˈoːˌzoːn] *n* : ozone *m*

P

p [ˈpiː] *n, pl* **p's** *or* **ps** [ˈpiːz] : p *m*, seizième lettre de l'alphabet
pace¹ [ˈpeɪs] *v* **paced; pacing** *vt* **1** : arpenter <to pace the room : arpenter la chambre> **2 to pace off** : mesurer en pas — *vi* **to pace to and fro** : faire les cent pas
pace² *n* **1** STEP : pas *m* **2** SPEED : allure *f*, vitesse *f* <to walk at a good pace : marcher à vive allure>
pacemaker [ˈpeɪsˌmeɪkər] *n* : stimulateur *m* cardiaque
pachyderm [ˈpækiˌdərm] *n* : pachyderme *m*
pacific [pəˈsɪfɪk] *adj* : pacifique
pacifier [ˈpæsəˌfaɪər] *n* : tétine *f*, sucette *f*
pacifism [ˈpæsəˌfɪzəm] *n* : pacifisme *m*
pacifist¹ [ˈpæsəfɪst] *or* **pacifistic** [ˌpæsəˈfɪstɪk] *adj* : pacifiste
pacifist² *n* : pacifiste *mf*
pacify [ˈpæsəˌfaɪ] *vt* **-fied; -fying** : pacifier, apaiser
pack¹ [ˈpæk] *vt* **1** PACKAGE : empaqueter, emballer **2** CRAM, FILL : entasser, empiler, remplir **3** : faire (sa valise, ses bagages) **4 to pack off** SEND : envoyer
pack² *n* **1** PACKAGE : paquet *m*, colis *m* **2** BUNDLE : balle *f*, baluchon *m* **3** BACKPACK : sac *m* à dos **4** GROUP : meute *f* (de chiens), bande *f* (de loups, etc.)
package¹ [ˈpækɪdʒ] *vt* **-aged; -aging** : empaqueter
package² *n* : paquet *m*, colis *m*
packet [ˈpækət] *n* : (petit) paquet *m*
pact [ˈpækt] *n* : pacte *m*
pad¹ [ˈpæd] *v* **padded; padding** *vt* **1** STUFF : rembourrer, matelasser **2** EXPAND : étoffer (une note de frais), délayer (un discours) — *vi* : marcher à pas feutrés
pad² *n* **1** CUSHION : coussin *m*, protection *f* (aux sports) <a shoulder pad : une épaulette> **2** TABLET : bloc *m* (de papier) **3** *or* **lily pad** : feuille *f* (de nénuphar) **4 ink pad** : tampon *m* encreur **5 launching pad** : rampe *m* de lancement
padding [ˈpædɪŋ] *n* **1** FILLING, STUFFING : rembourrage *m* **2** : remplissage *m*, délayage *m* (d'un discours)
paddle¹ [ˈpædəl] *v* **-dled; -dling** *vt* **1** : pagayer **2** SPANK : donner une fessée à — *vi* WADE : patauger, barboter
paddle² *n* : pagaie *f*, aube *f*, aviron *m* *Can*
paddock [ˈpædək] *n* : paddock *m*, enclos *m*
paddy [ˈpædi] *n, pl* **-dies** : rizière *f*
padlock¹ [ˈpædˌlɑk] *vt* : cadenasser
padlock² *n* : cadenas *m*
pagan¹ [ˈpeɪgən] *adj* : païen
pagan² *n* : païen *m*, païenne *f*
paganism [ˈpeɪgənˌɪzəm] *n* : paganisme *m*
page¹ [ˈpeɪdʒ] *v* **paged; paging** *vt* : appeler, demander — *vi* **to page through** : feuilleter
page² *n* **1** ATTENDANT, BELLHOP : chasseur *m* **2** : page *f* (d'un livre)
pageant [ˈpædʒənt] *n* **1** : reconstitution *f* historique (comme de Noël) **2**

SHOW, SPECTACLE : spectacle *m* fastueux

pageantry ['pædʒəntri] *n* : apparat *m*, pompe *f*

pagoda [pə'go:də] *n* : pagode *f*

paid → **pay**

pail ['peɪl] *n* : seau *m*

pain[1] ['peɪn] *vt* : peiner, faire souffrir

pain[2] *n* **1** : mal *m*, douleur *f* <back pains : maux de dos> **2** GRIEF : peine *f*, souffrance *f* **3 pains** *npl* : peine *f*, mal *m* <to take great pains : se donner beaucoup de mal>

painful ['peɪnfəl] *adj* : douloureux — **painfully** *adv*

painkiller ['peɪn,kɪlər] *n* : analgésique *m*

painkilling ['peɪn,kɪlɪŋ] *adj* : analgésique

painless ['peɪnləs] *adj* : indolore, sans douleur

painlessly ['peɪnləsli] *adv* : sans douleur, sans mal

painstaking ['peɪn,steɪkɪŋ] *adj* : soigneux, méticuleux — **painstakingly** *adv*

paint[1] ['peɪnt] *v* : peindre, peinturer *Can*

paint[2] *n* : peinture *f*

paintbrush ['peɪnt,brʌʃ] *n* : pinceau *m*, brosse *f*

painter ['peɪntər] *n* : peintre *m*

painting ['peɪntɪŋ] *n* : peinture *f*

pair[1] ['pær] *vi* **1** MATCH : apparier **2 to pair off** : se mettre par deux

pair[2] *n* **1** : paire *f* <a pair of gloves : une paire de gants> <a pair of pliers : une pince> **2** COUPLE : couple *m* (de personnes ou d'animaux)

pajamas *or Brit* **pyjamas** [pə'dʒɑməz, -'dʒæ-] *npl* : pyjama *m*

Pakistani[1] [,pækɪ'stæni, ,pɑkɪ'stɑni] *adj* : pakistanais

Pakistani[2] *n* : Pakistanais *m*, -naise *f*

pal ['pæl] *n* : copain *m*, -pine *f*

palace ['pæləs] *n* : palais *m*

palatable ['pælətəbəl] *adj* : savoureux

palate ['pælət] *n* : palais *m*

palatial [pə'leɪʃəl] *adj* : magnifique, somptueux

palaver[1] [pə'lævər, -'lɑ-] *vi* : palabrer, discuter

palaver[2] *n* : histoires *fpl*, palabres *fpl*

pale[1] ['peɪl] *vi* **paled; paling** : pâlir

pale[2] *adj* **paler; palest 1** PALLID : pâle, blême <to turn pale : pâlir> **2** : clair, pâle <pale bleu : bleu clair>

pale[3] *n* STAKE : pieu *m*

paleness ['peɪlnəs] *n* : pâleur *f*

Palestinian[1] [,pælə'stɪniən] *adj* : palestinien

Palestinian[2] *n* : Palestinien *m*, -nienne *f*

palette ['pælət] *n* : palette *f*

palisade [,pælə'seɪd] *n* **1** FENCE : palissade *f* **2** CLIFFS : ligne *f* de falaises

pall[1] ['pɔl] *vi* : perdre son charme, devenir ennuyeux

pall[2] *n* **1** : drap *m* mortuaire **2** CLOUD : voile *m* <a pall of smoke : un voile de fumée> <a pall of silence : un silence profond>

pallbearer ['pɔl,berər] *n* : porteur *m*, -teuse *f* de cercueil

pallet ['pælət] *n* **1** BED : grabat *m* **2** PLATFORM : palette *f*, plateau *m* de chargement

palliative ['pæli,eɪtɪv, 'pæljətɪv] *adj* : palliatif

pallid ['pælɪd] *adj* : pâle, blême

pallor ['pælər] *n* : pâleur *f*

palm[1] ['pɑm, 'pɑlm] *vt* **1** CONCEAL : escamoter (une carte, etc.) **2** *or* **to palm off** : refiler *fam*

palm[2] *n* **1** *or* **palm tree** : palmier *m* **2** : paume *f* (de la main)

Palm Sunday *n* : dimanche *m* des Rameaux

palomino [,pælə'mi:,no:] *n, pl* **-nos** : palomino *m*

palpable ['pælpəbəl] *adj* : palpable

palpitate ['pælpə,teɪt] *vi* **-tated; -tating** : palpiter

palpitation [,pælpə'teɪʃən] *n* : palpitation *f*

palsy ['pɔlzi] *n, pl* **-sies 1** : paralysie *f* **2 → cerebral palsy**

paltry ['pɔltri] *adj* **paltrier; -est** : dérisoire, piètre

pamper ['pæmpər] *vt* : choyer, dorloter

pamphlet ['pæmpflət] *n* : dépliant *m*, brochure *f*

pan[1] ['pæn] *vt* **panned; panning 1** *or* **to pan for** : chercher (de l'or, etc.) **2** CRITICIZE : éreinter (un spectacle)

pan[2] *n* **1** SAUCEPAN : casserole *f* **2** FRYING PAN : poêle *f*

panacea [,pænə'si:ə] *n* : panacée *f*

Panamanian[1] [,pænə'meɪniən] *adj* : panaméen

Panamanian[2] *n* : Panaméen *m*, -méenne *f*

pancake ['pæn,keɪk] *n* : crêpe *f*

pancreas ['pæŋkriəs, 'pæn-] *n* : pancréas *m*

panda ['pændə] *n* : panda *m*

pandemonium [,pændə'mo:niəm] *n* : brouhaha *m*, tumulte *m*

pander ['pændər] *vi* : flatter (bassement)

pane ['peɪn] *n* : vitre *f*, carreau *m*

panel[1] ['pænəl] *vt* **-eled** *or* **-elled; -eling** *or* **-elling** : recouvrir de panneaux

panel[2] *n* **1** : liste *f* (des jurés) **2** : panneau *m* <plywood panels : panneaux en contreplaqué> **3** COMMITTEE, GROUP : comité *m*, commission *f* **4** *or* **control panel** : tableau *m* (de bord)

paneling ['pænəlɪŋ] *n* : panneaux *mpl*

pang ['pæŋ] *n* **1** : tiraillement *m*, crampe *f* <hunger pangs : tiraillements d'estomac> **2** : serrement *m* de cœur <pangs of conscience : remords de conscience>

panic[1] ['pænɪk] *v* **-icked; -icking** *vt* : paniquer *fam* — *vi* : paniquer *fam*, s'affoler
panic[2] *n* : panique *f*, affolement *m*
panicky ['pænɪkɪ] *adj* : pris de panique
panorama [ˌpænə'ræmə, -'rɑ-] *n* : panorama *m*
panoramic [ˌpænə'ræmɪk, -'rɑ-] *adj* : panoramique
pansy ['pænzɪ] *n, pl* **-sies** : pensée *f*
pant[1] ['pænt] *vi* : haleter, souffler
pant[2] *n* : halètement *m*
pantaloons [ˌpæntə'lu:nz] → **pants**
panther ['pænθər] *n* **1** LEOPARD : panthère *f* **2** COUGAR, PUMA : puma *m*
panties ['pæntiz] *npl* : (petite) culotte *f*, slip *m France*
pantomime[1] ['pæntəˌmaɪm] *vt* **-mimed; -miming** : représenter par une pantomime
pantomime[2] *n* : pantomime *f*
pantry ['pæntrɪ] *n, pl* **-tries** : garde-manger *m*
pants ['pænts] *npl* **1** : pantalon *m* **2** → **panties**
panty hose ['pænti,ho:z] *npl* : collant *m*
pap ['pæp] *n* GRUEL : bouillie *f*
papal ['peɪpəl] *adj* : papal
papaya [pə'paɪə] *n* : papaye *f*
paper[1] ['peɪpər] *vt* WALLPAPER : tapisser
paper[2] *adj* : de papier, en papier
paper[3] *n* **1** : papier *m* <a sheet of paper : une feuille de papier> **2** DOCUMENT : document *m* **3** NEWSPAPER : journal *m* **4** WALLPAPER : papier *m* peint **5** : travail *m* (scolaire)
paperback ['peɪpərˌbæk] *n* : livre *m* de poche
paper clip *n* : trombone *m*
paperweight ['peɪpərˌweɪt] *n* : presse-papiers *m*
papery ['peɪpərɪ] *adj* : comme du papier
papier–mâché [ˌpeɪpərmə'ʃeɪ, ˌpæˌpjeɪ-mæ'ʃeɪ] *n* : papier *m* mâché
papoose [pæ'pu:s, pə-] *n* : enfant *mf* des Indiens nord-américains
paprika [pə'pri:kə, pæ-] *n* : paprika *m*
papyrus [pə'paɪrəs] *n, pl* **-ruses** *or* **-ri** [-ˌri, -ˌraɪ] : papyrus *m*
par ['pɑr] *n* **1** : pair *m* (en finances) <at par value : à la valeur au pair> **2** EQUALITY : égalité *f* <to be on a par with : être l'égal de> **3** : par *m* (au golf)
parable ['pærəbəl] *n* : parabole *f*
parachute[1] ['pærəˌʃu:t] *v* **-chuted; -chuting** *vt* : parachuter — *vi* : sauter en parachute
parachute[2] *n* : parachute *m*
parachutist ['pærəˌʃu:ɪst] *n* : parachutiste *mf*
parade[1] [pə'reɪd] *vi* **-raded; -rading 1** MARCH : défiler **2** SHOW OFF : parader, faire étalage
parade[2] *n* **1** : parade *f*, défilé *m* <circus parade : parade de cirque> **2** DISPLAY : étalage *m*
paradigm ['pærəˌdaɪm] *n* : paradigme *m*
paradise ['pærəˌdaɪs, -ˌdaɪz] *n* : paradis *m*
paradox ['pærəˌdɑks] *n* : paradoxe *m*
paradoxical [ˌpærə'dɑksɪkəl] *adj* : paradoxal — **paradoxically** [-klɪ] *adv*
paraffin ['pærəfən] *n* : paraffine *f*
paragon ['pærəˌgɑn, -gən] *n* : parangon *m*, modèle *m*
paragraph[1] ['pærəˌgræf] *vt* : diviser en paragraphes
paragraph[2] *n* : paragraphe *m*
Paraguayan[1] [ˌpærə'gwaɪən, -'gweɪ-] *adj* : paraguayen
Paraguayan[2] *n* : Paraguayen *m*, -guayenne *f*
parakeet ['pærəˌki:t] *n* : perruche *f*
parallel[1] ['pærəˌlɛl, -ləl] *vt* **1** EQUAL, MATCH : égaler, être équivalent à **2** : longer, être parallèle à <the road parallels the river : la route longe la rivière>
parallel[2] *adj* : parallèle
parallel[3] *n* **1** *or* **parallel line** : ligne *f* parallèle **2** : parallèle *m* (en géographie) **3** SIMILARITY : parallèle *m*, comparaison *f* <to be on a parallel with : être comparable à>
parallelogramme [ˌpærə'lɛləˌgræm] *n* : parallélogramme *m*
paralyse *Brit* → **paralyze**
paralysis [pə'ræləsɪs] *n, pl* **-yses** [-ˌsi:z] : paralysie *f*
paralyze *or Brit* **paralyse** ['pærəˌlaɪz] *vt* **-lyzed** *or Brit* **-lysed; -lyzing** *or Brit* **-lysing** : paralyser
parameter [pə'ræmətər] *n* : paramètre *m*
parametric [ˌpærə'mɛtrɪk] *adj* : paramétrique
paramount ['pærəˌmaʊnt] *adj* : suprême <of paramount importance : de la plus grande importance>
paranoia [ˌpærə'nɔɪə] *n* : paranoïa *f*
paranoid ['pærəˌnɔɪd] *adj* : paranoïaque
parapet ['pærəpət, -ˌpɛt] *n* : parapet *m*
paraphernalia [ˌpærəfə'neɪljə, -fər-] *ns & pl* : équipement *m*, attirail *m fam*
paraphrase[1] ['pærəˌfreɪz] *vt* **-phrased; -phrasing** : paraphraser
paraphrase[2] *n* : paraphrase *f*
paraplegic[1] ['pærə'pli:dʒɪk] *adj* : paraplégique
paraplegic[2] *n* : paraplégique *mf*
parasite ['pærəˌsaɪt] *n* : parasite *m*
parasitic [ˌpærə'sɪtɪk] *adj* : parasite, parasitaire
parasol ['pærəˌsɔl] *n* : ombrelle *f*, parasol *m*
paratrooper ['pærəˌtru:pər] *n* : parachutiste *m* (militaire)
parboil ['pɑrˌbɔɪl] *vt* : blanchir (des légumes)

parcel[1] ['pɑrsəl] *vt* **-celed** *or* **-celled; -celing** *or* **-celling** *or* **to parcel out** : diviser, répartir
parcel[2] *n* **1** PLOT : parcelle *f* (de terrain) **2** PACKAGE : paquet *m*, colis *m* **3 a parcel of lies** : un tissu de mensonges
parch ['pɑrtʃ] *vt* : dessécher
parchment ['pɑrtʃmənt] *n* : parchemin *m*
pardon[1] ['pɑrdən] *vt* **1** EXCUSE, FORGIVE : pardonner <pardon me : pardonnez-moi> **2** ABSOLVE : grâcier (en droit)
pardon[2] *n* **1** FORGIVENESS : pardon *m* <I beg your pardon : je vous demande pardon> **2** : pardon *m*, grâce *f* (en droit)
pardonable ['pɑrdənəbəl] *adj* : pardonnable
pare ['pær] *vt* **pared; paring 1** : peler (un fruit), éplucher (une pomme de terre), ronger (ses ongles) **2** REDUCE : réduire <to pare expenses : réduire les dépenses>
paregoric [ˌpærə'gɔrɪk] *n* : parégorique *m*
parent ['pærənt] *n* **1** : mère *f*, père *m* **2 parents** *npl* : parents *mpl*
parentage ['pærəntɪdʒ] *n* : ascendance *f*, origine *f*
parental [pə'rɛntəl] *adj* : parental
parenthesis [pə'rɛnθəsəs] *n, pl* **-theses** [-ˌsiːz] : parenthèse *f*
parenthetical [ˌpærən'θɛtɪkəl] *adj* : entre parenthèses
parenthetically [ˌpærən'θɛtɪkli] *adv* : entre parenthèses
parenthood ['pærənt,hʊd] *n* : maternité *f*, paternité *f*
parfait [pɑr'feɪ] *n* : parfait *m*
pariah [pə'raɪə] *n* : paria *m*
parish ['pærɪʃ] *n* : paroisse *f*
parishioner [pə'rɪʃənər] *n* : paroissien *m*, -sienne *f*
Parisian[1] [pə'rɪʒən, -'ri-] *adj* : parisien
Parisian[2] *n* : Parisien *m*, -sienne *f*
parity ['pærəṭi] *n, pl* **-ties** EQUALITY : parité *f*
park[1] ['pɑrk] *vt* : garer, stationner <to park a car : garer une voiture> — *vi* : se garer, se stationner
park[2] *n* : parc *m*, jardin *m* public
parka ['pɑrkə] *n* : parka *m*
parkway ['pɑrkˌweɪ] *n* : route *f* à paysage
parley[1] ['pɑrli] *vi* **-leyed; -leying** : parlementer
parley[2] *n, pl* **-leys** : pourparlers *mpl*
parliament ['pɑrləmənt] *n* : parlement *m*
parliamentarian [ˌpɑrləˌmen'teriən, -mən-] *n* : parlementaire *mf*
parliamentary [ˌpɑrlə'mɛntəri] *adj* : parlementaire
parlor *or Brit* **parlour** ['pɑrlər] *n* **1** : petit salon *m* (pour recevoir des invités) **2** : salon *m* <beauty parlor : salon de beauté> **3 funeral parlor** → **funeral home**
parochial [pə'roːkiəl] *adj* **1** : paroissial **2** PROVINCIAL : de clocher, provincial
parody[1] ['pærədi] *vt* **-died; -dying** : parodier
parody[2] *n, pl* **-dies** : parodie *f*
parole[1] [pə'roːl] *vt* **-roled; -roling** : mettre en liberté conditionnelle
parole[2] *n* : liberté *f* conditionnelle
parolee [pəˌroˈli, -'roːˌli] *n* : détenu *m* libéré sur parole
paroxysm ['pærəkˌsɪzəm, pə'rɑk-] *n* : quinte *f*, crise *f* <a paroxysm of coughing : une quinte de toux>
parquet ['pɑrˌkeɪ, pɑr'keɪ] *n* : parquet *m*
parrakeet → **parakeet**
parrot ['pærət] *n* : perroquet *m*
parry[1] ['pæri] *vt* **-ried; -rying 1** WARD OFF : esquiver, parer (un coup) **2** EVADE : éluder (une question)
parry[2] *n, pl* **-ries** : parade *f* (aux sports)
parse ['pɑrs] *vt* **parsed; parsing** : faire l'analyse grammaticale de
parsimonious [ˌpɑrsə'moːniəs] *adj* : parcimonieux — **parsimoniously** *adv*
parsley ['pɑrsli] *n* : persil *m*
parsnip ['pɑrsnɪp] *n* : panais *m*
parson ['pɑrsən] *n* : pasteur *m*, ecclésiastique *m*
part[1] ['pɑrt] *vi* **1** *or* **to part company** : se séparer, se quitter **2** BREAK : se rompre **3 to part with** : se défaire de — *vt* **1** SEPARATE : séparer **2 to part one's hair** : se faire une raie
part[2] *n* **1** : partie *f* <the best part : la meilleure partie> **2** DUTY : rôle *m*, fonction *f* **3** ROLE : rôle *m* (dans une pièce de théâtre) **4** : voix *f* <four-part harmony : harmonie à quatre voix> **5** SHARE : part *f* **6** SIDE : parti *m* <to take s.o.'s part : prendre le parti de qqn>
partake [pɑr'teɪk, pər-] *vi* **-took** [-'tʊk]; **-taken** [-'teɪkən]; **-taking 1 to partake in** : prendre part à, participer à (une activité) **2 to partake of** CONSUME : prendre, manger
partial ['pɑrʃəl] *adj* **1** : partiel <a partial solution : une solution partielle> **2** BIASED : partial — **partially** ['pɑrʃəli] *adv*
partiality [ˌpɑrʃi'æləṭi] *n, pl* **-ties** : partialité *f*
participant [pər'tɪsəpənt, pɑr-] *n* : participant *m*, -pante *f*
participate [pər'tɪsəˌpeɪt, pɑr-] *vi* **-pated; -pating** : participer
participation [pərˌtɪsə'peɪʃən, pɑr-] *n* : participation *f*
participial [ˌpɑrtə'sɪpiəl] *adj* : participial
participle ['pɑrṭəˌsɪpəl] *n* : participe *m* <past participle : participe passé>
particle ['pɑrṭɪkəl] *n* : particule *f*

particular[1] [pərˈtɪkjələr] *adj* **1** SPECIFIC : particulier, en particulier <one particular person : une personne en particulier> **2** SPECIAL : particulier <with particular care : avec un soin tout particulier> **3** FUSSY : tatillon, difficile

particular[2] *n* **1** : détail *m*, point *m* **2 in ~** : en particulier

particularly [pərˈtɪkjələrli] *adv* : particulièrement, spécialement

partisan[1] [ˈpərtəzən, -sən] *adj* : partisan

partisan[2] *n* SUPPORTER : partisan *m*, -sane *f*

partition[1] [pərˈtɪʃən, pɑr-] *vt* : morceler (un domaine), diviser, cloisonner (une pièce)

partition[2] *n* **1** DISTRIBUTION : division *f*, répartition *f* **2** DIVIDER : cloison *f* (d'une pièce, etc.)

partly [ˈpɑrtli] *adv* : en partie

partner [ˈpɑrtnər] *n* **1** ASSOCIATE : associé *m*, -ciée *f*; partenaire *mf* (en commerce) **2** : partenaire *mf* (aux sports, en danse) **3** COMPANION : compagnon *m*, compagne *f* **4** SPOUSE : époux *m*, épouse *f*

partnership [ˈpɑrtnərˌʃɪp] *n* : association *f*

part of speech *n* : partie *f* du discours

partridge [ˈpɑrtrɪdʒ] *n, pl* **-tridge** *or* **-tridges** : perdrix *f*

party [ˈpɑrti] *n, pl* **-ties 1** : parti *m* (politique) **2** PARTICIPANT : partie *f* **3** GROUP : groupe *m* <a mountain-climbing party : un groupe d'alpinisme> **4** GATHERING : fête *f*, party *m Can fam*

parvenu [ˈpɑrvəˌnuː, -ˌnjuː] *n* : parvenu *m*, -nue *f*

pass[1] [ˈpæs] *vi* **1** MOVE, PROCEED : passer **2** *or* **to pass away** DIE : mourir **3** : ne pas tenir compte de <I let his remark pass : je n'ai pas tenu compte de son commentaire> **4** TRANSFER : changer **5** OCCUR : se passer, avoir lieu **6** : passer (aux cartes) **7 to pass for** : se prendre pour — *vt* **1** : passer (une loi) **2** : dépasser (une voiture, etc.) **3** : passer (un examen) **4** : passer <pass the salt, please : passez-moi le sel, s'il vous plaît>

pass[2] *n* **1** CROSSING, GAP : col *m* **2** : mention *f* passable (à un examen) **3** PERMISSION, PERMIT : permis *m* **4** : laissez-passer *m* <season pass : laissez-passer saisonnier> **5** : passe *f* (aux sports)

passable [ˈpæsəbəl] *adj* **1** ACCEPTABLE : passable, acceptable **2** NEGOTIABLE : praticable, passable *Can* <passable roads : chemins praticables>

passably [ˈpæsəbli] *adv* : passablement

passage [ˈpæsɪdʒ] *n* **1** PASSAGEWAY : passage *m*, corridor *m*, couloir *m* **2** ENACTMENT : adoption *f* (d'une loi) **3** VOYAGE : voyage *m* **4** : passage *m*, extrait *m* (d'un livre)

passageway [ˈpæsɪdʒˌweɪ] *n* : passage *m*, corridor *m*, couloir *m*

passbook [ˈpæsˌbʊk] → **bankbook**

passé [pæˈseɪ] *adj* OUT-OF-DATE : dépassé, démodé

passenger [ˈpæsəndʒər] *n* : passager *m*, -gère *f*

passerby [ˌpæsərˈbaɪ, ˈpæsər,-] *n, pl* **passersby** : passant *m*, -sante *f*

passing [ˈpæsɪŋ] *n* DEATH : disparition *f*, mort *f*

passion [ˈpæʃən] *n* **1** LOVE : passion *f*, ardeur *f* **2** EMOTION : émotion *f* forte, passion *f* **3** ANGER : (accès *m* de) colère *f*

passionate [ˈpæʃənət] *adj* : passionné — **passionately** *adv*

passive[1] [ˈpæsɪv] *adj* : passif — **passively** *adv*

passive[2] *n or* **passive case** : passif *m* (en grammaire)

Passover [ˈpæsˌoːvər] *n* : Pâque *f* (juive)

passport [ˈpæsˌpɔrt] *n* : passeport *m*

password [ˈpæsˌwərd] *n* : mot *m* de passe

past[1] [ˈpæst] *adv* : devant <to run past : passer en courant>

past[2] *adj* **1** : dernier, passé <the past month : le mois dernier> **2** FORMER : ancien <a past president : un ancien président>

past[3] *n* **1** : passé *m* **2 in the past** : dans le passé, autrefois

past[4] *prep* **1** BEYOND : au-delà de <just past the corner : juste au-delà du coin> **2** (*in expressions of time*) <half past four : quatre heures et demie> **3 to go past** : passer

pasta [ˈpɑstə, ˈpæs-] *n* : pâtes *fpl* (alimentaires)

paste[1] [ˈpeɪst] *vt* **pasted; pasting** : coller

paste[2] *n* **1** : purée *f* <tomato paste : purée de tomates> **2** GLUE : colle *f*

pasteboard [ˈpeɪstˌbɔrd] → **cardboard**

pastel[1] [pæˈstɛl] *adj* : pastel

pastel[2] *n* : pastel *m*

pasteurization [ˌpæstʃərəˈzeɪʃən, ˌpæstjə-] *n* : pasteurisation *f*

pasteurize [ˈpæstʃəˌraɪz, ˈpæstjə-] *vt* **-ized; -izing** : pasteuriser

pastime [ˈpæsˌtaɪm] *n* : passe-temps *m*

pastor [ˈpæstər] *n* : pasteur *m*

pastoral [ˈpæstərəl] *adj* : pastoral

pastry [ˈpeɪstri] *n, pl* **-ries** : pâtisserie *f*

pasture[1] [ˈpæstʃər] *vt* **-tured; -turing** : faire paître

pasture[2] *n* : pâturage *m*

pasty [ˈpeɪsti] *adj* **pastier; -est 1** : pâteux <a pasty consistency : une consistance pâteuse> **2** PALLID : terreux (se dit du teint)

pat[1] [ˈpæt] *vt* **patted; patting** : tapoter

pat[2] *adv* : parfaitement <to have sth down pat : connaître par cœur qqch>

pat[3] *adj* **1** APT : convenable, approprié **2** GLIB : tout prêt

pat[4] *n* **1** TAP : (petite) tape *f* **2** : noix *f* (de beurre, etc.)

patch[1] ['pætʃ] *vt* **1** MEND, REPAIR : rapiécer, réparer **2 to patch up** : résoudre (des difficultés, etc.) <they patched things up : ils se sont réconciliés>
patch[2] *n* **1** : pièce *f* (d'étoffe) **2** : parcelle *f* (de terre) **3** : tache *f* <a patch of white : une tache blanche> **4** : plaque *f* <patches of ice : plaques de glace>
patchwork ['pætʃˌwərk] *n* : patchwork *m*
patchy ['pætʃi] *adj* **patchier; -est 1** : inégal, irrégulier **2** INCOMPLETE : incomplet
patent[1] ['pætənt] *vt* : breveter
patent[2] ['pætənt] *adj* **1** *or* **patented** [-təd] : breveté **2** ['pætənt, 'peɪt-] OBVIOUS : patent, évident
patent[3] ['pætənt] *n* : brevet *m*
paternal [pə'tərnəl] *adj* : paternel — **paternally** *adv*
paternity [pə'tərnəti] *n* : paternité *f*
path ['pæθ, 'paθ] *n* **1** : allée *f* (dans un jardin) **2** TRACK, TRAIL : chemin *m*, sentier *m* **3** COURSE, TRAJECTORY : trajectoire *f*
pathetic [pə'θɛtɪk] *adj* **1** PITIFUL : pitoyable **2** DEPLORABLE : minable *fam*, déplorable
pathological [ˌpæθə'lɑdʒɪkəl] *adj* : pathologique
pathologist [pə'θɑlədʒɪst] *n* : pathologiste *mf*
pathology [pə'θɑlədʒi] *n, pl* **-gies** : pathologie *f*
pathos ['peɪˌθɑs, 'pæ-, -ˌθɔs] *n* : pathos *m*
pathway ['pæθˌweɪ] *n* : sentier *m*, chemin *m*
patience ['peɪʃənts] *n* : patience *f*
patient[1] ['peɪʃənt] *adj* : patient
patient[2] *n* : patient *m*, -tiente *f*; malade *mf*
patiently ['peɪʃəntli] *adv* : patiemment
patina [pə'ti:nə, 'pætənə] *n, pl* **-nas** [-nəz] *or* **-nae** [-ˌni, -ˌnaɪ] : patine *f*
patio ['pætiˌo:, 'pɑt-] *n, pl* **-tios** : patio *m*
patriarch ['peɪtriˌɑrk] *n* : patriarche *m*
patrimony ['pætrəˌmo:ni] *n* : patrimoine *m*
patriot ['peɪtriət, -ˌɑt] *n* : patriote *mf*
patriotic [ˌpeɪtri'ɑtɪk] *adj* : patriote
patriotically [ˌpeɪtri'ɑtɪkli] *adv* : patriotiquement
patriotism ['peɪtriəˌtɪzəm] *n* : patriotisme *m*
patrol[1] [pə'tro:l] *vi* **-trolled; -trolling** : patrouiller
patrol[2] *n* : patrouille *f*
patrolman [pə'tro:lmən] *n, pl* **-men** [-mən, -ˌmɛn] : agent *m* de police
patron ['peɪtrən] *n* **1** SPONSOR, SUPPORTER : mécène *m* **2** CUSTOMER : client *m*, cliente *f*
patronage ['peɪtrənɪdʒ, 'pæ-] *n* **1** SPONSORSHIP : patronage *m* **2** CLIENTELE : clientèle *f* **3** : pouvoir *m* de nomination (en politique)
patronize ['peɪtrəˌnaɪz, 'pæ-] *vt* **-ized; -izing 1** SUPPORT : patronner, parrainer **2** : être un client de, fréquenter (un marché) **3** : traiter avec condescendance
patter[1] ['pætər] *vi* **1** TAP : tapoter **2** *or* **to patter about** : trottiner
patter[2] *n* **1** TALK : baratin *m* (d'un vendeur) **2** PAT, TAP : tapotement *m*
pattern[1] ['pætərn] *vt* : faire selon un motif, modeler
pattern[2] *n* **1** EXAMPLE, MODEL : modèle *m* **2** DESIGN : dessin *m*, motif *m* **3** NORM, STANDARD : mode *m*, norme *f*
patty ['pæti] *n, pl* **-ties 1** : petit pâté *m* **2** *or* **hamburger patty** : steak *m* haché
paucity ['pɔsəti] *n* : manque *m*, pénurie *f*
paunch ['pɔntʃ] *n* : ventre *m*, bedaine *f*
pauper ['pɔpər] *n* : pauvre *m*; indigent *m*, -gente *f*
pause[1] ['pɔz] *vi* **paused; pausing** : faire une pause
pause[2] *n* : pause *f*, arrêt *m*
pave ['peɪv] *vt* **paved; paving** : paver, revêtir (d'asphalte, etc.)
pavement ['peɪvmənt] *n* : revêtement *m* de la chaussée
pavilion [pə'vɪljən] *n* : pavillon *m*
paving ['peɪvɪŋ] → **pavement**
paw[1] ['pɔ] *vt* **1** TOUCH : tripoter, taponner *Can fam* **2** : donner un coup de patte à <the dog was pawing at my hand : le chien me donnait des coups de patte sur la main>
paw[2] *n* : patte *f* (d'un animal)
pawn[1] ['pɔn] *vt* : mettre en gage
pawn[2] *n* : gage *m*
pawnbroker ['pɔnˌbro:kər] *n* : prêteur *m*, -teuse *f* sur gages
pawnshop ['pɔnˌʃɑp] *n* : mont-de-piété *m France*
pay[1] ['peɪ] *v* **paid** ['peɪd]; **paying** *vt* **1** : payer (un compte, etc.) **2 to pay attention to** : prêter attention à **3 to pay back** : rembourser, s'acquitter de (une dette) **4 to pay one's respects to** : présenter ses respects à **5 to pay s.o. a visit** : aller voir qqn, rendre visite à qqn — *vi* : payer <crime doesn't pay : le crime ne paie pas>
pay[2] *n* : paie *f*, salaire *m*
payable ['peɪəbel] *adj* : payable
paycheck ['peɪˌtʃɛk] *n* : chèque *m* de paie
payee [peɪ'i:] *n* : bénéficiaire *mf*
payment ['peɪmənt] *n* : paiement *m*
PC [ˌpi:'si:] *n, pl* **PCs** *or* **PC's** : PC *m*, micro-ordinateur *m*
pea ['pi:] *n* : pois *m*
peace ['pi:s] *n* : paix *f*
peaceable ['pi:səbəl] *adj* : paisible — **peaceably** [-bli] *adv*

peaceful ['pi:sfəl] *adj* **1** PEACEABLE : de paix, paisible <peaceful times : temps de paix> **2** CALM : paisible, calme
peacefully ['pi:sfəli] *adv* : paisiblement, calmement
peacekeeper ['pi:s,ki:pər] *n* : soldat *m* de la paix
peacekeeping ['pi:s,ki:pɪŋ] *n* : maintien *m* de la paix
peacemaker ['pi:s,meɪkər] *n* : pacificateur *m*, -trice *f*; conciliateur *m*, -trice *f*
peach ['pi:tʃ] *n* : pêche *f*
peacock ['pi:,kɑk] *n* : paon *m*
peak¹ ['pi:k] *vi* : culminer, atteindre un sommet
peak² *adj* : maximal <peak performance : performance maximale>
peak³ *n* **1** CREST : sommet *m* (d'une colline) **2** *or* **mountain peak** : pic *m* **3** APEX : apogée *f* <at the peak of his glory : à l'apogée de sa gloire>
peaked ['pi:kəd] *adj* SICKLY : pâlot, malade
peal¹ ['pi:l] *vi* RESOUND : résonner
peal² *n* : carillonnement *m* (des cloches)
peanut ['pi:,nʌt] *n* **1** : cacahouète *f*, pinotte *f Can fam* (noix) **2** : arachide *f* (plante)
pear ['pær] *n* : poire *f*
pearl ['pərl] *n* : perle *f*
pearly ['pərli] *adj* **pearlier; -est** : nacré, perlé
peasant ['pɛzənt] *n* : paysan *m*, -sanne *f*
peat ['pi:t] *n* **1** : tourbe *f* **2 peat bog** → **bog**
pebble ['pɛbəl] *n* : caillou *m*
pecan [pi'kɑn, -'kæn, 'pi:,kæn] *n* : noix *f* de pécan *France*, noix *f* de pacane *Can*
peccadillo [,pɛkə'dɪlo] *n, pl* **-loes** *or* **-los** : peccadille *f*
peck¹ ['pɛk] *vt* : picorer, becqueter — *vi* **to peck at one's food** : manger du bout des dents
peck² *n* **1** : picotin *m* (mesure) **2** : coup *m* de bec (d'un oiseau) **3** KISS : bécot *m France fam*, bec *m Can fam*
pectoral ['pɛktərəl] *adj* : pectoral
peculiar [pɪ'kju:ljər] *adj* **1** DISTINCTIVE : particulier **2** STRANGE : étrange, bizarre
peculiarity [pɪ,kju:l'jærəṭi, -,kju:li'ær-] *n, pl* **-ties 1** DISTINCTIVENESS : particularité *f* **2** STRANGENESS : étrangeté *f*, bizarrerie *f*
peculiarly [pɪ'kju:ljərli] *adv* **1** PARTICULARLY : particulièrement **2** STRANGELY : de manière étrange, bizarrement
pecuniary [pɪ'kju:ni,ɛri] *adj* : pécuniaire
pedagogical [,pɛdə'gɑdʒɪkəl, -'go:-] *adj* : pédagogique
pedagogy ['pɛdə,go:dʒi, -,gɑ-] *n* : pédagogie *f*
pedal¹ ['pɛdəl] *vt* **-aled** *or* **-alled; -aling** *or* **-alling** : pédaler
pedal² *n* : pédale *f*
pedant ['pɛdənt] *n* : pédant *m*, -dante *f*
pedantic [pɪ'dæntɪk] *adj* : pédant
pedantry ['pɛdəntri] *n, pl* **-ries** : pédantisme *m*
peddle ['pɛdəl] *v* **-dled; -dling** *vt* : colporter — *vi* : faire du colportage
peddler ['pɛdlər] *n* : colporteur *m*, -teuse *f*
pedestal ['pɛdəstəl] *n* : piédestal *m*
pedestrian¹ [pə'destriən] *adj* **1** COMMONPLACE : prosaïque, commun **2** : piétonnier <pedestrian zone : zone piétonnière> <pedestrian crossing : passage pour piétons>
pedestrian² *n* : piéton *m*
pediatric [,pi:di'ætrɪk] *adj* : pédiatrique
pediatrician [,pi:diə'trɪʃən] *n* : pédiatre *mf*
pediatrics [,pi:di'ætrɪks] *ns & pl* : pédiatrie *f*
pedigree ['pɛdə,gri:] *n* **1** FAMILY TREE : arbre *m* généalogique **2** LINEAGE : pedigree *m* (d'un animal), lignée *f* (d'une personne)
pediment ['pɛdəmənt] *n* : fronton *m*
peek¹ ['pi:k] *vi* **1** PEEP : regarder furtivement **2** GLANCE : jeter un coup d'œil
peek² *n* : coup *m* d'œil furtif
peel¹ ['pi:l] *vt* **1** : peler (un fruit), éplucher (un oignon, etc.) **2** *or* **to peel off** : enlever (une étiquette, etc.) — *vi* **1** : peler, pleumer *Can fam* (se dit de la peau) **2** : s'écailler (se dit de la peinture)
peel² *n* : pelure *f* (d'une pomme), écorce *f* (d'une orange), épluchure *f* (de pommes de terre)
peeling → **peel²**
peep¹ ['pi:p] *vi* **1** : pépier, piauler (se dit d'un oiseau) **2** *or* **to peep through** EMERGE : apparaître, se montrer **3 to peep at** : jeter un coup d'œil à
peep² *n* **1** : pépiement *m* (d'un oiseau) **2** : coup *m* d'œil
peer¹ ['pɪr] *vi* : regarder attentivement
peer² *n* **1** EQUAL : pair *m*, égal *m* **2** NOBLEMAN : noble *m*, pair *m*
peerage ['pɪrɪdʒ] *n* : pairie *f*
peerless ['pɪrləs] *adj* : hors pair, sans égal
peeve¹ ['pi:v] *vt* **peeved; peeving** : mettre en rogne, irriter
peeve² *n or* **pet peeve** : bête *f* noire
peevish ['pi:vɪʃ] *adj* : grincheux, grognon
peg¹ ['pɛg] *vt* **pegged; pegging** ATTACH, FASTEN : accrocher, attacher
peg² *n* **1** HOOK : patère *f* (de bois), fiche *f* (de métal) **2** STAKE : piquet *m* (de tente)
peignoir [peɪn'wɑr, pɛn-] *n* : peignoir *m*, négligé *m*
pejorative [pɪ'dʒɔrəṭɪv] *adj* : péjoratif — **pejoratively** *adv*
pelican ['pɛlɪkən] *n* : pélican *m*
pellagra [pə'lægrə, -'leɪ-] *n* : pellagre *f*

pellet ['pɛlət] *n* **1** BALL : boulette *f* (de papier, etc.) **2** SHOT : plomb *m*
pell–mell ['pɛl'mɛl] *adv* : pêle-mêle
pelt¹ ['pɛlt] *vt* : cribler, bombarder <they pelted her with accusations : ils l'ont criblée d'accusations> <to pelt s.o. with stones : lancer des pierres à qqn>
pelt² *n* : peau *f* (d'un animal)
pelvic ['pɛlvɪk] *adj* : pelvien
pelvis ['pɛlvɪs] *n, pl* **-vises** [-vɪsəz] *or* **-ves** [-,vi:z] : bassin *m*, pelvis *m*
pen¹ ['pɛn] *vt* **penned; penning 1** : enfermer dans un abri ou un enclos **2** WRITE : écrire
pen² *n* **1** : enclos *m*, parc *m* (d'animaux) **2** : stylo *m* <ballpoint pen : stylo à bille>
penal ['pi:nəl] *adj* **1** : pénal <a penal offense : une offense pénale> **2** : pénitentiaire <a penal colony : une colonie pénitentiaire>
penalize ['pi:nəl,aɪz, 'pɛn-] *vt* **-ized; -izing** : pénaliser, punir *Can* (aux sports)
penalty ['pɛnəlti] *n, pl* **-ties 1** : peine *f* (en droit) **2** : pénalité *f*, pénalisation *f*, punition *f Can* (aux sports)
penance ['pɛnənʦ] *n* : pénitence *f*
pence ['pɛnʦ] → **penny**
penchant ['pɛnʧənt] *n* : penchant *m*
pencil¹ ['pɛnʦəl] *vt* **-ciled** *or* **-cilled; -ciling** *or* **-cilling** : écrire ou dessiner au crayon
pencil² *n* : crayon *m*
pencil sharpener *n* : taille-crayon *m*, aiguise-crayon *m Can*
pendant ['pɛndənt] *n* : pendentif *m*
pending¹ ['pɛndɪŋ] *adj* UNDECIDED : en instance
pending² *prep* **1** DURING : pendant **2** AWAITING : en attendant
pendulum ['pɛnʤələm, -djʊləm] *n* : pendule *m*
penetrate ['pɛnə,treɪt] *v* **-trated; -trating** *vt* : pénétrer — *vi* : pénétrer, s'infiltrer
penetration [,pɛnə'treɪʃən] *n* : pénétration *f*
penguin ['pɛŋgwɪn, 'pɛn-] *n* : manchot *m*
penicillin [,pɛnə'sɪlən] *n* : pénicilline *f*
peninsula [pə'nɪnʦələ, -'nɪnʃʊlə] *n* : péninsule *f*
penis ['pi:nəs] *n, pl* **-nes** [-,ni:z] *or* **-nises** : pénis *m*
penitence ['pɛnəɪʦənʦ] *n* : pénitence *f*
penitent¹ ['pɛnəɪʦənt] *adj* : pénitent, repentant
penitent² *n* : pénitent *m*, -tente *f*
penitential [,pɛnə'tɛntʃəl] *adj* : pénitentiel
penitentiary [,pɛnə'tɛntʃəri] *n, pl* **-ries** : pénitencier *m*, prison *f*
penmanship ['pɛnmənʃɪp] *n* : écriture *f*, calligraphie *f*
pen name *n* : nom *m* de plume, pseudonyme *m*
pennant ['pɛnənt] *n* : fanion *m*, flamme *f* (d'un navire)
penniless ['pɛnɪləs] *adj* : sans le sou
penny ['pɛni] *n, pl* **-nies** : centime *m*, cent *m*, sou *m Can*
pension¹ ['pɛnʃən] *vt* **1** : verser une pension à **2 to pension off** : mettre à la retraite
pension² *n* : pension *f*, retraite *f*
pensive ['pɛnʦɪv] *adj* : pensif, songeur — **pensively** *adv*
pent ['pɛnt] *adj* : réprimé <pent-up feelings : sentiments réprimés>
pentagon ['pɛntə,gɑn] *n* : pentagone *m*
pentagonal [pɛn'tɛgənəl] *adj* : pentagonal
penthouse ['pɛnt,haʊs] *n* : appartement *m* construit sur le toit d'un immeuble
penury ['pɛnjəri] *n* : indigence *f*
peon ['pi:,ɑn, -ən] *n, pl* **-ons** *or* **-ones** [pei'o:ni:z] : péon *m*
peony ['pi:əni] *n, pl* **-nies** : pivoine *f*
people¹ ['pi:pəl] *vt* **-pled; -pling** : peupler
people² *ns & pl* **1 people** *npl* : personnes *fpl*, gens *mfpl* <we met several people : nous avons rencontré plusieurs personnes> <old people : vieilles gens> **2** *pl* **peoples** : peuple *m* <the peoples of Africa : les peuples d'Afrique>
pep¹ ['pɛp] *vt* **pepped; pepping** *or* **to pep up** : remonter le moral à
pep² *n* : dynamisme *m*, entrain *m*
pepper¹ ['pɛpər] *vt* **1** : poivrer (en cuisine) **2** RIDDLE : cribler (de balles, etc.) **3** SPRINKLE : émailler <peppered with quotations : émaillé de citations>
pepper² *n* **1** : poivre *m* (condiment) **2** : poivron *m* <green pepper : poivron vert> **3** → **chili**
peppermint ['pɛpər,mɪnt] *n* : menthe *f* poivrée
peppery ['pɛpəri] *adj* : poivré
peppy ['pɛpi] *adj* **peppier; -est** : plein d'énergie, vivant
peptic ['pɛptɪk] *adj* **peptic ulcer** : ulcère *m* de l'estomac
per ['pər] *prep* **1** : par <ten dollars per day : dix dollars par jour> **2** ACCORDING TO : selon, conformément à <per instructions : selon les directives>
per annum [pər'ænəm] *adv* : par an, annuellement
percale [,pər'keɪl, 'pər-,; ,pər'kæl] *n* : percale *f*
perceive [pər'si:v] *vt* **-ceived; -ceiving** : percevoir
percent¹ [pər'sɛnt] *adv* : pour cent
percent² *n, pl* **-cent** *or* **-cents 1** : pour cent *m* <ten percent of the time : dix pour cent du temps> **2** PERCENTAGE : pourcentage *m* <a percent of his income : un pourcentage de son revenu>

percentage [pərˈsɛntɪdʒ] *n* : pourcentage *m*
perceptible [pərˈsɛptəbəl] *adj* : perceptible
perceptibly [pərˈsɛptəbli] *adv* : de manière perceptible
perception [pərˈsɛpʃən] *n* : perception *f*
perceptive [pərˈsɛptɪv] *adj* : perspicace
perceptively [pərˈsɛptɪvli] *adv* : avec perspicacité
perceptiveness [pərˈsɛptɪvnəs] *n* : perspicacité *f*
perch[1] [ˈpərtʃ] *vt* : percher — *vi* : se percher
perch[2] *n* **1** ROOST : perchoir *m* **2** *pl* **perch** *or* **perches** : perche *f* (poisson)
percolate [ˈpərkəˌleɪt] *v* **-lated; -lating** *vi* SEEP : filtrer, passer — *vt* : faire (du café) dans une cafetière
percolator [ˈpərkəˌleɪtər] *n* : cafetière *f* à pression
percussion [pərˈkʌʃən] *n* : percussion *f*
peremptory [pəˈrɛmptəri] *adj* : péremptoire
perennial[1] [pəˈrɛniəl] *adj* **1** : vivace <perennial flowers : fleurs vivaces> **2** RECURRING : perpétuel
perennial[2] *n* : plante *f* vivace
perennially [pəˈrɛniəli] *adv* : perpétuellement
perfect[1] [pərˈfɛkt] *vt* : perfectionner
perfect[2] [ˈpərfɪkt] *adj* : parfait — **perfectly** *adv*
perfectible [pərˈfɛktəbəl] *adj* : perfectible
perfection [pərˈfɛkʃən] *n* : perfection *f*
perfectionist[1] [pərˈfɛkʃənɪst] *or* **perfectionistic** [pərˌfɛkʃəˈnɪstɪk] *adj* : perfectionniste
perfectionist[2] *n* : perfectionniste *mf*
perfidious [pərˈfɪdiəs] *adj* : perfide
perforate [ˈpərfəˌreɪt] *vt* **-rated; -rating** : perforer
perforation [ˌpərfəˈreɪʃən] *n* : perforation *f*
perform [pərˈfɔrm] *vt* **1** CARRY OUT : réaliser, effectuer, accomplir **2** PRESENT : jouer, donner (une pièce de théâtre, etc.) — *vi* ACT : jouer (dans une pièce de théâtre, etc.)
performance [pərˈfɔrˌmənʧs] *n* **1** EXECUTION : rendement *m* **2** : interprétation *f* (d'un acteur, d'un comédien), performance *f* (d'une équipe) **3** PRESENTATION, SHOW : spectacle *m*
performer [pərˈfɔrmər] *n* : interprète *mf*
perfume[1] [pərˈfjuːm, ˈpər,-] *vt* **-fumed; -fuming** : parfumer
perfume[2] [ˈpərˌfjuːm, pərˈ-] *n* : parfum *m*
perfunctory [pərˈfʌŋktəri] *adj* : mécanique, sommaire
perhaps [pərˈhæps] *adv* : peut-être
peril [ˈpɛrəl] *n* : péril *m*, danger *m*
perilous [ˈpɛrələs] *adj* : périlleux, dangereux — **perilously** *adv*
perimeter [pəˈrɪmətər] *n* : périmètre *m*
period [ˈpɪriəd] *n* **1** : point *m* (signe de ponctuation) **2** INTERVAL, TIME : période *f* **3** EPOCH, ERA : ère *f*, période *f*, époque *f* **4** *or* **menstrual period** : règles *fpl*
periodic [ˌpɪriˈɑdɪk] *adj* : périodique — **periodically** [-dɪkli] *adv*
periodical [ˌpɪriˈɑdɪkəl] *n* : périodique *m*, journal *m*
peripheral [pəˈrɪfərəl] *adj* : périphérique
periphery [pəˈrɪfəri] *n, pl* **-eries** : périphérie *f*
periscope [ˈpɛrəˌskoːp] *n* : périscope *m*
perish [ˈpɛrɪʃ] *vi* DIE : périr
perishable [ˈpɛrɪʃəbəl] *adj* : périssable
perishables [ˈpɛrɪʃəbəlz] *npl* : denrées *fpl* périssables
perjure [ˈpərdʒər] *vt* **-jured; -juring** *or* **to perjure onself** : se parjurer
perjurer [ˈpərdʒərər] *n* : parjure *mf*
perjury [ˈpərdʒəri] *n* : faux témoignage *m*
perk[1] [ˈpərk] *vi* **to perk up** : se ragaillardir — *vt* **1** ENLIVEN, STIMULATE : revigorer **2** FRESHEN : égayer **3 to perk up one's ears** : dresser les oreilles
perk[2] *n* : avantage *m*, privilège *m* (d'un emploi)
perky [ˈpərki] *adj* **perkier; -est** : guilleret, fringant
permanence [ˈpərmənənʧs] *n* : permanence *f*
permanent[1] [ˈpərmənənt] *adj* : permanent
permanent[2] *n* : permanente *f*
permanently [ˈpərmənəntli] *adv* : de façon permanente, en permanence
permeable [ˈpərmiəbəl] *adj* : perméable
permeate [ˈpərmiˌeɪt] *v* **-ated; -ating** *vi* : se diffuser, se répandre — *vt* **1** IMPREGNATE : impregner <permeated with smoke : impregné de fumée> **2** PERVADE : s'infiltrer dans, se répandre dans
permissible [pərˈmɪsəbəl] *adj* : permis, admissible
permission [pərˈmɪʃən] *n* : permission *f*, autorisation *f*
permissive [pərˈmɪsɪv] *adj* : permissif — **permissively** *adv*
permit[1] [pərˈmɪt] *v* **-mitted; -mitting** *vt* : permettre, autoriser — *vi* ALLOW : permettre <if time permits : si le temps le permet>
permit[2] [ˈpərˌmɪt, pərˈ-] *n* : permis *m*, licence *f*
pernicious [pərˈnɪʃəs] *adj* : pernicieux — **perniciously** *adv*
peroxide [pəˈrɑkˌsaɪd] *n* : peroxyde *m*
perpendicular [ˌpərpənˈdɪkjələr] *adj* : perpendiculaire — **perpendicularly** *adv*
perpetrate [ˈpərpəˌtreɪt] *vt* **-trated; -trating** : perpétrer
perpetration [ˌpərpəˈtreɪʃən] *n* : perpétration *f*
perpetrator [ˈpərpəˌtreɪtər] *n* : auteur *m* (d'un délit)

perpetual [pərˈpɛtʃʊəl] *adj* : éternel, perpétuel
perpetually [pərˈpɛtʃʊəli, -tʃəli] *adv* : perpétuellement
perpetuate [pərˈpɛtʃʊˌeɪt] *vt* **-ated; -ating** : perpétuer
perpetuation [pərˌpɛtʃəˈweɪʃən] *n* : perpétuation *f*
perplex [pərˈplɛks] *vt* : laisser perplexe
perplexity [pərˈplɛksəti] *n, pl* **-ties** : perplexité *f*
persecute [ˈpərsɪˌkjuːt] *vt* **-cuted; -cuting** : persécuter
persecution [ˌpərsɪˈkjuːʃən] *n* : persécution *f*
persecutor [ˈpərsɪˌkjuːtər] *n* : persécuteur *m*, -trice *f*
perseverance [ˌpərsəˈvɪrənts] *n* : persévérance *f*
persevere [ˌpərsəˈvɪr] *vi* **-vered; -vering** : persévérer
Persian[1] [ˈpərʒən] *adj* : persan
Persian[2] *n* **1** : Persan *m*, -sane *f* **2** : persan *m* (langue)
persist [pərˈsɪst] *vi* : persister
persistence [pərˈsɪstənts] *n* : persistance *f*, persévérance *f*
persistent [pərˈsɪstənt] *adj* : persistant
persistently [pərˈsɪstəntli] *adv* : sans cesse, continuellement
person [ˈpərsən] *n* **1** INDIVIDUAL : personne *f*, individu *m* **2** : personne *f* (en grammaire) **3 in ~** : en personne
personable [ˈpərsənəbəl] *adj* : agréable, aimable
personage [ˈpərsənɪdʒ] *n* : personnage *m*, personne *f* haut placée
personal [ˈpərsənəl] *adj* **1** PRIVATE : personnel, privé <personal property : biens mobiliers personnels> <personal hygiene : hygiène personnelle> **2** : en personne <a personal visit : une visite en personne> **3** INTIMATE : personnel <a personal conversation : une conversation personnelle>
personality [ˌpərsənˈæləti] *n, pl* **-ties 1** CHARACTER, TEMPERAMENT : personnalité *f* **2** CELEBRITY : vedette *f*
personalize [ˈpərsənəˌlaɪz] *vt* **-ized; -izing** : personnaliser
personally [ˈpərsənəli] *adv* **1** : personnellement <I'll attend to the matter personally : je vais y voir personnellement> **2** DIRECTLY : en personne **3** INDIVIDUALLY : personnellement <not you personally : pas toi personnellement>
personification [pərˌsɑnəfəˈkeɪʃən] *n* : personnification *f*
personify [pərˈsɑnəˌfaɪ] *vt* **-fied; -fying** : personnifier
personnel [ˌpərsənˈɛl] *n* : personnel *m*
perspective [pərˈspɛktɪv] *n* : perspective *f*
perspicacious [ˌpərspəˈkeɪʃəs] *adj* : perspicace
perspicacity [ˌpərspəˈkæsəti] *n* : perspicacité *f*
perspiration [ˌpərspəˈreɪʃən] *n* : transpiration *f*, sueur *f*
perspire [pərˈspaɪr] *vi* **-spired; -spiring** : transpirer, suer
persuade [pərˈsweɪd] *vt* **-suaded; -suading** : persuader, convaincre
persuasion [pərˈsweɪʒən] *n* **1** : persuasion *f* <the power of persuasion : le pouvoir de persuasion> **2** BELIEF : conviction *f*
persuasive [pərˈsweɪsɪv, -zɪv] *adj* : persuasif, convaincant
persuasively [pərˈsweɪsɪvli, -zɪv-] *adv* : persuasivement
persuasiveness [pərˈsweɪsɪvnəs, -zɪv-] *n* : force *f* de persuasion
pert [ˈpərt] *adj* **1** FLIPPANT : effronté, insolent **2** JAUNTY : coquet
pertain [pərˈteɪn] *vi* **1** BELONG : se rapporter <duties pertaining to the office : des fonctions qui se rapportent au bureau> **2** RELATE : traiter, avoir rapport <books pertaining to birds : livres sur les oiseaux>
pertinence [ˈpərtənənts] *n* : pertinence *f*
pertinent [ˈpərtənənt] *adj* : pertinent
perturb [pərˈtərb] *vt* : troubler, inquiéter
perusal [pəˈruːzəl] *n* : lecture *f* attentive
peruse [pəˈruːz] *vt* **-rused; -rusing** : lire attentivement
Peruvian[1] [pəˈruːviən] *adj* : péruvien
Peruvian[2] *n* : Péruvien *m*, -vienne *f*
pervade [pərˈveɪd] *vt* **-vaded; -vading** : s'infiltrer à, se répandre dans
pervasive [pərˈveɪsɪv, -zɪv] *adj* : envahissant, pénétrant
perverse [pərˈvərs] *adj* **1** CORRUPT : pervers, vicieux **2** STUBBORN : obstiné, entêté
perversely [pərˈvərsli] *adv* **1** VICIOUSLY : avec un malin plaisir **2** STUBBORNLY : obstinément
perversion [pərˈvərʒən] *n* : perversion *f*
perversity [pərˈvərsəti] *n, pl* **-ties** : perversité *f*
pervert[1] [pərˈvərt] *vt* **1** CORRUPT : pervertir, corrompre **2** DISTORT : déformer
pervert[2] [ˈpərˌvərt] *n* : pervers *m*, -verse *f*
peso [ˈpeɪˌsoː] *n, pl* **-sos** : peso *m*
pessimism [ˈpɛsəˌmɪzəm] *n* : pessimisme *m*
pessimist [ˈpɛsəmɪst] *n* : pessimiste *mf*
pessimistic [ˌpɛsəˈmɪstɪk] *adj* : pessimiste
pest [ˈpɛst] *n* **1** NUISANCE : peste *f*, plaie *f fam* **2** : plante *f* ou animal *m* nuisible
pester [ˈpɛstər] *vt* **-tered; -tering** : importuner, harceler
pesticide [ˈpɛstəˌsaɪd] *n* : pesticide *m*
pestilence [ˈpɛstələnts] *n* : peste *f*, pestilence *f*
pestle [ˈpɛsəl, ˈpɛstəl] *n* : pilon *m*
pet[1] [ˈpɛt] *vt* **petted; petting** : caresser

pet[2] *n* **1** : animal *m* domestique **2** FAVORITE : chouchou *m fam*
petal ['pɛt̬əl] *n* : pétale *m*
petite [pə'tiːt] *adj* : menue, petite
petition[1] [pə'tɪʃən] *vi* : faire une pétition — *vt* : adresser une pétition à
petition[2] *n* : pétition *f*
petitioner [pə'tɪʃənər] *n* : pétitionnaire *mf*
petrify ['pɛtrə,faɪ] *vt* **-fied; -fying** : pétrifier
petroleum [pə'troːliəm] *n* : pétrole *m*
petticoat ['pɛt̬i,koːt] *n* : jupon *m*
pettiness ['pɛt̬inəs] *n* **1** INSIGNIFICANCE : insignifiance *f* **2** MEANNESS : mesquinerie *f*
petty ['pɛt̬i] *adj* **pettier; -est 1** MINOR : petit <petty cash : petite monnaie> **2** INSIGNIFICANT : sans importance, insignifiant **3** MEAN : mesquin
petty officer *n* : maître *m*
petulance ['pɛt̬ələnʦ] *n* : irritabilité *f*, irascibilité *f*
petulant ['pɛt̬ələnt] *adj* : irritable, irascible
petunia [pɪ'tuːnjə, -'tjuː-] *n* : pétunia *m*
pew ['pjuː] *n* : banc *m* d'église
pewter ['pjuːt̬ər] *n* : étain *m*
pH [,piːeɪt∫] *n* : pH *m*
phallic ['fælɪk] *adj* : phallique
phallus ['fæləs] *n, pl* **-li** ['fæ,laɪ] *or* **-luses** : phallus *m*
phantasy ['fæntəsi] → **fantasy**
phantom ['fæntəm] *n* : fantôme *m*
pharaoh ['fɛr,oː, 'fɛɪ,roː] *n* : pharaon *m*
pharmaceutical [,fɑrmə'suːt̬ɪkəl] *adj* : pharmaceutique
pharmacist [,fɑrməsɪst] *n* : pharmacien *m*, -cienne *f*
pharmacology [,fɑrmə'kɑlədʒi] *n* : pharmacologie *f*
pharmacy ['fɑrməsi] *n, pl* **-cies** : pharmacie *f*
pharynx ['færɪŋks] *n, pl* **pharynges** [fə'rɪn,dʒiːz] : pharynx *m*
phase[1] ['feɪz] *vt* **phased; phasing 1** SYNCHRONIZE : synchroniser **2 to phase in** : introduire graduellement **3 to phase out** : discontinuer progressivement
phase[2] *n* **1** : phase *f* (de la lune) **2** STAGE : phase *f*, stade *m*
pheasant ['fɛzənt] *n, pl* **-ant** *or* **-ants** : faisan *m*, -sane *f*
phenomenal [fɪ'nɑmənəl] *adj* : phénoménal — **phenomenally** *adv*
phenomenon [fɪ'nɑmə,nɑn, -nən] *n, pl* **-na** [-nə] *or* **-nons 1** EVENT, FACT : phénomène *m* **2** *pl* **-nons** PRODIGY : phénomène *m*
philanthropic [,fɪlən'θrɑpɪk] *adj* : philanthropique
philanthropist [fə'lænθrəpɪst] *n* : philanthrope *mf*
philanthropy [fə'lænθrəpi] *n, pl* **-pies** : philanthropie *f*
philately [fə'lætəli] *n* : philatélie *f*
philodendron [,fɪlə'dɛndrən] *n, pl* **-drons** *or* **-dra** [-drə] : philodendron *m*
philosopher [fə'lɑsəfər] *n* : philosophe *mf*
philosophical [,fɪlə'sɑfɪkəl] *adj* : philosophique — **philosophically** [-kli] *adv*
philosophize [fə'lɑsə,faɪz] *vt* **-phized; -phizing** : philosopher
philosophy [fə'lɑsəfi] *n, pl* **-phies** : philosophie *f*
phlebitis [flɪ'baɪt̬əs] *n* : phlébite *f*
phlegm ['flɛm] *n* : mucosité *f*
phlox ['flɑks] *n, pl* **phlox** *or* **phloxes** : phlox *m*
phobia ['foːbiə] *n* : phobie *f*
phoenix ['fiːnɪks] *n* : phénix *m*
phone[1] ['foːn] *v* → **telephone**[1]
phone[2] *n* → **telephone**[2]
phoneme ['foː,niːm] *n* : phonème *m*
phonetic [fə'nɛt̬ɪk] *adj* : phonétique
phonetics [fə'nɛt̬ɪks] *n* : phonétique *f*
phonics ['fɑnɪks] *n* : méthode *f* d'enseignement de la lecture par la phonétique
phonograph ['foːnə,græf] *n* : phonographe *m*
phony[1] *or* **phoney** ['foːni] *adj* **phonier; -est** : faux
phony[2] *or* **phoney** *n, pl* **-nies** : charlatan *m*
phosphate ['fɑs,feɪt] *n* : phosphate *m*
phosphorescence [,fɑsfə'rɛsənʦ] *n* : phosphorescence *f*
phosphorescent [,fɑsfə'rɛsənt] *adj* : phosphorescent
phosphorus ['fɑsfərəs] *n* : phosphore *m*
photo ['foːt̬oː] *n, pl* **-tos** : photo *f*
photocopy[1] ['foːt̬o,kɑpi] *vt* **-copied; -copying** : photocopier
photocopy[2] *n, pl* **-pies** : photocopie *f*
photoelectric [,foːt̬oɪ'lɛkt̬rɪk] *adj* : photoélectrique
photogenic [,foːt̬ə'dʒɛnɪk] *adj* : photogénique
photograph[1] ['foːt̬ə,græf] *vt* : photographier
photograph[2] *n* : photo *f*, photographie *f*
photographer [fə'tɑgrəfər] *n* : photographe *mf*
photographic [,foːt̬ə'græfɪk] *adj* : photographique — **photographically** [-fɪkli] *adv*
photography [fə'tɑgrəfi] *n* : photographie *f*
photosynthesis [,foːt̬osɪn'θəsəs] *n* : photosynthèse *f*
photosynthetic [,foːt̬osɪn'θɛt̬ɪk] *adj* : photosynthétique
phrase[1] ['freɪz] *vt* **phrased; phrasing** : formuler, exprimer
phrase[2] *n* **1** : expression *f*, locution *f* **2** : syntagme *m* (en grammaire)
phraseology [,freɪzi'ɑlədʒi] *n, pl* **-gies** : phraséologie *f*
phylum ['faɪləm] *n, pl* **-la** : phylum *m*

physical[1] ['fɪzɪkəl] *adj* : physique — **physically** [-kli] *adv*
physical[2] *n* : examen *m* médical
physician [fə'zɪʃən] *n* : médecin *mf*
physicist ['fɪzəsɪst] *n* : physicien *m*, -cienne *f*
physics ['fɪzɪks] *ns & pl* : physique *f*
physiognomy [ˌfɪzɪ'ɑgnəmɪ] *n, pl* **-mies** : physionomie *f*
physiological [ˌfɪziə'lɑdʒɪkəl] *or* **physiologic** [-dʒɪk] *adj* : physiologique
physiologist [ˌfɪzɪ'ɑlədʒɪst] *n* : physiologiste *mf*
physiology [ˌfɪzɪ'ɑlədʒi] *n* : physiologie *f*
physique [fə'zi:k] *n* : physique *m*
pi ['paɪ] *n, pl* **pis** ['paɪz] : pi *m*
pianist [pi'ænɪst, 'pi:ənɪst] *n* : pianiste *mf*
piano [pi'æno:] *n, pl* **-anos** : piano *m*
piazza [pi'æzə, -'ɑtsə] *n, pl* **-zas** *or* **-ze** [-'ɑtˌseɪ] : piazza *f*
picayune [ˌpɪki'ju:n] *adj* : insignifiant, sans valeur
piccolo ['pɪkəˌlo:] *n, pl* **-los** : piccolo *m*, picolo *m*
pick[1] ['pɪk] *vt* **1** : casser, percer (une surface) **2** : enlever <to pick meat from bones : enlever la viande des os> **3** : cueillir (des fleurs) **4** *or* **to pick out** SELECT : choisir **5 to pick a fight** : chercher la chicane **6 to pick a lock** : crocheter une serrure **7 to pick one's teeth** : se curer les dents **8 to pick pockets** : voler à la tire — *vi* **1 to pick at** NAG : critiquer **2 to pick at one's food** : manger du bout des doigts **3 to pick and choose** : faire le difficile
pick[2] *n* **1** : choix *m* <take your pick : faites votre choix> **2** : meilleur *m* <the pick of the herd : le meilleur du lot> **3** : pic *m* (outil)
pickax ['pɪkˌæks] *n* : pic *m*
pickerel ['pɪkərəl] *n, pl* **-el** *or* **-els** : espèce *f* de petit brochet
picket[1] ['pɪkət] *vi* : faire un piquet de grève, piqueter *Can*
picket[2] *n* **1** STAKE : piquet *m* (de clôture) **2** *or* **picket line** : piquet *m* de grève
pickle[1] ['pɪkəl] *vt* **-led; -ling** : conserver dans la saumure
pickle[2] *n* **1** BRINE : saumure *f* **2** GHERKIN : cornichon *m* **3** FIX, JAM : pétrin *m fam* <to be in a pickle : être dans le pétrin>
pickpocket ['pɪkˌpɑkət] *n* : voleur *m*, -leuse *f* à la tire
pickup ['pɪkˌəp] *n* **1** IMPROVEMENT : amélioration *f* **2** *or* **pickup truck** : pick-up *m*, camionnette *f*
pick up *vt* **1** GATHER, LIFT : ramasser, soulever, décrocher (le téléphone) <to pick oneself up : se relever> **2** CATCH, LEARN : saisir, comprendre (des renseignements) **3** RESUME : reprendre (une conversation, etc.) **4** TIDY : mettre en ordre **5 to pick up speed** : prendre de la vitesse — *vi* **1** IMPROVE : s'améliorer, remonter **2 to pick up after oneself** : se ramasser *Can*
picnic[1] ['pɪkˌnɪk] *vi* **-nicked; -nicking** : pique-niquer
picnic[2] *n* : pique-nique *m*
pictorial [pɪk'tori:əl] *adj* : illustré, pictural
picture[1] ['pɪktʃər] *vt* **-tured; -turing 1** DEPICT : dépeindre, décrire **2** IMAGINE : se représenter, s'imaginer
picture[2] *n* **1** : tableau *m*, image *f*, dessin *m* **2** DESCRIPTION : description *f* **3** IMAGE : image *f* <he's the picture of his father : il est l'image de son père> **4** MOVIE : film *m*
picturesque [ˌpɪktʃə'rɛsk] *adj* : pittoresque
pie ['paɪ] *n* **1** : tarte *f* <apple pie : tarte aux pommes> **2** : pâté *m*, tourte *f* *France* <meat pie : pâté à la viande>
piebald ['paɪˌbɔld] *adj* : pie (se dit d'un animal)
piece[1] ['pi:s] *vt* **pieced; piecing** *or* **to piece together** : rassembler, constituer
piece[2] *n* **1** FRAGMENT : bout *m*, morceau *m* <a piece of string : un bout de corde> **2** : pièce *f* (dans un jeu de société) **3** UNIT : objet *m*, chose *f*, pièce *f* <a piece of fruit : un fruit> <a piece of mail : du courrier> <a fifty-cent piece : une pièce de cinquante cents> **4** WORK : œuvre *f*, morceau *m* (de musique) **5** COMPONENT : pièce *f* <a three-piece suit : un costume de trois pièces>
piecemeal[1] ['pi:sˌmi:l] *adv* : graduellement
piecemeal[2] *adj* : fragmentaire <piecemeal reforms : réformes fragmentaires>
pied ['paɪd] *adj* : pie (se dit d'un cheval, etc.)
pier ['pɪr] *n* **1** JETTY : jetée *f* **2** : pile *f* (d'un pont) **3** COLUMN : pilier *m*
pierce ['pɪrs] *vt* **pierced; piercing 1** STAB : donner un coup de couteau à **2** PERFORATE : percer, transpercer **3** PENETRATE : pénétrer **4** DISCERN : comprendre, discerner
piety ['paɪəti] *n, pl* **-eties** : piété *f*
pig ['pɪg] *n* **1** : porc *m*, cochon *m* (animal) **2** SLOB : cochon *m*, -chonne *f* *fam* **3** CASTING : moulage *m* en fer
pigeon ['pɪdʒən] *n* : pigeon *m*
pigeonhole ['pɪdʒənˌho:l] *n* : casier *m*
piggish ['pɪgɪʃ] *adj* **1** GREEDY : goinfre, glouton **2** DIRTY : sale, cochon
piggyback ['pɪgiˌbæk] *adv & adj* : sur le dos
pigheaded ['pɪgˌhɛdəd] *adj* STUBBORN : têtu, obstiné
piglet ['pɪglət] *n* : porcelet *m*
pigment ['pɪgmənt] *n* : pigment *m*
pigmentation [ˌpɪgmən'teɪʃən] *n* : pigmentation *f*

pigmy → pygmy
pigpen ['pɪgˌpɛn] *n* : porcherie *f*, soue *f* *Can*
pigsty ['pɪgˌstaɪ] *n, pl* **-sties → pigpen**
pigtail ['pɪgˌteɪl] *n* : natte *f*
pike ['paɪk] *n* **1** WEAPON : pique *f* **2 → turnpike 3** *pl* **pike** *or* **pikes** : brochet *m* (poisson)
pilaf *or* **pilaff** [pɪ'lɑf, 'piˌlɑf] *or* **pilau** [pɪ'lo:, -'lɔ:, 'pilo, -lɔ] *n* : pilaf *m*
pile[1] ['paɪəl] *v* **piled; piling** *vt* **1** STACK : empiler **2** LOAD : remplir <he piled potatoes on his plate : il a rempli son assiette de pommes de terre> — *vi* **1** *or* **to pile up** : s'accumuler **2** CROWD : s'empiler <they piled into the car : ils se sont empilés dans la voiture>
pile[2] *n* **1** PILING, POST : pilotis *m*, pieu *m* **2** HEAP : pile *f*, tas *m* **3** NAP : poil *m* (d'un tapis, etc.)
piles ['paɪls] *npl* : hémorroïdes *fpl*
pilfer ['pɪlfər] *vt* : chaparder *fam*, dérober
pilgrim ['pɪlgrəm] *n* : pèlerin *m*, -rine *f*
pilgrimage ['pɪlgrəmɪdʒ] *n* : pèlerinage *m*
pill ['pɪl] *n* : pilule *f*, cachet *m*
pillage[1] ['pɪlɪdʒ] *vt* **-laged; -laging** : piller
pillage[2] *n* : pillage *m*
pillar ['pɪlər] *n* : pilier *m*, colonne *f*
pillbox ['pɪlˌbɑks] *n* : boîte *f* à pilules
pillory[1] ['pɪlərɪ] *vt* **-ried; -rying** : mettre au pilori
pillory[2] *n, pl* **-ries** : pilori *m*
pillow ['pɪlˌo:] *n* : oreiller *m*
pillowcase ['pɪloˌkeɪs] *n* : taie *f* d'oreiller
pilot[1] ['paɪlət] *vt* : piloter (un avion, un navire)
pilot[2] *n* : pilote *m*
pimento [pə'mɛnˌto:] *n, pl* **-tos** *or* **-to 1 → allspice 2 → pimiento**
pimiento [pə'mɛnˌto:, -'mjɛn-] *n, pl* **-tos** : piment *m* doux
pimp ['pɪmp] *n* : entremetteur *m*, souteneur *m*
pimple ['pɪmpəl] *n* : bouton *m*
pimply ['pɪmpəlɪ] *adj* **pimplier; -est** : boutonneux
pin[1] ['pɪn] *vt* **pinned; pinning 1** FASTEN : épingler **2** HOLD, IMMOBILIZE : fixer, immobiliser **3 to pin down** DEFINE, DETERMINE : définir, déterminer, cerner **4 to pin one's hopes on** : mettre tout son espoir dans
pin[2] *n* **1** : épingle *f* <safety pin : épingle de sûreté> **2** BROOCH : broche *f*, épinglette *f* *Can* **3** BADGE, INSIGNIA : insigne *m*, épinglette *f* **4** *or* **bowling pin** : quille *f*
pinafore ['pɪnəˌfor] *n* **1** APRON : tablier *m* **2** *or* **pinafore dress** : chasuble *f*
pincer ['pɪnʧər] *n* **1** : pince *f* (d'un homard) **2 pincers** *npl* : tenailles *fpl*, pinces *fpl*
pinch[1] ['pɪnʧ] *vt* **1** : pincer <to pinch oneself : se pincer> **2** STEAL : faucher *fam*, voler — *vi* : serrer, être étroit (se dit des chaussures)
pinch[2] *n* **1** SQUEEZE : pincement *m* **2** : pincée *f* <a pinch of salt : une pincée de sel> **3 in a pinch** : à la rigueur
pincushion ['pɪnˌkuʃən] *n* : pelote *f* (à épingles)
pine[1] ['paɪn] *vi* **pined; pining 1 to pine away** LANGUISH : languir **2 to pine for** : désirer ardemment
pine[2] *n* : pin *m*
pineapple ['paɪnˌæpəl] *n* : ananas *m*
pinecone ['paɪnˌko:n] *n* : pomme *f* de pin, cocotte *f* *Can*
pinion ['pɪnjən] *n* **1** : aileron *m* (d'un oiseau) **2** COGWHEEL : pignon *m*
pink[1] ['pɪŋk] *adj* : rose
pink[2] *n* **1** : œillet *m* (fleur) **2** : rose *m* (couleur) **3 to be in the pink** : être en pleine forme
pinkeye ['pɪŋkˌaɪ] *n* : conjonctivite *f*
pinkish ['pɪŋkɪʃ] *adj* : rosé
pinnacle ['pɪnɪkəl] *n* **1** : pinacle *m* (en architecture) **2** PEAK : sommet *m*, pic *m* **3** ACME : sommet *m*, comble *m* (d'une carrière, etc.)
pinpoint ['pɪnˌpɔɪnt] *vt* : indiquer, localiser avec précision
pint ['paɪnt] *n* : pinte *f*
pinto ['pɪnˌto:] *n, pl* **pintos** : cheval *m* pie
pinworm ['pɪnˌwərm] *n* : oxyure *m*
pioneer[1] [ˌpaɪə'nɪr] *vt* : être un innovateur de, mettre au point (des recherches, etc.)
pioneer[2] *n* : pionnier *m*, -nière *f*
pious ['paɪəs] *adj* : pieux, religieux
piously ['paɪəslɪ] *adv* : pieusement
pipe[1] ['paɪp] *v* **piped; piping** *vi* **1** : jouer de la cornemuse ou du pipeau **2** *or* **to pipe up** : se faire entendre, parler fort — *vt* *or* **to pipe in** : amener ou alimenter par tuyau (de l'eau, du pétrole, etc.)
pipe[2] *n* **1** FLUTE : pipeau *m* **2** BAGPIPE : cornemuse *f* **3** : tuyau *m*, conduit *m* (pour transporter un liquide, un gaz, etc.) **4** : pipe *f* (pour fumer du tabac) **5** : tuyau *m* (d'un orgue)
pipeline ['paɪpˌlaɪn] *n* **1** : pipeline *m* **2** CONDUIT : voie *f*, canal *m* <a pipeline for data : une voie de transmission pour les données>
piper ['paɪpər] *n* : joueur *m*, joueuse *f* (de cornemuse)
piping ['paɪpɪŋ] *n* **1** : musique *f* de cornemuse **2** TRIM : passepoil *m* (en couture)
piquancy ['pi:kənʧsi, 'pɪkwənʧsi] *n* SPICINESS : piquant *m*
piquant ['pi:kənt, 'pɪkwənt] *adj* : piquant
pique[1] ['pi:k] *vt* **piqued; piquing 1** IRRITATE : froisser, irriter **2** AROUSE : éveiller, susciter <to pique s.o.'s curiosity : éveiller la curiosité de qqn>
pique[2] *n* : ressentiment *m*, dépit *m*
piqué *or* **pique** [pɪ'keɪ, 'pi:ˌ-] *n* : piqué *m*

piracy ['paɪrəsi] *n, pl* **-cies 1** : piraterie *f* (sur un navire) **2** : piratage *m* <software piracy : piratage de logiciels>
piranha [pə'rɑnə, -'rɑnjə, -'rænjə] *n* : piranha *m*
pirate¹ ['paɪrət] *vt* **-rated; -rating** : pirater
pirate² *n* : pirate *m*
pirouette *n* : pirouette *f*
pis → pi
Pisces ['paɪˌsiːz] *n* : Poissons *mpl*
pistachio [pə'stæʃiˌoː, -'stɑ-] *n, pl* **-chios** : pistache *f* (noix)
pistil ['pɪstəl] *n* : pistil *m*
pistol ['pɪstəl] *n* : pistolet *m*
piston ['pɪstən] *n* : piston *m*
pit¹ ['pɪt] *vt* **pitted; pitting 1** : dénoyauter (un fruit) **2** RIDDLE : cribler <pitted by explosions : criblé par les explosions> **3** : marquer <a face pitted from smallpox : un visage marqué par la variole>
pit² *n* **1** HOLE : trou *m*, fosse *f* **2** MINE, SHAFT : mine *f*, puits *m* **3** : creux *m* (de l'estomac) **4** POCKMARK : marque *f* (sur la peau) **5** : noyau *m* (d'un fruit) **6** : fosse *f* <orchestra pit : fosse d'orchestre>
pitch¹ ['pɪtʃ] *vt* **1** ERECT : monter, dresser (une tente, etc.) **2** : jeter, fourcher <to pitch hay : fourcher du foin> **3** : lancer (une balle) **4** : donner le ton de (en musique) — *vi* **1** *or* **to pitch forward** : tomber **2** LURCH : tanguer (se dit d'un navire, etc.) **3** SLOPE : être incliné
pitch² *n* **1** THROWING : lancer *m*, lancement *m* **2** DEGREE, LEVEL : degré *m* (d'une pente), niveau *m* (d'enthousiasme, etc.) **3** TONE : ton *m* (en musique) **4** TAR : poix *f* **5** *or* **sales pitch** : boniment *m* de vente
pitcher ['pɪtʃər] *n* **1** JUG : cruche *f*, pichet *m* **2** : lanceur *m*, -ceuse *f*; artilleur *m Can* (au baseball)
pitchfork ['pɪtʃˌfɔrk] *n* : fourche *f*
pitfall ['pɪtˌfɔl] *n* : piège *m*, trappe *f*
pith ['pɪθ] *n* **1** : moelle *f* (d'une plante) **2** CORE : essence *f*, signification *f*
pithy ['pɪθi] *adj* **pithier; -est** : bref, incisif, concis
pitiable ['pɪtiəbəl] → **pitiful**
pitiful ['pɪtɪfəl] *adj* **1** : pitoyable <a pitiful cry : un cri pitoyable> **2** DEPLORABLE : lamentable, piteux <pitiful wages : salaires minables>
pitifully ['pɪtɪfli] *adv* : pitoyablement
pitiless ['pɪtɪləs] *adj* : impitoyable — **pitilessly** *adv*
pittance ['pɪtənts] *n* : somme *f* dérisoire
pituitary [pə'tuːəˌteri, -'tjuː-] *adj* : pituitaire
pity¹ ['pɪti] *vt* **pitied; pitying** : avoir pitié de
pity² *n, pl* **pities** : pitié *f* <to feel pity for : avoir pitié de> <what a pity! : quel dommage!>
pivot¹ ['pɪvət] *vi* : pivoter, tourner
pivot² *n* : pivot *m*
pivotal ['pɪvəṭəl] *adj* : crucial, essentiel
pixie *or* **pixy** ['pɪksi] *n, pl* **pixies** : lutin *m*
pizza ['piːtsə] *n* : pizza *f*
pizzazz *or* **pizazz** [pə'zæz] *n* : panache *m*
placard ['plækərd, -ˌkɑrd] *n* POSTER : affiche *f*, placard *m*
placate ['pleɪˌkeɪt, 'plæ-] *vt* **-cated; -cating** : apaiser, calmer
place¹ ['pleɪs] *v* **placed; placing** *vt* **1** PUT, SET : placer, mettre **2** APPOINT : placer (un employé) **3** RECOGNIZE : se rappeler de, remettre <I couldn't quite place her face : je n'arrivais pas à me rappeler d'elle> **4 to place an order** : passer une commande — *vi* RANK : se placer, se classer <he placed second : il est arrivé deuxième>
place² *n* **1** SPACE : place *f* <is this place taken? : cette place est-elle prise?> **2** LOCATION, SPOT : endroit *m*, lieu *m* **3** POSITION : place *f*, position *f* **4** RANK : place *f* <to take first place : prendre la première place> **5** SEAT : place *f*, siège *f* (au théâtre) **6** JOB : poste *m*, emploi *m* **7 in the first place** : tout d'abord **8 to take place** : avoir lieu
placebo [plə'siːˌboː] *n, pl* **-bos** : placebo *m*
placement ['pleɪsmənt] *n* : placement *m*
placenta [plə'sentə] *n, pl* **-tas** *or* **-tae** [-tiˌ, -ˌtaɪ] : placenta *m*
placid ['plæsəd] *adj* : placide, paisible — **placidly** *adv*
plagiarism ['pleɪdʒəˌrɪzəm] *n* : plagiat *m*
plagiarist ['pleɪdʒərɪst] *n* : plagiaire *mf*
plagiarize ['pleɪdʒəˌraɪz] *vt* **-rized; -rizing** : plagier
plague¹ ['pleɪg] *vt* **plagued; plaguing 1** AFFLICT : tourmenter **2** HARASS : harceler
plague² *n* **1** PESTILENCE : peste *f* **2** CALAMITY : fléau *m*, cataclysme *m*
plaid¹ ['plæd] *adj* : écossais
plaid² *n* : tissu *m* écossais
plain¹ ['pleɪn] *adj* **1** SIMPLE, UNADORNED : simple **2** CLEAR : clair, évident **3** FRANK : franc <plain speaking : le franc-parler> **4** HOMELY : sans attraits, ordinaire
plain² *n* : plaine *f*
plainly ['pleɪnli] *adv* **1** SIMPLY : simplement **2** CLEARLY : clairement, évidemment **3** FRANKLY : franchement
plaintiff ['pleɪntɪf] *n* : demandeur *m*, -deresse *f*; plaignant *m*, -nante *f*
plaintive ['pleɪntɪv] *adj* : plaintif — **plaintively** *adv*
plait¹ ['pleɪt, 'plæt] *vt* : natter, tresser
plait² *n* **1** PLEAT : pli *m* **2** BRAID : natte *f*, tresse *f*
plan¹ ['plæn] *v* **planned; planning** *vt* **1** : faire des plans pour, concevoir (un

édifice) **2** : organiser, planifier <to plan an outing : organiser une sortie> **3** INTEND : penser <I was planning to go : je pensais y aller> — *vi* : faire des projets

plan² *n* **1** DIAGRAM : plan *m*, dessin *m* **2** PROCEDURE : plan *m* <a plan of action : un plan d'action> **3** : régime *m*, plan *m* <pension plan : régime de retraite>

plane¹ ['pleɪn] *v* **planed; planing** *vt* : raboter, aplanir (une surface) — *vi* GLIDE : planer

plane² *adj* FLAT : plat

plane³ *n* **1** : rabot *m* (outil) **2** SURFACE : plan *m* <horizontal plane : plan horizontal> **3** LEVEL : plan *m* **4** → **airplane**

planet ['plænət] *n* : planète *f*

planetarium [ˌplænə'tɛriəm] *n, pl* **-iums** *or* **-ia** [-iə] : planétarium *m*

planetary ['plænəˌtɛri] *adj* : planétaire

plank ['plæŋk] *n* **1** : planche *f* (de bois) **2** : article *m* d'une plateforme électorale

plankton ['plæŋktən] *n* : plancton *m*

plant¹ ['plænt] *vt* **1** : planter (des graines, des fleurs, etc.) **2** AFFIX : planter, enfoncer

plant² *n* **1** : plante *f* <indoor plants : plantes d'intérieur> **2** FACTORY : usine *f* <an electric power plant : une centrale hydroélectrique> **3** EQUIPMENT : machinerie *f*, installations *fpl*

plantain ['plæntən] *n* : plantain *m* (arbre et fruit)

plantation [plæn'teɪʃən] *n* : plantation *f*

planter ['plæntər] *n* **1** : planteur *m*, -teuse *f* **2** : cache-pot *m* (pour des pots de fleurs)

plaque ['plæk] *n* **1** : plaque *f* <commemorative plaque : plaque commémorative> **2** : plaque *f* (dentaire)

plasma ['plæzmə] *n* : plasma *m*

plaster¹ ['plæstər] *vt* **1** : enduire (de plâtre) **2** COVER : couvrir <plastered with posters : couvert d'affiches>

plaster² *n* : plâtre *m*

plasterer ['plæstərər] *n* : plâtrier *m*

plastic¹ ['plæstɪk] *adj* **1** : de plastique, en plastique **2** FLEXIBLE : plastique, malléable

plastic² *n* : plastique *m*

plastic surgery *n* : chirurgie *f* plastique

plate¹ ['pleɪt] *vt* **plated; plating** : plaquer (avec un métal)

plate² *n* **1** SHEET : plaque *f* <steel plate : plaque d'acier> **2** DISH : assiette *f* **3** DENTURES : dentier *m* **4** ILLUSTRATION : planche *f* **5** *or* **license plate** : plaque *f* d'immatriculation

plateau [plæ'to:] *n, pl* **-teaus** *or* **-teaux** [-'to:z] : plateau *m*

platform ['plætˌfɔrm] *n* **1** STAGE : tribune *f*, estrade *f* **2** : quai *m* (d'un chemin de fer) **3** *or* **political platform** : plate-forme *f* (électorale)

plating ['pleɪtɪŋ] *n* : placage *m*

platinum ['plætənəm] *n* : platine *m*

platitude ['plætəˌtu:d, -ˌtju:d] *n* : platitude *f*, lieu *m* commun

platoon [plə'tu:n] *n* : section *f* (dans l'armée)

platter ['plætər] *n* : plateau *m* de service

platypus ['plætɪpəs, -ˌpʊs] *n* : ornithorynque *m*

plaudits ['plɔdəts] *npl* : applaudissements *mpl*

plausibility [ˌplɔzə'bɪləti] *n, pl* **-ties** : plausibilité *f*

plausible ['plɔzəbəl] *adj* : plausible, vraisemblable

plausibly ['plɔzəbli] *adv* : de façon convaincante, avec vraisemblance

play¹ ['pleɪ] *vi* **1** : s'amuser, jouer <come out to play : viens jouer> **2** : jouer (se dit d'un orchestre, etc.), se jouer (se dit d'une pièce de théâtre) **3** FIDDLE, TOY : jouer (avec qqch) **4 to play fair** : jouer franc jeu — *vt* **1** : jouer à (un jeu, un sport) **2** : jouer de (un instrument de musique) **3** PERFORM : jouer (une œuvre, un rôle) **4 to play a trick on** : jouer un tour à **5 to play up** EMPHASIZE : souligner, mettre en valeur

play² *n* **1** : jeu *m* (aux sports) **2** : jeu *m*, activité *f* <children at play : des enfants qui jouent> **3** : jeu *m* (de couleurs), mouvement *m* léger (du vent) **4** TURN : tour *m* <it's your play : c'est à ton tour> **5** : pièce *f* de théâtre

playacting ['pleɪˌæktɪŋ] *n* : comédie *f*, affectation *f*

player ['pleɪər] *n* : joueur *m*, joueuse *f*

playful ['pleɪfəl] *adj* : enjoué, gai

playfully ['pleɪfəli] *adv* : de façon enjouée

playfulness ['pleɪfəlnəs] *n* : enjouement *m*

playground ['pleɪˌgraʊnd] *n* : cour *f* de récréation

playhouse ['pleɪˌhaʊs] *n* **1** THEATER : théâtre *m* **2** : maison *f* de jeu pour les enfants

playing card *n* : carte *f* à jouer

playmate ['pleɪˌmeɪt] *n* : camarade *mf* de jeu

play-off ['pleɪˌɔf] *n* : finale *f* (de coupe), match *m* crucial

playpen ['pleɪˌpen] *n* : parc *m* (pour bébés)

plaything ['pleɪˌθɪŋ] *n* : jouet *m*

playwright ['pleɪˌraɪt] *n* : dramaturge *mf*, auteur *m* dramatique

plaza ['plæzə, 'plɑ-] *n* **1** : place *f* (publique) **2** *or* **shopping plaza** : centre *m* commercial

plea ['pli:] *n* **1** : défense *f* (en droit) **2** REQUEST : appel *m*, requête *f* <a plea for mercy : un appel à la clémence>

plead ['pliːd] *v* **pleaded** *or* **pled** ['pled]; **pleading** *vt* **1** : plaider (une cause) **2** (*used to introduce an excuse*) <I pleaded ignorance : j'ai prétendu que je ne savais rien> — *vi* **1** : plaider <to plead guilty : plaider coupable> **2** BEG : supplier, implorer
pleasant ['plezənt] *adj* : agréable, plaisant
pleasantly ['plezəntli] *adv* : agréablement, aimablement
pleasantness ['plezəntnəs] *n* : aimabilité *f*, agrément *m*
pleasantries ['plezəntriz] *npl* : plaisanteries *fpl*, civilités *fpl*
please[1] ['pliːz] *v* **pleased; pleasing** *vt* **1** GRATIFY : plaire à, faire plaisir à <to please everybody : faire plaisir à tout le monde> **2** SATISFY : contenter — *vi* **1** : plaire, faire plaisir <to be anxious to please : chercher à faire plaisir> **2** (*indicating choice*) <do as you please : fais comme il te plaît>
please[2] *adv* : s'il vous plaît, je vous en prie <please come in : rentrez, s'il vous plaît>
pleasing ['pliːzɪŋ] *adj* : agréable, plaisant — **pleasingly** *adv*
pleasurable ['pleʒərəbəl] *adj* : agréable, plaisant
pleasure ['pleʒər] *n* **1** DESIRE : gré *m*, guise *f* <at your pleasure : à votre guise> **2** ENJOYMENT : plaisir *m* **3** DELIGHT : plaisir *m*, bonheur *m* <it was a pleasure to see you again! : quel plaisir de vous revoir!>
pleat[1] ['pliːt] *vt* : plisser
pleat[2] *n* : pli *m*
plebeian [plɪ'biən] *adj* : plébéien
pledge[1] ['pledʒ] *vt* **pledged; pledging** **1** PAWN : mettre en gage **2** PROMISE : promettre
pledge[2] *n* **1** SECURITY : gage *m*, nantissement *m* **2** VOW : promesse *f* **3** TOKEN : gage *m* <a pledge of our love : un gage de notre amour>
plenteous ['plentiəs] → **plentiful**
plentiful ['plentɪfəl] *adj* : abondant — **plentifully** *adv*
plenty ['plenti] *n* **1** ABUNDANCE : abondance *f* **2** ~ **of** : beaucoup de <plenty of time : beaucoup de temps>
plethora ['pleθərə] *n* : pléthore *f*
pleurisy ['plʊrəsi] *n* : pleurésie *f*
pliable ['plaɪəbəl] *adj* : flexible, malléable
pliancy ['plaɪənt͡si] *n* : flexibilité *f*
pliant ['plaɪənt] → **pliable**
pliers ['plaɪərz] *npl* : pinces *fpl*
plight ['plaɪt] *n* : situation *f* difficile
plod ['plɑd] *vi* **plodded; plodding** **1** : marcher lourdement **2** DRUDGE : travailler laborieusement
plot[1] ['plɑt] *v* **plotted; plotting** *vt* : faire un plan de — *vi* CONSPIRE : comploter
plot[2] *n* **1** : lot *m*, parcelle *f* (de terre) **2** : plan *m* (d'un édifice) **3** : intrigue *f* (dans un livre, etc.) **4** CONSPIRACY : complot *m*, conspiration *f*
plotter ['plɑt̬ər] *n* : conspirateur *m*, -trice *f*; comploteur *m*, -teuse *f*
plover ['plə͡vər, 'ploːvər] *n, pl* **-ver** *or* **-vers** : pluvier *m*
plow[1] *or* **plough** ['plaʊ] *vt* **1** : labourer (la terre), creuser (un sillon) **2** : déneiger, déblayer <to plow the streets : déneiger les rues> — *vi* **1 to plow into** : percuter, heurter <the car plowed into the fence : la voiture a percuté la clôture> **2 to plow through** : avancer péniblement dans, éplucher <he plowed through a stack of letters : il a épluché une pile de lettres>
plow[2] *or* **plough** *n* : charrue *f*
plowshare ['plaʊ͡ʃer] *n* : soc *m* (de charrue)
ploy ['plɔɪ] *n* : manigance *f*, truc *m*
pluck[1] ['plʌk] *vt* **1** : cueillir <to pluck grapes : cueillir des raisins> **2** : plumer (un poulet), arracher (des plumes à) **3** : pincer les cordes de (un instrument de musique) **4 to pluck one's eyebrows** : s'épiler les sourcis
pluck[2] *n* COURAGE : courage *m*, audace *m*
plucky ['plʌki] *adj* **pluckier; -est** : courageux, fougueux
plug[1] ['plʌg] *v* **plugged; plugging** *vt* **1** BLOCK : boucher, obstruer **2** ADVERTISE : faire de la publicité pour **3 to plug in** : brancher <to plug in a lamp : brancher une lampe> — *vi or* **to plug away** : s'acharner
plug[2] *n* **1** STOPPER : bouchon *m*, tampon *m* **2** PUBLICITY : annonce *f* publicitaire **3** : fiche *f*, prise *f* (électrique) <telephone plug : prise téléphonique>
plum ['plʌm] *n* **1** : prune *f*, pruneau *m* *Can* (fruit) **2** PRIZE, REWARD : prix *m*, récompense *f*
plumage ['pluːmɪd͡ʒ] *n* : plumage *m*
plumb[1] ['plʌm] *vt* SOUND : sonder
plumb[2] *adv* **1** VERTICALLY : d'aplomb **2** ABSOLUTELY : complètement <plumb crazy : complètement cinglé>
plumb[3] *adj* : vertical, droit
plumber ['plʌmər] *n* : plombier *m*
plumbing ['plʌmɪŋ] *n* **1** : plomberie *f* (travail de plombier) **2** PIPES : tuyauterie *f*
plumb line *n* : fil *m* à plomb
plume ['pluːm] *n* **1** FEATHER : plume *f* **2** : plumet *m* (sur un chapeau)
plumed ['pluːmd] *adj* : aux plumes
plummet ['plʌmət] *vi* : descendre brusquement, tomber à pic (se dit d'un oiseau)
plump[1] ['plʌmp] *vi or* **to plump down** : s'affaler
plump[2] *adv* DIRECTLY : en plein, directement <he ran plump into the

wall : il a heurté le mur de plein fouet>

plump[3] *adj* : grassouillet, dodu

plumpness ['plʌmpnəs] *n* : embonpoint *m*, grosseur *f*

plunder[1] ['plʌndər] *vt* : piller

plunder[2] *n* : pillage *m*

plunderer ['plʌndərər] *n* : pillard *m*, -larde *f*

plunge[1] ['plʌndʒ] *v* **plunged; plunging** *vt* SUBMERGE : plonger, immerger — *vi* **1** DIVE : plonger **2** DESCEND : dévaler **3** RUSH : se précipiter, se lancer

plunge[2] *n* DIVE : plongeon *m*

plunger ['plʌndʒər] *n* : ventouse *f*

plural[1] ['plʊrəl] *adj* : pluriel

plural[2] *n* : pluriel *m*

plurality [plʊ'rælət̬i] *n, pl* **-ties** : pluralité *f*

pluralize ['plʊrə,laɪz] *vi* **-ized; -izing** : prendre le pluriel

plus[1] ['plʌs] *adj* : positif <a plus factor : un facteur positif>

plus[2] *n* **1** *or* **plus sign** : plus *m* **2** ADVANTAGE : plus *m*, avantage *m*

plus[3] *conj* AND : et

plus[4] *prep* : plus <six boys plus a girl : six garçons plus une fille> <4 plus 5 : 4 plus 5>

plush[1] ['plʌʃ] *adj* : luxueux, somptueux

plush[2] *n* : peluche *f*

plushy ['plʌʃi] *adj* **plushier; -est** : luxueux

Pluto ['pluːt̬oː] *n* : Pluton *f* (planète)

plutocracy [pluː'tɑkrəsi] *n, pl* **-cies** : ploutocratie *f*

plutonium [pluː'toːniəm] *n* : plutonium *m*

ply[1] ['plaɪ] *vt* **plied; plying 1** USE, WIELD : manier (un outil) **2** PRACTICE : pratiquer, exercer <to ply a trade : pratiquer un métier> **3 to ply s.o. with** : assaillir qqn de (questions, etc.)

ply[2] *n, pl* **plies 1** THICKNESS : épaisseur *f* **2** LAYER : pli *m* **3** STRAND : brin *m* (de laine)

plywood ['plaɪˌwʊd] *n* : contre-plaqué *m*

pneumatic [nʊ'mæt̬ɪk, njʊ-] *adj* : pneumatique

pneumonia [nʊ'moːnjə, njʊ-] *n* : pneumonie *f*

poach ['poːtʃ] *vt* **1** : pocher (des œufs) **2 to poach game** : braconner le gibier

poacher ['poːtʃər] *n* : braconnier *m*, -nière *f*

pock ['pɑk] *n* **1** PUSTULE : pustule *f* **2** → **pockmark**

pocket[1] ['pɑkət] *vt* **1** STEAL : empocher **2** : mettre dans sa poche <to pocket the change : mettre la monnaie dans sa poche>

pocket[2] *n* **1** : poche *f* (dans un vêtement) **2** : blouse *f* (au billard), poche *f* (marsupiale), poche *f* (d'or, d'eau, de gaz) **3** AREA : poche *f*, secteur *m* <pockets of unemployment : poches de chômage> **4** *or* **air pocket** : trou *m* d'air

pocketbook ['pɑkət̬bʊk] *n* **1** WALLET : portefeuille *m* **2** PURSE : sac *m* à main, sacoche *f* *Can* **3** INCOME : revenu *m*, ressources *fpl* financières

pocketknife ['pɑkət̬naɪf] *n* : canif *m*

pockmark ['pɑkˌmɑrk] *n* : cicatrice *f*

pod ['pɑd] *n* : cosse *f* <pea pod : cosse de pois>

podiatrist [pə'daɪət̬rɪst, po-] *n* : podologue *mf*

podiatry [pə'daɪət̬ri, po-] *n* : podologie *f*

podium ['poːdiəm] *n, pl* **-diums** *or* **-dia** [-iə] : podium *m*

poem ['poːəm] *n* : poème *m*

poet ['poːət] *n* : poète *mf*

poetic [poʊ'et̬ɪk,] *or* **poetical** [-ət̬ɪkəl] *adj* : poétique

poetry ['poːət̬ri] *n* : poésie *f*

pogrom ['poːgrəm, pə'grɑm, 'pɑgrəm] *n* : pogrom *m*

poignancy ['pɔɪnjənt̬si] *n, pl* **-cies** : caractère *m* poignant

poignant ['pɔɪnjənt] *adj* : poignant

poinsettia [pɔɪn'set̬iə, -'set̬ə] *n* : poinsettia *m*

point[1] ['pɔɪnt] *vt* **1** SHARPEN : aiguiser (un crayon, etc.) **2** AIM : pointer, montrer, braquer <to point one's finger at s.o. : montrer qqn du doigt> <to point a gun : braquer un fusil> **3** INDICATE : montrer, indiquer <to point the way : montrer la voie> **4 to point out** : signaler, remarquer — *vi* : tomber en arrêt (se dit d'un chien)

point[2] *n* **1** ITEM : point *m*, question *f* <the main points : les points principaux> **2** QUALITY : point *m*, force *f* <one of his strong points : un de ses points forts> **3** PURPOSE : utilité *f*, but *m* <there's no point in trying : il est inutile d'essayer> <what's the point? : où veux-tu en venir?> **4** PLACE : point *m*, endroit *m* <a distant point : un point distant> **5** MOMENT : moment *m*, instant *m* <at this point : à ce moment-là> **6** DEGREE, STAGE : point *m* <boiling point : point d'ébullition> **7** END, TIP : pointe *f* (d'un crayon, d'une épée) **8** VERGE : point *m* <at the point of death : au bord de la tombe> **9** HEADLAND : cap *m*, promontoire *m* **10** DOT, PERIOD : point *m* (signe de ponctuation) **11** : point *m* (aux sports) **12** → **decimal point**

point-blank[1] ['pɔɪnt'blæŋk] *adv* **1** : à bout portant <to shoot point-blank : tirer à bout portant> **2** ABSOLUTELY, BLUNTLY : catégoriquement

point-blank[2] *adj* **1** : à bout portant <point-blank shot : tir à bout portant> **2** BLUNT : catégorique <a point-blank refusal : un refus catégorique>

pointedly ['pɔɪnt̬ədli] *adv* : ostensiblement, de façon marquée

pointer ['pɔɪntər] *n* **1** ROD : baguette *f* **2** : chien *m* d'arrêt **3** TIP : conseil *m*, suggestion *f*
pointless ['pɔɪntləs] *adj* **1** SENSELESS : absurde **2** USELESS : inutile, futile <pointless attempts : tentatives inutiles>
point of view *n* : point *m* de vue
poise[1] ['pɔɪz] *vt* **poised; poising** BALANCE : tenir en équilibre
poise[2] *n* **1** EQUILIBRIUM : équilibre *m* **2** COMPOSURE : calme *m*, assurance *f*
poison[1] ['pɔɪzən] *vt* **1** : empoisonner <poisoned arrows : flèches empoisonnées> **2** CORRUPT : pervertir, corrompre <to poison s.o.'s mind : pervertir l'esprit de qqn>
poison[2] *n* : poison *m*
poison ivy *n* : sumac *m* vénéneux, herbe *f* à (la) puce *Can*
poisonous ['pɔɪzənəs] *adj* **1** : vénéneux (se dit d'une plante), vénimeux (se dit d'un serpent ou d'un insecte), toxique (se dit d'une émanation, d'une plante, etc.) **2** HARMFUL : destructeur, pernicieux
poke[1] ['poːk] *v* **poked; poking** *vt* **1** JAB : donner un coup de coude à (les côtes, etc.) **2** PROD : donner des petits coups à **3** THRUST : fourrer *fam*, passer <I poked my head out of the window : j'ai passé ma tête par la fenêtre> — *vi or* **to poke around** : fureter, fouiner *fam*
poke[2] *n* JAB : coup *m*
poker ['poːkər] *n* **1** : tisonnier *m* (pour le feu) **2** : poker *m* (jeu de cartes)
polar ['poːlər] *adj* : polaire
polar bear *n* : ours *m* polaire, ours *m* blanc
Polaris [poˈlæris, -ˈlɑr-] → **North Star**
polarize [ˈpoːləˌraɪz] *vt* **-ized; -izing** : polariser
pole ['poːl] *n* **1** ROD, STICK : perche *f* <a telephone pole : un poteau> <ski pole : bâton de ski> **2** : pôle *m* <the South Pole : le pôle Sud> **3** : pôle *m* (électrique)
Pole ['poːl] *n* : Polonais *m*, -naise *f*
polecat ['poːlˌkæt] *n, pl* **polecats** *or* **polecat 1** FERRET : putois *m* **2** SKUNK : mouffette *f*
polemical [pəˈlɛmɪkəl] *adj* : polémique
polemics [pəˈlɛmɪks] *ns & pl* : polémique *f*
police[1] [pəˈliːs] *vt* **-liced; -licing** : surveiller, maintenir l'ordre et la paix de
police[2] *ns & pl* **1** *or* **police force** : police *f*, gendarmerie *f* **2** POLICE OFFICERS : policiers *mpl*
policeman [pəˈliːsmən] *n, pl* **-men** [-mən, -ˌmɛn] : policier *m*
police officer *n* : policier *m*, agent *m* de police
policewoman [pəˈliːsˌwʊmən] *n, pl* **-women** [-ˌwɪmən] : femme *f* policier
policy [ˈpɑləsi] *n, pl* **-cies 1** : politique *f* <foreign policy : politique étrangère> **2** *or* **insurance policy** : police *f* d'assurance
policyholder [ˈpɑləsiˌhoːldər] *n* : assuré *m*, -rée *f*
polio [ˈpoːliˌoː] → **poliomyelitis**
poliomyelitis [ˌpoːliˌoːˌmaɪəˈlaɪtəs] *n* : poliomyélite *f*
polish[1] [ˈpɑlɪʃ] *vt* **1** : polir (une surface) **2** REFINE : parfaire, peaufiner
polish[2] *n* **1** LUSTER : poli *m*, éclat *m* **2** WAX : cire *f* (pour les meubles, etc.), cirage *m* (pour les chaussures) **3** REFINEMENT : perfection *f*, raffinement *m* **4 nail polish** : vernis *m* à ongles
Polish[1] [ˈpoːlɪʃ] *adj* : polonais
Polish[2] *n* : polonais *m* (langue)
polite [pəˈlaɪt] *adj* **politer; -est** : poli, courtois
politely [pəˈlaɪtli] *adv* : poliment
politeness [pəˈlaɪtnəs] *n* : politesse *f*
politic [ˈpɑləˌtɪk] *adj* : habile, diplomate
political [pəˈlɪtɪkəl] *adj* : politique — **politically** [-ˈtɪkli] *adv*
politician [ˌpɑləˈtɪʃən] *n* : politicien *m*, -cienne *f*
politics [ˈpɑləˌtɪks] *ns & pl* : politique *f*
polka [ˈpoːlkə, ˈpoːkə] *n* : polka *f*
polka dot *n* : pois *m*, picot *m Can*
poll[1] [ˈpoːl] *vt* **1** : obtenir, recueillir (des voix) **2** CANVASS : sonder — *vi* : voter
poll[2] *n* **1** SURVEY : sondage *m*, enquête *f* **2 polls** *npl* : urnes *fpl* <to go to the polls : aller aux urnes>
pollen [ˈpɑlən] *n* : pollen *m*
pollinate [ˈpɑləˌneɪt] *vt* **-nated; -nating** : polliniser
pollination [ˌpɑləˈneɪʃən] *n* : pollinisation *f*
pollster [ˈpoːlstər] *n* : sondeur *m*, -deuse *f*; enquêteur *m*, -teuse *f*
pollutant [pəˈluːtənt] *n* : polluant *m*
pollute [pəˈluːt] *vt* **-luted; -luting** : polluer
pollution [pəˈluːʃən] *n* : pollution *f*
pollywog *or* **polliwog** [ˈpɑliˌwɔg] *n* TADPOLE : têtard *m*
polo [ˈpoːˌloː] *n* : polo *m*
poltergeist [ˈpoːltərˌgaɪst] *n* : esprit *m* frappeur
polyester [ˈpɑliˌɛstər, ˌpɑliˈ-] *n* : polyester *m*
polygamist [pəˈlɪgəmɪst] *n* : polygame *mf*
polygamous [pəˈlɪgəməs] *adj* : polygame
polygamy [pəˈlɪgəmi] *n* : polygamie *f*
polygon [ˈpɑliˌgɑn] *n* : polygone *m*
polymer [ˈpɑləmər] *n* : polymère *m*
Polynesian[1] [ˌpɑləˈniːʒən, -ʃən] *adj* : polynésien
Polynesian[2] *n* **1** : Polynésien *m*, -sienne *f* **2** : polynésien *m* (langue)
polyp [ˈpɑləp] *n* : polype *m*
polytheism [ˈpɑliˌθiˌɪzəm] *n* : polythéisme *m*
polyunsaturated [ˌpɑliˌʌnˈsætʃəˌreɪtəd] *adj* : polyinsaturé

pomegranate [ˈpamə,grænət, ˈpam,græ-] *n* : grenade *f* (fruit)

pommel[1] [ˈpʌməl] *vt* → **pummel**

pommel[2] [ˈpʌməl, ˈpa-] *n* : pommeau *m* (sur une épée, d'une selle)

pomp [ˈpamp] *n* **1** SPLENDOR : pompe *f*, faste *m* **2** OSTENTATION : apparat *m*, ostentation *f*

pompous [ˈpampəs] *adj* : pompeux — **pompously** *adv*

poncho [ˈpan,ʃo:] *n, pl* **-chos** : poncho *m*

pond [ˈpand] *n* : étang *m*, mare *f*

ponder [ˈpandər] *vt* : évaluer, estimer — *vi* **to ponder over** : réfléchir à, méditer sur

ponderous [ˈpandərəs] *adj* : pesant, lourd

pontiff [ˈpantɪf] *n* : pontife *m*

pontifical [panˈtɪfɪkəl] *adj* : pontifical

pontificate [panˈtɪfə,keɪt] *vi* **-cated; -cating** : pontifier

pontoon [panˈtu:n] *n* : ponton *m*

pony [ˈpo:ni] *n, pl* **-nies** : poney *m*

ponytail [ˈpo:ni,teɪl] *n* : queue *f* de cheval

poodle [ˈpu:dəl] *n* : caniche *m*

pool[1] [ˈpu:l] *vt* : mettre en commun <to pool resources : mettre en commun des ressources>

pool[2] *n* **1** PUDDLE : flaque *f* (d'eau), mare *f* (de sang) **2** RESERVE : fonds *m* commun **3** BILLIARDS : billard *m* américain **4** *or* **swimming pool** : piscine *f*

poor [ˈpʊr, ˈpor] *adj* **1** : pauvre <poor people : gens pauvres> **2** : mauvais, piètre <a poor crop : une mauvaise récolte> <poor results : piètres résultats> <poor health : santé précaire> **3** BARREN : stérile, improductif <poor soil : terre stérile> **4** : pauvre <you poor thing! : pauvre de toi!> **5** UNFAVORABLE : défavorable

poorly [ˈpʊrli, ˈpor-] *adv* BADLY : mal

pop[1] [ˈpap] *v* **popped; popping** *vt* **1** BURST : faire éclater **2** PUT : mettre <he popped it into his mouth : il l'a mis dans sa bouche> — *vi* **1** BURST : éclater, exploser **2** *or* **to pop out** : sortir <his eyes were popping : les yeux lui sortaient de la tête> **3 to pop in** : faire une petite visite

pop[2] *adj* : pop <pop music : musique pop>

pop[3] *n* **1** : bruit *m* sec **2** SODA : boisson *f* gazeuse, liqueur *f Can*

popcorn [ˈpap,kɔrn] *n* : maïs *m* explosé, pop-corn *m*

pope [ˈpo:p] *n* : pape *m* <Pope Pius XII : le pape Pie XII>

poplar [ˈpaplər] *n* : peuplier *m*

poplin [ˈpaplɪn] *n* : popeline *f*

poppy [ˈpapi] *n, pl* **-pies** : coquelicot *m*

populace [ˈpapjələs] *n* **1** MASSES : masses *fpl*, peuple *m* **2** POPULATION : population *f*

popular [ˈpapjələr] *adj* **1** : populaire <popular government : gouvernement populaire> **2** PREVALENT, WIDESPREAD : répandu **3** : aimé, prisé, populaire <a popular destination : une destination prisée>

popularity [ˌpapjəˈlærəṭi] *n* : popularité *f*

popularize [ˈpapjələ,raɪz] *vt* **-ized; -izing** : populariser

popularly [ˈpapjələrli] *adv* : communément, généralement

populate [ˈpapjə,leɪt] *vt* **-lated; -lating** : peupler

population [ˌpapjəˈleɪʃən] *n* : population *f*

populous [ˈpapjələs] *adj* : populeux

porcelain [ˈporsələn] *n* : porcelaine *f*

porch [ˈport] *n* : véranda *f*, porche *m*, galerie *f Can*, perron *m Can*

porcupine [ˈpɔrkjə,paɪn] *n* : porc-épic *m*

pore[1] [ˈpor] *vi* **pored; poring** : lire attentivement, étudier de près

pore[2] *n* : pore *m* (de la peau)

pork [ˈpork] *n* : porc *m*

pornographic [ˌpɔrnəˈgræfɪk] *adj* : pornographique

pornography [pɔrˈnagrəfi] *n* : pornographie *f*

porous [ˈporəs] *adj* : poreux

porpoise [ˈpɔrpəs] *n* : marsouin *m*

porridge [ˈpɔrɪdʒ] *n* : porridge *m France*, gruau *m Can*

port[1] [ˈport] *adj* : portuaire

port[2] *n* **1** HARBOR : port *m*, ville *f* portuaire **2** ORIFICE : orifice *m* **3** PORTHOLE : hublot *m* **4** *or* **port side** : bâbord *m* (d'un navire) **5** *or* **port wine** : porto *m* **6** : port *m* (d'un ordinateur)

portable [ˈporṭəbəl] *adj* : portatif, portable <portable computer : ordinateur portable>

portal [ˈporṭəl] *n* : portail *m*

portend [pɔrˈtend] *vt* : présager, annoncer

portent [ˈpɔr,tent] *n* : présage *m*, prédiction *f*

portentous [pɔrˈtentəs] *adj* **1** : de mauvais augure **2** MARVELOUS : extraordinaire, prodigieux **3** GRAVE : grave, sérieux <portentous decisions : de graves décisions>

porter [ˈporṭər] *n* : porteur *m*, -teuse *f*

portfolio [portˈfo:li,o] *n, pl* **-lios 1** BRIEFCASE, FOLDER : porte-documents *m* **2** : dossier *m* (diplomatique) **3** *or* **investment portfolio** : portefeuille *m*

porthole [ˈport,ho:l] *n* : hublot *m*

portico [ˈporṭi,ko] *n, pl* **-coes** *or* **-cos** : portique *m*

portion[1] [ˈporʃən] *vt* : distribuer, diviser

portion[2] *n* PART, SHARE : portion *f*, part *m*

portly [ˈportli] *adj* **portlier; -est** : corpulent

portrait ['pɔrtrət, -ˌtreɪt] *n* : portrait *m*
portray [pɔr'treɪ] *vt* **1** DEPICT : représenter (par le dessin) **2** DESCRIBE : dépeindre (par la parole) **3** ENACT : jouer, interpréter (un rôle)
portrayal [pɔr'treɪəl] *n* **1** REPRESENTATION : représentation *f* **2** PORTRAIT : portrait *m*
Portuguese[1] ['pɔrtʃəˌgiːz, -ˌgiːs] *adj* : portugais
Portuguese[2] *n* **1** : Portugais *m*, -gaise *f* **2** : portugais *m* (langue)
pose[1] ['poːz] *v* **posed; posing** *vt* : poser (une question, etc.) — *vi* **1** : poser (se dit d'un modèle) **2 to pose as** : se faire passer pour
pose[2] *n* **1** : pose *f* <to strike a pose : adapter une pose> **2** PRETENSE : affectation *f*, faux-semblant *m*
posh ['pɑʃ] *adj* : chic, élégant
position[1] [pə'zɪʃən] *vt* : positionner
position[2] *n* **1** STANCE : position *f*, perspective *f* **2** LOCATION : position *f*, emplacement *m* **3** STATUS : position *f*, rang *m* **4** JOB : poste *m*
positive ['pɑzət̬ɪv] *adj* **1** DEFINITE : catégorique <a positive no : un non catégorique> **2** CONFIDENT : certain, convaincu **3** : positif (en grammaire, en mathématiques, en physique, etc.) **4** AFFIRMATIVE : positif
positively ['pɑzət̬ɪvli] *adv* **1** CERTAINLY : sans aucun doute, incontestablement **2** (*used for emphasis*) : réellement <positively surprised : réellement surpris>
possess [pə'zɛs] *vt* : posséder, détenir
possession [pə'zɛʃən] *n* **1** OWNERSHIP : possession *f* **2** PROPERTY : possession *f*, jouissance *f* (en droit) **3 possessions** *npl* BELONGINGS : biens *mpl*
possessive[1] [pə'zɛsɪv] *adj* **1** JEALOUS : possessif, jaloux **2** : possessif (en grammaire)
possessive[2] *n or* **possessive case** : possessif *m*
possessor [pə'zɛsər] *n* : possesseur *m*
possibility [ˌpɑsə'bɪləti] *n, pl* **-ties** : possibilité *f*
possible ['pɑsəbəl] *adj* : possible
possibly ['pɑsəbli] *adv* : peut-être, possiblement *Can*
possum ['pɑsəm] → **opossum**
post[1] ['poːst] *vt* **1** MAIL : poster (une lettre) **2** INFORM : tenir au courant, tenir informé <I'll keep you posted : je te tiendrai au courant> **3** STATION : poster <to post guards : poster des gardiens> **4** AFFIX : afficher, placarder
post[2] *n* **1** OFFICE, POSITION : poste *m* **2** POLE : poteau *m* **3** *Brit* → **mail**[2] **1, 2; postal service**
postage ['poːstɪdʒ] *n* : affranchissement *m*, tarifs *mpl* postaux
postal ['postəl] *adj* : postal
postal service *n* : courrier *m*, poste *f*
postcard ['poːstˌkɑrd] *n* : carte *f* postale
poster ['poːstər] *n* : poster *m*, affiche *f*
posterior[1] [pɑ'stɪriər, po-] *adj* : postérieur
posterior[2] *n* BUTTOCKS : postérieur *m fam*, derrière *m fam*
posterity [pɑ'stɛrət̬i] *n* : postérité *f*
postgraduate [ˌpoːst'grædʒʊət] *n* : étudiant *m*, -diante *f* de troisième cycle
posthaste ['poːst'heɪst] *adv* : en toute vitesse, en toute hâte
posthumous ['pɑstʃəməs] *adj* : posthume
posthumously ['pɑstʃəməsli] *adv* : après la mort
postman ['poːstmən, -ˌmæn] *n, pl* **-men** [-mən, -ˌmɛn] → **mailman**
postmark[1] ['poːstˌmɑrk] *vt* : oblitérer (un timbre)
postmark[2] *n* : cachet *m* de la poste
postmaster ['poːstˌmæstər] *n* : receveur *m* des Postes
postmortem [ˌpoːst'mɔrt̬əm] *n* : autopsie *f*
postnatal [ˌpoːst'neɪt̬əl] *adj* : postnatal
post office *n* : bureau *m* de poste
postoperative [ˌpoːst'ɑpərət̬ɪv, -ˌreɪ-] *adj* : postopératoire
postpaid [ˌpoːst'peɪd] *adj* : franco de port, port payé
postpone [ˌpoːst'poːn] *vt* **-poned; -poning** : reporter, remettre
postponement [ˌpoːst'poːnmənt] *n* : renvoi *m*, remise *f*
postscript ['poːstˌskrɪpt] *n* : post-scriptum *m*
postulate ['pɑstʃəˌleɪt] *vt* **-lated; -lating** : poser comme postulat
posture[1] ['pɑstʃər] *vi* **-tured; -turing** : poser, prendre des airs
posture[2] *n* : posture *f*
postwar [ˌpoːst'wɔr] *adj* : d'après-guerre
posy ['poːzi] *n, pl* **-sies 1** FLOWER : fleur *f* **2** BOUQUET : (petit) bouquet *m* de fleurs
pot[1] ['pɑt] *vt* **potted; potting** : empoter (une plante)
pot[2] *n* **1** POTFUL : pot *m* <a pot of soup : un pot de soupe> **2** *or* **cooking pot** : marmite *f*, casserole *f*
potable ['poːt̬əbəl] *adj* : potable
potash ['pɑtˌæʃ] *n* : potasse *f*
potassium [pə'tæsiəm] *n* : potassium *m*
potato [pə'teɪt̬o] *n, pl* **-toes** : pomme *f* de terre, patate *f fam*
potbellied ['pɑtˌbɛlɪd] *adj* : bedonnant
potbelly ['pɑtˌbɛli] *n, pl* **-lies** : bedaine *f*
potency ['poːtənsi] *n, pl* **-cies 1** POWER : puissance *f*, force *f* **2** EFFECTIVENESS : efficacité *f*
potent ['poːtənt] *adj* **1** POWERFUL : puissant **2** EFFECTIVE : efficace
potential[1] [pə'tɛnt̬ʃəl] *adj* : potentiel — **potentially** *adv*
potential[2] *n* : potentiel *m*
potful ['pɑtˌfʊl] *n* : pot *m*, contenu *m* d'un pot

pothole [ˈpɑtˌhoːl] *n* : nid-de-poule *m*
potion [ˈpoːʃən] *n* : potion *f*
potluck [ˈpɑtˌlʌk] *n or* **potluck supper** : souper *m* communautaire
potpourri [ˌpoːpuˈriː] *n* **1** : pot-pourri *m*, fleurs *fpl* séchées **2** COLLECTION : pot-pourri *m*, mélange *m*
potshot [ˈpɑtˌʃɑt] *n* **1** CRITICISM : commentaire *m* désobligeant **2 to take a potshot at** : tirer à vue sur
potter [ˈpɑtər] *n* : potier *m*, -tière *f*
pottery [ˈpɑtəri] *n, pl* **-teries** : poterie *f*
pouch [ˈpaʊtʃ] *n* **1** BAG : petit sac *m* **2** : poche *f* (des marsupiaux)
poultice [ˈpoːltəs] *n* : cataplasme *m*
poultry [ˈpoːltri] *n* : volaille *f*
pounce [ˈpaʊns] *vi* **pounced; pouncing 1** : sauter, bondir **2 to pounce upon** : attaquer, assaillir
pound¹ [ˈpaʊnd] *vt* **1** CRUSH : broyer, écraser **2** HAMMER : marteler **3** BEAT : battre, frapper <to pound one's chest : frapper la poitrine> **4 to pound the pavement** : battre le pavé — *vi* **1** BEAT : palpiter, battre <my heart was pounding : mon cœur battait la chamade> **2 to pound away at** : travailler avec acharnement à
pound² *n* **1** : livre *f* (unité de mesure) **2** : livre *f* sterling **3** SHELTER : fourrière *f* (pour des animaux)
pour [ˈpor] *vt* **1** : verser (des boissons) **2 to pour all one's energy into** : mettre toute son énergie dans — *vi* **1** FLOW : couler **2** RAIN : pleuvoir à verse
pout¹ [ˈpaʊt] *vi* : faire la moue
pout² *n* : moue *f*
poverty [ˈpɑvərti] *n* : pauvreté *f*
powder¹ [ˈpaʊdər] *vt* **1** : poudrer <to powder one's nose : se poudrer le nez> **2** CRUSH : pulvériser
powder² *n* : poudre *f*
powdery [ˈpaʊdəri] *adj* : poudreux
power¹ [ˈpaʊər] *vt* : faire fonctionner, faire marcher
power² *n* **1** AUTHORITY : pouvoir *m*, autorité *f* **2** ABILITY : capacité *f* **3** : puissance *f* <foreign power : puissance extérieure> **4** STRENGTH : force *f* (d'une personne), puissance *f* (d'une machine) **5** : énergie *f* (électrique)
powerful [ˈpaʊərfəl] *adj* : puissant, fort
powerfully [ˈpaʊərfəli] *adv* : puissamment, fortement
powerhouse [ˈpaʊərˌhaʊs] *n* : personne *f* très énergique
powerless [ˈpaʊərləs] *adj* : impuissant
powwow [ˈpaʊˌwaʊ] *n* : pow-wow *m* *Can*, assemblée *f* d'Amérindiens
pox [ˈpɑks] *n, pl* **pox** *or* **poxes 1 → chicken pox 2 → syphilis**
practicable [ˈpræktɪkəbəl] *adj* : praticable, réalisable
practical [ˈpræktɪkəl] *adj* : pratique
practically [ˈpræktɪkli] *adv* **1** : pratiquement, d'une façon pratique **2** ALMOST, NEARLY : presque, pratiquement
practice¹ *or* **practise** [ˈpræktəs] *v* **-ticed** *or* **-tised; -ticing** *or* **-tising** *vt* **1** : pratiquer (un sport, un métier) **2** CARRY OUT : pratiquer, mettre en application **3** OBSERVE : observer <to practice politeness : observer les règles de politesse> — *vi* : s'exercer, s'entraîner
practice² *n* **1** USE : pratique *f* <to put into practice : mettre en pratique> **2** CUSTOM, HABIT : coutume *f*, pratique *f* **3** : exercice *m* (d'une profession)
practitioner [prækˈtɪʃənər] *n* : praticien *m*, -cienne *f*
pragmatic [prægˈmæt̬ɪk] *adj* : pragmatique
pragmatism [ˈprægməˌtɪzəm] *n* : pragmatisme *m*
prairie [ˈprɛri] *n* : prairie *f*
praise¹ [ˈpreɪz] *vt* **praised; praising 1** COMMEND : louer, faire l'éloge de **2** GLORIFY : louer, glorifier
praise² *n* : louange *f*
praiseworthy [ˈpreɪzˌwərði] *adj* : louable, digne d'éloges
pram [ˈpræm] *n Brit* : voiture *f* d'enfant, landau *m France*
prance¹ [ˈprænʧ] *vt* **pranced; prancing** : caracoler (se dit d'un cheval), cabrioler (se dit d'une personne)
prance² *n* : cabriole *f*
prank [ˈpræŋk] *n* : farce *f*, tour *m*
prankster [ˈpræŋkstər] *n* : farceur *m*, -ceuse *f*
prattle¹ [ˈprætəl] *vi* **-tled; -tling** BABBLE : babiller, bavarder
prattle² *n* : bavardage *m*
prawn [ˈprɔn] *n* : crevette *f* (rose)
pray [ˈpreɪ] *vt* ENTREAT : supplier, implorer <pray be careful : je te prie de faire attention> — *vi* : prier (à Dieu)
prayer [ˈprɛr] *n* **1** : prière *f* <to say one's prayers : faire sa prière> <the Lord's Prayer : le Notre Père> <to kneel in prayer : prier à genoux> **2** WISH : désir *m*, souhait *m*
praying mantis → mantis
preach [ˈpriːʧ] *vt* **1** : prêcher <to preach the gospel : prêcher l'Évangile> **2** ADVOCATE : prêcher, prôner <to preach patience : prôner la patience> — *vi* : prêcher
preacher [ˈpriːʧər] *n* MINISTER : pasteur *m*
preamble [ˈpriːˌæmbəl] *n* : préambule *m*, introduction *f*
precarious [prɪˈkæriəs] *adj* : précaire — **precariously** *adv*
precariousness [prɪˈkæriəsnəs] *n* : précarité *f*
precaution [prɪˈkɔʃən] *n* : précaution *f*
precautionary [prɪˈkɔʃəˌnɛri] *adj* : de précaution, préventif
precede [prɪˈsiːd] *vt* **-ceded; -ceding** : précéder

precedence ['presədənts, pri'si:dənts] *n* **1** : préséance *f* <in order of precedence : par ordre de préséance> **2** PRIORITY : priorité *f* <to take precedence over : avoir la priorité sur>

precedent ['presədənt] *n* : précédent *m*

precept ['pri:,sɛpt] *n* : précepte *m*, principe *m*

precinct ['pri:,sɪŋkt] *n* **1** DISTRICT : arrondissement *m* (en France), circonscription *f* (au Canada) **2 precincts** *npl* : alentours *mpl*, environs *mpl*

precious ['prɛʃəs] *adj* **1** : précieux <precious stones : pierres précieuses> **2** CHERISHED, DEAR : cher **3** AFFECTED : affecté, forcé

precipice ['presəpəs] *n* : précipice *m*

precipitate[1] [pri'sɪpə,teɪt] *v* **-tated; -tating** *vt* **1** PROVOKE : provoquer **2** : condenser (un liquide) — *vi* : précipiter (en chimie)

precipitate[2] [pri'sɪpətət] *adj* **1** PRECIPITOUS : escarpé, à pic **2** RASH : précipité, prématuré

precipitate[3] [pri'sɪpətət, -,teɪt] *n* : précipité *m*

precipitation [pri,sɪpə'teɪʃən] *n* **1** HASTE : précipitation *f*, hâte *f* **2** : précipitations *fpl* (en météorologie)

precipitous [pri'sɪpəţəs] *adj* STEEP : à pic, abrupt

précis [preɪ'si:] *n, pl* **précis** [-'si:z] : précis *m*, résumé *m*

precise [pri'saɪs] *adj* : précis — **precisely** *adv*

preciseness [pri'saɪsnəs] *n* : précision *f*

precision [pri'sɪʒən] *n* : précision *f*

preclude [pri'klu:d] *vt* **-cluded; -cluding** : empêcher, prévenir

precocious [pri'ko:ʃəs] *adj* : précoce — **precociously** *adv*

precocity [pri'kɑsəţi] *n* : précocité *f*

preconceived [,pri:kən'si:vd] *adj* : préconçu

precondition [,pri:kən'dɪʃən] *n* : condition *f* préalable

precook [,pri:'kʊk] *vt* : précuire

precursor [pri'kərsər] *n* : précurseur *m*

predator ['prɛdəţər] *n* : prédateur *m*

predatory ['prɛdə,tori] *adj* : prédateur

predecessor ['prɛdə,sɛsər, 'pri:-] *n* : prédécesseur *m*

predestination [pri,dɛstə'neɪʃən] *n* : prédestination *f*

predestine [pri'dɛstən] *vt* **-tined; -tining** : prédestiner

predetermine [,pri:dɪ'tərmən] *vt* **-mined; -mining** : prédéterminer

predicament [pri'dɪkəmənt] *n* : situation *f* difficile

predicate[1] ['prɛdə,keɪt] *vt* **-cated; -cating 1** AFFIRM : affirmer, déclarer **2** BASE : fonder

predicate[2] ['prɛdɪkət] *n* : prédicat *m*

predict [pri'dɪkt] *vt* : prédire

predictability [pri,dɪktə'bɪləţi] *n* : prévisibilité *f*

predictable [pri'dɪktəbəl] *adj* : prévisible

predictably [pri'dɪktəbli] *adv* : comme prévu

prediction [pri'dɪkʃən] *n* : prédiction *f*

predilection [,prɛdəl'ɛkʃən, ,pri:-] *n* : prédilection *f*

predispose [,pri:dɪ'spo:z] *vt* : prédisposer

predisposition [,pri:,dɪspə'zɪʃən] *n* : prédisposition *f*

predominance [pri'dɑmənənts] *n* : prédominance *f*

predominant [pri'dɑmənənt] *adj* : prédominant

predominantly [pri'dɑmənəntli] *adv* MAINLY : principalement

predominate [pri'dɑmə,neɪt] *vt* **-nated; -nating** : prédominer

preeminence [pri'ɛmənənts] *n* : prééminence *f*

preeminent [pri'ɛmənənt] *adj* : prééminent

preeminently [pri'ɛmənəntli] *adv* : surtout, avant tout

preempt [pri'empt] *vt* **1** : préempter (un terrain) **2** APPROPRIATE : s'approprier, s'attribuer

preen ['pri:n] *vt* **1** : lisser (ses plumes) **2 to preen oneself** : se bichonner, se pomponner

prefabricated [,pri:'fæbrə,keɪţəd] *adj* : préfabriqué

preface[1] ['prɛfəs] *vt* **-aced; -acing** : préfacer (un livre), faire précéder (un discours, etc.)

preface[2] *n* : préface *f*

prefatory ['prɛfə,tori] *adj* : préliminaire

prefect ['pri,fɛkt] *n* : préfet *m*

prefer [pri'fər] *vt* **-ferred; -ferring 1** : préférer <he prefers sports to reading : il préfère les sports à la lecture> **2 to prefer charges** : porter plainte

preferable ['prɛfərəbəl] *adj* : préférable — **preferably** [-bli] *adv*

preference ['prɛfrənts, 'prɛfər-] *n* : préférence *f*, choix *m*

preferential [,prɛfə'rɛnʃəl] *adj* : préférentiel

prefigure [pri'fɪgjər] *vt* **-ured; -uring** : préfigurer, annoncer

prefix[1] ['pri:,fɪks, pri:'-] *vt* : préfixer (en linguistique)

prefix[2] ['pri:,fɪks] *n* : préfixe *m*

pregnancy ['prɛgnənţsi] *n, pl* **-cies** : grossesse *f*

pregnant ['prɛgnənt] *adj* **1** : enceinte, grosse **2** MEANINGFUL : profond, chargé de sens

preheat [,pri:'hi:ţ] *vt* : préchauffer

prehensile [pri'hɛnţəl, -'hɛn,saɪl] *adj* : préhensile

prehistoric [,pri:hɪs'ţɔrɪk] *or* **prehistorical** [-ɪkəl] *adj* : préhistorique

prejudge [,pri:'dʒʌdʒ] *vt* **-judged; -judging** : préjuger

prejudice[1] ['prɛdʒədəs] *vt* **-diced; -dicing 1** : porter préjudice à (en droit) **2 to be prejudiced against** : avoir des préjugés contre

prejudice[2] *n* **1** DAMAGES : préjudice *m*, dommage *m* **2** BIAS : préjugés *mpl*

prelate [ˈprɛlət] *n* : prélat *m*

preliminary[1] [prɪˈlɪməˌnɛri] *adj* : préliminaire

preliminary[2] *n, pl* **-naries** : préliminaire *m*

prelude [ˈprɛˌluːd, ˈprɛlˌjuːd; ˈpreɪˌluːd, ˈpriː-] *n* : prélude *m*

premarital [ˌpriːˈmærət̬əl] *adj* : avant le mariage, prénuptial

premature [ˌpriːməˈtʊr, -ˈtjʊr, -ˈtʃʊr] *adj* : prématuré — **prematurely** *adv*

premeditate [priˈmɛdəˌteɪt] *vt* **-tated; -tating** : préméditer

premeditation [priˌmɛdəˈteɪʃən] *n* : préméditation *f*

premenstrual [priˈmɛnt͡ʃstruəl] *adj* : prémenstruel

premier[1] [priˈmɪr, -ˈmjɪr; ˈpriːmiər] *adj* : premier

premier[2] → **prime minister**

premiere[1] [prɪˈmjɛr, -ˈmɪr] *vi* **-miered; -miering** : se donner en première

premiere[2] *n* : première *f* (d'un spectacle)

premise [ˈprɛmɪs] *n* **1** : prémisse *f* (d'un raisonnement) **2 premises** *npl* : lieux *mpl* <on the premises : sur les lieux>

premium [ˈpriːmiəm] *n* **1** BONUS : prime *f*, supplément *m* **2** *or* **insurance premium** : prime *f* d'assurance **3 to put a premium on** : mettre au premier plan **4 to sell at a premium** : vendre au-dessus du pair

premonition [ˌpriːməˈnɪʃən, ˌprɛmə-] *n* : prémonition *f*, pressentiment *m*

prenatal [ˌpriːˈneɪt̬əl] *adj* : prénatal

preoccupation [priˌɑkjəˈpeɪʃən] *n* : préoccupation *f*

preoccupied [priˈɑkjəˌpaɪd] *adj* : préoccupé, distrait

preoccupy [priˈɑkjəˌpaɪ] *vt* **-pied; -pying** : préoccuper

preparation [ˌprɛpəˈreɪʃən] *n* **1** PREPARING : préparation *f* <the preparation of meals : la préparation des repas> **2 preparations** *npl* : préparatifs *mpl*

preparatory [priˈpærəˌtori] *adj* : préparatoire

prepare [prɪˈpær] *v* **-pared; -paring** *vt* : préparer — *vi* : se préparer

prepay [ˌpriːˈpeɪ] *vt* **-paid; -paying** : payer d'avance

preponderance [prɪˈpɑndərən̪t͡s] *n* : prépondérance *f*

preponderant [prɪˈpɑndərən̪t] *adj* : prépondérant

preponderantly [prɪˈpɑndərən̪tli] *adv* : de façon prépondérante

preposition [ˌprɛpəˈzɪʃən] *n* : préposition *f*

prepositional [ˌprɛpəˈzɪʃən̪əl] *adj* : prépositionnel

prepossessing [ˌpriːpəˈzɛsɪŋ] *adj* : attrayant, avenant

preposterous [priˈpɑstərəs] *adj* : absurde, insensé

prerecorded [priːrɪˈkɔrdəd] *adj* : en différé

prerequisite[1] [priˈrɛkwəzət] *adj* : nécessaire au préalable

prerequisite[2] *n* : préalable *m*, prérequis *m Can*

prerogative [prɪˈrɑgət̬ɪv] *n* : prérogative *f*

presage[1] [ˈprɛsɪd͡ʒ, prɪˈseɪd͡ʒ] *vt* **-saged; -saging** : présager

presage[2] [ˈprɛsɪd͡ʒ] *n* : présage *m*

preschool [ˈpriːˌskuːl] *adj* : préscolaire

prescribe [priˈskraɪb] *vt* **-scribed; -scribing 1** RECOMMEND : préconiser, recommander **2** : prescrire (en médecine)

prescription [priˈskrɪpʃən] *n* : prescription *f*

presence [ˈprɛzən̪t͡s] *n* : présence *f*

present[1] [prɪˈzɛnt] *vt* **1** INTRODUCE : présenter **2** SHOW : présenter, donner, montrer <to present a play : présenter une pièce> **3** GIVE : offrir, présenter <the winner was presented with a medal : on a présenté une médaille au gagnant>

present[2] [ˈprɛzən̪t] *adj* **1** CURRENT : actuel <present conditions : conditions actuelles> **2** ATTENDING : présent

present[3] [ˈprɛzən̪t] *n* **1** GIFT : cadeau *m* **2** *or* **present time** : présent *m* <at present : actuellement>

presentation [ˌprizˌzɛnˈteɪʃən, ˌprɛzən-] *n* : présentation *f*

presentiment [prɪˈzɛnt̬əmən̪t] *n* : pressentiment *m*, prémonition *f*

presently [ˈprɛzən̪tli] *adv* **1** SOON : bientôt **2** NOW : à présent, en ce moment

present participle *n* : participe *m* présent

preservation [ˌprɛzərˈveɪʃən] *n* : préservation *f*, maintien *m*

preservative [priˈzərvət̬ɪv] *n* : agent *m* de conservation

preserve[1] [priˈzərv] *vt* **-served; -serving 1** PROTECT : préserver, protéger **2** MAINTAIN : garder, conserver <to preserve silence : garder le silence>

preserve[2] *n* **1** : chasse *f* réservée, réserve *f* <game preserve : chasse gardée> **2 preserves** *npl* : confitures *fpl*

preside [priˈzaɪd] *vi* **-sided; -siding 1 to preside over** : présider <to preside over a meeting : présider une réunion> **2 to preside over** OVERSEE : présider à

presidency [ˈprɛzədən̪t͡si] *n, pl* **-cies** : présidence *f*

president [ˈprɛzədən̪t] *n* : président *m*

presidential [ˌprɛzəˈdɛn̪t͡ʃəl] *adj* : présidentiel

press[1] [ˈprɛs] *vt* **1** PUSH : presser, appuyer sur **2** IRON : repasser **3** SQUEEZE : presser **4** URGE : presser, inciter — *vi* **1** PUSH : appuyer (sur un bouton, etc.) **2** CROWD : se presser **3 to press through** : se frayer un chemin dans

press[2] *n* **1** CROWD : foule *f* **2** *or* **printing press** : presse *f* <to go to press : mettre sous presse> **3** URGENCY : urgence *f* **4** : presse *f* <the story is getting good press : l'article a bonne presse> **5** PUBLISHER : maison *f* d'édition, presses *fpl* **6** PRINTER : imprimerie *f*

pressing [ˈprɛsɪŋ] *adj* : pressant, urgent

pressure[1] [ˈprɛʃər] *vt* **-sured; -suring** : pousser, faire pression sur

pressure[2] *n* **1** : pression *f* <to be under pressure : être sous pression> **2** → **blood pressure**

pressurize [ˈprɛʃəˌraɪz] *vt* **-ized; -izing** : pressuriser

prestidigitation [ˌprɛstəˌdɪdʒəˈteɪʃən] *n* SLEIGHT OF HAND : prestidigitation *f*

prestige [preˈstiːʒ, -ˈstiːdʒ] *n* : prestige *m*

prestigious [preˈstɪdʒəs, -ˈsti-, prə-] *adj* : prestigieux

presto [ˈprɛsˌtoː] *adv & interj* : presto!, tout de suite

presumably [priˈzuːməbli] adv : vraisemblablement, apparemment, présumément *Can*

presume [priˈzuːm] *vt* **-sumed; -suming** **1** DARE : se permettre <he presumed to contradict him : il s'est permis de le contredire> **2** ASSUME : présumer, supposer <to be presumed innocent : être présumé innocent> **3** IMPLY : présupposer, laisser supposer

presumption [priˈzʌmpʃən] *n* **1** EFFRONTERY : présomption *f*, arrogance *f* **2** ASSUMPTION : présomption *f*, supposition *f*

presumptuous [priˈzʌmptʃʊəs] *adj* : présomptueux, prétentieux

presuppose [ˌpriːsəˈpoːz] *vt* **-posed; -posing** : présupposer

presupposition [ˌpriːˌsəpəˈzɪʃən] *n* : présupposition *f*

pretend [priˈtɛnd] *vt* **1** PROFESS : prétendre <he doesn't pretend to be a psychiatrist : il ne prétend pas être psychiatre> **2** FEIGN : feindre, simuler <to pretend friendship : feindre l'amitié> — *vi* : faire semblant

pretense *or* **pretence** [ˈpriːˌtɛnts, priˈtɛnts] *n* **1** CLAIM : prétention *f* **2** : semblant *m*, simulacre *m* <to make a pretense of : faire semblant de> **3** SIMULATION : faux-semblant *m*

pretension [priˈtɛnʃən] *n* **1** CLAIM : prétention *f*, revendication *f* **2** PRETENTIOUSNESS : prétention *f* **3** ASPIRATION : ambition *f*, aspiration *f*

pretentious [priˈtɛntʃəs] *adj* : prétentieux — **pretentiously** *adv*

pretentiousness [priˈtɛntʃəsnəs] *n* : prétention *f*

pretext [ˈpriːˌtɛkst] *n* : prétexte *m*, excuse *f*

prettily [ˈprɪtəli] *adv* : joliment

prettiness [ˈprɪtɪnəs] *n* : beauté *f*

pretty[1] [ˈprɪti] *vt* **-tied; -tying** *or* **to pretty up** : enjoliver

pretty[2] *adv* FAIRLY : assez

pretty[3] *adj* **prettier; -est** : joli, beau <pretty flowers : de jolies fleurs> <it's not a pretty sight : ce n'est pas beau à voir>

pretzel [ˈprɛtsəl] *n* : bretzel *m*

prevail [priˈveɪl] *vi* **1** TRIUMPH : prévaloir, l'emporter **2** PREDOMINATE : prévaloir, prédominer **3 to prevail upon** : persuader

prevalence [ˈprɛvələnts] *n* : fréquence *f*, prédominance *f*, prévalence *f* (d'une maladie)

prevalent [ˈprɛvələnt] *adj* : répandu, commun

prevaricate [priˈværəˌkeɪt] *vi* **-cated; -cating** : tergiverser, user de détours

prevarication [priˌværəˈkeɪʃən] *n* : tergiversation *f*, faux-fuyant *m*

prevent [priˈvɛnt] *vt* **1** AVOID : prévenir, éviter **2** STOP : empêcher <bad weather prevented us from leaving : le mauvais temps nous a empêchés de partir>

preventable [priˈvɛntəbəl] *adj* : évitable

preventative [priˈvɛntəˌtɪv] → **preventive**

prevention [priˈvɛnʃən] *n* : prévention *f*

preventive [priˈvɛntɪv] *adj* : préventif

preview [ˈpriːˌvjuː] *n* : avant-première *f*

previous [ˈpriːviəs] *adj* : antérieur, précédent, initial <his previous position : sa position initiale> <a previous era : une époque antérieure> <the previous paragraph : le paragraphe précédent>

previously [ˈpriːviəsli] *adv* : antérieurement, auparavant

prewar [ˌpriːˈwɔr] *adj* : d'avant-guerre

prey[1] [preɪ] *vi* **1 to prey on** : faire sa proie de **2 to prey on s.o.'s mind** : ronger l'esprit à qqn

prey[2] *ns & pl* : proie *f*

price[1] [praɪs] *vt* **priced; pricing** : fixer un prix sur

price[2] *n* : prix *m*

priceless [ˈpraɪsləs] *adj* : inestimable

prick[1] [prɪk] *vt* **1** PIERCE : piquer, percer **2** GOAD : aiguillonner, piquer <guilt was pricking (at) his conscience : les remords aiguillonnaient sa conscience> **3 to prick up one's ears** : dresser l'oreille

prick[2] *n* : piqûre *f*

pricker [ˈprɪkər] *n* THORN : épine *f*

prickle[1] [ˈprɪkəl] *vt* **-led; -ling** : picoter

prickle[2] *n* **1** THORN : épine *f* (d'un rosier, etc.) **2** STING : picotement *m*

prickly [ˈprɪkəli] *adj* **pricklier; -est** **1** STINGING : épineux, piquant <a prickly sensation : une sensation de

picotement> **2** THORNY : épineux <prickly issues : questions épineuses>

pride[1] ['praɪd] *vt* **prided; priding** *or* **to pride oneself** : être fier

pride[2] *n* : fierté *f*, orgueil *m*

prideful ['praɪdfəl] *adj* : hautain, arrogant

priest ['pri:st] *n* : prêtre *m*

priestess ['pri:stɪs] *n* : prêtresse *f*

priesthood ['pri:st,hʊd] *n* : prêtrise *f*

priestly ['pri:stli] *adj* : sacerdotal

prim ['prɪm] *adj* **primmer; primmest** : collet monté, guindé

primarily [praɪ'merəli] *adv* **1** ORIGINALLY : d'abord, à l'origine **2** PRINCIPALLY : essentiellement, principalement

primary[1] ['praɪ,meri, 'praɪməri] *adj* **1** FIRST : primaire <primary education : enseignement primaire> **2** PRINCIPAL : principal **3** BASIC : fondamental, de base

primary[2] *n, pl* **-ries** : élection *f* primaire

primary school → **elementary school**

primate ['praɪ,meɪt, -mət] *n* : primate *m*

prime[1] ['praɪm] *vt* **primed; priming 1** FILL, LOAD : remplir, charger **2** PREPARE : apprêter (une surface, un mur) **3** COACH : préparer <to prime a witness : préparer un témoin>

prime[2] *adj* : de première qualité, de premier choix

prime[3] *n* **in the prime of one's life** : dans la force de l'âge

prime minister *n* : Premier ministre *m*

primer[1] ['prɪmər] *n* : premier livre *m* de lecture, abécédaire *m*

primer[2] ['praɪmər] *n* **1** : amorce *f* (d'un explosif) **2** *or* **prime coat** : apprêt *m*

primeval [praɪ'mi:vəl] *adj* : primitif

primitive ['prɪmətɪv] *adj* : primitif

primly ['prɪmli] *adv* : d'une façon guindée

primness ['prɪmnəs] *n* : air *m* collet monté

primordial [praɪ'mɔrdiəl] *adj* : primordial

primp ['prɪmp] *vt* : se pomponner, se bichonner

primrose ['prɪm,ro:z] *n* : primevère *f*

prince ['prɪnts] *n* : prince *m*

princely ['prɪntsli] *adj* : princier

princess ['prɪntsəs, 'prɪn,ses] *n* : princesse *f*

principal[1] ['prɪntsəpəl] *adj* : principal — **principally** *adv*

principal[2] *n* **1** : directeur *m*, -trice *f* <school principal : directeur d'école> **2** : principal *m* (d'une dette), capital *m* (d'une somme)

principality [,prɪntsə'pælətʲi] *n, pl* **-ties** : principauté *f*

principle ['prɪntsəpəl] *n* : principe *m*

print[1] ['prɪnt] *vt* : imprimer (un texte, etc.) — *vi* : écrire en lettres moulées

print[2] *n* **1** IMPRESSION, MARK : empreinte *f* **2** LETTER : caractère *m* <in fine print : en petits caractères> **3** ENGRAVING : gravure *f* **4** : imprimé *m* (d'un tissu) **5** : épreuve *f* (en photographie) **6 in ~** : disponible

printer ['prɪntər] *n* **1** : imprimeur *m* (personne) **2** : imprimante *f* (machine) <laser printer : imprimante laser>

printing ['prɪntɪŋ] *n* **1** : imprimerie *f* (technique) **2** IMPRESSION : impression *f* <the second printing : le second tirage> **3** LETTERING : écriture *f* en lettres moulées

printout ['prɪnt,aʊt] *n* : sortie *f* sur imprimante

print out *vt* : faire une sortie sur imprimante

prior ['praɪər] *adj* **1** PREVIOUS : antérieur, précédent **2** : qui prévaut, prioritaire <a prior claim : un droit de priorité>

priority [praɪ'ɔrəʲti] *n, pl* **-ties** : priorité *f*

priory ['praɪəri] *n, pl* **-ries** : prieuré *m*

prism ['prɪzəm] *n* : prisme *m*

prison ['prɪzən] *n* : prison *f*

prisoner ['prɪzənər] *n* : prisonnier *m*, -nière *f*

prissy ['prɪsi] *adj* **prissier; -est** : collet monté

pristine ['prɪsti:n, prɪs'-] *adj* : pur, immaculé

privacy ['praɪvəsi] *n, pl* **-cies 1** SECLUSION, SOLITUDE : intimité *f*, solitude *f* **2** : vie *f* privée <the right to privacy : le droit à la vie privée>

private[1] ['praɪvət] *adj* **1** : privé <private property : propriété privée> **2** PERSONAL : personnel, privé

private[2] *n* : soldat *m* de deuxième classe

privateer [,praɪvə'tɪr] *n* : corsaire *m*

privately ['praɪvətli] *adv* **1** SECRETLY : en privé **2 privately owned** : privé

privation [praɪ'veɪʃən] *n* : privation *f*

privilege ['prɪvlɪʤ, 'prɪvə-] *n* : privilège *m*

privileged ['prɪvlɪʤd, 'prɪvə-] *adj* : privilégié

privy ['prɪvi] *adj* **to be privy to** : être au courant de

prize[1] ['praɪz] *vt* **prized; prizing** : priser, chérir

prize[2] *adj* **1** PRIZEWINNING : primé **2** OUTSTANDING : remarquable, exceptionnel

prize[3] *n* : prix *m*

prizefight ['praɪz,faɪt] *n* : combat *m* de boxe

prizefighter ['praɪz,faɪʲtər] *n* : boxeur *m* professionnel

prizefighting ['praɪz,faɪʲtɪŋ] *n* : boxe *f* professionnelle

prizewinner ['praɪz,wɪnər] *n* : gagnant *m*, -gnante *f*

prizewinning ['praɪzˌwɪnɪŋ] *adj* : primé, qui remporte le prix
pro¹ ['pro:] *adv* **to argue pro** : argumenter en faveur
pro² *adj* → **professional**
pro³ *n* **1** → **professional 2 the pros and cons** : le pour et le contre
probability [ˌprɑbə'bɪləṭi] *n, pl* **-ties** : probabilité *f*
probable ['prɑbəbəl] *adj* : probable — **probably** [-bli] *adv*
probate¹ ['pro:ˌbeɪt] *vt* **-bated; -bating** : homologuer (un testament)
probate² *n* : homologation *f*
probation [pro'beɪʃən] *n* **1** *or* **probation period** : mise *f* à l'essai, probation *f* **2 on ~** : en sursis avec mise à l'épreuve (en droit)
probationary [pro'beɪʃəˌnɛri] *adj* **1** : d'essai <probationary period : période d'essai> **2** : de sursis, de probation (en droit)
probe¹ ['pro:b] *vt* **probed; probing 1** EXAMINE : sonder **2** INVESTIGATE : enquêter sur
probe² *n* **1** : sonde *f* (en médecine) **2** INVESTIGATION : enquête *f*, investigation *f*
probity ['pro:bəṭi] *n* : probité *f*
problem¹ ['prɑbləm] *adj* : difficile <a problem child : un enfant difficile>
problem² *n* : problème *m*
problematic [ˌprɑblə'mæṭɪk] *or* **problematical** [-ṭɪkəl] *adj* : problématique
proboscis [prə'bɑsɪs] *n, pl* **-cises** : trompe *f*
procedural [prə'si:dʒərəl] *adj* : de procédure
procedure [prə'si:dʒər] *n* : procédure *f*
proceed [pro'si:d] *vi* **1** ADVANCE : avancer, aller **2** ACT : procéder **3** CONTINUE : continuer, poursuivre **4 to proceed from** : provenir de
proceeding [pro'si:dɪŋ] *n* **1** : procédure *f* <a divorce proceeding : une procédure de divorce> **2** *or* **legal proceeding** : poursuite *f* judiciaire
proceeds ['pro:ˌsi:dz] *npl* : recette *f*, argent *m* recueilli
process¹ ['prɑˌsɛs, 'pro:-] *vt* **1** : traiter <to process one's request : traiter sa demande> **2** : traiter, transformer <processed cheese : fromage en tranches>
process² *n, pl* **-cesses** ['prɑˌsɛsəz, 'pro:-, -səsəz, -səˌsi:z] **1** : processus *m* <the process of growth : le processus de croissance> **2** METHOD : procédé *m* <a manufacturing process : un procédé de fabrication> **3** : procès *m* (en droit) **4** SUMMONS : citation *f* **5** PROJECTION : excroissance *f* (en biologie) **6 in the process of** : en train de
procession [prə'sɛʃən] *n* : procession *f*
processional [prə'sɛʃənəl] *n* : musique *f* processionnelle
processor ['prɑˌsɛsər, 'pro:-, -səsər] *n* : processeur *m* (en informatique)
proclaim [pro'kleɪm] *vt* : proclamer
proclamation [ˌprɑklə'meɪʃən] *n* : proclamation *f*
proclivity [pro'klɪvəṭi] *n, pl* **-ties** : propension *f*, tendance *f*, inclination *f*
procrastinate [prə'kræstəˌneɪt] *vi* **-nated; -nating** : remettre à plus tard, remettre au lendemain
procrastination [prəˌkræstə'neɪʃən] *n* : tendance *f* à tout remettre à plus tard
procreate ['pro:kriˌeɪt] *v* **-ated; -ating** *vt* : procréer — *vi* REPRODUCE : se reproduire
procreation [ˌpro:kri'eɪʃən] *n* : procréation *f*
proctor¹ ['prɑktər] *vt* : surveiller (un examen)
proctor² *n* : surveillant *m*, -lante *f* (à un examen)
procurable [prə'kjʊrəbəl] *adj* : que l'on peut se procurer
procure [prə'kjʊr] *vt* **-cured; -curing** : obtenir, se procurer
procurement [prə'kjʊrmənt] *n* : achat *m*, acquisition *f*
prod¹ ['prɑd] *vt* **prodded; prodding 1** POKE : pousser doucement, donner des petits coups à **2** GOAD, URGE : inciter
prod² *n* **1** POKE : petit coup *m*, poussée *f* **2** GOAD : aiguillon *m* <cattle prod : aiguillon pour le bétail>
prodigal¹ ['prɑdɪgəl] *adj* : prodigue
prodigal² *n* : prodigue *mf*
prodigality [ˌprɑdə'gæləṭi] *n* : prodigalité *f*
prodigious [prə'dɪdʒəs] *adj* **1** EXTRAORDINARY : prodigieux, extraordinaire **2** HUGE : énorme, monstre — **prodigiously** *adv*
prodigy ['prɑdədʒi] *n, pl* **-gies** : prodige *m*
produce¹ [prə'du:s, -'dju:s] *vt* **-duced; -ducing 1** : donner naissance à, engendrer (un enfant), produire (une œuvre), causer (un problème, etc.) **2** MAKE, MANUFACTURE : faire, produire, fabriquer **3** YIELD : produire, rapporter **4** EXHIBIT : présenter <to produce evidence : fournir des preuves> **5** STAGE : présenter, mettre en scène
produce² ['prɑˌdu:s, 'pro:-, -ˌdju:s] *n* : produits *mpl* agricoles
producer [prə'du:sər, -'dju:-] *n* : producteur *m*, -trice *f*
product ['prɑˌdʌkt] *n* : produit *m*
production [prə'dʌkʃən] *n* : production *f*
productive [prə'dʌktɪv] *adj* : productif
productivity [ˌpro:ˌdʌk'tɪvəṭi, ˌprɑ-] *n* : productivité *f*
profane¹ [pro'feɪn] *vt* **-faned; -faning** : profaner

profane[2] *adj* **1** SECULAR : profane **2** IRREVERENT : sacrilège, blasphématoire
profanity [prɔˈfænəṭi] *n, pl* **-ties 1** IRREVERENCE : impiété *f* **2** BLASPHEMY : blasphème *m*, juron *m*
profess [prəˈfɛs] *vt* **1** DECLARE : professer, affirmer **2** : professer (sa foi)
professedly [prəˈfɛsəd.li] *adv* **1** AVOWEDLY : de son propre aveu **2** ALLEGEDLY, SUPPOSEDLY : soi-disant, prétendument
profession [prəˈfɛʃən] *n* **1** DECLARATION : profession *f* (de foi, etc.) **2** OCCUPATION : profession *f*, occupation *f*
professional[1] [prəˈfɛʃənəl] *adj* : professionnel **— professionally** *adv*
professional[2] *n* : professionnel *m*, -nelle *f*
professionalism [prəˈfɛʃəna.lɪzəm] *n* : professionnalisme *m*
professor [prəˈfɛsər] *n* : professeur *m* (de faculté)
proffer [ˈprɑfər] *vt* **-fered; -fering** : tendre, offrir
proficiency [prəˈfɪʃənʃsi] *n, pl* **-cies** : compétence *f*, capacité *f*
proficient [prəˈfɪʃənt] *adj* : compétent, capable **— proficiently** *adv*
profile[1] [ˈpro.ˌfaɪl] *vt* **-filed; -filing** : profiler
profile[2] *n* : profil *m*
profit[1] [ˈprɑfət] *vi* **to profit from** : tirer profit de **—** *vt* BENEFIT : profiter à
profit[2] *n* **1** GAIN : profit *m*, bénéfice *m* <to make a profit : faire un bénéfice> <profit and loss : pertes et profits> **2** ADVANTAGE : avantage *m*, profit *m*
profitable [ˈprɑfətəbəl] *adj* : profitable **— profitably** [-bli] *adv*
profitless [ˈprɑfətləs] *adj* : qui ne rapporte pas de profits, sans profits
profligate [ˈprɑflɪgət, -.geɪt] *adj* **1** IMMORAL : licentieux, débauché **2** EXTRAVAGANT : prodigue, dépensier
profound [prəˈfaʊnd] *adj* : profond
profoundly [prəˈfaʊndli] *adv* : profondément
profundity [prəˈfʌndəṭi] *n, pl* **-ties** : profondeur *f*
profuse [prəˈfju:s] *adj* **1** BOUNTIFUL : abondant **2** LAVISH : prodigue <they were profuse in their thanks : ils se confondaient en remerciements>
profusely [prəˈfju:sli] *adv* : abondamment
profusion [prəˈfju:ʒən] *n* : profusion *f*, abondance *f*
progeny [ˈprɑdʒəni] *n, pl* **-nies** : progéniture *f*, descendance *f*
progesterone [proˈdʒɛstə.ro:n] *n* : progestérone *f*
prognosis [prɑgˈno:sɪs] *n, pl* **-noses** [-.si:z] : pronostic *m*
program[1] *or Brit* **programme** [ˈpro:-.ˌgræm, -grəm] *vt* **-grammed** *or* **-gramed; -gramming** *or* **-graming** : programmer
program[2] *or Brit* **programme** *n* **1** : programme *m* (d'un concert, etc.) **2** PLAN : programme *m*, plan *m* **3** : programme *m* (d'un ordinateur) **4** SHOW : émission *f* <television program : émission de télévision>
programmable [ˈpro.ˌgræməbəl] *adj* : programmable
programme *Brit* → **program**
programmer [ˈpro.ˌgræmər] *n* : programmeur *m*, -meuse *f*
progress[1] [prəˈgrɛs] *vi* **1** PROCEED : progresser, avancer **2** IMPROVE : progresser, s'améliorer
progress[2] [ˈprɑgrəs, -.grɛs] *n* : progrès *m*
progression [prəˈgrɛʃən] *n* **1** ADVANCE : progression *f*, avancement *m* **2** SERIES : progression *f*, suite *f*
progressive [prəˈgrɛsɪv] *adj* **1** : progressiste (en politique, etc.) **2** : progressif <a progressive city : une ville progressive> **3** GRADUAL : progressif, graduel
progressively [prəˈgrɛsɪvli] *adv* : progressivement
prohibit [proˈhɪbəṭ] *vt* **1** FORBID : interdire, défendre **2** PREVENT : empêcher, rendre impossible
prohibition [ˌpro:əˈbɪʃən, ˌpro:hə-] *n* **1** : interdiction *f*, défense *f* **2** : prohibition *f* (de l'alcool)
prohibitive [proˈhɪbəṭɪv] *adj* : prohibitif
project[1] [prəˈdʒɛkt] *vt* **1** DESIGN, PLAN : faire un plan de **2** HURL, THRUST : projeter, lancer **—** *vi* PROTRUDE : faire saillie
project[2] [ˈprɑ.dʒɛkt, -dʒɪkt] *n* **1** PLAN : projet *m*, plan *m* **2** *or* **research project** : étude *f* **3** *or* **school project** : travail *m* pratique
projectile [prəˈdʒɛktəl, -.taɪl] *n* : projectile *m*
projection [prəˈdʒɛkʃən] *n* **1** PROTRUSION : saillie *f* **2** : projection *f* (d'une image) **3** ESTIMATE : projection *f*, prévision *f*
projector [prəˈdʒɛktər] *n* : projecteur *m*
proletarian[1] [ˌpro:ləˈtɛriən] *adj* : prolétaire, prolétarien
proletarian[2] *n* : prolétaire *mf*
proletariat [ˌpro:ləˈtɛriət] *n* : prolétariat *m*
proliferate [prəˈlɪfə.reɪt] *vi* **-ated; -ating** : proliférer
proliferation [prə.lɪfəˈreɪʃən] *n* : prolifération *f*
prolific [prəˈlɪfɪk] *adj* : prolifique, fécond **— prolifically** [-fɪkli] *adv*
prologue [ˈpro:.lɔg, -.lɑg] *n* : prologue *m*, préface *f*
prolong [prəˈlɔŋ] *vt* : prolonger
prolongation [ˌpro:.lɔŋˈgeɪʃən] *n* : prolongation *f*
prom [ˈprɑm] *n* : bal *m* d'étudiants
promenade[1] [ˌprɑməˈneɪd, -ˈnɑd] *vi* **-naded; -nading** : se promener

promenade[2] *n* : promenade *f*
prominence [ˈpraːmənənts] *n* **1** PROTUBERANCE : proéminence *f* **2** EMINENCE : distinction *f*
prominent [ˈpraːmənənt] *adj* **1** PROTRUDING : proéminent **2** CONSPICUOUS : bien en vue **3** LEADING : de premier plan **4** WELL-KNOWN : connu, célèbre
prominently [ˈpraːmənənt̬li] *adv* : bien en vue, en évidence
promiscuity [ˌpraːmɪsˈkjuːət̬i] *n, pl* **-ties** : promiscuité *f* sexuelle
promiscuous [prəˈmɪskjʊəs] *adj* : de mœurs légères
promise[1] [ˈpraːməs] *v* **-mised; -mising** : promettre
promise[2] *n* : promesse *f*
promising [ˈpraːməsɪŋ] *adj* : prometteur
promissory [ˈpraːməˌsori] *adj* : à ordre <a promissory note : un billet à ordre>
promontory [ˈpraːmənˌtori] *n, pl* **-ries** : promontoire *m*
promote [prəˈmoːt] *vt* **-moted; -moting** **1** ADVANCE : promouvoir (un employé) **2** ADVERTISE : faire la promotion de **3** FURTHER : promouvoir, contribuer à
promoter [prəˈmoːt̬ər] *n* : promoteur *m*, -trice *f*
promotion [prəˈmoːʃən] *n* : promotion *f*
promotional [prəˈmoːʃənəl] *adj* : promotionnel
prompt[1] [ˈpraːmpt] *vt* **1** INCITE, INDUCE : inciter, pousser **2** CUE : souffler son rôle à (un acteur)
prompt[2] *adj* **1** PUNCTUAL : ponctuel **2** QUICK : prompt <to be prompt to answer : avoir la repartie prompte>
prompter [ˈpraːmptər] *n* : souffleur *m*, -fleuse *f* (au théâtre)
promptly [ˈpraːmptli] *adv* QUICKLY : immédiatement, sans délai
promptness [ˈpraːmptnəs] *n* : promptitude *f*
prone [ˈproːn] *adj* **1** APT : sujet, enclin <she's prone to forget names : elle a tendance à oublier les noms> <accident-prone : sujet aux accidents> **2** FLAT : à plat ventre <to lie prone : être allongé sur le ventre>
prong [ˈpraːŋ] *n* : dent *f*
pronged [ˈpraːŋd] *adj* : à dents
pronoun [ˈproːˌnaʊn] *n* : pronom *m*
pronounce [prəˈnaʊnts] *vt* **-nounced; -nouncing** **1** : prononcer, rendre (un jugement) **2** SAY : prononcer (un mot) **3** DECLARE : déclarer, prononcer
pronounced [prəˈnaʊnt̬st] *adj* DECIDED : prononcé, marqué
pronouncement [prəˈnaʊnt̬smənt] *n* : déclaration *f*
pronunciation [prəˌnʌnt̬siˈeɪʃən] *n* : prononciation *f*
proof[1] [ˈpruːf] *adj* : à l'épreuve <proof against tampering : à l'épreuve de l'altération>
proof[2] *n* **1** EVIDENCE : preuve *f* <proof of purchase : preuve d'achat> **2** PRINT : épreuve *f* (en photographie) **3 proofs** *npl* : épreuves *fpl* (d'un manuscrit)
proofread [ˈpruːfˌriːd] *vt* **-read** [-ˌred]; **-reading** : corriger les épreuves de
proofreader [ˈpruːfˌriːdər] *n* : correcteur *m*, -trice *f* d'épreuves
prop[1] [ˈpraːp] *vt* **propped; propping** **1** LEAN : appuyer **2 to prop up** SUPPORT, SUSTAIN : étayer, soutenir
prop[2] *n* **1** SUPPORT : étai *m* **2 props** *npl* : accessoires *mpl* (au théâtre)
propaganda [ˌpraːpəˈgændə, ˌproː-] *n* : propagande *f*
propagandize [ˌpraːpəˈgænˌdaɪz, ˌproː-] *vi* **-dized; -dizing** : faire de la propagande
propagate [ˈpraːpəˌgeɪt] *v* **-gated; -gating** *vt* : propager — *vi* : se propager
propagation [ˌpraːpəˈgeɪʃən] *n* : propagation *f*
propane [ˈproːˌpeɪn] *n* : propane *m*
propel [prəˈpel] *vt* **-pelled; -pelling** : propulser
propellant[1] [prəˈpelənt] *adj* : propulsif
propellant[2] *n* : propergol *m* (pour les roquettes), gaz *m* propulseur
propeller [prəˈpelər] *n* : hélice *f*
propensity [prəˈpent̬sət̬i] *n, pl* **-ties** : propension *f*, tendance *f*
proper [ˈpraːpər] *adj* **1** FIT : juste, approprié **2** : même, proprement dit <the city proper : la ville même> **3** CORRECT : correct, convenable
properly [ˈpraːpərli] *adv* **1** WELL : correctement, convenablement, comme du monde *Can* **2 properly speaking** : à proprement parler
property [ˈpraːpərt̬i] *n, pl* **-ties** **1** QUALITY : propriété *f*, qualité *f* **2** POSSESSIONS : biens *mpl* **3** REAL ESTATE : biens *mpl* immobiliers
prophecy [ˈpraːfəsi] *n, pl* **-cies** : prophétie *f*, prédiction *f*
prophesy [ˈpraːfəˌsaɪ] *vt* **-sied; -sying** : prophétiser, prédire
prophet [ˈpraːfət] *n* : prophète *m*, prophétesse *f*
prophetic [prəˈfet̬ɪk] *adj* : prophétique — **prophetically** [-ɪkli] *adv*
propitiate [proˈpɪʃiˌeɪt] *vt* **-ated; -ating** : se concilier, apaiser
propitious [prəˈpɪʃəs] *adj* : propice
proponent [prəˈpoːnənt] *n* : partisan *m*, -sane *f*
proportion[1] [prəˈporʃən] *vt* : proportionner
proportion[2] *n* **1** RATIO : proportion *f*, rapport *m* **2** SYMMETRY : proportion *f*, équilibre *m* <to be out of proportion : être disproportionné> **3** SHARE

: part *f* **4 proportions** *npl* SIZE : dimensions *fpl*

proportional [prə'porʃənəl] *adj* : proportionnel **— proportionally** *adv*

proportionate [prə'porʃənət] *adj* : proportionnel **— proportionately** *adv*

proposal [prə'poːzəl] *n* : proposition *f*

propose [prə'poːz] *v* **-posed; -posing** *vt* **1** SUGGEST : proposer, suggérer **2** INTEND : (se) proposer, penser **3** NOMINATE : proposer, présenter **—** *vi* : faire une demande en mariage

proposition [ˌprɑpə'zɪʃən] *n* **1** PROPOSAL : proposition *f* **2** AFFAIR, BUSINESS : affaire *f*, situation *f* <it's not a paying proposition : ce n'est pas une affaire payante>

propound [prə'paʊnd] *vt* : avancer, proposer

proprietary [prə'praɪəˌtɛri] *adj* **1** : du propriétaire **2 proprietary brand** : marque *f* déposée

proprietor [prə'praɪəṭər] *n* : propriétaire *mf*

propriety [prə'praɪəṭi] *n, pl* **-eties 1** APPROPRIATENESS : convenance *f* **2 proprieties** *npl* : bienséances *fpl*, convenances *fpl*

propulsion [prə'pʌlʃən] *n* : propulsion *f*

propulsive [prə'pʌlsɪv] *adj* : propulsif

prosaic [pro'zeɪɪk] *adj* : prosaïque

proscribe [pro'skraɪb] *vt* **-scribed; -scribing** : proscrire

proscription [pro'skrɪpʃən] *n* : proscription *f*

prose ['proːz] *n* : prose *f*

prosecute ['prɑsɪˌkjuːt] *v* **-cuted; -cuting** *vt* **1** CARRY OUT, PURSUE : poursuivre **2** : poursuivre en justice (en droit) **—** *vi* : engager des poursuites judiciaires

prosecution [ˌprɑsɪ'kjuːʃən] *n* **1** : poursuites *fpl* judiciaires **2** PROSECUTOR : avocat *m* de la partie civile, procureur *m*

prosecutor ['prɑsɪˌkjuːṭər] *n* : procureur *m*

prospect[1] ['prɑˌspɛkt] *vt* : prospecter

prospect[2] *n* **1** VIEW : vue *f* **2** POSSIBILITY : chance *f*, perspective *f* **3** BUYER : client *m* éventuel

prospective [prə'spɛktɪv, 'prɑˌspɛk-] *adj* **1** : éventuel, potentiel <a prospective buyer : un acheteur éventuel> **2** : futur <a prospective mother : une future mère>

prospector ['prɑˌspɛktər, prɑ'spɛk-] *n* : prospecteur *m*, -trice *f*

prospectus [prə'spɛktəs] *n* : prospectus *m* (d'une entreprise)

prosper ['prɑspər] *vt* **1** SUCCEED : prospérer, réussir **2** THRIVE : prospérer

prosperity [prɑ'spɛrəṭi] *n* : prospérité *f*

prosperous ['prɑspərəs] *adj* : prospère

prostate ['prɑˌstɛɪt] *n or* **prostate gland** : prostate *f*

prosthesis [prɑs'θiːsɪs, 'prɑsθə-] *n, pl* **-theses** [-ˌsiːz] : prothèse *f*

prostitute[1] ['prɑstəˌtuːt, -ˌtjuːt] *vt* **-tuted; -tuting 1** DEBASE : prostituer, dégrader **2 to prostitute oneself** : se prostituer

prostitute[2] *n* : prostituée *f*

prostitution [ˌprɑstə'tuːʃən, -'tjuː-] *n* : prostitution *f*

prostrate[1] ['prɑˌstreɪt] *vt* **-trated; -trating 1** OVERWHELM : abattre, accabler <prostrated with grief : accablé de chagrin> **2 to prostrate oneself** : se prosterner

prostrate[2] *adj* **1** : allongé à plat ventre **2** : accablé, prostré <prostrate from the heat : accablé par la chaleur>

prostration [prɑs'treɪʃən] *n* : prostration *f*

protagonist [pro'tɛgənɪst] *n* : protagoniste *mf*

protect [prə'tɛkt] *vt* : protéger

protection [prə'tɛkʃən] *n* : protection *f*

protective [prə'tɛktɪv] *adj* : protecteur

protector [prə'tɛktər] *n* **1** : protecteur *m*, -trice *f* **2** : dispositif *m* de protection (d'une machine)

protectorate [prə'tɛktərət] *n* : protectorat *m*

protégé ['proːṭəˌʒeɪ] *n* : protégé *m*, -gée *f*

protein ['proːˌtiːn] *n* : protéine *f*

protest[1] [pro'tɛst] *vt* **1** : protester de <to protest one's innocence : protester de son innocence> **2** *or* **to protest against** : protester contre **—** *vi* COMPLAIN : protester

protest[2] ['proːˌtɛst] *n* **1** DEMONSTRATION : manifestation *f* **2** OBJECTION : protestation *f*, plainte *f*

Protestant ['prɑṭəstənt] *n* : protestant *m*, -tante *f*

Protestantism ['prɑṭəstənˌtɪzəm] *n* : protestantisme *m*

protestation [ˌprɑṭəs'teɪʃən, ˌproː-, -ˌtɛs-] *n* : protestation *f*

protester *or* **protestor** [pro'ˌtɛstər, prə'-] *n* : manifestant *m*, -tante *f*

protocol ['proːṭəˌkɔl] *n* : protocole *m*

proton ['proːˌtɑn] *n* : proton *m*

protoplasm ['proːṭəˌplæzəm] *n* : protoplasme *m*

prototype ['proːṭəˌtaɪp] *n* : prototype *m*

protozoan [ˌproːṭə'zoːən] *n* : protozoaire *m*

protozoon [ˌproːṭə'zoːˌɑn] *n, pl* **-zoa** [-'zoə] → **protozoan**

protract [pro'trækt] *vt* : prolonger

protractor [pro'trækṭər] *n* : rapporteur *m* (en géométrie)

protrude [pro'truːd] *vi* **-truded; -truding** : dépasser, faire saillie

protrusion [pro'truːʒən] *n* : saillie *f*

protuberance [pro'tuːbərənṭs, -'tjuː-] *n* : protubérance *f*

protuberant [pro'tuːbərənt, -'tjuː-] *adj* : protubérant, saillant

proud ['praʊd] *adj* **1** HAUGHTY : fier, arrogant **2** PRIDEFUL : fier, orgueilleux <too proud to ask for help : trop fier pour demander de l'aide> **3** GLORIOUS : glorieux <the proudest moment in her life : le moment le plus glorieux de sa vie>

proudly ['praʊdli] *adv* : fièrement, orgueilleusement

prove ['pru:v] *v* **proved; proved** *or* **proven** ['pru:vən]; **proving** *vt* **1** TEST : confirmer, prouver <the exception proves the rule : l'exception confirme la règle> **2** ESTABLISH : prouver, établir — *vi* : s'avérer, se montrer

proverb ['prɑ,vərb] *n* : proverbe *m*, adage *m*

proverbial [prə'vərbiəl] *adj* : proverbial — **proverbially** *adv*

provide [prə'vaɪd] *v* **-vided; -viding** *vt* **1** SUPPLY : fournir, donner **2** STIPULATE : prévoir — *vi* **1 to provide against** : parer à **2 to provide for one's family** : subvenir aux besoins de sa famille

provided [prə'vaɪdəd] *conj* : pourvu que, à condition que <provided (that) you agree : à condition que tu sois d'accord>

providence ['prɑvədənʦ] *n* **1** FORESIGHT : prévoyance *f* **2** *or* **Providence** : providence *f* <divine providence : la divine providence> **3 Providence** GOD : Providence *f*

provident ['prɑvədənt] *adj* **1** PRUDENT : prévoyant **2** THRIFTY : économe

providential [ˌprɑvə'dɛnʧəl] *adj* : providentiel

provider [prə'vaɪdər] *n* BREADWINNER : soutien *m* de famille

providing → **provided**

province ['prɑvɪnʦ] *n* **1** : province *f* <the province of Quebec : la province de Québec> <to live in the provinces : vivre dans les provinces> **2** SPHERE : domaine *m*, sphère *f* <the province of science : le domaine des sciences>

provincial [prə'vɪnʃəl] *adj* **1** RURAL : provincial **2** NARROW : provincial, peu raffiné **3** : provincial *Can* <the provincial government : le gouvernement provincial>

provincialism [prə'vɪnʃəˌlɪzəm] *n* : provincialisme *m*

provision[1] [prə'vɪʒən] *vt* : approvisionner, ravitailler

provision[2] *n* **1** SUPPLYING : approvisionnement *m*, ravitaillement *m* **2** PREPARATION : dispositions *fpl* <to make provision for : prendre des dispositions pour> **3** PROVISO : stipulation *f* **4 provisions** *npl* : provisions *fpl*, vivres *mpl*

provisional [prə'vɪʒənəl] *adj* : provisoire, temporaire — **provisionally** *adv*

proviso [prə'vaɪˌzo:] *n*, *pl* **-sos** *or* **-soes** : stipulation *f*, clause *f*

provocation [ˌprɑvə'keɪʃən] *n* : provocation *f*

provocative [prə'vɑkəʧɪv] *adj* : provocant, provocateur

provoke [prə'vo:k] *vt* **-voked; -voking** : provoquer

prow ['praʊ] *n* : proue *f*

prowess ['praʊəs] *n* **1** VALOR : bravoure *f*, vaillance *f* **2** SKILL : habileté *f*, prouesses *fpl*

prowl[1] ['praʊl] *vi* : rôder, errer

prowl[2] *n* **to be on the prowl** : rôder

prowler ['praʊlər] *n* : rôdeur *m*, -deuse *f*

proximate ['prɑksəmət] *adj* : direct

proximity [prɑk'sɪməʧi] *n* : proximité *f*

proxy ['prɑksi] *n*, *pl* **proxies** : procuration *f* <to vote by proxy : voter par procuration>

prude ['pru:d] *n* : prude *f*

prudence ['pru:dənʦ] *n* : prudence *f*

prudent ['pru:dənt] *adj* **1** SHREWD : astucieux **2** CAUTIOUS : prudent, avisé **3** THRIFTY : économe

prudential [pru:'dɛnʧəl] *adj* : prudent

prudently [pru:dəntli] *adv* : prudemment

prudery ['pru:dəri] *n*, *pl* **-eries** : pruderie *f*

prudish ['pru:dɪʃ] *adj* : pudibond, prude

prune[1] ['pru:n] *vt* **pruned; pruning 1** : élaguer, tailler (un arbre, etc.) **2** : élaguer (un texte)

prune[2] *n* : pruneau *m*

prurient ['prʊriənt] *adj* : lubrique, luxurieux

pry ['praɪ] *v* **pried; prying** *vi* **to pry into** : mettre son nez dans — *vt* **1** *or* **to pry up** RAISE : forcer avec un levier **2 to pry sth out of s.o.** : soutirer qqch à qqn

psalm ['sɑm, 'sɑlm] *n* : psaume *m*

pseudonym ['su:dəˌnɪm] *n* : pseudonyme *m*

pseudonymous [su:'dɑnəməs] *adj* : pseudonyme

psoriasis [sə'raɪəsəs] *n* : psoriasis *m*

psyche ['saɪki] *n* : psychisme *m*, psyché *f*

psychiatric [ˌsaɪki'ætrɪk] *adj* : psychiatrique

psychiatrist [sə'kaɪətrɪst, saɪ-] *n* : psychiatre *mf*

psychiatry [sə'kaɪətri, saɪ-] *n* : psychiatrie *f*

psychic ['saɪkɪk] *adj* : psychique

psychoanalysis [ˌsaɪkoə'næləsɪs] *n* : psychanalyse *f*

psychoanalyst [ˌsaɪko'ænəlɪst] *n* : psychanalyste *mf*

psychoanalytic [ˌsaɪkoˌænəl'ɪṭɪk] *adj* : psychanalytique

psychoanalyze [ˌsaɪko'ænəlˌaɪz] *vt* **-lyzed; -lyzing** : psychanalyser

psychological [ˌsaɪkə'lɑdʒɪkəl] *adj* : psychologique — **psychologically** *adv*

psychologist [saɪ'kɑlədʒɪst] *n* : psychologue *mf*

psychology [saɪˈkɒlədʒi] *n, pl* **-gies** : psychologie *f*
psychopath [ˈsaɪkəˌpæθ] *n* : psychopathe *mf*
psychopathic [ˌsaɪkəˈpæθɪk] *adj* : psychopathe
psychosis [saɪˈkoːsɪs] *n, pl* **-choses** [-ˈkoːˌsiz] : psychose *f*
psychosomatic [ˌsaɪkəsəˈmæṭɪk] *adj* : psychosomatique
psychotherapist [ˌsaɪkoˈθɛrəpɪst] *n* : psychothérapeute *mf*
psychotherapy [ˌsaɪkoˈθɛrəpi] *n* : psychothérapie *f*
psychotic[1] [saɪˈkoṭɪk] *adj* : psychotique
psychotic[2] *n* : psychotique *mf*
pub [ˈpʌb] *n Brit* : pub *m*
puberty [ˈpjuːbərṭi] *n* : puberté *f*
pubic [ˈpjuːbɪk] *adj* : pubien
public[1] [ˈpʌblɪk] *adj* : public
public[2] *n* : public *m*
publication [ˌpʌbləˈkeɪʃən] *n* : publication *f*
publicist [ˈpʌbləsɪst] *n* : agent *m* publicitaire
publicity [pəˈblɪsəṭi] *n* : publicité *f*
publicize [ˈpʌbləˌsaɪz] *vt* **-cized; -cizing** : rendre public, faire connaître
publicly [ˈpʌblɪkli] *adv* : publiquement
publish [ˈpʌblɪʃ] *vt* **1** ANNOUNCE : faire connaître, déclarer **2** : publier (un livre)
publisher [ˈpʌblɪʃər] *n* **1** : éditeur *m*, -trice *f* **2** : maison *f* d'édition (entreprise)
puck [ˈpʌk] *n* : palet *m*, rondelle *f Can* (au hockey)
pucker[1] [ˈpʌkər] *vt* : plisser — *vi* : se plisser
pucker[2] *n* : pli *m*
pudding [ˈpʊdɪŋ] *n* : pudding *m*, pouding *m*
puddle [ˈpʌdəl] *n* : flaque *f* (d'eau)
pudgy [ˈpʌdʒi] *adj* **pudgier; -est** : grassouillet, potelé
puerile [ˈpjʊrəl, -ˌaɪl] *adj* : puéril
Puerto Rican[1] [ˌpwɛrṭəˈriːkən, ˌporṭə-] *adj* : portoricain
Puerto Rican[2] *n* : Portoricain *m*, -caine *f*
puff[1] [ˈpʌf] *vi* **1** BLOW : souffler **2** PANT : haleter **3 to puff up** SWELL : enfler, bouffir — *vt* **1** *or* **to puff out** : envoyer des bouffées de (la fumée, etc.) **2** *or* **to puff up** INFLATE : gonfler
puff[2] *n* **1** : bouffée *f* <a puff of air : une bouffée d'air> <to take a puff : tirer une bouffée> **2** SWELLING : bouffissure *f* **3 cream puff** : feuilleté *m* à la crème **4** *or* **powder puff** : houppette *f*
puffy [ˈpʌfi] *adj* **puffier; -est** : enflé, bouffi
pug [ˈpʌg] *n* : carlin *m*
pugilism [ˈpjuːdʒəˌlɪzəm] *n* : pugilat *m*
pugnacious [pʌgˈneɪʃəs] *adj* : combatif, pugnace
puke [ˈpjuːk] *vt* **puked; puking** : vomir, renvoyer *Can fam*
pull[1] [ˈpʊl, ˈpʌl] *vt* **1** : tirer <to pull a rope : tirer une corde> **2** STRAIN : se froisser (un muscle, etc.) **3** EXTRACT : arracher, extraire **4** DRAW : sortir <to pull a gun : sortir un fusil> **5** COMMIT : perpétrer (un crime) **6 to pull off** : enlever **7 to pull oneself together** : se ressaisir, se reprendre **8 to pull up** : remonter — *vi* **1 to pull away** WITHDRAW : se retirer **2 to pull out of** : quitter <the train was pulling out of the station : le train quittait la gare> **3 to pull through** : s'en tirer **4 to pull together** COOPERATE : agir en concert
pull[2] *n* **1** TUG : (petit) coup *m* **2** CLOUT : influence *f*, pouvoir *m* **3** EFFORT : effort *m* <a long uphill pull : une montée pénible> **4** ATTRACTION : force *f*, attrait *m* <the pull of gravity : la force gravitationnelle>
pullet [ˈpʊlət] *n* : poulette *f*
pulley [ˈpʊli] *n, pl* **-leys** : poulie *f*
pullover [ˈpʊlˌoːvər] *n* : chandail *m*, pullover *m France*
pulmonary [ˈpʊlməˌnɛri, ˈpʌl-] *adj* : pulmonaire
pulp [ˈpʌlp] *n* **1** : pulpe *f*, chair *f* (d'un fruit, etc.) **2** *or* **paper pulp** : pâte *f* à papier
pulpit [ˈpʊlˌpɪt] *n* : chaire *f*
pulsate [ˈpʌlˌseɪt] *vi* **-sated; -sating 1** BEAT : battre, palpiter **2** VIBRATE : vibrer
pulsation [ˌpʌlˈseɪʃən] *n* : battement *m*, pulsation *f*
pulse [ˈpʌls] *n* : pouls *m* <to take s.o.'s pulse : tâter le pouls de qqn>
pulverize [ˈpʌlvəˌraɪz] *vt* **-ized; -izing** : pulvériser
puma [ˈpuːmə, ˈpjuː-] *n* : puma *m*, cougar *m*
pumice [ˈpʌməs] *n or* **pumice stone** : pierre *f* ponce
pummel [ˈpʌməl] *vt* **-meled; -meling** : battre, rouer de coups
pump[1] [ˈpʌmp] *vt* **1** : pomper (de l'eau) **2 to pump through** : faire circuler (un gaz, un liquide, du sang) **3 to pump up** : gonfler (un pneu)
pump[2] *n* **1** : pompe *f* <bicycle pump : pompe à bicyclette> **2** : escarpin *m* (chaussure)
pumpernickel [ˈpʌmpərˌnɪkəl] *n* : pain *m* noir
pumpkin [ˈpʌmpkɪn, ˈpʌŋkən] *n* : citrouille *f*, potiron *m France*
pun[1] [ˈpʌn] *vi* **punned; punning** : faire des jeux de mots
pun[2] *n* : jeu *m* de mots, calembour *m*
punch[1] [ˈpʌntʃ] *vt* **1** : donner un coup de poing à **2** PERFORATE : poinçonner, perforer
punch[2] *n* **1** BLOW : coup *m* de poing **2** *or* **hole punch** : poinçonneuse *f* **3**

: punch *m* <fruit punch : punch aux fruits>

punctilious [pəŋk'tɪliəs] *adj* : pointilleux, méticuleux

punctual ['pʌŋktʃʊəl] *adj* : ponctuel — **punctually** *adv*

punctuality [ˌpʌŋktʃʊ'æləṭi] *n* : ponctualité *f*

punctuate ['pʌŋktʃʊˌeɪt] *vt* **-ated; -ating** : ponctuer

punctuation [ˌpʌŋktʃʊ'eɪʃən] *n* : ponctuation *f*

puncture[1] ['pʌŋktʃər] *vt* **-tured; -turing** **1** PIERCE : perforer **2** : crever (un ballon, un pneu, etc.)

puncture[2] *n* **1** HOLE : perforation *f* **2** PRICK : piqûre *f*

pundit ['pʌndɪt] *n* EXPERT : critique *mf;* expert *m,* -perte *f*

pungency ['pʌndʒənṭsi] *n* : piquant *m,* âpreté *f*

pungent ['pʌndʒənt] *adj* **1** BITING, SHARP : âcre, piquant **2** CAUSTIC : mordant

punish ['pʌnɪʃ] *vt* : punir

punishable ['pʌnɪʃəbəl] *adj* : punissable

punishment ['pʌnɪʃmənt] *n* : punition *f*

punitive ['pju:nəṭɪv] *adj* : punitif

punt[1] ['pʌnt] *vt* : faire avancer (une barque) à la perche — *vi* KICK : envoyer d'un coup de volée

punt[2] *n* **1** : barque *f* (à fond plat) **2** KICK : coup *m* de volée

puny ['pju:ni] *adj* **punier; -est** : malingre, chétif

pup ['pʌp] *n* : chiot *m,* jeune animal *m*

pupa ['pju:pə] *n, pl* **-pae** [-pi, -ˌpaɪ] *or* **-pas** : pupe *f,* chrysalide *f*

pupil ['pju:pəl] *n* **1** : élève *mf* (à l'école) **2** : pupille *f* (de l'œil)

puppet ['pʌpəṭ] *n* : marionnette *f*

puppeteer [ˌpʌpə'tɪr] *n* : marionnettiste *mf*

puppy ['pʌpi] *n, pl* **-pies** : chiot *m*

purchase[1] ['pərtʃəs] *vt* **-chased; -chasing** : acheter, acquérir

purchase[2] *n* **1** : achat *m,* acquisition *f* **2** GRASP : prise *f*

purchase order *n* : ordre *m* d'achat

purchaser ['pərtʃəsər] *n* : acheteur *m,* -teuse *f*

pure ['pjʊr] *adj* **purer; purest** : pur

puree[1] [pjʊ'reɪ, -'ri:] *vt* **-reed; -reeing** : réduire en purée

puree[2] *n* : purée *f*

purely ['pjʊrli] *adv* : purement

purgative[1] ['pərgəṭɪv] *adj* : purgatif

purgative[2] *n* LAXATIVE : purgatif *m*

purgatory ['pərgəˌtori] *n, pl* **-ries** : purgatoire *m*

purge[1] ['pərdʒ] *vt* **purged; purging** : purger

purge[2] *n* : purge *f* (des intestins), épuration *f* (en politique)

purification [ˌpjʊrəfə'keɪʃən] *n* : purification *f*

purifier ['pjʊrəˌfaɪər] *n* : purificateur *m* <air purifier : purificateur d'air>

purify ['pjʊrəˌfaɪ] *vt* **-fied; -fying** : purifier

puritan ['pju:rəṭən] *n* : puritain *m,* -taine *f*

puritanical [ˌpju:rə'tænɪkəl] *adj* : puritain

purity ['pjʊrəṭi] *n* : pureté *f*

purl[1] ['pərl] *vt* : tricoter à l'envers

purl[2] *n* : maille *f* à l'envers

purloin [pər'lɔɪn, 'pərˌlɔɪn] *vt* : dérober, voler

purple ['pərpəl] *n* : violet *m,* pourpre *m*

purplish ['pərpəlɪʃ] *adj* : violacé

purport [pər'port] *vt* : prétendre <to purport to be : prétendre être, se faire passer pour>

purportedly [pər'portədli] *adv* : prétendument

purpose ['pərpəs] *n* **1** AIM : intention *f,* but *m* **2** DETERMINATION : résolution *f* <to have a sense of purpose : être résolu> **3 for this purpose** : à cet effet, à cette fin **4 on ~** : exprès

purposeful ['pərpəsfəl] *adj* **1** MEANINGFUL : significatif **2** INTENTIONAL : prémédité, réfléchi **3** DETERMINED : résolu, décidé

purposefully ['pərpəsfəli] *adv* : résolument

purposeless ['pərpəsləs] *adj* MEANINGLESS : vide de sens

purposely ['pərpəsli] *adv* : délibérément, intentionnellement

purr[1] ['pər] *vi* : ronronner

purr[2] *n* : ronronnement *m*

purse[1] ['pərs] *vt* **pursed; pursing** : pincer, serrer <to purse one's lips : pincer les lèvres>

purse[2] *n* **1** *or* **change purse** : porte-monnaie *m* **2** HANDBAG : sac *m* à main, sacoche *f Can* **3** FUNDS, RESOURCES : moyens *mpl* **4** PRIZE : prix *m,* récompense *f*

pursue [pər'su:] *vt* **-sued; -suing** **1** CHASE : poursuivre, pourchasser **2** SEEK : poursuivre <to pursue a goal : poursuivre un but> **3** CARRY ON : poursuivre, continuer, conduire <to pursue a career : faire carrière>

pursuer [pər'su:ər] *n* : poursuivant *m,* -vante *f*

pursuit [pər'su:t] *n* **1** CHASE : poursuite *f* **2** ACTIVITY, OCCUPATION : activité *f,* occupation *f* **3** SEARCH : poursuite *f,* recherche *f* <the pursuit of happiness : la recherche du bonheur>

purvey [pər'veɪ] *vt* **-veyed; -veying** : fournir (des provisions, etc.)

purveyor [pər'veɪər] *n* : fournisseur *m,* -seuse *f*

pus ['pʌs] *n* : pus *m*

push[1] ['pʊʃ] *vt* **1** : pousser <to push a cart : pousser un chariot> <to push the door open : ouvrir la porte> **2** THRUST : enfoncer **3** *or* **to push up** RAISE : augmenter **4** URGE : pousser, inciter **5** APPROACH : approcher, friser <she must be pushing sixty

: elle doit approcher de la soixantaine> **6 to push away** : repousser — *vi* **1 to push for** : demander, réclamer **2 to push on** : continuer, persévérer **3 to push (oneself)** : s'exercer

push[2] *n* **1** SHOVE : poussée *f* <I gave him a push : je l'ai poussé> **2** DRIVE : effort *m* **3** IMPETUS : poussée *f*, impulsion *f*

pushcart [ˈpʊʃˌkɑrt] *n* : charrette *f* à bras

pushy [ˈpʊʃi] *adj* **pushier; -est** : arriviste

pussy [ˈpʊsi] *n, pl* **pussies** : minet *m*, minou *m fam*

pustule [ˈpʌsˌtʃuːl] *n* : pustule *f*

put [ˈpʊt] *vt* **put; putting 1** PLACE : mettre <put it on the table : mets-le sur la table> **2** INSERT : insérer, introduire **3** (*indicating causation of a state or feeling*) : mettre <it puts her in a good mood : ça la met de bonne humeur> **4** IMPOSE : infliger, imposer (une taxe, etc.) **5** SUBJECT : mettre <to put to the test : mettre à l'épreuve> <to put to death : mettre à mort> **6** EXPRESS : exprimer, dire <to put it mildly : c'est peu dire> **7** APPLY : mettre, appliquer <if you put your minds to it : si vous vous y mettez> **8** SET : mettre <to put to work : employer, mettre au travail> **9** ATTACH : attribuer, attacher <to put great value on : attacher beaucoup d'importance à> **10** PRESENT : soumettre, présenter <they put their case well : ils ont bien présenté leur cas> **11 to put forward** PROPOSE : avancer, proposer — *vi* **1 to put to sea** : lever l'ancre **2 to put up with** TOLERATE : supporter

put away *vt* **1** STORE : ranger **2** DISCARD, RENOUNCE : renoncer à (des idées, des émotions, etc.) **3** CONSUME : avaler, engloutir (de la nourriture) **4** CONFINE : enfermer, mettre sous les verrous

put by *vt* SAVE : économiser, mettre de côté

put down *vt* **1** SUPPRESS : réprimer **2** WRITE : écrire, mettre (par écrit) **3** ASCRIBE : mettre sur le compte <I put it down to luck : je l'ai mis sur le compte de la chance>

put off *vt* POSTPONE : remettre à plus tard, retarder

put on *vt* **1** ASSUME : prendre, assumer **2** PRESENT : monter (un spectacle, etc.) **3** WEAR : mettre (des vêtements)

put out *vt* **1** EXTINGUISH, TURN OFF : éteindre **2** INCONVENIENCE : déranger, importuner **3** ANNOY : contrarier, fâcher

putrefaction [ˌpjuːtrəˈfækʃən] *n* : putréfaction *f*

putrefy [ˈpjuːtrəˌfaɪ] *v* **-fied; -fying** *vt* : putréfier — *vi* : se putréfier

putrid [ˈpjuːtrɪd] *adj* : putride

putty[1] [ˈpʌt̬i] *vt* **-tied; -tying** : mastiquer

putty[2] *n, pl* **-ties** : mastic *m*

put up *vt* **1** ACCOMMODATE, LODGE : loger, héberger **2** BUILD : construire, ériger **3** NOMINATE : proposer (un candidat) **4** CONTRIBUTE : contribuer

puzzle[1] [ˈpʌzəl] *vt* **-zled; -zling 1** CONFUSE : intriguer, laisser perplexe **2 to puzzle out** SOLVE : résoudre, deviner

puzzle[2] *n* **1** : casse-tête *m* **2** *or* **jigsaw puzzle** : puzzle *m* **3** MYSTERY : énigme *f*, mystère *m*

puzzlement [ˈpʌzəlmənt] *n* : perplexité *f*

pygmy[1] [ˈpɪgmi] *adj* : pygmée

pygmy[2] *n, pl* **-mies 1** DWARF : pygmée *m* **2 Pygmy** : Pygmée *mf*

pyjamas *Brit* → **pajamas**

pylon [ˈpaɪˌlɑn, -lən] *n* : pylône *m*

pyramid [ˈpɪrəˌmɪd] *n* : pyramide *f*

pyre [ˈpaɪr] *n* : bûcher *m*

pyromania [ˌpaɪroˈmeɪniə] *n* : pyromanie *f*

pyromaniac [ˌpaɪroˈmeɪniˌæk] *n* : pyromane *mf*

pyrotechnics [ˌpaɪrəˈtɛknɪks] *npl* : pyrotechnie *f*

python [ˈpaɪˌθɑn, -θən] *n* : python *m*

Q

q [ˈkjuː] *n, pl* **q's** *or* **qs** [ˈkjuːz] : q *m*, dix-septième lettre de l'alphabet

quack[1] [ˈkwæk] *vi* : faire des coin-coin, cancaner

quack[2] *n* **1** : coin-coin *m* (d'un canard) **2** CHARLATAN : charlatan *m*

quadrangle [ˈkwɑˌdræŋgəl] *n* **1** COURTYARD : cour *f* (rectangulaire), patio *m* **2** → **quadrilateral**

quadrant [ˈkwɑdrənt] *n* : quadrant *m*

quadrilateral [ˌkwɑdrəˈlæt̬ərəl] *n* : quadrilatère *m*

quadruped [ˈkwɑdrəˌpɛd] *n* : quadrupède *m*

quadruple[1] [kwɑˈdruːpəl, -ˈdrʌ-; ˈkwɑdrə-] *vt* **-pled; -pling** : quadrupler

quadruple[2] *adj* : quadruple

quadruplet [kwɑˈdruːplət, -ˈdrʌ-; ˈkwɑdrə-] *n* : quadruplé *m*, -plée *f*

quagmire [ˈkwægˌmaɪr, ˈkwɑg-] *n* : bourbier *m*

quail[1] [ˈkweɪl] *vi* : trembler <to quail before : perdre courage devant>

quail[2] *n, pl* **quail** *or* **quails** : caille *f*

quaint ['kweɪnt] *adj* **1** ODD : étrange, bizarre **2** PICTURESQUE : pittoresque
quaintly ['kweɪntli] *adv* **1** : étrangement, bizarrement **2** : de façon pittoresque
quake[1] ['kweɪk] *vi* **quaked; quaking** : frémir, trembler
quake[2] *n* EARTHQUAKE : tremblement *m* de terre
qualification [ˌkwɑləfəˈkeɪʃən] *n* **1** QUALIFYING : qualification *f* **2** LIMITATION : réserve *f*, restriction *f* <without qualification : sans réserve> **3** SKILL : compétence *f*, aptitude *f*
qualified ['kwɑləˌfaɪd] *adj* : qualifié, compétent
qualify ['kwɑləˌfaɪ] *v* **-fied; -fying** *vt* **1** LIMIT, MODIFY : nuancer, préciser, poser des conditions sur **2** : qualifier, rendre compétent <to be qualified for : être habilité à> **3** MODERATE : adoucir, mitiger — *vi* : se qualifier, remplir les conditions requises
quality ['kwɑləti] *n, pl* **-ties 1** GRADE : qualité *f*, excellence *f* **2** CHARACTERISTIC : qualité *f*, attribut *m*, propriété *f*
qualm ['kwɑm, 'kwɑlm, 'kwɔm] *n* : scrupule *m*, doute *m* <to have no qualms about : ne pas avoir le moindre scrupule à>
quandary ['kwɑndri] *n, pl* **-ries** : doute *m*, confusion *f* <to be in a quandary : ne pas savoir que faire>
quantity ['kwɑntəti] *n, pl* **-ties** : quantité *f*
quantum theory ['kwɑntəm] *n* : théorie *f* des quanta
quarantine[1] ['kwɔrənˌtiːn] *vt* **-tined; -tining** : mettre en quarantaine
quarantine[2] *n* : quarantaine *f*
quarrel[1] ['kwɔrəl] *vi* **-reled** *or* **-relled; -reling** *or* **-relling** : se quereller, se disputer
quarrel[2] *n* : dispute *f*, querelle *f*
quarrelsome ['kwɔrəlsəm] *adj* : querelleur
quarry[1] ['kwɔri] *vt* **quarried; quarrying 1** EXTRACT : extraire <to quarry marble : extraire du marbre> **2** EXCAVATE : excaver
quarry[2] *n, pl* **quarries 1** PREY : proie *f* **2** EXCAVATION : carrière *f*
quart ['kwɔrt] *n* : quart *m* de gallon
quarter[1] ['kwɔrtər] *vt* : diviser en quatre
quarter[2] *n* **1** : quart *m* **2** (*used in expressions of time*) <a quarter after three : trois heures et quart> **3** : (pièce de) vingt-cinq cents *m*, trente-sous *m Can fam* **4** DISTRICT : quartier *m* (d'une ville) **5** : trimestre *m* (de l'année fiscale) **6 quarters** *npl* LODGINGS : logement *m*
quarterly[1] ['kwɔrtərli] *adv* : tous les trois mois, trimestriellement
quarterly[2] *adj* : trimestriel
quarterly[3] *n, pl* **-lies** : publication *f* trimestrielle
quartermaster ['kwɔrtərˌmæstər] *n* : intendant *m* militaire
quartet [kwɔrˈtet] *n* : quatuor *m* <string quartet : quatuor à cordes>
quartz ['kwɔrts] *n* : quartz *m*
quash ['kwɑʃ, 'kwɔʃ] *vt* **1** : annuler (un jugement) **2** SUPPRESS : étouffer, refouler (ses émotions)
quaver[1] ['kweɪvər] *vi* : trembloter, chevroter (se dit de la voix)
quaver[2] *n* : tremblement *m*, chevrotement *m*
quay ['kiː, 'keɪ, 'kweɪ] *n* WHARF : quai *m*
queasiness ['kwiːzinəs] *n* : nausée *f*
queasy ['kwiːzi] *adj* **queasier; -est** : nauséeux <to feel queasy : avoir mal au cœur>
Quebecer *or* **Quebecker** [kwɪˈbekər] *n* : Québécois *m*, -coise *f*
Quebecois *or* **Québécois** [kebeˈkwɑː] *n* : Québécois *m*, -coise *f*
queen ['kwiːn] *n* : reine *f*
queenly ['kwiːnli] *adj* : de reine
queer ['kwɪr] *adj* : étrange, bizarre — **queerly** *adv*
quell ['kwel] *vt* : réprimer, étouffer
quench ['kwentʃ] *vt* **1** EXTINGUISH : éteindre (un feu) **2** SATISFY : apaiser, étancher (la soif)
querulous ['kwerələs, -jələs] *adj* : plaintif, grincheux
querulously ['kwerələsli, -jələs-] *adv* : plaintivement
query[1] ['kwɪri, 'kwɪr-] *vt* **-ried; -rying 1** ASK : poser une question à **2** QUESTION : mettre en doute, poser des questions sur
query[2] *n, pl* **-ries** : question *f*
quest[1] ['kwest] *vi* **to quest for** : être en quête de, être à la recherche de
quest[2] *n* : quête *f*, recherche *f*
question[1] ['kwestʃən] *vt* **1** INTERROGATE : questionner, interroger **2** DISPUTE : mettre en doute
question[2] *n* **1** : question *f*, interrogation *f* **2** MATTER : question *f*, problème *m* **3 without ~** : sans l'ombre d'un doute
questionable ['kwestʃənəbəl] *adj* DUBIOUS : contestable, discutable, douteux
questioner ['kwestʃənər] *n* : interrogateur *m*, -trice *f*
question mark *n* : point *m* d'interrogation
questionnaire [ˌkwestʃəˈnær] *n* : questionnaire *m*
queue[1] ['kjuː] *vi* **queued; queuing** *or* **queueing** : faire la queue
queue[2] *n* **1** PIGTAIL : tresse *f* (de cheveux) **2** LINE : queue *f*, file *f* (d'attente)
quibble[1] ['kwɪbəl] *vi* **-bled; -bling** : chicaner
quibble[2] *n* : chicane *f*

quick[1] ['kwɪk] *adv* : rapidement
quick[2] *adj* **1** FAST : rapide **2** ALERT : vif, éveillé **3 to have a quick temper** : s'emporter facilement
quick[3] *n* **1** : chair *f* vive <his nails were bitten to the quick : il se rongeait les ongles jusqu'au sang> **2 to cut to the quick** : piquer au vif
quicken ['kwɪkən] *vt* **1** HASTEN : accélérer **2** AROUSE : stimuler
quickly ['kwɪkli] *adv* : rapidement, vite
quickness ['kwɪknəs] *n* : rapidité *f*, vitesse *f*
quicksand ['kwɪkˌsænd] *n* : sables *mpl* mouvants
quicksilver ['kwɪkˌsɪlvər] *n* : mercure *m*, vif-argent *m*
quick–tempered ['kwɪk'tɛmpərd] *adj* : coléreux, irascible
quick–witted ['kwɪk'wɪt̬əd] *adj* : à l'esprit vif
quiet[1] ['kwaɪət] *vt* : calmer <to quiet the crowd : calmer la foule> — *vi* **to quiet down** : se calmer
quiet[2] *adj* **1** CALM : tranquille **2** EASY-GOING : doux **3** STILL : tranquille, silencieux **4** : sobre, simple <quiet clothes : vêtements sobres> **5** SECLUDED : tranquille, retiré <a quiet nook : un coin tranquille>
quiet[3] *n* : tranquillité *f*, calme *m* <the quiet before the storm : le calme avant la tempête>
quietly ['kwaɪətli] *adv* **1** : sans bruit **2** CALMLY : tranquillement, paisiblement
quietness ['kwaɪətnəs] *n* : tranquillité *f*, silence *f*
quietude ['kwaɪəˌtu:d, -ˌtju:d] *n* : quiétude *f*
quill ['kwɪl] *n* **1** : piquant *m* (d'un porc-épic, etc.) **2** *or* **quill pen** : penne *f*, plume *f* d'oie
quilt[1] ['kwɪlt] *vt* : matelasser, piquer
quilt[2] *n* : courtepointe *f*, édredon *m* (piqué)
quince ['kwɪnts] *n* : coing *m* (fruit), cognassier *m* (arbre)
quinine ['kwaɪˌnaɪn] *n* : quinine *f*
quintessence [kwɪn'tɛsənts] *n* : quintessence *f*
quintet [kwɪn'tɛt] *n* : quintette *m*
quintuple [kwɪn'tu:pəl, -'tju:-, -'tʌ-; 'kwɪntə-] *adj* : quintuple
quintuplet [kwɪn'tʌplət, -'tu:-, -'tju:-; 'kwɪntə-] *n* : quintuplé *m*, -plée *f*
quip[1] ['kwɪp] *vi* **quipped; quipping** : lancer des mots piquants
quip[2] *n* : mot *m* piquant, trait *m* d'esprit
quirk ['kwərk] *n* : excentricité *f*, bizarrerie *f*
quirky ['kwərki] *adj* **quirkier; -iest** : excentrique
quit ['kwɪt] *v* **quit; quitting** *vt* **1** STOP : arrêter <quit fooling around : arrête de faire l'imbécile> **2** LEAVE : quitter, cesser <to quit school : quitter l'école> — *vi* **1** GIVE UP : abandonner, renoncer **2** RESIGN : démissionner
quite ['kwaɪt] *adv* **1** COMPLETELY : tout à fait **2** RATHER : assez <quite near : assez proche> **3** POSITIVELY : vraiment <I'm quite sure : je suis vraiment certaine>
quits ['kwɪts] *adj* : quitte <to be quits with s.o. : être quitte envers qqn> <let's call it quits! : restons-en là!>
quitter ['kwɪt̬ər] *n* : personne *f* qui abandonne facilement
quiver[1] ['kwɪvər] *vi* : trembler, frémir
quiver[2] *n* **1** : carquois *m* (pour des flèches) **2** TREMOR : tremblement *m*
quixotic [kwɪk'sɑt̬ɪk] *adj* : chimérique, utopique
quiz[1] ['kwɪz] *vt* **quizzed; quizzing** : questionner, interroger
quiz[2] *n, pl* **quizzes** : petit examen *m*, épreuve *f*
quizzical ['kwɪzɪkəl] *adj* **1** TEASING : moqueur, taquin, ironique **2** PUZZLED : perplexe
quorum ['kworəm] *n* : quorum *m*
quota ['kwoʊt̬ə] *n* : quota *m*
quotable ['kwoʊt̬əbəl] *adj* : qui peut être cité
quotation [kwo'teɪʃən] *n* **1** CITATION : citation *f* **2** ESTIMATE : devis *m* **3** : cote *f*, cotation *f* (à la Bourse)
quotation marks *npl* : guillemets *mpl*
quote[1] ['kwoʊt] *vt* **quoted; quoting 1** : citer <to quote a poem : citer un poème> **2** STATE : donner, soumettre (un prix) **3** : coter (un prix à la Bourse)
quote[2] *n* **1** → **quotation 2 quotes** *npl* → **quotation marks**
quotient ['kwoʊʃənt] *n* : quotient *m*

R

r ['ɑr] *n, pl* **r's** *or* **rs** ['ɑrz] : r *m*, dix-huitième lettre de l'alphabet
rabbi ['ræˌbaɪ] *n* : rabbin *m*
rabbit ['ræbət] *n, pl* **-bit** *or* **-bits** : lapin *m*, -pine *f*
rabble ['ræbəl] *n* **1** CROWD, MOB : cohue *f*, foule *f* **2** MASSES : populace *f*, masses *fpl*
rabid ['ræbɪd] *adj* **1** FURIOUS : furieux **2** FANATICAL : zélé, fanatique **3** : enragé (se dit d'un chien)
rabies ['reɪbi:z] *ns & pl* : rage *f*
raccoon [ræ'ku:n] *n, pl* **-coon** *or* **-coons** : raton *m* laveur, chat *m* sauvage *Can*
race[1] ['reɪs] *vi* **raced; racing 1** : faire une course **2** RUSH : courir, se hâter

race² *n* **1** CURRENT : courant *m*, cours *m* (d'eau) **2** : course *f* <horse race : course de chevaux> <presidential race : course à la présidence> **3** : race *f* <the white race : la race blanche>
racecourse ['reɪs,kors] *n* : champ *m* de courses
racehorse ['reɪs,hors] *n* : cheval *m* de course
racer ['reɪsər] *n* : coureur *m*, -reuse *f*
racetrack ['reɪs,træk] *n* : champ *m* de courses
racial ['reɪʃəl] *adj* : racial — **racially** *adv*
racism ['reɪ,sɪzəm] *n* : racisme *m*
racist ['reɪsɪst] *n* : raciste *mf*
rack¹ ['ræk] *vt* : torturer <to be racked with pain : être torturé par la douleur> <to rack one's brains : se creuser la tête>
rack² *n* **1** SHELF : étagère *f* <a luggage rack : un porte-bagages> <a roof rack : une galerie> <a clothes rack : un portemanteau> **2** : chevalet *m* (instrument de torture)
racket ['rækət] *n* **1** : raquette *f* <tennis racket : raquette de tennis> **2** CLAMOR : vacarme *m* **3** FRAUD : escroquerie *f*, racket *m*
racketeer [,rækə'tɪr] *n* : racketteur *m*
racketeering [,rækə'tɪrɪŋ] *n* : racket *m*
raconteur [,ræ,kɑn'tər] *n* STORYTELLER : raconteur *m*, -teuse *f*
racy ['reɪsi] *adj* **racier; -est 1** LIVELY : plein de verve **2** RISQUÉ : osé
radar ['reɪ,dɑr] *n* : radar *m*
radial ['reɪdiəl] *adj* : radial
radiance ['reɪdiənts] *n* : éclat *m*, rayonnement *m*
radiant ['reɪdiənt] *adj* **1** GLOWING : éclatant, brillant **2** : radieux, rayonnant <a radiant smile : un sourire radieux> **3** : radiant (en physique)
radiantly ['reɪdiəntli] *adv* : d'un air radieux
radiate ['reɪdi,eɪt] *v* **-ated; -ating** *vi* SHINE : briller, rayonner — *vt* **1** IRRADIATE : irradier **2** EMIT : dégager, émettre <to radiate heat : dégager de la chaleur>
radiation [,reɪdi'eɪʃən] *n* : rayonnement *m*, radiation *f*
radiator ['reɪdi,eɪtər] *n* : radiateur *m*, calorifère *m Can*
radical¹ ['rædɪkəl] *adj* : radical — **radically** ['rædɪkli] *adv*
radical² *n* : radical *m*, -cale *f*
radii → **radius**
radio¹ ['reɪdi,o:] *vt* : envoyer (un message) par radio
radio² *n*, *pl* **-dios** : radio *f*
radioactive [,reɪdio'æktɪv] *adj* : radioactif
radioactivity [,reɪdio,æk'tɪvəṭi] *n* : radioactivité *f*
radiologist [,reɪdi'ɑlədʒɪst] *n* : radiologiste *mf*, radiologue *mf*
radiology [,reɪdi'ɑlədʒi] *n* : radiologie *f*
radish ['rædɪʃ] *n* : radis *m*
radium ['reɪdiəm] *n* : radium *m*
radius ['reɪdiəs] *n*, *pl* **-dii** [-di,aɪ] : rayon *m*
radon ['reɪ,dɑn] *n* : radon *m*
raffle¹ ['ræfəl] *vt* **-fled; -fling** : mettre en tombola
raffle² *n* : tombola *f*
raft¹ ['ræft] *vt* : transporter par radeau
raft² *n* **1** : radeau *m* **2** SLEW : tas *m*, multitude *f* <a raft of errors : un tas d'erreurs>
rafter ['ræftər] *n* : chevron *m*
rag ['ræg] *n* **1** : chiffon *m*, guenille *f* *Can* **2 rags** *npl* : haillons *mpl*, guenilles *fpl* <clothed in rags : vêtu de haillons> **3** → **ragtime**
ragamuffin ['rægə,mʌfən] *n* : va-nu-pieds *m*
rage¹ ['reɪdʒ] *vi* **raged; raging 1** : être enragé (se dit d'une personne) **2** : faire rage <the fire raged for hours : le feu a fait rage pendant des heures>
rage² *n* **1** FURY : rage *f* **2 to be all the rage** : faire fureur
ragged ['rægəd] *adj* **1** : inégal <ragged cliffs : falaises inégales> **2** TATTERED : en loques, en lambeaux **3** DISCONNECTED, DISJOINTED : décousu
ragout [ræ'gu:] *n* : ragoût *m*
ragtime ['ræg,taɪm] *n* : ragtime *m*
ragweed ['ræg,wi:d] *n* : ambroisie *f*
raid¹ ['reɪd] *vt* : faire un raid (militaire) sur, faire une descente (policière) dans
raid² *n* **1** INCURSION : raid *m* (militaire) **2** *or* **police raid** : descente *f*, rafle *f*
raider ['reɪdər] *n* **1** : membre *m* d'un commando **2** LOOTER, MARAUDER : pillard *m*, -larde *f*
rail¹ ['reɪl] *vi* **to rail at** : invectiver contre
rail² *n* **1** RAILING : rampe *f* (d'un escalier), balustrade *f* (d'un balcon) **2** TRACK : rail *m* (d'une voie ferrée) **3** RAILROAD : train *m*, chemin *m* de fer <by rail : par train>
railing ['reɪlɪŋ] *n* : rampe *f*, balustrade *f*
raillery ['reɪləri] *n*, *pl* **-leries** : raillerie *f*
railroad ['reɪl,ro:d] *n* : chemin *m* de fer
railway ['reɪl,weɪ] → **railroad**
raiment ['reɪmənt] *n* : habits *mpl*, vêtements *mpl*
rain¹ ['reɪn] *vi* : pleuvoir
rain² *n* : pluie *f*
rainbow ['reɪn,bo:] *n* : arc-en-ciel *m*
raincoat ['reɪn,ko:t] *n* : imperméable *m*
raindrop ['reɪn,drɑp] *n* : goutte *f* de pluie
rainfall ['reɪn,fɔl] *n* : précipitations *fpl*
rainstorm ['reɪn,stɔrm] *n* : pluie *f* torrentielle
rainwater ['reɪn,wɔṭər] *n* : eau *f* de pluie

rainy ['reɪnɪ] *adj* **rainier; -est** : pluvieux
raise[1] ['reɪz] *vt* **raised; raising 1** LIFT : lever **2** AWAKEN : ressusciter **3** BUILD : ériger **4** COLLECT : collecter (des fonds) **5** GROW : cultiver (des produits agricoles) **6** REAR : élever **7** BRING UP : soulever (une question, etc.) **8** INCREASE : augmenter **9** PROVOKE : susciter, provoquer <to raise a commotion : susciter un émoi>
raise[2] *n* : augmentation *f* (de salaire)
raisin ['reɪzən] *n* : raisin *m* sec
raja *or* **rajah** ['rɑdʒə, -ˌdʒɑ, -ʒɑ] *n* : rajah *m*
rake[1] ['reɪk] *vt* **raked; raking 1** : ratisser, râteler (des feuilles) **2 to rake with gunfire** : balayer avec une mitrailleuse
rake[2] *n* **1** : râteau *m* **2** LIBERTINE : débauché *m*
rakish ['reɪkɪʃ] *adj* **1** JAUNTY : gaillard **2** WILD : libertin, dissolu
rally[1] ['ræli] *v* **-lied; -lying** *vt* MOBILIZE : rallier, rassembler — *vi* **1** : se rallier **2** RECOVER : retrouver ses forces, se remettre
rally[2] *n, pl* **-lies** : ralliement *m*, rassemblement *m*
ram[1] ['ræm] *vt* **rammed; ramming 1** HIT : heurter, percuter **2** CRAM : fourrer, entasser **3 to ram home** : forcer l'acceptation de (une idée, un projet de loi, etc.)
ram[2] *n* **1** : bélier *m* (mouton) **2 → battering ram**
RAM ['ræm] *n* : RAM *f*, mémoire *f* vive
ramble[1] ['ræmbəl] *vi* **-bled; -ling 1** ROAM : flâner, se balader **2** *or* **to ramble on** : discourir, pérorer
ramble[2] *n* : randonnée *f*, balade *f*
rambler ['ræmblər] *n* WALKER : randonneur *m*, -neuse *f*
rambunctious [ræmˈbʌŋkʃəs] *adj* : exubérant, turbulent
ramification [ˌræməfəˈkeɪʃən] *n* : ramification *f*
ramify ['ræməˌfaɪ] *vi* **-fied; -fying** : se ramifier
ramp ['ræmp] *n* **1** : rampe *f* **2** : passerelle *f* (pour accéder à un avion)
rampage[1] ['ræmˌpeɪdʒ, ræmˈpeɪdʒ] *vi* **-paged; -paging** : se déchaîner, donner libre cours à
rampage[2] ['ræmˌpeɪdʒ] *n* **to go on a rampage** : se livrer à des actes de destruction
rampant ['ræmpənt] *adj* WIDESPREAD : endémique, qui sévit
rampart ['ræmˌpɑrt] *n* : rempart *m*
ramrod ['ræmˌrɑd] *n* : baguette *f* (d'une arme à feu)
ramshackle ['ræmˌʃækəl] *adj* : délabré, en mauvais état
ran → run[1]
ranch[1] ['ræntʃ] *vi* : exploiter un ranch
ranch[2] *n* : ranch *m*
rancher ['ræntʃər] *n* : propriétaire *mf* de ranch
rancid ['ræn(t)sɪd] *adj* : rance
rancor *or Brit* **rancour** ['ræŋkər] *n* : rancœur *f*, rancune *f*
random ['rændəm] *adj* **1** : aléatoire <random process : processus aléatoire> **2 at ~** : au hasard
randomly ['rændəmlɪ] *adv* : au hasard
rang → ring[1]
range[1] ['reɪndʒ] *v* **ranged; ranging** *vt* ARRANGE : classer, ranger — *vi* **1** WANDER : vagabonder, errer **2 to range from** : varier entre, aller de
range[2] *n* **1** ROW : rangée *f* **2** PRAIRIE : prairie *f* **3** : chaîne *f* (de montagnes) **4** STOVE : cuisinière *f* **5** SERIES, SPREAD : éventail *m*, gamme *f* **6** *or* **shooting range** : champ *m* de tir **7** SCOPE : champ *m*, étendue *f* **8** VARIETY : variété *f* (de couleurs, de motifs)
ranger ['reɪndʒər] *n or* **forest ranger** : garde *m* forestier
rangy ['reɪndʒɪ] *adj* **rangier; -est** : élancé
rank[1] ['ræŋk] *vt* **1** ARRANGE : placer, ranger **2** CLASSIFY : classer — *vi* : se classer, compter <he ranks among the best in his class : il se classe parmi les meilleurs de sa classe>
rank[2] *adj* **1** : luxuriant (se dit de la végétation), envahissant (se dit des mauvais herbes) **2** MALODOROUS : fétide, nauséabond **3** FLAGRANT : complet, flagrant <rank disloyalty : déloyauté flagrante>
rank[3] *n* **1** LINE, ROW : rang *m* <to close ranks : serrer les rangs> **2** GRADE, POSITION : rang *m*, grade *m* <to pull rank : abuser de son rang> **3** CLASS : rang *m*, condition *f* (sociale) **4 ranks** *npl* : rangs *mpl* (militaires), échelons *mpl*
rank and file *n* **1** : hommes *mpl* du rang (dans les forces armées) **2** : base *f* (politique)
rankle ['ræŋkəl] *vi* **-kled; -kling** : rester sur le cœur, laisser une rancœur
ransack ['ræn(t)ˌsæk] *vt* **1** SEARCH : fouiller **2** PLUNDER : saccager, piller
ransom[1] ['ræn(t)səm] *vt* : payer une rançon pour, rançonner
ransom[2] *n* : rançon *f*
rant ['ræn(t)] *vi or* **to rant and rave** : tempêter, fulminer
rap[1] ['ræp] *v* **rapped; rapping** *vt* **1** STRIKE : frapper, taper **2** CRITICIZE : critiquer, réprimander — *vi* **1** KNOCK : frapper **2** CHAT : causer, bavarder
rap[2] *n* **1** BLOW, TAP : coup *m* sec, tape *f* **2** CHAT : causerie *f*, bavardage *m* **3** *or* **rap music** : rap *m* **4 to beat the rap** : échapper à la justice
rapacious [rəˈpeɪʃəs] *adj* **1** GREEDY : rapace, avide **2** RAVENOUS : rapace, vorace

rape[1] ['reɪp] *vt* **raped; raping** : violer
rape[2] *n* **1** : viol *m* **2** : colza *m* (plante)
rapid ['ræpɪd] *adj* : rapide
rapidity [rə'pɪdəṭi] *n* : rapidité *f*
rapids ['ræpɪdz] *ns & pl* : rapides *mpl*
rapier ['reɪpiər] *n* : rapière *f*
rapist ['reɪpɪst] *n* : violeur *m*
rapport [ræ'por] *n* : rapport *m*, relation *f*
rapt ['ræpt] *adj* : captivé, transporté
rapture ['ræptʃər] *n* : extase *f*, ravissement *m*
rapturous ['ræptʃərəs] *adj* : extasié, extatique
rare ['rær] *adj* **rarer; rarest 1** RAREFIED : raréfié (se dit de l'air) **2** DISTINCTIVE, FINE : extraordinaire, exceptionnel <a rare June day : une de ces journées extraordinaires du mois de juin> **3** UNCOMMON : rare **4** : saignant (se dit de la viande)
rarefy ['rærəˌfaɪ] *v* **-fied; -fying** *vt* : raréfier — *vi* : se raréfier
rarely ['rærli] *adv* SELDOM : rarement
raring ['rærən, -ɪŋ] *adj* : impatient <raring to go : impatient de partir>
rarity ['rærəṭi] *n, pl* **-ties** : rareté *f*
rascal ['ræskəl] *n* **1** : polisson *m*, -sonne *f* **2** ROGUE : scélérat *m*, -rate *f*
rash[1] ['ræʃ] *adj* : irréfléchi, téméraire
rash[2] *n* : rougeurs *fpl*
rashly ['ræʃli] *adv* : sans réfléchir, imprudemment
rasp[1] ['ræsp] *vt* **1** SCRAPE : râper **2** IRRITATE : irriter **3 to rasp out** : dire d'une voix rauque
rasp[2] *n* : râpe *f*
raspberry ['ræzˌberi] *n, pl* **-ries** : framboise *f*
rat ['ræt] *n* : rat *m*
ratchet ['rætʃəṭ] *n or* **ratchet wheel** : roue *f* à rochet
rate[1] ['reɪt] *vt* **rated; rating 1** APPRAISE : estimer, évaluer **2** REGARD : considérer, estimer <she is rated an excellent pianist : on la considère comme une excellente pianiste> **3** DESERVE : mériter
rate[2] *n* **1** : taux *m* <interest rate : taux d'intérêt> **2** PRICE : tarif *m* <hotel rates : tarifs hôteliers> **3** PACE : rythme *m*, train *m* <at a rate of 40 miles per hour : à un rythme de 40 milles à l'heure> **4 at any rate** : en tous cas
rather ['ræðər, 'rʌ-, 'rɑ-] *adv* **1** PREFERABLY : mieux <I'd rather not go : j'aimerais mieux ne pas y aller> **2** : plutôt <my father, or rather my stepfather : mon père, ou plutôt mon beau-père> **3** SOMEWHAT : assez, plutôt
ratification [ˌræṭəfə'keɪʃən] *n* : ratification *f*
ratify ['ræṭəˌfaɪ] *vt* **-fied; -fying** : ratifier
rating ['reɪṭɪŋ] *n* **1** STANDING : classement *m*, cote *f* **2 ratings** *npl* : indice *m* d'écoute
ratio ['reɪʃio] *n, pl* **-tios** : rapport *m*, proportion *f*
ration[1] ['ræʃən, 'reɪʃən] *vt* **rationed; rationing** : rationner
ration[2] *n* **1** : ration *f* **2 rations** *npl* PROVISIONS : rations *fpl*, provisions *fpl*
rational ['ræʃənəl] *adj* : raisonnable, sensé, logique
rationale [ˌræʃə'næl] *n* **1** EXPLANATION : raisons *fpl*, logique *f* **2** BASIS : justification *f*, raison *f* d'être
rationalization [ˌræʃənələ'zeɪʃən] *n* : justification *f*, rationalisation *f*
rationalize ['ræʃənəˌlaɪz] *vt* **-ized; -izing** : justifier, rationaliser
rationally ['ræʃənəli] *adv* : rationnellement
rattle[1] ['ræṭəl] *v* **-tled; -tling** *vi* : faire du bruit, vibrer — *vt* **1** UPSET : ébranler, secouer **2 to rattle off** : débiter à toute vitesse
rattle[2] *n* **1** : cliquetis *m*, bruit *m* **2** *or* **baby's rattle** : hochet *m* **3** : grelot *m* (d'un serpent à sonnettes)
rattler ['ræṭələr] → **rattlesnake**
rattlesnake ['ræṭəlˌsneɪk] *n* : serpent *m* à sonnettes, crotale *m*
ratty ['ræṭi] *adj* **rattier; -est** : miteux, misérable
raucous ['rɔkəs] *adj* **1** HARSH : rauque (se dit de la voix) **2** BOISTEROUS : bruyant — **raucously** *adv*
ravage ['rævɪdʒ] *vt* **-aged; -aging** : ravager
ravages ['rævɪdʒəz] *npl* : ravages *mpl*
rave ['reɪv] *vi* **raved; raving 1** : délirer (se dit d'un malade) **2 to rave about** : s'extasier sur, s'emballer au sujet de
ravel[1] ['rævəl] *v* **-eled** *or* **-elled; -eling** *or* **-elling** *vt* UNRAVEL : défaire (un tricot) — *vi* FRAY : s'effilocher
ravel[2] *n* : effiloche *f*
raven ['reɪvən] *n* : grand corbeau *m*
ravenous ['rævənəs] *adj* **1** HUNGRY : affamé <to be ravenous : avoir une faim de loup> **2** RAPACIOUS : vorace
ravenously ['rævənəsli] *adv* : voracement
ravine [rə'viːn] *n* : ravin *m*, coulée *f* *Can*
ravish ['rævɪʃ] *vt* **1** SEIZE : ravir, emporter de force **2** DELIGHT : ravir, enchanter **3** RAPE : violer
raw ['rɔ] *adj* **rawer; rawest 1** UNCOOKED : cru **2** UNTREATED : brut, écru (se dit des étoffes) <raw silk : soie grège> **3** INEXPERIENCED : inexpérimenté **4** OPEN : à vif, ouvert <a raw wound : une plaie ouverte> **5** : froid et humide, cru <a raw day : une journée crue> **6** COARSE, VULGAR : grossier, obscène **7 raw material** : matière *f* première **8 to get a raw deal** : être traité injustement
rawhide ['rɔˌhaɪd] *n* : cuir *m* brut

ray ['reɪ] *n* **1** : rayon *m* (de lumière) **2** BIT, GLIMMER : lueur *f* <a ray of hope : une lueur d'espoir>
rayon ['reɪˌɑn] *n* : rayonne *f*
raze ['reɪz] *vt* **razed; razing** : raser, détruire
razor ['reɪzər] *n* : rasoir *m*
reach[1] ['riːtʃ] *vt* **1** EXTEND : tendre, étendre <to reach out one's hand : tendre la main> **2** GRASP, TOUCH : atteindre **3** : arriver à, aller jusqu'à <his shadow reached the wall : son ombre arrivait jusqu'au mur> **4** : parvenir à <to reach an agreement : parvenir à une entente> **5** CONTACT : rejoindre — *vi* EXTEND : s'étendre
reach[2] *n* : portée *f* <within reach : à portée de la main>
react [riˈækt] *vi* : réagir
reaction [riˈækʃən] *n* : réaction *f*
reactionary[1] [riˈækʃəˌnɛri] *adj* : réactionnaire
reactionary[2] *n, pl* **-ries** : réactionnaire *mf*
reactor [riˈæktər] *n* : réacteur *m* <nuclear reactor : réacteur nucléaire>
read[1] ['riːd] *v* **read** ['rɛd]; **reading** *vt* **1** : lire <to read a book : lire un livre> **2** INTERPRET : interpréter, reconnaître <to read nature's signs : interpréter les signes de la nature> **3** UNDERSTAND : connaître, comprendre <she reads him like a book : elle connaît ses moindres réactions> **4** STUDY : faire, étudier <she reads law : elle fait son droit> **5** INDICATE : indiquer, montrer <the thermometer reads 10° : le thermomètre indique 10°> — *vi* : se lire <this book reads smoothly : ce livre se lit facilement>
read[2] ['rɛd] *adj* **well read** : instruit, informé
readable ['riːdəbəl] *adj* : lisible
reader ['riːdər] *n* : lecteur *m*, -trice *f*
readily ['rɛdəli] *adv* **1** WILLINGLY : avec empressement, volontiers **2** EASILY : facilement
readiness ['rɛdinəs] *n* **1** ALACRITY : empressement *m* **2** EASE : facilité *f*, aisance *f*
reading ['riːdɪŋ] *n* **1** : lecture *f* (d'un livre) **2** : indication *f* (d'un instrument), relevé *m* (d'un compteur) <to take a reading : faire un relevé>
readjust [ˌriːəˈdʒʌst] *vt* : rajuster, réajuster — *vi* : se réadapter
readjustment [ˌriːəˈdʒʌstmənt] *n* : réajustement *m*
ready[1] ['rɛdi] *vt* **readied; readying** : préparer
ready[2] *adj* **readier; -est 1** : prêt <dinner is ready : le dîner est prêt> <ready to cry : au bord des larmes> **2** WILLING : prêt <always ready to help : toujours prêt à aider> **3 to have a ready wit** : avoir la repartie facile **4 ready money** : argent *m* liquide
ready–made [ˌrɛdiˈmeɪd] *adj* : de prêt-à-porter (se dit des vêtements)
reaffirm [ˌriːəˈfərm] *vt* : réaffirmer
real[1] ['riːl] *adv* VERY : vraiment
real[2] *adj* **1** : réel <real income : revenu réel> **2** GENUINE : vrai, véritable **3** ACTUAL : réel, vrai <in real life : en réalité> **4 for ~** : pour de vrai
real estate *n* : biens *mpl* immobiliers
realism ['riːəˌlɪzəm] *n* : réalisme *m*
realist ['riːəlɪst] *n* : réaliste *mf*
realistic [ˌriːəˈlɪstɪk] *adj* : réaliste
realistically [ˌriːəˈlɪstɪkli] *adv* : de façon réaliste
reality [riˈæləṭi] *n, pl* **-ties** : réalité *f*
realization [ˌriːələˈzeɪʃən] *n* : réalisation *f*
realize ['riːəˌlaɪz] *vt* **-ized; -izing 1** ACCOMPLISH : réaliser **2** GAIN, OBTAIN : réaliser (un profit) **3** UNDERSTAND : se rendre compte de, comprendre
really ['rɪli, 'rɪ-] *adv* **1** ACTUALLY : vraiment <I didn't really mean it : je n'étais pas vraiment sérieux> **2** TRULY : incontestablement, vraiment **3** (*used as an intensifier*) <really, you're being ridiculous : vraiment, tu es ridicule>
realm ['rɛlm] *n* **1** KINGDOM : royaume *m* **2** SPHERE : domaine *m*
ream[1] ['riːm] *vt* : fraiser
ream[2] *n* : rame *f* (de papier)
reap ['riːp] *vt* **1** : moissonner, faucher (des récoltes) **2** HARVEST : récolter <he reaped a rich reward : il a récolté une riche récompense>
reaper ['riːpər] *n* : moissonneuse *f* (machine)
reappear [ˌriːəˈpɪr] *vi* : réapparaître, reparaître
rear[1] ['rɪr] *vt* **1** RAISE : lever, relever **2** BREED, BRING UP : élever (des animaux ou des enfants) — *vi* : se cabrer (se dit d'un cheval)
rear[2] *adj* : derrière
rear[3] *n* **1** BACK : derrière *m* **2** BUTTOCKS : derrière *m fam*, arrière-train *m fam*
rear admiral *n* : contre-amiral *m*
rearrange [ˌriːəˈreɪndʒ] *vt* **-ranged; -ranging** : réarranger
reason[1] ['riːzən] *vi* : raisonner
reason[2] *n* **1** EXPLANATION : raison *f* **2** BASIS : motif *m*, raisons *fpl* **3** CAUSE : cause *f*, raison *f* **4** COMMON SENSE : raison *f*, bon sens *m*
reasonable ['riːzənəbəl] *adj* **1** : raisonnable, sensé **2** AFFORDABLE : raisonnable, abordable
reasonably ['riːzənəbli] *adv* : raisonnablement
reasoning ['riːzənɪŋ] *n* : raisonnement *m*
reassess [ˌriːəˈsɛs] *vt* : réexaminer
reassurance [ˌriːəˈʃʊrənʦ] *n* **1** ASSURANCE : assurance *f* **2** COMFORTING : réconfort *m*
reassure [ˌriːəˈʃʊr] *vt* **-sured; -suring** : rassurer

reawaken [ˌriːəˈweɪkən] *vt* : réveiller
rebate[1] ['riːˌbeɪt] *vt* **-bated; -bating** : donner une ristourne à
rebate[2] *n* : ristourne *f*
rebel[1] [rɪˈbɛl] *vi* **-belled; -belling** : se rebeller, se révolter
rebel[2] ['rɛbəl] *adj* : rebelle
rebel[3] ['rɛbəl] *n* : rebelle *mf*
rebellion [rɪˈbɛljən] *n* : rébellion *f*, révolte *f*
rebellious [rɪˈbɛljəs] *adj* : rebelle
rebirth [ˌriːˈbərθ] *n* : renaissance *f*
reboot [ˌriːˈbuːt] *v* : redémarrer
rebound[1] ['riːˌbaʊnd, rɪˈbaʊnd] *vi* **1** : rebondir (se dit d'un ballon) **2** RECOVER : rebondir, repartir à zéro
rebound[2] ['riːˌbaʊnd] *n* : rebond *m*
rebuff[1] [rɪˈbʌf] *vt* : mal accueillir
rebuff[2] *n* : rebuffade *f*
rebuild [ˌriːˈbɪld] *vt* **-built** [-ˈbɪlt]; **-building** : reconstruire
rebuke[1] [rɪˈbjuːk] *vt* **-buked; -buking** : reprocher, réprimander
rebuke[2] *n* : reproche *m*, réprimande *f*
rebut [rɪˈbʌt] *vt* **-butted; -butting** : réfuter
rebuttal [rɪˈbʌtəl] *n* : réfutation *f*
recalcitrant [rɪˈkælsətrənt] *adj* : récalcitrant
recall[1] [rɪˈkɔl] *vt* **1** : rappeler <to be recalled to duty : être rappelé au devoir> **2** REMEMBER : se rappeler, se souvenir de **3** CANCEL, REVOKE : révoquer, annuler
recall[2] [rɪˈkɔl, ˈriːˌkɔl] *n* **1** : rappel *m* (de personnes ou de marchandises) **2** MEMORY : mémoire *f* **3** REVOCATION : révocation *f*, annulation *f*
recant [rɪˈkænt] *vt* : rétracter (une opinion) — *vi* : abjurer
recapitulate [ˌriːkəˈpɪtʃəˌleɪt] *vt* **-lated; -lating** : récapituler, résumer
recapitulation [ˌriːkəˌpɪtʃəˈleɪʃən] *n* : récapitulation *f*
recapture [ˌriːˈkæptʃər] *vt* **-tured; -turing 1** : reprendre (une ville, etc.) **2** RECOVER : recréer <to recapture the past : recréer le passé>
recede [rɪˈsiːd] *vi* **-ceded; -ceding 1** WITHDRAW : s'éloigner, redescendre (se dit de la marée), refluer (se dit des eaux) **2** DIMINISH : diminuer, baisser <to recede into the distance : disparaître dans le lointain>
receipt [rɪˈsiːt] *n* **1** : reçu *m*, récépissé *m* **2 receipts** *npl* : recettes *fpl*
receivable [rɪˈsiːvəbəl] *adj* : à recevoir <accounts receivable : comptes clients>
receive [rɪˈsiːv] *vt* **-ceived; -ceiving 1** GET : recevoir <to receive a gift : recevoir un cadeau> **2** GREET : accueillir (des visiteurs) **3** : recevoir, capter (des ondes radio)
receiver [rɪˈsiːvər] *n* **1** : receveur *m*, -veuse *f* (personne) **2** : récepteur *m* (de radio), combiné *m* (téléphonique)
recent ['riːsənt] *adj* : récent
recently ['riːsəntli] *adv* : récemment
receptacle [rɪˈsɛptɪkəl] *n* : récipient *m*
reception [rɪˈsɛpʃən] *n* : réception *f*
receptionist [rɪˈsɛpʃənɪst] *n* : réceptionniste *mf*
receptive [rɪˈsɛptɪv] *adj* : réceptif
receptivity [ˌriːsɛpˈtɪvəṭi] *n* : réceptivité *f*
recess[1] ['riːˌsɛs, rɪˈsɛs] *vt* : encastrer <recessed lighting : éclairage encastré> — *vi* : suspendre les séances
recess[2] *n* **1** ALCOVE : recoin *m*, alcôve *f* **2** BREAK : récréation *f* (scolaire)
recession [rɪˈsɛʃən] *n* : récession *f*
recharge [ˌriːˈtʃɑrdʒ] *vt* **-charged; -charging** : recharger
rechargeable [ˌriːˈtʃɑrdʒəbəl] *adj* : rechargeable
recipe ['rɛsəˌpiː] *n* : recette *f*
recipient [rɪˈsɪpiənt] *n* : destinataire *mf* (d'une lettre), récipiendaire *m* (d'un prix, d'un diplôme, etc.)
reciprocal [rɪˈsɪprəkəl] *adj* : réciproque — **reciprocally** *adv*
reciprocate [rɪˈsɪprəˌkeɪt] *v* **-cated; -cating** *vt* : retourner (un service) — *vi* : rendre la pareille, en faire autant
reciprocity [ˌrɛsəˈprɑsəṭi] *n, pl* **-ties** : réciprocité *f*
recital [rɪˈsaɪṭəl] *n* **1** NARRATIVE : narration *f*, énumération *f* **2** : récital *m* <dance recital : récital de danse>
recitation [ˌrɛsəˈteɪʃən] *n* : récitation *f*
recite [rɪˈsaɪt] *vt* **-cited; -citing 1** : réciter (un poème, etc.) **2** RECOUNT : relater, raconter
reckless ['rɛkləs] *adj* : imprudent, irréfléchi, téméraire
recklessly ['rɛkləsli] *adv* : imprudemment, sans réfléchir
recklessness ['rɛkləsnəs] *n* : imprudence *f*, témérité *f*
reckon ['rɛkən] *vt* **1** CALCULATE, COUNT : compter **2** CONSIDER : estimer, considérer
reckoning ['rɛkənɪŋ] *n* **1** CALCULATION : compte *m*, calcul *m* **2** ESTIMATION : estimation *f*, calculs *mpl* <according to his reckoning : selon ses calculs>
reclaim [rɪˈkleɪm] *vt* **1** : mettre en valeur (un terrain) **2** RECYCLE : recycler **3** RECOVER : récupérer
recline [rɪˈklaɪn] *vi* **-clined; -clining 1** LIE : être couché, être allongé **2** : s'incliner (se dit d'un siège)
recluse ['rɛˌkluːs, rɪˈkluːs] *n* : reclus *m*, -cluse *f*
recognition [ˌrɛkɪgˈnɪʃən] *n* : reconnaissance *f*
recognizable ['rɛkəgˌnaɪzəbəl] *adj* : reconnaissable
recognizably ['rɛkəgˌnaɪzəbli] *adv* : manifestement, d'une façon reconnaissable
recognize ['rɛkɪgˌnaɪz] *vt* **-nized; -nizing** : reconnaître

recoil[1] [rɪ'kɔɪl] *vi* : reculer
recoil[2] ['ri:,kɔɪl, rɪ'-] *n* : recul *m*, mouvement *m* de recul
recollect [,rɛkə'lɛkt] *vt* : se souvenir de, se rappeler — *vi* : se souvenir
recollection [,rɛkə'lɛkʃən] *n* : souvenir *m*
recommend [,rɛkə'mɛnd] *vt* : recommander
recommendation [,rɛkəmən'deɪʃən] *n* : recommandation *f*
recompense[1] ['rɛkəm,pɛnts] *vt* **-pensed; -pensing 1** REWARD : récompenser **2** COMPENSATE : dédommager, compenser
recompense[2] *n* **1** REWARD : récompense *f* **2** COMPENSATION : dédommagement *m*
reconcile ['rɛkən,saɪl] *v* **-ciled; -ciling** *vt* **1** : réconcilier **2 to reconcile oneself to** : se résigner à — *vi* MAKE UP : se réconcilier
reconciliation [,rɛkən,sɪli'eɪʃən] *n* : réconciliation *f*
recondite ['rɛkən,daɪt, rɪ'kɑn-] *adj* : abstrus, obscur
recondition [,ri:kən,dɪʃən] *vt* : remettre à neuf
reconnaissance [rɪ'kɑnəzənts, -sənts] *n* : reconnaissance *f*
reconnoiter *or* **reconnoitre** [,ri:kə-'nɔɪtər, ,rɛkə-] *v* **-tered** *or* **-tred; -tering** *or* **-tring** *vt* : reconnaître — *vi* : faire une reconnaissance
reconsider [,ri:kən'sɪdər] *vt* : réexaminer (un plan, une décision) — *vi* : repenser <I asked him to reconsider : je lui ai demandé d'y repenser>
reconsideration [,ri:kən,sɪdə'reɪʃən] *n* : révision *f*, réexamen *m*
reconstruct [,ri:kən'strʌkt] *vt* : reconstruire
record[1] [rɪ'kɔrd] *vt* **1** WRITE DOWN : noter, enregistrer **2** REGISTER : enregistrer **3** INDICATE : indiquer (la température, etc.) **4** TAPE : enregistrer (une émission)
record[2] ['rɛkərd] *n* **1** DOCUMENT : document *m*, écrit *m* **2** HISTORY, REPORT : compte rendu *m*, récit *m* (des événements, etc.) **3** : record *m* <the world record : le record mondial> **4** : disque *m* (de musique) **5** *or* **school record** : dossier *m* (scolaire) **6** *or* **police record** : casier *m* judiciaire
recorder [rɪ'kɔrdər] *n* **1** *or* **tape recorder** : magnétophone *m* **2** : flûte *f* à bec (instrument de musique)
recount [rɪ'kaʊnt] *vt* **1** NARRATE : raconter, conter **2** [,ri:-] : recompter (des votes, etc.), compter de nouveau
recoup [rɪ'ku:p] *vt* : recouvrer, récupérer
recourse ['ri:,kɔrs, rɪ'-] *n* : recours *m*
recover [rɪ'kʌvər] *vt* **1** REGAIN : retrouver, récupérer **2** RECOUP : recouvrer — *vi* RECUPERATE : se remettre, se rétablir
recovery [rɪ'kʌvəri] *n, pl* **-ries** : rétablissement *m*
re–create [,ri:kri'eɪt] *vt* **-ated; -ating** : recréer
recreation [,rɛkri'eɪʃən] *n* : loisirs *mpl*, récréation *f*
recreational [,rɛkri'eɪʃənəl] *adj* : récréatif
recriminate [rɪ'krɪmə,neɪt] *vi* **-nated; -nating** : récriminer <to recriminate against : récriminer contre>
recrimination [rɪ,krɪmə'neɪʃən] *n* : récrimination *f*
recruit[1] [rɪ'kru:t] *vt* : recruter
recruit[2] *n* : recrue *f*
recruitment [rɪ'kru:tmənt] *n* : recrutement *m*
rectal ['rɛktəl] *adj* : rectal
rectangle ['rɛk,tæŋgəl] *n* : rectangle *m*
rectangular [rɛk'tæŋgjələr] *adj* : rectangulaire
rectify ['rɛktə,faɪ] *vt* **-fied; -fying** : rectifier
rectitude ['rɛktə,tu:d, -,tju:d] *n* : rectitude *f*
rector ['rɛktər] *n* : pasteur *m*
rectory ['rɛktəri] *n, pl* **-ries** : presbytère *m*
rectum ['rɛktəm] *n, pl* **-tums** *or* **-ta** [-tə] : rectum *m*
recumbent [rɪ'kəmbənt] *adj* : couché, étendu
recuperate [rɪ'ku:pə,reɪt, -'kju:-] *v* **-ated; -ating** *vi* : se rétablir, se remettre — *vt* REGAIN : retrouver (ses forces), récupérer (ses débours)
recuperation [rɪ,ku:pə'reɪʃən, -,kju:-] *n* : rétablissement *m* (de la santé), recouvrement *m* (d'une dette, etc.)
recur [rɪ'kər] *vi* **-curred; -curring** : réapparaître
recurrence [rɪ'kərənts] *n* : réapparition *f*, retour *m*
recurrent [rɪ'kərənt] *adj* : récurrent, fréquent
recyclable [rɪ'saɪkələbəl] *adj* : recyclable
recycle [rɪ'saɪkəl] *vt* **-cled; -cling** : recycler
red[1] ['rɛd] *adj* : rouge
red[2] *n* **1** : rouge *m* **2 Red** : communiste *mf*, rouge *mf* **3 in the red** : dans le rouge, en déficit
red blood cell *n* : globule *m* rouge
red–blooded ['rɛd'blʌdəd] *adj* : vigoureux
redcap ['rɛd,kæp] → **porter**
redden ['rɛdən] *vt* : rougir — *vi* BLUSH : rougir
reddish ['rɛdɪʃ] *adj* : rougeâtre
redecorate [,ri:'dɛkə,reɪt] *vt* **-rated; -rating** : repeindre et retapisser
redeem [ri'di:m] *vt* **1** RESCUE, SAVE : racheter, sauver <to redeem oneself : se racheter> **2** REPAY, REPURCHASE : rembourser (une dette), racheter (une propriété chez un prêteur sur gages) **3** EXCHANGE : échanger <to

redeem savings bonds : échanger des bons d'épargne> **4** : racheter (en religion)
redeemer [rɪ'di:mər] *n* : rédempteur *m*
redemption [rɪ'dempʃən] *n* : rédemption *f*
red-handed ['rɛd'hændəd] *adv* : la main dans le sac
redhead ['rɛd,hɛd] *n* : roux *m*, rousse *f*
rediscover [,ri:di'skʌvər] *vt* : redécouvrir
redistribute [,ri:di'strɪ,bju:t] *vt* **-uted; -uting** : redistribuer
redness ['rɛdnəs] *n* : rougeur *f*
redo [,ri:'du:] *vt* **-did** [-dɪd]; **-done** [-'dʌn]; **-doing 1** : refaire **2** → **redecorate**
redolence ['rɛdələnʊs] *n* : arôme *m*, parfum *m*
redolent ['rɛdələnt] *adj* **1** FRAGRANT : aromatique, parfumé **2** SUGGESTIVE : évocateur **3** ~ **of** *or* ~ **with** : qui sent de, qui dégage (une odeur)
redouble [rɪ'dʌbəl] *vt* **-bled; -bling** : redoubler
redoubtable [rɪ'daʊtəbəl] *adj* : redoutable, formidable
redress [rɪ'drɛs] *vt* : redresser, réparer
red tape *n* : lenteurs *fpl* bureaucratiques, paperasserie *f*
reduce [rɪ'du:s, -'dju:s] *v* **-duced; -ducing** *vt* **1** LESSEN : réduire, diminuer **2** LOWER : baisser (des prix, etc.) **3** DEMOTE : rétrograder **4 to reduce to tears** : faire pleurer — *vi* : maigrir, perdre du poids
reduction [rɪ'dʌkʃən] *n* : réduction *f*, diminution *f*
redundant [rɪ'dʌndənt] *adj* : superflu, redondant
redwood ['rɛd,wʊd] *n* : séquoia *m*
reed ['ri:d] *n* **1** : roseau *m* **2** : anche *f* (d'un instrument de musique)
reef ['ri:f] *n* : récif *m*, écueil *m*
reek[1] ['ri:k] *vi* : empester, puer
reek[2] *n* : puanteur *f*
reel[1] ['ri:l] *vt* **1 to reel in** : enrouler (une ligne de pêche, etc.), ramener (un poisson) **2 to reel off** : débiter (un discours, etc.) — *vi* **1** SPIN, WHIRL : tournoyer <her head was reeling : elle avait la tête qui tournait> **2** STAGGER : chanceler, tituber
reel[2] *n* **1** : bobine *f*, rouleau *m*, moulinet *m* (de pêche) **2** : quadrille *m* écossais (danse)
reelect [,ri:rɪ'lɛkt] *vt* : réélire
reenact [,ri:rɪ'nækt] *vt* : reconstituer, reproduire
reenter [,ri:'ɛntər] *vt* : entrer à nouveau
reestablish [,ri:rɪ'stæblɪʃ] *vt* : rétablir
reevaluate [,ri:rɪ'væljʊ,eɪt] *vt* **-ated; -ating** : réévaluer
reexamine [,ri:ɪg'zæmən] *vt* **-ined; -ining** : réexaminer
refer [rɪ'fər] *v* **-ferred; -ferring** *vt* **1** DIRECT : envoyer, diriger <to refer a patient to a specialist : diriger un patient à un spécialiste> **2** SUBMIT : soumettre, présenter <to refer a proposal to a committee : soumettre un plan à un comité> — *vi* **to refer to** MENTION : faire allusion à, mentionner
referee[1] [,rɛfə'ri:] *v* **-eed; -eeing** : arbitrer
referee[2] *n* : arbitre *m*
reference ['rɛfərənʊs] *n* **1** *or* **reference book** : ouvrage *m* de référence **2** ALLUSION : allusion *f* **3** RECOMMENDATION : référence *f* **4 in reference to** : en ce qui concerne
referendum [,rɛfə'rɛndəm] *n, pl* **-da** [-də] *or* **-dums** : référendum *m*
refill[1] [,ri:'fɪl] *vt* : remplir à nouveau
refill[2] ['ri:,fɪl] *n* : recharge *f* (de stylo), cartouche *f* (d'encre)
refine [rɪ'faɪn] *vt* **-fined; -fining 1** : raffiner (le sucre, le pétrole, etc.) **2** IMPROVE, PERFECT : peaufiner, perfectionner
refinement [rɪ'faɪnmənt] *n* **1** : raffinage *m* (du pétrole, du sucre, etc.) **2** CULTIVATION, ELEGANCE : raffinement *m* **3** IMPROVEMENT : amélioration *f*, perfectionnement *m*
refinery [rɪ'faɪnəri] *n, pl* **-eries** : raffinerie *f*
reflect [rɪ'flɛkt] *vt* **1** : réfléchir (la lumière), renvoyer (des sons, de la chaleur, etc.) **2** : refléter (une image, des idées, des émotions, etc.) <art reflects life : l'art reflète la vie> — *vi* **1** PONDER : réfléchir **2 to reflect badly on** : faire du tort à **3 to reflect well on** : faire honneur à
reflection [rɪ'flɛkʃən] *n* **1** : réflexion *f* (de la lumière, des sons, etc.) **2** IMAGE : reflet *m*, image *f* **3** THOUGHT : réflexion *f*, pensée *f*
reflective [rɪ'flɛktɪv] *adj* **1** : réfléchissant (en physique) **2** THOUGHTFUL : pensif, songeur
reflector [rɪ'flɛktər] *n* : réflecteur *m*
reflex[1] ['ri:,flɛks] *adj* : réflexe
reflex[2] *n* : réflexe *m*
reflexive[1] [rɪ'flɛksɪv] *adj* : réfléchi <reflexive pronoun : pronom réfléchi>
reflexive[2] *n or* **reflexive verb** : verbe *m* réfléchi
reform[1] [rɪ'fɔrm] *vt* : réformer — *vi* : se réformer
reform[2] *n* : réforme *f* — **reformable** *adj*
reformation [,rɛfər'meɪʃən] *n* **1** : réforme *f* **2 the Reformation** : la Réforme
reformatory [rɪ'fɔrmə,tori] *n, pl* **-ries** : maison *f* de correction
reformer [rɪ'fɔrmər] *n* : réformateur *m*, -trice *f*
refract [rɪ'frækt] *vt* : réfracter — *vi* : se réfracter
refraction [rɪ'frækʃən] *n* : réfraction *f*
refractory [rɪ'fræktəri] *adj* : réfractaire
refrain[1] [rɪ'freɪn] *vi* **to refrain from** : se retenir de, s'empêcher de

refrain[2] *n* : refrain *m* (en musique)
refresh [rɪˈfreʃ] *vt* **1** RESTORE, REVIVE : rafraîchir <to refresh oneself : se rafraîchir> **2 to refresh s.o.'s memory** : rafraîchir la mémoire de qqn
refreshment [rɪˈfreʃmənt] *n* **1** REST : repos *m* **2 refreshments** *npl* : rafraîchissements *mpl*
refrigerate [rɪˈfrɪdʒəˌreɪt] *vt* **-ated; -ating** : réfrigérer, frigorifier
refrigeration [rɪˌfrɪdʒəˈreɪʃən] *n* : réfrigération *f*
refrigerator [rɪˈfrɪdʒəˌreɪtər] *n* : réfrigérateur *m*
refuel [riːˈfjuːəl] *v* **-eled** *or* **-elled; -eling** *or* **-elling** *vt* : ravitailler — *vi* : se ravitailler
refuge [ˈrɛˌfjuːdʒ] *n* : refuge *m*, abri *m*
refugee [ˌrɛfjʊˈdʒiː] *n* : réfugié *m*, -giée *f*
refund[1] [rɪˈfʌnd, ˈriːˌfʌnd] *vt* : rembourser (de l'argent)
refund[2] [ˈriːˌfʌnd] *n* : remboursement *m*, ristourne *f*
refundable [rɪˈfʌndəbəl] *adj* : remboursable
refurbish [rɪˈfərbɪʃ] *vt* : remettre à neuf, réaménager
refusal [rɪˈfjuːzəl] *n* : refus *m*
refuse[1] [rɪˈfjuːz] *vt* **-fused; -fusing 1** REJECT : refuser **2** DENY : refuser <they were refused admittance : on leur a refusé l'entrée> **3 to refuse to do sth** : se refuser à faire qqch
refuse[2] [ˈrɛˌfjuːs, -ˌfjuːz] *n* : ordures *fpl*, déchets *mpl*
refutation [ˌrɛfjʊˈteɪʃən] *n* : réfutation *f*
refute [rɪˈfjuːt] *vt* **-futed; -futing** : réfuter
regal [ˈriːgəl] *adj* : royal, majestueux
regale [rɪˈgeɪl] *vt* **-galed; -galing** : régaler
regalia [rɪˈgeɪljə] *npl* **1** INSIGNIA : insignes *mpl* **2** FINERY : atours *mpl*, accoutrement *m*
regard[1] [rɪˈgɑrd] *vt* **1** CONSIDER : considérer <I regard her as my sister : je la considère comme une sœur> **2** HEED : tenir compte de **3** OBSERVE : observer, considérer avec attention **4** RESPECT : respecter <highly regarded : très estimé>
regard[2] *n* **1** CONSIDERATION : égard *m*, considération *f* <without regard for : sans égard pour> **2** ESTEEM : respect *m*, estime *f* **3 regards** *npl* : amitiés *fpl* <send him my regards : transmettez-lui mes amitiés> **4 as regards** *or* **with regard to** : en ce qui concerne
regarding [rɪˈgɑrdɪŋ] *prep* : concernant
regardless [rɪˈgɑrdləs] *adv* : malgré tout, quand même
regardless of *prep* : sans tenir compte de
regenerate [rɪˈdʒɛnəˌreɪt] *v* **-ated; -ating** *vt* : régénérer — *vi* : se régénérer
regeneration [rɪˌdʒɛnəˈreɪʃən] *n* : régénération *f*
regent [ˈriːdʒənt] *n* : régent *m*, -gente *f*
regime [reɪˈʒiːm, rɪ-] *n* : régime *m*
regimen [ˈrɛdʒəmən] *n* : régime *m*
regiment[1] [ˈrɛdʒəˌmɛnt] *vt* : enrégimenter
regiment[2] [ˈrɛdʒəmənt] *n* : régiment *m*
region [ˈriːdʒən] *n* : région *f*
regional [ˈriːdʒənəl] *adj* : régional — **regionally** *adv*
register[1] [ˈrɛdʒəstər] *vt* **1** RECORD : inscrire, enregistrer **2** : immatriculer (un véhicule) **3** : enregistrer (une lettre) **4** SHOW : exprimer <to register surprise : exprimer la surprise> **5** : indiquer (la température, etc.) — *vi* ENROLL : s'inscrire
register[2] *n* **1** RECORD : registre *m* <a register of births : un registre des naissances> **2** RANGE : registre *m* (de la voix) **3 → cash register**
registrar [ˈrɛdʒəˌstrɑr] *n* : chef *m* de la division des inscriptions (dans une université)
registration [ˌrɛdʒəˈstreɪʃən] *n* **1** : enregistrement *m* (de bagages), immatriculation *f* (d'un véhicule) **2** ENROLLMENT : inscription *f*
registry [ˈrɛdʒəstri] *n, pl* **-tries 1** REGISTRATION : enregistrement *m* **2** : bureau *m* d'enregistrement
regress [rɪˈgrɛs] *vi* : régresser
regression [rɪˈgrɛʃən] *n* : régression *f*
regressive [rɪˈgrɛsɪv] *adj* : régressif
regret[1] [rɪˈgrɛt] *vt* **-gretted; -gretting** : regretter
regret[2] *n* **1** SORROW : regret *m* **2** REMORSE : remords *mpl*, regrets *mpl* **3 regrets** *npl* : excuses *fpl* <to send one's regrets to s.o. : s'excuser auprès de qqn>
regretful [rɪˈgrɛtfəl] *adj* : plein de regrets
regretfully [rɪˈgrɛtfəli] *adv* : avec regret
regrettable [rɪˈgrɛtəbəl] *adj* : regrettable
regrettably [rɪˈgrɛtəbli] *adv* : malheureusement
regular[1] [ˈrɛgjələr] *adj* **1** SYMMETRICAL : régulier **2** NORMAL : régulier, normal **3** STEADY : régulier, égal <a regular pace : un pas régulier> **4** ORDERLY : fixe <regular habits : habitudes fixes>
regular[2] *n* : habitué *m*, -tuée *f*
regularity [ˌrɛgjəˈlærətɪ] *n, pl* **-ties** : régularité *f*
regularly [ˈrɛgjələrli] *adv* : régulièrement
regulate [ˈrɛgjəˌleɪt] *vt* **-lated; -lating** : régler
regulation [ˌrɛgjəˈleɪʃən] *n* **1** RULE : règlement *m*, règle *f* <safety regulations : règlements de sécurité> **2** CONTROL : réglementation *f*
regurgitate [rɪˈgərdʒəˌteɪt] *vt* **-tated; -tating** : régurgiter
rehabilitate [ˌriːhəˈbɪləˌteɪt] *vt* **-tated; -tating 1** REINSTATE : réhabiliter **2**

RESTORE : rénover, réhabiliter (un quartier) **3** : rééduquer (un patient), réhabiliter (un détenu, un toxicomane, etc.)

rehabilitation [ˌriːhəˈbɪləˈteɪʃən] *n* : réhabilitation *f*

rehearsal [rɪˈhərsəl] *n* : répétition *f* (au théâtre)

rehearse [rɪˈhərs] *vt* **-hearsed; -hearsing** : répéter, répéter

reheat [riːˈhiːt] *vt* : réchauffer

reign[1] [ˈreɪn] *vi* **1** RULE : régner **2** PREVAIL : régner, prédominer

reign[2] *n* : règne *m*

reimburse [ˌriːəmˈbərs] *vt* **-bursed; -bursing** : rembourser

reimbursement [ˌriːəmˈbərsmənt] *n* : remboursement *m*

rein[1] [ˈreɪn] *vt* **1** : serrer la bride à (un cheval) **2 to rein in** CHECK : contenir, maîtriser (des émotions, etc.)

rein[2] *n* **1** : rêne *f*, bride *f* (d'un cheval) **2 to give full rein to** : donner libre cours à **3 to keep a tight rein on** : tenir la bride serrée à

reincarnate [ˌriːɪnˈkɑrˌneɪt] *vt* **-nated; -nating** : réincarner

reincarnation [ˌriːɪnˌkɑrˈneɪʃən] *n* : réincarnation *f*

reindeer [ˈreɪnˌdɪr] *n* : renne *f*

reinforce [ˌriːənˈfɔrs] *vt* **-forced; -forcing** : renforcer

reinforcement [ˌriːənˈfɔrsmənt] *n* : renforcement *m*

reinstate [ˌriːənˈsteɪt] *vt* **-stated; -stating** : réintégrer, rétablir

reinstatement [ˌriːənˈsteɪtmənt] *n* : réintégration *f*, rétablissement *m*

reiterate [riːˈɪtəˌreɪt] *vt* **-ated; -ating** : réitérer, répéter

reiteration [riːˌɪtəˈreɪʃən] *n* : réitération *f*, répétition *f*

reject[1] [rɪˈdʒɛkt] *vt* : rejeter

reject[2] [ˈriːˌdʒɛkt] *n* **1** : marchandise *f* de second choix **2** : personne *f* méprisée

rejection [rɪˈdʒɛkʃən] *n* : rejet *m*

rejoice [rɪˈdʒɔɪs] *vi* **-joiced; -joicing** : se réjouir

rejoin *vt* **1** [riːˈdʒɔɪn] : rejoindre <he rejoined the company : il a rejoint la compagnie> **2** [rɪˈ-] RETORT : répliquer, rétorquer

rejoinder [rɪˈdʒɔɪndər] *n* : réplique *f*

rejuvenate [rɪˈdʒuːvəˌneɪt] *vt* **-nated; -nating** : rajeunir

rejuvenation [rɪˌdʒuːvəˈneɪʃən] *n* : rajeunissement *m*

rekindle [ˌriːˈkɪndəl] *vt* **-dled; -dling** : raviver, ranimer (un feu, l'espoir etc.)

relapse[1] [rɪˈlæps] *vi* **-lapsed; -lapsing** : retomber, rechuter

relapse[2] [ˈriːˌlæps, rɪˈlæps] *n* : rechute *f* (en médecine)

relate [rɪˈleɪt] *v* **-lated; -lating** *vt* **1** TELL : raconter **2** ASSOCIATE : établir un lien entre, relier <to relate crime to poverty : relier le crime à la pauvreté> — *vi* **1** CONNECT : se rapporter **2** INTERACT : communiquer (avec) **3 to relate to** APPRECIATE, UNDERSTAND : apprécier

related [rɪˈleɪtəd] *adj* : apparenté

relation [rɪˈleɪʃən] *n* **1** NARRATION : récit *m* **2** CONNECTION, RELATIONSHIP : rapport *m* <in relation to : par rapport à> **3** RELATIVE : parent *m*, -rente *f* **4 relations** *npl* : rapports *mpl*, relations *fpl* <sexual relations : relations sexuelles> <foreign relations : affaires étrangères>

relationship [rɪˈleɪʃənˌʃɪp] *n* **1** CONNECTION : rapport *m*, relations *fpl* **2** KINSHIP : liens *mpl* de parenté

relative[1] [ˈrɛləˌtɪv] *adj* : relatif — **relatively** *adv*

relative[2] *n* : parent *m*, -rente *f*

relativity [ˌrɛləˈtɪvəˌti] *n* : relativité *f*

relax [rɪˈlæks] *vt* **1** SLACKEN : relâcher, desserrer **2** MODIFY : assouplir <to relax immigration laws : assouplir les lois d'immigration> — *vi* REST : se détendre, se reposer

relaxation [ˌriːˌlækˈseɪʃən] *n* **1** RELAXING : relâchement *m*, desserrement *m* **2** DIVERSION : détente *f*

relay[1] [ˈriːˌleɪ, rɪˈleɪ] *vt* **-layed; -laying** : relayer

relay[2] *n* **1 relay race** *or* : course *f* de relais

release[1] [rɪˈliːs] *vt* **-leased; -leasing 1** FREE : libérer **2** RELINQUISH : renoncer à (une réclamation, etc.) **3** RELIEVE : dégager <she was released from her promise : elle s'est dégagée de sa promesse> **4** : publier (un livre), sortir (un nouveau film), rendre public (un document, etc.) **5** LET GO, LOOSEN : desserrer, déclencher <to release the clutch : débrayer>

release[2] *n* **1** RELIEF : soulagement *m* (à la douleur) **2** LIBERATION : libération *f*, mise *f* en liberté **3** ISSUE : sortie *f* (d'un film), parution *f* (d'un livre) **4** : déclenchement *m* (d'un mécanisme) **5** *or* **news release** : communiqué *m*

relegate [ˈrɛləˌgeɪt] *vt* **-gated; -gating** : reléguer

relent [rɪˈlɛnt] *vi* **1** GIVE IN : se rendre **2** ABATE : se calmer

relentless [rɪˈlɛntləs] *adj* : implacable, impitoyable — **relentlessly** *adv*

relevance [ˈrɛləvənts] *n* : pertinence *f*

relevant [ˈrɛləvənt] *adj* : pertinent

relevantly [ˈrɛləvəntli] *adv* : pertinemment

reliability [rɪˌlaɪəˈbɪləˌti] *n*, *pl* **-ties 1** : sérieux *m*, intégrité *f* (d'une personne) **2** : fiabilité *f* (d'information, d'une machine, etc.)

reliable [rɪˈlaɪəbəl] *adj* : fiable, sûr

reliance [rɪˈlaɪənts] *n* **1** DEPENDENCE : dépendance *f* **2** TRUST : confiance *f*

reliant [rɪˈlaɪənt] *adj* **1** DEPENDENT : dépendant **2** TRUSTING : confiant

relic [ˈrɛlɪk] *n* **1** : relique *f* **2 relics** *mpl* : vestiges *mpl* (du passé)

relief [rɪˈliːf] *n* **1** : soulagement *m* <much to my relief : à mon grand soulagement> **2** AID, WELFARE : aide *f* (sociale) **3** : relief *m* <a relief map : une carte en relief> **4** REPLACEMENT : relève *f*, équipe *f* de relève

relieve [rɪˈliːv] *vt* **-lieved; -lieving 1** MITIGATE : soulager, alléger **2** UNBURDEN : libérer, débarrasser <to relieve s.o. of his suitcase : débarrasser qqn de ses valises> <to be relieved of a command : être relevé d'une fonction> **3** AID : secourir, venir en aide à **4** ALLEVIATE : briser (la monotonie), dissiper (la mélancolie), égayer (la noirceur d'un événement, etc.)

religion [rɪˈlɪdʒən] *n* : religion *f*

religious [rɪˈlɪdʒəs] *adj* : religieux — **religiously** *adv*

relinquish [rɪˈlɪŋkwɪʃ, -ˈlɪn-] *vt* **1** GIVE UP : renoncer à, abandonner **2** RELEASE : relâcher

relish[1] [ˈrɛlɪʃ] *vt* **1** : savourer (le boire et le manger) **2** ENJOY : se réjouir de, savourer (une idée, etc.)

relish[2] *n* **1** ENJOYMENT : plaisir *m*, délectation *f* **2** : condiment *m* à base de cornichons et de vinaigre, relish *f* *Can*

relive [ˌriːˈlɪv] *vi* **-lived; -living** : revivre

relocate [ˌriːloˌkeɪt, ˌriːloˈkeɪt] *v* **-cated; -cating** *vt* : muter, transférer <to relocate an employee : muter un employé> — *vi* : déménager, s'établir ailleurs

relocation [ˌriːloˈkeɪʃən] *n* **1** : mutation *f*, transfert *m* (d'un employé) **2** : déménagement *m* (d'une firme, etc.)

reluctance [rɪˈlʌktənts] *n* : réticence *f*, répugnance *f*

reluctant [rɪˈlʌktənt] *adj* **to be reluctant to** : être peu enclin à, être peu disposé à

reluctantly [rɪˈlʌktəntli] *adv* : à contrecœur

rely [rɪˈlaɪ] *vi* **-lied; -lying 1** DEPEND : compter (sur), dépendre (de) **2** TRUST : se fier (à)

remain [rɪˈmeɪn] *vi* **1** : rester <only ruins remain : il ne reste que des ruines> **2** STAY : rester, demeurer **3 it remains to be seen** : il reste à voir **4 the fact remains that** : toujours est-il que

remainder [rɪˈmeɪndər] *n* : reste *m*, restant *m*

remains [rɪˈmeɪnz] *npl* **1** : restes *mpl* <the remains of a meal : les restes d'un repas> **2** *or* **last remains** : restes *mpl*, dépouille *f* mortelle

remark[1] [rɪˈmɑrk] *vt* **1** NOTICE : remarquer, constater **2** SAY : remarquer, mentionner — *vi* **to remark on** : faire des remarques sur

remark[2] *n* : remarque *f*, observation *f*

remarkable [rɪˈmɑrkəbəl] *adj* : remarquable, extraordinaire — **remarkably** [-bli] *adv*

remedial [rɪˈmiːdiəl] *adj* : de rattrapage

remedy[1] [ˈrɛmədi] *vt* **-died; -dying** : remédier à

remedy[2] *n, pl* **-dies** : remède *m* (en médecine)

remember [rɪˈmɛmbər] *vt* **1** RECOLLECT : se rappeler, se souvenir de **2** : penser à, ne pas oublier de <remember to open the window : pensez à ouvrir la fenêtre, n'oubliez pas d'ouvrir la fenêtre> **3** COMMEMORATE : commémorer **4 remember me to your sister** : rappelez-moi au bon souvenir de votre sœur

remembrance [rɪˈmɛmbrənts] *n* **1** RECOLLECTION : mémoire *f*, souvenir *m* **2** KEEPSAKE : souvenir *m*

remind [rɪˈmaɪnd] *vt* : rappeler <remind me to do it : rappelle-moi de le faire>

reminder [rɪˈmaɪndər] *n* : rappel *m*

reminisce [ˌrɛməˈnɪs] *vi* : évoquer ses souvenirs

reminiscence [ˌrɛməˈnɪsənts] *n* **1** MEMORY : souvenir *m* **2** RECALLING : réminiscence *f*

reminiscent [ˌrɛməˈnɪsənt] *adj* **1** NOSTALGIC : nostalgique **2 ~ of** : qui rappelle, qui fait penser à

remiss [rɪˈmɪs] *adj* : négligent, inattentif

remission [rɪˈmɪʃən] *n* : rémission *f*

remit [rɪˈmɪt] *vt* **-mitted; -mitting 1** PARDON : remettre <to remit s.o.'s debt : remettre la dette de qqn> **2** SEND : envoyer (de l'argent)

remittance [rɪˈmɪtənts] *n* : paiement *m*, envoi *m*

remnant [ˈrɛmnənt] *n* : reste *m*, restant *m*

remodel [rɪˈmɑdəl] *vt* **-eled** *or* **-elled; -eling** *or* **-elling** : remodeler

remonstrate [rɪˈmɑnˌstreɪt, rɪˈmɑn-] *vi* **-strated; -strating** : protester <to remonstrate with : faire des remontrances à>

remorse [rɪˈmɔrs] *n* : remords *m*

remorseful [rɪˈmɔrsfəl] *adj* : plein de remords, contrit

remorseless [rɪˈmɔrsləs] *adj* **1** MERCILESS : sans remords, sans pitié **2** RELENTLESS : impitoyable, implacable

remote [rɪˈmoːt] *adj* **remoter; -est 1** : lointain, éloigné <the remote past : le passé lointain> **2** SECLUDED : retiré, isolé **3** : à distance <remote control : commande à distance> **4** SLIGHT : petit, faible <there's a remote chance : c'est très peu probable> **5** ALOOF : indifférent

remotely [rɪˈmoːtli] *adv* SLIGHTLY : faiblement, vaguement

remoteness [rɪˈmoːtnəs] *n* : isolement *m*, éloignement *m*

removable [rɪˈmuːvəbəl] *adj* : amovible

removal [rɪ'mu:vəl] *n* **1** ELIMINATION : suppression *f* (d'abus, etc.), enlèvement *m* (de tâches) **2** : ablation *f* (en médecine) **3** : renvoi (d'un employé), révocation *f* (d'un fonctionnaire)

remove [rɪ'mu:v] *vt* **-moved; -moving 1** : enlever, ôter <remove the lid : enlevez le couvercle> <to remove one's coat : ôter son manteau> **2** DISMISS : renvoyer (un employé), démettre (un fonctionnaire) **3** ELIMINATE : supprimer (une menace), écarter (un obstacle), dissiper (la peur)

remunerate [rɪ'mju:nəˌreɪt] *vt* **-ated; -ating** : rémunérer

remuneration [rɪˌmju:nə'reɪʃən] *n* : rémunération *f*

remunerative [rɪ'mju:nərətɪv, -ˌreɪ-] *adj* : rémunérateur, lucratif

renaissance [ˌrenə'sɑnts, -'zɑnts; 'renəˌ-] *n* **1** : renaissance *f* **2 the Renaissance** : la Renaissance

renal ['ri:nəl] *adj* : rénal

rename [ˌri:'neɪm] *vt* **-named; -naming** : rebaptiser

rend ['rend] *vt* **rent** ['rent]; **rending** : déchirer

render ['rendər] *vt* **1** EXTRACT : fondre (de la graisse) **2** GIVE UP : rendre, retourner **3** : rendre (un service), prêter (de l'aide) **4** MAKE : laisser, rendre <she was rendered helpless by the blow : le coup l'a laissée complètement impuissante> **5** PERFORM : interpréter (une chanson, etc.)

rendezvous ['rɑndɪˌvu:, -deɪ-] *ns & pl* : rendez-vous *m*

rendition [ren'dɪʃən] *n* : interprétation *f*

renegade ['renɪˌgeɪd] *n* : renégat *m*, -gate *f*

renege [rɪ'nɪg, -'neg] *vi* **-neged; -neging** : revenir (sur une promesse, etc.)

renew [rɪ'nu:, -'nju:] *vt* **1** REVIVE : raviver (la force, le courage, etc.) **2** RESUME : renouveler, reprendre <to renew one's efforts : renouveler ses efforts> **3** EXTEND : renouveler (un passeport, un abonnement, etc.)

renewable [rɪ'nu:əbəl, -'nju:-] *adj* : renouvelable

renewal [rɪ'nu:əl, -'nju:-] *n* : renouvellement *m*

renounce [rɪ'naʊnts] *vt* **-nounced; -nouncing 1** : renoncer à, abandonner <to renounce the throne : renoncer au trône> **2** REPUDIATE : renier, rejeter

renovate ['renəˌveɪt] *vt* **-vated; -vating** : rénover

renovation [ˌrenə'veɪʃən] *n* : rénovation *f*, restoration *f*

renown [rɪ'naʊn] *n* : renommée *f*, renom *m*

renowned [rɪ'naʊnd] *adj* : renommé, célèbre

rent¹ ['rent] *vt* : louer

rent² *n* **1** : loyer *m* (somme d'argent) **2** TEAR : déchirure *f* **3 for ~** : à louer

rental¹ ['rentəl] *adj* : de location <rental car : voiture de location>

rental² *n* **1** : location *f* <film rentals : location de films> **2** RENT : loyer *m*

renter ['rentər] *n* : locataire *mf*

renunciation [rɪˌnʌntsɪ'eɪʃən] *n* : renonciation *f*

repair¹ [rɪ'pær] *vt* : réparer

repair² *n* **1** : réparation *f* <car repair : réparation de voiture> **2** CONDITION : état *m*, condition *f* <in bad repair : en mauvais état>

reparations [ˌrepə'reɪʃənz] *npl* DAMAGES : réparations *fpl*

repartee [ˌrepər'ti:, -ˌpɑr-, -'teɪ] *n* : repartie *f*, réplique *f*

repast [rɪ'pæst, 'ri:ˌpæst] *n* : repas *m*

repatriate [rɪ'peɪtriˌeɪt] *vt* **-ated; -ating** : rapatrier

repay [rɪ'peɪ] *vt* **-paid; -paying** : rembourser (un emprunt), rendre (une faveur, etc.)

repeal¹ [rɪ'pi:l] *vt* : abroger

repeal² *n* : abrogation *f*

repeat¹ [rɪ'pi:t] *vt* : répéter — *vi* : se répéter

repeat² *n* **1** REPETITION : répétition *f* **2** : rediffusion *f*, reprise *f* <the show is a repeat : l'émission est en rediffusion>

repeatedly [rɪ'pi:ˌtədli] *adv* : à plusieurs reprises

repel [rɪ'pel] *vt* **-pelled; -pelling 1** : repousser (l'ennemi, etc.) **2** REJECT : rejeter **3** RESIST : résister à **4** DISGUST : repousser, répugner

repellent¹ [rɪ'pelənt] *adj* : repoussant, répugnant

repellent² *n or* **insect repellent** : insectifuge *m*

repent [rɪ'pent] *vi* : se repentir

repentance [rɪ'pentənts] *n* : repentir *m*

repentant [rɪ'pentənt] *adj* : repentant

repercussion [ˌri:pər'kʌʃən, ˌrepər-] *n* : répercussion *f*

repertoire ['repərˌtwɑr] *n* : répertoire *m*

repertory ['repərˌtori] *n, pl* **-ries 1** → **repertoire 2** *or* **repertory theater** : théâtre *m* de répertoire

repetition [ˌrepə'tɪʃən] *n* : répétition *f*

repetitious [ˌrepə'tɪʃəs] *adj* : répétitif

repetitive [rɪ'peɪˌəˌtɪv] *adj* : répétitif

repetitively [rɪ'peɪˌəˌtɪvli] *adv* : de façon répétitive

replace [rɪ'pleɪs] *vt* **-placed; -placing 1** RESTORE : remettre **2** SUBSTITUTE : remplacer, substituer

replaceable [rɪ'pleɪsəbəl] *adj* : remplaçable

replacement [rɪ'pleɪsmənt] *n* **1** REPLACING : remplacement *m* **2** SUBSTITUTE : remplaçant *m*, -çante *f*

replenish [rɪ'plenɪʃ] *vt* : remplir (de nouveau)

replenishment [rɪ'plenɪʃmənt] *n* : remplissage *m*
replete [rɪ'pli:t] *adj* **1** FULL : rempli <replete with details : rempli de détails> **2** SATIATED : rassasié
replica ['rɛplɪkə] *n* : copie *f* exacte, réplique *f*
replicate ['rɛpləˌkeɪt] *vt* **-cated; -cating** : reproduire, faire un double de
reply[1] [rɪ'plaɪ] *vi* **-plied; -plying** : répondre, répliquer
reply[2] *n, pl* **-plies** : réponse *f*, réplique *f*
report[1] [rɪ'port] *vt* **1** RELATE : raconter, faire le compte rendu de **2** : faire un reportage sur (en journalisme) **3** : signaler (un feu, un crime, etc.), dénoncer (un malfaiteur) — *vi* **1** : faire un rapport **2** : se présenter <to report for duty : se présenter au travail>
report[2] *n* **1** RUMOR : rumeur *f* **2** REPUTE : réputation *f* <of good report : de bonne réputation> **3** ACCOUNT : rapport *m*, compte rendu *m* **4** : détonation *f* (d'un fusil) **5** : bulletin *m* <weather report : bulletin météorologique> **6** *or* **news report** : reportage *m*
report card *n* : bulletin *m* scolaire
reportedly [rɪ'portədlɪ] *adv* : à ce que l'on dit
reporter [rɪ'porṭər] *n* : journaliste *mf*, reporter *m*
repose[1] [rɪ'po:z] *vi* **-posed; -posing** : se reposer, relaxer
repose[2] *n* **1** REST : repos *m* **2** PEACE : tranquillité *f*, calme *f*
repository [rɪ'pɑzəˌtorɪ] *n, pl* **-ries** : dépôt *m*, entrepôt *m*
repossess [ˌri:pə'zɛs] *vt* : reprendre possession de, saisir
repossession [ˌri:pə'zɛʃən] *n* : reprise *f* de possession
reprehend [ˌrɛprɪ'hɛnd] *vt* : réprimander, critiquer
reprehensible [ˌrɛprɪ'hɛnṭsəbəl] *adj* : répréhensible
reprehensibly [ˌrɛprɪ'hɛnṭsəblɪ] *adv* : de façon répréhensible
represent [ˌrɛprɪ'zɛnt] *vt* **1** PORTRAY : représenter, dépeindre **2** SYMBOLIZE : représenter <the flag represents our country : le drapeau représente notre pays> **3** : représenter <an attorney who represents his client : un avocat qui représente son client>
representation [ˌrɛprɪˌzɛn'teɪʃən, -zən-] *n* : représentation *f*
representative[1] [ˌrɛprɪ'zɛntəṭɪv] *adj* : représentatif
representative[2] *n* : représentant *m*, -tante *f*
repress [rɪ'prɛs] *vt* : réprimer
repression [rɪ'prɛʃən] *n* : répression *f*
repressive [rɪ'prɛsɪv] *adj* : répressif
reprieve[1] [rɪ'pri:v] *vt* **-prievd; -prieving** : accorder un sursis à
reprieve[2] *n* **1** : remise *f* de peine (en droit) **2** RESPITE : délai *m*, sursis *m*, répit *m*
reprimand[1] ['rɛprəˌmænd] *vt* : réprimander
reprimand[2] *n* : réprimande *f*
reprint[1] [rɪ'prɪnt] *vt* : réimprimer
reprint[2] ['ri:ˌprɪnt, rɪ'prɪnt] *n* : réimpression *f*
reprisal [rɪ'praɪzəl] *n* : représailles *fpl*
reproach[1] [rɪ'pro:tʃ] *vt* : reprocher à, faire des reproches à
reproach[2] *n* **1** REBUKE : reproche *m* **2 beyond ~** : irréprochable, au-dessus de tout reproche
reproachful [rɪ'pro:tʃfəl] *adj* : de reproche, réprobateur
reproachfully [rɪ'pro:tʃfəlɪ] *adv* : d'un ton réprobateur
reproduce [ˌri:prə'du:s, -'djuːs] *v* **-duced; -ducing** *vt* : reproduire — *vi* : se reproduire
reproduction [ˌri:prə'dʌkʃən] *n* : reproduction *f*
reproductive [ˌri:prə'dʌkṭɪv] *adj* : reproducteur
reproof [rɪ'pru:f] *n* : réprimande *f*
reprove [rɪ'pru:v] *vt* **-proved; -proving** : réprimander, réprouver
reptile ['rɛpˌtaɪl] *n* : reptile *m*
republic [rɪ'pʌblɪk] *n* : république *f*
republican[1] [rɪ'pʌblɪkən] *adj* : républicain
republican[2] *n* : républicain *m*, -caine *f*
repudiate [rɪ'pju:diˌeɪt] *vt* **-ated; -ating 1** DISOWN : répudier, rejeter **2** : refuser d'honorer (une dette, etc.)
repudiation [rɪˌpju:di'eɪʃən] *n* **1** : répudiation *f*, désaveu *m* **2** : refus *m* d'honerer (une dette)
repugnance [rɪ'pʌgnənṭs] *n* : répugnance *f*, aversion *f*
repugnant [rɪ'pʌgnənt] *adj* : répugnant
repulse[1] [rɪ'pʌls] *vt* **-pulsed; -pulsing 1** REBUFF, REPEL : repousser **2** DISGUST : repousser, dégoûter
repulse[2] *n* REBUFF : rejet *m*, rebuffade *f*
repulsive [rɪ'pʌlsɪv] *adj* : repoussant, répugnant
repulsively [rɪ'pʌlsɪvlɪ] *adv* : de façon répugnante
reputable ['rɛpjəṭəbəl] *adj* : de bonne réputation
reputation [ˌrɛpjə'teɪʃən] *n* : réputation *f*
repute [rɪ'pju:t] *n* **1** : réputation *f* **2 to hold s.o. in high repute** : tenir qqn en haute estime
reputed [rɪ'pju:ṭəd] *adj* **1** CONSIDERED : réputé **2 to be reputed to be** : avoir la réputation d'être
reputedly [rɪ'pju:ṭədlɪ] *adv* : d'après ce que l'on dit
request[1] [rɪ'kwɛst] *vt* ASK : demander
request[2] *n* : demande *f*, requête *f*
requiem ['rɛkwɪəm, 'reɪ-] *n* : requiem *m*

require [rɪˈkwaɪr] *vt* **-quired; -quiring 1** CALL FOR : demander, exiger **2** NEED : avoir besoin de

requirement [rɪˈkwaɪrmənt] *n* **1** NEED : besoin *m* **2** CONDITION : exigence *f*, condition *f*

requisite[1] [ˈrɛkwəzɪt] *adj* : nécessaire, essentiel

requisite[2] *n* : nécessité *f*

requisition[1] [ˌrɛkwəˈzɪʃən] *vt* : réquisitionner

requisition[2] *n* : réquisition *f*

reread [ˌriːˈriːd] *vt* **-read** [-ˈrɛd]; **-reading** : relire

reroute [ˌriːˈruːt, -ˈraʊt] *vt* **-routed; -routing** : dérouter, changer l'itinéraire de

resale [ˈriːˌseɪl, ˌriːˈseɪl] *n* : revente *f*

reschedule [riːˈskɛˌdʒuːl, -dʒəl] *vt* **-uled; -uling** : changer l'heure ou la date de

rescind [rɪˈsɪnd] *vt* : annuler (une commande), résilier (un contrat)

rescue[1] [ˈrɛsˌkjuː] *vt* **-cued; -cuing** : sauver, secourir

rescue[2] *n* : sauvetage *m*

rescuer [ˈrɛsˌkjuər] *n* : sauveteur *m*, secouriste *mf*

research[1] [rɪˈsərtʃ, ˈriːˌsərtʃ] *vt* : faire des recherches sur

research[2] *n* : recherches *fpl*

researcher [rɪˈsərtʃər, ˈriːˌ-] *n* : chercheur *m*, -cheuse *f*

resemblance [rɪˈzɛmbləns] *n* : ressemblance *f*

resemble [rɪˈzɛmbəl] *vt* **-sembled; -sembling** : ressembler à

resent [rɪˈzɛnt] *vt* : en vouloir à, éprouver de l'amertume envers

resentful [rɪˈzɛntfəl] *adj* : plein de ressentiment

resentfully [rɪˈzɛntfəli] *adv* : avec ressentiment

resentment [rɪˈzɛntmənt] *n* : ressentiment *m*

reservation [ˌrɛzərˈveɪʃən] *n* **1** RESERVING : réservation *f* **2** : réserve *f* <Indian reservation : réserve indienne> **3 without ~** : sans réserve

reserve[1] [rɪˈzərv] *vt* **-served; -serving** : réserver

reserve[2] *n* **1** SUPPLY : réserve *f*, provision *f* **2** : réserve *f* (dans les forces armées) **3** RESTRAINT : réserve *f*, discrétion *f*

reserved [rɪˈzərvd] *adj* : réservé, discret

reservoir [ˈrɛzərˌvwɑr, -ˌvwɔr, -ˌvɔr] *n* : réservoir *m*

reset [ˌriːˈsɛt] *vt* **-set; -setting** : remettre à l'heure (une montre), remettre à zéro (un compteur)

reside [rɪˈzaɪd] *vi* **-sided; -siding 1** DWELL : résider **2 to reside in** : résider dans

residence [ˈrɛzədəns] *n* **1** DWELLING : résidence *f*, demeure *f* **2** *or* **residence hall** : résidence *f* (universitaire)

resident[1] [ˈrɛzədənt] *adj* **1** RESIDING : résidant **2** : à demeure <resident doctors : médecins à demeure>

resident[2] *n* : résident *m*, -dente *f*

residential [ˌrɛzəˈdɛnʃəl] *adj* : résidentiel

residual [rɪˈzɪdʒʊəl] *adj* : résiduel

residue [ˈrɛzəˌduː, -ˌdjuː] *n* : résidu *m*, reste *m*

resign [riˈzaɪn] *vi* QUIT : démissionner — *vt* **to resign oneself to** : se résigner à

resignation [ˌrɛzɪgˈneɪʃən] *n* **1** RESIGNING : démission *f*, résignation *f* **2** ACCEPTANCE : résignation *f*

resignedly [rɪˈzaɪnədli] *adv* : avec résignation

resilience [rɪˈzɪljənts] *n* : élasticité *f*, résistance *f*

resilient [rɪˈzɪljənt] *adj* **1** STRONG : résistant, fort **2** ELASTIC : élastique

resin [ˈrɛzən] *n* : résine *f*

resinous [ˈrɛzənəs] *adj* : résineux

resist [rɪˈzɪst] *vt* **1** WITHSTAND : résister à <to resist disease : résister à la maladie> **2** OPPOSE : s'opposer à, résister à

resistance [rɪˈzɪstənts] *n* : résistance *f*

resistant [rɪˈzɪstənt] *adj* : résistant <fire-resistant : qui résiste au feu>

resolute [ˈrɛzəˌluːt] *adj* : résolu, décidé — **resolutely** *adv*

resolution [ˌrɛzəˈluːʃən] *n* **1** SOLUTION : résolution *f* <conflict resolution : résolution de conflits> **2** RESOLVE : détermination *f*, résolution *f* **3** DECISION, PROMISE : résolution *f* <New Year's resolutions : résolutions du nouvel an> **4** MOTION, PROPOSAL : motion *f*, résolution *f* (legislative)

resolve[1] [rɪˈzɑlv] *v* **-solved; -solving** *vt* **1** SOLVE : résoudre (un problème) **2** DECIDE : (se) résoudre, décider — *vi* : se résoudre

resolve[2] *n* : résolution *f*, détermination *f*

resonance [ˈrɛzənənts] *n* : résonance *f*

resonant [ˈrɛzənənt] *adj* **1** : résonant (en physique) **2** : sonore (se dit des sons, des voix, etc.)

resort[1] [rɪˈzɔrt] *vi* **to resort to** : recourir à, avoir recours à

resort[2] *n* **1** RESOURCE : recours *m* <as a last resort : en dernier recours> **2** HAUNT : endroit *m* préféré, repaire *m* **3** : station *f* <ski resort : station de ski> <vacation resorts : lieux de villégiature>

resound [rɪˈzaʊnd] *vi* : résonner, retentir

resounding [rɪˈzaʊndɪŋ] *adj* : retentissant, éclatant <a resounding success : un succès retentissant>

resource [ˈriːˌsɔrs, riˈsɔrs] *n* : ressource *f* <natural resources : ressources naturelles> <to be left to one's own resources : être livré à soi-même>

resourceful [rɪ'sorsfəl, -'zors-] *adj* : ingénieux, plein de ressources
resourcefulness [rɪ'sorsfəlnəs, -'zors-] *n* : ingéniosité *f*
respect[1] [rɪ'spɛkt] *vt* : respecter
respect[2] *n* **1** ESTEEM : respect *m*, estime *f* **2** CONSIDERATION : considération *f*, respect *m* **3** DETAIL : respect *m*, égard *m* <in some respects : à certains égards> **4 respects** *npl* : respects *mpl*, hommages *mpl* <to pay one's respects to s.o. : présenter ses respects à qqn> **5 in respect to** : en ce qui concerne
respectability [rɪˌspɛktə'bɪləṭi] *n* : respectabilité *f*
respectable [rɪ'spɛktəbəl] *adj* **1** PROPER : respectable, correct <respectable people : gens respectables> **2** CONSIDERABLE : respectable, considérable, assez bon <a respectable amount : une somme respectable>
respectably [rɪ'spɛktəbli] *adv* : respectablement, convenablement
respectful [rɪ'spɛktfəl] *adj* : respectueux — **respectfully** *adv*
respective [rɪ'spɛktɪv] *adj* : respectif — **respectively** *adv*
respiration [ˌrɛspə'reɪʃən] *n* : respiration *f*
respirator ['rɛspəˌreiṭər] *n* : respirateur *m*
respiratory ['rɛspərəˌtori, rɪ'spaɪrə-] *adj* : respiratoire
respite ['rɛspət] *n* : répit *m*, sursis *m*
resplendent [rɪ'splɛndənt] *adj* : resplendissant
respond [rɪ'spɑnd] *vi* **1** ANSWER : répondre **2** REACT : réagir <I didn't respond well to the surgery : j'ai mal réagi à la chirurgie> <to respond to pressure : céder aux pressions>
response [rɪ'spɑnts] *n* **1** ANSWER : réponse *f* **2** REACTION : réaction *f*, réponse *f*
responsibility [rɪˌspɑntsə'bɪləṭi] *n, pl* **-ties** : responsabilité *f*
responsible [rɪ'spɑntsəbəl] *adj* : responsable
responsibly [rɪ'spɑntsəbli] *adv* : de manière responsable
responsive [rɪ'spɑntsɪv] *adj* : sensible, réceptif
rest[1] ['rɛst] *vi* **1** RELAX, REPOSE : se reposer <to rest easy : être tranquille> **2** DEPEND : reposer, dépendre <the decision rests with me : la décision dépend de moi> **3 to rest on** *or* **to rest against** : reposer sur, être appuyé sur — *vt* **1** : reposer <rest your eyes now and then : reposez-vous la vue de temps à autre> **2** PLACE : placer, mettre <I rest all my hopes in him : je place tous mes espoirs en lui>
rest[2] *n* **1** REPOSE : repos *m* **2** BREAK : repos *m*, pause *f* **3** SUPPORT : appui *m*, support *m* **4** REMAINDER : reste *m* **5** : pause *f* (en musique) **6 rest area** : aire *f* de repos, halte *f* routière *Can*
restart [ri:'stɑrt] *vt* : remettre en marche (un moteur)
restaurant ['rɛstəˌrɑnt, -rənt] *n* : restaurant *m*
restful ['rɛstfəl] *adj* : reposant
restitution [ˌrɛstə'tu:ʃən, -'tju:-] *n* : restitution *f*
restive ['rɛstɪv] *adj* : agité, nerveux
restless ['rɛstləs] *adj* : agité, nerveux, impatient <a restless night : une nuit agitée>
restlessly ['rɛstləsli] *adv* : nerveusement, avec impatience
restlessness ['rɛstləsnəs] *n* : nervosité *f*, agitation *f*
restoration [ˌrɛstə'reɪʃən] *n* **1** : restitution *f*, rétablissement *m* (de la paix, de l'ordre, etc.) **2** : restauration *f* (d'une peinture, d'un édifice, etc.)
restore [rɪ'stor] *vt* **-stored; -storing 1** RETURN : rendre, restituer **2** RENOVATE : restaurer, rénover **3** REESTABLISH : rétablir, retrouver <to restore peace : rétablir la paix> <to be restored to health : être rétabli> <to have one's sight restored : recouvrer la vue>
restrain [rɪ'streɪn] *vt* **1** PREVENT : empêcher, retenir **2** CURB : contenir, refréner
restrained [rɪ'streɪnd] *adj* **1** : sobre <restrained style : style sobre> **2** RESERVED : réservé, contenu
restraining order *n* : injonction *f*
restraint [rɪ'streɪnt] *n* **1** RESTRICTION : restriction *f*, contrainte *f* **2** RESERVE, SELF-CONTROL : retenue *f*, mesure *f*
restrict [rɪ'strɪkt] *vt* : restreindre, limiter
restricted [rɪ'strɪktəd] *adj* **1** LIMITED : restreint, limité **2** CLASSIFIED : secret, confidentiel
restriction [rɪ'strɪkʃən] *n* : restriction *f*, limitation *f*
restrictive [rɪ'strɪktɪv] *adj* : restrictif
restructure [ri:'strʌktʃər] *vt* **-tured; -turing** : restructurer
result[1] [rɪ'zʌlt] *vi* **1 to result from** : résulter de, provenir de **2 to result in** : avoir pour résultat, aboutir à
result[2] *n* : résultat *m*, conséquence *f*
resultant [rɪ'zʌlṭənt] *adj* : résultant
resume [rɪ'zu:m] *v* **-sumed; -suming** *vt* : reprendre — *vi* : reprendre, recommencer, continuer
résumé *or* **resume** *or* **resumé** ['rɛzəˌmeɪ, ˌrɛzə'-] *n* **1** SUMMARY : résumé *m* **2** : curriculum *m* vitæ
resumption [rɪ'zʌmpʃən] *n* : reprise *f*
resurface [ˌri:'sərfəs] *vt* **-faced; -facing** : refaire le revêtement de (une route)
resurgence [rɪ'sərdʒənts] *n* : résurgence *f*, réapparition *f*
resurgent [rɪ'sərdʒənt] *adj* : renaissant

resurrect [ˌrɛzəˈrɛkt] *vt* : ressusciter
resurrection [ˌrɛzəˈrɛkʃən] *n* : résurrection *f*
resuscitate [rɪˈsʌsəˌteɪt] *vt* **-tated; -tating** : réanimer
resuscitation [rɪˌsʌsəˈteɪʃən, ˌri-] *n* : réanimation *f*
retail[1] [ˈriːˌteɪl] *vt* : vendre au détail
retail[2] *adv* : au détail
retail[3] *adj* : de détail <retail store : magasin de détail>
retail[4] *n* : vente *f* au détail
retailer [ˈriːˌteɪlər] *n* : détaillant *m*, -lante *f*
retain [rɪˈteɪn] *vt* **1** KEEP : garder, retenir **2** HOLD : retenir, conserver <lead retains heat : le plomb conserve la chaleur> **3** ENGAGE : engager (les services de qqn)
retainer [rɪˈteɪnər] *n* **1** SERVANT : domestique *mf* **2** ADVANCE : provision *f*
retaliate [rɪˈtæliˌeɪt] *vi* **-ated; -ating** : riposter, se venger <to retaliate against : user de représailles envers>
retaliation [rɪˌtæliˈeɪʃən] *n* : riposte *f*, représailles *fpl*
retard [rɪˈtɚd] *vt* : retarder
retarded [rɪˈtɚdəd] *adj* : arriéré
retch [ˈrɛtʃ] *vi* : avoir des haut-le-cœur
retention [rɪˈtɛnʃən] *n* : rétention *f*
retentive [rɪˈtɛntɪv] *adj* : qui retient bien <a retentive memory : une mémoire fidèle>
reticence [ˈrɛtəsənts] *n* : réticence *f*, hésitation *f*
reticent [ˈrɛtəsənt] *adj* : réticent, hésitant
reticently [ˈrɛtəsəntli] *adv* : avec réticence
retina [ˈrɛtənə] *n, pl* **-nas** *or* **-nae** [-ənˌiː, -ənˌaɪ] : rétine *f*
retinue [ˈrɛtənˌuː, -juː] *n* : suite *f*, escorte *f*
retire [rɪˈtaɪr] *vi* **-tired; -tiring 1** WITHDRAW : se retirer, partir **2** : prendre sa retraite <he retired at 65 : il a pris sa retraite à 65 ans> **3** : aller se coucher
retiree [rɪˌtaɪˈriː] *n* : retraité *m*, -tée *f*
retirement [rɪˈtaɪrmənt] *n* : retraite *f*
retiring [rɪˈtaɪrɪŋ] *adj* : réservé, timide
retort[1] [rɪˈtɔrt] *vt* : rétorquer, riposter
retort[2] *n* : réplique *f*, riposte *f*
retrace [ˌriːˈtreɪs] *vt* **-traced; -tracing** : reconstituer <to retrace one's steps : revenir sur ses pas>
retract [rɪˈtrækt] *vt* **1** : rétracter (ses griffes, ses cornes etc.) **2** WITHDRAW : rétracter, retirer — *vi* : se rétracter
retractable [rɪˈtræktəbəl] *adj* : escamotable
retrain [ˌriːˈtreɪn] *vt* : recycler
retreat[1] [rɪˈtriːt] *vi* : se retirer, reculer
retreat[2] *n* **1** WITHDRAWAL : retraite *f*, recul *m* **2** REFUGE : retraite *f*, abri *m*
retrench [rɪˈtrɛntʃ] *vt* : réduire, restreindre (les dépenses) — *vi* : faire des économies
retribution [ˌrɛtrəˈbjuːʃən] *n* : châtiment *m*, punition *f*
retrieval [rɪˈtriːvəl] *n* : récupération *f* <text retrieval : récupération d'un texte> <beyond retrieval : irrécupérable>
retrieve [rɪˈtriːv] *vt* **-trieved; -trieving 1** : rapporter <to retrieve game : rapporter du gibier> **2** RECOVER : récupérer
retriever [rɪˈtriːvər] *n* : chien *m* d'arrêt
retroactive [ˌrɛtroˈæktɪv] *adj* : rétroactif — **retroactively** *adv*
retrograde [ˈrɛtrəˌgreɪd] *adj* : rétrograde
retrospect [ˈrɛtrəˌspɛkt] *n* **in ~** : rétrospectivement
retrospective [ˌrɛtrəˈspɛktɪv] *adj* : rétrospectif — **retrospectively** *adv*
return[1] [rɪˈtɚn] *vi* **1** : retourner, rentrer <to return home : retourner à la maison> **2 to return to** : reprendre, revenir à <she returned to her old habits : elle a repris ses vieilles habitudes> — *vt* **1** RESTORE : rapporter, rendre <to return a book to the library : retourner un livre à la bibliothèque> **2** REPLACE : remettre **3** ANSWER : répondre, répliquer **4** YIELD : rapporter, produire **5** REPAY : retourner, rendre <to return the compliment : retourner le compliment> <to return a favor : en faire autant> **6** : rendre, prononcer <to return a verdict : rendre un verdict>
return[2] *adj* : aller et retour <a return ticket : un billet aller et retour>
return[3] *n* **1** : retour *m* <on their return : à leur retour> **2** YIELD : rapport *m*, rendement *m* **3** RETURNING : renvoi *m*, retour *m* (de marchandise) **4** *or* **income tax return** : déclaration *f* de revenus **5 returns** *npl* : résultats *mpl* (d'une élection)
reunion [riˈjuːnjən] *n* : réunion *f* <family reunion : réunion familiale>
reuse [riˈjuːz] *vt* **-used; -using** : réutiliser
revamp [ˌriːˈvæmp] *vt* : retaper (une maison), réviser (un texte)
reveal [rɪˈviːl] *vt* **1** DIVULGE : révéler, dévoiler (un secret) **2** SHOW : révéler, laisser voir
reveille [ˈrɛvəli] *n* : réveil *m* (dans les forces armées)
revel[1] [ˈrɛvəl] *vi* **-eled** *or* **-elled; -eling** *or* **-elling 1** : faire la fête **2 to revel in** : se délecter de
revel[2] *n* : festivités *fpl*
revelation [ˌrɛvəˈleɪʃən] *n* : révélation *f*
reveler *or* **reveller** [ˈrɛvələr] *n* : fêtard *m*, -tarde *f fam*
revelry [ˈrɛvəlri] *n* : festivités *fpl*, réjouissances *fpl*

revenge[1] [rɪ'vɛnʤ] *vt* **-venged; -venging** : venger <to revenge oneself on : se venger sur>
revenge[2] *n* : vengeance *f*
revenue ['rɛvə,nu:, -,nju:] *n* : revenu *m*
reverberate [rɪ'vərbə,reɪt] *vi* **-ated; -ating** : retentir, résonner
reverberation [rɪ,vərbə'reɪʃən] *n* : réverbération *f*, retentissement *m*
revere [rɪ'vɪr] *vt* **-vered; -vering** : révérer, vénérer
reverence ['rɛvərənʦ] *n* : révérence *f*, vénération *f*
reverend ['rɛvərənd] *adj* **1** REVERED : vénérable **2** : révérend (en religion) <the Reverend Richard Parker : le révérend Richard Parker>
reverent ['rɛvərənt] *adj* : respectueux — **reverently** *adv*
reverie ['rɛvərɪ] *n, pl* **-eries** : rêverie *f*
reversal [rɪ'vərsəl] *n* : revirement *m* (d'opinion), renversement *m* (d'une situation)
reverse[1] [rɪ'vərs] *v* **-versed; -versing** *vt* **1** INVERT : inverser **2** CHANGE : renverser, retourner **3** ANNUL : annuler — *vi* : faire marche arrière (se dit d'une voiture)
reverse[2] *adj* : inverse, opposé <in reverse order : en ordre inverse>
reverse[3] *n* **1** OPPOSITE : contraire *m* **2** SETBACK : revers *m*, épreuve *f* **3** BACK : envers *m* **4** *or* **reverse gear** : marche *f* arrière
reversible [rɪ'vərsəbəl] *adj* : réversible
reversion [rɪ'vərʒən] *n* **1** : retour *m* <a reversion to paganism : un retour au paganisme> **2** : réversion *f* (en biologie)
revert [rɪ'vərt] *vi* **to revert to** : revenir à, retourner à
review[1] [rɪ'vju:] *vt* **1** REEXAMINE : revoir, réviser **2** CRITICIZE : faire la critique de (un roman, etc.) **3** ASSESS, EXAMINE : examiner, faire le bilan de **4 to review the troops** : passer les troupes en revue
review[2] *n* **1** REAPPRAISAL : révision *f* **2** INSPECTION : revue *f* (militaire) **3** ANALYSIS, OVERVIEW : bilan *m*, examen *m* <to pass one's life in review : faire le bilan de sa vie> **4** EVALUATION : critique *f* **5** → **revue**
reviewer [rɪ'vjuər] *n* : critique *mf* <book reviewer : critique littéraire>
revile [rɪ'vaɪl] *vt* **-viled; -viling** : injurier, vilipender
revise [rɪ'vaɪz] *vt* **-vised; -vising 1** CORRECT : réviser, revoir (un manuscrit, etc.) **2** UPDATE : réviser, mettre à jour **3** ALTER : réviser (une idée, une politique, etc.)
reviser *or* **revisor** [rɪ'vaɪzər] *n* : réviseur *m*; correcteur *m*, -trice *f*
revision [rɪ'vɪʒən] *n* : révision *f*
revival [rɪ'vaɪvəl] *n* **1** : renouveau *m*, renaissance *f* (d'intérêt, d'idées, etc.) **2** : rétablissement *m* (des coutumes) **3** : reprise *f* (en médecine) **4** *or* **revival meeting** : réunion *f* pour le renouveau de la foi
revive [rɪ'vaɪv] *v* **-vived; -viving** *vt* **1** RESTABLISH : rétablir (une tradition, etc.) **2** REAWAKEN : ranimer, raviver — *vi* **1** COME TO : reprendre connaissance **2** : renaître, se réveiller <hope revived in him : l'espoir renaissait en lui>
revoke [rɪ'vo:k] *vt* **-voked; -voking** : révoquer, annuler
revolt[1] [rɪ'vo:lt] *vt* DISGUST : révolter, dégoûter — *vi* **to revolt against** : se révolter contre
revolt[2] *n* : révolte *f*, insurrection *f*
revolting [rɪ'vo:ltɪŋ] *adj* : révoltant, dégoûtant
revolution [,rɛvə'lu:ʃən] *n* **1** ROTATION : révolution *f*, tour *m* **2** : révolution *f* <the French Revolution : la Révolution française> <a technological revolution : une révolution technologique>
revolutionary[1] [,rɛvə'lu:ʃən,ɛri] *adj* : révolutionnaire
revolutionary[2] *n* : révolutionnaire *mf*
revolutionize [,rɛvə'lu:ʃən,aɪz] *vt* **-ized; -izing** : révolutionner
revolve [rɪ'vɑlv] *v* **-volved; -volving** *vt* ROTATE : faire tourner — *vi* **1** TURN : tourner <to revolve around : tourner autour> **2 to revolve around s.o.** : dépendre de qqn **3 to revolve in one's mind** : tourner et retourner dans son esprit
revolver [rɪ'vɑlvər] *n* : revolver *m*
revue [rɪ'vju:] *n* : revue *f* (au théâtre)
revulsion [rɪ'vʌlʃən] *n* REPUGNANCE : répulsion *f*, répugnance *f*
reward[1] [rɪ'wərd] *vt* : récompenser
reward[2] *n* : récompense *f*
rewind [,ri:'waɪnd] *vt* **-wound** [-'waʊnd]; **-winding** : rembobiner
rewrite [,ri:'raɪt] *vt* **-wrote** [-'ro:t]; **-written** [-'rɪtən]; **-writing** : récrire
rhapsody ['ræpsədi] *n, pl* **-dies 1** : rhapsodie *f* (en musique, en poésie) **2** RAPTURE : extase *f*
rhetoric ['rɛtərɪk] *n* : rhétorique *f*
rhetorical [rɪ'tɔrɪkəl] *adj* : rhétorique
rheumatic [rʊ'mæṭɪk] *adj* : rhumatismal
rheumatism ['ru:mə,tɪzəm, 'rʊ-] *n* : rhumatisme *m*
rhinestone ['raɪn,sto:n] *n* : faux diamant *m*
rhino ['raɪ,no:] *n, pl* **rhino** *or* **rhinos** → **rhinoceros**
rhinoceros [raɪ'nɑsərəs] *n, pl* **-eroses** *or* **-eros** *or* **-eri** [-,raɪ] : rhinocéros *m*
rhododendron [,ro:də'dɛndrən] *n* : rhododendron *m*
rhombus ['rɑmbəs] *n, pl* **-buses** *or* **-bi** [-,baɪ, -bi] : losange *m*
rhubarb ['ru:,bɑrb] *n* : rhubarbe *f*
rhyme[1] ['raɪm] *v* **rhymed; rhyming** *vt* : faire rimer — *vi* : rimer

rhyme² *n* **1** : rime *m* **2** VERSE : vers *m* (en poésie)
rhythm ['rɪðəm] *n* : rythme *m*
rhythmic ['rɪðmɪk] *or* **rhythmical** [-mɪkəl] *adj* : rythmique — **rythmically** [-mɪkli] *adv*
rib¹ ['rɪb] *vt* **ribbed; ribbing 1** : faire aux côtes <ribbed fabric : tissu à côtes> **2** TEASE : taquiner
rib² *n* **1** : côte *f* (en anatomie) **2** : baleine *f* (d'un parapluie), nervure *f* (d'une feuille, en architecture, etc.), côte *f* (d'un tricot)
ribald ['rɪbəld] *adj* : grivois, paillard
ribbon ['rɪbən] *n* **1** : ruban *m* <silk ribbon : ruban de soie> <typewriter ribbon : ruban d'une machine à écrire> **2 in ribbons** : en lambeaux
rice ['raɪs] *n* : riz *m*
rich ['rɪtʃ] *adj* **1** WEALTHY : riche, aisé **2** SUMPTUOUS : somptueux, riche **3** : riche <rich food : aliments riches> **4** ABUNDANT : abondant **5** FERTILE : fertile, riche
riches ['rɪtʃəz] *npl* : richesses *fpl*
richly ['rɪtʃli] *adv* : richement, somptueusement
richness ['rɪtʃnəs] *n* : richesse *f*
rickets ['rɪkəts] *n* : rachitisme *m*
rickety ['rɪkəṭi] *adj* : branlant
ricksha *or* **rickshaw** ['rɪkˌʃɔ] *n* : pousse-pousse *m*
ricochet¹ ['rɪkəˌʃeɪ] *vi* **-cheted** [-ˌʃeɪd] *or* **-chetted** [-ˌʃeṭəd]; **-cheting** [-ʃeɪɪŋ] *or* **-chetting** [-ʃeṭɪŋ] : ricocher
ricochet² *n* : ricochet *m*
rid ['rɪd] *vt* **rid; ridding 1** : débarrasser <to rid a dog of fleas : débarrasser un chien de ses puces> **2 to rid oneself of** : se débarrasser de
riddance ['rɪdənṭs] *n* : débarras *m* <good riddance! : bon débarras!>
riddle¹ ['rɪdəl] *vt* **-dled; -dling** : cribler <to riddle with bullets : cribler de balles> <riddled with errors : plein de fautes>
riddle² *n* : énigme *f*, devinette *f*
ride¹ ['raɪd] *v* **rode** ['ro:d]; **ridden** ['rɪdən]; **riding** *vt* **1** : monter à (un cheval), monter sur (une bicyclette), prendre (le bus, un taxi, etc.) **2** TRAVERSE : parcourir <he rode the countryside : il a parcouru tout le pays> **3** TEASE : taquiner **4** *or* **to ride out** WEATHER : réchapper à, surmonter **5 to ride the waves** : voguer sur les vagues (se dit d'une navire) — *vi* **1** : monter à cheval, aller à bicyclette **2** TRAVEL : aller <to ride in a bus : aller en autobus> **3 to ride at anchor** : être ancré **4 to let things ride** : laisser courir
ride² *n* **1** : tour *m*, promenade *f* <to go for a ride : aller faire un tour> **2** : manège *m* (à la foire) **3 to give s.o. a ride** : conduire qqn en voiture
rider ['raɪdər] *n* **1** HORSEMAN : cavalier *m*, -ière *f* **2** CYCLIST : cycliste *mf*, motocycliste *mf* **3** ANNEX : annexe *f* (en droit)
ridge ['rɪdʒ] *n* : chaîne *f* (de montagnes), crête *f* (d'un toit), billon *m* (dans un champ)
ridicule¹ ['rɪdəˌkju:l] *vt* **-culed; -culing** : ridiculiser, tourner en ridicule
ridicule² *n* : moquerie *f*, dérision *f*
ridiculous [rə'dɪkjələs] *adj* : ridicule, absurde — **ridiculously** *adv*
rife ['raɪf] *adj* : abondant, répandu <to be rife with : être abondant en> <rumor was rife : les rumeurs allaient bon train>
riffraff ['rɪfˌræf] *n* : racaille *f*, canaille *f*
rifle¹ ['raɪfəl] *v* **-fled; -fling** *vt* RANSACK : fouiller — *vi* **to rifle through** : fouiller dans
rifle² *n* : carabine *f*, fusil *m*
rift ['rɪft] *n* **1** FISSURE : fente *f*, fissure *f* **2** BREACH : désaccord *m*, rupture *f* (entre personnes)
rig¹ ['rɪg] *vt* **rigged; rigging 1** : gréer (un navire) **2** CLOTHE, DRESS : habiller **3** FIX : truquer (les élections, etc.) **4** *or* **to rig up** : bricoler, monter <to rig up a shelter : bricoler un abri> **5 to rig out** EQUIP : équiper
rig² *n* **1** RIGGING : gréement *m* (d'un navire) **2** *or* **oil rig** : plate-forme *f* pétrolière
rigging ['rɪgɪŋ, -gən] *n* : gréement *m*
right¹ ['raɪt] *vt* **1** RESTORE : redresser <to right the economy : redresser l'économie> **2** REDRESS : réparer <to right a wrong : réparer un tort>
right² *adv* **1** CORRECTLY : bien, comme il faut <to answer right : bien répondre> <you're not doing it right : tu ne le fais pas comme il faut> **2** EXACTLY : exactement, précisément <the book is right where you left it : le livre est juste là, où tu l'as laissé> <right here : ici même> **3** DIRECTLY : directement <he went right home : il est rentré directement chez lui> **4** IMMEDIATELY : tout de suite <right after lunch : tout de suite après le déjeuner> **5** COMPLETELY : tout à fait, complètement <he felt right at home : il se sentait tout à fait à l'aise> <right to the end : jusqu'au bout> **6** : à droite <turn right : tournez à droite>
right³ *adj* **1** JUST, PROPER : juste, bien <it's not right : ce n'est pas bien> **2** CORRECT : bon, juste <the right answer : la bonne réponse> **3** SUITABLE : approprié, convenable <the right person for the job : la personne qui convient le mieux pour l'emploi> **4** STRAIGHT : droit <a right line : une ligne droite> **5** HEALTHY, SOUND : bien <she's not in her right mind : elle n'a pas toute sa raison> <the patient didn't look right : le patient n'avait pas l'air bien> **6** : droit <the right side : le côté droit>

right[4] *n* **1** GOOD : bien *m* <right against wrong : le bien contre le mal> **2** : droite *f* <to be on the right : être à droite> **3** ENTITLEMENT : droit *m* <to exercise a right : exercer un droit> <women's rights : les droits de la femme> **4 rights** *npl* : droits *mpl* <film rights : droits d'adaptation cinématographique> <all rights reserved : tous droits réservés>
right angle *n* : angle *m* droit
right–angled ['raɪt'æŋgəld] *or* **right–angle** [-gəl] *adj* : à angle droit
righteous ['raɪtʃəs] *adj* : juste, vertueux — **righteously** *adv*
righteousness ['raɪtʃəsnəs] *n* : droiture *f*
rightful ['raɪtfəl] *adj* LAWFUL : légitime, véritable
rightfully ['raɪtfəli] *adv* : à juste titre, légitimement
right–hand ['raɪt'hænd] *adj* **1** : du côté droit **2** RIGHT-HANDED : de la main droite **3 right–hand man** : bras *m* droit
right–handed ['raɪt'hændəd] *adj* **1** : droitier <a right-handed pitcher : un lanceur droitier> **2** : de la main droite <a right-handed glove : un gant de la main droite>
rightly ['raɪtli] *adv* **1** FAIRLY : à juste titre **2** FITTINGLY : de façon appropriée **3** CORRECTLY : exactement, au juste
right–of–way [ˌraɪtəˈweɪ, -əv-] *n, pl* **rights–of–way** : priorité *f* (sur la route), droit *m* de passage (sur un terrain)
rightward ['raɪtwərd] *adv* : vers la droite
right–wing ['raɪt'wɪŋ] *adj* : de droite (en politique)
right wing *n* **the right wing** : la droite
right–winger ['raɪt'wɪŋər] *n* : personne *f* de droite
rigid ['rɪdʒɪd] *adj* **1** STIFF : rigide, raide **2** STRICT : rigide, sévère
rigidity [rɪ'dʒɪdəṭi] *n, pl* **-ties 1** STIFFNESS : rigidité *f* **2** STRICTNESS : rigidité *f*, inflexibilité *f*
rigmarole ['rɪgmərˌoːl, 'rɪgə-] *n* **1** NONSENSE : galimatias *m* **2** PROCEDURE : procédure *f* compliquée
rigor *or Brit* **rigour** ['rɪgər] *n* **1** SEVERITY : rigueur *f*, sévérité *f* **2** EXACTNESS : rigueur *f*, précision *f* **3 rigors** *npl* HARSHNESS : rigueurs *fpl*, intempéries *fpl* <the rigors of winter : les rigueurs de l'hiver>
rigorous ['rɪgərəs] *adj* **1** STRICT : rigoureux, sévère **2** HARSH : rigoureux, rude
rigorously ['rɪgərəsli] *adv* : rigoureusement, sévèrement
rile ['raɪl] *vt* **riled; riling** : énerver, mettre en colère
rill ['rɪl] *n* : ruisselet *m*
rim[1] ['rɪm] *vt* **rimmed; rimming** BORDER : border, entourer
rim[2] *n* **1** : bord *m* <the rim of a cup : le bord d'une tasse> **2** : jante *f* (d'une roue)
rime ['raɪm] *n* : givre *m*
rind ['raɪnd] *n* : écorce *f*
ring[1] ['rɪŋ] *vt* **ringed; ringing** SURROUND : encercler
ring[2] *v* **rang** ['ræŋ]; **rung** ['rʌŋ]; **ringing** *vi* **1** : sonner <the doorbell rang : on a sonné à la porte> **2** RESOUND : résonner **3 to ring true** : sonner vrai — *vt* : sonner <to ring the alarm : sonner l'alarme>
ring[3] *n* **1** : bague *f*, anneau *m* <engagement ring : bague de fiançailles> **2** : rond *m* <smoke rings : ronds de fumée> **3** ARENA : ring *m* (de boxe), piste *f* (d'un cirque) **4** GANG : cercle *m*, gang *m* **5** SOUND : son *m*, tintement *m* **6** RINGING : sonnerie *f* (du téléphone, etc.) **7** CALL : coup *m* de téléphone <give me a ring in the morning : appelle-moi dans la matinée>
ringer ['rɪŋər] *n* **to be a dead ringer for** : être le sosie de
ringleader ['rɪŋˌliːdər] *n* : meneur *m*, -neuse *f*
ringlet ['rɪŋlət] *n* : boucle *f* (de cheveux)
ringworm ['rɪŋˌwərm] *n* : teigne *f*
rink ['rɪŋk] *n* : patinoire *f*
rinse[1] ['rɪnts] *vt* **rinsed; rinsing 1** : rincer <to rinse the dishes : rincer la vaisselle> **2** : se rincer <to rinse one's mouth : se rincer la bouche>
rinse[2] *n* : rinçage *m*
riot[1] ['raɪət] *vi* : faire une émeute, manifester avec violence
riot[2] *n* : émeute *f*
rioter ['raɪəṭər] *n* : émeutier *m*, -tière *f*
riotous ['raɪəṭəs] *adj* **1** NOISY, ROWDY : tapageur, bruyant **2** ABUNDANT : abondant, exubérant
rip[1] ['rɪp] *v* **ripped; ripping** *vt* : déchirer — *vi* : se déchirer
rip[2] *n* : déchirure *f*
ripe ['raɪp] *adj* **riper; ripest 1** MATURE : mûr <a ripe pear : une poire mûre> **2** READY : prêt
ripen ['raɪpən] *v* : mûrir
ripeness ['raɪpnəs] *n* : maturité *f*
rip–off ['rɪpˌɔf] *n* SWINDLE, THEFT : escroquerie *f*, vol *m*, arnaque *f fam*
rip off *vt* : escroquer, arnaquer *fam*
ripple[1] ['rɪpəl] *v* **-pled; -pling** *vi* : onduler, se rider — *vt* : rider
ripple[2] *n* **1** : ondulation *f*, ride *f* **2** EFFECT, REPERCUSSION : répercussion *f* **3 a ripple of laughter** : une cascade de rires
rise[1] ['raɪz] *vi* **rose** ['roːz]; **risen** ['rɪzən]; **rising 1** ARISE : se lever <to rise to one's feet : se lever, se mettre debout> <to rise from the dead : ressusciter (des morts)> **2** : s'élever, se dresser <mountains rising in the distance : des montagnes qui s'élèvent au loin> **3** : se lever (se dit du soleil,

de la lune) **4** : monter <smoke rises : la fumée monte> **5** INCREASE : augmenter, monter **6** ORIGINATE : prendre sa source (dans) **7 to rise from the ranks** : sortir du rang **8 to rise to the occasion** : se montrer à la hauteur de la situation **9 to rise up** REBEL : se soulever (contre), se révolter

rise[2] *n* **1** ASCENT : lever *m* (du soleil), montée *f*, ascension *f* **2** ORIGIN : début *m*, source *f* **3** ELEVATION : élévation *f* <the rise of a step : l'élévation d'une marche> **4** INCREASE : augmentation *f*, hausse *f* **5** INCLINE : montée *f*, pente *f*

riser ['raɪzər] *n* **1** : contremarche *f* (d'un escalier) **2 early riser** : lève-tôt *mf* **3 late riser** : lève-tard *mf*

risk[1] ['rɪsk] *vt* : risquer

risk[2] *n* : risque *m*, danger *m*

riskiness ['rɪskinəs] *n* : risques *mpl*

risky ['rɪski] *adj* **riskier; -est** : risqué, hasardeux

risqué [rɪ'ske1] *adj* : risqué, osé

rite ['raɪt] *n* : rite *m*

ritual[1] ['rɪtʃʊəl] *adj* : rituel

ritual[2] *n* : rituel *m*

rival[1] ['raɪvəl] *vt* **-valed** *or* **-valled; -valing** *or* **-valling** : rivaliser avec

rival[2] *adj* : rival <rival factions : factions rivales>

rival[3] *n* : rival *m*, -vale *f*; compétiteur *m*, -trice *f*

rivalry ['raɪvəlri] *n, pl* **-ries** : rivalité *f*

river ['rɪvər] *n* : rivière *f*, fleuve *m*

riverbank ['rɪvər,bæŋk] *n* : rive *f*, berge *f*

riverbed ['rɪvər,bɛd] *n* : lit *m* de rivière

riverside ['rɪvər,saɪd] *n* : rive *f*, bord *m* d'une rivière

rivet[1] ['rɪvət] *vt* **1** : riveter, river **2 to be riveted to the spot** : être cloué sur place

rivet[2] *n* : rivet *m*

rivulet ['rɪvjələt] *n* : ruisselet *m*

roach ['ro:tʃ] → **cockroach**

road ['ro:d] *n* **1** : route *f*, rue *f* **2** PATH, WAY : chemin *m*, voie *f* <on the road to success : sur le chemin de la réussite>

roadblock ['ro:d,blɑk] *n* : barrage *m* routier

roadrunner ['ro:d,rʌnər] *n* : coucou *m* terrestre

roadside ['ro:d,saɪd] *n* : bord *m* de la route

roadway ['ro:d,we1] *n* : chaussée *f*

roam ['ro:m] *vi* WANDER : errer, rôder

roan[1] ['ro:n] *adj* : rouan

roan[2] *n* : rouan *m*, rouanne *f*

roar[1] ['ror] *vi* **1** : rugir (se dit d'un lion), mugir (se dit du vent, de la mer, etc.), gronder (se dit d'un moteur, du tonnerre, etc.) **2** : éclater, hurler <to roar with laughter : hurler de rire> — *vt* : hurler, vociférer <he roared approval : il a hurlé son approbation>

roar[2] *n* **1** : rugissement *m* (d'un lion) **2** : hurlement *m*, cri *m* <a roar of pain : un hurlement de douleur> **3** : vrombissement *m* (d'un moteur), grondement *m* (du tonnerre)

roast[1] ['ro:st] *vt* : rôtir (de la viande, etc.), griller (des noix), torréfier (du café)

roast[2] *adj* : rôti <roast beef : rôti de bœuf>

roast[3] *n* : rôti *m*

rob ['rɑb] *vt* **robbed; robbing 1** : dévaliser (une banque, etc.), cambrioler (une maison) **2** STEAL : voler <to rob jewelry : voler des bijoux>

robber ['rɑbər] *n* : voleur *m*, -leuse *f*

robbery ['rɑbəri] *n, pl* **-beries** : vol *m* <armed robbery : vol à main armé>

robe[1] ['ro:b] *vt* **robed; robing** : vêtir, habiller

robe[2] *n* **1** : toge *f* (d'un juge) **2** → **bathrobe**

robin ['rɑbən] *n* : rouge-gorge *m*

robot ['ro:,bɑt, -bət] *n* : robot *m*

robust [ro'bʌst, 'ro:,bʌst] *adj* : robuste, vigoureux — **robustly** *adv*

rock[1] ['rɑk] *vt* **1** : balancer (un berceau), bercer (un enfant) **2** SHAKE : ébranler, secouer — *vi* SWAY : se balancer

rock[2] *n* **1** STONE : roche *f*, roc *m* **2** BOULDER : rocher *m* **3** ROCKING : mouvement *m* de va-et-vient **4** : rock *m* (musique)

rocker ['rɑkər] *n* **1** : bascule *f* (d'un fauteuil) **2** → **rocking chair**

rocket[1] ['rɑkət] *vi* : monter en flèche

rocket[2] *n* : fusée *f*

rocking chair *n* : fauteuil *m* à bascule, chaise *f* berçante *Can*

rocking horse *n* : cheval *m* à bascule

rock salt *n* : sel *m* gemme

rocky ['rɑki] *adj* **rockier; -est** : rocheux

rod ['rɑd] *n* **1** STICK : baguette *f* **2** : tige *f*, tringle *f* <iron rod : tige de fer> **3** : unité *f* de mesure qui équivaut à 16,5 pieds **4** *or* **fishing rod** : canne *f* à pêche

rode → **ride**[1]

rodent ['ro:dənt] *n* : rongeur *m*

rodeo ['ro:di,o:, ro'de1,o:] *n, pl* **-deos** : rodéo *m*

roe ['ro:] *n* : œufs *mpl* de poisson

roe deer *n* : chevreuil *m*

rogue ['ro:g] *n* SCOUNDREL : escroc *m*, fripouille *f fam*

roguish ['ro:gɪʃ] *adj* : espiègle, coquin

role ['ro:l] *n* **1** PART : rôle *m* (dans une pièce de théâtre) **2** FUNCTION : rôle *m*, fonction *f*

roll[1] ['ro:l] *vt* **1** : rouler <to roll a barrel : rouler un tonneau> <to roll cigarettes : rouler des cigarettes> **2** FLATTEN : étendre (de la pâte) **3** : faire tourner <to roll the cameras : faire tourner les caméras> **4 to roll out** : dérouler (un tapis) **5 to roll up one's sleeves** : retrousser ses manches — *vi* **1** : se rouler <the children were rolling in the grass : les enfants se roulaient dans l'herbe> **2** : tanguer, faire du roulis (se dit d'un bateau) **3 to roll in** : affluer <money was rolling in : l'argent affluait> **4 to roll on** ELAPSE : passer **5 to roll over** : se retourner

roll[2] *n* **1** LIST : liste *f* <class roll : liste des élèves> <to call the roll : faire l'appel> **2** : rouleau *m* (de papier, etc.), liasse *f* (d'argent) **3** BUN : petit pain *m* **4** RUMBLE : roulement *m* (de tambour), grondement *m* (du tonnerre) **5** ROLLING : roulis *m* (d'un navire), lancement *m* (de dés), balancement *m* (des hanches, etc.)

roller ['ro:lər] *n* : rouleau *m*

roller coaster ['ro:lər,ko:stər] *n* : montagnes *fpl* russes

roller–skate ['ro:lər,skeɪt] *vi* **-skated; -skating** : faire du patin à roulettes

roller skate *n* : patin *m* à roulettes

rollicking ['rɑlɪkɪŋ] *adj* : joyeux, exubérant

rolling pin *n* : rouleau *m* à pâtisserie

Roman[1] ['ro:mən] *adj* : romain

Roman[2] *n* : Romain *m*, -maine *f*

Roman Catholic[1] *adj* : catholique

Roman Catholic[2] *n* : catholique *mf*

romance[1] [ro'mænʦ, 'ro:,mænʦ] *vi* **-manced; -mancing** : exagérer, fabuler

romance[2] *n* **1** : roman *m* du Moyen Âge **2** : histoire *f* d'amour **3** AFFAIR : liaison *f* amoureuse **4** APPEAL : charme *m*, attrait *m* <the romance of the sea : l'attrait de la mer>

Romanian[1] [ro'meɪniən, ro-] *adj* : roumain

Romanian[2] *n* **1** : Roumain *m*, -maine *f* **2** : roumain *m* (langue)

romantic [ro'mæntɪk] *adj* : romantique

romantically [ro'mæntɪkli] *adv* : de façon romantique

romp[1] ['rɑmp] *vi* : s'ébattre, folâtrer

romp[2] *n* : ébats *mpl*, jeux *mpl* folâtres

roof[1] ['ru:f, 'rʊf] *vt* : couvrir d'un toit

roof[2] *n, pl* **roofs** ['ru:fs, 'rʊfs; 'ru:vz, 'rʊvz] : toit *m*

roofing ['ru:fɪŋ, 'rʊfɪŋ] *n* : toiture *f*, couverture *f*

rooftop ['ru:f,tɑp, 'rʊf-] *n* ROOF : toit *m*

rook[1] ['rʊk] *vt* CHEAT : frauder, escroquer

rook[2] *n* **1** : freux *m*, corbeau *m* (oiseau) **2** : tour *f* (en échecs)

rookie ['rʊki] *n* : novice *mf*

room[1] ['ru:m, 'rʊm] *vi* : loger <to room with s.o. : partager un logement avec qqn>

room[2] *n* **1** SPACE : espace *m*, place *f* <there's not enough room : il manque d'espace> **2** : chambre *f* (d'hôtel), pièce *f* (d'une maison), salle *f* (de conférence) **3** OPPORTUNITY : chance *f*, possibilité *f* <there was no room for doubt : il n'y avait aucun doute possible>

roomer ['ru:mər, 'rʊmər] *n* : pensionnaire *mf*; chambreur *m*, -breuse *f Can*

rooming house *n* : immeuble *m* locatif

roommate ['ru:m,meɪt, 'rʊm-] *n* : camarade *mf* de chambre, colocataire *mf Can*

roomy ['ru:mi, 'rʊmi] *adj* **roomier; -est** : spacieux, vaste

roost[1] ['ru:st] *vi* : se percher

roost[2] *n* : perchoir *m*

rooster ['ru:stər, 'rʊs-] *n* : coq *m*

root[1] ['ru:t, 'rʊt] *vi* **1** : s'enraciner (se dit d'une plante) **2** : fouiller (se dit des cochons) **3 to root for** CHEER : encourager, applaudir — *vt* **1 to root out** UNCOVER : découvrir, déterrer **2 to root out** ERADICATE : extirper

root[2] *n* **1** : racine *f* (d'une plante) **2** : racine *f*, base *f* (d'une dent) **3** SOURCE : origine *f*, source *f* <the root of evil : l'origine du mal> **4** CORE : fond *m*, cœur *m* <let's get to the root of the matter : allons au fond des choses>

rootless ['ru:tləs, 'rʊt-] *adj* : sans racines

rope[1] ['ro:p] *vt* **roped; roping 1** TIE : attacher (avec une corde) **2** LASSO : prendre au lasso **3 to rope off** : interdire l'accès à, délimiter par une corde

rope[2] *n* : corde *f*

rosary ['ro:zəri] *n, pl* **-ries** : chapelet *m*

rose[1] → **rise**[1]

rose[2] ['ro:z] *adj* : (de couleur) rose

rose[3] *n* : rose *f* (fleur), rose *m* (couleur)

rosebud ['ro:z,bʌd] *n* : bouton *m* de rose

rosebush ['ro:z,bʊʃ] *n* : rosier *m*

rosemary ['ro:z,meri] *n, pl* **-maries** : romarin *m*

rosette [ro'zet] *n* : rosette *f* (fait de rubans), rosace *f* (en architecture)

Rosh Hashanah [,rɑʃhə'ʃɑnə, ,ro:ʃ-] *n* : Rosh Hashana *m*, fête *f* du nouvel an juif

rosin ['rɑzən] *n* : colophane *f*

roster ['rɑstər] *n* : tableau *m*, liste *f* <roster of duties : tableau de services>

rostrum ['rɑstrəm] *n, pl* **-trums** *or* **-tra** [-trə] : tribune *f*, estrade *f*

rosy ['ro:zi] *adj* **rosier; -est 1** : rose, rosé <rosy cheeks : joues rosées> **2** HOPEFUL : prometteur

rot[1] ['rɑt] *v* **rotted; rotting** *vt* : pourrir — *vi* : pourrir, se décomposer

rot[2] *n* : pourriture *f*

rotary[1] ['ro:ʧəri] *adj* : rotatif

rotary[2] *n* : rond-point *m*

rotate ['ro:,teɪt] *v* **-tated; -tating** *vi* REVOLVE : tourner — *vt* **1** TURN : faire tourner **2** ALTERNATE : alterner (des cultures agricoles)

rotation [ro'teɪʃən] *n* : rotation *f*

rote ['ro:t] *n* **by ~** : par cœur, machinalement

rotor ['ro:tər] *n* : rotor *m*

rotten ['rɑtən] *adj* **1** : pourri <rotten wood : bois pourri> **2** CORRUPT : pourri, corrumpu (se dit d'une personne) **3** BAD : pourri, mauvais <rotten weather : temps pourri>

rottenness [ˈrɒtənnəs] *n* : pourriture *f*
rotund [roˈtʌnd] *adj* : rondelet, potelé
rotunda [roˈtʌndə] *n* : rotonde *f*
rouge [ˈruːʒ] *n* : rouge *m* à joues
rough[1] [ˈrʌf] *vt* **1** → **roughen 2** *or* **to rough out** : ébaucher, esquisser **3** *or* **to rough up** MANHANDLE : tabasser *fam,* battre
rough[2] *adj* **1** : rugueux, rude <a rough surface : une surface rugueuse> **2** : inégal, accidenté <rough terrain : terrain inégal> **3** TURBULENT : agité **4** HARSH : rude, violent **5** UNCOUTH : rude, fruste **6** APPROXIMATE : approximatif, sommaire <a rough estimate : une estimation approximative>
rough[3] *n* : rough *m* (au golf)
roughage [ˈrʌfɪdʒ] *n* : fibres *mpl* alimentaires
roughen [ˈrʌfən] *vt* : rendre rude, rendre rugueux
roughly [ˈrʌfli] *adv* **1** HARSHLY : rudement, brutalement **2** IMPERFECTLY : grossièrement **3** NEARLY : à peu près, environ <roughly 20 percent : environ 20 pour cent>
roughneck [ˈrʌfˌnek] *n* : dur *m fam*
roughness [ˈrʌfnəs] *n* : rudesse *f,* rugosité *f*
roulette [ˌruːˈlet] *n* : roulette *f* (au casino)
round[1] [ˈraʊnd] *vt* **1** : arrondir <to round the lips : arrondir les lèvres> **2** TURN : tourner <she rounded the corner : elle a tourné au coin> **3 to round off** : arrondir (un chiffre) **4 to round out** COMPLETE : compléter **5 to round up** GATHER : rassembler
round[2] *adv* → **around**[1]
round[3] *adj* **1** : rond <a round face : un visage rond> <to have round shoulders : avoir le dos voûté> **2** COMPLETE, FULL : exact, tout rond <a round dozen : une douzaine tout rond>
round[4] *n* **1** CIRCLE : rond *m,* cercle *m* **2** : série *f* <a round of talks : une série de négociations> <the daily round : la routine quotidienne> **3** : manche *f* (d'un match), partie *f* (de golf) **4** : cartouche *f* (d'une arme à feu) **5 round of applause** : salve *f* d'applaudissements **6 round of drinks** : tournée *f fam* **7 rounds** *npl* : tournée *f* (de ses amis), ronde *f* (d'un lieu), visites *fpl* (d'un médecin)
round[5] *prep* → **around**[2]
roundabout [ˈraʊndəˌbaʊt] *adj* : détourné, indirect
roundness [ˈraʊndnəs] *n* : rondeur *f*
round–trip [ˈraʊndˌtrɪp] *n* : voyage *m* aller et retour
roundup [ˈraʊndˌʌp] *n* **1** : rassemblement *m* (de bétail, de personnes, etc.) **2** SUMMARY : rappel *m,* résumé *m*
round up *vt* GATHER : rassembler, regrouper
roundworm [ˈraʊndˌwərm] *n* : ascaride *m*
rouse [ˈraʊz] *v* **roused; rousing** *vt* **1** : réveiller **2** EXCITE : éveiller, susciter <to rouse s.o. to fury : éveiller la furie en qqn> — *vi* AWAKEN : se réveiller
rout[1] [ˈraʊt] *vt* **1** : mettre en déroute **2 to rout out** : expulser, déloger
rout[2] *n* : déroute *f,* débâcle *f*
route[1] [ˈruːt, ˈraʊt] *vt* **routed; routing** DIRECT : fixer l'itinéraire de, diriger
route[2] *n* **1** HIGHWAY : route *f* **2** LINE : parcours *m,* trajet *m* <bus route : parcours d'autobus> **3** : chemin *m,* itinéraire *m* <the best route : le meilleur chemin> **4 newspaper route** : tournée *f* de livraison
routine[1] [ruːˈtiːn] *adj* : routinier
routine[2] *n* : routine *f*
routinely [ruːˈtiːnli] *adv* : systématiquement
rove [ˈroːv] *v* **roved; roving** *vi* ROAM : errer, vagabonder — *vt* : rôder dans, parcourir
rover [ˈroːvər] *n* : vagabond *m,* -bonde *f*
row[1] [ˈroː] *vi* : ramer — *vt* : transporter par canot
row[2] [ˈroː] *n* **1** LINE, RANK : rang *m,* rangée *f* <a row of houses : une rangée de maisons> <to stand in a row : être debout en rang> **2** : excursion *f* en bateau **3** SUCCESSION : série *f* <twice in a row : deux fois de suite> **4** [ˈraʊ] QUARREL : altercation *f,* dispute *f*
rowboat [ˈroːˌboːt] *n* : bateau *m* à rames
rowdiness [ˈraʊdinəs] *n* : tapage *m,* vacarme *m*
rowdy[1] [ˈraʊdi] *adj* **rowdier; -est** : tapageur, bruyant
rowdy[2] *n, pl* **-dies** : voyou *m*
royal[1] [ˈrɔɪəl] *adj* : royal — **royally** *adv*
royal[2] *n* : membre *m* d'une famille royale
royalty [ˈrɔɪəlti] *n, pl* **-ties 1** : membres *m* d'une famille royale **2** : royauté *f* (position) **3 royalties** *npl* : droits *mpl* d'auteur
rub[1] [ˈrʌb] *v* **rubbed; rubbing** *vt* **1** : frotter, se frotter <to rub one's hands together : se frotter les mains> **2** MASSAGE : frictionner **3** CHAFE : frotter contre, blesser **4** POLISH : frotter, polir **5 to rub shoulders with s.o.** : coudoyer qqn **6 to rub s.o. the wrong way** : prendre qqn à rebrousse-poil — *vi* : frotter
rub[2] *n* **1** : friction *f,* frottement *m* <an alcohol rub : une friction à l'alcool> **2** OBSTACLE : obstacle *m,* difficulté *f*
rubber[1] [ˈrʌbər] *adj* : en caoutchouc
rubber[2] *n* **1** : caoutchouc *m* **2 rubbers** *npl* : caoutchoucs *mpl,* claques *fpl Can,* pardessus *m Can*
rubber band *n* : élastique *m*

rubber–stamp [ˈrʌbərˈstæmp] *vt* : tamponner
rubber stamp *n* : tampon *m* (de caoutchouc)
rubbery [ˈrʌbəri] *adj* : caoutchouteux
rubbish [ˈrʌbɪʃ] *n* : ordures *fpl*, déchets *mpl*
rubble [ˈrʌbəl] *n* : décombres *mpl*
ruble [ˈruːbəl] *n* : rouble *m*
ruby[1] [ˈruːbi] *adj* : vermeil (couleur)
ruby[2] *n, pl* **-bies 1** : rubis *m* **2** : couleur *f* rubis, couleur *f* vermeille
rudder [ˈrʌdər] *n* : gouvernail *m*
ruddy [ˈrʌdi] *adj* **ruddier; -est** : rougeâtre, rougeaud
rude [ˈruːd] *adj* **ruder; rudest 1** CRUDE : grossier, rudimentaire **2** UNDEVELOPED : primitif, rude **3** IMPOLITE : grossier, insolent
rudely [ˈruːdli] *adv* : impoliment, grossièrement
rudeness [ˈruːdnəs] *n* : impolitesse *f*, grossièreté *f*
rudiment [ˈruːdəmənt] *n* : rudiment *m*
rudimentary [ˌruːdəˈmentəri] *adj* : rudimentaire
rue [ˈruː] *vt* **rued; ruing** : regretter
rueful [ˈruːfəl] *adj* : triste, chagrin, attristé
ruffian [ˈrʌfiən] *n* : voyou *m*
ruffle[1] [ˈrʌfəl] *vt* **-fled; -fling 1** : hérisser (ses plumes), ébouriffer (ses cheveux) **2** TROUBLE, VEX : décontenancer, troubler, énerver
ruffle[2] *n* : ruche *f*
rug [ˈrʌg] *n* : tapis *m*, carpette *f*
rugged [ˈrʌgəd] *adj* **1** : accidenté <rugged landscape : paysage accidenté> **2** JAGGED : en dents de scie (se dit des montagnes) **3** HARSH : sévère, exigeant **4** STURDY : robuste, fort
ruin[1] [ˈruːən] *vt* **1** DESTROY : ruiner, anéantir **2** DAMAGE : abîmer **3** BANKRUPT : ruiner
ruin[2] *n* : ruine *f* <to be in ruins : être en ruines>
ruinous [ˈruːənəs] *adj* : ruineux
rule[1] [ˈruːl] *v* **ruled; ruling** *vt* **1** GOVERN : régner sur, gouverner (un pays, etc.) **2** DOMINATE : dominer, maîtriser (les émotions, etc.) **3** DRAW : tirer (à la règle) **4** DECREE, JUDGE : décréter, décider, juger — *vi* : régner
rule[2] *n* **1** : règle *f*, règlement *m* <as a rule : en règle générale> **2** CUSTOM : coutume *f*, habitude *f* **3** DOMINION : autorité *f*, gouvernement *m* **4** → **ruler**
ruler [ˈruːlər] *n* : règle *f* (pour mesurer)
rum [ˈrʌm] *n* : rhum *m*
Rumanian [ruˈmeɪniən] → **Romanian**
rumble[1] [ˈrʌmbəl] *vi* **-bled; -bling 1** ROAR : gronder (se dit du tonnerre, etc.) **2** : gargouiller (se dit de l'estomac)
rumble[2] *n* : grondement *m* (du tonnerre, etc.), gargouillement *m* (de l'estomac)
ruminant[1] [ˈruːmənənt] *adj* : ruminant
ruminant[2] *n* : ruminant *m*
ruminate [ˈruːmə,neɪt] *vi* **-nated; -nating 1** : ruminer (se dit d'une vâche) **2** MUSE : ruminer, réfléchir
rummage [ˈrʌmɪdʒ] *vi* **-maged; -maging** : fouiller, fourrager
rummy [ˈrʌmi] *n* : rami *m* (jeu de cartes)
rumor[1] *or Brit* **rumour** [ˈruːmər] *vt* **it is rumored that** : le bruit court que, il paraît que
rumor[2] *or Brit* **rumour** *n* : rumeur *f*, bruit *m*
rump [ˈrʌmp] *n* **1** : croupe *f* (d'un animal) **2** *or* **rump steak** : romsteck *m*
rumple [ˈrʌmpəl] *vt* **-pled; -pling 1** TOUSLE : ébouriffer **2** WRINKLE : froisser, friper
rumpus [ˈrʌmpəs] *n* : vacarme *m*, boucan *m*
run[1] [ˈrʌn] *v* **ran** [ˈræn]; **run; running** *vi* **1** : courir <he ran home : il est rentré chez lui en courant> **2** : être candidat <to run for the presidency : être candidat à la présidence> **3** FLOW : couler **4** FUNCTION, OPERATE : tourner <the engine was running : le moteur tournait> **5** BE : être <profits were running high : les profits étaient élevés> <I was running late : j'étais en retard> **6** : faire le service, circuler <the train runs between Washington and New York : le train fait le service entre Washington et New York> **7** OCCUR : être courant <it runs in our family : c'est courant dans notre famille> **8** : déteindre (se dit des couleurs) **9** EXTEND : passer **10 to run away** : s'enfuir, se sauver **11 to run out** EXPIRE : expirer **12 to run out of** : manquer — *vt* **1** : courir <to run the marathon : courir le marathon> **2** : faire, effectuer <to run errands : faire des courses> **3** OPERATE : faire marcher **4** INCUR : courir <to run a risk : courir un risque> **5** MANAGE : gérer, diriger **6** CHASE : chasser <we ran the thieves out of town : les bandits ont été chassés de la ville> **7 to run a fever** : faire de la température **8 to run a red light** : brûler un feu rouge **9 to run one's car off the road** : perdre la maîtrise de son véhicule
run[2] *n* **1** : course *f* <a three-mile run : une course de trois milles> <to break into a run : se mettre à courir> **2** SERIES : succession *f*, série *f* <a run of cloudy days : une succession de journées nuageuses> **3** RIDE : tour *m*, promenade *f* <a run in the car : un tour en voiture> **4** TRIP : trajet *m*, parcours *m* <the New York run : le trajet jusqu'à New York> **5** : maille *f* filée, échelle *f* (dans les bas) **6** SLOPE : pente *f* <ski run : pente de ski> **7** DEMAND, RUSH : ruée *f* (sur la

banque, etc.) **8** : point *m* (aux sports) **9** : enclos *m* (pour des animaux) **10** : tirage *m* (en imprimerie) **11 to have the run of the house** : avoir la maison à sa disposition **12 on the run** : en fuite, en cavale

runaway[1] [ˈrʌnəˌweɪ] *adj* : fugueur (se dit d'un enfant), emballé (se dit d'un cheval), incontrôlé (se dit d'un véhicule)

runaway[2] *n* : fugitif *m*, -tive *f*; fugueur *m*, -geuse *f*

run–down [ˈrʌnˈdaʊn] *adj* **1** DILAPIDATED : délabré **2** EXHAUSTED, WORN-OUT : fatigué, éreinté

rung[1] → **ring**[2]

rung[2] [ˈrʌŋ] *n* : barreau *m* (d'une échelle, d'une chaise, etc.)

runner [ˈrʌnər] *n* **1** RACER : coureur *m*, -reuse *f* **2** BLADE : lame *f* (d'un patin) **3** TRACK : glissière *f* (d'une porte, etc.), coulisse *f* **4** : coulant *m*, stolon *m* (d'une plante) **5** MESSENGER : coursier *m*, -sière *f*

runner–up [ˌrʌnərˈʌp] *n, pl* **runners–up** : second *m*, -conde *f*

running [ˈrʌnɪŋ] *adj* **1** FLOWING : courant <running water : eau courante> **2** CONTINUOUS : continuel <a running battle : une bataille continuelle> **3** CONSECUTIVE : de suite <three days running : trois jours consécutifs>

runt [ˈrʌnt] *n* : avorton *m*

runway [ˈrʌnˌweɪ] *n* : piste *f* d'envol, piste *f* d'atterrissage

rupee [ruːˈpiː, ˈruː,-] *n* : roupie *f*

rupture[1] [ˈrʌptʃər] *v* **-tured; -turing** *vt* BREAK, BURST : rompre — *vi* : se rompre

rupture[2] *n* **1** BREACH, BREAK : rupture *f* **2** HERNIA : hernie *f*

rural [ˈrʊrəl] *adj* : rural

ruse [ˈruːs, ˈruːz] *n* : ruse *f*, stratagème *m*

rush[1] [rʌʃ] *vi* HURRY : se précipiter, se dépêcher <to rush toward s.o. : se précipiter vers qqn> — *vt* **1** HURRY, PRESS : presser, bousculer **2** *or* **to rush through** : expédier <to rush one's work : expédier son travail> **3** ATTACK : attaquer, agresser **4** TRANSPORT : transporter d'urgence (à l'hôpital, etc.)

rush[2] *adj* : urgent <a rush order : une commande urgente>

rush[3] *n* **1** : jonc *m* (plante) **2** : ruée *f* <a rush towards the exit : une ruée vers la sortie> **3** HASTE : hâte *f*, empressement *m*

rush hour *n* : heure *f* de pointe

russet[1] [ˈrʌsət] *adj* : roussâtre, roux

russet[2] *n* : roux *m* (couleur)

Russian[1] [ˈrʌʃən] *adj* : russe

Russian[2] *n* **1** : Russe *mf* **2** : russe *m* (langue)

rust[1] [ˈrʌst] *vt* : rouiller — *vi* : se rouiller

rust[2] *n* **1** : rouille *f* (sur métal) **2** : couleur *f* rouille

rustic[1] [ˈrʌstɪk] *adj* : rustique, champêtre

rustic[2] *n* : campagnard *m*, -gnarde *f*

rustle[1] [ˈrʌsəl] *v* **-tled; -tling** *vi* : bruire <the pine needles rustled : on entendait bruire les aiguilles de pin> — *vt* STEAL : voler (du bétail)

rustle[2] *n* : bruissement *m*, froissement

rusty [ˈrʌsti] *adj* **rustier; -est 1** : rouillé <a rusty nail : un clou rouillé> **2** SLOW : rouillé, peu agile

rut [ˈrʌt] *n* **1** TRACK : ornière *f* **2 to be in a rut** : s'enliser dans une routine

ruthless [ˈruːθləs] *adj* : impitoyable, cruel — **ruthlessly** *adv*

ruthlessness [ˈruːθləsnəs] *n* : caractère *m* impitoyable

Rwandan[1] [rʊˈɑndən] *adj* : rwandais

Rwandan[2] *n* : Rwandais *m*, -daise *f*

rye [ˈraɪ] *n* **1** : seigle *m* <rye bread : pain de seigle> **2** *or* **rye whiskey** : whisky *m* (de seigle)

S

s [ˈɛs] *n, pl* **s's** *or* **ss** [ˈɛsəz] : s *m*, dix-neuvième lettre de l'alphabet

Sabbath [ˈsæbəθ] *n* : sabbat *m* (en judaïsme), dimanche *m* (en christianisme)

saber [ˈseɪbər] *n* : sabre *m*

sable [ˈseɪbəl] *n* **1** BLACK : noir *m* **2** : zibeline *f* (animal)

sabotage[1] [ˈsæbəˌtɑʒ] *vt* **-taged; -taging** : saboter

sabotage[2] *n* : sabotage *m*

saboteur [ˌsæbəˈtər, -ˈtʊr, -ˈtjʊr] *n* : saboteur *m*, -teuse *f*

sac [ˈsæk] *n* : sac *m*

saccharin [ˈsækərən] *n* : saccharine *f*

saccharine [ˈsækərən, -ˌriːn, -ˌraɪn] *adj* : mielleux, doucereux (se dit d'un sourire, etc.)

sachet [sæˈʃeɪ] *n* : sachet *m*

sack[1] [ˈsæk] *vt* **1** PLUNDER : mettre à sac **2** DISMISS, FIRE : virer, congédier

sack[2] *n* BAG : sac *m*

sacrament [ˈsækrəmənt] *n* : sacrement *m*

sacramental [ˌsækrəˈmɛntəl] *adj* : sacramentel

sacred [ˈseɪkrəd] *adj* : sacré

sacrifice[1] [ˈsækrəˌfaɪs] *vt* **-ficed; -ficing 1** : sacrifier **2 to sacrifice oneself** : se sacrifier

sacrifice[2] *n* : sacrifice *m*

sacrificial [ˌsækrəˈfɪʃəl] *adj* : sacrificiel
sacrilege [ˈsækrəlɪdʒ] *n* : sacrilège *m*
sacrilegious [ˌsækrəˈlɪdʒəs, -ˈliː-] *adj* : sacrilège
sacrosanct [ˈsækroˌsæŋkt] *adj* : sacro-saint
sad [ˈsæd] *adj* **sadder; saddest** : triste
sadden [ˈsædən] *vt* : attrister
saddle[1] [ˈsædəl] *vt* **-dled; -dling** : seller
saddle[2] *n* : selle *f* <in the saddle : en selle>
sadism [ˈseɪˌdɪzəm, ˈsæ-] *n* : sadisme *m*
sadist [ˈseɪdɪst, ˈsæ-] *n* : sadiste *mf*
sadistic [səˈdɪstɪk] *adj* : sadique — **sadistically** [-tɪkli] *adv*
sadly [ˈsædli] *adv* **1** SORROWFULLY : tristement **2** UNFORTUNATELY : malheureusement **3** (*used for emphasis*) <you are sadly mistaken : vous vous trompez fort>
sadness [ˈsædnəs] *n* : tristesse *f*
safari [səˈfɑri, -ˈfær-] *n* : safari *m*
safe[1] [ˈseɪf] *adj* **safer; safest 1** PROTECTED : en sécurité, à l'abri <safe and sound : sain et sauf> **2** SECURE : sûr **3 to play it safe** : ne prendre aucun risque
safe[2] *n* : coffre-fort *m*
safeguard[1] [ˈseɪfˌgɑrd] *vt* : sauvegarder
safeguard[2] *n* : sauvegarde *f*
safekeeping [ˈseɪfˈkiːpɪŋ] *n* : bonne garde *f*
safely [ˈseɪfli] *adv* **1** : sans incident, sûrement <the plane landed safely : l'avion a atterri sans incident> <to arrive safely : bien arriver> **2** SECURELY : en sécurité, à l'abri **3** CAREFULLY : prudemment
safety [ˈseɪfti] *n, pl* **-ties** : sécurité *f*
safety belt *n* : ceinture *f* de sécurité
safety pin *n* : épingle *f* de sûreté
saffron [ˈsæfrən] *n* : safran *m*
sag[1] [ˈsæg] *vi* **sagged; sagging** : s'affaisser
sag[2] *n* : affaissement *m*
saga [ˈsɑgə, ˈsæ-] *n* : saga *f*
sagacious [səˈgeɪʃəs] *adj* : sagace
sage[1] [ˈseɪdʒ] *adj* **sager; -est** : sage, avisé
sage[2] *n* **1** : sage *m* (personne) **2** : sauge *f* (plante)
sagebrush [ˈseɪdʒˌbrʌʃ] *n* : armoise *f*
sagely [ˈseɪdʒli] *adv* : avec sagesse
Sagittarius [ˌsædʒəˈtɛriəs] *n* : Sagittaire *m*
said → **say**[1]
sail[1] [ˈseɪl] *vi* **1** : voyager en bateau **2** *or* **to go sailing** : faire de la voile **3** : aller facilement <we sailed right in : nous sommes entrés sans problème> — *vt* **1** : naviguer, manœuvrer (un bateau) **2** CROSS : traverser, parcourir <to sail the seas : parcourir les mers>
sail[2] *n* **1** : voile *f* (d'un bateau) **2** : promenade *f* en bateau **3 to set sail** : appareiller, prendre la mer
sailboat [ˈseɪlˌboːt] *n* : bateau *m* à voiles, voilier *m*
sailor [ˈseɪlər] *n* : marin *m*, matelot *m*
saint [ˈseɪnt, *before a name* ˌseɪnt *or* sənt] *n* : saint *m*, sainte *f*
saintliness [ˈseɪntlinəs] *n* : sainteté *f*
saintly [ˈseɪntli] *adj* **saintlier; -est** : saint
sake [ˈseɪk] *n* **1** BENEFIT : bien *m* <for the children's sake : pour le bien des enfants> **2** (*indicating an end or purpose*) <art for art's sake : l'art pour l'art> <for the sake of money : pour l'argent> **3 for goodness' sake!** : pour l'amour de Dieu!
salacious [səˈleɪʃəs] *adj* : salace
salad [ˈsæləd] *n* : salade *f*
salamander [ˈsæləˌmændər] *n* : salamandre *f*
salami [səˈlɑmi] *n* : salami *m*, saucisson *m* sec
salary [ˈsæləri] *n, pl* **-ries** : salaire *m*
sale [ˈseɪl] *n* **1** SELLING : vente *f* <for sale : à vendre> **2** : solde *m* <on sale : en solde> **3 sales** *npl or* **sales department** : service *m* des ventes
salesman [ˈseɪlzmən] *n, pl* **-men** [-mən, -ˌmɛn] **1** : vendeur *m* **2 traveling salesman** : représentant *m* (de commerce)
salesperson [ˈseɪlzˌpərsən] *n* : vendeur *m*, -deuse *f*; représentant *m*, -tante *f* des ventes
saleswoman [ˈseɪlzˌwʊmən] *n, pl* **-women** [-ˌwɪmən] **1** : vendeuse *f* **2 traveling saleswoman** : représentante *f* (de commerce)
salient [ˈseɪljənt] *adj* : saillant
saline [ˈseɪˌlin, -ˌlaɪn] *adj* : salin
saliva [səˈlaɪvə] *n* : salive *f*
salivary [ˈsæləˌvɛri] *adj* : salivaire
salivate [ˈsæləˌveɪt] *vi* **-vated; -vating** : saliver
sallow [ˈsæloː] *adj* : jaunâtre
sally[1] [ˈsæli] *vi* **-lied; -lying** SET OUT : sortir
sally[2] *n, pl* **-lies 1** : sortie *f* (militaire) **2** EXCURSION : sortie *f* **3** QUIP : saillie *f*
salmon [ˈsæmən] *ns & pl* : saumon *m*
salon [səˈlɑn, ˈsæˌlɑn, sæˈlɔ̃] *n* : salon *m* <beauty salon : salon de beauté>
saloon [səˈluːn] *n* **1** : salon *m* (dans un navire) **2** BARROOM : bar *m*
salsa [ˈsɔlsə, ˈsɑl-] *n* **1** : sauce *f* pimentée **2** : salsa *f* (musique)
salt[1] [ˈsɔlt] *vt* : saler
salt[2] *adj* : salé
salt[3] *n* : sel *m*
saltshaker [ˈsɔltˌʃeɪkər] *n* : salière *f*
saltwater [ˈsɔltˌwɔtər, -ˌwɑ-] *adj* : de mer
salty [ˈsɔlti] *adj* **saltier; -est** : salé
salubrious [səˈluːbriəs] *adj* : salubre
salutary [ˈsæljəˌtɛri] *adj* : salutaire
salutation [ˌsæljəˈteɪʃən] *n* : salutation *f*
salute[1] [səˈluːt] *v* **-luted; -luting** *vt* : saluer — *vi* : faire un salut
salute[2] *n* **1** : salut *m* (avec la main), salve *f* (de canon) <twenty-one gun

salute : salve de vingt et un coups> **2** TRIBUTE : hommage *m*

salvage[1] ['sælvɪdʒ] *vt* **-vaged; -vaging** : sauver, récupérer

salvage[2] *n* : sauvetage *m*

salvation [sæl'veɪʃən] *n* : salut *m*

salve[1] ['sæv, 'sav] *vt* **salved; salving** : adoucir, apaiser, soulager

salve[2] *n* : onguent *m*, pommade *f*

salvo ['sæl,vo:] *n, pl* **-vos** *or* **-voes** : salve *f*

same[1] ['seɪm] *adj* : même <he's reading the same book : il lit le même livre> <same time, same place : à la même heure, au même endroit>

same[2] *pron* : même <she's never been the same since : elle n'est plus la même depuis> <I'll have the same : je prends la même chose>

sameness ['seɪmnəs] *n* **1** SIMILARITY : similitude *f* **2** MONOTONY : monotonie *f*

sample[1] ['sæmpəl] *vt* **-pled; -pling** : goûter (des mets, etc.), essayer (des produits)

sample[2] *n* : échantillon *m*

sampler ['sæmplər] *n* : modèle *m* de broderie

sanatorium [,sænə'toriəm] *n, pl* **-riums** *or* **-ria** [-iə] : sanatorium *m*

sanctify ['sæŋktə,faɪ] *vt* **-fied; -fying** : sanctifier

sanctimonious [,sæŋktə'mo:niəs] *adj* : moralisateur

sanction[1] ['sæŋkʃən] *vt* : sanctionner, approuver

sanction[2] *n* **1** APPROVAL : sanction *f* **2 sanctions** *npl* : sanctions *fpl* <to impose sanctions on : prendre des sanctions à l'encontre de>

sanctity ['sæŋktəṭi] *n, pl* **-ties** : sainteté *f*

sanctuary ['sæŋktʃu,ɛri] *n, pl* **-aries 1** : sanctuaire *m* (d'une église) **2** REFUGE : refuge *m*

sand[1] ['sænd] *vt* **1** : sabler <to sand the driveway : sabler la voie> **2** SMOOTH : poncer

sand[2] *n* : sable *m*

sandal ['sændəl] *n* : sandale *f*

sandbank ['sænd,bæŋk] *n* : banc *m* de sable

sandbar ['sænd,bɑr] *n* : barre *f*, batture *f Can*

sandpaper[1] ['sænd,peɪpər] *vt* : poncer (au papier de verre)

sandpaper[2] *n* : papier *m* de verre, papier *m* sablé *Can*

sandpiper ['sænd,paɪpər] *n* : bécasseau *m*

sandstone ['sænd,sto:n] *n* : grès *m*

sandstorm ['sænd,stɔrm] *n* : tempête *f* de sable

sandwich[1] ['sænd,wɪtʃ] *vt* WEDGE : prendre en sandwich, coincer

sandwich[2] *n* : sandwich *m*

sandy ['sændi] *adj* **sandier; -est** : sableux, sablonneux

sane ['seɪn] *adj* **saner; sanest 1** : sain d'esprit **2** SENSIBLE : raisonnable, sensé

sang → **sing**

sanguine ['sæŋgwən] *adj* **1** RUDDY : rubicond, sanguin **2** HOPEFUL : optimiste, confiant

sanitarium [,sænə'teriəm] *n, pl* **-iums** *or* **-ia** [-iə] → **sanatorium**

sanitary ['sænəteri] *adj* **1** : sanitaire <sanitary conditions : conditions sanitaires> **2** HYGIENIC : hygiénique

sanitary napkin *n* : serviette *f* hygiénique

sanitation [,sænə'teɪʃən] *n* : hygiène *f* publique

sanity ['sænəṭi] *n* : santé *f* mentale

sank → **sink**[1]

sap[1] ['sæp] *vt* **sapped; sapping** UNDERMINE : saper, miner

sap[2] *n* **1** : sève *f* (d'un arbre) **2** FOOL : nigaud *m*, -gaude *f*; andouille *f fam*

sapling ['sæplɪŋ] *n* : jeune arbre *m*

sapphire ['sæ,faɪr] *n* : saphir *m*

sarcasm ['sɑr,kæzəm] *n* : sarcasme *m*

sarcastic [sɑr'kæstɪk] *adj* : sarcastique **— sarcastically** [-ṭɪkli] *adv*

sarcophagus [sɑr'kɑfəgəs] *n, pl* **-gi** [-,gaɪ, -,dʒaɪ] : sarcophage *m*

sardine [sɑr'di:n] *n* : sardine *f*

sardonic [sɑr'dɑnɪk] *adj* : sardonique **— sardonically** [-nɪkli] *adv*

sarsaparilla [,sæspə'rɪlə, ,sɑrs-] *n* : salsepareille *f*

sartorial [sɑr'toriəl, sər-, -'tɔr-] *adj* : vestimentaire

sash ['sæʃ] *n* **1** : large ceinture *f* (d'une robe), écharpe *f* (insigne) **2** *pl* **sash** : châssis *m* (d'une fenêtre)

sassafras ['sæsə,fræs] *n* : sassafras *m*

sassy ['sæsi] *adj* **sassier; -est** → **saucy**

sat → **sit**

Satan ['seɪṭən] *n* : Satan *m*

satanic [sə'tænɪk, seɪ-] *adj* : satanique **— satanically** [-nɪkli] *adv*

satchel ['sæṭʃəl] *n* : sacoche *f*

sate ['seɪṭ] *vt* **sated; sating** : rassasier, assouvir

satellite ['sæṭə,laɪṭ] *n* : satellite *m*

satiate ['seɪʃi,eɪṭ] *vt* **-ated; -ating** : rassasier, assouvir

satin ['sæṭən] *n* : satin *m*

satire ['sæ,ṭaɪr] *n* : satire *f*

satiric [sə'tɪrɪk] *or* **satirical** [-ɪkəl] *adj* : satirique

satirize ['sæṭə,raɪz] *vt* **-rized; -rizing** : satiriser

satisfaction [,sæṭəs'fækʃən] *n* : satisfaction *f*

satisfactorily [,sæṭəs'fæktərəli] *adv* : de façon satisfaisante

satisfactory [,sæṭəs'fæktəri] *adj* : satisfaisant

satisfy ['sæṭəs,faɪ] *v* **-fied; -fying** *vt* **1** PLEASE : satisfaire, contenter **2** CONVINCE : convaincre, persuader **3** FULFILL : satisfaire à, répondre à, remplir <to satisfy the demand for

: répondre à la demande de> <to satisfy our needs : satisfaire à nos besoins> — *vi* SUFFICE : suffir

satisfying ['sætəs,faɪɪŋ] *adj* : satisfaisant

saturate ['sætʃə,reɪt] *vt* **-rated; -rating** : saturer

saturation [,sætʃə'reɪʃən] *n* : saturation *f*

Saturday ['sætər,deɪ, -di] *n* : samedi *m*

Saturn ['sætərn] *n* : Saturne *f* (planète)

satyr ['seɪtər, 'sæ-] *n* : satyre *m*

sauce ['sɔs] *n* : sauce *f*

saucepan ['sɔs,pæn] *n* : casserole *f*

saucer ['sɔsər] *n* : soucoupe *f*

saucily ['sɔsəli] *adv* : avec impertinence

sauciness ['sɔsinəs] *n* : impertinence *f*

saucy ['sɔsi] *adj* **saucier; -est** : impertinent

Saudi[1] ['saʊdi] *or* **Saudi Arabian** ['saʊdiə'reɪbiən] *adj* : saoudien

Saudi[2] *or* **Saudi Arabian** *n* : Saoudien *m*, -dienne *f*

sauerkraut ['saʊər,kraʊt] *n* : choucroute *f*

sauna ['sɔnə, 'saʊnə] *n* : sauna *m*

saunter ['sɔntər, 'sɑn-] *vi* : flâner, marcher d'un pas nonchalant

sausage ['sɔsɪdʒ] *n* : saucisse *f* (crue), saucisson *m* (cuit)

sauté [sɔ'teɪ, so-] *vt* **-téed** *or* **-téd; -téing** : faire sauter

savage[1] ['sævɪdʒ] *adj* : féroce, sauvage, brutal — **savagely** *adv*

savage[2] *n* : sauvage *mf*

savagery ['sævɪdʒri] *n, pl* **-ries** : sauvagerie *f*

save[1] ['seɪv] *v* **saved; saving** *vt* **1** RESCUE : sauver **2** KEEP, RESERVE : mettre de côté, garder (des biens, une place, etc.), économiser (de l'argent) **3** SPARE : épargner <she saved me an unnecessary trip : elle m'a épargné un déplacement inutile> **4** : sauvegarder (en informatique) — *vi* : économiser

save[2] *n* : arrêt *m* (aux sports)

save[3] *prep* EXCEPT : sauf, excepté

savior ['seɪvjər] *n* : sauveur *m*

savor[1] ['seɪvər] *vt* : savourer

savor[2] *n* : saveur *f*

savory ['seɪvəri] *adj* : savoureux

saw[1] → **see**[1]

saw[2] ['sɔ] *vt* **sawed; sawed** *or* **sawn** ['sɔn]; **sawing** : scier

saw[3] *n* : scie *f*

sawdust ['sɔ,dʌst] *n* : sciure *f*

sawhorse ['sɔ,hɔrs] *n* : chevalet *m*

sawmill *n* ['sɔ,mɪl] : scierie *f*

saxophone ['sæksə,foːn] *n* : saxophone *m*

say[1] ['seɪ] *v* **said** ['sɛd]; **saying; says** ['sɛz] *vt* **1** SPEAK, UTTER : dire <to say no : dire non> <it goes without saying that . . . : il va sans dire que . . .> <say your prayers : fais tes prières> **2** EXPRESS, INDICATE : exprimer, indiquer, dire <my watch says three o'clock : ma montre indique trois heures> **3** ALLEGE : dire <it's said that she's pretty : l'on dit qu'elle est belle> — *vi* : dire <I'd rather not say : je préfère ne pas le dire> <that is to say : c'est-à-dire>

say[2] *n, pl* **says** ['seɪz] : mot *m*, voix *f* <to have no say : ne pas avoir voix au chapitre> <to have one's say : dire son mot, dire ce qu'on a à dire>

saying ['seɪɪŋ] *n* : dicton *m*, proverbe *m*

scab ['skæb] *n* **1** : croûte *f*, gale *f* *Can* **2** STRIKEBREAKER : jaune *mf*

scabbard ['skæbərd] *n* : fourreau *m*

scabby ['skæbi] *adj* **scabbier; -est** : croûteux

scaffold ['skæfəld, -,foːld] *n* **1** *or* **scaffolding** : échafaudage *m* **2** : échafaud *m* (pour exécutions)

scald ['skɔld] *vt* **1** BURN : ébouillanter **2** HEAT : échauder

scale[1] ['skeɪl] *v* **scaled; scaling** *vt* **1** : écailler (un poisson) **2** CLIMB : escalader **3 to scale down** : réduire — *vi* WEIGH : peser <he scaled in at 200 pounds : il pesait 200 livres>

scale[2] *n* **1** *or* **scales** : pèse-personne *m*, balance *f* **2** : écaille *f* (d'un poisson) **3** EXTENT : étendue *f*, échelle *f* <on a large scale : sur une grande échelle> **4** : échelle *f* <drawn to scale : dessiné à l'échelle> **5** : gamme *f* (en musique)

scallion ['skæljən] *n* : ciboule *f*, échalote *f*

scallop ['skɑləp, 'skæ-] *n* **1** : coquille *f* Saint-Jacques **2** : feston *m* (en couture)

scalp[1] ['skælp] *vt* : scalper

scalp[2] *n* : cuir *m* chevelu

scalpel ['skælpəl] *n* : scalpel *m*

scaly ['skeɪli] *adj* **scalier; -est** : écailleux

scamp ['skæmp] *n* : polisson *m*, -sonne *f*; galopin *m*

scamper ['skæmpər] *vi* : gambader, galoper

scan[1] ['skæn] *v* **scanned; scanning** *vt* **1** : scander (un vers) **2** SCRUTINIZE : scruter <to scan the horizon : scruter l'horizon> **3** PERUSE : parcourir rapidement (un texte), feuilleter (une revue) **4** : examiner au scanner (en médecine) **5** : balayer (en électronique) — *vi* : se scander (se dit d'un vers)

scan[2] *n* **1** : balayage *m* (électronique) **2** : scanographie *f*, échographie *f* (ultrasonore) **3** : scansion *f* (littéraire)

scandal [,skændəl] *n* **1** DISGRACE : scandale *m* **2** GOSSIP : médisance *f*

scandalize ['skændəl,aɪz] *vt* **-ized; -izing** : scandaliser

scandalous ['skændələs] *adj* : scandaleux

Scandinavian[1] [,skændə'neɪviən] *adj* : scandinave

Scandinavian[2] *n* : Scandinave *mf*
scanner ['skænər] *n* : scanner *m*
scant ['skænt] *adj* : maigre, insuffisant
scanty ['skænti] *adj* **scantier; -est 1** : maigre, insuffisant <a scanty meal : un repas insuffisant> **2** BRIEF : léger (se dit des vêtements)
scapegoat ['skeɪpˌgo:t] *n* : bouc *m* émissaire
scapula ['skæpjələ] *n, pl* **-lae** [-ˌli:, -ˌlaɪ] *or* **-las** : omoplate *f*
scar[1] ['skɑr] *v* **scarred; scarring** *vt* : marquer d'une cicatrice — *vi* : se cicatriser
scar[2] *n* : cicatrice *f*
scarab ['skærəb] *n* : scarabée *m*
scarce ['skɛrs] *adj* **scarcer; -est** : rare
scarcely ['skɛrsli] *adv* **1** BARELY : à peine <he can scarcely read : il sait à peine lire> **2** HARDLY : difficilement <I can scarcely blame him : je peux difficilement le reprocher>
scarcity ['skɛrsəṭi] *n, pl* **-ties** : rareté *f*, manque *m*
scare[1] ['skɛr] *vt* **scared; scaring** : faire peur à, effrayer
scare[2] *n* **1** FRIGHT : peur *f* **2** ALARM : alerte *f*
scarecrow ['skɛrˌkro:] *n* : épouvantail *m*
scarf ['skɑrf] *n, pl* **scarves** ['skɑrvz] *or* **scarfs** : écharpe *f* (longue), foulard *m* (carré)
scarlet[1] ['skɑrlət] *adj* : écarlate
scarlet[2] *n* : écarlate *f*
scarlet fever *n* : scarlatine *f*
scary ['skɛri] *adj* **scarier, -est** : qui fait peur, effrayant, épeurant *Can*
scathing ['skeɪðɪŋ] *adj* : cinglant, mordant
scatter ['skætər] *vt* : disperser, éparpiller — *vi* DISPERSE : se disperser
scavenge ['skævəndʒ] *v* **-venged; -venging** *vt* : récupérer — *vi* : fouiller
scavenger ['skævəndʒər] *n* : charognard *m* (animal), pilleur *m* de poubelles (personne)
scenario [sə'næri,o:, -'nɑr-] *n, pl* **-ios** : scénario *m*
scene ['si:n] *n* **1** : scène *f* <the political scene : la scène politique> **2** SCENERY, SET : décor *m* **3** VIEW : vue *f* **4** LOCATION : lieu *m* <the scene of the crime : le lieu du crime>
scenery ['si:nəri] *n, pl* **-eries 1** : décor *m* **2** LANDSCAPE : paysages *mpl*
scenic ['si:nɪk] *adj* : pittoresque
scent[1] ['sɛnt] *vt* **1** SMELL : flairer (le gibier, le danger, etc.) **2** PERFUME : parfumer
scent[2] *n* **1** ODOR : odeur *f*, senteur *f* **2** NOSE, SMELLING : odorat *m*, flair *m* <a dog with a keen scent : un chien qui a du flair> **3** PERFUME : parfum *m*
scented ['sɛntəd] *adj* : parfumé
scepter ['sɛptər] *n* : sceptre *m*
sceptic ['skɛptɪk] → **skeptic**
schedule[1] ['skeˌdʒu:l, -dʒəl *esp Brit* ʃɛd,ju:l] *vt* **-uled; -uling** : prévoir, programmer
schedule[2] *n* **1** LIST : liste *f* **2** TIMETABLE : horaire *m* **3** PLAN : programme *m*, plan *m*
schematic [ski'mæṭɪk] *adj* : schématique
scheme[1] ['ski:m] *vi* **schemed; scheming** : intriguer, comploter
scheme[2] *n* **1** PLAN : projet *m*, plan *m* **2** PLOT : complot *m*, intrigue *f* **3** SYSTEM : système *m*
schemer ['ski:mər] *n* : intrigant *m*, -gante *f*
schism ['sɪzəm, 'skɪ-] *n* : schisme *m*
schizophrenia [ˌskɪtsə'fri:niə, ˌskɪzə-, -'frɛ-] *n* : schizophrénie *f*
schizophrenic [ˌskɪtsə'frɛnɪk, ˌskɪzə-] *adj* : schizophrène
scholar ['skɑlər] *n* **1** STUDENT : étudiant *m*, -diante *f*; élève *mf* **2** EXPERT : spécialiste *mf*; savant *m*, -vante *f*; érudit *m*, -dite *f*
scholarly ['skɑlərli] *adj* : savant, érudit
scholarship ['skɑlərˌʃɪp] *n* **1** LEARNING : érudition *f* **2** GRANT : bourse *f*
scholastic [skə'læstɪk] *adj* : scolaire
school[1] ['sku:l] *vt* : instruire, entraîner
school[2] *n* **1** : école *f* (institution) <elementary school : école primaire> **2** : école *f* (en peinture, etc.) <the Flemish school : l'école flamande> **3** COLLEGE : faculté *f* <medical school : faculté de médecine> **4** *or* **school of fish** : banc *m*
schoolboy ['sku:lˌbɔɪ] *n* : écolier *m*
schoolgirl ['sku:lˌgərl] *n* : écolière *f*
schoolhouse ['sku:lˌhaʊs] *n* : école *f*
schoolmate ['sku:lˌmeɪt] *n* : camarade *mf* de classe
schoolroom ['sku:lˌru:m] *n* : salle *f* de classe
schoolteacher ['sku:lˌti:tʃər] *n* : instituteur *m*, -trice *f*; enseignant *m*, -gnante *f*
schooner ['sku:nər] *n* : schooner *m*, goélette *f*
science ['saɪənʌs] *n* : science *f*
scientific [ˌsaɪən'tɪfɪk] *adj* : scientifique — **scientifically** [-fɪkli] *adv*
scientist ['saɪəntɪst] *n* : scientifique *mf*
scintillate ['sɪntəˌleɪt] *vi* **-lated; -lating** : scintiller
scintillating ['sɪntəˌleɪtɪŋ] *adj* : scintillant
scissors ['sɪzərz] *ns & pl* : ciseaux *mpl*
scoff ['skɑf] *vi* **to scoff at** : se moquer de
scold ['sko:ld] *vt* : gronder, réprimander
scoop[1] ['sku:p] *vt* **1 to scoop out** : évider, creuser **2 to scoop up** : prendre, ramasser (à la pelle)
scoop[2] *n* **1** SHOVEL : pelle *f* **2** *or* **ice cream scoop** : cuillère *f* à glace **3** : exclusivité *f* (en journalisme)
scoot ['sku:t] *vi* : filer *fam*

scooter ['skuːtər] *n* **1** : trottinette *f* **2** *or* **motor scooter** : scooter *m*
scope ['skoːp] *n* **1** EXTENT : étendue *f*, limites *fpl* **2** OPPORTUNITY : possibilité *f*, occasion *f*
scorch ['skɔrtʃ] *vt* : roussir
score[1] ['skɔr] *v* **scored; scoring** *vt* **1** RECORD : enregistrer **2** MARK, SCRATCH : marquer, rayer **3** : marquer (aux sports) **4** GRADE : noter **5** ORCHESTRATE : orchestrer, arranger — *vi* **1** : marquer des points (aux sports) **2** : obtenir une note (sur un examen)
score[2] *n, pl* **scores 1** *or pl* **score** TWENTY : vingt *m*, vingtaine *f* **2** : score *m*, marque *f*, pointage *m Can* (aux sports) **3** LINE, SCRATCH : rayure *f*, entaille *f* **4** ACCOUNT : compte *m*, point *m* <to settle a score : régler un compte> <on that score : sur ce point> **5** : partition *f* (en musique)
scorekeeper ['skɔrˌkiːpər] *n* : marqueur *m*, -queuse *f*; pointeur *m*, -teuse *f Can*
scorn[1] ['skɔrn] *vt* : mépriser
scorn[2] *n* : mépris *m*, dédain *m*
scornful ['skɔrnfəl] *adj* : méprisant — **scornfully** *adv*
Scorpio ['skɔrpiˌoː] *n* : Scorpion *m*
scorpion ['skɔrpjən] *n* : scorpion *m*
Scot ['skɑt] *n* : Écossais *m*, -saise *f*
Scotch[1] ['skɑtʃ] *adj* → **Scottish**[1]
Scotch[2] *n* **1** *or* **Scotch whiskey** : scotch *m* **2 the Scotch** : les Écossais
scot-free ['skɑtˈfriː] *adj* **to get off scot-free** : s'en tirer sans être puni
Scots ['skɑts] *n* : écossais *m* (langue)
Scottish[1] ['skɑtɪʃ] *adj* : écossais
Scottish[2] *n* → **Scots**
scoundrel ['skaʊndrəl] *n* : scélérat *m*, vaurien *m*
scour ['skaʊər] *vt* : récurer
scourge[1] ['skərdʒ] *vt* **scourged; scourging 1** WHIP : fouetter **2** PUNISH : châtier
scourge[2] *n* **1** WHIP : fouet *m* **2** BANE : fléau *m*
scout[1] ['skaʊt] *vi* **1** RECONNOITER : aller en reconnaissance **2 to scout around for** : aller à la recherche de
scout[2] *n* **1** : éclaireur *m*, -reuse *f*; scout *m*, scoute *f* **2** *or* **talent scout** : découvreur *m*, -vreuse *f* de nouveaux talents
scow ['skaʊ] *n* : chaland *m*
scowl[1] ['skaʊl] *vi* : se renfrogner, faire la grimace
scowl[2] *n* : mine *f* renfrognée
scraggly ['skrægli] *adj* UNKEMPT : en bataille (se dit d'une barbe, etc.)
scram ['skræm] *vi* **scrammed; scramming** : filer *fam*
scramble[1] ['skræmbəl] *v* **-bled; -bling** *vi* **1** CLAMBER : grimper <to scramble over : escalader> **2 to scramble for** : se bousculer pour, se disputer — *vt* : brouiller <to scramble eggs : faire des œufs brouillés>
scramble[2] *n* : bousculade *f*
scrap[1] ['skræp] *v* **scrapped; scrapping** *vt* DISCARD : mettre au rebut <we scrapped that idea : nous avons laissé tomber cette idée-là> — *vi* FIGHT : se battre
scrap[2] *n* **1** FRAGMENT : bout *m*, fragment *m* **2** FIGHT : bagarre *f* **3** *or* **scrap metal** : ferraille *f* **4 scraps** *npl* LEFTOVERS : restes *mpl*
scrapbook ['skræpˌbʊk] *n* : album *m*
scrape[1] ['skreɪp] *v* **scraped; scraping** *vt* **1** SCRATCH : écorcher, érafler <to scrape one's knees : s'écorcher les genoux> **2** CLEAN : gratter <to scrape mud off : décrotter> **3 to scrape up** *or* **to scrape together** : réunir, rassembler — *vi* **1** RUB : frotter **2 to scrape by** : se débrouiller
scrape[2] *n* **1** SCRAPING : grattement *m* **2** SCRATCH : éraflure *f* **3** PREDICAMENT : embarras *m*
scraper ['skreɪpər] *n* : grattoir *m*
scratch[1] ['skræt͡ʃ] *vt* **1** : gratter <to scratch one's head : se gratter la tête> **2** MARK : rayer **3** DELETE : supprimer **4** WOUND : écorcher, griffer, grafigner *Can* — *vi* **1** : se gratter <stop scratching! : arrête de te gratter!> **2** : griffer (se dit d'un chat)
scratch[2] *n* **1** SCRAPE : éraflure *f*, égratignure *f*, grafignure *f Can* **2** SCRATCHING : grattement *m*
scratchy ['skræt͡ʃi] *adj* **scratchier; -est** : rêche <a scratchy sweater : un pull qui gratte>
scrawl[1] ['skrɔl] *v* : griffonner, gribouiller
scrawl[2] *n* : griffonnage *m*, gribouillage *m*
scrawny ['skrɔni] *adj* **scrawnier; -est** : maigre, décharné
scream[1] ['skriːm] *v* : hurler, crier
scream[2] *n* : hurlement *m*, cri *m* perçant
screech[1] ['skriːt͡ʃ] *vi* **1** CRY, SCREAM : crier, hurler **2** : crisser (se dit des pneus, etc.)
screech[2] *n* **1** : cri *m* **2** : crissement *m* <the screech of tires : le crissement des pneus>
screen[1] ['skriːn] *vt* **1** SHIELD : protéger **2** CONCEAL : cacher **3** EXAMINE : trier, passer au crible **4** PROJECT : projeter, passer (un film)
screen[2] *n* **1** : écran *m* <smoke screen : écran de fumée> **2** PARTITION : paravent *m* **3** SIEVE : crible *m* **4** MOVIES : cinéma *m* **5** *or* **window screen** : moustiquaire *f*
screening ['skriːnɪŋ] *n* **1** SHOWING : projection *f* **2** SELECTION : sélection *f* **3** TEST : (test *m* de) dépistage *m* <cancer screening : dépistage du cancer>
screenplay ['skriːnˌpleɪ] *n* : scénario *m*
screw[1] ['skruː] *vt* **1** : visser **2 to screw together** : se visser l'un à l'autre

screw[2] *n* **1** : vis *f* **2** PROPELLER : hélice *f*
screwdriver ['skru:ˌdraɪvər] *n* : tournevis *m*
scribble[1] ['skrɪbəl] *v* **-bled; -bling** : gribouiller, griffonner
scribble[2] *n* : gribouillage *m*, griffonnage *m*
scribe ['skraɪb] *n* : scribe *m*
scrimp ['skrɪmp] *vi* : économiser, faire des économies
script ['skrɪpt] *n* **1** HANDWRITING : écriture *f* **2** TEXT : scénario *m*, script *m*
scriptural ['skrɪptʃərəl] *adj* : biblique
scripture ['skrɪptʃər] *n* **1** : texte *m* sacré **2 the Holy Scripture(s)** : l'Écriture *f* sainte, les Saintes Écritures
scroll[1] ['skro:l] *vi* : défiler (en informatique)
scroll[2] *n* : rouleau *m*
scrotum ['skro:ʈəm] *n, pl* **scrota** [-ʈə] *or* **scrotums** : scrotum *m*
scrounge ['skraʊnʤ] *v* **scrounged; scrounging** *vt* **1** CADGE : quémander **2** BORROW : emprunter — *vi* **1 to scrounge around for** : chercher **2 to scrounge off s.o.** : vivre aux crochets de qqn
scrub[1] ['skrʌb] *vt* **scrubbed; scrubbing 1** CLEAN : frotter, nettoyer à la brosse **2** SCRAP : laisser tomber, annuler
scrub[2] *n* **1** UNDERBRUSH : broussailles *fpl* **2** CLEANING : nettoyage *m*
scrubby ['skrʌbi] *adj* **scrubbier; -est 1** STUNTED : rabougri **2** OVERGROWN : broussailleux
scruff ['skrʌf] *n* **by the scruff of the neck** : par la peau du cou
scrumptious ['skrəmpʃəs] *adj* : délicieux
scruple ['skru:pəl] *n* : scrupule *m*
scrupulous ['skru:pjələs] *adj* : scrupuleux — **scrupulously** *adv*
scrutinize ['skru:ʈənˌaɪz] *vt* **-nized; -nizing** : scruter
scrutiny ['skru:ʈəni] *n, pl* **-nies** : examen *m* (approfondi)
scuff ['skʌf] *vt* **1** SCRAPE : érafler **2 to scuff one's feet** : traîner les pieds
scuffle[1] ['skʌfəl] *vi* **-fled; -fling** TUSSLE : se bagarrer
scuffle[2] *n* : bagarre *f*
scull[1] ['skʌl] *vi* : godiller, ramer
scull[2] *n* PADDLE : godille *f*
sculpt ['skʌlpt] *vt* : sculpter
sculptor ['skʌlptər] *n* : sculpteur *m*
sculpture[1] ['skəlpʧər] *vt* **-tured; -turing** : sculpter
sculpture[2] *n* : sculpture *f*
scum ['skʌm] *n* FROTH : écume *f*
scurrilous ['skərələs] *adj* : calomnieux
scurry ['skəri] *vi* **-ried; -rying** : se précipiter
scurvy ['skərvi] *n* : scorbut *m*
scuttle[1] ['skʌʈəl] *v* **-tled; -tling** *vt* : saborder (un navire) — *vi* : courir à toute vitesse, se précipiter
scuttle[2] *n or* **coal scuttle** : seau *m* à charbon
scythe ['saɪð] *n* : faux *f*
sea[1] ['si:] *adj* : de mer
sea[2] *n* **1** OCEAN : mer *f* **2** MASS : multitude *f*
seabird ['si:ˌbərd] *n* : oiseau *m* de mer
seaboard ['si:ˌbɔrd] *n* : littoral *m*
seacoast ['si:ˌko:st] *n* : côte *f* (de la mer)
seafarer ['si:ˌfærər] *n* : marin *m*
seafaring[1] ['si:ˌfærɪŋ] *adj* : maritime
seafaring[2] *n* : navigation *f*
seafood ['si:ˌfu:d] *n* : fruits *mpl* de mer
seagull ['si:ˌgʌl] *n* : mouette *f*
sea horse ['si:ˌhɔrs] *n* : hippocampe *m*
seal[1] ['si:l] *vt* : sceller
seal[2] *n* **1** STAMP : sceau *m*, cachet *m* **2** CLOSURE : fermeture *f* **3** GASKET : joint *m* étanche **4** : phoque *m*, loup-marin *m Can* (animal)
sea level *n* : niveau *m* de la mer
sea lion *n* : otarie *f*
sealskin ['si:lˌskɪn] *n* : peau *f* de phoque
seam[1] ['si:m] *vt* **1** STITCH : coudre **2** MARK : marquer <a face seamed with wrinkles : un visage marqué de rides>
seam[2] *n* **1** STITCHING : couture *f* **2** VEIN, LODE : veine *f*, filon *m*
seaman ['si:mən] *n, pl* **-men** [-mən, -ˌmɛn] : marin *m*
seamless ['si:mləs] *adj* : sans couture
seamstress ['si:mpstrəs] *n* : couturière *f*
seamy ['si:mi] *adj* **seamier; -est** : sordide
séance ['seɪˌɑnʦ] *n* : séance *f* de spiritisme
seaplane ['si:ˌpleɪn] *n* : hydravion *m*
seaport ['si:ˌport] *n* : port *m* maritime
sear ['sɪr] *vt* **1** PARCH, WITHER : dessécher, flétrir **2** BURN, SCORCH : calciner, brûler
search[1] ['sərʧ] *vt* **1** : chercher dans, fouiller (dans) <I searched the house : j'ai cherché dans la maison> <to search a suspect : fouiller un suspect> **2** : rechercher dans (en informatique) — *vi* **to search for** : chercher
search[2] *n* **1** EXAMINATION : fouille *f* **2** QUEST : recherche *f*
searcher ['sərʧər] *n* : chercheur *m*, -cheuse *f*
searchlight ['sərʧˌlaɪt] *n* : projecteur *m*
seashell ['si:ˌʃɛl] *n* : coquillage *m*
seashore ['si:ˌʃor] *n* : bord *m* de la mer
seasick ['si:ˌsɪk] *adj* **to be seasick** : avoir le mal de mer
seasickness ['si:ˌsɪknəs] *n* : mal *m* de mer
seaside ['si:ˌsaɪd] → **seacoast**
season[1] ['si:zən] *vt* **1** FLAVOR, SPICE : assaisonner, épicer **2** CURE : sécher (du bois)
season[2] *n* : saison *f*
seasonable ['si:zənəbəl] *adj* : de saison
seasonal ['si:zənəl] *adj* : saisonnier

seasonally [ˈsiːzənəli] *adv* : de façon saisonnière
seasoned [ˈsiːzənd] *adj* **1** SPICED : assaisonné **2** EXPERIENCED : expérimenté, éprouvé **3** : desséché (se dit du bois)
seasoning [ˈsiːzənɪŋ] *n* : assaisonnement *m*
seat[1] [ˈsiːt] *vt* **1** SIT : faire asseoir <please be seated : veuillez vous asseoir> **2** ACCOMMODATE, HOLD : avoir des places assises pour, tenir <this car seats five : on tient à cinq dans cette voiture>
seat[2] *n* **1** CHAIR : siège *m* **2** ACCOMMODATION, PLACE : place *f* **3** : fond *m* (de pantalon) **4** CENTER : centre *m*, siège *m* (du gouvernement, etc.)
seat belt *n* : ceinture *f* de sécurité
sea urchin *n* : oursin *m*
seawall [ˈsiːˌwɑl] *n* : digue *f*
seawater *n* [ˈsiːˌwɔṭər, -ˌwɑ-] : eau *f* de mer
seaweed *n* [ˈsiːˌwiːd] : algue *f*
seaworthy [ˈsiːˌwərði] *adj* : en état de naviguer
secede [sɪˈsiːd] *vi* **-ceded; -ceding** : se séparer, faire sécession
seclude [sɪˈkluːd] *vt* **-cluded; -cluding** : isoler
secluded *adj* : isolé, retiré, à l'écart
seclusion [sɪˈkluːʒən] *n* : isolement *m*, solitude *f*
second[1] [ˈsɛkənd] *vt* : affirmer, appuyer (une motion)
second[2] *or* **secondly** [ˈsɛkəndli] *adv* : deuxièmement, en second lieu
second[3] *adj* : second, deuxième <in the second place : en deuxième lieu> <a second chance : une seconde chance>
second[4] *n* **1** MOMENT : seconde *f* **2** : deuxième *mf*; second *m*, -conde *f* <the second of June : le deux juin> **3** : soigneur *m* (à la boxe), témoin *m* (dans un duel) **4** *or* **factory second** : articles *mpl* de second choix
secondary [ˈsɛkənˌdɛri] *adj* : secondaire
secondhand [ˈsɛkəndˈhænd] *adj* : d'occasion
second lieutenant *n* : sous-lieutenant *m*
secrecy [ˈsiːkrəsi] *n, pl* **-cies** : secret *m* <to swear to secrecy : faire jurer le secret>
secret[1] [ˈsiːkrət] *adj* : secret
secret[2] *n* : secret *m*
secretarial [ˌsɛkrəˈtɛriəl] *adj* : de secrétaire
secretariat [ˌsɛkrəˈtɛriət] *n* : secrétariat *m*
secretary [ˈsɛkrəˌtɛri] *n, pl* **-taries** : secrétaire *mf*
secrete [sɪˈkriːt] *vt* **-creted; -creting 1** EXUDE : sécréter **2** HIDE : cacher
secretion [sɪˈkriːʃən] *n* : sécrétion *f*
secretive [ˈsiːkrəṭɪv, sɪˈkriːṭɪv] *adj* : cachottier, secret
secretly [ˈsiːkrəṭli] *adv* : secrètement
sect [ˈsɛkt] *n* : secte *f*
sectarian [sɛkˈtɛriən] *adj* : sectaire
section [ˈsɛkʃən] *n* : section *f*, partie *f*
sectional [ˈsɛkʃənəl] *adj* **1** : en coupe, en profil <a sectional diagram : un schéma en coupe> **2** FACTIONAL : d'un groupe **3** MODULAR : à éléments
sector [ˈsɛktər] *n* : secteur *m*
secular [ˈsɛkjələr] *adj* **1** : séculaire, laïque **2** : profane (se dit de la musique, etc.)
secure[1] [sɪˈkjʊr] *vt* **-cured; -curing 1** FASTEN : fixer **2** OBTAIN : procurer **3** GUARANTEE : assurer
secure[2] *adj* **securer; -est** : sûr, en sécurité
securely [sɪˈkjʊrli] *adv* **1** FIRMLY : fermement, solidement, bien **2** SAFELY : en sécurité
security [sɪˈkjʊrəṭi] *n, pl* **-ties 1** SAFETY : sécurité *f* **2** GUARANTEE : garantie *f* **3 securities** *npl* : titres *mpl*, valeurs *fpl*, actions *fpl*
sedan [sɪˈdæn] *n* : berline *f*
sedate[1] [sɪˈdeɪṭ] *vt* **-dated; -dating** : tranquilliser, mettre sous calmants
sedate[2] *adj* : posé, calme — **sedately** *adv*
sedation [sɪˈdeɪʃən] *n* : sédation *f*
sedative[1] [ˈsɛdəṭɪv] *adj* : sédatif
sedative[2] *n* : calmant *m*, sédatif *m*
sedentary [ˈsɛdənˌtɛri] *adj* : sédentaire
sedge [ˈsɛdʒ] *n* : laîche *f*
sediment [ˈsɛdəmənt] *n* : sédiment *m*
sedimentary [ˌsɛdəˈmentəri] *adj* : sédimentaire
sedition [sɪˈdɪʃən] *n* : sédition *f*
seditious [sɪˈdɪʃəs] *adj* : séditieux
seduce [sɪˈduːs, -ˈdjuːs] *vt* **-duced; -ducing** : séduire
seduction [sɪˈdʌkʃən] *n* : séduction *f*
seductive [sɪˈdʌktɪv] *adj* : séduisant
see[1] [ˈsiː] *v* **saw** [ˈsɔ] ; **seen** [ˈsiːn]; **seeing** *vt* **1** : voir <I saw a dog : j'ai vu un chien> <see you later! : au revoir!> **2** EXPERIENCE : connaître, voir **3** UNDERSTAND : voir, comprendre **4** *or* **to see that** ENSURE : s'assurer, veiller à **5** ACCOMPANY : accompagner <he'll see me home : il me raccompagnera chez moi> — *vi* **1** : voir <seeing is believing : voir c'est croire> **2** UNDERSTAND : comprendre, voir **3** CONSIDER : voir <let's see : voyons> **4 to see to** : s'occuper de
see[2] *n* : évêché *m*
seed[1] [ˈsiːd] *vt* **1** SOW : semer **2** : épépiner, enlever la graine de <to seed grapes : épépiner des raisins>
seed[2] *n, pl* **seed** *or* **seeds 1** : graine *f* **2** SOURCE : germe *m*
seedless [ˈsiːdləs] *adj* : sans pépins
seedling [ˈsiːdlɪŋ] *n* : semis *m*, jeune plant *m*

seedy ['si:di] *adj* **seedier; -est 1** : plein de graines **2** SHABBY : miteux
seek ['si:k] *v* **sought** ['sɔt]; **seeking** *vt* **1** : chercher **2** REQUEST : demander — *vi* **to seek after** : rechercher, chercher
seem ['si:m] *vi* : paraître, sembler, avoir l'air <she seems tired : elle a l'air fatiguée> <it would seem not : il paraît que non>
seemingly ['si:mɪŋli] *adv* : apparemment
seemly ['si:mli] *adj* **seemlier; -est** : convenable
seep ['si:p] *vi* : suinter
seepage ['si:pɪdʒ] *n* : suintement *m*
seer ['si:ər] *n* : voyant *m*, voyante *f*
seesaw[1] ['si:,sɔ] *vi* **1** : jouer à la bascule **2** VACILLATE : balancer, osciller
seesaw[2] *n* : balançoire *f*, bascule *f*
seethe ['si:ð] *vi* **seethed; seething** : bouillonner
segment ['sɛgmənt] *n* : segment *m*
segmented [ˈsɛgˌmɛntəd, sɛgˈmɛn-] *adj* : segmentaire
segregate ['sɛgrɪˌgeɪt] *vt* **-gated; -gating** : séparer, isoler
segregation [ˌsɛgrɪˈgeɪʃən] *n* : ségrégation *f*
seismic ['saɪzmɪk, 'saɪs-] *adj* : sismique
seize ['si:z] *v* **seized; seizing** *vt* **1** CAPTURE : se saisir de, capturer, appréhender **2** GRASP : saisir, s'emparer de — *vi or* **to seize up** : se gripper
seizure ['si:ʒər] *n* **1** CAPTURE : prise *f*, saisie *f* **2** ARREST : arrestation *f* **3** ATTACK : attaque *f*, crise *f* <epileptic seizure : crise d'épilepsie>
seldom ['sɛldəm] *adv* : rarement
select[1] [sə'lɛkt] *vt* : choisir, sélectionner
select[2] *adj* : privilégié, sélect *fam*, choisi <a select few : seulement quelques privilégiés>
selection [sə'lɛkʃən] *n* : sélection *f*
selective [sə'lɛktɪv] *adj* : sélectif
self ['sɛlf] *n, pl* **selves** ['sɛlvz] **1** : moi *m*, être *m* <with his whole self : avec tout son être> <the self : le moi> **2** SIDE : côté *m* <his better self : son meilleur côté>
self-addressed envelope [ˌsɛlfə'drɛst] *n* : enveloppe *f* à mon (son) nom et adresse
self-appointed [ˌsɛlfə'pɔɪntəd] *adj* : qui s'est nommé
self-assurance [ˌsɛlfə'ʃʊrənts] *n* : assurance *f*, confiance *f* en soi
self-assured [ˌsɛlfə'ʃʊrd] *adj* : sûr de soi
self-centered [ˌsɛlf'sɛntərd] *adj* : égocentrique
self-confidence [ˌsɛlf'kɑnfədents] *n* : confiance *f* en soi
self-confident [ˌsɛlf'kɑnfədənt] *adj* : sûr de soi
self-conscious [ˌsɛlf'kɑnʃəs] *adj* **1** EMBARRASSED : timide, gêné **2** DELIBERATE : appuyé
self-consciously [ˌsɛlf'kɑnʃəsli] *adv* : timidement
self-consciousness [ˌsɛlf'kɑnʃəsnəs] *n* : timidité *f*, gêne *f*
self-contained [ˌsɛlfkən'teɪnd] *adj* : indépendant
self-control [ˌsɛlfkən'tro:l] *n* : maîtrise *f* de soi
self-defense [ˌsɛlfdɪ'fɛnts] *n* : légitime défense *f*
self-denial [ˌsɛlfdɪ'naɪəl] *n* : abnégation *f*
self-destructive [ˌsɛlfdɪ'strʌktɪv] *adj* : autodestructeur
self-determination [ˌsɛlfdɪˌtərmə'neɪʃən] *n* : autodétermination *f*
self-discipline [ˌsɛlf'dɪsəplən] *n* : autodiscipline *f*
self-employed [ˌsɛlfɪm'plɔɪd] *adj* : indépendant <she's self-employed : elle travaille à son compte>
self-esteem [ˌsɛlfɪ'sti:m] *n* : respect *m* de soi, amour-propre *m*
self-evident [ˌsɛlf'ɛvədənt] *adj* : évident
self-explanatory [ˌsɛlfɪk'splænəˌtori] *adj* : évident, explicite
self-expression [ˌsɛlfɪk'spreʃən] *n* : expression *f* libre
self-government [ˌsɛlf'gʌvərmənt, -vəm-] *n* : autonomie *f*
self-help [ˌsɛlf'hɛlp] *n* : initiative *f* personnelle <self-help group : groupe d'entraide>
self-important [ˌsɛlfɪm'pɔrtənt] *adj* : vaniteux, suffisant
self-indulgent [ˌsɛlfɪn'dʌldʒənt] *adj* : complaisant, qui ne se refuse rien
self-inflicted [ˌsɛlfɪn'flɪktəd] *adj* : auto-infligé
self-interest [ˌsɛlf'ɪntrəst, -təˌrɛst] *n* : intérêt *m* personnel
selfish ['sɛlfɪʃ] *adj* : égoïste
selfishly ['sɛlfɪʃli] *adv* : égoïstement
selfishness ['sɛlfɪʃnəs] *n* : égoïsme *m*
selfless ['sɛlfləs] *adj* UNSELFISH : désintéressé, altruiste
self-made [ˌsɛlf'meɪd] *adj* : qui a réussi tout seul <a self-made man : un self-made-man>
self-pity [ˌsɛlf'pɪti] *n, pl* **-ties** : apitoiement *m* sur soi-même
self-portrait [ˌsɛlf'pɔrtrət] *n* : autoportrait *m*
self-propelled [ˌsɛlfpro'pɛld] *adj* : autopropulsé
self-reliance [ˌsɛlfrɪ'laɪənts] *n* : autosuffisance *f*
self-respect [ˌsɛlfrɪ'spɛkt] *n* : respect *m* de soi
self-restraint [ˌsɛlfrɪ'streɪnt] *n* : retenue *f*
self-righteous [ˌsɛlf'raɪtʃəs] *adj* : suffisant
self-sacrifice [ˌsɛlf'sækrəˌfaɪs] *n* : abnégation *f*
selfsame ['sɛlf,seɪm] *adj* : même

self–service [ˌselfˈsɜrvəs] *n* : libre-service *m*
self–sufficiency [ˌselfsəˈfɪʃənt͡si] *n* : autosuffisance *f*, indépendance *f*
self–sufficient [ˌselfsəˈfɪʃənt] *adj* : autosuffisant, indépendant
self–taught [ˌselfˈtɔt] *adj* : autodidacte
sell ['sɛl] *v* **sold** ['so:ld]; **selling** *vt* : vendre — *vi* : se vendre
seller ['sɛlər] *n* : vendeur *m*, -deuse *f*
selves → **self**
semantic [sɪˈmæntɪk] *adj* : sémantique
semantics [sɪˈmæntɪks] *ns & pl* : sémantique *f*
semaphore ['sɛməˌfor] *n* : sémaphore *m*
semblance ['sɛmblən͡ts] *n* : semblant *m*, apparence *f*
semen ['si:mən] *n* : sperme *m*
semester [səˈmɛstər] *n* : semestre *m*
semicolon ['sɛmiˌko:lən, 'sɛˌmaɪ-] *n* : point-virgule *m*
semiconductor ['sɛmikənˌdʌktər, 'sɛˌmaɪ-] *n* : semiconducteur *m*
semifinal ['sɛmiˌfaɪnəl, 'sɛˌmaɪ-] *n* : demi-finale *f*
seminal ['sɛmənəl] *adj* : séminal
seminar ['sɛməˌnɑr] *n* : séminaire *m*
seminary ['sɛməˌnɛri] *n, pl* **-naries** : séminaire *m*
senate ['sɛnət] *n* : sénat *m*
senator ['sɛnətər] *n* **1** : sénateur *m* **2** : sénateur *m*, -trice *f Can*
send ['sɛnd] *vt* **sent** ['sɛnt]; **sending 1** : envoyer, expédier <he was sent to prison : on l'a envoyé en prison> <to send a letter : expédier une lettre> <to send word : faire dire> **2** PROPEL : pousser, envoyer **3 to send away for** : se faire envoyer, commander par correspondance **4 to send for** : appeler, faire venir
sender ['sɛndər] *n* : expéditeur *m*, -trice *f*
Senegalese[1] [ˌsɛnəgəˈli:z, -ˈli:s] *adj* : sénégalais
Senegalese[2] *n* : Sénégalais *m*, -laise *f*
senile ['si:ˌnaɪl] *adj* : sénile
senility [sɪˈnɪləţi] *n* : sénilité *f*
senior[1] ['si:njər] *adj* **1** ELDER : aîné, plus âgé <John Durant, Senior : John Durant, père> **2** : supérieur <a senior official : un officiel supérieur, un haut fonctionnaire>
senior[2] *n* **1** : aîné *m*, aînée *f* **2** *or* **high school senior** : élève *mf* de terminale **3** *or* **college senior** : étudiant *m*, -diante *f* de licence **4 to be s.o.'s senior** : être plus âgé que qqn <he is six years my senior : il a six ans de plus que moi>
seniority [ˌsi:ˈnjɔrəţi] *n* : ancienneté *f*, priorité *f* d'âge
sensation [sɛnˈseɪʃən] *n* : sensation *f*
sensational [sɛnˈseɪʃənəl] *adj* : sensationnel
sense[1] ['sɛn͡ts] *vt* **sensed; sensing** : sentir <he sensed danger : il a senti le danger>
sense[2] *n* **1** FACULTY : sens *m* <sense of touch : sens du toucher> **2** MEANING : sens *m*, signification *f* **3** SENSATION : sensation *f*, sentiment *m* <a sense of guilt : un sentiment de culpabilité> **4** WISDOM : sens *m* <common sense : bon sens> **5 to make sense** : avoir du sens
senseless ['sɛn͡tsləs] *adj* **1** MEANINGLESS : insensé **2** UNCONSCIOUS : sans connaissance
senselessly ['sɛn͡tsləsli] *adv* : stupidement, de manière insensée
sensibility [ˌsɛn͡tsəˈbɪləţi] *n, pl* **-ties** : sensibilité *f*
sensible ['sɛn͡tsəbəl] *adj* **1** PERCEPTIBLE : sensible **2** AWARE : conscient **3** REASONABLE : raisonnable
sensibly ['sɛn͡tsəbli] *adv* **1** PERCEPTIBLY : sensiblement, perceptiblement **2** REASONABLY : raisonnablement, de façon raisonnable
sensitive ['sɛn͡tsəţɪv] *adj* **1** : sensible <sensitive skin : peau sensible> **2** DELICATE : délicat **3** AWARE : conscient, sensibilisé
sensitiveness ['sɛn͡tsəţɪvnəs] → **sensitivity**
sensitivity [ˌsɛn͡tsəˈtɪvəţi] *n, pl* **-ties** : sensibilité *f*
sensitize ['sɛn͡tsəˌtaɪz] *vt* **-tized; -tizing** : sensibiliser
sensor ['sɛnˌsɔr, 'sɛn͡tsər] *n* : détecteur *m*
sensory ['sɛn͡tsəri] *adj* : sensoriel
sensual ['sɛn͡tʃʊəl] *adj* : sensuel — **sensually** *adv*
sensuality [ˌsɛnʃəˈwæləţi] *n* : sensualité *f*
sensuous ['sɛnʃʊəs] *adj* : sensuel
sent → **send**
sentence[1] ['sɛnţən͡ts, -ənz] *vt* **-tenced; -tencing** : condamner
sentence[2] *n* **1** : phrase *f* (en grammaire) **2** JUDGMENT : sentence *f*, condamnation *f*
sentiment ['sɛnţəmənt] *n* **1** BELIEF : avis *m* **2** FEELING : sentiment *m* **3** → **sentimentality**
sentimental [ˌsɛnţəˈmɛnţəl] *adj* : sentimental
sentimentality [ˌsɛnţəˌmɛnˈtæləţi] *n, pl* **-ties** : sentimentalité *f*, sensiblerie *f*
sentinel ['sɛnţənəl] *n* : sentinelle *f*, factionnaire *m*
sentry ['sɛntri] *n, pl* **-tries** : sentinelle *f*, factionnaire *m*
separate[1] ['sɛpəˌreɪţ] *v* **-rated; -rating** *vt* **1** DETACH, SEVER : séparer, détacher **2** DISTINGUISH : distinguer — *vi* : se séparer
separate[2] ['sɛpərəţ] *adj* **1** INDIVIDUAL : séparé **2** DISTINCT : distinct
separately ['sɛpərəţli] *adv* : séparément
separation [ˌsɛpəˈreɪʃən] *n* : séparation *f*
sepia ['si:piə] *n* : sépia *f*

September [sɛp'tɛmbər] *n* : septembre *m*
sepulchre ['sɛpəlkər] *n* : sépulcre *m*
sequel ['si:kwəl] *n* **1** CONSEQUENCE : conséquence *f* **2** CONTINUATION : suite *f* (d'un roman, d'un film, etc.)
sequence ['si:kwənts] *n* **1** SERIES : série *f*, succession *f* **2** ORDER : ordre *m*, suite *f*
sequential [sɪ'kwɛntʃəl] *adj* : séquentiel
sequester [sɪ'kwɛstər] *vt* : séquestrer
sequin ['si:kwən] *n* : paillette *f*, sequin *m*
sequoia [sɪ'kwɔɪə] *n* : séquoia *m*
sera → serum
Serb[1] ['sərb] *adj* : serbe
Serb[2] *n* **1** : Serbe *mf* **2 → Serbian**
Serbian ['sərbiən] *n* **1** : serbe *m* (langue) **2 → Serb**[2]
Serbo–Croatian[1] [,sərbokro'eɪʃən] *adj* : serbo-croate
Serbo–Croatian[2] *n* : serbo-croate *m* (langue)
serenade[1] [,sɛrə'neɪd] *vt* **-naded; -nading** : donner une sérénade à
serenade[2] *n* : sérénade *f*
serene [sə'ri:n] *adj* : serein **— serenely** *adv*
serenity [sə'rɛnəṭi] *n* : sérénité *f*
serf ['sərf] *n* : serf *m*, serve *f*
serge ['sərdʒ] *n* : serge *f*
sergeant ['sɑrdʒənt] *n* : sergent *m*
serial[1] ['sɪriəl] *adj* : en série, d'une série <serial number : numéro de série>
serial[2] *n* **1** : feuilleton *m* (histoire) **2** PERIODICAL : périodique *m*
serially ['sɪriəli] *adv* : en série
series ['sɪri:z] *ns & pl* : série *f*
serious ['sɪriəs] *adj* **1** SOBER : sérieux **2** DEDICATED, EARNEST : sérieux, dédié **3** SIGNIFICANT : important, considérable <serious damage : dommages importants> **4** GRAVE : grave, sérieux
seriously ['sɪriəsli] *adv* **1** : sérieusement <to take oneself too seriously : se prendre trop au sérieux> **2** GRAVELY : gravement
seriousness ['sɪriəsnəs] *n* : sérieux *m*
sermon ['sərmən] *n* : sermon *m*
serpent ['sərpənt] *n* : serpent *m*
serum ['sɪrəm] *n, pl* **serums** *or* **sera** ['sɪrə] : sérum *m*
servant ['sərvənt] *n* : domestique *mf*
serve[1] ['sərv] *v* **served; serving** *vi* **1** : servir <to serve in the navy : servir dans la marine> <to serve on a committee : être membre d'un comité> **2 to serve as** : servir de **3 to serve to** : servir à **—** *vt* **1** : servir <to serve one's country : servir son pays> **2** : desservir <a train serving the public : un train qui dessert le public> **3** PROVIDE, SUPPLY : alimenter (des services publiques) **4 to serve a sentence** : purger une peine **5 to serve a summons to** : remettre une assignation à
serve[2] *n* : service *m* (aux sports)
server ['sərvər] *n* **1** WAITER : serveur *m*, -veuse *f* **2** : serveur *m* (en informatique)
service[1] ['sərvəs] *vt* **-viced; -vicing 1** MAINTAIN : réviser, entretenir <to service a car : réviser une voiture> **2** REPAIR : réparer
service[2] *n* **1** : service *m* <to do s.o. a service : rendre un service à qqn> **2** CEREMONY : office *m* (en religion) **3** FACILITY : service *m* <social services : services sociaux> <train service : service de train> **4** SET : service *m* <tea service : service à thé> **5** MAINTENANCE : entretien *m*, révision *f* (d'une voiture, etc.) **6 services** *npl or* **armed services** : forces *fpl* armées
serviceable ['sərvəsəbəl] *adj* USABLE : utilisable
serviceman ['sərvəs,mæn, -mən] *n, pl* **-men** [-mən, -,men] : militaire *m*
service station *n* : station-service *f*, poste *m* d'essence
servicewoman ['sərvəs,wʊmən] *n, pl* **-women** [-,wɪmən] : femme *f* soldat
servile ['sərvəl, -,vaɪl] *adj* : servile
serving ['sərvɪŋ] *n* HELPING : portion *f*
servitude ['sərvə,tu:d, -,tju:d] *n* : servitude *f*
sesame ['sɛsəmi] *n* : sésame *m*
session ['sɛʃən] *n* : séance *f*, session *f*
set[1] ['sɛt] *v* **set; setting** *vt* **1** *or* **to set down** PLACE : placer, mettre, poser **2** SITUATE : disposer, situer <she set the story in France : elle a situé l'histoire en France> **3** PREPARE : mettre, tendre, dresser <to set the table : mettre la table> <to set a trap : tendre un piège> **4** FIX, ESTABLISH : fixer, établir <to set a time : fixer l'heure> <to set prices : fixer les prix> <to set a record : établir un record> **5** (*indicating the cause of a certain condition*) <to set fire to : mettre le feu à> <he set it free : il l'a libéré> **6** SOLIDIFY : faire prendre **—** *vi* **1** SOLIDIFY : durcir, prendre **2** : se coucher (se dit du soleil et de la lune)
set[2] *adj* **1** ESTABLISHED, SETTLED : fixe, établi **2** READY : prêt, préparé **3** DETERMINED : résolu, déterminé
set[3] *n* **1** COLLECTION : ensemble *m*, série *f* <chess set : jeu d'échecs> **2** GROUP : cercle *m*, milieu *m* (social) **3** *or* **stage set** : scène *f*, plateau *m*, décor *m* **4** APPARATUS : appareil *m*, poste *m* <television set : poste de télévision> **5** SERVICE : service *m* (à thé, à café, etc.) **6** : set *m* (aux sports) **7** : ensemble *m* (en mathématiques)
setback ['sɛt,bæk] *n* : revers *m*
set off *vt* **1** PROVOKE : déclencher, provoquer **2** EXPLODE : faire exploser **3** HIGHLIGHT : mettre en valeur **—** *vi or* **to set forth** : se mettre en route

set out *vt* **1** ARRANGE : disposer, étaler (des marchandises, etc.) **2** PRESENT : présenter, exposer (des idées) — *vi* **1** LEAVE : se mettre en route **2 to set out to do** : avoir pour but de faire

settee [seˈtiː] *n* : canapé *m*

setter [ˈsɛtər] *n* : setter *m* <Irish setter : setter irlandais>

setting [ˈsɛtɪŋ] *n* **1** SURROUNDINGS : cadre *m*, décor *m* **2** MOUNTING : monture *f* (d'un bijou) **3** : réglage *m* (d'une machine) **4** : coucher *m* (du soleil)

settle [ˈsɛt͡əl] *v* **settled; settling** *vi* **1** LAND : poser (se dit des oiseaux), laisser tomber (se dit de la poussière) **2** SINK : s'effondrer (se dit des bâtiments) **3** : s'installer (dans une maison, dans un fauteuil), se fixer (dans une région, dans un pays, etc.) **4 to settle down** : se calmer **5 to settle for** : accepter, se contenter de **6 to settle over** : descendre sur — *vt* **1** ARRANGE, RESOLVE : résoudre, régler **2** DETERMINE : décider, fixer **3** CALM : calmer, apaiser **4** PAY : payer, régler (une dette) **5** COLONIZE : coloniser

settlement [ˈsɛt͡əlmənt] *n* **1** PAYMENT : règlement *m* **2** COLONY : colonie *f* **3** RESOLUTION : résolution *f*, accord *m*

settler [ˈsɛt͡ələr] *n* : colonisateur *m*, -trice *f*; colon *m*

set up *vt* **1** ASSEMBLE : installer **2** ERECT : monter **3** ESTABLISH : établir

seven[1] [ˈsɛvən] *adj* : sept

seven[2] *n* : sept *m*

seventeen[1] [ˌsɛvənˈtiːn] *adj* : dix-sept

seventeen[2] *n* : dix-sept *m*

seventeenth[1] [ˌsɛvənˈtiːnθ] *adj* : dix-septième

seventeenth[2] *n* **1** : dix-septième *mf* (dans une série) **2** : dix-septième *m* (en mathématiques) **3** (*used in dates*) <the seventeenth of January : le dix-sept janvier>

seventh[1] [ˌsɛvənθ] *adj* : septième

seventh[2] *n* **1** : septième *mf* (dans une série) **2** : septième *m* (en mathématiques) **3** (*used in dates*) <the seventh of March : le sept Mars>

seventieth[1] [ˈsɛvəntiəθ] *adj* : soixante-dixième, septantième *Bel, Switz*

seventieth[2] *n* **1** : soixante-dixième *mf*, septantième *mf Bel, Switz* (dans une série) **2** : soixante-dixième *m* (en mathématiques)

seventy[1] [ˈsɛvənti] *adj* : soixante-dix, septante *Bel, Switz*

seventy[2] *n, pl* **-ties** : soixante-dix *m*, septante *mf Bel, Switz*

sever [ˈsɛvər] *vt* **-ered; -ering 1** CUT : couper **2** BREAK : rompre, cesser <to sever ties with : rompre les liens avec>

several[1] [ˈsɛvrəl, ˈsɛvə-] *adj* : plusieurs

several[2] *pron* : plusieurs

severance [ˈsɛvrənt͡s, ˈsɛvə-] *n* **1** : rupture *f* **2 severance pay** : indemnité *f* de départ

severe [səˈvɪr] *adj* **severer; -est 1** STRICT : sévère **2** AUSTERE : austère, sévère **3** SERIOUS : grave **4** DIFFICULT : dur, rigoureux

severely [səˈvɪrli] *adv* **1** HARSHLY : durement, sévèrement **2** SERIOUSLY : gravement, sérieusement **3** AUSTERELY : d'une façon austère

severity [səˈvɛrət͡i] *n* **1** HARSHNESS : sévérité *f* **2** SERIOUSNESS : gravité *f*

sew [ˈsoː] *v* **sewed; sewn** [ˈsoːn] *or* **sewed; sewing** : coudre

sewage [ˈsuːɪd͡ʒ] *n*.: eaux *fpl* d'égout

sewer[1] [ˈsoːər] *n* : couseur *m*, -seuse *f*

sewer[2] [ˈsuːər] *n* : égout *m*

sewing [ˈsoːɪŋ] *n* : couture *f*

sex [ˈsɛks] *n* **1** GENDER : sexe *m* **2** COPULATION : rapports *mpl* sexuels

sexism [ˈsɛkˌsɪzəm] *n* : sexisme *m*

sexist[1] [ˈsɛksɪst] *adj* : sexiste

sexist[2] *n* : sexiste *mf*

sextant [ˈsɛkstənt] *n* : sextant *m*

sextet [sɛkˈstɛt] *n* : sextuor *m*

sexton [ˈsɛkstən] *n* : sacristain *m*

sexual [ˈsɛkʃʊəl] *adj* : sexuel — **sexually** *adv*

sexuality [ˌsɛkʃʊˈælət͡i] *n* : sexualité *f*

sexy [ˈsɛksi] *adj* **sexier; -est** : sexy

shabbily [ˈʃæbəli] *adv* **1** POORLY : pauvrement **2** MEANLY : mesquinement

shabbiness [ˈʃæbinəs] *n* **1** : pauvreté *f*, délabrement *m* **2** MEANNESS : mesquinerie *f*

shabby [ˈʃæbi] *adj* **shabbier; -est 1** WORN : usé, miteux **2** MEAN : vilain, mesquin

shack [ˈʃæk] *n* : cabane *f*, hutte *f*

shackle [ˈʃækəl] *vt* **-led; -ling 1** BIND : enchaîner, mettre aux fers **2** HAMPER : entraver

shackles [ˈʃækəlz] *npl* : chaînes *fpl*, fers *mpl*

shad [ˈʃæd] *n* : alose *f*

shade[1] [ˈʃeɪd] *v* **shaded; shading** *vt* **1** : ombrager <the trees shade the courtyard : les arbres ombragent la cour> **2** SCREEN : abriter, donner de l'ombre à, protéger <to shade one's eyes : s'abriter les yeux> **3** *or* **to shade in** : hachurer — *vi* **to shade into** : se fondre en

shade[2] *n* **1** : ombre *f* <in the shade : à l'ombre> **2** GRADATION : ton *m*, nuance *f* **3** BIT : peu *m* <a shade larger : un peu plus grand>

shadow[1] [ˈʃædoː] *vt* **1** DARKEN : ombrager **2** FOLLOW : filer

shadow[2] *n* **1** : ombre *f* **2 to cast a shadow over** : projeter une ombre sur

shadowy [ˈʃædowi] *adj* **1** DARK : sombre **2** INDISTINCT : vague **3** MYSTERIOUS : mystérieux

shady ['ʃeɪdi] *adj* **shadier; -est 1** : ombragé **2** DISREPUTABLE : louche
shaft ['ʃæft] *n* **1** : arbre *m* (d'un moteur) **2** *or* **mine shaft** : puits *m* **3** *or* **shaft of light** : rai *m* **4** HANDLE, STEM : manche *m* (d'un outil), tige *f* (d'une flèche) **5 elevator shaft** : cage *f*
shaggy ['ʃægi] *adj* **shaggier; -est 1** HAIRY : poilu, broussailleux **2** UNKEMPT : débraillé
shake[1] ['ʃeɪk] *v* **shook** ['ʃʊk]; **shaken** ['ʃeɪkən]; **shaking** *vt* **1** : secouer <he shook his head : il a secoué la tête> **2** UPSET : ébranler <shaken by the news : ébranlé par la nouvelle> **3 to shake hands with s.o.** : serrer la main à qqn — *vi* TREMBLE : trembler
shake[2] *n* : secousse *f*, ébranlement *m*
shaker ['ʃeɪkər] *n* **1** → **saltshaker 2 pepper shaker** : poivrier *m* **3 cocktail shaker** : shaker *m*
shake-up ['ʃeɪkˌʌp] *n* : réorganisation *f*
shake up *vt* : secouer, agiter
shakily ['ʃeɪkəli] *adv* **1** : en tremblant **2** UNSTEADILY : à pas chancelants **3** WEAKLY : faiblement
shaky ['ʃeɪki] *adj* **shakier; -est 1** TREMBLING : tremblant **2** UNSTEADY : branlant **3** UNCERTAIN : chancelant, incertain
shale ['ʃeɪl] *n* : schiste *m* argileux
shall ['ʃæl] *v aux, past* **should** ['ʃʊd]; *pres sing & pl* **shall 1** (*used to express a command*) <you shall do as I say : vous ferez comme je vous dis> **2** (*used to express futurity*) <what shall we do? : que ferons-nous?> <I shall have finished it : je l'aurai fini> **3** (*used to express determination*) <you shall have the money : vous aurez l'argent>
shallow ['ʃæloː] *adj* **1** : peu profond **2** SUPERFICIAL : superficiel
shallows ['ʃæloːz] *npl* : haut-fond *m*, bas-fond *m*
sham[1] ['ʃæm] *v* **shammed; shamming** *vt* : feindre, faire semblant de — *vi* : faire semblant
sham[2] *adj* : faux
sham[3] *n* **1** PRETENSE : faux-semblant *m*, comédie *f* **2** IMPOSTER : imposteur *m*
shamble ['ʃæmbəl] *vi* **-bled; -bling** : marcher en traînant les pieds
shambles ['ʃæmbəlz] *ns & pl* : désordre *m*
shame[1] ['ʃeɪm] *vt* **shamed; shaming** : faire honte à
shame[2] *n* **1** : honte *f* **2** PITY : dommage *m* <what a shame! : quel dommage!>
shamefaced ['ʃeɪmˌfeɪst] *adj* : penaud, honteux
shameful ['ʃeɪmfəl] *adj* : honteux — **shamefully** *adv*
shameless ['ʃeɪmləs] *adj* : éhonté
shamelessly ['ʃeɪmləsli] *adv* : sans vergogne, sans honte
shampoo[1] [ʃæm'puː] *vt* : faire un shampooing à
shampoo[2] *n, pl* **-poos** : shampooing *m*
shamrock ['ʃæmˌrɑk] *n* : trèfle *m*
shank ['ʃæŋk] *n* **1** LEG : jambe *f*, canon *m* (d'un cheval) **2** SHAFT : tige *f*
shan't ['ʃænt] (*contraction of* **shall not**) → **shall**
shanty ['ʃænti] *n, pl* **-ties** : cabane *f*
shape[1] ['ʃeɪp] *v* **shaped; shaping** *vt* **1** MOLD : façonner, modeler **2** DETERMINE : former — *vi or* **to shape up** : prendre forme
shape[2] *n* **1** : forme *f* <in the shape of a circle : en forme de cercle> **2** CONDITION : forme *f*, état *m* <to be in good shape : être en bonne forme>
shapeless ['ʃeɪpləs] *adj* : informe, sans forme
shapely ['ʃeɪpli] *adj* **shapelier; -est** : bien fait, bien tourné
shard ['ʃɑrd] *n* : tesson *m*
share[1] ['ʃer] *v* **shared; sharing** *vt* : partager <to share the work : partager le travail> <they share the responsibility : ils se partagent la responsabilité> — *vi* **to share in** : prendre part à
share[2] *n* **1** PORTION : portion *f*, part *f* **2** STOCK : action *f*
sharecropper ['ʃerˌkrɑpər] *n* : métayer *m*, -tayère *f*
shareholder ['ʃerˌhoːldər] *n* : actionnaire *mf*
shark ['ʃɑrk] *n* : requin *m*
sharp[1] ['ʃɑrp] *adv* **1** PRECISELY : précisément, pile <at five o'clock sharp : à cinq heures pile> **2** ABRUPTLY : brusquement
sharp[2] *adj* **1** : aigu, tranchant, affilé <a sharp knife : un couteau tranchant> **2** CLEVER : vif **3** POINTED : pointu **4** INTENSE : vif, fort <a sharp pain : une douleur vive> **5** SUDDEN : brusque **6** DISTINCT : net, distinct **7** : dièse (en musique) **8** STYLISH : chic **9** KEEN : perçant, fin
sharp[3] *n* : dièse *m* (en musique)
sharpen ['ʃɑrpən] *vt* : aiguiser, affiler
sharpener ['ʃɑrpənər] *n* **1** *or* **knife sharpener** : aiguisoir *m* **2** → **pencil sharpener**
sharply ['ʃɑrpli] *adv* **1** ABRUPTLY : brusquement **2** DISTINCTLY : nettement, clairement **3** HARSHLY : sévèrement
sharpness ['ʃɑrpnəs] *n* **1** : tranchant *m* (d'un couteau, etc.) **2** ACUTENESS : acuité *f* **3** ABRUPTNESS : brusquerie *f* **4** INTENSITY : intensité *f* **5** HARSHNESS : sévérité *f* **6** CLARITY : netteté *f*
sharpshooter ['ʃɑrpˌʃuːtər] *n* : tireur *m* d'élite
shatter ['ʃæt̬ər] *vt* : briser, fracasser — *vi* : se briser, se fracasser

shave[1] ['ʃeɪv] *v* **shaved; shaved** *or* **shaven** ['ʃeɪvən]; **shaving** *vt* **1** : raser **2** PLANE : raboter, planer — *vi* : se raser
shave[2] *n* : rasage *m*
shaver ['ʃeɪvər] *n or* **electric shaver** : rasoir *m* électrique
shawl ['ʃɔl] *n* : châle *m*
she ['ʃi:] *pron* : elle
sheaf ['ʃi:f] *n, pl* **sheaves** ['ʃi:vz] : gerbe *f* (de céréales), liasse *f* (de papier)
shear ['ʃɪr] *vt* **sheared; sheared** *or* **shorn** [ʃɔrn]; **shearing** : tondre
shears ['ʃɪrz] *npl* **1** SCISSORS : cisailles *fpl* **2** CLIPPERS : tondeuse *f*
sheath ['ʃi:θ] *n, pl* **sheaths** ['ʃi:ðz, 'ʃi:θs] : fourreau *m* (d'épée), gaine *f* (de poignard, des plantes)
sheathe ['ʃi:ð] *vt* **sheathed; sheathing** : rengainer
shed[1] ['ʃed] *v* **shed; shedding** *vt* **1** : verser (des larmes, du sang) **2** : perdre (des feuilles, du poids) **3 to shed light on** : éclairer, éclaircir — *vi* : perdre ses poils
shed[2] *n* : abri *m*, remise *f*
she'd ['ʃi:d] (*contraction of* **she had** *or* **she would**) → **have, would**
sheen ['ʃi:n] *n* : lustre *m*, éclat *m*
sheep ['ʃi:p] *ns & pl* : mouton *m*
sheepfold ['ʃi:p,fo:ld] *n* : parc *m* à moutons
sheepish ['ʃi:pɪʃ] *adj* : penaud
sheepskin ['ʃi:p,skɪn] *n* **1** : peau *f* de mouton **2** DIPLOMA : diplôme *m*
sheer[1] ['ʃɪr] *adv* : à pic, abruptement
sheer[2] *adj* **1** PURE : pur **2** STEEP : à pic, abrupt **3** TRANSPARENT : transparent, fin
sheet ['ʃi:t] *n* **1** *or* **bedsheet** ['bed,ʃi:t] : drap *m* **2** : feuille *f* (de papier) **3** : plaque *f* <baking sheet : plaque de four>
sheikh *or* **sheik** ['ʃi:k, 'ʃeɪk] *n* : cheikh *m*
shelf ['ʃelf] *n, pl* **shelves** ['ʃelvz] **1** : étagère *f*, rayon *m* **2** : rebord *m*, saillie *f* (en géologie) <continental shelf : plate-forme continentale>
shell[1] ['ʃel] *vt* **1** : décortiquer (des noix), écosser (des pois) **2** BOMBARD : bombarder
shell[2] *n* **1** : coquille *f*, coque *f*, carapace *f* (de tortue, de homard) **2** SEASHELL : coquillage *m* **3** MISSILE : obus *m* **4** CARTRIDGE : cartouche *f* **5** *or* **racing shell** : canot *m*
she'll ['ʃi:l, ʃɪl] (*contraction of* **she shall** *or* **she will**) → **shall, will**
shellac[1] [ʃə'læk] *vt* **-lacked; -lacking 1** : laquer **2** DEFEAT : piler *fam*
shellac[2] *n* : laque *f*
shellfish ['ʃel,fɪʃ] *n* : crustacé *m*
shelter[1] ['ʃeltər] *vt* **1** PROTECT : abriter, protéger **2** HARBOR : donner asile à, recueillir
shelter[2] *n* : abri *m*
shelve ['ʃelv] *vt* **shelved; shelving 1** : mettre sur les rayons **2** DEFER : remettre
shenanigans [ʃə'nænɪgənz] *npl* **1** TRICKERY : manigances *fpl* **2** MISCHIEF : espièglerie *f*
shepherd[1] ['ʃepərd] *vt* **1** GUARD : surveiller, garder **2** GUIDE : guider, conduire
shepherd[2] *n* : berger *m*
shepherdess ['ʃepərdəs] *n* : bergère *f*
sherbet ['ʃərbət] *n* : sorbet *m*
sheriff ['ʃerɪf] *n* : shérif *m*
sherry ['ʃeri] *n, pl* **-ries** : xérès *m*
she's ['ʃi:z] (*contraction of* **she is** *or* **she has**) → **be, have**
shield[1] ['ʃi:ld] *vt* **1** PROTECT : protéger **2** CONCEAL : couvrir
shield[2] *n* **1** : bouclier *m* **2** PROTECTION : protection *f*
shier, shiest → **shy**
shift[1] ['ʃɪft] *vt* **1** CHANGE : changer de <to shift gears : changer de vitesse> **2** MOVE : déplacer — *vi* **1** CHANGE : changer **2** MOVE : se déplacer, bouger
shift[2] *n* **1** CHANGE : changement *m* <a shift in priorities : un changement de priorités> **2** : poste *m*, équipe *f* <night shift : équipe de nuit> **3** *or* **shift dress** : robe *f* fourreau **4** → **gearshift**
shiftless ['ʃɪftləs] *adj* : fainéant, paresseux
shifty ['ʃɪfti] *adj* **shiftier; -est** : sournois, rusé
shilling ['ʃɪlɪŋ] *n* : shilling *m*
shimmer ['ʃɪmər] *vi* GLIMMER : chatoyer, miroiter
shin[1] ['ʃɪn] *vi* **shinned; shinning** : grimper <she shinned up a tree : elle a grimpé à un arbre>
shin[2] *n* : tibia *m*
shine[1] ['ʃaɪn] *v* **shone** ['ʃo:n, *esp Brit and Can* 'ʃɔn] *or* **shined; shining** *vi* **1** : briller, luire **2** EXCEL : briller — *vt* **1** AIM : braquer, diriger <he shined the flashlight at the dog : il a braqué la lampe de poche sur le chien> **2** POLISH : astiquer, cirer (des chaussures)
shine[2] *n* : éclat *m*, lustre *m*
shingle[1] ['ʃɪŋgəl] *vt* **-gled; -gling** : couvrir de bardeaux
shingle[2] *n* : bardeau *m*
shingles ['ʃɪŋgəlz] *npl* : zona *m*
shinny ['ʃɪni] *vi* **-nied; -nying** → **shin**[1]
shiny ['ʃaɪni] *adj* **shinier; -est** : luisant, brillant
ship[1] ['ʃɪp] *vt* **shipped; shipping 1** LOAD : embarquer, mettre à bord **2** SEND : expédier (par bateau), transporter (par avion)
ship[2] *n* **1** : navire *m*, bateau *m* **2** → **spaceship**
shipboard ['ʃɪp,bord] *n* **on ~** : à bord
shipbuilder ['ʃɪp,bɪldər] *n* : constructeur *m*, -trice *f* de navires

shipment ['ʃɪpmənt] *n* **1** SHIPPING : expédition *f*, transport *m* **2** CARGO : cargaison *f* (par mer), chargement *m* (terrestre)

shipping ['ʃɪpɪŋ] *n* **1** SHIPS : navires *mpl* **2** TRANSPORT : transport *m* (maritime)

shipshape ['ʃɪpˈʃeɪp] *adj* : en bon ordre

shipwreck[1] ['ʃɪpˌrek] *vt* **to be shipwrecked** : faire naufrage

shipwreck[2] *n* : naufrage *m*

shipyard ['ʃɪpˌjɑrd] *n* : chantier *m* naval

shirk ['ʃərk] *vt* : se dérober à, esquiver <to shirk one's duties : se dérober à ses responsabilités>

shirt ['ʃərt] *n* : chemise *f*

shiver[1] ['ʃɪvər] *vi* : frissonner

shiver[2] *n* : frisson *m*

shoal ['ʃoːl] *n* **1** : banc *m* (de poissons) **2** SANDBANK : banc *m* de sable

shock[1] ['ʃɑk] *vt* : choquer

shock[2] *n* **1** : choc *m* <in a state of shock : en état de choc> **2** *or* **electric shock** : décharge *f* (électrique) **3 shock of hair** : tignasse *f*

shock absorber *n* : amortisseur *m*

shoddy ['ʃɑdi] *adj* **shoddier; -est** : de mauvaise qualité

shoe[1] ['ʃuː] *vt* **shod** ['ʃɑd]; **shoeing** : ferrer (un cheval)

shoe[2] *n* **1** : chaussure *f* **2 → horseshoe 3 brake shoe** : sabot *m* (de frein)

shoelace ['ʃuːˌleɪs] *n* : lacet *m*

shoemaker ['ʃuːˌmeɪkər] *n* : cordonnier *m*, -nière *f*

shone → shine[1]

shook → shake[1]

shoot[1] ['ʃuːt] *v* **shot** ['ʃɑt]; **shooting** *vt* **1** FIRE : tirer (une balle ou une flèche), lancer (un missile) **2** : tirer sur (une personne) <to shoot s.o. dead : abattre qqn> **3** : jouer, marquer (aux sports) <to shoot a basket : marquer un panier> **4** FILM : tourner **5** PHOTOGRAPH : prendre (en photo) **6** DIRECT : décocher, lancer (un regard) **—** *vi* **1** : tirer <to shoot to kill : tirer pour tuer> **2** DART : se précipiter **3** FILM : tourner

shoot[2] *n* : rejeton *m*, pousse *f* (d'une plante)

shooter ['ʃuːtər] *n* : tireur *m*, -reuse *f*

shooting star *n* : étoile *f* filante

shop[1] ['ʃɑp] *vi* **shopped; shopping** : faire des courses

shop[2] *n* **1** STORE : magasin *m*, boutique *f* **2 → workshop**

shopkeeper ['ʃɑpˌkiːpər] *n* : commerçant *m*, -çante *f*; marchand *m*, -chande *f*

shoplift ['ʃɑpˌlɪft] *vt* : voler à l'étalage

shoplifter ['ʃɑpˌlɪftər] *n* : voleur *m*, -leuse *f* à l'étalage

shopper ['ʃɑpər] *n* : personne *f* qui fait ses courses

shopping ['ʃɑpɪŋ] *n* : courses *fpl*, magasinage *m* *Can* <to go shopping : faire des courses>

shopwindow ['ʃɑpˌwɪndoː] *n* : vitrine *f*, devanture *f*

shore[1] ['ʃor] *vt* **shored; shoring** *or* **to shore up** : étayer

shore[2] *n* **1** : rivage *m*, bord *m* <on shore : à terre> **2** PROP : étai *m*

shorebird ['ʃorˌbərd] *n* : oiseau *m* des rivages

shoreline ['ʃorˌlaɪn] *n* : côte *f*, littoral *m*

shorn → shear

short[1] ['ʃɔrt] *adv* : court, de court <to fall short of : ne pas répondre à, ne pas atteindre>

short[2] *adj* **1** : court <a short dress : une robe courte> **2** : petit, de petite taille (se dit d'une personne) **3** BRIEF : bref <for a short time : pendant peu de temps> **4** CURT : brusque **5** INSUFFICIENT : insuffisant

short[3] *n* **1 → short circuit 2 shorts** *pl* : short *m* <tennis shorts : short de tennis> **3 in short** : en bref

shortage ['ʃɔrtɪdʒ] *n* : manque *m*, insuffisance *f*

shortcake ['ʃɔrtˌkeɪk] *n* : tarte *f* sablée

shortchange ['ʃɔrtˈtʃeɪndʒ] *vt* **-changed; -changing 1** : ne pas rendre assez de monnaie à **2** SWINDLE : escroquer

short–circuit ['ʃɔrtˈsərkət] *vt* : court-circuiter

short circuit *n* : court-circuit *m*

shortcoming ['ʃɔrtˌkʌmɪŋ] *n* : défaut *m*

shortcut ['ʃɔrtˌkʌt] *n* : raccourci *m*

shorten ['ʃɔrtən] *vt* : raccourcir

shorthand ['ʃɔrtˌhænd] *n* : sténographie *f*

short–lived ['ʃɔrtˈlɪvd, -ˈlaɪvd] *adj* : éphémère

shortly ['ʃɔrtli] *adv* **1** BRIEFLY : brièvement **2** SOON : bientôt

shortness ['ʃɔrtnəs] *n* **1** : petite taille *f* **2** BREVITY : brièveté *f*, petite durée *f* **3** CURTNESS : brusquerie *f* **4 shortness of breath** : manque *m* de souffle

shortsighted ['ʃɔrtˌsaɪtəd] **→ nearsighted**

shortstop ['ʃɔrtˌstɑp] *n* : arrêt-court *m* *Can*

shot[1] ['ʃɑt] *n* **1** : tir *m*, coup *m* <to fire a shot : tirer un coup> **2** ATTEMPT : essai *m*, tentative *f* <to give it one's best shot : faire de son mieux> **3** PELLETS : plombs *mpl* **4** PHOTOGRAPH : photo *f* **5** INJECTION : piqûre *f* **6** MARKSMAN : tireur *m*, -reuse *f* **7** SCENE : plan *m* (au cinéma)

shot[2] **→ shoot**[1]

shotgun ['ʃɑtˌgʌn] *n* : fusil *m* de chasse

should ['ʃʊd] *past of* **shall 1** (*used to express obligation*) : devoir <you should go : tu devrais y aller> **2** (*used to express probability*) <he should be here soon : il devrait être arrivé bientôt> **3** (*used in conditional sentences*) <if

he should die : s'il mourrait> <if you should change your mind : si vous changez d'avis>
shoulder[1] ['ʃo:ldər] *vt* **1** PUSH : pousser **2 to shoulder the responsibility** : endosser
shoulder[2] *n* **1** : épaule *f* (d'une personne) **2** : accotement *m* (d'une chaussée) <soft shoulder : accotement non stabilisé>
shoulder blade *n* : omoplate *f*
shouldn't ['ʃudənt] (*contraction of* **should not**) → **should**
shout[1] ['ʃaʊt] *v* : crier, hurler
shout[2] *n* : cri *m*, hurlement *m*
shove[1] ['ʃʌv] *v* **shoved; shoving** *vt* **1** PUSH : pousser **2** JOSTLE : bousculer — *vi* **to shove off** : s'en aller
shove[2] *n* : poussée *f*
shovel[1] ['ʃʌvəl] *vt* **-veled** *or* **-velled; -veling** *or* **-velling** : pelleter, enlever à la pelle
shovel[2] *n* : pelle *f*
show[1] ['ʃo:] *v* **showed; shown** ['ʃo:n] *or* **showed; showing** *vt* **1** DISPLAY, PRESENT : montrer, présenter **2** REVEAL : révéler **3** DEMONSTRATE, TEACH : montrer, indiquer **4** PROVE : prouver, démontrer **5** CONDUCT : conduire <he showed her to the door : il l'a conduite à la porte> — *vi* : se voir
show[2] *n* **1** DEMONSTRATION : démonstration *f*, manifestation *f* <a show of strength : une manifestation de force> **2** EXHIBITION : exposition *f* **3** : spectacle *m* (de théâtre), émission *f* (de télévision, de radio, etc.), séance *f* (de cinéma)
showcase ['ʃo:ˌkeɪs] *n* : vitrine *f*
showdown ['ʃo:ˌdaʊn] *n* : confrontation *f*
shower[1] ['ʃaʊər] *vt* **1** WET : doucher **2 to shower sth on** : faire pleuvoir qqch sur **3 to shower s.o. with** : couvrir qqn de <they showered him with gifts : ils l'ont couvert de cadeaux> — *vi* **1** BATHE : prendre une douche **2** RAIN : pleuvoir
shower[2] *n* **1** : averse *f* <snow showers : averses de neige> **2** : douche *f* <he's in the shower : il est sous la douche> **3** PARTY : fête *f* (donnée à l'occasion d'un mariage ou d'une naissance)
show off *vt* : faire valoir, faire parade de — *vi* : faire l'intéressant
show up *vi* **1** ARRIVE : arriver **2** APPEAR : ressortir, se voir — *vt* EXPOSE : démasquer
showy ['ʃo:i] *adj* **showier; -est** : tapageur, voyant
shrapnel ['ʃræpnəl] *ns & pl* : shrapnel *m*
shred[1] ['ʃred] *vt* **shredded; shredding** : déchirer, déchiqueter (le papier, le tissu), râper (les aliments)
shred[2] *n* **1** : lambeau *m* <to be in shreds : être en lambeaux> **2** BIT : brin *m*, parcelle *f* <not a shred of evidence : pas une parcelle d'évidence>
shrew ['ʃru:] *n* **1** : musaraigne *f* (animal) **2** : mégère *f* (femme)
shrewd ['ʃru:d] *adj* : habile, sagace
shrewdly ['ʃru:dli] *adv* : avec perspicacité, avec sagacité
shrewdness ['ʃru:dnəs] *n* : perspicacité *f*, astuce *f*, sagacité *f*
shriek[1] ['ʃri:k] *vi* : hurler, crier, pousser un cri perçant
shriek[2] *n* : cri *m* perçant
shrill ['ʃrɪl] *adj* : aigu, perçant, strident
shrilly ['ʃrɪli] *adv* : d'un ton aigu
shrimp ['ʃrɪmp] *n* : crevette *f*
shrine ['ʃraɪn] *n* **1** TOMB : tombeau *m* (d'un saint) **2** SANCTUARY : sanctuaire *m*, lieu *m* saint
shrink ['ʃrɪŋk] *v* **shrank** ['ʃræŋk]; **shrunk** ['ʃrʌŋk] *or* **shrunken** ['ʃrʌŋkən]; **shrinking** *vi* **1** RECOIL : reculer **2** : rétrécir, fouler *Can* (se dit des vêtements) **3** DWINDLE : rétrécir, diminuer — *vt* : rétrécir
shrinkage ['ʃrɪŋkɪdʒ] *n* : rétrécissement *m*
shrivel ['ʃrɪvəl] *v* **-eled** *or* **-elled; -eling** *or* **-elling** *vt* : ratatiner, dessécher — *vi* : se ratatiner
shroud[1] ['ʃraʊd] *vt* : envelopper, voiler
shroud[2] *n* **1** : linceul *m* **2** COVERING, VEIL : voile *m* <a shroud of mystery : un voile de mystère>
shrub ['ʃrʌb] *n* : arbuste *m*, arbrisseau *m*
shrubbery ['ʃrʌbəri] *n, pl* **-beries** : massif *m* d'arbustes, arbustes *mpl*
shrug[1] ['ʃrʌg] *v* **shrugged; shrugging** *vt* : hausser (les épaules) — *vi* : hausser les épaules
shrug[2] *n* : haussement *m* d'épaules
shuck[1] ['ʃʌk] *vt* : écosser (des légumes), écaler, décortiquer (des noix) <to shuck corn : enlever l'enveloppe de maïs>
shuck[2] *n* : cosse *f* (de légumes), écale *f* (de noix), enveloppe *f* (de maïs)
shudder[1] ['ʃʌdər] *vi* : frissonner, frémir
shudder[2] *n* : frisson *m*, frémissement *m*
shuffle[1] ['ʃʌfəl] *v* **-fled; -fling** *vt* MIX : mêler, battre (des cartes) — *vi* : marcher en traînant les pieds
shuffle[2] *n* **1** : pas *m* traînant **2** : battage *m* (des cartes) **3** JUMBLE : confusion *f*
shun ['ʃʌn] *vt* **shunned; shunning** : éviter
shunt ['ʃʌnt] *vt* : aiguiller, manœuvrer (un train)
shut[1] ['ʃʌt] *v* **shut; shutting** *vt* **1** CLOSE : fermer **2 to shut in** *or* **to shut up** CONFINE : enfermer **3 to shut off** : couper **4 to shut out** EXCLUDE : exclure — *vi* **1** : (se) fermer <the door is shutting : la porte se ferme> **2** : fermer <the store shuts at noon : le magasin ferme à midi>
shut[2] *adj* : fermé

shut–in ['ʃʌt,ɪn] *n* : invalide *mf*
shutout ['ʃʌt,aʊt] *n* : victoire *f* écrasante, blanchissage *m Can*
shutter ['ʃʌtər] *n* **1** : volet *m* (d'une fenêtre) **2** : obturateur *m* (d'un appareil photo)
shuttle[1] ['ʃʌt̬əl] *v* **-tled; -tling** *vi* : faire la navette — *vt* : transporter
shuttle[2] *n* : navette *f*
shuttlecock ['ʃʌt̬əl,kɑk] *n* : volant *m*
shut up *vi* : se taire <shut up! : taistoi!> — *vt* SILENCE : faire taire
shy[1] ['ʃaɪ] *vi* **shied; shying** *or* **to shy away** : reculer
shy[2] *adj* **shier** *or* **shyer** ['ʃaɪər]; **shiest** *or* **shyest** ['ʃaɪəst] **1** TIMID : timide, gêné *Can* **2** WARY : peureux **3** (*indicating a lack*) <I'm two dollars shy of my goal : il me manque deux dollars pour atteindre mon objectif> <he's shy of ideas : il est à court d'idées>
shyly ['ʃaɪlɪ] *adv* : timidement
shyness ['ʃaɪnəs] *n* : timidité *f*
sibling ['sɪblɪŋ] *n* : frère *m*, sœur *f*
sick ['sɪk] *adj* **1** ILL : malade **2** (*indicating nausea*) <to feel sick : avoir mal au cœur> <to get sick : vomir> **3 I'm sick of it** : j'en ai marre, j'en ai assez
sickbed ['sɪk,bɛd] *n* : lit *m* de malade
sicken ['sɪkən] *vt* : rendre malade — *vi* : tomber malade
sickening ['sɪkənɪŋ] *adj* : écœurant, nauséabond
sickle ['sɪkəl] *n* : faucille *f*
sickly ['sɪkli] *adj* **sicklier; -est** : maladif
sickness ['sɪknəs] *n* : maladie *f*
side ['saɪd] *n* **1** : côté *m* (d'une personne), flanc *m* (d'un animal) **2** EDGE : bord *m* **3** FACTION, GROUP : camp *m*, côté *m* <to take sides : prendre parti> **4** ASPECT : facette *f*, aspect *m*
sideboard ['saɪd,bɔrd] *n* : buffet *m*
sideburns ['saɪd,bərnz] *npl* : favoris *mpl*
sided ['saɪdəd] *adj* : à côtés <three-sided : à trois côtés>
side effect *n* : effet *m* secondaire
sideline ['saɪd,laɪn] *n* **1** : activité *f* secondaire **2** : ligne *f* de côté, ligne *f* de touche (aux sports)
sidelong ['saɪd,lɔŋ] *adj* : de côté, oblique
sideshow ['saɪd,ʃoː] *n* : attraction *f*
sidestep ['saɪd,stɛp] *v* **-stepped; -stepping** *vi* : faire un pas de côté — *vt* AVOID : éviter
sidetrack ['saɪd,trɛk] *vt* : détourner l'attention de, faire dévier de son sujet
sidewalk ['saɪd,wɔk] *n* : trottoir *m*
sideways[1] ['saɪd,weɪz] *adv* : de côté, en travers, latéralement
sideways[2] *adj* : de côté, oblique, latéral
siding ['saɪdɪŋ] *n* **1** : voie *f* de garage (pour trains) **2** : revêtement *m* extérieur (d'un édifice)
sidle ['saɪdəl] *vi* **-dled; -dling** : avancer de biais, marcher de côté
siege ['siːdʒ, 'siːʒ] *n* : siège *m*
siesta [siːˈɛstə] *n* : sieste *f*
sieve ['sɪv] *n* : tamis *m*, crible *m*
sift ['sɪft] *vt* **1** : tamiser, passer au tamis **2** *or* **to sift through** : passer au crible
sifter ['sɪftər] *n* : tamis *m*
sigh[1] ['saɪ] *vi* : soupirer
sigh[2] *n* : soupir *m*
sight[1] ['saɪt] *vt* : apercevoir
sight[2] *n* **1** : vue *f* <out of sight : hors de vue> <at first sight : à première vue> **2** SPECTACLE : spectacle *m* **3** : viseur *m* (d'une arme à feu)
sightless ['saɪtləs] *adj* : aveugle
sightseer ['saɪt,siːər] *n* : touriste *mf*
sign[1] ['saɪn] *vt* **1** : signer <to sign a check : signer un chèque> **2** *or* **to sign on** HIRE : engager — *vi* **1** : signer **2** SIGNAL : faire signe **3** *or* **to sign on** JOIN : s'engager
sign[2] *n* **1** SYMBOL : signe *m* **2** GESTURE : geste *m*, signe *m* **3** : panneau *m*, enseigne *f* <traffic signs : panneaux de signalisation> <neon sign : enseigne au néon> **4** TRACE : trace *f*
signal[1] ['sɪgnəl] *v* **-naled** *or* **-nalled; -naling** *or* **-nalling** *vt* **1** INDICATE : signaler, indiquer **2** : envoyer un signal à <to signal s.o. : faire signe à qqn> — *vi* : donner un signal
signal[2] *adj* NOTABLE : insigne
signal[3] *n* : signal *m*
signature ['sɪgnə,tʃʊr] *n* : signature *f*
signet ['sɪgnət] *n* : sceau *m*
significance [sɪg'nɪfɪkənts] *n* **1** MEANING : signification *f*, sens *m* **2** IMPORTANCE : importance *f*, portée *f*
significant [sɪg'nɪfɪkənt] *adj* **1** MEANINGFUL : significatif **2** IMPORTANT : important
significantly [sɪg'nɪfɪkəntli] *adv* **1** CONSIDERABLY : considérablement, sensiblement **2** MEANINGFULLY : de façon significative
signify ['sɪgnə,faɪ] *vt* **-fied; -fying 1** INDICATE : signaler, indiquer **2** MEAN : signifier
sign language *n* : langage *m* des signes
signpost ['saɪn,poːst] *n* **1** : poteau *m* indicateur **2** INDICATION : indication *f*, indice *m*
silence[1] ['saɪlənts] *vt* **-lenced; -lencing** : faire taire, réduire au silence
silence[2] *n* : silence *m*
silent ['saɪlənt] *adj* : silencieux — **silently** *adv*
silhouette[1] [ˌsɪləˈwɛt] *vt* **-etted; -etting** : silhouetter <to be silhouetted against : se découper contre, se profiler sur>
silhouette[2] *n* : silhouette *f*
silica ['sɪlɪkə] *n* : silice *f*
silicon ['sɪlɪkən, -ˌkɑn] *n* : silicium *m*
silk ['sɪlk] *n* : soie *f*
silken ['sɪlkən] *adj* **1** : de soie **2** SILKY : soyeux

silkworm ['sɪlkˌwərm] *n* : ver *m* à soie
silky ['sɪlki] *adj* **silkier; -est** : soyeux
sill ['sɪl] *n* : rebord *m* (d'une fenêtre), seuil *m* (d'une porte)
silliness ['sɪlinəs] *n* : sottise *f*, stupidité *f*
silly ['sɪli] *adj* **sillier; -est 1** STUPID : sot, niais **2** RIDICULOUS : fou, ridicule
silo ['saɪˌlo:] *n, pl* **silos** : silo *m*
silt ['sɪlt] *n* : limon *m*
silver[1] ['sɪlvər] *adj* **1** : d'argent, en argent <a silver spoon : une cuillère d'argent> **2 → silvery**
silver[2] *n* **1** : argent *m* **2 → silverware 3** : couleur *f* argent
silverware ['sɪlvərˌwær] *n* : argenterie *f*, coutellerie *f Can*
silvery ['sɪlvəri] *adj* : argenté
similar ['sɪmələr] *adj* : semblable, similaire
similarity [ˌsɪmə'lærəṭi] *n, pl* **-ties** : ressemblance *f*, similarité *f*
similarly ['sɪmələrli] *adv* : de la même façon
simile ['sɪməˌli:] *n* : comparaison *f*
simmer ['sɪmər] *vi* : cuire à feu doux, frémir — *vt* : faire cuire à feu doux, laisser frémir
simper[1] ['sɪmpər] *vi* : minauder
simper[2] *n* : sourire *m* affecté
simple ['sɪmpəl] *adj* **simpler; -plest** : simple
simpleton ['sɪmpəltən] *n* : nigaud *m*, -gaude *f*
simplicity [sɪm'plɪsəṭi] *n* : simplicité *f*
simplification [ˌsɪmpləfə'keɪʃən] *n* : simplification *f*
simplify ['sɪmpləˌfaɪ] *vt* **-fied; -fying** : simplifier
simply ['sɪmpli] *adv* : simplement
simulate ['sɪmjəˌleɪt] *vt* **-lated; -lating** : simuler
simultaneous [ˌsaɪməl'teɪniəs] *adj* : simultané — **simultaneously** *adv*
sin[1] ['sɪn] *vi* **sinned; sinning** : pécher
sin[2] *n* : péché *m*
since[1] ['sɪnʃ] *adv* **1** : depuis <they've been friends ever since : ils sont amis depuis> <she's since become mayor : elle est devenue maire depuis> **2 long since** : il y a longtemps **3 not long since** : il y a peu de temps
since[2] *conj* **1** : depuis que <since I've been here : depuis que je suis là> **2** BECAUSE, INASMUCH AS : puisque, comme
since[3] *prep* : depuis
sincere [sɪn'sɪr] *adj* **sincerer; -est** : sincère — **sincerely** *adv*
sincerity [sɪn'sɛrəṭi] *n* : sincérité *f*
sinew ['sɪnˌju:, 'sɪˌnu:] *n* **1** TENDON : tendon *m* **2** POWER : force *f*
sinewy ['sɪnjʊi, 'sɪnʊi] *adj* **1** : tendineux **2** MUSCLED : musclé
sinful ['sɪnfəl] *adj* : coupable, honteux
sing ['sɪŋ] *v* **sang** ['sæŋ] *or* **sung** ['sʌŋ]; **sung; singing** : chanter
Singaporean[1] [ˌsɪŋə'poriən, -'pɔr-] *adj* : singapourien
Singaporean[2] *n* : Singapourien *m*, -rienne *f*
singe ['sɪndʒ] *vt* **singed; singeing** : brûler légèrement, roussir
singer ['sɪŋər] *n* : chanteur *m*, -teuse *f*
single[1] ['sɪŋgəl] *vt* **-gled; -gling** *or* **to single out 1** SELECT : choisir, sélectionner **2** DISTINGUISH : distinguer
single[2] *adj* **1** SOLE : seul <not a single one : pas un seul> **2** UNMARRIED : célibataire
single[3] *n* **1** *or* **single room** : chambre *f* simple **2** : simple *m Can* (au baseball) **3 singles** *npl* : simple *m* (au tennis)
singly ['sɪŋgli] *adv* : séparément, individuellement
singular[1] ['sɪŋgjələr] *adj* **1** : singulier (en grammaire) **2** OUTSTANDING : remarquable **3** STRANGE : étrange
singular[2] *n* : singulier *m*
singularly ['sɪŋgjələrli] *adv* : singulièrement
sinister ['sɪnəstər] *adj* : sinistre
sink[1] ['sɪŋk] *v* **sank** ['sæŋk] *or* **sunk** ['sʌŋk]; **sunk; sinking** *vi* **1** : couler, sombrer <to sink into oblivion : sombrer dans l'oubli> **2** DROP, FALL : baisser **3** : s'enfoncer, s'affaisser <to sink into a chair : s'affaisser dans un fauteuil> — *vt* **1** : couler (un bateau, etc.) **2** LOWER : baisser **3** DRIVE, PLUNGE : enfoncer **4** EXCAVATE : creuser **5** INVEST : investir
sink[2] *n* **1 kitchen sink** : évier *m* **2 bathroom sink** : lavabo *m*
sinner ['sɪnər] *n* : pécheur *m*, -cheresse *f*
sinuous ['sɪnjʊəs] *adj* : sinueux
sinus ['saɪnəs] *n* : sinus *m*
sip[1] ['sɪp] *vt* **sipped; sipping** : boire à petites gorgées, siroter *fam*
sip[2] *n* : petite gorgée *f*
siphon[1] ['saɪfən] *vt* : siphonner
siphon[2] *n* : siphon *m*
sir ['sər] *n* **1** (*as a form of address*) : monsieur *m* <Dear Sir : Monsieur> <yes, sir! : oui, monsieur!> **2** (*in titles*) : sir *m*
sire[1] ['saɪr] *vt* **sired; siring** : engendrer
sire[2] *n* **1** : père *m* **2** (*as a form of address*) : sire *m*
siren ['saɪrən] *n* : sirène *f*
sirloin ['sərˌlɔɪn] *n* : aloyau *m*
sirup → syrup
sisal ['saɪsəl, -zəl] *n* : sisal *m*
sissy ['sɪsi] *n, pl* **-sies** : poule *f* mouillée *fam*
sister ['sɪstər] *n* **1** : sœur *f* **2** *Brit* **→ nurse**[2]
sisterhood ['sɪstərˌhʊd] *n* **1** : communauté *f* de femmes (religieuses) **2** : solidarité *f* féminine
sister-in-law ['sɪstərɪnˌlɔ] *n, pl* **sisters-in-law** : belle-sœur *f*
sisterly ['sɪstərli] *adj* : de sœur
sit ['sɪt] *v* **sat** ['sæt]; **sitting** *vi* **1** *or* **to sit down** : s'asseoir **2** ROOST : se percher

3 MEET : siéger, se réunir <the legislature is sitting : le corps législatif siège> 4 POSE : poser 5 REMAIN : rester <the mail sits unopened : le courrier reste fermé> 6 : se trouver, être <the house sits on a hill : la maison se trouve sur une colline> — *vt* 1 PLACE : placer, installer 2 SEAT : (faire) asseoir

site ['saɪt] *n* : site *m*

sitter ['sɪtɚ] → **baby–sitter**

sitting room → **living room**

situated [ˌsɪtʃuˈeɪtəd] *adj* LOCATED : situé

situation [ˌsɪtʃuˈeɪʃən] *n* 1 LOCATION : situation *f*, emplacement *m* 2 CIRCUMSTANCES : situation *f* 3 JOB : emploi *m*, situation *f*

six[1] ['sɪks] *adj* : six

six[2] *n* : six *m*

six–gun ['sɪksˌɡʌn] *n* : revolver *m* (à six coups)

six–shooter ['sɪksˌʃuːtɚ] → **six–gun**

sixteen[1] [ˌsɪksˈtiːn] *adj* : seize

sixteen[2] *n* : seize *m*

sixteenth[1] [ˌsɪksˈtiːnθ] *adj* : seizième

sixteenth[2] *n* 1 : seizième *mf* (dans une série) 2 : seizième *m* (en mathématiques) 3 (*used in dates*) <the sixteenth of May : le seize mai>

sixth[1] ['sɪksθ, 'sɪkst] *adj* : sixième

sixth[2] *n* 1 : sixième *mf* (dans une série) 2 : sixième *m* (en mathématiques) 3 (*used in dates*) <the sixth of July : le six juillet>

sixtieth[1] ['sɪkstiəθ] *adj* : soixantième

sixtieth[2] *n* 1 : soixantième *mf* (dans une série) 2 : soixantième *m* (en mathématiques)

sixty[1] ['sɪksti] *adj* : soixante

sixty[2] *n, pl* **-ties** : soixante *m*

sizable *or* **sizeable** ['saɪzəbəl] *adj* : assez grand

size[1] ['saɪz] *vt* **sized; sizing** 1 : classer selon la grosseur 2 **to size up** : jauger, évaluer

size[2] *n* 1 DIMENSIONS : grandeur *f*, taille *f* 2 : taille *f*, pointure *f* (de chaussures, de gants, etc.) <what is your size? : quelle est votre taille?> 3 MAGNITUDE : ampleur *f*, taille *f*

sizzle ['sɪzəl] *vi* **-zled; -zling** : grésiller

skate[1] ['skeɪt] *vi* **skated; skating** : patiner, faire du patin

skate[2] *n* 1 : patin *m* 2 : raie *f* (poisson)

skater ['skeɪtɚ] *n* : patineur *m*, -neuse *f*

skein ['skeɪn] *n* : écheveau *m*

skeletal ['skɛlətəl] *adj* : squelettique

skeleton ['skɛlətən] *n* : squelette *m*

skeptic ['skɛptɪk] *n* : sceptique *mf*

skeptical ['skɛptɪkəl] *adj* : sceptique

skepticism ['skɛptəˌsɪzəm] *n* : scepticisme *m*

sketch[1] ['skɛtʃ] *vt* : esquisser — *vi* : faire des esquisses

sketch[2] *n* : esquisse *f*, croquis *m*

sketchy ['skɛtʃi] *adj* **sketchier; -est** : imprécis, vague

skewer[1] ['skjuːər] *vt* : embrocher

skewer[2] *n* : brochette *f*

ski[1] ['skiː] *vi* **skied; skiing** : faire du ski

ski[2] *n, pl* **skis** : ski *m*

skid[1] ['skɪd] *vi* **skidded; skidding** : draper

skid[2] *n* : dérapage *m*

skier ['skiːər] *n* : skieur *m*, skieuse *f*

skiff ['skɪf] *n* : skiff *m*

skilful *Brit* → **skillful**

skill ['skɪl] *n* 1 CAPABILITY : habileté *f*, adresse *f*, compétence *f* 2 TRADE : métier *m* 3 **skills** : capacités *fpl*, compétences *fpl*

skilled ['skɪld] *adj* : habile, expérimenté

skillet ['skɪlət] *n* : poêle *f* (à frire)

skillful *or Brit* **skilful** ['skɪlfəl] *adj* : habile, adroit

skim[1] ['skɪm] *vt* **skimmed; skimming** 1 *or* **to skim off** : écumer, écrémer (le lait) 2 : parcourir (un livre, un journal, etc.) 3 : effleurer, raser (une surface)

skim[2] *adj* : écrémé <skim milk : lait écrémé>

skimp ['skɪmp] *vi* **to skimp on** : lésiner sur

skimpy ['skɪmpi] *adj* **skimpier; -est** : étriqué

skin[1] ['skɪn] *vt* **skinned; skinning** 1 : écorcher, dépouiller 2 PEEL : peler, éplucher

skin[2] *n* 1 : peau *f* 2 RIND : pelure *f*

skin diving *n* : plongée *f* sous-marine

skinflint ['skɪnˌflɪnt] *n* : grippe-sou *m*

skinned ['skɪnd] *adj* 1 : à (la) peau <fair-skinned : à peau claire> 2 → **thick–skinned, thin–skinned**

skinny ['skɪni] *adj* **skinnier; -est** : maigre

skip[1] ['skɪp] *v* **skipped; skipping** *vi* : sautiller, gambader — *vt* MISS, OMIT : sauter

skip[2] *n* : petit saut *m*, petit bond *m*

skipper ['skɪpɚ] *n* : capitaine *m*, skipper *m*

skirmish[1] ['skɚmɪʃ] *vi* : s'engager dans une escarmouche

skirmish[2] *n* : escarmouche *f*

skirt[1] ['skɚt] *vt* : contourner

skirt[2] *n* : jupe *f*

skit ['skɪt] *n* : sketch *m* (satirique)

skittish ['skɪtɪʃ] *adj* : ombrageux, difficile (se dit d'un cheval, etc.)

skulk ['skʌlk] *vi* : rôder

skull ['skʌl] *n* 1 : crâne *m* 2 **skull and crossbones** : tête *f* de mort

skunk ['skʌŋk] *n* : mouffette *f*

sky ['skaɪ] *n, pl* **skies** : ciel *m*

skylark ['skaɪˌlɑrk] *n* : alouette *f* des champs

skylight ['skaɪˌlaɪt] *n* : lucarne *f*

skyline ['skaɪˌlaɪn] *n* : ligne *f* d'horizon

skyrocket ['skaɪˌrɑkət] *vi* : monter en flèche

skyscraper ['skaɪˌskreɪpər] *n* : gratte-ciel *m*
skyward ['skaɪwərd] *adv* : vers le ciel
slab ['slæb] *n* : dalle *f*, bloc *m*
slack[1] ['slæk] *adj* **1** CARELESS : négligent **2** LOOSE : mou, lâche **3** SLOW : calme, stagnant <business is slack : les affaires marchent au ralenti>
slack[2] *n* **1** LOOSENESS : mou *m* **2 slacks** *npl* : pantalon *m*
slacken ['slækən] *vt* : relâcher — *vi* : se relâcher, ralentir
slag ['slæg] *n* : scories *fpl*
slain → **slay**
slake ['sleɪk] *vt* **slaked; slaking** : étancher (la soif), assouvir (les désirs)
slam[1] ['slæm] *v* **slammed; slamming** *vt* **1** : claquer <he slammed the door : il a claqué la porte> **2** HIT : frapper — *vi* : claquer
slam[2] *n* : claquement *m*
slander[1] ['slændər] *vt* : calomnier, diffamer
slander[2] *n* : calomnie *f*, diffamation *f*
slanderous ['slændərəs] *adj* : calomnieux, diffamatoire
slang ['slæŋ] *n* : argot *m*
slant[1] ['slænt] *vi* : pencher, s'incliner — *vt* : faire pencher, incliner
slant[2] *n* **1** : pente *f*, inclinaison *f* **2** POINT OF VIEW : point *m* de vue, perspective *f*
slap[1] ['slæp] *vt* **slapped; slapping** : gifler, donner une claque à
slap[2] *n* : gifle *f*, claque *f*
slash[1] ['slæʃ] *vt* **1** CUT : entailler **2** REDUCE : réduire
slash[2] *n* GASH : entaille *f*
slat ['slæt] *n* : lame *f*, lamelle *f*
slate ['sleɪt] *n* **1** : ardoise *f* <a slate roof : un toit d'ardoise> **2** LIST : liste *f* (de candidats)
slaughter[1] ['slɔtər] *vt* **1** : abattre (des animaux) **2** MASSACRE : massacrer (des personnes)
slaughter[2] *n* **1** : abattage *m* (d'animaux) **2** MASSACRE : massacre *m*
slaughterhouse ['slɔtərˌhaʊs] *n* : abattoir *m*
Slav ['slɑv, 'slæv] *n* : Slave *mf*
slave[1] ['sleɪv] *vi* **slaved; slaving** : travailler comme un esclave, trimer *fam*
slave[2] *n* : esclave *mf*
slaver ['slævər, 'sleɪ-] *vi* : baver
slavery ['sleɪvəri] *n* : esclavage *m*
slavish ['sleɪvɪʃ] *adj* : servile
slay ['sleɪ] *vt* **slew** ['slu:]; **slain** ['sleɪn]; **slaying** : tuer
slayer ['sleɪər] *n* : tueur *m*, tueuse *f*
sleazy ['sli:zi] *adj* **sleazier; -est 1** SHODDY : de mauvaise qualité **2** SQUALID : miteux, sordide **3** DISREPUTABLE : mal famé
sled[1] ['sled] *vi* **sledded; sledding** : faire du traîneau, faire de la luge
sled[2] *n* : traîneau *m*, luge *f*
sledge ['sledʒ] *n* **1** : traîneau *m* **2** → **sledgehammer**
sledgehammer ['sledʒˌhæmər] *n* : masse *f*
sleek[1] ['sli:k] *vt or* **to sleek down** : se lisser (les cheveux, etc.)
sleek[2] *adj* : lisse
sleep[1] ['sli:p] *vi* **slept** ['slɛpt]; **sleeping** : dormir
sleep[2] *n* **1** : sommeil *m* **2 to go to sleep** : s'endormir
sleeper ['sli:pər] *n* : dormeur *m*, -meuse *f*
sleepily ['sli:pəli] *adv* : d'un air endormi
sleepiness ['sli:pinəs] *n* : somnolence *f*, torpeur *f*
sleepless ['sli:pləs] *adj* : sans sommeil
sleepwalker ['sli:pˌwɔkər] *n* : somnambule *mf*
sleepy ['sli:pi] *adj* **sleepier; -est 1** DROWSY : somnolent <to be sleepy : avoir sommeil> **2** QUIET : endormi, somnolent <a sleepy town : une ville somnolente>
sleet[1] ['sli:t] *vi* : grésiller
sleet[2] *n* : grésil *m*
sleeve ['sli:v] *n* : manche *f*
sleeveless ['sli:vləs] *adj* : sans manches
sleigh ['sleɪ] *n* : traîneau *m*, carriole *f* *Can*
sleight of hand ['slaɪtəvˈhænd] *n* : tour *m* de passe-passe
slender ['slɛndər] *adj* **1** SLIM : mince **2** FEEBLE : faible <a slender hope : une faible espérance>
sleuth ['slu:θ] *n* : détective *m*, limier *m*
slew ['slu:] → **slay**
slice[1] ['slaɪs] *vt* **sliced; slicing** : trancher, découper en tranches
slice[2] *n* : tranche *f*, rondelle *f* (de saucisson)
slick[1] ['slɪk] *vt* : lisser
slick[2] *adj* **1** SLIPPERY : lisse **2** CRAFTY : habile
slicker ['slɪkər] *n* : imperméable *m*, ciré *m*
slide[1] ['slaɪd] *v* **slid** ['slɪd]; **sliding** ['slaɪdɪŋ] *vi* **1** : glisser **2** DECLINE : baisser <to let things slide : laisser aller> — *vt* : faire glisser
slide[2] *n* **1** SLIP : glissade *f* **2** : toboggan *m* (dans un terrain de jeu) **3** TRANSPARENCY : diapositive *f* **4** DECLINE : baisse *f*
slier, sliest → **sly**
slight[1] ['slaɪt] *vt* : offenser
slight[2] *adj* **1** SLENDER : mince **2** FRAIL : frêle **3** TRIFLING : léger <a slight injury : une légère blessure> **4** SMALL : menu <slight mishaps : menues méchancetés>
slight[3] *n* : affront *m*
slightly ['slaɪtli] *adv* **1** : légèrement, un peu, moindrement *Can* **2 slightly built** : mince

slim¹ ['slɪm] *v* **slimmed; slimming** *vi* : maigrir — *vt* : faire maigrir, amincir
slim² *adj* **slimmer; slimmest 1** SLENDER : svelte, élancé, mince **2** FAINT, SLIGHT : faible, mince <she has only a slim chance : elle n'a que de faibles chances>
slime ['slaɪm] *n* **1** : bave *f* (sécrétée par un escargot) **2** MUD : vase *f*, boue *f*
slimy ['slaɪmi] *adj* **slimier; -est** : visqueux
sling¹ ['slɪŋ] *vt* **slung** ['slʌŋ]; **slinging 1** THROW : lancer, jeter **2** HANG : suspendre
sling² *n* **1** : écharpe *f* <his arm is in a sling : son bras est en écharpe> **2** STRAP : bretelle *f* **3** → **slingshot**
slingshot ['slɪŋˌʃɑt] *n* : fronde *f*, lance-pierres *m*
slink ['slɪŋk] *vi* **slunk** ['slʌŋk]; **slinking 1** : entrer ou sortir furtivement **2 to slink away** : s'éclipser, s'éloigner furtivement
slip¹ ['slɪp] *v* **slipped; slipping** *vi* **1** SLIDE : glisser <he slipped on the sidewalk : il a glissé sur le trottoir> **2** DECLINE : décliner **3 to let slip** : laisser échapper **4 to slip away** : partir furtivement — *vt* **1** PASS : glisser <I slipped him ten dollars : j'ai glissé dix dollars dans sa main> **2** ESCAPE : échapper à **3 it slipped his mind** : ça lui est sorti de la tête, ça lui a échappé
slip² *n* **1** : glissade *f* **2** BERTH : slip *m* (de bateaux) **3** MISTAKE : erreur *f* <a slip of the tongue : un lapsus> **4** PETTICOAT : jupon *m* **5** CUTTING : bouture *f* (d'une plante)
slipcover ['slɪpˌkʌvər] *n* : housse *f*
slipper ['slɪpər] *n* : pantoufle *f*
slipperiness ['slɪpərinəs] *n* : état *m* glissant
slippery ['slɪpəri] *adj* **slipperier; -est 1** : glissant **2** TRICKY : rusé **3** EVASIVE : fuyant
slipshod ['slɪpˌʃɑd] *adj* : négligent
slip up *vi* : faire une gaffe
slit¹ ['slɪt] *vt* **slit; slitting 1** SPLIT : fendre **2** CUT : couper, inciser
slit² *n* **1** OPENING : fente *f* **2** CUT : coupure *f*, incision *f*
slither ['slɪðər] *vi* : ramper
sliver ['slɪvər] *n* **1** : éclat *m* (de bois) **2** SLICE : petite tranche *f*, petit morceau *m*
slob ['slɑb] *n* : personne *f* débraillée
slobber¹ ['slɑbər] *vi* : baver
slobber² *n* : bave *f*
slogan ['slo:gən] *n* : slogan *m*
sloop ['slu:p] *n* : sloop *m*
slop¹ ['slɑp] *v* **slopped; slopping** *vt* : renverser, répandre — *vi or* **to slop over** : se répandre, déborder
slop² *n* : pâtée *f*
slope¹ ['slo:p] *vi* **sloped; sloping** : pencher, être en pente
slope² *n* : pente *f*
sloppy ['slɑpi] *adj* **sloppier; -est 1** MUDDY : boueux, mouillé **2** UNTIDY : négligé **3** CARELESS : bâclé
slot ['slɑt] *n* **1** : fente *f* **2** GROOVE : rainure *f* **3** *or* **time slot** : créneau *m*, tranche *f* horaire
sloth ['slɔθ, 'slo:θ] *n*, **1** LAZINESS : paresse *f* **2** : paresseux *m* (animal)
slouch¹ ['slaʊtʃ] *vi* : être avachi, ne pas se tenir droit
slouch² *n* **1 to walk with a slouch** : marcher le dos voûté **2 he's no slouch** : il n'est pas empoté
slough¹ ['slʌf] *vt or* **to slough off** : se débarrasser de
slough² ['slu:, 'slaʊ] *n* SWAMP : bourbier *m*, marécage *m*
Slovak ['slo:ˌvɑk, -ˌvæk] *or* **Slovakian** [ˌslo:ˈvɑkiən, -ˈvæ-] *adj* : slovaque
Slovakian *n* : Slovaque *mf*
Slovene ['slo:ˌvi:n] *or* **Slovenian** [slo:-ˈvi:niən] *adj* : slovène
Slovenian *n* : Slovène *mf*
slovenly ['slʌvənli, 'slʌv-] *adj* **1** : négligé, sale **2** CARELESS : bâclé
slow¹ ['slo:] *vt* **1** : ralentir **2** DELAY : retarder — *vi* : ralentir
slow² *adv* : lentement
slow³ *adj* **1** : lent <a slow process : un processus lent> <my watch is five minutes slow : ma montre retarde de cinq minutes> **2** STUPID : peu intelligent, lent **3** SLACK : calme, stagnant <sales are slow : les ventes ne marchent pas fort> **4** SLUGGISH : léthargique, lent
slowly ['slo:li] *adv* : lentement
slowness ['slo:nəs] *n* : lenteur *f*, lourdeur *m*
slowpoke ['slo:ˌpo:k] *n* : traînard *m*, -narde *f*; lambineux *m*, -neuse *f* *Can fam*
sludge ['slʌdʒ] *n* : boue *f*, vase *f*
slug¹ ['slʌg] *vt* **slugged; slugging** : assommer
slug² *n* **1** : limace *f* (mollusque) **2** BULLET : balle *f* **3** TOKEN : jeton *m* **4** BLOW : coup *m*
sluggish ['slʌgɪʃ] *adj* : léthargique, lent
sluice¹ ['slu:s] *vt* **sluiced; sluicing** *or* **to sluice down** : laver à grande eau
sluice² *n* : vanne *f*
slum ['slʌm] *n* : taudis *m*, quartier *m* pauvre
slumber¹ ['slʌmbər] *vi* : dormir, sommeiller
slumber² *n* : sommeil *m*
slump¹ ['slʌmp] *vi* **1** DECLINE, DROP : baisser **2** SLOUCH : être avachi
slump² *n* : baisse *f*, crise *f* (économique)
slung → **sling¹**
slunk → **slink**
slur¹ ['slər] *vt* **slurred; slurring 1** : mal articuler (les mots) **2** : lier (en musique)

slur[2] *n* : affront *m*, insulte *f* <racial slur : insulte raciste>
slurp ['slərp] *v* : boire avec bruit
slush ['slʌʃ] *n* : neige *f* fondue, sloche *f Can*, gadoue *f Can*
slut ['slʌt] *n* PROSTITUTE : prostituée *f*
sly ['slaɪ] *adj* **slier** ['slaɪər]; **sliest** ['slaɪəst] **1** CUNNING : rusé **2** UNDERHANDED : sournois
slyly ['slaɪli] *adv* **1** CUNNINGLY : de façon rusée **2** UNDERHANDEDLY : sournoisement
slyness ['slaɪnəs] *n* CUNNING : ruse *f*
smack[1] ['smæk] *vi* **to smack of** : sentir — *vt* **1** KISS : donner un baiser à **2** SLAP : gifler, claquer **3 to smack one's lips** : se lécher les babines
smack[2] *adv* **smack in the middle** : en plein milieu
smack[3] *n* **1** TASTE, TRACE : soupçon *m* **2** KISS : gros baiser *m* **3** SLAP : gifle *f*, claque *f*
small ['smɔl] *adj* **1** : petit <a small house : une petite maison> <small change : petite monnaie> **2** TRIVIAL : insignifiant, peu important
smallness ['smɔlnəs] *n* : petitesse *f*
smallpox ['smɔlˌpɑks] *n* : variole *f*
smart[1] ['smɑrt] *vi* **1** STING : brûler, piquer **2** : être piqué au vif (par l'insulte)
smart[2] *adj* **1** INTELLIGENT : intelligent **2** STYLISH : chic
smart[3] *n* : douleur *f* cuisante
smartly ['smɑrtli] *adv* **1** CLEVERLY : habilement, astucieusement **2** STYLISHLY : avec beaucoup de chic **3** QUICKLY : vivement
smartness ['smɑrtnəs] *n* **1** INTELLIGENCE : intelligence *f* **2** ELEGANCE : élégance *f*
smash[1] ['smæʃ] *vt* **1** BREAK : briser **2** CRASH : écraser **3** SHATTER : fracasser, briser — *vi* **1** SHATTER : se briser, se fracasser **2** COLLIDE, CRASH : s'écraser
smash[2] *n* **1** BLOW : coup *m*, gifle *f* **2** COLLISION : collision *f* **3** BANG, CRASH : fracas *m*
smattering ['smætəɹɪŋ] *n* : notions *fpl* vagues, rudiments *mpl* <a smattering of French : quelques notions de français> <a smattering of spectators : quelques spectateurs>
smear[1] ['smɪr] *vt* **1** SMUDGE : faire des taches sur, barbouiller **2** SLANDER : diffamer
smear[2] *n* **1** STAIN : tache *f* **2** SLANDER : diffamation *f*
smell[1] ['smɛl] *v* **smelled** ['smɛld] *or* **smelt** ['smɛlt]; **smelling** *vt* : sentir <to smell danger : sentir le danger> — *vi* : sentir <to smell good : sentir bon>
smell[2] *n* **1** : odorat *m* (sens) **2** ODOR : odeur *f*
smelly ['smɛli] *adj* **smellier; -est** : malodorant <it's smelly in here : ça sent mauvais ici>
smelt[1] ['smɛlt] *vt* : fondre
smelt[2] *n, pl* **smelts** *or* **smelt** : éperlan *m* (poisson)
smile[1] ['smaɪl] *vi* **smiled; smiling** : sourire
smile[2] *n* : sourire *m*
smirk[1] ['smərk] *vi* : sourire d'un air satisfait
smirk[2] *n* : petit sourire *m* satisfait
smite ['smaɪt] *vt* **smote** ['smoːt]; **smitten** ['smɪtən] *or* **smote; smiting 1** STRIKE : frapper **2 to be smitten with** : être pris de <smitten with remorse : accablé de remords>
smith ['smɪθ] *n* : forgeron *m*
smithy ['smɪθi] *n, pl* **smithies** : forge *f*
smock ['smɑk] *n* : blouse *f*, sarrau *m*
smog ['smɑg, 'smɔg] *n* : smog *m*
smoke[1] ['smoːk] *v* **smoked; smoking** *vt* : fumer <to smoke a cigarette : fumer une cigarette> — *vi* : fumer
smoke[2] *n* : fumée *f*, boucane *f Can*
smoke detector *n* : détecteur *m* de fumée
smoker ['smoːkər] *n* : fumeur *m*, -meuse *f*
smokestack ['smoːkˌstæk] *n* : cheminée *f*
smoky ['smoːki] *adj* **smokier; -est** : enfumé
smolder ['smoːldər] *vi* : couver
smooth[1] ['smuːð] *vt* : lisser
smooth[2] *adj* **1** : lisse <smooth skin : peau lisse> **2** CALM : calme <a smooth landing : un atterrissage en douceur> **3** MILD : doux **4** FLOWING : fluide <smooth writing : écriture fluide>
smoothly ['smuːðli] *adv* **1** GENTLY, SOFTLY : doucement **2** EASILY : facilement
smoothness ['smuːðnəs] *n* : douceur *f*
smother ['smʌðər] *vt* **1** SUFFOCATE : étouffer **2** COVER : recouvrir (un feu) — *vi* : être étouffé
smudge[1] ['smʌdʒ] *v* **smudged; smudging** *vt* : salir, faire des taches sur — *vi* : se salir, s'étaler
smudge[2] *n* : tache *f*, bavure *f*
smug ['smʌg] *adj* **smugger; smuggest** : suffisant, content de soi
smuggle ['smʌgəl] *v* **-gled; -gling** *vt* : faire passer en contrebande — *vi* : faire de la contrebande
smuggler ['smʌgələr] *n* : contrebandier *m*, -dière *f*
smugly ['smʌgli] *adv* : avec suffisance
smut ['smʌt] *n* **1** SOOT : tache *f* de suie **2** OBSCENITY : cochonnerie *f* **3** FUNGUS : charbon *m* (du blé)
smutty ['smʌti] *adj* **smuttier; -est 1** SOOTY : noirci, sali **2** OBSCENE : cochon, ordurier
snack ['snæk] *n* : casse-croûte *m*
snag[1] ['snæg] *v* **snagged; snagging** *vt* : accrocher — *vi* : s'accrocher
snag[2] *n* : accroc *m*

snail ['sneɪl] *n* : escargot *m*
snake ['sneɪk] *n* : serpent *m*
snakebite ['sneɪkˌbaɪt] *n* : morsure *f* de serpent
snap[1] ['snæp] *v* **snapped; snapping** *vi* **1** CLICK : claquer **2** : essayer de mordre (se dit d'un chien, etc.) **3** BREAK : se casser, se briser **4** : parler d'un ton brusque — *vt* **1** CLICK : faire claquer **2** BREAK : casser, briser **3 to snap up** : arracher, saisir
snap[2] *n* **1** CLICK : claquement *m* **2** BREAK : cassure *f* **3** FASTENER : bouton-pression *m* **4** CINCH : quelque chose *f* de facile <it's a snap! : c'est du gâteau!>
snapdragon ['snæpˌdrægən] *n* : gueule-de-loup *f*
snapper ['snæpər] *n* : lutjanidé *m* (poisson)
snappy ['snæpi] *adj* **snappier; -est 1** FAST : vite <make it snappy! : fais ça vite!> **2** LIVELY : vif **3** STYLISH : chic
snapshot ['snæpˌʃɑt] *n* : instantané *m*
snare[1] ['snær] *vt* **snared; snaring** : attraper, prendre au piège
snare[2] *n* : piège *m*, collet *m*
snare drum *n* : caisse *f* claire
snarl[1] ['snɑrl] *vi* **1** TANGLE : enchevêtrer **2** GROWL : grogner
snarl[2] *n* **1** TANGLE : enchevêtrement *m* **2** GROWL : grognement *m*
snatch[1] ['snætʃ] *vt* : saisir
snatch[2] *n* : fragment *m*, bribe *f* <snatches of conversation : bribes de conversation>
sneak[1] ['sni:k] *vi* : se glisser, se faufiler — *vt* : faire furtivement <to sneak a look : jeter un coup d'œil> <he sneaked a smoke : il a fumé en cachette>
sneak[2] *n* : sournois *m*, -noise *f*; cafard *m*, -farde *f France fam*
sneakers ['sni:kərz] *npl* : tennis *mpl France*, espadrilles *fpl Can*
sneaky ['sni:ki] *adj* **sneakier; -est** : sournois
sneer[1] ['snɪr] *vi* : ricaner, sourire d'un air méprisant
sneer[2] *n* : ricanement *m*
sneeze[1] ['sni:z] *vi* **sneezed; sneezing** : éternuer
sneeze[2] *n* : éternuement *m*
snicker[1] ['snɪkər] *vi* : rire doucement, rire dans sa barbe
snicker[2] *n* : rire *m* étouffé
snide ['snaɪd] *adj* : narquois
sniff[1] ['snɪf] *vi* **1** : renifler **2 to sniff at** : dédaigner, faire la grimace à — *vt* **1** SMELL : sentir, humer **2 to sniff out** : flairer
sniff[2] *n* : reniflement *m*
sniffle[1] ['snɪfəl] *vi* **-fled; -fling** : renifler
sniffle[2] *n* **1** SNIFF : reniflement *m* **2 sniffles** *npl* : petit rhume *m* <to have the sniffles : être enrhumé>
snip[1] ['snɪp] *vt* **snipped; snipping** : couper
snip[2] *n* **1** CUT : coupure *f* **2** FRAGMENT, PIECE : petit bout *m*
snipe[1] ['snaɪp] *vi* **sniped; sniping 1 to snipe at** SHOOT : tirer sur **2 to snipe at** CRITICIZE : critiquer par en-dessous
snipe[2] *n, pl* **snipes** *or* **snipe** : bécassine *f* (oiseau)
sniper ['snaɪpər] *n* : tireur *m* embusqué
snivel ['snɪvəl] *vi* **-eled** *or* **-elled; -eling** *or* **-elling 1 → snuffle 2** WHINE : pleurnicher *fam*, chialer *fam*
snob ['snɑb] *n* : snob *mf*
snobbery ['snɑbəri] *n, pl* **-beries** : snobisme *m*
snobbish ['snɑbɪʃ] *adj* : snob
snobbishness ['snɑbɪʃnəs] *n* : snobisme *m*
snoop[1] ['snu:p] *vi* **1 to snoop around** : fouiner, fureter **2 to snoop on s.o.** : espionner qqn
snoop[2] *n* **1** : espion *m*, -pionne *f*; fouineur *m*, -neuse *f* **2 to have a snoop around** : fureter discrètement dans
snooze[1] ['snu:z] *vi* **snoozed; snoozing** : sommeiller
snooze[2] *n* : petit somme *m*
snore[1] ['snor] *vi* **snored; snoring** : ronfler
snore[2] *n* : ronflement *m*
snort[1] ['snɔrt] *vi* : grogner (se dit d'une personne ou d'un cochon), s'ébrouer (se dit d'un cheval)
snort[2] *n* : grognement *m*, ébrouement *m*
snout ['snaʊt] *n* : museau *m*, groin *m* (d'un porc)
snow[1] ['sno:] *vi* : neiger
snow[2] *n* : neige *f*
snowball ['sno:ˌbɔl] *n* : boule *f* de neige, pelote *f* de neige *Can*
snowbank ['sno:ˌbæŋk] *n* : congère *f France*, banc *m* de neige *Can*
snowblower ['sno:ˌblo:ər] *n* : souffleuse *f* (à neige) *Can*
snowdrift ['sno:ˌdrɪft] *n* : congère *f France*, banc *m* de neige *Can*
snowfall ['sno:ˌfɔl] *n* : chute *f* de neige
snowplow ['sno:ˌplaʊ] *n* : chasse-neige *m*, gratte *f Can*
snowshoes ['sno:ˌʃu:z] *npl* : raquettes *fpl*
snowstorm ['sno:ˌstɔrm] *n* : tempête *f* de neige, bordée *f* de neige *Can*
snowy ['sno:i] *adj* **snowier; -est** : neigeux
snub[1] ['snʌb] *vt* **snubbed; snubbing** : rabrouer
snub[2] *n* : rebuffade *f*
snub-nosed ['snʌbˌno:zd] *adj* : au nez retroussé
snuff[1] ['snʌf] *vt* **1** EXTINGUISH : moucher **2** SNIFF : renifler
snuff[2] *n* : tabac *m* à priser
snuffle ['snʌfəl] *vi* **-fled; -fling** : renifler

snug [ˈsnʌg] *adj* **snugger; snuggest 1** COMFORTABLE : confortable **2** TIGHT : bien ajusté

snuggle [ˈsnʌgəl] *vi* **-gled; -gling** : se pelotonner

snugly [ˈsnʌgli] *adv* **1** COMFORTABLY : confortablement **2** WELL : bien <the dress fits snugly : la robe est parfaitement ajustée>

so¹ [ˈsoː] *adv* **1** (*referring to something indicated or suggested*) <do you think so? : tu crois?> <so be it : ainsi soit-il> <I told her so : je le lui ai dit> **2** : si, tellement <it's so hot : il fait si chaud> <they were so late : ils ont été tellement en retard> **3** ALSO : aussi <so do I : moi aussi> **4** THUS : ainsi <it would seem so : il paraîtrait ainsi> <do it like so : fais-le ainsi> **5** AS : aussi <he'd never been so happy : il n'a jamais été aussi content> **6 is that so?** : c'est vrai?

so² *conj* **1** THEREFORE : donc, alors **2** *or* **so that** : afin de **3 so what?** : et alors?

soak¹ [ˈsoːk] *vi* : tremper — *vt* **1** WET : tremper **2** IMMERSE : faire tremper (la lessive, etc.) **3 to soak up** ABSORB : absorber

soak² *n* : trempage *m*

soap¹ [ˈsoːp] *vt* : savonner

soap² *n* : savon *m*

soapsuds [ˈsoːpˌsʌdz] → **suds**

soapy [ˈsoːpi] *adj* **soapier; -est** : savonneux

soar [ˈsor] *vi* **1** GLIDE : planer **2** TOWER : se dresser (vers le ciel), s'élever **3** RISE : monter (en flèche) <prices have soared : les prix ont monté> <my spirits soared : mon moral est remonté en flèche>

sob¹ [ˈsɑb] *vi* **sobbed; sobbing** : sangloter

sob² *n* : sanglot *m*

sober [ˈsoːbər] *adj* **1** : sobre <he's perfectly sober : il est parfaitement sobre> **2** SERIOUS : sérieux

soberly [ˈsoːbərli] *adv* **1** : avec sobriété, sobrement **2** SERIOUSLY : sérieusement

sobriety [səˈbraiəṭi, so-] *n* : sobriété *f*

soccer [ˈsɑkər] *n* : football *m France*, soccer *m Can*

sociability [ˌsoːʃəˈbɪləṭi] *n* : sociabilité *f*

sociable [ˈsoːʃəbəl] *adj* : sociable

social¹ [ˈsoːʃəl] *adj* : social — **socially** *adv*

social² *n* **1** PARTY : soirée *f* **2** GATHERING : réunion *f*

socialism [ˈsoːʃəˌlɪzəm] *n* : socialisme *m*

socialist¹ [ˈsoːʃəlɪst] *adj* : socialiste

socialist² *n* : socialiste *mf*

socialize [ˈsoːʃəˌlaɪz] *v* **-ized; -izing** *vt* : socialiser — *vi* : fréquenter des gens

social work *n* : travail *m* social

society [səˈsaiəṭi] *n, pl* **-eties 1** COMPANIONSHIP : compagnie *f* **2** : société *f* <a democratic society : une société démocratique> <high society : haute société> **3** ASSOCIATION : association *f*, société *f*

sociological [ˌsoːsiəˈlɑdʒɪkəl] *adj* : sociologique

sociologist [ˌsoːsiˈɑlədʒɪst] *n* : sociologue *mf*

sociology [ˌsoːsiˈɑlədʒi] *n* : sociologie *f*

sock¹ [ˈsɑk] *vt* : donner un coup de poing à

sock² *n* **1** PUNCH : coup *m*, beigne *f fam* **2** *pl* **socks** *or* **sox** : chaussette *f*

socket [ˈsɑkəṭ] *n* **1** : cavité *f* **2** *or* **electric socket** : prise *f* de courant **3 eye socket** : orbite *f*

sod¹ [ˈsɑd] *vt* **sodded; sodding** : gazonner

sod² *n* TURF : gazon *m*, motte *f* (de gazon)

soda [ˈsoːdə] *n* **1** *or* **soda pop** : boisson *f* gazeuse, soda *m France*, liqueur *f Can* **2** : soude *f* <baking soda : bicarbonate de soude>

sodden [ˈsɑdən] *adj* SOGGY : trempé, détrempé

sodium [ˈsoːdiəm] *n* : sodium *m*

sofa [ˈsoːfə] *n* : canapé *m*

soft [ˈsɔft] *adj* **1** : mou <a soft pillow : un mol oreiller> **2** SMOOTH : doux <soft to the touch : doux au toucher> <a soft ride : un roulement doux>

softball [ˈsɔftˌbɔl] *n* : balle-molle *f Can*, softball *m Can*

soft drink *n* : boisson *f* non alcoolisée, boisson *f* gazeuse

soften [ˈsɔfən] *vt* : amollir, adoucir (la peau), ramollir (le beurre, etc.) — *vi* : s'adoucir, se ramollir

softly [ˈsɔftli] *adv* : doucement, mollement

softness [ˈsɔftnəs] *n* : douceur *f*, mollesse *f*

software [ˈsɔftˌwær] *n* : logiciel *m*, software *m*

soggy [ˈsɑgi] *adj* **soggier; -est** : détrempé, trempé

soil¹ [ˈsɔɪl] *vt* : salir, souiller <he soiled his hands : il s'est sali les mains> — *vi* : se salir

soil² *n* **1** DIRT, EARTH : sol *m*, terre *f* **2** COUNTRY : sol *m*, terre *f* <her native soil : sa terre natale>

sojourn¹ [ˈsoːˌdʒərn, soːˈdʒərn] *vi* : séjourner

sojourn² *n* : séjour *m*

solace [ˈsɑləs] *n* : consolation *f*

solar [ˈsoːlər] *adj* : solaire

sold → **sell**

solder¹ [ˈsɑdər, ˈsɔ-] *vt* : souder

solder² *n* : soudure *f*

soldier¹ [ˈsoːldʒər] *vi* **1** : être soldat **2 to soldier on** : persévérer

soldier² *n* : soldat *m*, femme soldat *f*, militaire *m*

sole¹ [ˈsoːl] *adj* : seul

sole² *n* **1** : plante *f* (du pied) **2** : sole *f* (poisson)

solemn ['sɑləm] *adj* : solonnel — **solemnly** *adv*
solemnity [sə'lɛmnəṭi] *n, pl* **-ties** : solennité *f*
solicit [sə'lɪsəṭ] *vt* : solliciter
solicitous [sə'lɪsəṭəs] *adj* : plein de sollicitude
solicitude [sə'lɪsəˌtu:d, -ˌtju:d] *n* : sollicitude *f*
solid[1] ['sɑləd] *adj* **1** : solide <solid food : aliments solides> **2** : plein, massif <solid gold : or massif> <a solid rubber ball : un ballon plein en caoutchouc> **3** CONTINUOUS : de suite <two solid hours : deux heures de suite>
solid[2] *n* : solide *m*
solidarity [ˌsɑlə'dærəṭi] *n* : solidarité *f*
solidify [sə'lɪdəˌfaɪ] *v* **-fied; -fying** *vt* : solidifier — *vi* : se solidifier
solidity [sə'lɪdəṭi] *n, pl* **-ties** : solidité *f*
solidly ['sɑlədli] *adv* : solidement
soliloquy [sə'lɪləkwi] *n, pl* **-quies** : soliloque *m*
solitaire ['sɑləˌtɛr] *n* : solitaire *m*
solitary ['sɑləˌtɛri] *adj* **1** ALONE : solitaire **2** SINGLE : seul
solitude ['sɑləˌtu:d, -ˌtju:d] *n* : solitude *f*
solo[1] ['so:ˌlo:] *vi* : jouer en solo
solo[2] *adv* : en solo
solo[3] *adj* : solo
solo[4] *n, pl* **solos** : solo *m*
soloist ['so:ˌloɪst] *n* : soliste *mf*
solstice ['sɑlstɪs] *n* : solstice *m*
soluble ['sɑljəbəl] *adj* : soluble
solution [sə'lu:ʃən] *n* : solution *f*
solve ['sɑlv] *vt* **solved; solving** : résoudre, trouver la solution de
solvency ['sɑlvənsi] *n* : solvabilité *f*
solvent[1] ['sɑlvənt] *adj* : solvable
solvent[2] *n* : solvant *m*, dissolvant *m*
Somali[1] [so'mɑli, sə-] *adj* : somali
Somali[2] *n* : Somali *m*, -lie *f*
Somalian[1] [so'mɑliən, -ljən, sə-] *adj* : somalien
Somalian[2] *n* : Somalien *m*, -lienne *f*
somber ['sɑmbər] *adj* : sombre
sombrero [səm'brɛr,o:] *n, pl* **-ros** : sombrero *m*
some[1] ['sʌm] *adj* **1** (*being an amount*) : de <some water : de l'eau> <do you want some apples? : voulez-vous des pommes?> **2** (*being an unspecified or indefinite number*) : certains <he read some books : il a lu certains livres> **3** SEVERAL : quelques <some good candidates : quelques bons candidats> <some years ago : il y a quelques années> **4** (*being an unspecified individual or thing*) : un, une, quelque <some lady stopped me : une dame m'a arrêté> <some distant galaxy : quelque galaxie lointaine>
some[2] *pron* **1** : certains *mpl*, certaines *fpl*, quelques-uns *mpl*, quelques-unes *fpl* <some left, others stayed : certains sont partis, d'autres sont restés> **2** : un peu, en <there's some left : il en reste un peu> <do you want some? : en voulez-vous?>
somebody ['sʌmbədi, -ˌbɑdi] *pron* : quelqu'un, on
someday ['sʌmˌdeɪ] *adv* : un jour
somehow ['sʌmˌhaʊ] *adv* **1** : de quelque manière <somehow or other : d'une manière ou d'une autre> **2** : pour quelque raison <somehow I don't trust him : pour quelque raison je ne lui fais pas confiance>
someone ['sʌmˌwʌn] *pron* : quelqu'un, on
somersault[1] ['sʌmərˌsɔlt] *vi* : faire une culbute
somersault[2] *n* : culbute *f*
something ['sʌmθɪŋ] *pron* : quelque chose <something happened : quelque chose est arrivé> <something else : autre chose>
sometime ['sʌmˌtaɪm] *adv* **1** (*indicating a time in the future*) : un jour, un de ces jours <you should try it sometime : tu devrais l'essayer un jour> **2** (*indicating a time in the past*) <she called sometime last week : elle a téléphoné au cours de la semaine passée>
sometimes ['sʌmˌtaɪmz] *adv* : quelquefois, parfois
somewhat ['sʌmˌhwʌt, -ˌhwɑt] *adv* : un peu, quelque peu, assez
somewhere ['sʌmˌhwɛr] *adv* **1** : quelque part **2 somewhere else** : ailleurs, autre part
son ['sʌn] *n* : fils *m*
sonar ['so:ˌnɑr] *n* : sonar *m*
sonata [sə'nɑṭə] *n* : sonate *f*
song ['sɔŋ] *n* : chanson *f*
songbird ['sɔŋˌbərd] *n* : oiseau *m* chanteur
sonic ['sɑnɪk] *adj* : sonique
son-in-law ['sʌnɪnˌlɔ] *n, pl* **sons-in-law** : gendre *m*, beau-fils *m*
sonnet ['sɑnət] *n* : sonnet *m*
sonorous ['sɑnərəs, sə'norəs] *adj* : sonore
soon ['su:n] *adv* **1** : bientôt <he'll arrive soon : il arrivera bientôt> <soon after : peu après> **2** QUICKLY : vite <as soon as possible : le plus tôt possible>
soot ['sʊt, 'su:t, 'sʌt] *n* : suie *f*
soothe ['su:ð] *v* **soothed; soothing 1** CALM : calmer, apaiser **2** RELIEVE : soulager
soothsayer ['su:θˌseɪər] *n* : devin *m*, -vineresse *f*
sooty ['sʊṭi, 'su:-, 'sʌ-] *adj* **sootier; -est** : couvert de suie
sop[1] ['sɑp] *vt* **sopped; sopping 1** SOAK : tremper **2 to sop up** : éponger
sop[2] *n* : concession *f* (symbolique) <as a sop to his pride : pour flatter son orgueil>
sophisticated [sə'fɪstəˌkeɪṭəd] *adj* **1** COMPLEX : compliqué **2** WORLDLY : raffiné, sophistiqué
sophistication [səˌfɪstə'keɪʃən] *n* **1** WORLDLINESS : sophistication *f* **2**

COMPLEXITY : sophistication *f*, perfectionnement *m* **3** REFINEMENT, URBANITY : raffinement *m*

sophomore [ˈsɑfˌmor, ˈsɑfəˌmor] *n* : étudiant *m*, -diante *f* de seconde année

soporific [ˌsɑpəˈrɪfɪk, ˌsoː-] *adj* : soporifique

soprano [səˈpræˌnoː] *n, pl* **-nos** : soprano *mf* (personne), soprano *m* (voix)

sorcerer [ˈsɔrsərər] *n* : sorcier *m*

sorceress [ˈsɔrsərəs] *n* : sorcière *f*

sorcery [ˈsɔrsəri] *n* : sorcellerie *f*

sordid [ˈsɔrdɪd] *adj* : sordide

sore¹ [ˈsor] *adj* **sorer; sorest 1** PAINFUL : douloureux **2** GREAT : grand <to be in sore need of : avoir grand besoin de> **3** ANGRY : fâché, vexé

sore² *n* : plaie *f*

sorely [ˈsorli] *adv* : gravement, grandement, extrêmement

soreness [ˈsorməs] *n* : douleur *f*

sorghum [ˈsɔrgəm] *n* : sorgho *m*

sorority [səˈrɔrəṭi] *n, pl* **-ties** : club *m* d'étudiantes

sorrel [ˈsɔrəl] *n* **1** : oseille *f* (plante) **2** : brun *m* roux (couleur)

sorrow [ˈsɑrˌoː] *n* : chagrin *m*, peine *f*, tristesse *f*

sorrowful [ˈsɑrofəl] *adj* : triste

sorrowfully [ˈsɑrofəli] *adv* : tristement

sorry [ˈsɑri] *adj* **sorrier; -est 1** PITIFUL : piteux <in a sorry state : dans un piteux état> **2 to be sorry** : être désolé, regretter <I'm sorry : je suis désolé> **3 to feel sorry for** : plaindre <I don't feel sorry for him : je ne le plains pas>

sort¹ [ˈsɔrt] *vt* : trier

sort² *n* **1** KIND : genre *m*, sorte *f* **2 out of sorts** : de mauvaise humeur

sortie [ˈsɔrṭi, sɔrˈtiː] *n* : sortie *f*

SOS [ˌɛsˌoːˈɛs] *n* : S.O.S. *m*

so–so¹ [ˈsoːˈsoː] *adv* : comme ci comme ça

so–so² *adj* : moyen

soufflé [suːˈfleɪ] *n* : soufflé *m*

sought → **seek**

soul [ˈsoːl] *n* **1** SPIRIT : âme *f* **2** ESSENCE : essence *f* **3** PERSON : âme *f*, personne *f* <not a soul : pas âme qui vive>

soulful [ˈsoːlfəl] *adj* : attendrissant, émouvant, sentimental

sound¹ [ˈsɑʊnd] *vt* **1** : sonner <to sound the alarm : sonner l'alarme> <to sound the horn : klaxonner> **2** *or* **to sound out** PROBE : sonder — *vi* **1** : sonner **2** SEEM : sembler, paraître

sound² *adj* **1** HEALTHY : sain <safe and sound : sain et sauf> **2** FIRM, SOLID : solide **3** SENSIBLE : raisonnable **4** DEEP : profond <a sound sleep : un sommeil profond>

sound³ *n* **1** : son *m* **2** NOISE : bruit *m* **3** CHANNEL : détroit *m*, bras *m* de mer

soundless [ˈsɑʊndləs] *adj* : silencieux — **soundlessly** *adv*

soundly [ˈsɑʊndli] *adv* **1** SOLIDLY : solidement **2** SENSIBLY : judicieusement **3** DEEPLY : profondément <to sleep soundly : dormir profondément>

soundness [ˈsɑʊndnəs] *n* **1** SOLIDITY : solidité *f* **2** SENSE, WISDOM : sagesse *f*, bon sens *m*, justesse *f*

soundproof [ˈsɑʊndˌpruːf] *adj* : insonorisé

soup [ˈsuːp] *n* : soupe *f* <vegetable soup : soupe aux légumes>

sour¹ [ˈsɑʊər] *v* : aigrir

sour² *adj* **1** ACID : aigre, sur **2** DISAGREEABLE : revêche, acerbe

source [ˈsɔrs] *n* : source *f*

sourness [ˈsɑʊərnəs] *n* : aigreur *f*

south¹ [ˈsɑʊθ] *adv* : au sud, vers le sud <further south : plus au sud>

south² *adj* : sud, du sud <the south entrance : l'entrée sud> <South America : Amérique du Sud>

south³ *n* : sud *m*

South African¹ *adj* : sud-africain

South African² *n* : Sud-Africain *m*, -caine *f*

South American¹ *adj* : sud-américain

South American² *n* : Sud-Américain *m*, -caine *f*

southbound [ˈsɑʊθˌbɑʊnd] *adj* : qui va vers le sud

southeast¹ [sɑʊˈθiːst, *as a nautical term often* sɑʊˈiːst] *adj* : sud-est

southeast² *n* : sud-est *m*

southeasterly¹ [sɑʊˈθiːstərli] *adv* : vers le sud-est

southeasterly² *adj* : du sud-est

southeastern [sɑʊˈθiːstərn] → **southeast¹**

southerly¹ [ˈsʌðərli] *adv* : vers le sud

southerly² *adj* : du sud

southern [ˈsʌðərn] *adj* : du sud

Southerner [ˈsʌðərnər] *n* : habitant *m*, -tante *f* du Sud

south pole *n* : pôle *m* Sud

southward¹ [ˈsɑʊθwərd] *or* **southwards** [-wərdz] *adv* : vers le sud

southward² *or* **southwards** *adj* : au sud, du sud

southwest¹ [sɑʊθˈwest, *as a nautical term often* sɑʊˈwest] *adj* : sud-ouest

southwest² *n* : sud-ouest *m*

southwesterly¹ [sɑʊθˈwestərli] *adv* : vers le sud-ouest

southwesterly² *adj* : du sud-ouest

southwestern [sɑʊθˈwestərn] → **southwest¹**

souvenir [ˌsuːvəˈnɪr, ˈsuːvəˌ-] *n* : souvenir *m*

sovereign¹ [ˈsɑvərən] *adj* : souverain

sovereign² *n* **1** MONARCH : souverain *m*, -raine *f* **2** : souverain *m* (pièce de monnaie)

sovereignty [ˈsɑvərənti] *n, pl* **-ties** : souveraineté *f*

Soviet [ˈsoːviˌɛt, ˈsɑ-, -viət] *adj* : soviétique

sow¹ ['so:] *vt* **sowed; sown** ['so:n] *or* **sowed; sowing** : semer
sow² ['saʊ] *n* : truie *f*
sox → sock²
soybean ['sɔɪˌbi:n] *n* : graine *f* de soja
spa ['spɑ] *n* : station *f* thermale
space¹ ['speɪs] *vt* **spaced; spacing** *or* **to space out** : espacer, étaler, échelonner
space² *n* **1** *or* **outer space** : espace *m* **2** INTERVAL : espace *m* <in the space of a few days : en l'espace de quelques jours> **3** ROOM : place *f* <there's no more space : il n'y a plus de place> **4** : espace *f* (typographique)
spacecraft ['speɪsˌkræft] *n* : vaisseau *m* spatial
spaceflight ['speɪsˌflaɪt] *n* : vol *m* spatial
spaceman ['speɪsmən, -ˌmæn] *n, pl* **-men** [-mən, -ˌmen] : astronaute *mf*, cosmonaute *mf*
spaceship ['speɪsˌʃɪp] *n* : vaisseau *m* spatial
space shuttle *n* : navette *f* spatiale
space suit *n* : combinaison *f* spatiale
spacious ['speɪʃəs] *adj* : spacieux
spade¹ ['speɪd] *vt* **spaded; spading** : bêcher, pelleter
spade² *n* **1** SHOVEL : bêche *f*, pelle *f* **2** : pique *f* (aux cartes)
spaghetti [spə'geṭi] *n* : spaghetti *mpl*, spaghettis *mpl*
span¹ ['spæn] *vt* **spanned; spanning 1** CROSS : franchir, enjamber **2** ENCOMPASS : embrasser, comprendre
span² *n* **1** WIDTH : envergure *f*, portée *f*, travée *f* **2** DURATION : durée *f*
spangle ['spæŋgəl] *n* : paillette *f*
Spaniard ['spænjərd] *n* : Espagnol *m*, -gnole *f*
spaniel ['spænjəl] *n* : épagneul *m*
Spanish¹ ['spænɪʃ] *adj* : espagnol
Spanish² *n* **1** : espagnol *m* (langue) **2 the Spanish** : les Espagnols
spank ['spæŋk] *vt* : fesser
spanking¹ ['spæŋkɪŋ] *adj* BRISK : vif
spanking² *n* : fessée *f*
spanner ['spænər] *Brit* → **wrench² 3**
spar¹ ['spɑr] *vi* **sparred; sparring** : s'entraîner à la boxe
spar² *n* : espar *m*, verge *f Can*
spare¹ ['spɛr] *vt* **spared; sparing 1** SAVE : épargner <to spare s.o.'s life : épargner la vie de qqn> <to spare oneself the trouble of : s'épargner l'ennui de> **2** DISPENSE WITH : se passer de <we can't spare him : nous ne pouvons pas nous passer de lui> <can you spare me $10? : est-ce que tu as 10 $ à me passer?> **3 to spare no effort** : faire tout son possible
spare² *adj* **1** : de réserve **2** EXTRA, SURPLUS : de trop <a spare moment : un moment de libre> **3** LEAN : maigre
spare³ *n* **1** *or* **spare part** : pièce *f* de rechange **2** *or* **spare tire** : pneu *m* de rechange
sparing ['spɛrɪŋ] *adj* : économe
sparingly ['spɛrɪŋli] *adv* : avec modération, frugalement
spark¹ ['spɑrk] *vi* : émettre des étincelles — *vt* **1** PROVOKE : déclencher <to spark a dispute : déclencher une dispute> **2** AWAKEN : éveiller <to spark the curiosity of : éveiller la curiosité de>
spark² *n* : étincelle *f*
sparkle¹ ['sparkəl] *vi* **-kled; -kling 1** FLASH : étinceler, scintiller **2** EFFERVESCE : pétiller
sparkle² *n* : scintillement *m*, éclat *m*
sparkler ['sparklər] *n* : cierge *m* magique
spark plug *n* : bougie *f*
sparrow ['spɛro:] *n* : moineau *m*
sparse ['spɑrs] *adj* **sparser; -est** : clairsemé, épars
sparsely ['spɑrsli] *adv* : peu <sparsely furnished : peu meublé>
spasm ['spæzəm] *n* **1** : spasme *m* **2** FIT : accès *m*
spasmodic [spæz'mɑdɪk] *adj* **1** : spasmodique (se dit de la douleur, etc.) **2** SPORADIC : intermittent
spasmodically [spæz'mɑdɪkli] *adv* : par à-coups
spastic ['spæstɪk] *adj* : spasmodique, handicapé moteur
spat¹ ['spæt] → **spit¹**
spat² *n* **1** QUARREL : prise *f* de bec **2 spats** *npl* : guêtres *fpl*
spatial ['speɪʃəl] *adj* : spatial
spatter¹ ['spæṭər] *vt* : éclabousser — *vi* : crépiter, gicler
spatter² *n* : éclaboussure *f*
spatula ['spætʃələ] *n* : spatule *f*
spawn¹ ['spɔn] *vi* : frayer — *vt* GENERATE : engendrer
spawn² *n* : frai *m*
spay ['speɪ] *vt* : châtrer
speak ['spi:k] *v* **spoke** ['spo:k]; **spoken** ['spo:kən]; **speaking** *vi* **1** TALK : parler <to speak to s.o. : parler à qqn> <to speak well of : dire du bien de> <strictly speaking : à proprement parler> <so to speak : pour ainsi dire> **2 to speak out** : parler clairement **3 to speak out against** : s'élever contre **4 to speak up** : parler plus fort **5 to speak up for** : soutenir, défendre — *vt* **1** SAY : dire <she spoke her mind : elle a dit sa pensée> **2** : parler (une langue)
speaker ['spi:kər] *n* **1** : personne *f* qui parle **2** ORATOR : orateur *m*, -trice *f*; conférencier *m*, -cière *f* **3** LOUDSPEAKER : haut-parleur *m*, enceinte *f* acoustique (d'une chaîne stéréo)
spear¹ ['spɪr] *vt* : transpercer d'un coup de lance
spear² *n* : lance *f*
spearhead¹ ['spɪrˌhɛd] *vt* : être le fer de lance de, mener
spearhead² *n* : fer *m* de lance

spearmint ['spɪr,mɪnt] *n* : menthe *f* verte
special ['spɛʃəl] *adj* : spécial, particulier <nothing special : rien de particulier>
specialist ['spɛʃəlɪst] *n* : spécialiste *mf*
specialization [,spɛʃələ'zeɪʃən] *n* : spécialisation *f*
specialize ['spɛʃə,laɪz] *vi* **-ized; -izing** : se spécialiser
specially ['spɛʃəli] *adv* **1** PARTICULARLY : spécialement, particulièrement **2** SPECIFICALLY : exprès, spécialement
specialty ['spɛʃəlti] *n, pl* **-ties** : spécialité *f*
species ['spi:,ʃi:z, -,si:z] *ns & pl* : espèce *f*
specific [spɪ'sɪfɪk] *adj* **1** EXPLICIT : précis, explicite **2** : spécifique (en biologie, en médecine, etc.)
specifically [spɪ'sɪfɪkli] *adv* **1** EXPLICITLY : précisément, explicitement **2** PARTICULARLY : spécialement, en particulier
specification [,spɛsəfə'keɪʃən] *n* : spécification *f*
specify ['spɛsə,faɪ] *vt* **-fied; -fying** : spécifier
specimen ['spɛsəmən] *n* **1** SAMPLE : échantillon *m* **2** EXAMPLE : spécimen *m*, exemplaire *m*
speck ['spɛk] *n* **1** SPOT : tache *f* **2** BIT, TRACE : grain *m* <a speck of dust : un grain de poussière>
speckled ['spɛkəld] *adj* : tacheté, moucheté
spectacle ['spɛktɪkəl] *n* **1** : spectacle *m* **2 spectacles** *npl* GLASSES : lunettes *fpl*
spectacular [spɛk'tækjələr] *adj* : spectaculaire
spectator ['spɛk,teɪtər] *n* : spectateur *m*, -trice *f*
specter ['spɛktər] *n* : spectre *m*
spectrum ['spɛktrəm] *n, pl* **spectra** [-trə] *or* **spectrums 1** : spectre *m* <the visible spectrum : le spectre visible> **2** RANGE : gamme *f*
speculate ['spɛkjə,leɪt] *vi* **-lated; -lating** : spéculer
speculation [,spɛkjə'leɪʃən] *n* : conjectures *fpl*, spéculations *fpl*
speculative ['spɛkjə,leɪtɪv] *adj* : spéculatif
speculator ['spɛkjə,leɪtər] *n* : spéculateur *m*, -trice *f*
speech ['spi:tʃ] *n* **1** : parole *f* <to lose the power of speech : perdre la parole> **2** ADDRESS : discours *m*
speechless ['spi:tʃləs] *adj* : muet
speed[1] ['spi:d] *v* **sped** ['spɛd] *or* **speeded; speeding** *vi* **1** : aller à toute allure, aller à toute vitesse <he sped off : il est parti à toute allure> **2** : rouler trop vite (dans une voiture) <a ticket for speeding : une contravention pour excès de vitesse> — *vt or* **to speed up** : accélérer
speed[2] *n* **1** SWIFTNESS : vitesse *f* **2** VELOCITY : vélocité *f*
speedboat ['spi:d,bo:t] *n* : vedette *f* (rapide), hors-bord *m*
speed bump *n* : casse-vitesse *m*
speed limit *n* : limite *f* de vitesse
speedometer [spɪ'dɑmətər] *n* : compteur *m* de vitesse
speedup ['spi:d,ʌp] *n* : accélération *f*
speedy ['spi:di] *adj* **speedier; -est** : rapide — **speedily** [-dəli] *adv*
spell[1] ['spɛl] *vt* **1** : écrire, orthographier <how do you spell it? : comment est-ce que ça s'écrit?> **2** MEAN : signifier <that could spell trouble : on pourrait avoir des ennuis> **3** RELIEVE : relayer, relever — *vi* : connaître l'orthographe
spell[2] *n* **1** TURN : tour *m* **2** PERIOD : période *f* **3** ENCHANTMENT : charme *m*, sortilège *m*
spellbound ['spɛl,baʊnd] *adj* : captivé
speller ['spɛlər] *n* **to be a good speller** : être forte en orthographe
spelling ['spɛlɪŋ] *n* : orthographe *f*
spell out *vt* **1** : épeler (les lettres d'un mot) **2** EXPLAIN : expliquer
spend ['spɛnd] *vt* **spent** ['spɛnt]; **spending 1** : dépenser (de l'argent) **2** PASS : passer <to spend time on : passer son temps à>
spendthrift ['spɛnd,θrɪft] *n* : dépensier *m*, -sière *f*
sperm ['spərm] *n, pl* **sperm** *or* **sperms** : sperme *m*
spew ['spju:] *vt or* **to spew out** : vomir (de la fumée, de la lave, etc.) — *vi* : jaillir, gicler
sphere ['sfɪr] *n* : sphère *f*
spherical ['sfɪrɪkəl, 'sfɛr-] *adj* : sphérique
spice[1] ['spaɪs] *vt* **spiced; spicing 1** SEASON : épicer **2** *or* **to spice up** : pimenter
spice[2] *n* **1** : épice *f* **2** EXCITEMENT, PIQUANCY : piquant *m*
spick-and-span ['spɪkəndˈspæn] *adj* : impeccable
spicy ['spaɪsi] *adj* **spicier; -est 1** SPICED : épicé **2** RACY : pimenté, piquant
spider ['spaɪdər] *n* : araignée *f*
spigot ['spɪgət, -kət] *n* : robinet *m*
spike[1] ['spaɪk] *vt* **spiked; spiking 1** FASTEN : clouer **2** PIERCE : transpercer **3** : corser (de l'alcool)
spike[2] *n* **1** NAIL : (gros) clou *m* **2** : pointe *f* (d'une chaussure), épi *m* (des cheveux), épine *f* (d'un cactus)
spill[1] ['spɪl] *vt* **1** : renverser, répandre <to spill blood : verser du sang> **2** DIVULGE : révéler — *vi* : se répandre
spill[2] *n* **1** SPILLING : renversement *m* **2** FALL : chute *f*, culbute *f*
spin[1] ['spɪn] *v* **spun** ['spʌn]; **spinning** *vi* **1** ROTATE : tourner, tournoyer <my head is spinning : j'ai la tête qui tourne> **2** : filer (avec un rouet) —

vt **1** : faire tourner **2** : filer <to spin wool : filer de la laine>

spin² *n* : tour *m* <to go for a spin : faire un petit tour>

spinach ['spɪnɪtʃ] *n* : épinards *mpl*

spinal column ['spaɪnəl] *adj* BACKBONE : colonne *f* vertébrale

spinal cord *n* : moelle *f* épinière

spindle ['spɪndəl] *n* **1** : fuseau *m*, broche *f* (pour filer) **2** AXLE : axe *m*

spindly ['spɪndlɪ] *adj* : grêle (se dit des jambes), étiolé (se dit d'une plante)

spine ['spaɪn] *n* **1** BACKBONE : colonne *f* vertébrale **2** QUILL : piquant *m* (d'un animal) **3** THORN : épine *f* **4** : dos *m* (d'un livre)

spineless ['spaɪnləs] *adj* **1** : sans piquants, sans épines **2** INVERTEBRATE : invertébré **3** COWARDLY, WEAK : lâche, mou

spinet ['spɪnət] *n* : épinette *f*

spinster ['spɪnʃtər] *n* : célibataire *f*, vieille fille *f*

spiny ['spaɪnɪ] *adj* **spinier; -est** : couvert de piquants (se dit des animaux), épineux (se dit des plantes)

spiral¹ ['spaɪrəl] *vi* **-raled** *or* **-ralled; -raling** *or* **-ralling** : aller en spirale

spiral² *adj* : spirale, en spirale <spiral staircase : escalier en spirale>

spiral³ *n* : spirale *f*

spire ['spaɪr] *n* : flèche *f*

spirit¹ ['spɪrət] *vt* **to spirit away** : faire disparaître

spirit² *n* **1** : esprit *m* <in the spirit of friendship : dans l'esprit de l'amitié> **2** GHOST : esprit *m*, spectre *m*, fantôme *m* **3** ENTHUSIASM, VIVACITY : entrain *m* **4 spirits** *npl* MOOD : humeur *f* <to be in good spirits : être de bonne humeur> **5 spirits** *npl* LIQUORS : spiritueux *mpl*

spirited ['spɪrəṭəd] *adj* : animé, vif

spiritless ['spɪrətləs] *adj* : sans vie, sans entrain

spiritual¹ ['spɪrɪtʃʊəl, -tʃəl] *adj* : spirituel — **spiritually** *adv*

spiritual² *n* : spiritual *m*

spiritualism ['spɪrɪtʃʊəˌlɪzəm, -tʃə-] *n* : spiritisme *m*

spirituality [ˌspɪrɪtʃʊˈæləṭɪ] *n* : spiritualité *f*

spit¹ ['spɪt] *v* **spit** *or* **spat** ['spæt]; **spitting** : cracher

spit² *n* **1** SALIVA : crachat *m*, salive *f* **2** ROTISSERIE : broche *f* **3** POINT : pointe *f* (de terre)

spite¹ ['spaɪt] *vt* **spited; spiting** : contrarier

spite² *n* **1** : dépit *m*, malveillance *f* **2 in spite of** : en dépit de, malgré

spiteful ['spaɪtfəl] *adj* : malveillant

spittle ['spɪṭəl] *n* : salive *f*

splash¹ ['splæʃ] *vt* : éclabousser — *vi* **1** *or* **to splash about** : barboter, patauger **2 to splash through** : traverser en faisant des éclaboussures

splash² *n* **1** SPLASHING : éclaboussement *m* **2** SQUIRT : goutte *f* **3** SPOT : tache *f*, éclaboussure *f* **4 to make a splash** : faire sensation

splatter ['splætər] → **spatter**

splay ['spleɪ] *vt* : écarter (des doigts, des jambes) — *vi* : s'écarter

spleen ['spliːn] *n* **1** : rate *f* (organe) **2** ANGER, SPITE : mauvaise humeur *f*

splendid ['splendəd] *adj* : splendide, superbe

splendidly ['splendədlɪ] *adv* : superbement, magnifiquement

splendor *or Brit* **splendour** ['splendər] *n* : splendeur *f*

splice¹ ['splaɪs] *vt* **spliced; splicing** : épisser, coller

splice² *n* : épissure *f*

splint ['splɪnt] *n* : attelle *f*

splinter¹ ['splɪntər] *vt* : briser en éclats — *vi* : se briser en éclats

splinter² *n* : éclat *m*

split¹ ['splɪt] *v* **split; splitting** *vt* **1** CLEAVE : fendre, couper <to split wood : fendre du bois> **2** TEAR : déchirer **3** SHARE : partager **4** DIVIDE : diviser — *vi* **1** CRACK : se fendre **2** TEAR : se déchirer **3** DIVIDE, SEPARATE : se diviser

split² *n* **1** CRACK : fente *f* **2** TEAR : déchirure *f* **3** DIVISION : division *f*, scission *f*

splurge¹ ['splərdʒ] *v* **splurged; splurging** *vi* : faire des folles dépenses — *vt* : dépenser

splurge² *n* : folles dépenses *fpl*

spoil ['spɔɪl] *v* **spoiled** ['spɔɪld, 'spɔɪlt] *or* **spoilt** ['spɔɪlt]; **spoiling 1** PILLAGE : piller **2** RUIN : gâcher, abîmer **3** PAMPER : gâter — *vi* : se gâter, s'abîmer

spoils ['spɔɪlz] *npl* PLUNDER : butin *m*, dépouilles *fpl*

spoke¹ → **speak**

spoke² ['spoːk] *n* : rayon *m*

spoken → **speak**

spokesman ['spoːksmən] *n, pl* **-men** [-mən, -ˌmen] : porte-parole *m*

spokeswoman ['spoːksˌwʊmən] *n, pl* **-women** [-ˌwɪmən] : porte-parole *m*

sponge¹ ['spʌnʤ] *vt* **sponged; sponging** : éponger

sponge² *n* : éponge *f*

spongy ['spʌnʤɪ] *adj* **spongier; -est** : spongieux

sponsor¹ ['spɑnʃər] *vt* : patronner, sponsoriser

sponsor² *n* : sponsor *m*, commanditaire *m*, parrain *m*

sponsorship ['spɑnʃərˌʃɪp] *n* : parrainage *m*, patronage *m*

spontaneity [ˌspɑntəˈneiəṭi, -ˈneɪ-] *n* : spontanéité *f*

spontaneous [spɑnˈteɪnɪəs] *adj* : spontané — **spontaneously** *adv*

spoof ['spuːf] *n* : parodie *f*

spook¹ ['spuːk] *vt* : faire peur à

spook² *n* : fantôme *m*

spooky ['spu:ki] *adj* **spookier; -est** : sinistre, qui fait froid dans le dos
spool ['spu:l] *n* : bobine *f*
spoon[1] ['spu:n] *vt* : servir, verser (avec une cuillère)
spoon[2] *n* : cuillère *f*, cuiller *f*
spoonful ['spu:n,fʊl] *n* : cuillerée *f*
spoor ['spʊr, 'spɔr] *n* : piste *f*, trace *f*
sporadic [spə'rædɪk] *adj* : sporadique — **sporadically** [-dɪkli] *adv*
spore ['spɔr] *n* : spore *f*
sport[1] ['spɔrt] *vi* FROLIC : s'amuser — *vt* WEAR : arborer, porter
sport[2] *n* **1** : sport *m* **2** JEST : jeu *m* **3 to be a good sport** : être beau joueur
sportsman ['spɔrtsmən] *n, pl* **-men** [-mən, -,mɛn] : sportif *m*
sportsmanship ['spɔrtsmən,ʃɪp] *n* : sportivité *f*
sportswoman ['spɔrts,wʊmən] *n, pl* **-women** [-,wɪmən] : sportive *f*
sporty ['spɔrṭi] *adj* **sportier; -est** : sportif
spot[1] ['spɑt] *v* **spotted; spotting** *vt* **1** STAIN : tacher **2** NOTICE : apercevoir, repérer <to spot an error : apercevoir une erreur> — *vi* : se tacher
spot[2] *adj* : fait au hasard <a spot check : un contrôle au hasard>
spot[3] *n* **1** STAIN : tache *f* **2** DOT : pois *m* **3** PREDICAMENT : situation *f* difficile **4** PLACE : endroit *m*, lieu *m*, <on the spot : sur place>
spotless ['spɑtləs] *adj* : sans tache
spotlessly ['spɑtləsli] *adv* **spotlessly clean** : impeccable, reluisant de propreté
spotlight[1] ['spɑt,laɪt] *vt* **-lighted** *or* **-lit** [-,lɪt]; **-lighting 1** LIGHT : diriger les projecteurs sur **2** HIGHLIGHT : mettre en lumière
spotlight[2] *n* **1** : projecteur *m*, spot *m* **2 to be in the spotlight** : être en vedette
spotty ['spɑṭi] *adj* **spottier; -est 1** SPOTTED : tacheté **2** UNEVEN : irrégulier
spouse ['spaʊs] *n* : époux *m*, épouse *f*
spout[1] ['spaʊt] *vt* **1** : faire jaillir **2** DECLAIM : déclamer — *vi* : jaillir
spout[2] *n* **1** : bec *m* verseur **2** STREAM : jet *m*
sprain[1] ['spreɪn] *vt* : faire une entorse à, fouler
sprain[2] *n* : entorse *f*, foulure *f*
sprawl[1] ['prɔl] *vi* **1** : être affalé (se dit d'une personne) **2** SPREAD : s'étaler
sprawl[2] *n* **1** : position *f* affalée **2** EXTENT, SPREAD : étendue *f*
spray[1] ['spreɪ] *vt* : atomiser, vaporiser, arroser (un jardin)
spray[2] *n* **1** BOUQUET : bouquet *m* **2** MIST : gouttelettes *fpl* fines, embruns *mpl* (de la mer) **3** ATOMIZER : atomiseur *m*, vaporisateur *m*, bombe *f*
spray gun *n* : pistolet *m* (à peinture)
spread[1] ['spred] *v* **spread; spreading** *vt* **1** *or* **to spread out** : étendre **2** : étaler, tartiner <to spread butter : étaler du beurre> **3** DISSEMINATE : répandre, propager — *vi* **1** EXTEND : s'étendre, s'étaler **2** : se répandre, se propager <the disease is spreading : la maladie se répand>
spread[2] *n* **1** EXTENT, RANGE : éventail *m*, envergure *f* **2** → **bedspread 3** PASTE : pâte *f* à tartiner <cheese spread : fromage à tartiner> **4** PROPAGATION : propagation *f*
spreadsheet ['spred,ʃi:t] *n* : tableur *m*
spree ['spri] *n* : fête *f* <to go on a spending spree : faire de folles dépenses>
sprig ['sprɪg] *n* : brin *m*
sprightly ['spraɪtli] *adj* **sprightlier; -est** : vif, alerte
spring[1] ['sprɪŋ] *v* **sprang** ['spræŋ] *or* **sprung** ['spraŋ]; **sprung; springing** *vi* **1** LEAP : sauter, bondir **2** (*indicating rapid movement*) <to spring to s.o.'s aid : se précipiter pour aider qqn> <tears sprang to my eyes : les larmes me sont montées aux yeux> **3 to spring up** : surgir — *vt* **1** RELEASE : déclencher, faire jouer <to spring a trap : faire jouer un piège> **2** : annoncer (une nouvelle, etc.), poser (une question) <to spring the news on s.o. : surprendre qqn avec les nouvelles> **3 to spring a leak** : commencer à fuir
spring[2] *n* **1** SOURCE : source *f* **2** : printemps *m* (saison) <in the spring : au printemps> **3** COIL : ressort *m* **4** LEAP : bond *m*, saut *m* **5** RESILIENCE : élasticité *f*
springboard ['sprɪŋ,bɔrd] *n* : tremplin *m*
springtime ['sprɪŋ,taɪm] *n* : printemps *m*
springy ['sprɪŋi] *adj* **springier; -est 1** RESILIENT : élastique **2** LIVELY : énergique
sprinkle[1] ['sprɪŋkəl] *v* **-kled; -kling** *vt* **1** : saupoudrer <sprinkle with oregano : saupoudrez d'oregano> **2** : asperger, arroser <to sprinkle the lawn : arroser la pelouse> — *vi* : tomber des gouttes (se dit de la pluie)
sprinkle[2] *n* **1** PINCH : pincée *f*, petite quantité *f* **2** RAIN : petite pluie *f*
sprinkler ['sprɪŋkələr] *n* : arroseur *m*
sprint[1] ['sprɪnt] *vi* : sprinter
sprint[2] *n* : sprint *m*
sprite ['spraɪt] *n* **1** : lutin *m* **2** *or* **water sprite** : naïade *f*
sprocket ['prɑkət] *n* : pignon *m*
sprout[1] ['spraʊt] *v* : pousser
sprout[2] *n* : pousse *f*
spruce[1] ['spru:s] *vt* **spruced; sprucing 1** *or* **to spruce up** : faire beau (un enfant, etc.), astiquer (une maison) **2 to spruce oneself up** : se faire beau
spruce[2] *adj* **sprucer; sprucest** : pimpant
spruce[3] *n* : sapinette *f*, épicéa *m* *France*, épinette *f* *Can*
spry ['spraɪ] *adj* **sprier** *or* **spryer** ['spraɪər]; **spriest** *or* **spryest** ['spraɪəst] : alerte, plein d'entrain

spun → spin¹

spunk ['spʌŋk] *n* : courage *m*, cran *m* *fam*

spunky ['spʌŋki] *adj* **spunkier; -est** : courageux

spur¹ ['spər] *vt* **spurred; spurring** *or* **to spur on** : éperonner (un cheval), aiguillonner (une personne)

spur² *n* **1** : éperon *m* **2** STIMULUS : stimulant *m*, aiguillon *m* **3** RIDGE : éperon *m*, contrefort *m* **4 on the spur of the moment** : sur le coup, sur l'impulsion du moment

spurious ['spjʊriəs] *adj* : faux, fallacieux

spurn ['spərn] *vt* : rejeter

spurt¹ ['spərt] *vt* SQUIRT : faire gicler — *vi* : jaillir, gicler

spurt² *n* **1** BURST : sursaut *m*, bourrée *f* *Can* <a spurt of enthusiasm : un sursaut d'enthousiasme> **2** GUSH, JET : jaillissement *m*

sputter¹ ['spʌtər] *vi* **1** JABBER, MUTTER : bredouiller **2** : grésiller, crépiter (se dit d'un feu), tousser (se dit d'un moteur)

sputter² *n* **1** JABBERING, MUTTERING : bredouillement *m* **2** : crépitement *m* (d'un feu), raté *m* (d'un moteur)

spy¹ ['spaɪ] *v* **spied; spying** *vt* SEE : apercevoir, discerner — *vi* **1** : faire de l'espionnage **2 to spy on s.o.** : espionner qqn

spy² *n* : espion *m*

squab ['skwɑb] *n, pl* **squabs** *or* **squab** : pigeonneau *m*

squabble¹ ['skwɑbəl] *vi* **-bled; -bling** : se disputer, se chamailler

squabble² *n* : dispute *f*, querelle *f*

squad ['skwɑd] *n* : équipe *f*, peloton *m* (militaire), brigade *f* (de police)

squadron ['skwɑdrən] *n* : escadron *m*

squalid ['skwɑlɪd] *adj* : sordide

squall ['skwɔl] *n* : bourrasque *f* <snow squall : bourrasque de neige>

squalor ['skwɑlər] *n* : conditions *fpl* sordides, misère *f*

squander ['skwɑndər] *vt* : gaspiller

square¹ ['skwær] *v* **squared; squaring** *vt* **1** : équarrir, carrer **2** : carrer (en mathématiques) **3** *or* **to square away** SETTLE : régler — *vi* **to square with** : cadrer avec, coïncider avec

square² *adj* **squarer; -est 1** : carré <a square house : une maison carrée> **2** RIGHT-ANGLED : à angle droit **3** : carré (en mathématiques) <a square meter : un mètre carré> **4** HONEST : honnête

square³ *n* **1** : équerre *f* (instrument) **2** : carré *m* <to fold into squares : plier en forme de carré> **3** : place *f* (d'une ville) **4** : carré *m* (en mathématiques)

squarely ['skwærli] *adv* **1** EXACTLY : carrément **2** HONESTLY : honnêtement

square root *n* : racine *f* carrée

squash¹ ['skwɑʃ, 'skwɔʃ] *vt* **1** CRUSH : écraser, aplatir, écrapoutir *Can* **2** SUPPRESS : remettre à sa place (une personne), réduire à néant (des espoirs), réprimer (une révolte) — *vi* : s'écraser

squash² *n, pl* **squashes** *or* **squash 1** : courge *f* **2** *or* **squash rackets** : squash *m*

squat¹ ['skwɑt] *vi* **squatted; squatting 1** CROUCH : s'accroupir **2 to squat in** : squatter (un bâtiment, etc.)

squat² *adj* **squatter; squattest** : trapu

squat³ *n* **1** : position *f* accroupie **2** : squat *m* (dans un bâtiment)

squaw ['skwɔ] *n* : squaw *f*

squawk¹ ['skwɔk] *vi* : criailler

squawk² *n* : criaillement *m* (d'un oiseau), cri *m* rauque (d'une personne)

squeak¹ ['skwiːk] *vi* : grincer, couiner

squeak² *n* : grincement *m*, couinement *m*

squeaky ['skwiːki] *adj* **squeakier; -est** : grinçant, aigu <a squeaky voice : une voix aiguë> <squeaky shoes : des chaussures qui craquent>

squeal¹ ['skwiːl] *vi* **1** : pousser des cris aigus (se dit des personnes et des animaux), crisser (se dit des pneus), grincer (se dit des freins) **2 to squeal on** : dénoncer

squeal² *n* **1** : cri *m* aigu **2** SCREECH : crissement *m* (de pneus), grincement *m* (de freins)

squeamish ['skwiːmɪʃ] *adj* : délicat, sensible, facilement dégoûté

squeeze¹ ['skwiːz] *v* **squeezed; squeezing** *vt* **1** PRESS : presser, serrer **2** EXTRACT : exprimer **3** EXTORT : extorquer, soutirer — *vi* : se glisser <he squeezed into the room : il s'est glissé dans la salle>

squeeze² *n* : pression *f*, resserrement *m*

squelch ['skwɛlʧ] *vt* : écraser, étouffer, aplatir

squid ['skwɪd] *n, pl* **squid** *or* **squids** : calmar *m*, encornet *m*

squint¹ ['skwɪnt] *vi* : plisser les yeux, loucher

squint² *adj* *or* **squint-eyed** : qui louche

squint³ *n* : strabisme *m*

squire ['skwaɪr] *n* **1** LANDOWNER : propriétaire *mf* **2** : écuyer *m* (d'un chevalier)

squirm ['skwərm] *vi* : se tortiller

squirrel ['skwərəl] *n* : écureuil *m*

squirt¹ ['skwərt] *vt* : faire gicler — *vi* : gicler

squirt² *n* : jet *m*, giclée *f*

Sri Lankan¹ [ˌsriːˈlæŋkən] *adj* : sri lankais

Sri Lankan² *n* : Sri Lankais *m*, -kaise *f*

stab¹ ['stæb] *vt* **stabbed; stabbing 1** KNIFE : poignarder **2** STICK : piquer

stab² *n* **1** : coup *m* de couteau **2 to take a stab at** : essayer, tenter

stability [stə'bɪləti] *n, pl* **-ties** : stabilité *f*
stabilize ['steɪbə,laɪz] *v* **-lized; -lizing** *vt* : stabiliser — *vi* : se stabiliser
stable[1] ['steɪbəl] *vt* **-bled; -bling** : mettre à l'écurie
stable[2] *adj* **-bler; -blest 1** FIXED, STEADY : stable, fixe **2** LASTING : stable, durable **3** : équilibré (en psychologie), stationnaire (en médicine)
stable[3] *n* : écurie *f*
staccato [stə'kɑtoː] *adj* : staccato
stack[1] ['stæk] *vi* **1** PILE : entasser, empiler, mettre en meule (se dit du foin) **2** FILL : remplir <the table was stacked with books : la table était remplie de livres>
stack[2] *n* **1** PILE : tas *m*, pile *f* **2** → **smokestack**
stadium ['steɪdiəm] *n, pl* **-dia** [-diə] *or* **-diums** : stade *m*
staff[1] ['stæf] *vt* : pourvoir en personnel
staff[2] *n, pl* **staffs** ['stæfs, 'stævz] *or* **staves** ['stævz, 'steɪvz] **1** STICK : bâton *m* **2** *pl* **staffs** PERSONNEL : personnel *m* **3** : portée *f* (en musique)
stag[1] ['stæg] *adv* : seul <to go stag : aller sans compagne>
stag[2] *adj* : entre hommes
stag[3] *n, pl* **stags** *or* **stag** : cerf *m*
stage[1] ['steɪdʒ] *vt* **staged; staging 1** ORGANIZE : organiser (une manifestation, etc.) **2** : monter, mettre en scène (une pièce de théâtre)
stage[2] *n* **1** PLATFORM : estrade *f*, scène *f* (au théâtre) **2** PHASE : stade *m*, phase *f*, étape *f* **3 the stage** : le théâtre
stagecoach ['steɪdʒ,koːtʃ] *n* : diligence *f*
stagger[1] ['stægər] *vi* TOTTER : tituber, chanceler — *vt* **1** SPACE OUT : échelonner, étaler **2** AMAZE : stupéfier
stagger[2] *n* : pas *m* chancelant
staggering ['stægərɪŋ] *adj* : stupéfiant
stagnant ['stægnənt] *adj* : stagnant
stagnate ['stæg,neɪt] *vi* **-nated; -nating** : stagner
stagnation [stæg'neɪʃən] *n* : stagnation *f*
staid ['steɪd] *adj* : collet monté, guindé
stain[1] ['steɪn] *vt* **1** DISCOLOR : tacher **2** DYE : teindre, teinter **3** SULLY : souiller — *vi* : se tacher
stain[2] *n* **1** SPOT : tache *f* **2** DYE : teinture *f* **3** BLEMISH : souillure *f*
stainless ['steɪnləs] *adj* : inoxydable <stainless steel : acier inoxydable>
stair ['stær] *n* **1** STEP : marche *f* **2 stairs** *npl* : escalier *m*
staircase ['stær,keɪs] *n* : escalier *m*
stairway ['stær,weɪ] *n* : escalier *m*
stairwell ['steɪr,wel] *n* : cage *f* d'escalier
stake[1] ['steɪk] *vt* **staked; staking 1** *or* **to stake out** : jalonner, marquer (une ligne frontière), délimiter (un espace) **2** BET : miser, parier **3 to stake a claim to** : établir son droit à, revendiquer
stake[2] *n* **1** POST : poteau *m*, pieu *m*, piquet *m* **2** BET : enjeu *m* <to be at stake : être en jeu> **3** INTEREST, SHARE : intérêt *m*, part *f*
stalactite [stə'læk,taɪt] *n* : stalactite *f*
stalagmite [stə'læg,maɪt] *n* : stalagmite *f*
stale ['steɪl] *adj* **staler; stalest** : vieux, rassis (se dit du pain), éventé (se dit d'une boisson)
stalemate ['steɪl,meɪt] *n* : pat *m*, impasse *f*
stalk[1] ['stɔk] *vt* **1** TRACK : traquer **2** PROWL : rôder dans <to stalk the countryside : rôder dans les campagnes> — *vi* : marcher fièrement <to stalk out : sortir d'un air hautain>
stalk[2] *n* : tige *f* (d'une plante)
stall[1] ['stɔl] *vt* **1** : faire caler (un moteur) **2** DELAY : retarder, bloquer — *vi* **1** : caler (se dit d'un moteur) **2** *or* **to stall for time** : essayer de gagner du temps
stall[2] *n* **1** : stalle *f* (d'un cheval, etc.) **2** BOOTH : stand *m*, étal *m*
stallion ['stæljən] *n* : étalon *m*
stalwart ['stɔlwərt] *adj* **1** STRONG : robuste <a stalwart supporter : un supporter inconditionnel> **2** BRAVE : vaillant, brave
stamen ['steɪmən] *n* : étamine *f*
stamina ['stæmənə] *n* : vigueur *f*, résistance *f*
stammer[1] ['stæmər] *v* : bégayer
stammer[2] *n* : bégaiement *m*
stamp[1] ['stæmp] *vt* **1** IMPRESS, IMPRINT : frapper, estamper (le métal, etc.) **2** : timbrer, affranchir (le courrier), viser (un passeport) **3 to stamp one's feet** : taper des pieds
stamp[2] *n* **1** IMPRESSION, MARK : cachet *m*, tampon *m* **2** *or* **postage stamp** : timbre *m* **3** → **rubber stamp 4** HALLMARK, TRAIT : empreinte *f*, marque *f* <to bear the stamp of s.o. : avoir la marque de qqn>
stampede[1] [stæm'piːd] *vi* **-peded; -peding** : s'enfuir à la débandade
stampede[2] *n* : débandade *f*
stance ['stænts] *n* : position *f*
stanch ['stɔntʃ, 'stɑntʃ] *vt* : étancher
stand[1] ['stænd] *v* **stood** ['stʊd]; **standing** *vi* **1** : être debout **2** *or* **to stand up** : se mettre debout, se lever **3** (*indicating a specified position or location*) <the machines are standing idle : les machines restent inutilisées> **4** (*referring to an opinion*) <where does he stand on the matter? : quelle est sa position là-dessus?> **5** BE : être, se trouver <the house stands on a hill : la maison se trouve sur une colline> **6** CONTINUE : rester valable <the offer stands : l'offre reste valable> **7** REMAIN, REST : reposer <the statue stands on a pedestal : la statue repose sur un piédestal> — *vt* **1** PLACE, SET

: mettre **2** ENDURE, TOLERATE : supporter <I can't stand it any longer : je ne peux plus supporter ça>

stand[2] *n* **1** RESISTANCE : résistance *f* (militaire) **2** BOOTH, STALL : stand *m*, étal *m* **3** BASE : pied *m*, piédestal *m* **4** GROVE : bosquet *m* (d' arbres) **5** POSITION : position *f* **6 stands** *npl* GRANDSTAND : tribune *f*

standard[1] ['stændərd] *adj* **1** ESTABLISHED : établi <standard English : l'anglais correct> **2** NORMAL : normal, standard **3** CLASSIC : classique <a standard work : une œuvre classique>

standard[2] *n* **1** BANNER : étendard *m* **2** CRITERION, NORM : critère *m*, norme *f*, étalon *m* <the gold standard : l'étalon-or> **3** LEVEL : niveau *m* <standard of living : niveau de vie> **4** SUPPORT : pied *m*, poteau *m*

standardize ['stændərˌdaɪz] *vt* **-ized; -izing** : standardiser

standard time *n* : heure *f* légale

stand by *vt* **1** SUPPORT : soutenir **2** MAINTAIN : tenir, s'en tenir à (une promesse, une opinion, etc.) — *vi* **1** : rester là <to stand by and do nothing : rester là sans rien faire> **2** : être prêt, se tenir prêt

stand for *vt* **1** REPRESENT : représenter **2** PERMIT, TOLERATE : supporter, tolérer

standing ['stændɪŋ] *n* **1** POSITION, RANK : position *f*, standing *m*, cote *f* **2** DURATION : durée *f* <of long standing : de longue date>

stand out *vi* **1** : ressortir, se détacher <she stands out from her colleagues : elle se détache de ses collègues> **2 to stand out against** RESIST : s'opposer à

standpoint ['stændˌpɔɪnt] *n* : point *m* de vue

standstill ['stændˌstɪl] *n* **1** STOP : arrêt *m* <to come to a standstill : s'arrêter> **2** DEADLOCK : impasse *f*

stand up *vt* **1** : mettre debout **2 to stand s.o. up** : poser un lapin à qqn *fam* — *vi* **1** ENDURE : tenir **2 to stand up for** : défendre **3 to stand up to** : résister à

stank → **stink**[1]

stanza ['stænzə] *n* : strophe *f*

staple[1] ['steɪpəl] *vt* **-pled; -pling** : agrafer

staple[2] *adj* : principal, de base <staple foods : denrées de base>

staple[3] *n* : agrafe *f*

stapler ['steɪplər] *n* : agrafeuse *f*

star[1] ['stɑr] *v* **starred; starring** *vt* **1** : marquer d'une étoile ou d'un astérisque **2** FEATURE : avoir pour vedette — *vi* : être la vedette

star[2] *n* **1** : étoile *f* **2** : vedette *f*, étoile *f*, star *f* <a movie star : une vedette de cinéma>

starboard ['stɑrbərd] *n* : tribord *m*

starch[1] ['stɑrtʃ] *vt* : amidonner

starch[2] *n* **1** : amidon *m* **2 starches** *npl* : féculents *mpl* (aliments)

starchy ['stɑrtʃi] *adj* **starchier; -est** : féculent <a starchy diet : un régime riche en féculents>

stardom ['stɑrdəm] *n* : célébrité *f*

stare[1] ['stɛr] *vi* **stared; staring** : regarder fixement

stare[2] *n* : regard *m* fixe

starfish ['stɑrˌfɪʃ] *n* : étoile *f* de mer

stark[1] ['stɑrk] *adv* : complètement <stark raving mad : complètement fou> <stark naked : tout nu>

stark[2] *adj* **1** ABSOLUTE : absolu, pur **2** BARREN, DESOLATE : désolé, dénudé **3** BLUNT, HARSH : cru, catégorique, dur <the stark realities : les dures réalités>

starlight ['stɑrˌlaɪt] *n* : lumière *f* des étoiles

starling ['stɑrlɪŋ] *n* : étourneau *m*

starry ['stɑri] *adj* **starrier; -est** : étoilé

start[1] ['stɑrt] *vi* **1** JUMP : sursauter **2** BEGIN : commencer **3** DEPART : partir (en voyage, etc.) **4** : démarrer (se dit d'un moteur) — *vt* **1** BEGIN : commencer, se mettre à **2** CAUSE : provoquer **3** ESTABLISH : établir, créer <to start a business : établir une entreprise> **4** : mettre en marche, démarrer <to start the car : démarrer la voiture>

start[2] *n* **1** JUMP : sursaut *m* **2** BEGINNING : commencement *m*, début *m* <to get an early start : commencer tôt>

starter ['stɑrtər] *n* **1** ENTRANT : partant *m*, -tante *f*; participant *m*, -pante *f* (aux sports) **2** APPETIZER : hors-d'œuvre *m*, entrée *f* **3** : démarreur *m* (d'un véhicule)

startle ['stɑrtəl] *vt* **-tled; -tling** : surprendre, alarmer, faire tressaillir

starve ['stɑrv] *v* **starved; starving** *vi* : mourir de faim — *vt* : affamer, faire mourir de faim

stash ['stæʃ] *vt* : cacher, mettre de côté

state[1] ['steɪt] *vt* **stated; stating 1** REPORT : exposer, déclarer **2** SPECIFY : spécifier, indiquer <as stated above : ainsi qu'il est indiqué plus haut>

state[2] *n* **1** CONDITION : état *m* **2** NATION : état *m*, nation *f* **3** : état *m* (d'un pays) **4 the States** : les États-Unis

stateliness ['steɪtlinəs] *n* : majesté *f*, grandeur *f*

stately ['steɪtli] *adj* **statelier; -est** : majestueux, imposant

statement ['steɪtmənt] *n* **1** DECLARATION : déclaration *f* **2** *or* **bank statement** : relevé *m* de compte

stateroom ['steɪtˌru:m] *n* : cabine *f* de luxe

statesman ['steɪtsmən] *n, pl* **-men** [-mən, -ˌmɛn] : homme *m* d'État

static[1] ['stæɪɪk] *adj* : statique

static[2] *n* **1** : parasites *mpl* (de radio, de télévision) **2** *or* **static electricity** : électricité *f* statique
station[1] ['steɪʃən] *vt* : poster, placer
station[2] *n* **1** : gare *f* (de train), station *f* (de métro) **2** RANK, STANDING : rang *m* **3** : station *f* (de radio), chaîne *f* (de télévision) **4 police station** : poste *m* de police **5 fire station** : caserne *f* de pompiers **6 → service station**
stationary ['steɪʃə,nɛri] *adj* **1** IMMOBILE : stationnaire, immobile **2** UNCHANGING : fixe
stationery ['steɪʃə,nɛri] *n* : papeterie *f*, papier *m* à lettres
station wagon *n* : familiale *f*
statistic [stə'tɪstɪk] *n* : statistique *f*
statistical [stə'tɪstɪkəl] *adj* : statistique, de statistique
statue ['stæ,tʃu:] *n* : statue *f*
statuesque [,stæt'ʃʊ'ɛsk] *adj* : sculptural
statuette [,stæt'ʃʊ'ɛt] *n* : statuette *f*
stature ['stætʃər] *n* **1** HEIGHT : stature *f*, taille *f* **2** CALIBRE, STATUS : stature *f*, envergure *f*, calibre *m*
status ['steɪtəs, 'stæ-] *n* **1** : situation *f* (légale), statut *m* <marital status : situation de famille> **2** PRESTIGE : prestige *m*, standing *m* **3** POSITION : position *f*, rang *m* (social)
statute ['stæ,tʃu:t] *n* : loi *f*, règle *f*
staunch ['stɔntʃ] *adj* : dévoué, loyal <a staunch supporter : un fidèle>
staunchly ['stɔntʃli] *adv* : avec dévouement, loyalement
stave[1] ['steɪv] *vt* **staved** *or* **stove** ['stov]; **staving 1 to stave in** : enfoncer **2 to stave off** : écarter, tromper (la faim, etc.), éviter
stave[2] *n* : douve *f* (d'un tonneau)
staves → staff[2]
stay[1] ['steɪ] *vi* **1** REMAIN : rester, demeurer <to stay in : rester à la maison> <he stays in the city : il demeure en ville> **2** CONTINUE : rester <to stay awake : rester éveillé> **3** LODGE : loger — *vt* **1** HALT : arrêter, surseoir à (en droit) **2 to stay the course** : tenir jusqu'au bout
stay[2] *n* **1** SOJOURN : séjour *m* **2** SUPPORT : soutien *m*
stead ['stɛd] *n* **1** : place *f* <she went in his stead : elle est allée à sa place> **2 to stand s.o. in good stead** : être utile à qqn
steadfast ['stɛd,fæst] *adj* **1** IMMOVABLE : fixe **2** FIRM : ferme, résolu **3** LOYAL : dévoué <a steadfast friend : un fidèle ami>
steadily ['stɛdəli] *adv* **1** CONSTANTLY : régulièrement, sans arrêt **2** FIRMLY : fermement **3** FIXEDLY : fixement **4** GRADUALLY : progressivement
steady[1] ['stɛdi] *v* **steadied; steadying** *vt* : stabiliser <she steadied herself : elle a retrouvé son équilibre> — *vi* : se stabiliser
steady[2] *adj* **steadier; -est 1** FIRM, SURE : ferme, sûr **2** REGULAR, CONSTANT : régulier, constant **3** CALM : calme **4** STABLE : stable
steak ['steɪk] *n* : bifteck *m*, steak *m*
steal ['sti:l] *v* **stole** ['sto:l]; **stolen** ['stolən]; **stealing** *vt* : voler — *vi* **1** : voler <thou shalt not steal : tu ne voleras point> **2** CREEP, SLIP : se glisser **3 to steal away** : s'esquiver
stealth ['stɛlθ] *n* : discrétion *f* <by stealth : furtivement>
stealthily ['stɛlθəli] *adv* : furtivement
stealthy ['stɛlθi] *adj* **stealthier; -est** : furtif
steam[1] ['sti:m] *vi* **1** : fumer **2 to steam ahead** : avancer — *vt* **1** : cuire à la vapeur **2 to steam open** : décacheter à la vapeur
steam[2] *n* : vapeur *f*
steamboat ['sti:m,bo:t] → **steamship**
steam engine *n* : moteur *m* à vapeur
steamroller ['sti:m,ro:lər] *n* : rouleau *m* compresseur
steamship ['sti:m,ʃɪp] *n* : paquebot *m*, navire *m* à vapeur
steamy ['sti:mi] *adj* **steamier; -est 1** : plein de vapeur, embué **2** EROTIC : érotique
steed ['sti:d] *n* : coursier *m*
steel[1] ['sti:l] *vt* **1 to steel oneself** : s'armer de courage **2 to steel oneself against** : se cuirasser contre
steel[2] *adj* : en acier, d'acier
steel[3] *n* : acier *m*
steely ['sti:li] *adj* **steelier; -est** : d'acier <a steely gaze : un regard d'acier> <steely determination : une volonté de fer>
steep[1] ['sti:p] *vt* : tremper, faire tremper
steep[2] *adj* **1** : raide, à pic **2** SHARP : fort <a steep increase : une forte augmentation> **3** EXCESSIVE : excessif <steep prices : des prix exorbitants>
steeple ['sti:pəl] *n* : clocher *m*, flèche *f*
steeplechase ['sti:pəl,tʃeɪs] *n* : course *f* d'obstacles
steeply ['sti:pli] *adv* **1** : à pic, abruptement, en pente raide **2 to rise steeply** : monter en flèche (se dit des prix)
steer[1] ['stɪr] *vt* **1** : conduire (une voiture), gouverner (un navire) **2** GUIDE : diriger, guider
steer[2] *n* : bœuf *m*
steering wheel *n* : volant *m*
stein ['staɪn] *n* : chope *f*
stellar ['stɛlər] *adj* **1** : stellaire **2** SUPERB : superbe
stem[1] ['stɛm] *v* **stemmed; stemming** *vt* : arrêter, contenir, endiguer <to stem the tide : endiguer le flot> — *vi* **to stem from** : provenir de
stem[2] *n* : tige *f* (d'une plante)
stench ['stɛntʃ] *n* : puanteur *f*
stencil[1] ['stɛnɪsəl] *vt* **-ciled** *or* **-cilled; -ciling** *or* **-cilling** : dessiner au pochoir

stencil[2] *n* : pochoir *m*
stenographer [stə'nɑgrəfər] *n* : sténographe *mf*
stenographic [ˌstenə'græfɪk] *adj* : sténographique
stenography [stə'nɑgrəfi] *n* : sténographie *f*
step[1] ['step] *vi* **stepped; stepping 1** : aller, marcher <step this way, please : par ici, s'il vous plaît> <he stepped outside : il est sorti> **2 to step on** : marcher sur
step[2] *n* **1** : pas *m* <step by step : pas à pas> <with a quick step : d'un pas rapide> **2** STAIR : marche *f* **3** RUNG : échelon *m*, barreau *m* **4** MEASURE : mesure *f*, disposition *f* <to take steps : prendre des mesures> **5** MOVE : pas *m* <a step in the right direction : un pas dans la bonne voie>
stepbrother ['stepˌbrʌðər] *n* : beau-frère *m*
stepdaughter ['stepˌdɔṭər] *n* : belle-fille *f*
stepfather ['stepˌfɑðər, -ˌfa-] *n* : beau-père *m*
stepladder ['stepˌlædər] *n* : escabeau *m*
stepmother ['stepˌmʌðər] *n* : belle-mère *f*
steppe ['step] *n* : steppe *f*
stepson ['stepˌsʌn] *n* : beau-fils *m*
step up *vt* INCREASE : intensifier
stereo[1] ['sterio:, 'stɪr-] *adj* : stéréo
stereo[2] *n, pl* **stereos 1** : stéréo *f* <in stereo : en stéréo> **2** *or* **stereo system** : chaîne *f* stéréo
stereophonic [ˌsterio'fɑnɪk, ˌstɪr-] *adj* : stéréophonique
stereotype[1] ['sterioˌtaɪp, 'stɪr-] *vt* **-typed; -typing** : stéréotyper
stereotype[2] *n* : stéréotype *m*
sterile ['sterəl] *adj* : stérile
sterility [stə'rɪlə̰ṭi] *n* : stérilité *f*
sterilization [ˌsterələ'zeɪʃən] *n* : stérilisation *f*
sterilize ['sterəˌlaɪz] *vt* **-ized; -izing** : stériliser
sterling ['stərlɪŋ] *adj* **1** : fin (se dit de l'argent) **2** EXCELLENT : excellent, de premier ordre
stern[1] ['stərn] *adj* : sévère — **sternly** *adv*
stern[2] *n* : arrière *m*, poupe *f*
sternness ['stərnnəs] *n* : sévérité *f*
sternum ['stərnəm] *n, pl* **sternums** *or* **sterna** [-nə] : sternum *m*
stethoscope ['steθəˌskoːp] *n* : stéthoscope *m*
stevedore ['stiːvəˌdor] *n* : docker *m*
stew[1] ['stuː, 'stjuː] *vt* : cuire, faire cuire (en ragoût) — *vi* **1** : cuire (se dit des fruits), cuire en ragoût, mijoter (se dit de la viande) **2** FRET : être dans tous ses états
stew[2] *n* **1** : ragoût *m* **2 to be in a stew** : être dans tous ses états
steward ['stuːərd, 'stjuː-] *n* **1** MANAGER : régisseur *m* (d'un domaine) **2** : steward *m* (d'un avion, etc.)
stewardess ['stuːərdəs, 'stjuː-] *n* : hôtesse *f*
stick[1] ['stɪk] *v* **stuck** ['stʌk]; **sticking** *vt* **1** STAB : piquer, enfoncer **2** AFFIX : coller **3** PUT : mettre, insérer <to stick one's head out the window : passer la tête par la fenêtre> **4 to stick out** : sortir, tirer (la langue) **5 to stick up** ROB : dévaliser — *vi* **1** ADHERE : coller **2** : se planter, s'enfoncer <the nail stuck in my hand : je me suis planté le clou dans la main> **3** JAM : se coincer, se bloquer **4 to stick around** : attendre **5 to stick out** PROTRUDE : faire saillie, dépasser (d'une superficie), ressortir (d'un contexte) **6 to stick to** : ne pas abandonner <to stick to one's guns : ne pas en démordre> **7 to stick up** : se dresser (se dit des cheveux, etc.), dépasser, sortir **8 to stick with** : rester avec
stick[2] *n* **1** BRANCH : bâton *m* **2** : crosse *f* (aux sports) **3** → **walking stick**
sticker ['stɪkər] *n* : autocollant *m*, collant *m Can*
stickler ['stɪklər] *n* : personne *f* exigeante <to be a stickler for : être à cheval sur>
sticky ['stɪki] *adj* **stickier; -est 1** : collant **2** MUGGY : humide **3** DIFFICULT : difficile
stiff ['stɪf] *adj* **1** RIGID : rigide, raide <a stiff dough : une pâte ferme> **2** : ankylosé, courbaturé <stiff muscles : des muscles courbaturés> **3** FORMAL : guindé **4** STRONG : fort (se dit du vent, etc.) **5** DIFFICULT, SEVERE : sévère, difficile
stiffen ['stɪfən] *vt* **1** STRENGTHEN : renforcer **2** THICKEN : donner de la consistance à (des œufs, une sauce) **3** : courbaturer (les muscles) — *vi* **1** HARDEN : se durcir, se raidir **2** THICKEN : devenir ferme, épaisser **3** : s'ankyloser (se dit des articulations, etc.)
stiffly ['stɪfli] *adv* **1** RIGIDLY : avec raideur, rigidement **2** COLDLY : avec froideur
stiffness ['stɪfnəs] *n* **1** RIGIDITY : raideur *f*, rigidité *f* **2** COLDNESS : froideur *f* **3** SEVERITY : sévérité *f*
stifle ['staɪfəl] *vt* **-fled; -fling** SMOTHER, SUPPRESS : étouffer, réprimer, retenir <to stifle a yawn : retenir un bâillement>
stigma ['stɪgmə] *n, pl* **stigmata** [stɪg'mɑtə, 'stɪgmə̰tə] *or* **stigmas** : stigmate *m*
stigmatize ['stɪgmaˌtaɪz] *vt* **-tized; -tizing** : stigmatiser
stile ['staɪl] *n* : échalier *m*
stiletto [stə'leṭoː] *n, pl* **-tos** *or* **-toes 1** : stylet *m* **2** *or* **stiletto heel** : talon *m* aiguille

still¹ ['stɪl] *vt* CALM : calmer — *vi* : se calmer
still² *adv* **1** MOTIONLESSLY : sans bouger <sit still! : reste tranquille!> **2** : encore, toujours <she still lives there : elle y habite toujours> <it's still the same : c'est toujours pareille> **3** : quand même, tout de même <he still has doubts : il a quand même des doutes> <I still prefer that you stay : je préfère tout de même que tu restes>
still³ *adj* **1** MOTIONLESS : immobile **2** CALM : tranquille **3** SILENT : silencieux
still⁴ *n* **1** SILENCE : silence *m* **2** : alambic *m* (pour distiller l'alcool)
stillborn ['stɪlˌbɔrn] *adj* : mort-né
stillness ['stɪlnəs] *n* : calme *m*, tranquillité *f*
stilt ['stɪlt] *n* : échasse *f*
stilted ['stɪltəd] *adj* : guindé
stimulant ['stɪmjələnt] *n* : stimulant *m*
stimulate ['stɪmjəˌleɪt] *vt* **-lated; -lating** : stimuler
stimulation [ˌstɪmjə'leɪʃən] *n* **1** STIMULATING : stimulation *f* **2** STIMULUS : stimulant *m*
stimulus ['stɪmjələs] *n, pl* **-li** [-ˌlaɪ] **1** : stimulus *m* (en physiologie) **2** INCENTIVE : stimulant *m*
sting¹ ['stɪŋ] *v* **stung** ['stʌŋ]; **stinging** *vt* **1** : piquer <a bee stung him : une abeille l'a piqué> **2** HURT : blesser, piquer au vif
sting² *n* : piqûre *f*
stinger ['stɪŋər] *n* : dard *m*, aiguillon *m*
stinginess ['stɪndʒɪnəs] *n* : avarice *f*, pingrerie *f*
stingy ['stɪndʒi] *adj* **stingier; -est** : avare, pingre
stink¹ ['stɪŋk] *vi* **stank** ['stæŋk] *or* **stunk** ['stʌŋk]; **stunk; stinking** : puer
stink² *n* : puanteur *f*
stint¹ ['stɪnt] *vt* DEPRIVE : priver — *vi* **to stint on** : lésiner sur
stint² *n* : période *f* (de travail)
stipend ['staɪˌpend, -pənd] *n* : traitement *m*
stipulate ['stɪpjəˌleɪt] *vt* **-lated; -lating** : stipuler
stipulation [ˌstɪpjə'leɪʃən] *n* : stipulation *f*
stir¹ ['stər] *v* **stirred; stirring** *vt* **1** AGITATE : agiter **2** MIX : remuer **3** INCITE : inciter **4** MOVE : émouvoir (une personne), exciter (la curiosité, etc.) **5** *or* **to stir up** PROVOKE : susciter (un sentiment, etc.), provoquer (la colère, etc.) — *vi* : bouger
stir² *n* **1** MOTION : mouvement *m* **2** COMMOTION : agitation *f*
stirrup ['stərəp, 'stɪr-] *n* : étrier *m*
stitch¹ ['stɪtʃ] *vt* : coudre, suturer (en médecine) — *vi* : coudre
stitch² *n* **1** : point *m* **2** TWINGE : point *m* (au côté)
stock¹ ['stɑk] *vt* **1** SUPPLY : approvisionner **2** SELL : avoir pour vendre — *vi* **to stock up** : s'approvisionner
stock² *n* **1** SUPPLY : réserve *f*, stock *m* <to be out of stock : être épuisé> **2** LIVESTOCK : bétail *m* **3** ANCESTRY : lignée *f*, souche *f* **4** BROTH : bouillon *m* **5** STANDING : cote *f* **6 stocks** *npl* SECURITIES : actions *fpl*, valeurs *fpl* **7 to take stock** : évaluer, faire le point
stockade [stɑ'keɪd] *n* : palissade *f*
stockbroker ['stɑkˌbroːkər] *n* : agent *m* de change
stockholder ['stɑkˌhoːldər] *n* : actionnaire *mf*
stocking ['stɑkɪŋ] *n* : bas *m* <a pair of stockings : une paire de bas>
stock market *n* : Bourse *f*
stockpile¹ ['stɑkˌpaɪl] *vt* **-piled; -piling** : stocker, amasser
stockpile² *n* : stock *m*, réserve *f*
stocky ['stɑki] *adj* **stockier; -est** : trapu
stockyard ['stɑkˌjɑrd] *n* : parc *m* à bétail
stodgy ['stɑdʒi] *adj* **stodgier; -est 1** DULL : ennuyeux, lourd **2** HIDEBOUND : borné, rigide
stoic¹ ['stoːɪk] *or* **stoical** [-ɪkəl] *adj* : stoïque — **stoically** [-ɪkli] *adv*
stoic² *n* : stoïque *mf*
stoicism ['stoːəˌsɪzəm] *n* : stoïcisme *m*
stoke ['stoːk] *vt* **stoked; stoking** : alimenter, entretenir
stole¹ → **steal**
stole² ['stoːl] *n* : étole *f*
stolen → **steal**
stolid ['stɑlɪd] *adj* : impassible — **stolidly** *adv*
stomach¹ ['stʌmɪk] *vt* : supporter, tolérer
stomach² *n* **1** : estomac *m* **2** BELLY : ventre *m* <to have a fat stomach : avoir du ventre> **3** DESIRE : envie *f* <to have no stomach for : n'avoir aucune envie de>
stomachache ['stʌmɪkˌeɪk] *n* : mal *m* de ventre
stomp ['stɑmp, 'stɔmp] *vt* : piétiner — *vi* : marcher d'un pas lourd
stone¹ ['stoːn] *vt* **stoned; stoning** : jeter des pierres sur
stone² *n* **1** : pierre *f* **2** PIT : noyau *m* (d'un fruit)
Stone Age *n* : âge *m* de pierre
stony ['stoːni] *adj* **stonier; -est 1** ROCKY : pierreux **2** UNFEELING : insensible, glacial <a stony stare : un regard glacial>
stood → **stand¹**
stool ['stuːl] *n* **1** SEAT : tabouret *m*, escabeau *m* **2** FOOTSTOOL : tabouret *m* **3** FECES : selle *f*
stoop¹ ['stuːp] *vi* **1** CROUCH : se baisser, se pencher **2 to stoop to** : s'abaisser à

stoop[2] *n* **1** : dos *m* voûté <to have a stoop : avoir le dos voûté> **2** PORCH, VERANDA : porche *m*, véranda *f*

stop[1] ['stɑp] *v* **stopped; stopping** *vt* **1** *or* **to stop up** PLUG : boucher **2** PREVENT : empêcher <she stopped me from leaving : elle m'a empêché de partir> **3** HALT : arrêter, stopper **4** CEASE : arrêter, cesser <he stopped talking : il a cessé de parler> — *vi* **1** HALT : s'arrêter, stopper **2** CEASE : cesser, s'arrêter <the rain won't stop : la pluie n'arrête pas> **3** STAY : rester **4 to stop by** : passer <stop by at my house : passe chez moi>

stop[2] *n* **1** STOPPER : bouchon *m* **2** HALT : arrêt *m*, halte *f* <to come to a stop : s'arrêter> <to put a stop to : mettre fin à> **3** : arrêt *m* <bus stop : arrêt de bus>

stopgap ['stɑpˌgæp] *n* : bouche-trou *m*

stoplight ['stɑpˌlaɪt] *n* : feu *m* rouge

stoppage ['stɑpɪdʒ] *n* : arrêt *m*, suspension *f* <work stoppage : arrêt de travail>

stopper ['stɑpər] *n* : bouchon *m*

storage ['stɔrɪdʒ] *n* **1** : emmagasinage *m*, entreposage *m* **2** : stockage *m* (des données)

storage battery *n* : accumulateur *m*

store[1] ['stɔr] *vt* **stored; storing** : emmagasiner, entreposer

store[2] *n* **1** RESERVE, SUPPLY : réserve *f*, provision *f* **2** SHOP : magasin *m* **3 to have in store** : avoir en réserve

storehouse ['stɔrˌhaʊs] *n* : entrepôt *m*

storekeeper ['stɔrˌkiːpər] *n* : commerçant *m*, -çante *f*

storeroom ['stɔrˌruːm, -ˌrʊm] *n* : magasin *m*, réserve *f*

stork ['stɔrk] *n* : cigogne *f*

storm[1] ['stɔrm] *vi* **1** : faire rage (se dit d'une tempête) **2** RAGE : tempêter, fulminer <to storm out : sortir comme un ouragan, partir furieux> — *vt* ATTACK : prendre d'assaut

storm[2] *n* **1** : orage *m*, tempête *f* **2** UPROAR : tempête *f* <a storm of abuse : une tempête d'injures>

stormy ['stɔrmi] *adj* **stormier; -est** : orageux

story ['stori] *n, pl* **stories 1** NARRATIVE : histoire *f* **2** ACCOUNT : article *m* (en journalisme) **3** PLOT : intrigue *f*, scénario *m* **4** FLOOR : étage *m*

stout ['staʊt] *adj* **1** FIRM, RESOLUTE : ferme, résolu **2** STURDY : solide **3** FAT : corpulent, gros

stove[1] ['stoːv] *n* : poêle *m* (pour chauffer), cuisinière *f* (pour cuisiner)

stove[2] → **stave**[1]

stow ['stoː] *vt* **1** STORE : ranger, emmagasiner, arrimer (la cargaison) **2** LOAD : remplir — *vi* **to stow away** : s'embarquer clandestinement

straddle ['strædəl] *vt* **-dled; -dling 1** : enfourcher (un cheval, une bicyclette) **2** SPAN : enjamber

straggle ['strægəl] *vi* **-gled; -gling** : traîner

straggler ['strægələr] *n* : traînard *m*, -narde *f*

straight[1] ['streɪt] *adv* **1** : droit <go straight, then turn right : allez tout droit, puis tournez à droite> **2** HONESTLY : honnêtement <to go straight : vivre honnêtement> **3** CLEARLY : clairement **4** DIRECTLY : directement **5** FRANKLY : franchement

straight[2] *adj* **1** : droit, d'aplomb (se dit d'un objet vertical), raide (se dit des cheveux), sec (se dit d'une boisson alcoolisée) **2** HONEST, JUST : honnête, juste **3** NEAT, ORDERLY : en ordre **4** DIRECT : direct

straightaway [ˌstreɪtəˈweɪ] *adv* : immédiatement

straighten ['streɪtən] *vt* **1** : redresser, rendre droit **2** *or* **to straighten up** ORGANIZE : mettre en ordre, ranger

straightforward [streɪtˈfɔrwərd] *adj* **1** FRANK : franc, honnête **2** CLEAR, PRECISE : clair, simple

strain[1] ['streɪn] *vt* **1** EXERT, STRETCH : tendre, forcer <to strain oneself : faire un grand effort> **2** FILTER : filtrer **3** INJURE : froisser, fatiguer <to strain a muscle : se froisser un muscle>

strain[2] *n* **1** LINEAGE : lignée *f* **2** EFFORT : effort *m* **3** VARIETY : variété *f* **4** STRESS : stress *m*, tension *f* **5** SPRAIN : foulure *f* **6 strains** *npl* TUNE : air *m*, accents *mpl*

strainer ['streɪnər] *n* : passoire *f*

strait ['streɪt] *n* **1** : détroit *m* **2 straits** *npl* DISTRESS : gêne *f* <in dire straits : aux abois>

straitened ['streɪtənd] *adj* **in straitened circumstances** : dans le besoin

strand[1] ['strænd] *vt* **1** : échouer **2 to be left stranded** : être abandonné

strand[2] *n* **1** : toron *m*, brin *m* <a strand of hair : un cheveu> **2** BEACH : plage *f*

strange ['streɪndʒ] *adj* **stranger; -est 1** QUEER, UNUSUAL : étrange, bizarre **2** UNFAMILIAR : inconnu

strangely ['streɪndʒli] *adv* : étrangement, bizarrement <to behave strangely : se comporter de façon étrange> <strangely, he didn't call : curieusement, il n'a pas téléphoné>

strangeness ['streɪndʒnəs] *n* : étrangeté *f*

stranger ['streɪndʒər] *n* : étranger *m*, -gère *f*

strangle ['stræŋgəl] *vt* **-gled; -gling** : étrangler

strangler ['stræŋglər] *n* : étrangleur *m*, -gleuse *f*

strap[1] ['stræp] *vt* **strapped; strapping 1** FASTEN : attacher **2** FLOG : fouetter

strap[2] *n* **1** : courroie *f*, sangle *f* **2 shoulder strap** : bretelle *f*

strapless ['stræpləs] *n* : sans bretelles
strapping ['stræpɪŋ] *adj* : robuste, costaud *fam*
stratagem ['strætəˌdʒəm, -ˌdʒɛm] *n* : stratagème *m*
strategic [strə'ti:dʒɪk] *adj* : stratégique
strategy ['strætəˌdʒi] *n, pl* **-gies** : stratégie *f*
stratified ['strætəˌfaɪd] *adj* : stratifié
stratosphere ['strætəˌsfɪr] *n* : stratosphère *f*
stratum ['streɪtəm, 'stræ-] *n, pl* **strata** [-tə] : strate *f*, couche *f*
straw ['strɔ] *n* : paille *f*
strawberry ['strɔˌbɛri] *n, pl* **-ries** : fraise *f*
stray[1] ['streɪ] *vi* **1** WANDER : errer, s'égarer <the cattle strayed away : les bœufs se sont égarés> **2** : errer, vagabonder (se dit des pensées, des yeux, etc.) <to stray from the point : s'éloigner du sujet>
stray[2] *adj* : errant, perdu
stray[3] *n* : animal *m* errant
streak[1] ['stri:k] *vt* : rayer <blue streaked with grey : bleu rayé de gris> — *vi* DASH, RUSH : s'élancer
streak[2] *n* **1** LINE : raie *f*, bande *f*, mèche *f* (dans les cheveux) **2** TENDENCY : tendance *f*, côté *m* <a stubborn streak : un côté obstiné> **3** TRACE : trace *f* **4** PERIOD : période *f*, passe *f* <a streak of luck : une bonne passe>
stream[1] ['stri:m] *vi* : couler, ruisseler <tears streamed from his eyes : des larmes ruisselaient de ses yeux> — *vt* : ruisseler de <to stream blood : ruisseler de sang>
stream[2] *n* **1** BROOK : ruisseau *m* **2** FLOW : courant *m*, flot *m*
streamer ['stri:mər] *n* **1** BANNER : banderole *f* **2** RIBBON : serpentin *m* (de papier)
streamlined ['stri:mˌlaɪnd] *adj* **1** : aérodynamique **2** EFFICIENT : rationalisé, dégraissé
street ['stri:t] *n* : rue *f*
streetcar ['stri:tˌkɑr] *n* : tramway *m*
strength ['strɛŋkθ] *n* **1** POWER : force *f*, puissance *f* **2** SOLIDITY : solidité *f* **3** INTENSITY : intensité *f*, force *f* **4** NUMBERS : effectif *m* <we're at full strength : nos effectifs sont au complet> **5** : qualité *f* <strengths and weaknesses : qualités et faiblesses>
strengthen ['strɛŋkθən] *vt* **1** : fortifier (les muscles, etc.), raffermir **2** REINFORCE : renforcer **3** INTENSIFY : intensifier
strenuous ['strɛnjuəs] *adj* **1** VIGOROUS : vigoureux, énergique **2** ARDUOUS : ardu, fatiguant
strenuously ['strɛnjuəsli] *adv* : vigoureusement
stress[1] ['stres] *vt* **1** : charger, mettre sous tension **2** EMPHASIZE : mettre l'accent sur, souligner, accentuer (en prononciation) **3 to stress out** : stresser
stress[2] *n* **1** PRESSURE : contrainte *f*, effort *m* **2** EMPHASIS : accent *m*, insistance *f* **3** TENSION : tension *f*, stress *m*
stressful ['stresfəl] *adj* : stressant
stretch[1] ['stretʃ] *vt* **1** EXTEND : tendre, allonger **2** : distendre, étirer (les muscles) **3** PROLONG : prolonger, faire durer **4 to stretch the truth** : exagérer — *vi* : s'étirer
stretch[2] *n* **1** STRETCHING : extension *f*, étirement *m* (des muscles) **2** ELASTICITY : élasticité *f* **3** EXPANSE : étendue *f* <the home stretch : la ligne d'arrivée> **4** PERIOD : période *f* (de temps)
stretcher ['stretʃər] *n* : civière *f*, brancard *m*
strew ['stru:] *vt* **strewed; strewed** *or* **strewn** ['stru:n]; **strewing 1** SCATTER : répandre **2 to be strewn with** : être jonché de
stricken ['strɪkən] *adj* **stricken with** : affligé de (une émotion), atteint de (une maladie)
strict ['strɪkt] *adj* : strict — **strictly** *adv*
strictness ['strɪktli] *n* **1** SEVERITY : sévérité *f* **2** RIGOR : rigueur *f*
stricture ['strɪktʃər] *n* **1** NARROWING : rétrécissement *m* (en médecine) **2** CENSURE : critique *f* (sévère) **3** RESTRICTION : contrainte *f*
stride[1] ['straɪd] *vi* **strode** ['stro:d]; **stridden** ['strɪdən]; **striding** : marcher à grands pas, marcher à grandes enjambées
stride[2] *n* **1** : grand pas *m*, enjambée *f* **2 to make great strides** : faire de grands progrès
strident ['straɪdənt] *adj* : strident
strife ['straɪf] *n* : conflit *m*, lutte *f*
strike[1] ['straɪk] *v* **struck** ['strʌk]; **struck; striking** *vt* **1** HIT : frapper **2** DELETE : rayer **3** COIN, MINT : frapper **4** : sonner (l'heure) **5** AFFLICT : frapper <he was stricken with a fever : il a eu une poussée de fièvre> **6** IMPRESS : impressionner <her voice struck me : sa voix m'a impressionné> <it struck him as funny : ça lui a paru drôle> **7** : frotter (une allumette) **8** FIND : trouver, découvrir (de l'or, du pétrole) **9** ADOPT : adopter, prendre (une pose, une attitude) — *vi* **1** HIT : frapper **2** ATTACK : attaquer **3** *or* **to go on strike** : faire grève
strike[2] *n* **1** BLOW : coup *m* **2** : grève *f* <to be on strike : faire grève> **3** ATTACK : attaque *f* **4** : prise *f* *Can* (au baseball)
strikebreaker ['straɪkˌbreɪkər] *n* : briseur *m*, -seuse *f* de grève, jaune *mf*
strike out *vi* **1** GO : aller, partir **2** : retirer *Can* (au baseball)
striker ['straɪkər] *n* : gréviste *mf*; piqueteur *m*, -teuse *f*

strike up *vt* START : commencer
striking ['straɪkɪŋ] *adj* : frappant, saisissant <a striking beauty : une beauté frappante>
strikingly ['straɪkɪŋli] *adv* : de manière frappante, remarquablement
string[1] ['strɪŋ] *vt* **strung** ['strʌŋ]; **stringing 1** : mettre des cordes à, monter (une guitare, etc.) **2** : enfiler (des perles) **3** HANG : suspendre
string[2] *n* **1** CORD : ficelle *f*, cordon *m* **2** SERIES : suite *f* **3 strings** *npl* : cordes *fpl* (d'un orchestre)
string bean *n* : haricot *m* vert
stringent ['strɪndʒənt] *adj* : rigoureux, strict
stringy ['strɪŋi] *adj* **stringier; -est** : fibreux, filandreux (se dit des viandes, des légumes, etc.)
strip[1] ['strɪp] *v* **stripped; stripping** *vt* **1** REMOVE : enlever **2** UNDRESS : déshabiller — *vi* : se déshabiller
strip[2] *n* : bande *f* <a strip of land : une bande de terre>
stripe[1] ['straɪp] *vt* **striped** ['straɪpt]; **striping** : marquer avec rayures
stripe[2] *n* **1** : rayure *f*, bande *f* **2** CHEVRON : chevron *m*, galon *m*
striped ['straɪpt, 'straɪpəd] *adj* : rayé, à rayures
strive ['straɪv] *vi* **strove** ['stro:v]; **striven** ['strɪvən] *or* **strived; striving 1** to **strive for** : lutter pour **2 to strive to** : s'efforcer de
strode → stride[1]
stroke[1] ['stro:k] *vt* **stroked; stroking** : caresser
stroke[2] *n* **1** MOVEMENT : coup *m* <stroke of luck : coup de chance> **2** *or* **brush stroke** : trait *m* (de pinceau) **3** : attaque *f* (en médecine)
stroll[1] ['stro:l] *vi* : se promener
stroll[2] *n* : promenade *f*, petit tour *m*
stroller ['stro:lər] *n* : poussette *f* (pour enfants), carrosse *m Can*
strong ['strɔŋ] *adj* **1** : fort **2** HEALTHY : robuste, en forme **3** ZEALOUS : acharné, fervent
stronghold ['strɔŋho:ld] *n* : forteresse *f*, bastion *m* <a cultural stronghold : un bastion de la culture>
strongly ['strɔŋli] *adv* **1** POWERFULLY : fortement **2** STURDILY : solidement **3** INTENSELY : intensément **4** WHOLEHEARTEDLY : vivement, fermement
struck → strike[1]
structural ['strʌktʃərəl] *adj* : structural, de construction
structure[1] ['strʌktʃər] *vt* **-tured; -turing** : structurer
structure[2] *n* **1** BUILDING : construction *f* **2** ARRANGEMENT, FRAMEWORK : structure *f*
struggle[1] ['strʌgəl] *vi* **-gled; -gling 1** CONTEND : lutter, se débattre **2** : faire avec difficulté <she struggled forward : elle s'est avancée avec difficulté>
struggle[2] *n* : lutte *f*
strum ['strʌm] *v* **strummed; strumming** *vt* : gratter de — *vi* **to strum on** : gratter sur
strung → string[1]
strut[1] ['strʌt] *vi* **strutted; strutting** : se pavaner
strut[2] *n* **1** SWAGGER : démarche *f* arrogante **2** SUPPORT : étai *m*, support *m*
strychnine ['strɪkˌnaɪn, -nən, -ˌni:n] *n* : strychnine *f*
stub[1] ['stʌb] *vt* **stubbed; stubbing 1 to stub one's toe** : se cogner le doigt de pied **2 to stub out** : écraser
stub[2] *n* : mégot *m* (de cigarette), bout *m* (de crayon, etc.), talon *m* (de chèque)
stubble ['stʌbəl] *n* **1** : chaume *m* (de plantes) **2** : barbe *f* de plusieurs jours
stubborn ['stʌbərn] *adj* **1** OBSTINATE : obstiné, têtu **2** PERSISTENT : tenace
stubbornly ['stʌbərnli] *adv* : obstinément, de façon têtue
stubbornness ['stʌbərnnəs] *n* : entêtement *m*
stubby ['stʌbi] **stubbier; -est** *adj* : gros et court, trapu (se dit d'une personne) <stubby fingers : doigts épais>
stucco ['stʌko:] *n, pl* **stuccos** *or* **stuccoes** : stuc *m*
stuck → stick[1]
stuck-up ['stʌkˈʌp] *adj* : bêcheur, prétentieux, snob
stud[1] ['stʌd] *vt* **studded; studding** : clouter
stud[2] *n* **1** *or* **stud horse** : étalon *m* **2** UPRIGHT : montant *m* **3** HOBNAIL : caboche *f* **4** *or* **collar stud** : bouton *m* de col
student ['stu:dənt, 'stju:-] *n* : étudiant *m*, -diante *f*
studied ['stʌdi:d] *adj* : étudié, calculé, recherché
studio ['stu:diˌo:, 'stju:-] *n, pl* **-dios** : studio *m*, atelier *m* (d'un artist, etc.)
studious ['stu:diəs, 'stju:-] *adj* **1** : studieux **2** DELIBERATE : étudié, délibéré
studiously ['stu:diəsli, 'stju:-] *adv* : délibérément
study[1] ['stʌdi] *v* **studied; studying** *vt* **1** : étudier, faire des études de **2** EXAMINE : examiner — *vi* : étudier, faire ses études
study[2] *n, pl* **studies 1** : étude *f* **2** OFFICE : bureau *m*, cabinet *m* de travail
stuff[1] ['stʌf] *vt* **1** FILL : rembourrer (un meuble, etc.), empailler (en taxidermie), farcir (en cuisine) **2** SHOVE : fourrer <I stuffed it in my pocket : je l'ai fourré dans ma poche>
stuff[2] *n* **1** POSSESSIONS : affaires *fpl*, choses *fpl* **2** ESSENCE : essence *f*, étoffe *f* **3** SUBSTANCE : substance *f*, matière *f* <some sticky stuff : une

substance collante> <she knows her stuff : elle s'y connaît>

stuffing [ˈstʌfɪŋ] *n* **1** FILLING, PADDING : rembourrage *m*, bourrure *f Can* **2** : farce *f* (en cuisine)

stuffy [ˈstʌfi] *adj* **stuffier; -est 1** CLOSE : mal aéré **2** BLOCKED : bouché (se dit du nez) **3** STODGY : ennuyeux

stumble[1] [ˈstʌmbəl] *vi* **-bled; -bling 1** TRIP : trébucher **2 to stumble across** *or* **to stumble upon** : tomber sur

stumble[2] *n* : trébuchement *m*

stump[1] [ˈstʌmp] *vt* BAFFLE : déconcerter, laisser perplexe

stump[2] *n* **1** : bout *m*, moignon *m* (d'un membre) **2** *or* **tree stump** : souche *f*

stun [ˈstʌn] *vt* **stunned; stunning 1** : assommer (avec un coup) **2** ASTONISH : étonner, stupéfier

stung → sting[1]

stunk → stink[1]

stunning [ˈstʌnɪŋ] *adj* **1** ASTONISHING : épatant **2** STRIKING : ravissant, sensationnel

stunt[1] [ˈstʌnt] *vt* : retarder <to stunt s.o.'s growth : retarder la croissance de qqn>

stunt[2] *n* **1** : cascade *f*, acrobatie *f* **2** *or* **publicity stunt** : coup *m* de publicité

stupefy [ˈstuːpəˌfaɪ, ˈstjuː-] *vt* **-fied; -fying 1** : abrutir (avec des drogues, etc.) **2** AMAZE : stupéfier, abasourdir

stupendous [stuˈpendəs, stjuː-] *adj* : prodigieux, extraordinaire — **stupendously** *adv*

stupid [ˈstuːpəd, ˈstjuː-] *adj* **1** IDIOTIC, SILLY : idiot, bête **2** DULL, OBTUSE : stupide, bête, nounoune *Can*

stupidity [stuˈpidəṭi, stjuː-] *n, pl* **-ties** : stupidité *f*, bêtise *f*

stupidly [ˈstuːpədli, ˈstjuː-] *adv* : stupidement

stupor [ˈstuːpər, ˈstjuː-] *n* : stupeur *f*

sturdily [ˈstərdəli] *adv* : solidement

sturdiness [ˈstərdinəs] *n* : solidité *f*, robustesse *f*

sturdy [ˈstərdi] *adj* **sturdier; -est** : solide, robuste

sturgeon [ˈstərdʒən] *n* : esturgeon *m*

stutter[1] [ˈstʌṭər] *v* : bégayer

stutter[2] *n* : bégaiement *m*

sty [ˈstaɪ] *n* **1** *pl* **sties** PIGPEN : porcherie *f*, soue *f Can* **2** *pl* **sties** *or* **styes** : orgelet *m* (dans l'œil)

style[1] [ˈstaɪl] *vt* **styled; styling 1** NAME : appeler, dénommer **2** DESIGN : dessiner, concevoir, créer <carefully styled prose : prose conçue avec soin> **3** : coiffer (les cheveux)

style[2] *n* **1** : style *m*, manière *f* <that's just his style : c'est bien son genre> **2** FASHION : mode *f* **3** ELEGANCE : élégance *f*, style *m* <to live in style : mener grand train, vivre dans le luxe>

stylish [ˈstaɪlɪʃ] *adj* : chic, élégant

stylishly [ˈstaɪlɪʃli] *adv* : avec chic, élégamment

stylishness [ˈstaɪlɪʃnəs] *n* : chic *m*, élégance *f*

stylize [ˈstaɪəˌlaɪz] *vt* **-lized; -lizing** : styliser

stylus [ˈstaɪləs] *n, pl* **styli** [ˈstaɪˌlaɪ] **1** PEN : style *m* **2** NEEDLE : saphir *m* (d'un tourne-disque)

stymie [ˈstaɪmi] *vt* **-mied; -mieing** : coincer

suave [ˈswɑv] *adj* : suave

sub[1] [ˈsʌb] *vi* **subbed; subbing → substitute**[1]

sub[2] *n* **1 → substitute**[2] **2 → submarine**[2]

subcommittee [ˈsʌbkəˌmɪṭi] *n* : sous-comité *m*

subconscious[1] [ˌsʌbˈkɑnʃəs] *adj* : subconscient

subconscious[2] *n* : subconscient *m*

subconsciously [ˌsʌbˈkɑnʃəsli] *adv* : inconsciemment, de façon subconsciente

subcontract [ˌsʌbˈkɑnˌtrækt] *vt* : sous-traiter

subdivide [ˌsʌbdəˈvaɪd, ˈsʌbdəˌ-] *vt* **-vided; -viding** : subdiviser

subdivision [ˈsʌbdəˌvɪʒən] *n* : subdivision *f*

subdue [səbˈduː, -ˈdjuː] *vt* **-dued; -duing 1** OVERCOME : subjuguer, soumettre **2** CONTROL : maîtriser, réprimer **3** SOFTEN : adoucir, atténuer

subhead [ˈsʌbˌhɛd] *or* **subheading** [-ˌhɛdɪŋ] *n* : sous-titre *m*

subject[1] [səbˈdʒɛkt] *vt* **1** CONTROL, DOMINATE : soumettre, assujettir **2 to subject to** : exposer à, soumettre à

subject[2] [ˈsʌbdʒɪkt] *adj* **1** : sujet, soumis **2** PRONE : sujet <subject to colds : sujet aux rhumes> **3 subject to** : à condition de, sous réserve de <subject to change : sous réserve de modification>

subject[3] *n* **1** : sujet *m*, -jette *f* **2** TOPIC : sujet *m* **3** : sujet *m* (en grammaire)

subjection [səbˈdʒɛkʃən] *n* : sujétion *f*, soumission *f*

subjective [səbˈdʒɛkṭɪv] *adj* : subjectif — **subjectively** *adv*

subjectivity [ˌsʌbˌdʒɛkˈtɪvəṭi] *n* : subjectivité *f*

subjugate [ˈsʌbdʒɪˌgeɪt] *vt* **-gated; -gating** : subjuguer, soumettre

subjunctive[1] [səbˈdʒʌnkṭɪv] *adj* : subjonctif

subjunctive[2] *n* : subjonctif *m*

sublet [ˈsʌbˌlɛṭ] *vt* **-let; -letting** : sous-louer

sublime [səˈblaɪm] *adj* : sublime

sublimely [səˈblaɪmli] *adv* **1** : de manière sublime **2** UTTERLY : suprêmement

submarine[1] [ˈsʌbməˌriːn, ˌsʌbməˈ-] *adj* : sous-marin

submarine[2] *n* : sous-marin *m*

submerge [səbˈmərdʒ] *v* **-merged; -merging** *vt* : submerger, immerger — *vi* : s'immerger

submission [səb'mɪʃən] *n* **1** OBEDIENCE : soumission *f* **2** PRESENTATION : présentation *f*, soumission *f*
submissive [səb'mɪsɪv] *adj* : soumis
submit [səb'mɪt] *v* **-mitted; -mitting** *vi* YIELD : se soumettre — *vt* PRESENT : présenter, soumettre
subnormal [ˌsʌb'nɔrməl] *adj* : au-dessous de la normale
subordinate[1] [sə'bɔrdənˌeɪt] *vt* **-nated; -nating** : subordonner
subordinate[2] [sə'bɔrdənət] *adj* : subalterne, inférieur
subordinate[3] *n* : subordonné *m*, -née *f*
subordination [səˌbɔrdən'eɪʃən] *n* : subordination *f*
subpoena[1] [sə'piːnə] *vt* **-naed; -naing** : citer
subpoena[2] *n* : assignation *f*, citation *f*
subscribe [səb'skraɪb] *vi* **-scribed; -scribing 1** : s'abonner (à un magazine) **2 to subscribe to** : souscrire à, être d'accord avec (un point de vue, etc.)
subscriber [səb'skraɪbər] *n* : abonné *m*, -née *f*
subscription [səb'skrɪpʃən] *n* : abonnement *m*
subsequent ['sʌbsɪkwənt, -səˌkwɛnt] *adj* : subséquent, suivant
subsequently ['sʌbsɪˌkwɛntli, -ˌkwənt-] *adv* : par la suite, plus tard
subservient [səb'sərviənt] *adj* : servile
subside [səb'saɪd] *vi* **-sided; -siding 1** SINK : s'affaisser **2** ABATE : s'apaiser, se calmer
subsidiary[1] [səb'sɪdiˌɛri] *adj* : subsidiaire
subsidiary[2] *n, pl* **-ries** *or* **subsidiary company** : filiale *f*
subsidize ['sʌbsəˌdaɪz] *vt* **-dized; -dizing** : subventionner
subsidy ['sʌbsədi] *n, pl* **-dies** : subvention *f*
subsist [səb'sɪst] *vi* : subsister
subsistence [səb'sɪstənts] *n* : subsistance *f*
substance ['sʌbstənts] *n* **1** ESSENCE : substance *f*, essentiel *m* **2** MATERIAL : substance *f* **3** WEALTH : richesses *fpl* <a man of substance : un homme riche>
substandard [ˌsʌb'stændərd] *adj* : inférieur
substantial [səb'stænt͡ʃəl] *adj* **1** ABUNDANT : substantiel, copieux **2** CONSIDERABLE : considérable, appréciable
substantially [səb'stænt͡ʃəli] *adv* : considérablement
substantiate [səb'stænt͡ʃiˌeɪt] *vt* **-ated; -ating** : confirmer
substitute[1] ['sʌbstəˌtuːt, -ˌtjuːt] *v* **-tuted; -tuting** *vt* : substituer, remplacer — *vi* **to substitute for** : remplacer
substitute[2] *n* **1** ALTERNATE, STAND-IN : remplaçant *m*, -çante *f* **2** : produit *m* de remplacement, succédané *m* <sugar substitute : succédané de sucre>
substitute teacher *n* : suppléant *m*, -pléante *f*
substitution [ˌsʌbstə'tuːʃən, -'tjuː-] *n* : substitution *f*
subterfuge ['sʌbtərˌfjuːdʒ] *n* : subterfuge *m*
subterranean [ˌsʌbtə'reɪniən] *adj* : souterrain
subtitle ['sʌbˌtaɪt͡l] *n* : sous-titre *m*
subtle ['sʌt͡l] *adj* **-tler; -tlest** : subtil
subtlety ['sʌt͡lti] *n, pl* **-ties** : subtilité *f*
subtly ['sʌt͡li] *adv* : subtilement
subtotal ['sʌbˌtoːt͡əl] *n* : total *m* partiel
subtract [səb'trækt] *vt* : soustraire — *vi* : faire des soustractions
subtraction [səb'ræk͡ʃən] *n* : soustraction *f*
suburb ['sʌˌbərb] *n* : banlieue *f*
suburban [sə'bərbən] *adj* : de banlieue
subversion [səb'vərʒən] *n* : subversion *f*
subversive [səb'vərsɪv] *adj* : subversif
subway ['səbˌweɪ] *n* : métro *m*
succeed [sək'siːd] *vt* FOLLOW : succéder à — *vi* : réussir <she succeeded in finishing : elle a réussi à terminer>
success [sək'sɛs] *n* : réussite *f*, succès *m*
successful [sək'sɛsfəl] *adj* : réussi, courronné de succès
successfully [sək'sɛsfəli] *adv* : avec succès
succession [sək'sɛʃən] *n* : succession *f*
successive [sək'sɛsɪv] *adj* : successif — **successively** *adv*
successor [sək'sɛsər] *n* : successeur *m*
succinct [sək'sɪŋkt, sə'sɪŋkt] *adj* : succinct — **succinctly** *adv*
succor[1] *or Brit* **succour** ['sʌkər] *vt* : secourir, aider
succor[2] *or Brit* **succour** *n* : secours *m*, aide *f*
succotash ['sʌkəˌtæʃ] *n* : plat *m* de maïs et de fèves
succour *Brit* → **succor**
succulent[1] ['sʌkjələnt] *adj* : succulent
succulent[2] *n* : plante *f* grasse
succumb [sə'kʌm] *vi* : succomber
such[1] ['sʌt͡ʃ] *adv* **1** SO : aussi <such tall buildings : des bâtiments aussi grands> **2** VERY : si, tellement <he's not in such good shape : il n'est pas en tellement bonne forme> **3** SUCH THAT : de telle manière que
such[2] *adj* : tel, pareil <there's no such thing : une telle chose n'existe pas> <in such a case : dans un cas pareil> <animals such as cows and sheep : des animaux tels que les moutons et les vaches>
such[3] *pron* **1** : tel <such is the result : tel est le résultat> <he's a child, and acts as such : c'est un enfant et il se comporte comme tel> **2** : choses *fpl* semblables <books, papers, and such

: des livres, des papiers, et autres choses de ce genre> **3 as such** : en soi, comme tel

suck[1] ['sʌk] *vt* **1** : sucer (par la bouche) **2** PULL : aspirer (avec une machine, etc.) **3 to get sucked into sth** : être entraîné dans qqch — *vi* : têter (se dit d'un enfant) <to suck at : sucer>

suck[2] *n* : action *f* de sucer

sucker ['sʌkər] *n* **1** : suçoir *m* (d'un insecte), drageon *m* (d'une plante) **2** → **lollipop 3** FOOL : poire *f fam*, gogo *m fam*

suckle ['sʌkəl] *v* **-led; -ling** *vt* : allaiter — *vi* : têter

suckling ['sʌklɪŋ] *n* : nourrisson *m*

sucrose ['su:ˌkro:s, -ˌkro:z] *n* : saccharose *f*

suction ['sʌkʃən] *n* : succion *f*

Sudanese[1] [ˌsu:dən'i:z] *adj* : soudanais

Sudanese[2] *n* : Soudanais *m*, -naise *f*

sudden ['sʌdən] *adj* **1** : soudain, subit <all of a sudden : tout à coup> **2** UNEXPECTED : imprévu, inattendu **3** ABRUPT, HASTY : brusque

suddenly ['sʌdənli] *adv* **1** : soudainement, subitement, tout à coup **2** ABRUPTLY : brusquement

suddenness ['sʌdənnəs] *n* **1** : soudaineté *f* **2** ABRUPTNESS : brusquerie *f*

suds ['sʌdz] *npl* : mousse *f* (de savon)

sue ['su:] *v* **sued; suing** *vt* : intenter un procès à, poursuivre en justice — *vi* **to sue for** : solliciter

suede ['sweɪd] *n* : daim *m*, suède *m*

suet ['su:ət] *n* : graisse *f* de rognon (de bœuf)

suffer ['sʌfər] *vi* : souffrir — *vt* **1** UNDERGO : souffrir, subir **2** PERMIT : permettre, souffrir **3** TOLERATE : tolérer, supporter

sufferer ['sʌfərər] *n* : victime *f*, malade *mf*

suffering ['sʌfərɪŋ] *n* : souffrance *f*

suffice [sə'faɪs] *vi* **-ficed; -ficing** : être suffisant, suffir

sufficient [sə'fɪʃənt] *adj* : suffisant

sufficiently [sə'fɪʃəntli] *adv* : suffisamment

suffix ['sʌˌfɪks] *n* : suffixe *m*

suffocate ['sʌfəˌkeɪt] *v* **-cated; -cating** : suffoquer

suffocation [ˌsʌfə'keɪʃən] *n* : suffocation *f*

suffrage ['sʌfrɪdʒ] *n* : suffrage *m*

suffuse [sə'fju:z] *vt* **-fused; -fusing** : se répandre sur, baigner

sugar[1] ['ʃʊgər] *vt* : sucrer

sugar[2] *n* : sucre *m*

sugarcane ['ʃʊgərˌkeɪn] *n* : canne *f* à sucre

sugarhouse ['ʃʊgərˌhaʊs] *n* : cabane *f* (à sucre) *Can*

sugary ['ʃʊgəri] *adj* : sucré

suggest [səg'dʒest, sə-] *vt* **1** PROPOSE : proposer, suggérer **2** INDICATE : sembler indiquer, laisser supposer **3** EVOKE : évoquer, suggérer

suggestible [səg'dʒestəbəl, sə-] *adj* : influençable, suggestible

suggestion [səg'dʒestʃən, sə-] *n* **1** PROPOSAL : suggestion *f*, proposition *f* **2** INDICATION : indication *f* **3** HINT, TRACE : soupçon *m* **4 the power of suggestion** : la force de suggestion

suggestive [səg'dʒestɪv, sə-] *adj* : suggestif

suggestively [səg'dʒestɪvli, sə-] *adv* : de façon suggestive

suicidal [ˌsu:ə'saɪdəl] *adj* : suicidaire

suicide ['su:əˌsaɪd] *n* **1** : suicide *m* (acte) **2** : suicidé *m*, -dée *f* (personne)

suit[1] ['su:t] *vt* **1** ADAPT : accommoder, adapter **2** BECOME, BEFIT : convenir à, aller à <the dress suits you : la robe te va bien> **3** PLEASE : convenir à, arranger <does Friday suit you? : est-ce que vendredi t'arrange?> <suit yourself! : faites comme vous voulez!>

suit[2] *n* **1** → **lawsuit 2** : costume *m*, complet *m* (d'homme), tailleur *m* (de femme) **3** : couleur *f* (aux cartes)

suitability [ˌsu:ɨə'bɪləɨi] *n* : caractère *m* convenable, pertinence *f*, aptitude *f* (d'une personne)

suitable ['su:ɨəbəl] *adj* : convenable, approprié

suitably ['su:ɨəbli] *adv* : convenablement

suitcase ['su:tˌkeɪs] *n* : valise *f*

suite ['swi:t, *for 2 also* 'su:t] *n* **1** : suite *f* **2** : mobilier *m* <dining-room suite : mobilier de salle à manger>

suitor ['su:tər] *n* : prétendant *m*

sulfur *or Brit* **sulphur** ['sʌlfər] *n* : soufre *m*

sulfuric acid *or Brit* **sulphuric acid** [ˌsʌl'fjʊrɪk] *adj* : acide *m* sulfurique

sulfurous *or Brit* **sulphurous** [ˌsʌl'fjʊrəs, 'sʌlfərəs, 'sʌlfjə-] *adj* : sulfureux

sulk[1] ['sʌlk] *vi* : bouder

sulk[2] *n* : bouderie *f*

sulky ['sʌlki] *adj* **sulkier; -est** : boudeur

sullen ['sʌlən] *adj* **1** MOROSE : maussade, morose, renfrogné **2** GLOOMY : maussade, morne <sullen clouds : des nuages menaçants>

sullenly ['sʌlənli] *adv* : d'un air maussade, d'un air renfrogné

sully ['sʌli] *vt* **sullied; sullying** : souiller

sulphur *Brit* → **sulfur**

sultan ['sʌltən] *n* : sultan *m*

sultry ['sʌltri] *adj* **sultrier; -est 1** : étouffant <sultry weather : temps lourd> **2** SENSUAL : sensuel

sum[1] ['sʌm] *vt* **summed; summing 1** ADD : additionner **2** → **sum up**

sum[2] *n* **1** AMOUNT : somme *f* **2** TOTAL : total *m*, tout *m* **3** : calcul *m* (en mathématiques)

sumac ['ʃu:ˌmæk, 'su:-] *n* : sumac *m*

summarize ['sʌməˌraɪz] *v* **-rized; -rizing** *vt* : résumer — *vi* : se résumer

summary[1] ['sʌmərɪ] *adj* : sommaire
summary[2] *n, pl* **-ries** : sommaire *m*
summer ['sʌmər] *n* : été *m*
summery ['sʌmərɪ] *adj* : d'été
summit ['sʌmət] *n* **1** : sommet *m*, cime *f* **2** *or* **summit conference** : conférence *f* au sommet
summon ['sʌmən] *vt* **1** CALL : appeler, convoquer (une réunion, etc.) **2** : sommer de comparaître (en droit) **3 to summon up** : rassembler, faire appel à <to summon up one's strength : rassembler ses forces>
summons ['sʌmənz] *n, pl* **summonses 1** SUPOENA : assignation *f* **2** CALL : appel *m*
sumptuous ['sʌmptʃʊəs] *adj* : somptueux
sum up *vt* **1** SUMMARIZE : résumer **2** ASSESS : apprécier, jauger
sun[1] ['sʌn] *vt* **sunned; sunning 1** : exposer au soleil **2 to sun oneself** : prendre le soleil
sun[2] *n* **1** : soleil *m* **2** → **sunshine**
sunbeam ['sʌnˌbiːm] *n* : rayon *m* de soleil
sunblock ['sʌnˌblɑk] *n* : écran *m* total
sunburn[1] ['sʌnˌbərn] *vi* **-burned** *or* **-burnt** [-ˌbərnt]; **-burning** : prendre un coup de soleil
sunburn[2] *n* : coup *m* de soleil
sundae ['sʌndi] *n* : sundae *m Can*
Sunday ['sʌnˌdeɪ, -di] *n* : dimanche *m*
sundial ['sʌnˌdaɪəl] *n* : cadran *m* solaire
sundown ['sʌnˌdaʊn] → **sunset**
sundries ['sʌndriz] *npl* : articles *mpl* divers
sundry ['sʌndrɪ] *adj* : divers
sunflower ['sʌnˌflaʊər] *n* : tournesol *m*
sung → **sing**
sunglasses ['sʌnˌglæsəz] *npl* : lunettes *fpl* de soleil
sunk → **sink**[1]
sunken ['sʌŋkən] *adj* **1** HOLLOW : creux **2** SUBMERGED : submergé
sunlight ['sʌnˌlaɪt] *n* : soleil *m*, lumière *f* du soleil
sunny ['sʌnɪ] *adj* **sunnier; -est 1** : ensoleillé **2** CHEERFUL : heureux
sunrise ['sʌnˌraɪz] *n* : lever *m* du soleil
sunset ['sʌnˌsɛt] *n* : coucher *m* du soleil
sunshine ['sʌnˌʃaɪn] *n* : lumière *f* du soleil
sunspot ['sʌnˌspɑt] *n* : tache *f* solaire
sunstroke ['sʌnˌstroːk] *n* : insolation *f*
suntan ['sʌnˌtæn] *n* : hâle *m*, bronzage *m*
super ['suːpər] *adj* **1** GREAT, TERRIFIC : super *fam*, génial **2** SUPERIOR : supérieur
superabundance [ˌsuːpərə'bʌndənʦ] *n* : surabondance *f*
superb [su'pərb] *adj* : superbe — **superbly** *adv*
supercilious [ˌsuːpər'sɪliəs] *adj* : hautain, dédaigneux
superficial [ˌsuːpər'fɪʃəl] *adj* : superficiel — **superficially** *adv*
superfluous [su'pərflʊəs] *adj* : superflu
superhuman [ˌsuːpər'hjuːmən] *adj* : surhumain
superimpose [ˌsuːpərɪm'poːz] *vt* **-posed; -posing** : superposer
superintend [ˌsuːpərɪn'tɛnd] *vt* : surveiller
superintendent [ˌsuːpərɪn'tɛndənt] *n* **1** : directeur *m*, -trice *f* **2** : concierge *mf* (d'un immeuble) **3** : inspecteur *m*, -trice *f* (d'école)
superior[1] [su'pɪriər] *adj* : supérieur
superior[2] *n* : supérieur *m*, -rieure *f*
superiority [suˌpɪri'ɔrəʧi] *n, pl* **-ties** : supériorité *f*
superlative[1] [su'pərləʧɪv] *adj* **1** : superlatif (en grammaire) **2** SUPREME : suprême **3** EXCELLENT, OUTSTANDING : superbe, exceptionnel, sans pareil
superlative[2] *n* : superlatif *m*
supermarket ['suːpərˌmɑrkət] *n* : supermarché *m*
supernatural [ˌsuːpər'nætʃərəl] *adj* : surnaturel
supernaturally [ˌsuːpər'nætʃərəli] *adv* : de manière surnaturelle
superpower ['suːpərˌpaʊər] *n* : superpuissance *f*
supersede [ˌsuːpər'siːd] *vt* **-seded; -seding** : remplacer, supplanter
supersonic [ˌsuːpər'sɑnɪk] *adj* : supersonique
superstition [ˌsuːpər'stɪʃən] *n* : superstition *f*
superstitious [ˌsuːpər'stɪʃəs] *adj* : superstitieux
superstructure ['suːpərˌstrʌktʃər] *n* : superstructure *f*
supervise ['suːpərˌvaɪz] *vt* **-vised; -vising** : surveiller, superviser
supervision [ˌsuːpər'vɪʒən] *n* : surveillance *f*, supervision *f*
supervisor ['suːpərˌvaɪzər] *n* : surveillant *m*, -lante *f*
supervisory [ˌsuːpər'vaɪzərɪ] *adj* : de surveillance
supine [su'paɪn] *adj* **1** : couché sur le dos **2** INDOLENT, SLACK : indolent, mou
supper ['sʌpər] *n* : dîner *m*, souper *m Can*
supplant [sə'plænt] *vt* : supplanter
supple ['sʌpəl] *adj* **-pler; -plest** : souple
supplement[1] ['sʌpləˌmənt] *vt* : compléter, augmenter
supplement[2] *n* : supplément *m*
supplementary [ˌsʌpləˈmɛntərɪ] *adj* : supplémentaire
supplicate ['sʌpləˌkeɪt] *vt* **-cated; -cating** : supplier, implorer
supplier [sə'plaɪər] *n* : fournisseur *m*, -seuse *f*
supply[1] [sə'plaɪ] *vt* **-plied; -plying** : fournir, munir, approvisionner
supply[2] *n, pl* **-plies 1** PROVISION : fourniture *f*, approvisionnement *m* **2** STOCK : provision *f*, réserve *f* **3 sup-**

plies *npl* : provisions *fpl,* approvisionnements *mpl,* vivres *mpl*

support[1] [sə'port] *vt* **1** BACK : soutenir, appuyer **2** MAINTAIN : maintenir, entretenir **3** PROP UP : supporter, soutenir

support[2] *n* **1** BACKING : appui *m,* soutien *m* **2** PROP : support *m,* appui *m*

supporter [sə'portər] *n* **1** : partisan *m,* -sane *f* **2** FAN : supporter *m*

suppose [sə'poːz] **vt -posed; -posing 1** ASSUME : supposer **2** BELIEVE : croire **3 to be supposed to do sth** : être censé faire qqch

supposedly [sə'poːzədli] *adv* : censément

supposition [ˌsʌpə'zɪʃən] *n* : supposition *f*

suppository [sə'pɑzəˌtori] *n, pl* **-ries** : suppositoire *m*

suppress [sə'pres] *vt* **1** SUBDUE : maîtriser, réprimer (une révolte, etc.) **2** WITHHOLD : supprimer **3** REPRESS : étouffer, réprimer <to suppress a yawn : étouffer un bâillement>

suppression [sə'preʃən] *n* **1** SUBDUING : répression *f* **2** : suppression *f* (d'information) **3** REPRESSION : étouffement *m,* refoulement *m*

supremacy [sʊ'preməsi] *n, pl* **-cies** : suprématie *f*

supreme [sʊ'priːm] *adj* : suprême — **supremely** *adv*

Supreme Being *n* GOD : Être *m* suprême

surcharge ['sərˌtʃɑrdʒ] *n* : surcharge *f*

sure[1] ['ʃʊr] *adv* **1** ALL RIGHT : bien sûr **2** (*used as an intensifier*) : vraiment, drôlement <it sure is hot! : il fait drôlement chaud!> <she sure is pretty! : qu'est-ce qu'elle est belle!>

sure[2] *adj* **surer; -est** : sûr <I'm sure of it : j'en suis sûr> <she's sure to succeed : elle va sûrement réussir> <for sure : pour sûr>

surely ['ʃʊrli] *adv* **1** CERTAINLY : sûrement **2** (*used as an intensifier*) <you surely don't mean that! : tu ne peux pas vouloir dire cela!>

sureness ['ʃʊrnəs] *n* : sûreté *f*

surety ['ʃʊrəti] *n, pl* **-ties 1** GUARANTOR : garant *m,* -rante *f* **2** COLLATERAL : sûreté *f,* caution *f*

surf ['sərf] *n* **1** WAVES : vagues *fpl* (déferlantes) **2** FOAM : écume *f*

surface[1] ['sərfəs] *v* **-faced; -facing** *vi* : faire surface, remonter à la surface — *vt* : revêtir (une chaussée)

surface[2] *n* : surface *f*

surfboard ['sərfˌbɔrd] *n* : planche *f* de surf

surfeit ['sərfət] *n* : excès *m*

surfing ['sərfɪŋ] *n* : surf *m*

surge[1] ['sərdʒ] *vi* **surged; surging 1** SWELL : s'enfler, déferler (se dit de la mer) **2** INCREASE : monter **3** SWARM : se presser, déferler (se dit d'une foule, etc.)

surge[2] *n* **1** RUSH : brusque montée *f* (de la mer), ruée *f* (de personnes) **2** FLUSH : vague *f,* accès *m* (de colère, etc.) **3** INCREASE : augmentation *f,* surtension *f* (de l'électricité)

surgeon ['sərdʒən] *n* : chirurgien *m,* -gienne *f*

surgery ['sərdʒəri] *n, pl* **-geries** : chirurgie *f*

surgical ['sərdʒɪkəl] *adj* : chirurgical

surgically ['sərdʒɪkli] *adv* : par opération, par intervention chirurgicale

Surinamese[1] [ˌsʊrənə'miːz, -'miːs] *adj* : surinamien

Surinamese[2] *n* : Surinamien *m,* -mienne *f*

surly ['sərli] *adj* **surlier; -est** : revêche, bourru, hargneux

surmise[1] [sər'maɪz] *v* **-mised; -mising** : conjecturer, présumer

surmise[2] *n* : conjecture *f,* hypothèse *f*

surmount [sər'maʊnt] *vt* **1** OVERCOME : surmonter, vaincre **2** CAP, TOP : surmonter

surname ['sərˌneɪm] *n* : nom *m* de famille

surpass [sər'pæs] *vt* : surpasser, dépasser

surplus ['sərˌplʌs] *n* : excédent *m,* surplus *m*

surprise[1] [sə'praɪz, sər-] *vt* **-prised; -prising** : surprendre

surprise[2] *n* : surprise *f* <to take by surprise : prendre au dépourvu>

surprising [sə'praɪzɪŋ, sər-] *adj* : surprenant, étonnant

surprisingly [sə'praɪzɪŋli, sər-] *adv* : étonnamment, incroyablement

surrender[1] [sə'rendər] *vt* **1** : rendre, livrer, céder **2 to surrender oneself to** : se livrer à — *vi* : se rendre, capituler

surrender[2] *n* : capitulation *f,* reddition *f*

surreptitious [ˌsərəp'tɪʃəs] *adj* : subreptice, furtif — **surreptitiously** *adv*

surrogate ['sərəgət, -ˌgeɪt] *n* : substitut *m;* remplaçant *m,* -çante *f*

surround [sə'raʊnd] *vt* : entourer, cerner

surroundings [sə'raʊndɪŋz] *npl* : environs *mpl,* alentours *mpl*

surveillance [sər'veɪlənts, -'veɪljənts, -'veɪənts] *n* : surveillance *f*

survey[1] [sər'veɪ] *vt* **-veyed; -veying 1** : arpenter (un terrain) **2** EXAMINE : examiner, inspecter **3** POLL : sonder

survey[2] ['sərˌveɪ] *n, pl* **-veys 1** INSPECTION : inspection *f* **2** : arpentage *m* (d'un terrain) **3** POLL : sondage *m*

surveyor [sər'veɪər] *n* : arpenteur *m,* -teuse *f*

survival [sər'vaɪvəl] *n* **1** : survie *f* (d'une personne, d'un animal, d'une plante) **2** REMAINDER, VESTIGE : survivance *f,* vestige *m*

survive [sər'vaɪv] *v* **-vived; -viving** *vi* : survivre — *vt* OUTLIVE : survivre à

survivor [sər'vaɪvər] *n* : survivant *m*, -vante *f*
susceptibility [sə,septə'bɪləṭi] *n, pl* **-ties** : susceptibilité *f*
susceptible [sə'septəbəl] *adj* : sensible, susceptible
suspect[1] [sə'spekt] *vt* **1** DISTRUST : douter de, se méfier de **2** : soupçonner (d'un crime) **3** IMAGINE, THINK : imaginer, soupçonner
suspect[2] ['sʌs,pekt, sə'spekt] *adj* : suspect
suspect[3] ['sʌs,pekt] *n* : suspect *m*, -pecte *f*
suspend [sə'spend] *vt* : suspendre
suspenders [sə'spendərz] *npl* : bretelles *fpl*
suspense [sə'spenʦ] *n* : attente *f*, suspense *m* <to keep in suspense : laisser dans l'incertitude>
suspenseful [sə'spenʦfəl] *adj* : plein de suspense
suspension [sə'spenʃən] *n* : suspension *f*
suspicion [sə'spɪʃən] *n* : soupçon *m*, méfiance *f*
suspicious [sə'spɪʃəs] *adj* **1** QUESTIONABLE : suspect **2** DISTRUSTFUL : méfiant, soupçonneux
suspiciously [sə'spɪʃəsli] *adv* **1** : d'une manière suspecte **2** WARILY : d'un air soupçonneux, avec méfiance
sustain [sə'steɪn] *vt* **1** NOURISH : nourrir **2** MAINTAIN : maintenir, entretenir **3** SUFFER : éprouver <to sustain an injury : recevoir une blessure> **4** SUPPORT : soutenir
sustenance ['sʌsṭənənʦ] *n* **1** NOURISHMENT : nourriture *f* **2** LIVELIHOOD, SUBSISTENCE : (moyens *mpl* de) subsistance *f*
svelte ['sfɛlt] *adj* : svelte
swab[1] ['swɑb] *vt* **swabbed; swabbing 1** CLEAN : nettoyer **2** *or* **to swab down** MOP : laver
swab[2] *n or* **cotton swab** : tampon *m*
swaddle ['swɑdəl] *vt* **-dled; -dling** [-dəlɪŋ] WRAP : emmitoufler, envelopper
swagger[1] ['swægər] *vi* **-gered; -gering** : se pavaner
swagger[2] *n* : démarche *f* arrogante
swallow[1] ['swɑlo:] *vt* **1** : avaler **2** *or* **to swallow up** ENGULF : engloutir **3** REPRESS : ravaler — *vi* : avaler, déglutir
swallow[2] *n* **1** GULP : gorgée *f* **2** : hirondelle *f* (oiseau)
swam → **swim**[1]
swamp[1] ['swɑmp] *vi* : inonder
swamp[2] *n* : marais *m*, marécage *m*, savane *f Can*
swampy ['swɑmpi] *adj* **swampier; -est** : marécageux
swan ['swɑn] *n* : cygne *m*
swap[1] ['swɑp] *vt* **swapped; swapping** : échanger
swap[2] *n* : échange *m*
swarm[1] ['swɔrm] *vi* **1** : essaimer (se dit des abeilles) **2** TEEM, THRONG : grouiller, se presser <to be swarming with people : grouiller de gens>
swarm[2] *n* **1** : essaim *m* (d'abeilles) **2** : masse *f*, essaim *m* (de personnes)
swarthy ['swɔrði, -θi] *adj* **swarthier; -est** : basané
swashbuckling ['swɑʃ,bʌklɪŋ] *adj* : de cape et d'épée (se dit d'un film, etc.)
swat[1] ['swɑt] *vt* **swatted; swatting** : écraser (un insecte), frapper (une personne)
swat[2] *n* : tape *f*
swatch ['swɑtʃ] *n* : échantillon *m* (de tissu)
swath ['swɑθ, 'swɔθ,] *or* **swathe** ['swɑð, 'swɔð, 'sweɪð] *n* : andain *m* (en agriculture), bande *f* (de terre)
swathe ['swɑð, 'swɔð, 'sweɪð] *vt* **swathed; swathing** : emmailloter, envelopper
swatter ['swɑṭər] → **flyswatter**
sway[1] ['sweɪ] *vi* : se balancer — *vt* **1** INFLUENCE : influencer **2** ROCK : balancer
sway[2] *n* **1** SWINGING : balancement *m* **2** INFLUENCE : influence *f*
swear ['swær] *v* **swore** ['swɔr]; **sworn** ['swɔrn]; **swearing** *vi* **1** VOW : jurer <to swear on the Bible> **2** CURSE : jurer, injurier — *vt* : jurer <to swear allegiance : jurer allégeance> <to swear an oath : prêter serment>
swearword ['swær,wərd] *n* : juron *m*, grossièreté *f*
sweat[1] ['swet] *vi* **sweat** *or* **sweated; sweating 1** PERSPIRE : transpirer **2** OOZE : suinter, suer **3 to sweat over** : suer sur
sweat[2] *n* : sueur *f*, transpiration *f*
sweater ['sweṭər] *n* : pull-over *m France*, chandail *m*
sweatshirt ['swet,ʃərt] *n* : sweat-shirt *m*
sweaty ['sweṭi] *adj* **sweatier; -est** : couvert de sueur
Swede ['swi:d] *n* : Suédois *m*, -doise *f*
Swedish[1] ['swi:dɪʃ] *adj* : suédois
Swedish[2] *n* **1** : suédois *m* (langue) **2 the Swedish** : les Suédois
sweep[1] ['swi:p] *v* **swept** ['swept]; **sweeping** *vt* **1** : balayer **2** *or* **to sweep away** : emporter, entraîner **3** *or* **to sweep through** : gagner, s'emparer de <panic swept the city : la panique s'est emparée de la ville> — *vi* **1** : balayer **2** EXTEND : s'étendre, décrire (une courbe) <the sun swept across the sky : le soleil a décrit une courbe dans le ciel>
sweep[2] *n* **1** : coup *m* de balai **2** : mouvement *m* circulaire (de la main, etc.) **3** SCOPE : étendue *f*
sweeper ['swi:pər] *n* : balayeur *m*, balayeuse *f*
sweeping ['swi:pɪŋ] *adj* **1** WIDE : large **2** EXTENSIVE : considérable, radical **3**

INDISCRIMINATE : péremptoire, trop général
sweepstakes ['swi:pˌsteɪks] *ns & pl* : sweepstake *m*
sweet[1] ['swi:t] *adj* **1** : doux, sucré <sweet desserts : desserts sucrés> **2** FRESH : frais (se dit de l'eau, etc.) **3** : sans sel (se dit du beurre) **4** KIND, PLEASANT : agréable, gentil **5** CUTE, PRETTY : mignon, adorable
sweet[2] *n* : bonbon *m*, dessert *m*
sweeten ['swi:tən] *vt* : sucrer
sweetener ['swi:tənər] *n* : édulcorant *m*
sweetheart ['swi:tˌhɑrt] *n* **1** : petit ami *m*, petite amie *f* **2** (*used as a term of address*) : chéri *m*, chérie *f*
sweetly ['swi:tli] *adv* : doucement
sweetness ['swi:tnəs] *n* : douceur *f*
sweet potato *n* : patate *f* douce
swell[1] ['swɛl] *vi* **swelled; swelled** *or* **swollen** ['swo:lən]; **swelling 1** *or* **to swell up** : enfler, gonfler <her ankle swelled : sa cheville enflait> **2** INCREASE : augmenter, grossir
swell[2] *n* **1** : houle *f* (de la mer) **2** INCREASE : augmentation *f*
swelling ['swɛlɪŋ] *n* : enflure *f*, gonflement *m*
swelter ['swɛltər] *vi* : étouffer de chaleur
swept → **sweep**[1]
swerve[1] ['swərv] *vi* **swerved; swerving** : faire une embardée
swerve[2] *n* : embardée *f*
swift[1] ['swɪft] *adj* **1** FAST : rapide **2** PROMPT : prompt — **swiftly** *adv*
swift[2] *n* : martinet *m* (oiseau)
swiftness ['swɪftnəs] *n* **1** SPEED : rapidité *f* **2** PROMPTNESS : promptitude *f*
swig[1] ['swɪg] *vi* **swigged; swigging** : boire à grands traits, siffler *fam*
swig[2] *n* : lampée *f fam*, gorgée *f*
swill[1] ['swɪl] *vt or* **to swill down** : lamper, écluser *fam*
swill[2] *n* **1** SLOP : pâtée *f* **2** GARBAGE : ordures *fpl*
swim[1] ['swɪm] *vi* **swam** ['swæm]; **swum** ['swʌm]; **swimming 1** : nager, faire de la natation, se baigner **2** FLOAT : flotter **3** REEL : tourner <his head was swimming : il avait la tête qui tournait>
swim[2] *n* : baignade *f* <to go for a swim : aller se baigner>
swimmer ['swɪmər] *n* : nageur *m*, -geuse *f*
swindle[1] ['swɪndəl] *vt* **-dled; -dling** : escroquer
swindle[2] *n* : escroquerie *f*
swindler ['swɪndələr] *n* : escroc *m*
swine ['swaɪn] *ns & pl* : porc *m*
swing[1] ['swɪŋ] *v* **swung** ['swʌŋ]; **swinging** *vt* **1** : balancer (les bras, etc.), faire osciller **2** : décrire une courbe avec, brandir <he swung his ax : il a brandi sa hache> <to swing into the saddle : sauter en selle> **3** SUSPEND : suspendre — *vi* **1** SWAY : se balancer **2** CHANGE : virer, passer <to swing from enthusiasm to disappointment : passer de l'enthousiasme à la déception> **3** SWIVEL : tourner, pivoter <the door swung shut : la porte s'est refermée>
swing[2] *n* **1** SWINGING : balancement *m*, oscillation *f* **2** CHANGE, SHIFT : revirement *m* **3** : balançoire *f* (pour les enfants)
swipe[1] ['swaɪp] *v* **swiped; swiping** *vi* **to swipe at** : essayer de frapper, donner un coup pour frapper — *vt* STEAL : chiper *fam*, faucher *fam*
swipe[2] *n* : grand coup *m*
swirl[1] ['swərl] *vi* : tourbillonner
swirl[2] *n* : tourbillon *m*
swish[1] ['swɪʃ] *vi* : siffler (se dit d'un fouet, etc.), bruire (se dit de l'eau), froufrouter (se dit d'une étoffe)
swish[2] *n* : sifflement *m*, bruissement *m*, froufrou *m*
Swiss[1] ['swɪs] *adj* : suisse
Swiss[2] *ns & pl* : Suisse *m*, Suissesse *f*
switch[1] ['swɪtʃ] *vt* **1** LASH, WHIP : fouetter **2** CHANGE : changer de **3 to switch on** : ouvrir, allumer **4 to switch off** : couper, fermer, éteindre — *vi* **1** CHANGE : changer **2** SWAP : échanger
switch[2] *n* **1** CANE, STICK : badine *f* **2** CHANGE, SHIFT : changement *m* **3** : interrupteur *m* (d'électricité), bouton *m* (d'une radio ou d'une télévision)
switchboard ['swɪtʃˌbɔrd] *n or* **telephone switchboard** : standard *m*
swivel[1] ['swɪvəl] *vi* **-eled** *or* **-elled; -eling** *or* **-elling** : pivoter
swivel[2] *n* : pivot *m*
swollen → **swell**[1]
swoon[1] ['swu:n] *vi* **1** FAINT : s'évanouir **2 to swoon over** : se pâmer devant
swoon[2] *n* **1** FAINT : évanouissement *m* **2** DAZE, RAPTURE : pâmoison *f*
swoop[1] ['swu:p] *vi* : fondre, piquer
swoop[2] *n* : descente *f* en piqué
sword ['sɔrd] *n* : épée *f*
swordfish ['sɔrdˌfɪʃ] *n* : espadon *m*
swore, sworn → **swear**
swum → **swim**[1]
swung → **swing**[1]
sycamore ['sɪkəˌmor] *n* : sycomore *m*
sycophant ['sɪkəfənt, -ˌfænt] *n* : flagorneur *m*, -neuse *f*
syllabic [sə'læbɪk] *adj* : syllabique
syllable ['sɪləbəl] *n* : syllabe *f*
syllabus ['sɪləbəs] *n, pl* **-bi** [-ˌbaɪ] *or* **-buses** : programme *m*
symbol ['sɪmbəl] *n* : symbole *m*
symbolic [sɪm'bɑlɪk] *adj* : symbolique — **symbolically** [-kli] *adv*
symbolism ['sɪmbəˌlɪzəm] *n* : symbolisme *m*
symbolize ['sɪmbəˌlaɪz] *vt* **-ized; -izing** : symboliser

symmetrical [sə'mɛtrɪkəl] *adj* : symétrique — **symmetrically** [-kli] *adv*
symmetry ['sɪmətri] *n, pl* **-tries** : symétrie *f*
sympathetic [ˌsɪmpə'θɛtɪk] *adj* **1** PLEASING : agréable, sympathique **2** RECEPTIVE : bien disposé **3** COMPASSIONATE, UNDERSTANDING : compatissant, compréhensif
sympathetically [ˌsɪmpə'θɛtɪkli] *adv* : avec compassion, avec compréhension
sympathize ['sɪmpəˌθaɪz] *vi* **-thized; -thizing 1** : compatir, comprendre <I sympathize with him : je le plains> **2 to sympathize with** SUPPORT : sympathiser avec
sympathizer ['sɪmpəˌθaɪzər] *n* : sympathisant *m*, -sante *f*
sympathy ['sɪmpəθi] *n, pl* **-thies 1** COMPASSION : compassion *f*, sympathie *f* **2** UNDERSTANDING : compréhension *f* **3** AGREEMENT : approbation *f*, sympathie *f*
symphonic [sɪm'fɑnɪk] *adj* : symphonique
symphony ['sɪmˌfəni] *n, pl* **-nies** : symphonie *f*
symposium [sɪm'poːziəm] *n, pl* **-sia** [-ziə] *or* **-siums** : symposium *m*
symptom ['sɪmptəm] *n* : symptôme *m*
symptomatic [ˌsɪmptə'mætɪk] *adj* : symptomatique
synagogue ['sɪnəˌgɑg, -ˌgɔg] *n* : synagogue *f*
synchronize ['sɪŋkrəˌnaɪz, 'sɪn-] *v* **-nized; -nizing** *vt* : synchroniser — *vi* : être synchrone
syndicate[1] ['sɪndɪˌkeɪt] *v* **-cated; -cating** *vi* UNITE : se syndiquer — *vt* : publier simultanément dans plusieurs journaux
syndicate[2] ['sɪndɪkət] *n* : syndicat *m*
syndrome ['sɪnˌdroːm] *n* : syndrome *m*
synonym ['sɪnəˌnɪm] *n* : synonyme *m*
synonymous [sə'nɑnəməs] *adj* : synonyme
synopsis [sə'nɑpsɪs] *n, pl* **-opses** [-ˌsiːz] : résumé *m*
syntax ['sɪnˌtæks] *n* : syntaxe *f*
synthesis ['sɪnθəsəs] *n, pl* **-theses** [-ˌsiːz] : synthèse *f*
synthesize ['sɪnθəˌsaɪz] *vt* **-sized; -sizing** : synthétiser
synthetic[1] [sɪn'θɛtɪk] *adj* : synthétique — **synthetically** [-ɡɪkli] *adv*
synthetic[2] *n* : produit *m* synthétique
syphilis ['sɪfələs] *n* : syphilis *f*
Syrian[1] ['sɪriən] *adj* : syrien
Syrian[2] *n* : Syrien *m*, -rienne *f*
syringe [sə'rɪndʒ, 'sɪrɪndʒ] *n* : seringue *f*
syrup ['sərəp, 'sɪrəp] *n* : sirop *m*
system ['sɪstəm] *n* **1** METHOD : système *m*, méthode *f* **2** STRUCTURE : système *m* <the solar system : le système solaire> **3** APPARATUS : appareil *m*, système *m* <digestive system : appareil digestif> **4** BODY : organisme *m* **5** NETWORK : réseau *m*
systematic [ˌsɪstə'mætɪk] *adj* : systématique — **systematically** [-ɡɪkli] *adv*
systematize ['sɪstəməˌtaɪz] *vt* **-tized; -tizing** : systématiser
systemic [sɪs'tɛmɪk] *adj* : du système, systémique

T

t ['tiː] *n, pl* **t's** *or* **ts** ['tiːz] : t *m*, vingtième lettre de l'alphabet
tab [tæb] *n* **1** FLAP : patte *f* **2** BILL, CHECK : note *f*, addition *f* **3** LOOP : attache *f* **4 to keep tabs on s.o.** : surveiller qqn, garder qqn à l'œil
tabby ['tæbi] *n, pl* **-bies** : chat *m* tigré, chatte *f* tigrée
tabernacle ['tæbərˌnækəl] *n* : tabernacle *m*
table ['teɪbəl] *n* **1** : table *f* <kitchen table : table de cuisine> **2** MEAL : table *f* <to serve a good table : servir une bonne table> **3** CHART : table *f*, tableau *m* **4 table of contents** : table *f* des matières
tableau [tæ'bloː, 'tæˌ-] *n, pl* **tableaux** [tæ'bloːz, 'tæˌbloːz] : tableau *m*
tablecloth ['teɪbəlˌklɔθ] *n* : nappe *f*
tablespoon ['teɪbəlˌspuːn] *n* : cuillère *f* à soupe
tablespoonful ['teɪbəlˌspuːnˌfʊl] *n* : cuillère *f* à soupe
tablet ['tæblət] *n* **1** PLAQUE : plaque *f*, tablette *f* (de pierre) **2** NOTEPAD : bloc-notes *m*, tablette *f Can* **3** PILL : comprimé *m* <aspirin tablet : comprimé d'aspirine>
table tennis *n* : tennis *m* de table
tabletop ['teɪbəlˌtɑp] *n* : dessus *m* de table
tableware ['teɪbəlˌweɪr] *n* : vaisselle *f*
tabloid ['tæˌblɔɪd] *n* : quotidien *m* populaire, tabloïde *m*
taboo[1] [tə'buː, tæ-] *adj* : tabou, interdit
taboo[2] *n, pl* **taboos** : tabou *m*
tabular ['tæbjələr] *adj* : tabulaire
tabulate ['tæbjəˌleɪt] *vt* **-lated; -lating** : mettre sous forme de tableau
tabulator ['tæbjəˌleɪtər] *n* : tabulateur *m*
tacit ['tæsɪt] *adj* : tacite, implicite — **tacitly** *adv*
taciturn ['tæsɪˌtərn] *adj* : taciturne
tack[1] ['tæk] *vt* **1** ATTACH : clouer, fixer <to tack down a carpet : clouer un

tapis> **2 to tack on** ADD : ajouter, rajouter — *vi* : faire une bordée (se dit d'un navire)

tack[2] *n* **1** BRAD : semence *f*, clou *m* **2 → thumbtack 3** COURSE : voie *f*, tactique *f* <to change tack : changer de voie>

tackle[1] ['takəl] *vt* **-led; -ling 1** : plaquer (au football) **2** : s'attaquer à <to tackle a problem : s'attaquer à un problème>

tackle[2] *n* **1** GEAR : équipement *m*, matériel *m* <fishing tackle : matériel de pêche> **2** PULLEYS : appareil *m* de levage **3** : plaquage *m* (au football)

tacky ['tæki] *adj* **tackier; -est 1** STICKY : collant **2** SHABBY : moche, minable **3** TASTELESS : de mauvais goût

tact ['tækt] *n* : tact *m*, diplomatie *f*

tactful ['tæktfəl] *adj* : plein de tact

tactfully ['tæktfəli] *adv* : avec tact, avec diplomatie

tactic ['tæktɪk] *n* : tactique *f*, plan *m*

tactical ['tæktɪkəl] *adj* : tactique

tactics ['tæktɪks] *ns & pl* : tactique *f*

tactile ['tæktəl, -ˌtaɪl] *adj* : tactile

tactless ['tæktləs] *adj* : qui manque de tact

tactlessly ['tæktləsli] *adv* : sans tact

tadpole ['tædˌpoːl] *n* : têtard *m*

taffeta ['tæfəṭə] *n* : taffetas *m*

taffy ['tæfi] *n, pl* **-fies** : bonbon *m* au caramel

tag[1] ['tæg] *v* **tagged; tagging** *vt* **1** LABEL : étiqueter **2** TOUCH : toucher (au jeu de chat, au baseball, etc.) — *vi* **to tag along behind** : suivre

tag[2] *n* **1** : jeu *m* de chat **2** *or* **price tag** : étiquette *f*

Tahitian[1] [tə'hiːʃən] *adj* : tahitien

Tahitian[2] *n* : Tahitien, -tienne *f*

tail[1] ['teɪl] *vt* FOLLOW : suivre de près

tail[2] *n* **1** : queue *f* (d'un animal) **2** : queue *f* (d'un avion, d'une comète, etc.) **3 tails** *npl* : pile *f* (d'une pièce de monnaie) <heads or tails? : pile ou face?>

tailgate[1] ['teɪlˌgeɪt] *vt* **-gated; -gating** : coller au pare-chocs de

tailgate[2] *n* : hayon *m*

taillight ['teɪlˌlaɪt] *n* : feu *m* arrière (d'un véhicule)

tailor[1] ['teɪlər] *vt* **1** : faire sur mesure, confectionner (un vêtement) **2** ADAPT : faire, concevoir, adapter

tailor[2] *n* : tailleur *m*

tailpipe ['teɪlˌpaɪp] *n* : tuyau *m* d'échappement

tailspin ['teɪlˌspɪn] *n* : vrille *f* (d'un avion)

taint[1] ['teɪnt] *vt* **1** SULLY : entacher, souiller (une reputation, etc.) **2** SPOIL : gâter (des aliments)

taint[2] *n* : souillure *f*

Taiwanese[1] [ˌtaɪwə'niːz, -'niːs] *adj* : taiwanais

Taiwanese[2] *n* : Taiwanais *m*, -naise *f*

take[1] ['teɪk] *v* **took** ['tʊk]; **taken** ['teɪkən]; **taking** *vt* **1** CAPTURE : prendre, retenir **2** GRASP : prendre, saisir **3** CAPTIVATE : éprendre **4** INGEST : prendre <take your medicine : prends tes medicaments> **5** ACCEPT : entrer, accepter, prendre <to take office : entrer en fonction> <to take a job : accepter un emploi> **6** ASSUME : prendre, s'attribuer <she took all the credit : elle s'est attribuée tout le mérite> **7** BRING : porter, apporter <he took his father some coffee : il a apporté du café à son père> **8** WIN : remporter **9** SELECT : prendre, choisir **10** : prendre <she takes the train : elle prend le train> <take a seat : asseyez-vous> **11** FOLLOW : prendre, emprunter <they took a different route : ils ont pris un autre chemin> **12** CONDUCT : mener, conduire, emmener <the bus will take you there : l'autobus vous y mènera> **13 to take apart** DISMANTLE : démonter, démancher *Can* **14 to take place** HAPPEN : avoir lieu **15 to take s.o.'s side** : prendre parti pour qqn — *vi* **1** : faire effet <the vaccination took : le vaccin a fait effet> **2** BECOME, FALL : tomber <he took ill : il est tombé malade>

take[2] *n* : prise *f*

take back *vt* : retirer

take in *vt* **1** : reprendre (un vêtement) **2** INCLUDE : inclure, couvrir **3** ATTEND : aller à <let's take in a movie : allons au cinéma> **4** UNDERSTAND : saisir, comprendre **5** DECEIVE : tromper, se faire avoir

takeoff ['teɪkˌɔf] *n* **1** : décollage *m* (d'un avion) **2** PARODY : parodie *f*, imitation *f*

take off *vt* **1** REMOVE : enlever, ôter <take your shoes off : enlevez vos chaussures> **2** DEDUCT : déduire, soustraire **3** TAKE : prendre <he took two weeks off : il a pris deux semaines de vacances> — *vi* **1** DEPART : s'en aller, décamper **2** : décoller (se dit d'un avion)

take on *vt* **1** ACCEPT : assumer, prendre, accepter (des responsabilités, etc.) **2** : jouer contre <he took on the champion : il a joué contre le champion> **3** ADOPT : arborer, prendre <the city took on a festive air : la ville arborait un air de fête> **4** HIRE : engager, embaucher

takeover ['teɪkˌoːvər] *n* : prise *f* de pouvoir

take over *vt* : prendre le pouvoir, prendre la relève

taker ['teɪkər] *n* : preneur *m*, -neuse *f*

take up *vt* **1** LIFT : enlever, prendre **2** BEGIN : faire <to take up painting : faire de la peinture> **3** RESUME

: reprendre **4** SHORTEN : raccourcir (une jupe, une robe etc.)

takings ['teɪkɪŋz] *npl Brit* : recette *f*

talc ['tælk] → **talcum powder**

talcum powder ['tælkəm] *n* : talc *m*

tale ['teɪl] *n* **1** STORY : conte *m*, récit *m* **2** FALSEHOOD : histoires *fpl*, mensonge *m*

talent ['tælənt] *n* : talent *m*

talented ['tæləntəd] *adj* : talentueux, doué

talisman ['tæləsmən, -ləz-] *n, pl* **-mans** : talisman *m*

talk[1] ['tɔk] *vt* **1** SPEAK : parler <to talk French : parler français> **2** DISCUSS : parler (de) <to talk business : parler affaires> **3 to talk s.o. into doing sth** : persuader qqn de faire qqch — *vi* **1** CHAT : parler, causer **2** LECTURE : parler, discourir **3** GOSSIP : cancaner, jaser

talk[2] *n* **1** TALKING : paroles *fpl*, propos *mpl* **2** CONVERSATION, DISCUSSION : entretien *m*, conversation *f* <I had a talk with him : j'ai discuté avec lui> **3** RUMOR : racontars *mpl*, commérage *m fam* <it's the talk of the town : on ne parle que de ça> **4** SPEECH : discours *m*, exposé *m*

talkative ['tɔkəʧɪv] *adj* : bavard, loquace

talker ['tɔkər] *n* **he's a talker** : il est bavard

tall ['tɔl] *adj* **1** : grand <she's six feet tall : elle mesure six pieds> **2** : haut, élevé <a building two meters tall : un édifice haut de deux mètres> **3 a tall tale** : une histoire invraisemblable

tallness ['tɔlnəs] *n* : hauteur *f* (d'un édifice, etc.), taille *f* (d'une personne)

tallow ['tæloː] *n* : suif *m*

tally[1] ['tæli] *v* **-lied; -lying** *vt* RECORD : tenir le compte de — *vi* MATCH : correspondre

tally[2] *n, pl* **-lies** : compte *m*, pointage *m*

talon ['tælən] *n* : serre *f* (d'aigle)

tambourine [ˌtæmbəˈriːn] *n* : tambourin *m*

tame[1] ['teɪm] *vt* **tamed; taming** : apprivoiser, domestiquer

tame[2] *adj* **tamer; tamest 1** DOMESTICATED : apprivoisé **2** SUBDUED : docile, soumis **3** DULL : fade, terne

tamely ['teɪmli] *adv* : docilement

tamer ['teɪmər] *n* : dompteur *m*, -teuse *f* (de lions, etc.)

tamp ['tæmp] *vt* **to tamp down** : damer, tasser

tamper ['tæmpər] *vi* **1 to tamper with** ALTER : altérer, falsifier **2 to tamper with** BRIBE : suborner <to tamper with a witness : suborner un témoin>

tampon ['tæmˌpɑn] *n* : tampon *m* (hygiénique)

tan[1] ['tæn] *v* **tanned; tanning** *vt* : tanner <to tan hides : tanner des peaux> — *vi* : bronzer

tan[2] *n* **1** SUNTAN : bronzage *m* <to get a tan : se faire bronzer> **2** : brun *m* clair (couleur)

tandem[1] ['tændəm] *adv* **to ride tandem** : se promener en tandem

tandem[2] *n* : tandem *m*

tang ['tæŋ] *n* : goût *m* piquant

tangent ['tænʤənt] *n* **1** : tangente *f* (en mathématiques) **2** DIGRESSION : digression *f* <to go off on a tangent : partir dans une digression>

tangerine ['tænʤəˌriːn, ˌtænʤəˈ-] *n* : mandarine *f*

tangible ['tænʤəbəl] *adj* : tangible, palpable

tangibly ['tænʤəbli] *adv* : manifestement, de manière tangible

tangle[1] ['tæŋgəl] *v* **-gled; -gling** *vt* : emmêler, enchevêtrer — *vi* : s'emmêler

tangle[2] *n* **1** : enchevêtrement *m* **2** MUDDLE : confusion *f*, fouillis *m*

tango[1] ['tæŋgoː] *vi* : danser le tango

tango[2] *n, pl* **-gos** : tango *m*

tangy['tæŋi] *adj* **tangier; tangiest** : acidulé

tank ['tæŋk] *n* **1** : réservoir *m*, citerne *f*, cuve *f* <gas tank : réservoir à essence> **2** : char *m* (militaire)

tankard ['tæŋkərd] *n* : chope *f*

tanker ['tæŋkər] *n* **1** : navire-citern *m*, camion-citern *m* **2** *or* **oil tanker** : pétrolier *m*

tanner ['tænər] *n* : tanneur *m*

tannery ['tænəri] *n, pl* **-neries** : tannerie *f*

tannin ['tænən] *n* : tanin *m*

tantalize ['tæntəˌlaɪz] *vt* **-lized; -lizing** : tourmenter, allécher

tantalizing ['tæntəˌlaɪzɪŋ] *adj* : tentant, alléchant

tantamount ['tæntəˌmaʊnt] *adj* **~ to** : équivalent à

tantrum ['tæntrəm] *n* : accès *m* de colère, crise *f* <to throw a tantrum : piquer une crise>

Tanzanian[1] [ˌtænzəˈniːən] *adj* : tanzanien

Tanzanian[2] *n* : Tanzanien *m*, -nienne *f*

tap[1] ['tæp] *v* **tapped; tapping** *vt* **1** : percer (un tonneau), inciser (des arbres) **2** PAT, TOUCH : tapoter, taper <he tapped me on the shoulder : il me tapotait sur l'épaule> **3 to tap a phone** : mettre un téléphone sur écoute — *vi* : taper légèrement

tap[2] *n* **1** FAUCET : robinet *m* <beer on tap : bière en fût> **2** PAT, TOUCH : petit coup *m*, petite tape *f* <a sharp tap : un coup sec>

tape[1] ['teɪp] *vt* **taped; taping 1** : coller avec un ruban adhésif **2** RECORD : enregistrer (une cassette)

tape[2] *n* **1** STRIP : bande *f*, ruban *m* **2** *or* **adhesive tape** : ruban *m* adhésif **3** → **magnetic tape, tape measure**

tape measure *n* : mètre *m* ruban *France*, ruban *m* à mesurer *Can*
taper[1] ['teɪpər] *vt* : effiler, tailler en pointe — *vi* : s'effiler, se terminer en pointe
taper[2] *n* **1** CANDLE : cierge *m* **2** TAPERING : forme *f* effilée
tapestry ['tæpəstri] *n, pl* **-tries** : tapisserie *f*
tapeworm ['teɪpˌwərm] *n* : ténia *m*, ver *m* solitaire
tapioca [ˌtæpi'o:kə] *n* : tapioca *m*
tar[1] ['tɑr] *vt* **tarred; tarring** : goudronner
tar[2] *n* : goudron *m*
tarantula [tə'ræntʃələ, -'ræntələ] *n* : tarentule *f*
tardily ['tɑrdəli] *adv* : tardivement
tardiness ['tɑrdinəs] *n* : retard *m*
tardy ['tɑrdi] *adj* **tardier; -est** : tardif, en retard
target[1] ['tɑrgət] *vt* : viser, cibler
target[2] *n* **1** : cible *f* **2** GOAL : objectif *m*, but *m*
tariff ['tærɪf] *n* : tarif *m* douanier
tarnish[1] ['tɑrnɪʃ] *vt* : ternir
tarnish[2] *n* : ternissure *f*
tarpaulin [tɑr'pɔlən, 'tɑrpə-] *n* : bâche *f*
tarry[1] ['tæri] *vi* **-ried; -rying** : tarder
tarry[2] ['tɑri] *adj* : goudronneux, couvert de goudron
tart[1] ['tɑrt] *adj* **1** SOUR : aigre, âpre **2** CAUSTIC : aigre, acrimonieux
tart[2] *n* : tartelette *f*
tartan ['tɑrtən] *n* : tartan *m*, tissu *m* écossais
tartar ['tɑrtər] *n* **1** : tartre *m* (sur les dents) **2 tartar sauce** : sauce *f* tartare
tartness ['tɑrtnəs] *n* **1** SOURNESS : aigreur *f*, acidité *f* **2** ACRIMONY : acrimonie *f*
task ['tæsk] *n* : tâche *f*
taskmaster ['tæskˌmæstər] *n* **to be a hard taskmaster** : être très exigeant
tassel ['tæsəl] *n* : gland *m* (ornement)
taste[1] ['teɪst] *v* **tasted; tasting** *vt* **1** : goûter (à) <taste the sauce : goûte la sauce> **2** : sentir le goût de <you can't taste the pepper : on ne sent pas le goût du poivre> — *vi* : goûter <to taste sour : goûter amère> <to taste good : avoir bon goût>
taste[2] *n* **1** : goût *m* (sens) **2** FLAVOR : goût *m*, saveur *f* **3** BIT, SAMPLE : aperçu *m* <a taste of high life : un aperçu de la grande vie> **4** INCLINATION : goût *m*, penchant *m*
taste bud *n* : papille *f* gustative
tasteful ['teɪstfəl] *adj* : de bon goût
tastefully ['teɪstfəli] *adv* : avec goût
tasteless ['teɪstləs] *adj* **1** FLAVORLESS : insipide, qui n'a aucun goût **2** : de mauvais goût <a tasteless joke : une blague de mauvais goût>
taster ['teɪstər] *n* : dégustateur *m*, -trice *f*
tastiness ['teɪstinəs] *n* : saveur *f* agréable, bon goût *m*
tasty ['teɪsti] *adj* **tastier; -est** : savoureux, délicieux
tattered ['tæt̬ərd] *adj* : en lambeaux, en loques
tatters ['tæt̬ərz] *npl* **to be in tatters** : être en loques
tattle ['tæt̬əl] *vi* **-tled; -tling 1** CHATTER : jaser **2 to tattle on s.o.** : dénoncer qqn
tattletale ['tæt̬əlˌteɪl] *n* : rapporteur *m*, -teuse *f*
tattoo[1] [tæ'tu:] *vt* : tatouer
tattoo[2] *n* **1** : tatouage *m* **2 to beat a tattoo on** : tambouriner sur
taught → **teach**
taunt[1] ['tɔnt] *vt* : ridiculiser, railler
taunt[2] *n* : raillerie *f*, insulte *f*
Taurus [tɔrəs] *n* : Taureau *m*
taut ['tɔt] *adj* : tendu, raide
tautly ['tɔtli] *adv* : de façon tendue
tautness ['tɔtnəs] *n* : tension *f*, raideur *f*
tavern ['tævərn] *n* : taverne *f*
tawdry ['tɔdri] *adj* **tawdrier; -est** : tape-à-l'œil, criard, tapageur
tawny ['tɔni] *adj* **tawnier; -est** : fauve (couleur)
tax[1] ['tæks] *vt* **1** : imposer (une personne), taxer (des marchandises) **2** CHARGE : accuser <he taxed them with carelessness : il les a accusés d'être négligents> **3** TRY : mettre à l'épreuve <the job taxed her strength : l'emploi la fatiguait>
tax[2] *n* **1** : taxe *f* <sales tax : taxe à l'achat> **2** : impôt *m* <income tax : impôt sur le revenu> **3** STRAIN : fardeau *m*, poids *m*
taxable ['tæksəbəl] *adj* : imposable
taxation [tæk'seɪʃən] *n* : taxation *f*, imposition *f*
tax–exempt ['tæksɪg'zɛmpt, -ɛg-] *adj* : exempt d'impôts
taxi[1] ['tæksi] *vi* **taxied; taxiing** *or* **taxying; taxis** *or* **taxies 1** : transporter par taxi **2** : rouler au sol (se dit d'un avion)
taxi[2] *n, pl* **taxis** : taxi *m*
taxicab ['tæksiˌkæb] → **taxi**[2]
taxidermist ['tæksəˌdərmɪst] *n* : taxidermiste *mf*
taxidermy ['tæksəˌdərmi] *n* : taxidermie *f*
taxpayer ['tækspeɪər] *n* : contribuable *mf*
TB [ˌti:'bi:] → **tuberculosis**
tea ['ti:] *n* : thé *m*
teach ['ti:tʃ] *v* **taught** ['tɔt]; **teaching** *vt* **1** : apprendre, montrer <he's teaching me to drive : il m'apprend à conduire> **2** : enseigner, faire cours à <she teaches French : elle enseigne le français> **3 to teach s.o. a lesson** : servir de leçon à qqn — *vi* : enseigner
teacher ['ti:tʃər] *n* : enseignant *m*, -nante *f*; professeur *m*

teaching [ˈtiːtʃɪŋ] *n* : enseignement *m*
teacup [ˈtiːˌkʌp] *n* : tasse *f* à thé
teak [ˈtiːk] *n* : teck *m*
teakettle [ˈtiːˌketəl] *n* : bouilloire *f*
teal [ˈtiːl] *n, pl* **teal** *or* **teals** : sarcelle *f* (canard)
team[1] [ˈtiːm] *vi* **to team up with** : faire équipe avec
team[2] *adj* : d'équipe <a team effort : un effort d'équipe>
team[3] *n* **1** : attelage *m* (d'animaux) **2** : équipe *f* (aux sports, etc.)
teammate [ˈtiːmˌmeɪt] *n* : coéquipier *m*, -pière *f*
teamster [ˈtiːmstər] *n* : camionneur *m*, -neuse *f*; routier *m*
teamwork [ˈtiːmˌwərk] *n* : travail *m* d'équipe
teapot [ˈtiːˌpɑt] *n* : théière *f*
tear[1] [ˈtɛr] *v* **tore** [ˈtɔr]; **torn** [ˈtɔrn]; **tearing** *vt* **1** RIP : déchirer (un papier, etc.), se dechirer (un muscle) <to tear to shreds : mettre en lambeaux> **2** LACERATE : blesser (la peau) **3** REMOVE, SNATCH : arracher **4** *or* **to tear apart** DIVIDE : déchirer **5 to tear down** : démolir — *vi* **1** : se déchirer <this cloth tears easily : ce tissu se déchire facilement> **2** RUSH : se précipiter <he tore out of the house : il est sorti en trombe de la maison>
tear[2] *n* : déchirure *f*
tear[3] [ˈtɪr] *n* : larme *f* <to break into tears : fondre en larmes>
teardrop [ˈtɪrˌdrɑp] → **tear**[3]
tearful [ˈtɪrfəl] *adj* : larmoyant
tearfully [ˈtɪrfəli] *adv* : en pleurant, les larmes aux yeux
tease[1] [ˈtiːz] *vt* **teased; teasing** : taquiner
tease[2] *n* : taquin *m*, -quine *f*
teaspoon [ˈtiːˌspuːn] *n* : petite cuillère *f*, cuillère *f* à café
teaspoonful [ˈtiːˌspuːnˌfʊl] *n* : cuillerée *f* à café
teat [ˈtiːt] *n* : tétine *f*
technical [ˈtɛknɪkəl] *adj* : technique — **technically** [-kli] *adv*
technicality [ˌtɛknəˈkæləṭi] *n, pl* **-ties** : détail *m* technique
technician [tɛkˈnɪʃən] *n* : technicien *m*, -cienne *f*
technique [tɛkˈniːk] *n* : technique *f*
technological [ˌtɛknəˈlɑdʒɪkəl] *adj* : technologique
technology [tɛkˈnɑlədʒi] *n, pl* **-gies** : technologie *f*
tedious [ˈtiːdiəs] *adj* : fastidieux, ennuyeux
tediously [ˈtiːdiəsli] *adv* : fastidieusement, de façon ennuyeuse
tediousness [ˈtiːdiəsnəs] *n* : ennui *m*
tedium [ˈtiːdiəm] → **tediousness**
tee [ˈtiː] *n* : tee *m* (au golf)
teem [ˈtiːm] *vi* **to teem with** : foisonner de, abonder en
teenage [ˈtiːnˌeɪdʒ] *or* **teenaged** [-ˌeɪdʒd] *adj* : jeune, adolescent, d'adolescence
teenager [ˈtiːnˌeɪdʒər] *n* : adolescent *m*, -cente *f*
teens [ˈtiːnz] *npl* : adolescence *f*
teepee → **tepee**
teeter[1] [ˈtiːṭər] *vi* **1** WAVER : vaciller, chanceler **2** SEESAW : balancer, basculer
teeter[2] *n or* **teeter–totter** [ˈtiːṭər-ˌtɑṭər] → **seesaw**
teeth → **tooth**
teethe [ˈtiːð] *vi* **teethed; teething** : faire ses dents
telecast[1] [ˈtɛləˌkæst] *vt* **-cast; -casting** : téléviser, diffuser
telecast[2] *n* : émission *f* de télévision
telecommunication [ˌtɛləkəˌmjuːnəˈkeɪʃən] *n* : télécommunication *f*
telegram [ˈtɛləˌgræm] *n* : télégramme *m*
telegraph[1] [ˈtɛləˌgræf] *v* : télégraphier
telegraph[2] *n* : télégraphe *m*
telepathic [ˌtɛləˈpæθɪk] *adj* : télépathique
telepathy [təˈlɛpəθi] *n* : télépathie *f*
telephone[1] [ˈtɛləˌfoːn] *v* **-phoned; -phoning** *vt* : téléphoner à — *vi* : appeler, téléphoner
telephone[2] *n* : téléphone *m*
telescope[1] [ˈtɛləˌskoːp] *v* **-scoped; -scoping** *vi* : se télescoper — *vt* CONDENSE : comprimer, condenser
telescope[2] *n* : télescope *m*
telescopic [ˌtɛləˈskɑpɪk] *adj* : télescopique
televise [ˈtɛləˌvaɪz] *vt* **-vised; -vising** : téléviser
television [ˈtɛləˌvɪʒən] *n* **1** : télévision *f* **2** *or* **television set** : téléviseur *m*
tell [ˈtɛl] *v* **told** [ˈtoːld]; **telling** *vt* **1** COUNT : compter, être en tout <all told there were 27 of us : nous étions 27 en tout> **2** NARRATE : raconter, conter **3** REVEAL : divulguer, dévoiler **4** ORDER : dire à <they told me to wait : ils m'ont dit d'attendre> **5** RECOGNIZE : voir, lire <you can tell it's a masterpiece : on voit bien que c'est un chef-d'œuvre> <to tell time : lire l'heure> — *vi* **1** SAY : dire **2** KNOW : savoir <as far as I can tell : pour autant que je sache> **3** SHOW : se faire sentir <the tension began to tell : la tension a commencé à se faire sentir>
teller [ˈtɛlər] *n* **1** NARRATOR : conteur *m*, -teuse *f* **2** *or* **bank teller** : caissier *m*, -sière *f*
temerity [təˈmɛrəṭi] *n, pl* **-ties** : témérité *f*, audace *f*
temp [ˈtɛmp] *n* : intérimaire *mf*; occasionnel *m*, -nelle *f Can*
temper[1] [ˈtɛmpər] *vt* **1** MODERATE : tempérer **2** TOUGHEN : endurcir
temper[2] *n* **1** HARDNESS : trempe *f* (de métal) **2** DISPOSITION : tempérament

m, caractère *m* **3 to lose one's temper** : se mettre en colère, s'emporter
temperament |ˈtɛmpərmənt, -prə-, -pərə-| *n* : tempérament *m*, nature *f*
temperamental |ˌtɛmpərˈmɛntəl, -prə-, -pərə-| *adj* : capricieux
temperance |ˈtɛmprənts| *n* : tempérance *f*, modération *f*
temperate |ˈtɛmpərət| *adj* **1** MILD : tempéré <temperate climate : climat tempéré> **2** MODERATE : modéré <to be a temperate drinker : boire modérément>
temperature |ˈtɛmpərˌtʃʊr, -prə-, -tʃər| *n* **1** : température *f* **2** FEVER : température *f*, fièvre *f* <to run a temperature : faire de la température>
tempest |ˈtɛmpəst| *n* **1** STORM : tempête *f*, orage *m* **2** UPROAR : tumulte *m*, chahut *m*
tempestuous |tɛmˈpɛstʃʊəs| *adj* **1** STORMY : tempétueux **2** ARDENT, RAGING : impétueux, fougueux
temple |ˈtɛmpəl| *n* **1** : temple *m* (religieux) **2** : tempe *f* (en anatomie)
tempo |ˈtɛmˌpoː| *n, pl* **-pi** |-ˌpiː| *or* **-pos** : tempo *m*
temporal |ˈtɛmpərəl| *adj* : temporel
temporary |ˈtɛmpəˌrɛri| *adj* : temporaire — **temporarily** |ˌtɛmpəˈrɛrəli| *adv*
tempt |ˈtɛmpt| *vt* : tenter
temptation |tɛmpˈteɪʃən| *n* : tentation *f*
tempter |ˈtɛmptər| *n* : tentateur *m*
temptress |ˈtɛmptrəs| *n* : tentatrice *f*
ten[1] |ˈtɛn| *adj* : dix
ten[2] *n* **1** : dix *m* **2** : dizaine *f* <there were tens of them : il y en avait des dizaines>
tenable |ˈtɛnəbəl| *adj* : soutenable, défendable
tenacious |təˈneɪʃəs| *adj* : tenace
tenaciously |təˈneɪʃəsli| *adv* : avec ténacité
tenacity |təˈnæsəṭi| *n* : ténacité *f*, opiniâtreté *f*
tenancy |ˈtɛnənt͡si| *n, pl* **-cies 1** : location *f* <terms of tenancy : conditions de location> **2** : période *f* d'occupation (d'un logement)
tenant |ˈtɛnənt| *n* : locataire *mf*
tend |ˈtɛnd| *vi* **1** : se diriger <we cannot tell where society is tending : on ne peut pas dire où notre société se dirige> **2 to tend to** : avoir tendance à, être enclin à <she tends to be pessimistic : elle a tendance à être pessimiste> — *vt* : surveiller, s'occuper de <to tend the plants : s'occuper des plantes>
tendency |ˈtɛndənt͡si| *n, pl* **-cies** : tendance *f*
tender[1] |ˈtɛndər| *vt* OFFER : donner, offrir <I tendered my resignation : j'ai donné ma démission> <to tender thanks : offrir ses remerciements>
tender[2] *adj* **1** DELICATE : tendre, fragile **2** LOVING : tendre, affectueux **3** SORE : sensible **4** YOUNG : tendre <a tender age : un âge tendre> **5** SUCCULENT : tendre <a tender steak : un steak tendre>
tender[3] *n* **1** OFFER : soumission *f*, offre *f* **2 legal tender** : cours *m* légal
tenderize |ˈtɛndəˌraɪz| *vt* **-ized; -izing** : attendrir (de la viande)
tenderloin |ˈtɛndərˌlɔɪn| *n* : filet *m* (de bœuf, de porc, etc.)
tenderly |ˈtɛndərli| *adv* : tendrement, avec tendresse
tenderness |ˈtɛndərnəs| *n* : tendresse *f*
tendon |ˈtɛndən| *n* : tendon *m*
tendril |ˈtɛndrɪl| *n* : vrille *f* (d'une plante)
tenement |ˈtɛnəmənt| *n or* **tenement house** : immeuble *m*
tenet |ˈtɛnət| *n* : principe *m*, croyance *f*
tennis |ˈtɛnəs| *n* : tennis *m*
tenor |ˈtɛnər| *n* **1** DRIFT, GIST : contenu *m*, sens *m* général (d'une conversation, etc.) **2** : ténor *m* <tenor voice : voix de ténor>
tenpins |ˈtɛnˌpɪnz| *n* : bowling *m*
tense[1] |ˈtɛnt͡s| *vi* **tensed; tensing** *or* **to tense up** : se raidir, se tendre
tense[2] *adj* **tenser; tensest 1** RIGID : tendu, raide **2** UPTIGHT : tendu, stressé
tense[3] *n* : temps *m* (en grammaire) <the past tense : le passé composé>
tensely |ˈtɛnt͡sli| *adv* : de façon tendue
tenseness |ˈtɛnt͡snəs| *n* : tension *f*
tensile |ˈtɛnt͡səl, ˈtɛnˌsaɪl| *adj* : extensible
tension |ˈtɛnt͡ʃən| *n* **1** TAUTNESS : tension *f*, raideur *f* **2** STRESS : tension *f*, stress *m*
tent |ˈtɛnt| *n* : tente *f*
tentacle |ˈtɛntɪkəl| *n* : tentacule *m*
tentative |ˈtɛntəṭɪv| *adj* **1** : provisoire <tentative plans : plans provisoires> **2** HESITANT : hésitant, indécis <tentative steps : pas hésitants>
tentatively |ˈtɛntəṭɪvli| *adv* **1** : provisoirement **2** HESITANTLY : incertainement, timidement
tenth[1] |ˈtɛnθ| *adv & adj* : dixième
tenth[2] *n* **1** : dizième *mf* (dans une série) **2** : dizième *m* (en mathématiques) **3** (*used in dates*) <the tenth of May : le dix mai>
tenuous |ˈtɛnjʊəs| *adj* : précaire, ténu
tenuously |ˈtɛnjʊəsli| *adv* : de manière ténue
tenure |ˈtɛnjər| *n* : période *f* de jouissance (en droit), titularisation *f* (à un poste universitaire)
tenured |ˈtɛnjərd| *adj* : titulaire
tepee |ˈtiːˌpiː| *n* : tipi *m*
tepid |ˈtɛpɪd| *adj* : tiède
term[1] |ˈtərm| *vt* : appeler, nommer
term[2] *n* **1** PERIOD : terme *m* **2** : terme *m* (en mathématiques) **3** WORD : terme *m*, expression *f* **4 terms** *npl* CONDITIONS : termes *mpl*, conditions *fpl* **5 terms** *npl* RELATIONS : termes

mpl, rapports *mpl* <on good terms with : en bons termes avec>
terminal[1] ['tərmənəl] *adj* : terminal
terminal[2] *n* **1** : borne *f* (en électricité) **2** *or* **computer terminal** : terminal *m* **3** : terminus *m* (de train, de bus)
terminate ['tərmə,neɪt] *v* **-nated; -nating** *vt* : mettre fin à — *vi* : se terminer
termination [,tərmə'neɪʃən] *n* **1** END : fin *f* **2** ENDING : terminaison *f* (en grammaire)
terminology [,tərmə'nɑlədʒi] *n, pl* **-gies** : terminologie *f*
terminus ['tərmənəs] *n, pl* **-ni** [-,naɪ] *or* **-nuses 1** END : bout *m,* fin *f* **2** TERMINAL : terminus *m*
termite ['tər,maɪt] *n* : termite *m*
tern ['tərn] *n* : hirondelle *f* de mer, sterne *f*
terrace[1] ['terəs] *vt* **-raced; -racing** : aménager en terrasses
terrace[2] *n* **1** PATIO : terrasse *f* **2** EMBANKMENT : terre-plein *m* **3** : terrasse *f* (en agriculture) **4** *or* **terraced houses** : rangée *f* de maisons
terra–cotta [,terə'kɑtə] *n* : terre *f* cuite
terrain [tə'reɪn] *n* : terrain *m*
terrapin ['terəpɪn] *n* : tortue *f* d'eau douce
terrarium [tə'ræriəm] *n, pl* **-ia** [-iə] *or* **-iums** : vivarium *m* (pour les animaux), serre *f* miniature (pour les plantes)
terrestrial [tə'restriəl] *adj* : terrestre
terrible ['terəbəl] *adj* : terrible, épouvantable
terribly ['terəbli] *adv* **1** VERY : terriblement, vraiment <I'm terribly sorry : je suis vraiment désolée> **2** BADLY : terriblement, affreusement mal <terribly ill : terriblement malade>
terrier ['teriər] *n* : terrier *m*
terrific [tə'rɪfɪk] *adj* **1** FRIGHTFUL : terrible, terrifiant **2** EXTRAORDINARY : terrible, extrême <a terrific speed : une allure vertigineuse> **3** EXCELLENT : formidable, épatant *fam* <we had a terrific time : nous nous sommes vraiment amusés>
terrify ['terə,faɪ] *vt* **-fied; -fying** : terrifier
terrifying ['terə,faɪɪŋ] *adj* : terrifiant, effroyable
territorial [,terə'toriəl] *adj* : territorial
territory ['terə,tori] *n, pl* **-ries** : territoire *m*
terror ['terər] *n* : terreur *f*
terrorism ['terər,ɪzəm] *n* : terrorisme *m*
terrorist[1] ['terərɪst] *adj* : terroriste
terrorist[2] *n* : terroriste *mf*
terrorize ['terər,aɪz] *vt* **-ized; -izing** : terroriser
terry ['teri] *n, pl* **-ries** *or* **terry cloth** : tissu *m* éponge, ratine *f Can*
terse ['tərs] *adj* **terser; tersest** : concis, succinct
tersely ['tərsli] *adv* : succinctement, brièvement
tertiary ['tərʃi,eri] *adj* : tertiaire
test[1] ['test] *vt* : examiner, tester — *vi* **to test for** : faire une recherche de
test[2] *n* **1** : examen *m* (scolaire), test *m* **2** TRIAL : épreuve *f* **3** : analyse *f,* examen *m* <blood test : analyse de sang>
testament ['testəmənt] *n* **1** WILL : testament *m* **2** : Testament *m* <the New Testament : le Nouveau Testament>
testicle ['testɪkəl] *n* : testicule *m*
testify ['testə,faɪ] *v* **-fied; -fying** : témoigner
testimonial [,testə'moːniəl] *n* **1** RECOMMENDATION : recommandation *f,* attestation *f* **2** TRIBUTE : témoignage *m*
testimony ['testə,moːni] *n, pl* **-nies** : témoignage *m,* déposition *f*
testy ['testi] *adj* **testier; -est** : irritable, irascible
tetanus ['tetənəs] *n* : tétanos *m*
tête–à–tête [,teɪtə'tet, ,teɪtə'teɪt] *n* : tête-à-tête *m*
tether[1] ['teðər] *vt* : attacher (un animal)
tether[2] *n* **1** : longe *f* **2 at the end of one's tether** : à bout de patience
text ['tekst] *n* **1** : texte *m* **2** TOPIC : thème *m,* sujet *m* **3** → **textbook**
textbook ['tekst,bʊk] *n* : manuel *m* scolaire
textile ['tek,staɪl, 'tekstəl] *n* : textile *m*
textual ['tekstʃʊəl] *adj* : textuel
texture ['tekstʃər] *n* : texture *f*
Thai[1] ['taɪ] *adj* : thaïlandais
Thai[2] *n* : Thaïlandais *m,* -daise *f*
than[1] ['ðæn] *conj* : que <older than I am : plus âgé que moi> <nothing is worse than boredom : rien n'est pire que l'ennui> <he'd do anything rather than lie : il ferait tout plutôt que mentir>
than[2] *prep* : que, de <thinner than me : plus mince que moi> <fewer than 10 : moins de 10>
thank ['θæŋk] *vt* : remercier
thankful ['θæŋkfəl] *adj* : reconnaissant
thankfully ['θæŋkfəli] *adv* **1** GRATEFULLY : avec reconnaissance, avec gratitude **2** FORTUNATELY : heureusement
thankfulness ['θæŋkfəlnəs] *n* : reconnaissance *f,* gratitude *f*
thankless ['θæŋkləs] *adj* : ingrat
thanks ['θæŋks] *npl* **1** : remerciements *mpl* **2** ~ **to** : grâce à
Thanksgiving [θæŋks'gɪvɪŋ, 'θæŋks,-] *n* : jour *m* d'Action de Grâces
that[1] ['ðæt] *adv* **1** : comme ça <a nail about that long : un clou environ long comme ça> **2** VERY : tellement, très <he did not take his classes that seriously : il ne prenait pas ses cours tellement au sérieux>
that[2] *adj, pl* **those** : ce, cet, cette, ces <that girl : cette fille> <those people : ces gens-là>
that[3] *conj* **1** : que <she said that she was busy : elle a dit qu'elle était oc-

cupée> <it's unlikely that he'll be there : il y a peu de chances qu'il soit là> **2** SO : afin que <he shouted that all might hear : il a crié afin que tout le monde puisse entendre>

that[4] *pron, pl* **those** [ˈðoːz] **1** (*used to introduce relative clauses*) : que <the house that we built : la maison que nous avons construite> **2** WHO : qui <the person that won the race : la personne qui a gagné la course> **3** : celui-là, celle-là <do you prefer this or that? : préférez-vous celui-ci ou celui-là?> **4** : cela, ce, ça <is that you? : c'est toi?> <after that : après cela>

thatch[1] [ˈθætʃ] *vt* : couvrir (un toit) de chaume

thatch[2] *n* : chaume *m*

thaw[1] [ˈθɔ] *vt* : dégeler — *vi* : fondre

thaw[2] *n* : dégel *m*

the[1] [ðə, *before vowel sounds usu* ðiː] *adv* : le <the sooner the better : le plus tôt sera le mieux>

the[2] *art* **1** : le, la, l', les <let the cat out : laisse le chat sortir> <the right answer : la bonne réponse> <the elite : l'élite> <the English : les Anglais> **2** EACH : le, la <forty cookies the box : quarante biscuits la boîte>

theater *or* **theatre** [ˈθiːəʲtər] *n* **1** : théâtre *m* (édifice) **2** DRAMA : théâtre *m*, art *m* dramatique **3** : théâtre *m* (de la guerre, etc.)

theatrical [θiˈætrɪkəl] *adj* : théâtral

thee [ðiː] *pron* : te, toi

theft [ˈθeft] *n* : vol *m*

their [ðer] *adj* : leur <their notebooks : leurs cahiers>

theirs [ðerz] *pron* : le leur, la leur, les leurs <the red house is theirs : la maison rouge est la leur>

them [ðem] *pron* **1** (*as a direct object*) : les <in order to understand them : afin de les comprendre> **2** (*as an indirect object*) : leur <we sent them a present : nous leur avons envoyé un cadeau> **3** (*as the object of a preposition*) : eux, elles <he thought of them : il a pensé à eux> <some of them : quelques-unes d'entre elles>

theme [ˈθiːm] *n* **1** TOPIC : thème *m* **2** COMPOSITION : composition *f* **3** : thème *m* (musical)

themselves [ðəmˈselvz, ðem-] *pron* **1** (*used reflexively*) : se <they hurt themselves : ils se sont blessés> **2** (*used for emphasis*) : eux-mêmes, elles-mêmes <they made the dresses themselves : elles ont fait les robes elles-mêmes> **3** (*used after a preposition*) : eux, elles, eux-mêmes, elles-mêmes <they talked among themselves : ils discutaient entre eux> **4 by themselves** : tous seuls, toutes seules

then[1] [ðen] *adv* **1** : alors, à ce moment-là <from then on : à partir de ce moment-là> **2** : ensuite, puis <he answered the questions and then he left : il a répondu aux questions, puis il est parti> **3** BESIDES : et puis <then there is the interest to be paid : et puis il y a l'intérêt à payer> **4** : donc, alors <take it, then, if you want it so much : prends-le, alors, si tu le veux tant> **5** CONSEQUENTLY : donc

then[2] *adj* : d'alors, de l'époque <the then treasurer : le trésorier d'alors>

then[3] *n* : ce temps-là <since then : depuis ce temps-là>

thence [ˈðenʦ, ˈθenʦ] *adv* : de là

theologian [ˌθiːəˈloːʤən] *n* : théologien *m*, -gienne *f*

theological [ˌθiːəˈlɑdʒɪkəl] *adj* : théologique

theology [θiˈɑlədʒi] *n, pl* **-gies** : théologie *f*

theorem [ˈθiːərəm, ˈθɪrəm] *n* : théorème *m*

theoretical [ˌθiːəˈretɪkəl] *adj* : théorique — **theoretically** *adv*

theorize [ˈθiːəˌraɪz] *vi* **-rized; -rizing** : théoriser

theory [ˈθiːəri, ˈθɪri] *n, pl* **-ries** : théorie *f*

therapeutic [ˌθerəˈpjuːʲɪk] *adj* : thérapeutique — **therapeutically** *adv*

therapist [ˈθerəpɪst] *n* : thérapeute *mf*

therapy [ˈθerəpi] *n, pl* **-pies** : thérapie *f*

there[1] [ðær] *adv* **1** : là, là-bas, y <stand over there : mettez-vous debout là-bas> <he went there after class : il s'y est rendu après ses cours> **2** (*used for emphasis*) : voilà <there's where I disagree : voilà où je ne suis pas d'accord> <there, I'm finished! : voilà, j'ai terminé!>

there[2] *pron* **1** (*used as a function word to introduce a sentence or clause*) <there shall come a time : le jour viendra> **2** (*used as an indefinite substitute for a name*) <hi there! : salut, toi!> **3 there is** : il y a <there's someone waiting for you : il y a quelqu'un qui t'attend>

thereabouts [ðærəˈbaʊʦ, ˈðærəˌ-] *or* **thereabout** [ðærəˈbaʊt, ˈðærəˌ-] *adv* **1** NEARBY : dans les environs, par là **2** : environ <a boy of 18 or thereabouts : un garçon d'environ 18 ans>

thereafter [ðærˈæftər] *adv* : par la suite

thereby [ðærˈbaɪ, ˈðærˌbaɪ] *adv* **1** THUS : ainsi <she thereby lost her chance to win : elle a ainsi perdu sa chance de gagner> **2 thereby hangs a tale** : c'est toute une histoire

therefore [ˈðærˌfor] *adv* : donc, par conséquent

therein [ðærˈɪn] *adv* **1** : dedans, à l'intérieur <the box and the jewels therein : la boîte et les bijoux qui étaient dedans> **2** : là <therein lies the problem : là réside le problème>

thereof [ðærˈʌv, -ˈɑv] *adv* : de cela, en

thereupon [ˈðerəˌpɑn, -ˌpɔn; ˌðerəˈpɑn, -ˈpɔn] *adv* : sur ce

therewith [ðərˈwɪð, -ˈwɪθ] *adv* : avec cela
thermal [ˈθərməl] *adj* : thermal, thermique <thermal spring : source thermale> <thermal power station : centrale thermique>
thermodynamics [ˌθərmodaˈnæmɪks] *ns & pl* : thermodynamique *f*
thermometer [θərˈmɑmət̬ər] *n* : thermomètre *m*
thermos [ˈθərməs] *n* : thermos *mf*
thermostat [ˈθərmə,stæt] *n* : thermostat *m*
thesaurus [θiˈsɔrəs] *n, pl* **-sauri** [-ˈsɔr,aɪ] *or* **-sauruses** [-ˈsɔrəsəz] : dictionnaire *m* analogique, dictionnaire *m* des synonymes
these → this², **this³**
thesis [ˈθiːsɪs] *n, pl* **theses** [ˈθi,siːz] : thèse *f*
they [ˈðeɪ] *pron* **1** : ils, elles <they dance well : ils dansent bien> <there they are : les voici> **2** (*used for emphasis*) : eux, elles <*they* won't be coming : ils ne viennent pas, eux> **3** PEOPLE : on <they say she's pretty : on dit qu'elle est belle>
thiamine [ˈθaɪəmɪn, -ˌmiːn] *n* : thiamine *f*
thick¹ [ˈθɪk] *adj* **1** : épais <a thick plank : une planche épaisse> <two millimeters thick : deux millimètres d'épaisseur> **2** : dense, épais <thick fog : brume épaisse> **3** STUPID : bête, obtus **4 to be thick with** : être rempli de
thick² *n* **1 in the thick of** : au plus fort de (une bataille, etc.) **2 through thick and thin** : contre vents et marées
thicken [ˈθɪkən] *vi* : s'épaissir — *vt* : épaissir (une sauce, etc.)
thickener [ˈθɪkənər] *n* : épaississant *m*
thicket [ˈθɪkət] *n* : fourré *m*, hallier *m*
thickly [ˈθɪkli] *adv* **1** : en couche épaisse, en tranches épaisses **2** DENSELY : dru <snow was falling thickly : la neige tombait dru> <thickly wooded : très boisé>
thickness [ˈθɪknəs] *n* : épaisseur *f*, grosseur *f*
thick–skinned [ˈθɪkˈskɪnd] *adj* : dur, insensible
thief [ˈθiːf] *n, pl* **thieves** [ˈθiːvz] : voleur *m*, -leuse *f*
thieve [ˈθiːv] *v* **thieved; thieving** : voler
thigh [ˈθaɪ] *n* : cuisse *f*
thighbone [ˈθaɪ,boːn] *n* : fémur *m*
thimble [ˈθɪmbəl] *n* : dé *m* à coudre
thin¹ [ˈθɪn] *v* **thinned; thinning** *vt* : allonger, diluer (un liquide) — *vi* : se dissiper (se dit du brouillard, etc.), se disperser (se dit d'une foule) <his hair was thinning : il perdait ses cheveux>
thin² *adj* **thinner; thinnest 1** : fin, mince <thin paper : papier fin> **2** LEAN, SLIM : mince, maigre **3** SPARSE : clairsemé <thin hair : cheveux clairsemés> **4** : raréfié (de l'air), clair (d'un potage)
thing [ˈθɪŋ] *n* **1** OBJECT : chose *f*, objet *m*, truc *m fam* <a thing of beauty : une belle chose> **2** ACTIVITY, EVENT : chose *f* <the first thing to do : la première chose à faire> <it was a terrible thing : c'était une chose épouvantable> **3 things** *npl* BELONGINGS : affaires *fpl*, effets *mpl* personnels <to pack one's things : faire ses valises> <I don't have a thing to wear : je n'ai rien à me mettre>
think [ˈθɪŋk] *v* **thought** [ˈθɔt]; **thinking** *vt* **1** INTEND : penser <he thought to return early : il a pensé revenir tôt> **2** BELIEVE : penser, croire **3** PONDER : penser à, réfléchir à <to think things out : bien réfléchir> **4** REMEMBER : penser à, se rappeler <I didn't think to ask him : je n'ai pas pensé à lui demander> **5 to think up** : inventer — *vi* **1** REASON : penser, raisonner **2 to think of** CONSIDER : penser à, considérer <think of your family first : pense à ta famille en premier>
thinker [ˈθɪŋkər] *n* : penseur *m*, -seuse *f*
thinly [ˈθɪnli] *adv* **1** LIGHTLY : légèrement **2 to cut thinly** : couper en tranches minces **3 to spread thinly** : étaler en couche mince **4 thinly populated** : à la population éparse
thinness [ˈθɪnnəs] *n* : minceur *f*
thin–skinned [ˈθɪnˈskɪnd] *adj* : susceptible, sensible
third¹ [ˈθərd] *or* **thirdly** [-li] *adv* : troisième, troisièmement, en troisième place
third² *adj* : troisième
third³ *n* **1** : troisième *mf* (dans une série) **2** : tiers *m* (en mathématiques) **3** (*used in dates*) <the third of December : le trois décembre>
Third World *n* : le tiers-monde *m*
thirst¹ [ˈθərst] *vi* **to thirst for** : avoir soif de
thirst² *n* : soif *f*
thirsty [ˈθərsti] *adj* **thirstier; -est** : assoiffé
thirteen¹ [ˌθərˈtiːn] *adj* : treize
thirteen² *n* : treize *m*
thirteenth¹ [ˌθərˈtiːnθ] *adj* : treizième
thirteenth² *n* **1** : treizième *mf* (dans une série) **2** : treizième *m* (en mathématiques) **3** (*used in dates*) <the thirteenth of January : le treize janvier>
thirtieth¹ [ˈθərt̬iəθ] *adj* : trentième
thirtieth² *n* **1** : trentième *mf* (dans une série) **2** : trentième *m* (en mathématiques)
thirty¹ [ˈθərt̬i] *adj* : trente
thirty² *n, pl* **thirties** : trente *m*
this¹ [ˈðɪs] *adv* : si, aussi <it was this big : c'était aussi grand que ça>

this[2] *adj, pl* **these** [ˈðiːz] **1** : ce, cet, cette, ces <this morning : ce matin> <all these years : toutes ces années> **2** : ce . . . -ci, cet . . . -ci, cette . . . -ci, ces . . . -ci <this car or that one : cette voiture-ci ou celle-là>
this[3] *pron, pl* **these 1** : voici <this is your book : voici ton livre> **2** : ce, ceci <who is this? : qui est-ce?> <after this, he left : après ceci, il est parti> <this is my sister : je vous présente ma sœur>
thistle [ˈθɪsəl] *n* : chardon *m*
thong [ˈθɔŋ] *n* : lanière *f* (de cuir, etc.)
thorax [ˈθorˌæks] *n, pl* **-raxes** *or* **-races** [ˈθoraˌsiːz] : thorax *m*
thorn [ˈθɔrn] *n* : épine *f*
thorny [ˈθɔrni] *adj* **thornier; -est** : épineux
thorough [ˈθəˌroː] *adj* **1** COMPLETE : approfondi **2** PAINSTAKING : consciencieux, minutieux
thoroughbred [ˈθəroˌbrɛd] *adj* : de pure race
Thoroughbred *n* : pur-sang *m*
thoroughfare [ˈθəroˌfær] *n* : voie *f* de communication, rue *f*
thoroughly [ˈθərəli] *adv* **1** METICULOUSLY : minutieusement, à fond **2** COMPLETELY : tout à fait, absolument
those → that[2], **that**[4]
thou [ˈðaʊ] *pron* : tu
though[1] [ˈðoː] *adv* HOWEVER : cependant, pourtant
though[2] *conj* : bien que, quoique
thought[1] [ˈθɔt] **→ think**
thought[2] *n* **1** THINKING : pensée *f* <Western thought : la pensée de l'Ouest> **2** CONSIDERATION : réflexion *f* <after much thought : après mûre réflexion> **3** IDEA : pensée *f*, idée *f*
thoughtful [ˈθɔtfəl] *adj* **1** PENSIVE : pensif, songeur **2** CONSIDERATE : attentionné, prévenant **3** REASONED : réfléchi, sérieux <a thoughtful essay : une composition réfléchie>
thoughtfully [ˈθɔtfəli] *adv* **1** PENSIVELY : pensivement **2** CONSIDERATELY : avec prévenance **3** REFLECTIVELY : de façon réfléchie
thoughtfulness [ˈθɔtfəlnəs] *n* : considération *f*, attention *f*
thoughtless [ˈθɔtləs] *adj* **1** RASH : irréfléchi, hâtif **2** INCONSIDERATE : irréfléchi, inconsidéré
thoughtlessly [ˈθɔtləsli] *adv* : inconsidérément
thousand[1] [ˈθaʊzənd] *adj* : mille
thousand[2] *n, pl* **-sands** *or* **-sand** : mille *m* <two thousand : deux mille>
thousandth[1] [ˈθaʊzənθ] *adj* : millième
thousandth[2] *n* **1** : millième *mf* (dans une série) **2** : millième *m* (en mathématiques)
thrash [ˈθræʃ] *vt* **1** THRESH : battre (le grain) **2** BEAT : battre — *vi or* **to thrash about** : se débattre
thread[1] *vt* **1** : enfiler (une aiguille, des perles) **2 to thread one's way through** : se faufiler entre
thread[2] [ˈθrɛd] *n* **1** : fil *m* (en couture) **2** : fil *m*, cours *m* <the thread of the story : le fil de l'histoire> **3** TRICKLE, WISP : filet *m* <a thread of smoke : un filet de fumée>
threadbare [ˈθrɛdˌbær] *adj* **1** WORN : usé jusqu'à la corde, élimé **2** TRITE : usé, banal
threat [ˈθrɛt] *n* : menace *f*
threaten [ˈθrɛtən] *v* : menacer
threateningly [ˈθrɛtəniŋli] *adv* : de façon menaçante
three[1] [ˈθriː] *adj* : trois
three[2] *n* : trois *m*
threefold[1] [ˈθriːˌfoːld] *adv* : trois fois autant
threefold[2] *adj* : triple
threescore [ˈθriːˈskor] *adj* : soixante
thresh [ˈθrɛʃ] *vt* : battre (le grain)
thresher [ˈθrɛʃər] *n or* **threshing machine** : batteuse *f*
threshold [ˈθrɛʃˌhoːld, -ˌoːld] *n* : seuil *m*
threw → throw[1]
thrice [ˈθraɪs] *adv* : trois fois
thrift [ˈθrɪft] *n* : économie *f*
thriftless [ˈθrɪftləs] *adj* : dépensier
thrifty [ˈθrɪfti] *adj* **thriftier; -est** : économe
thrill[1] [ˈθrɪl] *vt* : électriser, transporter (d'émotion) — *vi* : frissonner
thrill[2] *n* : frisson *m*, émotion *f*
thriller [ˈθrɪlər] *n* : thriller *m*, roman *m* ou film *m* à suspense
thrive [ˈθraɪv] *vi* **throve** [ˈθroːv] *or* **thrived; thriven** [ˈθrɪvən] **1** FLOURISH : bien pousser, bien se porter **2** PROSPER : prospérer, réussir
throat [ˈθroːt] *n* : gorge *f* <sore throat : mal de gorge> <to clear one's throat : s'éclaircir la voix>
throaty [ˈθroːti] *adj* **throatier; -est** : rauque, guttural
throb[1] [ˈθrɑb] *vi* **throbbed; throbbing 1** PALPITATE : battre, palpiter (se dit du cœur) **2** : vibrer (se dit d'un moteur) **3 to throb with pain** : lanciner <my head was throbbing : j'avais mal à la tête>
throb[2] *n* **1** BEAT : battement *m*, pulsation *f* (cardiaque) **2** VIBRATION : vibration *f*, vrombissement *m* (d'un moteur, etc.) **3** : élancement *m* <a throb of pain : un élancement de douleur>
throe [ˈθroː] *n* **1** PANG : agonie *f* <the throes of childbirth : les douleurs de l'enfantement> **2 in the throes of** : en proie à
throne [ˈθroːn] *n* : trône *m*
throng[1] [ˈθrɔŋ] *vt* CROWD : se presser dans, remplir — *vi* : se presser
throng[2] *n* : foule *f*

throttle[1] ['θrɑtəl] *vt* **-tled; -tling 1** CHOKE : étrangler **2 to throttle down** : mettre au ralenti (un moteur)
throttle[2] *n* **1** : accélérateur *m* (d'une voiture) **2** *or* **throttle valve** : papillon *m* des gaz
through[1] ['θru:] *adv* **1** : à travers, d'un côté à l'autre <let me through : laissez-moi passer> **2** : d'un trait, jusqu'au bout <I read the book through : j'ai lu le livre d'un trait> **3** THOROUGHLY : complètement <soaked through : complètement mouillé>
through[2] *adj* **1** DIRECT : direct <a through road : une route directe> **2** : en transit <through traffic : trafic en transit> **3** FINISHED : fini, terminé <are you through? : as-tu fini?>
through[3] *prep* **1** (*indicating movement from one side to the other*) : à travers <the bullet went right through his arm : la balle lui a transpercé le bras> **2** (*indicating passage*) : par <he got in through the window : il est rentré par la fenêtre> <she went through a red light : elle a brûlé un feu rouge> **3** (*indicating a period of time*) <through the whole night : pendant toute la nuit> <from Monday through Friday : du lundi au vendredi)
throughout[1] [θru:'aʊt] *adv* **1** EVERYWHERE : partout <one color throughout : d'une seule couleur> **2** : toujours <he remained loyal throughout : il est toujours demeuré fidèle>
throughout[2] *prep* **1** : partout dans <he traveled throughout the country : il voyageait partout dans le pays> **2** : tout au long de <throughout her life : tout au long de sa vie>
throve → **thrive**
throw[1] ['θro:] *vt* **threw** ['θru:]; **thrown** ['θro:n]; **throwing 1** : lancer <to throw a ball : lancer une balle> **2** *or* **to throw down** : jeter à terre, envoyer au tapis **3** CAST : jeter, projeter <she threw her arms around him : elle s'est jetée à son cou> <to throw a shadow : projeter une ombre> **4 to throw a party** : organiser une fête **5 to throw a tantrum** : piquer une crise **6 to throw sth into confusion** : semer la confusion dans qqch **7 to throw away, to throw out** : jeter
throw[2] *n* TOSS : lancer *m*, jet *m*
thrower ['θro:ər] *n* : lanceur *m*, -ceuse *f*
throw up *vt* : vomir, renvoyer *Can fam*, restituer *Can fam*
thrush ['θrʌʃ] *n* : grive *f* (oiseau)
thrust[1] ['θrʌst] *vt* **thrust; thrusting 1** SHOVE : pousser violemment **2** PLUNGE, STAB : enfoncer, planter **3 to thrust upon** : imposer à
thrust[2] *n* **1** PUSH : poussée *f* **2** STAB : coup *m* (de couteau, d'épée, etc.) **3** AIM, POINT : portée *f*, sens *m* (d'un argument, etc.)
thud[1] ['θʌd] *vi* **thudded; thudding** : faire un bruit sourd
thud[2] *n* : bruit *m* sourd
thug ['θʌg] *n* : voyou *m*
thumb[1] ['θʌm] *vt or* **to thumb through** : feuilleter (un livre, etc.)
thumb[2] *n* : pouce *m*
thumbnail ['θʌm,neɪl] *n* : ongle *m* du pouce
thumbtack ['θʌm,tæk] *n* : punaise *f*
thump[1] ['θʌmp] *vt* POUND : cogner à, frapper sur — *vi* : battre fort (se dit du cœur)
thump[2] *n* **1** BLOW : coup *m* **2** THUD : bruit *m* sourd
thunder[1] ['θʌndər] *vi* **1** : tonner <it was thundering : il tonnait> **2** BOOM, RESOUND : gronder, retentir — *vt* ROAR : vociférer <they thundered their disapproval : ils ont vociféré leur désaccord>
thunder[2] *n* **1** : tonnerre *m* **2** RUMBLE : tonnerre *m*, bruit *m* assourdissant
thunderbolt ['θʌndər,bo:lt] *n* : foudre *f*
thunderclap ['θʌndər,klæp] *n* : coup *m* de tonnerre
thunderous ['θəndərəs] *adj* : étourdissant <thunderous applause : un tonnerre d'applaudissements>
thundershower ['θʌndər,ʃaʊər] → **thunderstorm**
thunderstorm ['θʌndər,storm] *n* : orage *m*
thunderstruck ['θʌndər,strʌk] *adj* : abasourdi, stupéfié
Thursday ['θərz,deɪ, -di] *n* : jeudi *m*
thus [ðʌs] *adv* **1** SO : ainsi, donc, par conséquent **2 thus far** : jusqu'à présent, jusqu'ici
thwart ['θwɔrt] *vt* : contrecarrer, contrarier
thy ['ðaɪ] *adj* : ton, ta, tes
thyme ['taɪm, 'θaɪm] *n* : thym *m*
thyroid ['θaɪ,rɔɪd] *n or* **thyroid gland** : thyroïde *f*
thyself [ðaɪ'sɛlf] *pron* : toi-même
tiara [ti'ærə, -'ɑr-] *n* : diadème *m*
Tibetan[1] [tə'bɛtən] *adj* : tibétain
Tibetan[2] *n* **1** : Tibétain *m*, -taine *f* **2** : tibétain *m* (langue)
tibia ['tɪbiə] *n, pl* **-iae** [-bi,i:] : tibia *m*
tic ['tɪk] *n* : tic *m* (nerveux)
tick[1] ['tɪk] *vi* **1** : faire tic-tac (se dit d'une horloge) **2** OPERATE, RUN : tourner (se dit d'un moteur) — *vt or* **to tick off** CHECK : cocher, marquer
tick[2] *n* **1** : tique *f* (insecte) **2** : tic-tac *m* (d'une horloge) **3** CHECK : coche *f*
ticket[1] ['tɪkət] *vt* **1** LABEL : étiqueter **2** : donner une contravention à (un automobiliste)
ticket[2] *n* **1** TAG : étiquette *f* **2** : billet *m*, ticket *m* <bus ticket : billet d'autobus> **3** : contravention *f* <a speeding ticket : une contravention pour

excès de vitesse> **4** SLATE : liste *f* (électorale)

tickle[1] ['tɪkəl] *v* **-led; -ling** *vt* **1** : chatouiller <don't tickle my feet : ne me chatouillez pas les pieds> **2** PLEASE : chatouiller, émouvoir **3** AMUSE : amuser — *vi* : chatouiller, piquer

tickle[2] *n* : chatouillement *m*

ticklish ['tɪkəlɪʃ] *adj* **1** : chatouilleux **2** DELICATE, TRICKY : épineux, délicat

tidal ['taɪdəl] *adj* : des marées

tidal wave *n* : raz-de-marée *m*

tidbit ['tɪd,bɪt] *n* **1** : détail *m* intéressant **2** DELICACY : gâterie *f*

tide[1] ['taɪd] *vt* **tided; tiding** *or* **to tide over** : dépanner

tide[2] *n* : marée *f*

tidewater ['taɪdˌwɔṭər, -ˌwɑ-] *n* : eaux *nfpl* de marée

tidiness ['taɪdinəs] *n* : ordre *m*, propreté *f*

tidings ['taɪdɪŋz] *npl* : nouvelles *fpl* <good tidings : de bonnes nouvelles>

tidy[1] ['taɪdi] *vt* **or to tidy up** : ranger — *vi* **or to tidy up** : tout ranger, faire du rangement

tidy[2] *adj* **tidier; -est 1** NEAT : bien rangé, propre **2** LARGE : joli *fam*, coquet *fam* <a tidy sum : une jolie somme>

tie[1] ['taɪ] *v* **tied; tying** *or* **tieing** *vt* **1** : attacher, nouer <tie your shoelaces : attache tes lacets> **2** CONNECT : unir, lier — *vi* **1** FASTEN : s'attacher, se nouer **2** : faire match nul, être ex æquo <to tie for third place : être troisième ex æquo>

tie[2] *n* **1** FASTENER : attache *f* **2** *or* **railroad tie** : traverse *f* **3** BOND : lien *m*, nœud *m* <family ties : liens familiaux> **4** : match *m* nul, égalité *f* (aux sports) **5** NECKTIE : cravate *f*

tier ['tɪr] *n* : étage *m* (d'un gâteau), gradin *m* (au théâtre)

tiff ['tɪf] *n* : chicane *f*, dispute *f*

tiger ['taɪgər] *n* : tigre *m*

tight[1] ['taɪt] *adv* **1** TIGHTLY : bien, fermement <is the door shut tight? : la porte est-elle bien fermée?> <hold on tight : tenez-vous bien> **2** DEEPLY : profondément <to sleep tight : dormir profondément>

tight[2] *adj* **1** : étanche, hermétique <a tight seal : une fermeture étanche> **2** SNUG : serré, étriqué **3** TAUT : tendu, raide **4** DIFFICULT : difficile <to be in a tight spot : être dans une situation difficile> **5** STINGY : avare **6** CLOSE : serré <a tight game : un match serré> **7** SCARCE : juste, serré <money is a bit tight : les finances sont un peu justes>

tighten ['taɪtən] *vt* : serrer, resserrer

tightly ['taɪtli] *adv* : fermement, bien

tightness ['taɪtnəs] *n* **1** : étroitesse *f* (d'un vêtement, etc.) **2** STRICTNESS : sévérite *f*, rigueur *f* **3** TAUTNESS : tension *f*, raideur *f*

tightrope ['taɪtˌroːp] *n* : corde *f* raide

tights ['taɪts] *npl* : collants *mpl*

tightwad ['taɪtˌwɑd] *n* : grippe-sou *mf fam*

tigress ['taɪgrəs] *n* : tigresse *f*

tile[1] ['taɪl] *vt* **tiled; tiling** : poser des tuiles sur, carreler

tile[2] *n* : tuile *f*

till[1] ['tɪl] *vt* : labourer

till[2] *n* : tiroir-caisse *m*

till[3] *conj & prep* → **until**

tiller ['tɪlər] *n* **1** : cultivateur *m*, -trice *f* **2** : barre *f*, gouvernail *m* (d'un bateau)

tilt[1] ['tɪlt] *vt* SLANT : pencher, incliner — *vi* : se pencher, s'incliner

tilt[2] *n* **1** SLOPE : inclinaison *f* **2 at full tilt** : à toute vitesse

timber ['tɪmbər] *n* **1** : bois *m* de construction **2** BEAM : poutre *f*, madrier *m*

timberland ['tɪmbərˌlænd] *n* : terrain *m* forestier (exploitable)

timbre ['tæmbər, 'tɪm-] *n* : timbre *m* (de la voix)

time[1] ['taɪm] *vt* **timed; timing 1** SCHEDULE : prévoir, fixer **2** : minuter, chronométrer <to time a race : chronométrer une course>

time[2] *n* **1** : temps *m* <it's a matter of time : c'est une question de temps> <to find time for : trouver du temps pour> <time flies : le temps passe vite> **2** OCCASION : fois *f* **3** AGE : époque *f*, temps *m* **4** TEMPO : mesure *f*, rythme *m* **5** : heure *f* <what time is it? : quelle heure est-il?> <she arrived on time : elle est arrivée à l'heure> <on company time : pendant les heures de travail> **6** : temps *m* (de l'année) <it's very hot for this time of year : il fait très chaud pour la saison> **7** PERIOD : moment *m*, période *f* <hard times : des moments difficiles> **8 times** *npl* : fois *f* <you've told me several times : tu me l'as dit plusieurs fois> **9 at times** : parfois **10 for the time being** : pour le moment **11 from time to time** : de temps à autre **12 time and time again** : maintes et maintes fois

timekeeper ['taɪmˌkiːpər] *n* : chronométreur *m*, -treuse *f*

timeless ['taɪmləs] *adj* : éternel

timely ['taɪmli] *adj* **-lier; -est** : opportun, propice

timepiece ['taɪmˌpiːs] *n* : montre *f*, horloge *f*

timer ['taɪmər] *n* **1** TIMEKEEPER : chronométreur *m*, -treuse *f* **2** STOPWATCH : chronomètre *m* **3** : minuteur *m* (en cuisine)

times ['taɪmz] *prep* : fois (en mathématiques) <seven times two is fourteen : sept fois deux font quatorze>

timetable ['taɪmˌteɪbəl] *n* **1** : horaire *m* (de trains, d'autobus, etc.) **2** SCHEDULE : programme *m*, horaire *m*

timid [ˈtɪmɪd] *adj* : timide — **timidly** *adv*
timidity [təˈmɪdəṭi] *n* : timidité *f*
timorous [ˈtɪmərəs] *adj* FEARFUL : timoré
timpani [ˈtɪmpəni] *npl* : timbales *fpl*
tin [ˈtɪn] *n* **1** : étain *m* (métal) **2** *or* **tin can** : boîte *f* de conserve
tincture [ˈtɪŋktʃər] *n* : teinture *f*
tinder [ˈtɪndər] *n* : amadou *m*, petit bois *m*
tine [ˈtaɪn] *n* : dent *f* (d'une fourchette, etc.)
tinfoil [ˈtɪnˌfɔɪl] *n* : papier *m* d'aluminium
tinge[1] [ˈtɪndʒ] *vt* **tinged; tingeing** *or* **tinging** [ˈtɪndʒɪŋ] : teinter
tinge[2] *n* : teinte *f*, nuance *f*
tingle[1] [ˈtɪŋgəl] *vi* **-gled; -gling** : picoter, fourmiller
tingle[2] *n* : picotement *m*
tinker [ˈtɪŋkər] *vi* : bricoler
tinkle[1] [ˈtɪŋkəl] *v* **-kled; -kling** *vi* : tinter, sonner — *vt* : faire tinter
tinkle[2] *n* : tintement *m*
tinsel [ˈtɪnsəl] *n* : guirlandes *fpl* (de Noël)
tint[1] [ˈtɪnt] *vt* : teinter
tint[2] *n* : teinte *f*, nuance *f*
tiny [ˈtaɪni] *adj* **tinier; -est** : minuscule, tout petit
tip[1] [ˈtɪp] *v* **tipped; tipping** *vt* **1** : mettre un embout à (une canne, etc.) **2** OVERTURN : chavirer, renverser **3** TILT : pencher, incliner **4** : donner un pourboire à (un serveur) **5 to tip off** : donner un tuyau à, renseigner — *vi* TILT : pencher, basculer
tip[2] *n* **1** END : pointe *f*, bout *m* (d'un crayon) <the tip of the island : la pointe de l'île> **2** GRATUITY : pourboire *m* **3** INFORMATION : conseil *m*, tuyau *m fam*
tip–off [ˈtɪpˌɔf] *n* : tuyau *m fam*
tipple [ˈtɪpəl] *vi* **-pled; -pling** : prendre un coup *fam*, picoler *fam*
tipsy [ˈtɪpsi] *adj* **tipsier; -est** : pompette *fam*, éméché *fam*
tiptoe[1] [ˈtɪpˌto:] *vi* **-toed; -toeing** : marcher sur la pointe des pieds
tiptoe[2] *n* **on ~** : sur la pointe des pieds
tip–top[1] [ˈtɪpˌto:] *adj* : excellent <in tip-top shape : en excellente forme>
tip–top[2] *n* : sommet *m*, haut *m*
tirade [ˈtaɪˌreɪd] *n* : tirade *f*, diatribe *f*
tire[1] [ˈtaɪr] *v* **tired; tiring** *vt* **1** FATIGUE : fatiguer **2** BORE : fatiguer, lasser — *vi* : se fatiguer
tire[2] *n* : pneu *m*
tired [ˈtaɪrd] *adj* : fatigué, las
tireless [ˈtaɪrləs] *adj* : infatigable, inlassable
tirelessly [ˈtaɪrləsli] *adv* : infatigablement, sans relâche
tiresome [ˈtaɪrsəm] *adj* : ennuyeux, fastidieux, agaçant
tiresomely [ˈtaɪrsəmli] *adv* : fastidieusement, de façon agaçante
tissue [ˈtɪˌʃu:] *n* **1** : mouchoir *m* en papier, papier *m* mouchoir *Can* **2** : tissu *m* (en biologie)
titanic [taɪˈtænɪk, tə-] *adj* : titanesque, colossal
titanium [taɪˈteɪniəm, tə-] *n* : titane *m*
titillate [ˈtɪtəlˌeɪt] *vt* **-lated; -lating** : titiller
title[1] [ˈtaɪṭəl] **-tled; -tling** *vt* : intituler
title[2] *n* : titre *m*
titter[1] [ˈtɪṭər] *vi* : rire nerveusement
titter[2] *n* : petit rire *m* nerveux
tizzy [ˈtɪzi] *n, pl* **tizzies** : panique *f*, agitation *f* <to be in a tizzy : être dans tous ses états>
TNT [ˌti:ˌenˈti:] *n* : TNT *m*
to[1] [ˈtu:] *adv* **1 to come to** : reprendre connaissance **2 to run to and fro** : aller et venir
to[2] *prep* **1** (*indicating movement or direction*) : à, en <I walk to school : je vais à l'école à pied> <we drove to town : nous sommes allés en ville en voiture> **2** TOWARD : vers <his back was turned to the door : il avait le dos tourné vers la porte> **3** AGAINST, ON : sur <she put her hand to her heart : elle a placé sa main sur son cœur> **4** (*indicating intent*) : à <he came to our aid : il est venu à notre aide> **5** (*indicating a point or position*) : à, de <100 miles to the nearest town : à 100 milles de la ville la plus proche> <perpendicular to the floor : perpendiculaire au plancher> **6** (*in expressions of time*) : moins <five minutes to five : cinq heures moins cinq> **7** UNTIL : à, jusqu'à <from Monday to Friday : du lundi au vendredi> **8** FOR : de, pour <the key to the door : la clé de la porte> **9** (*indicating comparison or proportion*) : à <similar to that one : semblable à celui-là> <we won ten to six : nous avons gagné dix à six> **10** (*indicating agreement or conformity*) : à <add salt to taste : salez au goût> <to my knowledge : à ma connaissance> **11** (*used to form the infinitive*) <I like to swim : j'aime nager> <he wants to go there : il veut y aller>
toad [ˈto:d] *n* : crapaud *m*
toadstool [ˈto:dˌstu:l] *n* : champignon *m* vénéneux
toady [ˈto:di] *n, pl* **toadies** : flagorneur *m*, -neuse *f*; flatteur *m*, -teuse *f*
toast[1] [ˈto:st] *vt* **1** : griller (du pain), toaster *Can* **2** : boire à la santé de (un invité) — *vi* WARM : chauffer <to toast oneself : se réchauffer>
toast[2] *n* **1** : toast *m*, pain *m* grillé, rôtie *f* **2** : toast *m* <to drink a toast to : porter un toast à>
toaster [ˈto:stər] *n* : grille-pain *m*
tobacco [təˈbæˌko:] *n, pl* **-cos** : tabac *m*
toboggan[1] [təˈbɑgən] *vi* : faire du toboggan
toboggan[2] *n* : toboggan *m*, traîne *f Can*

today¹ [tə'deɪ] *adv* **1** : aujourd'hui **2** NOWADAYS : de nos jours
today² *n* : aujourd'hui *m*
toddle ['tɑdəl] *vi* **-dled; -dling** : marcher d'un pas chancelant
toddler ['tɑdələr] *n* : bambin *m*, -bine *f*
to–do [tə'du:] *n, pl* **to–dos** [-'du:z] FUSS : agitation *f*, remue-ménage *m*
toe ['to:] *n* : orteil *m*, doigt *m* de pied
toenail ['to:ˌneɪl] *n* : ongle *m* d'orteil
toffee ['tɔfi, 'tɑ-] *n, pl* **toffees** : caramel *m*
toga ['to:gə] *n* : toge *f*
together [tə'geðər] *adv* **1** : ensemble <let's go together : allons-y ensemble> **2** SIMULTANEOUSLY : en même temps, simultanément **3 together with** : ainsi que, avec, en même temps que
togetherness [tə'geðərnəs] *n* : unité *f*, camaraderie *f*
Togolese¹ [ˌto:gə'li:z, -ˌli:s] *adj* : togolais
Togolese² *n* : Togolais *m*, -laise *f*
togs ['tɑgz, 'tɔgz] *npl* : fringues *fpl fam*
toil¹ ['tɔɪl] *vi* **1** : travailler dur, peiner **2** PLOD : marcher péniblement
toil² *n* : labeur *m*, dur travail *m*
toilet ['tɔɪlət] *n* **1** DRESSING, GROOMING : toilette *f* **2** BATHROOM : toilettes *fpl*, toilette *f Can* <to go to the toilet : aller aux toilettes>
toilet paper *n* : papier *m* hygiénique
token ['to:kən] *n* **1** SIGN, SYMBOL : signe *m*, marque *f*, témoignage *m* <as a token of our friendship : en signe de notre amitié> **2** : jeton *m* <subway token : jeton de métro>
told → tell
tolerable ['tɑlərəbəl] *adj* **1** : tolérable, supportable <tolerable pain : douleur tolérable> **2** PASSABLE : pas (trop) mal, acceptable
tolerably ['tɑlərəbli] *adv* : passablement, acceptablement
tolerance ['tɑlərənts] *n* **1** ENDURANCE : tolérance *f* <to have a high tolerance for pain : tolérer bien la douleur> **2** OPEN-MINDEDNESS : tolérance *f*, indulgence *f*
tolerant ['tɑlərənt] *adj* : tolérant, libéral
tolerantly ['tɑlərəntli] *adv* : avec tolérance
tolerate ['tɑləˌreɪt] *vt* **-ated; -ating** : tolérer
toleration [ˌtɑlə'reɪʃən] *n* : tolérance *f*
toll¹ ['to:l] *vt* : sonner (une cloche) — *vi* : sonner
toll² *n* **1** : péage *m* (sur une autoroute) **2 death toll** : nombre *m* de victimes **3 to take its toll** : avoir des conséquences néfastes
tollbooth ['to:lˌbu:θ] *n* : poste *m* de péage
tollgate ['to:lˌgeɪt] *n* : barrière *f* de péage
tomahawk ['tɑməˌhɔk] *n* : tomahawk *m*
tomato [tə'meɪˌto, -'mɑ-] *n, pl* **-toes** : tomate *f*
tomb ['tu:m] *n* : tombeau *m*, tombe *f*
tomboy ['tɑmˌbɔɪ] *n* : garçon *m* manqué
tombstone ['tu:mˌsto:n] *n* : pierre *f* tombale
tomcat ['tɑmˌkæt] *n* : matou *m*
tome ['to:m] *n* : gros volume *m*
tomorrow¹ [tə'mɑro] *adv* : demain
tomorrow² *n* : demain *m*
tom–tom ['tɑmˌtɑm] *n* : tam-tam *m*
ton ['tən] *n* : tonne *f*
tonality [to'nælətˌi] *n* : tonalité *f*
tone¹ ['to:n] *vt* **toned; toning** *or* **to tone down** : atténuer
tone² *n* **1** : sonorité *f*, ton *m* (en musique) **2** : ton *m*, intonation *f* <in a friendly tone : d'un ton chaleureux> <to speak in low tones : parler d'une voix basse>
tongs ['tɑŋz, 'tɔŋz] *npl* : pinces *fpl*, pincettes *fpl*
tongue ['tʌŋ] *n* **1** : langue *f* (de la bouche) **2** LANGUAGE : langue *f* <mother tongue : langue maternelle> **3** FLAP : languette *f* (d'un soulier)
tongue–tied ['tʌŋˌtaɪd] *adj* **1** : muet **2 to get tongue–tied** : ne plus savoir que dire
tonic¹ ['tɑnɪk] *adj* : tonique
tonic² *n* : tonique *m*
tonight¹ [tə'naɪt] *adv* : ce soir
tonight² *n* : ce soir, cette nuit <tonight's party : la fête de ce soir>
tonsil ['tɑntsəl] *n* : amygdale *f*
tonsillitis [ˌtɑntsə'laɪtəs] *n* : amygdalite *f*
too ['tu:] *adv* **1** ALSO, BESIDES : aussi **2** VERY : très <he didn't seem too interested : il ne semblait pas très intéressé> <not too bad : pas trop mal>
took → take¹
tool¹ ['tu:l] *vt* : travailler, ouvrager
tool² *n* : outil *m*, instrument *m*
toolbar ['tu:lˌbɑr] *n* : barre *f* d'outils (en informatique)
toolbox ['tu:lˌbɑks] *n* : boîte *f* à outils
toot¹ ['tu:t] *vi* : klaxonner (se dit d'une voiture), siffler (se dit d'un train) — *vt* **to toot one's horn** : donner un coup de klaxon
toot² *n* : coup *m* de klaxon, coup *m* de sifflet
tooth ['tu:θ] *n, pl* **teeth** ['ti:θ] **1** : dent *f* <to brush one's teeth : se brosser les dents> **2** : dent *f* (d'un peigne, d'une roue, etc.)
toothache ['tu:θˌeɪk] *n* : mal *m* de dents
toothbrush ['tu:θˌbrʌʃ] *n* : brosse *f* à dents
toothless ['tu:θləs] *adj* : édenté
toothpaste ['tu:θˌpeɪst] *n* : dentifrice *m*
toothpick ['tu:θˌpɪk] *n* : cure-dents *m*
top¹ ['tɑp] *vt* **topped; topping 1** CAP, CROWN : couvrir, recouvrir **2** SURPASS : dépasser, surpasser **3** HEAD : être en tête de (une liste, etc.)
top² *adj* **1** : dernier <the top floor : le dernier étage> **2** CHIEF, LEADING : premier, prinicipal, de tête

top³ *n* **1** SUMMIT : haut *m*, cime *f*, tête *f* <at the top of one's class : à la tête de sa classe> **2** : dessus *m* <the top of the table : le dessus de la table> **3** LID : couvercle *m* **4** : toupie *f* (jouet) **5 on top of** : sur

topaz ['to:ˌpæz] *n* : topaze *f*

topcoat ['tɑpˌko:t] *n* : pardessus *m*

topic ['tɑpɪk] *n* : sujet *m*, thème *m*

topical ['tɑpɪkəl] *adj* **1** LOCAL : à usage local (en médecine) **2** CURRENT : d'actualité

topmost ['tɑpˌmo:st] *adj* : le plus haut

top–notch ['tɑpˈnɑtʃ] *adj* : excellent, de premier ordre

topographic [ˌtɑpəˈgræfɪk] *or* **topographical** [-fɪkəl] *adj* : topographique

topography [tə'pɑgrəfi] *n* : topographie *f*

topple ['tɑpəl] *v* **-pled; -pling** *vt* : renverser, faire tomber — *vi or* **to topple over** : basculer, se renverser

topsy–turvy [ˌtɑpsiˈtərvi] *adv & adj* : sens dessus dessous, à l'envers

torch ['tɔrtʃ] *n* : torche *f*, flambeau *m*

tore → **tear¹**

torment¹ ['tɔrˌment, tɔrˈ-] *vt* : tourmenter, torturer

torment² ['tɔrˌment] *n* : tourment *m*, supplice *m*

tormentor ['tɔrˌmentər, tɔrˈ-] *n* : persécuteur *m*, -trice *f*; bourreau *m*

torn → **tear¹**

tornado [tɔrˈneɪdo] *n, pl* **-does** *or* **-dos** : tornade *f*

torpedo¹ [tɔrˈpi:do] *vt* : torpiller

torpedo² *n, pl* **-does** : torpille *f*

torpid ['tɔrpɪd] *adj* : léthargique, torpide, engourdi

torpor ['tɔrpər] *n* : torpeur *f*, léthargie *f*

torrent ['tɔrənt] *n* : torrent *m*

torrential [tɔˈrentʃəl, tə-] *adj* : torrentiel

torrid ['tɔrɪd] *adj* : torride

torso ['tɔrˌso:] *n, pl* **-sos** *or* **-si** [-ˌsi:] : torse *m*

tortilla [tɔrˈti:jə] *n* : tortilla *f*

tortoise ['tɔrtəs] *n* : tortue *f*

tortoiseshell ['tɔrtəsˌʃel] *n* : écaille *f*

tortuous ['tɔrtʃʊəs] *adj* : tortueux

torture¹ ['tɔrtʃər] *vt* **-tured; -turing** : torturer

torture² *n* : torture *f*

torturer ['tɔrtʃərər] *n* : tortionnaire *mf*

toss¹ ['tɔs, 'tɑs] *vt* **1** THROW : lancer, jeter **2** *or* **to toss about** AGITATE : ballotter, secouer **3 to toss a coin** : jouer à pile ou face — *vi* **to toss and turn** : s'agiter, se tourner et se retourner

toss² *n* THROW : lancer *m*, lancement *m*

toss–up ['tɔsˌʌp] *n* : chances *fpl* égales

tot ['tɑt] *n* : petit enfant *m*

total¹ ['to:təl] *vt* **-taled** *or* **-talled; -taling** *or* **-talling** : totaliser

total² *adj* : total

total³ *n* : total *m*

totalitarian [ˌto:ˌtælə'teriən] *adj* : totalitaire

totalitarianism [ˌto:ˌtælə'teriəˌnɪzəm] *n* : totalitarisme *m*

totality [to'tælətɪ] *n, pl* **-ties** : totalité *f*

totally ['to:təli] *adv* : totalement, entièrement, complètement

tote ['to:t] *vt* **toted; toting** : porter, transporter

totem ['to:təm] *n* : totem *m*

totter ['tɑtər] *vi* : chanceler, tituber

touch¹ ['tʌtʃ] *vt* **1** FEEL, HANDLE : toucher **2** : toucher à <he never touches alcohol : il ne touche jamais à l'alcool> **3** HARM : toucher **4** AFFECT, MOVE : émouvoir, toucher — *vi* : se toucher, être en contact

touch² *n* **1** : toucher *m* (sens) **2** FEEL : toucher *m* <soft to the touch : doux au toucher> **3** DETAIL : touche *f* <a touch of color : une touche de couleur> **4** HINT, TRACE : touche *f*, pointe *f* **5** CONTACT : contact *m* <to keep in touch with : rester en contact avec>

touchdown ['tʌtʃˌdaʊn] *n* **1** : atterrissage *m* (d'un avion) **2** : but *m* (au football américain)

touch up *vt* : faire des retouches à, retoucher

touchy ['tʌtʃi] *adj* **touchier; -est 1** : susceptible (se dit des personnes) **2** : délicat, épineux <a touchy subject : un sujet épineux>

tough¹ ['tʌf] *adj* **1** HARDY : robuste, résistant **2** : dur, coriace (se dit de la viande) **3** STRICT : strict, sévère **4** DIFFICULT : difficile, pénible **5** STUBBORN : inflexible, dur **6** ROUGH : dur <a tough neighbourhood : un quartier dur> **7 tough luck!** : tant pis pour toi!

tough² *n* : dur *m fam*

toughen ['tʌfən] *vt* : endurcir, rendre plus résistant — *vi* : s'endurcir

toughness ['tʌfnəs] *n* : résistance *f*

toupee [tu:ˈpeɪ] *n* : postiche *m*

tour¹ ['tʊr] *vt* : visiter <we toured the city : nous avons visité la ville> — *vi* : faire du tourisme, voyager

tour² *n* **1** : tour *m* (d'une ville, etc.), visite *f* (d'un édifice) <a bus tour : une excursion en autobus> **2 to go on tour** : faire une tournée

tourist ['tʊrɪst, 'tər-] *n* : touriste *mf*

tournament ['tərnəmənt, 'tʊr-] *n* : tournoi *m*

tourniquet ['tərnɪkət, 'tʊr-] *n* : garrot *m*, tourniquet *m*

tousle ['taʊzəl] *vt* **-sled; -sling** : ébouriffer (les cheveux)

tout ['taʊt] *vt* : vanter les mérites de

tow¹ ['to:] *vt* : remorquer (une voiture)

tow² *n* : remorquage *m* <he gave me a tow : il m'a remorqué>

toward ['tɔrd, tə'wɔrd] *or* **towards** ['tɔrdz, tə'wɔrdz] *prep* **1** : vers, dans la direction de <toward the river : vers

la rivière> <their backs were toward me : ils étaient dos à moi> **2** : envers <his attitude toward life : son attitude envers la vie> **3** : pour <she put $100 toward a new car : elle a mis 100 $ de côté pour une nouvelle voiture> **4** NEAR : vers <toward the middle : vers le milieu>

towel ['taʊəl] *n* : serviette *f*

tower[1] ['taʊər] *vi* **to tower over** : dominer

tower[2] *n* : tour *f*

towering ['taʊərɪŋ] *adj* **1** IMPOSING : imposant, très haut **2** EXCESSIVE : sans bornes, démesuré <towering ambition : ambition démesurée>

town ['taʊn] *n* : ville *f* <to go to town : aller en ville> <to be out of town : être en déplacement>

township ['taʊnˌʃɪp] *n* **1** : commune *f*, municipalité *f* **2** : canton *m Can* (division territoriale)

tow truck ['toˌtrʌk] *n* : dépanneuse *f*, remorqueuse *f Can*

toxic ['tɑksɪk] *adj* : toxique

toxicity [tɑk'sɪsəṭi] *n, pl* **-ties** : toxicité *f*

toxin ['tɑksɪn] *n* : toxine *f*

toy[1] ['tɔɪ] *vi* **to toy with** : jouer avec

toy[2] *adj* : de jeu <toy soldiers : soldats de plomb> <a toy house : une maison miniature>

toy[3] *n* : jouet *m*

trace[1] ['treɪs] *vt* **traced; tracing 1** OUTLINE, SKETCH : tracer, dessiner **2** FOLLOW : suivre (la trace de) **3** LOCATE : retrouver, localiser

trace[2] *n* **1** TRACK : trace *f*, empreinte *f* **2** VESTIGE : trace *f* <traces of blood : traces de sang> **3** HINT : soupçon *m*, pointe *f* <a trace of a smile : un léger sourire> <without a trace of anger : sans la moindre colère> **4** : trait *m* (d'un harnais)

trachea ['treɪkiə] *n, pl* **-cheae** [-ki,i:] : trachée *f*

track[1] ['træk] *vt* : suivre la trace de, suivre la piste de

track[2] *n* **1** MARK, TRAIL : trace *f*, piste *f* <rabbit tracks : traces de lapin> **2** PATH, TRAJECTORY : piste *f*, trajectoire *f* **3** : piste *f* (aux sports) **4** → **racetrack 5** *or* **railroad track** : voie *f* ferrée **6 to keep track of** : faire attention à

track–and–field [ˌtrækənd'fi:ld] *adj* : d'athlétisme <track-and-field events : événements d'athlétisme>

tract ['trækt] *n* **1** AREA : étendue *f* (de terre) **2** : appareil *m*, voie *f* (en physiologie) <respiratory tract : appareil respiratoire> **3** PAMPHLET : tract *m*, brochure *f*

tractable ['trækṭəbəl] *adj* **1** DOCILE : docile (se dit d'un animal) **2** MALLEABLE : malléable

traction ['trækʃən] *n* : traction *f*

tractor ['trækṭər] *n* : tracteur *m*

trade[1] ['treɪd] *v* **traded; trading** *vt* EXCHANGE : échanger, troquer — *vi* : faire du commerce

trade[2] *n* **1** : commerce *m*, industrie *f* <the tourist trade : l'industrie touristique> <foreign trade : commerce extérieur> **2** OCCUPATION : métier *m*, profession *f*

trade–in ['treɪdˌɪn] *n* : reprise *f*

trade in *vt* : faire reprendre <to trade in a car : échanger une vieille voiture pour une neuve>

trademark[1] ['treɪdˌmɑrk] *vt* : déposer une marque sur

trademark[2] *n* : marque *f* de fabrique

tradesman ['treɪdzmən] *n, pl* **-men** [-mən, -ˌmɛn] : commerçant *m*, -çante *f*

trade wind *n* : alizé *m*

tradition [trə'diʃən] *n* : tradition *f*

traditional [trə'diʃənəl] *adj* : traditionnel — **traditionally** *adv*

traffic[1] ['træfɪk] *vi* **trafficked; trafficking** : trafiquer <to traffic in : faire le trafic de>

traffic[2] *n* **1** TRADE : commerce *m*, trafic *m* <the drug traffic : le trafic de drogue> **2** : circulation *f*, trafic *m* <road traffic : circulation routière> <air traffic : trafic aérien>

traffic circle *n* : rond-point *m*

trafficker ['træfɪkər] *n* : trafiquant *m*, -quante *f*

traffic light *n* : feu *m* de signalisation

tragedy ['trædʒədi] *n, pl* **-dies** : tragédie *f*

tragic ['trædʒɪk] *adj* : tragique — **tragically** [-dʒɪkəli] *adv*

trail[1] ['treɪl] *vi* **1** DRAG, HANG : traîner, pendre **2** *or* **to trail behind** LAG : traîner, être à la traîne **3 to trail away** *or* **to trail off** : s'estomper, diminuer <the sound trailed off : le bruit s'estompait> — *vt* **1** DRAG : traîner, tirer **2** FOLLOW : suivre, poursuivre

trail[2] *n* **1** PATH : chemin *m*, sentier *m*, piste *f* <ski trail : piste de ski> **2** TRACK : trace *f*, piste *f* <to be on one's trail : être sur sa trace> **3** MARK, TRACE : traînée *f*, trace *f* <a trail of smoke : une traînée de fumée>

trailer ['treɪlər] *n* **1** : remorque *f* (de camion, etc.) **2** : caravane *f*, roulotte *f Can* <he toured the country in a trailer : il a fait le tour du pays en caravane>

train[1] ['treɪn] *vt* **1** : palisser (une vigne, etc.), former, entraîner (du personnel) **2** AIM, DIRECT : pointer, diriger — *vi* : recevoir une formation, s'entraîner

train[2] *n* **1** : traîne *f* (d'une robe) **2** PROCESSION : cortège *m*, file *f* **3** SUCCESSION : suite *f*, série *f*, fil *m* <train of thought : fil des pensées> **4** : train *m* <train de banlieue : commuter train>

trainee [treɪ'ni:] *n* : apprenti *m*, -tie *f*; stagiaire *mf*
trainer [ˈtreɪnər] *n* **1** : entraîneur *m*, -neuse *f* (aux sports) **2** : dresseur *m*, -seuse *f* (d'animaux)
traipse [ˈtreɪps] *vi* **traipsed; traipsing** : traîner <to traipse in : entrer en traînassant>
trait [ˈtreɪt] *n* : trait *m*, qualité *f*
traitor [ˈtreɪtər] *n* : traître *m*, -tresse *f*
traitorous [ˈtreɪtərəs] *adj* : traître
trajectory [trəˈdʒɛktəri] *n, pl* **-ries** : trajectoire *f*
tram [ˈtræm] *n Brit* : tramway *m*
tramp[1] [ˈtræmp] *vi* : marcher d'un pas lourd — *vt* : parcourir à pied
tramp[2] *n* : clochard *m*, -charde *f*; vagabond *m*, -bonde *f*
trample [ˈtræmpəl] *vt* **-pled; -pling** : fouler aux pieds, piétiner
trampoline [ˌtræmpəˈliːn, ˈtræmpəˌ-] *n* : trampoline *m*
trance [ˈtræns] *n* : transe *f*
tranquil [ˈtræŋkwəl] *adj* : tranquille, paisible — **tranquilly** *adv*
tranquilize [ˈtræŋkwəˌlaɪz] *vt* **-ized; -izing** : tranquilliser
tranquilizer [ˈtræŋkwəˌlaɪzər] *n* : tranquillisant *m*
tranquillity *or* **tranquility** [trəŋˈkwɪləti] *n* : tranquillité *f*
transact [trænˈzækt] *vt* : négocier, régler (des affaires)
transaction [trænˈzækʃən] *n* **1** : transaction *f*, opération *f* <market transactions : opérations de la Bourse> **2 transactions** *npl* : actes *mpl* (d'une société)
transcend [trænˈsɛnd] *vt* : transcender
transcribe [trænˈskraɪb] *vt* **-scribed; -scribing** : transcrire
transcript [ˈtræn,skrɪpt] *n* : transcription *f*
transcription [trænˈskrɪpʃən] *n* : transcription *f*
transfer[1] [trænsˈfər, ˈtræns,fər] *v* **-ferred; -ferring** *vt* **1** : transférer, transmettre <to transfer a title : transférer un titre> **2** : transférer, muter (un employé) **3** : transborder (des marchandises) — *vi* : être transféré, être muté
transfer[2] [ˈtræns,fər] *n* **1** : transfert *m*, mutation *f* (d'un employé), cession *f* (de propriété), virement *m* (de fonds) **2** TICKET : billet *m* de correspondance **3** DECAL : décalcomanie *f*
transferable [trænsˈfərəbəl] *adj* : transmissible
transference [trænsˈfərəns] *n* : transfert *m*
transfiguration [ˌtræns,fɪgjəˈreɪʃən] *n* : transfiguration *f*
transfigure [trænsˈfɪgjər] *vt* **-ured; -uring** : transfigurer
transfix [trænsˈfɪks] *vt* **1** PIERCE : transpercer **2** IMMOBILIZE : paralyser, figer
transform [trænsˈfɔrm] *vt* : transformer
transformation [ˌtræns,fərˈmeɪʃən] *n* : transformation *f*
transformer [trænsˈfɔrmər] *n* : transformateur *m*
transfusion [trænsˈfjuːʒən] *n* : transfusion *f*
transgress [trænsˈgrɛs, trænz-] *vt* : transgresser
transgression [trænsˈgrɛʃən, trænz-] *n* : transgression *f*
transient[1] [ˈtrænʃənt, ˈtrænsiənt] *adj* : transitoire, passager
transient[2] *n* : personne *f* de passage
transistor [trænˈzɪstər, -ˈsɪs-] *n* : transistor *m*
transit [ˈtrænsɪt, ˈtrænzɪt] *n* **1** : transit *m* <in transit : en transit> **2** TRANSPORTATION : transit *m*, transport *m* (de marchandises) **3** : théodolite *m* (instrument d'arpenteur)
transition [trænˈsɪʃən, -ˈzɪʃ-] *n* : transition *f*
transitional [trænˈsɪʃənəl, -ˈzɪʃ-] *adj* : transitoire, de transition
transitive [ˈtrænsəṭɪv, ˈtrænzə-] *adj* : transitif
transitory [ˈtrænsəˌtori, ˈtrænzə-] *adj* : transitoire, passager
translate [trænsˈleɪt, trænz-; ˈtræns,-, ˈtrænz,-] *v* **-lated; -lating** *vt* : traduire — *vi* : se traduire
translation [trænsˈleɪʃən, trænz-] *n* : traduction *f*
translator [trænsˈleɪtər, trænz-; ˈtræns,-, ˈtrænz,-] *n* : traducteur *m*, -trice *f*
translucent [trænsˈluːsənt, trænz-] *adj* : translucide
transmissible [trænsˈmɪsəbəl, trænz-] *adj* : transmissible
transmission [trænsˈmɪʃən, trænz-] *n* **1** TRANSMITTING : transmission *f* (d'une maladie, etc.) **2** : transmission *f* (d'une voiture)
transmit [trænsˈmɪt, trænz-] *v* **-mitted; -mitting** *vt* : transmettre — *vi* : émettre, diffuser (se dit de la radio, de la télévision, etc.)
transmitter [trænsˈmɪṭər, trænz-; ˈtræns,-, ˈtrænz,-] *n* : émetteur *m*
transom [ˈtrænsəm] *n* : traverse *f*
transparency [trænsˈpærənsi] *n, pl* **-cies 1** : transparence *f* **2** SLIDE : diapositive *f*, acétate *f Can*
transparent [trænsˈpærənt] *adj* : transparent
transpiration [ˌtrænspəˈreɪʃən] *n* : transpiration *f*
transpire [trænsˈpaɪr] *v* **-spired; -spiring** *vt* : transpirer — *vi* OCCUR : arriver, se passer
transplant[1] [trænsˈplænt] *vt* : transplanter
transplant[2] [ˈtræns,plænt] *n* : transplantation *f*
transport[1] [trænsˈport, ˈtræns,-] *vt* : transporter

transport[2] ['trænˌspɔrt] *n* **1** TRANSPORTATION : transport *m* <public transport : transports en commun> **2** *or* **transport ship** : navire *m* de transport **3 transports** *npl* : transports *mpl* (de joie), accès *mpl* (de colère, etc.)
transportation [ˌtrænˌspɔr'teɪʃən] *n* : transport *m*
transpose [trænˌs'poːz] *vt* **-posed; -posing** : transposer
transposition [ˌtrænˌspə'zɪʃən] *n* : transposition *f*
transverse [trænˌs'vərs, trænz-] *adj* : transversal — **transversely** *adv*
trap[1] ['træp] *vt* **trapped; trapping** : prendre au piège, attraper
trap[2] *n* **1** : piège *m* <to set a trap : tendre un piège> **2** : siphon *m* <the trap in a drainpipe : le siphon dans un tuyau d'écoulement>
trapdoor ['træp'dɔr] *n* : trappe *f*
trapeze [trə'piːz] *n* : trapèze *m*
trapezoid ['trəpəˌzɔɪd] *n* : trapèze *m*
trapper ['trəpər] *n* : trappeur *m*
trappings ['trəpɪŋz] *npl* **1** : caparaçon *m* (d'un cheval) **2** SIGNS : attributs *mpl* <the trappings of success : les signes extérieurs de la réussite>
trash ['træʃ] *n* : déchets *mpl*, ordures *fpl*
trauma ['trɔmə, 'traʊ-] *n* : traumatisme *m*
traumatic [trɔ'mæt̬ɪk, trɔ-, traʊ-] *adj* : traumatisant
traumatize ['trɔməˌtaɪz, traʊ-] *vt* : traumatiser
travel[1] ['trævəl] *v* **-eled** *or* **-elled; -eling** *or* **-elling** *vi* **1** JOURNEY : faire un voyage, voyager **2** SPREAD : circuler, se répandre <news traveled fast : les nouvelles circulaient vite> **3** GO, MOVE : aller, rouler <the train traveled at 60 miles per hour : le train roulait à 60 milles à l'heure> — *vt* : parcourir <to travel the countryside : parcourir la campagne>
travel[2] *n* : voyages *mpl*
traveler *or* **traveller** ['trævələr] *n* : voyageur *m*, -geuse *f*
traverse ['trəˈvərs, træˈvərs, 'trævərs] *vt* **-versed; -versing** : traverser, franchir
travesty ['trævəsti] *n, pl* **-ties** : parodie *f*
trawl[1] ['trɔl] *vi* : pêcher au chalut
trawl[2] *n* : chalut *m*
trawler ['trɔlər] *n* : chalutier *m*
tray ['treɪ] *n* : plateau *m*
treacherous ['trɛtʃərəs] *adj* **1** : traître, déloyal **2** UNRELIABLE : infidèle, incertain **3** DANGEROUS : dangereux, périlleux
treacherously ['trɛtʃərəsli] *adv* : traîtreusement
treachery ['trɛtʃəri] *n, pl* **-eries** : traîtrise *f*, déloyauté *f*
tread[1] ['trɛd] *v* **trod** ['trɑd]; **trodden** ['trɑdən] *or* **trod; treading** *vi* **1** WALK : marcher **2 to tread on** : marcher sur, piétiner — *vt* BEAT : tracer <to tread a path : tracer un chemin>
tread[2] *n* **1** FOOTSTEP : pas *m*, trace *f* de pas **2** : bande *f* de roulement (d'un pneu), semelle *f* (d'un soulier) **3** *or* **stair tread** : dessus *m* (d'une marche)
treadle ['trɛdəl] *n* : pédale *f*
treadmill ['trɛdˌmɪl] *n* **1** : exerciseur *m* **2** ROUTINE : engrenage *m*, train-train *m*
treason ['triːzən] *n* : trahison *f*
treasure[1] ['trɛʒər, 'treɪ-] *vt* **-sured; -suring** CHERISH : tenir beaucoup à
treasure[2] *n* : trésor *m*
treasurer ['trɛʒərər, 'treɪ-] *n* : trésorier *m*, -rière *f*
treasury ['trɛʒəri, 'treɪ-] *n, pl* **-suries 1** : trésorerie *f* (édifice) **2 Treasury** : ministère *m* des Finances
treat[1] ['triːt] *vi or* **to treat of** : traiter de, parler de <a book treating of animals : un livre qui traite des animaux> — *vt* **1** DEAL WITH, HANDLE : traiter <he treated him as inferior : il le traitait en inférieur> **2** PROCESS : traiter <to treat soil with lime : traiter le sol avec du chaux> **3** : traiter, soigner (en médecine) **4 to treat s.o. to sth** : payer qqch à qqn, offrir qqch à qqn
treat[2] *n* : cadeau *m* spécial, (petit) plaisir *m* <let's give him a treat : faisons-lui un plaisir> <it's my treat : c'est moi qui paie>
treatise ['triːt̬əs] *n* : traité *m*
treatment ['triːtmənt] *n* **1** HANDLING : traitement *m* **2** : soins *mpl*, traitement *m* (en médecine)
treaty ['triːt̬i] *n, pl* **-ties** : traité *m*
treble[1] ['trɛbəl] *v* **-bled; -bling** : tripler
treble[2] *adj* **1 → triple 2** : de soprano
treble[3] *n* : soprano *m*
treble clef *n* : clé *f* de sol
tree ['triː] *n* : arbre *m*
treeless ['triːləs] *adj* : sans arbres, dénué d'arbres
trek[1] ['trɛk] *vi* **trekked; trekking** : faire une longue randonnée, avancer avec peine
trek[2] *n* : randonnée *f*, marche *f* pénible
trellis ['trɛlɪs] *n* : treillis *m*, treillage *m*
tremble ['trɛmbəl] *vi* **-bled; -bling 1** SHIVER : trembler, frissonner **2** VIBRATE : trembler, vibrer (se dit de la voix)
tremendous [trɪ'mɛndəs] *adj* : énorme, immense
tremendously [trɪ'mɛndəsli] *adv* : extrêmement, énormément
tremor ['trɛmər] *n* **1** TREMBLING : tremblement *m*, frisson *m* **2** : secousse *f* sismique (en géologie)
tremulous ['trɛmjələs] *adj* **1** : tremblant, frémissant **2** TIMID : timide
trench ['trɛntʃ] *n* : tranchée *f*
trenchant ['trɛntʃənt] *adj* : incisif, tranchant

trend [ˈtrɛnd] *n* : tendance *f*, mode *f* <to set a trend : lancer une mode> <a downward trend : une tendance à la baisse>
trendy [ˈtrɛndi] *adj* **trendier; -est** : branché *fam*, à la mode <a trendy spot : un endroit branché> <trendy clothes : vêtements dernier cri>
trepidation [ˌtrɛpəˈdeɪʃən] *n* : appréhension *f*, inquiétude *f*
trespass[1] [ˈtrɛspəs, -ˌpæs] *vi* **1** SIN : offenser **2** : s'introduire illégalement <no trespassing : défense d'entrer>
trespass[2] *n* **1** SIN : offense *f*, péché *m* **2** : entrée *f* non autorisée
tress [ˈtrɛs] *n* : mèche *f* de cheveux, boucle *f* de cheveux
trestle [ˈtrɛsəl] *n* **1** : tréteau *m*, chevalet *m* **2** *or* **trestle bridge** : pont *m* sur chevalets
triad [ˈtraɪˌæd] *n* : triade *f*
trial[1] [ˈtraɪəl] *adj* : d'essai <trial period : période d'essai>
trial[2] *n* **1** HEARING : procès *m* **2** TEST : essai *m* **3** ORDEAL : épreuve *f*, difficulté *f* <the trials of youth : les épreuves de la jeunesse>
triangle [ˈtraɪˌæŋgəl] *n* : triangle *m*
triangular [traɪˈæŋgjələr] *adj* : triangulaire
tribal [ˈtraɪbəl] *adj* : tribal
tribe [ˈtraɪb] *n* : tribu *f*
tribesman [ˈtraɪbzmən] *n, pl* **-men** [-mən, -ˌmɛn] : membre *m* d'une tribu
tribulation [ˌtrɪbjəˈleɪʃən] *n* : affliction *f*, tourment *m*
tribunal [traɪˈbjuːnəl, trɪ-] *n* : tribunal *m*
tributary [ˈtrɪbjəˌtɛri] *n, pl* **-taries** : affluent *m*
tribute [ˈtrɪbjuːt] *n* : tribut *m*, hommage *m* <to pay tribute to s.o. : rendre hommage à qqn>
trick[1] [ˈtrɪk] *vt* : attraper, rouler *fam* <to trick s.o. : jouer un tour à qqn>
trick[2] *n* **1** RUSE : tour *m*, artifice *m*, ruse *f* **2** PRANK : farce *f*, tour *m* <to play a trick on : jouer un tour à> **3** *or* **magic trick** : tour *m* **4** MANNERISM : manie *f*, habitude *f* **5** KNACK : don *m*, truc *m* **6** : pli *m*, levée *f* (de cartes) <to take a trick : faire un pli>
trickery [ˈtrɪkəri] *n* : supercherie *f*, tromperie *f*
trickle[1] [ˈtrɪkəl] *vi* **-led; -ling 1** DRIP : dégouliner, couler **2** *or* **to trickle away** : se dissiper petit à petit
trickle[2] *n* : filet *m* (d'eau), écoulement *m* (de sable, etc.)
trickster [ˈtrɪkstər] *n* : filou *m*, escroc *m*
tricky [ˈtrɪki] *adj* **trickier; -est 1** SLY : rusé, fourbe **2** DIFFICULT : difficile, délicat, épineux
tricycle [ˈtraɪəkəl, -ˌsɪkəl] *n* : tricycle *m*
trident [ˈtraɪdənt] *n* : trident *m*
triennial [ˌtraɪˈɛniəl] *adj* : triennal
trifle[1] [ˈtraɪfəl] *vi* **-fled; -fling 1** TOY : jouer **2 to trifle with** : jouer avec (les sentiments de qqn), traîter (une personne) à la légère
trifle[2] *n* : bagatelle *f*, rien *m* <it's a mere trifle : c'est peu de chose>
trifling [ˈtraɪflɪŋ] *adj* : insignifiant, peu important
trigger[1] [ˈtrɪgər] *vt* : déclencher
trigger[2] *n* : détente *f*, gâchette *f* <to pull the trigger : appuyer sur la détente>
trigonometry [ˌtrɪgəˈnɑmətri] *n* : trigonométrie *f*
trill[1] [ˈtrɪl] *vi* : triller (en musique) — *vt* : triller, rouler <to trill one's *r*'s : rouler les *r*>
trill[2] *n* **1** : trille *m* (en musique) **2** : consonne *f* roulée (en linguistique)
trillion [ˈtrɪljən] *n* : billion *m*
trilogy [ˈtrɪlədʒi] *n, pl* **-gies** : trilogie *f*
trim[1] [ˈtrɪm] *vt* **trimmed; trimming 1** DECORATE : décorer, orner **2** CUT : tailler, couper (une haie, une barbe, etc.) **3** REDUCE : limiter
trim[2] *adj* **trimmer; trimmest 1** NEAT : soigné, bien tenu **2** SLIM : svelte, mince
trim[3] *n* **1** CONDITION, FITNESS : forme *f* <to keep in good trim : se maintenir en bonne forme> **2** CUT : coupe *f* d'entretien (des cheveux) **3** TRIMMING : garniture *f*
trimming [ˈtrɪmɪŋ] *n* **1** : parement *m* (en couture), garniture *f* **2 trimmings** *npl* : garniture *f* (en cuisine) **3 trimmings** *npl* SCRAPS : rognures *fpl*, chutes *fpl*
Trinidadian[1] [ˌtrɪnəˈdædiən] *adj* : trinidadien
Trinidadian[2] *n* : Trinidadien *m*, -dienne *f*
Trinity [ˈtrɪnəṭi] *n* : Trinité *f*
trinket [ˈtrɪŋkət] *n* : babiole *f*, colifichet *m*
trio [ˈtriˌoː] *n, pl* **trios** : trio *m*
trip[1] [ˈtrɪp] *v* **tripped; tripping** *vi* **1** : marcher d'un pas léger **2** STUMBLE : trébucher, s'enfarger *Can* **3** *or* **to trip up** ERR : trébucher, faire un faux pas — *vt* **1** : faire trébucher (une personne) **2** : déclencher (un mécanisme) **3 to trip up** DISCONCERT, TRAP : désarçonner
trip[2] *n* **1** JOURNEY : voyage *m*, excursion *f*, tour *m* **2** STUMBLE : trébuchement *m*
tripartite [traɪˈpɑrˌtaɪt] *adj* : tripartite
tripe [ˈtraɪp] *n* **1** : tripes *fpl* (d'un animal) **2** NONSENSE : bêtises *fpl*
triple[1] [ˈtrɪpəl] *v* **-pled; -pling** : tripler
triple[2] *adj* : triple
triple[3] *n* : triple *m*
triplet [ˈtrɪplət] *n* **1** : triolet *m* (en musique) **2 triplets** *npl* : triplés *mpl*
triplicate [ˈtrɪplɪkət] *n* **in ~** : en trois exemplaires
tripod [ˈtraɪˌpɑd] *n* : trépied *m*
trite [ˈtraɪt] *adj* **triter; tritest** : banal
triumph[1] [ˈtraɪəmpf] *vi* : triompher
triumph[2] *n* : triomphe *m*

triumphal [traɪˈʌmpfəl] *adj* : triomphal
triumphant [traɪˈʌmpfənt] *adj* : triomphant
triumphantly [traɪˈʌmpfəntli] *adv* : triomphalement, en triomphe
trivia [ˈtrɪviə] *ns & pl* : futilités *fpl*, bagatelles *fpl*
trivial [ˈtrɪviəl] *adj* : sans importance, insignifiant
triviality [ˌtrɪviˈæləṭi] *n, pl* **-ties** : banalité *f*, insignifiance *f*
trod, trodden → **tread**[1]
troll [ˈtroːl] *n* : troll *m*
trolley [ˈtrɑli] *n, pl* **trolleys** : tramway *m*
trombone [trɑmˈboːn] *n* : trombone *m*
trombonist [trɑmˈboːnɪst] *n* : tromboniste *mf*
troop[1] [ˈtruːp] *vi* : aller en bande <to troop by : passer en troupe>
troop[2] *n* **1** GROUP : bande *f*, groupe *m* **2 troops** *npl* : troupes *fpl*, soldats *mpl*
trooper [ˈtruːpər] *n* **1** : soldat *m* de cavalerie **2** *or* **state trooper** : gendarme *m France*, policier *m*
trophy [ˈtroːfi] *n, pl* **-phies** : trophée *m*
tropic[1] [ˈtrɑpɪk] *or* **tropical** [ˈtrɑpɪkəl] *adj* : tropical
tropic[2] *n* : tropique *m* <Tropic of Cancer : tropique du Cancer>
trot[1] [ˈtrɑt] *vi* **trotted; trotting** : trotter
trot[2] *n* : trot *m*
trouble[1] [ˈtrʌbəl] *vt* **-bled; -bling 1** UPSET, WORRY : troubler, inquiéter **2** AFFLICT : faire mal à <to be troubled by a headache : être incommodé par un mal de tête> **3** BOTHER : déranger <please don't trouble yourself : je vous en prie, ne vous dérangez pas>
trouble[2] *n* **1** PROBLEMS : ennuis *mpl*, difficultés *fpl* <to get into trouble : avoir des ennuis> <he has trouble reading : il a de la difficulté à lire> <back trouble : problèmes de dos> **2** EFFORT : mal *m*, peine *f* <to take the trouble : se donner la peine>
troublemaker [ˈtrʌbəlˌmeɪkər] *n* : fauteur *m*, -trice *f* de troubles; provocateur *m*, -trice *f*
troublesome [ˈtrʌbəlsəm] *adj* : difficile, gênant, pénible
trough [ˈtrɔf] *n, pl* **troughs** [ˈtrɔfs, ˈtrɔvz] **1** : abreuvoir *m* (pour les animaux) **2** CHANNEL, DEPRESSION : chenal *m*, creux *m*
trounce [ˈtraʊnʃs] *vt* **trounced; trouncing 1** THRASH : battre, rosser **2** DEFEAT : battre à plates coutures, écraser
troupe [ˈtruːp] *n* : troupe *f*
trousers [ˈtraʊzərz] *npl* : pantalon *m*
trout [ˈtraʊt] *ns & pl* : truite *f*
trowel [ˈtraʊəl] *n* **1** : truelle *f* (pour étendre le mortier) **2** : déplantoir *m* (pour le jardinage)
truant [ˈtruːənt] *n* : élève *mf* absentéiste <to play truant : faire l'école buissonnière>
truce [ˈtruːs] *n* : trêve *f*
truck[1] [ˈtrʌk] *vt* : camionner
truck[2] *n* **1** : camion *m* **2** DEALINGS : association *f*, relations *fpl* <to have no truck with : ne rien avoir à faire avec>
trucker [ˈtrʌkər] *n* : camionneur *m*, -neuse *f*; routier *m*
truculent [ˈtrʌkjələnt] *adj* : agressif
trudge [ˈtrʌdʒ] *vi* **trudged; trudging** : marcher péniblement, marcher lourdement
true[1] [ˈtruː] *vt* **trued; trueing** : ajuster, aligner <to true up a board : aligner une planche>
true[2] *adv* **1** TRUTHFULLY : honnêtement **2** ACCURATELY : juste
true[3] *adj* **truer; truest 1** LOYAL : fidèle, sincère **2** ACCURATE : juste, vrai, exact **3** GENUINE : vrai, véritable <a true love : un véritable amour> **4** RIGHTFUL : légitime
true–blue [ˈtruːˈbluː] *adj* : loyal, fidèle
truffle [ˈtrʌfəl] *n* : truffe *f*
truism [ˈtruːˌɪzəm] *n* : truisme *m*
truly [ˈtruːli] *adv* **1** INDEED : vraiment, réellement **2 Yours truly** : Veuillez agréer l'expression de mes sentiments distingués
trump[1] [ˈtrʌmp] *vt* : couper (une carte), jouer atout sur
trump[2] *n* : atout *m*
trumped–up [ˈtrʌmptˈʌp] *adj* : inventé de toutes parts
trumpet[1] [ˈtrʌmpət] *vi* **1** : sonner de la trompette **2** : barrir (se dit d'un éléphant) — *vt* : claironner (des nouvelles, etc.)
trumpet[2] *n* : trompette *f*
trumpeter [ˈtrʌmpəṭər] *n* : trompettiste *mf*
truncate [ˈtrʌŋkeɪt, ˈtrʌn-] *vt* **-cated; -cating** : tronquer
trundle [ˈtrʌndəl] *v* **-dled; -dling** *vi* ROLL : rouler — *vt* WHEEL : pousser, faire rouler (bruyamment)
trunk [ˈtrʌŋk] *n* **1** : tronc *m* (du corps, d'un arbre, etc.) **2** : trompe *f* (d'un éléphant) **3** : coffre *m* (d'une voiture), malle *f* (pour voyager) **4 trunks** *npl* *or* **bathing trunks** : maillot *m* de bain
truss[1] [ˈtrʌs] *vt* **1** BIND : trousser (une volaille) **2** REINFORCE : armer
truss[2] *n* **1** : bandage *m* herniaire **2** FRAMEWORK : armature *f*
trust[1] [ˈtrʌst] *vi* **to trust in** : croire en (Dieu), faire confiance à (une personne) — *vt* **1** ENTRUST : confier **2** : avoir confiance en <I trust his judgment : j'ai confiance en son jugement>
trust[2] *n* **1** : confiance *f* <breach of trust : abus de confiance> **2** HOPE : espoir *m*, espérance *f* **3** CARTEL : trust *m* **4** : fidéicommis *m* <to hold sth in trust : tenir qqch par fidéicommis> **5** CARE, CUSTODY : charge *f*

trustee [ˌtrʌsˈtiː] *n* : fiduciaire *mf*, fidéicommissaire *mf*

trustful [ˈtrʌstfəl] *adj* : qui a confiance, confiant

trustfully [ˈtrʌstfəli] *adv* : avec confiance

trustworthiness [ˈtrʌstˌwərðinəs] *n* : loyauté *f*, fiabilité *f*

trustworthy [ˈtrʌstˌwərði] *adj* : digne de confiance, loyal

trusty [ˈtrʌsti] *adj* **trustier; -est** : loyal, fidèle

truth [ˈtruːθ] *n, pl* **truths** [ˈtruːðz, ˈtruːθs] : vérité *f*

truthful [ˈtruːθfəl] *adj* **1** HONEST : honnête **2** ACCURATE : exact, vrai

truthfully [ˈtruːθfəli] *adv* : sans mentir, sincèrement

truthfulness [ˈtruːθfəlnəs] *n* : véracité *f*, honnêteté *f*

try[1] [ˈtraɪ] *v* **tried; trying** *vt* **1** : juger (un accusé) **2** ATTEMPT : essayer, tenter <try to understand : essayez de comprendre> <to try one's luck : tenter sa chance> **3** TEST : éprouver, mettre à l'épreuve <to try one's patience : mettre sa patience à l'épreuve> **4** SAMPLE : goûter à, essayer — *vi* : essayer

try[2] *n, pl* **tries** : essai *m*, tentative *f*

tryout [ˈtraɪˌaʊt] *n* : essai *m*

try out *vt* : essayer, faire l'essai de

tsar [ˈzɑr, ˈtsɑr, ˈsɑr] → **czar**

T–shirt [ˈtiːˌʃərt] *n* : tee-shirt *m*, t-shirt *m*

tub [ˈtʌb] *n* **1** VAT : cuve *f*, bac *m* **2** CONTAINER : contenant *m*, pot *m* <a tub of margarine : un contenant de margarine> **3** → **bathtub**

tuba [ˈtuːbə, ˈtjuː-] *n* : tuba *m*

tube [ˈtuːb, ˈtjuːb] *n* **1** CYLINDER : tube *m*, cylindre *m* **2** : tube *m* (de dentifrice, etc.) **3** *or* **inner tube** : chambre *f* à air **4** *or* **cathode-ray tube** : tube *m* (cathodique)

tuber [ˈtuːbər, ˈtjuː-] *n* : tubercule *m*

tubercular [tʊˈbərkjələr, tjʊ-] *adj* : tuberculeux

tuberculosis [tuˌbərkjəˈloːsəs, tjʊ-] *n, pl* **-loses** [-ˌsiːz] : tuberculose *f*

tuberculous [tʊˈbərkjələs, tjʊ-] *adj* : tuberculeux

tubing [ˈtuːbɪŋ, ˈtjuː-] *n* : tubes *mpl*

tubular [ˈtubjələr, ˈtjuː-] *adj* : tubulaire

tuck[1] [ˈtʌk] *vt* **1** *or* **to tuck away** : cacher, ranger <to tuck away one's money : mettre son argent en sécurité> **2 to tuck in** : rentrer (sa chemise), border (un enfant) — *vi* **to tuck into** : manger ou boire avec appétit

tuck[2] *n* : pli *m*

tucker [ˈtʌkər] *vt or* **to tucker out** : fatiguer, épuiser

Tuesday [ˈtuːzˌdeɪ, ˈtjuːz-, -di] *n* : mardi *m*

tuft [ˈtʌft] *n* : touffe *f* (de cheveux, de plantes, etc.)

tug[1] [ˈtʌg] *v* **tugged; tugging** *vt* **1** TOW : remorquer **2** LUG : tirer, traîner — *vi* **to tug at** : tirer sur

tug[2] *n* **1** : petit coup *m* **2** → **tugboat**

tugboat [ˈtʌgˌboːt] *n* : remorqueur *m*

tug–of–war [ˌtʌgəˈwɔr] *n, pl* **tugs–of–war** : lutte *f* à la corde

tuition [tuːˈɪʃən, ˈtjuː-] *n* : frais *mpl* de scolarité

tulip [ˈtuːlɪp, ˈtjuː-] *n* : tulipe *f*

tumble[1] [ˈtəmbəl] *v* **-bled; -bling** *vi* **1** FALL : tomber, dégringoler **2** : faire des culbutes, culbuter (en gymnastique) **3** PLUMMET : chuter (se dit des prix, etc.) — *vt* **1** TOPPLE : faire tomber, renverser **2** *or* **to tumble together** : mélanger

tumble[2] *n* **1** : culbute *f* (en gymnastique) **2** FALL : chute *f*

tumbler [ˈtʌmblər] *n* **1** ACROBAT : acrobate *mf* **2** GLASS : verre *m* droit **3** : gorge *f* (de serrure)

tummy [ˈtʌmi] *n, pl* **-mies** : ventre *m*

tumor *or Brit* **tumour** [ˈtuːmər, ˈtjuː-] *n* : tumeur *f*

tumult [ˈtuːˌmʌlt ˈtjuː-] *n* **1** COMMOTION : tumulte *m*, vacarme *m* **2** CONFUSION : agitation *f*, tumulte *m*

tumultuous [tʊˈmʌltʃʊəs, tjuː-] *adj* : tumultueux

tuna [ˈtuːnə ˈtjuː-] *n, pl* **-na** *or* **-nas** : thon *m*

tundra [ˈtʌndrə] *n* : toundra *f*

tune[1] [ˈtuːn, ˈtjuːn] *v* **tuned; tuning** *vt* **1** : accorder (un instrument de musique) **2** *or* **to tune up** : régler, mettre au point (un moteur) — *vi* **to tune in to** : se mettre à l'écoute de

tune[2] *n* **1** MELODY : air *m*, mélodie *f* **2 to be in tune** : être accordé (se dit d'un instrument), chanter juste **3 to be out of tune** : être désaccordé (se dit d'un instrument), chanter faux **4 to be in tune with** : être en accord avec

tuneful [ˈtuːnfəl, ˈtjuːn-] *adj* : mélodieux, harmonieux

tuner [ˈtuːnər, ˈtjuː-] *n* **1** : accordeur *m* <piano tuner : accordeur de piano> **2** : tuner *m* (de radio, etc.)

tungsten [ˈtʌŋkstən] *n* : tungstène *m*

tunic [ˈtuːnɪk, ˈtjuː-] *n* : tunique *f*

tuning fork *n* : diapason *m*

Tunisian[1] [tuːˈniʒən, tjuːˈnɪziən] *adj* : tunisien

Tunisian[2] *n* : Tunisien *m*, -sienne *f*

tunnel[1] [ˈtʌnəl] *vi* **-neled** *or* **-nelled; -neling** *or* **-nelling** : creuser un tunnel

tunnel[2] *n* : tunnel *m*

turban [ˈtərbən] *n* : turban *m*

turbid [ˈtərbɪd] *adj* : turbide, trouble

turbine [ˈtərbən, -ˌbaɪn] *n* : turbine *f*

turboprop [ˈtərboːˌprɑp] *n* : turbopropulseur *m* (moteur), avion *m* à turbopropulseur

turbulence [ˈtərbjələnʦ] *n* : turbulence *f*

turbulent [ˈtərbjələnt] *adj* : turbulent, agité
turbulently [ˈtərbjələntli] *adv* : avec turbulence
tureen [təˈriːn, tjʊ-] *n* : soupière *f*
turf [ˈtərf] *n* : gazon *m*, motte *f* de gazon
turgid [ˈtərdʒəd] *adj* **1** SWOLLEN : enflé, gonflé **2** BOMBASTIC : pompeux
Turk [ˈtərk] *n* : Turc *m*, Turque *f*
turkey [ˈtərki] *n, pl* **-keys** : dinde *f*
Turkish[1] [ˈtərkiʃ] *adj* : turc
Turkish[2] *n* : turc *m* (langue)
turmoil [ˈtər,mɔɪl] *n* : désarroi *m*, confusion *f*
turn[1] [ˈtərn] *vt* **1** : tourner <to turn a wheel : tourner une roue> <turn the doorknob : tourne la poignée> **2** TWIST : tordre <to turn one's ankle : se tordre la cheville> **3** : tourner, retourner, changer de direction <she turned her chair toward the fire : elle a tourné sa chaise pour faire face au feu> <I turned the child over in bed : j'ai retourné l'enfant dans son lit> **4 to turn one's stomach** : se soulever le cœur **5 to turn over** PONDER : réfléchir à, tourner et retourner (un problème, une question, etc.) — *vi* **1** SPOIL : tourner, cailler **2** CHANGE : se transformer **3** BECOME : devenir <his hair turned gray : ses cheveux sont devenus gris> **4** : se tourner <he turned to them for help : il s'est tourné vers eux en espérant obtenir de l'aide> **5** HEAD : se diriger <we turned toward home : nous nous sommes dirigés vers la maison>
turn[2] *n* **1** ROTATION : tour *m* **2** CHANGE : amélioration *f*, tournure *f* <to take a turn for the better : s'être amélioré> **3** BEND : virage *m*, tournant *m* <a sharp turn : un brusque virage> <to make a right turn : tourner à droite> **4** DEED : service *m* <to do a good turn to : rendre service à> **5** : tour *m* <wait your turn : attendez votre tour> **6** STROLL : tour *m*, promenade *f*
turn away *vt* **1** AVERT : détourner (les yeux) **2 to turn s.o. away** : renvoyer qqn, refuser qqn — *vi* : se détourner
turncoat [ˈtərn,koːt] *n* : renégat *m*, -gate *f*
turn down *vt* **1** : retourner (une carte), rabattre (un collet) **2** LOWER : baisser (le volume) **3** REFUSE : refuser, décliner
turn in *vi* : se coucher <I turned in early : je me suis couché tôt> — *vt* **1** : rendre, remettre <she turned in her paper : elle a remis son devoir> **2** DELIVER : livrer <we turned him in to police : nous l'avons livré à la police>
turnip [ˈtərnəp] *n* : navet *m*
turn off : éteindre (la lumière), fermer (une radio, etc.), arrêter (un moteur)
turnout [ˈtərn,aʊt] *n* : participation *f*
turn out *vt* **1** EVICT : expulser, mettre à la porte **2** TURN OFF : éteindre — *vi* **1** COME : venir, se présenter <voters turned out in droves : les électeurs se sont présentés en grands nombres> **2 to turn out to be** : s'avérer, se révéler <the outing turned out to be a disaster : la sortie s'est révélée désastreuse>
turnover [ˈtərn,oːvər] *n* **1** REVERSAL : renversement *m* **2** : chausson *m* <apple turnover : chausson aux pommes> **3** : roulement *m* (du personnel)
turn over *vt* **1** TRANSFER : remettre, rendre **2** : tourner, retourner <to turn over a playing card : retourner une carte> — *vi* **1** : se retourner (se dit d'une personne) **2** : commencer à tourner (se dit d'un moteur)
turnpike [ˈtərn,paɪk] *n* : autoroute *f* à péage
turnstile [ˈtərn,staɪl] *n* : tourniquet *m*
turntable [ˈtərn,teɪbəl] *n* : platine *f* (d'un tourne-disque)
turn up *vt* **1** : mettre plus fort (la lumière, etc.), augmenter (le volume) **2** DISCOVER : découvrir **3** : retrousser (ses manches), relever (son collet) — *vi* **1** APPEAR, ARRIVE : arriver, apparaître **2** HAPPEN : survenir, se passer
turpentine [ˈtərpən,taɪn] *n* : térébenthine *f*
turquoise [ˈtər,kɔɪz, -,kwɔɪz] *n* : turquoise *f* (minéral), turquoise *m* (couleur)
turret [ˈtərət] *n* : tourelle *f*
turtle [ˈtərṭəl] *n* : tortue *f*
turtledove [ˈtərṭəl,dʌv] *n* : tourterelle *f*
turtleneck [ˈtərṭəl,nɛk] *n* : col *m* roulé, col *m* montant
tusk [ˈtʌsk] *n* : défense *f* (d'un animal)
tussle[1] [ˈtʌsəl] *vi* : se bagarrer, se battre
tussle[2] *n* : bagarre *f*, mêlée *f*
tutor[1] [ˈtuːṭər, ˈtjuː-] *vt* : donner des cours particuliers à
tutor[2] *n* : précepteur *m*, -trice *f*; professeur *m* particulier
tuxedo [ˌtəkˈsiːdoː] *n, pl* **-dos** *or* **-does** : smoking *m*
TV [ˌtiːˈviː, ˈtiːˌviː] *n* : TV *m*
twain [ˈtweɪn] *n* : deux *m*
twang[1] [ˈtwæŋ] *vt* : pincer les cordes de (un instrument) — *vi* : vibrer
twang[2] *n* **1** : ton *m* nasillard (de la voix) **2** : son *m* de corde pincée
tweak[1] [ˈtwiːk] *vt* : tirer, tordre
tweak[2] *n* : petit coup *m* sec
tweed [ˈtwiːd] *n* : tweed *m*
tweet[1] [ˈtwiːṭ] *vi* : pépier, gazouiller
tweet[2] *n* : pépiement *m*
tweezers [ˈtwiːzərz] *ns & pl* : pince *f* à épiler
twelfth[1] [ˈtwɛlfθ] *adj* : douzième
twelfth[2] *n* **1** : douzième *mf* (dans une série) **2** : douzième *m* (en mathé-

matiques) **3** (*used in dates*) <the twelfth of June : le douze juin>
twelve[1] ['twɛlv] *adj* : douze
twelve[2] *n* : douze *m*
twentieth[1] ['twʌntiəθ, 'twɛn-] *adj* : vingtième
twentieth[2] *n* **1** : vingtième *mf* (dans une série) **2** : vingtième *m* (en mathématiques) **3** (*used in dates*) <the twentieth of June : le vingt juin>
twenty[1] ['twʌnti, 'twɛn-] *adj* : vingt
twenty[2] *n, pl* **-ties** : vingt *m*
twenty–twenty *or* **20/20** *adj* **to have twenty–twenty vision** : avoir dix dixièmes à chaque œil
twice ['twaɪs] *adv* : deux fois <twice as much : deux fois plus>
twig ['twɪg] *n* : petite branche *f*, brindille *f*
twilight ['twaɪˌlaɪt] *n* : crépuscule *m* (du soir), aube *f* (du matin)
twill ['twɪl] *n* : sergé *m*
twin[1] ['twɪn] *adj* : jumeau <twin sister : sœur jumelle>
twin[2] *n* : jumeau *m*, -melle *f*
twine[1] ['twaɪn] *v* **twined; twining** *vt* : enrouler — *vi* : s'enrouler
twine[2] *n* : ficelle *f*
twinge ['twɪndʒ] *n* : élancement *m* (de douleur)
twinkle[1] ['twɪŋkəl] *vi* **-kled; -kling 1** : briller, scintiller (se dit des étoiles, etc.) **2** : pétiller (se dit des yeux)
twinkle[2] *n* : scintillement *m* (des étoiles), pétillement *m* (des yeux)
twirl[1] ['twərl] *vi* : tournoyer — *vt* : faire tournoyer
twirl[2] *n* : tournoiement *m*
twist[1] ['twɪst] *vt* **1** : tourner, tordre <to twist one's ankle : se tordre la cheville> **2** DISTORT : déformer, pervertir <to twist the facts : déformer les faits> — *vi* **1** : serpenter (se dit d'une route) **2** ENTWINE : s'enrouler **3 to twist and turn** : se tortiller
twist[2] *n* **1** TURN : tour *m*, torsion *f* **2** BEND : tournant *m* (d'une route, etc.) **3** COIL : tortillon *m*, rouleau *m* <a twist of lemon : un zeste de citron> **4** : rebondissement *m*, tournure *f* (des événements) <a twist of fate : un coup du sort>
twister ['twɪstər] *n* **1** → **tornado 2** → **waterspout**
twitch[1] ['twɪtʃ] *vi* **1** QUIVER : trembloter, avoir un mouvement convulsif **2** : se convulser, se contracter (se dit d'un muscle)
twitch[2] *n* **1** JERK : saccade *f*, coup *m* sec **2** SPASM : spasme *m* **3** *or* **nervous twitch** : tic *m* (nerveux)
twitter[1] ['twɪtər] *vi* **1** CHIRP : pépier, gazouiller **2** CHATTER : jacasser **3** *or* **to twitter about** : s'agiter (nerveusement)
twitter[2] *n* : pépiement *m*, gazouillement *m* (d'un oiseau)
two[1] ['tu:] *adj* : deux
two[2] *n, pl* **twos** : deux *m*
twofold[1] ['tu:fo:ld] *adv* : doublement
twofold[2] *adj* : double
twosome ['tu:səm] *n* : couple *m*
tycoon [taɪ'ku:n] *n* : magnat *m*
tying → **tie**[1]
type[1] ['taɪp] *v* **typed; typing** *vt* **1** : taper (une lettre, etc.) **2** CATEGORIZE : classifier, déterminer le type de — *vi* : taper (à la machine)
type[2] *n* **1** KIND : genre *m*, sorte *f*, type *m* **2** *or* **printing type** : caractère *m* (d'imprimerie)
typewriter ['taɪpˌraɪtər] *n* : machine *f* à écrire, dactylo *f Can*
typhoid ['taɪˌfɔɪd, taɪ'-] *n or* **typhoid fever** : typhoïde *f*, fièvre *f* typhoïde
typhoon [taɪ'fu:n] *n* : typhon *m*
typhus ['taɪfəs] *n* : typhus *m*
typical ['tɪpɪkəl] *adj* : typique, caractéristique
typically ['tɪpɪkli] *adv* **1** : typiquement <typically American : typiquement américain> **2** USUALLY : d'habitude
typify ['tɪpəˌfaɪ] *vt* **-fied; -fying** : représenter, être typique de
typist ['taɪpɪst] *n* : dactylo *mf*
typographic [ˌtaɪpə'græfɪk] *or* **typographical** [-fɪkəl] *adj* : typographique — **typographically** [-fɪkli] *adv*
typography [taɪ'pɑgrəfi] *n* : typographie *f*
tyrannical [tə'rænɪkəl, taɪ-] *adj* : tyrannique — **tyrannically** [-nɪkli] *adv*
tyrannize ['tɪrəˌnaɪz] *vt* **-nized; -nizing** : tyranniser
tyranny ['tɪrəni] *n, pl* **-nies** : tyrannie *f*
tyrant ['taɪrənt] *n* : tyran *m*
tzar ['zɑr, 'tsɑr, 'sɑr] → **czar**

U

u ['ju:] *n, pl* **u's** *or* **us** ['ju:z] : u *m*, vingt et unième lettre de l'alphabet
ubiquitous [ju:'bɪkwəˌtəs] *adj* : omniprésent
ubiquity [ju:'bɪkwəˌti] *n* : omniprésence *f*, ubiquité *f*
udder ['ʌdər] *n* : pis *m* (d'une vache)
Ugandan[1] [ju:'gændən, -'gɑn-; u:'gɑn-] *adj* : ougandais
Ugandan[2] *n* : Ougandais *m*, -daise *f*
ugliness ['ʌglinəs] *n* : laideur *f*
ugly ['ʌgli] *adj* **uglier; -est 1** : laid <an ugly color : une couleur laide> **2** DISAGREEABLE, FOUL : mauvais,

désagréable, vilain <ugly weather : du temps vilain> **3** QUARRELSOME : agressif, querelleur <the crowd turned ugly : la foule est devenue agressive>

Ukrainian[1] [ju:'kreɪniən, -'kraɪ-] *adj* : ukrainien

Ukrainian[2] *n* **1** : Ukrainien *m*, -nienne *f* **2** : ukrainien *m* (langue)

ukulele [ˌju:kə'leɪli] *n* : guitare *f* hawaïenne

ulcer ['ʌlsər] *n* : ulcère *f*

ulcerate ['ʌlsəˌreɪt] *vt* **-ated; -ating** : ulcérer

ulceration [ˌʌlsə'reɪʃən] *n* : ulcération *f*

ulcerous [ˌʌlsərəs] *adj* : ulcéreux

ulna ['ʌlnə] *n* : cubitus *m*

ulterior [ˌʌl'tɪriər] *adj* HIDDEN : secret, inavoué <to have ulterior motives : avoir des arrière-pensées>

ultimate[1] ['ʌltəmət] *adj* **1** FINAL : ultime, final **2** SUPREME : suprême **3** FUNDAMENTAL : absolu, fondamental

ultimate[2] *n* : summum *m* <the ultimate in modernity : le summum de la modernité>

ultimately ['ʌltəmətli] *adv* : en fin de compte, finalement

ultimatum [ˌʌltə'meɪtəm, -'mɑ-] *n, pl* **-tums** *or* **-ta** [-tə] : ultimatum *m* <to deliver an ultimatum : adresser un ultimatum>

ultraviolet [ˌʌltrə'vaɪələt] *adj* : ultraviolet

umbilical cord [ʌm'bɪlɪkəl] : cordon *m* ombilical

umbrage ['ʌmbrɪdʒ] *n* **to take umbrage at** : prendre ombrage de, s'offenser de

umbrella [ˌʌm'brɛlə] *n* : parapluie *m*

umpire[1] ['ʌmˌpaɪr] *v* **-pired; -piring** *vt* : arbitrer (aux sports) — *vi* : servir d'arbitre

umpire[2] *n* : arbitre *m*

umpteen [ˌʌmˌpti:n, ˌʌmp'-] *adj* : des tas de

umpteenth [ˌʌmˌptinθ, ˌʌmp'-] *adj* : énième

unable [ˌʌn'eɪbəl] *adj* **to be unable to** : ne pas pouvoir, être incapable de

unabridged [ˌʌnə'brɪdʒd] *adj* : intégral

unacceptable [ˌʌnɪk'sɛptəbəl] *adj* : inacceptable, inadmissible

unaccompanied [ˌʌnə'kʌmpənɪd] *adj* : non accompagné

unaccountable [ˌʌnə'kaʊntəbəl] *adj* : inexplicable — **unaccountably** [-bli] *adv*

unaccounted [ˌʌnə'kaʊntəd] *adj* **~ for** : introuvable (se dit des choses), pas retrouvé (se dit des personnes)

unaccustomed [ˌʌnə'kʌstəmd] *adj* **1** UNCHARACTERISTIC : inaccoutumé, inhabituel **2 to be unaccustomed to** : ne pas avoir l'habitude de

unacquainted [ˌʌnə'kweɪntəd] *adj* **to be unacquainted with** : ne pas connaître

unadorned [ˌʌnə'dɔrnd] *adj* : sans ornement

unadulterated [ˌʌnə'dʌltəˌreɪtəd] *adj* **1** PURE : pur, naturel **2** : pur (et simple) <unadulterated nonsense : de la pure bêtise>

unaffected [ˌʌnə'fɛktəd] *adj* **1** : qui n'est pas affecté <I was unaffected by his plea : sa demande m'a laissé indifférent> **2** NATURAL : naturel, sincère, sans affectation

unaffectedly [ˌʌnə'fɛktədli] *adv* : sans affectation

unafraid [ˌʌnə'freɪd] *adj* : sans peur

unaided [ˌʌn'eɪdəd] *adj* : sans aide, tout seul

unalike [ˌʌnə'laɪk] *adj* : peu ressemblant, différent

unambiguous [ˌʌnæm'bɪgjʊəs] *adj* : non équivoque

unanimity [ˌju:nə'nɪmət̬i] *n* : unanimité *f*

unanimous [jʊ'nænəməs] *adj* : unanime

unanimously [jʊ'nænəməsli] *adv* : à l'unanimité, unanimement

unannounced [ˌʌnə'naʊnst] *adj* : inattendu, sans se faire annoncer

unanswered [ˌʌn'ænsərd] *adj* : qui reste sans réponse

unappealing [ˌʌnə'pi:lɪŋ] *adj* : peu attirant

unappetizing [ˌʌn'æpəˌtaɪzɪŋ] *adj* : peu appétissant

unarguable [ˌʌn'ɑrgjuəbəl] *adj* : incontestable

unarmed [ˌʌn'ɑrmd] *adj* : non armé, sans armes

unassuming [ˌʌnə'su:mɪŋ] *adj* : modeste, sans prétention

unattached [ˌʌnə'tætʃt] *adj* **1** : détaché, indépendant <unattached buildings : bâtiments détachés> **2** : libre (se dit d'une personne célibataire)

unattractive [ˌʌnə'trækɪv] *adj* : peu attrayant

unauthorized [ˌʌn'ɔθəˌraɪzd] *adj* : non autorisé

unavailable [ˌʌnə'veɪləbəl] *adj* : indisponible

unavoidable [ˌʌnə'vɔɪdəbəl] *adj* : inévitable

unaware[1] [ˌʌnə'wær] *adv* → **unawares**

unaware[2] *adj* : qui n'est pas conscient, qui ignore <unaware of the danger : inconscient du danger>

unawares [ˌʌnə'wærz] *adv* **1** UNEXPECTEDLY : soudainement, à l'improviste <to take unawares : prendre au dépourvu> **2** UNINTENTIONALLY : par mégarde, inconsciemment

unbalanced [ˌʌn'bælənʧt] *adj* **1** LOPSIDED : qui n'est pas équilibré **2** UNSTABLE : déséquilibré (se dit d'une personne)

unbearable [ˌʌn'bærəbəl] *adj* : insupportable, insoutenable

unbeaten [ˌʌn'bi:tən] *adj* : invaincu

unbecoming [ˌʌnbɪˈkʌmɪŋ] *adj* **1** UNFLATTERING : peu seyant, peu flatteur **2** UNSEEMLY : inconvenant
unbelievable [ˌʌnbəˈliːvəbəl] *adj* : incroyable — **unbelievably** [-bli] *adv*
unbend [ˌʌnˈbɛnd] *v* **-bent; -bending** *vt* : détordre (un fil, etc.) — *vi* RELAX : se détendre
unbending [ˌʌnˈbɛndɪŋ] *adj* : inflexible
unbiased [ˌʌnˈbaɪəst] *adj* : impartial
unbind [ˌʌnˈbaɪnd] *vt* **-bound; -binding** **1** UNTIE : délier, détacher **2** RELEASE : libérer
unbolt [ˌʌnˈboːlt] *vt* : déverrouiller
unborn [ˌʌnˈbɔrn] *adj* : qui n'est pas encore né
unbosom [ˌʌnˈbʊzəm, -ˈbuː-] *vt* **to unbosom oneself to** : se confier à
unbreakable [ˌʌnˈbreɪkəbəl] *adj* : incassable
unbridled [ˌʌnˈbraɪdəld] *adj* UNRESTRAINED : débridé, déchaîné, non contenu
unbroken [ˌʌnˈbroːkən] *adj* **1** WHOLE : intact, qui n'est pas brisé **2** UNTAMED : indompté **3** UNINTERRUPTED : continu
unbuckle [ˌʌnˈbʌkəl] *vt* **-led; -ling** : déboucler
unburden [ˌʌnˈbərdən] *vt* **1** RELIEVE : décharger (d'un fardeau) **2 to unburden oneself** : se confier, s'épancher
unbutton [ˌʌnˈbʌtən] *vt* : déboutonner
uncalled-for [ˌʌnˈkɔld,fɔr] *adj* : déplacé, injustifié
uncannily [ənˈkænəli] *adv* : étrangement
uncanny [ənˈkæni] *adj* **1** EERIE, STRANGE : mystérieux, troublant, étrange **2** REMARKABLE : extraordinaire
unceasing [ˌʌnˈsiːsɪŋ] *adj* : incessant, continu
unceasingly [ˌʌnˈsiːsɪŋli] *adv* : sans cesse
unceremonious [ˌʌnsɛrəˈmoːniəs] *adj* **1** INFORMAL : informel, sans façon **2** ABRUPT : précipité, brusque <an unceremonious dismissal : un licenciement précipité>
unceremoniously [ˌʌnsɛrəˈmoːniəsli] *adv* : sans façon, sans cérémonie
uncertain [ˌʌnˈsərtən] *adj* **1** INDEFINITE, UNKNOWN : incertain, inconnu **2** CHANGEABLE : incertain, variable <uncertain weather : du temps incertain> **3** UNSURE : incertain
uncertainly [ˌʌnˈsərtənli] *adv* : avec hésitation, d'un air hésitant
uncertainty [ˌʌnˈsərtənti] *n, pl* **-ties** : incertitude *f*, doute *m*
unchangeable [ˌʌnˈtʃeɪndʒəbəl] *adj* : immuable, invariable
unchanged [ˌʌnˈtʃeɪndʒd] *adj* : inchangé
unchanging [ˌʌnˈtʃeɪndʒɪŋ] *adj* : immuable
uncharacteristic [ˌʌnˌkærɪktəˈrɪstɪk] *adj* : peu habituel, peu typique
uncharged [ˌʌnˈtʃɑrdʒd] *adj* : qui n'a pas de charge électrique
uncivilized [ˌʌnˈsɪvəˌlaɪzd] *adj* **1** WILD : non civilisé (se dit d'un endroit) **2** BARBAROUS : barbare, sauvage
uncle [ˈʌŋkəl] *n* : oncle *m*
unclean [ˌʌnˈkliːn] *adj* **1** IMPURE : impur **2** DIRTY : malpropre, sale
uncleanliness [ˌʌnˈklɛnlinəs] *n* : malpropreté *f*, saleté *f*
unclear [ˌʌnˈklɪr] *adj* : peu clair, incertain
unclog [ˌʌnˈklɑg] *vt* **-clogged; -clogging** : déboucher (un évier, etc.)
unclothed [ˌʌnˈkloːðd] *adj* : nu, dévêtu
unclouded [ˌʌnˈklaʊdəd] *adj* : limpide, sans nuages
uncomfortable [ˌʌnˈkʌmfərtəbəl] *adj* **1** : inconfortable (se dit d'une chaise, etc.) **2** UNEASY : mal à l'aise, gêné (se dit d'une personne)
uncomfortably [ˌʌnˈkʌmfərtəbli] *adv* **1** DISAGREEABLY : désagréablement, inconfortablement **2** UNEASILY : avec gêne, avec inquiétude
uncommitted [ˌʌnkəˈmɪtəd] *adj* : non engagé
uncommon [ˌʌnˈkɑmən] *adj* **1** UNUSUAL : rare, peu commun **2** REMARKABLE : remarquable, extraordinaire
uncommonly [ˌʌnˈkɑmənli] *adv* : extraordinairement, exceptionnellement
uncompromising [ˌʌnˈkɑmprəˈmaɪzɪŋ] *adj* : intransigeant, inflexible
unconcerned [ˌʌnkənˈsərnd] *adj* **1** UNINTERESTED : indifférent **2** UNWORRIED : insouciant, imperturbable
unconditional [ˌʌnkənˈdɪʃənəl] *adj* : inconditionnel — **unconditionally** *adv*
unconscious[1] [ˌʌnˈkɑnʃəs] *adj* **1** UNAWARE : inconscient **2** INSENSIBLE : sans connaissance
unconscious[2] *n* : inconscient *m*
unconsciously [ˌʌnˈkɑnʃəsli] *adv* : inconsciemment
unconsciousness [ˌʌnˈkɑnʃəsnəs] *n* : inconscience *f*
unconstitutional [ˌʌnˈkɑnɪstəˈtuːʃənəl, -ˈtjuː-] *adj* : inconstitutionnel
uncontrollable [ˌʌnkənˈtroːləbəl] *adj* : incontrôlable, irrésistible
uncontrollably [ˌʌnkənˈtroːləbli] *adv* : irrésistiblement <to laugh uncontrollably : rire sans pouvoir se contrôler>
uncontrolled [ˌʌnkənˈtroːld] *adj* : incontrôlé, non maîtrisé
unconventional [ˌʌnkənˈvɛnʃənəl] *adj* : peu conventionnel
unconvincing [ˌʌnkənˈvɪnɪsɪŋ] *adj* : peu convaincant
uncouth [ˌʌnˈkuːθ] *adj* : grossier, fruste
uncover [ˌʌnˈkʌvər] *vt* : découvrir
uncultivated [ˌʌnˈkʌlṭəˌveɪṭəd] *adj* : inculte
unctuous [ˈʌŋktʃʊəs] *adj* : onctueux, mielleux
uncut [ˌʌnˈkʌt] *adj* **1** : non coupé (se dit des cheveux), non taillé (se dit d'une

pierre précieuse) **2** UNABRIDGED : intégral

undaunted [ʌn'dɔnɪ̯təd] *adj* : imperturbable

undecided [ʌndɪ'saɪdəd] *adj* **1** IRRESOLUTE : indécis, incertain **2** UNRESOLVED : non résolu

undefeated [ʌndɪ'fi:ɪ̯təd] *adj* : invaincu

undeniable [ʌndɪ'naɪəbəl] *adj* : indéniable — **undeniably** [-bli] *adv*

under[1] ['ʌndər] *adv* **1** : en dessous <the diver went under again : le plongeur est retourné sous l'eau> **2** LESS : moins <$10 or under : 10 $ ou moins> **3 to put under** : anesthésier, endormir

under[2] *adj* **1** LOWER : inférieur **2** SUBORDINATE : subordonné **3** INSUFFICIENT : insuffisant <an under dose of medicine : une dose insuffisante du médicament>

under[3] *prep* **1** BELOW, BENEATH : sous <under a tree : sous un arbre> <we walked under the ladder : nous avons passé sous l'échelle> <it's under there : c'est là-dessous> **2** UNDERNEATH : sous, en dessous de <I wore a sweater under my coat : je portais un chandail sous mon manteau> **3** (*indicating rank or authority*) : sous, sous la direction de <to serve under the general : servir sous le général> **4** : moins de <under two pounds : moins de deux livres> **5** ACCORDING TO : d'après, selon <under the terms of the contract : selon les modalités du contrat> **6 under lock and key** : sous clef

underage [ʌndər'eɪdʒ] *adj* : mineur, sous l'âge réglementaire

underbrush ['ʌndər,brəʃ] *n* : sous-bois *m*, broussailles *fpl*

undercarriage ['ʌndər,kærɪdʒ] *n* **1** : châssis *m* (d'une voiture) **2** *Brit* : train *m* d'atterrissage (d'un avion)

underclothes ['ʌndər,klo:z, -,klo:ðz] *npl* → **underwear**

underclothing ['ʌndər,kloðɪŋ] → **underwear**

undercover [ʌndər'kʌvər] *adj* : secret, clandestin <an undercover agent : un agent secret>

undercurrent ['ʌndər,kərənt] *n* **1** : courant *m* sous-marin **2** : sentiment *m* sous-jacent <an undercurrent of resentment : un ressentiment sous-jacent>

undercut [ʌndər'kʌt] *vt* **-cut; -cutting 1** : vendre moins cher que **2** UNDERMINE : amoindrir, saper

underdeveloped [ʌndərdɪ'vɛləpt] *adj* : sous-développé

underdog ['ʌndər,dɔg] *n* **1** : celui *m* que l'on donne perdant **2** : opprimé *m*, -mée *f*

underdone [ʌndər'dʌn] *adj* : pas assez cuit

underestimate [ʌndər'estə,meɪt] *vt* **-mated; -mating** : sous-estimer

underexpose [ʌndərɪk'spo:z] *vt* **-posed; -posing** : sous-exposer (une photo)

underexposure [ʌndərɪk'spo:ʒər] *n* : sous-exposition *f* (en photographie)

underfoot [ʌndər'fʊt] *adv* **1** : sous les pieds <warm sand underfoot : du sable chaud sous les pieds> **2 to be underfoot** : être dans les jambes

undergarment ['ʌndər,gɑrmənt] *n* : sous-vêtement *m*

undergo [ʌndər'go:] *vt* **-went** [-'wɛnt]; **-gone** [-'gɔn]; **-going** : éprouver (des souffrances), subir (une opération, des examens, etc.)

undergraduate [ʌndər'grædʒʊət] *n* : étudiant *m*, -diante *f* de premier cycle; étudiant *m*, -diante *f* qui prépare une licence *France*

underground[1] [ʌndər'graʊnd] *adv* **1** : sous terre **2** SECRETLY : clandestinement, secrètement <to go underground : passer dans la clandestinité>

underground[2] ['ʌndər,graʊnd] *adj* **1** SUBTERRANEAN : souterrain **2** SECRET : clandestin, secret

underground[3] ['ʌndər,graʊnd] *n* **1** SUBWAY : métro *m* **2** : résistance *f* (en politique)

undergrowth ['ʌndər'gro:θ] *n* : sous-bois *m*, broussailles *fpl*, fardoches *fpl Can*

underhand[1] ['ʌndər,hænd] *adv* **1** SECRETLY, SLYLY : sournoisement, en sous-main **2** : par en dessous <to throw underhand : lancer par en dessous>

underhand[2] *adj* **1** SLY : sournois **2** : par en dessous <an underhand throw : un lancer par en dessous>

underhanded[1] [ʌndər'hændəd] *adv* → **underhand**[1]

underhanded[2] *adj* SECRET : clandestin <underhanded dealings : transactions en sous-main>

underline ['ʌndər,laɪn] *vt* **-lined; -lining 1** : souligner (un mot) **2** STRESS : souligner, mettre l'accent sur

underling ['ʌndərlɪŋ] *n* : subordonné *m*, -née *f*; subalterne *mf*

underlying [ʌndər'laɪɪŋ] *adj* **1** : sous-jacent <underlying strata : strates sous-jacentes> **2** FUNDAMENTAL : fondamental, sous-jacent

undermine [ʌndər'maɪn] *vt* **-mined; -mining 1** : saper, miner (un escarpement, une construction, etc.) **2** SAP, WEAKEN : saper, amoindrir <to undermine one's confidence : saper sa confiance>

underneath[1] ['ʌndər'ni:θ] *adv* : en dessous, dessous <the part underneath : la partie d'en dessous>

underneath[2] *prep* : sous, au-dessous de

undernourished [ʌndər'nərɪʃt] *adj* : sous-alimenté

undernourishment [ˌʌndərˈnərɪʃmənt] *n* : sous-alimentation *f*
underpants [ˈʌndərˌpænts] *npl* : slip *m France,* caleçon *m,* petite culotte *f Can*
underpass [ˈʌndərˌpæs] *n* : voie *f* inférieure (de l'autoroute), passage *m* souterrain (pour les piétons)
underprivileged [ˌʌndərˈprɪvɪlɪdʒd] *adj* : défavorisé, déshérité
underrate [ˌʌndərˈreɪt] *vt* **-rated; -rating** : sous-estimer
underscore [ˈʌndərˌskor] *vt* **-scored -scoring** → **underline**
undersea[1] [ˌʌndərˈsiː] *or* **underseas** [-ˈsiːz] *adv* : sous la mer
undersea[2] *adj* : sous-marin
undersecretary [ˌʌndərˈsekrəˌteri] *n, pl* **-taries** : sous-secrétaire *mf*
undersell [ˌʌndərˈsel] *vt* **-sold** [-ˈsoːld]; **-selling** : vendre moins cher que
undershirt [ˈʌndərˌʃərt] *n* : maillot *m* de corps, camisole *f Can*
undershorts [ˈʌndərˌʃɔrts] *npl* : caleçon *m*
underside [ˈʌndərˌsaɪd, ˌʌndərˈsaɪd] *n* : dessous *m*
undersized [ˌʌndərˈsaɪzd] *adj* : trop petit
understand [ˌʌndərˈstænd] *v* **-stood** [-ˈstʊd]; **-standing** *vt* **1** COMPREHEND : comprendre <I don't understand : je ne comprends pas> <to make oneself understood : se faire comprendre> **2** BELIEVE : croire, comprendre <I understand that he is sick : je crois qu'il est malade> **3** INFER : entendre <to let it be understood that : laisser entendre que> — *vi* : comprendre
understandable [ˌʌndərˈstændəbəl] *adj* : compréhensible <that's understandable : ça se comprend>
understandably [ˌʌndərˈstændəbli] *adv* : naturellement
understanding[1] [ˌʌndərˈstændɪŋ] *adj* : compréhensif, bienveillant
understanding[2] *n* **1** GRASP : compréhension *f,* entendement *m,* intelligence *f* **2** AGREEMENT : entente *f,* accord *m* **3** INTERPRETATION : interprétation *f* <my understanding was that : j'ai compris que> **4** SYMPATHY : compréhension *f*
understate [ˌʌndərˈsteɪt] *vt* **-stated; -stating** : minimiser, réduire l'importance de
understatement [ˌʌndərˈsteɪtmənt] *n* : affirmation *f* en dessous de la vérité <that's an understatement! : c'est peu dire!>
understudy [ˈʌndərˌstʌdi] *n, pl* **-dies** : doublure *f* (au théâtre)
undertake [ˌʌndərˈteɪk] *vt* **-took** [-ˈtʊk]; **-taken** [-ˈteɪkən]; **-taking 1** : entreprendre (une tâche), assumer (une responsabilité) **2** GUARANTEE : s'engager à, promettre (de faire quelque chose)
undertaker [ˈʌndərˌteɪkər] *n* : entrepreneur *m* de pompes funèbres
undertaking [ˈʌndərˌteɪkɪŋ, ˌʌndərˈ-] *n* **1** ENTERPRISE, VENTURE : entreprise *f* **2** PLEDGE : promesse *f,* garantie *f*
undertone [ˈʌndərˌtoːn] *n* **1** : voix *f* basse <to speak in an undertone : parler à mi-voix, parler à voix basse> **2** HINT, UNDERCURRENT : pointe *f,* note *f*
undertow [ˈʌndərˌtoː] *n* : courant *m* sous-marin
undervalue [ˌʌndərˈvælˌjuː] *vt* **-ued; -uing** : sous-évaluer, sous-estimer
underwater[1] [ˌʌndərˈwɔtər, -ˈwɑ-] *adv* : sous l'eau
underwater[2] *adj* : sous-marin <underwater plants : plantes sous-marines>
under way [ˌʌndərˈweɪ] *adv* : en cours, en route <to get under way : se mettre en route>
underwear [ˈʌndərˌwær] *n* : sous-vêtements *mpl*
underworld [ˈʌndərˌwərld] *n* **1** *or* **criminal underworld** : milieu *m,* pègre *f* **2 the underworld** HELL : les enfers
underwrite [ˈʌndərˌraɪt, ˌʌndərˈ-] *vt* **-wrote** [-ˌroːt, -ˈroːt]; **-written** [-ˌrɪtən, -ˈrɪtən]; **-writing 1** FINANCE : soutenir financièrement **2** INSURE : garantir, souscrire (une police d'assurance)
underwriter [ˈʌndərˌraɪtər, ˌʌndərˈ-] *n* INSURER : assureur *m*
undeserving [ˌʌndɪˈzərvɪŋ] *adj* : peu méritant
undesirable [ˌʌndɪˈzaɪrəbəl] *adj* : indésirable
undeveloped [ˌʌndɪˈveləpt] *adj* : non développé, inexploité
undies [ˈʌndiːz] *npl* → **underwear**
undignified [ˌʌnˈdɪgnəfaɪd] *adj* : indigne, qui manque de dignité
undiluted [ˌʌndarˈluːt̬əd, -də-] *adj* : non dilué, sans mélange
undiscovered [ˌʌndɪˈskʌvərd] *adj* : non découvert
undisputed [ˌʌndɪˈspjuːt̬əd] *adj* : incontesté
undisturbed [ˌʌndɪˈstərbd] *adj* **1** PEACEFUL : tranquille **2** UNTOUCHED : intact, non dérangé
undivided [ˌʌndɪˈvaɪdəd] *adj* : entier <your undivided attention : toute votre attention>
undo [ˌʌnˈduː] *vt* **-did; -done; -doing 1** UNTIE : défaire **2** UNWRAP : déballer **3** REVERSE : retourner, réparer (les dommages) **4** RUIN : détruire
undoing [ˌʌnˈduːɪŋ] *n* RUIN : ruine *f,* perte *f*
undoubted [ˌʌnˈdaʊt̬əd] *adj* : indubitable, certain
undoubtedly [ˌʌnˈdaʊt̬ədli] *adv* : indubitablement, sans aucun doute
undress [ˌʌnˈdres] *vt* : déshabiller, dévêtir — *vi* : se déshabiller, se dévêtir

undrinkable [ˌʌnˈdrɪŋkəbəl] *adj* : non potable
undue [ˌʌnˈduː, -ˈdjuː] *adj* : excessif, démesuré — **unduly** [ˌʌnˈduːli] *adv*
undulate [ˈʌndʒəˌleɪt] *vi* **-lated; -lating** : onduler
undulation [ˌʌndʒəˈleɪʃən] *n* : ondulation *f*
undying [ˌʌnˈdaɪɪŋ] *adj* : éternel, perpétuel <undying love : amour éternel>
unearth [ˌʌnˈɛrθ] *vt* **1** EXHUME : déterrer, exhumer **2** DISCOVER : dénicher, découvrir
unearthly [ˌʌnˈɛrθli] *adj* **1** STRANGE, WEIRD : surnaturel, étrange **2** UNGODLY : indu <at an unearthly hour : à une heure indue>
uneasily [ˌʌnˈiːzəli] *adv* **1** UNCOMFORTABLY : d'un air gêné **2** APPREHENSIVELY : avec inquiétude
uneasiness [ˌʌnˈiːzinəs] *n* : inquiétude *f*, malaise *m*
uneasy [ˌʌnˈiːzi] *adj* **1** AWKWARD, EMBARRASSED : mal à l'aise, gêné **2** RESTLESS : agité, inquiet **3** UNSTABLE : précaire <an uneasy truce : une trêve précaire>
uneducated [ˌʌnˈɛdʒəˌkeɪtəd] *adj* : sans éducation
unemployed [ˌʌnɪmˈplɔɪd] *adj* : en chômage, sans travail
unemployment [ˌʌnɪmˈplɔɪmənt] *n* : chômage *m*
unending [ˌʌnˈendɪŋ] *adj* : sans fin, interminable
unendurable [ˌʌnɪnˈdʊrəbəl] *adj* : intolérable
unequal [ˌʌnˈiːkwəl] *adj* **1** : inégal **2 to be unequal to a task** : ne pas être à la hauteur d'une tâche
unequaled *or* **unequalled** [ˌʌnˈiːkwəld] *adj* : inégalé, sans égal
unequally [ˌʌnˈiːkwəli] *adv* : de manière inégale
unequivocal [ˌʌnɪˈkwɪvəkəl] *adj* : explicite, sans équivoque, clair
unequivocally [ˌʌnɪˈkwɪvəkəli] *adv* : explicitement
unerring [ˌʌnˈɛrɪŋ, -ˈər-] *adj* : infaillible
uneven [ˌʌnˈiːvən] *adj* **1** ODD : impair <uneven numbers : chiffres impairs> **2** : inégal <uneven terrain : terrain inégal> <an uneven performance : une performance inégale> **3** IRREGULAR : inégal, irrégulier <uneven teeth : dentition irrégulière>
unevenly [ˌʌnˈiːvənli] *adv* **1** : de façon inégale **2** IRREGULARLY : de façon irrégulière
unevenness [ˌʌnˈiːvənnəs] *n* : inégalité *f*, irrégularité *f*
uneventful [ˌʌnɪˈventfəl] *adj* : sans histoires, peu mouvementé
uneventfully [ˌʌnɪˈventfəli] *adv* : sans incidents
unexpected [ˌʌnɪkˈspektəd] *adj* : inattendu, imprévu
unexpectedly [ˌʌnɪkˈspektədli] *adv* : à l'improviste, contre toute attente
unexplained [ˌʌnɪkˈspleɪnd] *adj* : inexpliqué
unfailing [ˌʌnˈfeɪlɪŋ] *adj* **1** CONSTANT : inaltérable, invariable <unfailing courtesy : courtoisie inaltérable> **2** INEXHAUSTIBLE : inépuisable, infini **3** SURE : infaillible, sûr
unfailingly [ˌʌnˈfeɪlɪŋli] *adv* : invariablement, inlassablement
unfair [ˌʌnˈfær] *adj* : injuste — **unfairly** *adj*
unfairness [ˌʌnˈfærnəs] *n* : injustice *f*
unfaithful [ˌʌnˈfeɪθfəl] *adj* : infidèle — **unfaithfully** *adv*
unfaithfulness [ˌʌnˈfeɪθfəlnəs] *n* : infidélité *f*
unfamiliar [ˌʌnfəˈmɪljər] *adj* **1** : inconnu, peu familier **2 to be unfamiliar with sth** : mal connaître qqch
unfamiliarity [ˌʌnfəˌmɪliˈærəṭi] *n, pl* **-ties** : caractère *m* peu connu, connaissance *f* limitée
unfasten [ˌʌnˈfæsən] *vt* : déboucler (une ceinture), défaire (un bouton)
unfavorable [ˌʌnˈfeɪvərəbəl] *adj* : défavorable — **unfavorably** [-bli] *adv*
unfeeling [ˌʌnˈfiːlɪŋ] *adj* : insensible, froid
unfeelingly [ˌʌnˈfiːlɪŋli] *adv* : froidement, sans pitié
unfinished [ˌʌnˈfɪnɪʃd] *adj* : inachevé, en cours
unfit [ˌʌnˈfɪt] *adj* **1** UNSUITABLE : inapte, impropre <unfit for consumption : impropre à la consommation> **2** UNSUITED : inapte, incapable **3** : qui n'est pas en forme <he's physically unfit : physiquement, il n'est pas en forme>
unflappable [ˌʌnˈflæpəbəl] *adj* : imperturbable
unflattering [ˌʌnˈflæṭərɪŋ] *adj* : peu flatteur
unfold [ˌʌnˈfoːld] *vt* **1** EXPAND : déplier <to unfold a map : déplier une carte> **2** REVEAL : exposer, dévoiler (un plan, etc.) — *vi* **1** DEVELOP : se dérouler, évoluer <the story unfolded : l'histoire s'est déroulée> **2** : se dévoiler, se manifester <a panorama unfolded before their eyes : un panorama se dévoilait devant leurs yeux>
unforeseeable [ˌʌnfɔrˈsiəbəl] *adj* : imprévisible
unforeseen [ˌʌnfɔrˈsiːn] *adj* : imprévu, inattendu
unforgettable [ˌʌnfərˈgeṭəbəl] *adj* : inoubliable, mémorable — **unforgettably** [-bli] *adv*
unforgivable [ˌʌnfərˈgɪvəbəl] *adj* : impardonnable, inexcusable
unfortunate[1] [ˌʌnˈfɔrtʃənəṭ] *adj* **1** UNLUCKY : malchanceux **2** REGRETTABLE : malheureux, fâcheux <how unfortunate! : quel dommage!>

unfortunate[2] *n* : malheureux *m*, -reuse *f*
unfortunately [ʌnˈfɔrtʃənətli] *adv* : malheureusement
unfounded [ʌnˈfaʊndəd] *adj* : sans fondement
unfreeze [ʌnˈfriːz] *vt* **-froze; -frozen; -freezing 1** THAW : dégeler **2** : débloquer <to unfreeze prices : débloquer les prix>
unfriendliness [ʌnˈfrɛndlinəs] *n* : froideur *f*
unfriendly [ʌnˈfrɛndli] *adj* : peu amical, peu sympathique, froid
unfurl [ʌnˈfərl] *vt* : dérouler, déployer — *vi* : se déployer
unfurnished [ʌnˈfərnɪʃt] *adj* : non meublé
ungainly [ʌnˈgeɪnli] *adj* AWKWARD, CLUMSY : gauche, maladroit
ungodly [ʌnˈgɔdli, -ˈgɑd-] *adj* **1** IMPIOUS : impie (en religion) **2** WICKED : mauvais, honteux **3** OUTRAGEOUS : indu, impossible <at an ungodly hour : à une heure indue>
ungracious [ʌnˈgreɪʃəs] *adj* : désobligeant, désagréable
ungrateful [ʌnˈgreɪtfəl] *adj* : ingrat
ungratefully [ʌnˈgreɪtfəli] *adv* : avec ingratitude
ungratefulness [ʌnˈgreɪtfəlnəs] *n* : ingratitude *f*
unhappily [ʌnˈhæpəli] *adv* **1** UNFORTUNATELY : malheureusement **2** SADLY : tristement
unhappiness [ʌnˈhæpinəs] *n* : tristesse *f*, peine *f*
unhappy [ʌnˈhæpi] *adj* **-happier; -est 1** UNFORTUNATE : malheureux, regrettable **2** SAD : malheureux, triste **3** DISSATISFIED : mécontent
unhealthy [ʌnˈhɛlθi] *adj* **-healthier; -est 1** UNWHOLESOME : insalubre, malsain <an unhealthy climate : un climat malsain> **2** SICKLY : malade, maladif **3** MORBID : morbid, malsain (se dit de la curiosité, etc.)
unheard–of [ʌnˈhərdəv] *adj* : sans précédent, inconnu
unhinge [ʌnˈhɪndʒ] *vt* **-hinged; -hinging 1** : démonter, enlever de ses gonds (une porte, une fenêtre) **2** UNBALANCE, UNSETTLE : déstabiliser, déséquilibrer (une personne)
unhitch [ʌnˈhɪtʃ] *vt* : détacher, décrocher
unholy [ʌnˈhoːli] *adj* **-holier; -est 1** : impie (en religion) **2** OUTRAGEOUS, SHOCKING : scandaleux, épouvantable <an unholy hour : une heure indue>
unhook [ʌnˈhʊk] *vt* : décrocher (un tableau, etc.), dégrafer (un vêtement)
unhurried [ʌnˈhʌrɪd] *adj* : qui ne se presse pas, tranquille
unhurt [ʌnˈhərt] *adj* : indemne
unicorn [ˈjuːnəˌkɔrn] *n* : licorne *f*
unidentified [ʌnaɪˈdɛntəˌfaɪd] *adj* : non identifié <unidentified flying object : objet volant non identifié>
unification [ˌjuːnəfəˈkeɪʃən] *n* : unification *f*
uniform[1] [ˈjuːnəˌfɔrm] *adj* **1** CONSTANT, UNCHANGING : uniforme, constant **2** IDENTICAL : identique
uniform[2] *n* : uniforme *m* <military uniform : uniforme militaire>
uniformity [ˌjuːnəˈfɔrmət̬i] *n, pl* **-ties** : uniformité *f*
uniformly [ˈjuːnəˌfɔrmli] *adv* : uniformément
unify [ˈjuːnəˌfaɪ] *vt* **-fied; -fying** : unifier
unilateral [ˌjuːnəˈlæt̬ərəl] *adj* : unilatéral — **unilaterally** *adv*
unimaginable [ʌnɪˈmædʒənəbəl] *adj* : inconcevable, inimaginable
unimportant [ʌnɪmˈpɔrtənt] *adj* : sans importance
uninhabited [ʌnɪnˈhæbət̬əd] *adj* : inhabité
uninhibited [ʌnɪnˈhɪbət̬əd] *adj* : sans inhibitions, sans complexes
uninstall [ʌnɪnˈstɔl] *vt* : désinstaller
unintelligent [ʌnɪnˈteledʒənt] *adj* : inintelligent
unintelligible [ʌnɪnˈteledʒəbəl] *adj* : inintelligible
unintentional [ʌnɪnˈtɛntʃənəl] *adj* : involontaire — **unintentionally** *adv*
uninterested [ʌnˈɪntəˌrestəd, -trəstəd] *adj* : indifférent
uninteresting [ʌnˈɪntəˌrestɪŋ, -trəstɪŋ] *adj* : intéressant, sans intérêt
uninterrupted [ʌnˌɪntəˈrʌpt̬əd] *adj* : ininterrompu, continu
union [ˈjuːnjən] *n* **1** : union *f* **2** *or* **labor union** : syndicat *m*
unionize [ˈjuːnjəˌnaɪz] *v* **-ized; -izing** *vt* : syndiquer, syndicaliser — *vi* : se syndicaliser
unique [juˈniːk] *adj* **1** SOLE : unique, seul <his unique concern : son seul souci> **2** UNUSUAL : unique, particulier **3** UNEQUALED : exceptionnel, sans égal
uniquely [juˈniːkli] *adv* **1** EXCLUSIVELY : uniquement, exclusivement **2** EXCEPTIONALLY : exceptionnellement
uniqueness [juˈniːknəs] *n* : originalité *f*, caractère *m* unique
unison [ˈjuːnəsən, -zən] *n* **1** : unisson *m* <to sing in unison : chanter à l'unisson> **2 to act in unison** : agir de concert
unit[1] [ˈjuːnɪt] *adj* : unitaire <unit price : prix unitaire>
unit[2] *n* **1** ONE : unité *f* **2** : unité *f* <unit of measurement : unité de mesure> **3** GROUP : groupe *m*, unité *f* <research unit : groupe de recherche> **4** PART : élément *m*
unite [juˈnaɪt] *v* **united; uniting** *vt* **1** JOIN, LINK : unir **2** UNIFY : unifier — *vi* : s'unir

unity ['juːnəti] *n, pl* **-ties 1** ONENESS : unité *f* **2** HARMONY : unité *f*, harmonie *f*
universal [ˌjuːnə'vərsəl] *adj* **1** GENERAL : universel, général <universal rules : des règles universelles> **2** WORLD-WIDE : universel, mondial
universally [ˌjuːnə'vərsəli] *adv* : universellement
universe ['juːnəˌvərs] *n* : univers *m*
university [juːnə'vərsəti] *n, pl* **-ties** : université *f*
unjust [ˌʌn'dʒʌst] *adj* : injuste — **unjustly** *adv*
unjustifiable [ˌʌnˌdʒʌstə'faɪəbəl] *adj* : injustifiable
unjustified [ˌʌn'dʒʌstəˌfaɪd] *adj* : injustifié
unkempt [ˌʌn'kɛmpt] *adj* : en désordre, négligé, ébouriffé (se dit des cheveux)
unkind [ˌʌn'kaɪnd] *adj* : peu aimable, pas gentil
unkindly [ˌʌn'kaɪndli] *adv* : méchamment
unkindness [ˌʌn'kaɪndnəs] *n* : manque *m* de gentillesse, méchanceté *f*
unknowing [ˌʌn'noːɪŋ] *adj* : inconscient
unknowingly [ˌʌn'noːɪŋli] *adv* : sans le savoir
unknown [ˌʌn'noːn] *adj* : inconnu
unlawful [ˌʌn'lɔfəl] *adj* : illégal, illicite — **unlawfully** *adv*
unleash [ˌʌn'liːʃ] *vt* **1** RELEASE : libérer, lâcher **2** : déchaîner (des passions, de la furie, etc.)
unless [ən'lɛs] *conj* : à moins que, à moins de
unlike[1] [ˌʌn'laɪk] *adj* **1** DIFFERENT : dissemblable, différent **2** UNEQUAL : inégal
unlike[2] *prep* **1** : différent de <he's very unlike his brother : il est très différent de son frère> **2** : contrairement à, à la différence de <unlike him, she enjoys her work : contrairement à lui, elle aime son travail> **3** (*indicating an uncharacteristic state or action*) <it's unlike them to be late : ça n'est pas dans leur habitude d'être en retard>
unlikelihood [ˌʌn'laɪkliˌhʊd] *n* : improbabilité *f*
unlikely [ˌʌn'laɪkli] *adj* **-likelier; -est 1** IMPROBABLE : improbable, peu probable **2** UNPROMISING : peu prometteur
unlimited [ˌʌn'lɪmətəd] *adj* : illimité
unload [ˌʌn'loːd] *vt* **1** : décharger (un bateau, un fusil, de la cargaison, etc.) **2** DISPOSE OF, DUMP : se débarrasser de, se défaire de — *vi* : être déchargé
unlock [ˌʌn'lɑk] *vt* **1** : ouvrir, débarrer *Can* (une porte, etc.) **2** DISCLOSE, REVEAL : découvrir, révéler
unluckily [ˌʌn'lʌkəli] *adv* : malheureusement
unlucky [ˌʌn'lʌki] *adj* **-luckier; -est 1** : malchanceux <an unlucky year : une année malchanceuse> **2** INAUSPICIOUS : qui porte malheur **3** REGRETTABLE : malencontreux, regrettable
unmanageable [ˌʌn'mænɪdʒəbəl] *adj* : difficile à manier, peu maniable
unmarried [ˌʌn'mærɪd] *adj* : non marié, célibataire
unmask [ˌʌn'mæsk] *vt* : démasquer
unmatched [ˌʌn'mætʃt] *adj* : sans égal, incomparable
unmerciful [ˌʌn'mərsɪfəl] *adj* : sans merci, impitoyable
unmercifully [ˌʌn'mərsɪfəli] *adv* : impitoyablement
unmistakable [ˌʌnmɪ'steɪkəbəl] *adj* : évident, indubitable
unmistakably [ˌʌnmɪ'steɪkəbli] *adv* : indubitablement
unmoved [ˌʌn'muːvd] *adj* : indifférent, insensible
unnatural [ˌʌn'nætʃərəl] *adj* **1** ABNORMAL, UNUSUAL : anormal, peu naturel **2** AFFECTED : artificiel, affecté **3** PERVERSE : pervers, contre nature
unnaturally [ˌʌn'nætʃərəli] *adv* : anormalement, de façon peu naturelle
unnecessarily [ˌʌnˌnɛsə'sɛrəli] *adv* : inutilement, sans raison
unnecessary [ˌʌn'nɛsəˌseri] *adj* : inutile, superflu
unnerve [ˌʌn'nərv] *vt* **-nerved; -nerving** : décontenancer, déconcerter, rendre nerveux
unnoticeable [ˌʌn'noːtəsəbəl] *adj* : imperceptible
unnoticed [ˌʌn'noːtəst] *adj* : inaperçu
unobstructed [ˌʌnəb'strʌktəd] *adj* : non obstrué, dégagé
unobtainable [ˌʌnəb'teɪnəbəl] *adj* : introuvable, impossible à obtenir
unobtrusive [ˌʌnəb'truːsɪv] *adj* : discret, pas trop visible
unoccupied [ˌʌn'ɑkjəˌpaɪd] *adj* **1** IDLE : inoccupé, oisif **2** EMPTY : libre, vacant
unofficial [ˌʌnə'fɪʃəl] *adj* : officieux, non officiel
unorganized [ˌʌn'ɔrgəˌnaɪzd] *adj* : mal organisé, inorganisé
unorthodox [ˌʌn'ɔrθəˌdɑks] *adj* : peu orthodoxe
unpack [ˌʌn'pæk] *vt* : défaire, déballer <to unpack one's suitcase : défaire sa valise> — *vi* : défaire ses bagages
unpaid [ˌʌn'peɪd] *adj* **1** : impayé (se dit d'une facture), non acquitté (se dit d'une dette) **2** : bénévole, non rémunéré <unpaid assistants : assistants bénévoles>
unparalleled [ˌʌn'pærəˌlɛld] *adj* : sans égal, sans pareil
unpatriotic [ˌʌnˌpeɪtri'ɑtɪk] *adj* : peu patriote
unpleasant [ˌʌn'plɛzənt] *adj* : désagréable, déplaisant

unpleasantly [ʌn'plɛzəntli] *adv* : désagréablement, de façon déplaisante
unplug [ʌn'plʌg] *vt* **-plugged; -plugging 1** UNCLOG : déboucher **2** DISCONNECT : débrancher, déconnecter
unpopular [ʌn'pɑpjələr] *adj* : impopulaire, peu populaire
unpopularity [ʌnˌpɑpjə'lærəṭi] *n* : impopularité *f*
unprecedented [ʌn'prɛsəˌdɛntəd] *adj* : sans précédent
unpredictable [ˌʌnpri'dɪktəbəl] *adj* : imprévisible
unprejudiced [ʌn'prɛdʒədəst] *adj* : sans préjugés, sans parti pris, impartial
unprepared [ˌʌnpri'pærd] *adj* : mal préparé
unpretentious [ˌʌnpri'tɛnʃəs] *adj* : sans prétention
unprincipled [ʌn'prɪnṭsəpəld] *adj* : sans scrupules
unproductive [ˌʌnprə'dʌktɪv] *adj* : improductif
unprofitable [ʌn'prɑfəṭəbəl] *adj* **1** : non rentable (se dit d'une entreprise, etc.) **2** VAIN : peu profitable, inutile
unpromising [ʌn'prɑməsɪŋ] *adj* : peu prometteur
unprotected [ˌʌnprə'tɛktəd] *adj* **1** : sans protection **2** EXPOSED : exposé
unprovoked [ˌʌnprə'vo:kt] *adj* : sans provocation, délibéré
unpunished [ʌn'pʌnɪʃt] *adj* : impuni <to go unpunished : rester impuni>
unqualified [ʌn'kwɑləˌfaɪd] *adj* **1** UNFIT : non qualifié, incompétent **2** COMPLETE : sans réserve, inconditionnel <an unqualified denial : un démenti sans réserve>
unquestionable [ʌn'kwɛstʃənəbəl] *adj* : incontestable, indéniable
unquestionably [ʌn'kwɛstʃənəbli] *adv* : incontestablement, sans aucun doute
unquestioning [ʌn'kwɛstʃənɪŋ] *adj* : inconditionnel, absolu
unravel [ʌn'rævəl] *v* **-eled** *or* **-elled; -eling** *or* **elling** *vt* **1** DISENTANGLE : démêler **2** SOLVE : résoudre, éclaircir <to unravel a mystery : résoudre un mystère> — *vi* : se démêler
unreal [ʌn'ri:l] *adj* : irréel
unrealistic [ˌʌnˌri:ə'lɪstɪk] *adj* : peu réaliste, irréaliste
unreality [ˌʌnri'æləṭi] *n* : irréalité *f*
unreasonable [ʌn'ri:zənəbel] *adj* **1** SENSELESS : déraisonnable **2** EXCESSIVE : excessif, démesuré
unreasonably [ʌn'ri:zənəbli] *adv* **1** SENSELESSLY : déraisonnablement **2** EXCESSIVELY : excessivement
unrelated [ˌʌnri'leiṭəd] *adj* : sans rapport
unrelenting [ˌʌnri'lɛntɪŋ] *adj* **1** STERN : dur, implacable **2** CONSTANT : continuel
unrelentingly [ˌʌnri'lɛntɪŋli] *adv* : sans répit
unreliable [ˌʌnri'laɪəbəl] *adj* : peu fidèle, peu sûr
unrepentant [ˌʌnri'pɛntənt] *adj* : impénitent
unresolved [ˌʌnri'zɑlvd] *adj* : non résolu
unrest [ʌn'rɛst] *n* : agitation *f*, troubles *mpl* <social unrest : malaise social>
unrestrained [ˌʌnri'streɪnd] *adj* : effréné, non contenu
unrestricted [ˌʌnri'strɪktəd] *adj* : libre, illimité <unrestricted access : libre accès>
unrewarding [ˌʌnri'wɔrdɪŋ] *adj* THANKLESS : ingrat
unripe [ʌn'raɪp] *adj* : pas mûr, vert
unrivaled *or* **unrivalled** [ʌn'raɪvəld] *adj* : sans égal, incomparable
unroll [ʌn'ro:l] *vt* : dérouler — *vi* : se dérouler
unruffled [ʌn'rʌfəld] *adj* **1** : imperturbable (se dit d'une personne) **2** SMOOTH : calme <unruffled waters : eaux calmes>
unruly [ʌn'ru:li] *adj* : indiscipliné
unsafe [ʌn'seɪf] *adj* **1** DANGEROUS : dangereux **2 to feel unsafe** : ne pas se sentir en sécurité, se sentir en danger
unsaid [ʌn'sɛd] *adj* : inexprimé, non dit <to leave unsaid : passer sous silence>
unsanitary [ʌn'sænəˌṭɛri] *adj* : peu hygiénique
unsatisfactory [ˌʌnˌsætəs'fæktəri] *adj* : peu satisfaisant
unsatisfied [ʌn'sætəsˌfaɪd] *adj* : peu satisfait, insatisfait
unsavory [ʌn'seɪvəri] *adj* **1** TASTELESS : peu savoureux, insipide **2** DISTASTEFUL : désagréable
unscathed [ʌn'skeɪðd] *adj* UNHARMED : indemne
unscheduled [ʌn'skɛˌdʒu:ld] *adj* : imprévu
unscientific [ˌʌnˌsaɪən'tɪfɪk] *adj* : non scientifique
unscrew [ʌn'skru:] *vt* : dévisser
unscrupulous [ʌn'skru:pjələs] *adj* : sans scrupules, peu scrupuleux
unscrupulously [ʌn'skru:pjələsli] *adv* : sans scrupules, peu scrupuleusement
unseal [ʌn'si:l] *vt* : décacheter (une enveloppe, etc.)
unseasonable [ʌn'si:zənəbəl] *adj* **1** UNTIMELY : inopportun, mal choisi **2** : hors de saison <unseasonable weather : température qui n'est pas de saison>
unseemly [ʌn'si:mli] *adj* **-seemlier; -est 1** UNBECOMING : inconvenant **2** INAPPROPRIATE : inapproprié
unseen [ʌn'si:n] *adj* : invisible, inaperçu
unselfish [ʌn'sɛlfɪʃ] *adj* : désintéressé, généreux

unselfishly [ˌʌnˈselfɪʃli] *adv* : généreusement, de façon désintéressée
unselfishness [ˌʌnˈselfɪʃnəs] *n* : générosité *f*, désintéressement *m*
unsettle [ˌʌnˈsɛʧəl] *vt* **-tled; -tling 1** UPSET : déranger (l'estomac) **2** DISTURB : perturber, troubler
unsettled [ˌʌnˈsɛtəld] *adj* **1** DISTURBED : perturbé, troublé **2** VARIABLE : changeant, variable <unsettled weather : temps variable> **3** DOUBTFUL, UNDECIDED : incertain, non résolu **4** UNPAID : impayé, non réglé **5** UNINHABITED : inhabité
unsightly [ˌʌnˈsaɪtli] *adj* : laid, disgracieux
unskilled [ˌʌnˈskɪld] *adj* : non qualifié, non spécialisé
unskillful [ˌʌnˈskɪlfəl] *adj* : malhabile, inexpert
unsociable [ˌʌnˈsoːʃəbəl] *adj* : peu sociable, insociable
unsolved [ˌʌnˈsɑlvd] *adj* : non résolu
unsophisticated [ˌʌnsəˈfɪstəˌkeɪʧəd] *adj* : peu sophistiqué, simple
unsound [ˌʌnˈsaʊnd] *adj* **1** : peu judicieux (se dit d'une idée), instable (se dit d'une structure) **2 to be of unsound mind** : ne pas avoir toute sa raison
unspeakable [ˌʌnˈspiːkəbəl] *adj* **1** INEXPRESSIBLE : indescriptible, indicible **2** ATROCIOUS : innommable, atroce
unspeakably [ˌʌnˈspiːkəbli] *adv* **1** INEXPRESSIBLY : indiciblement **2** ATROCIOUSLY : atrocement
unspecified [ˌʌnˈspesəˌfaɪd] *adj* : non spécifié
unspoiled [ˌʌnˈspɔɪld] *adj* **1** : qui n'a pas été gâté (se dit d'un enfant) **2** : intact, naturel, vierge <unspoiled scenery : paysage intact>
unstable [ˌʌnˈsteɪbəl] *adj* : instable
unsteadily [ˌʌnˈstɛdəli] *adv* : d'un pas chancelant, d'une main tremblante, d'une voix mal assurée
unsteady [ˌʌnˈstɛdi] *adj* **1** : instable, branlant (se dit d'une structure, etc.) **2** SHAKY : tremblant, chancelant, mal assuré **3** IRREGULAR : irrégulier
unstoppable [ˌʌnˈstɑpəbəl] *adj* : irrésistible, qu'on ne peut pas arrêter
unsubstantiated [ˌʌnsəbˈstænˌʃiˌeɪʧəd] *adj* : non confirmé, non corroboré
unsuccessful [ˌʌnsəkˈsɛsfəl] *adj* : infructueux, qui n'a pas réussi
unsuitable [ˌʌnˈsuːʧəbəl] *adj* : qui ne convient pas, inconvenant, inapproprié <an unsuitable time : un moment inopportun>
unsuited [ˌʌnˈsuːʧəd] *adj* : inadapté, mal adapté, inapproprié
unsung [ˌʌnˈsʌŋ] *adj* : méconnu
unsure [ˌʌnˈʃʊr] *adj* : incertain, pas sûr <to be unsure of oneself : manquer de confiance en soi>
unsurpassed [ˌʌnsərˈpæst] *adj* : sans pareil, sans égal
unsuspecting [ˌʌnsəˈspɛktɪŋ] *adj* : qui ne se doute de rien, sans méfiance
unsympathetic [ˌʌnˌsɪmpəˈθeʧɪk] *adj* : incompréhensif, peu compatissant
untangle [ˌʌnˈtæŋgəl] *vt* **-gled; -gling 1** : démêler (des fils, etc.), débrouiller (un problème, un mystère)
unthinkable [ˌʌnˈθɪŋkəbəl] *adj* : impensable, inconcevable
unthinking [ˌʌnˈθɪŋkɪŋ] *adj* : irréfléchi, inconsidéré
unthinkingly [ˌʌnˈθɪŋkɪŋli] *adv* : inconsidérément, sans réfléchir
untidy [ˌʌnˈtaɪdi] *adj* **-tidier; -est 1** : désordonné, débraillé (se dit d'une personne) **2** : en désordre <an untidy room : une chambre en désordre>
untie [ˌʌnˈtaɪ] *vt* **-tied; -tying** *or* **-tieing 1** : défaire, dénouer <to untie a knot : défaire un nœud> **2** : délier, détacher (des mains, un prisonnier, etc.)
until[1] [ˌʌnˈtɪl] *conj* : jusqu'à ce que, avant que, avant de <boil the eggs until cooked : bouillez les œufs jusqu'à ce qu'ils soient cuits> <don't speak until I tell you to : ne parlez pas avant que je ne vous le dise> <until I saw him : avant de l'avoir vu> <wait until I call : attend que j'appelle>
until[2] *prep* **1** UP TO : jusqu'à <I worked until noon : j'ai travaillé jusqu'à midi> **2** BEFORE : avant <it won't be available until tomorrow : ça ne sera pas disponible avant demain> <we don't open until ten : nous ouvrons à dix heures seulement>
untimely [ˌʌnˈtaɪmli] *adj* **1** PREMATURE : précoce, prématuré <an untimely death : une mort prématurée> **2** INOPPORTUNE : inopportun, déplacé
untold [ˌʌnˈtoːld] *adj* **1** : jamais raconté <untold stories : des histoires jamais racontées> **2** VAST : incalculable, indicible
untouched [ˌʌnˈtʌʃt] *adj* **1** INTACT : intact, qui n'a pas été touché **2** UNHARMED : indemne **3** UNAFFECTED : non affecté
untoward [ˌʌnˈtɔrd, -ˈtoːərd, -təˈwɔrd] *adj* **1** UNFORTUNATE : fâcheux, malencontreux **2** UNSEEMLY : inconvenant
untrained [ˌʌnˈtreɪnd] *adj* **1** : sans formation **2 to the untrained eye** : pour un œil inexercé
untreated [ˌʌnˈtriːʧəd] *adj* : non traité
untroubled [ˌʌnˈtrʌbəld] *adj* **1** : paisible, tranquille <untroubled waters : eaux paisibles> **2 to be untroubled by** : ne pas être affecté par
untrue [ˌʌnˈtruː] *adj* **1** DISLOYAL : infidèle, déloyal **2** FALSE : faux, erroné
untruth [ˌʌnˈtruːθ, ˈʌn-] *n* **1** FALSITY : fausseté *f* **2** LIE : mensonge *m*

untruthful [ʌn'tru:θfəl] *adj* **1** FALSE : faux, inexact **2** DISHONEST : malhonnête
unusable [ʌn'ju:zəbəl] *adj* : inutilisable
unused *adj* [ʌn'ju:zd, *in sense* **1** *usually* -'ju:st] **1** UNACCUSTOMED : pas habitué **2** NEW : neuf, nouveau **3** IDLE : inutilisé **4** ACCRUED : cumulé
unusual [ʌn'ju:ʒʊəl] *adj* : peu commun, rare
unusually [ʌn'ju:ʒʊəli] *adv* : exceptionnellement
unwanted [ʌn'wɑntəd] *adj* : non désiré, superflu
unwarranted [ʌn'wɔrəntəd] *adj* : injustifié
unwary [ʌn'wæri] *adj* : qui ne se méfie pas, sans méfiance
unwavering [ʌn'weɪvəriŋ] *adj* : ferme, inébranlable <an unwavering gaze : un regard fixe>
unwelcome [ʌn'wɛlkəm] *adj* : inopportun, fâcheux
unwell [ʌn'wɛl] *adj* : souffrant, malade, mal-en-train *Can*
unwholesome [ʌn'ho:lsəm] *adj* **1** UNHEALTHY : malsain, insalubre **2** PERNICIOUS : pernicieux, nocif
unwieldy [ʌn'wi:ldi] *adj* CUMBERSOME : difficile à manier, encombrant
unwilling [ʌn'wɪliŋ] *adj* : réticent, peu disposé
unwillingly [ʌn'wɪliŋli] *adv* : à contrecœur
unwind [ʌn'waɪnd] *v* **-wound; -winding** *vt* UNROLL : dérouler — *vi* **1** : se dérouler **2** RELAX : se détendre
unwise [ʌn'waɪz] *adj* : imprudent, peu judicieux
unwisely [ʌn'waɪzli] *adv* : imprudemment
unwitting [ʌn'wɪṭɪŋ] *adj* **1** UNAWARE : inconscient **2** INADVERTENT : involontaire
unwittingly [ʌn'wɪṭɪŋli] *adv* **1** UNCONSCIOUSLY : inconsciemment **2** INADVERTENTLY : involontairement
unworthiness [ʌn'wərðinəs] *n* : indignité *f*
unworthy [ʌn'wərði] *adj* **1** UNDESERVING : indigne **2** UNMERITED : peu méritant
unwrap [ʌn'ræp] *vt* **-wrapped; -wrapped** : déballer
unwritten [ʌn'rɪtən] *adj* : tacite, non écrit
unyielding [ʌn'ji:ldiŋ] *adj* **1** STIFF : dur, ferme **2** ADAMANT : qui ne cède pas, inflexible
unzip [ʌn'zɪp] *vt* **-zipped; -zipping** : défaire la fermeture à glissière de
up[1] ['ʌp] *v* **upped; upping** *vt* **1** INCREASE : augmenter <they upped the prices : ils ont augmenté les prix> — *vi* (*used with* and *and another verb to indicate surprising or abrupt action*) <she up and left : elle est partie sans mot dire> <he up and married her : il l'a épousée sur-le-champ>
up[2] *adv* **1** (*in or to a higher position or level*) <the oil shot up 200 feet : le pétrole jaillissait du sol et atteignait 200 pieds de hauteur> **2** (*from beneath a surface or level*) <the fish swam up : les poissons montaient à la surface de l'eau> **3** (*in or into an upright position*) <we stayed up all night : nous avons veillé toute la nuit> <get up! : levez-vous!> **4** (*with greater intensity*) <speak up! : parlez plus fort!> **5** (*in continuance from a point or to a point*) <from third grade up : à partir de la troisième année> <at prices of $10 and up : à des prix de 10 $ et plus> <up until now : jusqu'à maintenant> **6** (*into existence, evidence, prominence, or prevalence*) <they put up several new buildings : ils ont construit plusieurs nouveaux immeubles> **7** (*into consideration or attention*) <we brought the matter up : nous avons soulevé la question> **8** COMPLETELY, ENTIRELY : au complet <button up your coat : boutonne ton manteau jusqu'au cou> **9** (*used as an intensifier*) <we cleaned up the house : nous avons nettoyé la maison> **10** (*so as to arrive or approach*) <he walked up to me and said "hello" : il s'est approché de moi et m'a dit «bonjour»> **11** (*in or into parts*) <she tore up the paper : elle a déchiré le papier en petits morceaux> **12** (*to a stop*) <he pulled up to the curb : il s'est garé le long de la courbe> **13** (*for each side*) <the score was 15 up : le score était nul avec 15 points pour chaque équipe>
up[3] *adj* **1** RISEN : levé (se dit du soleil) **2** RISING : en crue (se dit d'une rivière) **3** AWAKE, STANDING : levé, debout <he's up at 6 o'clock : il se lève à 6h> **4** LIFTED : levé, ouvert <the windows were up : les fenêtres étaient ouvertes> **5** BUILT : construit <the houses are up : la construction des maisons est terminée> **6** : qui pousse <the corn was up : le maïs poussait> **7** : qui monte <the up escalator : l'escalier mécanique qui monte> **8** INCREASING : qui augmente <attendance is up at the meetings : le nombre de personnes qui assiste aux réunions a augmenté> <the wind is up : le vent s'est levé> **9** READY : prêt <the team was up for the game : l'équipe était prête pour le match> **10** : qui se passe <what's up? : qu'est-ce qui se passe?> **11** UP-TO-DATE : au courant, à jour <to be up on the news : être au courant des nouvelles> <he was up on his homework : il était à jour dans ses devoirs> **12** EXPIRED : expiré, terminé <the

contract was up in June : le contrat s'est terminé en juin>

up[4] *n* **1 to be on the up** : être en train d'augmenter **2 ups and downs** : fluctuations *fpl*

up[5] *prep* **1** (*to, toward, or at a higher point of*) <she went up the stairs : elle a monté l'escalier> **2** (*to or toward the source of*) <to sail up the river : remonter la rivière en bateau> **3** (*near or toward the end of*) <to walk up the street : monter la rue> <we live a few miles up the coast : nous demeurons à quelques milles de la côte> **4 → up to**

upbraid [ˌʌpˈbreɪd] *vt* : reprocher, réprimander

upbringing [ˈʌpˌbrɪŋɪŋ] *n* : éducation *f*

upcoming [ˌʌpˈkʌmɪŋ] *adj* : prochain, à venir

update[1] [ˌʌpˈdeɪt] *vt* **-dated; -dating** : mettre à jour, actualiser

update[2] [ˈʌpˌdeɪt] *n* : mise *f* à jour

upend [ˌʌpˈend] *vt* **1** : mettre debout **2** OVERTURN : retourner, renverser

upgrade[1] [ˈʌpˌgreɪd, ˌʌpˈ-] *vt* **-graded; -grading** : améliorer (un produit), promouvoir (un employé)

upgrade[2] [ˈʌpˌgreɪd] *n* **1** SLOPE : pente *f* ascendante, montée *f* **2 to be on the upgrade** : monter, être en hausse

upheaval [ˌʌpˈhiːvəl] *n* **1** : soulèvement *m* (de la croûte terrestre) **2** COMMOTION : bouleversement *m*, remue-ménage *m*

uphill[1] [ˌʌpˈhɪl] *adv* **to go uphill** : monter, aller en montant

uphill[2] [ˈʌpˌhɪl] *adj* **1** ASCENDING : montant, qui monte **2** DIFFICULT : pénible, difficile

uphold [ˌʌpˈhoːld] *vt* **-held; -holding 1** SUPPORT : soutenir, défendre **2** RAISE : soutenir, élever **3** CONFIRM : confirmer, maintenir (en droit)

upholster [ˌʌpˈhoːlstər] *vt* **1** STUFF : rembourrer **2** COVER : tapisser, recouvrir

upholsterer [ˌʌpˈhoːlstərər] *n* : tapissier *m*, -sière *f*

upholstery [ˌʌpˈhoːlstəri] *n, pl* **-steries 1** STUFFING : rembourrage *m* **2** COVERING : tissu *m* d'ameublement, revêtement *m*

upkeep [ˈʌpˌkiːp] *n* : entretien *m*

upland [ˈʌplənd, -ˈlænd] *n* **1** : plateau *m* **2 the uplands** : les hautes terres

uplift[1] [ˌʌpˈlɪft] *vt* **1** RAISE : soulever, élever **2** : remonter, encourager <to uplift s.o.'s spirits : remonter le moral de qqn>

uplift[2] [ˈʌpˌlɪft] *n* **1** : élévation *f*, soulèvement *m* **2** IMPROVEMENT : amélioration *f*

upon [əˈpɔn, əˈpɑn] *prep* : sur, à <upon the table : sur la table> <upon our departure : à notre départ> <questions upon questions : des questions et des questions>

upper[1] [ˈʌpər] *adj* **1** : supérieur <the upper lip : la lèvre supérieure> **2** : plus haut, plus élevé <the upper classes : l'aristocratie> **3** NORTHERN : haut (en géographie) <the upper Mississippi : la haute Mississippi>

upper[2] *n* : empeigne *f* (d'un soulier)

upper hand *n* **to have the upper hand** : avoir le dessus

uppermost [ˈʌpərˌmoːst] *adj* **1** HIGHEST : le plus haut, le plus élevé **2** : de la plus haute importance <it was uppermost in my mind : ça me préoccupait par-dessus tout>

upright[1] [ˈʌpˌraɪt] *adv* : droit <to stand upright : se tenir droit>

upright[2] *adj* **1** PERPENDICULAR : vertical **2** ERECT : debout, droit <an upright freezer : un congélateur armoire> **3** JUST : honnête, droit

upright[3] *n* **1** : montant *m* (en construction) **2** *or* **upright piano** : piano *m* droit

uprightly [ˈʌpˌraɪtli] *adv* : honnêtement

uprising [ˈʌpˌraɪzɪŋ] *n* : soulèvement *m*, révolte *f*

uproar [ˈʌpˌroːr] *n* : tumulte *m*, vacarme *m*

uproarious [ˌʌpˈroriəs] *adj* **1** NOISY : bruyant **2** HILARIOUS : désopilant, comique

uproariously [ˌʌpˈroriəsli] *adv* : aux éclats

uproot [ˌʌpˈruːt, -ˈrʊt] *vt* : déraciner

upset[1] [ˌʌpˈset] *vt* **-set; -setting 1** OVERTURN : renverser **2** DISTURB, TROUBLE : déranger, perturber **3** SICKEN : rendre malade <the food upset my stomach : la nourriture m'a dérangé l'estomac> **4** DISRUPT : déranger, bouleverser (des plans, etc.)

upset[2] *adj* **1** DISTRESSED : attristé, peiné **2** ANNOYED : ennuyé, contrarié **3** : dérangé (se dit de l'estomac)

upset[3] [ˈʌpˌset] *n* **1** OVERTURNING : renversement *m* **2** DISRUPTION : bouleversement *m* (des plans) **3** DEFEAT : revers *m* (aux sports)

upshot [ˈʌpˌʃɑt] *n* : résultat *m*

upside–down [ˌʌpˌsaɪdˈdaʊn] *adj* : à l'envers

upside down *adv* **1** : à l'envers <turn the card upside down : tournez la carte à l'envers> **2** : sens dessus dessous <she turned the room upside down : elle a mis la pièce sens dessus dessous>

upstairs[1] [ˌʌpˈstærz] *adv* : en haut

upstairs[2] [ˈʌpˌstærz, ˌʌpˈ-] *adj* : d'en haut, à l'étage

upstairs[3] [ˈʌpˌstærz, ˌʌpˈ-] *ns & pl* : étage *m* (du haut)

upstanding [ˌʌpˈstændɪŋ, ˈʌpˌ-] *adj* : honnête, intègre

upstart [ˈʌpˌstɑrt] *n* : parvenu *m*, -nue *f*; arriviste *mf*

upstream [ˈʌpˈstriːm] *adv* : en amont

upswing ['ʌpˌswɪŋ] *n* **1** : mouvement *m* ascendant **2** IMPROVEMENT : amélioration *f* notable
uptight [ˌʌpˈtaɪt] *adj* **1** TENSE : tendu, crispé, pogné *Can* **2** INDIGNANT : indigné, outré **3** REPRESSED : coincé *fam*
up to *prep* **1** : jusqu'à <in water up to my ankles : dans l'eau jusqu'aux chevilles> <up to here : jusqu'ici> **2 to be up to** : être à <if it were up to me : si c'était à moi de décider> **3 to be up to** : être capable de <he's not up to studying : il n'est pas en état d'étudier>
up–to–date [ˌʌptəˈdeɪt] *adj* **1** CURRENT : à jour <up-to-date maps : des cartes à jour> <to stay up-to-date : se tenir au courant> **2** MODERN : moderne
uptown ['ʌpˈtaʊn] *adv* : dans les quartiers résidentiels
upturn ['ʌpˌtɜrn] *n* : amélioration *f*, reprise *f* (économique)
upward[1] ['ʌpwərd] *or* **upwards** [-wərdz] *adv* **1** : vers le haut, en montant **2** (*used to express continuance from a point*) <from $ 5 upward : à partir de 5 $>
upward[2] *adj* ASCENDING : ascendant <upward mobility : ascension sociale>
upwardly ['ʌpwərdli] *adv* : vers le haut
upwind[1] [ˌʌpˈwɪnd] *adv* : contre le vent
upwind[2] *adj* **to be upwind of** : être dans le vent par rapport à
uranium [jʊˈreɪniəm] *n* : uranium *m*
Uranus [jʊˈreɪnəs, ˈjʊrənəs] *n* : Uranus *f*
urban ['ərbən] *adj* : urbain, de ville
urbane [ˌərˈbeɪn] *adj* : raffiné, courtois
urchin ['ərtʃən] *n* : polisson *m*, -sonne *f*
urethra [jʊˈriːθrə] *n, pl* **-thras** *or* **-thrae** [-ˌθriː] : urètre *m*
urge[1] ['ərdʒ] *vt* **urged; urging 1** PUSH : pousser <we urged him to tell the truth : nous l'avons poussé à dire la vérité> **2** ADVOCATE : conseiller, préconiser **3 to urge on** : presser, faire avancer
urge[2] *n* : désir *m*, (forte) envie *f*
urgency ['ərdʒənt͡si] *n, pl* **-cies** : urgence *f*
urgent ['ərdʒənt] *adj* **1** PRESSING : urgent, pressant **2** INSISTENT : insistant
urgently ['ərdʒəntli] *adv* : d'urgence
urinal ['jʊrənəl, *esp Brit* jʊˈraɪnəl] *n* : urinoir *m*
urinary ['jʊrəˌnɛri] *adj* : urinaire
urinate ['jʊrəˌneɪt] *vi* **-nated; -nating** : uriner
urination [ˌjʊrəˈneɪʃən] *n* : urination *f*
urine ['jʊrən] *n* : urine *f*
urn ['ərn] *n* **1** VASE : urne *f* **2** : fontaine *f* (à café)
Uruguayan[1] [ˌjʊrəˈgwaɪən, ˌjʊr-, -ˈgweɪ-] *adj* : uruguayen
Uruguayan[2] *n* : Uruguayen *m*, -guayenne *f*

us ['ʌs] *pron* **1** (*used as a direct object of a verb*) <they were visiting us : ils nous rendaient visite> **2** (*used as an indirect object of a verb*) <give us some time : donnez-nous du temps> **3** (*used as the object of a preposition*) <in front of us : devant nous>
usable ['juːzəbəl] *adj* : utilisable
usage ['juːsɪdʒ, -zɪdʒ] *n* **1** HABIT, PRACTICE : usage *m*, coutume *f* **2** : usage *m* (en linguistique) **3** USE : utilisation *f*, consommation *f*
use[1] ['juːz] *v* **used** ['juːzd; *in phrase "used to" usually* 'juːstuː]; **using** *vt* **1** EMPLOY : utiliser, se servir de **2** CONSUME : consommer <use before April : à consommer avant avril> **3** TREAT : traiter <they used the prisoners cruelly : ils ont traité les prisonniers avec cruauté> **4** EXPLOIT : se servir de, profiter de <he used his friends to get ahead : il s'est servi de ses amis afin d'avancer> **5 to use up** : épuiser, consommer — *vi* (*used in the past tense with* to *to indicate a former fact or state*) <she didn't use to smoke : elle ne fumait pas avant>
use[2] ['juːs] *n* **1** APPLICATION, EMPLOYMENT : utilisation *f* **2** : usage *m*, jouissance *f* (d'un bien) <to have use of the beach : avoir la jouissance de la plage> <to lose the use of a limb : perdre l'usage d'un membre> **3** USEFULNESS : utilité *f* <it's no use : c'est inutile, ça ne sert à rien> <what's the use of complaining : à quoi bon se plaindre> **4** NEED : usage *m*, besoin *m* <they didn't have use for it : ils n'en avaient pas besoin>
used ['juːzd] *adj* **1** SECONDHAND : usagé, de seconde main **2** ACCUSTOMED : habitué <not used to all the attention : pas habitué à recevoir autant d'attention>
useful ['juːsfəl] *adj* : utile, pratique
usefully ['juːsfəli] *adv* : utilement
usefulness ['juːsfəlnəs] *n* : utilité *f*
useless ['juːsləs] *adj* : inutile — **uselessly** *adv*
uselessness ['juːsləsnəs] *n* : inutilité *f*
user ['juːzər] *n* : usager *m*; utilisateur *m*, -trice *f* (d'un ordinateur)
user–friendly [ˌjuːzərˈfrendɪli] *adj* : facile à utiliser, convivial (en informatique)
usher[1] ['ʌʃər] *vt* **1** ESCORT : conduire, accompagner <to usher s.o. in : faire entrer qqn> **2 to usher in** : inaugurer
usher[2] *n* : huissier *m* (à un tribunal); placeur *m*, -ceuse *f* (au théâtre)
usherette [ˌʌʃəˈrɛt] *n* : ouvreuse *f*
usual ['juːʒʊəl] *adj* : CUSTOMARY, NORMAL : habituel <our usual route : notre chemin habituel> <more than usual : plus que d'habitude> <as usual : comme d'habitude>

usually ['juːʒʊəli] *adv* : habituellement, d'habitude, normalement
usurp [jʊˈsɜrp, -ˈzərp] *vt* : usurper
usurper [jʊˈsərpər, -ˈzər-] *n* : usurpateur *m*, -trice *f*
utensil [juˈtentsəl] *n* : ustensile *m* (de cuisine, de jardinage, etc.)
uterine ['juːtəˌraɪn, -rən] *adj* : utérin
uterus ['juːtərəs] *n, pl* **uteri** [-ˌraɪ] : utérus *m*
utilitarian [juːˌtɪləˈteriən] *adj* : utilitaire
utility [juːˈtɪləti] *n, pl* **-ties 1** USEFULNESS : utilité *f* **2** *or* **public utility** : service *m* public
utilization [ˌjuːtələˈzeɪʃən] *n* : utilisation *f*
utilize ['juːtəˌlaɪz] *vt* **-lized; -lizing** : utiliser
utmost[1] ['ʌtˌmoːst] *adj* **1** EXTREME : extrême <the utmost point of the earth : le bout de la terre> **2** : capital, important <a matter of utmost concern : une question de la plus haute importance>
utmost[2] *n* **1** : plus haut degré *m*, plus haut point *m* <the utmost in reliability : ce qu'il y a de plus fiable> **2 to do one's utmost** : faire son possible
utopia [juˈtoːpiə] *n* : utopie *f*
utopian [juˈtoːpiən] *adj* : utopique
utter[1] ['ʌtər] *vt* : exprimer, prononcer (un mot), pousser (un cri)
utter[2] *adj* : absolu, total, complet <utter darkness : obscurité totale>
utterly ['ʌtərli] *adv* : complètement
utterance ['ʌtərənts] *n* : déclaration *f*, paroles *fpl*

V

v ['viː] *n, pl* **v's** *or* **vs** ['viːz] : v *m*, vingt-deuxième lettre de l'alphabet
vacancy ['veɪkənsi] *n, pl* **-cies 1** : chambre *f* disponible (dans un hôtel) <no vacancies : complet> **2** : poste *m* vacant <to fill a vacancy : pourvoir un poste> **3** EMPTINESS : vide *m*
vacant ['veɪkənt] *adj* **1** EMPTY : vide, inoccupé **2** UNOCCUPIED : libre (se dit d'une chambre), vacant (se dit d'un poste) **3** DISTRACTED : distrait, absent <a vacant smile : un sourire absent>
vacate ['veɪˌkeɪt] *vt* **-cated; -cating** : quitter, libérer (une chambre) <to vacate the premises : vider les lieux>
vacation[1] [veɪˈkeɪʃən, və-] *vi* : prendre des vacances
vacation[2] *n* : vacances *fpl*, congé *m*
vacationer [veɪˈkeɪʃənər, və-] *n* : vacancier *m*, -cière *f*
vaccinate ['vækseˌneɪt] *vt* **-nated; -nating** : vacciner
vaccination [ˌvæksəˈneɪʃən] *n* : vaccination *f*
vaccine [vækˈsiːn, ˈvækˌ-] *n* : vaccin *m*
vacillate ['væsəˌleɪt] *vi* **-lated; -lating 1** SWAY : vaciller, perdre son équilibre **2** HESITATE : hésiter
vacillation [ˌvæsəˈleɪʃən] *n* : hésitation *f*, indécision *f*
vacuous ['vækjʊəs] *adj* **1** BLANK, EMPTY : vide **2** INANE : stupide, idiot
vacuum[1] ['væˌkjuːm, -kjəm] *vt* : passer l'aspirateur dans (un tapis, etc.)
vacuum[2] *n, pl* **vacuums** *or* **vacua** ['vækjʊə] **1** VOID : vide *m* **2** → **vacuum cleaner**
vacuum cleaner *n* : aspirateur *m*, balayeuse *f Can*
vagabond[1] ['vægəˌbɑnd] *adj* : vagabond, errant
vagabond[2] *n* : vagabond *m*, -bonde *f*
vagary ['veɪgəri, vəˈgeri] *n, pl* **-ries** : caprice *m*
vagina [vəˈdʒaɪnə] *n, pl* **-nae** [-ˌniː, -ˌnaɪ] *or* **-nas** : vagin *m*
vaginal ['vædʒənəl] *adj* : vaginal
vagrancy ['veɪgrənsi] *n, pl* **-cies** : vagabondage *m*
vagrant[1] ['veɪgrənt] *adj* : vagabond
vagrant[2] *n* : clochard *m*, -charde *f*; itinérant *m*, -rante *f Can*
vague ['veɪg] *adj* **vaguer; vaguest 1** IMPRECISE : vague, imprécis **2** SLIGHT : moindre <I haven't the vaguest idea : je n'en ai pas la moindre idée> **3** INDISTINCT : vague, flou **4** ABSENT-MINDED : distrait
vaguely ['veɪgli] *adv* : vaguement
vain ['veɪn] *adj* **1** WORTHLESS : sans valeur **2** FUTILE : inutile, futile **3** CONCEITED : vaniteux **4 in ~** : en vain
vainglorious [ˌveɪnˈgloriəs] *adj* PROUD : orgueilleux, vaniteux
vainly ['veɪnli] *adv* **1** UNSUCCESSFULLY : vainement, inutilement **2** CONCEITEDLY : avec vanité, vaniteusement
valance ['vælənts, 'veɪ-] *n* : lambrequin *m* (d'un lit), cantonnière *f* (pour des rideaux)
vale ['veɪl] *n* : val *m*, vallée *f*
valedictorian [ˌvæləˌdɪkˈtoriən] *n* : étudiant *m*, -diante *f* qui prononce un discours lors d'une cérémonie de graduation
valedictory[1] [ˌvæləˈdɪktəri] *adj* : d'adieu
valedictory[2] *n, pl* **-ries** : discours *m* d'adieu
valentine ['vælənˌtaɪn] *n* : carte *f* de Saint-Valentin, valentin *m Can*
valet ['væˌleɪ, væˈleɪ, 'vælət] *n* : valet *m* de chambre

valiant ['vælɪənt] *adj* : vaillant, courageux
valiantly ['vælɪəntlɪ] *adv* : vaillamment, courageusement
valid ['vælɪd] *adj* **1** : valid <a valid contract : un contrat valide> **2** : bien fondé, valable <valid arguments : raisonnements bien fondés>
validate ['vælə,deɪt] *vt* **-dated; -dating** : valider (un document), confirmer (une théorie, etc.)
validation [,vælə'deɪʃən] *n* : validation *f*
validity [və'lɪdəṭi, væ-] *n* : validité *f*
valise [və'li:s] *n* : mallette *f*, sac *m* de voyage
valley ['vælɪ] *n, pl* **-leys** : vallée *f*
valor *or Brit* **valour** ['vælər] *n* : bravoure *f*, héroïsme *m*
valorous ['vælərəs] *adj* : valeureux
valour *Brit* → **valor**
valuable ['vælɪjuəbəl, -jəbəl] *adj* **1** EXPENSIVE : de valeur **2** WORTHWHILE : précieux <a valuable friendship : une amitié précieuse>
valuables ['vælɪjuəbəlz, -jəbəlz]*npl* : objets *mpl* de valeur
valuation [,vælɪju'eɪʃən] *n* **1** APPRAISAL : évaluation *f*, estimation *f* **2** WORTH : valeur *f*, prix *m*
value[1] ['vælˌju:] *vt* **valued; valuing 1** APPRAISE : estimer, évaluer **2** APPRECIATE, ESTEEM : apprécier, estimer
value[2] *n* **1** : valeur *f* <of no value : sans valeur> <to be of great value : valoir cher> **2** IMPORTANCE, MERIT : valeur *f*, mérite *m* <to place a high value on : attacher beaucoup d'importance à> **3 values** *npl* : valeurs *fpl* <family values : valeurs familiales>
valueless ['vælˌju:ləs] *adj* : sans valeur
valve ['vælv] *n* **1** : valve *f*, soupape *f* (en mécanique) **2** : valvule *f* (en anatomie)
vampire ['væmˌpaɪr] *n* : vampire *m*
van ['væn] *n* **1** : camionnette *f*, fourgonnette *f* (voiture) **2** → **vanguard**
vanadium [və'neɪdɪəm] *n* : vanadium *m*
vandal ['vændəl] *n* : vandale *mf*
vandalism ['vændəlˌɪzəm] *n* : vandalisme *m*
vandalize ['vændəlˌaɪz] *vt* **-ized; -izing** : saccager
vane ['veɪn] *n or* **weather vane** : girouette *f*
vanguard ['vænˌgɑrd] *n* : avant-garde *f*
vanilla [və'nɪlə, -ne-] *n* : vanille *f*
vanish ['vænɪʃ] *vi* : disparaître
vanity ['vænəṭi] *n, pl* **-ties 1** FUTILITY : futilité *f* **2** CONCEIT : vanité *f*, orgueil *m* **3** *or* **vanity table** : coiffeuse *f*
vanquish ['væŋkwɪʃ, 'væn-] *vt* : vaincre
vantage point ['væntɪdʒ] *n* : point *m* de vue, perspective *f*
vapid ['væpɪd, 'veɪ-] *adj* : insipide, fade
vapor ['veɪpər] *n* : vapeur *f*
vaporize ['veɪpəˌraɪz] *vt* **-ized; -izing** : vaporiser
vaporizer ['veɪpəˌraɪzər] *n* : vaporisateur *m*
variability [,veriə'bɪləṭi] *n, pl* **-ties** : variabilité *f*
variable[1] ['veriəbəl] *adj* : variable
variable[2] *n* : variable *f*
variance ['veriənts] *n* **1** DIFFERENCE : différence *f*, écart *m* **2** DISAGREEMENT : désaccord *m* <to be at variance with s.o. : être en désaccord avec qqn>
variant[1] ['veriənt] *adj* : différent
variant[2] *n* : variante *f*
variation [,veri'eɪʃən] *n* : variation *f*, différence *f*
varicose ['verəˌko:s] *adj* : variqueux
varicose veins *npl* : varices *fpl*
varied ['verɪd] *adj* : varié, divers
variegated ['veriəˌgeɪṭəd] *adj* **1** MULTICOLORED : bigarré, bariolé **2** : panaché (en botanique)
variety [və'raɪəṭi] *n, pl* **-eties 1** DIVERSITY : variété *f*, diversité *f* **2** ASSORTMENT : variété *f*, quantité *f* <a wide variety of : un grand nombre de> **3** TYPE : espèce *f*, sorte *f* **4** : variété *f* (en botanique)
various ['veriəs] *adj* : divers, varié
varnish[1] ['vɑrnɪʃ] *vt* **1** : vernir (du bois) **2** GLOSS : voiler, embellir
varnish[2] *n* : vernis *m*
varsity ['vɑrsəṭi] *n, pl* **-ties** : équipe *f* universitaire
vary ['veri] *v* **varied; varying** *vi* **1** CHANGE : varier, changer, se modifier **2** DIFFER : varier — *vt* : varier, diversifier
vascular ['væskjələr] *adj* : vasculaire
vase ['veɪs, 'veɪz, 'vɑz] *n* : vase *m*
vast ['væst] *adj* : vaste, énorme
vastly ['væstlɪ] *adv* : immensément, énormément
vastness ['væstnəs] *n* : immensité *f*, grandeur *f*
vat ['væt] *n* : cuve *f*, bac *m*
vaudeville ['vɔdvəl, -ˌvɪl; 'vɔdəˌvɪl] *n* : vaudeville *m*
vault[1] ['vɔlt] *vt* : sauter par-dessus — *vi* : sauter
vault[2] *n* **1** JUMP : saut *m* **2** DOME : voûte *f* **3** : cave *f* (à vin), chambre *f* forte (d'une banque) **4** *or* **burial vault** : caveau *m*
vaulted ['vɔltəd] *adj* : voûté
vaunted ['vɔntəd] *adj* : vanté <her much-vaunted beauty : sa beauté tant vantée>
VCR [,vi:ˌsi:'ar] *n* : magnétoscope *m*
veal ['vi:l] *n* : veau *m*
veer ['vɪr] *vi* : tourner, virer (se dit d'un bateau, du vent, etc.)
vegetable[1] ['vedʒəṭəbəl, 'vedʒəṭə-] *adj* **1** : végétal <vegetable oil : huile végétale> **2** : de légumes <vegetable broth : bouillon de légumes>
vegetable[2] *n* **1** : végétal *m* (en botanique) **2** : légume *m* <fruits and vegetables : les fruits et les légumes>

vegetarian[1] [ˌvɛdʒəˈtɛriən] *adj* : végétarien
vegetarian[2] *n* : végétarien *m*, -rienne *f*
vegetarianism [ˌvɛdʒəˈtɛriəˌnɪzəm] *n* : végétarisme *m*
vegetate [ˈvɛdʒəˌtɛɪt] *vi* **-tated; -tating** : végéter
vegetation [ˌvɛdʒəˈteɪʃən] *n* : végétation *f*
vegetative [ˈvɛdʒəˌtɛɪtɪv] *adj* : végétatif
vehemence [ˈviːəmənts] *n* : véhémence *f*, intensité *f*
vehement [ˈviːəmənt] *adj* : ardent, véhément
vehemently [ˈviːəməntli] *adv* : avec véhémence
vehicle [ˈviəkəl, ˈviːˌhɪkəl] *n* **1** CARRIER, MEDIUM : véhicule *m* **2** *or* **motor vehicle** : véhicule *m* (routier)
vehicular [viˈhɪkjələr, və-] *adj* : de véhicules <vehicular accidents : accidents de la route>
veil[1] [ˈveɪl] *vt* **1** CONCEAL : voiler, masquer **2** : couvrir d'un voile <to veil one's face : se voiler>
veil[2] *n* : voile *m* <bridal veil : voile de mariée> <veil of secrecy : voile du secret>
vein [ˈveɪn] *n* **1** : veine *f* (en anatomie) **2** LODE : filon *m*, veine *f* **3** : nervure *f* (d'une feuille) **4** STYLE : veine *f*, esprit *m* <in the same vein : dans le même esprit>
veined [ˈveɪnd] *adj* : veiné (se dit des minéraux, etc.), nervuré (se dit d'une feuille)
velocity [vəˈlɑsəti] *n, pl* **-ties** : vélocité *f*, vitesse *f*
velour [vəˈlʊr] *or* **velours** [-ˈlʊrz] *n, pl* **velours** : velours *m*
velvet[1] [ˈvɛlvət] *adj* **1** : de velours **2** → **velvety**
velvet[2] *n* : velours *m*
velvety [ˈvɛlvəti] *adj* : velouté
venal [ˈviːnəl] *adj* : vénal
vend [ˈvɛnd] *vt* : vendre
vendetta [vɛnˈdɛtə] *n* : vendetta *f*
vending machine *n* : distributeur *m* automatique
vendor [ˈvɛndər] *n* **1** : vendeur *m*, -deuse *f*; marchand *m*, -chande *f* **2** → **vending machine**
veneer[1] [vəˈnɪr] *vt* : plaquer
veneer[2] *n* **1** : placage *m* (du bois) **2** APPEARANCE, FACADE : vernis *m*, fausse *f* apparence
venerable [ˈvɛnərəbəl] *adj* : vénérable
venerate [ˈvɛnəˌreɪt] *vt* **-ated; -ating** : vénérer
veneration [ˌvɛnəˈreɪʃən] *n* : vénération *f*
venereal disease [vəˈnɪriəl] *n* : maladie *f* vénérienne
venetian blind [vəˈniːʃən] : store *m* vénitien
Venezuelan[1] [ˌvɛnəˈzweɪlən, -zuˈeɪ-] *adj* : vénézuélien
Venezuelan[2] *n* : Vénézuélien *m*, -lienne *f*
vengeance [ˈvɛndʒənts] *n* : vengeance *f* <to take vengeance on s.o. : se venger sur qqn>
vengeful [ˈvɛndʒfəl] *adj* : vengeur, vindicatif
venial [ˈviːniəl] *adj* : véniel <venial sins : péchés véniels>
venison [ˈvɛnəsən, -zən] *n* : venaison *f*
venom [ˈvɛnəm] *n* **1** : venin *m* (de serpent) **2** ILL WILL : venin *m*, malveillance *f*
venomous [ˈvɛnəməs] *adj* **1** : venimeux (se dit d'un serpent) **2** SPITEFUL : venimeux, haineux
vent[1] [ˈvɛnt] *vt* **1** EXPEL : évacuer, laisser échapper (de la fumée, etc.) **2** : décharger, donner libre cours à (ses émotions)
vent[2] *n* **1** OUTLET : orifice *m*, conduit *m*, bouche *f* d'aération **2 to give vent to** : donner libre cours à
ventilate [ˈvɛntəlˌeɪt] *vt* **-lated; -lating** : ventiler, aérer
ventilation [ˌvɛntəlˈeɪʃən] *n* : ventilation *f*, aération *f*
ventilator [ˈvɛntəlˌeɪtər] *n* : ventilateur *m*
ventricle [ˈvɛntrɪkəl] *n* : ventricule *m*
ventriloquism [vɛnˈtrɪləˌkwɪzəm] *n* : ventriloquie *f*
ventriloquist [vɛnˈtrɪləˌkwɪst] *n* : ventriloque *mf*
venture[1] [ˈvɛntʃər] *v* **-tured; -turing** *vt* **1** RISK : risquer, hasarder **2** OFFER : hasarder, avancer <to venture an opinion : hasarder une opinion> — *vi* : s'embarquer, s'aventurer
venture[2] *n* **1** UNDERTAKING : entreprise *f* risquée, affaire *f* **2** STAKE : enjeu *m*
venturesome [ˈvɛntʃərsəm] *adj* **1** HAZARDOUS : dangereux, périlleux **2** DARING : audacieux, brave
venue [ˈvɛnˌjuː] *n* : lieu *m* (de rencontre)
Venus [ˈviːnəs] *n* : Vénus *f* (planète)
veracity [vəˈræsəti] *n, pl* **-ties** : véracité *f*
veranda *or* **verandah** [vəˈrændə] *n* : véranda *f*
verb [ˈvərb] *n* : verbe *m*
verbal [ˈvərbəl] *adj* : verbal
verbalize [ˈvərbəˌlaɪz] *vt* **-ized; -izing** : rendre par des mots, verbaliser
verbally [ˈvərbəli] *adv* : verbalement
verbatim[1] [vərˈbeɪtəm] *adv* : textuellement
verbatim[2] *adj* : mot pour mot, textuel
verbose [vərˈboːs] *adj* : verbeux, prolixe
verdant [ˈvərdənt] *adj* : verdoyant
verdict [ˈvərdɪkt] *n* **1** : verdict *m* (en droit) **2** JUDGMENT, OPINION : opinion *f*, jugement *m*
verdure [ˈvərdʒər, -djər] *n* : verdure *f*

verge[1] ['vərdʒ] *vi* **verged; verging 1** : être au bord **2 to verge on** : s'approcher de, friser
verge[2] *n* **1** EDGE, RIM : bord *m* **2 to be on the verge of** : être sur le bord de, être sur le point de
verifiable [,vɛrə'faɪəbəl] *adj* : vérifiable
verification [,vɛrəfə'keɪʃən] *n* : vérification *f*
verify ['vɛrə,faɪ] *vt* **-fied; -fying** : vérifier
veritable ['vɛrəṭəbəl] *adj* : véritable — **veritably** [-bli] *adv*
vermicelli [,vərmə'tʃeli, -'sɛli] *n* : vermicelle *m*
vermin ['vərmən] *ns & pl* : vermine *f*, animaux *mpl* nuisibles
vermouth [vər'mu:θ] *n* : vermouth *m*
vernacular[1] [vər'nækjələr] *adj* : vernaculaire, du pays
vernacular[2] *n* : langage *m* vernaculaire
versatile ['vərsəṭəl] *adj* **1** : aux talents divers (se dit d'une personne) **2** MULTIPURPOSE : polyvalent, aux usages multiples
versatility [,vərsə'tɪləṭi] *n* : souplesse *f* (de l'esprit), polyvalence *f* (d'un outil, etc.)
verse ['vərs] *n* **1** STANZA : strophe *f* **2** POETRY : vers *mpl*, poésie *f* **3** : verset *m* (de la Bible)
versed ['vərst] *adj* **to be well versed in** : être très versé dans
version ['vərʒən] *n* : version *f*
versus ['vərsəs] *prep* : contre, par rapport à
vertebra ['vərtəbrə] *n, pl* **-brae** [-,breɪ, -,bri:] *or* **-bras** : vertèbre *f*
vertebral [vər'tibrəl, 'vərtə-] *adj* : vertébral
vertebrate[1] ['vərtəbrət, -,breɪt] *adj* : vertébré
vertebrate[2] *n* : vertébré *m*
vertex ['vər,teks] *n, pl* **vertices** ['vərtə,si:z] **1** : vertex *m* (en anatomie), sommet *m* (d'un angle) **2** SUMMIT, TOP : sommet *m*
vertical[1] ['vərtɪkəl] *adj* : vertical — **vertically** *adv*
vertical[2] *n* : verticale *f*
vertigo ['vərtɪ,go:] *n, pl* **-goes** *or* **-gos** : vertige *m*
verve ['vərv] *n* : verve *f*, brio *m*
very[1] ['veri] *adv* **1** TRULY : vraiment, exactement <the very same story : exactement la même histoire> <at the very least : tout au moins> **2** EXCEEDINGLY : très, vraiment, tellement <very hot : très chaud> <it didn't hurt very much : ça ne m'a pas fait tellement mal>
very[2] *adj* **1** EXACT : même, précis <the very heart of the city : le cœur même de la ville> **2** PERFECT : parfait <the very tool for the job : le parfait outil pour le travail> **3** BARE, MERE : seul <the very thought of leaving : la seule idée de partir> **4** SELFSAME : même, identique <he's the very man I saw : c'est justement l'homme que j'ai vu>
vesicle ['vɛsɪkəl] *n* : vésicule *f*
vespers ['vɛspərz] *npl* : vêpres *fpl*
vessel ['vɛsəl] *n* **1** CONTAINER : récipient *m*, contenant *m* **2** SHIP : vaisseau *m* **3 → blood vessel**
vest[1] ['vɛst] *vt* **1** : investir <to vest a deputy with authority : investir un député d'autorité> **2** CLOTHE : vêtir
vest[2] *n* : gilet *m*, veste *f Can*
vestibule ['vɛstə,bju:l] *n* : vestibule *m*
vestige ['vɛstɪdʒ] *n* : vestige *m*, trace *f*
vestment ['vɛstmənt] *n* : vêtement *m* sacerdotal
vestry ['vɛstri] *n, pl* **-tries** : sacristie *f*
veteran[1] ['vɛṭərən, 'vɛtrən] *adj* : chevronné
veteran[2] *n* : ancien combattant *m*, vétéran *m*
veterinarian [,vɛṭərə'nɛriən, ,vɛṭrə-] *n* : vétérinaire *mf*
veterinary ['vɛṭərə,nɛri, 'vɛtrə-] *adj* : vétérinaire
veto[1] ['vi:ṭo] *vt* **1** PROHIBIT : interdire, défendre **2** : mettre son veto à, opposer son veto à (une loi)
veto[2] *n, pl* **-toes 1** PROHIBITION : interdiction *f*, prohibition *f* **2** : veto *m* <right of veto : droit de veto>
vex ['vɛks] *vt* **vexed; vexing 1** UPSET : vexer, froisser **2** ANNOY : contrarier, ennuyer
vexation [vɛk'seɪʃən] *n* IRRITATION : contrariété *f*, agacement *m*
via ['vaɪə, 'viə] *prep* : via, par
viability [,vaɪə'bɪləṭi] *n* : viabilité *f*
viable ['vaɪəbəl] *adj* : viable
viaduct ['vaɪə,dʌkt] *n* : viaduc *m*
vial ['vaɪəl] *n* : fiole *f*
vibrant ['vaɪbrənt] *adj* **1** BRIGHT : vif <a vibrant red : un rouge vif> **2** RESONANT : vibrant, résonant **3** LIVELY : vivant, animé
vibrate ['vaɪ,breɪt] *v* **-brated; -brating** *vt* : faire vibrer — *vi* **1** OSCILLATE : vibrer, osciller **2** QUIVER, THRILL : frémir, vibrer
vibration [vaɪ'breɪʃən] *n* : vibration *f*
vicar ['vɪkər] *n* : vicaire *m*
vicarious [vaɪ'kæriəs, vɪ-] *adj* **1** DELEGATED : délégué **2** INDIRECT : indirect <vicarious experiences : expériences vécues indirectement>
vicariously [vaɪ'kæriəsli, vɪ-] *adv* : indirectement
vice ['vaɪs] *n* **1** : vice *m* **2** *Brit* **→ vise**
vice admiral *n* : vice-amiral *m*
vice president *n* : vice-président *m*, -dente *f*
viceroy ['vaɪs,rɔɪ] *n* : vice-roi *m*
vice versa [,vaɪsɪ'vərsə, ,vaɪs'vər-] *adv* : vice versa
vicinity [və'sɪnəṭi] *n, pl* **-ties 1** NEARNESS : proximité *f* **2** NEIGHBORHOOD

: quartier *m*, voisinage *m*, environs *mpl*

vicious [ˈvɪʃəs] *adj* **1** DEPRAVED : vicieux, corrompu **2** SAVAGE : méchant <a vicious dog : un chien méchant> **3** SPITEFUL : malveillant, méchant

viciously [ˈvɪʃəsli] *adv* **1** SAVAGELY : brutalement, violemment **2** SPITEFULLY : méchamment, cruellement

viciousness [ˈvɪʃəsnəs] *n* **1** : brutalité *f*, violence *f* **2** MEANNESS : méchanceté *f*, cruauté *f*

vicissitude [vəˈsɪsəˌtuːd, vaɪ-, -ˌtjuːd] *n* : vicissitude *f*

victim [ˈvɪktəm] *n* : victime *f*

victimize [ˈvɪktəˌmaɪz] *vt* **-ized; -izing** : persécuter, faire une victime de

victor [ˈvɪktər] *n* : vainqueur *m*

Victorian [vɪkˈtoːriən] *adj* : victorien

victorious [vɪkˈtoːriəs] *adj* : victorieux **— victoriously** *adv*

victory [ˈvɪktəri] *n, pl* **-ries** : victoire *f*

victuals [ˈvɪtəlz] *npl* : victuailles *fpl*

video[1] [ˈvɪdiˌoː] *adj* : vidéo

video[2] *n* **1** : vidéo *f* **2** → **videotape**[2]

videocassette [ˌvɪdiokəˈset] *n* : vidéocassette *f*

videotape[1] [ˈvɪdioˌteɪp] **-taped; -taping** *vt* : enregistrer (sur magnétoscope)

videotape[2] *n* : bande *f* vidéo

vie [ˈvaɪ] *vi* **vied; vying** [ˈvaɪɪŋ] : rivaliser, être en compétition

Vietnamese[1] [viˌɛtnəˈmiːz, -ˈmiːs] *adj* : vietnamien

Vietnamese[2] *n* **1** : Vietnamien *m*, -mienne *f* **2** : vietnamien *m* (langue)

view[1] [ˈvjuː] *vt* **1** EXAMINE : examiner, inspecter **2** SEE, WATCH : regarder, voir (un film, etc.) **3** CONSIDER : étudier, peser <to view all sides of a question : étudier tous les aspects d'un problème>

view[2] *n* **1** SIGHT : vue *f* <to come into view : apparaître> **2** ATTITUDE, OPINION : opinion *f*, avis *m* <in my view : d'après moi, à mon avis> **3** PROSPECT : vue *f*, panorama *m* <a room with a view : une chambre avec vue> **4** INTENTION : intention *f*, vue *f* <with a view to : dans l'intention de, en vue de> **5 in view of** : vu, étant donné

viewer [ˈvjuːər] *n* **1** *or* **television viewer** : téléspectateur *m*, -trice *f* **2** : visionneuse *f* (en photographie)

viewpoint [ˈvjuːˌpɔɪnt] *n* : point *m* de vue

vigil [ˈvɪdʒəl] *n* **1** : vigile *f* (en religion) **2** WAKEFULNESS, WATCH : veille *f* <to keep a vigil : veiller>

vigilance [ˈvɪdʒələnts] *n* : vigilance *f*

vigilant [ˈvɪdʒələnt] *adj* : vigilant, attentif

vigilante [ˌvɪdʒəˈlæn,tiː] *n* : membre *m* d'un groupe qui lutte contre le crime

vigilantly [ˈvɪdʒələntli] *adv* : avec vigilance

vigor *or Brit* **vigour** [ˈvɪgər] *n* : vigueur *f*, énergie *f*

vigorous [ˈvɪgərəs] *adj* : vigoureux, énergique **— vigorously** *adv*

vigour *Brit* → **vigor**

Viking [ˈvaɪkɪŋ] *n* : Viking *mf*

vile [ˈvaɪl] *adj* **viler; vilest 1** BASE : vil, ignoble **2** REVOLTING : abominable, écœurant **3** AWFUL, FOUL : exécrable, massacrant <in a vile temper : d'une humeur massacrante> <vile weather : sale temps>

vilely [ˈvaɪəlli] *adv* : vilement, ignoblement

vileness [ˈvaɪlnəs] *n* : caractère *m* ignoble

vilification [ˌvɪləfəˈkeɪʃən] *n* : diffamation *f*, calomnie *f*

vilify [ˈvɪləˌfaɪ] *vt* **-fied; -fying** : diffamer, calomnier

villa [ˈvɪlə] *n* : villa *f*

village [ˈvɪlɪdʒ] *n* : village *m*

villager [ˈvɪlɪdʒər] *n* : villageois *m*, -geoise *f*

villain [ˈvɪlən] *n* : scélérat *m*, -rate *f*; méchant *m*, -chante *f* (dans un livre, un film, etc.)

villainous [ˈvɪlənəs] *adj* : vil, ignoble, infâme

villainy [ˈvɪləni] *n, pl* **-lainies** : vilenie *f*, infamie *f*

vim [ˈvɪm] *n* : énergie *f*, vitalité *f*, entrain *m*

vindicate [ˈvɪndəˌkeɪt] *vt* **-cated; -cating 1** EXONERATE : innocenter **2** JUSTIFY : justifier

vindication [ˌvɪndəˈkeɪʃən] *n* : justification *f*

vindictive [vɪnˈdɪktɪv] *adj* : vindicatif, rancunier

vindictiveness [vɪnˈdɪktɪvnəs] *n* : esprit *m* rancunier

vine [ˈvaɪn] *n* **1** GRAPEVINE : vigne *f* **2** : plante *f* grimpante

vinegar [ˈvɪnɪgər] *n* : vinaigre *m*

vineyard [ˈvɪnjərd] *n* : vignoble *m*

vintage[1] [ˈvɪntɪdʒ] *adj* **1** : millésimé (se dit du vin) **2** CLASSIC : d'époque **3** : à son meilleur <vintage Shaw : du Shaw à son meilleur>

vintage[2] *n* **1** HARVEST : vendange *f* (en viticulture) **2** PERIOD : époque *f* <a piano of 1845 vintage : un piano qui date de 1845> **3** *or* **vintage wine** : vin *m* de grand cru **4** *or* **vintage year** : millésime *m*

vinyl [ˈvaɪnəl] *n* : vinyle *m*

viola [viˈoːlə] *n* : alto *m*

violate [ˈvaɪəˌleɪt] *vt* **-lated; -lating 1** BREAK : transgresser, enfreindre <to violate the law : enfreindre la loi> **2** RAPE : violer **3** DESECRATE : profaner

violation [ˌvaɪəˈleɪʃən] *n* **1** INFRINGEMENT : infraction *f*, transgression *f* <traffic violation : infraction au code de la route> **2** RAPE : viol *m* **3** DESECRATION : profanation *f*, viol *m*

violator [ˈvaɪəˌleɪtər] *n* : violateur *m*, -trice *f*

violence ['vaɪələnʧs] *n* : violence *f*
violent ['vaɪələnt] *adj* : violent
violently ['vaɪələntli] *adv* : violemment, avec violence
violet ['vaɪələt] *n* **1** : violette *f* (plante) **2** : violet *m* (couleur)
violin [ˌvaɪə'lɪn] *n* : violon *m*
violincello [ˌvaɪə'lən'ʧeˌloː, ˌviː-] → **cello**
violinist [ˌvaɪə'lɪnɪst] *n* : violoniste *mf*
VIP [ˌviːˌaɪ'piː] *n, pl* **VIPs** [-'piːz] : V.I.P. *m fam*, personnalité *f* de marque
viper ['vaɪpər] *n* : vipère *f*
viral ['vaɪrəl] *adj* : viral
virgin[1] ['vərʤən] *adj* **1** CHASTE : vierge **2** UNSPOILED : vierge, intact
virgin[2] *n* **1** : vierge *f* **2 the Virgin Mary** : la Vierge Marie
virginity [vər'ʤɪnəṭi] *n, pl* **-ties** : virginité *f*
Virgo ['vərˌgoː, 'vɪr-] *n* : Vierge *f*
virile ['vɪrəl, -ˌaɪl] *adj* : viril
virility [və'rɪləṭi] *n* : virilité *f*
virtual ['vərʧʊəl] *adj* **1** : en pratique, de fait <a virtual leader : un chef de fait> **2** NEAR : quasi-total <a virtual impossibility : une quasi-impossibilité> <it's a virtual certainty : c'est presque certain> **3** : virtuel (en informatique)
virtually ['vərʧʊəli] *adv* : pratiquement, presque
virtue ['vərˌʧuː] *n* **1** GOODNESS : vertu *f* **2** MERIT : avantage *m*, mérite *m* **3 by virtue of** : en raison de, en vertu de
virtuosity [ˌvərʧʊ'ɑsəṭi] *n, pl* **-ties** : virtuosité *f*
virtuoso [ˌvərʧʊ'oːˌsoː, -ˌzoː] *n, pl* **-sos** *or* **-si** [-ˌsiː, -ˌziː] : virtuose *mf*
virtuous ['vərʧʊəs] *adj* : vertueux — **virtuously** ['vərʧʊəsli] *adv*
virulence ['vɪrələnʦ, -jələnʦ] *n* : virulence *f*
virulent ['vɪrələnt, -jələnt] *adj* : virulent
virulently ['vɪrələntli, -jələnt-] *adv* : avec virulence
virus ['vaɪrəs] *n* : virus *m* (en médecine, en informatique, etc.)
visa ['viːzə, -sə] *n* : visa *m*
visage ['vɪzɪʤ] *n* : physionomie *f*
vis-à-vis [ˌviːzə'viː, -sə-] *prep* : vis-a-vis de, par rapport à
viscera ['vɪsərə] *npl* : viscères *mpl*
visceral ['vɪsərəl] *adj* : viscéral
viscosity [vɪs'kɑsəṭi] *n, pl* **-ties** : viscosité *f*
viscount ['vaɪˌkaʊnt] *n* : vicomte *m*
viscountess ['vaɪˌkaʊntəs] *n* : vicomtesse *f*
viscous ['vɪskəs] *adj* : visqueux
vise *or Brit* **vice** ['vaɪs] *n* : étau *m*
visibility [ˌvɪzə'bɪləṭi] *n, pl* **-ties** : visibilité *f*
visible ['vɪzəbəl] *adj* **1** : visible <visible stars : étoiles visibles> **2** OBVIOUS : visible, manifeste, apparent
visibly ['vɪzəbli] *adv* : visiblement
vision ['vɪʒən] *n* **1** EYESIGHT : vision *f*, vue *f* **2** APPARITION : apparition *f*, vision *f* **3** FORESIGHT : vision *f* (de l'avenir), prévoyance *f*, imagination *f* **4** IMAGE : image *f* <a vision of beauty : une image de la beauté>
visionary[1] ['vɪʒəˌnɛri] *adj* **1** FARSIGHTED : visionnaire **2** UTOPIAN : utopique, irréel
visionary[2] *n, pl* **-aries** : visionnaire *mf*
visit[1] ['vɪzəṭ] *vt* **1** : rendre visite à, aller voir (une personne) **2** : visiter, faire visite à (un lieu) **3 to be visited by** : être éprouvé par (des difficultés, etc.)
visit[2] *n* : visite *f*
visitor ['vɪzəṭər] *n* : visiteur *m*, -teuse *f*
visor ['vaɪzər] *n* **1** : visière *f* (d'un casque) **2** *or* **sun visor** : pare-soleil *m*
vista ['vɪstə] *n* : vue *f*, perspective *f*
visual ['vɪʒʊəl] *adj* : visuel — **visually** *adv*
visualize ['vɪʒʊəˌlaɪz] *vt* **-ized; -izing 1** IMAGINE : visualiser, s'imaginer **2** ENVISAGE : prévoir, envisager
vital ['vaɪṭəl] *adj* **1** : vital <vital organs : organes vitaux> **2** LIVELY : vivant, dynamique **3** ESSENTIAL : vital, indispensable, essentiel <to be of vital importance : être indispensable>
vitality [vaɪ'tæləṭi] *n, pl* **-ties** : vitalité *f*
vitally ['vaɪṭəli] *adv* : extrêmement, très
vital statistics *n* : statistiques *fpl* démographiques
vitamin ['vaɪṭəmən] *n* : vitamine *f*
vitreous ['vɪtriəs] *adj* : vitreux
vitriolic [ˌvɪtri'ɑlɪk] *adj* : au vitriol, venimeux
vituperate [vaɪ'tuːpəˌreɪt, və-, -'tjuː-] *vt* **-ated; -ating** : vitupérer
vituperation [vaɪˌtuːpə'reɪʃən, və-, -ˌtjuː-] *n* : vitupération *f*
vivacious [və'veɪʃəs, vaɪ-] *adj* : vif, animé, plein d'entrain
vivaciously [və'veɪʃəsli, vaɪ-] *adv* : avec vivacité
vivacity [və'væsəṭi, vaɪ-] *n* : vivacité *f*, entrain *m*
vivid ['vɪvəd] *adj* **1** FRESH, LIVELY : vivant, vif <a vivid imagination : une vive imagination> **2** BRIGHT : vif, éclatant <a vivid blue : un bleu vif> **3** SHARP : vivant, frappant <a vivid description : une description vivante>
vividly ['vɪvədli] *adv* : de façon éclatante, de façon vivante
vividness ['vɪvədnəs] *n* **1** BRIGHTNESS : éclat *m* **2** CLARITY, SHARPNESS : clarté *f*, vivacité *f*
vivisection [ˌvɪvə'sɛkʃən, 'vɪvəˌ-] *n* : vivisection *f*
vixen ['vɪksən] *n* : renarde *f*
vocabulary [voː'kæbjəˌlɛri] *n, pl* **-laries 1** LEXICON : vocabulaire *m*, lexique *m* **2** : vocabulaire *m* (de la langue)

vocal [ˈvoːkəl] *adj* **1** : vocal **2** OUTSPOKEN : franc, qui se fait bien entendre
vocal cords *npl* : cordes *fpl* vocales
vocalist [ˈvoːkəlɪst] *n* : chanteur *m*, -teuse *f*
vocalize [ˈvoːkəlˌaɪz] *v* **-ized; -izing** *vt* UTTER : exprimer — *vi* : vocaliser (en musique)
vocation [voˈkeɪʃən] *n* **1** : vocation *f* (religieuse) **2** OCCUPATION : emploi *m*, profession *f*
vocational [voˈkeɪʃənəl] *adj* : professionnel <vocational guidance : orientation professionnelle>
vociferous [voˈsɪfərəs] *adj* : véhément, bruyant
vociferously [voˈsɪfərəsli] *adv* : avec véhémence, bruyamment
vodka [ˈvɑdkə] *n* : vodka *m*
vogue [ˈvoːg] *n* : vogue *f*, mode *f* <to be in vogue : être à la mode>
voice[1] [ˈvɔɪs] *vt* **voiced; voicing** : exprimer, formuler
voice[2] *n* **1** : voix *f* <a booming voice : une voix retentissante> <fear took his voice away : la peur l'avait rendu muet> **2** : voix *f* (en grammaire)
voice box → larynx
voiced [ˈvɔɪst] *adj* : sonore
void[1] [ˈvɔɪd] *vt* **1** DISCHARGE : évacuer (en physiologie) **2** ANNUL : annuler
void[2] *adj* **1** EMPTY : vide <void of common sense : dépourvu de bon sens> **2** NULL : nul
void[3] *n* : vide *m*
volatile [ˈvɑləṭəl] *adj* : volatil, instable
volatility [ˌvɑləˈtɪləṭi] *n* : volatilité *f*, instabilité *f*
volcanic [vɑlˈkænɪk, vɔl-] *adj* : volcanique
volcano [vɑlˈkeɪˌno:, vɔl-] *n, pl* **-noes** *or* **-nos** : volcan *m*
vole [ˈvoːl] *n* : campagnol *m*
volition [voˈlɪʃən] *n* : volonté *f* <of one's own volition : de son propre gré>
volley [ˈvɑli] *n, pl* **-leys 1** : volée *f* (de missiles), salve *f* (d'applaudissements) **2** : bordée *f* <a volley of insults : une bordée d'injures> **3** : volée *f* (aux sports)
volleyball [ˈvɑliˌbɔl] *n* : volley *m*, volley-ball *m*
volt [ˈvoːlt] *n* : volt *m*
voltage [ˈvoːltɪdʒ] *n* : voltage *m*, tension *f*
voluble [ˈvɑljəbəl] *adj* : volubile
volume [ˈvɑljəm, -juːm] *n* **1** BOOK : volume *m* **2** CAPACITY : capacité *f*, volume *m* (cubique) **3** AMOUNT : volume *m*, quantité *f* <a high volume of traffic : beaucoup de circulation> **4** LOUDNESS : volume *m* **5 to speak volumes** : être révélateur, en dire long
voluminous [vəˈluːmənəs] *adj* : volumineux
voluntarily [ˌvɑlənˈtɛrəli] *adv* : volontairement
voluntary [ˈvɑlənˌtɛri] *adj* : volontaire
volunteer[1] [ˌvɑlənˈtɪr] *vt* : offrir, donner volontairement — *vi* : se porter volontaire
volunteer[2] *adj* : bénévole
volunteer[3] *n* : volontaire *mf*, bénévole *mf*
voluptuous [vəˈlʌpṭʃuəs] *adj* : voluptueux — **voluptuously** *adv*
voluptuousness [vəˈlʌpṭʃuəsnəs] *n* : volupté *f*
vomit[1] [ˈvɑmət] *v* : vomir
vomit[2] *n* : vomi *m*
voodoo [ˈvuːˌduː] *n, pl* **voodoos** : vaudou *m*
voracious [vɔˈreɪʃəs, və-] *adj* : vorace, avide
voraciously [vɔˈreɪʃəsli, və-] *adv* : voracement, avec voracité
voracity [vɔˈræsəṭi, və-] *n* : voracité *f*
vortex [ˈvɔrˌṭɛks] *n, pl* **vortices** [ˈvɔrṭəˌsiːz] : tourbillon *m*
vote[1] [ˈvoːt] *v* **voted; voting** : voter
vote[2] *n* **1** : vote *m* **2** FRANCHISE : vote *m*, droit *m* de vote
voter [ˈvoːṭər] *n* : électeur *m*, -trice *f*
voting [ˈvoːṭɪŋ] *n* : scrutin *m*, vote *m*
vouch [ˈvaʊtʃ] *vi* **to vouch for** : répondre de, se porter garant de
voucher [ˈvaʊtʃər] *n* **1** RECEIPT : récépissé *m*, reçu *m* **2** *or* **credit voucher** : bon *m*
vouchsafe [vaʊtʃˈseɪf] *vt* **-safed; -safing 1** GRANT : octroyer, accorder **2 to vouchsafe to do** : s'engager à faire
vow[1] [vaʊ] *vt* : jurer, promettre
vow[2] *n* **1** : serment *m*, promesse *f* **2** : vœu *m* (en religion)
vowel [ˈvaʊəl] *n* : voyelle *f*
voyage[1] [ˈvɔɪɪdʒ] *vi* **-aged; -aging** : voyager
voyage[2] *n* : voyage *m*
voyager [ˈvɔɪɪdʒər] *n* : voyageur *m*, -geuse *f*
vulcanize [ˈvʌlkəˌnaɪz] *vt* **-nized; -nizing** : vulcaniser
vulgar [ˈvʌlgər] *adj* **1** COMMON, PLEBEIAN : vulgaire, commun **2** COARSE, CRUDE : vulgaire, grossier
vulgarity [ˌvʌlˈgærəṭi] *n, pl* **-ties** : vulgarité *f*
vulgarly [ˈvʌlgərli] *adv* : vulgairement
vulnerability [ˌvʌlnərəˈbɪləṭi] *n* : vulnérabilité *f*
vulnerable [ˈvʌlnərəbəl] *adj* : vulnérable
vulture [ˈvʌlṭʃər] *n* : vautour *m*
vulva [ˈvʌlvə] *n, pl* **-vae** [-ˌviː, -ˌvaɪ] : vulve *f*
vying → vie

W

w [ˈdʌbəljuː] *n, pl* **w's** *or* **ws** [-juːz] : w *m,* vingt-troisième lettre de l'alphabet

wad¹ [ˈwɑd] *vt* **wadded; wadding 1** : bourrer (un fusil) **2** *or* **to wad up** : faire un tampon de

wad² *n* **1** : tampon *m* (d'ouate, etc.), bourre *f* de fusil 2 BUNDLE : liasse *f,* paquet *m* <wad of money : liasse de billets>

waddle¹ [ˈwɑdəl] *vi* **-dled; -dling** : se dandiner

waddle² *n* : dandinement *m*

wade [ˈweɪd] *vi* **waded; wading 1** : patauger, avancer dans l'eau **2 to wade through** : accomplir péniblement <to wade through an assignment : faire un travail avec beaucoup de mal>

wading bird *n* : échassier *m*

wafer [ˈweɪfər] *n* : gaufrette *f*

waffle [ˈwɑfəl] *n* : gaufre *f*

waffle iron *n* : gaufrier *m*

waft [ˈwɑft, ˈwæft] *vi* : flotter <to waft through the air : flotter dans l'air> — *vt* CARRY : apporter, transporter

wag¹ [ˈwæg] *v* **wagged; wagging** *vt* : agiter, remuer (la queue) — *vi* : frétiller, remuer

wag² *n* **1** : frétillement *m* (de la queue) **2** JOKER, WIT : farceur *m,* -ceuse *f*

wage¹ [ˈweɪdʒ] *vt* **waged; waging** : faire (la guerre), mener (une campagne)

wage² *n* **1** PAY : salaire *m,* paie *f* <hourly wage : salaire horaire> **2 wages** *ns & pl* REWARD : récompense *f* <the wages of sin is death : la mort est le prix du péché>

wager¹ [ˈweɪdʒər] *v* : parier

wager² *n* : pari *m*

waggish [ˈwægɪʃ] *adj* : facétieux, humoristique

waggle [ˈwæɡəl] *vt* **-gled; -gling** WAG : remuer, agiter

wagon [ˈwæɡən] *n* **1** : chariot *m* (tiré par des chevaux) **2** CART : chariot *m* **3 → station wagon**

waif [ˈweɪf] *n* : enfant *m* abandonné, enfant *f* abandonnée

wail¹ [ˈweɪl] *vi* **1** : gémir, pleurer (se dit d'une personne) **2** : gémir (se dit du vent), hurler (se dit d'une sirène)

wail² *n* : gémissement *m*

wainscot [ˈweɪnskət, -ˌskɑt, -ˌskoːt] *or* **wainscoting** [-skəɾɪŋ, -ˌskɑ-, -ˌskoː-] *n* : lambris *m,* boiseries *fpl*

waist [ˈweɪst] *n* : taille *f*

waistline [ˈweɪstˌlaɪn] *n* : taille *f*

wait¹ [ˈweɪt] *vt* **1** AWAIT : attendre <wait your turn : attendez votre tour> **2** DELAY : retarder (le dîner, etc.) <don't wait lunch for me : ne m'attendez pas pour déjeuner> **3** SERVE : servir <to wait tables : servir à table> — *vi* : attendre

wait² *n* **1** : attente *f* **2 to lie in wait for** : guetter, attendre

waiter [ˈweɪɾər] *n* : serveur *m,* garçon *m*

waiting room *n* : salle *f* d'attente

waitress [ˈweɪtrəs] *n* : serveuse *f*

waive [ˈweɪv] *vt* **waived; waiving** : renoncer à (un droit), déroger à (une règle), supprimer (une condition)

waiver [ˈweɪvər] *n* : renonciation *f,* abandon *m*

wake¹ [ˈweɪk] *v* **woke** [ˈwoːk]; **woken** [ˈwoːkən] *or* **waked; waking** *vi or* **to wake up** : se réveiller — *vt* : réveiller <to wake s.o. up : réveiller qqn>

wake² *n* **1** WATCH : veillée *f* funèbre **2** : sillage *m* (laissé par un bateau) **3 in the wake of** : à la suite de

wakeful [ˈweɪkfəl] *adj* : éveillé, alerte

waken [ˈweɪkən] *vi* AWAKE : se réveiller

walk¹ [ˈwɔk] *vi* **1** : marcher <to walk back and forth : marcher de long en large> **2** : aller à pied, se promener <he walks to school : il se rend à l'école à pied> — *vt* **1** TRAVERSE : faire à pied, parcourir <we walked the streets : nous parcourions les rues> **2** ACCOMPANY : raccompagner <she walked him home : elle l'a raccompagné chez lui> **3** : faire marcher, promener <to walk the dog : promener le chien>

walk² *n* **1** : marche *f,* promenade *f* <to go for a short walk : se promener quelques minutes> **2** PATH : chemin *m,* allée *f,* promenade *f* **3** GAIT : démarche *f* (d'une personne), pas *m* (d'un animal) **4 from all walks of life** : de tous les milieux

walker [ˈwɔkər] *n* **1** : marcheur *m,* -cheuse *f;* promeneur *m,* -neuse *f* **2** *or* **baby walker** : trotteur *m*

walking stick *n* : canne *f*

walkout [ˈwɔkˌaʊt] *n* STRIKE : grève *f*

walk out *vi* **1** STRIKE : se mettre en grève **2** LEAVE : partir, sortir **3 to walk out on** ABANDON : quitter, abandonner

wall¹ [ˈwɔl] *vt* **1 to wall in** : entourer d'un mur **2 to wall off** : séparer par un mur **3 to wall up** : murer

wall² *n* **1** : mur *m* (d'un édifice, d'une pièce, etc.) <a wall of silence : un mur de silence> **2** SIDE : paroi *f* <the wall of a container : la paroi d'un récipient> <heart walls : parois du cœur> **3** : paroi *f,* face *f* (d'une montagne)

wallaby [ˈwɑləbi] *n, pl* **-bies** : wallaby *m*

wallet [ˈwɑlət] *n* : portefeuille *m*

wallflower [ˈwɔlˌflaʊər] *n* **1** : giroflée *f* **2 to be a wallflower** : faire tapisserie

Walloon¹ [wɑˈluːn] *adj* : wallon

Walloon² *n* **1** : Wallon *m,* -lonne *f* **2** : wallon *m* (langue)

wallop[1] ['wɑləp] *vt* **1** BEAT : donner une raclée à **2** DEFEAT : battre à plates coutures **3** HIT : taper sur (une balle, etc.)

wallop[2] *n* BLOW : coup *m* fort, raclée *f*

wallow[1] ['wɑˌlo:] *vi* **1** : se vautrer, s'étaler (se dit d'un animal) **2** INDULGE : se vautrer <to wallow in self-pity : s'apitoyer sur son sort>

wallow[2] *n* : bauge *f* (pour des animaux)

wallpaper[1] ['wɔlˌpeɪpər] *vt* : tapisser

wallpaper[2] *n* : tapisserie *f*

walnut ['wɔlˌnʌt] *n* : noyer *m* (arbre et bois), noix *f* (fruit)

walrus ['wɔlrəs, 'wɑl-] *n, pl* **-rus** *or* **-ruses** : morse *m*

waltz[1] ['wɔlts] *vi* **1** : valser **2 to waltz in** : entrer d'un pas désinvolte

waltz[2] *n* : valse *f*

wampum ['wɑmpəm] *n* : wampum *m*

wan ['wɑn] *adj* **wanner; wannest 1** PALLID : blême, pâle **2** DIM, FAINT : faible <a wan smile : un faible sourire>

wand ['wɑnd] *n* : baguette *f* (magique)

wander ['wɑndər] *vi* **1** RAMBLE : se promener, se balader **2** STRAY : errer, s'égarer **3** : vagabonder <his thoughts were wandering : ses pensées vagabondaient>

wanderer ['wɑndərər] *n* : vagabond *m*, -bonde *f*

wanderlust ['wɑndərˌlʌst] *n* : envie *f* de voyager

wane[1] ['weɪn] *vi* **waned; waning 1** : décroître (se dit de la lune) **2** DECLINE : décliner, diminuer

wane[2] *n* : déclin *m*, décroissance *f* <to be on the wane : décliner>

wangle ['wæŋgəl] *vt* **-gled; -gling** FINAGLE : se débrouiller pour obtenir

wanly ['wɑnli] *adv* : faiblement

want[1] ['wɑnt, 'wɔnt] *vt* **1** DESIRE : vouloir, désirer **2** NEED, REQUIRE : avoir besoin de **3** REQUEST : demander <you're wanted on the phone : on vous demande au téléphone> **4** SEEK : rechercher <to be wanted for murder : être recherché pour meurtre> — *vi* **1 to want for** LACK : manquer de **2 to want in** : vouloir entrer

want[2] *n* **1** LACK : manque *m* **2** DESIRE, NEED : besoin *m* **3** POVERTY : misère *f*, indigence *f* <to be in want : être dans le besoin>

wanting[1] ['wɑntɪŋ, 'wɔnt-] *adj* **1** ABSENT : absent **2 to be wanting in** : manquer de

wanting[2] *prep* **1** LESS : moins <a month wanting two days : un mois moins deux jours> **2** WITHOUT : sans <a book wanting a cover : un livre sans couverture>

wanton ['wɑntən, 'wɔn-] *adj* **1** PLAYFUL : capricieux <a wanton breeze : une brise capricieuse> **2** LEWD : impudique, licencieux **3** MALICIOUS : cruel, injustifié

wapiti ['wɑpəţi] *n, pl* **-ti** *or* **-tis** : wapiti *m*

war[1] ['wɔr] *vi* **warred; warring** : faire la guerre

war[2] *n* : guerre *f* <to go to war with : entrer en guerre avec>

warble[1] ['wɔrbəl] *vi* **-bled; -bling** : gazouiller

warble[2] *n* : gazouillis *m*

warbler ['wɔrblər] *n* : fauvette *f*

ward[1] ['wɔrd] *vt or* **to ward off** : parer, éviter

ward[2] *n* **1** *or* **ward of the court** : pupille *f* **2** : salle *f* (d'un hôpital), quartier *m* (d'une prison) **3** : circonscription *f* électorale (d'une ville)

warden ['wɔrdən] *n* **1** KEEPER : gardien *m*, -dienne *f* (de parcs, etc.) **2** *or* **prison warden** : directeur *m*, -trice *f* de prison

wardrobe ['wɔrdˌro:b] *n* **1** CLOSET : armoire *f*, penderie *f*, garde-robe *mf* *Can* **2** CLOTHES : garde-robe *f*

ware ['wær] *n* **1** POTTERY : poterie *f* **2 wares** *npl* GOODS : marchandises *fpl*

warehouse ['wærˌhaʊs] *n* : entrepôt *m*, magasin *m*

warfare ['wɔrˌfær] *n* **1** WAR : guerre *f* **2** STRUGGLE : lutte *f*, guerre *f* <class warfare : lutte de classes>

warhead ['wɔrˌhed] *n* : ogive *f*

warily ['wærəli] *adv* : avec prudence, avec précaution

wariness ['wærinəs] *n* : circonspection *f*, prudence *f*

warlike ['wɔrˌlaɪk] *adj* : guerrier, belliqueux

warm[1] ['wɔrm] *vi* **1** : chauffer **2 to warm to** : se montrer intéressé envers, être sympathique envers — *vt* **1** HEAT : chauffer, réchauffer **2 to warm oneself** : se réchauffer

warm[2] *adj* **1** LUKEWARM : tiède <warm milk : lait tiède> **2** : chaud <warm clothing : vêtements chauds> <it's warm today : il fait chaud aujourd'hui> **3** CORDIAL, ENTHUSIASTIC : chaleureux, amical <a warm welcome : un accueil chaleureux> **4** : chaud (se dit des couleurs) **5** FRESH : récent <a warm trail : une piste récente> **6** (*used in guessing games*) <you're getting warm! : tu chauffes!>

warm-blooded ['wɔrmˈblʌdəd] *adj* : à sang chaud

warmhearted ['wɔrmˈhɑrţəd] *adj* : chaleureux, affectueux

warmly ['wɔrmli] *adv* **1** : chaudement <warmly dressed : habillé chaudement> **2** ENTHUSIASTICALLY : chaleureusement, amicalement

warmonger ['wɔrˌmɑŋgər, -ˌmʌŋ-] *n* : belliciste *mf*

warmth ['wɔrmpθ] *n* **1** : chaleur *f* <the warmth of the sun : la chaleur du

soleil> **2** ENTHUSIASM : chaleur *f*, enthousiasme *m*, cordialité *f*

warm–up [ˈwɔrmˌʌp] *n* : échauffement *m*

warm up *vi* : s'échauffer (aux sports) — *vt* **1** : réchauffer <to warm up the leftovers : réchauffer les restes> **2** : faire chauffer (le moteur)

warn [ˈwɔrn] *vt* **1** CAUTION : avertir, prévenir **2** INFORM : aviser

warning[1] [ˈwɔrnɪŋ] *adj* : d'alarme, d'alerte <a warning bell : une sonnette d'alarme>

warning[2] *n* **1** CAUTION : avertissement *m* <without warning : sans prévenir> **2** NOTICE : avis *m* <gale warning : avis de vents violents>

warp[1] [ˈwɔrp] *vt* **1** : voiler, gauchir (le bois, etc.) **2** DISTORT, PERVERT : pervertir, fausser — *vi* : gauchir, se voiler, coffrer *Can* (se dit du bois)

warp[2] *n* **1** : chaîne *f* (en tissage) **2** DISTORTION : déformation *f*, gauchissement *m* (du bois, du métal)

warrant[1] [ˈwɔrənt] *vt* **1** : être certain que, parier <I warrant he'll be here by noon : je suis certain qu'il sera ici à midi> **2** GUARANTEE : garantir **3** JUSTIFY, MERIT : mériter

warrant[2] *n* **1** JUSTIFICATION : justification *f*, droit *m* **2** AUTHORIZATION : mandat *m* <search warrant : mandat de perquisition>

warrant officer *n* : adjudant *m* (dans les forces armées)

warranty [ˈwɔrənti, ˌwɔrənˈtiː] *n, pl* **-ties** : garantie *f*

warren [ˈwɔrən] *n* : garenne *f*

warrior [ˈwɔriər] *n* : guerrier *m*, -rière *f*

warship [ˈwɔrˌʃɪp] *n* : navire *m* de guerre

wart [ˈwɔrt] *n* : verrue *f*

wartime [ˈwɔrˌtaɪm] *n* : temps *m* de guerre

wary [ˈwæri] *adj* **warier; -est** : prudent, circonspect <to be wary of : se méfier de>

was → be

wash[1] [ˈwɔʃ, ˈwɑʃ] *vt* **1** CLEAN : laver <to wash clothes : laver des vêtements> <to wash one's hands : se laver les mains> **2** LAP : baigner <waves washing the shore : des vagues qui baignent la côte> **3** CARRY, DRAG : entraîner, emporter <to be washed out to sea : être entraîné par la mer> **4 to wash away** : emporter (un pont, etc.) — *vi* **1** : se laver (se dit d'une personne ou des vêtements) **2** WORK : marcher <her story just doesn't wash : son histoire ne marche pas, son histoire ne tient pas debout>

wash[2] *n* **1** : lavage *m*, lessive *f* <the clothes are in the wash : le linge est au lavage> <to do the wash : faire la lessive> **2** CLEANING, WASHING : lavage *m*, nettoyage *m* <to give sth a wash : laver qqch> **3** : remous *m* (d'un bateau)

washable [ˈwɔʃəbəl, ˈwɑʃ-] *adj* : lavable

washboard [ˈwɔʃˌbɔrd, ˈwɑʃ-] *n* : planche *f* à laver

washbowl [ˈwɔʃˌboːl, ˈwɑʃ-] *n* : cuvette *f*, bassine *f*

washcloth [ˈwɔʃˌklɔθ, ˈwɑʃ-] *n* : gant *m* de toilette, débarbouillette *f Can*

washed–out [ˈwɔʃtˈaʊt, ˈwɑʃt-] *adj* **1** FADED : délavé, décoloré **2** EXHAUSTED : épuisé

washed–up [ˈwɔʃtˈʌp, ˈwɑʃt-] *adj* : fichu *fam*, ruiné

washer [ˈwɔʃər, ˈwɑ-] *n* **1** : rondelle *f*, joint *m* (en technologie) **2 → washing machine**

washing [ˈwɔʃɪŋ, ˈwɑ-] *n* WASH : lavage *m*, lessive *f*

washing machine *n* : machine *f* à laver, laveuse *f Can*

washout [ˈwɔʃˌaʊt, ˈwɑʃ-] *n* **1** : érosion *f* (dû à la pluie) **2** FAILURE : fiasco *m*, échec *m*

washroom [ˈwɔʃˌruːm, ˈwɑʃ-, -ˌrʊm] *n* : toilettes *fpl*

wasn't [ˈwʌzənt] (*contraction of* **was not**) **→ be**

wasp [ˈwɑsp] *n* : guêpe *f*

waspish [ˈwɑspɪʃ] *adj* : irritable, qui a mauvais caractère

waste[1] *v* **wasted; wasting** [ˈweɪst] *vt* **1** DEVASTATE : dévaster, ravager **2** SQUANDER : gaspiller (de l'argent) <to waste one's time : perdre son temps> — *vi or* **to waste away** : dépérir

waste[2] *adj* **1** DESOLATE : désert, désolé **2** DISCARDED : de rebut, usé **3** *or* **waste material** : déchets *mpl*

waste[3] *n* **1 → wasteland 2** MISUSE : perte *f*, gaspillage *m* <a waste of time : une perte de temps> **3** REFUSE : déchets *mpl*, ordures *fpl* <nuclear waste : déchets nucléaires> <household wastes : ordures ménagères> **4** EXCREMENT : excrément *m*

wastebasket [ˈweɪstˌbæskət] *n* : corbeille *f* à papier

wasteful [ˈweɪstfəl] *adj* : gaspilleur, dépensier

wastefulness [ˈweɪstfəlnəs] *n* : gaspillage *m*

wasteland [ˈweɪstˌlænd, -lənd] *n* : terrain *m* vague, désert *m*

watch[1] [ˈwɑtʃ] *vi* **1** *or* **to keep watch** : veiller **2** LOOK : regarder **3 to watch for** AWAIT : guetter, attendre **4 to watch out** : faire attention — *vt* **1** OBSERVE : regarder, surveiller **2** *or* **to watch over** : veiller sur, garder **3** : faire attention à <watch what you are doing! : faites attention à ce que vous faites!>

watch[2] *n* **1** SURVEILLANCE : surveillance *f* <to keep a close watch on : surveiller de près> **2** LOOKOUT, SEN-

TRY : sentinelle *m*, homme *m* de quart (sur un navire) **3** TIMEPIECE : montre *f*

watchdog ['wɑtʃˌdɔg] *n* : chien *m* de garde, chienne *f* de garde

watcher ['wɑtʃər] *n* : spectateur *m*, -trice *f*; observateur *m*, -trice *f*

watchful ['wɑtʃfəl] *adj* : attentif, vigilant

watchfully ['wɑtʃfəli] *adv* : attentivement, de façon vigilante

watchman ['wɑtʃmən] *n, pl* **-men** [-mən, -ˌmɛn] : gardien *m*

watchword ['wɑtʃˌwərd] *n* **1** PASSWORD : mot *m* de passe **2** SLOGAN : mot *m* d'ordre, slogan *m*

water[1] ['wɔṭər, 'wɑ-] *vt* **1** : arroser (un jardin, etc.) **2** : donner à boire à (des animaux) **3** *or* **to water down** DILUTE : couper (d'eau) — *vi* **1** : larmoyer (se dit des yeux) **2** : avoir l'eau à la bouche <to make one's mouth water : faire venir l'eau à la bouche>

water[2] *n* **1** : eau *f* <fresh water : eau douce> **2 waters** *npl* : eaux *fpl* <in Canadian waters : dans les eaux territoriales canadiennes>

water buffalo *n* : buffle *m*

watercolor ['wɔṭərˌkʌlər, 'wɑ-] *n* **1** : couleur *f* pour aquarelle **2** *or* **watercolor painting** : aquarelle *f*

watercourse ['wɔṭərˌkɔrs, 'wɑ-] *n* : cours *m* d'eau

watercress ['wɔṭərˌkrɛs, 'wɑ-] *n* : cresson *m*

waterfall ['wɔṭərˌfɔl, 'wɑ-] *n* : chute *f* (d'eau), cascade *f*

waterfowl ['wɔṭərˌfaʊl, 'wɑ-] *ns & pl* **1** : oiseau *m* aquatique **2 waterfowl** *npl* : gibier *m* d'eau

waterfront ['wɔṭərˌfrʌnt, 'wɑ-] *n* : front *m* de mer

water lily *n* : nénuphar *m*

waterlogged ['wɔṭərˌlɔgd, -ˌlɑgd] *adj* : imprégné d'eau, détrempé (se dit de la terre)

watermark ['wɔṭərˌmɑrk, 'wɑ-] *n* **1** : laisse *f* de haute mer (en navigation) **2** : filigrane *m* (du papier)

watermelon ['wɔṭərˌmɛlən, 'wɑ-] *n* : pastèque *f*, melon *m* d'eau

water moccasin → **moccasin**

waterpower ['wɔṭərˌpaʊər, 'wɑ-] *n* : énergie *f* hydraulique

waterproof[1] ['wɔṭərˌpruːf, 'wɑ-] *vt* : imperméabiliser

waterproof[2] *adj* : imperméable

watershed ['wɔṭərˌʃɛd, 'wɑ-] *n* : ligne *m* de partage des eaux

water–ski ['wɔṭərˌskiː, 'wɑ-] *vi* : faire du ski nautique

water ski *n* : ski *m* nautique

waterskiing ['wɔṭərˌskiːɪŋ, 'wɑ-] *n* : ski *m* nautique

waterspout ['wɔṭərˌspaʊt, 'wɑ-] *n* **1** : gouttière *f*, tuyau *m* de descente **2** : trombe *f* (en météorologie)

watertight ['wɔṭərˌtaɪt, 'wɑ-] *adj* **1** : étanche <a watertight joint : un raccord étanche> **2** : inattaquable, incontestable <a watertight argument : un argument inattaquable>

waterway ['wɔṭərˌweɪ, 'wɑ-] *n* : cours *m* d'eau navigable

waterworks ['wɔṭərˌwərks, 'wɑ-] *npl* : système *m* hydraulique

watery ['wɔṭəri, 'wɑ-] *adj* **1** : larmoyant (se dit des yeux) **2** THIN, WEAK : faible, liquide <watery soup : soupe trop liquide> **3** SOGGY : détrempé

watt ['wɑt] *n* : watt *m*

wattage ['wɑṭɪdʒ] *n* : consommation *f* en watts

wattle ['wɑṭəl] *n* : caroncule *f* (d'un oiseau)

wave[1] ['weɪv] *v* **waved; waving** *vi* **1** FLUTTER : flotter, ondoyer **2** : faire un signe de la main <to wave goodbye : faire au revoir de la main> **3** UNDULATE : onduler — *vt* **1** SHAKE : agiter **2** BRANDISH : brandir **3** CURL : onduler (ses cheveux) **4** SIGNAL : faire signe à <I waved down the passing car : j'ai fait signe à la voiture d'arrêter>

wave[2] *n* **1** : vague *f* (d'eau) **2** CURL : ondulation *f* (des cheveux) **3** GREETING : geste *m* de la main **4** FLOW, GUSH : vague *f*, déferlement *m* <a wave of anger : une vague de colère> **5** : onde *f* (en physique)

wavelength ['weɪvˌlɛŋkθ] *n* : longueur *f* d'onde (en physique)

waver ['weɪvər] *vi* **1** VACILLATE : vaciller, hésiter **2** FLICKER : vaciller **3** FALTER : chanceler, trembloter (se dit de la voix)

wavy ['weɪvi] *adj* **wavier; -est** : ondulé

wax[1] ['wæks] *vt* : cirer (le plancher, etc.), farter (des skis) — *vi* **1** : croître (se dit de la lune) **2** BECOME : devenir, se montrer <to wax indignant : se montrer indigné>

wax[2] *n* **1** : cire *f* (pour les planchers, les meubles, etc.) **2** → **beeswax 3** → **earwax**

waxen ['wæksən] *adj* : cireux

waxy ['wæksi] *adj* **waxier; -est** : cireux

way ['weɪ] *n* **1** PATH, STREET : chemin *m* **2** ROUTE : chemin *m*, passage *m* <the way back : le chemin du retour> <it's the only way out : c'est la seule façon de s'en sortir> **3** MEANS, RESPECT : façon *f*, manière *f* <a new way of thinking : une nouvelle façon de penser> <in no way does he resemble his mother : il ne ressemble aucunement à sa mère> **4** FACILITY : talent *m*, habileté *f* <he has a way with children : il s'y prend bien avec les enfants> **5** MANNER, STYLE : façon *f* de vivre, manières *fpl* <it's just her way : c'est sa façon de vivre habituelle> **6** CONDITION, STATE : état *m*, situation *f* <it's the way

things are : c'est ainsi> **7** DISTANCE : distance *f* <we walked a long way : nous avons marché longtemps> **8** DIRECTION : direction *f*, sens *m* <he was looking my way : il regardait dans ma direction> <she's coming this way : elle vient par ici> **9 by the way** : à propos **10 by way of** VIA : par, via **11 in a way** : dans un certain sens **12 in the way of** : en fait de <he had little in the way of help : il n'était pas choyé en fait d'aide> **13 out of the way** : éloigné, isolé **14** → **under way**

wayfarer ['weɪˌfærər] *n* : voyageur *m*, -geuse *f*

waylay ['weɪˌleɪ] *vt* **-laid** [-ˌleɪd]; **-laying** : attaquer, attirer dans une embuscade

wayside ['weɪˌsaɪd] *n* **1** : bord *m* de la route **2 to fall by the wayside** : tomber à l'eau, tomber en désuétude

wayward ['weɪwərd] *adj* **1** UNRULY : rebelle, capricieux **2** UNPREDICTABLE : imprévisible **3** UNTOWARD : malencontreux

we ['wi:] *pron* : nous <we're ready : nous sommes prêts> <as we say in Canada : comme on dit au Canada>

weak ['wi:k] *adj* **1** FEEBLE : faible, fragile (se dit des personnes) **2** : peu solide, fragile (se dit des structures, etc.) **3** UNCONVINCING : peu convaincant, faible <a weak argument : un argument réfutable> **4** DEFICIENT : faible **5** DILUTED : faible, léger, dilué **6** FAINT : faible (se dit des couleurs, des sons, de la lumière, etc.)

weaken ['wi:kən] *vt* : affaiblir — *vi* : s'affaiblir, faiblir

weakling ['wi:klɪŋ] *n* : gringalet *m*

weakly ['wi:kli] *adv* : faiblement

weakness ['wi:knəs] *n* **1** : faiblesse *f*, point *m* faible <in a moment of weakness : dans un moment de faiblesse> **2** FAULT : défaut *m* **3** PARTIALITY : faible *m*, penchant *m* <a weakness for luxury : un faible pour le luxe>

wealth ['welθ] *n* **1** RICHES : richesse *f*, fortune *f* **2** PROFUSION : abondance *f*, profusion *f*

wealthy ['welθi] *adj* **wealthier; -est** : riche

wean ['wi:n] *vt* **1** : sevrer (un bébé) **2 to wean s.o. away from** : détacher qqn de, détourner qqn de

weapon ['wepən] *n* : arme *f*

wear[1] ['wær] *v* **wore** ['wor]; **worn** ['worn]; **wearing** *vt* **1** : porter (des vêtements, des lunettes, etc.) **2** EXHIBIT, PRESENT : arborer <to wear a happy smile : arborer un large sourire> **3 to wear away** : ronger, éroder (des roches, etc.) **4** *or* **to wear out** : user **5** EXHAUST : épuiser — *vi* **1** LAST : durer **2** *or* **to wear out** : s'user, se détériorer **3 to wear off** : diminuer

wear[2] *n* **1** USE : port *m* <for everyday wear : de tous les jours> **2** CLOTHES : vêtements *mpl* **3** *or* **wear and tear** : usure *f*

wearable ['wærəbəl] *adj* : mettable, portable

wearily ['wɪrəli] *adv* : d'un air las

weariness ['wɪrinəs] *n* : lassitude *f*

wearisome ['wɪrisəm] *adj* : fastidieux, fatigant

weary[1] ['wɪri] *v* **-ried; -rying** *vt* : lasser, fatiguer — *vi* : se lasser

weary[2] *adj* **wearier; -est** : fatigué, las

weasel ['wi:zəl] *n* : belette *f*

weather[1] ['weðər] *vt* **1** : exposer (le bois, etc.) aux intempéries **2** ENDURE : se tirer de, surmonter — *vi* : s'éroder (se dit des roches)

weather[2] *n* : temps *m*

weather-beaten ['weðərˌbi:tən] *adj* **1** : battu, usé (par les intempéries) **2** : hâlé <a weather-beaten face : un visage hâlé>

weatherman ['weðərˌmæn] *n, pl* **-men** : météorologiste *mf*

weatherproof[1] ['weðərˌpru:f] *vt* : imperméabiliser

weatherproof[2] *adj* : imperméable, étanche

weather vane → **vane**

weave[1] ['wi:v] *v* **wove** ['wo:v] *or* **weaved; woven** ['wo:vən] *or* **weaved; weaving** *vt* **1** : tisser **2** INTERLACE : entrelacer, tresser **3 to weave a tale** : inventer une histoire **4 to weave one's way through** : se faufiler à travers — *vi* **1** : tisser **2** WIND : serpenter

weave[2] *n* : tissage *m*

weaver ['wi:vər] *n* : tisserand *m*, -rande *f*

web ['web] *n* **1** COBWEB : toile *f* (d'araignée) **2** : palmure *f* (d'un oiseau) **3** ENTANGLEMENT : tissu *m*, réseau *m* <a web of lies : un tissu de mensonges> **4** NETWORK : réseau *m* **5 Web** → **World Wide Web**

webbed ['webd] *adj* : palmé <webbed feet : pattes palmées>

webmaster ['webˌmæstər] *n* : webmaster *m*, webmestre *m*

Web site *n* : site *m* Web

wed ['wed] *vt* **wedded; wedding 1** MARRY : se marier à, épouser **2** UNITE : allier

we'd ['wi:d] (*contraction of* **we had, we should,** *or* **we would**) → **have, should, would**

wedding ['wedɪŋ] *n* : mariage *m*, noces *fpl*

wedge[1] ['wedʒ] *vt* **wedged; wedging 1** : caler, fixer (avec une cale) **2** CRAM : enfoncer, coincer

wedge[2] *n* **1** : cale *f* (pour tenir ouverte une porte, etc.), coin *m* (pour enfoncer dans une bûche) **2** PIECE : morceau *m*, part *m* (de gâteau, etc.)

wedlock ['wedˌlɑk] *n* : mariage *m*

Wednesday ['wenzˌdeɪ, -di] *n* : mercredi *m*

wee [ˈwiː] *adj* : tout petit <in the wee hours of the morning : aux petites heures du matin>
weed¹ [ˈwiːd] *vi* : désherber, enlever les mauvaises herbes — *vt* **1** : désherber (un jardin) **2 to weed out** : se débarrasser de, éliminer
weed² *n* : mauvaise herbe *f*
weedy [ˈwiːdi] *adj* **weedier; -est 1** : couvert de mauvaises herbes **2** LANKY, SCRAWNY : dégingandé, décharné
week [ˈwiːk] *n* : semaine *f*
weekday [ˈwiːkˌdeɪ] *n* : jour *m* de semaine
weekend [ˈwiːkˌend] *n* : fin *f* de semaine, week-end *m*
weekly¹ [ˈwiːkli] *adv* : à la semaine, chaque semaine
weekly² *adj* : hebdomadaire
weekly³ *n, pl* **-lies** : hebdomadaire *m*, journal *m* hebdomadaire
weep [ˈwiːp] *vi* **wept** [ˈwɛpt]; **weeping** : pleurer
weeping willow *n* : saule *m* pleureur
weepy [ˈwiːpi] *adj* **weepier; -est** : larmoyant, au bord des larmes
weevil [ˈwiːvəl] *n* : charançon *m*
weft [ˈwɛft] *n* : trame *f*
weigh [ˈweɪ] *vt* **1** : peser **2** CONSIDER : peser, considérer **3 to weigh anchor** : lever l'ancre **4 to weigh down** : surcharger (un véhicule, etc.), accabler (une personne) — *vi* **1** : peser <she weighs 100 pounds : elle pèse 100 livres> **2** COUNT : compter, avoir de l'importance <to weigh against : jouer contre> **3 to weigh on s.o.'s mind** : préoccuper qqn
weight¹ [ˈweɪt] *vt* **1** LOAD : charger, lester **2** *or* **to weight down** BURDEN : alourdir, charger
weight² *n* **1** HEAVINESS : poids *m* <to lose weight : perdre du poids> <to sell by weight : vendre au poids> **2** : poids *m* <weights and measures : poids et mesures> **3** : poids *m* <to lift weights : soulever des poids> **4** BURDEN : poids *m*, pesanteur *f* <it's a weight on my mind : cela me pèse beaucoup> **5** IMPORTANCE : influence *f*, importance *f* <to throw one's weight around : essayer de faire l'important>
weightlessness [ˈweɪtləsnəs] *n* : apesanteur *f*
weighty [ˈweɪti] *adj* **weightier; -est 1** HEAVY : pesant, lourd **2** POWERFUL : important, de poids
weird [ˈwɪrd] *adj* **1** UNEARTHLY : surnaturel, mystérieux **2** STRANGE : étrange, bizarre
weirdly [ˈwɪrdli] *adv* **1** MYSTERIOUSLY : mystérieusement **2** STRANGELY : étrangement, bizarrement
welcome¹ [ˈwɛlkəm] *vt* **-comed; -coming 1** GREET : accueillir, souhaiter la bienvenue à **2** ACCEPT : accepter avec plaisir, être heureux de recevoir
welcome² *adj* **1** : bienvenu <they are always welcome : ils sont toujours les bienvenus> <you're welcome to come and go : vous pouvez aller et venir à votre guise> **2** PLEASING : bienvenu, agréable <a welcome relief : un vrai soulagement> **3 you're welcome** : de rien, je vous en prie
welcome³ *n* : accueil *m*
weld¹ [ˈwɛld] *vi* : souder — *vt* **1** : souder **2** UNITE : unir
weld² *n* : soudure *f*
welder [ˈwɛldər] *n* : soudeur *m*, -deuse *f*
welfare [ˈwɛlˌfær] *n* **1** WELL-BEING : bien-être *m* **2** AID : aide *f* sociale, assistance *f* publique
well¹ [ˈwɛl] *vi or* **to well up** : monter
well² *adv* **better** [ˈbɛṭər]; **best** [ˈbɛst] **1** : bien <he did well in his classes : il réussissait bien dans ses cours> **2** HIGHLY : bien <to speak well of s.o. : dire du bien de qqn> <to think well of : avoir de l'estime pour> **3** COMPLETELY, FULLY : tout à fait <to be well aware of : être tout à fait conscient de> <it's well worth the price : cela vaut bien le prix> **4** INTIMATELY : bien, intimement <I know him well : je le connais bien> **5** CONSIDERABLY, FAR : considérablement, bien <well over one million dollars : bien au-delà d'un million de dollars> **6** DEFINITELY, EXACTLY : clairement, bien <she remembered it well : elle s'en souvenait très clairement> **7 as well** ALSO : aussi **8 → as well as 9 it may well be that** : il se pourrait bien que
well³ *adj* **1** PLEASING, SATISFACTORY : bien <all's well that ends well : tout est bien qui finit bien> **2** DESIRABLE : désirable, souhaitable <it would be well for you to leave : il vaudrait mieux pour vous de partir> **3** HEALTHY : bien portant <she's not well : elle ne se porte pas bien>
well⁴ *n* **1** : puits *m* (d'eau, de pétrole, etc.) **2** ORIGIN, SOURCE : source *f*, fontaine *f* **3 → stairwell**
well⁵ *interj* **1** (*used to express surprise or doubt*) : ça alors!, eh bien! **2** (*used to begin or resume a conversation*) : bon, bien, enfin
we'll [ˈwiːl, wɪl] (*contraction of* **we shall** *or* **we will**) **→ shall, will**
well–adjusted [ˌwɛlə̆ˈdʒʌstəd] *adj* : équilibré, bien adapté
well–advised [ˌwɛlə̆dˈvaɪzd] *adj* : prudent, sage
well–being [ˈwɛlˈbiːɪŋ] *n* : bien-être *m*
well–bred [ˈwɛlˈbrɛd] *adj* : bien élevé, poli
well–done [ˈwɛlˈdʌn] *adj* **1** : bien fait **2** : bien cuit (en cuisine)
well–known [ˈwɛlˈnoːn] *adj* : bien connu

well-meaning ['wɛlˈmiːnɪŋ] *adj* : bien intentionné
well-nigh ['wɛlˈnaɪ] *adv* : presque, quasi <well-nigh impossible : quasi impossible>
well-off ['wɛlˈɔf] → **well-to-do**
well-rounded ['wɛlˈraʊndəd] *adj* : complet
well-to-do [ˌwɛltəˈduː] *adj* : prospère, aisé, riche
Welsh[1] ['wɛlʃ, 'wɛltʃ] *adj* : gallois
Welsh[2] *n* **1** : gallois *m* (langue) **2 the Welsh** : les Gallois *mpl*
welt ['wɛlt] *n* **1** : trépointe *f* (de chaussures) **2** : zébrure *f*, marque *f* (sur la peau)
welter[1] ['wɛltər] *vi* : se rouler, se vautrer
welter[2] *n* JUMBLE : fatras *m*, fouillis *m*
wend ['wɛnd] *vi* **to wend one's way towards** : s'acheminer vers, se diriger vers
went → **go**[1]
wept → **weep**
were → **be**
we're ['wɪr, 'wər, 'wiːər] (*contraction of* **we are**) → **be**
werewolf ['wɪrˌwʊlf, 'wɛr-, 'wər-, -ˌwʌlf] *n, pl* **-wolves** [-ˌwʊlvz, -ˌwʌlvz] : loup-garou *m*
west[1] ['wɛst] *adv* : à l'ouest, vers l'ouest
west[2] *adj* : ouest, d'ouest
west[3] *n* **1** : ouest *m* **2 the West** : l'Ouest *m*, l'Occident *m*
westerly[1] ['wɛstərli] *adv* : vers l'ouest
westerly[2] *adj* : à l'ouest, d'ouest
western ['wɛstərn] *adj* **1** : ouest, de l'ouest, occidental **2 Western** : de l'Ouest, occidental <Western Europe : l'Europe occidentale>
Westerner ['wɛstərnər] *n* : habitant *m*, -tante *f* de l'Ouest
West Indian[1] *adj* : antillais
West Indian[2] *n* : Antillais, -laise *f*
westward ['wɛstwərd] *adj & adv* : vers l'ouest
westwards ['wɛstwərdz] *adv* : vers l'ouest
wet[1] ['wɛt] *vt* **wet** *or* **wetted; wetting** : mouiller
wet[2] *adj* **wetter; wettest 1** : mouillé, humide <a wet cloth : un chiffon humide> **2** RAINY : pluvieux **3** : frais <wet paint : peinture fraîche>
wet[3] *n* **1** WATER : eau *f* **2** MOISTURE : humidité *f* **3** RAIN : pluie *f*
we've ['wiːv] (*contraction of* **we have**) → **have**
whack[1] ['ʰwæk] *vt* : donner une claque à, donner un grand coup à
whack[2] *n* **1** BLOW : coup *m*, claque *f* **2** TRY : essai *m* <to have a whack at sth : essayer (de faire) qqch>
whale[1] ['ʰweɪl] *v* **whaled; whaling** *vi* : pêcher la baleine
whale[2] *n, pl* **whales** *or* **whale** : baleine *f*
whaleboat ['ʰweɪlˌboːt] *n* : baleinière *f*, baleinier *m*
whalebone ['ʰweɪlˌboːn] *n* : fanon *m* de baleine
whaler ['ʰweɪlər] *n* **1** : baleinier *m* (personne) **2** → **whaleboat**
wharf ['ʰwɔrf] *n, pl* **wharves** ['ʰwɔrvz] : quai *m*
what[1] ['ʰwɑt, 'ʰwʌt] *adv* **1** (*used in rhetorical questions*) <what does it matter : qu'est-ce que ça fait> **2** (*used to introduce prepositional phrases*) <what with one thing and another : avec ceci et cela>
what[2] *adj* **1** (*used in questions*) : quel <what book are you reading? : quel livre lisez-vous?> **2** (*used in exclamations*) <what an idea! : quelle idée!> <what fun we had! : le plaisir qu'on a eu ensemble!> **3** ANY, WHATEVER : le peu de, tout <what money he had : tout l'argent qu'il avait>
what[3] *pron* **1** : qu'est-ce que, qu'est-ce qui <what is this? : qu'est-ce que c'est?> <what's happening? : qu'est-ce qui se passe?> **2** : ce que, ce qui <I know what you want : je sais ce que vous voulez> **3** (*used in interrogative sentences or to express surprise*) : quoi <what's new? : quoi de neuf?> <what, no breakfast? : quoi, vous ne déjeunez pas?> **4** WHATEVER : (tout) ce que <say what you want : dites ce que vous voulez> **5 what for** WHY : pourquoi <what did you do that for? : pourquoi as-tu fait ça?> **6 what if** : et si <what if they find out? : et s'ils l'apprenaient?>
whatever[1] [ˌʰwɑtˈɛvər, ˌʰwʌt-] *adj* **1** : n'importe quel, tout <take whatever seat : prenez n'importe quel siège> **2** (*in negative constructions*) <we had no food whatever : nous n'avions pas la moindre nourriture> <nothing whatever : rien du tout>
whatever[2] *pron* **1** ANYTHING : (tout) ce que <I'll do whatever you ask : je ferai tout ce que vous me demandez> **2** : quoi que <whatever it may be : quoi que ce soit> **3** WHAT : qu'est-ce que, qu'est-ce qui <whatever do you mean? : qu'est-ce que vous voulez dire?>
whatsoever [ˌʰwɑtsoˈɛvər, ˌʰwʌt-] *pron & adj* → **whatever**
wheal ['ʰwiːl] *n* : marque *f* (sur la peau)
wheat ['ʰwiːt] *n* : blé *m*
wheaten ['ʰwiːtən] *adj* : de blé
wheedle ['ʰwiːdəl] *vt* **-dled; -dling** : cajoler, enjôler <to wheedle money out of s.o. : soutirer de l'argent à qqn par des cajoleries>
wheel[1] ['ʰwiːl] *vi* **1** REVOLVE : tourner **2** *or* **to wheel around** TURN : faire demi-tour — *vt* : pousser <they wheeled in the patient : ils ont fait entrer le patient sur un lit roulant>

wheel[2] *n* **1** : roue *f* (d'un véhicule), roulette *f* (d'un meuble, etc.) **2** → **steering wheel 3 wheels** *npl* WORKINGS : rouages *mpl* <wheels of government : rouages du gouvernement>
wheelbarrow [ˈhwiːlˌbæro:] *n* : brouette *f*
wheelchair [ˈhwiːlˌtʃær] *n* : fauteuil *m* roulant
wheeze[1] [ˈhwiːz] *vi* **wheezed; wheezing** : respirer péniblement et bruyamment
wheeze[2] *n* : respiration *f* sifflante
whelk [ˈhwɛlk] *n* : buccin *m*
whelp[1] [ˈhwɛlp] *v* : mettre bas
whelp[2] *n* : petit *m* (d'un animal)
when[1] [ˈhwɛn] *adv* **1** (*used in direct and indirect questions*) : quand <when did you return? : quand êtes-vous revenu?> <he asked me when I did it : il m'a demandé quand je l'ai fait> **2** : où <at a time when things were better : à une époque où les choses allaient mieux>
when[2] *conj* **1** (*referring to a specified time*) : quand, lorsque <when he was a boy : quand il était garçon> <I smiled when he said it : j'ai souri lorsqu'il l'a dit> **2** IF, WHENEVER : quand, si <you're disqualified when you cheat : vous serez disqualifié si vous trichez> **3** ALTHOUGH : alors que, quand, si <why do you tease me, when you know it's wrong? : pourquoi me taquines-tu alors que tu sais que c'est mal?>
when[3] *pron* **1 by when** : avant quand **2 since when** : depuis quand
whence [ˈhwɛnʦ] *adv & conj* : d'où
whenever[1] [hwɛnˈɛvər] *adv* : quand
whenever[2] *conj* : chaque fois que
where[1] [ˈhwɛr] *adv* **1** (*at what place*) : où <where are they? : où sont-ils?> **2** (*at which part*) : où <where did I go wrong? : où est-ce que je me suis trompée?>
where[2] *conj* **1** : où <he knows where the house is : il sait où se trouve la maison> <stay where you are : restez où vous êtes> **2** WHEREVER : où que, partout où <she goes where he likes to go : elle va partout où il aime aller>
where[3] *pron* : où <the town where she was born : la ville où elle est née>
whereabouts[1] [ˈhwɛrəˌbaʊʦ] *adv* : où <whereabouts is the house? : où est la maison?>
whereabouts[2] *ns & pl* **to know s.o.'s whereabouts** : savoir où se trouve qqn
whereas [hwɛrˈæz] *conj* **1** : alors que, tandis que <I like the sea whereas she likes the mountains : j'aime la mer alors qu'elle aime les montagnes> **2** SINCE : attendu que (en droit)
whereby [hwɛrˈbaɪ] *conj* : par lequel, selon lequel
wherefore[1] [ˈhwɛrˌfor] *adv* **1** WHY : pourquoi **2** THEREFORE : donc
wherefore[2] *n* **the whys and wherefores** : le pourquoi et le comment
wherein [hwɛrˈɪn] *adv* : en quoi
whereof [hwɛrˈʌv, -ɑv] *conj* : de quoi
whereupon [ˈhwɛrəˌpɑn, -ˌpɔn] *conj* : sur quoi, sur ce
wherever[1] [hwɛrˈɛvər] *adv* **1** (*used for emphasis*) : mais où, où donc <wherever did you get that tie? : mais où donc as-tu déniché cette cravate?> **2 or wherever** : Dieu sait où
wherever[2] *conj* : où que, partout où <wherever you go : où que tu ailles>
wherewithal [ˈhwɛrwɪˌðɔl, -ˌðɔl] *n* : ressources *fpl*, moyens *mpl*
whet [ˈhwɛt] *vt* **whetted; whetting 1** SHARPEN : affûter, aiguiser (un couteau) **2** STIMULATE : stimuler <to whet one's appetite : ouvrir l'appétit>
whether [ˈhwɛðər] *conj* **1** IF : si <see whether they've left : vérifie s'ils sont partis> **2** (*used to introduce alternatives*) <the game will be played whether it rains or not : nous allons jouer la partie qu'il pleuve ou non> <whether before or after : soit avant soit après>
whetstone [ˈhwɛtˌsto:n] *n* : pierre *f* à aiguiser
whey [ˈhwɛɪ] *n* : petit-lait *m*
which[1] [ˈhwɪʧ] *adj* : quel <which shirt should I wear? : quelle chemise devrais-je porter?> <which ones? : lesquels?>
which[2] *pron* **1** : lequel, quel <which of the answers is right? : laquelle des réponses est la bonne?> <he wondered which would be better : il se demandait quel serait mieux> **2** (*used as a function word to introduce a relative clause*) : qui, que <the suggestion which you made : la suggestion que vous avez faite>
whichever[1] [hwɪtʃˈɛvər] *adj* : peu importe quel <whichever way you go : peu importe quel chemin vous empruntez>
whichever[2] *pron* : quel que <whichever you prefer : quelle que soit votre préférence>
whiff[1] [ˈhwɪf] *vi* **1** PUFF : souffler **2** : respirer une odeur
whiff[2] *n* **1** GUST, PUFF : bouffée *f* **2** SMELL, TRACE : odeur *f* <to catch a whiff of : sentir l'odeur de>
while[1] [ˈhwaɪl] *vt* **whiled; whiling** : (faire) passer <to while away the time : passer le temps>
while[2] *n* **1** : temps *m*, moment *m* <after a while : au bout d'un moment> <once in a while : de temps en temps> <a long while ago : il y a longtemps> **2 to be worth one's while** : valoir la peine
while[3] *conj* **1** : pendant que <while you're at it : pendant que vous y êtes>

<while you were out : pendant votre absence> **2** ALTHOUGH : bien que <while respected, he is not liked : bien que respecté, il n'est pas aimé> **3** WHEREAS : tandis que, alors que

whim [ˈhwɪm] *n* : caprice *m*, lubie *f*

whimper[1] [ˈhwɪmpər] *vi* : gémir, pleurnicher *fam*

whimper[2] *n* : gémissement *m*

whimsical [ˈhwɪmzɪkəl] *adj* **1** CAPRICIOUS : capricieux, fantasque **2** ERRATIC : changeant, imprévisible

whimsically [ˈhwɪmzɪkəli] *adv* : curieusement, de façon saugrenue

whimsy [ˈhwɪmzi] *n, pl* **1** → **whim 2** : fantaisie *f*, caractère *m* fantasque

whine[1] [ˈhwaɪn] *vi* **whined; whining 1** WHIMPER : gémir, geindre **2** COMPLAIN : se plaindre, se lamenter

whine[2] *n* : gémissement *m*

whinny[1] [ˈhwɪni] *vi* **-nied; -nying** : hennir

whinny[2] *n* : hennissement *m*

whip[1] [ˈhwɪp] *v* **whipped; whipping** *vt* **1** SNATCH : tirer brusquement, arracher <she whipped off the tablecloth : elle a brusquement arraché la nappe> **2** LASH : fouetter **3** DEFEAT : vaincre, battre à plates coutures **4** BEAT : battre (des œufs, etc.) **5 to whip up** INCITE : attiser (une émotion), susciter (de l'intérêt) — *vi* **1** LASH : battre <the rain whipped against the shutters : la pluie battait contre les volets> **2** : aller rapidement <to whip along : filer à toute allure>

whip[2] *n* **1** : fouet *m*, cravache *f* (d'équitation) **2** : député *m* d'un parti législatif qui réglemente la discipline et les votes de son parti **3** : mousse *f* <prune whip : mousse aux pruneaux>

whiplash [ˈhwɪpˌlæʃ] *n or* **whiplash injury** : coup *m* du lapin

whippet [ˈhwɪpət] *n* : whippet *m*

whippoorwill [ˈhwɪpərˌwɪl] *n* : engoulevent *m* (de l'Amérique du Nord)

whir[1] [ˈhwər] *vi* **whirred; whirring 1** : bruire (se dit des ailes) **2** : ronronner, vrombir (se dit d'un moteur, d'un ventilateur, etc.)

whir[2] *n* **1** : bruissement *m* (de feuilles, d'ailes) **2** : ronronnement *m*, vrombissement *m* <the whir of propellers : le vrombissement des hélices>

whirl[1] [ˈhwərl] *vi* **1** SPIN : tournoyer, tourbillonner **2** REEL : tourner <my head was whirling : la tête me tournait> **3 to whirl around** : se retourner **4 to whirl by** : aller à toute vitesse, filer à toute allure — *vi* : faire tournoyer, faire tourbillonner

whirl[2] *n* **1** WHIRLING : tournoiement *m* **2** BUSTLE : tourbillon *m* **3 to give sth a whirl** : s'essayer à qqch

whirlpool [ˈhwərlˌpuːl] *n* : tourbillon *m* (d'eau)

whirlwind [ˈhwərlˌwɪnd] *n* : tourbillon *m* (de vent), trombe *f*

whisk[1] [ˈhwɪsk] *vt* **1** : faire rapidement <I whisked it out of my purse : je l'ai brusquement sorti de mon sac à main> **2** BEAT : battre (des œufs) **3** *or* **to whisk away** : enlever d'un geste rapide — *vi* : aller vite

whisk[2] *n* **1** WHISKING : coup *m* léger **2** : fouet *m* (en cuisine)

whisk broom *n* : époussette *f*

whisker [ˈhwɪskər] *n* **1** : poil *m* de barbe <to win by a whisker : gagner d'un poil> **2 whiskers** *npl* : barbe *f* (d'un homme), moustaches *fpl* (d'un chat, etc.)

whiskey *or* **whisky** [ˈhwɪski] *n, pl* **-keys** *or* **-kies** : whisky *m*

whisper[1] [ˈhwɪspər] *vi* : chuchoter, parler à voix basse — *vt* : chuchoter, dire à voix basse

whisper[2] *n* **1** : chuchotement *m* <to speak in whispers : parler tout bas> **2** RUMOR : rumeur *f*, bruit *m* **3** HINT : soupçon *m*, trace *f*

whistle[1] [ˈhwɪsəl] *vi* **-tled; -tling 1** : siffler **2 to whistle by** : passer en sifflant — *vt* : siffler

whistle[2] *n* **1** WHISTLING : sifflement *m* **2** : sifflet *m* <to blow a whistle : donner un coup de sifflet>

whit [ˈhwɪt] *n* BIT : brin *m*, petit peu *m*

white[1] [ˈhwaɪt] *adj* **whiter; -est** : blanc

white[2] *n* **1** : blanc *m* (couleur) **2** *or* **egg white** : blanc *m* d'œuf **3** : Blanc *m*, Blanche *f* (personne)

white blood cell *n* : globule *m* blanc

whitecaps [ˈhwaɪtˌkæps] *npl* : moutons *mpl*

white–collar [ˈhwaɪtˈkɑlər] *adj* : de bureau, de col blanc

whitefish [ˈhwaɪtˌfɪʃ] *n* : corégone *m*

whiten [ˈhwaɪtən] *v* : blanchir

whiteness [ˈhwaɪtnəs] *n* : blancheur *f*

white–tailed deer [ˈhwaɪtˈteɪld] *n* : cerf *m* de Virginie, chevreuil *m Can*

whitewash[1] [ˈhwaɪtˌwɔʃ] *vt* **1** : blanchir (une clôture, etc.) à la chaux **2** CONCEAL : camoufler, dissimuler

whitewash[2] *n* **1** : lait *m* de chaux **2** COVER-UP : dissimulation *f*, camouflage *m*

whither [ˈhwɪðər] *adv* : où

whiting [ˈhwaɪtɪŋ] *n* : merlan *m* (poisson)

whitish [ˈhwaɪtɪʃ] *adj* : blanchâtre

whittle [ˈhwɪtəl] *vt* **-tled; -tling 1** : tailler au couteau, gosser *Can fam* **2** PARE, REDUCE : réduire, amoindrir

whiz[1] *or* **whizz** [ˈhwɪz] *vi* **whizzed; whizzing 1** BUZZ, HISS : bourdonner, siffler **2** *or* **to whiz by** : passer à toute vitesse, passer en sifflant

whiz[2] *or* **whizz** *n* **1** BUZZ : bourdonnement *m*, sifflement *m* **2** : expert *m*, as *m* <a computer whiz : un expert en informatique>

who [ˈhu:] *pron* **1** (*used as an interrogative*) : qui <who was elected? : qui a été élu?> <do you know who the message was from? : savez-vous qui a écrit le message?> **2** WHOEVER : qui, qui que ce soit **3** (*used to introduce a relative clause*) : qui <my father, who was a lawyer : mon père, qui était avocat>

whodunit [hu:ˈdʌnɪt] *n* : roman *m* policier

whoever [hu:ˈɛvər] *pron* **1** : qui que ce soit, n'importe qui <whoever told you that, he's wrong : qui que ce soit qui te l'a dit il se trompe> **2** : celui qui, quiconque <whoever wants to participate : quiconque veut participer> **3** (*used to express astonishment or perplexity*) <whoever can that be? : qui est-ce que ça peut bien être?>

whole[1] [ˈho:l] *adj* **1** : entier <whole milk : lait entier> **2** INTACT : complet, intact **3** COMPLETE, ENTIRE : au complet, tout <she owns the whole island : l'île au complet lui appartient> <his whole attention : toute son attention> **4 a whole lot** : beaucoup

whole[2] *n* **1** : tout *m*, ensemble *m* **2 as a whole** : dans son ensemble, entièrement **3 on the whole** : en général, dans l'ensemble

wholehearted [ˈho:lˈhɑrt̬əd] *adj* : de bon cœur, sans réserve

whole number *n* : nombre *m* entier

wholesale[1] [ˈho:lˌseɪl] *v* **-saled; -saling** *vt* : vendre au prix de gros — *vi* : se vendre au prix de gros

wholesale[2] *adv* : en gros

wholesale[3] *adj* **1** : de gros <wholesale prices : prix de gros> **2** : en masse <wholesale slaughter : massacre en masse>

wholesale[4] *n* : vente *f* en gros

wholesaler [ˈho:lˌseɪlər] *n* : grossiste *mf*

wholesome [ˈho:lsəm] *adj* **1** HEALTHY, SOUND : sain, en santé **2** HEALTHFUL : sain, salubre

whole wheat *adj* : de blé entier

wholly [ˈho:li] *adv* **1** COMPLETELY : complètement, entièrement **2** SOLELY : exclusivement

whom [ˈhu:m] *pron* **1** (*used as an interrogative*) <whom did he fight? : avec qui s'est-il battu?> **2** (*used as a relative pronoun*) <two professors whom I met in Italy : deux professeurs que j'ai rencontrés en Italie> **3** (*used as the object of a preposition*) <the politician to whom you wrote : le politicien à qui vous avez écrit>

whomever [hu:mˈɛvər] → **whoever**

whoop[1] [ˈhwu:p, ˈhwʊp] *vi* : pousser des cris

whoop[2] *n* : cri *m*

whooping cough *n* : coqueluche *f*

whopper [ˈhwɑpər] *n* **1** : chose *f* énorme **2** LIE : bobard *m fam*, gros mensonge *m*

whopping [ˈhwɑpɪŋ] *adj* : colossal, monstre

whore [ˈhor] *n* : prostituée *f*

whorl [ˈhwɔrl, ˈhwərl] *n* **1** : spire *f* (d'un coquillage), verticille *m* (de pétales), volute *f* (d'un doigt) **2** SWIRL : spirale *f*, volute *f* <a whorl of smoke : une spirale de fumée>

whose[1] [ˈhu:z] *adj* **1** (*used in questions*) : de qui, à qui <whose daughter is she? : de qui est-elle la fille?> <whose fault is it? : à qui la faute?> **2** (*used in relative clauses*) : dont <a friend whose husband works with me : une amie dont le mari travaille avec moi>

whose[2] *pron* : à qui <whose is this? : à qui est ceci?>

why[1] [ˈhwaɪ] *adv* : pourquoi <why did you do it? : pourquoi l'as-tu fait?>

why[2] *n, pl* **whys** : pourquoi *m*

why[3] *conj* **1** : pourquoi <I know why he did it : je sais pourquoi il l'a fait> **2** : pour lequel <the reason why he accepted : la raison pour laquelle il a accepté>

why[4] *interj* : mais!, tiens!

wick [ˈwɪk] *n* : mèche *f*

wicked [ˈwɪkəd] *adj* **1** EVIL : corrompu, méchant **2** MISCHIEVOUS : espiègle, malicieux **3** TERRIBLE : mauvais, épouvantable

wickedly [ˈwɪkədli] *adv* **1** : avec méchanceté **2** MISCHIEVOUSLY : malicieusement

wickedness [ˈwɪkədnəs] *n* : méchanceté *f*, vilenie *f*

wicker[1] [ˈwɪkər] *adj* : en osier

wicker[2] *n* **1** : osier *m* **2** → **wickerwork**

wickerwork [ˈwɪkərˌwərk] *n* : vannerie *f*

wicket [ˈwɪkət] *n* : guichet *m*

wide[1] [ˈwaɪd] *adv* **wider; widest 1** : partout <to search far and wide : chercher partout> **2** FULLY : complètement <she opened her eyes wide : elle a ouvert grand les yeux>

wide[2] *adj* **wider; widest 1** EXTENSIVE, VAST : vaste, étendu <a wide area : une vaste superficie> <to have wide experience : avoir une grande expérience> **2** : dé large <3 feet wide : trois pieds de large> **3** BROAD : large **4 to be wide of the mark** : être loin de la vérité

wide-awake [ˈwaɪdəˈweɪk] *adj* : éveillé, alerte

wide-eyed [ˈwaɪdˈaɪd] *adj* **1** : aux yeux écarquillés **2** AMAZED : étonné, stupéfait **3** NAIVE : naïf, crédule

widely [ˈwaɪdli] *adv* **1** EXTENSIVELY : largement, beaucoup **2** SIGNIFICANTLY : considérablement

widen [ˈwaɪdən] *vt* : élargir — *vi* : s'élargir

widespread ['waɪdˈspɛd] *adj* **1** EXTENDED, SPREAD : déployé, étendu **2** EXTENSIVE : diffus, répandu
widow¹ ['wɪˌdo:] *vt* **to be widowed** : devenir veuf, devenir veuve
widow² *n* : veuve *f*
widower ['wɪdowər] *n* : veuf *m*
width ['wɪdθ] *n* : largeur *f*
wield ['wi:ld] *vt* **1** : brandir <to wield a broom : brandir un balai> **2** EXERT : exercer (de l'influence, etc.)
wiener ['wi:nər] → **frankfurter**
wife ['waɪf] *n, pl* **wives** ['waɪvz] : femme *f*, épouse *f*
wifely ['waɪfli] *adj* : d'épouse
wig ['wɪg] *n* : perruque *f*, postiche *m*
wiggle¹ ['wɪgəl] *v* **-gled; -gling** *vi* **1** JIGGLE : remuer (se dit des personnes), branler (se dit des choses) **2** WRIGGLE : se tortiller — *vt* : faire branler, faire bouger
wiggle² *n* : tortillement *m*
wiggly ['wɪgəli] *adj* **wigglier; -est 1** : qui se tortille **2** WAVY : ondulé, sinueux
wigwam ['wɪgˌwɑm] *n* : wigwam *m*
wild¹ ['waɪld] *adv* **1 to go wild** : devenir fou **2 to grow wild** : pousser à l'état sauvage **3 to run wild** : courir en liberté (se dit des animaux)
wild² *adj* **1** : sauvage <wild ducks : canards sauvages> **2** UNRULY : dissolu, indiscipliné **3** TURBULENT : violent, déchaîné **4** CRAZY : insensé, fou <wild ideas : idées insensées> **5** UNCIVILIZED : sauvage, fruste **6** ERRATIC : imprévisible, inattendu <to take a wild guess : deviner au hasard>
wild³ *n* → **wilderness**
wild boar *n* : sanglier *m*
wildcat ['waɪldˌkæt] *n* **1** : chat *m* sauvage **2** BOBCAT : lynx *m*
wilderness ['wɪldərnəs] *n* : région *f* sauvage
wildfire ['waɪldˌfaɪr] *n* **1** : feu *m* de forêt incontrôlé **2 to spread like wildfire** : se répandre comme une traînée de poudre
wildflower ['waɪldˌflɑʊər] *n* : fleur *f* des champs
wildfowl ['waɪldˌfaʊl] *ns & pl* : oiseaux *mpl* sauvages
wildlife ['waɪldˌlaɪf] *n* : faune *f*
wildly ['waɪldli] *adv* **1** FRANTICALLY : de façon agitée **2** EXTREMELY : extrêmement, immensément
wile¹ ['waɪl] *vt* **wiled; wiling** LURE : attirer
wile² *n* : ruse *f*, artifice *m*
will¹ ['wɪl] *v, past* **would** ['wʊd]; *pres sing & pl* **will** *vt* WISH : vouloir <say what you will : dis ce que tu veux> — *v aux* **1** (*used to express willingness*) <no one would take the job : personne ne voulait l'emploi> **2** (*used to express habitual action*) <he'll get angry over nothing : il se fâche pour des riens> **3** (*used to express futurity*) <tomorrow we will go swimming : demain nous irons nous baigner> **4** (*used to express capacity*) <the back seat will hold three people : le siège arrière peut accommoder trois personnes> **5** (*used to express probability*) <that will be the mailman : ça doit être le facteur> **6** (*used to express determination*) <I won't give in : je refuse d'abandonner> **7** (*used to express a command*) <you will do as I say : je t'ordonne de faire ce que je te dis>
will² *vt* **1** ORDAIN : vouloir <if the Lord willed it : si le Seigneur l'a voulu ainsi> **2** : vouloir très fort <to will s.o.'s success : souhaiter ardemment la réussite de qqn> **3** BEQUEATH : léguer
will³ *n* **1** DESIRE, WISH : désir *m*, envie *f* **2** INCLINATION : volonté *f*, détermination *f* <where there's a will there's a way : quand on veut on peut> **3** VOLITION : gré *m*, volonté *f* <of her own free will : de son propre gré> **4** : volonté *f*, résolution *f* <an iron will : une volonté de fer> **5** : testament *m* <to make a will : faire un testament>
willful *or* **wilful** ['wɪlfəl] *adj* **1** STUBBORN : volontaire, obstiné **2** INTENTIONAL : délibéré, voulu
willfully ['wɪlfəli] *adv* **1** STUBBORNLY : obstinément **2** INTENTIONALLY : délibérément, intentionnellement
willing ['wɪlɪŋ] *adj* **1** INCLINED, READY : prêt, disposé <willing to help : prêt à aider> **2** EAGER : empressé, de bonne volonté <willing workers : travailleurs empressés> **3** VOLUNTARY : volontaire <a willing sacrifice : un sacrifice volontaire>
willingly ['wɪlɪŋli] *adv* **1** GLADLY : volontiers, de bon cœur **2** VOLUNTARILY : volontairement
willingness ['wɪlɪŋnəs] *n* **1** ENTHUSIASM : empressement *m*, bonne volonté *f* **2** READINESS : volonté *f*
willow ['wɪˌlo:] *n* : saule *m*
willowy ['wɪlowi] *adj* : svelte, élancé
willpower ['wɪlˌpaʊər] *n* : volonté *f*
willy–nilly [ˌwɪliˈnɪli] *adv & adj* : bon gré mal gré
wilt ['wɪlt] *vi* **1** : se faner (se dit des fleurs) **2** LANGUISH : dépérir, languir
wily ['waɪli] *adj* **wilier; -est** : rusé, malin
win¹ ['wɪn] *v* **won** ['wʌn]; **winning** *vt* **1** : gagner, remporter <to win the war : gagner la guerre> <to win a prize : remporter un prix> **2** GAIN : obtenir, s'attirer **3 to win over** : convaincre, rallier — *vi* : gagner
win² *n* : victoire *f*
wince¹ ['wɪnʃ] *vi* **winced; wincing** : tressaillir
wince² *n* : tressaillement *m*
winch¹ ['wɪntʃ] *vt or* **to winch up** : hisser à l'aide d'un treuil
winch² *n* : treuil *m*

wind[1] ['wɪnd] *vt* : faire perdre le souffle à, couper la respiration à
wind[2] *n* **1** : vent *m* **2** BREATH : souffle *m* **3** FLATULENCE : gaz *mpl* intestinaux **4 to get wind of** : avoir vent de
wind[3] ['waɪnd] *v* **wound** ['waʊnd]; **winding** *vt* **1** COIL : enrouler **2** WRAP : envelopper **3** : remonter (une horloge) — *vi* MEANDER : serpenter
wind[4] ['waɪnd] *n* BEND : tournant *m*, courbe *f*
windbreak ['wɪnd,breɪk] *n* : brise-vent *m*
windbreaker ['wɪnd,breɪkər] *n* : coupe-vent *m*
windfall ['wɪnd,fɔl] *n* **1** : fruits *mpl* tombés **2** BENEFIT, GAIN : aubaine *f*, chance *f*
wind instrument *n* : instrument *m* à vent
windlass ['wɪndləs] *n* : guindeau *m*
windmill ['wɪnd,mɪl] *n* : moulin *m* à vent
window ['wɪn,do:] *n* **1** : fenêtre *f* (d'une maison), vitre *f* (d'une voiture), guichet *m* (dans une banque, etc.) **2** GAP, INTERVAL : espace *m*, créneau *m* <a window of time : un espace de temps> **3** : fenêtre *f* (en informatique) **4 → shopwindow, windowpane**
windowpane ['wɪn,do:,peɪn] *n* : vitre *f*, carreau *m*
window-shop ['wɪndo,ʃɑp] *vi* **-shopped; -shopping** : faire du lèche-vitrines
windpipe ['wɪnd,paɪp] *n* : trachée *f*
windshield ['wɪnd,ʃi:ld] *n* : pare-brise *m*
windshield wiper → wiper
windup ['waɪnd,ʌp] *n* : fin *f*, conclusion *f*
wind up *vt* : terminer, conclure — *vi* : finir
windward[1] ['wɪndwərd] *adj* : contre le vent, au vent
windward[2] *n* : côté *m* du vent
windy ['wɪndi] *adj* **windier; -est 1** : venteux **2** BOMBASTIC : verbeux, grandiloquent
wine[1] ['waɪn] *vt* **to wine and dine s.o.** : inviter qqn dans les bons restaurants
wine[2] *n* : vin *m*
wing[1] ['wɪŋ] *vt* **1** WOUND : blesser (un oiseau) **2 to wing it** : improviser — *vi* FLY : voler, s'envoler
wing[2] *n* **1** : aile *f* (d'un oiseau) **2** : aile *f* (d'un édifice), pavillon *m* (d'un hôpital) **3** FACTION : aile *f*, partie *f* **4** : ailier *m* (aux sports) **5 on the wing** : en vol **6 to take s.o. under one's wing** : prendre qqn sous son aile **7 wings** *npl* : coulisses *fpl* (au théâtre)
winged ['wɪnd, 'wɪnəd] *adj* : ailé
wink[1] ['wɪŋk] *vi* **1** : faire un clin d'œil **2** BLINK : cligner des yeux **3** TWINKLE : clignoter, scintiller
wink[2] *n* **1** : clin *m* d'œil **2** NAP : sieste *f*, somme *m* <I didn't get a wink of sleep : je n'ai pas fermé l'œil> **3 quick as a wink** : en un clin d'œil
winner ['wɪnər] *n* : gagnant *m*, -gnante *f*
winning ['wɪnɪŋ] *adj* **1** VICTORIOUS : gagnant **2** CHARMING : séduisant, engageant
winnings ['wɪnɪŋz] *npl* : gains *mpl*
winnow ['wɪno] *vt* **1** : vanner (en agriculture) **2** SEPARATE : trier, passer au crible
winsome ['wɪnsəm] *adj* : charmant, engageant
winter[1] ['wɪntər] *adj* : d'hiver
winter[2] *n* : hiver *m*
wintergreen ['wɪntər,gri:n] *n* : gaulthérie *f*
wintertime ['wɪntər,taɪm] *n* : hiver *m*
wintry ['wɪntri] *adj* **wintrier; -est 1** : hivernal <wintry weather : temps hivernal> **2** COLD : froid, glacial <a wintry welcome : un accueil froid>
wipe[1] ['waɪp] *vt* **wiped; wiping 1** : essuyer <to wipe the dishes : essuyer la vaisselle> **2** *or* **to wipe away** : essuyer (des larmes), effacer (un souvenir, etc.) **3 to wipe out** : détruire
wipe[2] *n* : coup *m* d'éponge, coup *m* de torchon
wiper ['waɪpər] *n or* **windshield wiper** : essuie-glace *m*
wire[1] ['waɪr] *vt* **wired; wiring 1** : faire l'installation électrique de **2** BIND, CONNECT : relier, attacher (avec du fil métallique) **3** TELEGRAPH : envoyer un télégramme à
wire[2] *n* **1** : fil *m* métallique, broche *f* *Can* <barbed wire : fil de fer barbelé> **2** TELEGRAM : télégramme *m*
wireless ['waɪrləs] *adj* : sans fil
wiretapping ['waɪr,tæpɪŋ] *n* : mise *f* sur écoute téléphonique
wiring ['waɪrɪŋ] *n* : installation *f* électrique
wiry ['waɪri] *adj* **wirier** ['waɪrɪər]; **-est 1** : raide (se dit des cheveux, etc.) **2** SINEWY : mince et musclé
wisdom ['wɪzdəm] *n* **1** KNOWLEDGE : sagesse *f*, connaissances *fpl* **2** JUDGMENT : sagesse *f*, discernement *m*
wisdom tooth *n* : dent *f* de sagesse
wise[1] ['waɪz] *adj* **wiser; wisest 1** LEARNED : sage **2** PRUDENT, SENSIBLE : sage, prudent, judicieux **3 to be wise to** : être au courant de
wise[2] *n* : manière *f*, façon *f* <in no wise : en aucune façon>
wisecrack ['waɪz,kræk] *n* : blague *f*, vanne *f* *fam*
wisely ['waɪzli] *adv* : sagement, avec sagesse
wish[1] ['wɪʃ] *vt* **1** WANT : souhaiter, désirer **2 to wish (something) for** : souhaiter <we wished her a happy birthday : nous lui avons souhaité bonne fête> <she wished me good night : elle m'a dit bonsoir> — *vi* : souhaiter, vouloir <as you wish : comme vous voulez>

wish[2] *n* **1** : souhait *m*, désir *m*, vœu *m* <make a wish : fais un vœu> **2 wishes** *npl* : vœux *mpl*, amitiés *fpl* <best wishes : meilleurs vœux>
wishbone [ˈwɪʃˌboːn] *n* : bréchet *m*, fourchette *f*
wishful [ˈwɪʃfəl] *adj* **1** HOPEFUL : désireux **2 it's wishful thinking** : c'est prendre ses désirs pour des réalités
wishy–washy [ˈwɪʃiˌwɔʃi, -ˌwɑʃi] *adj* **1** INEFFECTUAL : incapable, incompétent **2** WEAK : faible, insipide
wisp [ˈwɪsp] *n* **1** : mèche *f* (de cheveux), volute *f* (de fumée), brin *m* (de foin) **2** HINT : trace *f*, soupçon *m*
wispy [ˈwɪspi] *adj* **wispier; -est** : fin, épars
wisteria [wɪsˈtɪriə] *n* : glycine *f*
wistful [ˈwɪstfəl] *adj* : mélancolique, pensif — **wistfully** *adv*
wistfulness [ˈwɪstfəlnəs] *n* : mélancolie *f*
wit [ˈwɪt] *n* **1** MIND : esprit *m*, intelligence *f* **2** CLEVERNESS, HUMOR : esprit *m* <to have a quick wit : avoir l'esprit vif> **3** JOKER : farceur *m*, -ceuse *f* **4 wits** *npl* : sens *m*, raison *f* <to be at one's wits' end : ne plus savoir que faire> <you scared me out of my wits : tu m'as fait une de ces peurs>
witch [ˈwɪtʃ] *n* : sorcière *f*
witchcraft [ˈwɪtʃˌkræft] *n* : sorcellerie *f*
witch doctor *n* : sorcier *m*, -cière *f*
witchery [ˈwɪtʃəri] *n, pl* **-eries 1** → **witchcraft 2** CHARM : ensorcellement *m*
witch hazel [ˈwɪtʃˌheɪzəl] *n* : hamamélis *m*
witch–hunt [ˈwɪtʃˌhʌnt] *n* **1** : chasse *f* aux sorcières **2** : persécution *f* (politique)
with [ˈwɪð, ˈwɪθ] *prep* **1** (*indicating accompaniment*) : avec <I'm going with you : je vais avec vous> **2** AGAINST : avec, contre <he had a fight with his brother : il s'est chicané avec son frère> <to be angry with s.o. : être fâché contre qqn> **3** (*used in descriptions*) : à <the girl with red hair : la fille aux cheveux roux> **4** (*indicating manner, means, or cause*) : avec <to cut with a knife : couper avec un couteau> <with any luck : avec un peu de chance> **5** DESPITE : malgré <with all her faults, she's still my friend : malgré tous ses défauts, elle est quand même mon amie> <with all your money . . . : il a beau avoir de l'argent . . .> **6** REGARDING, TOWARD : avec <be patient with the children : soyez patient avec les enfants> <it's a habit with her : c'est une habitude chez elle> **7** ACCORDING TO : avec <it varies with the season : ça change avec la saison> **8** (*indicating support or understanding*) : avec <I'm with you all the way : je suis avec vous cent pour cent>
withdraw [wɪðˈdrɔ, wɪθ-] *v* **-drew** [-ˈdruː]; **-drawn** [-ˈdrɔn]; **-drawing** *vt* **1** REMOVE : retirer <to withdraw money : retirer de l'argent> **2** RETRACT : retirer, rétracter (une parole, etc.) — *vi* LEAVE, RETREAT : se retirer
withdrawal [wɪðˈdrɔəl, wɪθ-] *n* **1** : retrait *m* (de fonds, des troupes) **2** RETRACTION : rétraction *f* **3** *or* **withdrawal symptoms** : symptômes *mpl* de manque
withdrawn [wɪðˈdrɔn, wɪθ-] *adj* : renfermé, replié sur soi-même
wither [ˈwɪðər] *vi* **1** WILT : se faner, se flétrir **2 to wither away** : s'évanouir
withers [ˈwɪðərz] *npl* : garrot *m* (d'un cheval)
withhold [wɪθˈhoːld, wɪð-] *vt* **-held** [-ˈhɛld]; **-holding** : retenir (des fonds), refuser (la permission, etc.), cacher (des faits, la vérité)
within[1] [wɪðˈɪn, wɪθ-] *adv* : à l'intérieur
within[2] *prep* **1** INSIDE : dans, à l'intérieur de <within the building : à l'intérieur de l'édifice> **2** (*indicating limitation*) <to live within one's income : vivre selon ses moyens> <within reach : à (la) portée de la main> **3** (*indicating distance*) <within a mile of the city : à moins d'un mille de la ville> **4** (*indicating time*) <within a month : en moins d'un mois> <within the time limit : dans les temps impartis>
without[1] [wɪðˈaʊt, wɪθ-] *adv* **1** OUTSIDE : à l'extérieur, au dehors **2 to do without** : se passer de
without[2] *prep* **1** OUTSIDE : à l'extérieur de **2** : sans <I spoke without thinking : j'ai parlé sans réfléchir> <without a doubt : sans aucun doute>
withstand [wɪθˈstænd, wɪð-] *vt* **-stood** [-ˈstʊd]; **-standing 1** BEAR : supporter **2** RESIST : résister à
witless [ˈwɪtləs] *adj* : stupide, sans génie
witness[1] [ˈwɪtnəs] *vt* **1** SEE : être témoin de, assister à **2** : servir de témoin de (une signature) — *vi* TESTIFY : témoigner
witness[2] *n* **1** TESTIMONY : témoignage *m* <to bear false witness : donner un faux témoignage> **2** : témoin *m* <to call as a witness : citer comme témoin>
witticism [ˈwɪtəˌsɪzəm] *n* : bon mot *m*, mot *m* d'esprit
witty [ˈwɪti] *adj* **wittier; -est** : humoristique, amusant
wives → **wife**
wizard [ˈwɪzərd] *n* **1** SORCERER : magicien *m*, sorcier *m* **2** : génie *m* <a math wizard : un génie des mathématiques>
wizardry [ˈwɪzərdri] *n* : sorcellerie *f*
wizened [ˈwɪzənd, ˈwiːz-] *adj* : desséché, ratatiné
wobble[1] [ˈwɑbəl] *vi* **-bled; -bling** : branler, osciller, trembler

wobble[2] *n* : branlement *m*
wobbly ['wɑbəli] *adj* : vacillant, branlant
woe ['wo:] *n* **1** SORROW : chagrin *m* **2 woes** *npl* MISFORTUNE : malheur *m*
woeful ['wo:fəl] *adj* **1** SORROWFUL : désolé, affligé, triste **2** DEPLORABLE, UNFORTUNATE : lamentable, malheureux
woefully ['wo:fəli] *adv* **1** SADLY : tristement **2** DEPLORABLY : lamentablement
woke, woken → **wake**[1]
wolf[1] ['wʊlf] *vt or* **to wolf down** : engloutir, engouffrer
wolf[2] *n, pl* **wolves** ['wʊlvz] : loup *m*, louve *f*
wolfish ['wʊlfɪʃ] *adj* : féroce
wolfram ['wʊlfrəm] → **tungsten**
wolverine [ˌwʊlvə'ri:n] *n, pl* **-ines** : glouton *m*
woman ['wʊmən] *n, pl* **women** ['wɪmən] : femme *f*
womanhood ['wʊmənˌhʊd] *n* **1** : féminité *f* **2** WOMEN : femmes *fpl*
womanly ['wʊmənli] *adj* : féminin, de femme
womb ['wu:m] *n* : utérus *m*
won → **win**[1]
wonder[1] ['wʌndər] *vi* **1** MARVEL : s'émerveiller, s'étonner **2** SPECULATE : penser, songer — *vt* : se demander <I wondered why : je me suis demandé pourquoi>
wonder[2] *n* **1** MARVEL : merveille *f* <to work wonders : faire des merveilles> <it's a wonder that : c'est étonnant que> **2** ASTONISHMENT : émerveillement *m*
wonderful ['wʌndərfəl] *adj* : merveilleux, formidable
wonderfully ['wʌndərfəli] *adv* : merveilleusement, à merveille
wonderland ['wʌndərˌlænd, -lənd] *n* : pays *m* des merveilles, pays *m* enchanté
wonderment ['wʌndərmənt] *n* : émerveillement *m*, étonnement *m*
wondrous ['wəndrəs] → **wonderful**
wont[1] ['wɔnt, 'wo:nt] *adj* : habitué <to be wont to do : avoir coutume de faire>
wont[2] *n* : habitude *f*, coutume *f*
won't ['wo:nt] (*contraction of* **will not**) → **will**[1]
woo ['wu:] *vt* **1** COURT : courtiser, faire la cour à **2** : rechercher les faveurs de (des clients, etc.)
wood[1] ['wʊd] *adj* : de bois, en bois
wood[2] *n* **1** : bois *m* <solid wood : bois massif> **2** *or* **woods** *npl* FOREST : bois *m*, boisé *m Can*
woodchuck ['wʊdˌtʃʌk] *n* : marmotte *f* d'Amérique
woodcraft ['wʊdˌkræft] *n* **1** : connaissance *f* des bois **2** : art *m* de travailler le bois
woodcut ['wʊdˌkʌt] *n* : gravure *f* sur bois
woodcutter ['wʊdˌkʌtər] *n* : bûcheron *m*, -ronne *f*
wooded ['wʊdəd] *adj* : boisé
wooden ['wʊdən] *adj* **1** : en bois, de bois **2** STIFF : raide, qui manque de nature!
woodland ['wʊdlənd, -ˌlænd] *n* : région *f* boisée, bois *m*
woodpecker ['wʊdˌpɛkər] *n* : pic *m*, pic-bois *m Can*
woodpile ['wʊdˌpaɪl] *n* : tas *m* de bois
woodshed ['wʊdˌʃɛd] *n* : bûcher *m*, remise *f* à bois
woodsman ['wʊdzmən] *n, pl* **-men** [-mən, -ˌmɛn] **1** → **woodcutter 2** FORESTER : forestier *m*, -tière *f*
woodwind ['wʊdˌwɪnd] *n* : bois *m* (en musique)
woodwork ['wʊdˌwərk] *n* : boiseries *fpl* (dans une maison)
woodworking ['wʊdˌwərkɪŋ] *n* CARPENTRY : menuiserie *f*, ébénisterie *f*
woody ['wʊdi] *adj* **woodier; -est 1** WOODED : boisé **2** : ligneux (se dit des plantes)
woof ['wʊf] → **weft**
wool ['wʊl] *n* : laine *f*
woolen[1] *or* **woollen** ['wʊlən] *adj* : de laine, en laine
woolen[2] *n* **1** : tissu *m* en laine **2 woolens** *npl* : vêtements *mpl* de laine
woolly ['wʊli] *adj* **woolier; -est 1** : de laine, en laine **2** : laineux (se dit d'un animal) **3** CONFUSED, VAGUE : confus, flou
woozy ['wu:zi] *adj* **woozier; -est** : écœuré, qui a la tête qui tourne <to feel woozy : avoir mal au cœur>
word[1] ['wərd] *vt* : formuler, rédiger
word[2] *n* **1** : mot *m*, parole *f* <word for word : mot pour mot> <in a word, no : en un mot, non> <in word and deed : en paroles et en fait> <what is the word for . . . ? : comment dit-on . . . ?> **2** TALK : parole *f* <to have a word with s.o. : parler avec qqn> **3** COMMAND : ordre *m*, mot *m* d'ordre <to give the word : donner l'ordre> **4** MESSAGE, NEWS : nouvelles *fpl* <there's no word from Marie : on est sans nouvelles de Marie> <to send word : envoyer un mot> **5** PROMISE : parole *f* <to keep one's word : tenir (sa) parole> **6 words** *npl* QUARREL : dispute *f* <to have words with : se disputer avec> **7 words** *npl* : texte *m*, paroles *fpl* (en musique)
wordiness ['wərdinəs] *n* : verbosité *f*
wording ['wərdɪŋ] *n* : termes *mpl* (d'un document), formulation *f* (d'une invitation, etc.)
wordless ['wərdləs] *adj* : muet
word processing *n* : traitement *m* de texte
word processor *n* : machine *f* de traitement de textes

wore → **wear**[1]

work[1] ['wərk] *v* **worked** ['wərkt] *or* **wrought** ['rɔt]; **working** *vt* **1** EFFECT : faire <to work miracles : faire des miracles> **2** FORGE, SHAPE : travailler (le fer, l'acier, etc.) **3** OPERATE : faire marcher, activer **4** EXPLOIT : faire travailler **5** ARRANGE : arranger, organiser **6** EXCITE, PROVOKE : provoquer, exciter <I worked myself into a rage : la rage montait en moi> — *vi* **1** LABOR : travailler **2** SUCCEED : fonctionner, réussir

work[2] *adj* : de travail <work clothes : vêtements de travail>

work[3] *n* **1** LABOR : travail *m* **2** EMPLOYMENT : travail *m*, emploi *m* **3** TASK : travail *m*, ouvrage *m* **4** WORKMANSHIP : travail *m*, exécution *f* **5** : œuvre *f*, ouvrage *m* <a work of art : une œuvre d'art> **6 works** *npl* FACTORY : usine *f* **7 works** *npl* : travaux *mpl* <public works : travaux publics> **8 works** *npl* MECHANISM : rouages *mpl* (d'une horloge, etc.) **9 in the works** : en train de se faire

workable ['wərkəbəl] *adj* **1** : exploitable (se dit d'une mine, etc.) **2** PRACTICABLE : possible, réalisable

workaday ['wərkəˌdeɪ] *adj* : commun, ordinaire

workbench ['wərkˌbɛnt∫] *n* : établi *m*

workday ['wərkˌdeɪ] *n* **1** : journée *f* de travail **2** *or* **working day** : jour *m* ouvrable

worker ['wərkər] *n* **1** : travailleur *m*, -leuse *f*; employé *m*, -ployée *f* <he's a hard worker : c'est un grand travailleur> <white-collar workers : employés de bureau> **2** LABORER : ouvrier *m*, -vrière *f*

working ['wərkɪŋ] *adj* **1** : qui travaille <working people : gens qui travaillent> **2** : de bureau, de travail <during working hours : pendant les heures de bureau> **3** FUNCTIONING : qui fonctionne, qui marche <in working order : en état de marche> **4** SUFFICIENT : suffisant <a working knowledge : une connaissance adéquate>

workingman ['wərkɪŋˌmæn] *n, pl* **-men** [-mən, -ˌmɛn] : ouvrier *m*

workman ['wərkmən] *n, pl* **-men** [-mən, -ˌmɛn] **1** → **workingman** **2** ARTISAN : artisan *m*

workmanlike ['wərkmənˌlaɪk] *adj* **1** : professionnel, consciencieux (se dit d'une personne) **2** : bien fait (se dit d'un objet)

workmanship ['wərkmənˌ∫ɪp] *n* **1** SKILL : habileté *f* **2** QUALITY : qualité *f*, exécution *f*

workout ['wərkˌaʊt] *n* : séance *f* d'entraînement

work out *vt* **1** SOLVE : résoudre (un problème) **2** DEVELOP : développer, élaborer (un plan, etc.) — *vi* **1** SUCCEED, WORK : marcher, fonctionner, réussir **2** EXERCISE : s'entraîner, faire de l'exercice

workroom ['wərkˌru:m, -ˌrʊm] *n* : salle *f* de travail

workshop ['wərkˌ∫ɑp] *n* **1** SHOP : atelier *m* **2** SEMINAR : atelier *m*, groupe *m* de travail

world[1] ['wərld] *adj* : du monde, mondial

world[2] *n* **1** : monde *m* <around the world : autour du monde> <that makes a world of difference : cela fait un monde de différence> <to think the world of s.o. : penser le plus grand bien de qqn> **2** PEOPLE : monde *m*, société *f* <in the eyes of the world : aux yeux du monde> <the academic world : le monde académique>

worldly ['wərldli] *adj* **1** : matériel, de ce monde **2** → **worldly-wise**

worldly–wise ['wərldliˌwaɪz] *adj* : qui a l'expérience du monde

worldwide[1] ['wərldˈwaɪd] *adv* : dans le monde entier, partout dans le monde

worldwide[2] *adj* : mondial, universel

World Wide Web *n* WEB : Web *m*, Toile *f*

worm[1] ['wərm] *vt* **1** : débarrasser (un animal) de ses vers **2 to worm one's way into** : s'insinuer dans **3 to worm one's way through** : se faufiler à travers

worm[2] *n* **1** : ver *m* **2 worms** *npl* : vers *mpl* (intestinaux)

wormy ['wərmi] *adj* **wormier; -est** : véreux

worn ['wɔrn] → **wear**[1]

worn–out ['wɔrnˈaʊt] *adj* **1** : usé, fini (se dit d'un objet) **2** EXHAUSTED : épuisé, éreinté (se dit d'une personne)

worried ['wərid] *adj* : inquiet, soucieux

worrier ['wəriər] *n* : personne *f* qui s'inquiète

worrisome ['wərisəm] *adj* : inquiétant, préoccupant

worry[1] ['wəri] *v* **-ried; -rying** *vt* : inquiéter, tracasser — *vi* FRET : s'inquiéter

worry[2] *n, pl* **-ries** **1** ANXIETY : inquiétude *f* **2** DIFFICULTY : problème *m*, ennui *m*

worse[1] ['wərs] *adv* (*comparative of* **bad** *or of* **ill**) : moins bien, plus mal <we sleep worse in the warm weather : nous dormons moins bien quand il fait chaud>

worse[2] *adj* (*comparative of* **bad** *or of* **ill**) **1** : pire <it's worse than ever : c'est pire que jamais, c'est pire qu'avant> **2** : plus mal, plus malade <to feel worse : se sentir encore plus mal>

worse[3] *n* : pire *m* <to take a turn for the worse : s'aggraver, empirer> <none the worse : pas plus mal>

worsen ['wərsən] *vi* : empirer, se détériorer, rempirer *Can fam* — *vt* : aggraver, rendre pire

worship[1] ['wərʃəp] *v* **-shiped** *or* **-shipped; -shiping** *or* **-shipping** *vt* : adorer, vénérer — *vi* : faire ses dévotions

worship[2] *n* **1** : culte *m* <a place of worship : un lieu consacré au culte> **2** REVERENCE : adoration *f*, vénération *f*

worshiper *or* **worshipper** ['wərʃəpər] *n* : adorateur *m*, -trice *f*

worst[1] ['wərst] *vt* DEFEAT : battre, vaincre

worst[2] *adv* (*superlative of* **bad** *or of* **ill**) : plus mal <the worst dressed : le plus mal habillé>

worst[3] *adj* (*superlative of* **bad** *or of* **ill**) : pire, plus mauvais <the worst fate : le pire sort>

worst[4] *n* : pire *m* <to fear the worst : craindre le pire>

worsted ['wʊstəd, 'wərstəd] *n* : laine *f* peignée

worth[1] ['wərθ] *n* **1** : valeur *f* (monétaire) <what is its worth? : quelle est sa valeur?> **2** EXCELLENCE : valeur *f*, mérite *m*

worth[2] *prep* **to be worth** : valoir <he's worth thousands : il vaut des milliers> <to be well worth the effort : valoir bien l'effort>

worthiness ['wərðinəs] *n* : dignité *f*, mérite *m*

worthless ['wərθləs] *adj* : sans valeur

worthwhile ['wərθ'ʰwaɪl] *adj* : qui en vaut la peine

worthy ['wərði] *adj* **worthier; -est** : digne, méritant

would ['wʊd] *past of* **will 1** (*used to express preference*) <I would rather stay here : je préférerais rester ici> **2** (*used to express a wish, desire, or intent*) <those who would forbid gambling : ceux qui interdiraient les jeux d'argent> **3** (*used to express a plan*) <I said we would go : j'ai dit que nous irions> **4** (*used to express consent or choice*) <she would put off her work if she could : elle remettrait son travail à plus tard si elle pouvait> **5** (*used to express contingency*) <if they were coming, they would be here by now : s'ils venaient, ils seraient déjà arrivés> **6** (*used in a noun clause*) <we wish that he would go : nous aimerions qu'il parte> **7** (*used to express probability*) <I would have won if I had not tripped : j'aurais gagné si je n'avais pas trébuché> **8** (*used to express a request*) <would you please help us? : pourriez-vous nous aider s'il vous plaît?>

would-be ['wʊd'biː] *adj* : soi-disant, prétendu

wouldn't ['wʊdənt] (*contraction of* **would** *and* **not**) → **would**

wound[1] ['wuːnd] *vt* : blesser

wound[2] *n* : blessure *f*

wound[3] ['waʊnd] → **wind**[3]

wove, woven → **weave**[1]

wrangle[1] ['ræŋgəl] *vi* **-gled; -gling** : se quereller, se disputer <to wrangle over : se disputer à propos de>

wrangle[2] *n* : querelle *f*, dispute *f*, chicane *f*

wrap[1] ['ræp] *v* **wrapped; wrapping** *vt* **1** COVER : envelopper, emballer <to wrap a present : envelopper un cadeau> **2** SURROUND : envelopper, entourer <wrapped in mystery : entouré de mystère> **3** WIND : enrouler **4** *or* **to wrap up** SUMMARIZE : résumer — *vi* **to wrap up** DRESS : se couvrir, s'habiller

wrap[2] *n* **1** → **wrapper 2** SHAWL : châle *m*

wrapper ['ræpər] *n* **1** : papier *m*, emballage *m* <candy wrapper : papier de bonbon> **2** : jaquette *f* (de livre), bande *f* (de journal)

wrapping ['ræpɪŋ] *n* **1** : emballage *m* **2 wrapping paper** : papier d'emballage

wrath ['ræθ] *n* : furie *f*, colère *f*

wrathful ['ræθfəl] *adj* : courroucé, en colère

wreak ['riːk] *vt* **1** INFLICT : infliger (une punition, etc.) **2 to wreak havoc** : faire des ravages, dévaster

wreath ['riːθ] *n, pl* **wreaths** ['riːðz, 'riːθs] : couronne *f* (de fleurs, etc.)

wreathe ['riːð] *vt* **wreathed; wreathing 1** ADORN : couronner, orner **2** ENVELOP : envelopper <wreathed in mist : enveloppé de brume>

wreck[1] ['rɛk] *vt* **1** : provoquer le naufrage de (un navire), faire dérailler (un train), détruire (une voiture) **2** DESTROY, RUIN : détruire, miner, briser (un mariage, etc.) <to wreck one's chances : anéantir ses chances>

wreck[2] *n* **1** WRECKAGE : épave *f* (d'un navire), voiture *f* accidentée **2** ACCIDENT : accident *m* (de voiture), écrasement *m* (d'avion) **3 to be a wreck** : être à bout, être une épave

wreckage ['rɛkɪdʒ] *n* **1** : épave *f* (d'un navire), voiture *f* accidentée **2** REMAINS : décombres *mpl*, débris *mpl*

wrecker ['rɛkər] *n* **1** : destructeur *m*, -trice *f* **2** TOW TRUCK : dépanneuse *f*

wren ['rɛn] *n* : roitelet *m*

wrench[1] ['rɛntʃ] *vt* **1** PULL : tirer brusquement sur <to wrench sth away from s.o. : arracher qqch des mains de qqn> **2** TWIST : tordre <to wrench one's ankle : se tordre la cheville> — *vi* **to wrench free** : se dégager

wrench[2] *n* **1** PULL : mouvement *m* violent, secousse *f* (de torsion) **2** SPRAIN : foulure *f*, entorse *f* **3** : clef *f* (outil)

wrest ['rɛst] *vt* : arracher

wrestle[1] ['rɛsəl] *v* **-tled; -tling** *vi* **1** : lutter, pratiquer la lutte (aux sports) **2**

STRUGGLE : lutter <to wrestle with one's conscience : se débattre avec sa conscience> — *vt* : lutter contre

wrestle[2] *n* STRUGGLE : lutte *f*

wrestler ['rɛsələr] *n* : lutteur *m*, -teuse *f*

wrestling ['rɛsəlɪŋ] *n* : lutte *f* (sport)

wretch ['rɛtʃ] *n* **1** : misérable *mf* <a poor wretch : un pauvre misérable> **2** ROGUE : scélérat *m*

wretched ['rɛtʃəd] *adj* **1** POOR : misérable <wretched slums : taudis misérables> **2** MISERABLE, UNHAPPY : misérable, malheureux <to feel wretched : se sentir très mal> **3** AWFUL : affreux, déplorable <wretched weather : temps affreux>

wretchedly ['rɛtʃədli] *adv* : misérablement

wretchedness ['rɛtʃədnəs] *n* : misère *f*

wriggle ['rɪgəl] *v* **-gled; -gling** *vt* **1** SQUIRM, WIGGLE : gigoter, remuer **2 to wriggle one's way** : s'avancer en se tortillant — *vi* **to wriggle out of** : s'extirper de

wring ['rɪŋ] *vt* **wrung** ['rʌŋ]; **wringing 1** *or* **to wring out** : essorer, tordre (le linge) **2** TWIST : tordre <to wring s.o.'s neck : tordre le cou à qqn> <to wring one's hands : se tordre les mains> **3** EXTRACT : arracher (un aveu, etc.) **4 to wring one's heart** : se fendre le cœur

wringer ['rɪŋər] *n* : essoreuse *f*

wrinkle[1] ['rɪŋkəl] *v* **-kled; -kling** *vi* : se rider (se dit de la peau), se froisser (se dit des vêtements) — *vt* **1** : rider (la peau) **2** : plisser, faire des plis dans (des vêtements) <to wrinkle one's brow : plisser le front>

wrinkle[2] *n* : pli *m* (de vêtements), ride *f* (sur la peau)

wrinkly ['rɪŋkəli] *adj* : ridé

wrist ['rɪst] *n* : poignet *m*

wristband ['rɪstˌbænd] *n* **1** CUFF : poignet *m* (d'une chemise, etc.) **2** : bracelet *m* (d'une montre)

wristwatch ['rɪstˌwɑtʃ] *n* : montre-bracelet *f*

writ ['rɪt] *n* : ordonnance *f* (en droit)

write ['raɪt] *v* **wrote** ['roːt]; **written** ['rɪtən]; **writing** : écrire

write down *vt* : mettre par écrit, noter

write off *vt* CANCEL : annuler

writer ['raɪtər] *n* : écrivain *m*, écrivaine *f Can*

writhe ['raɪð] *vi* **writhed; writhing** : se tordre, se tortiller

writing ['raɪtɪŋ] *n* **1** : écriture *f* <to put in writing : mettre par écrit> **2** HANDWRITING : écriture *f* **3 writings** *npl* : écrits *mpl*, œuvres *fpl*

wrong[1] ['rɔŋ] *vt* **wronged; wronging 1** HARM, INJURE : faire du tort à **2** CHEAT : frauder

wrong[2] *adv* **1** WRONGLY : à tort **2** INCORRECTLY : mal <I guessed wrong : j'ai mal deviné>

wrong[3] *adj* **wronger; wrongest 1** SINFUL : mal, immoral **2** UNSUITABLE : mal, peu convenable, inapproprié **3** INCORRECT : mauvais, erroné <the wrong answer : la mauvaise réponse> **4 to be wrong** : se tromper, avoir tort

wrong[4] *n* **1** EVIL : mal *m* **2** INJUSTICE : tort *m*, injustice *f*

wrongdoer ['rɔŋˌduːər] *n* : malfaiteur *m*

wrongdoing ['rɔŋˌduːɪŋ] *n* : méfait *m*, mal *m*

wrongful ['rɔŋfəl] *adj* **1** UNJUST, WRONG : mal, injustifié **2** UNLAWFUL : illégal <wrongful arrest : arrestation arbitraire>

wrongfully ['rɔŋfəli] *adv* : injustement, à tort

wrongly ['rɔŋli] *adv* : à tort <wrongly accused : accusé à tort>

wrote → write

wrought[1] **→ work**[1]

wrought[2] ['rɔt] *adj* **1** SHAPED, WORKED : travaillé, ouvré <wrought iron : fer forgé> **2 to be wrought up** : être énervé, être très tendu

wrung → wring

wry ['raɪ] *adj* **wrier** ['raɪər]; **wriest** ['raɪəst] **1** : forcé <a wry smile : un sourire forcé> **2** TWISTED : tordu <to have a wry neck : avoir un torticolis> **3** SARDONIC : ironique, moqueur

X

x[1] ['ɛks] *n, pl* **x's** *or* **xs** ['ɛksəz] **1** : x *m*, vingt-quatrième lettre de l'alphabet **2** : x *m* (en mathématiques)

x[2] ['ɛks] *vt* **x–ed** ['ɛkst]; **x–ing** *or* **x'ing** ['ɛksɪŋ] DELETE: barrer, rayer

xenon ['ziːˌnɑn, 'zɛ-] *n* : xénon *m*

xenophobia [ˌzɛnəˈfoːbiə, ˌziː-] *n* : xénophobie *f*

xenophobic [ˌzɛnəˈfoːbɪk, ˈziː-] *adj* : xénophobe

xerography [zəˈrɑgrəfi] *n* : photocopie *f*

xerox ['zɪrɑks] *vt* : photocopier

Xmas ['krɪsməs] → **Christmas**

x–ray ['ɛksˌreɪ] *vt* : radiographier

X ray ['ɛksˌreɪ] *n* **1** : rayon *m* X **2** *or* **X–ray photograph** : radiographie *f*

xylophone ['zaɪləˌfoːn] *n* : xylophone *m*

xylophonist ['zaɪləˌfoːnɪst] *n* : xylophoniste *mf*

Y

y ['waɪ] *n, pl* **y's** *or* **ys** ['waɪz] : y *m*, vingt-cinquième lettre de l'alphabet
yacht[1] ['jɑt] *vi* : faire du yachting
yacht[2] *n* : yacht *m*
yak ['jæk] *n* : yack *m*
yam ['jæm] *n* **1** : igname *f* (plante) **2** SWEET POTATO : patate *f* douce
yank[1] ['jæŋk] *vt* : tirer d'un coup sec
yank[2] *n* : coup *m* sec
Yankee ['jæŋki] *n* : Yankee *mf*
yap[1] ['jæp] *vi* **yapped; yapping 1** YELP : japper (se dit d'un chien) **2** CHATTER : jacasser
yap[2] *n* : jappement *m*
yard ['jɑrd] *n* **1** : yard *m*, verge *f Can* (unité de mesure) **2** SPAR : vergue *f* (d'un navire) **3** COURTYARD : cour *f* (d'immeuble) **4** : jardin *m* (d'une maison) **5** : chantier *m* (de construction), dépôt *m* (de marchandises)
yardage ['jɑrdɪdʒ] *n* : longueur *f* en yards, longueur *f* en verges *Can*
yardarm ['jɑrdˌɑrm] *n* : bout *m* de vergue
yardstick ['jɑrdˌstɪk] *n* **1** : mètre *m* **2** : CRITERION : critère *m*, point *m* de référence
yarn ['jɑrn] *n* **1** : fil *m* (à tisser) **2** TALE : histoire *f* <to spin a yarn : raconter des histoires>
yawl ['jɔl] *n* : yawl *m*
yawn[1] ['jɔn] *vi* : bâiller
yawn[2] *n* : bâillement *m*
ye ['jiː] *pron* : vous
yea[1] ['jeɪ] *adv* YES : oui
yea[2] *n* : vote *m* affirmatif, oui *m* <the yeas and the nays : les oui et les non>
year ['jɪr] *n* **1** : an *m*, année *f* <next year : l'an prochain> <the school year : l'année scolaire> **2** : an *m* <their son is seven years olds : leur fils a sept ans> **3 years** *npl* AGE : âge *m* <she's getting on in years : elle prend de l'âge>
yearbook ['jɪrˌbʊk] *n* : recueil *m* annuel, annuaire *m*
yearling ['jɪrlɪŋ, 'jərlən] *n* : animal *m* d'un an
yearly[1] ['jɪrli] *adv* : annuellement
yearly[2] *adj* : annuel
yearn ['jərn] *vi* **to yearn for** : désirer ardemment, aspirer à
yearning ['jərnɪŋ] *n* : désir *m* ardent
yeast ['jiːst] *n* : levure *f*
yell[1] ['jɛl] *vi* : crier — *vt* SHOUT : crier, hurler
yell[2] *n* : cri *m*, hurlement *m*
yellow[1] ['jɛlo] *v* : jaunir
yellow[2] *adj* **1** : jaune **2** COWARDLY : lâche, peureux
yellow[3] *n* **1** : jaune *m* (couleur) **2** YOLK : jaune *m* d'œuf
yellow fever *n* : fièvre *f* jaune
yellowish ['jɛloɪʃ] *adj* : jaunâtre
yellow jacket *n* : guêpe *f*
yelp[1] ['jɛlp] *vi* : glapir
yelp[2] *n* : glapissement *m*
Yemeni[1] ['jɛməni] *adj* : yéménite
Yemeni[2] *n* : Yéménite *mf*
yen ['jɛn] *n* : désir *m*, envie *f*
yeoman ['joːmən] *n, pl* **-men** [-mən, -ˌmɛn] : sous-officier *m* de la marine
yes[1] ['jɛs] *adv* **1** (*used in general statements*) : oui <are you ready? yes, I am : êtes-vous prêt? oui, je suis prêt> **2** (*used after a negative question*) : si <you're not ready, are you? yes, I am : vous n'êtes pas prêt? mais si, je le suis>
yes[2] *n* : oui *m*
yesterday[1] ['jɛstərˌdeɪ, -di] *adv* : hier
yesterday[2] *n* **1** : hier *m* **2 the day before yesterday** : avant-hier *m*
yet[1] ['jɛt] *adv* **1** BESIDES : de plus, encore <yet another excuse : encore une autre excuse> <yet again : encore une fois> **2** SO FAR : jusqu'à présent, jusqu'ici <the best yet : le mieux jusqu'ici> **3** (*used in negative phrases*) : encore <not yet : pas encore> **4** EVENTUALLY, STILL : encore <they may yet return : ils pourraient encore revenir> **5** NEVERTHELESS : néanmoins
yet[2] *conj* BUT : mais
yew ['juː] *n* : if *m*
yield[1] ['jiːld] *vt* **1** SURRENDER : rendre, céder <to yield the right of way : céder le passage> **2** PRODUCE : produire, donner, rapporter — *vi* **1** GIVE : céder, fléchir <to yield under pressure : céder sous la pression> **2** GIVE IN, SURRENDER : se rendre, céder
yield[2] *n* : rendement *m*, rapport *m*, récolte *f* (en agriculture)
yodel ['joːdəl] *vi* **-deled** *or* **-delled; -deling** *or* **-delling** : iodler
yoga ['joːgə] *n* : yoga *m*
yogurt ['joːgərt] *n* : yaourt *m*, yogourt *m*
yoke[1] ['joːk] *vt* **yoked; yoking 1** : atteler (des animaux) **2** JOIN : joindre
yoke[2] *n* **1** : joug *m* (d'animaux) **2** DOMINION : joug *m* <the yoke of slavery : le joug de l'esclavage> **3** TEAM : attelage *m* **4** : empiècement *m* (d'un vêtement)
yokel ['joːkəl] *n* : rustre *mf;* plouc *mf France fam;* péquenaud *m*, -naude *f France fam*
yolk ['joːk] *n* : jaune *m* d'œuf
Yom Kippur [ˌjoːmkɪˈpʊr, ˌjɑm-, -ˈkɪpər] *n* : Yom Kippour *m*
yonder ['jɑndər] *adv & adj* : là-bas
yore ['joːr] *n* **of ~** : d'antan <in days of yore : au temps jadis>
you ['juː] *pron* **1** (*used as subject — singular*) : tu (familier), vous (forme polie) <you may sit in the armchair : tu peux t'asseoir dans le fauteuil> <you were right : vous aviez raison> **2** (*used as subject — plural*) : vous

<you are my friends : vous êtes mes amis> **3** (*used as the direct or indirect object of a verb*) : te (familier), vous (forme polie), vous (pluriel) <can I pour you a cup of tea? : puis-je vous verser une tasse de thé?> <I will help you : je t'aiderai> **4** (*used as the object of a preposition*) : toi (familier), vous (forme polie), vous (pluriel) <bring the children with you : amenez les enfants avec toi> **5** ONE : on <you never know what's going to happen : on ne sait jamais ce qui va arriver>

you'd ['jʊd] (*contraction of* **you had** *or* **you would**) → **have, would**

you'll ['ju:l, 'jʊl] (*contraction of* **you shall** *or* **you will**) → **shall, will**

young[1] ['jʌŋ] *adj* **younger** ['jʌŋgər]; **youngest** ['jʌŋgəst] **1** : jeune <very young children : enfants tout jeunes> **2** NEW : jeune <a young industry : une industrie jeune> **3** YOUTHFUL : jeune, jeune de cœur <to look young : avoir l'air jeune>

young[2] *ns & pl* **the young** : les jeunes (personnes), les petits (animaux)

youngish ['jʌŋɪʃ] *adj* : assez jeune, plutôt jeune

youngster ['jʌŋkstər] *n* **1** : jeune *mf* **2** CHILD : enfant *mf*

your ['jʊr, 'jo:r, jər] *adj* **1** (*familiar singular*) : ta, ton <your book : ton livre> **2** (*formal singular*) : votre <it's your money : c'est votre argent> **3** (*familiar and formal plural*) : tes, vos <your teeth : tes dents> <your contributions : vos contributions> **4** (*impersonal*) : votre, vos <the house is at your right : la maison est à votre droite> <it's good for your health : c'est bon pour la santé> **5** (*used as an equivalent to the definite article* the) <he's different from your average teacher : il se démarque des autres professeurs> **6** (*used before a title*) : Votre <Your Majesty : Votre Majesté>

yours ['jʊrz, 'jo:rz] *pron* **1** (*familiar singular*) : le tien, la tienne <is it yours? : est-ce que c'est le tien?> <the bike is yours : la bicyclette est à toi> **2** (*formal singular*) : le vôtre, la vôtre <a friend of yours : un de vos amis> **3** (*familiar plural*) : les tiens, les tiennes **4** (*formal plural*) : les vôtres <ours are here; yours are there : les nôtres sont ici, les vôtres sont là>

yourself [jər'sɛlf] *pron, pl* **yourselves** [jər'sɛlvz] **1** (*used reflexively*) : tu (familier), vous (forme polie), vous (pluriel) <you'll hurt yourself if you're not careful : tu te feras mal si tu ne fais pas attention> <please help yourself : servez-vous s'il vous plaît> **2** (*used for emphasis*) : toi-même (familier), vous-même (forme polie), vous-mêmes (pluriel) <carry them yourselves : emportez-les vous-mêmes>

youth ['ju:θ] *n, pl* **youths** ['ju:ðz, 'ju:θs] **1** : jeunesse *f* <to regain one's youth : retrouver sa jeunesse> **2** ADOLESCENT : jeune homme *m* **3** : jeunes *mf*, jeunesse *f* <the youth of today : les jeunes d'aujourd'hui>

youthful ['ju:θfəl] *adj* **1** : de jeunesse **2** YOUNG : jeune <to look youthful : avoir l'air jeune> **3** JUVENILE : juvénile

youthfulness ['ju:θfəlnəs] *n* : jeunesse *f*

you've ['ju:v] (*contraction of* **you have**) → **have**

yowl[1] ['jæʊl] *vi* : miauler (se dit d'un chat), hurler (se dit d'un chien ou d'une personne)

yowl[2] *n* : miaulement *m* (d'un chat) hurlement *m* (d'un chien ou d'une personne)

yo-yo ['jo:ˌjo:] *n, pl* **yo-yos** : yo-yo *m*

yucca ['jʌkə] *n* : yucca *m*

Yugoslav[1] ['ju:go,slav] *or* **Yugoslavian** [ˌju:go'slaviən] *adj* : yougoslave

Yugoslav[2] *or* **Yugoslavian** *n* : Yougoslave *mf*

yule ['ju:l] *n* : Noël *m*

yuletide ['ju:lˌtaɪd] *n* : époque *f* de Noël

Z

z ['zi:] *n, pl* **z's** *or* **zs** : z *m*, vingt-sixième lettre de l'alphabet

Zairian[1] [za'riən] *adj* : zaïrois

Zairian[2] *n* : Zaïrois *m*, -roise *f*

Zambian[1] ['zæmbiən] *adj* : zambien

Zambian[2] *n* : Zambien *m*, -bienne *f*

zany[1] ['zeɪni] *adj* **zanier; -est** : farfelu *fam*, loufoque *fam*

zany[2] *n, pl* **-nies** BUFFOON : bouffon *m*

zeal ['zi:l] *n* : zèle *m*, enthousiasme *m*

zealot ['zɛlət] *n* : fanatique *mf*; zélateur *m*, -trice *f*

zealous ['zɛləs] *adj* : zélé, dévoué

zealously ['zɛləsli] *adv* : avec zèle

zebra ['zi:brə] *n* : zèbre *m*

zed ['zɛd] *Brit* → **z**

zenith ['zi:nəθ] *n* : zénith *m*, apogée *m*

zephyr ['zɛfər] *n* : zéphyr *m*

zeppelin ['zɛplən, -pəlɪn] *n* : zeppelin *m*

zero[1] ['zi:ro, 'zɪro] *vi* **to zero in on** : se diriger droit sur, faire porter tous ses efforts sur

zero[2] *adj* : zéro, nul <zero growth : croissance zéro>

zero[3] *n, pl* **-ros** : zéro *m*

zest ['zest] *n* **1** GUSTO : enthousiasme

m, entrain *m* **2** FLAVOR, PIQUANCY : saveur *f*, piquant *m*
zestful [ˈzɛstfəl] *adj* : enthousiaste, passionné
zestfully [ˈzɛstfəli] *adv* : avec enthousiasme
zigzag[1] [ˈzɪgˌzæg] *vi* **-zagged; -zagging** : zigzaguer
zigzag[2] *adj & adv* : en zigzag
zigzag[3] *n* : zigzag *m*
Zimbabwean[1] [zɪmˈbɑbwiən, -bweɪ-] *adj* : zimbabwéen
Zimbabwean[2] *n* : Zimbabwéen *m*, -wéenne *f*
zinc [ˈzɪŋk] *n* : zinc *m*
zing [ˈzɪŋ] *n* **1** HISS, HUM : sifflement *m* **2** ZEST : entrain *m*
zinnia [ˈzɪniə, ˈziː-, -njə] *n* : zinnia *m*
zip[1] [ˈzɪp] *v* **zipped; zipping** *vt or* **to zip up** : fermer avec une fermeture à glissière — *vi* **1** DASH : filer à toute allure **2 to zip by** *or* **to zip past** : passer comme une flèche **3** : siffler (se dit d'une balle, etc.)
zip[2] *n* **1** ENERGY, VIM : vitalité *f*, entrain *m* **2** HISSING, HUMMING : sifflement *m*
zip code *n* : code *m* postal
zipper [ˈzɪpər] *n* : fermeture *f* à glissière
zippy [ˈzɪpi] *adj* **zippier; -est** LIVELY : vif, entraînant
zircon [ˈzərˌkɑn] *n* : zircon *m*
zirconium [ˌzərˈkoːniəm] *n* : zirconium *m*
zither [ˈzɪðər, -θər] *n* : cithare *f*
zodiac [ˈzoːdiˌæk] *n* : zodiaque *m*
zombie [ˈzɑmbi] *n* : zombie *m*
zone[1] [ˈzoːn] *vt* **zoned; zoning 1** : diviser en zones **2 to be zoned for business** : être réservé à l'entreprise
zone[2] *n* : zone *f*
zoo [ˈzuː] *n, pl* **zoos** : zoo *m*
zookeeper [ˈzuːˌkiːpər] *n* : gardien *m*, -dienne *f* de zoo
zoological [ˌzoːəˈlɑdʒɪkəl, ˌzuːə-] *adj* : zoologique
zoologist [zoˈɑlədʒɪst, zuː-] *n* : zoologiste *mf*
zoology [zoˈɑlədʒi, zuː-] *n* : zoologie *f*
zoom[1] [ˈzuːm] *vi* **1** : aller à toute allure <to zoom past : passer comme une trombe> <the plane zoomed up : l'avion a monté en chandelle> **2 to zoom in** : faire un zoom (en photographie)
zoom[2] *n* **1** : bourdonnement *m* (d'un moteur) **2** *or* **zoom lens** : zoom *m*
zucchini [zoˈkiːni] *n, pl* **-ni** *or* **-nis** : courgette *f*
zwieback [ˈswiːˌbɑk, ˈswaɪ-, ˈzwiː-, ˈzwaɪ-] *n* : biscotte *f*
zygote [ˈzaɪˌgoːt] *n* : zygote *m*

Common French Abbreviations

FRENCH ABBREVIATION AND EXPANSION		ENGLISH EQUIVALENT	
AB, Alb.	Alberta	**AB, Alta.**	Alberta
ALÉNA	Accord de libre-échange nord-américain	**NAFTA**	North American Free Trade Agreement
AP	assistance publique (France)	**—**	welfare services
ap. J.-C.	après Jésus-Christ	**AD**	anno Domini
a/s	aux soins de	**c/o**	care of
A.T.	Ancien Testament	**O.T.**	Old Testament
av.	avenue	**ave.**	avenue
av. J.-C.	avant Jésus-Christ	**BC**	before Christ
avr.	avril	**Apr.**	April
BC	Colombie-Britannique	**BC, B.C.**	British Columbia
bd	boulevard	**blvd.**	boulevard
BD	bande dessinée	**—**	comic strip
BN	Bibliothèque nationale	**—**	national library
BP	boîte postale	**P.O.B.**	post office box
B.S.	bien-être social (Canada)	**—**	welfare services
c	centime	**c, ct.**	cent
C	centigrade, Celsius	**C**	centigrade, Celsius
CA	comptable agréé (Canada)	**CPA**	certified public accountant
CA	courant alternatif	**AC**	alternating current
c.-à-d.	c'est-à-dire	**i.e.**	that is
Cap.	capitaine	**Capt.**	captain
C.-B.	Colombie-Britannique	**BC, B.C.**	British Columbia
CC	courant continu	**DC**	direct current
CE	Communauté européenne	**EC**	European Community
CEE	Communauté européenne économique	**EEC**	European Economic Community
cf.	confer	**cf.**	compare
cg	centigramme	**cg**	centigram
chap.	chapitre	**ch., chap.**	chapter
Cie	compagnie	**Co.**	company
cm	centimètre	**cm**	centimeter
col.	colonne	**col.**	column
Col.	colonel	**Col.**	colonel
C.P.	case postale (Canada)	**P.O.B**	post office box
CV	curriculum vitae	**CV**	curriculum vitae
déc.	décembre	**Dec.**	December
dép., dépt.	département	**dept.**	department
DG	directeur général	**CEO**	chief executive officer
dim.	dimanche	**Sun.**	Sunday
dir.	directeur	**dir.**	director

FRENCH ABBREVIATION AND EXPANSION		ENGLISH EQUIVALENT	
DOM	Département(s) d'outre-mer	—	French overseas department
dr.	droite	**rt.**	right
Dr	docteur	**Dr.**	doctor
E	Est, est	**E**	East, east
ECG	électrocardiogramme	**EKG**	electrocardiogram
éd.	édition	**ed.**	edition
EPS	éducation physique et sportive	**PE**	physical education
etc.	et caetera, et cetera	**etc.**	et cetera
É.-U.	États-Unis	**US**	United States
F	Fahrenheit	**F**	Fahrenheit
F	franc	**fr.**	franc
FAB	franco à bord	**FOB**	free on board
FB	franc belge	—	Belgian franc
févr.	février	**Feb.**	February
FF	franc français	—	French franc
FMI	Fonds monétaire international	**IMF**	International Monetary Fund
g	gauche	**l., L**	left
g	gramme	**g**	gram
Gén.	général	**Gen.**	general
h	heure(s)	**hr.**	hour
ha	hectare	**ha**	hectare
HS	hors service	—	out of order
i.e.	c'est-à-dire	**i.e.**	that is
IPC	indice des prix à la consommation	**CPI**	consumer price index
Î.P.-É	île-du-Prince-Édouard	**PE, P.E.I.**	Prince Edward Island
janv.	janvier	**Jan.**	January
jeu.	jeudi	**Thurs.**	Thursday
juill.	juillet	**Jul.**	July
kg	kilogramme	**kg**	kilogram
km	kilomètre	**km**	kilometer
l	litre	**l**	liter
lun.	lundi	**Mon.**	Monday
m	mètre	**m.**	meter
M.	monsieur	—	Mr., mister
mar.	mardi	**Tues.**	Tuesday
MB, Man.	Manitoba	**MB, Man.**	Manitoba
mer.	mercredi	**Wed.**	Wednesday
Mgr.	Monseigneur	**Mgr., Msgr.**	Monsignor, Monseigneur
min	minute	**min.**	minute
MLF	mouvement de libération des femmes	—	—
Mlle	Mademoiselle	—	Ms., Miss
Mme	Madame	—	Ms., Mrs.
MST	maladie sexuellement transmissible	**STD**	sexually transmitted disease

FRENCH ABBREVIATION AND EXPANSION		ENGLISH EQUIVALENT	
N	Nord, nord	**N**	North, north
N°, n°	numéro	**no.**	number
NB, N.-B.	Nouveau-Brunswick	**NB, N.B.**	New Brunswick
n.d.	non daté	**n.d.**	no date, not dated
n.d.	non disponible	**NA**	not available
NF	Terre-Neuve	**NF, Nfld.**	Newfoundland
nov.	novembre	**Nov.**	November
NS, N.-É.	Nouvelle-Écosse	**NS, N.S.**	Nova Scotia
N.T.	Nouveau Testament	**N.T.**	New Testament
NT	Territoires du Nord-Ouest	**NT, N.T.**	Northwest Territories
O	Ouest, ouest	**W**	West, west
oc	ondes courtes	**s-w**	short wave
oct.	octobre	**Oct.**	October
OIT	Organisation internationale du travail	**ILO**	International Labor Organization
OMS	Organisation mondiale de la santé	**WHO**	World Health Organization
ON	Ontario	**ON, Ont.**	Ontario
ONG	organisation non gouvernementale	**NGO**	nongovernmental organization
Ont.	Ontario	**ON**	Ontario
ONU	Organisation des Nations Unies	**UN**	United Nations
OTAN	Organisation du traité de l'Atlantique Nord	**NATO**	North Atlantic Treaty Organization
OVNI, ovni	objet volant non identifié	**UFO**	unidentified flying object
p.	page	**p.**	page
P.	Père	**Fr.**	Father
PCV	paiement contre vérification	**—**	collect call
PDG	président-directeur général	**CEO**	chief executive officer
p.-ê.	peut-être	**—**	maybe
PE	Île-du-Prince-Édouard	**PE, P.E.I.**	Prince Edward Island
p. ex.	par exemple	**e.g.**	for example
PIB	produit intérieur brut	**GDP**	gross domestic product
PNB	produit national brut	**GNP**	gross national product
P.-S.	post-scriptum	**P.S.**	postscript
QC	Québec	**QC, Que.**	Quebec
QG	quartier général	**HQ**	headquarters
QI	quotient intellectuel	**IQ**	intelligence quotient
R-D	recherche-développement	**R and D**	research and development
réf.	référence	**ref.**	reference
RF	République Française	**—**	France
RN	route nationale	**—**	interstate highway
RV	rendez-vous	**rdv., R.V.**	rendezvous

FRENCH ABBREVIATION AND EXPANSION		ENGLISH EQUIVALENT	
s.	siècle	**c., cent.**	century
S	Sud, sud	**S, so.**	South, south
SA	société anonyme	**Inc.**	incorporated (company)
sam.	samedi	**Sat.**	Saturday
SARL	société à responsabilité limitée	**Ltd.**	limited (corporation)
Sask.	Saskatchewan	**SK, Sask.**	Saskatchewan
SDF	sans domicile fixe	**—**	homeless (person)
sept.	septembre	**Sept.**	September
Sgt.	sergent	**Sgt.**	sergeant
SK	Saskatchewan	**SK, Sask.**	Saskatchewan
SM	Sa Majesté	**HM**	His Majesty, Her Majesty
SME	Système monétaire européen	**—**	European Monetary System
S.S.	Sa Sainteté	**H.H.**	His Holiness
St	saint	**St.**	Saint
Ste	sainte	**St.**	Saint
SVP	s'il vous plaît	**pls.**	please
t	tonne	**t., tn.**	ton
tél.	téléphone	**tel.**	telephone
T.-N.	Terre-Neuve	**NF, Nfld.**	Newfoundland
T.N.-O.	Territoires du Nord-Ouest	**NT, N.T.**	Northwest Territories
TVA	taxe à valeur ajoutée	**VAT**	value-added tax
UE	Union européenne	**EU**	European Union
univ.	université	**U., univ.**	university
V., v.	voir	**vid.**	see
ven.	vendredi	**Fri.**	Friday
vol.	volume	**vol.**	volume
VPC	vente par correspondance	**—**	mail-order selling
vs	versus	**v., vs.**	versus
W-C	water closet	**w.c.**	water closet
YT, Yuk.	Yukon	**YT, Y.T.**	Yukon Territory

French Numbers

Cardinal Numbers

1	un	33	trente-trois
2	deux	34	trente-quatre
3	trois	35	trente-cinq
4	quatre	36	trente-six
5	cinq	37	trente-sept
6	six	38	trente-huit
7	sept	39	trente-neuf
8	huit	40	quarante
9	neuf	41	quarante et un
10	dix	50	cinquante
11	onze	60	soixante
12	douze	70	soixante-dix
13	treize	80	quatre-vingts
14	quatorze	90	quatre-vingt-dix
15	quinze	100	cent
16	seize	101	cent un
17	dix-sept	102	cent deux
18	dix-huit	200	deux cents
19	dix-neuf	300	trois cents
20	vingt	400	quatre cents
21	vingt et un	500	cinq cents
22	vingt-deux	600	six cents
23	vingt-trois	700	sept cents
24	vingt-quatre	800	huit cents
25	vingt-cinq	900	neuf cents
26	vingt-six	1 000	mille
27	vingt-sept	1 001	mille un
28	vingt-huit	2 000	deux mille
29	vingt-neuf	100 000	cent mille
30	trente	1 000 000	un million
31	trente et un	1 000 000 000	un milliard
32	trente-deux		

Ordinal Numbers

1st	premier, première	16th	seizième
2nd	deuxième *or* second	17th	dix-septième
3rd	troisième	18th	dix-huitième
4th	quatrième	19th	dix-neuvième
5th	cinquième	20th	vingtième
6th	sixième	21st	vingt et unième
7th	septième	22nd	vingt-deuxième
8th	huitième	30th	trentième
9th	neuvième	40th	quarantième
10th	dixième	50th	cinquantième
11th	onzième	60th	soixantième
12th	douzième	70th	soixante-dixième
13th	treizième	80th	quatre-vingtième
14th	quatorzième	90th	quatre-vingt-dixième
15th	quinzième	100th	centième